Collins

OFFICIAL
SCRABBLE™
BRAND Crossword Game
WORDS

S
1

Published by Collins
An imprint of HarperCollins Publishers
Westerhill Road
Bishopbriggs
Glasgow G64 2QT

Fifth Edition 2020

10 9 8 7 6 5 4 3 2 1

© HarperCollins Publishers 2004, 2005,
2006, 2007, 2011, 2015, 2020

ISBN 978-0-00-832013-3

www.harpercollins.co.uk/scrabble

Typeset by Davidson Publishing Solutions,
Glasgow

Printed and bound in Great Britain by
CPI Group (UK) Ltd, Croydon CR0 4YY

If you would like to comment on any aspect
of this book, please contact us at the given
address or online.
E-mail: puzzles@harpercollins.co.uk
 facebook.com/collinsdictionary
 @collinsdict

MIX
Paper from
responsible sources
FSC™ C007454

FSC
www.fsc.org

Contents

Scrabble Consultants
Darryl Francis
David Sutton

Editor
Mary O'Neill

Computing Support
Claire Dimeo

For the Publisher
Gerry Breslin
Kerry Ferguson

Foreword by Philip Nelkon

Is it already four years since we got to play *lolz* and *xed* on a Scrabble board? Congratulations to the Collins team led by Darryl Francis and David Sutton for the hard work they have done in identifying nearly 3,000 new words for us to use and abuse in this new edition of *Collins Official Scrabble Words* (OSW). Now, for the first time, there is a word to describe OSW aficionados – *wordies*! There's also *boardies*, which would be a great collective noun for Scrabble fanatics, though it's actually an Australian term for men's shorts.

There's more good news. We all know that 2-letter words are the lifeblood of high-score Scrabble, enabling us to make those high-scoring parallel plays involving many words. Now, for the first time since 2007, there are three new 2-letter words to enhance our Scrabble firepower. If you've been following the media, you'll have seen that one of these – *ok* – has been the source of much controversy. Well, the word list compilers have gone *judgy* and made their decision – it's in.

A fair smattering of words that I have seen played incorrectly over the board in the past make it, at last, into this edition, words like *zen*, *earnt* and *laxed*. On publication of the last list, I was personally accosted by two irate elderly gentlemen who were fans of 'figgy pie' and couldn't believe that *figgy* wasn't allowed, but the word has now been included. That's the sort of passion Scrabble can engender. You might also be getting emotional over the political situation at the moment but there is one incontestable benefit of Brexit (not shown due to being a proper noun) – *remainer* has finally made it into the Dictionary.

With all these new terms, it's tempting to fantasize over their source. A couple of editions ago, a large number of cricketing terms appeared, this time it's the turn of obscure currencies. The undoubted star is *qapik*, from Azerbaijan, that's going to be helpful if you don't have a U with your Q. There's also *thetri*, *togrog*, *metica*, *maraca* and even *kopiyky*, though I think that one is unlikely to come in useful on a regular basis. Another regular contributor is food, which gives us a couple of potentially fruitful 3's – *bao* and *ume*. There are other foodie terms like *nduja*, *jollof*, *labneh* and *arancini*, which I predict will start to appear regularly on Scrabble boards in the future.

What else will enhance our play? Well, there are some useful 7- and 8-letter words; these are the most effective for playing all your tiles in one go and getting a 50-point bonus. *Rendang* could have been included in the food section and also has a high probability of turning up on your rack, as do *galants*, *othered*, *roguier* and *telogen*. Amongst 8-letter words there are *transmen*, *nonstate* and *sonliest*.

No matter how you enjoy your Scrabble – in tournaments, online or at home – this is the go-to book for adjudication and for adding ammunition to your Scrabble armoury.

Philip Nelkon
Four-time National Scrabble Champion

Introduction

This new edition of *Collins Official Scrabble Words* marks the completion of an epic amount of work carried out by the World English-Language Scrabble Players Association (WESPA) Dictionary Committee, comprising Darryl Francis, Chairman, with David Sutton and others, working in tandem with Collins lexicographers. The team at Collins had just completed work on the largest single-volume English dictionary in print, *Collins English Dictionary*, and presented the WESPA Dictionary Committee with a huge selection task to identify the candidates for inclusion according to the rules that apply to the Scrabble word list, which now boasts 279,496 word forms and will be officially adopted for use in WESPA tournaments by 1st July 2019.

Rules for the Scrabble word list

- Only includes words of between 2 and 15 letters in length
- Does not include proper nouns, place names, and words with an initial capital letter, unless such words can also be spelt with a lowercase initial letter
- Does not include abbreviations, prefixes, suffixes, words requiring apostrophes or hyphens
- Includes foreign words that are considered to have been absorbed into the English language
- Includes inflected forms, such as plurals and verb forms, eg plumb, plumbs, plumbed, plumbing
- Includes words that are old, obsolete, dialectal, historical and/or literary
- Includes World English, including spelling and variants from the US, South Africa, Australia, New Zealand, etc
- Includes words that are denoted contractions, short forms and slang
- Includes words which may be deemed rude or offensive

Disclaimer

The words in this list are published in accordance with the rules of the WESPA Dictionary Committee and based on the strict criteria above. They are valid for use in Scrabble games under the aegis of WESPA, and no word is excluded on the grounds of religion, gender, race, or for any reason other than that it is an invalid word form for the game of Scrabble. The presence or exclusion of any word does not in any way represent the views of WESPA or the Publisher, HarperCollins.

The Collins Editorial Team and WESPA

Other Scrabble resources

Associations

World English-Language Scrabble Players Association (WESPA) –
www.wespa.org

The WESPA website also provides access to resources for national associations,
tournament organizers, players and youth players.

Association of British Scrabble Players (ABSP) – www.absp.org.uk

The ABSP website includes details of UK Scrabble clubs and UK tournaments.

North American Scrabble Players Association (NASPA) –
www.scrabbleplayers.org

The NASPA website contains numerous word lists and lists of further
Scrabble resources.

Mindsports Academy – www.mindsportsacademy.com

Facebook

Several Scrabble groups, including:

World English-Language Scrabble Players Association

Scrabble International

Scrabble Snippetz

Collins Scrabble Players

Mindsports Academy

Interactive Scrabble games

Internet Scrabble Club (ISC) – www.isc.ro

Mobile phone – Real Networks

Sky Interactive – Sky TV platform

iTouch / iPhone / Android / iPad – Electronic Arts (EA)

Collins Scrabble App

Download the Collins Official SCRABBLE™ app from the App Store.

Perfect for adjudication, solving and training.

Collins Scrabble Tools online

www.collinsdictionary.com/scrabble/scrabble-tools

Tools and tips, plus *Collins Scrabble Word Finder*, giving instant access to all official playable Scrabble words and scores.

Alphabetical list of two-letter words

AA	EA	IN	OD	TA
AB	ED	IO	OE	TE
AD	EE	IS	OF	TI
AE	EF	IT	OH	TO
AG	EH	JA	OI	UG
AH	EL	JO	OK	UH
AI	EM	KA	OM	UM
AL	EN	KI	ON	UN
AM	ER	KO	OO	UP
AN	ES	KY	OP	UR
AR	ET	LA	OR	US
AS	EW	LI	OS	UT
AT	EX	LO	OU	WE
AW	FA	MA	OW	WO
AX	FE	ME	OX	XI
AY	FY	MI	OY	XU
BA	GI	MM	PA	YA
BE	GO	MO	PE	YE
BI	GU	MU	PI	YO
BO	HA	MY	PO	YU
BY	HE	NA	QI	ZA
CH	HI	NE	RE	ZE
DA	HM	NO	SH	ZO
DE	HO	NU	SI	
DI	ID	NY	SO	
DO	IF	OB	ST	

Alphabetical list of three-letter words

AAH	AJI	ARE	BAC	BOB
AAL	AKA	ARF	BAD	BOD
AAS	AKE	ARK	BAE	BOG
ABA	ALA	ARM	BAG	BOH
ABB	ALB	ARS	BAH	BOI
ABO	ALE	ART	BAL	BOK
ABS	ALF	ARY	BAM	BON
ABY	ALL	ASH	BAN	BOO
ACE	ALP	ASK	BAO	BOP
ACH	ALS	ASP	BAP	BOR
ACT	ALT	ASS	BAR	BOS
ADD	ALU	ATE	BAS	BOT
ADO	AMA	ATS	BAT	BOW
ADS	AME	ATT	BAY	BOX
ADZ	AMI	AUA	BED	BOY
AFF	AMP	AUE	BEE	BRA
AFT	AMU	AUF	BEG	BRO
AGA	ANA	AUK	BEL	BRR
AGE	AND	AVA	BEN	BRU
AGO	ANE	AVE	BES	BUB
AGS	ANI	AVO	BET	BUD
AHA	ANN	AWA	BEY	BUG
AHI	ANS	AWE	BEZ	BUM
AHS	ANT	AWK	BIB	BUN
AIA	ANY	AWL	BID	BUR
AID	APE	AWN	BIG	BUS
AIL	APO	AXE	BIN	BUT
AIM	APP	AYE	BIO	BUY
AIN	APT	AYS	BIS	BYE
AIR	ARB	AYU	BIT	BYS
AIS	ARC	AZO	BIZ	CAA
AIT	ARD	BAA	BOA	CAB

CAD	COX	DEP	DRY	EGO
CAF	COY	DEV	DSO	EHS
CAG	COZ	DEW	DUB	EIK
CAL	CRU	DEX	DUD	EKE
CAM	CRY	DEY	DUE	ELD
CAN	CUB	DIB	DUG	ELF
CAP	CUD	DID	DUH	ELK
CAR	CUE	DIE	DUI	ELL
CAT	CUM	DIF	DUM	ELM
CAW	CUP	DIG	DUN	ELS
CAY	CUR	DIM	DUO	ELT
CAZ	CUT	DIN	DUP	EME
CEE	CUZ	DIP	DUX	EMO
CEL	CWM	DIS	DYE	EMS
CEP	DAB	DIT	DZO	EMU
CHA	DAD	DIV	EAN	END
CHE	DAE	DOB	EAR	ENE
CHI	DAG	DOC	EAS	ENG
CID	DAH	DOD	EAT	ENS
CIG	DAK	DOE	EAU	EON
CIS	DAL	DOF	EBB	ERA
CIT	DAM	DOG	ECH	ERE
CLY	DAN	DOH	ECO	ERF
COB	DAP	DOL	ECU	ERG
COD	DAS	DOM	EDH	ERK
COG	DAW	DON	EDS	ERM
COL	DAY	DOO	EEK	ERN
CON	DEB	DOP	EEL	ERR
COO	DEE	DOR	EEN	ERS
COP	DEF	DOS	EEW	ESS
COR	DEG	DOT	EFF	EST
COS	DEI	DOW	EFS	ETA
COT	DEL	DOX	EFT	ETH
COW	DEN	DOY	EGG	EUK

EVE	FIB	GAE	GNU	HAO
EVO	FID	GAG	GOA	HAP
EWE	FIE	GAK	GOB	HAS
EWK	FIG	GAL	GOD	HAT
EWT	FIL	GAM	GOE	HAW
EXO	FIN	GAN	GON	HAY
EYE	FIR	GAP	GOO	HEH
FAA	FIT	GAR	GOR	HEM
FAB	FIX	GAS	GOS	HEN
FAD	FIZ	GAT	GOT	HEP
FAE	FLU	GAU	GOV	HER
FAG	FLY	GAW	GOX	HES
FAH	FOB	GAY	GOY	HET
FAN	FOE	GED	GRR	HEW
FAP	FOG	GEE	GUB	HEX
FAR	FOH	GEL	GUE	HEY
FAS	FON	GEM	GUL	HIC
FAT	FOO	GEN	GUM	HID
FAW	FOP	GEO	GUN	HIE
FAX	FOR	GER	GUP	HIM
FAY	FOU	GET	GUR	HIN
FED	FOX	GEY	GUS	HIP
FEE	FOY	GHI	GUT	HIS
FEG	FRA	GIB	GUV	HIT
FEH	FRO	GID	GUY	HMM
FEM	FRY	GIE	GYM	HOA
FEN	FUB	GIF	GYP	HOB
FER	FUD	GIG	HAD	HOC
FES	FUG	GIN	HAE	HOD
FET	FUM	GIO	HAG	HOE
FEU	FUN	GIP	HAH	HOG
FEW	FUR	GIS	HAJ	HOH
FEY	GAB	GIT	HAM	HOI
FEZ	GAD	GJU	HAN	HOM

HON	INS	JOT	KIS	LES
HOO	ION	JOW	KIT	LET
HOP	IOS	JOY	KOA	LEU
HOS	IRE	JUD	KOB	LEV
HOT	IRK	JUG	KOI	LEW
HOW	ISH	JUN	KON	LEX
HOX	ISM	JUS	KOP	LEY
HOY	ISO	JUT	KOR	LEZ
HUB	ITA	KAB	KOS	LIB
HUE	ITS	KAE	KOW	LID
HUG	IVY	KAF	KUE	LIE
HUH	IWI	KAI	KYE	LIG
HUI	JAB	KAK	KYU	LIN
HUM	JAG	KAM	LAB	LIP
HUN	JAI	KAS	LAC	LIS
HUP	JAK	KAT	LAD	LIT
HUT	JAM	KAW	LAG	LOB
HYE	JAP	KAY	LAH	LOD
HYP	JAR	KEA	LAM	LOG
ICE	JAW	KEB	LAP	LOO
ICH	JAY	KED	LAR	LOP
ICK	JEE	KEF	LAS	LOR
ICY	JET	KEG	LAT	LOS
IDE	JEU	KEN	LAV	LOT
IDS	JEW	KEP	LAW	LOU
IFF	JIB	KET	LAX	LOW
IFS	JIG	KEX	LAY	LOX
IGG	JIN	KEY	LEA	LOY
ILK	JIZ	KHI	LED	LUD
ILL	JOB	KID	LEE	LUG
IMP	JOE	KIF	LEG	LUM
ING	JOG	KIN	LEI	LUN
INK	JOL	KIP	LEK	LUR
INN	JOR	KIR	LEP	LUV

LUX	MID	MUT	NOD	ODD
LUZ	MIG	MUX	NOG	ODE
LYE	MIL	MYC	NOH	ODS
LYM	MIM	NAB	NOM	OES
MAA	MIR	NAE	NON	OFF
MAC	MIS	NAG	NOO	OFT
MAD	MIX	NAH	NOR	OHM
MAE	MIZ	NAM	NOS	OHO
MAG	MMM	NAN	NOT	OHS
MAK	MNA	NAP	NOW	OIK
MAL	MOA	NAS	NOX	OIL
MAM	MOB	NAT	NOY	OIS
MAN	MOC	NAV	NTH	OKA
MAP	MOD	NAW	NUB	OKE
MAR	MOE	NAY	NUG	OLD
MAS	MOG	NEB	NUN	OLE
MAT	MOI	NED	NUR	OLM
MAW	MOL	NEE	NUS	OMA
MAX	MOM	NEF	NUT	OMS
MAY	MON	NEG	NYE	ONE
MED	MOO	NEK	NYM	ONO
MEE	MOP	NEP	NYS	ONS
MEG	MOR	NET	OAF	ONY
MEH	MOS	NEW	OAK	OOF
MEL	MOT	NIB	OAR	OOH
MEM	MOU	NID	OAT	OOM
MEN	MOW	NIE	OBA	OON
MES	MOY	NIL	OBE	OOP
MET	MOZ	NIM	OBI	OOR
MEU	MUD	NIP	OBO	OOS
MEW	MUG	NIS	OBS	OOT
MHO	MUM	NIT	OCA	OPA
MIB	MUN	NIX	OCH	OPE
MIC	MUS	NOB	ODA	OPS

OPT	PAR	PLU	PYX	REW
ORA	PAS	PLY	QAT	REX
ORB	PAT	POA	QIN	REZ
ORC	PAV	POD	QIS	RHO
ORD	PAW	POH	QUA	RHY
ORE	PAX	POI	RAD	RIA
ORF	PAY	POL	RAG	RIB
ORG	PEA	POM	RAH	RID
ORS	PEC	POO	RAI	RIF
ORT	PED	POP	RAJ	RIG
OSE	PEE	POS	RAM	RIM
OUD	PEG	POT	RAN	RIN
OUK	PEH	POW	RAP	RIP
OUP	PEL	POX	RAS	RIT
OUR	PEN	POZ	RAT	RIZ
OUS	PEP	PRE	RAV	ROB
OUT	PER	PRO	RAW	ROC
OVA	PES	PRY	RAX	ROD
OWE	PET	PSI	RAY	ROE
OWL	PEW	PST	REB	ROK
OWN	PHI	PUB	REC	ROM
OWT	PHO	PUD	RED	ROO
OXO	PHT	PUG	REE	ROT
OXY	PIA	PUH	REF	ROW
OYE	PIC	PUL	REG	RUB
OYS	PIE	PUN	REH	RUC
PAC	PIG	PUP	REI	RUD
PAD	PIN	PUR	REM	RUE
PAH	PIP	PUS	REN	RUG
PAK	PIR	PUT	REO	RUM
PAL	PIS	PUY	REP	RUN
PAM	PIT	PWN	RES	RUT
PAN	PIU	PYA	RET	RYA
PAP	PIX	PYE	REV	RYE

RYU	SHA	SOU	TAO	TIT
SAB	SHE	SOV	TAP	TIX
SAC	SHH	SOW	TAR	TIZ
SAD	SHO	SOX	TAS	TOC
SAE	SHY	SOY	TAT	TOD
SAG	SIB	SOZ	TAU	TOE
SAI	SIC	SPA	TAV	TOG
SAL	SIF	SPY	TAW	TOM
SAM	SIG	SRI	TAX	TON
SAN	SIK	STY	TAY	TOO
SAP	SIM	SUB	TEA	TOP
SAR	SIN	SUD	TEC	TOR
SAT	SIP	SUE	TED	TOT
SAU	SIR	SUG	TEE	TOW
SAV	SIS	SUI	TEF	TOY
SAW	SIT	SUK	TEG	TRY
SAX	SIX	SUM	TEL	TSK
SAY	SKA	SUN	TEN	TUB
SAZ	SKI	SUP	TES	TUG
SEA	SKY	SUQ	TET	TUI
SEC	SLY	SUR	TEW	TUM
SED	SMA	SUS	TEX	TUN
SEE	SNY	SWY	THE	TUP
SEG	SOB	SYE	THO	TUT
SEI	SOC	SYN	THY	TUX
SEL	SOD	TAB	TIC	TWA
SEN	SOG	TAD	TID	TWO
SER	SOH	TAE	TIE	TWP
SET	SOL	TAG	TIG	TYE
SEV	SOM	TAI	TIK	TYG
SEW	SON	TAJ	TIL	UDO
SEX	SOP	TAK	TIN	UDS
SEY	SOS	TAM	TIP	UEY
SEZ	SOT	TAN	TIS	UFO

UGH	VAW	WAX	WYE	YOU
UGS	VAX	WAY	WYN	YOW
UKE	VEE	WAZ	XED	YUG
ULE	VEG	WEB	XIS	YUK
ULU	VET	WED	YAD	YUM
UME	VEX	WEE	YAE	YUP
UMM	VIA	WEM	YAG	YUS
UMP	VID	WEN	YAH	ZAG
UMS	VIE	WET	YAK	ZAP
UMU	VIG	WEX	YAM	ZAS
UNI	VIM	WEY	YAP	ZAX
UNS	VIN	WHA	YAR	ZEA
UPO	VIS	WHO	YAS	ZED
UPS	VLY	WHY	YAW	ZEE
URB	VOE	WIG	YAY	ZEK
URD	VOG	WIN	YEA	ZEL
URE	VOL	WIS	YEH	ZEN
URN	VOM	WIT	YEN	ZEP
URP	VOR	WIZ	YEP	ZEX
USE	VOW	WOE	YER	ZHO
UTA	VOX	WOF	YES	ZIG
UTE	VUG	WOG	YET	ZIN
UTS	VUM	WOK	YEW	ZIP
UTU	WAB	WON	YEX	ZIT
UVA	WAD	WOO	YEZ	ZIZ
VAC	WAE	WOP	YGO	ZOA
VAE	WAG	WOS	YID	ZOL
VAG	WAI	WOT	YIN	ZOO
VAN	WAN	WOW	YIP	ZOS
VAR	WAP	WOX	YOB	ZUZ
VAS	WAR	WRY	YOD	ZZZ
VAT	WAS	WUD	YOK	
VAU	WAT	WUS	YOM	
VAV	WAW	WUZ	YON	

two to nine letter words

AA	ABAND	ABATTISES	ABDOMINA	ABESSIVES
AAH	ABANDED	ABATTOIR	ABDOMINAL	ABET
AAHED	ABANDING	ABATTOIRS	ABDUCE	ABETMENT
AAHING	ABANDON	ABATTU	ABDUCED	ABETMENTS
AAHS	ABANDONED	ABATURE	ABDUCENS	ABETS
AAL	ABANDONEE	ABATURES	ABDUCENT	ABETTAL
AALII	ABANDONER	ABAXIAL	ABDUCES	ABETTALS
AALIIS	ABANDONS	ABAXILE	ABDUCING	ABETTED
AALS	ABANDS	ABAYA	ABDUCT	ABETTER
AARDVARK	ABAPICAL	ABAYAS	ABDUCTED	ABETTERS
AARDVARKS	ABAS	ABB	ABDUCTEE	ABETTING
AARDWOLF	ABASE	ABBA	ABDUCTEES	ABETTOR
AARGH	ABASED	ABBACIES	ABDUCTING	ABETTORS
AARRGH	ABASEDLY	ABBACY	ABDUCTION	ABEYANCE
AARRGHH	ABASEMENT	ABBAS	ABDUCTOR	ABEYANCES
AARTI	ABASER	ABBATIAL	ABDUCTORS	ABEYANCY
AARTIS	ABASERS	ABBE	ABDUCTS	ABEYANT
AAS	ABASES	ABBED	ABEAM	ABFARAD
AASVOGEL	ABASH	ABBES	ABEAR	ABFARADS
AASVOGELS	ABASHED	ABBESS	ABEARING	ABHENRIES
AB	ABASHEDLY	ABBESSES	ABEARS	ABHENRY
ABA	ABASHES	ABBEY	ABED	ABHENRYS
ABAC	ABASHING	ABBEYS	ABEGGING	ABHOR
ABACA	ABASHLESS	ABBOT	ABEIGH	ABHORRED
ABACAS	ABASHMENT	ABBOTCIES	ABELE	ABHORRENT
ABACI	ABASIA	ABBOTCY	ABELES	ABHORRER
ABACK	ABASIAS	ABBOTS	ABELIA	ABHORRERS
ABACS	ABASING	ABBOTSHIP	ABELIAN	ABHORRING
ABACTINAL	ABASK	ABBS	ABELIAS	ABHORS
ABACTOR	ABATABLE	ABCEE	ABELMOSK	ABID
ABACTORS	ABATE	ABCEES	ABELMOSKS	ABIDANCE
ABACUS	ABATED	ABCOULOMB	ABER	ABIDANCES
ABACUSES	ABATEMENT	ABDABS	ABERNETHY	ABIDDEN
ABAFT	ABATER	ABDICABLE	ABERRANCE	ABIDE
ABAKA	ABATERS	ABDICANT	ABERRANCY	ABIDED
ABAKAS	ABATES	ABDICANTS	ABERRANT	ABIDER
ABALONE	ABATING	ABDICATE	ABERRANTS	ABIDERS
ABALONES	ABATIS	ABDICATED	ABERRATE	ABIDES
ABAMP	ABATISES	ABDICATES	ABERRATED	ABIDING
ABAMPERE	ABATOR	ABDICATOR	ABERRATES	ABIDINGLY
ABAMPERES	ABATORS	ABDOMEN	ABERS	ABIDINGS
ABAMPS	ABATTIS	ABDOMENS	ABESSIVE	ABIES

ABIETES	ABLEISTS	ABOLITION	ABOUNDED	ABRIDGER
ABIETIC	ABLER	ABOLLA	ABOUNDING	ABRIDGERS
ABIGAIL	ABLES	ABOLLAE	ABOUNDS	ABRIDGES
ABIGAILS	ABLEST	ABOLLAS	ABOUT	ABRIDGING
ABILITIES	ABLET	ABOMA	ABOUTS	ABRIM
ABILITY	ABLETS	ABOMAS	ABOVE	ABRIN
ABIOGENIC	ABLING	ABOMASA	ABOVES	ABRINS
ABIOSES	ABLINGS	ABOMASAL	ABRACHIA	ABRIS
ABIOSIS	ABLINS	ABOMASI	ABRACHIAS	ABROACH
ABIOTIC	ABLOOM	ABOMASUM	ABRADABLE	ABROAD
ABITUR	ABLOW	ABOMASUS	ABRADANT	ABROADS
ABITURS	ABLUENT	ABOMINATE	ABRADANTS	ABROGABLE
ABJECT	ABLUENTS	ABONDANCE	ABRADE	ABROGATE
ABJECTED	ABLUSH	ABOON	ABRADED	ABROGATED
ABJECTING	ABLUTED	ABORAL	ABRADER	ABROGATES
ABJECTION	ABLUTION	ABORALLY	ABRADERS	ABROGATOR
ABJECTLY	ABLUTIONS	ABORD	ABRADES	ABROOKE
ABJECTS	ABLY	ABORDED	ABRADING	ABROOKED
ABJOINT	ABMHO	ABORDING	ABRAID	ABROOKES
ABJOINTED	ABMHOS	ABORDS	ABRAIDED	ABROOKING
ABJOINTS	ABNEGATE	ABORE	ABRAIDING	ABROSIA
ABJURE	ABNEGATED	ABORIGEN	ABRAIDS	ABROSIAS
ABJURED	ABNEGATES	ABORIGENS	ABRAM	ABRUPT
ABJURER	ABNEGATOR	ABORIGIN	ABRASAX	ABRUPTER
ABJURERS	ABNORMAL	ABORIGINE	ABRASAXES	ABRUPTEST
ABJURES	ABNORMALS	ABORIGINS	ABRASION	ABRUPTION
ABJURING	ABNORMITY	ABORNE	ABRASIONS	ABRUPTLY
ABLATE	ABNORMOUS	ABORNING	ABRASIVE	ABRUPTS
ABLATED	ABO	ABORT	ABRASIVES	ABS
ABLATES	ABOARD	ABORTED	ABRAXAS	ABSCESS
ABLATING	ABODE	ABORTEE	ABRAXASES	ABSCESSED
ABLATION	ABODED	ABORTEES	ABRAY	ABSCESSES
ABLATIONS	ABODEMENT	ABORTER	ABRAYED	ABSCIND
ABLATIVAL	ABODES	ABORTERS	ABRAYING	ABSCINDED
ABLATIVE	ABODING	ABORTING	ABRAYS	ABSCINDS
ABLATIVES	ABOHM	ABORTION	ABRAZO	ABSCISE
ABLATOR	ABOHMS	ABORTIONS	ABRAZOS	ABSCISED
ABLATORS	ABOIDEAU	ABORTIVE	ABREACT	ABSCISES
ABLAUT	ABOIDEAUS	ABORTS	ABREACTED	ABSCISIC
ABLAUTS	ABOIDEAUX	ABORTUARY	ABREACTS	ABSCISIN
ABLAZE	ABOIL	ABORTUS	ABREAST	ABSCISING
ABLE	ABOITEAU	ABORTUSES	ABREGE	ABSCISINS
ABLED	ABOITEAUS	ABOS	ABREGES	ABSCISS
ABLEGATE	ABOITEAUX	ABOUGHT	ABRI	ABSCISSA
ABLEGATES	ABOLISH	ABOULIA	ABRICOCK	ABSCISSAE
ABLEISM	ABOLISHED	ABOULIAS	ABRICOCKS	ABSCISSAS
ABLEISMS	ABOLISHER	ABOULIC	ABRIDGE	ABSCISSE
ABLEIST	ABOLISHES	ABOUND	ABRIDGED	ABSCISSES

ABSCISSIN	ABSORBING	ABUSIONS	ACAJOUS	ACAUDATE
ABSCOND	ABSORBS	ABUSIVE	ACALCULIA	ACAULINE
ABSCONDED	ABSTAIN	ABUSIVELY	ACALEPH	ACAULOSE
ABSCONDER	ABSTAINED	ABUT	ACALEPHAE	ACAULOUS
ABSCONDS	ABSTAINER	ABUTILON	ACALEPHAN	ACCA
ABSEIL	ABSTAINS	ABUTILONS	ACALEPHE	ACCABLE
ABSEILED	ABSTERGE	ABUTMENT	ACALEPHES	ACCAS
ABSEILER	ABSTERGED	ABUTMENTS	ACALEPHS	ACCEDE
ABSEILERS	ABSTERGES	ABUTS	ACANTH	ACCEDED
ABSEILING	ABSTINENT	ABUTTAL	ACANTHA	ACCEDENCE
ABSEILS	ABSTRACT	ABUTTALS	ACANTHAE	ACCEDER
ABSENCE	ABSTRACTS	ABUTTED	ACANTHAS	ACCEDERS
ABSENCES	ABSTRICT	ABUTTER	ACANTHI	ACCEDES
ABSENT	ABSTRICTS	ABUTTERS	ACANTHIN	ACCEDING
ABSENTED	ABSTRUSE	ABUTTING	ACANTHINE	ACCEND
ABSENTEE	ABSTRUSER	ABUZZ	ACANTHINS	ACCENDED
ABSENTEES	ABSURD	ABVOLT	ACANTHOID	ACCENDING
ABSENTER	ABSURDER	ABVOLTS	ACANTHOUS	ACCENDS
ABSENTERS	ABSURDEST	ABWATT	ACANTHS	ACCENSION
ABSENTING	ABSURDISM	ABWATTS	ACANTHUS	ACCENT
ABSENTLY	ABSURDIST	ABY	ACAPNIA	ACCENTED
ABSENTS	ABSURDITY	ABYE	ACAPNIAS	ACCENTING
ABSEY	ABSURDLY	ABYEING	ACARBOSE	ACCENTOR
ABSEYS	ABSURDS	ABYES	ACARBOSES	ACCENTORS
ABSINTH	ABTHANE	ABYING	ACARI	ACCENTS
ABSINTHE	ABTHANES	ABYS	ACARIAN	ACCENTUAL
ABSINTHES	ABUBBLE	ABYSM	ACARIASES	ACCEPT
ABSINTHS	ABUILDING	ABYSMAL	ACARIASIS	ACCEPTANT
ABSIT	ABULIA	ABYSMALLY	ACARICIDE	ACCEPTED
ABSITS	ABULIAS	ABYSMS	ACARID	ACCEPTEE
ABSOLUTE	ABULIC	ABYSS	ACARIDAN	ACCEPTEES
ABSOLUTER	ABUNA	ABYSSAL	ACARIDANS	ACCEPTER
ABSOLUTES	ABUNAS	ABYSSES	ACARIDEAN	ACCEPTERS
ABSOLVE	ABUNDANCE	ACACIA	ACARIDIAN	ACCEPTING
ABSOLVED	ABUNDANCY	ACACIAS	ACARIDS	ACCEPTIVE
ABSOLVENT	ABUNDANT	ACADEME	ACARINE	ACCEPTOR
ABSOLVER	ABUNE	ACADEMES	ACARINES	ACCEPTORS
ABSOLVERS	ABURST	ACADEMIA	ACAROID	ACCEPTS
ABSOLVES	ABUSABLE	ACADEMIAS	ACAROLOGY	ACCESS
ABSOLVING	ABUSAGE	ACADEMIC	ACARPOUS	ACCESSARY
ABSONANT	ABUSAGES	ACADEMICS	ACARUS	ACCESSED
ABSORB	ABUSE	ACADEMIES	ACATER	ACCESSES
ABSORBANT	ABUSED	ACADEMISM	ACATERS	ACCESSING
ABSORBATE	ABUSER	ACADEMIST	ACATES	ACCESSION
ABSORBED	ABUSERS	ACADEMY	ACATHISIA	ACCESSORY
ABSORBENT	ABUSES	ACAI	ACATOUR	ACCIDENCE
ABSORBER	ABUSING	ACAIS	ACATOURS	ACCIDENT
ABSORBERS	ABUSION	ACAJOU	ACAUDAL	ACCIDENTS

A

ACCIDIA	ACCOST	ACCURST	ACESCENCY	ACHENE
ACCIDIAS	ACCOSTED	ACCUSABLE	ACESCENT	ACHENES
ACCIDIE	ACCOSTING	ACCUSABLY	ACESCENTS	ACHENIA
ACCIDIES	ACCOSTS	ACCUSAL	ACETA	ACHENIAL
ACCINGE	ACCOUNT	ACCUSALS	ACETABULA	ACHENIUM
ACCINGED	ACCOUNTED	ACCUSANT	ACETAL	ACHENIUMS
ACCINGES	ACCOUNTS	ACCUSANTS	ACETALS	ACHES
ACCINGING	ACCOURAGE	ACCUSE	ACETAMID	ACHIER
ACCIPITER	ACCOURT	ACCUSED	ACETAMIDE	ACHIEST
ACCITE	ACCOURTED	ACCUSER	ACETAMIDS	ACHIEVE
ACCITED	ACCOURTS	ACCUSERS	ACETATE	ACHIEVED
ACCITES	ACCOUTER	ACCUSES	ACETATED	ACHIEVER
ACCITING	ACCOUTERS	ACCUSING	ACETATES	ACHIEVERS
ACCLAIM	ACCOUTRE	ACCUSTOM	ACETIC	ACHIEVES
ACCLAIMED	ACCOUTRED	ACCUSTOMS	ACETIFIED	ACHIEVING
ACCLAIMER	ACCOUTRES	ACE	ACETIFIER	ACHILLEA
ACCLAIMS	ACCOY	ACED	ACETIFIES	ACHILLEAS
ACCLIMATE	ACCOYED	ACEDIA	ACETIFY	ACHIMENES
ACCLIVITY	ACCOYING	ACEDIAS	ACETIN	ACHINESS
ACCLIVOUS	ACCOYLD	ACELDAMA	ACETINS	ACHING
ACCLOY	ACCOYS	ACELDAMAS	ACETONE	ACHINGLY
ACCLOYED	ACCREDIT	ACELLULAR	ACETONES	ACHINGS
ACCLOYING	ACCREDITS	ACENTRIC	ACETONIC	ACHIOTE
ACCLOYS	ACCRETE	ACENTRICS	ACETOSE	ACHIOTES
ACCOAST	ACCRETED	ACEPHALIC	ACETOUS	ACHIRAL
ACCOASTED	ACCRETES	ACEQUIA	ACETOXYL	ACHKAN
ACCOASTS	ACCRETING	ACEQUIAS	ACETOXYLS	ACHKANS
ACCOIED	ACCRETION	ACER	ACETUM	ACHOLIA
ACCOIL	ACCRETIVE	ACERATE	ACETYL	ACHOLIAS
ACCOILS	ACCREW	ACERATED	ACETYLATE	ACHOO
ACCOLADE	ACCREWED	ACERB	ACETYLENE	ACHOOS
ACCOLADED	ACCREWING	ACERBATE	ACETYLIC	ACHROMAT
ACCOLADES	ACCREWS	ACERBATED	ACETYLIDE	ACHROMATS
ACCOMPANY	ACCROIDES	ACERBATES	ACETYLS	ACHROMIC
ACCOMPT	ACCRUABLE	ACERBER	ACH	ACHROMOUS
ACCOMPTED	ACCRUAL	ACERBEST	ACHAENIA	ACHY
ACCOMPTS	ACCRUALS	ACERBIC	ACHAENIUM	ACICLOVIR
ACCORAGE	ACCRUE	ACERBITY	ACHAGE	ACICULA
ACCORAGED	ACCRUED	ACEROLA	ACHAGES	ACICULAE
ACCORAGES	ACCRUES	ACEROLAS	ACHALASIA	ACICULAR
ACCORD	ACCRUING	ACEROSE	ACHAR	ACICULAS
ACCORDANT	ACCUMBENT	ACEROUS	ACHARNE	ACICULATE
ACCORDED	ACCURACY	ACERS	ACHARS	ACICULUM
ACCORDER	ACCURATE	ACERVATE	ACHARYA	ACICULUMS
ACCORDERS	ACCURSE	ACERVULI	ACHARYAS	ACID
ACCORDING	ACCURSED	ACERVULUS	ACHATES	ACIDEMIA
ACCORDION	ACCURSES	ACES	ACHE	ACIDEMIAS
ACCORDS	ACCURSING	ACESCENCE	ACHED	ACIDER

ACIDEST	ACKNOWS	ACQUIGHTS	ACROBATIC	ACTA
ACIDHEAD	ACLINIC	ACQUIRAL	ACROBATS	ACTABLE
ACIDHEADS	ACMATIC	ACQUIRALS	ACRODONT	ACTANT
ACIDIC	ACME	ACQUIRE	ACRODONTS	ACTANTS
ACIDIER	ACMES	ACQUIRED	ACRODROME	ACTED
ACIDIEST	ACMIC	ACQUIREE	ACROGEN	ACTIN
ACIDIFIED	ACMITE	ACQUIREES	ACROGENIC	ACTINAL
ACIDIFIER	ACMITES	ACQUIRER	ACROGENS	ACTINALLY
ACIDIFIES	ACNE	ACQUIRERS	ACROLECT	ACTING
ACIDIFY	ACNED	ACQUIRES	ACROLECTS	ACTINGS
ACIDITIES	ACNES	ACQUIRING	ACROLEIN	ACTINIA
ACIDITY	ACNODAL	ACQUIS	ACROLEINS	ACTINIAE
ACIDLY	ACNODE	ACQUIST	ACROLITH	ACTINIAN
ACIDNESS	ACNODES	ACQUISTS	ACROLITHS	ACTINIANS
ACIDOPHIL	ACOCK	ACQUIT	ACROMIA	ACTINIAS
ACIDOSES	ACOELOUS	ACQUITE	ACROMIAL	ACTINIC
ACIDOSIS	ACOEMETI	ACQUITES	ACROMION	ACTINIDE
ACIDOTIC	ACOLD	ACQUITING	ACRONIC	ACTINIDES
ACIDS	ACOLUTHIC	ACQUITS	ACRONICAL	ACTINISM
ACIDULATE	ACOLYTE	ACQUITTAL	ACRONYCAL	ACTINISMS
ACIDULENT	ACOLYTES	ACQUITTED	ACRONYM	ACTINIUM
ACIDULOUS	ACOLYTH	ACQUITTER	ACRONYMIC	ACTINIUMS
ACIDURIA	ACOLYTHS	ACRASIA	ACRONYMS	ACTINOID
ACIDURIAS	ACONITE	ACRASIAS	ACROPETAL	ACTINOIDS
ACIDY	ACONITES	ACRASIN	ACROPHOBE	ACTINON
ACIERAGE	ACONITIC	ACRASINS	ACROPHONY	ACTINONS
ACIERAGES	ACONITINE	ACRATIC	ACROPOLIS	ACTINOPOD
ACIERATE	ACONITUM	ACRAWL	ACROS	ACTINS
ACIERATED	ACONITUMS	ACRE	ACROSOMAL	ACTION
ACIERATES	ACORN	ACREAGE	ACROSOME	ACTIONED
ACIFORM	ACORNED	ACREAGES	ACROSOMES	ACTIONER
ACINAR	ACORNS	ACRED	ACROSPIRE	ACTIONERS
ACING	ACOSMISM	ACRES	ACROSS	ACTIONING
ACINI	ACOSMISMS	ACRID	ACROSTIC	ACTIONIST
ACINIC	ACOSMIST	ACRIDER	ACROSTICS	ACTIONS
ACINIFORM	ACOSMISTS	ACRIDEST	ACROTER	ACTIVATE
ACINOSE	ACOUCHI	ACRIDIN	ACROTERIA	ACTIVATED
ACINOUS	ACOUCHIES	ACRIDINE	ACROTERS	ACTIVATES
ACINUS	ACOUCHIS	ACRIDINES	ACROTIC	ACTIVATOR
ACKEE	ACOUCHY	ACRIDINS	ACROTISM	ACTIVE
ACKEES	ACOUSTIC	ACRIDITY	ACROTISMS	ACTIVELY
ACKER	ACOUSTICS	ACRIDLY	ACRYLATE	ACTIVES
ACKERS	ACQUAINT	ACRIDNESS	ACRYLATES	ACTIVISE
ACKNEW	ACQUAINTS	ACRIMONY	ACRYLIC	ACTIVISED
ACKNOW	ACQUEST	ACRITARCH	ACRYLICS	ACTIVISES
ACKNOWING	ACQUESTS	ACRITICAL	ACRYLYL	ACTIVISM
ACKNOWN	ACQUIESCE	ACRO	ACRYLYLS	ACTIVISMS
ACKNOWNE	ACQUIGHT	ACROBAT	ACT	ACTIVIST

ACTIVISTS	ACUMENS	ADAPTIVE	ADDITIVES	ADENOIDAL
ACTIVITY	ACUMINATE	ADAPTOGEN	ADDITORY	ADENOIDS
ACTIVIZE	ACUMINOUS	ADAPTOR	ADDLE	ADENOMA
ACTIVIZED	ACUPOINT	ADAPTORS	ADDLED	ADENOMAS
ACTIVIZES	ACUPOINTS	ADAPTS	ADDLEMENT	ADENOMATA
ACTON	ACUSHLA	ADAW	ADDLES	ADENOSES
ACTONS	ACUSHLAS	ADAWED	ADDLING	ADENOSINE
ACTOR	ACUTANCE	ADAWING	ADDOOM	ADENOSIS
ACTORISH	ACUTANCES	ADAWS	ADDOOMED	ADENYL
ACTORLIER	ACUTE	ADAXIAL	ADDOOMING	ADENYLATE
ACTORLY	ACUTELY	ADAYS	ADDOOMS	ADENYLIC
ACTORS	ACUTENESS	ADBOT	ADDORSED	ADENYLS
ACTRESS	ACUTER	ADBOTS	ADDRESS	ADEPT
ACTRESSES	ACUTES	ADD	ADDRESSED	ADEPTER
ACTRESSY	ACUTEST	ADDABLE	ADDRESSEE	ADEPTEST
ACTS	ACYCLIC	ADDAX	ADDRESSER	ADEPTLY
ACTUAL	ACYCLOVIR	ADDAXES	ADDRESSES	ADEPTNESS
ACTUALISE	ACYL	ADDEBTED	ADDRESSOR	ADEPTS
ACTUALIST	ACYLATE	ADDED	ADDREST	ADEQUACY
ACTUALITE	ACYLATED	ADDEDLY	ADDS	ADEQUATE
ACTUALITY	ACYLATES	ADDEEM	ADDUCE	ADERMIN
ACTUALIZE	ACYLATING	ADDEEMED	ADDUCED	ADERMINS
ACTUALLY	ACYLATION	ADDEEMING	ADDUCENT	ADESPOTA
ACTUALS	ACYLOIN	ADDEEMS	ADDUCER	ADESSIVE
ACTUARIAL	ACYLOINS	ADDEND	ADDUCERS	ADESSIVES
ACTUARIES	ACYLS	ADDENDA	ADDUCES	ADHAN
ACTUARY	AD	ADDENDS	ADDUCIBLE	ADHANS
ACTUATE	ADAGE	ADDENDUM	ADDUCING	ADHARMA
ACTUATED	ADAGES	ADDENDUMS	ADDUCT	ADHARMAS
ACTUATES	ADAGIAL	ADDER	ADDUCTED	ADHERABLE
ACTUATING	ADAGIO	ADDERBEAD	ADDUCTING	ADHERE
ACTUATION	ADAGIOS	ADDERS	ADDUCTION	ADHERED
ACTUATOR	ADAMANCE	ADDERWORT	ADDUCTIVE	ADHERENCE
ACTUATORS	ADAMANCES	ADDIBLE	ADDUCTOR	ADHEREND
ACTURE	ADAMANCY	ADDICT	ADDUCTORS	ADHERENDS
ACTURES	ADAMANT	ADDICTED	ADDUCTS	ADHERENT
ACUATE	ADAMANTLY	ADDICTING	ADDY	ADHERENTS
ACUATED	ADAMANTS	ADDICTION	ADEEM	ADHERER
ACUATES	ADAMSITE	ADDICTIVE	ADEEMED	ADHERERS
ACUATING	ADAMSITES	ADDICTS	ADEEMING	ADHERES
ACUITIES	ADAPT	ADDIES	ADEEMS	ADHERING
ACUITY	ADAPTABLE	ADDING	ADELGID	ADHESION
ACULEATE	ADAPTED	ADDINGS	ADELGIDS	ADHESIONS
ACULEATED	ADAPTER	ADDIO	ADEMPTION	ADHESIVE
ACULEATES	ADAPTERS	ADDIOS	ADENINE	ADHESIVES
ACULEI	ADAPTING	ADDITION	ADENINES	ADHIBIT
ACULEUS	ADAPTION	ADDITIONS	ADENITIS	ADHIBITED
ACUMEN	ADAPTIONS	ADDITIVE	ADENOID	ADHIBITS

ADHOCRACY	ADJURING	ADMITTEES	ADOPTIVE	ADSORBATE
ADIABATIC	ADJUROR	ADMITTER	ADOPTS	ADSORBED
ADIAPHORA	ADJURORS	ADMITTERS	ADORABLE	ADSORBENT
ADIEU	ADJUST	ADMITTING	ADORABLY	ADSORBER
ADIEUS	ADJUSTED	ADMIX	ADORATION	ADSORBERS
ADIEUX	ADJUSTER	ADMIXED	ADORE	ADSORBING
ADIOS	ADJUSTERS	ADMIXES	ADORED	ADSORBS
ADIOSES	ADJUSTING	ADMIXING	ADORER	ADSPEAK
ADIPIC	ADJUSTIVE	ADMIXT	ADORERS	ADSPEAKS
ADIPOCERE	ADJUSTOR	ADMIXTURE	ADORES	ADSUKI
ADIPOCYTE	ADJUSTORS	ADMONISH	ADORING	ADSUKIS
ADIPOSE	ADJUSTS	ADMONITOR	ADORINGLY	ADSUM
ADIPOSES	ADJUTAGE	ADNASCENT	ADORKABLE	ADUKI
ADIPOSIS	ADJUTAGES	ADNATE	ADORN	ADUKIS
ADIPOSITY	ADJUTANCY	ADNATION	ADORNED	ADULARIA
ADIPOUS	ADJUTANT	ADNATIONS	ADORNER	ADULARIAS
ADIPSIA	ADJUTANTS	ADNEXA	ADORNERS	ADULATE
ADIPSIAS	ADJUVANCY	ADNEXAL	ADORNING	ADULATED
ADIT	ADJUVANT	ADNOMINAL	ADORNMENT	ADULATES
ADITS	ADJUVANTS	ADNOUN	ADORNS	ADULATING
ADJACENCE	ADLAND	ADNOUNS	ADOS	ADULATION
ADJACENCY	ADLANDS	ADO	ADOWN	ADULATOR
ADJACENT	ADMAN	ADOBE	ADOZE	ADULATORS
ADJACENTS	ADMASS	ADOBELIKE	ADPRESS	ADULATORY
ADJECTIVE	ADMASSES	ADOBES	ADPRESSED	ADULT
ADJIGO	ADMEASURE	ADOBO	ADPRESSES	ADULTERER
ADJIGOS	ADMEN	ADOBOS	ADRAD	ADULTERY
ADJOIN	ADMIN	ADONIS	ADRATE	ADULTHOOD
ADJOINED	ADMINICLE	ADONISE	ADRATES	ADULTLIKE
ADJOINING	ADMINS	ADONISED	ADREAD	ADULTLY
ADJOINS	ADMIRABLE	ADONISES	ADREADED	ADULTNESS
ADJOINT	ADMIRABLY	ADONISING	ADREADING	ADULTRESS
ADJOINTS	ADMIRAL	ADONIZE	ADREADS	ADULTS
ADJOURN	ADMIRALS	ADONIZED	ADRED	ADUMBRAL
ADJOURNED	ADMIRALTY	ADONIZES	ADRENAL	ADUMBRATE
ADJOURNS	ADMIRANCE	ADONIZING	ADRENALIN	ADUNC
ADJUDGE	ADMIRE	ADOORS	ADRENALLY	ADUNCATE
ADJUDGED	ADMIRED	ADOPT	ADRENALS	ADUNCATED
ADJUDGES	ADMIRER	ADOPTABLE	ADRIFT	ADUNCITY
ADJUDGING	ADMIRERS	ADOPTED	ADROIT	ADUNCOUS
ADJUNCT	ADMIRES	ADOPTEE	ADROITER	ADUST
ADJUNCTLY	ADMIRING	ADOPTEES	ADROITEST	ADUSTED
ADJUNCTS	ADMISSION	ADOPTER	ADROITLY	ADUSTING
ADJURE	ADMISSIVE	ADOPTERS	ADRY	ADUSTS
ADJURED	ADMIT	ADOPTING	ADS	ADVANCE
ADJURER	ADMITS	ADOPTION	ADSCRIPT	ADVANCED
ADJURERS	ADMITTED	ADOPTIONS	ADSCRIPTS	ADVANCER
ADJURES	ADMITTEE	ADOPTIOUS	ADSORB	ADVANCERS

ADVANCES	ADVISERS	AEDICULES	AERIE	AEROLOGIC
ADVANCING	ADVISES	AEDILE	AERIED	AEROLOGY
ADVANTAGE	ADVISING	AEDILES	AERIER	AEROMANCY
ADVECT	ADVISINGS	AEDINE	AERIES	AEROMETER
ADVECTED	ADVISOR	AEFALD	AERIEST	AEROMETRY
ADVECTING	ADVISORS	AEFAULD	AERIFIED	AEROMOTOR
ADVECTION	ADVISORY	AEGIRINE	AERIFIES	AERONAUT
ADVECTIVE	ADVOCAAT	AEGIRINES	AERIFORM	AERONAUTS
ADVECTS	ADVOCAATS	AEGIRITE	AERIFY	AERONOMER
ADVENE	ADVOCACY	AEGIRITES	AERIFYING	AERONOMIC
ADVENED	ADVOCATE	AEGIS	AERILY	AERONOMY
ADVENES	ADVOCATED	AEGISES	AERO	AEROPAUSE
ADVENING	ADVOCATES	AEGLOGUE	AEROBAT	AEROPHAGY
ADVENT	ADVOCATOR	AEGLOGUES	AEROBATIC	AEROPHOBE
ADVENTIVE	ADVOUTRER	AEGROTAT	AEROBATS	AEROPHONE
ADVENTS	ADVOUTRY	AEGROTATS	AEROBE	AEROPHORE
ADVENTURE	ADVOWSON	AEMULE	AEROBES	AEROPHYTE
ADVERB	ADVOWSONS	AEMULED	AEROBIA	AEROPLANE
ADVERBIAL	ADWARD	AEMULES	AEROBIC	AEROPULSE
ADVERBS	ADWARDED	AEMULING	AEROBICS	AEROS
ADVERSARY	ADWARDING	AENEOUS	AEROBIONT	AEROSAT
ADVERSE	ADWARDS	AENEUS	AEROBIUM	AEROSATS
ADVERSELY	ADWARE	AENEUSES	AEROBOMB	AEROSCOPE
ADVERSER	ADWARES	AEOLIAN	AEROBOMBS	AEROSHELL
ADVERSEST	ADWOMAN	AEOLIPILE	AEROBOT	AEROSOL
ADVERSITY	ADWOMEN	AEOLIPYLE	AEROBOTS	AEROSOLS
ADVERT	ADYNAMIA	AEON	AEROBRAKE	AEROSPACE
ADVERTED	ADYNAMIAS	AEONIAN	AEROBUS	AEROSPIKE
ADVERTENT	ADYNAMIC	AEONIC	AEROBUSES	AEROSTAT
ADVERTING	ADYTA	AEONS	AERODART	AEROSTATS
ADVERTISE	ADYTUM	AEPYORNIS	AERODARTS	AEROTAXES
ADVERTIZE	ADZ	AEQUORIN	AERODROME	AEROTAXIS
ADVERTS	ADZE	AEQUORINS	AERODUCT	AEROTONE
ADVEW	ADZED	AERADIO	AERODUCTS	AEROTONES
ADVEWED	ADZELIKE	AERADIOS	AERODYNE	AEROTRAIN
ADVEWING	ADZES	AERATE	AERODYNES	AERUGO
ADVEWS	ADZING	AERATED	AEROFOIL	AERUGOS
ADVICE	ADZUKI	AERATES	AEROFOILS	AERY
ADVICEFUL	ADZUKIS	AERATING	AEROGEL	AESC
ADVICES	AE	AERATION	AEROGELS	AESCES
ADVISABLE	AECIA	AERATIONS	AEROGRAM	AESCULIN
ADVISABLY	AECIAL	AERATOR	AEROGRAMS	AESCULINS
ADVISE	AECIDIA	AERATORS	AEROGRAPH	AESIR
ADVISED	AECIDIAL	AERIAL	AEROLITE	AESTHESES
ADVISEDLY	AECIDIUM	AERIALIST	AEROLITES	AESTHESIA
ADVISEE	AECIUM	AERIALITY	AEROLITH	AESTHESIS
ADVISEES	AEDES	AERIALLY	AEROLITHS	AESTHETE
ADVISER	AEDICULE	AERIALS	AEROLITIC	AESTHETES

AESTHETIC	AFFERENTS	AFFLUX	AFIRE	AFTERTAX
AESTIVAL	AFFIANCE	AFFLUXES	AFLAJ	AFTERTIME
AESTIVATE	AFFIANCED	AFFLUXION	AFLAME	AFTERWARD
AETATIS	AFFIANCES	AFFOGATO	AFLATOXIN	AFTERWORD
AETHER	AFFIANT	AFFOGATOS	AFLOAT	AFTMOST
AETHEREAL	AFFIANTS	AFFOORD	AFLUTTER	AFTOSA
AETHERIC	AFFICHE	AFFOORDED	AFOCAL	AFTOSAS
AETHERS	AFFICHES	AFFOORDS	AFOOT	AG
AETIOLOGY	AFFIDAVIT	AFFORCE	AFORE	AGA
AFALD	AFFIED	AFFORCED	AFOREHAND	AGACANT
AFAR	AFFIES	AFFORCES	AFORESAID	AGACANTE
AFARA	AFFILIATE	AFFORCING	AFORETIME	AGACERIE
AFARAS	AFFINAL	AFFORD	AFOUL	AGACERIES
AFARS	AFFINE	AFFORDED	AFRAID	AGAIN
AFAWLD	AFFINED	AFFORDING	AFREET	AGAINST
AFEAR	AFFINELY	AFFORDS	AFREETS	AGALACTIA
AFEARD	AFFINES	AFFOREST	AFRESH	AGALLOCH
AFEARED	AFFINITY	AFFORESTS	AFRIT	AGALLOCHS
AFEARING	AFFIRM	AFFRAP	AFRITS	AGALWOOD
AFEARS	AFFIRMANT	AFFRAPPED	AFRO	AGALWOODS
AFEBRILE	AFFIRMED	AFFRAPS	AFRONT	AGAMA
AFF	AFFIRMER	AFFRAY	AFROS	AGAMAS
AFFABLE	AFFIRMERS	AFFRAYED	AFT	AGAMETE
AFFABLY	AFFIRMING	AFFRAYER	AFTER	AGAMETES
AFFAIR	AFFIRMS	AFFRAYERS	AFTERBODY	AGAMI
AFFAIRE	AFFIX	AFFRAYING	AFTERBURN	AGAMIC
AFFAIRES	AFFIXABLE	AFFRAYS	AFTERCARE	AGAMID
AFFAIRS	AFFIXAL	AFFRENDED	AFTERCLAP	AGAMIDS
AFFEAR	AFFIXED	AFFRET	AFTERDAMP	AGAMIS
AFFEARD	AFFIXER	AFFRETS	AFTERDECK	AGAMOGONY
AFFEARE	AFFIXERS	AFFRICATE	AFTEREYE	AGAMOID
AFFEARED	AFFIXES	AFFRIGHT	AFTEREYED	AGAMOIDS
AFFEARES	AFFIXIAL	AFFRIGHTS	AFTEREYES	AGAMONT
AFFEARING	AFFIXING	AFFRONT	AFTERGAME	AGAMONTS
AFFEARS	AFFIXMENT	AFFRONTE	AFTERGLOW	AGAMOUS
AFFECT	AFFIXTURE	AFFRONTED	AFTERHEAT	AGAPAE
AFFECTED	AFFLATED	AFFRONTEE	AFTERINGS	AGAPAI
AFFECTER	AFFLATION	AFFRONTS	AFTERLIFE	AGAPE
AFFECTERS	AFFLATUS	AFFUSION	AFTERMAST	AGAPEIC
AFFECTING	AFFLICT	AFFUSIONS	AFTERMATH	AGAPES
AFFECTION	AFFLICTED	AFFY	AFTERMOST	AGAR
AFFECTIVE	AFFLICTER	AFFYDE	AFTERNOON	AGARIC
AFFECTS	AFFLICTS	AFFYING	AFTERPAIN	AGARICS
AFFEER	AFFLUENCE	AFGHAN	AFTERPEAK	AGAROSE
AFFEERED	AFFLUENCY	AFGHANI	AFTERS	AGAROSES
AFFEERING	AFFLUENT	AFGHANIS	AFTERSHOW	AGARS
AFFEERS	AFFLUENTS	AFGHANS	AFTERSUN	AGARWOOD
AFFERENT	AFFLUENZA	AFIELD	AFTERSUNS	AGARWOODS

AGAS	AGENE	AGGRACING	AGISTERS	AGNAIL
AGAST	AGENES	AGGRADE	AGISTING	AGNAILS
AGASTED	AGENESES	AGGRADED	AGISTMENT	AGNAME
AGASTING	AGENESIA	AGGRADES	AGISTOR	AGNAMED
AGASTS	AGENESIAS	AGGRADING	AGISTORS	AGNAMES
AGATE	AGENESIS	AGGRATE	AGISTS	AGNATE
AGATES	AGENETIC	AGGRATED	AGITA	AGNATES
AGATEWARE	AGENISE	AGGRATES	AGITABLE	AGNATHAN
AGATISE	AGENISED	AGGRATING	AGITANS	AGNATHANS
AGATISED	AGENISES	AGGRAVATE	AGITAS	AGNATHOUS
AGATISES	AGENISING	AGGREGATE	AGITATE	AGNATIC
AGATISING	AGENIZE	AGGRESS	AGITATED	AGNATICAL
AGATIZE	AGENIZED	AGGRESSED	AGITATES	AGNATION
AGATIZED	AGENIZES	AGGRESSES	AGITATING	AGNATIONS
AGATIZES	AGENIZING	AGGRESSOR	AGITATION	AGNISE
AGATIZING	AGENT	AGGRI	AGITATIVE	AGNISED
AGATOID	AGENTED	AGGRIEVE	AGITATO	AGNISES
AGAVE	AGENTIAL	AGGRIEVED	AGITATOR	AGNISING
AGAVES	AGENTING	AGGRIEVES	AGITATORS	AGNIZE
AGAZE	AGENTINGS	AGGRO	AGITPOP	AGNIZED
AGAZED	AGENTIVAL	AGGROS	AGITPOPS	AGNIZES
AGE	AGENTIVE	AGGRY	AGITPROP	AGNIZING
AGED	AGENTIVES	AGHA	AGITPROPS	AGNOLOTTI
AGEDLY	AGENTRIES	AGHAS	AGLARE	AGNOMEN
AGEDNESS	AGENTRY	AGHAST	AGLEAM	AGNOMENS
AGEE	AGENTS	AGILA	AGLEE	AGNOMINA
AGEING	AGER	AGILAS	AGLET	AGNOMINAL
AGEINGS	AGERATUM	AGILE	AGLETS	AGNOSIA
AGEISM	AGERATUMS	AGILELY	AGLEY	AGNOSIAS
AGEISMS	AGERS	AGILENESS	AGLIMMER	AGNOSIC
AGEIST	AGES	AGILER	AGLITTER	AGNOSTIC
AGEISTS	AGEUSIA	AGILEST	AGLOO	AGNOSTICS
AGELAST	AGEUSIAS	AGILITIES	AGLOOS	AGO
AGELASTIC	AGFLATION	AGILITY	AGLOSSAL	AGOG
AGELASTS	AGGADA	AGIN	AGLOSSATE	AGOGE
AGELESS	AGGADAH	AGING	AGLOSSIA	AGOGES
AGELESSLY	AGGADAHS	AGINGS	AGLOSSIAS	AGOGIC
AGELONG	AGGADAS	AGINNER	AGLOW	AGOGICS
AGEMATE	AGGADIC	AGINNERS	AGLU	AGOING
AGEMATES	AGGADOT	AGIO	AGLUS	AGON
AGEN	AGGADOTH	AGIOS	AGLY	AGONAL
AGENCIES	AGGER	AGIOTAGE	AGLYCON	AGONE
AGENCY	AGGERS	AGIOTAGES	AGLYCONE	AGONES
AGENDA	AGGIE	AGISM	AGLYCONES	AGONIC
AGENDAS	AGGIES	AGISMS	AGLYCONS	AGONIES
AGENDER	AGGRACE	AGIST	AGMA	AGONISE
AGENDUM	AGGRACED	AGISTED	AGMAS	AGONISED
AGENDUMS	AGGRACES	AGISTER	AGMINATE	AGONISES

AGONISING	AGREMENT	AGUISING	AIDA	AILS
AGONISM	AGREMENTS	AGUIZE	AIDANCE	AIM
AGONISMS	AGRESTAL	AGUIZED	AIDANCES	AIMED
AGONIST	AGRESTIAL	AGUIZES	AIDANT	AIMER
AGONISTES	AGRESTIC	AGUIZING	AIDANTS	AIMERS
AGONISTIC	AGRIA	AGUNA	AIDAS	AIMFUL
AGONISTS	AGRIAS	AGUNAH	AIDE	AIMFULLY
AGONIZE	AGRIMONY	AGUNOT	AIDED	AIMING
AGONIZED	AGRIN	AGUNOTH	AIDER	AIMLESS
AGONIZES	AGRINS	AGUTI	AIDERS	AIMLESSLY
AGONIZING	AGRIOLOGY	AGUTIS	AIDES	AIMS
AGONS	AGRISE	AGYRIA	AIDFUL	AIN
AGONY	AGRISED	AGYRIAS	AIDING	AINE
AGOOD	AGRISES	AH	AIDLESS	AINEE
AGORA	AGRISING	AHA	AIDMAN	AINGA
AGORAE	AGRIZE	AHCHOO	AIDMEN	AINGAS
AGORAS	AGRIZED	AHEAD	AIDOI	AINS
AGOROT	AGRIZES	AHEAP	AIDOS	AINSELL
AGOROTH	AGRIZING	AHED	AIDS	AINSELLS
AGOUTA	AGRO	AHEIGHT	AIERIES	AIOLI
AGOUTAS	AGRODOLCE	AHEM	AIERY	AIOLIS
AGOUTI	AGROLOGIC	AHEMERAL	AIGA	AIR
AGOUTIES	AGROLOGY	AHENT	AIGAS	AIRBAG
AGOUTIS	AGRONOMIC	AHI	AIGHT	AIRBAGS
AGOUTY	AGRONOMY	AHIGH	AIGLET	AIRBALL
AGRAFE	AGROS	AHIMSA	AIGLETS	AIRBALLED
AGRAFES	AGROUND	AHIMSAS	AIGRET	AIRBALLS
AGRAFFE	AGRYPNIA	AHIND	AIGRETS	AIRBASE
AGRAFFES	AGRYPNIAS	AHING	AIGRETTE	AIRBASES
AGRAPHA	AGRYZE	AHINT	AIGRETTES	AIRBOARD
AGRAPHIA	AGRYZED	AHIS	AIGUILLE	AIRBOARDS
AGRAPHIAS	AGRYZES	AHISTORIC	AIGUILLES	AIRBOAT
AGRAPHIC	AGRYZING	AHOLD	AIKIDO	AIRBOATS
AGRAPHON	AGS	AHOLDS	AIKIDOS	AIRBORNE
AGRARIAN	AGTERSKOT	AHORSE	AIKONA	AIRBOUND
AGRARIANS	AGUACATE	AHOY	AIL	AIRBRICK
AGRASTE	AGUACATES	AHS	AILANTHIC	AIRBRICKS
AGRAVIC	AGUE	AHULL	AILANTHUS	AIRBRUSH
AGREE	AGUED	AHUNGERED	AILANTO	AIRBURST
AGREEABLE	AGUELIKE	AHUNGRY	AILANTOS	AIRBURSTS
AGREEABLY	AGUES	AHURU	AILED	AIRBUS
AGREED	AGUEWEED	AHURUHURU	AILERON	AIRBUSES
AGREEING	AGUEWEEDS	AHURUS	AILERONS	AIRBUSSES
AGREEMENT	AGUISE	AI	AILETTE	AIRCHECK
AGREES	AGUISED	AIA	AILETTES	AIRCHECKS
AGREGE	AGUISES	AIAS	AILING	AIRCOACH
AGREGES	AGUISH	AIBLINS	AILMENT	AIRCON
AGREMENS	AGUISHLY	AID	AILMENTS	AIRCONS

AIRCRAFT	AIRLINE	AIRSIDE	AIT	AKENES
AIRCREW	AIRLINER	AIRSIDES	AITCH	AKENIAL
AIRCREWS	AIRLINERS	AIRSOME	AITCHBONE	AKES
AIRDATE	AIRLINES	AIRSPACE	AITCHES	AKHARA
AIRDATES	AIRLOCK	AIRSPACES	AITS	AKHARAS
AIRDRAWN	AIRLOCKS	AIRSPEED	AITU	AKIMBO
AIRDROME	AIRMAIL	AIRSPEEDS	AITUS	AKIN
AIRDROMES	AIRMAILED	AIRSTOP	AIVER	AKINESES
AIRDROP	AIRMAILS	AIRSTOPS	AIVERS	AKINESIA
AIRDROPS	AIRMAN	AIRSTREAM	AIYEE	AKINESIAS
AIRED	AIRMEN	AIRSTRIKE	AIZLE	AKINESIS
AIRER	AIRMOBILE	AIRSTRIP	AIZLES	AKINETIC
AIRERS	AIRN	AIRSTRIPS	AJAR	AKING
AIREST	AIRNED	AIRT	AJEE	AKIRAHO
AIRFARE	AIRNING	AIRTED	AJI	AKIRAHOS
AIRFARES	AIRNS	AIRTH	AJIES	AKITA
AIRFIELD	AIRPARK	AIRTHED	AJIS	AKITAS
AIRFIELDS	AIRPARKS	AIRTHING	AJIVA	AKKAS
AIRFLOW	AIRPLANE	AIRTHS	AJIVAS	AKOLUTHOS
AIRFLOWS	AIRPLANES	AIRTIGHT	AJOWAN	AKRASIA
AIRFOIL	AIRPLAY	AIRTIME	AJOWANS	AKRASIAS
AIRFOILS	AIRPLAYS	AIRTIMES	AJUGA	AKRATIC
AIRFRAME	AIRPORT	AIRTING	AJUGAS	AKVAVIT
AIRFRAMES	AIRPORTS	AIRTRAM	AJUTAGE	AKVAVITS
AIRGAP	AIRPOST	AIRTRAMS	AJUTAGES	AL
AIRGAPS	AIRPOSTS	AIRTS	AJWAN	ALA
AIRGLOW	AIRPOWER	AIRVAC	AJWANS	ALAAP
AIRGLOWS	AIRPOWERS	AIRVACS	AKA	ALAAPS
AIRGRAPH	AIRPROOF	AIRWARD	AKARYOTE	ALABAMINE
AIRGRAPHS	AIRPROOFS	AIRWARDS	AKARYOTES	ALABASTER
AIRGUN	AIRPROX	AIRWAVE	AKARYOTIC	ALACHLOR
AIRGUNS	AIRPROXES	AIRWAVES	AKAS	ALACHLORS
AIRHEAD	AIRS	AIRWAY	AKATEA	ALACK
AIRHEADED	AIRSCAPE	AIRWAYS	AKATEAS	ALACKADAY
AIRHEADS	AIRSCAPES	AIRWISE	AKATHISIA	ALACRITY
AIRHOLE	AIRSCREW	AIRWOMAN	AKE	ALAE
AIRHOLES	AIRSCREWS	AIRWOMEN	AKEAKE	ALAIMENT
AIRIER	AIRSHAFT	AIRWORTHY	AKEAKES	ALAIMENTS
AIRIEST	AIRSHAFTS	AIRY	AKEBIA	ALALAGMOI
AIRILY	AIRSHED	AIS	AKEBIAS	ALALAGMOS
AIRINESS	AIRSHEDS	AISLE	AKED	ALALIA
AIRING	AIRSHIP	AISLED	AKEDAH	ALALIAS
AIRINGS	AIRSHIPS	AISLELESS	AKEDAHS	ALAMEDA
AIRLESS	AIRSHOT	AISLES	AKEE	ALAMEDAS
AIRLIFT	AIRSHOTS	AISLEWAY	AKEES	ALAMO
AIRLIFTED	AIRSHOW	AISLEWAYS	AKELA	ALAMODE
AIRLIFTS	AIRSHOWS	AISLING	AKELAS	ALAMODES
AIRLIKE	AIRSICK	AISLINGS	AKENE	ALAMORT

ALAMOS	ALATION	ALBITIZE	ALCHYMY	ALECITHAL
ALAN	ALATIONS	ALBITIZED	ALCID	ALECK
ALAND	ALAY	ALBITIZES	ALCIDINE	ALECKS
ALANDS	ALAYED	ALBIZIA	ALCIDS	ALECOST
ALANE	ALAYING	ALBIZIAS	ALCO	ALECOSTS
ALANG	ALAYS	ALBIZZIA	ALCOHOL	ALECS
ALANGS	ALB	ALBIZZIAS	ALCOHOLIC	ALECTRYON
ALANIN	ALBA	ALBRICIAS	ALCOHOLS	ALEE
ALANINE	ALBACORE	ALBS	ALCOLOCK	ALEF
ALANINES	ALBACORES	ALBUGO	ALCOLOCKS	ALEFS
ALANINS	ALBARELLI	ALBUGOS	ALCOOL	ALEFT
ALANNAH	ALBARELLO	ALBUM	ALCOOLS	ALEGAR
ALANNAHS	ALBAS	ALBUMEN	ALCOPOP	ALEGARS
ALANS	ALBATA	ALBUMENS	ALCOPOPS	ALEGGE
ALANT	ALBATAS	ALBUMIN	ALCORZA	ALEGGED
ALANTS	ALBATROSS	ALBUMINS	ALCORZAS	ALEGGES
ALANYL	ALBE	ALBUMOSE	ALCOS	ALEGGING
ALANYLS	ALBEDO	ALBUMOSES	ALCOVE	ALEHOUSE
ALAP	ALBEDOES	ALBUMS	ALCOVED	ALEHOUSES
ALAPA	ALBEDOS	ALBURNOUS	ALCOVES	ALEMBIC
ALAPAS	ALBEE	ALBURNUM	ALDEA	ALEMBICS
ALAPS	ALBEIT	ALBURNUMS	ALDEAS	ALEMBROTH
ALAR	ALBERGHI	ALBUTEROL	ALDEHYDE	ALENCON
ALARM	ALBERGO	ALCADE	ALDEHYDES	ALENCONS
ALARMABLE	ALBERT	ALCADES	ALDEHYDIC	ALENGTH
ALARMED	ALBERTITE	ALCAHEST	ALDER	ALEPH
ALARMEDLY	ALBERTS	ALCAHESTS	ALDERFLY	ALEPHS
ALARMING	ALBESCENT	ALCAIC	ALDERMAN	ALEPINE
ALARMISM	ALBESPINE	ALCAICS	ALDERMEN	ALEPINES
ALARMISMS	ALBESPYNE	ALCAIDE	ALDERN	ALERCE
ALARMIST	ALBICORE	ALCAIDES	ALDERS	ALERCES
ALARMISTS	ALBICORES	ALCALDE	ALDICARB	ALERION
ALARMS	ALBINAL	ALCALDES	ALDICARBS	ALERIONS
ALARUM	ALBINESS	ALCARRAZA	ALDOL	ALERT
ALARUMED	ALBINIC	ALCATRAS	ALDOLASE	ALERTED
ALARUMING	ALBINISM	ALCAYDE	ALDOLASES	ALERTER
ALARUMS	ALBINISMS	ALCAYDES	ALDOLS	ALERTEST
ALARY	ALBINO	ALCAZAR	ALDOSE	ALERTING
ALAS	ALBINOISM	ALCAZARS	ALDOSES	ALERTLY
ALASKA	ALBINOS	ALCHEMIC	ALDOXIME	ALERTNESS
ALASKAS	ALBINOTIC	ALCHEMIES	ALDOXIMES	ALERTS
ALASTOR	ALBITE	ALCHEMISE	ALDRIN	ALES
ALASTORS	ALBITES	ALCHEMIST	ALDRINS	ALETHIC
ALASTRIM	ALBITIC	ALCHEMIZE	ALE	ALEURON
ALASTRIMS	ALBITICAL	ALCHEMY	ALEATORIC	ALEURONE
ALATE	ALBITISE	ALCHERA	ALEATORY	ALEURONES
ALATED	ALBITISED	ALCHERAS	ALEBENCH	ALEURONIC
ALATES	ALBITISES	ALCHYMIES	ALEC	ALEURONS

ALEVIN	ALGAS	ALIBIING	ALIGNS	ALKALI
ALEVINS	ALGATE	ALIBIS	ALIKE	ALKALIC
ALEW	ALGATES	ALIBLE	ALIKENESS	ALKALIES
ALEWASHED	ALGEBRA	ALICANT	ALIMENT	ALKALIFY
ALEWIFE	ALGEBRAIC	ALICANTS	ALIMENTAL	ALKALIN
ALEWIVES	ALGEBRAS	ALICYCLIC	ALIMENTED	ALKALINE
ALEWS	ALGERINE	ALIDAD	ALIMENTS	ALKALIS
ALEXANDER	ALGERINES	ALIDADE	ALIMONIED	ALKALISE
ALEXIA	ALGESES	ALIDADES	ALIMONIES	ALKALISED
ALEXIAS	ALGESIA	ALIDADS	ALIMONY	ALKALISER
ALEXIC	ALGESIAS	ALIEN	ALINE	ALKALISES
ALEXIN	ALGESIC	ALIENABLE	ALINED	ALKALIZE
ALEXINE	ALGESIS	ALIENAGE	ALINEMENT	ALKALIZED
ALEXINES	ALGETIC	ALIENAGES	ALINER	ALKALIZER
ALEXINIC	ALGICIDAL	ALIENATE	ALINERS	ALKALIZES
ALEXINS	ALGICIDE	ALIENATED	ALINES	ALKALOID
ALEYE	ALGICIDES	ALIENATES	ALINING	ALKALOIDS
ALEYED	ALGID	ALIENATOR	ALIPED	ALKALOSES
ALEYES	ALGIDITY	ALIENED	ALIPEDS	ALKALOSIS
ALEYING	ALGIDNESS	ALIENEE	ALIPHATIC	ALKALOTIC
ALF	ALGIN	ALIENEES	ALIQUANT	ALKANE
ALFA	ALGINATE	ALIENER	ALIQUOT	ALKANES
ALFAKI	ALGINATES	ALIENERS	ALIQUOTS	ALKANET
ALFAKIS	ALGINIC	ALIENING	ALISMA	ALKANETS
ALFALFA	ALGINS	ALIENISM	ALISMAS	ALKANNIN
ALFALFAS	ALGOID	ALIENISMS	ALISON	ALKANNINS
ALFAQUI	ALGOLOGY	ALIENIST	ALISONS	ALKENE
ALFAQUIN	ALGOMETER	ALIENISTS	ALIST	ALKENES
ALFAQUINS	ALGOMETRY	ALIENLY	ALIT	ALKIE
ALFAQUIS	ALGOR	ALIENNESS	ALITERACY	ALKIES
ALFAS	ALGORISM	ALIENOR	ALITERATE	ALKINE
ALFERECES	ALGORISMS	ALIENORS	ALIUNDE	ALKINES
ALFEREZ	ALGORITHM	ALIENS	ALIVE	ALKO
ALFILARIA	ALGORS	ALIF	ALIVENESS	ALKOS
ALFILERIA	ALGUACIL	ALIFORM	ALIYA	ALKOXIDE
ALFORJA	ALGUACILS	ALIFS	ALIYAH	ALKOXIDES
ALFORJAS	ALGUAZIL	ALIGARTA	ALIYAHS	ALKOXY
ALFREDO	ALGUAZILS	ALIGARTAS	ALIYAS	ALKY
ALFRESCO	ALGUM	ALIGHT	ALIYOS	ALKYD
ALFS	ALGUMS	ALIGHTED	ALIYOT	ALKYDS
ALGA	ALIAS	ALIGHTING	ALIYOTH	ALKYL
ALGAE	ALIASED	ALIGHTS	ALIZARI	ALKYLATE
ALGAECIDE	ALIASES	ALIGN	ALIZARIN	ALKYLATED
ALGAL	ALIASING	ALIGNED	ALIZARINE	ALKYLATES
ALGAROBA	ALIASINGS	ALIGNER	ALIZARINS	ALKYLIC
ALGAROBAS	ALIBI	ALIGNERS	ALIZARIS	ALKYLS
ALGARROBA	ALIBIED	ALIGNING	ALKAHEST	ALKYNE
ALGARROBO	ALIBIES	ALIGNMENT	ALKAHESTS	ALKYNES

ALL	ALLELUIAH	ALLNESS	ALLOTS	ALLUSIVE
ALLANITE	ALLELUIAS	ALLNESSES	ALLOTTED	ALLUVIA
ALLANITES	ALLEMANDE	ALLNIGHT	ALLOTTEE	ALLUVIAL
ALLANTOIC	ALLENARLY	ALLOBAR	ALLOTTEES	ALLUVIALS
ALLANTOID	ALLERGEN	ALLOBARS	ALLOTTER	ALLUVION
ALLANTOIN	ALLERGENS	ALLOCABLE	ALLOTTERS	ALLUVIONS
ALLANTOIS	ALLERGIC	ALLOCARPY	ALLOTTERY	ALLUVIUM
ALLATIVE	ALLERGICS	ALLOCATE	ALLOTTING	ALLUVIUMS
ALLATIVES	ALLERGIES	ALLOCATED	ALLOTYPE	ALLY
ALLAY	ALLERGIN	ALLOCATES	ALLOTYPES	ALLYING
ALLAYED	ALLERGINS	ALLOCATOR	ALLOTYPIC	ALLYL
ALLAYER	ALLERGIST	ALLOD	ALLOTYPY	ALLYLIC
ALLAYERS	ALLERGY	ALLODIA	ALLOVER	ALLYLS
ALLAYING	ALLERION	ALLODIAL	ALLOVERS	ALLYOU
ALLAYINGS	ALLERIONS	ALLODIUM	ALLOW	ALMA
ALLAYMENT	ALLETHRIN	ALLODIUMS	ALLOWABLE	ALMAGEST
ALLAYS	ALLEVIANT	ALLODS	ALLOWABLY	ALMAGESTS
ALLCOMERS	ALLEVIATE	ALLODYNIA	ALLOWANCE	ALMAH
ALLEDGE	ALLEY	ALLOGAMY	ALLOWED	ALMAHS
ALLEDGED	ALLEYCAT	ALLOGENIC	ALLOWEDLY	ALMAIN
ALLEDGES	ALLEYCATS	ALLOGRAFT	ALLOWING	ALMAINS
ALLEDGING	ALLEYED	ALLOGRAPH	ALLOWS	ALMANAC
ALLEE	ALLEYS	ALLOMERIC	ALLOXAN	ALMANACK
ALLEES	ALLEYWAY	ALLOMETRY	ALLOXANS	ALMANACKS
ALLEGE	ALLEYWAYS	ALLOMONE	ALLOY	ALMANACS
ALLEGED	ALLHEAL	ALLOMONES	ALLOYED	ALMANDINE
ALLEGEDLY	ALLHEALS	ALLOMORPH	ALLOYING	ALMANDITE
ALLEGER	ALLIABLE	ALLONGE	ALLOYS	ALMAS
ALLEGERS	ALLIAK	ALLONGED	ALLOZYME	ALME
ALLEGES	ALLIAKS	ALLONGES	ALLOZYMES	ALMEH
ALLEGGE	ALLIANCE	ALLONGING	ALLS	ALMEHS
ALLEGGED	ALLIANCES	ALLONS	ALLSEED	ALMEMAR
ALLEGGES	ALLICE	ALLONYM	ALLSEEDS	ALMEMARS
ALLEGGING	ALLICES	ALLONYMS	ALLSORTS	ALMERIES
ALLEGIANT	ALLICHOLY	ALLOPATH	ALLSPICE	ALMERY
ALLEGING	ALLICIN	ALLOPATHS	ALLSPICES	ALMES
ALLEGORIC	ALLICINS	ALLOPATHY	ALLUDE	ALMIGHTY
ALLEGORY	ALLIED	ALLOPATRY	ALLUDED	ALMIRAH
ALLEGRO	ALLIES	ALLOPHANE	ALLUDES	ALMIRAHS
ALLEGROS	ALLIGARTA	ALLOPHONE	ALLUDING	ALMNER
ALLEL	ALLIGATE	ALLOPLASM	ALLURE	ALMNERS
ALLELE	ALLIGATED	ALLOSAUR	ALLURED	ALMOND
ALLELES	ALLIGATES	ALLOSAURS	ALLURER	ALMONDIER
ALLELIC	ALLIGATOR	ALLOSTERY	ALLURERS	ALMONDITE
ALLELISM	ALLIS	ALLOT	ALLURES	ALMONDS
ALLELISMS	ALLISES	ALLOTMENT	ALLURING	ALMONDY
ALLELS	ALLIUM	ALLOTROPE	ALLUSION	ALMONER
ALLELUIA	ALLIUMS	ALLOTROPY	ALLUSIONS	ALMONERS

ALMONRIES	ALONELY	ALS	ALTIPLANO	ALUMSTONE
ALMONRY	ALONENESS	ALSIKE	ALTISSIMO	ALUNITE
ALMOST	ALONG	ALSIKES	ALTITUDE	ALUNITES
ALMOUS	ALONGSIDE	ALSO	ALTITUDES	ALURE
ALMS	ALONGST	ALSOON	ALTO	ALURES
ALMSGIVER	ALOO	ALSOONE	ALTOIST	ALUS
ALMSHOUSE	ALOOF	ALT	ALTOISTS	ALVAR
ALMSMAN	ALOOFLY	ALTAR	ALTOS	ALVARS
ALMSMEN	ALOOFNESS	ALTARAGE	ALTRICES	ALVEARIES
ALMSWOMAN	ALOOS	ALTARAGES	ALTRICIAL	ALVEARY
ALMSWOMEN	ALOPECIA	ALTARS	ALTRUISM	ALVEATED
ALMUCE	ALOPECIAS	ALTARWISE	ALTRUISMS	ALVEOLAR
ALMUCES	ALOPECIC	ALTER	ALTRUIST	ALVEOLARS
ALMUD	ALOPECOID	ALTERABLE	ALTRUISTS	ALVEOLATE
ALMUDE	ALOUD	ALTERABLY	ALTS	ALVEOLE
ALMUDES	ALOW	ALTERANT	ALU	ALVEOLES
ALMUDS	ALOWE	ALTERANTS	ALUDEL	ALVEOLI
ALMUG	ALP	ALTERCATE	ALUDELS	ALVEOLUS
ALMUGS	ALPACA	ALTERED	ALULA	ALVINE
ALNAGE	ALPACAS	ALTERER	ALULAE	ALWAY
ALNAGER	ALPACCA	ALTERERS	ALULAR	ALWAYS
ALNAGERS	ALPACCAS	ALTERING	ALULAS	ALYSSUM
ALNAGES	ALPARGATA	ALTERITY	ALUM	ALYSSUMS
ALNICO	ALPEEN	ALTERN	ALUMIN	AM
ALNICOS	ALPEENS	ALTERNANT	ALUMINA	AMA
ALOCASIA	ALPENGLOW	ALTERNAT	ALUMINAS	AMABILE
ALOCASIAS	ALPENHORN	ALTERNATE	ALUMINATE	AMADAVAT
ALOD	ALPHA	ALTERNATS	ALUMINE	AMADAVATS
ALODIA	ALPHABET	ALTERNE	ALUMINES	AMADODA
ALODIAL	ALPHABETS	ALTERNES	ALUMINIC	AMADOU
ALODIUM	ALPHAS	ALTERS	ALUMINIDE	AMADOUS
ALODIUMS	ALPHASORT	ALTESSE	ALUMINISE	AMAH
ALODS	ALPHATEST	ALTESSES	ALUMINIUM	AMAHS
ALOE	ALPHORN	ALTEZA	ALUMINIZE	AMAIN
ALOED	ALPHORNS	ALTEZAS	ALUMINOUS	AMAKHOSI
ALOES	ALPHOSIS	ALTEZZA	ALUMINS	AMAKOSI
ALOESWOOD	ALPHYL	ALTEZZAS	ALUMINUM	AMALGAM
ALOETIC	ALPHYLS	ALTHAEA	ALUMINUMS	AMALGAMS
ALOETICS	ALPINE	ALTHAEAS	ALUMISH	AMANDINE
ALOFT	ALPINELY	ALTHEA	ALUMIUM	AMANDINES
ALOGIA	ALPINES	ALTHEAS	ALUMIUMS	AMANDLA
ALOGIAS	ALPINISM	ALTHO	ALUMNA	AMANDLAS
ALOGICAL	ALPINISMS	ALTHORN	ALUMNAE	AMANITA
ALOHA	ALPINIST	ALTHORNS	ALUMNI	AMANITAS
ALOHAS	ALPINISTS	ALTHOUGH	ALUMNUS	AMANITIN
ALOIN	ALPS	ALTIGRAPH	ALUMROOT	AMANITINS
ALOINS	ALREADY	ALTIMETER	ALUMROOTS	AMARACUS
ALONE	ALRIGHT	ALTIMETRY	ALUMS	AMARANT

AMARANTH	AMAZED	AMBIENT	AMBULETTE	AMENDS
AMARANTHS	AMAZEDLY	AMBIENTS	AMBUSCADE	AMENE
AMARANTIN	AMAZEMENT	AMBIGUITY	AMBUSCADO	AMENED
AMARANTS	AMAZES	AMBIGUOUS	AMBUSH	AMENING
AMARELLE	AMAZING	AMBIPOLAR	AMBUSHED	AMENITIES
AMARELLES	AMAZINGLY	AMBIT	AMBUSHER	AMENITY
AMARETTI	AMAZON	AMBITION	AMBUSHERS	AMENS
AMARETTO	AMAZONIAN	AMBITIONS	AMBUSHES	AMENT
AMARETTOS	AMAZONITE	AMBITIOUS	AMBUSHING	AMENTA
AMARNA	AMAZONS	AMBITS	AME	AMENTAL
AMARONE	AMBACH	AMBITTY	AMEARST	AMENTIA
AMARONES	AMBACHES	AMBIVERT	AMEBA	AMENTIAS
AMARYLLID	AMBAGE	AMBIVERTS	AMEBAE	AMENTS
AMARYLLIS	AMBAGES	AMBLE	AMEBAN	AMENTUM
AMAS	AMBAGIOUS	AMBLED	AMEBAS	AMERCE
AMASS	AMBAN	AMBLER	AMEBEAN	AMERCED
AMASSABLE	AMBANS	AMBLERS	AMEBIASES	AMERCER
AMASSED	AMBARI	AMBLES	AMEBIASIS	AMERCERS
AMASSER	AMBARIES	AMBLING	AMEBIC	AMERCES
AMASSERS	AMBARIS	AMBLINGS	AMEBOCYTE	AMERCING
AMASSES	AMBARY	AMBLYOPIA	AMEBOID	AMERICIUM
AMASSING	AMBASSAGE	AMBLYOPIC	AMEER	AMES
AMASSMENT	AMBASSIES	AMBO	AMEERATE	AMESACE
AMATE	AMBASSY	AMBOINA	AMEERATES	AMESACES
AMATED	AMBATCH	AMBOINAS	AMEERS	AMETHYST
AMATES	AMBATCHES	AMBONES	AMEIOSES	AMETHYSTS
AMATEUR	AMBEER	AMBOS	AMEIOSIS	AMETROPIA
AMATEURS	AMBEERS	AMBOYNA	AMELCORN	AMETROPIC
AMATING	AMBER	AMBOYNAS	AMELCORNS	AMI
AMATION	AMBERED	AMBRIES	AMELIA	AMIA
AMATIONS	AMBERGRIS	AMBROID	AMELIAS	AMIABLE
AMATIVE	AMBERIER	AMBROIDS	AMEN	AMIABLY
AMATIVELY	AMBERIES	AMBROSIA	AMENABLE	AMIANTHUS
AMATOL	AMBERIEST	AMBROSIAL	AMENABLY	AMIANTUS
AMATOLS	AMBERINA	AMBROSIAN	AMENAGE	AMIAS
AMATORIAL	AMBERINAS	AMBROSIAS	AMENAGED	AMICABLE
AMATORIAN	AMBERITE	AMBROTYPE	AMENAGES	AMICABLY
AMATORY	AMBERITES	AMBRY	AMENAGING	AMICE
AMAUROSES	AMBERJACK	AMBSACE	AMENAUNCE	AMICES
AMAUROSIS	AMBEROID	AMBSACES	AMEND	AMICI
AMAUROTIC	AMBEROIDS	AMBULACRA	AMENDABLE	AMICUS
AMAUT	AMBEROUS	AMBULANCE	AMENDE	AMID
AMAUTI	AMBERS	AMBULANT	AMENDED	AMIDASE
AMAUTIK	AMBERY	AMBULANTS	AMENDER	AMIDASES
AMAUTIKS	AMBIANCE	AMBULATE	AMENDERS	AMIDE
AMAUTIS	AMBIANCES	AMBULATED	AMENDES	AMIDES
AMAUTS	AMBIENCE	AMBULATES	AMENDING	AMIDIC
AMAZE	AMBIENCES	AMBULATOR	AMENDMENT	AMIDIN

AMIDINE	AMITY	AMNESTIED	AMORETTI	AMPED
AMIDINES	AMLA	AMNESTIES	AMORETTO	AMPERAGE
AMIDINS	AMLAS	AMNESTY	AMORETTOS	AMPERAGES
AMIDMOST	AMMAN	AMNIA	AMORINI	AMPERE
AMIDO	AMMANS	AMNIC	AMORINO	AMPERES
AMIDOGEN	AMMETER	AMNIO	AMORISM	AMPERSAND
AMIDOGENS	AMMETERS	AMNION	AMORISMS	AMPERZAND
AMIDOL	AMMINE	AMNIONIC	AMORIST	AMPHIBIA
AMIDOLS	AMMINES	AMNIONS	AMORISTIC	AMPHIBIAN
AMIDONE	AMMINO	AMNIOS	AMORISTS	AMPHIBOLE
AMIDONES	AMMIRAL	AMNIOTE	AMORNINGS	AMPHIBOLY
AMIDS	AMMIRALS	AMNIOTES	AMOROSA	AMPHIGORY
AMIDSHIP	AMMO	AMNIOTIC	AMOROSAS	AMPHIOXI
AMIDSHIPS	AMMOCETE	AMNIOTOMY	AMOROSITY	AMPHIOXUS
AMIDST	AMMOCETES	AMOEBA	AMOROSO	AMPHIPATH
AMIE	AMMOCOETE	AMOEBAE	AMOROSOS	AMPHIPOD
AMIES	AMMOLITE	AMOEBAEAN	AMOROUS	AMPHIPODS
AMIGA	AMMOLITES	AMOEBAN	AMOROUSLY	AMPHOLYTE
AMIGAS	AMMON	AMOEBAS	AMORPHISM	AMPHORA
AMIGO	AMMONAL	AMOEBEAN	AMORPHOUS	AMPHORAE
AMIGOS	AMMONALS	AMOEBIC	AMORT	AMPHORAL
AMILDAR	AMMONATE	AMOEBOID	AMORTISE	AMPHORAS
AMILDARS	AMMONATES	AMOK	AMORTISED	AMPHORIC
AMIN	AMMONIA	AMOKS	AMORTISES	AMPING
AMINE	AMMONIAC	AMOKURA	AMORTIZE	AMPLE
AMINES	AMMONIACS	AMOKURAS	AMORTIZED	AMPLENESS
AMINIC	AMMONIAS	AMOLE	AMORTIZES	AMPLER
AMINITIES	AMMONIATE	AMOLES	AMOSITE	AMPLEST
AMINITY	AMMONIC	AMOMUM	AMOSITES	AMPLEXUS
AMINO	AMMONICAL	AMOMUMS	AMOTION	AMPLIDYNE
AMINOS	AMMONIFY	AMONG	AMOTIONS	AMPLIFIED
AMINS	AMMONITE	AMONGST	AMOUNT	AMPLIFIER
AMIR	AMMONITES	AMOOVE	AMOUNTED	AMPLIFIES
AMIRATE	AMMONITIC	AMOOVED	AMOUNTING	AMPLIFY
AMIRATES	AMMONIUM	AMOOVES	AMOUNTS	AMPLITUDE
AMIRS	AMMONIUMS	AMOOVING	AMOUR	AMPLOSOME
AMIS	AMMONO	AMORAL	AMOURETTE	AMPLY
AMISES	AMMONOID	AMORALISM	AMOURS	AMPOULE
AMISS	AMMONOIDS	AMORALIST	AMOVE	AMPOULES
AMISSES	AMMONS	AMORALITY	AMOVED	AMPS
AMISSIBLE	AMMOS	AMORALLY	AMOVES	AMPUL
AMISSING	AMNESIA	AMORANCE	AMOVING	AMPULE
AMITIES	AMNESIAC	AMORANCES	AMOWT	AMPULES
AMITOSES	AMNESIACS	AMORANT	AMOWTS	AMPULLA
AMITOSIS	AMNESIAS	AMORCE	AMP	AMPULLAE
AMITOTIC	AMNESIC	AMORCES	AMPACITY	AMPULLAR
AMITROLE	AMNESICS	AMORET	AMPASSIES	AMPULLARY
AMITROLES	AMNESTIC	AMORETS	AMPASSY	AMPULS

AMPUTATE	AMYGDALE	ANACONDA	ANALOGIES	ANAPESTIC
AMPUTATED	AMYGDALES	ANACONDAS	ANALOGISE	ANAPESTS
AMPUTATES	AMYGDALIN	ANACRUSES	ANALOGISM	ANAPHASE
AMPUTATOR	AMYGDALS	ANACRUSIS	ANALOGIST	ANAPHASES
AMPUTEE	AMYGDULE	ANADEM	ANALOGIZE	ANAPHASIC
AMPUTEES	AMYGDULES	ANADEMS	ANALOGON	ANAPHOR
AMREETA	AMYL	ANAEMIA	ANALOGONS	ANAPHORA
AMREETAS	AMYLASE	ANAEMIAS	ANALOGOUS	ANAPHORAL
AMRIT	AMYLASES	ANAEMIC	ANALOGS	ANAPHORAS
AMRITA	AMYLENE	ANAEROBE	ANALOGUE	ANAPHORIC
AMRITAS	AMYLENES	ANAEROBES	ANALOGUES	ANAPHORS
AMRITS	AMYLIC	ANAEROBIA	ANALOGY	ANAPLASIA
AMSINCKIA	AMYLOGEN	ANAEROBIC	ANALYSAND	ANAPLASTY
AMTMAN	AMYLOGENS	ANAGEN	ANALYSE	ANAPTYXES
AMTMANS	AMYLOID	ANAGENS	ANALYSED	ANAPTYXIS
AMTRAC	AMYLOIDAL	ANAGLYPH	ANALYSER	ANARCH
AMTRACK	AMYLOIDS	ANAGLYPHS	ANALYSERS	ANARCHAL
AMTRACKS	AMYLOPSIN	ANAGLYPHY	ANALYSES	ANARCHIAL
AMTRACS	AMYLOSE	ANAGOGE	ANALYSING	ANARCHIC
AMTRAK	AMYLOSES	ANAGOGES	ANALYSIS	ANARCHIES
AMTRAKS	AMYLS	ANAGOGIC	ANALYST	ANARCHISE
AMU	AMYLUM	ANAGOGIES	ANALYSTS	ANARCHISM
AMUCK	AMYLUMS	ANAGOGY	ANALYTE	ANARCHIST
AMUCKS	AMYOTONIA	ANAGRAM	ANALYTES	ANARCHIZE
AMULET	AMYTAL	ANAGRAMS	ANALYTIC	ANARCHS
AMULETIC	AMYTALS	ANAL	ANALYTICS	ANARCHY
AMULETS	AN	ANALCIME	ANALYZE	ANARTHRIA
AMUS	ANA	ANALCIMES	ANALYZED	ANARTHRIC
AMUSABLE	ANABAENA	ANALCIMIC	ANALYZER	ANAS
AMUSE	ANABAENAS	ANALCITE	ANALYZERS	ANASARCA
AMUSEABLE	ANABANTID	ANALCITES	ANALYZES	ANASARCAS
AMUSED	ANABAS	ANALECTA	ANALYZING	ANASTASES
AMUSEDLY	ANABASES	ANALECTIC	ANAMNESES	ANASTASIS
AMUSEMENT	ANABASIS	ANALECTS	ANAMNESIS	ANASTATIC
AMUSER	ANABATIC	ANALEMMA	ANAMNIOTE	ANATA
AMUSERS	ANABIOSES	ANALEMMAS	ANAN	ANATAS
AMUSES	ANABIOSIS	ANALEPTIC	ANANA	ANATASE
AMUSETTE	ANABIOTIC	ANALGESIA	ANANAS	ANATASES
AMUSETTES	ANABLEPS	ANALGESIC	ANANASES	ANATEXES
AMUSIA	ANABOLIC	ANALGETIC	ANANDA	ANATEXIS
AMUSIAS	ANABOLISM	ANALGIA	ANANDAS	ANATHEMA
AMUSIC	ANABOLITE	ANALGIAS	ANANDROUS	ANATHEMAS
AMUSING	ANABRANCH	ANALITIES	ANANKE	ANATMAN
AMUSINGLY	ANACHARIS	ANALITY	ANANKES	ANATMANS
AMUSIVE	ANACLINAL	ANALLY	ANANTHOUS	ANATOMIC
AMYGDAL	ANACLISES	ANALOG	ANAPAEST	ANATOMIES
AMYGDALA	ANACLISIS	ANALOGA	ANAPAESTS	ANATOMISE
AMYGDALAE	ANACLITIC	ANALOGIC	ANAPEST	ANATOMIST

ANATOMIZE	ANCILLAS	ANEARING	ANETIC	ANGIOLOGY
ANATOMY	ANCIPITAL	ANEARS	ANEUPLOID	ANGIOMA
ANATOXIN	ANCLE	ANEATH	ANEURIN	ANGIOMAS
ANATOXINS	ANCLES	ANECDOTA	ANEURINS	ANGIOMATA
ANATROPY	ANCOME	ANECDOTAL	ANEURISM	ANGISHORE
ANATTA	ANCOMES	ANECDOTE	ANEURISMS	ANGKLUNG
ANATTAS	ANCON	ANECDOTES	ANEURYSM	ANGKLUNGS
ANATTO	ANCONAL	ANECDOTIC	ANEURYSMS	ANGLE
ANATTOS	ANCONE	ANECDYSES	ANEW	ANGLED
ANAXIAL	ANCONEAL	ANECDYSIS	ANGA	ANGLEDUG
ANBURIES	ANCONES	ANECHOIC	ANGAKOK	ANGLEDUGS
ANBURY	ANCONOID	ANELACE	ANGAKOKS	ANGLEPOD
ANCE	ANCORA	ANELACES	ANGARIA	ANGLEPODS
ANCESTOR	ANCRESS	ANELASTIC	ANGARIAS	ANGLER
ANCESTORS	ANCRESSES	ANELE	ANGARIES	ANGLERS
ANCESTRAL	AND	ANELED	ANGARY	ANGLES
ANCESTRY	ANDANTE	ANELES	ANGAS	ANGLESITE
ANCHO	ANDANTES	ANELING	ANGASHORE	ANGLEWISE
ANCHOR	ANDANTINI	ANELLI	ANGEKKOK	ANGLEWORM
ANCHORAGE	ANDANTINO	ANEMIA	ANGEKKOKS	ANGLICE
ANCHORED	ANDESINE	ANEMIAS	ANGEKOK	ANGLICISE
ANCHORESS	ANDESINES	ANEMIC	ANGEKOKS	ANGLICISM
ANCHORET	ANDESITE	ANEMOGRAM	ANGEL	ANGLICIST
ANCHORETS	ANDESITES	ANEMOLOGY	ANGELED	ANGLICIZE
ANCHORING	ANDESITIC	ANEMONE	ANGELFISH	ANGLIFIED
ANCHORITE	ANDESYTE	ANEMONES	ANGELHOOD	ANGLIFIES
ANCHORMAN	ANDESYTES	ANEMOSES	ANGELIC	ANGLIFY
ANCHORMEN	ANDIRON	ANEMOSIS	ANGELICA	ANGLING
ANCHORS	ANDIRONS	ANENST	ANGELICAL	ANGLINGS
ANCHOS	ANDOUILLE	ANENT	ANGELICAS	ANGLIST
ANCHOVETA	ANDRADITE	ANERGIA	ANGELING	ANGLISTS
ANCHOVIES	ANDRO	ANERGIAS	ANGELS	ANGLO
ANCHOVY	ANDROECIA	ANERGIC	ANGELUS	ANGLOPHIL
ANCHUSA	ANDROGEN	ANERGIES	ANGELUSES	ANGLOS
ANCHUSAS	ANDROGENS	ANERGY	ANGER	ANGOLA
ANCHUSIN	ANDROGYNE	ANERLY	ANGERED	ANGOPHORA
ANCHUSINS	ANDROGYNY	ANEROID	ANGERING	ANGORA
ANCHYLOSE	ANDROID	ANEROIDS	ANGERLESS	ANGORAS
ANCIENT	ANDROIDS	ANES	ANGERLY	ANGOSTURA
ANCIENTER	ANDROLOGY	ANESTRA	ANGERS	ANGRIER
ANCIENTLY	ANDROMEDA	ANESTRI	ANGICO	ANGRIES
ANCIENTRY	ANDROS	ANESTROUS	ANGICOS	ANGRIEST
ANCIENTS	ANDS	ANESTRUM	ANGINA	ANGRILY
ANCILE	ANDVILE	ANESTRUS	ANGINAL	ANGRINESS
ANCILIA	ANDVILES	ANETHOL	ANGINAS	ANGRY
ANCILLA	ANE	ANETHOLE	ANGINOSE	ANGST
ANCILLAE	ANEAR	ANETHOLES	ANGINOUS	ANGSTIER
ANCILLARY	ANEARED	ANETHOLS	ANGIOGRAM	ANGSTIEST

ANGSTROM	ANILINS	ANIMUSES	ANLAGES	ANNONAS
ANGSTROMS	ANILITIES	ANION	ANLAS	ANNOTATE
ANGSTS	ANILITY	ANIONIC	ANLASES	ANNOTATED
ANGSTY	ANILS	ANIONS	ANN	ANNOTATES
ANGUIFORM	ANIMA	ANIRIDIA	ANNA	ANNOTATOR
ANGUINE	ANIMACIES	ANIRIDIAS	ANNAL	ANNOUNCE
ANGUIPED	ANIMACY	ANIRIDIC	ANNALISE	ANNOUNCED
ANGUIPEDE	ANIMAL	ANIS	ANNALISED	ANNOUNCER
ANGUIPEDS	ANIMALIAN	ANISE	ANNALISES	ANNOUNCES
ANGUISH	ANIMALIC	ANISEED	ANNALIST	ANNOY
ANGUISHED	ANIMALIER	ANISEEDS	ANNALISTS	ANNOYANCE
ANGUISHES	ANIMALISE	ANISES	ANNALIZE	ANNOYED
ANGULAR	ANIMALISM	ANISETTE	ANNALIZED	ANNOYER
ANGULARLY	ANIMALIST	ANISETTES	ANNALIZES	ANNOYERS
ANGULATE	ANIMALITY	ANISIC	ANNALS	ANNOYING
ANGULATED	ANIMALIZE	ANISOGAMY	ANNAS	ANNOYS
ANGULATES	ANIMALLY	ANISOLE	ANNAT	ANNS
ANGULOSE	ANIMALS	ANISOLES	ANNATES	ANNUAL
ANGULOUS	ANIMAS	ANKER	ANNATS	ANNUALISE
ANHEDONIA	ANIMATE	ANKERITE	ANNATTA	ANNUALIZE
ANHEDONIC	ANIMATED	ANKERITES	ANNATTAS	ANNUALLY
ANHEDRAL	ANIMATELY	ANKERS	ANNATTO	ANNUALS
ANHEDRALS	ANIMATER	ANKH	ANNATTOS	ANNUITANT
ANHINGA	ANIMATERS	ANKHS	ANNEAL	ANNUITIES
ANHINGAS	ANIMATES	ANKLE	ANNEALED	ANNUITISE
ANHUNGRED	ANIMATEUR	ANKLEBONE	ANNEALER	ANNUITIZE
ANHYDRASE	ANIMATI	ANKLED	ANNEALERS	ANNUITY
ANHYDRIDE	ANIMATIC	ANKLES	ANNEALING	ANNUL
ANHYDRITE	ANIMATICS	ANKLET	ANNEALS	ANNULAR
ANHYDROUS	ANIMATING	ANKLETS	ANNECTENT	ANNULARLY
ANI	ANIMATION	ANKLING	ANNELID	ANNULARS
ANICCA	ANIMATISM	ANKLONG	ANNELIDAN	ANNULATE
ANICCAS	ANIMATIST	ANKLONGS	ANNELIDS	ANNULATED
ANICONIC	ANIMATO	ANKLUNG	ANNEX	ANNULATES
ANICONISM	ANIMATOR	ANKLUNGS	ANNEXABLE	ANNULET
ANICONIST	ANIMATORS	ANKUS	ANNEXE	ANNULETS
ANICUT	ANIMATOS	ANKUSES	ANNEXED	ANNULI
ANICUTS	ANIME	ANKUSH	ANNEXES	ANNULLED
ANIDROSES	ANIMES	ANKUSHES	ANNEXING	ANNULLING
ANIDROSIS	ANIMI	ANKYLOSE	ANNEXION	ANNULMENT
ANIGH	ANIMIS	ANKYLOSED	ANNEXIONS	ANNULOSE
ANIGHT	ANIMISM	ANKYLOSES	ANNEXMENT	ANNULS
ANIL	ANIMISMS	ANKYLOSIS	ANNEXURE	ANNULUS
ANILE	ANIMIST	ANKYLOTIC	ANNEXURES	ANNULUSES
ANILIN	ANIMISTIC	ANLACE	ANNICUT	ANOA
ANILINE	ANIMISTS	ANLACES	ANNICUTS	ANOAS
ANILINES	ANIMOSITY	ANLAGE	ANNO	ANOBIID
ANILINGUS	ANIMUS	ANLAGEN	ANNONA	ANOBIIDS

ANODAL	ANONYMAS	ANSAPHONE	ANTEFIXES	ANTHOLOGY
ANODALLY	ANONYMISE	ANSATE	ANTEING	ANTHOTAXY
ANODE	ANONYMITY	ANSATED	ANTELOPE	ANTHOZOAN
ANODES	ANONYMIZE	ANSATZ	ANTELOPES	ANTHOZOIC
ANODIC	ANONYMOUS	ANSATZES	ANTELUCAN	ANTHRACES
ANODISE	ANONYMS	ANSERINE	ANTENATAL	ANTHRACIC
ANODISED	ANOOPSIA	ANSERINES	ANTENATI	ANTHRAX
ANODISER	ANOOPSIAS	ANSEROUS	ANTENNA	ANTHRAXES
ANODISERS	ANOPHELES	ANSWER	ANTENNAE	ANTHRO
ANODISES	ANOPIA	ANSWERED	ANTENNAL	ANTHROPIC
ANODISING	ANOPIAS	ANSWERER	ANTENNARY	ANTHROS
ANODIZE	ANOPSIA	ANSWERERS	ANTENNAS	ANTHURIUM
ANODIZED	ANOPSIAS	ANSWERING	ANTENNULE	ANTI
ANODIZER	ANORAK	ANSWERS	ANTEPAST	ANTIABUSE
ANODIZERS	ANORAKS	ANT	ANTEPASTS	ANTIACNE
ANODIZES	ANORECTAL	ANTA	ANTERIOR	ANTIAGING
ANODIZING	ANORECTIC	ANTACID	ANTEROOM	ANTIAIR
ANODONTIA	ANORETIC	ANTACIDS	ANTEROOMS	ANTIALIEN
ANODYNE	ANORETICS	ANTAE	ANTES	ANTIAR
ANODYNES	ANOREXIA	ANTALGIC	ANTETYPE	ANTIARIN
ANODYNIC	ANOREXIAS	ANTALGICS	ANTETYPES	ANTIARINS
ANOESES	ANOREXIC	ANTALKALI	ANTEVERT	ANTIARMOR
ANOESIS	ANOREXICS	ANTAR	ANTEVERTS	ANTIARS
ANOESTRA	ANOREXIES	ANTARA	ANTHELIA	ANTIATOM
ANOESTRI	ANOREXY	ANTARAS	ANTHELION	ANTIATOMS
ANOESTRUM	ANORTHIC	ANTARCTIC	ANTHELIX	ANTIAUXIN
ANOESTRUS	ANORTHITE	ANTARS	ANTHEM	ANTIBIAS
ANOETIC	ANOSMATIC	ANTAS	ANTHEMED	ANTIBLACK
ANOINT	ANOSMIA	ANTBEAR	ANTHEMIA	ANTIBODY
ANOINTED	ANOSMIAS	ANTBEARS	ANTHEMIC	ANTIBOSS
ANOINTER	ANOSMIC	ANTBIRD	ANTHEMING	ANTIBUG
ANOINTERS	ANOTHER	ANTBIRDS	ANTHEMION	ANTIBUSER
ANOINTING	ANOUGH	ANTE	ANTHEMIS	ANTIC
ANOINTS	ANOUROUS	ANTEATER	ANTHEMS	ANTICAL
ANOLE	ANOVULANT	ANTEATERS	ANTHER	ANTICALLY
ANOLES	ANOVULAR	ANTECEDE	ANTHERAL	ANTICAR
ANOLYTE	ANOW	ANTECEDED	ANTHERID	ANTICHLOR
ANOLYTES	ANOXAEMIA	ANTECEDES	ANTHERIDS	ANTICISE
ANOMALIES	ANOXAEMIC	ANTECHOIR	ANTHERS	ANTICISED
ANOMALOUS	ANOXEMIA	ANTED	ANTHESES	ANTICISES
ANOMALY	ANOXEMIAS	ANTEDATE	ANTHESIS	ANTICITY
ANOMIC	ANOXEMIC	ANTEDATED	ANTHILL	ANTICIVIC
ANOMIE	ANOXIA	ANTEDATES	ANTHILLS	ANTICIZE
ANOMIES	ANOXIAS	ANTEED	ANTHOCARP	ANTICIZED
ANOMY	ANOXIC	ANTEFIX	ANTHOCYAN	ANTICIZES
ANON	ANS	ANTEFIXA	ANTHODIA	ANTICK
ANONYM	ANSA	ANTEFIXAE	ANTHODIUM	ANTICKE
ANONYMA	ANSAE	ANTEFIXAL	ANTHOID	ANTICKED

ANVILLED

A

ANTICKES	ANTIJAM	ANTIPATHY	ANTISHARK	ANTIWOMAN
ANTICKING	ANTIKING	ANTIPHON	ANTISHIP	ANTIWORLD
ANTICKS	ANTIKINGS	ANTIPHONS	ANTISHOCK	ANTLER
ANTICLINE	ANTIKNOCK	ANTIPHONY	ANTISKID	ANTLERED
ANTICLING	ANTILABOR	ANTIPILL	ANTISLEEP	ANTLERS
ANTICLY	ANTILEAK	ANTIPODAL	ANTISLIP	ANTLIA
ANTICODON	ANTILEFT	ANTIPODE	ANTISMOG	ANTLIAE
ANTICOLD	ANTILIFE	ANTIPODES	ANTISMOKE	ANTLIATE
ANTICOUS	ANTILIFER	ANTIPOLAR	ANTISMUT	ANTLIKE
ANTICRACK	ANTILOCK	ANTIPOLE	ANTISNOB	ANTLION
ANTICRIME	ANTILOG	ANTIPOLES	ANTISNOBS	ANTLIONS
ANTICS	ANTILOGS	ANTIPOPE	ANTISOLAR	ANTONYM
ANTICULT	ANTILOGY	ANTIPOPES	ANTISPAM	ANTONYMIC
ANTICULTS	ANTIMACHO	ANTIPORN	ANTISPAST	ANTONYMS
ANTIDORA	ANTIMALE	ANTIPOT	ANTISTAT	ANTONYMY
ANTIDORON	ANTIMAN	ANTIPRESS	ANTISTATE	ANTPITTA
ANTIDOTAL	ANTIMASK	ANTIPYIC	ANTISTATS	ANTPITTAS
ANTIDOTE	ANTIMASKS	ANTIPYICS	ANTISTICK	ANTRA
ANTIDOTED	ANTIMEN	ANTIQUARK	ANTISTORY	ANTRAL
ANTIDOTES	ANTIMERE	ANTIQUARY	ANTISTYLE	ANTRE
ANTIDRAFT	ANTIMERES	ANTIQUATE	ANTITANK	ANTRES
ANTIDRUG	ANTIMERIC	ANTIQUE	ANTITAX	ANTRORSE
ANTIDUNE	ANTIMINE	ANTIQUED	ANTITHEFT	ANTRUM
ANTIDUNES	ANTIMONIC	ANTIQUELY	ANTITHET	ANTRUMS
ANTIELITE	ANTIMONY	ANTIQUER	ANTITHETS	ANTS
ANTIENT	ANTIMONYL	ANTIQUERS	ANTITOXIC	ANTSIER
ANTIENTS	ANTIMUON	ANTIQUES	ANTITOXIN	ANTSIEST
ANTIFA	ANTIMUONS	ANTIQUEY	ANTITRADE	ANTSINESS
ANTIFAS	ANTIMUSIC	ANTIQUIER	ANTITRAGI	ANTSY
ANTIFAT	ANTIMYCIN	ANTIQUING	ANTITRUST	ANTWACKIE
ANTIFLU	ANTING	ANTIQUITY	ANTITUMOR	ANUCLEATE
ANTIFOAM	ANTINGS	ANTIRADAR	ANTITYPAL	ANURA
ANTIFOG	ANTINODAL	ANTIRAPE	ANTITYPE	ANURAL
ANTIFRAUD	ANTINODE	ANTIRED	ANTITYPES	ANURAN
ANTIFUR	ANTINODES	ANTIRIOT	ANTITYPIC	ANURANS
ANTIGANG	ANTINOISE	ANTIROCK	ANTIULCER	ANURESES
ANTIGAY	ANTINOME	ANTIROLL	ANTIUNION	ANURESIS
ANTIGEN	ANTINOMES	ANTIROYAL	ANTIURBAN	ANURETIC
ANTIGENE	ANTINOMIC	ANTIRUST	ANTIVAX	ANURIA
ANTIGENES	ANTINOMY	ANTIRUSTS	ANTIVAXER	ANURIAS
ANTIGENIC	ANTINOVEL	ANTIS	ANTIVENIN	ANURIC
ANTIGENS	ANTINUKE	ANTISAG	ANTIVENOM	ANUROUS
ANTIGLARE	ANTINUKER	ANTISCIAN	ANTIVIRAL	ANUS
ANTIGRAFT	ANTINUKES	ANTISENSE	ANTIVIRUS	ANUSES
ANTIGUN	ANTIPAPAL	ANTISERA	ANTIWAR	ANVIL
ANTIHELIX	ANTIPARTY	ANTISERUM	ANTIWEAR	ANVILED
ANTIHERO	ANTIPASTI	ANTISEX	ANTIWEED	ANVILING
ANTIHUMAN	ANTIPASTO	ANTISHAKE	ANTIWHITE	ANVILLED

ANVILLING	APAGOGIC	APERS	APHIDES	APICULATE
ANVILS	APAID	APERT	APHIDIAN	APICULI
ANVILTOP	APANAGE	APERTNESS	APHIDIANS	APICULUS
ANVILTOPS	APANAGED	APERTURAL	APHIDIOUS	APIECE
ANXIETIES	APANAGES	APERTURE	APHIDS	APIEZON
ANXIETY	APAREJO	APERTURED	APHIS	APIMANIA
ANXIOUS	APAREJOS	APERTURES	APHOLATE	APIMANIAS
ANXIOUSLY	APART	APERY	APHOLATES	APING
ANY	APARTHEID	APES	APHONIA	APIOL
ANYBODIES	APARTMENT	APESHIT	APHONIAS	APIOLOGY
ANYBODY	APARTNESS	APETALIES	APHONIC	APIOLS
ANYHOW	APATETIC	APETALOUS	APHONICS	APISH
ANYMORE	APATHATON	APETALY	APHONIES	APISHLY
ANYON	APATHETIC	APEX	APHONOUS	APISHNESS
ANYONE	APATHIES	APEXES	APHONY	APISM
ANYONES	APATHY	APGAR	APHORISE	APISMS
ANYONS	APATITE	APHAGIA	APHORISED	APIVOROUS
ANYPLACE	APATITES	APHAGIAS	APHORISER	APLANAT
ANYROAD	APATOSAUR	APHAKIA	APHORISES	APLANATIC
ANYTHING	APAY	APHAKIAS	APHORISM	APLANATS
ANYTHINGS	APAYD	APHANITE	APHORISMS	APLANETIC
ANYTIME	APAYING	APHANITES	APHORIST	APLASIA
ANYWAY	APAYS	APHANITIC	APHORISTS	APLASIAS
ANYWAYS	APE	APHASIA	APHORIZE	APLASTIC
ANYWHEN	APEAK	APHASIAC	APHORIZED	APLENTY
ANYWHERE	APED	APHASIACS	APHORIZER	APLITE
ANYWHERES	APEDOM	APHASIAS	APHORIZES	APLITES
ANYWISE	APEDOMS	APHASIC	APHOTIC	APLITIC
ANZIANI	APEEK	APHASICS	APHRODITE	APLOMB
AORIST	APEHOOD	APHELIA	APHTHA	APLOMBS
AORISTIC	APEHOODS	APHELIAN	APHTHAE	APLUSTRE
AORISTS	APELIKE	APHELION	APHTHOUS	APLUSTRES
AORTA	APEMAN	APHELIONS	APHYLLIES	APNEA
AORTAE	APEMEN	APHERESES	APHYLLOUS	APNEAL
AORTAL	APEPSIA	APHERESIS	APHYLLY	APNEAS
AORTAS	APEPSIAS	APHERETIC	APIACEOUS	APNEIC
AORTIC	APEPSIES	APHESES	APIAN	APNEUSES
AORTITIS	APEPSY	APHESIS	APIARIAN	APNEUSIS
AOUDAD	APER	APHETIC	APIARIANS	APNEUSTIC
AOUDADS	APERCU	APHETISE	APIARIES	APNOEA
APACE	APERCUS	APHETISED	APIARIST	APNOEAL
APACHE	APERIENT	APHETISES	APIARISTS	APNOEAS
APACHES	APERIENTS	APHETIZE	APIARY	APNOEIC
APADANA	APERIES	APHETIZED	APICAL	APO
APADANAS	APERIODIC	APHETIZES	APICALLY	APOAPSES
APAGE	APERITIF	APHICIDE	APICALS	APOAPSIS
APAGOGE	APERITIFS	APHICIDES	APICES	APOCARP
APAGOGES	APERITIVE	APHID	APICIAN	APOCARPS

APOCARPY
APOCOPATE
APOCOPE
APOCOPES
APOCOPIC
APOCRINE
APOCRYPHA
APOD
APODAL
APODE
APODES
APODICTIC
APODOSES
APODOSIS
APODOUS
APODS
APOENZYME
APOGAEIC
APOGAMIC
APOGAMIES
APOGAMOUS
APOGAMY
APOGEAL
APOGEAN
APOGEE
APOGEES
APOGEIC
APOGRAPH
APOGRAPHS
APOLLO
APOLLOS
APOLOG
APOLOGAL
APOLOGIA
APOLOGIAE
APOLOGIAS
APOLOGIES
APOLOGISE
APOLOGIST
APOLOGIZE
APOLOGS
APOLOGUE
APOLOGUES
APOLOGY
APOLUNE
APOLUNES
APOMICT
APOMICTIC

APOMICTS
APOMIXES
APOMIXIS
APOOP
APOPHASES
APOPHASIS
APOPHATIC
APOPHENIA
APOPHONY
APOPHYGE
APOPHYGES
APOPHYSES
APOPHYSIS
APOPLAST
APOPLASTS
APOPLEX
APOPLEXED
APOPLEXES
APOPLEXY
APOPTOSES
APOPTOSIS
APOPTOTIC
APORETIC
APORIA
APORIAS
APORT
APOS
APOSITIA
APOSITIAS
APOSITIC
APOSPORIC
APOSPORY
APOSTACY
APOSTASY
APOSTATE
APOSTATES
APOSTATIC
APOSTIL
APOSTILLE
APOSTILS
APOSTLE
APOSTLES
APOSTOLIC
APOTHECE
APOTHECES
APOTHECIA
APOTHEGM
APOTHEGMS

APOTHEM
APOTHEMS
APOZEM
APOZEMS
APP
APPAID
APPAIR
APPAIRED
APPAIRING
APPAIRS
APPAL
APPALL
APPALLED
APPALLING
APPALLS
APPALOOSA
APPALS
APPALTI
APPALTO
APPANAGE
APPANAGED
APPANAGES
APPARAT
APPARATS
APPARATUS
APPAREL
APPARELED
APPARELS
APPARENCY
APPARENT
APPARENTS
APPARITOR
APPAY
APPAYD
APPAYING
APPAYS
APPEACH
APPEACHED
APPEACHES
APPEAL
APPEALED
APPEALER
APPEALERS
APPEALING
APPEALS
APPEAR
APPEARED
APPEARER

APPEARERS
APPEARING
APPEARS
APPEASE
APPEASED
APPEASER
APPEASERS
APPEASES
APPEASING
APPEL
APPELLANT
APPELLATE
APPELLEE
APPELLEES
APPELLOR
APPELLORS
APPELS
APPEND
APPENDAGE
APPENDANT
APPENDED
APPENDENT
APPENDING
APPENDIX
APPENDS
APPERIL
APPERILL
APPERILLS
APPERILS
APPERTAIN
APPESTAT
APPESTATS
APPETENCE
APPETENCY
APPETENT
APPETIBLE
APPETISE
APPETISED
APPETISER
APPETISES
APPETITE
APPETITES
APPETIZE
APPETIZED
APPETIZER
APPETIZES
APPLAUD
APPLAUDED

APPLAUDER
APPLAUDS
APPLAUSE
APPLAUSES
APPLE
APPLECART
APPLEJACK
APPLES
APPLET
APPLETINI
APPLETS
APPLEY
APPLIABLE
APPLIANCE
APPLICANT
APPLICATE
APPLIED
APPLIER
APPLIERS
APPLIES
APPLIEST
APPLIQUE
APPLIQUED
APPLIQUES
APPLY
APPLYING
APPOINT
APPOINTED
APPOINTEE
APPOINTER
APPOINTOR
APPOINTS
APPORT
APPORTION
APPORTS
APPOSABLE
APPOSE
APPOSED
APPOSER
APPOSERS
APPOSING
APPOSITE
APPRAISAL
APPRAISE
APPRAISED
APPRAISEE
APPRAISER

APPRAISES	APRICATED	APTOTE	AQUATINT	ARACHISES
APPREHEND	APRICATES	APTOTES	AQUATINTA	ARACHNID
APPRESS	APRICOCK	APTOTIC	AQUATINTS	ARACHNIDS
APPRESSED	APRICOCKS	APTS	AQUATONE	ARACHNOID
APPRESSES	APRICOT	APYRASE	AQUATONES	ARAGONITE
APPRISE	APRICOTS	APYRASES	AQUAVIT	ARAHUANA
APPRISED	APRIORISM	APYRETIC	AQUAVITS	ARAHUANAS
APPRISER	APRIORIST	APYREXIA	AQUEDUCT	ARAISE
APPRISERS	APRIORITY	APYREXIAS	AQUEDUCTS	ARAISED
APPRISES	APRON	AQUA	AQUEOUS	ARAISES
APPRISING	APRONED	AQUABATIC	AQUEOUSLY	ARAISING
APPRIZE	APRONFUL	AQUABOARD	AQUIFER	ARAK
APPRIZED	APRONFULS	AQUACADE	AQUIFERS	ARAKS
APPRIZER	APRONING	AQUACADES	AQUILEGIA	ARALIA
APPRIZERS	APRONLIKE	AQUADROME	AQUILINE	ARALIAS
APPRIZES	APRONS	AQUAE	AQUILON	ARAME
APPRIZING	APROPOS	AQUAFABA	AQUILONS	ARAMES
APPRO	APROTIC	AQUAFABAS	AQUIVER	ARAMID
APPROACH	APSARAS	AQUAFARM	AR	ARAMIDS
APPROBATE	APSARASES	AQUAFARMS	ARAARA	ARANCINI
APPROOF	APSE	AQUAFER	ARAARAS	ARANEID
APPROOFS	APSES	AQUAFERS	ARABA	ARANEIDAN
APPROS	APSIDAL	AQUAFIT	ARABAS	ARANEIDS
APPROVAL	APSIDES	AQUAFITS	ARABESK	ARANEOUS
APPROVALS	APSIDIOLE	AQUALUNG	ARABESKS	ARAPAIMA
APPROVE	APSIS	AQUALUNGS	ARABESQUE	ARAPAIMAS
APPROVED	APSO	AQUANAUT	ARABIC	ARAPONGA
APPROVER	APSOS	AQUANAUTS	ARABICA	ARAPONGAS
APPROVERS	APT	AQUAPHOBE	ARABICAS	ARAPUNGA
APPROVES	APTAMER	AQUAPLANE	ARABICISE	ARAPUNGAS
APPROVING	APTAMERS	AQUAPORIN	ARABICIZE	ARAR
APPS	APTED	AQUARELLE	ARABILITY	ARAROBA
APPUI	APTER	AQUARIA	ARABIN	ARAROBAS
APPUIED	APTERAL	AQUARIAL	ARABINOSE	ARARS
APPUIS	APTERIA	AQUARIAN	ARABINS	ARAUCARIA
APPULSE	APTERISM	AQUARIANS	ARABIS	ARAWANA
APPULSES	APTERISMS	AQUARIIST	ARABISE	ARAWANAS
APPULSIVE	APTERIUM	AQUARIST	ARABISED	ARAYSE
APPUY	APTEROUS	AQUARISTS	ARABISES	ARAYSED
APPUYED	APTERYX	AQUARIUM	ARABISING	ARAYSES
APPUYING	APTERYXES	AQUARIUMS	ARABIZE	ARAYSING
APPUYS	APTEST	AQUAROBIC	ARABIZED	ARB
APRACTIC	APTING	AQUAS	ARABIZES	ARBA
APRAXIA	APTITUDE	AQUASCAPE	ARABIZING	ARBALEST
APRAXIAS	APTITUDES	AQUASHOW	ARABLE	ARBALESTS
APRAXIC	APTLY	AQUASHOWS	ARABLES	ARBALIST
APRES	APTNESS	AQUATIC	ARACEOUS	ARBALISTS
APRICATE	APTNESSES	AQUATICS	ARACHIS	ARBAS

ARBELEST	ARCADE	ARCHDUKES	ARCHONTIC	ARDOURS
ARBELESTS	ARCADED	ARCHEAN	ARCHOSAUR	ARDRI
ARBITER	ARCADES	ARCHED	ARCHRIVAL	ARDRIGH
ARBITERS	ARCADIA	ARCHEI	ARCHSTONE	ARDRIGHS
ARBITRAGE	ARCADIAN	ARCHENEMY	ARCHWAY	ARDRIS
ARBITRAL	ARCADIANS	ARCHER	ARCHWAYS	ARDS
ARBITRARY	ARCADIAS	ARCHERESS	ARCHWISE	ARDUOUS
ARBITRATE	ARCADING	ARCHERIES	ARCIFORM	ARDUOUSLY
ARBITRESS	ARCADINGS	ARCHERS	ARCING	ARE
ARBITRIUM	ARCANA	ARCHERY	ARCINGS	AREA
ARBLAST	ARCANAS	ARCHES	ARCKED	AREACH
ARBLASTER	ARCANE	ARCHEST	ARCKING	AREACHED
ARBLASTS	ARCANELY	ARCHETYPE	ARCKINGS	AREACHES
ARBOR	ARCANIST	ARCHEUS	ARCMIN	AREACHING
ARBOREAL	ARCANISTS	ARCHFIEND	ARCMINS	AREAD
ARBORED	ARCANUM	ARCHFOE	ARCMINUTE	AREADING
ARBOREOUS	ARCANUMS	ARCHFOES	ARCO	AREADS
ARBORES	ARCATURE	ARCHFOOL	ARCOGRAPH	AREAE
ARBORET	ARCATURES	ARCHFOOLS	ARCOLOGY	AREAL
ARBORETA	ARCCOSINE	ARCHI	ARCOS	AREALLY
ARBORETS	ARCED	ARCHICARP	ARCS	AREAR
ARBORETUM	ARCH	ARCHIL	ARCSEC	AREARS
ARBORIO	ARCHAEA	ARCHILOWE	ARCSECOND	AREAS
ARBORIOS	ARCHAEAL	ARCHILS	ARCSECS	AREAWAY
ARBORISE	ARCHAEAN	ARCHIMAGE	ARCSINE	AREAWAYS
ARBORISED	ARCHAEANS	ARCHINE	ARCSINES	ARECA
ARBORISES	ARCHAEI	ARCHINES	ARCTIC	ARECAS
ARBORIST	ARCHAEON	ARCHING	ARCTICS	ARECOLINE
ARBORISTS	ARCHAEUS	ARCHINGS	ARCTIID	ARED
ARBORIZE	ARCHAIC	ARCHITECT	ARCTIIDS	AREDD
ARBORIZED	ARCHAICAL	ARCHITYPE	ARCTOID	AREDE
ARBORIZES	ARCHAISE	ARCHIVAL	ARCTOPHIL	AREDES
ARBOROUS	ARCHAISED	ARCHIVE	ARCUATE	AREDING
ARBORS	ARCHAISER	ARCHIVED	ARCUATED	AREFIED
ARBOUR	ARCHAISES	ARCHIVES	ARCUATELY	AREFIES
ARBOURED	ARCHAISM	ARCHIVING	ARCUATION	AREFY
ARBOURS	ARCHAISMS	ARCHIVIST	ARCUS	AREFYING
ARBOVIRAL	ARCHAIST	ARCHIVOLT	ARCUSES	AREG
ARBOVIRUS	ARCHAISTS	ARCHLET	ARD	AREIC
ARBS	ARCHAIZE	ARCHLETS	ARDEB	ARENA
ARBUSCLE	ARCHAIZED	ARCHLIKE	ARDEBS	ARENAS
ARBUSCLES	ARCHAIZER	ARCHLUTE	ARDENCIES	ARENATION
ARBUTE	ARCHAIZES	ARCHLUTES	ARDENCY	ARENE
ARBUTEAN	ARCHANGEL	ARCHLY	ARDENT	ARENES
ARBUTES	ARCHDRUID	ARCHNESS	ARDENTLY	ARENITE
ARBUTUS	ARCHDUCAL	ARCHOLOGY	ARDOR	ARENITES
ARBUTUSES	ARCHDUCHY	ARCHON	ARDORS	ARENITIC
ARC	ARCHDUKE	ARCHONS	ARDOUR	ARENOSE

ARENOUS	ARGENTS	ARGUMENTS	ARILS	ARMCHAIRS
AREOLA	ARGENTUM	ARGUS	ARIOSE	ARMED
AREOLAE	ARGENTUMS	ARGUSES	ARIOSI	ARMER
AREOLAR	ARGH	ARGUTE	ARIOSO	ARMERIA
AREOLAS	ARGHAN	ARGUTELY	ARIOSOS	ARMERIAS
AREOLATE	ARGHANS	ARGYLE	ARIOT	ARMERS
AREOLATED	ARGIL	ARGYLES	ARIPPLE	ARMET
AREOLE	ARGILLITE	ARGYLL	ARIS	ARMETS
AREOLES	ARGILS	ARGYLLS	ARISE	ARMFUL
AREOLOGY	ARGINASE	ARGYRIA	ARISEN	ARMFULS
AREOMETER	ARGINASES	ARGYRIAS	ARISES	ARMGAUNT
AREOMETRY	ARGININE	ARGYRITE	ARISH	ARMGUARD
AREOSTYLE	ARGININES	ARGYRITES	ARISHES	ARMGUARDS
AREPA	ARGLE	ARHAT	ARISING	ARMHOLE
AREPAS	ARGLED	ARHATS	ARISTA	ARMHOLES
ARERE	ARGLES	ARHATSHIP	ARISTAE	ARMIES
ARES	ARGLING	ARHYTHMIA	ARISTAS	ARMIGER
ARET	ARGOL	ARHYTHMIC	ARISTATE	ARMIGERAL
ARETE	ARGOLS	ARIA	ARISTO	ARMIGERO
ARETES	ARGON	ARIARIES	ARISTOS	ARMIGEROS
ARETHUSA	ARGONAUT	ARIARY	ARISTOTLE	ARMIGERS
ARETHUSAS	ARGONAUTS	ARIAS	ARK	ARMIL
ARETS	ARGONON	ARID	ARKED	ARMILLA
ARETT	ARGONONS	ARIDER	ARKING	ARMILLAE
ARETTED	ARGONS	ARIDEST	ARKITE	ARMILLARY
ARETTING	ARGOSIES	ARIDITIES	ARKITES	ARMILLAS
ARETTS	ARGOSY	ARIDITY	ARKOSE	ARMILS
AREW	ARGOT	ARIDLY	ARKOSES	ARMING
ARF	ARGOTIC	ARIDNESS	ARKOSIC	ARMINGS
ARFS	ARGOTS	ARIEL	ARKS	ARMISTICE
ARGAL	ARGUABLE	ARIELS	ARLE	ARMLESS
ARGALA	ARGUABLY	ARIETTA	ARLED	ARMLET
ARGALAS	ARGUE	ARIETTAS	ARLES	ARMLETS
ARGALI	ARGUED	ARIETTE	ARLING	ARMLIKE
ARGALIS	ARGUER	ARIETTES	ARM	ARMLOAD
ARGALS	ARGUERS	ARIGHT	ARMADA	ARMLOADS
ARGAN	ARGUES	ARIKI	ARMADAS	ARMLOCK
ARGAND	ARGUFIED	ARIKIS	ARMADILLO	ARMLOCKED
ARGANDS	ARGUFIER	ARIL	ARMAGNAC	ARMLOCKS
ARGANS	ARGUFIERS	ARILED	ARMAGNACS	ARMOIRE
ARGEMONE	ARGUFIES	ARILLARY	ARMAMENT	ARMOIRES
ARGEMONES	ARGUFY	ARILLATE	ARMAMENTS	ARMONICA
ARGENT	ARGUFYING	ARILLATED	ARMATURE	ARMONICAS
ARGENTAL	ARGUING	ARILLI	ARMATURED	ARMOR
ARGENTIC	ARGULI	ARILLODE	ARMATURES	ARMORED
ARGENTINE	ARGULUS	ARILLODES	ARMBAND	ARMORER
ARGENTITE	ARGUMENT	ARILLOID	ARMBANDS	ARMORERS
ARGENTOUS	ARGUMENTA	ARILLUS	ARMCHAIR	ARMORIAL

ARMORIALS
ARMORIES
ARMORING
ARMORIST
ARMORISTS
ARMORLESS
ARMORS
ARMORY
ARMOUR
ARMOURED
ARMOURER
ARMOURERS
ARMOURIES
ARMOURING
ARMOURS
ARMOURY
ARMOZEEN
ARMOZEENS
ARMOZINE
ARMOZINES
ARMPIT
ARMPITS
ARMREST
ARMRESTS
ARMS
ARMSFUL
ARMURE
ARMURES
ARMY
ARMYWORM
ARMYWORMS
ARNA
ARNAS
ARNATTO
ARNATTOS
ARNICA
ARNICAS
ARNOTTO
ARNOTTOS
ARNUT
ARNUTS
AROBA
AROBAS
AROHA
AROHAS
AROID
AROIDS
AROINT

AROINTED
AROINTING
AROINTS
AROLLA
AROLLAS
AROMA
AROMAS
AROMATASE
AROMATIC
AROMATICS
AROMATISE
AROMATIZE
AROSE
AROUND
AROUSABLE
AROUSAL
AROUSALS
AROUSE
AROUSED
AROUSER
AROUSERS
AROUSES
AROUSING
AROW
AROWANA
AROWANAS
AROYNT
AROYNTED
AROYNTING
AROYNTS
ARPA
ARPAS
ARPEGGIO
ARPEGGIOS
ARPEN
ARPENS
ARPENT
ARPENTS
ARPILLERA
ARQUEBUS
ARRACACHA
ARRACK
ARRACKS
ARRAH
ARRAIGN
ARRAIGNED
ARRAIGNER
ARRAIGNS

ARRANGE
ARRANGED
ARRANGER
ARRANGERS
ARRANGES
ARRANGING
ARRANT
ARRANTLY
ARRAS
ARRASED
ARRASENE
ARRASENES
ARRASES
ARRAUGHT
ARRAY
ARRAYAL
ARRAYALS
ARRAYED
ARRAYER
ARRAYERS
ARRAYING
ARRAYMENT
ARRAYS
ARREAR
ARREARAGE
ARREARS
ARRECT
ARREEDE
ARREEDES
ARREEDING
ARREST
ARRESTANT
ARRESTED
ARRESTEE
ARRESTEES
ARRESTER
ARRESTERS
ARRESTING
ARRESTIVE
ARRESTOR
ARRESTORS
ARRESTS
ARRET
ARRETS
ARRHIZAL
ARRIAGE
ARRIAGES
ARRIBA

ARRIDE
ARRIDED
ARRIDES
ARRIDING
ARRIERE
ARRIERO
ARRIEROS
ARRIS
ARRISES
ARRISH
ARRISHES
ARRIVAL
ARRIVALS
ARRIVANCE
ARRIVANCY
ARRIVE
ARRIVED
ARRIVER
ARRIVERS
ARRIVES
ARRIVING
ARRIVISME
ARRIVISTE
ARROBA
ARROBAS
ARROCES
ARROGANCE
ARROGANCY
ARROGANT
ARROGATE
ARROGATED
ARROGATES
ARROGATOR
ARROW
ARROWED
ARROWHEAD
ARROWIER
ARROWIEST
ARROWING
ARROWLESS
ARROWLIKE
ARROWROOT
ARROWS
ARROWWOOD
ARROWWORM
ARROWY
ARROYO
ARROYOS

ARROZ
ARROZES
ARS
ARSE
ARSED
ARSEHOLE
ARSEHOLED
ARSEHOLES
ARSENAL
ARSENALS
ARSENATE
ARSENATES
ARSENIATE
ARSENIC
ARSENICAL
ARSENICS
ARSENIDE
ARSENIDES
ARSENIOUS
ARSENITE
ARSENITES
ARSENO
ARSENOUS
ARSES
ARSEY
ARSHEEN
ARSHEENS
ARSHIN
ARSHINE
ARSHINES
ARSHINS
ARSIER
ARSIEST
ARSINE
ARSINES
ARSING
ARSINO
ARSIS
ARSON
ARSONIST
ARSONISTS
ARSONITE
ARSONITES
ARSONOUS
ARSONS
ARSY
ART
ARTAL

ARTEFACT	ARTIST	ARYTHMIAS	ASCITES	ASHED
ARTEFACTS	ARTISTE	ARYTHMIC	ASCITIC	ASHEN
ARTEL	ARTISTES	AS	ASCITICAL	ASHERIES
ARTELS	ARTISTIC	ASAFETIDA	ASCLEPIAD	ASHERY
ARTEMISIA	ARTISTRY	ASANA	ASCLEPIAS	ASHES
ARTERIAL	ARTISTS	ASANAS	ASCOCARP	ASHET
ARTERIALS	ARTLESS	ASAR	ASCOCARPS	ASHETS
ARTERIES	ARTLESSLY	ASARUM	ASCOGONIA	ASHFALL
ARTERIOLE	ARTMAKER	ASARUMS	ASCON	ASHFALLS
ARTERITIS	ARTMAKERS	ASBESTIC	ASCONCE	ASHIER
ARTERY	ARTMAKING	ASBESTINE	ASCONOID	ASHIEST
ARTESIAN	ARTS	ASBESTOS	ASCONS	ASHINE
ARTFUL	ARTSIE	ASBESTOUS	ASCORBATE	ASHINESS
ARTFULLY	ARTSIER	ASBESTUS	ASCORBIC	ASHING
ARTHOUSE	ARTSIES	ASCARED	ASCOSPORE	ASHIVER
ARTHOUSES	ARTSIEST	ASCARID	ASCOT	ASHKEY
ARTHRITIC	ARTSINESS	ASCARIDES	ASCOTS	ASHKEYS
ARTHRITIS	ARTSMAN	ASCARIDS	ASCRIBE	ASHLAR
ARTHRODIA	ARTSMEN	ASCARIS	ASCRIBED	ASHLARED
ARTHROPOD	ARTSY	ASCARISES	ASCRIBES	ASHLARING
ARTHROSES	ARTWORK	ASCAUNT	ASCRIBING	ASHLARS
ARTHROSIS	ARTWORKS	ASCEND	ASCUS	ASHLER
ARTI	ARTY	ASCENDANT	ASDIC	ASHLERED
ARTIC	ARUANA	ASCENDED	ASDICS	ASHLERING
ARTICHOKE	ARUANAS	ASCENDENT	ASEA	ASHLERS
ARTICLE	ARUGOLA	ASCENDER	ASEISMIC	ASHLESS
ARTICLED	ARUGOLAS	ASCENDERS	ASEITIES	ASHMAN
ARTICLES	ARUGULA	ASCENDEUR	ASEITY	ASHMEN
ARTICLING	ARUGULAS	ASCENDING	ASEMANTIC	ASHORE
ARTICS	ARUHE	ASCENDS	ASEPALOUS	ASHPAN
ARTICULAR	ARUHES	ASCENSION	ASEPSES	ASHPANS
ARTIER	ARUM	ASCENSIVE	ASEPSIS	ASHPLANT
ARTIES	ARUMS	ASCENT	ASEPTATE	ASHPLANTS
ARTIEST	ARUSPEX	ASCENTS	ASEPTIC	ASHRAF
ARTIFACT	ARUSPICES	ASCERTAIN	ASEPTICS	ASHRAM
ARTIFACTS	ARVAL	ASCESES	ASEXUAL	ASHRAMA
ARTIFICE	ARVEE	ASCESIS	ASEXUALLY	ASHRAMAS
ARTIFICER	ARVEES	ASCETIC	ASH	ASHRAMITE
ARTIFICES	ARVICOLE	ASCETICAL	ASHAKE	ASHRAMS
ARTIGI	ARVICOLES	ASCETICS	ASHAME	ASHTANGA
ARTIGIS	ARVO	ASCI	ASHAMED	ASHTANGAS
ARTILLERY	ARVOS	ASCIAN	ASHAMEDLY	ASHTRAY
ARTILY	ARY	ASCIANS	ASHAMES	ASHTRAYS
ARTINESS	ARYBALLOS	ASCIDIA	ASHAMING	ASHY
ARTIS	ARYL	ASCIDIAN	ASHCAKE	ASIAGO
ARTISAN	ARYLS	ASCIDIANS	ASHCAKES	ASIAGOS
ARTISANAL	ARYTENOID	ASCIDIATE	ASHCAN	ASIDE
ARTISANS	ARYTHMIA	ASCIDIUM	ASHCANS	ASIDES

ASSIGNING

ASINICO ASPECTED ASPHYXIES ASS ASSENTIVE
ASINICOS ASPECTING ASPHYXY ASSAGAI ASSENTOR
ASININE ASPECTS ASPIC ASSAGAIED ASSENTORS
ASININELY ASPECTUAL ASPICK ASSAGAIS ASSENTS
ASININITY ASPEN ASPICKS ASSAI ASSERT
ASK ASPENS ASPICS ASSAIL ASSERTED
ASKANCE ASPER ASPIDIA ASSAILANT ASSERTER
ASKANCED ASPERATE ASPIDIOID ASSAILED ASSERTERS
ASKANCES ASPERATED ASPIDIUM ASSAILER ASSERTING
ASKANCING ASPERATES ASPIE ASSAILERS ASSERTION
ASKANT ASPERGE ASPIES ASSAILING ASSERTIVE
ASKANTED ASPERGED ASPINE ASSAILS ASSERTOR
ASKANTING ASPERGER ASPINES ASSAIS ASSERTORS
ASKANTS ASPERGERS ASPIRANT ASSAM ASSERTORY
ASKARI ASPERGES ASPIRANTS ASSAMS ASSERTS
ASKARIS ASPERGILL ASPIRATA ASSART ASSES
ASKED ASPERGING ASPIRATAE ASSARTED ASSESS
ASKER ASPERITY ASPIRATE ASSARTING ASSESSED
ASKERS ASPERMIA ASPIRATED ASSARTS ASSESSES
ASKESES ASPERMIAS ASPIRATES ASSASSIN ASSESSING
ASKESIS ASPEROUS ASPIRATOR ASSASSINS ASSESSOR
ASKEW ASPERS ASPIRE ASSAULT ASSESSORS
ASKEWNESS ASPERSE ASPIRED ASSAULTED ASSET
ASKING ASPERSED ASPIRER ASSAULTER ASSETLESS
ASKINGS ASPERSER ASPIRERS ASSAULTS ASSETS
ASKLENT ASPERSERS ASPIRES ASSAY ASSEVER
ASKOI ASPERSES ASPIRIN ASSAYABLE ASSEVERED
ASKOS ASPERSING ASPIRING ASSAYED ASSEVERS
ASKS ASPERSION ASPIRINS ASSAYER ASSEZ
ASLAKE ASPERSIVE ASPIS ASSAYERS ASSHOLE
ASLAKED ASPERSOIR ASPISES ASSAYING ASSHOLES
ASLAKES ASPERSOR ASPISH ASSAYINGS ASSIDUITY
ASLAKING ASPERSORS ASPLENIUM ASSAYS ASSIDUOUS
ASLANT ASPERSORY ASPORT ASSEGAAI ASSIEGE
ASLEEP ASPHALT ASPORTED ASSEGAAIS ASSIEGED
ASLOPE ASPHALTED ASPORTING ASSEGAI ASSIEGES
ASLOSH ASPHALTER ASPORTS ASSEGAIED ASSIEGING
ASMEAR ASPHALTIC ASPOUT ASSEGAIS ASSIENTO
ASMOULDER ASPHALTS ASPRAWL ASSEMBLE ASSIENTOS
ASOCIAL ASPHALTUM ASPREAD ASSEMBLED ASSIGN
ASOCIALS ASPHERIC ASPRO ASSEMBLER ASSIGNAT
ASP ASPHERICS ASPROS ASSEMBLES ASSIGNATS
ASPARAGUS ASPHODEL ASPROUT ASSEMBLY ASSIGNED
ASPARKLE ASPHODELS ASPS ASSENT ASSIGNEE
ASPARTAME ASPHYXIA ASQUAT ASSENTED ASSIGNEES
ASPARTATE ASPHYXIAL ASQUINT ASSENTER ASSIGNER
ASPARTIC ASPHYXIAS ASRAMA ASSENTERS ASSIGNERS
ASPECT ASPHYXIED ASRAMAS ASSENTING ASSIGNING

two to nine letter words | 31

ASSIGNOR	ASSUAGES	ASTATINES	ASTONED	ASTUNS
ASSIGNORS	ASSUAGING	ASTATKI	ASTONES	ASTUTE
ASSIGNS	ASSUASIVE	ASTATKIS	ASTONIED	ASTUTELY
ASSIST	ASSUETUDE	ASTEISM	ASTONIES	ASTUTER
ASSISTANT	ASSUMABLE	ASTEISMS	ASTONING	ASTUTEST
ASSISTED	ASSUMABLY	ASTELIC	ASTONISH	ASTYLAR
ASSISTER	ASSUME	ASTELIES	ASTONY	ASUDDEN
ASSISTERS	ASSUMED	ASTELY	ASTONYING	ASUNDER
ASSISTING	ASSUMEDLY	ASTER	ASTOOP	ASURA
ASSISTIVE	ASSUMER	ASTERIA	ASTOUND	ASURAS
ASSISTOR	ASSUMERS	ASTERIAS	ASTOUNDED	ASWARM
ASSISTORS	ASSUMES	ASTERID	ASTOUNDS	ASWAY
ASSISTS	ASSUMING	ASTERIDS	ASTRACHAN	ASWIM
ASSIZE	ASSUMINGS	ASTERISK	ASTRADDLE	ASWING
ASSIZED	ASSUMPSIT	ASTERISKS	ASTRAGAL	ASWIRL
ASSIZER	ASSURABLE	ASTERISM	ASTRAGALI	ASWOON
ASSIZERS	ASSURANCE	ASTERISMS	ASTRAGALS	ASYLA
ASSIZES	ASSURE	ASTERN	ASTRAKHAN	ASYLEE
ASSIZING	ASSURED	ASTERNAL	ASTRAL	ASYLEES
ASSLIKE	ASSUREDLY	ASTEROID	ASTRALLY	ASYLLABIC
ASSOCIATE	ASSUREDS	ASTEROIDS	ASTRALS	ASYLUM
ASSOIL	ASSURER	ASTERS	ASTRAND	ASYLUMS
ASSOILED	ASSURERS	ASTERT	ASTRANTIA	ASYMMETRY
ASSOILING	ASSURES	ASTERTED	ASTRAY	ASYMPTOTE
ASSOILS	ASSURGENT	ASTERTING	ASTRICT	ASYNAPSES
ASSOILZIE	ASSURING	ASTERTS	ASTRICTED	ASYNAPSIS
ASSONANCE	ASSUROR	ASTHANGA	ASTRICTS	ASYNDETA
ASSONANT	ASSURORS	ASTHANGAS	ASTRIDE	ASYNDETIC
ASSONANTS	ASSWAGE	ASTHENIA	ASTRINGE	ASYNDETON
ASSONATE	ASSWAGED	ASTHENIAS	ASTRINGED	ASYNERGIA
ASSONATED	ASSWAGES	ASTHENIC	ASTRINGER	ASYNERGY
ASSONATES	ASSWAGING	ASTHENICS	ASTRINGES	ASYSTOLE
ASSORT	ASSWIPE	ASTHENIES	ASTROCYTE	ASYSTOLES
ASSORTED	ASSWIPES	ASTHENY	ASTRODOME	ASYSTOLIC
ASSORTER	ASTABLE	ASTHMA	ASTROFELL	AT
ASSORTERS	ASTANGA	ASTHMAS	ASTROID	ATAATA
ASSORTING	ASTANGAS	ASTHMATIC	ASTROIDS	ATAATAS
ASSORTIVE	ASTARE	ASTHORE	ASTROLABE	ATABAL
ASSORTS	ASTART	ASTHORES	ASTROLOGY	ATABALS
ASSOT	ASTARTED	ASTICHOUS	ASTRONAUT	ATABEG
ASSOTS	ASTARTING	ASTIGMIA	ASTRONOMY	ATABEGS
ASSOTT	ASTARTS	ASTIGMIAS	ASTROPHEL	ATABEK
ASSOTTED	ASTASIA	ASTILBE	ASTRUT	ATABEKS
ASSOTTING	ASTASIAS	ASTILBES	ASTUCIOUS	ATABRIN
ASSUAGE	ASTATIC	ASTIR	ASTUCITY	ATABRINE
ASSUAGED	ASTATIDE	ASTOMATAL	ASTUN	ATABRINES
ASSUAGER	ASTATIDES	ASTOMOUS	ASTUNNED	ATABRINS
ASSUAGERS	ASTATINE	ASTONE	ASTUNNING	ATACAMITE

A

ATACTIC	ATHAMES	ATHLETICS	ATOM	ATOPIC
ATAGHAN	ATHANASY	ATHODYD	ATOMIC	ATOPIES
ATAGHANS	ATHANOR	ATHODYDS	ATOMICAL	ATOPY
ATALAYA	ATHANORS	ATHRILL	ATOMICITY	ATRAMENT
ATALAYAS	ATHEISE	ATHROB	ATOMICS	ATRAMENTS
ATAMAN	ATHEISED	ATHROCYTE	ATOMIES	ATRAZINE
ATAMANS	ATHEISES	ATHWART	ATOMISE	ATRAZINES
ATAMASCO	ATHEISING	ATIGI	ATOMISED	ATREMBLE
ATAMASCOS	ATHEISM	ATIGIS	ATOMISER	ATRESIA
ATAP	ATHEISMS	ATILT	ATOMISERS	ATRESIAS
ATAPS	ATHEIST	ATIMIES	ATOMISES	ATRESIC
ATARACTIC	ATHEISTIC	ATIMY	ATOMISING	ATRETIC
ATARAXIA	ATHEISTS	ATINGLE	ATOMISM	ATRIA
ATARAXIAS	ATHEIZE	ATISHOO	ATOMISMS	ATRIAL
ATARAXIC	ATHEIZED	ATISHOOS	ATOMIST	ATRIP
ATARAXICS	ATHEIZES	ATLANTES	ATOMISTIC	ATRIUM
ATARAXIES	ATHEIZING	ATLAS	ATOMISTS	ATRIUMS
ATARAXY	ATHELING	ATLASES	ATOMIZE	ATROCIOUS
ATAVIC	ATHELINGS	ATLATL	ATOMIZED	ATROCITY
ATAVISM	ATHEMATIC	ATLATLS	ATOMIZER	ATROPHIA
ATAVISMS	ATHENAEUM	ATMA	ATOMIZERS	ATROPHIAS
ATAVIST	ATHENEUM	ATMAN	ATOMIZES	ATROPHIC
ATAVISTIC	ATHENEUMS	ATMANS	ATOMIZING	ATROPHIED
ATAVISTS	ATHEOLOGY	ATMAS	ATOMS	ATROPHIES
ATAXIA	ATHEOUS	ATMOLOGY	ATOMY	ATROPHY
ATAXIAS	ATHERINE	ATMOLYSE	ATONABLE	ATROPIA
ATAXIC	ATHERINES	ATMOLYSED	ATONAL	ATROPIAS
ATAXICS	ATHEROMA	ATMOLYSES	ATONALISM	ATROPIN
ATAXIES	ATHEROMAS	ATMOLYSIS	ATONALIST	ATROPINE
ATAXY	ATHETESES	ATMOLYZE	ATONALITY	ATROPINES
ATCHIEVE	ATHETESIS	ATMOLYZED	ATONALLY	ATROPINS
ATCHIEVED	ATHETISE	ATMOLYZES	ATONE	ATROPISM
ATCHIEVES	ATHETISED	ATMOMETER	ATONEABLE	ATROPISMS
ATE	ATHETISES	ATMOMETRY	ATONED	ATROPOUS
ATEBRIN	ATHETIZE	ATMOS	ATONEMENT	ATS
ATEBRINS	ATHETIZED	ATMOSES	ATONER	ATT
ATECHNIC	ATHETIZES	ATOC	ATONERS	ATTABOY
ATECHNICS	ATHETOID	ATOCIA	ATONES	ATTABOYS
ATELIC	ATHETOSES	ATOCIAS	ATONIA	ATTACH
ATELIER	ATHETOSIC	ATOCS	ATONIAS	ATTACHE
ATELIERS	ATHETOSIS	ATOK	ATONIC	ATTACHED
ATEMOYA	ATHETOTIC	ATOKAL	ATONICITY	ATTACHER
ATEMOYAS	ATHIRST	ATOKE	ATONICS	ATTACHERS
ATEMPORAL	ATHLETA	ATOKES	ATONIES	ATTACHES
ATENOLOL	ATHLETAS	ATOKOUS	ATONING	ATTACHING
ATENOLOLS	ATHLETE	ATOKS	ATONINGLY	ATTACK
ATES	ATHLETES	ATOLL	ATONY	ATTACKED
ATHAME	ATHLETIC	ATOLLS	ATOP	ATTACKER

ATTACKERS	ATTERCOP	ATTRACTED	AUBERGINE	AUDITABLE
ATTACKING	ATTERCOPS	ATTRACTER	AUBRETIA	AUDITED
ATTACKMAN	ATTEST	ATTRACTOR	AUBRETIAS	AUDITEE
ATTACKMEN	ATTESTANT	ATTRACTS	AUBRIETA	AUDITEES
ATTACKS	ATTESTED	ATTRAHENS	AUBRIETAS	AUDITING
ATTAGIRL	ATTESTER	ATTRAHENT	AUBRIETIA	AUDITINGS
ATTAIN	ATTESTERS	ATTRAP	AUBURN	AUDITION
ATTAINDER	ATTESTING	ATTRAPPED	AUBURNS	AUDITIONS
ATTAINED	ATTESTOR	ATTRAPS	AUCEPS	AUDITIVE
ATTAINER	ATTESTORS	ATTRIBUTE	AUCEPSES	AUDITIVES
ATTAINERS	ATTESTS	ATTRIST	AUCTION	AUDITOR
ATTAINING	ATTIC	ATTRISTED	AUCTIONED	AUDITORIA
ATTAINS	ATTICISE	ATTRISTS	AUCTIONS	AUDITORS
ATTAINT	ATTICISED	ATTRIT	AUCTORIAL	AUDITORY
ATTAINTED	ATTICISES	ATTRITE	AUCUBA	AUDITRESS
ATTAINTS	ATTICISM	ATTRITED	AUCUBAS	AUDITS
ATTAP	ATTICISMS	ATTRITES	AUDACIOUS	AUE
ATTAPS	ATTICIST	ATTRITING	AUDACITY	AUF
ATTAR	ATTICISTS	ATTRITION	AUDAD	AUFGABE
ATTARS	ATTICIZE	ATTRITIVE	AUDADS	AUFGABES
ATTASK	ATTICIZED	ATTRITS	AUDIAL	AUFS
ATTASKED	ATTICIZES	ATTRITTED	AUDIBLE	AUGEND
ATTASKING	ATTICS	ATTUENT	AUDIBLED	AUGENDS
ATTASKS	ATTIRE	ATTUITE	AUDIBLES	AUGER
ATTASKT	ATTIRED	ATTUITED	AUDIBLING	AUGERS
ATTEMPER	ATTIRES	ATTUITES	AUDIBLY	AUGH
ATTEMPERS	ATTIRING	ATTUITING	AUDIENCE	AUGHT
ATTEMPT	ATTIRINGS	ATTUITION	AUDIENCES	AUGHTS
ATTEMPTED	ATTITUDE	ATTUITIVE	AUDIENCIA	AUGITE
ATTEMPTER	ATTITUDES	ATTUNE	AUDIENT	AUGITES
ATTEMPTS	ATTOLASER	ATTUNED	AUDIENTS	AUGITIC
ATTEND	ATTOLLENS	ATTUNES	AUDILE	AUGMENT
ATTENDANT	ATTOLLENT	ATTUNING	AUDILES	AUGMENTED
ATTENDED	ATTOMETER	ATUA	AUDING	AUGMENTER
ATTENDEE	ATTOMETRE	ATUAS	AUDINGS	AUGMENTOR
ATTENDEES	ATTONCE	ATWAIN	AUDIO	AUGMENTS
ATTENDER	ATTONE	ATWEEL	AUDIOBOOK	AUGUR
ATTENDERS	ATTONED	ATWEEN	AUDIOGRAM	AUGURAL
ATTENDING	ATTONES	ATWITTER	AUDIOLOGY	AUGURED
ATTENDS	ATTONING	ATWIXT	AUDIOPHIL	AUGURER
ATTENT	ATTORN	ATYPIC	AUDIOS	AUGURERS
ATTENTAT	ATTORNED	ATYPICAL	AUDIOTAPE	AUGURIES
ATTENTATS	ATTORNEY	AUA	AUDIPHONE	AUGURING
ATTENTION	ATTORNEYS	AUAS	AUDISM	AUGURS
ATTENTIVE	ATTORNING	AUBADE	AUDISMS	AUGURSHIP
ATTENTS	ATTORNS	AUBADES	AUDIST	AUGURY
ATTENUANT	ATTOTESLA	AUBERGE	AUDISTS	AUGUST
ATTENUATE	ATTRACT	AUBERGES	AUDIT	AUGUSTE

AUGUSTER	AURAL	AURORALLY	AUTHORING	AUTOFLARE
AUGUSTES	AURALITY	AURORAS	AUTHORISE	AUTOFOCUS
AUGUSTEST	AURALLY	AUROREAN	AUTHORISH	AUTOGAMIC
AUGUSTLY	AURAR	AUROUS	AUTHORISM	AUTOGAMY
AUGUSTS	AURAS	AURUM	AUTHORITY	AUTOGENIC
AUK	AURATE	AURUMS	AUTHORIZE	AUTOGENY
AUKLET	AURATED	AUSFORM	AUTHORS	AUTOGIRO
AUKLETS	AURATES	AUSFORMED	AUTISM	AUTOGIROS
AUKS	AUREATE	AUSFORMS	AUTISMS	AUTOGRAFT
AULA	AUREATELY	AUSLANDER	AUTIST	AUTOGRAPH
AULARIAN	AUREI	AUSPEX	AUTISTIC	AUTOGUIDE
AULARIANS	AUREITIES	AUSPICATE	AUTISTICS	AUTOGYRO
AULAS	AUREITY	AUSPICE	AUTISTS	AUTOGYROS
AULD	AURELIA	AUSPICES	AUTO	AUTOHARP
AULDER	AURELIAN	AUSTENITE	AUTOBAHN	AUTOHARPS
AULDEST	AURELIANS	AUSTERE	AUTOBAHNS	AUTOICOUS
AULIC	AURELIAS	AUSTERELY	AUTOBANK	AUTOING
AULNAGE	AUREOLA	AUSTERER	AUTOBANKS	AUTOLATRY
AULNAGER	AUREOLAE	AUSTEREST	AUTOBODY	AUTOLOAD
AULNAGERS	AUREOLAS	AUSTERITY	AUTOBUS	AUTOLOADS
AULNAGES	AUREOLE	AUSTRAL	AUTOBUSES	AUTOLOGY
AULOI	AUREOLED	AUSTRALES	AUTOCADE	AUTOLYSE
AULOS	AUREOLES	AUSTRALIS	AUTOCADES	AUTOLYSED
AUMAIL	AUREOLING	AUSTRALS	AUTOCAR	AUTOLYSES
AUMAILED	AURES	AUSUBO	AUTOCARP	AUTOLYSIN
AUMAILING	AUREUS	AUSUBOS	AUTOCARPS	AUTOLYSIS
AUMAILS	AURIC	AUTACOID	AUTOCARS	AUTOLYTIC
AUMBRIES	AURICLE	AUTACOIDS	AUTOCIDAL	AUTOLYZE
AUMBRY	AURICLED	AUTARCH	AUTOCLAVE	AUTOLYZED
AUMIL	AURICLES	AUTARCHIC	AUTOCOID	AUTOLYZES
AUMILS	AURICULA	AUTARCHS	AUTOCOIDS	AUTOMAGIC
AUNE	AURICULAE	AUTARCHY	AUTOCRACY	AUTOMAKER
AUNES	AURICULAR	AUTARKIC	AUTOCRAT	AUTOMAN
AUNT	AURICULAS	AUTARKIES	AUTOCRATS	AUTOMAT
AUNTER	AURIFIED	AUTARKIST	AUTOCRIME	AUTOMATA
AUNTERS	AURIFIES	AUTARKY	AUTOCRINE	AUTOMATE
AUNTHOOD	AURIFORM	AUTECIOUS	AUTOCROSS	AUTOMATED
AUNTHOODS	AURIFY	AUTECISM	AUTOCUE	AUTOMATES
AUNTIE	AURIFYING	AUTECISMS	AUTOCUES	AUTOMATIC
AUNTIES	AURIS	AUTEUR	AUTOCUTIE	AUTOMATON
AUNTLIER	AURISCOPE	AUTEURISM	AUTOCYCLE	AUTOMATS
AUNTLIEST	AURIST	AUTEURIST	AUTODIAL	AUTOMEN
AUNTLIKE	AURISTS	AUTEURS	AUTODIALS	AUTOMETER
AUNTLY	AUROCHS	AUTHENTIC	AUTODROME	AUTONOMIC
AUNTS	AUROCHSES	AUTHOR	AUTODYNE	AUTONOMY
AUNTY	AURORA	AUTHORED	AUTODYNES	AUTONYM
AURA	AURORAE	AUTHORESS	AUTOECISM	AUTONYMS
AURAE	AURORAL	AUTHORIAL	AUTOED	AUTOPEN

AUTOPENS

AUTOPENS	AUTUMN	AVAS	AVERRED	AVIDER
AUTOPHAGY	AUTUMNAL	AVASCULAR	AVERRING	AVIDEST
AUTOPHOBY	AUTUMNIER	AVAST	AVERS	AVIDIN
AUTOPHONY	AUTUMNS	AVATAR	AVERSE	AVIDINS
AUTOPHYTE	AUTUMNY	AVATARS	AVERSELY	AVIDITIES
AUTOPILOT	AUTUNITE	AVAUNT	AVERSION	AVIDITY
AUTOPISTA	AUTUNITES	AVAUNTED	AVERSIONS	AVIDLY
AUTOPOINT	AUXESES	AVAUNTING	AVERSIVE	AVIDNESS
AUTOPSIA	AUXESIS	AVAUNTS	AVERSIVES	AVIETTE
AUTOPSIAS	AUXETIC	AVE	AVERT	AVIETTES
AUTOPSIC	AUXETICS	AVEL	AVERTABLE	AVIFAUNA
AUTOPSIED	AUXILIAR	AVELLAN	AVERTED	AVIFAUNAE
AUTOPSIES	AUXILIARS	AVELLANE	AVERTEDLY	AVIFAUNAL
AUTOPSIST	AUXILIARY	AVELS	AVERTER	AVIFAUNAS
AUTOPSY	AUXIN	AVENGE	AVERTERS	AVIFORM
AUTOPTIC	AUXINIC	AVENGED	AVERTIBLE	AVIGATOR
AUTOPUT	AUXINS	AVENGEFUL	AVERTING	AVIGATORS
AUTOPUTS	AUXOCYTE	AVENGER	AVERTS	AVINE
AUTOREPLY	AUXOCYTES	AVENGERS	AVES	AVION
AUTOROUTE	AUXOMETER	AVENGES	AVGAS	AVIONIC
AUTOS	AUXOSPORE	AVENGING	AVGASES	AVIONICS
AUTOSAVE	AUXOTONIC	AVENIR	AVGASSES	AVIONS
AUTOSAVED	AUXOTROPH	AVENIRS	AVIAN	AVIRULENT
AUTOSAVES	AVA	AVENS	AVIANISE	AVISANDUM
AUTOSCOPY	AVADAVAT	AVENSES	AVIANISED	AVISE
AUTOSOMAL	AVADAVATS	AVENTAIL	AVIANISES	AVISED
AUTOSOME	AVAIL	AVENTAILE	AVIANIZE	AVISEMENT
AUTOSOMES	AVAILABLE	AVENTAILS	AVIANIZED	AVISES
AUTOSPORE	AVAILABLY	AVENTRE	AVIANIZES	AVISING
AUTOSPORT	AVAILE	AVENTRED	AVIANS	AVISO
AUTOTELIC	AVAILED	AVENTRES	AVIARIES	AVISOS
AUTOTEST	AVAILES	AVENTRING	AVIARIST	AVITAL
AUTOTESTS	AVAILFUL	AVENTURE	AVIARISTS	AVIZANDUM
AUTOTIMER	AVAILING	AVENTURES	AVIARY	AVIZE
AUTOTOMIC	AVAILS	AVENTURIN	AVIATE	AVIZED
AUTOTOMY	AVAL	AVENUE	AVIATED	AVIZEFULL
AUTOTOXIC	AVALANCHE	AVENUES	AVIATES	AVIZES
AUTOTOXIN	AVALE	AVER	AVIATIC	AVIZING
AUTOTROPH	AVALED	AVERAGE	AVIATING	AVO
AUTOTUNE	AVALEMENT	AVERAGED	AVIATION	AVOCADO
AUTOTUNES	AVALES	AVERAGELY	AVIATIONS	AVOCADOES
AUTOTYPE	AVALING	AVERAGER	AVIATOR	AVOCADOS
AUTOTYPED	AVANT	AVERAGERS	AVIATORS	AVOCATION
AUTOTYPES	AVANTI	AVERAGES	AVIATRESS	AVOCET
AUTOTYPIC	AVANTIST	AVERAGING	AVIATRICE	AVOCETS
AUTOTYPY	AVANTISTS	AVERMENT	AVIATRIX	AVODIRE
AUTOVAC	AVARICE	AVERMENTS	AVICULAR	AVODIRES
AUTOVACS	AVARICES	AVERRABLE	AVID	AVOID

AVOIDABLE	AVULSING	AWATOS	AWKWARD	AXIAL
AVOIDABLY	AVULSION	AWAVE	AWKWARDER	AXIALITY
AVOIDANCE	AVULSIONS	AWAY	AWKWARDLY	AXIALLY
AVOIDANT	AVUNCULAR	AWAYDAY	AWL	AXIL
AVOIDED	AVYZE	AWAYDAYS	AWLBIRD	AXILE
AVOIDER	AVYZED	AWAYES	AWLBIRDS	AXILEMMA
AVOIDERS	AVYZES	AWAYNESS	AWLESS	AXILEMMAS
AVOIDING	AVYZING	AWAYS	AWLS	AXILLA
AVOIDS	AW	AWDL	AWLWORT	AXILLAE
AVOISION	AWA	AWDLS	AWLWORTS	AXILLAR
AVOISIONS	AWAIT	AWE	AWMOUS	AXILLARS
AVOPARCIN	AWAITED	AWEARIED	AWMRIE	AXILLARY
AVOS	AWAITER	AWEARY	AWMRIES	AXILLAS
AVOSET	AWAITERS	AWEATHER	AWMRY	AXILS
AVOSETS	AWAITING	AWED	AWN	AXING
AVOUCH	AWAITS	AWEE	AWNED	AXINITE
AVOUCHED	AWAKE	AWEEL	AWNER	AXINITES
AVOUCHER	AWAKED	AWEIGH	AWNERS	AXIOLOGY
AVOUCHERS	AWAKEN	AWEING	AWNIER	AXIOM
AVOUCHES	AWAKENED	AWELESS	AWNIEST	AXIOMATIC
AVOUCHING	AWAKENER	AWES	AWNING	AXIOMS
AVOURE	AWAKENERS	AWESOME	AWNINGED	AXION
AVOURES	AWAKENING	AWESOMELY	AWNINGS	AXIONS
AVOUTERER	AWAKENS	AWESTRIKE	AWNLESS	AXIS
AVOUTRER	AWAKES	AWESTRUCK	AWNS	AXISED
AVOUTRERS	AWAKING	AWETO	AWNY	AXISES
AVOUTRIES	AWAKINGS	AWETOS	AWOKE	AXITE
AVOUTRY	AWANTING	AWFUL	AWOKEN	AXITES
AVOW	AWARD	AWFULLER	AWOL	AXLE
AVOWABLE	AWARDABLE	AWFULLEST	AWOLS	AXLED
AVOWABLY	AWARDED	AWFULLY	AWORK	AXLES
AVOWAL	AWARDEE	AWFULNESS	AWRACK	AXLETREE
AVOWALS	AWARDEES	AWFY	AWRONG	AXLETREES
AVOWED	AWARDER	AWHAPE	AWRY	AXLIKE
AVOWEDLY	AWARDERS	AWHAPED	AWSOME	AXMAN
AVOWER	AWARDING	AWHAPES	AX	AXMEN
AVOWERS	AWARDS	AWHAPING	AXAL	AXOID
AVOWING	AWARE	AWHATO	AXE	AXOIDS
AVOWRIES	AWARENESS	AWHATOS	AXEBIRD	AXOLEMMA
AVOWRY	AWARER	AWHEEL	AXEBIRDS	AXOLEMMAS
AVOWS	AWAREST	AWHEELS	AXED	AXOLOTL
AVOYER	AWARN	AWHETO	AXEL	AXOLOTLS
AVOYERS	AWARNED	AWHETOS	AXELIKE	AXON
AVRUGA	AWARNING	AWHILE	AXELS	AXONAL
AVRUGAS	AWARNS	AWHIRL	AXEMAN	AXONE
AVULSE	AWASH	AWING	AXEMEN	AXONEMAL
AVULSED	AWATCH	AWK	AXENIC	AXONEME
AVULSES	AWATO	AWKS	AXES	AXONEMES

AXONES

AXONES	AYONT	AZIDO	AZOTED	AZURE
AXONIC	AYRE	AZIMUTH	AZOTEMIA	AZUREAN
AXONS	AYRES	AZIMUTHAL	AZOTEMIAS	AZURES
AXOPLASM	AYRIE	AZIMUTHS	AZOTEMIC	AZURIES
AXOPLASMS	AYRIES	AZINE	AZOTES	AZURINE
AXSEED	AYS	AZINES	AZOTH	AZURINES
AXSEEDS	AYU	AZIONE	AZOTHS	AZURITE
AY	AYURVEDA	AZIONES	AZOTIC	AZURITES
AYAH	AYURVEDAS	AZLON	AZOTISE	AZURN
AYAHS	AYURVEDIC	AZLONS	AZOTISED	AZURY
AYAHUASCA	AYUS	AZO	AZOTISES	AZYGIES
AYAHUASCO	AYWORD	AZOIC	AZOTISING	AZYGOS
AYATOLLAH	AYWORDS	AZOLE	AZOTIZE	AZYGOSES
AYAYA	AZALEA	AZOLES	AZOTIZED	AZYGOUS
AYAYAS	AZALEAS	AZOLLA	AZOTIZES	AZYGOUSLY
AYE	AZAN	AZOLLAS	AZOTIZING	AZYGY
AYELP	AZANS	AZON	AZOTOUS	AZYM
AYENBITE	AZEDARACH	AZONAL	AZOTURIA	AZYME
AYENBITES	AZEOTROPE	AZONIC	AZOTURIAS	AZYMES
AYES	AZEOTROPY	AZONS	AZUKI	AZYMITE
AYGRE	AZERTY	AZOTAEMIA	AZUKIS	AZYMITES
AYIN	AZIDE	AZOTAEMIC	AZULEJO	AZYMOUS
AYINS	AZIDES	AZOTE	AZULEJOS	AZYMS

B

BA
BAA
BAAED
BAAING
BAAINGS
BAAL
BAALEBOS
BAALIM
BAALISM
BAALISMS
BAALS
BAAS
BAASES
BAASKAAP
BAASKAAPS
BAASKAP
BAASKAPS
BAASSKAP
BAASSKAPS
BABA
BABACO
BABACOOTE
BABACOS
BABACU
BABACUS
BABALAS
BABAS
BABASSU
BABASSUS
BABBELAS
BABBITRY
BABBITT
BABBITTED
BABBITTRY
BABBITTS
BABBLE
BABBLED
BABBLER
BABBLERS
BABBLES
BABBLIER
BABBLIEST

BABBLING
BABBLINGS
BABBLY
BABE
BABEL
BABELDOM
BABELDOMS
BABELISH
BABELISM
BABELISMS
BABELS
BABES
BABESIA
BABESIAE
BABESIAS
BABICHE
BABICHES
BABIED
BABIER
BABIES
BABIEST
BABIRUSA
BABIRUSAS
BABIRUSSA
BABKA
BABKAS
BABLAH
BABLAHS
BABOO
BABOOL
BABOOLS
BABOON
BABOONERY
BABOONISH
BABOONS
BABOOS
BABOOSH
BABOOSHES
BABOUCHE
BABOUCHES
BABU
BABUCHE

BABUCHES
BABUDOM
BABUDOMS
BABUISM
BABUISMS
BABUL
BABULS
BABUS
BABUSHKA
BABUSHKAS
BABY
BABYCCINO
BABYCINO
BABYCINOS
BABYDADDY
BABYDOLL
BABYDOLLS
BABYFOOD
BABYFOODS
BABYHOOD
BABYHOODS
BABYING
BABYISH
BABYISHLY
BABYLIKE
BABYMOON
BABYMOONS
BABYPROOF
BABYSAT
BABYSIT
BABYSITS
BAC
BACALAO
BACALAOS
BACALHAU
BACALHAUS
BACCA
BACCAE
BACCALA
BACCALAS
BACCARA
BACCARAS

BACCARAT
BACCARATS
BACCARE
BACCAS
BACCATE
BACCATED
BACCHANAL
BACCHANT
BACCHANTE
BACCHANTS
BACCHIAC
BACCHIAN
BACCHIC
BACCHII
BACCHIUS
BACCIES
BACCIFORM
BACCO
BACCOES
BACCOS
BACCY
BACH
BACHA
BACHARACH
BACHAS
BACHATA
BACHATAS
BACHCHA
BACHCHAS
BACHED
BACHELOR
BACHELORS
BACHES
BACHING
BACHS
BACILLAR
BACILLARY
BACILLI
BACILLUS
BACK
BACKACHE
BACKACHES

BACKACTER
BACKARE
BACKBAND
BACKBANDS
BACKBAR
BACKBARS
BACKBEAT
BACKBEATS
BACKBENCH
BACKBEND
BACKBENDS
BACKBIT
BACKBITE
BACKBITER
BACKBITES
BACKBLOCK
BACKBOARD
BACKBOND
BACKBONDS
BACKBONE
BACKBONED
BACKBONES
BACKBURN
BACKBURNS
BACKCAST
BACKCASTS
BACKCHAT
BACKCHATS
BACKCHECK
BACKCLOTH
BACKCOMB
BACKCOMBS
BACKCOURT
BACKCROSS
BACKDATE
BACKDATED
BACKDATES
BACKDOOR
BACKDOWN
BACKDOWNS
BACKDRAFT
BACKDROP

BACKDROPS	BACKLIST	BACKSPIN	BACONER	BADIOUS
BACKDROPT	BACKLISTS	BACKSPINS	BACONERS	BADLAND
BACKED	BACKLIT	BACKSPLIT	BACONS	BADLANDS
BACKER	BACKLOAD	BACKSTAB	BACRONYM	BADLY
BACKERS	BACKLOADS	BACKSTABS	BACRONYMS	BADMAN
BACKET	BACKLOG	BACKSTAGE	BACS	BADMASH
BACKETS	BACKLOGS	BACKSTAIR	BACTERIA	BADMASHES
BACKFALL	BACKLOT	BACKSTALL	BACTERIAL	BADMEN
BACKFALLS	BACKLOTS	BACKSTAMP	BACTERIAN	BADMINTON
BACKFAT	BACKMOST	BACKSTAY	BACTERIAS	BADMOUTH
BACKFATS	BACKOUT	BACKSTAYS	BACTERIC	BADMOUTHS
BACKFIELD	BACKOUTS	BACKSTOP	BACTERIN	BADNESS
BACKFILE	BACKPACK	BACKSTOPS	BACTERINS	BADNESSES
BACKFILES	BACKPACKS	BACKSTORY	BACTERISE	BADS
BACKFILL	BACKPEDAL	BACKSTRAP	BACTERIUM	BADWARE
BACKFILLS	BACKPIECE	BACKSWEPT	BACTERIZE	BADWARES
BACKFIRE	BACKPLANE	BACKSWING	BACTEROID	BAE
BACKFIRED	BACKPLATE	BACKSWORD	BACULA	BAEL
BACKFIRES	BACKRA	BACKTALK	BACULINE	BAELS
BACKFISCH	BACKRAS	BACKTALKS	BACULITE	BAES
BACKFIT	BACKREST	BACKTRACK	BACULITES	BAETYL
BACKFITS	BACKRESTS	BACKUP	BACULUM	BAETYLS
BACKFLIP	BACKRONYM	BACKUPS	BACULUMS	BAFF
BACKFLIPS	BACKROOM	BACKVELD	BAD	BAFFED
BACKFLOW	BACKROOMS	BACKVELDS	BADASS	BAFFIES
BACKFLOWS	BACKRUSH	BACKWALL	BADASSED	BAFFING
BACKHAND	BACKS	BACKWALLS	BADASSES	BAFFLE
BACKHANDS	BACKSAW	BACKWARD	BADDER	BAFFLED
BACKHAUL	BACKSAWS	BACKWARDS	BADDEST	BAFFLEGAB
BACKHAULS	BACKSEAT	BACKWASH	BADDIE	BAFFLER
BACKHOE	BACKSEATS	BACKWATER	BADDIES	BAFFLERS
BACKHOED	BACKSET	BACKWIND	BADDISH	BAFFLES
BACKHOES	BACKSETS	BACKWINDS	BADDY	BAFFLING
BACKHOUSE	BACKSEY	BACKWOOD	BADE	BAFFS
BACKIE	BACKSEYS	BACKWOODS	BADGE	BAFFY
BACKIES	BACKSHISH	BACKWORD	BADGED	BAFT
BACKING	BACKSHORE	BACKWORDS	BADGELESS	BAFTS
BACKINGS	BACKSIDE	BACKWORK	BADGER	BAG
BACKLAND	BACKSIDES	BACKWORKS	BADGERED	BAGARRE
BACKLANDS	BACKSIGHT	BACKWRAP	BADGERING	BAGARRES
BACKLASH	BACKSLAP	BACKWRAPS	BADGERLY	BAGASS
BACKLESS	BACKSLAPS	BACKYARD	BADGERS	BAGASSE
BACKLIFT	BACKSLASH	BACKYARDS	BADGES	BAGASSES
BACKLIFTS	BACKSLID	BACLAVA	BADGING	BAGATELLE
BACKLIGHT	BACKSLIDE	BACLAVAS	BADINAGE	BAGEL
BACKLINE	BACKSPACE	BACLOFEN	BADINAGED	BAGELED
BACKLINER	BACKSPEER	BACLOFENS	BADINAGES	BAGELING
BACKLINES	BACKSPEIR	BACON	BADINERIE	BAGELLED

BAGELLING	BAGWASH	BAILMENTS	BAJUS	BALANCER
BAGELS	BAGWASHES	BAILOR	BAKE	BALANCERS
BAGFUL	BAGWIG	BAILORS	BAKEAPPLE	BALANCES
BAGFULS	BAGWIGS	BAILOUT	BAKEBOARD	BALANCING
BAGGAGE	BAGWORM	BAILOUTS	BAKED	BALANITIS
BAGGAGES	BAGWORMS	BAILS	BAKEHOUSE	BALAS
BAGGED	BAH	BAILSMAN	BAKELITE	BALASES
BAGGER	BAHADA	BAILSMEN	BAKELITES	BALATA
BAGGERS	BAHADAS	BAININ	BAKEMEAT	BALATAS
BAGGIE	BAHADUR	BAININS	BAKEMEATS	BALAYAGE
BAGGIER	BAHADURS	BAINITE	BAKEN	BALAYAGED
BAGGIES	BAHOOKIE	BAINITES	BAKEOFF	BALAYAGES
BAGGIEST	BAHOOKIES	BAIRN	BAKEOFFS	BALBOA
BAGGILY	BAHT	BAIRNISH	BAKER	BALBOAS
BAGGINESS	BAHTS	BAIRNLIER	BAKERIES	BALCONET
BAGGING	BAHU	BAIRNLIKE	BAKERS	BALCONETS
BAGGINGS	BAHUS	BAIRNLY	BAKERY	BALCONIED
BAGGIT	BAHUT	BAIRNS	BAKES	BALCONIES
BAGGITS	BAHUTS	BAISA	BAKESHOP	BALCONY
BAGGY	BAHUVRIHI	BAISAS	BAKESHOPS	BALD
BAGH	BAIDAR	BAISEMAIN	BAKESTONE	BALDACHIN
BAGHOUSE	BAIDARKA	BAIT	BAKEWARE	BALDAQUIN
BAGHOUSES	BAIDARKAS	BAITED	BAKEWARES	BALDED
BAGHS	BAIDARS	BAITER	BAKGAT	BALDER
BAGIE	BAIGNOIRE	BAITERS	BAKHSHISH	BALDEST
BAGIES	BAIL	BAITFISH	BAKING	BALDFACED
BAGLESS	BAILABLE	BAITH	BAKINGS	BALDHEAD
BAGLIKE	BAILBOND	BAITING	BAKKIE	BALDHEADS
BAGMAN	BAILBONDS	BAITINGS	BAKKIES	BALDICOOT
BAGMEN	BAILED	BAITS	BAKLAVA	BALDIE
BAGNETTE	BAILEE	BAIZA	BAKLAVAS	BALDIER
BAGNETTES	BAILEES	BAIZAS	BAKLAWA	BALDIES
BAGNIO	BAILER	BAIZE	BAKLAWAS	BALDIEST
BAGNIOS	BAILERS	BAIZED	BAKRA	BALDING
BAGPIPE	BAILEY	BAIZES	BAKRAS	BALDISH
BAGPIPED	BAILEYS	BAIZING	BAKSHEESH	BALDLY
BAGPIPER	BAILIE	BAJADA	BAKSHISH	BALDMONEY
BAGPIPERS	BAILIES	BAJADAS	BAL	BALDNESS
BAGPIPES	BAILIFF	BAJAN	BALACLAVA	BALDPATE
BAGPIPING	BAILIFFS	BAJANS	BALADIN	BALDPATED
BAGS	BAILING	BAJILLION	BALADINE	BALDPATES
BAGSFUL	BAILIWICK	BAJRA	BALADINES	BALDRIC
BAGUET	BAILLI	BAJRAS	BALADINS	BALDRICK
BAGUETS	BAILLIAGE	BAJREE	BALAFON	BALDRICKS
BAGUETTE	BAILLIE	BAJREES	BALAFONS	BALDRICS
BAGUETTES	BAILLIES	BAJRI	BALALAIKA	BALDS
BAGUIO	BAILLIS	BAJRIS	BALANCE	BALDY
BAGUIOS	BAILMENT	BAJU	BALANCED	BALE

BALECTION	BALLADING	BALLISTA	BALLYHOOS	BAMBINO
BALED	BALLADINS	BALLISTAE	BALLYRAG	BAMBINOS
BALEEN	BALLADIST	BALLISTAS	BALLYRAGS	BAMBIS
BALEENS	BALLADRY	BALLISTIC	BALM	BAMBOO
BALEFIRE	BALLADS	BALLIUM	BALMACAAN	BAMBOOS
BALEFIRES	BALLAN	BALLIUMS	BALMED	BAMBOOZLE
BALEFUL	BALLANS	BALLOCKS	BALMIER	BAMMED
BALEFULLY	BALLANT	BALLON	BALMIEST	BAMMER
BALER	BALLANTED	BALLONET	BALMILY	BAMMERS
BALERS	BALLANTS	BALLONETS	BALMINESS	BAMMING
BALES	BALLAST	BALLONNE	BALMING	BAMPOT
BALING	BALLASTED	BALLONNES	BALMLIKE	BAMPOTS
BALINGS	BALLASTER	BALLONS	BALMORAL	BAMS
BALISAUR	BALLASTS	BALLOON	BALMORALS	BAN
BALISAURS	BALLAT	BALLOONED	BALMS	BANAK
BALISE	BALLATED	BALLOONS	BALMY	BANAKS
BALISES	BALLATING	BALLOT	BALNEAL	BANAL
BALISTA	BALLATS	BALLOTED	BALNEARY	BANALER
BALISTAE	BALLBOY	BALLOTEE	BALONEY	BANALEST
BALISTAS	BALLBOYS	BALLOTEES	BALONEYS	BANALISE
BALK	BALLCLAY	BALLOTER	BALOO	BANALISED
BALKANISE	BALLCLAYS	BALLOTERS	BALOOS	BANALISES
BALKANIZE	BALLCOCK	BALLOTING	BALS	BANALITY
BALKED	BALLCOCKS	BALLOTINI	BALSA	BANALIZE
BALKER	BALLED	BALLOTS	BALSAM	BANALIZED
BALKERS	BALLER	BALLOW	BALSAMED	BANALIZES
BALKIER	BALLERINA	BALLOWS	BALSAMIC	BANALLY
BALKIEST	BALLERINE	BALLPARK	BALSAMIER	BANANA
BALKILY	BALLERS	BALLPARKS	BALSAMING	BANANAS
BALKINESS	BALLET	BALLPEEN	BALSAMS	BANAUSIAN
BALKING	BALLETED	BALLPOINT	BALSAMY	BANAUSIC
BALKINGLY	BALLETIC	BALLROOM	BALSAS	BANC
BALKINGS	BALLETING	BALLROOMS	BALSAWOOD	BANCO
BALKLINE	BALLETS	BALLS	BALTHASAR	BANCOS
BALKLINES	BALLFIELD	BALLSED	BALTHAZAR	BANCS
BALKS	BALLGAME	BALLSES	BALTI	BAND
BALKY	BALLGAMES	BALLSIER	BALTIC	BANDA
BALL	BALLGIRL	BALLSIEST	BALTIS	BANDAGE
BALLABILE	BALLGIRLS	BALLSING	BALU	BANDAGED
BALLABILI	BALLGOWN	BALLSY	BALUN	BANDAGER
BALLAD	BALLGOWNS	BALLUP	BALUNS	BANDAGERS
BALLADE	BALLHAWK	BALLUPS	BALUS	BANDAGES
BALLADED	BALLHAWKS	BALLUTE	BALUSTER	BANDAGING
BALLADEER	BALLIER	BALLUTES	BALUSTERS	BANDAID
BALLADES	BALLIES	BALLY	BALZARINE	BANDALORE
BALLADIC	BALLIEST	BALLYARD	BAM	BANDANA
BALLADIN	BALLING	BALLYARDS	BAMBI	BANDANAS
BALLADINE	BALLINGS	BALLYHOO	BAMBINI	BANDANNA

BANDANNAS
BANDAR
BANDARI
BANDARIS
BANDARS
BANDAS
BANDBOX
BANDBOXES
BANDBRAKE
BANDEAU
BANDEAUS
BANDEAUX
BANDED
BANDEIRA
BANDEIRAS
BANDELET
BANDELETS
BANDELIER
BANDER
BANDEROL
BANDEROLE
BANDEROLS
BANDERS
BANDFISH
BANDH
BANDHS
BANDICOOT
BANDIED
BANDIER
BANDIES
BANDIEST
BANDINESS
BANDING
BANDINGS
BANDIT
BANDITO
BANDITOS
BANDITRY
BANDITS
BANDITTI
BANDITTIS
BANDLIKE
BANDMATE
BANDMATES
BANDOBAST
BANDOBUST
BANDOG
BANDOGS

BANDOLEER
BANDOLEON
BANDOLERO
BANDOLIER
BANDOLINE
BANDONEON
BANDONION
BANDOOK
BANDOOKS
BANDORA
BANDORAS
BANDORE
BANDORES
BANDPASS
BANDROL
BANDROLS
BANDS
BANDSAW
BANDSAWED
BANDSAWS
BANDSHELL
BANDSMAN
BANDSMEN
BANDSTAND
BANDSTER
BANDSTERS
BANDURA
BANDURAS
BANDURIST
BANDWAGON
BANDWIDTH
BANDY
BANDYING
BANDYINGS
BANDYMAN
BANDYMEN
BANE
BANEBERRY
BANED
BANEFUL
BANEFULLY
BANES
BANG
BANGALAY
BANGALAYS
BANGALORE
BANGALOW
BANGALOWS

BANGBELLY
BANGED
BANGER
BANGERS
BANGING
BANGKOK
BANGKOKS
BANGLE
BANGLED
BANGLES
BANGS
BANGSRING
BANGSTER
BANGSTERS
BANGTAIL
BANGTAILS
BANI
BANIA
BANIAN
BANIANS
BANIAS
BANING
BANISH
BANISHED
BANISHER
BANISHERS
BANISHES
BANISHING
BANISTER
BANISTERS
BANJAX
BANJAXED
BANJAXES
BANJAXING
BANJO
BANJOES
BANJOIST
BANJOISTS
BANJOLELE
BANJOS
BANJULELE
BANK
BANKABLE
BANKBOOK
BANKBOOKS
BANKCARD
BANKCARDS
BANKED

BANKER
BANKERLY
BANKERS
BANKET
BANKETS
BANKING
BANKINGS
BANKIT
BANKITS
BANKNOTE
BANKNOTES
BANKROLL
BANKROLLS
BANKRUPT
BANKRUPTS
BANKS
BANKSIA
BANKSIAS
BANKSIDE
BANKSIDES
BANKSMAN
BANKSMEN
BANKSTER
BANKSTERS
BANLIEUE
BANLIEUES
BANNABLE
BANNED
BANNER
BANNERALL
BANNERED
BANNERET
BANNERETS
BANNERING
BANNEROL
BANNEROLS
BANNERS
BANNET
BANNETS
BANNING
BANNINGS
BANNISTER
BANNOCK
BANNOCKS
BANNS
BANOFFEE
BANOFFEES
BANOFFI

BANOFFIS
BANQUET
BANQUETED
BANQUETER
BANQUETS
BANQUETTE
BANS
BANSELA
BANSELAS
BANSHEE
BANSHEES
BANSHIE
BANSHIES
BANT
BANTAM
BANTAMS
BANTED
BANTENG
BANTENGS
BANTER
BANTERED
BANTERER
BANTERERS
BANTERING
BANTERS
BANTIES
BANTING
BANTINGS
BANTLING
BANTLINGS
BANTS
BANTU
BANTUS
BANTY
BANXRING
BANXRINGS
BANYA
BANYAN
BANYANS
BANYAS
BANZAI
BANZAIS
BAO
BAOBAB
BAOBABS
BAOS
BAP
BAPS

BAPTISE	BARBECUE	BARCA	BAREHAND	BARHOPPED
BAPTISED	BARBECUED	BARCAROLE	BAREHANDS	BARHOPS
BAPTISER	BARBECUER	BARCAS	BAREHEAD	BARIATRIC
BAPTISERS	BARBECUES	BARCHAN	BARELAND	BARIC
BAPTISES	BARBED	BARCHANE	BARELY	BARILLA
BAPTISIA	BARBEL	BARCHANES	BARENESS	BARILLAS
BAPTISIAS	BARBELL	BARCHANS	BARER	BARING
BAPTISING	BARBELLS	BARCODE	BARES	BARISH
BAPTISM	BARBELS	BARCODED	BARESARK	BARISTA
BAPTISMAL	BARBEQUE	BARCODES	BARESARKS	BARISTAS
BAPTISMS	BARBEQUED	BARD	BAREST	BARITE
BAPTIST	BARBEQUES	BARDASH	BARF	BARITES
BAPTISTRY	BARBER	BARDASHES	BARFED	BARITONAL
BAPTISTS	BARBERED	BARDE	BARFI	BARITONE
BAPTIZE	BARBERING	BARDED	BARFING	BARITONES
BAPTIZED	BARBERRY	BARDES	BARFIS	BARIUM
BAPTIZER	BARBERS	BARDIC	BARFLIES	BARIUMS
BAPTIZERS	BARBES	BARDIE	BARFLY	BARK
BAPTIZES	BARBET	BARDIER	BARFS	BARKAN
BAPTIZING	BARBETS	BARDIES	BARFUL	BARKANS
BAPU	BARBETTE	BARDIEST	BARGAIN	BARKED
BAPUS	BARBETTES	BARDING	BARGAINED	BARKEEP
BAR	BARBICAN	BARDISM	BARGAINER	BARKEEPER
BARACAN	BARBICANS	BARDISMS	BARGAINS	BARKEEPS
BARACANS	BARBICEL	BARDLING	BARGANDER	BARKEN
BARACHOIS	BARBICELS	BARDLINGS	BARGE	BARKENED
BARAGOUIN	BARBIE	BARDO	BARGED	BARKENING
BARASINGA	BARBIES	BARDOS	BARGEE	BARKENS
BARATHEA	BARBING	BARDS	BARGEES	BARKER
BARATHEAS	BARBITAL	BARDSHIP	BARGEESE	BARKERS
BARATHRUM	BARBITALS	BARDSHIPS	BARGELIKE	BARKHAN
BARAZA	BARBITONE	BARDY	BARGELLO	BARKHANS
BARAZAS	BARBLESS	BARE	BARGELLOS	BARKIER
BARB	BARBOLA	BAREBACK	BARGEMAN	BARKIEST
BARBAL	BARBOLAS	BAREBACKS	BARGEMEN	BARKING
BARBARIAN	BARBOT	BAREBOAT	BARGEPOLE	BARKLESS
BARBARIC	BARBOTINE	BAREBOATS	BARGES	BARKLIKE
BARBARISE	BARBOTS	BAREBONE	BARGEST	BARKS
BARBARISM	BARBOTTE	BAREBONED	BARGESTS	BARKY
BARBARITY	BARBOTTES	BAREBONES	BARGHEST	BARLEDUC
BARBARIZE	BARBS	BARED	BARGHESTS	BARLEDUCS
BARBAROUS	BARBULE	BAREFACED	BARGING	BARLESS
BARBASCO	BARBULES	BAREFIT	BARGOON	BARLEY
BARBASCOS	BARBUT	BAREFOOT	BARGOONS	BARLEYS
BARBASTEL	BARBUTS	BAREGE	BARGOOSE	BARLOW
BARBATE	BARBWIRE	BAREGES	BARGUEST	BARLOWS
BARBATED	BARBWIRES	BAREGINE	BARGUESTS	BARM
BARBE	BARBY	BAREGINES	BARHOP	BARMAID

B

BARMAIDS	BAROMETER	BARRAGE	BARRICOES	BARWOODS
BARMAN	BAROMETRY	BARRAGED	BARRICOS	BARYE
BARMBRACK	BAROMETZ	BARRAGES	BARRIE	BARYES
BARMEN	BARON	BARRAGING	BARRIER	BARYON
BARMIE	BARONAGE	BARRANCA	BARRIERED	BARYONIC
BARMIER	BARONAGES	BARRANCAS	BARRIERS	BARYONS
BARMIEST	BARONESS	BARRANCO	BARRIES	BARYTA
BARMILY	BARONET	BARRANCOS	BARRIEST	BARYTAS
BARMINESS	BARONETCY	BARRAS	BARRING	BARYTE
BARMKIN	BARONETS	BARRASWAY	BARRINGS	BARYTES
BARMKINS	BARONG	BARRAT	BARRIO	BARYTIC
BARMPOT	BARONGS	BARRATED	BARRIOS	BARYTON
BARMPOTS	BARONIAL	BARRATER	BARRIQUE	BARYTONE
BARMS	BARONIES	BARRATERS	BARRIQUES	BARYTONES
BARMY	BARONNE	BARRATING	BARRISTER	BARYTONS
BARN	BARONNES	BARRATOR	BARRO	BAS
BARNACLE	BARONS	BARRATORS	BARROOM	BASAL
BARNACLED	BARONY	BARRATRY	BARROOMS	BASALLY
BARNACLES	BAROPHILE	BARRATS	BARROW	BASALT
BARNBOARD	BAROQUE	BARRE	BARROWFUL	BASALTES
BARNBRACK	BAROQUELY	BARRED	BARROWS	BASALTIC
BARNED	BAROQUES	BARREED	BARRULET	BASALTINE
BARNET	BAROSAUR	BARREFULL	BARRULETS	BASALTS
BARNETS	BAROSAURS	BARREING	BARRY	BASAN
BARNEY	BAROSCOPE	BARREL	BARS	BASANITE
BARNEYED	BAROSTAT	BARRELAGE	BARSTOOL	BASANITES
BARNEYING	BAROSTATS	BARRELED	BARSTOOLS	BASANS
BARNEYS	BAROTITIS	BARRELFUL	BARTEND	BASANT
BARNIER	BAROUCHE	BARRELING	BARTENDED	BASANTS
BARNIEST	BAROUCHES	BARRELLED	BARTENDER	BASCINET
BARNING	BARP	BARRELS	BARTENDS	BASCINETS
BARNLIKE	BARPERSON	BARREN	BARTER	BASCULE
BARNS	BARPS	BARRENER	BARTERED	BASCULES
BARNSTORM	BARQUE	BARRENEST	BARTERER	BASE
BARNWOOD	BARQUES	BARRENLY	BARTERERS	BASEBALL
BARNWOODS	BARQUETTE	BARRENS	BARTERING	BASEBALLS
BARNY	BARRA	BARRES	BARTERS	BASEBAND
BARNYARD	BARRABLE	BARRET	BARTISAN	BASEBANDS
BARNYARDS	BARRACAN	BARRETOR	BARTISANS	BASEBOARD
BAROCCO	BARRACANS	BARRETORS	BARTIZAN	BASEBORN
BAROCCOS	BARRACE	BARRETRY	BARTIZANS	BASED
BAROCK	BARRACES	BARRETS	BARTON	BASEEJ
BAROCKS	BARRACK	BARRETTE	BARTONS	BASEHEAD
BAROGRAM	BARRACKED	BARRETTER	BARTSIA	BASEHEADS
BAROGRAMS	BARRACKER	BARRETTES	BARTSIAS	BASELARD
BAROGRAPH	BARRACKS	BARRICADE	BARWARE	BASELARDS
BAROLO	BARRACOON	BARRICADO	BARWARES	BASELESS
BAROLOS	BARRACUDA	BARRICO	BARWOOD	BASELINE

BASELINER	BASIFIED	BASNET	BASTA	BATCHING
BASELINES	BASIFIER	BASNETS	BASTARD	BATCHINGS
BASELOAD	BASIFIERS	BASOCHE	BASTARDLY	BATE
BASELOADS	BASIFIES	BASOCHES	BASTARDRY	BATEAU
BASELY	BASIFIXED	BASON	BASTARDS	BATEAUX
BASEMAN	BASIFUGAL	BASONS	BASTARDY	BATED
BASEMEN	BASIFY	BASOPHIL	BASTE	BATELESS
BASEMENT	BASIFYING	BASOPHILE	BASTED	BATELEUR
BASEMENTS	BASIJ	BASOPHILS	BASTER	BATELEURS
BASEN	BASIL	BASQUE	BASTERS	BATEMENT
BASENESS	BASILAR	BASQUED	BASTES	BATEMENTS
BASENJI	BASILARY	BASQUES	BASTI	BATES
BASENJIS	BASILECT	BASQUINE	BASTIDE	BATFISH
BASEPATH	BASILECTS	BASQUINES	BASTIDES	BATFISHES
BASEPATHS	BASILIC	BASS	BASTILE	BATFOWL
BASEPLATE	BASILICA	BASSE	BASTILES	BATFOWLED
BASER	BASILICAE	BASSED	BASTILLE	BATFOWLER
BASES	BASILICAL	BASSER	BASTILLES	BATFOWLS
BASEST	BASILICAN	BASSERS	BASTINADE	BATGIRL
BASH	BASILICAS	BASSES	BASTINADO	BATGIRLS
BASHAW	BASILICON	BASSEST	BASTING	BATH
BASHAWISM	BASILISK	BASSET	BASTINGS	BATHCUBE
BASHAWS	BASILISKS	BASSETED	BASTION	BATHCUBES
BASHED	BASILS	BASSETING	BASTIONED	BATHE
BASHER	BASIN	BASSETS	BASTIONS	BATHED
BASHERS	BASINAL	BASSETT	BASTIS	BATHER
BASHES	BASINED	BASSETTED	BASTLE	BATHERS
BASHFUL	BASINET	BASSETTS	BASTLES	BATHES
BASHFULLY	BASINETS	BASSI	BASTO	BATHETIC
BASHING	BASINFUL	BASSIER	BASTOS	BATHHOUSE
BASHINGS	BASINFULS	BASSIEST	BASTS	BATHING
BASHLESS	BASING	BASSINET	BASUCO	BATHINGS
BASHLIK	BASINLIKE	BASSINETS	BASUCOS	BATHLESS
BASHLIKS	BASINS	BASSING	BAT	BATHMAT
BASHLYK	BASION	BASSIST	BATABLE	BATHMATS
BASHLYKS	BASIONS	BASSISTS	BATARD	BATHMIC
BASHMENT	BASIPETAL	BASSLINE	BATARDS	BATHMISM
BASHMENTS	BASIS	BASSLINES	BATATA	BATHMISMS
BASHO	BASK	BASSLY	BATATAS	BATHOLITE
BASHTAG	BASKED	BASSNESS	BATAVIA	BATHOLITH
BASHTAGS	BASKET	BASSO	BATAVIAS	BATHORSE
BASIC	BASKETFUL	BASSOON	BATBOY	BATHORSES
BASICALLY	BASKETRY	BASSOONS	BATBOYS	BATHOS
BASICITY	BASKETS	BASSOS	BATCH	BATHOSES
BASICS	BASKING	BASSWOOD	BATCHED	BATHROBE
BASIDIA	BASKS	BASSWOODS	BATCHER	BATHROBES
BASIDIAL	BASMATI	BASSY	BATCHERS	BATHROOM
BASIDIUM	BASMATIS	BAST	BATCHES	BATHROOMS

BATHS	BATTED	BATTS	BAULKS	BAWNS
BATHTUB	BATTEL	BATTU	BAULKY	BAWR
BATHTUBS	BATTELED	BATTUE	BAUR	BAWRS
BATHWATER	BATTELER	BATTUES	BAURS	BAWSUNT
BATHYAL	BATTELERS	BATTUTA	BAUSOND	BAWTIE
BATHYBIUS	BATTELING	BATTUTAS	BAUXITE	BAWTIES
BATHYLITE	BATTELLED	BATTUTO	BAUXITES	BAWTY
BATHYLITH	BATTELS	BATTUTOS	BAUXITIC	BAXTER
BATIK	BATTEMENT	BATTY	BAVARDAGE	BAXTERS
BATIKED	BATTEN	BATWING	BAVAROIS	BAY
BATIKING	BATTENED	BATWOMAN	BAVIN	BAYADEER
BATIKS	BATTENER	BATWOMEN	BAVINED	BAYADEERS
BATING	BATTENERS	BAUBEE	BAVINING	BAYADERE
BATISTE	BATTENING	BAUBEES	BAVINS	BAYADERES
BATISTES	BATTENS	BAUBLE	BAWBEE	BAYAMO
BATLER	BATTER	BAUBLES	BAWBEES	BAYAMOS
BATLERS	BATTERED	BAUBLING	BAWBLE	BAYARD
BATLET	BATTERER	BAUCHLE	BAWBLES	BAYARDS
BATLETS	BATTERERS	BAUCHLED	BAWCOCK	BAYBERRY
BATLIKE	BATTERIE	BAUCHLES	BAWCOCKS	BAYE
BATMAN	BATTERIES	BAUCHLING	BAWD	BAYED
BATMEN	BATTERING	BAUD	BAWDIER	BAYER
BATOLOGY	BATTERO	BAUDEKIN	BAWDIES	BAYES
BATON	BATTEROS	BAUDEKINS	BAWDIEST	BAYEST
BATONED	BATTERS	BAUDRIC	BAWDILY	BAYFRONT
BATONING	BATTERY	BAUDRICK	BAWDINESS	BAYFRONTS
BATONNIER	BATTIER	BAUDRICKE	BAWDKIN	BAYING
BATONS	BATTIES	BAUDRICKS	BAWDKINS	BAYLE
BATOON	BATTIEST	BAUDRICS	BAWDRIC	BAYLES
BATOONED	BATTIK	BAUDRONS	BAWDRICS	BAYMAN
BATOONING	BATTIKS	BAUDS	BAWDRIES	BAYMEN
BATOONS	BATTILL	BAUERA	BAWDRY	BAYNODDY
BATRACHIA	BATTILLED	BAUERAS	BAWDS	BAYONET
BATS	BATTILLS	BAUHINIA	BAWDY	BAYONETED
BATSHIT	BATTILY	BAUHINIAS	BAWK	BAYONETS
BATSMAN	BATTINESS	BAUK	BAWKS	BAYOU
BATSMEN	BATTING	BAUKED	BAWL	BAYOUS
BATSWING	BATTINGS	BAUKING	BAWLED	BAYS
BATSWOMAN	BATTLE	BAUKS	BAWLER	BAYSIDE
BATSWOMEN	BATTLEAX	BAULK	BAWLERS	BAYSIDES
BATT	BATTLEAXE	BAULKED	BAWLEY	BAYT
BATTA	BATTLEBUS	BAULKER	BAWLEYS	BAYTED
BATTALIA	BATTLED	BAULKERS	BAWLING	BAYTING
BATTALIAS	BATTLER	BAULKIER	BAWLINGS	BAYTS
BATTALION	BATTLERS	BAULKIEST	BAWLS	BAYWOOD
BATTAS	BATTLES	BAULKILY	BAWN	BAYWOODS
BATTEAU	BATTLING	BAULKING	BAWNEEN	BAYWOP
BATTEAUX	BATTOLOGY	BAULKLINE	BAWNEENS	BAYWOPS

BAYYAN
BAYYANS
BAZAAR
BAZAARS
BAZAR
BAZARS
BAZAZZ
BAZAZZES
BAZILLION
BAZOO
BAZOOKA
BAZOOKAS
BAZOOM
BAZOOMS
BAZOOS
BAZOUKI
BAZOUKIS
BAZZ
BAZZAZZ
BAZZAZZES
BAZZED
BAZZES
BAZZING
BDELLIUM
BDELLIUMS
BE
BEACH
BEACHBALL
BEACHBOY
BEACHBOYS
BEACHCOMB
BEACHED
BEACHES
BEACHGOER
BEACHHEAD
BEACHIER
BEACHIEST
BEACHING
BEACHSIDE
BEACHWEAR
BEACHY
BEACON
BEACONED
BEACONING
BEACONS
BEAD
BEADBLAST
BEADED

BEADER
BEADERS
BEADHOUSE
BEADIER
BEADIEST
BEADILY
BEADINESS
BEADING
BEADINGS
BEADLE
BEADLEDOM
BEADLES
BEADLIKE
BEADMAN
BEADMEN
BEADROLL
BEADROLLS
BEADS
BEADSMAN
BEADSMEN
BEADWORK
BEADWORKS
BEADY
BEAGLE
BEAGLED
BEAGLER
BEAGLERS
BEAGLES
BEAGLING
BEAGLINGS
BEAK
BEAKED
BEAKER
BEAKERFUL
BEAKERS
BEAKIER
BEAKIEST
BEAKLESS
BEAKLIKE
BEAKS
BEAKY
BEAL
BEALING
BEALINGS
BEALS
BEAM
BEAMED
BEAMER

BEAMERS
BEAMIER
BEAMIEST
BEAMILY
BEAMINESS
BEAMING
BEAMINGLY
BEAMINGS
BEAMISH
BEAMISHLY
BEAMLESS
BEAMLET
BEAMLETS
BEAMLIKE
BEAMS
BEAMY
BEAN
BEANBAG
BEANBAGS
BEANBALL
BEANBALLS
BEANED
BEANERIES
BEANERY
BEANFEAST
BEANIE
BEANIES
BEANING
BEANLIKE
BEANO
BEANOS
BEANPOLE
BEANPOLES
BEANS
BEANSTALK
BEANY
BEAR
BEARABLE
BEARABLY
BEARBERRY
BEARBINE
BEARBINES
BEARCAT
BEARCATS
BEARD
BEARDED
BEARDIE
BEARDIER

BEARDIES
BEARDIEST
BEARDING
BEARDLESS
BEARDLIKE
BEARDS
BEARDY
BEARE
BEARED
BEARER
BEARERS
BEARES
BEARGRASS
BEARHUG
BEARHUGS
BEARING
BEARINGS
BEARISH
BEARISHLY
BEARLIKE
BEARNAISE
BEARPAW
BEARPAWS
BEARS
BEARSKIN
BEARSKINS
BEARWARD
BEARWARDS
BEARWOOD
BEARWOODS
BEAST
BEASTED
BEASTHOOD
BEASTIE
BEASTIES
BEASTILY
BEASTING
BEASTINGS
BEASTLIER
BEASTLIKE
BEASTLY
BEASTS
BEAT
BEATABLE
BEATBOX
BEATBOXED
BEATBOXER
BEATBOXES

BEATDOWN
BEATDOWNS
BEATEN
BEATER
BEATERS
BEATH
BEATHED
BEATHING
BEATHS
BEATIER
BEATIEST
BEATIFIC
BEATIFIED
BEATIFIES
BEATIFY
BEATING
BEATINGS
BEATITUDE
BEATLESS
BEATNIK
BEATNIKS
BEATS
BEATY
BEAU
BEAUCOUP
BEAUCOUPS
BEAUFET
BEAUFETS
BEAUFFET
BEAUFFETS
BEAUFIN
BEAUFINS
BEAUISH
BEAUS
BEAUT
BEAUTEOUS
BEAUTER
BEAUTEST
BEAUTIED
BEAUTIES
BEAUTIFUL
BEAUTIFY
BEAUTS
BEAUTY
BEAUTYING
BEAUX
BEAUXITE
BEAUXITES

BEAVER	BECHARM	BECRIME	BEDAZING	BEDEWS
BEAVERED	BECHARMED	BECRIMED	BEDAZZLE	BEDFAST
BEAVERIES	BECHARMS	BECRIMES	BEDAZZLED	BEDFELLOW
BEAVERING	BECK	BECRIMING	BEDAZZLES	BEDFRAME
BEAVERS	BECKE	BECROWD	BEDBATH	BEDFRAMES
BEAVERY	BECKED	BECROWDED	BEDBATHS	BEDGOWN
BEBEERINE	BECKES	BECROWDS	BEDBOARD	BEDGOWNS
BEBEERU	BECKET	BECRUST	BEDBOARDS	BEDHEAD
BEBEERUS	BECKETS	BECRUSTED	BEDBUG	BEDHEADS
BEBLOOD	BECKING	BECRUSTS	BEDBUGS	BEDIAPER
BEBLOODED	BECKON	BECUDGEL	BEDCHAIR	BEDIAPERS
BEBLOODS	BECKONED	BECUDGELS	BEDCHAIRS	BEDIDE
BEBOP	BECKONER	BECURL	BEDCOVER	BEDIGHT
BEBOPPED	BECKONERS	BECURLED	BEDCOVERS	BEDIGHTED
BEBOPPER	BECKONING	BECURLING	BEDDABLE	BEDIGHTS
BEBOPPERS	BECKONS	BECURLS	BEDDED	BEDIM
BEBOPPING	BECKS	BECURSE	BEDDER	BEDIMMED
BEBOPS	BECLAMOR	BECURSED	BEDDERS	BEDIMMING
BEBUNG	BECLAMORS	BECURSES	BEDDING	BEDIMPLE
BEBUNGS	BECLAMOUR	BECURSING	BEDDINGS	BEDIMPLED
BECALL	BECLASP	BECURST	BEDE	BEDIMPLES
BECALLED	BECLASPED	BED	BEDEAFEN	BEDIMS
BECALLING	BECLASPS	BEDABBLE	BEDEAFENS	BEDIRTIED
BECALLS	BECLOAK	BEDABBLED	BEDECK	BEDIRTIES
BECALM	BECLOAKED	BEDABBLES	BEDECKED	BEDIRTY
BECALMED	BECLOAKS	BEDAD	BEDECKING	BEDIZEN
BECALMING	BECLOG	BEDAGGLE	BEDECKS	BEDIZENED
BECALMS	BECLOGGED	BEDAGGLED	BEDEGUAR	BEDIZENS
BECAME	BECLOGS	BEDAGGLES	BEDEGUARS	BEDLAM
BECAP	BECLOTHE	BEDAMN	BEDEHOUSE	BEDLAMER
BECAPPED	BECLOTHED	BEDAMNED	BEDEL	BEDLAMERS
BECAPPING	BECLOTHES	BEDAMNING	BEDELL	BEDLAMISM
BECAPS	BECLOUD	BEDAMNS	BEDELLS	BEDLAMITE
BECARPET	BECLOUDED	BEDARKEN	BEDELS	BEDLAMP
BECARPETS	BECLOUDS	BEDARKENS	BEDELSHIP	BEDLAMPS
BECASSE	BECLOWN	BEDASH	BEDEMAN	BEDLAMS
BECASSES	BECLOWNED	BEDASHED	BEDEMEN	BEDLESS
BECAUSE	BECLOWNS	BEDASHES	BEDERAL	BEDLIKE
BECCACCIA	BECOME	BEDASHING	BEDERALS	BEDLINER
BECCAFICO	BECOMES	BEDAUB	BEDES	BEDLINERS
BECHALK	BECOMING	BEDAUBED	BEDESMAN	BEDMAKER
BECHALKED	BECOMINGS	BEDAUBING	BEDESMEN	BEDMAKERS
BECHALKS	BECOWARD	BEDAUBS	BEDEVIL	BEDMATE
BECHAMEL	BECOWARDS	BEDAWIN	BEDEVILED	BEDMATES
BECHAMELS	BECQUEREL	BEDAWINS	BEDEVILS	BEDOTTED
BECHANCE	BECRAWL	BEDAZE	BEDEW	BEDOUIN
BECHANCED	BECRAWLED	BEDAZED	BEDEWED	BEDOUINS
BECHANCES	BECRAWLS	BEDAZES	BEDEWING	BEDPAN

BEDPANS
BEDPLATE
BEDPLATES
BEDPOST
BEDPOSTS
BEDQUILT
BEDQUILTS
BEDRAGGLE
BEDRAIL
BEDRAILS
BEDRAL
BEDRALS
BEDRAPE
BEDRAPED
BEDRAPES
BEDRAPING
BEDRENCH
BEDREST
BEDRESTS
BEDRID
BEDRIDDEN
BEDRIGHT
BEDRIGHTS
BEDRITE
BEDRITES
BEDRIVEL
BEDRIVELS
BEDROCK
BEDROCKS
BEDROLL
BEDROLLS
BEDROOM
BEDROOMED
BEDROOMS
BEDROP
BEDROPPED
BEDROPS
BEDROPT
BEDRUG
BEDRUGGED
BEDRUGS
BEDS
BEDSHEET
BEDSHEETS
BEDSIDE
BEDSIDES
BEDSIT
BEDSITS

BEDSITTER
BEDSKIRT
BEDSKIRTS
BEDSOCK
BEDSOCKS
BEDSONIA
BEDSONIAS
BEDSORE
BEDSORES
BEDSPREAD
BEDSPRING
BEDSTAND
BEDSTANDS
BEDSTEAD
BEDSTEADS
BEDSTRAW
BEDSTRAWS
BEDTICK
BEDTICKS
BEDTIME
BEDTIMES
BEDU
BEDUCK
BEDUCKED
BEDUCKING
BEDUCKS
BEDUIN
BEDUINS
BEDUMB
BEDUMBED
BEDUMBING
BEDUMBS
BEDUNCE
BEDUNCED
BEDUNCES
BEDUNCING
BEDUNG
BEDUNGED
BEDUNGING
BEDUNGS
BEDUST
BEDUSTED
BEDUSTING
BEDUSTS
BEDWARD
BEDWARDS
BEDWARF
BEDWARFED

BEDWARFS
BEDWARMER
BEDWETTER
BEDYDE
BEDYE
BEDYED
BEDYEING
BEDYES
BEE
BEEBEE
BEEBEES
BEEBREAD
BEEBREADS
BEECH
BEECHEN
BEECHES
BEECHIER
BEECHIEST
BEECHMAST
BEECHNUT
BEECHNUTS
BEECHWOOD
BEECHY
BEEDI
BEEDIE
BEEDIES
BEEF
BEEFALO
BEEFALOES
BEEFALOS
BEEFCAKE
BEEFCAKES
BEEFEATER
BEEFED
BEEFIER
BEEFIEST
BEEFILY
BEEFINESS
BEEFING
BEEFLESS
BEEFS
BEEFSTEAK
BEEFWOOD
BEEFWOODS
BEEFY
BEEGAH
BEEGAHS
BEEHIVE

BEEHIVED
BEEHIVES
BEEKEEPER
BEELIKE
BEELINE
BEELINED
BEELINES
BEELINING
BEEN
BEENAH
BEENAHS
BEENTO
BEENTOS
BEEP
BEEPED
BEEPER
BEEPERS
BEEPING
BEEPS
BEER
BEERAGE
BEERAGES
BEERFEST
BEERFESTS
BEERHALL
BEERHALLS
BEERIER
BEERIEST
BEERILY
BEERINESS
BEERMAT
BEERMATS
BEERNUT
BEERNUTS
BEERS
BEERSIES
BEERY
BEES
BEESOME
BEESTING
BEESTINGS
BEESTUNG
BEESWAX
BEESWAXED
BEESWAXES
BEESWING
BEESWINGS
BEET

BEETED
BEETFLIES
BEETFLY
BEETING
BEETLE
BEETLED
BEETLER
BEETLERS
BEETLES
BEETLING
BEETROOT
BEETROOTS
BEETS
BEEVES
BEEYARD
BEEYARDS
BEEZER
BEEZERS
BEFALL
BEFALLEN
BEFALLING
BEFALLS
BEFANA
BEFANAS
BEFELD
BEFELL
BEFFANA
BEFFANAS
BEFINGER
BEFINGERS
BEFINNED
BEFIT
BEFITS
BEFITTED
BEFITTING
BEFLAG
BEFLAGGED
BEFLAGS
BEFLEA
BEFLEAED
BEFLEAING
BEFLEAS
BEFLECK
BEFLECKED
BEFLECKS
BEFLOWER
BEFLOWERS
BEFLUM

B

BEFLUMMED	BEGEMMED	BEGLADS	BEGUINE	BEHOLDER
BEFLUMS	BEGEMMING	BEGLAMOR	BEGUINES	BEHOLDERS
BEFOAM	BEGEMS	BEGLAMORS	BEGUINS	BEHOLDING
BEFOAMED	BEGET	BEGLAMOUR	BEGULF	BEHOLDS
BEFOAMING	BEGETS	BEGLERBEG	BEGULFED	BEHOOF
BEFOAMS	BEGETTER	BEGLOOM	BEGULFING	BEHOOFS
BEFOG	BEGETTERS	BEGLOOMED	BEGULFS	BEHOOVE
BEFOGGED	BEGETTING	BEGLOOMS	BEGUM	BEHOOVED
BEFOGGING	BEGGAR	BEGNAW	BEGUMS	BEHOOVES
BEFOGS	BEGGARDOM	BEGNAWED	BEGUN	BEHOOVING
BEFOOL	BEGGARED	BEGNAWING	BEGUNK	BEHOTE
BEFOOLED	BEGGARIES	BEGNAWS	BEGUNKED	BEHOTES
BEFOOLING	BEGGARING	BEGO	BEGUNKING	BEHOTING
BEFOOLS	BEGGARLY	BEGOES	BEGUNKS	BEHOVE
BEFORE	BEGGARS	BEGOGGLED	BEHALF	BEHOVED
BEFORTUNE	BEGGARY	BEGOING	BEHALVES	BEHOVEFUL
BEFOUL	BEGGED	BEGONE	BEHAPPEN	BEHOVELY
BEFOULED	BEGGING	BEGONIA	BEHAPPENS	BEHOVES
BEFOULER	BEGGINGLY	BEGONIAS	BEHATTED	BEHOVING
BEFOULERS	BEGGINGS	BEGORAH	BEHAVE	BEHOWL
BEFOULING	BEGHARD	BEGORED	BEHAVED	BEHOWLED
BEFOULS	BEGHARDS	BEGORRA	BEHAVER	BEHOWLING
BEFRET	BEGIFT	BEGORRAH	BEHAVERS	BEHOWLS
BEFRETS	BEGIFTED	BEGOT	BEHAVES	BEIGE
BEFRETTED	BEGIFTING	BEGOTTEN	BEHAVING	BEIGEL
BEFRIEND	BEGIFTS	BEGRIM	BEHAVIOR	BEIGELS
BEFRIENDS	BEGILD	BEGRIME	BEHAVIORS	BEIGER
BEFRINGE	BEGILDED	BEGRIMED	BEHAVIOUR	BEIGES
BEFRINGED	BEGILDING	BEGRIMES	BEHEAD	BEIGEST
BEFRINGES	BEGILDS	BEGRIMING	BEHEADAL	BEIGIER
BEFUDDLE	BEGILT	BEGRIMMED	BEHEADALS	BEIGIEST
BEFUDDLED	BEGIN	BEGRIMS	BEHEADED	BEIGNE
BEFUDDLES	BEGINNE	BEGROAN	BEHEADER	BEIGNES
BEG	BEGINNER	BEGROANED	BEHEADERS	BEIGNET
BEGAD	BEGINNERS	BEGROANS	BEHEADING	BEIGNETS
BEGALL	BEGINNES	BEGRUDGE	BEHEADS	BEIGY
BEGALLED	BEGINNING	BEGRUDGED	BEHELD	BEIN
BEGALLING	BEGINS	BEGRUDGER	BEHEMOTH	BEINED
BEGALLS	BEGIRD	BEGRUDGES	BEHEMOTHS	BEING
BEGAN	BEGIRDED	BEGS	BEHEST	BEINGLESS
BEGAR	BEGIRDING	BEGUILE	BEHESTS	BEINGNESS
BEGARS	BEGIRDLE	BEGUILED	BEHIGHT	BEINGS
BEGAT	BEGIRDLED	BEGUILER	BEHIGHTED	BEINING
BEGAZE	BEGIRDLES	BEGUILERS	BEHIGHTS	BEINKED
BEGAZED	BEGIRDS	BEGUILES	BEHIND	BEINNESS
BEGAZES	BEGIRT	BEGUILING	BEHINDS	BEINS
BEGAZING	BEGLAD	BEGUIN	BEHOLD	BEJABBERS
BEGEM	BEGLADDED	BEGUINAGE	BEHOLDEN	BEJABERS

BEJADE	BELADY	BELFRIED	BELLHOP	BELOVES
BEJADED	BELADYING	BELFRIES	BELLHOPS	BELOVING
BEJADES	BELAH	BELFRY	BELLIBONE	BELOW
BEJADING	BELAHS	BELGA	BELLICOSE	BELOWS
BEJANT	BELAMIES	BELGARD	BELLIED	BELS
BEJANTS	BELAMOUR	BELGARDS	BELLIES	BELT
BEJASUS	BELAMOURE	BELGAS	BELLING	BELTED
BEJASUSES	BELAMOURS	BELGICISM	BELLINGS	BELTER
BEJEEBERS	BELAMY	BELIE	BELLINI	BELTERS
BEJEEZUS	BELAR	BELIED	BELLINIS	BELTING
BEJESUIT	BELARS	BELIEF	BELLMAN	BELTINGS
BEJESUITS	BELATE	BELIEFS	BELLMEN	BELTLESS
BEJESUS	BELATED	BELIER	BELLOCK	BELTLIKE
BEJESUSES	BELATEDLY	BELIERS	BELLOCKED	BELTLINE
BEJEWEL	BELATES	BELIES	BELLOCKS	BELTLINES
BEJEWELED	BELATING	BELIEVE	BELLOW	BELTMAN
BEJEWELS	BELAUD	BELIEVED	BELLOWED	BELTMEN
BEJUMBLE	BELAUDED	BELIEVER	BELLOWER	BELTS
BEJUMBLED	BELAUDING	BELIEVERS	BELLOWERS	BELTWAY
BEJUMBLES	BELAUDS	BELIEVES	BELLOWING	BELTWAYS
BEKAH	BELAY	BELIEVING	BELLOWS	BELUGA
BEKAHS	BELAYED	BELIKE	BELLPULL	BELUGAS
BEKISS	BELAYER	BELIQUOR	BELLPULLS	BELVEDERE
BEKISSED	BELAYERS	BELIQUORS	BELLS	BELYING
BEKISSES	BELAYING	BELITTLE	BELLWORT	BEMA
BEKISSING	BELAYS	BELITTLED	BELLWORTS	BEMAD
BEKNAVE	BELCH	BELITTLER	BELLY	BEMADAM
BEKNAVED	BELCHED	BELITTLES	BELLYACHE	BEMADAMED
BEKNAVES	BELCHER	BELIVE	BELLYBAND	BEMADAMS
BEKNAVING	BELCHERS	BELL	BELLYBOAT	BEMADDED
BEKNIGHT	BELCHES	BELLBIND	BELLYFLOP	BEMADDEN
BEKNIGHTS	BELCHING	BELLBINDS	BELLYFUL	BEMADDENS
BEKNOT	BELDAM	BELLBIRD	BELLYFULS	BEMADDING
BEKNOTS	BELDAME	BELLBIRDS	BELLYING	BEMADS
BEKNOTTED	BELDAMES	BELLBOY	BELLYINGS	BEMAS
BEKNOWN	BELDAMS	BELLBOYS	BELLYLIKE	BEMATA
BEL	BELEAGUER	BELLBUOY	BELOMANCY	BEMAUL
BELABOR	BELEAP	BELLBUOYS	BELON	BEMAULED
BELABORED	BELEAPED	BELLCAST	BELONG	BEMAULING
BELABORS	BELEAPING	BELLCOTE	BELONGED	BEMAULS
BELABOUR	BELEAPS	BELLCOTES	BELONGER	BEMAZED
BELABOURS	BELEAPT	BELLE	BELONGERS	BEMBEX
BELACE	BELEE	BELLED	BELONGING	BEMBEXES
BELACED	BELEED	BELLEEK	BELONGS	BEMBIX
BELACES	BELEEING	BELLEEKS	BELONS	BEMBIXES
BELACING	BELEES	BELLES	BELOVE	BEMEAN
BELADIED	BELEMNITE	BELLETER	BELOVED	BEMEANED
BELADIES	BELEMNOID	BELLETERS	BELOVEDS	BEMEANING

B

BEMEANS	BEMUDDLES	BENDIEST	BENIGNEST	BENZAL
BEMEANT	BEMUDS	BENDINESS	BENIGNITY	BENZALS
BEMEDAL	BEMUFFLE	BENDING	BENIGNLY	BENZENE
BEMEDALED	BEMUFFLED	BENDINGLY	BENIS	BENZENES
BEMEDALS	BEMUFFLES	BENDINGS	BENISEED	BENZENOID
BEMETE	BEMURMUR	BENDLET	BENISEEDS	BENZIDIN
BEMETED	BEMURMURS	BENDLETS	BENISON	BENZIDINE
BEMETES	BEMUSE	BENDS	BENISONS	BENZIDINS
BEMETING	BEMUSED	BENDWAYS	BENITIER	BENZIL
BEMINGLE	BEMUSEDLY	BENDWISE	BENITIERS	BENZILS
BEMINGLED	BEMUSES	BENDY	BENJ	BENZIN
BEMINGLES	BEMUSING	BENDYS	BENJAMIN	BENZINE
BEMIRE	BEMUZZLE	BENE	BENJAMINS	BENZINES
BEMIRED	BEMUZZLED	BENEATH	BENJES	BENZINS
BEMIRES	BEMUZZLES	BENEDICK	BENNE	BENZOATE
BEMIRING	BEN	BENEDICKS	BENNES	BENZOATES
BEMIST	BENADRYL	BENEDICT	BENNET	BENZOIC
BEMISTED	BENADRYLS	BENEDICTS	BENNETS	BENZOIN
BEMISTING	BENAME	BENEDIGHT	BENNI	BENZOINS
BEMISTS	BENAMED	BENEFACT	BENNIES	BENZOL
BEMIX	BENAMES	BENEFACTS	BENNIS	BENZOLE
BEMIXED	BENAMING	BENEFIC	BENNY	BENZOLES
BEMIXES	BENCH	BENEFICE	BENOMYL	BENZOLINE
BEMIXING	BENCHED	BENEFICED	BENOMYLS	BENZOLS
BEMIXT	BENCHER	BENEFICES	BENS	BENZOYL
BEMOAN	BENCHERS	BENEFIT	BENT	BENZOYLS
BEMOANED	BENCHES	BENEFITED	BENTGRASS	BENZYL
BEMOANER	BENCHIER	BENEFITER	BENTHAL	BENZYLIC
BEMOANERS	BENCHIEST	BENEFITS	BENTHIC	BENZYLS
BEMOANING	BENCHING	BENEMPT	BENTHOAL	BEPAINT
BEMOANS	BENCHLAND	BENEMPTED	BENTHON	BEPAINTED
BEMOCK	BENCHLESS	BENES	BENTHONIC	BEPAINTS
BEMOCKED	BENCHMARK	BENET	BENTHONS	BEPAT
BEMOCKING	BENCHTOP	BENETS	BENTHOS	BEPATCHED
BEMOCKS	BENCHTOPS	BENETTED	BENTHOSES	BEPATS
BEMOIL	BENCHY	BENETTING	BENTIER	BEPATTED
BEMOILED	BEND	BENGA	BENTIEST	BEPATTING
BEMOILING	BENDABLE	BENGALINE	BENTO	BEPEARL
BEMOILS	BENDAY	BENGAS	BENTONITE	BEPEARLED
BEMONSTER	BENDAYED	BENI	BENTOS	BEPEARLS
BEMOUTH	BENDAYING	BENIGHT	BENTS	BEPELT
BEMOUTHED	BENDAYS	BENIGHTED	BENTWOOD	BEPELTED
BEMOUTHS	BENDED	BENIGHTEN	BENTWOODS	BEPELTING
BEMUD	BENDEE	BENIGHTER	BENTY	BEPELTS
BEMUDDED	BENDEES	BENIGHTS	BENUMB	BEPEPPER
BEMUDDING	BENDER	BENIGN	BENUMBED	BEPEPPERS
BEMUDDLE	BENDERS	BENIGNANT	BENUMBING	BEPESTER
BEMUDDLED	BENDIER	BENIGNER	BENUMBS	BEPESTERS

BEPIMPLE

BEPIMPLE	BERBERIS	BERGYLT	BERRIGAN	BESEECHED
BEPIMPLED	BERBERS	BERGYLTS	BERRIGANS	BESEECHER
BEPIMPLES	BERBICE	BERHYME	BERRY	BESEECHES
BEPITIED	BERCEAU	BERHYMED	BERRYING	BESEEING
BEPITIES	BERCEAUX	BERHYMES	BERRYINGS	BESEEKE
BEPITY	BERCEUSE	BERHYMING	BERRYLESS	BESEEKES
BEPITYING	BERCEUSES	BERIBERI	BERRYLIKE	BESEEKING
BEPLASTER	BERDACHE	BERIBERIS	BERSEEM	BESEEM
BEPLUMED	BERDACHES	BERIMBAU	BERSEEMS	BESEEMED
BEPOMMEL	BERDASH	BERIMBAUS	BERSERK	BESEEMING
BEPOMMELS	BERDASHES	BERIME	BERSERKER	BESEEMLY
BEPOWDER	BERE	BERIMED	BERSERKLY	BESEEMS
BEPOWDERS	BEREAVE	BERIMES	BERSERKS	BESEEN
BEPRAISE	BEREAVED	BERIMING	BERTH	BESEES
BEPRAISED	BEREAVEN	BERINGED	BERTHA	BESES
BEPRAISES	BEREAVER	BERK	BERTHAGE	BESET
BEPROSE	BEREAVERS	BERKELIUM	BERTHAGES	BESETMENT
BEPROSED	BEREAVES	BERKO	BERTHAS	BESETS
BEPROSES	BEREAVING	BERKS	BERTHE	BESETTER
BEPROSING	BEREFT	BERLEY	BERTHED	BESETTERS
BEPUFF	BERES	BERLEYED	BERTHES	BESETTING
BEPUFFED	BERET	BERLEYING	BERTHING	BESHADOW
BEPUFFING	BERETS	BERLEYS	BERTHINGS	BESHADOWS
BEPUFFS	BERETTA	BERLIN	BERTHS	BESHAME
BEQUEATH	BERETTAS	BERLINE	BERYL	BESHAMED
BEQUEATHS	BERG	BERLINES	BERYLINE	BESHAMES
BEQUEST	BERGALL	BERLINS	BERYLLIA	BESHAMING
BEQUESTS	BERGALLS	BERM	BERYLLIAS	BESHINE
BERAKE	BERGAMA	BERME	BERYLLIUM	BESHINES
BERAKED	BERGAMAS	BERMED	BERYLS	BESHINING
BERAKES	BERGAMASK	BERMES	BES	BESHIVER
BERAKING	BERGAMOT	BERMING	BESAINT	BESHIVERS
BERASCAL	BERGAMOTS	BERMS	BESAINTED	BESHONE
BERASCALS	BERGANDER	BERMUDAS	BESAINTS	BESHOUT
BERATE	BERGEN	BERNICLE	BESANG	BESHOUTED
BERATED	BERGENIA	BERNICLES	BESAT	BESHOUTS
BERATES	BERGENIAS	BEROB	BESAW	BESHREW
BERATING	BERGENS	BEROBBED	BESCATTER	BESHREWED
BERAY	BERGERE	BEROBBING	BESCORCH	BESHREWS
BERAYED	BERGERES	BEROBED	BESCOUR	BESHROUD
BERAYING	BERGFALL	BEROBS	BESCOURED	BESHROUDS
BERAYS	BERGFALLS	BEROUGED	BESCOURS	BESIDE
BERBER	BERGHAAN	BERRET	BESCRAWL	BESIDES
BERBERE	BERGHAANS	BERRETS	BESCRAWLS	BESIEGE
BERBERES	BERGMEHL	BERRETTA	BESCREEN	BESIEGED
BERBERIN	BERGMEHLS	BERRETTAS	BESCREENS	BESIEGER
BERBERINE	BERGOMASK	BERRIED	BESEE	BESIEGERS
BERBERINS	BERGS	BERRIES	BESEECH	BESIEGES

BESIEGING	BESNOWS	BESPOTTED	BESTOWER	BETEEM
BESIGH	BESOGNIO	BESPOUSE	BESTOWERS	BETEEME
BESIGHED	BESOGNIOS	BESPOUSED	BESTOWING	BETEEMED
BESIGHING	BESOIN	BESPOUSES	BESTOWS	BETEEMES
BESIGHS	BESOINS	BESPOUT	BESTREAK	BETEEMING
BESING	BESOM	BESPOUTED	BESTREAKS	BETEEMS
BESINGING	BESOMED	BESPOUTS	BESTREW	BETEL
BESINGS	BESOMING	BESPREAD	BESTREWED	BETELNUT
BESIT	BESOMS	BESPREADS	BESTREWN	BETELNUTS
BESITS	BESONIAN	BESPRENT	BESTREWS	BETELS
BESITTING	BESONIANS	BEST	BESTRID	BETES
BESLAVE	BESOOTHE	BESTAD	BESTRIDE	BETH
BESLAVED	BESOOTHED	BESTADDE	BESTRIDES	BETHANK
BESLAVER	BESOOTHES	BESTAIN	BESTRODE	BETHANKED
BESLAVERS	BESORT	BESTAINED	BESTROW	BETHANKIT
BESLAVES	BESORTED	BESTAINS	BESTROWED	BETHANKS
BESLAVING	BESORTING	BESTAR	BESTROWN	BETHEL
BESLIME	BESORTS	BESTARRED	BESTROWS	BETHELS
BESLIMED	BESOT	BESTARS	BESTS	BETHESDA
BESLIMES	BESOTS	BESTEAD	BESTUCK	BETHESDAS
BESLIMING	BESOTTED	BESTEADED	BESTUD	BETHINK
BESLOBBER	BESOTTING	BESTEADS	BESTUDDED	BETHINKS
BESLUBBER	BESOUGHT	BESTED	BESTUDS	BETHORN
BESMEAR	BESOULED	BESTEST	BESUITED	BETHORNED
BESMEARED	BESPAKE	BESTI	BESUNG	BETHORNS
BESMEARER	BESPANGLE	BESTIAL	BESWARM	BETHOUGHT
BESMEARS	BESPAT	BESTIALLY	BESWARMED	BETHRALL
BESMILE	BESPATE	BESTIALS	BESWARMS	BETHRALLS
BESMILED	BESPATTER	BESTIARY	BET	BETHS
BESMILES	BESPEAK	BESTICK	BETA	BETHUMB
BESMILING	BESPEAKS	BESTICKS	BETACISM	BETHUMBED
BESMIRCH	BESPECKLE	BESTIE	BETACISMS	BETHUMBS
BESMOKE	BESPED	BESTIES	BETAINE	BETHUMP
BESMOKED	BESPEED	BESTILL	BETAINES	BETHUMPED
BESMOKES	BESPEEDS	BESTILLED	BETAKE	BETHUMPS
BESMOKING	BESPICE	BESTILLS	BETAKEN	BETHWACK
BESMOOTH	BESPICED	BESTING	BETAKES	BETHWACKS
BESMOOTHS	BESPICES	BESTIR	BETAKING	BETID
BESMUDGE	BESPICING	BESTIRRED	BETAS	BETIDE
BESMUDGED	BESPIT	BESTIRS	BETATOPIC	BETIDED
BESMUDGES	BESPITS	BESTIS	BETATRON	BETIDES
BESMUT	BESPOKE	BESTORM	BETATRONS	BETIDING
BESMUTCH	BESPOKEN	BESTORMED	BETATTER	BETIGHT
BESMUTS	BESPORT	BESTORMS	BETATTERS	BETIME
BESMUTTED	BESPORTED	BESTOW	BETAXED	BETIMED
BESNOW	BESPORTS	BESTOWAL	BETCHA	BETIMES
BESNOWED	BESPOT	BESTOWALS	BETE	BETIMING
BESNOWING	BESPOTS	BESTOWED	BETED	BETING

BETISE
BETISES
BETITLE
BETITLED
BETITLES
BETITLING
BETOIL
BETOILED
BETOILING
BETOILS
BETOKEN
BETOKENED
BETOKENS
BETON
BETONIES
BETONS
BETONY
BETOOK
BETOSS
BETOSSED
BETOSSES
BETOSSING
BETRAY
BETRAYAL
BETRAYALS
BETRAYED
BETRAYER
BETRAYERS
BETRAYING
BETRAYS
BETREAD
BETREADS
BETRIM
BETRIMMED
BETRIMS
BETROD
BETRODDEN
BETROTH
BETROTHAL
BETROTHED
BETROTHS
BETS
BETTA
BETTAS
BETTED
BETTER
BETTERED
BETTERING

BETTERS
BETTIES
BETTING
BETTINGS
BETTONG
BETTONGS
BETTOR
BETTORS
BETTY
BETUMBLED
BETWEEN
BETWEENS
BETWIXT
BEUNCLED
BEURRE
BEURRES
BEVATRON
BEVATRONS
BEVEL
BEVELED
BEVELER
BEVELERS
BEVELING
BEVELLED
BEVELLER
BEVELLERS
BEVELLING
BEVELMENT
BEVELS
BEVER
BEVERAGE
BEVERAGES
BEVERED
BEVERING
BEVERS
BEVIES
BEVOMIT
BEVOMITED
BEVOMITS
BEVOR
BEVORS
BEVUE
BEVUES
BEVVIED
BEVVIES
BEVVY
BEVVYING
BEVY

BEWAIL
BEWAILED
BEWAILER
BEWAILERS
BEWAILING
BEWAILS
BEWARE
BEWARED
BEWARES
BEWARING
BEWEARIED
BEWEARIES
BEWEARY
BEWEEP
BEWEEPING
BEWEEPS
BEWENT
BEWEPT
BEWET
BEWETS
BEWETTED
BEWETTING
BEWHORE
BEWHORED
BEWHORES
BEWHORING
BEWIG
BEWIGGED
BEWIGGING
BEWIGS
BEWILDER
BEWILDERS
BEWINGED
BEWITCH
BEWITCHED
BEWITCHER
BEWITCHES
BEWORM
BEWORMED
BEWORMING
BEWORMS
BEWORRIED
BEWORRIES
BEWORRY
BEWRAP
BEWRAPPED
BEWRAPS
BEWRAPT

BEWRAY
BEWRAYED
BEWRAYER
BEWRAYERS
BEWRAYING
BEWRAYS
BEY
BEYLIC
BEYLICS
BEYLIK
BEYLIKS
BEYOND
BEYONDS
BEYS
BEZ
BEZANT
BEZANTS
BEZAZZ
BEZAZZES
BEZEL
BEZELLESS
BEZELS
BEZES
BEZIL
BEZILS
BEZIQUE
BEZIQUES
BEZOAR
BEZOARDIC
BEZOARS
BEZONIAN
BEZONIANS
BEZZANT
BEZZANTS
BEZZAZZ
BEZZAZZES
BEZZIE
BEZZIES
BEZZLE
BEZZLED
BEZZLES
BEZZLING
BEZZY
BHAGEE
BHAGEES
BHAI
BHAIS
BHAJAN

BHAJANS
BHAJEE
BHAJEES
BHAJI
BHAJIA
BHAJIS
BHAKTA
BHAKTAS
BHAKTI
BHAKTIS
BHANG
BHANGRA
BHANGRAS
BHANGS
BHARAL
BHARALS
BHAT
BHATS
BHAVAN
BHAVANS
BHAWAN
BHAWANS
BHEESTIE
BHEESTIES
BHEESTY
BHEL
BHELPURI
BHELPURIS
BHELS
BHIKHU
BHIKHUS
BHIKKHUNI
BHINDI
BHINDIS
BHISHTI
BHISHTIS
BHISTEE
BHISTEES
BHISTI
BHISTIE
BHISTIES
BHISTIS
BHOONA
BHOONAS
BHOOT
BHOOTS
BHUNA
BHUNAS

BHUT	BIBBS	BICOASTAL	BIDERS	BIFIDITY
BHUTS	BIBCOCK	BICOLOR	BIDES	BIFIDLY
BI	BIBCOCKS	BICOLORED	BIDET	BIFIDUM
BIACETYL	BIBE	BICOLORS	BIDETS	BIFIDUMS
BIACETYLS	BIBELOT	BICOLOUR	BIDI	BIFIDUS
BIACH	BIBELOTS	BICOLOURS	BIDING	BIFIDUSES
BIACHES	BIBES	BICONCAVE	BIDINGS	BIFILAR
BIALI	BIBFUL	BICONVEX	BIDIS	BIFILARLY
BIALIES	BIBFULS	BICORN	BIDON	BIFLEX
BIALIS	BIBIMBAP	BICORNATE	BIDONS	BIFOCAL
BIALY	BIBIMBAPS	BICORNE	BIDS	BIFOCALED
BIALYS	BIBLE	BICORNES	BIELD	BIFOCALS
BIANNUAL	BIBLES	BICORNS	BIELDED	BIFOLD
BIANNUALS	BIBLESS	BICRON	BIELDIER	BIFOLDS
BIAS	BIBLICAL	BICRONS	BIELDIEST	BIFOLIATE
BIASED	BIBLICISM	BICURIOUS	BIELDING	BIFORATE
BIASEDLY	BIBLICIST	BICUSPID	BIELDS	BIFORKED
BIASES	BIBLIKE	BICUSPIDS	BIELDY	BIFORM
BIASING	BIBLIOTIC	BICYCLE	BIEN	BIFORMED
BIASINGS	BIBLIST	BICYCLED	BIENNALE	BIFTAH
BIASNESS	BIBLISTS	BICYCLER	BIENNALES	BIFTAHS
BIASSED	BIBS	BICYCLERS	BIENNIA	BIFTER
BIASSEDLY	BIBULOUS	BICYCLES	BIENNIAL	BIFTERS
BIASSES	BICAMERAL	BICYCLIC	BIENNIALS	BIFURCATE
BIASSING	BICARB	BICYCLING	BIENNIUM	BIG
BIATCH	BICARBS	BICYCLIST	BIENNIUMS	BIGA
BIATCHES	BICAUDAL	BID	BIER	BIGAE
BIATHLETE	BICCIES	BIDARKA	BIERS	BIGAMIES
BIATHLON	BICCY	BIDARKAS	BIERWURST	BIGAMIST
BIATHLONS	BICE	BIDARKEE	BIESTINGS	BIGAMISTS
BIAXAL	BICENTRIC	BIDARKEES	BIFACE	BIGAMOUS
BIAXIAL	BICEP	BIDDABLE	BIFACES	BIGAMY
BIAXIALLY	BICEPS	BIDDABLY	BIFACIAL	BIGARADE
BIB	BICEPSES	BIDDEN	BIFARIOUS	BIGARADES
BIBACIOUS	BICES	BIDDER	BIFF	BIGAROON
BIBASIC	BICHIR	BIDDERS	BIFFED	BIGAROONS
BIBATION	BICHIRS	BIDDIES	BIFFER	BIGARREAU
BIBATIONS	BICHORD	BIDDING	BIFFERS	BIGEMINAL
BIBB	BICHROME	BIDDINGS	BIFFIES	BIGEMINY
BIBBED	BICIPITAL	BIDDY	BIFFIN	BIGENER
BIBBER	BICKER	BIDE	BIFFING	BIGENERIC
BIBBERIES	BICKERED	BIDED	BIFFINS	BIGENERS
BIBBERS	BICKERER	BIDENT	BIFFO	BIGEYE
BIBBERY	BICKERERS	BIDENTAL	BIFFOS	BIGEYES
BIBBING	BICKERING	BIDENTALS	BIFFS	BIGFEET
BIBBINGS	BICKERS	BIDENTATE	BIFFY	BIGFOOT
BIBBLE	BICKIE	BIDENTS	BIFID	BIGFOOTED
BIBBLES	BICKIES	BIDER	BIFIDA	BIGFOOTS

BIGG
BIGGED
BIGGER
BIGGEST
BIGGETIER
BIGGETY
BIGGIE
BIGGIES
BIGGIN
BIGGING
BIGGINGS
BIGGINS
BIGGISH
BIGGITIER
BIGGITY
BIGGON
BIGGONS
BIGGS
BIGGY
BIGHA
BIGHAS
BIGHEAD
BIGHEADED
BIGHEADS
BIGHORN
BIGHORNS
BIGHT
BIGHTED
BIGHTING
BIGHTS
BIGLY
BIGMOUTH
BIGMOUTHS
BIGNESS
BIGNESSES
BIGNONIA
BIGNONIAS
BIGOS
BIGOSES
BIGOT
BIGOTED
BIGOTEDLY
BIGOTRIES
BIGOTRY
BIGOTS
BIGS
BIGSTICK
BIGTIME

BIGUANIDE
BIGUINE
BIGUINES
BIGWIG
BIGWIGS
BIHOURLY
BIJECTION
BIJECTIVE
BIJOU
BIJOUS
BIJOUX
BIJUGATE
BIJUGOUS
BIJURAL
BIJWONER
BIJWONERS
BIKE
BIKED
BIKER
BIKERS
BIKES
BIKEWAY
BIKEWAYS
BIKIE
BIKIES
BIKING
BIKINGS
BIKINI
BIKINIED
BIKINIS
BIKKIE
BIKKIES
BILABIAL
BILABIALS
BILABIATE
BILANDER
BILANDERS
BILATERAL
BILAYER
BILAYERS
BILBERRY
BILBIES
BILBO
BILBOA
BILBOAS
BILBOES
BILBOS
BILBY

BILE
BILECTION
BILED
BILES
BILESTONE
BILEVEL
BILEVELS
BILGE
BILGED
BILGES
BILGIER
BILGIEST
BILGING
BILGY
BILHARZIA
BILIAN
BILIANS
BILIARIES
BILIARY
BILIMBI
BILIMBING
BILIMBIS
BILINEAR
BILING
BILINGUAL
BILIOUS
BILIOUSLY
BILIRUBIN
BILITERAL
BILK
BILKED
BILKER
BILKERS
BILKING
BILKS
BILL
BILLABLE
BILLABONG
BILLBOARD
BILLBOOK
BILLBOOKS
BILLBUG
BILLBUGS
BILLED
BILLER
BILLERS
BILLET
BILLETED

BILLETEE
BILLETEES
BILLETER
BILLETERS
BILLETING
BILLETS
BILLFISH
BILLFOLD
BILLFOLDS
BILLHEAD
BILLHEADS
BILLHOOK
BILLHOOKS
BILLIARD
BILLIARDS
BILLIE
BILLIES
BILLING
BILLINGS
BILLION
BILLIONS
BILLIONTH
BILLMAN
BILLMEN
BILLON
BILLONS
BILLOW
BILLOWED
BILLOWIER
BILLOWING
BILLOWS
BILLOWY
BILLS
BILLY
BILLYBOY
BILLYBOYS
BILLYCAN
BILLYCANS
BILLYCOCK
BILLYO
BILLYOH
BILLYOHS
BILLYOS
BILOBAR
BILOBATE
BILOBATED
BILOBED
BILOBULAR

BILOCULAR
BILSTED
BILSTEDS
BILTONG
BILTONGS
BIMA
BIMAH
BIMAHS
BIMANAL
BIMANOUS
BIMANUAL
BIMAS
BIMBASHI
BIMBASHIS
BIMBETTE
BIMBETTES
BIMBLE
BIMBO
BIMBOES
BIMBOS
BIMENSAL
BIMESTER
BIMESTERS
BIMETAL
BIMETALS
BIMETHYL
BIMETHYLS
BIMINI
BIMINIS
BIMODAL
BIMONTHLY
BIMORPH
BIMORPHS
BIN
BINAL
BINARIES
BINARISM
BINARISMS
BINARY
BINATE
BINATELY
BINAURAL
BIND
BINDABLE
BINDER
BINDERIES
BINDERS
BINDERY

BINDHI	BINMAN	BIOFILM	BIONOMICS	BIOTERROR
BINDHIS	BINMEN	BIOFILMS	BIONOMIES	BIOTIC
BINDI	BINNACLE	BIOFOULER	BIONOMIST	BIOTICAL
BINDING	BINNACLES	BIOFUEL	BIONOMY	BIOTICS
BINDINGLY	BINNED	BIOFUELED	BIONT	BIOTIN
BINDINGS	BINNING	BIOFUELS	BIONTIC	BIOTINS
BINDIS	BINOCLE	BIOG	BIONTS	BIOTITE
BINDLE	BINOCLES	BIOGAS	BIOPARENT	BIOTITES
BINDLES	BINOCS	BIOGASES	BIOPHILIA	BIOTITIC
BINDS	BINOCULAR	BIOGASSES	BIOPHOR	BIOTOPE
BINDWEED	BINOMIAL	BIOGEN	BIOPHORE	BIOTOPES
BINDWEEDS	BINOMIALS	BIOGENIC	BIOPHORES	BIOTOXIN
BINE	BINOMINAL	BIOGENIES	BIOPHORS	BIOTOXINS
BINER	BINOVULAR	BIOGENOUS	BIOPIC	BIOTRON
BINERS	BINS	BIOGENS	BIOPICS	BIOTRONS
BINERVATE	BINT	BIOGENY	BIOPIRACY	BIOTROPH
BINES	BINTS	BIOGRAPH	BIOPIRATE	BIOTROPHS
BING	BINTURONG	BIOGRAPHS	BIOPLASM	BIOTURBED
BINGE	BINUCLEAR	BIOGRAPHY	BIOPLASMS	BIOTYPE
BINGEABLE	BIO	BIOGS	BIOPLAST	BIOTYPES
BINGED	BIOACTIVE	BIOHACKER	BIOPLASTS	BIOTYPIC
BINGEING	BIOASSAY	BIOHAZARD	BIOPLAY	BIOVULAR
BINGEINGS	BIOASSAYS	BIOHERM	BIOPLAYS	BIOWASTE
BINGER	BIOBANK	BIOHERMS	BIOPSIC	BIOWASTES
BINGERS	BIOBANKS	BIOLOGIC	BIOPSIED	BIOWEAPON
BINGES	BIOBLAST	BIOLOGICS	BIOPSIES	BIPACK
BINGHI	BIOBLASTS	BIOLOGIES	BIOPSY	BIPACKS
BINGHIS	BIOCENOSE	BIOLOGISM	BIOPSYING	BIPAROUS
BINGIES	BIOCHEMIC	BIOLOGIST	BIOPTIC	BIPARTED
BINGING	BIOCHIP	BIOLOGY	BIOREGION	BIPARTITE
BINGINGS	BIOCHIPS	BIOLYSES	BIORHYTHM	BIPARTY
BINGLE	BIOCIDAL	BIOLYSIS	BIOS	BIPED
BINGLED	BIOCIDE	BIOLYTIC	BIOSAFETY	BIPEDAL
BINGLES	BIOCIDES	BIOMARKER	BIOSCOPE	BIPEDALLY
BINGLING	BIOCLEAN	BIOMASS	BIOSCOPES	BIPEDS
BINGO	BIOCYCLE	BIOMASSES	BIOSCOPY	BIPHASIC
BINGOED	BIOCYCLES	BIOME	BIOSENSOR	BIPHENYL
BINGOES	BIODATA	BIOMES	BIOSOCIAL	BIPHENYLS
BINGOING	BIODIESEL	BIOMETER	BIOSOLID	BIPINNATE
BINGOS	BIODOT	BIOMETERS	BIOSOLIDS	BIPLANE
BINGS	BIODOTS	BIOMETRIC	BIOSPHERE	BIPLANES
BINGY	BIOENERGY	BIOMETRY	BIOSTABLE	BIPOD
BINIOU	BIOETHIC	BIOMINING	BIOSTATIC	BIPODS
BINIOUS	BIOETHICS	BIOMORPH	BIOSTROME	BIPOLAR
BINIT	BIOFACT	BIOMORPHS	BIOTA	BIPRISM
BINITS	BIOFACTS	BIONIC	BIOTAS	BIPRISMS
BINK	BIOFIBERS	BIONICS	BIOTECH	BIPYRAMID
BINKS	BIOFIBRES	BIONOMIC	BIOTECHS	BIRACIAL

BIRADIAL

BIRADIAL	BIRDSEEDS	BIRSE	BISERIATE	BISTOURY
BIRADICAL	BIRDSEYE	BIRSED	BISERRATE	BISTRE
BIRAMOSE	BIRDSEYES	BIRSES	BISES	BISTRED
BIRAMOUS	BIRDSFOOT	BIRSIER	BISEXUAL	BISTRES
BIRCH	BIRDSHOT	BIRSIEST	BISEXUALS	BISTRO
BIRCHBARK	BIRDSHOTS	BIRSING	BISH	BISTROIC
BIRCHED	BIRDSONG	BIRSLE	BISHES	BISTROS
BIRCHEN	BIRDSONGS	BIRSLED	BISHOP	BISULCATE
BIRCHES	BIRDWATCH	BIRSLES	BISHOPDOM	BISULFATE
BIRCHING	BIRDWING	BIRSLING	BISHOPED	BISULFIDE
BIRCHINGS	BIRDWINGS	BIRSY	BISHOPESS	BISULFITE
BIRCHIR	BIREME	BIRTH	BISHOPING	BIT
BIRCHIRS	BIREMES	BIRTHDATE	BISHOPRIC	BITABLE
BIRCHWOOD	BIRETTA	BIRTHDAY	BISHOPS	BITCH
BIRD	BIRETTAS	BIRTHDAYS	BISK	BITCHED
BIRDBATH	BIRIANI	BIRTHDOM	BISKS	BITCHEN
BIRDBATHS	BIRIANIS	BIRTHDOMS	BISMAR	BITCHERY
BIRDBRAIN	BIRIYANI	BIRTHED	BISMARCK	BITCHES
BIRDCAGE	BIRIYANIS	BIRTHER	BISMARCKS	BITCHFEST
BIRDCAGES	BIRK	BIRTHERS	BISMARS	BITCHIER
BIRDCALL	BIRKEN	BIRTHING	BISMILLAH	BITCHIEST
BIRDCALLS	BIRKIE	BIRTHINGS	BISMUTH	BITCHILY
BIRDDOG	BIRKIER	BIRTHMARK	BISMUTHAL	BITCHING
BIRDDOGS	BIRKIES	BIRTHNAME	BISMUTHIC	BITCHY
BIRDED	BIRKIEST	BIRTHRATE	BISMUTHS	BITCOIN
BIRDER	BIRKS	BIRTHROOT	BISNAGA	BITCOINS
BIRDERS	BIRL	BIRTHS	BISNAGAS	BITE
BIRDFARM	BIRLE	BIRTHWORT	BISOM	BITEABLE
BIRDFARMS	BIRLED	BIRYANI	BISOMS	BITEPLATE
BIRDFEED	BIRLER	BIRYANIS	BISON	BITER
BIRDFEEDS	BIRLERS	BIS	BISONS	BITERS
BIRDHOUSE	BIRLES	BISCACHA	BISONTINE	BITES
BIRDIE	BIRLIEMAN	BISCACHAS	BISPHENOL	BITESIZE
BIRDIED	BIRLIEMEN	BISCOTTI	BISQUE	BITEWING
BIRDIEING	BIRLING	BISCOTTO	BISQUES	BITEWINGS
BIRDIES	BIRLINGS	BISCUIT	BISSON	BITING
BIRDING	BIRLINN	BISCUITS	BISSONED	BITINGLY
BIRDINGS	BIRLINNS	BISCUITY	BISSONING	BITINGS
BIRDLIFE	BIRLS	BISE	BISSONS	BITLESS
BIRDLIFES	BIRO	BISECT	BIST	BITMAP
BIRDLIKE	BIROS	BISECTED	BISTABLE	BITMAPPED
BIRDLIME	BIRR	BISECTING	BISTABLES	BITMAPS
BIRDLIMED	BIRRED	BISECTION	BISTATE	BITO
BIRDLIMES	BIRRETTA	BISECTOR	BISTER	BITONAL
BIRDMAN	BIRRETTAS	BISECTORS	BISTERED	BITOS
BIRDMEN	BIRRING	BISECTRIX	BISTERS	BITOU
BIRDS	BIRROTCH	BISECTS	BISTORT	BITRATE
BIRDSEED	BIRRS	BISERIAL	BISTORTS	BITRATES

BITS	BITURBOS	BIZZES	BLACKJACK	BLAFFED
BITSER	BITWISE	BIZZIES	BLACKLAND	BLAFFING
BITSERS	BIUNIQUE	BIZZO	BLACKLEAD	BLAFFS
BITSIER	BIVALENCE	BIZZOS	BLACKLEG	BLAG
BITSIEST	BIVALENCY	BIZZY	BLACKLEGS	BLAGGED
BITSTOCK	BIVALENT	BLAB	BLACKLIST	BLAGGER
BITSTOCKS	BIVALENTS	BLABBED	BLACKLY	BLAGGERS
BITSTREAM	BIVALVATE	BLABBER	BLACKMAIL	BLAGGING
BITSY	BIVALVE	BLABBERED	BLACKNESS	BLAGGINGS
BITT	BIVALVED	BLABBERS	BLACKOUT	BLAGS
BITTACLE	BIVALVES	BLABBIER	BLACKOUTS	BLAGUE
BITTACLES	BIVARIANT	BLABBIEST	BLACKPOLL	BLAGUER
BITTE	BIVARIATE	BLABBING	BLACKS	BLAGUERS
BITTED	BIVIA	BLABBINGS	BLACKSPOT	BLAGUES
BITTEN	BIVINYL	BLABBY	BLACKTAIL	BLAGUEUR
BITTER	BIVINYLS	BLABS	BLACKTIP	BLAGUEURS
BITTERED	BIVIOUS	BLACK	BLACKTIPS	BLAH
BITTERER	BIVIUM	BLACKBALL	BLACKTOP	BLAHED
BITTEREST	BIVOUAC	BLACKBAND	BLACKTOPS	BLAHER
BITTERING	BIVOUACKS	BLACKBIRD	BLACKWASH	BLAHEST
BITTERISH	BIVOUACS	BLACKBODY	BLACKWOOD	BLAHING
BITTERLY	BIVVIED	BLACKBOY	BLAD	BLAHS
BITTERN	BIVVIES	BLACKBOYS	BLADDED	BLAIN
BITTERNS	BIVVY	BLACKBUCK	BLADDER	BLAINS
BITTERNUT	BIVVYING	BLACKBUTT	BLADDERED	BLAISE
BITTERS	BIWEEKLY	BLACKCAP	BLADDERS	BLAIZE
BITTIE	BIYEARLY	BLACKCAPS	BLADDERY	BLAM
BITTIER	BIZ	BLACKCOCK	BLADDING	BLAMABLE
BITTIES	BIZARRE	BLACKDAMP	BLADE	BLAMABLY
BITTIEST	BIZARRELY	BLACKED	BLADED	BLAME
BITTILY	BIZARRES	BLACKEN	BLADELESS	BLAMEABLE
BITTINESS	BIZARRO	BLACKENED	BLADELIKE	BLAMEABLY
BITTING	BIZARROS	BLACKENER	BLADER	BLAMED
BITTINGS	BIZAZZ	BLACKENS	BLADERS	BLAMEFUL
BITTOCK	BIZAZZES	BLACKER	BLADES	BLAMELESS
BITTOCKS	BIZCACHA	BLACKEST	BLADEWORK	BLAMER
BITTOR	BIZCACHAS	BLACKFACE	BLADIER	BLAMERS
BITTORS	BIZE	BLACKFIN	BLADIEST	BLAMES
BITTOUR	BIZES	BLACKFINS	BLADING	BLAMING
BITTOURS	BIZJET	BLACKFISH	BLADINGS	BLAMMED
BITTS	BIZJETS	BLACKFLY	BLADS	BLAMMING
BITTUR	BIZNAGA	BLACKGAME	BLADY	BLAMS
BITTURS	BIZNAGAS	BLACKGUM	BLAE	BLANCH
BITTY	BIZONAL	BLACKGUMS	BLAEBERRY	BLANCHED
BITUMED	BIZONE	BLACKHEAD	BLAER	BLANCHER
BITUMEN	BIZONES	BLACKING	BLAES	BLANCHERS
BITUMENS	BIZZAZZ	BLACKINGS	BLAEST	BLANCHES
BITURBO	BIZZAZZES	BLACKISH	BLAFF	BLANCHING

BLANCO	BLASHING	BLATT	BLEAKER	BLELLUM
BLANCOED	BLASHY	BLATTANT	BLEAKEST	BLELLUMS
BLANCOING	BLASPHEME	BLATTED	BLEAKISH	BLEMISH
BLANCOS	BLASPHEMY	BLATTER	BLEAKLY	BLEMISHED
BLAND	BLAST	BLATTERED	BLEAKNESS	BLEMISHER
BLANDED	BLASTED	BLATTERS	BLEAKS	BLEMISHES
BLANDER	BLASTEMA	BLATTING	BLEAKY	BLENCH
BLANDEST	BLASTEMAL	BLATTS	BLEAR	BLENCHED
BLANDING	BLASTEMAS	BLAUBOK	BLEARED	BLENCHER
BLANDISH	BLASTEMIC	BLAUBOKS	BLEARER	BLENCHERS
BLANDLY	BLASTER	BLAUD	BLEAREST	BLENCHES
BLANDNESS	BLASTERS	BLAUDED	BLEAREYED	BLENCHING
BLANDS	BLASTHOLE	BLAUDING	BLEARIER	BLEND
BLANK	BLASTIE	BLAUDS	BLEARIEST	BLENDABLE
BLANKED	BLASTIER	BLAW	BLEARILY	BLENDE
BLANKER	BLASTIES	BLAWED	BLEARING	BLENDED
BLANKEST	BLASTIEST	BLAWING	BLEARS	BLENDER
BLANKET	BLASTING	BLAWN	BLEARY	BLENDERS
BLANKETED	BLASTINGS	BLAWORT	BLEAT	BLENDES
BLANKETS	BLASTMENT	BLAWORTS	BLEATED	BLENDING
BLANKETY	BLASTOFF	BLAWS	BLEATER	BLENDINGS
BLANKIE	BLASTOFFS	BLAY	BLEATERS	BLENDS
BLANKIES	BLASTOID	BLAYS	BLEATING	BLENNIES
BLANKING	BLASTOIDS	BLAZAR	BLEATINGS	BLENNIOID
BLANKINGS	BLASTOMA	BLAZARS	BLEATS	BLENNY
BLANKLY	BLASTOMAS	BLAZE	BLEB	BLENT
BLANKNESS	BLASTOPOR	BLAZED	BLEBBIER	BLEOMYCIN
BLANKS	BLASTS	BLAZER	BLEBBIEST	BLERT
BLANKY	BLASTULA	BLAZERED	BLEBBING	BLERTS
BLANQUET	BLASTULAE	BLAZERS	BLEBBINGS	BLESBOK
BLANQUETS	BLASTULAR	BLAZES	BLEBBY	BLESBOKS
BLARE	BLASTULAS	BLAZING	BLEBS	BLESBUCK
BLARED	BLASTY	BLAZINGLY	BLECH	BLESBUCKS
BLARES	BLAT	BLAZON	BLED	BLESS
BLARING	BLATANCY	BLAZONED	BLEE	BLESSED
BLARNEY	BLATANT	BLAZONER	BLEED	BLESSEDER
BLARNEYED	BLATANTLY	BLAZONERS	BLEEDER	BLESSEDLY
BLARNEYS	BLATE	BLAZONING	BLEEDERS	BLESSER
BLART	BLATED	BLAZONRY	BLEEDING	BLESSERS
BLARTED	BLATER	BLAZONS	BLEEDINGS	BLESSES
BLARTING	BLATES	BLEACH	BLEEDS	BLESSING
BLARTS	BLATEST	BLEACHED	BLEEP	BLESSINGS
BLASE	BLATHER	BLEACHER	BLEEPED	BLEST
BLASH	BLATHERED	BLEACHERS	BLEEPER	BLET
BLASHED	BLATHERER	BLEACHERY	BLEEPERS	BLETHER
BLASHES	BLATHERS	BLEACHES	BLEEPING	BLETHERED
BLASHIER	BLATING	BLEACHING	BLEEPS	BLETHERER
BLASHIEST	BLATS	BLEAK	BLEES	BLETHERS

BLETS	BLINDS	BLIT	BLOCKAGES	BLOND
BLETTED	BLINDSIDE	BLITE	BLOCKBUST	BLONDE
BLETTING	BLINDWORM	BLITES	BLOCKED	BLONDER
BLEUATRE	BLING	BLITHE	BLOCKER	BLONDES
BLEW	BLINGED	BLITHEFUL	BLOCKERS	BLONDEST
BLEWART	BLINGER	BLITHELY	BLOCKHEAD	BLONDINE
BLEWARTS	BLINGEST	BLITHER	BLOCKHOLE	BLONDINED
BLEWIT	BLINGIER	BLITHERED	BLOCKIE	BLONDINES
BLEWITS	BLINGIEST	BLITHERS	BLOCKIER	BLONDING
BLEWITSES	BLINGING	BLITHEST	BLOCKIES	BLONDINGS
BLEY	BLINGLISH	BLITS	BLOCKIEST	BLONDISH
BLEYS	BLINGS	BLITTED	BLOCKING	BLONDNESS
BLIGHT	BLINGY	BLITTER	BLOCKINGS	BLONDS
BLIGHTED	BLINI	BLITTERS	BLOCKISH	BLOOD
BLIGHTER	BLINIS	BLITTING	BLOCKS	BLOODBATH
BLIGHTERS	BLINK	BLITZ	BLOCKSHIP	BLOODED
BLIGHTIES	BLINKARD	BLITZED	BLOCKWORK	BLOODFIN
BLIGHTING	BLINKARDS	BLITZER	BLOCKY	BLOODFINS
BLIGHTS	BLINKED	BLITZERS	BLOCS	BLOODIED
BLIGHTY	BLINKER	BLITZES	BLOG	BLOODIER
BLIKSEM	BLINKERED	BLITZING	BLOGGABLE	BLOODIES
BLIMBING	BLINKERS	BLIVE	BLOGGED	BLOODIEST
BLIMBINGS	BLINKING	BLIZZARD	BLOGGER	BLOODILY
BLIMEY	BLINKS	BLIZZARDS	BLOGGERS	BLOODING
BLIMP	BLINNED	BLIZZARDY	BLOGGIER	BLOODINGS
BLIMPED	BLINNING	BLOAT	BLOGGIEST	BLOODLESS
BLIMPERY	BLINS	BLOATED	BLOGGING	BLOODLIKE
BLIMPING	BLINTZ	BLOATER	BLOGGINGS	BLOODLINE
BLIMPISH	BLINTZE	BLOATERS	BLOGGY	BLOODLUST
BLIMPS	BLINTZES	BLOATING	BLOGPOST	BLOODRED
BLIMY	BLINY	BLOATINGS	BLOGPOSTS	BLOODROOT
BLIN	BLIP	BLOATS	BLOGRING	BLOODS
BLIND	BLIPPED	BLOATWARE	BLOGRINGS	BLOODSHED
BLINDAGE	BLIPPING	BLOB	BLOGROLL	BLOODSHOT
BLINDAGES	BLIPS	BLOBBED	BLOGROLLS	BLOODWOOD
BLINDED	BLIPVERT	BLOBBIER	BLOGS	BLOODWORM
BLINDER	BLIPVERTS	BLOBBIEST	BLOKART	BLOODWORT
BLINDERS	BLISS	BLOBBING	BLOKARTS	BLOODY
BLINDEST	BLISSED	BLOBBY	BLOKE	BLOODYING
BLINDFISH	BLISSES	BLOBS	BLOKEDOM	BLOOEY
BLINDFOLD	BLISSFUL	BLOC	BLOKEDOMS	BLOOIE
BLINDGUT	BLISSING	BLOCK	BLOKEISH	BLOOK
BLINDGUTS	BLISSLESS	BLOCKABLE	BLOKES	BLOOKS
BLINDING	BLIST	BLOCKADE	BLOKEY	BLOOM
BLINDINGS	BLISTER	BLOCKADED	BLOKIER	BLOOMED
BLINDLESS	BLISTERED	BLOCKADER	BLOKIEST	BLOOMER
BLINDLY	BLISTERS	BLOCKADES	BLOKISH	BLOOMERS
BLINDNESS	BLISTERY	BLOCKAGE	BLONCKET	BLOOMERY

BLOOMIER	BLOUBOKS	BLOWLAMP	BLUDGER	BLUEING
BLOOMIEST	BLOUSE	BLOWLAMPS	BLUDGERS	BLUEINGS
BLOOMING	BLOUSED	BLOWN	BLUDGES	BLUEISH
BLOOMINGS	BLOUSES	BLOWOFF	BLUDGING	BLUEJACK
BLOOMLESS	BLOUSIER	BLOWOFFS	BLUDIE	BLUEJACKS
BLOOMS	BLOUSIEST	BLOWOUT	BLUDIER	BLUEJAY
BLOOMY	BLOUSILY	BLOWOUTS	BLUDIEST	BLUEJAYS
BLOOP	BLOUSING	BLOWPIPE	BLUDS	BLUEJEANS
BLOOPED	BLOUSON	BLOWPIPES	BLUDY	BLUELINE
BLOOPER	BLOUSONS	BLOWS	BLUE	BLUELINER
BLOOPERS	BLOUSY	BLOWSE	BLUEBACK	BLUELINES
BLOOPIER	BLOVIATE	BLOWSED	BLUEBACKS	BLUELY
BLOOPIEST	BLOVIATED	BLOWSES	BLUEBALL	BLUEMOUTH
BLOOPING	BLOVIATES	BLOWSIER	BLUEBALLS	BLUENESS
BLOOPS	BLOW	BLOWSIEST	BLUEBEARD	BLUENOSE
BLOOPY	BLOWBACK	BLOWSILY	BLUEBEAT	BLUENOSED
BLOOSME	BLOWBACKS	BLOWSY	BLUEBEATS	BLUENOSES
BLOOSMED	BLOWBALL	BLOWTORCH	BLUEBELL	BLUEPOINT
BLOOSMES	BLOWBALLS	BLOWTUBE	BLUEBELLS	BLUEPRINT
BLOOSMING	BLOWBY	BLOWTUBES	BLUEBERRY	BLUER
BLOOTERED	BLOWBYS	BLOWUP	BLUEBILL	BLUES
BLOQUISTE	BLOWDART	BLOWUPS	BLUEBILLS	BLUESHIFT
BLORE	BLOWDARTS	BLOWY	BLUEBIRD	BLUESIER
BLORES	BLOWDOWN	BLOWZE	BLUEBIRDS	BLUESIEST
BLOSSOM	BLOWDOWNS	BLOWZED	BLUEBLOOD	BLUESMAN
BLOSSOMED	BLOWED	BLOWZES	BLUEBOOK	BLUESMEN
BLOSSOMS	BLOWER	BLOWZIER	BLUEBOOKS	BLUEST
BLOSSOMY	BLOWERS	BLOWZIEST	BLUEBUCK	BLUESTEM
BLOT	BLOWFISH	BLOWZILY	BLUEBUCKS	BLUESTEMS
BLOTCH	BLOWFLIES	BLOWZY	BLUEBUSH	BLUESTONE
BLOTCHED	BLOWFLY	BLUB	BLUECAP	BLUESY
BLOTCHES	BLOWGUN	BLUBBED	BLUECAPS	BLUET
BLOTCHIER	BLOWGUNS	BLUBBER	BLUECOAT	BLUETICK
BLOTCHILY	BLOWHARD	BLUBBERED	BLUECOATS	BLUETICKS
BLOTCHING	BLOWHARDS	BLUBBERER	BLUECURLS	BLUETIT
BLOTCHY	BLOWHOLE	BLUBBERS	BLUED	BLUETITS
BLOTLESS	BLOWHOLES	BLUBBERY	BLUEFIN	BLUETS
BLOTS	BLOWIE	BLUBBING	BLUEFINS	BLUETTE
BLOTTED	BLOWIER	BLUBS	BLUEFISH	BLUETTES
BLOTTER	BLOWIES	BLUCHER	BLUEGILL	BLUEWEED
BLOTTERS	BLOWIEST	BLUCHERS	BLUEGILLS	BLUEWEEDS
BLOTTIER	BLOWINESS	BLUD	BLUEGOWN	BLUEWING
BLOTTIEST	BLOWING	BLUDE	BLUEGOWNS	BLUEWINGS
BLOTTING	BLOWINGS	BLUDES	BLUEGRASS	BLUEWOOD
BLOTTINGS	BLOWJOB	BLUDGE	BLUEGUM	BLUEWOODS
BLOTTO	BLOWJOBS	BLUDGED	BLUEGUMS	BLUEY
BLOTTY	BLOWKART	BLUDGEON	BLUEHEAD	BLUEYS
BLOUBOK	BLOWKARTS	BLUDGEONS	BLUEHEADS	BLUFF

B

BLUFFABLE	BLUNTISH	BOAB	BOATFULS	BOBBITTED
BLUFFED	BLUNTLY	BOABS	BOATHOOK	BOBBITTS
BLUFFER	BLUNTNESS	BOAK	BOATHOOKS	BOBBLE
BLUFFERS	BLUNTS	BOAKED	BOATHOUSE	BOBBLED
BLUFFEST	BLUR	BOAKING	BOATIE	BOBBLES
BLUFFING	BLURB	BOAKS	BOATIES	BOBBLIER
BLUFFLY	BLURBED	BOAR	BOATING	BOBBLIEST
BLUFFNESS	BLURBING	BOARD	BOATINGS	BOBBLING
BLUFFS	BLURBIST	BOARDABLE	BOATLIFT	BOBBLY
BLUGGIER	BLURBISTS	BOARDED	BOATLIFTS	BOBBY
BLUGGIEST	BLURBS	BOARDER	BOATLIKE	BOBBYSOCK
BLUGGY	BLURRED	BOARDERS	BOATLOAD	BOBBYSOX
BLUID	BLURREDLY	BOARDIES	BOATLOADS	BOBCAT
BLUIDIER	BLURRIER	BOARDING	BOATMAN	BOBCATS
BLUIDIEST	BLURRIEST	BOARDINGS	BOATMEN	BOBECHE
BLUIDS	BLURRILY	BOARDLIKE	BOATNECK	BOBECHES
BLUIDY	BLURRING	BOARDMAN	BOATNECKS	BOBFLOAT
BLUIER	BLURRY	BOARDMEN	BOATPORT	BOBFLOATS
BLUIEST	BLURS	BOARDROOM	BOATPORTS	BOBLET
BLUING	BLURT	BOARDS	BOATS	BOBLETS
BLUINGS	BLURTED	BOARDWALK	BOATSMAN	BOBO
BLUISH	BLURTER	BOARFISH	BOATSMEN	BOBOL
BLUME	BLURTERS	BOARHOUND	BOATSWAIN	BOBOLINK
BLUMED	BLURTING	BOARISH	BOATTAIL	BOBOLINKS
BLUMES	BLURTINGS	BOARISHLY	BOATTAILS	BOBOLLED
BLUMING	BLURTS	BOARS	BOATYARD	BOBOLLING
BLUNDER	BLUSH	BOART	BOATYARDS	BOBOLS
BLUNDERED	BLUSHED	BOARTS	BOB	BOBOS
BLUNDERER	BLUSHER	BOAS	BOBA	BOBOTIE
BLUNDERS	BLUSHERS	BOAST	BOBAC	BOBOTIES
BLUNGE	BLUSHES	BOASTED	BOBACS	BOBOWLER
BLUNGED	BLUSHET	BOASTER	BOBAK	BOBOWLERS
BLUNGER	BLUSHETS	BOASTERS	BOBAKS	BOBS
BLUNGERS	BLUSHFUL	BOASTFUL	BOBAS	BOBSKATE
BLUNGES	BLUSHING	BOASTING	BOBBED	BOBSKATES
BLUNGING	BLUSHINGS	BOASTINGS	BOBBEJAAN	BOBSLED
BLUNK	BLUSHLESS	BOASTLESS	BOBBER	BOBSLEDS
BLUNKED	BLUSTER	BOASTS	BOBBERIES	BOBSLEIGH
BLUNKER	BLUSTERED	BOAT	BOBBERS	BOBSTAY
BLUNKERS	BLUSTERER	BOATABLE	BOBBERY	BOBSTAYS
BLUNKING	BLUSTERS	BOATBILL	BOBBIES	BOBTAIL
BLUNKS	BLUSTERY	BOATBILLS	BOBBIN	BOBTAILED
BLUNT	BLUSTROUS	BOATED	BOBBINET	BOBTAILS
BLUNTED	BLUTWURST	BOATEL	BOBBINETS	BOBWEIGHT
BLUNTER	BLYPE	BOATELS	BOBBING	BOBWHEEL
BLUNTEST	BLYPES	BOATER	BOBBINS	BOBWHEELS
BLUNTHEAD	BO	BOATERS	BOBBISH	BOBWHITE
BLUNTING	BOA	BOATFUL	BOBBITT	BOBWHITES

BOBWIG	BODGING	BOERBUL	BOGGIEST	BOHEMIANS
BOBWIGS	BODHI	BOERBULL	BOGGINESS	BOHEMIAS
BOCACCIO	BODHIS	BOERBULLS	BOGGING	BOHO
BOCACCIOS	BODHRAN	BOERBULS	BOGGISH	BOHOS
BOCAGE	BODHRANS	BOEREWORS	BOGGLE	BOHRIUM
BOCAGES	BODICE	BOERTJIE	BOGGLED	BOHRIUMS
BOCCA	BODICES	BOERTJIES	BOGGLER	BOHS
BOCCAS	BODIED	BOET	BOGGLERS	BOHUNK
BOCCE	BODIES	BOETS	BOGGLES	BOHUNKS
BOCCES	BODIKIN	BOEUF	BOGGLING	BOI
BOCCI	BODIKINS	BOEUFS	BOGGY	BOIL
BOCCIA	BODILESS	BOFF	BOGHEAD	BOILABLE
BOCCIAS	BODILY	BOFFED	BOGHOLE	BOILED
BOCCIE	BODING	BOFFIN	BOGHOLES	BOILER
BOCCIES	BODINGLY	BOFFING	BOGIE	BOILERIES
BOCCIS	BODINGS	BOFFINIER	BOGIED	BOILERMAN
BOCHE	BODKIN	BOFFINS	BOGIEING	BOILERMEN
BOCHES	BODKINS	BOFFINY	BOGIES	BOILERS
BOCK	BODLE	BOFFO	BOGLAND	BOILERY
BOCKED	BODLES	BOFFOLA	BOGLANDS	BOILING
BOCKEDY	BODRAG	BOFFOLAS	BOGLE	BOILINGLY
BOCKING	BODRAGS	BOFFOS	BOGLED	BOILINGS
BOCKS	BODS	BOFFS	BOGLES	BOILOFF
BOCONCINI	BODY	BOG	BOGLING	BOILOFFS
BOD	BODYBOARD	BOGAN	BOGMAN	BOILOVER
BODACH	BODYBUILD	BOGANS	BOGMEN	BOILOVERS
BODACHS	BODYBUILT	BOGART	BOGOAK	BOILS
BODACIOUS	BODYCHECK	BOGARTED	BOGOAKS	BOING
BODDLE	BODYGUARD	BOGARTING	BOGONG	BOINGED
BODDLES	BODYING	BOGARTS	BOGONGS	BOINGING
BODE	BODYLINE	BOGBEAN	BOGS	BOINGS
BODED	BODYLINES	BOGBEANS	BOGUE	BOINK
BODEFUL	BODYMAN	BOGEY	BOGUES	BOINKED
BODEGA	BODYMEN	BOGEYED	BOGUS	BOINKING
BODEGAS	BODYSHELL	BOGEYING	BOGUSLY	BOINKS
BODEGUERO	BODYSIDE	BOGEYISM	BOGUSNESS	BOIS
BODEMENT	BODYSIDES	BOGEYISMS	BOGWOOD	BOISERIE
BODEMENTS	BODYSUIT	BOGEYMAN	BOGWOODS	BOISERIES
BODES	BODYSUITS	BOGEYMEN	BOGY	BOITE
BODGE	BODYSURF	BOGEYS	BOGYISM	BOITES
BODGED	BODYSURFS	BOGGARD	BOGYISMS	BOK
BODGER	BODYWASH	BOGGARDS	BOGYMAN	BOKE
BODGERS	BODYWORK	BOGGART	BOGYMEN	BOKED
BODGES	BODYWORKS	BOGGARTS	BOH	BOKEH
BODGIE	BOEHMITE	BOGGED	BOHEA	BOKEHS
BODGIER	BOEHMITES	BOGGER	BOHEAS	BOKES
BODGIES	BOEP	BOGGERS	BOHEMIA	BOKING
BODGIEST	BOEPS	BOGGIER	BOHEMIAN	BOKKEN

BOKKENS	BOLLARD	BOLTHOLE	BOMBO	BONDMAN
BOKO	BOLLARDS	BOLTHOLES	BOMBORA	BONDMEN
BOKOS	BOLLED	BOLTING	BOMBORAS	BONDS
BOKS	BOLLEN	BOLTINGS	BOMBOS	BONDSMAN
BOLA	BOLLETRIE	BOLTLESS	BOMBPROOF	BONDSMEN
BOLAR	BOLLING	BOLTLIKE	BOMBS	BONDSTONE
BOLAS	BOLLIX	BOLTONIA	BOMBSHELL	BONDUC
BOLASES	BOLLIXED	BOLTONIAS	BOMBSIGHT	BONDUCS
BOLD	BOLLIXES	BOLTROPE	BOMBSITE	BONDWOMAN
BOLDED	BOLLIXING	BOLTROPES	BOMBSITES	BONDWOMEN
BOLDEN	BOLLOCK	BOLTS	BOMBYCID	BONE
BOLDENED	BOLLOCKED	BOLUS	BOMBYCIDS	BONEBED
BOLDENING	BOLLOCKS	BOLUSES	BOMBYCOID	BONEBEDS
BOLDENS	BOLLOX	BOMA	BOMBYX	BONEBLACK
BOLDER	BOLLOXED	BOMAS	BOMBYXES	BONED
BOLDEST	BOLLOXES	BOMB	BOMMIE	BONEFISH
BOLDFACE	BOLLOXING	BOMBABLE	BOMMIES	BONEHEAD
BOLDFACED	BOLLS	BOMBARD	BON	BONEHEADS
BOLDFACES	BOLLWORM	BOMBARDE	BONA	BONELESS
BOLDING	BOLLWORMS	BOMBARDED	BONACI	BONELIKE
BOLDLY	BOLO	BOMBARDER	BONACIS	BONEMEAL
BOLDNESS	BOLOGNA	BOMBARDES	BONAMANI	BONEMEALS
BOLDS	BOLOGNAS	BOMBARDON	BONAMANO	BONER
BOLE	BOLOGNESE	BOMBARDS	BONAMIA	BONERS
BOLECTION	BOLOGRAPH	BOMBASINE	BONAMIAS	BONES
BOLERO	BOLOMETER	BOMBAST	BONANZA	BONESET
BOLEROS	BOLOMETRY	BOMBASTED	BONANZAS	BONESETS
BOLES	BOLONEY	BOMBASTER	BONASSUS	BONETIRED
BOLETE	BOLONEYS	BOMBASTIC	BONASUS	BONEY
BOLETES	BOLOS	BOMBASTS	BONASUSES	BONEYARD
BOLETI	BOLSHEVIK	BOMBAX	BONBON	BONEYARDS
BOLETUS	BOLSHIE	BOMBAXES	BONBONS	BONEYER
BOLETUSES	BOLSHIER	BOMBAZINE	BONCE	BONEYEST
BOLIDE	BOLSHIES	BOMBE	BONCES	BONFIRE
BOLIDES	BOLSHIEST	BOMBED	BOND	BONFIRES
BOLINE	BOLSHY	BOMBER	BONDABLE	BONG
BOLINES	BOLSON	BOMBERS	BONDAGE	BONGED
BOLIVAR	BOLSONS	BOMBES	BONDAGER	BONGING
BOLIVARES	BOLSTER	BOMBESIN	BONDAGERS	BONGO
BOLIVARS	BOLSTERED	BOMBESINS	BONDAGES	BONGOES
BOLIVIA	BOLSTERER	BOMBILATE	BONDED	BONGOIST
BOLIVIANO	BOLSTERS	BOMBINATE	BONDER	BONGOISTS
BOLIVIAS	BOLT	BOMBING	BONDERS	BONGOS
BOLIX	BOLTED	BOMBINGS	BONDING	BONGRACE
BOLIXED	BOLTER	BOMBLET	BONDINGS	BONGRACES
BOLIXES	BOLTERS	BOMBLETS	BONDLESS	BONGS
BOLIXING	BOLTHEAD	BOMBLOAD	BONDMAID	BONHAM
BOLL	BOLTHEADS	BOMBLOADS	BONDMAIDS	BONHAMS

BONHOMIE	BONNY	BOOBOISIE	BOOGYING	BOOKLORES
BONHOMIES	BONOBO	BOOBOO	BOOGYMAN	BOOKLOUSE
BONHOMMIE	BONOBOS	BOOBOOK	BOOGYMEN	BOOKMAKER
BONHOMOUS	BONSAI	BOOBOOKS	BOOH	BOOKMAN
BONIATO	BONSELA	BOOBOOS	BOOHAI	BOOKMARK
BONIATOS	BONSELAS	BOOBS	BOOHAIS	BOOKMARKS
BONIBELL	BONSELLA	BOOBY	BOOHED	BOOKMEN
BONIBELLS	BONSELLAS	BOOBYISH	BOOHING	BOOKOO
BONIE	BONSOIR	BOOBYISM	BOOHOO	BOOKOOS
BONIER	BONSPELL	BOOBYISMS	BOOHOOED	BOOKPLATE
BONIEST	BONSPELLS	BOOCOO	BOOHOOING	BOOKRACK
BONIFACE	BONSPIEL	BOOCOOS	BOOHOOS	BOOKRACKS
BONIFACES	BONSPIELS	BOODIE	BOOHS	BOOKREST
BONILASSE	BONTBOK	BOODIED	BOOING	BOOKRESTS
BONINESS	BONTBOKS	BOODIES	BOOINGS	BOOKS
BONING	BONTEBOK	BOODLE	BOOJUM	BOOKSHELF
BONINGS	BONTEBOKS	BOODLED	BOOJUMS	BOOKSHOP
BONISM	BONUS	BOODLER	BOOK	BOOKSHOPS
BONISMS	BONUSED	BOODLERS	BOOKABLE	BOOKSIE
BONIST	BONUSES	BOODLES	BOOKBAG	BOOKSIER
BONISTS	BONUSING	BOODLING	BOOKBAGS	BOOKSIEST
BONITA	BONUSINGS	BOODY	BOOKCASE	BOOKSTALL
BONITAS	BONUSSED	BOODYING	BOOKCASES	BOOKSTAND
BONITO	BONUSSES	BOOED	BOOKED	BOOKSTORE
BONITOES	BONUSSING	BOOFHEAD	BOOKEND	BOOKSY
BONITOS	BONXIE	BOOFHEADS	BOOKENDED	BOOKWORK
BONJOUR	BONXIES	BOOFIER	BOOKENDS	BOOKWORKS
BONK	BONY	BOOFIEST	BOOKER	BOOKWORM
BONKED	BONZA	BOOFY	BOOKERS	BOOKWORMS
BONKERS	BONZE	BOOGALOO	BOOKFUL	BOOKY
BONKING	BONZER	BOOGALOOS	BOOKFULS	BOOL
BONKINGS	BONZES	BOOGER	BOOKIE	BOOLED
BONKS	BOO	BOOGERMAN	BOOKIER	BOOLING
BONNE	BOOAI	BOOGERMEN	BOOKIES	BOOLS
BONNES	BOOAIS	BOOGERS	BOOKIEST	BOOM
BONNET	BOOAY	BOOGEY	BOOKING	BOOMBOX
BONNETED	BOOAYS	BOOGEYED	BOOKINGS	BOOMBOXES
BONNETING	BOOB	BOOGEYING	BOOKISH	BOOMBURB
BONNETS	BOOBED	BOOGEYMAN	BOOKISHLY	BOOMBURBS
BONNIBELL	BOOBHEAD	BOOGEYMEN	BOOKLAND	BOOMED
BONNIE	BOOBHEADS	BOOGEYS	BOOKLANDS	BOOMER
BONNIER	BOOBIALLA	BOOGIE	BOOKLESS	BOOMERANG
BONNIES	BOOBIE	BOOGIED	BOOKLET	BOOMERS
BONNIEST	BOOBIES	BOOGIEING	BOOKLETS	BOOMIER
BONNILY	BOOBING	BOOGIEMAN	BOOKLICE	BOOMIEST
BONNINESS	BOOBIRD	BOOGIEMEN	BOOKLIGHT	BOOMING
BONNOCK	BOOBIRDS	BOOGIES	BOOKLIKE	BOOMINGLY
BONNOCKS	BOOBISH	BOOGY	BOOKLORE	BOOMINGS

BOOMKIN	BOOT	BOPPED	BORDERING	BORN
BOOMKINS	BOOTABLE	BOPPER	BORDERS	BORNA
BOOMLET	BOOTBLACK	BOPPERS	BORDES	BORNE
BOOMLETS	BOOTCUT	BOPPIER	BORDS	BORNEOL
BOOMS	BOOTED	BOPPIEST	BORDURE	BORNEOLS
BOOMSLANG	BOOTEE	BOPPING	BORDURES	BORNITE
BOOMSTICK	BOOTEES	BOPPISH	BORE	BORNITES
BOOMTOWN	BOOTERIES	BOPPY	BOREAL	BORNITIC
BOOMTOWNS	BOOTERY	BOPS	BOREALIS	BORNYL
BOOMY	BOOTH	BOR	BOREAS	BORNYLS
BOON	BOOTHOSE	BORA	BOREASES	BORON
BOONDOCK	BOOTHS	BORACES	BORECOLE	BORONIA
BOONDOCKS	BOOTIE	BORACHIO	BORECOLES	BORONIAS
BOONER	BOOTIES	BORACHIOS	BORED	BORONIC
BOONERS	BOOTIKIN	BORACIC	BOREDOM	BORONS
BOONEST	BOOTIKINS	BORACITE	BOREDOMS	BOROUGH
BOONG	BOOTING	BORACITES	BOREE	BOROUGHS
BOONGA	BOOTJACK	BORAGE	BOREEN	BORREL
BOONGARY	BOOTJACKS	BORAGES	BOREENS	BORRELIA
BOONGAS	BOOTLACE	BORAK	BOREES	BORRELIAS
BOONGS	BOOTLACES	BORAKS	BOREHOLE	BORRELL
BOONIES	BOOTLAST	BORAL	BOREHOLES	BORROW
BOONLESS	BOOTLASTS	BORALS	BOREL	BORROWED
BOONS	BOOTLEG	BORANE	BORELS	BORROWER
BOOR	BOOTLEGS	BORANES	BORER	BORROWERS
BOORD	BOOTLESS	BORAS	BORERS	BORROWING
BOORDE	BOOTLICK	BORATE	BORES	BORROWS
BOORDES	BOOTLICKS	BORATED	BORESCOPE	BORS
BOORDS	BOOTMAKER	BORATES	BORESOME	BORSCH
BOORISH	BOOTS	BORATING	BORGHETTO	BORSCHES
BOORISHLY	BOOTSTRAP	BORAX	BORGO	BORSCHT
BOORKA	BOOTY	BORAXES	BORGOS	BORSCHTS
BOORKAS	BOOZE	BORAZON	BORIC	BORSHCH
BOORS	BOOZED	BORAZONS	BORIDE	BORSHCHES
BOORTREE	BOOZER	BORD	BORIDES	BORSHT
BOORTREES	BOOZERS	BORDAR	BORING	BORSHTS
BOOS	BOOZES	BORDARS	BORINGLY	BORSIC
BOOSE	BOOZEY	BORDE	BORINGS	BORSICS
BOOSED	BOOZIER	BORDEAUX	BORK	BORSTAL
BOOSES	BOOZIEST	BORDEL	BORKED	BORSTALL
BOOSHIT	BOOZILY	BORDELLO	BORKING	BORSTALLS
BOOSING	BOOZINESS	BORDELLOS	BORKINGS	BORSTALS
BOOST	BOOZING	BORDELS	BORKS	BORT
BOOSTED	BOOZINGS	BORDER	BORLOTTI	BORTIER
BOOSTER	BOOZY	BORDEREAU	BORM	BORTIEST
BOOSTERS	BOP	BORDERED	BORMED	BORTS
BOOSTING	BOPEEP	BORDERER	BORMING	BORTSCH
BOOSTS	BOPEEPS	BORDERERS	BORMS	BORTSCHES

BORTY	BOSQUE	BOTANISTS	BOTONE	BOUCHE
BORTZ	BOSQUES	BOTANIZE	BOTONEE	BOUCHEE
BORTZES	BOSQUET	BOTANIZED	BOTONNEE	BOUCHEES
BORZOI	BOSQUETS	BOTANIZER	BOTOXED	BOUCHES
BORZOIS	BOSS	BOTANIZES	BOTRYOID	BOUCLE
BOS	BOSSBOY	BOTANY	BOTRYOSE	BOUCLEE
BOSBERAAD	BOSSBOYS	BOTARGO	BOTRYTIS	BOUCLEES
BOSBOK	BOSSDOM	BOTARGOES	BOTS	BOUCLES
BOSBOKS	BOSSDOMS	BOTARGOS	BOTT	BOUDERIE
BOSCAGE	BOSSED	BOTAS	BOTTARGA	BOUDERIES
BOSCAGES	BOSSER	BOTCH	BOTTARGAS	BOUDIN
BOSCHBOK	BOSSES	BOTCHED	BOTTE	BOUDINS
BOSCHBOKS	BOSSEST	BOTCHEDLY	BOTTED	BOUDOIR
BOSCHE	BOSSET	BOTCHER	BOTTEGA	BOUDOIRS
BOSCHES	BOSSETS	BOTCHERS	BOTTEGAS	BOUFFANT
BOSCHVARK	BOSSIER	BOTCHERY	BOTTES	BOUFFANTS
BOSCHVELD	BOSSIES	BOTCHES	BOTTINE	BOUFFE
BOSH	BOSSIEST	BOTCHIER	BOTTINES	BOUFFES
BOSHBOK	BOSSILY	BOTCHIEST	BOTTING	BOUGE
BOSHBOKS	BOSSINESS	BOTCHILY	BOTTLE	BOUGED
BOSHES	BOSSING	BOTCHING	BOTTLED	BOUGES
BOSHTA	BOSSINGS	BOTCHINGS	BOTTLEFUL	BOUGET
BOSHTER	BOSSISM	BOTCHY	BOTTLER	BOUGETS
BOSHVARK	BOSSISMS	BOTE	BOTTLERS	BOUGH
BOSHVARKS	BOSSY	BOTEL	BOTTLES	BOUGHED
BOSIE	BOSTANGI	BOTELS	BOTTLING	BOUGHLESS
BOSIES	BOSTANGIS	BOTES	BOTTLINGS	BOUGHPOT
BOSK	BOSTHOON	BOTFLIES	BOTTOM	BOUGHPOTS
BOSKAGE	BOSTHOONS	BOTFLY	BOTTOMED	BOUGHS
BOSKAGES	BOSTON	BOTH	BOTTOMER	BOUGHT
BOSKER	BOSTONS	BOTHAN	BOTTOMERS	BOUGHTEN
BOSKET	BOSTRYX	BOTHANS	BOTTOMING	BOUGHTS
BOSKETS	BOSTRYXES	BOTHER	BOTTOMRY	BOUGIE
BOSKIER	BOSUN	BOTHERED	BOTTOMS	BOUGIES
BOSKIEST	BOSUNS	BOTHERING	BOTTOMSET	BOUGING
BOSKINESS	BOT	BOTHERS	BOTTONY	BOUILLI
BOSKS	BOTA	BOTHIE	BOTTS	BOUILLIS
BOSKY	BOTANIC	BOTHIES	BOTTY	BOUILLON
BOSOM	BOTANICA	BOTHOLE	BOTULIN	BOUILLONS
BOSOMED	BOTANICAL	BOTHOLES	BOTULINAL	BOUK
BOSOMIER	BOTANICAS	BOTHRIA	BOTULINS	BOUKS
BOSOMIEST	BOTANICS	BOTHRIUM	BOTULINUM	BOULDER
BOSOMING	BOTANIES	BOTHRIUMS	BOTULINUS	BOULDERED
BOSOMS	BOTANISE	BOTHY	BOTULISM	BOULDERER
BOSOMY	BOTANISED	BOTHYMAN	BOTULISMS	BOULDERS
BOSON	BOTANISER	BOTHYMEN	BOUBOU	BOULDERY
BOSONIC	BOTANISES	BOTNET	BOUBOUS	BOULE
BOSONS	BOTANIST	BOTNETS		BOULES

BOULEVARD	BOURD	BOUTIQUEY	BOWGETS	BOWSERS
BOULLE	BOURDED	BOUTON	BOWHEAD	BOWSES
BOULLES	BOURDER	BOUTONNE	BOWHEADS	BOWSEY
BOULT	BOURDERS	BOUTONNEE	BOWHUNT	BOWSEYS
BOULTED	BOURDING	BOUTONS	BOWHUNTED	BOWSHOT
BOULTER	BOURDON	BOUTS	BOWHUNTER	BOWSHOTS
BOULTERS	BOURDONS	BOUVARDIA	BOWHUNTS	BOWSIE
BOULTING	BOURDS	BOUVIER	BOWIE	BOWSIES
BOULTINGS	BOURG	BOUVIERS	BOWING	BOWSING
BOULTS	BOURGEOIS	BOUZOUKI	BOWINGLY	BOWSMAN
BOUN	BOURGEON	BOUZOUKIA	BOWINGS	BOWSMEN
BOUNCE	BOURGEONS	BOUZOUKIS	BOWKNOT	BOWSPRIT
BOUNCED	BOURGS	BOVATE	BOWKNOTS	BOWSPRITS
BOUNCER	BOURKHA	BOVATES	BOWL	BOWSTRING
BOUNCERS	BOURKHAS	BOVID	BOWLDER	BOWSTRUNG
BOUNCES	BOURLAW	BOVIDS	BOWLDERS	BOWWOOD
BOUNCIER	BOURLAWS	BOVINE	BOWLED	BOWWOODS
BOUNCIEST	BOURN	BOVINELY	BOWLEG	BOWWOW
BOUNCILY	BOURNE	BOVINES	BOWLEGGED	BOWWOWED
BOUNCING	BOURNES	BOVINITY	BOWLEGS	BOWWOWING
BOUNCY	BOURNS	BOVVER	BOWLER	BOWWOWS
BOUND	BOURREE	BOVVERS	BOWLERS	BOWYANG
BOUNDABLE	BOURREES	BOW	BOWLESS	BOWYANGS
BOUNDARY	BOURRIDE	BOWAT	BOWLFUL	BOWYER
BOUNDED	BOURRIDES	BOWATS	BOWLFULS	BOWYERS
BOUNDEN	BOURSE	BOWBENT	BOWLIKE	BOX
BOUNDER	BOURSES	BOWED	BOWLINE	BOXBALL
BOUNDERS	BOURSIER	BOWEL	BOWLINES	BOXBALLS
BOUNDING	BOURSIERS	BOWELED	BOWLING	BOXBERRY
BOUNDLESS	BOURSIN	BOWELING	BOWLINGS	BOXBOARD
BOUNDNESS	BOURSINS	BOWELLED	BOWLLIKE	BOXBOARDS
BOUNDS	BOURTREE	BOWELLESS	BOWLS	BOXCAR
BOUNED	BOURTREES	BOWELLING	BOWMAN	BOXCARS
BOUNING	BOUSE	BOWELS	BOWMEN	BOXED
BOUNS	BOUSED	BOWER	BOWNE	BOXEN
BOUNTEOUS	BOUSES	BOWERBIRD	BOWNED	BOXER
BOUNTIED	BOUSIER	BOWERED	BOWNES	BOXERCISE
BOUNTIES	BOUSIEST	BOWERIES	BOWNING	BOXERS
BOUNTIFUL	BOUSING	BOWERING	BOWPOT	BOXES
BOUNTREE	BOUSOUKI	BOWERS	BOWPOTS	BOXFISH
BOUNTREES	BOUSOUKIA	BOWERY	BOWR	BOXFISHES
BOUNTY	BOUSOUKIS	BOWES	BOWRS	BOXFUL
BOUNTYHED	BOUSY	BOWET	BOWS	BOXFULS
BOUQUET	BOUT	BOWETS	BOWSAW	BOXHAUL
BOUQUETS	BOUTADE	BOWFIN	BOWSAWS	BOXHAULED
BOURASQUE	BOUTADES	BOWFINS	BOWSE	BOXHAULS
BOURBON	BOUTIQUE	BOWFRONT	BOWSED	BOXIER
BOURBONS	BOUTIQUES	BOWGET	BOWSER	BOXIEST

BOXILY	BOYKIE	BRACHIAL	BRAGGED	BRAINIER
BOXINESS	BOYKIES	BRACHIALS	BRAGGER	BRAINIEST
BOXING	BOYLA	BRACHIATE	BRAGGERS	BRAININLY
BOXINGS	BOYLAS	BRACHIUM	BRAGGEST	BRAINING
BOXKEEPER	BOYO	BRACHIUMS	BRAGGIER	BRAINISH
BOXLA	BOYOS	BRACHOT	BRAGGIEST	BRAINLESS
BOXLAS	BOYS	BRACHS	BRAGGING	BRAINPAN
BOXLIKE	BOYSHORTS	BRACING	BRAGGINGS	BRAINPANS
BOXPLOT	BOYSIER	BRACINGLY	BRAGGY	BRAINS
BOXPLOTS	BOYSIEST	BRACINGS	BRAGLY	BRAINSICK
BOXROOM	BOYSY	BRACIOLA	BRAGS	BRAINSTEM
BOXROOMS	BOZO	BRACIOLAS	BRAHMA	BRAINWASH
BOXTHORN	BOZOS	BRACIOLE	BRAHMAN	BRAINWAVE
BOXTHORNS	BOZZETTI	BRACIOLES	BRAHMANI	BRAINWORK
BOXTIES	BOZZETTO	BRACK	BRAHMANIS	BRAINY
BOXTY	BRA	BRACKEN	BRAHMANS	BRAIRD
BOXWALLAH	BRAAI	BRACKENS	BRAHMAS	BRAIRDED
BOXWOOD	BRAAIED	BRACKET	BRAHMIN	BRAIRDING
BOXWOODS	BRAAIING	BRACKETED	BRAHMINS	BRAIRDS
BOXY	BRAAIS	BRACKETS	BRAID	BRAISE
BOY	BRAATA	BRACKISH	BRAIDE	BRAISED
BOYAR	BRAATAS	BRACKS	BRAIDED	BRAISES
BOYARD	BRAATASES	BRACONID	BRAIDER	BRAISING
BOYARDS	BRABBLE	BRACONIDS	BRAIDERS	BRAIZE
BOYARISM	BRABBLED	BRACT	BRAIDEST	BRAIZES
BOYARISMS	BRABBLER	BRACTEAL	BRAIDING	BRAK
BOYARS	BRABBLERS	BRACTEATE	BRAIDINGS	BRAKE
BOYAU	BRABBLES	BRACTED	BRAIDS	BRAKEAGE
BOYAUX	BRABBLING	BRACTEOLE	BRAIL	BRAKEAGES
BOYCHICK	BRACCATE	BRACTLESS	BRAILED	BRAKED
BOYCHICKS	BRACCIA	BRACTLET	BRAILING	BRAKELESS
BOYCHIK	BRACCIO	BRACTLETS	BRAILLE	BRAKEMAN
BOYCHIKS	BRACE	BRACTS	BRAILLED	BRAKEMEN
BOYCOTT	BRACED	BRAD	BRAILLER	BRAKES
BOYCOTTED	BRACELET	BRADAWL	BRAILLERS	BRAKESMAN
BOYCOTTER	BRACELETS	BRADAWLS	BRAILLES	BRAKESMEN
BOYCOTTS	BRACER	BRADDED	BRAILLING	BRAKIER
BOYED	BRACERO	BRADDING	BRAILLIST	BRAKIEST
BOYF	BRACEROS	BRADOON	BRAILS	BRAKING
BOYFRIEND	BRACERS	BRADOONS	BRAIN	BRAKINGS
BOYFS	BRACES	BRADS	BRAINBOX	BRAKS
BOYG	BRACH	BRAE	BRAINCASE	BRAKY
BOYGS	BRACHAH	BRAEHEID	BRAINDEAD	BRALESS
BOYHOOD	BRACHAHS	BRAEHEIDS	BRAINED	BRAMBLE
BOYHOODS	BRACHES	BRAES	BRAINFART	BRAMBLED
BOYING	BRACHET	BRAG	BRAINFOOD	BRAMBLES
BOYISH	BRACHETS	BRAGGART	BRAINIAC	BRAMBLIER
BOYISHLY	BRACHIA	BRAGGARTS	BRAINIACS	BRAMBLING

BRAMBLY
BRAME
BRAMES
BRAN
BRANCARD
BRANCARDS
BRANCH
BRANCHED
BRANCHER
BRANCHERS
BRANCHERY
BRANCHES
BRANCHIA
BRANCHIAE
BRANCHIAL
BRANCHIER
BRANCHING
BRANCHLET
BRANCHY
BRAND
BRANDADE
BRANDADES
BRANDED
BRANDER
BRANDERED
BRANDERS
BRANDIED
BRANDIES
BRANDING
BRANDINGS
BRANDISE
BRANDISES
BRANDISH
BRANDLESS
BRANDLING
BRANDRETH
BRANDS
BRANDY
BRANDYING
BRANE
BRANES
BRANGLE
BRANGLED
BRANGLES
BRANGLING
BRANK
BRANKED
BRANKIER

BRANKIEST
BRANKING
BRANKS
BRANKY
BRANLE
BRANLES
BRANNED
BRANNER
BRANNERS
BRANNIER
BRANNIEST
BRANNIGAN
BRANNING
BRANNY
BRANS
BRANSLE
BRANSLES
BRANT
BRANTAIL
BRANTAILS
BRANTLE
BRANTLES
BRANTS
BRAP
BRAS
BRASCO
BRASCOS
BRASERO
BRASEROS
BRASES
BRASH
BRASHED
BRASHER
BRASHES
BRASHEST
BRASHIER
BRASHIEST
BRASHING
BRASHLY
BRASHNESS
BRASHY
BRASIER
BRASIERS
BRASIL
BRASILEIN
BRASILIN
BRASILINS
BRASILS

BRASS
BRASSAGE
BRASSAGES
BRASSARD
BRASSARDS
BRASSART
BRASSARTS
BRASSED
BRASSERIE
BRASSES
BRASSET
BRASSETS
BRASSICA
BRASSICAS
BRASSIE
BRASSIER
BRASSIERE
BRASSIES
BRASSIEST
BRASSILY
BRASSING
BRASSISH
BRASSWARE
BRASSY
BRAST
BRASTING
BRASTS
BRAT
BRATCHET
BRATCHETS
BRATLING
BRATLINGS
BRATPACK
BRATPACKS
BRATS
BRATTICE
BRATTICED
BRATTICES
BRATTIER
BRATTIEST
BRATTISH
BRATTLE
BRATTLED
BRATTLES
BRATTLING
BRATTY
BRATWURST
BRAUNCH

BRAUNCHED
BRAUNCHES
BRAUNITE
BRAUNITES
BRAVA
BRAVADO
BRAVADOED
BRAVADOES
BRAVADOS
BRAVAS
BRAVE
BRAVED
BRAVELY
BRAVENESS
BRAVER
BRAVERIES
BRAVERS
BRAVERY
BRAVES
BRAVEST
BRAVI
BRAVING
BRAVO
BRAVOED
BRAVOES
BRAVOING
BRAVOS
BRAVURA
BRAVURAS
BRAVURE
BRAW
BRAWER
BRAWEST
BRAWL
BRAWLED
BRAWLER
BRAWLERS
BRAWLIE
BRAWLIER
BRAWLIEST
BRAWLING
BRAWLINGS
BRAWLS
BRAWLY
BRAWN
BRAWNED
BRAWNIER
BRAWNIEST

BRAWNILY
BRAWNS
BRAWNY
BRAWS
BRAXIES
BRAXY
BRAY
BRAYED
BRAYER
BRAYERS
BRAYING
BRAYS
BRAZA
BRAZAS
BRAZE
BRAZED
BRAZELESS
BRAZEN
BRAZENED
BRAZENING
BRAZENLY
BRAZENRY
BRAZENS
BRAZER
BRAZERS
BRAZES
BRAZIER
BRAZIERS
BRAZIERY
BRAZIL
BRAZILEIN
BRAZILIN
BRAZILINS
BRAZILS
BRAZING
BREACH
BREACHED
BREACHER
BREACHERS
BREACHES
BREACHING
BREAD
BREADBIN
BREADBINS
BREADBOX
BREADED
BREADHEAD
BREADIER

BREADIEST	BREASTFED	BREEM	BRENNE	BREWERY
BREADING	BREASTING	BREENGE	BRENNES	BREWHOUSE
BREADLESS	BREASTPIN	BREENGED	BRENNING	BREWING
BREADLIKE	BREASTS	BREENGES	BRENS	BREWINGS
BREADLINE	BREATH	BREENGING	BRENT	BREWIS
BREADNUT	BREATHE	BREER	BRENTER	BREWISES
BREADNUTS	BREATHED	BREERED	BRENTEST	BREWPUB
BREADROOM	BREATHER	BREERING	BRENTS	BREWPUBS
BREADROOT	BREATHERS	BREERS	BRER	BREWS
BREADS	BREATHES	BREES	BRERE	BREWSKI
BREADTH	BREATHFUL	BREESE	BRERES	BREWSKIES
BREADTHS	BREATHIER	BREESES	BRERS	BREWSKIS
BREADY	BREATHILY	BREEST	BRESAOLA	BREWSTER
BREAK	BREATHING	BREESTS	BRESAOLAS	BREWSTERS
BREAKABLE	BREATHS	BREEZE	BRETASCHE	BREY
BREAKAGE	BREATHY	BREEZED	BRETESSE	BREYED
BREAKAGES	BRECCIA	BREEZES	BRETESSES	BREYING
BREAKAWAY	BRECCIAL	BREEZEWAY	BRETHREN	BREYS
BREAKBACK	BRECCIAS	BREEZIER	BRETON	BRIAR
BREAKBEAT	BRECCIATE	BREEZIEST	BRETONS	BRIARD
BREAKBONE	BRECHAM	BREEZILY	BRETTICE	BRIARDS
BREAKDOWN	BRECHAMS	BREEZING	BRETTICED	BRIARED
BREAKER	BRECHAN	BREEZY	BRETTICES	BRIARIER
BREAKERS	BRECHANS	BREGMA	BREVE	BRIARIEST
BREAKEVEN	BRED	BREGMAS	BREVES	BRIARROOT
BREAKFAST	BREDE	BREGMATA	BREVET	BRIARS
BREAKING	BREDED	BREGMATE	BREVETCY	BRIARWOOD
BREAKINGS	BREDES	BREGMATIC	BREVETE	BRIARY
BREAKNECK	BREDIE	BREHON	BREVETED	BRIBABLE
BREAKOFF	BREDIES	BREHONS	BREVETING	BRIBE
BREAKOFFS	BREDING	BREI	BREVETS	BRIBEABLE
BREAKOUT	BREDREN	BREID	BREVETTED	BRIBED
BREAKOUTS	BREDRENS	BREIDS	BREVIARY	BRIBEE
BREAKS	BREDRIN	BREIING	BREVIATE	BRIBEES
BREAKTIME	BREDRINS	BREINGE	BREVIATES	BRIBER
BREAKUP	BREDS	BREINGED	BREVIER	BRIBERIES
BREAKUPS	BREE	BREINGES	BREVIERS	BRIBERS
BREAKWALL	BREECH	BREINGING	BREVIS	BRIBERY
BREAM	BREECHED	BREIS	BREVISES	BRIBES
BREAMED	BREECHES	BREIST	BREVITIES	BRIBING
BREAMING	BREECHING	BREISTS	BREVITY	BRICABRAC
BREAMS	BREED	BREKKIE	BREW	BRICHT
BREARE	BREEDER	BREKKIES	BREWAGE	BRICHTER
BREARES	BREEDERS	BREKKY	BREWAGES	BRICHTEST
BREASKIT	BREEDING	BRELOQUE	BREWED	BRICK
BREASKITS	BREEDINGS	BRELOQUES	BREWER	BRICKBAT
BREAST	BREEDS	BREME	BREWERIES	BRICKBATS
BREASTED	BREEKS	BREN	BREWERS	BRICKCLAY

BRICKED	BRIDLEWAY	BRIGUES	BRINIER	BRISKS
BRICKEN	BRIDLING	BRIGUING	BRINIES	BRISKY
BRICKIE	BRIDOON	BRIGUINGS	BRINIEST	BRISLING
BRICKIER	BRIDOONS	BRIK	BRININESS	BRISLINGS
BRICKIES	BRIE	BRIKI	BRINING	BRISS
BRICKIEST	BRIEF	BRIKIS	BRINISH	BRISSES
BRICKING	BRIEFCASE	BRIKS	BRINJAL	BRISTLE
BRICKINGS	BRIEFED	BRILL	BRINJALS	BRISTLED
BRICKKILN	BRIEFER	BRILLER	BRINJARRY	BRISTLES
BRICKLE	BRIEFERS	BRILLEST	BRINK	BRISTLIER
BRICKLES	BRIEFEST	BRILLIANT	BRINKMAN	BRISTLING
BRICKLIKE	BRIEFING	BRILLO	BRINKMEN	BRISTLY
BRICKS	BRIEFINGS	BRILLOS	BRINKS	BRISTOL
BRICKWALL	BRIEFLESS	BRILLS	BRINNIES	BRISTOLS
BRICKWORK	BRIEFLY	BRIM	BRINNY	BRISURE
BRICKY	BRIEFNESS	BRIMFUL	BRINS	BRISURES
BRICKYARD	BRIEFS	BRIMFULL	BRINY	BRIT
BRICOLAGE	BRIER	BRIMFULLY	BRIO	BRITANNIA
BRICOLE	BRIERED	BRIMING	BRIOCHE	BRITCHES
BRICOLES	BRIERIER	BRIMINGS	BRIOCHES	BRITH
BRICOLEUR	BRIERIEST	BRIMLESS	BRIOLETTE	BRITHS
BRIDAL	BRIERROOT	BRIMMED	BRIONIES	BRITS
BRIDALLY	BRIERS	BRIMMER	BRIONY	BRITSCHKA
BRIDALS	BRIERWOOD	BRIMMERS	BRIOS	BRITSKA
BRIDE	BRIERY	BRIMMING	BRIQUET	BRITSKAS
BRIDECAKE	BRIES	BRIMS	BRIQUETS	BRITT
BRIDED	BRIG	BRIMSTONE	BRIQUETTE	BRITTANIA
BRIDEMAID	BRIGADE	BRIMSTONY	BRIS	BRITTLE
BRIDEMAN	BRIGADED	BRIN	BRISANCE	BRITTLED
BRIDEMEN	BRIGADES	BRINDED	BRISANCES	BRITTLELY
BRIDES	BRIGADIER	BRINDISI	BRISANT	BRITTLER
BRIDESMAN	BRIGADING	BRINDISIS	BRISE	BRITTLES
BRIDESMEN	BRIGALOW	BRINDLE	BRISES	BRITTLEST
BRIDEWELL	BRIGALOWS	BRINDLED	BRISK	BRITTLING
BRIDGABLE	BRIGAND	BRINDLES	BRISKED	BRITTLY
BRIDGE	BRIGANDRY	BRINE	BRISKEN	BRITTS
BRIDGED	BRIGANDS	BRINED	BRISKENED	BRITZKA
BRIDGES	BRIGHT	BRINELESS	BRISKENS	BRITZKAS
BRIDGING	BRIGHTEN	BRINER	BRISKER	BRITZSKA
BRIDGINGS	BRIGHTENS	BRINERS	BRISKEST	BRITZSKAS
BRIDIE	BRIGHTER	BRINES	BRISKET	BRIZE
BRIDIES	BRIGHTEST	BRING	BRISKETS	BRIZES
BRIDING	BRIGHTISH	BRINGDOWN	BRISKIER	BRO
BRIDLE	BRIGHTLY	BRINGER	BRISKIEST	BROACH
BRIDLED	BRIGHTS	BRINGERS	BRISKING	BROACHED
BRIDLER	BRIGS	BRINGING	BRISKISH	BROACHER
BRIDLERS	BRIGUE	BRINGINGS	BRISKLY	BROACHERS
BRIDLES	BRIGUED	BRINGS	BRISKNESS	BROACHES

BROACHING	BROCHED	BROIDERED	BROMIC	BRONZER
BROAD	BROCHES	BROIDERER	BROMID	BRONZERS
BROADAX	BROCHETTE	BROIDERS	BROMIDE	BRONZES
BROADAXE	BROCHING	BROIDERY	BROMIDES	BRONZIER
BROADAXES	BROCHO	BROIL	BROMIDIC	BRONZIEST
BROADBAND	BROCHOS	BROILED	BROMIDS	BRONZIFY
BROADBEAN	BROCHS	BROILER	BROMIN	BRONZING
BROADBILL	BROCHURE	BROILERS	BROMINATE	BRONZINGS
BROADBRIM	BROCHURES	BROILING	BROMINE	BRONZITE
BROADCAST	BROCK	BROILS	BROMINES	BRONZITES
BROADEN	BROCKAGE	BROKAGE	BROMINISM	BRONZY
BROADENED	BROCKAGES	BROKAGES	BROMINS	BROO
BROADENER	BROCKED	BROKE	BROMISE	BROOCH
BROADENS	BROCKET	BROKED	BROMISED	BROOCHED
BROADER	BROCKETS	BROKEN	BROMISES	BROOCHES
BROADEST	BROCKIT	BROKENLY	BROMISING	BROOCHING
BROADISH	BROCKRAM	BROKER	BROMISM	BROOD
BROADLEAF	BROCKRAMS	BROKERAGE	BROMISMS	BROODED
BROADLINE	BROCKS	BROKERED	BROMIZE	BROODER
BROADLOOM	BROCOLI	BROKERIES	BROMIZED	BROODERS
BROADLY	BROCOLIS	BROKERING	BROMIZES	BROODIER
BROADNESS	BROD	BROKERS	BROMIZING	BROODIEST
BROADS	BRODDED	BROKERY	BROMMER	BROODILY
BROADSIDE	BRODDING	BROKES	BROMMERS	BROODING
BROADTAIL	BRODDLE	BROKING	BROMO	BROODINGS
BROADWAY	BRODDLED	BROKINGS	BROMOFORM	BROODLESS
BROADWAYS	BRODDLES	BROLGA	BROMOS	BROODMARE
BROADWISE	BRODDLING	BROLGAS	BRONC	BROODS
BROAST	BRODEKIN	BROLLIES	BRONCHI	BROODY
BROASTED	BRODEKINS	BROLLY	BRONCHIA	BROOK
BROASTING	BRODKIN	BROMAL	BRONCHIAL	BROOKABLE
BROASTS	BRODKINS	BROMALS	BRONCHIUM	BROOKED
BROCADE	BRODS	BROMANCE	BRONCHO	BROOKIE
BROCADED	BROEKIES	BROMANCES	BRONCHOS	BROOKIES
BROCADES	BROG	BROMANTIC	BRONCHUS	BROOKING
BROCADING	BROGAN	BROMATE	BRONCO	BROOKITE
BROCAGE	BROGANS	BROMATED	BRONCOS	BROOKITES
BROCAGES	BROGGED	BROMATES	BRONCS	BROOKLET
BROCARD	BROGGING	BROMATING	BROND	BROOKLETS
BROCARDS	BROGH	BROME	BRONDE	BROOKLIKE
BROCATEL	BROGHS	BROMELAIN	BRONDER	BROOKLIME
BROCATELS	BROGS	BROMELIA	BRONDES	BROOKS
BROCCOLI	BROGUE	BROMELIAD	BRONDEST	BROOKWEED
BROCCOLIS	BROGUEISH	BROMELIAS	BRONDS	BROOL
BROCH	BROGUERY	BROMELIN	BRONDYRON	BROOLS
BROCHAN	BROGUES	BROMELINS	BRONZE	BROOM
BROCHANS	BROGUISH	BROMEOSIN	BRONZED	BROOMBALL
BROCHE	BROIDER	BROMES	BRONZEN	BROOMCORN

BROOMED	BROWED	BRUCITE	BRUNETS	BRUTALISE
BROOMIER	BROWLESS	BRUCITES	BRUNETTE	BRUTALISM
BROOMIEST	BROWN	BRUCKLE	BRUNETTES	BRUTALIST
BROOMING	BROWNED	BRUGH	BRUNG	BRUTALITY
BROOMRAPE	BROWNER	BRUGHS	BRUNIZEM	BRUTALIZE
BROOMS	BROWNERS	BRUHAHA	BRUNIZEMS	BRUTALLY
BROOMY	BROWNEST	BRUHAHAS	BRUNT	BRUTE
BROOS	BROWNIE	BRUILZIE	BRUNTED	BRUTED
BROOSE	BROWNIER	BRUILZIES	BRUNTING	BRUTELIKE
BROOSES	BROWNIES	BRUIN	BRUNTS	BRUTELY
BROS	BROWNIEST	BRUINS	BRUS	BRUTENESS
BROSE	BROWNING	BRUISE	BRUSH	BRUTER
BROSES	BROWNINGS	BRUISED	BRUSHABLE	BRUTERS
BROSIER	BROWNISH	BRUISER	BRUSHBACK	BRUTES
BROSIEST	BROWNNESS	BRUISERS	BRUSHED	BRUTEST
BROSY	BROWNNOSE	BRUISES	BRUSHER	BRUTIFIED
BROTH	BROWNOUT	BRUISING	BRUSHERS	BRUTIFIES
BROTHA	BROWNOUTS	BRUISINGS	BRUSHES	BRUTIFY
BROTHAS	BROWNS	BRUIT	BRUSHFIRE	BRUTING
BROTHEL	BROWNTAIL	BRUITED	BRUSHIER	BRUTINGS
BROTHELS	BROWNY	BRUITER	BRUSHIEST	BRUTISH
BROTHER	BROWRIDGE	BRUITERS	BRUSHING	BRUTISHLY
BROTHERED	BROWS	BRUITING	BRUSHINGS	BRUTISM
BROTHERLY	BROWSABLE	BRUITS	BRUSHLAND	BRUTISMS
BROTHERS	BROWSE	BRULE	BRUSHLESS	BRUTS
BROTHIER	BROWSED	BRULES	BRUSHLIKE	BRUX
BROTHIEST	BROWSER	BRULOT	BRUSHMARK	BRUXED
BROTHS	BROWSERS	BRULOTS	BRUSHOFF	BRUXES
BROTHY	BROWSES	BRULYIE	BRUSHOFFS	BRUXING
BROUGH	BROWSIER	BRULYIES	BRUSHUP	BRUXISM
BROUGHAM	BROWSIEST	BRULZIE	BRUSHUPS	BRUXISMS
BROUGHAMS	BROWSING	BRULZIES	BRUSHWOOD	BRYOLOGY
BROUGHS	BROWSINGS	BRUMAL	BRUSHWORK	BRYONIES
BROUGHT	BROWST	BRUMBIES	BRUSHY	BRYONY
BROUGHTA	BROWSTS	BRUMBY	BRUSK	BRYOPHYTE
BROUGHTAS	BROWSY	BRUME	BRUSKER	BRYOZOAN
BROUHAHA	BRR	BRUMES	BRUSKEST	BRYOZOANS
BROUHAHAS	BRRR	BRUMMAGEM	BRUSQUE	BUAT
BROUZE	BRU	BRUMMER	BRUSQUELY	BUATS
BROUZES	BRUCELLA	BRUMMERS	BRUSQUER	BUAZE
BROW	BRUCELLAE	BRUMOUS	BRUSQUEST	BUAZES
BROWALLIA	BRUCELLAS	BRUNCH	BRUSSELS	BUB
BROWBAND	BRUCHID	BRUNCHED	BRUSSEN	BUBA
BROWBANDS	BRUCHIDS	BRUNCHER	BRUST	BUBAL
BROWBEAT	BRUCIN	BRUNCHERS	BRUSTING	BUBALE
BROWBEATS	BRUCINE	BRUNCHES	BRUSTS	BUBALES
BROWBONE	BRUCINES	BRUNCHING	BRUT	BUBALINE
BROWBONES	BRUCINS	BRUNET	BRUTAL	BUBALIS

BUBALISES

BUBALISES	BUCKAROO	BUCKRAS	BUDGED	BUFFERS
BUBALS	BUCKAROOS	BUCKS	BUDGER	BUFFEST
BUBAS	BUCKAYRO	BUCKSAW	BUDGEREE	BUFFET
BUBBA	BUCKAYROS	BUCKSAWS	BUDGERO	BUFFETED
BUBBAS	BUCKBEAN	BUCKSHEE	BUDGEROS	BUFFETER
BUBBE	BUCKBEANS	BUCKSHEES	BUDGEROW	BUFFETERS
BUBBES	BUCKBOARD	BUCKSHISH	BUDGEROWS	BUFFETING
BUBBIE	BUCKBRUSH	BUCKSHOT	BUDGERS	BUFFETS
BUBBIES	BUCKED	BUCKSHOTS	BUDGES	BUFFI
BUBBLE	BUCKEEN	BUCKSKIN	BUDGET	BUFFIER
BUBBLED	BUCKEENS	BUCKSKINS	BUDGETARY	BUFFIEST
BUBBLEGUM	BUCKER	BUCKSOM	BUDGETED	BUFFING
BUBBLER	BUCKEROO	BUCKTAIL	BUDGETEER	BUFFINGS
BUBBLERS	BUCKEROOS	BUCKTAILS	BUDGETER	BUFFO
BUBBLES	BUCKERS	BUCKTEETH	BUDGETERS	BUFFOON
BUBBLIER	BUCKET	BUCKTHORN	BUDGETING	BUFFOONS
BUBBLIES	BUCKETED	BUCKTOOTH	BUDGETS	BUFFOS
BUBBLIEST	BUCKETFUL	BUCKU	BUDGIE	BUFFS
BUBBLING	BUCKETING	BUCKUS	BUDGIES	BUFFY
BUBBLY	BUCKETS	BUCKWHEAT	BUDGING	BUFO
BUBBY	BUCKEYE	BUCKYBALL	BUDI	BUFOS
BUBINGA	BUCKEYES	BUCKYTUBE	BUDIS	BUFOTALIN
BUBINGAS	BUCKHORN	BUCOLIC	BUDLESS	BUFTIE
BUBKES	BUCKHORNS	BUCOLICAL	BUDLIKE	BUFTIES
BUBKIS	BUCKHOUND	BUCOLICS	BUDMASH	BUFTY
BUBO	BUCKIE	BUD	BUDMASHES	BUG
BUBOED	BUCKIES	BUDA	BUDO	BUGABOO
BUBOES	BUCKING	BUDAS	BUDOS	BUGABOOS
BUBONIC	BUCKINGS	BUDDED	BUDS	BUGBANE
BUBS	BUCKISH	BUDDER	BUDTENDER	BUGBANES
BUBU	BUCKISHLY	BUDDERS	BUDWOOD	BUGBEAR
BUBUKLE	BUCKLE	BUDDHA	BUDWOODS	BUGBEARS
BUBUKLES	BUCKLED	BUDDHAS	BUDWORM	BUGEYE
BUBUS	BUCKLER	BUDDIED	BUDWORMS	BUGEYES
BUCARDO	BUCKLERED	BUDDIER	BUFF	BUGGAN
BUCARDOS	BUCKLERS	BUDDIES	BUFFA	BUGGANE
BUCATINI	BUCKLES	BUDDIEST	BUFFABLE	BUGGANES
BUCCAL	BUCKLING	BUDDING	BUFFALO	BUGGANS
BUCCALLY	BUCKLINGS	BUDDINGS	BUFFALOED	BUGGED
BUCCANEER	BUCKO	BUDDLE	BUFFALOES	BUGGER
BUCCANIER	BUCKOES	BUDDLED	BUFFALOS	BUGGERED
BUCCINA	BUCKOS	BUDDLEIA	BUFFAS	BUGGERIES
BUCCINAS	BUCKRA	BUDDLEIAS	BUFFE	BUGGERING
BUCELLAS	BUCKRAKE	BUDDLES	BUFFED	BUGGERS
BUCENTAUR	BUCKRAKES	BUDDLING	BUFFEL	BUGGERY
BUCHU	BUCKRAM	BUDDY	BUFFER	BUGGIER
BUCHUS	BUCKRAMED	BUDDYING	BUFFERED	BUGGIES
BUCK	BUCKRAMS	BUDGE	BUFFERING	BUGGIEST

BUGGIN	BUILDERS	BULGIER	BULLCOOK	BULLNECK
BUGGINESS	BUILDING	BULGIEST	BULLCOOKS	BULLNECKS
BUGGING	BUILDINGS	BULGINE	BULLDIKE	BULLNOSE
BUGGINGS	BUILDOUT	BULGINES	BULLDIKES	BULLNOSED
BUGGINS	BUILDOUTS	BULGINESS	BULLDOG	BULLNOSES
BUGGY	BUILDS	BULGING	BULLDOGS	BULLOCK
BUGHOUSE	BUILDUP	BULGINGLY	BULLDOZE	BULLOCKED
BUGHOUSES	BUILDUPS	BULGUR	BULLDOZED	BULLOCKS
BUGLE	BUILT	BULGURS	BULLDOZER	BULLOCKY
BUGLED	BUIRDLIER	BULGY	BULLDOZES	BULLOSA
BUGLER	BUIRDLY	BULIMIA	BULLDUST	BULLOUS
BUGLERS	BUIST	BULIMIAC	BULLDUSTS	BULLPEN
BUGLES	BUISTED	BULIMIACS	BULLDYKE	BULLPENS
BUGLET	BUISTING	BULIMIAS	BULLDYKES	BULLPOUT
BUGLETS	BUISTS	BULIMIC	BULLED	BULLPOUTS
BUGLEWEED	BUKE	BULIMICS	BULLER	BULLRING
BUGLING	BUKES	BULIMIES	BULLERED	BULLRINGS
BUGLOSS	BUKKAKE	BULIMUS	BULLERING	BULLRUSH
BUGLOSSES	BUKKAKES	BULIMUSES	BULLERS	BULLS
BUGONG	BUKSHEE	BULIMY	BULLET	BULLSEYE
BUGONGS	BUKSHEES	BULK	BULLETED	BULLSEYES
BUGOUT	BUKSHI	BULKAGE	BULLETIN	BULLSHAT
BUGOUTS	BUKSHIS	BULKAGES	BULLETING	BULLSHIT
BUGS	BULB	BULKED	BULLETINS	BULLSHITS
BUGSEED	BULBAR	BULKER	BULLETRIE	BULLSHOT
BUGSEEDS	BULBED	BULKERS	BULLETS	BULLSHOTS
BUGSHA	BULBEL	BULKHEAD	BULLEY	BULLSNAKE
BUGSHAS	BULBELS	BULKHEADS	BULLEYS	BULLWADDY
BUGWORT	BULBIL	BULKIER	BULLFIGHT	BULLWEED
BUGWORTS	BULBILS	BULKIEST	BULLFINCH	BULLWEEDS
BUHL	BULBING	BULKILY	BULLFROG	BULLWHACK
BUHLS	BULBLET	BULKINESS	BULLFROGS	BULLWHIP
BUHLWORK	BULBLETS	BULKING	BULLGINE	BULLWHIPS
BUHLWORKS	BULBOSITY	BULKINGS	BULLGINES	BULLY
BUHR	BULBOUS	BULKS	BULLHEAD	BULLYBOY
BUHRS	BULBOUSLY	BULKY	BULLHEADS	BULLYBOYS
BUHRSTONE	BULBS	BULL	BULLHORN	BULLYCIDE
BUHUND	BULBUL	BULLA	BULLHORNS	BULLYING
BUHUNDS	BULBULS	BULLACE	BULLIED	BULLYINGS
BUIBUI	BULGAR	BULLACES	BULLIER	BULLYISM
BUIBUIS	BULGARS	BULLAE	BULLIES	BULLYISMS
BUIK	BULGE	BULLARIES	BULLIEST	BULLYRAG
BUIKS	BULGED	BULLARY	BULLING	BULLYRAGS
BUILD	BULGER	BULLATE	BULLINGS	BULNBULN
BUILDABLE	BULGERS	BULLBARS	BULLION	BULNBULNS
BUILDDOWN	BULGES	BULLBAT	BULLIONS	BULRUSH
BUILDED	BULGHUR	BULLBATS	BULLISH	BULRUSHES
BUILDER	BULGHURS	BULLBRIER	BULLISHLY	BULRUSHY

BULSE	BUMMED	BUNCES	BUNDYING	BUNKERS
BULSES	BUMMEL	BUNCH	BUNFIGHT	BUNKHOUSE
BULWADDEE	BUMMELS	BUNCHED	BUNFIGHTS	BUNKIE
BULWADDY	BUMMER	BUNCHER	BUNG	BUNKIES
BULWARK	BUMMERS	BUNCHERS	BUNGALOID	BUNKING
BULWARKED	BUMMEST	BUNCHES	BUNGALOW	BUNKMATE
BULWARKS	BUMMING	BUNCHIER	BUNGALOWS	BUNKMATES
BUM	BUMMLE	BUNCHIEST	BUNGED	BUNKO
BUMALO	BUMMLED	BUNCHILY	BUNGEE	BUNKOED
BUMALOTI	BUMMLES	BUNCHING	BUNGEES	BUNKOING
BUMALOTIS	BUMMLING	BUNCHINGS	BUNGER	BUNKOS
BUMBAG	BUMMOCK	BUNCHY	BUNGERS	BUNKS
BUMBAGS	BUMMOCKS	BUNCING	BUNGEY	BUNKUM
BUMBAZE	BUMP	BUNCO	BUNGEYS	BUNKUMS
BUMBAZED	BUMPED	BUNCOED	BUNGHOLE	BUNN
BUMBAZES	BUMPER	BUNCOES	BUNGHOLES	BUNNET
BUMBAZING	BUMPERED	BUNCOING	BUNGIE	BUNNETS
BUMBLE	BUMPERING	BUNCOMBE	BUNGIES	BUNNIA
BUMBLEBEE	BUMPERS	BUNCOMBES	BUNGING	BUNNIAS
BUMBLED	BUMPH	BUNCOS	BUNGLE	BUNNIES
BUMBLEDOM	BUMPHS	BUND	BUNGLED	BUNNS
BUMBLER	BUMPIER	BUNDE	BUNGLER	BUNNY
BUMBLERS	BUMPIEST	BUNDED	BUNGLERS	BUNODONT
BUMBLES	BUMPILY	BUNDH	BUNGLES	BUNRAKU
BUMBLING	BUMPINESS	BUNDHS	BUNGLING	BUNRAKUS
BUMBLINGS	BUMPING	BUNDIED	BUNGLINGS	BUNS
BUMBO	BUMPINGS	BUNDIES	BUNGS	BUNSEN
BUMBOAT	BUMPKIN	BUNDING	BUNGWALL	BUNSENS
BUMBOATS	BUMPKINLY	BUNDIST	BUNGWALLS	BUNT
BUMBOS	BUMPKINS	BUNDISTS	BUNGY	BUNTAL
BUMBOY	BUMPOLOGY	BUNDLE	BUNHEAD	BUNTALS
BUMBOYS	BUMPS	BUNDLED	BUNHEADS	BUNTED
BUMELIA	BUMPTIOUS	BUNDLER	BUNIA	BUNTER
BUMELIAS	BUMPY	BUNDLERS	BUNIAS	BUNTERS
BUMF	BUMS	BUNDLES	BUNION	BUNTIER
BUMFLUFF	BUMSTER	BUNDLING	BUNIONS	BUNTIEST
BUMFLUFFS	BUMSTERS	BUNDLINGS	BUNJE	BUNTING
BUMFS	BUMSUCKER	BUNDOBUST	BUNJEE	BUNTINGS
BUMFUCK	BUMWAD	BUNDOOK	BUNJEES	BUNTLINE
BUMFUCKS	BUMWADS	BUNDOOKS	BUNJES	BUNTLINES
BUMFUZZLE	BUN	BUNDS	BUNJIE	BUNTS
BUMKIN	BUNA	BUNDT	BUNJIES	BUNTY
BUMKINS	BUNAS	BUNDTS	BUNJY	BUNYA
BUMMALO	BUNBURIED	BUNDU	BUNK	BUNYAS
BUMMALOS	BUNBURIES	BUNDUS	BUNKED	BUNYIP
BUMMALOTI	BUNBURY	BUNDWALL	BUNKER	BUNYIPS
BUMMAREE	BUNCE	BUNDWALLS	BUNKERED	BUOY
BUMMAREES	BUNCED	BUNDY	BUNKERING	BUOYAGE

B

BUOYAGES	BURDENOUS	BURGONETS	BURLESQUE	BURP
BUOYANCE	BURDENS	BURGOO	BURLETTA	BURPED
BUOYANCES	BURDIE	BURGOOS	BURLETTAS	BURPEE
BUOYANCY	BURDIES	BURGOUT	BURLEY	BURPEES
BUOYANT	BURDIZZO	BURGOUTS	BURLEYCUE	BURPING
BUOYANTLY	BURDIZZOS	BURGRAVE	BURLEYED	BURPS
BUOYED	BURDOCK	BURGRAVES	BURLEYING	BURQA
BUOYING	BURDOCKS	BURGS	BURLEYS	BURQAS
BUOYS	BURDS	BURGUNDY	BURLIER	BURQUINI
BUPKES	BUREAU	BURHEL	BURLIEST	BURQUINIS
BUPKIS	BUREAUS	BURHELS	BURLIKE	BURR
BUPKUS	BUREAUX	BURIAL	BURLILY	BURRAMYS
BUPLEVER	BURET	BURIALS	BURLINESS	BURRATA
BUPLEVERS	BURETS	BURIED	BURLING	BURRATAS
BUPPIE	BURETTE	BURIER	BURLS	BURRAWANG
BUPPIES	BURETTES	BURIERS	BURLY	BURRED
BUPPY	BURFI	BURIES	BURN	BURREL
BUPRESTID	BURFIS	BURIN	BURNABLE	BURRELL
BUPROPION	BURG	BURINIST	BURNABLES	BURRELLS
BUQSHA	BURGAGE	BURINISTS	BURNED	BURRELS
BUQSHAS	BURGAGES	BURINS	BURNER	BURRER
BUR	BURGANET	BURITI	BURNERS	BURRERS
BURA	BURGANETS	BURITIS	BURNET	BURRFISH
BURAN	BURGEE	BURK	BURNETS	BURRHEL
BURANS	BURGEES	BURKA	BURNIE	BURRHELS
BURAS	BURGEON	BURKAS	BURNIES	BURRIER
BURB	BURGEONED	BURKE	BURNING	BURRIEST
BURBLE	BURGEONS	BURKED	BURNINGLY	BURRING
BURBLED	BURGER	BURKER	BURNINGS	BURRITO
BURBLER	BURGERS	BURKERS	BURNISH	BURRITOS
BURBLERS	BURGESS	BURKES	BURNISHED	BURRO
BURBLES	BURGESSES	BURKHA	BURNISHER	BURROS
BURBLIER	BURGH	BURKHAS	BURNISHES	BURROW
BURBLIEST	BURGHAL	BURKING	BURNOOSE	BURROWED
BURBLING	BURGHER	BURKINI	BURNOOSED	BURROWER
BURBLINGS	BURGHERS	BURKINIS	BURNOOSES	BURROWERS
BURBLY	BURGHS	BURKITE	BURNOUS	BURROWING
BURBOT	BURGHUL	BURKITES	BURNOUSE	BURROWS
BURBOTS	BURGHULS	BURKS	BURNOUSED	BURRS
BURBS	BURGLAR	BURL	BURNOUSES	BURRSTONE
BURD	BURGLARED	BURLADERO	BURNOUT	BURRY
BURDASH	BURGLARS	BURLAP	BURNOUTS	BURS
BURDASHES	BURGLARY	BURLAPS	BURNS	BURSA
BURDEN	BURGLE	BURLED	BURNSIDE	BURSAE
BURDENED	BURGLED	BURLER	BURNSIDES	BURSAL
BURDENER	BURGLES	BURLERS	BURNT	BURSAR
BURDENERS	BURGLING	BURLESK	BUROO	BURSARIAL
BURDENING	BURGONET	BURLESKS	BUROOS	BURSARIES

BURSARS	BUSHBABY	BUSHTITS	BUSTARDS	BUTCHERED
BURSARY	BUSHBUCK	BUSHVELD	BUSTED	BUTCHERER
BURSAS	BUSHBUCKS	BUSHVELDS	BUSTEE	BUTCHERLY
BURSATE	BUSHCRAFT	BUSHWA	BUSTEES	BUTCHERS
BURSE	BUSHED	BUSHWAH	BUSTER	BUTCHERY
BURSEED	BUSHEL	BUSHWAHS	BUSTERS	BUTCHES
BURSEEDS	BUSHELED	BUSHWALK	BUSTI	BUTCHEST
BURSERA	BUSHELER	BUSHWALKS	BUSTIC	BUTCHING
BURSES	BUSHELERS	BUSHWAS	BUSTICATE	BUTCHINGS
BURSICON	BUSHELFUL	BUSHWHACK	BUSTICS	BUTCHNESS
BURSICONS	BUSHELING	BUSHWOMAN	BUSTIER	BUTE
BURSIFORM	BUSHELLED	BUSHWOMEN	BUSTIERS	BUTENE
BURSITIS	BUSHELLER	BUSHY	BUSTIEST	BUTENES
BURST	BUSHELMAN	BUSIED	BUSTINESS	BUTEO
BURSTED	BUSHELMEN	BUSIER	BUSTING	BUTEONINE
BURSTEN	BUSHELS	BUSIES	BUSTINGS	BUTEOS
BURSTER	BUSHER	BUSIEST	BUSTIS	BUTES
BURSTERS	BUSHERS	BUSILY	BUSTLE	BUTLE
BURSTIER	BUSHES	BUSINESS	BUSTLED	BUTLED
BURSTIEST	BUSHFIRE	BUSINESSY	BUSTLER	BUTLER
BURSTING	BUSHFIRES	BUSING	BUSTLERS	BUTLERAGE
BURSTONE	BUSHFLIES	BUSINGS	BUSTLES	BUTLERED
BURSTONES	BUSHFLY	BUSK	BUSTLINE	BUTLERIES
BURSTS	BUSHGOAT	BUSKED	BUSTLINES	BUTLERING
BURSTY	BUSHGOATS	BUSKER	BUSTLING	BUTLERS
BURTHEN	BUSHIDO	BUSKERS	BUSTS	BUTLERY
BURTHENED	BUSHIDOS	BUSKET	BUSTY	BUTLES
BURTHENS	BUSHIE	BUSKETS	BUSULFAN	BUTLING
BURTON	BUSHIER	BUSKIN	BUSULFANS	BUTMENT
BURTONS	BUSHIES	BUSKINED	BUSUUTI	BUTMENTS
BURWEED	BUSHIEST	BUSKING	BUSUUTIS	BUTOH
BURWEEDS	BUSHILY	BUSKINGS	BUSY	BUTOHS
BURY	BUSHINESS	BUSKINS	BUSYBODY	BUTS
BURYING	BUSHING	BUSKS	BUSYING	BUTSUDAN
BUS	BUSHINGS	BUSKY	BUSYNESS	BUTSUDANS
BUSBAR	BUSHLAND	BUSLOAD	BUSYWORK	BUTT
BUSBARS	BUSHLANDS	BUSLOADS	BUSYWORKS	BUTTALS
BUSBIES	BUSHLESS	BUSMAN	BUT	BUTTE
BUSBOY	BUSHLIKE	BUSMEN	BUTADIENE	BUTTED
BUSBOYS	BUSHLOT	BUSS	BUTANE	BUTTER
BUSBY	BUSHLOTS	BUSSED	BUTANES	BUTTERBUR
BUSED	BUSHMAN	BUSSES	BUTANOIC	BUTTERCUP
BUSERA	BUSHMEAT	BUSSING	BUTANOL	BUTTERED
BUSERAS	BUSHMEATS	BUSSINGS	BUTANOLS	BUTTERFAT
BUSES	BUSHMEN	BUSSU	BUTANONE	BUTTERFLY
BUSGIRL	BUSHPIG	BUSSUS	BUTANONES	BUTTERIER
BUSGIRLS	BUSHPIGS	BUST	BUTCH	BUTTERIES
BUSH	BUSHTIT	BUSTARD	BUTCHER	BUTTERINE

BUTTERING
BUTTERNUT
BUTTERS
BUTTERY
BUTTES
BUTTHEAD
BUTTHEADS
BUTTIES
BUTTING
BUTTINSKI
BUTTINSKY
BUTTLE
BUTTLED
BUTTLES
BUTTLING
BUTTOCK
BUTTOCKED
BUTTOCKS
BUTTON
BUTTONED
BUTTONER
BUTTONERS
BUTTONIER
BUTTONING
BUTTONS
BUTTONY
BUTTRESS
BUTTS
BUTTSTOCK
BUTTY
BUTTYMAN
BUTTYMEN
BUTUT
BUTUTS
BUTYL
BUTYLATE
BUTYLATED
BUTYLATES
BUTYLENE
BUTYLENES

BUTYLS
BUTYRAL
BUTYRALS
BUTYRATE
BUTYRATES
BUTYRIC
BUTYRIN
BUTYRINS
BUTYROUS
BUTYRYL
BUTYRYLS
BUVETTE
BUVETTES
BUXOM
BUXOMER
BUXOMEST
BUXOMLY
BUXOMNESS
BUY
BUYABLE
BUYABLES
BUYBACK
BUYBACKS
BUYER
BUYERS
BUYING
BUYINGS
BUYOFF
BUYOFFS
BUYOUT
BUYOUTS
BUYS
BUZKASHI
BUZKASHIS
BUZUKI
BUZUKIA
BUZUKIS
BUZZ
BUZZARD
BUZZARDS

BUZZBAIT
BUZZBAITS
BUZZCUT
BUZZCUTS
BUZZED
BUZZER
BUZZERS
BUZZES
BUZZIER
BUZZIEST
BUZZING
BUZZINGLY
BUZZINGS
BUZZKILL
BUZZKILLS
BUZZSAW
BUZZSAWS
BUZZWIG
BUZZWIGS
BUZZWORD
BUZZWORDS
BUZZY
BWANA
BWANAS
BWAZI
BWAZIS
BY
BYCATCH
BYCATCHES
BYCOKET
BYCOKETS
BYDE
BYDED
BYDES
BYDING
BYE
BYELAW
BYELAWS
BYES
BYGONE

BYGONES
BYKE
BYKED
BYKES
BYKING
BYLANDER
BYLANDERS
BYLANE
BYLANES
BYLAW
BYLAWS
BYLINE
BYLINED
BYLINER
BYLINERS
BYLINES
BYLINING
BYLIVE
BYNAME
BYNAMES
BYNEMPT
BYPASS
BYPASSED
BYPASSES
BYPASSING
BYPAST
BYPATH
BYPATHS
BYPLACE
BYPLACES
BYPLAY
BYPLAYS
BYPRODUCT
BYRE
BYREMAN
BYREMEN
BYRES
BYREWOMAN
BYREWOMEN
BYRL

BYRLADY
BYRLAKIN
BYRLAW
BYRLAWS
BYRLED
BYRLING
BYRLS
BYRNIE
BYRNIES
BYROAD
BYROADS
BYROOM
BYROOMS
BYS
BYSSAL
BYSSI
BYSSINE
BYSSOID
BYSSUS
BYSSUSES
BYSTANDER
BYSTREET
BYSTREETS
BYTALK
BYTALKS
BYTE
BYTES
BYTOWNITE
BYWAY
BYWAYS
BYWONER
BYWONERS
BYWORD
BYWORDS
BYWORK
BYWORKS
BYZANT
BYZANTINE
BYZANTS

C

CAA	CABBED	CABOBBED	CACA	CACKIEST
CAAED	CABBIE	CABOBBING	CACAFOGO	CACKING
CAAING	CABBIES	CABOBS	CACAFOGOS	CACKLE
CAAS	CABBING	CABOC	CACAFUEGO	CACKLED
CAATINGA	CABBY	CABOCEER	CACAO	CACKLER
CAATINGAS	CABDRIVER	CABOCEERS	CACAOS	CACKLERS
CAB	CABER	CABOCHED	CACAS	CACKLES
CABA	CABERNET	CABOCHON	CACHACA	CACKLING
CABAL	CABERNETS	CABOCHONS	CACHACAS	CACKS
CABALA	CABERS	CABOCS	CACHAEMIA	CACKY
CABALAS	CABESTRO	CABOMBA	CACHAEMIC	CACODEMON
CABALETTA	CABESTROS	CABOMBAS	CACHALOT	CACODOXY
CABALETTE	CABEZON	CABOODLE	CACHALOTS	CACODYL
CABALISM	CABEZONE	CABOODLES	CACHE	CACODYLIC
CABALISMS	CABEZONES	CABOOSE	CACHECTIC	CACODYLS
CABALIST	CABEZONS	CABOOSES	CACHED	CACOEPIES
CABALISTS	CABILDO	CABOSHED	CACHEPOT	CACOEPY
CABALLED	CABILDOS	CABOTAGE	CACHEPOTS	CACOETHES
CABALLER	CABIN	CABOTAGES	CACHES	CACOETHIC
CABALLERO	CABINED	CABOVER	CACHET	CACOGENIC
CABALLERS	CABINET	CABOVERS	CACHETED	CACOLET
CABALLINE	CABINETRY	CABRE	CACHETING	CACOLETS
CABALLING	CABINETS	CABRESTA	CACHETS	CACOLOGY
CABALS	CABINING	CABRESTAS	CACHEXIA	CACOMIXL
CABANA	CABINMATE	CABRESTO	CACHEXIAS	CACOMIXLE
CABANAS	CABINS	CABRESTOS	CACHEXIC	CACOMIXLS
CABARET	CABLE	CABRETTA	CACHEXIES	CACONYM
CABARETS	CABLECAST	CABRETTAS	CACHEXY	CACONYMS
CABAS	CABLED	CABRIE	CACHING	CACONYMY
CABBAGE	CABLEGRAM	CABRIES	CACHOLONG	CACOON
CABBAGED	CABLER	CABRILLA	CACHOLOT	CACOONS
CABBAGES	CABLERS	CABRILLAS	CACHOLOTS	CACOPHONY
CABBAGEY	CABLES	CABRIO	CACHOU	CACOTOPIA
CABBAGIER	CABLET	CABRIOLE	CACHOUS	CACTI
CABBAGING	CABLETS	CABRIOLES	CACHUCHA	CACTIFORM
CABBAGY	CABLEWAY	CABRIOLET	CACHUCHAS	CACTOID
CABBALA	CABLEWAYS	CABRIOS	CACIQUE	CACTUS
CABBALAH	CABLING	CABRIT	CACIQUES	CACTUSES
CABBALAHS	CABLINGS	CABRITS	CACIQUISM	CACUMEN
CABBALAS	CABMAN	CABS	CACK	CACUMENS
CABBALISM	CABMEN	CABSTAND	CACKED	CACUMINA
CABBALIST	CABOB	CABSTANDS	CACKIER	CACUMINAL

CAD	CADETSHIP	CAESTUS	CAGEYNESS	CAIRNGORM
CADAGA	CADGE	CAESTUSES	CAGIER	CAIRNIER
CADAGAS	CADGED	CAESURA	CAGIEST	CAIRNIEST
CADAGI	CADGER	CAESURAE	CAGILY	CAIRNS
CADAGIS	CADGERS	CAESURAL	CAGINESS	CAIRNY
CADASTER	CADGES	CAESURAS	CAGING	CAISSON
CADASTERS	CADGIER	CAESURIC	CAGMAG	CAISSONS
CADASTRAL	CADGIEST	CAF	CAGMAGGED	CAITIFF
CADASTRE	CADGING	CAFARD	CAGMAGS	CAITIFFS
CADASTRES	CADGY	CAFARDS	CAGOT	CAITIVE
CADAVER	CADI	CAFE	CAGOTS	CAITIVES
CADAVERIC	CADIE	CAFES	CAGOUL	CAJAPUT
CADAVERS	CADIES	CAFETERIA	CAGOULE	CAJAPUTS
CADDICE	CADIS	CAFETIERE	CAGOULES	CAJEPUT
CADDICES	CADMIC	CAFETORIA	CAGOULS	CAJEPUTS
CADDIE	CADMIUM	CAFF	CAGS	CAJOLE
CADDIED	CADMIUMS	CAFFEIN	CAGY	CAJOLED
CADDIES	CADRANS	CAFFEINE	CAGYNESS	CAJOLER
CADDIS	CADRANSES	CAFFEINES	CAHIER	CAJOLERS
CADDISED	CADRE	CAFFEINIC	CAHIERS	CAJOLERY
CADDISES	CADRES	CAFFEINS	CAHOOT	CAJOLES
CADDISFLY	CADS	CAFFEISM	CAHOOTS	CAJOLING
CADDISH	CADUAC	CAFFEISMS	CAHOUN	CAJON
CADDISHLY	CADUACS	CAFFILA	CAHOUNS	CAJONES
CADDY	CADUCEAN	CAFFILAS	CAHOW	CAJUN
CADDYING	CADUCEI	CAFFS	CAHOWS	CAJUPUT
CADDYSS	CADUCEUS	CAFILA	CAID	CAJUPUTS
CADDYSSES	CADUCITY	CAFILAS	CAIDS	CAKE
CADE	CADUCOUS	CAFS	CAILLACH	CAKEAGE
CADEAU	CAECA	CAFTAN	CAILLACHS	CAKEAGES
CADEAUX	CAECAL	CAFTANED	CAILLE	CAKEBOX
CADEE	CAECALLY	CAFTANS	CAILLEACH	CAKEBOXES
CADEES	CAECILIAN	CAG	CAILLES	CAKED
CADELLE	CAECITIS	CAGANER	CAILLIACH	CAKEHOLE
CADELLES	CAECUM	CAGANERS	CAIMAC	CAKEHOLES
CADENCE	CAEOMA	CAGE	CAIMACAM	CAKES
CADENCED	CAEOMAS	CAGED	CAIMACAMS	CAKEWALK
CADENCES	CAERULE	CAGEFUL	CAIMACS	CAKEWALKS
CADENCIES	CAERULEAN	CAGEFULS	CAIMAN	CAKEY
CADENCING	CAESAR	CAGELIKE	CAIMANS	CAKIER
CADENCY	CAESAREAN	CAGELING	CAIN	CAKIEST
CADENT	CAESARIAN	CAGELINGS	CAINS	CAKINESS
CADENTIAL	CAESARISM	CAGER	CAIQUE	CAKING
CADENZA	CAESARS	CAGERS	CAIQUES	CAKINGS
CADENZAS	CAESE	CAGES	CAIRD	CAKY
CADES	CAESIOUS	CAGEWORK	CAIRDS	CAL
CADET	CAESIUM	CAGEWORKS	CAIRN	CALABASH
CADETS	CAESIUMS	CAGEY	CAIRNED	CALABAZA

CALABAZAS

CALABAZAS	CALCAR	CALDRONS	CALICOS	CALLALOOS
CALABOGUS	CALCARATE	CALECHE	CALICULAR	CALLALOU
CALABOOSE	CALCARIA	CALECHES	CALID	CALLALOUS
CALABRESE	CALCARINE	CALEFIED	CALIDITY	CALLAN
CALADIUM	CALCARS	CALEFIES	CALIF	CALLANS
CALADIUMS	CALCEATE	CALEFY	CALIFATE	CALLANT
CALALOO	CALCEATED	CALEFYING	CALIFATES	CALLANTS
CALALOOS	CALCEATES	CALEMBOUR	CALIFONT	CALLAS
CALALU	CALCED	CALENDAL	CALIFONTS	CALLBACK
CALALUS	CALCEDONY	CALENDAR	CALIFS	CALLBACKS
CALAMANCO	CALCES	CALENDARS	CALIGO	CALLBOARD
CALAMANSI	CALCIC	CALENDER	CALIGOES	CALLBOY
CALAMAR	CALCICOLE	CALENDERS	CALIGOS	CALLBOYS
CALAMARI	CALCIFIC	CALENDRER	CALIMA	CALLED
CALAMARIS	CALCIFIED	CALENDRIC	CALIMAS	CALLEE
CALAMARS	CALCIFIES	CALENDRY	CALIMOCHO	CALLEES
CALAMARY	CALCIFUGE	CALENDS	CALIOLOGY	CALLER
CALAMATA	CALCIFY	CALENDULA	CALIPASH	CALLERS
CALAMATAS	CALCIMINE	CALENTURE	CALIPEE	CALLET
CALAMI	CALCINE	CALESA	CALIPEES	CALLETS
CALAMINE	CALCINED	CALESAS	CALIPER	CALLID
CALAMINED	CALCINES	CALESCENT	CALIPERED	CALLIDITY
CALAMINES	CALCINING	CALF	CALIPERS	CALLIGRAM
CALAMINT	CALCITE	CALFDOZER	CALIPH	CALLING
CALAMINTS	CALCITES	CALFHOOD	CALIPHAL	CALLINGS
CALAMITE	CALCITIC	CALFHOODS	CALIPHATE	CALLIOPE
CALAMITES	CALCIUM	CALFLESS	CALIPHS	CALLIOPES
CALAMITY	CALCIUMS	CALFLICK	CALISAYA	CALLIPASH
CALAMUS	CALCRETE	CALFLICKS	CALISAYAS	CALLIPEE
CALAMUSES	CALCRETES	CALFLIKE	CALIVER	CALLIPEES
CALANDO	CALCSPAR	CALFS	CALIVERS	CALLIPER
CALANDRIA	CALCSPARS	CALFSKIN	CALIX	CALLIPERS
CALANTHE	CALCTUFA	CALFSKINS	CALIXES	CALLOP
CALANTHES	CALCTUFAS	CALIATOUR	CALK	CALLOPS
CALASH	CALCTUFF	CALIBER	CALKED	CALLOSE
CALASHES	CALCTUFFS	CALIBERED	CALKER	CALLOSES
CALATHEA	CALCULAR	CALIBERS	CALKERS	CALLOSITY
CALATHEAS	CALCULARY	CALIBRATE	CALKIN	CALLOUS
CALATHI	CALCULATE	CALIBRE	CALKING	CALLOUSED
CALATHOS	CALCULI	CALIBRED	CALKINGS	CALLOUSES
CALATHUS	CALCULOSE	CALIBRES	CALKINS	CALLOUSLY
CALAVANCE	CALCULOUS	CALICES	CALKS	CALLOUT
CALCANEA	CALCULUS	CALICHE	CALL	CALLOUTS
CALCANEAL	CALDARIA	CALICHES	CALLA	CALLOW
CALCANEAN	CALDARIUM	CALICLE	CALLABLE	CALLOWER
CALCANEI	CALDERA	CALICLES	CALLAIDES	CALLOWEST
CALCANEUM	CALDERAS	CALICO	CALLAIS	CALLOWLY
CALCANEUS	CALDRON	CALICOES	CALLALOO	CALLOWS

CALLS	CALOTYPES	CALVERING	CAMASES	CAMELLIA
CALLTIME	CALOYER	CALVERS	CAMASH	CAMELLIAS
CALLTIMES	CALOYERS	CALVES	CAMASHES	CAMELLIKE
CALLUNA	CALP	CALVING	CAMASS	CAMELOID
CALLUNAS	CALPA	CALVITIES	CAMASSES	CAMELOIDS
CALLUS	CALPAC	CALX	CAMBER	CAMELOT
CALLUSED	CALPACK	CALXES	CAMBERED	CAMELOTS
CALLUSES	CALPACKS	CALYCATE	CAMBERING	CAMELRIES
CALLUSING	CALPACS	CALYCEAL	CAMBERS	CAMELRY
CALM	CALPAIN	CALYCES	CAMBIA	CAMELS
CALMANT	CALPAINS	CALYCINAL	CAMBIAL	CAMEO
CALMANTS	CALPAS	CALYCINE	CAMBIFORM	CAMEOED
CALMATIVE	CALPS	CALYCLE	CAMBISM	CAMEOING
CALMED	CALQUE	CALYCLED	CAMBISMS	CAMEOS
CALMER	CALQUED	CALYCLES	CAMBIST	CAMERA
CALMEST	CALQUES	CALYCOID	CAMBISTRY	CAMERAE
CALMIER	CALQUING	CALYCULAR	CAMBISTS	CAMERAL
CALMIEST	CALS	CALYCULE	CAMBIUM	CAMERAMAN
CALMING	CALTHA	CALYCULES	CAMBIUMS	CAMERAMEN
CALMINGLY	CALTHAS	CALYCULI	CAMBOGE	CAMERAS
CALMINGS	CALTHROP	CALYCULUS	CAMBOGES	CAMERATED
CALMLY	CALTHROPS	CALYPSO	CAMBOGIA	CAMES
CALMNESS	CALTRAP	CALYPSOES	CAMBOGIAS	CAMESE
CALMS	CALTRAPS	CALYPSOS	CAMBOOSE	CAMESES
CALMSTANE	CALTROP	CALYPTER	CAMBOOSES	CAMI
CALMSTONE	CALTROPS	CALYPTERA	CAMBREL	CAMION
CALMY	CALUMBA	CALYPTERS	CAMBRELS	CAMIONS
CALO	CALUMBAS	CALYPTRA	CAMBRIC	CAMIS
CALOMEL	CALUMET	CALYPTRAS	CAMBRICS	CAMISA
CALOMELS	CALUMETS	CALYX	CAMCORD	CAMISADE
CALORIC	CALUMNIED	CALYXES	CAMCORDED	CAMISADES
CALORICS	CALUMNIES	CALZONE	CAMCORDER	CAMISADO
CALORIE	CALUMNY	CALZONES	CAMCORDS	CAMISADOS
CALORIES	CALUTRON	CALZONI	CAME	CAMISAS
CALORIFIC	CALUTRONS	CAM	CAMEL	CAMISE
CALORISE	CALVADOS	CAMA	CAMELBACK	CAMISES
CALORISED	CALVARIA	CAMAIEU	CAMELEER	CAMISIA
CALORISES	CALVARIAE	CAMAIEUX	CAMELEERS	CAMISIAS
CALORIST	CALVARIAL	CAMAIL	CAMELEON	CAMISOLE
CALORISTS	CALVARIAN	CAMAILED	CAMELEONS	CAMISOLES
CALORIZE	CALVARIAS	CAMAILS	CAMELHAIR	CAMLET
CALORIZED	CALVARIES	CAMAN	CAMELIA	CAMLETS
CALORIZES	CALVARIUM	CAMANACHD	CAMELIAS	CAMMED
CALORY	CALVARY	CAMANS	CAMELID	CAMMIE
CALOS	CALVE	CAMARILLA	CAMELIDS	CAMMIES
CALOTTE	CALVED	CAMARON	CAMELINE	CAMMING
CALOTTES	CALVER	CAMARONS	CAMELINES	CAMO
CALOTYPE	CALVERED	CAMAS	CAMELISH	CAMOGIE

CAMOGIES	CAMPHONES	CAMSTONES	CANCEL	CANDLING
CAMOMILE	CAMPHOR	CAMUS	CANCELBOT	CANDOCK
CAMOMILES	CAMPHORIC	CAMUSES	CANCELED	CANDOCKS
CAMOODI	CAMPHORS	CAMWHORE	CANCELEER	CANDOR
CAMOODIS	CAMPI	CAMWHORED	CANCELER	CANDORS
CAMORRA	CAMPIER	CAMWHORES	CANCELERS	CANDOUR
CAMORRAS	CAMPIEST	CAMWOOD	CANCELIER	CANDOURS
CAMORRIST	CAMPILY	CAMWOODS	CANCELING	CANDY
CAMOS	CAMPINESS	CAN	CANCELLED	CANDYGRAM
CAMOTE	CAMPING	CANADA	CANCELLER	CANDYING
CAMOTES	CAMPINGS	CANADAS	CANCELLI	CANDYMAN
CAMOUFLET	CAMPION	CANAIGRE	CANCELS	CANDYMEN
CAMP	CAMPIONS	CANAIGRES	CANCER	CANDYTUFT
CAMPAGNA	CAMPLE	CANAILLE	CANCERATE	CANE
CAMPAGNAS	CAMPLED	CANAILLES	CANCERED	CANEBRAKE
CAMPAGNE	CAMPLES	CANAKIN	CANCEROUS	CANED
CAMPAIGN	CAMPLING	CANAKINS	CANCERS	CANEFRUIT
CAMPAIGNS	CAMPLY	CANAL	CANCHA	CANEGRUB
CAMPANA	CAMPNESS	CANALBOAT	CANCHAS	CANEGRUBS
CAMPANAS	CAMPO	CANALED	CANCRINE	CANEH
CAMPANERO	CAMPODEID	CANALING	CANCROID	CANEHS
CAMPANILE	CAMPONG	CANALISE	CANCROIDS	CANELLA
CAMPANILI	CAMPONGS	CANALISED	CANDELA	CANELLAS
CAMPANIST	CAMPOREE	CANALISES	CANDELAS	CANELLINI
CAMPANULA	CAMPOREES	CANALIZE	CANDENT	CANEPHOR
CAMPCRAFT	CAMPOS	CANALIZED	CANDID	CANEPHORA
CAMPEACHY	CAMPOUT	CANALIZES	CANDIDA	CANEPHORE
CAMPEADOR	CAMPOUTS	CANALLED	CANDIDACY	CANEPHORS
CAMPED	CAMPS	CANALLER	CANDIDAL	CANER
CAMPER	CAMPSHIRT	CANALLERS	CANDIDAS	CANERS
CAMPERIES	CAMPSITE	CANALLING	CANDIDATE	CANES
CAMPERS	CAMPSITES	CANALS	CANDIDER	CANESCENT
CAMPERY	CAMPSTOOL	CANAPE	CANDIDEST	CANEWARE
CAMPESINO	CAMPUS	CANAPES	CANDIDLY	CANEWARES
CAMPEST	CAMPUSED	CANARD	CANDIDS	CANFIELD
CAMPFIRE	CAMPUSES	CANARDS	CANDIE	CANFIELDS
CAMPFIRES	CAMPUSING	CANARIED	CANDIED	CANFUL
CAMPHANE	CAMPY	CANARIES	CANDIES	CANFULS
CAMPHANES	CAMS	CANARY	CANDIRU	CANG
CAMPHENE	CAMSHAFT	CANARYING	CANDIRUS	CANGLE
CAMPHENES	CAMSHAFTS	CANASTA	CANDLE	CANGLED
CAMPHINE	CAMSHO	CANASTAS	CANDLED	CANGLES
CAMPHINES	CAMSHOCH	CANASTER	CANDLELIT	CANGLING
CAMPHIRE	CAMSTAIRY	CANASTERS	CANDLENUT	CANGS
CAMPHIRES	CAMSTANE	CANBANK	CANDLEPIN	CANGUE
CAMPHOL	CAMSTANES	CANBANKS	CANDLER	CANGUES
CAMPHOLS	CAMSTEARY	CANCAN	CANDLERS	CANICULAR
CAMPHONE	CAMSTONE	CANCANS	CANDLES	CANID

CANIDS	CANNIER	CANONISER	CANTERED	CANTONISE
CANIER	CANNIEST	CANONISES	CANTERING	CANTONIZE
CANIEST	CANNIKIN	CANONIST	CANTERS	CANTONS
CANIKIN	CANNIKINS	CANONISTS	CANTEST	CANTOR
CANIKINS	CANNILY	CANONIZE	CANTHAL	CANTORIAL
CANINE	CANNINESS	CANONIZED	CANTHARI	CANTORIS
CANINES	CANNING	CANONIZER	CANTHARID	CANTORS
CANING	CANNINGS	CANONIZES	CANTHARIS	CANTOS
CANINGS	CANNISTER	CANONRIES	CANTHARUS	CANTRAIP
CANINITY	CANNOLI	CANONRY	CANTHI	CANTRAIPS
CANISTEL	CANNOLIS	CANONS	CANTHIC	CANTRAP
CANISTELS	CANNON	CANOODLE	CANTHITIS	CANTRAPS
CANISTER	CANNONADE	CANOODLED	CANTHOOK	CANTRED
CANISTERS	CANNONED	CANOODLER	CANTHOOKS	CANTREDS
CANITIES	CANNONEER	CANOODLES	CANTHUS	CANTREF
CANKER	CANNONIER	CANOPIC	CANTIC	CANTREFS
CANKERED	CANNONING	CANOPIED	CANTICLE	CANTRIP
CANKERIER	CANNONRY	CANOPIES	CANTICLES	CANTRIPS
CANKERING	CANNONS	CANOPY	CANTICO	CANTS
CANKEROUS	CANNOT	CANOPYING	CANTICOED	CANTUS
CANKERS	CANNS	CANOROUS	CANTICOS	CANTUSES
CANKERY	CANNULA	CANS	CANTICOY	CANTY
CANKLE	CANNULAE	CANSFUL	CANTICOYS	CANULA
CANKLES	CANNULAR	CANSO	CANTICUM	CANULAE
CANN	CANNULAS	CANSOS	CANTICUMS	CANULAR
CANNA	CANNULATE	CANST	CANTIER	CANULAS
CANNABIC	CANNY	CANSTICK	CANTIEST	CANULATE
CANNABIN	CANOE	CANSTICKS	CANTILENA	CANULATED
CANNABINS	CANOEABLE	CANT	CANTILY	CANULATES
CANNABIS	CANOED	CANTABANK	CANTINA	CANVAS
CANNACH	CANOEING	CANTABILE	CANTINAS	CANVASED
CANNACHS	CANOEINGS	CANTAL	CANTINESS	CANVASER
CANNAE	CANOEIST	CANTALA	CANTING	CANVASERS
CANNAS	CANOEISTS	CANTALAS	CANTINGLY	CANVASES
CANNED	CANOEMAN	CANTALOUP	CANTINGS	CANVASING
CANNEL	CANOEMEN	CANTALS	CANTION	CANVASS
CANNELON	CANOER	CANTAR	CANTIONS	CANVASSED
CANNELONI	CANOERS	CANTARS	CANTLE	CANVASSER
CANNELONS	CANOES	CANTATA	CANTLED	CANVASSES
CANNELS	CANOEWOOD	CANTATAS	CANTLES	CANY
CANNELURE	CANOLA	CANTATE	CANTLET	CANYON
CANNER	CANOLAS	CANTATES	CANTLETS	CANYONEER
CANNERIES	CANON	CANTDOG	CANTLING	CANYONING
CANNERS	CANONESS	CANTDOGS	CANTO	CANYONS
CANNERY	CANONIC	CANTED	CANTON	CANZONA
CANNIBAL	CANONICAL	CANTEEN	CANTONAL	CANZONAS
CANNIBALS	CANONISE	CANTEENS	CANTONED	CANZONE
CANNIE	CANONISED	CANTER	CANTONING	CANZONES

CANZONET	CAPHS	CAPONATA	CAPRIFY	CAPTAINS
CANZONETS	CAPI	CAPONATAS	CAPRINE	CAPTAN
CANZONI	CAPIAS	CAPONIER	CAPRIOLE	CAPTANS
CAP	CAPIASES	CAPONIERE	CAPRIOLED	CAPTCHA
CAPA	CAPICHE	CAPONIERS	CAPRIOLES	CAPTCHAS
CAPABLE	CAPICOLLA	CAPONISE	CAPRIS	CAPTION
CAPABLER	CAPICOLLO	CAPONISED	CAPROATE	CAPTIONED
CAPABLEST	CAPILLARY	CAPONISES	CAPROATES	CAPTIONS
CAPABLY	CAPING	CAPONIZE	CAPROCK	CAPTIOUS
CAPACIOUS	CAPISCE	CAPONIZED	CAPROCKS	CAPTIVATE
CAPACITOR	CAPISH	CAPONIZES	CAPROIC	CAPTIVE
CAPACITY	CAPITA	CAPONS	CAPRYLATE	CAPTIVED
CAPARISON	CAPITAL	CAPORAL	CAPRYLIC	CAPTIVES
CAPAS	CAPITALLY	CAPORALS	CAPS	CAPTIVING
CAPCOM	CAPITALS	CAPOS	CAPSAICIN	CAPTIVITY
CAPCOMS	CAPITAN	CAPOT	CAPSICIN	CAPTOPRIL
CAPE	CAPITANI	CAPOTASTO	CAPSICINS	CAPTOR
CAPED	CAPITANO	CAPOTE	CAPSICUM	CAPTORS
CAPEESH	CAPITANOS	CAPOTES	CAPSICUMS	CAPTURE
CAPELAN	CAPITANS	CAPOTS	CAPSID	CAPTURED
CAPELANS	CAPITATE	CAPOTTED	CAPSIDAL	CAPTURER
CAPELET	CAPITATED	CAPOTTING	CAPSIDS	CAPTURERS
CAPELETS	CAPITATES	CAPOUCH	CAPSIZAL	CAPTURES
CAPELIKE	CAPITAYN	CAPOUCHES	CAPSIZALS	CAPTURING
CAPELIN	CAPITAYNS	CAPPED	CAPSIZE	CAPUCCIO
CAPELINE	CAPITELLA	CAPPER	CAPSIZED	CAPUCCIOS
CAPELINES	CAPITOL	CAPPERS	CAPSIZES	CAPUCHE
CAPELINS	CAPITOLS	CAPPING	CAPSIZING	CAPUCHED
CAPELLET	CAPITULA	CAPPINGS	CAPSOMER	CAPUCHES
CAPELLETS	CAPITULAR	CAPRATE	CAPSOMERE	CAPUCHIN
CAPELLINE	CAPITULUM	CAPRATES	CAPSOMERS	CAPUCHINS
CAPELLINI	CAPIZ	CAPRESE	CAPSTAN	CAPUERA
CAPER	CAPIZES	CAPRESES	CAPSTANS	CAPUERAS
CAPERED	CAPLE	CAPRI	CAPSTONE	CAPUL
CAPERER	CAPLES	CAPRIC	CAPSTONES	CAPULS
CAPERERS	CAPLESS	CAPRICCI	CAPSULAR	CAPUT
CAPERING	CAPLET	CAPRICCIO	CAPSULARY	CAPYBARA
CAPERS	CAPLETS	CAPRICE	CAPSULATE	CAPYBARAS
CAPES	CAPLIKE	CAPRICES	CAPSULE	CAR
CAPESKIN	CAPLIN	CAPRID	CAPSULED	CARABAO
CAPESKINS	CAPLINS	CAPRIDS	CAPSULES	CARABAOS
CAPEWORK	CAPMAKER	CAPRIFIED	CAPSULING	CARABID
CAPEWORKS	CAPMAKERS	CAPRIFIES	CAPSULISE	CARABIDS
CAPEX	CAPO	CAPRIFIG	CAPSULIZE	CARABIN
CAPEXES	CAPOCCHIA	CAPRIFIGS	CAPTAIN	CARABINE
CAPFUL	CAPOEIRA	CAPRIFOIL	CAPTAINCY	CARABINER
CAPFULS	CAPOEIRAS	CAPRIFOLE	CAPTAINED	CARABINES
CAPH	CAPON	CAPRIFORM	CAPTAINRY	CARABINS

CARACAL	CARAVANCE	CARBONIC	CARDAMONS	CARE
CARACALS	CARAVANED	CARBONISE	CARDAMUM	CARED
CARACARA	CARAVANER	CARBONIUM	CARDAMUMS	CAREEN
CARACARAS	CARAVANS	CARBONIZE	CARDAN	CAREENAGE
CARACK	CARAVEL	CARBONOUS	CARDBOARD	CAREENED
CARACKS	CARAVELLE	CARBONS	CARDCASE	CAREENER
CARACOL	CARAVELS	CARBONYL	CARDCASES	CAREENERS
CARACOLE	CARAWAY	CARBONYLS	CARDECU	CAREENING
CARACOLED	CARAWAYS	CARBORA	CARDECUE	CAREENS
CARACOLER	CARB	CARBORAS	CARDECUES	CAREER
CARACOLES	CARBACHOL	CARBORNE	CARDECUS	CAREERED
CARACOLS	CARBAMATE	CARBOS	CARDED	CAREERER
CARACT	CARBAMIC	CARBOXYL	CARDER	CAREERERS
CARACTS	CARBAMIDE	CARBOXYLS	CARDERS	CAREERING
CARACUL	CARBAMINO	CARBOY	CARDI	CAREERISM
CARACULS	CARBAMOYL	CARBOYED	CARDIA	CAREERIST
CARAFE	CARBAMYL	CARBOYS	CARDIAC	CAREERS
CARAFES	CARBAMYLS	CARBS	CARDIACAL	CAREFREE
CARAGANA	CARBANION	CARBUNCLE	CARDIACS	CAREFUL
CARAGANAS	CARBARN	CARBURATE	CARDIAE	CAREFULLY
CARAGEEN	CARBARNS	CARBURET	CARDIALGY	CAREGIVER
CARAGEENS	CARBARYL	CARBURETS	CARDIAS	CARELESS
CARAMBA	CARBARYLS	CARBURISE	CARDIE	CARELINE
CARAMBOLA	CARBAZOLE	CARBURIZE	CARDIES	CARELINES
CARAMBOLE	CARBEEN	CARBY	CARDIGAN	CAREME
CARAMEL	CARBEENS	CARCAJOU	CARDIGANS	CAREMES
CARAMELS	CARBENE	CARCAJOUS	CARDINAL	CARER
CARANGID	CARBENES	CARCAKE	CARDINALS	CARERS
CARANGIDS	CARBIDE	CARCAKES	CARDING	CARES
CARANGOID	CARBIDES	CARCANET	CARDINGS	CARESS
CARANNA	CARBIDOPA	CARCANETS	CARDIO	CARESSED
CARANNAS	CARBIES	CARCASE	CARDIOID	CARESSER
CARAP	CARBINE	CARCASED	CARDIOIDS	CARESSERS
CARAPACE	CARBINEER	CARCASES	CARDIOS	CARESSES
CARAPACED	CARBINES	CARCASING	CARDIS	CARESSING
CARAPACES	CARBINIER	CARCASS	CARDITIC	CARESSIVE
CARAPAX	CARBINOL	CARCASSED	CARDITIS	CARET
CARAPAXES	CARBINOLS	CARCASSES	CARDON	CARETAKE
CARAPS	CARBO	CARCEL	CARDONS	CARETAKEN
CARASSOW	CARBOLIC	CARCELS	CARDOON	CARETAKER
CARASSOWS	CARBOLICS	CARCERAL	CARDOONS	CARETAKES
CARAT	CARBOLISE	CARCINOID	CARDPHONE	CARETOOK
CARATE	CARBOLIZE	CARCINOMA	CARDPUNCH	CARETS
CARATES	CARBON	CARD	CARDS	CAREWARE
CARATS	CARBONADE	CARDAMINE	CARDSHARP	CAREWARES
CARAUNA	CARBONADO	CARDAMOM	CARDUUS	CAREWORN
CARAUNAS	CARBONARA	CARDAMOMS	CARDUUSES	CAREX
CARAVAN	CARBONATE	CARDAMON	CARDY	CARFARE

CARFARES
CARFAX
CARFOX
CARFOXES
CARFUFFLE
CARFUL
CARFULS
CARGEESE
CARGO
CARGOED
CARGOES
CARGOING
CARGOOSE
CARGOS
CARHOP
CARHOPPED
CARHOPS
CARIACOU
CARIACOUS
CARIAMA
CARIAMAS
CARIBE
CARIBES
CARIBOO
CARIBOOS
CARIBOU
CARIBOUS
CARICES
CARIED
CARIERE
CARIERES
CARIES
CARILLON
CARILLONS
CARINA
CARINAE
CARINAL
CARINAS
CARINATE
CARINATED
CARING
CARINGLY
CARINGS
CARIOCA
CARIOCAS
CARIOLE
CARIOLES

CARIOSE
CARIOSITY
CARIOUS
CARITAS
CARITASES
CARITATES
CARJACK
CARJACKED
CARJACKER
CARJACKS
CARJACOU
CARJACOUS
CARK
CARKED
CARKING
CARKS
CARL
CARLE
CARLES
CARLESS
CARLIN
CARLINE
CARLINES
CARLING
CARLINGS
CARLINS
CARLISH
CARLOAD
CARLOADS
CARLOCK
CARLOCKS
CARLOT
CARLOTS
CARLS
CARMAKER
CARMAKERS
CARMAN
CARMELITE
CARMEN
CARMINE
CARMINES
CARN
CARNAGE
CARNAGES
CARNAHUBA
CARNAL
CARNALISE
CARNALISM

CARNALIST
CARNALITY
CARNALIZE
CARNALLED
CARNALLY
CARNALS
CARNAROLI
CARNATION
CARNAUBA
CARNAUBAS
CARNELIAN
CARNEOUS
CARNET
CARNETS
CARNEY
CARNEYED
CARNEYING
CARNEYS
CARNIE
CARNIED
CARNIER
CARNIES
CARNIEST
CARNIFEX
CARNIFIED
CARNIFIES
CARNIFY
CARNITINE
CARNIVAL
CARNIVALS
CARNIVORA
CARNIVORE
CARNIVORY
CARNOSAUR
CARNOSE
CARNOSITY
CARNOTITE
CARNS
CARNY
CARNYING
CARNYX
CARNYXES
CAROACH
CAROACHES
CAROB
CAROBS
CAROCH
CAROCHE

CAROCHES
CAROL
CAROLED
CAROLER
CAROLERS
CAROLI
CAROLING
CAROLINGS
CAROLLED
CAROLLER
CAROLLERS
CAROLLING
CAROLS
CAROLUS
CAROLUSES
CAROM
CAROMED
CAROMEL
CAROMELS
CAROMING
CAROMS
CARON
CARONS
CAROTENE
CAROTENES
CAROTID
CAROTIDAL
CAROTIDS
CAROTIN
CAROTINS
CAROUSAL
CAROUSALS
CAROUSE
CAROUSED
CAROUSEL
CAROUSELS
CAROUSER
CAROUSERS
CAROUSES
CAROUSING
CARP
CARPACCIO
CARPAL
CARPALE
CARPALES
CARPALIA
CARPALS
CARPED

CARPEL
CARPELS
CARPENTER
CARPENTRY
CARPER
CARPERS
CARPET
CARPETBAG
CARPETED
CARPETING
CARPETS
CARPHONE
CARPHONES
CARPI
CARPING
CARPINGLY
CARPINGS
CARPLIKE
CARPOLOGY
CARPOOL
CARPOOLED
CARPOOLER
CARPOOLS
CARPORT
CARPORTS
CARPS
CARPUS
CARR
CARRACK
CARRACKS
CARRACT
CARRACTS
CARRAGEEN
CARRAT
CARRATS
CARRAWAY
CARRAWAYS
CARRECT
CARRECTS
CARREFOUR
CARREL
CARRELL
CARRELLS
CARRELS
CARRIAGE
CARRIAGES
CARRICK
CARRIED

CARRIER
CARRIERS
CARRIES
CARRIOLE
CARRIOLES
CARRION
CARRIONS
CARRITCH
CARROCH
CARROCHES
CARROM
CARROMED
CARROMING
CARROMS
CARRON
CARRONADE
CARROT
CARROTIER
CARROTIN
CARROTINS
CARROTS
CARROTTOP
CARROTY
CARROUSEL
CARRS
CARRY
CARRYALL
CARRYALLS
CARRYBACK
CARRYCOT
CARRYCOTS
CARRYING
CARRYON
CARRYONS
CARRYOUT
CARRYOUTS
CARRYOVER
CARRYTALE
CARS
CARSE
CARSES
CARSEY
CARSEYS
CARSHARE
CARSHARED
CARSHARES
CARSICK
CARSPIEL

CARSPIELS
CART
CARTA
CARTABLE
CARTAGE
CARTAGES
CARTAS
CARTE
CARTED
CARTEL
CARTELISE
CARTELISM
CARTELIST
CARTELIZE
CARTELS
CARTER
CARTERS
CARTES
CARTFUL
CARTFULS
CARTHORSE
CARTILAGE
CARTING
CARTLOAD
CARTLOADS
CARTOGRAM
CARTOLOGY
CARTON
CARTONAGE
CARTONED
CARTONING
CARTONS
CARTOON
CARTOONED
CARTOONS
CARTOONY
CARTOP
CARTOPPER
CARTOUCH
CARTOUCHE
CARTRIDGE
CARTROAD
CARTROADS
CARTS
CARTULARY
CARTWAY
CARTWAYS
CARTWHEEL

CARUCAGE
CARUCAGES
CARUCATE
CARUCATES
CARUNCLE
CARUNCLES
CARVACROL
CARVE
CARVED
CARVEL
CARVELS
CARVEN
CARVER
CARVERIES
CARVERS
CARVERY
CARVES
CARVIES
CARVING
CARVINGS
CARVY
CARWASH
CARWASHES
CARYATIC
CARYATID
CARYATIDS
CARYOPSES
CARYOPSIS
CARYOTIN
CARYOTINS
CASA
CASABA
CASABAS
CASAS
CASAVA
CASAVAS
CASBAH
CASBAHS
CASCABEL
CASCABELS
CASCABLE
CASCABLES
CASCADE
CASCADED
CASCADES
CASCADING
CASCADURA
CASCARA

CASCARAS
CASCHROM
CASCHROMS
CASCO
CASCOS
CASE
CASEASE
CASEASES
CASEATE
CASEATED
CASEATES
CASEATING
CASEATION
CASEBOOK
CASEBOOKS
CASEBOUND
CASED
CASEFIED
CASEFIES
CASEFY
CASEFYING
CASEIC
CASEIN
CASEINATE
CASEINS
CASELAW
CASELAWS
CASELOAD
CASELOADS
CASEMAKER
CASEMAN
CASEMATE
CASEMATED
CASEMATES
CASEMEN
CASEMENT
CASEMENTS
CASEMIX
CASEMIXES
CASEOSE
CASEOSES
CASEOUS
CASERN
CASERNE
CASERNES
CASERNS
CASES
CASETTE

CASETTES
CASEVAC
CASEVACED
CASEVACS
CASEWORK
CASEWORKS
CASEWORM
CASEWORMS
CASH
CASHABLE
CASHAW
CASHAWS
CASHBACK
CASHBACKS
CASHBOOK
CASHBOOKS
CASHBOX
CASHBOXES
CASHED
CASHES
CASHEW
CASHEWS
CASHIER
CASHIERED
CASHIERER
CASHIERS
CASHING
CASHLESS
CASHMERE
CASHMERES
CASHOO
CASHOOS
CASHPOINT
CASHSPIEL
CASIMERE
CASIMERES
CASIMIRE
CASIMIRES
CASING
CASINGS
CASINI
CASINO
CASINOS
CASITA
CASITAS
CASK
CASKED
CASKET

CASKETED	CASSONADE	CASTRATO	CATALYSED	CATCALLED
CASKETING	CASSONE	CASTRATOR	CATALYSER	CATCALLER
CASKETS	CASSONES	CASTRATOS	CATALYSES	CATCALLS
CASKIER	CASSOULET	CASTS	CATALYSIS	CATCH
CASKIEST	CASSOWARY	CASUAL	CATALYST	CATCHABLE
CASKING	CASSPIR	CASUALISE	CATALYSTS	CATCHALL
CASKS	CASSPIRS	CASUALISM	CATALYTIC	CATCHALLS
CASKSTAND	CAST	CASUALIZE	CATALYZE	CATCHCRY
CASKY	CASTABLE	CASUALLY	CATALYZED	CATCHED
CASPASE	CASTANET	CASUALS	CATALYZER	CATCHEN
CASPASES	CASTANETS	CASUALTY	CATALYZES	CATCHER
CASQUE	CASTAWAY	CASUARINA	CATAMARAN	CATCHERS
CASQUED	CASTAWAYS	CASUIST	CATAMENIA	CATCHES
CASQUES	CASTE	CASUISTIC	CATAMITE	CATCHFLY
CASSABA	CASTED	CASUISTRY	CATAMITES	CATCHIER
CASSABAS	CASTEISM	CASUISTS	CATAMOUNT	CATCHIEST
CASSAREEP	CASTEISMS	CASUS	CATAPAN	CATCHILY
CASSATA	CASTELESS	CAT	CATAPANS	CATCHING
CASSATAS	CASTELLA	CATABASES	CATAPHOR	CATCHINGS
CASSATION	CASTELLAN	CATABASIS	CATAPHORA	CATCHLINE
CASSAVA	CASTELLUM	CATABATIC	CATAPHORS	CATCHMENT
CASSAVAS	CASTER	CATABOLIC	CATAPHYLL	CATCHPOLE
CASSENA	CASTERED	CATACLASM	CATAPLASM	CATCHPOLL
CASSENAS	CASTERS	CATACLYSM	CATAPLEXY	CATCHT
CASSENE	CASTES	CATACOMB	CATAPULT	CATCHUP
CASSENES	CASTIGATE	CATACOMBS	CATAPULTS	CATCHUPS
CASSEROLE	CASTING	CATAFALCO	CATARACT	CATCHWEED
CASSETTE	CASTINGS	CATAGEN	CATARACTS	CATCHWORD
CASSETTES	CASTLE	CATAGENS	CATARHINE	CATCHY
CASSIA	CASTLED	CATALASE	CATARRH	CATCLAW
CASSIAS	CASTLES	CATALASES	CATARRHAL	CATCLAWS
CASSIE	CASTLING	CATALATIC	CATARRHS	CATCON
CASSIES	CASTLINGS	CATALEPSY	CATASTA	CATCONS
CASSIMERE	CASTOCK	CATALEXES	CATASTAS	CATE
CASSINA	CASTOCKS	CATALEXIS	CATATONIA	CATECHIN
CASSINAS	CASTOFF	CATALO	CATATONIC	CATECHINS
CASSINE	CASTOFFS	CATALOES	CATATONY	CATECHISE
CASSINES	CASTOR	CATALOG	CATAWBA	CATECHISM
CASSINGLE	CASTOREUM	CATALOGED	CATAWBAS	CATECHIST
CASSINO	CASTORIES	CATALOGER	CATBIRD	CATECHIZE
CASSINOS	CASTORS	CATALOGIC	CATBIRDS	CATECHOL
CASSIOPE	CASTORY	CATALOGNE	CATBOAT	CATECHOLS
CASSIOPES	CASTRAL	CATALOGS	CATBOATS	CATECHU
CASSIS	CASTRATE	CATALOGUE	CATBRIAR	CATECHUS
CASSISES	CASTRATED	CATALOS	CATBRIARS	CATEGORIC
CASSOCK	CASTRATER	CATALPA	CATBRIER	CATEGORY
CASSOCKED	CASTRATES	CATALPAS	CATBRIERS	CATELOG
CASSOCKS	CASTRATI	CATALYSE	CATCALL	CATELOGS

CATENA	CATHECTIC	CATNAPPED	CATWORM	CAULICULI
CATENAE	CATHECTS	CATNAPPER	CATWORMS	CAULIFORM
CATENANE	CATHEDRA	CATNAPS	CAUCHEMAR	CAULINARY
CATENANES	CATHEDRAE	CATNEP	CAUCUS	CAULINE
CATENARY	CATHEDRAL	CATNEPS	CAUCUSED	CAULIS
CATENAS	CATHEDRAS	CATNIP	CAUCUSES	CAULK
CATENATE	CATHEPSIN	CATNIPS	CAUCUSING	CAULKED
CATENATED	CATHEPTIC	CATOLYTE	CAUCUSSED	CAULKER
CATENATES	CATHETER	CATOLYTES	CAUCUSSES	CAULKERS
CATENOID	CATHETERS	CATOPTRIC	CAUDA	CAULKING
CATENOIDS	CATHETUS	CATRIGGED	CAUDAD	CAULKINGS
CATER	CATHEXES	CATS	CAUDAE	CAULKS
CATERAN	CATHEXIS	CATSKIN	CAUDAL	CAULOME
CATERANS	CATHINONE	CATSKINS	CAUDALLY	CAULOMES
CATERED	CATHISMA	CATSPAW	CAUDATE	CAULS
CATERER	CATHISMAS	CATSPAWS	CAUDATED	CAUM
CATERERS	CATHODAL	CATSUIT	CAUDATES	CAUMED
CATERESS	CATHODE	CATSUITS	CAUDATION	CAUMING
CATERING	CATHODES	CATSUP	CAUDEX	CAUMS
CATERINGS	CATHODIC	CATSUPS	CAUDEXES	CAUMSTANE
CATERS	CATHOLE	CATTABU	CAUDICES	CAUMSTONE
CATERWAUL	CATHOLES	CATTABUS	CAUDICLE	CAUP
CATES	CATHOLIC	CATTAIL	CAUDICLES	CAUPS
CATFACE	CATHOLICS	CATTAILS	CAUDILLO	CAURI
CATFACES	CATHOLYTE	CATTALO	CAUDILLOS	CAURIS
CATFACING	CATHOOD	CATTALOES	CAUDLE	CAUSA
CATFALL	CATHOODS	CATTALOS	CAUDLED	CAUSABLE
CATFALLS	CATHOUSE	CATTED	CAUDLES	CAUSAE
CATFIGHT	CATHOUSES	CATTERIES	CAUDLING	CAUSAL
CATFIGHTS	CATION	CATTERY	CAUDRON	CAUSALGIA
CATFISH	CATIONIC	CATTIE	CAUDRONS	CAUSALGIC
CATFISHED	CATIONS	CATTIER	CAUF	CAUSALITY
CATFISHES	CATJANG	CATTIES	CAUGHT	CAUSALLY
CATFLAP	CATJANGS	CATTIEST	CAUK	CAUSALS
CATFLAPS	CATKIN	CATTILY	CAUKER	CAUSATION
CATFOOD	CATKINATE	CATTINESS	CAUKERS	CAUSATIVE
CATFOODS	CATKINS	CATTING	CAUKS	CAUSE
CATGUT	CATLIKE	CATTISH	CAUL	CAUSED
CATGUTS	CATLIN	CATTISHLY	CAULD	CAUSELESS
CATHARISE	CATLING	CATTLE	CAULDER	CAUSEN
CATHARIZE	CATLINGS	CATTLEMAN	CAULDEST	CAUSER
CATHARSES	CATLINITE	CATTLEMEN	CAULDRIFE	CAUSERIE
CATHARSIS	CATLINS	CATTLEYA	CAULDRON	CAUSERIES
CATHARTIC	CATMINT	CATTLEYAS	CAULDRONS	CAUSERS
CATHEAD	CATMINTS	CATTY	CAULDS	CAUSES
CATHEADS	CATNAP	CATWALK	CAULES	CAUSEWAY
CATHECT	CATNAPER	CATWALKS	CAULICLE	CAUSEWAYS
CATHECTED	CATNAPERS	CATWORKS	CAULICLES	CAUSEY

CAUSEYED	CAVEATORS	CAVING	CEASINGS	CEES
CAUSEYS	CAVEATS	CAVINGS	CEAZE	CEIBA
CAUSING	CAVED	CAVITARY	CEAZED	CEIBAS
CAUSTIC	CAVEFISH	CAVITATE	CEAZES	CEIL
CAUSTICAL	CAVEL	CAVITATED	CEAZING	CEILED
CAUSTICS	CAVELIKE	CAVITATES	CEBADILLA	CEILER
CAUTEL	CAVELS	CAVITIED	CEBID	CEILERS
CAUTELOUS	CAVEMAN	CAVITIES	CEBIDS	CEILI
CAUTELS	CAVEMEN	CAVITY	CEBOID	CEILIDH
CAUTER	CAVENDISH	CAVORT	CEBOIDS	CEILIDHS
CAUTERANT	CAVEOLA	CAVORTED	CECA	CEILING
CAUTERIES	CAVEOLAE	CAVORTER	CECAL	CEILINGED
CAUTERISE	CAVEOLAR	CAVORTERS	CECALLY	CEILINGS
CAUTERISM	CAVER	CAVORTING	CECILS	CEILIS
CAUTERIZE	CAVERN	CAVORTS	CECITIES	CEILS
CAUTERS	CAVERNED	CAVY	CECITIS	CEINTURE
CAUTERY	CAVERNING	CAW	CECITISES	CEINTURES
CAUTION	CAVERNOUS	CAWED	CECITY	CEL
CAUTIONED	CAVERNS	CAWING	CECROPIA	CELADON
CAUTIONER	CAVERS	CAWINGS	CECROPIAS	CELADONS
CAUTIONRY	CAVES	CAWK	CECROPIN	CELANDINE
CAUTIONS	CAVESSON	CAWKER	CECROPINS	CELEB
CAUTIOUS	CAVESSONS	CAWKERS	CECUM	CELEBRANT
CAUVES	CAVETTI	CAWKS	CEDAR	CELEBRATE
CAVA	CAVETTO	CAWS	CEDARBIRD	CELEBRITY
CAVALCADE	CAVETTOS	CAXON	CEDARED	CELEBS
CAVALERO	CAVIAR	CAXONS	CEDARIER	CELECOXIB
CAVALEROS	CAVIARE	CAY	CEDARIEST	CELERIAC
CAVALETTI	CAVIARES	CAYENNE	CEDARN	CELERIACS
CAVALIER	CAVIARIE	CAYENNED	CEDARS	CELERIES
CAVALIERS	CAVIARIES	CAYENNES	CEDARWOOD	CELERITY
CAVALLA	CAVIARS	CAYMAN	CEDARY	CELERY
CAVALLAS	CAVICORN	CAYMANS	CEDE	CELESTA
CAVALLIES	CAVICORNS	CAYS	CEDED	CELESTAS
CAVALLY	CAVIE	CAYUSE	CEDER	CELESTE
CAVALRIES	CAVIER	CAYUSES	CEDERS	CELESTES
CAVALRY	CAVIERS	CAZ	CEDES	CELESTIAL
CAVAS	CAVIES	CAZH	CEDI	CELESTINE
CAVASS	CAVIL	CAZIQUE	CEDILLA	CELESTITE
CAVASSES	CAVILED	CAZIQUES	CEDILLAS	CELIAC
CAVATINA	CAVILER	CEANOTHUS	CEDING	CELIACS
CAVATINAS	CAVILERS	CEAS	CEDIS	CELIBACY
CAVATINE	CAVILING	CEASE	CEDRATE	CELIBATE
CAVE	CAVILLED	CEASED	CEDRATES	CELIBATES
CAVEAT	CAVILLER	CEASEFIRE	CEDRINE	CELIBATIC
CAVEATED	CAVILLERS	CEASELESS	CEDULA	CELL
CAVEATING	CAVILLING	CEASES	CEDULAS	CELLA
CAVEATOR	CAVILS	CEASING	CEE	CELLAE

CELLAR	CELSITUDE	CENSURED	CENTNER	CENTURIAL
CELLARAGE	CELT	CENSURER	CENTNERS	CENTURIES
CELLARED	CELTS	CENSURERS	CENTO	CENTURION
CELLARER	CEMBALI	CENSURES	CENTOIST	CENTURY
CELLARERS	CEMBALIST	CENSURING	CENTOISTS	CEORL
CELLARET	CEMBALO	CENSUS	CENTONATE	CEORLISH
CELLARETS	CEMBALOS	CENSUSED	CENTONEL	CEORLS
CELLARING	CEMBRA	CENSUSES	CENTONELL	CEP
CELLARIST	CEMBRAS	CENSUSING	CENTONELLS	CEPACEOUS
CELLARMAN	CEMENT	CENT	CENTONES	CEPAGE
CELLARMEN	CEMENTA	CENTAGE	CENTONIST	CEPAGES
CELLAROUS	CEMENTED	CENTAGES	CENTOS	CEPE
CELLARS	CEMENTER	CENTAI	CENTRA	CEPES
CELLARWAY	CEMENTERS	CENTAL	CENTRAL	CEPHALAD
CELLBLOCK	CEMENTING	CENTALS	CENTRALER	CEPHALATE
CELLED	CEMENTITE	CENTARE	CENTRALLY	CEPHALIC
CELLI	CEMENTS	CENTARES	CENTRALS	CEPHALICS
CELLING	CEMENTUM	CENTAS	CENTRE	CEPHALIN
CELLINGS	CEMENTUMS	CENTAUR	CENTRED	CEPHALINS
CELLIST	CEMETERY	CENTAUREA	CENTREING	CEPHALOUS
CELLISTS	CEMITARE	CENTAURIC	CENTREMAN	CEPHEID
CELLMATE	CEMITARES	CENTAURS	CENTREMEN	CEPHEIDS
CELLMATES	CENACLE	CENTAURY	CENTRES	CEPS
CELLO	CENACLES	CENTAVO	CENTRIC	CERACEOUS
CELLOIDIN	CENDRE	CENTAVOS	CENTRICAL	CERAMAL
CELLOS	CENOBITE	CENTENARY	CENTRIES	CERAMALS
CELLOSE	CENOBITES	CENTENIER	CENTRING	CERAMIC
CELLOSES	CENOBITIC	CENTER	CENTRINGS	CERAMICS
CELLPHONE	CENOTAPH	CENTERED	CENTRIOLE	CERAMIDE
CELLS	CENOTAPHS	CENTERING	CENTRISM	CERAMIDES
CELLULAR	CENOTE	CENTERS	CENTRISMS	CERAMIST
CELLULARS	CENOTES	CENTESES	CENTRIST	CERAMISTS
CELLULASE	CENOZOIC	CENTESIMI	CENTRISTS	CERASIN
CELLULE	CENS	CENTESIMO	CENTRODE	CERASINS
CELLULES	CENSE	CENTESIS	CENTRODES	CERASTES
CELLULITE	CENSED	CENTIARE	CENTROID	CERASTIUM
CELLULOID	CENSER	CENTIARES	CENTROIDS	CERATE
CELLULOSE	CENSERS	CENTIGRAM	CENTRUM	CERATED
CELLULOUS	CENSES	CENTILE	CENTRUMS	CERATES
CELOM	CENSING	CENTILES	CENTRY	CERATIN
CELOMATA	CENSOR	CENTIME	CENTS	CERATINS
CELOMIC	CENSORED	CENTIMES	CENTU	CERATITIS
CELOMS	CENSORIAL	CENTIMO	CENTUM	CERATODUS
CELOSIA	CENSORIAN	CENTIMOS	CENTUMS	CERATOID
CELOSIAS	CENSORING	CENTINEL	CENTUMVIR	CERBEREAN
CELOTEX	CENSORS	CENTINELL	CENTUPLE	CERBERIAN
CELOTEXES	CENSUAL	CENTINELS	CENTUPLED	CERCAL
CELS	CENSURE	CENTIPEDE	CENTUPLES	CERCARIA

CERCARIAE	CERITE	CERUMEN	CESTODES	CHABUKS
CERCARIAL	CERITES	CERUMENS	CESTOI	CHACE
CERCARIAN	CERIUM	CERUSE	CESTOID	CHACED
CERCARIAS	CERIUMS	CERUSES	CESTOIDS	CHACES
CERCI	CERMET	CERUSITE	CESTOS	CHACHKA
CERCIS	CERMETS	CERUSITES	CESTOSES	CHACHKAS
CERCISES	CERNE	CERUSSITE	CESTUI	CHACING
CERCLAGE	CERNED	CERVELAS	CESTUIS	CHACK
CERCLAGES	CERNES	CERVELAT	CESTUS	CHACKED
CERCOPID	CERNING	CERVELATS	CESTUSES	CHACKING
CERCOPIDS	CERNUOUS	CERVEZA	CESURA	CHACKS
CERCUS	CERO	CERVEZAS	CESURAE	CHACMA
CERE	CEROC	CERVICAL	CESURAL	CHACMAS
CEREAL	CEROCS	CERVICES	CESURAS	CHACO
CEREALIST	CEROGRAPH	CERVICUM	CESURE	CHACOES
CEREALS	CEROMANCY	CERVICUMS	CESURES	CHACONINE
CEREBELLA	CEROON	CERVID	CETACEAN	CHACONNE
CEREBRA	CEROONS	CERVIDS	CETACEANS	CHACONNES
CEREBRAL	CEROS	CERVINE	CETACEOUS	CHACOS
CEREBRALS	CEROTIC	CERVIX	CETANE	CHAD
CEREBRATE	CEROTYPE	CERVIXES	CETANES	CHADAR
CEREBRIC	CEROTYPES	CESAREAN	CETE	CHADARIM
CEREBROID	CEROUS	CESAREANS	CETERACH	CHADARS
CEREBRUM	CERRADO	CESAREVNA	CETERACHS	CHADDAR
CEREBRUMS	CERRADOS	CESARIAN	CETES	CHADDARS
CERECLOTH	CERRIAL	CESARIANS	CETOLOGY	CHADDOR
CERED	CERRIS	CESIOUS	CETRIMIDE	CHADDORS
CEREMENT	CERRISES	CESIUM	CETUXIMAB	CHADLESS
CEREMENTS	CERT	CESIUMS	CETYL	CHADO
CEREMONY	CERTAIN	CESPITOSE	CETYLS	CHADOR
CEREOUS	CERTAINER	CESS	CETYWALL	CHADORS
CERES	CERTAINLY	CESSATION	CETYWALLS	CHADOS
CERESIN	CERTAINTY	CESSE	CEVADILLA	CHADRI
CERESINE	CERTES	CESSED	CEVAPCICI	CHADS
CERESINES	CERTIE	CESSER	CEVICHE	CHAEBOL
CERESINS	CERTIFIED	CESSERS	CEVICHES	CHAEBOLS
CEREUS	CERTIFIER	CESSES	CEVITAMIC	CHAETA
CEREUSES	CERTIFIES	CESSING	CEYLANITE	CHAETAE
CERGE	CERTIFY	CESSION	CEYLONITE	CHAETAL
CERGES	CERTITUDE	CESSIONS	CEZVE	CHAETODON
CERIA	CERTS	CESSPIT	CEZVES	CHAETOPOD
CERIAS	CERTY	CESSPITS	CH	CHAFE
CERIC	CERULE	CESSPOOL	CHA	CHAFED
CERING	CERULEAN	CESSPOOLS	CHABAZITE	CHAFER
CERIPH	CERULEANS	CESTA	CHABLIS	CHAFERS
CERIPHS	CERULEIN	CESTAS	CHABOUK	CHAFES
CERISE	CERULEINS	CESTI	CHABOUKS	CHAFF
CERISES	CERULEOUS	CESTODE	CHABUK	CHAFFED

CHAFFER	CHAIRMANS	CHALKS	CHAMFERS	CHANA
CHAFFERED	CHAIRMEN	CHALKY	CHAMFRAIN	CHANAS
CHAFFERER	CHAIRS	CHALLA	CHAMFRON	CHANCE
CHAFFERS	CHAIS	CHALLAH	CHAMFRONS	CHANCED
CHAFFERY	CHAISE	CHALLAHS	CHAMISA	CHANCEFUL
CHAFFIER	CHAISES	CHALLAN	CHAMISAL	CHANCEL
CHAFFIEST	CHAKALAKA	CHALLANS	CHAMISALS	CHANCELS
CHAFFINCH	CHAKRA	CHALLAS	CHAMISAS	CHANCER
CHAFFING	CHAKRAS	CHALLENGE	CHAMISE	CHANCERS
CHAFFINGS	CHAL	CHALLIE	CHAMISES	CHANCERY
CHAFFRON	CHALAH	CHALLIES	CHAMISO	CHANCES
CHAFFRONS	CHALAHS	CHALLIS	CHAMISOS	CHANCEY
CHAFFS	CHALAN	CHALLISES	CHAMLET	CHANCIER
CHAFFY	CHALANED	CHALLOT	CHAMLETS	CHANCIEST
CHAFING	CHALANING	CHALLOTH	CHAMMIED	CHANCILY
CHAFT	CHALANNED	CHALLY	CHAMMIES	CHANCING
CHAFTS	CHALANS	CHALONE	CHAMMY	CHANCRE
CHAGAN	CHALAZA	CHALONES	CHAMMYING	CHANCRES
CHAGANS	CHALAZAE	CHALONIC	CHAMOIS	CHANCROID
CHAGRIN	CHALAZAL	CHALOT	CHAMOISED	CHANCROUS
CHAGRINED	CHALAZAS	CHALOTH	CHAMOISES	CHANCY
CHAGRINS	CHALAZIA	CHALS	CHAMOIX	CHANDELLE
CHAI	CHALAZION	CHALUMEAU	CHAMOMILE	CHANDLER
CHAIN	CHALCID	CHALUPA	CHAMP	CHANDLERS
CHAINE	CHALCIDS	CHALUPAS	CHAMPAC	CHANDLERY
CHAINED	CHALCOGEN	CHALUTZ	CHAMPACA	CHANFRON
CHAINER	CHALDER	CHALUTZES	CHAMPACAS	CHANFRONS
CHAINERS	CHALDERS	CHALUTZIM	CHAMPACS	CHANG
CHAINES	CHALDRON	CHALYBEAN	CHAMPAGNE	CHANGA
CHAINFALL	CHALDRONS	CHALYBITE	CHAMPAIGN	CHANGE
CHAINING	CHALEH	CHAM	CHAMPAK	CHANGED
CHAINLESS	CHALEHS	CHAMADE	CHAMPAKS	CHANGEFUL
CHAINLET	CHALET	CHAMADES	CHAMPART	CHANGER
CHAINLETS	CHALETS	CHAMBER	CHAMPARTS	CHANGERS
CHAINMAN	CHALICE	CHAMBERED	CHAMPAS	CHANGES
CHAINMEN	CHALICED	CHAMBERER	CHAMPED	CHANGEUP
CHAINS	CHALICES	CHAMBERS	CHAMPER	CHANGEUPS
CHAINSAW	CHALK	CHAMBRAY	CHAMPERS	CHANGING
CHAINSAWS	CHALKED	CHAMBRAYS	CHAMPERTY	CHANGS
CHAINSHOT	CHALKFACE	CHAMBRE	CHAMPIER	CHANK
CHAINWORK	CHALKIER	CHAMELEON	CHAMPIEST	CHANKS
CHAIR	CHALKIEST	CHAMELOT	CHAMPING	CHANNEL
CHAIRBACK	CHALKING	CHAMELOTS	CHAMPION	CHANNELED
CHAIRDAYS	CHALKLAND	CHAMETZ	CHAMPIONS	CHANNELER
CHAIRED	CHALKLIKE	CHAMETZES	CHAMPLEVE	CHANNELS
CHAIRING	CHALKMARK	CHAMFER	CHAMPS	CHANNER
CHAIRLIFT	CHALKPIT	CHAMFERED	CHAMPY	CHANNERS
CHAIRMAN	CHALKPITS	CHAMFERER	CHAMS	CHANOYO

CHANOYOS	CHAPELESS	CHARACID	CHARISMA	CHARQUID
CHANOYU	CHAPELRY	CHARACIDS	CHARISMAS	CHARQUIS
CHANOYUS	CHAPELS	CHARACIN	CHARISMS	CHARR
CHANSON	CHAPERON	CHARACINS	CHARITIES	CHARREADA
CHANSONS	CHAPERONE	CHARACT	CHARITY	CHARRED
CHANT	CHAPERONS	CHARACTER	CHARIVARI	CHARRIER
CHANTABLE	CHAPES	CHARACTS	CHARK	CHARRIEST
CHANTAGE	CHAPESS	CHARADE	CHARKA	CHARRING
CHANTAGES	CHAPESSES	CHARADES	CHARKAS	CHARRO
CHANTED	CHAPITER	CHARANGA	CHARKED	CHARROS
CHANTER	CHAPITERS	CHARANGAS	CHARKHA	CHARRS
CHANTERS	CHAPKA	CHARANGO	CHARKHAS	CHARRY
CHANTEUSE	CHAPKAS	CHARANGOS	CHARKING	CHARS
CHANTEY	CHAPLAIN	CHARAS	CHARKS	CHART
CHANTEYS	CHAPLAINS	CHARASES	CHARLADY	CHARTA
CHANTIE	CHAPLESS	CHARBROIL	CHARLATAN	CHARTABLE
CHANTIES	CHAPLET	CHARCOAL	CHARLEY	CHARTAS
CHANTILLY	CHAPLETED	CHARCOALS	CHARLEYS	CHARTED
CHANTING	CHAPLETS	CHARCOALY	CHARLIE	CHARTER
CHANTINGS	CHAPMAN	CHARD	CHARLIER	CHARTERED
CHANTOR	CHAPMEN	CHARDS	CHARLIES	CHARTERER
CHANTORS	CHAPPAL	CHARE	CHARLOCK	CHARTERS
CHANTRESS	CHAPPALS	CHARED	CHARLOCKS	CHARTING
CHANTRIES	CHAPPATI	CHARES	CHARLOTTE	CHARTISM
CHANTRY	CHAPPATIS	CHARET	CHARM	CHARTISMS
CHANTS	CHAPPED	CHARETS	CHARMED	CHARTIST
CHANTY	CHAPPESS	CHARETTE	CHARMER	CHARTISTS
CHANUKIAH	CHAPPIE	CHARETTES	CHARMERS	CHARTLESS
CHAO	CHAPPIER	CHARGE	CHARMEUSE	CHARTS
CHAOLOGY	CHAPPIES	CHARGED	CHARMFUL	CHARVER
CHAORDIC	CHAPPIEST	CHARGEFUL	CHARMING	CHARVERS
CHAOS	CHAPPING	CHARGER	CHARMLESS	CHARWOMAN
CHAOSES	CHAPPY	CHARGERS	CHARMONIA	CHARWOMEN
CHAOTIC	CHAPRASSI	CHARGES	CHARMS	CHARY
CHAP	CHAPS	CHARGING	CHARNECO	CHAS
CHAPARRAL	CHAPSTICK	CHARGINGS	CHARNECOS	CHASE
CHAPATI	CHAPT	CHARGRILL	CHARNEL	CHASEABLE
CHAPATIES	CHAPTER	CHARIDEE	CHARNELS	CHASED
CHAPATIS	CHAPTERAL	CHARIDEES	CHAROSET	CHASEPORT
CHAPATTI	CHAPTERED	CHARIER	CHAROSETH	CHASER
CHAPATTIS	CHAPTERS	CHARIEST	CHAROSETS	CHASERS
CHAPBOOK	CHAPTREL	CHARILY	CHARPAI	CHASES
CHAPBOOKS	CHAPTRELS	CHARINESS	CHARPAIS	CHASING
CHAPE	CHAQUETA	CHARING	CHARPIE	CHASINGS
CHAPEAU	CHAQUETAS	CHARIOT	CHARPIES	CHASM
CHAPEAUS	CHAR	CHARIOTED	CHARPOY	CHASMAL
CHAPEAUX	CHARA	CHARIOTS	CHARPOYS	CHASMED
CHAPEL	CHARABANC	CHARISM	CHARQUI	CHASMIC

CHASMIER	CHATTAS	CHAUSSURE	CHEAPER	CHECKOUT
CHASMIEST	CHATTED	CHAUVIN	CHEAPEST	CHECKOUTS
CHASMS	CHATTEL	CHAUVINS	CHEAPIE	CHECKRAIL
CHASMY	CHATTELS	CHAV	CHEAPIES	CHECKREIN
CHASSE	CHATTER	CHAVE	CHEAPING	CHECKROOM
CHASSED	CHATTERED	CHAVENDER	CHEAPISH	CHECKROW
CHASSEED	CHATTERER	CHAVETTE	CHEAPJACK	CHECKROWS
CHASSEING	CHATTERS	CHAVETTES	CHEAPLY	CHECKS
CHASSEPOT	CHATTERY	CHAVISH	CHEAPNESS	CHECKSTOP
CHASSES	CHATTI	CHAVS	CHEAPO	CHECKSUM
CHASSEUR	CHATTIER	CHAVVIER	CHEAPOS	CHECKSUMS
CHASSEURS	CHATTIES	CHAVVIEST	CHEAPS	CHECKUP
CHASSIS	CHATTIEST	CHAVVY	CHEAPSHOT	CHECKUPS
CHASTE	CHATTILY	CHAW	CHEAPY	CHECKY
CHASTELY	CHATTING	CHAWBACON	CHEAT	CHEDARIM
CHASTEN	CHATTIS	CHAWDRON	CHEATABLE	CHEDDAR
CHASTENED	CHATTY	CHAWDRONS	CHEATED	CHEDDARS
CHASTENER	CHAUFE	CHAWED	CHEATER	CHEDDARY
CHASTENS	CHAUFED	CHAWER	CHEATERS	CHEDDITE
CHASTER	CHAUFER	CHAWERS	CHEATERY	CHEDDITES
CHASTEST	CHAUFERS	CHAWING	CHEATING	CHEDER
CHASTISE	CHAUFES	CHAWK	CHEATINGS	CHEDERS
CHASTISED	CHAUFF	CHAWKS	CHEATS	CHEDITE
CHASTISER	CHAUFFED	CHAWS	CHEBEC	CHEDITES
CHASTISES	CHAUFFER	CHAY	CHEBECS	CHEECHAKO
CHASTITY	CHAUFFERS	CHAYA	CHECHAKO	CHEEK
CHASUBLE	CHAUFFEUR	CHAYAS	CHECHAKOS	CHEEKBONE
CHASUBLES	CHAUFFING	CHAYOTE	CHECHAQUO	CHEEKED
CHAT	CHAUFFS	CHAYOTES	CHECHIA	CHEEKFUL
CHATBOT	CHAUFING	CHAYROOT	CHECHIAS	CHEEKFULS
CHATBOTS	CHAUMER	CHAYROOTS	CHECK	CHEEKIER
CHATCHKA	CHAUMERS	CHAYS	CHECKABLE	CHEEKIEST
CHATCHKAS	CHAUNCE	CHAZAN	CHECKBOOK	CHEEKILY
CHATCHKE	CHAUNCED	CHAZANIM	CHECKBOX	CHEEKING
CHATCHKES	CHAUNCES	CHAZANS	CHECKED	CHEEKLESS
CHATEAU	CHAUNCING	CHAZZAN	CHECKER	CHEEKS
CHATEAUS	CHAUNGE	CHAZZANIM	CHECKERED	CHEEKY
CHATEAUX	CHAUNGED	CHAZZANS	CHECKERS	CHEEP
CHATELAIN	CHAUNGES	CHAZZEN	CHECKIER	CHEEPED
CHATLINE	CHAUNGING	CHAZZENIM	CHECKIEST	CHEEPER
CHATLINES	CHAUNT	CHAZZENS	CHECKING	CHEEPERS
CHATON	CHAUNTED	CHE	CHECKINGS	CHEEPING
CHATONS	CHAUNTER	CHEAP	CHECKLESS	CHEEPS
CHATOYANT	CHAUNTERS	CHEAPED	CHECKLIST	CHEER
CHATROOM	CHAUNTING	CHEAPEN	CHECKMARK	CHEERED
CHATROOMS	CHAUNTRY	CHEAPENED	CHECKMATE	CHEERER
CHATS	CHAUNTS	CHEAPENER	CHECKOFF	CHEERERS
CHATTA	CHAUSSES	CHEAPENS	CHECKOFFS	CHEERFUL

CHEERIER	CHELAS	CHEMPADUK	CHERTS	CHEVALET
CHEERIEST	CHELASHIP	CHEMS	CHERTY	CHEVALETS
CHEERILY	CHELATE	CHEMSEX	CHERUB	CHEVALIER
CHEERING	CHELATED	CHEMSEXES	CHERUBIC	CHEVELURE
CHEERINGS	CHELATES	CHEMTRAIL	CHERUBIM	CHEVEN
CHEERIO	CHELATING	CHEMURGIC	CHERUBIMS	CHEVENS
CHEERIOS	CHELATION	CHEMURGY	CHERUBIN	CHEVEREL
CHEERLEAD	CHELATOR	CHENAR	CHERUBINS	CHEVERELS
CHEERLED	CHELATORS	CHENARS	CHERUBS	CHEVERIL
CHEERLESS	CHELICERA	CHENET	CHERUP	CHEVERILS
CHEERLY	CHELIFORM	CHENETS	CHERUPED	CHEVERON
CHEERO	CHELIPED	CHENILLE	CHERUPING	CHEVERONS
CHEEROS	CHELIPEDS	CHENILLES	CHERUPS	CHEVERYE
CHEERS	CHELLUP	CHENIX	CHERVIL	CHEVERYES
CHEERY	CHELLUPS	CHENIXES	CHERVILS	CHEVET
CHEESE	CHELOID	CHENOPOD	CHESHIRE	CHEVETS
CHEESED	CHELOIDAL	CHENOPODS	CHESHIRES	CHEVIED
CHEESES	CHELOIDS	CHEONGSAM	CHESIL	CHEVIES
CHEESEVAT	CHELONE	CHEQUE	CHESILS	CHEVILLE
CHEESIER	CHELONES	CHEQUER	CHESNUT	CHEVILLES
CHEESIEST	CHELONIAN	CHEQUERED	CHESNUTS	CHEVIN
CHEESILY	CHELP	CHEQUERS	CHESS	CHEVINS
CHEESING	CHELPED	CHEQUES	CHESSEL	CHEVIOT
CHEESY	CHELPING	CHEQUIER	CHESSELS	CHEVIOTS
CHEETAH	CHELPS	CHEQUIEST	CHESSES	CHEVRE
CHEETAHS	CHEM	CHEQUING	CHESSMAN	CHEVRES
CHEEWINK	CHEMIC	CHEQUY	CHESSMEN	CHEVRET
CHEEWINKS	CHEMICAL	CHER	CHEST	CHEVRETS
CHEF	CHEMICALS	CHERALITE	CHESTED	CHEVRETTE
CHEFDOM	CHEMICKED	CHERE	CHESTFUL	CHEVRON
CHEFDOMS	CHEMICS	CHERIMOYA	CHESTFULS	CHEVRONED
CHEFED	CHEMISE	CHERISH	CHESTIER	CHEVRONS
CHEFFED	CHEMISES	CHERISHED	CHESTIEST	CHEVRONY
CHEFFIER	CHEMISM	CHERISHER	CHESTILY	CHEVROTIN
CHEFFIEST	CHEMISMS	CHERISHES	CHESTING	CHEVY
CHEFFING	CHEMISORB	CHERMOULA	CHESTNUT	CHEVYING
CHEFFY	CHEMIST	CHERNOZEM	CHESTNUTS	CHEW
CHEFING	CHEMISTRY	CHEROOT	CHESTS	CHEWABLE
CHEFS	CHEMISTS	CHEROOTS	CHESTY	CHEWED
CHEGOE	CHEMITYPE	CHERRIED	CHETAH	CHEWER
CHEGOES	CHEMITYPY	CHERRIER	CHETAHS	CHEWERS
CHEILITIS	CHEMMIES	CHERRIES	CHETH	CHEWET
CHEKA	CHEMMY	CHERRIEST	CHETHS	CHEWETS
CHEKAS	CHEMO	CHERRY	CHETNIK	CHEWIE
CHEKIST	CHEMOKINE	CHERRYING	CHETNIKS	CHEWIER
CHEKISTS	CHEMOS	CHERT	CHETRUM	CHEWIES
CHELA	CHEMOSORB	CHERTIER	CHETRUMS	CHEWIEST
CHELAE	CHEMOSTAT	CHERTIEST	CHEVAL	CHEWINESS

CHEWING	CHICANE	CHID	CHIKARA	CHILLAXES
CHEWINK	CHICANED	CHIDDEN	CHIKARAS	CHILLED
CHEWINKS	CHICANER	CHIDE	CHIKHOR	CHILLER
CHEWS	CHICANERS	CHIDED	CHIKHORS	CHILLERS
CHEWY	CHICANERY	CHIDER	CHIKOR	CHILLEST
CHEZ	CHICANES	CHIDERS	CHIKORS	CHILLI
CHHERTUM	CHICANING	CHIDES	CHIKS	CHILLIER
CHI	CHICANO	CHIDING	CHILBLAIN	CHILLIES
CHIA	CHICANOS	CHIDINGLY	CHILD	CHILLIEST
CHIACK	CHICAS	CHIDINGS	CHILDBED	CHILLILY
CHIACKED	CHICCORY	CHIDLINGS	CHILDBEDS	CHILLING
CHIACKING	CHICER	CHIEF	CHILDCARE	CHILLINGS
CHIACKS	CHICEST	CHIEFDOM	CHILDE	CHILLIS
CHIANTI	CHICH	CHIEFDOMS	CHILDED	CHILLNESS
CHIANTIS	CHICHA	CHIEFER	CHILDER	CHILLS
CHIAO	CHICHAS	CHIEFERY	CHILDES	CHILLUM
CHIAOS	CHICHES	CHIEFESS	CHILDHOOD	CHILLUMS
CHIAREZZA	CHICHI	CHIEFEST	CHILDING	CHILLY
CHIAREZZE	CHICHIER	CHIEFLESS	CHILDISH	CHILOPOD
CHIAS	CHICHIEST	CHIEFLING	CHILDLESS	CHILOPODS
CHIASM	CHICHIS	CHIEFLY	CHILDLIER	CHILTEPIN
CHIASMA	CHICK	CHIEFRIES	CHILDLIKE	CHIMAERA
CHIASMAL	CHICKADEE	CHIEFRY	CHILDLY	CHIMAERAS
CHIASMAS	CHICKAREE	CHIEFS	CHILDNESS	CHIMAERIC
CHIASMATA	CHICKEE	CHIEFSHIP	CHILDREN	CHIMAR
CHIASMI	CHICKEES	CHIEFTAIN	CHILDS	CHIMARS
CHIASMIC	CHICKEN	CHIEL	CHILE	CHIMB
CHIASMS	CHICKENED	CHIELD	CHILES	CHIMBLEY
CHIASMUS	CHICKENS	CHIELDS	CHILI	CHIMBLEYS
CHIASTIC	CHICKLING	CHIELS	CHILIAD	CHIMBLIES
CHIAUS	CHICKORY	CHIFFON	CHILIADAL	CHIMBLY
CHIAUSED	CHICKPEA	CHIFFONS	CHILIADIC	CHIMBS
CHIAUSES	CHICKPEAS	CHIFFONY	CHILIADS	CHIME
CHIAUSING	CHICKS	CHIGETAI	CHILIAGON	CHIMED
CHIB	CHICKWEED	CHIGETAIS	CHILIARCH	CHIMENEA
CHIBBED	CHICLE	CHIGGA	CHILIASM	CHIMENEAS
CHIBBING	CHICLES	CHIGGAS	CHILIASMS	CHIMER
CHIBOL	CHICLY	CHIGGER	CHILIAST	CHIMERA
CHIBOLS	CHICNESS	CHIGGERS	CHILIASTS	CHIMERAS
CHIBOUK	CHICO	CHIGNON	CHILIDOG	CHIMERE
CHIBOUKS	CHICON	CHIGNONED	CHILIDOGS	CHIMERES
CHIBOUQUE	CHICONS	CHIGNONS	CHILIES	CHIMERIC
CHIBS	CHICORIES	CHIGOE	CHILIS	CHIMERID
CHIC	CHICORY	CHIGOES	CHILL	CHIMERIDS
CHICA	CHICOS	CHIGRE	CHILLADA	CHIMERISM
CHICALOTE	CHICOT	CHIGRES	CHILLADAS	CHIMERS
CHICANA	CHICOTS	CHIHUAHUA	CHILLAX	CHIMES
CHICANAS	CHICS	CHIK	CHILLAXED	CHIMINEA

CHIMINEAS	CHINKIER	CHIPPERER	CHIRPY	CHITTERED
CHIMING	CHINKIES	CHIPPERS	CHIRR	CHITTERS
CHIMLA	CHINKIEST	CHIPPIE	CHIRRE	CHITTIER
CHIMLAS	CHINKING	CHIPPIER	CHIRRED	CHITTIES
CHIMLEY	CHINKS	CHIPPIES	CHIRREN	CHITTIEST
CHIMLEYS	CHINKY	CHIPPIEST	CHIRRES	CHITTING
CHIMNEY	CHINLESS	CHIPPING	CHIRRING	CHITTY
CHIMNEYED	CHINNED	CHIPPINGS	CHIRRS	CHIV
CHIMNEYS	CHINNING	CHIPPY	CHIRRUP	CHIVALRIC
CHIMO	CHINO	CHIPS	CHIRRUPED	CHIVALRY
CHIMP	CHINOIS	CHIPSET	CHIRRUPER	CHIVAREE
CHIMPS	CHINOISES	CHIPSETS	CHIRRUPS	CHIVAREED
CHIN	CHINONE	CHIRAGRA	CHIRRUPY	CHIVAREES
CHINA	CHINONES	CHIRAGRAS	CHIRT	CHIVARI
CHINAMAN	CHINOOK	CHIRAGRIC	CHIRTED	CHIVARIED
CHINAMEN	CHINOOKS	CHIRAL	CHIRTING	CHIVARIES
CHINAMPA	CHINOS	CHIRALITY	CHIRTS	CHIVE
CHINAMPAS	CHINOVNIK	CHIRIMOYA	CHIRU	CHIVED
CHINAR	CHINS	CHIRK	CHIRUS	CHIVES
CHINAROOT	CHINSE	CHIRKED	CHIS	CHIVIED
CHINARS	CHINSED	CHIRKER	CHISEL	CHIVIES
CHINAS	CHINSES	CHIRKEST	CHISELED	CHIVING
CHINAWARE	CHINSING	CHIRKING	CHISELER	CHIVS
CHINBONE	CHINSTRAP	CHIRKS	CHISELERS	CHIVVED
CHINBONES	CHINTS	CHIRL	CHISELING	CHIVVIED
CHINCAPIN	CHINTSES	CHIRLED	CHISELLED	CHIVVIES
CHINCH	CHINTZ	CHIRLING	CHISELLER	CHIVVING
CHINCHED	CHINTZES	CHIRLS	CHISELS	CHIVVY
CHINCHES	CHINTZIER	CHIRM	CHIT	CHIVVYING
CHINCHIER	CHINTZILY	CHIRMED	CHITAL	CHIVY
CHINCHING	CHINTZY	CHIRMING	CHITALS	CHIVYING
CHINCHY	CHINWAG	CHIRMS	CHITCHAT	CHIWEENIE
CHINCOUGH	CHINWAGS	CHIRO	CHITCHATS	CHIYOGAMI
CHINDIT	CHIP	CHIROLOGY	CHITIN	CHIZ
CHINDITS	CHIPBOARD	CHIRONOMY	CHITINOID	CHIZZ
CHINE	CHIPMAKER	CHIROPODY	CHITINOUS	CHIZZED
CHINED	CHIPMUCK	CHIROPTER	CHITINS	CHIZZES
CHINES	CHIPMUCKS	CHIROS	CHITLIN	CHIZZING
CHINESE	CHIPMUNK	CHIRP	CHITLING	CHLAMYDES
CHING	CHIPMUNKS	CHIRPED	CHITLINGS	CHLAMYDIA
CHINGS	CHIPOCHIA	CHIRPER	CHITLINS	CHLAMYS
CHINING	CHIPOLATA	CHIRPERS	CHITON	CHLAMYSES
CHINK	CHIPOTLE	CHIRPIER	CHITONS	CHLOASMA
CHINKAPIN	CHIPOTLES	CHIRPIEST	CHITOSAN	CHLOASMAS
CHINKARA	CHIPPABLE	CHIRPILY	CHITOSANS	CHLORACNE
CHINKARAS	CHIPPED	CHIRPING	CHITS	CHLORAL
CHINKED	CHIPPER	CHIRPINGS	CHITTED	CHLORALS
CHINKIE	CHIPPERED	CHIRPS	CHITTER	CHLORATE

CHLORATES	CHOCO	CHOKIEST	CHOMPED	CHOPINS
CHLORDAN	CHOCOLATE	CHOKING	CHOMPER	CHOPLOGIC
CHLORDANE	CHOCOLATY	CHOKINGLY	CHOMPERS	CHOPPED
CHLORDANS	CHOCOS	CHOKO	CHOMPING	CHOPPER
CHLORELLA	CHOCS	CHOKOS	CHOMPS	CHOPPERED
CHLORIC	CHOCTAW	CHOKRA	CHON	CHOPPERS
CHLORID	CHOCTAWS	CHOKRAS	CHONDRAL	CHOPPIER
CHLORIDE	CHODE	CHOKRI	CHONDRE	CHOPPIEST
CHLORIDES	CHOENIX	CHOKRIS	CHONDRES	CHOPPILY
CHLORIDIC	CHOENIXES	CHOKY	CHONDRI	CHOPPING
CHLORIDS	CHOG	CHOLA	CHONDRIFY	CHOPPINGS
CHLORIN	CHOGS	CHOLAEMIA	CHONDRIN	CHOPPY
CHLORINE	CHOICE	CHOLAEMIC	CHONDRINS	CHOPS
CHLORINES	CHOICEFUL	CHOLAS	CHONDRITE	CHOPSOCKY
CHLORINS	CHOICELY	CHOLATE	CHONDROID	CHOPSTICK
CHLORITE	CHOICER	CHOLATES	CHONDROMA	CHORAGI
CHLORITES	CHOICES	CHOLECYST	CHONDRULE	CHORAGIC
CHLORITIC	CHOICEST	CHOLELITH	CHONDRUS	CHORAGUS
CHLOROSES	CHOIL	CHOLEMIA	CHONS	CHORAL
CHLOROSIS	CHOILS	CHOLEMIAS	CHOOF	CHORALE
CHLOROTIC	CHOIR	CHOLENT	CHOOFED	CHORALES
CHLOROUS	CHOIRBOY	CHOLENTS	CHOOFING	CHORALIST
CHOANA	CHOIRBOYS	CHOLER	CHOOFS	CHORALLY
CHOANAE	CHOIRED	CHOLERA	CHOOK	CHORALS
CHOBDAR	CHOIRGIRL	CHOLERAIC	CHOOKED	CHORD
CHOBDARS	CHOIRING	CHOLERAS	CHOOKIE	CHORDA
CHOC	CHOIRLIKE	CHOLERIC	CHOOKIES	CHORDAE
CHOCCIER	CHOIRMAN	CHOLEROID	CHOOKING	CHORDAL
CHOCCIES	CHOIRMEN	CHOLERS	CHOOKS	CHORDATE
CHOCCIEST	CHOIRS	CHOLI	CHOOM	CHORDATES
CHOCCY	CHOKE	CHOLIAMB	CHOOMS	CHORDED
CHOCHO	CHOKEABLE	CHOLIAMBS	CHOON	CHORDEE
CHOCHOS	CHOKEBORE	CHOLIC	CHOONS	CHORDEES
CHOCK	CHOKECOIL	CHOLINE	CHOOSE	CHORDING
CHOCKED	CHOKED	CHOLINES	CHOOSER	CHORDINGS
CHOCKER	CHOKEDAMP	CHOLIS	CHOOSERS	CHORDLIKE
CHOCKERS	CHOKEHOLD	CHOLLA	CHOOSES	CHORDS
CHOCKFUL	CHOKER	CHOLLAS	CHOOSEY	CHORDWISE
CHOCKFULL	CHOKERMAN	CHOLLERS	CHOOSIER	CHORE
CHOCKIE	CHOKERMEN	CHOLO	CHOOSIEST	CHOREA
CHOCKIER	CHOKERS	CHOLOS	CHOOSILY	CHOREAL
CHOCKIES	CHOKES	CHOLTRIES	CHOOSING	CHOREAS
CHOCKIEST	CHOKEY	CHOLTRY	CHOOSY	CHOREATIC
CHOCKING	CHOKEYS	CHOMETZ	CHOP	CHOREBOY
CHOCKO	CHOKIDAR	CHOMETZES	CHOPHOUSE	CHOREBOYS
CHOCKOS	CHOKIDARS	CHOMMIE	CHOPIN	CHORED
CHOCKS	CHOKIER	CHOMMIES	CHOPINE	CHOREE
CHOCKY	CHOKIES	CHOMP	CHOPINES	CHOREES

CHOREGI	CHORUS	CHOWSE	CHROMISE	CHUCKLE
CHOREGIC	CHORUSED	CHOWSED	CHROMISED	CHUCKLED
CHOREGUS	CHORUSES	CHOWSES	CHROMISES	CHUCKLER
CHOREIC	CHORUSING	CHOWSING	CHROMITE	CHUCKLERS
CHOREMAN	CHORUSSED	CHOWTIME	CHROMITES	CHUCKLES
CHOREMEN	CHORUSSES	CHOWTIMES	CHROMIUM	CHUCKLING
CHOREOID	CHOSE	CHRESARD	CHROMIUMS	CHUCKS
CHORES	CHOSEN	CHRESARDS	CHROMIZE	CHUCKY
CHOREUS	CHOSES	CHRISM	CHROMIZED	CHUDDAH
CHOREUSES	CHOTA	CHRISMA	CHROMIZES	CHUDDAHS
CHORIA	CHOTT	CHRISMAL	CHROMO	CHUDDAR
CHORIAL	CHOTTS	CHRISMALS	CHROMOGEN	CHUDDARS
CHORIAMB	CHOU	CHRISMON	CHROMOLY	CHUDDER
CHORIAMBI	CHOUGH	CHRISMONS	CHROMOLYS	CHUDDERS
CHORIAMBS	CHOUGHS	CHRISMS	CHROMOS	CHUDDIES
CHORIC	CHOULTRY	CHRISOM	CHROMOUS	CHUDDY
CHORINE	CHOUNTER	CHRISOMS	CHROMY	CHUFA
CHORINES	CHOUNTERS	CHRISTEN	CHROMYL	CHUFAS
CHORING	CHOUSE	CHRISTENS	CHROMYLS	CHUFF
CHORIOID	CHOUSED	CHRISTIAN	CHRONAXIE	CHUFFED
CHORIOIDS	CHOUSER	CHRISTIE	CHRONAXY	CHUFFER
CHORION	CHOUSERS	CHRISTIES	CHRONIC	CHUFFEST
CHORIONIC	CHOUSES	CHRISTOM	CHRONICAL	CHUFFIER
CHORIONS	CHOUSH	CHRISTOMS	CHRONICLE	CHUFFIEST
CHORISES	CHOUSHES	CHRISTY	CHRONICS	CHUFFING
CHORISIS	CHOUSING	CHROMA	CHRONON	CHUFFS
CHORISM	CHOUT	CHROMAKEY	CHRONONS	CHUFFY
CHORISMS	CHOUTS	CHROMAS	CHRYSALID	CHUG
CHORIST	CHOUX	CHROMATE	CHRYSALIS	CHUGALUG
CHORISTER	CHOW	CHROMATES	CHRYSANTH	CHUGALUGS
CHORISTS	CHOWCHOW	CHROMATIC	CHTHONIAN	CHUGGED
CHORIZO	CHOWCHOWS	CHROMATID	CHTHONIC	CHUGGER
CHORIZONT	CHOWDER	CHROMATIN	CHUB	CHUGGERS
CHORIZOS	CHOWDERED	CHROME	CHUBASCO	CHUGGING
CHOROID	CHOWDERS	CHROMED	CHUBASCOS	CHUGGINGS
CHOROIDAL	CHOWDOWN	CHROMEL	CHUBBIER	CHUGS
CHOROIDS	CHOWDOWNS	CHROMELS	CHUBBIEST	CHUKAR
CHOROLOGY	CHOWED	CHROMENE	CHUBBILY	CHUKARS
CHORRIE	CHOWHOUND	CHROMENES	CHUBBY	CHUKKA
CHORRIES	CHOWING	CHROMES	CHUBS	CHUKKAR
CHORTEN	CHOWK	CHROMIC	CHUCK	CHUKKARS
CHORTENS	CHOWKIDAR	CHROMIDE	CHUCKED	CHUKKAS
CHORTLE	CHOWKS	CHROMIDES	CHUCKER	CHUKKER
CHORTLED	CHOWRI	CHROMIDIA	CHUCKERS	CHUKKERS
CHORTLER	CHOWRIES	CHROMIER	CHUCKHOLE	CHUKOR
CHORTLERS	CHOWRIS	CHROMIEST	CHUCKIE	CHUKORS
CHORTLES	CHOWRY	CHROMING	CHUCKIES	CHUM
CHORTLING	CHOWS	CHROMINGS	CHUCKING	CHUMASH

CHUMASHES	CHUPPAHS	CHUTING	CIAO	CIDE
CHUMASHIM	CHUPPAS	CHUTIST	CIBATION	CIDED
CHUMLEY	CHUPPOT	CHUTISTS	CIBATIONS	CIDER
CHUMLEYS	CHUPPOTH	CHUTNEE	CIBOL	CIDERIER
CHUMMAGE	CHUPRASSY	CHUTNEES	CIBOLS	CIDERIEST
CHUMMAGES	CHUR	CHUTNEY	CIBORIA	CIDERKIN
CHUMMED	CHURCH	CHUTNEYS	CIBORIUM	CIDERKINS
CHUMMIER	CHURCHED	CHUTS	CIBORIUMS	CIDERS
CHUMMIES	CHURCHES	CHUTZPA	CIBOULE	CIDERY
CHUMMIEST	CHURCHIER	CHUTZPAH	CIBOULES	CIDES
CHUMMILY	CHURCHING	CHUTZPAHS	CICADA	CIDING
CHUMMING	CHURCHISM	CHUTZPAS	CICADAE	CIDS
CHUMMY	CHURCHLY	CHYACK	CICADAS	CIEL
CHUMP	CHURCHMAN	CHYACKED	CICALA	CIELED
CHUMPED	CHURCHMEN	CHYACKING	CICALAS	CIELING
CHUMPING	CHURCHWAY	CHYACKS	CICALE	CIELINGS
CHUMPINGS	CHURCHY	CHYLDE	CICATRICE	CIELS
CHUMPS	CHURIDAR	CHYLE	CICATRISE	CIERGE
CHUMS	CHURIDARS	CHYLES	CICATRIX	CIERGES
CHUMSHIP	CHURINGA	CHYLIFIED	CICATRIZE	CIG
CHUMSHIPS	CHURINGAS	CHYLIFIES	CICELIES	CIGAR
CHUNDER	CHURL	CHYLIFY	CICELY	CIGARET
CHUNDERED	CHURLISH	CHYLOUS	CICERO	CIGARETS
CHUNDERS	CHURLS	CHYLURIA	CICERONE	CIGARETTE
CHUNK	CHURN	CHYLURIAS	CICERONED	CIGARILLO
CHUNKED	CHURNED	CHYME	CICERONES	CIGARLIKE
CHUNKIER	CHURNER	CHYMES	CICERONI	CIGARS
CHUNKIEST	CHURNERS	CHYMIC	CICEROS	CIGGIE
CHUNKILY	CHURNING	CHYMICS	CICHLID	CIGGIES
CHUNKING	CHURNINGS	CHYMIFIED	CICHLIDAE	CIGGY
CHUNKINGS	CHURNMILK	CHYMIFIES	CICHLIDS	CIGS
CHUNKS	CHURNS	CHYMIFY	CICHLOID	CIGUATERA
CHUNKY	CHURR	CHYMIST	CICINNUS	CILANTRO
CHUNNEL	CHURRED	CHYMISTRY	CICISBEI	CILANTROS
CHUNNELS	CHURRING	CHYMISTS	CICISBEO	CILIA
CHUNNER	CHURRO	CHYMOSIN	CICISBEOS	CILIARY
CHUNNERED	CHURROS	CHYMOSINS	CICLATON	CILIATE
CHUNNERS	CHURRS	CHYMOUS	CICLATONS	CILIATED
CHUNTER	CHURRUS	CHYND	CICLATOUN	CILIATELY
CHUNTERED	CHURRUSES	CHYPRE	CICOREE	CILIATES
CHUNTERS	CHUSE	CHYPRES	CICOREES	CILIATION
CHUPATI	CHUSED	CHYRON	CICUTA	CILICE
CHUPATIS	CHUSES	CHYRONS	CICUTAS	CILICES
CHUPATTI	CHUSING	CHYTRID	CICUTINE	CILICIOUS
CHUPATTIS	CHUT	CHYTRIDS	CICUTINES	CILIOLATE
CHUPATTY	CHUTE	CIABATTA	CID	CILIUM
CHUPPA	CHUTED	CIABATTAS	CIDARIS	CILL
CHUPPAH	CHUTES	CIABATTE	CIDARISES	CILLS

CIMAR	CINERAMIC	CIRCA	CIRROSE	CITADELS
CIMARS	CINERARIA	CIRCADIAN	CIRROUS	CITAL
CIMBALOM	CINERARY	CIRCAR	CIRRUS	CITALS
CIMBALOMS	CINERATOR	CIRCARS	CIRRUSES	CITATION
CIMELIA	CINEREA	CIRCINATE	CIRSOID	CITATIONS
CIMEX	CINEREAL	CIRCITER	CIS	CITATOR
CIMICES	CINEREAS	CIRCLE	CISALPINE	CITATORS
CIMIER	CINEREOUS	CIRCLED	CISCO	CITATORY
CIMIERS	CINERIN	CIRCLER	CISCOES	CITE
CIMINITE	CINERINS	CIRCLERS	CISCOS	CITEABLE
CIMINITES	CINES	CIRCLES	CISELEUR	CITED
CIMMERIAN	CINGULA	CIRCLET	CISELEURS	CITER
CIMOLITE	CINGULAR	CIRCLETS	CISELURE	CITERS
CIMOLITES	CINGULATE	CIRCLING	CISELURES	CITES
CINCH	CINGULUM	CIRCLINGS	CISGENDER	CITESS
CINCHED	CINNABAR	CIRCLIP	CISLUNAR	CITESSES
CINCHES	CINNABARS	CIRCLIPS	CISPADANE	CITHARA
CINCHING	CINNAMIC	CIRCS	CISPLATIN	CITHARAS
CINCHINGS	CINNAMON	CIRCUIT	CISSIER	CITHARIST
CINCHONA	CINNAMONS	CIRCUITAL	CISSIES	CITHER
CINCHONAS	CINNAMONY	CIRCUITED	CISSIEST	CITHERN
CINCHONIC	CINNAMYL	CIRCUITRY	CISSIFIED	CITHERNS
CINCINNUS	CINNAMYLS	CIRCUITS	CISSING	CITHERS
CINCT	CINQ	CIRCUITY	CISSINGS	CITHREN
CINCTURE	CINQS	CIRCULAR	CISSOID	CITHRENS
CINCTURED	CINQUAIN	CIRCULARS	CISSOIDS	CITIED
CINCTURES	CINQUAINS	CIRCULATE	CISSUS	CITIES
CINDER	CINQUE	CIRCUS	CISSUSES	CITIFIED
CINDERED	CINQUES	CIRCUSES	CISSY	CITIFIES
CINDERIER	CION	CIRCUSIER	CIST	CITIFY
CINDERING	CIONS	CIRCUSSY	CISTED	CITIFYING
CINDEROUS	CIOPPINO	CIRCUSY	CISTERN	CITIGRADE
CINDERS	CIOPPINOS	CIRE	CISTERNA	CITING
CINDERY	CIPAILLE	CIRES	CISTERNAE	CITIZEN
CINE	CIPAILLES	CIRL	CISTERNAL	CITIZENLY
CINEAST	CIPHER	CIRLS	CISTERNS	CITIZENRY
CINEASTE	CIPHERED	CIRQUE	CISTIC	CITIZENS
CINEASTES	CIPHERER	CIRQUES	CISTRON	CITO
CINEASTS	CIPHERERS	CIRRATE	CISTRONIC	CITOLA
CINEMA	CIPHERING	CIRRHOSED	CISTRONS	CITOLAS
CINEMAS	CIPHERS	CIRRHOSES	CISTS	CITOLE
CINEMATIC	CIPHONIES	CIRRHOSIS	CISTUS	CITOLES
CINEOL	CIPHONY	CIRRHOTIC	CISTUSES	CITRAL
CINEOLE	CIPOLIN	CIRRI	CISTVAEN	CITRALS
CINEOLES	CIPOLINS	CIRRIFORM	CISTVAENS	CITRANGE
CINEOLS	CIPOLLINO	CIRRIPED	CIT	CITRANGES
CINEPHILE	CIPPI	CIRRIPEDE	CITABLE	CITRATE
CINEPLEX	CIPPUS	CIRRIPEDS	CITADEL	CITRATED

CITRATES	CIVILISTS	CLADISTS	CLAMORED	CLANSHIPS
CITREOUS	CIVILITY	CLADODE	CLAMORER	CLANSMAN
CITRIC	CIVILIZE	CLADODES	CLAMORERS	CLANSMEN
CITRIN	CIVILIZED	CLADODIAL	CLAMORING	CLAP
CITRINE	CIVILIZER	CLADOGRAM	CLAMOROUS	CLAPBOARD
CITRINES	CIVILIZES	CLADS	CLAMORS	CLAPBREAD
CITRININ	CIVILLY	CLAES	CLAMOUR	CLAPDISH
CITRININS	CIVILNESS	CLAFOUTI	CLAMOURED	CLAPNET
CITRINS	CIVILS	CLAFOUTIS	CLAMOURER	CLAPNETS
CITRON	CIVISM	CLAG	CLAMOURS	CLAPPED
CITRONS	CIVISMS	CLAGGED	CLAMP	CLAPPER
CITROUS	CIVVIES	CLAGGIER	CLAMPDOWN	CLAPPERED
CITRUS	CIVVY	CLAGGIEST	CLAMPED	CLAPPERS
CITRUSES	CIZERS	CLAGGING	CLAMPER	CLAPPING
CITRUSIER	CLABBER	CLAGGY	CLAMPERED	CLAPPINGS
CITRUSSY	CLABBERED	CLAGS	CLAMPERS	CLAPS
CITRUSY	CLABBERS	CLAIM	CLAMPING	CLAPT
CITS	CLACH	CLAIMABLE	CLAMPINGS	CLAPTRAP
CITTERN	CLACHAN	CLAIMANT	CLAMPS	CLAPTRAPS
CITTERNS	CLACHANS	CLAIMANTS	CLAMS	CLAQUE
CITY	CLACHED	CLAIMED	CLAMSHELL	CLAQUER
CITYFIED	CLACHES	CLAIMER	CLAMWORM	CLAQUERS
CITYFIES	CLACHING	CLAIMERS	CLAMWORMS	CLAQUES
CITYFY	CLACHS	CLAIMING	CLAN	CLAQUEUR
CITYFYING	CLACK	CLAIMS	CLANG	CLAQUEURS
CITYSCAPE	CLACKBOX	CLAM	CLANGBOX	CLARAIN
CITYWARD	CLACKDISH	CLAMANCY	CLANGED	CLARAINS
CITYWIDE	CLACKED	CLAMANT	CLANGER	CLARENCE
CIVE	CLACKER	CLAMANTLY	CLANGERS	CLARENCES
CIVES	CLACKERS	CLAMBAKE	CLANGING	CLARENDON
CIVET	CLACKING	CLAMBAKES	CLANGINGS	CLARET
CIVETLIKE	CLACKS	CLAMBE	CLANGOR	CLARETED
CIVETS	CLAD	CLAMBER	CLANGORED	CLARETING
CIVIC	CLADDAGH	CLAMBERED	CLANGORS	CLARETS
CIVICALLY	CLADDAGHS	CLAMBERER	CLANGOUR	CLARIES
CIVICISM	CLADDED	CLAMBERS	CLANGOURS	CLARIFIED
CIVICISMS	CLADDER	CLAME	CLANGS	CLARIFIER
CIVICS	CLADDERS	CLAMES	CLANK	CLARIFIES
CIVIE	CLADDIE	CLAMLIKE	CLANKED	CLARIFY
CIVIES	CLADDIES	CLAMMED	CLANKIER	CLARINET
CIVIL	CLADDING	CLAMMER	CLANKIEST	CLARINETS
CIVILIAN	CLADDINGS	CLAMMERS	CLANKING	CLARINI
CIVILIANS	CLADE	CLAMMIER	CLANKINGS	CLARINO
CIVILISE	CLADES	CLAMMIEST	CLANKS	CLARINOS
CIVILISED	CLADISM	CLAMMILY	CLANKY	CLARION
CIVILISER	CLADISMS	CLAMMING	CLANNISH	CLARIONED
CIVILISES	CLADIST	CLAMMY	CLANS	CLARIONET
CIVILIST	CLADISTIC	CLAMOR	CLANSHIP	CLARIONS

CLARITIES	CLASSILY	CLAUSULAE	CLAYED	CLEARCUT
CLARITY	CLASSING	CLAUSULAR	CLAYEY	CLEARCUTS
CLARKIA	CLASSINGS	CLAUT	CLAYIER	CLEARED
CLARKIAS	CLASSIS	CLAUTED	CLAYIEST	CLEARER
CLARO	CLASSISM	CLAUTING	CLAYING	CLEARERS
CLAROES	CLASSISMS	CLAUTS	CLAYISH	CLEAREST
CLAROS	CLASSIST	CLAVATE	CLAYLIKE	CLEAREYED
CLARSACH	CLASSISTS	CLAVATED	CLAYMORE	CLEARING
CLARSACHS	CLASSLESS	CLAVATELY	CLAYMORES	CLEARINGS
CLART	CLASSMAN	CLAVATION	CLAYPAN	CLEARLY
CLARTED	CLASSMATE	CLAVE	CLAYPANS	CLEARNESS
CLARTHEAD	CLASSMEN	CLAVECIN	CLAYS	CLEAROUT
CLARTIER	CLASSON	CLAVECINS	CLAYSTONE	CLEAROUTS
CLARTIEST	CLASSONS	CLAVER	CLAYTONIA	CLEARS
CLARTING	CLASSROOM	CLAVERED	CLAYWARE	CLEARSKIN
CLARTS	CLASSWORK	CLAVERING	CLAYWARES	CLEARWAY
CLARTY	CLASSY	CLAVERS	CLEAN	CLEARWAYS
CLARY	CLAST	CLAVES	CLEANABLE	CLEARWEED
CLASH	CLASTIC	CLAVI	CLEANED	CLEARWING
CLASHED	CLASTICS	CLAVICLE	CLEANER	CLEAT
CLASHER	CLASTS	CLAVICLES	CLEANERS	CLEATED
CLASHERS	CLAT	CLAVICORN	CLEANEST	CLEATING
CLASHES	CLATCH	CLAVICULA	CLEANING	CLEATS
CLASHING	CLATCHED	CLAVIE	CLEANINGS	CLEAVABLE
CLASHINGS	CLATCHES	CLAVIER	CLEANISH	CLEAVAGE
CLASP	CLATCHING	CLAVIERS	CLEANLIER	CLEAVAGES
CLASPED	CLATHRATE	CLAVIES	CLEANLILY	CLEAVE
CLASPER	CLATS	CLAVIFORM	CLEANLY	CLEAVED
CLASPERS	CLATTED	CLAVIGER	CLEANNESS	CLEAVER
CLASPING	CLATTER	CLAVIGERS	CLEANOUT	CLEAVERS
CLASPINGS	CLATTERED	CLAVIS	CLEANOUTS	CLEAVES
CLASPS	CLATTERER	CLAVULATE	CLEANS	CLEAVING
CLASPT	CLATTERS	CLAVUS	CLEANSE	CLEAVINGS
CLASS	CLATTERY	CLAW	CLEANSED	CLECHE
CLASSABLE	CLATTING	CLAWBACK	CLEANSER	CLECK
CLASSED	CLAUCHT	CLAWBACKS	CLEANSERS	CLECKED
CLASSER	CLAUCHTED	CLAWED	CLEANSES	CLECKIER
CLASSERS	CLAUCHTS	CLAWER	CLEANSING	CLECKIEST
CLASSES	CLAUGHT	CLAWERS	CLEANSKIN	CLECKING
CLASSIBLE	CLAUGHTED	CLAWING	CLEANTECH	CLECKINGS
CLASSIC	CLAUGHTS	CLAWLESS	CLEANUP	CLECKS
CLASSICAL	CLAUSAL	CLAWLIKE	CLEANUPS	CLECKY
CLASSICO	CLAUSE	CLAWS	CLEAR	CLEEK
CLASSICS	CLAUSES	CLAXON	CLEARABLE	CLEEKED
CLASSIER	CLAUSTRA	CLAXONS	CLEARAGE	CLEEKING
CLASSIEST	CLAUSTRAL	CLAY	CLEARAGES	CLEEKIT
CLASSIFIC	CLAUSTRUM	CLAYBANK	CLEARANCE	CLEEKS
CLASSIFY	CLAUSULA	CLAYBANKS	CLEARCOLE	CLEEP

CLEEPED
CLEEPING
CLEEPS
CLEEVE
CLEEVES
CLEF
CLEFS
CLEFT
CLEFTED
CLEFTING
CLEFTS
CLEG
CLEGS
CLEIDOIC
CLEIK
CLEIKS
CLEITHRAL
CLEM
CLEMATIS
CLEMENCY
CLEMENT
CLEMENTLY
CLEMMED
CLEMMING
CLEMS
CLENCH
CLENCHED
CLENCHER
CLENCHERS
CLENCHES
CLENCHING
CLEOME
CLEOMES
CLEOPATRA
CLEPE
CLEPED
CLEPES
CLEPING
CLEPSYDRA
CLEPT
CLERGIES
CLERGY
CLERGYMAN
CLERGYMEN
CLERIC
CLERICAL
CLERICALS
CLERICATE

CLERICITY
CLERICS
CLERID
CLERIDS
CLERIHEW
CLERIHEWS
CLERISIES
CLERISY
CLERK
CLERKDOM
CLERKDOMS
CLERKED
CLERKESS
CLERKING
CLERKISH
CLERKLIER
CLERKLIKE
CLERKLING
CLERKLY
CLERKS
CLERKSHIP
CLERUCH
CLERUCHIA
CLERUCHS
CLERUCHY
CLEUCH
CLEUCHS
CLEUGH
CLEUGHS
CLEVE
CLEVEITE
CLEVEITES
CLEVER
CLEVERER
CLEVEREST
CLEVERISH
CLEVERLY
CLEVES
CLEVIS
CLEVISES
CLEW
CLEWED
CLEWING
CLEWS
CLIANTHUS
CLICHE
CLICHED
CLICHEED

CLICHES
CLICK
CLICKABLE
CLICKBAIT
CLICKED
CLICKER
CLICKERS
CLICKET
CLICKETED
CLICKETS
CLICKING
CLICKINGS
CLICKLESS
CLICKS
CLICKWRAP
CLIED
CLIENT
CLIENTAGE
CLIENTAL
CLIENTELE
CLIENTS
CLIES
CLIFF
CLIFFED
CLIFFHANG
CLIFFHUNG
CLIFFIER
CLIFFIEST
CLIFFLIKE
CLIFFS
CLIFFSIDE
CLIFFTOP
CLIFFTOPS
CLIFFY
CLIFT
CLIFTED
CLIFTIER
CLIFTIEST
CLIFTS
CLIFTY
CLIMACTIC
CLIMATAL
CLIMATE
CLIMATED
CLIMATES
CLIMATIC
CLIMATING
CLIMATISE

CLIMATIZE
CLIMATURE
CLIMAX
CLIMAXED
CLIMAXES
CLIMAXING
CLIMB
CLIMBABLE
CLIMBDOWN
CLIMBED
CLIMBER
CLIMBERS
CLIMBING
CLIMBINGS
CLIMBS
CLIME
CLIMES
CLINAL
CLINALLY
CLINAMEN
CLINAMENS
CLINCH
CLINCHED
CLINCHER
CLINCHERS
CLINCHES
CLINCHING
CLINE
CLINES
CLING
CLINGED
CLINGER
CLINGERS
CLINGFILM
CLINGFISH
CLINGIER
CLINGIEST
CLINGING
CLINGS
CLINGWRAP
CLINGY
CLINIC
CLINICAL
CLINICIAN
CLINICS
CLINIQUE
CLINIQUES
CLINK

CLINKED
CLINKER
CLINKERED
CLINKERS
CLINKING
CLINKS
CLINOAXES
CLINOAXIS
CLINOSTAT
CLINQUANT
CLINT
CLINTONIA
CLINTS
CLIOMETRY
CLIP
CLIPART
CLIPARTS
CLIPBOARD
CLIPE
CLIPED
CLIPES
CLIPING
CLIPPABLE
CLIPPED
CLIPPER
CLIPPERS
CLIPPIE
CLIPPIES
CLIPPING
CLIPPINGS
CLIPS
CLIPSHEAR
CLIPSHEET
CLIPT
CLIQUE
CLIQUED
CLIQUES
CLIQUEY
CLIQUIER
CLIQUIEST
CLIQUING
CLIQUISH
CLIQUISM
CLIQUISMS
CLIQUY
CLIT
CLITELLA
CLITELLAR

CLITELLUM	CLODDED	CLONE	CLOSETED	CLOUDED
CLITHRAL	CLODDIER	CLONED	CLOSETFUL	CLOUDIER
CLITIC	CLODDIEST	CLONER	CLOSETING	CLOUDIEST
CLITICISE	CLODDING	CLONERS	CLOSETS	CLOUDILY
CLITICIZE	CLODDISH	CLONES	CLOSEUP	CLOUDING
CLITICS	CLODDY	CLONIC	CLOSEUPS	CLOUDINGS
CLITORAL	CLODLY	CLONICITY	CLOSING	CLOUDLAND
CLITORIC	CLODPATE	CLONIDINE	CLOSINGS	CLOUDLESS
CLITORIS	CLODPATED	CLONING	CLOSURE	CLOUDLET
CLITS	CLODPATES	CLONINGS	CLOSURED	CLOUDLETS
CLITTER	CLODPOLE	CLONISM	CLOSURES	CLOUDLIKE
CLITTERED	CLODPOLES	CLONISMS	CLOSURING	CLOUDS
CLITTERS	CLODPOLL	CLONK	CLOT	CLOUDTOWN
CLIVERS	CLODPOLLS	CLONKED	CLOTBUR	CLOUDY
CLIVIA	CLODS	CLONKIER	CLOTBURS	CLOUGH
CLIVIAS	CLOFF	CLONKIEST	CLOTE	CLOUGHS
CLOACA	CLOFFS	CLONKING	CLOTES	CLOUR
CLOACAE	CLOG	CLONKS	CLOTH	CLOURED
CLOACAL	CLOGDANCE	CLONKY	CLOTHE	CLOURING
CLOACAS	CLOGGED	CLONS	CLOTHED	CLOURS
CLOACINAL	CLOGGER	CLONUS	CLOTHES	CLOUS
CLOACITIS	CLOGGERS	CLONUSES	CLOTHIER	CLOUT
CLOAK	CLOGGIER	CLOOP	CLOTHIERS	CLOUTED
CLOAKED	CLOGGIEST	CLOOPS	CLOTHING	CLOUTER
CLOAKING	CLOGGILY	CLOOT	CLOTHINGS	CLOUTERLY
CLOAKROOM	CLOGGING	CLOOTIE	CLOTHLIKE	CLOUTERS
CLOAKS	CLOGGINGS	CLOOTS	CLOTHS	CLOUTING
CLOAM	CLOGGY	CLOP	CLOTPOLL	CLOUTS
CLOAMS	CLOGMAKER	CLOPPED	CLOTPOLLS	CLOVE
CLOBBER	CLOGS	CLOPPING	CLOTS	CLOVEN
CLOBBERED	CLOISON	CLOPS	CLOTTED	CLOVER
CLOBBERS	CLOISONNE	CLOQUE	CLOTTER	CLOVERED
CLOCHARD	CLOISONS	CLOQUES	CLOTTERED	CLOVERIER
CLOCHARDS	CLOISTER	CLOSABLE	CLOTTERS	CLOVERS
CLOCHE	CLOISTERS	CLOSE	CLOTTIER	CLOVERY
CLOCHES	CLOISTRAL	CLOSEABLE	CLOTTIEST	CLOVES
CLOCK	CLOKE	CLOSED	CLOTTING	CLOVIS
CLOCKED	CLOKED	CLOSEDOWN	CLOTTINGS	CLOW
CLOCKER	CLOKES	CLOSEHEAD	CLOTTISH	CLOWDER
CLOCKERS	CLOKING	CLOSELY	CLOTTY	CLOWDERS
CLOCKFACE	CLOMB	CLOSENESS	CLOTURE	CLOWED
CLOCKING	CLOMP	CLOSEOUT	CLOTURED	CLOWING
CLOCKINGS	CLOMPED	CLOSEOUTS	CLOTURES	CLOWN
CLOCKLIKE	CLOMPING	CLOSER	CLOTURING	CLOWNED
CLOCKS	CLOMPS	CLOSERS	CLOU	CLOWNERY
CLOCKWISE	CLON	CLOSES	CLOUD	CLOWNFISH
CLOCKWORK	CLONAL	CLOSEST	CLOUDAGE	CLOWNING
CLOD	CLONALLY	CLOSET	CLOUDAGES	CLOWNINGS

CLOWNISH	CLUBMAN	CLUMPY	CLYSTERS	COADUNATE
CLOWNS	CLUBMATE	CLUMSIER	CNEMIAL	COADY
CLOWS	CLUBMATES	CLUMSIEST	CNEMIDES	COAEVAL
CLOY	CLUBMEN	CLUMSILY	CNEMIS	COAEVALS
CLOYE	CLUBMOSS	CLUMSY	CNIDA	COAGENCY
CLOYED	CLUBROOM	CLUNCH	CNIDAE	COAGENT
CLOYES	CLUBROOMS	CLUNCHES	CNIDARIAN	COAGENTS
CLOYING	CLUBROOT	CLUNG	COACH	COAGULA
CLOYINGLY	CLUBROOTS	CLUNK	COACHABLE	COAGULANT
CLOYLESS	CLUBRUSH	CLUNKED	COACHDOG	COAGULASE
CLOYMENT	CLUBS	CLUNKER	COACHDOGS	COAGULATE
CLOYMENTS	CLUBWOMAN	CLUNKERS	COACHED	COAGULUM
CLOYS	CLUBWOMEN	CLUNKIER	COACHEE	COAGULUMS
CLOYSOME	CLUCK	CLUNKIEST	COACHEES	COAITA
CLOZAPINE	CLUCKED	CLUNKING	COACHER	COAITAS
CLOZE	CLUCKER	CLUNKS	COACHERS	COAL
CLOZES	CLUCKERS	CLUNKY	COACHES	COALA
CLUB	CLUCKIER	CLUPEID	COACHIER	COALAS
CLUBABLE	CLUCKIEST	CLUPEIDS	COACHIES	COALBALL
CLUBBABLE	CLUCKING	CLUPEOID	COACHIEST	COALBALLS
CLUBBED	CLUCKS	CLUPEOIDS	COACHING	COALBIN
CLUBBER	CLUCKY	CLUSIA	COACHINGS	COALBINS
CLUBBERS	CLUDGIE	CLUSIAS	COACHLINE	COALBOX
CLUBBIER	CLUDGIES	CLUSTER	COACHLOAD	COALBOXES
CLUBBIEST	CLUE	CLUSTERED	COACHMAN	COALDUST
CLUBBILY	CLUED	CLUSTERS	COACHMEN	COALDUSTS
CLUBBING	CLUEING	CLUSTERY	COACHROOF	COALED
CLUBBINGS	CLUELESS	CLUTCH	COACHWHIP	COALER
CLUBBISH	CLUES	CLUTCHED	COACHWOOD	COALERS
CLUBBISM	CLUEY	CLUTCHES	COACHWORK	COALESCE
CLUBBISMS	CLUIER	CLUTCHIER	COACHY	COALESCED
CLUBBIST	CLUIEST	CLUTCHING	COACT	COALESCES
CLUBBISTS	CLUING	CLUTCHY	COACTED	COALFACE
CLUBBY	CLUMBER	CLUTTER	COACTING	COALFACES
CLUBFACE	CLUMBERS	CLUTTERED	COACTION	COALFIELD
CLUBFACES	CLUMP	CLUTTERS	COACTIONS	COALFISH
CLUBFEET	CLUMPED	CLUTTERY	COACTIVE	COALHOLE
CLUBFOOT	CLUMPER	CLY	COACTOR	COALHOLES
CLUBHAND	CLUMPERED	CLYING	COACTORS	COALHOUSE
CLUBHANDS	CLUMPERS	CLYPE	COACTS	COALIER
CLUBHAUL	CLUMPET	CLYPEAL	COADAPTED	COALIEST
CLUBHAULS	CLUMPETS	CLYPEATE	COADIES	COALIFIED
CLUBHEAD	CLUMPIER	CLYPED	COADJUTOR	COALIFIES
CLUBHEADS	CLUMPIEST	CLYPEI	COADMIRE	COALIFY
CLUBHOUSE	CLUMPING	CLYPES	COADMIRED	COALING
CLUBLAND	CLUMPISH	CLYPEUS	COADMIRES	COALISE
CLUBLANDS	CLUMPLIKE	CLYPING	COADMIT	COALISED
CLUBLIKE	CLUMPS	CLYSTER	COADMITS	COALISES

COALISING	COASSUME	COAXER	COBURG	COCHINS
COALITION	COASSUMED	COAXERS	COBURGS	COCHLEA
COALIZE	COASSUMES	COAXES	COBWEB	COCHLEAE
COALIZED	COAST	COAXIAL	COBWEBBED	COCHLEAR
COALIZES	COASTAL	COAXIALLY	COBWEBBY	COCHLEARE
COALIZING	COASTALLY	COAXING	COBWEBS	COCHLEARS
COALLESS	COASTED	COAXINGLY	COBZA	COCHLEAS
COALMAN	COASTER	COAXINGS	COBZAS	COCHLEATE
COALMEN	COASTERS	COB	COCA	COCINERA
COALMINE	COASTING	COBAEA	COCAIN	COCINERAS
COALMINER	COASTINGS	COBAEAS	COCAINE	COCK
COALMINES	COASTLAND	COBALAMIN	COCAINES	COCKADE
COALPIT	COASTLINE	COBALT	COCAINISE	COCKADED
COALPITS	COASTS	COBALTIC	COCAINISM	COCKADES
COALS	COASTWARD	COBALTINE	COCAINIST	COCKAMAMY
COALSACK	COASTWISE	COBALTITE	COCAINIZE	COCKAPOO
COALSACKS	COAT	COBALTOUS	COCAINS	COCKAPOOS
COALSHED	COATDRESS	COBALTS	COCAPTAIN	COCKATEEL
COALSHEDS	COATE	COBB	COCAS	COCKATIEL
COALY	COATED	COBBED	COCCAL	COCKATOO
COALYARD	COATEE	COBBER	COCCI	COCKATOOS
COALYARDS	COATEES	COBBERS	COCCIC	COCKBILL
COAMING	COATER	COBBIER	COCCID	COCKBILLS
COAMINGS	COATERS	COBBIEST	COCCIDIA	COCKBIRD
COANCHOR	COATES	COBBING	COCCIDIAN	COCKBIRDS
COANCHORS	COATI	COBBLE	COCCIDIUM	COCKBOAT
COANNEX	COATING	COBBLED	COCCIDS	COCKBOATS
COANNEXED	COATINGS	COBBLER	COCCO	COCKCROW
COANNEXES	COATIS	COBBLERS	COCCOID	COCKCROWS
COAPPEAR	COATLESS	COBBLERY	COCCOIDAL	COCKED
COAPPEARS	COATLIKE	COBBLES	COCCOIDS	COCKER
COAPT	COATRACK	COBBLING	COCCOLITE	COCKERED
COAPTED	COATRACKS	COBBLINGS	COCCOLITH	COCKEREL
COAPTING	COATROOM	COBBS	COCCOS	COCKERELS
COAPTS	COATROOMS	COBBY	COCCOUS	COCKERING
COARB	COATS	COBIA	COCCUS	COCKERS
COARBS	COATSTAND	COBIAS	COCCYGEAL	COCKET
COARCTATE	COATTAIL	COBLE	COCCYGES	COCKETS
COARSE	COATTAILS	COBLES	COCCYGIAN	COCKEYE
COARSELY	COATTEND	COBLOAF	COCCYX	COCKEYED
COARSEN	COATTENDS	COBLOAVES	COCCYXES	COCKEYES
COARSENED	COATTEST	COBNUT	COCH	COCKFIGHT
COARSENS	COATTESTS	COBNUTS	COCHAIR	COCKHORSE
COARSER	COAUTHOR	COBRA	COCHAIRED	COCKIER
COARSEST	COAUTHORS	COBRAS	COCHAIRS	COCKIES
COARSISH	COAX	COBRIC	COCHES	COCKIEST
COASSIST	COAXAL	COBRIFORM	COCHIN	COCKILY
COASSISTS	COAXED	COBS	COCHINEAL	COCKINESS

COCKING	COCOA	CODDED	CODGER	COEDS
COCKISH	COCOANUT	CODDER	CODGERS	COEFFECT
COCKLE	COCOANUTS	CODDERS	CODICES	COEFFECTS
COCKLEBUR	COCOAS	CODDING	CODICIL	COEHORN
COCKLED	COCOBOLA	CODDLE	CODICILS	COEHORNS
COCKLEERT	COCOBOLAS	CODDLED	CODIFIED	COELIAC
COCKLEMAN	COCOBOLO	CODDLER	CODIFIER	COELIACS
COCKLEMEN	COCOBOLOS	CODDLERS	CODIFIERS	COELOM
COCKLER	COCOMAT	CODDLES	CODIFIES	COELOMATA
COCKLERS	COCOMATS	CODDLING	CODIFY	COELOMATE
COCKLES	COCONUT	CODE	CODIFYING	COELOME
COCKLIKE	COCONUTS	CODEBOOK	CODILLA	COELOMES
COCKLING	COCONUTTY	CODEBOOKS	CODILLAS	COELOMIC
COCKLINGS	COCOON	CODEBTOR	CODILLE	COELOMS
COCKLOFT	COCOONED	CODEBTORS	CODILLES	COELOSTAT
COCKLOFTS	COCOONER	CODEC	CODING	COEMBODY
COCKMATCH	COCOONERS	CODECS	CODINGS	COEMPLOY
COCKNEY	COCOONERY	CODED	CODIRECT	COEMPLOYS
COCKNEYFY	COCOONING	CODEIA	CODIRECTS	COEMPT
COCKNEYS	COCOONS	CODEIAS	CODIST	COEMPTED
COCKNIFY	COCOPAN	CODEIN	CODISTS	COEMPTING
COCKPIT	COCOPANS	CODEINA	CODLIN	COEMPTION
COCKPITS	COCOPLUM	CODEINAS	CODLING	COEMPTS
COCKROACH	COCOPLUMS	CODEINE	CODLINGS	COENACLE
COCKS	COCOS	CODEINES	CODLINS	COENACLES
COCKSCOMB	COCOTTE	CODEINS	CODOLOGY	COENACT
COCKSFOOT	COCOTTES	CODELESS	CODOMAIN	COENACTED
COCKSHIES	COCOUNSEL	CODEN	CODOMAINS	COENACTS
COCKSHOT	COCOYAM	CODENAME	CODON	COENAMOR
COCKSHOTS	COCOYAMS	CODENAMES	CODONS	COENAMORS
COCKSHUT	COCOZELLE	CODENS	CODPIECE	COENAMOUR
COCKSHUTS	COCREATE	CODER	CODPIECES	COENDURE
COCKSHY	COCREATED	CODERIVE	CODRIVE	COENDURED
COCKSIER	COCREATES	CODERIVED	CODRIVEN	COENDURES
COCKSIEST	COCREATOR	CODERIVES	CODRIVER	COENOBIA
COCKSMAN	COCTILE	CODERS	CODRIVERS	COENOBITE
COCKSMEN	COCTION	CODES	CODRIVES	COENOBIUM
COCKSPUR	COCTIONS	CODESIGN	CODRIVING	COENOCYTE
COCKSPURS	COCULTURE	CODESIGNS	CODROVE	COENOSARC
COCKSURE	COCURATE	CODETTA	CODS	COENURE
COCKSWAIN	COCURATED	CODETTAS	COECILIAN	COENURES
COCKSY	COCURATES	CODEVELOP	COED	COENURI
COCKTAIL	COCURATOR	CODEWORD	COEDIT	COENURUS
COCKTAILS	COCUSWOOD	CODEWORDS	COEDITED	COENZYME
COCKUP	COD	CODEX	COEDITING	COENZYMES
COCKUPS	CODA	CODEXES	COEDITOR	COEQUAL
COCKY	CODABLE	CODFISH	COEDITORS	COEQUALLY
COCO	CODAS	CODFISHES	COEDITS	COEQUALS

COEQUATE	COFFIN	COGITATED	COHABITER	COHOSTED
COEQUATED	COFFINED	COGITATES	COHABITOR	COHOSTESS
COEQUATES	COFFING	COGITATOR	COHABITS	COHOSTING
COERCE	COFFINING	COGITO	COHABS	COHOSTS
COERCED	COFFINITE	COGITOS	COHEAD	COHOUSING
COERCER	COFFINS	COGNAC	COHEADED	COHUNE
COERCERS	COFFLE	COGNACS	COHEADING	COHUNES
COERCES	COFFLED	COGNATE	COHEADS	COHYPONYM
COERCIBLE	COFFLES	COGNATELY	COHEIR	COIF
COERCIBLY	COFFLING	COGNATES	COHEIRESS	COIFED
COERCING	COFFRET	COGNATION	COHEIRS	COIFFE
COERCION	COFFRETS	COGNISANT	COHEN	COIFFED
COERCIONS	COFFS	COGNISE	COHENS	COIFFES
COERCIVE	COFINANCE	COGNISED	COHERE	COIFFEUR
COERECT	COFIRING	COGNISER	COHERED	COIFFEURS
COERECTED	COFIRINGS	COGNISERS	COHERENCE	COIFFEUSE
COERECTS	COFOUND	COGNISES	COHERENCY	COIFFING
COESITE	COFOUNDED	COGNISING	COHERENT	COIFFURE
COESITES	COFOUNDER	COGNITION	COHERER	COIFFURED
COETERNAL	COFOUNDS	COGNITIVE	COHERERS	COIFFURES
COEVAL	COFT	COGNIZANT	COHERES	COIFING
COEVALITY	COG	COGNIZE	COHERING	COIFS
COEVALLY	COGENCE	COGNIZED	COHERITOR	COIGN
COEVALS	COGENCES	COGNIZER	COHESIBLE	COIGNE
COEVOLVE	COGENCIES	COGNIZERS	COHESION	COIGNED
COEVOLVED	COGENCY	COGNIZES	COHESIONS	COIGNES
COEVOLVES	COGENER	COGNIZING	COHESIVE	COIGNING
COEXERT	COGENERS	COGNOMEN	COHIBIT	COIGNS
COEXERTED	COGENT	COGNOMENS	COHIBITED	COIL
COEXERTS	COGENTLY	COGNOMINA	COHIBITS	COILED
COEXIST	COGGED	COGNOSCE	COHO	COILER
COEXISTED	COGGER	COGNOSCED	COHOBATE	COILERS
COEXISTS	COGGERS	COGNOSCES	COHOBATED	COILING
COEXTEND	COGGIE	COGNOVIT	COHOBATES	COILS
COEXTENDS	COGGIES	COGNOVITS	COHOE	COIN
COFACTOR	COGGING	COGON	COHOES	COINABLE
COFACTORS	COGGINGS	COGONS	COHOG	COINAGE
COFEATURE	COGGLE	COGS	COHOGS	COINAGES
COFF	COGGLED	COGUE	COHOLDER	COINCIDE
COFFED	COGGLES	COGUES	COHOLDERS	COINCIDED
COFFEE	COGGLIER	COGWAY	COHORN	COINCIDES
COFFEEPOT	COGGLIEST	COGWAYS	COHORNS	COINED
COFFEES	COGGLING	COGWHEEL	COHORT	COINER
COFFER	COGGLY	COGWHEELS	COHORTS	COINERS
COFFERDAM	COGIE	COHAB	COHOS	COINFECT
COFFERED	COGIES	COHABIT	COHOSH	COINFECTS
COFFERING	COGITABLE	COHABITED	COHOSHES	COINFER
COFFERS	COGITATE	COHABITEE	COHOST	COINFERS

COINHERE	COKESES	COLESSOR	COLLAPSED	COLLIERS
COINHERED	COKIER	COLESSORS	COLLAPSES	COLLIERY
COINHERES	COKIEST	COLETIT	COLLAR	COLLIES
COINING	COKING	COLETITS	COLLARD	COLLIGATE
COININGS	COKINGS	COLEUS	COLLARDS	COLLIMATE
COINMATE	COKULORIS	COLEUSES	COLLARED	COLLINEAR
COINMATES	COKY	COLEWORT	COLLARET	COLLING
COINOP	COL	COLEWORTS	COLLARETS	COLLINGS
COINS	COLA	COLEY	COLLARING	COLLINS
COINSURE	COLANDER	COLEYS	COLLARS	COLLINSES
COINSURED	COLANDERS	COLIBRI	COLLATE	COLLINSIA
COINSURER	COLAS	COLIBRIS	COLLATED	COLLISION
COINSURES	COLBIES	COLIC	COLLATES	COLLOCATE
COINTER	COLBY	COLICIN	COLLATING	COLLODION
COINTERS	COLBYS	COLICINE	COLLATION	COLLODIUM
COINTREAU	COLCANNON	COLICINES	COLLATIVE	COLLOGUE
COINVENT	COLCHICA	COLICINS	COLLATOR	COLLOGUED
COINVENTS	COLCHICUM	COLICKIER	COLLATORS	COLLOGUES
COINVEST	COLCOTHAR	COLICKY	COLLEAGUE	COLLOID
COINVESTS	COLD	COLICROOT	COLLECT	COLLOIDAL
COIR	COLDBLOOD	COLICS	COLLECTED	COLLOIDS
COIRS	COLDCOCK	COLICWEED	COLLECTOR	COLLOP
COISTREL	COLDCOCKS	COLIES	COLLECTS	COLLOPS
COISTRELS	COLDER	COLIFORM	COLLED	COLLOQUE
COISTRIL	COLDEST	COLIFORMS	COLLEEN	COLLOQUED
COISTRILS	COLDHOUSE	COLIN	COLLEENS	COLLOQUES
COIT	COLDIE	COLINEAR	COLLEGE	COLLOQUIA
COITAL	COLDIES	COLINS	COLLEGER	COLLOQUY
COITALLY	COLDISH	COLIPHAGE	COLLEGERS	COLLOTYPE
COITION	COLDLY	COLISEUM	COLLEGES	COLLOTYPY
COITIONAL	COLDNESS	COLISEUMS	COLLEGIA	COLLS
COITIONS	COLDS	COLISTIN	COLLEGIAL	COLLUDE
COITS	COLE	COLISTINS	COLLEGIAN	COLLUDED
COITUS	COLEAD	COLITIC	COLLEGIUM	COLLUDER
COITUSES	COLEADER	COLITIS	COLLET	COLLUDERS
COJOIN	COLEADERS	COLITISES	COLLETED	COLLUDES
COJOINED	COLEADING	COLL	COLLETING	COLLUDING
COJOINING	COLEADS	COLLAB	COLLETS	COLLUSION
COJOINS	COLECTOMY	COLLABS	COLLICULI	COLLUSIVE
COJONES	COLED	COLLAGE	COLLIDE	COLLUVIA
COKE	COLEOPTER	COLLAGED	COLLIDED	COLLUVIAL
COKED	COLES	COLLAGEN	COLLIDER	COLLUVIES
COKEHEAD	COLESEED	COLLAGENS	COLLIDERS	COLLUVIUM
COKEHEADS	COLESEEDS	COLLAGES	COLLIDES	COLLY
COKELIKE	COLESLAW	COLLAGING	COLLIDING	COLLYING
COKERNUT	COLESLAWS	COLLAGIST	COLLIE	COLLYRIA
COKERNUTS	COLESSEE	COLLAPSAR	COLLIED	COLLYRIUM
COKES	COLESSEES	COLLAPSE	COLLIER	COLOBI

COLOBID	COLORABLY	COLOURED	COLUMELLA	COMBATERS
COLOBIDS	COLORADO	COLOUREDS	COLUMELS	COMBATING
COLOBOMA	COLORANT	COLOURER	COLUMN	COMBATIVE
COLOBOMAS	COLORANTS	COLOURERS	COLUMNAL	COMBATS
COLOBUS	COLORBRED	COLOURFUL	COLUMNALS	COMBATTED
COLOBUSES	COLORCAST	COLOURIER	COLUMNAR	COMBE
COLOCATE	COLORED	COLOURING	COLUMNEA	COMBED
COLOCATED	COLOREDS	COLOURISE	COLUMNEAS	COMBER
COLOCATES	COLORER	COLOURISM	COLUMNED	COMBERS
COLOCYNTH	COLORERS	COLOURIST	COLUMNIST	COMBES
COLOG	COLORFAST	COLOURIZE	COLUMNS	COMBI
COLOGNE	COLORFUL	COLOURMAN	COLURE	COMBIER
COLOGNED	COLORIER	COLOURMEN	COLURES	COMBIES
COLOGNES	COLORIEST	COLOURS	COLY	COMBIEST
COLOGS	COLORIFIC	COLOURWAY	COLZA	COMBINATE
COLOMBARD	COLORING	COLOURY	COLZAS	COMBINE
COLON	COLORINGS	COLPITIS	COMA	COMBINED
COLONE	COLORISE	COLPOTOMY	COMADE	COMBINEDS
COLONEL	COLORISED	COLS	COMAE	COMBINER
COLONELCY	COLORISER	COLT	COMAKE	COMBINERS
COLONELS	COLORISES	COLTAN	COMAKER	COMBINES
COLONES	COLORISM	COLTANS	COMAKERS	COMBING
COLONI	COLORISMS	COLTED	COMAKES	COMBINGS
COLONIAL	COLORIST	COLTER	COMAKING	COMBINING
COLONIALS	COLORISTS	COLTERS	COMAL	COMBIS
COLONIC	COLORIZE	COLTHOOD	COMANAGE	COMBLE
COLONICS	COLORIZED	COLTHOODS	COMANAGED	COMBLES
COLONIES	COLORIZER	COLTING	COMANAGER	COMBLESS
COLONISE	COLORIZES	COLTISH	COMANAGES	COMBLIKE
COLONISED	COLORLESS	COLTISHLY	COMARB	COMBO
COLONISER	COLORMAN	COLTS	COMARBS	COMBOS
COLONISES	COLORMEN	COLTSFOOT	COMART	COMBOVER
COLONIST	COLORS	COLTWOOD	COMARTS	COMBOVERS
COLONISTS	COLORWASH	COLTWOODS	COMAS	COMBRETUM
COLONITIS	COLORWAY	COLUBRIAD	COMATE	COMBS
COLONIZE	COLORWAYS	COLUBRID	COMATES	COMBUST
COLONIZED	COLORY	COLUBRIDS	COMATIC	COMBUSTED
COLONIZER	COLOSSAL	COLUBRINE	COMATIK	COMBUSTOR
COLONIZES	COLOSSEUM	COLUGO	COMATIKS	COMBUSTS
COLONNADE	COLOSSI	COLUGOS	COMATOSE	COMBWISE
COLONS	COLOSSUS	COLUMBARY	COMATULA	COMBY
COLONUS	COLOSTOMY	COLUMBATE	COMATULAE	COME
COLONY	COLOSTRAL	COLUMBIC	COMATULID	COMEBACK
COLOPHON	COLOSTRIC	COLUMBINE	COMB	COMEBACKS
COLOPHONS	COLOSTRUM	COLUMBITE	COMBAT	COMEDDLE
COLOPHONY	COLOTOMY	COLUMBIUM	COMBATANT	COMEDDLED
COLOR	COLOUR	COLUMBOUS	COMBATED	COMEDDLES
COLORABLE	COLOURANT	COLUMEL	COMBATER	COMEDIAN

C

COMEDIANS	COMICS	COMMERGE	COMMOTS	COMPANDOR
COMEDIC	COMING	COMMERGED	COMMOVE	COMPANDS
COMEDIES	COMINGLE	COMMERGES	COMMOVED	COMPANIED
COMEDIST	COMINGLED	COMMERS	COMMOVES	COMPANIES
COMEDISTS	COMINGLES	COMMIE	COMMOVING	COMPANING
COMEDO	COMINGS	COMMIES	COMMS	COMPANION
COMEDONES	COMIQUE	COMMINATE	COMMUNAL	COMPANY
COMEDOS	COMIQUES	COMMINGLE	COMMUNARD	COMPARE
COMEDOWN	COMITADJI	COMMINUTE	COMMUNE	COMPARED
COMEDOWNS	COMITAL	COMMIS	COMMUNED	COMPARER
COMEDY	COMITATUS	COMMISH	COMMUNER	COMPARERS
COMELIER	COMITIA	COMMISHES	COMMUNERS	COMPARES
COMELIEST	COMITIAL	COMMISSAR	COMMUNES	COMPARING
COMELILY	COMITIAS	COMMIT	COMMUNING	COMPART
COMELY	COMITIES	COMMITS	COMMUNION	COMPARTED
COMEMBER	COMITY	COMMITTAL	COMMUNISE	COMPARTS
COMEMBERS	COMIX	COMMITTED	COMMUNISM	COMPAS
COMEOVER	COMM	COMMITTEE	COMMUNIST	COMPASS
COMEOVERS	COMMA	COMMITTER	COMMUNITY	COMPASSED
COMER	COMMAND	COMMIX	COMMUNIZE	COMPASSES
COMERS	COMMANDED	COMMIXED	COMMUTATE	COMPAST
COMES	COMMANDER	COMMIXES	COMMUTE	COMPEAR
COMET	COMMANDO	COMMIXING	COMMUTED	COMPEARED
COMETARY	COMMANDOS	COMMIXT	COMMUTER	COMPEARS
COMETH	COMMANDS	COMMO	COMMUTERS	COMPED
COMETHER	COMMAS	COMMODE	COMMUTES	COMPEER
COMETHERS	COMMATA	COMMODES	COMMUTING	COMPEERED
COMETIC	COMMENCE	COMMODIFY	COMMUTUAL	COMPEERS
COMETS	COMMENCED	COMMODITY	COMMY	COMPEL
COMFIER	COMMENCER	COMMODO	COMODO	COMPELLED
COMFIEST	COMMENCES	COMMODORE	COMONOMER	COMPELLER
COMFILY	COMMEND	COMMON	COMORBID	COMPELS
COMFINESS	COMMENDAM	COMMONAGE	COMOSE	COMPEND
COMFIT	COMMENDED	COMMONED	COMOUS	COMPENDIA
COMFITS	COMMENDER	COMMONER	COMP	COMPENDS
COMFITURE	COMMENDS	COMMONERS	COMPACT	COMPER
COMFORT	COMMENSAL	COMMONEST	COMPACTED	COMPERE
COMFORTED	COMMENT	COMMONEY	COMPACTER	COMPERED
COMFORTER	COMMENTED	COMMONEYS	COMPACTLY	COMPERES
COMFORTS	COMMENTER	COMMONING	COMPACTOR	COMPERING
COMFREY	COMMENTOR	COMMONLY	COMPACTS	COMPERS
COMFREYS	COMMENTS	COMMONS	COMPADRE	COMPESCE
COMFY	COMMER	COMMORANT	COMPADRES	COMPESCED
COMIC	COMMERCE	COMMOS	COMPAGE	COMPESCES
COMICAL	COMMERCED	COMMOT	COMPAGES	COMPETE
COMICALLY	COMMERCES	COMMOTE	COMPAND	COMPETED
COMICE	COMMERE	COMMOTES	COMPANDED	COMPETENT
COMICES	COMMERES	COMMOTION	COMPANDER	COMPETES

COMPETING	COMPONY	COMPUTANT	CONCEDERS	CONCHOS
COMPILE	COMPORT	COMPUTE	CONCEDES	CONCHS
COMPILED	COMPORTED	COMPUTED	CONCEDING	CONCHY
COMPILER	COMPORTS	COMPUTER	CONCEDO	CONCIERGE
COMPILERS	COMPOS	COMPUTERS	CONCEIT	CONCILIAR
COMPILES	COMPOSE	COMPUTES	CONCEITED	CONCISE
COMPILING	COMPOSED	COMPUTING	CONCEITS	CONCISED
COMPING	COMPOSER	COMPUTIST	CONCEITY	CONCISELY
COMPINGS	COMPOSERS	COMRADE	CONCEIVE	CONCISER
COMPITAL	COMPOSES	COMRADELY	CONCEIVED	CONCISES
COMPLAIN	COMPOSING	COMRADERY	CONCEIVER	CONCISEST
COMPLAINS	COMPOSITE	COMRADES	CONCEIVES	CONCISING
COMPLAINT	COMPOST	COMS	CONCENT	CONCISION
COMPLEAT	COMPOSTED	COMSAT	CONCENTER	CONCLAVE
COMPLEATS	COMPOSTER	COMSATS	CONCENTRE	CONCLAVES
COMPLECT	COMPOSTS	COMSYMP	CONCENTS	CONCLUDE
COMPLECTS	COMPOSURE	COMSYMPS	CONCENTUS	CONCLUDED
COMPLETE	COMPOT	COMTE	CONCEPT	CONCLUDER
COMPLETED	COMPOTE	COMTES	CONCEPTI	CONCLUDES
COMPLETER	COMPOTES	COMUS	CONCEPTS	CONCOCT
COMPLETES	COMPOTIER	COMUSES	CONCEPTUS	CONCOCTED
COMPLEX	COMPOTS	CON	CONCERN	CONCOCTER
COMPLEXED	COMPOUND	CONACRE	CONCERNED	CONCOCTOR
COMPLEXER	COMPOUNDS	CONACRED	CONCERNS	CONCOCTS
COMPLEXES	COMPRADOR	CONACRES	CONCERT	CONCOLOR
COMPLEXLY	COMPRESS	CONACRING	CONCERTED	CONCORD
COMPLEXUS	COMPRINT	CONARIA	CONCERTI	CONCORDAL
COMPLIANT	COMPRINTS	CONARIAL	CONCERTO	CONCORDAT
COMPLICE	COMPRISAL	CONARIUM	CONCERTOS	CONCORDED
COMPLICES	COMPRISE	CONATION	CONCERTS	CONCORDS
COMPLICIT	COMPRISED	CONATIONS	CONCETTI	CONCOURS
COMPLIED	COMPRISES	CONATIVE	CONCETTO	CONCOURSE
COMPLIER	COMPRIZE	CONATUS	CONCH	CONCREATE
COMPLIERS	COMPRIZED	CONCAUSE	CONCHA	CONCRETE
COMPLIES	COMPRIZES	CONCAUSES	CONCHAE	CONCRETED
COMPLIN	COMPS	CONCAVE	CONCHAL	CONCRETES
COMPLINE	COMPT	CONCAVED	CONCHAS	CONCREW
COMPLINES	COMPTABLE	CONCAVELY	CONCHATE	CONCREWED
COMPLINS	COMPTED	CONCAVES	CONCHE	CONCREWS
COMPLISH	COMPTER	CONCAVING	CONCHED	CONCUBINE
COMPLOT	COMPTERS	CONCAVITY	CONCHES	CONCUPIES
COMPLOTS	COMPTIBLE	CONCEAL	CONCHIE	CONCUPY
COMPLUVIA	COMPTING	CONCEALED	CONCHIES	CONCUR
COMPLY	COMPTROLL	CONCEALER	CONCHING	CONCURRED
COMPLYING	COMPTS	CONCEALS	CONCHITIS	CONCURS
COMPO	COMPULSE	CONCEDE	CONCHO	CONCUSS
COMPONE	COMPULSED	CONCEDED	CONCHOID	CONCUSSED
COMPONENT	COMPULSES	CONCEDER	CONCHOIDS	CONCUSSES

C

CONCYCLIC	CONDUCT	CONFESSED	CONFORMED	CONGESTS
COND	CONDUCTED	CONFESSES	CONFORMER	CONGIARY
CONDEMN	CONDUCTI	CONFESSOR	CONFORMS	CONGII
CONDEMNED	CONDUCTOR	CONFEST	CONFOUND	CONGIUS
CONDEMNER	CONDUCTS	CONFESTLY	CONFOUNDS	CONGLOBE
CONDEMNOR	CONDUCTUS	CONFETTI	CONFRERE	CONGLOBED
CONDEMNS	CONDUIT	CONFETTO	CONFRERES	CONGLOBES
CONDENSE	CONDUITS	CONFIDANT	CONFRERIE	CONGO
CONDENSED	CONDYLAR	CONFIDE	CONFRONT	CONGOES
CONDENSER	CONDYLE	CONFIDED	CONFRONTE	CONGOS
CONDENSES	CONDYLES	CONFIDENT	CONFRONTS	CONGOU
CONDER	CONDYLOID	CONFIDER	CONFS	CONGOUS
CONDERS	CONDYLOMA	CONFIDERS	CONFUSE	CONGRATS
CONDIDDLE	CONE	CONFIDES	CONFUSED	CONGREE
CONDIE	CONED	CONFIDING	CONFUSES	CONGREED
CONDIES	CONELESS	CONFIGURE	CONFUSING	CONGREES
CONDIGN	CONELIKE	CONFINE	CONFUSION	CONGREET
CONDIGNLY	CONELRAD	CONFINED	CONFUTE	CONGREETS
CONDIMENT	CONELRADS	CONFINER	CONFUTED	CONGRESS
CONDITION	CONENOSE	CONFINERS	CONFUTER	CONGRUE
CONDO	CONENOSES	CONFINES	CONFUTERS	CONGRUED
CONDOES	CONEPATE	CONFINING	CONFUTES	CONGRUENT
CONDOLE	CONEPATES	CONFIRM	CONFUTING	CONGRUES
CONDOLED	CONEPATL	CONFIRMED	CONGA	CONGRUING
CONDOLENT	CONEPATLS	CONFIRMEE	CONGAED	CONGRUITY
CONDOLER	CONES	CONFIRMER	CONGAING	CONGRUOUS
CONDOLERS	CONEY	CONFIRMOR	CONGAS	CONI
CONDOLES	CONEYS	CONFIRMS	CONGE	CONIA
CONDOLING	CONF	CONFISEUR	CONGEAL	CONIAS
CONDOM	CONFAB	CONFIT	CONGEALED	CONIC
CONDOMS	CONFABBED	CONFITEOR	CONGEALER	CONICAL
CONDONE	CONFABS	CONFITS	CONGEALS	CONICALLY
CONDONED	CONFECT	CONFITURE	CONGED	CONICINE
CONDONER	CONFECTED	CONFIX	CONGEE	CONICINES
CONDONERS	CONFECTS	CONFIXED	CONGEED	CONICITY
CONDONES	CONFER	CONFIXES	CONGEEING	CONICS
CONDONING	CONFEREE	CONFIXING	CONGEES	CONIDIA
CONDOR	CONFEREES	CONFLATE	CONGEING	CONIDIAL
CONDORES	CONFERRAL	CONFLATED	CONGENER	CONIDIAN
CONDORS	CONFERRED	CONFLATES	CONGENERS	CONIDIUM
CONDOS	CONFERREE	CONFLICT	CONGENIAL	CONIES
CONDUCE	CONFERRER	CONFLICTS	CONGENIC	CONIFER
CONDUCED	CONFERS	CONFLUENT	CONGER	CONIFERS
CONDUCER	CONFERVA	CONFLUX	CONGERIES	CONIFORM
CONDUCERS	CONFERVAE	CONFLUXES	CONGERS	CONIINE
CONDUCES	CONFERVAL	CONFOCAL	CONGES	CONIINES
CONDUCING	CONFERVAS	CONFORM	CONGEST	CONIMA
CONDUCIVE	CONFESS	CONFORMAL	CONGESTED	CONIMAS

CONIN	CONKS	CONOID	CONSOLES	CONSULTED
CONINE	CONKY	CONOIDAL	CONSOLING	CONSULTEE
CONINES	CONLANG	CONOIDIC	CONSOLS	CONSULTER
CONING	CONLANGER	CONOIDS	CONSOLUTE	CONSULTOR
CONINS	CONLANGS	CONOMINEE	CONSOMME	CONSULTS
CONIOLOGY	CONMAN	CONQUER	CONSOMMES	CONSUME
CONIOSES	CONMEN	CONQUERED	CONSONANT	CONSUMED
CONIOSIS	CONN	CONQUERER	CONSONOUS	CONSUMER
CONIUM	CONNATE	CONQUEROR	CONSORT	CONSUMERS
CONIUMS	CONNATELY	CONQUERS	CONSORTED	CONSUMES
CONJECT	CONNATION	CONQUEST	CONSORTER	CONSUMING
CONJECTED	CONNATURE	CONQUESTS	CONSORTIA	CONSUMPT
CONJECTS	CONNE	CONQUIAN	CONSORTS	CONSUMPTS
CONJEE	CONNECT	CONQUIANS	CONSPIRE	CONTACT
CONJEED	CONNECTED	CONS	CONSPIRED	CONTACTED
CONJEEING	CONNECTER	CONSCIENT	CONSPIRER	CONTACTEE
CONJEES	CONNECTOR	CONSCIOUS	CONSPIRES	CONTACTOR
CONJOIN	CONNECTS	CONSCRIBE	CONSPUE	CONTACTS
CONJOINED	CONNED	CONSCRIPT	CONSPUED	CONTADINA
CONJOINER	CONNER	CONSEIL	CONSPUES	CONTADINE
CONJOINS	CONNERS	CONSEILS	CONSPUING	CONTADINI
CONJOINT	CONNES	CONSENSUS	CONSTABLE	CONTADINO
CONJUGAL	CONNEXION	CONSENT	CONSTANCY	CONTAGIA
CONJUGANT	CONNEXIVE	CONSENTED	CONSTANT	CONTAGION
CONJUGATE	CONNIE	CONSENTER	CONSTANTS	CONTAGIUM
CONJUNCT	CONNIES	CONSENTS	CONSTATE	CONTAIN
CONJUNCTS	CONNING	CONSERVE	CONSTATED	CONTAINED
CONJUNTO	CONNINGS	CONSERVED	CONSTATES	CONTAINER
CONJUNTOS	CONNIVE	CONSERVER	CONSTER	CONTAINS
CONJURE	CONNIVED	CONSERVES	CONSTERED	CONTANGO
CONJURED	CONNIVENT	CONSIDER	CONSTERS	CONTANGOS
CONJURER	CONNIVER	CONSIDERS	CONSTRAIN	CONTE
CONJURERS	CONNIVERS	CONSIGN	CONSTRICT	CONTECK
CONJURES	CONNIVERY	CONSIGNED	CONSTRUAL	CONTECKS
CONJURIES	CONNIVES	CONSIGNEE	CONSTRUCT	CONTEMN
CONJURING	CONNIVING	CONSIGNER	CONSTRUE	CONTEMNED
CONJUROR	CONNOR	CONSIGNOR	CONSTRUED	CONTEMNER
CONJURORS	CONNORS	CONSIGNS	CONSTRUER	CONTEMNOR
CONJURY	CONNOTATE	CONSIST	CONSTRUES	CONTEMNS
CONK	CONNOTE	CONSISTED	CONSUL	CONTEMPER
CONKED	CONNOTED	CONSISTS	CONSULAGE	CONTEMPO
CONKER	CONNOTES	CONSOCIES	CONSULAR	CONTEMPT
CONKERS	CONNOTING	CONSOL	CONSULARS	CONTEMPTS
CONKIER	CONNOTIVE	CONSOLATE	CONSULATE	CONTEND
CONKIEST	CONNS	CONSOLE	CONSULS	CONTENDED
CONKING	CONNUBIAL	CONSOLED	CONSULT	CONTENDER
CONKOUT	CONODONT	CONSOLER	CONSULTA	CONTENDS
CONKOUTS	CONODONTS	CONSOLERS	CONSULTAS	CONTENT

C

CONTENTED, CONTENTLY, CONTENTS, CONTES, CONTESSA, CONTESSAS, CONTEST, CONTESTED, CONTESTER, CONTESTS, CONTEXT, CONTEXTS, CONTICENT, CONTINENT, CONTINUA, CONTINUAL, CONTINUE, CONTINUED, CONTINUER, CONTINUES, CONTINUO, CONTINUOS, CONTINUUM, CONTLINE, CONTLINES, CONTO, CONTORNI, CONTORNO, CONTORNOS, CONTORT, CONTORTED, CONTORTS, CONTOS, CONTOUR, CONTOURED, CONTOURS, CONTRA, CONTRACT, CONTRACTS, CONTRAIL, CONTRAILS, CONTRAIR, CONTRALTI, CONTRALTO, CONTRARY, CONTRAS, CONTRAST, CONTRASTS

CONTRASTY, CONTRAT, CONTRATE, CONTRATS, CONTRIST, CONTRISTS, CONTRITE, CONTRIVE, CONTRIVED, CONTRIVER, CONTRIVES, CONTROL, CONTROLE, CONTROLS, CONTROUL, CONTROULS, CONTUMACY, CONTUMELY, CONTUND, CONTUNDED, CONTUNDS, CONTUSE, CONTUSED, CONTUSES, CONTUSING, CONTUSION, CONTUSIVE, CONUNDRUM, CONURBAN, CONURBIA, CONURBIAS, CONURE, CONURES, CONUS, CONVECT, CONVECTED, CONVECTOR, CONVECTS, CONVENE, CONVENED, CONVENER, CONVENERS, CONVENES, CONVENING, CONVENOR, CONVENORS, CONVENT, CONVENTED

CONVENTS, CONVERGE, CONVERGED, CONVERGES, CONVERSE, CONVERSED, CONVERSER, CONVERSES, CONVERSO, CONVERSOS, CONVERT, CONVERTED, CONVERTER, CONVERTOR, CONVERTS, CONVEX, CONVEXED, CONVEXES, CONVEXING, CONVEXITY, CONVEXLY, CONVEY, CONVEYAL, CONVEYALS, CONVEYED, CONVEYER, CONVEYERS, CONVEYING, CONVEYOR, CONVEYORS, CONVEYS, CONVICT, CONVICTED, CONVICTS, CONVINCE, CONVINCED, CONVINCER, CONVINCES, CONVIVE, CONVIVED, CONVIVES, CONVIVIAL, CONVIVING, CONVO, CONVOCATE, CONVOKE, CONVOKED, CONVOKER

CONVOKERS, CONVOKES, CONVOKING, CONVOLUTE, CONVOLVE, CONVOLVED, CONVOLVES, CONVOS, CONVOY, CONVOYED, CONVOYING, CONVOYS, CONVULSE, CONVULSED, CONVULSES, CONWOMAN, CONWOMEN, CONY, COO, COOCH, COOCHES, COOCOO, COOED, COOEE, COOEED, COOEEING, COOEES, COOER, COOERS, COOEY, COOEYED, COOEYING, COOEYS, COOF, COOFS, COOING, COOINGLY, COOINGS, COOK, COOKABLE, COOKABLES, COOKBOOK, COOKBOOKS, COOKED, COOKER, COOKERIES, COOKERS, COOKERY

COOKEY, COOKEYS, COOKHOUSE, COOKIE, COOKIES, COOKING, COOKINGS, COOKLESS, COOKMAID, COOKMAIDS, COOKOFF, COOKOFFS, COOKOUT, COOKOUTS, COOKROOM, COOKROOMS, COOKS, COOKSHACK, COOKSHOP, COOKSHOPS, COOKSTOVE, COOKTOP, COOKTOPS, COOKWARE, COOKWARES, COOKY, COOL, COOLABAH, COOLABAHS, COOLAMON, COOLAMONS, COOLANT, COOLANTS, COOLDOWN, COOLDOWNS, COOLED, COOLER, COOLERS, COOLEST, COOLHOUSE, COOLIBAH, COOLIBAHS, COOLIBAR, COOLIBARS, COOLIE, COOLIES, COOLING, COOLINGLY

COOLINGS	COOPTED	COPARENTS	COPLOTTED	COPS
COOLISH	COOPTING	COPARTNER	COPOLYMER	COPSE
COOLIST	COOPTION	COPASETIC	COPOUT	COPSED
COOLISTS	COOPTIONS	COPASTOR	COPOUTS	COPSES
COOLLY	COOPTS	COPASTORS	COPPED	COPSEWOOD
COOLNESS	COORDINAL	COPATAINE	COPPER	COPSHOP
COOLS	COORIE	COPATRIOT	COPPERAH	COPSHOPS
COOLTH	COORIED	COPATRON	COPPERAHS	COPSIER
COOLTHS	COORIEING	COPATRONS	COPPERAS	COPSIEST
COOLY	COORIES	COPAY	COPPERED	COPSING
COOM	COOS	COPAYMENT	COPPERIER	COPSY
COOMB	COOSEN	COPAYS	COPPERING	COPTER
COOMBE	COOSENED	COPE	COPPERISH	COPTERS
COOMBES	COOSENING	COPECK	COPPERS	COPUBLISH
COOMBS	COOSENS	COPECKS	COPPERY	COPULA
COOMED	COOSER	COPED	COPPICE	COPULAE
COOMIER	COOSERS	COPEMATE	COPPICED	COPULAR
COOMIEST	COOSIN	COPEMATES	COPPICES	COPULAS
COOMING	COOSINED	COPEN	COPPICING	COPULATE
COOMS	COOSINING	COPENS	COPPIES	COPULATED
COOMY	COOSINS	COPEPOD	COPPIN	COPULATES
COON	COOST	COPEPODS	COPPING	COPURIFY
COONCAN	COOT	COPER	COPPINS	COPY
COONCANS	COOTCH	COPERED	COPPLE	COPYABLE
COONDOG	COOTCHED	COPERING	COPPLES	COPYBOOK
COONDOGS	COOTCHES	COPERS	COPPRA	COPYBOOKS
COONHOUND	COOTCHING	COPES	COPPRAS	COPYBOY
COONS	COOTER	COPESETIC	COPPY	COPYBOYS
COONSHIT	COOTERS	COPESTONE	COPRA	COPYCAT
COONSHITS	COOTIE	COPIABLE	COPRAEMIA	COPYCATS
COONSKIN	COOTIES	COPIED	COPRAEMIC	COPYDESK
COONSKINS	COOTIKIN	COPIER	COPRAH	COPYDESKS
COONTIE	COOTIKINS	COPIERS	COPRAHS	COPYEDIT
COONTIES	COOTS	COPIES	COPRAS	COPYEDITS
COONTY	COOZE	COPIHUE	COPREMIA	COPYFIGHT
COOP	COOZES	COPIHUES	COPREMIAS	COPYGIRL
COOPED	COP	COPILOT	COPREMIC	COPYGIRLS
COOPER	COPACETIC	COPILOTED	COPRESENT	COPYGRAPH
COOPERAGE	COPAIBA	COPILOTS	COPRINCE	COPYHOLD
COOPERATE	COPAIBAS	COPING	COPRINCES	COPYHOLDS
COOPERED	COPAIVA	COPINGS	COPRODUCE	COPYING
COOPERIES	COPAIVAS	COPIOUS	COPRODUCT	COPYINGS
COOPERING	COPAL	COPIOUSLY	COPROLITE	COPYISM
COOPERS	COPALM	COPITA	COPROLITH	COPYISMS
COOPERY	COPALMS	COPITAS	COPROLOGY	COPYIST
COOPING	COPALS	COPLANAR	COPROSMA	COPYISTS
COOPS	COPARCENY	COPLOT	COPROSMAS	COPYLEFT
COOPT	COPARENT	COPLOTS	COPROZOIC	COPYLEFTS

COPYREAD	CORBEIL	CORDOTOMY	CORIXIDS	CORNBRASH
COPYREADS	CORBEILLE	CORDOVAN	CORK	CORNBREAD
COPYRIGHT	CORBEILS	CORDOVANS	CORKAGE	CORNCAKE
COPYTAKER	CORBEL	CORDS	CORKAGES	CORNCAKES
COQUET	CORBELED	CORDUROY	CORKBOARD	CORNCOB
COQUETRY	CORBELING	CORDUROYS	CORKBORER	CORNCOBS
COQUETS	CORBELLED	CORDWAIN	CORKED	CORNCRAKE
COQUETTE	CORBELS	CORDWAINS	CORKER	CORNCRIB
COQUETTED	CORBES	CORDWOOD	CORKERS	CORNCRIBS
COQUETTES	CORBICULA	CORDWOODS	CORKIER	CORNEA
COQUI	CORBIE	CORDYLINE	CORKIEST	CORNEAE
COQUILLA	CORBIES	CORE	CORKINESS	CORNEAL
COQUILLAS	CORBINA	CORED	CORKING	CORNEAS
COQUILLE	CORBINAS	COREDEEM	CORKIR	CORNED
COQUILLES	CORBY	COREDEEMS	CORKIRS	CORNEITIS
COQUINA	CORCASS	COREGENT	CORKLIKE	CORNEL
COQUINAS	CORCASSES	COREGENTS	CORKS	CORNELIAN
COQUIS	CORD	COREIGN	CORKSCREW	CORNELS
COQUITO	CORDAGE	COREIGNS	CORKTREE	CORNEMUSE
COQUITOS	CORDAGES	CORELATE	CORKTREES	CORNEOUS
COR	CORDATE	CORELATED	CORKWING	CORNER
CORACLE	CORDATELY	CORELATES	CORKWINGS	CORNERED
CORACLES	CORDED	CORELESS	CORKWOOD	CORNERING
CORACOID	CORDELLE	CORELLA	CORKWOODS	CORNERMAN
CORACOIDS	CORDELLED	CORELLAS	CORKY	CORNERMEN
CORAGGIO	CORDELLES	COREMIA	CORM	CORNERS
CORAL	CORDER	COREMIUM	CORMEL	CORNET
CORALLA	CORDERS	COREOPSIS	CORMELS	CORNETCY
CORALLINE	CORDGRASS	CORER	CORMIDIA	CORNETIST
CORALLITE	CORDIAL	CORERS	CORMIDIUM	CORNETS
CORALLOID	CORDIALLY	CORES	CORMLET	CORNETT
CORALLUM	CORDIALS	COREY	CORMLETS	CORNETTI
CORALROOT	CORDIFORM	COREYS	CORMLIKE	CORNETTO
CORALS	CORDINER	CORF	CORMOID	CORNETTOS
CORALWORT	CORDINERS	CORFHOUSE	CORMORANT	CORNETTS
CORAM	CORDING	CORGI	CORMOUS	CORNFED
CORAMINE	CORDINGS	CORGIS	CORMS	CORNFIELD
CORAMINES	CORDITE	CORIA	CORMUS	CORNFLAG
CORANACH	CORDITES	CORIANDER	CORMUSES	CORNFLAGS
CORANACHS	CORDLESS	CORIES	CORN	CORNFLAKE
CORANTO	CORDLIKE	CORING	CORNACRE	CORNFLIES
CORANTOES	CORDOBA	CORIOUS	CORNACRES	CORNFLOUR
CORANTOS	CORDOBAS	CORIUM	CORNAGE	CORNFLY
CORBAN	CORDON	CORIUMS	CORNAGES	CORNHUSK
CORBANS	CORDONED	CORIVAL	CORNBALL	CORNHUSKS
CORBE	CORDONING	CORIVALRY	CORNBALLS	CORNI
CORBEAU	CORDONNET	CORIVALS	CORNBORER	CORNICE
CORBEAUS	CORDONS	CORIXID	CORNBRAID	CORNICED

CORNICES	CORNUAL	COROTATE	CORRIDORS	CORSLET
CORNICHE	CORNUS	COROTATED	CORRIE	CORSLETED
CORNICHES	CORNUSES	COROTATES	CORRIES	CORSLETS
CORNICHON	CORNUTE	COROZO	CORRIGENT	CORSNED
CORNICING	CORNUTED	COROZOS	CORRIVAL	CORSNEDS
CORNICLE	CORNUTES	CORPORA	CORRIVALS	CORSO
CORNICLES	CORNUTING	CORPORAL	CORRODANT	CORSOS
CORNICULA	CORNUTO	CORPORALE	CORRODE	CORTEGE
CORNIER	CORNUTOS	CORPORALS	CORRODED	CORTEGES
CORNIEST	CORNWORM	CORPORAS	CORRODENT	CORTEX
CORNIFIC	CORNWORMS	CORPORATE	CORRODER	CORTEXES
CORNIFIED	CORNY	CORPOREAL	CORRODERS	CORTICAL
CORNIFIES	COROCORE	CORPORIFY	CORRODES	CORTICATE
CORNIFORM	COROCORES	CORPOSANT	CORRODIES	CORTICES
CORNIFY	COROCORO	CORPS	CORRODING	CORTICOID
CORNILY	COROCOROS	CORPSE	CORRODY	CORTICOSE
CORNINESS	CORODIES	CORPSED	CORROSION	CORTILE
CORNING	CORODY	CORPSES	CORROSIVE	CORTILI
CORNIST	COROLLA	CORPSING	CORRUGATE	CORTIN
CORNISTS	COROLLARY	CORPSMAN	CORRUPT	CORTINA
CORNLAND	COROLLAS	CORPSMEN	CORRUPTED	CORTINAS
CORNLANDS	COROLLATE	CORPULENT	CORRUPTER	CORTINS
CORNLOFT	COROLLINE	CORPUS	CORRUPTLY	CORTISOL
CORNLOFTS	CORONA	CORPUSCLE	CORRUPTOR	CORTISOLS
CORNMEAL	CORONACH	CORPUSES	CORRUPTS	CORTISONE
CORNMEALS	CORONACHS	CORRADE	CORS	CORULER
CORNMILL	CORONAE	CORRADED	CORSAC	CORULERS
CORNMILLS	CORONAL	CORRADES	CORSACS	CORUNDUM
CORNMOTH	CORONALLY	CORRADING	CORSAGE	CORUNDUMS
CORNMOTHS	CORONALS	CORRAL	CORSAGES	CORUSCANT
CORNO	CORONARY	CORRALLED	CORSAIR	CORUSCATE
CORNOPEAN	CORONAS	CORRALS	CORSAIRS	CORVEE
CORNPIPE	CORONATE	CORRASION	CORSE	CORVEES
CORNPIPES	CORONATED	CORRASIVE	CORSELET	CORVES
CORNPONE	CORONATES	CORREA	CORSELETS	CORVET
CORNPONES	CORONEL	CORREAS	CORSES	CORVETED
CORNRENT	CORONELS	CORRECT	CORSET	CORVETING
CORNRENTS	CORONER	CORRECTED	CORSETED	CORVETS
CORNROW	CORONERS	CORRECTER	CORSETIER	CORVETTE
CORNROWED	CORONET	CORRECTLY	CORSETING	CORVETTED
CORNROWS	CORONETED	CORRECTOR	CORSETRY	CORVETTES
CORNS	CORONETS	CORRECTS	CORSETS	CORVID
CORNSILK	CORONIAL	CORRELATE	CORSEY	CORVIDS
CORNSILKS	CORONIS	CORRETTO	CORSEYS	CORVINA
CORNSTALK	CORONISES	CORRETTOS	CORSITE	CORVINAS
CORNSTONE	CORONIUM	CORRIDA	CORSITES	CORVINE
CORNU	CORONIUMS	CORRIDAS	CORSIVE	CORVUS
CORNUA	CORONOID	CORRIDOR	CORSIVES	CORVUSES

CORY	COSHES	COSPHERED	COSTRELS	COTINGA
CORYBANT	COSHING	COSPLAY	COSTS	COTINGAS
CORYBANTS	COSIE	COSPLAYS	COSTUME	COTININE
CORYDALIS	COSIED	COSPONSOR	COSTUMED	COTININES
CORYLUS	COSIER	COSS	COSTUMER	COTISE
CORYLUSES	COSIERS	COSSACK	COSTUMERS	COTISED
CORYMB	COSIES	COSSACKS	COSTUMERY	COTISES
CORYMBED	COSIEST	COSSES	COSTUMES	COTISING
CORYMBOSE	COSIGN	COSSET	COSTUMEY	COTLAND
CORYMBOUS	COSIGNED	COSSETED	COSTUMIER	COTLANDS
CORYMBS	COSIGNER	COSSETING	COSTUMING	COTQUEAN
CORYPHAEI	COSIGNERS	COSSETS	COSTUS	COTQUEANS
CORYPHE	COSIGNING	COSSETTED	COSTUSES	COTRUSTEE
CORYPHEE	COSIGNS	COSSIE	COSY	COTS
CORYPHEES	COSILY	COSSIES	COSYING	COTT
CORYPHENE	COSINE	COST	COT	COTTA
CORYPHES	COSINES	COSTA	COTAN	COTTABUS
CORYZA	COSINESS	COSTAE	COTANGENT	COTTAE
CORYZAL	COSING	COSTAL	COTANS	COTTAGE
CORYZAS	COSMEA	COSTALGIA	COTE	COTTAGED
COS	COSMEAS	COSTALLY	COTEAU	COTTAGER
COSCRIPT	COSMESES	COSTALS	COTEAUS	COTTAGERS
COSCRIPTS	COSMESIS	COSTAR	COTEAUX	COTTAGES
COSE	COSMETIC	COSTARD	COTED	COTTAGEY
COSEC	COSMETICS	COSTARDS	COTELETTE	COTTAGIER
COSECANT	COSMIC	COSTARRED	COTELINE	COTTAGING
COSECANTS	COSMICAL	COSTARS	COTELINES	COTTAR
COSECH	COSMID	COSTATE	COTENANCY	COTTARS
COSECHS	COSMIDS	COSTATED	COTENANT	COTTAS
COSECS	COSMIN	COSTE	COTENANTS	COTTED
COSED	COSMINE	COSTEAN	COTERIE	COTTER
COSEISMAL	COSMINES	COSTEANED	COTERIES	COTTERED
COSEISMIC	COSMINS	COSTEANS	COTES	COTTERING
COSES	COSMISM	COSTED	COTH	COTTERS
COSET	COSMISMS	COSTER	COTHS	COTTID
COSETS	COSMIST	COSTERS	COTHURN	COTTIDS
COSEY	COSMISTS	COSTES	COTHURNAL	COTTIER
COSEYS	COSMOCRAT	COSTING	COTHURNI	COTTIERS
COSH	COSMOGENY	COSTINGS	COTHURNS	COTTING
COSHED	COSMOGONY	COSTIVE	COTHURNUS	COTTISE
COSHER	COSMOID	COSTIVELY	COTICULAR	COTTISED
COSHERED	COSMOLINE	COSTLESS	COTIDAL	COTTISES
COSHERER	COSMOLOGY	COSTLIER	COTIJA	COTTISING
COSHERERS	COSMONAUT	COSTLIEST	COTIJAS	COTTOID
COSHERIES	COSMORAMA	COSTLY	COTILLION	COTTON
COSHERING	COSMOS	COSTMARY	COTILLON	COTTONADE
COSHERS	COSMOSES	COSTOTOMY	COTILLONS	COTTONED
COSHERY	COSMOTRON	COSTREL	COTING	COTTONIER

COTTONING	COULD	COUNTROL	COURED	COUSINRY
COTTONS	COULDEST	COUNTROLS	COURES	COUSINS
COTTONY	COULDST	COUNTRY	COURGETTE	COUTA
COTTOWN	COULEE	COUNTS	COURIE	COUTAS
COTTOWNS	COULEES	COUNTSHIP	COURIED	COUTEAU
COTTS	COULIBIAC	COUNTY	COURIEING	COUTEAUX
COTTUS	COULIS	COUP	COURIER	COUTER
COTTUSES	COULISSE	COUPE	COURIERED	COUTERS
COTURNIX	COULISSES	COUPED	COURIERS	COUTH
COTWAL	COULOIR	COUPEE	COURIES	COUTHER
COTWALS	COULOIRS	COUPEES	COURING	COUTHEST
COTYLAE	COULOMB	COUPER	COURLAN	COUTHIE
COTYLE	COULOMBIC	COUPERS	COURLANS	COUTHIER
COTYLEDON	COULOMBS	COUPES	COURS	COUTHIEST
COTYLES	COULTER	COUPING	COURSE	COUTHS
COTYLOID	COULTERS	COUPLE	COURSED	COUTHY
COTYLOIDS	COUMARIC	COUPLED	COURSER	COUTIL
COTYPE	COUMARIN	COUPLEDOM	COURSERS	COUTILLE
COTYPES	COUMARINS	COUPLER	COURSES	COUTILLES
COUCAL	COUMARONE	COUPLERS	COURSING	COUTILS
COUCALS	COUMAROU	COUPLES	COURSINGS	COUTURE
COUCH	COUMAROUS	COUPLET	COURT	COUTURES
COUCHANT	COUNCIL	COUPLETS	COURTED	COUTURIER
COUCHE	COUNCILOR	COUPLING	COURTEOUS	COUVADE
COUCHED	COUNCILS	COUPLINGS	COURTER	COUVADES
COUCHEE	COUNSEL	COUPON	COURTERS	COUVERT
COUCHEES	COUNSELED	COUPONING	COURTESAN	COUVERTS
COUCHER	COUNSELEE	COUPONS	COURTESY	COUZIN
COUCHERS	COUNSELOR	COUPS	COURTEZAN	COUZINS
COUCHES	COUNSELS	COUPURE	COURTIER	COVALENCE
COUCHETTE	COUNT	COUPURES	COURTIERS	COVALENCY
COUCHING	COUNTABLE	COUR	COURTING	COVALENT
COUCHINGS	COUNTABLY	COURAGE	COURTINGS	COVARIANT
COUDE	COUNTBACK	COURAGES	COURTLET	COVARIATE
COUDES	COUNTDOWN	COURANT	COURTLETS	COVARIED
COUGAN	COUNTED	COURANTE	COURTLIER	COVARIES
COUGANS	COUNTER	COURANTES	COURTLIKE	COVARY
COUGAR	COUNTERED	COURANTO	COURTLING	COVARYING
COUGARS	COUNTERS	COURANTOS	COURTLY	COVE
COUGH	COUNTESS	COURANTS	COURTROOM	COVED
COUGHED	COUNTIAN	COURB	COURTS	COVELET
COUGHER	COUNTIANS	COURBARIL	COURTSHIP	COVELETS
COUGHERS	COUNTIES	COURBED	COURTSIDE	COVELLINE
COUGHING	COUNTING	COURBETTE	COURTYARD	COVELLITE
COUGHINGS	COUNTINGS	COURBING	COUSCOUS	COVEN
COUGHS	COUNTLESS	COURBS	COUSIN	COVENANT
COUGUAR	COUNTLINE	COURD	COUSINAGE	COVENANTS
COUGUARS	COUNTRIES	COURE	COUSINLY	COVENS

COZENAGES

COVENT	COVINOUS	COWHAGE	COWPEAS	COXCOMBS
COVENTS	COVINS	COWHAGES	COWPED	COXED
COVER	COVYNE	COWHAND	COWPIE	COXES
COVERABLE	COVYNES	COWHANDS	COWPIES	COXIB
COVERAGE	COW	COWHEARD	COWPING	COXIBS
COVERAGES	COWABUNGA	COWHEARDS	COWPLOP	COXIER
COVERALL	COWAGE	COWHEEL	COWPLOPS	COXIEST
COVERALLS	COWAGES	COWHEELS	COWPOKE	COXINESS
COVERED	COWAL	COWHERB	COWPOKES	COXING
COVERER	COWALS	COWHERBS	COWPOX	COXITIDES
COVERERS	COWAN	COWHERD	COWPOXES	COXITIS
COVERING	COWANS	COWHERDS	COWPS	COXLESS
COVERINGS	COWARD	COWHIDE	COWPUNK	COXSACKIE
COVERLESS	COWARDED	COWHIDED	COWPUNKS	COXSWAIN
COVERLET	COWARDICE	COWHIDES	COWRIE	COXSWAINS
COVERLETS	COWARDING	COWHIDING	COWRIES	COXY
COVERLID	COWARDLY	COWHOUSE	COWRITE	COY
COVERLIDS	COWARDRY	COWHOUSES	COWRITER	COYAU
COVERS	COWARDS	COWIER	COWRITERS	COYAUS
COVERSED	COWBANE	COWIEST	COWRITES	COYDOG
COVERSINE	COWBANES	COWING	COWRITING	COYDOGS
COVERSLIP	COWBELL	COWINNER	COWRITTEN	COYED
COVERT	COWBELLS	COWINNERS	COWROTE	COYER
COVERTER	COWBERRY	COWISH	COWRY	COYEST
COVERTEST	COWBIND	COWISHES	COWS	COYING
COVERTLY	COWBINDS	COWITCH	COWSHED	COYISH
COVERTS	COWBIRD	COWITCHES	COWSHEDS	COYISHLY
COVERTURE	COWBIRDS	COWK	COWSKIN	COYLY
COVERUP	COWBOY	COWKED	COWSKINS	COYNESS
COVERUPS	COWBOYED	COWKING	COWSLIP	COYNESSES
COVES	COWBOYING	COWKS	COWSLIPS	COYOTE
COVET	COWBOYS	COWL	COWTOWN	COYOTES
COVETABLE	COWED	COWLED	COWTOWNS	COYOTILLO
COVETED	COWEDLY	COWLICK	COWTREE	COYPOU
COVETER	COWER	COWLICKS	COWTREES	COYPOUS
COVETERS	COWERED	COWLIKE	COWY	COYPU
COVETING	COWERING	COWLING	COX	COYPUS
COVETISE	COWERS	COWLINGS	COXA	COYS
COVETISES	COWFEEDER	COWLS	COXAE	COYSTREL
COVETOUS	COWFISH	COWLSTAFF	COXAL	COYSTRELS
COVETS	COWFISHES	COWMAN	COXALGIA	COYSTRIL
COVEY	COWFLAP	COWMEN	COXALGIAS	COYSTRILS
COVEYS	COWFLAPS	COWORKER	COXALGIC	COZ
COVIN	COWFLOP	COWORKERS	COXALGIES	COZE
COVINE	COWFLOPS	COWP	COXALGY	COZED
COVINES	COWGIRL	COWPAT	COXCOMB	COZEN
COVING	COWGIRLS	COWPATS	COXCOMBIC	COZENAGE
COVINGS	COWGRASS	COWPEA	COXCOMBRY	COZENAGES

COZENED	CRACHACH	CRAFTERS	CRAMOISIE	CRANKCASE
COZENER	CRACK	CRAFTIER	CRAMOISY	CRANKED
COZENERS	CRACKA	CRAFTIEST	CRAMP	CRANKER
COZENING	CRACKAS	CRAFTILY	CRAMPBARK	CRANKEST
COZENS	CRACKBACK	CRAFTING	CRAMPED	CRANKIER
COZES	CRACKDOWN	CRAFTLESS	CRAMPER	CRANKIEST
COZEY	CRACKED	CRAFTS	CRAMPERS	CRANKILY
COZEYS	CRACKER	CRAFTSMAN	CRAMPET	CRANKING
COZIE	CRACKERS	CRAFTSMEN	CRAMPETS	CRANKISH
COZIED	CRACKET	CRAFTWORK	CRAMPFISH	CRANKLE
COZIER	CRACKETS	CRAFTY	CRAMPIER	CRANKLED
COZIERS	CRACKHEAD	CRAG	CRAMPIEST	CRANKLES
COZIES	CRACKIE	CRAGFAST	CRAMPING	CRANKLING
COZIEST	CRACKIER	CRAGGED	CRAMPIT	CRANKLY
COZILY	CRACKIES	CRAGGER	CRAMPITS	CRANKNESS
COZINESS	CRACKIEST	CRAGGERS	CRAMPON	CRANKOUS
COZING	CRACKING	CRAGGIER	CRAMPONED	CRANKPIN
COZY	CRACKINGS	CRAGGIEST	CRAMPONS	CRANKPINS
COZYING	CRACKJAW	CRAGGILY	CRAMPOON	CRANKS
COZZES	CRACKJAWS	CRAGGY	CRAMPOONS	CRANKY
COZZIE	CRACKLE	CRAGS	CRAMPS	CRANNIED
COZZIES	CRACKLED	CRAGSMAN	CRAMPY	CRANNIES
CRAAL	CRACKLES	CRAGSMEN	CRAMS	CRANNOG
CRAALED	CRACKLIER	CRAIC	CRAN	CRANNOGE
CRAALING	CRACKLING	CRAICS	CRANACHAN	CRANNOGES
CRAALS	CRACKLY	CRAIG	CRANAGE	CRANNOGS
CRAB	CRACKNEL	CRAIGS	CRANAGES	CRANNY
CRABAPPLE	CRACKNELS	CRAKE	CRANAPPLE	CRANNYING
CRABBED	CRACKPOT	CRAKED	CRANBERRY	CRANREUCH
CRABBEDLY	CRACKPOTS	CRAKES	CRANCH	CRANS
CRABBER	CRACKS	CRAKING	CRANCHED	CRANTS
CRABBERS	CRACKSMAN	CRAM	CRANCHES	CRANTSES
CRABBIER	CRACKSMEN	CRAMBE	CRANCHING	CRAP
CRABBIEST	CRACKUP	CRAMBES	CRANE	CRAPAUD
CRABBILY	CRACKUPS	CRAMBO	CRANED	CRAPAUDS
CRABBING	CRACKY	CRAMBOES	CRANEFLY	CRAPE
CRABBIT	CRACOWE	CRAMBOS	CRANELIKE	CRAPED
CRABBY	CRACOWES	CRAME	CRANES	CRAPELIKE
CRABEATER	CRADLE	CRAMES	CRANIA	CRAPES
CRABGRASS	CRADLED	CRAMESIES	CRANIAL	CRAPIER
CRABLIKE	CRADLER	CRAMESY	CRANIALLY	CRAPIEST
CRABMEAT	CRADLERS	CRAMFULL	CRANIATE	CRAPING
CRABMEATS	CRADLES	CRAMMABLE	CRANIATES	CRAPLE
CRABS	CRADLING	CRAMMED	CRANING	CRAPLES
CRABSTICK	CRADLINGS	CRAMMER	CRANIUM	CRAPOLA
CRABWISE	CRAFT	CRAMMERS	CRANIUMS	CRAPOLAS
CRABWOOD	CRAFTED	CRAMMING	CRANK	CRAPPED
CRABWOODS	CRAFTER	CRAMMINGS	CRANKBAIT	CRAPPER

CRAPPERS
CRAPPIE
CRAPPIER
CRAPPIES
CRAPPIEST
CRAPPING
CRAPPY
CRAPS
CRAPSHOOT
CRAPULENT
CRAPULOUS
CRAPY
CRARE
CRARES
CRASES
CRASH
CRASHED
CRASHER
CRASHERS
CRASHES
CRASHING
CRASHPAD
CRASHPADS
CRASIS
CRASS
CRASSER
CRASSEST
CRASSLY
CRASSNESS
CRATCH
CRATCHES
CRATE
CRATED
CRATEFUL
CRATEFULS
CRATER
CRATERED
CRATERING
CRATERLET
CRATEROUS
CRATERS
CRATES
CRATHUR
CRATHURS
CRATING
CRATON
CRATONIC
CRATONS

CRATUR
CRATURS
CRAUNCH
CRAUNCHED
CRAUNCHES
CRAUNCHY
CRAVAT
CRAVATE
CRAVATES
CRAVATS
CRAVATTED
CRAVE
CRAVED
CRAVEN
CRAVENED
CRAVENER
CRAVENEST
CRAVENING
CRAVENLY
CRAVENS
CRAVER
CRAVERS
CRAVES
CRAVING
CRAVINGS
CRAW
CRAWDAD
CRAWDADDY
CRAWDADS
CRAWFISH
CRAWL
CRAWLED
CRAWLER
CRAWLERS
CRAWLIER
CRAWLIEST
CRAWLING
CRAWLINGS
CRAWLS
CRAWLWAY
CRAWLWAYS
CRAWLY
CRAWS
CRAY
CRAYER
CRAYERS
CRAYEST
CRAYFISH

CRAYON
CRAYONED
CRAYONER
CRAYONERS
CRAYONING
CRAYONIST
CRAYONS
CRAYS
CRAYTHUR
CRAYTHURS
CRAZE
CRAZED
CRAZES
CRAZIER
CRAZIES
CRAZIEST
CRAZILY
CRAZINESS
CRAZING
CRAZINGS
CRAZY
CRAZYWEED
CREACH
CREACHS
CREAGH
CREAGHS
CREAK
CREAKED
CREAKIER
CREAKIEST
CREAKILY
CREAKING
CREAKS
CREAKY
CREAM
CREAMCUPS
CREAMED
CREAMER
CREAMERS
CREAMERY
CREAMIER
CREAMIEST
CREAMILY
CREAMING
CREAMLAID
CREAMLIKE
CREAMPUFF
CREAMS

CREAMWARE
CREAMWOVE
CREAMY
CREANCE
CREANCES
CREANT
CREASE
CREASED
CREASER
CREASERS
CREASES
CREASIER
CREASIEST
CREASING
CREASOTE
CREASOTED
CREASOTES
CREASY
CREATABLE
CREATE
CREATED
CREATES
CREATIC
CREATIN
CREATINE
CREATINES
CREATING
CREATINS
CREATION
CREATIONS
CREATIVE
CREATIVES
CREATOR
CREATORS
CREATRESS
CREATRIX
CREATURAL
CREATURE
CREATURES
CRECHE
CRECHES
CRED
CREDAL
CREDENCE
CREDENCES
CREDENDA
CREDENDUM
CREDENT

CREDENZA
CREDENZAS
CREDIBLE
CREDIBLY
CREDIT
CREDITED
CREDITING
CREDITOR
CREDITORS
CREDITS
CREDO
CREDOS
CREDS
CREDULITY
CREDULOUS
CREE
CREED
CREEDAL
CREEDS
CREEING
CREEK
CREEKIER
CREEKIEST
CREEKS
CREEKSIDE
CREEKY
CREEL
CREELED
CREELING
CREELS
CREEP
CREEPAGE
CREEPAGES
CREEPED
CREEPER
CREEPERED
CREEPERS
CREEPIE
CREEPIER
CREEPIES
CREEPIEST
CREEPILY
CREEPING
CREEPMICE
CREEPS
CREEPY
CREES
CREESE

CREESED
CREESES
CREESH
CREESHED
CREESHES
CREESHIER
CREESHING
CREESHY
CREESING
CREM
CREMAINS
CREMANT
CREMASTER
CREMATE
CREMATED
CREMATES
CREMATING
CREMATION
CREMATOR
CREMATORS
CREMATORY
CREME
CREMES
CREMINI
CREMINIS
CREMOCARP
CREMONA
CREMONAS
CREMOR
CREMORNE
CREMORNES
CREMORS
CREMOSIN
CREMS
CREMSIN
CRENA
CRENAS
CRENATE
CRENATED
CRENATELY
CRENATION
CRENATURE
CRENEL
CRENELATE
CRENELED
CRENELING
CRENELLE
CRENELLED

CRENELLES
CRENELS
CRENSHAW
CRENSHAWS
CRENULATE
CREODONT
CREODONTS
CREOLE
CREOLES
CREOLIAN
CREOLIANS
CREOLISE
CREOLISED
CREOLISES
CREOLIST
CREOLISTS
CREOLIZE
CREOLIZED
CREOLIZES
CREOPHAGY
CREOSOL
CREOSOLS
CREOSOTE
CREOSOTED
CREOSOTES
CREOSOTIC
CREPANCE
CREPANCES
CREPE
CREPED
CREPELIKE
CREPERIE
CREPERIES
CREPES
CREPEY
CREPIER
CREPIEST
CREPINESS
CREPING
CREPITANT
CREPITATE
CREPITUS
CREPOLINE
CREPON
CREPONS
CREPS
CREPT
CREPUSCLE

CREPY
CRESCENDI
CRESCENDO
CRESCENT
CRESCENTS
CRESCIVE
CRESOL
CRESOLS
CRESS
CRESSES
CRESSET
CRESSETS
CRESSIER
CRESSIEST
CRESSY
CREST
CRESTA
CRESTAL
CRESTALS
CRESTED
CRESTING
CRESTINGS
CRESTLESS
CRESTON
CRESTONS
CRESTS
CRESYL
CRESYLIC
CRESYLS
CRETIC
CRETICS
CRETIN
CRETINISE
CRETINISM
CRETINIZE
CRETINOID
CRETINOUS
CRETINS
CRETISM
CRETISMS
CRETONNE
CRETONNES
CRETONS
CREUTZER
CREUTZERS
CREVALLE
CREVALLES
CREVASSE

CREVASSED
CREVASSES
CREVETTE
CREVETTES
CREVICE
CREVICED
CREVICES
CREW
CREWCUT
CREWCUTS
CREWE
CREWED
CREWEL
CREWELIST
CREWELLED
CREWELS
CREWES
CREWING
CREWLESS
CREWMAN
CREWMATE
CREWMATES
CREWMEN
CREWNECK
CREWNECKS
CREWS
CRIA
CRIANT
CRIAS
CRIB
CRIBBAGE
CRIBBAGES
CRIBBED
CRIBBER
CRIBBERS
CRIBBING
CRIBBINGS
CRIBBLE
CRIBBLED
CRIBBLES
CRIBBLING
CRIBELLA
CRIBELLAR
CRIBELLUM
CRIBLE
CRIBLES
CRIBRATE
CRIBROSE

CRIBROUS
CRIBS
CRIBWORK
CRIBWORKS
CRICETID
CRICETIDS
CRICK
CRICKED
CRICKET
CRICKETED
CRICKETER
CRICKETS
CRICKEY
CRICKING
CRICKS
CRICKY
CRICOID
CRICOIDS
CRIED
CRIER
CRIERS
CRIES
CRIKEY
CRIM
CRIME
CRIMED
CRIMEFUL
CRIMELESS
CRIMEN
CRIMES
CRIMEWAVE
CRIMINA
CRIMINAL
CRIMINALS
CRIMINATE
CRIMINE
CRIMING
CRIMINI
CRIMINIS
CRIMINOUS
CRIMINY
CRIMMER
CRIMMERS
CRIMP
CRIMPED
CRIMPER
CRIMPERS
CRIMPIER

CRIMPIEST	CRIOLLO	CRIT	CROCINE	CROMLECHS
CRIMPING	CRIOLLOS	CRITERIA	CROCK	CROMORNA
CRIMPLE	CRIOS	CRITERIAL	CROCKED	CROMORNAS
CRIMPLED	CRIOSES	CRITERION	CROCKERY	CROMORNE
CRIMPLES	CRIP	CRITERIUM	CROCKET	CROMORNES
CRIMPLING	CRIPE	CRITH	CROCKETED	CRON
CRIMPS	CRIPES	CRITHS	CROCKETS	CRONE
CRIMPY	CRIPPLE	CRITIC	CROCKING	CRONES
CRIMS	CRIPPLED	CRITICAL	CROCKPOT	CRONET
CRIMSON	CRIPPLER	CRITICISE	CROCKPOTS	CRONETS
CRIMSONED	CRIPPLERS	CRITICISM	CROCKS	CRONIES
CRIMSONS	CRIPPLES	CRITICIZE	CROCODILE	CRONISH
CRINAL	CRIPPLING	CRITICS	CROCOITE	CRONK
CRINATE	CRIPS	CRITIQUE	CROCOITES	CRONKER
CRINATED	CRIS	CRITIQUED	CROCOSMIA	CRONKEST
CRINE	CRISE	CRITIQUES	CROCS	CRONS
CRINED	CRISES	CRITS	CROCUS	CRONY
CRINES	CRISIC	CRITTER	CROCUSES	CRONYISM
CRINGE	CRISIS	CRITTERS	CROFT	CRONYISMS
CRINGED	CRISP	CRITTUR	CROFTED	CROODLE
CRINGER	CRISPATE	CRITTURS	CROFTER	CROODLED
CRINGERS	CRISPATED	CRIVENS	CROFTERS	CROODLES
CRINGES	CRISPED	CRIVVENS	CROFTING	CROODLING
CRINGEY	CRISPEN	CROAK	CROFTINGS	CROOK
CRINGIER	CRISPENED	CROAKED	CROFTS	CROOKBACK
CRINGIEST	CRISPENS	CROAKER	CROG	CROOKED
CRINGING	CRISPER	CROAKERS	CROGGED	CROOKEDER
CRINGINGS	CRISPERS	CROAKIER	CROGGIES	CROOKEDLY
CRINGLE	CRISPEST	CROAKIEST	CROGGING	CROOKER
CRINGLES	CRISPHEAD	CROAKILY	CROGGY	CROOKERY
CRINGY	CRISPIER	CROAKING	CROGS	CROOKEST
CRINING	CRISPIES	CROAKINGS	CROISSANT	CROOKING
CRINITE	CRISPIEST	CROAKS	CROJIK	CROOKNECK
CRINITES	CRISPILY	CROAKY	CROJIKS	CROOKS
CRINKLE	CRISPIN	CROC	CROKINOLE	CROOL
CRINKLED	CRISPING	CROCEATE	CROMACK	CROOLED
CRINKLES	CRISPINS	CROCEIN	CROMACKS	CROOLING
CRINKLIER	CRISPLY	CROCEINE	CROMB	CROOLS
CRINKLIES	CRISPNESS	CROCEINES	CROMBEC	CROON
CRINKLING	CRISPS	CROCEINS	CROMBECS	CROONED
CRINKLY	CRISPY	CROCEOUS	CROMBED	CROONER
CRINOID	CRISSA	CROCHE	CROMBING	CROONERS
CRINOIDAL	CRISSAL	CROCHES	CROMBS	CROONIER
CRINOIDS	CRISSUM	CROCHET	CROME	CROONIEST
CRINOLINE	CRISTA	CROCHETED	CROMED	CROONING
CRINOSE	CRISTAE	CROCHETER	CROMES	CROONINGS
CRINUM	CRISTATE	CROCHETS	CROMING	CROONS
CRINUMS	CRISTATED	CROCI	CROMLECH	CROONY

CROOVE	CROSSCUT	CROTALA	CROUTONS	CROWS
CROOVES	CROSSCUTS	CROTALE	CROUTS	CROWSFEET
CROP	CROSSE	CROTALES	CROW	CROWSFOOT
CROPBOUND	CROSSED	CROTALINE	CROWBAIT	CROWSTEP
CROPFUL	CROSSER	CROTALISM	CROWBAITS	CROWSTEPS
CROPFULL	CROSSERS	CROTALS	CROWBAR	CROZE
CROPFULLS	CROSSES	CROTALUM	CROWBARS	CROZER
CROPFULS	CROSSEST	CROTCH	CROWBERRY	CROZERS
CROPLAND	CROSSETTE	CROTCHED	CROWBOOT	CROZES
CROPLANDS	CROSSFALL	CROTCHES	CROWBOOTS	CROZIER
CROPLESS	CROSSFIRE	CROTCHET	CROWD	CROZIERS
CROPPED	CROSSFISH	CROTCHETS	CROWDED	CROZZLED
CROPPER	CROSSHAIR	CROTCHETY	CROWDEDLY	CRU
CROPPERS	CROSSHEAD	CROTON	CROWDER	CRUBEEN
CROPPIE	CROSSING	CROTONBUG	CROWDERS	CRUBEENS
CROPPIES	CROSSINGS	CROTONIC	CROWDFUND	CRUCES
CROPPING	CROSSISH	CROTONS	CROWDIE	CRUCIAL
CROPPINGS	CROSSJACK	CROTTLE	CROWDIES	CRUCIALLY
CROPPY	CROSSLET	CROTTLES	CROWDING	CRUCIAN
CROPS	CROSSLETS	CROUCH	CROWDS	CRUCIANS
CROPSICK	CROSSLIKE	CROUCHED	CROWDY	CRUCIATE
CROQUANTE	CROSSLY	CROUCHES	CROWEA	CRUCIATES
CROQUET	CROSSNESS	CROUCHING	CROWEAS	CRUCIBLE
CROQUETED	CROSSOVER	CROUP	CROWED	CRUCIBLES
CROQUETS	CROSSPLY	CROUPADE	CROWER	CRUCIFER
CROQUETTE	CROSSROAD	CROUPADES	CROWERS	CRUCIFERS
CROQUIS	CROSSRUFF	CROUPE	CROWFEET	CRUCIFIED
CRORE	CROSSTALK	CROUPED	CROWFOOT	CRUCIFIER
CROREPATI	CROSSTIE	CROUPER	CROWFOOTS	CRUCIFIES
CRORES	CROSSTIED	CROUPERS	CROWING	CRUCIFIX
CROSIER	CROSSTIES	CROUPES	CROWINGLY	CRUCIFORM
CROSIERED	CROSSTOWN	CROUPIER	CROWINGS	CRUCIFY
CROSIERS	CROSSTREE	CROUPIERS	CROWLIKE	CRUCK
CROSS	CROSSWALK	CROUPIEST	CROWN	CRUCKS
CROSSABLE	CROSSWAY	CROUPILY	CROWNED	CRUD
CROSSARM	CROSSWAYS	CROUPING	CROWNER	CRUDDED
CROSSARMS	CROSSWIND	CROUPON	CROWNERS	CRUDDIER
CROSSBAND	CROSSWIRE	CROUPONS	CROWNET	CRUDDIEST
CROSSBAR	CROSSWISE	CROUPOUS	CROWNETS	CRUDDING
CROSSBARS	CROSSWORD	CROUPS	CROWNING	CRUDDLE
CROSSBEAM	CROSSWORT	CROUPY	CROWNINGS	CRUDDLED
CROSSBILL	CROST	CROUSE	CROWNLAND	CRUDDLES
CROSSBIT	CROSTATA	CROUSELY	CROWNLESS	CRUDDLING
CROSSBITE	CROSTATAS	CROUSTADE	CROWNLET	CRUDDY
CROSSBOW	CROSTINI	CROUT	CROWNLETS	CRUDE
CROSSBOWS	CROSTINIS	CROUTE	CROWNLIKE	CRUDELY
CROSSBRED	CROSTINO	CROUTES	CROWNS	CRUDENESS
CROSSBUCK	CROTAL	CROUTON	CROWNWORK	CRUDER

CRUDES
CRUDEST
CRUDIER
CRUDIEST
CRUDITES
CRUDITIES
CRUDITY
CRUDO
CRUDOS
CRUDS
CRUDY
CRUE
CRUEL
CRUELER
CRUELEST
CRUELLER
CRUELLEST
CRUELLS
CRUELLY
CRUELNESS
CRUELS
CRUELTIES
CRUELTY
CRUES
CRUET
CRUETS
CRUFT
CRUFTS
CRUISE
CRUISED
CRUISER
CRUISERS
CRUISES
CRUISEWAY
CRUISEY
CRUISIE
CRUISIER
CRUISIES
CRUISIEST
CRUISING
CRUISINGS
CRUISY
CRUIVE
CRUIVES
CRUIZIE
CRUIZIES
CRULLER
CRULLERS

CRUMB
CRUMBED
CRUMBER
CRUMBERS
CRUMBIER
CRUMBIEST
CRUMBING
CRUMBLE
CRUMBLED
CRUMBLES
CRUMBLIER
CRUMBLIES
CRUMBLING
CRUMBLY
CRUMBS
CRUMBUM
CRUMBUMS
CRUMBY
CRUMEN
CRUMENAL
CRUMENALS
CRUMENS
CRUMHORN
CRUMHORNS
CRUMMACK
CRUMMACKS
CRUMMIE
CRUMMIER
CRUMMIES
CRUMMIEST
CRUMMILY
CRUMMOCK
CRUMMOCKS
CRUMMY
CRUMP
CRUMPED
CRUMPER
CRUMPEST
CRUMPET
CRUMPETS
CRUMPIER
CRUMPIEST
CRUMPING
CRUMPLE
CRUMPLED
CRUMPLES
CRUMPLIER
CRUMPLING

CRUMPLY
CRUMPS
CRUMPY
CRUNCH
CRUNCHED
CRUNCHER
CRUNCHERS
CRUNCHES
CRUNCHIE
CRUNCHIER
CRUNCHIES
CRUNCHILY
CRUNCHING
CRUNCHY
CRUNK
CRUNKED
CRUNKLE
CRUNKLED
CRUNKLES
CRUNKLING
CRUNKS
CRUNODAL
CRUNODE
CRUNODES
CRUOR
CRUORES
CRUORS
CRUPPER
CRUPPERS
CRURA
CRURAL
CRUS
CRUSADE
CRUSADED
CRUSADER
CRUSADERS
CRUSADES
CRUSADING
CRUSADO
CRUSADOES
CRUSADOS
CRUSE
CRUSES
CRUSET
CRUSETS
CRUSH
CRUSHABLE
CRUSHED

CRUSHER
CRUSHERS
CRUSHES
CRUSHING
CRUSHINGS
CRUSIAN
CRUSIANS
CRUSIE
CRUSIES
CRUSILY
CRUST
CRUSTA
CRUSTACEA
CRUSTAE
CRUSTAL
CRUSTAS
CRUSTATE
CRUSTATED
CRUSTED
CRUSTIER
CRUSTIES
CRUSTIEST
CRUSTILY
CRUSTING
CRUSTLESS
CRUSTLIKE
CRUSTOSE
CRUSTS
CRUSTY
CRUSY
CRUTCH
CRUTCHED
CRUTCHES
CRUTCHING
CRUVE
CRUVES
CRUX
CRUXES
CRUZADO
CRUZADOES
CRUZADOS
CRUZEIRO
CRUZEIROS
CRUZIE
CRUZIES
CRWTH
CRWTHS
CRY

CRYBABIES
CRYBABY
CRYER
CRYERS
CRYING
CRYINGLY
CRYINGS
CRYOBANK
CRYOBANKS
CRYOCABLE
CRYOGEN
CRYOGENIC
CRYOGENS
CRYOGENY
CRYOLITE
CRYOLITES
CRYOMETER
CRYOMETRY
CRYONIC
CRYONICS
CRYOPHYTE
CRYOPROBE
CRYOSCOPE
CRYOSCOPY
CRYOSTAT
CRYOSTATS
CRYOTRON
CRYOTRONS
CRYPT
CRYPTADIA
CRYPTAL
CRYPTIC
CRYPTICAL
CRYPTO
CRYPTOGAM
CRYPTON
CRYPTONS
CRYPTONYM
CRYPTOS
CRYPTS
CRYSTAL
CRYSTALS
CSARDAS
CSARDASES
CTENE
CTENES
CTENIDIA
CTENIDIUM

C

CTENIFORM
CTENOID
CUADRILLA
CUATRO
CUATROS
CUB
CUBAGE
CUBAGES
CUBANE
CUBANELLE
CUBANES
CUBATURE
CUBATURES
CUBBED
CUBBIER
CUBBIES
CUBBIEST
CUBBING
CUBBINGS
CUBBISH
CUBBISHLY
CUBBY
CUBBYHOLE
CUBE
CUBEB
CUBEBS
CUBED
CUBELIKE
CUBER
CUBERS
CUBES
CUBHOOD
CUBHOODS
CUBIC
CUBICA
CUBICAL
CUBICALLY
CUBICAS
CUBICITY
CUBICLE
CUBICLES
CUBICLY
CUBICS
CUBICULA
CUBICULUM
CUBIFORM
CUBING
CUBISM

CUBISMS
CUBIST
CUBISTIC
CUBISTS
CUBIT
CUBITAL
CUBITI
CUBITS
CUBITUS
CUBITUSES
CUBLESS
CUBOID
CUBOIDAL
CUBOIDS
CUBS
CUCKING
CUCKOLD
CUCKOLDED
CUCKOLDLY
CUCKOLDOM
CUCKOLDRY
CUCKOLDS
CUCKOO
CUCKOOED
CUCKOOING
CUCKOOS
CUCULLATE
CUCUMBER
CUCUMBERS
CUCURBIT
CUCURBITS
CUD
CUDBEAR
CUDBEARS
CUDDEN
CUDDENS
CUDDIE
CUDDIES
CUDDIN
CUDDINS
CUDDLE
CUDDLED
CUDDLER
CUDDLERS
CUDDLES
CUDDLIER
CUDDLIEST
CUDDLING

CUDDLY
CUDDY
CUDGEL
CUDGELED
CUDGELER
CUDGELERS
CUDGELING
CUDGELLED
CUDGELLER
CUDGELS
CUDGERIE
CUDGERIES
CUDS
CUDWEED
CUDWEEDS
CUE
CUED
CUEING
CUEINGS
CUEIST
CUEISTS
CUES
CUESTA
CUESTAS
CUFF
CUFFABLE
CUFFED
CUFFIN
CUFFING
CUFFINS
CUFFLE
CUFFLED
CUFFLES
CUFFLESS
CUFFLING
CUFFLINK
CUFFLINKS
CUFFO
CUFFS
CUFFUFFLE
CUIF
CUIFS
CUING
CUIRASS
CUIRASSED
CUIRASSES
CUISH
CUISHES

CUISINART
CUISINE
CUISINES
CUISINIER
CUISSE
CUISSER
CUISSERS
CUISSES
CUIT
CUITER
CUITERED
CUITERING
CUITERS
CUITIKIN
CUITIKINS
CUITS
CUITTLE
CUITTLED
CUITTLES
CUITTLING
CUKE
CUKES
CULCH
CULCHES
CULCHIE
CULCHIER
CULCHIES
CULCHIEST
CULET
CULETS
CULEX
CULEXES
CULICES
CULICID
CULICIDS
CULICINE
CULICINES
CULINARY
CULL
CULLAY
CULLAYS
CULLED
CULLENDER
CULLER
CULLERS
CULLET
CULLETS
CULLIED

CULLIES
CULLING
CULLINGS
CULLION
CULLIONLY
CULLIONS
CULLIS
CULLISES
CULLS
CULLY
CULLYING
CULLYISM
CULLYISMS
CULM
CULMED
CULMEN
CULMINA
CULMINANT
CULMINATE
CULMING
CULMS
CULOTTE
CULOTTES
CULPA
CULPABLE
CULPABLY
CULPAE
CULPATORY
CULPRIT
CULPRITS
CULSHIE
CULSHIER
CULSHIES
CULSHIEST
CULT
CULTCH
CULTCHES
CULTER
CULTERS
CULTI
CULTIC
CULTIER
CULTIEST
CULTIGEN
CULTIGENS
CULTISH
CULTISHLY
CULTISM

CULTISMS	CUMEC	CUNNERS	CUPPIER	CURASSOW
CULTIST	CUMECS	CUNNING	CUPPIEST	CURASSOWS
CULTISTS	CUMIN	CUNNINGER	CUPPING	CURAT
CULTIVAR	CUMINS	CUNNINGLY	CUPPINGS	CURATE
CULTIVARS	CUMMED	CUNNINGS	CUPPY	CURATED
CULTIVATE	CUMMER	CUNT	CUPREOUS	CURATES
CULTLIKE	CUMMERS	CUNTS	CUPRESSUS	CURATING
CULTRATE	CUMMIN	CUP	CUPRIC	CURATION
CULTRATED	CUMMING	CUPBEARER	CUPRITE	CURATIONS
CULTS	CUMMINS	CUPBOARD	CUPRITES	CURATIVE
CULTURAL	CUMQUAT	CUPBOARDS	CUPROUS	CURATIVES
CULTURATI	CUMQUATS	CUPCAKE	CUPRUM	CURATOR
CULTURE	CUMS	CUPCAKES	CUPRUMS	CURATORS
CULTURED	CUMSHAW	CUPEL	CUPS	CURATORY
CULTURES	CUMSHAWS	CUPELED	CUPSFUL	CURATRIX
CULTURING	CUMULATE	CUPELER	CUPULA	CURATS
CULTURIST	CUMULATED	CUPELERS	CUPULAE	CURB
CULTUS	CUMULATES	CUPELING	CUPULAR	CURBABLE
CULTUSES	CUMULET	CUPELLED	CUPULATE	CURBED
CULTY	CUMULETS	CUPELLER	CUPULE	CURBER
CULVER	CUMULI	CUPELLERS	CUPULES	CURBERS
CULVERIN	CUMULOSE	CUPELLING	CUR	CURBING
CULVERINS	CUMULOUS	CUPELS	CURABLE	CURBINGS
CULVERS	CUMULUS	CUPFERRON	CURABLY	CURBLESS
CULVERT	CUMULUSES	CUPFUL	CURACAO	CURBS
CULVERTED	CUNABULA	CUPFULS	CURACAOS	CURBSIDE
CULVERTS	CUNCTATOR	CUPGALL	CURACIES	CURBSIDES
CUM	CUNDIES	CUPGALLS	CURACOA	CURBSTONE
CUMACEAN	CUNDUM	CUPHEAD	CURACOAS	CURCH
CUMACEANS	CUNDUMS	CUPHEADS	CURACY	CURCHEF
CUMARIC	CUNDY	CUPHOLDER	CURAGH	CURCHEFS
CUMARIN	CUNEAL	CUPID	CURAGHS	CURCHES
CUMARINS	CUNEATE	CUPIDITY	CURANDERA	CURCULIO
CUMARONE	CUNEATED	CUPIDS	CURANDERO	CURCULIOS
CUMARONES	CUNEATELY	CUPLIKE	CURARA	CURCUMA
CUMBENT	CUNEATIC	CUPMAN	CURARAS	CURCUMAS
CUMBER	CUNEI	CUPMEN	CURARE	CURCUMIN
CUMBERED	CUNEIFORM	CUPOLA	CURARES	CURCUMINE
CUMBERER	CUNETTE	CUPOLAED	CURARI	CURCUMINS
CUMBERERS	CUNETTES	CUPOLAING	CURARINE	CURD
CUMBERING	CUNEUS	CUPOLAR	CURARINES	CURDED
CUMBERS	CUNIFORM	CUPOLAS	CURARIS	CURDIER
CUMBIA	CUNIFORMS	CUPOLATED	CURARISE	CURDIEST
CUMBIAS	CUNIT	CUPPA	CURARISED	CURDINESS
CUMBRANCE	CUNITS	CUPPAS	CURARISES	CURDING
CUMBROUS	CUNJEVOI	CUPPED	CURARIZE	CURDLE
CUMBUNGI	CUNJEVOIS	CUPPER	CURARIZED	CURDLED
CUMBUNGIS	CUNNER	CUPPERS	CURARIZES	CURDLER

CURDLERS

CURDLERS	CURLER	CURRICULA	CURT	CURVETTED
CURDLES	CURLERS	CURRIE	CURTAIL	CURVEY
CURDLING	CURLEW	CURRIED	CURTAILED	CURVIER
CURDS	CURLEWS	CURRIER	CURTAILER	CURVIEST
CURDY	CURLI	CURRIERS	CURTAILS	CURVIFORM
CURE	CURLICUE	CURRIERY	CURTAIN	CURVINESS
CURED	CURLICUED	CURRIES	CURTAINED	CURVING
CURELESS	CURLICUES	CURRIJONG	CURTAINS	CURVITAL
CURER	CURLIER	CURRING	CURTAL	CURVITIES
CURERS	CURLIES	CURRISH	CURTALAX	CURVITY
CURES	CURLIEST	CURRISHLY	CURTALAXE	CURVY
CURET	CURLILY	CURRS	CURTALS	CUSCUS
CURETS	CURLINESS	CURRY	CURTANA	CUSCUSES
CURETTAGE	CURLING	CURRYCOMB	CURTANAS	CUSEC
CURETTE	CURLINGS	CURRYING	CURTATE	CUSECS
CURETTED	CURLPAPER	CURRYINGS	CURTATION	CUSH
CURETTES	CURLS	CURS	CURTAXE	CUSHAT
CURETTING	CURLY	CURSAL	CURTAXES	CUSHATS
CURF	CURLYCUE	CURSE	CURTER	CUSHAW
CURFEW	CURLYCUES	CURSED	CURTEST	CUSHAWS
CURFEWS	CURN	CURSEDER	CURTESIES	CUSHES
CURFS	CURNEY	CURSEDEST	CURTESY	CUSHIE
CURFUFFLE	CURNIER	CURSEDLY	CURTILAGE	CUSHIER
CURIA	CURNIEST	CURSENARY	CURTLY	CUSHIES
CURIAE	CURNS	CURSER	CURTNESS	CUSHIEST
CURIAL	CURNY	CURSERS	CURTSEY	CUSHILY
CURIALISM	CURPEL	CURSES	CURTSEYED	CUSHINESS
CURIALIST	CURPELS	CURSI	CURTSEYS	CUSHION
CURIAS	CURR	CURSILLO	CURTSIED	CUSHIONED
CURIE	CURRACH	CURSILLOS	CURTSIES	CUSHIONET
CURIES	CURRACHS	CURSING	CURTSY	CUSHIONS
CURIET	CURRAGH	CURSINGS	CURTSYING	CUSHIONY
CURIETS	CURRAGHS	CURSITOR	CURULE	CUSHTY
CURING	CURRAJONG	CURSITORS	CURVATE	CUSHY
CURINGS	CURRAN	CURSITORY	CURVATED	CUSK
CURIO	CURRANS	CURSIVE	CURVATION	CUSKS
CURIOS	CURRANT	CURSIVELY	CURVATIVE	CUSP
CURIOSA	CURRANTS	CURSIVES	CURVATURE	CUSPAL
CURIOSITY	CURRANTY	CURSOR	CURVE	CUSPATE
CURIOUS	CURRAWONG	CURSORARY	CURVEBALL	CUSPATED
CURIOUSER	CURRED	CURSORES	CURVED	CUSPED
CURIOUSLY	CURREJONG	CURSORIAL	CURVEDLY	CUSPID
CURITE	CURRENCY	CURSORILY	CURVES	CUSPIDAL
CURITES	CURRENT	CURSORS	CURVESOME	CUSPIDATE
CURIUM	CURRENTLY	CURSORY	CURVET	CUSPIDES
CURIUMS	CURRENTS	CURST	CURVETED	CUSPIDOR
CURL	CURRICLE	CURSTNESS	CURVETING	CUSPIDORE
CURLED	CURRICLES	CURSUS	CURVETS	CUSPIDORS

CUSPIDS	CUTAWAY	CUTLAS	CUTWATERS	CYANO
CUSPIER	CUTAWAYS	CUTLASES	CUTWORK	CYANOGEN
CUSPIEST	CUTBACK	CUTLASS	CUTWORKS	CYANOGENS
CUSPIS	CUTBACKS	CUTLASSES	CUTWORM	CYANOSE
CUSPLIKE	CUTBANK	CUTLER	CUTWORMS	CYANOSED
CUSPS	CUTBANKS	CUTLERIES	CUVEE	CYANOSES
CUSPY	CUTBLOCK	CUTLERS	CUVEES	CYANOSIS
CUSS	CUTBLOCKS	CUTLERY	CUVETTE	CYANOTIC
CUSSED	CUTCH	CUTLET	CUVETTES	CYANOTYPE
CUSSEDLY	CUTCHA	CUTLETS	CUZ	CYANS
CUSSER	CUTCHERRY	CUTLETTE	CUZES	CYANURATE
CUSSERS	CUTCHERY	CUTLETTES	CUZZES	CYANURET
CUSSES	CUTCHES	CUTLINE	CUZZIE	CYANURETS
CUSSING	CUTDOWN	CUTLINES	CUZZIES	CYANURIC
CUSSO	CUTDOWNS	CUTOFF	CWM	CYATHI
CUSSOS	CUTE	CUTOFFS	CWMS	CYATHIA
CUSSWORD	CUTELY	CUTOUT	CWTCH	CYATHIUM
CUSSWORDS	CUTENESS	CUTOUTS	CWTCHED	CYATHUS
CUSTARD	CUTER	CUTOVER	CWTCHES	CYBER
CUSTARDS	CUTES	CUTOVERS	CWTCHING	CYBERCAFE
CUSTARDY	CUTESIE	CUTPURSE	CYAN	CYBERCAST
CUSTOCK	CUTESIER	CUTPURSES	CYANAMID	CYBERNATE
CUSTOCKS	CUTESIEST	CUTS	CYANAMIDE	CYBERNAUT
CUSTODE	CUTEST	CUTSCENE	CYANAMIDS	CYBERPET
CUSTODES	CUTESY	CUTSCENES	CYANATE	CYBERPETS
CUSTODIAL	CUTEY	CUTTABLE	CYANATES	CYBERPORN
CUSTODIAN	CUTEYS	CUTTAGE	CYANIC	CYBERPUNK
CUSTODIER	CUTGLASS	CUTTAGES	CYANID	CYBERSEX
CUSTODIES	CUTGRASS	CUTTER	CYANIDE	CYBERWAR
CUSTODY	CUTICLE	CUTTERS	CYANIDED	CYBERWARS
CUSTOM	CUTICLES	CUTTHROAT	CYANIDES	CYBORG
CUSTOMARY	CUTICULA	CUTTIER	CYANIDING	CYBORGS
CUSTOMED	CUTICULAE	CUTTIES	CYANIDS	CYBRARIAN
CUSTOMER	CUTICULAR	CUTTIEST	CYANIN	CYBRID
CUSTOMERS	CUTIE	CUTTING	CYANINE	CYBRIDS
CUSTOMISE	CUTIES	CUTTINGLY	CYANINES	CYCAD
CUSTOMIZE	CUTIKIN	CUTTINGS	CYANINS	CYCADEOID
CUSTOMS	CUTIKINS	CUTTLE	CYANISE	CYCADS
CUSTOS	CUTIN	CUTTLED	CYANISED	CYCAS
CUSTREL	CUTINISE	CUTTLES	CYANISES	CYCASES
CUSTRELS	CUTINISED	CUTTLING	CYANISING	CYCASIN
CUSTUMAL	CUTINISES	CUTTO	CYANITE	CYCASINS
CUSTUMALS	CUTINIZE	CUTTOE	CYANITES	CYCLAMATE
CUSTUMARY	CUTINIZED	CUTTOES	CYANITIC	CYCLAMEN
CUSUM	CUTINIZES	CUTTY	CYANIZE	CYCLAMENS
CUSUMS	CUTINS	CUTUP	CYANIZED	CYCLAMIC
CUT	CUTIS	CUTUPS	CYANIZES	CYCLASE
CUTANEOUS	CUTISES	CUTWATER	CYANIZING	CYCLASES

CYCLE	CYCLOPIAN	CYMENE	CYPRINIDS	CYTOLOGIC
CYCLECAR	CYCLOPIC	CYMENES	CYPRINOID	CYTOLOGY
CYCLECARS	CYCLOPS	CYMES	CYPRIS	CYTOLYSES
CYCLED	CYCLORAMA	CYMLIN	CYPRUS	CYTOLYSIN
CYCLEPATH	CYCLOS	CYMLING	CYPRUSES	CYTOLYSIS
CYCLER	CYCLOSES	CYMLINGS	CYPSELA	CYTOLYTIC
CYCLERIES	CYCLOSIS	CYMLINS	CYPSELAE	CYTOMETER
CYCLERS	CYCLOTRON	CYMOGENE	CYST	CYTOMETRY
CYCLERY	CYCLUS	CYMOGENES	CYSTEIN	CYTON
CYCLES	CYCLUSES	CYMOGRAPH	CYSTEINE	CYTONS
CYCLEWAY	CYDER	CYMOID	CYSTEINES	CYTOPATHY
CYCLEWAYS	CYDERS	CYMOL	CYSTEINIC	CYTOPENIA
CYCLIC	CYESES	CYMOLS	CYSTEINS	CYTOPLASM
CYCLICAL	CYESIS	CYMOPHANE	CYSTIC	CYTOPLAST
CYCLICALS	CYGNET	CYMOSE	CYSTID	CYTOSINE
CYCLICISM	CYGNETS	CYMOSELY	CYSTIDEAN	CYTOSINES
CYCLICITY	CYLICES	CYMOUS	CYSTIDS	CYTOSOL
CYCLICLY	CYLIKES	CYNANCHE	CYSTIFORM	CYTOSOLIC
CYCLIN	CYLINDER	CYNANCHES	CYSTINE	CYTOSOLS
CYCLING	CYLINDERS	CYNEGETIC	CYSTINES	CYTOSOME
CYCLINGS	CYLINDRIC	CYNIC	CYSTITIS	CYTOSOMES
CYCLINS	CYLIX	CYNICAL	CYSTOCARP	CYTOTAXES
CYCLISE	CYMA	CYNICALLY	CYSTOCELE	CYTOTAXIS
CYCLISED	CYMAE	CYNICISM	CYSTOID	CYTOTOXIC
CYCLISES	CYMAGRAPH	CYNICISMS	CYSTOIDS	CYTOTOXIN
CYCLISING	CYMAR	CYNICS	CYSTOLITH	CZAPKA
CYCLIST	CYMARS	CYNODONT	CYSTOTOMY	CZAPKAS
CYCLISTS	CYMAS	CYNODONTS	CYSTS	CZAR
CYCLITOL	CYMATIA	CYNOMOLGI	CYTASE	CZARDAS
CYCLITOLS	CYMATICS	CYNOSURAL	CYTASES	CZARDASES
CYCLIZE	CYMATIUM	CYNOSURE	CYTASTER	CZARDOM
CYCLIZED	CYMBAL	CYNOSURES	CYTASTERS	CZARDOMS
CYCLIZES	CYMBALEER	CYPHER	CYTE	CZAREVICH
CYCLIZINE	CYMBALER	CYPHERED	CYTES	CZAREVNA
CYCLIZING	CYMBALERS	CYPHERING	CYTIDINE	CZAREVNAS
CYCLO	CYMBALIST	CYPHERS	CYTIDINES	CZARINA
CYCLOGIRO	CYMBALO	CYPRES	CYTIDYLIC	CZARINAS
CYCLOID	CYMBALOES	CYPRESES	CYTISI	CZARISM
CYCLOIDAL	CYMBALOM	CYPRESS	CYTISINE	CZARISMS
CYCLOIDS	CYMBALOMS	CYPRESSES	CYTISINES	CZARIST
CYCLOLITH	CYMBALOS	CYPRIAN	CYTISUS	CZARISTS
CYCLONAL	CYMBALS	CYPRIANS	CYTODE	CZARITSA
CYCLONE	CYMBIDIA	CYPRID	CYTODES	CZARITSAS
CYCLONES	CYMBIDIUM	CYPRIDES	CYTOGENY	CZARITZA
CYCLONIC	CYMBIFORM	CYPRIDS	CYTOID	CZARITZAS
CYCLONITE	CYMBLING	CYPRINE	CYTOKINE	CZARS
CYCLOPEAN	CYMBLINGS	CYPRINES	CYTOKINES	
CYCLOPES	CYME	CYPRINID	CYTOKININ	

D

DA	DACOITS	DADS	DAGGERING	DAIDLES
DAAL	DACOITY	DAE	DAGGERS	DAIDLING
DAALS	DACQUOISE	DAEDAL	DAGGIER	DAIDZEIN
DAB	DACRON	DAEDALEAN	DAGGIEST	DAIDZEINS
DABBA	DACRONS	DAEDALIAN	DAGGING	DAIKER
DABBAS	DACTYL	DAEDALIC	DAGGINGS	DAIKERED
DABBED	DACTYLAR	DAEING	DAGGLE	DAIKERING
DABBER	DACTYLI	DAEMON	DAGGLED	DAIKERS
DABBERS	DACTYLIC	DAEMONES	DAGGLES	DAIKO
DABBING	DACTYLICS	DAEMONIC	DAGGLING	DAIKON
DABBITIES	DACTYLIST	DAEMONS	DAGGY	DAIKONS
DABBITY	DACTYLS	DAES	DAGLOCK	DAIKOS
DABBLE	DACTYLUS	DAFF	DAGLOCKS	DAILIES
DABBLED	DAD	DAFFED	DAGO	DAILINESS
DABBLER	DADA	DAFFIER	DAGOBA	DAILY
DABBLERS	DADAH	DAFFIES	DAGOBAS	DAILYNESS
DABBLES	DADAHS	DAFFIEST	DAGOES	DAIMEN
DABBLING	DADAISM	DAFFILY	DAGOS	DAIMIO
DABBLINGS	DADAISMS	DAFFINESS	DAGS	DAIMIOS
DABCHICK	DADAIST	DAFFING	DAGWOOD	DAIMOKU
DABCHICKS	DADAISTIC	DAFFINGS	DAGWOODS	DAIMOKUS
DABS	DADAISTS	DAFFODIL	DAH	DAIMON
DABSTER	DADAS	DAFFODILS	DAHABEAH	DAIMONES
DABSTERS	DADBOD	DAFFS	DAHABEAHS	DAIMONIC
DACE	DADBODS	DAFFY	DAHABEEAH	DAIMONS
DACES	DADCHELOR	DAFT	DAHABIAH	DAIMYO
DACHA	DADDED	DAFTAR	DAHABIAHS	DAIMYOS
DACHAS	DADDIES	DAFTARS	DAHABIEH	DAINE
DACHSHUND	DADDING	DAFTER	DAHABIEHS	DAINED
DACITE	DADDLE	DAFTEST	DAHABIYA	DAINES
DACITES	DADDLED	DAFTIE	DAHABIYAH	DAINING
DACK	DADDLES	DAFTIES	DAHABIYAS	DAINT
DACKED	DADDLING	DAFTLY	DAHABIYEH	DAINTTER
DACKER	DADDOCK	DAFTNESS	DAHL	DAINTIES
DACKERED	DADDOCKS	DAG	DAHLIA	DAINTIEST
DACKERING	DADDY	DAGABA	DAHLIAS	DAINTILY
DACKERS	DADGUM	DAGABAS	DAHLS	DAINTS
DACKING	DADO	DAGGA	DAHOON	DAINTY
DACKS	DADOED	DAGGAS	DAHOONS	DAIQUIRI
DACOIT	DADOES	DAGGED	DAHS	DAIQUIRIS
DACOITAGE	DADOING	DAGGER	DAIDLE	DAIRIES
DACOITIES	DADOS	DAGGERED	DAIDLED	DAIRY

DAIRYING	DALLIANCE	DAME	DAMPENER	DANDER
DAIRYINGS	DALLIED	DAMEHOOD	DAMPENERS	DANDERED
DAIRYMAID	DALLIER	DAMEHOODS	DAMPENING	DANDERING
DAIRYMAN	DALLIERS	DAMES	DAMPENS	DANDERS
DAIRYMEN	DALLIES	DAMEWORT	DAMPER	DANDIACAL
DAIS	DALLOP	DAMEWORTS	DAMPERS	DANDIER
DAISES	DALLOPS	DAMFOOL	DAMPEST	DANDIES
DAISHIKI	DALLY	DAMFOOLS	DAMPIER	DANDIEST
DAISHIKIS	DALLYING	DAMIANA	DAMPIEST	DANDIFIED
DAISIED	DALMAHOY	DAMIANAS	DAMPING	DANDIFIES
DAISIES	DALMAHOYS	DAMMAR	DAMPINGS	DANDIFY
DAISY	DALMATIAN	DAMMARS	DAMPISH	DANDILY
DAISYLIKE	DALMATIC	DAMME	DAMPLY	DANDIPRAT
DAK	DALMATICS	DAMMED	DAMPNESS	DANDLE
DAKER	DALS	DAMMER	DAMPS	DANDLED
DAKERED	DALT	DAMMERS	DAMPY	DANDLER
DAKERHEN	DALTON	DAMMING	DAMS	DANDLERS
DAKERHENS	DALTONIAN	DAMMIT	DAMSEL	DANDLES
DAKERING	DALTONIC	DAMN	DAMSELFLY	DANDLING
DAKERS	DALTONISM	DAMNABLE	DAMSELS	DANDRIFF
DAKOIT	DALTONS	DAMNABLY	DAMSON	DANDRIFFS
DAKOITI	DALTS	DAMNATION	DAMSONS	DANDRUFF
DAKOITIES	DAM	DAMNATORY	DAN	DANDRUFFS
DAKOITIS	DAMAGE	DAMNDEST	DANAZOL	DANDRUFFY
DAKOITS	DAMAGED	DAMNDESTS	DANAZOLS	DANDY
DAKOITY	DAMAGER	DAMNED	DANCE	DANDYFUNK
DAKS	DAMAGERS	DAMNEDER	DANCEABLE	DANDYISH
DAL	DAMAGES	DAMNEDEST	DANCECORE	DANDYISM
DALAPON	DAMAGING	DAMNER	DANCED	DANDYISMS
DALAPONS	DAMAN	DAMNERS	DANCEHALL	DANDYPRAT
DALASI	DAMANS	DAMNEST	DANCELIKE	DANEGELD
DALASIS	DAMAR	DAMNESTS	DANCER	DANEGELDS
DALE	DAMARS	DAMNIFIED	DANCERS	DANEGELT
DALED	DAMASCENE	DAMNIFIES	DANCES	DANEGELTS
DALEDH	DAMASK	DAMNIFY	DANCETTE	DANELAGH
DALEDHS	DAMASKED	DAMNING	DANCETTEE	DANELAGHS
DALEDS	DAMASKEEN	DAMNINGLY	DANCETTES	DANELAW
DALES	DAMASKIN	DAMNS	DANCETTY	DANELAWS
DALESMAN	DAMASKING	DAMOISEL	DANCEWEAR	DANEWEED
DALESMEN	DAMASKINS	DAMOISELS	DANCEY	DANEWEEDS
DALETH	DAMASKS	DAMOSEL	DANCICAL	DANEWORT
DALETHS	DAMASQUIN	DAMOSELS	DANCICALS	DANEWORTS
DALGYTE	DAMASSIN	DAMOZEL	DANCIER	DANG
DALGYTES	DAMASSINS	DAMOZELS	DANCIEST	DANGED
DALI	DAMBOARD	DAMP	DANCING	DANGER
DALIS	DAMBOARDS	DAMPED	DANCINGS	DANGERED
DALLE	DAMBROD	DAMPEN	DANCY	DANGERING
DALLES	DAMBRODS	DAMPENED	DANDELION	DANGEROUS

DANGERS	DAPHNIAS	DARING	DARNEDER	DAS
DANGEST	DAPHNID	DARINGLY	DARNEDEST	DASH
DANGING	DAPHNIDS	DARINGS	DARNEL	DASHBOARD
DANGLE	DAPPED	DARIOLE	DARNELS	DASHCAM
DANGLED	DAPPER	DARIOLES	DARNER	DASHCAMS
DANGLER	DAPPERER	DARIS	DARNERS	DASHED
DANGLERS	DAPPEREST	DARK	DARNEST	DASHEEN
DANGLES	DAPPERLY	DARKED	DARNESTS	DASHEENS
DANGLIER	DAPPERS	DARKEN	DARNING	DASHEKI
DANGLIEST	DAPPING	DARKENED	DARNINGS	DASHEKIS
DANGLING	DAPPLE	DARKENER	DARNS	DASHER
DANGLINGS	DAPPLED	DARKENERS	DAROGHA	DASHERS
DANGLY	DAPPLES	DARKENING	DAROGHAS	DASHES
DANGS	DAPPLING	DARKENS	DARRAIGN	DASHI
DANIO	DAPS	DARKER	DARRAIGNE	DASHIER
DANIOS	DAPSONE	DARKEST	DARRAIGNS	DASHIEST
DANISH	DAPSONES	DARKEY	DARRAIN	DASHIKI
DANISHES	DAQUIRI	DARKEYS	DARRAINE	DASHIKIS
DANK	DAQUIRIS	DARKFIELD	DARRAINED	DASHING
DANKER	DARAF	DARKIE	DARRAINES	DASHINGLY
DANKEST	DARAFS	DARKIES	DARRAINS	DASHIS
DANKISH	DARB	DARKING	DARRAYN	DASHLIGHT
DANKLY	DARBAR	DARKISH	DARRAYNED	DASHPOT
DANKNESS	DARBARS	DARKLE	DARRAYNS	DASHPOTS
DANKS	DARBIES	DARKLED	DARRE	DASHY
DANNEBROG	DARBS	DARKLES	DARRED	DASSIE
DANNIES	DARCIES	DARKLIER	DARRES	DASSIES
DANNY	DARCY	DARKLIEST	DARRING	DASTARD
DANS	DARCYS	DARKLING	DARSHAN	DASTARDLY
DANSAK	DARE	DARKLINGS	DARSHANS	DASTARDS
DANSAKS	DARED	DARKLY	DART	DASTARDY
DANSEUR	DAREDEVIL	DARKMANS	DARTBOARD	DASYMETER
DANSEURS	DAREFUL	DARKNESS	DARTED	DASYPOD
DANSEUSE	DARER	DARKNET	DARTER	DASYPODS
DANSEUSES	DARERS	DARKNETS	DARTERS	DASYURE
DANT	DARES	DARKROOM	DARTING	DASYURES
DANTED	DARESAY	DARKROOMS	DARTINGLY	DATA
DANTHONIA	DARG	DARKS	DARTITIS	DATABANK
DANTING	DARGA	DARKSOME	DARTLE	DATABANKS
DANTON	DARGAH	DARKY	DARTLED	DATABASE
DANTONED	DARGAHS	DARLING	DARTLES	DATABASED
DANTONING	DARGAS	DARLINGLY	DARTLING	DATABASES
DANTONS	DARGLE	DARLINGS	DARTRE	DATABLE
DANTS	DARGLES	DARN	DARTRES	DATABUS
DAP	DARGS	DARNATION	DARTROUS	DATABUSES
DAPHNE	DARI	DARNDEST	DARTS	DATACARD
DAPHNES	DARIC	DARNDESTS	DARZI	DATACARDS
DAPHNIA	DARICS	DARNED	DARZIS	DATACOMMS

DATAFLOW	DAUBE	DAURS	DAWNERING	DAYGLOWS
DATAGLOVE	DAUBED	DAUT	DAWNERS	DAYLIGHT
DATAGRAM	DAUBER	DAUTED	DAWNEY	DAYLIGHTS
DATAGRAMS	DAUBERIES	DAUTIE	DAWNING	DAYLILIES
DATAL	DAUBERS	DAUTIES	DAWNINGS	DAYLILY
DATALLER	DAUBERY	DAUTING	DAWNLIKE	DAYLIT
DATALLERS	DAUBES	DAUTS	DAWNS	DAYLONG
DATALS	DAUBIER	DAVEN	DAWS	DAYMARE
DATARIA	DAUBIEST	DAVENED	DAWSONITE	DAYMARES
DATARIAS	DAUBING	DAVENING	DAWT	DAYMARK
DATARIES	DAUBINGLY	DAVENPORT	DAWTED	DAYMARKS
DATARY	DAUBINGS	DAVENS	DAWTIE	DAYNT
DATCHA	DAUBRIES	DAVIDIA	DAWTIES	DAYNTS
DATCHAS	DAUBRY	DAVIDIAS	DAWTING	DAYPACK
DATE	DAUBS	DAVIES	DAWTS	DAYPACKS
DATEABLE	DAUBY	DAVIT	DAY	DAYROOM
DATEBOOK	DAUD	DAVITS	DAYAN	DAYROOMS
DATEBOOKS	DAUDED	DAVY	DAYANIM	DAYS
DATED	DAUDING	DAW	DAYANS	DAYSACK
DATEDLY	DAUDS	DAWAH	DAYBED	DAYSACKS
DATEDNESS	DAUGHTER	DAWAHS	DAYBEDS	DAYSAIL
DATELESS	DAUGHTERS	DAWBAKE	DAYBOAT	DAYSAILED
DATELINE	DAULT	DAWBAKES	DAYBOATS	DAYSAILER
DATELINED	DAULTS	DAWBRIES	DAYBOOK	DAYSAILOR
DATELINES	DAUNDER	DAWBRY	DAYBOOKS	DAYSAILS
DATER	DAUNDERED	DAWCOCK	DAYBOY	DAYSHELL
DATERS	DAUNDERS	DAWCOCKS	DAYBOYS	DAYSHELLS
DATES	DAUNER	DAWD	DAYBREAK	DAYSIDE
DATING	DAUNERED	DAWDED	DAYBREAKS	DAYSIDES
DATINGS	DAUNERING	DAWDING	DAYCARE	DAYSMAN
DATIVAL	DAUNERS	DAWDLE	DAYCARES	DAYSMEN
DATIVE	DAUNT	DAWDLED	DAYCATION	DAYSPRING
DATIVELY	DAUNTED	DAWDLER	DAYCENTRE	DAYSTAR
DATIVES	DAUNTER	DAWDLERS	DAYCH	DAYSTARS
DATO	DAUNTERS	DAWDLES	DAYCHED	DAYTALE
DATOLITE	DAUNTING	DAWDLING	DAYCHES	DAYTALER
DATOLITES	DAUNTLESS	DAWDLINGS	DAYCHING	DAYTALERS
DATOS	DAUNTON	DAWDS	DAYDREAM	DAYTALES
DATTO	DAUNTONED	DAWED	DAYDREAMS	DAYTIME
DATTOS	DAUNTONS	DAWEN	DAYDREAMT	DAYTIMES
DATUM	DAUNTS	DAWING	DAYDREAMY	DAYWEAR
DATUMS	DAUPHIN	DAWISH	DAYFLIES	DAYWEARS
DATURA	DAUPHINE	DAWK	DAYFLOWER	DAYWORK
DATURAS	DAUPHINES	DAWKS	DAYFLY	DAYWORKER
DATURIC	DAUPHINS	DAWN	DAYGIRL	DAYWORKS
DATURINE	DAUR	DAWNED	DAYGIRLS	DAZE
DATURINES	DAURED	DAWNER	DAYGLO	DAZED
DAUB	DAURING	DAWNERED	DAYGLOW	DAZEDLY

DAZEDNESS	DEADLIFTS	DEALIGNS	DEASIL	DEBARKING
DAZER	DEADLIGHT	DEALING	DEASILS	DEBARKS
DAZERS	DEADLINE	DEALINGS	DEASIUL	DEBARMENT
DAZES	DEADLINED	DEALMAKER	DEASIULS	DEBARRASS
DAZING	DEADLINES	DEALS	DEASOIL	DEBARRED
DAZZLE	DEADLOCK	DEALT	DEASOILS	DEBARRING
DAZZLED	DEADLOCKS	DEAMINASE	DEATH	DEBARS
DAZZLER	DEADLY	DEAMINATE	DEATHBED	DEBASE
DAZZLERS	DEADMAN	DEAMINISE	DEATHBEDS	DEBASED
DAZZLES	DEADMEN	DEAMINIZE	DEATHBLOW	DEBASER
DAZZLING	DEADNESS	DEAN	DEATHCARE	DEBASERS
DAZZLINGS	DEADPAN	DEANED	DEATHCUP	DEBASES
DE	DEADPANS	DEANER	DEATHCUPS	DEBASING
DEACIDIFY	DEADS	DEANERIES	DEATHFUL	DEBATABLE
DEACON	DEADSTOCK	DEANERS	DEATHIER	DEBATABLY
DEACONED	DEADWATER	DEANERY	DEATHIEST	DEBATE
DEACONESS	DEADWOOD	DEANING	DEATHLESS	DEBATED
DEACONING	DEADWOODS	DEANS	DEATHLIER	DEBATEFUL
DEACONRY	DEAERATE	DEANSHIP	DEATHLIKE	DEBATER
DEACONS	DEAERATED	DEANSHIPS	DEATHLY	DEBATERS
DEAD	DEAERATES	DEAR	DEATHS	DEBATES
DEADBEAT	DEAERATOR	DEARE	DEATHSMAN	DEBATING
DEADBEATS	DEAF	DEARED	DEATHSMEN	DEBATINGS
DEADBOLT	DEAFBLIND	DEARER	DEATHTRAP	DEBAUCH
DEADBOLTS	DEAFEN	DEARES	DEATHWARD	DEBAUCHED
DEADBOY	DEAFENED	DEAREST	DEATHY	DEBAUCHEE
DEADBOYS	DEAFENING	DEARESTS	DEAVE	DEBAUCHER
DEADED	DEAFENS	DEARIE	DEAVED	DEBAUCHES
DEADEN	DEAFER	DEARIES	DEAVES	DEBBIER
DEADENED	DEAFEST	DEARING	DEAVING	DEBBIES
DEADENER	DEAFISH	DEARLING	DEAW	DEBBIEST
DEADENERS	DEAFLY	DEARLINGS	DEAWED	DEBBY
DEADENING	DEAFNESS	DEARLY	DEAWIE	DEBE
DEADENS	DEAIR	DEARN	DEAWING	DEBEAK
DEADER	DEAIRED	DEARNED	DEAWS	DEBEAKED
DEADERS	DEAIRING	DEARNESS	DEAWY	DEBEAKING
DEADEST	DEAIRS	DEARNFUL	DEB	DEBEAKS
DEADEYE	DEAL	DEARNING	DEBACLE	DEBEARD
DEADEYES	DEALATE	DEARNLY	DEBACLES	DEBEARDED
DEADFALL	DEALATED	DEARNS	DEBAG	DEBEARDS
DEADFALLS	DEALATES	DEARS	DEBAGGED	DEBEL
DEADHEAD	DEALATION	DEARTH	DEBAGGING	DEBELLED
DEADHEADS	DEALBATE	DEARTHS	DEBAGS	DEBELLING
DEADHOUSE	DEALER	DEARY	DEBAR	DEBELS
DEADING	DEALERS	DEASH	DEBARK	DEBENTURE
DEADLIER	DEALFISH	DEASHED	DEBARKED	DEBES
DEADLIEST	DEALIGN	DEASHES	DEBARKER	DEBILE
DEADLIFT	DEALIGNED	DEASHING	DEBARKERS	DEBILITY

DEBIT	DEBUDDED	DECAFF	DECARBING	DECENTERS
DEBITED	DEBUDDING	DECAFFS	DECARBS	DECENTEST
DEBITING	DEBUDS	DECAFS	DECARE	DECENTLY
DEBITOR	DEBUG	DECAGON	DECARES	DECENTRE
DEBITORS	DEBUGGED	DECAGONAL	DECASTERE	DECENTRED
DEBITS	DEBUGGER	DECAGONS	DECASTICH	DECENTRES
DEBONAIR	DEBUGGERS	DECAGRAM	DECASTYLE	DECEPTION
DEBONAIRE	DEBUGGING	DECAGRAMS	DECATHLON	DECEPTIVE
DEBONE	DEBUGS	DECAHEDRA	DECAUDATE	DECEPTORY
DEBONED	DEBUNK	DECAL	DECAY	DECERN
DEBONER	DEBUNKED	DECALCIFY	DECAYABLE	DECERNED
DEBONERS	DEBUNKER	DECALED	DECAYED	DECERNING
DEBONES	DEBUNKERS	DECALING	DECAYER	DECERNS
DEBONING	DEBUNKING	DECALITER	DECAYERS	DECERTIFY
DEBOSH	DEBUNKS	DECALITRE	DECAYING	DECESSION
DEBOSHED	DEBUR	DECALLED	DECAYLESS	DECHEANCE
DEBOSHES	DEBURR	DECALLING	DECAYS	DECIARE
DEBOSHING	DEBURRED	DECALOG	DECCIE	DECIARES
DEBOSS	DEBURRING	DECALOGS	DECCIES	DECIBEL
DEBOSSED	DEBURRS	DECALOGUE	DECEASE	DECIBELS
DEBOSSES	DEBURS	DECALS	DECEASED	DECIDABLE
DEBOSSING	DEBUS	DECAMETER	DECEASEDS	DECIDE
DEBOUCH	DEBUSED	DECAMETRE	DECEASES	DECIDED
DEBOUCHE	DEBUSES	DECAMP	DECEASING	DECIDEDLY
DEBOUCHED	DEBUSING	DECAMPED	DECEDENT	DECIDER
DEBOUCHES	DEBUSSED	DECAMPING	DECEDENTS	DECIDERS
DEBRIDE	DEBUSSES	DECAMPS	DECEIT	DECIDES
DEBRIDED	DEBUSSING	DECAN	DECEITFUL	DECIDING
DEBRIDES	DEBUT	DECANAL	DECEITS	DECIDUA
DEBRIDING	DEBUTANT	DECANALLY	DECEIVE	DECIDUAE
DEBRIEF	DEBUTANTE	DECANE	DECEIVED	DECIDUAL
DEBRIEFED	DEBUTANTS	DECANES	DECEIVER	DECIDUAS
DEBRIEFER	DEBUTED	DECANI	DECEIVERS	DECIDUATE
DEBRIEFS	DEBUTING	DECANOIC	DECEIVES	DECIDUOUS
DEBRIS	DEBUTS	DECANS	DECEIVING	DECIGRAM
DEBRUISE	DEBYE	DECANT	DECELERON	DECIGRAMS
DEBRUISED	DEBYES	DECANTATE	DECEMVIR	DECILE
DEBRUISES	DECACHORD	DECANTED	DECEMVIRI	DECILES
DEBS	DECAD	DECANTER	DECEMVIRS	DECILITER
DEBT	DECADAL	DECANTERS	DECENARY	DECILITRE
DEBTED	DECADE	DECANTING	DECENCIES	DECILLION
DEBTEE	DECADENCE	DECANTS	DECENCY	DECIMAL
DEBTEES	DECADENCY	DECAPOD	DECENNARY	DECIMALLY
DEBTLESS	DECADENT	DECAPODAL	DECENNIA	DECIMALS
DEBTOR	DECADENTS	DECAPODAN	DECENNIAL	DECIMATE
DEBTORS	DECADES	DECAPODS	DECENNIUM	DECIMATED
DEBTS	DECADS	DECARB	DECENT	DECIMATES
DEBUD	DECAF	DECARBED	DECENTER	DECIMATOR

DECIME	DECLAW	DECOMMITS	DECRIAL	DEDICATE
DECIMES	DECLAWED	DECOMPLEX	DECRIALS	DEDICATED
DECIMETER	DECLAWING	DECOMPOSE	DECRIED	DEDICATEE
DECIMETRE	DECLAWS	DECONGEST	DECRIER	DEDICATES
DECIPHER	DECLINAL	DECONTROL	DECRIERS	DEDICATOR
DECIPHERS	DECLINALS	DECOR	DECRIES	DEDIMUS
DECISION	DECLINANT	DECORATE	DECROWN	DEDIMUSES
DECISIONS	DECLINATE	DECORATED	DECROWNED	DEDUCE
DECISIVE	DECLINE	DECORATES	DECROWNS	DEDUCED
DECISORY	DECLINED	DECORATOR	DECRY	DEDUCES
DECISTERE	DECLINER	DECOROUS	DECRYING	DEDUCIBLE
DECK	DECLINERS	DECORS	DECRYPT	DEDUCIBLY
DECKCHAIR	DECLINES	DECORUM	DECRYPTED	DEDUCING
DECKED	DECLINING	DECORUMS	DECRYPTS	DEDUCT
DECKEL	DECLINIST	DECOS	DECTET	DEDUCTED
DECKELS	DECLIVITY	DECOUPAGE	DECTETS	DEDUCTING
DECKER	DECLIVOUS	DECOUPLE	DECUBITAL	DEDUCTION
DECKERS	DECLUTCH	DECOUPLED	DECUBITI	DEDUCTIVE
DECKHAND	DECLUTTER	DECOUPLER	DECUBITUS	DEDUCTS
DECKHANDS	DECO	DECOUPLES	DECUMAN	DEE
DECKHOUSE	DECOCT	DECOY	DECUMANS	DEED
DECKING	DECOCTED	DECOYED	DECUMBENT	DEEDED
DECKINGS	DECOCTING	DECOYER	DECUPLE	DEEDER
DECKLE	DECOCTION	DECOYERS	DECUPLED	DEEDEST
DECKLED	DECOCTIVE	DECOYING	DECUPLES	DEEDFUL
DECKLES	DECOCTS	DECOYS	DECUPLING	DEEDIER
DECKLESS	DECOCTURE	DECREASE	DECURIA	DEEDIEST
DECKO	DECODABLE	DECREASED	DECURIAS	DEEDILY
DECKOED	DECODE	DECREASES	DECURIES	DEEDING
DECKOING	DECODED	DECREE	DECURION	DEEDLESS
DECKOS	DECODER	DECREED	DECURIONS	DEEDS
DECKS	DECODERS	DECREEING	DECURRENT	DEEDY
DECLAIM	DECODES	DECREER	DECURSION	DEEING
DECLAIMED	DECODING	DECREERS	DECURSIVE	DEEJAY
DECLAIMER	DECODINGS	DECREES	DECURVE	DEEJAYED
DECLAIMS	DECOHERER	DECREET	DECURVED	DEEJAYING
DECLARANT	DECOKE	DECREETS	DECURVES	DEEJAYS
DECLARE	DECOKED	DECREMENT	DECURVING	DEEK
DECLARED	DECOKES	DECREPIT	DECURY	DEELY
DECLARER	DECOKING	DECRETAL	DECUSSATE	DEEM
DECLARERS	DECOLLATE	DECRETALS	DEDAL	DEEMED
DECLARES	DECOLLETE	DECRETIST	DEDALIAN	DEEMING
DECLARING	DECOLOR	DECRETIVE	DEDANS	DEEMS
DECLASS	DECOLORED	DECRETORY	DEDENDA	DEEMSTER
DECLASSE	DECOLORS	DECREW	DEDENDUM	DEEMSTERS
DECLASSED	DECOLOUR	DECREWED	DEDENDUMS	DEEN
DECLASSEE	DECOLOURS	DECREWING	DEDICANT	DEENS
DECLASSES	DECOMMIT	DECREWS	DEDICANTS	DEEP

DEEPEN

DEEPEN
DEEPENED
DEEPENER
DEEPENERS
DEEPENING
DEEPENS
DEEPER
DEEPEST
DEEPFELT
DEEPFROZE
DEEPIE
DEEPIES
DEEPLY
DEEPMOST
DEEPNESS
DEEPS
DEEPWATER
DEER
DEERBERRY
DEERE
DEERES
DEERFLIES
DEERFLY
DEERGRASS
DEERHORN
DEERHORNS
DEERHOUND
DEERLET
DEERLETS
DEERLIKE
DEERS
DEERSKIN
DEERSKINS
DEERWEED
DEERWEEDS
DEERYARD
DEERYARDS
DEES
DEET
DEETS
DEEV
DEEVE
DEEVED
DEEVES
DEEVING
DEEVS
DEEWAN
DEEWANS

DEF
DEFACE
DEFACED
DEFACER
DEFACERS
DEFACES
DEFACING
DEFAECATE
DEFALCATE
DEFAME
DEFAMED
DEFAMER
DEFAMERS
DEFAMES
DEFAMING
DEFAMINGS
DEFANG
DEFANGED
DEFANGING
DEFANGS
DEFAST
DEFASTE
DEFAT
DEFATS
DEFATTED
DEFATTING
DEFAULT
DEFAULTED
DEFAULTER
DEFAULTS
DEFEAT
DEFEATED
DEFEATER
DEFEATERS
DEFEATING
DEFEATISM
DEFEATIST
DEFEATS
DEFEATURE
DEFECATE
DEFECATED
DEFECATES
DEFECATOR
DEFECT
DEFECTED
DEFECTING
DEFECTION
DEFECTIVE

DEFECTOR
DEFECTORS
DEFECTS
DEFENCE
DEFENCED
DEFENCES
DEFENCING
DEFEND
DEFENDANT
DEFENDED
DEFENDER
DEFENDERS
DEFENDING
DEFENDS
DEFENSE
DEFENSED
DEFENSES
DEFENSING
DEFENSIVE
DEFER
DEFERABLE
DEFERENCE
DEFERENT
DEFERENTS
DEFERMENT
DEFERRAL
DEFERRALS
DEFERRED
DEFERRER
DEFERRERS
DEFERRING
DEFERS
DEFFER
DEFFEST
DEFFLY
DEFFO
DEFI
DEFIANCE
DEFIANCES
DEFIANT
DEFIANTLY
DEFICIENT
DEFICIT
DEFICITS
DEFIED
DEFIER
DEFIERS
DEFIES

DEFILADE
DEFILADED
DEFILADES
DEFILE
DEFILED
DEFILER
DEFILERS
DEFILES
DEFILING
DEFINABLE
DEFINABLY
DEFINE
DEFINED
DEFINER
DEFINERS
DEFINES
DEFINIENS
DEFINING
DEFINITE
DEFINITES
DEFIS
DEFLATE
DEFLATED
DEFLATER
DEFLATERS
DEFLATES
DEFLATING
DEFLATION
DEFLATOR
DEFLATORS
DEFLEA
DEFLEAED
DEFLEAING
DEFLEAS
DEFLECT
DEFLECTED
DEFLECTOR
DEFLECTS
DEFLEX
DEFLEXED
DEFLEXES
DEFLEXING
DEFLEXION
DEFLEXURE
DEFLORATE
DEFLOWER
DEFLOWERS
DEFLUENT

DEFLUXION
DEFO
DEFOAM
DEFOAMED
DEFOAMER
DEFOAMERS
DEFOAMING
DEFOAMS
DEFOCUS
DEFOCUSED
DEFOCUSES
DEFOG
DEFOGGED
DEFOGGER
DEFOGGERS
DEFOGGING
DEFOGS
DEFOLIANT
DEFOLIATE
DEFORCE
DEFORCED
DEFORCER
DEFORCERS
DEFORCES
DEFORCING
DEFOREST
DEFORESTS
DEFORM
DEFORMED
DEFORMER
DEFORMERS
DEFORMING
DEFORMITY
DEFORMS
DEFOUL
DEFOULED
DEFOULING
DEFOULS
DEFRAG
DEFRAGGED
DEFRAGGER
DEFRAGS
DEFRAUD
DEFRAUDED
DEFRAUDER
DEFRAUDS
DEFRAY
DEFRAYAL

DEFRAYALS	DEGAGE	DEGS	DEIDER	DEIXISES
DEFRAYED	DEGAME	DEGU	DEIDEST	DEJECT
DEFRAYER	DEGAMES	DEGUM	DEIDS	DEJECTA
DEFRAYERS	DEGAMI	DEGUMMED	DEIF	DEJECTED
DEFRAYING	DEGAMIS	DEGUMMING	DEIFER	DEJECTING
DEFRAYS	DEGARNISH	DEGUMS	DEIFEST	DEJECTION
DEFREEZE	DEGAS	DEGUS	DEIFIC	DEJECTORY
DEFREEZES	DEGASES	DEGUST	DEIFICAL	DEJECTS
DEFRIEND	DEGASSED	DEGUSTATE	DEIFIED	DEJEUNE
DEFRIENDS	DEGASSER	DEGUSTED	DEIFIER	DEJEUNER
DEFROCK	DEGASSERS	DEGUSTING	DEIFIERS	DEJEUNERS
DEFROCKED	DEGASSES	DEGUSTS	DEIFIES	DEJEUNES
DEFROCKS	DEGASSING	DEHAIR	DEIFORM	DEKAGRAM
DEFROST	DEGAUSS	DEHAIRED	DEIFY	DEKAGRAMS
DEFROSTED	DEGAUSSED	DEHAIRING	DEIFYING	DEKALITER
DEFROSTER	DEGAUSSER	DEHAIRS	DEIGN	DEKALITRE
DEFROSTS	DEGAUSSES	DEHISCE	DEIGNED	DEKALOGY
DEFROZE	DEGEARING	DEHISCED	DEIGNING	DEKAMETER
DEFROZEN	DEGENDER	DEHISCENT	DEIGNS	DEKAMETRE
DEFT	DEGENDERS	DEHISCES	DEIL	DEKARE
DEFTER	DEGERM	DEHISCING	DEILS	DEKARES
DEFTEST	DEGERMED	DEHORN	DEINDEX	DEKE
DEFTLY	DEGERMING	DEHORNED	DEINDEXED	DEKED
DEFTNESS	DEGERMS	DEHORNER	DEINDEXES	DEKEING
DEFUEL	DEGGED	DEHORNERS	DEINOSAUR	DEKES
DEFUELED	DEGGING	DEHORNING	DEIONISE	DEKING
DEFUELING	DEGLAZE	DEHORNS	DEIONISED	DEKKO
DEFUELLED	DEGLAZED	DEHORS	DEIONISER	DEKKOED
DEFUELS	DEGLAZES	DEHORT	DEIONISES	DEKKOING
DEFUNCT	DEGLAZING	DEHORTED	DEIONIZE	DEKKOS
DEFUNCTS	DEGOUT	DEHORTER	DEIONIZED	DEL
DEFUND	DEGOUTED	DEHORTERS	DEIONIZER	DELAINE
DEFUNDED	DEGOUTING	DEHORTING	DEIONIZES	DELAINES
DEFUNDING	DEGOUTS	DEHORTS	DEIPAROUS	DELAPSE
DEFUNDS	DEGRADE	DEHYDRATE	DEISEAL	DELAPSED
DEFUSE	DEGRADED	DEI	DEISEALS	DELAPSES
DEFUSED	DEGRADER	DEICE	DEISHEAL	DELAPSING
DEFUSER	DEGRADERS	DEICED	DEISHEALS	DELAPSION
DEFUSERS	DEGRADES	DEICER	DEISM	DELATE
DEFUSES	DEGRADING	DEICERS	DEISMS	DELATED
DEFUSING	DEGRAS	DEICES	DEIST	DELATES
DEFUZE	DEGREASE	DEICIDAL	DEISTIC	DELATING
DEFUZED	DEGREASED	DEICIDE	DEISTICAL	DELATION
DEFUZES	DEGREASER	DEICIDES	DEISTS	DELATIONS
DEFUZING	DEGREASES	DEICING	DEITIES	DELATOR
DEFY	DEGREE	DEICTIC	DEITY	DELATORS
DEFYING	DEGREED	DEICTICS	DEIXES	DELAY
DEG	DEGREES	DEID	DEIXIS	DELAYABLE

DELAYED	DELICATES	DELOPE	DELUSTRE	DEMEAN
DELAYER	DELICE	DELOPED	DELUSTRED	DEMEANE
DELAYERS	DELICES	DELOPES	DELUSTRES	DEMEANED
DELAYING	DELICIOUS	DELOPING	DELUXE	DEMEANES
DELAYS	DELICT	DELOS	DELVE	DEMEANING
DELE	DELICTS	DELOUSE	DELVED	DEMEANOR
DELEAD	DELIGHT	DELOUSED	DELVER	DEMEANORS
DELEADED	DELIGHTED	DELOUSER	DELVERS	DEMEANOUR
DELEADING	DELIGHTER	DELOUSERS	DELVES	DEMEANS
DELEADS	DELIGHTS	DELOUSES	DELVING	DEMENT
DELEAVE	DELIME	DELOUSING	DEMAGOG	DEMENTATE
DELEAVED	DELIMED	DELPH	DEMAGOGED	DEMENTED
DELEAVES	DELIMES	DELPHIC	DEMAGOGIC	DEMENTI
DELEAVING	DELIMING	DELPHIN	DEMAGOGS	DEMENTIA
DELEBLE	DELIMIT	DELPHINIA	DEMAGOGUE	DEMENTIAL
DELECTATE	DELIMITED	DELPHINS	DEMAGOGY	DEMENTIAS
DELED	DELIMITER	DELPHS	DEMAIN	DEMENTING
DELEGABLE	DELIMITS	DELS	DEMAINE	DEMENTIS
DELEGACY	DELINEATE	DELT	DEMAINES	DEMENTS
DELEGATE	DELINK	DELTA	DEMAINS	DEMERARA
DELEGATED	DELINKED	DELTAIC	DEMAN	DEMERARAN
DELEGATEE	DELINKING	DELTAS	DEMAND	DEMERARAS
DELEGATES	DELINKS	DELTIC	DEMANDANT	DEMERGE
DELEGATOR	DELIQUIUM	DELTOID	DEMANDED	DEMERGED
DELEING	DELIRIA	DELTOIDEI	DEMANDER	DEMERGER
DELENDA	DELIRIANT	DELTOIDS	DEMANDERS	DEMERGERS
DELES	DELIRIOUS	DELTS	DEMANDING	DEMERGES
DELETABLE	DELIRIUM	DELUBRA	DEMANDS	DEMERGING
DELETE	DELIRIUMS	DELUBRUM	DEMANNED	DEMERIT
DELETED	DELIS	DELUBRUMS	DEMANNING	DEMERITED
DELETES	DELISH	DELUDABLE	DEMANS	DEMERITS
DELETING	DELIST	DELUDE	DEMANTOID	DEMERSAL
DELETION	DELISTED	DELUDED	DEMARCATE	DEMERSE
DELETIONS	DELISTING	DELUDER	DEMARCHE	DEMERSED
DELETIVE	DELISTS	DELUDERS	DEMARCHES	DEMERSES
DELETORY	DELIVER	DELUDES	DEMARK	DEMERSING
DELF	DELIVERED	DELUDING	DEMARKED	DEMERSION
DELFS	DELIVERER	DELUGE	DEMARKET	DEMES
DELFT	DELIVERLY	DELUGED	DEMARKETS	DEMESNE
DELFTS	DELIVERS	DELUGES	DEMARKING	DEMESNES
DELFTWARE	DELIVERY	DELUGING	DEMARKS	DEMETON
DELI	DELL	DELUNDUNG	DEMAST	DEMETONS
DELIBATE	DELLIER	DELUSION	DEMASTED	DEMIC
DELIBATED	DELLIES	DELUSIONS	DEMASTING	DEMIES
DELIBATES	DELLIEST	DELUSIVE	DEMASTS	DEMIGOD
DELIBLE	DELLS	DELUSORY	DEMAYNE	DEMIGODS
DELICACY	DELLY	DELUSTER	DEMAYNES	DEMIJOHN
DELICATE	DELO	DELUSTERS	DEME	DEMIJOHNS

DEMILUNE	DEMOCRATY	DEMPT	DENDRONS	DENS
DEMILUNES	DEMODE	DEMULCENT	DENE	DENSE
DEMIMONDE	DEMODED	DEMULSIFY	DENERVATE	DENSELY
DEMINER	DEMOED	DEMUR	DENES	DENSENESS
DEMINERS	DEMOI	DEMURE	DENET	DENSER
DEMINING	DEMOING	DEMURED	DENETS	DENSEST
DEMININGS	DEMOLISH	DEMURELY	DENETTED	DENSIFIED
DEMIPIQUE	DEMOLOGY	DEMURER	DENETTING	DENSIFIER
DEMIREP	DEMON	DEMURES	DENGUE	DENSIFIES
DEMIREPS	DEMONESS	DEMUREST	DENGUES	DENSIFY
DEMISABLE	DEMONIAC	DEMURING	DENI	DENSITIES
DEMISE	DEMONIACS	DEMURRAGE	DENIABLE	DENSITY
DEMISED	DEMONIAN	DEMURRAL	DENIABLY	DENT
DEMISES	DEMONIC	DEMURRALS	DENIAL	DENTAL
DEMISING	DEMONICAL	DEMURRED	DENIALIST	DENTALIA
DEMISS	DEMONISE	DEMURRER	DENIALS	DENTALISE
DEMISSION	DEMONISED	DEMURRERS	DENIED	DENTALITY
DEMISSIVE	DEMONISES	DEMURRING	DENIER	DENTALIUM
DEMISSLY	DEMONISM	DEMURS	DENIERS	DENTALIZE
DEMIST	DEMONISMS	DEMY	DENIES	DENTALLY
DEMISTED	DEMONIST	DEMYSHIP	DENIGRATE	DENTALS
DEMISTER	DEMONISTS	DEMYSHIPS	DENIM	DENTARIA
DEMISTERS	DEMONIZE	DEMYSTIFY	DENIMED	DENTARIAS
DEMISTING	DEMONIZED	DEMYTHIFY	DENIMS	DENTARIES
DEMISTS	DEMONIZES	DEN	DENIS	DENTARY
DEMIT	DEMONRIES	DENAR	DENITRATE	DENTATE
DEMITASSE	DEMONRY	DENARI	DENITRIFY	DENTATED
DEMITS	DEMONS	DENARIES	DENIZEN	DENTATELY
DEMITTED	DEMONYM	DENARII	DENIZENED	DENTATION
DEMITTING	DEMONYMS	DENARIUS	DENIZENS	DENTED
DEMIURGE	DEMOS	DENARS	DENNED	DENTEL
DEMIURGES	DEMOSCENE	DENARY	DENNET	DENTELLE
DEMIURGIC	DEMOSES	DENATURE	DENNETS	DENTELLES
DEMIURGUS	DEMOTE	DENATURED	DENNING	DENTELS
DEMIVEG	DEMOTED	DENATURES	DENOMINAL	DENTEX
DEMIVEGES	DEMOTES	DENAY	DENOTABLE	DENTEXES
DEMIVOLT	DEMOTIC	DENAYED	DENOTATE	DENTICARE
DEMIVOLTE	DEMOTICS	DENAYING	DENOTATED	DENTICLE
DEMIVOLTS	DEMOTING	DENAYS	DENOTATES	DENTICLES
DEMIWORLD	DEMOTION	DENAZIFY	DENOTE	DENTIFORM
DEMO	DEMOTIONS	DENCH	DENOTED	DENTIL
DEMOB	DEMOTIST	DENDRIMER	DENOTES	DENTILED
DEMOBBED	DEMOTISTS	DENDRITE	DENOTING	DENTILS
DEMOBBING	DEMOUNT	DENDRITES	DENOTIVE	DENTIN
DEMOBS	DEMOUNTED	DENDRITIC	DENOUNCE	DENTINAL
DEMOCRACY	DEMOUNTS	DENDROID	DENOUNCED	DENTINE
DEMOCRAT	DEMPSTER	DENDROIDS	DENOUNCER	DENTINES
DEMOCRATS	DEMPSTERS	DENDRON	DENOUNCES	DENTING

DENTINS	DEPAINTS	DEPLANE	DEPOSE	DEPURANTS
DENTIST	DEPANNEUR	DEPLANED	DEPOSED	DEPURATE
DENTISTRY	DEPART	DEPLANES	DEPOSER	DEPURATED
DENTISTS	DEPARTED	DEPLANING	DEPOSERS	DEPURATES
DENTITION	DEPARTEDS	DEPLENISH	DEPOSES	DEPURATOR
DENTOID	DEPARTEE	DEPLETE	DEPOSING	DEPUTABLE
DENTS	DEPARTEES	DEPLETED	DEPOSIT	DEPUTE
DENTULOUS	DEPARTER	DEPLETER	DEPOSITED	DEPUTED
DENTURAL	DEPARTERS	DEPLETERS	DEPOSITOR	DEPUTES
DENTURE	DEPARTING	DEPLETES	DEPOSITS	DEPUTIES
DENTURES	DEPARTS	DEPLETING	DEPOT	DEPUTING
DENTURISM	DEPARTURE	DEPLETION	DEPOTS	DEPUTISE
DENTURIST	DEPASTURE	DEPLETIVE	DEPRAVE	DEPUTISED
DENUDATE	DEPECHE	DEPLETORY	DEPRAVED	DEPUTISES
DENUDATED	DEPECHED	DEPLORE	DEPRAVER	DEPUTIZE
DENUDATES	DEPECHES	DEPLORED	DEPRAVERS	DEPUTIZED
DENUDE	DEPECHING	DEPLORER	DEPRAVES	DEPUTIZES
DENUDED	DEPEINCT	DEPLORERS	DEPRAVING	DEPUTY
DENUDER	DEPEINCTS	DEPLORES	DEPRAVITY	DEQUEUE
DENUDERS	DEPEND	DEPLORING	DEPRECATE	DEQUEUED
DENUDES	DEPENDANT	DEPLOY	DEPREDATE	DEQUEUES
DENUDING	DEPENDED	DEPLOYED	DEPREHEND	DEQUEUING
DENY	DEPENDENT	DEPLOYER	DEPRENYL	DERACINE
DENYING	DEPENDING	DEPLOYERS	DEPRENYLS	DERACINES
DENYINGLY	DEPENDS	DEPLOYING	DEPRESS	DERAIGN
DEODAND	DEPEOPLE	DEPLOYS	DEPRESSED	DERAIGNED
DEODANDS	DEPEOPLED	DEPLUME	DEPRESSES	DERAIGNS
DEODAR	DEPEOPLES	DEPLUMED	DEPRESSOR	DERAIL
DEODARA	DEPERM	DEPLUMES	DEPRIME	DERAILED
DEODARAS	DEPERMED	DEPLUMING	DEPRIMED	DERAILER
DEODARS	DEPERMING	DEPOLISH	DEPRIMES	DERAILERS
DEODATE	DEPERMS	DEPONE	DEPRIMING	DERAILING
DEODATES	DEPICT	DEPONED	DEPRIVAL	DERAILS
DEODORANT	DEPICTED	DEPONENT	DEPRIVALS	DERANGE
DEODORISE	DEPICTER	DEPONENTS	DEPRIVE	DERANGED
DEODORIZE	DEPICTERS	DEPONES	DEPRIVED	DERANGER
DEONTIC	DEPICTING	DEPONING	DEPRIVER	DERANGERS
DEONTICS	DEPICTION	DEPORT	DEPRIVERS	DERANGES
DEORBIT	DEPICTIVE	DEPORTED	DEPRIVES	DERANGING
DEORBITED	DEPICTOR	DEPORTEE	DEPRIVING	DERAT
DEORBITS	DEPICTORS	DEPORTEES	DEPROGRAM	DERATE
DEOXIDATE	DEPICTS	DEPORTER	DEPS	DERATED
DEOXIDISE	DEPICTURE	DEPORTERS	DEPSIDE	DERATES
DEOXIDIZE	DEPIGMENT	DEPORTING	DEPSIDES	DERATING
DEOXY	DEPILATE	DEPORTS	DEPTH	DERATINGS
DEP	DEPILATED	DEPOSABLE	DEPTHLESS	DERATION
DEPAINT	DEPILATES	DEPOSAL	DEPTHS	DERATIONS
DEPAINTED	DEPILATOR	DEPOSALS	DEPURANT	DERATS

DERATTED	DERMA	DESALTER	DESERT	DESIRERS
DERATTING	DERMAL	DESALTERS	DESERTED	DESIRES
DERAY	DERMAS	DESALTING	DESERTER	DESIRING
DERAYED	DERMATIC	DESALTS	DESERTERS	DESIROUS
DERAYING	DERMATOID	DESAND	DESERTIC	DESIS
DERAYS	DERMATOME	DESANDED	DESERTIFY	DESIST
DERBIES	DERMESTID	DESANDING	DESERTING	DESISTED
DERBY	DERMIC	DESANDS	DESERTION	DESISTING
DERE	DERMIS	DESCALE	DESERTS	DESISTS
DERECHO	DERMISES	DESCALED	DESERVE	DESK
DERECHOS	DERMOID	DESCALER	DESERVED	DESKBOUND
DERED	DERMOIDS	DESCALERS	DESERVER	DESKFAST
DERELICT	DERMS	DESCALES	DESERVERS	DESKFASTS
DERELICTS	DERN	DESCALING	DESERVES	DESKILL
DEREPRESS	DERNED	DESCANT	DESERVING	DESKILLED
DERES	DERNFUL	DESCANTED	DESEX	DESKILLS
DERHAM	DERNIER	DESCANTER	DESEXED	DESKING
DERHAMS	DERNIES	DESCANTS	DESEXES	DESKINGS
DERIDE	DERNING	DESCEND	DESEXING	DESKMAN
DERIDED	DERNLY	DESCENDED	DESHI	DESKMEN
DERIDER	DERNS	DESCENDER	DESHIS	DESKNOTE
DERIDERS	DERNY	DESCENDS	DESI	DESKNOTES
DERIDES	DERNYS	DESCENT	DESICCANT	DESKS
DERIDING	DERO	DESCENTS	DESICCATE	DESKTOP
DERIG	DEROGATE	DESCHOOL	DESIGN	DESKTOPS
DERIGGED	DEROGATED	DESCHOOLS	DESIGNATE	DESMAN
DERIGGING	DEROGATES	DESCRIBE	DESIGNED	DESMANS
DERIGS	DEROS	DESCRIBED	DESIGNEE	DESMID
DERING	DERRICK	DESCRIBER	DESIGNEES	DESMIDIAN
DERINGER	DERRICKED	DESCRIBES	DESIGNER	DESMIDS
DERINGERS	DERRICKS	DESCRIED	DESIGNERS	DESMINE
DERISIBLE	DERRIERE	DESCRIER	DESIGNFUL	DESMINES
DERISION	DERRIERES	DESCRIERS	DESIGNING	DESMODIUM
DERISIONS	DERRIES	DESCRIES	DESIGNS	DESMOID
DERISIVE	DERRINGER	DESCRIVE	DESILVER	DESMOIDS
DERISORY	DERRIS	DESCRIVED	DESILVERS	DESMOSOME
DERIVABLE	DERRISES	DESCRIVES	DESINE	DESNOOD
DERIVABLY	DERRO	DESCRY	DESINED	DESNOODED
DERIVATE	DERROS	DESCRYING	DESINENCE	DESNOODS
DERIVATED	DERRY	DESECRATE	DESINENT	DESOEUVRE
DERIVATES	DERTH	DESEED	DESINES	DESOLATE
DERIVE	DERTHS	DESEEDED	DESINING	DESOLATED
DERIVED	DERV	DESEEDER	DESIPIENT	DESOLATER
DERIVER	DERVISH	DESEEDERS	DESIRABLE	DESOLATES
DERIVERS	DERVISHES	DESEEDING	DESIRABLY	DESOLATOR
DERIVES	DERVS	DESEEDS	DESIRE	DESORB
DERIVING	DESALT	DESELECT	DESIRED	DESORBED
DERM	DESALTED	DESELECTS	DESIRER	DESORBER

DESORBERS	DESTEMPER	DETAILING	DETERRER	DETRACTS
DESORBING	DESTINATE	DETAILS	DETERRERS	DETRAIN
DESORBS	DESTINE	DETAIN	DETERRING	DETRAINED
DESOXY	DESTINED	DETAINED	DETERS	DETRAINS
DESPAIR	DESTINES	DETAINEE	DETERSION	DETRAQUE
DESPAIRED	DESTINIES	DETAINEES	DETERSIVE	DETRAQUEE
DESPAIRER	DESTINING	DETAINER	DETEST	DETRAQUES
DESPAIRS	DESTINY	DETAINERS	DETESTED	DETRIMENT
DESPATCH	DESTITUTE	DETAINING	DETESTER	DETRITAL
DESPERADO	DESTOCK	DETAINS	DETESTERS	DETRITION
DESPERATE	DESTOCKED	DETANGLE	DETESTING	DETRITUS
DESPIGHT	DESTOCKS	DETANGLED	DETESTS	DETRUDE
DESPIGHTS	DESTREAM	DETANGLER	DETHATCH	DETRUDED
DESPISAL	DESTREAMS	DETANGLES	DETHRONE	DETRUDES
DESPISALS	DESTRESS	DETASSEL	DETHRONED	DETRUDING
DESPISE	DESTRIER	DETASSELS	DETHRONER	DETRUSION
DESPISED	DESTRIERS	DETECT	DETHRONES	DETRUSOR
DESPISER	DESTROY	DETECTED	DETICK	DETRUSORS
DESPISERS	DESTROYED	DETECTER	DETICKED	DETUNE
DESPISES	DESTROYER	DETECTERS	DETICKER	DETUNED
DESPISING	DESTROYS	DETECTING	DETICKERS	DETUNES
DESPITE	DESTRUCT	DETECTION	DETICKING	DETUNING
DESPITED	DESTRUCTO	DETECTIVE	DETICKS	DEUCE
DESPITES	DESTRUCTS	DETECTOR	DETINUE	DEUCED
DESPITING	DESUETUDE	DETECTORS	DETINUES	DEUCEDLY
DESPOIL	DESUGAR	DETECTS	DETONABLE	DEUCES
DESPOILED	DESUGARED	DETENT	DETONATE	DEUCING
DESPOILER	DESUGARS	DETENTE	DETONATED	DEUDDARN
DESPOILS	DESULFUR	DETENTES	DETONATES	DEUDDARNS
DESPOND	DESULFURS	DETENTION	DETONATOR	DEUS
DESPONDED	DESULPHUR	DETENTIST	DETORSION	DEUTERATE
DESPONDS	DESULTORY	DETENTS	DETORT	DEUTERIC
DESPOT	DESYATIN	DETENU	DETORTED	DEUTERIDE
DESPOTAT	DESYATINS	DETENUE	DETORTING	DEUTERIUM
DESPOTATE	DESYNE	DETENUES	DETORTION	DEUTERON
DESPOTATS	DESYNED	DETENUS	DETORTS	DEUTERONS
DESPOTIC	DESYNES	DETER	DETOUR	DEUTON
DESPOTISM	DESYNING	DETERGE	DETOURED	DEUTONS
DESPOTS	DETACH	DETERGED	DETOURING	DEUTZIA
DESPUMATE	DETACHED	DETERGENT	DETOURS	DEUTZIAS
DESSE	DETACHER	DETERGER	DETOX	DEV
DESSERT	DETACHERS	DETERGERS	DETOXED	DEVA
DESSERTS	DETACHES	DETERGES	DETOXES	DEVALL
DESSES	DETACHING	DETERGING	DETOXIFY	DEVALLED
DESSYATIN	DETAIL	DETERMENT	DETOXING	DEVALLING
DESTAIN	DETAILED	DETERMINE	DETRACT	DEVALLS
DESTAINED	DETAILER	DETERRED	DETRACTED	DEVALUATE
DESTAINS	DETAILERS	DETERRENT	DETRACTOR	DEVALUE

DEVALUED	DEVILDOMS	DEVOIRS	DEWATERER	DEXTER
DEVALUES	DEVILED	DEVOLVE	DEWATERS	DEXTERITY
DEVALUING	DEVILESS	DEVOLVED	DEWAX	DEXTEROUS
DEVAS	DEVILET	DEVOLVES	DEWAXED	DEXTERS
DEVASTATE	DEVILETS	DEVOLVING	DEWAXES	DEXTRAL
DEVEIN	DEVILFISH	DEVON	DEWAXING	DEXTRALLY
DEVEINED	DEVILING	DEVONIAN	DEWBERRY	DEXTRALS
DEVEINING	DEVILINGS	DEVONPORT	DEWCLAW	DEXTRAN
DEVEINS	DEVILISH	DEVONS	DEWCLAWED	DEXTRANS
DEVEL	DEVILISM	DEVORE	DEWCLAWS	DEXTRIN
DEVELED	DEVILISMS	DEVORES	DEWDROP	DEXTRINE
DEVELING	DEVILKIN	DEVOS	DEWDROPS	DEXTRINES
DEVELLED	DEVILKINS	DEVOT	DEWED	DEXTRINS
DEVELLING	DEVILLED	DEVOTE	DEWFALL	DEXTRO
DEVELOP	DEVILLING	DEVOTED	DEWFALLS	DEXTRORSE
DEVELOPE	DEVILMENT	DEVOTEDLY	DEWFULL	DEXTROSE
DEVELOPED	DEVILRIES	DEVOTEE	DEWIER	DEXTROSES
DEVELOPER	DEVILRY	DEVOTEES	DEWIEST	DEXTROUS
DEVELOPES	DEVILS	DEVOTES	DEWILY	DEXY
DEVELOPPE	DEVILSHIP	DEVOTING	DEWINESS	DEY
DEVELOPS	DEVILTRY	DEVOTION	DEWING	DEYS
DEVELS	DEVILWOOD	DEVOTIONS	DEWITT	DEZINC
DEVERBAL	DEVIOUS	DEVOTS	DEWITTED	DEZINCED
DEVERBALS	DEVIOUSLY	DEVOUR	DEWITTING	DEZINCING
DEVEST	DEVIS	DEVOURED	DEWITTS	DEZINCKED
DEVESTED	DEVISABLE	DEVOURER	DEWLAP	DEZINCS
DEVESTING	DEVISAL	DEVOURERS	DEWLAPPED	DHABA
DEVESTS	DEVISALS	DEVOURING	DEWLAPS	DHABAS
DEVI	DEVISE	DEVOURS	DEWLAPT	DHAK
DEVIANCE	DEVISED	DEVOUT	DEWLESS	DHAKS
DEVIANCES	DEVISEE	DEVOUTER	DEWOOL	DHAL
DEVIANCY	DEVISEES	DEVOUTEST	DEWOOLED	DHALS
DEVIANT	DEVISER	DEVOUTLY	DEWOOLING	DHAMMA
DEVIANTS	DEVISERS	DEVS	DEWOOLS	DHAMMAS
DEVIATE	DEVISES	DEVVEL	DEWORM	DHANSAK
DEVIATED	DEVISING	DEVVELLED	DEWORMED	DHANSAKS
DEVIATES	DEVISOR	DEVVELS	DEWORMER	DHARMA
DEVIATING	DEVISORS	DEW	DEWORMERS	DHARMAS
DEVIATION	DEVITRIFY	DEWAN	DEWORMING	DHARMIC
DEVIATIVE	DEVLING	DEWANI	DEWORMS	DHARMSALA
DEVIATOR	DEVLINGS	DEWANIS	DEWPOINT	DHARNA
DEVIATORS	DEVO	DEWANNIES	DEWPOINTS	DHARNAS
DEVIATORY	DEVOICE	DEWANNY	DEWS	DHIKR
DEVICE	DEVOICED	DEWANS	DEWY	DHIKRS
DEVICEFUL	DEVOICES	DEWAR	DEX	DHIMMI
DEVICES	DEVOICING	DEWARS	DEXES	DHIMMIS
DEVIL	DEVOID	DEWATER	DEXIE	DHOBI
DEVILDOM	DEVOIR	DEWATERED	DEXIES	DHOBIS

DHOL	DIABOLO	DIAL	DIALYSIS	DIAPHONE
DHOLAK	DIABOLOGY	DIALECT	DIALYTIC	DIAPHONES
DHOLAKS	DIABOLOS	DIALECTAL	DIALYZATE	DIAPHONIC
DHOLE	DIACETYL	DIALECTIC	DIALYZE	DIAPHONY
DHOLES	DIACETYLS	DIALECTS	DIALYZED	DIAPHRAGM
DHOLL	DIACHRONY	DIALED	DIALYZER	DIAPHYSES
DHOLLS	DIACHYLON	DIALER	DIALYZERS	DIAPHYSIS
DHOLS	DIACHYLUM	DIALERS	DIALYZES	DIAPIR
DHOOLIES	DIACID	DIALING	DIALYZING	DIAPIRIC
DHOOLY	DIACIDIC	DIALINGS	DIAMAGNET	DIAPIRISM
DHOORA	DIACIDS	DIALIST	DIAMANTE	DIAPIRS
DHOORAS	DIACODION	DIALISTS	DIAMANTES	DIAPSID
DHOOTI	DIACODIUM	DIALLAGE	DIAMETER	DIAPSIDS
DHOOTIE	DIACONAL	DIALLAGES	DIAMETERS	DIAPYESES
DHOOTIES	DIACONATE	DIALLAGIC	DIAMETRAL	DIAPYESIS
DHOOTIS	DIACRITIC	DIALLED	DIAMETRIC	DIAPYETIC
DHOTI	DIACT	DIALLEL	DIAMIDE	DIARCH
DHOTIS	DIACTINAL	DIALLELS	DIAMIDES	DIARCHAL
DHOURRA	DIACTINE	DIALLER	DIAMIN	DIARCHIC
DHOURRAS	DIACTINES	DIALLERS	DIAMINE	DIARCHIES
DHOW	DIACTINIC	DIALLING	DIAMINES	DIARCHY
DHOWS	DIACTS	DIALLINGS	DIAMINS	DIARIAL
DHURNA	DIADEM	DIALLIST	DIAMOND	DIARIAN
DHURNAS	DIADEMED	DIALLISTS	DIAMONDED	DIARIES
DHURRA	DIADEMING	DIALOG	DIAMONDS	DIARISE
DHURRAS	DIADEMS	DIALOGED	DIAMYL	DIARISED
DHURRIE	DIADOCHI	DIALOGER	DIANDRIES	DIARISES
DHURRIES	DIADOCHY	DIALOGERS	DIANDROUS	DIARISING
DHUTI	DIADROM	DIALOGIC	DIANDRY	DIARIST
DHUTIS	DIADROMS	DIALOGING	DIANE	DIARISTIC
DHYANA	DIAERESES	DIALOGISE	DIANODAL	DIARISTS
DHYANAS	DIAERESIS	DIALOGISM	DIANOETIC	DIARIZE
DI	DIAERETIC	DIALOGIST	DIANOIA	DIARIZED
DIABASE	DIAGLYPH	DIALOGITE	DIANOIAS	DIARIZES
DIABASES	DIAGLYPHS	DIALOGIZE	DIANTHUS	DIARIZING
DIABASIC	DIAGNOSE	DIALOGS	DIAPASE	DIARRHEA
DIABETES	DIAGNOSED	DIALOGUE	DIAPASES	DIARRHEAL
DIABETIC	DIAGNOSES	DIALOGUED	DIAPASON	DIARRHEAS
DIABETICS	DIAGNOSIS	DIALOGUER	DIAPASONS	DIARRHEIC
DIABLE	DIAGONAL	DIALOGUES	DIAPAUSE	DIARRHOEA
DIABLERIE	DIAGONALS	DIALS	DIAPAUSED	DIARY
DIABLERY	DIAGRAM	DIALYSATE	DIAPAUSES	DIASCIA
DIABLES	DIAGRAMED	DIALYSE	DIAPENTE	DIASCIAS
DIABOLIC	DIAGRAMS	DIALYSED	DIAPENTES	DIASCOPE
DIABOLISE	DIAGRAPH	DIALYSER	DIAPER	DIASCOPES
DIABOLISM	DIAGRAPHS	DIALYSERS	DIAPERED	DIASPORA
DIABOLIST	DIAGRID	DIALYSES	DIAPERING	DIASPORAS
DIABOLIZE	DIAGRIDS	DIALYSING	DIAPERS	DIASPORE

DIASPORES	DIAZINONS	DICES	DICKTIEST	DIDACTS
DIASPORIC	DIAZINS	DICEY	DICKTY	DIDACTYL
DIASTASE	DIAZO	DICH	DICKY	DIDACTYLS
DIASTASES	DIAZOES	DICHASIA	DICKYBIRD	DIDAKAI
DIASTASIC	DIAZOLE	DICHASIAL	DICLINIES	DIDAKAIS
DIASTASIS	DIAZOLES	DICHASIUM	DICLINISM	DIDAKEI
DIASTATIC	DIAZONIUM	DICHOGAMY	DICLINOUS	DIDAKEIS
DIASTEM	DIAZOS	DICHONDRA	DICLINY	DIDAPPER
DIASTEMA	DIAZOTISE	DICHOPTIC	DICOT	DIDAPPERS
DIASTEMAS	DIAZOTIZE	DICHORD	DICOTS	DIDDER
DIASTEMS	DIB	DICHORDS	DICOTYL	DIDDERED
DIASTER	DIBASIC	DICHOTIC	DICOTYLS	DIDDERING
DIASTERS	DIBBED	DICHOTOMY	DICROTAL	DIDDERS
DIASTOLE	DIBBER	DICHROIC	DICROTIC	DIDDICOY
DIASTOLES	DIBBERS	DICHROISM	DICROTISM	DIDDICOYS
DIASTOLIC	DIBBING	DICHROITE	DICROTOUS	DIDDIER
DIASTRAL	DIBBLE	DICHROMAT	DICT	DIDDIES
DIASTYLE	DIBBLED	DICHROMIC	DICTA	DIDDIEST
DIASTYLES	DIBBLER	DICHT	DICTATE	DIDDLE
DIATHERMY	DIBBLERS	DICHTED	DICTATED	DIDDLED
DIATHESES	DIBBLES	DICHTING	DICTATES	DIDDLER
DIATHESIS	DIBBLING	DICHTS	DICTATING	DIDDLERS
DIATHETIC	DIBBS	DICIER	DICTATION	DIDDLES
DIATOM	DIBBUK	DICIEST	DICTATOR	DIDDLEY
DIATOMIC	DIBBUKIM	DICING	DICTATORS	DIDDLEYS
DIATOMIST	DIBBUKKIM	DICINGS	DICTATORY	DIDDLIES
DIATOMITE	DIBBUKS	DICK	DICTATRIX	DIDDLING
DIATOMS	DIBROMIDE	DICKED	DICTATURE	DIDDLY
DIATONIC	DIBS	DICKENS	DICTED	DIDDUMS
DIATREME	DIBUTYL	DICKENSES	DICTIER	DIDDY
DIATREMES	DICACIOUS	DICKER	DICTIEST	DIDELPHIC
DIATRETA	DICACITY	DICKERED	DICTING	DIDELPHID
DIATRETUM	DICACODYL	DICKERER	DICTION	DIDICOI
DIATRIBE	DICALCIUM	DICKERERS	DICTIONAL	DIDICOIS
DIATRIBES	DICAMBA	DICKERING	DICTIONS	DIDICOY
DIATRON	DICAMBAS	DICKERS	DICTS	DIDICOYS
DIATRONS	DICAST	DICKEY	DICTUM	DIDIE
DIATROPIC	DICASTERY	DICKEYS	DICTUMS	DIDIES
DIAXON	DICASTIC	DICKHEAD	DICTY	DIDJERIDU
DIAXONS	DICASTS	DICKHEADS	DICTYOGEN	DIDO
DIAZEPAM	DICE	DICKIE	DICUMAROL	DIDOES
DIAZEPAMS	DICED	DICKIER	DICYCLIC	DIDOS
DIAZEUXES	DICELIKE	DICKIES	DICYCLIES	DIDRACHM
DIAZEUXIS	DICENTRA	DICKIEST	DICYCLY	DIDRACHMA
DIAZIN	DICENTRAS	DICKING	DID	DIDRACHMS
DIAZINE	DICENTRIC	DICKINGS	DIDACT	DIDST
DIAZINES	DICER	DICKS	DIDACTIC	DIDY
DIAZINON	DICERS	DICKTIER	DIDACTICS	DIDYMIUM

DIDYMIUMS	DIESTERS	DIFFUSER	DIGIPACKS	DIGYNIAN
DIDYMO	DIESTOCK	DIFFUSERS	DIGIT	DIGYNOUS
DIDYMOS	DIESTOCKS	DIFFUSES	DIGITAL	DIHEDRA
DIDYMOUS	DIESTROUS	DIFFUSING	DIGITALIN	DIHEDRAL
DIDYNAMY	DIESTRUM	DIFFUSION	DIGITALIS	DIHEDRALS
DIE	DIESTRUMS	DIFFUSIVE	DIGITALLY	DIHEDRON
DIEB	DIESTRUS	DIFFUSOR	DIGITALS	DIHEDRONS
DIEBACK	DIET	DIFFUSORS	DIGITATE	DIHYBRID
DIEBACKS	DIETARIAN	DIFS	DIGITATED	DIHYBRIDS
DIEBS	DIETARIES	DIG	DIGITISE	DIHYDRIC
DIECIOUS	DIETARILY	DIGAMIES	DIGITISED	DIKA
DIED	DIETARY	DIGAMIST	DIGITISER	DIKAS
DIEDRAL	DIETED	DIGAMISTS	DIGITISES	DIKAST
DIEDRALS	DIETER	DIGAMMA	DIGITIZE	DIKASTS
DIEDRE	DIETERS	DIGAMMAS	DIGITIZED	DIKDIK
DIEDRES	DIETETIC	DIGAMOUS	DIGITIZER	DIKDIKS
DIEGESES	DIETETICS	DIGAMY	DIGITIZES	DIKE
DIEGESIS	DIETHER	DIGASTRIC	DIGITONIN	DIKED
DIEGETIC	DIETHERS	DIGENESES	DIGITOXIN	DIKER
DIEHARD	DIETHYL	DIGENESIS	DIGITRON	DIKERS
DIEHARDS	DIETHYLS	DIGENETIC	DIGITRONS	DIKES
DIEING	DIETICIAN	DIGERATI	DIGITS	DIKETONE
DIEL	DIETINE	DIGEST	DIGITULE	DIKETONES
DIELDRIN	DIETINES	DIGESTANT	DIGITULES	DIKEY
DIELDRINS	DIETING	DIGESTED	DIGLOSSIA	DIKIER
DIELS	DIETINGS	DIGESTER	DIGLOSSIC	DIKIEST
DIELYTRA	DIETIST	DIGESTERS	DIGLOT	DIKING
DIELYTRAS	DIETISTS	DIGESTIF	DIGLOTS	DIKKOP
DIEMAKER	DIETITIAN	DIGESTIFS	DIGLOTTIC	DIKKOPS
DIEMAKERS	DIETS	DIGESTING	DIGLYPH	DIKTAT
DIENE	DIF	DIGESTION	DIGLYPHS	DIKTATS
DIENES	DIFF	DIGESTIVE	DIGNIFIED	DILATABLE
DIEOFF	DIFFER	DIGESTOR	DIGNIFIES	DILATABLY
DIEOFFS	DIFFERED	DIGESTORS	DIGNIFY	DILATANCY
DIERESES	DIFFERENT	DIGESTS	DIGNITARY	DILATANT
DIERESIS	DIFFERING	DIGGABLE	DIGNITIES	DILATANTS
DIERETIC	DIFFERS	DIGGED	DIGNITY	DILATATE
DIES	DIFFICILE	DIGGER	DIGONAL	DILATATOR
DIESEL	DIFFICULT	DIGGERS	DIGOXIN	DILATE
DIESELED	DIFFIDENT	DIGGING	DIGOXINS	DILATED
DIESELING	DIFFLUENT	DIGGINGS	DIGRAPH	DILATER
DIESELISE	DIFFORM	DIGHT	DIGRAPHIC	DILATERS
DIESELIZE	DIFFRACT	DIGHTED	DIGRAPHS	DILATES
DIESELS	DIFFRACTS	DIGHTING	DIGRESS	DILATING
DIESES	DIFFS	DIGHTS	DIGRESSED	DILATION
DIESINKER	DIFFUSE	DIGICAM	DIGRESSER	DILATIONS
DIESIS	DIFFUSED	DIGICAMS	DIGRESSES	DILATIVE
DIESTER	DIFFUSELY	DIGIPACK	DIGS	DILATOR

DILATORS	DILUVIUM	DIMOUTS	DINGEY	DINNA
DILATORY	DILUVIUMS	DIMP	DINGEYS	DINNAE
DILDO	DIM	DIMPLE	DINGHIES	DINNED
DILDOE	DIMBLE	DIMPLED	DINGHY	DINNER
DILDOES	DIMBLES	DIMPLES	DINGIED	DINNERED
DILDOS	DIMBO	DIMPLIER	DINGIER	DINNERING
DILEMMA	DIMBOES	DIMPLIEST	DINGIES	DINNERS
DILEMMAS	DIMBOS	DIMPLING	DINGIEST	DINNING
DILEMMIC	DIME	DIMPLY	DINGILY	DINNLE
DILIGENCE	DIMENSION	DIMPS	DINGINESS	DINNLED
DILIGENT	DIMER	DIMPSIES	DINGING	DINNLES
DILL	DIMERIC	DIMPSY	DINGLE	DINNLING
DILLED	DIMERISE	DIMS	DINGLES	DINO
DILLI	DIMERISED	DIMWIT	DINGO	DINOCERAS
DILLIER	DIMERISES	DIMWITS	DINGOED	DINOMANIA
DILLIES	DIMERISM	DIMWITTED	DINGOES	DINOS
DILLIEST	DIMERISMS	DIMYARIAN	DINGOING	DINOSAUR
DILLING	DIMERIZE	DIMYARY	DINGOS	DINOSAURS
DILLINGS	DIMERIZED	DIN	DINGS	DINOTHERE
DILLIS	DIMERIZES	DINAR	DINGUS	DINS
DILLS	DIMEROUS	DINARCHY	DINGUSES	DINT
DILLWEED	DIMERS	DINARS	DINGY	DINTED
DILLWEEDS	DIMES	DINDLE	DINGYING	DINTING
DILLY	DIMETER	DINDLED	DINIC	DINTLESS
DILSCOOP	DIMETERS	DINDLES	DINICS	DINTS
DILSCOOPS	DIMETHYL	DINDLING	DINING	DIOBOL
DILTIAZEM	DIMETHYLS	DINE	DININGS	DIOBOLON
DILUENT	DIMETRIC	DINED	DINITRO	DIOBOLONS
DILUENTS	DIMIDIATE	DINER	DINK	DIOBOLS
DILUTABLE	DIMINISH	DINERIC	DINKED	DIOCESAN
DILUTE	DIMISSORY	DINERO	DINKER	DIOCESANS
DILUTED	DIMITIES	DINEROS	DINKEST	DIOCESE
DILUTEE	DIMITY	DINERS	DINKEY	DIOCESES
DILUTEES	DIMLY	DINES	DINKEYS	DIODE
DILUTER	DIMMABLE	DINETTE	DINKIE	DIODES
DILUTERS	DIMMED	DINETTES	DINKIER	DIOECIES
DILUTES	DIMMER	DINFUL	DINKIES	DIOECIOUS
DILUTING	DIMMERS	DING	DINKIEST	DIOECISM
DILUTION	DIMMEST	DINGBAT	DINKING	DIOECISMS
DILUTIONS	DIMMING	DINGBATS	DINKLIER	DIOECY
DILUTIVE	DIMMINGS	DINGDONG	DINKLIEST	DIOESTRUS
DILUTOR	DIMMISH	DINGDONGS	DINKLY	DIOICOUS
DILUTORS	DIMNESS	DINGE	DINKS	DIOL
DILUVIA	DIMNESSES	DINGED	DINKUM	DIOLEFIN
DILUVIAL	DIMORPH	DINGER	DINKUMS	DIOLEFINS
DILUVIAN	DIMORPHIC	DINGERS	DINKY	DIOLS
DILUVION	DIMORPHS	DINGES	DINMONT	DIONYSIAC
DILUVIONS	DIMOUT	DINGESES	DINMONTS	DIONYSIAN

D

DIOPSIDE	DIPLEGIAS	DIPOLAR	DIRDAMS	DIRKS
DIOPSIDES	DIPLEGIC	DIPOLE	DIRDUM	DIRL
DIOPSIDIC	DIPLEX	DIPOLES	DIRDUMS	DIRLED
DIOPTASE	DIPLEXER	DIPPABLE	DIRE	DIRLING
DIOPTASES	DIPLEXERS	DIPPED	DIRECT	DIRLS
DIOPTER	DIPLOE	DIPPER	DIRECTED	DIRNDL
DIOPTERS	DIPLOES	DIPPERFUL	DIRECTER	DIRNDLS
DIOPTRAL	DIPLOGEN	DIPPERS	DIRECTEST	DIRT
DIOPTRATE	DIPLOGENS	DIPPIER	DIRECTING	DIRTBAG
DIOPTRE	DIPLOIC	DIPPIEST	DIRECTION	DIRTBAGS
DIOPTRES	DIPLOID	DIPPINESS	DIRECTIVE	DIRTBALL
DIOPTRIC	DIPLOIDIC	DIPPING	DIRECTLY	DIRTBALLS
DIOPTRICS	DIPLOIDS	DIPPINGS	DIRECTOR	DIRTED
DIORAMA	DIPLOIDY	DIPPY	DIRECTORS	DIRTIED
DIORAMAS	DIPLOMA	DIPROTIC	DIRECTORY	DIRTIER
DIORAMIC	DIPLOMACY	DIPS	DIRECTRIX	DIRTIES
DIORISM	DIPLOMAED	DIPSADES	DIRECTS	DIRTIEST
DIORISMS	DIPLOMAS	DIPSAS	DIREFUL	DIRTILY
DIORISTIC	DIPLOMAT	DIPSHIT	DIREFULLY	DIRTINESS
DIORITE	DIPLOMATA	DIPSHITS	DIRELY	DIRTING
DIORITES	DIPLOMATE	DIPSO	DIREMPT	DIRTS
DIORITIC	DIPLOMATS	DIPSOS	DIREMPTED	DIRTY
DIOSGENIN	DIPLON	DIPSTICK	DIREMPTS	DIRTYING
DIOTA	DIPLONEMA	DIPSTICKS	DIRENESS	DIS
DIOTAS	DIPLONS	DIPSWITCH	DIRER	DISA
DIOXAN	DIPLONT	DIPT	DIREST	DISABLE
DIOXANE	DIPLONTIC	DIPTERA	DIRGE	DISABLED
DIOXANES	DIPLONTS	DIPTERAL	DIRGEFUL	DISABLER
DIOXANS	DIPLOPIA	DIPTERAN	DIRGELIKE	DISABLERS
DIOXID	DIPLOPIAS	DIPTERANS	DIRGES	DISABLES
DIOXIDE	DIPLOPIC	DIPTERAS	DIRHAM	DISABLING
DIOXIDES	DIPLOPOD	DIPTERIST	DIRHAMS	DISABLISM
DIOXIDS	DIPLOPODS	DIPTEROI	DIRHEM	DISABLIST
DIOXIN	DIPLOSES	DIPTERON	DIRHEMS	DISABUSAL
DIOXINS	DIPLOSIS	DIPTERONS	DIRIGE	DISABUSE
DIP	DIPLOTENE	DIPTEROS	DIRIGENT	DISABUSED
DIPCHICK	DIPLOZOA	DIPTEROUS	DIRIGES	DISABUSES
DIPCHICKS	DIPLOZOIC	DIPTYCA	DIRIGIBLE	DISACCORD
DIPEPTIDE	DIPLOZOON	DIPTYCAS	DIRIGISM	DISADORN
DIPHASE	DIPNET	DIPTYCH	DIRIGISME	DISADORNS
DIPHASIC	DIPNETS	DIPTYCHS	DIRIGISMS	DISAFFECT
DIPHENYL	DIPNETTED	DIQUARK	DIRIGISTE	DISAFFIRM
DIPHENYLS	DIPNOAN	DIQUARKS	DIRIMENT	DISAGREE
DIPHONE	DIPNOANS	DIQUAT	DIRK	DISAGREED
DIPHONES	DIPNOOUS	DIQUATS	DIRKE	DISAGREES
DIPHTHONG	DIPODIC	DIRAM	DIRKED	DISALLIED
DIPHYSITE	DIPODIES	DIRAMS	DIRKES	DISALLIES
DIPLEGIA	DIPODY	DIRDAM	DIRKING	DISALLOW

DISALLOWS	DISBUDS	DISCING	DISCROWN	DISFAVOUR
DISALLY	DISBURDEN	DISCIPLE	DISCROWNS	DISFIGURE
DISANCHOR	DISBURSAL	DISCIPLED	DISCS	DISFLESH
DISANNEX	DISBURSE	DISCIPLES	DISCUMBER	DISFLUENT
DISANNUL	DISBURSED	DISCLAIM	DISCURE	DISFOREST
DISANNULS	DISBURSER	DISCLAIMS	DISCURED	DISFORM
DISANOINT	DISBURSES	DISCLESS	DISCURES	DISFORMED
DISAPPEAR	DISC	DISCLIKE	DISCURING	DISFORMS
DISAPPLY	DISCAGE	DISCLIMAX	DISCURSUS	DISFROCK
DISARM	DISCAGED	DISCLOSE	DISCUS	DISFROCKS
DISARMED	DISCAGES	DISCLOSED	DISCUSES	DISGAVEL
DISARMER	DISCAGING	DISCLOSER	DISCUSS	DISGAVELS
DISARMERS	DISCAL	DISCLOSES	DISCUSSED	DISGEST
DISARMING	DISCALCED	DISCLOST	DISCUSSER	DISGESTED
DISARMS	DISCANDIE	DISCO	DISCUSSES	DISGESTS
DISARRAY	DISCANDY	DISCOBOLI	DISDAIN	DISGODDED
DISARRAYS	DISCANT	DISCOED	DISDAINED	DISGORGE
DISAS	DISCANTED	DISCOER	DISDAINS	DISGORGED
DISASTER	DISCANTER	DISCOERS	DISEASE	DISGORGER
DISASTERS	DISCANTS	DISCUES	DISEASED	DISGORGES
DISATTIRE	DISCARD	DISCOID	DISEASES	DISGOWN
DISATTUNE	DISCARDED	DISCOIDAL	DISEASING	DISGOWNED
DISAVOUCH	DISCARDER	DISCOIDS	DISEDGE	DISGOWNS
DISAVOW	DISCARDS	DISCOING	DISEDGED	DISGRACE
DISAVOWAL	DISCASE	DISCOLOGY	DISEDGES	DISGRACED
DISAVOWED	DISCASED	DISCOLOR	DISEDGING	DISGRACER
DISAVOWER	DISCASES	DISCOLORS	DISEMBARK	DISGRACES
DISAVOWS	DISCASING	DISCOLOUR	DISEMBODY	DISGRADE
DISBAND	DISCED	DISCOMFIT	DISEMPLOY	DISGRADED
DISBANDED	DISCEPT	DISCOMMON	DISENABLE	DISGRADES
DISBANDS	DISCEPTED	DISCORD	DISENDOW	DISGUISE
DISBAR	DISCEPTS	DISCORDED	DISENDOWS	DISGUISED
DISBARK	DISCERN	DISCORDS	DISENGAGE	DISGUISER
DISBARKED	DISCERNED	DISCOS	DISENROL	DISGUISES
DISBARKS	DISCERNER	DISCOUNT	DISENROLS	DISGUST
DISBARRED	DISCERNS	DISCOUNTS	DISENTAIL	DISGUSTED
DISBARS	DISCERP	DISCOURE	DISENTOMB	DISGUSTS
DISBELIEF	DISCERPED	DISCOURED	DISESTEEM	DISH
DISBENCH	DISCERPS	DISCOURES	DISEUR	DISHABIT
DISBODIED	DISCHARGE	DISCOURSE	DISEURS	DISHABITS
DISBOSOM	DISCHURCH	DISCOVER	DISEUSE	DISHABLE
DISBOSOMS	DISCI	DISCOVERS	DISEUSES	DISHABLED
DISBOUND	DISCIDE	DISCOVERT	DISFAME	DISHABLES
DISBOWEL	DISCIDED	DISCOVERY	DISFAMED	DISHALLOW
DISBOWELS	DISCIDES	DISCREDIT	DISFAMES	DISHCLOTH
DISBRANCH	DISCIDING	DISCREET	DISFAMING	DISHCLOUT
DISBUD	DISCIFORM	DISCRETE	DISFAVOR	DISHDASH
DISBUDDED	DISCINCT	DISCRETER	DISFAVORS	DISHDASHA

DISHED	DISIMMURE	DISLIKENS	DISMAYLED	DISPARTS
DISHELM	DISINFECT	DISLIKER	DISMAYLS	DISPATCH
DISHELMED	DISINFEST	DISLIKERS	DISMAYS	DISPATHY
DISHELMS	DISINFORM	DISLIKES	DISME	DISPAUPER
DISHERIT	DISINHUME	DISLIKING	DISMEMBER	DISPEACE
DISHERITS	DISINTER	DISLIMB	DISMES	DISPEACES
DISHES	DISINTERS	DISLIMBED	DISMISS	DISPEL
DISHEVEL	DISINURE	DISLIMBS	DISMISSAL	DISPELLED
DISHEVELS	DISINURED	DISLIMN	DISMISSED	DISPELLER
DISHFUL	DISINURES	DISLIMNED	DISMISSES	DISPELS
DISHFULS	DISINVENT	DISLIMNS	DISMODED	DISPENCE
DISHIER	DISINVEST	DISLINK	DISMOUNT	DISPENCED
DISHIEST	DISINVITE	DISLINKED	DISMOUNTS	DISPENCES
DISHING	DISJASKIT	DISLINKS	DISNATURE	DISPEND
DISHINGS	DISJECT	DISLOAD	DISNEST	DISPENDED
DISHLIKE	DISJECTED	DISLOADED	DISNESTED	DISPENDS
DISHMOP	DISJECTS	DISLOADS	DISNESTS	DISPENSE
DISHMOPS	DISJOIN	DISLOCATE	DISOBEY	DISPENSED
DISHOARD	DISJOINED	DISLODGE	DISOBEYED	DISPENSER
DISHOARDS	DISJOINS	DISLODGED	DISOBEYER	DISPENSES
DISHOME	DISJOINT	DISLODGES	DISOBEYS	DISPEOPLE
DISHOMED	DISJOINTS	DISLOIGN	DISOBLIGE	DISPERSAL
DISHOMES	DISJUNCT	DISLOIGNS	DISODIUM	DISPERSE
DISHOMING	DISJUNCTS	DISLOYAL	DISOMIC	DISPERSED
DISHONEST	DISJUNE	DISLUSTRE	DISOMIES	DISPERSER
DISHONOR	DISJUNED	DISMAL	DISOMY	DISPERSES
DISHONORS	DISJUNES	DISMALER	DISORBED	DISPIRIT
DISHONOUR	DISJUNING	DISMALEST	DISORDER	DISPIRITS
DISHORN	DISK	DISMALITY	DISORDERS	DISPLACE
DISHORNED	DISKED	DISMALLER	DISORIENT	DISPLACED
DISHORNS	DISKER	DISMALLY	DISOWN	DISPLACER
DISHORSE	DISKERS	DISMALS	DISOWNED	DISPLACES
DISHORSED	DISKETTE	DISMAN	DISOWNER	DISPLANT
DISHORSES	DISKETTES	DISMANNED	DISOWNERS	DISPLANTS
DISHOUSE	DISKING	DISMANS	DISOWNING	DISPLAY
DISHOUSED	DISKLESS	DISMANTLE	DISOWNS	DISPLAYED
DISHOUSES	DISKLIKE	DISMASK	DISPACE	DISPLAYER
DISHPAN	DISKS	DISMASKED	DISPACED	DISPLAYS
DISHPANS	DISLEAF	DISMASKS	DISPACES	DISPLE
DISHRAG	DISLEAFED	DISMAST	DISPACING	DISPLEASE
DISHRAGS	DISLEAFS	DISMASTED	DISPARAGE	DISPLED
DISHTOWEL	DISLEAL	DISMASTS	DISPARATE	DISPLES
DISHUMOUR	DISLEAVE	DISMAY	DISPARITY	DISPLING
DISHWARE	DISLEAVED	DISMAYD	DISPARK	DISPLODE
DISHWARES	DISLEAVES	DISMAYED	DISPARKED	DISPLODED
DISHWATER	DISLIKE	DISMAYFUL	DISPARKS	DISPLODES
DISHY	DISLIKED	DISMAYING	DISPART	DISPLUME
DISILLUDE	DISLIKEN	DISMAYL	DISPARTED	DISPLUMED

DISPLUMES	DISPUNGE	DISSEAT	DISSOLVES	DISTORTER
DISPONDEE	DISPUNGED	DISSEATED	DISSONANT	DISTORTS
DISPONE	DISPUNGES	DISSEATS	DISSUADE	DISTRACT
DISPONED	DISPURSE	DISSECT	DISSUADED	DISTRACTS
DISPONEE	DISPURSED	DISSECTED	DISSUADER	DISTRAIL
DISPONEES	DISPURSES	DISSECTOR	DISSUADES	DISTRAILS
DISPONER	DISPURVEY	DISSECTS	DISSUNDER	DISTRAIN
DISPONERS	DISPUTANT	DISSED	DISTAFF	DISTRAINS
DISPONES	DISPUTE	DISSEISE	DISTAFFS	DISTRAINT
DISPONGE	DISPUTED	DISSEISED	DISTAIN	DISTRAIT
DISPONGED	DISPUTER	DISSEISEE	DISTAINED	DISTRAITE
DISPONGES	DISPUTERS	DISSEISES	DISTAINS	DISTRESS
DISPONING	DISPUTES	DISSEISIN	DISTAL	DISTRICT
DISPORT	DISPUTING	DISSEISOR	DISTALLY	DISTRICTS
DISPORTED	DISQUIET	DISSEIZE	DISTANCE	DISTRIX
DISPORTS	DISQUIETS	DISSEIZED	DISTANCED	DISTRIXES
DISPOSAL	DISRANK	DISSEIZEE	DISTANCES	DISTRUST
DISPOSALS	DISRANKED	DISSEIZES	DISTANT	DISTRUSTS
DISPOSE	DISRANKS	DISSEIZIN	DISTANTLY	DISTUNE
DISPOSED	DISRATE	DISSEIZOR	DISTASTE	DISTUNED
DISPOSER	DISRATED	DISSEMBLE	DISTASTED	DISTUNES
DISPOSERS	DISRATES	DISSEMBLY	DISTASTES	DISTUNING
DISPOSES	DISRATING	DISSENSUS	DISTAVES	DISTURB
DISPOSING	DISREGARD	DISSENT	DISTEMPER	DISTURBED
DISPOST	DISRELISH	DISSENTED	DISTEND	DISTURBER
DISPOSTED	DISREPAIR	DISSENTER	DISTENDED	DISTURBS
DISPOSTS	DISREPUTE	DISSENTS	DISTENDER	DISTYLE
DISPOSURE	DISROBE	DISSERT	DISTENDS	DISTYLES
DISPRAD	DISROBED	DISSERTED	DISTENT	DISULFATE
DISPRAISE	DISROBER	DISSERTS	DISTENTS	DISULFID
DISPREAD	DISROBERS	DISSERVE	DISTHENE	DISULFIDE
DISPREADS	DISROBES	DISSERVED	DISTHENES	DISULFIDS
DISPRED	DISROBING	DISSERVES	DISTHRONE	DISUNION
DISPREDS	DISROOT	DISSES	DISTICH	DISUNIONS
DISPRISON	DISROOTED	DISSEVER	DISTICHAL	DISUNITE
DISPRIZE	DISROOTS	DISSEVERS	DISTICHS	DISUNITED
DISPRIZED	DISRUPT	DISSHIVER	DISTIL	DISUNITER
DISPRIZES	DISRUPTED	DISSIDENT	DISTILL	DISUNITES
DISPROFIT	DISRUPTER	DISSIGHT	DISTILLED	DISUNITY
DISPROOF	DISRUPTOR	DISSIGHTS	DISTILLER	DISUSAGE
DISPROOFS	DISRUPTS	DISSIMILE	DISTILLS	DISUSAGES
DISPROOVE	DISS	DISSING	DISTILS	DISUSE
DISPROVAL	DISSAVE	DISSIPATE	DISTINCT	DISUSED
DISPROVE	DISSAVED	DISSOCIAL	DISTINGUE	DISUSES
DISPROVED	DISSAVER	DISSOLUTE	DISTOME	DISUSING
DISPROVEN	DISSAVERS	DISSOLVE	DISTOMES	DISVALUE
DISPROVER	DISSAVES	DISSOLVED	DISTORT	DISVALUED
DISPROVES	DISSAVING	DISSOLVER	DISTORTED	DISVALUES

DISVOUCH	DITSINESS	DIVAS	DIVIDIVI	DIVS
DISYOKE	DITSY	DIVE	DIVIDIVIS	DIVULGATE
DISYOKED	DITT	DIVEBOMB	DIVIDUAL	DIVULGE
DISYOKES	DITTANDER	DIVEBOMBS	DIVIDUOUS	DIVULGED
DISYOKING	DITTANIES	DIVED	DIVIED	DIVULGER
DIT	DITTANY	DIVELLENT	DIVINABLE	DIVULGERS
DITA	DITTAY	DIVER	DIVINATOR	DIVULGES
DITAL	DITTAYS	DIVERGE	DIVINE	DIVULGING
DITALS	DITTED	DIVERGED	DIVINED	DIVULSE
DITAS	DITTIED	DIVERGENT	DIVINELY	DIVULSED
DITCH	DITTIES	DIVERGES	DIVINER	DIVULSES
DITCHED	DITTING	DIVERGING	DIVINERS	DIVULSING
DITCHER	DITTIT	DIVERS	DIVINES	DIVULSION
DITCHERS	DITTO	DIVERSE	DIVINEST	DIVULSIVE
DITCHES	DITTOED	DIVERSED	DIVING	DIVVIED
DITCHING	DITTOING	DIVERSELY	DIVINGS	DIVVIER
DITCHLESS	DITTOLOGY	DIVERSES	DIVINIFY	DIVVIES
DITE	DITTOS	DIVERSIFY	DIVINING	DIVVIEST
DITED	DITTS	DIVERSING	DIVINISE	DIVVY
DITES	DITTY	DIVERSION	DIVINISED	DIVVYING
DITHECAL	DITTYING	DIVERSITY	DIVINISES	DIVYING
DITHECOUS	DITZ	DIVERSLY	DIVINITY	DIWAN
DITHEISM	DITZES	DIVERT	DIVINIZE	DIWANS
DITHEISMS	DITZIER	DIVERTED	DIVINIZED	DIXI
DITHEIST	DITZIEST	DIVERTER	DIVINIZES	DIXIE
DITHEISTS	DITZINESS	DIVERTERS	DIVIS	DIXIES
DITHELETE	DITZY	DIVERTING	DIVISIBLE	DIXIT
DITHELISM	DIURESES	DIVERTIVE	DIVISIBLY	DIXITS
DITHER	DIURESIS	DIVERTS	DIVISIM	DIXY
DITHERED	DIURETIC	DIVES	DIVISION	DIYA
DITHERER	DIURETICS	DIVEST	DIVISIONS	DIYAS
DITHERERS	DIURNAL	DIVESTED	DIVISIVE	DIZAIN
DITHERIER	DIURNALLY	DIVESTING	DIVISOR	DIZAINS
DITHERING	DIURNALS	DIVESTS	DIVISORS	DIZEN
DITHERS	DIURON	DIVESTURE	DIVNA	DIZENED
DITHERY	DIURONS	DIVI	DIVO	DIZENING
DITHIOL	DIUTURNAL	DIVIDABLE	DIVORCE	DIZENMENT
DITHIOLS	DIV	DIVIDANT	DIVORCED	DIZENS
DITHIONIC	DIVA	DIVIDE	DIVORCEE	DIZYGOTIC
DITHYRAMB	DIVAGATE	DIVIDED	DIVORCEES	DIZYGOUS
DITING	DIVAGATED	DIVIDEDLY	DIVORCER	DIZZARD
DITOKOUS	DIVAGATES	DIVIDEND	DIVORCERS	DIZZARDS
DITONE	DIVALENCE	DIVIDENDS	DIVORCES	DIZZIED
DITONES	DIVALENCY	DIVIDER	DIVORCING	DIZZIER
DITROCHEE	DIVALENT	DIVIDERS	DIVORCIVE	DIZZIES
DITS	DIVALENTS	DIVIDES	DIVOS	DIZZIEST
DITSIER	DIVAN	DIVIDING	DIVOT	DIZZILY
DITSIEST	DIVANS	DIVIDINGS	DIVOTS	DIZZINESS

DIZZY	DOBLA	DOCKISES	DODDERIER	DOESKINS
DIZZYING	DOBLAS	DOCKISING	DODDERING	DOEST
DJEBEL	DOBLON	DOCKIZE	DODDERS	DOETH
DJEBELS	DOBLONES	DOCKIZED	DODDERY	DOF
DJELLABA	DOBLONS	DOCKIZES	DODDIER	DOFF
DJELLABAH	DOBRA	DOCKIZING	DODDIES	DOFFED
DJELLABAS	DOBRAS	DOCKLAND	DODDIEST	DOFFER
DJEMBE	DOBRO	DOCKLANDS	DODDING	DOFFERS
DJEMBES	DOBROS	DOCKS	DODDIPOLL	DOFFING
DJIBBA	DOBS	DOCKSIDE	DODDLE	DOFFS
DJIBBAH	DOBSON	DOCKSIDES	DODDLES	DOG
DJIBBAHS	DOBSONFLY	DOCKYARD	DODDY	DOGAN
DJIBBAS	DOBSONS	DOCKYARDS	DODDYPOLL	DOGANS
DJIN	DOBY	DOCO	DODECAGON	DOGARESSA
DJINN	DOC	DOCOS	DODGE	DOGATE
DJINNI	DOCENT	DOCQUET	DODGEBALL	DOGATES
DJINNS	DOCENTS	DOCQUETED	DODGED	DOGBANE
DJINNY	DOCETIC	DOCQUETS	DODGEM	DOGBANES
DJINS	DOCHMIAC	DOCS	DODGEMS	DOGBERRY
DO	DOCHMIACS	DOCTOR	DODGER	DOGBOLT
DOAB	DOCHMII	DOCTORAL	DODGERIES	DOGBOLTS
DOABLE	DOCHMIUS	DOCTORAND	DODGERS	DOGCART
DOABS	DOCHT	DOCTORATE	DODGERY	DOGCARTS
DOAT	DOCIBLE	DOCTORED	DODGES	DOGDOM
DOATED	DOCILE	DOCTORESS	DODGIER	DOGDOMS
DOATER	DOCILELY	DOCTORIAL	DODGIEST	DOGE
DOATERS	DOCILER	DOCTORING	DODGINESS	DOGEAR
DOATING	DOCILEST	DOCTORLY	DODGING	DOGEARED
DOATINGS	DOCILITY	DOCTORS	DODGINGS	DOGEARING
DOATS	DOCIMASY	DOCTRESS	DODGY	DOGEARS
DOB	DOCK	DOCTRINAL	DODKIN	DOGEATE
DOBBED	DOCKAGE	DOCTRINE	DODKINS	DOGEATES
DOBBER	DOCKAGES	DOCTRINES	DODMAN	DOGEDOM
DOBBERS	DOCKED	DOCU	DODMANS	DOGEDOMS
DOBBIE	DOCKEN	DOCUDRAMA	DODO	DOGES
DOBBIES	DOCKENS	DOCUMENT	DODOES	DOGESHIP
DOBBIN	DOCKER	DOCUMENTS	DODOISM	DOGESHIPS
DOBBING	DOCKERS	DOCUS	DODOISMS	DOGEY
DOBBINS	DOCKET	DOCUSOAP	DODOS	DOGEYS
DOBBY	DOCKETED	DOCUSOAPS	DODS	DOGFACE
DOBCHICK	DOCKETING	DOD	DOE	DOGFACES
DOBCHICKS	DOCKETS	DODDARD	DOEK	DOGFIGHT
DOBE	DOCKHAND	DODDARDS	DOEKS	DOGFIGHTS
DOBES	DOCKHANDS	DODDED	DOEN	DOGFISH
DOBHASH	DOCKING	DODDER	DOER	DOGFISHES
DOBHASHES	DOCKINGS	DODDERED	DOERS	DOGFOOD
DOBIE	DOCKISE	DODDERER	DOES	DOGFOODS
DOBIES	DOCKISED	DODDERERS	DOESKIN	DOGFOUGHT

D

DOGFOX	DOGMAS	DOGWATCH	DOLINAS	DOLORS
DOGFOXES	DOGMATA	DOGWOOD	DOLINE	DOLOS
DOGGED	DOGMATIC	DOGWOODS	DOLINES	DOLOSSE
DOGGEDER	DOGMATICS	DOGY	DOLING	DOLOSTONE
DOGGEDEST	DOGMATISE	DOH	DOLIUM	DOLOUR
DOGGEDLY	DOGMATISM	DOHS	DOLL	DOLOURS
DOGGER	DOGMATIST	DOHYO	DOLLAR	DOLPHIN
DOGGEREL	DOGMATIZE	DOHYOS	DOLLARED	DOLPHINET
DOGGERELS	DOGMATORY	DOILED	DOLLARISE	DOLPHINS
DOGGERIES	DOGMEN	DOILIED	DOLLARIZE	DOLS
DOGGERMAN	DOGNAP	DOILIES	DOLLARS	DOLT
DOGGERMEN	DOGNAPED	DOILT	DOLLDOM	DOLTISH
DOGGERS	DOGNAPER	DOILTER	DOLLDOMS	DOLTISHLY
DOGGERY	DOGNAPERS	DOILTEST	DOLLED	DOLTS
DOGGESS	DOGNAPING	DOILY	DOLLHOOD	DOM
DOGGESSES	DOGNAPPED	DOING	DOLLHOODS	DOMAIN
DOGGIE	DOGNAPPER	DOINGS	DOLLHOUSE	DOMAINAL
DOGGIER	DOGNAPS	DOIT	DOLLIED	DOMAINE
DOGGIES	DOGPILE	DOITED	DOLLIER	DOMAINES
DOGGIEST	DOGPILES	DOITIT	DOLLIERS	DOMAINS
DOGGINESS	DOGREL	DOITKIN	DOLLIES	DOMAL
DOGGING	DOGRELS	DOITKINS	DOLLINESS	DOMANIAL
DOGGINGS	DOGROBBER	DOITS	DOLLING	DOMATIA
DOGGISH	DOGS	DOJO	DOLLISH	DOMATIUM
DOGGISHLY	DOGSBODY	DOJOS	DOLLISHLY	DOME
DOGGO	DOGSHIP	DOL	DOLLOP	DOMED
DOGGONE	DOGSHIPS	DOLABRATE	DOLLOPED	DOMELIKE
DOGGONED	DOGSHORES	DOLCE	DOLLOPING	DOMES
DOGGONER	DOGSHOW	DOLCES	DOLLOPS	DOMESDAY
DOGGONES	DOGSHOWS	DOLCETTO	DOLLS	DOMESDAYS
DOGGONEST	DOGSKIN	DOLCETTOS	DOLLY	DOMESTIC
DOGGONING	DOGSKINS	DOLCI	DOLLYBIRD	DOMESTICS
DOGGREL	DOGSLED	DOLDRUMS	DOLLYING	DOMETT
DOGGRELS	DOGSLEDS	DOLE	DOLMA	DOMETTS
DOGGY	DOGSLEEP	DOLED	DOLMADES	DOMIC
DOGHANGED	DOGSLEEPS	DOLEFUL	DOLMAN	DOMICAL
DOGHOLE	DOGSTAIL	DOLEFULLY	DOLMANS	DOMICALLY
DOGHOLES	DOGSTAILS	DOLENT	DOLMAS	DOMICIL
DOGHOUSE	DOGTAIL	DOLENTE	DOLMEN	DOMICILE
DOGHOUSES	DOGTAILS	DOLERITE	DOLMENIC	DOMICILED
DOGIE	DOGTEETH	DOLERITES	DOLMENS	DOMICILES
DOGIES	DOGTOOTH	DOLERITIC	DOLOMITE	DOMICILS
DOGLEG	DOGTOWN	DOLES	DOLOMITES	DOMIER
DOGLEGGED	DOGTOWNS	DOLESOME	DOLOMITIC	DOMIEST
DOGLEGS	DOGTROT	DOLIA	DOLOR	DOMINANCE
DOGLIKE	DOGTROTS	DOLICHOS	DOLORIFIC	DOMINANCY
DOGMA	DOGVANE	DOLICHURI	DOLOROSO	DOMINANT
DOGMAN	DOGVANES	DOLINA	DOLOROUS	DOMINANTS

D

DOMINATE	DONATORS	DONNES	DOODAHS	DOOMSMEN
DOMINATED	DONATORY	DONNICKER	DOODIES	DOOMSTER
DOMINATES	DONDER	DONNIES	DOODLE	DOOMSTERS
DOMINATOR	DONDERED	DONNIKER	DOODLEBUG	DOOMWATCH
DOMINE	DONDERING	DONNIKERS	DOODLED	DOOMY
DOMINEE	DONDERS	DONNING	DOODLER	DOON
DOMINEER	DONE	DONNISH	DOODLERS	DOONA
DOMINEERS	DONEE	DONNISHLY	DOODLES	DOONAS
DOMINEES	DONEES	DONNISM	DOODLING	DOOR
DOMINES	DONEGAL	DONNISMS	DOODOO	DOORBELL
DOMING	DONEGALS	DONNOT	DOODOOS	DOORBELLS
DOMINICAL	DONENESS	DONNOTS	DOODY	DOORCASE
DOMINICK	DONEPEZIL	DONNY	DOOFER	DOORCASES
DOMINICKS	DONER	DONOR	DOOFERS	DOORED
DOMINIE	DONERS	DONORS	DOOFUS	DOORFRAME
DOMINIES	DONG	DONORSHIP	DOOFUSES	DOORJAMB
DOMINION	DONGA	DONS	DOOHICKEY	DOORJAMBS
DOMINIONS	DONGAS	DONSHIP	DOOK	DOORKNOB
DOMINIQUE	DONGED	DONSHIPS	DOOKED	DOORKNOBS
DOMINIUM	DONGING	DONSIE	DOOKET	DOORKNOCK
DOMINIUMS	DONGLE	DONSIER	DOOKETS	DOORLESS
DOMINO	DONGLES	DONSIEST	DOOKING	DOORLIKE
DOMINOES	DONGOLA	DONSY	DOOKS	DOORMAN
DOMINOS	DONGOLAS	DONUT	DOOL	DOORMAT
DOMOIC	DONGS	DONUTS	DOOLALLY	DOORMATS
DOMS	DONING	DONUTTED	DOOLAN	DOORMEN
DOMY	DONINGS	DONUTTING	DOOLANS	DOORN
DON	DONJON	DONZEL	DOOLE	DOORNAIL
DONA	DONJONS	DONZELS	DOOLEE	DOORNAILS
DONAH	DONKEY	DOO	DOOLEES	DOORNBOOM
DONAHS	DONKEYMAN	DOOB	DOOLES	DOORNS
DONAIR	DONKEYMEN	DOOBIE	DOOLIE	DOORPLATE
DONAIRS	DONKEYS	DOOBIES	DOOLIES	DOORPOST
DONARIES	DONKO	DOOBREY	DOOLS	DOORPOSTS
DONARY	DONKOS	DOOBREYS	DOOLY	DOORS
DONAS	DONNA	DOOBRIE	DOOM	DOORSILL
DONATARY	DONNARD	DOOBRIES	DOOMED	DOORSILLS
DONATE	DONNART	DOOBRY	DOOMFUL	DOORSMAN
DONATED	DONNAS	DOOBS	DOOMFULLY	DOORSMEN
DONATES	DONNAT	DOOCE	DOOMIER	DOORSTEP
DONATING	DONNATS	DOOCED	DOOMIEST	DOORSTEPS
DONATION	DONNE	DOOCES	DOOMILY	DOORSTONE
DONATIONS	DONNED	DOOCING	DOOMING	DOORSTOP
DONATISM	DONNEE	DOOCOT	DOOMS	DOORSTOPS
DONATISMS	DONNEES	DOOCOTS	DOOMSAYER	DOORWAY
DONATIVE	DONNERD	DOODAD	DOOMSDAY	DOORWAYS
DONATIVES	DONNERED	DOODADS	DOOMSDAYS	DOORWOMAN
DONATOR	DONNERT	DOODAH	DOOMSMAN	DOORWOMEN

DOORYARD	DOPPING	DORMANT	DORTERS	DOSSIERS
DOORYARDS	DOPPINGS	DORMANTS	DORTIER	DOSSIL
DOOS	DOPPIO	DORMER	DORTIEST	DOSSILS
DOOSES	DOPPIOS	DORMERED	DORTINESS	DOSSING
DOOSRA	DOPS	DORMERS	DORTING	DOST
DOOSRAS	DOPY	DORMICE	DORTOUR	DOT
DOOWOP	DOR	DORMIE	DORTOURS	DOTAGE
DOOWOPS	DORAD	DORMIENT	DORTS	DOTAGES
DOOZER	DORADO	DORMIN	DORTY	DOTAL
DOOZERS	DORADOS	DORMINS	DORY	DOTANT
DOOZIE	DORADS	DORMITION	DORYMAN	DOTANTS
DOOZIES	DORB	DORMITIVE	DORYMEN	DOTARD
DOOZY	DORBA	DORMITORY	DOS	DOTARDLY
DOP	DORBAS	DORMOUSE	DOSA	DOTARDS
DOPA	DORBEETLE	DORMS	DOSAGE	DOTATION
DOPAMINE	DORBS	DORMY	DOSAGES	DOTATIONS
DOPAMINES	DORBUG	DORNECK	DOSAI	DOTCOM
DOPANT	DORBUGS	DORNECKS	DOSAS	DOTCOMMER
DOPANTS	DORE	DORNICK	DOSE	DOTCOMS
DOPAS	DOREE	DORNICKS	DOSED	DOTE
DOPATTA	DOREES	DORNOCK	DOSEH	DOTED
DOPATTAS	DORES	DORNOCKS	DOSEHS	DOTER
DOPE	DORHAWK	DORONICUM	DOSEMETER	DOTERS
DOPED	DORHAWKS	DORP	DOSER	DOTES
DOPEHEAD	DORIC	DORPER	DOSERS	DOTH
DOPEHEADS	DORIDOID	DORPERS	DOSES	DOTIER
DOPER	DORIDOIDS	DORPS	DOSH	DOTIEST
DOPERS	DORIES	DORR	DOSHA	DOTING
DOPES	DORIS	DORRED	DOSHAS	DOTINGLY
DOPESHEET	DORISE	DORRING	DOSHES	DOTINGS
DOPEST	DORISED	DORRS	DOSIMETER	DOTISH
DOPESTER	DORISES	DORS	DOSIMETRY	DOTS
DOPESTERS	DORISING	DORSA	DOSING	DOTTED
DOPEY	DORIZE	DORSAD	DOSIOLOGY	DOTTEL
DOPEYNESS	DORIZED	DORSAL	DOSOLOGY	DOTTELS
DOPIAZA	DORIZES	DORSALLY	DOSS	DOTTER
DOPIAZAS	DORIZING	DORSALS	DOSSAL	DOTTEREL
DOPIER	DORK	DORSE	DOSSALS	DOTTERELS
DOPIEST	DORKIER	DORSEL	DOSSED	DOTTERS
DOPILY	DORKIEST	DORSELS	DOSSEL	DOTTIER
DOPINESS	DORKINESS	DORSER	DOSSELS	DOTTIEST
DOPING	DORKISH	DORSERS	DOSSER	DOTTILY
DOPINGS	DORKS	DORSES	DOSSERET	DOTTINESS
DOPPED	DORKY	DORSIFLEX	DOSSERETS	DOTTING
DOPPER	DORLACH	DORSUM	DOSSERS	DOTTLE
DOPPERS	DORLACHS	DORT	DOSSES	DOTTLED
DOPPIE	DORM	DORTED	DOSSHOUSE	DOTTLER
DOPPIES	DORMANCY	DORTER	DOSSIER	DOTTLES

DOTTLEST	DOUCEURS	DOURAS	DOVIE	DOWLE
DOTTREL	DOUCHE	DOURER	DOVIER	DOWLES
DOTTRELS	DOUCHEBAG	DOUREST	DOVIEST	DOWLIER
DOTTY	DOUCHED	DOURINE	DOVING	DOWLIEST
DOTY	DOUCHES	DOURINES	DOVISH	DOWLNE
DOUANE	DOUCHING	DOURLY	DOVISHLY	DOWLNES
DOUANES	DOUCHINGS	DOURNESS	DOW	DOWLNEY
DOUANIER	DOUCINE	DOUSE	DOWABLE	DOWLS
DOUANIERS	DOUCINES	DOUSED	DOWAGER	DOWLY
DOUAR	DOUCS	DOUSER	DOWAGERS	DOWN
DOUARS	DOUGH	DOUSERS	DOWAR	DOWNA
DOUBLE	DOUGHBALL	DOUSES	DOWARS	DOWNBEAT
DOUBLED	DOUGHBOY	DOUSING	DOWD	DOWNBEATS
DOUBLER	DOUGHBOYS	DOUT	DOWDIER	DOWNBOUND
DOUBLERS	DOUGHFACE	DOUTED	DOWDIES	DOWNBOW
DOUBLES	DOUGHIER	DOUTER	DOWDIEST	DOWNBOWS
DOUBLET	DOUGHIEST	DOUTERS	DOWDILY	DOWNBURST
DOUBLETON	DOUGHLIKE	DOUTING	DOWDINESS	DOWNCAST
DOUBLETS	DOUGHNUT	DOUTS	DOWDS	DOWNCASTS
DOUBLING	DOUGHNUTS	DOUX	DOWDY	DOWNCOME
DOUBLINGS	DOUGHS	DOUZEPER	DOWDYISH	DOWNCOMER
DOUBLOON	DOUGHT	DOUZEPERS	DOWDYISM	DOWNCOMES
DOUBLOONS	DOUGHTIER	DOVE	DOWDYISMS	DOWNCOURT
DOUBLURE	DOUGHTILY	DOVECOT	DOWED	DOWNCRIED
DOUBLURES	DOUGHTY	DOVECOTE	DOWEL	DOWNCRIES
DOUBLY	DOUGHY	DOVECOTES	DOWELED	DOWNCRY
DOUBT	DOUK	DOVECOTS	DOWELING	DOWNDRAFT
DOUBTABLE	DOUKED	DOVED	DOWELINGS	DOWNED
DOUBTABLY	DOUKING	DOVEISH	DOWELLED	DOWNER
DOUBTED	DOUKS	DOVEISHLY	DOWELLING	DOWNERS
DOUBTER	DOULA	DOVEKEY	DOWELS	DOWNFALL
DOUBTERS	DOULAS	DOVEKEYS	DOWER	DOWNFALLS
DOUBTFUL	DOULEIA	DOVEKIE	DOWERED	DOWNFIELD
DOUBTFULS	DOULEIAS	DOVEKIES	DOWERIES	DOWNFLOW
DOUBTING	DOUM	DOVELET	DOWERING	DOWNFLOWS
DOUBTINGS	DOUMA	DOVELETS	DOWERLESS	DOWNFORCE
DOUBTLESS	DOUMAS	DOVELIKE	DOWERS	DOWNGRADE
DOUBTS	DOUMS	DOVEN	DOWERY	DOWNHAUL
DOUC	DOUN	DOVENED	DOWF	DOWNHAULS
DOUCE	DOUP	DOVENING	DOWFNESS	DOWNHILL
DOUCELY	DOUPIONI	DOVENS	DOWIE	DOWNHILLS
DOUCENESS	DOUPIONIS	DOVER	DOWIER	DOWNHOLE
DOUCEPERE	DOUPPIONI	DOVERED	DOWIEST	DOWNIER
DOUCER	DOUPS	DOVERING	DOWING	DOWNIES
DOUCEST	DOUR	DOVERS	DOWITCHER	DOWNIEST
DOUCET	DOURA	DOVES	DOWL	DOWNILY
DOUCETS	DOURAH	DOVETAIL	DOWLAS	DOWNINESS
DOUCEUR	DOURAHS	DOVETAILS	DOWLASES	DOWNING

DOWNLAND	DOWNTIMES	DOXOLOGY	DRABETTE	DRAFTY
DOWNLANDS	DOWNTOWN	DOXY	DRABETTES	DRAG
DOWNLESS	DOWNTOWNS	DOY	DRABLER	DRAGEE
DOWNLIGHT	DOWNTREND	DOYEN	DRABLERS	DRAGEES
DOWNLIKE	DOWNTROD	DOYENNE	DRABLY	DRAGGED
DOWNLINK	DOWNTURN	DOYENNES	DRABNESS	DRAGGER
DOWNLINKS	DOWNTURNS	DOYENS	DRABS	DRAGGERS
DOWNLOAD	DOWNVOTE	DOYLEY	DRAC	DRAGGIER
DOWNLOADS	DOWNVOTED	DOYLEYS	DRACAENA	DRAGGIEST
DOWNLOW	DOWNVOTES	DOYLIES	DRACAENAS	DRAGGING
DOWNLOWS	DOWNWARD	DOYLY	DRACENA	DRAGGINGS
DOWNMOST	DOWNWARDS	DOYS	DRACENAS	DRAGGLE
DOWNPIPE	DOWNWARP	DOZE	DRACHM	DRAGGLED
DOWNPIPES	DOWNWARPS	DOZED	DRACHMA	DRAGGLES
DOWNPLAY	DOWNWASH	DOZEN	DRACHMAE	DRAGGLING
DOWNPLAYS	DOWNWIND	DOZENED	DRACHMAI	DRAGGY
DOWNPOUR	DOWNY	DOZENING	DRACHMAS	DRAGHOUND
DOWNPOURS	DOWNZONE	DOZENS	DRACHMS	DRAGLINE
DOWNRANGE	DOWNZONED	DOZENTH	DRACK	DRAGLINES
DOWNRATE	DOWNZONES	DOZENTHS	DRACO	DRAGNET
DOWNRATED	DOWP	DOZER	DRACONE	DRAGNETS
DOWNRATES	DOWPS	DOZERS	DRACONES	DRAGOMAN
DOWNRIGHT	DOWRIES	DOZES	DRACONIAN	DRAGOMANS
DOWNRIVER	DOWRY	DOZIER	DRACONIC	DRAGOMEN
DOWNRUSH	DOWS	DOZIEST	DRACONISM	DRAGON
DOWNS	DOWSABEL	DOZILY	DRACONTIC	DRAGONESS
DOWNSCALE	DOWSABELS	DOZINESS	DRAD	DRAGONET
DOWNSHIFT	DOWSE	DOZING	DRAFF	DRAGONETS
DOWNSIDE	DOWSED	DOZINGS	DRAFFIER	DRAGONFLY
DOWNSIDES	DOWSER	DOZY	DRAFFIEST	DRAGONISE
DOWNSIZE	DOWSERS	DRAB	DRAFFISH	DRAGONISH
DOWNSIZED	DOWSES	DRABBED	DRAFFS	DRAGONISM
DOWNSIZER	DOWSET	DRABBER	DRAFFY	DRAGONIZE
DOWNSIZES	DOWSETS	DRABBERS	DRAFT	DRAGONNE
DOWNSLIDE	DOWSING	DRABBEST	DRAFTABLE	DRAGONS
DOWNSLOPE	DOWSINGS	DRABBET	DRAFTED	DRAGOON
DOWNSPIN	DOWT	DRABBETS	DRAFTEE	DRAGOONED
DOWNSPINS	DOWTS	DRABBIER	DRAFTEES	DRAGOONS
DOWNSPOUT	DOX	DRABBIEST	DRAFTER	DRAGROPE
DOWNSTAGE	DOXAPRAM	DRABBING	DRAFTERS	DRAGROPES
DOWNSTAIR	DOXAPRAMS	DRABBISH	DRAFTIER	DRAGS
DOWNSTATE	DOXASTIC	DRABBLE	DRAFTIEST	DRAGSMAN
DOWNSWEPT	DOXASTICS	DRABBLED	DRAFTILY	DRAGSMEN
DOWNSWING	DOXED	DRABBLER	DRAFTING	DRAGSTER
DOWNTHROW	DOXES	DRABBLERS	DRAFTINGS	DRAGSTERS
DOWNTICK	DOXIE	DRABBLES	DRAFTS	DRAGSTRIP
DOWNTICKS	DOXIES	DRABBLING	DRAFTSMAN	DRAGWAY
DOWNTIME	DOXING	DRABBY	DRAFTSMEN	DRAGWAYS

DRAIL	DRANTS	DRAWBORE	DREADFUL	DREDGED
DRAILED	DRAP	DRAWBORES	DREADFULS	DREDGER
DRAILING	DRAPABLE	DRAWCARD	DREADING	DREDGERS
DRAILS	DRAPE	DRAWCARDS	DREADLESS	DREDGES
DRAIN	DRAPEABLE	DRAWCORD	DREADLOCK	DREDGING
DRAINABLE	DRAPED	DRAWCORDS	DREADLY	DREDGINGS
DRAINAGE	DRAPER	DRAWDOWN	DREADS	DREE
DRAINAGES	DRAPERIED	DRAWDOWNS	DREAM	DREED
DRAINED	DRAPERIES	DRAWEE	DREAMBOAT	DREEING
DRAINER	DRAPERS	DRAWEES	DREAMED	DREER
DRAINERS	DRAPERY	DRAWER	DREAMER	DREES
DRAINING	DRAPES	DRAWERFUL	DREAMERS	DREEST
DRAINPIPE	DRAPET	DRAWERS	DREAMERY	DREG
DRAINS	DRAPETS	DRAWING	DREAMFUL	DREGGIER
DRAISENE	DRAPEY	DRAWINGS	DREAMHOLE	DREGGIEST
DRAISENES	DRAPIER	DRAWKNIFE	DREAMIER	DREGGISH
DRAISINE	DRAPIERS	DRAWL	DREAMIEST	DREGGY
DRAISINES	DRAPIEST	DRAWLED	DREAMILY	DREGS
DRAKE	DRAPING	DRAWLER	DREAMING	DREICH
DRAKES	DRAPPED	DRAWLERS	DREAMINGS	DREICHER
DRAM	DRAPPIE	DRAWLIER	DREAMLAND	DREICHEST
DRAMA	DRAPPIES	DRAWLIEST	DREAMLESS	DREIDEL
DRAMADIES	DRAPPING	DRAWLING	DREAMLIKE	DREIDELS
DRAMADY	DRAPPY	DRAWLS	DREAMS	DREIDL
DRAMAS	DRAPS	DRAWLY	DREAMT	DREIDLS
DRAMATIC	DRASTIC	DRAWN	DREAMTIME	DREIGH
DRAMATICS	DRASTICS	DRAWNWORK	DREAMY	DREIGHER
DRAMATISE	DRAT	DRAWPLATE	DREAR	DREIGHEST
DRAMATIST	DRATCHELL	DRAWS	DREARE	DREK
DRAMATIZE	DRATS	DRAWSHAVE	DREARER	DREKKIER
DRAMATURG	DRATTED	DRAWTUBE	DREARES	DREKKIEST
DRAMEDIES	DRATTING	DRAWTUBES	DREAREST	DREKKY
DRAMEDY	DRAUGHT	DRAY	DREARIER	DREKS
DRAMMACH	DRAUGHTED	DRAYAGE	DREARIES	DRENCH
DRAMMACHS	DRAUGHTER	DRAYAGES	DREARIEST	DRENCHED
DRAMMED	DRAUGHTS	DRAYED	DREARILY	DRENCHER
DRAMMING	DRAUGHTY	DRAYHORSE	DREARING	DRENCHERS
DRAMMOCK	DRAUNT	DRAYING	DREARINGS	DRENCHES
DRAMMOCKS	DRAUNTED	DRAYMAN	DREARS	DRENCHING
DRAMS	DRAUNTING	DRAYMEN	DREARY	DRENT
DRAMSHOP	DRAUNTS	DRAYS	DRECK	DREPANID
DRAMSHOPS	DRAVE	DRAZEL	DRECKIER	DREPANIDS
DRANGWAY	DRAW	DRAZELS	DRECKIEST	DREPANIUM
DRANGWAYS	DRAWABLE	DREAD	DRECKISH	DRERE
DRANK	DRAWBACK	DREADED	DRECKS	DRERES
DRANT	DRAWBACKS	DREADER	DRECKSILL	DRERIHEAD
DRANTED	DRAWBAR	DREADERS	DRECKY	DRESS
DRANTING	DRAWBARS	DREADEST	DREDGE	DRESSAGE

DRESSAGES	DRIFTAGE	DRIPSTONE	DROILS	DRONY
DRESSED	DRIFTAGES	DRIPT	DROIT	DROOB
DRESSER	DRIFTED	DRISHEEN	DROITS	DROOBS
DRESSERS	DRIFTER	DRISHEENS	DROKE	DROOG
DRESSES	DRIFTERS	DRIVABLE	DROKES	DROOGISH
DRESSIER	DRIFTIER	DRIVE	DROLE	DROOGS
DRESSIEST	DRIFTIEST	DRIVEABLE	DROLER	DROOK
DRESSILY	DRIFTING	DRIVEL	DROLES	DROOKED
DRESSING	DRIFTINGS	DRIVELED	DROLEST	DROOKING
DRESSINGS	DRIFTLESS	DRIVELER	DROLL	DROOKINGS
DRESSMADE	DRIFTNET	DRIVELERS	DROLLED	DROOKIT
DRESSMAKE	DRIFTNETS	DRIVELINE	DROLLER	DROOKS
DRESSY	DRIFTPIN	DRIVELING	DROLLERY	DROOL
DREST	DRIFTPINS	DRIVELLED	DROLLEST	DROOLED
DREVILL	DRIFTS	DRIVELLER	DROLLING	DROOLIER
DREVILLS	DRIFTWOOD	DRIVELS	DROLLINGS	DROOLIEST
DREW	DRIFTY	DRIVEN	DROLLISH	DROOLING
DREY	DRILL	DRIVER	DROLLNESS	DROOLS
DREYS	DRILLABLE	DRIVERS	DROLLS	DROOLY
DRIB	DRILLED	DRIVES	DROLLY	DROOME
DRIBBED	DRILLER	DRIVEWAY	DROME	DROOMES
DRIBBER	DRILLERS	DRIVEWAYS	DROMEDARE	DROOP
DRIBBERS	DRILLHOLE	DRIVING	DROMEDARY	DROOPED
DRIBBING	DRILLING	DRIVINGLY	DROMES	DROOPIER
DRIBBLE	DRILLINGS	DRIVINGS	DROMIC	DROOPIEST
DRIBBLED	DRILLS	DRIZZLE	DROMICAL	DROOPILY
DRIBBLER	DRILLSHIP	DRIZZLED	DROMOI	DROOPING
DRIBBLERS	DRILY	DRIZZLES	DROMON	DROOPS
DRIBBLES	DRINK	DRIZZLIER	DROMOND	DROOPY
DRIBBLET	DRINKABLE	DRIZZLING	DROMONDS	DROP
DRIBBLETS	DRINKABLY	DRIZZLY	DROMONS	DROPCLOTH
DRIBBLIER	DRINKER	DROGER	DROMOS	DROPDOWN
DRIBBLING	DRINKERS	DROGERS	DRONE	DROPDOWNS
DRIBBLY	DRINKING	DROGHER	DRONED	DROPFLIES
DRIBLET	DRINKINGS	DROGHERS	DRONER	DROPFLY
DRIBLETS	DRINKS	DROGUE	DRONERS	DROPFORGE
DRIBS	DRIP	DROGUES	DRONES	DROPHEAD
DRICE	DRIPLESS	DROGUET	DRONGO	DROPHEADS
DRICES	DRIPPED	DROGUETS	DRONGOES	DROPKICK
DRICKSIE	DRIPPER	DROICH	DRONGOS	DROPKICKS
DRICKSIER	DRIPPERS	DROICHIER	DRONIER	DROPLET
DRIED	DRIPPIER	DROICHS	DRONIEST	DROPLETS
DRIEGH	DRIPPIEST	DROICHY	DRONING	DROPLIGHT
DRIER	DRIPPILY	DROID	DRONINGLY	DROPLIKE
DRIERS	DRIPPING	DROIDS	DRONISH	DROPLOCK
DRIES	DRIPPINGS	DROIL	DRONISHLY	DROPLOCKS
DRIEST	DRIPPY	DROILED	DRONKLAP	DROPOUT
DRIFT	DRIPS	DROILING	DRONKLAPS	DROPOUTS

DROPPABLE	DROUTH	DRUDGISM	DRUMLIN	DRYAS
DROPPED	DROUTHIER	DRUDGISMS	DRUMLINS	DRYASDUST
DROPPER	DROUTHS	DRUG	DRUMLY	DRYBEAT
DROPPERS	DROUTHY	DRUGGED	DRUMMED	DRYBEATEN
DROPPING	DROVE	DRUGGER	DRUMMER	DRYBEATS
DROPPINGS	DROVED	DRUGGERS	DRUMMERS	DRYER
DROPPLE	DROVER	DRUGGET	DRUMMIES	DRYERS
DROPPLES	DROVERS	DRUGGETS	DRUMMING	DRYEST
DROPS	DROVES	DRUGGIE	DRUMMINGS	DRYING
DROPSEED	DROVING	DRUGGIER	DRUMMOCK	DRYINGS
DROPSEEDS	DROVINGS	DRUGGIES	DRUMMOCKS	DRYISH
DROPSHOT	DROW	DRUGGIEST	DRUMMY	DRYLAND
DROPSHOTS	DROWN	DRUGGING	DRUMROLL	DRYLANDS
DROPSICAL	DROWND	DRUGGIST	DRUMROLLS	DRYLOT
DROPSIED	DROWNDED	DRUGGISTS	DRUMS	DRYLOTS
DROPSIES	DROWNDING	DRUGGY	DRUMSTICK	DRYLY
DROPSONDE	DROWNDS	DRUGLESS	DRUNK	DRYMOUTH
DROPSTONE	DROWNED	DRUGLORD	DRUNKARD	DRYMOUTHS
DROPSY	DROWNER	DRUGLORDS	DRUNKARDS	DRYNESS
DROPT	DROWNERS	DRUGMAKER	DRUNKEN	DRYNESSES
DROPTOP	DROWNING	DRUGS	DRUNKENLY	DRYPOINT
DROPTOPS	DROWNINGS	DRUGSTER	DRUNKER	DRYPOINTS
DROPWISE	DROWNS	DRUGSTERS	DRUNKEST	DRYS
DROPWORT	DROWS	DRUGSTORE	DRUNKISH	DRYSALTER
DROPWORTS	DROWSE	DRUID	DRUNKS	DRYSTONE
DROSERA	DROWSED	DRUIDESS	DRUPE	DRYSUIT
DROSERAS	DROWSES	DRUIDIC	DRUPEL	DRYSUITS
DROSHKIES	DROWSIER	DRUIDICAL	DRUPELET	DRYWALL
DROSHKY	DROWSIEST	DRUIDISM	DRUPELETS	DRYWALLED
DROSKIES	DROWSIHED	DRUIDISMS	DRUPELS	DRYWALLER
DROSKY	DROWSILY	DRUIDRIES	DRUPES	DRYWALLS
DROSS	DROWSING	DRUIDRY	DRUSE	DRYWELL
DROSSES	DROWSY	DRUIDS	DRUSEN	DRYWELLS
DROSSIER	DRUB	DRUM	DRUSES	DSO
DROSSIEST	DRUBBED	DRUMBEAT	DRUSIER	DSOBO
DROSSY	DRUBBER	DRUMBEATS	DRUSIEST	DSOBOS
DROSTDIES	DRUBBERS	DRUMBLE	DRUSY	DSOMO
DROSTDY	DRUBBING	DRUMBLED	DRUTHER	DSOMOS
DROSTDYS	DRUBBINGS	DRUMBLES	DRUTHERS	DSOS
DROUGHT	DRUBS	DRUMBLING	DRUXIER	DUAD
DROUGHTS	DRUCKEN	DRUMFIRE	DRUXIEST	DUADS
DROUGHTY	DRUDGE	DRUMFIRES	DRUXY	DUAL
DROUK	DRUDGED	DRUMFISH	DRY	DUALIN
DROUKED	DRUDGER	DRUMHEAD	DRYABLE	DUALINS
DROUKING	DRUDGERS	DRUMHEADS	DRYAD	DUALISE
DROUKINGS	DRUDGERY	DRUMLIER	DRYADES	DUALISED
DROUKIT	DRUDGES	DRUMLIEST	DRYADIC	DUALISES
DROUKS	DRUDGING	DRUMLIKE	DRYADS	DUALISING

DUALISM	DUBITATES	DUCKTAIL	DUDISM	DUETTOS
DUALISMS	DUBNIUM	DUCKTAILS	DUDISMS	DUETTS
DUALIST	DUBNIUMS	DUCKWALK	DUDS	DUFF
DUALISTIC	DUBONNET	DUCKWALKS	DUE	DUFFED
DUALISTS	DUBONNETS	DUCKWEED	DUECENTO	DUFFEL
DUALITIES	DUBS	DUCKWEEDS	DUECENTOS	DUFFELS
DUALITY	DUBSTEP	DUCKY	DUED	DUFFER
DUALIZE	DUBSTEPS	DUCT	DUEFUL	DUFFERDOM
DUALIZED	DUCAL	DUCTAL	DUEL	DUFFERISM
DUALIZES	DUCALLY	DUCTED	DUELED	DUFFERS
DUALIZING	DUCAT	DUCTILE	DUELER	DUFFEST
DUALLED	DUCATOON	DUCTILELY	DUELERS	DUFFING
DUALLIE	DUCATOONS	DUCTILITY	DUELING	DUFFINGS
DUALLIES	DUCATS	DUCTING	DUELINGS	DUFFLE
DUALLING	DUCDAME	DUCTINGS	DUELIST	DUFFLES
DUALLY	DUCE	DUCTLESS	DUELISTS	DUFFS
DUALS	DUCES	DUCTS	DUELLED	DUFUS
DUAN	DUCHESS	DUCTULE	DUELLER	DUFUSES
DUANS	DUCHESSE	DUCTULES	DUELLERS	DUG
DUAR	DUCHESSED	DUCTWORK	DUELLI	DUGITE
DUARCHIES	DUCHESSES	DUCTWORKS	DUELLING	DUGITES
DUARCHY	DUCHIES	DUD	DUELLINGS	DUGONG
DUARS	DUCHY	DUDDER	DUELLIST	DUGONGS
DUATHLETE	DUCI	DUDDERED	DUELLISTS	DUGOUT
DUATHLON	DUCK	DUDDERIES	DUELLO	DUGOUTS
DUATHLONS	DUCKBILL	DUDDERING	DUELLOS	DUGS
DUB	DUCKBILLS	DUDDERS	DUELS	DUH
DUBBED	DUCKBOARD	DUDDERY	DUELSOME	DUHKHA
DUBBER	DUCKED	DUDDIE	DUENDE	DUHKHAS
DUBBERS	DUCKER	DUDDIER	DUENDES	DUI
DUBBIN	DUCKERS	DUDDIES	DUENESS	DUIKER
DUBBINED	DUCKFOOT	DUDDIEST	DUENESSES	DUIKERBOK
DUBBING	DUCKIE	DUDDY	DUENNA	DUIKERS
DUBBINGS	DUCKIER	DUDE	DUENNAS	DUING
DUBBINING	DUCKIES	DUDED	DUES	DUIT
DUBBINS	DUCKIEST	DUDEEN	DUET	DUITS
DUBBO	DUCKING	DUDEENS	DUETED	DUKA
DUBBOS	DUCKINGS	DUDENESS	DUETING	DUKAS
DUBIETIES	DUCKISH	DUDES	DUETS	DUKE
DUBIETY	DUCKISHES	DUDETTE	DUETT	DUKED
DUBIOSITY	DUCKLING	DUDETTES	DUETTED	DUKEDOM
DUBIOUS	DUCKLINGS	DUDGEON	DUETTI	DUKEDOMS
DUBIOUSLY	DUCKMOLE	DUDGEONS	DUETTING	DUKELING
DUBITABLE	DUCKMOLES	DUDHEEN	DUETTINO	DUKELINGS
DUBITABLY	DUCKPIN	DUDHEENS	DUETTINOS	DUKERIES
DUBITANCY	DUCKPINS	DUDING	DUETTIST	DUKERY
DUBITATE	DUCKS	DUDISH	DUETTISTS	DUKES
DUBITATED	DUCKSHOVE	DUDISHLY	DUETTO	DUKESHIP

DUKESHIPS	DULLNESS	DUMKY	DUNAMS	DUNKED
DUKING	DULLS	DUMMERER	DUNCE	DUNKER
DUKKA	DULLY	DUMMERERS	DUNCEDOM	DUNKERS
DUKKAH	DULNESS	DUMMIED	DUNCEDOMS	DUNKING
DUKKAHS	DULNESSES	DUMMIER	DUNCELIKE	DUNKINGS
DUKKAS	DULOCRACY	DUMMIES	DUNCERIES	DUNKS
DUKKHA	DULOSES	DUMMIEST	DUNCERY	DUNLIN
DUKKHAS	DULOSIS	DUMMINESS	DUNCES	DUNLINS
DULCAMARA	DULOTIC	DUMMKOPF	DUNCH	DUNNAGE
DULCE	DULSE	DUMMKOPFS	DUNCHED	DUNNAGES
DULCES	DULSES	DUMMY	DUNCHES	DUNNAKIN
DULCET	DULY	DUMMYING	DUNCHING	DUNNAKINS
DULCETLY	DUM	DUMOSE	DUNCICAL	DUNNART
DULCETS	DUMA	DUMOSITY	DUNCISH	DUNNARTS
DULCIAN	DUMAIST	DUMOUS	DUNCISHLY	DUNNED
DULCIANA	DUMAISTS	DUMP	DUNDER	DUNNER
DULCIANAS	DUMAS	DUMPBIN	DUNDERS	DUNNESS
DULCIANS	DUMB	DUMPBINS	DUNE	DUNNESSES
DULCIFIED	DUMBBELL	DUMPCART	DUNELAND	DUNNEST
DULCIFIES	DUMBBELLS	DUMPCARTS	DUNELANDS	DUNNIER
DULCIFY	DUMBCANE	DUMPED	DUNELIKE	DUNNIES
DULCIMER	DUMBCANES	DUMPEE	DUNES	DUNNIEST
DULCIMERS	DUMBED	DUMPEES	DUNG	DUNNING
DULCIMORE	DUMBER	DUMPER	DUNGAREE	DUNNINGS
DULCINEA	DUMBEST	DUMPERS	DUNGAREED	DUNNISH
DULCINEAS	DUMBFOUND	DUMPIER	DUNGAREES	DUNNITE
DULCITE	DUMBHEAD	DUMPIES	DUNGED	DUNNITES
DULCITES	DUMBHEADS	DUMPIEST	DUNGEON	DUNNO
DULCITOL	DUMBING	DUMPILY	DUNGEONED	DUNNOCK
DULCITOLS	DUMBLY	DUMPINESS	DUNGEONER	DUNNOCKS
DULCITUDE	DUMBNESS	DUMPING	DUNGEONS	DUNNY
DULCOSE	DUMBO	DUMPINGS	DUNGER	DUNS
DULCOSES	DUMBOS	DUMPISH	DUNGERS	DUNSH
DULE	DUMBS	DUMPISHLY	DUNGHEAP	DUNSHED
DULES	DUMBSHIT	DUMPLE	DUNGHEAPS	DUNSHES
DULIA	DUMBSHITS	DUMPLED	DUNGHILL	DUNSHING
DULIAS	DUMBSHOW	DUMPLES	DUNGHILLS	DUNT
DULL	DUMBSHOWS	DUMPLING	DUNGIER	DUNTED
DULLARD	DUMBSIZE	DUMPLINGS	DUNGIEST	DUNTING
DULLARDS	DUMBSIZED	DUMPS	DUNGING	DUNTS
DULLED	DUMBSIZES	DUMPSITE	DUNGMERE	DUO
DULLER	DUMDUM	DUMPSITES	DUNGMERES	DUOBINARY
DULLEST	DUMDUMS	DUMPSTER	DUNGS	DUODECIMO
DULLIER	DUMELA	DUMPSTERS	DUNGY	DUODENA
DULLIEST	DUMFOUND	DUMPTRUCK	DUNITE	DUODENAL
DULLING	DUMFOUNDS	DUMPY	DUNITES	DUODENARY
DULLISH	DUMKA	DUN	DUNITIC	DUODENUM
DULLISHLY	DUMKAS	DUNAM	DUNK	DUODENUMS

DUOLOG	DUPPED	DURMASTS	DUSKLY	DUTEOUSLY
DUOLOGS	DUPPIES	DURN	DUSKNESS	DUTIABLE
DUOLOGUE	DUPPING	DURNDEST	DUSKS	DUTIED
DUOLOGUES	DUPPY	DURNED	DUSKY	DUTIES
DUOMI	DUPS	DURNEDER	DUST	DUTIFUL
DUOMO	DURA	DURNEDEST	DUSTBALL	DUTIFULLY
DUOMOS	DURABLE	DURNING	DUSTBALLS	DUTY
DUOPOLIES	DURABLES	DURNS	DUSTBIN	DUUMVIR
DUOPOLIST	DURABLY	DURO	DUSTBINS	DUUMVIRAL
DUOPOLY	DURAL	DUROC	DUSTCART	DUUMVIRI
DUOPSONY	DURALS	DUROCS	DUSTCARTS	DUUMVIRS
DUOS	DURALUMIN	DUROMETER	DUSTCLOTH	DUVET
DUOTONE	DURAMEN	DUROS	DUSTCOAT	DUVETINE
DUOTONES	DURAMENS	DUROY	DUSTCOATS	DUVETINES
DUP	DURANCE	DUROYS	DUSTCOVER	DUVETS
DUPABLE	DURANCES	DURR	DUSTED	DUVETYN
DUPATTA	DURANT	DURRA	DUSTER	DUVETYNE
DUPATTAS	DURANTS	DURRAS	DUSTERS	DUVETYNES
DUPE	DURAS	DURRIE	DUSTHEAP	DUVETYNS
DUPED	DURATION	DURRIES	DUSTHEAPS	DUX
DUPER	DURATIONS	DURRS	DUSTIER	DUXELLES
DUPERIES	DURATIVE	DURRY	DUSTIEST	DUXES
DUPERS	DURATIVES	DURST	DUSTILY	DUYKER
DUPERY	DURBAR	DURUKULI	DUSTINESS	DUYKERS
DUPES	DURBARS	DURUKULIS	DUSTING	DVANDVA
DUPING	DURDUM	DURUM	DUSTINGS	DVANDVAS
DUPINGS	DURDUMS	DURUMS	DUSTLESS	DVORNIK
DUPION	DURE	DURZI	DUSTLIKE	DVORNIKS
DUPIONS	DURED	DURZIS	DUSTMAN	DWAAL
DUPLE	DUREFUL	DUSH	DUSTMEN	DWAALS
DUPLET	DURES	DUSHED	DUSTOFF	DWALE
DUPLETS	DURESS	DUSHES	DUSTOFFS	DWALES
DUPLEX	DURESSE	DUSHING	DUSTPAN	DWALM
DUPLEXED	DURESSES	DUSK	DUSTPANS	DWALMED
DUPLEXER	DURGAH	DUSKED	DUSTPROOF	DWALMING
DUPLEXERS	DURGAHS	DUSKEN	DUSTRAG	DWALMS
DUPLEXES	DURGAN	DUSKENED	DUSTRAGS	DWAM
DUPLEXING	DURGANS	DUSKENING	DUSTS	DWAMMED
DUPLEXITY	DURGIER	DUSKENS	DUSTSHEET	DWAMMING
DUPLICAND	DURGIEST	DUSKER	DUSTSTORM	DWAMS
DUPLICATE	DURGY	DUSKEST	DUSTUP	DWANG
DUPLICITY	DURIAN	DUSKIER	DUSTUPS	DWANGS
DUPLIED	DURIANS	DUSKIEST	DUSTY	DWARF
DUPLIES	DURICRUST	DUSKILY	DUTCH	DWARFED
DUPLY	DURING	DUSKINESS	DUTCHES	DWARFER
DUPLYING	DURION	DUSKING	DUTCHMAN	DWARFEST
DUPONDII	DURIONS	DUSKISH	DUTCHMEN	DWARFING
DUPONDIUS	DURMAST	DUSKISHLY	DUTEOUS	DWARFISH

DWARFISM	DYARCHY	DYNAMISED	DYSGENIC	DYSPNOIC
DWARFISMS	DYBBUK	DYNAMISES	DYSGENICS	DYSPRAXIA
DWARFLIKE	DYBBUKIM	DYNAMISM	DYSLALIA	DYSPRAXIC
DWARFNESS	DYBBUKKIM	DYNAMISMS	DYSLALIAS	DYSTAXIA
DWARFS	DYBBUKS	DYNAMIST	DYSLECTIC	DYSTAXIAS
DWARVES	DYE	DYNAMISTS	DYSLEXIA	DYSTAXIC
DWAUM	DYEABLE	DYNAMITE	DYSLEXIAS	DYSTECTIC
DWAUMED	DYED	DYNAMITED	DYSLEXIC	DYSTHESIA
DWAUMING	DYEING	DYNAMITER	DYSLEXICS	DYSTHETIC
DWAUMS	DYEINGS	DYNAMITES	DYSLOGIES	DYSTHYMIA
DWEEB	DYELINE	DYNAMITIC	DYSLOGY	DYSTHYMIC
DWEEBIER	DYELINES	DYNAMIZE	DYSMELIA	DYSTOCIA
DWEEBIEST	DYER	DYNAMIZED	DYSMELIAS	DYSTOCIAL
DWEEBISH	DYERS	DYNAMIZES	DYSMELIC	DYSTOCIAS
DWEEBS	DYES	DYNAMO	DYSODIL	DYSTONIA
DWEEBY	DYESTER	DYNAMOS	DYSODILE	DYSTONIAS
DWELL	DYESTERS	DYNAMOTOR	DYSODILES	DYSTONIC
DWELLED	DYESTUFF	DYNAST	DYSODILS	DYSTOPIA
DWELLER	DYESTUFFS	DYNASTIC	DYSODYLE	DYSTOPIAN
DWELLERS	DYEWEED	DYNASTIES	DYSODYLES	DYSTOPIAS
DWELLING	DYEWEEDS	DYNASTS	DYSPATHY	DYSTROPHY
DWELLINGS	DYEWOOD	DYNASTY	DYSPEPSIA	DYSURIA
DWELLS	DYEWOODS	DYNATRON	DYSPEPSY	DYSURIAS
DWELT	DYEWORKS	DYNATRONS	DYSPEPTIC	DYSURIC
DWILE	DYING	DYNE	DYSPHAGIA	DYSURIES
DWILES	DYINGLY	DYNEIN	DYSPHAGIC	DYSURY
DWINDLE	DYINGNESS	DYNEINS	DYSPHAGY	DYTISCID
DWINDLED	DYINGS	DYNEL	DYSPHASIA	DYTISCIDS
DWINDLES	DYKE	DYNELS	DYSPHASIC	DYVOUR
DWINDLING	DYKED	DYNES	DYSPHONIA	DYVOURIES
DWINE	DYKES	DYNODE	DYSPHONIC	DYVOURS
DWINED	DYKEY	DYNODES	DYSPHORIA	DYVOURY
DWINES	DYKIER	DYNORPHIN	DYSPHORIC	DZEREN
DWINING	DYKIEST	DYSBINDIN	DYSPLASIA	DZERENS
DYABLE	DYKING	DYSCHROA	DYSPNEA	DZHO
DYAD	DYKON	DYSCHROAS	DYSPNEAL	DZHOS
DYADIC	DYKONS	DYSCHROIA	DYSPNEAS	DZIGGETAI
DYADICS	DYNAMETER	DYSCRASIA	DYSPNEIC	DZO
DYADS	DYNAMIC	DYSCRASIC	DYSPNOEA	DZOS
DYARCHAL	DYNAMICAL	DYSCRATIC	DYSPNOEAL	
DYARCHIC	DYNAMICS	DYSENTERY	DYSPNOEAS	
DYARCHIES	DYNAMISE	DYSFLUENT	DYSPNOEIC	

E

EA	EARBOB	EARLYWOOD	EARTHIEST	EASEMENT
EACH	EARBOBS	EARMARK	EARTHILY	EASEMENTS
EACHWHERE	EARBUD	EARMARKED	EARTHING	EASER
EADISH	EARBUDS	EARMARKS	EARTHLIER	EASERS
EADISHES	EARCON	EARMUFF	EARTHLIES	EASES
EAGER	EARCONS	EARMUFFS	EARTHLIKE	EASIED
EAGERER	EARD	EARN	EARTHLING	EASIER
EAGEREST	EARDED	EARNED	EARTHLY	EASIES
EAGERLY	EARDING	EARNER	EARTHMAN	EASIEST
EAGERNESS	EARDROP	EARNERS	EARTHMEN	EASILY
EAGERS	EARDROPS	EARNEST	EARTHNUT	EASINESS
EAGLE	EARDRUM	EARNESTLY	EARTHNUTS	EASING
EAGLED	EARDRUMS	EARNESTS	EARTHPEA	EASINGS
EAGLEHAWK	EARDS	EARNING	EARTHPEAS	EASLE
EAGLES	EARED	EARNINGS	EARTHRISE	EASLES
EAGLET	EARFLAP	EARNS	EARTHS	EASSEL
EAGLETS	EARFLAPS	EARNT	EARTHSET	EASSIL
EAGLEWOOD	EARFUL	EARPHONE	EARTHSETS	EAST
EAGLING	EARFULS	EARPHONES	EARTHSTAR	EASTABOUT
EAGRE	EARHOLE	EARPICK	EARTHWARD	EASTBOUND
EAGRES	EARHOLES	EARPICKS	EARTHWAX	EASTED
EALDORMAN	EARING	EARPIECE	EARTHWOLF	EASTER
EALDORMEN	EARINGS	EARPIECES	EARTHWORK	EASTERLY
EALE	EARL	EARPLUG	EARTHWORM	EASTERN
EALED	EARLAP	EARPLUGS	EARTHY	EASTERNER
EALES	EARLAPS	EARRING	EARWAX	EASTERS
EALING	EARLDOM	EARRINGED	EARWAXES	EASTING
EAN	EARLDOMS	EARRINGS	EARWIG	EASTINGS
EANED	EARLESS	EARS	EARWIGGED	EASTLAND
EANING	EARLIER	EARSHOT	EARWIGGY	EASTLANDS
EANLING	EARLIES	EARSHOTS	EARWIGS	EASTLIN
EANLINGS	EARLIEST	EARST	EARWORM	EASTLING
EANS	EARLIKE	EARSTONE	EARWORMS	EASTLINGS
EAR	EARLINESS	EARSTONES	EAS	EASTLINS
EARACHE	EARLOBE	EARTH	EASE	EASTMOST
EARACHES	EARLOBES	EARTHBORN	EASED	EASTS
EARBALL	EARLOCK	EARTHED	EASEFUL	EASTWARD
EARBALLS	EARLOCKS	EARTHEN	EASEFULLY	EASTWARDS
EARBASH	EARLS	EARTHFALL	EASEL	EASY
EARBASHED	EARLSHIP	EARTHFAST	EASELED	EASYGOING
EARBASHER	EARLSHIPS	EARTHFLAX	EASELESS	EASYING
EARBASHES	EARLY	EARTHIER	EASELS	EAT

EATABLE
EATABLES
EATAGE
EATAGES
EATCHE
EATCHES
EATEN
EATER
EATERIE
EATERIES
EATERS
EATERY
EATH
EATHE
EATHLY
EATING
EATINGS
EATS
EAU
EAUS
EAUX
EAVE
EAVED
EAVES
EAVESDRIP
EAVESDROP
EAVING
EBAUCHE
EBAUCHES
EBAYER
EBAYERS
EBAYING
EBAYINGS
EBB
EBBED
EBBET
EBBETS
EBBING
EBBLESS
EBBS
EBENEZER
EBENEZERS
EBENISTE
EBENISTES
EBIONISE
EBIONISED
EBIONISES
EBIONISM

EBIONISMS
EBIONITIC
EBIONIZE
EBIONIZED
EBIONIZES
EBON
EBONICS
EBONIES
EBONISE
EBONISED
EBONISES
EBONISING
EBONIST
EBONISTS
EBONITE
EBONITES
EBONIZE
EBONIZED
EBONIZES
EBONIZING
EBONS
EBONY
EBOOK
EBOOKS
EBRIATE
EBRIATED
EBRIETIES
EBRIETY
EBRILLADE
EBRIOSE
EBRIOSITY
EBULLIENT
EBURNEAN
EBURNEOUS
ECAD
ECADS
ECARINATE
ECARTE
ECARTES
ECAUDATE
ECBOLE
ECBOLES
ECBOLIC
ECBOLICS
ECCE
ECCENTRIC
ECCLESIA
ECCLESIAE

ECCLESIAL
ECCO
ECCRINE
ECCRISES
ECCRISIS
ECCRITIC
ECCRITICS
ECDEMIC
ECDYSES
ECDYSIAL
ECDYSIAST
ECDYSIS
ECDYSISES
ECDYSON
ECDYSONE
ECDYSONES
ECDYSONS
ECESIC
ECESIS
ECESISES
ECH
ECHAPPE
ECHAPPES
ECHARD
ECHARDS
ECHE
ECHED
ECHELLE
ECHELLES
ECHELON
ECHELONED
ECHELONS
ECHES
ECHEVERIA
ECHIDNA
ECHIDNAE
ECHIDNAS
ECHIDNINE
ECHINACEA
ECHINATE
ECHINATED
ECHING
ECHINI
ECHINOID
ECHINOIDS
ECHINUS
ECHINUSES
ECHIUM

ECHIUMS
ECHIURAN
ECHIURANS
ECHIUROID
ECHO
ECHOED
ECHOER
ECHOERS
ECHOES
ECHOEY
ECHOGRAM
ECHOGRAMS
ECHOGRAPH
ECHOIC
ECHOIER
ECHOIEST
ECHOING
ECHOISE
ECHOISED
ECHOISES
ECHOISING
ECHOISM
ECHOISMS
ECHOIST
ECHOISTS
ECHOIZE
ECHOIZED
ECHOIZES
ECHOIZING
ECHOLALIA
ECHOLALIC
ECHOLESS
ECHOS
ECHOVIRUS
ECHT
ECLAIR
ECLAIRS
ECLAMPSIA
ECLAMPSY
ECLAMPTIC
ECLAT
ECLATS
ECLECTIC
ECLECTICS
ECLIPSE
ECLIPSED
ECLIPSER
ECLIPSERS

ECLIPSES
ECLIPSING
ECLIPSIS
ECLIPTIC
ECLIPTICS
ECLOGITE
ECLOGITES
ECLOGUE
ECLOGUES
ECLOSE
ECLOSED
ECLOSES
ECLOSING
ECLOSION
ECLOSIONS
ECO
ECOCIDAL
ECOCIDE
ECOCIDES
ECOD
ECOFREAK
ECOFREAKS
ECOGIFT
ECOGIFTS
ECOLODGE
ECOLODGES
ECOLOGIC
ECOLOGIES
ECOLOGIST
ECOLOGY
ECOMAP
ECOMAPS
ECOMMERCE
ECOMUSEUM
ECONOBOX
ECONOMIC
ECONOMICS
ECONOMIES
ECONOMISE
ECONOMISM
ECONOMIST
ECONOMIZE
ECONOMY
ECONUT
ECONUTS
ECOPHOBIA
ECORCHE
ECORCHES

ECOREGION	ECTOCRINE	EDACIOUS	EDICTALLY	EDUCTION
ECOS	ECTODERM	EDACITIES	EDICTS	EDUCTIONS
ECOSPHERE	ECTODERMS	EDACITY	EDIFICE	EDUCTIVE
ECOSSAISE	ECTOGENE	EDAMAME	EDIFICES	EDUCTOR
ECOSTATE	ECTOGENES	EDAMAMES	EDIFICIAL	EDUCTORS
ECOSYSTEM	ECTOGENIC	EDAPHIC	EDIFIED	EDUCTS
ECOTAGE	ECTOGENY	EDDIED	EDIFIER	EE
ECOTAGES	ECTOMERE	EDDIES	EDIFIERS	EECH
ECOTARIAN	ECTOMERES	EDDISH	EDIFIES	EECHED
ECOTONAL	ECTOMERIC	EDDISHES	EDIFY	EECHES
ECOTONE	ECTOMORPH	EDDO	EDIFYING	EECHING
ECOTONES	ECTOPHYTE	EDDOES	EDILE	EEEW
ECOTOPIA	ECTOPIA	EDDY	EDILES	EEJIT
ECOTOPIAS	ECTOPIAS	EDDYING	EDIT	EEJITS
ECOTOUR	ECTOPIC	EDELWEISS	EDITABLE	EEK
ECOTOURED	ECTOPIES	EDEMA	EDITED	EEL
ECOTOURS	ECTOPLASM	EDEMAS	EDITING	EELFARE
ECOTOXIC	ECTOPROCT	EDEMATA	EDITINGS	EELFARES
ECOTYPE	ECTOPY	EDEMATOSE	EDITION	EELGRASS
ECOTYPES	ECTOSARC	EDEMATOUS	EDITIONED	EELIER
ECOTYPIC	ECTOSARCS	EDENIC	EDITIONS	EELIEST
ECOZONE	ECTOTHERM	EDENTAL	EDITOR	EELING
ECOZONES	ECTOZOA	EDENTATE	EDITORIAL	EELINGS
ECPHRASES	ECTOZOAN	EDENTATES	EDITORS	EELLIKE
ECPHRASIS	ECTOZOANS	EDGE	EDITRESS	EELPOUT
ECRASEUR	ECTOZOIC	EDGEBONE	EDITRICES	EELPOUTS
ECRASEURS	ECTOZOON	EDGEBONES	EDITRIX	EELS
ECRITOIRE	ECTROPIC	EDGED	EDITRIXES	EELWORM
ECRU	ECTROPION	EDGELESS	EDITS	EELWORMS
ECRUS	ECTROPIUM	EDGER	EDS	EELWRACK
ECSTASES	ECTYPAL	EDGERS	EDUCABLE	EELWRACKS
ECSTASIED	ECTYPE	EDGES	EDUCABLES	EELY
ECSTASIES	ECTYPES	EDGEWAYS	EDUCATE	EEN
ECSTASIS	ECU	EDGEWISE	EDUCATED	EENSIER
ECSTASISE	ECUELLE	EDGIER	EDUCATES	EENSIEST
ECSTASIZE	ECUELLES	EDGIEST	EDUCATING	EENSY
ECSTASY	ECUMENE	EDGILY	EDUCATION	EERIE
ECSTATIC	ECUMENES	EDGINESS	EDUCATIVE	EERIER
ECSTATICS	ECUMENIC	EDGING	EDUCATOR	EERIEST
ECTASES	ECUMENICS	EDGINGS	EDUCATORS	EERILY
ECTASIA	ECUMENISM	EDGY	EDUCATORY	EERINESS
ECTASIAS	ECUMENIST	EDH	EDUCE	EERY
ECTASIS	ECURIE	EDHS	EDUCED	EEVEN
ECTATIC	ECURIES	EDIBILITY	EDUCEMENT	EEVENS
ECTHYMA	ECUS	EDIBLE	EDUCES	EEVN
ECTHYMAS	ECZEMA	EDIBLES	EDUCIBLE	EEVNING
ECTHYMATA	ECZEMAS	EDICT	EDUCING	EEVNINGS
ECTOBLAST	ED	EDICTAL	EDUCT	EEVNS

EEW	EFFLUENTS	EGENCY	EGGWHISKS	EGRET
EF	EFFLUVIA	EGER	EGGY	EGRETS
EFF	EFFLUVIAL	EGERS	EGIS	EGYPTIAN
EFFABLE	EFFLUVIUM	EGEST	EGISES	EGYPTIANS
EFFACE	EFFLUX	EGESTA	EGLANTINE	EH
EFFACED	EFFLUXES	EGESTED	EGLATERE	EHED
EFFACER	EFFLUXION	EGESTING	EGLATERES	EHING
EFFACERS	EFFORCE	EGESTION	EGLOMISE	EHS
EFFACES	EFFORCED	EGESTIONS	EGLOMISES	EIDE
EFFACING	EFFORCES	EGESTIVE	EGMA	EIDENT
EFFECT	EFFORCING	EGESTS	EGMAS	EIDER
EFFECTED	EFFORT	EGG	EGO	EIDERDOWN
EFFECTER	EFFORTFUL	EGGAR	EGOISM	EIDERS
EFFECTERS	EFFORTS	EGGARS	EGOISMS	EIDETIC
EFFECTING	EFFRAIDE	EGGBEATER	EGOIST	EIDETICS
EFFECTIVE	EFFRAY	EGGCORN	EGOISTIC	EIDOGRAPH
EFFECTOR	EFFRAYS	EGGCORNS	EGOISTS	EIDOLA
EFFECTORS	EFFS	EGGCUP	EGOITIES	EIDOLIC
EFFECTS	EFFULGE	EGGCUPS	EGOITY	EIDOLON
EFFECTUAL	EFFULGED	EGGED	EGOLESS	EIDOLONS
EFFED	EFFULGENT	EGGER	EGOMANIA	EIDOS
EFFEIR	EFFULGES	EGGERIES	EGOMANIAC	EIGENMODE
EFFEIRED	EFFULGING	EGGERS	EGOMANIAS	EIGENTONE
EFFEIRING	EFFUSE	EGGERY	EGOS	EIGHT
EFFEIRS	EFFUSED	EGGFRUIT	EGOSURF	EIGHTBALL
EFFENDI	EFFUSES	EGGFRUITS	EGOSURFED	EIGHTEEN
EFFENDIS	EFFUSING	EGGHEAD	EGOSURFS	EIGHTEENS
EFFERE	EFFUSION	EGGHEADED	EGOTHEISM	EIGHTFOIL
EFFERED	EFFUSIONS	EGGHEADS	EGOTISE	EIGHTFOLD
EFFERENCE	EFFUSIVE	EGGIER	EGOTISED	EIGHTFOOT
EFFERENT	EFS	EGGIEST	EGOTISES	EIGHTH
EFFERENTS	EFT	EGGING	EGOTISING	EIGHTHLY
EFFERES	EFTEST	EGGLER	EGOTISM	EIGHTHS
EFFERING	EFTS	EGGLERS	EGOTISMS	EIGHTIES
EFFETE	EFTSOON	EGGLESS	EGOTIST	EIGHTIETH
EFFETELY	EFTSOONS	EGGLIKE	EGOTISTIC	EIGHTS
EFFICACY	EGAD	EGGMASS	EGOTISTS	EIGHTSMAN
EFFICIENT	EGADS	EGGMASSES	EGOTIZE	EIGHTSMEN
EFFIERCE	EGAL	EGGNOG	EGOTIZED	EIGHTSOME
EFFIERCED	EGALITE	EGGNOGS	EGOTIZES	EIGHTVO
EFFIERCES	EGALITES	EGGPLANT	EGOTIZING	EIGHTVOS
EFFIGIAL	EGALITIES	EGGPLANTS	EGREGIOUS	EIGHTY
EFFIGIES	EGALITY	EGGS	EGRESS	EIGNE
EFFIGY	EGALLY	EGGSHELL	EGRESSED	EIK
EFFING	EGAREMENT	EGGSHELLS	EGRESSES	EIKED
EFFINGS	EGENCE	EGGWASH	EGRESSING	EIKING
EFFLUENCE	EGENCES	EGGWASHES	EGRESSION	EIKON
EFFLUENT	EGENCIES	EGGWHISK	EGRESSIVE	EIKONES

EIKONS

EIKONS	EKISTIC	ELASTOMER	ELECT	ELEGISTS
EIKS	EKISTICAL	ELATE	ELECTABLE	ELEGIT
EILD	EKISTICS	ELATED	ELECTED	ELEGITS
EILDING	EKKA	ELATEDLY	ELECTEE	ELEGIZE
EILDINGS	EKKAS	ELATER	ELECTEES	ELEGIZED
EILDS	EKLOGITE	ELATERID	ELECTING	ELEGIZES
EINA	EKLOGITES	ELATERIDS	ELECTION	ELEGIZING
EINE	EKPHRASES	ELATERIN	ELECTIONS	ELEGY
EINKORN	EKPHRASIS	ELATERINS	ELECTIVE	ELEMENT
EINKORNS	EKPWELE	ELATERITE	ELECTIVES	ELEMENTAL
EINSTEIN	EKPWELES	ELATERIUM	ELECTOR	ELEMENTS
EINSTEINS	EKTEXINE	ELATERS	ELECTORAL	ELEMI
EIRACK	EKTEXINES	ELATES	ELECTORS	ELEMIS
EIRACKS	EKUELE	ELATING	ELECTRESS	ELENCH
EIRENIC	EL	ELATION	ELECTRET	ELENCHI
EIRENICAL	ELABORATE	ELATIONS	ELECTRETS	ELENCHIC
EIRENICON	ELAEAGNUS	ELATIVE	ELECTRIC	ELENCHS
EIRENICS	ELAEOLITE	ELATIVES	ELECTRICS	ELENCHTIC
EISEGESES	ELAIN	ELBOW	ELECTRIFY	ELENCHUS
EISEGESIS	ELAINS	ELBOWED	ELECTRISE	ELENCTIC
EISEL	ELAIOSOME	ELBOWING	ELECTRIZE	ELEOPTENE
EISELL	ELAN	ELBOWINGS	ELECTRO	ELEPHANT
EISELLS	ELANCE	ELBOWROOM	ELECTRODE	ELEPHANTS
EISELS	ELANCED	ELBOWS	ELECTROED	ELEPIDOTE
EISH	ELANCES	ELCHEE	ELECTRON	ELEUTHERI
EISWEIN	ELANCING	ELCHEES	ELECTRONS	ELEVATE
EISWEINS	ELAND	ELCHI	ELECTROS	ELEVATED
EITHER	ELANDS	ELCHIS	ELECTRUM	ELEVATEDS
EJACULATE	ELANET	ELD	ELECTRUMS	ELEVATES
EJECT	ELANETS	ELDER	ELECTS	ELEVATING
EJECTA	ELANS	ELDERCARE	ELECTUARY	ELEVATION
EJECTABLE	ELAPHINE	ELDERLIES	ELEDOISIN	ELEVATOR
EJECTED	ELAPID	ELDERLY	ELEGANCE	ELEVATORS
EJECTING	ELAPIDS	ELDERS	ELEGANCES	ELEVATORY
EJECTION	ELAPINE	ELDERSHIP	ELEGANCY	ELEVEN
EJECTIONS	ELAPSE	ELDEST	ELEGANT	ELEVENS
EJECTIVE	ELAPSED	ELDESTS	ELEGANTLY	ELEVENSES
EJECTIVES	ELAPSES	ELDIN	ELEGIAC	ELEVENTH
EJECTMENT	ELAPSING	ELDING	ELEGIACAL	ELEVENTHS
EJECTOR	ELASTANCE	ELDINGS	ELEGIACS	ELEVON
EJECTORS	ELASTANE	ELDINS	ELEGIAST	ELEVONS
EJECTS	ELASTANES	ELDORADO	ELEGIASTS	ELF
EJIDO	ELASTASE	ELDORADOS	ELEGIES	ELFED
EJIDOS	ELASTASES	ELDRESS	ELEGISE	ELFHOOD
EKE	ELASTIC	ELDRESSES	ELEGISED	ELFHOODS
EKED	ELASTICS	ELDRICH	ELEGISES	ELFIN
EKES	ELASTIN	ELDRITCH	ELEGISING	ELFING
EKING	ELASTINS	ELDS	ELEGIST	ELFINS

ELFISH	ELLAGIC	ELONGATE	ELUTED	EMANATE
ELFISHES	ELLIPSE	ELONGATED	ELUTES	EMANATED
ELFISHLY	ELLIPSES	ELONGATES	ELUTING	EMANATES
ELFLAND	ELLIPSIS	ELOPE	ELUTION	EMANATING
ELFLANDS	ELLIPSOID	ELOPED	ELUTIONS	EMANATION
ELFLIKE	ELLIPTIC	ELOPEMENT	ELUTOR	EMANATIST
ELFLOCK	ELLOPS	ELOPER	ELUTORS	EMANATIVE
ELFLOCKS	ELLOPSES	ELOPERS	ELUTRIATE	EMANATOR
ELFS	ELLS	ELOPES	ELUVIA	EMANATORS
ELHI	ELLWAND	ELOPING	ELUVIAL	EMANATORY
ELIAD	ELLWANDS	ELOPS	ELUVIATE	EMBACE
ELIADS	ELM	ELOPSES	ELUVIATED	EMBACES
ELICHE	ELMEN	ELOQUENCE	ELUVIATES	EMBACING
ELICHES	ELMIER	ELOQUENT	ELUVIUM	EMBAIL
ELICIT	ELMIEST	ELPEE	ELUVIUMS	EMBAILED
ELICITED	ELMS	ELPEES	ELVAN	EMBAILING
ELICITING	ELMWOOD	ELS	ELVANITE	EMBAILS
ELICITOR	ELMWOODS	ELSE	ELVANITES	EMBALE
ELICITORS	ELMY	ELSEWHERE	ELVANS	EMBALED
ELICITS	ELOCUTE	ELSEWISE	ELVEN	EMBALES
ELIDE	ELOCUTED	ELSHIN	ELVER	EMBALING
ELIDED	ELOCUTES	ELSHINS	ELVERS	EMBALL
ELIDES	ELOCUTING	ELSIN	ELVES	EMBALLED
ELIDIBLE	ELOCUTION	ELSINS	ELVISH	EMBALLING
ELIDING	ELOCUTORY	ELT	ELVISHES	EMBALLS
ELIGIBLE	ELODEA	ELTCHI	ELVISHLY	EMBALM
ELIGIBLES	ELODEAS	ELTCHIS	ELYSIAN	EMBALMED
ELIGIBLY	ELOGE	ELTS	ELYTRA	EMBALMER
ELIMINANT	ELOGES	ELUANT	ELYTRAL	EMBALMERS
ELIMINATE	ELOGIES	ELUANTS	ELYTROID	EMBALMING
ELINT	ELOGIST	ELUATE	ELYTRON	EMBALMS
ELINTS	ELOGISTS	ELUATES	ELYTROUS	EMBANK
ELISION	ELOGIUM	ELUCIDATE	ELYTRUM	EMBANKED
ELISIONS	ELOGIUMS	ELUDE	EM	EMBANKER
ELITE	ELOGY	ELUDED	EMACIATE	EMBANKERS
ELITES	ELOIGN	ELUDER	EMACIATED	EMBANKING
ELITISM	ELOIGNED	ELUDERS	EMACIATES	EMBANKS
ELITISMS	ELOIGNER	ELUDES	EMACS	EMBAR
ELITIST	ELOIGNERS	ELUDIBLE	EMACSEN	EMBARGO
ELITISTS	ELOIGNING	ELUDING	EMAIL	EMBARGOED
ELIXIR	ELOIGNS	ELUENT	EMAILABLE	EMBARGOES
ELIXIRS	ELOIN	ELUENTS	EMAILED	EMBARK
ELK	ELOINED	ELUSION	EMAILER	EMBARKED
ELKHORN	ELOINER	ELUSIONS	EMAILERS	EMBARKING
ELKHOUND	ELOINERS	ELUSIVE	EMAILING	EMBARKS
ELKHOUNDS	ELOINING	ELUSIVELY	EMAILINGS	EMBARRAS
ELKS	ELOINMENT	ELUSORY	EMAILS	EMBARRASS
ELL	ELOINS	ELUTE	EMANANT	EMBARRED

EMBARRING	EMBLEM	EMBORDER	EMBRASOR	EMBUSSED
EMBARS	EMBLEMA	EMBORDERS	EMBRASORS	EMBUSSES
EMBASE	EMBLEMATA	EMBOSCATA	EMBRASURE	EMBUSSING
EMBASED	EMBLEMED	EMBOSK	EMBRAVE	EMBUSY
EMBASES	EMBLEMING	EMBOSKED	EMBRAVED	EMBUSYING
EMBASING	EMBLEMISE	EMBOSKING	EMBRAVES	EMCEE
EMBASSADE	EMBLEMIZE	EMBOSKS	EMBRAVING	EMCEED
EMBASSAGE	EMBLEMS	EMBOSOM	EMBRAZURE	EMCEEING
EMBASSIES	EMBLIC	EMBOSOMED	EMBREAD	EMCEES
EMBASSY	EMBLICS	EMBOSOMS	EMBREADED	EMDASH
EMBASTE	EMBLOOM	EMBOSS	EMBREADS	EMDASHES
EMBATHE	EMBLOOMED	EMBOSSED	EMBREATHE	EME
EMBATHED	EMBLOOMS	EMBOSSER	EMBRITTLE	EMEER
EMBATHES	EMBLOSSOM	EMBOSSERS	EMBROCATE	EMEERATE
EMBATHING	EMBODIED	EMBOSSES	EMBROGLIO	EMEERATES
EMBATTLE	EMBODIER	EMBOSSING	EMBROIDER	EMEERS
EMBATTLED	EMBODIERS	EMBOST	EMBROIL	EMEND
EMBATTLES	EMBODIES	EMBOUND	EMBROILED	EMENDABLE
EMBAY	EMBODY	EMBOUNDED	EMBROILER	EMENDALS
EMBAYED	EMBODYING	EMBOUNDS	EMBROILS	EMENDATE
EMBAYING	EMBOG	EMBOW	EMBROWN	EMENDATED
EMBAYLD	EMBOGGED	EMBOWED	EMBROWNED	EMENDATES
EMBAYMENT	EMBOGGING	EMBOWEL	EMBROWNS	EMENDATOR
EMBAYS	EMBOGS	EMBOWELED	EMBRUE	EMENDED
EMBED	EMBOGUE	EMBOWELS	EMBRUED	EMENDER
EMBEDDED	EMBOGUED	EMBOWER	EMBRUES	EMENDERS
EMBEDDING	EMBOGUES	EMBOWERED	EMBRUING	EMENDING
EMBEDMENT	EMBOGUING	EMBOWERS	EMBRUTE	EMENDS
EMBEDS	EMBOIL	EMBOWING	EMBRUTED	EMERALD
EMBELLISH	EMBOILED	EMBOWMENT	EMBRUTES	EMERALDS
EMBER	EMBOILING	EMBOWS	EMBRUTING	EMERAUDE
EMBERS	EMBOILS	EMBOX	EMBRYO	EMERAUDES
EMBEZZLE	EMBOLDEN	EMBOXED	EMBRYOID	EMERG
EMBEZZLED	EMBOLDENS	EMBOXES	EMBRYOIDS	EMERGE
EMBEZZLER	EMBOLI	EMBOXING	EMBRYON	EMERGED
EMBEZZLES	EMBOLIC	EMBRACE	EMBRYONAL	EMERGENCE
EMBIGGEN	EMBOLIES	EMBRACED	EMBRYONIC	EMERGENCY
EMBIGGENS	EMBOLISE	EMBRACEOR	EMBRYONS	EMERGENT
EMBITTER	EMBOLISED	EMBRACER	EMBRYOS	EMERGENTS
EMBITTERS	EMBOLISES	EMBRACERS	EMBRYOTIC	EMERGES
EMBLAZE	EMBOLISM	EMBRACERY	EMBUS	EMERGING
EMBLAZED	EMBOLISMS	EMBRACES	EMBUSED	EMERGS
EMBLAZER	EMBOLIZE	EMBRACING	EMBUSES	EMERIED
EMBLAZERS	EMBOLIZED	EMBRACIVE	EMBUSIED	EMERIES
EMBLAZES	EMBOLIZES	EMBRAID	EMBUSIES	EMERITA
EMBLAZING	EMBOLUS	EMBRAIDED	EMBUSING	EMERITAE
EMBLAZON	EMBOLUSES	EMBRAIDS	EMBUSQUE	EMERITAS
EMBLAZONS	EMBOLY	EMBRANGLE	EMBUSQUES	EMERITI

EMERITUS	EMINENCY	EMODINS	EMPANOPLY	EMPHASIS
EMEROD	EMINENT	EMOJI	EMPARE	EMPHASISE
EMERODS	EMINENTLY	EMOJIS	EMPARED	EMPHASIZE
EMEROID	EMIR	EMOLLIATE	EMPARES	EMPHATIC
EMEROIDS	EMIRATE	EMOLLIENT	EMPARING	EMPHATICS
EMERSE	EMIRATES	EMOLUMENT	EMPARL	EMPHLYSES
EMERSED	EMIRS	EMONG	EMPARLED	EMPHLYSIS
EMERSION	EMISSARY	EMONGES	EMPARLING	EMPHYSEMA
EMERSIONS	EMISSILE	EMONGEST	EMPARLS	EMPIERCE
EMERY	EMISSION	EMONGST	EMPART	EMPIERCED
EMERYING	EMISSIONS	EMOS	EMPARTED	EMPIERCES
EMES	EMISSIVE	EMOTE	EMPARTING	EMPIGHT
EMESES	EMIT	EMOTED	EMPARTS	EMPIGHTED
EMESIS	EMITS	EMOTER	EMPATHIC	EMPIGHTS
EMESISES	EMITTANCE	EMOTERS	EMPATHIES	EMPIRE
EMETIC	EMITTED	EMOTES	EMPATHISE	EMPIRES
EMETICAL	EMITTER	EMOTICON	EMPATHIST	EMPIRIC
EMETICS	EMITTERS	EMOTICONS	EMPATHIZE	EMPIRICAL
EMETIN	EMITTING	EMOTING	EMPATHY	EMPIRICS
EMETINE	EMLETS	EMOTION	EMPATRON	EMPLACE
EMETINES	EMMA	EMOTIONAL	EMPATRONS	EMPLACED
EMETINS	EMMARBLE	EMOTIONS	EMPAYRE	EMPLACES
EMEU	EMMARBLED	EMOTIVE	EMPAYRED	EMPLACING
EMEUS	EMMARBLES	EMOTIVELY	EMPAYRES	EMPLANE
EMEUTE	EMMAS	EMOTIVISM	EMPAYRING	EMPLANED
EMEUTES	EMMER	EMOTIVITY	EMPEACH	EMPLANES
EMIC	EMMERS	EMOVE	EMPEACHED	EMPLANING
EMICANT	EMMESH	EMOVED	EMPEACHES	EMPLASTER
EMICATE	EMMESHED	EMOVES	EMPENNAGE	EMPLASTIC
EMICATED	EMMESHES	EMOVING	EMPEOPLE	EMPLASTRA
EMICATES	EMMESHING	EMPACKET	EMPEOPLED	EMPLEACH
EMICATING	EMMET	EMPACKETS	EMPEOPLES	EMPLECTON
EMICATION	EMMETROPE	EMPAESTIC	EMPERCE	EMPLECTUM
EMICS	EMMETS	EMPAIRE	EMPERCED	EMPLONGE
EMICTION	EMMEW	EMPAIRED	EMPERCES	EMPLONGED
EMICTIONS	EMMEWED	EMPAIRES	EMPERCING	EMPLONGES
EMICTORY	EMMEWING	EMPAIRING	EMPERIES	EMPLOY
EMIGRANT	EMMEWS	EMPALE	EMPERISE	EMPLOYE
EMIGRANTS	EMMOVE	EMPALED	EMPERISED	EMPLOYED
EMIGRATE	EMMOVED	EMPALER	EMPERISES	EMPLOYEE
EMIGRATED	EMMOVES	EMPALERS	EMPERISH	EMPLOYEES
EMIGRATES	EMMOVING	EMPALES	EMPERIZE	EMPLOYER
EMIGRE	EMMY	EMPALING	EMPERIZED	EMPLOYERS
EMIGREE	EMMYS	EMPANADA	EMPERIZES	EMPLOYES
EMIGREES	EMO	EMPANADAS	EMPEROR	EMPLOYING
EMIGRES	EMOCORE	EMPANEL	EMPERORS	EMPLOYS
EMINENCE	EMOCORES	EMPANELED	EMPERY	EMPLUME
EMINENCES	EMODIN	EMPANELS	EMPHASES	EMPLUMED

EMPLUMES	EMPYEMA	EMUNGING	ENAMORED	ENCASTRE
EMPLUMING	EMPYEMAS	EMURE	ENAMORING	ENCAUSTIC
EMPOISON	EMPYEMATA	EMURED	ENAMORS	ENCAVE
EMPOISONS	EMPYEMIC	EMURES	ENAMOUR	ENCAVED
EMPOLDER	EMPYESES	EMURING	ENAMOURED	ENCAVES
EMPOLDERS	EMPYESIS	EMUS	ENAMOURS	ENCAVING
EMPORIA	EMPYREAL	EMYD	ENANTHEMA	ENCEINTE
EMPORIUM	EMPYREAN	EMYDE	ENARCH	ENCEINTES
EMPORIUMS	EMPYREANS	EMYDES	ENARCHED	ENCEPHALA
EMPOWER	EMPYREUMA	EMYDS	ENARCHES	ENCHAFE
EMPOWERED	EMS	EMYS	ENARCHING	ENCHAFED
EMPOWERS	EMU	EN	ENARGITE	ENCHAFES
EMPRESS	EMULATE	ENABLE	ENARGITES	ENCHAFING
EMPRESSE	EMULATED	ENABLED	ENARM	ENCHAIN
EMPRESSES	EMULATES	ENABLER	ENARMED	ENCHAINED
EMPRISE	EMULATING	ENABLERS	ENARMING	ENCHAINS
EMPRISES	EMULATION	ENABLES	ENARMS	ENCHANT
EMPRIZE	EMULATIVE	ENABLING	ENATE	ENCHANTED
EMPRIZES	EMULATOR	ENACT	ENATES	ENCHANTER
EMPT	EMULATORS	ENACTABLE	ENATIC	ENCHANTS
EMPTED	EMULE	ENACTED	ENATION	ENCHARGE
EMPTIABLE	EMULED	ENACTING	ENATIONS	ENCHARGED
EMPTIED	EMULES	ENACTION	ENAUNTER	ENCHARGES
EMPTIER	EMULGE	ENACTIONS	ENCAENIA	ENCHARM
EMPTIERS	EMULGED	ENACTIVE	ENCAENIAS	ENCHARMED
EMPTIES	EMULGENCE	ENACTMENT	ENCAGE	ENCHARMS
EMPTIEST	EMULGENT	ENACTOR	ENCAGED	ENCHASE
EMPTILY	EMULGES	ENACTORS	ENCAGES	ENCHASED
EMPTINESS	EMULGING	ENACTORY	ENCAGING	ENCHASER
EMPTING	EMULING	ENACTS	ENCALM	ENCHASERS
EMPTINGS	EMULOUS	ENACTURE	ENCALMED	ENCHASES
EMPTINS	EMULOUSLY	ENACTURES	ENCALMING	ENCHASING
EMPTION	EMULSIBLE	ENALAPRIL	ENCALMS	ENCHEASON
EMPTIONAL	EMULSIFY	ENALLAGE	ENCAMP	ENCHEER
EMPTIONS	EMULSIN	ENALLAGES	ENCAMPED	ENCHEERED
EMPTS	EMULSINS	ENAMEL	ENCAMPING	ENCHEERS
EMPTY	EMULSION	ENAMELED	ENCAMPS	ENCHILADA
EMPTYING	EMULSIONS	ENAMELER	ENCANTHIS	ENCHORIAL
EMPTYINGS	EMULSIVE	ENAMELERS	ENCAPSULE	ENCHORIC
EMPTYSES	EMULSOID	ENAMELING	ENCARPUS	ENCIERRO
EMPTYSIS	EMULSOIDS	ENAMELIST	ENCASE	ENCIERROS
EMPURPLE	EMULSOR	ENAMELLED	ENCASED	ENCINA
EMPURPLED	EMULSORS	ENAMELLER	ENCASES	ENCINAL
EMPURPLES	EMUNCTION	ENAMELS	ENCASH	ENCINAS
EMPUSA	EMUNCTORY	ENAMINE	ENCASHED	ENCIPHER
EMPUSAS	EMUNGE	ENAMINES	ENCASHES	ENCIPHERS
EMPUSE	EMUNGED	ENAMOR	ENCASHING	ENCIRCLE
EMPUSES	EMUNGES	ENAMORADO	ENCASING	ENCIRCLED

ENCIRCLES	ENCORES	ENDARTS	ENDITING	ENDORSING
ENCLASP	ENCORING	ENDASH	ENDIVE	ENDORSIVE
ENCLASPED	ENCOUNTER	ENDASHES	ENDIVES	ENDORSOR
ENCLASPS	ENCOURAGE	ENDBRAIN	ENDLANG	ENDORSORS
ENCLAVE	ENCRADLE	ENDBRAINS	ENDLEAF	ENDOSARC
ENCLAVED	ENCRADLED	ENDCAP	ENDLEAFS	ENDOSARCS
ENCLAVES	ENCRADLES	ENDCAPS	ENDLEAVES	ENDOSCOPE
ENCLAVING	ENCRATIES	ENDEAR	ENDLESS	ENDOSCOPY
ENCLISES	ENCRATY	ENDEARED	ENDLESSLY	ENDOSMOS
ENCLISIS	ENCREASE	ENDEARING	ENDLONG	ENDOSMOSE
ENCLITIC	ENCREASED	ENDEARS	ENDMOST	ENDOSOME
ENCLITICS	ENCREASES	ENDEAVOR	ENDNOTE	ENDOSOMES
ENCLOSE	ENCRIMSON	ENDEAVORS	ENDNOTES	ENDOSPERM
ENCLOSED	ENCRINAL	ENDEAVOUR	ENDOBLAST	ENDOSPORE
ENCLOSER	ENCRINIC	ENDECAGON	ENDOCARP	ENDOSS
ENCLOSERS	ENCRINITE	ENDED	ENDOCARPS	ENDOSSED
ENCLOSES	ENCROACH	ENDEICTIC	ENDOCAST	ENDOSSES
ENCLOSING	ENCRUST	ENDEIXES	ENDOCASTS	ENDOSSING
ENCLOSURE	ENCRUSTED	ENDEIXIS	ENDOCRINE	ENDOSTEA
ENCLOTHE	ENCRUSTS	ENDEMIAL	ENDOCYTIC	ENDOSTEAL
ENCLOTHED	ENCRYPT	ENDEMIC	ENDODERM	ENDOSTEUM
ENCLOTHES	ENCRYPTED	ENDEMICAL	ENDODERMS	ENDOSTYLE
ENCLOUD	ENCRYPTS	ENDEMICS	ENDODYNE	ENDOTHERM
ENCLOUDED	ENCUMBER	ENDEMISM	ENDOERGIC	ENDOTOXIC
ENCLOUDS	ENCUMBERS	ENDEMISMS	ENDOGAMIC	ENDOTOXIN
ENCODABLE	ENCURTAIN	ENDENIZEN	ENDOGAMY	ENDOW
ENCODE	ENCYCLIC	ENDER	ENDOGEN	ENDOWED
ENCODED	ENCYCLICS	ENDERMIC	ENDOGENIC	ENDOWER
ENCODER	ENCYST	ENDERON	ENDOGENS	ENDOWERS
ENCODERS	ENCYSTED	ENDERONS	ENDOGENY	ENDOWING
ENCODES	ENCYSTING	ENDERS	ENDOLYMPH	ENDOWMENT
ENCODING	ENCYSTS	ENDEW	ENDOMIXES	ENDOWS
ENCODINGS	END	ENDEWED	ENDOMIXIS	ENDOZOA
ENCOLOUR	ENDAMAGE	ENDEWING	ENDOMORPH	ENDOZOIC
ENCOLOURS	ENDAMAGED	ENDEWS	ENDOPHAGY	ENDOZOON
ENCOLPIA	ENDAMAGES	ENDEXINE	ENDOPHYTE	ENDPAPER
ENCOLPION	ENDAMEBA	ENDEXINES	ENDOPLASM	ENDPAPERS
ENCOLPIUM	ENDAMEBAE	ENDGAME	ENDOPOD	ENDPLATE
ENCOLURE	ENDAMEBAS	ENDGAMES	ENDOPODS	ENDPLATES
ENCOLURES	ENDAMEBIC	ENDGATE	ENDOPROCT	ENDPLAY
ENCOMIA	ENDAMOEBA	ENDGATES	ENDORPHIN	ENDPLAYED
ENCOMIAST	ENDANGER	ENDING	ENDORSE	ENDPLAYS
ENCOMION	ENDANGERS	ENDINGS	ENDORSED	ENDPOINT
ENCOMIUM	ENDARCH	ENDIRON	ENDORSEE	ENDPOINTS
ENCOMIUMS	ENDARCHY	ENDIRONS	ENDORSEES	ENDRIN
ENCOMPASS	ENDART	ENDITE	ENDORSER	ENDRINS
ENCORE	ENDARTED	ENDITED	ENDORSERS	ENDS
ENCORED	ENDARTING	ENDITES	ENDORSES	ENDSHIP

ENDSHIPS	ENERVE	ENFLAMES	ENGAOL	ENGORED
ENDUE	ENERVED	ENFLAMING	ENGAOLED	ENGORES
ENDUED	ENERVES	ENFLESH	ENGAOLING	ENGORGE
ENDUES	ENERVING	ENFLESHED	ENGAOLS	ENGORGED
ENDUING	ENES	ENFLESHES	ENGARLAND	ENGORGES
ENDUNGEON	ENEW	ENFLOWER	ENGENDER	ENGORGING
ENDURABLE	ENEWED	ENFLOWERS	ENGENDERS	ENGORING
ENDURABLY	ENEWING	ENFOLD	ENGENDURE	ENGOULED
ENDURANCE	ENEWS	ENFOLDED	ENGILD	ENGOUMENT
ENDURE	ENFACE	ENFOLDER	ENGILDED	ENGRACE
ENDURED	ENFACED	ENFOLDERS	ENGILDING	ENGRACED
ENDURER	ENFACES	ENFOLDING	ENGILDS	ENGRACES
ENDURERS	ENFACING	ENFOLDS	ENGILT	ENGRACING
ENDURES	ENFANT	ENFORCE	ENGINE	ENGRAFF
ENDURING	ENFANTS	ENFORCED	ENGINED	ENGRAFFED
ENDURO	ENFEEBLE	ENFORCER	ENGINEER	ENGRAFFS
ENDUROS	ENFEEBLED	ENFORCERS	ENGINEERS	ENGRAFT
ENDWAYS	ENFEEBLER	ENFORCES	ENGINER	ENGRAFTED
ENDWISE	ENFEEBLES	ENFORCING	ENGINERS	ENGRAFTS
ENDYSES	ENFELON	ENFOREST	ENGINERY	ENGRAIL
ENDYSIS	ENFELONED	ENFORESTS	ENGINES	ENGRAILED
ENDZONE	ENFELONS	ENFORM	ENGINING	ENGRAILS
ENDZONES	ENFEOFF	ENFORMED	ENGINOUS	ENGRAIN
ENE	ENFEOFFED	ENFORMING	ENGIRD	ENGRAINED
ENEMA	ENFEOFFS	ENFORMS	ENGIRDED	ENGRAINER
ENEMAS	ENFESTED	ENFRAME	ENGIRDING	ENGRAINS
ENEMATA	ENFETTER	ENFRAMED	ENGIRDLE	ENGRAM
ENEMIES	ENFETTERS	ENFRAMES	ENGIRDLED	ENGRAMMA
ENEMY	ENFEVER	ENFRAMING	ENGIRDLES	ENGRAMMAS
ENERGETIC	ENFEVERED	ENFREE	ENGIRDS	ENGRAMME
ENERGIC	ENFEVERS	ENFREED	ENGIRT	ENGRAMMES
ENERGID	ENFIERCE	ENFREEDOM	ENGLACIAL	ENGRAMMIC
ENERGIDS	ENFIERCED	ENFREEING	ENGLISH	ENGRAMS
ENERGIES	ENFIERCES	ENFREES	ENGLISHED	ENGRASP
ENERGISE	ENFILADE	ENFREEZE	ENGLISHES	ENGRASPED
ENERGISED	ENFILADED	ENFREEZES	ENGLOBE	ENGRASPS
ENERGISER	ENFILADES	ENFROSEN	ENGLOBED	ENGRAVE
ENERGISES	ENFILED	ENFROZE	ENGLOBES	ENGRAVED
ENERGIZE	ENFIRE	ENFROZEN	ENGLOBING	ENGRAVEN
ENERGIZED	ENFIRED	ENG	ENGLOOM	ENGRAVER
ENERGIZER	ENFIRES	ENGAGE	ENGLOOMED	ENGRAVERS
ENERGIZES	ENFIRING	ENGAGED	ENGLOOMS	ENGRAVERY
ENERGUMEN	ENFIX	ENGAGEDLY	ENGLUT	ENGRAVES
ENERGY	ENFIXED	ENGAGEE	ENGLUTS	ENGRAVING
ENERVATE	ENFIXES	ENGAGER	ENGLUTTED	ENGRENAGE
ENERVATED	ENFIXING	ENGAGERS	ENGOBE	ENGRIEVE
ENERVATES	ENFLAME	ENGAGES	ENGOBES	ENGRIEVED
ENERVATOR	ENFLAMED	ENGAGING	ENGORE	ENGRIEVES

ENGROOVE	ENISLES	ENLIGHTS	ENNOBLE	ENPLANES
ENGROOVED	ENISLING	ENLINK	ENNOBLED	ENPLANING
ENGROOVES	ENJAMB	ENLINKED	ENNOBLER	ENPRINT
ENGROSS	ENJAMBED	ENLINKING	ENNOBLERS	ENPRINTS
ENGROSSED	ENJAMBING	ENLINKS	ENNOBLES	ENQUEUE
ENGROSSER	ENJAMBS	ENLIST	ENNOBLING	ENQUEUED
ENGROSSES	ENJOIN	ENLISTED	ENNOG	ENQUEUES
ENGS	ENJOINDER	ENLISTEE	ENNOGS	ENQUEUING
ENGUARD	ENJOINED	ENLISTEES	ENNUI	ENQUIRE
ENGUARDED	ENJOINER	ENLISTER	ENNUIED	ENQUIRED
ENGUARDS	ENJOINERS	ENLISTERS	ENNUIS	ENQUIRER
ENGULF	ENJOINING	ENLISTING	ENNUYE	ENQUIRERS
ENGULFED	ENJOINS	ENLISTS	ENNUYED	ENQUIRES
ENGULFING	ENJOY	ENLIT	ENNUYEE	ENQUIRIES
ENGULFS	ENJOYABLE	ENLIVEN	ENNUYING	ENQUIRING
ENGULPH	ENJOYABLY	ENLIVENED	ENODAL	ENQUIRY
ENGULPHED	ENJOYED	ENLIVENER	ENOKI	ENRACE
ENGULPHS	ENJOYER	ENLIVENS	ENOKIDAKE	ENRACED
ENGYSCOPE	ENJOYERS	ENLOCK	ENOKIS	ENRACES
ENHALO	ENJOYING	ENLOCKED	ENOKITAKE	ENRACING
ENHALOED	ENJOYMENT	ENLOCKING	ENOL	ENRAGE
ENHALOES	ENJOYS	ENLOCKS	ENOLASE	ENRAGED
ENHALOING	ENKERNEL	ENLUMINE	ENOLASES	ENRAGEDLY
ENHALOS	ENKERNELS	ENLUMINED	ENOLIC	ENRAGES
ENHANCE	ENKINDLE	ENLUMINES	ENOLOGIES	ENRAGING
ENHANCED	ENKINDLED	ENMESH	ENOLOGIST	ENRANCKLE
ENHANCER	ENKINDLER	ENMESHED	ENOLOGY	ENRANGE
ENHANCERS	ENKINDLES	ENMESHES	ENOLS	ENRANGED
ENHANCES	ENLACE	ENMESHING	ENOMOTIES	ENRANGES
ENHANCING	ENLACED	ENMEW	ENOMOTY	ENRANGING
ENHANCIVE	ENLACES	ENMEWED	ENOPHILE	ENRANK
ENHEARSE	ENLACING	ENMEWING	ENOPHILES	ENRANKED
ENHEARSED	ENLARD	ENMEWS	ENORM	ENRANKING
ENHEARSES	ENLARDED	ENMITIES	ENORMITY	ENRANKS
ENHEARTEN	ENLARDING	ENMITY	ENORMOUS	ENRAPT
ENHUNGER	ENLARDS	ENMOSSED	ENOSES	ENRAPTURE
ENHUNGERS	ENLARGE	ENMOVE	ENOSIS	ENRAUNGE
ENHYDRITE	ENLARGED	ENMOVED	ENOSISES	ENRAUNGED
ENHYDROS	ENLARGEN	ENMOVES	ENOUGH	ENRAUNGES
ENHYDROUS	ENLARGENS	ENMOVING	ENOUGHS	ENRAVISH
ENIAC	ENLARGER	ENNAGE	ENOUNCE	ENRHEUM
ENIACS	ENLARGERS	ENNAGES	ENOUNCED	ENRHEUMED
ENIGMA	ENLARGES	ENNEAD	ENOUNCES	ENRHEUMS
ENIGMAS	ENLARGING	ENNEADIC	ENOUNCING	ENRICH
ENIGMATA	ENLEVE	ENNEADS	ENOW	ENRICHED
ENIGMATIC	ENLIGHT	ENNEAGON	ENOWS	ENRICHER
ENISLE	ENLIGHTED	ENNEAGONS	ENPLANE	ENRICHERS
ENISLED	ENLIGHTEN	ENNEAGRAM	ENPLANED	ENRICHES

ENRICHING	ENSEAM	ENSKY	ENSURERS	ENTERED
ENRIDGED	ENSEAMED	ENSKYED	ENSURES	ENTERER
ENRING	ENSEAMING	ENSKYING	ENSURING	ENTERERS
ENRINGED	ENSEAMS	ENSLAVE	ENSWATHE	ENTERIC
ENRINGING	ENSEAR	ENSLAVED	ENSWATHED	ENTERICS
ENRINGS	ENSEARED	ENSLAVER	ENSWATHES	ENTERING
ENRIVEN	ENSEARING	ENSLAVERS	ENSWEEP	ENTERINGS
ENROBE	ENSEARS	ENSLAVES	ENSWEEPS	ENTERITIS
ENROBED	ENSEMBLE	ENSLAVING	ENSWEPT	ENTERON
ENROBER	ENSEMBLES	ENSNARE	ENTAIL	ENTERONS
ENROBERS	ENSERF	ENSNARED	ENTAILED	ENTERS
ENROBES	ENSERFED	ENSNARER	ENTAILER	ENTERTAIN
ENROBING	ENSERFING	ENSNARERS	ENTAILERS	ENTERTAKE
ENROL	ENSERFS	ENSNARES	ENTAILING	ENTERTOOK
ENROLL	ENSEW	ENSNARING	ENTAILS	ENTETE
ENROLLED	ENSEWED	ENSNARL	ENTAME	ENTETEE
ENROLLEE	ENSEWING	ENSNARLED	ENTAMEBA	ENTHALPY
ENROLLEES	ENSEWS	ENSNARLS	ENTAMEBAE	ENTHETIC
ENROLLER	ENSHEATH	ENSORCEL	ENTAMEBAS	ENTHRAL
ENROLLERS	ENSHEATHE	ENSORCELL	ENTAMED	ENTHRALL
ENROLLING	ENSHEATHS	ENSORCELS	ENTAMES	ENTHRALLS
ENROLLS	ENSHELL	ENSOUL	ENTAMING	ENTHRALS
ENROLMENT	ENSHELLED	ENSOULED	ENTAMOEBA	ENTHRONE
ENROLS	ENSHELLS	ENSOULING	ENTANGLE	ENTHRONED
ENROOT	ENSHELTER	ENSOULS	ENTANGLED	ENTHRONES
ENROOTED	ENSHIELD	ENSPHERE	ENTANGLER	ENTHUSE
ENROOTING	ENSHIELDS	ENSPHERED	ENTANGLES	ENTHUSED
ENROOTS	ENSHRINE	ENSPHERES	ENTASES	ENTHUSES
ENROUGH	ENSHRINED	ENSTAMP	ENTASIA	ENTHUSING
ENROUGHED	ENSHRINEE	ENSTAMPED	ENTASIAS	ENTHYMEME
ENROUGHS	ENSHRINES	ENSTAMPS	ENTASIS	ENTIA
ENROUND	ENSHROUD	ENSTATITE	ENTASTIC	ENTICE
ENROUNDED	ENSHROUDS	ENSTEEP	ENTAYLE	ENTICED
ENROUNDS	ENSIFORM	ENSTEEPED	ENTAYLED	ENTICER
ENS	ENSIGN	ENSTEEPS	ENTAYLES	ENTICERS
ENSAMPLE	ENSIGNCY	ENSTYLE	ENTAYLING	ENTICES
ENSAMPLED	ENSIGNED	ENSTYLED	ENTELECHY	ENTICING
ENSAMPLES	ENSIGNING	ENSTYLES	ENTELLUS	ENTICINGS
ENSATE	ENSIGNS	ENSTYLING	ENTENDER	ENTIRE
ENSCONCE	ENSILAGE	ENSUE	ENTENDERS	ENTIRELY
ENSCONCED	ENSILAGED	ENSUED	ENTENTE	ENTIRES
ENSCONCES	ENSILAGES	ENSUES	ENTENTES	ENTIRETY
ENSCROLL	ENSILE	ENSUING	ENTER	ENTITIES
ENSCROLLS	ENSILED	ENSUITE	ENTERA	ENTITLE
ENSEAL	ENSILES	ENSUITES	ENTERABLE	ENTITLED
ENSEALED	ENSILING	ENSURE	ENTERAL	ENTITLES
ENSEALING	ENSKIED	ENSURED	ENTERALLY	ENTITLING
ENSEALS	ENSKIES	ENSURER	ENTERATE	ENTITY

ENTOBLAST	ENTRECHAT	ENURES	ENVOY	EOCENE
ENTODERM	ENTRECOTE	ENURESES	ENVOYS	EOHIPPUS
ENTODERMS	ENTREE	ENURESIS	ENVOYSHIP	EOLIAN
ENTOIL	ENTREES	ENURETIC	ENVY	EOLIENNE
ENTOILED	ENTREMES	ENURETICS	ENVYING	EOLIENNES
ENTOILING	ENTREMETS	ENURING	ENVYINGLY	EOLIPILE
ENTOILS	ENTRENCH	ENURN	ENVYINGS	EOLIPILES
ENTOMB	ENTREPOT	ENURNED	ENWALL	EOLITH
ENTOMBED	ENTREPOTS	ENURNING	ENWALLED	EOLITHIC
ENTOMBING	ENTRESOL	ENURNS	ENWALLING	EOLITHS
ENTOMBS	ENTRESOLS	ENVASSAL	ENWALLOW	EOLOPILE
ENTOMIC	ENTREZ	ENVASSALS	ENWALLOWS	EOLOPILES
ENTOPHYTE	ENTRIES	ENVAULT	ENWALLS	EON
ENTOPIC	ENTRISM	ENVAULTED	ENWHEEL	EONIAN
ENTOPROCT	ENTRISMS	ENVAULTS	ENWHEELED	EONISM
ENTOPTIC	ENTRIST	ENVEIGLE	ENWHEELS	EONISMS
ENTOPTICS	ENTRISTS	ENVEIGLED	ENWIND	EONS
ENTOTIC	ENTROLD	ENVEIGLES	ENWINDING	EORL
ENTOURAGE	ENTROPIC	ENVELOP	ENWINDS	EORLS
ENTOZOA	ENTROPIES	ENVELOPE	ENWOMB	EOSIN
ENTOZOAL	ENTROPION	ENVELOPED	ENWOMBED	EOSINE
ENTOZOAN	ENTROPIUM	ENVELOPER	ENWOMBING	EOSINES
ENTOZOANS	ENTROPY	ENVELOPES	ENWOMBS	EOSINIC
ENTOZOIC	ENTRUST	ENVELOPS	ENWOUND	EOSINS
ENTOZOON	ENTRUSTED	ENVENOM	ENWRAP	EOTHEN
ENTRAIL	ENTRUSTS	ENVENOMED	ENWRAPPED	EPACRID
ENTRAILED	ENTRY	ENVENOMS	ENWRAPS	EPACRIDS
ENTRAILS	ENTRYISM	ENVERMEIL	ENWRAPT	EPACRIS
ENTRAIN	ENTRYISMS	ENVIABLE	ENWREATH	EPACRISES
ENTRAINED	ENTRYIST	ENVIABLY	ENWREATHE	EPACT
ENTRAINER	ENTRYISTS	ENVIED	ENWREATHS	EPACTS
ENTRAINS	ENTRYWAY	ENVIER	ENZIAN	EPAENETIC
ENTRALL	ENTRYWAYS	ENVIERS	ENZIANS	EPAGOGE
ENTRALLES	ENTS	ENVIES	ENZONE	EPAGOGES
ENTRAMMEL	ENTWINE	ENVIOUS	ENZONED	EPAGOGIC
ENTRANCE	ENTWINED	ENVIOUSLY	ENZONES	EPANODOS
ENTRANCED	ENTWINES	ENVIRO	ENZONING	EPARCH
ENTRANCES	ENTWINING	ENVIRON	ENZOOTIC	EPARCHATE
ENTRANT	ENTWIST	ENVIRONED	ENZOOTICS	EPARCHIAL
ENTRANTS	ENTWISTED	ENVIRONS	ENZYM	EPARCHIES
ENTRAP	ENTWISTS	ENVIROS	ENZYMATIC	EPARCHS
ENTRAPPED	ENUCLEATE	ENVISAGE	ENZYME	EPARCHY
ENTRAPPER	ENUF	ENVISAGED	ENZYMES	EPATANT
ENTRAPS	ENUMERATE	ENVISAGES	ENZYMIC	EPATER
ENTREAT	ENUNCIATE	ENVISION	ENZYMS	EPATERED
ENTREATED	ENURE	ENVISIONS	EOAN	EPATERING
ENTREATS	ENURED	ENVOI	EOBIONT	EPATERS
ENTREATY	ENUREMENT	ENVOIS	EOBIONTS	EPAULE

EPAULES

EPAULES	EPHEMERID	EPICISTS	EPIGENIC	EPIMERISE
EPAULET	EPHEMERIS	EPICLESES	EPIGENIST	EPIMERISM
EPAULETED	EPHEMERON	EPICLESIS	EPIGENOME	EPIMERIZE
EPAULETS	EPHIALTES	EPICLIKE	EPIGENOUS	EPIMERS
EPAULETTE	EPHOD	EPICORMIC	EPIGEOUS	EPIMYSIA
EPAXIAL	EPHODS	EPICOTYL	EPIGON	EPIMYSIUM
EPAZOTE	EPHOR	EPICOTYLS	EPIGONE	EPINAOI
EPAZOTES	EPHORAL	EPICRANIA	EPIGONES	EPINAOS
EPEDAPHIC	EPHORALTY	EPICRISES	EPIGONI	EPINASTIC
EPEE	EPHORATE	EPICRISIS	EPIGONIC	EPINASTY
EPEEIST	EPHORATES	EPICRITIC	EPIGONISM	EPINEURAL
EPEEISTS	EPHORI	EPICS	EPIGONOUS	EPINEURIA
EPEES	EPHORS	EPICURE	EPIGONS	EPINICIAN
EPEIRA	EPIBIOSES	EPICUREAN	EPIGONUS	EPINICION
EPEIRAS	EPIBIOSIS	EPICURES	EPIGRAM	EPINIKIAN
EPEIRIC	EPIBIOTIC	EPICURISE	EPIGRAMS	EPINIKION
EPEIRID	EPIBLAST	EPICURISM	EPIGRAPH	EPINOSIC
EPEIRIDS	EPIBLASTS	EPICURIZE	EPIGRAPHS	EPIPHANIC
EPENDYMA	EPIBLEM	EPICYCLE	EPIGRAPHY	EPIPHANY
EPENDYMAL	EPIBLEMS	EPICYCLES	EPIGYNIES	EPIPHRAGM
EPENDYMAS	EPIBOLIC	EPICYCLIC	EPIGYNOUS	EPIPHYSES
EPEOLATRY	EPIBOLIES	EPIDEMIC	EPIGYNY	EPIPHYSIS
EPERDU	EPIBOLY	EPIDEMICS	EPILATE	EPIPHYTAL
EPERDUE	EPIC	EPIDERM	EPILATED	EPIPHYTE
EPERGNE	EPICAL	EPIDERMAL	EPILATES	EPIPHYTES
EPERGNES	EPICALLY	EPIDERMIC	EPILATING	EPIPHYTIC
EPHA	EPICALYX	EPIDERMIS	EPILATION	EPIPLOA
EPHAH	EPICANTHI	EPIDERMS	EPILATOR	EPIPLOIC
EPHAHS	EPICARDIA	EPIDICTIC	EPILATORS	EPIPLOON
EPHAS	EPICARP	EPIDOSITE	EPILEPSY	EPIPLOONS
EPHEBE	EPICARPS	EPIDOTE	EPILEPTIC	EPIPOLIC
EPHEBES	EPICEDE	EPIDOTES	EPILIMNIA	EPIPOLISM
EPHEBI	EPICEDES	EPIDOTIC	EPILITHIC	EPIROGENY
EPHEBIC	EPICEDIA	EPIDURAL	EPILOBIUM	EPIRRHEMA
EPHEBOI	EPICEDIAL	EPIDURALS	EPILOG	EPISCIA
EPHEBOS	EPICEDIAN	EPIFAUNA	EPILOGIC	EPISCIAS
EPHEBUS	EPICEDIUM	EPIFAUNAE	EPILOGISE	EPISCOPAL
EPHEDRA	EPICENE	EPIFAUNAL	EPILOGIST	EPISCOPE
EPHEDRAS	EPICENES	EPIFAUNAS	EPILOGIZE	EPISCOPES
EPHEDRIN	EPICENISM	EPIFOCAL	EPILOGS	EPISCOPY
EPHEDRINE	EPICENTER	EPIGAEAL	EPILOGUE	EPISEMON
EPHEDRINS	EPICENTRA	EPIGAEAN	EPILOGUED	EPISEMONS
EPHELIDES	EPICENTRE	EPIGAEOUS	EPILOGUES	EPISODAL
EPHELIS	EPICIER	EPIGAMIC	EPIMER	EPISODE
EPHEMERA	EPICIERS	EPIGEAL	EPIMERASE	EPISODES
EPHEMERAE	EPICISM	EPIGEAN	EPIMERE	EPISODIAL
EPHEMERAL	EPICISMS	EPIGEIC	EPIMERES	EPISODIC
EPHEMERAS	EPICIST	EPIGENE	EPIMERIC	EPISOMAL

EPISOME	EPITHET	EPOPT	EQUALIZE	EQUIPPERS
EPISOMES	EPITHETED	EPOPTS	EQUALIZED	EQUIPPING
EPISPERM	EPITHETIC	EPOS	EQUALIZER	EQUIPS
EPISPERMS	EPITHETON	EPOSES	EQUALIZES	EQUISETA
EPISPORE	EPITHETS	EPOXIDE	EQUALLED	EQUISETIC
EPISPORES	EPITOME	EPOXIDES	EQUALLING	EQUISETUM
EPISTASES	EPITOMES	EPOXIDISE	EQUALLY	EQUITABLE
EPISTASIS	EPITOMIC	EPOXIDIZE	EQUALNESS	EQUITABLY
EPISTASY	EPITOMISE	EPOXIED	EQUALS	EQUITANT
EPISTATIC	EPITOMIST	EPOXIES	EQUANT	EQUITES
EPISTAXES	EPITOMIZE	EPOXY	EQUANTS	EQUITIES
EPISTAXIS	EPITONIC	EPOXYED	EQUATABLE	EQUITY
EPISTEMIC	EPITOPE	EPOXYING	EQUATE	EQUIVALVE
EPISTERNA	EPITOPES	EPRIS	EQUATED	EQUIVOCAL
EPISTLE	EPITRITE	EPRISE	EQUATES	EQUIVOKE
EPISTLED	EPITRITES	EPSILON	EQUATING	EQUIVOKES
EPISTLER	EPIZEUXES	EPSILONIC	EQUATION	EQUIVOQUE
EPISTLERS	EPIZEUXIS	EPSILONS	EQUATIONS	ER
EPISTLES	EPIZOA	EPSOMITE	EQUATIVE	ERA
EPISTLING	EPIZOAN	EPSOMITES	EQUATOR	ERADIATE
EPISTOLER	EPIZOANS	EPUISE	EQUATORS	ERADIATED
EPISTOLET	EPIZOIC	EPUISEE	EQUERRIES	ERADIATES
EPISTOLIC	EPIZOISM	EPULARY	EQUERRY	ERADICANT
EPISTOME	EPIZOISMS	EPULATION	EQUES	ERADICATE
EPISTOMES	EPIZOITE	EPULIDES	EQUID	ERAS
EPISTYLE	EPIZOITES	EPULIS	EQUIDS	ERASABLE
EPISTYLES	EPIZOON	EPULISES	EQUIFINAL	ERASE
EPITAPH	EPIZOOTIC	EPULOTIC	EQUIMOLAL	ERASED
EPITAPHED	EPIZOOTY	EPULOTICS	EQUIMOLAR	ERASEMENT
EPITAPHER	EPOCH	EPURATE	EQUINAL	ERASER
EPITAPHIC	EPOCHA	EPURATED	EQUINE	ERASERS
EPITAPHS	EPOCHAL	EPURATES	EQUINELY	ERASES
EPITASES	EPOCHALLY	EPURATING	EQUINES	ERASING
EPITASIS	EPOCHAS	EPURATION	EQUINIA	ERASION
EPITAXES	EPOCHS	EPYLLIA	EQUINIAS	ERASIONS
EPITAXIAL	EPODE	EPYLLION	EQUINITY	ERASURE
EPITAXIC	EPODES	EPYLLIONS	EQUINOX	ERASURES
EPITAXIES	EPODIC	EQUABLE	EQUINOXES	ERATHEM
EPITAXIS	EPONYM	EQUABLY	EQUIP	ERATHEMS
EPITAXY	EPONYMIC	EQUAL	EQUIPAGE	ERBIA
EPITHECA	EPONYMIES	EQUALED	EQUIPAGED	ERBIAS
EPITHECAE	EPONYMOUS	EQUALI	EQUIPAGES	ERBIUM
EPITHELIA	EPONYMS	EQUALING	EQUIPE	ERBIUMS
EPITHEM	EPONYMY	EQUALISE	EQUIPES	ERE
EPITHEMA	EPOPEE	EQUALISED	EQUIPMENT	ERECT
EPITHEMS	EPOPEES	EQUALISER	EQUIPOISE	ERECTABLE
EPITHESES	EPOPOEIA	EQUALISES	EQUIPPED	ERECTED
EPITHESIS	EPOPOEIAS	EQUALITY	EQUIPPER	ERECTER

ERECTERS

ERECTERS	ERGOGRAMS	ERISTICS	EROTETIC	ERRORS
ERECTILE	ERGOGRAPH	ERK	EROTIC	ERRS
ERECTING	ERGOMANIA	ERKS	EROTICA	ERS
ERECTION	ERGOMETER	ERLANG	EROTICAL	ERSATZ
ERECTIONS	ERGOMETRY	ERLANGS	EROTICAS	ERSATZES
ERECTIVE	ERGON	ERLKING	EROTICISE	ERSES
ERECTLY	ERGONOMIC	ERLKINGS	EROTICISM	ERST
ERECTNESS	ERGONS	ERM	EROTICIST	ERSTWHILE
ERECTOR	ERGOS	ERMELIN	EROTICIZE	ERUCIC
ERECTORS	ERGOT	ERMELINS	EROTICS	ERUCIFORM
ERECTS	ERGOTIC	ERMINE	EROTISE	ERUCT
ERED	ERGOTISE	ERMINED	EROTISED	ERUCTATE
ERELONG	ERGOTISED	ERMINES	EROTISES	ERUCTATED
EREMIC	ERGOTISES	ERN	EROTISING	ERUCTATES
EREMITAL	ERGOTISM	ERNE	EROTISM	ERUCTED
EREMITE	ERGOTISMS	ERNED	EROTISMS	ERUCTING
EREMITES	ERGOTIZE	ERNES	EROTIZE	ERUCTS
EREMITIC	ERGOTIZED	ERNING	EROTIZED	ERUDITE
EREMITISH	ERGOTIZES	ERNS	EROTIZES	ERUDITELY
EREMITISM	ERGOTS	ERODABLE	EROTIZING	ERUDITES
EREMURI	ERGS	ERODE	EROTOLOGY	ERUDITION
EREMURUS	ERHU	ERODED	ERR	ERUGO
ERENOW	ERHUS	ERODENT	ERRABLE	ERUGOS
EREPSIN	ERIACH	ERODENTS	ERRANCIES	ERUMPENT
EREPSINS	ERIACHS	ERODES	ERRANCY	ERUPT
ERES	ERIC	ERODIBLE	ERRAND	ERUPTED
ERETHIC	ERICA	ERODING	ERRANDS	ERUPTIBLE
ERETHISM	ERICAS	ERODIUM	ERRANT	ERUPTING
ERETHISMS	ERICK	ERODIUMS	ERRANTLY	ERUPTION
ERETHITIC	ERICKS	EROGENIC	ERRANTRY	ERUPTIONS
EREV	ERICOID	EROGENOUS	ERRANTS	ERUPTIVE
EREVS	ERICS	EROS	ERRATA	ERUPTIVES
EREWHILE	ERIGERON	EROSE	ERRATAS	ERUPTS
EREWHILES	ERIGERONS	EROSELY	ERRATIC	ERUV
ERF	ERING	EROSES	ERRATICAL	ERUVIM
ERG	ERINGO	EROSIBLE	ERRATICS	ERUVIN
ERGASTIC	ERINGOES	EROSION	ERRATUM	ERUVS
ERGATANER	ERINGOS	EROSIONAL	ERRED	ERVALENTA
ERGATE	ERINITE	EROSIONS	ERRHINE	ERVEN
ERGATES	ERINITES	EROSIVE	ERRHINES	ERVIL
ERGATIVE	ERINUS	EROSIVITY	ERRING	ERVILS
ERGATIVES	ERINUSES	EROSTRATE	ERRINGLY	ERYNGIUM
ERGATOID	ERIOMETER	EROTEMA	ERRINGS	ERYNGIUMS
ERGATOIDS	ERIONITE	EROTEMAS	ERRONEOUS	ERYNGO
ERGO	ERIONITES	EROTEME	ERROR	ERYNGOES
ERGODIC	ERIOPHYID	EROTEMES	ERRORIST	ERYNGOS
ERGOGENIC	ERISTIC	EROTESES	ERRORISTS	ERYTHEMA
ERGOGRAM	ERISTICAL	EROTESIS	ERRORLESS	ERYTHEMAL

ERYTHEMAS	ESCAROLE	ESCROLS	ESPALIERS	ESSAYISH
ERYTHEMIC	ESCAROLES	ESCROW	ESPANOL	ESSAYIST
ERYTHRINA	ESCARP	ESCROWED	ESPANOLES	ESSAYISTS
ERYTHRISM	ESCARPED	ESCROWING	ESPARTO	ESSAYS
ERYTHRITE	ESCARPING	ESCROWS	ESPARTOS	ESSE
ERYTHROID	ESCARPS	ESCUAGE	ESPECIAL	ESSENCE
ERYTHRON	ESCARS	ESCUAGES	ESPERANCE	ESSENCES
ERYTHRONS	ESCHALOT	ESCUDO	ESPIAL	ESSENTIAL
ES	ESCHALOTS	ESCUDOS	ESPIALS	ESSES
ESCABECHE	ESCHAR	ESCULENT	ESPIED	ESSIVE
ESCALADE	ESCHARS	ESCULENTS	ESPIEGLE	ESSIVES
ESCALADED	ESCHEAT	ESEMPLASY	ESPIER	ESSOIN
ESCALADER	ESCHEATED	ESERINE	ESPIERS	ESSOINED
ESCALADES	ESCHEATOR	ESERINES	ESPIES	ESSOINER
ESCALADO	ESCHEATS	ESES	ESPIONAGE	ESSOINERS
ESCALATE	ESCHEW	ESILE	ESPLANADE	ESSOINING
ESCALATED	ESCHEWAL	ESILES	ESPOIR	ESSOINS
ESCALATES	ESCHEWALS	ESKAR	ESPOIRS	ESSONITE
ESCALATOR	ESCHEWED	ESKARS	ESPOUSAL	ESSONITES
ESCALIER	ESCHEWER	ESKER	ESPOUSALS	ESSOYNE
ESCALIERS	ESCHEWERS	ESKERS	ESPOUSE	ESSOYNES
ESCALLOP	ESCHEWING	ESKIES	ESPOUSED	EST
ESCALLOPS	ESCHEWS	ESKY	ESPOUSER	ESTABLISH
ESCALOP	ESCLANDRE	ESLOIN	ESPOUSERS	ESTACADE
ESCALOPE	ESCOLAR	ESLOINED	ESPOUSES	ESTACADES
ESCALOPED	ESCOLARS	ESLOINING	ESPOUSING	ESTAFETTE
ESCALOPES	ESCOPETTE	ESLOINS	ESPRESSO	ESTAMINET
ESCALOPS	ESCORT	ESLOYNE	ESPRESSOS	ESTANCIA
ESCAPABLE	ESCORTAGE	ESLOYNED	ESPRIT	ESTANCIAS
ESCAPADE	ESCORTED	ESLOYNES	ESPRITS	ESTATE
ESCAPADES	ESCORTING	ESLOYNING	ESPUMOSO	ESTATED
ESCAPADO	ESCORTS	ESNE	ESPUMOSOS	ESTATES
ESCAPADOS	ESCOT	ESNECIES	ESPY	ESTATING
ESCAPE	ESCOTED	ESNECY	ESPYING	ESTEEM
ESCAPED	ESCOTING	ESNES	ESQUIRE	ESTEEMED
ESCAPEE	ESCOTS	ESOPHAGI	ESQUIRED	ESTEEMING
ESCAPEES	ESCOTTED	ESOPHAGUS	ESQUIRES	ESTEEMS
ESCAPER	ESCOTTING	ESOTERIC	ESQUIRESS	ESTER
ESCAPERS	ESCRIBANO	ESOTERICA	ESQUIRING	ESTERASE
ESCAPES	ESCRIBE	ESOTERIES	ESQUISSE	ESTERASES
ESCAPING	ESCRIBED	ESOTERISM	ESQUISSES	ESTERIFY
ESCAPISM	ESCRIBES	ESOTERY	ESS	ESTERS
ESCAPISMS	ESCRIBING	ESOTROPIA	ESSAY	ESTHESES
ESCAPIST	ESCROC	ESOTROPIC	ESSAYED	ESTHESIA
ESCAPISTS	ESCROCS	ESPADA	ESSAYER	ESTHESIAS
ESCAR	ESCROL	ESPADAS	ESSAYERS	ESTHESIS
ESCARGOT	ESCROLL	ESPAGNOLE	ESSAYETTE	ESTHETE
ESCARGOTS	ESCROLLS	ESPALIER	ESSAYING	ESTHETES

ESTHETIC	ESTRICH	ETAPE	ETHANOLS	ETHICIZES
ESTHETICS	ESTRICHES	ETAPES	ETHANOYL	ETHICS
ESTIMABLE	ESTRIDGE	ETAS	ETHANOYLS	ETHINYL
ESTIMABLY	ESTRIDGES	ETAT	ETHE	ETHINYLS
ESTIMATE	ESTRILDID	ETATISM	ETHENE	ETHION
ESTIMATED	ESTRIN	ETATISME	ETHENES	ETHIONINE
ESTIMATES	ESTRINS	ETATISMES	ETHEPHON	ETHIONS
ESTIMATOR	ESTRIOL	ETATISMS	ETHEPHONS	ETHIOPS
ESTIVAL	ESTRIOLS	ETATIST	ETHER	ETHIOPSES
ESTIVATE	ESTRO	ETATISTE	ETHERCAP	ETHMOID
ESTIVATED	ESTROGEN	ETATISTES	ETHERCAPS	ETHMOIDAL
ESTIVATES	ESTROGENS	ETATS	ETHEREAL	ETHMOIDS
ESTIVATOR	ESTRONE	ETCETERA	ETHEREOUS	ETHNARCH
ESTOC	ESTRONES	ETCETERAS	ETHERIAL	ETHNARCHS
ESTOCS	ESTROS	ETCH	ETHERIC	ETHNARCHY
ESTOILE	ESTROUS	ETCHANT	ETHERICAL	ETHNE
ESTOILES	ESTRUAL	ETCHANTS	ETHERIFY	ETHNIC
ESTOP	ESTRUM	ETCHED	ETHERION	ETHNICAL
ESTOPPAGE	ESTRUMS	ETCHER	ETHERIONS	ETHNICISM
ESTOPPED	ESTRUS	ETCHERS	ETHERISE	ETHNICITY
ESTOPPEL	ESTRUSES	ETCHES	ETHERISED	ETHNICS
ESTOPPELS	ESTS	ETCHING	ETHERISER	ETHNOCIDE
ESTOPPING	ESTUARIAL	ETCHINGS	ETHERISES	ETHNOGENY
ESTOPS	ESTUARIAN	ETEN	ETHERISH	ETHNOLOGY
ESTOVER	ESTUARIES	ETENS	ETHERISM	ETHNONYM
ESTOVERS	ESTUARINE	ETERNAL	ETHERISMS	ETHNONYMS
ESTRADE	ESTUARY	ETERNALLY	ETHERIST	ETHNOS
ESTRADES	ESURIENCE	ETERNALS	ETHERISTS	ETHNOSES
ESTRADIOL	ESURIENCY	ETERNE	ETHERIZE	ETHOGRAM
ESTRAGON	ESURIENT	ETERNISE	ETHERIZED	ETHOGRAMS
ESTRAGONS	ET	ETERNISED	ETHERIZER	ETHOLOGIC
ESTRAL	ETA	ETERNISES	ETHERIZES	ETHOLOGY
ESTRANGE	ETACISM	ETERNITY	ETHERS	ETHONONE
ESTRANGED	ETACISMS	ETERNIZE	ETHIC	ETHONONES
ESTRANGER	ETAERIO	ETERNIZED	ETHICAL	ETHOS
ESTRANGES	ETAERIOS	ETERNIZES	ETHICALLY	ETHOSES
ESTRAPADE	ETAGE	ETESIAN	ETHICALS	ETHOXIDE
ESTRAY	ETAGERE	ETESIANS	ETHICIAN	ETHOXIDES
ESTRAYED	ETAGERES	ETH	ETHICIANS	ETHOXIES
ESTRAYING	ETAGES	ETHAL	ETHICISE	ETHOXY
ESTRAYS	ETALAGE	ETHALS	ETHICISED	ETHOXYL
ESTREAT	ETALAGES	ETHANAL	ETHICISES	ETHOXYLS
ESTREATED	ETALON	ETHANALS	ETHICISM	ETHS
ESTREATS	ETALONS	ETHANE	ETHICISMS	ETHYL
ESTREPE	ETAMIN	ETHANES	ETHICIST	ETHYLATE
ESTREPED	ETAMINE	ETHANOATE	ETHICISTS	ETHYLATED
ESTREPES	ETAMINES	ETHANOIC	ETHICIZE	ETHYLATES
ESTREPING	ETAMINS	ETHANOL	ETHICIZED	ETHYLENE

ETHYLENES	ETYMIC	EUGENIA	EULOGY	EUPHONY
ETHYLENIC	ETYMOLOGY	EUGENIAS	EUMELANIN	EUPHORBIA
ETHYLIC	ETYMON	EUGENIC	EUMERISM	EUPHORIA
ETHYLS	ETYMONS	EUGENICAL	EUMERISMS	EUPHORIAS
ETHYNE	ETYPIC	EUGENICS	EUMONG	EUPHORIC
ETHYNES	ETYPICAL	EUGENISM	EUMONGS	EUPHORIES
ETHYNYL	EUCAIN	EUGENISMS	EUMUNG	EUPHORY
ETHYNYLS	EUCAINE	EUGENIST	EUMUNGS	EUPHOTIC
ETIC	EUCAINES	EUGENISTS	EUNUCH	EUPHRASIA
ETICS	EUCAINS	EUGENOL	EUNUCHISE	EUPHRASY
ETIOLATE	EUCALYPT	EUGENOLS	EUNUCHISM	EUPHROE
ETIOLATED	EUCALYPTI	EUGH	EUNUCHIZE	EUPHROES
ETIOLATES	EUCALYPTS	EUGHEN	EUNUCHOID	EUPHUISE
ETIOLIN	EUCARYON	EUGHS	EUNUCHS	EUPHUISED
ETIOLINS	EUCARYONS	EUGLENA	EUOI	EUPHUISES
ETIOLOGIC	EUCARYOT	EUGLENAS	EUONYMIN	EUPHUISM
ETIOLOGY	EUCARYOTE	EUGLENID	EUONYMINS	EUPHUISMS
ETIQUETTE	EUCARYOTS	EUGLENIDS	EUONYMUS	EUPHUIST
ETNA	EUCHARIS	EUGLENOID	EUOUAE	EUPHUISTS
ETNAS	EUCHLORIC	EUK	EUOUAES	EUPHUIZE
ETOILE	EUCHLORIN	EUKARYON	EUPAD	EUPHUIZED
ETOILES	EUCHOLOGY	EUKARYONS	EUPADS	EUPHUIZES
ETOUFFEE	EUCHRE	EUKARYOT	EUPATRID	EUPLASTIC
ETOUFFEES	EUCHRED	EUKARYOTE	EUPATRIDS	EUPLOID
ETOURDI	EUCHRES	EUKARYOTS	EUPEPSIA	EUPLOIDS
ETOURDIE	EUCHRING	EUKED	EUPEPSIAS	EUPLOIDY
ETRANGER	EUCLASE	EUKING	EUPEPSIES	EUPNEA
ETRANGERE	EUCLASES	EUKS	EUPEPSY	EUPNEAS
ETRANGERS	EUCLIDEAN	EULACHAN	EUPEPTIC	EUPNEIC
ETRENNE	EUCLIDIAN	EULACHANS	EUPHAUSID	EUPNOEA
ETRENNES	EUCRITE	EULACHON	EUPHEMISE	EUPNOEAS
ETRIER	EUCRITES	EULACHONS	EUPHEMISM	EUPNOEIC
ETRIERS	EUCRITIC	EULOGIA	EUPHEMIST	EUREKA
ETTERCAP	EUCRYPHIA	EULOGIAE	EUPHEMIZE	EUREKAS
ETTERCAPS	EUCYCLIC	EULOGIAS	EUPHENIC	EURHYTHMY
ETTIN	EUDAEMON	EULOGIES	EUPHENICS	EURIPI
ETTINS	EUDAEMONS	EULOGISE	EUPHOBIA	EURIPUS
ETTLE	EUDAEMONY	EULOGISED	EUPHOBIAS	EURIPUSES
ETTLED	EUDAIMON	EULOGISER	EUPHON	EURO
ETTLES	EUDAIMONS	EULOGISES	EUPHONIA	EUROBOND
ETTLING	EUDEMON	EULOGIST	EUPHONIAS	EUROBONDS
ETUDE	EUDEMONIA	EULOGISTS	EUPHONIC	EUROCRAT
ETUDES	EUDEMONIC	EULOGIUM	EUPHONIES	EUROCRATS
ETUI	EUDEMONS	EULOGIUMS	EUPHONISE	EUROCREEP
ETUIS	EUDIALYTE	EULOGIZE	EUPHONISM	EUROKIES
ETWEE	EUGARIE	EULOGIZED	EUPHONIUM	EUROKOUS
ETWEES	EUGARIES	EULOGIZER	EUPHONIZE	EUROKY
ETYMA	EUGE	EULOGIZES	EUPHONS	EUROLAND

EUROLANDS	EUTHANISE	EVANISH	EVERGLADE	EVILDOING
EURONOTE	EUTHANIZE	EVANISHED	EVERGREEN	EVILER
EURONOTES	EUTHENICS	EVANISHES	EVERMORE	EVILEST
EUROPHILE	EUTHENIST	EVANITION	EVERNET	EVILLER
EUROPIUM	EUTHERIAN	EVAPORATE	EVERNETS	EVILLEST
EUROPIUMS	EUTHYMIA	EVAPORITE	EVERSIBLE	EVILLY
EUROPOP	EUTHYMIAS	EVASIBLE	EVERSION	EVILNESS
EUROPOPS	EUTHYROID	EVASION	EVERSIONS	EVILS
EUROS	EUTRAPELY	EVASIONAL	EVERT	EVINCE
EUROZONE	EUTROPHIC	EVASIONS	EVERTED	EVINCED
EUROZONES	EUTROPHY	EVASIVE	EVERTING	EVINCES
EURYBATH	EUTROPIC	EVASIVELY	EVERTOR	EVINCIBLE
EURYBATHS	EUTROPIES	EVE	EVERTORS	EVINCIBLY
EURYOKIES	EUTROPOUS	EVECTION	EVERTS	EVINCING
EURYOKOUS	EUTROPY	EVECTIONS	EVERWHERE	EVINCIVE
EURYOKY	EUXENITE	EVEJAR	EVERWHICH	EVIRATE
EURYTHERM	EUXENITES	EVEJARS	EVERY	EVIRATED
EURYTHMIC	EVACUANT	EVEN	EVERYBODY	EVIRATES
EURYTHMY	EVACUANTS	EVENED	EVERYDAY	EVIRATING
EURYTOPIC	EVACUATE	EVENEMENT	EVERYDAYS	EVITABLE
EUSOCIAL	EVACUATED	EVENER	EVERYMAN	EVITATE
EUSOL	EVACUATES	EVENERS	EVERYMEN	EVITATED
EUSOLS	EVACUATOR	EVENEST	EVERYONE	EVITATES
EUSTACIES	EVACUEE	EVENFALL	EVERYWAY	EVITATING
EUSTACY	EVACUEES	EVENFALLS	EVERYWHEN	EVITATION
EUSTASIES	EVADABLE	EVENING	EVES	EVITE
EUSTASY	EVADE	EVENINGS	EVET	EVITED
EUSTATIC	EVADED	EVENLY	EVETS	EVITERNAL
EUSTELE	EVADER	EVENNESS	EVHOE	EVITES
EUSTELES	EVADERS	EVENS	EVICT	EVITING
EUSTRESS	EVADES	EVENSONG	EVICTED	EVO
EUSTYLE	EVADIBLE	EVENSONGS	EVICTEE	EVOCABLE
EUSTYLES	EVADING	EVENT	EVICTEES	EVOCATE
EUTAXIA	EVADINGLY	EVENTED	EVICTING	EVOCATED
EUTAXIAS	EVAGATION	EVENTER	EVICTION	EVOCATES
EUTAXIES	EVAGINATE	EVENTERS	EVICTIONS	EVOCATING
EUTAXITE	EVALUABLE	EVENTFUL	EVICTOR	EVOCATION
EUTAXITES	EVALUATE	EVENTIDE	EVICTORS	EVOCATIVE
EUTAXITIC	EVALUATED	EVENTIDES	EVICTS	EVOCATOR
EUTAXY	EVALUATES	EVENTING	EVIDENCE	EVOCATORS
EUTECTIC	EVALUATOR	EVENTINGS	EVIDENCED	EVOCATORY
EUTECTICS	EVANESCE	EVENTIVE	EVIDENCES	EVOE
EUTECTOID	EVANESCED	EVENTLESS	EVIDENT	EVOHE
EUTEXIA	EVANESCES	EVENTRATE	EVIDENTLY	EVOKE
EUTEXIAS	EVANGEL	EVENTS	EVIDENTS	EVOKED
EUTHANASE	EVANGELIC	EVENTUAL	EVIL	EVOKER
EUTHANASY	EVANGELS	EVENTUATE	EVILDOER	EVOKERS
EUTHANAZE	EVANGELY	EVER	EVILDOERS	EVOKES

EVOKING	EX	EXAMPLE	EXCEPTING	EXCITE
EVOLUE	EXABYTE	EXAMPLED	EXCEPTION	EXCITED
EVOLUES	EXABYTES	EXAMPLES	EXCEPTIVE	EXCITEDLY
EVOLUTE	EXACT	EXAMPLING	EXCEPTOR	EXCITER
EVOLUTED	EXACTA	EXAMS	EXCEPTORS	EXCITERS
EVOLUTES	EXACTABLE	EXANIMATE	EXCEPTS	EXCITES
EVOLUTING	EXACTAS	EXANTHEM	EXCERPT	EXCITING
EVOLUTION	EXACTED	EXANTHEMA	EXCERPTA	EXCITON
EVOLUTIVE	EXACTER	EXANTHEMS	EXCERPTED	EXCITONIC
EVOLVABLE	EXACTERS	EXAPTED	EXCERPTER	EXCITONS
EVOLVE	EXACTEST	EXAPTIVE	EXCERPTOR	EXCITOR
EVOLVED	EXACTING	EXARATE	EXCERPTS	EXCITORS
EVOLVENT	EXACTION	EXARATION	EXCERPTUM	EXCLAIM
EVOLVENTS	EXACTIONS	EXARCH	EXCESS	EXCLAIMED
EVOLVER	EXACTLY	EXARCHAL	EXCESSED	EXCLAIMER
EVOLVERS	EXACTMENT	EXARCHATE	EXCESSES	EXCLAIMS
EVOLVES	EXACTNESS	EXARCHIES	EXCESSING	EXCLAVE
EVOLVING	EXACTOR	EXARCHIST	EXCESSIVE	EXCLAVES
EVONYMUS	EXACTORS	EXARCHS	EXCHANGE	EXCLOSURE
EVOS	EXACTRESS	EXARCHY	EXCHANGED	EXCLUDE
EVOVAE	EXACTS	EXCAMB	EXCHANGER	EXCLUDED
EVOVAES	EXACUM	EXCAMBED	EXCHANGES	EXCLUDEE
EVULGATE	EXACUMS	EXCAMBING	EXCHEAT	EXCLUDEES
EVULGATED	EXAHERTZ	EXCAMBION	EXCHEATS	EXCLUDER
EVULGATES	EXALT	EXCAMBIUM	EXCHEQUER	EXCLUDERS
EVULSE	EXALTED	EXCAMBS	EXCIDE	EXCLUDES
EVULSED	EXALTEDLY	EXCARNATE	EXCIDED	EXCLUDING
EVULSES	EXALTER	EXCAUDATE	EXCIDES	EXCLUSION
EVULSING	EXALTERS	EXCAVATE	EXCIDING	EXCLUSIVE
EVULSION	EXALTING	EXCAVATED	EXCIMER	EXCLUSORY
EVULSIONS	EXALTS	EXCAVATES	EXCIMERS	EXCORIATE
EVZONE	EXAM	EXCAVATOR	EXCIPIENT	EXCREMENT
EVZONES	EXAMEN	EXCEED	EXCIPLE	EXCRETA
EW	EXAMENS	EXCEEDED	EXCIPLES	EXCRETAL
EWE	EXAMETRE	EXCEEDER	EXCISABLE	EXCRETE
EWER	EXAMETRES	EXCEEDERS	EXCISE	EXCRETED
EWERS	EXAMINANT	EXCEEDING	EXCISED	EXCRETER
EWES	EXAMINATE	EXCEEDS	EXCISEMAN	EXCRETERS
EWEST	EXAMINE	EXCEL	EXCISEMEN	EXCRETES
EWFTES	EXAMINED	EXCELLED	EXCISES	EXCRETING
EWGHEN	EXAMINEE	EXCELLENT	EXCISING	EXCRETION
EWHOW	EXAMINEES	EXCELLING	EXCISION	EXCRETIVE
EWK	EXAMINER	EXCELS	EXCISIONS	EXCRETORY
EWKED	EXAMINERS	EXCELSIOR	EXCITABLE	EXCUBANT
EWKING	EXAMINES	EXCENTRIC	EXCITABLY	EXCUDIT
EWKS	EXAMINING	EXCEPT	EXCITANCY	EXCULPATE
EWT	EXAMPLAR	EXCEPTANT	EXCITANT	EXCURRENT
EWTS	EXAMPLARS	EXCEPTED	EXCITANTS	EXCURSE

EXCURSED	EXEEMING	EXERTS	EXIGENCES	EXODERMAL
EXCURSES	EXEEMS	EXES	EXIGENCY	EXODERMIS
EXCURSING	EXEGESES	EXEUNT	EXIGENT	EXODERMS
EXCURSION	EXEGESIS	EXFIL	EXIGENTLY	EXODES
EXCURSIVE	EXEGETE	EXFILLED	EXIGENTS	EXODIC
EXCURSUS	EXEGETES	EXFILLING	EXIGIBLE	EXODIST
EXCUSABLE	EXEGETIC	EXFILS	EXIGUITY	EXODISTS
EXCUSABLY	EXEGETICS	EXFOLIANT	EXIGUOUS	EXODOI
EXCUSAL	EXEGETIST	EXFOLIATE	EXILABLE	EXODONTIA
EXCUSALS	EXEME	EXHALABLE	EXILE	EXODOS
EXCUSE	EXEMED	EXHALANT	EXILED	EXODUS
EXCUSED	EXEMES	EXHALANTS	EXILEMENT	EXODUSES
EXCUSER	EXEMING	EXHALE	EXILER	EXOENZYME
EXCUSERS	EXEMPLA	EXHALED	EXILERS	EXOERGIC
EXCUSES	EXEMPLAR	EXHALENT	EXILES	EXOGAMIC
EXCUSING	EXEMPLARS	EXHALENTS	EXILIAN	EXOGAMIES
EXCUSIVE	EXEMPLARY	EXHALES	EXILIC	EXOGAMOUS
EXEAT	EXEMPLE	EXHALING	EXILING	EXOGAMY
EXEATS	EXEMPLES	EXHAUST	EXILITIES	EXOGEN
EXEC	EXEMPLIFY	EXHAUSTED	EXILITY	EXOGENIC
EXECRABLE	EXEMPLUM	EXHAUSTER	EXIMIOUS	EXOGENISM
EXECRABLY	EXEMPT	EXHAUSTS	EXINE	EXOGENOUS
EXECRATE	EXEMPTED	EXHEDRA	EXINES	EXOGENS
EXECRATED	EXEMPTING	EXHEDRAE	EXING	EXOME
EXECRATES	EXEMPTION	EXHIBIT	EXIST	EXOMES
EXECRATOR	EXEMPTIVE	EXHIBITED	EXISTED	EXOMION
EXECS	EXEMPTS	EXHIBITER	EXISTENCE	EXOMIONS
EXECUTANT	EXEQUATUR	EXHIBITOR	EXISTENT	EXOMIS
EXECUTARY	EXEQUIAL	EXHIBITS	EXISTENTS	EXOMISES
EXECUTE	EXEQUIES	EXHORT	EXISTING	EXON
EXECUTED	EXEQUY	EXHORTED	EXISTS	EXONERATE
EXECUTER	EXERCISE	EXHORTER	EXIT	EXONEREE
EXECUTERS	EXERCISED	EXHORTERS	EXITANCE	EXONEREES
EXECUTES	EXERCISER	EXHORTING	EXITANCES	EXONIC
EXECUTING	EXERCISES	EXHORTS	EXITED	EXONS
EXECUTION	EXERCYCLE	EXHUMATE	EXITING	EXONUMIA
EXECUTIVE	EXERGIES	EXHUMATED	EXITLESS	EXONUMIST
EXECUTOR	EXERGONIC	EXHUMATES	EXITS	EXONYM
EXECUTORS	EXERGUAL	EXHUME	EXO	EXONYMS
EXECUTORY	EXERGUE	EXHUMED	EXOCARP	EXOPHAGY
EXECUTRIX	EXERGUES	EXHUMER	EXOCARPS	EXOPHORIC
EXECUTRY	EXERGY	EXHUMERS	EXOCRINE	EXOPLANET
EXED	EXERT	EXHUMES	EXOCRINES	EXOPLASM
EXEDRA	EXERTED	EXHUMING	EXOCYCLIC	EXOPLASMS
EXEDRAE	EXERTING	EXIES	EXOCYTIC	EXOPOD
EXEDRAS	EXERTION	EXIGEANT	EXOCYTOSE	EXOPODITE
EXEEM	EXERTIONS	EXIGEANTE	EXODE	EXOPODS
EXEEMED	EXERTIVE	EXIGENCE	EXODERM	EXORABLE

EXORATION	EXPANDING	EXPERTING	EXPLOITS	EXPRESSOS
EXORCISE	EXPANDOR	EXPERTISE	EXPLORE	EXPUGN
EXORCISED	EXPANDORS	EXPERTISM	EXPLORED	EXPUGNED
EXORCISER	EXPANDS	EXPERTIZE	EXPLORER	EXPUGNING
EXORCISES	EXPANSE	EXPERTLY	EXPLORERS	EXPUGNS
EXORCISM	EXPANSES	EXPERTS	EXPLORES	EXPULSE
EXORCISMS	EXPANSILE	EXPIABLE	EXPLORING	EXPULSED
EXORCIST	EXPANSION	EXPIATE	EXPLOSION	EXPULSES
EXORCISTS	EXPANSIVE	EXPIATED	EXPLOSIVE	EXPULSING
EXORCIZE	EXPAT	EXPIATES	EXPO	EXPULSION
EXORCIZED	EXPATIATE	EXPIATING	EXPONENT	EXPULSIVE
EXORCIZER	EXPATS	EXPIATION	EXPONENTS	EXPUNCT
EXORCIZES	EXPECT	EXPIATOR	EXPONIBLE	EXPUNCTED
EXORDIA	EXPECTANT	EXPIATORS	EXPORT	EXPUNCTS
EXORDIAL	EXPECTED	EXPIATORY	EXPORTED	EXPUNGE
EXORDIUM	EXPECTER	EXPIRABLE	EXPORTER	EXPUNGED
EXORDIUMS	EXPECTERS	EXPIRANT	EXPORTERS	EXPUNGER
EXOSMIC	EXPECTING	EXPIRANTS	EXPORTING	EXPUNGERS
EXOSMOSE	EXPECTS	EXPIRE	EXPORTS	EXPUNGES
EXOSMOSES	EXPEDIENT	EXPIRED	EXPOS	EXPUNGING
EXOSMOSIS	EXPEDITE	EXPIRER	EXPOSABLE	EXPURGATE
EXOSMOTIC	EXPEDITED	EXPIRERS	EXPOSAL	EXPURGE
EXOSPHERE	EXPEDITER	EXPIRES	EXPOSALS	EXPURGED
EXOSPORAL	EXPEDITES	EXPIRIES	EXPOSE	EXPURGES
EXOSPORE	EXPEDITOR	EXPIRING	EXPOSED	EXPURGING
EXOSPORES	EXPEL	EXPIRY	EXPOSER	EXQUISITE
EXOSPORIA	EXPELLANT	EXPISCATE	EXPOSERS	EXSCIND
EXOSTOSES	EXPELLED	EXPLAIN	EXPOSES	EXSCINDED
EXOSTOSIS	EXPELLEE	EXPLAINED	EXPOSING	EXSCINDS
EXOTERIC	EXPELLEES	EXPLAINER	EXPOSIT	EXSECANT
EXOTIC	EXPELLENT	EXPLAINS	EXPOSITED	EXSECANTS
EXOTICA	EXPELLER	EXPLANT	EXPOSITOR	EXSECT
EXOTICISE	EXPELLERS	EXPLANTED	EXPOSITS	EXSECTED
EXOTICISM	EXPELLING	EXPLANTS	EXPOSOME	EXSECTING
EXOTICIST	EXPELS	EXPLETIVE	EXPOSOMES	EXSECTION
EXOTICIZE	EXPEND	EXPLETORY	EXPOSTURE	EXSECTS
EXOTICS	EXPENDED	EXPLICATE	EXPOSURE	EXSERT
EXOTISM	EXPENDER	EXPLICIT	EXPOSURES	EXSERTED
EXOTISMS	EXPENDERS	EXPLICITS	EXPOUND	EXSERTILE
EXOTOXIC	EXPENDING	EXPLODE	EXPOUNDED	EXSERTING
EXOTOXIN	EXPENDS	EXPLODED	EXPOUNDER	EXSERTION
EXOTOXINS	EXPENSE	EXPLODER	EXPOUNDS	EXSERTS
EXOTROPIA	EXPENSED	EXPLODERS	EXPRESS	EXSICCANT
EXOTROPIC	EXPENSES	EXPLODES	EXPRESSED	EXSICCATE
EXPAND	EXPENSING	EXPLODING	EXPRESSER	EXSTROPHY
EXPANDED	EXPENSIVE	EXPLOIT	EXPRESSES	EXSUCCOUS
EXPANDER	EXPERT	EXPLOITED	EXPRESSLY	EXTANT
EXPANDERS	EXPERTED	EXPLOITER	EXPRESSO	EXTASIES

EXTASY	EXTOLLING	EXTROPIAN	EXUVIATE	EYELASH
EXTATIC	EXTOLLS	EXTROPIES	EXUVIATED	EYELASHES
EXTEMPORE	EXTOLMENT	EXTROPY	EXUVIATES	EYELESS
EXTEND	EXTOLS	EXTRORSAL	EXUVIUM	EYELET
EXTENDANT	EXTORSIVE	EXTRORSE	EYALET	EYELETED
EXTENDED	EXTORT	EXTROVERT	EYALETS	EYELETEER
EXTENDER	EXTORTED	EXTRUDE	EYAS	EYELETING
EXTENDERS	EXTORTER	EXTRUDED	EYASES	EYELETS
EXTENDING	EXTORTERS	EXTRUDER	EYASS	EYELETTED
EXTENDS	EXTORTING	EXTRUDERS	EYASSES	EYELEVEL
EXTENSE	EXTORTION	EXTRUDES	EYE	EYELIAD
EXTENSES	EXTORTIVE	EXTRUDING	EYEABLE	EYELIADS
EXTENSILE	EXTORTS	EXTRUSILE	EYEBALL	EYELID
EXTENSION	EXTRA	EXTRUSION	EYEBALLED	EYELIDS
EXTENSITY	EXTRABOLD	EXTRUSIVE	EYEBALLS	EYELIFT
EXTENSIVE	EXTRACT	EXTRUSORY	EYEBANK	EYELIFTS
EXTENSOR	EXTRACTED	EXTUBATE	EYEBANKS	EYELIKE
EXTENSORS	EXTRACTOR	EXTUBATED	EYEBAR	EYELINE
EXTENT	EXTRACTS	EXTUBATES	EYEBARS	EYELINER
EXTENTS	EXTRADITE	EXUBERANT	EYEBATH	EYELINERS
EXTENUATE	EXTRADOS	EXUBERATE	EYEBATHS	EYELINES
EXTERIOR	EXTRAIT	EXUDATE	EYEBEAM	EYEN
EXTERIORS	EXTRAITS	EXUDATES	EYEBEAMS	EYEOPENER
EXTERMINE	EXTRALITY	EXUDATION	EYEBLACK	EYEPATCH
EXTERN	EXTRANET	EXUDATIVE	EYEBLACKS	EYEPIECE
EXTERNAL	EXTRANETS	EXUDE	EYEBLINK	EYEPIECES
EXTERNALS	EXTRAPOSE	EXUDED	EYEBLINKS	EYEPOINT
EXTERNAT	EXTRAS	EXUDES	EYEBOLT	EYEPOINTS
EXTERNATS	EXTRAUGHT	EXUDING	EYEBOLTS	EYEPOPPER
EXTERNE	EXTRAVERT	EXUL	EYEBRIGHT	EYER
EXTERNES	EXTREAT	EXULLED	EYEBROW	EYERS
EXTERNS	EXTREATED	EXULLING	EYEBROWED	EYES
EXTINCT	EXTREATS	EXULS	EYEBROWS	EYESHADE
EXTINCTED	EXTREMA	EXULT	EYECUP	EYESHADES
EXTINCTS	EXTREMAL	EXULTANCE	EYECUPS	EYESHADOW
EXTINE	EXTREMALS	EXULTANCY	EYED	EYESHINE
EXTINES	EXTREME	EXULTANT	EYEDNESS	EYESHINES
EXTIRP	EXTREMELY	EXULTED	EYEDROPS	EYESHOT
EXTIRPATE	EXTREMER	EXULTING	EYEFOLD	EYESHOTS
EXTIRPED	EXTREMES	EXULTS	EYEFOLDS	EYESIGHT
EXTIRPING	EXTREMEST	EXURB	EYEFUL	EYESIGHTS
EXTIRPS	EXTREMISM	EXURBAN	EYEFULS	EYESOME
EXTOL	EXTREMIST	EXURBIA	EYEGLASS	EYESORE
EXTOLD	EXTREMITY	EXURBIAS	EYEHOLE	EYESORES
EXTOLL	EXTREMUM	EXURBS	EYEHOLES	EYESPOT
EXTOLLED	EXTREMUMS	EXUVIA	EYEHOOK	EYESPOTS
EXTOLLER	EXTRICATE	EXUVIAE	EYEHOOKS	EYESTALK
EXTOLLERS	EXTRINSIC	EXUVIAL	EYEING	EYESTALKS

EYESTONE	EYEWASHES	EYEWINKS	EYOTS	EYRIES
EYESTONES	EYEWATER	EYING	EYRA	EYRIR
EYESTRAIN	EYEWATERS	EYLIAD	EYRAS	EYRY
EYETEETH	EYEWEAR	EYLIADS	EYRE	EZINE
EYETOOTH	EYEWEARS	EYNE	EYRES	EZINES
EYEWASH	EYEWINK	EYOT	EYRIE	

E

F

FA	FABULISTS	FACETIAE	FACTIVE	FADDISTS
FAA	FABULIZE	FACETIME	FACTOID	FADDLE
FAAING	FABULIZED	FACETIMED	FACTOIDAL	FADDLED
FAAN	FABULIZES	FACETIMES	FACTOIDS	FADDLES
FAAS	FABULOUS	FACETING	FACTOR	FADDLING
FAB	FABURDEN	FACETINGS	FACTORAGE	FADDY
FABACEOUS	FABURDENS	FACETIOUS	FACTORED	FADE
FABBER	FACADE	FACETS	FACTORIAL	FADEAWAY
FABBEST	FACADES	FACETTED	FACTORIES	FADEAWAYS
FABBIER	FACE	FACETTING	FACTORING	FADED
FABBIEST	FACEABLE	FACEUP	FACTORISE	FADEDLY
FABBY	FACEBAR	FACIA	FACTORIZE	FADEDNESS
FABLE	FACEBARS	FACIAE	FACTORS	FADEIN
FABLED	FACEBOOK	FACIAL	FACTORY	FADEINS
FABLER	FACEBOOKS	FACIALIST	FACTOTUM	FADELESS
FABLERS	FACECLOTH	FACIALLY	FACTOTUMS	FADEOUT
FABLES	FACED	FACIALS	FACTS	FADEOUTS
FABLET	FACEDOWN	FACIAS	FACTSHEET	FADER
FABLETS	FACEDOWNS	FACIEND	FACTUAL	FADERS
FABLIAU	FACELESS	FACIENDS	FACTUALLY	FADES
FABLIAUX	FACELIFT	FACIES	FACTUM	FADEUR
FABLING	FACELIFTS	FACILE	FACTUMS	FADEURS
FABLINGS	FACEMAIL	FACILELY	FACTURE	FADGE
FABRIC	FACEMAILS	FACILITY	FACTURES	FADGED
FABRICANT	FACEMAN	FACING	FACULA	FADGES
FABRICATE	FACEMASK	FACINGS	FACULAE	FADGING
FABRICKED	FACEMASKS	FACONNE	FACULAR	FADIER
FABRICS	FACEMEN	FACONNES	FACULTIES	FADIEST
FABRIQUE	FACEOFF	FACSIMILE	FACULTY	FADING
FABRIQUES	FACEOFFS	FACT	FACUNDITY	FADINGS
FABS	FACEPALM	FACTA	FAD	FADLIKE
FABULAR	FACEPALMS	FACTFUL	FADABLE	FADO
FABULATE	FACEPLANT	FACTICE	FADAISE	FADOMETER
FABULATED	FACEPLATE	FACTICES	FADAISES	FADOS
FABULATES	FACEPRINT	FACTICITY	FADDIER	FADS
FABULATOR	FACER	FACTION	FADDIEST	FADY
FABULISE	FACERS	FACTIONAL	FADDINESS	FAE
FABULISED	FACES	FACTIONS	FADDISH	FAECAL
FABULISES	FACET	FACTIOUS	FADDISHLY	FAECES
FABULISM	FACETE	FACTIS	FADDISM	FAENA
FABULISMS	FACETED	FACTISES	FADDISMS	FAENAS
FABULIST	FACETELY	FACTITIVE	FADDIST	FAERIE

FAERIES	FAIBLE	FAINTLY	FAITOUR	FALCONETS
FAERY	FAIBLES	FAINTNESS	FAITOURS	FALCONINE
FAFF	FAIENCE	FAINTS	FAIX	FALCONOID
FAFFED	FAIENCES	FAINTY	FAJITA	FALCONRY
FAFFIER	FAIK	FAIR	FAJITAS	FALCONS
FAFFIEST	FAIKED	FAIRED	FAKE	FALCULA
FAFFING	FAIKES	FAIRER	FAKED	FALCULAE
FAFFS	FAIKING	FAIREST	FAKEER	FALCULAS
FAFFY	FAIKS	FAIRFACED	FAKEERS	FALCULATE
FAG	FAIL	FAIRGOER	FAKEMENT	FALDAGE
FAGACEOUS	FAILED	FAIRGOERS	FAKEMENTS	FALDAGES
FAGGED	FAILING	FAIRIER	FAKER	FALDERAL
FAGGERIES	FAILINGLY	FAIRIES	FAKERIES	FALDERALS
FAGGERY	FAILINGS	FAIRIEST	FAKERS	FALDEROL
FAGGIER	FAILLE	FAIRILY	FAKERY	FALDEROLS
FAGGIEST	FAILLES	FAIRING	FAKES	FALDETTA
FAGGING	FAILOVER	FAIRINGS	FAKEST	FALDETTAS
FAGGINGS	FAILOVERS	FAIRISH	FAKEY	FALDSTOOL
FAGGOT	FAILS	FAIRISHLY	FAKEYS	FALL
FAGGOTED	FAILURE	FAIRLEAD	FAKIE	FALLACIES
FAGGOTIER	FAILURES	FAIRLEADS	FAKIER	FALLACY
FAGGOTING	FAIN	FAIRLY	FAKIES	FALLAL
FAGGOTRY	FAINE	FAIRNESS	FAKIEST	FALLALERY
FAGGOTS	FAINEANCE	FAIRS	FAKING	FALLALISH
FAGGOTY	FAINEANCY	FAIRWAY	FAKIR	FALLALS
FAGGY	FAINEANT	FAIRWAYS	FAKIRISM	FALLAWAY
FAGIN	FAINEANTS	FAIRY	FAKIRISMS	FALLAWAYS
FAGINS	FAINED	FAIRYDOM	FAKIRS	FALLBACK
FAGOT	FAINER	FAIRYDOMS	FALAFEL	FALLBACKS
FAGOTED	FAINES	FAIRYHOOD	FALAFELS	FALLBOARD
FAGOTER	FAINEST	FAIRYISM	FALAJ	FALLEN
FAGOTERS	FAINING	FAIRYISMS	FALANGISM	FALLER
FAGOTING	FAINITES	FAIRYLAND	FALANGIST	FALLERS
FAGOTINGS	FAINLY	FAIRYLIKE	FALBALA	FALLFISH
FAGOTS	FAINNE	FAIRYTALE	FALBALAS	FALLIBLE
FAGOTTI	FAINNES	FAITH	FALCADE	FALLIBLY
FAGOTTIST	FAINNESS	FAITHCURE	FALCADES	FALLING
FAGOTTO	FAINS	FAITHED	FALCATE	FALLINGS
FAGOTTOS	FAINT	FAITHER	FALCATED	FALLOFF
FAGS	FAINTED	FAITHERS	FALCATION	FALLOFFS
FAH	FAINTER	FAITHFUL	FALCES	FALLOUT
FAHLBAND	FAINTERS	FAITHFULS	FALCHION	FALLOUTS
FAHLBANDS	FAINTEST	FAITHING	FALCHIONS	FALLOW
FAHLERZ	FAINTIER	FAITHINGS	FALCIFORM	FALLOWED
FAHLERZES	FAINTIEST	FAITHLESS	FALCON	FALLOWER
FAHLORE	FAINTING	FAITHS	FALCONER	FALLOWEST
FAHLORES	FAINTINGS	FAITOR	FALCONERS	FALLOWING
FAHS	FAINTISH	FAITORS	FALCONET	FALLOWS

F

FALLS	FAMILY	FANDOMS	FANKS	FANTASY
FALSE	FAMINE	FANDS	FANLIGHT	FANTEEG
FALSED	FAMINES	FANE	FANLIGHTS	FANTEEGS
FALSEFACE	FAMING	FANEGA	FANLIKE	FANTIGUE
FALSEHOOD	FAMISH	FANEGADA	FANNED	FANTIGUES
FALSELY	FAMISHED	FANEGADAS	FANNEL	FANTOD
FALSENESS	FAMISHES	FANEGAS	FANNELL	FANTODS
FALSER	FAMISHING	FANES	FANNELLS	FANTOM
FALSERS	FAMOUS	FANFARADE	FANNELS	FANTOMS
FALSES	FAMOUSED	FANFARE	FANNER	FANTOOSH
FALSEST	FAMOUSES	FANFARED	FANNERS	FANUM
FALSETTO	FAMOUSING	FANFARES	FANNIED	FANUMS
FALSETTOS	FAMOUSLY	FANFARING	FANNIES	FANWISE
FALSEWORK	FAMULI	FANFARON	FANNING	FANWORT
FALSIE	FAMULUS	FANFARONA	FANNINGS	FANWORTS
FALSIES	FAN	FANFARONS	FANNY	FANZINE
FALSIFIED	FANAL	FANFIC	FANNYING	FANZINES
FALSIFIER	FANALS	FANFICS	FANO	FAP
FALSIFIES	FANATIC	FANFOLD	FANON	FAQIR
FALSIFY	FANATICAL	FANFOLDED	FANONS	FAQIRS
FALSING	FANATICS	FANFOLDS	FANOS	FAQUIR
FALSISH	FANBASE	FANG	FANS	FAQUIRS
FALSISM	FANBASES	FANGA	FANSITE	FAR
FALSISMS	FANBOY	FANGAS	FANSITES	FARAD
FALSITIES	FANBOYS	FANGED	FANSUB	FARADAIC
FALSITY	FANCIABLE	FANGING	FANSUBS	FARADAY
FALTBOAT	FANCIED	FANGIRL	FANTAD	FARADAYS
FALTBOATS	FANCIER	FANGIRLS	FANTADS	FARADIC
FALTER	FANCIERS	FANGLE	FANTAIL	FARADISE
FALTERED	FANCIES	FANGLED	FANTAILED	FARADISED
FALTERER	FANCIEST	FANGLES	FANTAILS	FARADISER
FALTERERS	FANCIFIED	FANGLESS	FANTASIA	FARADISES
FALTERING	FANCIFIES	FANGLIKE	FANTASIAS	FARADISM
FALTERS	FANCIFUL	FANGLING	FANTASIE	FARADISMS
FALX	FANCIFY	FANGO	FANTASIED	FARADIZE
FAME	FANCILESS	FANGOS	FANTASIES	FARADIZED
FAMED	FANCILY	FANGS	FANTASISE	FARADIZER
FAMELESS	FANCINESS	FANION	FANTASIST	FARADIZES
FAMES	FANCY	FANIONS	FANTASIZE	FARADS
FAMILIAL	FANCYING	FANJET	FANTASM	FARAND
FAMILIAR	FANCYWORK	FANJETS	FANTASMAL	FARANDINE
FAMILIARS	FAND	FANK	FANTASMIC	FARANDOLE
FAMILIES	FANDANGLE	FANKED	FANTASMS	FARANG
FAMILISM	FANDANGO	FANKING	FANTASQUE	FARANGS
FAMILISMS	FANDANGOS	FANKLE	FANTAST	FARAWAY
FAMILIST	FANDED	FANKLED	FANTASTIC	FARAWAYS
FAMILLE	FANDING	FANKLES	FANTASTRY	FARCE
FAMILLES	FANDOM	FANKLING	FANTASTS	FARCED

FARCEMEAT	FARINA	FARRANT	FASCICULE	FASTEST
FARCER	FARINAS	FARRED	FASCICULI	FASTI
FARCERS	FARING	FARREN	FASCIITIS	FASTIE
FARCES	FARINHA	FARRENS	FASCINATE	FASTIES
FARCEUR	FARINHAS	FARRIER	FASCINE	FASTIGIUM
FARCEURS	FARINOSE	FARRIERS	FASCINES	FASTING
FARCEUSE	FARL	FARRIERY	FASCIO	FASTINGS
FARCEUSES	FARLE	FARRING	FASCIOLA	FASTISH
FARCI	FARLES	FARRO	FASCIOLAS	FASTLY
FARCICAL	FARLS	FARROS	FASCIOLE	FASTNESS
FARCIE	FARM	FARROW	FASCIOLES	FASTS
FARCIED	FARMABLE	FARROWED	FASCIS	FASTUOUS
FARCIES	FARMED	FARROWING	FASCISM	FAT
FARCIFIED	FARMER	FARROWS	FASCISMI	FATAL
FARCIFIES	FARMERESS	FARRUCA	FASCISMO	FATALISM
FARCIFY	FARMERIES	FARRUCAS	FASCISMS	FATALISMS
FARCIN	FARMERS	FARS	FASCIST	FATALIST
FARCING	FARMERY	FARSE	FASCISTA	FATALISTS
FARCINGS	FARMHAND	FARSED	FASCISTI	FATALITY
FARCINS	FARMHANDS	FARSEEING	FASCISTIC	FATALLY
FARCY	FARMHOUSE	FARSES	FASCISTS	FATALNESS
FARD	FARMING	FARSIDE	FASCITIS	FATBACK
FARDAGE	FARMINGS	FARSIDES	FASH	FATBACKS
FARDAGES	FARMLAND	FARSING	FASHED	FATBERG
FARDED	FARMLANDS	FART	FASHERIES	FATBERGS
FARDEL	FARMOST	FARTED	FASHERY	FATBIRD
FARDELS	FARMS	FARTHEL	FASHES	FATBIRDS
FARDEN	FARMSTEAD	FARTHELS	FASHING	FATE
FARDENS	FARMWIFE	FARTHER	FASHION	FATED
FARDING	FARMWIVES	FARTHEST	FASHIONED	FATEFUL
FARDINGS	FARMWORK	FARTHING	FASHIONER	FATEFULLY
FARDS	FARMWORKS	FARTHINGS	FASHIONS	FATES
FARE	FARMYARD	FARTING	FASHIONY	FATHEAD
FAREBOX	FARMYARDS	FARTLEK	FASHIOUS	FATHEADED
FAREBOXES	FARNARKEL	FARTLEKS	FAST	FATHEADS
FARED	FARNESOL	FARTS	FASTBACK	FATHER
FARER	FARNESOLS	FAS	FASTBACKS	FATHERED
FARERS	FARNESS	FASCES	FASTBALL	FATHERING
FARES	FARNESSES	FASCI	FASTBALLS	FATHERLY
FAREWELL	FARO	FASCIA	FASTED	FATHERS
FAREWELLS	FAROLITO	FASCIAE	FASTEN	FATHOM
FARFAL	FAROLITOS	FASCIAL	FASTENED	FATHOMED
FARFALLE	FAROS	FASCIAS	FASTENER	FATHOMER
FARFALLES	FAROUCHE	FASCIATE	FASTENERS	FATHOMERS
FARFALS	FARRAGO	FASCIATED	FASTENING	FATHOMING
FARFEL	FARRAGOES	FASCICLE	FASTENS	FATHOMS
FARFELS	FARRAGOS	FASCICLED	FASTER	FATIDIC
FARFET	FARRAND	FASCICLES	FASTERS	FATIDICAL

FATIGABLE	FATUITOUS	FAUNIST	FAVISM	FAYALITES
FATIGATE	FATUITY	FAUNISTIC	FAVISMS	FAYED
FATIGATED	FATUOUS	FAUNISTS	FAVONIAN	FAYENCE
FATIGATES	FATUOUSLY	FAUNLIKE	FAVOR	FAYENCES
FATIGUE	FATWA	FAUNS	FAVORABLE	FAYER
FATIGUED	FATWAED	FAUNULA	FAVORABLY	FAYEST
FATIGUES	FATWAH	FAUNULAE	FAVORED	FAYING
FATIGUING	FATWAHED	FAUNULE	FAVORER	FAYNE
FATING	FATWAHING	FAUNULES	FAVORERS	FAYNED
FATISCENT	FATWAHS	FAUR	FAVORING	FAYNES
FATLESS	FATWAING	FAURD	FAVORITE	FAYNING
FATLIKE	FATWAS	FAURER	FAVORITES	FAYRE
FATLING	FATWOOD	FAUREST	FAVORLESS	FAYRES
FATLINGS	FATWOODS	FAUSTIAN	FAVORS	FAYS
FATLY	FAUBOURG	FAUT	FAVOSE	FAZE
FATNESS	FAUBOURGS	FAUTED	FAVOUR	FAZED
FATNESSES	FAUCAL	FAUTEUIL	FAVOURED	FAZENDA
FATS	FAUCALS	FAUTEUILS	FAVOURER	FAZENDAS
FATSIA	FAUCES	FAUTING	FAVOURERS	FAZES
FATSIAS	FAUCET	FAUTOR	FAVOURING	FAZING
FATSO	FAUCETRY	FAUTORS	FAVOURITE	FE
FATSOES	FAUCETS	FAUTS	FAVOURS	FEAGUE
FATSOS	FAUCHION	FAUVE	FAVOUS	FEAGUED
FATSTOCK	FAUCHIONS	FAUVES	FAVRILE	FEAGUES
FATSTOCKS	FAUCHON	FAUVETTE	FAVRILES	FEAGUING
FATTED	FAUCHONS	FAUVETTES	FAVUS	FEAL
FATTEN	FAUCIAL	FAUVISM	FAVUSES	FEALED
FATTENED	FAUGH	FAUVISMS	FAW	FEALING
FATTENER	FAULCHION	FAUVIST	FAWN	FEALS
FATTENERS	FAULD	FAUVISTS	FAWNED	FEALTIES
FATTENING	FAULDS	FAUX	FAWNER	FEALTY
FATTENS	FAULT	FAUXMANCE	FAWNERS	FEAR
FATTER	FAULTED	FAVA	FAWNIER	FEARE
FATTEST	FAULTFUL	FAVAS	FAWNIEST	FEARED
FATTIER	FAULTIER	FAVE	FAWNING	FEARER
FATTIES	FAULTIEST	FAVEL	FAWNINGLY	FEARERS
FATTIEST	FAULTILY	FAVELA	FAWNINGS	FEARES
FATTILY	FAULTING	FAVELAS	FAWNLIKE	FEARFUL
FATTINESS	FAULTLESS	FAVELL	FAWNS	FEARFULLY
FATTING	FAULTLINE	FAVELLA	FAWNY	FEARING
FATTISH	FAULTS	FAVELLAS	FAWS	FEARLESS
FATTISM	FAULTY	FAVELS	FAX	FEARS
FATTISMS	FAUN	FAVEOLATE	FAXABLE	FEARSOME
FATTIST	FAUNA	FAVER	FAXED	FEART
FATTISTS	FAUNAE	FAVES	FAXES	FEASANCE
FATTRELS	FAUNAL	FAVEST	FAXING	FEASANCES
FATTY	FAUNALLY	FAVICON	FAY	FEASE
FATUITIES	FAUNAS	FAVICONS	FAYALITE	FEASED

FEASES	FECES	FEDS	FEEN	FEINTING
FEASIBLE	FECHT	FEE	FEENS	FEINTS
FEASIBLY	FECHTER	FEEB	FEER	FEIRIE
FEASING	FECHTERS	FEEBLE	FEERED	FEIRIER
FEAST	FECHTING	FEEBLED	FEERIE	FEIRIEST
FEASTED	FECHTS	FEEBLER	FEERIES	FEIS
FEASTER	FECIAL	FEEBLES	FEERIN	FEISEANNA
FEASTERS	FECIALS	FEEBLEST	FEERING	FEIST
FEASTFUL	FECIT	FEEBLING	FEERINGS	FEISTIER
FEASTING	FECK	FEEBLISH	FEERINS	FEISTIEST
FEASTINGS	FECKED	FEEBLY	FEERS	FEISTILY
FEASTLESS	FECKIN	FEEBS	FEES	FEISTS
FEASTS	FECKING	FEED	FEESE	FEISTY
FEAT	FECKLESS	FEEDABLE	FEESED	FELAFEL
FEATED	FECKLY	FEEDBACK	FEESES	FELAFELS
FEATEOUS	FECKS	FEEDBACKS	FEESING	FELCH
FEATER	FECULA	FEEDBAG	FEET	FELCHED
FEATEST	FECULAE	FEEDBAGS	FEETFIRST	FELCHES
FEATHER	FECULAS	FEEDBOX	FEETLESS	FELCHING
FEATHERED	FECULENCE	FEEDBOXES	FEEZE	FELDGRAU
FEATHERS	FECULENCY	FEEDER	FEEZED	FELDGRAUS
FEATHERY	FECULENT	FEEDERS	FEEZES	FELDSCHAR
FEATING	FECUND	FEEDGRAIN	FEEZING	FELDSCHER
FEATLIER	FECUNDATE	FEEDHOLE	FEG	FELDSHER
FEATLIEST	FECUNDITY	FEEDHOLES	FEGARIES	FELDSHERS
FEATLY	FED	FEEDING	FEGARY	FELDSPAR
FEATOUS	FEDARIE	FEEDINGS	FEGS	FELDSPARS
FEATS	FEDARIES	FEEDLOT	FEH	FELDSPATH
FEATUOUS	FEDAYEE	FEEDLOTS	FEHM	FELICIA
FEATURE	FEDAYEEN	FEEDPIPE	FEHME	FELICIAS
FEATURED	FEDELINI	FEEDPIPES	FEHMIC	FELICIFIC
FEATURELY	FEDELINIS	FEEDS	FEHS	FELICITER
FEATURES	FEDERACY	FEEDSTOCK	FEIGN	FELICITY
FEATURING	FEDERAL	FEEDSTUFF	FEIGNED	FELID
FEAZE	FEDERALLY	FEEDWATER	FEIGNEDLY	FELIDS
FEAZED	FEDERALS	FEEDYARD	FEIGNER	FELINE
FEAZES	FEDERARIE	FEEDYARDS	FEIGNERS	FELINELY
FEAZING	FEDERARY	FEEING	FEIGNING	FELINES
FEBLESSE	FEDERATE	FEEL	FEIGNINGS	FELINITY
FEBLESSES	FEDERATED	FEELBAD	FEIGNS	FELL
FEBRICITY	FEDERATES	FEELER	FEIJOA	FELLA
FEBRICULA	FEDERATOR	FEELERS	FEIJOADA	FELLABLE
FEBRICULE	FEDEX	FEELESS	FEIJOADAS	FELLAH
FEBRIFIC	FEDEXED	FEELGOOD	FEIJOAS	FELLAHEEN
FEBRIFUGE	FEDEXES	FEELING	FEINT	FELLAHIN
FEBRILE	FEDEXING	FEELINGLY	FEINTED	FELLAHS
FEBRILITY	FEDORA	FEELINGS	FEINTER	FELLAS
FECAL	FEDORAS	FEELS	FEINTEST	FELLATE

FELLATED	FELTER	FEMINIZE	FENESTRAS	FEOFFS
FELLATES	FELTERED	FEMINIZED	FENI	FER
FELLATING	FELTERING	FEMINIZES	FENING	FERACIOUS
FELLATIO	FELTERS	FEMITER	FENINGA	FERACITY
FELLATION	FELTIER	FEMITERS	FENINGS	FERAL
FELLATIOS	FELTIEST	FEMME	FENIS	FERALISED
FELLATOR	FELTING	FEMMES	FENITAR	FERALIZED
FELLATORS	FELTINGS	FEMMIER	FENITARS	FERALS
FELLATRIX	FELTLIKE	FEMMIEST	FENKS	FERBAM
FELLED	FELTS	FEMMY	FENLAND	FERBAMS
FELLER	FELTY	FEMORA	FENLANDS	FERE
FELLERS	FELUCCA	FEMORAL	FENMAN	FERER
FELLEST	FELUCCAS	FEMS	FENMEN	FERES
FELLFIELD	FELWORT	FEMUR	FENNEC	FEREST
FELLIES	FELWORTS	FEMURS	FENNECS	FERETORY
FELLING	FEM	FEN	FENNEL	FERIA
FELLINGS	FEMAL	FENAGLE	FENNELS	FERIAE
FELLNESS	FEMALE	FENAGLED	FENNIER	FERIAL
FELLOE	FEMALES	FENAGLES	FENNIES	FERIAS
FELLOES	FEMALITY	FENAGLING	FENNIEST	FERINE
FELLOW	FEMALS	FENCE	FENNING	FERITIES
FELLOWED	FEME	FENCED	FENNISH	FERITY
FELLOWING	FEMERALL	FENCELESS	FENNY	FERLIE
FELLOWLY	FEMERALLS	FENCELIKE	FENS	FERLIED
FELLOWMAN	FEMERELL	FENCELINE	FENT	FERLIER
FELLOWMEN	FEMERELLS	FENCER	FENTANYL	FERLIES
FELLOWS	FEMES	FENCEROW	FENTANYLS	FERLIEST
FELLS	FEMETARY	FENCEROWS	FENTHION	FERLY
FELLY	FEMICIDAL	FENCERS	FENTHIONS	FERLYING
FELON	FEMICIDE	FENCES	FENTS	FERM
FELONIES	FEMICIDES	FENCEWIRE	FENUGREEK	FERMATA
FELONIOUS	FEMINACY	FENCIBLE	FENURON	FERMATAS
FELONOUS	FEMINAL	FENCIBLES	FENURONS	FERMATE
FELONRIES	FEMINAZI	FENCING	FEOD	FERMENT
FELONRY	FEMINAZIS	FENCINGS	FEODAL	FERMENTED
FELONS	FEMINEITY	FEND	FEODARIES	FERMENTER
FELONY	FEMINIE	FENDED	FEODARY	FERMENTOR
FELQUISTE	FEMINIES	FENDER	FEODS	FERMENTS
FELSIC	FEMININE	FENDERED	FEOFF	FERMI
FELSITE	FEMININES	FENDERS	FEOFFED	FERMION
FELSITES	FEMINISE	FENDIER	FEOFFEE	FERMIONIC
FELSITIC	FEMINISED	FENDIEST	FEOFFEES	FERMIONS
FELSPAR	FEMINISES	FENDING	FEOFFER	FERMIS
FELSPARS	FEMINISM	FENDS	FEOFFERS	FERMIUM
FELSTONE	FEMINISMS	FENDY	FEOFFING	FERMIUMS
FELSTONES	FEMINIST	FENESTRA	FEOFFMENT	FERMS
FELT	FEMINISTS	FENESTRAE	FEOFFOR	FERN
FELTED	FEMINITY	FENESTRAL	FEOFFORS	FERNALLY

FERNBIRD	FERRUGO	FESSES	FETIALIS	FETTLERS
FERNBIRDS	FERRUGOS	FESSING	FETIALS	FETTLES
FERNERIES	FERRULE	FESSWISE	FETICH	FETTLING
FERNERY	FERRULED	FEST	FETICHE	FETTLINGS
FERNIER	FERRULES	FESTA	FETICHES	FETTS
FERNIEST	FERRULING	FESTAL	FETICHISE	FETTUCINE
FERNING	FERRUM	FESTALLY	FETICHISM	FETTUCINI
FERNINGS	FERRUMS	FESTALS	FETICHIST	FETUS
FERNINST	FERRY	FESTAS	FETICHIZE	FETUSES
FERNLESS	FERRYBOAT	FESTER	FETICIDAL	FETWA
FERNLIKE	FERRYING	FESTERED	FETICIDE	FETWAS
FERNS	FERRYMAN	FESTERING	FETICIDES	FEU
FERNSHAW	FERRYMEN	FESTERS	FETID	FEUAR
FERNSHAWS	FERTIGATE	FESTIER	FETIDER	FEUARS
FERNTICLE	FERTILE	FESTIEST	FETIDEST	FEUD
FERNY	FERTILELY	FESTILOGY	FETIDITY	FEUDAL
FEROCIOUS	FERTILER	FESTINATE	FETIDLY	FEUDALISE
FEROCITY	FERTILEST	FESTIVAL	FETIDNESS	FEUDALISM
FERRATE	FERTILISE	FESTIVALS	FETING	FEUDALIST
FERRATES	FERTILITY	FESTIVE	FETISH	FEUDALITY
FERREL	FERTILIZE	FESTIVELY	FETISHES	FEUDALIZE
FERRELED	FERULA	FESTIVITY	FETISHISE	FEUDALLY
FERRELING	FERULAE	FESTIVOUS	FETISHISM	FEUDARIES
FERRELLED	FERULAS	FESTOLOGY	FETISHIST	FEUDARY
FERRELS	FERULE	FESTOON	FETISHIZE	FEUDATORY
FERREOUS	FERULED	FESTOONED	FETLOCK	FEUDED
FERRET	FERULES	FESTOONS	FETLOCKED	FEUDING
FERRETED	FERULING	FESTS	FETLOCKS	FEUDINGS
FERRETER	FERVENCY	FESTY	FETOLOGY	FEUDIST
FERRETERS	FERVENT	FET	FETOR	FEUDISTS
FERRETIER	FERVENTER	FETA	FETORS	FEUDS
FERRETING	FERVENTLY	FETAL	FETOSCOPE	FEUED
FERRETS	FERVID	FETAS	FETOSCOPY	FEUILLETE
FERRETY	FERVIDER	FETATION	FETS	FEUING
FERRIAGE	FERVIDEST	FETATIONS	FETT	FEUS
FERRIAGES	FERVIDITY	FETCH	FETTA	FEUTRE
FERRIC	FERVIDLY	FETCHED	FETTAS	FEUTRED
FERRIED	FERVOR	FETCHER	FETTED	FEUTRES
FERRIES	FERVOROUS	FETCHERS	FETTER	FEUTRING
FERRITE	FERVORS	FETCHES	FETTERED	FEVER
FERRITES	FERVOUR	FETCHING	FETTERER	FEVERED
FERRITIC	FERVOURS	FETE	FETTERERS	FEVERFEW
FERRITIN	FES	FETED	FETTERING	FEVERFEWS
FERRITINS	FESCUE	FETERITA	FETTERS	FEVERING
FERROCENE	FESCUES	FETERITAS	FETTING	FEVERISH
FERROGRAM	FESS	FETES	FETTLE	FEVERLESS
FERROTYPE	FESSE	FETIAL	FETTLED	FEVEROUS
FERROUS	FESSED	FETIALES	FETTLER	FEVERROOT

FEVERS	FIB	FIBROLITE	FICUS	FIEFS
FEVERWEED	FIBBED	FIBROMA	FICUSES	FIELD
FEVERWORT	FIBBER	FIBROMAS	FID	FIELDBOOT
FEW	FIBBERIES	FIBROMATA	FIDDIOUS	FIELDED
FEWER	FIBBERS	FIBROS	FIDDLE	FIELDER
FEWEST	FIBBERY	FIBROSE	FIDDLED	FIELDERS
FEWMET	FIBBING	FIBROSED	FIDDLER	FIELDFARE
FEWMETS	FIBER	FIBROSES	FIDDLERS	FIELDING
FEWNESS	FIBERED	FIBROSING	FIDDLES	FIELDINGS
FEWNESSES	FIBERFILL	FIBROSIS	FIDDLEY	FIELDMICE
FEWS	FIBERISE	FIBROTIC	FIDDLEYS	FIELDS
FEWTER	FIBERISED	FIBROUS	FIDDLIER	FIELDSMAN
FEWTERED	FIBERISES	FIBROUSLY	FIDDLIEST	FIELDSMEN
FEWTERING	FIBERIZE	FIBS	FIDDLING	FIELDVOLE
FEWTERS	FIBERIZED	FIBSTER	FIDDLINGS	FIELDWARD
FEWTRILS	FIBERIZES	FIBSTERS	FIDDLY	FIELDWORK
FEY	FIBERLESS	FIBULA	FIDEISM	FIEND
FEYED	FIBERLIKE	FIBULAE	FIDEISMS	FIENDISH
FEYER	FIBERS	FIBULAR	FIDEIST	FIENDLIKE
FEYEST	FIBRANNE	FIBULAS	FIDEISTIC	FIENDS
FEYING	FIBRANNES	FICAIN	FIDEISTS	FIENT
FEYLY	FIBRATE	FICAINS	FIDELISMO	FIENTS
FEYNESS	FIBRATES	FICE	FIDELISTA	FIER
FEYNESSES	FIBRE	FICES	FIDELITY	FIERCE
FEYS	FIBRED	FICHE	FIDES	FIERCELY
FEZ	FIBREFILL	FICHES	FIDGE	FIERCER
FEZES	FIBRELESS	FICHU	FIDGED	FIERCEST
FEZZED	FIBRELIKE	FICHUS	FIDGES	FIERE
FEZZES	FIBRES	FICIN	FIDGET	FIERES
FEZZY	FIBRIFORM	FICINS	FIDGETED	FIERIER
FIACRE	FIBRIL	FICKLE	FIDGETER	FIERIEST
FIACRES	FIBRILAR	FICKLED	FIDGETERS	FIERILY
FIANCE	FIBRILLA	FICKLER	FIDGETIER	FIERINESS
FIANCEE	FIBRILLAE	FICKLES	FIDGETING	FIERS
FIANCEES	FIBRILLAR	FICKLEST	FIDGETS	FIERY
FIANCES	FIBRILLIN	FICKLING	FIDGETY	FIEST
FIAR	FIBRILS	FICKLY	FIDGING	FIESTA
FIARS	FIBRIN	FICO	FIDIBUS	FIESTAS
FIASCHI	FIBRINOID	FICOES	FIDIBUSES	FIFE
FIASCO	FIBRINOUS	FICOS	FIDO	FIFED
FIASCOES	FIBRINS	FICTILE	FIDOS	FIFER
FIASCOS	FIBRO	FICTION	FIDS	FIFERS
FIAT	FIBROCYTE	FICTIONAL	FIDUCIAL	FIFES
FIATED	FIBROID	FICTIONS	FIDUCIARY	FIFI
FIATING	FIBROIDS	FICTIVE	FIE	FIFING
FIATS	FIBROIN	FICTIVELY	FIEF	FIFIS
FIAUNT	FIBROINS	FICTOR	FIEFDOM	FIFTEEN
FIAUNTS	FIBROLINE	FICTORS	FIEFDOMS	FIFTEENER

F

FIFTEENS	FIGURE	FILASSES	FILIFORM	FILMCARD
FIFTEENTH	FIGURED	FILATORY	FILIGRAIN	FILMCARDS
FIFTH	FIGUREDLY	FILATURE	FILIGRANE	FILMDOM
FIFTHLY	FIGURER	FILATURES	FILIGREE	FILMDOMS
FIFTHS	FIGURERS	FILAZER	FILIGREED	FILMED
FIFTIES	FIGURES	FILAZERS	FILIGREES	FILMER
FIFTIETH	FIGURINE	FILBERD	FILII	FILMERS
FIFTIETHS	FIGURINES	FILBERDS	FILING	FILMFEST
FIFTY	FIGURING	FILBERT	FILINGS	FILMFESTS
FIFTYFOLD	FIGURIST	FILBERTS	FILIOQUE	FILMGOER
FIFTYISH	FIGURISTS	FILCH	FILIOQUES	FILMGOERS
FIG	FIGWORT	FILCHED	FILISTER	FILMGOING
FIGEATER	FIGWORTS	FILCHER	FILISTERS	FILMI
FIGEATERS	FIKE	FILCHERS	FILIUS	FILMIC
FIGGED	FIKED	FILCHES	FILK	FILMIER
FIGGERIES	FIKERIES	FILCHING	FILKS	FILMIEST
FIGGERY	FIKERY	FILCHINGS	FILL	FILMILY
FIGGIER	FIKES	FILE	FILLABLE	FILMINESS
FIGGIEST	FIKIER	FILEABLE	FILLAGREE	FILMING
FIGGING	FIKIEST	FILECARD	FILLE	FILMINGS
FIGGY	FIKING	FILECARDS	FILLED	FILMIS
FIGHT	FIKISH	FILED	FILLER	FILMISH
FIGHTABLE	FIKY	FILEFISH	FILLERS	FILMLAND
FIGHTBACK	FIL	FILEMOT	FILLES	FILMLANDS
FIGHTER	FILA	FILEMOTS	FILLESTER	FILMLESS
FIGHTERS	FILABEG	FILENAME	FILLET	FILMLIKE
FIGHTING	FILABEGS	FILENAMES	FILLETED	FILMMAKER
FIGHTINGS	FILACEOUS	FILER	FILLETER	FILMS
FIGHTS	FILACER	FILERS	FILLETERS	FILMSET
FIGJAM	FILACERS	FILES	FILLETING	FILMSETS
FIGJAMS	FILAGGRIN	FILET	FILLETS	FILMSTRIP
FIGLIKE	FILAGREE	FILETED	FILLIBEG	FILMY
FIGMENT	FILAGREED	FILETING	FILLIBEGS	FILO
FIGMENTS	FILAGREES	FILETS	FILLIES	FILOPLUME
FIGO	FILAMENT	FILFOT	FILLING	FILOPODIA
FIGOS	FILAMENTS	FILFOTS	FILLINGS	FILOS
FIGS	FILANDER	FILIAL	FILLIP	FILOSE
FIGTREE	FILANDERS	FILIALLY	FILLIPED	FILOSELLE
FIGTREES	FILAR	FILIATE	FILLIPEEN	FILOVIRUS
FIGULINE	FILAREE	FILIATED	FILLIPING	FILS
FIGULINES	FILAREES	FILIATES	FILLIPS	FILTER
FIGURABLE	FILARIA	FILIATING	FILLISTER	FILTERED
FIGURAL	FILARIAE	FILIATION	FILLO	FILTERER
FIGURALLY	FILARIAL	FILIBEG	FILLOS	FILTERERS
FIGURANT	FILARIAN	FILIBEGS	FILLS	FILTERING
FIGURANTE	FILARIID	FILICIDAL	FILLY	FILTERS
FIGURANTS	FILARIIDS	FILICIDE	FILM	FILTH
FIGURATE	FILASSE	FILICIDES	FILMABLE	FILTHIER

FILTHIEST	FINANCING	FINGANS	FINLIKE	FIQUE
FILTHILY	FINBACK	FINGER	FINLIT	FIQUES
FILTHS	FINBACKS	FINGERED	FINLITS	FIR
FILTHY	FINCA	FINGERER	FINMARK	FIRE
FILTRABLE	FINCAS	FINGERERS	FINMARKS	FIREABLE
FILTRATE	FINCH	FINGERING	FINNAC	FIREARM
FILTRATED	FINCHED	FINGERS	FINNACK	FIREARMED
FILTRATES	FINCHES	FINGERTIP	FINNACKS	FIREARMS
FILTRE	FINCHLIKE	FINI	FINNACS	FIREBACK
FILUM	FIND	FINIAL	FINNAN	FIREBACKS
FIMBLE	FINDABLE	FINIALED	FINNANS	FIREBALL
FIMBLES	FINDER	FINIALS	FINNED	FIREBALLS
FIMBRIA	FINDERS	FINICAL	FINNER	FIREBASE
FIMBRIAE	FINDING	FINICALLY	FINNERS	FIREBASES
FIMBRIAL	FINDINGS	FINICKETY	FINNESKO	FIREBIRD
FIMBRIATE	FINDRAM	FINICKIER	FINNICKY	FIREBIRDS
FIN	FINDRAMS	FINICKIN	FINNIER	FIREBOARD
FINABLE	FINDS	FINICKING	FINNIEST	FIREBOAT
FINAGLE	FINE	FINICKY	FINNING	FIREBOATS
FINAGLED	FINEABLE	FINIKIN	FINNMARK	FIREBOMB
FINAGLER	FINED	FINIKING	FINNMARKS	FIREBOMBS
FINAGLERS	FINEER	FINING	FINNOCHIO	FIREBOX
FINAGLES	FINEERED	FININGS	FINNOCK	FIREBOXES
FINAGLING	FINEERING	FINIS	FINNOCKS	FIREBRAND
FINAL	FINEERS	FINISES	FINNSKO	FIREBRAT
FINALE	FINEISH	FINISH	FINNY	FIREBRATS
FINALES	FINELESS	FINISHED	FINO	FIREBREAK
FINALIS	FINELY	FINISHER	FINOCCHIO	FIREBRICK
FINALISE	FINENESS	FINISHERS	FINOCHIO	FIREBUG
FINALISED	FINER	FINISHES	FINOCHIOS	FIREBUGS
FINALISER	FINERIES	FINISHING	FINOS	FIREBUSH
FINALISES	FINERS	FINITE	FINS	FIRECLAY
FINALISM	FINERY	FINITELY	FINSKO	FIRECLAYS
FINALISMS	FINES	FINITES	FINTECH	FIRECREST
FINALIST	FINESPUN	FINITISM	FINTECHS	FIRED
FINALISTS	FINESSE	FINITISMS	FIORATURA	FIREDAMP
FINALITY	FINESSED	FINITIST	FIORD	FIREDAMPS
FINALIZE	FINESSER	FINITISTS	FIORDS	FIREDOG
FINALIZED	FINESSERS	FINITO	FIORIN	FIREDOGS
FINALIZER	FINESSES	FINITUDE	FIORINS	FIREDRAKE
FINALIZES	FINESSING	FINITUDES	FIORITURA	FIREFANG
FINALLY	FINEST	FINJAN	FIORITURE	FIREFANGS
FINALS	FINESTS	FINJANS	FIPPENCE	FIREFIGHT
FINANCE	FINFISH	FINK	FIPPENCES	FIREFLIES
FINANCED	FINFISHES	FINKED	FIPPLE	FIREFLOAT
FINANCES	FINFOOT	FINKING	FIPPLES	FIREFLOOD
FINANCIAL	FINFOOTS	FINKS	FIQH	FIREFLY
FINANCIER	FINGAN	FINLESS	FIQHS	FIREGUARD

FIREHALL	FIREWATER	FIRSTHAND	FISHIFIED	FISSIPEDE
FIREHALLS	FIREWEED	FIRSTLING	FISHIFIES	FISSIPEDS
FIREHOSE	FIREWEEDS	FIRSTLY	FISHIFY	FISSIVE
FIREHOSES	FIREWOMAN	FIRSTNESS	FISHILY	FISSLE
FIREHOUSE	FIREWOMEN	FIRSTS	FISHINESS	FISSLED
FIRELESS	FIREWOOD	FIRTH	FISHING	FISSLES
FIRELIGHT	FIREWOODS	FIRTHS	FISHINGS	FISSLING
FIRELIT	FIREWORK	FIRWOOD	FISHKILL	FISSURAL
FIRELOCK	FIREWORKS	FIRWOODS	FISHKILLS	FISSURE
FIRELOCKS	FIREWORM	FISC	FISHLESS	FISSURED
FIREMAN	FIREWORMS	FISCAL	FISHLIKE	FISSURES
FIREMANIC	FIRIE	FISCALIST	FISHLINE	FISSURING
FIREMARK	FIRIES	FISCALLY	FISHLINES	FIST
FIREMARKS	FIRING	FISCALS	FISHMEAL	FISTED
FIREMEN	FIRINGS	FISCS	FISHMEALS	FISTFIGHT
FIREPAN	FIRK	FISGIG	FISHNET	FISTFUL
FIREPANS	FIRKED	FISGIGS	FISHNETS	FISTFULS
FIREPINK	FIRKIN	FISH	FISHPLATE	FISTIANA
FIREPINKS	FIRKING	FISHABLE	FISHPOLE	FISTIANAS
FIREPIT	FIRKINS	FISHBALL	FISHPOLES	FISTIC
FIREPITS	FIRKS	FISHBALLS	FISHPOND	FISTICAL
FIREPLACE	FIRLOT	FISHBOAT	FISHPONDS	FISTICUFF
FIREPLUG	FIRLOTS	FISHBOATS	FISHSKIN	FISTIER
FIREPLUGS	FIRM	FISHBOLT	FISHSKINS	FISTIEST
FIREPOT	FIRMAMENT	FISHBOLTS	FISHTAIL	FISTING
FIREPOTS	FIRMAN	FISHBONE	FISHTAILS	FISTINGS
FIREPOWER	FIRMANS	FISHBONES	FISHWAY	FISTMELE
FIREPROOF	FIRMED	FISHBOWL	FISHWAYS	FISTMELES
FIRER	FIRMER	FISHBOWLS	FISHWIFE	FISTNOTE
FIREREEL	FIRMERS	FISHCAKE	FISHWIVES	FISTNOTES
FIREREELS	FIRMEST	FISHCAKES	FISHWORM	FISTS
FIREROOM	FIRMING	FISHED	FISHWORMS	FISTULA
FIREROOMS	FIRMLESS	FISHER	FISHY	FISTULAE
FIRERS	FIRMLY	FISHERIES	FISHYBACK	FISTULAR
FIRES	FIRMNESS	FISHERMAN	FISK	FISTULAS
FIRESCAPE	FIRMS	FISHERMEN	FISKED	FISTULATE
FIRESHIP	FIRMWARE	FISHERS	FISKING	FISTULOSE
FIRESHIPS	FIRMWARES	FISHERY	FISKS	FISTULOUS
FIRESIDE	FIRN	FISHES	FISNOMIE	FISTY
FIRESIDES	FIRNS	FISHEYE	FISNOMIES	FIT
FIRESTONE	FIRRIER	FISHEYES	FISSATE	FITCH
FIRESTORM	FIRRIEST	FISHFUL	FISSILE	FITCHE
FIRETHORN	FIRRING	FISHGIG	FISSILITY	FITCHEE
FIRETRAP	FIRRINGS	FISHGIGS	FISSION	FITCHES
FIRETRAPS	FIRRY	FISHHOOK	FISSIONAL	FITCHET
FIRETRUCK	FIRS	FISHHOOKS	FISSIONED	FITCHETS
FIREWALL	FIRST	FISHIER	FISSIONS	FITCHEW
FIREWALLS	FIRSTBORN	FISHIEST	FISSIPED	FITCHEWS

FITCHY	FIXED	FLABBIER	FLAGON	FLAMELETS
FITFUL	FIXEDLY	FLABBIEST	FLAGONS	FLAMELIKE
FITFULLY	FIXEDNESS	FLABBILY	FLAGPOLE	FLAMEN
FITLIER	FIXER	FLABBY	FLAGPOLES	FLAMENCO
FITLIEST	FIXERS	FLABELLA	FLAGRANCE	FLAMENCOS
FITLY	FIXES	FLABELLUM	FLAGRANCY	FLAMENS
FITMENT	FIXING	FLABS	FLAGRANT	FLAMEOUT
FITMENTS	FIXINGS	FLACCID	FLAGS	FLAMEOUTS
FITNA	FIXIT	FLACCIDER	FLAGSHIP	FLAMER
FITNAS	FIXITIES	FLACCIDLY	FLAGSHIPS	FLAMERS
FITNESS	FIXITS	FLACK	FLAGSTAFF	FLAMES
FITNESSES	FIXITY	FLACKED	FLAGSTICK	FLAMFEW
FITS	FIXIVE	FLACKER	FLAGSTONE	FLAMFEWS
FITT	FIXT	FLACKERED	FLAIL	FLAMIER
FITTABLE	FIXTURE	FLACKERS	FLAILED	FLAMIEST
FITTE	FIXTURES	FLACKERY	FLAILING	FLAMINES
FITTED	FIXURE	FLACKET	FLAILS	FLAMING
FITTER	FIXURES	FLACKETED	FLAIR	FLAMINGLY
FITTERS	FIZ	FLACKETS	FLAIRS	FLAMINGO
FITTES	FIZGIG	FLACKING	FLAK	FLAMINGOS
FITTEST	FIZGIGGED	FLACKS	FLAKE	FLAMM
FITTING	FIZGIGS	FLACON	FLAKED	FLAMMABLE
FITTINGLY	FIZZ	FLACONS	FLAKER	FLAMMED
FITTINGS	FIZZED	FLAFF	FLAKERS	FLAMMING
FITTS	FIZZEN	FLAFFED	FLAKES	FLAMMS
FIVE	FIZZENS	FLAFFER	FLAKEY	FLAMMULE
FIVEFOLD	FIZZER	FLAFFERED	FLAKIER	FLAMMULES
FIVEPENCE	FIZZERS	FLAFFERS	FLAKIES	FLAMS
FIVEPENNY	FIZZES	FLAFFING	FLAKIEST	FLAMY
FIVEPIN	FIZZGIG	FLAFFS	FLAKILY	FLAN
FIVEPINS	FIZZGIGS	FLAG	FLAKINESS	FLANCARD
FIVER	FIZZIER	FLAGELLA	FLAKING	FLANCARDS
FIVERS	FIZZIEST	FLAGELLAR	FLAKS	FLANCH
FIVES	FIZZILY	FLAGELLIN	FLAKY	FLANCHED
FIX	FIZZINESS	FLAGELLUM	FLAM	FLANCHES
FIXABLE	FIZZING	FLAGEOLET	FLAMBE	FLANCHING
FIXATE	FIZZINGS	FLAGGED	FLAMBEAU	FLANE
FIXATED	FIZZLE	FLAGGER	FLAMBEAUS	FLANED
FIXATES	FIZZLED	FLAGGERS	FLAMBEAUX	FLANERIE
FIXATIF	FIZZLES	FLAGGIER	FLAMBEE	FLANERIES
FIXATIFS	FIZZLING	FLAGGIEST	FLAMBEED	FLANES
FIXATING	FIZZY	FLAGGING	FLAMBEES	FLANEUR
FIXATION	FJELD	FLAGGINGS	FLAMBEING	FLANEURS
FIXATIONS	FJELDS	FLAGGY	FLAMBES	FLANGE
FIXATIVE	FJORD	FLAGITATE	FLAME	FLANGED
FIXATIVES	FJORDIC	FLAGLESS	FLAMED	FLANGER
FIXATURE	FJORDS	FLAGMAN	FLAMELESS	FLANGERS
FIXATURES	FLAB	FLAGMEN	FLAMELET	FLANGES

FLANGING	FLARIEST	FLATFEET	FLATTOP	FLAVONE
FLANGINGS	FLARING	FLATFISH	FLATTOPS	FLAVONES
FLANING	FLARINGLY	FLATFOOT	FLATTY	FLAVONOID
FLANK	FLARY	FLATFOOTS	FLATULENT	FLAVONOL
FLANKED	FLASER	FLATFORM	FLATUOUS	FLAVONOLS
FLANKEN	FLASERS	FLATFORMS	FLATUS	FLAVOR
FLANKENS	FLASH	FLATHEAD	FLATUSES	FLAVORED
FLANKER	FLASHBACK	FLATHEADS	FLATWARE	FLAVORER
FLANKERED	FLASHBANG	FLATIRON	FLATWARES	FLAVORERS
FLANKERS	FLASHBULB	FLATIRONS	FLATWASH	FLAVORFUL
FLANKING	FLASHCARD	FLATLAND	FLATWATER	FLAVORIER
FLANKS	FLASHCUBE	FLATLANDS	FLATWAYS	FLAVORING
FLANNEL	FLASHED	FLATLET	FLATWISE	FLAVORIST
FLANNELED	FLASHER	FLATLETS	FLATWORK	FLAVOROUS
FLANNELET	FLASHERS	FLATLINE	FLATWORKS	FLAVORS
FLANNELLY	FLASHES	FLATLINED	FLATWORM	FLAVORY
FLANNELS	FLASHEST	FLATLINER	FLATWORMS	FLAVOUR
FLANNEN	FLASHGUN	FLATLINES	FLAUGHT	FLAVOURED
FLANNENS	FLASHGUNS	FLATLING	FLAUGHTED	FLAVOURER
FLANNIE	FLASHIER	FLATLINGS	FLAUGHTER	FLAVOURS
FLANNIES	FLASHIEST	FLATLONG	FLAUGHTS	FLAVOURY
FLANNY	FLASHILY	FLATLY	FLAUNCH	FLAW
FLANS	FLASHING	FLATMATE	FLAUNCHED	FLAWED
FLAP	FLASHINGS	FLATMATES	FLAUNCHES	FLAWIER
FLAPERON	FLASHLAMP	FLATNESS	FLAUNE	FLAWIEST
FLAPERONS	FLASHOVER	FLATPACK	FLAUNES	FLAWING
FLAPJACK	FLASHTUBE	FLATPACKS	FLAUNT	FLAWLESS
FLAPJACKS	FLASHY	FLATPICK	FLAUNTED	FLAWN
FLAPLESS	FLASK	FLATPICKS	FLAUNTER	FLAWNS
FLAPLIKE	FLASKET	FLATS	FLAUNTERS	FLAWS
FLAPPABLE	FLASKETS	FLATSHARE	FLAUNTIER	FLAWY
FLAPPED	FLASKS	FLATSTICK	FLAUNTILY	FLAX
FLAPPER	FLAT	FLATTED	FLAUNTING	FLAXEN
FLAPPERS	FLATBACK	FLATTEN	FLAUNTS	FLAXES
FLAPPIER	FLATBACKS	FLATTENED	FLAUNTY	FLAXIER
FLAPPIEST	FLATBED	FLATTENER	FLAUTA	FLAXIEST
FLAPPING	FLATBEDS	FLATTENS	FLAUTAS	FLAXLIKE
FLAPPINGS	FLATBOAT	FLATTER	FLAUTIST	FLAXSEED
FLAPPY	FLATBOATS	FLATTERED	FLAUTISTS	FLAXSEEDS
FLAPS	FLATBREAD	FLATTERER	FLAVA	FLAXY
FLAPTRACK	FLATBROD	FLATTERS	FLAVANOL	FLAY
FLARE	FLATBRODS	FLATTERY	FLAVANOLS	FLAYED
FLAREBACK	FLATCAP	FLATTEST	FLAVANONE	FLAYER
FLARED	FLATCAPS	FLATTIE	FLAVAS	FLAYERS
FLARES	FLATCAR	FLATTIES	FLAVIN	FLAYING
FLAREUP	FLATCARS	FLATTING	FLAVINE	FLAYS
FLAREUPS	FLATETTE	FLATTINGS	FLAVINES	FLAYSOME
FLARIER	FLATETTES	FLATTISH	FLAVINS	FLEA

FLEABAG	FLEECHED	FLENCHED	FLEW	FLICKING
FLEABAGS	FLEECHES	FLENCHER	FLEWED	FLICKS
FLEABANE	FLEECHING	FLENCHERS	FLEWS	FLICS
FLEABANES	FLEECIE	FLENCHES	FLEX	FLIED
FLEABITE	FLEECIER	FLENCHING	FLEXAGON	FLIER
FLEABITES	FLEECIES	FLENSE	FLEXAGONS	FLIERS
FLEADH	FLEECIEST	FLENSED	FLEXED	FLIES
FLEADHS	FLEECILY	FLENSER	FLEXES	FLIEST
FLEAM	FLEECING	FLENSERS	FLEXI	FLIGHT
FLEAMS	FLEECY	FLENSES	FLEXIBLE	FLIGHTED
FLEAPIT	FLEEING	FLENSING	FLEXIBLY	FLIGHTIER
FLEAPITS	FLEEK	FLEROVIUM	FLEXILE	FLIGHTILY
FLEAS	FLEEKS	FLESH	FLEXING	FLIGHTING
FLEASOME	FLEER	FLESHED	FLEXION	FLIGHTS
FLEAWORT	FLEERED	FLESHER	FLEXIONAL	FLIGHTY
FLEAWORTS	FLEERER	FLESHERS	FLEXIONS	FLIM
FLECHE	FLEERERS	FLESHHOOD	FLEXIS	FLIMFLAM
FLECHES	FLEERING	FLESHIER	FLEXITIME	FLIMFLAMS
FLECHETTE	FLEERINGS	FLESHIEST	FLEXO	FLIMP
FLECK	FLEERS	FLESHILY	FLEXOR	FLIMPED
FLECKED	FLEES	FLESHING	FLEXORS	FLIMPING
FLECKER	FLEET	FLESHINGS	FLEXOS	FLIMPS
FLECKERED	FLEETED	FLESHLESS	FLEXTIME	FLIMS
FLECKERS	FLEETER	FLESHLIER	FLEXTIMER	FLIMSIER
FLECKIER	FLEETERS	FLESHLING	FLEXTIMES	FLIMSIES
FLECKIEST	FLEETEST	FLESHLY	FLEXUOSE	FLIMSIEST
FLECKING	FLEETING	FLESHMENT	FLEXUOUS	FLIMSILY
FLECKLESS	FLEETLY	FLESHPOT	FLEXURAL	FLIMSY
FLECKS	FLEETNESS	FLESHPOTS	FLEXURE	FLINCH
FLECKY	FLEETS	FLESHWORM	FLEXURES	FLINCHED
FLECTION	FLEG	FLESHY	FLEXWING	FLINCHER
FLECTIONS	FLEGGED	FLETCH	FLEXWINGS	FLINCHERS
FLED	FLEGGING	FLETCHED	FLEY	FLINCHES
FLEDGE	FLEGS	FLETCHER	FLEYED	FLINCHING
FLEDGED	FLEHMEN	FLETCHERS	FLEYING	FLINDER
FLEDGES	FLEHMENED	FLETCHES	FLEYS	FLINDERED
FLEDGIER	FLEHMENS	FLETCHING	FLIBBERT	FLINDERS
FLEDGIEST	FLEISHIG	FLETTON	FLIBBERTS	FLING
FLEDGING	FLEISHIK	FLETTONS	FLIC	FLINGER
FLEDGLING	FLEME	FLEUR	FLICHTER	FLINGERS
FLEDGY	FLEMED	FLEURET	FLICHTERS	FLINGING
FLEE	FLEMES	FLEURETS	FLICK	FLINGS
FLEECE	FLEMING	FLEURETTE	FLICKABLE	FLINKITE
FLEECED	FLEMISH	FLEURON	FLICKED	FLINKITES
FLEECER	FLEMISHED	FLEURONS	FLICKER	FLINT
FLEECERS	FLEMISHES	FLEURS	FLICKERED	FLINTED
FLEECES	FLEMIT	FLEURY	FLICKERS	FLINTHEAD
FLEECH	FLENCH		FLICKERY	FLINTIER

FLINTIEST	FLISKY	FLOB	FLOODLIT	FLORALLY
FLINTIFY	FLIT	FLOBBED	FLOODMARK	FLORALS
FLINTILY	FLITCH	FLOBBING	FLOODS	FLORAS
FLINTING	FLITCHED	FLOBS	FLOODTIDE	FLOREANT
FLINTLIKE	FLITCHES	FLOC	FLOODWALL	FLOREAT
FLINTLOCK	FLITCHING	FLOCCED	FLOODWAY	FLOREATED
FLINTS	FLITE	FLOCCI	FLOODWAYS	FLORENCE
FLINTY	FLITED	FLOCCING	FLOOEY	FLORENCES
FLIP	FLITES	FLOCCOSE	FLOOIE	FLORET
FLIPBOARD	FLITING	FLOCCULAR	FLOOR	FLORETS
FLIPBOOK	FLITS	FLOCCULE	FLOORAGE	FLORIATED
FLIPBOOKS	FLITT	FLOCCULES	FLOORAGES	FLORICANE
FLIPCHART	FLITTED	FLOCCULI	FLOORED	FLORID
FLIPFLOP	FLITTER	FLOCCULUS	FLOORER	FLORIDEAN
FLIPFLOPS	FLITTERED	FLOCCUS	FLOORERS	FLORIDER
FLIPPANCY	FLITTERN	FLOCK	FLOORHEAD	FLORIDEST
FLIPPANT	FLITTERNS	FLOCKED	FLOORING	FLORIDITY
FLIPPED	FLITTERS	FLOCKIER	FLOORINGS	FLORIDLY
FLIPPER	FLITTING	FLOCKIEST	FLOORLESS	FLORIER
FLIPPERS	FLITTINGS	FLOCKING	FLOORPAN	FLORIEST
FLIPPEST	FLITTS	FLOCKINGS	FLOORPANS	FLORIFORM
FLIPPIER	FLIVVER	FLOCKLESS	FLOORS	FLORIGEN
FLIPPIEST	FLIVVERS	FLOCKS	FLOORSHOW	FLORIGENS
FLIPPING	FLIX	FLOCKY	FLOOSIE	FLORIN
FLIPPINGS	FLIXED	FLOCS	FLOOSIES	FLORINS
FLIPPY	FLIXES	FLOE	FLOOSY	FLORIST
FLIPS	FLIXING	FLOES	FLOOZIE	FLORISTIC
FLIPSIDE	FLIXWEED	FLOG	FLOOZIES	FLORISTRY
FLIPSIDES	FLIXWEEDS	FLOGGABLE	FLOOZY	FLORISTS
FLIR	FLOAT	FLOGGED	FLOP	FLORS
FLIRS	FLOATABLE	FLOGGER	FLOPHOUSE	FLORUIT
FLIRT	FLOATAGE	FLOGGERS	FLOPOVER	FLORUITS
FLIRTED	FLOATAGES	FLOGGING	FLOPOVERS	FLORULA
FLIRTER	FLOATANT	FLOGGINGS	FLOPPED	FLORULAE
FLIRTERS	FLOATANTS	FLOGS	FLOPPER	FLORULE
FLIRTIER	FLOATBASE	FLOKATI	FLOPPERS	FLORULES
FLIRTIEST	FLOATCUT	FLOKATIS	FLOPPIER	FLORY
FLIRTING	FLOATED	FLONG	FLOPPIES	FLOSCULAR
FLIRTINGS	FLOATEL	FLONGS	FLOPPIEST	FLOSCULE
FLIRTISH	FLOATELS	FLOOD	FLOPPILY	FLOSCULES
FLIRTS	FLOATER	FLOODABLE	FLOPPING	FLOSH
FLIRTY	FLOATERS	FLOODED	FLOPPY	FLOSHES
FLISK	FLOATIER	FLOODER	FLOPS	FLOSS
FLISKED	FLOATIEST	FLOODERS	FLOPTICAL	FLOSSED
FLISKIER	FLOATING	FLOODGATE	FLOR	FLOSSER
FLISKIEST	FLOATINGS	FLOODING	FLORA	FLOSSERS
FLISKING	FLOATS	FLOODINGS	FLORAE	FLOSSES
FLISKS	FLOATY	FLOODLESS	FLORAL	FLOSSIE

FLOSSIER	FLOUSING	FLUE	FLUIDIZES	FLUORESCE
FLOSSIES	FLOUT	FLUED	FLUIDLIKE	FLUORIC
FLOSSIEST	FLOUTED	FLUELLEN	FLUIDLY	FLUORID
FLOSSILY	FLOUTER	FLUELLENS	FLUIDNESS	FLUORIDE
FLOSSING	FLOUTERS	FLUELLIN	FLUIDRAM	FLUORIDES
FLOSSINGS	FLOUTING	FLUELLINS	FLUIDRAMS	FLUORIDS
FLOSSY	FLOUTS	FLUENCE	FLUIDS	FLUORIN
FLOTA	FLOW	FLUENCES	FLUIER	FLUORINE
FLOTAGE	FLOWABLE	FLUENCIES	FLUIEST	FLUORINES
FLOTAGES	FLOWAGE	FLUENCY	FLUISH	FLUORINS
FLOTANT	FLOWAGES	FLUENT	FLUKE	FLUORITÉ
FLOTAS	FLOWCHART	FLUENTLY	FLUKED	FLUORITES
FLOTATION	FLOWED	FLUENTS	FLUKES	FLUOROSES
FLOTE	FLOWER	FLUERIC	FLUKEY	FLUOROSIS
FLOTED	FLOWERAGE	FLUERICS	FLUKIER	FLUOROTIC
FLOTEL	FLOWERBED	FLUES	FLUKIEST	FLUORS
FLOTELS	FLOWERED	FLUEWORK	FLUKILY	FLUORSPAR
FLOTES	FLOWERER	FLUEWORKS	FLUKINESS	FLURR
FLOTILLA	FLOWERERS	FLUEY	FLUKING	FLURRED
FLOTILLAS	FLOWERET	FLUFF	FLUKY	FLURRIED
FLOTING	FLOWERETS	FLUFFBALL	FLUME	FLURRIES
FLOTSAM	FLOWERFUL	FLUFFED	FLUMED	FLURRING
FLOTSAMS	FLOWERIER	FLUFFER	FLUMES	FLURRS
FLOUNCE	FLOWERILY	FLUFFERS	FLUMING	FLURRY
FLOUNCED	FLOWERING	FLUFFIER	FLUMMERY	FLURRYING
FLOUNCES	FLOWERPOT	FLUFFIEST	FLUMMOX	FLUS
FLOUNCIER	FLOWERS	FLUFFILY	FLUMMOXED	FLUSH
FLOUNCING	FLOWERY	FLUFFING	FLUMMOXES	FLUSHABLE
FLOUNCY	FLOWING	FLUFFS	FLUMP	FLUSHED
FLOUNDER	FLOWINGLY	FLUFFY	FLUMPED	FLUSHER
FLOUNDERS	FLOWMETER	FLUGEL	FLUMPING	FLUSHERS
FLOUR	FLOWN	FLUGELMAN	FLUMPS	FLUSHES
FLOURED	FLOWS	FLUGELMEN	FLUNG	FLUSHEST
FLOURIER	FLOWSTONE	FLUGELS	FLUNK	FLUSHIER
FLOURIEST	FLOX	FLUID	FLUNKED	FLUSHIEST
FLOURING	FLU	FLUIDAL	FLUNKER	FLUSHING
FLOURISH	FLUATE	FLUIDALLY	FLUNKERS	FLUSHINGS
FLOURISHY	FLUATES	FLUIDIC	FLUNKEY	FLUSHNESS
FLOURLESS	FLUB	FLUIDICS	FLUNKEYS	FLUSHWORK
FLOURS	FLUBBED	FLUIDIFY	FLUNKIE	FLUSHY
FLOURY	FLUBBER	FLUIDISE	FLUNKIES	FLUSTER
FLOUSE	FLUBBERS	FLUIDISED	FLUNKING	FLUSTERED
FLOUSED	FLUBBING	FLUIDISER	FLUNKS	FLUSTERS
FLOUSES	FLUBDUB	FLUIDISES	FLUNKY	FLUSTERY
FLOUSH	FLUBDUBS	FLUIDITY	FLUNKYISM	FLUSTRATE
FLOUSHED	FLUBS	FLUIDIZE	FLUOR	FLUTE
FLOUSHES	FLUCTUANT	FLUIDIZED	FLUORENE	FLUTED
FLOUSHING	FLUCTUATE	FLUIDIZER	FLUORENES	FLUTELIKE

FLUTER	FLYBLOWS	FLYSPECKS	FOCALISE	FOETORS
FLUTERS	FLYBOAT	FLYSPRAY	FOCALISED	FOETUS
FLUTES	FLYBOATS	FLYSPRAYS	FOCALISES	FOETUSES
FLUTEY	FLYBOOK	FLYSTRIKE	FOCALIZE	FOG
FLUTEYER	FLYBOOKS	FLYTE	FOCALIZED	FOGASH
FLUTEYEST	FLYBOY	FLYTED	FOCALIZES	FOGASHES
FLUTIER	FLYBOYS	FLYTES	FOCALLY	FOGBOUND
FLUTIEST	FLYBRIDGE	FLYTIER	FOCI	FOGBOW
FLUTINA	FLYBY	FLYTIERS	FOCIMETER	FOGBOWS
FLUTINAS	FLYBYS	FLYTING	FOCOMETER	FOGDOG
FLUTING	FLYER	FLYTINGS	FOCUS	FOGDOGS
FLUTINGS	FLYERS	FLYTRAP	FOCUSABLE	FOGEY
FLUTIST	FLYEST	FLYTRAPS	FOCUSED	FOGEYDOM
FLUTISTS	FLYFISHER	FLYWAY	FOCUSER	FOGEYDOMS
FLUTTER	FLYHAND	FLYWAYS	FOCUSERS	FOGEYISH
FLUTTERED	FLYHANDS	FLYWEIGHT	FOCUSES	FOGEYISM
FLUTTERER	FLYING	FLYWHEEL	FOCUSING	FOGEYISMS
FLUTTERS	FLYINGS	FLYWHEELS	FOCUSINGS	FOGEYS
FLUTTERY	FLYLEAF	FOAL	FOCUSLESS	FOGFRUIT
FLUTY	FLYLEAVES	FOALED	FOCUSSED	FOGFRUITS
FLUVIAL	FLYLESS	FOALFOOT	FOCUSSES	FOGGAGE
FLUVIATIC	FLYLINE	FOALFOOTS	FOCUSSING	FOGGAGES
FLUX	FLYLINES	FOALING	FODDER	FOGGED
FLUXED	FLYMAKER	FOALINGS	FODDERED	FOGGER
FLUXES	FLYMAKERS	FOALS	FODDERER	FOGGERS
FLUXGATE	FLYMAN	FOAM	FODDERERS	FOGGIER
FLUXGATES	FLYMEN	FOAMABLE	FODDERING	FOGGIEST
FLUXING	FLYOFF	FOAMED	FODDERS	FOGGILY
FLUXION	FLYOFFS	FOAMER	FODGEL	FOGGINESS
FLUXIONAL	FLYOVER	FOAMERS	FOE	FOGGING
FLUXIONS	FLYOVERS	FOAMIER	FOEDARIE	FOGGINGS
FLUXIVE	FLYPAPER	FOAMIEST	FOEDARIES	FOGGY
FLUXMETER	FLYPAPERS	FOAMILY	FOEDERATI	FOGHORN
FLUYT	FLYPAST	FOAMINESS	FOEFIE	FOGHORNS
FLUYTS	FLYPASTS	FOAMING	FOEHN	FOGIE
FLY	FLYPE	FOAMINGLY	FOEHNS	FOGIES
FLYABLE	FLYPED	FOAMINGS	FOEMAN	FOGLE
FLYAWAY	FLYPES	FOAMLESS	FOEMEN	FOGLES
FLYAWAYS	FLYPING	FOAMLIKE	FOEN	FOGLESS
FLYBACK	FLYPITCH	FOAMS	FOES	FOGLIGHT
FLYBACKS	FLYPOSTER	FOAMY	FOETAL	FOGLIGHTS
FLYBANE	FLYRODDER	FOB	FOETATION	FOGMAN
FLYBANES	FLYSCH	FOBBED	FOETICIDE	FOGMEN
FLYBELT	FLYSCHES	FOBBING	FOETID	FOGOU
FLYBELTS	FLYSCREEN	FOBS	FOETIDER	FOGOUS
FLYBLEW	FLYSHEET	FOCACCIA	FOETIDEST	FOGRAM
FLYBLOW	FLYSHEETS	FOCACCIAS	FOETIDLY	FOGRAMITE
FLYBLOWN	FLYSPECK	FOCAL	FOETOR	FOGRAMITY

FOGRAMS	FOLDBACKS	FOLKINESS	FOMENTERS	FONTLET
FOGS	FOLDBOAT	FOLKISH	FOMENTING	FONTLETS
FOGY	FOLDBOATS	FOLKLAND	FOMENTS	FONTS
FOGYDOM	FOLDED	FOLKLANDS	FOMES	FOO
FOGYDOMS	FOLDER	FOLKLIFE	FOMITE	FOOBAR
FOGYISH	FOLDEROL	FOLKLIFES	FOMITES	FOOD
FOGYISM	FOLDEROLS	FOLKLIKE	FON	FOODBANK
FOGYISMS	FOLDERS	FOLKLIVES	FOND	FOODBANKS
FOH	FOLDING	FOLKLORE	FONDA	FOODBORNE
FOHN	FOLDINGS	FOLKLORES	FONDANT	FOODERIES
FOHNS	FOLDOUT	FOLKLORIC	FONDANTS	FOODERY
FOIBLE	FOLDOUTS	FOLKMOOT	FONDAS	FOODFUL
FOIBLES	FOLDS	FOLKMOOTS	FONDED	FOODIE
FOID	FOLDUP	FOLKMOT	FONDER	FOODIES
FOIDS	FOLDUPS	FOLKMOTE	FONDEST	FOODISM
FOIL	FOLEY	FOLKMOTES	FONDING	FOODISMS
FOILABLE	FOLEYS	FOLKMOTS	FONDLE	FOODLAND
FOILBORNE	FOLIA	FOLKS	FONDLED	FOODLANDS
FOILED	FOLIAGE	FOLKSIER	FONDLER	FOODLESS
FOILING	FOLIAGED	FOLKSIEST	FONDLERS	FOODOIR
FOILINGS	FOLIAGES	FOLKSILY	FONDLES	FOODOIRS
FOILIST	FOLIAR	FOLKSONG	FONDLING	FOODS
FOILISTS	FOLIATE	FOLKSONGS	FONDLINGS	FOODSHED
FOILS	FOLIATED	FOLKSY	FONDLY	FOODSHEDS
FOILSMAN	FOLIATES	FOLKTALE	FONDNESS	FOODSTUFF
FOILSMEN	FOLIATING	FOLKTALES	FONDS	FOODWAYS
FOIN	FOLIATION	FOLKWAY	FONDU	FOODY
FOINED	FOLIATURE	FOLKWAYS	FONDUE	FOOFARAW
FOINING	FOLIC	FOLKY	FONDUED	FOOFARAWS
FOININGLY	FOLIE	FOLLES	FONDUEING	FOOL
FOINS	FOLIES	FOLLICLE	FONDUES	FOOLED
FOISON	FOLIO	FOLLICLES	FONDUING	FOOLERIES
FOISONS	FOLIOED	FOLLIED	FONDUS	FOOLERY
FOIST	FOLIOING	FOLLIES	FONE	FOOLFISH
FOISTED	FOLIOLATE	FOLLIS	FONES	FOOLHARDY
FOISTER	FOLIOLE	FOLLOW	FONLY	FOOLING
FOISTERS	FOLIOLES	FOLLOWED	FONNED	FOOLINGS
FOISTING	FOLIOLOSE	FOLLOWER	FONNING	FOOLISH
FOISTS	FOLIOS	FOLLOWERS	FONS	FOOLISHER
FOLACIN	FOLIOSE	FOLLOWING	FONT	FOOLISHLY
FOLACINS	FOLIOUS	FOLLOWS	FONTAL	FOOLPROOF
FOLATE	FOLIUM	FOLLOWUP	FONTANEL	FOOLS
FOLATES	FOLIUMS	FOLLOWUPS	FONTANELS	FOOLSCAP
FOLD	FOLK	FOLLY	FONTANGE	FOOLSCAPS
FOLDABLE	FOLKIE	FOLLYING	FONTANGES	FOOS
FOLDAWAY	FOLKIER	FOMENT	FONTICULI	FOOSBALL
FOLDAWAYS	FOLKIES	FOMENTED	FONTINA	FOOSBALLS
FOLDBACK	FOLKIEST	FOMENTER	FONTINAS	FOOT

F

FOOTAGE	FOOTLONGS	FOOTSTONE	FORASMUCH	FORCIBLY
FOOTAGES	FOOTLOOSE	FOOTSTOOL	FORAY	FORCING
FOOTBAG	FOOTMAN	FOOTSY	FORAYED	FORCINGLY
FOOTBAGS	FOOTMARK	FOOTWALL	FORAYER	FORCIPATE
FOOTBALL	FOOTMARKS	FOOTWALLS	FORAYERS	FORCIPES
FOOTBALLS	FOOTMEN	FOOTWAY	FORAYING	FORD
FOOTBAR	FOOTMUFF	FOOTWAYS	FORAYS	FORDABLE
FOOTBARS	FOOTMUFFS	FOOTWEAR	FORB	FORDED
FOOTBATH	FOOTNOTE	FOOTWEARS	FORBAD	FORDID
FOOTBATHS	FOOTNOTED	FOOTWEARY	FORBADE	FORDING
FOOTBED	FOOTNOTES	FOOTWELL	FORBARE	FORDLESS
FOOTBEDS	FOOTPACE	FOOTWELLS	FORBEAR	FORDO
FOOTBOARD	FOOTPACES	FOOTWORK	FORBEARER	FORDOES
FOOTBOY	FOOTPAD	FOOTWORKS	FORBEARS	FORDOING
FOOTBOYS	FOOTPADS	FOOTWORN	FORBID	FORDONE
FOOTBRAKE	FOOTPAGE	FOOTY	FORBIDAL	FORDONNE
FOOTCLOTH	FOOTPAGES	FOOZLE	FORBIDALS	FORDS
FOOTED	FOOTPATH	FOOZLED	FORBIDDAL	FORE
FOOTER	FOOTPATHS	FOOZLER	FORBIDDEN	FOREANENT
FOOTERED	FOOTPLATE	FOOZLERS	FORBIDDER	FOREARM
FOOTERING	FOOTPOST	FOOZLES	FORBIDS	FOREARMED
FOOTERS	FOOTPOSTS	FOOZLING	FORBODE	FOREARMS
FOOTFALL	FOOTPRINT	FOOZLINGS	FORBODED	FOREBAY
FOOTFALLS	FOOTPUMP	FOP	FORBODES	FOREBAYS
FOOTFAULT	FOOTPUMPS	FOPLING	FORBODING	FOREBEAR
FOOTGEAR	FOOTRA	FOPLINGS	FORBORE	FOREBEARS
FOOTGEARS	FOOTRACE	FOPPED	FORBORNE	FOREBITT
FOOTHILL	FOOTRACES	FOPPERIES	FORBS	FOREBITTS
FOOTHILLS	FOOTRAS	FOPPERY	FORBY	FOREBODE
FOOTHOLD	FOOTREST	FOPPING	FORBYE	FOREBODED
FOOTHOLDS	FOOTRESTS	FOPPISH	FORCAT	FOREBODER
FOOTIE	FOOTROPE	FOPPISHLY	FORCATS	FOREBODES
FOOTIER	FOOTROPES	FOPS	FORCE	FOREBODY
FOOTIES	FOOTRULE	FOR	FORCEABLE	FOREBOOM
FOOTIEST	FOOTRULES	FORA	FORCEABLY	FOREBOOMS
FOOTING	FOOTS	FORAGE	FORCED	FOREBRAIN
FOOTINGS	FOOTSAL	FORAGED	FORCEDLY	FOREBY
FOOTLE	FOOTSALS	FORAGER	FORCEFUL	FOREBYE
FOOTLED	FOOTSIE	FORAGERS	FORCELESS	FORECABIN
FOOTLER	FOOTSIES	FORAGES	FORCEMEAT	FORECADDY
FOOTLERS	FOOTSLOG	FORAGING	FORCEOUT	FORECAR
FOOTLES	FOOTSLOGS	FORAM	FORCEOUTS	FORECARS
FOOTLESS	FOOTSORE	FORAMEN	FORCEPS	FORECAST
FOOTLIGHT	FOOTSTALK	FORAMENS	FORCEPSES	FORECASTS
FOOTLIKE	FOOTSTALL	FORAMINA	FORCER	FORECHECK
FOOTLING	FOOTSTEP	FORAMINAL	FORCERS	FORECLOSE
FOOTLINGS	FOOTSTEPS	FORAMS	FORCES	FORECLOTH
FOOTLONG	FOOTSTOCK	FORANE	FORCIBLE	FORECOURT

FOREDATE	FOREKNOW	FOREPAST	FORESLACK	FOREWIND
FOREDATED	FOREKNOWN	FOREPAW	FORESLOW	FOREWINDS
FOREDATES	FOREKNOWS	FOREPAWS	FORESLOWS	FOREWING
FOREDECK	FOREL	FOREPEAK	FORESPAKE	FOREWINGS
FOREDECKS	FORELADY	FOREPEAKS	FORESPEAK	FOREWOMAN
FOREDID	FORELAID	FOREPLAN	FORESPEND	FOREWOMEN
FOREDO	FORELAIN	FOREPLANS	FORESPENT	FOREWORD
FOREDOES	FORELAND	FOREPLAY	FORESPOKE	FOREWORDS
FOREDOING	FORELANDS	FOREPLAYS	FOREST	FOREWORN
FOREDONE	FORELAY	FOREPOINT	FORESTAGE	FOREX
FOREDOOM	FORELAYS	FORERAN	FORESTAIR	FOREXES
FOREDOOMS	FORELEG	FORERANK	FORESTAL	FOREYARD
FOREFACE	FORELEGS	FORERANKS	FORESTALL	FOREYARDS
FOREFACES	FORELEND	FOREREACH	FORESTAY	FORFAIR
FOREFEEL	FORELENDS	FOREREAD	FORESTAYS	FORFAIRED
FOREFEELS	FORELENT	FOREREADS	FORESTEAL	FORFAIRN
FOREFEET	FORELIE	FORERUN	FORESTED	FORFAIRS
FOREFELT	FORELIES	FORERUNS	FORESTER	FORFAITER
FOREFEND	FORELIFT	FORES	FORESTERS	FORFAULT
FOREFENDS	FORELIFTS	FORESAID	FORESTIAL	FORFAULTS
FOREFOOT	FORELIMB	FORESAIL	FORESTINE	FORFEIT
FOREFRONT	FORELIMBS	FORESAILS	FORESTING	FORFEITED
FOREGLEAM	FORELLED	FORESAW	FORESTRY	FORFEITER
FOREGO	FORELLING	FORESAY	FORESTS	FORFEITS
FOREGOER	FORELOCK	FORESAYS	FORESWEAR	FORFEND
FOREGOERS	FORELOCKS	FORESEE	FORESWORE	FORFENDED
FOREGOES	FORELS	FORESEEN	FORESWORN	FORFENDS
FOREGOING	FORELYING	FORESEER	FORETASTE	FORFEX
FOREGONE	FOREMAN	FORESEERS	FORETEACH	FORFEXES
FOREGUT	FOREMAST	FORESEES	FORETEETH	FORFICATE
FOREGUTS	FOREMASTS	FORESHANK	FORETELL	FORFOCHEN
FOREHAND	FOREMEAN	FORESHEET	FORETELLS	FORGAT
FOREHANDS	FOREMEANS	FORESHEW	FORETHINK	FORGATHER
FOREHEAD	FOREMEANT	FORESHEWN	FORETIME	FORGAVE
FOREHEADS	FOREMEN	FORESHEWS	FORETIMES	FORGE
FOREHENT	FOREMILK	FORESHIP	FORETOKEN	FORGEABLE
FOREHENTS	FOREMILKS	FORESHIPS	FORETOLD	FORGED
FOREHOCK	FOREMOST	FORESHOCK	FORETOOTH	FORGEMAN
FOREHOCKS	FORENAME	FORESHORE	FORETOP	FORGEMEN
FOREHOOF	FORENAMED	FORESHOW	FORETOPS	FORGER
FOREHOOFS	FORENAMES	FORESHOWN	FOREVER	FORGERIES
FOREIGN	FORENIGHT	FORESHOWS	FOREVERS	FORGERS
FOREIGNER	FORENOON	FORESIDE	FOREWARD	FORGERY
FOREIGNLY	FORENOONS	FORESIDES	FOREWARDS	FORGES
FOREJUDGE	FORENSIC	FORESIGHT	FOREWARN	FORGET
FOREKING	FORENSICS	FORESKIN	FOREWARNS	FORGETFUL
FOREKINGS	FOREPART	FORESKINS	FOREWEIGH	FORGETIVE
FOREKNEW	FOREPARTS	FORESKIRT	FOREWENT	FORGETS

FORGETTER	FORKFUL	FORMATE	FORNENST	FORSPENT
FORGING	FORKFULS	FORMATED	FORNENT	FORSPOKE
FORGINGS	FORKHEAD	FORMATES	FORNICAL	FORSPOKEN
FORGIVE	FORKHEADS	FORMATING	FORNICATE	FORSWATT
FORGIVEN	FORKIER	FORMATION	FORNICES	FORSWEAR
FORGIVER	FORKIEST	FORMATIVE	FORNIX	FORSWEARS
FORGIVERS	FORKINESS	FORMATS	FORPET	FORSWINK
FORGIVES	FORKING	FORMATTED	FORPETS	FORSWINKS
FORGIVING	FORKLESS	FORMATTER	FORPINE	FORSWONCK
FORGO	FORKLIFT	FORME	FORPINED	FORSWORE
FORGOER	FORKLIFTS	FORMED	FORPINES	FORSWORN
FORGOERS	FORKLIKE	FORMEE	FORPINING	FORSWUNK
FORGOES	FORKS	FORMEES	FORPIT	FORSYTHIA
FORGOING	FORKSFUL	FORMER	FORPITS	FORT
FORGONE	FORKTAIL	FORMERLY	FORRAD	FORTALICE
FORGOT	FORKTAILS	FORMERS	FORRADER	FORTE
FORGOTTEN	FORKY	FORMES	FORRADS	FORTED
FORHAILE	FORLANA	FORMFUL	FORRARDER	FORTES
FORHAILED	FORLANAS	FORMIATE	FORRAY	FORTH
FORHAILES	FORLEND	FORMIATES	FORRAYED	FORTHCAME
FORHENT	FORLENDS	FORMIC	FORRAYING	FORTHCOME
FORHENTS	FORLENT	FORMICA	FORRAYS	FORTHINK
FORHOO	FORLESE	FORMICANT	FORREN	FORTHINKS
FORHOOED	FORLESES	FORMICARY	FORRIT	FORTHWITH
FORHOOIE	FORLESING	FORMICAS	FORSAID	FORTHY
FORHOOIED	FORLORE	FORMICATE	FORSAKE	FORTIES
FORHOOIES	FORLORN	FORMING	FORSAKEN	FORTIETH
FORHOOING	FORLORNER	FORMINGS	FORSAKER	FORTIETHS
FORHOOS	FORLORNLY	FORMLESS	FORSAKERS	FORTIFIED
FORHOW	FORLORNS	FORMOL	FORSAKES	FORTIFIER
FORHOWED	FORM	FORMOLS	FORSAKING	FORTIFIES
FORHOWING	FORMABLE	FORMS	FORSAY	FORTIFY
FORHOWS	FORMABLY	FORMULA	FORSAYING	FORTILAGE
FORINSEC	FORMAL	FORMULAE	FORSAYS	FORTING
FORINT	FORMALIN	FORMULAIC	FORSLACK	FORTIS
FORINTS	FORMALINE	FORMULAR	FORSLACKS	FORTITUDE
FORJASKIT	FORMALINS	FORMULARS	FORSLOE	FORTLET
FORJESKIT	FORMALISE	FORMULARY	FORSLOED	FORTLETS
FORJUDGE	FORMALISM	FORMULAS	FORSLOES	FORTNIGHT
FORJUDGED	FORMALIST	FORMULATE	FORSLOW	FORTRESS
FORJUDGES	FORMALITY	FORMULISE	FORSLOWED	FORTS
FORK	FORMALIZE	FORMULISM	FORSLOWS	FORTUITY
FORKBALL	FORMALLY	FORMULIST	FORSOOK	FORTUNATE
FORKBALLS	FORMALS	FORMULIZE	FORSOOTH	FORTUNE
FORKED	FORMAMIDE	FORMWORK	FORSPEAK	FORTUNED
FORKEDLY	FORMANT	FORMWORKS	FORSPEAKS	FORTUNES
FORKER	FORMANTS	FORMYL	FORSPEND	FORTUNING
FORKERS	FORMAT	FORMYLS	FORSPENDS	FORTUNISE

FORTUNIZE	FOSSILS	FOULED	FOURSES	FOWLPOX
FORTY	FOSSOR	FOULER	FOURSOME	FOWLPOXES
FORTYFOLD	FOSSORIAL	FOULES	FOURSOMES	FOWLS
FORTYISH	FOSSORS	FOULEST	FOURTEEN	FOWTH
FORUM	FOSSULA	FOULIE	FOURTEENS	FOWTHS
FORUMS	FOSSULAE	FOULIES	FOURTH	FOX
FORWANDER	FOSSULATE	FOULING	FOURTHLY	FOXBERRY
FORWARD	FOSTER	FOULINGS	FOURTHS	FOXED
FORWARDED	FOSTERAGE	FOULLY	FOUS	FOXES
FORWARDER	FOSTERED	FOULMART	FOUSSA	FOXFIRE
FORWARDLY	FOSTERER	FOULMARTS	FOUSSAS	FOXFIRES
FORWARDS	FOSTERERS	FOULNESS	FOUSTIER	FOXFISH
FORWARN	FOSTERING	FOULS	FOUSTIEST	FOXFISHES
FORWARNED	FOSTERS	FOUMART	FOUSTY	FOXGLOVE
FORWARNS	FOSTRESS	FOUMARTS	FOUTER	FOXGLOVES
FORWASTE	FOTHER	FOUND	FOUTERED	FOXHOLE
FORWASTED	FOTHERED	FOUNDED	FOUTERING	FOXHOLES
FORWASTES	FOTHERING	FOUNDER	FOUTERS	FOXHOUND
FORWEARY	FOTHERS	FOUNDERED	FOUTH	FOXHOUNDS
FORWENT	FOU	FOUNDERS	FOUTHS	FOXHUNT
FORWHY	FOUAT	FOUNDING	FOUTRA	FOXHUNTED
FORWORN	FOUATS	FOUNDINGS	FOUTRAS	FOXHUNTER
FORZA	FOUD	FOUNDLING	FOUTRE	FOXHUNTS
FORZANDI	FOUDRIE	FOUNDRESS	FOUTRED	FOXIE
FORZANDO	FOUDRIES	FOUNDRIES	FOUTRES	FOXIER
FORZANDOS	FOUDS	FOUNDRY	FOUTRING	FOXIES
FORZATI	FOUER	FOUNDS	FOVEA	FOXIEST
FORZATO	FOUEST	FOUNT	FOVEAE	FOXILY
FORZATOS	FOUET	FOUNTAIN	FOVEAL	FOXINESS
FORZE	FOUETS	FOUNTAINS	FOVEAS	FOXING
FOSCARNET	FOUETTE	FOUNTFUL	FOVEATE	FOXINGS
FOSS	FOUETTES	FOUNTS	FOVEATED	FOXLIKE
FOSSA	FOUGADE	FOUR	FOVEIFORM	FOXSHARK
FOSSAE	FOUGADES	FOURBALL	FOVEOLA	FOXSHARKS
FOSSAS	FOUGASSE	FOURBALLS	FOVEOLAE	FOXSHIP
FOSSATE	FOUGASSES	FOURCHEE	FOVEOLAR	FOXSHIPS
FOSSE	FOUGHT	FOURCHEES	FOVEOLAS	FOXSKIN
FOSSED	FOUGHTEN	FOUREYED	FOVEOLATE	FOXSKINS
FOSSES	FOUGHTIER	FOURFOLD	FOVEOLE	FOXTAIL
FOSSETTE	FOUGHTY	FOURGON	FOVEOLES	FOXTAILS
FOSSETTES	FOUL	FOURGONS	FOVEOLET	FOXTROT
FOSSICK	FOULARD	FOURPENCE	FOVEOLETS	FOXTROTS
FOSSICKED	FOULARDS	FOURPENNY	FOWL	FOXY
FOSSICKER	FOULBROOD	FOURPLAY	FOWLED	FOY
FOSSICKS	FOULDER	FOURPLAYS	FOWLER	FOYBOAT
FOSSIL	FOULDERED	FOURPLEX	FOWLERS	FOYBOATS
FOSSILISE	FOULDERS	FOURS	FOWLING	FOYER
FOSSILIZE	FOULE	FOURSCORE	FOWLINGS	FOYERS

FOYLE	FRAENA	FRAMERS	FRANZIEST	FRAUGHTED
FOYLED	FRAENUM	FRAMES	FRANZY	FRAUGHTER
FOYLES	FRAENUMS	FRAMEWORK	FRAP	FRAUGHTS
FOYLING	FRAG	FRAMING	FRAPE	FRAULEIN
FOYNE	FRAGGED	FRAMINGS	FRAPEAGE	FRAULEINS
FOYNED	FRAGGING	FRAMPAL	FRAPEAGES	FRAUS
FOYNES	FRAGGINGS	FRAMPLER	FRAPED	FRAUTAGE
FOYNING	FRAGILE	FRAMPLERS	FRAPES	FRAUTAGES
FOYS	FRAGILELY	FRAMPOLD	FRAPING	FRAWZEY
FOZIER	FRAGILER	FRANC	FRAPPANT	FRAWZEYS
FOZIEST	FRAGILEST	FRANCHISE	FRAPPE	FRAY
FOZINESS	FRAGILITY	FRANCISE	FRAPPED	FRAYED
FOZY	FRAGMENT	FRANCISED	FRAPPEE	FRAYING
FRA	FRAGMENTS	FRANCISES	FRAPPES	FRAYINGS
FRAB	FRAGOR	FRANCIUM	FRAPPING	FRAYS
FRABBED	FRAGORS	FRANCIUMS	FRAPS	FRAZIL
FRABBING	FRAGRANCE	FRANCIZE	FRAS	FRAZILS
FRABBIT	FRAGRANCY	FRANCIZED	FRASCATI	FRAZZLE
FRABJOUS	FRAGRANT	FRANCIZES	FRASCATIS	FRAZZLED
FRABS	FRAGS	FRANCO	FRASS	FRAZZLES
FRACAS	FRAICHEUR	FRANCOLIN	FRASSES	FRAZZLING
FRACASES	FRAIL	FRANCS	FRAT	FREAK
FRACK	FRAILER	FRANGER	FRATCH	FREAKED
FRACKED	FRAILEST	FRANGERS	FRATCHES	FREAKERY
FRACKER	FRAILISH	FRANGIBLE	FRATCHETY	FREAKFUL
FRACKERS	FRAILLY	FRANGLAIS	FRATCHIER	FREAKIER
FRACKING	FRAILNESS	FRANION	FRATCHING	FREAKIEST
FRACKINGS	FRAILS	FRANIONS	FRATCHY	FREAKILY
FRACKS	FRAILTEE	FRANK	FRATE	FREAKING
FRACT	FRAILTEES	FRANKABLE	FRATER	FREAKISH
FRACTAL	FRAILTIES	FRANKED	FRATERIES	FREAKOUT
FRACTALS	FRAILTY	FRANKER	FRATERNAL	FREAKOUTS
FRACTED	FRAIM	FRANKERS	FRATERS	FREAKS
FRACTI	FRAIMS	FRANKEST	FRATERY	FREAKY
FRACTING	FRAISE	FRANKFORT	FRATI	FRECKLE
FRACTION	FRAISED	FRANKFURT	FRATRIES	FRECKLED
FRACTIONS	FRAISES	FRANKING	FRATRY	FRECKLES
FRACTIOUS	FRAISING	FRANKLIN	FRATS	FRECKLIER
FRACTS	FRAKTUR	FRANKLINS	FRAU	FRECKLING
FRACTUR	FRAKTURS	FRANKLY	FRAUD	FRECKLY
FRACTURAL	FRAMABLE	FRANKNESS	FRAUDFUL	FREDAINE
FRACTURE	FRAMBESIA	FRANKS	FRAUDS	FREDAINES
FRACTURED	FRAMBOISE	FRANKUM	FRAUDSMAN	FREE
FRACTURER	FRAME	FRANKUMS	FRAUDSMEN	FREEBASE
FRACTURES	FRAMEABLE	FRANSERIA	FRAUDSTER	FREEBASED
FRACTURS	FRAMED	FRANTIC	FRAUGHAN	FREEBASER
FRACTUS	FRAMELESS	FRANTICLY	FRAUGHANS	FREEBASES
FRAE	FRAMER	FRANZIER	FRAUGHT	FREEBEE

FREEBEES

FREEBEES FREESTYLE FRENNES FRESHMAN FRICATIVE
FREEBIE FREET FRENULA FRESHMEN FRICHT
FREEBIES FREETIER FRENULAR FRESHNESS FRICHTED
FREEBOARD FREETIEST FRENULUM FRESNEL FRICHTING
FREEBOOT FREETS FRENULUMS FRESNELS FRICHTS
FREEBOOTS FREETY FRENUM FRET FRICKING
FREEBOOTY FREEWARE FRENUMS FRETBOARD FRICOT
FREEBORN FREEWARES FRENZICAL FRETFUL FRICOTS
FREECYCLE FREEWAY FRENZIED FRETFULLY FRICTION
FREED FREEWAYS FRENZIES FRETLESS FRICTIONS
FREEDIVER FREEWHEEL FRENZILY FRETS FRIDGE
FREEDMAN FREEWILL FRENZY FRETSAW FRIDGED
FREEDMEN FREEWOMAN FRENZYING FRETSAWS FRIDGES
FREEDOM FREEWOMEN FREON FRETSOME FRIDGING
FREEDOMS FREEWRITE FREONS FRETTED FRIED
FREEFALL FREEWROTE FREQUENCE FRETTER FRIEDCAKE
FREEFORM FREEZABLE FREQUENCY FRETTERS FRIEND
FREEGAN FREEZE FREQUENT FRETTIER FRIENDED
FREEGANS FREEZER FREQUENTS FRETTIEST FRIENDING
FREEHAND FREEZERS FRERE FRETTING FRIENDLY
FREEHOLD FREEZES FRERES FRETTINGS FRIENDS
FREEHOLDS FREEZING FRESCADE FRETTY FRIER
FREEING FREEZINGS FRESCADES FRETWORK FRIERS
FREEKEH FREIGHT FRESCO FRETWORKS FRIES
FREEKEHS FREIGHTED FRESCOED FRIABLE FRIEZE
FREELANCE FREIGHTER FRESCOER FRIAND FRIEZED
FREELOAD FREIGHTS FRESCOERS FRIANDE FRIEZES
FREELOADS FREIT FRESCOES FRIANDES FRIEZING
FREELY FREITIER FRESCOING FRIANDS FRIG
FREEMAN FREITIEST FRESCOIST FRIAR FRIGATE
FREEMASON FREITS FRESCOS FRIARBIRD FRIGATES
FREEMEN FREITY FRESH FRIARIES FRIGATOON
FREEMIUM FREMD FRESHED FRIARLY FRIGES
FREEMIUMS FREMDS FRESHEN FRIARS FRIGGED
FREENESS FREMIT FRESHENED FRIARY FRIGGER
FREEPHONE FREMITS FRESHENER FRIB FRIGGERS
FREEPOST FREMITUS FRESHENS FRIBBLE FRIGGING
FREEPOSTS FRENA FRESHER FRIBBLED FRIGGINGS
FREER FRENCH FRESHERS FRIBBLER FRIGHT
FREERIDE FRENCHED FRESHES FRIBBLERS FRIGHTED
FREERIDES FRENCHES FRESHEST FRIBBLES FRIGHTEN
FREERS FRENCHIFY FRESHET FRIBBLING FRIGHTENS
FREES FRENCHING FRESHETS FRIBBLISH FRIGHTFUL
FREESHEET FRENEMIES FRESHIE FRIBS FRIGHTING
FREESIA FRENEMY FRESHIES FRICADEL FRIGHTS
FREESIAS FRENETIC FRESHING FRICADELS FRIGID
FREEST FRENETICS FRESHISH FRICANDO FRIGIDER
FREESTONE FRENNE FRESHLY FRICASSEE FRIGIDEST

FRIGIDITY	FRISK	FRIULANO	FROCKLESS	FRONDENT
FRIGIDLY	FRISKA	FRIULANOS	FROCKS	FRONDEUR
FRIGOT	FRISKAS	FRIVOL	FROE	FRONDEURS
FRIGOTS	FRISKED	FRIVOLED	FROES	FRONDLESS
FRIGS	FRISKER	FRIVOLER	FROG	FRONDOSE
FRIJOL	FRISKERS	FRIVOLERS	FROGBIT	FRONDOUS
FRIJOLE	FRISKET	FRIVOLING	FROGBITS	FRONDS
FRIJOLES	FRISKETS	FRIVOLITY	FROGEYE	FRONS
FRIKKADEL	FRISKFUL	FRIVOLLED	FROGEYED	FRONT
FRILL	FRISKIER	FRIVOLLER	FROGEYES	FRONTAGE
FRILLED	FRISKIEST	FRIVOLOUS	FROGFISH	FRONTAGER
FRILLER	FRISKILY	FRIVOLS	FROGGED	FRONTAGES
FRILLERS	FRISKING	FRIZ	FROGGERY	FRONTAL
FRILLERY	FRISKINGS	FRIZADO	FROGGIER	FRONTALLY
FRILLIER	FRISKS	FRIZADOS	FROGGIEST	FRONTALS
FRILLIES	FRISKY	FRIZE	FROGGING	FRONTED
FRILLIEST	FRISSON	FRIZED	FROGGINGS	FRONTENIS
FRILLING	FRISSONS	FRIZER	FROGGY	FRONTER
FRILLINGS	FRIST	FRIZERS	FROGLET	FRONTERS
FRILLS	FRISTED	FRIZES	FROGLETS	FRONTES
FRILLY	FRISTING	FRIZETTE	FROGLIKE	FRONTEST
FRINGE	FRISTS	FRIZETTES	FROGLING	FRONTIER
FRINGED	FRISURE	FRIZING	FROGLINGS	FRONTIERS
FRINGES	FRISURES	FRIZZ	FROGMAN	FRONTING
FRINGIER	FRIT	FRIZZANTE	FROGMARCH	FRONTLESS
FRINGIEST	FRITES	FRIZZED	FROGMEN	FRONTLET
FRINGING	FRITFLIES	FRIZZER	FROGMOUTH	FRONTLETS
FRINGINGS	FRITFLY	FRIZZERS	FROGS	FRONTLINE
FRINGY	FRITH	FRIZZES	FROGSPAWN	FRONTLIST
FRIPON	FRITHBORH	FRIZZIER	FROIDEUR	FRONTMAN
FRIPONS	FRITHS	FRIZZIES	FROIDEURS	FRONTMEN
FRIPPER	FRITS	FRIZZIEST	FROING	FRONTON
FRIPPERER	FRITT	FRIZZILY	FROINGS	FRONTONS
FRIPPERS	FRITTATA	FRIZZING	FROISE	FRONTOON
FRIPPERY	FRITTATAS	FRIZZLE	FROISES	FRONTOONS
FRIPPET	FRITTED	FRIZZLED	FROLIC	FRONTPAGE
FRIPPETS	FRITTER	FRIZZLER	FROLICKED	FRONTS
FRIS	FRITTERED	FRIZZLERS	FROLICKER	FRONTWARD
FRISBEE	FRITTERER	FRIZZLES	FROLICKY	FRONTWAYS
FRISBEES	FRITTERS	FRIZZLIER	FROLICS	FRONTWISE
FRISE	FRITTING	FRIZZLING	FROM	FRORE
FRISEE	FRITTS	FRIZZLY	FROMAGE	FROREN
FRISEES	FRITURE	FRIZZY	FROMAGES	FRORN
FRISES	FRITURES	FRO	FROMENTY	FRORNE
FRISETTE	FRITZ	FROCK	FROND	FRORY
FRISETTES	FRITZED	FROCKED	FRONDAGE	FROS
FRISEUR	FRITZES	FROCKING	FRONDAGES	FROSH
FRISEURS	FRITZING	FROCKINGS	FRONDED	FROSHES

FROST	FROW	FRUGAL	FRUMPS	FUCHSINES
FROSTBIT	FROWARD	FRUGALIST	FRUMPY	FUCHSINS
FROSTBITE	FROWARDLY	FRUGALITY	FRUSEMIDE	FUCHSITE
FROSTED	FROWARDS	FRUGALLY	FRUSH	FUCHSITES
FROSTEDS	FROWIE	FRUGGED	FRUSHED	FUCI
FROSTFISH	FROWIER	FRUGGING	FRUSHES	FUCK
FROSTIER	FROWIEST	FRUGIVORE	FRUSHING	FUCKED
FROSTIEST	FROWN	FRUGS	FRUST	FUCKER
FROSTILY	FROWNED	FRUICT	FRUSTA	FUCKERS
FROSTING	FROWNER	FRUICTS	FRUSTRATE	FUCKFACE
FROSTINGS	FROWNERS	FRUIT	FRUSTS	FUCKFACES
FROSTLESS	FROWNIER	FRUITAGE	FRUSTULE	FUCKHEAD
FROSTLIKE	FROWNIEST	FRUITAGES	FRUSTULES	FUCKHEADS
FROSTLINE	FROWNING	FRUITCAKE	FRUSTUM	FUCKING
FROSTNIP	FROWNS	FRUITED	FRUSTUMS	FUCKINGS
FROSTNIPS	FROWNY	FRUITER	FRUTEX	FUCKOFF
FROSTS	FROWS	FRUITERER	FRUTICES	FUCKOFFS
FROSTWORK	FROWSIER	FRUITERS	FRUTICOSE	FUCKS
FROSTY	FROWSIEST	FRUITERY	FRUTIFIED	FUCKUP
FROTH	FROWSILY	FRUITFUL	FRUTIFIES	FUCKUPS
FROTHED	FROWST	FRUITIER	FRUTIFY	FUCKWIT
FROTHER	FROWSTED	FRUITIEST	FRY	FUCKWITS
FROTHERS	FROWSTER	FRUITILY	FRYABLE	FUCOID
FROTHERY	FROWSTERS	FRUITING	FRYBREAD	FUCOIDAL
FROTHIER	FROWSTIER	FRUITINGS	FRYBREADS	FUCOIDS
FROTHIEST	FROWSTING	FRUITION	FRYER	FUCOSE
FROTHILY	FROWSTS	FRUITIONS	FRYERS	FUCOSES
FROTHING	FROWSTY	FRUITIVE	FRYING	FUCOUS
FROTHINGS	FROWSY	FRUITLESS	FRYINGS	FUCUS
FROTHLESS	FROWY	FRUITLET	FRYPAN	FUCUSED
FROTHS	FROWZIER	FRUITLETS	FRYPANS	FUCUSES
FROTHY	FROWZIEST	FRUITLIKE	FUB	FUD
FROTTAGE	FROWZILY	FRUITS	FUBAR	FUDDIER
FROTTAGES	FROWZY	FRUITWOOD	FUBBED	FUDDIES
FROTTEUR	FROZE	FRUITWORM	FUBBERIES	FUDDIEST
FROTTEURS	FROZEN	FRUITY	FUBBERY	FUDDLE
FROUFROU	FROZENLY	FRUMENTY	FUBBIER	FUDDLED
FROUFROUS	FRUCTAN	FRUMP	FUBBIEST	FUDDLER
FROUGHIER	FRUCTANS	FRUMPED	FUBBING	FUDDLERS
FROUGHY	FRUCTED	FRUMPIER	FUBBY	FUDDLES
FROUNCE	FRUCTIFY	FRUMPIEST	FUBS	FUDDLING
FROUNCED	FRUCTIVE	FRUMPILY	FUBSIER	FUDDLINGS
FROUNCES	FRUCTOSE	FRUMPING	FUBSIEST	FUDDY
FROUNCING	FRUCTOSES	FRUMPISH	FUBSY	FUDGE
FROUZIER	FRUCTUARY	FRUMPLE	FUCHSIA	FUDGED
FROUZIEST	FRUCTUATE	FRUMPLED	FUCHSIAS	FUDGES
FROUZILY	FRUCTUOUS	FRUMPLES	FUCHSIN	FUDGIER
FROUZY	FRUG	FRUMPLING	FUCHSINE	FUDGIEST

FUDGING	FUGLE	FULHAMS	FUMADO	FUMOSITY
FUDGY	FUGLED	FULL	FUMADOES	FUMOUS
FUDS	FUGLEMAN	FULLAGE	FUMADOS	FUMS
FUEHRER	FUGLEMEN	FULLAGES	FUMAGE	FUMULI
FUEHRERS	FUGLES	FULLAM	FUMAGES	FUMULUS
FUEL	FUGLIER	FULLAMS	FUMARASE	FUMY
FUELED	FUGLIEST	FULLAN	FUMARASES	FUN
FUELER	FUGLING	FULLANS	FUMARATE	FUNBOARD
FUELERS	FUGLY	FULLBACK	FUMARATES	FUNBOARDS
FUELING	FUGS	FULLBACKS	FUMARIC	FUNCKIA
FUELLED	FUGU	FULLBLOOD	FUMAROLE	FUNCKIAS
FUELLER	FUGUE	FULLED	FUMAROLES	FUNCTION
FUELLERS	FUGUED	FULLER	FUMAROLIC	FUNCTIONS
FUELLING	FUGUELIKE	FULLERED	FUMATORIA	FUNCTOR
FUELS	FUGUES	FULLERENE	FUMATORY	FUNCTORS
FUELWOOD	FUGUING	FULLERIDE	FUMBLE	FUND
FUELWOODS	FUGUIST	FULLERIES	FUMBLED	FUNDABLE
FUERO	FUGUISTS	FULLERING	FUMBLER	FUNDAMENT
FUEROS	FUGUS	FULLERITE	FUMBLERS	FUNDED
FUFF	FUHRER	FULLERS	FUMBLES	FUNDER
FUFFED	FUHRERS	FULLERY	FUMBLING	FUNDERS
FUFFIER	FUJI	FULLEST	FUME	FUNDI
FUFFIEST	FUJIS	FULLFACE	FUMED	FUNDIC
FUFFING	FULCRA	FULLFACES	FUMELESS	FUNDIE
FUFFS	FULCRATE	FULLING	FUMELIKE	FUNDIES
FUFFY	FULCRUM	FULLISH	FUMER	FUNDING
FUG	FULCRUMS	FULLNESS	FUMEROLE	FUNDINGS
FUGACIOUS	FULFIL	FULLS	FUMEROLES	FUNDIS
FUGACITY	FULFILL	FULLY	FUMERS	FUNDLESS
FUGAL	FULFILLED	FULMAR	FUMES	FUNDRAISE
FUGALLY	FULFILLER	FULMARS	FUMET	FUNDS
FUGATO	FULFILLS	FULMINANT	FUMETS	FUNDUS
FUGATOS	FULFILS	FULMINATE	FUMETTE	FUNDY
FUGGED	FULGENCY	FULMINE	FUMETTES	FUNEBRAL
FUGGIER	FULGENT	FULMINED	FUMETTI	FUNEBRE
FUGGIEST	FULGENTLY	FULMINES	FUMETTO	FUNEBRIAL
FUGGILY	FULGID	FULMINIC	FUMETTOS	FUNERAL
FUGGINESS	FULGOR	FULMINING	FUMIER	FUNERALS
FUGGING	FULGOROUS	FULMINOUS	FUMIEST	FUNERARY
FUGGY	FULGORS	FULNESS	FUMIGANT	FUNEREAL
FUGHETTA	FULGOUR	FULNESSES	FUMIGANTS	FUNEST
FUGHETTAS	FULGOURS	FULSOME	FUMIGATE	FUNFAIR
FUGIE	FULGURAL	FULSOMELY	FUMIGATED	FUNFAIRS
FUGIES	FULGURANT	FULSOMER	FUMIGATES	FUNFEST
FUGIO	FULGURATE	FULSOMEST	FUMIGATOR	FUNFESTS
FUGIOS	FULGURITE	FULVID	FUMING	FUNG
FUGITIVE	FULGUROUS	FULVOUS	FUMINGLY	FUNGAL
FUGITIVES	FULHAM	FUM	FUMITORY	FUNGALS

FUNGI	FUNNELLED	FURCRAEAS	FURMITIES	FURTH
FUNGIBLE	FUNNELS	FURCULA	FURMITY	FURTHER
FUNGIBLES	FUNNER	FURCULAE	FURNACE	FURTHERED
FUNGIC	FUNNEST	FURCULAR	FURNACED	FURTHERER
FUNGICIDE	FUNNIER	FURCULUM	FURNACES	FURTHERS
FUNGIFORM	FUNNIES	FURDER	FURNACING	FURTHEST
FUNGISTAT	FUNNIEST	FUREUR	FURNIMENT	FURTIVE
FUNGO	FUNNILY	FUREURS	FURNISH	FURTIVELY
FUNGOED	FUNNINESS	FURFAIR	FURNISHED	FURUNCLE
FUNGOES	FUNNING	FURFAIRS	FURNISHER	FURUNCLES
FUNGOID	FUNNY	FURFUR	FURNISHES	FURY
FUNGOIDAL	FUNNYMAN	FURFURAL	FURNITURE	FURZE
FUNGOIDS	FUNNYMEN	FURFURALS	FUROL	FURZES
FUNGOING	FUNPLEX	FURFURAN	FUROLE	FURZIER
FUNGOS	FUNPLEXES	FURFURANS	FUROLES	FURZIEST
FUNGOSITY	FUNS	FURFURES	FUROLS	FURZY
FUNGOUS	FUNSTER	FURFUROL	FUROR	FUSAIN
FUNGS	FUNSTERS	FURFUROLE	FURORE	FUSAINS
FUNGUS	FUR	FURFUROLS	FURORES	FUSARIA
FUNGUSES	FURACIOUS	FURFUROUS	FURORS	FUSARIUM
FUNHOUSE	FURACITY	FURFURS	FURPHIES	FUSARIUMS
FUNHOUSES	FURAL	FURIBUND	FURPHY	FUSAROL
FUNICLE	FURALS	FURIES	FURPIECE	FUSAROLE
FUNICLES	FURAN	FURIOSITY	FURPIECES	FUSAROLES
FUNICULAR	FURANE	FURIOSO	FURR	FUSAROLS
FUNICULI	FURANES	FURIOSOS	FURRED	FUSBALL
FUNICULUS	FURANOSE	FURIOUS	FURRIER	FUSBALLS
FUNK	FURANOSES	FURIOUSLY	FURRIERS	FUSC
FUNKED	FURANS	FURKID	FURRIERY	FUSCOUS
FUNKER	FURBALL	FURKIDS	FURRIES	FUSE
FUNKERS	FURBALLS	FURL	FURRIEST	FUSED
FUNKHOLE	FURBEARER	FURLABLE	FURRILY	FUSEE
FUNKHOLES	FURBELOW	FURLANA	FURRINER	FUSEES
FUNKIA	FURBELOWS	FURLANAS	FURRINERS	FUSEL
FUNKIAS	FURBISH	FURLED	FURRINESS	FUSELAGE
FUNKIER	FURBISHED	FURLER	FURRING	FUSELAGES
FUNKIEST	FURBISHER	FURLERS	FURRINGS	FUSELESS
FUNKILY	FURBISHES	FURLESS	FURROW	FUSELIKE
FUNKINESS	FURCA	FURLIKE	FURROWED	FUSELS
FUNKING	FURCAE	FURLING	FURROWER	FUSES
FUNKS	FURCAL	FURLONG	FURROWERS	FUSHION
FUNKSTER	FURCATE	FURLONGS	FURROWIER	FUSHIONS
FUNKSTERS	FURCATED	FURLOUGH	FURROWING	FUSIBLE
FUNKY	FURCATELY	FURLOUGHS	FURROWS	FUSIBLY
FUNNED	FURCATES	FURLS	FURROWY	FUSIDIC
FUNNEL	FURCATING	FURMENTY	FURRS	FUSIFORM
FUNNELED	FURCATION	FURMETIES	FURRY	FUSIL
FUNNELING	FURCRAEA	FURMETY	FURS	FUSILE

FUSILEER
FUSILEERS
FUSILIER
FUSILIERS
FUSILLADE
FUSILLI
FUSILLIS
FUSILS
FUSING
FUSION
FUSIONAL
FUSIONISM
FUSIONIST
FUSIONS
FUSK
FUSKED
FUSKER
FUSKERED
FUSKERING
FUSKERS
FUSKING
FUSKS
FUSS
FUSSBALL
FUSSBALLS
FUSSED
FUSSER
FUSSERS

FUSSES
FUSSIER
FUSSIEST
FUSSILY
FUSSINESS
FUSSING
FUSSPOT
FUSSPOTS
FUSSY
FUST
FUSTED
FUSTET
FUSTETS
FUSTIAN
FUSTIANS
FUSTIC
FUSTICS
FUSTIER
FUSTIEST
FUSTIGATE
FUSTILUGS
FUSTILY
FUSTINESS
FUSTING
FUSTOC
FUSTOCS
FUSTS
FUSTY

FUSULINID
FUSUMA
FUSUMAS
FUTCHEL
FUTCHELS
FUTHARC
FUTHARCS
FUTHARK
FUTHARKS
FUTHORC
FUTHORCS
FUTHORK
FUTHORKS
FUTILE
FUTILELY
FUTILER
FUTILEST
FUTILITY
FUTON
FUTONS
FUTSAL
FUTSALS
FUTTOCK
FUTTOCKS
FUTURAL
FUTURE
FUTURES
FUTURISM

FUTURISMS
FUTURIST
FUTURISTS
FUTURITY
FUTZ
FUTZED
FUTZES
FUTZING
FUZE
FUZED
FUZEE
FUZEES
FUZELESS
FUZES
FUZIL
FUZILS
FUZING
FUZZ
FUZZBALL
FUZZBALLS
FUZZBOX
FUZZBOXES
FUZZED
FUZZES
FUZZIER
FUZZIEST
FUZZILY
FUZZINESS

FUZZING
FUZZLE
FUZZLED
FUZZLES
FUZZLING
FUZZTONE
FUZZTONES
FUZZY
FY
FYCE
FYCES
FYKE
FYKED
FYKES
FYKING
FYLE
FYLES
FYLFOT
FYLFOTS
FYNBOS
FYNBOSES
FYRD
FYRDS
FYTTE
FYTTES

F

G

GAB
GABARDINE
GABBA
GABBARD
GABBARDS
GABBART
GABBARTS
GABBAS
GABBED
GABBER
GABBERS
GABBIER
GABBIEST
GABBINESS
GABBING
GABBLE
GABBLED
GABBLER
GABBLERS
GABBLES
GABBLING
GABBLINGS
GABBRO
GABBROIC
GABBROID
GABBROS
GABBY
GABELLE
GABELLED
GABELLER
GABELLERS
GABELLES
GABERDINE
GABFEST
GABFESTS
GABIES
GABION
GABIONADE
GABIONAGE
GABIONED
GABIONS
GABLE

GABLED
GABLELIKE
GABLES
GABLET
GABLETS
GABLING
GABNASH
GABNASHES
GABOON
GABOONS
GABS
GABY
GACH
GACHED
GACHER
GACHERS
GACHES
GACHING
GAD
GADABOUT
GADABOUTS
GADARENE
GADDED
GADDER
GADDERS
GADDI
GADDING
GADDIS
GADE
GADES
GADFLIES
GADFLY
GADGE
GADGES
GADGET
GADGETEER
GADGETIER
GADGETRY
GADGETS
GADGETY
GADGIE
GADGIES

GADI
GADID
GADIDS
GADIS
GADJE
GADJES
GADJO
GADJOS
GADLING
GADLINGS
GADMAN
GADMEN
GADOID
GADOIDS
GADOLINIC
GADROON
GADROONED
GADROONS
GADS
GADSMAN
GADSMEN
GADSO
GADWALL
GADWALLS
GADZOOKS
GAE
GAED
GAEING
GAELICISE
GAELICISM
GAELICIZE
GAEN
GAES
GAFF
GAFFE
GAFFED
GAFFER
GAFFERS
GAFFES
GAFFING
GAFFINGS
GAFFS

GAFFSAIL
GAFFSAILS
GAG
GAGA
GAGAKU
GAGAKUS
GAGE
GAGEABLE
GAGEABLY
GAGED
GAGER
GAGERS
GAGES
GAGGED
GAGGER
GAGGERIES
GAGGERS
GAGGERY
GAGGING
GAGGLE
GAGGLED
GAGGLES
GAGGLING
GAGGLINGS
GAGING
GAGMAN
GAGMEN
GAGS
GAGSTER
GAGSTERS
GAHNITE
GAHNITES
GAID
GAIDS
GAIETIES
GAIETY
GAIJIN
GAILLARD
GAILLARDE
GAILY
GAIN
GAINABLE

GAINED
GAINER
GAINERS
GAINEST
GAINFUL
GAINFULLY
GAINING
GAININGS
GAINLESS
GAINLIER
GAINLIEST
GAINLY
GAINS
GAINSAID
GAINSAY
GAINSAYER
GAINSAYS
GAINST
GAIR
GAIRFOWL
GAIRFOWLS
GAIRS
GAIT
GAITA
GAITAS
GAITED
GAITER
GAITERED
GAITERS
GAITING
GAITS
GAITT
GAITTS
GAJO
GAJOS
GAK
GAKS
GAL
GALA
GALABEA
GALABEAH
GALABEAHS

GALABEAS	GALEIFORM	GALLEONS	GALLIVAT	GALOP
GALABIA	GALENA	GALLERIA	GALLIVATS	GALOPADE
GALABIAH	GALENAS	GALLERIAS	GALLIWASP	GALOPADES
GALABIAHS	GALENGALE	GALLERIED	GALLIZE	GALOPED
GALABIAS	GALENIC	GALLERIES	GALLIZED	GALOPIN
GALABIEH	GALENICAL	GALLERIST	GALLIZES	GALOPING
GALABIEHS	GALENITE	GALLERY	GALLIZING	GALOPINS
GALABIYA	GALENITES	GALLET	GALLNUT	GALOPPED
GALABIYAH	GALENOID	GALLETA	GALLNUTS	GALOPPING
GALABIYAS	GALERE	GALLETAS	GALLOCK	GALOPS
GALACTIC	GALERES	GALLETED	GALLON	GALORE
GALACTICO	GALES	GALLETING	GALLONAGE	GALORES
GALACTOSE	GALETTE	GALLETS	GALLONS	GALOSH
GALAGE	GALETTES	GALLEY	GALLOON	GALOSHE
GALAGES	GALILEE	GALLEYS	GALLOONED	GALOSHED
GALAGO	GALILEES	GALLFLIES	GALLOONS	GALOSHES
GALAGOS	GALING	GALLFLY	GALLOOT	GALOSHING
GALAH	GALINGALE	GALLIARD	GALLOOTS	GALOWSES
GALAHS	GALIONGEE	GALLIARDS	GALLOP	GALRAVAGE
GALANGA	GALIOT	GALLIASS	GALLOPADE	GALS
GALANGAL	GALIOTS	GALLIC	GALLOPED	GALTONIA
GALANGALS	GALIPOT	GALLICA	GALLOPER	GALTONIAS
GALANGAS	GALIPOTS	GALLICAN	GALLOPERS	GALUMPH
GALANT	GALIVANT	GALLICAS	GALLOPING	GALUMPHED
GALANTINE	GALIVANTS	GALLICISE	GALLOPS	GALUMPHER
GALANTS	GALL	GALLICISM	GALLOUS	GALUMPHS
GALANTY	GALLABEA	GALLICIZE	GALLOW	GALUT
GALAPAGO	GALLABEAH	GALLIED	GALLOWAY	GALUTH
GALAPAGOS	GALLABEAS	GALLIER	GALLOWAYS	GALUTHS
GALAS	GALLABIA	GALLIES	GALLOWED	GALUTS
GALATEA	GALLABIAH	GALLIEST	GALLOWING	GALVANIC
GALATEAS	GALLABIAS	GALLINAZO	GALLOWS	GALVANISE
GALAVANT	GALLABIEH	GALLING	GALLOWSES	GALVANISM
GALAVANTS	GALLABIYA	GALLINGLY	GALLS	GALVANIST
GALAX	GALLAMINE	GALLINULE	GALLSTONE	GALVANIZE
GALAXES	GALLANT	GALLIOT	GALLUMPH	GALVO
GALAXIES	GALLANTED	GALLIOTS	GALLUMPHS	GALVOS
GALAXY	GALLANTER	GALLIPOT	GALLUS	GALYAC
GALBANUM	GALLANTLY	GALLIPOTS	GALLUSED	GALYACS
GALBANUMS	GALLANTRY	GALLISE	GALLUSES	GALYAK
GALDRAGON	GALLANTS	GALLISED	GALLY	GALYAKS
GALE	GALLATE	GALLISES	GALLYING	GAM
GALEA	GALLATES	GALLISING	GALOCHE	GAMA
GALEAE	GALLEASS	GALLISISE	GALOCHED	GAMAHUCHE
GALEAS	GALLED	GALLISIZE	GALOCHES	GAMARUCHE
GALEATE	GALLEIN	GALLIUM	GALOCHING	GAMAS
GALEATED	GALLEINS	GALLIUMS	GALOOT	GAMASH
GALED	GALLEON	GALLIVANT	GALOOTS	GAMASHES

G

GAMAY
GAMAYS
GAMB
GAMBA
GAMBADE
GAMBADES
GAMBADO
GAMBADOED
GAMBADOES
GAMBADOS
GAMBAS
GAMBE
GAMBES
GAMBESON
GAMBESONS
GAMBET
GAMBETS
GAMBETTA
GAMBETTAS
GAMBIA
GAMBIAS
GAMBIER
GAMBIERS
GAMBIR
GAMBIRS
GAMBIST
GAMBISTS
GAMBIT
GAMBITED
GAMBITING
GAMBITS
GAMBLE
GAMBLED
GAMBLER
GAMBLERS
GAMBLES
GAMBLING
GAMBLINGS
GAMBO
GAMBOES
GAMBOGE
GAMBOGES
GAMBOGIAN
GAMBOGIC
GAMBOL
GAMBOLED
GAMBOLING
GAMBOLLED

GAMBOLS
GAMBOS
GAMBREL
GAMBRELS
GAMBROON
GAMBROONS
GAMBS
GAMBUSIA
GAMBUSIAS
GAME
GAMEBAG
GAMEBAGS
GAMEBOOK
GAMEBOOKS
GAMECOCK
GAMECOCKS
GAMED
GAMEFISH
GAMEFOWL
GAMEFOWLS
GAMELAN
GAMELANS
GAMELIKE
GAMELY
GAMENESS
GAMEPLAY
GAMEPLAYS
GAMER
GAMERS
GAMES
GAMESHOW
GAMESHOWS
GAMESIER
GAMESIEST
GAMESMAN
GAMESMEN
GAMESOME
GAMEST
GAMESTER
GAMESTERS
GAMESY
GAMETAL
GAMETE
GAMETES
GAMETIC
GAMEY
GAMEYNESS
GAMGEE

GAMIC
GAMIER
GAMIEST
GAMIFIED
GAMIFIES
GAMIFY
GAMIFYING
GAMILY
GAMIN
GAMINE
GAMINERIE
GAMINES
GAMINESS
GAMING
GAMINGS
GAMINS
GAMMA
GAMMADIA
GAMMADION
GAMMAS
GAMMAT
GAMMATIA
GAMMATION
GAMMATS
GAMME
GAMMED
GAMMER
GAMMERS
GAMMES
GAMMIER
GAMMIEST
GAMMING
GAMMOCK
GAMMOCKED
GAMMOCKS
GAMMON
GAMMONED
GAMMONER
GAMMONERS
GAMMONING
GAMMONS
GAMMY
GAMODEME
GAMODEMES
GAMONE
GAMONES
GAMP
GAMPISH

GAMPS
GAMS
GAMUT
GAMUTS
GAMY
GAMYNESS
GAN
GANACHE
GANACHES
GANCH
GANCHED
GANCHES
GANCHING
GANDER
GANDERED
GANDERING
GANDERISM
GANDERS
GANDY
GANE
GANEF
GANEFS
GANEV
GANEVS
GANG
GANGBANG
GANGBANGS
GANGBO
GANGBOARD
GANGBOS
GANGED
GANGER
GANGERS
GANGING
GANGINGS
GANGLAND
GANGLANDS
GANGLE
GANGLED
GANGLES
GANGLIA
GANGLIAL
GANGLIAR
GANGLIATE
GANGLIER
GANGLIEST
GANGLING
GANGLION

GANGLIONS
GANGLY
GANGPLANK
GANGPLOW
GANGPLOWS
GANGREL
GANGRELS
GANGRENE
GANGRENED
GANGRENES
GANGS
GANGSHAG
GANGSHAGS
GANGSMAN
GANGSMEN
GANGSTA
GANGSTAS
GANGSTER
GANGSTERS
GANGUE
GANGUES
GANGWAY
GANGWAYS
GANISTER
GANISTERS
GANJA
GANJAH
GANJAHS
GANJAS
GANNED
GANNET
GANNETRY
GANNETS
GANNING
GANNISTER
GANOF
GANOFS
GANOID
GANOIDS
GANOIN
GANOINE
GANOINES
GANOINS
GANS
GANSEY
GANSEYS
GANT
GANTED

GANTELOPE	GAPPED	GARBOILS	GARGOYLED	GAROTTED
GANTING	GAPPER	GARBOLOGY	GARGOYLES	GAROTTER
GANTLET	GAPPERS	GARBOS	GARI	GAROTTERS
GANILETED	GAPPIER	GARBS	GARIAL	GAROTTES
GANTLETS	GAPPIEST	GARBURE	GARIALS	GAROTTING
GANTLINE	GAPPING	GARBURES	GARIBALDI	GAROUPA
GANTLINES	GAPPINGS	GARCINIA	GARIGUE	GAROUPAS
GANTLOPE	GAPPY	GARCINIAS	GARIGUES	GARPIKE
GANTLOPES	GAPS	GARCON	GARIS	GARPIKES
GANTRIES	GAPY	GARCONS	GARISH	GARRAN
GANTRY	GAR	GARDA	GARISHED	GARRANS
GANTS	GARAGE	GARDAI	GARISHES	GARRE
GANYMEDE	GARAGED	GARDANT	GARISHING	GARRED
GANYMEDES	GARAGEMAN	GARDANTS	GARISHLY	GARRES
GANZFELD	GARAGEMEN	GARDEN	GARJAN	GARRET
GANZFELDS	GARAGES	GARDENED	GARJANS	GARRETED
GAOL	GARAGEY	GARDENER	GARLAND	GARRETEER
GAOLBIRD	GARAGIER	GARDENERS	GARLANDED	GARRETS
GAOLBIRDS	GARAGIEST	GARDENFUL	GARLANDRY	GARRIGUE
GAOLBREAK	GARAGING	GARDENIA	GARLANDS	GARRIGUES
GAOLBROKE	GARAGINGS	GARDENIAS	GARLIC	GARRING
GAOLED	GARAGIST	GARDENING	GARLICKED	GARRISON
GAOLER	GARAGISTE	GARDENS	GARLICKY	GARRISONS
GAOLERESS	GARAGISTS	GARDEROBE	GARLICS	GARRON
GAOLERS	GARB	GARDYLOO	GARMENT	GARRONS
GAOLING	GARBAGE	GARDYLOOS	GARMENTED	GARROT
GAOLLESS	GARBAGES	GARE	GARMENTS	GARROTE
GAOLS	GARBAGEY	GAREFOWL	GARMS	GARROTED
GAP	GARBAGIER	GAREFOWLS	GARNER	GARROTER
GAPE	GARBAGY	GARES	GARNERED	GARROTERS
GAPED	GARBANZO	GARFISH	GARNERING	GARROTES
GAPER	GARBANZOS	GARFISHES	GARNERS	GARROTING
GAPERS	GARBE	GARGANEY	GARNET	GARROTS
GAPES	GARBED	GARGANEYS	GARNETS	GARROTTE
GAPESEED	GARBES	GARGANTUA	GARNI	GARROTTED
GAPESEEDS	GARBING	GARGARISE	GARNISH	GARROTTER
GAPEWORM	GARBLE	GARGARISM	GARNISHED	GARROTTES
GAPEWORMS	GARBLED	GARGARIZE	GARNISHEE	GARRULITY
GAPIER	GARBLER	GARGET	GARNISHER	GARRULOUS
GAPIEST	GARBLERS	GARGETS	GARNISHES	GARRYA
GAPING	GARBLES	GARGETY	GARNISHOR	GARRYAS
GAPINGLY	GARBLESS	GARGLE	GARNISHRY	GARRYOWEN
GAPINGS	GARBLING	GARGLED	GARNITURE	GARS
GAPLESS	GARBLINGS	GARGLER	GAROTE	GART
GAPO	GARBO	GARGLERS	GAROTED	GARTER
GAPOS	GARBOARD	GARGLES	GAROTES	GARTERED
GAPOSIS	GARBOARDS	GARGLING	GAROTING	GARTERING
GAPOSISES	GARBOIL	GARGOYLE	GAROTTE	GARTERS

GARTH	GASIFIES	GASSIEST	GATECRASH	GAUCIER
GARTHS	GASIFORM	GASSILY	GATED	GAUCIEST
GARUDA	GASIFY	GASSINESS	GATEFOLD	GAUCY
GARUDAS	GASIFYING	GASSING	GATEFOLDS	GAUD
GARUM	GASKET	GASSINGS	GATEHOUSE	GAUDEAMUS
GARUMS	GASKETED	GASSY	GATELEG	GAUDED
GARVEY	GASKETS	GAST	GATELEGS	GAUDERIES
GARVEYS	GASKIN	GASTED	GATELESS	GAUDERY
GARVIE	GASKING	GASTER	GATELIKE	GAUDGIE
GARVIES	GASKINGS	GASTERED	GATEMAN	GAUDGIES
GARVOCK	GASKINS	GASTERING	GATEMEN	GAUDIER
GARVOCKS	GASLESS	GASTERS	GATEPOST	GAUDIES
GAS	GASLIGHT	GASTFULL	GATEPOSTS	GAUDIEST
GASAHOL	GASLIGHTS	GASTHAUS	GATER	GAUDILY
GASAHOLS	GASLIT	GASTIGHT	GATERS	GAUDINESS
GASALIER	GASMAN	GASTING	GATES	GAUDING
GASALIERS	GASMEN	GASTNESS	GATEWAY	GAUDS
GASBAG	GASOGENE	GASTNESSE	GATEWAYS	GAUDY
GASBAGGED	GASOGENES	GASTRAEA	GATH	GAUFER
GASBAGS	GASOHOL	GASTRAEAS	GATHER	GAUFERS
GASCON	GASOHOLS	GASTRAEUM	GATHERED	GAUFFER
GASCONADE	GASOLENE	GASTRAL	GATHERER	GAUFFERED
GASCONISM	GASOLENES	GASTREA	GATHERERS	GAUFFERS
GASCONS	GASOLIER	GASTREAS	GATHERING	GAUFRE
GASEITIES	GASOLIERS	GASTRIC	GATHERS	GAUFRES
GASEITY	GASOLINE	GASTRIN	GATHS	GAUGE
GASELIER	GASOLINES	GASTRINS	GATING	GAUGEABLE
GASELIERS	GASOLINIC	GASTRITIC	GATINGS	GAUGEABLY
GASEOUS	GASOMETER	GASTRITIS	GATLING	GAUGED
GASES	GASOMETRY	GASTROPOD	GATOR	GAUGER
GASFIELD	GASP	GASTROPUB	GATORS	GAUGERS
GASFIELDS	GASPED	GASTRULA	GATS	GAUGES
GASH	GASPER	GASTRULAE	GATVOL	GAUGING
GASHED	GASPEREAU	GASTRULAR	GAU	GAUGINGS
GASHER	GASPERS	GASTRULAS	GAUCH	GAUJE
GASHES	GASPIER	GASTS	GAUCHE	GAUJES
GASHEST	GASPIEST	GASWORKS	GAUCHED	GAULEITER
GASHFUL	GASPINESS	GAT	GAUCHELY	GAULT
GASHING	GASPING	GATCH	GAUCHER	GAULTER
GASHLIER	GASPINGLY	GATCHED	GAUCHERIE	GAULTERS
GASHLIEST	GASPINGS	GATCHER	GAUCHERS	GAULTS
GASHLY	GASPS	GATCHERS	GAUCHES	GAUM
GASHOLDER	GASPY	GATCHES	GAUCHESCO	GAUMED
GASHOUSE	GASSED	GATCHING	GAUCHEST	GAUMIER
GASHOUSES	GASSER	GATE	GAUCHING	GAUMIEST
GASIFIED	GASSERS	GATEAU	GAUCHO	GAUMING
GASIFIER	GASSES	GATEAUS	GAUCHOS	GAUMLESS
GASIFIERS	GASSIER	GATEAUX	GAUCIE	GAUMS

GAUMY	GAVELKIND	GAWS	GAZETTE	GEARHEADS
GAUN	GAVELLED	GAWSIE	GAZETTED	GEARING
GAUNCH	GAVELLING	GAWSIER	GAZETTEER	GEARINGS
GAUNCHED	GAVELMAN	GAWSIEST	GAZETTES	GEARLESS
GAUNCHES	GAVELMEN	GAWSY	GAZETTING	GEARS
GAUNCHING	GAVELOCK	GAY	GAZIER	GEARSHIFT
GAUNT	GAVELOCKS	GAYAL	GAZIEST	GEARSTICK
GAUNTED	GAVELS	GAYALS	GAZILLION	GEARWHEEL
GAUNTER	GAVIAL	GAYCATION	GAZING	GEASON
GAUNTEST	GAVIALOID	GAYDAR	GAZINGS	GEAT
GAUNTING	GAVIALS	GAYDARS	GAZOGENE	GEATS
GAUNTLET	GAVOT	GAYER	GAZOGENES	GEBUR
GAUNTLETS	GAVOTS	GAYEST	GAZON	GEBURS
GAUNTLY	GAVOTTE	GAYETIES	GAZONS	GECK
GAUNTNESS	GAVOTTED	GAYETY	GAZOO	GECKED
GAUNTREE	GAVOTTES	GAYLY	GAZOOKA	GECKING
GAUNTREES	GAVOTTING	GAYNESS	GAZOOKAS	GECKO
GAUNTRIES	GAW	GAYNESSES	GAZOON	GECKOES
GAUNTRY	GAWCIER	GAYS	GAZOONS	GECKOS
GAUNTS	GAWCIEST	GAYSOME	GAZOOS	GECKS
GAUP	GAWCY	GAYWINGS	GAZPACHO	GED
GAUPED	GAWD	GAZABO	GAZPACHOS	GEDACT
GAUPER	GAWDS	GAZABOES	GAZUMP	GEDACTS
GAUPERS	GAWK	GAZABOS	GAZUMPED	GEDDIT
GAUPING	GAWKED	GAZAL	GAZUMPER	GEDECKT
GAUPS	GAWKER	GAZALS	GAZUMPERS	GEDECKTS
GAUPUS	GAWKERS	GAZANG	GAZUMPING	GEDS
GAUPUSES	GAWKIER	GAZANGED	GAZUMPS	GEE
GAUR	GAWKIES	GAZANGING	GAZUNDER	GEEBAG
GAURS	GAWKIEST	GAZANGS	GAZUNDERS	GEEBAGS
GAUS	GAWKIHOOD	GAZANIA	GAZY	GEEBUNG
GAUSS	GAWKILY	GAZANIAS	GEAL	GEEBUNGS
GAUSSES	GAWKINESS	GAZAR	GEALED	GEECHEE
GAUSSIAN	GAWKING	GAZARS	GEALING	GEECHEES
GAUZE	GAWKISH	GAZE	GEALOUS	GEED
GAUZELIKE	GAWKISHLY	GAZEBO	GEALOUSY	GEEGAW
GAUZES	GAWKS	GAZEBOES	GEALS	GEEGAWS
GAUZIER	GAWKY	GAZEBOS	GEAN	GEEING
GAUZIEST	GAWMOGE	GAZED	GEANS	GEEK
GAUZILY	GAWMOGES	GAZEFUL	GEAR	GEEKDOM
GAUZINESS	GAWP	GAZEHOUND	GEARBOX	GEEKDOMS
GAUZY	GAWPED	GAZELLE	GEARBOXES	GEEKED
GAVAGE	GAWPER	GAZELLES	GEARCASE	GEEKERIES
GAVAGES	GAWPERS	GAZEMENT	GEARCASES	GEEKERY
GAVE	GAWPING	GAZEMENTS	GEARE	GEEKIER
GAVEL	GAWPS	GAZER	GEARED	GEEKIEST
GAVELED	GAWPUS	GAZERS	GEARES	GEEKINESS
GAVELING	GAWPUSES	GAZES	GEARHEAD	GEEKISH

GEEKISM	GELATIN	GEMCLIPS	GEMSBUCKS	GENETS
GEEKISMS	GELATINE	GEMEL	GEMSHORN	GENETTE
GEEKS	GELATINES	GEMELS	GEMSHORNS	GENETTES
GEEKSPEAK	GELATING	GEMFISH	GEMSTONE	GENEVA
GEEKY	GELATINS	GEMFISHES	GEMSTONES	GENEVAS
GEELBEK	GELATION	GEMINAL	GEMUTLICH	GENIAL
GEELBEKS	GELATIONS	GEMINALLY	GEN	GENIALISE
GEEP	GELATIS	GEMINATE	GENA	GENIALITY
GEEPOUND	GELATO	GEMINATED	GENAL	GENIALIZE
GEEPOUNDS	GELATOS	GEMINATES	GENAPPE	GENIALLY
GEEPS	GELCAP	GEMINI	GENAPPES	GENIC
GEES	GELCAPS	GEMINIES	GENAS	GENICALLY
GEESE	GELCOAT	GEMINOUS	GENDARME	GENICULAR
GEEST	GELCOATS	GEMINY	GENDARMES	GENIE
GEESTS	GELD	GEMLIKE	GENDER	GENIES
GEEZ	GELDED	GEMMA	GENDERED	GENII
GEEZAH	GELDER	GEMMAE	GENDERING	GENIP
GEEZAHS	GELDERS	GEMMAN	GENDERISE	GENIPAP
GEEZER	GELDING	GEMMATE	GENDERIZE	GENIPAPO
GEEZERS	GELDINGS	GEMMATED	GENDERS	GENIPAPOS
GEFILTE	GELDS	GEMMATES	GENE	GENIPAPS
GEFUFFLE	GELEE	GEMMATING	GENEALOGY	GENIPS
GEFUFFLED	GELEES	GEMMATION	GENERA	GENISTA
GEFUFFLES	GELID	GEMMATIVE	GENERABLE	GENISTAS
GEFULLTE	GELIDER	GEMMED	GENERAL	GENISTEIN
GEGGIE	GELIDEST	GEMMEN	GENERALCY	GENITAL
GEGGIES	GELIDITY	GEMMEOUS	GENERALE	GENITALIA
GEHLENITE	GELIDLY	GEMMERIES	GENERALIA	GENITALIC
GEISHA	GELIDNESS	GEMMERY	GENERALLY	GENITALLY
GEISHAS	GELIGNITE	GEMMIER	GENERALS	GENITALS
GEIST	GELLANT	GEMMIEST	GENERANT	GENITIVAL
GEISTS	GELLANTS	GEMMILY	GENERANTS	GENITIVE
GEIT	GELLED	GEMMINESS	GENERATE	GENITIVES
GEITED	GELLIES	GEMMING	GENERATED	GENITOR
GEITING	GELLING	GEMMOLOGY	GENERATES	GENITORS
GEITS	GELLY	GEMMULE	GENERATOR	GENITRIX
GEL	GELOSIES	GEMMULES	GENERIC	GENITURE
GELABLE	GELOSY	GEMMY	GENERICAL	GENITURES
GELADA	GELS	GEMOLOGY	GENERICS	GENIUS
GELADAS	GELSEMIA	GEMONY	GENEROUS	GENIUSES
GELANDE	GELSEMINE	GEMOT	GENES	GENIZAH
GELANT	GELSEMIUM	GEMOTE	GENESES	GENIZAHS
GELANTS	GELT	GEMOTES	GENESIS	GENIZOT
GELASTIC	GELTS	GEMOTS	GENET	GENIZOTH
GELATE	GEM	GEMS	GENETIC	GENLOCK
GELATED	GEMATRIA	GEMSBOK	GENETICAL	GENLOCKED
GELATES	GEMATRIAS	GEMSBOKS	GENETICS	GENLOCKS
GELATI	GEMCLIP	GEMSBUCK	GENETRIX	GENNAKER

GENNAKERS	GENTILIC	GEODESICS	GEOPHAGIA	GERENT
GENNED	GENTILISE	GEODESIES	GEOPHAGY	GERENTS
GENNEL	GENTILISH	GEODESIST	GEOPHILIC	GERENUK
GENNELS	GENTILISM	GEODESY	GEOPHONE	GERENUKS
GENNET	GENTILITY	GEODETIC	GEOPHONES	GERES
GENNETS	GENTILIZE	GEODETICS	GEOPHYTE	GERFALCON
GENNIES	GENTLE	GEODIC	GEOPHYTES	GERIATRIC
GENNING	GENTLED	GEODUCK	GEOPHYTIC	GERLE
GENNY	GENTLEMAN	GEODUCKS	GEOPONIC	GERLES
GENOA	GENTLEMEN	GEOFACT	GEOPONICS	GERM
GENOAS	GENTLER	GEOFACTS	GEOPROBE	GERMAIN
GENOCIDAL	GENTLES	GEOGENIES	GEOPROBES	GERMAINE
GENOCIDE	GENTLEST	GEOGENY	GEORGETTE	GERMAINES
GENOCIDES	GENTLING	GEOGNOSES	GEORGIC	GERMAINS
GENOGRAM	GENTLY	GEOGNOSIS	GEORGICAL	GERMAN
GENOGRAMS	GENTOO	GEOGNOST	GEORGICS	GERMANDER
GENOISE	GENTOOS	GEOGNOSTS	GEOS	GERMANE
GENOISES	GENTRICE	GEOGNOSY	GEOSPHERE	GERMANELY
GENOM	GENTRICES	GEOGONIC	GEOSTATIC	GERMANIC
GENOME	GENTRIES	GEOGONIES	GEOTACTIC	GERMANISE
GENOMES	GENTRIFY	GEOGONY	GEOTAG	GERMANITE
GENOMIC	GENTRY	GEOGRAPHY	GEOTAGGED	GERMANIUM
GENOMICS	GENTS	GEOID	GEOTAGS	GERMANIZE
GENOMS	GENTY	GEOIDAL	GEOTAXES	GERMANOUS
GENOTOXIC	GENU	GEOIDS	GEOTAXIS	GERMANS
GENOTYPE	GENUA	GEOLATRY	GEOTHERM	GERMED
GENOTYPED	GENUFLECT	GEOLOGER	GEOTHERMS	GERMEN
GENOTYPES	GENUINE	GEOLOGERS	GEOTROPIC	GERMENS
GENOTYPIC	GENUINELY	GEOLOGIAN	GER	GERMFREE
GENRE	GENUS	GEOLOGIC	GERAH	GERMICIDE
GENRES	GENUSES	GEOLOGIES	GERAHS	GERMIER
GENRO	GEO	GEOLOGISE	GERANIAL	GERMIEST
GENROS	GEOBOTANY	GEOLOGIST	GERANIALS	GERMIN
GENS	GEOCACHE	GEOLOGIZE	GERANIOL	GERMINA
GENSENG	GEOCACHED	GEOLOGY	GERANIOLS	GERMINAL
GENSENGS	GEOCACHER	GEOMANCER	GERANIUM	GERMINANT
GENT	GEOCACHES	GEOMANCY	GERANIUMS	GERMINATE
GENTEEL	GEOCARPIC	GEOMANT	GERARDIA	GERMINESS
GENTEELER	GEOCARPY	GEOMANTIC	GERARDIAS	GERMING
GENTEELLY	GEOCODE	GEOMANTS	GERBE	GERMINS
GENTES	GEOCODED	GEOMATICS	GERBERA	GERMLIKE
GENTIAN	GEOCODES	GEOMETER	GERBERAS	GERMPLASM
GENTIANS	GEOCODING	GEOMETERS	GERBES	GERMPROOF
GENTIER	GEOCORONA	GEOMETRIC	GERBIL	GERMS
GENTIEST	GEODATA	GEOMETRID	GERBILLE	GERMY
GENTIL	GEODE	GEOMETRY	GERBILLES	GERNE
GENTILE	GEODES	GEOMYOID	GERBILS	GERNED
GENTILES	GEODESIC	GEONOMICS	GERE	GERNES

GERNING
GERONIMO
GERONTIC
GEROPIGA
GEROPIGAS
GERS
GERT
GERTCHA
GERUND
GERUNDIAL
GERUNDIVE
GERUNDS
GESNERIA
GESNERIAD
GESNERIAS
GESSAMINE
GESSE
GESSED
GESSES
GESSING
GESSO
GESSOED
GESSOES
GEST
GESTALT
GESTALTEN
GESTALTS
GESTANT
GESTAPO
GESTAPOS
GESTATE
GESTATED
GESTATES
GESTATING
GESTATION
GESTATIVE
GESTATORY
GESTE
GESTES
GESTIC
GESTICAL
GESTS
GESTURAL
GESTURE
GESTURED
GESTURER
GESTURERS
GESTURES

GESTURING
GET
GETA
GETABLE
GETAS
GETATABLE
GETAWAY
GETAWAYS
GETOUT
GETOUTS
GETS
GETTABLE
GETTER
GETTERED
GETTERING
GETTERS
GETTING
GETTINGS
GETUP
GETUPS
GEUM
GEUMS
GEWGAW
GEWGAWED
GEWGAWS
GEY
GEYAN
GEYER
GEYEST
GEYSER
GEYSERED
GEYSERING
GEYSERITE
GEYSERS
GHARIAL
GHARIALS
GHARRI
GHARRIES
GHARRIS
GHARRY
GHAST
GHASTED
GHASTFUL
GHASTING
GHASTLIER
GHASTLY
GHASTNESS
GHASTS

GHAT
GHATS
GHAUT
GHAUTS
GHAZAL
GHAZALS
GHAZEL
GHAZELS
GHAZI
GHAZIES
GHAZIS
GHEE
GHEES
GHERAO
GHERAOED
GHERAOES
GHERAOING
GHERAOS
GHERKIN
GHERKINS
GHESSE
GHESSED
GHESSES
GHESSING
GHEST
GHETTO
GHETTOED
GHETTOES
GHETTOING
GHETTOISE
GHETTOIZE
GHETTOS
GHI
GHIBLI
GHIBLIS
GHILGAI
GHILGAIS
GHILLIE
GHILLIED
GHILLIES
GHILLYING
GHIS
GHOST
GHOSTED
GHOSTIER
GHOSTIEST
GHOSTING
GHOSTINGS

GHOSTLIER
GHOSTLIKE
GHOSTLY
GHOSTS
GHOSTY
GHOUL
GHOULIE
GHOULIES
GHOULISH
GHOULS
GHRELIN
GHRELINS
GHUBAR
GHYLL
GHYLLS
GI
GIAMBEUX
GIANT
GIANTESS
GIANTHOOD
GIANTISM
GIANTISMS
GIANTLIER
GIANTLIKE
GIANTLY
GIANTRIES
GIANTRY
GIANTS
GIANTSHIP
GIAOUR
GIAOURS
GIARDIA
GIARDIAS
GIB
GIBBED
GIBBER
GIBBERED
GIBBERING
GIBBERISH
GIBBERS
GIBBET
GIBBETED
GIBBETING
GIBBETS
GIBBETTED
GIBBING
GIBBON
GIBBONS

GIBBOSE
GIBBOSITY
GIBBOUS
GIBBOUSLY
GIBBSITE
GIBBSITES
GIBE
GIBED
GIBEL
GIBELS
GIBER
GIBERS
GIBES
GIBING
GIBINGLY
GIBLET
GIBLETS
GIBLI
GIBLIS
GIBS
GIBSON
GIBSONS
GIBUS
GIBUSES
GID
GIDDAP
GIDDAY
GIDDIED
GIDDIER
GIDDIES
GIDDIEST
GIDDILY
GIDDINESS
GIDDUP
GIDDY
GIDDYAP
GIDDYING
GIDDYUP
GIDGEE
GIDGEES
GIDJEE
GIDJEES
GIDS
GIE
GIED
GIEING
GIEN
GIES

GIF	GIGGLERS	GILLAROOS	GIMMALS	GINGES
GIFS	GIGGLES	GILLED	GIMME	GINGHAM
GIFT	GIGGLIER	GILLER	GIMMER	GINGHAMS
GIFTABLE	GIGGLIEST	GILLERS	GIMMERS	GINGILI
GIFTABLES	GIGGLING	GILLET	GIMMES	GINGILIS
GIFTED	GIGGLINGS	GILLETS	GIMMICK	GINGILLI
GIFTEDLY	GIGGLY	GILLFLIRT	GIMMICKED	GINGILLIS
GIFTEE	GIGHE	GILLIE	GIMMICKRY	GINGIVA
GIFTEES	GIGLET	GILLIED	GIMMICKS	GINGIVAE
GIFTING	GIGLETS	GILLIES	GIMMICKY	GINGIVAL
GIFTINGS	GIGLOT	GILLING	GIMMIE	GINGKO
GIFTLESS	GIGLOTS	GILLION	GIMMIES	GINGKOES
GIFTS	GIGMAN	GILLIONS	GIMMOR	GINGKOS
GIFTSHOP	GIGMANITY	GILLNET	GIMMORS	GINGLE
GIFTSHOPS	GIGMEN	GILLNETS	GIMP	GINGLES
GIFTWARE	GIGOLO	GILLS	GIMPED	GINGLYMI
GIFTWARES	GIGOLOS	GILLY	GIMPIER	GINGLYMUS
GIFTWRAP	GIGOT	GILLYING	GIMPIEST	GINGS
GIFTWRAPS	GIGOTS	GILLYVOR	GIMPING	GINHOUSE
GIG	GIGS	GILLYVORS	GIMPS	GINHOUSES
GIGA	GIGUE	GILPEY	GIMPY	GINK
GIGABIT	GIGUES	GILPEYS	GIN	GINKGO
GIGABITS	GILA	GILPIES	GINCH	GINKGOES
GIGABYTE	GILAS	GILPY	GINCHES	GINKGOS
GIGABYTES	GILBERT	GILRAVAGE	GING	GINKS
GIGACYCLE	GILBERTS	GILSONITE	GINGAL	GINN
GIGAFLOP	GILCUP	GILT	GINGALL	GINNED
GIGAFLOPS	GILCUPS	GILTCUP	GINGALLS	GINNEL
GIGAHERTZ	GILD	GILTCUPS	GINGALS	GINNELS
GIGANTEAN	GILDED	GILTHEAD	GINGE	GINNER
GIGANTIC	GILDEN	GILTHEADS	GINGELEY	GINNERIES
GIGANTISM	GILDER	GILTS	GINGELEYS	GINNERS
GIGAS	GILDERS	GILTWOOD	GINGELI	GINNERY
GIGATON	GILDHALL	GIMBAL	GINGELIES	GINNIER
GIGATONS	GILDHALLS	GIMBALED	GINGELIS	GINNIEST
GIGAVOLT	GILDING	GIMBALING	GINGELLI	GINNING
GIGAVOLTS	GILDINGS	GIMBALLED	GINGELLIS	GINNINGS
GIGAWATT	GILDS	GIMBALS	GINGELLY	GINNY
GIGAWATTS	GILDSMAN	GIMCRACK	GINGELY	GINORMOUS
GIGGED	GILDSMEN	GIMCRACKS	GINGER	GINS
GIGGING	GILET	GIMEL	GINGERADE	GINSENG
GIGGIT	GILETS	GIMELS	GINGERED	GINSENGS
GIGGITED	GILGAI	GIMLET	GINGERIER	GINSHOP
GIGGITING	GILGAIS	GIMLETED	GINGERING	GINSHOPS
GIGGITS	GILGIE	GIMLETING	GINGERLY	GINZO
GIGGLE	GILGIES	GIMLETS	GINGEROUS	GINZOES
GIGGLED	GILL	GIMMAL	GINGERS	GINZOS
GIGGLER	GILLAROO	GIMMALLED	GINGERY	GIO

GIOCOSO	GIRDLE	GIRTED	GIVEBACKS	GLADDEN
GIOS	GIRDLED	GIRTH	GIVED	GLADDENED
GIP	GIRDLER	GIRTHED	GIVEN	GLADDENER
GIPON	GIRDLERS	GIRTHING	GIVENNESS	GLADDENS
GIPONS	GIRDLES	GIRTHLINE	GIVENS	GLADDER
GIPPED	GIRDLING	GIRTHS	GIVER	GLADDEST
GIPPER	GIRDS	GIRTING	GIVERS	GLADDIE
GIPPERS	GIRKIN	GIRTLINE	GIVES	GLADDIES
GIPPIES	GIRKINS	GIRTLINES	GIVING	GLADDING
GIPPING	GIRL	GIRTS	GIVINGS	GLADDON
GIPPO	GIRLHOOD	GIS	GIZMO	GLADDONS
GIPPOES	GIRLHOODS	GISARME	GIZMOLOGY	GLADE
GIPPOS	GIRLIE	GISARMES	GIZMOS	GLADELIKE
GIPPY	GIRLIER	GISM	GIZZ	GLADES
GIPS	GIRLIES	GISMO	GIZZARD	GLADFUL
GIPSEN	GIRLIEST	GISMOLOGY	GIZZARDS	GLADIATE
GIPSENS	GIRLISH	GISMOS	GIZZEN	GLADIATOR
GIPSIED	GIRLISHLY	GISMS	GIZZENED	GLADIER
GIPSIES	GIRLOND	GIST	GIZZENING	GLADIEST
GIPSY	GIRLONDS	GISTS	GIZZENS	GLADIOLA
GIPSYDOM	GIRLS	GIT	GIZZES	GLADIOLAR
GIPSYDOMS	GIRLY	GITANA	GJETOST	GLADIOLAS
GIPSYHOOD	GIRN	GITANAS	GJETOSTS	GLADIOLE
GIPSYING	GIRNED	GITANO	GJU	GLADIOLES
GIPSYISH	GIRNEL	GITANOS	GJUS	GLADIOLI
GIPSYISM	GIRNELS	GITCH	GLABELLA	GLADIOLUS
GIPSYISMS	GIRNER	GITCHES	GLABELLAE	GLADIUS
GIPSYWORT	GIRNERS	GITE	GLABELLAR	GLADIUSES
GIRAFFE	GIRNIE	GITES	GLABRATE	GLADLIER
GIRAFFES	GIRNIER	GITS	GLABROUS	GLADLIEST
GIRAFFID	GIRNIEST	GITTARONE	GLACE	GLADLY
GIRAFFIDS	GIRNING	GITTED	GLACED	GLADNESS
GIRAFFINE	GIRNS	GITTERN	GLACEED	GLADS
GIRAFFISH	GIRO	GITTERNED	GLACEING	GLADSOME
GIRAFFOID	GIROLLE	GITTERNS	GLACES	GLADSOMER
GIRANDOLA	GIROLLES	GITTIN	GLACIAL	GLADSTONE
GIRANDOLE	GIRON	GITTING	GLACIALLY	GLADWRAP
GIRASOL	GIRONIC	GIUST	GLACIALS	GLADWRAPS
GIRASOLE	GIRONNY	GIUSTED	GLACIATE	GLADY
GIRASOLES	GIRONS	GIUSTING	GLACIATED	GLAIK
GIRASOLS	GIROS	GIUSTO	GLACIATES	GLAIKET
GIRD	GIROSOL	GIUSTS	GLACIER	GLAIKIT
GIRDED	GIROSOLS	GIVABLE	GLACIERED	GLAIKS
GIRDER	GIRR	GIVE	GLACIERS	GLAIR
GIRDERS	GIRRS	GIVEABLE	GLACIS	GLAIRE
GIRDING	GIRSH	GIVEAWAY	GLACISES	GLAIRED
GIRDINGLY	GIRSHES	GIVEAWAYS	GLAD	GLAIREOUS
GIRDINGS	GIRT	GIVEBACK	GLADDED	GLAIRES

GLAIRIER	GLANS	GLAURIEST	GLEDE	GLEY
GLAIRIEST	GLARE	GLAURS	GLEDES	GLEYED
GLAIRIN	GLAREAL	GLAURY	GLEDGE	GLEYING
GLAIRING	GLARED	GLAZE	GLEDGED	GLEYINGS
GLAIRINS	GLARELESS	GLAZED	GLEDGES	GLEYS
GLAIRS	GLAREOUS	GLAZEN	GLEDGING	GLIA
GLAIRY	GLARES	GLAZER	GLEDS	GLIADIN
GLAIVE	GLARIER	GLAZERS	GLEE	GLIADINE
GLAIVED	GLARIEST	GLAZES	GLEED	GLIADINES
GLAIVES	GLARINESS	GLAZIER	GLEEDS	GLIADINS
GLAM	GLARING	GLAZIERS	GLEEFUL	GLIAL
GLAMMED	GLARINGLY	GLAZIERY	GLEEFULLY	GLIAS
GLAMMER	GLARY	GLAZIEST	GLEEING	GLIB
GLAMMEST	GLASNOST	GLAZILY	GLEEK	GLIBBED
GLAMMIER	GLASNOSTS	GLAZINESS	GLEEKED	GLIBBER
GLAMMIEST	GLASS	GLAZING	GLEEKING	GLIBBERY
GLAMMING	GLASSED	GLAZINGS	GLEEKS	GLIBBEST
GLAMMY	GLASSEN	GLAZY	GLEEMAN	GLIBBING
GLAMOR	GLASSES	GLEAM	GLEEMEN	GLIBLY
GLAMORED	GLASSFUL	GLEAMED	GLEENIE	GLIBNESS
GLAMORING	GLASSFULS	GLEAMER	GLEENIES	GLIBS
GLAMORISE	GLASSIE	GLEAMERS	GLEES	GLID
GLAMORIZE	GLASSIER	GLEAMIER	GLEESOME	GLIDDER
GLAMOROUS	GLASSIES	GLEAMIEST	GLEET	GLIDDERY
GLAMORS	GLASSIEST	GLEAMING	GLEETED	GLIDDEST
GLAMOUR	GLASSIFY	GLEAMINGS	GLEETIER	GLIDE
GLAMOURED	GLASSILY	GLEAMS	GLEETIEST	GLIDED
GLAMOURS	GLASSINE	GLEAMY	GLEETING	GLIDEPATH
GLAMPING	GLASSINES	GLEAN	GLEETS	GLIDER
GLAMPINGS	GLASSING	GLEANABLE	GLEETY	GLIDERS
GLAMS	GLASSLESS	GLEANED	GLEG	GLIDES
GLANCE	GLASSLIKE	GLEANER	GLEGGER	GLIDING
GLANCED	GLASSMAN	GLEANERS	GLEGGEST	GLIDINGLY
GLANCER	GLASSMEN	GLEANING	GLEGLY	GLIDINGS
GLANCERS	GLASSWARE	GLEANINGS	GLEGNESS	GLIFF
GLANCES	GLASSWORK	GLEANS	GLEI	GLIFFING
GLANCING	GLASSWORM	GLEAVE	GLEIS	GLIFFINGS
GLANCINGS	GLASSWORT	GLEAVES	GLEN	GLIFFS
GLAND	GLASSY	GLEBA	GLENGARRY	GLIFT
GLANDERED	GLAUCOMA	GLEBAE	GLENLIKE	GLIFTS
GLANDERS	GLAUCOMAS	GLEBE	GLENOID	GLIKE
GLANDES	GLAUCOUS	GLEBELESS	GLENOIDAL	GLIKES
GLANDLESS	GLAUM	GLEBES	GLENOIDS	GLIM
GLANDLIKE	GLAUMED	GLEBIER	GLENS	GLIME
GLANDS	GLAUMING	GLEBIEST	GLENT	GLIMED
GLANDULAR	GLAUMS	GLEBOUS	GLENTED	GLIMES
GLANDULE	GLAUR	GLEBY	GLENTING	GLIMING
GLANDULES	GLAURIER	GLED	GLENTS	GLIMMER

G

GLIMMERED	GLITZ	GLOBOSITY	GLOOPIER	GLOSSISTS
GLIMMERS	GLITZED	GLOBOUS	GLOOPIEST	GLOSSITIC
GLIMMERY	GLITZES	GLOBS	GLOOPING	GLOSSITIS
GLIMPSE	GLITZIER	GLOBULAR	GLOOPS	GLOSSLESS
GLIMPSED	GLITZIEST	GLOBULARS	GLOOPY	GLOSSY
GLIMPSER	GLITZILY	GLOBULE	GLOP	GLOST
GLIMPSERS	GLITZING	GLOBULES	GLOPPED	GLOSTS
GLIMPSES	GLITZY	GLOBULET	GLOPPIER	GLOTTAL
GLIMPSING	GLOAM	GLOBULETS	GLOPPIEST	GLOTTIC
GLIMS	GLOAMING	GLOBULIN	GLOPPING	GLOTTIDES
GLINT	GLOAMINGS	GLOBULINS	GLOPPY	GLOTTIS
GLINTED	GLOAMS	GLOBULITE	GLOPS	GLOTTISES
GLINTIER	GLOAT	GLOBULOUS	GLORIA	GLOUT
GLINTIEST	GLOATED	GLOBUS	GLORIAS	GLOUTED
GLINTING	GLOATER	GLOBY	GLORIED	GLOUTING
GLINTS	GLOATERS	GLOCHID	GLORIES	GLOUTS
GLINTY	GLOATING	GLOCHIDIA	GLORIFIED	GLOVE
GLIOMA	GLOATINGS	GLOCHIDS	GLORIFIER	GLOVEBOX
GLIOMAS	GLOATS	GLODE	GLORIFIES	GLOVED
GLIOMATA	GLOB	GLOGG	GLORIFY	GLOVELESS
GLIOSES	GLOBAL	GLOGGS	GLORIOLE	GLOVELIKE
GLIOSIS	GLOBALISE	GLOIRE	GLORIOLES	GLOVER
GLISK	GLOBALISM	GLOIRES	GLORIOSA	GLOVERS
GLISKS	GLOBALIST	GLOM	GLORIOSAS	GLOVES
GLISSADE	GLOBALIZE	GLOMERA	GLORIOUS	GLOVING
GLISSADED	GLOBALLY	GLOMERATE	GLORY	GLOVINGS
GLISSADER	GLOBATE	GLOMERULE	GLORYING	GLOW
GLISSADES	GLOBATED	GLOMERULI	GLOSS	GLOWED
GLISSANDI	GLOBBIER	GLOMMED	GLOSSA	GLOWER
GLISSANDO	GLOBBIEST	GLOMMING	GLOSSAE	GLOWERED
GLISSE	GLOBBY	GLOMS	GLOSSAL	GLOWERING
GLISSES	GLOBE	GLOMUS	GLOSSARY	GLOWERS
GLISTEN	GLOBED	GLONOIN	GLOSSAS	GLOWFLIES
GLISTENED	GLOBEFISH	GLONOINS	GLOSSATOR	GLOWFLY
GLISTENS	GLOBELIKE	GLOOM	GLOSSED	GLOWING
GLISTER	GLOBES	GLOOMED	GLOSSEME	GLOWINGLY
GLISTERED	GLOBESITY	GLOOMFUL	GLOSSEMES	GLOWLAMP
GLISTERS	GLOBETROT	GLOOMIER	GLOSSER	GLOWLAMPS
GLIT	GLOBI	GLOOMIEST	GLOSSERS	GLOWS
GLITCH	GLOBIER	GLOOMILY	GLOSSES	GLOWSTICK
GLITCHES	GLOBIEST	GLOOMING	GLOSSIER	GLOWWORM
GLITCHIER	GLOBIN	GLOOMINGS	GLOSSIES	GLOWWORMS
GLITCHY	GLOBING	GLOOMLESS	GLOSSIEST	GLOXINIA
GLITS	GLOBINS	GLOOMS	GLOSSILY	GLOXINIAS
GLITTER	GLOBOID	GLOOMSTER	GLOSSINA	GLOZE
GLITTERED	GLOBOIDS	GLOOMY	GLOSSINAS	GLOZED
GLITTERS	GLOBOSE	GLOOP	GLOSSING	GLOZES
GLITTERY	GLOBOSELY	GLOOPED	GLOSSIST	GLOZING

GLOZINGS

GLUCAGON

GLUCAGONS

GLUCAN

GLUCANS

GLUCINA

GLUCINAS

GLUCINIC

GLUCINIUM

GLUCINUM

GLUCINUMS

GLUCONATE

GLUCONIC

GLUCOSE

GLUCOSES

GLUCOSIC

GLUCOSIDE

GLUE

GLUEBALL

GLUEBALLS

GLUED

GLUEING

GLUEISH

GLUELIKE

GLUEPOT

GLUEPOTS

GLUER

GLUERS

GLUES

GLUEY

GLUEYNESS

GLUG

GLUGGABLE

GLUGGED

GLUGGING

GLUGS

GLUHWEIN

GLUHWEINS

GLUIER

GLUIEST

GLUILY

GLUINESS

GLUING

GLUISH

GLUM

GLUME

GLUMELIKE

GLUMELLA

GLUMELLAS

GLUMES

GLUMLY

GLUMMER

GLUMMEST

GLUMNESS

GLUMPIER

GLUMPIEST

GLUMPILY

GLUMPISH

GLUMPS

GLUMPY

GLUMS

GLUNCH

GLUNCHED

GLUNCHES

GLUNCHING

GLUON

GLUONS

GLURGE

GLURGES

GLUT

GLUTAEAL

GLUTAEI

GLUTAEUS

GLUTAMATE

GLUTAMIC

GLUTAMINE

GLUTCH

GLUTCHED

GLUTCHES

GLUTCHING

GLUTE

GLUTEAL

GLUTEI

GLUTELIN

GLUTELINS

GLUTEN

GLUTENIN

GLUTENINS

GLUTENOUS

GLUTENS

GLUTES

GLUTEUS

GLUTINOUS

GLUTS

GLUTTED

GLUTTING

GLUTTON

GLUTTONS

GLUTTONY

GLYCAEMIA

GLYCAEMIC

GLYCAN

GLYCANS

GLYCATION

GLYCEMIA

GLYCEMIAS

GLYCEMIC

GLYCERIA

GLYCERIAS

GLYCERIC

GLYCERIDE

GLYCERIN

GLYCERINE

GLYCERINS

GLYCEROL

GLYCEROLS

GLYCERYL

GLYCERYLS

GLYCIN

GLYCINE

GLYCINES

GLYCINS

GLYCOCOLL

GLYCOGEN

GLYCOGENS

GLYCOL

GLYCOLIC

GLYCOLLIC

GLYCOLS

GLYCONIC

GLYCONICS

GLYCOSE

GLYCOSES

GLYCOSIDE

GLYCOSYL

GLYCOSYLS

GLYCYL

GLYCYLS

GLYPH

GLYPHIC

GLYPHS

GLYPTAL

GLYPTALS

GLYPTIC

GLYPTICS

GMELINITE

GNAMMA

GNAR

GNARL

GNARLED

GNARLIER

GNARLIEST

GNARLING

GNARLS

GNARLY

GNARR

GNARRED

GNARRING

GNARRS

GNARS

GNASH

GNASHED

GNASHER

GNASHERS

GNASHES

GNASHING

GNASHINGS

GNAT

GNATHAL

GNATHIC

GNATHION

GNATHIONS

GNATHITE

GNATHITES

GNATHONIC

GNATLIKE

GNATLING

GNATLINGS

GNATS

GNATTIER

GNATTIEST

GNATTY

GNATWREN

GNATWRENS

GNAW

GNAWABLE

GNAWED

GNAWER

GNAWERS

GNAWING

GNAWINGLY

GNAWINGS

GNAWN

GNAWS

GNEISS

GNEISSES

GNEISSIC

GNEISSOID

GNEISSOSE

GNOCCHI

GNOMAE

GNOME

GNOMELIKE

GNOMES

GNOMIC

GNOMICAL

GNOMISH

GNOMIST

GNOMISTS

GNOMON

GNOMONIC

GNOMONICS

GNOMONS

GNOSES

GNOSIS

GNOSTIC

GNOSTICAL

GNOSTICS

GNOW

GNOWS

GNU

GNUS

GO

GOA

GOAD

GOADED

GOADING

GOADLIKE

GOADS

GOADSMAN

GOADSMEN

GOADSTER

GOADSTERS

GOAF

GOAFS

GOAL

GOALBALL

GOALBALLS

GOALED

GOALIE

G

GOALIES	GOBBIEST	GODDESSES	GOELS	GOITRE
GOALING	GOBBING	GODDING	GOER	GOITRED
GOALLESS	GOBBLE	GODET	GOERS	GOITRES
GOALMOUTH	GOBBLED	GODETIA	GOES	GOITROGEN
GOALPOST	GOBBLER	GODETIAS	GOEST	GOITROUS
GOALPOSTS	GOBBLERS	GODETS	GOETH	GOJI
GOALS	GOBBLES	GODFATHER	GOETHITE	GOJIS
GOALWARD	GOBBLING	GODHEAD	GOETHITES	GOLCONDA
GOALWARDS	GOBBO	GODHEADS	GOETIC	GOLCONDAS
GOANNA	GOBBY	GODHOOD	GOETIES	GOLD
GOANNAS	GOBI	GODHOODS	GOETY	GOLDARN
GOARY	GOBIES	GODLESS	GOEY	GOLDARNED
GOAS	GOBIID	GODLESSLY	GOFER	GOLDARNS
GOAT	GOBIIDS	GODLIER	GOFERS	GOLDBRICK
GOATEE	GOBIOID	GODLIEST	GOFF	GOLDBUG
GOATEED	GOBIOIDS	GODLIKE	GOFFED	GOLDBUGS
GOATEES	GOBIS	GODLILY	GOFFER	GOLDCREST
GOATFISH	GOBLET	GODLINESS	GOFFERED	GOLDEN
GOATHERD	GOBLETS	GODLING	GOFFERING	GOLDENED
GOATHERDS	GOBLIN	GODLINGS	GOFFERS	GOLDENER
GOATIER	GOBLINS	GODLY	GOFFING	GOLDENEST
GOATIES	GOBO	GODMOTHER	GOFFS	GOLDENEYE
GOATIEST	GOBOES	GODOWN	GOGGA	GOLDENING
GOATISH	GOBONEE	GODOWNS	GOGGAS	GOLDENLY
GOATISHLY	GOBONY	GODPARENT	GOGGLE	GOLDENROD
GOATLIKE	GOBOS	GODROON	GOGGLEBOX	GOLDENS
GOATLING	GOBS	GODROONED	GOGGLED	GOLDER
GOATLINGS	GOBSHITE	GODROONS	GOGGLER	GOLDEST
GOATS	GOBSHITES	GODS	GOGGLERS	GOLDEYE
GOATSE	GOBURRA	GODSEND	GOGGLES	GOLDEYES
GOATSES	GOBURRAS	GODSENDS	GOGGLIER	GOLDFIELD
GOATSKIN	GOBY	GODSHIP	GOGGLIEST	GOLDFINCH
GOATSKINS	GOCHUJANG	GODSHIPS	GOGGLING	GOLDFINNY
GOATWEED	GOD	GODSLOT	GOGGLINGS	GOLDFISH
GOATWEEDS	GODAWFUL	GODSLOTS	GOGGLY	GOLDIER
GOATY	GODCHILD	GODSO	GOGLET	GOLDIES
GOB	GODDAM	GODSON	GOGLETS	GOLDIEST
GOBAN	GODDAMMED	GODSONS	GOGO	GOLDISH
GOBANG	GODDAMMIT	GODSPEED	GOGOS	GOLDLESS
GOBANGS	GODDAMN	GODSPEEDS	GOHONZON	GOLDMINER
GOBANS	GODDAMNED	GODSQUAD	GOHONZONS	GOLDS
GOBAR	GODDAMNIT	GODSQUADS	GOIER	GOLDSINNY
GOBBED	GODDAMNS	GODWARD	GOIEST	GOLDSIZE
GOBBELINE	GODDAMS	GODWARDS	GOING	GOLDSIZES
GOBBET	GODDED	GODWIT	GOINGS	GOLDSMITH
GOBBETS	GODDEN	GODWITS	GOITER	GOLDSPINK
GOBBI	GODDENS	GOE	GOITERED	GOLDSTICK
GOBBIER	GODDESS	GOEL	GOITERS	GOLDSTONE

GOLDTAIL	GOLLIWOGG	GOMUTOS	GONOCOCCI	GOODSIRE
GOLDTONE	GOLLIWOGS	GON	GONOCYTE	GOODSIRES
GOLDTONES	GOLLOP	GONAD	GONOCYTES	GOODTIME
GOLDURN	GOLLOPED	GONADAL	GONODUCT	GOODWIFE
GOLDURNS	GOLLOPER	GONADIAL	GONODUCTS	GOODWILL
GOLDWORK	GOLLOPERS	GONADIC	GONOF	GOODWILLS
GOLDWORKS	GOLLOPING	GONADS	GONOFS	GOODWIVES
GOLDY	GOLLOPS	GONCH	GONOPH	GOODY
GOLE	GOLLY	GONCHES	GONOPHORE	GOODYEAR
GOLEM	GOLLYING	GONDELAY	GONOPHS	GOODYEARS
GOLEMS	GOLLYWOG	GONDELAYS	GONOPOD	GOOEY
GOLES	GOLLYWOGS	GONDOLA	GONOPODS	GOOEYNESS
GOLF	GOLOMYNKA	GONDOLAS	GONOPORE	GOOF
GOLFED	GOLOSH	GONDOLIER	GONOPORES	GOOFBALL
GOLFER	GOLOSHE	GONE	GONORRHEA	GOOFBALLS
GOLFERS	GOLOSHED	GONEF	GONOSOME	GOOFED
GOLFIANA	GOLOSHES	GONEFS	GONOSOMES	GOOFIER
GOLFIANAS	GOLOSHING	GONENESS	GONS	GOOFIEST
GOLFING	GOLOSHOES	GONER	GONYS	GOOFILY
GOLFINGS	GOLP	GONERS	GONYSES	GOOFINESS
GOLFS	GOLPE	GONFALON	GONZO	GOOFING
GOLGOTHA	GOLPES	GONFALONS	GONZOS	GOOFS
GOLGOTHAS	GOLPS	GONFANON	GOO	GOOFUS
GOLIARD	GOMBEEN	GONFANONS	GOOBER	GOOFUSES
GOLIARDIC	GOMBEENS	GONG	GOOBERS	GOOFY
GOLIARDS	GOMBO	GONGED	GOOBIES	GOOG
GOLIARDY	GOMBOS	GONGING	GOOBY	GOOGLE
GOLIAS	GOMBRO	GONGLIKE	GOOD	GOOGLED
GOLIASED	GOMBROON	GONGS	GOODBY	GOOGLES
GOLIASES	GOMBROONS	GONGSTER	GOODBYE	GOOGLIES
GOLIASING	GOMBROS	GONGSTERS	GOODBYES	GOOGLING
GOLIATH	GOMER	GONGYO	GOODBYS	GOOGLY
GOLIATHS	GOMERAL	GONGYOS	GOODFACED	GOOGOL
GOLLAN	GOMERALS	GONIA	GOODFELLA	GOOGOLS
GOLLAND	GOMEREL	GONIATITE	GOODIE	GOOGS
GOLLANDS	GOMERELS	GONIDIA	GOODIER	GOOIER
GOLLANS	GOMERIL	GONIDIAL	GOODIES	GOOIEST
GOLLAR	GOMERILS	GONIDIC	GOODIEST	GOOILY
GOLLARED	GOMERS	GONIDIUM	GOODINESS	GOOINESS
GOLLARING	GOMOKU	GONIF	GOODISH	GOOK
GOLLARS	GOMOKUS	GONIFF	GOODLIER	GOOKIER
GOLLER	GOMPA	GONIFFS	GOODLIEST	GOOKIEST
GOLLERED	GOMPAS	GONIFS	GOODLY	GOOKS
GOLLERING	GOMPHOSES	GONION	GOODMAN	GOOKY
GOLLERS	GOMPHOSIS	GONIUM	GOODMEN	GOOL
GOLLIED	GOMUTI	GONK	GOODNESS	GOOLD
GOLLIES	GOMUTIS	GONKS	GOODNIGHT	GOOLDS
GOLLIWOG	GOMUTO	GONNA	GOODS	GOOLEY

GOOLEYS	GOOSEHERD	GORGE	GORMY	GOSSE
GOOLIE	GOOSELIKE	GORGEABLE	GORP	GOSSED
GOOLIES	GOOSENECK	GORGED	GORPED	GOSSES
GOOLS	GOOSERIES	GORGEDLY	GORPING	GOSSIB
GOOLY	GOOSERY	GORGEOUS	GORPS	GOSSIBS
GOOMBAH	GOOSES	GORGER	GORS	GOSSING
GOOMBAHS	GOOSEY	GORGERIN	GORSE	GOSSIP
GOOMBAY	GOOSEYS	GORGERINS	GORSEDD	GOSSIPED
GOOMBAYS	GOOSIER	GORGERS	GORSEDDS	GOSSIPER
GOON	GOOSIES	GORGES	GORSES	GOSSIPERS
GOONDA	GOOSIEST	GORGET	GORSIER	GOSSIPIER
GOONDAS	GOOSINESS	GORGETED	GORSIEST	GOSSIPING
GOONERIES	GOOSING	GORGETS	GORSOON	GOSSIPPED
GOONERY	GOOSY	GORGIA	GORSOONS	GOSSIPPER
GOONEY	GOPAK	GORGIAS	GORSY	GOSSIPRY
GOONEYS	GOPAKS	GORGING	GORY	GOSSIPS
GOONIE	GOPHER	GORGIO	GOS	GOSSIPY
GOONIER	GOPHERED	GORGIOS	GOSH	GOSSOON
GOONIES	GOPHERING	GORGON	GOSHAWK	GOSSOONS
GOONIEST	GOPHERS	GORGONEIA	GOSHAWKS	GOSSYPINE
GOONS	GOPIK	GORGONIAN	GOSHT	GOSSYPOL
GOONY	GOPIKS	GORGONISE	GOSHTS	GOSSYPOLS
GOOP	GOPURA	GORGONIZE	GOSLARITE	GOSTER
GOOPED	GOPURAM	GORGONS	GOSLET	GOSTERED
GOOPIER	GOPURAMS	GORHEN	GOSLETS	GOSTERING
GOOPIEST	GOPURAS	GORHENS	GOSLING	GOSTERS
GOOPINESS	GOR	GORI	GOSLINGS	GOT
GOOPS	GORA	GORIER	GOSPEL	GOTCH
GOOPY	GORAL	GORIEST	GOSPELER	GOTCHA
GOOR	GORALS	GORILLA	GOSPELERS	GOTCHAS
GOORAL	GORAMIES	GORILLAS	GOSPELISE	GOTCHES
GOORALS	GORAMY	GORILLIAN	GOSPELIZE	GOTCHIES
GOORIE	GORAS	GORILLINE	GOSPELLED	GOTH
GOORIES	GORBELLY	GORILLOID	GOSPELLER	GOTHIC
GOOROO	GORBLIMEY	GORILY	GOSPELLY	GOTHICISE
GOOROOS	GORBLIMY	GORINESS	GOSPELS	GOTHICISM
GOORS	GORCOCK	GORING	GOSPODA	GOTHICIZE
GOORY	GORCOCKS	GORINGS	GOSPODAR	GOTHICS
GOOS	GORCROW	GORIS	GOSPODARS	GOTHIER
GOOSANDER	GORCROWS	GORM	GOSPODIN	GOTHIEST
GOOSE	GORDITA	GORMAND	GOSPORT	GOTHITE
GOOSED	GORDITAS	GORMANDS	GOSPORTS	GOTHITES
GOOSEFISH	GORE	GORMED	GOSS	GOTHS
GOOSEFOOT	GORED	GORMIER	GOSSAMER	GOTHY
GOOSEGOB	GOREFEST	GORMIEST	GOSSAMERS	GOTTA
GOOSEGOBS	GOREFESTS	GORMING	GOSSAMERY	GOTTEN
GOOSEGOG	GOREHOUND	GORMLESS	GOSSAN	GOUACHE
GOOSEGOGS	GORES	GORMS	GOSSANS	GOUACHES

GOUCH	GOUTINESS	GOWNING	GRACILIS	GRADUATOR
GOUCHED	GOUTS	GOWNMAN	GRACILITY	GRADUS
GOUCHES	GOUTTE	GOWNMEN	GRACING	GRADUSES
GOUCHING	GOUTTES	GOWNS	GRACIOSO	GRAECISE
GOUGE	GOUTWEED	GOWNSMAN	GRACIOSOS	GRAECISED
GOUGED	GOUTWEEDS	GOWNSMEN	GRACIOUS	GRAECISES
GOUGER	GOUTWORT	GOWPEN	GRACKLE	GRAECIZE
GOUGERE	GOUTWORTS	GOWPENFUL	GRACKLES	GRAECIZED
GOUGERES	GOUTY	GOWPENS	GRAD	GRAECIZES
GOUGERS	GOV	GOX	GRADABLE	GRAFF
GOUGES	GOVERN	GOXES	GRADABLES	GRAFFED
GOUGING	GOVERNALL	GOY	GRADATE	GRAFFING
GOUJEERS	GOVERNED	GOYIM	GRADATED	GRAFFITI
GOUJON	GOVERNESS	GOYISCH	GRADATES	GRAFFITIS
GOUJONS	GOVERNING	GOYISH	GRADATIM	GRAFFITO
GOUK	GOVERNOR	GOYISHE	GRADATING	GRAFFS
GOUKS	GOVERNORS	GOYLE	GRADATION	GRAFT
GOULASH	GOVERNS	GOYLES	GRADATORY	GRAFTAGE
GOULASHES	GOVS	GOYS	GRADDAN	GRAFTAGES
GOURA	GOWAN	GOZZAN	GRADDANED	GRAFTED
GOURAMI	GOWANED	GOZZANS	GRADDANS	GRAFTER
GOURAMIES	GOWANS	GRAAL	GRADE	GRAFTERS
GOURAMIS	GOWANY	GRAALS	GRADED	GRAFTING
GOURAS	GOWD	GRAB	GRADELESS	GRAFTINGS
GOURD	GOWDER	GRABBABLE	GRADELIER	GRAFTS
GOURDE	GOWDEST	GRABBED	GRADELY	GRAHAM
GOURDES	GOWDS	GRABBER	GRADER	GRAHAMS
GOURDFUL	GOWDSPINK	GRABBERS	GRADERS	GRAIL
GOURDFULS	GOWF	GRABBIER	GRADES	GRAILE
GOURDIER	GOWFED	GRABBIEST	GRADIENT	GRAILES
GOURDIEST	GOWFER	GRABBING	GRADIENTS	GRAILS
GOURDLIKE	GOWFERS	GRABBLE	GRADIN	GRAIN
GOURDS	GOWFING	GRABBLED	GRADINE	GRAINAGE
GOURDY	GOWFS	GRABBLER	GRADINES	GRAINAGES
GOURMAND	GOWK	GRABBLERS	GRADING	GRAINE
GOURMANDS	GOWKS	GRABBLES	GRADINGS	GRAINED
GOURMET	GOWL	GRABBLING	GRADINI	GRAINER
GOURMETS	GOWLAN	GRABBY	GRADINO	GRAINERS
GOUSTIER	GOWLAND	GRABEN	GRADINS	GRAINES
GOUSTIEST	GOWLANDS	GRABENS	GRADS	GRAINIER
GOUSTROUS	GOWLANS	GRABS	GRADUAL	GRAINIEST
GOUSTY	GOWLED	GRACE	GRADUALLY	GRAINING
GOUT	GOWLING	GRACED	GRADUALS	GRAININGS
GOUTFLIES	GOWLS	GRACEFUL	GRADUAND	GRAINLESS
GOUTFLY	GOWN	GRACELESS	GRADUANDS	GRAINS
GOUTIER	GOWNBOY	GRACES	GRADUATE	GRAINY
GOUTIEST	GOWNBOYS	GRACILE	GRADUATED	GRAIP
GOUTILY	GOWNED	GRACILES	GRADUATES	GRAIPS

GRAITH
GRAITHED
GRAITHING
GRAITHLY
GRAITHS
GRAKLE
GRAKLES
GRALLOCH
GRALLOCHS
GRAM
GRAMA
GRAMARIES
GRAMARY
GRAMARYE
GRAMARYES
GRAMAS
GRAMASH
GRAMASHES
GRAME
GRAMERCY
GRAMES
GRAMMA
GRAMMAGE
GRAMMAGES
GRAMMAR
GRAMMARS
GRAMMAS
GRAMMATIC
GRAMME
GRAMMES
GRAMOCHE
GRAMOCHES
GRAMP
GRAMPA
GRAMPAS
GRAMPIES
GRAMPS
GRAMPUS
GRAMPUSES
GRAMPY
GRAMS
GRAN
GRANA
GRANARIES
GRANARY
GRAND
GRANDAD
GRANDADDY

GRANDADS
GRANDAM
GRANDAME
GRANDAMES
GRANDAMS
GRANDAUNT
GRANDBABY
GRANDDAD
GRANDDADS
GRANDDAM
GRANDDAMS
GRANDE
GRANDEE
GRANDEES
GRANDER
GRANDEST
GRANDEUR
GRANDEURS
GRANDIOSE
GRANDIOSO
GRANDKID
GRANDKIDS
GRANDLY
GRANDMA
GRANDMAMA
GRANDMAS
GRANDNESS
GRANDPA
GRANDPAPA
GRANDPAS
GRANDS
GRANDSIR
GRANDSIRE
GRANDSIRS
GRANDSON
GRANDSONS
GRANFER
GRANFERS
GRANGE
GRANGER
GRANGERS
GRANGES
GRANITA
GRANITAS
GRANITE
GRANITES
GRANITIC
GRANITISE

GRANITITE
GRANITIZE
GRANITOID
GRANIVORE
GRANNAM
GRANNAMS
GRANNIE
GRANNIED
GRANNIES
GRANNOM
GRANNOMS
GRANNY
GRANNYING
GRANNYISH
GRANOLA
GRANOLAS
GRANOLITH
GRANS
GRANT
GRANTABLE
GRANTED
GRANTEE
GRANTEES
GRANTER
GRANTERS
GRANTING
GRANTOR
GRANTORS
GRANTS
GRANTSMAN
GRANTSMEN
GRANULAR
GRANULARY
GRANULATE
GRANULE
GRANULES
GRANULITE
GRANULOMA
GRANULOSE
GRANULOUS
GRANUM
GRANUMS
GRAPE
GRAPED
GRAPELESS
GRAPELICE
GRAPELIKE
GRAPERIES

GRAPERY
GRAPES
GRAPESEED
GRAPESHOT
GRAPETREE
GRAPEVINE
GRAPEY
GRAPH
GRAPHED
GRAPHEME
GRAPHEMES
GRAPHEMIC
GRAPHENE
GRAPHENES
GRAPHIC
GRAPHICAL
GRAPHICLY
GRAPHICS
GRAPHING
GRAPHITE
GRAPHITES
GRAPHITIC
GRAPHIUM
GRAPHIUMS
GRAPHS
GRAPIER
GRAPIEST
GRAPINESS
GRAPING
GRAPLE
GRAPLES
GRAPLIN
GRAPLINE
GRAPLINES
GRAPLINS
GRAPNEL
GRAPNELS
GRAPPA
GRAPPAS
GRAPPLE
GRAPPLED
GRAPPLER
GRAPPLERS
GRAPPLES
GRAPPLING
GRAPY
GRASP
GRASPABLE

GRASPED
GRASPER
GRASPERS
GRASPING
GRASPLESS
GRASPS
GRASS
GRASSBIRD
GRASSED
GRASSER
GRASSERS
GRASSES
GRASSHOOK
GRASSIER
GRASSIEST
GRASSILY
GRASSING
GRASSINGS
GRASSLAND
GRASSLESS
GRASSLIKE
GRASSPLOT
GRASSQUIT
GRASSROOT
GRASSUM
GRASSUMS
GRASSY
GRASTE
GRAT
GRATE
GRATED
GRATEFUL
GRATELESS
GRATER
GRATERS
GRATES
GRATICULE
GRATIFIED
GRATIFIER
GRATIFIES
GRATIFY
GRATIN
GRATINATE
GRATINE
GRATINEE
GRATINEED
GRATINEES
GRATING

GRATINGLY	GRAVIDLY	GRAYMAILS	GREBE	GREENER
GRATINGS	GRAVIES	GRAYNESS	GREBES	GREENERS
GRATINS	GRAVING	GRAYOUT	GREBO	GREENERY
GRATIS	GRAVINGS	GRAYOUTS	GREBOES	GREENEST
GRATITUDE	GRAVIS	GRAYS	GREBOS	GREENEYE
GRATTOIR	GRAVITAS	GRAYSCALE	GRECE	GREENEYES
GRATTOIRS	GRAVITATE	GRAYSTONE	GRECES	GREENFLY
GRATUITY	GRAVITIES	GRAYWACKE	GRECIAN	GREENGAGE
GRATULANT	GRAVITINO	GRAYWATER	GRECIANS	GREENHAND
GRATULATE	GRAVITON	GRAZABLE	GRECISE	GREENHEAD
GRAUNCH	GRAVITONS	GRAZE	GRECISED	GREENHORN
GRAUNCHED	GRAVITY	GRAZEABLE	GRECISES	GREENIE
GRAUNCHER	GRAVLAKS	GRAZED	GRECISING	GREENIER
GRAUNCHES	GRAVLAX	GRAZER	GRECIZE	GREENIES
GRAUPEL	GRAVLAXES	GRAZERS	GRECIZED	GREENIEST
GRAUPELS	GRAVS	GRAZES	GRECIZES	GREENING
GRAV	GRAVURE	GRAZIER	GRECIZING	GREENINGS
GRAVADLAX	GRAVURES	GRAZIERS	GRECQUE	GREENISH
GRAVAMEN	GRAVY	GRAZING	GRECQUES	GREENLET
GRAVAMENS	GRAWLIX	GRAZINGLY	GREE	GREENLETS
GRAVAMINA	GRAWLIXES	GRAZINGS	GREEBO	GREENLING
GRAVE	GRAY	GRAZIOSO	GREEBOES	GREENLIT
GRAVED	GRAYBACK	GREASE	GREEBOS	GREENLY
GRAVEL	GRAYBACKS	GREASED	GREECE	GREENMAIL
GRAVELED	GRAYBEARD	GREASER	GREECES	GREENNESS
GRAVELESS	GRAYED	GREASERS	GREED	GREENROOM
GRAVELIKE	GRAYER	GREASES	GREEDHEAD	GREENS
GRAVELING	GRAYEST	GREASIER	GREEDIER	GREENSAND
GRAVELISH	GRAYFISH	GREASIES	GREEDIEST	GREENSICK
GRAVELLED	GRAYFLIES	GREASIEST	GREEDILY	GREENSOME
GRAVELLY	GRAYFLY	GREASILY	GREEDLESS	GREENTH
GRAVELS	GRAYHEAD	GREASING	GREEDS	GREENTHS
GRAVELY	GRAYHEADS	GREASY	GREEDSOME	GREENWASH
GRAVEN	GRAYHEN	GREAT	GREEDY	GREENWAY
GRAVENESS	GRAYHENS	GREATCOAT	GREEGREE	GREENWAYS
GRAVER	GRAYHOUND	GREATEN	GREEGREES	GREENWEED
GRAVERS	GRAYING	GREATENED	GREEING	GREENWING
GRAVES	GRAYISH	GREATENS	GREEK	GREENWOOD
GRAVESIDE	GRAYLAG	GREATER	GREEKED	GREENY
GRAVESITE	GRAYLAGS	GREATEST	GREEKING	GREES
GRAVEST	GRAYLE	GREATESTS	GREEKINGS	GREESE
GRAVEWARD	GRAYLES	GREATLY	GREEN	GREESES
GRAVEYARD	GRAYLING	GREATNESS	GREENBACK	GREESING
GRAVID	GRAYLINGS	GREATS	GREENBELT	GREESINGS
GRAVIDA	GRAYLIST	GREAVE	GREENBONE	GREET
GRAVIDAE	GRAYLISTS	GREAVED	GREENBUG	GREETE
GRAVIDAS	GRAYLY	GREAVES	GREENBUGS	GREETED
GRAVIDITY	GRAYMAIL	GREAVING	GREENED	GREETER

GREETERS

GREETERS	GRESSINGS	GRIDDED	GRIFFONS	GRIMIEST
GREETES	GREVE	GRIDDER	GRIFFS	GRIMILY
GREETING	GREVES	GRIDDERS	GRIFT	GRIMINESS
GREETINGS	GREVILLEA	GRIDDING	GRIFTED	GRIMING
GREETS	GREW	GRIDDLE	GRIFTER	GRIMLY
GREFFIER	GREWED	GRIDDLED	GRIFTERS	GRIMMER
GREFFIERS	GREWHOUND	GRIDDLES	GRIFTING	GRIMMEST
GREGALE	GREWING	GRIDDLING	GRIFTS	GRIMNESS
GREGALES	GREWS	GRIDE	GRIG	GRIMOIRE
GREGARIAN	GREWSOME	GRIDED	GRIGGED	GRIMOIRES
GREGARINE	GREWSOMER	GRIDELIN	GRIGGING	GRIMY
GREGATIM	GREX	GRIDELINS	GRIGRI	GRIN
GREGE	GREXES	GRIDES	GRIGRIS	GRINCH
GREGED	GREY	GRIDING	GRIGS	GRINCHES
GREGES	GREYBACK	GRIDIRON	GRIKE	GRIND
GREGING	GREYBACKS	GRIDIRONS	GRIKES	GRINDED
GREGO	GREYBEARD	GRIDLOCK	GRILL	GRINDELIA
GREGOS	GREYED	GRIDLOCKS	GRILLADE	GRINDER
GREIGE	GREYER	GRIDS	GRILLADES	GRINDERS
GREIGES	GREYEST	GRIECE	GRILLAGE	GRINDERY
GREIN	GREYHEAD	GRIECED	GRILLAGES	GRINDING
GREINED	GREYHEADS	GRIECES	GRILLE	GRINDINGS
GREINING	GREYHEN	GRIEF	GRILLED	GRINDS
GREINS	GREYHENS	GRIEFER	GRILLER	GRINGA
GREISEN	GREYHOUND	GRIEFERS	GRILLERS	GRINGAS
GREISENS	GREYING	GRIEFFUL	GRILLERY	GRINGO
GREISLY	GREYINGS	GRIEFLESS	GRILLES	GRINGOS
GREMIAL	GREYISH	GRIEFS	GRILLING	GRINNED
GREMIALS	GREYLAG	GRIESIE	GRILLINGS	GRINNER
GREMLIN	GREYLAGS	GRIESLY	GRILLION	GRINNERS
GREMLINS	GREYLIST	GRIESY	GRILLIONS	GRINNING
GREMMIE	GREYLISTS	GRIEVANCE	GRILLROOM	GRINNINGS
GREMMIES	GREYLY	GRIEVANT	GRILLS	GRINS
GREMMY	GREYNESS	GRIEVANTS	GRILLWORK	GRIOT
GREMOLATA	GREYS	GRIEVE	GRILSE	GRIOTS
GREN	GREYSCALE	GRIEVED	GRILSES	GRIP
GRENACHE	GREYSTONE	GRIEVER	GRIM	GRIPE
GRENACHES	GREYWACKE	GRIEVERS	GRIMACE	GRIPED
GRENADE	GRIBBLE	GRIEVES	GRIMACED	GRIPER
GRENADES	GRIBBLES	GRIEVING	GRIMACER	GRIPERS
GRENADIER	GRICE	GRIEVINGS	GRIMACERS	GRIPES
GRENADINE	GRICED	GRIEVOUS	GRIMACES	GRIPEY
GRENNED	GRICER	GRIFF	GRIMACING	GRIPIER
GRENNING	GRICERS	GRIFFE	GRIMALKIN	GRIPIEST
GRENS	GRICES	GRIFFES	GRIME	GRIPING
GRESE	GRICING	GRIFFIN	GRIMED	GRIPINGLY
GRESES	GRICINGS	GRIFFINS	GRIMES	GRIPINGS
GRESSING	GRID	GRIFFON	GRIMIER	GRIPLE

GRIPMAN	GRISTLY	GROCERS	GROOFS	GROSSEST
GRIPMEN	GRISTMILL	GROCERY	GROOLIER	GROSSING
GRIPPE	GRISTS	GROCKED	GROOLIEST	GROSSLY
GRIPPED	GRISY	GROCKING	GROOLY	GROSSNESS
GRIPPER	GRIT	GROCKLE	GROOM	GROSSULAR
GRIPPERS	GRITH	GROCKLES	GROOMED	GROSZ
GRIPPES	GRITHS	GRODIER	GROOMER	GROSZE
GRIPPIER	GRITLESS	GRODIEST	GROOMERS	GROSZY
GRIPPIEST	GRITS	GRODY	GROOMING	GROT
GRIPPING	GRITSTONE	GROG	GROOMINGS	GROTESQUE
GRIPPLE	GRITTED	GROGGED	GROOMS	GROTS
GRIPPLES	GRITTER	GROGGERY	GROOMSMAN	GROTTIER
GRIPPY	GRITTERS	GROGGIER	GROOMSMEN	GROTTIEST
GRIPS	GRITTEST	GROGGIEST	GROOVE	GROTTO
GRIPSACK	GRITTIER	GROGGILY	GROOVED	GROTTOED
GRIPSACKS	GRITTIEST	GROGGING	GROOVER	GROTTOES
GRIPT	GRITTILY	GROGGY	GROOVERS	GROTTOS
GRIPTAPE	GRITTING	GROGRAM	GROOVES	GROTTY
GRIPTAPES	GRITTINGS	GROGRAMS	GROOVIER	GROUCH
GRIPY	GRITTY	GROGS	GROOVIEST	GROUCHED
GRIS	GRIVATION	GROGSHOP	GROOVILY	GROUCHES
GRISAILLE	GRIVET	GROGSHOPS	GROOVING	GROUCHIER
GRISE	GRIVETS	GROIN	GROOVY	GROUCHILY
GRISED	GRIZ	GROINED	GROPE	GROUCHING
GRISELY	GRIZE	GROINING	GROPED	GROUCHY
GRISEOUS	GRIZES	GROININGS	GROPER	GROUF
GRISES	GRIZZES	GROINS	GROPERS	GROUFS
GRISETTE	GRIZZLE	GROK	GROPES	GROUGH
GRISETTES	GRIZZLED	GROKED	GROPING	GROUGHS
GRISGRIS	GRIZZLER	GROKING	GROPINGLY	GROUND
GRISING	GRIZZLERS	GROKKED	GROSBEAK	GROUNDAGE
GRISKIN	GRIZZLES	GROKKING	GROSBEAKS	GROUNDED
GRISKINS	GRIZZLIER	GROKS	GROSCHEN	GROUNDEN
GRISLED	GRIZZLIES	GROMA	GROSCHENS	GROUNDER
GRISLIER	GRIZZLING	GROMAS	GROSER	GROUNDERS
GRISLIES	GRIZZLY	GROMET	GROSERS	GROUNDHOG
GRISLIEST	GROAN	GROMETS	GROSERT	GROUNDING
GRISLY	GROANED	GROMMET	GROSERTS	GROUNDMAN
GRISON	GROANER	GROMMETED	GROSET	GROUNDMEN
GRISONS	GROANERS	GROMMETS	GROSETS	GROUNDNUT
GRISSINI	GROANFUL	GROMWELL	GROSGRAIN	GROUNDOUT
GRISSINO	GROANING	GROMWELLS	GROSS	GROUNDS
GRIST	GROANINGS	GRONE	GROSSART	GROUNDSEL
GRISTER	GROANS	GRONED	GROSSARTS	GROUP
GRISTERS	GROAT	GRONEFULL	GROSSED	GROUPABLE
GRISTLE	GROATS	GRONES	GROSSER	GROUPAGE
GRISTLES	GROCER	GRONING	GROSSERS	GROUPAGES
GRISTLIER	GROCERIES	GROOF	GROSSES	GROUPED

GROUPER	GROVIEST	GRUBBLING	GRUGRUS	GRUNGEY
GROUPERS	GROVY	GRUBBY	GRUIFORM	GRUNGIER
GROUPIE	GROW	GRUBS	GRUING	GRUNGIEST
GROUPIES	GROWABLE	GRUBSTAKE	GRUM	GRUNGY
GROUPING	GROWER	GRUBWORM	GRUMBLE	GRUNION
GROUPINGS	GROWERS	GRUBWORMS	GRUMBLED	GRUNIONS
GROUPIST	GROWING	GRUDGE	GRUMBLER	GRUNT
GROUPISTS	GROWINGLY	GRUDGED	GRUMBLERS	GRUNTED
GROUPLET	GROWINGS	GRUDGEFUL	GRUMBLES	GRUNTER
GROUPLETS	GROWL	GRUDGER	GRUMBLIER	GRUNTERS
GROUPOID	GROWLED	GRUDGERS	GRUMBLING	GRUNTING
GROUPOIDS	GROWLER	GRUDGES	GRUMBLY	GRUNTINGS
GROUPS	GROWLERS	GRUDGING	GRUME	GRUNTLE
GROUPWARE	GROWLERY	GRUDGINGS	GRUMES	GRUNTLED
GROUPWORK	GROWLIER	GRUE	GRUMLY	GRUNTLES
GROUPY	GROWLIEST	GRUED	GRUMMER	GRUNTLING
GROUSE	GROWLING	GRUEING	GRUMMEST	GRUNTS
GROUSED	GROWLINGS	GRUEL	GRUMMET	GRUPPETTI
GROUSER	GROWLS	GRUELED	GRUMMETED	GRUPPETTO
GROUSERS	GROWLY	GRUELER	GRUMMETS	GRUSHIE
GROUSES	GROWN	GRUELERS	GRUMNESS	GRUTCH
GROUSEST	GROWNUP	GRUELING	GRUMOSE	GRUTCHED
GROUSING	GROWNUPS	GRUELINGS	GRUMOUS	GRUTCHES
GROUT	GROWS	GRUELLED	GRUMP	GRUTCHING
GROUTED	GROWTH	GRUELLER	GRUMPED	GRUTTEN
GROUTER	GROWTHIER	GRUELLERS	GRUMPH	GRUYERE
GROUTERS	GROWTHIST	GRUELLING	GRUMPHED	GRUYERES
GROUTIER	GROWTHS	GRUELS	GRUMPHIE	GRYCE
GROUTIEST	GROWTHY	GRUES	GRUMPHIES	GRYCES
GROUTING	GROYNE	GRUESOME	GRUMPHING	GRYDE
GROUTINGS	GROYNES	GRUESOMER	GRUMPHS	GRYDED
GROUTS	GROZING	GRUFE	GRUMPHY	GRYDES
GROUTY	GRR	GRUFES	GRUMPIER	GRYDING
GROVE	GRRL	GRUFF	GRUMPIES	GRYESY
GROVED	GRRLS	GRUFFED	GRUMPIEST	GRYFON
GROVEL	GRRRL	GRUFFER	GRUMPILY	GRYFONS
GROVELED	GRRRLS	GRUFFEST	GRUMPING	GRYKE
GROVELER	GRUB	GRUFFIER	GRUMPISH	GRYKES
GROVELERS	GRUBBED	GRUFFIEST	GRUMPS	GRYPE
GROVELESS	GRUBBER	GRUFFILY	GRUMPY	GRYPES
GROVELING	GRUBBERS	GRUFFING	GRUND	GRYPHON
GROVELLED	GRUBBIER	GRUFFISH	GRUNDIES	GRYPHONS
GROVELLER	GRUBBIEST	GRUFFLY	GRUNDLE	GRYPT
GROVELS	GRUBBILY	GRUFFNESS	GRUNDLES	GRYSBOK
GROVES	GRUBBING	GRUFFS	GRUNGE	GRYSBOKS
GROVET	GRUBBLE	GRUFFY	GRUNGER	GRYSELY
GROVETS	GRUBBLED	GRUFTED	GRUNGERS	GRYSIE
GROVIER	GRUBBLES	GRUGRU	GRUNGES	GU

GUACAMOLE	GUARANAS	GUBERNIYA	GUESSING	GUIDEWORD
GUACHARO	GUARANI	GUBS	GUESSINGS	GUIDING
GUACHAROS	GUARANIES	GUCK	GUESSWORK	GUIDINGS
GUACO	GUARANIS	GUCKIER	GUEST	GUIDON
GUACOS	GUARANTEE	GUCKIEST	GUESTBOOK	GUIDONS
GUAIAC	GUARANTOR	GUCKS	GUESTED	GUIDS
GUAIACOL	GUARANTY	GUCKY	GUESTEN	GUILD
GUAIACOLS	GUARD	GUDDLE	GUESTENED	GUILDER
GUAIACS	GUARDABLE	GUDDLED	GUESTENS	GUILDERS
GUAIACUM	GUARDAGE	GUDDLES	GUESTING	GUILDHALL
GUAIACUMS	GUARDAGES	GUDDLING	GUESTS	GUILDRIES
GUAIOCUM	GUARDANT	GUDE	GUESTWISE	GUILDRY
GUAIOCUMS	GUARDANTS	GUDEMAN	GUFF	GUILDS
GUAN	GUARDDOG	GUDEMEN	GUFFAW	GUILDSHIP
GUANA	GUARDDOGS	GUDES	GUFFAWED	GUILDSMAN
GUANABANA	GUARDED	GUDESIRE	GUFFAWING	GUILDSMEN
GUANACO	GUARDEDLY	GUDESIRES	GUFFAWS	GUILE
GUANACOS	GUARDEE	GUDEWIFE	GUFFIE	GUILED
GUANAS	GUARDEES	GUDEWIVES	GUFFIES	GUILEFUL
GUANASE	GUARDER	GUDGEON	GUFFS	GUILELESS
GUANASES	GUARDERS	GUDGEONED	GUGA	GUILER
GUANAY	GUARDIAN	GUDGEONS	GUGAS	GUILERS
GUANAYS	GUARDIANS	GUE	GUGGLE	GUILES
GUANAZOLO	GUARDING	GUELDER	GUGGLED	GUILING
GUANGO	GUARDLESS	GUENON	GUGGLES	GUILLEMET
GUANGOS	GUARDLIKE	GUENONS	GUGGLING	GUILLEMOT
GUANIDIN	GUARDRAIL	GUERDON	GUGLET	GUILLOCHE
GUANIDINE	GUARDROOM	GUERDONED	GUGLETS	GUILT
GUANIDINS	GUARDS	GUERDONER	GUICHET	GUILTED
GUANIN	GUARDSHIP	GUERDONS	GUICHETS	GUILTIER
GUANINE	GUARDSMAN	GUEREZA	GUID	GUILTIEST
GUANINES	GUARDSMEN	GUEREZAS	GUIDABLE	GUILTILY
GUANINS	GUARISH	GUERIDON	GUIDAGE	GUILTING
GUANO	GUARISHED	GUERIDONS	GUIDAGES	GUILTLESS
GUANOS	GUARISHES	GUERILLA	GUIDANCE	GUILTS
GUANOSINE	GUARS	GUERILLAS	GUIDANCES	GUILTY
GUANS	GUAVA	GUERITE	GUIDE	GUIMBARD
GUANXI	GUAVAS	GUERITES	GUIDEBOOK	GUIMBARDS
GUANXIS	GUAYABERA	GUERNSEY	GUIDED	GUIMP
GUANYLIC	GUAYULE	GUERNSEYS	GUIDELESS	GUIMPE
GUAR	GUAYULES	GUERRILLA	GUIDELINE	GUIMPED
GUARACHA	GUB	GUES	GUIDEPOST	GUIMPES
GUARACHAS	GUBBAH	GUESS	GUIDER	GUIMPING
GUARACHE	GUBBAHS	GUESSABLE	GUIDERS	GUIMPS
GUARACHES	GUBBED	GUESSED	GUIDES	GUINEA
GUARACHI	GUBBING	GUESSER	GUIDESHIP	GUINEAS
GUARACHIS	GUBBINS	GUESSERS	GUIDEWAY	GUINEP
GUARANA	GUBBINSES	GUESSES	GUIDEWAYS	GUINEPS

GUIPURE	GULLABLE	GUMBOTILS	GUMSUCKER	GUNLOCKS
GUIPURES	GULLABLY	GUMDROP	GUMTREE	GUNMAKER
GUIRO	GULLED	GUMDROPS	GUMTREES	GUNMAKERS
GUIROS	GULLER	GUMLANDS	GUMWEED	GUNMAN
GUISARD	GULLERIES	GUMLESS	GUMWEEDS	GUNMEN
GUISARDS	GULLERS	GUMLIKE	GUMWOOD	GUNMETAL
GUISE	GULLERY	GUMLINE	GUMWOODS	GUNMETALS
GUISED	GULLET	GUMLINES	GUN	GUNNAGE
GUISER	GULLETS	GUMMA	GUNBOAT	GUNNAGES
GUISERS	GULLEY	GUMMAS	GUNBOATS	GUNNED
GUISES	GULLEYED	GUMMATA	GUNCOTTON	GUNNEL
GUISING	GULLEYING	GUMMATOUS	GUNDIES	GUNNELS
GUISINGS	GULLEYS	GUMMED	GUNDOG	GUNNEN
GUITAR	GULLIBLE	GUMMER	GUNDOGS	GUNNER
GUITARIST	GULLIBLY	GUMMERS	GUNDY	GUNNERA
GUITARS	GULLIED	GUMMI	GUNFIGHT	GUNNERAS
GUITGUIT	GULLIES	GUMMIER	GUNFIGHTS	GUNNERIES
GUITGUITS	GULLING	GUMMIES	GUNFIRE	GUNNERS
GUIZER	GULLISH	GUMMIEST	GUNFIRES	GUNNERY
GUIZERS	GULLS	GUMMILY	GUNFLINT	GUNNIES
GUL	GULLWING	GUMMINESS	GUNFLINTS	GUNNING
GULA	GULLY	GUMMING	GUNFOUGHT	GUNNINGS
GULAG	GULLYING	GUMMINGS	GUNG	GUNNY
GULAGS	GULOSITY	GUMMIS	GUNGE	GUNNYBAG
GULAR	GULP	GUMMITE	GUNGED	GUNNYBAGS
GULARS	GULPED	GUMMITES	GUNGES	GUNNYSACK
GULAS	GULPER	GUMMOSE	GUNGIER	GUNPAPER
GULCH	GULPERS	GUMMOSES	GUNGIEST	GUNPAPERS
GULCHED	GULPH	GUMMOSIS	GUNGING	GUNPLAY
GULCHES	GULPHS	GUMMOSITY	GUNGY	GUNPLAYS
GULCHING	GULPIER	GUMMOUS	GUNHOUSE	GUNPOINT
GULDEN	GULPIEST	GUMMY	GUNHOUSES	GUNPOINTS
GULDENS	GULPING	GUMNUT	GUNITE	GUNPORT
GULE	GULPINGLY	GUMNUTS	GUNITES	GUNPORTS
GULES	GULPS	GUMP	GUNK	GUNPOWDER
GULET	GULPY	GUMPED	GUNKED	GUNROOM
GULETS	GULS	GUMPHION	GUNKHOLE	GUNROOMS
GULF	GULY	GUMPHIONS	GUNKHOLED	GUNRUNNER
GULFED	GUM	GUMPING	GUNKHOLES	GUNS
GULFIER	GUMBALL	GUMPS	GUNKIER	GUNSEL
GULFIEST	GUMBALLS	GUMPTION	GUNKIEST	GUNSELS
GULFING	GUMBO	GUMPTIONS	GUNKING	GUNSHIP
GULFLIKE	GUMBOIL	GUMPTIOUS	GUNKS	GUNSHIPS
GULFS	GUMBOILS	GUMS	GUNKY	GUNSHOT
GULFWEED	GUMBOOT	GUMSHIELD	GUNLAYER	GUNSHOTS
GULFWEEDS	GUMBOOTS	GUMSHOE	GUNLAYERS	GUNSIGHT
GULFY	GUMBOS	GUMSHOED	GUNLESS	GUNSIGHTS
GULL	GUMBOTIL	GUMSHOES	GUNLOCK	GUNSMITH

GUNSMITHS	GURLIEST	GUSLE	GUTSES	GUYLES
GUNSTICK	GURLING	GUSLES	GUTSFUL	GUYLINE
GUNSTICKS	GURLS	GUSLI	GUTSFULS	GUYLINER
GUNSTOCK	GURLY	GUSLIS	GUTSIER	GUYLINERS
GUNSTOCKS	GURN	GUSSET	GUTSIEST	GUYLINES
GUNSTONE	GURNARD	GUSSETED	GUTSILY	GUYLING
GUNSTONES	GURNARDS	GUSSETING	GUTSINESS	GUYOT
GUNTER	GURNED	GUSSETS	GUTSING	GUYOTS
GUNTERS	GURNET	GUSSIE	GUTSY	GUYS
GUNWALE	GURNETS	GUSSIED	GUTTA	GUYSE
GUNWALES	GURNEY	GUSSIES	GUTTAE	GUYSES
GUNYAH	GURNEYS	GUSSY	GUTTAS	GUZZLE
GUNYAHS	GURNING	GUSSYING	GUTTATE	GUZZLED
GUP	GURNS	GUST	GUTTATED	GUZZLER
GUPPIES	GURRAH	GUSTABLE	GUTTATES	GUZZLERS
GUPPY	GURRAHS	GUSTABLES	GUTTATING	GUZZLES
GUPS	GURRIER	GUSTATION	GUTTATION	GUZZLING
GUQIN	GURRIERS	GUSTATIVE	GUTTED	GWEDUC
GUQINS	GURRIES	GUSTATORY	GUTTER	GWEDUCK
GUR	GURRY	GUSTED	GUTTERED	GWEDUCKS
GURAMI	GURS	GUSTFUL	GUTTERIER	GWEDUCS
GURAMIS	GURSH	GUSTIE	GUTTERING	GWINE
GURDIES	GURSHES	GUSTIER	GUTTERS	GWINIAD
GURDWARA	GURU	GUSTIEST	GUTTERY	GWINIADS
GURDWARAS	GURUDOM	GUSTILY	GUTTIER	GWYNIAD
GURDY	GURUDOMS	GUSTINESS	GUTTIES	GWYNIADS
GURGE	GURUISM	GUSTING	GUTTIEST	GYAL
GURGED	GURUISMS	GUSTLESS	GUTTING	GYALS
GURGES	GURUS	GUSTO	GUTTLE	GYAN
GURGING	GURUSHIP	GUSTOES	GUTTLED	GYANS
GURGLE	GURUSHIPS	GUSTOS	GUTTLER	GYBE
GURGLED	GUS	GUSTS	GUTTLERS	GYBED
GURGLES	GUSH	GUSTY	GUTTLES	GYBES
GURGLET	GUSHED	GUT	GUTTLING	GYBING
GURGLETS	GUSHER	GUTBUCKET	GUTTURAL	GYELD
GURGLIER	GUSHERS	GUTCHER	GUTTURALS	GYELDS
GURGLIEST	GUSHES	GUTCHERS	GUTTY	GYLDEN
GURGLING	GUSHIER	GUTFUL	GUTZER	GYM
GURGLY	GUSHIEST	GUTFULS	GUTZERS	GYMBAL
GURGOYLE	GUSHILY	GUTLESS	GUV	GYMBALS
GURGOYLES	GUSHINESS	GUTLESSLY	GUVS	GYMKHANA
GURJUN	GUSHING	GUTLIKE	GUY	GYMKHANAS
GURJUNS	GUSHINGLY	GUTROT	GUYED	GYMMAL
GURL	GUSHY	GUTROTS	GUYING	GYMMALS
GURLED	GUSLA	GUTS	GUYLE	GYMNASIA
GURLET	GUSLAR	GUTSED	GUYLED	GYMNASIAL
GURLETS	GUSLARS	GUTSER	GUYLER	GYMNASIC
GURLIER	GUSLAS	GUTSERS	GUYLERS	GYMNASIEN

G

G

GYMNASIUM	GYNECIC	GYPPIE	GYRASES	GYRONIC
GYMNAST	GYNECIUM	GYPPIES	GYRATE	GYRONNY
GYMNASTIC	GYNECOID	GYPPING	GYRATED	GYRONS
GYMNASTS	GYNIATRY	GYPPO	GYRATES	GYROPILOT
GYMNIC	GYNIE	GYPPOS	GYRATING	GYROPLANE
GYMNOSOPH	GYNIES	GYPPY	GYRATION	GYROS
GYMP	GYNNEY	GYPS	GYRATIONS	GYROSCOPE
GYMPED	GYNNEYS	GYPSEIAN	GYRATOR	GYROSE
GYMPIE	GYNNIES	GYPSEOUS	GYRATORS	GYROSTAT
GYMPIES	GYNNY	GYPSIED	GYRATORY	GYROSTATS
GYMPING	GYNO	GYPSIES	GYRE	GYROUS
GYMPS	GYNOCRACY	GYPSTER	GYRED	GYROVAGUE
GYMS	GYNOECIA	GYPSTERS	GYRENE	GYRUS
GYMSLIP	GYNOECIUM	GYPSUM	GYRENES	GYRUSES
GYMSLIPS	GYNOPHOBE	GYPSUMS	GYRES	GYTE
GYMSUIT	GYNOPHORE	GYPSY	GYRFALCON	GYTES
GYMSUITS	GYNOS	GYPSYDOM	GYRI	GYTRASH
GYNAE	GYNY	GYPSYDOMS	GYRING	GYTRASHES
GYNAECEA	GYOZA	GYPSYHOOD	GYRO	GYTTJA
GYNAECEUM	GYOZAS	GYPSYING	GYROCAR	GYTTJAS
GYNAECIA	GYP	GYPSYISH	GYROCARS	GYVE
GYNAECIUM	GYPLURE	GYPSYISM	GYRODYNE	GYVED
GYNAECOID	GYPLURES	GYPSYISMS	GYRODYNES	GYVES
GYNAES	GYPO	GYPSYWORT	GYROIDAL	GYVING
GYNANDRY	GYPOS	GYRAL	GYROLITE	
GYNARCHIC	GYPPED	GYRALLY	GYROLITES	
GYNARCHY	GYPPER	GYRANT	GYROMANCY	
GYNECIA	GYPPERS	GYRASE	GYRON	

H

HA
HAAF
HAAFS
HAANEPOOT
HAAR
HAARS
HABANERA
HABANERAS
HABANERO
HABANEROS
HABDABS
HABDALAH
HABDALAHS
HABENDUM
HABENDUMS
HABERDINE
HABERGEON
HABILABLE
HABILE
HABIT
HABITABLE
HABITABLY
HABITAN
HABITANS
HABITANT
HABITANTS
HABITAT
HABITATS
HABITED
HABITING
HABITS
HABITUAL
HABITUALS
HABITUATE
HABITUDE
HABITUDES
HABITUE
HABITUES
HABITUS
HABITUSES
HABLE
HABOOB

HABOOBS
HABU
HABUS
HACEK
HACEKS
HACENDADO
HACHIS
HACHURE
HACHURED
HACHURES
HACHURING
HACIENDA
HACIENDAS
HACK
HACKABLE
HACKAMORE
HACKBERRY
HACKBOLT
HACKBOLTS
HACKBUT
HACKBUTS
HACKED
HACKEE
HACKEES
HACKER
HACKERIES
HACKERS
HACKERY
HACKETTE
HACKETTES
HACKIE
HACKIES
HACKING
HACKINGS
HACKLE
HACKLED
HACKLER
HACKLERS
HACKLES
HACKLET
HACKLETS
HACKLIER

HACKLIEST
HACKLING
HACKLY
HACKMAN
HACKMEN
HACKNEY
HACKNEYED
HACKNEYS
HACKS
HACKSAW
HACKSAWED
HACKSAWN
HACKSAWS
HACKWORK
HACKWORKS
HACQUETON
HAD
HADAL
HADARIM
HADAWAY
HADDEN
HADDEST
HADDIE
HADDIES
HADDING
HADDOCK
HADDOCKS
HADE
HADED
HADEDAH
HADEDAHS
HADES
HADING
HADITH
HADITHS
HADJ
HADJEE
HADJEES
HADJES
HADJI
HADJIS
HADROME

HADROMES
HADRON
HADRONIC
HADRONS
HADROSAUR
HADS
HADST
HAE
HAECCEITY
HAED
HAEING
HAEM
HAEMAL
HAEMATAL
HAEMATEIN
HAEMATIC
HAEMATICS
HAEMATIN
HAEMATINS
HAEMATITE
HAEMATOID
HAEMATOMA
HAEMIC
HAEMIN
HAEMINS
HAEMOCOEL
HAEMOCYTE
HAEMOID
HAEMOLYSE
HAEMOLYZE
HAEMONIES
HAEMONY
HAEMOSTAT
HAEMS
HAEN
HAEREDES
HAEREMAI
HAEREMAIS
HAERES
HAES
HAET
HAETS

HAFF
HAFFET
HAFFETS
HAFFIT
HAFFITS
HAFFLIN
HAFFLINS
HAFFS
HAFIZ
HAFIZES
HAFNIUM
HAFNIUMS
HAFT
HAFTARA
HAFTARAH
HAFTARAHS
HAFTARAS
HAFTAROS
HAFTAROT
HAFTAROTH
HAFTED
HAFTER
HAFTERS
HAFTING
HAFTORAH
HAFTORAHS
HAFTOROS
HAFTOROT
HAFTOROTH
HAFTS
HAG
HAGADIC
HAGADIST
HAGADISTS
HAGBERRY
HAGBOLT
HAGBOLTS
HAGBORN
HAGBUSH
HAGBUSHES
HAGBUT
HAGBUTEER

HAGBUTS	HAGS	HAIRBANDS	HAIRWORMS	HALAKISTS
HAGBUTTER	HAH	HAIRBELL	HAIRY	HALAKOTH
HAGDEN	HAHA	HAIRBELLS	HAIRYBACK	HALAL
HAGDENS	HAHAS	HAIRBRUSH	HAITH	HALALA
HAGDON	HAHNIUM	HAIRCAP	HAJ	HALALAH
HAGDONS	HAHNIUMS	HAIRCAPS	HAJES	HALALAHS
HAGDOWN	HAHS	HAIRCLOTH	HAJI	HALALAS
HAGDOWNS	HAICK	HAIRCUT	HAJIS	HALALLED
HAGFISH	HAICKS	HAIRCUTS	HAJJ	HALALLING
HAGFISHES	HAIDUK	HAIRDO	HAJJAH	HALALS
HAGG	HAIDUKS	HAIRDOS	HAJJAHS	HALATION
HAGGADA	HAIK	HAIRDRIER	HAJJES	HALATIONS
HAGGADAH	HAIKA	HAIRDRYER	HAJJI	HALAVAH
HAGGADAHS	HAIKAI	HAIRED	HAJJIS	HALAVAHS
HAGGADAS	HAIKS	HAIRGRIP	HAKA	HALAZONE
HAGGADIC	HAIKU	HAIRGRIPS	HAKAM	HALAZONES
HAGGADIST	HAIKUS	HAIRIER	HAKAMS	HALBERD
HAGGADOT	HAIL	HAIRIEST	HAKARI	HALBERDS
HAGGADOTH	HAILED	HAIRIF	HAKARIS	HALBERT
HAGGARD	HAILER	HAIRIFS	HAKAS	HALBERTS
HAGGARDLY	HAILERS	HAIRILY	HAKE	HALCYON
HAGGARDS	HAILIER	HAIRINESS	HAKEA	HALCYONIC
HAGGED	HAILIEST	HAIRING	HAKEAS	HALCYONS
HAGGING	HAILING	HAIRLESS	HAKEEM	HALE
HAGGIS	HAILS	HAIRLIKE	HAKEEMS	HALED
HAGGISES	HAILSHOT	HAIRLINE	HAKES	HALENESS
HAGGISH	HAILSHOTS	HAIRLINES	HAKIM	HALER
HAGGISHLY	HAILSTONE	HAIRLOCK	HAKIMS	HALERS
HAGGLE	HAILSTORM	HAIRLOCKS	HAKU	HALERU
HAGGLED	HAILY	HAIRNET	HAKUS	HALES
HAGGLER	HAIMISH	HAIRNETS	HALACHA	HALEST
HAGGLERS	HAIN	HAIRPIECE	HALACHAS	HALF
HAGGLES	HAINCH	HAIRPIN	HALACHIC	HALFA
HAGGLING	HAINCHED	HAIRPINS	HALACHIST	HALFAS
HAGGLINGS	HAINCHES	HAIRS	HALACHOT	HALFBACK
HAGGS	HAINCHING	HAIRSPRAY	HALACHOTH	HALFBACKS
HAGIARCHY	HAINED	HAIRST	HALAKAH	HALFBEAK
HAGIOLOGY	HAINING	HAIRSTED	HALAKAHS	HALFBEAKS
HAGLET	HAININGS	HAIRSTING	HALAKHA	HALFEN
HAGLETS	HAINS	HAIRSTS	HALAKHAH	HALFLIFE
HAGLIKE	HAINT	HAIRSTYLE	HALAKHAHS	HALFLIN
HAGRIDDEN	HAINTS	HAIRTAIL	HALAKHAS	HALFLING
HAGRIDE	HAIQUE	HAIRTAILS	HALAKHIC	HALFLINGS
HAGRIDER	HAIQUES	HAIRWING	HALAKHIST	HALFLINS
HAGRIDERS	HAIR	HAIRWINGS	HALAKHOT	HALFLIVES
HAGRIDES	HAIRBALL	HAIRWORK	HALAKHOTH	HALFNESS
HAGRIDING	HAIRBALLS	HAIRWORKS	HALAKIC	HALFPACE
HAGRODE	HAIRBAND	HAIRWORM	HALAKIST	HALFPACES

HALFPENCE	HALLALIS	HALLWAYS	HALTINGS	HAME
HALFPENNY	HALLALLED	HALLYON	HALTLESS	HAMED
HALFPIPE	HALLALOO	HALLYONS	HALTS	HAMES
HALFPIPES	HALLALOOS	HALM	HALUTZ	HAMEWITH
HALFS	HALLALS	HALMA	HALUTZIM	HAMFAT
HALFTIME	HALLAN	HALMAS	HALVA	HAMFATS
HALFTIMES	HALLANS	HALMS	HALVAH	HAMFATTER
HALFTONE	HALLEL	HALO	HALVAHS	HAMING
HALFTONES	HALLELS	HALOBIONT	HALVAS	HAMLET
HALFTRACK	HALLIAN	HALOCLINE	HALVE	HAMLETS
HALFWAY	HALLIANS	HALOED	HALVED	HAMMADA
HALFWIT	HALLIARD	HALOES	HALVER	HAMMADAS
HALFWITS	HALLIARDS	HALOGEN	HALVERS	HAMMAL
HALIBUT	HALLING	HALOGENIC	HALVES	HAMMALS
HALIBUTS	HALLINGS	HALOGENS	HALVING	HAMMAM
HALICORE	HALLION	HALOGETON	HALVINGS	HAMMAMS
HALICORES	HALLIONS	HALOID	HALWA	HAMMED
HALID	HALLMARK	HALOIDS	HALWAS	HAMMER
HALIDE	HALLMARKS	HALOING	HALYARD	HAMMERED
HALIDES	HALLO	HALOLIKE	HALYARDS	HAMMERER
HALIDOM	HALLOA	HALON	HAM	HAMMERERS
HALIDOME	HALLOAED	HALONS	HAMADA	HAMMERING
HALIDOMES	HALLOAING	HALOPHILE	HAMADAS	HAMMERKOP
HALIDOMS	HALLOAS	HALOPHILY	HAMADRYAD	HAMMERMAN
HALIDS	HALLOED	HALOPHOBE	HAMADRYAS	HAMMERMEN
HALIER	HALLOES	HALOPHYTE	HAMAL	HAMMERS
HALIEROV	HALLOING	HALOS	HAMALS	HAMMERTOE
HALIERS	HALLOO	HALOSERE	HAMAMELIS	HAMMIER
HALIEUTIC	HALLOOED	HALOSERES	HAMARTIA	HAMMIES
HALIMOT	HALLOOING	HALOTHANE	HAMARTIAS	HAMMIEST
HALIMOTE	HALLOOS	HALOUMI	HAMATE	HAMMILY
HALIMOTES	HALLOS	HALOUMIS	HAMATES	HAMMINESS
HALIMOTS	HALLOT	HALSE	HAMATSA	HAMMING
HALING	HALLOTH	HALSED	HAMATSAS	HAMMOCK
HALIOTIS	HALLOUMI	HALSER	HAMAUL	HAMMOCKS
HALITE	HALLOUMIS	HALSERS	HAMAULS	HAMMY
IIALITES	HALLOW	HALSES	HAMBA	HAMOSE
HALITOSES	HALLOWED	HALSING	HAMBLE	HAMOUS
HALITOSIS	HALLOWER	HALT	HAMBLED	HAMPER
HALITOTIC	HALLOWERS	HALTED	HAMBLES	HAMPERED
HALITOUS	HALLOWING	HALTER	HAMBLING	HAMPERER
HALITUS	HALLOWS	HALTERE	HAMBONE	HAMPERERS
HALITUSES	HALLS	HALTERED	HAMBONED	HAMPERING
HALL	HALLSTAND	HALTERES	HAMBONES	HAMPERS
HALLAH	HALLUCAL	HALTERING	HAMBONING	HAMPSTER
HALLAHS	HALLUCES	HALTERS	HAMBURG	HAMPSTERS
HALLAL	HALLUX	HALTING	HAMBURGER	HAMS
HALLALI	HALLWAY	HALTINGLY	HAMBURGS	HAMSTER

HAMSTERS	HANDCUFF	HANDLING	HANDSY	HANGS
HAMSTRING	HANDCUFFS	HANDLINGS	HANDTOWEL	HANGTAG
HAMSTRUNG	HANDED	HANDLIST	HANDWHEEL	HANGTAGS
HAMULAR	HANDER	HANDLISTS	HANDWORK	HANGUL
HAMULATE	HANDERS	HANDLOOM	HANDWORKS	HANGULS
HAMULI	HANDFAST	HANDLOOMS	HANDWOVEN	HANGUP
HAMULOSE	HANDFASTS	HANDMADE	HANDWRIT	HANGUPS
HAMULOUS	HANDFED	HANDMAID	HANDWRITE	HANIWA
HAMULUS	HANDFEED	HANDMAIDS	HANDWROTE	HANIWAS
HAMZA	HANDFEEDS	HANDOFF	HANDY	HANJAR
HAMZAH	HANDFUL	HANDOFFS	HANDYMAN	HANJARS
HAMZAHS	HANDFULS	HANDOUT	HANDYMEN	HANK
HAMZAS	HANDGLASS	HANDOUTS	HANDYWORK	HANKED
HAN	HANDGRIP	HANDOVER	HANEPOOT	HANKER
HANAP	HANDGRIPS	HANDOVERS	HANEPOOTS	HANKERED
HANAPER	HANDGUN	HANDPASS	HANG	HANKERER
HANAPERS	HANDGUNS	HANDPHONE	HANGABLE	HANKERERS
HANAPS	HANDHELD	HANDPICK	HANGAR	HANKERING
HANCE	HANDHELDS	HANDPICKS	HANGARAGE	HANKERS
HANCES	HANDHOLD	HANDPLAY	HANGARED	HANKIE
HANCH	HANDHOLDS	HANDPLAYS	HANGARING	HANKIES
HANCHED	HANDICAP	HANDPRESS	HANGARS	HANKING
HANCHES	HANDICAPS	HANDPRINT	HANGBIRD	HANKS
HANCHING	HANDIER	HANDRAIL	HANGBIRDS	HANKY
HAND	HANDIEST	HANDRAILS	HANGDOG	HANSA
HANDAX	HANDILY	HANDROLL	HANGDOGS	HANSAS
HANDAXE	HANDINESS	HANDROLLS	HANGED	HANSE
HANDAXES	HANDING	HANDS	HANGER	HANSEATIC
HANDBAG	HANDISM	HANDSAW	HANGERS	HANSEL
HANDBAGS	HANDISMS	HANDSAWS	HANGFIRE	HANSELED
HANDBALL	HANDIWORK	HANDSEL	HANGFIRES	HANSELING
HANDBALLS	HANDJAR	HANDSELED	HANGI	HANSELLED
HANDBELL	HANDJARS	HANDSELS	HANGING	HANSELS
HANDBELLS	HANDJOB	HANDSET	HANGINGS	HANSES
HANDBILL	HANDJOBS	HANDSETS	HANGIS	HANSOM
HANDBILLS	HANDKNIT	HANDSEWN	HANGMAN	HANSOMS
HANDBLOWN	HANDKNITS	HANDSFUL	HANGMEN	HANT
HANDBOOK	HANDLE	HANDSHAKE	HANGNAIL	HANTED
HANDBOOKS	HANDLEBAR	HANDSIER	HANGNAILS	HANTING
HANDBRAKE	HANDLED	HANDSIEST	HANGNEST	HANTLE
HANDCAR	HANDLER	HANDSOME	HANGNESTS	HANTLES
HANDCARS	HANDLERS	HANDSOMER	HANGOUT	HANTS
HANDCART	HANDLES	HANDSOMES	HANGOUTS	HANUKIAH
HANDCARTS	HANDLESS	HANDSPIKE	HANGOVER	HANUKIAHS
HANDCLAP	HANDLIKE	HANDSTAFF	HANGOVERS	HANUMAN
HANDCLAPS	HANDLINE	HANDSTAMP	HANGRIER	HANUMANS
HANDCLASP	HANDLINER	HANDSTAND	HANGRIEST	HAO
HANDCRAFT	HANDLINES	HANDSTURN	HANGRY	HAOLE

HAOLES	HAPPOSHUS	HARBORED	HARDGRASS	HARDWARES
HAOMA	HAPPY	HARBORER	HARDHACK	HARDWIRE
HAOMAS	HAPPYING	HARBORERS	HARDHACKS	HARDWIRED
HAOS	HAPS	HARBORFUL	HARDHAT	HARDWIRES
HAP	HAPTEN	HARBORING	HARDHATS	HARDWOOD
HAPAX	HAPTENE	HARBOROUS	HARDHEAD	HARDWOODS
HAPAXES	HAPTENES	HARBORS	HARDHEADS	HARDY
HAPHAZARD	HAPTENIC	HARBOUR	HARDIER	HARE
HAPHTARA	HAPTENS	HARBOURED	HARDIES	HAREBELL
HAPHTARAH	HAPTERON	HARBOURER	HARDIEST	HAREBELLS
HAPHTARAS	HAPTERONS	HARBOURS	HARDIHEAD	HARED
HAPHTAROT	HAPTIC	HARD	HARDIHOOD	HAREEM
HAPKIDO	HAPTICAL	HARDASS	HARDILY	HAREEMS
HAPKIDOS	HAPTICS	HARDASSES	HARDIMENT	HARELD
HAPLESS	HAPU	HARDBACK	HARDINESS	HARELDS
HAPLESSLY	HAPUKA	HARDBACKS	HARDISH	HARELIKE
HAPLITE	HAPUKAS	HARDBAG	HARDLINE	HARELIP
HAPLITES	HAPUKU	HARDBAGS	HARDLINER	HARELIPS
HAPLITIC	HAPUKUS	HARDBAKE	HARDLY	HAREM
HAPLOID	HAPUS	HARDBAKES	HARDMAN	HAREMS
HAPLOIDIC	HAQUETON	HARDBALL	HARDMEN	HARES
HAPLOIDS	HAQUETONS	HARDBALLS	HARDNESS	HARESTAIL
HAPLOIDY	HARAAM	HARDBEAM	HARDNOSE	HAREWOOD
HAPLOLOGY	HARAKEKE	HARDBEAMS	HARDNOSED	HAREWOODS
HAPLONT	HARAKEKES	HARDBOARD	HARDNOSES	HARIANA
HAPLONTIC	HARAM	HARDBODY	HARDOKE	HARIANAS
HAPLONTS	HARAMBEE	HARDBOOT	HARDOKES	HARICOT
HAPLOPIA	HARAMBEES	HARDBOOTS	HARDPACK	HARICOTS
HAPLOPIAS	HARAMDA	HARDBOUND	HARDPACKS	HARIGALDS
HAPLOSES	HARAMDAS	HARDCASE	HARDPAN	HARIGALS
HAPLOSIS	HARAMDI	HARDCASES	HARDPANS	HARIJAN
HAPLOTYPE	HARAMDIS	HARDCORE	HARDPARTS	HARIJANS
HAPLY	HARAMS	HARDCORES	HARDROCK	HARIM
HAPPED	HARAMZADA	HARDCOURT	HARDROCKS	HARIMS
HAPPEN	HARAMZADI	HARDCOVER	HARDS	HARING
HAPPENED	HARANGUE	HARDEDGE	HARDSCAPE	HARIOLATE
HAPPENING	HARANGUED	HARDEDGES	HARDSET	HARIRA
HAPPENS	HARANGUER	HARDEN	HARDSHELL	HARIRAS
HAPPI	HARANGUES	HARDENED	HARDSHIP	HARISH
HAPPIED	HARASS	HARDENER	HARDSHIPS	HARISSA
HAPPIER	HARASSED	HARDENERS	HARDSTAND	HARISSAS
HAPPIES	HARASSER	HARDENING	HARDTACK	HARK
HAPPIEST	HARASSERS	HARDENS	HARDTACKS	HARKED
HAPPILY	HARASSES	HARDER	HARDTAIL	HARKEN
HAPPINESS	HARASSING	HARDEST	HARDTAILS	HARKENED
HAPPING	HARBINGER	HARDFACE	HARDTOP	HARKENER
HAPPIS	HARBOR	HARDFACES	HARDTOPS	HARKENERS
HAPPOSHU	HARBORAGE	HARDGOODS	HARDWARE	HARKENING

HARKENS	HARMS	HARSH	HASHISH	HASTINESS
HARKING	HARN	HARSHED	HASHISHES	HASTING
HARKS	HARNESS	HARSHEN	HASHMARK	HASTINGS
HARL	HARNESSED	HARSHENED	HASHMARKS	HASTY
HARLED	HARNESSER	HARSHENS	HASHTAG	HAT
HARLEQUIN	HARNESSES	HARSHER	HASHTAGS	HATABLE
HARLING	HARNS	HARSHES	HASHY	HATBAND
HARLINGS	HARO	HARSHEST	HASK	HATBANDS
HARLOT	HAROS	HARSHING	HASKS	HATBOX
HARLOTRY	HAROSET	HARSHLY	HASLET	HATBOXES
HARLOTS	HAROSETH	HARSHNESS	HASLETS	HATBRUSH
HARLS	HAROSETHS	HARSLET	HASP	HATCH
HARM	HAROSETS	HARSLETS	HASPED	HATCHABLE
HARMALA	HARP	HART	HASPING	HATCHBACK
HARMALAS	HARPED	HARTAL	HASPS	HATCHECK
HARMALIN	HARPER	HARTALS	HASS	HATCHECKS
HARMALINE	HARPERS	HARTBEES	HASSAR	HATCHED
HARMALINS	HARPIES	HARTBEEST	HASSARS	HATCHEL
HARMAN	HARPIN	HARTELY	HASSEL	HATCHELED
HARMANS	HARPING	HARTEN	HASSELS	HATCHELS
HARMATTAN	HARPINGS	HARTENED	HASSES	HATCHER
HARMDOING	HARPINS	HARTENING	HASSIUM	HATCHERS
HARMED	HARPIST	HARTENS	HASSIUMS	HATCHERY
HARMEL	HARPISTS	HARTLESSE	HASSLE	HATCHES
HARMELS	HARPOON	HARTS	HASSLED	HATCHET
HARMER	HARPOONED	HARTSHORN	HASSLES	HATCHETS
HARMERS	HARPOONER	HARUMPH	HASSLING	HATCHETY
HARMFUL	HARPOONS	HARUMPHED	HASSOCK	HATCHING
HARMFULLY	HARPS	HARUMPHS	HASSOCKS	HATCHINGS
HARMIN	HARPY	HARUSPEX	HASSOCKY	HATCHLING
HARMINE	HARPYLIKE	HARUSPICY	HAST	HATCHMENT
HARMINES	HARQUEBUS	HARVEST	HASTA	HATCHWAY
HARMING	HARRIDAN	HARVESTED	HASTATE	HATCHWAYS
HARMINS	HARRIDANS	HARVESTER	HASTATED	HATE
HARMLESS	HARRIED	HARVESTS	HASTATELY	HATEABLE
HARMONIC	HARRIER	HAS	HASTE	HATED
HARMONICA	HARRIERS	HASBIAN	HASTED	HATEFUL
HARMONICS	HARRIES	HASBIANS	HASTEFUL	HATEFULLY
HARMONIES	HARROW	HASH	HASTEN	HATELESS
HARMONISE	HARROWED	HASHED	HASTENED	HATER
HARMONIST	HARROWER	HASHEESH	HASTENER	HATERENT
HARMONIUM	HARROWERS	HASHES	HASTENERS	HATERENTS
HARMONIZE	HARROWING	HASHHEAD	HASTENING	HATERS
HARMONY	HARROWS	HASHHEADS	HASTENS	HATES
HARMOST	HARRUMPH	HASHIER	HASTES	HATFUL
HARMOSTS	HARRUMPHS	HASHIEST	HASTIER	HATFULS
HARMOSTY	HARRY	HASHING	HASTIEST	HATGUARD
HARMOTOME	HARRYING	HASHINGS	HASTILY	HATGUARDS

HATH	HAULBACK	HAUT	HAVOCKERS	HAWS
HATHA	HAULBACKS	HAUTBOIS	HAVOCKING	HAWSE
HATINATOR	HAULD	HAUTBOY	HAVOCS	HAWSED
HATING	HAULDS	HAUTBOYS	HAW	HAWSEHOLE
HATLESS	HAULED	HAUTE	HAWALA	HAWSEPIPE
HATLIKE	HAULER	HAUTER	HAWALAS	HAWSER
HATMAKER	HAULERS	HAUTEST	HAWBUCK	HAWSERS
HATMAKERS	HAULIER	HAUTEUR	HAWBUCKS	HAWSES
HATPEG	HAULIERS	HAUTEURS	HAWEATER	HAWSING
HATPEGS	HAULING	HAUYNE	HAWEATERS	HAWTHORN
HATPIN	HAULINGS	HAUYNES	HAWED	HAWTHORNS
HATPINS	HAULM	HAVARTI	HAWFINCH	HAWTHORNY
HATRACK	HAULMIER	HAVARTIS	HAWING	HAY
HATRACKS	HAULMIEST	HAVDALAH	HAWK	HAYBAND
HATRED	HAULMS	HAVDALAHS	HAWKBELL	HAYBANDS
HATREDS	HAULMY	HAVDOLOH	HAWKBELLS	HAYBOX
HATS	HAULOUT	HAVDOLOHS	HAWKBILL	HAYBOXES
HATSFUL	HAULOUTS	HAVE	HAWKBILLS	HAYCATION
HATSTAND	HAULS	HAVELOCK	HAWKBIT	HAYCOCK
HATSTANDS	HAULST	HAVELOCKS	HAWKBITS	HAYCOCKS
HATTED	HAULT	HAVEN	HAWKED	HAYED
HATTER	HAULYARD	HAVENED	HAWKER	HAYER
HATTERED	HAULYARDS	HAVENING	HAWKERS	HAYERS
HATTERIA	HAUN	HAVENLESS	HAWKEY	HAYEY
HATTERIAS	HAUNCH	HAVENS	HAWKEYED	HAYFIELD
HATTERING	HAUNCHED	HAVEOUR	HAWKEYS	HAYFIELDS
HATTERS	HAUNCHES	HAVEOURS	HAWKIE	HAYFORK
HATTING	HAUNCHING	HAVER	HAWKIES	HAYFORKS
HATTINGS	HAUNS	HAVERED	HAWKING	HAYIER
HATTOCK	HAUNT	HAVEREL	HAWKINGS	HAYIEST
HATTOCKS	HAUNTED	HAVERELS	HAWKISH	HAYING
HAUBERK	HAUNTER	HAVERING	HAWKISHLY	HAYINGS
HAUBERKS	HAUNTERS	HAVERINGS	HAWKIT	HAYLAGE
HAUBOIS	HAUNTING	HAVERS	HAWKLIKE	HAYLAGES
HAUD	HAUNTINGS	HAVERSACK	HAWKMOTH	HAYLE
HAUDING	HAUNTS	HAVERSINE	HAWKMOTHS	HAYLES
HAUDS	HAURIANT	HAVES	HAWKNOSE	HAYLOFT
HAUF	HAURIENT	HAVILDAR	HAWKNOSES	HAYLOFTS
HAUFS	HAUSE	HAVILDARS	HAWKS	HAYMAKER
HAUGH	HAUSED	HAVING	HAWKSBILL	HAYMAKERS
HAUGHS	HAUSEN	HAVINGS	HAWKSHAW	HAYMAKING
HAUGHT	HAUSENS	HAVIOR	HAWKSHAWS	HAYMOW
HAUGHTIER	HAUSES	HAVIORS	HAWKWEED	HAYMOWS
HAUGHTILY	HAUSFRAU	HAVIOUR	HAWKWEEDS	HAYRACK
HAUGHTY	HAUSFRAUS	HAVIOURS	HAWM	HAYRACKS
HAUL	HAUSING	HAVOC	HAWMED	HAYRAKE
HAULAGE	HAUSTELLA	HAVOCKED	HAWMING	HAYRAKES
HAULAGES	HAUSTORIA	HAVOCKER	HAWMS	HAYRICK

HAYRICKS	HAZZAN	HEADINGS	HEADSCARF	HEALTH
HAYRIDE	HAZZANIM	HEADLAMP	HEADSET	HEALTHFUL
HAYRIDES	HAZZANS	HEADLAMPS	HEADSETS	HEALTHIER
HAYS	HE	HEADLAND	HEADSHAKE	HEALTHILY
HAYSEED	HEAD	HEADLANDS	HEADSHIP	HEALTHISM
HAYSEEDS	HEADACHE	HEADLEASE	HEADSHIPS	HEALTHS
HAYSEL	HEADACHES	HEADLESS	HEADSHOT	HEALTHY
HAYSELS	HEADACHEY	HEADLIGHT	HEADSHOTS	HEAME
HAYSTACK	HEADACHY	HEADLIKE	HEADSMAN	HEAP
HAYSTACKS	HEADAGE	HEADLINE	HEADSMEN	HEAPED
HAYWARD	HEADAGES	HEADLINED	HEADSPACE	HEAPER
HAYWARDS	HEADBAND	HEADLINER	HEADSTALL	HEAPERS
HAYWIRE	HEADBANDS	HEADLINES	HEADSTAND	HEAPIER
HAYWIRES	HEADBANG	HEADLOCK	HEADSTAY	HEAPIEST
HAZAN	HEADBANGS	HEADLOCKS	HEADSTAYS	HEAPING
HAZANIM	HEADBOARD	HEADLONG	HEADSTICK	HEAPS
HAZANS	HEADCASE	HEADMAN	HEADSTOCK	HEAPSTEAD
HAZARD	HEADCASES	HEADMARK	HEADSTONE	HEAPY
HAZARDED	HEADCHAIR	HEADMARKS	HEADWALL	HEAR
HAZARDER	HEADCLOTH	HEADMEN	HEADWALLS	HEARABLE
HAZARDERS	HEADCOUNT	HEADMOST	HEADWARD	HEARD
HAZARDING	HEADDRESS	HEADNOTE	HEADWARDS	HEARDS
HAZARDIZE	HEADED	HEADNOTES	HEADWATER	HEARE
HAZARDOUS	HEADEND	HEADPEACE	HEADWAY	HEARER
HAZARDRY	HEADENDS	HEADPHONE	HEADWAYS	HEARERS
HAZARDS	HEADER	HEADPIECE	HEADWIND	HEARES
HAZE	HEADERS	HEADPIN	HEADWINDS	HEARIE
HAZED	HEADFAST	HEADPINS	HEADWORD	HEARING
HAZEL	HEADFASTS	HEADPOND	HEADWORDS	HEARINGS
HAZELHEN	HEADFIRST	HEADPONDS	HEADWORK	HEARKEN
HAZELHENS	HEADFISH	HEADRACE	HEADWORKS	HEARKENED
HAZELLY	HEADFRAME	HEADRACES	HEADY	HEARKENER
HAZELNUT	HEADFUCK	HEADRAIL	HEAL	HEARKENS
HAZELNUTS	HEADFUCKS	HEADRAILS	HEALABLE	HEARS
HAZELS	HEADFUL	HEADREACH	HEALD	HEARSAY
HAZELWOOD	HEADFULS	HEADREST	HEALDED	HEARSAYS
HAZER	HEADGATE	HEADRESTS	HEALDING	HEARSE
HAZERS	HEADGATES	HEADRIG	HEALDS	HEARSED
HAZES	HEADGEAR	HEADRIGS	HEALED	HEARSES
HAZIER	HEADGEARS	HEADRING	HEALEE	HEARSIER
HAZIEST	HEADGUARD	HEADRINGS	HEALEES	HEARSIEST
HAZILY	HEADHUNT	HEADROOM	HEALER	HEARSING
HAZINESS	HEADHUNTS	HEADROOMS	HEALERS	HEARSY
HAZING	HEADIER	HEADROPE	HEALING	HEART
HAZINGS	HEADIEST	HEADROPES	HEALINGLY	HEARTACHE
HAZMAT	HEADILY	HEADS	HEALINGS	HEARTBEAT
HAZMATS	HEADINESS	HEADSAIL	HEALS	HEARTBURN
HAZY	HEADING	HEADSAILS	HEALSOME	HEARTED

HEARTEN	HEATHER	HEBES	HEDARIM	HEEDING
HEARTENED	HEATHERED	HEBETANT	HEDDLE	HEEDLESS
HEARTENER	HEATHERS	HEBETATE	HEDDLED	HEEDS
HEARTENS	HEATHERY	HEBETATED	HEDDLES	HEEDY
HEARTFELT	HEATHFOWL	HEBETATES	HEDDLING	HEEHAW
HEARTFREE	HEATHIER	HEBETIC	HEDER	HEEHAWED
HEARTH	HEATHIEST	HEBETUDE	HEDERA	HEEHAWING
HEARTHRUG	HEATHLAND	HEBETUDES	HEDERAL	HEEHAWS
HEARTHS	HEATHLESS	HEBONA	HEDERAS	HEEL
HEARTIER	HEATHLIKE	HEBONAS	HEDERATED	HEELBALL
HEARTIES	HEATHS	HEBRAISE	HEDERS	HEELBALLS
HEARTIEST	HEATHY	HEBRAISED	HEDGE	HEELBAR
HEARTIKIN	HEATING	HEBRAISES	HEDGEBILL	HEELBARS
HEARTILY	HEATINGS	HEBRAIZE	HEDGED	HEELED
HEARTING	HEATLESS	HEBRAIZED	HEDGEHOG	HEELER
HEARTLAND	HEATPROOF	HEBRAIZES	HEDGEHOGS	HEELERS
HEARTLESS	HEATS	HECATOMB	HEDGEHOP	HEELING
HEARTLET	HEATSPOT	HECATOMBS	HEDGEHOPS	HEELINGS
HEARTLETS	HEATSPOTS	HECH	HEDGEPIG	HEELLESS
HEARTLING	HEATWAVE	HECHT	HEDGEPIGS	HEELPIECE
HEARTLY	HEATWAVES	HECHTING	HEDGER	HEELPLATE
HEARTPEA	HEAUME	HECHTS	HEDGEROW	HEELPOST
HEARTPEAS	HEAUMES	HECK	HEDGEROWS	HEELPOSTS
HEARTS	HEAVE	HECKLE	HEDGERS	HEELS
HEARTSEED	HEAVED	HECKLED	HEDGES	HEELTAP
HEARTSICK	HEAVEN	HECKLER	HEDGIER	HEELTAPS
HEARTSINK	HEAVENLY	HECKLERS	HEDGIEST	HEEZE
HEARTSOME	HEAVENS	HECKLES	HEDGING	HEEZED
HEARTSORE	HEAVER	HECKLING	HEDGINGLY	HEEZES
HEARTWOOD	HEAVERS	HECKLINGS	HEDGINGS	HEEZIE
HEARTWORM	HEAVES	HECKS	HEDGY	HEEZIES
HEARTY	HEAVIER	HECKUVA	HEDONIC	HEEZING
HEAST	HEAVIES	HECOGENIN	HEDONICS	HEFT
HEASTE	HEAVIEST	HECTARE	HEDONISM	HEFTE
HEASTES	HEAVILY	HECTARES	HEDONISMS	HEFTED
HEASTS	HEAVINESS	HECTIC	HEDONIST	HEFTER
HEAT	HEAVING	HECTICAL	HEDONISTS	HEFTERS
HEATABLE	HEAVINGS	HECTICLY	HEDYPHANE	HEFTIER
HEATED	HEAVY	HECTICS	HEDYSARUM	HEFTIEST
HEATEDLY	HEAVYISH	HECTOGRAM	HEED	HEFTILY
HEATER	HEAVYSET	HECTOR	HEEDED	HEFTINESS
HEATERS	HEBDOMAD	HECTORED	HEEDER	HEFTING
HEATH	HEBDOMADS	HECTORER	HEEDERS	HEFTS
HEATHBIRD	HEBE	HECTORERS	HEEDFUL	HEFTY
HEATHCOCK	HEBEN	HECTORING	HEEDFULLY	HEGARI
HEATHEN	HEBENON	HECTORISM	HEEDIER	HEGARIS
HEATHENRY	HEBENONS	HECTORLY	HEEDIEST	HEGEMON
HEATHENS	HEBENS	HECTORS	HEEDINESS	HEGEMONIC

HEGEMONS	HEIRSHIPS	HELICOPTS	HELLDIVER	HELMINTHS
HEGEMONY	HEISHI	HELICTITE	HELLEBORE	HELMLESS
HEGIRA	HEIST	HELIDECK	HELLED	HELMS
HEGIRAS	HEISTED	HELIDECKS	HELLENISE	HELMSMAN
HEGUMEN	HEISTER	HELIDROME	HELLENIZE	HELMSMEN
HEGUMENE	HEISTERS	HELILIFT	HELLER	HELO
HEGUMENES	HEISTING	HELILIFTS	HELLERI	HELOPHYTE
HEGUMENOI	HEISTS	HELIMAN	HELLERIES	HELOS
HEGUMENOS	HEITIKI	HELIMEN	HELLERIS	HELOT
HEGUMENS	HEITIKIS	HELING	HELLERS	HELOTAGE
HEGUMENY	HEJAB	HELIO	HELLERY	HELOTAGES
HEH	HEJABS	HELIODOR	HELLFIRE	HELOTISM
HEHS	HEJIRA	HELIODORS	HELLFIRES	HELOTISMS
HEID	HEJIRAS	HELIOGRAM	HELLHOLE	HELOTRIES
HEIDS	HEJRA	HELIOLOGY	HELLHOLES	HELOTRY
HEIDUC	HEJRAS	HELIOPSES	HELLHOUND	HELOTS
HEIDUCS	HEKETARA	HELIOPSIS	HELLICAT	HELP
HEIFER	HEKETARAS	HELIOS	HELLICATS	HELPABLE
HEIFERS	HEKTARE	HELIOSES	HELLIER	HELPDESK
HEIGH	HEKTARES	HELIOSIS	HELLIERS	HELPDESKS
HEIGHT	HEKTOGRAM	HELIOSTAT	HELLING	HELPED
HEIGHTEN	HELCOID	HELIOTYPE	HELLION	HELPER
HEIGHTENS	HELD	HELIOTYPY	HELLIONS	HELPERS
HEIGHTH	HELE	HELIOZOAN	HELLISH	HELPFUL
HEIGHTHS	HELED	HELIOZOIC	HELLISHLY	HELPFULLY
HEIGHTISM	HELENIUM	HELIPAD	HELLKITE	HELPING
HEIGHTS	HELENIUMS	HELIPADS	HELLKITES	HELPINGS
HEIL	HELES	HELIPILOT	HELLO	HELPLESS
HEILED	HELIAC	HELIPORT	HELLOED	HELPLINE
HEILING	HELIACAL	HELIPORTS	HELLOES	HELPLINES
HEILS	HELIAST	HELISKI	HELLOING	HELPMATE
HEIMISH	HELIASTS	HELISKIED	HELLOS	HELPMATES
HEINIE	HELIBORNE	HELISKIS	HELLOVA	HELPMEET
HEINIES	HELIBUS	HELISTOP	HELLS	HELPMEETS
HEINOUS	HELIBUSES	HELISTOPS	HELLSCAPE	HELPS
HEINOUSLY	HELICAL	HELITACK	HELLUVA	HELVE
HEIR	HELICALLY	HELITACKS	HELLWARD	HELVED
HEIRDOM	HELICASE	HELIUM	HELLWARDS	HELVES
HEIRDOMS	HELICASES	HELIUMS	HELM	HELVETIUM
HEIRED	HELICES	HELIX	HELMED	HELVING
HEIRESS	HELICITY	HELIXES	HELMER	HEM
HEIRESSES	HELICLINE	HELL	HELMERS	HEMAGOG
HEIRING	HELICOID	HELLBENT	HELMET	HEMAGOGS
HEIRLESS	HELICOIDS	HELLBOX	HELMETED	HEMAGOGUE
HEIRLOOM	HELICON	HELLBOXES	HELMETING	HEMAL
HEIRLOOMS	HELICONIA	HELLBROTH	HELMETS	HEMATAL
HEIRS	HELICONS	HELLCAT	HELMING	HEMATEIN
HEIRSHIP	HELICOPT	HELLCATS	HELMINTH	HEMATEINS

HEMATIC	HEMISPACE	HEN	HENNISH	HEPTAGON
HEMATICS	HEMISTICH	HENBANE	HENNISHLY	HEPTAGONS
HEMATIN	HEMITROPE	HENBANES	HENNY	HEPTANE
HEMATINE	HEMITROPY	HENBIT	HENOTIC	HEPTANES
HEMATINES	HEMLINE	HENBITS	HENPECK	HEPTAPODY
HEMATINIC	HEMLINES	HENCE	HENPECKED	HEPTARCH
HEMATINS	HEMLOCK	HENCH	HENPECKS	HEPTARCHS
HEMATITE	HEMLOCKS	HENCHER	HENRIES	HEPTARCHY
HEMATITES	HEMMED	HENCHEST	HENRY	HEPTOSE
HEMATITIC	HEMMER	HENCHMAN	HENRYS	HEPTOSES
HEMATOID	HEMMERS	HENCHMEN	HENS	HER
HEMATOMA	HEMMING	HENCOOP	HENT	HERALD
HEMATOMAS	HEMOCOEL	HENCOOPS	HENTED	HERALDED
HEMATOSES	HEMOCOELS	HEND	HENTING	HERALDIC
HEMATOSIS	HEMOCONIA	HENDED	HENTS	HERALDING
HEMATOZOA	HEMOCYTE	HENDIADYS	HEP	HERALDIST
HEMATURIA	HEMOCYTES	HENDING	HEPAR	HERALDRY
HEMATURIC	HEMOID	HENDS	HEPARIN	HERALDS
HEME	HEMOLYMPH	HENEQUEN	HEPARINS	HERB
HEMELYTRA	HEMOLYSE	HENEQUENS	HEPARS	HERBAGE
HEMES	HEMOLYSED	HENEQUIN	HEPATIC	HERBAGED
HEMIALGIA	HEMOLYSES	HENEQUINS	HEPATICA	HERBAGES
HEMIC	HEMOLYSIN	HENGE	HEPATICAE	HERBAL
HEMICYCLE	HEMOLYSIS	HENGES	HEPATICAL	HERBALISM
HEMIHEDRA	HEMOLYTIC	HENHOUSE	HEPATICAS	HERBALIST
HEMIHEDRY	HEMOLYZE	HENHOUSES	HEPATICS	HERBALS
HEMIN	HEMOLYZED	HENIQUEN	HEPATISE	HERBAR
HEMINA	HEMOLYZES	HENIQUENS	HEPATISED	HERBARIA
HEMINAS	HEMOPHILE	HENIQUIN	HEPATISES	HERBARIAL
HEMINS	HEMOSTAT	HENIQUINS	HEPATITE	HERBARIAN
HEMIOLA	HEMOSTATS	HENLEY	HEPATITES	HERBARIES
HEMIOLAS	HEMOTOXIC	HENLEYS	HEPATITIS	HERBARIUM
HEMIOLIA	HEMOTOXIN	HENLIKE	HEPATIZE	HERBARS
HEMIOLIAS	HEMP	HENNA	HEPATIZED	HERBARY
HEMIOLIC	HEMPEN	HENNAED	HEPATIZES	HERBED
HEMIONE	HEMPIE	HENNAING	HEPATOMA	HERBELET
HEMIONES	HEMPIER	HENNAS	HEPATOMAS	HERBELETS
HEMIONUS	HEMPIES	HENNED	HEPCAT	HERBICIDE
HEMIOPIA	HEMPIEST	HENNER	HEPCATS	HERBIER
HEMIOPIAS	HEMPLIKE	HENNERIES	HEPPER	HERBIEST
HEMIOPIC	HEMPS	HENNERS	HEPPEST	HERBIST
HEMIOPSIA	HEMPSEED	HENNERY	HEPS	HERBISTS
HEMIPOD	HEMPSEEDS	HENNIER	HEPSTER	HERBIVORA
HEMIPODE	HEMPWEED	HENNIES	HEPSTERS	HERBIVORE
HEMIPODES	HEMPWEEDS	HENNIEST	HEPT	HERBIVORY
HEMIPODS	HEMPY	HENNIN	HEPTAD	HERBLESS
HEMIPTER	HEMS	HENNING	HEPTADS	HERBLET
HEMIPTERS	HEMSTITCH	HENNINS	HEPTAGLOT	HERBLETS

HERBLIKE	HEREOF	HERMITISM	HEROSHIP	HESPS
HERBOLOGY	HEREON	HERMITRY	HEROSHIPS	HESSIAN
HERBORISE	HERES	HERMITS	HERPES	HESSIANS
HERBORIST	HERESIES	HERMS	HERPESES	HESSITE
HERBORIZE	HERESY	HERN	HERPETIC	HESSITES
HERBOSE	HERETIC	HERNIA	HERPETICS	HESSONITE
HERBOUS	HERETICAL	HERNIAE	HERPETOID	HEST
HERBS	HERETICS	HERNIAL	HERPTILE	HESTERNAL
HERBY	HERETO	HERNIAS	HERRIED	HESTS
HERCOGAMY	HERETRIX	HERNIATE	HERRIES	HET
HERCULEAN	HEREUNDER	HERNIATED	HERRIMENT	HETAERA
HERCULES	HEREUNTO	HERNIATES	HERRING	HETAERAE
HERCYNITE	HEREUPON	HERNS	HERRINGER	HETAERAS
HERD	HEREWITH	HERNSHAW	HERRINGS	HETAERIC
HERDBOY	HERIED	HERNSHAWS	HERRY	HETAERISM
HERDBOYS	HERIES	HERO	HERRYING	HETAERIST
HERDED	HERIOT	HEROES	HERRYMENT	HETAIRA
HERDEN	HERIOTS	HEROIC	HERS	HETAIRAI
HERDENS	HERISSE	HEROICAL	HERSALL	HETAIRAS
HERDER	HERISSON	HEROICISE	HERSALLS	HETAIRIA
HERDERS	HERISSONS	HEROICIZE	HERSE	HETAIRIAS
HERDESS	HERITABLE	HEROICLY	HERSED	HETAIRIC
HERDESSES	HERITABLY	HEROICS	HERSELF	HETAIRISM
HERDIC	HERITAGE	HEROIN	HERSES	HETAIRIST
HERDICS	HERITAGES	HEROINE	HERSHIP	HETE
HERDING	HERITOR	HEROINES	HERSHIPS	HETERO
HERDINGS	HERITORS	HEROINISM	HERSTORY	HETERODOX
HERDLIKE	HERITRESS	HEROINS	HERTZ	HETERONYM
HERDMAN	HERITRIX	HEROISE	HERTZES	HETEROPOD
HERDMEN	HERKOGAMY	HEROISED	HERY	HETEROS
HERDS	HERL	HEROISES	HERYE	HETEROSES
HERDSMAN	HERLING	HEROISING	HERYED	HETEROSIS
HERDSMEN	HERLINGS	HEROISM	HERYES	HETEROTIC
HERDWICK	HERLS	HEROISMS	HERYING	HETES
HERDWICKS	HERM	HEROIZE	HES	HETH
HERE	HERMA	HEROIZED	HESITANCE	HETHER
HEREABOUT	HERMAE	HEROIZES	HESITANCY	HETHS
HEREAFTER	HERMAEAN	HEROIZING	HESITANT	HETING
HEREAT	HERMAI	HERON	HESITATE	HETMAN
HEREAWAY	HERMANDAD	HERONRIES	HESITATED	HETMANATE
HEREAWAYS	HERMETIC	HERONRY	HESITATER	HETMANS
HEREBY	HERMETICS	HERONS	HESITATES	HETMEN
HEREDES	HERMETISM	HERONSEW	HESITATOR	HETS
HEREDITY	HERMETIST	HERONSEWS	HESP	HETTIE
HEREFROM	HERMIT	HERONSHAW	HESPED	HETTIES
HEREIN	HERMITAGE	HEROON	HESPERID	HEUCH
HEREINTO	HERMITESS	HEROONS	HESPERIDS	HEUCHERA
HERENESS	HERMITIC	HEROS	HESPING	HEUCHERAS

HEUCHS	HEXANOIC	HIATAL	HIDDEN	HIES
HEUGH	HEXAPLA	HIATUS	HIDDENITE	HIFALUTIN
HEUGHS	HEXAPLAR	HIATUSES	HIDDENLY	HIGGLE
HEUREKA	HEXAPLAS	HIBACHI	HIDDER	HIGGLED
HEUREKAS	HEXAPLOID	HIBACHIS	HIDDERS	HIGGLER
HEURETIC	HEXAPOD	HIBAKUSHA	HIDE	HIGGLERS
HEURETICS	HEXAPODAL	HIBERNAL	HIDEAWAY	HIGGLES
HEURISM	HEXAPODIC	HIBERNATE	HIDEAWAYS	HIGGLING
HEURISMS	HEXAPODS	HIBERNISE	HIDEBOUND	HIGGLINGS
HEURISTIC	HEXAPODY	HIBERNIZE	HIDED	HIGH
HEVEA	HEXARCH	HIBISCUS	HIDELESS	HIGHBALL
HEVEAS	HEXARCHY	HIC	HIDEOSITY	HIGHBALLS
HEW	HEXASTICH	HICATEE	HIDEOUS	HIGHBORN
HEWABLE	HEXASTYLE	HICATEES	HIDEOUSLY	HIGHBOY
HEWED	HEXATHLON	HICCATEE	HIDEOUT	HIGHBOYS
HEWER	HEXED	HICCATEES	HIDEOUTS	HIGHBRED
HEWERS	HEXENE	HICCOUGH	HIDER	HIGHBROW
HEWGH	HEXENES	HICCOUGHS	HIDERS	HIGHBROWS
HEWING	HEXER	HICCUP	HIDES	HIGHBUSH
HEWINGS	HEXEREI	HICCUPED	HIDING	HIGHCHAIR
HEWN	HEXEREIS	HICCUPIER	HIDINGS	HIGHED
HEWS	HEXERS	HICCUPING	HIDLING	HIGHER
HEX	HEXES	HICCUPPED	HIDLINGS	HIGHERED
HEXACHORD	HEXING	HICCUPS	HIDLINS	HIGHERING
HEXACT	HEXINGS	HICCUPY	HIDROSES	HIGHERS
HEXACTS	HEXONE	HICK	HIDROSIS	HIGHEST
HEXAD	HEXONES	HICKER	HIDROTIC	HIGHFLIER
HEXADE	HEXOSAN	HICKEST	HIDROTICS	HIGHFLYER
HEXADECYL	HEXOSANS	HICKEY	HIE	HIGHING
HEXADES	HEXOSE	HICKEYS	HIED	HIGHISH
HEXADIC	HEXOSES	HICKIE	HIEING	HIGHJACK
HEXADS	HEXYL	HICKIES	HIELAMAN	HIGHJACKS
HEXAFOIL	HEXYLENE	HICKISH	HIELAMANS	HIGHJINKS
HEXAFOILS	HEXYLENES	HICKORIES	HIELAND	HIGHLAND
HEXAGLOT	HEXYLIC	HICKORY	HIEMAL	HIGHLANDS
HEXAGLOTS	HEXYLS	HICKS	HIEMS	HIGHLIFE
HEXAGON	HEY	HICKWALL	HIERACIUM	HIGHLIFES
HEXAGONAL	HEYDAY	HICKWALLS	HIERARCH	HIGHLIGHT
HEXAGONS	HEYDAYS	HICKYMAL	HIERARCHS	HIGHLY
HEXAGRAM	HEYDEY	HICKYMALS	HIERARCHY	HIGHMAN
HEXAGRAMS	HEYDEYS	HID	HIERATIC	HIGHMEN
HEXAHEDRA	HEYDUCK	HIDABLE	HIERATICA	HIGHMOST
HEXAMERAL	HEYDUCKS	HIDAGE	HIERATICS	HIGHNESS
HEXAMETER	HEYED	HIDAGES	HIEROCRAT	HIGHRISE
HEXAMINE	HEYING	HIDALGA	HIERODULE	HIGHRISES
HEXAMINES	HEYS	HIDALGAS	HIEROGRAM	HIGHROAD
HEXANE	HI	HIDALGO	HIEROLOGY	HIGHROADS
HEXANES	HIANT	HIDALGOS	HIERURGY	HIGHS

HIGHSPOT	HILCHING	HIMATIA	HINGES	HIPPIN
HIGHSPOTS	HILD	HIMATION	HINGING	HIPPINESS
HIGHT	HILDING	HIMATIONS	HINGS	HIPPING
HIGHTAIL	HILDINGS	HIMBO	HINKIER	HIPPINGS
HIGHTAILS	HILI	HIMBOS	HINKIEST	HIPPINS
HIGHTED	HILL	HIMS	HINKY	HIPPISH
HIGHTH	HILLBILLY	HIMSELF	HINNIE	HIPPO
HIGHTHS	HILLCREST	HIN	HINNIED	HIPPOCRAS
HIGHTING	HILLED	HINAHINA	HINNIES	HIPPODAME
HIGHTINGS	HILLER	HINAHINAS	HINNY	HIPPOLOGY
HIGHTOP	HILLERS	HINAU	HINNYING	HIPPOS
HIGHTOPS	HILLFOLK	HINAUS	HINS	HIPPURIC
HIGHTS	HILLFORT	HIND	HINT	HIPPURITE
HIGHVELD	HILLFORTS	HINDBERRY	HINTED	HIPPUS
HIGHVELDS	HILLIER	HINDBRAIN	HINTER	HIPPUSES
HIGHWAY	HILLIEST	HINDCAST	HINTERS	HIPPY
HIGHWAYS	HILLINESS	HINDCASTS	HINTING	HIPPYDOM
HIJAB	HILLING	HINDER	HINTINGLY	HIPPYDOMS
HIJABS	HILLINGS	HINDERED	HINTINGS	HIPPYISH
HIJACK	HILLMEN	HINDERER	HINTS	HIPS
HIJACKED	HILLO	HINDERERS	HIOI	HIPSHOT
HIJACKER	HILLOA	HINDERING	HIOIS	HIPSTER
HIJACKERS	HILLOAED	HINDERS	HIP	HIPSTERS
HIJACKING	HILLOAING	HINDFEET	HIPBONE	HIPT
HIJACKS	HILLOAS	HINDFOOT	HIPBONES	HIRABLE
HIJINKS	HILLOCK	HINDGUT	HIPHUGGER	HIRAGANA
HIJRA	HILLOCKED	HINDGUTS	HIPLESS	HIRAGANAS
HIJRAH	HILLOCKS	HINDHEAD	HIPLIKE	HIRAGE
HIJRAHS	HILLOCKY	HINDHEADS	HIPLINE	HIRAGES
HIJRAS	HILLOED	HINDLEG	HIPLINES	HIRCINE
HIKE	HILLOES	HINDLEGS	HIPLY	HIRCOSITY
HIKED	HILLOING	HINDMILK	HIPNESS	HIRE
HIKER	HILLOS	HINDMILKS	HIPNESSES	HIREABLE
HIKERS	HILLS	HINDMOST	HIPPARCH	HIREAGE
HIKES	HILLSIDE	HINDRANCE	HIPPARCHS	HIREAGES
HIKING	HILLSIDES	HINDS	HIPPED	HIRED
HIKINGS	HILLSLOPE	HINDSHANK	HIPPEN	HIREE
HIKOI	HILLTOP	HINDSIGHT	HIPPENS	HIREES
HIKOIED	HILLTOPS	HINDWARD	HIPPER	HIRELING
HIKOIING	HILLY	HINDWING	HIPPEST	HIRELINGS
HIKOIS	HILT	HINDWINGS	HIPPIATRY	HIRER
HILA	HILTED	HING	HIPPIC	HIRERS
HILAR	HILTING	HINGE	HIPPIE	HIRES
HILARIOUS	HILTLESS	HINGED	HIPPIEDOM	HIRING
HILARITY	HILTS	HINGELESS	HIPPIEISH	HIRINGS
HILCH	HILUM	HINGELIKE	HIPPIER	HIRLING
HILCHED	HILUS	HINGER	HIPPIES	HIRLINGS
HILCHES	HIM	HINGERS	HIPPIEST	HIRPLE

HIRPLED	HISTIDINE	HITMEN	HOARFROST	HOBBLERS
HIRPLES	HISTIDINS	HITS	HOARHEAD	HOBBLES
HIRPLING	HISTIE	HITTABLE	HOARHEADS	HOBBLING
HIRRIENT	HISTING	HITTER	HOARHOUND	HOBBLINGS
HIRRIENTS	HISTIOID	HITTERS	HOARIER	HOBBY
HIRSEL	HISTOGEN	HITTING	HOARIEST	HOBBYISM
HIRSELED	HISTOGENS	HIVE	HOARILY	HOBBYISMS
HIRSELING	HISTOGENY	HIVED	HOARINESS	HOBBYIST
HIRSELLED	HISTOGRAM	HIVELESS	HOARING	HOBBYISTS
HIRSELS	HISTOID	HIVELIKE	HOARS	HOBBYLESS
HIRSLE	HISTOLOGY	HIVEMIND	HOARSE	HOBDAY
HIRSLED	HISTONE	HIVEMINDS	HOARSELY	HOBDAYED
HIRSLES	HISTONES	HIVER	HOARSEN	HOBDAYING
HIRSLING	HISTORIAN	HIVERS	HOARSENED	HOBDAYS
HIRSTIE	HISTORIC	HIVES	HOARSENS	HOBGOBLIN
HIRSUTE	HISTORIED	HIVEWARD	HOARSER	HOBJOB
HIRSUTISM	HISTORIES	HIVEWARDS	HOARSEST	HOBJOBBED
HIRUDIN	HISTORIFY	HIVING	HOARY	HOBJOBBER
HIRUDINS	HISTORISM	HIYA	HOAS	HOBJOBS
HIRUNDINE	HISTORY	HIZEN	HOAST	HOBLIKE
HIS	HISTRIO	HIZENS	HOASTED	HOBNAIL
HISH	HISTRION	HIZZ	HOASTING	HOBNAILED
HISHED	HISTRIONS	HIZZED	HOASTMAN	HOBNAILS
HISHES	HISTRIOS	HIZZES	HOASTMEN	HOBNOB
HISHING	HISTS	HIZZING	HOASTS	HOBNOBBED
HISN	HIT	HIZZONER	HOATCHING	HOBNOBBER
HISPANISM	HITCH	HIZZONERS	HOATZIN	HOBNOBBY
HISPID	HITCHED	HM	HOATZINES	HOBNOBS
HISPIDITY	HITCHER	HMM	HOATZINS	HOBO
HISS	HITCHERS	HMMM	HOAX	HOBODOM
HISSED	HITCHES	HO	HOAXED	HOBODOMS
HISSELF	HITCHHIKE	HOA	HOAXER	HOBOED
HISSER	HITCHIER	HOACTZIN	HOAXERS	HOBOES
HISSERS	HITCHIEST	HOACTZINS	HOAXES	HOBOING
HISSES	HITCHILY	HOAED	HOAXING	HOBOISM
HISSIER	HITCHING	HOAGIE	HOB	HOBOISMS
HISSIES	HITCHY	HOAGIES	HOBBED	HOBOS
HISSIEST	HITHE	HOAGY	HOBBER	HOBS
HISSING	HITHER	HOAING	HOBBERS	HOC
HISSINGLY	HITHERED	HOAR	HOBBIES	HOCK
HISSINGS	HITHERING	HOARD	HOBBING	HOCKED
HISSY	HITHERS	HOARDED	HOBBISH	HOCKER
HIST	HITHERTO	HOARDER	HOBBIT	HOCKERS
HISTAMIN	HITHES	HOARDERS	HOBBITRY	HOCKEY
HISTAMINE	HITLESS	HOARDING	HOBBITS	HOCKEYS
HISTAMINS	HITMAKER	HOARDINGS	HOBBLE	HOCKING
HISTED	HITMAKERS	HOARDS	HOBBLED	HOCKLE
HISTIDIN	HITMAN	HOARED	HOBBLER	HOCKLED

HOCKLES	HOES	HOGTIEING	HOISTMEN	HOLDS
HOCKLING	HOG	HOGTIES	HOISTS	HOLDUP
HOCKS	HOGAN	HOGTYING	HOISTWAY	HOLDUPS
HOCKSHOP	HOGANS	HOGWARD	HOISTWAYS	HOLE
HOCKSHOPS	HOGBACK	HOGWARDS	HOKA	HOLED
HOCUS	HOGBACKS	HOGWASH	HOKAS	HOLELESS
HOCUSED	HOGEN	HOGWASHES	HOKE	HOLES
HOCUSES	HOGENS	HOGWEED	HOKED	HOLESOM
HOCUSING	HOGFISH	HOGWEEDS	HOKES	HOLESOME
HOCUSSED	HOGFISHES	HOH	HOKEY	HOLEY
HOCUSSES	HOGG	HOHA	HOKEYNESS	HOLEYER
HOCUSSING	HOGGED	HOHED	HOKI	HOLEYEST
HOD	HOGGER	HOHING	HOKIER	HOLIBUT
HODAD	HOGGEREL	HOHS	HOKIEST	HOLIBUTS
HODADDIES	HOGGERELS	HOI	HOKILY	HOLIDAY
HODADDY	HOGGERIES	HOICK	HOKINESS	HOLIDAYED
HODADS	HOGGERS	HOICKED	HOKING	HOLIDAYER
HODDED	HOGGERY	HOICKING	HOKIS	HOLIDAYS
HODDEN	HOGGET	HOICKS	HOKKU	HOLIER
HODDENS	HOGGETS	HOICKSED	HOKONUI	HOLIES
HODDIN	HOGGIN	HOICKSES	HOKONUIS	HOLIEST
HODDING	HOGGING	HOICKSING	HOKUM	HOLILY
HODDINS	HOGGINGS	HOIDEN	HOKUMS	HOLINESS
HODDLE	HOGGINS	HOIDENED	HOKYPOKY	HOLING
HODDLED	HOGGISH	HOIDENING	HOLANDRIC	HOLINGS
HODDLES	HOGGISHLY	HOIDENISH	HOLARCHY	HOLISM
HODDLING	HOGGS	HOIDENS	HOLARD	HOLISMS
HODIERNAL	HOGH	HOIED	HOLARDS	HOLIST
HODJA	HOGHOOD	HOIING	HOLD	HOLISTIC
HODJAS	HOGHOODS	HOIK	HOLDABLE	HOLISTS
HODMAN	HOGHS	HOIKED	HOLDALL	HOLK
HODMANDOD	HOGLIKE	HOIKING	HOLDALLS	HOLKED
HODMEN	HOGMANAY	HOIKS	HOLDBACK	HOLKING
HODOGRAPH	HOGMANAYS	HOING	HOLDBACKS	HOLKS
HODOMETER	HOGMANE	HOIS	HOLDDOWN	HOLLA
HODOMETRY	HOGMANES	HOISE	HOLDDOWNS	HOLLAED
HODOSCOPE	HOGMENAY	HOISED	HOLDEN	HOLLAING
HODS	HOGMENAYS	HOISES	HOLDER	HOLLAND
HOE	HOGNOSE	HOISIN	HOLDERBAT	HOLLANDS
HOECAKE	HOGNOSED	HOISING	HOLDERS	HOLLAS
HOECAKES	HOGNOSES	HOISINS	HOLDFAST	HOLLER
HOED	HOGNUT	HOIST	HOLDFASTS	HOLLERED
HOEDOWN	HOGNUTS	HOISTED	HOLDING	HOLLERING
HOEDOWNS	HOGS	HOISTER	HOLDINGS	HOLLERS
HOEING	HOGSHEAD	HOISTERS	HOLDOUT	HOLLIDAM
HOELIKE	HOGSHEADS	HOISTING	HOLDOUTS	HOLLIDAMS
HOER	HOGTIE	HOISTINGS	HOLDOVER	HOLLIES
HOERS	HOGTIED	HOISTMAN	HOLDOVERS	HOLLO

HOLLOA	HOLOPTIC	HOMEBOY	HOMESITE	HOMINIZE
HOLLOAED	HOLOS	HOMEBOYS	HOMESITES	HOMINIZED
HOLLOAING	HOLOTYPE	HOMEBRED	HOMESPUN	HOMINIZES
HOLLOAS	HOLOTYPES	HOMEBREDS	HOMESPUNS	HOMINOID
HOLLOED	HOLOTYPIC	HOMEBREW	HOMESTALL	HOMINOIDS
HOLLOES	HOLOZOIC	HOMEBREWS	HOMESTAND	HOMINY
HOLLOING	HOLP	HOMEBUILT	HOMESTAY	HOMME
HOLLOO	HOLPEN	HOMEBUYER	HOMESTAYS	HOMMES
HOLLOOED	HOLS	HOMECOMER	HOMESTEAD	HOMMOCK
HOLLOOING	HOLSTEIN	HOMECRAFT	HOMESTYLE	HOMMOCKS
HOLLOOS	HOLSTEINS	HOMED	HOMETOWN	HOMMOS
HOLLOS	HOLSTER	HOMEFELT	HOMETOWNS	HOMMOSES
HOLLOW	HOLSTERED	HOMEGIRL	HOMEWARD	HOMO
HOLLOWARE	HOLSTERS	HOMEGIRLS	HOMEWARDS	HOMOCERCY
HOLLOWED	HOLT	HOMEGROWN	HOMEWARE	HOMODONT
HOLLOWER	HOLTS	HOMELAND	HOMEWARES	HOMODYNE
HOLLOWEST	HOLUBTSI	HOMELANDS	HOMEWORK	HOMOEOBOX
HOLLOWING	HOLY	HOMELESS	HOMEWORKS	HOMOEOSES
HOLLOWLY	HOLYDAM	HOMELIER	HOMEY	HOMOEOSIS
HOLLOWS	HOLYDAME	HOMELIEST	HOMEYNESS	HOMOEOTIC
HOLLY	HOLYDAMES	HOMELIKE	HOMEYS	HOMOGAMIC
HOLLYHOCK	HOLYDAMS	HOMELILY	HOMICIDAL	HOMOGAMY
HOLM	HOLYDAY	HOMELY	HOMICIDE	HOMOGENY
HOLME	HOLYDAYS	HOMELYN	HOMICIDES	HOMOGONY
HOLMES	HOLYSTONE	HOMELYNS	HOMIE	HOMOGRAFT
HOLMIA	HOLYTIDE	HOMEMADE	HOMIER	HOMOGRAPH
HOLMIAS	HOLYTIDES	HOMEMAKER	HOMIES	HOMOLOG
HOLMIC	HOM	HOMEOBOX	HOMIEST	HOMOLOGIC
HOLMIUM	HOMA	HOMEOMERY	HOMILETIC	HOMOLOGS
HOLMIUMS	HOMAGE	HOMEOPATH	HOMILIES	HOMOLOGUE
HOLMS	HOMAGED	HOMEOSES	HOMILIST	HOMOLOGY
HOLO	HOMAGER	HOMEOSIS	HOMILISTS	HOMOLYSES
HOLOCAINE	HOMAGERS	HOMEOTIC	HOMILY	HOMOLYSIS
HOLOCAUST	HOMAGES	HOMEOWNER	HOMINES	HOMOLYTIC
HOLOCENE	HOMAGING	HOMEPAGE	HOMINESS	HOMOMORPH
HOLOCRINE	HOMALOID	HOMEPAGES	HOMING	HOMONYM
HOLOGAMY	HOMALOIDS	HOMEPLACE	HOMINGS	HOMONYMIC
HOLOGRAM	HOMAS	HOMEPORT	HOMINIAN	HOMONYMS
HOLOGRAMS	HOMBRE	HOMEPORTS	HOMINIANS	HOMONYMY
HOLOGRAPH	HOMBRES	HOMER	HOMINID	HOMOPHILE
HOLOGYNIC	HOMBURG	HOMERED	HOMINIDS	HOMOPHOBE
HOLOGYNY	HOMBURGS	HOMERIC	HOMINIES	HOMOPHONE
HOLOHEDRA	HOME	HOMERING	HOMININ	HOMOPHONY
HOLON	HOMEBIRD	HOMEROOM	HOMININE	HOMOPHYLY
HOLONIC	HOMEBIRDS	HOMEROOMS	HOMININS	HOMOPLASY
HOLONS	HOMEBIRTH	HOMERS	HOMINISE	HOMOPOLAR
HOLOPHOTE	HOMEBODY	HOMES	HOMINISED	HOMOS
HOLOPHYTE	HOMEBOUND	HOMESICK	HOMINISES	HOMOSEX

HOMOSEXES	HONEWORTS	HONORARY	HOODWINK	HOOLACHAN
HOMOSPORY	HONEY	HONORED	HOODWINKS	HOOLEY
HOMOSTYLY	HONEYBEE	HONOREE	HOODY	HOOLEYS
HOMOTAXES	HONEYBEES	HONOREES	HOOEY	HOOLICAN
HOMOTAXIC	HONEYBELL	HONORER	HOOEYS	HOOLICANS
HOMOTAXIS	HONEYBUN	HONORERS	HOOF	HOOLIE
HOMOTONIC	HONEYBUNS	HONORIFIC	HOOFBEAT	HOOLIER
HOMOTONY	HONEYCOMB	HONORING	HOOFBEATS	HOOLIES
HOMOTYPAL	HONEYDEW	HONORLESS	HOOFBOUND	HOOLIEST
HOMOTYPE	HONEYDEWS	HONORS	HOOFED	HOOLIGAN
HOMOTYPES	HONEYED	HONOUR	HOOFER	HOOLIGANS
HOMOTYPIC	HONEYEDLY	HONOURARY	HOOFERS	HOOLOCK
HOMOTYPY	HONEYFUL	HONOURED	HOOFING	HOOLOCKS
HOMOUSIAN	HONEYING	HONOUREE	HOOFLESS	HOOLY
HOMS	HONEYLESS	HONOUREES	HOOFLIKE	HOON
HOMUNCLE	HONEYMOON	HONOURER	HOOFPRINT	HOONED
HOMUNCLES	HONEYPOT	HONOURERS	HOOFROT	HOONING
HOMUNCULE	HONEYPOTS	HONOURING	HOOFROTS	HOONS
HOMUNCULI	HONEYS	HONOURS	HOOFS	HOOP
HOMY	HONEYTRAP	HONS	HOOK	HOOPED
HON	HONG	HOO	HOOKA	HOOPER
HONAN	HONGI	HOOCH	HOOKAH	HOOPERS
HONANS	HONGIED	HOOCHES	HOOKAHS	HOOPING
HONCHO	HONGIES	HOOCHIE	HOOKAS	HOOPLA
HONCHOED	HONGIING	HOOCHIES	HOOKCHECK	HOOPLAS
HONCHOES	HONGING	HOOD	HOOKED	HOOPLESS
HONCHOING	HONGIS	HOODED	HOOKER	HOOPLIKE
HONCHOS	HONGS	HOODIA	HOOKERS	HOOPOE
HOND	HONIED	HOODIAS	HOOKEY	HOOPOES
HONDA	HONIEDLY	HOODIE	HOOKEYS	HOOPOO
HONDAS	HONING	HOODIER	HOOKIER	HOOPOOS
HONDLE	HONK	HOODIES	HOOKIES	HOOPS
HONDLED	HONKED	HOODIEST	HOOKIEST	HOOPSKIRT
HONDLES	HONKER	HOODING	HOOKING	HOOPSTER
HONDLING	HONKERS	HOODLESS	HOOKINGS	HOOPSTERS
HONDS	HONKEY	HOODLIKE	HOOKLESS	HOOR
HONE	HONKEYS	HOODLUM	HOOKLET	HOORAH
HONED	HONKIE	HOODLUMS	HOOKLETS	HOORAHED
HONER	HONKIES	HOODMAN	HOOKLIKE	HOORAHING
HONERS	HONKING	HOODMEN	HOOKNOSE	HOORAHS
HONES	HONKS	HOODMOLD	HOOKNOSED	HOORAY
HONEST	HONKY	HOODMOLDS	HOOKNOSES	HOORAYED
HONESTER	HONOR	HOODOO	HOOKS	HOORAYING
HONESTEST	HONORABLE	HOODOOED	HOOKUP	HOORAYS
HONESTIES	HONORABLY	HOODOOING	HOOKUPS	HOORD
HONESTLY	HONORAND	HOODOOISM	HOOKWORM	HOORDS
HONESTY	HONORANDS	HOODOOS	HOOKWORMS	HOOROO
HONEWORT	HONORARIA	HOODS	HOOKY	HOOROOED

HOOROOING	HOPERS	HORDING	HORNFELS	HOROLOGY
HOOROOS	HOPES	HORDOCK	HORNFISH	HOROMETRY
HOORS	HOPFIELD	HORDOCKS	HORNFUL	HOROPITO
HOOSEGOW	HOPFIELDS	HORE	HORNFULS	HOROPITOS
HOOSEGOWS	HOPHEAD	HOREHOUND	HORNGELD	HOROPTER
HOOSGOW	HOPHEADS	HORI	HORNGELDS	HOROPTERS
HOOSGOWS	HOPING	HORIATIKI	HORNIER	HOROSCOPE
HOOSH	HOPINGLY	HORIS	HORNIEST	HOROSCOPY
HOOSHED	HOPLITE	HORIZON	HORNILY	HORRENT
HOOSHES	HOPLITES	HORIZONAL	HORNINESS	HORRIBLE
HOOSHING	HOPLITIC	HORIZONS	HORNING	HORRIBLES
HOOT	HOPLOLOGY	HORK	HORNINGS	HORRIBLY
HOOTCH	HOPPED	HORKED	HORNISH	HORRID
HOOTCHES	HOPPER	HORKEY	HORNIST	HORRIDER
HOOTED	HOPPERCAR	HORKEYS	HORNISTS	HORRIDEST
HOOTER	HOPPERS	HORKING	HORNITO	HORRIDLY
HOOTERS	HOPPIER	HORKS	HORNITOS	HORRIFIC
HOOTIER	HOPPIEST	HORLICKS	HORNLESS	HORRIFIED
HOOTIEST	HOPPINESS	HORME	HORNLET	HORRIFIES
HOOTING	HOPPING	HORMES	HORNLETS	HORRIFY
HOOTNANNY	HOPPINGS	HORMESES	HORNLIKE	HORROR
HOOTS	HOPPLE	HORMESIS	HORNPIPE	HORRORS
HOOTY	HOPPLED	HORMETIC	HORNPIPES	HORS
HOOVE	HOPPLER	HORMIC	HORNPOUT	HORSE
HOOVED	HOPPLERS	HORMONAL	HORNPOUTS	HORSEBACK
HOOVEN	HOPPLES	HORMONE	HORNS	HORSEBEAN
HOOVER	HOPPLING	HORMONES	HORNSTONE	HORSEBOX
HOOVERED	HOPPUS	HORMONIC	HORNTAIL	HORSECAR
HOOVERING	HOPPY	HORN	HORNTAILS	HORSECARS
HOOVERS	HOPS	HORNBAG	HORNWORK	HORSED
HOOVES	HOPSACK	HORNBAGS	HORNWORKS	HORSEFLY
HOOVING	HOPSACKS	HORNBEAK	HORNWORM	HORSEHAIR
HOP	HOPSCOTCH	HORNBEAKS	HORNWORMS	HORSEHEAD
HOPAK	HOPTOAD	HORNBEAM	HORNWORT	HORSEHIDE
HOPAKS	HOPTOADS	HORNBEAMS	HORNWORTS	HORSELESS
HOPBIND	HORA	HORNBILL	HORNWRACK	HORSELIKE
HOPBINDS	HORAH	HORNBILLS	HORNY	HORSEMAN
HOPBINE	HORAHS	HORNBOOK	HORNYHEAD	HORSEMEAT
HOPBINES	HORAL	HORNBOOKS	HORNYWINK	HORSEMEN
HOPDOG	HORARY	HORNBUG	HOROEKA	HORSEMINT
HOPDOGS	HORAS	HORNBUGS	HOROEKAS	HORSEPLAY
HOPE	HORDE	HORNDOG	HOROKAKA	HORSEPOND
HOPED	HORDED	HORNDOGS	HOROKAKAS	HORSEPOX
HOPEFUL	HORDEIN	HORNED	HOROLOGE	HORSERACE
HOPEFULLY	HORDEINS	HORNER	HOROLOGER	HORSES
HOPEFULS	HORDEOLA	HORNERS	HOROLOGES	HORSESHIT
HOPELESS	HORDEOLUM	HORNET	HOROLOGIA	HORSESHOD
HOPER	HORDES	HORNETS	HOROLOGIC	HORSESHOE

HORSETAIL	HOSIER	HOSTRIES	HOTLINERS	HOUGHING
HORSEWAY	HOSIERIES	HOSTRY	HOTLINES	HOUGHS
HORSEWAYS	HOSIERS	HOSTS	HOTLINK	HOUHERE
HORSEWEED	HOSIERY	HOT	HOTLINKS	HOUHERES
HORSEWHIP	HOSING	HOTBED	HOTLY	HOUMMOS
HORSEY	HOSPICE	HOTBEDS	HOTNESS	HOUMMOSES
HORSIE	HOSPICES	HOTBLOOD	HOTNESSES	HOUMOUS
HORSIER	HOSPITAGE	HOTBLOODS	HOTPLATE	HOUMOUSES
HORSIES	HOSPITAL	HOTBOX	HOTPLATES	HOUMUS
HORSIEST	HOSPITALE	HOTBOXED	HOTPOT	HOUMUSES
HORSILY	HOSPITALS	HOTBOXES	HOTPOTS	HOUND
HORSINESS	HOSPITIA	HOTBOXING	HOTPRESS	HOUNDED
HORSING	HOSPITIUM	HOTCAKE	HOTROD	HOUNDER
HORSINGS	HOSPODAR	HOTCAKES	HOTRODS	HOUNDERS
HORSON	HOSPODARS	HOTCH	HOTS	HOUNDFISH
HORSONS	HOSS	HOTCHED	HOTSHOT	HOUNDING
HORST	HOSSES	HOTCHES	HOTSHOTS	HOUNDS
HORSTE	HOST	HOTCHING	HOTSPOT	HOUNGAN
HORSTES	HOSTA	HOTCHPOT	HOTSPOTS	HOUNGANS
HORSTS	HOSTAGE	HOTCHPOTS	HOTSPUR	HOUR
HORSY	HOSTAGES	HOTDOG	HOTSPURS	HOURGLASS
HORTATION	HOSTAS	HOTDOGGED	HOTTED	HOURI
HORTATIVE	HOSTED	HOTDOGGER	HOTTENTOT	HOURIS
HORTATORY	HOSTEL	HOTDOGS	HOTTER	HOURLIES
HORTENSIA	HOSTELED	HOTE	HOTTERED	HOURLONG
HOS	HOSTELER	HOTEL	HOTTERING	HOURLY
HOSANNA	HOSTELERS	HOTELDOM	HOTTERS	HOURPLATE
HOSANNAED	HOSTELING	HOTELDOMS	HOTTEST	HOURS
HOSANNAH	HOSTELLED	HOTELIER	HOTTIE	HOUSE
HOSANNAHS	HOSTELLER	HOTELIERS	HOTTIES	HOUSEBOAT
HOSANNAS	HOSTELRY	HOTELING	HOTTING	HOUSEBOY
HOSE	HOSTELS	HOTELINGS	HOTTINGS	HOUSEBOYS
HOSED	HOSTESS	HOTELLING	HOTTISH	HOUSECARL
HOSEL	HOSTESSED	HOTELMAN	HOTTY	HOUSECOAT
HOSELIKE	HOSTESSES	HOTELMEN	HOUDAH	HOUSED
HOSELS	HOSTIE	HOTELS	HOUDAHS	HOUSEFLY
HOSEMAN	HOSTIES	HOTEN	HOUDAN	HOUSFFUL
HOSEMEN	HOSTILE	HOTFOOT	HOUDANS	HOUSEFULS
HOSEN	HOSTILELY	HOTFOOTED	HOUF	HOUSEHOLD
HOSEPIPE	HOSTILES	HOTFOOTS	HOUFED	HOUSEKEEP
HOSEPIPES	HOSTILITY	HOTHEAD	HOUFF	HOUSEKEPT
HOSER	HOSTING	HOTHEADED	HOUFFED	HOUSEL
HOSERS	HOSTINGS	HOTHEADS	HOUFFING	HOUSELED
HOSES	HOSTLER	HOTHOUSE	HOUFFS	HOUSELEEK
HOSEY	HOSTLERS	HOTHOUSED	HOUFING	HOUSELESS
HOSEYED	HOSTLESS	HOTHOUSES	HOUFS	HOUSELIKE
HOSEYING	HOSTLESSE	HOTLINE	HOUGH	HOUSELINE
HOSEYS	HOSTLY	HOTLINER	HOUGHED	HOUSELING

HOUSELLED	HOVERFLY	HOWRE	HUBBUBS	HUFFING
HOUSELS	HOVERING	HOWRES	HUBBY	HUFFINGS
HOUSEMAID	HOVERPORT	HOWS	HUBCAP	HUFFISH
HOUSEMAN	HOVERS	HOWSO	HUBCAPS	HUFFISHLY
HOUSEMATE	HOVES	HOWSOEVER	HUBLESS	HUFFKIN
HOUSEMEN	HOVING	HOWTOWDIE	HUBRIS	HUFFKINS
HOUSER	HOW	HOWZAT	HUBRISES	HUFFS
HOUSEROOM	HOWBE	HOWZIT	HUBRISTIC	HUFFY
HOUSERS	HOWBEIT	HOX	HUBS	HUG
HOUSES	HOWDAH	HOXED	HUCK	HUGE
HOUSESAT	HOWDAHS	HOXES	HUCKABACK	HUGELY
HOUSESIT	HOWDIE	HOXING	HUCKED	HUGENESS
HOUSESITS	HOWDIED	HOY	HUCKERY	HUGEOUS
HOUSETOP	HOWDIES	HOYA	HUCKING	HUGEOUSLY
HOUSETOPS	HOWDY	HOYAS	HUCKLE	HUGER
HOUSEWIFE	HOWDYING	HOYDEN	HUCKLED	HUGEST
HOUSEWORK	HOWE	HOYDENED	HUCKLES	HUGGABLE
HOUSEWRAP	HOWES	HOYDENING	HUCKLING	HUGGED
HOUSEY	HOWEVER	HOYDENISH	HUCKS	HUGGER
HOUSIER	HOWF	HOYDENISM	HUCKSTER	HUGGERS
HOUSIEST	HOWFED	HOYDENS	HUCKSTERS	HUGGIER
HOUSING	HOWFF	HOYED	HUCKSTERY	HUGGIEST
HOUSINGS	HOWFFED	HOYING	HUDDEN	HUGGING
HOUSLING	HOWFFING	HOYLE	HUDDLE	HUGGY
HOUSLINGS	HOWFFS	HOYLES	HUDDLED	HUGS
HOUSTONIA	HOWFING	HOYS	HUDDLER	HUGY
HOUT	HOWFS	HRYVNA	HUDDLERS	HUH
HOUTED	HOWITZER	HRYVNAS	HUDDLES	HUHU
HOUTING	HOWITZERS	HRYVNIA	HUDDLING	HUHUS
HOUTINGS	HOWK	HRYVNIAS	HUDDUP	HUI
HOUTS	HOWKED	HRYVNYA	HUDNA	HUIA
HOVE	HOWKER	HRYVNYAS	HUDNAS	HUIAS
HOVEA	HOWKERS	HUANACO	HUDUD	HUIC
HOVEAS	HOWKING	HUANACOS	HUDUDS	HUIPIL
HOVED	HOWKS	HUAQUERO	HUE	HUIPILES
HOVEL	HOWL	HUAQUEROS	HUED	HUIPILS
HOVELED	HOWLBACK	HUARACHE	HUELESS	HUIS
HOVELING	HOWLBACKS	HUARACHES	HUER	HUISACHE
HOVELLED	HOWLED	HUARACHO	HUERS	HUISACHES
HOVELLER	HOWLER	HUARACHOS	HUES	HUISSIER
HOVELLERS	HOWLERS	HUB	HUFF	HUISSIERS
HOVELLING	HOWLET	HUBBIES	HUFFED	HUITAIN
HOVELS	HOWLETS	HUBBLIER	HUFFER	HUITAINS
HOVEN	HOWLING	HUBBLIEST	HUFFERS	HULA
HOVER	HOWLINGLY	HUBBLY	HUFFIER	HULAS
HOVERED	HOWLINGS	HUBBUB	HUFFIEST	HULE
HOVERER	HOWLROUND	HUBBUBOO	HUFFILY	HULES
HOVERERS	HOWLS	HUBBUBOOS	HUFFINESS	HULK

HULKED	HUMANIZES	HUMFED	HUMMOCK	HUMPING
HULKIER	HUMANKIND	HUMFING	HUMMOCKED	HUMPLESS
HULKIEST	HUMANLIKE	HUMFS	HUMMOCKS	HUMPLIKE
HULKING	HUMANLY	HUMHUM	HUMMOCKY	HUMPS
HULKS	HUMANNESS	HUMHUMS	HUMMUM	HUMPTIES
HULKY	HUMANOID	HUMIC	HUMMUMS	HUMPTY
HULL	HUMANOIDS	HUMICOLE	HUMMUS	HUMPY
HULLED	HUMANS	HUMICOLES	HUMMUSES	HUMS
HULLER	HUMAS	HUMID	HUMOGEN	HUMSTRUM
HULLERS	HUMATE	HUMIDER	HUMOGENS	HUMSTRUMS
HULLIER	HUMATES	HUMIDEST	HUMONGOUS	HUMUNGOUS
HULLIEST	HUMBLE	HUMIDEX	HUMOR	HUMUS
HULLING	HUMBLEBEE	HUMIDEXES	HUMORAL	HUMUSES
HULLO	HUMBLED	HUMIDICES	HUMORALLY	HUMUSIER
HULLOA	HUMBLER	HUMIDIFY	HUMORED	HUMUSIEST
HULLOAED	HUMBLERS	HUMIDITY	HUMORESK	HUMUSY
HULLOAING	HUMBLES	HUMIDLY	HUMORESKS	HUMVEE
HULLOAS	HUMBLESSE	HUMIDNESS	HUMORFUL	HUMVEES
HULLOED	HUMBLEST	HUMIDOR	HUMORING	HUN
HULLOES	HUMBLING	HUMIDORS	HUMORIST	HUNCH
HULLOING	HUMBLINGS	HUMIFIED	HUMORISTS	HUNCHBACK
HULLOO	HUMBLY	HUMIFIES	HUMORLESS	HUNCHED
HULLOOED	HUMBUCKER	HUMIFY	HUMOROUS	HUNCHES
HULLOOING	HUMBUG	HUMIFYING	HUMORS	HUNCHING
HULLOOS	HUMBUGGED	HUMILIANT	HUMORSOME	HUNDRED
HULLOS	HUMBUGGER	HUMILIATE	HUMOUR	HUNDREDER
HULLS	HUMBUGS	HUMILITY	HUMOURED	HUNDREDOR
HULLY	HUMBUZZ	HUMINT	HUMOURFUL	HUNDREDS
HUM	HUMBUZZES	HUMINTS	HUMOURING	HUNDREDTH
HUMA	HUMDINGER	HUMITE	HUMOURS	HUNG
HUMAN	HUMDRUM	HUMITES	HUMOUS	HUNGAN
HUMANE	HUMDRUMS	HUMITURE	HUMOUSES	HUNGANS
HUMANELY	HUMECT	HUMITURES	HUMP	HUNGER
HUMANER	HUMECTANT	HUMLIE	HUMPBACK	HUNGERED
HUMANEST	HUMECTATE	HUMLIES	HUMPBACKS	HUNGERFUL
HUMANHOOD	HUMECTED	HUMMABLE	HUMPED	HUNGERING
HUMANISE	HUMECTING	HUMMAUM	HUMPEN	HUNGERLY
HUMANISED	HUMECTIVE	HUMMAUMS	HUMPENS	HUNGERS
HUMANISER	HUMECTS	HUMMED	HUMPER	HUNGOVER
HUMANISES	HUMEFIED	HUMMEL	HUMPERS	HUNGRIER
HUMANISM	HUMEFIES	HUMMELLED	HUMPH	HUNGRIEST
HUMANISMS	HUMEFY	HUMMELLER	HUMPHED	HUNGRILY
HUMANIST	HUMEFYING	HUMMELS	HUMPHING	HUNGRY
HUMANISTS	HUMERAL	HUMMER	HUMPHS	HUNH
HUMANITY	HUMERALS	HUMMERS	HUMPIER	HUNK
HUMANIZE	HUMERI	HUMMING	HUMPIES	HUNKER
HUMANIZED	HUMERUS	HUMMINGS	HUMPIEST	HUNKERED
HUMANIZER	HUMF	HUMMLE	HUMPINESS	HUNKERING

HUNKERS	HURDS	HURTLING	HUSSIFS	HYACINE
HUNKEY	HURL	HURTS	HUSSY	HYACINES
HUNKEYS	HURLBAT	HUSBAND	HUSTINGS	HYACINTH
HUNKIE	HURLBATS	HUSBANDED	HUSTLE	HYACINTHS
HUNKIER	HURLED	HUSBANDER	HUSTLED	HYAENA
HUNKIES	HURLER	HUSBANDLY	HUSTLER	HYAENAS
HUNKIEST	HURLERS	HUSBANDRY	HUSTLERS	HYAENIC
HUNKS	HURLEY	HUSBANDS	HUSTLES	HYALIN
HUNKSES	HURLEYS	HUSH	HUSTLING	HYALINE
HUNKY	HURLIES	HUSHABIED	HUSTLINGS	HYALINES
HUNNISH	HURLING	HUSHABIES	HUSWIFE	HYALINISE
HUNS	HURLINGS	HUSHABY	HUSWIFES	HYALINIZE
HUNT	HURLS	HUSHABYE	HUSWIVES	HYALINS
HUNTABLE	HURLY	HUSHED	HUT	HYALITE
HUNTAWAY	HURRA	HUSHEDLY	HUTCH	HYALITES
HUNTAWAYS	HURRAED	HUSHER	HUTCHED	HYALOGEN
HUNTED	HURRAH	HUSHERED	HUTCHES	HYALOGENS
HUNTEDLY	HURRAHED	HUSHERING	HUTCHIE	HYALOID
HUNTER	HURRAHING	HUSHERS	HUTCHIES	HYALOIDS
HUNTERS	HURRAHS	HUSHES	HUTCHING	HYALONEMA
HUNTING	HURRAING	HUSHFUL	HUTIA	HYBRID
HUNTINGS	HURRAS	HUSHIER	HUTIAS	HYBRIDISE
HUNTRESS	HURRAY	HUSHIEST	HUTLIKE	HYBRIDISM
HUNTS	HURRAYED	HUSHING	HUTMENT	HYBRIDIST
HUNTSMAN	HURRAYING	HUSHPUPPY	HUTMENTS	HYBRIDITY
HUNTSMEN	HURRAYS	HUSHY	HUTS	HYBRIDIZE
HUP	HURRICANE	HUSK	HUTTED	HYBRIDOMA
HUPIRO	HURRICANO	HUSKED	HUTTING	HYBRIDOUS
HUPIROS	HURRIED	HUSKER	HUTTINGS	HYBRIDS
HUPPAH	HURRIEDLY	HUSKERS	HUTZPA	HYBRIS
HUPPAHS	HURRIER	HUSKIER	HUTZPAH	HYBRISES
HUPPED	HURRIERS	HUSKIES	HUTZPAHS	HYBRISTIC
HUPPING	HURRIES	HUSKIEST	HUTZPAS	HYDANTOIN
HUPPOT	HURRY	HUSKILY	HUZOOR	HYDATHODE
HUPPOTH	HURRYING	HUSKINESS	HUZOORS	HYDATID
HUPS	HURRYINGS	HUSKING	HUZZA	HYDATIDS
HURCHEON	HURST	HUSKINGS	HUZZAED	HYDATOID
HURCHEONS	HURSTS	HUSKLIKE	HUZZAH	HYDRA
HURDEN	HURT	HUSKS	HUZZAHED	HYDRACID
HURDENS	HURTER	HUSKY	HUZZAHING	HYDRACIDS
HURDIES	HURTERS	HUSO	HUZZAHS	HYDRAE
HURDLE	HURTFUL	HUSOS	HUZZAING	HYDRAEMIA
HURDLED	HURTFULLY	HUSS	HUZZAS	HYDRAGOG
HURDLER	HURTING	HUSSAR	HUZZIES	HYDRAGOGS
HURDLERS	HURTLE	HUSSARS	HUZZY	HYDRANGEA
HURDLES	HURTLED	HUSSES	HWAN	HYDRANT
HURDLING	HURTLES	HUSSIES	HWYL	HYDRANTH
HURDLINGS	HURTLESS	HUSSIF	HWYLS	HYDRANTHS

HYDRANTS	HYDRONAUT	HYGIEIST	HYMENEALS	HYPERBOLE
HYDRAS	HYDRONIC	HYGIEISTS	HYMENEAN	HYPERCUBE
HYDRASE	HYDRONIUM	HYGIENE	HYMENEANS	HYPEREMIA
HYDRASES	HYDROPATH	HYGIENES	HYMENIA	HYPEREMIC
HYDRASTIS	HYDROPIC	HYGIENIC	HYMENIAL	HYPERER
HYDRATE	HYDROPS	HYGIENICS	HYMENIUM	HYPEREST
HYDRATED	HYDROPSES	HYGIENIST	HYMENIUMS	HYPERFINE
HYDRATES	HYDROPSY	HYGRISTOR	HYMENS	HYPERGAMY
HYDRATING	HYDROPTIC	HYGRODEIK	HYMN	HYPERGOL
HYDRATION	HYDROPULT	HYGROLOGY	HYMNAL	HYPERGOLS
HYDRATOR	HYDROS	HYGROMA	HYMNALS	HYPERICIN
HYDRATORS	HYDROSERE	HYGROMAS	HYMNARIES	HYPERICUM
HYDRAULIC	HYDROSKI	HYGROMATA	HYMNARY	HYPERLINK
HYDRAZIDE	HYDROSKIS	HYGROPHIL	HYMNBOOK	HYPERMART
HYDRAZINE	HYDROSOL	HYGROSTAT	HYMNBOOKS	HYPERNOVA
HYDRAZOIC	HYDROSOLS	HYING	HYMNED	HYPERNYM
HYDREMIA	HYDROSOMA	HYKE	HYMNIC	HYPERNYMS
HYDREMIAS	HYDROSOME	HYKES	HYMNING	HYPERNYMY
HYDRIA	HYDROSTAT	HYLA	HYMNIST	HYPERON
HYDRIAE	HYDROUS	HYLAS	HYMNISTS	HYPERONS
HYDRIC	HYDROVANE	HYLDING	HYMNLESS	HYPEROPE
HYDRID	HYDROXIDE	HYLDINGS	HYMNLIKE	HYPEROPES
HYDRIDE	HYDROXIUM	HYLE	HYMNODIES	HYPEROPIA
HYDRIDES	HYDROXY	HYLEG	HYMNODIST	HYPEROPIC
HYDRIDS	HYDROXYL	HYLEGS	HYMNODY	HYPERPNEA
HYDRILLA	HYDROXYLS	HYLES	HYMNOLOGY	HYPERPURE
HYDRILLAS	HYDROZOA	HYLIC	HYMNS	HYPERREAL
HYDRIODIC	HYDROZOAN	HYLICISM	HYNDE	HYPERS
HYDRO	HYDROZOON	HYLICISMS	HYNDES	HYPERTEXT
HYDROCAST	HYDYNE	HYLICIST	HYOID	HYPES
HYDROCELE	HYDYNES	HYLICISTS	HYOIDAL	HYPESTER
HYDROFOIL	HYE	HYLISM	HYOIDEAN	HYPESTERS
HYDROGEL	HYED	HYLISMS	HYOIDS	HYPETHRAL
HYDROGELS	HYEING	HYLIST	HYOSCINE	HYPHA
HYDROGEN	HYEN	HYLISTS	HYOSCINES	HYPHAE
HYDROGENS	HYENA	HYLOBATE	HYP	HYPHAL
HYDROID	HYENAS	HYLOBATES	HYPALGIA	HYPHEMIA
HYDROIDS	HYENIC	HYLOIST	HYPALGIAS	HYPHEMIAS
HYDROLASE	HYENINE	HYLOISTS	HYPALLAGE	HYPHEN
HYDROLOGY	HYENOID	HYLOPHYTE	HYPANTHIA	HYPHENATE
HYDROLYSE	HYENS	HYLOZOIC	HYPATE	HYPHENED
HYDROLYTE	HYES	HYLOZOISM	HYPATES	HYPHENIC
HYDROLYZE	HYETAL	HYLOZOIST	HYPE	HYPHENING
HYDROMA	HYETOLOGY	HYMEN	HYPED	HYPHENISE
HYDROMAS	HYGEIST	HYMENAEAL	HYPER	HYPHENISM
HYDROMATA	HYGEISTS	HYMENAEAN	HYPERACID	HYPHENIZE
HYDROMEL	HYGGE	HYMENAL	HYPERARID	HYPHENS
HYDROMELS	HYGGES	HYMENEAL	HYPERBOLA	HYPHIES

HYPHY	HYPNOTOID	HYPOGEA	HYPOPLOID	HYPPING
HYPING	HYPNUM	HYPOGEAL	HYPOPNEA	HYPS
HYPINGS	HYPNUMS	HYPOGEAN	HYPOPNEAS	HYPURAL
HYPINOSES	HYPO	HYPOGENE	HYPOPNEIC	HYRACES
HYPINOSIS	HYPOACID	HYPOGENIC	HYPOPNOEA	HYRACOID
HYPNIC	HYPOBARIC	HYPOGEOUS	HYPOPYON	HYRACOIDS
HYPNICS	HYPOBLAST	HYPOGEUM	HYPOPYONS	HYRAX
HYPNOGENY	HYPOBOLE	HYPOGYNY	HYPOS	HYRAXES
HYPNOID	HYPOBOLES	HYPOID	HYPOSTOME	HYSON
HYPNOIDAL	HYPOCAUST	HYPOIDS	HYPOSTYLE	HYSONS
HYPNOLOGY	HYPOCIST	HYPOING	HYPOTAXES	HYSSOP
HYPNONE	HYPOCISTS	HYPOMANIA	HYPOTAXIS	HYSSOPS
HYPNONES	HYPOCOTYL	HYPOMANIC	HYPOTHEC	HYSTERIA
HYPNOSES	HYPOCRISY	HYPOMORPH	HYPOTHECA	HYSTERIAS
HYPNOSIS	HYPOCRITE	HYPONASTY	HYPOTHECS	HYSTERIC
HYPNOTEE	HYPODERM	HYPONEA	HYPOTONIA	HYSTERICS
HYPNOTEES	HYPODERMA	HYPONEAS	HYPOTONIC	HYSTEROID
HYPNOTIC	HYPODERMS	HYPONOIA	HYPOXEMIA	HYTE
HYPNOTICS	HYPOED	HYPONOIAS	HYPOXEMIC	HYTHE
HYPNOTISE	HYPOGAEA	HYPONYM	HYPOXIA	HYTHES
HYPNOTISM	HYPOGAEAL	HYPONYMS	HYPOXIAS	
HYPNOTIST	HYPOGAEAN	HYPONYMY	HYPOXIC	
HYPNOTIZE	HYPOGAEUM	HYPOPHYGE	HYPPED	

H

I

IAMB	ICECAP	ICHNOLITE	ICONISED	IDEALIZER
IAMBI	ICECAPPED	ICHNOLOGY	ICONISES	IDEALIZES
IAMBIC	ICECAPS	ICHOR	ICONISING	IDEALLESS
IAMBICS	ICED	ICHOROUS	ICONIZE	IDEALLY
IAMBIST	ICEFALL	ICHORS	ICONIZED	IDEALNESS
IAMBISTS	ICEFALLS	ICHS	ICONIZES	IDEALOGUE
IAMBS	ICEFIELD	ICHTHIC	ICONIZING	IDEALOGY
IAMBUS	ICEFIELDS	ICHTHYIC	ICONOLOGY	IDEALS
IAMBUSES	ICEFISH	ICHTHYOID	ICONOSTAS	IDEAS
IANTHINE	ICEFISHED	ICHTHYS	ICONS	IDEATA
IATRIC	ICEFISHES	ICHTHYSES	ICTAL	IDEATE
IATRICAL	ICEHOUSE	ICICLE	ICTERIC	IDEATED
IATROGENY	ICEHOUSES	ICICLED	ICTERICAL	IDEATES
IBADAH	ICEKHANA	ICICLES	ICTERICS	IDEATING
IBADAT	ICEKHANAS	ICIER	ICTERID	IDEATION
IBERIS	ICELESS	ICIEST	ICTERIDS	IDEATIONS
IBERISES	ICELIKE	ICILY	ICTERINE	IDEATIVE
IBEX	ICEMAKER	ICINESS	ICTERUS	IDEATUM
IBEXES	ICEMAKERS	ICINESSES	ICTERUSES	IDEE
IBICES	ICEMAN	ICING	ICTIC	IDEES
IBIDEM	ICEMEN	ICINGS	ICTUS	IDEM
IBIS	ICEPACK	ICK	ICTUSES	IDENT
IBISES	ICEPACKS	ICKER	ICY	IDENTIC
IBOGAINE	ICER	ICKERS	ID	IDENTICAL
IBOGAINES	ICERS	ICKIER	IDANT	IDENTIFY
IBRIK	ICES	ICKIEST	IDANTS	IDENTIKIT
IBRIKS	ICESCAPE	ICKILY	IDE	IDENTITY
IBUPROFEN	ICESCAPES	ICKINESS	IDEA	IDENTS
ICE	ICESTONE	ICKLE	IDEAED	IDEOGRAM
ICEBALL	ICESTONES	ICKLER	IDEAL	IDEOGRAMS
ICEBALLS	ICEWINE	ICKLEST	IDEALESS	IDEOGRAPH
ICEBERG	ICEWINES	ICKS	IDEALISE	IDEOLOGIC
ICEBERGS	ICEWORM	ICKY	IDEALISED	IDEOLOGUE
ICEBLINK	ICEWORMS	ICON	IDEALISER	IDEOLOGY
ICEBLINKS	ICH	ICONES	IDEALISES	IDEOMOTOR
ICEBOAT	ICHABOD	ICONIC	IDEALISM	IDEOPHONE
ICEBOATED	ICHED	ICONICAL	IDEALISMS	IDEOPOLIS
ICEBOATER	ICHES	ICONICITY	IDEALIST	IDES
ICEBOATS	ICHING	ICONIFIED	IDEALISTS	IDIOBLAST
ICEBOUND	ICHNEUMON	ICONIFIES	IDEALITY	IDIOCIES
ICEBOX	ICHNITE	ICONIFY	IDEALIZE	IDIOCY
ICEBOXES	ICHNITES	ICONISE	IDEALIZED	IDIOGRAM

IDIOGRAMS	IDOLISERS	IGLOO	IGUANA	ILLAPSED
IDIOGRAPH	IDOLISES	IGLOOS	IGUANAS	ILLAPSES
IDIOLECT	IDOLISING	IGLU	IGUANIAN	ILLAPSING
IDIOLECTS	IDOLISM	IGLUS	IGUANIANS	ILLATION
IDIOM	IDOLISMS	IGNARO	IGUANID	ILLATIONS
IDIOMATIC	IDOLIST	IGNAROES	IGUANIDS	ILLATIVE
IDIOMS	IDOLISTS	IGNAROS	IGUANODON	ILLATIVES
IDIOPATHY	IDOLIZE	IGNATIA	IHRAM	ILLAWARRA
IDIOPHONE	IDOLIZED	IGNATIAS	IHRAMS	ILLEGAL
IDIOPLASM	IDOLIZER	IGNEOUS	IJTIHAD	ILLEGALLY
IDIOT	IDOLIZERS	IGNESCENT	IJTIHADS	ILLEGALS
IDIOTCIES	IDOLIZES	IGNIFIED	IKAN	ILLEGIBLE
IDIOTCY	IDOLIZING	IGNIFIES	IKANS	ILLEGIBLY
IDIOTIC	IDOLON	IGNIFY	IKAT	ILLER
IDIOTICAL	IDOLS	IGNIFYING	IKATS	ILLEST
IDIOTICON	IDOLUM	IGNITABLE	IKEBANA	ILLIAD
IDIOTISH	IDONEITY	IGNITE	IKEBANAS	ILLIADS
IDIOTISM	IDONEOUS	IGNITED	IKON	ILLIBERAL
IDIOTISMS	IDS	IGNITER	IKONS	ILLICIT
IDIOTS	IDYL	IGNITERS	ILEA	ILLICITLY
IDIOTYPE	IDYLIST	IGNITES	ILEAC	ILLIMITED
IDIOTYPES	IDYLISTS	IGNITIBLE	ILEAL	ILLINIUM
IDIOTYPIC	IDYLL	IGNITING	ILEITIDES	ILLINIUMS
IDLE	IDYLLIAN	IGNITION	ILEITIS	ILLIPE
IDLED	IDYLLIC	IGNITIONS	ILEITISES	ILLIPES
IDLEHOOD	IDYLLIST	IGNITOR	ILEOSTOMY	ILLIQUID
IDLEHOODS	IDYLLISTS	IGNITORS	ILEUM	ILLISION
IDLENESS	IDYLLS	IGNITRON	ILEUS	ILLISIONS
IDLER	IDYLS	IGNITRONS	ILEUSES	ILLITE
IDLERS	IF	IGNOBLE	ILEX	ILLITES
IDLES	IFF	IGNOBLER	ILEXES	ILLITIC
IDLESSE	IFFIER	IGNOBLEST	ILIA	ILLNESS
IDLESSES	IFFIEST	IGNOBLY	ILIAC	ILLNESSES
IDLEST	IFFILY	IGNOMIES	ILIACI	ILLOGIC
IDLING	IFFINESS	IGNOMINY	ILIACUS	ILLOGICAL
IDLY	IFFY	IGNOMY	ILIACUSES	ILLOGICS
IDOCRASE	IFS	IGNORABLE	ILIAD	ILLS
IDOCRASES	IFTAR	IGNORAMI	ILIADS	ILLTH
IDOL	IFTARS	IGNORAMUS	ILIAL	ILLTHS
IDOLA	IGAD	IGNORANCE	ILICES	ILLUDE
IDOLATER	IGAPO	IGNORANT	ILIUM	ILLUDED
IDOLATERS	IGAPOS	IGNORANTS	ILK	ILLUDES
IDOLATOR	IGARAPE	IGNORE	ILKA	ILLUDING
IDOLATORS	IGARAPES	IGNORED	ILKADAY	ILLUME
IDOLATRY	IGG	IGNORER	ILKADAYS	ILLUMED
IDOLISE	IGGED	IGNORERS	ILKS	ILLUMES
IDOLISED	IGGING	IGNORES	ILL	ILLUMINE
IDOLISER	IGGS	IGNORING	ILLAPSE	ILLUMINED

ILLUMINER	IMAMATES	IMBLAZE	IMBURSE	IMMEDIATE
ILLUMINES	IMAMS	IMBLAZED	IMBURSED	IMMENSE
ILLUMING	IMARET	IMBLAZES	IMBURSES	IMMENSELY
ILLUPI	IMARETS	IMBLAZING	IMBURSING	IMMENSER
ILLUPIS	IMARI	IMBODIED	IMID	IMMENSEST
ILLUSION	IMARIS	IMBODIES	IMIDAZOLE	IMMENSITY
ILLUSIONS	IMAUM	IMBODY	IMIDE	IMMERGE
ILLUSIVE	IMAUMS	IMBODYING	IMIDES	IMMERGED
ILLUSORY	IMBALANCE	IMBOLDEN	IMIDIC	IMMERGES
ILLUVIA	IMBALM	IMBOLDENS	IMIDO	IMMERGING
ILLUVIAL	IMBALMED	IMBORDER	IMIDS	IMMERSE
ILLUVIATE	IMBALMER	IMBORDERS	IMINAZOLE	IMMERSED
ILLUVIUM	IMBALMERS	IMBOSK	IMINE	IMMERSER
ILLUVIUMS	IMBALMING	IMBOSKED	IMINES	IMMERSERS
ILLY	IMBALMS	IMBOSKING	IMINO	IMMERSES
ILMENITE	IMBAR	IMBOSKS	IMINOUREA	IMMERSING
ILMENITES	IMBARK	IMBOSOM	IMIPENEM	IMMERSION
IMAGE	IMBARKED	IMBOSOMED	IMIPENEMS	IMMERSIVE
IMAGEABLE	IMBARKING	IMBOSOMS	IMITABLE	IMMESH
IMAGED	IMBARKS	IMBOSS	IMITANCY	IMMESHED
IMAGELESS	IMBARRED	IMBOSSED	IMITANT	IMMESHES
IMAGER	IMBARRING	IMBOSSES	IMITANTS	IMMESHING
IMAGERIES	IMBARS	IMBOSSING	IMITATE	IMMEW
IMAGERS	IMBASE	IMBOWER	IMITATED	IMMEWED
IMAGERY	IMBASED	IMBOWERED	IMITATES	IMMEWING
IMAGES	IMBASES	IMBOWERS	IMITATING	IMMEWS
IMAGINAL	IMBASING	IMBRANGLE	IMITATION	IMMIES
IMAGINARY	IMBATHE	IMBRAST	IMITATIVE	IMMIGRANT
IMAGINE	IMBATHED	IMBREX	IMITATOR	IMMIGRATE
IMAGINED	IMBATHES	IMBRICATE	IMITATORS	IMMINENCE
IMAGINEER	IMBATHING	IMBRICES	IMMANACLE	IMMINENCY
IMAGINER	IMBECILE	IMBROGLIO	IMMANE	IMMINENT
IMAGINERS	IMBECILES	IMBROWN	IMMANELY	IMMINGLE
IMAGINES	IMBECILIC	IMBROWNED	IMMANENCE	IMMINGLED
IMAGING	IMBED	IMBROWNS	IMMANENCY	IMMINGLES
IMAGINGS	IMBEDDED	IMBRUE	IMMANENT	IMMINUTE
IMAGINING	IMBEDDING	IMBRUED	IMMANITY	IMMISSION
IMAGINIST	IMBEDS	IMBRUES	IMMANTLE	IMMIT
IMAGISM	IMBIBE	IMBRUING	IMMANTLED	IMMITS
IMAGISMS	IMBIBED	IMBRUTE	IMMANTLES	IMMITTED
IMAGIST	IMBIBER	IMBRUTED	IMMASK	IMMITTING
IMAGISTIC	IMBIBERS	IMBRUTES	IMMASKED	IMMIX
IMAGISTS	IMBIBES	IMBRUTING	IMMASKING	IMMIXED
IMAGO	IMBIBING	IMBUE	IMMASKS	IMMIXES
IMAGOES	IMBITTER	IMBUED	IMMATURE	IMMIXING
IMAGOS	IMBITTERS	IMBUEMENT	IMMATURER	IMMIXTURE
IMAM	IMBIZO	IMBUES	IMMATURES	IMMOBILE
IMAMATE	IMBIZOS	IMBUING	IMMEDIACY	IMMODEST

IMMODESTY	IMPAINT	IMPASTOED	IMPERFECT	IMPLEADER
IMMOLATE	IMPAINTED	IMPASTOS	IMPERIA	IMPLEADS
IMMOLATED	IMPAINTS	IMPATIENS	IMPERIAL	IMPLED
IMMOLATES	IMPAIR	IMPATIENT	IMPERIALS	IMPLEDGE
IMMOLATOR	IMPAIRED	IMPAVE	IMPERIL	IMPLEDGED
IMMOMENT	IMPAIRER	IMPAVED	IMPERILED	IMPLEDGES
IMMORAL	IMPAIRERS	IMPAVES	IMPERILS	IMPLEMENT
IMMORALLY	IMPAIRING	IMPAVID	IMPERIOUS	IMPLETE
IMMORTAL	IMPAIRS	IMPAVIDLY	IMPERIUM	IMPLETED
IMMORTALS	IMPALA	IMPAVING	IMPERIUMS	IMPLETES
IMMOTILE	IMPALAS	IMPAWN	IMPETICOS	IMPLETING
IMMOVABLE	IMPALE	IMPAWNED	IMPETIGO	IMPLETION
IMMOVABLY	IMPALED	IMPAWNING	IMPETIGOS	IMPLEX
IMMUNE	IMPALER	IMPAWNS	IMPETRATE	IMPLEXES
IMMUNER	IMPALERS	IMPEACH	IMPETUOUS	IMPLEXION
IMMUNES	IMPALES	IMPEACHED	IMPETUS	IMPLICATE
IMMUNEST	IMPALING	IMPEACHER	IMPETUSES	IMPLICIT
IMMUNISE	IMPANATE	IMPEACHES	IMPHEE	IMPLICITY
IMMUNISED	IMPANEL	IMPEARL	IMPHEES	IMPLIED
IMMUNISER	IMPANELED	IMPEARLED	IMPI	IMPLIEDLY
IMMUNISES	IMPANELS	IMPEARLS	IMPIES	IMPLIES
IMMUNITY	IMPANNEL	IMPECCANT	IMPIETIES	IMPLODE
IMMUNIZE	IMPANNELS	IMPED	IMPIETY	IMPLODED
IMMUNIZED	IMPARITY	IMPEDANCE	IMPING	IMPLODENT
IMMUNIZER	IMPARK	IMPEDE	IMPINGE	IMPLODES
IMMUNIZES	IMPARKED	IMPEDED	IMPINGED	IMPLODING
IMMUNOGEN	IMPARKING	IMPEDER	IMPINGENT	IMPLORE
IMMURE	IMPARKS	IMPEDERS	IMPINGER	IMPLORED
IMMURED	IMPARL	IMPEDES	IMPINGERS	IMPLORER
IMMURES	IMPARLED	IMPEDING	IMPINGES	IMPLORERS
IMMURING	IMPARLING	IMPEDOR	IMPINGING	IMPLORES
IMMUTABLE	IMPARLS	IMPEDORS	IMPINGS	IMPLORING
IMMUTABLY	IMPART	IMPEL	IMPIOUS	IMPLOSION
IMMY	IMPARTED	IMPELLED	IMPIOUSLY	IMPLOSIVE
IMP	IMPARTER	IMPELLENT	IMPIS	IMPLUNGE
IMPACABLE	IMPARTERS	IMPELLER	IMPISH	IMPLUNGED
IMPACT	IMPARTIAL	IMPELLERS	IMPISHLY	IMPLUNGES
IMPACTED	IMPARTING	IMPELLING	IMPLANT	IMPLUVIA
IMPACTER	IMPARTS	IMPELLOR	IMPLANTED	IMPLUVIUM
IMPACTERS	IMPASSE	IMPELLORS	IMPLANTER	IMPLY
IMPACTFUL	IMPASSES	IMPELS	IMPLANTS	IMPLYING
IMPACTING	IMPASSION	IMPEND	IMPLATE	IMPOCKET
IMPACTION	IMPASSIVE	IMPENDED	IMPLATED	IMPOCKETS
IMPACTITE	IMPASTE	IMPENDENT	IMPLATES	IMPOLDER
IMPACTIVE	IMPASTED	IMPENDING	IMPLATING	IMPOLDERS
IMPACTOR	IMPASTES	IMPENDS	IMPLEACH	IMPOLICY
IMPACTORS	IMPASTING	IMPENNATE	IMPLEAD	IMPOLITE
IMPACTS	IMPASTO	IMPERATOR	IMPLEADED	IMPOLITER

IMPOLITIC	IMPRECATE	IMPUGNING	INANITY	INBY
IMPONE	IMPRECISE	IMPUGNS	INAPT	INBYE
IMPONED	IMPREGN	IMPULSE	INAPTER	INCAGE
IMPONENT	IMPREGNED	IMPULSED	INAPTEST	INCAGED
IMPONENTS	IMPREGNS	IMPULSES	INAPTLY	INCAGES
IMPONES	IMPRESA	IMPULSING	INAPTNESS	INCAGING
IMPONING	IMPRESARI	IMPULSION	INARABLE	INCANT
IMPOROUS	IMPRESAS	IMPULSIVE	INARCH	INCANTED
IMPORT	IMPRESE	IMPUNDULU	INARCHED	INCANTING
IMPORTANT	IMPRESES	IMPUNITY	INARCHES	INCANTS
IMPORTED	IMPRESS	IMPURE	INARCHING	INCAPABLE
IMPORTER	IMPRESSE	IMPURELY	INARM	INCAPABLY
IMPORTERS	IMPRESSED	IMPURER	INARMED	INCARNATE
IMPORTING	IMPRESSER	IMPUREST	INARMING	INCASE
IMPORTS	IMPRESSES	IMPURITY	INARMS	INCASED
IMPORTUNE	IMPREST	IMPURPLE	INASMUCH	INCASES
IMPOSABLE	IMPRESTS	IMPURPLED	INAUDIBLE	INCASING
IMPOSE	IMPRIMIS	IMPURPLES	INAUDIBLY	INCAUTION
IMPOSED	IMPRINT	IMPUTABLE	INAUGURAL	INCAVE
IMPOSER	IMPRINTED	IMPUTABLY	INAURATE	INCAVED
IMPOSERS	IMPRINTER	IMPUTE	INAURATED	INCAVES
IMPOSES	IMPRINTS	IMPUTED	INAURATES	INCAVI
IMPOSEX	IMPRISON	IMPUTER	INBEING	INCAVING
IMPOSEXES	IMPRISONS	IMPUTERS	INBEINGS	INCAVO
IMPOSING	IMPRO	IMPUTES	INBENT	INCEDE
IMPOST	IMPROBITY	IMPUTING	INBOARD	INCEDED
IMPOSTED	IMPROMPTU	IMSHI	INBOARDS	INCEDES
IMPOSTER	IMPROPER	IMSHY	INBORN	INCEDING
IMPOSTERS	IMPROS	IN	INBOUND	INCEL
IMPOSTING	IMPROV	INABILITY	INBOUNDED	INCELS
IMPOSTOR	IMPROVE	INACTION	INBOUNDS	INCENSE
IMPOSTORS	IMPROVED	INACTIONS	INBOX	INCENSED
IMPOSTS	IMPROVER	INACTIVE	INBOXES	INCENSER
IMPOSTUME	IMPROVERS	INAIDABLE	INBREAK	INCENSERS
IMPOSTURE	IMPROVES	INAMORATA	INBREAKS	INCENSES
IMPOT	IMPROVING	INAMORATI	INBREATHE	INCENSING
IMPOTENCE	IMPROVISE	INAMORATO	INBRED	INCENSOR
IMPOTENCY	IMPROVS	INANE	INBREDS	INCENSORS
IMPOTENT	IMPRUDENT	INANELY	INBREED	INCENSORY
IMPOTENTS	IMPS	INANENESS	INBREEDER	INCENT
IMPOTS	IMPSONITE	INANER	INBREEDS	INCENTED
IMPOUND	IMPUDENCE	INANES	INBRING	INCENTER
IMPOUNDED	IMPUDENCY	INANEST	INBRINGS	INCENTERS
IMPOUNDER	IMPUDENT	INANGA	INBROUGHT	INCENTING
IMPOUNDS	IMPUGN	INANGAS	INBUILT	INCENTIVE
IMPOWER	IMPUGNED	INANIMATE	INBURNING	INCENTRE
IMPOWERED	IMPUGNER	INANITIES	INBURST	INCENTRES
IMPOWERS	IMPUGNERS	INANITION	INBURSTS	INCENTS

INDICIUMS

INCEPT	INCISORY	INCOME	INCULT	INDELIBLE
INCEPTED	INCISURAL	INCOMER	INCUMBENT	INDELIBLY
INCEPTING	INCISURE	INCOMERS	INCUMBER	INDEMNIFY
INCEPTION	INCISURES	INCOMES	INCUMBERS	INDEMNITY
INCEPTIVE	INCITABLE	INCOMING	INCUNABLE	INDENE
INCEPTOR	INCITANT	INCOMINGS	INCUR	INDENES
INCEPTORS	INCITANTS	INCOMMODE	INCURABLE	INDENT
INCEPTS	INCITE	INCOMPACT	INCURABLY	INDENTED
INCERTAIN	INCITED	INCONDITE	INCURIOUS	INDENTER
INCESSANT	INCITER	INCONIE	INCURRED	INDENTERS
INCEST	INCITERS	INCONNU	INCURRENT	INDENTING
INCESTS	INCITES	INCONNUE	INCURRING	INDENTION
INCH	INCITING	INCONNUES	INCURS	INDENTOR
INCHASE	INCIVIL	INCONNUS	INCURSION	INDENTORS
INCHASED	INCIVISM	INCONY	INCURSIVE	INDENTS
INCHASES	INCIVISMS	INCORPSE	INCURVATE	INDENTURE
INCHASING	INCLASP	INCORPSED	INCURVE	INDEVOUT
INCHED	INCLASPED	INCORPSES	INCURVED	INDEW
INCHER	INCLASPS	INCORRECT	INCURVES	INDEWED
INCHERS	INCLE	INCORRUPT	INCURVING	INDEWING
INCHES	INCLEMENT	INCREASE	INCURVITY	INDEWS
INCHING	INCLES	INCREASED	INCUS	INDEX
INCHMEAL	INCLINE	INCREASER	INCUSE	INDEXABLE
INCHOATE	INCLINED	INCREASES	INCUSED	INDEXAL
INCHOATED	INCLINER	INCREATE	INCUSES	INDEXED
INCHOATES	INCLINERS	INCREMATE	INCUSING	INDEXER
INCHPIN	INCLINES	INCREMENT	INCUT	INDEXERS
INCHPINS	INCLINING	INCRETION	INCUTS	INDEXES
INCHTAPE	INCLIP	INCRETORY	INDABA	INDEXICAL
INCHTAPES	INCLIPPED	INCROSS	INDABAS	INDEXING
INCHWORM	INCLIPS	INCROSSED	INDAGATE	INDEXINGS
INCHWORMS	INCLOSE	INCROSSES	INDAGATED	INDEXLESS
INCIDENCE	INCLOSED	INCRUST	INDAGATES	INDIA
INCIDENT	INCLOSER	INCRUSTED	INDAGATOR	INDIAS
INCIDENTS	INCLOSERS	INCRUSTS	INDAMIN	INDICAN
INCIPIENT	INCLOSES	INCUBATE	INDAMINE	INDICANS
INCIPIT	INCLOSING	INCUBATED	INDAMINES	INDICANT
INCIPITS	INCLOSURE	INCUBATES	INDAMINS	INDICANTS
INCISAL	INCLUDE	INCUBATOR	INDART	INDICATE
INCISE	INCLUDED	INCUBI	INDARTED	INDICATED
INCISED	INCLUDES	INCUBOUS	INDARTING	INDICATES
INCISES	INCLUDING	INCUBUS	INDARTS	INDICATOR
INCISING	INCLUSION	INCUBUSES	INDEBTED	INDICES
INCISION	INCLUSIVE	INCUDAL	INDECENCY	INDICIA
INCISIONS	INCOG	INCUDATE	INDECENT	INDICIAL
INCISIVE	INCOGNITA	INCUDES	INDECORUM	INDICIAS
INCISOR	INCOGNITO	INCULCATE	INDEED	INDICIUM
INCISORS	INCOGS	INCULPATE	INDEEDY	INDICIUMS

INDICT	INDOCIBLE	INDUCTILE	INEBRIATE	INFAMING
INDICTED	INDOCILE	INDUCTING	INEBRIETY	INFAMISE
INDICTEE	INDOL	INDUCTION	INEBRIOUS	INFAMISED
INDICTEES	INDOLE	INDUCTIVE	INEDIBLE	INFAMISES
INDICTER	INDOLENCE	INDUCTOR	INEDIBLY	INFAMIZE
INDICTERS	INDOLENCY	INDUCTORS	INEDITA	INFAMIZED
INDICTING	INDOLENT	INDUCTS	INEDITED	INFAMIZES
INDICTION	INDOLES	INDUE	INEFFABLE	INFAMOUS
INDICTOR	INDOLS	INDUED	INEFFABLY	INFAMY
INDICTORS	INDOOR	INDUES	INELASTIC	INFANCIES
INDICTS	INDOORS	INDUING	INELEGANT	INFANCY
INDIE	INDORSE	INDULGE	INEPT	INFANT
INDIES	INDORSED	INDULGED	INEPTER	INFANTA
INDIGEN	INDORSEE	INDULGENT	INEPTEST	INFANTAS
INDIGENCE	INDORSEES	INDULGER	INEPTLY	INFANTE
INDIGENCY	INDORSER	INDULGERS	INEPTNESS	INFANTEER
INDIGENE	INDORSERS	INDULGES	INEQUABLE	INFANTES
INDIGENES	INDORSES	INDULGING	INEQUITY	INFANTILE
INDIGENS	INDORSING	INDULIN	INERM	INFANTINE
INDIGENT	INDORSOR	INDULINE	INERMOUS	INFANTRY
INDIGENTS	INDORSORS	INDULINES	INERRABLE	INFANTS
INDIGEST	INDOW	INDULINS	INERRABLY	INFARCT
INDIGESTS	INDOWED	INDULT	INERRANCY	INFARCTED
INDIGN	INDOWING	INDULTS	INERRANT	INFARCTS
INDIGNANT	INDOWS	INDUMENTA	INERT	INFARE
INDIGNIFY	INDOXYL	INDUNA	INERTER	INFARES
INDIGNITY	INDOXYLS	INDUNAS	INERTEST	INFATUATE
INDIGNLY	INDRAFT	INDURATE	INERTIA	INFAUNA
INDIGO	INDRAFTS	INDURATED	INERTIAE	INFAUNAE
INDIGOES	INDRAUGHT	INDURATES	INERTIAL	INFAUNAL
INDIGOID	INDRAWN	INDUSIA	INERTIAS	INFAUNAS
INDIGOIDS	INDRENCH	INDUSIAL	INERTLY	INFAUST
INDIGOS	INDRI	INDUSIATE	INERTNESS	INFECT
INDIGOTIC	INDRIS	INDUSIUM	INERTS	INFECTANT
INDIGOTIN	INDRISES	INDUSTRY	INERUDITE	INFECTED
INDINAVIR	INDUBIOUS	INDUVIAE	INESSIVE	INFECTER
INDIRECT	INDUCE	INDUVIAL	INESSIVES	INFECTERS
INDIRUBIN	INDUCED	INDUVIATE	INEXACT	INFECTING
INDISPOSE	INDUCER	INDWELL	INEXACTLY	INFECTION
INDITE	INDUCERS	INDWELLER	INEXPERT	INFECTIVE
INDITED	INDUCES	INDWELLS	INEXPERTS	INFECTOR
INDITER	INDUCIAE	INDWELT	INFALL	INFECTORS
INDITERS	INDUCIBLE	INDYREF	INFALLING	INFECTS
INDITES	INDUCING	INDYREFS	INFALLS	INFECUND
INDITING	INDUCT	INEARTH	INFAME	INFEED
INDIUM	INDUCTED	INEARTHED	INFAMED	INFEEDS
INDIUMS	INDUCTEE	INEARTHS	INFAMES	INFEFT
INDIVIDUA	INDUCTEES	INEBRIANT	INFAMIES	INFEFTED

INFEFTING	INFINITE	INFLOW	INFRUGAL	INGLOBE
INFEFTS	INFINITES	INFLOWING	INFULA	INGLOBED
INFELT	INFINITY	INFLOWS	INFULAE	INGLOBES
INFEOFF	INFIRM	INFLUENCE	INFURIATE	INGLOBING
INFEOFFED	INFIRMARY	INFLUENT	INFUSCATE	INGLUVIAL
INFEOFFS	INFIRMED	INFLUENTS	INFUSE	INGLUVIES
INFER	INFIRMER	INFLUENZA	INFUSED	INGO
INFERABLE	INFIRMEST	INFLUX	INFUSER	INGOES
INFERABLY	INFIRMING	INFLUXES	INFUSERS	INGOING
INFERE	INFIRMITY	INFLUXION	INFUSES	INGOINGS
INFERENCE	INFIRMLY	INFO	INFUSIBLE	INGOT
INFERIAE	INFIRMS	INFOBAHN	INFUSING	INGOTED
INFERIBLE	INFIX	INFOBAHNS	INFUSION	INGOTING
INFERIOR	INFIXED	INFOLD	INFUSIONS	INGOTS
INFERIORS	INFIXES	INFOLDED	INFUSIVE	INGRAFT
INFERNAL	INFIXING	INFOLDER	INFUSORIA	INGRAFTED
INFERNO	INFIXION	INFOLDERS	INFUSORY	INGRAFTS
INFERNOS	INFIXIONS	INFOLDING	ING	INGRAIN
INFERRED	INFLAME	INFOLDS	INGAN	INGRAINED
INFERRER	INFLAMED	INFOMANIA	INGANS	INGRAINER
INFERRERS	INFLAMER	INFORCE	INGATE	INGRAINS
INFERRING	INFLAMERS	INFORCED	INGATES	INGRAM
INFERS	INFLAMES	INFORCES	INGATHER	INGRAMS
INFERTILE	INFLAMING	INFORCING	INGATHERS	INGRATE
INFEST	INFLATE	INFORM	INGENER	INGRATELY
INFESTANT	INFLATED	INFORMAL	INGENERS	INGRATES
INFESTED	INFLATER	INFORMANT	INGENIOUS	INGRESS
INFESTER	INFLATERS	INFORMED	INGENIUM	INGRESSES
INFESTERS	INFLATES	INFORMER	INGENIUMS	INGROOVE
INFESTING	INFLATING	INFORMERS	INGENU	INGROOVED
INFESTS	INFLATION	INFORMING	INGENUE	INGROOVES
INFICETE	INFLATIVE	INFORMS	INGENUES	INGROSS
INFIDEL	INFLATOR	INFORTUNE	INGENUITY	INGROSSED
INFIDELIC	INFLATORS	INFOS	INGENUOUS	INGROSSES
INFIDELS	INFLATUS	INFOTECH	INGENUS	INGROUND
INFIELD	INFLECT	INFOTECHS	INGEST	INGROUNDS
INFIELDER	INFLECTED	INFOUGHT	INGESTA	INGROUP
INFIELDS	INFLECTOR	INFRA	INGESTED	INGROUPS
INFIGHT	INFLECTS	INFRACT	INGESTING	INGROWING
INFIGHTER	INFLEXED	INFRACTED	INGESTION	INGROWN
INFIGHTS	INFLEXION	INFRACTOR	INGESTIVE	INGROWTH
INFILL	INFLEXURE	INFRACTS	INGESTS	INGROWTHS
INFILLED	INFLICT	INFRARED	INGINE	INGRUM
INFILLING	INFLICTED	INFRAREDS	INGINES	INGRUMS
INFILLS	INFLICTER	INFRINGE	INGLE	INGS
INFIMA	INFLICTOR	INFRINGED	INGLENEUK	INGUINAL
INFIMUM	INFLICTS	INFRINGER	INGLENOOK	INGULF
INFIMUMS	INFLIGHT	INFRINGES	INGLES	INGULFED

INGULFING	INHIBIN	INJECTING	INKLES	INLOCKS
INGULFS	INHIBINS	INJECTION	INKLESS	INLY
INGULPH	INHIBIT	INJECTIVE	INKLIKE	INLYING
INGULPHED	INHIBITED	INJECTOR	INKLING	INMATE
INGULPHS	INHIBITER	INJECTORS	INKLINGS	INMATES
INHABIT	INHIBITOR	INJECTS	INKOSI	INMESH
INHABITED	INHIBITS	INJELLIED	INKOSIS	INMESHED
INHABITER	INHOLDER	INJELLIES	INKPAD	INMESHES
INHABITOR	INHOLDERS	INJELLY	INKPADS	INMESHING
INHABITS	INHOLDING	INJERA	INKPOT	INMIGRANT
INHALABLE	INHOOP	INJERAS	INKPOTS	INMOST
INHALANT	INHOOPED	INJOINT	INKS	INN
INHALANTS	INHOOPING	INJOINTED	INKSPOT	INNAGE
INHALATOR	INHOOPS	INJOINTS	INKSPOTS	INNAGES
INHALE	INHUMAN	INJUNCT	INKSTAIN	INNARDS
INHALED	INHUMANE	INJUNCTED	INKSTAINS	INNATE
INHALER	INHUMANER	INJUNCTS	INKSTAND	INNATELY
INHALERS	INHUMANLY	INJURABLE	INKSTANDS	INNATIVE
INHALES	INHUMATE	INJURE	INKSTONE	INNED
INHALING	INHUMATED	INJURED	INKSTONES	INNER
INHARMONY	INHUMATES	INJURER	INKWELL	INNERLY
INHAUL	INHUME	INJURERS	INKWELLS	INNERMOST
INHAULER	INHUMED	INJURES	INKWOOD	INNERNESS
INHAULERS	INHUMER	INJURIES	INKWOODS	INNERS
INHAULS	INHUMERS	INJURING	INKY	INNERSOLE
INHAUST	INHUMES	INJURIOUS	INLACE	INNERVATE
INHAUSTED	INHUMING	INJURY	INLACED	INNERVE
INHAUSTS	INIA	INJUSTICE	INLACES	INNERVED
INHEARSE	INIMICAL	INK	INLACING	INNERVES
INHEARSED	INION	INKBERRY	INLAID	INNERVING
INHEARSES	INIONS	INKBLOT	INLAND	INNERWEAR
INHERCE	INIQUITY	INKBLOTS	INLANDER	INNING
INHERCED	INISLE	INKED	INLANDERS	INNINGS
INHERCES	INISLED	INKER	INLANDS	INNINGSES
INHERCING	INISLES	INKERS	INLAY	INNIT
INHERE	INISLING	INKHOLDER	INLAYER	INNKEEPER
INHERED	INITIAL	INKHORN	INLAYERS	INNLESS
INHERENCE	INITIALED	INKHORNS	INLAYING	INNOCENCE
INHERENCY	INITIALER	INKHOSI	INLAYINGS	INNOCENCY
INHERENT	INITIALLY	INKHOSIS	INLAYS	INNOCENT
INHERES	INITIALS	INKIER	INLET	INNOCENTS
INHERING	INITIATE	INKIEST	INLETS	INNOCUITY
INHERIT	INITIATED	INKINESS	INLETTING	INNOCUOUS
INHERITED	INITIATES	INKING	INLIER	INNOVATE
INHERITOR	INITIATOR	INKJET	INLIERS	INNOVATED
INHERITS	INJECT	INKJETS	INLOCK	INNOVATES
INHESION	INJECTANT	INKLE	INLOCKED	INNOVATOR
INHESIONS	INJECTED	INKLED	INLOCKING	INNOXIOUS

INNS	INQUIET	INSCULPS	INSHRINES	INSOMUCH
INNUENDO	INQUIETED	INSCULPT	INSIDE	INSOOTH
INNUENDOS	INQUIETLY	INSEAM	INSIDER	INSOUL
INNYARD	INQUIETS	INSEAMED	INSIDERS	INSOULED
INNYARDS	INQUILINE	INSEAMING	INSIDES	INSOULING
INOCULA	INQUINATE	INSEAMS	INSIDIOUS	INSOULS
INOCULANT	INQUIRE	INSECT	INSIGHT	INSOURCE
INOCULATE	INQUIRED	INSECTAN	INSIGHTS	INSOURCED
INOCULUM	INQUIRER	INSECTARY	INSIGNE	INSOURCES
INOCULUMS	INQUIRERS	INSECTEAN	INSIGNIA	INSPAN
INODOROUS	INQUIRES	INSECTILE	INSIGNIAS	INSPANNED
INOPINATE	INQUIRIES	INSECTION	INSINCERE	INSPANS
INORB	INQUIRING	INSECTS	INSINEW	INSPECT
INORBED	INQUIRY	INSECURE	INSINEWED	INSPECTED
INORBING	INQUORATE	INSECURER	INSINEWS	INSPECTOR
INORBS	INRO	INSEEM	INSINUATE	INSPECTS
INORGANIC	INROAD	INSEEMED	INSIPID	INSPHERE
INORNATE	INROADS	INSEEMING	INSIPIDER	INSPHERED
INOSINE	INRUN	INSEEMS	INSIPIDLY	INSPHERES
INOSINES	INRUNS	INSELBERG	INSIPIENT	INSPIRE
INOSITE	INRUSH	INSENSATE	INSIST	INSPIRED
INOSITES	INRUSHES	INSERT	INSISTED	INSPIRER
INOSITOL	INRUSHING	INSERTED	INSISTENT	INSPIRERS
INOSITOLS	INS	INSERTER	INSISTER	INSPIRES
INOTROPE	INSANE	INSERTERS	INSISTERS	INSPIRING
INOTROPES	INSANELY	INSERTING	INSISTING	INSPIRIT
INOTROPIC	INSANER	INSERTION	INSISTS	INSPIRITS
INPATIENT	INSANEST	INSERTS	INSNARE	INSPO
INPAYMENT	INSANIE	INSET	INSNARED	INSPOS
INPHASE	INSANIES	INSETS	INSNARER	INSTABLE
INPOUR	INSANITY	INSETTED	INSNARERS	INSTAGRAM
INPOURED	INSATIATE	INSETTER	INSNARES	INSTAL
INPOURING	INSATIETY	INSETTERS	INSNARING	INSTALL
INPOURS	INSCAPE	INSETTING	INSOFAR	INSTALLED
INPUT	INSCAPES	INSHALLAH	INSOLATE	INSTALLER
INPUTS	INSCIENCE	INSHEATH	INSOLATED	INSTALLS
INPUTTED	INSCIENT	INSHEATHE	INSOLATES	INSTALS
INPUTTER	INSCONCE	INSHEATHS	INSOLE	INSTANCE
INPUTTERS	INSCONCED	INSHELL	INSOLENCE	INSTANCED
INPUTTING	INSCONCES	INSHELLED	INSOLENT	INSTANCES
INQILAB	INSCRIBE	INSHELLS	INSOLENTS	INSTANCY
INQILABS	INSCRIBED	INSHELTER	INSOLES	INSTANT
INQUERE	INSCRIBER	INSHIP	INSOLUBLE	INSTANTER
INQUERED	INSCRIBES	INSHIPPED	INSOLUBLY	INSTANTLY
INQUERES	INSCROLL	INSHIPS	INSOLVENT	INSTANTS
INQUERING	INSCROLLS	INSHORE	INSOMNIA	INSTAR
INQUEST	INSCULP	INSHRINE	INSOMNIAC	INSTARRED
INQUESTS	INSCULPED	INSHRINED	INSOMNIAS	INSTARS

INSTATE	INSURANTS	INTENSATE	INTERFOLD	INTERNET
INSTATED	INSURE	INTENSE	INTERFUSE	INTERNETS
INSTATES	INSURED	INTENSELY	INTERGANG	INTERNING
INSTATING	INSUREDS	INTENSER	INTERGREW	INTERNIST
INSTEAD	INSURER	INTENSEST	INTERGROW	INTERNODE
INSTEP	INSURERS	INTENSIFY	INTERIM	INTERNS
INSTEPS	INSURES	INTENSION	INTERIMS	INTERPAGE
INSTIGATE	INSURGENT	INTENSITY	INTERIOR	INTERPLAY
INSTIL	INSURING	INTENSIVE	INTERIORS	INTERPLED
INSTILL	INSWATHE	INTENT	INTERJECT	INTERPONE
INSTILLED	INSWATHED	INTENTION	INTERJOIN	INTERPOSE
INSTILLER	INSWATHES	INTENTIVE	INTERKNIT	INTERPRET
INSTILLS	INSWEPT	INTENTLY	INTERKNOT	INTERRACE
INSTILS	INSWING	INTENTS	INTERLACE	INTERRAIL
INSTINCT	INSWINGER	INTER	INTERLAID	INTERRED
INSTINCTS	INSWINGS	INTERACT	INTERLAP	INTERREX
INSTITUTE	INTACT	INTERACTS	INTERLAPS	INTERRING
INSTRESS	INTACTLY	INTERAGE	INTERLARD	INTERROW
INSTROKE	INTAGLI	INTERARCH	INTERLAY	INTERRUPT
INSTROKES	INTAGLIO	INTERBANK	INTERLAYS	INTERS
INSTRUCT	INTAGLIOS	INTERBED	INTERLEAF	INTERSECT
INSTRUCTS	INTAKE	INTERBEDS	INTERLEND	INTERSERT
INSUCKEN	INTAKES	INTERBRED	INTERLENT	INTERSEX
INSULA	INTARSIA	INTERCEDE	INTERLINE	INTERTERM
INSULAE	INTARSIAS	INTERCELL	INTERLINK	INTERTEXT
INSULANT	INTEGER	INTERCEPT	INTERLOAN	INTERTIE
INSULANTS	INTEGERS	INTERCITY	INTERLOCK	INTERTIES
INSULAR	INTEGRAL	INTERCLAN	INTERLOOP	INTERTILL
INSULARLY	INTEGRALS	INTERCLUB	INTERLOPE	INTERUNIT
INSULARS	INTEGRAND	INTERCOM	INTERLUDE	INTERVAL
INSULATE	INTEGRANT	INTERCOMS	INTERMALE	INTERVALE
INSULATED	INTEGRATE	INTERCOOL	INTERMAT	INTERVALS
INSULATES	INTEGRIN	INTERCROP	INTERMATS	INTERVEIN
INSULATOR	INTEGRINS	INTERCUT	INTERMENT	INTERVENE
INSULIN	INTEGRITY	INTERCUTS	INTERMESH	INTERVIEW
INSULINS	INTEL	INTERDASH	INTERMIT	INTERWAR
INSULSE	INTELLECT	INTERDEAL	INTERMITS	INTERWEB
INSULSITY	INTELS	INTERDICT	INTERMIX	INTERWEBS
INSULT	INTENABLE	INTERDINE	INTERMONT	INTERWIND
INSULTANT	INTEND	INTERESS	INTERMURE	INTERWORD
INSULTED	INTENDANT	INTERESSE	INTERN	INTERWORK
INSULTER	INTENDED	INTEREST	INTERNAL	INTERWOVE
INSULTERS	INTENDEDS	INTERESTS	INTERNALS	INTERZONE
INSULTING	INTENDER	INTERFACE	INTERNE	INTESTACY
INSULTS	INTENDERS	INTERFERE	INTERNED	INTESTATE
INSURABLE	INTENDING	INTERFILE	INTERNEE	INTESTINE
INSURANCE	INTENDS	INTERFIRM	INTERNEES	INTHRAL
INSURANT	INTENIBLE	INTERFLOW	INTERNES	INTHRALL

INTHRALLS	INTONATES	INTROITUS	INUKSUK	INVASION
INTHRALS	INTONATOR	INTROJECT	INUKSUKS	INVASIONS
INTHRONE	INTONE	INTROLD	INULA	INVASIVE
INTHRONED	INTONED	INTROMIT	INULAS	INVEAGLE
INTHRONES	INTONER	INTROMITS	INULASE	INVEAGLED
INTI	INTONERS	INTRON	INULASES	INVEAGLES
INTIFADA	INTONES	INTRONIC	INULIN	INVECKED
INTIFADAH	INTONING	INTRONS	INULINS	INVECTED
INTIFADAS	INTONINGS	INTRORSE	INUMBRATE	INVECTIVE
INTIFADEH	INTORSION	INTROS	INUNCTION	INVEIGH
INTIL	INTORT	INTROVERT	INUNDANT	INVEIGHED
INTIMA	INTORTED	INTRUDE	INUNDATE	INVEIGHER
INTIMACY	INTORTING	INTRUDED	INUNDATED	INVEIGHS
INTIMAE	INTORTION	INTRUDER	INUNDATES	INVEIGLE
INTIMAL	INTORTS	INTRUDERS	INUNDATOR	INVEIGLED
INTIMAS	INTOWN	INTRUDES	INURBANE	INVEIGLER
INTIMATE	INTRA	INTRUDING	INURE	INVEIGLES
INTIMATED	INTRACITY	INTRUSION	INURED	INVENIT
INTIMATER	INTRADA	INTRUSIVE	INUREMENT	INVENT
INTIMATES	INTRADAS	INTRUST	INURES	INVENTED
INTIME	INTRADAY	INTRUSTED	INURING	INVENTER
INTIMISM	INTRADOS	INTRUSTS	INURN	INVENTERS
INTIMISMS	INTRANET	INTUBATE	INURNED	INVENTING
INTIMIST	INTRANETS	INTUBATED	INURNING	INVENTION
INTIMISTE	INTRANT	INTUBATES	INURNMENT	INVENTIVE
INTIMISTS	INTRANTS	INTUIT	INURNS	INVENTOR
INTIMITY	INTREAT	INTUITED	INUSITATE	INVENTORS
INTINE	INTREATED	INTUITING	INUST	INVENTORY
INTINES	INTREATS	INTUITION	INUSTION	INVENTS
INTIRE	INTRENCH	INTUITIVE	INUSTIONS	INVERITY
INTIS	INTREPID	INTUITS	INUTILE	INVERNESS
INTITLE	INTRICACY	INTUMESCE	INUTILELY	INVERSE
INTITLED	INTRICATE	INTURN	INUTILITY	INVERSED
INTITLES	INTRIGANT	INTURNED	INVADABLE	INVERSELY
INTITLING	INTRIGUE	INTURNS	INVADE	INVERSES
INTITULE	INTRIGUED	INTUSE	INVADED	INVERSING
INTITULED	INTRIGUER	INTUSES	INVADER	INVERSION
INTITULES	INTRIGUES	INTWINE	INVADERS	INVERSIVE
INTO	INTRINCE	INTWINED	INVADES	INVERT
INTOED	INTRINSIC	INTWINES	INVADING	INVERTASE
INTOMB	INTRO	INTWINING	INVALID	INVERTED
INTOMBED	INTRODUCE	INTWIST	INVALIDED	INVERTER
INTOMBING	INTROFIED	INTWISTED	INVALIDER	INVERTERS
INTOMBS	INTROFIES	INTWISTS	INVALIDLY	INVERTIN
INTONACO	INTROFY	INUKSHUIT	INVALIDS	INVERTING
INTONACOS	INTROIT	INUKSHUK	INVAR	INVERTINS
INTONATE	INTROITAL	INUKSHUKS	INVARIANT	INVERTOR
INTONATED	INTROITS	INUKSUIT	INVARS	INVERTORS

INVERTS	INVOLUTES	IODATING	IONICS	IRATELY
INVEST	INVOLVE	IODATION	IONISABLE	IRATENESS
INVESTED	INVOLVED	IODATIONS	IONISE	IRATER
INVESTING	INVOLVER	IODIC	IONISED	IRATEST
INVESTOR	INVOLVERS	IODID	IONISER	IRE
INVESTORS	INVOLVES	IODIDE	IONISERS	IRED
INVESTS	INVOLVING	IODIDES	IONISES	IREFUL
INVEXED	INWALL	IODIDS	IONISING	IREFULLY
INVIABLE	INWALLED	IODIN	IONIUM	IRELESS
INVIABLY	INWALLING	IODINATE	IONIUMS	IRENIC
INVIDIOUS	INWALLS	IODINATED	IONIZABLE	IRENICAL
INVIOLACY	INWARD	IODINATES	IONIZE	IRENICISM
INVIOLATE	INWARDLY	IODINE	IONIZED	IRENICON
INVIOUS	INWARDS	IODINES	IONIZER	IRENICONS
INVIRILE	INWEAVE	IODINS	IONIZERS	IRENICS
INVISCID	INWEAVED	IODISE	IONIZES	IRENOLOGY
INVISIBLE	INWEAVES	IODISED	IONIZING	IRES
INVISIBLY	INWEAVING	IODISER	IONOGEN	IRID
INVITAL	INWICK	IODISERS	IONOGENIC	IRIDAL
INVITE	INWICKED	IODISES	IONOGENS	IRIDEAL
INVITED	INWICKING	IODISING	IONOMER	IRIDES
INVITEE	INWICKS	IODISM	IONOMERS	IRIDIAL
INVITEES	INWIND	IODISMS	IONONE	IRIDIAN
INVITER	INWINDING	IODIZE	IONONES	IRIDIC
INVITERS	INWINDS	IODIZED	IONOPAUSE	IRIDISE
INVITES	INWIT	IODIZER	IONOPHORE	IRIDISED
INVITING	INWITH	IODIZERS	IONOSONDE	IRIDISES
INVITINGS	INWITS	IODIZES	IONOTROPY	IRIDISING
INVOCABLE	INWORK	IODIZING	IONS	IRIDIUM
INVOCATE	INWORKED	IODOFORM	IOPANOIC	IRIDIUMS
INVOCATED	INWORKING	IODOFORMS	IOS	IRIDIZE
INVOCATES	INWORKS	IODOMETRY	IOTA	IRIDIZED
INVOCATOR	INWORN	IODOPHILE	IOTACISM	IRIDIZES
INVOICE	INWOUND	IODOPHOR	IOTACISMS	IRIDIZING
INVOICED	INWOVE	IODOPHORS	IOTAS	IRIDOCYTE
INVOICES	INWOVEN	IODOPSIN	IPECAC	IRIDOLOGY
INVOICING	INWRAP	IODOPSINS	IPECACS	IRIDOTOMY
INVOKE	INWRAPPED	IODOUS	IPOMOEA	IRIDS
INVOKED	INWRAPS	IODURET	IPOMOEAS	IRING
INVOKER	INWRAPT	IODURETS	IPPON	IRIS
INVOKERS	INWREATHE	IODYRITE	IPPONS	IRISATE
INVOKES	INWROUGHT	IODYRITES	IPRINDOLE	IRISATED
INVOKING	INYALA	IOLITE	IRACUND	IRISATES
INVOLUCEL	INYALAS	IOLITES	IRADE	IRISATING
INVOLUCRA	IO	ION	IRADES	IRISATION
INVOLUCRE	IODATE	IONIC	IRASCIBLE	IRISCOPE
INVOLUTE	IODATED	IONICALLY	IRASCIBLY	IRISCOPES
INVOLUTED	IODATES	IONICITY	IRATE	IRISED

IRISES	IRONSIDES	IS	ISLEMEN	ISOCHRONE
IRISING	IRONSMITH	ISABEL	ISLES	ISOCHRONS
IRITIC	IRONSTONE	ISABELLA	ISLESMAN	ISOCLINAL
IRITIS	IRONWARE	ISABELLAS	ISLESMEN	ISOCLINE
IRITISES	IRONWARES	ISABELS	ISLET	ISOCLINES
IRK	IRONWEED	ISAGOGE	ISLETED	ISOCLINIC
IRKED	IRONWEEDS	ISAGOGES	ISLETS	ISOCRACY
IRKING	IRONWOMAN	ISAGOGIC	ISLING	ISOCRATIC
IRKS	IRONWOMEN	ISAGOGICS	ISLOMANIA	ISOCRYMAL
IRKSOME	IRONWOOD	ISALLOBAR	ISM	ISOCRYME
IRKSOMELY	IRONWOODS	ISARITHM	ISMATIC	ISOCRYMES
IROKO	IRONWORK	ISARITHMS	ISMATICAL	ISOCYANIC
IROKOS	IRONWORKS	ISATIN	ISMS	ISOCYCLIC
IRON	IRONY	ISATINE	ISNA	ISODICA
IRONBARK	IRRADIANT	ISATINES	ISNAE	ISODICON
IRONBARKS	IRRADIATE	ISATINIC	ISO	ISODOMA
IRONBOUND	IRREAL	ISATINS	ISOAMYL	ISODOMON
IRONCLAD	IRREALITY	ISBA	ISOAMYLS	ISODOMOUS
IRONCLADS	IRREDENTA	ISBAS	ISOBAR	ISODOMUM
IRONE	IRREGULAR	ISCHAEMIA	ISOBARE	ISODONT
IRONED	IRRELATED	ISCHAEMIC	ISOBARES	ISODONTAL
IRONER	IRRIDENTA	ISCHEMIA	ISOBARIC	ISODONTS
IRONERS	IRRIGABLE	ISCHEMIAS	ISOBARISM	ISODOSE
IRONES	IRRIGABLY	ISCHEMIC	ISOBARS	ISODOSES
IRONIC	IRRIGATE	ISCHIA	ISOBASE	ISOENZYME
IRONICAL	IRRIGATED	ISCHIADIC	ISOBASES	ISOETES
IRONIER	IRRIGATES	ISCHIAL	ISOBATH	ISOFORM
IRONIES	IRRIGATOR	ISCHIATIC	ISOBATHIC	ISOFORMS
IRONIEST	IRRIGUOUS	ISCHIUM	ISOBATHS	ISOGAMETE
IRONING	IRRISION	ISCHURIA	ISOBRONT	ISOGAMIC
IRONINGS	IRRISIONS	ISCHURIAS	ISOBRONTS	ISOGAMIES
IRONISE	IRRISORY	ISEIKONIA	ISOBUTANE	ISOGAMOUS
IRONISED	IRRITABLE	ISEIKONIC	ISOBUTENE	ISOGAMY
IRONISES	IRRITABLY	ISENERGIC	ISOBUTYL	ISOGENEIC
IRONISING	IRRITANCY	ISH	ISOBUTYLS	ISOGENIC
IRONIST	IRRITANT	ISHES	ISOCHASM	ISOGENIES
IRONISTS	IRRITANTS	ISINGLASS	ISOCHASMS	ISOGENOUS
IRONIZE	IRRITATE	ISIT	ISOCHEIM	ISOGENY
IRONIZED	IRRITATED	ISLAND	ISOCHEIMS	ISOGLOSS
IRONIZES	IRRITATES	ISLANDED	ISOCHIMAL	ISOGON
IRONIZING	IRRITATOR	ISLANDER	ISOCHIME	ISOGONAL
IRONLESS	IRRUPT	ISLANDERS	ISOCHIMES	ISOGONALS
IRONLIKE	IRRUPTED	ISLANDING	ISOCHOR	ISOGONE
IRONMAN	IRRUPTING	ISLANDS	ISOCHORE	ISOGONES
IRONMEN	IRRUPTION	ISLE	ISOCHORES	ISOGONIC
IRONNESS	IRRUPTIVE	ISLED	ISOCHORIC	ISOGONICS
IRONS	IRRUPTS	ISLELESS	ISOCHORS	ISOGONIES
IRONSIDE	IRUKANDJI	ISLEMAN	ISOCHRON	ISOGONS

ISOGONY	ISOMETRIC	ISOTHERES	ITA	ITINERACY
ISOGRAFT	ISOMETRY	ISOTHERM	ITACISM	ITINERANT
ISOGRAFTS	ISOMORPH	ISOTHERMS	ITACISMS	ITINERARY
ISOGRAM	ISOMORPHS	ISOTONE	ITACONIC	ITINERATE
ISOGRAMS	ISONIAZID	ISOTONES	ITALIC	ITS
ISOGRAPH	ISONOME	ISOTONIC	ITALICISE	ITSELF
ISOGRAPHS	ISONOMES	ISOTOPE	ITALICIZE	IURE
ISOGRIV	ISONOMIC	ISOTOPES	ITALICS	IVIED
ISOGRIVS	ISONOMIES	ISOTOPIC	ITAS	IVIES
ISOHEL	ISONOMOUS	ISOTOPIES	ITCH	IVORIED
ISOHELS	ISONOMY	ISOTOPY	ITCHED	IVORIER
ISOHYDRIC	ISOOCTANE	ISOTRON	ITCHES	IVORIES
ISOHYET	ISOPACH	ISOTRONS	ITCHIER	IVORIEST
ISOHYETAL	ISOPACHS	ISOTROPIC	ITCHIEST	IVORIST
ISOHYETS	ISOPHONE	ISOTROPY	ITCHILY	IVORISTS
ISOKONT	ISOPHONES	ISOTYPE	ITCHINESS	IVORY
ISOKONTAN	ISOPHOTAL	ISOTYPES	ITCHING	IVORYBILL
ISOKONTS	ISOPHOTE	ISOTYPIC	ITCHINGS	IVORYLIKE
ISOLABLE	ISOPHOTES	ISOZYME	ITCHWEED	IVORYWOOD
ISOLATE	ISOPLETH	ISOZYMES	ITCHWEEDS	IVRESSE
ISOLATED	ISOPLETHS	ISOZYMIC	ITCHY	IVRESSES
ISOLATES	ISOPOD	ISPAGHULA	ITEM	IVY
ISOLATING	ISOPODAN	ISSEI	ITEMED	IVYLEAF
ISOLATION	ISOPODANS	ISSEIS	ITEMING	IVYLIKE
ISOLATIVE	ISOPODOUS	ISSUABLE	ITEMISE	IWI
ISOLATOR	ISOPODS	ISSUABLY	ITEMISED	IWIS
ISOLATORS	ISOPOLITY	ISSUANCE	ITEMISER	IXIA
ISOLEAD	ISOPRENE	ISSUANCES	ITEMISERS	IXIAS
ISOLEADS	ISOPRENES	ISSUANT	ITEMISES	IXNAY
ISOLEX	ISOPROPYL	ISSUE	ITEMISING	IXODIASES
ISOLEXES	ISOPTERAN	ISSUED	ITEMIZE	IXODIASIS
ISOLINE	ISOPYCNAL	ISSUELESS	ITEMIZED	IXODID
ISOLINES	ISOPYCNIC	ISSUER	ITEMIZER	IXODIDS
ISOLOG	ISOS	ISSUERS	ITEMIZERS	IXORA
ISOLOGOUS	ISOSCELES	ISSUES	ITEMIZES	IXORAS
ISOLOGS	ISOSMOTIC	ISSUING	ITEMIZING	IXTLE
ISOLOGUE	ISOSPIN	ISTANA	ITEMS	IXTLES
ISOLOGUES	ISOSPINS	ISTANAS	ITERANCE	IZAR
ISOMER	ISOSPORY	ISTHMI	ITERANCES	IZARD
ISOMERASE	ISOSTACY	ISTHMIAN	ITERANT	IZARDS
ISOMERE	ISOSTASY	ISTHMIANS	ITERATE	IZARS
ISOMERES	ISOSTATIC	ISTHMIC	ITERATED	IZVESTIA
ISOMERIC	ISOSTERIC	ISTHMOID	ITERATES	IZVESTIAS
ISOMERISE	ISOTACH	ISTHMUS	ITERATING	IZVESTIYA
ISOMERISM	ISOTACHS	ISTHMUSES	ITERATION	IZZARD
ISOMERIZE	ISOTACTIC	ISTLE	ITERATIVE	IZZARDS
ISOMEROUS	ISOTHERAL	ISTLES	ITERUM	IZZAT
ISOMERS	ISOTHERE	IT	ITHER	IZZATS

J

JA	JACKAL	JACKSCREW	JADISHLY	JAGRA
JAAP	JACKALLED	JACKSHAFT	JADITIC	JAGRAS
JAAPS	JACKALOPE	JACKSIE	JAEGER	JAGS
JAB	JACKALS	JACKSIES	JAEGERS	JAGUAR
JABBED	JACKAROO	JACKSMELT	JAFA	JAGUARS
JABBER	JACKAROOS	JACKSMITH	JAFAS	JAI
JABBERED	JACKASS	JACKSNIPE	JAFFA	JAIL
JABBERER	JACKASSES	JACKSTAFF	JAFFAS	JAILABLE
JABBERERS	JACKBOOT	JACKSTAY	JAG	JAILBAIT
JABBERING	JACKBOOTS	JACKSTAYS	JAGA	JAILBAITS
JABBERS	JACKDAW	JACKSTONE	JAGAED	JAILBIRD
JABBING	JACKDAWS	JACKSTRAW	JAGAING	JAILBIRDS
JABBINGLY	JACKED	JACKSY	JAGAS	JAILBREAK
JABBLE	JACKEEN	JACKY	JAGDWURST	JAILBROKE
JABBLED	JACKEENS	JACOBIN	JAGER	JAILED
JABBLES	JACKER	JACOBINS	JAGERS	JAILER
JABBLING	JACKEROO	JACOBUS	JAGG	JAILERESS
JABERS	JACKEROOS	JACOBUSES	JAGGARIES	JAILERS
JABIRU	JACKERS	JACONET	JAGGARY	JAILHOUSE
JABIRUS	JACKET	JACONETS	JAGGED	JAILING
JABORANDI	JACKETED	JACQUARD	JAGGEDER	JAILLESS
JABOT	JACKETING	JACQUARDS	JAGGEDEST	JAILOR
JABOTS	JACKETS	JACQUERIE	JAGGEDLY	JAILORESS
JABS	JACKFISH	JACTATION	JAGGER	JAILORS
JACAL	JACKFRUIT	JACULATE	JAGGERIES	JAILS
JACALES	JACKIES	JACULATED	JAGGERS	JAK
JACALS	JACKING	JACULATES	JAGGERY	JAKE
JACAMAR	JACKINGS	JACULATOR	JAGGHERY	JAKER
JACAMARS	JACKKNIFE	JACUZZI	JAGGIER	JAKES
JACANA	JACKLEG	JACUZZIS	JAGGIES	JAKESES
JACANAS	JACKLEGS	JADE	JAGGIEST	JAKEST
JACARANDA	JACKLIGHT	JADED	JAGGING	JAKEY
JACARE	JACKLING	JADEDLY	JAGGS	JAKEYS
JACARES	JACKLINGS	JADEDNESS	JAGGY	JAKFRUIT
JACCHUS	JACKMAN	JADEITE	JAGHIR	JAKFRUITS
JACCHUSES	JACKMEN	JADEITES	JAGHIRDAR	JAKS
JACENT	JACKPLANE	JADELIKE	JAGHIRE	JALABIB
JACINTH	JACKPOT	JADERIES	JAGHIRES	JALAP
JACINTHE	JACKPOTS	JADERY	JAGHIRS	JALAPENO
JACINTHES	JACKROLL	JADES	JAGIR	JALAPENOS
JACINTHS	JACKROLLS	JADING	JAGIRS	JALAPIC
JACK	JACKS	JADISH	JAGLESS	JALAPIN

JALAPINS	JAMBO	JANES	JAPANIZE	JARINAS
JALAPS	JAMBOK	JANGLE	JAPANIZED	JARK
JALEBI	JAMBOKKED	JANGLED	JAPANIZES	JARKMAN
JALEBIS	JAMBOKS	JANGLER	JAPANNED	JARKMEN
JALFREZI	JAMBOLAN	JANGLERS	JAPANNER	JARKS
JALFREZIS	JAMBOLANA	JANGLES	JAPANNERS	JARL
JALLEBI	JAMBOLANS	JANGLIER	JAPANNING	JARLDOM
JALLEBIS	JAMBONE	JANGLIEST	JAPANS	JARLDOMS
JALOP	JAMBONES	JANGLING	JAPE	JARLS
JALOPIES	JAMBOOL	JANGLINGS	JAPED	JARLSBERG
JALOPPIES	JAMBOOLS	JANGLY	JAPER	JAROOL
JALOPPY	JAMBOREE	JANIFORM	JAPERIES	JAROOLS
JALOPS	JAMBOREES	JANISARY	JAPERS	JAROSITE
JALOPY	JAMBS	JANISSARY	JAPERY	JAROSITES
JALOUSE	JAMBU	JANITOR	JAPES	JAROVISE
JALOUSED	JAMBUL	JANITORS	JAPING	JAROVISED
JALOUSES	JAMBULS	JANITRESS	JAPINGLY	JAROVISES
JALOUSIE	JAMBUS	JANITRIX	JAPINGS	JAROVIZE
JALOUSIED	JAMBUSTER	JANIZAR	JAPONICA	JAROVIZED
JALOUSIES	JAMDANI	JANIZARS	JAPONICAS	JAROVIZES
JALOUSING	JAMDANIS	JANIZARY	JAPPED	JARP
JAM	JAMES	JANKER	JAPPING	JARPED
JAMAAT	JAMESES	JANKERS	JAPS	JARPING
JAMAATS	JAMJAR	JANN	JAR	JARPS
JAMADAR	JAMJARS	JANNEY	JARARACA	JARRAH
JAMADARS	JAMLIKE	JANNEYED	JARARACAS	JARRAHS
JAMB	JAMMABLE	JANNEYING	JARARAKA	JARRED
JAMBALAYA	JAMMED	JANNEYS	JARARAKAS	JARRING
JAMBART	JAMMER	JANNIED	JARFUL	JARRINGLY
JAMBARTS	JAMMERS	JANNIES	JARFULS	JARRINGS
JAMBE	JAMMIER	JANNOCK	JARGON	JARS
JAMBEAU	JAMMIES	JANNOCKS	JARGONED	JARSFUL
JAMBEAUS	JAMMIEST	JANNS	JARGONEER	JARTA
JAMBEAUX	JAMMING	JANNY	JARGONEL	JARTAS
JAMBED	JAMMINGS	JANNYING	JARGONELS	JARUL
JAMBEE	JAMMY	JANNYINGS	JARGONIER	JARULS
JAMBEES	JAMON	JANSKY	JARGONISE	JARVEY
JAMBER	JAMPACKED	JANSKYS	JARGONING	JARVEYS
JAMBERS	JAMPAN	JANTEE	JARGONISH	JARVIE
JAMBES	JAMPANEE	JANTIER	JARGONIST	JARVIES
JAMBEUX	JAMPANEES	JANTIES	JARGONIZE	JASEY
JAMBIER	JAMPANI	JANTIEST	JARGONS	JASEYS
JAMBIERS	JAMPANIS	JANTY	JARGONY	JASIES
JAMBING	JAMPANS	JAP	JARGOON	JASMIN
JAMBIYA	JAMPOT	JAPAN	JARGOONS	JASMINE
JAMBIYAH	JAMPOTS	JAPANISE	JARHEAD	JASMINES
JAMBIYAHS	JAMS	JAPANISED	JARHEADS	JASMINS
JAMBIYAS	JANE	JAPANISES	JARINA	JASMONATE

JASP	JAUNTILY	JAYBIRD	JEATS	JEHADI
JASPE	JAUNTING	JAYBIRDS	JEBEL	JEHADIS
JASPER	JAUNTS	JAYCEE	JEBELS	JEHADISM
JASPERIER	JAUNTY	JAYCEES	JEDI	JEHADISMS
JASPERISE	JAUP	JAYGEE	JEDIS	JEHADIST
JASPERIZE	JAUPED	JAYGEES	JEE	JEHADISTS
JASPEROUS	JAUPING	JAYHAWKER	JEED	JEHADS
JASPERS	JAUPS	JAYS	JEEING	JEHU
JASPERY	JAVA	JAYVEE	JEEL	JEHUS
JASPES	JAVAS	JAYVEES	JEELED	JEJUNA
JASPIDEAN	JAVEL	JAYWALK	JEELIE	JEJUNAL
JASPILITE	JAVELIN	JAYWALKED	JEELIED	JEJUNE
JASPIS	JAVELINA	JAYWALKER	JEELIEING	JEJUNELY
JASPISES	JAVELINAS	JAYWALKS	JEELIES	JEJUNITY
JASPS	JAVELINED	JAZERANT	JEELING	JEJUNUM
JASS	JAVELINS	JAZERANTS	JEELS	JEJUNUMS
JASSES	JAVELLE	JAZIES	JEELY	JELAB
JASSID	JAVELS	JAZY	JEELYING	JELABS
JASSIDS	JAW	JAZZ	JEEP	JELL
JASY	JAWAN	JAZZBO	JEEPED	JELLABA
JATAKA	JAWANS	JAZZBOS	JEEPERS	JELLABAH
JATAKAS	JAWARI	JAZZED	JEEPING	JELLABAHS
JATO	JAWARIS	JAZZER	JEEPNEY	JELLABAS
JATOS	JAWBATION	JAZZERS	JEEPNEYS	JELLED
JATROPHA	JAWBONE	JAZZES	JEEPS	JELLIED
JATROPHAS	JAWBONED	JAZZIER	JEER	JELLIES
JAUK	JAWBONER	JAZZIEST	JEERED	JELLIFIED
JAUKED	JAWBONERS	JAZZILY	JEERER	JELLIFIES
JAUKING	JAWBONES	JAZZINESS	JEERERS	JELLIFY
JAUKS	JAWBONING	JAZZING	JEERING	JELLING
JAUNCE	JAWBOX	JAZZLIKE	JEERINGLY	JELLO
JAUNCED	JAWBOXES	JAZZMAN	JEERINGS	JELLOS
JAUNCES	JAWED	JAZZMEN	JEERS	JELLS
JAUNCING	JAWFALL	JAZZY	JEES	JELLY
JAUNDICE	JAWFALLS	JEALOUS	JEESLY	JELLYBEAN
JAUNDICED	JAWHOLE	JEALOUSE	JEEZ	JELLYFISH
JAUNDICES	JAWHOLES	JEALOUSED	JEEZE	JELLYING
JAUNSE	JAWING	JEALOUSER	JEEZELY	JELLYLIKE
JAUNSED	JAWINGS	JEALOUSES	JEEZLY	JELLYROLL
JAUNSES	JAWLESS	JEALOUSLY	JEFE	JELUTONG
JAUNSING	JAWLIKE	JEALOUSY	JEFES	JELUTONGS
JAUNT	JAWLINE	JEAN	JEFF	JEMADAR
JAUNTED	JAWLINES	JEANED	JEFFED	JEMADARS
JAUNTEE	JAWS	JEANETTE	JEFFING	JEMBE
JAUNTIE	JAXIE	JEANETTES	JEFFS	JEMBES
JAUNTIER	JAXIES	JEANS	JEGGINGS	JEMIDAR
JAUNTIES	JAXY	JEANSWEAR	JEHAD	JEMIDARS
JAUNTIEST	JAY	JEAT	JEHADEEN	JEMIMA

J

JEMIMAS	JERKINGLY	JESTFUL	JETTONS	JIBBED
JEMMIED	JERKINGS	JESTING	JETTY	JIBBER
JEMMIER	JERKINS	JESTINGLY	JETTYING	JIBBERED
JEMMIES	JERKS	JESTINGS	JETWAY	JIBBERING
JEMMIEST	JERKWATER	JESTS	JETWAYS	JIBBERS
JEMMINESS	JERKY	JESUIT	JEU	JIBBING
JEMMY	JEROBOAM	JESUITIC	JEUNE	JIBBINGS
JEMMYING	JEROBOAMS	JESUITISM	JEUX	JIBBONS
JENNET	JERQUE	JESUITRY	JEW	JIBBOOM
JENNETING	JERQUED	JESUITS	JEWED	JIBBOOMS
JENNETS	JERQUER	JESUS	JEWEL	JIBBS
JENNIES	JERQUERS	JET	JEWELED	JIBE
JENNY	JERQUES	JETBEAD	JEWELER	JIBED
JEOFAIL	JERQUING	JETBEADS	JEWELERS	JIBER
JEOFAILS	JERQUINGS	JETE	JEWELFISH	JIBERS
JEON	JERREED	JETES	JEWELING	JIBES
JEONS	JERREEDS	JETFOIL	JEWELLED	JIBING
JEOPARD	JERRICAN	JETFOILS	JEWELLER	JIBINGLY
JEOPARDED	JERRICANS	JETLAG	JEWELLERS	JIBS
JEOPARDER	JERRID	JETLAGS	JEWELLERY	JICAMA
JEOPARDS	JERRIDS	JETLIKE	JEWELLIKE	JICAMAS
JEOPARDY	JERRIES	JETLINER	JEWELLING	JICKAJOG
JEQUERITY	JERRY	JETLINERS	JEWELRIES	JICKAJOGS
JEQUIRITY	JERRYCAN	JETON	JEWELRY	JIFF
JERBIL	JERRYCANS	JETONS	JEWELS	JIFFIES
JERBILS	JERSEY	JETPACK	JEWELWEED	JIFFS
JERBOA	JERSEYED	JETPACKS	JEWFISH	JIFFY
JERBOAS	JERSEYS	JETPORT	JEWFISHES	JIG
JEREED	JESS	JETPORTS	JEWIE	JIGABOO
JEREEDS	JESSAMIES	JETS	JEWIES	JIGABOOS
JEREMIAD	JESSAMINE	JETSAM	JEWING	JIGAJIG
JEREMIADS	JESSAMY	JETSAMS	JEWS	JIGAJIGS
JEREPIGO	JESSANT	JETSOM	JEZAIL	JIGAJOG
JEREPIGOS	JESSE	JETSOMS	JEZAILS	JIGAJOGS
JERFALCON	JESSED	JETSON	JEZEBEL	JIGAMAREE
JERID	JESSERANT	JETSONS	JEZEBELS	JIGGED
JERIDS	JESSES	JETSTREAM	JHALA	JIGGER
JERK	JESSIE	JETTATURA	JHALAS	JIGGERED
JERKED	JESSIES	JETTED	JHATKA	JIGGERING
JERKER	JESSING	JETTIED	JHATKAS	JIGGERS
JERKERS	JEST	JETTIER	JIAO	JIGGIER
JERKIER	JESTBOOK	JETTIES	JIAOS	JIGGIEST
JERKIES	JESTBOOKS	JETTIEST	JIB	JIGGING
JERKIEST	JESTED	JETTINESS	JIBB	JIGGINGS
JERKILY	JESTEE	JETTING	JIBBA	JIGGISH
JERKIN	JESTEES	JETTISON	JIBBAH	JIGGLE
JERKINESS	JESTER	JETTISONS	JIBBAHS	JIGGLED
JERKING	JESTERS	JETTON	JIBBAS	JIGGLES

JIGGLIER	JIMINY	JINJILIS	JITTERY	JOBNAME
JIGGLIEST	JIMJAM	JINK	JIUJITSU	JOBNAMES
JIGGLING	JIMJAMS	JINKED	JIUJITSUS	JOBS
JIGGLY	JIMMIE	JINKER	JIUJUTSU	JOBSEEKER
JIGGUMBOB	JIMMIED	JINKERED	JIUJUTSUS	JOBSHARE
JIGGY	JIMMIES	JINKERING	JIVE	JOBSHARES
JIGJIG	JIMMINY	JINKERS	JIVEASS	JOBSWORTH
JIGJIGS	JIMMY	JINKING	JIVEASSES	JOCK
JIGLIKE	JIMMYING	JINKS	JIVED	JOCKDOM
JIGOT	JIMP	JINN	JIVER	JOCKDOMS
JIGOTS	JIMPER	JINNE	JIVERS	JOCKETTE
JIGS	JIMPEST	JINNEE	JIVES	JOCKETTES
JIGSAW	JIMPIER	JINNI	JIVEST	JOCKEY
JIGSAWED	JIMPIEST	JINNIS	JIVEY	JOCKEYED
JIGSAWING	JIMPLY	JINNS	JIVIER	JOCKEYING
JIGSAWN	JIMPNESS	JINRIKSHA	JIVIEST	JOCKEYISH
JIGSAWS	JIMPSON	JINS	JIVING	JOCKEYISM
JIHAD	JIMPY	JINX	JIVY	JOCKEYS
JIHADEEN	JIMSON	JINXED	JIZ	JOCKIER
JIHADI	JIMSONS	JINXES	JIZZ	JOCKIEST
JIHADIS	JIN	JINXING	JIZZES	JOCKISH
JIHADISM	JINGAL	JIPIJAPA	JNANA	JOCKNEY
JIHADISMS	JINGALL	JIPIJAPAS	JNANAS	JOCKNEYS
JIHADIST	JINGALLS	JIPYAPA	JO	JOCKO
JIHADISTS	JINGALS	JIPYAPAS	JOANNA	JOCKOS
JIHADS	JINGBANG	JIRBLE	JOANNAS	JOCKS
JILBAB	JINGBANGS	JIRBLED	JOANNES	JOCKSTRAP
JILBABS	JINGKO	JIRBLES	JOANNESES	JOCKTELEG
JILGIE	JINGKOES	JIRBLING	JOB	JOCKY
JILGIES	JINGLE	JIRD	JOBATION	JOCO
JILL	JINGLED	JIRDS	JOBATIONS	JOCOS
JILLAROO	JINGLER	JIRGA	JOBBED	JOCOSE
JILLAROOS	JINGLERS	JIRGAS	JOBBER	JOCOSELY
JILLET	JINGLES	JIRKINET	JOBBERIES	JOCOSER
JILLETS	JINGLET	JIRKINETS	JOBBERS	JOCOSEST
JILLFLIRT	JINGLETS	JIRRE	JOBBERY	JOCOSITY
JILLION	JINGLIER	JISM	JOBBIE	JOCULAR
JILLIONS	JINGLIEST	JISMS	JOBBIES	JOCULARLY
JILLIONTH	JINGLING	JISSOM	JOBBING	JOCULATOR
JILLS	JINGLY	JISSOMS	JOBBINGS	JOCUND
JILT	JINGO	JITNEY	JOBCENTRE	JOCUNDER
JILTED	JINGOES	JITNEYS	JOBE	JOCUNDEST
JILTER	JINGOISH	JITTER	JOBED	JOCUNDITY
JILTERS	JINGOISM	JITTERBUG	JOBERNOWL	JOCUNDLY
JILTING	JINGOISMS	JITTERED	JOBES	JODEL
JILTS	JINGOIST	JITTERIER	JOBHOLDER	JODELLED
JIMCRACK	JINGOISTS	JITTERING	JOBING	JODELLING
JIMCRACKS	JINJILI	JITTERS	JOBLESS	JODELS

JODHPUR	JOINTERS	JOLLEY	JOMOS	JOSSES
JODHPURS	JOINTING	JOLLEYER	JONCANOE	JOSTLE
JOE	JOINTINGS	JOLLEYERS	JONCANOES	JOSTLED
JOES	JOINTLESS	JOLLEYING	JONES	JOSTLER
JOEY	JOINTLY	JOLLEYS	JONESED	JOSTLERS
JOEYS	JOINTNESS	JOLLIED	JONESES	JOSTLES
JOG	JOINTRESS	JOLLIER	JONESING	JOSTLING
JOGGED	JOINTS	JOLLIERS	JONG	JOSTLINGS
JOGGER	JOINTURE	JOLLIES	JONGLEUR	JOT
JOGGERS	JOINTURED	JOLLIEST	JONGLEURS	JOTA
JOGGING	JOINTURES	JOLLIFIED	JONGS	JOTAS
JOGGINGS	JOINTWEED	JOLLIFIES	JONNOCK	JOTS
JOGGLE	JOINTWORM	JOLLIFY	JONNYCAKE	JOTTED
JOGGLED	JOIST	JOLLILY	JONQUIL	JOTTER
JOGGLER	JOISTED	JOLLIMENT	JONQUILS	JOTTERS
JOGGLERS	JOISTING	JOLLINESS	JONTIES	JOTTIER
JOGGLES	JOISTS	JOLLING	JONTY	JOTTIEST
JOGGLING	JOJOBA	JOLLITIES	JOOK	JOTTING
JOGPANTS	JOJOBAS	JOLLITY	JOOKED	JOTTINGS
JOGS	JOKE	JOLLOF	JOOKERIES	JOTTY
JOGTROT	JOKED	JOLLOP	JOOKERY	JOTUN
JOGTROTS	JOKER	JOLLOPS	JOOKING	JOTUNN
JOHANNES	JOKERS	JOLLS	JOOKS	JOTUNNS
JOHN	JOKES	JOLLY	JOR	JOTUNS
JOHNBOAT	JOKESMITH	JOLLYBOAT	JORAM	JOUAL
JOHNBOATS	JOKESOME	JOLLYER	JORAMS	JOUALS
JOHNNIE	JOKESTER	JOLLYERS	JORDAN	JOUGS
JOHNNIES	JOKESTERS	JOLLYHEAD	JORDANS	JOUISANCE
JOHNNY	JOKEY	JOLLYING	JORDELOO	JOUK
JOHNS	JOKIER	JOLLYINGS	JORDELOOS	JOUKED
JOHNSON	JOKIEST	JOLS	JORS	JOUKERIES
JOHNSONS	JOKILY	JOLT	JORUM	JOUKERY
JOIN	JOKINESS	JOLTED	JORUMS	JOUKING
JOINABLE	JOKING	JOLTER	JOSEPH	JOUKS
JOINDER	JOKINGLY	JOLTERS	JOSEPHS	JOULE
JOINDERS	JOKINGS	JOLTHEAD	JOSH	JOULED
JOINED	JOKOL	JOLTHEADS	JOSHED	JOULES
JOINER	JOKY	JOLTIER	JOSHER	JOULING
JOINERIES	JOL	JOLTIEST	JOSHERS	JOUNCE
JOINERS	JOLE	JOLTILY	JOSHES	JOUNCED
JOINERY	JOLED	JOLTING	JOSHING	JOUNCES
JOINING	JOLES	JOLTINGLY	JOSHINGLY	JOUNCIER
JOININGS	JOLING	JOLTINGS	JOSHINGS	JOUNCIEST
JOINS	JOLIOTIUM	JOLTS	JOSKIN	JOUNCING
JOINT	JOLL	JOLTY	JOSKINS	JOUNCY
JOINTED	JOLLED	JOMO	JOSS	JOUR
JOINTEDLY	JOLLER	JOMON	JOSSER	JOURNAL
JOINTER	JOLLERS	JOMONS	JOSSERS	JOURNALED

JOURNALS	JOYOUSLY	JUDGEABLE	JUGGINGS	JUJUS
JOURNEY	JOYPAD	JUDGED	JUGGINS	JUJUTSU
JOURNEYED	JOYPADS	JUDGELESS	JUGGINSES	JUJUTSUS
JOURNEYER	JOYPOP	JUDGELIKE	JUGGLE	JUKE
JOURNEYS	JOYPOPPED	JUDGEMENT	JUGGLED	JUKEBOX
JOURNO	JOYPOPPER	JUDGER	JUGGLER	JUKEBOXES
JOURNOS	JOYPOPS	JUDGERS	JUGGLERS	JUKED
JOURS	JOYRIDDEN	JUDGES	JUGGLERY	JUKES
JOUST	JOYRIDE	JUDGESHIP	JUGGLES	JUKING
JOUSTED	JOYRIDER	JUDGEY	JUGGLING	JUKSKEI
JOUSTER	JOYRIDERS	JUDGIER	JUGGLINGS	JUKSKEIS
JOUSTERS	JOYRIDES	JUDGIEST	JUGHEAD	JUKU
JOUSTING	JOYRIDING	JUDGING	JUGHEADS	JUKUS
JOUSTINGS	JOYRODE	JUDGINGLY	JUGLET	JULEP
JOUSTS	JOYS	JUDGINGS	JUGLETS	JULEPS
JOVIAL	JOYSTICK	JUDGMATIC	JUGS	JULIENNE
JOVIALITY	JOYSTICKS	JUDGMENT	JUGSFUL	JULIENNED
JOVIALLY	JUBA	JUDGMENTS	JUGULA	JULIENNES
JOVIALTY	JUBAS	JUDGY	JUGULAR	JULIET
JOW	JUBATE	JUDICABLE	JUGULARS	JULIETS
JOWAR	JUBBAH	JUDICARE	JUGULATE	JUMAR
JOWARI	JUBBAHS	JUDICARES	JUGULATED	JUMARED
JOWARIS	JUBE	JUDICATOR	JUGULATES	JUMARING
JOWARS	JUBES	JUDICIAL	JUGULUM	JUMARRED
JOWED	JUBHAH	JUDICIARY	JUGUM	JUMARRING
JOWING	JUBHAHS	JUDICIOUS	JUGUMS	JUMARS
JOWL	JUBILANCE	JUDIES	JUICE	JUMART
JOWLED	JUBILANCY	JUDO	JUICED	JUMARTS
JOWLER	JUBILANT	JUDOGI	JUICEHEAD	JUMBAL
JOWLERS	JUBILATE	JUDOGIS	JUICELESS	JUMBALS
JOWLIER	JUBILATED	JUDOIST	JUICER	JUMBIE
JOWLIEST	JUBILATES	JUDOISTS	JUICERS	JUMBIES
JOWLINESS	JUBILE	JUDOKA	JUICES	JUMBLE
JOWLING	JUBILEE	JUDOKAS	JUICIER	JUMBLED
JOWLS	JUBILEES	JUDOS	JUICIEST	JUMBLER
JOWLY	JUBILES	JUDS	JUICILY	JUMBLERS
JOWS	JUCO	JUDY	JUICINESS	JUMBLES
JOY	JUCOS	JUG	JUICING	JUMBLIER
JOYANCE	JUD	JUGA	JUICY	JUMBLIEST
JOYANCES	JUDAS	JUGAAD	JUJITSU	JUMBLING
JOYED	JUDASES	JUGAADS	JUJITSUS	JUMBLY
JOYFUL	JUDDER	JUGAL	JUJU	JUMBO
JOYFULLER	JUDDERED	JUGALS	JUJUBE	JUMBOISE
JOYFULLY	JUDDERIER	JUGATE	JUJUBES	JUMBOISED
JOYING	JUDDERING	JUGFUL	JUJUISM	JUMBOISES
JOYLESS	JUDDERS	JUGFULS	JUJUISMS	JUMBOIZE
JOYLESSLY	JUDDERY	JUGGED	JUJUIST	JUMBOIZED
JOYOUS	JUDGE	JUGGING	JUJUISTS	JUMBOIZES

JUMBOS	JUNCTURAL	JUNKETING	JURELS	JUSTING
JUMBUCK	JUNCTURE	JUNKETS	JURES	JUSTLE
JUMBUCKS	JUNCTURES	JUNKETTED	JURIDIC	JUSTLED
JUMBY	JUNCUS	JUNKETTER	JURIDICAL	JUSTLES
JUMELLE	JUNCUSES	JUNKIE	JURIED	JUSTLING
JUMELLES	JUNEATING	JUNKIER	JURIES	JUSTLY
JUMP	JUNGLE	JUNKIES	JURIST	JUSTNESS
JUMPABLE	JUNGLED	JUNKIEST	JURISTIC	JUSTS
JUMPED	JUNGLEGYM	JUNKINESS	JURISTS	JUT
JUMPER	JUNGLES	JUNKING	JUROR	JUTE
JUMPERS	JUNGLI	JUNKMAN	JURORS	JUTELIKE
JUMPIER	JUNGLIER	JUNKMEN	JURY	JUTES
JUMPIEST	JUNGLIEST	JUNKS	JURYING	JUTS
JUMPILY	JUNGLIS	JUNKY	JURYLESS	JUTTED
JUMPINESS	JUNGLIST	JUNKYARD	JURYMAN	JUTTIED
JUMPING	JUNGLISTS	JUNKYARDS	JURYMAST	JUTTIER
JUMPINGLY	JUNGLY	JUNTA	JURYMASTS	JUTTIES
JUMPINGS	JUNIOR	JUNTAS	JURYMEN	JUTTIEST
JUMPOFF	JUNIORATE	JUNTO	JURYWOMAN	JUTTING
JUMPOFFS	JUNIORED	JUNTOS	JURYWOMEN	JUTTINGLY
JUMPROPE	JUNIORING	JUPATI	JUS	JUTTY
JUMPROPES	JUNIORITY	JUPATIS	JUSSIVE	JUTTYING
JUMPS	JUNIORS	JUPE	JUSSIVES	JUVE
JUMPSHOT	JUNIPER	JUPES	JUST	JUVENAL
JUMPSHOTS	JUNIPERS	JUPON	JUSTED	JUVENALS
JUMPSIES	JUNK	JUPONS	JUSTER	JUVENILE
JUMPSUIT	JUNKANOO	JURA	JUSTERS	JUVENILES
JUMPSUITS	JUNKANOOS	JURAL	JUSTEST	JUVENILIA
JUMPY	JUNKED	JURALLY	JUSTICE	JUVES
JUN	JUNKER	JURANT	JUSTICER	JUVIE
JUNCATE	JUNKERDOM	JURANTS	JUSTICERS	JUVIES
JUNCATES	JUNKERS	JURASSIC	JUSTICES	JUXTAPOSE
JUNCO	JUNKET	JURAT	JUSTICIAR	JYMOLD
JUNCOES	JUNKETED	JURATORY	JUSTIFIED	JYNX
JUNCOS	JUNKETEER	JURATS	JUSTIFIER	JYNXES
JUNCTION	JUNKETER	JURE	JUSTIFIES	
JUNCTIONS	JUNKETERS	JUREL	JUSTIFY	

K

KA	KABOB	KAF	KAIES	KAJEPUTS
KAAL	KABOBBED	KAFFIR	KAIF	KAK
KAAMA	KABOBBING	KAFFIRS	KAIFS	KAKA
KAAMAS	KABOBS	KAFFIYAH	KAIK	KAKAPO
KAAS	KABOCHA	KAFFIYAHS	KAIKA	KAKAPOS
KAB	KABOCHAS	KAFFIYEH	KAIKAI	KAKARIKI
KABAB	KABOODLE	KAFFIYEHS	KAIKAIS	KAKARIKIS
KABABBED	KABOODLES	KAFILA	KAIKAS	KAKAS
KABABBING	KABOOM	KAFILAS	KAIKAWAKA	KAKEMONO
KABABS	KABOOMS	KAFIR	KAIKOMAKO	KAKEMONOS
KABADDI	KABS	KAFIRS	KAIKS	KAKI
KABADDIS	KABUKI	KAFS	KAIL	KAKIEMON
KABAKA	KABUKIS	KAFTAN	KAILS	KAKIEMONS
KABAKAS	KACCHA	KAFTANS	KAILYAIRD	KAKIS
KABALA	KACCHAS	KAFUFFLE	KAILYARD	KAKIVAK
KABALAS	KACHA	KAFUFFLES	KAILYARDS	KAKIVAKS
KABALISM	KACHAHRI	KAGO	KAIM	KAKODYL
KABALISMS	KACHAHRIS	KAGOOL	KAIMAKAM	KAKODYLS
KABALIST	KACHCHA	KAGOOLS	KAIMAKAMS	KAKS
KABALISTS	KACHERI	KAGOS	KAIMS	KAKURO
KABAR	KACHERIS	KAGOUL	KAIN	KAKUROS
KABARS	KACHINA	KAGOULE	KAING	KALAM
KABAYA	KACHINAS	KAGOULES	KAINGA	KALAMANSI
KABAYAS	KACHORI	KAGOULS	KAINGAS	KALAMATA
KABBALA	KACHORIS	KAGU	KAINIT	KALAMATAS
KABBALAH	KACHUMBER	KAGUS	KAINITE	KALAMDAN
KABBALAHS	KACK	KAHAL	KAINITES	KALAMDANS
KABBALAS	KACKS	KAHALS	KAINITS	KALAMKARI
KABBALISM	KADAI	KAHAWAI	KAINS	KALAMS
KABBALIST	KADAIS	KAHAWAIS	KAIROMONE	KALANCHOE
KABELE	KADAITCHA	KAHIKATEA	KAIS	KALE
KABELES	KADDISH	KAHIKATOA	KAISER	KALENDAR
KABELJOU	KADDISHES	KAHUNA	KAISERDOM	KALENDARS
KABELJOUS	KADDISHIM	KAHUNAS	KAISERIN	KALENDS
KABELJOUW	KADE	KAI	KAISERINS	KALES
KABIKI	KADES	KAIAK	KAISERISM	KALEWIFE
KABIKIS	KADI	KAIAKED	KAISERS	KALEWIVES
KABLOOEY	KADIS	KAIAKING	KAIZEN	KALEYARD
KABLOOIE	KAE	KAIAKS	KAIZENS	KALEYARDS
KABLOONA	KAED	KAID	KAJAWAH	KALI
KABLOONAS	KAEING	KAIDS	KAJAWAHS	KALIAN
KABLOONAT	KAES	KAIE	KAJEPUT	KALIANS

KALIF	KAMAHI	KANBANS	KAOLINS	KARATEKAS
KALIFATE	KAMAHIS	KANDIES	KAON	KARATES
KALIFATES	KAMALA	KANDY	KAONIC	KARATS
KALIFS	KAMALAS	KANE	KAONS	KAREAREA
KALIMBA	KAMAS	KANEH	KAPA	KAREAREAS
KALIMBAS	KAME	KANEHS	KAPAS	KARENGO
KALINITE	KAMEES	KANES	KAPEEK	KARENGOS
KALINITES	KAMEESES	KANG	KAPEYKA	KARITE
KALIPH	KAMEEZ	KANGA	KAPH	KARITES
KALIPHATE	KAMEEZES	KANGAROO	KAPHS	KARK
KALIPHS	KAMELA	KANGAROOS	KAPOK	KARKED
KALIS	KAMELAS	KANGAS	KAPOKS	KARKING
KALIUM	KAMERAD	KANGHA	KAPOW	KARKS
KALIUMS	KAMERADED	KANGHAS	KAPOWS	KARMA
KALLIDIN	KAMERADS	KANGS	KAPPA	KARMAS
KALLIDINS	KAMES	KANJI	KAPPAS	KARMIC
KALLITYPE	KAMI	KANJIS	KAPU	KARN
KALMIA	KAMICHI	KANS	KAPUKA	KARNS
KALMIAS	KAMICHIS	KANSES	KAPUKAS	KARO
KALONG	KAMIK	KANT	KAPUS	KAROO
KALONGS	KAMIKAZE	KANTAR	KAPUT	KAROOS
KALOOKI	KAMIKAZES	KANTARS	KAPUTT	KARORO
KALOOKIE	KAMIKS	KANTED	KARA	KAROROS
KALOOKIES	KAMILA	KANTELA	KARABINER	KAROS
KALOOKIS	KAMILAS	KANTELAS	KARAHI	KAROSHI
KALOTYPE	KAMIS	KANTELE	KARAHIS	KAROSHIS
KALOTYPES	KAMISES	KANTELES	KARAISM	KAROSS
KALPA	KAMME	KANTEN	KARAISMS	KAROSSES
KALPAC	KAMOKAMO	KANTENS	KARAIT	KARRI
KALPACS	KAMOKAMOS	KANTHA	KARAITS	KARRIS
KALPAK	KAMOTIK	KANTHAS	KARAKA	KARROO
KALPAKS	KAMOTIKS	KANTIKOY	KARAKAS	KARROOS
KALPAS	KAMOTIQ	KANTIKOYS	KARAKIA	KARSEY
KALPIS	KAMOTIQS	KANTING	KARAKIAS	KARSEYS
KALPISES	KAMPONG	KANTS	KARAKUL	KARSIES
KALSOMINE	KAMPONGS	KANUKA	KARAKULS	KARST
KALUKI	KAMSEEN	KANUKAS	KARAMU	KARSTIC
KALUKIS	KAMSEENS	KANZU	KARAMUS	KARSTIFY
KALUMPIT	KAMSIN	KANZUS	KARANGA	KARSTS
KALUMPITS	KAMSINS	KAOLIANG	KARANGAED	KARSY
KALYPTRA	KANA	KAOLIANGS	KARANGAS	KART
KALYPTRAS	KANAE	KAOLIN	KARAOKE	KARTER
KAM	KANAES	KAOLINE	KARAOKES	KARTERS
KAMA	KANAKA	KAOLINES	KARAS	KARTING
KAMAAINA	KANAKAS	KAOLINIC	KARAT	KARTINGS
KAMAAINAS	KANAMYCIN	KAOLINISE	KARATE	KARTS
KAMACITE	KANAS	KAOLINITE	KARATEIST	KARYOGAMY
KAMACITES	KANBAN	KAOLINIZE	KARATEKA	KARYOGRAM

KARYOLOGY	KATHARSIS	KAWAIIS	KEAVIES	KEDGIEST
KARYON	KATHODAL	KAWAKAWA	KEB	KEDGING
KARYONS	KATHODE	KAWAKAWAS	KEBAB	KEDGY
KARYOSOME	KATHODES	KAWAS	KEBABBED	KEDS
KARYOTIN	KATHODIC	KAWAU	KEBABBING	KEECH
KARYOTINS	KATHUMP	KAWAUS	KEBABS	KEECHES
KARYOTYPE	KATHUMPS	KAWED	KEBAR	KEEF
KARZIES	KATI	KAWING	KEBARS	KEEFS
KARZY	KATION	KAWS	KEBBED	KEEK
KAS	KATIONS	KAY	KEBBIE	KEEKED
KASBAH	KATIPO	KAYAK	KEBBIES	KEEKER
KASBAHS	KATIPOS	KAYAKED	KEBBING	KEEKERS
KASHA	KATIS	KAYAKER	KEBBOCK	KEEKING
KASHAS	KATORGA	KAYAKERS	KEBBOCKS	KEEKS
KASHER	KATORGAS	KAYAKING	KEBBUCK	KEEL
KASHERED	KATS	KAYAKINGS	KEBBUCKS	KEELAGE
KASHERING	KATSINA	KAYAKS	KEBELE	KEELAGES
KASHERS	KATSINAM	KAYLE	KEBELES	KEELBOAT
KASHMIR	KATSINAS	KAYLES	KEBLAH	KEELBOATS
KASHMIRS	KATSURA	KAYLIED	KEBLAHS	KEELED
KASHRUS	KATSURAS	KAYO	KEBOB	KEELER
KASHRUSES	KATTI	KAYOED	KEBOBBED	KEELERS
KASHRUT	KATTIS	KAYOES	KEBOBBING	KEELHALE
KASHRUTH	KATYDID	KAYOING	KEBOBS	KEELHALED
KASHRUTHS	KATYDIDS	KAYOINGS	KEBS	KEELHALES
KASHRUTS	KAUGH	KAYOS	KECK	KEELHAUL
KASME	KAUGHS	KAYS	KECKED	KEELHAULS
KAT	KAUMATUA	KAZACHKI	KECKING	KEELIE
KATA	KAUMATUAS	KAZACHOC	KECKLE	KEELIES
KATABASES	KAUPAPA	KAZACHOCS	KECKLED	KEELING
KATABASIS	KAUPAPAS	KAZACHOK	KECKLES	KEELINGS
KATABATIC	KAURI	KAZACHOKS	KECKLING	KEELIVINE
KATABOLIC	KAURIES	KAZATSKI	KECKLINGS	KEELLESS
KATAKANA	KAURIS	KAZATSKY	KECKS	KEELMAN
KATAKANAS	KAURU	KAZATZKA	KECKSES	KEELMEN
KATAL	KAURUS	KAZATZKAS	KECKSIES	KEELS
KATALS	KAURY	KAZI	KECKSY	KEELSON
KATANA	KAVA	KAZILLION	KED	KEELSONS
KATANAS	KAVAKAVA	KAZIS	KEDDAH	KEELYVINE
KATAS	KAVAKAVAS	KAZOO	KEDDAHS	KEEMA
KATCHINA	KAVAL	KAZOOS	KEDGE	KEEMAS
KATCHINAS	KAVALS	KBAR	KEDGED	KEEN
KATCINA	KAVAS	KBARS	KEDGER	KEENED
KATCINAS	KAVASS	KEA	KEDGEREE	KEENER
KATHAK	KAVASSES	KEAS	KEDGEREES	KEENERS
KATHAKALI	KAW	KEASAR	KEDGERS	KEENEST
KATHAKS	KAWA	KEASARS	KEDGES	KEENING
KATHARSES	KAWAII	KEAVIE	KEDGIER	KEENINGS

KEENLY	KEGLING	KELSONS	KENNELMEN	KERATIN
KEENNESS	KEGLINGS	KELT	KENNELS	KERATINS
KEENO	KEGS	KELTER	KENNER	KERATITIS
KEENOS	KEHUA	KELTERS	KENNERS	KERATOID
KEENS	KEHUAS	KELTIE	KENNET	KERATOMA
KEEP	KEIGHT	KELTIES	KENNETS	KERATOMAS
KEEPABLE	KEIR	KELTS	KENNETT	KERATOSE
KEEPER	KEIREN	KELTY	KENNETTED	KERATOSES
KEEPERS	KEIRENS	KELVIN	KENNETTS	KERATOSIC
KEEPING	KEIRETSU	KELVINS	KENNING	KERATOSIS
KEEPINGS	KEIRETSUS	KEMB	KENNINGS	KERATOTIC
KEEPNET	KEIRIN	KEMBED	KENO	KERB
KEEPNETS	KEIRINS	KEMBING	KENOS	KERBAYA
KEEPS	KEIRS	KEMBLA	KENOSES	KERBAYAS
KEEPSAKE	KEISTER	KEMBLAS	KENOSIS	KERBED
KEEPSAKES	KEISTERS	KEMBO	KENOSISES	KERBING
KEEPSAKY	KEITLOA	KEMBOED	KENOTIC	KERBINGS
KEESHOND	KEITLOAS	KEMBOING	KENOTICS	KERBLOOEY
KEESHONDS	KEKENO	KEMBOS	KENOTRON	KERBS
KEESTER	KEKENOS	KEMBS	KENOTRONS	KERBSIDE
KEESTERS	KEKERENGU	KEMP	KENS	KERBSIDES
KEET	KEKS	KEMPED	KENSPECK	KERBSTONE
KEETS	KEKSYE	KEMPER	KENT	KERCHIEF
KEEVE	KEKSYES	KEMPERS	KENTE	KERCHIEFS
KEEVES	KELEP	KEMPIER	KENTED	KERCHOO
KEF	KELEPS	KEMPIEST	KENTES	KEREL
KEFFEL	KELIM	KEMPING	KENTIA	KERELS
KEFFELS	KELIMS	KEMPINGS	KENTIAS	KERERU
KEFFIYAH	KELL	KEMPLE	KENTING	KERERUS
KEFFIYAHS	KELLAUT	KEMPLES	KENTLEDGE	KERF
KEFFIYEH	KELLAUTS	KEMPS	KENTS	KERFED
KEFFIYEHS	KELLIES	KEMPT	KEP	KERFING
KEFIR	KELLS	KEMPY	KEPHALIC	KERFLOOEY
KEFIRS	KELLY	KEN	KEPHALICS	KERFS
KEFS	KELOID	KENAF	KEPHALIN	KERFUFFLE
KEFTEDES	KELOIDAL	KENAFS	KEPHALINS	KERKIER
KEFUFFLE	KELOIDS	KENCH	KEPHIR	KERKIEST
KEFUFFLED	KELP	KENCHES	KEPHIRS	KERKY
KEFUFFLES	KELPED	KENDO	KEPI	KERMA
KEG	KELPER	KENDOIST	KEPIS	KERMAS
KEGELER	KELPERS	KENDOISTS	KEPPED	KERMES
KEGELERS	KELPFISH	KENDOS	KEPPEN	KERMESES
KEGGED	KELPIE	KENNED	KEPPING	KERMESITE
KEGGER	KELPIES	KENNEL	KEPPIT	KERMESS
KEGGERS	KELPING	KENNELED	KEPS	KERMESSE
KEGGING	KELPS	KENNELING	KEPT	KERMESSES
KEGLER	KELPY	KENNELLED	KERAMIC	KERMIS
KEGLERS	KELSON	KENNELMAN	KERAMICS	KERMISES

KERMODE	KESTRELS	KEVILS	KEYSTERS	KHANSAMAS
KERMODES	KESTS	KEWL	KEYSTONE	KHANUM
KERN	KET	KEWLER	KEYSTONED	KHANUMS
KERNE	KETA	KEWLEST	KEYSTONES	KHAPH
KERNED	KETAINE	KEWPIE	KEYSTROKE	KHAPHS
KERNEL	KETAMINE	KEWPIES	KEYWAY	KHARIF
KERNELED	KETAMINES	KEX	KEYWAYS	KHARIFS
KERNELING	KETAS	KEXES	KEYWORD	KHAT
KERNELLED	KETCH	KEY	KEYWORDS	KHATS
KERNELLY	KETCHES	KEYBOARD	KEYWORKER	KHAYA
KERNELS	KETCHING	KEYBOARDS	KGOTLA	KHAYAL
KERNES	KETCHUP	KEYBUGLE	KGOTLAS	KHAYALS
KERNING	KETCHUPS	KEYBUGLES	KHADDAR	KHAYAS
KERNINGS	KETCHUPY	KEYBUTTON	KHADDARS	KHAZEN
KERNISH	KETE	KEYCARD	KHADI	KHAZENIM
KERNITE	KETENE	KEYCARDS	KHADIS	KHAZENS
KERNITES	KETENES	KEYED	KHAF	KHAZI
KERNS	KETES	KEYER	KHAFS	KHAZIS
KERO	KETMIA	KEYERS	KHAKI	KHEDA
KEROGEN	KETMIAS	KEYEST	KHAKILIKE	KHEDAH
KEROGENS	KETO	KEYFRAME	KHAKIS	KHEDAHS
KEROS	KETOGENIC	KEYFRAMES	KHALAT	KHEDAS
KEROSENE	KETOL	KEYHOLE	KHALATS	KHEDIVA
KEROSENES	KETOLS	KEYHOLES	KHALIF	KHEDIVAL
KEROSINE	KETONE	KEYING	KHALIFA	KHEDIVAS
KEROSINES	KETONEMIA	KEYINGS	KHALIFAH	KHEDIVATE
KERPLUNK	KETONES	KEYLESS	KHALIFAHS	KHEDIVE
KERPLUNKS	KETONIC	KEYLINE	KHALIFAS	KHEDIVES
KERRIA	KETONURIA	KEYLINES	KHALIFAT	KHEDIVIAL
KERRIAS	KETOSE	KEYLOGGER	KHALIFATE	KHET
KERRIES	KETOSES	KEYNOTE	KHALIFATS	KHETH
KERRY	KETOSIS	KEYNOTED	KHALIFS	KHETHS
KERSEY	KETOTIC	KEYNOTER	KHAMSEEN	KHETS
KERSEYS	KETOXIME	KEYNOTERS	KHAMSEENS	KHI
KERVE	KETOXIMES	KEYNOTES	KHAMSIN	KHILAFAT
KERVED	KETS	KEYNOTING	KHAMSINS	KHILAFATS
KERVES	KETTLE	KEYPAD	KHAN	KHILAT
KERVING	KETTLED	KEYPADS	KHANATE	KHILATS
KERYGMA	KETTLEFUL	KEYPAL	KHANATES	KHILIM
KERYGMAS	KETTLES	KEYPALS	KHANDA	KHILIMS
KERYGMATA	KETTLING	KEYPRESS	KHANDAS	KHIMAR
KESAR	KETUBAH	KEYPUNCH	KHANGA	KHIMARS
KESARS	KETUBAHS	KEYRING	KHANGAS	KHIRKAH
KESH	KETUBOT	KEYRINGS	KHANJAR	KHIRKAHS
KESHES	KETUBOTH	KEYS	KHANJARS	KHIS
KEST	KEVEL	KEYSET	KHANS	KHODJA
KESTING	KEVELS	KEYSETS	KHANSAMA	KHODJAS
KESTREL	KEVIL	KEYSTER	KHANSAMAH	KHOJA

KHOJAS	KIBITKAS	KICKUP	KIDNAPPEE	KILDERKIN
KHOR	KIBITZ	KICKUPS	KIDNAPPER	KILERG
KHORS	KIBITZED	KICKY	KIDNAPS	KILERGS
KHOTBAH	KIBITZER	KID	KIDNEY	KILEY
KHOTBAHS	KIBITZERS	KIDDED	KIDNEYS	KILEYS
KHOTBEH	KIBITZES	KIDDER	KIDOLOGY	KILIKITI
KHOTBEHS	KIBITZING	KIDDERS	KIDS	KILIKITIS
KHOUM	KIBLA	KIDDIE	KIDSKIN	KILIM
KHOUMS	KIBLAH	KIDDIED	KIDSKINS	KILIMS
KHUD	KIBLAHS	KIDDIER	KIDSTAKES	KILL
KHUDS	KIBLAS	KIDDIERS	KIDULT	KILLABLE
KHURTA	KIBOSH	KIDDIES	KIDULTS	KILLADAR
KHURTAS	KIBOSHED	KIDDING	KIDVID	KILLADARS
KHUSKHUS	KIBOSHES	KIDDINGLY	KIDVIDS	KILLAS
KHUTBAH	KIBOSHING	KIDDINGS	KIEF	KILLASES
KHUTBAHS	KICK	KIDDISH	KIEFS	KILLCOW
KI	KICKABLE	KIDDLE	KIEKIE	KILLCOWS
KIAAT	KICKABOUT	KIDDLES	KIEKIES	KILLCROP
KIAATS	KICKBACK	KIDDO	KIELBASA	KILLCROPS
KIACK	KICKBACKS	KIDDOES	KIELBASAS	KILLDEE
KIACKS	KICKBALL	KIDDOS	KIELBASI	KILLDEER
KIANG	KICKBALLS	KIDDUSH	KIELBASY	KILLDEERS
KIANGS	KICKBOARD	KIDDUSHES	KIER	KILLDEES
KIAUGH	KICKBOX	KIDDY	KIERIE	KILLED
KIAUGHS	KICKBOXED	KIDDYING	KIERIES	KILLER
KIBBE	KICKBOXER	KIDDYWINK	KIERS	KILLERS
KIBBEH	KICKBOXES	KIDEL	KIESELGUR	KILLICK
KIBBEHS	KICKDOWN	KIDELS	KIESERITE	KILLICKS
KIBBES	KICKDOWNS	KIDGE	KIESTER	KILLIE
KIBBI	KICKED	KIDGIE	KIESTERS	KILLIES
KIBBIS	KICKER	KIDGIER	KIEV	KILLIFISH
KIBBITZ	KICKERS	KIDGIEST	KIEVE	KILLING
KIBBITZED	KICKFLIP	KIDGLOVE	KIEVES	KILLINGLY
KIBBITZER	KICKFLIPS	KIDLET	KIEVS	KILLINGS
KIBBITZES	KICKIER	KIDLETS	KIF	KILLJOY
KIBBLE	KICKIEST	KIDLIKE	KIFF	KILLJOYS
KIBBLED	KICKING	KIDLING	KIFS	KILLOCK
KIBBLES	KICKINGS	KIDLINGS	KIGHT	KILLOCKS
KIBBLING	KICKOFF	KIDLIT	KIGHTS	KILLOGIE
KIBBUTZ	KICKOFFS	KIDLITS	KIKE	KILLOGIES
KIBBUTZIM	KICKOUT	KIDNAP	KIKES	KILLS
KIBE	KICKOUTS	KIDNAPED	KIKOI	KILLUT
KIBEI	KICKPLATE	KIDNAPEE	KIKOIS	KILLUTS
KIBEIS	KICKS	KIDNAPEES	KIKUMON	KILN
KIBES	KICKSHAW	KIDNAPER	KIKUMONS	KILNED
KIBIBYTE	KICKSHAWS	KIDNAPERS	KIKUYU	KILNING
KIBIBYTES	KICKSTAND	KIDNAPING	KIKUYUS	KILNS
KIBITKA	KICKSTART	KIDNAPPED	KILD	KILO

KILOBAR	KILTS	KINDLY	KINGLIEST	KINSWOMEN
KILOBARS	KILTY	KINDNESS	KINGLIKE	KINTLEDGE
KILOBASE	KIMBO	KINDRED	KINGLING	KIORE
KILOBASES	KIMBOED	KINDREDS	KINGLINGS	KIORES
KILOBAUD	KIMBOING	KINDS	KINGLY	KIOSK
KILOBAUDS	KIMBOS	KINDY	KINGMAKER	KIOSKS
KILOBIT	KIMCHEE	KINE	KINGPIN	KIP
KILOBITS	KIMCHEES	KINEMA	KINGPINS	KIPE
KILOBYTE	KIMCHI	KINEMAS	KINGPOST	KIPES
KILOBYTES	KIMCHIS	KINEMATIC	KINGPOSTS	KIPP
KILOCURIE	KIMMER	KINES	KINGS	KIPPA
KILOCYCLE	KIMMERS	KINESCOPE	KINGSHIP	KIPPAGE
KILOGAUSS	KIMONO	KINESES	KINGSHIPS	KIPPAGES
KILOGRAM	KIMONOED	KINESIC	KINGSIDE	KIPPAH
KILOGRAMS	KIMONOS	KINESICS	KINGSIDES	KIPPAHS
KILOGRAY	KIN	KINESIS	KINGSNAKE	KIPPAS
KILOGRAYS	KINA	KINESISES	KINGWOOD	KIPPED
KILOHERTZ	KINAKINA	KINETIC	KINGWOODS	KIPPEN
KILOJOULE	KINAKINAS	KINETICAL	KININ	KIPPER
KILOLITER	KINARA	KINETICS	KININS	KIPPERED
KILOLITRE	KINARAS	KINETIN	KINK	KIPPERER
KILOMETER	KINAS	KINETINS	KINKAJOU	KIPPERERS
KILOMETRE	KINASE	KINFOLK	KINKAJOUS	KIPPERING
KILOMOLE	KINASES	KINFOLKS	KINKED	KIPPERS
KILOMOLES	KINCHIN	KING	KINKIER	KIPPING
KILOPOND	KINCHINS	KINGBIRD	KINKIEST	KIPPS
KILOPONDS	KINCOB	KINGBIRDS	KINKILY	KIPS
KILORAD	KINCOBS	KINGBOLT	KINKINESS	KIPSKIN
KILORADS	KIND	KINGBOLTS	KINKING	KIPSKINS
KILOS	KINDA	KINGCRAFT	KINKLE	KIPUNJI
KILOTON	KINDED	KINGCUP	KINKLES	KIPUNJIS
KILOTONNE	KINDER	KINGCUPS	KINKS	KIR
KILOTONS	KINDERS	KINGDOM	KINKY	KIRANA
KILOVOLT	KINDEST	KINGDOMED	KINLESS	KIRANAS
KILOVOLTS	KINDIE	KINGDOMS	KINO	KIRBEH
KILOWATT	KINDIES	KINGED	KINONE	KIRBEHS
KILOWATTS	KINDING	KINGFISH	KINONES	KIRBIGRIP
KILP	KINDLE	KINGHOOD	KINOS	KIRBY
KILPS	KINDLED	KINGHOODS	KINRED	KIRIGAMI
KILT	KINDLER	KINGING	KINREDS	KIRIGAMIS
KILTED	KINDLERS	KINGKLIP	KINS	KIRIMON
KILTER	KINDLES	KINGKLIPS	KINSFOLK	KIRIMONS
KILTERS	KINDLESS	KINGLE	KINSFOLKS	KIRK
KILTIE	KINDLIER	KINGLES	KINSHIP	KIRKED
KILTIES	KINDLIEST	KINGLESS	KINSHIPS	KIRKING
KILTING	KINDLILY	KINGLET	KINSMAN	KIRKINGS
KILTINGS	KINDLING	KINGLETS	KINSMEN	KIRKMAN
KILTLIKE	KINDLINGS	KINGLIER	KINSWOMAN	KIRKMEN

KIRKS

KIRKS
KIRKTON
KIRKTONS
KIRKWARD
KIRKYAIRD
KIRKYARD
KIRKYARDS
KIRMESS
KIRMESSES
KIRN
KIRNED
KIRNING
KIRNS
KIRPAN
KIRPANS
KIRRI
KIRRIS
KIRS
KIRSCH
KIRSCHES
KIRTAN
KIRTANS
KIRTLE
KIRTLED
KIRTLES
KIS
KISAN
KISANS
KISH
KISHES
KISHKA
KISHKAS
KISHKE
KISHKES
KISKADEE
KISKADEES
KISMAT
KISMATS
KISMET
KISMETIC
KISMETS
KISS
KISSABLE
KISSABLY
KISSAGRAM
KISSED
KISSEL
KISSELS

KISSER
KISSERS
KISSES
KISSIER
KISSIEST
KISSING
KISSINGS
KISSOGRAM
KISSY
KIST
KISTED
KISTFUL
KISTFULS
KISTING
KISTS
KISTVAEN
KISTVAENS
KIT
KITBAG
KITBAGS
KITCHEN
KITCHENED
KITCHENER
KITCHENET
KITCHENS
KITE
KITEBOARD
KITED
KITELIKE
KITENGE
KITENGES
KITER
KITERS
KITES
KITH
KITHARA
KITHARAS
KITHE
KITHED
KITHES
KITHING
KITHS
KITING
KITINGS
KITLING
KITLINGS
KITS
KITSCH

KITSCHES
KITSCHIER
KITSCHIFY
KITSCHILY
KITSCHY
KITSET
KITSETS
KITTED
KITTEL
KITTELS
KITTEN
KITTENED
KITTENIER
KITTENING
KITTENISH
KITTENS
KITTENY
KITTIES
KITTING
KITTIWAKE
KITTLE
KITTLED
KITTLER
KITTLES
KITTLEST
KITTLIER
KITTLIEST
KITTLING
KITTLY
KITTUL
KITTULS
KITTY
KITUL
KITULS
KIVA
KIVAS
KIWI
KIWIFRUIT
KIWIS
KLANG
KLANGS
KLAP
KLAPPED
KLAPPING
KLAPS
KLATCH
KLATCHES
KLATSCH

KLATSCHES
KLAVERN
KLAVERNS
KLAVIER
KLAVIERS
KLAXON
KLAXONED
KLAXONING
KLAXONS
KLEAGLE
KLEAGLES
KLEENEX
KLEENEXES
KLEFTIKO
KLEFTIKOS
KLENDUSIC
KLEPHT
KLEPHTIC
KLEPHTISM
KLEPHTS
KLEPTO
KLEPTOS
KLETT
KLETTS
KLEZMER
KLEZMERS
KLEZMORIM
KLICK
KLICKS
KLIEG
KLIEGS
KLIK
KLIKS
KLINKER
KLINKERS
KLINOSTAT
KLIPDAS
KLIPDASES
KLISTER
KLISTERS
KLONDIKE
KLONDIKED
KLONDIKER
KLONDIKES
KLONDYKE
KLONDYKED
KLONDYKER
KLONDYKES

KLONG
KLONGS
KLOOCH
KLOOCHES
KLOOCHMAN
KLOOCHMEN
KLOOF
KLOOFS
KLOOTCH
KLOOTCHES
KLUDGE
KLUDGED
KLUDGES
KLUDGEY
KLUDGIER
KLUDGIEST
KLUDGING
KLUDGY
KLUGE
KLUGED
KLUGES
KLUGING
KLUTZ
KLUTZES
KLUTZIER
KLUTZIEST
KLUTZY
KLYSTRON
KLYSTRONS
KNACK
KNACKED
KNACKER
KNACKERED
KNACKERS
KNACKERY
KNACKIER
KNACKIEST
KNACKING
KNACKISH
KNACKS
KNACKY
KNAG
KNAGGIER
KNAGGIEST
KNAGGY
KNAGS
KNAIDEL
KNAIDELS

KNAIDLACH	KNEEBOARD	KNIFEMAN	KNOBBLING	KNOTTIER
KNAP	KNEECAP	KNIFEMEN	KNOBBLY	KNOTTIEST
KNAPPED	KNEECAPS	KNIFER	KNOBBY	KNOTTILY
KNAPPER	KNEED	KNIFEREST	KNOBHEAD	KNOTTING
KNAPPERS	KNEEHOLE	KNIFERS	KNOBHEADS	KNOTTINGS
KNAPPING	KNEEHOLES	KNIFES	KNOBLIKE	KNOTTY
KNAPPLE	KNEEING	KNIFING	KNOBS	KNOTWEED
KNAPPLED	KNEEJERK	KNIFINGS	KNOBSTICK	KNOTWEEDS
KNAPPLES	KNEEL	KNIGHT	KNOCK	KNOTWORK
KNAPPLING	KNEELED	KNIGHTAGE	KNOCKBACK	KNOTWORKS
KNAPS	KNEELER	KNIGHTED	KNOCKDOWN	KNOUT
KNAPSACK	KNEELERS	KNIGHTING	KNOCKED	KNOUTED
KNAPSACKS	KNEELIKE	KNIGHTLY	KNOCKER	KNOUTING
KNAPWEED	KNEELING	KNIGHTS	KNOCKERS	KNOUTS
KNAPWEEDS	KNEELS	KNIPHOFIA	KNOCKING	KNOW
KNAR	KNEEPAD	KNISH	KNOCKINGS	KNOWABLE
KNARL	KNEEPADS	KNISHES	KNOCKLESS	KNOWE
KNARLIER	KNEEPAN	KNIT	KNOCKOFF	KNOWER
KNARLIEST	KNEEPANS	KNITBONE	KNOCKOFFS	KNOWERS
KNARLS	KNEEPIECE	KNITBONES	KNOCKOUT	KNOWES
KNARLY	KNEEROOM	KNITCH	KNOCKOUTS	KNOWHOW
KNARRED	KNEEROOMS	KNITCHES	KNOCKS	KNOWHOWS
KNARRIER	KNEES	KNITS	KNOLL	KNOWING
KNARRIEST	KNEESIES	KNITTABLE	KNOLLED	KNOWINGER
KNARRING	KNEESOCK	KNITTED	KNOLLER	KNOWINGLY
KNARRY	KNEESOCKS	KNITTER	KNOLLERS	KNOWINGS
KNARS	KNEIDEL	KNITTERS	KNOLLIER	KNOWLEDGE
KNAUR	KNEIDELS	KNITTING	KNOLLIEST	KNOWN
KNAURS	KNEIDLACH	KNITTINGS	KNOLLING	KNOWNS
KNAVE	KNELL	KNITTLE	KNOLLS	KNOWS
KNAVERIES	KNELLED	KNITTLES	KNOLLY	KNUB
KNAVERY	KNELLING	KNITWEAR	KNOP	KNUBBIER
KNAVES	KNELLS	KNITWEARS	KNOPPED	KNUBBIEST
KNAVESHIP	KNELT	KNIVE	KNOPS	KNUBBLE
KNAVISH	KNESSET	KNIVED	KNOSP	KNUBBLED
KNAVISHLY	KNESSETS	KNIVES	KNOSPS	KNUBBLES
KNAWE	KNEVELL	KNIVING	KNOT	KNUBBLIER
KNAWEL	KNEVELLED	KNOB	KNOTGRASS	KNUBBLING
KNAWELS	KNEVELLS	KNOBBED	KNOTHEAD	KNUBBLY
KNAWES	KNEW	KNOBBER	KNOTHEADS	KNUBBY
KNEAD	KNICKER	KNOBBERS	KNOTHOLE	KNUBS
KNEADABLE	KNICKERED	KNOBBIER	KNOTHOLES	KNUCKLE
KNEADED	KNICKERS	KNOBBIEST	KNOTLESS	KNUCKLED
KNEADER	KNICKS	KNOBBING	KNOTLIKE	KNUCKLER
KNEADERS	KNIFE	KNOBBLE	KNOTS	KNUCKLERS
KNEADING	KNIFED	KNOBBLED	KNOTTED	KNUCKLES
KNEADS	KNIFELESS	KNOBBLES	KNOTTER	KNUCKLIER
KNEE	KNIFELIKE	KNOBBLIER	KNOTTERS	KNUCKLING

K

KNUCKLY	KOFTWORK	KOLBASSAS	KONK	KORARIS
KNUR	KOFTWORKS	KOLBASSI	KONKED	KORAS
KNURL	KOGAL	KOLBASSIS	KONKING	KORAT
KNURLED	KOGALS	KOLHOZ	KONKS	KORATS
KNURLIER	KOHA	KOLHOZES	KONNING	KORE
KNURLIEST	KOHANIM	KOLHOZY	KONS	KORERO
KNURLING	KOHAS	KOLINSKI	KOODOO	KOREROED
KNURLINGS	KOHEKOHE	KOLINSKY	KOODOOS	KOREROING
KNURLS	KOHEKOHES	KOLKHOS	KOOK	KOREROS
KNURLY	KOHEN	KOLKHOSES	KOOKED	KORES
KNURR	KOHL	KOLKHOSY	KOOKIE	KORFBALL
KNURRS	KOHLRABI	KOLKHOZ	KOOKIER	KORFBALLS
KNURS	KOHLRABIS	KOLKHOZES	KOOKIEST	KORIMAKO
KNUT	KOHLS	KOLKHOZY	KOOKILY	KORIMAKOS
KNUTS	KOI	KOLKOZ	KOOKINESS	KORKIR
KO	KOINE	KOLKOZES	KOOKING	KORKIRS
KOA	KOINES	KOLKOZY	KOOKS	KORMA
KOALA	KOIS	KOLO	KOOKUM	KORMAS
KOALAS	KOJI	KOLOS	KOOKUMS	KORO
KOAN	KOJIS	KOMATIK	KOOKY	KOROMIKO
KOANS	KOKA	KOMATIKS	KOOLAH	KOROMIKOS
KOAP	KOKAKO	KOMBU	KOOLAHS	KORORA
KOAPS	KOKAKOS	KOMBUS	KOORI	KORORAS
KOAS	KOKAM	KOMISSAR	KOORIES	KOROS
KOB	KOKAMS	KOMISSARS	KOORIS	KOROWAI
KOBAN	KOKANEE	KOMITAJI	KOP	KOROWAIS
KOBANG	KOKANEES	KOMITAJIS	KOPASETIC	KORS
KOBANGS	KOKAS	KOMONDOR	KOPECK	KORU
KOBANS	KOKER	KOMONDORS	KOPECKS	KORUN
KOBO	KOKERS	KOMPROMAT	KOPEK	KORUNA
KOBOLD	KOKIRI	KON	KOPEKS	KORUNAS
KOBOLDS	KOKIRIS	KONAKI	KOPH	KORUNY
KOBOS	KOKOBEH	KONAKIS	KOPHS	KORUS
KOBS	KOKOPU	KONBU	KOPIYKA	KOS
KOCHIA	KOKOPUS	KONBUS	KOPIYKAS	KOSES
KOCHIAS	KOKOWAI	KOND	KOPIYKY	KOSHER
KOEKOEA	KOKOWAIS	KONDO	KOPIYOK	KOSHERED
KOEKOEAS	KOKRA	KONDOS	KOPJE	KOSHERING
KOEL	KOKRAS	KONEKE	KOPJES	KOSHERS
KOELS	KOKUM	KONEKES	KOPPA	KOSMOS
KOFF	KOKUMS	KONFYT	KOPPAS	KOSMOSES
KOFFS	KOLA	KONFYTS	KOPPIE	KOSS
KOFTA	KOLACKIES	KONGONI	KOPPIES	KOSSES
KOFTAS	KOLACKY	KONIMETER	KOPS	KOTARE
KOFTGAR	KOLAS	KONINI	KOR	KOTARES
KOFTGARI	KOLBASI	KONINIS	KORA	KOTCH
KOFTGARIS	KOLBASIS	KONIOLOGY	KORAI	KOTCHED
KOFTGARS	KOLBASSA	KONISCOPE	KORARI	KOTCHES

KOTCHING	KRAB	KREUTZER	KRYPSES	KULBASA
KOTO	KRABS	KREUTZERS	KRYPSIS	KULBASAS
KOTOS	KRAFT	KREUZER	KRYPTON	KULFI
KOTOW	KRAFTS	KREUZERS	KRYPTONS	KULFIS
KOTOWED	KRAI	KREWE	KRYTRON	KULTUR
KOTOWER	KRAIS	KREWES	KRYTRONS	KULTURS
KOTOWERS	KRAIT	KRILL	KSAR	KUMARA
KOTOWING	KRAITS	KRILLS	KSARS	KUMARAHOU
KOTOWS	KRAKEN	KRIMMER	KUBASA	KUMARAS
KOTTABOS	KRAKENS	KRIMMERS	KUBASAS	KUMARI
KOTUKU	KRAKOWIAK	KRIS	KUBIE	KUMARIS
KOTUKUS	KRAMERIA	KRISED	KUBIES	KUMBALOI
KOTWAL	KRAMERIAS	KRISES	KUCCHA	KUMERA
KOTWALS	KRANG	KRISING	KUCCHAS	KUMERAS
KOULAN	KRANGS	KROMESKY	KUCHCHA	KUMIKUMI
KOULANS	KRANS	KRONA	KUCHEN	KUMIKUMIS
KOUMIS	KRANSES	KRONE	KUCHENS	KUMIS
KOUMISES	KRANTZ	KRONEN	KUDLIK	KUMISES
KOUMISS	KRANTZES	KRONER	KUDLIKS	KUMISS
KOUMISSES	KRANZ	KRONOR	KUDO	KUMISSES
KOUMYS	KRANZES	KRONUR	KUDOS	KUMITE
KOUMYSES	KRATER	KROON	KUDOSES	KUMITES
KOUMYSS	KRATERS	KROONI	KUDU	KUMKUM
KOUMYSSES	KRAUT	KROONS	KUDUS	KUMKUMS
KOUPREY	KRAUTROCK	KRUBI	KUDZU	KUMMEL
KOUPREYS	KRAUTS	KRUBIS	KUDZUS	KUMMELS
KOURA	KRAY	KRUBUT	KUE	KUMQUAT
KOURAS	KRAYS	KRUBUTS	KUEH	KUMQUATS
KOURBASH	KREASOTE	KRULLER	KUES	KUMYS
KOUROI	KREASOTED	KRULLERS	KUFI	KUMYSES
KOUROS	KREASOTES	KRUMHORN	KUFIS	KUNA
KOUSKOUS	KREATINE	KRUMHORNS	KUFIYAH	KUNDALINI
KOUSSO	KREATINES	KRUMKAKE	KUFIYAHS	KUNE
KOUSSOS	KREEP	KRUMKAKES	KUGEL	KUNEKUNE
KOW	KREEPS	KRUMMHOLZ	KUGELS	KUNEKUNES
KOWHAI	KREESE	KRUMMHORN	KUIA	KUNJOOS
KUWHAIS	KREESED	KRUMPER	KUIAS	KUNKAR
KOWS	KREESES	KRUMPERS	KUKRI	KUNKARS
KOWTOW	KREESING	KRUMPING	KUKRIS	KUNKUR
KOWTOWED	KREMLIN	KRUMPINGS	KUKU	KUNKURS
KOWTOWER	KREMLINS	KRUNK	KUKUS	KUNZITE
KOWTOWERS	KRENG	KRUNKED	KULA	KUNZITES
KOWTOWING	KRENGS	KRUNKS	KULAK	KURBASH
KOWTOWS	KREOSOTE	KRYOLITE	KULAKI	KURBASHED
KRAAL	KREOSOTED	KRYOLITES	KULAKS	KURBASHES
KRAALED	KREOSOTES	KRYOLITH	KULAN	KURFUFFLE
KRAALING	KREPLACH	KRYOLITHS	KULANS	KURGAN
KRAALS	KREPLECH	KRYOMETER	KULAS	KURGANS

KURI	KUTCHES	KWACHAS	KYAT	KYMOGRAPH
KURIS	KUTI	KWAITO	KYATS	KYND
KURRAJONG	KUTIS	KWAITOS	KYBO	KYNDE
KURRE	KUTU	KWANZA	KYBOS	KYNDED
KURRES	KUTUS	KWANZAS	KYBOSH	KYNDES
KURSAAL	KUVASZ	KWELA	KYBOSHED	KYNDING
KURSAALS	KUVASZOK	KWELAS	KYBOSHES	KYNDS
KURTA	KUZU	KY	KYBOSHING	KYNE
KURTAS	KUZUS	KYACK	KYDST	KYOGEN
KURTOSES	KVAS	KYACKS	KYE	KYOGENS
KURTOSIS	KVASES	KYAK	KYES	KYPE
KURU	KVASS	KYAKS	KYLE	KYPES
KURUS	KVASSES	KYANG	KYLES	KYPHOSES
KURUSH	KVELL	KYANGS	KYLICES	KYPHOSIS
KURUSHES	KVELLED	KYANISE	KYLIE	KYPHOTIC
KURVEY	KVELLING	KYANISED	KYLIES	KYRIE
KURVEYED	KVELLS	KYANISES	KYLIKES	KYRIELLE
KURVEYING	KVETCH	KYANISING	KYLIN	KYRIELLES
KURVEYOR	KVETCHED	KYANITE	KYLINS	KYRIES
KURVEYORS	KVETCHER	KYANITES	KYLIX	KYTE
KURVEYS	KVETCHERS	KYANITIC	KYLIXES	KYTES
KUSSO	KVETCHES	KYANIZE	KYLLOSES	KYTHE
KUSSOS	KVETCHIER	KYANIZED	KYLLOSIS	KYTHED
KUTA	KVETCHILY	KYANIZES	KYLOE	KYTHES
KUTAS	KVETCHING	KYANIZING	KYLOES	KYTHING
KUTCH	KVETCHY	KYAR	KYMOGRAM	KYU
KUTCHA	KWACHA	KYARS	KYMOGRAMS	KYUS

L

LA	LABIATED	LABRIDS	LACEWORK	LACQUEYS
LAAGER	LABIATES	LABROID	LACEWORKS	LACRIMAL
LAAGERED	LABILE	LABROIDS	LACEY	LACRIMALS
LAAGERING	LABILITY	LABROSE	LACHES	LACRIMARY
LAAGERS	LABIS	LABRUM	LACHESES	LACRIMOSO
LAARI	LABISES	LABRUMS	LACHRYMAL	LACROSSE
LAARIS	LABIUM	LABRUSCA	LACIER	LACROSSES
LAB	LABLAB	LABRUSCAS	LACIEST	LACRYMAL
LABARA	LABLABS	LABRYS	LACILY	LACRYMALS
LABARUM	LABNEH	LABRYSES	LACINESS	LACS
LABARUMS	LABNEHS	LABS	LACING	LACTAM
LABDA	LABOR	LABURNUM	LACINGS	LACTAMS
LABDACISM	LABORED	LABURNUMS	LACINIA	LACTARIAN
LABDANUM	LABOREDLY	LABYRINTH	LACINIAE	LACTARY
LABDANUMS	LABORER	LAC	LACINIATE	LACTASE
LABDAS	LABORERS	LACCOLITE	LACK	LACTASES
LABEL	LABORING	LACCOLITH	LACKADAY	LACTATE
LABELABLE	LABORIOUS	LACE	LACKED	LACTATED
LABELED	LABORISM	LACEBARK	LACKER	LACTATES
LABELER	LABORISMS	LACEBARKS	LACKERED	LACTATING
LABELERS	LABORIST	LACED	LACKERING	LACTATION
LABELING	LABORISTS	LACELESS	LACKERS	LACTEAL
LABELLA	LABORITE	LACELIKE	LACKEY	LACTEALLY
LABELLATE	LABORITES	LACEMAKER	LACKEYED	LACTEALS
LABELLED	LABORS	LACER	LACKEYING	LACTEAN
LABELLER	LABORSOME	LACERABLE	LACKEYS	LACTEOUS
LABELLERS	LABOUR	LACERANT	LACKING	LACTIC
LABELLING	LABOURED	LACERATE	LACKLAND	LACTIFIC
LABELLIST	LABOURER	LACERATED	LACKLANDS	LACTITOL
LABELLOID	LABOURERS	LACERATES	LACKS	LACTITOLS
LABELLUM	LABOURING	LACERS	LACMUS	LACTIVISM
LABELMATE	LABOURISM	LACERTIAN	LACMUSES	LACTIVIST
LABELS	LABOURIST	LACERTID	LACONIC	LACTONE
LABIA	LABOURITE	LACERTIDS	LACONICAL	LACTONES
LABIAL	LABOURS	LACERTINE	LACONISM	LACTONIC
LABIALISE	LABRA	LACES	LACONISMS	LACTOSE
LABIALISM	LABRADOR	LACET	LACQUER	LACTOSES
LABIALITY	LABRADORS	LACETS	LACQUERED	LACTULOSE
LABIALIZE	LABRAL	LACEWING	LACQUERER	LACUNA
LABIALLY	LABRET	LACEWINGS	LACQUERS	LACUNAE
LABIALS	LABRETS	LACEWOOD	LACQUEY	LACUNAL
LABIATE	LABRID	LACEWOODS	LACQUEYED	LACUNAR

LACUNARIA	LADINOS	LAERS	LAH	LAIR
LACUNARS	LADLE	LAESIE	LAHAL	LAIRAGE
LACUNARY	LADLED	LAETARE	LAHALS	LAIRAGES
LACUNAS	LADLEFUL	LAETARES	LAHAR	LAIRD
LACUNATE	LADLEFULS	LAETRILE	LAHARS	LAIRDLIER
LACUNE	LADLER	LAETRILES	LAHS	LAIRDLY
LACUNES	LADLERS	LAEVIGATE	LAIC	LAIRDS
LACUNOSE	LADLES	LAEVO	LAICAL	LAIRDSHIP
LACY	LADLING	LAEVULIN	LAICALLY	LAIRED
LAD	LADRON	LAEVULINS	LAICH	LAIRIER
LADANUM	LADRONE	LAEVULOSE	LAICHS	LAIRIEST
LADANUMS	LADRONES	LAG	LAICISE	LAIRING
LADDER	LADRONS	LAGAN	LAICISED	LAIRISE
LADDERED	LADS	LAGANS	LAICISES	LAIRISED
LADDERIER	LADY	LAGENA	LAICISING	LAIRISES
LADDERING	LADYBIRD	LAGENAS	LAICISM	LAIRISING
LADDERS	LADYBIRDS	LAGEND	LAICISMS	LAIRIZE
LADDERY	LADYBOY	LAGENDS	LAICITIES	LAIRIZED
LADDIE	LADYBOYS	LAGER	LAICITY	LAIRIZES
LADDIER	LADYBUG	LAGERED	LAICIZE	LAIRIZING
LADDIES	LADYBUGS	LAGERING	LAICIZED	LAIRS
LADDIEST	LADYCOW	LAGERS	LAICIZES	LAIRY
LADDISH	LADYCOWS	LAGGARD	LAICIZING	LAISSE
LADDISHLY	LADYFIED	LAGGARDLY	LAICS	LAISSES
LADDISM	LADYFIES	LAGGARDS	LAID	LAITANCE
LADDISMS	LADYFISH	LAGGED	LAIDED	LAITANCES
LADDY	LADYFLIES	LAGGEN	LAIDING	LAITH
LADE	LADYFLY	LAGGENS	LAIDLIER	LAITHLY
LADED	LADYFY	LAGGER	LAIDLIEST	LAITIES
LADEN	LADYFYING	LAGGERS	LAIDLY	LAITY
LADENED	LADYHOOD	LAGGIN	LAIDS	LAKE
LADENING	LADYHOODS	LAGGING	LAIGH	LAKEBED
LADENS	LADYISH	LAGGINGLY	LAIGHER	LAKEBEDS
LADER	LADYISM	LAGGINGS	LAIGHEST	LAKED
LADERS	LADYISMS	LAGGINS	LAIGHS	LAKEFILL
LADES	LADYKIN	LAGNAPPE	LAIK	LAKEFILLS
LADETTE	LADYKINS	LAGNAPPES	LAIKA	LAKEFRONT
LADETTES	LADYLIKE	LAGNIAPPE	LAIKAS	LAKEHEAD
LADHOOD	LADYLOVE	LAGOMORPH	LAIKED	LAKEHEADS
LADHOODS	LADYLOVES	LAGOON	LAIKER	LAKELAND
LADIES	LADYNESS	LAGOONAL	LAIKERS	LAKELANDS
LADIFIED	LADYPALM	LAGOONS	LAIKING	LAKELET
LADIFIES	LADYPALMS	LAGRIMOSO	LAIKS	LAKELETS
LADIFY	LADYSHIP	LAGS	LAIN	LAKELIKE
LADIFYING	LADYSHIPS	LAGUNA	LAIPSE	LAKEPORT
LADING	LAER	LAGUNAS	LAIPSED	LAKEPORTS
LADINGS	LAERED	LAGUNE	LAIPSES	LAKER
LADINO	LAERING	LAGUNES	LAIPSING	LAKERS

LAKES	LAMBADAS	LAMELLATE	LAMMER	LAMPUKAS
LAKESHORE	LAMBAST	LAMELLOID	LAMMERS	LAMPUKI
LAKESIDE	LAMBASTE	LAMELLOSE	LAMMIE	LAMPUKIS
LAKESIDES	LAMBASTED	LAMELY	LAMMIES	LAMPYRID
LAKEVIEW	LAMBASTES	LAMENESS	LAMMIGER	LAMPYRIDS
LAKEWARD	LAMBASTS	LAMENT	LAMMIGERS	LAMS
LAKEWARDS	LAMBDA	LAMENTED	LAMMING	LAMSTER
LAKH	LAMBDAS	LAMENTER	LAMMINGS	LAMSTERS
LAKHS	LAMBDOID	LAMENTERS	LAMMY	LANA
LAKIER	LAMBED	LAMENTING	LAMP	LANAI
LAKIEST	LAMBENCY	LAMENTS	LAMPAD	LANAIS
LAKIN	LAMBENT	LAMER	LAMPADARY	LANAS
LAKING	LAMBENTLY	LAMES	LAMPADIST	LANATE
LAKINGS	LAMBER	LAMEST	LAMPADS	LANATED
LAKINS	LAMBERS	LAMETER	LAMPAS	LANCE
LAKISH	LAMBERT	LAMETERS	LAMPASES	LANCED
LAKSA	LAMBERTS	LAMIA	LAMPASSE	LANCEGAY
LAKSAS	LAMBIE	LAMIAE	LAMPASSES	LANCEGAYS
LAKY	LAMBIER	LAMIAS	LAMPBLACK	LANCEJACK
LALANG	LAMBIES	LAMIGER	LAMPBRUSH	LANCELET
LALANGS	LAMBIEST	LAMIGERS	LAMPED	LANCELETS
LALDIE	LAMBING	LAMINA	LAMPER	LANCELIKE
LALDIES	LAMBINGS	LAMINABLE	LAMPERN	LANCEOLAR
LALDY	LAMBITIVE	LAMINAE	LAMPERNS	LANCER
LALIQUE	LAMBKILL	LAMINAL	LAMPERS	LANCERS
LALIQUES	LAMBKILLS	LAMINALS	LAMPERSES	LANCES
LALL	LAMBKIN	LAMINAR	LAMPHOLE	LANCET
LALLAN	LAMBKINS	LAMINARIA	LAMPHOLES	LANCETED
LALLAND	LAMBLIKE	LAMINARIN	LAMPING	LANCETS
LALLANDS	LAMBLING	LAMINARY	LAMPINGS	LANCEWOOD
LALLANS	LAMBLINGS	LAMINAS	LAMPION	LANCH
LALLATION	LAMBOYS	LAMINATE	LAMPIONS	LANCHED
LALLED	LAMBRUSCO	LAMINATED	LAMPLESS	LANCHES
LALLING	LAMBS	LAMINATES	LAMPLIGHT	LANCHING
LALLINGS	LAMBSKIN	LAMINATOR	LAMPLIT	LANCIERS
LALLS	LAMBSKINS	LAMING	LAMPOON	LANCIFORM
LALLYGAG	LAMBSWOOL	LAMINGTON	LAMPOONED	LANCINATE
LALLYGAGS	LAMBY	LAMININ	LAMPOONER	LANCING
LAM	LAME	LAMININS	LAMPOONS	LAND
LAMA	LAMEBRAIN	LAMINITIS	LAMPPOST	LANDAMMAN
LAMAISTIC	LAMED	LAMINOSE	LAMPPOSTS	LANDAU
LAMANTIN	LAMEDH	LAMINOUS	LAMPREY	LANDAULET
LAMANTINS	LAMEDHS	LAMISH	LAMPREYS	LANDAUS
LAMAS	LAMEDS	LAMISTER	LAMPS	LANDBOARD
LAMASERAI	LAMELLA	LAMISTERS	LAMPSHADE	LANDDAMNE
LAMASERY	LAMELLAE	LAMITER	LAMPSHELL	LANDDROS
LAMB	LAMELLAR	LAMITERS	LAMPSTAND	LANDDROST
LAMBADA	LAMELLAS	LAMMED	LAMPUKA	LANDE

LANDED	LANDSLIDE	LANGUES	LANTHANON	LAPPER
LANDER	LANDSLIP	LANGUET	LANTHANUM	LAPPERED
LANDERS	LANDSLIPS	LANGUETS	LANTHORN	LAPPERING
LANDES	LANDSMAN	LANGUETTE	LANTHORNS	LAPPERS
LANDFALL	LANDSMEN	LANGUID	LANTS	LAPPET
LANDFALLS	LANDWARD	LANGUIDLY	LANTSKIP	LAPPETED
LANDFAST	LANDWARDS	LANGUISH	LANTSKIPS	LAPPETS
LANDFILL	LANDWASH	LANGUOR	LANUGO	LAPPIE
LANDFILLS	LANDWIND	LANGUORS	LANUGOS	LAPPIES
LANDFORCE	LANDWINDS	LANGUR	LANX	LAPPING
LANDFORM	LANE	LANGURS	LANYARD	LAPPINGS
LANDFORMS	LANELY	LANIARD	LANYARDS	LAPS
LANDGRAB	LANES	LANIARDS	LAODICEAN	LAPSABLE
LANDGRABS	LANEWAY	LANIARIES	LAOGAI	LAPSANG
LANDGRAVE	LANEWAYS	LANIARY	LAOGAIS	LAPSANGS
LANDING	LANG	LANITAL	LAP	LAPSE
LANDINGS	LANGAHA	LANITALS	LAPBOARD	LAPSED
LANDLADY	LANGAHAS	LANK	LAPBOARDS	LAPSER
LANDLER	LANGAR	LANKED	LAPDOG	LAPSERS
LANDLERS	LANGARS	LANKER	LAPDOGS	LAPSES
LANDLESS	LANGER	LANKEST	LAPEL	LAPSIBLE
LANDLINE	LANGERED	LANKIER	LAPELED	LAPSING
LANDLINES	LANGERS	LANKIEST	LAPELLED	LAPSTONE
LANDLOPER	LANGEST	LANKILY	LAPELS	LAPSTONES
LANDLORD	LANGLAUF	LANKINESS	LAPFUL	LAPSTRAKE
LANDLORDS	LANGLAUFS	LANKING	LAPFULS	LAPSTREAK
LANDMAN	LANGLEY	LANKLY	LAPHELD	LAPSUS
LANDMARK	LANGLEYS	LANKNESS	LAPIDARY	LAPTOP
LANDMARKS	LANGOUSTE	LANKS	LAPIDATE	LAPTOPS
LANDMASS	LANGRAGE	LANKY	LAPIDATED	LAPTRAY
LANDMEN	LANGRAGES	LANNER	LAPIDATES	LAPTRAYS
LANDMINE	LANGREL	LANNERET	LAPIDEOUS	LAPWING
LANDMINED	LANGRELS	LANNERETS	LAPIDES	LAPWINGS
LANDMINES	LANGRIDGE	LANNERS	LAPIDIFIC	LAPWORK
LANDOWNER	LANGSHAN	LANOLATED	LAPIDIFY	LAPWORKS
LANDRACE	LANGSHANS	LANOLIN	LAPIDIST	LAQUEARIA
LANDRACES	LANGSPEL	LANOLINE	LAPIDISTS	LAR
LANDRAIL	LANGSPELS	LANOLINES	LAPILLI	LARBOARD
LANDRAILS	LANGSPIEL	LANOLINS	LAPILLUS	LARBOARDS
LANDS	LANGSPIL	LANOSE	LAPIN	LARCENER
LANDSCAPE	LANGSPILS	LANOSITY	LAPINS	LARCENERS
LANDSHARK	LANGSYNE	LANT	LAPIS	LARCENIES
LANDSIDE	LANGSYNES	LANTANA	LAPISES	LARCENIST
LANDSIDES	LANGUAGE	LANTANAS	LAPJE	LARCENOUS
LANDSKIP	LANGUAGED	LANTERLOO	LAPJES	LARCENY
LANDSKIPS	LANGUAGES	LANTERN	LAPPED	LARCH
LANDSLEIT	LANGUE	LANTERNED	LAPPEL	LARCHEN
LANDSLID	LANGUED	LANTERNS	LAPPELS	LARCHES

LARCHWOOD	LARINE	LARVATED	LASSIE	LATEENER
LARD	LARIS	LARVICIDE	LASSIES	LATEENERS
LARDALITE	LARK	LARVIFORM	LASSIS	LATEENS
LARDED	LARKED	LARVIKITE	LASSITUDE	LATELY
LARDER	LARKER	LARYNGAL	LASSLORN	LATEN
LARDERER	LARKERS	LARYNGALS	LASSO	LATENCE
LARDERERS	LARKIER	LARYNGEAL	LASSOCK	LATENCES
LARDERS	LARKIEST	LARYNGES	LASSOCKS	LATENCIES
LARDIER	LARKINESS	LARYNX	LASSOED	LATENCY
LARDIEST	LARKING	LARYNXES	LASSOER	LATENED
LARDING	LARKISH	LAS	LASSOERS	LATENESS
LARDLIKE	LARKS	LASAGNA	LASSOES	LATENING
LARDON	LARKSOME	LASAGNAS	LASSOING	LATENS
LARDONS	LARKSPUR	LASAGNE	LASSOINGS	LATENT
LARDOON	LARKSPURS	LASAGNES	LASSOS	LATENTLY
LARDOONS	LARKY	LASCAR	LASSU	LATENTS
LARDS	LARMIER	LASCARS	LASSUS	LATER
LARDY	LARMIERS	LASE	LASSY	LATERAD
LARE	LARN	LASED	LAST	LATERAL
LAREE	LARNAKES	LASER	LASTAGE	LATERALED
LAREES	LARNAX	LASERDISC	LASTAGES	LATERALLY
LARES	LARNED	LASERDISK	LASTBORN	LATERALS
LARGANDO	LARNEY	LASERED	LASTBORNS	LATERBORN
LARGE	LARNEYS	LASERING	LASTED	LATERISE
LARGELY	LARNIER	LASERS	LASTER	LATERISED
LARGEN	LARNIEST	LASERWORT	LASTERS	LATERISES
LARGENED	LARNING	LASES	LASTING	LATERITE
LARGENESS	LARNS	LASH	LASTINGLY	LATERITES
LARGENING	LARNT	LASHED	LASTINGS	LATERITIC
LARGENS	LAROID	LASHER	LASTLY	LATERIZE
LARGER	LARRIGAN	LASHERS	LASTS	LATERIZED
LARGES	LARRIGANS	LASHES	LAT	LATERIZES
LARGESS	LARRIKIN	LASHING	LATAH	LATESCENT
LARGESSE	LARRIKINS	LASHINGLY	LATAHS	LATEST
LARGESSES	LARRUP	LASHINGS	LATAKIA	LATESTS
LARGEST	LARRUPED	LASHINS	LATAKIAS	LATEWAKE
LARGHETTO	LARRUPER	LASHKAR	LATCH	LATEWAKES
LARGISH	LARRUPERS	LASHKARS	LATCHED	LATEWOOD
LARGITION	LARRUPING	LASHLESS	LATCHES	LATEWOODS
LARGO	LARRUPS	LASING	LATCHET	LATEX
LARGOS	LARS	LASINGS	LATCHETS	LATEXES
LARI	LARUM	LASKET	LATCHING	LATH
LARIAT	LARUMS	LASKETS	LATCHKEY	LATHE
LARIATED	LARVA	LASQUE	LATCHKEYS	LATHED
LARIATING	LARVAE	LASQUES	LATE	LATHEE
LARIATS	LARVAL	LASS	LATECOMER	LATHEES
LARIGAN	LARVAS	LASSES	LATED	LATHEN
LARIGANS	LARVATE	LASSI	LATEEN	LATHER

LATHERED	LATITATS	LAUDATORS	LAURAS	LAVENDERS
LATHERER	LATITUDE	LAUDATORY	LAUREATE	LAVER
LATHERERS	LATITUDES	LAUDED	LAUREATED	LAVEROCK
LATHERIER	LATKE	LAUDER	LAUREATES	LAVEROCKS
LATHERING	LATKES	LAUDERS	LAUREL	LAVERS
LATHERS	LATOSOL	LAUDING	LAURELED	LAVES
LATHERY	LATOSOLIC	LAUDS	LAURELING	LAVING
LATHES	LATOSOLS	LAUF	LAURELLED	LAVISH
LATHI	LATRANT	LAUFS	LAURELS	LAVISHED
LATHIER	LATRATION	LAUGH	LAURIC	LAVISHER
LATHIEST	LATRIA	LAUGHABLE	LAURYL	LAVISHERS
LATHING	LATRIAS	LAUGHABLY	LAURYLS	LAVISHES
LATHINGS	LATRINE	LAUGHED	LAUWINE	LAVISHEST
LATHIS	LATRINES	LAUGHER	LAUWINES	LAVISHING
LATHLIKE	LATROCINY	LAUGHERS	LAV	LAVISHLY
LATHS	LATRON	LAUGHFUL	LAVA	LAVOLT
LATHWORK	LATRONS	LAUGHIER	LAVABO	LAVOLTA
LATHWORKS	LATS	LAUGHIEST	LAVABOES	LAVOLTAED
LATHY	LATTE	LAUGHING	LAVABOS	LAVOLTAS
LATHYRISM	LATTEN	LAUGHINGS	LAVAFORM	LAVOLTED
LATHYRUS	LATTENS	LAUGHLINE	LAVAGE	LAVOLTING
LATI	LATTER	LAUGHS	LAVAGES	LAVOLTS
LATICES	LATTERLY	LAUGHSOME	LAVAL	LAVRA
LATICIFER	LATTERS	LAUGHTER	LAVALAVA	LAVRAS
LATICLAVE	LATTES	LAUGHTERS	LAVALAVAS	LAVROCK
LATIFONDI	LATTICE	LAUGHY	LAVALIER	LAVROCKS
LATIFONDO	LATTICED	LAUNCE	LAVALIERE	LAVS
LATIGO	LATTICES	LAUNCED	LAVALIERS	LAVVIES
LATIGOES	LATTICING	LAUNCES	LAVALIKE	LAVVY
LATIGOS	LATTICINI	LAUNCH	LAVANDIN	LAW
LATILLA	LATTICINO	LAUNCHED	LAVANDINS	LAWBOOK
LATILLAS	LATTIN	LAUNCHER	LAVAS	LAWBOOKS
LATIMERIA	LATTINS	LAUNCHERS	LAVASH	LAWCOURT
LATINA	LATU	LAUNCHES	LAVASHES	LAWCOURTS
LATINAS	LATUS	LAUNCHING	LAVATERA	LAWED
LATINISE	LAUAN	LAUNCHPAD	LAVATERAS	LAWER
LATINISED	LAUANS	LAUNCING	LAVATION	LAWEST
LATINISES	LAUCH	LAUND	LAVATIONS	LAWFARE
LATINITY	LAUCHING	LAUNDER	LAVATORY	LAWFARES
LATINIZE	LAUCHS	LAUNDERED	LAVE	LAWFUL
LATINIZED	LAUD	LAUNDERER	LAVED	LAWFULLY
LATINIZES	LAUDABLE	LAUNDERS	LAVEER	LAWGIVER
LATINO	LAUDABLY	LAUNDRESS	LAVEERED	LAWGIVERS
LATINOS	LAUDANUM	LAUNDRIES	LAVEERING	LAWGIVING
LATISH	LAUDANUMS	LAUNDRY	LAVEERS	LAWIN
LATITANCY	LAUDATION	LAUNDS	LAVEMENT	LAWINE
LATITANT	LAUDATIVE	LAURA	LAVEMENTS	LAWINES
LATITAT	LAUDATOR	LAURAE	LAVENDER	LAWING

LAWINGS	LAXITY	LAYUP	LEACHIER	LEAFINESS
LAWINS	LAXLY	LAYUPS	LEACHIEST	LEAFING
LAWK	LAXNESS	LAYWOMAN	LEACHING	LEAFLESS
LAWKS	LAXNESSES	LAYWOMEN	LEACHINGS	LEAFLET
LAWLAND	LAY	LAZAR	LEACHOUR	LEAFLETED
LAWLANDS	LAYABOUT	LAZARET	LEACHOURS	LEAFLETER
LAWLESS	LAYABOUTS	LAZARETS	LEACHY	LEAFLETS
LAWLESSLY	LAYAWAY	LAZARETTE	LEAD	LEAFLIKE
LAWLIKE	LAYAWAYS	LAZARETTO	LEADABLE	LEAFMOLD
LAWMAKER	LAYBACK	LAZARS	LEADED	LEAFMOLDS
LAWMAKERS	LAYBACKED	LAZE	LEADEN	LEAFROLL
LAWMAKING	LAYBACKS	LAZED	LEADENED	LEAFROLLS
LAWMAN	LAYDEEZ	LAZES	LEADENING	LEAFS
LAWMEN	LAYED	LAZIED	LEADENLY	LEAFSTALK
LAWMONGER	LAYER	LAZIER	LEADENS	LEAFWORM
LAWN	LAYERAGE	LAZIES	LEADER	LEAFWORMS
LAWNED	LAYERAGES	LAZIEST	LEADERENE	LEAFY
LAWNIER	LAYERED	LAZILY	LEADERS	LEAGUE
LAWNIEST	LAYERING	LAZINESS	LEADIER	LEAGUED
LAWNING	LAYERINGS	LAZING	LEADIEST	LEAGUER
LAWNMOWER	LAYERS	LAZO	LEADING	LEAGUERED
LAWNS	LAYETTE	LAZOED	LEADINGLY	LEAGUERS
LAWNY	LAYETTES	LAZOES	LEADINGS	LEAGUES
LAWS	LAYIN	LAZOING	LEADLESS	LEAGUING
LAWSUIT	LAYING	LAZOS	LEADMAN	LEAK
LAWSUITS	LAYINGS	LAZULI	LEADMEN	LEAKAGE
LAWYER	LAYINS	LAZULIS	LEADOFF	LEAKAGES
LAWYERED	LAYLOCK	LAZULITE	LEADOFFS	LEAKED
LAWYERING	LAYLOCKS	LAZULITES	LEADPLANT	LEAKER
LAWYERLY	LAYMAN	LAZURITE	LEADS	LEAKERS
LAWYERS	LAYMANISE	LAZURITES	LEADSCREW	LEAKIER
LAX	LAYMANIZE	LAZY	LEADSMAN	LEAKIEST
LAXATION	LAYMEN	LAZYBONES	LEADSMEN	LEAKILY
LAXATIONS	LAYOFF	LAZYING	LEADWORK	LEAKINESS
LAXATIVE	LAYOFFS	LAZYISH	LEADWORKS	LEAKING
LAXATIVES	LAYOUT	LAZZARONE	LEADWORT	LEAKLESS
LAXATOR	LAYOUTS	LAZZARONI	LEADWORTS	LEAKPROOF
LAXATORS	LAYOVER	LAZZI	LEADY	LEAKS
LAXED	LAYOVERS	LAZZO	LEAF	LEAKY
LAXER	LAYPEOPLE	LEA	LEAFAGE	LEAL
LAXES	LAYPERSON	LEACH	LEAFAGES	LEALER
LAXEST	LAYS	LEACHABLE	LEAFBUD	LEALEST
LAXING	LAYSHAFT	LEACHATE	LEAFBUDS	LEALLY
LAXISM	LAYSHAFTS	LEACHATES	LEAFED	LEALTIES
LAXISMS	LAYSTALL	LEACHED	LEAFERIES	LEALTY
LAXIST	LAYSTALLS	LEACHER	LEAFERY	LEAM
LAXISTS	LAYTIME	LEACHERS	LEAFIER	LEAMED
LAXITIES	LAYTIMES	LEACHES	LEAFIEST	LEAMING

LEAMS

LEAMS	LEASEBACK	LEAZE	LECTURNS	LEERINESS
LEAN	LEASED	LEAZES	LECYTHI	LEERING
LEANED	LEASEHOLD	LEBBEK	LECYTHIS	LEERINGLY
LEANER	LEASER	LEBBEKS	LECYTHUS	LEERINGS
LEANERS	LEASERS	LEBEN	LED	LEERS
LEANEST	LEASES	LEBENS	LEDDEN	LEERY
LEANING	LEASH	LEBKUCHEN	LEDDENS	LEES
LEANINGS	LEASHED	LECANORA	LEDE	LEESE
LEANLY	LEASHES	LECANORAS	LEDES	LEESES
LEANNESS	LEASHING	LECCIES	LEDGE	LEESING
LEANS	LEASING	LECCY	LEDGED	LEET
LEANT	LEASINGS	LECH	LEDGER	LEETLE
LEANY	LEASOW	LECHAIM	LEDGERED	LEETS
LEAP	LEASOWE	LECHAIMS	LEDGERING	LEETSPEAK
LEAPED	LEASOWED	LECHAYIM	LEDGERS	LEEWARD
LEAPER	LEASOWES	LECHAYIMS	LEDGES	LEEWARDLY
LEAPEROUS	LEASOWING	LECHED	LEDGIER	LEEWARDS
LEAPERS	LEASOWS	LECHER	LEDGIEST	LEEWAY
LEAPFROG	LEAST	LECHERED	LEDGY	LEEWAYS
LEAPFROGS	LEASTS	LECHERIES	LEDUM	LEEZE
LEAPING	LEASTWAYS	LECHERING	LEDUMS	LEFT
LEAPOROUS	LEASTWISE	LECHEROUS	LEE	LEFTE
LEAPROUS	LEASURE	LECHERS	LEEAR	LEFTER
LEAPS	LEASURES	LECHERY	LEEARS	LEFTEST
LEAPT	LEAT	LECHES	LEEBOARD	LEFTIE
LEAR	LEATHER	LECHING	LEEBOARDS	LEFTIES
LEARE	LEATHERED	LECHWE	LEECH	LEFTISH
LEARED	LEATHERN	LECHWES	LEECHDOM	LEFTISM
LEARES	LEATHERS	LECITHIN	LEECHDOMS	LEFTISMS
LEARIER	LEATHERY	LECITHINS	LEECHED	LEFTIST
LEARIEST	LEATS	LECTERN	LEECHEE	LEFTISTS
LEARINESS	LEAVE	LECTERNS	LEECHEES	LEFTMOST
LEARING	LEAVED	LECTIN	LEECHES	LEFTMOSTS
LEARN	LEAVEN	LECTINS	LEECHING	LEFTOVER
LEARNABLE	LEAVENED	LECTION	LEECHLIKE	LEFTOVERS
LEARNED	LEAVENER	LECTIONS	LEED	LEFTS
LEARNEDLY	LEAVENERS	LECTOR	LEEING	LEFTWARD
LEARNER	LEAVENING	LECTORATE	LEEK	LEFTWARDS
LEARNERS	LEAVENOUS	LECTORS	LEEKS	LEFTWING
LEARNING	LEAVENS	LECTOTYPE	LEEP	LEFTY
LEARNINGS	LEAVER	LECTRESS	LEEPED	LEG
LEARNS	LEAVERS	LECTURE	LEEPING	LEGACIES
LEARNT	LEAVES	LECTURED	LEEPS	LEGACY
LEARS	LEAVIER	LECTURER	LEER	LEGAL
LEARY	LEAVIEST	LECTURERS	LEERED	LEGALESE
LEAS	LEAVING	LECTURES	LEERIER	LEGALESES
LEASABLE	LEAVINGS	LECTURING	LEERIEST	LEGALISE
LEASE	LEAVY	LECTURN	LEERILY	LEGALISED

LEGALISER
LEGALISES
LEGALISM
LEGALISMS
LEGALIST
LEGALISTS
LEGALITY
LEGALIZE
LEGALIZED
LEGALIZER
LEGALIZES
LEGALLY
LEGALS
LEGATARY
LEGATE
LEGATED
LEGATEE
LEGATEES
LEGATES
LEGATINE
LEGATING
LEGATION
LEGATIONS
LEGATO
LEGATOR
LEGATORS
LEGATOS
LEGEND
LEGENDARY
LEGENDISE
LEGENDIST
LEGENDIZE
LEGENDRY
LEGENDS
LEGER
LEGERING
LEGERINGS
LEGERITY
LEGERS
LEGES
LEGGE
LEGGED
LEGGER
LEGGERS
LEGGES
LEGGIE
LEGGIER
LEGGIERO

LEGGIES
LEGGIEST
LEGGIN
LEGGINESS
LEGGING
LEGGINGED
LEGGINGS
LEGGINS
LEGGISM
LEGGISMS
LEGGO
LEGGY
LEGHOLD
LEGHOLDS
LEGHORN
LEGHORNS
LEGIBLE
LEGIBLY
LEGION
LEGIONARY
LEGIONED
LEGIONS
LEGISLATE
LEGIST
LEGISTS
LEGIT
LEGITIM
LEGITIMS
LEGITS
LEGLAN
LEGLANS
LEGLEN
LEGLENS
LEGLESS
LEGLET
LEGLETS
LEGLIKE
LEGLIN
LEGLINS
LEGMAN
LEGMEN
LEGONG
LEGONGS
LEGROOM
LEGROOMS
LEGS
LEGSIDE
LEGSIDES

LEGUAAN
LEGUAANS
LEGUAN
LEGUANS
LEGUME
LEGUMES
LEGUMIN
LEGUMINS
LEGWARMER
LEGWEAR
LEGWEARS
LEGWORK
LEGWORKS
LEHAIM
LEHAIMS
LEHAYIM
LEHAYIMS
LEHR
LEHRJAHRE
LEHRS
LEHUA
LEHUAS
LEI
LEIDGER
LEIDGERS
LEIGER
LEIGERS
LEIOMYOMA
LEIPOA
LEIPOAS
LEIR
LEIRED
LEIRING
LEIRS
LEIS
LEISH
LEISHER
LEISHEST
LEISLER
LEISLERS
LEISTER
LEISTERED
LEISTERS
LEISURE
LEISURED
LEISURELY
LEISURES
LEISURING

LEITMOTIF
LEITMOTIV
LEK
LEKE
LEKGOTLA
LEKGOTLAS
LEKKED
LEKKER
LEKKING
LEKKINGS
LEKS
LEKU
LEKVAR
LEKVARS
LEKYTHI
LEKYTHOI
LEKYTHOS
LEKYTHUS
LEMAN
LEMANS
LEME
LEMED
LEMEL
LEMELS
LEMES
LEMING
LEMMA
LEMMAS
LEMMATA
LEMMATISE
LEMMATIZE
LEMME
LEMMING
LEMMINGS
LEMNISCAL
LEMNISCI
LEMNISCUS
LEMON
LEMONADE
LEMONADES
LEMONED
LEMONFISH
LEMONIER
LEMONIEST
LEMONING
LEMONISH
LEMONLIKE
LEMONS

LEMONWOOD
LEMONY
LEMPIRA
LEMPIRAS
LEMUR
LEMURES
LEMURIAN
LEMURIANS
LEMURINE
LEMURINES
LEMURLIKE
LEMUROID
LEMUROIDS
LEMURS
LEND
LENDABLE
LENDER
LENDERS
LENDING
LENDINGS
LENDS
LENES
LENG
LENGED
LENGER
LENGEST
LENGING
LENGS
LENGTH
LENGTHEN
LENGTHENS
LENGTHFUL
LENGTHIER
LENGTHILY
LENGTHMAN
LENGTHMEN
LENGTHS
LENGTHY
LENIENCE
LENIENCES
LENIENCY
LENIENT
LENIENTLY
LENIENTS
LENIFIED
LENIFIES
LENIFY
LENIFYING

L

LENIS	LENVOY	LERED	LETDOWNS	LEUCINE
LENITE	LENVOYS	LERES	LETHAL	LEUCINES
LENITED	LEONE	LERING	LETHALITY	LEUCINS
LENITES	LEONES	LERNAEAN	LETHALLY	LEUCISM
LENITIES	LEONINE	LERP	LETHALS	LEUCISMS
LENITING	LEOPARD	LERPS	LETHARGIC	LEUCISTIC
LENITION	LEOPARDS	LES	LETHARGY	LEUCITE
LENITIONS	LEOTARD	LESBIAN	LETHE	LEUCITES
LENITIVE	LEOTARDED	LESBIANS	LETHEAN	LEUCITIC
LENITIVES	LEOTARDS	LESBIC	LETHEE	LEUCO
LENITY	LEP	LESBIGAY	LETHEES	LEUCOCYTE
LENO	LEPER	LESBIGAYS	LETHES	LEUCOMA
LENOS	LEPERS	LESBO	LETHIED	LEUCOMAS
LENS	LEPID	LESBOS	LETOUT	LEUCON
LENSE	LEPIDOTE	LESES	LETOUTS	LEUCONS
LENSED	LEPIDOTES	LESION	LETROZOLE	LEUCOSES
LENSES	LEPORID	LESIONED	LETS	LEUCOSIN
LENSING	LEPORIDAE	LESIONING	LETTABLE	LEUCOSINS
LENSINGS	LEPORIDS	LESIONS	LETTED	LEUCOSIS
LENSLESS	LEPORINE	LESPEDEZA	LETTER	LEUCOTIC
LENSLIKE	LEPPED	LESS	LETTERBOX	LEUCOTOME
LENSMAN	LEPPING	LESSEE	LETTERED	LEUCOTOMY
LENSMEN	LEPRA	LESSEES	LETTERER	LEUD
LENT	LEPRAS	LESSEN	LETTERERS	LEUDES
LENTANDO	LEPROSE	LESSENED	LETTERING	LEUDS
LENTEN	LEPROSERY	LESSENING	LETTERMAN	LEUGH
LENTI	LEPROSIES	LESSENS	LETTERMEN	LEUGHEN
LENTIC	LEPROSITY	LESSER	LETTERN	LEUKAEMIA
LENTICEL	LEPROSY	LESSES	LETTERNS	LEUKAEMIC
LENTICELS	LEPROTIC	LESSON	LETTERS	LEUKEMIA
LENTICLE	LEPROUS	LESSONED	LETTERSET	LEUKEMIAS
LENTICLES	LEPROUSLY	LESSONING	LETTING	LEUKEMIC
LENTICULE	LEPS	LESSONS	LETTINGS	LEUKEMICS
LENTIFORM	LEPT	LESSOR	LETTRE	LEUKEMOID
LENTIGO	LEPTA	LESSORS	LETTRES	LEUKOCYTE
LENTIL	LEPTIN	LEST	LETTUCE	LEUKOMA
LENTILS	LEPTINS	LESTED	LETTUCES	LEUKOMAS
LENTISC	LEPTOME	LESTING	LETUP	LEUKON
LENTISCS	LEPTOMES	LESTS	LETUPS	LEUKONS
LENTISK	LEPTON	LESULA	LEU	LEUKOSES
LENTISKS	LEPTONIC	LESULAS	LEUCAEMIA	LEUKOSIS
LENTO	LEPTONS	LET	LEUCAEMIC	LEUKOTIC
LENTOID	LEPTOPHOS	LETCH	LEUCEMIA	LEUKOTOME
LENTOIDS	LEPTOSOME	LETCHED	LEUCEMIAS	LEUKOTOMY
LENTOR	LEPTOTENE	LETCHES	LEUCEMIC	LEV
LENTORS	LEQUEAR	LETCHING	LEUCH	LEVA
LENTOS	LEQUEARS	LETCHINGS	LEUCHEN	LEVANT
LENTOUS	LERE	LETDOWN	LEUCIN	LEVANTED

LEVANTER	LEVIN	LEXEMES	LIASES	LIBERATE
LEVANTERS	LEVINS	LEXEMIC	LIASSIC	LIBERATED
LEVANTINE	LEVIRATE	LEXES	LIATRIS	LIBERATES
LEVANTING	LEVIRATES	LEXICA	LIATRISES	LIBERATOR
LEVANTS	LEVIRATIC	LEXICAL	LIB	LIBERO
LEVAS	LEVIS	LEXICALLY	LIBANT	LIBEROS
LEVATOR	LEVITATE	LEXICON	LIBATE	LIBERS
LEVATORES	LEVITATED	LEXICONS	LIBATED	LIBERTIES
LEVATORS	LEVITATES	LEXIGRAM	LIBATES	LIBERTINE
LEVE	LEVITATOR	LEXIGRAMS	LIBATING	LIBERTY
LEVEE	LEVITE	LEXIS	LIBATION	LIBIDINAL
LEVEED	LEVITES	LEXISES	LIBATIONS	LIBIDO
LEVEEING	LEVITIC	LEY	LIBATORY	LIBIDOS
LEVEES	LEVITICAL	LEYLANDI	LIBBARD	LIBKEN
LEVEL	LEVITIES	LEYLANDII	LIBBARDS	LIBKENS
LEVELED	LEVITY	LEYLANDIS	LIBBED	LIBLAB
LEVELER	LEVO	LEYS	LIBBER	LIBLABS
LEVELERS	LEVODOPA	LEZ	LIBBERS	LIBRA
LEVELING	LEVODOPAS	LEZES	LIBBING	LIBRAE
LEVELLED	LEVOGYRE	LEZZ	LIBECCHIO	LIBRAIRE
LEVELLER	LEVOGYRES	LEZZA	LIBECCIO	LIBRAIRES
LEVELLERS	LEVS	LEZZAS	LIBECCIOS	LIBRAIRIE
LEVELLEST	LEVULIN	LEZZES	LIBEL	LIBRARIAN
LEVELLING	LEVULINS	LEZZIE	LIBELANT	LIBRARIES
LEVELLY	LEVULOSE	LEZZIES	LIBELANTS	LIBRARY
LEVELNESS	LEVULOSES	LEZZY	LIBELED	LIBRAS
LEVELS	LEVY	LI	LIBELEE	LIBRATE
LEVER	LEVYING	LIABILITY	LIBELEES	LIBRATED
LEVERAGE	LEW	LIABLE	LIBELER	LIBRATES
LEVERAGED	LEWD	LIAISE	LIBELERS	LIBRATING
LEVERAGES	LEWDER	LIAISED	LIBELING	LIBRATION
LEVERED	LEWDEST	LIAISES	LIBELINGS	LIBRATORY
LEVERET	LEWDLY	LIAISING	LIBELIST	LIBRETTI
LEVERETS	LEWDNESS	LIAISON	LIBELISTS	LIBRETTO
LEVERING	LEWDSBIES	LIAISONS	LIBELLANT	LIBRETTOS
LEVERS	LEWDSBY	LIANA	LIBELLED	LIBRI
LEVES	LEWDSTER	LIANAS	LIBELLEE	LIBRIFORM
LEVIABLE	LEWDSTERS	LIANE	LIBELLEES	LIBS
LEVIATHAN	LEWIS	LIANES	LIBELLER	LICE
LEVIED	LEWISES	LIANG	LIBELLERS	LICENCE
LEVIER	LEWISIA	LIANGS	LIBELLING	LICENCED
LEVIERS	LEWISIAS	LIANOID	LIBELLOUS	LICENCEE
LEVIES	LEWISITE	LIAR	LIBELOUS	LICENCEES
LEVIGABLE	LEWISITES	LIARD	LIBELS	LICENCER
LEVIGATE	LEWISSON	LIARDS	LIBER	LICENCERS
LEVIGATED	LEWISSONS	LIARS	LIBERAL	LICENCES
LEVIGATES	LEX	LIART	LIBERALLY	LICENCING
LEVIGATOR	LEXEME	LIAS	LIBERALS	LICENSE

LICENSED	LICKED	LIENEE	LIFEWAY	LIGGES
LICENSEE	LICKER	LIENEES	LIFEWAYS	LIGGING
LICENSEES	LICKERISH	LIENOR	LIFEWORK	LIGGINGS
LICENSER	LICKERS	LIENORS	LIFEWORKS	LIGHT
LICENSERS	LICKING	LIENS	LIFEWORLD	LIGHTBULB
LICENSES	LICKINGS	LIENTERIC	LIFT	LIGHTED
LICENSING	LICKPENNY	LIENTERY	LIFTABLE	LIGHTEN
LICENSOR	LICKS	LIER	LIFTBACK	LIGHTENED
LICENSORS	LICKSPIT	LIERNE	LIFTBACKS	LIGHTENER
LICENSURE	LICKSPITS	LIERNES	LIFTBOY	LIGHTENS
LICENTE	LICORICE	LIERS	LIFTBOYS	LIGHTER
LICH	LICORICES	LIES	LIFTED	LIGHTERED
LICHANOS	LICTOR	LIEU	LIFTER	LIGHTERS
LICHEE	LICTORIAN	LIEUS	LIFTERS	LIGHTEST
LICHEES	LICTORS	LIEVE	LIFTGATE	LIGHTFACE
LICHEN	LID	LIEVER	LIFTGATES	LIGHTFAST
LICHENED	LIDAR	LIEVES	LIFTING	LIGHTFUL
LICHENIN	LIDARS	LIEVEST	LIFTMAN	LIGHTING
LICHENING	LIDDED	LIFE	LIFTMEN	LIGHTINGS
LICHENINS	LIDDING	LIFEBELT	LIFTOFF	LIGHTISH
LICHENISM	LIDDINGS	LIFEBELTS	LIFTOFFS	LIGHTLESS
LICHENIST	LIDGER	LIFEBLOOD	LIFTS	LIGHTLIED
LICHENOID	LIDGERS	LIFEBOAT	LIFULL	LIGHTLIES
LICHENOSE	LIDLESS	LIFEBOATS	LIG	LIGHTLY
LICHENOUS	LIDO	LIFEBUOY	LIGAMENT	LIGHTNESS
LICHENS	LIDOCAINE	LIFEBUOYS	LIGAMENTS	LIGHTNING
LICHES	LIDOS	LIFECARE	LIGAN	LIGHTS
LICHGATE	LIDS	LIFECARES	LIGAND	LIGHTSHIP
LICHGATES	LIE	LIFEFUL	LIGANDS	LIGHTSOME
LICHI	LIED	LIFEGUARD	LIGANS	LIGHTWAVE
LICHIS	LIEDER	LIFEHACK	LIGASE	LIGHTWOOD
LICHT	LIEF	LIFEHACKS	LIGASES	LIGNAGE
LICHTED	LIEFER	LIFEHOLD	LIGATE	LIGNAGES
LICHTER	LIEFEST	LIFELESS	LIGATED	LIGNALOES
LICHTEST	LIEFLY	LIFELIKE	LIGATES	LIGNAN
LICHTING	LIEFS	LIFELINE	LIGATING	LIGNANS
LICHTLIED	LIEGE	LIFELINES	LIGATION	LIGNE
LICHTLIES	LIEGEDOM	LIFELONG	LIGATIONS	LIGNEOUS
LICHTLY	LIEGEDOMS	LIFER	LIGATIVE	LIGNES
LICHTS	LIEGELESS	LIFERS	LIGATURE	LIGNICOLE
LICHWAKE	LIEGEMAN	LIFES	LIGATURED	LIGNIFIED
LICHWAKES	LIEGEMEN	LIFESAVER	LIGATURES	LIGNIFIES
LICHWAY	LIEGER	LIFESOME	LIGER	LIGNIFORM
LICHWAYS	LIEGERS	LIFESPAN	LIGERS	LIGNIFY
LICIT	LIEGES	LIFESPANS	LIGGE	LIGNIN
LICITLY	LIEN	LIFESTYLE	LIGGED	LIGNINS
LICITNESS	LIENABLE	LIFETIME	LIGGER	LIGNITE
LICK	LIENAL	LIFETIMES	LIGGERS	LIGNITES

LIGNITIC	LIKINS	LIMBERED	LIMINA	LIMPAS
LIGNOSE	LIKUTA	LIMBERER	LIMINAL	LIMPED
LIGNOSES	LILAC	LIMBEREST	LIMINESS	LIMPER
LIGNUM	LILACS	LIMBERING	LIMING	LIMPERS
LIGNUMS	LILANGENI	LIMBERLY	LIMINGS	LIMPEST
LIGROIN	LILIED	LIMBERS	LIMIT	LIMPET
LIGROINE	LILIES	LIMBI	LIMITABLE	LIMPETS
LIGROINES	LILL	LIMBIC	LIMITARY	LIMPID
LIGROINS	LILLED	LIMBIER	LIMITED	LIMPIDITY
LIGS	LILLING	LIMBIEST	LIMITEDLY	LIMPIDLY
LIGULA	LILLIPUT	LIMBING	LIMITEDS	LIMPING
LIGULAE	LILLIPUTS	LIMBLESS	LIMITER	LIMPINGLY
LIGULAR	LILLS	LIMBMEAL	LIMITERS	LIMPINGS
LIGULAS	LILO	LIMBO	LIMITES	LIMPKIN
LIGULATE	LILOS	LIMBOED	LIMITING	LIMPKINS
LIGULATED	LILT	LIMBOES	LIMITINGS	LIMPLY
LIGULE	LILTED	LIMBOING	LIMITLESS	LIMPNESS
LIGULES	LILTING	LIMBOS	LIMITS	LIMPS
LIGULOID	LILTINGLY	LIMBOUS	LIMMA	LIMPSEY
LIGURE	LILTS	LIMBS	LIMMAS	LIMPSIER
LIGURES	LILY	LIMBUS	LIMMER	LIMPSIEST
LIGUSTRUM	LILYLIKE	LIMBUSES	LIMMERS	LIMPSY
LIKABLE	LIMA	LIMBY	LIMN	LIMULI
LIKABLY	LIMACEL	LIME	LIMNAEID	LIMULOID
LIKE	LIMACELS	LIMEADE	LIMNAEIDS	LIMULOIDS
LIKEABLE	LIMACEOUS	LIMEADES	LIMNED	LIMULUS
LIKEABLY	LIMACES	LIMED	LIMNER	LIMULUSES
LIKED	LIMACINE	LIMEKILN	LIMNERS	LIMY
LIKELIER	LIMACON	LIMEKILNS	LIMNETIC	LIN
LIKELIEST	LIMACONS	LIMELESS	LIMNIC	LINABLE
LIKELY	LIMAIL	LIMELIGHT	LIMNING	LINAC
LIKEN	LIMAILS	LIMELIT	LIMNOLOGY	LINACS
LIKENED	LIMAN	LIMEN	LIMNS	LINAGE
LIKENESS	LIMANS	LIMENS	LIMO	LINAGES
LIKENING	LIMAS	LIMEPIT	LIMONENE	LINALOL
LIKENS	LIMATION	LIMEPITS	LIMONENES	LINALOLS
LIKER	LIMATIONS	LIMERENCE	LIMONITE	LINALOOL
LIKERS	LIMAX	LIMERICK	LIMONITES	LINALOOLS
LIKES	LIMB	LIMERICKS	LIMONITIC	LINCH
LIKEST	LIMBA	LIMES	LIMONIUM	LINCHES
LIKEWAKE	LIMBAS	LIMESCALE	LIMONIUMS	LINCHET
LIKEWAKES	LIMBATE	LIMESTONE	LIMOS	LINCHETS
LIKEWALK	LIMBEC	LIMEWASH	LIMOSES	LINCHPIN
LIKEWALKS	LIMBECK	LIMEWATER	LIMOSIS	LINCHPINS
LIKEWISE	LIMBECKS	LIMEY	LIMOUS	LINCRUSTA
LIKIN	LIMBECS	LIMEYS	LIMOUSINE	LINCTURE
LIKING	LIMBED	LIMIER	LIMP	LINCTURES
LIKINGS	LIMBER	LIMIEST	LIMPA	LINCTUS

LINCTUSES	LINERS	LINGUINI	LINKSPAN	LINTERS
LIND	LINES	LINGUINIS	LINKSPANS	LINTIE
LINDANE	LINESCORE	LINGUISA	LINKSTER	LINTIER
LINDANES	LINESMAN	LINGUISAS	LINKSTERS	LINTIES
LINDEN	LINESMEN	LINGUIST	LINKUP	LINTIEST
LINDENS	LINEUP	LINGUISTS	LINKUPS	LINTING
LINDIED	LINEUPS	LINGULA	LINKWORK	LINTINGS
LINDIES	LINEY	LINGULAE	LINKWORKS	LINTLESS
LINDS	LING	LINGULAR	LINKY	LINTOL
LINDWORM	LINGA	LINGULAS	LINN	LINTOLS
LINDWORMS	LINGAM	LINGULATE	LINNED	LINTS
LINDY	LINGAMS	LINGY	LINNET	LINTSEED
LINDYING	LINGAS	LINHAY	LINNETS	LINTSEEDS
LINE	LINGBERRY	LINHAYS	LINNEY	LINTSTOCK
LINEABLE	LINGCOD	LINIER	LINNEYS	LINTWHITE
LINEAGE	LINGCODS	LINIEST	LINNIES	LINTY
LINEAGES	LINGEL	LINIMENT	LINNING	LINUM
LINEAL	LINGELS	LINIMENTS	LINNS	LINUMS
LINEALITY	LINGER	LININ	LINNY	LINURON
LINEALLY	LINGERED	LINING	LINO	LINURONS
LINEAMENT	LINGERER	LININGS	LINOCUT	LINUX
LINEAR	LINGERERS	LININS	LINOCUTS	LINUXES
LINEARISE	LINGERIE	LINISH	LINOLEATE	LINY
LINEARITY	LINGERIES	LINISHED	LINOLEIC	LION
LINEARIZE	LINGERING	LINISHER	LINOLENIC	LIONCEL
LINEARLY	LINGERS	LINISHERS	LINOLEUM	LIONCELLE
LINEATE	LINGIER	LINISHES	LINOLEUMS	LIONCELS
LINEATED	LINGIEST	LINISHING	LINOS	LIONEL
LINEATION	LINGLE	LINK	LINOTYPE	LIONELS
LINEBRED	LINGLES	LINKABLE	LINOTYPED	LIONESS
LINECUT	LINGO	LINKAGE	LINOTYPER	LIONESSES
LINECUTS	LINGOES	LINKAGES	LINOTYPES	LIONET
LINED	LINGOS	LINKBOY	LINS	LIONETS
LINELESS	LINGOT	LINKBOYS	LINSANG	LIONFISH
LINELIKE	LINGOTS	LINKED	LINSANGS	LIONHEAD
LINEMAN	LINGS	LINKER	LINSEED	LIONHEADS
LINEMATE	LINGSTER	LINKERS	LINSEEDS	LIONISE
LINEMATES	LINGSTERS	LINKIER	LINSEY	LIONISED
LINEMEN	LINGUA	LINKIEST	LINSEYS	LIONISER
LINEN	LINGUAE	LINKING	LINSTOCK	LIONISERS
LINENFOLD	LINGUAL	LINKMAN	LINSTOCKS	LIONISES
LINENIER	LINGUALLY	LINKMEN	LINT	LIONISING
LINENIEST	LINGUALS	LINKROT	LINTED	LIONISM
LINENS	LINGUAS	LINKROTS	LINTEL	LIONISMS
LINENY	LINGUICA	LINKS	LINTELED	LIONIZE
LINEOLATE	LINGUICAS	LINKSLAND	LINTELLED	LIONIZED
LINER	LINGUINE	LINKSMAN	LINTELS	LIONIZER
LINERLESS	LINGUINES	LINKSMEN	LINTER	LIONIZERS

LIONIZES	LIPOMA	LIQUEFY	LISKS	LISTSERV
LIONIZING	LIPOMAS	LIQUESCE	LISLE	LISTSERVS
LIONLIER	LIPOMATA	LIQUESCED	LISLES	LIT
LIONLIEST	LIPOPLAST	LIQUESCES	LISP	LITAI
LIONLIKE	LIPOS	LIQUEUR	LISPED	LITANIES
LIONLY	LIPOSOMAL	LIQUEURED	LISPER	LITANY
LIONS	LIPOSOME	LIQUEURS	LISPERS	LITAS
LIP	LIPOSOMES	LIQUID	LISPING	LITCHI
LIPA	LIPOSUCK	LIQUIDATE	LISPINGLY	LITCHIS
LIPAEMIA	LIPOSUCKS	LIQUIDIER	LISPINGS	LITE
LIPAEMIAS	LIPOTROPY	LIQUIDISE	LISPOUND	LITED
LIPARITE	LIPPED	LIQUIDITY	LISPOUNDS	LITENESS
LIPARITES	LIPPEN	LIQUIDIZE	LISPS	LITER
LIPAS	LIPPENED	LIQUIDLY	LISPUND	LITERACY
LIPASE	LIPPENING	LIQUIDS	LISPUNDS	LITERAL
LIPASES	LIPPENS	LIQUIDUS	LISSES	LITERALLY
LIPE	LIPPER	LIQUIDY	LISSOM	LITERALS
LIPECTOMY	LIPPERED	LIQUIFIED	LISSOME	LITERARY
LIPEMIA	LIPPERING	LIQUIFIER	LISSOMELY	LITERATE
LIPEMIAS	LIPPERS	LIQUIFIES	LISSOMLY	LITERATES
LIPES	LIPPIE	LIQUIFY	LIST	LITERATI
LIPGLOSS	LIPPIER	LIQUITAB	LISTABLE	LITERATIM
LIPID	LIPPIES	LIQUITABS	LISTBOX	LITERATO
LIPIDE	LIPPIEST	LIQUOR	LISTBOXES	LITERATOR
LIPIDES	LIPPINESS	LIQUORED	LISTED	LITERATUS
LIPIDIC	LIPPING	LIQUORICE	LISTEE	LITEROSE
LIPIDOSES	LIPPINGS	LIQUORING	LISTEES	LITERS
LIPIDOSIS	LIPPITUDE	LIQUORISH	LISTEL	LITES
LIPIDS	LIPPY	LIQUORS	LISTELS	LITEST
LIPIN	LIPREAD	LIRA	LISTEN	LITH
LIPINS	LIPREADER	LIRAS	LISTENED	LITHARGE
LIPLESS	LIPREADS	LIRE	LISTENER	LITHARGES
LIPLIKE	LIPS	LIRI	LISTENERS	LITHATE
LIPLINER	LIPSALVE	LIRIOPE	LISTENING	LITHATES
LIPLINERS	LIPSALVES	LIRIOPES	LISTENS	LITHE
LIPO	LIPSTICK	LIRIPIPE	LISTER	LITHED
LIPOCYTE	LIPSTICKS	LIRIPIPES	LISTERIA	LITHELY
LIPOCYTES	LIPURIA	LIRIPOOP	LISTERIAL	LITHEMIA
LIPOGRAM	LIPURIAS	LIRIPOOPS	LISTERIAS	LITHEMIAS
LIPOGRAMS	LIQUABLE	LIRK	LISTERS	LITHEMIC
LIPOIC	LIQUATE	LIRKED	LISTETH	LITHENESS
LIPOID	LIQUATED	LIRKING	LISTFUL	LITHER
LIPOIDAL	LIQUATES	LIRKS	LISTICLE	LITHERLY
LIPOIDS	LIQUATING	LIROT	LISTICLES	LITHES
LIPOLITIC	LIQUATION	LIROTH	LISTING	LITHESOME
LIPOLYSES	LIQUEFIED	LIS	LISTINGS	LITHEST
LIPOLYSIS	LIQUEFIER	LISENTE	LISTLESS	LITHIA
LIPOLYTIC	LIQUEFIES	LISK	LISTS	LITHIAS

LITHIASES	LITTEN	LIVELOOD	LIVOR	LOAFINGS
LITHIASIS	LITTER	LIVELOODS	LIVORS	LOAFS
LITHIC	LITTERBAG	LIVELY	LIVRAISON	LOAM
LITHIFIED	LITTERBUG	LIVEN	LIVRE	LOAMED
LITHIFIES	LITTERED	LIVENED	LIVRES	LOAMIER
LITHIFY	LITTERER	LIVENER	LIVYER	LOAMIEST
LITHING	LITTERERS	LIVENERS	LIVYERS	LOAMINESS
LITHISTID	LITTERIER	LIVENESS	LIXIVIA	LOAMING
LITHITE	LITTERING	LIVENING	LIXIVIAL	LOAMLESS
LITHITES	LITTERS	LIVENS	LIXIVIATE	LOAMS
LITHIUM	LITTERY	LIVER	LIXIVIOUS	LOAMY
LITHIUMS	LITTLE	LIVERED	LIXIVIUM	LOAN
LITHO	LITTLER	LIVERIED	LIXIVIUMS	LOANABLE
LITHOCYST	LITTLES	LIVERIES	LIZARD	LOANBACK
LITHOED	LITTLEST	LIVERING	LIZARDS	LOANBACKS
LITHOES	LITTLIE	LIVERINGS	LIZZIE	LOANED
LITHOID	LITTLIES	LIVERISH	LIZZIES	LOANEE
LITHOIDAL	LITTLIN	LIVERLEAF	LLAMA	LOANEES
LITHOING	LITTLING	LIVERLESS	LLAMAS	LOANER
LITHOLOGY	LITTLINGS	LIVERS	LLANERO	LOANERS
LITHOPONE	LITTLINS	LIVERWORT	LLANEROS	LOANING
LITHOPS	LITTLISH	LIVERY	LLANO	LOANINGS
LITHOS	LITTORAL	LIVERYMAN	LLANOS	LOANS
LITHOSOL	LITTORALS	LIVERYMEN	LO	LOANSHIFT
LITHOSOLS	LITU	LIVES	LOACH	LOANWORD
LITHOTOME	LITURGIC	LIVEST	LOACHES	LOANWORDS
LITHOTOMY	LITURGICS	LIVESTOCK	LOAD	LOAST
LITHOTYPE	LITURGIES	LIVETRAP	LOADABLE	LOATH
LITHS	LITURGISM	LIVETRAPS	LOADED	LOATHE
LITIGABLE	LITURGIST	LIVEWARE	LOADEN	LOATHED
LITIGANT	LITURGY	LIVEWARES	LOADENED	LOATHER
LITIGANTS	LITUUS	LIVEWELL	LOADENING	LOATHERS
LITIGATE	LITUUSES	LIVEWELLS	LOADENS	LOATHES
LITIGATED	LIVABLE	LIVEYER	LOADER	LOATHEST
LITIGATES	LIVE	LIVEYERE	LOADERS	LOATHFUL
LITIGATOR	LIVEABLE	LIVEYERES	LOADING	LOATHING
LITIGIOUS	LIVEBLOG	LIVEYERS	LOADINGS	LOATHINGS
LITING	LIVEBLOGS	LIVID	LOADS	LOATHLIER
LITMUS	LIVED	LIVIDER	LOADSPACE	LOATHLY
LITMUSES	LIVEDO	LIVIDEST	LOADSTAR	LOATHNESS
LITORAL	LIVEDOS	LIVIDITY	LOADSTARS	LOATHSOME
LITOTES	LIVELIER	LIVIDLY	LOADSTONE	LOATHY
LITOTIC	LIVELIEST	LIVIDNESS	LOAF	LOAVE
LITRE	LIVELILY	LIVIER	LOAFED	LOAVED
LITREAGE	LIVELOD	LIVIERS	LOAFER	LOAVES
LITREAGES	LIVELODS	LIVING	LOAFERISH	LOAVING
LITRES	LIVELONG	LIVINGLY	LOAFERS	LOB
LITS	LIVELONGS	LIVINGS	LOAFING	LOBAR

LOBATE
LOBATED
LOBATELY
LOBATION
LOBATIONS
LOBBED
LOBBER
LOBBERS
LOBBIED
LOBBIES
LOBBING
LOBBY
LOBBYER
LOBBYERS
LOBBYGOW
LOBBYGOWS
LOBBYING
LOBBYINGS
LOBBYISM
LOBBYISMS
LOBBYIST
LOBBYISTS
LOBE
LOBECTOMY
LOBED
LOBEFIN
LOBEFINS
LOBELESS
LOBELET
LOBELETS
LOBELIA
LOBELIAS
LOBELIKE
LOBELINE
LOBELINES
LOBES
LOBI
LOBING
LOBINGS
LOBIPED
LOBLOLLY
LOBO
LOBOLA
LOBOLAS
LOBOLO
LOBOLOS
LOBOS
LOBOSE

LOBOTOMY
LOBS
LOBSCOUSE
LOBSTER
LOBSTERED
LOBSTERER
LOBSTERS
LOBSTICK
LOBSTICKS
LOBTAIL
LOBTAILED
LOBTAILS
LOBULAR
LOBULARLY
LOBULATE
LOBULATED
LOBULE
LOBULES
LOBULI
LOBULOSE
LOBULUS
LOBUS
LOBWORM
LOBWORMS
LOCA
LOCAL
LOCALE
LOCALES
LOCALISE
LOCALISED
LOCALISER
LOCALISES
LOCALISM
LOCALISMS
LOCALIST
LOCALISTS
LOCALITE
LOCALITES
LOCALITY
LOCALIZE
LOCALIZED
LOCALIZER
LOCALIZES
LOCALLY
LOCALNESS
LOCALS
LOCATABLE
LOCATE

LOCATED
LOCATER
LOCATERS
LOCATES
LOCATING
LOCATION
LOCATIONS
LOCATIVE
LOCATIVES
LOCATOR
LOCATORS
LOCAVORE
LOCAVORES
LOCELLATE
LOCH
LOCHAN
LOCHANS
LOCHE
LOCHES
LOCHIA
LOCHIAL
LOCHIAS
LOCHS
LOCI
LOCIE
LOCIES
LOCIS
LOCK
LOCKABLE
LOCKAGE
LOCKAGES
LOCKAWAY
LOCKAWAYS
LOCKBOX
LOCKBOXES
LOCKDOWN
LOCKDOWNS
LOCKED
LOCKER
LOCKERS
LOCKET
LOCKETS
LOCKFAST
LOCKFUL
LOCKFULS
LOCKHOUSE
LOCKING
LOCKINGS

LOCKJAW
LOCKJAWS
LOCKLESS
LOCKMAKER
LOCKMAN
LOCKMEN
LOCKNUT
LOCKNUTS
LOCKOUT
LOCKOUTS
LOCKPICK
LOCKPICKS
LOCKRAM
LOCKRAMS
LOCKS
LOCKSET
LOCKSETS
LOCKSMAN
LOCKSMEN
LOCKSMITH
LOCKSTEP
LOCKSTEPS
LOCKUP
LOCKUPS
LOCO
LOCOED
LOCOES
LOCOFOCO
LOCOFOCOS
LOCOING
LOCOISM
LOCOISMS
LOCOMAN
LOCOMEN
LOCOMOTE
LOCOMOTED
LOCOMOTES
LOCOMOTOR
LOCOPLANT
LOCOS
LOCOWEED
LOCOWEEDS
LOCULAR
LOCULATE
LOCULATED
LOCULE
LOCULED
LOCULES

LOCULI
LOCULUS
LOCUM
LOCUMS
LOCUPLETE
LOCUS
LOCUST
LOCUSTA
LOCUSTAE
LOCUSTAL
LOCUSTED
LOCUSTING
LOCUSTS
LOCUTION
LOCUTIONS
LOCUTORY
LOD
LODE
LODEN
LODENS
LODES
LODESMAN
LODESMEN
LODESTAR
LODESTARS
LODESTONE
LODGE
LODGEABLE
LODGED
LODGEMENT
LODGEPOLE
LODGER
LODGERS
LODGES
LODGING
LODGINGS
LODGMENT
LODGMENTS
LODICULA
LODICULAE
LODICULE
LODICULES
LODS
LOERIE
LOERIES
LOESS
LOESSAL
LOESSES

L

LOESSIAL	LOGICALLY	LOGOMACHY	LOLIGO	LONENESS
LOESSIC	LOGICIAN	LOGON	LOLIGOS	LONER
LOFT	LOGICIANS	LOGONS	LOLIUM	LONERS
LOFTED	LOGICISE	LOGOPEDIC	LOLIUMS	LONESOME
LOFTER	LOGICISED	LOGOPHILE	LOLL	LONESOMES
LOFTERS	LOGICISES	LOGORRHEA	LOLLED	LONG
LOFTIER	LOGICISM	LOGOS	LOLLER	LONGA
LOFTIEST	LOGICISMS	LOGOTHETE	LOLLERS	LONGAEVAL
LOFTILY	LOGICIST	LOGOTYPE	LOLLIES	LONGAN
LOFTINESS	LOGICISTS	LOGOTYPES	LOLLING	LONGANS
LOFTING	LOGICIZE	LOGOTYPY	LOLLINGLY	LONGAS
LOFTLESS	LOGICIZED	LOGOUT	LOLLIPOP	LONGBOARD
LOFTLIKE	LOGICIZES	LOGOUTS	LOLLIPOPS	LONGBOAT
LOFTS	LOGICLESS	LOGROLL	LOLLOP	LONGBOATS
LOFTSMAN	LOGICS	LOGROLLED	LOLLOPED	LONGBOW
LOFTSMEN	LOGIE	LOGROLLER	LOLLOPIER	LONGBOWS
LOFTY	LOGIER	LOGROLLS	LOLLOPING	LONGCASE
LOG	LOGIES	LOGS	LOLLOPS	LONGCLOTH
LOGAN	LOGIEST	LOGWAY	LOLLOPY	LONGE
LOGANIA	LOGILY	LOGWAYS	LOLLS	LONGED
LOGANIAS	LOGIN	LOGWOOD	LOLLY	LONGEING
LOGANS	LOGINESS	LOGWOODS	LOLLYGAG	LONGER
LOGAOEDIC	LOGINS	LOGY	LOLLYGAGS	LONGERON
LOGARITHM	LOGION	LOHAN	LOLLYPOP	LONGERONS
LOGBOARD	LOGIONS	LOHANS	LOLLYPOPS	LONGERS
LOGBOARDS	LOGISTIC	LOIASES	LOLOG	LONGES
LOGBOOK	LOGISTICS	LOIASIS	LOLOGS	LONGEST
LOGBOOKS	LOGJAM	LOIASISES	LOLZ	LONGEVAL
LOGE	LOGJAMMED	LOID	LOMA	LONGEVITY
LOGES	LOGJAMS	LOIDED	LOMAS	LONGEVOUS
LOGGAT	LOGJUICE	LOIDING	LOMATA	LONGFORM
LOGGATS	LOGJUICES	LOIDS	LOME	LONGHAIR
LOGGED	LOGLINE	LOIN	LOMED	LONGHAIRS
LOGGER	LOGLINES	LOINCLOTH	LOMEIN	LONGHAND
LOGGERS	LOGLOG	LOINS	LOMEINS	LONGHANDS
LOGGETS	LOGLOGS	LOIPE	LOMENT	LONGHEAD
LOGGIA	LOGNORMAL	LOIPEN	LOMENTA	LONGHEADS
LOGGIAS	LOGO	LOIR	LOMENTS	LONGHORN
LOGGIE	LOGOED	LOIRS	LOMENTUM	LONGHORNS
LOGGIER	LOGOFF	LOITER	LOMENTUMS	LONGHOUSE
LOGGIEST	LOGOFFS	LOITERED	LOMES	LONGICORN
LOGGING	LOGOGRAM	LOITERER	LOMING	LONGIES
LOGGINGS	LOGOGRAMS	LOITERERS	LOMPISH	LONGING
LOGGISH	LOGOGRAPH	LOITERING	LONE	LONGINGLY
LOGGY	LOGOGRIPH	LOITERS	LONELIER	LONGINGS
LOGIA	LOGOI	LOKE	LONELIEST	LONGISH
LOGIC	LOGOMACH	LOKES	LONELILY	LONGITUDE
LOGICAL	LOGOMACHS	LOKSHEN	LONELY	LONGJUMP

LONGJUMPS	LOOIE	LOOPHOLE	LOPES	LORDLY
LONGLEAF	LOOIES	LOOPHOLED	LOPGRASS	LORDOMA
LONGLINE	LOOING	LOOPHOLES	LOPHODONT	LORDOMAS
LONGLINER	LOOK	LOOPIER	LOPING	LORDOSES
LONGLINES	LOOKALIKE	LOOPIEST	LOPINGLY	LORDOSIS
LONGLIST	LOOKDOWN	LOOPILY	LOPOLITH	LORDOTIC
LONGLISTS	LOOKDOWNS	LOOPINESS	LOPOLITHS	LORDS
LONGLY	LOOKED	LOOPING	LOPPED	LORDSHIP
LONGNECK	LOOKER	LOOPINGS	LOPPER	LORDSHIPS
LONGNECKS	LOOKERS	LOOPLIKE	LOPPERED	LORDY
LONGNESS	LOOKIE	LOOPS	LOPPERING	LORE
LONGS	LOOKING	LOOPY	LOPPERS	LOREAL
LONGSHIP	LOOKISM	LOOR	LOPPET	LOREL
LONGSHIPS	LOOKISMS	LOORD	LOPPETS	LORELS
LONGSHORE	LOOKIST	LOORDS	LOPPIER	LORES
LONGSOME	LOOKISTS	LOOS	LOPPIES	LORETTE
LONGSPUR	LOOKIT	LOOSE	LOPPIEST	LORETTES
LONGSPURS	LOOKOUT	LOOSEBOX	LOPPING	LORGNETTE
LONGTIME	LOOKOUTS	LOOSED	LOPPINGS	LORGNON
LONGUEUR	LOOKOVER	LOOSELY	LOPPY	LORGNONS
LONGUEURS	LOOKOVERS	LOOSEN	LOPS	LORIC
LONGWALL	LOOKS	LOOSENED	LOPSIDED	LORICA
LONGWALLS	LOOKSISM	LOOSENER	LOPSTICK	LORICAE
LONGWAYS	LOOKSISMS	LOOSENERS	LOPSTICKS	LORICAS
LONGWISE	LOOKUP	LOOSENESS	LOQUACITY	LORICATE
LONGWORM	LOOKUPS	LOOSENING	LOQUAT	LORICATED
LONGWORMS	LOOKY	LOOSENS	LOQUATS	LORICATES
LONICERA	LOOM	LOOSER	LOQUITUR	LORICS
LONICERAS	LOOMED	LOOSES	LOR	LORIES
LOO	LOOMING	LOOSEST	LORAL	LORIKEET
LOOBIER	LOOMS	LOOSIE	LORAN	LORIKEETS
LOOBIES	LOON	LOOSIES	LORANS	LORIMER
LOOBIEST	LOONEY	LOOSING	LORATE	LORIMERS
LOOBILY	LOONEYS	LOOSINGS	LORAZEPAM	LORINER
LOOBY	LOONIE	LOOT	LORCHA	LORINERS
LOOED	LOONIER	LOOTED	LORCHAS	LORING
LOOEY	LOONIES	LOOTEN	LORD	LORINGS
LOOEYS	LOONIEST	LOOTER	LORDED	LORIOT
LOOF	LOONILY	LOOTERS	LORDING	LORIOTS
LOOFA	LOONINESS	LOOTING	LORDINGS	LORIS
LOOFAH	LOONING	LOOTINGS	LORDKIN	LORISES
LOOFAHS	LOONINGS	LOOTS	LORDKINS	LORN
LOOFAS	LOONS	LOOVES	LORDLESS	LORNER
LOOFFUL	LOONY	LOP	LORDLIER	LORNEST
LOOFFULS	LOOP	LOPE	LORDLIEST	LORNNESS
LOOFS	LOOPED	LOPED	LORDLIKE	LORRELL
LOOGIE	LOOPER	LOPER	LORDLING	LORRELLS
LOOGIES	LOOPERS	LOPERS	LORDLINGS	LORRIES

LORRY

LORRY
LORY
LOS
LOSABLE
LOSE
LOSED
LOSEL
LOSELS
LOSEN
LOSER
LOSERS
LOSES
LOSH
LOSING
LOSINGEST
LOSINGLY
LOSINGS
LOSLYF
LOSLYFS
LOSS
LOSSES
LOSSIER
LOSSIEST
LOSSLESS
LOSSMAKER
LOSSY
LOST
LOSTNESS
LOT
LOTA
LOTAH
LOTAHS
LOTAS
LOTE
LOTES
LOTH
LOTHARIO
LOTHARIOS
LOTHEFULL
LOTHER
LOTHEST
LOTHFULL
LOTHNESS
LOTHSOME
LOTI
LOTIC
LOTION
LOTIONS

LOTO
LOTOS
LOTOSES
LOTS
LOTSA
LOTTA
LOTTE
LOTTED
LOTTER
LOTTERIES
LOTTERS
LOTTERY
LOTTES
LOTTING
LOTTO
LOTTOS
LOTUS
LOTUSES
LOTUSLAND
LOU
LOUCHE
LOUCHELY
LOUCHER
LOUCHEST
LOUD
LOUDEN
LOUDENED
LOUDENING
LOUDENS
LOUDER
LOUDEST
LOUDISH
LOUDLIER
LOUDLIEST
LOUDLY
LOUDMOUTH
LOUDNESS
LOUED
LOUGH
LOUGHS
LOUIE
LOUIES
LOUING
LOUIS
LOUMA
LOUMAS
LOUN
LOUND

LOUNDED
LOUNDER
LOUNDERED
LOUNDERS
LOUNDING
LOUNDS
LOUNED
LOUNGE
LOUNGED
LOUNGER
LOUNGERS
LOUNGES
LOUNGEY
LOUNGIER
LOUNGIEST
LOUNGING
LOUNGINGS
LOUNGY
LOUNING
LOUNS
LOUP
LOUPE
LOUPED
LOUPEN
LOUPES
LOUPING
LOUPIT
LOUPS
LOUR
LOURE
LOURED
LOURES
LOURIE
LOURIER
LOURIES
LOURIEST
LOURING
LOURINGLY
LOURINGS
LOURS
LOURY
LOUS
LOUSE
LOUSED
LOUSER
LOUSERS
LOUSES
LOUSEWORT

LOUSIER
LOUSIEST
LOUSILY
LOUSINESS
LOUSING
LOUSINGS
LOUSY
LOUT
LOUTED
LOUTERIES
LOUTERY
LOUTING
LOUTISH
LOUTISHLY
LOUTS
LOUVAR
LOUVARS
LOUVER
LOUVERED
LOUVERS
LOUVRE
LOUVRED
LOUVRES
LOVABLE
LOVABLY
LOVAGE
LOVAGES
LOVAT
LOVATS
LOVE
LOVEABLE
LOVEABLY
LOVEBIRD
LOVEBIRDS
LOVEBITE
LOVEBITES
LOVEBUG
LOVEBUGS
LOVED
LOVEFEST
LOVEFESTS
LOVELESS
LOVELIER
LOVELIES
LOVELIEST
LOVELIGHT
LOVELILY
LOVELOCK

LOVELOCKS
LOVELORN
LOVELY
LOVEMAKER
LOVER
LOVERED
LOVERLESS
LOVERLY
LOVERS
LOVES
LOVESEAT
LOVESEATS
LOVESICK
LOVESOME
LOVEVINE
LOVEVINES
LOVEY
LOVEYS
LOVIE
LOVIER
LOVIES
LOVIEST
LOVING
LOVINGLY
LOVINGS
LOW
LOWAN
LOWANS
LOWBALL
LOWBALLED
LOWBALLS
LOWBORN
LOWBOY
LOWBOYS
LOWBRED
LOWBROW
LOWBROWED
LOWBROWS
LOWBUSH
LOWBUSHES
LOWDOWN
LOWDOWNS
LOWE
LOWED
LOWER
LOWERABLE
LOWERCASE
LOWERED

LOWERIER
LOWERIEST
LOWERING
LOWERINGS
LOWERMOST
LOWERS
LOWERY
LOWES
LOWEST
LOWING
LOWINGS
LOWISH
LOWLAND
LOWLANDER
LOWLANDS
LOWLIER
LOWLIEST
LOWLIFE
LOWLIFER
LOWLIFERS
LOWLIFES
LOWLIGHT
LOWLIGHTS
LOWLIHEAD
LOWLILY
LOWLINESS
LOWLIVES
LOWLY
LOWN
LOWND
LOWNDED
LOWNDING
LOWNDS
LOWNE
LOWNED
LOWNES
LOWNESS
LOWNESSES
LOWNING
LOWNS
LOWP
LOWPASS
LOWPED
LOWPING
LOWPS
LOWRIDER
LOWRIDERS
LOWRIE

LOWRIES
LOWRY
LOWS
LOWSE
LOWSED
LOWSENING
LOWSER
LOWSES
LOWSEST
LOWSING
LOWSIT
LOWT
LOWTED
LOWTING
LOWTS
LOWVELD
LOWVELDS
LOX
LOXED
LOXES
LOXING
LOXODROME
LOXODROMY
LOXYGEN
LOXYGENS
LOY
LOYAL
LOYALER
LOYALEST
LOYALISM
LOYALISMS
LOYALIST
LOYALISTS
LOYALLER
LOYALLEST
LOYALLY
LOYALNESS
LOYALTIES
LOYALTY
LOYS
LOZELL
LOZELLS
LOZEN
LOZENGE
LOZENGED
LOZENGES
LOZENGIER
LOZENGY

LOZENS
LUACH
LUAU
LUAUS
LUBBARD
LUBBARDS
LUBBER
LUBBERLY
LUBBERS
LUBE
LUBED
LUBES
LUBFISH
LUBFISHES
LUBING
LUBRA
LUBRAS
LUBRIC
LUBRICAL
LUBRICANT
LUBRICATE
LUBRICITY
LUBRICOUS
LUCARNE
LUCARNES
LUCE
LUCENCE
LUCENCES
LUCENCIES
LUCENCY
LUCENT
LUCENTLY
LUCERN
LUCERNE
LUCERNES
LUCERNS
LUCES
LUCHOT
LUCHOTH
LUCID
LUCIDER
LUCIDEST
LUCIDITY
LUCIDLY
LUCIDNESS
LUCIFER
LUCIFERIN
LUCIFERS

LUCIGEN
LUCIGENS
LUCITE
LUCITES
LUCK
LUCKED
LUCKEN
LUCKIE
LUCKIER
LUCKIES
LUCKIEST
LUCKILY
LUCKINESS
LUCKING
LUCKLESS
LUCKPENNY
LUCKS
LUCKY
LUCRATIVE
LUCRE
LUCRES
LUCTATION
LUCUBRATE
LUCULENT
LUCUMA
LUCUMAS
LUCUMO
LUCUMONES
LUCUMOS
LUD
LUDE
LUDERICK
LUDERICKS
LUDES
LUDIC
LUDICALLY
LUDICROUS
LUDO
LUDOS
LUDS
LUDSHIP
LUDSHIPS
LUES
LUETIC
LUETICS
LUFF
LUFFA
LUFFAS

LUFFED
LUFFING
LUFFS
LUG
LUGE
LUGED
LUGEING
LUGEINGS
LUGER
LUGERS
LUGES
LUGGABLE
LUGGABLES
LUGGAGE
LUGGAGES
LUGGED
LUGGER
LUGGERS
LUGGIE
LUGGIES
LUGGING
LUGHOLE
LUGHOLES
LUGING
LUGINGS
LUGS
LUGSAIL
LUGSAILS
LUGWORM
LUGWORMS
LUIT
LUITEN
LUKE
LUKEWARM
LULIBUB
LULIBUBS
LULL
LULLABIED
LULLABIES
LULLABY
LULLED
LULLER
LULLERS
LULLING
LULLINGLY
LULLS
LULU
LULUS

L

LULZ	LUMMOX	LUNATICS	LUNGYI	LURCHERS
LUM	LUMMOXES	LUNATION	LUNGYIS	LURCHES
LUMA	LUMMY	LUNATIONS	LUNIER	LURCHING
LUMAS	LUMP	LUNCH	LUNIES	LURDAN
LUMBAGO	LUMPED	LUNCHBOX	LUNIEST	LURDANE
LUMBAGOS	LUMPEN	LUNCHED	LUNINESS	LURDANES
LUMBANG	LUMPENLY	LUNCHEON	LUNISOLAR	LURDANS
LUMBANGS	LUMPENS	LUNCHEONS	LUNITIDAL	LURDEN
LUMBAR	LUMPER	LUNCHER	LUNK	LURDENS
LUMBARS	LUMPERS	LUNCHERS	LUNKER	LURE
LUMBER	LUMPFISH	LUNCHES	LUNKERS	LURED
LUMBERED	LUMPIA	LUNCHING	LUNKHEAD	LURER
LUMBERER	LUMPIAS	LUNCHMEAT	LUNKHEADS	LURERS
LUMBERERS	LUMPIER	LUNCHPAIL	LUNKS	LURES
LUMBERING	LUMPIEST	LUNCHROOM	LUNS	LUREX
LUMBERLY	LUMPILY	LUNCHTIME	LUNT	LUREXES
LUMBERMAN	LUMPINESS	LUNE	LUNTED	LURGI
LUMBERMEN	LUMPING	LUNES	LUNTING	LURGIES
LUMBERS	LUMPINGLY	LUNET	LUNTS	LURGIS
LUMBI	LUMPISH	LUNETS	LUNULA	LURGY
LUMBRICAL	LUMPISHLY	LUNETTE	LUNULAE	LURID
LUMBRICI	LUMPKIN	LUNETTES	LUNULAR	LURIDER
LUMBRICUS	LUMPKINS	LUNG	LUNULATE	LURIDEST
LUMBUS	LUMPS	LUNGAN	LUNULATED	LURIDLY
LUMEN	LUMPY	LUNGANS	LUNULE	LURIDNESS
LUMENAL	LUMS	LUNGE	LUNULES	LURING
LUMENS	LUN	LUNGED	LUNY	LURINGLY
LUMINA	LUNA	LUNGEE	LUNYIE	LURINGS
LUMINAIRE	LUNACIES	LUNGEES	LUNYIES	LURK
LUMINAL	LUNACY	LUNGEING	LUPANAR	LURKED
LUMINANCE	LUNANAUT	LUNGER	LUPANARS	LURKER
LUMINANT	LUNANAUTS	LUNGERS	LUPIN	LURKERS
LUMINANTS	LUNAR	LUNGES	LUPINE	LURKING
LUMINARIA	LUNARIAN	LUNGFISH	LUPINES	LURKINGLY
LUMINARY	LUNARIANS	LUNGFUL	LUPINS	LURKINGS
LUMINE	LUNARIES	LUNGFULS	LUPOID	LURKS
LUMINED	LUNARIST	LUNGI	LUPOUS	LURRIES
LUMINES	LUNARISTS	LUNGIE	LUPPEN	LURRY
LUMINESCE	LUNARNAUT	LUNGIES	LUPULIN	LURS
LUMINING	LUNARS	LUNGING	LUPULINE	LURVE
LUMINISM	LUNARY	LUNGIS	LUPULINIC	LURVES
LUMINISMS	LUNAS	LUNGLESS	LUPULINS	LUSCIOUS
LUMINIST	LUNATE	LUNGLIKE	LUPUS	LUSER
LUMINISTS	LUNATED	LUNGS	LUPUSES	LUSERS
LUMINOUS	LUNATELY	LUNGWORM	LUR	LUSH
LUMME	LUNATES	LUNGWORMS	LURCH	LUSHED
LUMMIER	LUNATIC	LUNGWORT	LURCHED	LUSHER
LUMMIEST	LUNATICAL	LUNGWORTS	LURCHER	LUSHERS

LUSHES	LUSTY	LUVVED	LYCHEE	LYNCHERS
LUSHEST	LUSUS	LUVVIE	LYCHEES	LYNCHES
LUSHIER	LUSUSES	LUVVIEDOM	LYCHES	LYNCHET
LUSHIES	LUTANIST	LUVVIES	LYCHGATE	LYNCHETS
LUSHIEST	LUTANISTS	LUVVING	LYCHGATES	LYNCHING
LUSHING	LUTE	LUVVY	LYCHNIS	LYNCHINGS
LUSHLY	LUTEA	LUX	LYCHNISES	LYNCHPIN
LUSHNESS	LUTEAL	LUXATE	LYCOPENE	LYNCHPINS
LUSHY	LUTECIUM	LUXATED	LYCOPENES	LYNE
LUSK	LUTECIUMS	LUXATES	LYCOPOD	LYNES
LUSKED	LUTED	LUXATING	LYCOPODS	LYNX
LUSKING	LUTEFISK	LUXATION	LYCOPSID	LYNXES
LUSKISH	LUTEFISKS	LUXATIONS	LYCOPSIDS	LYNXLIKE
LUSKS	LUTEIN	LUXE	LYCRA	LYOLYSES
LUST	LUTEINISE	LUXED	LYCRAS	LYOLYSIS
LUSTED	LUTEINIZE	LUXER	LYDDITE	LYOMEROUS
LUSTER	LUTEINS	LUXES	LYDDITES	LYONNAISE
LUSTERED	LUTELIKE	LUXEST	LYE	LYOPHIL
LUSTERING	LUTENIST	LUXING	LYES	LYOPHILE
LUSTERS	LUTENISTS	LUXMETER	LYFULL	LYOPHILED
LUSTFUL	LUTEOLIN	LUXMETERS	LYING	LYOPHILIC
LUSTFULLY	LUTEOLINS	LUXURIANT	LYINGLY	LYOPHOBE
LUSTICK	LUTEOLOUS	LUXURIATE	LYINGS	LYOPHOBIC
LUSTIER	LUTEOUS	LUXURIES	LYKEWAKE	LYRA
LUSTIEST	LUTER	LUXURIOUS	LYKEWAKES	LYRATE
LUSTIHEAD	LUTERS	LUXURIST	LYKEWALK	LYRATED
LUSTIHOOD	LUTES	LUXURISTS	LYKEWALKS	LYRATELY
LUSTILY	LUTESCENT	LUXURY	LYM	LYRE
LUSTINESS	LUTETIUM	LUZ	LYME	LYREBIRD
LUSTING	LUTETIUMS	LUZERN	LYMES	LYREBIRDS
LUSTIQUE	LUTEUM	LUZERNS	LYMITER	LYRES
LUSTLESS	LUTFISK	LUZZES	LYMITERS	LYRIC
LUSTRA	LUTFISKS	LWEI	LYMPH	LYRICAL
LUSTRAL	LUTHERN	LWEIS	LYMPHAD	LYRICALLY
LUSTRATE	LUTHERNS	LYAM	LYMPHADS	LYRICISE
LUSTRATED	LUTHIER	LYAMS	LYMPHATIC	LYRICISED
LUSTRATES	LUTHIERS	LYARD	LYMPHOID	LYRICISES
LUSTRE	LUTING	LYART	LYMPHOMA	LYRICISM
LUSTRED	LUTINGS	LYASE	LYMPHOMAS	LYRICISMS
LUSTRES	LUTIST	LYASES	LYMPHOUS	LYRICIST
LUSTRINE	LUTISTS	LYCAENID	LYMPHS	LYRICISTS
LUSTRINES	LUTITE	LYCAENIDS	LYMS	LYRICIZE
LUSTRING	LUTITES	LYCEA	LYNAGE	LYRICIZED
LUSTRINGS	LUTTEN	LYCEE	LYNAGES	LYRICIZES
LUSTROUS	LUTZ	LYCEES	LYNCEAN	LYRICON
LUSTRUM	LUTZES	LYCEUM	LYNCH	LYRICONS
LUSTRUMS	LUV	LYCEUMS	LYNCHED	LYRICS
LUSTS	LUVS	LYCH	LYNCHER	LYRIFORM

LYRISM

LYRISM
LYRISMS
LYRIST
LYRISTS
LYSATE
LYSATES
LYSE
LYSED
LYSERGIC

LYSERGIDE
LYSES
LYSIGENIC
LYSIMETER
LYSIN
LYSINE
LYSINES
LYSING
LYSINS

LYSIS
LYSOGEN
LYSOGENIC
LYSOGENS
LYSOGENY
LYSOL
LYSOLS
LYSOSOMAL
LYSOSOME

LYSOSOMES
LYSOZYME
LYSOZYMES
LYSSA
LYSSAS
LYTE
LYTED
LYTES
LYTHE

LYTHES
LYTHRUM
LYTHRUMS
LYTIC
LYTICALLY
LYTING
LYTTA
LYTTAE
LYTTAS

L

M

MA	MACARONI	MACHER	MACON	MACULATES
MAA	MACARONIC	MACHERS	MACONS	MACULE
MAAED	MACARONIS	MACHES	MACOYA	MACULED
MAAING	MACARONS	MACHETE	MACOYAS	MACULES
MAAR	MACAROON	MACHETES	MACRAME	MACULING
MAARE	MACAROONS	MACHI	MACRAMES	MACULOSE
MAARS	MACAS	MACHINATE	MACRAMI	MACUMBA
MAAS	MACASSAR	MACHINE	MACRAMIS	MACUMBAS
MAASES	MACASSARS	MACHINED	MACRO	MAD
MAATJES	MACAW	MACHINERY	MACROBIAN	MADAFU
MABE	MACAWS	MACHINES	MACROCODE	MADAFUS
MABELA	MACCABAW	MACHINIMA	MACROCOPY	MADAM
MABELAS	MACCABAWS	MACHINING	MACROCOSM	MADAME
MABES	MACCABOY	MACHINIST	MACROCYST	MADAMED
MAC	MACCABOYS	MACHISMO	MACROCYTE	MADAMES
MACA	MACCARONI	MACHISMOS	MACRODOME	MADAMING
MACABER	MACCHIA	MACHMETER	MACRODONT	MADAMS
MACABRE	MACCHIATO	MACHO	MACROGLIA	MADAROSES
MACABRELY	MACCHIE	MACHOISM	MACROLIDE	MADAROSIS
MACABRER	MACCOBOY	MACHOISMS	MACROLOGY	MADBRAIN
MACABREST	MACCOBOYS	MACHOS	MACROMERE	MADBRAINS
MACACO	MACE	MACHREE	MACROMOLE	MADCAP
MACACOS	MACED	MACHREES	MACRON	MADCAPS
MACADAM	MACEDOINE	MACHS	MACRONS	MADDED
MACADAMED	MACER	MACHZOR	MACROPOD	MADDEN
MACADAMIA	MACERAL	MACHZORIM	MACROPODS	MADDENED
MACADAMS	MACERALS	MACHZORS	MACROPSIA	MADDENING
MACAHUBA	MACERATE	MACING	MACROS	MADDENS
MACAHUBAS	MACERATED	MACINTOSH	MACROTOUS	MADDER
MACALLUM	MACERATER	MACK	MACRURAL	MADDERS
MACALLUMS	MACERATES	MACKEREL	MACRURAN	MADDEST
MACAQUE	MACERATOR	MACKERELS	MACRURANS	MADDING
MACAQUES	MACERS	MACKINAW	MACRUROID	MADDINGLY
MACARISE	MACES	MACKINAWS	MACRUROUS	MADDISH
MACARISED	MACH	MACKLE	MACS	MADDOCK
MACARISES	MACHACA	MACKLED	MACTATION	MADDOCKS
MACARISM	MACHACAS	MACKLES	MACULA	MADE
MACARISMS	MACHAIR	MACKLING	MACULAE	MADEFIED
MACARIZE	MACHAIRS	MACKS	MACULAR	MADEFIES
MACARIZED	MACHAN	MACLE	MACULAS	MADEFY
MACARIZES	MACHANS	MACLED	MACULATE	MADEFYING
MACARON	MACHE	MACLES	MACULATED	MADEIRA

MADEIRAS	MADS	MAFTIRS	MAGLEV	MAGNUM
MADELEINE	MADTOM	MAG	MAGLEVS	MAGNUMS
MADERISE	MADTOMS	MAGAININ	MAGMA	MAGNUS
MADERISED	MADURO	MAGAININS	MAGMAS	MAGOT
MADERISES	MADUROS	MAGALOG	MAGMATA	MAGOTS
MADERIZE	MADWOMAN	MAGALOGS	MAGMATIC	MAGPIE
MADERIZED	MADWOMEN	MAGALOGUE	MAGMATISM	MAGPIES
MADERIZES	MADWORT	MAGAZINE	MAGNALIUM	MAGS
MADEUPPY	MADWORTS	MAGAZINES	MAGNATE	MAGSMAN
MADGE	MADZOON	MAGDALEN	MAGNATES	MAGSMEN
MADGES	MADZOONS	MAGDALENE	MAGNES	MAGUEY
MADHOUSE	MAE	MAGDALENS	MAGNESES	MAGUEYS
MADHOUSES	MAELID	MAGE	MAGNESIA	MAGUS
MADID	MAELIDS	MAGENTA	MAGNESIAL	MAGYAR
MADISON	MAELSTROM	MAGENTAS	MAGNESIAN	MAHA
MADISONS	MAENAD	MAGES	MAGNESIAS	MAHANT
MADLING	MAENADES	MAGESHIP	MAGNESIC	MAHANTS
MADLINGS	MAENADIC	MAGESHIPS	MAGNESITE	MAHARAJA
MADLY	MAENADISM	MAGG	MAGNESIUM	MAHARAJAH
MADMAN	MAENADS	MAGGED	MAGNET	MAHARAJAS
MADMEN	MAERL	MAGGIE	MAGNETAR	MAHARANEE
MADNESS	MAERLS	MAGGIES	MAGNETARS	MAHARANI
MADNESSES	MAES	MAGGING	MAGNETIC	MAHARANIS
MADONNA	MAESTOSO	MAGGOT	MAGNETICS	MAHARISHI
MADONNAS	MAESTOSOS	MAGGOTIER	MAGNETISE	MAHATMA
MADOQUA	MAESTRI	MAGGOTS	MAGNETISM	MAHATMAS
MADOQUAS	MAESTRO	MAGGOTY	MAGNETIST	MAHEWU
MADRAS	MAESTROS	MAGGS	MAGNETITE	MAHEWUS
MADRASA	MAFFIA	MAGI	MAGNETIZE	MAHIMAHI
MADRASAH	MAFFIAS	MAGIAN	MAGNETO	MAHIMAHIS
MADRASAHS	MAFFICK	MAGIANISM	MAGNETON	MAHJONG
MADRASAS	MAFFICKED	MAGIANS	MAGNETONS	MAHJONGG
MADRASES	MAFFICKER	MAGIC	MAGNETOS	MAHJONGGS
MADRASSA	MAFFICKS	MAGICAL	MAGNETRON	MAHJONGS
MADRASSAH	MAFFLED	MAGICALLY	MAGNETS	MAHLSTICK
MADRASSAS	MAFFLIN	MAGICIAN	MAGNIFIC	MAHMAL
MADRE	MAFFLING	MAGICIANS	MAGNIFICO	MAHMALS
MADREPORE	MAFFLINGS	MAGICKED	MAGNIFIED	MAHOE
MADRES	MAFFLINS	MAGICKING	MAGNIFIER	MAHOES
MADRIGAL	MAFIA	MAGICS	MAGNIFIES	MAHOGANY
MADRIGALS	MAFIAS	MAGILP	MAGNIFY	MAHONIA
MADRILENE	MAFIC	MAGILPS	MAGNITUDE	MAHONIAS
MADRONA	MAFICS	MAGISM	MAGNOLIA	MAHOUT
MADRONAS	MAFIOSI	MAGISMS	MAGNOLIAS	MAHOUTS
MADRONE	MAFIOSO	MAGISTER	MAGNON	MAHSEER
MADRONES	MAFIOSOS	MAGISTERS	MAGNONS	MAHSEERS
MADRONO	MAFTED	MAGISTERY	MAGNOX	MAHSIR
MADRONOS	MAFTIR	MAGISTRAL	MAGNOXES	MAHSIRS

MAHUA
MAHUANG
MAHUANGS
MAHUAS
MAHWA
MAHWAS
MAHZOR
MAHZORIM
MAHZORS
MAIASAUR
MAIASAURA
MAIASAURS
MAID
MAIDAN
MAIDANS
MAIDED
MAIDEN
MAIDENISH
MAIDENLY
MAIDENS
MAIDHOOD
MAIDHOODS
MAIDING
MAIDISH
MAIDISM
MAIDISMS
MAIDLESS
MAIDS
MAIEUTIC
MAIEUTICS
MAIGRE
MAIGRES
MAIHEM
MAIHEMS
MAIK
MAIKO
MAIKOS
MAIKS
MAIL
MAILABLE
MAILBAG
MAILBAGS
MAILBOAT
MAILBOATS
MAILBOX
MAILBOXES
MAILCAR
MAILCARS

MAILCOACH
MAILE
MAILED
MAILER
MAILERS
MAILES
MAILGRAM
MAILGRAMS
MAILING
MAILINGS
MAILL
MAILLESS
MAILLOT
MAILLOTS
MAILLS
MAILMAN
MAILMEN
MAILMERGE
MAILPOUCH
MAILROOM
MAILROOMS
MAILS
MAILSACK
MAILSACKS
MAILSHOT
MAILSHOTS
MAILVAN
MAILVANS
MAIM
MAIMED
MAIMER
MAIMERS
MAIMING
MAIMINGS
MAIMS
MAIN
MAINBOOM
MAINBOOMS
MAINBRACE
MAINDOOR
MAINDOORS
MAINED
MAINER
MAINEST
MAINFRAME
MAINING
MAINLAND
MAINLANDS

MAINLINE
MAINLINED
MAINLINER
MAINLINES
MAINLY
MAINMAST
MAINMASTS
MAINOR
MAINORS
MAINOUR
MAINOURS
MAINPRISE
MAINS
MAINSAIL
MAINSAILS
MAINSHEET
MAINSTAGE
MAINSTAY
MAINSTAYS
MAINTAIN
MAINTAINS
MAINTOP
MAINTOPS
MAINYARD
MAINYARDS
MAIOLICA
MAIOLICAS
MAIR
MAIRE
MAIREHAU
MAIREHAUS
MAIRES
MAIRS
MAISE
MAISES
MAIST
MAISTER
MAISTERED
MAISTERS
MAISTRIES
MAISTRING
MAISTRY
MAISTS
MAIZE
MAIZES
MAJAGUA
MAJAGUAS
MAJESTIC

MAJESTIES
MAJESTY
MAJLIS
MAJLISES
MAJOLICA
MAJOLICAS
MAJOR
MAJORAT
MAJORATS
MAJORDOMO
MAJORED
MAJORETTE
MAJORING
MAJORITY
MAJORLY
MAJORS
MAJORSHIP
MAJUSCULE
MAK
MAKABLE
MAKAR
MAKARS
MAKE
MAKEABLE
MAKEABLES
MAKEBATE
MAKEBATES
MAKEFAST
MAKEFASTS
MAKELESS
MAKEOVER
MAKEOVERS
MAKER
MAKEREADY
MAKERS
MAKES
MAKESHIFT
MAKEUP
MAKEUPS
MAKHANI
MAKHANIS
MAKI
MAKIMONO
MAKIMONOS
MAKING
MAKINGS
MAKIS
MAKO

MAKOS
MAKS
MAKUTA
MAKUTU
MAKUTUED
MAKUTUING
MAKUTUS
MAL
MALA
MALACCA
MALACCAS
MALACHITE
MALACIA
MALACIAS
MALADIES
MALADROIT
MALADY
MALAGUENA
MALAISE
MALAISES
MALAM
MALAMS
MALAMUTE
MALAMUTES
MALANDER
MALANDERS
MALANGA
MALANGAS
MALAPERT
MALAPERTS
MALAPROP
MALAPROPS
MALAR
MALARIA
MALARIAL
MALARIAN
MALARIAS
MALARIOUS
MALARKEY
MALARKEYS
MALARKIES
MALARKY
MALAROMA
MALAROMAS
MALARS
MALAS
MALATE
MALATES

M

MALATHION	MALIGNER	MALLETS	MALTMEN	MAMBOED
MALAX	MALIGNERS	MALLEUS	MALTOL	MAMBOES
MALAXAGE	MALIGNING	MALLEUSES	MALTOLS	MAMBOING
MALAXAGES	MALIGNITY	MALLING	MALTOSE	MAMBOS
MALAXATE	MALIGNLY	MALLINGS	MALTOSES	MAMEE
MALAXATED	MALIGNS	MALLOW	MALTREAT	MAMEES
MALAXATES	MALIHINI	MALLOWS	MALTREATS	MAMELON
MALAXATOR	MALIHINIS	MALLS	MALTS	MAMELONS
MALAXED	MALIK	MALM	MALTSTER	MAMELUCO
MALAXES	MALIKS	MALMAG	MALTSTERS	MAMELUCOS
MALAXING	MALINE	MALMAGS	MALTWORM	MAMELUKE
MALE	MALINES	MALMIER	MALTWORMS	MAMELUKES
MALEATE	MALINGER	MALMIEST	MALTY	MAMEY
MALEATES	MALINGERS	MALMS	MALUS	MAMEYES
MALEDICT	MALINGERY	MALMSEY	MALUSES	MAMEYS
MALEDICTS	MALIS	MALMSEYS	MALVA	MAMIE
MALEFFECT	MALISM	MALMSTONE	MALVAS	MAMIES
MALEFIC	MALISMS	MALMY	MALVASIA	MAMILLA
MALEFICE	MALISON	MALODOR	MALVASIAN	MAMILLAE
MALEFICES	MALISONS	MALODORS	MALVASIAS	MAMILLAR
MALEIC	MALIST	MALODOUR	MALVESIE	MAMILLARY
MALEMIUT	MALKIN	MALODOURS	MALVESIES	MAMILLATE
MALEMIUTS	MALKINS	MALONATE	MALVOISIE	MAMLUK
MALEMUTE	MALL	MALONATES	MALWA	MAMLUKS
MALEMUTES	MALLAM	MALONIC	MALWARE	MAMMA
MALENESS	MALLAMS	MALOTI	MALWARES	MAMMAE
MALENGINE	MALLANDER	MALPIGHIA	MALWAS	MAMMAL
MALES	MALLARD	MALPOSED	MAM	MAMMALIAN
MALFED	MALLARDS	MALS	MAMA	MAMMALITY
MALFORMED	MALLCORE	MALSTICK	MAMAGUY	MAMMALOGY
MALGRADO	MALLCORES	MALSTICKS	MAMAGUYED	MAMMALS
MALGRE	MALLEABLE	MALT	MAMAGUYS	MAMMARIES
MALGRED	MALLEABLY	MALTALENT	MAMAKAU	MAMMARY
MALGRES	MALLEATE	MALTASE	MAMAKAUS	MAMMAS
MALGRING	MALLEATED	MALTASES	MAMAKO	MAMMATE
MALI	MALLEATES	MALTED	MAMAKOS	MAMMATI
MALIBU	MALLECHO	MALTEDS	MAMAKU	MAMMATUS
MALIC	MALLECHOS	MALTESE	MAMAKUS	MAMMEE
MALICE	MALLED	MALTHA	MAMALIGA	MAMMEES
MALICED	MALLEE	MALTHAS	MAMALIGAS	MAMMER
MALICES	MALLEES	MALTIER	MAMAS	MAMMERED
MALICHO	MALLEI	MALTIEST	MAMASAN	MAMMERING
MALICHOS	MALLEMUCK	MALTINESS	MAMASANS	MAMMERS
MALICING	MALLENDER	MALTING	MAMATEEK	MAMMET
MALICIOUS	MALLEOLAR	MALTINGS	MAMATEEKS	MAMMETRY
MALIGN	MALLEOLI	MALTIPOO	MAMBA	MAMMETS
MALIGNANT	MALLEOLUS	MALTIPOOS	MAMBAS	MAMMEY
MALIGNED	MALLET	MALTMAN	MAMBO	MAMMEYS

MAMMIE	MANANA	MANDI	MANET	MANGONEL
MAMMIES	MANANAS	MANDIBLE	MANEUVER	MANGONELS
MAMMIFER	MANAS	MANDIBLES	MANEUVERS	MANGOS
MAMMIFERS	MANAT	MANDILION	MANFUL	MANGOSTAN
MAMMIFORM	MANATEE	MANDIOC	MANFULLER	MANGOUSTE
MAMMILLA	MANATEES	MANDIOCA	MANFULLY	MANGROVE
MAMMILLAE	MANATI	MANDIOCAS	MANG	MANGROVES
MAMMILLAR	MANATIS	MANDIOCCA	MANGA	MANGS
MAMMITIS	MANATOID	MANDIOCS	MANGABEY	MANGULATE
MAMMOCK	MANATS	MANDIR	MANGABEYS	MANGY
MAMMOCKED	MANATU	MANDIRA	MANGABIES	MANHANDLE
MAMMOCKS	MANATUS	MANDIRAS	MANGABY	MANHATTAN
MAMMOGRAM	MANAWA	MANDIRS	MANGAL	MANHOLE
MAMMON	MANAWAS	MANDIS	MANGALS	MANHOLES
MAMMONISH	MANBAG	MANDOLA	MANGANATE	MANHOOD
MAMMONISM	MANBAGS	MANDOLAS	MANGANESE	MANHOODS
MAMMONIST	MANBAND	MANDOLIN	MANGANIC	MANHUNT
MAMMONITE	MANBANDS	MANDOLINE	MANGANIN	MANHUNTER
MAMMONS	MANCALA	MANDOLINS	MANGANINS	MANHUNTS
MAMMOTH	MANCALAS	MANDOM	MANGANITE	MANI
MAMMOTHS	MANCANDO	MANDOMS	MANGANOUS	MANIA
MAMMY	MANCHE	MANDORA	MANGAS	MANIAC
MAMPARA	MANCHEGO	MANDORAS	MANGE	MANIACAL
MAMPARAS	MANCHEGOS	MANDORLA	MANGEAO	MANIACS
MAMPOER	MANCHES	MANDORLAS	MANGEAOS	MANIAS
MAMPOERS	MANCHET	MANDRAKE	MANGED	MANIC
MAMS	MANCHETS	MANDRAKES	MANGEL	MANICALLY
MAMSELLE	MANCIPATE	MANDREL	MANGELS	MANICOTTI
MAMSELLES	MANCIPLE	MANDRELS	MANGER	MANICS
MAMZER	MANCIPLES	MANDRIL	MANGERS	MANICURE
MAMZERIM	MANCUS	MANDRILL	MANGES	MANICURED
MAMZERS	MANCUSES	MANDRILLS	MANGETOUT	MANICURES
MAN	MAND	MANDRILS	MANGEY	MANIES
MANA	MANDALA	MANDUCATE	MANGIER	MANIFEST
MANACLE	MANDALAS	MANDYLION	MANGIEST	MANIFESTO
MANACLED	MANDAIIC	MANE	MANGILY	MANIFESTS
MANACLES	MANDAMUS	MANEB	MANGINESS	MANIFOLD
MANACLING	MANDARIN	MANEBS	MANGING	MANIFOLDS
MANAGE	MANDARINE	MANED	MANGLE	MANIFORM
MANAGED	MANDARINS	MANEGE	MANGLED	MANIHOC
MANAGER	MANDATARY	MANEGED	MANGLER	MANIHOCS
MANAGERS	MANDATE	MANEGES	MANGLERS	MANIHOT
MANAGES	MANDATED	MANEGING	MANGLES	MANIHOTS
MANAGING	MANDATES	MANEH	MANGLING	MANIKIN
MANAIA	MANDATING	MANEHS	MANGO	MANIKINS
MANAIAS	MANDATOR	MANELESS	MANGOES	MANILA
MANAKIN	MANDATORS	MANENT	MANGOLD	MANILAS
MANAKINS	MANDATORY	MANES	MANGOLDS	MANILLA

MANILLAS	MANNERS	MANSE	MANTRAM	MANYFOLD
MANILLE	MANNIKIN	MANSES	MANTRAMS	MANYPLIES
MANILLES	MANNIKINS	MANSHIFT	MANTRAP	MANZANITA
MANIOC	MANNING	MANSHIFTS	MANTRAPS	MANZELLO
MANIOCA	MANNISH	MANSION	MANTRAS	MANZELLOS
MANIOCAS	MANNISHLY	MANSIONS	MANTRIC	MAOMAO
MANIOCS	MANNITE	MANSLAYER	MANTUA	MAOMAOS
MANIPLE	MANNITES	MANSONRY	MANTUAS	MAORMOR
MANIPLES	MANNITIC	MANSPLAIN	MANTY	MAORMORS
MANIPLIES	MANNITOL	MANSPREAD	MANTYHOSE	MAP
MANIPULAR	MANNITOLS	MANSUETE	MANUAL	MAPAU
MANIS	MANNOSE	MANSWORN	MANUALLY	MAPAUS
MANISES	MANNOSES	MANSWORNS	MANUALS	MAPLE
MANITO	MANO	MANTA	MANUARY	MAPLELIKE
MANITOS	MANOAO	MANTAS	MANUBRIA	MAPLES
MANITOU	MANOAOS	MANTEAU	MANUBRIAL	MAPLESS
MANITOUS	MANOES	MANTEAUS	MANUBRIUM	MAPLIKE
MANITU	MANOEUVER	MANTEAUX	MANUCODE	MAPMAKER
MANITUS	MANOEUVRE	MANTEEL	MANUCODES	MAPMAKERS
MANJACK	MANOMETER	MANTEELS	MANUHIRI	MAPMAKING
MANJACKS	MANOMETRY	MANTEL	MANUHIRIS	MAPPABLE
MANKIER	MANOR	MANTELET	MANUKA	MAPPED
MANKIEST	MANORIAL	MANTELETS	MANUKAS	MAPPEMOND
MANKIND	MANORS	MANTELS	MANUL	MAPPER
MANKINDS	MANOS	MANTES	MANULS	MAPPERIES
MANKINI	MANOSCOPY	MANTIC	MANUMATIC	MAPPERS
MANKINIS	MANPACK	MANTICORA	MANUMEA	MAPPERY
MANKY	MANPACKS	MANTICORE	MANUMEAS	MAPPING
MANLESS	MANPOWER	MANTID	MANUMIT	MAPPINGS
MANLIER	MANPOWERS	MANTIDS	MANUMITS	MAPPIST
MANLIEST	MANQUE	MANTIES	MANURANCE	MAPPISTS
MANLIKE	MANQUES	MANTILLA	MANURE	MAPS
MANLIKELY	MANRED	MANTILLAS	MANURED	MAPSTICK
MANLILY	MANREDS	MANTIS	MANURER	MAPSTICKS
MANLINESS	MANRENT	MANTISES	MANURERS	MAPWISE
MANLY	MANRENTS	MANTISSA	MANURES	MAQUETTE
MANMADE	MANRIDER	MANTISSAS	MANURIAL	MAQUETTES
MANNA	MANRIDERS	MANTLE	MANURING	MAQUI
MANNAN	MANRIDING	MANTLED	MANURINGS	MAQUILA
MANNANS	MANROPE	MANTLES	MANUS	MAQUILAS
MANNAS	MANROPES	MANTLET	MANWARD	MAQUIS
MANNED	MANS	MANTLETS	MANWARDS	MAQUISARD
MANNEQUIN	MANSARD	MANTLING	MANWISE	MAR
MANNER	MANSARDED	MANTLINGS	MANY	MARA
MANNERED	MANSARDS	MANTO	MANYATA	MARABI
MANNERISM	MANSCAPE	MANTOES	MANYATAS	MARABIS
MANNERIST	MANSCAPED	MANTOS	MANYATTA	MARABOU
MANNERLY	MANSCAPES	MANTRA	MANYATTAS	MARABOUS

MARABOUT	MARCASITE	MARGARINE	MARINAS	MARKKAA
MARABOUTS	MARCATO	MARGARINS	MARINATE	MARKKAS
MARABUNTA	MARCATOS	MARGARITA	MARINATED	MARKMAN
MARACA	MARCEL	MARGARITE	MARINATES	MARKMEN
MARACAS	MARCELLA	MARGATE	MARINE	MARKS
MARAE	MARCELLAS	MARGATES	MARINER	MARKSMAN
MARAES	MARCELLED	MARGAY	MARINERA	MARKSMEN
MARAGING	MARCELLER	MARGAYS	MARINERAS	MARKUP
MARAGINGS	MARCELS	MARGE	MARINERS	MARKUPS
MARAH	MARCH	MARGENT	MARINES	MARL
MARAHS	MARCHED	MARGENTED	MARINIERE	MARLE
MARAKA	MARCHEN	MARGENTS	MARIPOSA	MARLED
MARANATHA	MARCHER	MARGES	MARIPOSAS	MARLES
MARANTA	MARCHERS	MARGIN	MARISCHAL	MARLIER
MARANTAS	MARCHES	MARGINAL	MARISH	MARLIEST
MARARI	MARCHESA	MARGINALS	MARISHES	MARLIN
MARARIS	MARCHESAS	MARGINATE	MARITAGE	MARLINE
MARAS	MARCHESE	MARGINED	MARITAGES	MARLINES
MARASCA	MARCHESI	MARGINING	MARITAL	MARLING
MARASCAS	MARCHING	MARGINS	MARITALLY	MARLINGS
MARASMIC	MARCHLAND	MARGOSA	MARITIME	MARLINS
MARASMOID	MARCHLIKE	MARGOSAS	MARJORAM	MARLITE
MARASMUS	MARCHMAN	MARGRAVE	MARJORAMS	MARLITES
MARATHON	MARCHMEN	MARGRAVES	MARK	MARLITIC
MARATHONS	MARCHPANE	MARGS	MARKA	MARLS
MARAUD	MARCONI	MARIA	MARKAS	MARLSTONE
MARAUDED	MARCONIED	MARIACHI	MARKDOWN	MARLY
MARAUDER	MARCONIS	MARIACHIS	MARKDOWNS	MARM
MARAUDERS	MARCS	MARIALITE	MARKED	MARMALADE
MARAUDING	MARD	MARID	MARKEDLY	MARMALISE
MARAUDS	MARDIED	MARIDS	MARKER	MARMALIZE
MARAVEDI	MARDIER	MARIES	MARKERS	MARMARISE
MARAVEDIS	MARDIES	MARIGOLD	MARKET	MARMARIZE
MARBELISE	MARDIEST	MARIGOLDS	MARKETED	MARMELISE
MARBELIZE	MARDY	MARIGRAM	MARKETEER	MARMELIZE
MARBLE	MARDYING	MARIGRAMS	MARKETER	MARMEM
MARBLED	MARE	MARIGRAPH	MARKETERS	MARMITE
MARBLEISE	MAREMMA	MARIHUANA	MARKETING	MARMITES
MARBLEIZE	MAREMMAS	MARIJUANA	MARKETISE	MARMOREAL
MARBLER	MAREMME	MARIMBA	MARKETIZE	MARMOREAN
MARBLERS	MARENGO	MARIMBAS	MARKETS	MARMOSE
MARBLES	MARERO	MARIMBIST	MARKHOOR	MARMOSES
MARBLIER	MAREROS	MARINA	MARKHOORS	MARMOSET
MARBLIEST	MARES	MARINADE	MARKHOR	MARMOSETS
MARBLING	MARESCHAL	MARINADED	MARKHORS	MARMOT
MARBLINGS	MARG	MARINADES	MARKING	MARMOTS
MARBLY	MARGARIC	MARINARA	MARKINGS	MARMS
MARC	MARGARIN	MARINARAS	MARKKA	MAROCAIN

M

MAROCAINS	MARROWFAT	MARTELLO	MARVERS	MASHIE
MARON	MARROWIER	MARTELLOS	MARVIER	MASHIER
MARONS	MARROWING	MARTELS	MARVIEST	MASHIES
MAROON	MARROWISH	MARTEN	MARVY	MASHIEST
MAROONED	MARROWS	MARTENS	MARXISANT	MASHING
MAROONER	MARROWSKY	MARTEXT	MARY	MASHINGS
MAROONERS	MARROWY	MARTEXTS	MARYBUD	MASHLAM
MAROONING	MARRUM	MARTIAL	MARYBUDS	MASHLAMS
MAROONS	MARRUMS	MARTIALLY	MARYJANE	MASHLIM
MAROQUIN	MARRY	MARTIALS	MARYJANES	MASHLIMS
MAROQUINS	MARRYING	MARTIAN	MARZIPAN	MASHLIN
MAROR	MARRYINGS	MARTIANS	MARZIPANS	MASHLINS
MARORS	MARS	MARTIN	MAS	MASHLOCH
MARPLOT	MARSALA	MARTINET	MASA	MASHLOCHS
MARPLOTS	MARSALAS	MARTINETS	MASALA	MASHLUM
MARQUE	MARSE	MARTING	MASALAS	MASHLUMS
MARQUEE	MARSEILLE	MARTINGAL	MASAS	MASHMAN
MARQUEES	MARSES	MARTINI	MASCARA	MASHMEN
MARQUES	MARSH	MARTINIS	MASCARAED	MASHUA
MARQUESS	MARSHAL	MARTINS	MASCARAS	MASHUAS
MARQUETRY	MARSHALCY	MARTLET	MASCARON	MASHUP
MARQUIS	MARSHALED	MARTLETS	MASCARONS	MASHUPS
MARQUISE	MARSHALER	MARTS	MASCLE	MASHY
MARQUISES	MARSHALL	MARTYR	MASCLED	MASING
MARRA	MARSHALLS	MARTYRDOM	MASCLES	MASJID
MARRAM	MARSHALS	MARTYRED	MASCON	MASJIDS
MARRAMS	MARSHBUCK	MARTYRIA	MASCONS	MASK
MARRANO	MARSHED	MARTYRIES	MASCOT	MASKABLE
MARRANOS	MARSHES	MARTYRING	MASCOTS	MASKED
MARRAS	MARSHIER	MARTYRISE	MASCULINE	MASKEG
MARRED	MARSHIEST	MARTYRISH	MASCULIST	MASKEGS
MARRELS	MARSHLAND	MARTYRIUM	MASCULY	MASKER
MARRER	MARSHLIKE	MARTYRIZE	MASE	MASKERS
MARRERS	MARSHWORT	MARTYRLY	MASED	MASKING
MARRI	MARSHY	MARTYRS	MASER	MASKINGS
MARRIAGE	MARSPORT	MARTYRY	MASERS	MASKLIKE
MARRIAGES	MARSPORTS	MARVEL	MASES	MASKS
MARRIED	MARSQUAKE	MARVELED	MASH	MASLIN
MARRIEDS	MARSUPIA	MARVELER	MASHALLAH	MASLINS
MARRIER	MARSUPIAL	MARVELERS	MASHED	MASOCHISM
MARRIERS	MARSUPIAN	MARVELING	MASHER	MASOCHIST
MARRIES	MARSUPIUM	MARVELLED	MASHERS	MASON
MARRING	MART	MARVELLER	MASHES	MASONED
MARRIS	MARTAGON	MARVELOUS	MASHGIACH	MASONIC
MARRON	MARTAGONS	MARVELS	MASHGIAH	MASONING
MARRONS	MARTED	MARVER	MASHGIHIM	MASONITE
MARROW	MARTEL	MARVERED	MASHIACH	MASONITES
MARROWED	MARTELLED	MARVERING	MASHIACHS	MASONRIED

MASONRIES	MASSOOLAS	MASTOID	MATCHMADE	MATINEE
MASONRY	MASSTIGE	MASTOIDAL	MATCHMAKE	MATINEES
MASONS	MASSTIGES	MASTOIDS	MATCHMARK	MATINESS
MASOOLAH	MASSY	MASTOPEXY	MATCHPLAY	MATING
MASOOLAHS	MASSYMORE	MASTS	MATCHUP	MATINGS
MASQUE	MAST	MASTY	MATCHUPS	MATINS
MASQUER	MASTABA	MASU	MATCHWOOD	MATIPO
MASQUERS	MASTABAH	MASULA	MATE	MATIPOS
MASQUES	MASTABAHS	MASULAS	MATED	MATJES
MASS	MASTABAS	MASURIUM	MATELASSE	MATLESS
MASSA	MASTED	MASURIUMS	MATELESS	MATLO
MASSACRE	MASTER	MASUS	MATELOT	MATLOS
MASSACRED	MASTERATE	MAT	MATELOTE	MATLOW
MASSACRER	MASTERDOM	MATACHIN	MATELOTES	MATLOWS
MASSACRES	MASTERED	MATACHINA	MATELOTS	MATOKE
MASSAGE	MASTERFUL	MATACHINI	MATELOTTE	MATOKES
MASSAGED	MASTERIES	MATACHINS	MATER	MATOOKE
MASSAGER	MASTERING	MATADOR	MATERIAL	MATOOKES
MASSAGERS	MASTERLY	MATADORA	MATERIALS	MATRASS
MASSAGES	MASTERS	MATADORAS	MATERIEL	MATRASSES
MASSAGING	MASTERY	MATADORE	MATERIELS	MATRES
MASSAGIST	MASTFUL	MATADORES	MATERNAL	MATRIARCH
MASSAS	MASTHEAD	MATADORS	MATERNITY	MATRIC
MASSCULT	MASTHEADS	MATAGOURI	MATERS	MATRICE
MASSCULTS	MASTHOUSE	MATAI	MATES	MATRICES
MASSE	MASTIC	MATAIS	MATESHIP	MATRICIDE
MASSED	MASTICATE	MATAMATA	MATESHIPS	MATRICS
MASSEDLY	MASTICH	MATAMATAS	MATEY	MATRICULA
MASSES	MASTICHE	MATAMBALA	MATEYNESS	MATRILINY
MASSETER	MASTICHES	MATATA	MATEYS	MATRIMONY
MASSETERS	MASTICHS	MATATAS	MATFELLON	MATRIX
MASSEUR	MASTICOT	MATATU	MATFELON	MATRIXES
MASSEURS	MASTICOTS	MATATUS	MATFELONS	MATRON
MASSEUSE	MASTICS	MATCH	MATGRASS	MATRONAGE
MASSEUSES	MASTIER	MATCHA	MATH	MATRONAL
MASSICOT	MASTIEST	MATCHABLE	MATHESES	MATRONISE
MASSICOTS	MASTIFF	MATCHAS	MATHESIS	MATRONIZE
MASSIER	MASTIFFS	MATCHBOOK	MATHS	MATRONLY
MASSIEST	MASTING	MATCHBOX	MATICO	MATRONS
MASSIF	MASTITIC	MATCHED	MATICOS	MATROSS
MASSIFS	MASTITIS	MATCHER	MATIER	MATROSSES
MASSINESS	MASTIX	MATCHERS	MATIES	MATS
MASSING	MASTIXES	MATCHES	MATIEST	MATSAH
MASSIVE	MASTLESS	MATCHET	MATILDA	MATSAHS
MASSIVELY	MASTLIKE	MATCHETS	MATILDAS	MATSURI
MASSIVES	MASTODON	MATCHING	MATILY	MATSURIS
MASSLESS	MASTODONS	MATCHLESS	MATIN	MATSUTAKE
MASSOOLA	MASTODONT	MATCHLOCK	MATINAL	MATT

M

MATTAMORE	MATZAHS	MAUNDY	MAWGER	MAXIMINS
MATTE	MATZAS	MAUNGIER	MAWING	MAXIMISE
MATTED	MATZO	MAUNGIEST	MAWK	MAXIMISED
MATTEDLY	MATZOH	MAUNGY	MAWKIER	MAXIMISER
MATTER	MATZOHS	MAUNNA	MAWKIEST	MAXIMISES
MATTERED	MATZOON	MAURI	MAWKIN	MAXIMIST
MATTERFUL	MATZOONS	MAURIS	MAWKINS	MAXIMISTS
MATTERIER	MATZOS	MAUSIER	MAWKISH	MAXIMITE
MATTERING	MATZOT	MAUSIEST	MAWKISHLY	MAXIMITES
MATTERS	MATZOTH	MAUSOLEA	MAWKS	MAXIMIZE
MATTERY	MAUBIES	MAUSOLEAN	MAWKY	MAXIMIZED
MATTES	MAUBY	MAUSOLEUM	MAWMET	MAXIMIZER
MATTIE	MAUD	MAUSY	MAWMETRY	MAXIMIZES
MATTIES	MAUDLIN	MAUT	MAWMETS	MAXIMS
MATTIFIED	MAUDLINLY	MAUTHER	MAWN	MAXIMUM
MATTIFIES	MAUDS	MAUTHERS	MAWNS	MAXIMUMLY
MATTIFY	MAUGER	MAUTS	MAWPUS	MAXIMUMS
MATTIN	MAUGRE	MAUVAIS	MAWPUSES	MAXIMUS
MATTING	MAUGRED	MAUVAISE	MAWR	MAXIMUSES
MATTINGS	MAUGRES	MAUVE	MAWRS	MAXING
MATTINS	MAUGRING	MAUVEIN	MAWS	MAXIS
MATTOCK	MAUL	MAUVEINE	MAWSEED	MAXIXE
MATTOCKS	MAULED	MAUVEINES	MAWSEEDS	MAXIXES
MATTOID	MAULER	MAUVEINS	MAWTHER	MAXWELL
MATTOIDS	MAULERS	MAUVER	MAWTHERS	MAXWELLS
MATTRASS	MAULGRE	MAUVES	MAX	MAY
MATTRESS	MAULGRED	MAUVEST	MAXED	MAYA
MATTS	MAULGRES	MAUVIN	MAXES	MAYAN
MATURABLE	MAULGRING	MAUVINE	MAXI	MAYAPPLE
MATURATE	MAULING	MAUVINES	MAXIBOAT	MAYAPPLES
MATURATED	MAULINGS	MAUVINS	MAXIBOATS	MAYAS
MATURATES	MAULS	MAUZIER	MAXICOAT	MAYBE
MATURE	MAULSTICK	MAUZIEST	MAXICOATS	MAYBES
MATURED	MAULVI	MAUZY	MAXIDRESS	MAYBIRD
MATURELY	MAULVIS	MAVEN	MAXILLA	MAYBIRDS
MATURER	MAUMET	MAVENS	MAXILLAE	MAYBUSH
MATURERS	MAUMETRY	MAVERICK	MAXILLAR	MAYBUSHES
MATURES	MAUMETS	MAVERICKS	MAXILLARY	MAYDAY
MATUREST	MAUN	MAVIE	MAXILLAS	MAYDAYS
MATURING	MAUND	MAVIES	MAXILLULA	MAYED
MATURITY	MAUNDED	MAVIN	MAXIM	MAYEST
MATUTINAL	MAUNDER	MAVINS	MAXIMA	MAYFISH
MATUTINE	MAUNDERED	MAVIS	MAXIMAL	MAYFISHES
MATWEED	MAUNDERER	MAVISES	MAXIMALLY	MAYFLIES
MATWEEDS	MAUNDERS	MAVOURNIN	MAXIMALS	MAYFLOWER
MATY	MAUNDIES	MAW	MAXIMAND	MAYFLY
MATZA	MAUNDING	MAWBOUND	MAXIMANDS	MAYHAP
MATZAH	MAUNDS	MAWED	MAXIMIN	MAYHAPPEN

MAYHEM	MAZINESS	MEALS	MEASURE	MECHANIST
MAYHEMS	MAZING	MEALTIME	MEASURED	MECHANIZE
MAYING	MAZOURKA	MEALTIMES	MEASURER	MECHITZA
MAYINGS	MAZOURKAS	MEALWORM	MEASURERS	MECHITZAS
MAYO	MAZOUT	MEALWORMS	MEASURES	MECHITZOT
MAYOR	MAZOUTS	MEALY	MEASURING	MECHOUI
MAYORAL	MAZUMA	MEALYBUG	MEAT	MECHOUIS
MAYORALTY	MAZUMAS	MEALYBUGS	MEATAL	MECHS
MAYORESS	MAZURKA	MEAN	MEATAXE	MECK
MAYORS	MAZURKAS	MEANDER	MEATAXES	MECKS
MAYORSHIP	MAZUT	MEANDERED	MEATBALL	MECLIZINE
MAYOS	MAZUTS	MEANDERER	MEATBALLS	MECONATE
MAYPOLE	MAZY	MEANDERS	MEATED	MECONATES
MAYPOLES	MAZZARD	MEANDRIAN	MEATH	MECONIC
MAYPOP	MAZZARDS	MEANDROUS	MEATHE	MECONIN
MAYPOPS	MBAQANGA	MEANE	MEATHEAD	MECONINS
MAYS	MBAQANGAS	MEANED	MEATHEADS	MECONIUM
MAYST	MBIRA	MEANER	MEATHES	MECONIUMS
MAYSTER	MBIRAS	MEANERS	MEATHOOK	MED
MAYSTERS	ME	MEANES	MEATHOOKS	MEDACCA
MAYVIN	MEACOCK	MEANEST	MEATHS	MEDACCAS
MAYVINS	MEACOCKS	MEANIE	MEATIER	MEDAILLON
MAYWEED	MEAD	MEANIES	MEATIEST	MEDAKA
MAYWEEDS	MEADOW	MEANING	MEATILY	MEDAKAS
MAZAEDIA	MEADOWIER	MEANINGLY	MEATINESS	MEDAL
MAZAEDIUM	MEADOWS	MEANINGS	MEATLESS	MEDALED
MAZARD	MEADOWY	MEANLY	MEATLOAF	MEDALET
MAZARDS	MEADS	MEANNESS	MEATMAN	MEDALETS
MAZARINE	MEAGER	MEANS	MEATMEN	MEDALING
MAZARINES	MEAGERER	MEANT	MEATS	MEDALIST
MAZE	MEAGEREST	MEANTIME	MEATSPACE	MEDALISTS
MAZED	MEAGERLY	MEANTIMES	MEATUS	MEDALLED
MAZEDLY	MEAGRE	MEANWHILE	MEATUSES	MEDALLIC
MAZEDNESS	MEAGRELY	MEANY	MEATY	MEDALLING
MAZEFUL	MEAGRER	MEARE	MEAWES	MEDALLION
MAZELIKE	MEAGRES	MEARES	MEAZEL	MEDALLIST
MAZELTOV	MEAGREST	MEARING	MEAZELS	MEDALPLAY
MAZEMENT	MEAL	MEASE	MEBIBYTE	MEDALS
MAZEMENTS	MEALED	MEASED	MEBIBYTES	MEDCINAL
MAZER	MEALER	MEASES	MEBOS	MEDDLE
MAZERS	MEALERS	MEASING	MEBOSES	MEDDLED
MAZES	MEALIE	MEASLE	MECCA	MEDDLER
MAZEY	MEALIER	MEASLED	MECCAS	MEDDLERS
MAZHBI	MEALIES	MEASLES	MECH	MEDDLES
MAZHBIS	MEALIEST	MEASLIER	MECHANIC	MEDDLING
MAZIER	MEALINESS	MEASLIEST	MECHANICS	MEDDLINGS
MAZIEST	MEALING	MEASLING	MECHANISE	MEDEVAC
MAZILY	MEALLESS	MEASLY	MECHANISM	MEDEVACED

M

MEDEVACS	MEDICINAL	MEDULLATE	MEGABITS	MEGARONS
MEDFLIES	MEDICINE	MEDUSA	MEGABUCK	MEGASCOPE
MEDFLY	MEDICINED	MEDUSAE	MEGABUCKS	MEGASPORE
MEDIA	MEDICINER	MEDUSAL	MEGABYTE	MEGASS
MEDIACIES	MEDICINES	MEDUSAN	MEGABYTES	MEGASSE
MEDIACY	MEDICK	MEDUSANS	MEGACITY	MEGASSES
MEDIAD	MEDICKS	MEDUSAS	MEGACURIE	MEGASTAR
MEDIAE	MEDICO	MEDUSOID	MEGACYCLE	MEGASTARS
MEDIAEVAL	MEDICOS	MEDUSOIDS	MEGADEAL	MEGASTORE
MEDIAL	MEDICS	MEE	MEGADEALS	MEGASTORM
MEDIALLY	MEDIEVAL	MEED	MEGADEATH	MEGATHERE
MEDIALS	MEDIEVALS	MEEDS	MEGADOSE	MEGATON
MEDIAN	MEDIGAP	MEEK	MEGADOSES	MEGATONIC
MEDIANLY	MEDIGAPS	MEEKEN	MEGADYNE	MEGATONS
MEDIANS	MEDII	MEEKENED	MEGADYNES	MEGAVOLT
MEDIANT	MEDINA	MEEKENING	MEGAFARAD	MEGAVOLTS
MEDIANTS	MEDINAS	MEEKENS	MEGAFAUNA	MEGAWATT
MEDIAS	MEDIOCRE	MEEKER	MEGAFLOP	MEGAWATTS
MEDIATE	MEDITATE	MEEKEST	MEGAFLOPS	MEGILLA
MEDIATED	MEDITATED	MEEKLY	MEGAFLORA	MEGILLAH
MEDIATELY	MEDITATES	MEEKNESS	MEGAFOG	MEGILLAHS
MEDIATES	MEDITATOR	MEEMIE	MEGAFOGS	MEGILLAS
MEDIATING	MEDIUM	MEEMIES	MEGAGAUSS	MEGILLOTH
MEDIATION	MEDIUMS	MEER	MEGAHERTZ	MEGILP
MEDIATISE	MEDIUS	MEERCAT	MEGAHIT	MEGILPH
MEDIATIVE	MEDIUSES	MEERCATS	MEGAHITS	MEGILPHS
MEDIATIZE	MEDIVAC	MEERED	MEGAJOULE	MEGILPS
MEDIATOR	MEDIVACED	MEERING	MEGALITH	MEGOHM
MEDIATORS	MEDIVACS	MEERKAT	MEGALITHS	MEGOHMS
MEDIATORY	MEDLAR	MEERKATS	MEGALITRE	MEGRIM
MEDIATRIX	MEDLARS	MEERS	MEGALODON	MEGRIMS
MEDIC	MEDLE	MEES	MEGALOPIC	MEGS
MEDICABLE	MEDLED	MEET	MEGALOPS	MEH
MEDICABLY	MEDLES	MEETER	MEGAMALL	MEHNDI
MEDICAID	MEDLEY	MEETERS	MEGAMALLS	MEHNDIS
MEDICAIDS	MEDLEYS	MEETEST	MEGAPHONE	MEIBOMIAN
MEDICAL	MEDLING	MEETING	MEGAPHYLL	MEIKLE
MEDICALLY	MEDRESA	MEETINGS	MEGAPIXEL	MEIN
MEDICALS	MEDRESAS	MEETLY	MEGAPLEX	MEINED
MEDICANT	MEDRESE	MEETNESS	MEGAPOD	MEINEY
MEDICANTS	MEDRESES	MEETS	MEGAPODE	MEINEYS
MEDICARE	MEDRESSEH	MEFF	MEGAPODES	MEINIE
MEDICARES	MEDS	MEFFS	MEGAPODS	MEINIES
MEDICATE	MEDULLA	MEG	MEGAQUAKE	MEINING
MEDICATED	MEDULLAE	MEGA	MEGARA	MEINS
MEDICATES	MEDULLAR	MEGABAR	MEGARAD	MEINT
MEDICIDE	MEDULLARY	MEGABARS	MEGARADS	MEINY
MEDICIDES	MEDULLAS	MEGABIT	MEGARON	MEIOCYTE

MEIOCYTES	MELANIZED	MELITTIN	MELOID	MEMENTOES
MEIOFAUNA	MELANIZES	MELITTINS	MELOIDS	MEMENTOS
MEIONITE	MELANO	MELL	MELOMANIA	MEMES
MEIONITES	MELANOID	MELLAY	MELOMANIC	MEMETIC
MEIOSES	MELANOIDS	MELLAYS	MELON	MEMETICS
MEIOSIS	MELANOMA	MELLED	MELONGENE	MEMO
MEIOSPORE	MELANOMAS	MELLIFIC	MELONIER	MEMOIR
MEIOTIC	MELANOS	MELLING	MELONIEST	MEMOIRISM
MEISHI	MELANOSES	MELLITE	MELONS	MEMOIRIST
MEISHIS	MELANOSIS	MELLITES	MELONY	MEMOIRS
MEISTER	MELANOTIC	MELLITIC	MELOXICAM	MEMORABLE
MEISTERS	MELANOUS	MELLOTRON	MELPHALAN	MEMORABLY
MEITH	MELANURIA	MELLOW	MELS	MEMORANDA
MEITHS	MELANURIC	MELLOWED	MELT	MEMORIAL
MEJLIS	MELAPHYRE	MELLOWER	MELTABLE	MEMORIALS
MEJLISES	MELAS	MELLOWEST	MELTAGE	MEMORIES
MEKKA	MELASTOME	MELLOWIER	MELTAGES	MEMORISE
MEKKAS	MELATONIN	MELLOWING	MELTDOWN	MEMORISED
MEKOMETER	MELBA	MELLOWLY	MELTDOWNS	MEMORISER
MEL	MELD	MELLOWS	MELTED	MEMORISES
MELA	MELDED	MELLOWY	MELTEMI	MEMORITER
MELAENA	MELDER	MELLS	MELTEMIS	MEMORIZE
MELAENAS	MELDERS	MELOCOTON	MELTER	MEMORIZED
MELALEUCA	MELDING	MELODEON	MELTERS	MEMORIZER
MELAMDIM	MELDS	MELODEONS	MELTIER	MEMORIZES
MELAMED	MELEE	MELODIA	MELTIEST	MEMORY
MELAMINE	MELEES	MELODIAS	MELTING	MEMOS
MELAMINES	MELENA	MELODIC	MELTINGLY	MEMS
MELAMPODE	MELENAS	MELODICA	MELTINGS	MEMSAHIB
MELANGE	MELIC	MELODICAS	MELTITH	MEMSAHIBS
MELANGES	MELICK	MELODICS	MELTITHS	MEN
MELANIAN	MELICKS	MELODIES	MELTON	MENACE
MELANIANS	MELICS	MELODION	MELTONS	MENACED
MELANIC	MELIK	MELODIONS	MELTS	MENACER
MELANICS	MELIKS	MELODIOUS	MELTWATER	MENACERS
MELANIN	MELILITE	MELODISE	MELTY	MENACES
MELANINS	MELILITES	MELODISED	MELUNGEON	MENACING
MELANISE	MELILOT	MELODISER	MEM	MENAD
MELANISED	MELILOTS	MELODISES	MEMBER	MENADIONE
MELANISES	MELINITE	MELODIST	MEMBERED	MENADS
MELANISM	MELINITES	MELODISTS	MEMBERS	MENAGE
MELANISMS	MELIORATE	MELODIZE	MEMBRAL	MENAGED
MELANIST	MELIORISM	MELODIZED	MEMBRANAL	MENAGERIE
MELANISTS	MELIORIST	MELODIZER	MEMBRANE	MENAGES
MELANITE	MELIORITY	MELODIZES	MEMBRANED	MENAGING
MELANITES	MELISMA	MELODRAMA	MEMBRANES	MENARCHE
MELANITIC	MELISMAS	MELODRAME	MEME	MENARCHES
MELANIZE	MELISMATA	MELODY	MEMENTO	MENAZON

MENAZONS	MENOMINI	MENTHENES	MERCERISE	MERFOLK
MEND	MENOMINIS	MENTHOL	MERCERIZE	MERFOLKS
MENDABLE	MENOPAUSE	MENTHOLS	MERCERS	MERGANSER
MENDACITY	MENOPOLIS	MENTICIDE	MERCERY	MERGE
MENDED	MENOPOME	MENTION	MERCES	MERGED
MENDER	MENOPOMES	MENTIONED	MERCH	MERGEE
MENDERS	MENORAH	MENTIONER	MERCHANT	MERGEES
MENDICANT	MENORAHS	MENTIONS	MERCHANTS	MERGENCE
MENDICITY	MENORRHEA	MENTO	MERCHES	MERGENCES
MENDIGO	MENSA	MENTOR	MERCHET	MERGER
MENDIGOS	MENSAE	MENTORED	MERCHETS	MERGERS
MENDING	MENSAL	MENTORIAL	MERCHILD	MERGES
MENDINGS	MENSAS	MENTORING	MERCIABLE	MERGING
MENDS	MENSCH	MENTORS	MERCIES	MERGINGS
MENE	MENSCHEN	MENTOS	MERCIFIDE	MERGUEZ
MENED	MENSCHES	MENTUM	MERCIFIED	MERI
MENEER	MENSCHIER	MENU	MERCIFIES	MERICARP
MENEERS	MENSCHY	MENUDO	MERCIFUL	MERICARPS
MENES	MENSE	MENUDOS	MERCIFY	MERIDIAN
MENFOLK	MENSED	MENUISIER	MERCILESS	MERIDIANS
MENFOLKS	MENSEFUL	MENUS	MERCS	MERIL
MENG	MENSELESS	MENYIE	MERCURATE	MERILS
MENGE	MENSES	MENYIES	MERCURIAL	MERIMAKE
MENGED	MENSH	MEOU	MERCURIC	MERIMAKES
MENGES	MENSHED	MEOUED	MERCURIES	MERING
MENGING	MENSHEN	MEOUING	MERCURISE	MERINGS
MENGS	MENSHES	MEOUS	MERCURIZE	MERINGUE
MENHADEN	MENSHING	MEOW	MERCUROUS	MERINGUES
MENHADENS	MENSING	MEOWED	MERCURY	MERINO
MENHIR	MENSTRUA	MEOWING	MERCY	MERINOS
MENHIRS	MENSTRUAL	MEOWS	MERDE	MERIS
MENIAL	MENSTRUUM	MEPACRINE	MERDES	MERISES
MENIALLY	MENSUAL	MEPHITIC	MERE	MERISIS
MENIALS	MENSURAL	MEPHITIS	MERED	MERISM
MENILITE	MENSWEAR	MEPHITISM	MEREL	MERISMS
MENILITES	MENSWEARS	MERANTI	MERELL	MERISTEM
MENING	MENT	MERANTIS	MERELLS	MERISTEMS
MENINGEAL	MENTA	MERBROMIN	MERELS	MERISTIC
MENINGES	MENTAL	MERC	MERELY	MERIT
MENINX	MENTALESE	MERCADO	MERENGUE	MERITED
MENISCAL	MENTALISM	MERCADOS	MERENGUES	MERITING
MENISCATE	MENTALIST	MERCAPTAN	MEREOLOGY	MERITLESS
MENISCI	MENTALITY	MERCAPTO	MERER	MERITS
MENISCOID	MENTALLY	MERCAT	MERES	MERK
MENISCUS	MENTATION	MERCATS	MERESMAN	MERKIN
MENO	MENTEE	MERCENARY	MERESMEN	MERKINS
MENOLOGY	MENTEES	MERCER	MEREST	MERKS
MENOMINEE	MENTHENE	MERCERIES	MERESTONE	MERL

MERLE	MERYCISM	MESHWORK	MESOZOAN	MESTESO
MERLES	MERYCISMS	MESHWORKS	MESOZOANS	MESTESOES
MERLIN	MES	MESHY	MESOZOIC	MESTESOS
MERLING	MESA	MESIAD	MESPIL	MESTINO
MERLINGS	MESAIL	MESIAL	MESPILS	MESTINOES
MERLINS	MESAILS	MESIALLY	MESPRISE	MESTINOS
MERLON	MESAL	MESIAN	MESPRISES	MESTIZA
MERLONS	MESALLY	MESIC	MESPRIZE	MESTIZAS
MERLOT	MESARAIC	MESICALLY	MESPRIZES	MESTIZO
MERLOTS	MESARCH	MESMERIC	MESQUIN	MESTIZOES
MERLS	MESAS	MESMERISE	MESQUINE	MESTIZOS
MERMAID	MESCAL	MESMERISM	MESQUIT	MESTO
MERMAIDEN	MESCALIN	MESMERIST	MESQUITE	MESTOM
MERMAIDS	MESCALINE	MESMERIZE	MESQUITES	MESTOME
MERMAN	MESCALINS	MESNALTY	MESQUITS	MESTOMES
MERMEN	MESCALISM	MESNE	MESS	MESTOMS
MEROCRINE	MESCALS	MESNES	MESSAGE	MESTRANOL
MEROGONY	MESCLUM	MESOBLAST	MESSAGED	MET
MEROISTIC	MESCLUMS	MESOCARP	MESSAGES	META
MEROME	MESCLUN	MESOCARPS	MESSAGING	METABASES
MEROMES	MESCLUNS	MESOCRANY	MESSALINE	METABASIS
MERONYM	MESDAMES	MESODERM	MESSAN	METABATIC
MERONYMS	MESE	MESODERMS	MESSANS	METABOLIC
MERONYMY	MESEEMED	MESOGLEA	MESSED	METABOLY
MEROPIA	MESEEMETH	MESOGLEAL	MESSENGER	METACARPI
MEROPIAS	MESEEMS	MESOGLEAS	MESSES	METADATA
MEROPIC	MESEL	MESOGLOEA	MESSIAH	METADATAS
MEROPIDAN	MESELED	MESOLITE	MESSIAHS	METAFILE
MEROSOME	MESELS	MESOLITES	MESSIANIC	METAFILES
MEROSOMES	MESENTERA	MESOMERE	MESSIAS	METAGE
MEROZOITE	MESENTERY	MESOMERES	MESSIASES	METAGENIC
MERPEOPLE	MESES	MESOMORPH	MESSIER	METAGES
MERRIE	MESETA	MESON	MESSIEST	METAIRIE
MERRIER	MESETAS	MESONIC	MESSIEURS	METAIRIES
MERRIES	MESH	MESONS	MESSILY	METAL
MERRIEST	MESHED	MESOPAUSE	MESSINESS	METALED
MERRILY	MESHES	MESOPHILE	MESSING	METALHEAD
MERRIMENT	MESHIER	MESOPHYL	MESSMAN	METALING
MERRINESS	MESHIEST	MESOPHYLL	MESSMATE	METALISE
MERRY	MESHING	MESOPHYLS	MESSMATES	METALISED
MERRYMAN	MESHINGS	MESOPHYTE	MESSMEN	METALISES
MERRYMEN	MESHUGA	MESOSAUR	MESSUAGE	METALIST
MERSALYL	MESHUGAAS	MESOSAURS	MESSUAGES	METALISTS
MERSALYLS	MESHUGAH	MESOSCALE	MESSY	METALIZE
MERSE	MESHUGAS	MESOSOME	MESTEE	METALIZED
MERSES	MESHUGGA	MESOSOMES	MESTEES	METALIZES
MERSION	MESHUGGAH	MESOTRON	MESTER	METALLED
MERSIONS	MESHUGGE	MESOTRONS	MESTERS	METALLIC

M

METALLICS	METAZOIC	METHODISE	METOPIC	MEVE
METALLIKE	METAZOON	METHODISM	METOPISM	MEVED
METALLINE	METCAST	METHODIST	METOPISMS	MEVES
METALLING	METCASTS	METHODIZE	METOPON	MEVING
METALLISE	METE	METHODS	METOPONS	MEVROU
METALLIST	METED	METHOS	METOPRYL	MEVROUS
METALLIZE	METEOR	METHOUGHT	METOPRYLS	MEW
METALLOID	METEORIC	METHOXIDE	METRALGIA	MEWED
METALLY	METEORISM	METHOXIES	METRAZOL	MEWING
METALMARK	METEORIST	METHOXY	METRAZOLS	MEWL
METALS	METEORITE	METHOXYL	METRE	MEWLED
METALWARE	METEOROID	METHOXYLS	METRED	MEWLER
METALWORK	METEOROUS	METHS	METRES	MEWLERS
METAMALE	METEORS	METHYL	METRIC	MEWLING
METAMALES	METEPA	METHYLAL	METRICAL	MEWLS
METAMER	METEPAS	METHYLALS	METRICATE	MEWS
METAMERAL	METER	METHYLASE	METRICIAN	MEWSED
METAMERE	METERAGE	METHYLATE	METRICISE	MEWSES
METAMERES	METERAGES	METHYLENE	METRICISM	MEWSING
METAMERIC	METERED	METHYLIC	METRICIST	MEYNT
METAMERS	METERING	METHYLS	METRICIZE	MEZAIL
METAMICT	METERS	METHYSES	METRICS	MEZAILS
METANOIA	METES	METHYSIS	METRIFIED	MEZCAL
METANOIAS	METESTICK	METHYSTIC	METRIFIER	MEZCALINE
METAPELET	METESTRUS	METIC	METRIFIES	MEZCALS
METAPHASE	METEWAND	METICA	METRIFY	MEZE
METAPHOR	METEWANDS	METICAIS	METRING	MEZEREON
METAPHORS	METEYARD	METICAL	METRIST	MEZEREONS
METAPLASM	METEYARDS	METICALS	METRISTS	MEZEREUM
METAPLOT	METFORMIN	METICAS	METRITIS	MEZEREUMS
METARCHON	METH	METICS	METRO	MEZES
METASOMA	METHADON	METIER	METROLOGY	MEZQUIT
METASOMAS	METHADONE	METIERS	METRONOME	MEZQUITE
METATAG	METHADONS	METIF	METROPLEX	MEZQUITES
METATAGS	METHANAL	METIFS	METROS	MEZQUITS
METATARSI	METHANALS	METING	METS	MEZUZA
METATE	METHANE	METIS	METTLE	MEZUZAH
METATES	METHANES	METISSE	METTLED	MEZUZAHS
METAVERSE	METHANOIC	METISSES	METTLES	MEZUZAS
METAXYLEM	METHANOL	METOL	METUMP	MEZUZOT
METAYAGE	METHANOLS	METOLS	METUMPS	MEZUZOTH
METAYAGES	METHANOYL	METONYM	MEU	MEZZ
METAYER	METHEGLIN	METONYMIC	MEUNIERE	MEZZALUNA
METAYERS	METHINK	METONYMS	MEUS	MEZZANINE
METAZOA	METHINKS	METONYMY	MEUSE	MEZZE
METAZOAL	METHO	METOPAE	MEUSED	MEZZES
METAZOAN	METHOD	METOPE	MEUSES	MEZZO
METAZOANS	METHODIC	METOPES	MEUSING	MEZZOS

MEZZOTINT	MICELLAS	MICROBLOG	MICROTOME	MIDGETS
MGANGA	MICELLE	MICROBREW	MICROTOMY	MIDGIE
MGANGAS	MICELLES	MICROBUS	MICROTONE	MIDGIER
MHO	MICELLS	MICROCAP	MICROTUBE	MIDGIES
MHORR	MICH	MICROCAR	MICROVOLT	MIDGIEST
MHORRS	MICHAEL	MICROCARD	MICROWATT	MIDGUT
MHOS	MICHAELS	MICROCARS	MICROWAVE	MIDGUTS
MI	MICHE	MICROCHIP	MICROWIRE	MIDGY
MIAOU	MICHED	MICROCODE	MICRURGY	MIDI
MIAOUED	MICHER	MICROCOPY	MICS	MIDIBUS
MIAOUING	MICHERS	MICROCOSM	MICTION	MIDIBUSES
MIAOUS	MICHES	MICROCYTE	MICTIONS	MIDINETTE
MIAOW	MICHIGAN	MICRODONT	MICTURATE	MIDIRON
MIAOWED	MICHIGANS	MICRODOT	MID	MIDIRONS
MIAOWING	MICHING	MICRODOTS	MIDAIR	MIDIS
MIAOWS	MICHINGS	MICROFILM	MIDAIRS	MIDISKIRT
MIASM	MICHT	MICROFINE	MIDBAND	MIDLAND
MIASMA	MICHTS	MICROFORM	MIDBRAIN	MIDLANDER
MIASMAL	MICK	MICROGLIA	MIDBRAINS	MIDLANDS
MIASMAS	MICKERIES	MICROGRAM	MIDCALF	MIDLEG
MIASMATA	MICKERY	MICROHM	MIDCALVES	MIDLEGS
MIASMATIC	MICKEY	MICROHMS	MIDCAP	MIDLIFE
MIASMIC	MICKEYED	MICROINCH	MIDCOURSE	MIDLIFER
MIASMOUS	MICKEYING	MICROJET	MIDCULT	MIDLIFERS
MIASMS	MICKEYS	MICROJETS	MIDCULTS	MIDLINE
MIAUL	MICKIES	MICROLITE	MIDDAY	MIDLINES
MIAULED	MICKLE	MICROLITH	MIDDAYS	MIDLIST
MIAULING	MICKLER	MICROLOAN	MIDDEN	MIDLISTS
MIAULS	MICKLES	MICROLOGY	MIDDENS	MIDLIVES
MIB	MICKLEST	MICROLUX	MIDDEST	MIDMONTH
MIBS	MICKS	MICROMERE	MIDDIE	MIDMONTHS
MIBUNA	MICKY	MICROMESH	MIDDIES	MIDMOST
MIBUNAS	MICO	MICROMHO	MIDDLE	MIDMOSTS
MIC	MICOS	MICROMHOS	MIDDLED	MIDNIGHT
MICA	MICRA	MICROMINI	MIDDLEMAN	MIDNIGHTS
MICACEOUS	MICRIFIED	MICROMOLE	MIDDLEMEN	MIDNOON
MICAS	MICRIFIES	MICROMORT	MIDDLER	MIDNOONS
MICATE	MICRIFY	MICRON	MIDDLERS	MIDPAY
MICATED	MICRO	MICRONISE	MIDDLES	MIDPOINT
MICATES	MICROBAR	MICRONIZE	MIDDLING	MIDPOINTS
MICATING	MICROBARS	MICRONS	MIDDLINGS	MIDRANGE
MICAWBER	MICROBE	MICROPORE	MIDDORSAL	MIDRANGES
MICAWBERS	MICROBEAD	MICROPSIA	MIDDY	MIDRASH
MICE	MICROBEAM	MICROPUMP	MIDFIELD	MIDRASHIC
MICELL	MICROBES	MICROPYLE	MIDFIELDS	MIDRASHIM
MICELLA	MICROBIAL	MICROS	MIDGE	MIDRASHOT
MICELLAE	MICROBIAN	MICROSITE	MIDGES	MIDRIB
MICELLAR	MICROBIC	MICROSOME	MIDGET	MIDRIBS

M

MIDRIFF	MIEVE	MIHAS	MILDEWING	MILKED
MIDRIFFS	MIEVED	MIHI	MILDEWS	MILKEN
MIDS	MIEVES	MIHIED	MILDEWY	MILKER
MIDSEASON	MIEVING	MIHIING	MILDING	MILKERS
MIDSHIP	MIFF	MIHIS	MILDISH	MILKFISH
MIDSHIPS	MIFFED	MIHRAB	MILDLY	MILKIER
MIDSHORE	MIFFIER	MIHRABS	MILDNESS	MILKIEST
MIDSIZE	MIFFIEST	MIJNHEER	MILDS	MILKILY
MIDSIZED	MIFFILY	MIJNHEERS	MILE	MILKINESS
MIDSOLE	MIFFINESS	MIKADO	MILEAGE	MILKING
MIDSOLES	MIFFING	MIKADOS	MILEAGES	MILKINGS
MIDSPACE	MIFFS	MIKE	MILEPOST	MILKLESS
MIDSPACES	MIFFY	MIKED	MILEPOSTS	MILKLIKE
MIDST	MIFTY	MIKES	MILER	MILKMAID
MIDSTORY	MIG	MIKING	MILERS	MILKMAIDS
MIDSTREAM	MIGAWD	MIKRA	MILES	MILKMAN
MIDSTS	MIGG	MIKRON	MILESIAN	MILKMEN
MIDSUMMER	MIGGLE	MIKRONS	MILESIMO	MILKO
MIDTERM	MIGGLES	MIKVA	MILESIMOS	MILKOS
MIDTERMS	MIGGS	MIKVAH	MILESTONE	MILKS
MIDTHIGH	MIGHT	MIKVAHS	MILF	MILKSHAKE
MIDTHIGHS	MIGHTEST	MIKVAS	MILFOIL	MILKSHED
MIDTOWN	MIGHTFUL	MIKVEH	MILFOILS	MILKSHEDS
MIDTOWNS	MIGHTIER	MIKVEHS	MILFS	MILKSOP
MIDWATCH	MIGHTIEST	MIKVOS	MILIA	MILKSOPPY
MIDWATER	MIGHTILY	MIKVOT	MILIARIA	MILKSOPS
MIDWATERS	MIGHTS	MIKVOTH	MILIARIAL	MILKTOAST
MIDWAY	MIGHTST	MIL	MILIARIAS	MILKWEED
MIDWAYS	MIGHTY	MILADI	MILIARY	MILKWEEDS
MIDWEEK	MIGMATITE	MILADIES	MILIEU	MILKWOOD
MIDWEEKLY	MIGNON	MILADIS	MILIEUS	MILKWOODS
MIDWEEKS	MIGNONNE	MILADY	MILIEUX	MILKWORT
MIDWIFE	MIGNONNES	MILAGE	MILING	MILKWORTS
MIDWIFED	MIGNONS	MILAGES	MILINGS	MILKY
MIDWIFERY	MIGRAINE	MILCH	MILITANCE	MILL
MIDWIFES	MIGRAINES	MILCHIG	MILITANCY	MILLABLE
MIDWIFING	MIGRANT	MILCHIK	MILITANT	MILLAGE
MIDWINTER	MIGRANTS	MILD	MILITANTS	MILLAGES
MIDWIVE	MIGRATE	MILDED	MILITAR	MILLBOARD
MIDWIVED	MIGRATED	MILDEN	MILITARIA	MILLCAKE
MIDWIVES	MIGRATES	MILDENED	MILITARY	MILLCAKES
MIDWIVING	MIGRATING	MILDENING	MILITATE	MILLDAM
MIDYEAR	MIGRATION	MILDENS	MILITATED	MILLDAMS
MIDYEARS	MIGRATOR	MILDER	MILITATES	MILLE
MIELIE	MIGRATORS	MILDEST	MILITIA	MILLED
MIELIES	MIGRATORY	MILDEW	MILITIAS	MILLENARY
MIEN	MIGS	MILDEWED	MILIUM	MILLENNIA
MIENS	MIHA	MILDEWIER	MILK	MILLEPED

MILLEPEDE	MILLIPED	MILTS	MIMSY	MINED
MILLEPEDS	MILLIPEDE	MILTY	MIMULUS	MINEFIELD
MILLEPORE	MILLIPEDS	MILTZ	MIMULUSES	MINELAYER
MILLER	MILLIREM	MILTZES	MINA	MINEOLA
MILLERITE	MILLIREMS	MILVINE	MINABLE	MINEOLAS
MILLERS	MILLIVOLT	MIM	MINACIOUS	MINER
MILLES	MILLIWATT	MIMBAR	MINACITY	MINERAL
MILLET	MILLOCRAT	MIMBARS	MINAE	MINERALS
MILLETS	MILLPOND	MIME	MINAR	MINERS
MILLHAND	MILLPONDS	MIMED	MINARET	MINES
MILLHANDS	MILLRACE	MIMEO	MINARETED	MINESHAFT
MILLHOUSE	MILLRACES	MIMEOED	MINARETS	MINESTONE
MILLIAMP	MILLRIND	MIMEOING	MINARS	MINETTE
MILLIAMPS	MILLRINDS	MIMEOS	MINAS	MINETTES
MILLIARD	MILLRUN	MIMER	MINATORY	MINEVER
MILLIARDS	MILLRUNS	MIMERS	MINBAR	MINEVERS
MILLIARE	MILLS	MIMES	MINBARS	MING
MILLIARES	MILLSCALE	MIMESES	MINCE	MINGE
MILLIARY	MILLSTONE	MIMESIS	MINCED	MINGED
MILLIBAR	MILLTAIL	MIMESISES	MINCEMEAT	MINGER
MILLIBARS	MILLTAILS	MIMESTER	MINCER	MINGERS
MILLIE	MILLWHEEL	MIMESTERS	MINCERS	MINGES
MILLIEME	MILLWORK	MIMETIC	MINCES	MINGIER
MILLIEMES	MILLWORKS	MIMETICAL	MINCEUR	MINGIEST
MILLIER	MILNEB	MIMETITE	MINCIER	MINGILY
MILLIERS	MILNEBS	MIMETITES	MINCIEST	MINGINESS
MILLIES	MILO	MIMIC	MINCING	MINGING
MILLIGAL	MILOMETER	MIMICAL	MINCINGLY	MINGLE
MILLIGALS	MILOR	MIMICKED	MINCY	MINGLED
MILLIGRAM	MILORD	MIMICKER	MIND	MINGLER
MILLILUX	MILORDS	MIMICKERS	MINDED	MINGLERS
MILLIME	MILORS	MIMICKING	MINDEDLY	MINGLES
MILLIMES	MILOS	MIMICRIES	MINDER	MINGLING
MILLIMHO	MILPA	MIMICRY	MINDERS	MINGLINGS
MILLIMHOS	MILPAS	MIMICS	MINDFUCK	MINGS
MILLIMOLE	MILREIS	MIMING	MINDFUCKS	MINGY
MILLINE	MILS	MIMIVIRUS	MINDFUL	MINI
MILLINER	MILSEY	MIMMER	MINDFULLY	MINIATE
MILLINERS	MILSEYS	MIMMEST	MINDING	MINIATED
MILLINERY	MILT	MIMMICK	MINDINGS	MINIATES
MILLINES	MILTED	MIMMICKED	MINDLESS	MINIATING
MILLING	MILTER	MIMMICKS	MINDS	MINIATION
MILLINGS	MILTERS	MIMOSA	MINDSCAPE	MINIATURE
MILLIOHM	MILTIER	MIMOSAE	MINDSET	MINIBAR
MILLIOHMS	MILTIEST	MIMOSAS	MINDSETS	MINIBARS
MILLION	MILTING	MIMSEY	MINDSHARE	MINIBIKE
MILLIONS	MILTONIA	MIMSIER	MINE	MINIBIKER
MILLIONTH	MILTONIAS	MIMSIEST	MINEABLE	MINIBIKES

MINIBREAK	MINIMISES	MINIVET	MINTY	MIRACLES
MINIBUS	MINIMISM	MINIVETS	MINUEND	MIRADOR
MINIBUSES	MINIMISMS	MINK	MINUENDS	MIRADORS
MINICAB	MINIMIST	MINKE	MINUET	MIRAGE
MINICABS	MINIMISTS	MINKES	MINUETED	MIRAGES
MINICAM	MINIMIZE	MINKS	MINUETING	MIRANDISE
MINICAMP	MINIMIZED	MINNEOLA	MINUETS	MIRANDIZE
MINICAMPS	MINIMIZER	MINNEOLAS	MINUS	MIRBANE
MINICAMS	MINIMIZES	MINNICK	MINUSCULE	MIRBANES
MINICAR	MINIMOTO	MINNICKED	MINUSES	MIRCHI
MINICARS	MINIMOTOS	MINNICKS	MINUTE	MIRE
MINICOM	MINIMS	MINNIE	MINUTED	MIRED
MINICOMS	MINIMUM	MINNIES	MINUTELY	MIREPOIX
MINIDISC	MINIMUMS	MINNOCK	MINUTEMAN	MIRES
MINIDISCS	MINIMUS	MINNOCKED	MINUTEMEN	MIREX
MINIDISH	MINIMUSES	MINNOCKS	MINUTER	MIREXES
MINIDISK	MINING	MINNOW	MINUTES	MIRI
MINIDISKS	MININGS	MINNOWS	MINUTEST	MIRID
MINIDRESS	MINION	MINNY	MINUTIA	MIRIDS
MINIER	MINIONS	MINO	MINUTIAE	MIRIER
MINIEST	MINIPARK	MINOR	MINUTIAL	MIRIEST
MINIFIED	MINIPARKS	MINORCA	MINUTING	MIRIFIC
MINIFIES	MINIPILL	MINORCAS	MINUTIOSE	MIRIFICAL
MINIFY	MINIPILLS	MINORED	MINX	MIRIN
MINIFYING	MINIRUGBY	MINORING	MINXES	MIRINESS
MINIGOLF	MINIS	MINORITY	MINXISH	MIRING
MINIGOLFS	MINISCULE	MINORS	MINY	MIRINS
MINIKIN	MINISH	MINORSHIP	MINYAN	MIRITI
MINIKINS	MINISHED	MINOS	MINYANIM	MIRITIS
MINILAB	MINISHES	MINOTAUR	MINYANS	MIRK
MINILABS	MINISHING	MINOXIDIL	MIOCENE	MIRKER
MINIM	MINISKI	MINSHUKU	MIOMBO	MIRKEST
MINIMA	MINISKIRT	MINSHUKUS	MIOMBOS	MIRKIER
MINIMAL	MINISKIS	MINSTER	MIOSES	MIRKIEST
MINIMALLY	MINISODE	MINSTERS	MIOSIS	MIRKILY
MINIMALS	MINISODES	MINSTREL	MIOSISES	MIRKINESS
MINIMART	MINISTATE	MINSTRELS	MIOTIC	MIRKS
MINIMARTS	MINISTER	MINT	MIOTICS	MIRKY
MINIMAX	MINISTERS	MINTAGE	MIPS	MIRLIER
MINIMAXED	MINISTRY	MINTAGES	MIQUELET	MIRLIEST
MINIMAXES	MINITOWER	MINTED	MIQUELETS	MIRLIGOES
MINIMENT	MINITRACK	MINTER	MIR	MIRLITON
MINIMENTS	MINIUM	MINTERS	MIRABELLE	MIRLITONS
MINIMILL	MINIUMS	MINTIER	MIRABILIA	MIRLY
MINIMILLS	MINIVAN	MINTIEST	MIRABILIS	MIRO
MINIMISE	MINIVANS	MINTING	MIRABLE	MIROMIRO
MINIMISED	MINIVER	MINTLIKE	MIRACIDIA	MIROMIROS
MINIMISER	MINIVERS	MINTS	MIRACLE	MIROS

MIRROR	MISARRAY	MISCALLS	MISCREEDS	MISDRAWS
MIRRORED	MISARRAYS	MISCARRY	MISCUE	MISDREAD
MIRRORING	MISASSAY	MISCAST	MISCUED	MISDREADS
MIRRORS	MISASSAYS	MISCASTS	MISCUEING	MISDREW
MIRS	MISASSIGN	MISCEGEN	MISCUES	MISDRIVE
MIRTH	MISASSUME	MISCEGENE	MISCUING	MISDRIVEN
MIRTHFUL	MISATE	MISCEGENS	MISCUT	MISDRIVES
MIRTHLESS	MISATONE	MISCEGINE	MISCUTS	MISDROVE
MIRTHS	MISATONED	MISCH	MISDATE	MISE
MIRV	MISATONES	MISCHANCE	MISDATED	MISEASE
MIRVED	MISAUNTER	MISCHANCY	MISDATES	MISEASES
MIRVING	MISAVER	MISCHARGE	MISDATING	MISEAT
MIRVS	MISAVERS	MISCHIEF	MISDEAL	MISEATEN
MIRY	MISAVISED	MISCHIEFS	MISDEALER	MISEATING
MIRZA	MISAWARD	MISCHOICE	MISDEALS	MISEATS
MIRZAS	MISAWARDS	MISCHOOSE	MISDEALT	MISEDIT
MIS	MISBECAME	MISCHOSE	MISDEED	MISEDITED
MISACT	MISBECOME	MISCHOSEN	MISDEEDS	MISEDITS
MISACTED	MISBEGAN	MISCIBLE	MISDEEM	MISEMPLOY
MISACTING	MISBEGIN	MISCITE	MISDEEMED	MISENROL
MISACTS	MISBEGINS	MISCITED	MISDEEMS	MISENROLL
MISADAPT	MISBEGOT	MISCITES	MISDEFINE	MISENROLS
MISADAPTS	MISBEGUN	MISCITING	MISDEMEAN	MISENTER
MISADD	MISBEHAVE	MISCLAIM	MISDEMPT	MISENTERS
MISADDED	MISBELIEF	MISCLAIMS	MISDESERT	MISENTRY
MISADDING	MISBESEEM	MISCLASS	MISDIAL	MISER
MISADDS	MISBESTOW	MISCODE	MISDIALED	MISERABLE
MISADJUST	MISBIAS	MISCODED	MISDIALS	MISERABLY
MISADVICE	MISBIASED	MISCODES	MISDID	MISERE
MISADVISE	MISBIASES	MISCODING	MISDIET	MISERERE
MISAGENT	MISBILL	MISCOIN	MISDIETED	MISERERES
MISAGENTS	MISBILLED	MISCOINED	MISDIETS	MISERES
MISAIM	MISBILLS	MISCOINS	MISDIGHT	MISERIES
MISAIMED	MISBIND	MISCOLOR	MISDIGHTS	MISERLIER
MISAIMING	MISBINDS	MISCOLORS	MISDIRECT	MISERLY
MISAIMS	MISBIRTH	MISCOLOUR	MISDIVIDE	MISERS
MISALIGN	MISBIRTHS	MISCOOK	MISDO	MISERY
MISALIGNS	MISBORN	MISCOOKED	MISDOER	MISES
MISALLEGE	MISBOUND	MISCOOKS	MISDOERS	MISESTEEM
MISALLIED	MISBRAND	MISCOPIED	MISDOES	MISEVENT
MISALLIES	MISBRANDS	MISCOPIES	MISDOING	MISEVENTS
MISALLOT	MISBUILD	MISCOPY	MISDOINGS	MISFAITH
MISALLOTS	MISBUILDS	MISCOUNT	MISDONE	MISFAITHS
MISALLY	MISBUILT	MISCOUNTS	MISDONNE	MISFALL
MISALTER	MISBUTTON	MISCREANT	MISDOUBT	MISFALLEN
MISALTERS	MISCALL	MISCREATE	MISDOUBTS	MISFALLS
MISANDRY	MISCALLED	MISCREDIT	MISDRAW	MISFALNE
MISAPPLY	MISCALLER	MISCREED	MISDRAWN	MISFARE

M

MISFARED	MISGOING	MISJOIN	MISLEEKED	MISMOVE
MISFARES	MISGONE	MISJOINED	MISLEEKES	MISMOVED
MISFARING	MISGOTTEN	MISJOINS	MISLETOE	MISMOVES
MISFEASOR	MISGOVERN	MISJUDGE	MISLETOES	MISMOVING
MISFED	MISGRADE	MISJUDGED	MISLIE	MISNAME
MISFEED	MISGRADED	MISJUDGER	MISLIES	MISNAMED
MISFEEDS	MISGRADES	MISJUDGES	MISLIGHT	MISNAMES
MISFEIGN	MISGRAFF	MISKAL	MISLIGHTS	MISNAMING
MISFEIGNS	MISGRAFT	MISKALS	MISLIKE	MISNOMER
MISFELL	MISGRAFTS	MISKEEP	MISLIKED	MISNOMERS
MISFIELD	MISGREW	MISKEEPS	MISLIKER	MISNUMBER
MISFIELDS	MISGROW	MISKEN	MISLIKERS	MISO
MISFILE	MISGROWN	MISKENNED	MISLIKES	MISOCLERE
MISFILED	MISGROWS	MISKENS	MISLIKING	MISOGAMIC
MISFILES	MISGROWTH	MISKENT	MISLIPPEN	MISOGAMY
MISFILING	MISGUESS	MISKEPT	MISLIT	MISOGYNIC
MISFIRE	MISGUGGLE	MISKEY	MISLIVE	MISOGYNY
MISFIRED	MISGUIDE	MISKEYED	MISLIVED	MISOLOGY
MISFIRES	MISGUIDED	MISKEYING	MISLIVES	MISONEISM
MISFIRING	MISGUIDER	MISKEYS	MISLIVING	MISONEIST
MISFIT	MISGUIDES	MISKICK	MISLOCATE	MISORDER
MISFITS	MISHANDLE	MISKICKED	MISLODGE	MISORDERS
MISFITTED	MISHANTER	MISKICKS	MISLODGED	MISORIENT
MISFOCUS	MISHAP	MISKNEW	MISLODGES	MISOS
MISFOLD	MISHAPPED	MISKNOW	MISLUCK	MISPAGE
MISFOLDED	MISHAPPEN	MISKNOWN	MISLUCKED	MISPAGED
MISFOLDS	MISHAPS	MISKNOWS	MISLUCKS	MISPAGES
MISFORM	MISHAPT	MISLABEL	MISLYING	MISPAGING
MISFORMED	MISHEAR	MISLABELS	MISMADE	MISPAINT
MISFORMS	MISHEARD	MISLABOR	MISMAKE	MISPAINTS
MISFRAME	MISHEARS	MISLABORS	MISMAKES	MISPARSE
MISFRAMED	MISHEGAAS	MISLABOUR	MISMAKING	MISPARSED
MISFRAMES	MISHEGOSS	MISLAID	MISMANAGE	MISPARSES
MISGAGE	MISHIT	MISLAIN	MISMARK	MISPART
MISGAGED	MISHITS	MISLAY	MISMARKED	MISPARTED
MISGAGES	MISHMASH	MISLAYER	MISMARKS	MISPARTS
MISGAGING	MISHMEE	MISLAYERS	MISMARRY	MISPATCH
MISGAUGE	MISHMEES	MISLAYING	MISMATCH	MISPEN
MISGAUGED	MISHMI	MISLAYS	MISMATE	MISPENNED
MISGAUGES	MISHMIS	MISLEAD	MISMATED	MISPENS
MISGAVE	MISHMOSH	MISLEADER	MISMATES	MISPHRASE
MISGENDER	MISHUGAS	MISLEADS	MISMATING	MISPICKEL
MISGIVE	MISINFER	MISLEARED	MISMEET	MISPLACE
MISGIVEN	MISINFERS	MISLEARN	MISMEETS	MISPLACED
MISGIVES	MISINFORM	MISLEARNS	MISMET	MISPLACES
MISGIVING	MISINTEND	MISLEARNT	MISMETRE	MISPLAN
MISGO	MISINTER	MISLED	MISMETRED	MISPLANS
MISGOES	MISINTERS	MISLEEKE	MISMETRES	MISPLANT

MISPLANTS	MISRELY	MISSHAPEN	MISSTAMPS	MISTERMED
MISPLAY	MISRENDER	MISSHAPER	MISSTART	MISTERMS
MISPLAYED	MISREPORT	MISSHAPES	MISSTARTS	MISTERS
MISPLAYS	MISRHYMED	MISSHOD	MISSTATE	MISTERY
MISPLEAD	MISROUTE	MISSHOOD	MISSTATED	MISTEUK
MISPLEADS	MISROUTED	MISSHOODS	MISSTATES	MISTFUL
MISPLEASE	MISROUTES	MISSIER	MISSTEER	MISTHINK
MISPLED	MISRULE	MISSIES	MISSTEERS	MISTHINKS
MISPOINT	MISRULED	MISSIEST	MISSTEP	MISTHREW
MISPOINTS	MISRULES	MISSILE	MISSTEPS	MISTHROW
MISPOISE	MISRULING	MISSILEER	MISSTOP	MISTHROWN
MISPOISED	MISS	MISSILERY	MISSTOPS	MISTHROWS
MISPOISES	MISSA	MISSILES	MISSTRIKE	MISTICO
MISPRAISE	MISSABLE	MISSILRY	MISSTRUCK	MISTICOS
MISPRICE	MISSAE	MISSING	MISSTYLE	MISTIER
MISPRICED	MISSAID	MISSINGLY	MISSTYLED	MISTIEST
MISPRICES	MISSAL	MISSION	MISSTYLES	MISTIGRIS
MISPRINT	MISSALS	MISSIONAL	MISSUIT	MISTILY
MISPRINTS	MISSAW	MISSIONED	MISSUITED	MISTIME
MISPRISE	MISSAY	MISSIONER	MISSUITS	MISTIMED
MISPRISED	MISSAYING	MISSIONS	MISSUS	MISTIMES
MISPRISES	MISSAYS	MISSIS	MISSUSES	MISTIMING
MISPRIZE	MISSEAT	MISSISES	MISSY	MISTINESS
MISPRIZED	MISSEATED	MISSISH	MIST	MISTING
MISPRIZER	MISSEATS	MISSIVE	MISTAKE	MISTINGS
MISPRIZES	MISSED	MISSIVES	MISTAKEN	MISTITLE
MISPROUD	MISSEE	MISSOLD	MISTAKER	MISTITLED
MISQUOTE	MISSEEING	MISSORT	MISTAKERS	MISTITLES
MISQUOTED	MISSEEM	MISSORTED	MISTAKES	MISTLE
MISQUOTER	MISSEEMED	MISSORTS	MISTAKING	MISTLED
MISQUOTES	MISSEEMS	MISSOUND	MISTAL	MISTLES
MISRAISE	MISSEEN	MISSOUNDS	MISTALS	MISTLETOE
MISRAISED	MISSEES	MISSOUT	MISTAUGHT	MISTLING
MISRAISES	MISSEL	MISSOUTS	MISTBOW	MISTOLD
MISRATE	MISSELL	MISSPACE	MISTBOWS	MISTOOK
MISRATED	MISSELLS	MISSPACED	MISTEACH	MISTOUCH
MISRATES	MISSELS	MISSPACES	MISTED	MISTRACE
MISRATING	MISSEND	MISSPEAK	MISTELL	MISTRACED
MISREAD	MISSENDS	MISSPEAKS	MISTELLS	MISTRACES
MISREADS	MISSENSE	MISSPELL	MISTEMPER	MISTRAIN
MISRECKON	MISSENSED	MISSPELLS	MISTEND	MISTRAINS
MISRECORD	MISSENSES	MISSPELT	MISTENDED	MISTRAL
MISREFER	MISSENT	MISSPEND	MISTENDS	MISTRALS
MISREFERS	MISSES	MISSPENDS	MISTER	MISTREAT
MISREGARD	MISSET	MISSPENT	MISTERED	MISTREATS
MISRELATE	MISSETS	MISSPOKE	MISTERIES	MISTRESS
MISRELIED	MISSHAPE	MISSPOKEN	MISTERING	MISTRIAL
MISRELIES	MISSHAPED	MISSTAMP	MISTERM	MISTRIALS

MISTRUST	MISYOKING	MITSVAHS	MIZENMAST	MOATING
MISTRUSTS	MITCH	MITSVOTH	MIZENS	MOATLIKE
MISTRUTH	MITCHED	MITT	MIZMAZE	MOATS
MISTRUTHS	MITCHES	MITTEN	MIZMAZES	MOB
MISTRYST	MITCHING	MITTENED	MIZUNA	MOBBED
MISTRYSTS	MITE	MITTENS	MIZUNAS	MOBBER
MISTS	MITER	MITTIMUS	MIZZ	MOBBERS
MISTUNE	MITERED	MITTS	MIZZEN	MOBBIE
MISTUNED	MITERER	MITUMBA	MIZZENS	MOBBIES
MISTUNES	MITERERS	MITUMBAS	MIZZES	MOBBING
MISTUNING	MITERING	MITY	MIZZLE	MOBBINGS
MISTUTOR	MITERS	MITZVAH	MIZZLED	MOBBISH
MISTUTORS	MITERWORT	MITZVAHS	MIZZLES	MOBBISHLY
MISTY	MITES	MITZVOTH	MIZZLIER	MOBBISM
MISTYPE	MITHER	MIURUS	MIZZLIEST	MOBBISMS
MISTYPED	MITHERED	MIURUSES	MIZZLING	MOBBLE
MISTYPES	MITHERING	MIX	MIZZLINGS	MOBBLED
MISTYPING	MITHERS	MIXABLE	MIZZLY	MOBBLES
MISUNION	MITICIDAL	MIXDOWN	MIZZONITE	MOBBLING
MISUNIONS	MITICIDE	MIXDOWNS	MIZZY	MOBBY
MISUSAGE	MITICIDES	MIXED	MM	MOBCAP
MISUSAGES	MITIER	MIXEDLY	MMM	MOBCAPS
MISUSE	MITIEST	MIXEDNESS	MNA	MOBCAST
MISUSED	MITIGABLE	MIXEN	MNAS	MOBCASTED
MISUSER	MITIGANT	MIXENS	MNEME	MOBCASTS
MISUSERS	MITIGANTS	MIXER	MNEMES	MOBE
MISUSES	MITIGATE	MIXERS	MNEMIC	MOBES
MISUSING	MITIGATED	MIXES	MNEMON	MOBEY
MISUST	MITIGATES	MIXIBLE	MNEMONIC	MOBEYS
MISVALUE	MITIGATOR	MIXIER	MNEMONICS	MOBIE
MISVALUED	MITIS	MIXIEST	MNEMONIST	MOBIES
MISVALUES	MITISES	MIXING	MNEMONS	MOBILE
MISWEEN	MITOGEN	MIXINGS	MO	MOBILES
MISWEENED	MITOGENIC	MIXMASTER	MOA	MOBILISE
MISWEENS	MITOGENS	MIXOLOGY	MOAI	MOBILISED
MISWEND	MITOMYCIN	MIXT	MOAN	MOBILISER
MISWENDS	MITOSES	MIXTAPE	MOANED	MOBILISES
MISWENT	MITOSIS	MIXTAPES	MOANER	MOBILITY
MISWORD	MITOTIC	MIXTE	MOANERS	MOBILIZE
MISWORDED	MITRAILLE	MIXTION	MOANFUL	MOBILIZED
MISWORDS	MITRAL	MIXTIONS	MOANFULLY	MOBILIZER
MISWRIT	MITRE	MIXTURE	MOANING	MOBILIZES
MISWRITE	MITRED	MIXTURES	MOANINGLY	MOBISODE
MISWRITES	MITRES	MIXUP	MOANINGS	MOBISODES
MISWROTE	MITREWORT	MIXUPS	MOANS	MOBLE
MISYOKE	MITRIFORM	MIXY	MOAS	MOBLED
MISYOKED	MITRING	MIZ	MOAT	MOBLES
MISYOKES	MITSVAH	MIZEN	MOATED	MOBLING

MOBLOG
MOBLOGGER
MOBLOGS
MOBOCRACY
MOBOCRAT
MOBOCRATS
MOBS
MOBSMAN
MOBSMEN
MOBSTER
MOBSTERS
MOBY
MOC
MOCASSIN
MOCASSINS
MOCCASIN
MOCCASINS
MOCCIES
MOCH
MOCHA
MOCHAS
MOCHED
MOCHELL
MOCHELLS
MOCHI
MOCHIE
MOCHIER
MOCHIEST
MOCHILA
MOCHILAS
MOCHINESS
MOCHING
MOCHIS
MOCHS
MOCHY
MOCK
MOCKABLE
MOCKADO
MOCKADOES
MOCKAGE
MOCKAGES
MOCKED
MOCKER
MOCKERED
MOCKERIES
MOCKERING
MOCKERNUT
MOCKERS

MOCKERY
MOCKING
MOCKINGLY
MOCKINGS
MOCKNEY
MOCKNEYS
MOCKS
MOCKTAIL
MOCKTAILS
MOCKUP
MOCKUPS
MOCOCK
MOCOCKS
MOCS
MOCUCK
MOCUCKS
MOCUDDUM
MOCUDDUMS
MOD
MODAFINIL
MODAL
MODALISM
MODALISMS
MODALIST
MODALISTS
MODALITY
MODALLY
MODALS
MODDED
MODDER
MODDERS
MODDING
MODDINGS
MODE
MODEL
MODELED
MODELER
MODELERS
MODELING
MODELINGS
MODELIST
MODELISTS
MODELLED
MODELLER
MODELLERS
MODELLI
MODELLING
MODELLIST

MODELLO
MODELLOS
MODELS
MODEM
MODEMED
MODEMING
MODEMS
MODENA
MODENAS
MODER
MODERATE
MODERATED
MODERATES
MODERATO
MODERATOR
MODERATOS
MODERN
MODERNE
MODERNER
MODERNES
MODERNEST
MODERNISE
MODERNISM
MODERNIST
MODERNITY
MODERNIZE
MODERNLY
MODERNS
MODERS
MODES
MODEST
MODESTER
MODESTEST
MODESTIES
MODESTLY
MODESTY
MODGE
MODGED
MODGES
MODGING
MODI
MODICA
MODICUM
MODICUMS
MODIFIED
MODIFIER
MODIFIERS
MODIFIES

MODIFY
MODIFYING
MODII
MODILLION
MODIOLAR
MODIOLI
MODIOLUS
MODISH
MODISHLY
MODIST
MODISTE
MODISTES
MODISTS
MODIUS
MODIWORT
MODIWORTS
MODS
MODULAR
MODULARLY
MODULARS
MODULATE
MODULATED
MODULATES
MODULATOR
MODULE
MODULES
MODULI
MODULO
MODULUS
MODUS
MOE
MOELLON
MOELLONS
MOER
MOERED
MOERING
MOERS
MOES
MOFETTE
MOFETTES
MOFFETTE
MOFFETTES
MOFFIE
MOFFIES
MOFO
MOFOS
MOFUSSIL
MOFUSSILS

MOG
MOGGAN
MOGGANS
MOGGED
MOGGIE
MOGGIES
MOGGING
MOGGY
MOGHUL
MOGHULS
MOGS
MOGUL
MOGULED
MOGULS
MOHAIR
MOHAIRS
MOHALIM
MOHAWK
MOHAWKS
MOHEL
MOHELIM
MOHELS
MOHICAN
MOHICANS
MOHO
MOHOS
MOHR
MOHRS
MOHUA
MOHUAS
MOHUR
MOHURS
MOI
MOIDER
MOIDERED
MOIDERING
MOIDERS
MOIDORE
MOIDORES
MOIETIES
MOIETY
MOIL
MOILE
MOILED
MOILER
MOILERS
MOILES
MOILING

MOILINGLY	MOKOMOKO	MOLELIKE	MOLOSSUS	MOMZERIM
MOILS	MOKOMOKOS	MOLES	MOLS	MOMZERS
MOINEAU	MOKOPUNA	MOLESKIN	MOLT	MON
MOINEAUS	MOKOPUNAS	MOLESKINS	MOLTED	MONA
MOIRA	MOKORO	MOLEST	MOLTEN	MONACHAL
MOIRAI	MOKOROS	MOLESTED	MOLTENLY	MONACHISM
MOIRE	MOKOS	MOLESTER	MOLTER	MONACHIST
MOIRES	MOKSHA	MOLESTERS	MOLTERS	MONACID
MOISER	MOKSHAS	MOLESTFUL	MOLTING	MONACIDIC
MOISERS	MOL	MOLESTING	MOLTO	MONACIDS
MOIST	MOLA	MOLESTS	MOLTS	MONACT
MOISTED	MOLAL	MOLIES	MOLY	MONACTINE
MOISTEN	MOLALITY	MOLIMEN	MOLYBDATE	MONACTS
MOISTENED	MOLAR	MOLIMENS	MOLYBDIC	MONAD
MOISTENER	MOLARITY	MOLINE	MOLYBDOUS	MONADAL
MOISTENS	MOLARS	MOLINES	MOLYS	MONADES
MOISTER	MOLAS	MOLINET	MOM	MONADIC
MOISTEST	MOLASSE	MOLINETS	MOME	MONADICAL
MOISTFUL	MOLASSES	MOLING	MOMENT	MONADISM
MOISTIFY	MOLD	MOLL	MOMENTA	MONADISMS
MOISTING	MOLDABLE	MOLLA	MOMENTANY	MONADNOCK
MOISTLY	MOLDAVITE	MOLLAH	MOMENTARY	MONADS
MOISTNESS	MOLDBOARD	MOLLAHS	MOMENTLY	MONAL
MOISTS	MOLDED	MOLLAS	MOMENTO	MONALS
MOISTURE	MOLDER	MOLLIE	MOMENTOES	MONAMINE
MOISTURES	MOLDERED	MOLLIES	MOMENTOS	MONAMINES
MOIT	MOLDERING	MOLLIFIED	MOMENTOUS	MONANDRY
MOITHER	MOLDERS	MOLLIFIER	MOMENTS	MONARCH
MOITHERED	MOLDIER	MOLLIFIES	MOMENTUM	MONARCHAL
MOITHERS	MOLDIEST	MOLLIFY	MOMENTUMS	MONARCHIC
MOITS	MOLDINESS	MOLLITIES	MOMES	MONARCHS
MOJAHEDIN	MOLDING	MOLLS	MOMI	MONARCHY
MOJARRA	MOLDINGS	MOLLUSC	MOMISM	MONARDA
MOJARRAS	MOLDS	MOLLUSCA	MOMISMS	MONARDAS
MOJITO	MOLDWARP	MOLLUSCAN	MOMMA	MONAS
MOJITOS	MOLDWARPS	MOLLUSCS	MOMMAS	MONASES
MOJO	MOLDY	MOLLUSCUM	MOMMET	MONASTERY
MOJOES	MOLE	MOLLUSK	MOMMETS	MONASTIC
MOJOS	MOLECAST	MOLLUSKAN	MOMMIES	MONASTICS
MOKADDAM	MOLECASTS	MOLLUSKS	MOMMY	MONATOMIC
MOKADDAMS	MOLECULAR	MOLLY	MOMOIR	MONAUL
MOKE	MOLECULE	MOLLYHAWK	MOMOIRS	MONAULS
MOKES	MOLECULES	MOLLYMAWK	MOMS	MONAURAL
MOKI	MOLED	MOLOCH	MOMSER	MONAXIAL
MOKIHI	MOLEHILL	MOLOCHISE	MOMSERS	MONAXON
MOKIHIS	MOLEHILLS	MOLOCHIZE	MOMUS	MONAXONIC
MOKIS	MOLEHUNT	MOLOCHS	MOMUSES	MONAXONS
MOKO	MOLEHUNTS	MOLOSSI	MOMZER	MONAZITE

MONAZITES	MONGEESE	MONISTIC	MONOCOT	MONOLATER
MONDAIN	MONGER	MONISTS	MONOCOTS	MONOLATRY
MONDAINE	MONGERED	MONITION	MONOCOTYL	MONOLAYER
MONDAINES	MONGERIES	MONITIONS	MONOCRACY	MONOLINE
MONDAINS	MONGERING	MONITIVE	MONOCRAT	MONOLITH
MONDE	MONGERS	MONITOR	MONOCRATS	MONOLITHS
MONDES	MONGERY	MONITORED	MONOCROP	MONOLOG
MONDIAL	MONGO	MONITORS	MONOCROPS	MONOLOGIC
MONDO	MONGOE	MONITORY	MONOCULAR	MONOLOGS
MONDOS	MONGOES	MONITRESS	MONOCYCLE	MONOLOGUE
MONECIAN	MONGOL	MONK	MONOCYTE	MONOLOGY
MONECIOUS	MONGOLIAN	MONKERIES	MONOCYTES	MONOMACHY
MONELLIN	MONGOLISM	MONKERY	MONOCYTIC	MONOMANIA
MONELLINS	MONGOLOID	MONKEY	MONODIC	MONOMARK
MONEME	MONGOLS	MONKEYED	MONODICAL	MONOMARKS
MONEMES	MONGOOSE	MONKEYING	MONODIES	MONOMER
MONER	MONGOOSES	MONKEYISH	MONODIST	MONOMERIC
MONERA	MONGOS	MONKEYISM	MONODISTS	MONOMERS
MONERAN	MONGREL	MONKEYPOD	MONODONT	MONOMETER
MONERANS	MONGRELLY	MONKEYPOT	MONODRAMA	MONOMIAL
MONERGISM	MONGRELS	MONKEYPOX	MONODY	MONOMIALS
MONERON	MONGS	MONKEYS	MONOECIES	MONOMODE
MONETARY	MONGST	MONKFISH	MONOECISM	MONONYM
MONETH	MONIAL	MONKHOOD	MONOECY	MONONYMS
MONETHS	MONIALS	MONKHOODS	MONOESTER	MONOPHAGY
MONETISE	MONIC	MONKISH	MONOFIL	MONOPHASE
MONETISED	MONICKER	MONKISHLY	MONOFILS	MONOPHONY
MONETISES	MONICKERS	MONKS	MONOFUEL	MONOPHYLY
MONETIZE	MONIE	MONKSHOOD	MONOFUELS	MONOPITCH
MONETIZED	MONIED	MONO	MONOGAMIC	MONOPLANE
MONETIZES	MONIES	MONOACID	MONOGAMY	MONOPLOID
MONEY	MONIKER	MONOACIDS	MONOGENIC	MONOPOD
MONEYBAG	MONIKERED	MONOAMINE	MONOGENY	MONOPODE
MONEYBAGS	MONIKERS	MONOAO	MONOGERM	MONOPODES
MONEYBELT	MONILIA	MONOAOS	MONOGLOT	MONOPODIA
MONEYBOX	MONILIAE	MONOBASIC	MONOGLOTS	MONOPODS
MONEYED	MONILIAL	MONOBLOC	MONOGONY	MONOPODY
MONEYER	MONILIAS	MONOBROW	MONOGRAM	MONOPOLE
MONEYERS	MONIMENT	MONOBROWS	MONOGRAMS	MONOPOLES
MONEYLESS	MONIMENTS	MONOCARP	MONOGRAPH	MONOPOLY
MONEYMAN	MONIPLIES	MONOCARPS	MONOGYNY	MONOPRINT
MONEYMEN	MONISH	MONOCEROS	MONOHULL	MONOPSONY
MONEYS	MONISHED	MONOCHORD	MONOHULLS	MONOPTERA
MONEYWORT	MONISHES	MONOCLE	MONOICOUS	MONOPTOTE
MONG	MONISHING	MONOCLED	MONOKINE	MONOPULSE
MONGCORN	MONISM	MONOCLES	MONOKINES	MONORAIL
MONGCORNS	MONISMS	MONOCLINE	MONOKINI	MONORAILS
MONGED	MONIST	MONOCOQUE	MONOKINIS	MONORCHID

M

MONORHINE	MONSTERAS	MOO	MOONBEAMS	MOONROCKS
MONORHYME	MONSTERED	MOOBIES	MOONBLIND	MOONROOF
MONOS	MONSTERS	MOOBS	MOONBOOTS	MOONROOFS
MONOSEMIC	MONSTROUS	MOOCH	MOONBOW	MOONS
MONOSEMY	MONTADALE	MOOCHED	MOONBOWS	MOONSAIL
MONOSES	MONTAGE	MOOCHER	MOONCAKE	MOONSAILS
MONOSIES	MONTAGED	MOOCHERS	MOONCAKES	MOONSCAPE
MONOSIS	MONTAGES	MOOCHES	MOONCALF	MOONSEED
MONOSKI	MONTAGING	MOOCHING	MOONCHILD	MOONSEEDS
MONOSKIED	MONTAN	MOOD	MOONCRAFT	MOONSET
MONOSKIER	MONTANE	MOODIED	MOONDOG	MOONSETS
MONOSKIS	MONTANES	MOODIER	MOONDOGS	MOONSHEE
MONOSOME	MONTANT	MOODIES	MOONDUST	MOONSHEES
MONOSOMES	MONTANTO	MOODIEST	MOONDUSTS	MOONSHINE
MONOSOMIC	MONTANTOS	MOODILY	MOONED	MOONSHINY
MONOSOMY	MONTANTS	MOODINESS	MOONER	MOONSHIP
MONOSTELE	MONTARIA	MOODS	MOONERS	MOONSHIPS
MONOSTELY	MONTARIAS	MOODY	MOONEYE	MOONSHOT
MONOSTICH	MONTE	MOODYING	MOONEYES	MOONSHOTS
MONOSTOME	MONTEITH	MOOED	MOONFACE	MOONSTONE
MONOSTYLE	MONTEITHS	MOOI	MOONFACED	MOONWALK
MONOSY	MONTEM	MOOING	MOONFACES	MOONWALKS
MONOTASK	MONTEMS	MOOK	MOONFISH	MOONWARD
MONOTASKS	MONTERO	MOOKS	MOONG	MOONWARDS
MONOTINT	MONTEROS	MOOKTAR	MOONGATE	MOONWORT
MONOTINTS	MONTES	MOOKTARS	MOONGATES	MOONWORTS
MONOTONE	MONTH	MOOL	MOONIER	MOONY
MONOTONED	MONTHLIES	MOOLA	MOONIES	MOOP
MONOTONES	MONTHLING	MOOLAH	MOONIEST	MOOPED
MONOTONIC	MONTHLONG	MOOLAHS	MOONILY	MOOPING
MONOTONY	MONTHLY	MOOLAS	MOONINESS	MOOPS
MONOTREME	MONTHS	MOOLED	MOONING	MOOR
MONOTROCH	MONTICLE	MOOLEY	MOONISH	MOORAGE
MONOTYPE	MONTICLES	MOOLEYS	MOONISHLY	MOORAGES
MONOTYPES	MONTICULE	MOOLI	MOONLESS	MOORBURN
MONOTYPIC	MONTIES	MOOLIES	MOONLET	MOORBURNS
MONOVULAR	MONTRE	MOOLING	MOONLETS	MOORCOCK
MONOXIDE	MONTRES	MOOLIS	MOONLIGHT	MOORCOCKS
MONOXIDES	MONTURE	MOOLOO	MOONLIKE	MOORED
MONOXYLON	MONTURES	MOOLOOS	MOONLIT	MOORFOWL
MONS	MONTY	MOOLS	MOONPHASE	MOORFOWLS
MONSIEUR	MONUMENT	MOOLVI	MOONPORT	MOORHEN
MONSIGNOR	MONUMENTS	MOOLVIE	MOONPORTS	MOORHENS
MONSOON	MONURON	MOOLVIES	MOONQUAKE	MOORIER
MONSOONAL	MONURONS	MOOLVIS	MOONRAKER	MOORIEST
MONSOONS	MONY	MOOLY	MOONRISE	MOORILL
MONSTER	MONYPLIES	MOON	MOONRISES	MOORILLS
MONSTERA	MONZONITE	MOONBEAM	MOONROCK	MOORING

MOORINGS	MOPEHAWKS	MORALES	MORDANT	MORLINGS
MOORISH	MOPER	MORALISE	MORDANTED	MORMAOR
MOORLAND	MOPERIES	MORALISED	MORDANTLY	MORMAORS
MOORLANDS	MOPERS	MORALISER	MORDANTS	MORN
MOORLOG	MOPERY	MORALISES	MORDENT	MORNAY
MOORLOGS	MOPES	MORALISM	MORDENTS	MORNAYS
MOORMAN	MOPEY	MORALISMS	MORE	MORNE
MOORMEN	MOPHEAD	MORALIST	MOREEN	MORNED
MOORS	MOPHEADS	MORALISTS	MOREENS	MORNES
MOORVA	MOPIER	MORALITY	MOREISH	MORNING
MOORVAS	MOPIEST	MORALIZE	MOREL	MORNINGS
MOORWORT	MOPILY	MORALIZED	MORELLE	MORNS
MOORWORTS	MOPINESS	MORALIZER	MORELLES	MOROCCO
MOORY	MOPING	MORALIZES	MORELLO	MOROCCOS
MOOS	MOPINGLY	MORALL	MORELLOS	MORON
MOOSE	MOPISH	MORALLED	MORELS	MORONIC
MOOSEBIRD	MOPISHLY	MORALLER	MORENDO	MORONISM
MOOSEHAIR	MOPOKE	MORALLERS	MORENDOS	MORONISMS
MOOSEHIDE	MOPOKES	MORALLING	MORENESS	MORONITY
MOOSEWOOD	MOPPED	MORALLS	MOREOVER	MORONS
MOOSEYARD	MOPPER	MORALLY	MOREPORK	MOROSE
MOOT	MOPPERS	MORALS	MOREPORKS	MOROSELY
MOOTABLE	MOPPET	MORAS	MORES	MOROSER
MOOTED	MOPPETS	MORASS	MORESQUE	MOROSEST
MOOTER	MOPPIER	MORASSES	MORESQUES	MOROSITY
MOOTERS	MOPPIEST	MORASSIER	MORGAN	MORPH
MOOTEST	MOPPING	MORASSY	MORGANITE	MORPHEAN
MOOTING	MOPPY	MORAT	MORGANS	MORPHED
MOOTINGS	MOPS	MORATORIA	MORGAY	MORPHEME
MOOTMAN	MOPSIES	MORATORY	MORGAYS	MORPHEMES
MOOTMEN	MOPSTICK	MORATS	MORGEN	MORPHEMIC
MOOTNESS	MOPSTICKS	MORAY	MORGENS	MORPHETIC
MOOTS	MOPSY	MORAYS	MORGUE	MORPHEW
MOOVE	MOPUS	MORBID	MORGUES	MORPHEWS
MOOVED	MOPUSES	MORBIDER	MORIA	MORPHIA
MOOVES	MOPY	MORBIDEST	MORIAS	MORPHIAS
MOOVING	MOQUETTE	MORBIDITY	MOKIBUND	MORPHIC
MOP	MOQUETTES	MORBIDLY	MORICHE	MORPHIN
MOPANE	MOR	MORBIFIC	MORICHES	MORPHINE
MOPANES	MORA	MORBILLI	MORION	MORPHINES
MOPANI	MORACEOUS	MORBUS	MORIONS	MORPHING
MOPANIS	MORAE	MORBUSES	MORISCO	MORPHINGS
MOPBOARD	MORAINAL	MORCEAU	MORISCOES	MORPHINIC
MOPBOARDS	MORAINE	MORCEAUX	MORISCOS	MORPHINS
MOPE	MORAINES	MORCHA	MORISH	MORPHO
MOPED	MORAINIC	MORCHAS	MORKIN	MORPHOGEN
MOPEDS	MORAL	MORDACITY	MORKINS	MORPHOS
MOPEHAWK	MORALE	MORDANCY	MORLING	MORPHOSES

M

MORPHOSIS	MORTBELL	MOSASAUR	MOSSING	MOTI
MORPHOTIC	MORTBELLS	MOSASAURI	MOSSLAND	MOTIER
MORPHS	MORTCLOTH	MOSASAURS	MOSSLANDS	MOTIEST
MORRA	MORTGAGE	MOSCATO	MOSSLIKE	MOTIF
MORRAS	MORTGAGED	MOSCATOS	MOSSO	MOTIFIC
MORRELL	MORTGAGEE	MOSCHATE	MOSSPLANT	MOTIFS
MORRELLS	MORTGAGER	MOSCHATEL	MOSSY	MOTILE
MORRHUA	MORTGAGES	MOSCOVIUM	MOST	MOTILES
MORRHUAS	MORTGAGOR	MOSE	MOSTE	MOTILITY
MORRICE	MORTICE	MOSED	MOSTEST	MOTION
MORRICES	MORTICED	MOSELLE	MOSTESTS	MOTIONAL
MORRION	MORTICER	MOSELLES	MOSTLY	MOTIONED
MORRIONS	MORTICERS	MOSES	MOSTS	MOTIONER
MORRIS	MORTICES	MOSEY	MOSTWHAT	MOTIONERS
MORRISED	MORTICIAN	MOSEYED	MOT	MOTIONING
MORRISES	MORTICING	MOSEYING	MOTE	MOTIONIST
MORRISING	MORTIFIC	MOSEYS	MOTED	MOTIONS
MORRO	MORTIFIED	MOSH	MOTEL	MOTIS
MORROS	MORTIFIER	MOSHAV	MOTELIER	MOTIVATE
MORROW	MORTIFIES	MOSHAVIM	MOTELIERS	MOTIVATED
MORROWS	MORTIFY	MOSHED	MOTELS	MOTIVATES
MORS	MORTISE	MOSHER	MOTEN	MOTIVATOR
MORSAL	MORTISED	MOSHERS	MOTES	MOTIVE
MORSALS	MORTISER	MOSHES	MOTET	MOTIVED
MORSE	MORTISERS	MOSHING	MOTETS	MOTIVES
MORSEL	MORTISES	MOSHINGS	MOTETT	MOTIVIC
MORSELED	MORTISING	MOSING	MOTETTIST	MOTIVING
MORSELING	MORTLING	MOSK	MOTETTS	MOTIVITY
MORSELLED	MORTLINGS	MOSKONFYT	MOTEY	MOTLEY
MORSELS	MORTMAIN	MOSKS	MOTEYS	MOTLEYER
MORSES	MORTMAINS	MOSLINGS	MOTH	MOTLEYEST
MORSURE	MORTS	MOSQUE	MOTHBALL	MOTLEYS
MORSURES	MORTSAFE	MOSQUES	MOTHBALLS	MOTLIER
MORT	MORTSAFES	MOSQUITO	MOTHED	MOTLIEST
MORTAL	MORTUARY	MOSQUITOS	MOTHER	MOTMOT
MORTALISE	MORULA	MOSS	MOTHERED	MOTMOTS
MORTALITY	MORULAE	MOSSBACK	MOTHERESE	MOTOCROSS
MORTALIZE	MORULAR	MOSSBACKS	MOTHERIER	MOTOR
MORTALLY	MORULAS	MOSSED	MOTHERING	MOTORABLE
MORTALS	MORWONG	MOSSER	MOTHERLY	MOTORAIL
MORTAR	MORWONGS	MOSSERS	MOTHERS	MOTORAILS
MORTARED	MORYAH	MOSSES	MOTHERY	MOTORBIKE
MORTARIER	MOS	MOSSGROWN	MOTHIER	MOTORBOAT
MORTARING	MOSAIC	MOSSIE	MOTHIEST	MOTORBUS
MORTARMAN	MOSAICISM	MOSSIER	MOTHLIKE	MOTORCADE
MORTARMEN	MOSAICIST	MOSSIES	MOTHPROOF	MOTORCAR
MORTARS	MOSAICKED	MOSSIEST	MOTHS	MOTORCARS
MORTARY	MOSAICS	MOSSINESS	MOTHY	MOTORDOM

MOTORDOMS	MOTTS	MOULINETS	MOUSE	MOUTAN
MOTORED	MOTTY	MOULINS	MOUSEBIRD	MOUTANS
MOTORHOME	MOTU	MOULS	MOUSED	MOUTER
MOTORIAL	MOTUCA	MOULT	MOUSEKIN	MOUTERED
MOTORIC	MOTUCAS	MOULTED	MOUSEKINS	MOUTERER
MOTORICS	MOTUS	MOULTEN	MOUSELIKE	MOUTERERS
MOTORING	MOTZA	MOULTER	MOUSEMAT	MOUTERING
MOTORINGS	MOTZAS	MOULTERS	MOUSEMATS	MOUTERS
MOTORISE	MOU	MOULTING	MOUSEOVER	MOUTH
MOTORISED	MOUCH	MOULTINGS	MOUSEPAD	MOUTHABLE
MOTORISES	MOUCHARD	MOULTS	MOUSEPADS	MOUTHED
MOTORIST	MOUCHARDS	MOUND	MOUSER	MOUTHER
MOTORISTS	MOUCHED	MOUNDBIRD	MOUSERIES	MOUTHERS
MOTORIUM	MOUCHER	MOUNDED	MOUSERS	MOUTHFEEL
MOTORIUMS	MOUCHERS	MOUNDING	MOUSERY	MOUTHFUL
MOTORIZE	MOUCHES	MOUNDS	MOUSES	MOUTHFULS
MOTORIZED	MOUCHING	MOUNSEER	MOUSETAIL	MOUTHIER
MOTORIZES	MOUCHOIR	MOUNSEERS	MOUSETRAP	MOUTHIEST
MOTORLESS	MOUCHOIRS	MOUNT	MOUSEY	MOUTHILY
MOTORMAN	MOUDIWART	MOUNTABLE	MOUSIE	MOUTHING
MOTORMEN	MOUDIWORT	MOUNTAIN	MOUSIER	MOUTHLESS
MOTORS	MOUE	MOUNTAINS	MOUSIES	MOUTHLIKE
MOTORSHIP	MOUES	MOUNTAINY	MOUSIEST	MOUTHPART
MOTORWAY	MOUFFLON	MOUNTANT	MOUSILY	MOUTHS
MOTORWAYS	MOUFFLONS	MOUNTANTS	MOUSINESS	MOUTHWASH
MOTORY	MOUFLON	MOUNTED	MOUSING	MOUTHY
MOTOSCAFI	MOUFLONS	MOUNTER	MOUSINGS	MOUTON
MOTOSCAFO	MOUGHT	MOUNTERS	MOUSLE	MOUTONNEE
MOTS	MOUILLE	MOUNTING	MOUSLED	MOUTONS
MOTSER	MOUJIK	MOUNTINGS	MOUSLES	MOVABLE
MOTSERS	MOUJIKS	MOUNTS	MOUSLING	MOVABLES
MOTT	MOULAGE	MOUP	MOUSME	MOVABLY
MOTTE	MOULAGES	MOUPED	MOUSMEE	MOVANT
MOTTES	MOULD	MOUPING	MOUSMEES	MOVANTS
MOTTIER	MOULDABLE	MOUPS	MOUSMES	MOVE
MOTTIES	MOULDED	MOURN	MOUSSAKA	MOVEABLE
MOTTIEST	MOULDER	MOURNED	MOUSSAKAS	MOVEABLES
MOTTLE	MOULDERED	MOURNER	MOUSSE	MOVEABLY
MOTTLED	MOULDERS	MOURNERS	MOUSSED	MOVED
MOTTLER	MOULDIER	MOURNFUL	MOUSSES	MOVELESS
MOTTLERS	MOULDIEST	MOURNING	MOUSSEUX	MOVEMENT
MOTTLES	MOULDING	MOURNINGS	MOUSSING	MOVEMENTS
MOTTLING	MOULDINGS	MOURNIVAL	MOUST	MOVER
MOTTLINGS	MOULDS	MOURNS	MOUSTACHE	MOVERS
MOTTO	MOULDWARP	MOURVEDRE	MOUSTED	MOVES
MOTTOED	MOULDY	MOUS	MOUSTING	MOVIE
MOTTOES	MOULIN	MOUSAKA	MOUSTS	MOVIEDOM
MOTTOS	MOULINET	MOUSAKAS	MOUSY	MOVIEDOMS

MOVIEGOER	MOZED	MUCIGENS	MUCOSA	MUDEJAR
MOVIELAND	MOZES	MUCILAGE	MUCOSAE	MUDEJARES
MOVIEOKE	MOZETTA	MUCILAGES	MUCOSAL	MUDEYE
MOVIEOKES	MOZETTAS	MUCIN	MUCOSAS	MUDEYES
MOVIEOLA	MOZETTE	MUCINOGEN	MUCOSE	MUDFISH
MOVIEOLAS	MOZING	MUCINOID	MUCOSITY	MUDFISHES
MOVIES	MOZO	MUCINOUS	MUCOUS	MUDFLAP
MOVING	MOZOS	MUCINS	MUCRO	MUDFLAPS
MOVINGLY	MOZZ	MUCK	MUCRONATE	MUDFLAT
MOVIOLA	MOZZES	MUCKAMUCK	MUCRONES	MUDFLATS
MOVIOLAS	MOZZETTA	MUCKED	MUCROS	MUDFLOW
MOW	MOZZETTAS	MUCKENDER	MUCULENT	MUDFLOWS
MOWA	MOZZETTE	MUCKER	MUCUS	MUDGE
MOWAS	MOZZIE	MUCKERED	MUCUSES	MUDGED
MOWBURN	MOZZIES	MUCKERING	MUD	MUDGER
MOWBURNED	MOZZLE	MUCKERISH	MUDBANK	MUDGERS
MOWBURNS	MOZZLED	MUCKERS	MUDBANKS	MUDGES
MOWBURNT	MOZZLES	MUCKHEAP	MUDBATH	MUDGING
MOWDIE	MOZZLING	MUCKHEAPS	MUDBATHS	MUDGUARD
MOWDIES	MPRET	MUCKIER	MUDBUG	MUDGUARDS
MOWED	MPRETS	MUCKIEST	MUDBUGS	MUDHEN
MOWER	MRIDAMGAM	MUCKILY	MUDCAP	MUDHENS
MOWERS	MRIDANG	MUCKINESS	MUDCAPPED	MUDHOLE
MOWING	MRIDANGA	MUCKING	MUDCAPS	MUDHOLES
MOWINGS	MRIDANGAM	MUCKLE	MUDCAT	MUDHOOK
MOWN	MRIDANGAS	MUCKLER	MUDCATS	MUDHOOKS
MOWRA	MRIDANGS	MUCKLES	MUDDED	MUDHOPPER
MOWRAS	MU	MUCKLEST	MUDDER	MUDIR
MOWS	MUCATE	MUCKLUCK	MUDDERS	MUDIRIA
MOXA	MUCATES	MUCKLUCKS	MUDDIED	MUDIRIAS
MOXAS	MUCH	MUCKRAKE	MUDDIER	MUDIRIEH
MOXIE	MUCHACHA	MUCKRAKED	MUDDIES	MUDIRIEHS
MOXIES	MUCHACHAS	MUCKRAKER	MUDDIEST	MUDIRS
MOY	MUCHACHO	MUCKRAKES	MUDDILY	MUDLARK
MOYA	MUCHACHOS	MUCKS	MUDDINESS	MUDLARKED
MOYAS	MUCHEL	MUCKSWEAT	MUDDING	MUDLARKS
MOYGASHEL	MUCHELL	MUCKWORM	MUDDLE	MUDLOGGER
MOYITIES	MUCHELLS	MUCKWORMS	MUDDLED	MUDPACK
MOYITY	MUCHELS	MUCKY	MUDDLER	MUDPACKS
MOYL	MUCHES	MUCKYMUCK	MUDDLERS	MUDPIE
MOYLE	MUCHLY	MUCLUC	MUDDLES	MUDPIES
MOYLED	MUCHNESS	MUCLUCS	MUDDLIER	MUDPUPPY
MOYLES	MUCHO	MUCOID	MUDDLIEST	MUDRA
MOYLING	MUCIC	MUCOIDAL	MUDDLING	MUDRAS
MOYLS	MUCID	MUCOIDS	MUDDLINGS	MUDROCK
MOYS	MUCIDITY	MUCOLYTIC	MUDDLY	MUDROCKS
MOZ	MUCIDNESS	MUCOR	MUDDY	MUDROOM
MOZE	MUCIGEN	MUCORS	MUDDYING	MUDROOMS

MUDS	MUGGAR	MUJIK	MULLAHISM	MULTICAST
MUDSCOW	MUGGARS	MUJIKS	MULLAHS	MULTICELL
MUDSCOWS	MUGGAS	MUKHTAR	MULLARKY	MULTICIDE
MUDSILL	MUGGED	MUKHTARS	MULLAS	MULTICITY
MUDSILLS	MUGGEE	MUKLUK	MULLED	MULTICOPY
MUDSLIDE	MUGGEES	MUKLUKS	MULLEIN	MULTICORE
MUDSLIDES	MUGGER	MUKTUK	MULLEINS	MULTICULT
MUDSLING	MUGGERS	MUKTUKS	MULLEN	MULTIDAY
MUDSLINGS	MUGGIER	MULATRESS	MULLENS	MULTIDISC
MUDSLUNG	MUGGIEST	MULATTA	MULLER	MULTIDISK
MUDSTONE	MUGGILY	MULATTAS	MULLERED	MULTIDRUG
MUDSTONES	MUGGINESS	MULATTO	MULLERIAN	MULTIFID
MUDWORT	MUGGING	MULATTOES	MULLERING	MULTIFIL
MUDWORTS	MUGGINGS	MULATTOS	MULLERS	MULTIFILS
MUEDDIN	MUGGINS	MULBERRY	MULLET	MULTIFOIL
MUEDDINS	MUGGINSES	MULCH	MULLETS	MULTIFOLD
MUENSTER	MUGGISH	MULCHED	MULLEY	MULTIFORM
MUENSTERS	MUGGLE	MULCHES	MULLEYS	MULTIGENE
MUESLI	MUGGLES	MULCHING	MULLIGAN	MULTIGERM
MUESLIS	MUGGS	MULCT	MULLIGANS	MULTIGRID
MUEZZIN	MUGGUR	MULCTED	MULLING	MULTIGYM
MUEZZINS	MUGGURS	MULCTING	MULLION	MULTIGYMS
MUFF	MUGGY	MULCTS	MULLIONED	MULTIHUED
MUFFED	MUGHAL	MULE	MULLIONS	MULTIHULL
MUFFETTEE	MUGHALS	MULED	MULLITE	MULTIJET
MUFFIN	MUGS	MULES	MULLITES	MULTILANE
MUFFINEER	MUGSHOT	MULESED	MULLOCK	MULTILINE
MUFFING	MUGSHOTS	MULESES	MULLOCKS	MULTILOBE
MUFFINS	MUGWORT	MULESING	MULLOCKY	MULTIMODE
MUFFISH	MUGWORTS	MULESINGS	MULLOWAY	MULTIPACK
MUFFLE	MUGWUMP	MULETA	MULLOWAYS	MULTIPAGE
MUFFLED	MUGWUMPS	MULETAS	MULLS	MULTIPARA
MUFFLER	MUHLIES	MULETEER	MULMUL	MULTIPART
MUFFLERED	MUHLY	MULETEERS	MULMULL	MULTIPATH
MUFFLERS	MUID	MULEY	MULMULLS	MULTIPED
MUFFLES	MUIDS	MULEYS	MULMULS	MULTIPEDE
MUFFLING	MUIL	MULGA	MULSE	MULTIPEDS
MUFFS	MUILS	MULGAS	MULSES	MULTIPION
MUFLON	MUIR	MULIE	MULSH	MULTIPLE
MUFLONS	MUIRBURN	MULIES	MULSHED	MULTIPLES
MUFTI	MUIRBURNS	MULING	MULSHES	MULTIPLET
MUFTIS	MUIRS	MULISH	MULSHING	MULTIPLEX
MUG	MUIST	MULISHLY	MULTEITY	MULTIPLY
MUGEARITE	MUISTED	MULL	MULTIAGE	MULTIPOLE
MUGFUL	MUISTING	MULLA	MULTIATOM	MULTIPORT
MUGFULS	MUISTS	MULLAH	MULTIBAND	MULTIRISK
MUGG	MUJAHEDIN	MULLAHED	MULTIBANK	MULTIROLE
MUGGA	MUJAHIDIN	MULLAHING	MULTICAR	MULTIROOM

MULTISITE	MUMMIFIED	MUNDIC	MUNTERS	MURDERS
MULTISIZE	MUMMIFIES	MUNDICS	MUNTIN	MURE
MULTISTEP	MUMMIFORM	MUNDIFIED	MUNTINED	MURED
MULTITASK	MUMMIFY	MUNDIFIES	MUNTING	MUREIN
MULTITIER	MUMMING	MUNDIFY	MUNTINGS	MUREINS
MULTITON	MUMMINGS	MUNDUNGO	MUNTINS	MURENA
MULTITONE	MUMMOCK	MUNDUNGOS	MUNTJAC	MURENAS
MULTITOOL	MUMMOCKS	MUNDUNGUS	MUNTJACS	MURES
MULTITUDE	MUMMS	MUNG	MUNTJAK	MUREX
MULTIUNIT	MUMMY	MUNGA	MUNTJAKS	MUREXES
MULTIUSE	MUMMYING	MUNGAS	MUNTRIE	MURGEON
MULTIUSER	MUMP	MUNGCORN	MUNTRIES	MURGEONED
MULTIWALL	MUMPED	MUNGCORNS	MUNTS	MURGEONS
MULTIWAY	MUMPER	MUNGE	MUNTU	MURIATE
MULTIYEAR	MUMPERS	MUNGED	MUNTUS	MURIATED
MULTUM	MUMPING	MUNGES	MUON	MURIATES
MULTUMS	MUMPISH	MUNGING	MUONIC	MURIATIC
MULTURE	MUMPISHLY	MUNGO	MUONIUM	MURICATE
MULTURED	MUMPS	MUNGOES	MUONIUMS	MURICATED
MULTURER	MUMPSIMUS	MUNGOOSE	MUONS	MURICES
MULTURERS	MUMS	MUNGOOSES	MUPPET	MURID
MULTURES	MUMSIER	MUNGOS	MUPPETS	MURIDS
MULTURING	MUMSIES	MUNGS	MUQADDAM	MURIFORM
MUM	MUMSIEST	MUNI	MUQADDAMS	MURINE
MUMBLE	MUMSINESS	MUNICIPAL	MURA	MURINES
MUMBLED	MUMSY	MUNIFIED	MURAENA	MURING
MUMBLER	MUMU	MUNIFIES	MURAENAS	MURK
MUMBLERS	MUMUS	MUNIFY	MURAENID	MURKED
MUMBLES	MUN	MUNIFYING	MURAENIDS	MURKER
MUMBLIER	MUNCH	MUNIMENT	MURAGE	MURKEST
MUMBLIEST	MUNCHABLE	MUNIMENTS	MURAGES	MURKIER
MUMBLING	MUNCHED	MUNIS	MURAL	MURKIEST
MUMBLINGS	MUNCHER	MUNITE	MURALED	MURKILY
MUMBLY	MUNCHERS	MUNITED	MURALIST	MURKINESS
MUMCHANCE	MUNCHES	MUNITES	MURALISTS	MURKING
MUMM	MUNCHIE	MUNITING	MURALLED	MURKISH
MUMMED	MUNCHIER	MUNITION	MURALS	MURKLY
MUMMER	MUNCHIES	MUNITIONS	MURAS	MURKS
MUMMERED	MUNCHIEST	MUNNION	MURDABAD	MURKSOME
MUMMERIES	MUNCHING	MUNNIONS	MURDER	MURKY
MUMMERING	MUNCHKIN	MUNS	MURDERED	MURL
MUMMERS	MUNCHKINS	MUNSHI	MURDEREE	MURLAIN
MUMMERY	MUNCHY	MUNSHIS	MURDEREES	MURLAINS
MUMMIA	MUNDANE	MUNSTER	MURDERER	MURLAN
MUMMIAS	MUNDANELY	MUNSTERS	MURDERERS	MURLANS
MUMMICHOG	MUNDANER	MUNT	MURDERESS	MURLED
MUMMIED	MUNDANEST	MUNTED	MURDERING	MURLIER
MUMMIES	MUNDANITY	MUNTER	MURDEROUS	MURLIEST

MURLIN	MURRIS	MUSCOIDS	MUSICALES	MUSKRAT
MURLING	MURRS	MUSCOLOGY	MUSICALLY	MUSKRATS
MURLINS	MURRY	MUSCONE	MUSICALS	MUSKROOT
MURLS	MURSHID	MUSCONES	MUSICIAN	MUSKROOTS
MURLY	MURSHIDS	MUSCOSE	MUSICIANS	MUSKS
MURMUR	MURTHER	MUSCOVADO	MUSICK	MUSKY
MURMURED	MURTHERED	MUSCOVITE	MUSICKED	MUSLIN
MURMURER	MURTHERER	MUSCOVY	MUSICKER	MUSLINED
MURMURERS	MURTHERS	MUSCULAR	MUSICKERS	MUSLINET
MURMURING	MURTI	MUSCULOUS	MUSICKING	MUSLINETS
MURMUROUS	MURTIS	MUSE	MUSICKS	MUSLINS
MURMURS	MURVA	MUSED	MUSICLESS	MUSMON
MURPHIES	MURVAS	MUSEFUL	MUSICS	MUSMONS
MURPHY	MUS	MUSEFULLY	MUSIMON	MUSO
MURR	MUSACEOUS	MUSEOLOGY	MUSIMONS	MUSOS
MURRA	MUSANG	MUSER	MUSING	MUSPIKE
MURRAGH	MUSANGS	MUSERS	MUSINGLY	MUSPIKES
MURRAGHS	MUSAR	MUSES	MUSINGS	MUSQUASH
MURRAIN	MUSARS	MUSET	MUSIT	MUSROL
MURRAINED	MUSCA	MUSETS	MUSITS	MUSROLS
MURRAINS	MUSCADEL	MUSETTE	MUSIVE	MUSS
MURRAM	MUSCADELS	MUSETTES	MUSJID	MUSSE
MURRAMS	MUSCADET	MUSEUM	MUSJIDS	MUSSED
MURRAS	MUSCADETS	MUSEUMS	MUSK	MUSSEL
MURRAY	MUSCADIN	MUSH	MUSKED	MUSSELLED
MURRAYS	MUSCADINE	MUSHA	MUSKEG	MUSSELS
MURRE	MUSCADINS	MUSHED	MUSKEGS	MUSSES
MURREE	MUSCAE	MUSHER	MUSKET	MUSSIER
MURREES	MUSCARINE	MUSHERS	MUSKETEER	MUSSIEST
MURRELET	MUSCAT	MUSHES	MUSKETOON	MUSSILY
MURRELETS	MUSCATEL	MUSHIE	MUSKETRY	MUSSINESS
MURREN	MUSCATELS	MUSHIER	MUSKETS	MUSSING
MURRENS	MUSCATS	MUSHIES	MUSKIE	MUSSITATE
MURRES	MUSCAVADO	MUSHIEST	MUSKIER	MUSSY
MURREY	MUSCID	MUSHILY	MUSKIES	MUST
MURREYS	MUSCIDS	MUSHINESS	MUSKIEST	MUSTACHE
MURRHA	MUSCLE	MUSHING	MUSKILY	MUSTACHED
MURRHAS	MUSCLED	MUSHINGS	MUSKINESS	MUSTACHES
MURRHINE	MUSCLEMAN	MUSHMOUTH	MUSKING	MUSTACHIO
MURRHINES	MUSCLEMEN	MUSHRAT	MUSKIT	MUSTANG
MURRI	MUSCLES	MUSHRATS	MUSKITS	MUSTANGS
MURRIES	MUSCLEY	MUSHROOM	MUSKLE	MUSTARD
MURRIN	MUSCLIER	MUSHROOMS	MUSKLES	MUSTARDS
MURRINE	MUSCLIEST	MUSHROOMY	MUSKMELON	MUSTARDY
MURRINES	MUSCLING	MUSHY	MUSKONE	MUSTED
MURRINS	MUSCLINGS	MUSIC	MUSKONES	MUSTEE
MURRION	MUSCLY	MUSICAL	MUSKOX	MUSTEES
MURRIONS	MUSCOID	MUSICALE	MUSKOXEN	MUSTELID

MUSTELIDS	MUTELY	MUTUALIST	MWALIMUS	MYELITES
MUSTELINE	MUTENESS	MUTUALITY	MY	MYELITIS
MUSTER	MUTER	MUTUALIZE	MYAL	MYELOCYTE
MUSTERED	MUTES	MUTUALLY	MYALGIA	MYELOGRAM
MUSTERER	MUTEST	MUTUALS	MYALGIAS	MYELOID
MUSTERERS	MUTHA	MUTUCA	MYALGIC	MYELOMA
MUSTERING	MUTHAS	MUTUCAS	MYALISM	MYELOMAS
MUSTERS	MUTI	MUTUEL	MYALISMS	MYELOMATA
MUSTH	MUTICATE	MUTUELS	MYALIST	MYELON
MUSTHS	MUTICOUS	MUTULAR	MYALISTS	MYELONS
MUSTIER	MUTILATE	MUTULE	MYALL	MYGALE
MUSTIEST	MUTILATED	MUTULES	MYALLS	MYGALES
MUSTILY	MUTILATES	MUTUUM	MYASES	MYIASES
MUSTINESS	MUTILATOR	MUTUUMS	MYASIS	MYIASIS
MUSTING	MUTINE	MUUMUU	MYC	MYIOPHILY
MUSTS	MUTINED	MUUMUUS	MYCELE	MYLAR
MUSTY	MUTINEER	MUX	MYCELES	MYLARS
MUT	MUTINEERS	MUXED	MYCELIA	MYLODON
MUTABLE	MUTINES	MUXES	MYCELIAL	MYLODONS
MUTABLY	MUTING	MUXING	MYCELIAN	MYLODONT
MUTAGEN	MUTINIED	MUZAK	MYCELIUM	MYLODONTS
MUTAGENIC	MUTINIES	MUZAKIER	MYCELLA	MYLOHYOID
MUTAGENS	MUTINING	MUZAKIEST	MYCELLAS	MYLONITE
MUTANDA	MUTINOUS	MUZAKS	MYCELOID	MYLONITES
MUTANDUM	MUTINY	MUZAKY	MYCETES	MYLONITIC
MUTANT	MUTINYING	MUZHIK	MYCETOMA	MYNA
MUTANTS	MUTIS	MUZHIKS	MYCETOMAS	MYNAH
MUTASE	MUTISM	MUZJIK	MYCOBIONT	MYNAHS
MUTASES	MUTISMS	MUZJIKS	MYCOFLORA	MYNAS
MUTATE	MUTON	MUZZ	MYCOLOGIC	MYNHEER
MUTATED	MUTONS	MUZZED	MYCOLOGY	MYNHEERS
MUTATES	MUTOSCOPE	MUZZES	MYCOPHAGY	MYOBLAST
MUTATING	MUTS	MUZZIER	MYCOPHILE	MYOBLASTS
MUTATION	MUTT	MUZZIEST	MYCORHIZA	MYOCARDIA
MUTATIONS	MUTTER	MUZZILY	MYCOSES	MYOCLONIC
MUTATIVE	MUTTERED	MUZZINESS	MYCOSIS	MYOCLONUS
MUTATOR	MUTTERER	MUZZING	MYCOTIC	MYOFIBRIL
MUTATORS	MUTTERERS	MUZZLE	MYCOTOXIN	MYOGEN
MUTATORY	MUTTERING	MUZZLED	MYCOVIRUS	MYOGENIC
MUTCH	MUTTERS	MUZZLER	MYCS	MYOGENS
MUTCHED	MUTTON	MUZZLERS	MYDRIASES	MYOGLOBIN
MUTCHES	MUTTONIER	MUZZLES	MYDRIASIS	MYOGRAM
MUTCHING	MUTTONS	MUZZLING	MYDRIATIC	MYOGRAMS
MUTCHKIN	MUTTONY	MUZZY	MYELIN	MYOGRAPH
MUTCHKINS	MUTTS	MVULE	MYELINE	MYOGRAPHS
MUTE	MUTUAL	MVULES	MYELINES	MYOGRAPHY
MUTED	MUTUALISE	MWAH	MYELINIC	MYOID
MUTEDLY	MUTUALISM	MWALIMU	MYELINS	MYOIDS

MYOLOGIC	MYOSISES	MYRMIDON	MYSTICLY	MYTHOLOGY
MYOLOGIES	MYOSITIS	MYRMIDONS	MYSTICS	MYTHOMANE
MYOLOGIST	MYOSOTE	MYROBALAN	MYSTIFIED	MYTHOPEIC
MYOLOGY	MYOSOTES	MYRRH	MYSTIFIER	MYTHOPOET
MYOMA	MYOSOTIS	MYRRHIC	MYSTIFIES	MYTHOS
MYOMANCY	MYOSTATIN	MYRRHIER	MYSTIFY	MYTHS
MYOMANTIC	MYOTIC	MYRRHIEST	MYSTIQUE	MYTHUS
MYOMAS	MYOTICS	MYRRHINE	MYSTIQUES	MYTHY
MYOMATA	MYOTOME	MYRRHOL	MYTH	MYTILOID
MYOMATOUS	MYOTOMES	MYRRHOLS	MYTHI	MYXAMEBA
MYOMERE	MYOTONIA	MYRRHS	MYTHIC	MYXAMEBAE
MYOMERES	MYOTONIAS	MYRRHY	MYTHICAL	MYXAMEBAS
MYONEURAL	MYOTONIC	MYRTLE	MYTHICISE	MYXAMOEBA
MYOPATHIC	MYOTUBE	MYRTLES	MYTHICISM	MYXEDEMA
MYOPATHY	MYOTUBES	MYSELF	MYTHICIST	MYXEDEMAS
MYOPE	MYRBANE	MYSID	MYTHICIZE	MYXEDEMIC
MYOPES	MYRBANES	MYSIDS	MYTHIER	MYXO
MYOPHILY	MYRIAD	MYSOST	MYTHIEST	MYXOCYTE
MYOPIA	MYRIADS	MYSOSTS	MYTHISE	MYXOCYTES
MYOPIAS	MYRIADTH	MYSPACE	MYTHISED	MYXOEDEMA
MYOPIC	MYRIADTHS	MYSPACED	MYTHISES	MYXOID
MYOPICS	MYRIAPOD	MYSPACES	MYTHISING	MYXOMA
MYOPIES	MYRIAPODS	MYSPACING	MYTHISM	MYXOMAS
MYOPS	MYRICA	MYSTAGOG	MYTHISMS	MYXOMATA
MYOPSES	MYRICAS	MYSTAGOGS	MYTHIST	MYXOS
MYOPY	MYRINGA	MYSTAGOGY	MYTHISTS	MYXOVIRAL
MYOSCOPE	MYRINGAS	MYSTERIES	MYTHIZE	MYXOVIRUS
MYOSCOPES	MYRIOPOD	MYSTERY	MYTHIZED	MZEE
MYOSES	MYRIOPODS	MYSTIC	MYTHIZES	MZEES
MYOSIN	MYRIORAMA	MYSTICAL	MYTHIZING	MZUNGU
MYOSINS	MYRISTIC	MYSTICETE	MYTHMAKER	MZUNGUS
MYOSIS	MYRMECOID	MYSTICISM	MYTHOI	

M

N

NA
NAAM
NAAMS
NAAN
NAANS
NAARTJE
NAARTJES
NAARTJIE
NAARTJIES
NAB
NABBED
NABBER
NABBERS
NABBING
NABE
NABES
NABIS
NABK
NABKS
NABLA
NABLAS
NABOB
NABOBERY
NABOBESS
NABOBISH
NABOBISM
NABOBISMS
NABOBS
NABS
NACARAT
NACARATS
NACELLE
NACELLES
NACH
NACHAS
NACHE
NACHES
NACHO
NACHOS
NACHTMAAL
NACKET
NACKETS

NACRE
NACRED
NACREOUS
NACRES
NACRITE
NACRITES
NACROUS
NADA
NADAS
NADIR
NADIRAL
NADIRS
NADORS
NADS
NAE
NAEBODIES
NAEBODY
NAES
NAETHING
NAETHINGS
NAEVE
NAEVES
NAEVI
NAEVOID
NAEVUS
NAFF
NAFFED
NAFFER
NAFFEST
NAFFING
NAFFLY
NAFFNESS
NAFFS
NAG
NAGA
NAGANA
NAGANAS
NAGAPIE
NAGAPIES
NAGARI
NAGARIS
NAGAS

NAGGED
NAGGER
NAGGERS
NAGGIER
NAGGIEST
NAGGING
NAGGINGLY
NAGGINGS
NAGGY
NAGMAAL
NAGMAALS
NAGOR
NAGORS
NAGS
NAGWARE
NAGWARES
NAH
NAHAL
NAHALS
NAIAD
NAIADES
NAIADS
NAIANT
NAIF
NAIFER
NAIFEST
NAIFLY
NAIFNESS
NAIFS
NAIK
NAIKS
NAIL
NAILBITER
NAILBRUSH
NAILED
NAILER
NAILERIES
NAILERS
NAILERY
NAILFILE
NAILFILES
NAILFOLD

NAILFOLDS
NAILHEAD
NAILHEADS
NAILING
NAILINGS
NAILLESS
NAILS
NAILSET
NAILSETS
NAIN
NAINSELL
NAINSELLS
NAINSOOK
NAINSOOKS
NAIRA
NAIRAS
NAIRU
NAIRUS
NAISSANCE
NAISSANT
NAIVE
NAIVELY
NAIVENESS
NAIVER
NAIVES
NAIVEST
NAIVETE
NAIVETES
NAIVETIES
NAIVETY
NAIVIST
NAKED
NAKEDER
NAKEDEST
NAKEDLY
NAKEDNESS
NAKER
NAKERS
NAKFA
NAKFAS
NALA
NALAS

NALED
NALEDS
NALIDIXIC
NALLA
NALLAH
NALLAHS
NALLAS
NALOXONE
NALOXONES
NAM
NAMABLE
NAMASKAR
NAMASKARS
NAMASTE
NAMASTES
NAMAYCUSH
NAME
NAMEABLE
NAMECHECK
NAMED
NAMELESS
NAMELY
NAMEPLATE
NAMER
NAMERS
NAMES
NAMESAKE
NAMESAKES
NAMETAG
NAMETAGS
NAMETAPE
NAMETAPES
NAMING
NAMINGS
NAMMA
NAMS
NAMU
NAMUS
NAN
NANA
NANAS
NANCE

NANCES	NANOGRASS	NAPING	NARCOMATA	NARRASES
NANCIER	NANOMETER	NAPKIN	NARCOS	NARRATE
NANCIES	NANOMETRE	NAPKINS	NARCOSE	NARRATED
NANCIEST	NANOOK	NAPLESS	NARCOSES	NARRATER
NANCIFIED	NANOOKS	NAPOLEON	NARCOSIS	NARRATERS
NANCY	NANOPORE	NAPOLEONS	NARCOTIC	NARRATES
NANDIN	NANOPORES	NAPOO	NARCOTICS	NARRATING
NANDINA	NANOS	NAPOOED	NARCOTINE	NARRATION
NANDINAS	NANOSCALE	NAPOOING	NARCOTISE	NARRATIVE
NANDINE	NANOTECH	NAPOOS	NARCOTISM	NARRATOR
NANDINES	NANOTECHS	NAPPA	NARCOTIST	NARRATORS
NANDINS	NANOTESLA	NAPPAS	NARCOTIZE	NARRATORY
NANDOO	NANOTUBE	NAPPE	NARCS	NARRE
NANDOOS	NANOTUBES	NAPPED	NARD	NARROW
NANDU	NANOWATT	NAPPER	NARDED	NARROWED
NANDUS	NANOWATTS	NAPPERS	NARDINE	NARROWER
NANE	NANOWIRE	NAPPES	NARDING	NARROWEST
NANG	NANOWIRES	NAPPIE	NARDOO	NARROWING
NANISM	NANOWORLD	NAPPIER	NARDOOS	NARROWISH
NANISMS	NANS	NAPPIES	NARDS	NARROWLY
NANITE	NANUA	NAPPIEST	NARE	NARROWS
NANITES	NANUAS	NAPPINESS	NARES	NARTHEX
NANKEEN	NAOI	NAPPING	NARGHILE	NARTHEXES
NANKEENS	NAOS	NAPPY	NARGHILES	NARTJIE
NANKIN	NAOSES	NAPRON	NARGHILLY	NARTJIES
NANKINS	NAP	NAPRONS	NARGHILY	NARWAL
NANNA	NAPA	NAPROXEN	NARGILE	NARWALS
NANNAS	NAPALM	NAPROXENS	NARGILEH	NARWHAL
NANNIE	NAPALMED	NAPS	NARGILEHS	NARWHALE
NANNIED	NAPALMING	NARAS	NARGILES	NARWHALES
NANNIES	NAPALMS	NARASES	NARGILIES	NARWHALS
NANNY	NAPAS	NARC	NARGILY	NARY
NANNYGAI	NAPE	NARCEEN	NARGUILEH	NAS
NANNYGAIS	NAPED	NARCEENS	NARIAL	NASAL
NANNYING	NAPERIES	NARCEIN	NARIC	NASALISE
NANNYINGS	NAPERY	NARCEINE	NARICORN	NASALISED
NANNYISH	NAPES	NARCCINES	NARICORNS	NASALISES
NANO	NAPHTHA	NARCEINS	NARINE	NASALISM
NANOBE	NAPHTHAS	NARCISM	NARIS	NASALISMS
NANOBEE	NAPHTHENE	NARCISMS	NARK	NASALITY
NANOBEES	NAPHTHOL	NARCISSI	NARKED	NASALIZE
NANOBES	NAPHTHOLS	NARCISSUS	NARKIER	NASALIZED
NANOBOT	NAPHTHOUS	NARCIST	NARKIEST	NASALIZES
NANOBOTS	NAPHTHYL	NARCISTIC	NARKING	NASALLY
NANODOT	NAPHTHYLS	NARCISTS	NARKS	NASALS
NANODOTS	NAPHTOL	NARCO	NARKY	NASARD
NANOGRAM	NAPHTOLS	NARCOMA	NARQUOIS	NASARDS
NANOGRAMS	NAPIFORM	NARCOMAS	NARRAS	NASCENCE

two to nine letter words | 383

NASCENCES	NATIVISM	NAUNT	NAVICERTS	NEAFFE
NASCENCY	NATIVISMS	NAUNTS	NAVICULA	NEAFFES
NASCENT	NATIVIST	NAUPLIAL	NAVICULAR	NEAL
NASEBERRY	NATIVISTS	NAUPLII	NAVICULAS	NEALED
NASHGAB	NATIVITY	NAUPLIOID	NAVIES	NEALING
NASHGABS	NATRIUM	NAUPLIUS	NAVIGABLE	NEALS
NASHI	NATRIUMS	NAUSEA	NAVIGABLY	NEANIC
NASHIS	NATROLITE	NAUSEANT	NAVIGATE	NEAP
NASIAL	NATRON	NAUSEANTS	NAVIGATED	NEAPED
NASION	NATRONS	NAUSEAS	NAVIGATES	NEAPING
NASIONS	NATS	NAUSEATE	NAVIGATOR	NEAPS
NASSELLA	NATTER	NAUSEATED	NAVS	NEAR
NASTALIK	NATTERED	NAUSEATES	NAVVIED	NEARBY
NASTALIKS	NATTERER	NAUSEOUS	NAVVIES	NEARED
NASTIC	NATTERERS	NAUTCH	NAVVY	NEARER
NASTIER	NATTERIER	NAUTCHES	NAVVYING	NEAREST
NASTIES	NATTERING	NAUTIC	NAVY	NEARING
NASTIEST	NATTERS	NAUTICAL	NAW	NEARISH
NASTILY	NATTERY	NAUTICS	NAWAB	NEARLIER
NASTINESS	NATTIER	NAUTILI	NAWABS	NEARLIEST
NASTY	NATTIEST	NAUTILOID	NAY	NEARLY
NASUTE	NATTILY	NAUTILUS	NAYS	NEARNESS
NASUTES	NATTINESS	NAV	NAYSAID	NEARS
NAT	NATTY	NAVAID	NAYSAY	NEARSHORE
NATAL	NATURA	NAVAIDS	NAYSAYER	NEARSIDE
NATALITY	NATURAE	NAVAL	NAYSAYERS	NEARSIDES
NATANT	NATURAL	NAVALISM	NAYSAYING	NEAT
NATANTLY	NATURALLY	NAVALISMS	NAYSAYS	NEATEN
NATATION	NATURALS	NAVALLY	NAYTHLES	NEATENED
NATATIONS	NATURE	NAVAR	NAYWARD	NEATENING
NATATORIA	NATURED	NAVARCH	NAYWARDS	NEATENS
NATATORY	NATURES	NAVARCHS	NAYWORD	NEATER
NATCH	NATURING	NAVARCHY	NAYWORDS	NEATEST
NATCHES	NATURISM	NAVARHO	NAZE	NEATH
NATES	NATURISMS	NAVARHOS	NAZES	NEATHERD
NATHELESS	NATURIST	NAVARIN	NAZI	NEATHERDS
NATHEMO	NATURISTS	NAVARINS	NAZIFIED	NEATLY
NATHEMORE	NAUCH	NAVARS	NAZIFIES	NEATNESS
NATHLESS	NAUCHES	NAVE	NAZIFY	NEATNIK
NATIFORM	NAUGAHYDE	NAVEL	NAZIFYING	NEATNIKS
NATION	NAUGHT	NAVELS	NAZIR	NEATS
NATIONAL	NAUGHTIER	NAVELWORT	NAZIRS	NEB
NATIONALS	NAUGHTIES	NAVES	NAZIS	NEBBED
NATIONS	NAUGHTILY	NAVETTE	NDUJA	NEBBICH
NATIS	NAUGHTS	NAVETTES	NDUJAS	NEBBICHS
NATIVE	NAUGHTY	NAVEW	NE	NEBBING
NATIVELY	NAUMACHIA	NAVEWS	NEAFE	NEBBISH
NATIVES	NAUMACHY	NAVICERT	NEAFES	NEBBISHE

NEBBISHER	NECKERS	NECTARY	NEEMS	NEGOTIATE
NEBBISHES	NECKGEAR	NED	NEEP	NEGRESS
NEBBISHY	NECKGEARS	NEDDIER	NEEPS	NEGRESSES
NEBBUK	NECKING	NEDDIES	NEESBERRY	NEGRITUDE
NEBBUKS	NECKINGS	NEDDIEST	NEESE	NEGRO
NEBECK	NECKLACE	NEDDISH	NEESED	NEGROES
NEBECKS	NECKLACED	NEDDY	NEESES	NEGROHEAD
NEBEK	NECKLACES	NEDETTE	NEESING	NEGROID
NEBEKS	NECKLESS	NEDETTES	NEEZE	NEGROIDAL
NEBEL	NECKLET	NEDS	NEEZED	NEGROIDS
NEBELS	NECKLETS	NEE	NEEZES	NEGROISM
NEBENKERN	NECKLIKE	NEED	NEEZING	NEGROISMS
NEBISH	NECKLINE	NEEDED	NEF	NEGRONI
NEBISHES	NECKLINES	NEEDER	NEFANDOUS	NEGRONIS
NEBRIS	NECKPIECE	NEEDERS	NEFARIOUS	NEGROPHIL
NEBRISES	NECKS	NEEDFIRE	NEFAST	NEGS
NEBS	NECKSHOT	NEEDFIRES	NEFS	NEGUS
NEBULA	NECKSHOTS	NEEDFUL	NEG	NEGUSES
NEBULAE	NECKTIE	NEEDFULLY	NEGATE	NEIF
NEBULAR	NECKTIES	NEEDFULS	NEGATED	NEIFS
NEBULAS	NECKVERSE	NEEDIER	NEGATER	NEIGH
NEBULE	NECKWEAR	NEEDIEST	NEGATERS	NEIGHBOR
NEBULES	NECKWEARS	NEEDILY	NEGATES	NEIGHBORS
NEBULISE	NECKWEED	NEEDINESS	NEGATING	NEIGHBOUR
NEBULISED	NECKWEEDS	NEEDING	NEGATION	NEIGHED
NEBULISER	NECROLOGY	NEEDLE	NEGATIONS	NEIGHING
NEBULISES	NECROPHIL	NEEDLED	NEGATIVE	NEIGHINGS
NEBULIUM	NECROPOLI	NEEDLEFUL	NEGATIVED	NEIGHS
NEBULIUMS	NECROPSY	NEEDLER	NEGATIVES	NEINEI
NEBULIZE	NECROSE	NEEDLERS	NEGATON	NEINEIS
NEBULIZED	NECROSED	NEEDLES	NEGATONS	NEIST
NEBULIZER	NECROSES	NEEDLESS	NEGATOR	NEITHER
NEBULIZES	NECROSING	NEEDLIER	NEGATORS	NEIVE
NEBULOSE	NECROSIS	NEEDLIEST	NEGATORY	NEIVES
NEBULOUS	NECROTIC	NEEDLING	NEGATRON	NEK
NEBULY	NECROTISE	NEEDLINGS	NEGATRONS	NEKS
NECESSARY	NECROTI7F	NEEDLY	NEGLECT	NEKTON
NECESSITY	NECROTOMY	NEEDMENT	NEGLECTED	NEKTONIC
NECK	NECTAR	NEEDMENTS	NEGLECTER	NEKTONS
NECKATEE	NECTAREAL	NEEDS	NEGLECTOR	NELIES
NECKATEES	NECTAREAN	NEEDY	NEGLECTS	NELIS
NECKBAND	NECTARED	NEELD	NEGLIGE	NELLIE
NECKBANDS	NECTARIAL	NEELDS	NEGLIGEE	NELLIES
NECKBEEF	NECTARIED	NEELE	NEGLIGEES	NELLY
NECKBEEFS	NECTARIES	NEELES	NEGLIGENT	NELSON
NECKCLOTH	NECTARINE	NEEM	NEGLIGES	NELSONS
NECKED	NECTAROUS	NEEMB	NEGOCIANT	NELUMBIUM
NECKER	NECTARS	NEEMBS	NEGOTIANT	NELUMBO

NELUMBOS	NEOMORPH	NEP	NERDISH	NERVURE
NEMA	NEOMORPHS	NEPENTHE	NERDS	NERVURES
NEMAS	NEOMYCIN	NEPENTHES	NERDY	NERVY
NEMATIC	NEOMYCINS	NEPER	NEREID	NESCIENCE
NEMATICS	NEON	NEPERS	NEREIDES	NESCIENT
NEMATODE	NEONATAL	NEPETA	NEREIDS	NESCIENTS
NEMATODES	NEONATE	NEPETAS	NEREIS	NESH
NEMATOID	NEONATES	NEPHALISM	NERINE	NESHER
NEMERTEAN	NEONED	NEPHALIST	NERINES	NESHEST
NEMERTIAN	NEONOMIAN	NEPHELINE	NERITE	NESHNESS
NEMERTINE	NEONS	NEPHELITE	NERITES	NESS
NEMESES	NEOPAGAN	NEPHEW	NERITIC	NESSES
NEMESIA	NEOPAGANS	NEPHEWS	NERK	NEST
NEMESIAS	NEOPHILE	NEPHOGRAM	NERKA	NESTABLE
NEMESIS	NEOPHILES	NEPHOLOGY	NERKAS	NESTED
NEMN	NEOPHILIA	NEPHRALGY	NERKS	NESTER
NEMNED	NEOPHOBE	NEPHRIC	NEROL	NESTERS
NEMNING	NEOPHOBES	NEPHRIDIA	NEROLI	NESTFUL
NEMNS	NEOPHOBIA	NEPHRISM	NEROLIS	NESTFULS
NEMOPHILA	NEOPHOBIC	NEPHRISMS	NEROLS	NESTING
NEMORAL	NEOPHYTE	NEPHRITE	NERTS	NESTINGS
NEMOROUS	NEOPHYTES	NEPHRITES	NERTZ	NESTLE
NEMPT	NEOPHYTIC	NEPHRITIC	NERVAL	NESTLED
NENE	NEOPILINA	NEPHRITIS	NERVATE	NESTLER
NENES	NEOPLASIA	NEPHROID	NERVATION	NESTLERS
NENNIGAI	NEOPLASM	NEPHRON	NERVATURE	NESTLES
NENNIGAIS	NEOPLASMS	NEPHRONS	NERVE	NESTLIKE
NENUPHAR	NEOPLASTY	NEPHROSES	NERVED	NESTLING
NENUPHARS	NEOPRENE	NEPHROSIS	NERVELESS	NESTLINGS
NEOBLAST	NEOPRENES	NEPHROTIC	NERVELET	NESTMATE
NEOBLASTS	NEOSOUL	NEPIONIC	NERVELETS	NESTMATES
NEOCON	NEOSOULS	NEPIT	NERVER	NESTOR
NEOCONS	NEOTEINIA	NEPITS	NERVERS	NESTORS
NEOCORTEX	NEOTENIC	NEPOTIC	NERVES	NESTS
NEODYMIUM	NEOTENIES	NEPOTISM	NERVIER	NET
NEOGENE	NEOTENOUS	NEPOTISMS	NERVIEST	NETBALL
NEOGOTHIC	NEOTENY	NEPOTIST	NERVILY	NETBALLER
NEOLITH	NEOTERIC	NEPOTISTS	NERVINE	NETBALLS
NEOLITHIC	NEOTERICS	NEPS	NERVINES	NETBOOK
NEOLITHS	NEOTERISE	NEPTUNIUM	NERVINESS	NETBOOKS
NEOLOGIAN	NEOTERISM	NERAL	NERVING	NETE
NEOLOGIC	NEOTERIST	NERALS	NERVINGS	NETES
NEOLOGIES	NEOTERIZE	NERD	NERVOSITY	NETFUL
NEOLOGISE	NEOTOXIN	NERDIC	NERVOUS	NETFULS
NEOLOGISM	NEOTOXINS	NERDICS	NERVOUSLY	NETHEAD
NEOLOGIST	NEOTROPIC	NERDIER	NERVULAR	NETHEADS
NEOLOGIZE	NEOTYPE	NERDIEST	NERVULE	NETHELESS
NEOLOGY	NEOTYPES	NERDINESS	NERVULES	NETHER

NETIZEN	NEUME	NEURULAE	NEWELS	NEWSMAKER
NETIZENS	NEUMES	NEURULAR	NEWER	NEWSMAN
NETLESS	NEUMIC	NEURULAS	NEWEST	NEWSMEN
NETLIKE	NEUMS	NEUSTIC	NEWFANGLE	NEWSPAPER
NETMINDER	NEURAL	NEUSTICS	NEWFOUND	NEWSPEAK
NETOP	NEURALGIA	NEUSTON	NEWIE	NEWSPEAKS
NETOPS	NEURALGIC	NEUSTONIC	NEWIES	NEWSPRINT
NETROOT	NEURALLY	NEUSTONS	NEWING	NEWSREEL
NETROOTS	NEURATION	NEUTER	NEWISH	NEWSREELS
NETS	NEURAXON	NEUTERED	NEWISHLY	NEWSROOM
NETSPEAK	NEURAXONS	NEUTERING	NEWLY	NEWSROOMS
NETSPEAKS	NEURILITY	NEUTERS	NEWLYWED	NEWSSHEET
NETSUKE	NEURINE	NEUTRAL	NEWLYWEDS	NEWSSTAND
NETSUKES	NEURINES	NEUTRALLY	NEWMARKET	NEWSTRADE
NETSURF	NEURISM	NEUTRALS	NEWMOWN	NEWSWIRE
NETSURFED	NEURISMS	NEUTRETTO	NEWNESS	NEWSWIRES
NETSURFER	NEURITE	NEUTRINO	NEWNESSES	NEWSWOMAN
NETSURFS	NEURITES	NEUTRINOS	NEWS	NEWSWOMEN
NETT	NEURITIC	NEUTRON	NEWSAGENT	NEWSY
NETTABLE	NEURITICS	NEUTRONIC	NEWSBEAT	NEWT
NETTED	NEURITIS	NEUTRONS	NEWSBEATS	NEWTON
NETTER	NEUROCHIP	NEVE	NEWSBOY	NEWTONS
NETTERS	NEUROCOEL	NEVEL	NEWSBOYS	NEWTS
NETTIE	NEUROGLIA	NEVELLED	NEWSBREAK	NEWWAVER
NETTIER	NEUROGRAM	NEVELLING	NEWSCAST	NEWWAVERS
NETTIES	NEUROID	NEVELS	NEWSCASTS	NEXT
NETTIEST	NEUROIDS	NEVER	NEWSCLIP	NEXTDOOR
NETTING	NEUROLOGY	NEVERMIND	NEWSCLIPS	NEXTLY
NETTINGS	NEUROMA	NEVERMORE	NEWSDESK	NEXTNESS
NETTLE	NEUROMAS	NEVES	NEWSDESKS	NEXTS
NETTLED	NEUROMAST	NEVI	NEWSED	NEXUS
NETTLER	NEUROMATA	NEVOID	NEWSES	NEXUSES
NETTLERS	NEURON	NEVUS	NEWSFEED	NGAI
NETTLES	NEURONAL	NEW	NEWSFEEDS	NGAIO
NETTLIER	NEURONE	NEWB	NEWSFLASH	NGAIOS
NETTLIEST	NEURONES	NEWBIE	NEWSGIRL	NGANA
NETTLING	NEURONIC	NEWBIES	NEWSGIRLS	NGANAS
NETTLY	NEURONS	NEWBORN	NEWSGROUP	NGARARA
NETTS	NEUROPATH	NEWBORNS	NEWSHAWK	NGARARAS
NETTY	NEUROPIL	NEWBS	NEWSHAWKS	NGATI
NETWORK	NEUROPILS	NEWCOME	NEWSHOUND	NGATIS
NETWORKED	NEUROSAL	NEWCOMER	NEWSIE	NGOMA
NETWORKER	NEUROSES	NEWCOMERS	NEWSIER	NGOMAS
NETWORKS	NEUROSIS	NEWED	NEWSIES	NGULTRUM
NEUK	NEUROTIC	NEWEL	NEWSIEST	NGULTRUMS
NEUKS	NEUROTICS	NEWELL	NEWSINESS	NGWEE
NEUM	NEUROTOMY	NEWELLED	NEWSING	NGWEES
NEUMATIC	NEURULA	NEWELLS	NEWSLESS	NHANDU

NHANDUS	NICISH	NICOTINS	NIEFS	NIGGERING
NIACIN	NICK	NICTATE	NIELLATED	NIGGERISH
NIACINS	NICKAR	NICTATED	NIELLI	NIGGERISM
NIAGARA	NICKARS	NICTATES	NIELLIST	NIGGERS
NIAGARAS	NICKED	NICTATING	NIELLISTS	NIGGERY
NIAISERIE	NICKEL	NICTATION	NIELLO	NIGGLE
NIALAMIDE	NICKELED	NICTITANT	NIELLOED	NIGGLED
NIB	NICKELIC	NICTITATE	NIELLOING	NIGGLER
NIBBED	NICKELINE	NID	NIELLOS	NIGGLERS
NIBBING	NICKELING	NIDAL	NIENTE	NIGGLES
NIBBLE	NICKELISE	NIDAMENTA	NIES	NIGGLIER
NIBBLED	NICKELIZE	NIDATE	NIEVE	NIGGLIEST
NIBBLER	NICKELLED	NIDATED	NIEVEFUL	NIGGLING
NIBBLERS	NICKELOUS	NIDATES	NIEVEFULS	NIGGLINGS
NIBBLES	NICKELS	NIDATING	NIEVES	NIGGLY
NIBBLIES	NICKER	NIDATION	NIFE	NIGH
NIBBLING	NICKERED	NIDATIONS	NIFES	NIGHED
NIBBLINGS	NICKERING	NIDDERING	NIFF	NIGHER
NIBBLY	NICKERNUT	NIDDICK	NIFFED	NIGHEST
NIBLET	NICKERS	NIDDICKS	NIFFER	NIGHING
NIBLETS	NICKING	NIDE	NIFFERED	NIGHLY
NIBLICK	NICKLE	NIDED	NIFFERING	NIGHNESS
NIBLICKS	NICKLED	NIDERING	NIFFERS	NIGHS
NIBLIKE	NICKLES	NIDERINGS	NIFFIER	NIGHT
NIBS	NICKLING	NIDERLING	NIFFIEST	NIGHTBIRD
NICAD	NICKNACK	NIDES	NIFFING	NIGHTCAP
NICADS	NICKNACKS	NIDGET	NIFFNAFF	NIGHTCAPS
NICCOLITE	NICKNAME	NIDGETED	NIFFNAFFS	NIGHTCLUB
NICE	NICKNAMED	NIDGETING	NIFFS	NIGHTED
NICEISH	NICKNAMER	NIDGETS	NIFFY	NIGHTFALL
NICELY	NICKNAMES	NIDI	NIFTIER	NIGHTFIRE
NICENESS	NICKPOINT	NIDIFIED	NIFTIES	NIGHTGEAR
NICER	NICKS	NIDIFIES	NIFTIEST	NIGHTGLOW
NICEST	NICKSTICK	NIDIFY	NIFTILY	NIGHTGOWN
NICETIES	NICKUM	NIDIFYING	NIFTINESS	NIGHTHAWK
NICETY	NICKUMS	NIDING	NIFTY	NIGHTIE
NICHE	NICOISE	NIDINGS	NIGELLA	NIGHTIES
NICHED	NICOL	NIDOR	NIGELLAS	NIGHTJAR
NICHER	NICOLS	NIDOROUS	NIGER	NIGHTJARS
NICHERED	NICOMPOOP	NIDORS	NIGERS	NIGHTLESS
NICHERING	NICOTIAN	NIDS	NIGGARD	NIGHTLIFE
NICHERS	NICOTIANA	NIDUS	NIGGARDED	NIGHTLIKE
NICHES	NICOTIANS	NIDUSES	NIGGARDLY	NIGHTLONG
NICHING	NICOTIN	NIE	NIGGARDS	NIGHTLY
NICHROME	NICOTINE	NIECE	NIGGER	NIGHTMARE
NICHROMES	NICOTINED	NIECES	NIGGERDOM	NIGHTMARY
NICHT	NICOTINES	NIED	NIGGERED	NIGHTS
NICHTS	NICOTINIC	NIEF	NIGGERIER	NIGHTSIDE

NIGHTSPOT	NIM	NINETIES	NIPTER	NITID
NIGHTTIDE	NIMB	NINETIETH	NIPTERS	NITINOL
NIGHTTIME	NIMBED	NINETY	NIQAAB	NITINOLS
NIGHTWARD	NIMBI	NINHYDRIN	NIQAABS	NITON
NIGHTWEAR	NIMBLE	NINJA	NIQAB	NITONS
NIGHTY	NIMBLER	NINJAS	NIQABS	NITPICK
NIGIRI	NIMBLESSE	NINJITSU	NIRAMIAI	NITPICKED
NIGIRIS	NIMBLEST	NINJITSUS	NIRAMIAIS	NITPICKER
NIGRICANT	NIMBLEWIT	NINJUTSU	NIRL	NITPICKS
NIGRIFIED	NIMBLY	NINJUTSUS	NIRLED	NITPICKY
NIGRIFIES	NIMBS	NINNIES	NIRLIE	NITRAMINE
NIGRIFY	NIMBUS	NINNY	NIRLIER	NITRATE
NIGRITUDE	NIMBUSED	NINNYISH	NIRLIEST	NITRATED
NIGROSIN	NIMBUSES	NINON	NIRLING	NITRATES
NIGROSINE	NIMBYISM	NINONS	NIRLIT	NITRATINE
NIGROSINS	NIMBYISMS	NINTH	NIRLS	NITRATING
NIHIL	NIMBYNESS	NINTHLY	NIRLY	NITRATION
NIHILISM	NIMIETIES	NINTHS	NIRVANA	NITRATOR
NIHILISMS	NIMIETY	NIOBATE	NIRVANAS	NITRATORS
NIHILIST	NIMIOUS	NIOBATES	NIRVANIC	NITRE
NIHILISTS	NIMMED	NIOBIC	NIS	NITREOUS
NIHILITY	NIMMER	NIOBITE	NISBERRY	NITRES
NIHILS	NIMMERS	NIOBITES	NISEI	NITRIC
NIHONGA	NIMMING	NIOBIUM	NISEIS	NITRID
NIHONGAS	NIMONIC	NIOBIUMS	NISGUL	NITRIDE
NIHONIUM	NIMPS	NIOBOUS	NISGULS	NITRIDED
NIHONIUMS	NIMROD	NIP	NISH	NITRIDES
NIKAB	NIMRODS	NIPA	NISHES	NITRIDING
NIKABS	NIMS	NIPAS	NISI	NITRIDS
NIKAH	NINCOM	NIPCHEESE	NISSE	NITRIFIED
NIKAHS	NINCOMS	NIPPED	NISSES	NITRIFIER
NIKAU	NINCUM	NIPPER	NISUS	NITRIFIES
NIKAUS	NINCUMS	NIPPERED	NIT	NITRIFY
NIL	NINE	NIPPERING	NITCHIE	NITRIL
NILGAI	NINEBARK	NIPPERKIN	NITCHIES	NITRILE
NILGAIS	NINEBARKS	NIPPERS	NITE	NITRILES
NILGAU	NINEFOLD	NIPPIER	NITER	NITRILS
NTLGAUS	NINEHOLES	NIPPIEST	NITERIE	NITRITE
NILGHAI	NINEPENCE	NIPPILY	NITERIES	NITRITES
NILGHAIS	NINEPENNY	NIPPINESS	NITERS	NITRO
NILGHAU	NINEPIN	NIPPING	NITERY	NITROGEN
NILGHAUS	NINEPINS	NIPPINGLY	NITES	NITROGENS
NILL	NINER	NIPPLE	NITHER	NITROLIC
NILLED	NINERS	NIPPLED	NITHERED	NITROS
NILLING	NINES	NIPPLES	NITHERING	NITROSO
NILLS	NINESCORE	NIPPLING	NITHERS	NITROSYL
NILPOTENT	NINETEEN	NIPPY	NITHING	NITROSYLS
NILS	NINETEENS	NIPS	NITHINGS	NITROUS

NITROX	NOBBUT	NOCTUOID	NODULE	NOISES
NITROXES	NOBBY	NOCTUOIDS	NODULED	NOISETTE
NITROXYL	NOBELIUM	NOCTURIA	NODULES	NOISETTES
NITROXYLS	NOBELIUMS	NOCTURIAS	NODULOSE	NOISIER
NITRY	NOBILESSE	NOCTURN	NODULOUS	NOISIEST
NITRYL	NOBILIARY	NOCTURNAL	NODUS	NOISILY
NITRYLS	NOBILITY	NOCTURNE	NOEL	NOISINESS
NITS	NOBLE	NOCTURNES	NOELS	NOISING
NITTIER	NOBLEMAN	NOCTURNS	NOES	NOISOME
NITTIEST	NOBLEMEN	NOCUOUS	NOESES	NOISOMELY
NITTY	NOBLENESS	NOCUOUSLY	NOESIS	NOISY
NITWIT	NOBLER	NOD	NOESISES	NOLE
NITWITS	NOBLES	NODAL	NOETIC	NOLES
NITWITTED	NOBLESSE	NODALISE	NOG	NOLITION
NIVAL	NOBLESSES	NODALISED	NOGAKU	NOLITIONS
NIVATION	NOBLEST	NODALISES	NOGG	NOLL
NIVATIONS	NOBLY	NODALITY	NOGGED	NOLLS
NIVEOUS	NOBODIES	NODALIZE	NOGGIN	NOLO
NIX	NOBODY	NODALIZED	NOGGING	NOLOS
NIXE	NOBS	NODALIZES	NOGGINGS	NOM
NIXED	NOCAKE	NODALLY	NOGGINS	NOMA
NIXER	NOCAKES	NODATED	NOGGS	NOMAD
NIXERS	NOCEBO	NODATION	NOGOODNIK	NOMADE
NIXES	NOCEBOS	NODATIONS	NOGS	NOMADES
NIXIE	NOCENT	NODDED	NOH	NOMADIC
NIXIES	NOCENTLY	NODDER	NOHOW	NOMADIES
NIXING	NOCENTS	NODDERS	NOHOWISH	NOMADISE
NIXY	NOCHEL	NODDIER	NOIL	NOMADISED
NIZAM	NOCHELED	NODDIES	NOILIER	NOMADISES
NIZAMATE	NOCHELING	NODDIEST	NOILIES	NOMADISM
NIZAMATES	NOCHELLED	NODDING	NOILIEST	NOMADISMS
NIZAMS	NOCHELS	NODDINGLY	NOILS	NOMADIZE
NKOSI	NOCK	NODDINGS	NOILY	NOMADIZED
NKOSIS	NOCKED	NODDLE	NOINT	NOMADIZES
NO	NOCKET	NODDLED	NOINTED	NOMADS
NOAH	NOCKETS	NODDLES	NOINTER	NOMADY
NOAHS	NOCKING	NODDLING	NOINTERS	NOMARCH
NOB	NOCKS	NODDY	NOINTING	NOMARCHS
NOBBIER	NOCTILIO	NODE	NOINTS	NOMARCHY
NOBBIEST	NOCTILIOS	NODES	NOIR	NOMAS
NOBBILY	NOCTILUCA	NODI	NOIRISH	NOMBLES
NOBBINESS	NOCTUA	NODICAL	NOIRS	NOMBRIL
NOBBLE	NOCTUARY	NODOSE	NOISE	NOMBRILS
NOBBLED	NOCTUAS	NODOSITY	NOISED	NOME
NOBBLER	NOCTUID	NODOUS	NOISEFUL	NOMEN
NOBBLERS	NOCTUIDS	NODS	NOISELESS	NOMENS
NOBBLES	NOCTULE	NODULAR	NOISENIK	NOMES
NOBBLING	NOCTULES	NODULATED	NOISENIKS	NOMIC

NOMINA	NONANSWER	NONCOM	NONETTES	NONGOLFER
NOMINABLE	NONARABLE	NONCOMBAT	NONETTI	NONGRADED
NOMINAL	NONARIES	NONCOMS	NONETTO	NONGREASY
NOMINALLY	NONART	NONCONCUR	NONETTOS	NONGREEN
NOMINALS	NONARTIST	NONCORE	NONEVENT	NONGROWTH
NOMINATE	NONARTS	NONCOUNT	NONEVENTS	NONGS
NOMINATED	NONARY	NONCOUNTY	NONEXEMPT	NONGUEST
NOMINATES	NONAS	NONCREDIT	NONEXOTIC	NONGUESTS
NOMINATOR	NONATOMIC	NONCRIME	NONEXPERT	NONGUILT
NOMINEE	NONAUTHOR	NONCRIMES	NONEXTANT	NONGUILTS
NOMINEES	NONAVIAN	NONCRISES	NONFACT	NONHARDY
NOMISM	NONBANK	NONCRISIS	NONFACTOR	NONHEME
NOMISMS	NONBANKS	NONCYCLIC	NONFACTS	NONHERO
NOMISTIC	NONBASIC	NONDAIRY	NONFADING	NONHEROES
NOMOCRACY	NONBEING	NONDANCE	NONFAMILY	NONHEROIC
NOMOGENY	NONBEINGS	NONDANCER	NONFAN	NONHOME
NOMOGRAM	NONBELIEF	NONDANCES	NONFANS	NONHUMAN
NOMOGRAMS	NONBINARY	NONDEALER	NONFARM	NONHUMANS
NOMOGRAPH	NONBITING	NONDEGREE	NONFARMER	NONHUNTER
NOMOI	NONBLACK	NONDEMAND	NONFAT	NONI
NOMOLOGIC	NONBLACKS	NONDESERT	NONFATAL	NONIDEAL
NOMOLOGY	NONBODIES	NONDOCTOR	NONFATTY	NONILLION
NOMOS	NONBODY	NONDOLLAR	NONFEUDAL	NONIMAGE
NOMOTHETE	NONBONDED	NONDRIP	NONFILIAL	NONIMAGES
NOMS	NONBOOK	NONDRIVER	NONFINAL	NONIMMUNE
NON	NONBOOKS	NONDRUG	NONFINITE	NONIMPACT
NONA	NONBRAND	NONDRYING	NONFISCAL	NONINERT
NONACID	NONBUYING	NONE	NONFLUID	NONINJURY
NONACIDIC	NONCAKING	NONEDIBLE	NONFLUIDS	NONINSECT
NONACIDS	NONCAMPUS	NONEGO	NONFLYING	NONIONIC
NONACTING	NONCAREER	NONEGOS	NONFOCAL	NONIRON
NONACTION	NONCASH	NONELECT	NONFOOD	NONIS
NONACTIVE	NONCASUAL	NONELECTS	NONFOODS	NONISSUE
NONACTOR	NONCAUSAL	NONELITE	NONFORMAL	NONISSUES
NONACTORS	NONCE	NONEMPTY	NONFOSSIL	NONJOINER
NONADDICT	NONCEREAL	NONENDING	NONFROZEN	NONJURIES
NONADULT	NONCES	NONENERGY	NONFUEL	NONJURING
NONADULTS	NONCHURCH	NONENTITY	NONFUELS	NONJUROR
NONAGE	NONCLASS	NONENTRY	NONFUNDED	NONJURORS
NONAGED	NONCLING	NONEQUAL	NONG	NONJURY
NONAGES	NONCODING	NONEQUALS	NONGAME	NONKIN
NONAGON	NONCOITAL	NONEROTIC	NONGAY	NONKINS
NONAGONAL	NONCOKING	NONES	NONGAYS	NONKOSHER
NONAGONS	NONCOLA	NONESUCH	NONGHETTO	NONLABOR
NONANE	NONCOLAS	NONET	NONGLARE	NONLABOUR
NONANES	NONCOLOR	NONETHNIC	NONGLARES	NONLAWYER
NONANIMAL	NONCOLORS	NONETS	NONGLAZED	NONLEADED
NONANOIC	NONCOLOUR	NONETTE	NONGLOSSY	NONLEAFY

N

NONLEAGUE	NONNEWS	NONPROFIT	NONSOLIDS	NONUSABLE
NONLEGAL	NONNIES	NONPROS	NONSPEECH	NONUSE
NONLEGUME	NONNOBLE	NONPROVEN	NONSTAPLE	NONUSER
NONLETHAL	NONNORMAL	NONPUBLIC	NONSTATE	NONUSERS
NONLEVEL	NONNOVEL	NONQUOTA	NONSTATIC	NONUSES
NONLIABLE	NONNOVELS	NONRACIAL	NONSTEADY	NONUSING
NONLIFE	NONNY	NONRACISM	NONSTICK	NONVACANT
NONLINEAL	NONOBESE	NONRANDOM	NONSTICKY	NONVALID
NONLINEAR	NONOHMIC	NONRATED	NONSTOP	NONVECTOR
NONLIQUID	NONOILY	NONREADER	NONSTOPS	NONVENOUS
NONLIVES	NONORAL	NONRETURN	NONSTORY	NONVERBAL
NONLIVING	NONORALLY	NONRHOTIC	NONSTYLE	NONVESTED
NONLOCAL	NONOWNER	NONRIGID	NONSTYLES	NONVIABLE
NONLOCALS	NONOWNERS	NONRIOTER	NONSUCH	NONVIEWER
NONLOVING	NONPAGAN	NONRIVAL	NONSUCHES	NONVIRAL
NONLOYAL	NONPAGANS	NONRIVALS	NONSUGAR	NONVIRGIN
NONLYRIC	NONPAID	NONROYAL	NONSUGARS	NONVIRILE
NONMAJOR	NONPAPAL	NONROYALS	NONSUIT	NONVISUAL
NONMAJORS	NONPAPIST	NONRUBBER	NONSUITED	NONVITAL
NONMAN	NONPAR	NONRULING	NONSUITS	NONVOCAL
NONMANUAL	NONPAREIL	NONRUN	NONSYSTEM	NONVOCALS
NONMARKET	NONPARENT	NONRUNNER	NONTALKER	NONVOTER
NONMATURE	NONPARITY	NONRURAL	NONTARGET	NONVOTERS
NONMEAT	NONPAROUS	NONSACRED	NONTARIFF	NONVOTING
NONMEATS	NONPARTY	NONSALINE	NONTAX	NONWAGE
NONMEMBER	NONPAST	NONSCHOOL	NONTAXES	NONWAR
NONMEN	NONPASTS	NONSECRET	NONTHEISM	NONWARS
NONMENTAL	NONPAYING	NONSECURE	NONTHEIST	NONWHITE
NONMETAL	NONPEAK	NONSELF	NONTIDAL	NONWHITES
NONMETALS	NONPEAKS	NONSELVES	NONTITLE	NONWINGED
NONMETRIC	NONPERSON	NONSENSE	NONTONAL	NONWOODY
NONMETRO	NONPLANAR	NONSENSES	NONTONIC	NONWOOL
NONMOBILE	NONPLAY	NONSERIAL	NONTOXIC	NONWORD
NONMODAL	NONPLAYER	NONSEXIST	NONTOXICS	NONWORDS
NONMODERN	NONPLAYS	NONSEXUAL	NONTRAGIC	NONWORK
NONMONEY	NONPLIANT	NONSHRINK	NONTRIBAL	NONWORKER
NONMORAL	NONPLUS	NONSIGNER	NONTRUMP	NONWORKS
NONMORTAL	NONPLUSED	NONSKATER	NONTRUTH	NONWOVEN
NONMOTILE	NONPLUSES	NONSKED	NONTRUTHS	NONWOVENS
NONMOVING	NONPOETIC	NONSKEDS	NONUNION	NONWRITER
NONMUSIC	NONPOINT	NONSKID	NONUNIONS	NONYL
NONMUSICS	NONPOLAR	NONSKIER	NONUNIQUE	NONYLS
NONMUTANT	NONPOLICE	NONSKIERS	NONUPLE	NONZERO
NONMUTUAL	NONPOOR	NONSLIP	NONUPLES	NOO
NONNASAL	NONPOORS	NONSMOKER	NONUPLET	NOOB
NONNATIVE	NONPOROUS	NONSOCIAL	NONUPLETS	NOOBS
NONNAVAL	NONPOSTAL	NONSOLAR	NONURBAN	NOODGE
NONNEURAL	NONPRINT	NONSOLID	NONURGENT	NOODGED

NOODGES	NOPALITO	NORTENO	NOSH	NOTARIES
NOODGING	NOPALITOS	NORTENOS	NOSHED	NOTARISE
NOODLE	NOPALS	NORTH	NOSHER	NOTARISED
NOODLED	NOPE	NORTHEAST	NOSHERIE	NOTARISES
NOODLEDOM	NOPLACE	NORTHED	NOSHERIES	NOTARIZE
NOODLES	NOR	NORTHER	NOSHERS	NOTARIZED
NOODLING	NORDIC	NORTHERED	NOSHERY	NOTARIZES
NOODLINGS	NORDICITY	NORTHERLY	NOSHES	NOTARY
NOOGIE	NORI	NORTHERN	NOSHING	NOTATE
NOOGIES	NORIA	NORTHERNS	NOSIER	NOTATED
NOOIT	NORIAS	NORTHERS	NOSIES	NOTATES
NOOK	NORIMON	NORTHING	NOSIEST	NOTATING
NOOKIE	NORIMONS	NORTHINGS	NOSILY	NOTATION
NOOKIER	NORIS	NORTHLAND	NOSINESS	NOTATIONS
NOOKIES	NORITE	NORTHMOST	NOSING	NOTATOR
NOOKIEST	NORITES	NORTHS	NOSINGS	NOTATORS
NOOKLIKE	NORITIC	NORTHWARD	NOSODE	NOTCH
NOOKS	NORK	NORTHWEST	NOSODES	NOTCHBACK
NOOKY	NORKS	NORWARD	NOSOLOGIC	NOTCHED
NOOLOGIES	NORLAND	NORWARDS	NOSOLOGY	NOTCHEL
NOOLOGY	NORLANDS	NOS	NOSTALGIA	NOTCHELED
NOOMETRY	NORM	NOSE	NOSTALGIC	NOTCHELS
NOON	NORMA	NOSEAN	NOSTOC	NOTCHER
NOONDAY	NORMAL	NOSEANS	NOSTOCS	NOTCHERS
NOONDAYS	NORMALCY	NOSEBAG	NOSTOI	NOTCHES
NOONED	NORMALISE	NOSEBAGS	NOSTOLOGY	NOTCHIER
NOONER	NORMALITY	NOSEBAND	NOSTOS	NOTCHIEST
NOONERS	NORMALIZE	NOSEBANDS	NOSTRIL	NOTCHING
NOONING	NORMALLY	NOSEBLEED	NOSTRILS	NOTCHINGS
NOONINGS	NORMALS	NOSED	NOSTRO	NOTCHY
NOONS	NORMAN	NOSEDIVE	NOSTRUM	NOTE
NOONTIDE	NORMANDE	NOSEDIVED	NOSTRUMS	NOTEBANDI
NOONTIDES	NORMANDES	NOSEDIVES	NOSY	NOTEBOOK
NOONTIME	NORMANS	NOSEDOVE	NOT	NOTEBOOKS
NOONTIMES	NORMAS	NOSEGAY	NOTA	NOTECARD
NOOP	NORMATIVE	NOSEGAYS	NOTABILIA	NOTECARDS
NOOPS	NORMCORE	NOSEGUARD	NOTABLE	NOTECASE
NOOSE	NORMCORES	NOSELESS	NOTABLES	NOTECASES
NOOSED	NORMED	NOSELIKE	NOTABLY	NOTED
NOOSELIKE	NORMLESS	NOSELITE	NOTAEUM	NOTEDLY
NOOSER	NORMS	NOSELITES	NOTAEUMS	NOTEDNESS
NOOSERS	NOROVIRUS	NOSEPIECE	NOTAIRE	NOTELESS
NOOSES	NORSEL	NOSER	NOTAIRES	NOTELET
NOOSING	NORSELLED	NOSERS	NOTAL	NOTELETS
NOOSPHERE	NORSELLER	NOSES	NOTANDA	NOTEPAD
NOOTROPIC	NORSELS	NOSEWHEEL	NOTANDUM	NOTEPADS
NOPAL	NORTENA	NOSEY	NOTAPHILY	NOTEPAPER
NOPALES	NORTENAS	NOSEYS	NOTARIAL	NOTER

NOTERS	NOUMENON	NOVELDOM	NOW	NTH
NOTES	NOUN	NOVELDOMS	NOWADAYS	NU
NOTHER	NOUNAL	NOVELESE	NOWAY	NUANCE
NOTHING	NOUNALLY	NOVELESES	NOWAYS	NUANCED
NOTHINGS	NOUNIER	NOVELETTE	NOWCAST	NUANCES
NOTICE	NOUNIEST	NOVELISE	NOWCASTS	NUANCING
NOTICED	NOUNLESS	NOVELISED	NOWED	NUB
NOTICER	NOUNS	NOVELISER	NOWHENCE	NUBBED
NOTICERS	NOUNY	NOVELISES	NOWHERE	NUBBER
NOTICES	NOUP	NOVELISH	NOWHERES	NUBBERS
NOTICING	NOUPS	NOVELISM	NOWHITHER	NUBBIER
NOTIFIED	NOURICE	NOVELISMS	NOWISE	NUBBIEST
NOTIFIER	NOURICES	NOVELIST	NOWL	NUBBIN
NOTIFIERS	NOURISH	NOVELISTS	NOWLS	NUBBINESS
NOTIFIES	NOURISHED	NOVELIZE	NOWN	NUBBING
NOTIFY	NOURISHER	NOVELIZED	NOWNESS	NUBBINGS
NOTIFYING	NOURISHES	NOVELIZER	NOWNESSES	NUBBINS
NOTING	NOURITURE	NOVELIZES	NOWS	NUBBLE
NOTION	NOURSLE	NOVELLA	NOWT	NUBBLED
NOTIONAL	NOURSLED	NOVELLAE	NOWTIER	NUBBLES
NOTIONIST	NOURSLES	NOVELLAS	NOWTIEST	NUBBLIER
NOTIONS	NOURSLING	NOVELLE	NOWTS	NUBBLIEST
NOTITIA	NOUS	NOVELLY	NOWTY	NUBBLING
NOTITIAE	NOUSELL	NOVELS	NOWY	NUBBLY
NOTITIAS	NOUSELLED	NOVELTIES	NOX	NUBBY
NOTOCHORD	NOUSELLS	NOVELTY	NOXAL	NUBECULA
NOTORIETY	NOUSES	NOVEMBER	NOXES	NUBECULAE
NOTORIOUS	NOUSLE	NOVEMBERS	NOXIOUS	NUBIA
NOTORNIS	NOUSLED	NOVENA	NOXIOUSLY	NUBIAS
NOTOUR	NOUSLES	NOVENAE	NOY	NUBIFORM
NOTT	NOUSLING	NOVENARY	NOYADE	NUBILE
NOTTURNI	NOUT	NOVENAS	NOYADES	NUBILITY
NOTTURNO	NOUVEAU	NOVENNIAL	NOYANCE	NUBILOSE
NOTUM	NOUVEAUX	NOVERCAL	NOYANCES	NUBILOUS
NOUGAT	NOUVELLE	NOVERINT	NOYAU	NUBS
NOUGATINE	NOUVELLES	NOVERINTS	NOYAUS	NUBUCK
NOUGATS	NOVA	NOVICE	NOYAUX	NUBUCKS
NOUGHT	NOVAE	NOVICES	NOYED	NUCELLAR
NOUGHTIES	NOVALIA	NOVICHOK	NOYES	NUCELLI
NOUGHTS	NOVALIKE	NOVICHOKS	NOYESES	NUCELLUS
NOUL	NOVAS	NOVICIATE	NOYING	NUCHA
NOULD	NOVATE	NOVITIATE	NOYOUS	NUCHAE
NOULDE	NOVATED	NOVITIES	NOYS	NUCHAL
NOULE	NOVATES	NOVITY	NOYSOME	NUCHALS
NOULES	NOVATING	NOVOCAINE	NOZZER	NUCLEAL
NOULS	NOVATION	NOVODAMUS	NOZZERS	NUCLEAR
NOUMENA	NOVATIONS	NOVUM	NOZZLE	NUCLEASE
NOUMENAL	NOVEL	NOVUMS	NOZZLES	NUCLEASES

NUCLEATE	NUDISMS	NULLINGS	NUMERICAL	NUNNISH
NUCLEATED	NUDIST	NULLIPARA	NUMERICS	NUNNY
NUCLEATES	NUDISTS	NULLIPORE	NUMEROUS	NUNS
NUCLEATOR	NUDITIES	NULLITIES	NUMINA	NUNSHIP
NUCLEI	NUDITY	NULLITY	NUMINOUS	NUNSHIPS
NUCLEIC	NUDNICK	NULLNESS	NUMMARY	NUPTIAL
NUCLEIDE	NUDNICKS	NULLS	NUMMIER	NUPTIALLY
NUCLEIDES	NUDNIK	NUMB	NUMMIEST	NUPTIALS
NUCLEIN	NUDNIKS	NUMBAT	NUMMULAR	NUR
NUCLEINIC	NUDZH	NUMBATS	NUMMULARY	NURAGHE
NUCLEINS	NUDZHED	NUMBED	NUMMULINE	NURAGHI
NUCLEOID	NUDZHES	NUMBER	NUMMULITE	NURAGHIC
NUCLEOIDS	NUDZHING	NUMBERED	NUMMY	NURD
NUCLEOLAR	NUFF	NUMBERER	NUMNAH	NURDIER
NUCLEOLE	NUFFIN	NUMBERERS	NUMNAHS	NURDIEST
NUCLEOLES	NUFFINS	NUMBERING	NUMPKIN	NURDISH
NUCLEOLI	NUFFS	NUMBERS	NUMPKINS	NURDLE
NUCLEOLUS	NUG	NUMBEST	NUMPTIES	NURDLED
NUCLEON	NUGAE	NUMBFISH	NUMPTY	NURDLES
NUCLEONIC	NUGATORY	NUMBHEAD	NUMSKULL	NURDLING
NUCLEONS	NUGGAR	NUMBHEADS	NUMSKULLS	NURDS
NUCLEUS	NUGGARS	NUMBING	NUN	NURDY
NUCLEUSES	NUGGET	NUMBINGLY	NUNATAK	NURHAG
NUCLIDE	NUGGETED	NUMBLES	NUNATAKER	NURHAGS
NUCLIDES	NUGGETIER	NUMBLY	NUNATAKS	NURL
NUCLIDIC	NUGGETING	NUMBNESS	NUNCHAKU	NURLED
NUCULE	NUGGETS	NUMBNUT	NUNCHAKUS	NURLING
NUCULES	NUGGETTED	NUMBNUTS	NUNCHEON	NURLS
NUDATION	NUGGETY	NUMBS	NUNCHEONS	NURR
NUDATIONS	NUGS	NUMBSKULL	NUNCHUCK	NURRS
NUDDIES	NUISANCE	NUMCHUCK	NUNCHUCKS	NURS
NUDDY	NUISANCER	NUMCHUCKS	NUNCHUK	NURSE
NUDE	NUISANCES	NUMDAH	NUNCHUKS	NURSED
NUDELY	NUKE	NUMDAHS	NUNCIO	NURSELIKE
NUDENESS	NUKED	NUMEN	NUNCIOS	NURSELING
NUDER	NUKES	NUMERABLE	NUNCLE	NURSEMAID
NUDES	NUKING	NUMERABLY	NUNCLES	NURSER
NUDEST	NULL	NUMERACY	NUNCUPATE	NURSERIES
NUDGE	NULLA	NUMERAIRE	NUNDINAL	NURSERS
NUDGED	NULLAH	NUMERAL	NUNDINALS	NURSERY
NUDGER	NULLAHS	NUMERALLY	NUNDINE	NURSES
NUDGERS	NULLAS	NUMERALS	NUNDINES	NURSING
NUDGES	NULLED	NUMERARY	NUNHOOD	NURSINGS
NUDGING	NULLIFIED	NUMERATE	NUNHOODS	NURSLE
NUDICAUL	NULLIFIER	NUMERATED	NUNLIKE	NURSLED
NUDIE	NULLIFIES	NUMERATES	NUNNATION	NURSLES
NUDIES	NULLIFY	NUMERATOR	NUNNERIES	NURSLING
NUDISM	NULLING	NUMERIC	NUNNERY	NURSLINGS

NURTURAL	NUTHOUSES	NUTSHELLS	NYAFFING	NYMPHAEAS
NURTURANT	NUTJOB	NUTSIER	NYAFFS	NYMPHAEUM
NURTURE	NUTJOBBER	NUTSIEST	NYAH	NYMPHAL
NURTURED	NUTJOBS	NUTSO	NYALA	NYMPHALID
NURTURER	NUTLET	NUTSOS	NYALAS	NYMPHEAN
NURTURERS	NUTLETS	NUTSY	NYANZA	NYMPHED
NURTURES	NUTLIKE	NUTTED	NYANZAS	NYMPHET
NURTURING	NUTLOAF	NUTTER	NYAOPE	NYMPHETIC
NUS	NUTLOAVES	NUTTERIES	NYAOPES	NYMPHETS
NUT	NUTMEAL	NUTTERS	NYAS	NYMPHETTE
NUTANT	NUTMEALS	NUTTERY	NYASES	NYMPHIC
NUTARIAN	NUTMEAT	NUTTIER	NYBBLE	NYMPHICAL
NUTARIANS	NUTMEATS	NUTTIEST	NYBBLES	NYMPHING
NUTATE	NUTMEG	NUTTILY	NYCTALOPE	NYMPHISH
NUTATED	NUTMEGGED	NUTTINESS	NYCTALOPS	NYMPHLIER
NUTATES	NUTMEGGY	NUTTING	NYE	NYMPHLIKE
NUTATING	NUTMEGS	NUTTINGS	NYED	NYMPHLY
NUTATION	NUTPECKER	NUTTY	NYES	NYMPHO
NUTATIONS	NUTPICK	NUTWOOD	NYING	NYMPHOS
NUTBAR	NUTPICKS	NUTWOODS	NYLGHAI	NYMPHS
NUTBARS	NUTRIA	NUZZER	NYLGHAIS	NYS
NUTBROWN	NUTRIAS	NUZZERS	NYLGHAU	NYSSA
NUTBUTTER	NUTRIENT	NUZZLE	NYLGHAUS	NYSSAS
NUTCASE	NUTRIENTS	NUZZLED	NYLON	NYSTAGMIC
NUTCASES	NUTRIMENT	NUZZLER	NYLONED	NYSTAGMUS
NUTGALL	NUTRITION	NUZZLERS	NYLONS	NYSTATIN
NUTGALLS	NUTRITIVE	NUZZLES	NYM	NYSTATINS
NUTGRASS	NUTS	NUZZLING	NYMPH	
NUTHATCH	NUTSEDGE	NY	NYMPHA	
NUTHIN	NUTSEDGES	NYAFF	NYMPHAE	
NUTHOUSE	NUTSHELL	NYAFFED	NYMPHAEA	

O

OAF	OARS	OBDURATED	OBESE	OBJETS
OAFISH	OARSMAN	OBDURATES	OBESELY	OBJURE
OAFISHLY	OARSMEN	OBDURE	OBESENESS	OBJURED
OAFS	OARSWOMAN	OBDURED	OBESER	OBJURES
OAK	OARSWOMEN	OBDURES	OBESEST	OBJURGATE
OAKED	OARWEED	OBDURING	OBESITIES	OBJURING
OAKEN	OARWEEDS	OBE	OBESITY	OBLAST
OAKENSHAW	OARY	OBEAH	OBESOGEN	OBLASTI
OAKER	OASES	OBEAHED	OBESOGENS	OBLASTS
OAKERS	OASIS	OBEAHING	OBEY	OBLATE
OAKIER	OAST	OBEAHISM	OBEYABLE	OBLATELY
OAKIES	OASTHOUSE	OBEAHISMS	OBEYED	OBLATES
OAKIEST	OASTS	OBEAHS	OBEYER	OBLATION
OAKINESS	OAT	OBECHE	OBEYERS	OBLATIONS
OAKLEAF	OATCAKE	OBECHES	OBEYING	OBLATORY
OAKLEAVES	OATCAKES	OBEDIENCE	OBEYS	OBLIGABLE
OAKLIKE	OATEN	OBEDIENT	OBFUSCATE	OBLIGANT
OAKLING	OATER	OBEISANCE	OBI	OBLIGANTS
OAKLINGS	OATERS	OBEISANT	OBIA	OBLIGATE
OAKMOSS	OATH	OBEISM	OBIAS	OBLIGATED
OAKMOSSES	OATHABLE	OBEISMS	OBIED	OBLIGATES
OAKS	OATHS	OBELI	OBIING	OBLIGATI
OAKUM	OATIER	OBELIA	OBIISM	OBLIGATO
OAKUMS	OATIEST	OBELIAS	OBIISMS	OBLIGATOR
OAKWOOD	OATLIKE	OBELION	OBIIT	OBLIGATOS
OAKWOODS	OATMEAL	OBELISCAL	OBIS	OBLIGE
OAKY	OATMEALS	OBELISE	OBIT	OBLIGED
OANSHAGH	OATS	OBELISED	OBITAL	OBLIGEE
OANSHAGHS	OATY	OBELISES	OBITER	OBLIGEES
OAR	OAVES	OBELISING	OBITS	OBLIGER
OARAGE	OB	OBELISK	OBITUAL	OBLIGERS
OARAGES	OBA	OBELISKS	OBITUARY	OBLIGES
OARED	OBANG	OBELISM	OBJECT	OBLIGING
OARFISH	OBANGS	OBELISMS	OBJECTED	OBLIGOR
OARFISHES	OBAS	OBELIZE	OBJECTIFY	OBLIGORS
OARIER	OBBLIGATI	OBELIZED	OBJECTING	OBLIQUE
OARIEST	OBBLIGATO	OBELIZES	OBJECTION	OBLIQUED
OARING	OBCONIC	OBELIZING	OBJECTIVE	OBLIQUELY
OARLESS	OBCONICAL	OBELUS	OBJECTOR	OBLIQUER
OARLIKE	OBCORDATE	OBENTO	OBJECTORS	OBLIQUES
OARLOCK	OBDURACY	OBENTOS	OBJECTS	OBLIQUEST
OARLOCKS	OBDURATE	OBES	OBJET	OBLIQUID

OBLIQUING

OBLIQUING	OBSEQUIE	OBTENDED	OBVIATORS	OCCUPANTS
OBLIQUITY	OBSEQUIES	OBTENDING	OBVIOUS	OCCUPATE
OBLIVION	OBSEQUY	OBTENDS	OBVIOUSLY	OCCUPATED
OBLIVIONS	OBSERVANT	OBTENTION	OBVOLUTE	OCCUPATES
OBLIVIOUS	OBSERVE	OBTEST	OBVOLUTED	OCCUPIED
OBLONG	OBSERVED	OBTESTED	OBVOLVENT	OCCUPIER
OBLONGLY	OBSERVER	OBTESTING	OBVS	OCCUPIERS
OBLONGS	OBSERVERS	OBTESTS	OCA	OCCUPIES
OBLOQUIAL	OBSERVES	OBTRUDE	OCARINA	OCCUPY
OBLOQUIES	OBSERVING	OBTRUDED	OCARINAS	OCCUPYING
OBLOQUY	OBSESS	OBTRUDER	OCAS	OCCUR
OBNOXIOUS	OBSESSED	OBTRUDERS	OCCAM	OCCURRED
OBO	OBSESSES	OBTRUDES	OCCAMIES	OCCURRENT
OBOE	OBSESSING	OBTRUDING	OCCAMS	OCCURRING
OBOES	OBSESSION	OBTRUSION	OCCAMY	OCCURS
OBOIST	OBSESSIVE	OBTRUSIVE	OCCASION	OCCY
OBOISTS	OBSESSOR	OBTUND	OCCASIONS	OCEAN
OBOL	OBSESSORS	OBTUNDED	OCCIDENT	OCEANARIA
OBOLARY	OBSIDIAN	OBTUNDENT	OCCIDENTS	OCEANAUT
OBOLE	OBSIDIANS	OBTUNDING	OCCIES	OCEANAUTS
OBOLES	OBSIGN	OBTUNDITY	OCCIPITA	OCEANIC
OBOLI	OBSIGNATE	OBTUNDS	OCCIPITAL	OCEANID
OBOLS	OBSIGNED	OBTURATE	OCCIPUT	OCEANIDES
OBOLUS	OBSIGNING	OBTURATED	OCCIPUTS	OCEANIDS
OBOS	OBSIGNS	OBTURATES	OCCLUDE	OCEANS
OBOVATE	OBSOLESCE	OBTURATOR	OCCLUDED	OCEANSIDE
OBOVATELY	OBSOLETE	OBTUSE	OCCLUDENT	OCEANVIEW
OBOVOID	OBSOLETED	OBTUSELY	OCCLUDER	OCEANWARD
OBREPTION	OBSOLETES	OBTUSER	OCCLUDERS	OCELLAR
OBS	OBSTACLE	OBTUSEST	OCCLUDES	OCELLATE
OBSCENE	OBSTACLES	OBTUSITY	OCCLUDING	OCELLATED
OBSCENELY	OBSTETRIC	OBUMBRATE	OCCLUSAL	OCELLI
OBSCENER	OBSTINACY	OBVENTION	OCCLUSION	OCELLUS
OBSCENEST	OBSTINATE	OBVERSE	OCCLUSIVE	OCELOID
OBSCENITY	OBSTRUCT	OBVERSELY	OCCLUSOR	OCELOT
OBSCURANT	OBSTRUCTS	OBVERSES	OCCLUSORS	OCELOTS
OBSCURE	OBSTRUENT	OBVERSION	OCCULT	OCH
OBSCURED	OBTAIN	OBVERT	OCCULTED	OCHE
OBSCURELY	OBTAINED	OBVERTED	OCCULTER	OCHER
OBSCURER	OBTAINER	OBVERTING	OCCULTERS	OCHERED
OBSCURERS	OBTAINERS	OBVERTS	OCCULTING	OCHERIER
OBSCURES	OBTAINING	OBVIABLE	OCCULTISM	OCHERIEST
OBSCUREST	OBTAINS	OBVIATE	OCCULTIST	OCHERING
OBSCURING	OBTECT	OBVIATED	OCCULTLY	OCHERISH
OBSCURITY	OBTECTED	OBVIATES	OCCULTS	OCHEROID
OBSECRATE	OBTEMPER	OBVIATING	OCCUPANCE	OCHEROUS
OBSEQUENT	OBTEMPERS	OBVIATION	OCCUPANCY	OCHERS
OBSEQUIAL	OBTEND	OBVIATOR	OCCUPANT	OCHERY

OCHES	OCTANGLE	OCTOSTYLE	ODDLY	ODORFUL
OCHIDORE	OCTANGLES	OCTOTHORP	ODDMENT	ODORISE
OCHIDORES	OCTANOL	OCTROI	ODDMENTS	ODORISED
OCHLOCRAT	OCTANOLS	OCTROIS	ODDNESS	ODORISER
OCHONE	OCTANS	OCTUOR	ODDNESSES	ODORISERS
OCHRE	OCTANT	OCTUORS	ODDS	ODORISES
OCHREA	OCTANTAL	OCTUPLE	ODDSMAKER	ODORISING
OCHREAE	OCTANTS	OCTUPLED	ODDSMAN	ODORIZE
OCHREAS	OCTAPLA	OCTUPLES	ODDSMEN	ODORIZED
OCHREATE	OCTAPLAS	OCTUPLET	ODE	ODORIZER
OCHRED	OCTAPLOID	OCTUPLETS	ODEA	ODORIZERS
OCHREOUS	OCTAPODIC	OCTUPLEX	ODEON	ODORIZES
OCHRES	OCTAPODY	OCTUPLING	ODEONS	ODORIZING
OCHREY	OCTARCHY	OCTUPLY	ODES	ODORLESS
OCHRIER	OCTAROON	OCTYL	ODEUM	ODOROUS
OCHRIEST	OCTAROONS	OCTYLS	ODEUMS	ODOROUSLY
OCHRING	OCTAS	OCULAR	ODIC	ODORS
OCHROID	OCTASTICH	OCULARIST	ODIFEROUS	ODOUR
OCHROUS	OCTASTYLE	OCULARLY	ODIOUS	ODOURED
OCHRY	OCTAVAL	OCULARS	ODIOUSLY	ODOURFUL
OCICAT	OCTAVE	OCULATE	ODISM	ODOURLESS
OCICATS	OCTAVES	OCULATED	ODISMS	ODOURS
OCKER	OCTAVO	OCULI	ODIST	ODS
OCKERISM	OCTAVOS	OCULIST	ODISTS	ODSO
OCKERISMS	OCTENNIAL	OCULISTS	ODIUM	ODYL
OCKERS	OCTET	OCULUS	ODIUMS	ODYLE
OCKODOLS	OCTETS	OD	ODOGRAPH	ODYLES
OCOTILLO	OCTETT	ODA	ODOGRAPHS	ODYLISM
OCOTILLOS	OCTETTE	ODAH	ODOMETER	ODYLISMS
OCREA	OCTETTES	ODAHS	ODOMETERS	ODYLS
OCREAE	OCTETTS	ODAL	ODOMETRY	ODYSSEAN
OCREAS	OCTILLION	ODALIQUE	ODONATA	ODYSSEY
OCREATE	OCTOFID	ODALIQUES	ODONATE	ODYSSEYS
OCTA	OCTOHEDRA	ODALISK	ODONATES	ODZOOKS
OCTACHORD	OCTONARII	ODALISKS	ODONATIST	OE
OCTAD	OCTONARY	ODALISQUE	ODONTALGY	OECIST
OCTADIC	OCTOPI	ODALLER	ODONTIC	OECISTS
OCTADS	OCTOPLOID	ODALLERS	ODONTIST	OECOLOGIC
OCTAGON	OCTOPOD	ODALS	ODONTISTS	OECOLOGY
OCTAGONAL	OCTOPODAN	ODAS	ODONTOID	OECUMENIC
OCTAGONS	OCTOPODES	ODD	ODONTOIDS	OEDEMA
OCTAHEDRA	OCTOPODS	ODDBALL	ODONTOMA	OEDEMAS
OCTAL	OCTOPOID	ODDBALLS	ODONTOMAS	OEDEMATA
OCTALS	OCTOPUS	ODDER	ODOR	OEDIPAL
OCTAMETER	OCTOPUSES	ODDEST	ODORANT	OEDIPALLY
OCTAN	OCTOPUSH	ODDISH	ODORANTS	OEDIPEAN
OCTANE	OCTOROON	ODDITIES	ODORATE	OEDOMETER
OCTANES	OCTOROONS	ODDITY	ODORED	OEILLADE

OEILLADES	OFFED	OFFLOADED	OGDOADS	OHONE
OENANTHIC	OFFENCE	OFFLOADS	OGEE	OHS
OENOLOGY	OFFENCES	OFFPEAK	OGEED	OI
OENOMANCY	OFFEND	OFFPRINT	OGEES	OIDIA
OENOMANIA	OFFENDED	OFFPRINTS	OGGIN	OIDIOID
OENOMEL	OFFENDER	OFFPUT	OGGINS	OIDIUM
OENOMELS	OFFENDERS	OFFPUTS	OGHAM	OIK
OENOMETER	OFFENDING	OFFRAMP	OGHAMIC	OIKIST
OENOPHIL	OFFENDS	OFFRAMPS	OGHAMIST	OIKISTS
OENOPHILE	OFFENSE	OFFS	OGHAMISTS	OIKS
OENOPHILS	OFFENSES	OFFSADDLE	OGHAMS	OIL
OENOPHILY	OFFENSIVE	OFFSCREEN	OGIVAL	OILBIRD
OENOTHERA	OFFER	OFFSCUM	OGIVE	OILBIRDS
OERLIKON	OFFERABLE	OFFSCUMS	OGIVES	OILCAMP
OERLIKONS	OFFERED	OFFSEASON	OGLE	OILCAMPS
OERSTED	OFFEREE	OFFSET	OGLED	OILCAN
OERSTEDS	OFFEREES	OFFSETS	OGLER	OILCANS
OES	OFFERER	OFFSHOOT	OGLERS	OILCLOTH
OESOPHAGI	OFFERERS	OFFSHOOTS	OGLES	OILCLOTHS
OESTRAL	OFFERING	OFFSHORE	OGLING	OILCUP
OESTRIN	OFFERINGS	OFFSHORED	OGLINGS	OILCUPS
OESTRINS	OFFEROR	OFFSHORES	OGMIC	OILED
OESTRIOL	OFFERORS	OFFSIDE	OGRE	OILER
OESTRIOLS	OFFERS	OFFSIDER	OGREISH	OILERIES
OESTROGEN	OFFERTORY	OFFSIDERS	OGREISHLY	OILERS
OESTRONE	OFFHAND	OFFSIDES	OGREISM	OILERY
OESTRONES	OFFHANDED	OFFSPRING	OGREISMS	OILFIELD
OESTROUS	OFFICE	OFFSTAGE	OGRES	OILFIELDS
OESTRUAL	OFFICER	OFFSTAGES	OGRESS	OILFIRED
OESTRUM	OFFICERED	OFFTAKE	OGRESSES	OILGAS
OESTRUMS	OFFICERS	OFFTAKES	OGRISH	OILGASES
OESTRUS	OFFICES	OFFTRACK	OGRISHLY	OILHOLE
OESTRUSES	OFFICIAL	OFFY	OGRISM	OILHOLES
OEUVRE	OFFICIALS	OFLAG	OGRISMS	OILIER
OEUVRES	OFFICIANT	OFLAGS	OH	OILIEST
OF	OFFICIARY	OFT	OHED	OILILY
OFAY	OFFICIATE	OFTEN	OHIA	OILINESS
OFAYS	OFFICINAL	OFTENER	OHIAS	OILING
OFF	OFFICIOUS	OFTENEST	OHING	OILLET
OFFA	OFFIE	OFTENNESS	OHM	OILLETS
OFFAL	OFFIES	OFTER	OHMAGE	OILMAN
OFFALS	OFFING	OFTEST	OHMAGES	OILMEN
OFFBEAT	OFFINGS	OFTTIMES	OHMIC	OILNUT
OFFBEATS	OFFISH	OGAM	OHMICALLY	OILNUTS
OFFCAST	OFFISHLY	OGAMIC	OHMMETER	OILPAN
OFFCASTS	OFFKEY	OGAMS	OHMMETERS	OILPANS
OFFCUT	OFFLINE	OGANESSON	OHMS	OILPAPER
OFFCUTS	OFFLOAD	OGDOAD	OHO	OILPAPERS

OILPROOF	OKRAS	OLEINES	OLIPHANTS	OLYMPICS
OILS	OKTA	OLEINS	OLITORIES	OM
OILSEED	OKTAS	OLENT	OLITORY	OMA
OILSEEDS	OLD	OLEO	OLIVARY	OMADHAUN
OILSKIN	OLDE	OLEOGRAPH	OLIVE	OMADHAUNS
OILSKINS	OLDEN	OLEORESIN	OLIVENITE	OMAS
OILSTONE	OLDENED	OLEOS	OLIVER	OMASA
OILSTONES	OLDENING	OLES	OLIVERS	OMASAL
OILTIGHT	OLDENS	OLESTRA	OLIVES	OMASUM
OILWAY	OLDER	OLESTRAS	OLIVET	OMBER
OILWAYS	OLDEST	OLEUM	OLIVETS	OMBERS
OILY	OLDIE	OLEUMS	OLIVEWOOD	OMBRE
OINK	OLDIES	OLFACT	OLIVINE	OMBRELLA
OINKED	OLDISH	OLFACTED	OLIVINES	OMBRELLAS
OINKING	OLDNESS	OLFACTING	OLIVINIC	OMBRES
OINKS	OLDNESSES	OLFACTION	OLLA	OMBROPHIL
OINOLOGY	OLDS	OLFACTIVE	OLLAMH	OMBU
OINOMEL	OLDSQUAW	OLFACTORY	OLLAMHS	OMBUDSMAN
OINOMELS	OLDSQUAWS	OLFACTS	OLLAS	OMBUDSMEN
OINT	OLDSTER	OLIBANUM	OLLAV	OMBUS
OINTED	OLDSTERS	OLIBANUMS	OLLAVS	OMEGA
OINTING	OLDSTYLE	OLICOOK	OLLER	OMEGAS
OINTMENT	OLDSTYLES	OLICOOKS	OLLERS	OMELET
OINTMENTS	OLDWIFE	OLID	OLLIE	OMELETS
OINTS	OLDWIVES	OLIGAEMIA	OLLIED	OMELETTE
OIS	OLDY	OLIGAEMIC	OLLIEING	OMELETTES
OITICICA	OLE	OLIGARCH	OLLIES	OMEN
OITICICAS	OLEA	OLIGARCHS	OLM	OMENED
OJIME	OLEACEOUS	OLIGARCHY	OLMS	OMENING
OJIMES	OLEANDER	OLIGEMIA	OLOGIES	OMENS
OK	OLEANDERS	OLIGEMIAS	OLOGIST	OMENTA
OKA	OLEARIA	OLIGEMIC	OLOGISTS	OMENTAL
OKAPI	OLEARIAS	OLIGIST	OLOGOAN	OMENTUM
OKAPIS	OLEASTER	OLIGISTS	OLOGOANED	OMENTUMS
OKAS	OLEASTERS	OLIGOCENE	OLOGOANS	OMER
OKAY	OLEATE	OLIGOGENE	OLOGY	OMERS
OKAYED	OLEATES	OLIGOMER	OLOLIUQUI	OMERTA
OKAYING	OLECRANAL	OLIGOMERS	OLOROSO	OMERTAS
OKAYS	OLECRANON	OLIGOPOLY	OLOROSOS	OMICRON
OKE	OLEFIANT	OLIGURIA	OLPAE	OMICRONS
OKEH	OLEFIN	OLIGURIAS	OLPE	OMIGOD
OKEHS	OLEFINE	OLIGURIC	OLPES	OMIKRON
OKES	OLEFINES	OLINGO	OLYCOOK	OMIKRONS
OKEYDOKE	OLEFINIC	OLINGOS	OLYCOOKS	OMINOUS
OKEYDOKEY	OLEFINS	OLINGUITO	OLYKOEK	OMINOUSLY
OKIMONO	OLEIC	OLIO	OLYKOEKS	OMISSIBLE
OKIMONOS	OLEIN	OLIOS	OLYMPIAD	OMISSION
OKRA	OLEINE	OLIPHANT	OLYMPIADS	OMISSIONS

O

OMISSIVE	OMPHALI	ONCOSTMEN	ONIONIEST	ONSTEAD
OMIT	OMPHALIC	ONCOSTS	ONIONING	ONSTEADS
OMITS	OMPHALOI	ONCOTOMY	ONIONS	ONSTREAM
OMITTANCE	OMPHALOID	ONCOVIRUS	ONIONSKIN	ONTIC
OMITTED	OMPHALOS	ONCUS	ONIONY	ONTICALLY
OMITTER	OMRAH	ONDATRA	ONIRIC	ONTO
OMITTERS	OMRAHS	ONDATRAS	ONISCOID	ONTOGENIC
OMITTING	OMS	ONDINE	ONIUM	ONTOGENY
OMLAH	ON	ONDINES	ONIUMS	ONTOLOGIC
OMLAHS	ONAGER	ONDING	ONKUS	ONTOLOGY
OMMATEA	ONAGERS	ONDINGS	ONLAY	ONUS
OMMATEUM	ONAGRI	ONDOGRAM	ONLAYS	ONUSES
OMMATIDIA	ONANISM	ONDOGRAMS	ONLIEST	ONWARD
OMNEITIES	ONANISMS	ONDOGRAPH	ONLINE	ONWARDLY
OMNEITY	ONANIST	ONE	ONLINER	ONWARDS
OMNIANA	ONANISTIC	ONEFOLD	ONLINERS	ONY
OMNIANAS	ONANISTS	ONEIRIC	ONLOAD	ONYCHA
OMNIARCH	ONBEAT	ONELY	ONLOADED	ONYCHAS
OMNIARCHS	ONBEATS	ONENESS	ONLOADING	ONYCHIA
OMNIBUS	ONBOARD	ONENESSES	ONLOADS	ONYCHIAS
OMNIBUSES	ONBOARDED	ONER	ONLOOKER	ONYCHITE
OMNIETIES	ONBOARDS	ONERIER	ONLOOKERS	ONYCHITES
OMNIETY	ONCE	ONERIEST	ONLOOKING	ONYCHITIS
OMNIFIC	ONCER	ONEROUS	ONLY	ONYCHIUM
OMNIFIED	ONCERS	ONEROUSLY	ONNED	ONYCHIUMS
OMNIFIES	ONCES	ONERS	ONNING	ONYMOUS
OMNIFORM	ONCET	ONERY	ONO	ONYX
OMNIFY	ONCIDIUM	ONES	ONOMAST	ONYXES
OMNIFYING	ONCIDIUMS	ONESELF	ONOMASTIC	OO
OMNIMODE	ONCOGEN	ONESIE	ONOMASTS	OOBIT
OMNIRANGE	ONCOGENE	ONESIES	ONOS	OOBITS
OMNIUM	ONCOGENES	ONETIME	ONRUSH	OOCYST
OMNIUMS	ONCOGENIC	ONEYER	ONRUSHES	OOCYSTS
OMNIVORA	ONCOGENS	ONEYERS	ONRUSHING	OOCYTE
OMNIVORE	ONCOLOGIC	ONEYRE	ONS	OOCYTES
OMNIVORES	ONCOLOGY	ONEYRES	ONSCREEN	OODLES
OMNIVORY	ONCOLYSES	ONFALL	ONSET	OODLINS
OMOHYOID	ONCOLYSIS	ONFALLS	ONSETS	OOF
OMOHYOIDS	ONCOLYTIC	ONFLOW	ONSETTER	OOFIER
OMOPHAGIA	ONCOME	ONFLOWS	ONSETTERS	OOFIEST
OMOPHAGIC	ONCOMES	ONGAONGA	ONSETTING	OOFS
OMOPHAGY	ONCOMETER	ONGAONGAS	ONSHORE	OOFTISH
OMOPHORIA	ONCOMICE	ONGOING	ONSHORING	OOFTISHES
OMOPLATE	ONCOMING	ONGOINGS	ONSIDE	OOFY
OMOPLATES	ONCOMINGS	ONIE	ONSIDES	OOGAMETE
OMOV	ONCOMOUSE	ONION	ONSLAUGHT	OOGAMETES
OMOVS	ONCOST	ONIONED	ONST	OOGAMIES
OMPHACITE	ONCOSTMAN	ONIONIER	ONSTAGE	OOGAMOUS

OOGAMY	OOMPHS	OOZES	OPENINGS	OPHIDIAN
OOGENESES	OOMS	OOZIER	OPENLY	OPHIDIANS
OOGENESIS	OOMYCETE	OOZIEST	OPENNESS	OPHIOLITE
OOGENETIC	OOMYCETES	OOZILY	OPENS	OPHIOLOGY
OOGENIES	OON	OOZINESS	OPENSIDE	OPHITE
OOGENY	OONS	OOZING	OPENSIDES	OPHITES
OOGONIA	OONT	OOZY	OPENWORK	OPHITIC
OOGONIAL	OONTS	OP	OPENWORKS	OPHIURA
OOGONIUM	OOP	OPA	OPEPE	OPHIURAN
OOGONIUMS	OOPED	OPACIFIED	OPEPES	OPHIURANS
OOH	OOPHORON	OPACIFIER	OPERA	OPHIURAS
OOHED	OOPHORONS	OPACIFIES	OPERABLE	OPHIURID
OOHING	OOPHYTE	OPACIFY	OPERABLY	OPHIURIDS
OOHINGS	OOPHYTES	OPACITIES	OPERAGOER	OPHIUROID
OOHS	OOPHYTIC	OPACITY	OPERAND	OPIATE
OOIDAL	OOPING	OPACOUS	OPERANDS	OPIATED
OOLACHAN	OOPS	OPAH	OPERANT	OPIATES
OOLACHANS	OOR	OPAHS	OPERANTLY	OPIATING
OOLAKAN	OORALI	OPAL	OPERANTS	OPIFICER
OOLAKANS	OORALIS	OPALED	OPERAS	OPIFICERS
OOLICHAN	OORIAL	OPALESCE	OPERATE	OPINABLE
OOLICHANS	OORIALS	OPALESCED	OPERATED	OPINE
OOLITE	OORIE	OPALESCES	OPERATES	OPINED
OOLITES	OORIER	OPALINE	OPERATIC	OPINES
OOLITH	OORIEST	OPALINES	OPERATICS	OPING
OOLITHS	OOS	OPALISED	OPERATING	OPINICUS
OOLITIC	OOSE	OPALIZED	OPERATION	OPINING
OOLOGIC	OOSES	OPALS	OPERATISE	OPINION
OOLOGICAL	OOSIER	OPAQUE	OPERATIVE	OPINIONED
OOLOGIES	OOSIEST	OPAQUED	OPERATIZE	OPINIONS
OOLOGIST	OOSPERM	OPAQUELY	OPERATOR	OPIOID
OOLOGISTS	OOSPERMS	OPAQUER	OPERATORS	OPIOIDS
OOLOGY	OOSPHERE	OPAQUES	OPERCELE	OPIUM
OOLONG	OOSPHERES	OPAQUEST	OPERCELES	OPIUMISM
OOLONGS	OOSPORE	OPAQUING	OPERCULA	OPIUMISMS
OOM	OOSPORES	OPAS	OPERCULAR	OPIUMS
OOMIAC	OOSPORIC	OPCODE	OPERCULE	OPOBALSAM
OOMIACK	OOSPOROUS	OPCODES	OPERCULES	OPODELDOC
OOMIACKS	OOSY	OPE	OPERCULUM	OPOPANAX
OOMIACS	OOT	OPED	OPERETTA	OPORICE
OOMIAK	OOTHECA	OPEN	OPERETTAS	OPORICES
OOMIAKS	OOTHECAE	OPENABLE	OPERON	OPOSSUM
OOMPAH	OOTHECAL	OPENCAST	OPERONS	OPOSSUMS
OOMPAHED	OOTID	OPENED	OPEROSE	OPPIDAN
OOMPAHING	OOTIDS	OPENER	OPEROSELY	OPPIDANS
OOMPAHPAH	OOTS	OPENERS	OPEROSITY	OPPILANT
OOMPAHS	OOZE	OPENEST	OPES	OPPILATE
OOMPH	OOZED	OPENING	OPGEFOK	OPPILATED

O

OPPILATES	OPT	OPTOMETRY	ORALS	ORBIEST
OPPO	OPTANT	OPTOPHONE	ORANG	ORBING
OPPONENCY	OPTANTS	OPTRONIC	ORANGE	ORBIT
OPPONENS	OPTATIVE	OPTRONICS	ORANGEADE	ORBITA
OPPONENT	OPTATIVES	OPTS	ORANGER	ORBITAL
OPPONENTS	OPTED	OPULENCE	ORANGERIE	ORBITALLY
OPPORTUNE	OPTER	OPULENCES	ORANGERY	ORBITALS
OPPOS	OPTERS	OPULENCY	ORANGES	ORBITAS
OPPOSABLE	OPTIC	OPULENT	ORANGEST	ORBITED
OPPOSABLY	OPTICAL	OPULENTLY	ORANGEY	ORBITER
OPPOSE	OPTICALLY	OPULUS	ORANGIER	ORBITERS
OPPOSED	OPTICIAN	OPULUSES	ORANGIEST	ORBITIES
OPPOSER	OPTICIANS	OPUNTIA	ORANGISH	ORBITING
OPPOSERS	OPTICIST	OPUNTIAS	ORANGS	ORBITS
OPPOSES	OPTICISTS	OPUS	ORANGUTAN	ORBITY
OPPOSING	OPTICS	OPUSCLE	ORANGY	ORBLESS
OPPOSITE	OPTIMA	OPUSCLES	ORANT	ORBLIKE
OPPOSITES	OPTIMAL	OPUSCULA	ORANTS	ORBS
OPPRESS	OPTIMALLY	OPUSCULAR	ORARIA	ORBY
OPPRESSED	OPTIMATE	OPUSCULE	ORARIAN	ORC
OPPRESSES	OPTIMATES	OPUSCULES	ORARIANS	ORCA
OPPRESSOR	OPTIME	OPUSCULUM	ORARION	ORCAS
OPPUGN	OPTIMES	OPUSES	ORARIONS	ORCEIN
OPPUGNANT	OPTIMISE	OQUASSA	ORARIUM	ORCEINS
OPPUGNED	OPTIMISED	OQUASSAS	ORATE	ORCHARD
OPPUGNER	OPTIMISER	OR	ORATED	ORCHARDS
OPPUGNERS	OPTIMISES	ORA	ORATES	ORCHAT
OPPUGNING	OPTIMISM	ORACH	ORATING	ORCHATS
OPPUGNS	OPTIMISMS	ORACHE	ORATION	ORCHEL
OPS	OPTIMIST	ORACHES	ORATIONS	ORCHELLA
OPSIMATH	OPTIMISTS	ORACIES	ORATOR	ORCHELLAS
OPSIMATHS	OPTIMIZE	ORACLE	ORATORIAL	ORCHELS
OPSIMATHY	OPTIMIZED	ORACLED	ORATORIAN	ORCHESES
OPSIN	OPTIMIZER	ORACLES	ORATORIES	ORCHESIS
OPSINS	OPTIMIZES	ORACLING	ORATORIO	ORCHESTIC
OPSOMANIA	OPTIMUM	ORACULAR	ORATORIOS	ORCHESTRA
OPSONIC	OPTIMUMS	ORACULOUS	ORATORS	ORCHID
OPSONIFY	OPTING	ORACY	ORATORY	ORCHIDIST
OPSONIN	OPTION	ORAD	ORATRESS	ORCHIDS
OPSONINS	OPTIONAL	ORAGIOUS	ORATRICES	ORCHIL
OPSONISE	OPTIONALS	ORAL	ORATRIX	ORCHILLA
OPSONISED	OPTIONED	ORALISM	ORATRIXES	ORCHILLAS
OPSONISES	OPTIONEE	ORALISMS	ORATURE	ORCHILS
OPSONIUM	OPTIONEES	ORALIST	ORATURES	ORCHIS
OPSONIUMS	OPTIONING	ORALISTS	ORB	ORCHISES
OPSONIZE	OPTIONS	ORALITIES	ORBED	ORCHITIC
OPSONIZED	OPTOLOGY	ORALITY	ORBICULAR	ORCHITIS
OPSONIZES	OPTOMETER	ORALLY	ORBIER	ORCIN

ORCINE	ORDNANCES	ORGANISED	ORIBI	ORISHA
ORCINES	ORDO	ORGANISER	ORIBIS	ORISHAS
ORCINOL	ORDOS	ORGANISES	ORICALCHE	ORISON
ORCINOLS	ORDS	ORGANISM	ORICHALC	ORISONS
ORCINS	ORDURE	ORGANISMS	ORICHALCS	ORIXA
ORCS	ORDURES	ORGANIST	ORIEL	ORIXAS
ORD	ORDUROUS	ORGANISTS	ORIELLED	ORLE
ORDAIN	ORE	ORGANITY	ORIELS	ORLEANS
ORDAINED	OREAD	ORGANIZE	ORIENCIES	ORLEANSES
ORDAINER	OREADES	ORGANIZED	ORIENCY	ORLES
ORDAINERS	OREADS	ORGANIZER	ORIENT	ORLISTAT
ORDAINING	OREBODIES	ORGANIZES	ORIENTAL	ORLISTATS
ORDAINS	OREBODY	ORGANON	ORIENTALS	ORLON
ORDALIAN	ORECTIC	ORGANONS	ORIENTATE	ORLONS
ORDALIUM	ORECTIVE	ORGANOSOL	ORIENTATE	ORLOP
ORDALIUMS	OREGANO	ORGANOTIN	ORIENTED	ORLOPS
ORDEAL	OREGANOS	ORGANS	ORIENTEER	ORMER
ORDEALS	OREIDE	ORGANUM	ORIENTER	ORMERS
ORDER	OREIDES	ORGANUMS	ORIENTERS	ORMOLU
ORDERABLE	OREODONT	ORGANZA	ORIENTING	ORMOLUS
ORDERED	OREODONTS	ORGANZAS	ORIENTS	ORNAMENT
ORDERER	OREOLOGY	ORGANZINE	ORIFEX	ORNAMENTS
ORDERERS	OREPEARCH	ORGASM	ORIFEXES	ORNATE
ORDERING	ORES	ORGASMED	ORIFICE	ORNATELY
ORDERINGS	ORESTUNCK	ORGASMIC	ORIFICES	ORNATER
ORDERLESS	OREWEED	ORGASMING	ORIFICIAL	ORNATEST
ORDERLIES	OREWEEDS	ORGASMS	ORIFLAMME	ORNERIER
ORDERLY	OREXIN	ORGASTIC	ORIGAMI	ORNERIEST
ORDERS	OREXINS	ORGEAT	ORIGAMIS	ORNERY
ORDINAIRE	OREXIS	ORGEATS	ORIGAN	ORNIS
ORDINAL	OREXISES	ORGIA	ORIGANE	ORNISES
ORDINALLY	ORF	ORGIAC	ORIGANES	ORNITHES
ORDINALS	ORFE	ORGIAS	ORIGANS	ORNITHIC
ORDINANCE	ORFES	ORGIAST	ORIGANUM	ORNITHINE
ORDINAND	ORFRAY	ORGIASTIC	ORIGANUMS	ORNITHOID
ORDINANDS	ORFRAYS	ORGIASTS	ORIGIN	OROGEN
ORDINANT	ORFS	ORGIC	ORIGINAL	OROGENIC
ORDINANTS	ORG	ORGIES	ORIGINALS	OROGENIES
ORDINAR	ORGAN	ORGILLOUS	ORIGINARY	OROGENS
ORDINARS	ORGANA	ORGONE	ORIGINATE	OROGENY
ORDINARY	ORGANDIE	ORGONES	ORIGINS	OROGRAPHY
ORDINATE	ORGANDIES	ORGS	ORIHOU	OROIDE
ORDINATED	ORGANDY	ORGUE	ORIHOUS	OROIDES
ORDINATES	ORGANELLE	ORGUES	ORILLION	OROLOGIES
ORDINEE	ORGANIC	ORGULOUS	ORILLIONS	OROLOGIST
ORDINEES	ORGANICAL	ORGY	ORINASAL	OROLOGY
ORDINES	ORGANICS	ORIBATID	ORINASALS	OROMETER
ORDNANCE	ORGANISE	ORIBATIDS	ORIOLE	OROMETERS

ORONASAL	ORTHODOXY	OSCULES	OSPREYS	OSTEOID
OROPESA	ORTHOEPIC	OSCULUM	OSSA	OSTEOIDS
OROPESAS	ORTHOEPY	OSE	OSSARIUM	OSTEOLOGY
OROTUND	ORTHOPEDY	OSES	OSSARIUMS	OSTEOMA
OROTUNDLY	ORTHOPOD	OSETRA	OSSATURE	OSTEOMAS
ORPHAN	ORTHOPODS	OSETRAS	OSSATURES	OSTEOMATA
ORPHANAGE	ORTHOPTER	OSHAC	OSSEIN	OSTEOPATH
ORPHANED	ORTHOPTIC	OSHACS	OSSEINS	OSTEOSES
ORPHANING	ORTHOS	OSIER	OSSELET	OSTEOSIS
ORPHANISM	ORTHOSES	OSIERED	OSSELETS	OSTEOTOME
ORPHANS	ORTHOSIS	OSIERIES	OSSEOUS	OSTEOTOMY
ORPHARION	ORTHOTIC	OSIERS	OSSEOUSLY	OSTIA
ORPHIC	ORTHOTICS	OSIERY	OSSETER	OSTIAL
ORPHICAL	ORTHOTIST	OSMATE	OSSETERS	OSTIARIES
ORPHISM	ORTHOTONE	OSMATES	OSSETRA	OSTIARY
ORPHISMS	ORTHROS	OSMATIC	OSSETRAS	OSTIATE
ORPHREY	ORTHROSES	OSMETERIA	OSSIA	OSTINATI
ORPHREYED	ORTOLAN	OSMIATE	OSSIAS	OSTINATO
ORPHREYS	ORTOLANS	OSMIATES	OSSICLE	OSTINATOS
ORPIMENT	ORTS	OSMIC	OSSICLES	OSTIOLAR
ORPIMENTS	ORVAL	OSMICALLY	OSSICULAR	OSTIOLATE
ORPIN	ORVALS	OSMICS	OSSIFIC	OSTIOLE
ORPINE	ORYX	OSMIOUS	OSSIFIED	OSTIOLES
ORPINES	ORYXES	OSMIUM	OSSIFIER	OSTIUM
ORPINS	ORZO	OSMIUMS	OSSIFIERS	OSTLER
ORRA	ORZOS	OSMOL	OSSIFIES	OSTLERESS
ORRAMAN	OS	OSMOLAL	OSSIFRAGA	OSTLERS
ORRAMEN	OSAR	OSMOLAR	OSSIFRAGE	OSTMARK
ORRERIES	OSCAR	OSMOLE	OSSIFY	OSTMARKS
ORRERY	OSCARS	OSMOLES	OSSIFYING	OSTOMATE
ORRICE	OSCHEAL	OSMOLS	OSSOBUCO	OSTOMATES
ORRICES	OSCILLATE	OSMOMETER	OSSOBUCOS	OSTOMIES
ORRIS	OSCINE	OSMOMETRY	OSSUARIES	OSTOMY
ORRISES	OSCINES	OSMOSE	OSSUARY	OSTOSES
ORRISROOT	OSCININE	OSMOSED	OSTEAL	OSTOSIS
ORS	OSCITANCE	OSMOSES	OSTEITIC	OSTOSISES
ORSEILLE	OSCITANCY	OSMOSING	OSTEITIS	OSTRACA
ORSEILLES	OSCITANT	OSMOSIS	OSTENSIVE	OSTRACEAN
ORSELLIC	OSCITATE	OSMOTIC	OSTENSORY	OSTRACISE
ORT	OSCITATED	OSMOUS	OSTENT	OSTRACISM
ORTANIQUE	OSCITATES	OSMUND	OSTENTED	OSTRACIZE
ORTHIAN	OSCULA	OSMUNDA	OSTENTING	OSTRACOD
ORTHICON	OSCULANT	OSMUNDAS	OSTENTS	OSTRACODE
ORTHICONS	OSCULAR	OSMUNDINE	OSTEOCYTE	OSTRACODS
ORTHO	OSCULATE	OSMUNDS	OSTEODERM	OSTRACON
ORTHOAXES	OSCULATED	OSNABURG	OSTEOGEN	OSTRAKA
ORTHOAXIS	OSCULATES	OSNABURGS	OSTEOGENS	OSTRAKON
ORTHODOX	OSCULE	OSPREY	OSTEOGENY	OSTREGER

OSTREGERS	OTTAVAS	OUIJA	OUROLOGY	OUTBARKS
OSTRICH	OTTAVINO	OUIJAS	OUROSCOPY	OUTBARRED
OSTRICHES	OTTAVINOS	OUISTITI	OURS	OUTBARS
OTAKU	OTTER	OUISTITIS	OURSELF	OUTBAWL
OTAKUS	OTTERED	OUK	OURSELVES	OUTBAWLED
OTALGIA	OTTERING	OUKS	OUS	OUTBAWLS
OTALGIAS	OTTERS	OULACHON	OUSEL	OUTBEAM
OTALGIC	OTTO	OULACHONS	OUSELS	OUTBEAMED
OTALGIES	OTTOMAN	OULAKAN	OUST	OUTBEAMS
OTALGY	OTTOMANS	OULAKANS	OUSTED	OUTBEG
OTARID	OTTOS	OULD	OUSTER	OUTBEGGED
OTARIES	OTTRELITE	OULDER	OUSTERS	OUTBEGS
OTARINE	OU	OULDEST	OUSTING	OUTBID
OTARY	OUABAIN	OULK	OUSTITI	OUTBIDDEN
OTHER	OUABAINS	OULKS	OUSTITIS	OUTBIDDER
OTHERED	OUAKARI	OULONG	OUSTS	OUTBIDS
OTHERING	OUAKARIS	OULONGS	OUT	OUTBITCH
OTHERNESS	OUBAAS	OUMA	OUTA	OUTBLAZE
OTHERS	OUBAASES	OUMAS	OUTACT	OUTBLAZED
OTHERWISE	OUBIT	OUNCE	OUTACTED	OUTBLAZES
OTIC	OUBITS	OUNCES	OUTACTING	OUTBLEAT
OTIOSE	OUBLIETTE	OUNDIER	OUTACTS	OUTBLEATS
OTIOSELY	OUCH	OUNDIEST	OUTADD	OUTBLESS
OTIOSITY	OUCHED	OUNDY	OUTADDED	OUTBLOOM
OTITIC	OUCHES	OUP	OUTADDING	OUTBLOOMS
OTITIDES	OUCHING	OUPA	OUTADDS	OUTBLUFF
OTITIS	OUCHT	OUPAS	OUTAGE	OUTBLUFFS
OTITISES	OUCHTS	OUPED	OUTAGES	OUTBLUSH
OTOCYST	OUD	OUPH	OUTARGUE	OUTBOARD
OTOCYSTIC	OUDS	OUPHE	OUTARGUED	OUTBOARDS
OTOCYSTS	OUENS	OUPHES	OUTARGUES	OUTBOAST
OTOLITH	OUGHLIED	OUPHS	OUTASIGHT	OUTBOASTS
OTOLITHIC	OUGHLIES	OUPING	OUTASITE	OUTBOUGHT
OTOLITHS	OUGHLY	OUPS	OUTASK	OUTBOUND
OTOLOGIC	OUGHLYING	OUR	OUTASKED	OUTBOUNDS
OTOLOGIES	OUGHT	OURALI	OUTASKING	OUTBOX
OTOLOGIST	OUGHTED	OURALIS	OUTASKS	OUTBOXED
OTOLOGY	OUGHTING	OURANG	OUTATE	OUTBOXES
OTOPLASTY	OUGHTNESS	OURANGS	OUTBACK	OUTBOXING
OTORRHOEA	OUGHTS	OURARI	OUTBACKER	OUTBRAG
OTOSCOPE	OUGIYA	OURARIS	OUTBACKS	OUTBRAGS
OTOSCOPES	OUGIYAS	OUREBI	OUTBAKE	OUTBRAVE
OTOSCOPIC	OUGLIE	OUREBIS	OUTBAKED	OUTBRAVED
OTOSCOPY	OUGLIED	OURIE	OUTBAKES	OUTBRAVES
OTOTOXIC	OUGLIEING	OURIER	OUTBAKING	OUTBRAWL
OTTAR	OUGLIES	OURIEST	OUTBAR	OUTBRAWLS
OTTARS	OUGUIYA	OURN	OUTBARK	OUTBRAZEN
OTTAVA	OUGUIYAS	OUROBOROS	OUTBARKED	OUTBREAK

OUTBREAKS	OUTCHEATS	OUTDATES	OUTEARN	OUTFIRE
OUTBRED	OUTCHID	OUTDATING	OUTEARNED	OUTFIRED
OUTBREED	OUTCHIDE	OUTDAZZLE	OUTEARNS	OUTFIRES
OUTBREEDS	OUTCHIDED	OUTDEBATE	OUTEAT	OUTFIRING
OUTBRIBE	OUTCHIDES	OUTDESIGN	OUTEATEN	OUTFISH
OUTBRIBED	OUTCITIES	OUTDID	OUTEATING	OUTFISHED
OUTBRIBES	OUTCITY	OUTDO	OUTEATS	OUTFISHES
OUTBROKE	OUTCLASS	OUTDODGE	OUTECHO	OUTFIT
OUTBROKEN	OUTCLIMB	OUTDODGED	OUTECHOED	OUTFITS
OUTBUILD	OUTCLIMBS	OUTDODGES	OUTECHOES	OUTFITTED
OUTBUILDS	OUTCLOMB	OUTDOER	OUTED	OUTFITTER
OUTBUILT	OUTCOACH	OUTDOERS	OUTEDGE	OUTFLANK
OUTBULGE	OUTCOME	OUTDOES	OUTEDGES	OUTFLANKS
OUTBULGED	OUTCOMES	OUTDOING	OUTER	OUTFLASH
OUTBULGES	OUTCOOK	OUTDONE	OUTERCOAT	OUTFLEW
OUTBULK	OUTCOOKED	OUTDOOR	OUTERMOST	OUTFLIES
OUTBULKED	OUTCOOKS	OUTDOORS	OUTERS	OUTFLING
OUTBULKS	OUTCOUNT	OUTDOORSY	OUTERWEAR	OUTFLINGS
OUTBULLY	OUTCOUNTS	OUTDRAG	OUTFABLE	OUTFLOAT
OUTBURN	OUTCRAFTY	OUTDRAGS	OUTFABLED	OUTFLOATS
OUTBURNED	OUTCRAWL	OUTDRANK	OUTFABLES	OUTFLOW
OUTBURNS	OUTCRAWLS	OUTDRAW	OUTFACE	OUTFLOWED
OUTBURNT	OUTCRIED	OUTDRAWN	OUTFACED	OUTFLOWN
OUTBURST	OUTCRIES	OUTDRAWS	OUTFACES	OUTFLOWS
OUTBURSTS	OUTCROP	OUTDREAM	OUTFACING	OUTFLUNG
OUTBUY	OUTCROPS	OUTDREAMS	OUTFALL	OUTFLUSH
OUTBUYING	OUTCROSS	OUTDREAMT	OUTFALLS	OUTFLY
OUTBUYS	OUTCROW	OUTDRESS	OUTFAST	OUTFLYING
OUTBY	OUTCROWD	OUTDREW	OUTFASTED	OUTFOOL
OUTBYE	OUTCROWDS	OUTDRINK	OUTFASTS	OUTFOOLED
OUTCALL	OUTCROWED	OUTDRINKS	OUTFAWN	OUTFOOLS
OUTCALLED	OUTCROWS	OUTDRIVE	OUTFAWNED	OUTFOOT
OUTCALLS	OUTCRY	OUTDRIVEN	OUTFAWNS	OUTFOOTED
OUTCAPER	OUTCRYING	OUTDRIVES	OUTFEAST	OUTFOOTS
OUTCAPERS	OUTCURSE	OUTDROP	OUTFEASTS	OUTFOUGHT
OUTCAST	OUTCURSED	OUTDROPS	OUTFEEL	OUTFOUND
OUTCASTE	OUTCURSES	OUTDROVE	OUTFEELS	OUTFOX
OUTCASTED	OUTCURVE	OUTDRUNK	OUTFELT	OUTFOXED
OUTCASTES	OUTCURVES	OUTDUEL	OUTFENCE	OUTFOXES
OUTCASTS	OUTDANCE	OUTDUELED	OUTFENCED	OUTFOXING
OUTCATCH	OUTDANCED	OUTDUELS	OUTFENCES	OUTFROWN
OUTCAUGHT	OUTDANCES	OUTDURE	OUTFIELD	OUTFROWNS
OUTCAVIL	OUTDARE	OUTDURED	OUTFIELDS	OUTFUMBLE
OUTCAVILS	OUTDARED	OUTDURES	OUTFIGHT	OUTGAIN
OUTCHARGE	OUTDARES	OUTDURING	OUTFIGHTS	OUTGAINED
OUTCHARM	OUTDARING	OUTDWELL	OUTFIGURE	OUTGAINS
OUTCHARMS	OUTDATE	OUTDWELLS	OUTFIND	OUTGALLOP
OUTCHEAT	OUTDATED	OUTDWELT	OUTFINDS	OUTGAMBLE

OUTGAS	OUTGUIDED	OUTJINX	OUTLEAP	OUTMODED
OUTGASES	OUTGUIDES	OUTJINXED	OUTLEAPED	OUTMODES
OUTGASSED	OUTGUN	OUTJINXES	OUTLEAPS	OUTMODING
OUTGASSES	OUTGUNNED	OUTJOCKEY	OUTLEAPT	OUTMOST
OUTGATE	OUTGUNS	OUTJUGGLE	OUTLEARN	OUTMOVE
OUTGATES	OUTGUSH	OUTJUMP	OUTLEARNS	OUTMOVED
OUTGAVE	OUTGUSHED	OUTJUMPED	OUTLEARNT	OUTMOVES
OUTGAZE	OUTGUSHES	OUTJUMPS	OUTLED	OUTMOVING
OUTGAZED	OUTHANDLE	OUTJUT	OUTLER	OUTMUSCLE
OUTGAZES	OUTHARBOR	OUTJUTS	OUTLERS	OUTNAME
OUTGAZING	OUTHAUL	OUTJUTTED	OUTLET	OUTNAMED
OUTGIVE	OUTHAULER	OUTKEEP	OUTLETS	OUTNAMES
OUTGIVEN	OUTHAULS	OUTKEEPS	OUTLIE	OUTNAMING
OUTGIVES	OUTHEAR	OUTKEPT	OUTLIED	OUTNESS
OUTGIVING	OUTHEARD	OUTKICK	OUTLIER	OUTNESSES
OUTGLARE	OUTHEARS	OUTKICKED	OUTLIERS	OUTNIGHT
OUTGLARED	OUTHER	OUTKICKS	OUTLIES	OUTNIGHTS
OUTGLARES	OUTHIRE	OUTKILL	OUTLINE	OUTNUMBER
OUTGLEAM	OUTHIRED	OUTKILLED	OUTLINEAR	OUTOFFICE
OUTGLEAMS	OUTHIRES	OUTKILLS	OUTLINED	OUTPACE
OUTGLOW	OUTHIRING	OUTKISS	OUTLINER	OUTPACED
OUTGLOWED	OUTHIT	OUTKISSED	OUTLINERS	OUTPACES
OUTGLOWS	OUTHITS	OUTKISSES	OUTLINES	OUTPACING
OUTGNAW	OUTHOMER	OUTLAID	OUTLINING	OUTPAINT
OUTGNAWED	OUTHOMERS	OUTLAIN	OUTLIVE	OUTPAINTS
OUTGNAWN	OUTHOUSE	OUTLAND	OUTLIVED	OUTPART
OUTGNAWS	OUTHOUSES	OUTLANDER	OUTLIVER	OUTPARTS
OUTGO	OUTHOWL	OUTLANDS	OUTLIVERS	OUTPASS
OUTGOER	OUTHOWLED	OUTLASH	OUTLIVES	OUTPASSED
OUTGOERS	OUTHOWLS	OUTLASHED	OUTLIVING	OUTPASSES
OUTGOES	OUTHUMOR	OUTLASHES	OUTLOOK	OUTPEEP
OUTGOING	OUTHUMORS	OUTLAST	OUTLOOKED	OUTPEEPED
OUTGOINGS	OUTHUMOUR	OUTLASTED	OUTLOOKS	OUTPEEPS
OUTGONE	OUTHUNT	OUTLASTS	OUTLOVE	OUTPEER
OUTGREW	OUTHUNTED	OUTLAUGH	OUTLOVED	OUTPEERED
OUTGRIN	OUTHUNTS	OUTLAUGHS	OUTLOVES	OUTPEERS
OUTGRINS	OUTHUSTLE	OUTLAUNCE	OUTLOVING	OUTPEOPLE
OUTGROSS	OUTHYRE	OUTLAUNCH	OUTLUSTER	OUTPITCH
OUTGROUP	OUTHYRED	OUTLAW	OUTLUSTRE	OUTPITTED
OUTGROUPS	UUTHYRES	OUTLAWED	OUTLYING	OUTPITIES
OUTGROW	OUTHYRING	OUTLAWING	OUTMAN	OUTPITY
OUTGROWN	OUTING	OUTLAWRY	OUTMANNED	OUTPLACE
OUTGROWS	OUTINGS	OUTLAWS	OUTMANS	OUTPLACED
OUTGROWTH	OUTJEST	OUTLAY	OUTMANTLE	OUTPLACER
OUTGUARD	OUTJESTED	OUTLAYING	OUTMARCH	OUTPLACES
OUTGUARDS	OUTJESTS	OUTLAYS	OUTMASTER	OUTPLAN
OUTGUESS	OUTJET	OUTLEAD	OUTMATCH	OUTPLANS
OUTGUIDE	OUTJETS	OUTLEADS	OUTMODE	OUTPLAY

O

OUTPLAYED	OUTPUTS	OUTREMERS	OUTRUSHES	OUTSHOT
OUTPLAYS	OUTPUTTED	OUTRIDDEN	OUTS	OUTSHOTS
OUTPLOD	OUTQUOTE	OUTRIDE	OUTSAID	OUTSHOUT
OUTPLODS	OUTQUOTED	OUTRIDER	OUTSAIL	OUTSHOUTS
OUTPLOT	OUTQUOTES	OUTRIDERS	OUTSAILED	OUTSIDE
OUTPLOTS	OUTRACE	OUTRIDES	OUTSAILS	OUTSIDER
OUTPOINT	OUTRACED	OUTRIDING	OUTSANG	OUTSIDERS
OUTPOINTS	OUTRACES	OUTRIG	OUTSAT	OUTSIDES
OUTPOLL	OUTRACING	OUTRIGGED	OUTSAVOR	OUTSIGHT
OUTPOLLED	OUTRAGE	OUTRIGGER	OUTSAVORS	OUTSIGHTS
OUTPOLLS	OUTRAGED	OUTRIGHT	OUTSAVOUR	OUTSIN
OUTPORT	OUTRAGES	OUTRIGS	OUTSAW	OUTSING
OUTPORTER	OUTRAGING	OUTRING	OUTSAY	OUTSINGS
OUTPORTS	OUTRAISE	OUTRINGS	OUTSAYING	OUTSINNED
OUTPOST	OUTRAISED	OUTRIVAL	OUTSAYS	OUTSINS
OUTPOSTS	OUTRAISES	OUTRIVALS	OUTSCHEME	OUTSIT
OUTPOUR	OUTRAN	OUTRO	OUTSCOLD	OUTSITS
OUTPOURED	OUTRANCE	OUTROAR	OUTSCOLDS	OUTSIZE
OUTPOURER	OUTRANCES	OUTROARED	OUTSCOOP	OUTSIZED
OUTPOURS	OUTRANG	OUTROARS	OUTSCOOPS	OUTSIZES
OUTPOWER	OUTRANGE	OUTROCK	OUTSCORE	OUTSKATE
OUTPOWERS	OUTRANGED	OUTROCKED	OUTSCORED	OUTSKATED
OUTPRAY	OUTRANGES	OUTROCKS	OUTSCORES	OUTSKATES
OUTPRAYED	OUTRANK	OUTRODE	OUTSCORN	OUTSKIRT
OUTPRAYS	OUTRANKED	OUTROLL	OUTSCORNS	OUTSKIRTS
OUTPREACH	OUTRANKS	OUTROLLED	OUTSCREAM	OUTSLEEP
OUTPREEN	OUTRATE	OUTROLLS	OUTSEE	OUTSLEEPS
OUTPREENS	OUTRATED	OUTROOP	OUTSEEING	OUTSLEPT
OUTPRESS	OUTRATES	OUTROOPER	OUTSEEN	OUTSLICK
OUTPRICE	OUTRATING	OUTROOPS	OUTSEES	OUTSLICKS
OUTPRICED	OUTRAVE	OUTROOT	OUTSELL	OUTSMART
OUTPRICES	OUTRAVED	OUTROOTED	OUTSELLS	OUTSMARTS
OUTPRIZE	OUTRAVES	OUTROOTS	OUTSERT	OUTSMELL
OUTPRIZED	OUTRAVING	OUTROPE	OUTSERTS	OUTSMELLS
OUTPRIZES	OUTRE	OUTROPER	OUTSERVE	OUTSMELT
OUTPSYCH	OUTREACH	OUTROPERS	OUTSERVED	OUTSMILE
OUTPSYCHS	OUTREAD	OUTROPES	OUTSERVES	OUTSMILED
OUTPULL	OUTREADS	OUTROS	OUTSET	OUTSMILES
OUTPULLED	OUTREASON	OUTROW	OUTSETS	OUTSMOKE
OUTPULLS	OUTRECKON	OUTROWED	OUTSHAME	OUTSMOKED
OUTPUNCH	OUTRED	OUTROWING	OUTSHAMED	OUTSMOKES
OUTPUPIL	OUTREDDED	OUTROWS	OUTSHAMES	OUTSNORE
OUTPUPILS	OUTREDDEN	OUTRUN	OUTSHINE	OUTSNORED
OUTPURSUE	OUTREDS	OUTRUNG	OUTSHINED	OUTSNORES
OUTPUSH	OUTREIGN	OUTRUNNER	OUTSHINES	OUTSOAR
OUTPUSHED	OUTREIGNS	OUTRUNS	OUTSHONE	OUTSOARED
OUTPUSHES	OUTRELIEF	OUTRUSH	OUTSHOOT	OUTSOARS
OUTPUT	OUTREMER	OUTRUSHED	OUTSHOOTS	OUTSOLD

OUZO

OUTSOLE	OUTSTRIVE	OUTTHINK	OUTVYING	OUTWINDED
OUTSOLES	OUTSTRODE	OUTTHINKS	OUTWAIT	OUTWINDS
OUTSOURCE	OUTSTROKE	OUTTHREW	OUTWAITED	OUTWING
OUTSPAN	OUTSTROVE	OUTTHROB	OUTWAITS	OUTWINGED
OUTSPANS	OUTSTRUCK	OUTTHROBS	OUTWALK	OUTWINGS
OUTSPEAK	OUTSTUDY	OUTTHROW	OUTWALKED	OUTWINS
OUTSPEAKS	OUTSTUNT	OUTTHROWN	OUTWALKS	OUTWISH
OUTSPED	OUTSTUNTS	OUTTHROWS	OUTWAR	OUTWISHED
OUTSPEED	OUTSULK	OUTTHRUST	OUTWARD	OUTWISHES
OUTSPEEDS	OUTSULKED	OUTTOLD	OUTWARDLY	OUTWIT
OUTSPELL	OUTSULKS	OUTTONGUE	OUTWARDS	OUTWITH
OUTSPELLS	OUTSUM	OUTTOOK	OUTWARRED	OUTWITS
OUTSPELT	OUTSUMMED	OUTTOP	OUTWARS	OUTWITTED
OUTSPEND	OUTSUMS	OUTTOPPED	OUTWASH	OUTWON
OUTSPENDS	OUTSUNG	OUTTOPS	OUTWASHES	OUTWORE
OUTSPENT	OUTSWAM	OUTTOWER	OUTWASTE	OUTWORK
OUTSPOKE	OUTSWARE	OUTTOWERS	OUTWASTED	OUTWORKED
OUTSPOKEN	OUTSWEAR	OUTTRADE	OUTWASTES	OUTWORKER
OUTSPORT	OUTSWEARS	OUTTRADED	OUTWATCH	OUTWORKS
OUTSPORTS	OUTSWEEP	OUTTRADES	OUTWEAR	OUTWORN
OUTSPRANG	OUTSWEEPS	OUTTRAVEL	OUTWEARS	OUTWORTH
OUTSPREAD	OUTSWELL	OUTTRICK	OUTWEARY	OUTWORTHS
OUTSPRING	OUTSWELLS	OUTTRICKS	OUTWEED	OUTWOUND
OUTSPRINT	OUTSWEPT	OUTTROT	OUTWEEDED	OUTWREST
OUTSPRUNG	OUTSWIM	OUTTROTS	OUTWEEDS	OUTWRESTS
OUTSTAND	OUTSWIMS	OUTTRUMP	OUTWEEP	OUTWRIT
OUTSTANDS	OUTSWING	OUTTRUMPS	OUTWEEPS	OUTWRITE
OUTSTARE	OUTSWINGS	OUTTURN	OUTWEIGH	OUTWRITES
OUTSTARED	OUTSWORE	OUTTURNS	OUTWEIGHS	OUTWROTE
OUTSTARES	OUTSWORN	OUTVALUE	OUTWELL	OUTYELL
OUTSTART	OUTSWUM	OUTVALUED	OUTWELLED	OUTYELLED
OUTSTARTS	OUTSWUNG	OUTVALUES	OUTWELLS	OUTYELLS
OUTSTATE	OUTTA	OUTVAUNT	OUTWENT	OUTYELP
OUTSTATED	OUTTAKE	OUTVAUNTS	OUTWEPT	OUTYELPED
OUTSTATES	OUTTAKEN	OUTVENOM	OUTWHIRL	OUTYELPS
OUTSTAY	OUTTAKES	OUTVENOMS	OUTWHIRLS	OUTYIELD
OUTSTAYED	OUTTAKING	OUTVIE	OUTWICK	OUTYIELDS
OUTSTAYS	OUTTALK	OUTVIED	OUTWICKED	OUVERT
OUTSTEER	OUTTALKED	OUTVIES	OUTWICKS	OUVERTE
OUTSTEERS	OUTTALKS	OUTVOICE	OUTWILE	OUVRAGE
OUTSTEP	OUTTASK	OUTVOICED	OUTWILED	OUVRAGES
OUTSTEPS	OUTTASKED	OUTVOICES	OUTWILES	OUVRIER
OUTSTOOD	OUTTASKS	OUTVOTE	OUTWILING	OUVRIERE
OUTSTRAIN	OUTTELL	OUTVOTED	OUTWILL	OUVRIERES
OUTSTRIDE	OUTTELLS	OUTVOTER	OUTWILLED	OUVRIERS
OUTSTRIKE	OUTTHANK	OUTVOTERS	OUTWILLS	OUZEL
OUTSTRIP	OUTTHANKS	OUTVOTES	OUTWIN	OUZELS
OUTSTRIPS	OUTTHIEVE	OUTVOTING	OUTWIND	OUZO

O

OUZOS	OVERAGE	OVERBORE	OVERCOAT	OVERDRAFT
OVA	OVERAGED	OVERBORN	OVERCOATS	OVERDRANK
OVAL	OVERAGES	OVERBORNE	OVERCOLD	OVERDRAW
OVALBUMIN	OVERALERT	OVERBOUND	OVERCOLOR	OVERDRAWN
OVALITIES	OVERALL	OVERBRAKE	OVERCOME	OVERDRAWS
OVALITY	OVERALLED	OVERBRED	OVERCOMER	OVERDRESS
OVALLY	OVERALLS	OVERBREED	OVERCOMES	OVERDREW
OVALNESS	OVERAPT	OVERBRIEF	OVERCOOK	OVERDRIED
OVALS	OVERARCH	OVERBRIM	OVERCOOKS	OVERDRIES
OVARIAL	OVERARM	OVERBRIMS	OVERCOOL	OVERDRINK
OVARIAN	OVERARMED	OVERBROAD	OVERCOOLS	OVERDRIVE
OVARIES	OVERARMS	OVERBROW	OVERCOUNT	OVERDROVE
OVARIOLE	OVERATE	OVERBROWS	OVERCOVER	OVERDRUNK
OVARIOLES	OVERAWE	OVERBUILD	OVERCOY	OVERDRY
OVARIOUS	OVERAWED	OVERBUILT	OVERCRAM	OVERDUB
OVARITIS	OVERAWES	OVERBULK	OVERCRAMS	OVERDUBS
OVARY	OVERAWING	OVERBULKS	OVERCRAW	OVERDUE
OVATE	OVERBAKE	OVERBURN	OVERCRAWS	OVERDUST
OVATED	OVERBAKED	OVERBURNS	OVERCROP	OVERDUSTS
OVATELY	OVERBAKES	OVERBURNT	OVERCROPS	OVERDYE
OVATES	OVERBANK	OVERBUSY	OVERCROW	OVERDYED
OVATING	OVERBANKS	OVERBUY	OVERCROWD	OVERDYER
OVATION	OVERBEAR	OVERBUYS	OVERCROWS	OVERDYERS
OVATIONAL	OVERBEARS	OVERBY	OVERCURE	OVERDYES
OVATIONS	OVERBEAT	OVERCALL	OVERCURED	OVEREAGER
OVATOR	OVERBEATS	OVERCALLS	OVERCURES	OVEREASY
OVATORS	OVERBED	OVERCAME	OVERCUT	OVEREAT
OVEL	OVERBET	OVERCARRY	OVERCUTS	OVEREATEN
OVELS	OVERBETS	OVERCAST	OVERDARE	OVEREATER
OVEN	OVERBID	OVERCASTS	OVERDARED	OVEREATS
OVENABLE	OVERBIDS	OVERCATCH	OVERDARES	OVERED
OVENBIRD	OVERBIG	OVERCHEAP	OVERDATED	OVEREDIT
OVENBIRDS	OVERBILL	OVERCHECK	OVERDEAR	OVEREDITS
OVENED	OVERBILLS	OVERCHILL	OVERDECK	OVEREGG
OVENING	OVERBITE	OVERCIVIL	OVERDECKS	OVEREGGED
OVENLIKE	OVERBITES	OVERCLAD	OVERDID	OVEREGGS
OVENPROOF	OVERBLEW	OVERCLAIM	OVERDIGHT	OVEREMOTE
OVENS	OVERBLOW	OVERCLASS	OVERDO	OVEREQUIP
OVENWARE	OVERBLOWN	OVERCLEAN	OVERDOER	OVEREXERT
OVENWARES	OVERBLOWS	OVERCLEAR	OVERDOERS	OVEREYE
OVENWOOD	OVERBOARD	OVERCLOCK	OVERDOES	OVEREYED
OVENWOODS	OVERBOIL	OVERCLOSE	OVERDOG	OVEREYES
OVER	OVERBOILS	OVERCLOUD	OVERDOGS	OVEREYING
OVERABLE	OVERBOLD	OVERCLOY	OVERDOING	OVERFALL
OVERACT	OVERBOOK	OVERCLOYS	OVERDONE	OVERFALLS
OVERACTED	OVERBOOKS	OVERCLUB	OVERDOSE	OVERFAR
OVERACTS	OVERBOOT	OVERCLUBS	OVERDOSED	OVERFAST
OVERACUTE	OVERBOOTS	OVERCOACH	OVERDOSES	OVERFAT

OVERFAVOR	OVERGIVES	OVERHEAT	OVERLAID	OVERLY
OVERFEAR	OVERGLAD	OVERHEATS	OVERLAIN	OVERLYING
OVERFEARS	OVERGLAZE	OVERHELD	OVERLAND	OVERMAN
OVERFED	OVERGLOOM	OVERHENT	OVERLANDS	OVERMANS
OVERFEED	OVERGO	OVERHENTS	OVERLAP	OVERMANY
OVERFEEDS	OVERGOAD	OVERHIGH	OVERLAPS	OVERMAST
OVERFELL	OVERGOADS	OVERHIT	OVERLARD	OVERMASTS
OVERFILL	OVERGOES	OVERHITS	OVERLARDS	OVERMATCH
OVERFILLS	OVERGOING	OVERHOLD	OVERLARGE	OVERMEEK
OVERFINE	OVERGONE	OVERHOLDS	OVERLATE	OVERMELT
OVERFISH	OVERGORGE	OVERHOLY	OVERLAX	OVERMELTS
OVERFIT	OVERGOT	OVERHONOR	OVERLAY	OVERMEN
OVERFLEW	OVERGRADE	OVERHOPE	OVERLAYS	OVERMERRY
OVERFLIES	OVERGRAIN	OVERHOPED	OVERLEAF	OVERMILD
OVERFLOOD	OVERGRASS	OVERHOPES	OVERLEAP	OVERMILK
OVERFLOW	OVERGRAZE	OVERHOT	OVERLEAPS	OVERMILKS
OVERFLOWN	OVERGREAT	OVERHUNG	OVERLEAPT	OVERMINE
OVERFLOWS	OVERGREEN	OVERHUNT	OVERLEARN	OVERMINED
OVERFLUSH	OVERGREW	OVERHUNTS	OVERLEND	OVERMINES
OVERFLY	OVERGROW	OVERHYPE	OVERLENDS	OVERMIX
OVERFOCUS	OVERGROWN	OVERHYPED	OVERLENT	OVERMIXED
OVERFOLD	OVERGROWS	OVERHYPES	OVERLET	OVERMIXES
OVERFOLDS	OVERHAILE	OVERIDLE	OVERLETS	OVERMOUNT
OVERFOND	OVERHAIR	OVERING	OVERLEWD	OVERMUCH
OVERFOUL	OVERHAIRS	OVERINKED	OVERLIE	OVERNAME
OVERFRANK	OVERHALE	OVERISSUE	OVERLIER	OVERNAMED
OVERFREE	OVERHALED	OVERJOY	OVERLIERS	OVERNAMES
OVERFULL	OVERHALES	OVERJOYED	OVERLIES	OVERNEAR
OVERFUND	OVERHAND	OVERJOYS	OVERLIGHT	OVERNEAT
OVERFUNDS	OVERHANDS	OVERJUMP	OVERLIT	OVERNET
OVERFUSSY	OVERHANG	OVERJUMPS	OVERLIVE	OVERNETS
OVERGALL	OVERHANGS	OVERJUST	OVERLIVED	OVERNEW
OVERGALLS	OVERHAPPY	OVERKEEN	OVERLIVES	OVERNICE
OVERGANG	OVERHARD	OVERKEEP	OVERLOAD	OVERNIGHT
OVERGANGS	OVERHASTE	OVERKEEPS	OVERLOADS	OVERPACK
OVERGAVE	OVERHASTY	OVERKEPT	OVERLOCK	OVERPACKS
OVERGEAR	OVERHATE	OVERKEST	OVERLOCKS	OVERPAGE
OVERGEARS	OVERHATED	OVERKILL	OVERLONG	OVERPAID
OVERGET	OVERHATES	OVERKILLS	OVERLOOK	OVERPAINT
OVERGETS	OVERHAUL	OVERKIND	OVERLOOKS	OVERPART
OVERGILD	OVERHAULS	OVERKING	OVERLORD	OVERPARTS
OVERGILDS	OVERHEAD	OVERKINGS	OVERLORDS	OVERPASS
OVERGILT	OVERHEADS	OVERKNEE	OVERLOUD	OVERPAST
OVERGIRD	OVERHEAP	OVERLABOR	OVERLOVE	OVERPAY
OVERGIRDS	OVERHEAPS	OVERLADE	OVERLOVED	OVERPAYS
OVERGIRT	OVERHEAR	OVERLADED	OVERLOVES	OVERPEDAL
OVERGIVE	OVERHEARD	OVERLADEN	OVERLUSH	OVERPEER
OVERGIVEN	OVERHEARS	OVERLADES	OVERLUSTY	OVERPEERS

OVERPERCH	OVERRENS	OVERSEW	OVERSPENT	OVERTALK
OVERPERT	OVERRICH	OVERSEWED	OVERSPICE	OVERTALKS
OVERPITCH	OVERRIDE	OVERSEWN	OVERSPILL	OVERTAME
OVERPLAID	OVERRIDER	OVERSEWS	OVERSPILT	OVERTART
OVERPLAN	OVERRIDES	OVERSEXED	OVERSPIN	OVERTASK
OVERPLANS	OVERRIFE	OVERSHADE	OVERSPINS	OVERTASKS
OVERPLANT	OVERRIGID	OVERSHARE	OVERSTAFF	OVERTAX
OVERPLAST	OVERRIPE	OVERSHARP	OVERSTAIN	OVERTAXED
OVERPLAY	OVERRIPEN	OVERSHINE	OVERSTAND	OVERTAXES
OVERPLAYS	OVERROAST	OVERSHIRT	OVERSTANK	OVERTEACH
OVERPLIED	OVERRODE	OVERSHOE	OVERSTARE	OVERTEEM
OVERPLIES	OVERRUDE	OVERSHOES	OVERSTATE	OVERTEEMS
OVERPLOT	OVERRUFF	OVERSHONE	OVERSTAY	OVERTHICK
OVERPLOTS	OVERRUFFS	OVERSHOOT	OVERSTAYS	OVERTHIN
OVERPLUS	OVERRULE	OVERSHOT	OVERSTEER	OVERTHINK
OVERPLY	OVERRULED	OVERSHOTS	OVERSTEP	OVERTHINS
OVERPOISE	OVERRULER	OVERSICK	OVERSTEPS	OVERTHREW
OVERPOST	OVERRULES	OVERSIDE	OVERSTINK	OVERTHROW
OVERPOSTS	OVERRUN	OVERSIDES	OVERSTIR	OVERTIGHT
OVERPOWER	OVERRUNS	OVERSIGHT	OVERSTIRS	OVERTIME
OVERPRESS	OVERS	OVERSIZE	OVERSTOCK	OVERTIMED
OVERPRICE	OVERSAD	OVERSIZED	OVERSTOOD	OVERTIMER
OVERPRINT	OVERSAIL	OVERSIZES	OVERSTORY	OVERTIMES
OVERPRIZE	OVERSAILS	OVERSKATE	OVERSTREW	OVERTIMID
OVERPROOF	OVERSALE	OVERSKIP	OVERSTUDY	OVERTIP
OVERPROUD	OVERSALES	OVERSKIPS	OVERSTUFF	OVERTIPS
OVERPUMP	OVERSALT	OVERSKIRT	OVERSTUNK	OVERTIRE
OVERPUMPS	OVERSALTS	OVERSLEEP	OVERSUDS	OVERTIRED
OVERQUICK	OVERSAUCE	OVERSLEPT	OVERSUP	OVERTIRES
OVERRACK	OVERSAVE	OVERSLIP	OVERSUPS	OVERTLY
OVERRACKS	OVERSAVED	OVERSLIPS	OVERSURE	OVERTNESS
OVERRAKE	OVERSAVES	OVERSLIPT	OVERSWAM	OVERTOIL
OVERRAKED	OVERSAW	OVERSLOW	OVERSWAY	OVERTOILS
OVERRAKES	OVERSCALE	OVERSMAN	OVERSWAYS	OVERTONE
OVERRAN	OVERSCORE	OVERSMEN	OVERSWEAR	OVERTONES
OVERRANK	OVERSEA	OVERSMOKE	OVERSWEET	OVERTOOK
OVERRANKS	OVERSEAS	OVERSOAK	OVERSWELL	OVERTOP
OVERRASH	OVERSEE	OVERSOAKS	OVERSWIM	OVERTOPS
OVERRATE	OVERSEED	OVERSOFT	OVERSWIMS	OVERTOWER
OVERRATED	OVERSEEDS	OVERSOLD	OVERSWING	OVERTRADE
OVERRATES	OVERSEEN	OVERSOON	OVERSWORE	OVERTRAIN
OVERREACH	OVERSEER	OVERSOUL	OVERSWORN	OVERTREAT
OVERREACT	OVERSEERS	OVERSOULS	OVERSWUM	OVERTRICK
OVERREAD	OVERSEES	OVERSOW	OVERSWUNG	OVERTRIM
OVERREADS	OVERSELL	OVERSOWED	OVERT	OVERTRIMS
OVERRED	OVERSELLS	OVERSOWN	OVERTAKE	OVERTRIP
OVERREDS	OVERSET	OVERSOWS	OVERTAKEN	OVERTRIPS
OVERREN	OVERSETS	OVERSPEND	OVERTAKES	OVERTRUMP

OVERTRUST	OVERWISE	OVOLO	OWN	OXEN
OVERTURE	OVERWORD	OVOLOS	OWNABLE	OXER
OVERTURED	OVERWORDS	OVONIC	OWNED	OXERS
OVERTURES	OVERWORE	OVONICS	OWNER	OXES
OVERTURN	OVERWORK	OVOTESTES	OWNERLESS	OXEYE
OVERTURNS	OVERWORKS	OVOTESTIS	OWNERS	OXEYES
OVERTYPE	OVERWORN	OVULAR	OWNERSHIP	OXFORD
OVERTYPED	OVERWOUND	OVULARY	OWNING	OXFORDS
OVERTYPES	OVERWRAP	OVULATE	OWNS	OXGANG
OVERURGE	OVERWRAPS	OVULATED	OWNSOME	OXGANGS
OVERURGED	OVERWRAPT	OVULATES	OWNSOMES	OXGATE
OVERURGES	OVERWREST	OVULATING	OWRE	OXGATES
OVERUSE	OVERWRITE	OVULATION	OWRECAME	OXHEAD
OVERUSED	OVERWROTE	OVULATORY	OWRECOME	OXHEADS
OVERUSES	OVERYEAR	OVULE	OWRECOMES	OXHEART
OVERUSING	OVERYEARS	OVULES	OWRELAY	OXHEARTS
OVERVALUE	OVERZEAL	OVUM	OWRELAYS	OXHERD
OVERVEIL	OVERZEALS	OW	OWRES	OXHERDS
OVERVEILS	OVIBOS	OWCHE	OWREWORD	OXHIDE
OVERVIEW	OVIBOSES	OWCHES	OWREWORDS	OXHIDES
OVERVIEWS	OVIBOVINE	OWE	OWRIE	OXIC
OVERVIVID	OVICIDAL	OWED	OWRIER	OXID
OVERVOTE	OVICIDE	OWELTIES	OWRIEST	OXIDABLE
OVERVOTED	OVICIDES	OWELTY	OWSE	OXIDANT
OVERVOTES	OVIDUCAL	OWER	OWSEN	OXIDANTS
OVERWARM	OVIDUCT	OWERBY	OWT	OXIDASE
OVERWARMS	OVIDUCTAL	OWERLOUP	OWTS	OXIDASES
OVERWARY	OVIDUCTS	OWERLOUPS	OX	OXIDASIC
OVERWASH	OVIFEROUS	OWES	OXACILLIN	OXIDATE
OVERWATCH	OVIFORM	OWIE	OXALATE	OXIDATED
OVERWATER	OVIGEROUS	OWIES	OXALATED	OXIDATES
OVERWEAK	OVINE	OWING	OXALATES	OXIDATING
OVERWEAR	OVINES	OWL	OXALATING	OXIDATION
OVERWEARS	OVIPARA	OWLED	OXALIC	OXIDATIVE
OVERWEARY	OVIPARITY	OWLER	OXALIS	OXIDE
OVERWEEN	OVIPAROUS	OWLERIES	OXALISES	OXIDES
OVERWEENS	OVIPOSIT	OWLERS	OXAZEPAM	OXIDIC
OVERWEIGH	OVIPOSITS	OWLERY	OXAZEPAMS	OXIDISE
OVERWENT	OVIRAPTOR	OWLET	OXAZINE	OXIDISED
OVERWET	OVISAC	OWLETS	OXAZINES	OXIDISER
OVERWETS	OVISACS	OWLIER	OXAZOLE	OXIDISERS
OVERWHELM	OVIST	OWLIEST	OXAZOLES	OXIDISES
OVERWIDE	OVISTS	OWLING	OXBLOOD	OXIDISING
OVERWILY	OVOID	OWLISH	OXBLOODS	OXIDIZE
OVERWIND	OVOIDAL	OWLISHLY	OXBOW	OXIDIZED
OVERWINDS	OVOIDALS	OWLLIKE	OXBOWS	OXIDIZER
OVERWING	OVOIDS	OWLS	OXCART	OXIDIZERS
OVERWINGS	OVOLI	OWLY	OXCARTS	OXIDIZES

O

OXIDIZING

OXIDIZING	OXTERED	OXYPHIL	OYEZ	OZONATION
OXIDS	OXTERING	OXYPHILE	OYEZES	OZONE
OXIES	OXTERS	OXYPHILES	OYS	OZONES
OXIM	OXTONGUE	OXYPHILIC	OYSTER	OZONIC
OXIME	OXTONGUES	OXYPHILS	OYSTERED	OZONIDE
OXIMES	OXY	OXYSALT	OYSTERER	OZONIDES
OXIMETER	OXYACID	OXYSALTS	OYSTERERS	OZONISE
OXIMETERS	OXYACIDS	OXYSOME	OYSTERING	OZONISED
OXIMETRY	OXYANION	OXYSOMES	OYSTERMAN	OZONISER
OXIMS	OXYANIONS	OXYTOCIC	OYSTERMEN	OZONISERS
OXLAND	OXYCODONE	OXYTOCICS	OYSTERS	OZONISES
OXLANDS	OXYGEN	OXYTOCIN	OYSTRIGE	OZONISING
OXLIKE	OXYGENASE	OXYTOCINS	OYSTRIGES	OZONIZE
OXLIP	OXYGENATE	OXYTONE	OZAENA	OZONIZED
OXLIPS	OXYGENIC	OXYTONES	OZAENAS	OZONIZER
OXO	OXYGENISE	OXYTONIC	OZALID	OZONIZERS
OXONIUM	OXYGENIZE	OXYTROPE	OZALIDS	OZONIZES
OXONIUMS	OXYGENOUS	OXYTROPES	OZEKI	OZONIZING
OXPECKER	OXYGENS	OY	OZEKIS	OZONOUS
OXPECKERS	OXYMEL	OYE	OZOCERITE	OZZIE
OXSLIP	OXYMELS	OYER	OZOKERITE	OZZIES
OXSLIPS	OXYMORA	OYERS	OZONATE	
OXTAIL	OXYMORON	OYES	OZONATED	
OXTAILS	OXYMORONS	OYESES	OZONATES	
OXTER	OXYNTIC	OYESSES	OZONATING	

O

P

PA	PACHOULI	PACKFONG	PADDERS	PADRONE
PAAL	PACHOULIS	PACKFONGS	PADDIES	PADRONES
PAALS	PACHUCO	PACKFRAME	PADDING	PADRONI
PAAN	PACHUCOS	PACKHORSE	PADDINGS	PADRONISM
PAANS	PACHYDERM	PACKING	PADDLE	PADS
PABLUM	PACHYTENE	PACKINGS	PADDLED	PADSAW
PABLUMS	PACIER	PACKLY	PADDLER	PADSAWS
PABOUCHE	PACIEST	PACKMAN	PADDLERS	PADSHAH
PABOUCHES	PACIFIC	PACKMEN	PADDLES	PADSHAHS
PABULAR	PACIFICAE	PACKMULE	PADDLING	PADUASOY
PABULOUS	PACIFICAL	PACKMULES	PADDLINGS	PADUASOYS
PABULUM	PACIFIED	PACKNESS	PADDOCK	PADYMELON
PABULUMS	PACIFIER	PACKS	PADDOCKED	PAEAN
PAC	PACIFIERS	PACKSACK	PADDOCKS	PAEANISM
PACA	PACIFIES	PACKSACKS	PADDY	PAEANISMS
PACABLE	PACIFISM	PACKSHEET	PADDYWACK	PAEANS
PACAS	PACIFISMS	PACKSTAFF	PADELLA	PAEDERAST
PACATION	PACIFIST	PACKWAX	PADELLAS	PAEDEUTIC
PACATIONS	PACIFISTS	PACKWAXES	PADEMELON	PAEDIATRY
PACE	PACIFY	PACKWAY	PADERERO	PAEDO
PACED	PACIFYING	PACKWAYS	PADEREROS	PAEDOLOGY
PACEMAKER	PACING	PACO	PADI	PAEDOS
PACEMAN	PACINGS	PACOS	PADIS	PAELLA
PACEMEN	PACK	PACS	PADISHAH	PAELLAS
PACER	PACKABLE	PACT	PADISHAHS	PAENULA
PACERS	PACKAGE	PACTA	PADKOS	PAENULAE
PACES	PACKAGED	PACTION	PADLE	PAENULAS
PACEWAY	PACKAGER	PACTIONAL	PADLES	PAEON
PACEWAYS	PACKAGERS	PACTIONED	PADLOCK	PAEONIC
PACEY	PACKAGES	PACTIONS	PADLOCKED	PAEONICS
PACHA	PACKAGING	PACTS	PADLOCKS	PAEONIES
PACHADOM	PACKBOARD	PACTUM	PADMA	PAEONS
PACHADOMS	PACKCLOTH	PACY	PADMAS	PAEONY
PACHAK	PACKED	PACZKI	PADNAG	PAESAN
PACHAKS	PACKER	PACZKIS	PADNAGS	PAESANI
PACHALIC	PACKERS	PAD	PADOUK	PAESANO
PACHALICS	PACKET	PADANG	PADOUKS	PAESANOS
PACHAS	PACKETED	PADANGS	PADRE	PAESANS
PACHINKO	PACKETING	PADAUK	PADRES	PAGAN
PACHINKOS	PACKETISE	PADAUKS	PADRI	PAGANDOM
PACHISI	PACKETIZE	PADDED	PADRONA	PAGANDOMS
PACHISIS	PACKETS	PADDER	PADRONAS	PAGANISE

PAGANISED	PAGURIDS	PAINTERS	PAJOCKES	PALAS
PAGANISER	PAH	PAINTIER	PAJOCKS	PALASES
PAGANISES	PAHAUTEA	PAINTIEST	PAK	PALATABLE
PAGANISH	PAHAUTEAS	PAINTING	PAKAHI	PALATABLY
PAGANISM	PAHLAVI	PAINTINGS	PAKAHIS	PALATAL
PAGANISMS	PAHLAVIS	PAINTPOT	PAKAPOO	PALATALLY
PAGANIST	PAHOEHOE	PAINTPOTS	PAKAPOOS	PALATALS
PAGANISTS	PAHOEHOES	PAINTRESS	PAKEHA	PALATE
PAGANIZE	PAHS	PAINTS	PAKEHAS	PALATED
PAGANIZED	PAID	PAINTURE	PAKFONG	PALATES
PAGANIZER	PAIDEUTIC	PAINTURES	PAKFONGS	PALATIAL
PAGANIZES	PAIDLE	PAINTWORK	PAKIHI	PALATINE
PAGANS	PAIDLES	PAINTY	PAKIHIS	PALATINES
PAGE	PAIGLE	PAIOCK	PAKKA	PALATING
PAGEANT	PAIGLES	PAIOCKE	PAKOKO	PALAVER
PAGEANTRY	PAIK	PAIOCKES	PAKOKOS	PALAVERED
PAGEANTS	PAIKED	PAIOCKS	PAKORA	PALAVERER
PAGEBOY	PAIKING	PAIR	PAKORAS	PALAVERS
PAGEBOYS	PAIKS	PAIRE	PAKS	PALAY
PAGED	PAIL	PAIRED	PAKTHONG	PALAYS
PAGEFUL	PAILFUL	PAIRER	PAKTHONGS	PALAZZI
PAGEFULS	PAILFULS	PAIRES	PAKTONG	PALAZZO
PAGEHOOD	PAILLARD	PAIREST	PAKTONGS	PALAZZOS
PAGEHOODS	PAILLARDS	PAIRIAL	PAL	PALE
PAGER	PAILLASSE	PAIRIALS	PALABRA	PALEA
PAGERS	PAILLETTE	PAIRING	PALABRAS	PALEAE
PAGES	PAILLON	PAIRINGS	PALACE	PALEAL
PAGEVIEW	PAILLONS	PAIRS	PALACED	PALEATE
PAGEVIEWS	PAILS	PAIRWISE	PALACES	PALEBUCK
PAGINAL	PAILSFUL	PAIS	PALACINKE	PALEBUCKS
PAGINATE	PAIN	PAISA	PALADIN	PALED
PAGINATED	PAINCH	PAISAN	PALADINS	PALEFACE
PAGINATES	PAINCHES	PAISANA	PALAEOSOL	PALEFACES
PAGING	PAINED	PAISANAS	PALAESTRA	PALELY
PAGINGS	PAINFUL	PAISANO	PALAFITTE	PALEMPORE
PAGLE	PAINFULLY	PAISANOS	PALAGI	PALENESS
PAGLES	PAINIM	PAISANS	PALAGIS	PALEOCENE
PAGOD	PAINIMS	PAISAS	PALAIS	PALEOCON
PAGODA	PAINING	PAISE	PALAMA	PALEOCONS
PAGODAS	PAINLESS	PAISLEY	PALAMAE	PALEOGENE
PAGODITE	PAINS	PAISLEYS	PALAMATE	PALEOLITH
PAGODITES	PAINT	PAITRICK	PALAMINO	PALEOLOGY
PAGODS	PAINTABLE	PAITRICKS	PALAMINOS	PALEOSOL
PAGRI	PAINTBALL	PAJAMA	PALAMPORE	PALEOSOLS
PAGRIS	PAINTBOX	PAJAMAED	PALANKEEN	PALEOZOIC
PAGURIAN	PAINTED	PAJAMAS	PALANQUIN	PALER
PAGURIANS	PAINTER	PAJOCK	PALAPA	PALES
PAGURID	PAINTERLY	PAJOCKE	PALAPAS	PALEST

PALESTRA	PALLAE	PALMATION	PALPABLE	PALTRILY
PALESTRAE	PALLAH	PALMBALL	PALPABLY	PALTRY
PALESTRAL	PALLAHS	PALMBALLS	PALPAL	PALUDAL
PALESTRAS	PALLASITE	PALMED	PALPATE	PALUDIC
PALET	PALLED	PALMER	PALPATED	PALUDINAL
PALETOT	PALLET	PALMERS	PALPATES	PALUDINE
PALETOTS	PALLETED	PALMETTE	PALPATING	PALUDISM
PALETS	PALLETING	PALMETTES	PALPATION	PALUDISMS
PALETTE	PALLETISE	PALMETTO	PALPATOR	PALUDOSE
PALETTES	PALLETIZE	PALMETTOS	PALPATORS	PALUDOUS
PALEWAYS	PALLETS	PALMFUL	PALPATORY	PALUSTRAL
PALEWISE	PALLETTE	PALMFULS	PALPEBRA	PALY
PALFREY	PALLETTES	PALMHOUSE	PALPEBRAE	PAM
PALFREYED	PALLIA	PALMIE	PALPEBRAL	PAMPA
PALFREYS	PALLIAL	PALMIER	PALPEBRAS	PAMPAS
PALI	PALLIARD	PALMIERS	PALPED	PAMPASES
PALIER	PALLIARDS	PALMIES	PALPI	PAMPEAN
PALIEST	PALLIASSE	PALMIEST	PALPING	PAMPEANS
PALIFORM	PALLIATE	PALMIET	PALPITANT	PAMPER
PALIKAR	PALLIATED	PALMIETS	PALPITATE	PAMPERED
PALIKARS	PALLIATES	PALMING	PALPS	PAMPERER
PALILALIA	PALLIATOR	PALMIPED	PALPUS	PAMPERERS
PALILLOGY	PALLID	PALMIPEDE	PALPUSES	PAMPERING
PALIMONY	PALLIDER	PALMIPEDS	PALS	PAMPERO
PALING	PALLIDEST	PALMIST	PALSA	PAMPEROS
PALINGS	PALLIDITY	PALMISTER	PALSAS	PAMPERS
PALINKA	PALLIDLY	PALMISTRY	PALSGRAVE	PAMPHLET
PALINKAS	PALLIED	PALMISTS	PALSHIP	PAMPHLETS
PALINODE	PALLIER	PALMITATE	PALSHIPS	PAMPHREY
PALINODES	PALLIES	PALMITIC	PALSIED	PAMPHREYS
PALINODY	PALLIEST	PALMITIN	PALSIER	PAMPOEN
PALINOPIA	PALLING	PALMITINS	PALSIES	PAMPOENS
PALIS	PALLIUM	PALMLIKE	PALSIEST	PAMPOOTIE
PALISADE	PALLIUMS	PALMPRINT	PALSTAFF	PAMS
PALISADED	PALLONE	PALMS	PALSTAFFS	PAN
PALISADES	PALLONES	PALMTOP	PALSTAVE	PANACEA
PALISADO	PALLOR	PALMTOPS	PALSTAVES	PANACEAN
PALISH	PALLORS	PALMY	PALSY	PANACEAS
PALKEE	PALLS	PALMYRA	PALSYING	PANACHAEA
PALKEES	PALLY	PALMYRAS	PALSYLIKE	PANACHE
PALKI	PALLYING	PALOLO	PALTER	PANACHES
PALKIS	PALM	PALOLOS	PALTERED	PANADA
PALL	PALMAR	PALOMINO	PALTERER	PANADAS
PALLA	PALMARIAN	PALOMINOS	PALTERERS	PANAMA
PALLADIA	PALMARY	PALOOKA	PALTERING	PANAMAS
PALLADIC	PALMATE	PALOOKAS	PALTERS	PANARIES
PALLADIUM	PALMATED	PALOVERDE	PALTRIER	PANARY
PALLADOUS	PALMATELY	PALP	PALTRIEST	PANATELA

PANATELAS	PANDERERS	PANELLIST	PANICLED	PANNIKIN
PANATELLA	PANDERESS	PANELS	PANICLES	PANNIKINS
PANAX	PANDERING	PANES	PANICS	PANNING
PANAXES	PANDERISM	PANETELA	PANICUM	PANNINGS
PANBROIL	PANDERLY	PANETELAS	PANICUMS	PANNIST
PANBROILS	PANDEROUS	PANETELLA	PANIER	PANNISTS
PANCAKE	PANDERS	PANETTONE	PANIERS	PANNOSE
PANCAKED	PANDIED	PANETTONI	PANIM	PANNUS
PANCAKES	PANDIES	PANFISH	PANIMS	PANNUSES
PANCAKING	PANDIT	PANFISHED	PANING	PANOCHA
PANCE	PANDITS	PANFISHES	PANINI	PANOCHAS
PANCES	PANDOOR	PANFORTE	PANINIS	PANOCHE
PANCETTA	PANDOORS	PANFORTES	PANINO	PANOCHES
PANCETTAS	PANDORA	PANFRIED	PANISC	PANOISTIC
PANCHAX	PANDORAS	PANFRIES	PANISCS	PANOPLIED
PANCHAXES	PANDORE	PANFRY	PANISK	PANOPLIES
PANCHAYAT	PANDORES	PANFRYING	PANISKS	PANOPLY
PANCHEON	PANDOUR	PANFUL	PANISLAM	PANOPTIC
PANCHEONS	PANDOURS	PANFULS	PANISLAMS	PANORAMA
PANCHION	PANDOWDY	PANG	PANJANDRA	PANORAMAS
PANCHIONS	PANDROP	PANGA	PANKO	PANORAMIC
PANCOSMIC	PANDROPS	PANGAMIC	PANKOS	PANPIPE
PANCRATIA	PANDS	PANGAMIES	PANLIKE	PANPIPES
PANCRATIC	PANDURA	PANGAMY	PANLOGISM	PANS
PANCREAS	PANDURAS	PANGAS	PANMICTIC	PANSEXUAL
PAND	PANDURATE	PANGED	PANMIXES	PANSIED
PANDA	PANDY	PANGEN	PANMIXIA	PANSIES
PANDAN	PANDYING	PANGENE	PANMIXIAS	PANSOPHIC
PANDANI	PANE	PANGENES	PANMIXIS	PANSOPHY
PANDANIS	PANED	PANGENS	PANNAGE	PANSPERMY
PANDANS	PANEER	PANGING	PANNAGES	PANSTICK
PANDANUS	PANEERS	PANGLESS	PANNE	PANSTICKS
PANDAR	PANEGOISM	PANGOLIN	PANNED	PANSY
PANDARED	PANEGYRIC	PANGOLINS	PANNELLED	PANT
PANDARING	PANEGYRY	PANGRAM	PANNER	PANTABLE
PANDARS	PANEITIES	PANGRAMS	PANNERS	PANTABLES
PANDAS	PANEITY	PANGS	PANNES	PANTAGAMY
PANDATION	PANEL	PANHANDLE	PANNI	PANTALEON
PANDECT	PANELED	PANHUMAN	PANNICK	PANTALET
PANDECTS	PANELESS	PANIC	PANNICKS	PANTALETS
PANDEMIA	PANELING	PANICALLY	PANNICLE	PANTALON
PANDEMIAN	PANELINGS	PANICK	PANNICLES	PANTALONE
PANDEMIAS	PANELISED	PANICKED	PANNIER	PANTALONS
PANDEMIC	PANELIST	PANICKIER	PANNIERED	PANTALOON
PANDEMICS	PANELISTS	PANICKING	PANNIERS	PANTDRESS
PANDER	PANELIZED	PANICKS	PANNIKEL	PANTED
PANDERED	PANELLED	PANICKY	PANNIKELL	PANTER
PANDERER	PANELLING	PANICLE	PANNIKELS	PANTERS

PANTHEISM	PANZOOTIC	PAPERCLIP	PAPPADUM	PARABOLAE
PANTHEIST	PAOLI	PAPERED	PAPPADUMS	PARABOLAS
PANTHENOL	PAOLO	PAPERER	PAPPED	PARABOLE
PANTHEON	PAP	PAPERERS	PAPPI	PARABOLES
PANTHEONS	PAPA	PAPERGIRL	PAPPIER	PARABOLIC
PANTHER	PAPABLE	PAPERIER	PAPPIES	PARABRAKE
PANTHERS	PAPACIES	PAPERIEST	PAPPIEST	PARACHOR
PANTIE	PAPACY	PAPERING	PAPPING	PARACHORS
PANTIES	PAPADAM	PAPERINGS	PAPPOOSE	PARACHUTE
PANTIHOSE	PAPADAMS	PAPERLESS	PAPPOOSES	PARACLETE
PANTILE	PAPADOM	PAPERS	PAPPOSE	PARACME
PANTILED	PAPADOMS	PAPERWARE	PAPPOUS	PARACMES
PANTILES	PAPADUM	PAPERWORK	PAPPUS	PARACRINE
PANTILING	PAPADUMS	PAPERY	PAPPUSES	PARACUSES
PANTINE	PAPAIN	PAPES	PAPPY	PARACUSIS
PANTINES	PAPAINS	PAPETERIE	PAPRICA	PARADE
PANTING	PAPAL	PAPHIAN	PAPRICAS	PARADED
PANTINGLY	PAPALISE	PAPHIANS	PAPRIKA	PARADER
PANTINGS	PAPALISED	PAPILIO	PAPRIKAS	PARADERS
PANTLEG	PAPALISES	PAPILIOS	PAPRIKASH	PARADES
PANTLEGS	PAPALISM	PAPILLA	PAPS	PARADIGM
PANTLER	PAPALISMS	PAPILLAE	PAPULA	PARADIGMS
PANTLERS	PAPALIST	PAPILLAR	PAPULAE	PARADING
PANTO	PAPALISTS	PAPILLARY	PAPULAR	PARADISAL
PANTOFFLE	PAPALIZE	PAPILLATE	PAPULAS	PARADISE
PANTOFLE	PAPALIZED	PAPILLOMA	PAPULE	PARADISES
PANTOFLES	PAPALIZES	PAPILLON	PAPULES	PARADISIC
PANTOMIME	PAPALLY	PAPILLONS	PAPULOSE	PARADOR
PANTON	PAPARAZZI	PAPILLOSE	PAPULOUS	PARADORES
PANTONS	PAPARAZZO	PAPILLOTE	PAPYRAL	PARADORS
PANTOS	PAPAS	PAPILLOUS	PAPYRI	PARADOS
PANTOUFLE	PAPASAN	PAPILLULE	PAPYRIAN	PARADOSES
PANTOUM	PAPASANS	PAPISH	PAPYRINE	PARADOX
PANTOUMS	PAPAUMA	PAPISHER	PAPYRUS	PARADOXAL
PANTRIES	PAPAUMAS	PAPISHERS	PAPYRUSES	PARADOXER
PANTROPIC	PAPAVER	PAPISHES	PAR	PARADOXES
PANTRY	PAPAVERS	PAPISM	PARA	PARADOXY
PANTRYMAN	PAPAW	PAPISMS	PARABASES	PARADROP
PANTRYMEN	PAPAWS	PAPIST	PARABASIS	PARADROPS
PANTS	PAPAYA	PAPISTIC	PARABEMA	PARAE
PANTSUIT	PAPAYAN	PAPISTRY	PARABEN	PARAFFIN
PANTSUITS	PAPAYAS	PAPISTS	PARABENS	PARAFFINE
PANTUN	PAPE	PAPOOSE	PARABLAST	PARAFFINS
PANTUNS	PAPER	PAPOOSES	PARABLE	PARAFFINY
PANTY	PAPERBACK	PAPPADAM	PARABLED	PARAFFLE
PANTYHOSE	PAPERBARK	PAPPADAMS	PARABLES	PARAFFLES
PANZER	PAPERBOY	PAPPADOM	PARABLING	PARAFLE
PANZERS	PAPERBOYS	PAPPADOMS	PARABOLA	PARAFLES

PARAFOIL	PARAMESE	PARASANGS	PARCENER	PARELLA
PARAFOILS	PARAMESES	PARASCEVE	PARCENERS	PARELLAS
PARAFORM	PARAMETER	PARASHAH	PARCH	PARELLE
PARAFORMS	PARAMO	PARASHAHS	PARCHED	PARELLES
PARAGE	PARAMORPH	PARASHOT	PARCHEDLY	PAREN
PARAGES	PARAMOS	PARASHOTH	PARCHEESI	PARENESES
PARAGLIDE	PARAMOUNT	PARASITE	PARCHES	PARENESIS
PARAGOGE	PARAMOUR	PARASITES	PARCHESI	PARENS
PARAGOGES	PARAMOURS	PARASITIC	PARCHESIS	PARENT
PARAGOGIC	PARAMYLUM	PARASOL	PARCHING	PARENTAGE
PARAGOGUE	PARANETE	PARASOLED	PARCHISI	PARENTAL
PARAGON	PARANETES	PARASOLS	PARCHISIS	PARENTED
PARAGONED	PARANG	PARATAXES	PARCHMENT	PARENTING
PARAGONS	PARANGS	PARATAXIS	PARCIMONY	PARENTS
PARAGRAM	PARANOEA	PARATHA	PARCLOSE	PAREO
PARAGRAMS	PARANOEAS	PARATHAS	PARCLOSES	PAREOS
PARAGRAPH	PARANOEIC	PARATHION	PARD	PARER
PARAKEET	PARANOIA	PARATONIC	PARDAH	PARERA
PARAKEETS	PARANOIAC	PARATROOP	PARDAHS	PARERAS
PARAKELIA	PARANOIAS	PARAVAIL	PARDAL	PARERGA
PARAKITE	PARANOIC	PARAVANE	PARDALE	PARERGON
PARAKITES	PARANOICS	PARAVANES	PARDALES	PARERS
PARALALIA	PARANOID	PARAVANT	PARDALIS	PARES
PARALEGAL	PARANOIDS	PARAVANTS	PARDALOTE	PARESES
PARALEXIA	PARANYM	PARAVAUNT	PARDALS	PARESIS
PARALEXIC	PARANYMPH	PARAWING	PARDED	PARETIC
PARALLAX	PARANYMS	PARAWINGS	PARDEE	PARETICS
PARALLEL	PARAPARA	PARAXIAL	PARDI	PAREU
PARALLELS	PARAPARAS	PARAZOA	PARDIE	PAREUS
PARALOGIA	PARAPENTE	PARAZOAN	PARDINE	PAREV
PARALOGUE	PARAPET	PARAZOANS	PARDNER	PAREVE
PARALOGY	PARAPETED	PARAZOON	PARDNERS	PARFAIT
PARALYSE	PARAPETS	PARBAKE	PARDON	PARFAITS
PARALYSED	PARAPH	PARBAKED	PARDONED	PARFLECHE
PARALYSER	PARAPHED	PARBAKES	PARDONER	PARFLESH
PARALYSES	PARAPHING	PARBAKING	PARDONERS	PARFOCAL
PARALYSIS	PARAPHS	PARBOIL	PARDONING	PARGANA
PARALYTIC	PARAPODIA	PARBOILED	PARDONS	PARGANAS
PARALYZE	PARAQUAT	PARBOILS	PARDS	PARGASITE
PARALYZED	PARAQUATS	PARBREAK	PARDY	PARGE
PARALYZER	PARAQUET	PARBREAKS	PARE	PARGED
PARALYZES	PARAQUETS	PARBUCKLE	PARECIOUS	PARGES
PARAMATTA	PARAQUITO	PARCEL	PARECISM	PARGET
PARAMECIA	PARARHYME	PARCELED	PARECISMS	PARGETED
PARAMEDIC	PARAS	PARCELING	PARED	PARGETER
PARAMENT	PARASAIL	PARCELLED	PAREGORIC	PARGETERS
PARAMENTA	PARASAILS	PARCELS	PAREIRA	PARGETING
PARAMENTS	PARASANG	PARCENARY	PAREIRAS	PARGETS

PARGETTED	PARKERS	PARLORS	PAROSMIAS	PARRIER
PARGETTER	PARKETTE	PARLOUR	PAROTIC	PARRIERS
PARGING	PARKETTES	PARLOURS	PAROTID	PARRIES
PARGINGS	PARKI	PARLOUS	PAROTIDES	PARRING
PARGO	PARKIE	PARLOUSLY	PAROTIDS	PARRITCH
PARGOES	PARKIER	PARLY	PAROTIS	PARROCK
PARGOS	PARKIES	PARMA	PAROTISES	PARROCKED
PARGYLINE	PARKIEST	PARMAS	PAROTITIC	PARROCKS
PARHELIA	PARKIN	PARMESAN	PAROTITIS	PARROKET
PARHELIC	PARKING	PARMESANS	PAROTOID	PARROKETS
PARHELION	PARKINGS	PAROCHIAL	PAROTOIDS	PARROQUET
PARHYPATE	PARKINS	PAROCHIN	PAROUS	PARROT
PARIAH	PARKIS	PAROCHINE	PAROUSIA	PARROTED
PARIAHS	PARKISH	PAROCHINS	PAROUSIAS	PARROTER
PARIAL	PARKLAND	PARODIC	PAROXYSM	PARROTERS
PARIALS	PARKLANDS	PARODICAL	PAROXYSMS	PARROTIER
PARIAN	PARKLIKE	PARODIED	PARP	PARROTING
PARIANS	PARKLY	PARODIES	PARPANE	PARROTRY
PARIES	PARKOUR	PARODIST	PARPANES	PARROTS
PARIETAL	PARKOURS	PARODISTS	PARPED	PARROTY
PARIETALS	PARKS	PARODOI	PARPEN	PARRS
PARIETES	PARKWARD	PARODOS	PARPEND	PARRY
PARING	PARKWARDS	PARODY	PARPENDS	PARRYING
PARINGS	PARKWAY	PARODYING	PARPENS	PARS
PARIS	PARKWAYS	PAROECISM	PARPENT	PARSABLE
PARISCHAN	PARKY	PAROEMIA	PARPENTS	PARSE
PARISES	PARLANCE	PAROEMIAC	PARPING	PARSEC
PARISH	PARLANCES	PAROEMIAL	PARPOINT	PARSECS
PARISHAD	PARLANDO	PAROEMIAS	PARPOINTS	PARSED
PARISHADS	PARLANTE	PAROICOUS	PARPS	PARSER
PARISHEN	PARLAY	PAROL	PARQUET	PARSERS
PARISHENS	PARLAYED	PAROLABLE	PARQUETED	PARSES
PARISHES	PARLAYING	PAROLE	PARQUETRY	PARSIMONY
PARISON	PARLAYS	PAROLED	PARQUETS	PARSING
PARISONS	PARLE	PAROLEE	PARR	PARSINGS
PARITIES	PARLED	PAROLEES	PARRA	PARSLEY
PARITOR	PARLEMENT	PAROLES	PARRAKEET	PARSLEYED
PARITORS	PARLES	PAROLING	PARRAL	PARSLEYS
PARITY	PARLEY	PAROLS	PARRALS	PARSLIED
PARK	PARLEYED	PARONYM	PARRAS	PARSNEP
PARKA	PARLEYER	PARONYMIC	PARRED	PARSNEPS
PARKADE	PARLEYERS	PARONYMS	PARREL	PARSNIP
PARKADES	PARLEYING	PARONYMY	PARRELS	PARSNIPS
PARKAS	PARLEYS	PAROQUET	PARRHESIA	PARSON
PARKED	PARLEYVOO	PAROQUETS	PARRICIDE	PARSONAGE
PARKEE	PARLIES	PARORE	PARRIDGE	PARSONIC
PARKEES	PARLING	PARORES	PARRIDGES	PARSONISH
PARKER	PARLOR	PAROSMIA	PARRIED	PARSONS

PART	PARTOOK	PASEARED	PASSAGE	PASSKEYS
PARTAKE	PARTRIDGE	PASEARING	PASSAGED	PASSLESS
PARTAKEN	PARTS	PASEARS	PASSAGER	PASSMAN
PARTAKER	PARTURE	PASELA	PASSAGES	PASSMEN
PARTAKERS	PARTURES	PASELAS	PASSAGING	PASSMENT
PARTAKES	PARTWAY	PASEO	PASSALONG	PASSMENTS
PARTAKING	PARTWORK	PASEOS	PASSAMENT	PASSOUT
PARTAN	PARTWORKS	PASES	PASSANT	PASSOUTS
PARTANS	PARTY	PASH	PASSATA	PASSOVER
PARTED	PARTYER	PASHA	PASSATAS	PASSOVERS
PARTER	PARTYERS	PASHADOM	PASSBAND	PASSPORT
PARTERRE	PARTYGOER	PASHADOMS	PASSBANDS	PASSPORTS
PARTERRES	PARTYING	PASHALIC	PASSBOOK	PASSUS
PARTERS	PARTYINGS	PASHALICS	PASSBOOKS	PASSUSES
PARTI	PARTYISM	PASHALIK	PASSCODE	PASSWORD
PARTIAL	PARTYISMS	PASHALIKS	PASSCODES	PASSWORDS
PARTIALLY	PARULIDES	PASHAS	PASSE	PAST
PARTIALS	PARULIS	PASHED	PASSED	PASTA
PARTIBLE	PARULISES	PASHES	PASSEE	PASTALIKE
PARTICLE	PARURA	PASHIM	PASSEL	PASTANCE
PARTICLES	PARURAS	PASHIMS	PASSELS	PASTANCES
PARTIED	PARURE	PASHING	PASSEMENT	PASTAS
PARTIER	PARURES	PASHKA	PASSENGER	PASTE
PARTIERS	PARURESES	PASHKAS	PASSEPIED	PASTED
PARTIES	PARURESIS	PASHM	PASSER	PASTEDOWN
PARTIEST	PARURETIC	PASHMINA	PASSERBY	PASTEL
PARTIM	PARVE	PASHMINAS	PASSERINE	PASTELIKE
PARTING	PARVENU	PASHMS	PASSERS	PASTELIST
PARTINGS	PARVENUE	PASKA	PASSERSBY	PASTELS
PARTIS	PARVENUES	PASKAS	PASSES	PASTER
PARTISAN	PARVENUS	PASKHA	PASSIBLE	PASTERN
PARTISANS	PARVIS	PASKHAS	PASSIBLY	PASTERNS
PARTITA	PARVISE	PASODOBLE	PASSIM	PASTERS
PARTITAS	PARVISES	PASPALUM	PASSING	PASTES
PARTITE	PARVO	PASPALUMS	PASSINGLY	PASTEUP
PARTITION	PARVOLIN	PASPIES	PASSINGS	PASTEUPS
PARTITIVE	PARVOLINE	PASPY	PASSION	PASTICCI
PARTITURA	PARVOLINS	PASQUIL	PASSIONAL	PASTICCIO
PARTIZAN	PARVOS	PASQUILER	PASSIONED	PASTICHE
PARTIZANS	PAS	PASQUILS	PASSIONS	PASTICHES
PARTLET	PASCAL	PASS	PASSIVATE	PASTIE
PARTLETS	PASCALS	PASSABLE	PASSIVE	PASTIER
PARTLY	PASCHAL	PASSABLY	PASSIVELY	PASTIES
PARTNER	PASCHALS	PASSADE	PASSIVES	PASTIEST
PARTNERED	PASCUAL	PASSADES	PASSIVISM	PASTIL
PARTNERS	PASCUALS	PASSADO	PASSIVIST	PASTILLE
PARTON	PASE	PASSADOES	PASSIVITY	PASTILLES
PARTONS	PASEAR	PASSADOS	PASSKEY	PASTILS

PASTILY	PATAKA	PATEREROS	PATINISED	PATRONAL
PASTIME	PATAKAS	PATERNAL	PATINISES	PATRONESS
PASTIMES	PATAMAR	PATERNITY	PATINIZE	PATRONISE
PASTINA	PATAMARS	PATERS	PATINIZED	PATRONIZE
PASTINAS	PATBALL	PATES	PATINIZES	PATRONLY
PASTINESS	PATBALLS	PATH	PATINS	PATRONNE
PASTING	PATCH	PATHED	PATIO	PATRONNES
PASTINGS	PATCHABLE	PATHETIC	PATIOS	PATRONS
PASTIS	PATCHED	PATHETICS	PATISSIER	PATROON
PASTISES	PATCHER	PATHIC	PATKA	PATROONS
PASTITSIO	PATCHERS	PATHICS	PATKAS	PATS
PASTITSO	PATCHERY	PATHING	PATLY	PATSIES
PASTITSOS	PATCHES	PATHLESS	PATNESS	PATSY
PASTLESS	PATCHIER	PATHNAME	PATNESSES	PATTAMAR
PASTNESS	PATCHIEST	PATHNAMES	PATOIS	PATTAMARS
PASTOR	PATCHILY	PATHOGEN	PATONCE	PATTE
PASTORAL	PATCHING	PATHOGENE	PATOOT	PATTED
PASTORALE	PATCHINGS	PATHOGENS	PATOOTIE	PATTEE
PASTORALI	PATCHOCKE	PATHOGENY	PATOOTIES	PATTEN
PASTORALS	PATCHOULI	PATHOLOGY	PATOOTS	PATTENED
PASTORATE	PATCHOULY	PATHOS	PATRIAL	PATTENING
PASTORED	PATCHWORK	PATHOSES	PATRIALS	PATTENS
PASTORING	PATCHY	PATHS	PATRIARCH	PATTER
PASTORIUM	PATE	PATHWAY	PATRIATE	PATTERED
PASTORLY	PATED	PATHWAYS	PATRIATED	PATTERER
PASTORS	PATELLA	PATIBLE	PATRIATES	PATTERERS
PASTRAMI	PATELLAE	PATIENCE	PATRICIAN	PATTERING
PASTRAMIS	PATELLAR	PATIENCES	PATRICIDE	PATTERN
PASTRIES	PATELLAS	PATIENT	PATRICK	PATTERNED
PASTROMI	PATELLATE	PATIENTED	PATRICKS	PATTERNS
PASTROMIS	PATEN	PATIENTER	PATRICO	PATTERS
PASTRY	PATENCIES	PATIENTLY	PATRICOES	PATTES
PASTS	PATENCY	PATIENTS	PATRICOS	PATTEST
PASTURAGE	PATENS	PATIKI	PATRILINY	PATTIE
PASTURAL	PATENT	PATIKIS	PATRIMONY	PATTIES
PASTURE	PATENTED	PATIN	PATRIOT	PATTING
PASTURED	PATENTEE	PATINA	PATRIOTIC	PATTLE
PASTURER	PATENTEES	PATINAE	PATRIOTS	PATTLES
PASTURERS	PATENTING	PATINAED	PATRISTIC	PATTRESS
PASTURES	PATENTLY	PATINAS	PATROL	PATTY
PASTURING	PATENTOR	PATINATE	PATROLLED	PATTYPAN
PASTY	PATENTORS	PATINATED	PATROLLER	PATTYPANS
PAT	PATENTS	PATINATES	PATROLMAN	PATU
PATACA	PATER	PATINE	PATROLMEN	PATULENT
PATACAS	PATERA	PATINED	PATROLOGY	PATULIN
PATAGIA	PATERAE	PATINES	PATROLS	PATULINS
PATAGIAL	PATERCOVE	PATINING	PATRON	PATULOUS
PATAGIUM	PATERERO	PATINISE	PATRONAGE	PATUS

PATUTUKI	PAUSERS	PAVONINE	PAY	PAYSAGE
PATUTUKIS	PAUSES	PAVS	PAYABLE	PAYSAGES
PATY	PAUSING	PAW	PAYABLES	PAYSAGIST
PATZER	PAUSINGLY	PAWA	PAYABLY	PAYSD
PATZERS	PAUSINGS	PAWAS	PAYBACK	PAYSLIP
PAUA	PAV	PAWAW	PAYBACKS	PAYSLIPS
PAUAS	PAVAGE	PAWAWED	PAYCHECK	PAYWALL
PAUCAL	PAVAGES	PAWAWING	PAYCHECKS	PAYWALLS
PAUCALS	PAVAN	PAWAWS	PAYCHEQUE	PAZAZZ
PAUCITIES	PAVANE	PAWED	PAYDAY	PAZAZZES
PAUCITY	PAVANES	PAWER	PAYDAYS	PAZZAZZ
PAUGHTIER	PAVANS	PAWERS	PAYDOWN	PAZZAZZES
PAUGHTY	PAVE	PAWING	PAYDOWNS	PE
PAUL	PAVED	PAWK	PAYED	PEA
PAULDRON	PAVEED	PAWKIER	PAYEE	PEABERRY
PAULDRONS	PAVEMENT	PAWKIEST	PAYEES	PEABRAIN
PAULIN	PAVEMENTS	PAWKILY	PAYER	PEABRAINS
PAULINS	PAVEN	PAWKINESS	PAYERS	PEACE
PAULOWNIA	PAVENS	PAWKS	PAYESS	PEACEABLE
PAULS	PAVER	PAWKY	PAYFONE	PEACEABLY
PAUNCE	PAVERS	PAWL	PAYFONES	PEACED
PAUNCES	PAVES	PAWLS	PAYGRADE	PEACEFUL
PAUNCH	PAVID	PAWN	PAYGRADES	PEACELESS
PAUNCHED	PAVILION	PAWNABLE	PAYING	PEACENIK
PAUNCHES	PAVILIONS	PAWNAGE	PAYINGS	PEACENIKS
PAUNCHIER	PAVILLON	PAWNAGES	PAYLIST	PEACES
PAUNCHING	PAVILLONS	PAWNCE	PAYLISTS	PEACETIME
PAUNCHY	PAVIN	PAWNCES	PAYLOAD	PEACH
PAUPER	PAVING	PAWNED	PAYLOADS	PEACHBLOW
PAUPERDOM	PAVINGS	PAWNEE	PAYMASTER	PEACHED
PAUPERED	PAVINS	PAWNEES	PAYMENT	PEACHER
PAUPERESS	PAVIOR	PAWNER	PAYMENTS	PEACHERS
PAUPERING	PAVIORS	PAWNERS	PAYNIM	PEACHES
PAUPERISE	PAVIOUR	PAWNING	PAYNIMRY	PEACHICK
PAUPERISM	PAVIOURS	PAWNOR	PAYNIMS	PEACHICKS
PAUPERIZE	PAVIS	PAWNORS	PAYOFF	PEACHIER
PAUPERS	PAVISE	PAWNS	PAYOFFS	PEACHIEST
PAUPIETTE	PAVISER	PAWNSHOP	PAYOLA	PEACHILY
PAURAQUE	PAVISERS	PAWNSHOPS	PAYOLAS	PEACHING
PAURAQUES	PAVISES	PAWPAW	PAYOR	PEACHY
PAUROPOD	PAVISSE	PAWPAWS	PAYORS	PEACING
PAUROPODS	PAVISSES	PAWS	PAYOUT	PEACOAT
PAUSAL	PAVLOVA	PAX	PAYOUTS	PEACOATS
PAUSE	PAVLOVAS	PAXES	PAYPHONE	PEACOCK
PAUSED	PAVONAZZO	PAXIUBA	PAYPHONES	PEACOCKED
PAUSEFUL	PAVONE	PAXIUBAS	PAYROLL	PEACOCKS
PAUSELESS	PAVONES	PAXWAX	PAYROLLS	PEACOCKY
PAUSER	PAVONIAN	PAXWAXES	PAYS	PEACOD

PEACODS	PEARLIES	PEATIEST	PECK	PECULATE
PEAFOWL	PEARLIEST	PEATLAND	PECKE	PECULATED
PEAFOWLS	PEARLIN	PEATLANDS	PECKED	PECULATES
PEAG	PEARLING	PEATMAN	PECKER	PECULATOR
PEAGE	PEARLINGS	PEATMEN	PECKERS	PECULIA
PEAGES	PEARLINS	PEATS	PECKES	PECULIAR
PEAGS	PEARLISED	PEATSHIP	PECKIER	PECULIARS
PEAHEN	PEARLITE	PEATSHIPS	PECKIEST	PECULIUM
PEAHENS	PEARLITES	PEATY	PECKING	PECUNIARY
PEAK	PEARLITIC	PEAVEY	PECKINGS	PECUNIOUS
PEAKED	PEARLIZED	PEAVEYS	PECKISH	PED
PEAKIER	PEARLS	PEAVIES	PECKISHLY	PEDAGOG
PEAKIEST	PEARLWARE	PEAVY	PECKS	PEDAGOGIC
PEAKINESS	PEARLWORT	PEAZE	PECKY	PEDAGOGS
PEAKING	PEARLY	PEAZED	PECORINI	PEDAGOGUE
PEAKINGS	PEARMAIN	PEAZES	PECORINO	PEDAGOGY
PEAKISH	PEARMAINS	PEAZING	PECORINOS	PEDAL
PEAKLESS	PEARS	PEBA	PECS	PEDALBOAT
PEAKLIKE	PEARST	PEBAS	PECTASE	PEDALCAR
PEAKS	PEART	PEBBLE	PECTASES	PEDALCARS
PEAKY	PEARTER	PEBBLED	PECTATE	PEDALED
PEAL	PEARTEST	PEBBLES	PECTATES	PEDALER
PEALED	PEARTLY	PEBBLIER	PECTEN	PEDALERS
PEALIKE	PEARTNESS	PEBBLIEST	PECTENS	PEDALFER
PEALING	PEARWOOD	PEBBLING	PECTIC	PEDALFERS
PEALS	PEARWOODS	PEBBLINGS	PECTIN	PEDALIER
PEAN	PEAS	PEBBLY	PECTINAL	PEDALIERS
PEANED	PEASANT	PEBIBYTE	PECTINALS	PEDALING
PEANING	PEASANTRY	PEBIBYTES	PECTINATE	PEDALLED
PEANS	PEASANTS	PEBRINE	PECTINEAL	PEDALLER
PEANUT	PEASANTY	PEBRINES	PECTINEI	PEDALLERS
PEANUTS	PEASCOD	PEC	PECTINES	PEDALLING
PEANUTTY	PEASCODS	PECAN	PECTINEUS	PEDALO
PEAPOD	PEASE	PECANS	PECTINOUS	PEDALOES
PEAPODS	PEASECOD	PECCABLE	PECTINS	PEDALOS
PEAR	PEASECODS	PECCANCY	PECTISE	PEDALS
PEARCE	PEASED	PECCANT	PECTISED	PEDANT
PEARCED	PEASEN	PECCANTLY	PECTISES	PEDANTIC
PEARCES	PEASES	PECCARIES	PECTISING	PEDANTISE
PEARCING	PEASING	PECCARY	PECTIZE	PEDANTISM
PEARE	PEASON	PECCAVI	PECTIZED	PEDANTIZE
PEARES	PEASOUPER	PECCAVIS	PECTIZES	PEDANTRY
PEARL	PEAT	PECH	PECTIZING	PEDANTS
PEARLASH	PEATARIES	PECHAN	PECTOLITE	PEDATE
PEARLED	PEATARY	PECHANS	PECTORAL	PEDATELY
PEARLER	PEATERIES	PECHED	PECTORALS	PEDATIFID
PEARLERS	PEATERY	PECHING	PECTOSE	PEDDER
PEARLIER	PEATIER	PECHS	PECTOSES	PEDDERS

P

PEDDLE	PEDLER	PEELING	PEESWEEPS	PEINCTS
PEDDLED	PEDLERIES	PEELINGS	PEETWEET	PEINED
PEDDLER	PEDLERS	PEELS	PEETWEETS	PEINING
PEDDLERS	PEDLERY	PEEN	PEEVE	PEINS
PEDDLERY	PEDOCAL	PEENED	PEEVED	PEIRASTIC
PEDDLES	PEDOCALIC	PEENGE	PEEVER	PEISE
PEDDLING	PEDOCALS	PEENGED	PEEVERS	PEISED
PEDDLINGS	PEDOGENIC	PEENGEING	PEEVES	PEISES
PEDERAST	PEDOLOGIC	PEENGES	PEEVING	PEISHWA
PEDERASTS	PEDOLOGY	PEENGING	PEEVISH	PEISHWAH
PEDERASTY	PEDOMETER	PEENING	PEEVISHLY	PEISHWAHS
PEDERERO	PEDOPHILE	PEENINGS	PEEWEE	PEISHWAS
PEDEREROS	PEDORTHIC	PEENS	PEEWEES	PEISING
PEDES	PEDRAIL	PEEOY	PEEWIT	PEIZE
PEDESES	PEDRAILS	PEEOYS	PEEWITS	PEIZED
PEDESIS	PEDRERO	PEEP	PEG	PEIZES
PEDESTAL	PEDREROES	PEEPBO	PEGASUS	PEIZING
PEDESTALS	PEDREROS	PEEPBOS	PEGASUSES	PEJORATE
PEDETIC	PEDRO	PEEPE	PEGBOARD	PEJORATED
PEDI	PEDROS	PEEPED	PEGBOARDS	PEJORATES
PEDIATRIC	PEDS	PEEPER	PEGBOX	PEKAN
PEDICAB	PEDUNCLE	PEEPERS	PEGBOXES	PEKANS
PEDICABS	PEDUNCLED	PEEPES	PEGGED	PEKE
PEDICEL	PEDUNCLES	PEEPHOLE	PEGGIER	PEKEPOO
PEDICELS	PEDWAY	PEEPHOLES	PEGGIES	PEKEPOOS
PEDICLE	PEDWAYS	PEEPING	PEGGIEST	PEKES
PEDICLED	PEE	PEEPS	PEGGING	PEKIN
PEDICLES	PEEBEEN	PEEPSHOW	PEGGINGS	PEKINS
PEDICULAR	PEEBEENS	PEEPSHOWS	PEGGY	PEKOE
PEDICULI	PEECE	PEEPTOE	PEGH	PEKOES
PEDICULUS	PEECES	PEEPUL	PEGHED	PEL
PEDICURE	PEED	PEEPULS	PEGHING	PELA
PEDICURED	PEEING	PEER	PEGHS	PELAGE
PEDICURES	PEEK	PEERAGE	PEGLEGGED	PELAGES
PEDIFORM	PEEKABO	PEERAGES	PEGLESS	PELAGIAL
PEDIGREE	PEEKABOO	PEERED	PEGLIKE	PELAGIALS
PEDIGREED	PEEKABOOS	PEERESS	PEGMATITE	PELAGIAN
PEDIGREES	PEEKABOS	PEERESSES	PEGS	PELAGIANS
PEDIMENT	PEEKAPOO	PEERIE	PEGTOP	PELAGIC
PEDIMENTS	PEEKAPOOS	PEERIER	PEGTOPS	PELAGICS
PEDIPALP	PEEKED	PEERIES	PEH	PELAS
PEDIPALPI	PEEKING	PEERIEST	PEHS	PELAU
PEDIPALPS	PEEKS	PEERING	PEIGNOIR	PELAUS
PEDIS	PEEL	PEERLESS	PEIGNOIRS	PELE
PEDLAR	PEELABLE	PEERS	PEIN	PELECYPOD
PEDLARIES	PEELED	PEERY	PEINCT	PELERINE
PEDLARS	PEELER	PEES	PEINCTED	PELERINES
PEDLARY	PEELERS	PEESWEEP	PEINCTING	PELES

PELF	PELOLOGY	PEMBINAS	PEND	PENIES
PELFS	PELON	PEMBROKE	PENDANT	PENILE
PELHAM	PELONS	PEMBROKES	PENDANTLY	PENILL
PELHAMS	PELORIA	PEMICAN	PENDANTS	PENILLION
PELICAN	PELORIAN	PEMICANS	PENDED	PENING
PELICANS	PELORIAS	PEMMICAN	PENDENCY	PENINSULA
PELISSE	PELORIC	PEMMICANS	PENDENT	PENIS
PELISSES	PELORIES	PEMOLINE	PENDENTLY	PENISES
PELITE	PELORISED	PEMOLINES	PENDENTS	PENISTONE
PELITES	PELORISM	PEMPHIGI	PENDICLE	PENITENCE
PELITIC	PELORISMS	PEMPHIGUS	PENDICLER	PENITENCY
PELL	PELORIZED	PEMPHIX	PENDICLES	PENITENT
PELLACH	PELORUS	PEMPHIXES	PENDING	PENITENTS
PELLACHS	PELORUSES	PEN	PENDRAGON	PENK
PELLACK	PELORY	PENAL	PENDS	PENKNIFE
PELLACKS	PELOTA	PENALISE	PENDU	PENKNIVES
PELLAGRA	PELOTAS	PENALISED	PENDULAR	PENKS
PELLAGRAS	PELOTON	PENALISES	PENDULATE	PENLIGHT
PELLAGRIN	PELOTONS	PENALITY	PENDULE	PENLIGHTS
PELLED	PELS	PENALIZE	PENDULES	PENLIKE
PELLET	PELT	PENALIZED	PENDULINE	PENLITE
PELLETAL	PELTA	PENALIZES	PENDULOUS	PENLITES
PELLETED	PELTAE	PENALLY	PENDULUM	PENMAN
PELLETIFY	PELTAS	PENALTIES	PENDULUMS	PENMEN
PELLETING	PELTAST	PENALTY	PENE	PENNA
PELLETISE	PELTASTS	PENANCE	PENED	PENNAE
PELLETIZE	PELTATE	PENANCED	PENEPLAIN	PENNAL
PELLETS	PELTATELY	PENANCES	PENEPLANE	PENNALISM
PELLICLE	PELTATION	PENANCING	PENES	PENNALS
PELLICLES	PELTED	PENANG	PENETRANT	PENNAME
PELLING	PELTER	PENANGS	PENETRATE	PENNAMES
PELLITORY	PELTERED	PENATES	PENFOLD	PENNANT
PELLMELL	PELTERING	PENCE	PENFOLDS	PENNANTS
PELLMELLS	PELTERS	PENCEL	PENFRIEND	PENNATE
PELLOCK	PELTING	PENCELS	PENFUL	PENNATED
PELLOCKS	PELTINGLY	PENCES	PENFULS	PENNATULA
PELLS	PELTINGS	PENCHANT	PENGO	PENNE
PELLUCID	PELTLESS	PENCHANTS	PENGOS	PENNED
PELLUM	PELTRIES	PENCIL	PENGUIN	PENNEECH
PELLUMS	PELTRY	PENCILED	PENGUINRY	PENNEECHS
PELMA	PELTS	PENCILER	PENGUINS	PENNEECK
PELMANISM	PELVES	PENCILERS	PENHOLDER	PENNEECKS
PELMAS	PELVIC	PENCILING	PENI	PENNER
PELMATIC	PELVICS	PENCILLED	PENIAL	PENNERS
PELMET	PELVIFORM	PENCILLER	PENICIL	PENNES
PELMETS	PELVIS	PENCILS	PENICILLI	PENNI
PELOID	PELVISES	PENCRAFT	PENICILS	PENNIA
PELOIDS	PEMBINA	PENCRAFTS	PENIE	PENNIED

PENNIES	PENSTEMON	PENTITO	PEOPLE	PEPS
PENNIFORM	PENSTER	PENTODE	PEOPLED	PEPSI
PENNILESS	PENSTERS	PENTODES	PEOPLER	PEPSIN
PENNILL	PENSTOCK	PENTOMIC	PEOPLERS	PEPSINATE
PENNINE	PENSTOCKS	PENTOSAN	PEOPLES	PEPSINE
PENNINES	PENSUM	PENTOSANE	PEOPLING	PEPSINES
PENNING	PENSUMS	PENTOSANS	PEP	PEPSINS
PENNINITE	PENT	PENTOSE	PEPERINO	PEPSIS
PENNIS	PENTACLE	PENTOSES	PEPERINOS	PEPTALK
PENNON	PENTACLES	PENTOSIDE	PEPEROMIA	PEPTALKED
PENNONCEL	PENTACT	PENTOXIDE	PEPERONI	PEPTALKS
PENNONED	PENTACTS	PENTROOF	PEPERONIS	PEPTIC
PENNONS	PENTAD	PENTROOFS	PEPFUL	PEPTICITY
PENNY	PENTADIC	PENTS	PEPINO	PEPTICS
PENNYBOY	PENTADS	PENTYL	PEPINOS	PEPTID
PENNYBOYS	PENTAGON	PENTYLENE	PEPITA	PEPTIDASE
PENNYFEE	PENTAGONS	PENTYLS	PEPITAS	PEPTIDE
PENNYFEES	PENTAGRAM	PENUCHE	PEPLA	PEPTIDES
PENNYLAND	PENTALOGY	PENUCHES	PEPLOS	PEPTIDIC
PENNYWISE	PENTALPHA	PENUCHI	PEPLOSES	PEPTIDS
PENNYWORT	PENTAMERY	PENUCHIS	PEPLUM	PEPTISE
PENOCHE	PENTANE	PENUCHLE	PEPLUMED	PEPTISED
PENOCHES	PENTANES	PENUCHLES	PEPLUMS	PEPTISER
PENOLOGY	PENTANGLE	PENUCKLE	PEPLUS	PEPTISERS
PENONCEL	PENTANOIC	PENUCKLES	PEPLUSES	PEPTISES
PENONCELS	PENTANOL	PENULT	PEPO	PEPTISING
PENPOINT	PENTANOLS	PENULTIMA	PEPONIDA	PEPTIZE
PENPOINTS	PENTAPODY	PENULTS	PEPONIDAS	PEPTIZED
PENPUSHER	PENTARCH	PENUMBRA	PEPONIUM	PEPTIZER
PENS	PENTARCHS	PENUMBRAE	PEPONIUMS	PEPTIZERS
PENSEE	PENTARCHY	PENUMBRAL	PEPOS	PEPTIZES
PENSEES	PENTATHLA	PENUMBRAS	PEPPED	PEPTIZING
PENSEL	PENTEL	PENURIES	PEPPER	PEPTONE
PENSELS	PENTELS	PENURIOUS	PEPPERBOX	PEPTONES
PENSEROSO	PENTENE	PENURY	PEPPERED	PEPTONIC
PENSIL	PENTENES	PENWIPER	PEPPERER	PEPTONISE
PENSILE	PENTHIA	PENWIPERS	PEPPERERS	PEPTONIZE
PENSILITY	PENTHIAS	PENWOMAN	PEPPERIER	PEQUISTE
PENSILS	PENTHOUSE	PENWOMEN	PEPPERING	PEQUISTES
PENSION	PENTICE	PEON	PEPPERONI	PER
PENSIONE	PENTICED	PEONAGE	PEPPERS	PERACID
PENSIONED	PENTICES	PEONAGES	PEPPERY	PERACIDS
PENSIONER	PENTICING	PEONES	PEPPIER	PERACUTE
PENSIONES	PENTISE	PEONIES	PEPPIEST	PERAEA
PENSIONI	PENTISED	PEONISM	PEPPILY	PERAEON
PENSIONS	PENTISES	PEONISMS	PEPPINESS	PERAEONS
PENSIVE	PENTISING	PEONS	PEPPING	PERAEOPOD
PENSIVELY	PENTITI	PEONY	PEPPY	PERAI

PERAIS	PERCUSS	PERFECTO	PERIANTHS	PERIKARYA
PERBORATE	PERCUSSED	PERFECTOR	PERIAPSES	PERIL
PERBORIC	PERCUSSES	PERFECTOS	PERIAPSIS	PERILED
PERC	PERCUSSOR	PERFECTS	PERIAPT	PERILING
PERCALE	PERDENDO	PERFERVID	PERIAPTS	PERILLA
PERCALES	PERDIE	PERFERVOR	PERIBLAST	PERILLAS
PERCALINE	PERDITION	PERFET	PERIBLEM	PERILLED
PERCASE	PERDU	PERFIDIES	PERIBLEMS	PERILLING
PERCE	PERDUE	PERFIDY	PERIBOLI	PERILOUS
PERCEABLE	PERDUES	PERFIN	PERIBOLOI	PERILS
PERCEANT	PERDURE	PERFING	PERIBOLOS	PERILUNE
PERCED	PERDURED	PERFINGS	PERIBOLUS	PERILUNES
PERCEIVE	PERDURES	PERFINS	PERICARP	PERILYMPH
PERCEIVED	PERDURING	PERFORANS	PERICARPS	PERIMETER
PERCEIVER	PERDUS	PERFORANT	PERICLASE	PERIMETRY
PERCEIVES	PERDY	PERFORATE	PERICLINE	PERIMORPH
PERCEN	PERE	PERFORCE	PERICON	PERIMYSIA
PERCENT	PEREA	PERFORM	PERICONES	PERINAEUM
PERCENTAL	PEREGAL	PERFORMED	PERICOPAE	PERINATAL
PERCENTS	PEREGALS	PERFORMER	PERICOPAL	PERINEA
PERCEPT	PEREGRIN	PERFORMS	PERICOPE	PERINEAL
PERCEPTS	PEREGRINE	PERFUME	PERICOPES	PERINEUM
PERCES	PEREGRINS	PERFUMED	PERICOPIC	PERINEUMS
PERCH	PEREIA	PERFUMER	PERICYCLE	PERIOD
PERCHANCE	PEREION	PERFUMERS	PERIDERM	PERIODATE
PERCHED	PEREIONS	PERFUMERY	PERIDERMS	PERIODED
PERCHER	PEREIOPOD	PERFUMES	PERIDIA	PERIODIC
PERCHERON	PEREIRA	PERFUMIER	PERIDIAL	PERIODID
PERCHERS	PEREIRAS	PERFUMING	PERIDINIA	PERIODIDE
PERCHERY	PERENNATE	PERFUMY	PERIDIUM	PERIODIDS
PERCHES	PERENNIAL	PERFUSATE	PERIDIUMS	PERIODING
PERCHING	PERENNITY	PERFUSE	PERIDOT	PERIODISE
PERCHINGS	PERENTIE	PERFUSED	PERIDOTE	PERIODIZE
PERCID	PERENTIES	PERFUSES	PERIDOTES	PERIODS
PERCIDS	PERENTY	PERFUSING	PERIDOTIC	PERIOST
PERCIFORM	PEREON	PERFUSION	PERIDOTS	PERIOSTEA
PERCINE	PEREONS	PERFUSIVE	PERIDROME	PERIOSTS
PERCINES	PEREOPOD	PERGOLA	PERIGEAL	PERIOTIC
PERCING	PEREOPODS	PERGOLAS	PERIGEAN	PERIOTICS
PERCOCT	PERES	PERGUNNAH	PERIGEE	PERIPATUS
PERCOCTED	PERFAY	PERHAPS	PERIGEES	PERIPETIA
PERCOCTS	PERFECT	PERHAPSES	PERIGON	PERIPETY
PERCOID	PERFECTA	PERI	PERIGONE	PERIPHERY
PERCOIDS	PERFECTAS	PERIAGUA	PERIGONES	PERIPLASM
PERCOLATE	PERFECTED	PERIAGUAS	PERIGONIA	PERIPLAST
PERCOLIN	PERFECTER	PERIAKTOI	PERIGONS	PERIPLUS
PERCOLINS	PERFECTI	PERIAKTOS	PERIGYNY	PERIPROCT
PERCS	PERFECTLY	PERIANTH	PERIHELIA	PERIPTER

PERIPTERS	PERLITE	PEROG	PERRUQUE	PERSUADES
PERIPTERY	PERLITES	PEROGEN	PERRUQUES	PERSUE
PERIQUE	PERLITIC	PEROGI	PERRY	PERSUED
PERIQUES	PERLOUS	PEROGIE	PERSALT	PERSUES
PERIS	PERM	PEROGIES	PERSALTS	PERSUING
PERISARC	PERMABEAR	PEROGIS	PERSANT	PERSWADE
PERISARCS	PERMABULL	PEROGS	PERSAUNT	PERSWADED
PERISCIAN	PERMALINK	PEROGY	PERSE	PERSWADES
PERISCOPE	PERMALLOY	PERONE	PERSECUTE	PERT
PERISH	PERMANENT	PERONEAL	PERSEITY	PERTAIN
PERISHED	PERMATAN	PERONEI	PERSELINE	PERTAINED
PERISHER	PERMATANS	PERONES	PERSES	PERTAINS
PERISHERS	PERMEABLE	PERONEUS	PERSEVERE	PERTAKE
PERISHES	PERMEABLY	PERORAL	PERSICO	PERTAKEN
PERISHING	PERMEANCE	PERORALLY	PERSICOS	PERTAKES
PERISPERM	PERMEANT	PERORATE	PERSICOT	PERTAKING
PERISTOME	PERMEANTS	PERORATED	PERSICOTS	PERTER
PERISTYLE	PERMEASE	PERORATES	PERSIENNE	PERTEST
PERITI	PERMEASES	PERORATOR	PERSIMMON	PERTHITE
PERITONEA	PERMEATE	PEROVSKIA	PERSING	PERTHITES
PERITRACK	PERMEATED	PEROXID	PERSIST	PERTHITIC
PERITRICH	PERMEATES	PEROXIDE	PERSISTED	PERTINENT
PERITUS	PERMEATOR	PEROXIDED	PERSISTER	PERTLY
PERIWIG	PERMED	PEROXIDES	PERSISTS	PERTNESS
PERIWIGS	PERMIAN	PEROXIDIC	PERSON	PERTOOK
PERJINK	PERMIE	PEROXIDS	PERSONA	PERTS
PERJURE	PERMIES	PEROXO	PERSONAE	PERTURB
PERJURED	PERMING	PEROXY	PERSONAGE	PERTURBED
PERJURER	PERMIT	PERP	PERSONAL	PERTURBER
PERJURERS	PERMITS	PERPEND	PERSONALS	PERTURBS
PERJURES	PERMITTED	PERPENDED	PERSONAS	PERTUSATE
PERJURIES	PERMITTEE	PERPENDS	PERSONATE	PERTUSE
PERJURING	PERMITTER	PERPENT	PERSONIFY	PERTUSED
PERJUROUS	PERMS	PERPENTS	PERSONISE	PERTUSION
PERJURY	PERMUTATE	PERPETUAL	PERSONIZE	PERTUSSAL
PERK	PERMUTE	PERPLEX	PERSONNED	PERTUSSES
PERKED	PERMUTED	PERPLEXED	PERSONNEL	PERTUSSIS
PERKIER	PERMUTES	PERPLEXER	PERSONS	PERUKE
PERKIEST	PERMUTING	PERPLEXES	PERSPEX	PERUKED
PERKILY	PERN	PERPS	PERSPEXES	PERUKES
PERKIN	PERNANCY	PERRADIAL	PERSPIRE	PERUSABLE
PERKINESS	PERNED	PERRADII	PERSPIRED	PERUSAL
PERKING	PERNING	PERRADIUS	PERSPIRES	PERUSALS
PERKINS	PERNIO	PERRIER	PERSPIRY	PERUSE
PERKISH	PERNIONES	PERRIERS	PERST	PERUSED
PERKS	PERNOD	PERRIES	PERSUADE	PERUSER
PERKY	PERNODS	PERRON	PERSUADED	PERUSERS
PERLEMOEN	PERNS	PERRONS	PERSUADER	PERUSES

PERUSING	PESKILY	PETALLED	PETIT	PETTABLE
PERV	PESKINESS	PETALLIKE	PETITE	PETTED
PERVADE	PESKY	PETALODIC	PETITES	PETTEDLY
PERVADED	PESO	PETALODY	PETITIO	PETTER
PERVADER	PESOS	PETALOID	PETITION	PETTERS
PERVADERS	PESSARIES	PETALOUS	PETITIONS	PETTI
PERVADES	PESSARY	PETALS	PETITIOS	PETTICOAT
PERVADING	PESSIMA	PETAMETER	PETITORY	PETTIER
PERVASION	PESSIMAL	PETAMETRE	PETNAP	PETTIES
PERVASIVE	PESSIMISM	PETANQUE	PETNAPER	PETTIEST
PERVE	PESSIMIST	PETANQUES	PETNAPERS	PETTIFOG
PERVED	PESSIMUM	PETAR	PETNAPING	PETTIFOGS
PERVERSE	PEST	PETARA	PETNAPPED	PETTILY
PERVERSER	PESTER	PETARAS	PETNAPPER	PETTINESS
PERVERT	PESTERED	PETARD	PETNAPS	PETTING
PERVERTED	PESTERER	PETARDS	PETRALE	PETTINGS
PERVERTER	PESTERERS	PETARIES	PETRALES	PETTIS
PERVERTS	PESTERING	PETARS	PETRARIES	PETTISH
PERVES	PESTEROUS	PETARY	PETRARY	PETTISHLY
PERVIATE	PESTERS	PETASOS	PETRE	PETTITOES
PERVIATED	PESTFUL	PETASOSES	PETREL	PETTLE
PERVIATES	PESTHOLE	PETASUS	PETRELS	PETTLED
PERVICACY	PESTHOLES	PETASUSES	PETRES	PETTLES
PERVIER	PESTHOUSE	PETAURINE	PETRI	PETTLING
PERVIEST	PESTICIDE	PETAURIST	PETRICHOR	PETTO
PERVING	PESTIER	PETCHARY	PETRIFIC	PETTY
PERVIOUS	PESTIEST	PETCOCK	PETRIFIED	PETULANCE
PERVO	PESTILENT	PETCOCKS	PETRIFIER	PETULANCY
PERVOS	PESTLE	PETECHIA	PETRIFIES	PETULANT
PERVS	PESTLED	PETECHIAE	PETRIFY	PETUNIA
PERVY	PESTLES	PETECHIAL	PETROGENY	PETUNIAS
PES	PESTLING	PETER	PETROGRAM	PETUNTSE
PESADE	PESTO	PETERED	PETROL	PETUNTSES
PESADES	PESTOLOGY	PETERING	PETROLAGE	PETUNTZE
PESANT	PESTOS	PETERMAN	PETROLEUM	PETUNTZES
PESANTE	PESTS	PETERMEN	PETROLEUR	PEW
PESANTS	PESTY	PETERS	PETROLIC	PEWEE
PESAUNT	PET	PETERSHAM	PETROLLED	PEWEES
PESAUNTS	PETABYTE	PETHER	PETROLOGY	PEWHOLDER
PESETA	PETABYTES	PETHERS	PETROLS	PEWIT
PESETAS	PETAFLOP	PETHIDINE	PETRONEL	PEWITS
PESEWA	PETAFLOPS	PETILLANT	PETRONELS	PEWS
PESEWAS	PETAHERTZ	PETIOLAR	PETROSAL	PEWTER
PESHMERGA	PETAL	PETIOLATE	PETROSALS	PEWTERER
PESHWA	PETALED	PETIOLE	PETROUS	PEWTERERS
PESHWAS	PETALINE	PETIOLED	PETS	PEWTERIER
PESKIER	PETALISM	PETIOLES	PETSAI	PEWTERS
PESKIEST	PETALISMS	PETIOLULE	PETSAIS	PEWTERY

P

PEYOTE	PHALANGES	PHARMINGS	PHELLEMS	PHEON
PEYOTES	PHALANGID	PHARMS	PHELLOGEN	PHEONS
PEYOTISM	PHALANX	PHAROS	PHELLOID	PHERESES
PEYOTISMS	PHALANXES	PHAROSES	PHELONIA	PHERESIS
PEYOTIST	PHALAROPE	PHARYNGAL	PHELONION	PHEROMONE
PEYOTISTS	PHALLI	PHARYNGES	PHENACITE	PHESE
PEYOTL	PHALLIC	PHARYNX	PHENAKISM	PHESED
PEYOTLS	PHALLIN	PHARYNXES	PHENAKITE	PHESES
PEYSE	PHALLINS	PHASE	PHENATE	PHESING
PEYSED	PHALLISM	PHASEAL	PHENATES	PHEW
PEYSES	PHALLISMS	PHASED	PHENAZIN	PHI
PEYSING	PHALLIST	PHASEDOWN	PHENAZINE	PHIAL
PEYTRAL	PHALLISTS	PHASELESS	PHENAZINS	PHIALLED
PEYTRALS	PHALLOID	PHASEOLIN	PHENE	PHIALLING
PEYTREL	PHALLUS	PHASEOUT	PHENES	PHIALS
PEYTRELS	PHALLUSES	PHASEOUTS	PHENETIC	PHILABEG
PEZANT	PHANG	PHASER	PHENETICS	PHILABEGS
PEZANTS	PHANGED	PHASERS	PHENETOL	PHILAMOT
PEZIZOID	PHANGING	PHASES	PHENETOLE	PHILAMOTS
PFENNIG	PHANGS	PHASIC	PHENETOLS	PHILANDER
PFENNIGE	PHANSIGAR	PHASING	PHENGITE	PHILATELY
PFENNIGS	PHANTASIM	PHASINGS	PHENGITES	PHILAVERY
PFENNING	PHANTASM	PHASIS	PHENIC	PHILHORSE
PFENNINGS	PHANTASMA	PHASMID	PHENIX	PHILIBEG
PFFT	PHANTASMS	PHASMIDS	PHENIXES	PHILIBEGS
PFUI	PHANTAST	PHASOR	PHENOBARB	PHILIPPIC
PHABLET	PHANTASTS	PHASORS	PHENOCOPY	PHILISTIA
PHABLETS	PHANTASY	PHAT	PHENOGAM	PHILLABEG
PHACELIA	PHANTOM	PHATIC	PHENOGAMS	PHILLIBEG
PHACELIAS	PHANTOMS	PHATTER	PHENOL	PHILOGYNY
PHACOID	PHANTOMY	PHATTEST	PHENOLATE	PHILOLOGY
PHACOIDAL	PHANTOSME	PHEASANT	PHENOLIC	PHILOMATH
PHACOLITE	PHARAOH	PHEASANTS	PHENOLICS	PHILOMEL
PHACOLITH	PHARAOHS	PHEAZAR	PHENOLOGY	PHILOMELA
PHAEIC	PHARAONIC	PHEAZARS	PHENOLS	PHILOMELS
PHAEISM	PHARE	PHEER	PHENOM	PHILOMOT
PHAEISMS	PHARES	PHEERE	PHENOME	PHILOMOTS
PHAENOGAM	PHARISAIC	PHEERES	PHENOMENA	PHILOPENA
PHAETON	PHARISEE	PHEERS	PHENOMES	PHILTER
PHAETONS	PHARISEES	PHEESE	PHENOMS	PHILTERED
PHAGE	PHARM	PHEESED	PHENOTYPE	PHILTERS
PHAGEDENA	PHARMA	PHEESES	PHENOXIDE	PHILTRA
PHAGES	PHARMACY	PHEESING	PHENOXY	PHILTRE
PHAGOCYTE	PHARMAS	PHEEZE	PHENYL	PHILTRED
PHAGOSOME	PHARMED	PHEEZED	PHENYLENE	PHILTRES
PHALANGAL	PHARMER	PHEEZES	PHENYLIC	PHILTRING
PHALANGE	PHARMERS	PHEEZING	PHENYLS	PHILTRUM
PHALANGER	PHARMING	PHELLEM	PHENYTOIN	PHIMOSES

PHIMOSIS	PHOCOMELY	PHONINESS	PHOTINIAS	PHOTOTYPE
PHIMOTIC	PHOEBE	PHONING	PHOTINO	PHOTOTYPY
PHINNOCK	PHOEBES	PHONMETER	PHOTINOS	PHOTS
PHINNOCKS	PHOEBUS	PHONO	PHOTISM	PHPHT
PHIS	PHOEBUSES	PHONOGRAM	PHOTISMS	PHRASAL
PHISH	PHOENIX	PHONOLITE	PHOTO	PHRASALLY
PHISHED	PHOENIXES	PHONOLOGY	PHOTOBLOG	PHRASE
PHISHER	PHOH	PHONON	PHOTOBOMB	PHRASED
PHISHERS	PHOLADES	PHONONS	PHOTOCALL	PHRASEMAN
PHISHES	PHOLAS	PHONOPORE	PHOTOCARD	PHRASEMEN
PHISHING	PHON	PHONOS	PHOTOCELL	PHRASER
PHISHINGS	PHONAL	PHONOTYPE	PHOTOCOPY	PHRASERS
PHISNOMY	PHONATE	PHONOTYPY	PHOTODISK	PHRASES
PHIZ	PHONATED	PHONS	PHOTOED	PHRASIER
PHIZES	PHONATES	PHONY	PHOTOFIT	PHRASIEST
PHIZOG	PHONATHON	PHONYING	PHOTOFITS	PHRASING
PHIZOGS	PHONATING	PHOOEY	PHOTOG	PHRASINGS
PHIZZ	PHONATION	PHORATE	PHOTOGEN	PHRASY
PHIZZES	PHONATORY	PHORATES	PHOTOGENE	PHRATRAL
PHLEBITIC	PHONE	PHORESIES	PHOTOGENS	PHRATRIC
PHLEBITIS	PHONECAM	PHORESY	PHOTOGENY	PHRATRIES
PHLEGM	PHONECAMS	PHORETIC	PHOTOGRAM	PHRATRY
PHLEGMIER	PHONECARD	PHORMINX	PHOTOGS	PHREAK
PHLEGMON	PHONED	PHORMIUM	PHOTOING	PHREAKED
PHLEGMONS	PHONEME	PHORMIUMS	PHOTOLYSE	PHREAKER
PHLEGMS	PHONEMES	PHORONID	PHOTOLYZE	PHREAKERS
PHLEGMY	PHONEMIC	PHORONIDS	PHOTOMAP	PHREAKING
PHLOEM	PHONEMICS	PHOS	PHOTOMAPS	PHREAKS
PHLOEMS	PHONER	PHOSGENE	PHOTOMASK	PHREATIC
PHLOMIS	PHONERS	PHOSGENES	PHOTON	PHRENESES
PHLOMISES	PHONES	PHOSPHATE	PHOTONIC	PHRENESIS
PHLORIZIN	PHONETIC	PHOSPHENE	PHOTONICS	PHRENETIC
PHLOX	PHONETICS	PHOSPHID	PHOTONS	PHRENIC
PHLOXES	PHONETISE	PHOSPHIDE	PHOTOPHIL	PHRENICS
PHLYCTENA	PHONETISM	PHOSPHIDS	PHOTOPIA	PHRENISM
PHO	PHONETIST	PHOSPHIN	PHOTOPIAS	PHRENISMS
PHOBIA	PHONETIZE	PHOSPHINE	PHOTOPIC	PHRENITIC
PHOBIAS	PHONEY	PHOSPHINS	PHOTOPLAY	PHRENITIS
PHOBIC	PHONEYED	PHOSPHITE	PHOTOPSIA	PHRENSIED
PHOBICS	PHONEYING	PHOSPHOR	PHOTOPSY	PHRENSIES
PHOBISM	PHONEYS	PHOSPHORE	PHOTOS	PHRENSY
PHOBISMS	PHONIC	PHOSPHORI	PHOTOSCAN	PHRENTICK
PHOBIST	PHONICS	PHOSPHORS	PHOTOSET	PHRYGANA
PHOBISTS	PHONIED	PHOSSY	PHOTOSETS	PHRYGANAS
PHOCA	PHONIER	PHOT	PHOTOSHOP	PHT
PHOCAE	PHONIES	PHOTIC	PHOTOSTAT	PHTHALATE
PHOCAS	PHONIEST	PHOTICS	PHOTOTAXY	PHTHALEIN
PHOCINE	PHONILY	PHOTINIA	PHOTOTUBE	PHTHALIC

PHTHALIN	PHYLUM	PIAFFER	PIBROCHS	PICKADILS
PHTHALINS	PHYSALIA	PIAFFERS	PIC	PICKAPACK
PHTHISES	PHYSALIAS	PIAFFES	PICA	PICKAROON
PHTHISIC	PHYSALIS	PIAFFING	PICACHO	PICKAX
PHTHISICS	PHYSED	PIAL	PICACHOS	PICKAXE
PHTHISIS	PHYSEDS	PIAN	PICADILLO	PICKAXED
PHUT	PHYSES	PIANETTE	PICADOR	PICKAXES
PHUTS	PHYSETER	PIANETTES	PICADORES	PICKAXING
PHUTTED	PHYSETERS	PIANI	PICADORS	PICKBACK
PHUTTING	PHYSIATRY	PIANIC	PICAL	PICKBACKS
PHWOAH	PHYSIC	PIANINO	PICAMAR	PICKED
PHWOAR	PHYSICAL	PIANINOS	PICAMARS	PICKEER
PHYCOCYAN	PHYSICALS	PIANISM	PICANINNY	PICKEERED
PHYCOLOGY	PHYSICIAN	PIANISMS	PICANTE	PICKEERER
PHYLA	PHYSICISM	PIANIST	PICARA	PICKEERS
PHYLACTIC	PHYSICIST	PIANISTE	PICARAS	PICKER
PHYLAE	PHYSICKED	PIANISTES	PICARIAN	PICKEREL
PHYLAR	PHYSICKY	PIANISTIC	PICARIANS	PICKERELS
PHYLARCH	PHYSICS	PIANISTS	PICARO	PICKERIES
PHYLARCHS	PHYSIO	PIANO	PICAROON	PICKERS
PHYLARCHY	PHYSIOS	PIANOLA	PICAROONS	PICKERY
PHYLAXIS	PHYSIQUE	PIANOLAS	PICAROS	PICKET
PHYLE	PHYSIQUED	PIANOLESS	PICAS	PICKETED
PHYLESES	PHYSIQUES	PIANOLIST	PICAYUNE	PICKETER
PHYLESIS	PHYSIS	PIANOS	PICAYUNES	PICKETERS
PHYLETIC	PHYTANE	PIANS	PICCADILL	PICKETING
PHYLETICS	PHYTANES	PIARIST	PICCANIN	PICKETS
PHYLIC	PHYTIN	PIARISTS	PICCANINS	PICKIER
PHYLLARY	PHYTINS	PIAS	PICCATA	PICKIEST
PHYLLID	PHYTOGENY	PIASABA	PICCATAS	PICKILY
PHYLLIDS	PHYTOID	PIASABAS	PICCIES	PICKIN
PHYLLITE	PHYTOL	PIASAVA	PICCOLO	PICKINESS
PHYLLITES	PHYTOLITH	PIASAVAS	PICCOLOS	PICKING
PHYLLITIC	PHYTOLOGY	PIASSABA	PICCY	PICKINGS
PHYLLO	PHYTOLS	PIASSABAS	PICE	PICKINS
PHYLLODE	PHYTON	PIASSAVA	PICENE	PICKLE
PHYLLODES	PHYTONIC	PIASSAVAS	PICENES	PICKLED
PHYLLODIA	PHYTONS	PIASTER	PICEOUS	PICKLER
PHYLLODY	PHYTOSES	PIASTERS	PICHOLINE	PICKLERS
PHYLLOID	PHYTOSIS	PIASTRE	PICHURIM	PICKLES
PHYLLOIDS	PHYTOTOMY	PIASTRES	PICHURIMS	PICKLING
PHYLLOME	PHYTOTRON	PIAZZA	PICIFORM	PICKLOCK
PHYLLOMES	PI	PIAZZAS	PICINE	PICKLOCKS
PHYLLOMIC	PIA	PIAZZE	PICK	PICKMAW
PHYLLOPOD	PIACEVOLE	PIAZZIAN	PICKABACK	PICKMAWS
PHYLLOS	PIACULAR	PIBAL	PICKABLE	PICKNEY
PHYLOGENY	PIAFFE	PIBALS	PICKADIL	PICKNEYS
PHYLON	PIAFFED	PIBROCH	PICKADILL	PICKOFF

PICKOFFS	PICRATE	PIECENED	PIERIDINE	PIGFACE
PICKPROOF	PICRATED	PIECENER	PIERIDS	PIGFACES
PICKS	PICRATES	PIECENERS	PIERIS	PIGFEED
PICKTHANK	PICRIC	PIECENING	PIERISES	PIGFEEDS
PICKUP	PICRITE	PIECENS	PIEROG	PIGFISH
PICKUPS	PICRITES	PIECER	PIEROGEN	PIGFISHES
PICKWICK	PICRITIC	PIECERS	PIEROGI	PIGGED
PICKWICKS	PICS	PIECES	PIEROGIES	PIGGERIES
PICKY	PICTARNIE	PIECEWISE	PIEROGS	PIGGERY
PICLORAM	PICTOGRAM	PIECEWORK	PIERRETTE	PIGGIE
PICLORAMS	PICTORIAL	PIECING	PIERROT	PIGGIER
PICNIC	PICTURAL	PIECINGS	PIERROTS	PIGGIES
PICNICKED	PICTURALS	PIECRUST	PIERS	PIGGIEST
PICNICKER	PICTURE	PIECRUSTS	PIERST	PIGGIN
PICNICKY	PICTURED	PIED	PIERT	PIGGINESS
PICNICS	PICTURES	PIEDFORT	PIERTS	PIGGING
PICOCURIE	PICTURING	PIEDFORTS	PIES	PIGGINGS
PICOFARAD	PICTURISE	PIEDISH	PIET	PIGGINS
PICOGRAM	PICTURIZE	PIEDISHES	PIETA	PIGGISH
PICOGRAMS	PICUL	PIEDMONT	PIETAS	PIGGISHLY
PICOLIN	PICULET	PIEDMONTS	PIETIES	PIGGY
PICOLINE	PICULETS	PIEDNESS	PIETISM	PIGGYBACK
PICOLINES	PICULS	PIEFORT	PIETISMS	PIGHEADED
PICOLINIC	PIDDLE	PIEFORTS	PIETIST	PIGHT
PICOLINS	PIDDLED	PIEHOLE	PIETISTIC	PIGHTED
PICOMETER	PIDDLER	PIEHOLES	PIETISTS	PIGHTING
PICOMETRE	PIDDLERS	PIEING	PIETS	PIGHTLE
PICOMOLE	PIDDLES	PIEINGS	PIETY	PIGHTLES
PICOMOLES	PIDDLIER	PIEMAN	PIEZO	PIGHTS
PICONG	PIDDLIEST	PIEMEN	PIFFERARI	PIGLET
PICONGS	PIDDLING	PIEND	PIFFERARO	PIGLETS
PICOT	PIDDLY	PIENDS	PIFFERO	PIGLIKE
PICOTE	PIDDOCK	PIEPLANT	PIFFEROS	PIGLING
PICOTED	PIDDOCKS	PIEPLANTS	PIFFLE	PIGLINGS
PICOTEE	PIDGEON	PIEPOWDER	PIFFLED	PIGMAEAN
PICOTEES	PIDGEONS	PIER	PIFFLER	PIGMAN
PICOTING	PIDGIN	PIERAGE	PIFFLERS	PIGMEAN
PICOTITE	PIDGINISE	PIERAGES	PIFFLES	PIGMEAT
PICOTITES	PIDGINIZE	PIERCE	PIFFLING	PIGMEATS
PICOTS	PIDGINS	PIERCED	PIG	PIGMEN
PICOWAVE	PIE	PIERCER	PIGBOAT	PIGMENT
PICOWAVED	PIEBALD	PIERCERS	PIGBOATS	PIGMENTAL
PICOWAVES	PIEBALDS	PIERCES	PIGEON	PIGMENTED
PICQUET	PIECE	PIERCING	PIGEONED	PIGMENTS
PICQUETED	PIECED	PIERCINGS	PIGEONING	PIGMIES
PICQUETS	PIECELESS	PIERHEAD	PIGEONITE	PIGMOID
PICRA	PIECEMEAL	PIERHEADS	PIGEONRY	PIGMOIDS
PICRAS	PIECEN	PIERID	PIGEONS	PIGMY

PIGNERATE	PIKELET	PILED	PILLARIST	PILOTIS
PIGNOLI	PIKELETS	PILEI	PILLARS	PILOTLESS
PIGNOLIA	PIKELIKE	PILELESS	PILLAU	PILOTMAN
PIGNOLIAS	PIKEMAN	PILEOUS	PILLAUS	PILOTMEN
PIGNOLIS	PIKEMEN	PILER	PILLBOX	PILOTS
PIGNORA	PIKEPERCH	PILERS	PILLBOXES	PILOUS
PIGNORATE	PIKER	PILES	PILLBUG	PILOW
PIGNUS	PIKERS	PILEUM	PILLBUGS	PILOWS
PIGNUT	PIKES	PILEUP	PILLED	PILSENER
PIGNUTS	PIKESTAFF	PILEUPS	PILLHEAD	PILSENERS
PIGOUT	PIKEY	PILEUS	PILLHEADS	PILSNER
PIGOUTS	PIKEYS	PILEWORK	PILLICOCK	PILSNERS
PIGPEN	PIKI	PILEWORKS	PILLIE	PILULA
PIGPENS	PIKING	PILEWORT	PILLIES	PILULAE
PIGS	PIKINGS	PILEWORTS	PILLING	PILULAR
PIGSCONCE	PIKIS	PILFER	PILLINGS	PILULAS
PIGSKIN	PIKUL	PILFERAGE	PILLION	PILULE
PIGSKINS	PIKULS	PILFERED	PILLIONED	PILULES
PIGSNEY	PILA	PILFERER	PILLIONS	PILUM
PIGSNEYS	PILAE	PILFERERS	PILLOCK	PILUS
PIGSNIE	PILAF	PILFERIES	PILLOCKS	PILY
PIGSNIES	PILAFF	PILFERING	PILLORIED	PIMA
PIGSNY	PILAFFS	PILFERS	PILLORIES	PIMAS
PIGSTICK	PILAFS	PILFERY	PILLORISE	PIMENT
PIGSTICKS	PILAO	PILGARLIC	PILLORIZE	PIMENTO
PIGSTIES	PILAOS	PILGRIM	PILLORY	PIMENTON
PIGSTUCK	PILAR	PILGRIMED	PILLOW	PIMENTONS
PIGSTY	PILASTER	PILGRIMER	PILLOWED	PIMENTOS
PIGSWILL	PILASTERS	PILGRIMS	PILLOWIER	PIMENTS
PIGSWILLS	PILAU	PILI	PILLOWING	PIMIENTO
PIGTAIL	PILAUS	PILIER	PILLOWS	PIMIENTOS
PIGTAILED	PILAW	PILIEST	PILLOWY	PIMP
PIGTAILS	PILAWS	PILIFORM	PILLS	PIMPED
PIGWASH	PILCH	PILING	PILLWORM	PIMPERNEL
PIGWASHES	PILCHARD	PILINGS	PILLWORMS	PIMPING
PIGWEED	PILCHARDS	PILINUT	PILLWORT	PIMPINGS
PIGWEEDS	PILCHER	PILINUTS	PILLWORTS	PIMPLE
PIHOIHOI	PILCHERS	PILIS	PILOMOTOR	PIMPLED
PIHOIHOIS	PILCHES	PILL	PILONIDAL	PIMPLES
PIING	PILCORN	PILLAGE	PILOSE	PIMPLIER
PIKA	PILCORNS	PILLAGED	PILOSITY	PIMPLIEST
PIKAKE	PILCROW	PILLAGER	PILOT	PIMPLY
PIKAKES	PILCROWS	PILLAGERS	PILOTAGE	PIMPS
PIKAS	PILE	PILLAGES	PILOTAGES	PIN
PIKAU	PILEA	PILLAGING	PILOTED	PINA
PIKAUS	PILEAS	PILLAR	PILOTFISH	PINACEOUS
PIKE	PILEATE	PILLARED	PILOTING	PINACOID
PIKED	PILEATED	PILLARING	PILOTINGS	PINACOIDS

PINAFORE	PINDARIS	PINGOES	PINKINGS	PINOCHLE
PINAFORED	PINDER	PINGOS	PINKISH	PINOCHLES
PINAFORES	PINDERS	PINGPONG	PINKLY	PINOCLE
PINAKOID	PINDLING	PINGPONGS	PINKNESS	PINOCLES
PINAKOIDS	PINDOWN	PINGRASS	PINKO	PINOCYTIC
PINANG	PINDOWNS	PINGS	PINKOES	PINOLE
PINANGS	PINE	PINGUEFY	PINKOS	PINOLES
PINAS	PINEAL	PINGUID	PINKROOT	PINON
PINASTER	PINEALS	PINGUIN	PINKROOTS	PINONES
PINASTERS	PINEAPPLE	PINGUINS	PINKS	PINONS
PINATA	PINECONE	PINHEAD	PINKY	PINOT
PINATAS	PINECONES	PINHEADED	PINLESS	PINOTAGE
PINBALL	PINED	PINHEADS	PINNA	PINOTAGES
PINBALLED	PINEDROPS	PINHOLE	PINNACE	PINOTS
PINBALLS	PINELAND	PINHOLES	PINNACES	PINPOINT
PINBOARD	PINELANDS	PINHOOKER	PINNACLE	PINPOINTS
PINBOARDS	PINELIKE	PINIER	PINNACLED	PINPRICK
PINBONE	PINENE	PINIES	PINNACLES	PINPRICKS
PINBONES	PINENES	PINIEST	PINNAE	PINS
PINCASE	PINERIES	PINING	PINNAL	PINSCHER
PINCASES	PINERY	PINION	PINNAS	PINSCHERS
PINCER	PINES	PINIONED	PINNATE	PINSETTER
PINCERED	PINESAP	PINIONING	PINNATED	PINSPOT
PINCERING	PINESAPS	PINIONS	PINNATELY	PINSPOTS
PINCERS	PINETA	PINITE	PINNATION	PINSTRIPE
PINCH	PINETUM	PINITES	PINNED	PINSWELL
PINCHBECK	PINEWOOD	PINITOL	PINNER	PINSWELLS
PINCHBUG	PINEWOODS	PINITOLS	PINNERS	PINT
PINCHBUGS	PINEY	PINK	PINNET	PINTA
PINCHCOCK	PINFALL	PINKED	PINNETS	PINTABLE
PINCHECK	PINFALLS	PINKEN	PINNIE	PINTABLES
PINCHECKS	PINFISH	PINKENED	PINNIES	PINTADA
PINCHED	PINFISHES	PINKENING	PINNING	PINTADAS
PINCHER	PINFOLD	PINKENS	PINNINGS	PINTADERA
PINCHERS	PINFOLDED	PINKER	PINNIPED	PINTADO
PINCHES	PINFOLDS	PINKERS	PINNIPEDE	PINTADOES
PINCHFIST	PING	PINKERTON	PINNIPEDS	PINTADOS
PINCHGUT	PINGED	PINKEST	PINNOCK	PINTAIL
PINCHGUTS	PINGER	PINKEY	PINNOCKS	PINTAILED
PINCHING	PINGERS	PINKEYE	PINNOED	PINTAILS
PINCHINGS	PINGING	PINKEYES	PINNULA	PINTANO
PINCURL	PINGLE	PINKEYS	PINNULAE	PINTANOS
PINCURLS	PINGLED	PINKIE	PINNULAR	PINTAS
PINDAN	PINGLER	PINKIER	PINNULAS	PINTLE
PINDANS	PINGLERS	PINKIES	PINNULATE	PINTLES
PINDAREE	PINGLES	PINKIEST	PINNULE	PINTO
PINDAREES	PINGLING	PINKINESS	PINNULES	PINTOES
PINDARI	PINGO	PINKING	PINNY	PINTOS

PINTS	PIOUSLY	PIPIER	PIRANA	PISCATRIX
PINTSIZE	PIOUSNESS	PIPIEST	PIRANAS	PISCIFORM
PINTSIZED	PIOY	PIPINESS	PIRANHA	PISCINA
PINTUCK	PIOYE	PIPING	PIRANHAS	PISCINAE
PINTUCKED	PIOYES	PIPINGLY	PIRARUCU	PISCINAL
PINTUCKS	PIOYS	PIPINGS	PIRARUCUS	PISCINAS
PINUP	PIP	PIPIS	PIRATE	PISCINE
PINUPS	PIPA	PIPISTREL	PIRATED	PISCINES
PINWALE	PIPAGE	PIPIT	PIRATES	PISCIVORE
PINWALES	PIPAGES	PIPITS	PIRATIC	PISCO
PINWEED	PIPAL	PIPKIN	PIRATICAL	PISCOS
PINWEEDS	PIPALS	PIPKINS	PIRATING	PISE
PINWHEEL	PIPAS	PIPLESS	PIRATINGS	PISES
PINWHEELS	PIPE	PIPPED	PIRAYA	PISH
PINWORK	PIPEAGE	PIPPIER	PIRAYAS	PISHED
PINWORKS	PIPEAGES	PIPPIEST	PIRIFORM	PISHEOG
PINWORM	PIPECLAY	PIPPIN	PIRL	PISHEOGS
PINWORMS	PIPECLAYS	PIPPING	PIRLICUE	PISHER
PINWRENCH	PIPED	PIPPINS	PIRLICUED	PISHERS
PINXIT	PIPEFISH	PIPPY	PIRLICUES	PISHES
PINY	PIPEFUL	PIPS	PIRLS	PISHING
PINYIN	PIPEFULS	PIPSQUEAK	PIRN	PISHOGE
PINYINS	PIPELESS	PIPUL	PIRNIE	PISHOGES
PINYON	PIPELIKE	PIPULS	PIRNIES	PISHOGUE
PINYONS	PIPELINE	PIPY	PIRNIT	PISHOGUES
PIOLET	PIPELINED	PIQUANCE	PIRNS	PISIFORM
PIOLETS	PIPELINES	PIQUANCES	PIROG	PISIFORMS
PION	PIPER	PIQUANCY	PIROGEN	PISKIES
PIONED	PIPERIC	PIQUANT	PIROGHI	PISKY
PIONEER	PIPERINE	PIQUANTLY	PIROGI	PISMIRE
PIONEERED	PIPERINES	PIQUE	PIROGIES	PISMIRES
PIONEERS	PIPERONAL	PIQUED	PIROGUE	PISO
PIONER	PIPERS	PIQUES	PIROGUES	PISOLITE
PIONERS	PIPES	PIQUET	PIROJKI	PISOLITES
PIONEY	PIPESTEM	PIQUETED	PIROPLASM	PISOLITH
PIONEYS	PIPESTEMS	PIQUETING	PIROQUE	PISOLITHS
PIONIC	PIPESTONE	PIQUETS	PIROQUES	PISOLITIC
PIONIES	PIPET	PIQUILLO	PIROSHKI	PISOS
PIONING	PIPETS	PIQUILLOS	PIROUETTE	PISS
PIONINGS	PIPETTE	PIQUING	PIROZHKI	PISSANT
PIONS	PIPETTED	PIR	PIROZHOK	PISSANTS
PIONY	PIPETTES	PIRACETAM	PIRS	PISSED
PIOPIO	PIPETTING	PIRACIES	PIS	PISSER
PIOPIOS	PIPEWORK	PIRACY	PISCARIES	PISSERS
PIOSITIES	PIPEWORKS	PIRAGUA	PISCARY	PISSES
PIOSITY	PIPEWORT	PIRAGUAS	PISCATOR	PISSHEAD
PIOTED	PIPEWORTS	PIRAI	PISCATORS	PISSHEADS
PIOUS	PIPI	PIRAIS	PISCATORY	PISSHOLE

PISSHOLES	PITCHED	PITIFUL	PIVOT	PIZZELLES
PISSIER	PITCHER	PITIFULLY	PIVOTABLE	PIZZERIA
PISSIEST	PITCHERS	PITIKINS	PIVOTAL	PIZZERIAS
PISSING	PITCHES	PITILESS	PIVOTALLY	PIZZICATI
PISSOIR	PITCHFORK	PITLIKE	PIVOTED	PIZZICATO
PISSOIRS	PITCHIER	PITMAN	PIVOTER	PIZZLE
PISSY	PITCHIEST	PITMANS	PIVOTERS	PIZZLES
PISTACHE	PITCHILY	PITMEN	PIVOTING	PLAAS
PISTACHES	PITCHING	PITON	PIVOTINGS	PLAASES
PISTACHIO	PITCHINGS	PITONS	PIVOTMAN	PLACABLE
PISTAREEN	PITCHMAN	PITOT	PIVOTMEN	PLACABLY
PISTE	PITCHMEN	PITOTS	PIVOTS	PLACARD
PISTED	PITCHOUT	PITPROP	PIX	PLACARDED
PISTES	PITCHOUTS	PITPROPS	PIXEL	PLACARDS
PISTIL	PITCHPINE	PITS	PIXELATE	PLACATE
PISTILLAR	PITCHPIPE	PITSAW	PIXELATED	PLACATED
PISTILS	PITCHPOLE	PITSAWS	PIXELATES	PLACATER
PISTOL	PITCHY	PITTA	PIXELLATE	PLACATERS
PISTOLE	PITEOUS	PITTANCE	PIXELS	PLACATES
PISTOLED	PITEOUSLY	PITTANCES	PIXES	PLACATING
PISTOLEER	PITFALL	PITTAS	PIXIE	PLACATION
PISTOLERO	PITFALLS	PITTED	PIXIEISH	PLACATIVE
PISTOLES	PITH	PITTEN	PIXIES	PLACATORY
PISTOLET	PITHBALL	PITTER	PIXILATE	PLACCAT
PISTOLETS	PITHBALLS	PITTERED	PIXILATED	PLACCATE
PISTOLIER	PITHEAD	PITTERING	PIXILATES	PLACCATES
PISTOLING	PITHEADS	PITTERS	PIXILLATE	PLACCATS
PISTOLLED	PITHECOID	PITTING	PIXINESS	PLACE
PISTOLS	PITHED	PITTINGS	PIXY	PLACEABLE
PISTON	PITHFUL	PITTITE	PIXYISH	PLACEBO
PISTONS	PITHIER	PITTITES	PIZAZZ	PLACEBOES
PISTOU	PITHIEST	PITUITA	PIZAZZES	PLACEBOS
PISTOUS	PITHILY	PITUITARY	PIZAZZIER	PLACED
PIT	PITHINESS	PITUITAS	PIZAZZY	PLACEKICK
PITA	PITHING	PITUITE	PIZE	PLACELESS
PITAHAYA	PITHLESS	PITUITES	PIZED	PLACEMAN
PITAHAYAS	PITHLIKE	PITUITRIN	PIZES	PLACEMAT
PITAPAT	PITHOI	PITURI	PIZING	PLACEMATS
PITAPATS	PITHOS	PITURIS	PIZZA	PLACEMEN
PITARA	PITHS	PITY	PIZZAIOLA	PLACEMENT
PITARAH	PITHY	PITYING	PIZZALIKE	PLACENTA
PITARAHS	PITIABLE	PITYINGLY	PIZZAS	PLACENTAE
PITARAS	PITIABLY	PITYROID	PIZZAZ	PLACENTAL
PITAS	PITIED	PIU	PIZZAZES	PLACENTAS
PITAYA	PITIER	PIUM	PIZZAZZ	PLACER
PITAYAS	PITIERS	PIUMS	PIZZAZZES	PLACERS
PITCH	PITIES	PIUPIU	PIZZAZZY	PLACES
PITCHBEND	PITIETH	PIUPIUS	PIZZELLE	PLACET

P

PLACETS	PLAIDS	PLANE	PLANTAGE	PLASHING
PLACID	PLAIN	PLANED	PLANTAGES	PLASHINGS
PLACIDER	PLAINANT	PLANELOAD	PLANTAIN	PLASHY
PLACIDEST	PLAINANTS	PLANENESS	PLANTAINS	PLASM
PLACIDITY	PLAINED	PLANER	PLANTAR	PLASMA
PLACIDLY	PLAINER	PLANERS	PLANTAS	PLASMAGEL
PLACING	PLAINEST	PLANES	PLANTED	PLASMAS
PLACINGS	PLAINFUL	PLANESIDE	PLANTER	PLASMASOL
PLACIT	PLAINING	PLANET	PLANTERS	PLASMATIC
PLACITA	PLAININGS	PLANETARY	PLANTING	PLASMIC
PLACITORY	PLAINISH	PLANETIC	PLANTINGS	PLASMID
PLACITS	PLAINLY	PLANETOID	PLANTLESS	PLASMIDS
PLACITUM	PLAINNESS	PLANETS	PLANTLET	PLASMIN
PLACK	PLAINS	PLANFORM	PLANTLETS	PLASMINS
PLACKET	PLAINSMAN	PLANFORMS	PLANTLIKE	PLASMODIA
PLACKETS	PLAINSMEN	PLANGENCY	PLANTLING	PLASMOID
PLACKLESS	PLAINSONG	PLANGENT	PLANTS	PLASMOIDS
PLACKS	PLAINT	PLANIGRAM	PLANTSMAN	PLASMON
PLACODERM	PLAINTEXT	PLANING	PLANTSMEN	PLASMONS
PLACOID	PLAINTFUL	PLANISH	PLANTULE	PLASMS
PLACOIDS	PLAINTIFF	PLANISHED	PLANTULES	PLAST
PLAFOND	PLAINTIVE	PLANISHER	PLANULA	PLASTE
PLAFONDS	PLAINTS	PLANISHES	PLANULAE	PLASTER
PLAGAL	PLAINWORK	PLANK	PLANULAR	PLASTERED
PLAGE	PLAISTER	PLANKED	PLANULATE	PLASTERER
PLAGES	PLAISTERS	PLANKING	PLANULOID	PLASTERS
PLAGIARY	PLAIT	PLANKINGS	PLANURIA	PLASTERY
PLAGIUM	PLAITED	PLANKLIKE	PLANURIAS	PLASTIC
PLAGIUMS	PLAITER	PLANKS	PLANURIES	PLASTICKY
PLAGUE	PLAITERS	PLANKTER	PLANURY	PLASTICLY
PLAGUED	PLAITING	PLANKTERS	PLANXTIES	PLASTICS
PLAGUER	PLAITINGS	PLANKTIC	PLANXTY	PLASTID
PLAGUERS	PLAITS	PLANKTON	PLAP	PLASTIDS
PLAGUES	PLAN	PLANKTONS	PLAPPED	PLASTIQUE
PLAGUEY	PLANAR	PLANLESS	PLAPPING	PLASTISOL
PLAGUIER	PLANARIA	PLANNED	PLAPS	PLASTRAL
PLAGUIEST	PLANARIAN	PLANNER	PLAQUE	PLASTRON
PLAGUILY	PLANARIAS	PLANNERS	PLAQUES	PLASTRONS
PLAGUING	PLANARITY	PLANNING	PLAQUETTE	PLASTRUM
PLAGUY	PLANATE	PLANNINGS	PLASH	PLASTRUMS
PLAICE	PLANATION	PLANOGRAM	PLASHED	PLAT
PLAICES	PLANCH	PLANOSOL	PLASHER	PLATAN
PLAID	PLANCHE	PLANOSOLS	PLASHERS	PLATANE
PLAIDED	PLANCHED	PLANS	PLASHES	PLATANES
PLAIDING	PLANCHES	PLANT	PLASHET	PLATANNA
PLAIDINGS	PLANCHET	PLANTA	PLASHETS	PLATANNAS
PLAIDMAN	PLANCHETS	PLANTABLE	PLASHIER	PLATANS
PLAIDMEN	PLANCHING	PLANTAE	PLASHIEST	PLATBAND

P

PLATBANDS	PLATT	PLAYFIELD	PLEACHING	PLEBES
PLATE	PLATTED	PLAYFUL	PLEAD	PLEBIFIED
PLATEASM	PLATTER	PLAYFULLY	PLEADABLE	PLEBIFIES
PLATEASMS	PLATTERS	PLAYGIRL	PLEADED	PLEBIFY
PLATEAU	PLATTING	PLAYGIRLS	PLEADER	PLEBS
PLATEAUED	PLATTINGS	PLAYGOER	PLEADERS	PLECTRA
PLATEAUS	PLATY	PLAYGOERS	PLEADING	PLECTRE
PLATEAUX	PLATYFISH	PLAYGOING	PLEADINGS	PLECTRES
PLATED	PLATYPI	PLAYGROUP	PLEADS	PLECTRON
PLATEFUL	PLATYPUS	PLAYHOUSE	PLEAED	PLECTRONS
PLATEFULS	PLATYS	PLAYING	PLEAING	PLECTRUM
PLATELESS	PLATYSMA	PLAYINGS	PLEAS	PLECTRUMS
PLATELET	PLATYSMAS	PLAYLAND	PLEASABLE	PLED
PLATELETS	PLAUDIT	PLAYLANDS	PLEASANCE	PLEDGABLE
PLATELIKE	PLAUDITE	PLAYLESS	PLEASANT	PLEDGE
PLATEMAN	PLAUDITS	PLAYLET	PLEASE	PLEDGED
PLATEMARK	PLAUSIBLE	PLAYLETS	PLEASED	PLEDGEE
PLATEMEN	PLAUSIBLY	PLAYLIKE	PLEASEDLY	PLEDGEES
PLATEN	PLAUSIVE	PLAYLIST	PLEASEMAN	PLEDGEOR
PLATENS	PLAUSTRAL	PLAYLISTS	PLEASEMEN	PLEDGEORS
PLATER	PLAY	PLAYMAKER	PLEASER	PLEDGER
PLATERS	PLAYA	PLAYMATE	PLEASERS	PLEDGERS
PLATES	PLAYABLE	PLAYMATES	PLEASES	PLEDGES
PLATESFUL	PLAYACT	PLAYOFF	PLEASETH	PLEDGET
PLATFORM	PLAYACTED	PLAYOFFS	PLEASING	PLEDGETS
PLATFORMS	PLAYACTOR	PLAYPEN	PLEASINGS	PLEDGING
PLATIER	PLAYACTS	PLAYPENS	PLEASURE	PLEDGOR
PLATIES	PLAYAS	PLAYROOM	PLEASURED	PLEDGORS
PLATIEST	PLAYBACK	PLAYROOMS	PLEASURER	PLEIAD
PLATINA	PLAYBACKS	PLAYS	PLEASURES	PLEIADES
PLATINAS	PLAYBILL	PLAYSET	PLEAT	PLEIADS
PLATING	PLAYBILLS	PLAYSETS	PLEATED	PLEIOCENE
PLATINGS	PLAYBOOK	PLAYSLIP	PLEATER	PLEIOMERY
PLATINIC	PLAYBOOKS	PLAYSLIPS	PLEATERS	PLEIOTAXY
PLATINISE	PLAYBOY	PLAYSOME	PLEATHER	PLENA
PLATINIZE	PLAYBOYS	PLAYSUIT	PLEATHERS	PLENARIES
PLATINOID	PLAYBUS	PLAYSUITS	PLEATING	PLENARILY
PLATINOUS	PLAYBUSES	PLAYTHING	PLEATINGS	PLENARTY
PLATINUM	PLAYDATE	PLAYTIME	PLEATLESS	PLENARY
PLATINUMS	PLAYDATES	PLAYTIMES	PLEATS	PLENCH
PLATITUDE	PLAYDAY	PLAYWEAR	PLEB	PLENCHES
PLATONIC	PLAYDAYS	PLAYWEARS	PLEBBIER	PLENILUNE
PLATONICS	PLAYDOUGH	PLAZA	PLEBBIEST	PLENIPO
PLATONISM	PLAYDOWN	PLAZAS	PLEBBY	PLENIPOES
PLATOON	PLAYDOWNS	PLEA	PLEBE	PLENIPOS
PLATOONED	PLAYED	PLEACH	PLEBEAN	PLENISH
PLATOONS	PLAYER	PLEACHED	PLEBEIAN	PLENISHED
PLATS	PLAYERS	PLEACHES	PLEBEIANS	PLENISHER

PLENISHES	PLEURAS	PLIGHTFUL	PLODDED	PLOTFUL
PLENISM	PLEURISY	PLIGHTING	PLODDER	PLOTLESS
PLENISMS	PLEURITIC	PLIGHTS	PLODDERS	PLOTLINE
PLENIST	PLEURITIS	PLIM	PLODDING	PLOTLINES
PLENISTS	PLEURON	PLIMMED	PLODDINGS	PLOTS
PLENITUDE	PLEURONIA	PLIMMING	PLODGE	PLOTTAGE
PLENTEOUS	PLEUSTON	PLIMS	PLODGED	PLOTTAGES
PLENTIES	PLEUSTONS	PLIMSOL	PLODGES	PLOTTED
PLENTIFUL	PLEW	PLIMSOLE	PLODGING	PLOTTER
PLENTY	PLEWS	PLIMSOLES	PLODS	PLOTTERED
PLENUM	PLEX	PLIMSOLL	PLOGGING	PLOTTERS
PLENUMS	PLEXAL	PLIMSOLLS	PLOGGINGS	PLOTTIE
PLEON	PLEXED	PLIMSOLS	PLOIDIES	PLOTTIER
PLEONAL	PLEXES	PLING	PLOIDY	PLOTTIES
PLEONASM	PLEXIFORM	PLINGED	PLONG	PLOTTIEST
PLEONASMS	PLEXING	PLINGING	PLONGD	PLOTTING
PLEONAST	PLEXOR	PLINGS	PLONGE	PLOTTINGS
PLEONASTE	PLEXORS	PLINK	PLONGED	PLOTTY
PLEONASTS	PLEXURE	PLINKED	PLONGES	PLOTZ
PLEONEXIA	PLEXURES	PLINKER	PLONGING	PLOTZED
PLEONIC	PLEXUS	PLINKERS	PLONGS	PLOTZES
PLEONS	PLEXUSES	PLINKIER	PLONK	PLOTZING
PLEOPOD	PLIABLE	PLINKIEST	PLONKED	PLOUGH
PLEOPODS	PLIABLY	PLINKING	PLONKER	PLOUGHBOY
PLERION	PLIANCIES	PLINKINGS	PLONKERS	PLOUGHED
PLERIONS	PLIANCY	PLINKS	PLONKIER	PLOUGHER
PLEROMA	PLIANT	PLINKY	PLONKIEST	PLOUGHERS
PLEROMAS	PLIANTLY	PLINTH	PLONKING	PLOUGHING
PLEROME	PLICA	PLINTHS	PLONKINGS	PLOUGHMAN
PLEROMES	PLICAE	PLIOCENE	PLONKO	PLOUGHMEN
PLESH	PLICAL	PLIOFILM	PLONKOS	PLOUGHS
PLESHES	PLICAS	PLIOFILMS	PLONKS	PLOUK
PLESSOR	PLICATE	PLIOSAUR	PLONKY	PLOUKIE
PLESSORS	PLICATED	PLIOSAURS	PLOOK	PLOUKIER
PLETHORA	PLICATELY	PLIOTRON	PLOOKIE	PLOUKIEST
PLETHORAS	PLICATES	PLIOTRONS	PLOOKIER	PLOUKS
PLETHORIC	PLICATING	PLISKIE	PLOOKIEST	PLOUKY
PLEUCH	PLICATION	PLISKIER	PLOOKS	PLOUTER
PLEUCHED	PLICATURE	PLISKIES	PLOOKY	PLOUTERED
PLEUCHING	PLIE	PLISKIEST	PLOP	PLOUTERS
PLEUCHS	PLIED	PLISKY	PLOPPED	PLOVER
PLEUGH	PLIER	PLISSE	PLOPPING	PLOVERIER
PLEUGHED	PLIERS	PLISSES	PLOPS	PLOVERS
PLEUGHING	PLIES	PLOAT	PLOSION	PLOVERY
PLEUGHS	PLIGHT	PLOATED	PLOSIONS	PLOW
PLEURA	PLIGHTED	PLOATING	PLOSIVE	PLOWABLE
PLEURAE	PLIGHTER	PLOATS	PLOSIVES	PLOWBACK
PLEURAL	PLIGHTERS	PLOD	PLOT	PLOWBACKS

PLOWBOY	PLUG	PLUME	PLUMS	PLUSH
PLOWBOYS	PLUGBOARD	PLUMED	PLUMULA	PLUSHED
PLOWED	PLUGGED	PLUMELESS	PLUMULAE	PLUSHER
PLOWER	PLUGGER	PLUMELET	PLUMULAR	PLUSHES
PLOWERS	PLUGGERS	PLUMELETS	PLUMULATE	PLUSHEST
PLOWHEAD	PLUGGING	PLUMELIKE	PLUMULE	PLUSHIER
PLOWHEADS	PLUGGINGS	PLUMERIA	PLUMULES	PLUSHIEST
PLOWING	PLUGHOLE	PLUMERIAS	PLUMULOSE	PLUSHILY
PLOWINGS	PLUGHOLES	PLUMERIES	PLUMY	PLUSHLY
PLOWLAND	PLUGLESS	PLUMERY	PLUNDER	PLUSHNESS
PLOWLANDS	PLUGOLA	PLUMES	PLUNDERED	PLUSHY
PLOWMAN	PLUGOLAS	PLUMIER	PLUNDERER	PLUSING
PLOWMEN	PLUGS	PLUMIEST	PLUNDERS	PLUSSAGE
PLOWS	PLUGUGLY	PLUMING	PLUNGE	PLUSSAGES
PLOWSHARE	PLUM	PLUMIPED	PLUNGED	PLUSSED
PLOWSTAFF	PLUMAGE	PLUMIPEDS	PLUNGER	PLUSSES
PLOWTAIL	PLUMAGED	PLUMIST	PLUNGERS	PLUSSING
PLOWTAILS	PLUMAGES	PLUMISTS	PLUNGES	PLUTEAL
PLOWTER	PLUMATE	PLUMLIKE	PLUNGING	PLUTEI
PLOWTERED	PLUMB	PLUMMER	PLUNGINGS	PLUTEUS
PLOWTERS	PLUMBABLE	PLUMMEST	PLUNK	PLUTEUSES
PLOWWISE	PLUMBAGO	PLUMMET	PLUNKED	PLUTO
PLOY	PLUMBAGOS	PLUMMETED	PLUNKER	PLUTOCRAT
PLOYE	PLUMBATE	PLUMMETS	PLUNKERS	PLUTOED
PLOYED	PLUMBATES	PLUMMIER	PLUNKIER	PLUTOES
PLOYES	PLUMBED	PLUMMIEST	PLUNKIEST	PLUTOID
PLOYING	PLUMBEOUS	PLUMMY	PLUNKING	PLUTOIDS
PLOYS	PLUMBER	PLUMOSE	PLUNKS	PLUTOING
PLU	PLUMBERS	PLUMOSELY	PLUNKY	PLUTOLOGY
PLUCK	PLUMBERY	PLUMOSITY	PLUOT	PLUTON
PLUCKED	PLUMBIC	PLUMOUS	PLUOTS	PLUTONIAN
PLUCKER	PLUMBING	PLUMP	PLURAL	PLUTONIC
PLUCKERS	PLUMBINGS	PLUMPED	PLURALISE	PLUTONISM
PLUCKIER	PLUMBISM	PLUMPEN	PLURALISM	PLUTONIUM
PLUCKIEST	PLUMBISMS	PLUMPENED	PLURALIST	PLUTONOMY
PLUCKILY	PLUMBITE	PLUMPENS	PLURALITY	PLUTONS
PLUCKING	PLUMBITES	PLUMPER	PLURALIZE	PLUTOS
PLUCKS	PLUMBLESS	PLUMPERS	PLURALLY	PLUVIAL
PLUCKY	PLUMBNESS	PLUMPEST	PLURALS	PLUVIALS
PLUE	PLUMBOUS	PLUMPIE	PLURIPARA	PLUVIAN
PLUES	PLUMBS	PLUMPIER	PLURISIE	PLUVIANS
PLUFF	PLUMBUM	PLUMPIEST	PLURISIES	PLUVIOSE
PLUFFED	PLUMBUMS	PLUMPING	PLURRY	PLUVIOUS
PLUFFIER	PLUMCAKE	PLUMPISH	PLUS	PLUVIUS
PLUFFIEST	PLUMCAKES	PLUMPLY	PLUSAGE	PLY
PLUFFING	PLUMCOT	PLUMPNESS	PLUSAGES	PLYER
PLUFFS	PLUMCOTS	PLUMPS	PLUSED	PLYERS
PLUFFY	PLUMDAMAS	PLUMPY	PLUSES	PLYING

P

PLYINGLY	POCKETERS	PODESTAS	POEP	POGGES
PLYWOOD	POCKETFUL	PODEX	POEPED	POGIES
PLYWOODS	POCKETING	PODEXES	POEPING	POGO
PNEUMA	POCKETS	PODGE	POEPOL	POGOED
PNEUMAS	POCKIER	PODGES	POEPOLS	POGOER
PNEUMATIC	POCKIES	PODGIER	POEPS	POGOERS
PNEUMONIA	POCKIEST	PODGIEST	POESIED	POGOES
PNEUMONIC	POCKILY	PODGILY	POESIES	POGOING
PO	POCKING	PODGINESS	POESY	POGONIA
POA	POCKMANKY	PODGY	POESYING	POGONIAS
POACEOUS	POCKMARK	PODIA	POET	POGONIP
POACH	POCKMARKS	PODIAL	POETASTER	POGONIPS
POACHABLE	POCKPIT	PODIATRIC	POETASTRY	POGOS
POACHED	POCKPITS	PODIATRY	POETESS	POGROM
POACHER	POCKS	PODITE	POETESSES	POGROMED
POACHERS	POCKY	PODITES	POETIC	POGROMING
POACHES	POCO	PODITIC	POETICAL	POGROMIST
POACHIER	POCOSEN	PODIUM	POETICALS	POGROMS
POACHIEST	POCOSENS	PODIUMED	POETICISE	POGY
POACHING	POCOSIN	PODIUMING	POETICISM	POH
POACHINGS	POCOSINS	PODIUMS	POETICIZE	POHED
POACHY	POCOSON	PODLEY	POETICS	POHING
POAKA	POCOSONS	PODLEYS	POETICULE	POHIRI
POAKAS	POD	PODLIKE	POETISE	POHIRIS
POAKE	PODAGRA	PODOCARP	POETISED	POHS
POAKES	PODAGRAL	PODOCARPS	POETISER	POI
POAS	PODAGRAS	PODOLOGY	POETISERS	POIGNADO
POBLANO	PODAGRIC	PODOMERE	POETISES	POIGNANCE
POBLANOS	PODAGROUS	PODOMERES	POETISING	POIGNANCY
POBOY	PODAL	PODS	POETIZE	POIGNANT
POBOYS	PODALIC	PODSOL	POETIZED	POILU
POCHARD	PODARGUS	PODSOLIC	POETIZER	POILUS
POCHARDS	PODCAST	PODSOLISE	POETIZERS	POINADO
POCHAY	PODCASTED	PODSOLIZE	POETIZES	POINADOES
POCHAYED	PODCASTER	PODSOLS	POETIZING	POINCIANA
POCHAYING	PODCASTS	PODUNK	POETLESS	POIND
POCHAYS	PODDED	PODUNKS	POETLIKE	POINDED
POCHETTE	PODDIE	PODZOL	POETRESSE	POINDER
POCHETTES	PODDIER	PODZOLIC	POETRIES	POINDERS
POCHOIR	PODDIES	PODZOLISE	POETRY	POINDING
POCHOIRS	PODDIEST	PODZOLIZE	POETS	POINDINGS
POCK	PODDING	PODZOLS	POETSHIP	POINDS
POCKARD	PODDLE	POECHORE	POETSHIPS	POINT
POCKARDS	PODDLED	POECHORES	POFFLE	POINTABLE
POCKED	PODDLES	POEM	POFFLES	POINTE
POCKET	PODDLING	POEMATIC	POGEY	POINTED
POCKETED	PODDY	POEMS	POGEYS	POINTEDLY
POCKETER	PODESTA	POENOLOGY	POGGE	POINTEL

POINTELLE	POKEFUL	POLEAXE	POLING	POLLAXED
POINTELS	POKEFULS	POLEAXED	POLINGS	POLLAXES
POINTER	POKELOGAN	POLEAXES	POLIO	POLLAXING
POINTERS	POKER	POLEAXING	POLIOS	POLLED
POINTES	POKERISH	POLECAT	POLIS	POLLEE
POINTIER	POKEROOT	POLECATS	POLISES	POLLEES
POINTIEST	POKEROOTS	POLED	POLISH	POLLEN
POINTILLE	POKERS	POLEIS	POLISHED	POLLENATE
POINTING	POKERWORK	POLELESS	POLISHER	POLLENED
POINTINGS	POKES	POLEMARCH	POLISHERS	POLLENING
POINTLESS	POKEWEED	POLEMIC	POLISHES	POLLENS
POINTLIKE	POKEWEEDS	POLEMICAL	POLISHING	POLLENT
POINTMAN	POKEY	POLEMICS	POLITBURO	POLLER
POINTMEN	POKEYS	POLEMISE	POLITE	POLLERS
POINTS	POKIE	POLEMISED	POLITELY	POLLEX
POINTSMAN	POKIER	POLEMISES	POLITER	POLLICAL
POINTSMEN	POKIES	POLEMIST	POLITESSE	POLLICES
POINTY	POKIEST	POLEMISTS	POLITEST	POLLICIE
POIS	POKILY	POLEMIZE	POLITIC	POLLICIES
POISE	POKINESS	POLEMIZED	POLITICAL	POLLICY
POISED	POKING	POLEMIZES	POLITICK	POLLIES
POISER	POKY	POLENTA	POLITICKS	POLLINATE
POISERS	POL	POLENTAS	POLITICLY	POLLING
POISES	POLACCA	POLER	POLITICO	POLLINGS
POISHA	POLACCAS	POLERS	POLITICOS	POLLINIA
POISHAS	POLACK	POLES	POLITICS	POLLINIC
POISING	POLACKS	POLESTAR	POLITIES	POLLINISE
POISON	POLACRE	POLESTARS	POLITIQUE	POLLINIUM
POISONED	POLACRES	POLEWARD	POLITY	POLLINIZE
POISONER	POLAR	POLEY	POLJE	POLLIST
POISONERS	POLARISE	POLEYN	POLJES	POLLISTS
POISONING	POLARISED	POLEYNS	POLK	POLLIWIG
POISONOUS	POLARISER	POLEYS	POLKA	POLLIWIGS
POISONS	POLARISES	POLIANITE	POLKAED	POLLIWOG
POISSON	POLARITY	POLICE	POLKAING	POLLIWOGS
POISSONS	POLARIZE	POLICED	POLKAS	POLLMAN
POITIN	POLARIZED	POLICEMAN	POLKED	POLLMEN
POITINS	POLARIZER	POLICEMEN	POLKING	POLLOCK
POITREL	POLARIZES	POLICER	POLKS	POLLOCKS
POITRELS	POLARON	POLICERS	POLL	POLLS
POITRINE	POLARONS	POLICES	POLLACK	POLLSTER
POITRINES	POLARS	POLICIER	POLLACKS	POLLSTERS
POKABLE	POLDER	POLICIERS	POLLAN	POLLTAKER
POKAL	POLDERED	POLICIES	POLLANS	POLLUCITE
POKALS	POLDERING	POLICING	POLLARD	POLLUSION
POKE	POLDERS	POLICINGS	POLLARDED	POLLUTANT
POKEBERRY	POLE	POLICY	POLLARDS	POLLUTE
POKED	POLEAX	POLIES	POLLAXE	POLLUTED

POLLUTER	POLYAMORY	POLYLEMMA	POLYPNEAS	POMACEOUS
POLLUTERS	POLYANDRY	POLYMASTY	POLYPNEIC	POMACES
POLLUTES	POLYANTHA	POLYMATH	POLYPOD	POMADE
POLLUTING	POLYANTHI	POLYMATHS	POLYPODS	POMADED
POLLUTION	POLYARCH	POLYMATHY	POLYPODY	POMADES
POLLUTIVE	POLYARCHY	POLYMER	POLYPOID	POMADING
POLLY	POLYAXIAL	POLYMERIC	POLYPORE	POMANDER
POLLYANNA	POLYAXON	POLYMERS	POLYPORES	POMANDERS
POLLYWIG	POLYAXONS	POLYMERY	POLYPOSES	POMATO
POLLYWIGS	POLYBAG	POLYMORPH	POLYPOSIS	POMATOES
POLLYWOG	POLYBAGS	POLYMYXIN	POLYPOUS	POMATUM
POLLYWOGS	POLYBASIC	POLYNIA	POLYPS	POMATUMED
POLO	POLYBRID	POLYNIAS	POLYPTYCH	POMATUMS
POLOIDAL	POLYBRIDS	POLYNYA	POLYPUS	POMBE
POLOIST	POLYCARPY	POLYNYAS	POLYPUSES	POMBES
POLOISTS	POLYCHETE	POLYNYI	POLYS	POME
POLONAISE	POLYCONIC	POLYOL	POLYSEME	POMELIKE
POLONIE	POLYCOT	POLYOLS	POLYSEMES	POMELO
POLONIES	POLYCOTS	POLYOMA	POLYSEMIC	POMELOS
POLONISE	POLYDEMIC	POLYOMAS	POLYSEMY	POMEROY
POLONISED	POLYDRUG	POLYOMINO	POLYSOME	POMEROYS
POLONISES	POLYENE	POLYONYM	POLYSOMES	POMES
POLONISM	POLYENES	POLYONYMS	POLYSOMIC	POMFRET
POLONISMS	POLYENIC	POLYONYMY	POLYSOMY	POMFRETS
POLONIUM	POLYESTER	POLYP	POLYSTYLE	POMMEE
POLONIUMS	POLYGALA	POLYPARIA	POLYTENE	POMMEL
POLONIZE	POLYGALAS	POLYPARY	POLYTENY	POMMELE
POLONIZED	POLYGAM	POLYPE	POLYTHENE	POMMELED
POLONIZES	POLYGAMIC	POLYPED	POLYTONAL	POMMELING
POLONY	POLYGAMS	POLYPEDS	POLYTYPE	POMMELLED
POLOS	POLYGAMY	POLYPES	POLYTYPED	POMMELS
POLS	POLYGENE	POLYPHAGY	POLYTYPES	POMMETTY
POLT	POLYGENES	POLYPHASE	POLYTYPIC	POMMIE
POLTED	POLYGENIC	POLYPHON	POLYURIA	POMMIES
POLTFEET	POLYGENY	POLYPHONE	POLYURIAS	POMMY
POLTFOOT	POLYGLOT	POLYPHONS	POLYURIC	POMO
POLTING	POLYGLOTS	POLYPHONY	POLYVINYL	POMOERIUM
POLTROON	POLYGLOTT	POLYPI	POLYWATER	POMOLOGY
POLTROONS	POLYGON	POLYPIDE	POLYZOA	POMOS
POLTS	POLYGONAL	POLYPIDES	POLYZOAN	POMP
POLVERINE	POLYGONS	POLYPIDOM	POLYZOANS	POMPADOUR
POLY	POLYGONUM	POLYPILL	POLYZOARY	POMPANO
POLYACID	POLYGONY	POLYPILLS	POLYZOIC	POMPANOS
POLYACIDS	POLYGRAPH	POLYPINE	POLYZONAL	POMPELO
POLYACT	POLYGYNE	POLYPITE	POLYZOOID	POMPELOS
POLYADIC	POLYGYNY	POLYPITES	POLYZOON	POMPEY
POLYAMIDE	POLYHEDRA	POLYPLOID	POM	POMPEYED
POLYAMINE	POLYIMIDE	POLYPNEA	POMACE	POMPEYING

POMPEYS
POMPHOLYX
POMPIER
POMPIERS
POMPILID
POMPILIDS
POMPION
POMPIONS
POMPOM
POMPOMS
POMPON
POMPONS
POMPOON
POMPOONS
POMPOSITY
POMPOSO
POMPOUS
POMPOUSLY
POMPS
POMROY
POMROYS
POMS
POMWATER
POMWATERS
PONCE
PONCEAU
PONCEAUS
PONCEAUX
PONCED
PONCES
PONCEY
PONCHO
PONCHOED
PONCHOS
PONCIER
PONCIEST
PONCING
PONCY
POND
PONDAGE
PONDAGES
PONDED
PONDER
PONDERAL
PONDERATE
PONDERED
PONDERER
PONDERERS

PONDERING
PONDEROSA
PONDEROUS
PONDERS
PONDING
PONDOK
PONDOKKIE
PONDOKS
PONDS
PONDWEED
PONDWEEDS
PONE
PONENT
PONENTS
PONES
PONEY
PONEYS
PONG
PONGA
PONGAL
PONGALS
PONGAS
PONGED
PONGEE
PONGEES
PONGID
PONGIDS
PONGIER
PONGIEST
PONGING
PONGO
PONGOES
PONGOS
PONGS
PONGY
PONIARD
PONIARDED
PONIARDS
PONIED
PONIES
PONK
PONKED
PONKING
PONKS
PONS
PONT
PONTAGE
PONTAGES

PONTAL
PONTES
PONTIANAC
PONTIANAK
PONTIC
PONTIE
PONTIES
PONTIFEX
PONTIFF
PONTIFFS
PONTIFIC
PONTIFICE
PONTIFIED
PONTIFIES
PONTIFY
PONTIL
PONTILE
PONTILES
PONTILS
PONTINE
PONTLEVIS
PONTON
PONTONEER
PONTONIER
PONTONS
PONTOON
PONTOONED
PONTOONER
PONTOONS
PONTS
PONTY
PONY
PONYING
PONYSKIN
PONYSKINS
PONYTAIL
PONYTAILS
PONZU
PONZUS
POO
POOBAH
POOBAHS
POOCH
POOCHED
POOCHES
POOCHING
POOD
POODLE

POODLES
POODS
POOED
POOF
POOFIER
POOFIEST
POOFS
POOFTAH
POOFTAHS
POOFTER
POOFTERS
POOFY
POOGYE
POOGYES
POOH
POOHED
POOHING
POOHS
POOING
POOJA
POOJAH
POOJAHS
POOJAS
POOK
POOKA
POOKAS
POOKING
POOKIT
POOKS
POOL
POOLED
POOLER
POOLERS
POOLHALL
POOLHALLS
POOLING
POOLROOM
POOLROOMS
POOLS
POOLSIDE
POOLSIDES
POON
POONAC
POONACS
POONCE
POONCED
POONCES
POONCING

POONS
POONTANG
POONTANGS
POOP
POOPED
POOPER
POOPERS
POOPIER
POOPIEST
POOPING
POOPS
POOPY
POOR
POORBOX
POORBOXES
POORER
POOREST
POORHOUSE
POORI
POORIS
POORISH
POORLIER
POORLIEST
POORLY
POORMOUTH
POORNESS
POORT
POORTITH
POORTITHS
POORTS
POORWILL
POORWILLS
POOS
POOT
POOTED
POOTER
POOTERED
POOTERING
POOTERS
POOTING
POOTLE
POOTLED
POOTLES
POOTLING
POOTS
POOVE
POOVERIES
POOVERY

P

POOVES	POPLINS	POPSTER	PORIER	POROSCOPY
POOVIER	POPLITEAL	POPSTERS	PORIEST	POROSE
POOVIEST	POPLITEI	POPSTREL	PORIFER	POROSES
POOVY	POPLITEUS	POPSTRELS	PORIFERAL	POROSIS
POP	POPLITIC	POPSY	PORIFERAN	POROSITY
POPADUM	POPOUT	POPTASTIC	PORIFERS	POROUS
POPADUMS	POPOUTS	POPULACE	PORIN	POROUSLY
POPCORN	POPOVER	POPULACES	PORINA	PORPESS
POPCORNS	POPOVERS	POPULAR	PORINAS	PORPESSE
POPE	POPPA	POPULARLY	PORINESS	PORPESSES
POPEDOM	POPPADOM	POPULARS	PORING	PORPHYRIA
POPEDOMS	POPPADOMS	POPULATE	PORINS	PORPHYRIC
POPEHOOD	POPPADUM	POPULATED	PORISM	PORPHYRIN
POPEHOODS	POPPADUMS	POPULATES	PORISMS	PORPHYRIO
POPELESS	POPPAS	POPULISM	PORISTIC	PORPHYRY
POPELIKE	POPPED	POPULISMS	PORK	PORPOISE
POPELING	POPPER	POPULIST	PORKED	PORPOISED
POPELINGS	POPPERING	POPULISTS	PORKER	PORPOISES
POPERA	POPPERS	POPULOUS	PORKERS	PORPORATE
POPERAS	POPPET	PORAE	PORKIER	PORRECT
POPERIES	POPPETS	PORAES	PORKIES	PORRECTED
POPERIN	POPPIED	PORAL	PORKIEST	PORRECTS
POPERINS	POPPIER	PORANGI	PORKINESS	PORRENGER
POPERY	POPPIES	PORBEAGLE	PORKING	PORRIDGE
POPES	POPPIEST	PORCELAIN	PORKLING	PORRIDGES
POPESEYE	POPPING	PORCH	PORKLINGS	PORRIDGY
POPESHIP	POPPISH	PORCHED	PORKPIE	PORRIGO
POPESHIPS	POPPIT	PORCHES	PORKPIES	PORRIGOS
POPETTE	POPPITS	PORCHETTA	PORKS	PORRINGER
POPETTES	POPPLE	PORCHLESS	PORKWOOD	PORT
POPEYED	POPPLED	PORCINE	PORKWOODS	PORTA
POPGUN	POPPLES	PORCINI	PORKY	PORTABLE
POPGUNS	POPPLIER	PORCINIS	PORLOCK	PORTABLES
POPINAC	POPPLIEST	PORCINO	PORLOCKED	PORTABLY
POPINACK	POPPLING	PORCUPINE	PORLOCKS	PORTAGE
POPINACKS	POPPLY	PORCUPINY	PORN	PORTAGED
POPINACS	POPPY	PORE	PORNIER	PORTAGES
POPINJAY	POPPYCOCK	PORED	PORNIEST	PORTAGING
POPINJAYS	POPPYHEAD	PORER	PORNO	PORTAGUE
POPISH	POPPYSEED	PORERS	PORNOMAG	PORTAGUES
POPISHLY	POPRIN	PORES	PORNOMAGS	PORTAL
POPJOY	POPS	PORGE	PORNOS	PORTALED
POPJOYED	POPSICLE	PORGED	PORNS	PORTALS
POPJOYING	POPSICLES	PORGES	PORNY	PORTANCE
POPJOYS	POPSIE	PORGIE	POROGAMIC	PORTANCES
POPLAR	POPSIES	PORGIES	POROGAMY	PORTAPACK
POPLARS	POPSOCK	PORGING	POROMERIC	PORTAPAK
POPLIN	POPSOCKS	PORGY	POROSCOPE	PORTAPAKS

PORTAS	PORTLANDS	POSEURS	POSSER	POSTCODED
PORTASES	PORTLAST	POSEUSE	POSSERS	POSTCODES
PORTATE	PORTLASTS	POSEUSES	POSSES	POSTCOUP
PORTATILE	PORTLESS	POSEY	POSSESS	POSTCRASH
PORTATIVE	PORTLIER	POSH	POSSESSED	POSTDATE
PORTED	PORTLIEST	POSHED	POSSESSES	POSTDATED
PORTEND	PORTLY	POSHER	POSSESSOR	POSTDATES
PORTENDED	PORTMAN	POSHES	POSSET	POSTDIVE
PORTENDS	PORTMEN	POSHEST	POSSETED	POSTDOC
PORTENT	PORTOISE	POSHING	POSSETING	POSTDOCS
PORTENTS	PORTOISES	POSHLY	POSSETS	POSTDRUG
PORTEOUS	PORTOLAN	POSHNESS	POSSIBLE	POSTED
PORTER	PORTOLANI	POSHO	POSSIBLER	POSTEEN
PORTERAGE	PORTOLANO	POSHOS	POSSIBLES	POSTEENS
PORTERED	PORTOLANS	POSHTEEN	POSSIBLY	POSTER
PORTERESS	PORTOUS	POSHTEENS	POSSIE	POSTERED
PORTERING	PORTOUSES	POSIDRIVE	POSSIES	POSTERING
PORTERLY	PORTRAIT	POSIER	POSSING	POSTERIOR
PORTERS	PORTRAITS	POSIES	POSSUM	POSTERISE
PORTESS	PORTRAY	POSIEST	POSSUMED	POSTERITY
PORTESSE	PORTRAYAL	POSIGRADE	POSSUMING	POSTERIZE
PORTESSES	PORTRAYED	POSING	POSSUMS	POSTERN
PORTFIRE	PORTRAYER	POSINGLY	POST	POSTERNS
PORTFIRES	PORTRAYS	POSINGS	POSTAGE	POSTERS
PORTFOLIO	PORTREEVE	POSIT	POSTAGES	POSTFACE
PORTHOLE	PORTRESS	POSITED	POSTAL	POSTFACES
PORTHOLES	PORTS	POSITIF	POSTALLY	POSTFACT
PORTHORS	PORTSIDE	POSITIFS	POSTALS	POSTFAULT
PORTHOS	PORTULACA	POSITING	POSTANAL	POSTFIRE
PORTHOSES	PORTULAN	POSITION	POSTAXIAL	POSTFIX
PORTHOUSE	PORTULANS	POSITIONS	POSTBAG	POSTFIXAL
PORTICO	PORTY	POSITIVE	POSTBAGS	POSTFIXED
PORTICOED	PORWIGGLE	POSITIVER	POSTBASE	POSTFIXES
PORTICOES	PORY	POSITIVES	POSTBASES	POSTFORM
PORTICOS	POS	POSITON	POSTBOX	POSTFORMS
PORTIER	POSABLE	POSITONS	POSTBOXES	POSTGAME
PORTIERE	POSADA	POSITRON	POSTBOY	POSTGRAD
PORTIERED	POSADAS	POSITRONS	POSTBOYS	POSTGRADS
PORTIERES	POSAUNE	POSITS	POSTBURN	POSTHASTE
PORTIEST	POSAUNES	POSNET	POSTBUS	POSTHEAT
PORTIGUE	POSE	POSNEIS	POSTBUSES	POSTHEATS
PORTIGUES	POSEABLE	POSOLE	POSTCARD	POSTHOLE
PORTING	POSED	POSOLES	POSTCARDS	POSTHOLES
PORTION	POSER	POSOLOGIC	POSTCAVA	POSTHORSE
PORTIONED	POSERISH	POSOLOGY	POSTCAVAE	POSTHOUSE
PORTIONER	POSERS	POSS	POSTCAVAL	POSTICAL
PORTIONS	POSES	POSSE	POSTCAVAS	POSTICHE
PORTLAND	POSEUR	POSSED	POSTCODE	POSTICHES

P

POSTICOUS	POSTTEENS	POTATOBUG	POTHERING	POTSHARDS
POSTIE	POSTTEST	POTATOES	POTHERS	POTSHARE
POSTIES	POSTTESTS	POTATORY	POTHERY	POTSHARES
POSTIL	POSTTRIAL	POTBELLY	POTHOLDER	POTSHERD
POSTILED	POSTTRUTH	POTBOIL	POTHOLE	POTSHERDS
POSTILING	POSTULANT	POTBOILED	POTHOLED	POTSHOP
POSTILION	POSTULATA	POTBOILER	POTHOLER	POTSHOPS
POSTILLED	POSTULATE	POTBOILS	POTHOLERS	POTSHOT
POSTILLER	POSTURAL	POTBOUND	POTHOLES	POTSHOTS
POSTILS	POSTURE	POTBOY	POTHOLING	POTSIE
POSTIN	POSTURED	POTBOYS	POTHOOK	POTSIES
POSTING	POSTURER	POTCH	POTHOOKS	POTSTONE
POSTINGS	POSTURERS	POTCHE	POTHOS	POTSTONES
POSTINS	POSTURES	POTCHED	POTHOSES	POTSY
POSTIQUE	POSTURING	POTCHER	POTHOUSE	POTT
POSTIQUES	POSTURISE	POTCHERS	POTHOUSES	POTTABLE
POSTLIKE	POSTURIST	POTCHES	POTHUNTER	POTTAGE
POSTLUDE	POSTURIZE	POTCHING	POTICARY	POTTAGES
POSTLUDES	POSTVIRAL	POTE	POTICHE	POTTED
POSTMAN	POSTWAR	POTED	POTICHES	POTTEEN
POSTMARK	POSTWOMAN	POTEEN	POTIN	POTTEENS
POSTMARKS	POSTWOMEN	POTEENS	POTING	POTTER
POSTMEN	POSY	POTENCE	POTINS	POTTERED
POSTNASAL	POT	POTENCES	POTION	POTTERER
POSTNATAL	POTABLE	POTENCIES	POTIONS	POTTERERS
POSTNATI	POTABLES	POTENCY	POTJIE	POTTERIES
POSTOP	POTAE	POTENT	POTJIES	POTTERING
POSTOPS	POTAES	POTENTATE	POTLACH	POTTERS
POSTORAL	POTAGE	POTENTIAL	POTLACHE	POTTERY
POSTPAID	POTAGER	POTENTISE	POTLACHES	POTTIER
POSTPONE	POTAGERS	POTENTIZE	POTLATCH	POTTIES
POSTPONED	POTAGES	POTENTLY	POTLIKE	POTTIEST
POSTPONER	POTALE	POTENTS	POTLINE	POTTINESS
POSTPONES	POTALES	POTES	POTLINES	POTTING
POSTPOSE	POTAMIC	POTFUL	POTLUCK	POTTINGAR
POSTPOSED	POTASH	POTFULS	POTLUCKS	POTTINGER
POSTPOSES	POTASHED	POTGUN	POTMAN	POTTLE
POSTPUNK	POTASHES	POTGUNS	POTMEN	POTTLES
POSTPUNKS	POTASHING	POTHEAD	POTOMETER	POTTO
POSTRACE	POTASS	POTHEADS	POTOO	POTTOS
POSTRIDER	POTASSA	POTHECARY	POTOOS	POTTS
POSTRIOT	POTASSAS	POTHEEN	POTOROO	POTTY
POSTS	POTASSES	POTHEENS	POTOROOS	POTWALLER
POSTSHOW	POTASSIC	POTHER	POTPIE	POTZER
POSTSYNC	POTASSIUM	POTHERB	POTPIES	POTZERS
POSTSYNCS	POTATION	POTHERBS	POTPOURRI	POUCH
POSTTAX	POTATIONS	POTHERED	POTS	POUCHED
POSTTEEN	POTATO	POTHERIER	POTSHARD	POUCHES

POUCHFUL	POULP	POURING	POWAN	POWTERING
POUCHFULS	POULPE	POURINGLY	POWANS	POWTERS
POUCHIER	POULPES	POURINGS	POWDER	POWWAW
POUCHIEST	POULPS	POURPOINT	POWDERED	POWWOW
POUCHING	POULT	POURS	POWDERER	POWWOWED
POUCHLIKE	POULTER	POURSEW	POWDERERS	POWWOWING
POUCHY	POULTERER	POURSEWED	POWDERIER	POWWOWS
POUDER	POULTERS	POURSEWS	POWDERING	POX
POUDERS	POULTICE	POURSUE	POWDERMAN	POXED
POUDRE	POULTICED	POURSUED	POWDERMEN	POXES
POUDRES	POULTICES	POURSUES	POWDERS	POXIER
POUF	POULTRIES	POURSUING	POWDERY	POXIEST
POUFED	POULTRY	POURSUIT	POWELLISE	POXING
POUFF	POULTS	POURSUITS	POWELLITE	POXVIRUS
POUFFE	POUNCE	POURTRAY	POWELLIZE	POXY
POUFFED	POUNCED	POURTRAYD	POWER	POYNANT
POUFFES	POUNCER	POURTRAYS	POWERBAND	POYNT
POUFFIER	POUNCERS	POUSADA	POWERBOAT	POYNTED
POUFFIEST	POUNCES	POUSADAS	POWERED	POYNTING
POUFFING	POUNCET	POUSOWDIE	POWERFUL	POYNTS
POUFFS	POUNCETS	POUSSE	POWERING	POYOU
POUFFY	POUNCHING	POUSSES	POWERLESS	POYOUS
POUFING	POUNCING	POUSSETTE	POWERPLAY	POYSE
POUFS	POUND	POUSSIE	POWERS	POYSED
POUFTAH	POUNDAGE	POUSSIES	POWFAGGED	POYSES
POUFTAHS	POUNDAGES	POUSSIN	POWHIRI	POYSING
POUFTER	POUNDAL	POUSSINS	POWHIRIS	POYSON
POUFTERS	POUNDALS	POUT	POWIN	POYSONED
POUK	POUNDCAKE	POUTASSOU	POWINS	POYSONING
POUKE	POUNDED	POUTED	POWN	POYSONS
POUKES	POUNDER	POUTER	POWND	POZ
POUKING	POUNDERS	POUTERS	POWNDED	POZIDRIVE
POUKIT	POUNDING	POUTFUL	POWNDING	POZOLE
POUKS	POUNDINGS	POUTHER	POWNDS	POZOLES
POULAINE	POUNDS	POUTHERED	POWNEY	POZZ
POULAINES	POUPE	POUTHERS	POWNEYS	POZZIES
POULARD	POUPED	POUTIER	POWNIE	POZZOLAN
POULARDE	POUPES	POUTIEST	POWNIES	POZZOLANA
POULARDES	POUPING	POUTINE	POWNS	POZZOLANS
POULARDS	POUPT	POUTINES	POWNY	POZZY
POULDER	POUR	POUTING	POWRE	PRAAM
POULDERS	POURABLE	POUTINGLY	POWRED	PRAAMS
POULDRE	POURBOIRE	POUTINGS	POWRES	PRABBLE
POULDRES	POURED	POUTS	POWRING	PRABBLES
POULDRON	POURER	POUTY	POWS	PRACHARAK
POULDRONS	POURERS	POVERTIES	POWSOWDY	PRACTIC
POULE	POURIE	POVERTY	POWTER	PRACTICAL
POULES	POURIES	POW	POWTERED	PRACTICE

P

PRACTICED	PRAISINGS	PRAT	PRAXISES	PREAMBLES
PRACTICER	PRAJNA	PRATE	PRAY	PREAMP
PRACTICES	PRAJNAS	PRATED	PRAYED	PREAMPS
PRACTICK	PRALINE	PRATER	PRAYER	PREANAL
PRACTICKS	PRALINES	PRATERS	PRAYERFUL	PREAPPLY
PRACTICS	PRAM	PRATES	PRAYERS	PREARM
PRACTICUM	PRAMS	PRATFALL	PRAYING	PREARMED
PRACTIQUE	PRANA	PRATFALLS	PRAYINGLY	PREARMING
PRACTISE	PRANAS	PRATFELL	PRAYINGS	PREARMS
PRACTISED	PRANAYAMA	PRATIE	PRAYS	PREASE
PRACTISER	PRANCE	PRATIES	PRE	PREASED
PRACTISES	PRANCED	PRATING	PREABSORB	PREASES
PRACTIVE	PRANCER	PRATINGLY	PREACCUSE	PREASING
PRACTOLOL	PRANCERS	PRATINGS	PREACE	PREASSE
PRAD	PRANCES	PRATIQUE	PREACED	PREASSED
PRADHAN	PRANCING	PRATIQUES	PREACES	PREASSES
PRADHANS	PRANCINGS	PRATS	PREACH	PREASSIGN
PRADS	PRANCK	PRATT	PREACHED	PREASSING
PRAEAMBLE	PRANCKE	PRATTED	PREACHER	PREASSURE
PRAECIPE	PRANCKED	PRATTING	PREACHERS	PREATOMIC
PRAECIPES	PRANCKES	PRATTLE	PREACHES	PREATTUNE
PRAECOCES	PRANCKING	PRATTLED	PREACHIER	PREAUDIT
PRAEDIAL	PRANCKS	PRATTLER	PREACHIFY	PREAUDITS
PRAEDIALS	PRANDIAL	PRATTLERS	PREACHILY	PREAVER
PRAEFECT	PRANG	PRATTLES	PREACHING	PREAVERS
PRAEFECTS	PRANGED	PRATTLING	PREACHY	PREAXIAL
PRAELECT	PRANGING	PRATTS	PREACING	PREBADE
PRAELECTS	PRANGS	PRATY	PREACT	PREBAKE
PRAELUDIA	PRANK	PRAU	PREACTED	PREBAKED
PRAENOMEN	PRANKED	PRAUNCE	PREACTING	PREBAKES
PRAESES	PRANKFUL	PRAUNCED	PREACTS	PREBAKING
PRAESIDIA	PRANKIER	PRAUNCES	PREADAMIC	PREBASAL
PRAETOR	PRANKIEST	PRAUNCING	PREADAPT	PREBATTLE
PRAETORS	PRANKING	PRAUS	PREADAPTS	PREBEND
PRAGMATIC	PRANKINGS	PRAVITIES	PREADJUST	PREBENDAL
PRAHU	PRANKISH	PRAVITY	PREADMIT	PREBENDS
PRAHUS	PRANKLE	PRAWLE	PREADMITS	PREBID
PRAIRIE	PRANKLED	PRAWLES	PREADOPT	PREBIDDEN
PRAIRIED	PRANKLES	PRAWLIN	PREADOPTS	PREBIDS
PRAIRIES	PRANKLING	PRAWLINS	PREADULT	PREBILL
PRAISE	PRANKS	PRAWN	PREADULTS	PREBILLED
PRAISEACH	PRANKSOME	PRAWNED	PREAGED	PREBILLS
PRAISED	PRANKSTER	PRAWNER	PREALLOT	PREBIND
PRAISEFUL	PRANKY	PRAWNERS	PREALLOTS	PREBINDS
PRAISER	PRAO	PRAWNING	PREALTER	PREBIOTIC
PRAISERS	PRAOS	PRAWNS	PREALTERS	PREBIRTH
PRAISES	PRASE	PRAXES	PREAMBLE	PREBIRTHS
PRAISING	PRASES	PRAXIS	PREAMBLED	PREBLESS

PREBOARD	PRECES	PRECONISE	PREDESIGN	PREENACT
PREBOARDS	PRECESS	PRECONIZE	PREDEVOTE	PREENACTS
PREBOIL	PRECESSED	PRECOOK	PREDIAL	PREENED
PREBOILED	PRECESSES	PRECOOKED	PREDIALS	PREENER
PREBOILS	PRECHARGE	PRECOOKER	PREDICANT	PREENERS
PREBOOK	PRECHECK	PRECOOKS	PREDICATE	PREENING
PREBOOKED	PRECHECKS	PRECOOL	PREDICT	PREENS
PREBOOKS	PRECHILL	PRECOOLED	PREDICTED	PREERECT
PREBOOM	PRECHILLS	PRECOOLS	PREDICTER	PREERECTS
PREBORN	PRECHOOSE	PRECOUP	PREDICTOR	PREES
PREBOUGHT	PRECHOSE	PRECRASH	PREDICTS	PREEVE
PREBOUND	PRECHOSEN	PRECREASE	PREDIED	PREEVED
PREBUDGET	PRECIEUSE	PRECRISIS	PREDIES	PREEVES
PREBUILD	PRECIEUX	PRECURE	PREDIGEST	PREEVING
PREBUILDS	PRECINCT	PRECURED	PREDIKANT	PREEXCITE
PREBUILT	PRECINCTS	PRECURES	PREDILECT	PREEXEMPT
PREBUTTAL	PRECIOUS	PRECURING	PREDINNER	PREEXILIC
PREBUY	PRECIP	PRECURRER	PREDIVE	PREEXIST
PREBUYING	PRECIPE	PRECURSE	PREDOOM	PREEXISTS
PREBUYS	PRECIPES	PRECURSED	PREDOOMED	PREEXPOSE
PRECANCEL	PRECIPICE	PRECURSES	PREDOOMS	PREFAB
PRECANCER	PRECIPS	PRECURSOR	PREDRAFT	PREFABBED
PRECARIAT	PRECIS	PRECUT	PREDRAFTS	PREFABS
PRECAST	PRECISE	PRECUTS	PREDRIED	PREFACE
PRECASTS	PRECISED	PRECYCLE	PREDRIES	PREFACED
PRECATIVE	PRECISELY	PRECYCLED	PREDRILL	PREFACER
PRECATORY	PRECISER	PRECYCLES	PREDRILLS	PREFACERS
PRECAUDAL	PRECISES	PREDACITY	PREDRY	PREFACES
PRECAVA	PRECISEST	PREDATE	PREDRYING	PREFACIAL
PRECAVAE	PRECISIAN	PREDATED	PREDUSK	PREFACING
PRECAVAL	PRECISING	PREDATES	PREDUSKS	PREFADE
PRECAVALS	PRECISION	PREDATING	PREDY	PREFADED
PRECEDE	PRECISIVE	PREDATION	PREDYING	PREFADES
PRECEDED	PRECITED	PREDATISM	PREE	PREFADING
PRECEDENT	PRECLEAN	PREDATIVE	PREED	PREFARD
PRECEDES	PRECLEANS	PREDATOR	PREEDIT	PREFATORY
PRECEDING	PRECLEAR	PREDATORS	PREEDITED	PREFECT
PRECEESE	PRECLEARS	PREDATORY	PREEDITS	PREFECTS
PRECENSOR	PRECLUDE	PREDAWN	PREEING	PREFER
PRECENT	PRECLUDED	PREDAWNS	PREELECT	PREFERRED
PRECENTED	PRECLUDES	PREDEATH	PREELECTS	PREFERRER
PRECENTOR	PRECOCIAL	PREDEATHS	PREEMIE	PREFERS
PRECENTS	PRECOCITY	PREDEBATE	PREEMIES	PREFEUDAL
PRECEPIT	PRECODE	PREDEDUCT	PREEMPT	PREFIGHT
PRECEPITS	PRECODED	PREDEFINE	PREEMPTED	PREFIGURE
PRECEPT	PRECODES	PREDELLA	PREEMPTOR	PREFILE
PRECEPTOR	PRECODING	PREDELLAS	PREEMPTS	PREFILED
PRECEPTS	PRECOITAL	PREDELLE	PREEN	PREFILES

PREFILING	PREHARDEN	PRELECTED	PREMIERE	PRENATALS
PREFILLED	PREHEAT	PRELECTOR	PREMIERED	PRENEED
PREFIRE	PREHEATED	PRELECTS	PREMIERES	PRENOMEN
PREFIRED	PREHEATER	PRELEGAL	PREMIERS	PRENOMENS
PREFIRES	PREHEATS	PRELIFE	PREMIES	PRENOMINA
PREFIRING	PREHEND	PRELIM	PREMISE	PRENOON
PREFIX	PREHENDED	PRELIMIT	PREMISED	PRENOTIFY
PREFIXAL	PREHENDS	PRELIMITS	PREMISES	PRENOTION
PREFIXED	PREHENSOR	PRELIMS	PREMISING	PRENT
PREFIXES	PREHIRING	PRELIVES	PREMISS	PRENTED
PREFIXING	PREHNITE	PRELOAD	PREMISSED	PRENTICE
PREFIXION	PREHNITES	PRELOADED	PREMISSES	PRENTICED
PREFLAME	PREHUMAN	PRELOADS	PREMIUM	PRENTICES
PREFLIGHT	PREHUMANS	PRELOCATE	PREMIUMS	PRENTING
PREFOCUS	PREIF	PRELOVED	PREMIX	PRENTS
PREFORM	PREIFE	PRELUDE	PREMIXED	PRENUBILE
PREFORMAT	PREIFES	PRELUDED	PREMIXES	PRENUMBER
PREFORMED	PREIFS	PRELUDER	PREMIXING	PRENUP
PREFORMS	PREIMPOSE	PRELUDERS	PREMIXT	PRENUPS
PREFRANK	PREINFORM	PRELUDES	PREMODERN	PRENZIE
PREFRANKS	PREINSERT	PRELUDI	PREMODIFY	PREOBTAIN
PREFREEZE	PREINVITE	PRELUDIAL	PREMOLAR	PREOCCUPY
PREFROZE	PREJINK	PRELUDING	PREMOLARS	PREOCULAR
PREFROZEN	PREJUDGE	PRELUDIO	PREMOLD	PREON
PREFUND	PREJUDGED	PRELUDIOS	PREMOLDED	PREONS
PREFUNDED	PREJUDGER	PRELUNCH	PREMOLDS	PREOP
PREFUNDS	PREJUDGES	PRELUSION	PREMOLT	PREOPS
PREGAME	PREJUDICE	PRELUSIVE	PREMONISH	PREOPTION
PREGAMED	PREJUDIZE	PRELUSORY	PREMORAL	PREORAL
PREGAMES	PRELACIES	PREM	PREMORSE	PREORDAIN
PREGAMING	PRELACY	PREMADE	PREMOSAIC	PREORDER
PREGGERS	PRELATE	PREMAKE	PREMOTION	PREORDERS
PREGGIER	PRELATES	PREMAKES	PREMOTOR	PREOWNED
PREGGIEST	PRELATESS	PREMAKING	PREMOULD	PREP
PREGGO	PRELATIAL	PREMAN	PREMOULDS	PREPACK
PREGGY	PRELATIC	PREMARKET	PREMOULT	PREPACKED
PREGNABLE	PRELATIES	PREMATURE	PREMOVE	PREPACKS
PREGNANCE	PRELATION	PREMEAL	PREMOVED	PREPAID
PREGNANCY	PRELATISE	PREMED	PREMOVES	PREPARE
PREGNANT	PRELATISH	PREMEDIC	PREMOVING	PREPARED
PREGROWTH	PRELATISM	PREMEDICS	PREMS	PREPARER
PREGUIDE	PRELATIST	PREMEDS	PREMUNE	PREPARERS
PREGUIDED	PRELATIZE	PREMEET	PREMY	PREPARES
PREGUIDES	PRELATURE	PREMEN	PRENAME	PREPARING
PREHAB	PRELATY	PREMERGER	PRENAMES	PREPASTE
PREHABS	PRELAUNCH	PREMIA	PRENASAL	PREPASTED
PREHALLUX	PRELAW	PREMIE	PRENASALS	PREPASTES
PREHANDLE	PRELECT	PREMIER	PRENATAL	PREPAVE

PREPAVED	PREPUEBLO	PRESCRIPT	PRESIDIUM	PRESSURES
PREPAVES	PREPUNCH	PRESCUTA	PRESIFT	PRESSWORK
PREPAVING	PREPUPA	PRESCUTUM	PRESIFTED	PRESSY
PREPAY	PREPUPAE	PRESE	PRESIFTS	PREST
PREPAYING	PREPUPAL	PRESEASON	PRESIGNAL	PRESTAMP
PREPAYS	PREPUPAS	PRESELECT	PRESLEEP	PRESTAMPS
PREPENSE	PREPUTIAL	PRESELL	PRESLICE	PRESTED
PREPENSED	PREQUEL	PRESELLS	PRESLICED	PRESTER
PREPENSES	PREQUELS	PRESENCE	PRESLICES	PRESTERNA
PREPILL	PRERACE	PRESENCES	PRESOAK	PRESTERS
PREPLACE	PRERADIO	PRESENILE	PRESOAKED	PRESTIGE
PREPLACED	PRERECORD	PRESENT	PRESOAKS	PRESTIGES
PREPLACES	PRERECTAL	PRESENTED	PRESOLD	PRESTING
PREPLAN	PREREFORM	PRESENTEE	PRESOLVE	PRESTO
PREPLANS	PRERENAL	PRESENTER	PRESOLVED	PRESTORE
PREPLANT	PRERETURN	PRESENTLY	PRESOLVES	PRESTORED
PREPOLLEX	PREREVIEW	PRESENTS	PRESONG	PRESTORES
PREPONE	PRERINSE	PRESERVE	PRESORT	PRESTOS
PREPONED	PRERINSED	PRESERVED	PRESORTED	PRESTRESS
PREPONES	PRERINSES	PRESERVER	PRESORTS	PRESTRIKE
PREPONING	PRERIOT	PRESERVES	PRESPLIT	PRESTS
PREPOSE	PREROCK	PRESES	PRESS	PRESUME
PREPOSED	PRERUPT	PRESET	PRESSBACK	PRESUMED
PREPOSES	PRESA	PRESETS	PRESSED	PRESUMER
PREPOSING	PRESAGE	PRESETTLE	PRESSER	PRESUMERS
PREPOSTOR	PRESAGED	PRESHAPE	PRESSERS	PRESUMES
PREPOTENT	PRESAGER	PRESHAPED	PRESSES	PRESUMING
PREPPED	PRESAGERS	PRESHAPES	PRESSFAT	PRESUMMIT
PREPPIE	PRESAGES	PRESHIP	PRESSFATS	PRESURVEY
PREPPIER	PRESAGING	PRESHIPS	PRESSFUL	PRETAPE
PREPPIES	PRESALE	PRESHOW	PRESSFULS	PRETAPED
PREPPIEST	PRESALES	PRESHOWED	PRESSGANG	PRETAPES
PREPPILY	PRESBYOPE	PRESHOWN	PRESSIE	PRETAPING
PREPPING	PRESBYOPY	PRESHOWS	PRESSIES	PRETASTE
PREPPY	PRESBYTE	PRESHRANK	PRESSING	PRETASTED
PREPREG	PRESBYTER	PRESHRINK	PRESSINGS	PRETASTES
PREPREGS	PRESBYTES	PRESHRUNK	PRESSION	PRETAX
PREPRESS	PRESBYTIC	PRESIDE	PRESSIONS	PRETEEN
PREPRICE	PRESCHOOL	PRESIDED	PRESSMAN	PRETEENS
PREPRICED	PRESCIENT	PRESIDENT	PRESSMARK	PRETELL
PREPRICES	PRESCIND	PRESIDER	PRESSMEN	PRETELLS
PREPRINT	PRESCINDS	PRESIDERS	PRESSOR	PRETENCE
PREPRINTS	PRESCIOUS	PRESIDES	PRESSORS	PRETENCES
PREPS	PRESCORE	PRESIDIA	PRESSROOM	PRETEND
PREPUBES	PRESCORED	PRESIDIAL	PRESSRUN	PRETENDED
PREPUBIS	PRESCORES	PRESIDING	PRESSRUNS	PRETENDER
PREPUCE	PRESCREEN	PRESIDIO	PRESSURE	PRETENDS
PREPUCES	PRESCRIBE	PRESIDIOS	PRESSURED	PRETENSE

P

PRETENSES	PREUNITED	PREWARN	PRIAPUSES	PRIEF
PRETERIST	PREUNITES	PREWARNED	PRIBBLE	PRIEFE
PRETERIT	PREVAIL	PREWARNS	PRIBBLES	PRIEFES
PRETERITE	PREVAILED	PREWASH	PRICE	PRIEFS
PRETERITS	PREVAILER	PREWASHED	PRICEABLE	PRIER
PRETERM	PREVAILS	PREWASHES	PRICED	PRIERS
PRETERMIT	PREVALENT	PREWEANED	PRICELESS	PRIES
PRETERMS	PREVALUE	PREWEIGH	PRICER	PRIEST
PRETEST	PREVALUED	PREWEIGHS	PRICERS	PRIESTED
PRETESTED	PREVALUES	PREWIRE	PRICES	PRIESTESS
PRETESTS	PREVE	PREWIRED	PRICEY	PRIESTING
PRETEXT	PREVED	PREWIRES	PRICIER	PRIESTLY
PRETEXTED	PREVENE	PREWIRING	PRICIEST	PRIESTS
PRETEXTS	PREVENED	PREWORK	PRICILY	PRIEVE
PRETOLD	PREVENES	PREWORKED	PRICINESS	PRIEVED
PRETONIC	PREVENING	PREWORKS	PRICING	PRIEVES
PRETOR	PREVENT	PREWORN	PRICINGS	PRIEVING
PRETORIAL	PREVENTED	PREWRAP	PRICK	PRIG
PRETORIAN	PREVENTER	PREWRAPS	PRICKED	PRIGGED
PRETORS	PREVENTS	PREWRITE	PRICKER	PRIGGER
PRETRAIN	PREVERB	PREWRITES	PRICKERS	PRIGGERS
PRETRAINS	PREVERBAL	PREWROTE	PRICKET	PRIGGERY
PRETRAVEL	PREVERBS	PREWYN	PRICKETS	PRIGGING
PRETREAT	PREVES	PREWYNS	PRICKIER	PRIGGINGS
PRETREATS	PREVIABLE	PREX	PRICKIEST	PRIGGISH
PRETRIAL	PREVIEW	PREXES	PRICKING	PRIGGISM
PRETRIALS	PREVIEWED	PREXIE	PRICKINGS	PRIGGISMS
PRETRIM	PREVIEWER	PREXIES	PRICKLE	PRIGS
PRETRIMS	PREVIEWS	PREXY	PRICKLED	PRILL
PRETTIED	PREVING	PREY	PRICKLES	PRILLED
PRETTIER	PREVIOUS	PREYED	PRICKLIER	PRILLING
PRETTIES	PREVISE	PREYER	PRICKLING	PRILLS
PRETTIEST	PREVISED	PREYERS	PRICKLY	PRIM
PRETTIFY	PREVISES	PREYFUL	PRICKS	PRIMA
PRETTILY	PREVISING	PREYING	PRICKWOOD	PRIMACIES
PRETTY	PREVISION	PREYS	PRICKY	PRIMACY
PRETTYING	PREVISIT	PREZ	PRICY	PRIMAEVAL
PRETTYISH	PREVISITS	PREZES	PRIDE	PRIMAGE
PRETTYISM	PREVISOR	PREZZIE	PRIDED	PRIMAGES
PRETYPE	PREVISORS	PREZZIES	PRIDEFUL	PRIMAL
PRETYPED	PREVUE	PRIAL	PRIDELESS	PRIMALITY
PRETYPES	PREVUED	PRIALS	PRIDES	PRIMALLY
PRETYPING	PREVUES	PRIAPEAN	PRIDIAN	PRIMARIES
PRETZEL	PREVUING	PRIAPI	PRIDING	PRIMARILY
PRETZELS	PREWAR	PRIAPIC	PRIED	PRIMARY
PREUNION	PREWARM	PRIAPISM	PRIEDIEU	PRIMAS
PREUNIONS	PREWARMED	PRIAPISMS	PRIEDIEUS	PRIMATAL
PREUNITE	PREWARMS	PRIAPUS	PRIEDIEUX	PRIMATALS

PRIMATE	PRIMSIER	PRIOR	PRIVADO	PROBATE
PRIMATES	PRIMSIEST	PRIORATE	PRIVADOES	PROBATED
PRIMATIAL	PRIMULA	PRIORATES	PRIVADOS	PROBATES
PRIMATIC	PRIMULAS	PRIORESS	PRIVATE	PROBATING
PRIMAVERA	PRIMULINE	PRIORIES	PRIVATEER	PROBATION
PRIME	PRIMUS	PRIORITY	PRIVATELY	PROBATIVE
PRIMED	PRIMUSES	PRIORLY	PRIVATER	PROBATORY
PRIMELY	PRIMY	PRIORS	PRIVATES	PROBE
PRIMENESS	PRINCE	PRIORSHIP	PRIVATEST	PROBEABLE
PRIMER	PRINCED	PRIORY	PRIVATION	PROBED
PRIMERO	PRINCEDOM	PRISAGE	PRIVATISE	PROBER
PRIMEROS	PRINCEKIN	PRISAGES	PRIVATISM	PROBERS
PRIMERS	PRINCELET	PRISE	PRIVATIST	PROBES
PRIMES	PRINCELY	PRISED	PRIVATIVE	PROBING
PRIMETIME	PRINCES	PRISER	PRIVATIZE	PROBINGLY
PRIMEUR	PRINCESS	PRISERE	PRIVET	PROBINGS
PRIMEURS	PRINCESSE	PRISERES	PRIVETS	PROBIOTIC
PRIMEVAL	PRINCING	PRISERS	PRIVIER	PROBIT
PRIMI	PRINCIPAL	PRISES	PRIVIES	PROBITIES
PRIMINE	PRINCIPE	PRISING	PRIVIEST	PROBITS
PRIMINES	PRINCIPI	PRISM	PRIVILEGE	PROBITY
PRIMING	PRINCIPIA	PRISMATIC	PRIVILY	PROBLEM
PRIMINGS	PRINCIPLE	PRISMOID	PRIVITIES	PROBLEMS
PRIMIPARA	PRINCOCK	PRISMOIDS	PRIVITY	PROBOSCIS
PRIMITIAE	PRINCOCKS	PRISMS	PRIVY	PROBS
PRIMITIAL	PRINCOX	PRISMY	PRIZABLE	PROCACITY
PRIMITIAS	PRINCOXES	PRISON	PRIZE	PROCAINE
PRIMITIVE	PRINK	PRISONED	PRIZED	PROCAINES
PRIMLY	PRINKED	PRISONER	PRIZEMAN	PROCAMBIA
PRIMMED	PRINKER	PRISONERS	PRIZEMEN	PROCARP
PRIMMER	PRINKERS	PRISONING	PRIZER	PROCARPS
PRIMMERS	PRINKING	PRISONOUS	PRIZERS	PROCARYON
PRIMMEST	PRINKS	PRISONS	PRIZES	PROCEDURE
PRIMMING	PRINT	PRISS	PRIZING	PROCEED
PRIMNESS	PRINTABLE	PRISSED	PRO	PROCEEDED
PRIMO	PRINTED	PRISSES	PROA	PROCEEDER
PRIMORDIA	PRINTER	PRISSIER	PROACTION	PROCEEDS
PRIMOS	PRINTERS	PRISSIES	PROACTIVE	PROCERITY
PRIMP	PRINTERY	PRISSIEST	PROAS	PROCESS
PRIMPED	PRINTHEAD	PRISSILY	PROB	PROCESSED
PRIMPING	PRINTING	PRISSING	PROBABLE	PROCESSER
PRIMPS	PRINTINGS	PRISSY	PROBABLES	PROCESSES
PRIMROSE	PRINTLESS	PRISTANE	PROBABLY	PROCESSOR
PRIMROSED	PRINTOUT	PRISTANES	PROBALL	PROCHAIN
PRIMROSES	PRINTOUTS	PRISTINE	PROBAND	PROCHEIN
PRIMROSY	PRINTS	PRITHEE	PROBANDS	PROCHOICE
PRIMS	PRION	PRIVACIES	PROBANG	PROCHURCH
PRIMSIE	PRIONS	PRIVACY	PROBANGS	PROCIDENT

P

PROCINCT	PRODROMES	PROFILIST	PROIGN	PROLEPSIS
PROCINCTS	PRODROMI	PROFIT	PROIGNED	PROLEPTIC
PROCLAIM	PRODROMIC	PROFITED	PROIGNING	PROLER
PROCLAIMS	PRODROMUS	PROFITEER	PROIGNS	PROLERS
PROCLISES	PRODRUG	PROFITER	PROIN	PROLES
PROCLISIS	PRODRUGS	PROFITERS	PROINE	PROLETARY
PROCLITIC	PRODS	PROFITING	PROINED	PROLICIDE
PROCLIVE	PRODUCE	PROFITS	PROINES	PROLIFIC
PROCONSUL	PRODUCED	PROFLUENT	PROINING	PROLINE
PROCREANT	PRODUCER	PROFORMA	PROINS	PROLINES
PROCREATE	PRODUCERS	PROFORMAS	PROJECT	PROLING
PROCTAL	PRODUCES	PROFOUND	PROJECTED	PROLIX
PROCTITIS	PRODUCING	PROFOUNDS	PROJECTOR	PROLIXITY
PROCTODEA	PRODUCT	PROFS	PROJECTS	PROLIXLY
PROCTOR	PRODUCTS	PROFUSE	PROJET	PROLL
PROCTORED	PROEM	PROFUSELY	PROJETS	PROLLED
PROCTORS	PROEMBRYO	PROFUSER	PROKARYON	PROLLER
PROCURACY	PROEMIAL	PROFUSERS	PROKARYOT	PROLLERS
PROCURAL	PROEMS	PROFUSION	PROKE	PROLLING
PROCURALS	PROENZYME	PROFUSIVE	PROKED	PROLLS
PROCURE	PROESTRUS	PROG	PROKER	PROLLY
PROCURED	PROETTE	PROGENIES	PROKERS	PROLOG
PROCURER	PROETTES	PROGENY	PROKES	PROLOGED
PROCURERS	PROF	PROGERIA	PROKING	PROLOGING
PROCURES	PROFACE	PROGERIAS	PROLABOR	PROLOGISE
PROCURESS	PROFAMILY	PROGESTIN	PROLABOUR	PROLOGIST
PROCUREUR	PROFANE	PROGGED	PROLACTIN	PROLOGIZE
PROCURING	PROFANED	PROGGER	PROLAMIN	PROLOGS
PROCYONID	PROFANELY	PROGGERS	PROLAMINE	PROLOGUE
PROD	PROFANER	PROGGING	PROLAMINS	PROLOGUED
PRODDED	PROFANERS	PROGGINS	PROLAN	PROLOGUES
PRODDER	PROFANES	PROGNOSE	PROLANS	PROLONG
PRODDERS	PROFANING	PROGNOSED	PROLAPSE	PROLONGE
PRODDING	PROFANITY	PROGNOSES	PROLAPSED	PROLONGED
PRODDINGS	PROFESS	PROGNOSIS	PROLAPSES	PROLONGER
PRODIGAL	PROFESSED	PROGRADE	PROLAPSUS	PROLONGES
PRODIGALS	PROFESSES	PROGRADED	PROLATE	PROLONGS
PRODIGIES	PROFESSOR	PROGRADES	PROLATED	PROLUSION
PRODIGY	PROFFER	PROGRAM	PROLATELY	PROLUSORY
PRODITOR	PROFFERED	PROGRAMED	PROLATES	PROM
PRODITORS	PROFFERER	PROGRAMER	PROLATING	PROMACHOS
PRODITORY	PROFFERS	PROGRAMME	PROLATION	PROMENADE
PRODNOSE	PROFILE	PROGRAMS	PROLATIVE	PROMETAL
PRODNOSED	PROFILED	PROGRESS	PROLE	PROMETALS
PRODNOSES	PROFILER	PROGS	PROLED	PROMETRIC
PRODROMA	PROFILERS	PROGUN	PROLEG	PROMINE
PRODROMAL	PROFILES	PROHIBIT	PROLEGS	PROMINENT
PRODROME	PROFILING	PROHIBITS	PROLEPSES	PROMINES

PROMISE	PRONATING	PROP	PROPHECY	PROPYL
PROMISED	PRONATION	PROPAGATE	PROPHESY	PROPYLA
PROMISEE	PRONATOR	PROPAGE	PROPHET	PROPYLAEA
PROMISEES	PRONATORS	PROPAGED	PROPHETIC	PROPYLENE
PROMISER	PRONE	PROPAGES	PROPHETS	PROPYLIC
PROMISERS	PRONELY	PROPAGING	PROPHYLL	PROPYLITE
PROMISES	PRONENESS	PROPAGULA	PROPHYLLS	PROPYLON
PROMISING	PRONEPHRA	PROPAGULE	PROPINE	PROPYLONS
PROMISOR	PRONER	PROPALE	PROPINED	PROPYLS
PROMISORS	PRONES	PROPALED	PROPINES	PROPYNE
PROMISSOR	PRONEST	PROPALES	PROPINING	PROPYNES
PROMMER	PRONEUR	PROPALING	PROPIONIC	PRORATE
PROMMERS	PRONEURS	PROPANE	PROPJET	PRORATED
PROMO	PRONG	PROPANES	PROPJETS	PRORATES
PROMODERN	PRONGBUCK	PROPANOIC	PROPMAN	PRORATING
PROMOED	PRONGED	PROPANOL	PROPMEN	PRORATION
PROMOING	PRONGHORN	PROPANOLS	PROPODEON	PRORE
PROMOS	PRONGING	PROPANONE	PROPODEUM	PRORECTOR
PROMOTE	PRONGS	PROPEL	PROPOLIS	PROREFORM
PROMOTED	PRONK	PROPELLED	PROPONE	PRORES
PROMOTER	PRONKED	PROPELLER	PROPONED	PROROGATE
PROMOTERS	PRONKING	PROPELLOR	PROPONENT	PROROGUE
PROMOTES	PRONKINGS	PROPELS	PROPONES	PROROGUED
PROMOTING	PRONKS	PROPENAL	PROPONING	PROROGUES
PROMOTION	PRONOTA	PROPENALS	PROPOSAL	PROS
PROMOTIVE	PRONOTAL	PROPEND	PROPOSALS	PROSAIC
PROMOTOR	PRONOTUM	PROPENDED	PROPOSE	PROSAICAL
PROMOTORS	PRONOUN	PROPENDS	PROPOSED	PROSAISM
PROMPT	PRONOUNCE	PROPENE	PROPOSER	PROSAISMS
PROMPTED	PRONOUNS	PROPENES	PROPOSERS	PROSAIST
PROMPTER	PRONTO	PROPENOIC	PROPOSES	PROSAISTS
PROMPTERS	PRONUCLEI	PROPENOL	PROPOSING	PROSATEUR
PROMPTEST	PRONUNCIO	PROPENOLS	PROPOSITA	PROSCENIA
PROMPTING	PROO	PROPENSE	PROPOSITI	PROSCRIBE
PROMPTLY	PROOEMION	PROPENYL	PROPOUND	PROSCRIPT
PROMPTS	PROOEMIUM	PROPENYLS	PROPOUNDS	PROSE
PROMPTURE	PROOF	PROPER	PROPPANT	PROSECCO
PROMS	PROOFED	PROPERDIN	PROPPANTS	PROSECCOS
PROMULGE	PROOFER	PROPERER	PROPPED	PROSECT
PROMULGED	PROOFERS	PROPEREST	PROPPING	PROSECTED
PROMULGES	PROOFING	PROPERLY	PROPRETOR	PROSECTOR
PROMUSCES	PROOFINGS	PROPERS	PROPRIA	PROSECTS
PROMUSCIS	PROOFLESS	PROPERTY	PROPRIETY	PROSECUTE
PRONAOI	PROOFREAD	PROPHAGE	PROPRIUM	PROSED
PRONAOS	PROOFROOM	PROPHAGES	PROPS	PROSELIKE
PRONATE	PROOFS	PROPHASE	PROPTOSES	PROSELYTE
PRONATED	PROOTIC	PROPHASES	PROPTOSIS	PROSEMAN
PRONATES	PROOTICS	PROPHASIC	PROPULSOR	PROSEMEN

PROSER	PROSTRATE	PROTESTED	PROTRUDE	PROVES
PROSERS	PROSTYLE	PROTESTER	PROTRUDED	PROVIANT
PROSES	PROSTYLES	PROTESTOR	PROTRUDES	PROVIANTS
PROSEUCHA	PROSUMER	PROTESTS	PROTURAN	PROVIDE
PROSEUCHE	PROSUMERS	PROTEUS	PROTURANS	PROVIDED
PROSIER	PROSY	PROTEUSES	PROTYL	PROVIDENT
PROSIEST	PROTAMIN	PROTHALLI	PROTYLE	PROVIDER
PROSIFIED	PROTAMINE	PROTHESES	PROTYLES	PROVIDERS
PROSIFIES	PROTAMINS	PROTHESIS	PROTYLS	PROVIDES
PROSIFY	PROTANDRY	PROTHETIC	PROUD	PROVIDING
PROSILY	PROTANOPE	PROTHORAX	PROUDER	PROVIDOR
PROSIMIAN	PROTASES	PROTHYL	PROUDEST	PROVIDORS
PROSINESS	PROTASIS	PROTHYLS	PROUDFUL	PROVINCE
PROSING	PROTATIC	PROTIST	PROUDISH	PROVINCES
PROSINGS	PROTEA	PROTISTAN	PROUDLY	PROVINE
PROSIT	PROTEAN	PROTISTIC	PROUDNESS	PROVINED
PROSO	PROTEANS	PROTISTS	PROUL	PROVINES
PROSOCIAL	PROTEAS	PROTIUM	PROULED	PROVING
PROSODIAL	PROTEASE	PROTIUMS	PROULER	PROVINGS
PROSODIAN	PROTEASES	PROTO	PROULERS	PROVINING
PROSODIC	PROTECT	PROTOAVIS	PROULING	PROVIRAL
PROSODIES	PROTECTED	PROTOCOL	PROULS	PROVIRUS
PROSODIST	PROTECTER	PROTOCOLS	PROUNION	PROVISION
PROSODY	PROTECTOR	PROTODERM	PROUSTITE	PROVISO
PROSOMA	PROTECTS	PROTOGINE	PROVABLE	PROVISOES
PROSOMAL	PROTEGE	PROTOGYNY	PROVABLY	PROVISOR
PROSOMAS	PROTEGEE	PROTON	PROVAND	PROVISORS
PROSOMATA	PROTEGEES	PROTONATE	PROVANDS	PROVISORY
PROSOPON	PROTEGES	PROTONEMA	PROVANT	PROVISOS
PROSOPONS	PROTEI	PROTONIC	PROVANTED	PROVOCANT
PROSOS	PROTEID	PROTONS	PROVANTS	PROVOKE
PROSPECT	PROTEIDE	PROTOPOD	PROVE	PROVOKED
PROSPECTS	PROTEIDES	PROTOPODS	PROVEABLE	PROVOKER
PROSPER	PROTEIDS	PROTORE	PROVEABLY	PROVOKERS
PROSPERED	PROTEIN	PROTORES	PROVED	PROVOKES
PROSPERS	PROTEINIC	PROTOSTAR	PROVEDOR	PROVOKING
PROSS	PROTEINS	PROTOTYPE	PROVEDORE	PROVOLONE
PROSSES	PROTEND	PROTOXID	PROVEDORS	PROVOST
PROSSIE	PROTENDED	PROTOXIDE	PROVEN	PROVOSTRY
PROSSIES	PROTENDS	PROTOXIDS	PROVEND	PROVOSTS
PROST	PROTENSE	PROTOZOA	PROVENDER	PROW
PROSTATE	PROTENSES	PROTOZOAL	PROVENDS	PROWAR
PROSTATES	PROTEOME	PROTOZOAN	PROVENLY	PROWER
PROSTATIC	PROTEOMES	PROTOZOIC	PROVER	PROWESS
PROSTERNA	PROTEOMIC	PROTOZOON	PROVERB	PROWESSED
PROSTIE	PROTEOSE	PROTRACT	PROVERBED	PROWESSES
PROSTIES	PROTEOSES	PROTRACTS	PROVERBS	PROWEST
PROSTOMIA	PROTEST	PROTRADE	PROVERS	PROWL

PROWLED	PRUNELLOS	PSALMED	PSILOTIC	PSYLLID
PROWLER	PRUNER	PSALMIC	PSION	PSYLLIDS
PROWLERS	PRUNERS	PSALMING	PSIONIC	PSYLLIUM
PROWLING	PRUNES	PSALMIST	PSIONICS	PSYLLIUMS
PROWLINGS	PRUNEY	PSALMISTS	PSIONS	PSYOP
PROWLS	PRUNIER	PSALMODIC	PSIS	PSYOPS
PROWS	PRUNIEST	PSALMODY	PSOAE	PSYWAR
PROXEMIC	PRUNING	PSALMS	PSOAI	PSYWARS
PROXEMICS	PRUNINGS	PSALTER	PSOAS	PTARMIC
PROXIES	PRUNT	PSALTERIA	PSOASES	PTARMICS
PROXIMAL	PRUNTED	PSALTERS	PSOATIC	PTARMIGAN
PROXIMATE	PRUNTS	PSALTERY	PSOCID	PTERIA
PROXIMITY	PRUNUS	PSALTRESS	PSOCIDS	PTERIDINE
PROXIMO	PRUNUSES	PSALTRIES	PSORA	PTERIN
PROXY	PRURIENCE	PSALTRY	PSORALEA	PTERINS
PROYN	PRURIENCY	PSAMMITE	PSORALEAS	PTERION
PROYNE	PRURIENT	PSAMMITES	PSORALEN	PTEROIC
PROYNED	PRURIGO	PSAMMITIC	PSORALENS	PTEROPOD
PROYNES	PRURIGOS	PSAMMON	PSORAS	PTEROPODS
PROYNING	PRURITIC	PSAMMONS	PSORIASES	PTEROSAUR
PROYNS	PRURITUS	PSCHENT	PSORIASIS	PTERYGIA
PROZYMITE	PRUSIK	PSCHENTS	PSORIATIC	PTERYGIAL
PROZZIE	PRUSIKED	PSELLISM	PSORIC	PTERYGIUM
PROZZIES	PRUSIKING	PSELLISMS	PSST	PTERYGOID
PRUDE	PRUSIKS	PSEPHISM	PST	PTERYLA
PRUDENCE	PRUSSIAN	PSEPHISMS	PSYCH	PTERYLAE
PRUDENCES	PRUSSIATE	PSEPHITE	PSYCHE	PTILOSES
PRUDENT	PRUSSIC	PSEPHITES	PSYCHED	PTILOSIS
PRUDENTLY	PRUTA	PSEPHITIC	PSYCHES	PTISAN
PRUDERIES	PRUTAH	PSEUD	PSYCHIC	PTISANS
PRUDERY	PRUTOT	PSEUDAXES	PSYCHICAL	PTOMAIN
PRUDES	PRUTOTH	PSEUDAXIS	PSYCHICS	PTOMAINE
PRUDISH	PRY	PSEUDERY	PSYCHING	PTOMAINES
PRUDISHLY	PRYER	PSEUDISH	PSYCHISM	PTOMAINIC
PRUH	PRYERS	PSEUDO	PSYCHISMS	PTOMAINS
PRUINA	PRYING	PSEUDONYM	PSYCHIST	PTOOEY
PRUINAS	PRYINGLY	PSEUDOPOD	PSYCHISTS	PTOSES
PRUINE	PRYINGS	PSEUDOS	PSYCHO	PTOSIS
PRUINES	PRYS	PSEUDS	PSYCHOGAS	PTOTIC
PRUINOSE	PRYSE	PSHAW	PSYCHOID	PTUI
PRUNABLE	PRYSED	PSHAWED	PSYCHOIDS	PTYALIN
PRUNE	PRYSES	PSHAWING	PSYCHOS	PTYALINS
PRUNED	PRYSING	PSHAWS	PSYCHOSES	PTYALISE
PRUNELLA	PRYTANEA	PSI	PSYCHOSIS	PTYALISED
PRUNELLAS	PRYTANEUM	PSILOCIN	PSYCHOTIC	PTYALISES
PRUNELLE	PRYTHEE	PSILOCINS	PSYCHS	PTYALISM
PRUNELLES	PSALM	PSILOSES	PSYLLA	PTYALISMS
PRUNELLO	PSALMBOOK	PSILOSIS	PSYLLAS	PTYALIZE

PTYALIZED	PUCKA	PUDDOCK	PUFFBACK	PUGH
PTYALIZES	PUCKED	PUDDOCKS	PUFFBACKS	PUGIL
PTYXES	PUCKER	PUDDY	PUFFBALL	PUGILISM
PTYXIS	PUCKERED	PUDENCIES	PUFFBALLS	PUGILISMS
PTYXISES	PUCKERER	PUDENCY	PUFFBIRD	PUGILIST
PUB	PUCKERERS	PUDENDA	PUFFBIRDS	PUGILISTS
PUBBED	PUCKERIER	PUDENDAL	PUFFED	PUGILS
PUBBING	PUCKERIES	PUDENDOUS	PUFFER	PUGMARK
PUBBINGS	PUCKERING	PUDENDUM	PUFFERIES	PUGMARKS
PUBCO	PUCKEROOD	PUDENT	PUFFERS	PUGNACITY
PUBCOS	PUCKERS	PUDEUR	PUFFERY	PUGREE
PUBE	PUCKERY	PUDEURS	PUFFIER	PUGREES
PUBERAL	PUCKFIST	PUDGE	PUFFIEST	PUGS
PUBERTAL	PUCKFISTS	PUDGES	PUFFILY	PUH
PUBERTIES	PUCKING	PUDGIER	PUFFIN	PUHA
PUBERTY	PUCKISH	PUDGIEST	PUFFINESS	PUHAS
PUBES	PUCKISHLY	PUDGILY	PUFFING	PUIR
PUBESCENT	PUCKLE	PUDGINESS	PUFFINGLY	PUIRER
PUBIC	PUCKLES	PUDGY	PUFFINGS	PUIREST
PUBIS	PUCKOUT	PUDIBUND	PUFFINS	PUIRTITH
PUBISES	PUCKOUTS	PUDIC	PUFFS	PUIRTITHS
PUBLIC	PUCKS	PUDICITY	PUFFY	PUISNE
PUBLICAN	PUCKSTER	PUDOR	PUFTALOON	PUISNES
PUBLICANS	PUCKSTERS	PUDORS	PUG	PUISNY
PUBLICISE	PUD	PUDS	PUGAREE	PUISSANCE
PUBLICIST	PUDDEN	PUDSEY	PUGAREES	PUISSANT
PUBLICITY	PUDDENING	PUDSIER	PUGGAREE	PUISSAUNT
PUBLICIZE	PUDDENS	PUDSIES	PUGGAREES	PUJA
PUBLICLY	PUDDER	PUDSIEST	PUGGED	PUJAH
PUBLICS	PUDDERED	PUDSY	PUGGERIES	PUJAHS
PUBLISH	PUDDERING	PUDU	PUGGERY	PUJARI
PUBLISHED	PUDDERS	PUDUS	PUGGIE	PUJARIS
PUBLISHER	PUDDIER	PUEBLO	PUGGIER	PUJAS
PUBLISHES	PUDDIES	PUEBLOS	PUGGIES	PUKA
PUBS	PUDDIEST	PUER	PUGGIEST	PUKAS
PUCAN	PUDDING	PUERED	PUGGINESS	PUKATEA
PUCANS	PUDDINGS	PUERILE	PUGGING	PUKATEAS
PUCCOON	PUDDINGY	PUERILELY	PUGGINGS	PUKE
PUCCOONS	PUDDLE	PUERILISM	PUGGISH	PUKED
PUCE	PUDDLED	PUERILITY	PUGGLE	PUKEKO
PUCELAGE	PUDDLER	PUERING	PUGGLED	PUKEKOS
PUCELAGES	PUDDLERS	PUERPERA	PUGGLES	PUKER
PUCELLE	PUDDLES	PUERPERAE	PUGGLING	PUKERS
PUCELLES	PUDDLIER	PUERPERAL	PUGGREE	PUKES
PUCER	PUDDLIEST	PUERPERIA	PUGGREES	PUKEY
PUCES	PUDDLING	PUERS	PUGGRIES	PUKIER
PUCEST	PUDDLINGS	PUFF	PUGGRY	PUKIEST
PUCK	PUDDLY	PUFFA	PUGGY	PUKING

P

PUNCED

PUKKA	PULLING	PULPLESS	PULTRUDE	PUMICERS
PUKKAH	PULLMAN	PULPMILL	PULTRUDED	PUMICES
PUKU	PULLMANS	PULPMILLS	PULTRUDES	PUMICING
PUKUS	PULLORUM	PULPOUS	PULTUN	PUMICITE
PUKY	PULLOUT	PULPS	PULTUNS	PUMICITES
PUL	PULLOUTS	PULPSTONE	PULTURE	PUMIE
PULA	PULLOVER	PULPWOOD	PULTURES	PUMIES
PULAO	PULLOVERS	PULPWOODS	PULU	PUMMEL
PULAOS	PULLS	PULPY	PULUS	PUMMELED
PULAS	PULLULATE	PULQUE	PULVER	PUMMELING
PULDRON	PULLUP	PULQUES	PULVERED	PUMMELLED
PULDRONS	PULLUPS	PULS	PULVERINE	PUMMELO
PULE	PULLUS	PULSANT	PULVERING	PUMMELOS
PULED	PULLY	PULSAR	PULVERISE	PUMMELS
PULER	PULMO	PULSARS	PULVERIZE	PUMP
PULERS	PULMONARY	PULSATE	PULVEROUS	PUMPABLE
PULES	PULMONATE	PULSATED	PULVERS	PUMPED
PULI	PULMONES	PULSATES	PULVIL	PUMPER
PULICENE	PULMONIC	PULSATILE	PULVILIO	PUMPERS
PULICIDE	PULMONICS	PULSATING	PULVILIOS	PUMPHOOD
PULICIDES	PULMOTOR	PULSATION	PULVILLAR	PUMPHOODS
PULIER	PULMOTORS	PULSATIVE	PULVILLE	PUMPHOUSE
PULIEST	PULP	PULSATOR	PULVILLED	PUMPING
PULIK	PULPAL	PULSATORS	PULVILLES	PUMPINGS
PULING	PULPALLY	PULSATORY	PULVILLI	PUMPION
PULINGLY	PULPBOARD	PULSE	PULVILLIO	PUMPIONS
PULINGS	PULPED	PULSEBEAT	PULVILLUS	PUMPJACK
PULIS	PULPER	PULSED	PULVILS	PUMPJACKS
PULK	PULPERS	PULSEJET	PULVINAR	PUMPKIN
PULKA	PULPIER	PULSEJETS	PULVINARS	PUMPKING
PULKAS	PULPIEST	PULSELESS	PULVINATE	PUMPKINGS
PULKHA	PULPIFIED	PULSER	PULVINI	PUMPKINS
PULKHAS	PULPIFIES	PULSERS	PULVINULE	PUMPLESS
PULKS	PULPIFY	PULSES	PULVINUS	PUMPLIKE
PULL	PULPILY	PULSIDGE	PULWAR	PUMPS
PULLBACK	PULPINESS	PULSIDGES	PULWARS	PUMY
PULLBACKS	PULPING	PULSIFIC	PULY	PUN
PULLED	PULPINGS	PULSING	PUMA	PUNA
PULLER	PULPIT	PULSION	PUMAS	PUNAANI
PULLERS	PULPITAL	PULSIONS	PUMELO	PUNAANY
PULLET	PULPITED	PULSOJET	PUMELOS	PUNALUA
PULLETS	PULPITEER	PULSOJETS	PUMICATE	PUNALUAN
PULLEY	PULPITER	PULTAN	PUMICATED	PUNALUAS
PULLEYED	PULPITERS	PULTANS	PUMICATES	PUNANI
PULLEYING	PULPITRY	PULTON	PUMICE	PUNANY
PULLEYS	PULPITS	PULTONS	PUMICED	PUNAS
PULLI	PULPITUM	PULTOON	PUMICEOUS	PUNCE
PULLIES	PULPITUMS	PULTOONS	PUMICER	PUNCED

P

PUNCES	PUNGENCES	PUNKS	PUPILAGE	PURDONIUM
PUNCH	PUNGENCY	PUNKY	PUPILAGES	PURE
PUNCHBAG	PUNGENT	PUNNED	PUPILAR	PUREBLOOD
PUNCHBAGS	PUNGENTLY	PUNNER	PUPILARY	PUREBRED
PUNCHBALL	PUNGLE	PUNNERS	PUPILLAGE	PUREBREDS
PUNCHBOWL	PUNGLED	PUNNET	PUPILLAR	PURED
PUNCHED	PUNGLES	PUNNETS	PUPILLARY	PUREE
PUNCHEON	PUNGLING	PUNNIER	PUPILLATE	PUREED
PUNCHEONS	PUNGS	PUNNIEST	PUPILS	PUREEING
PUNCHER	PUNIER	PUNNING	PUPILSHIP	PUREES
PUNCHERS	PUNIEST	PUNNINGLY	PUPPED	PURELY
PUNCHES	PUNILY	PUNNINGS	PUPPET	PURENESS
PUNCHIER	PUNINESS	PUNNY	PUPPETEER	PURER
PUNCHIEST	PUNISH	PUNS	PUPPETRY	PURES
PUNCHILY	PUNISHED	PUNSTER	PUPPETS	PUREST
PUNCHING	PUNISHER	PUNSTERS	PUPPIED	PURFLE
PUNCHLESS	PUNISHERS	PUNT	PUPPIES	PURFLED
PUNCHLINE	PUNISHES	PUNTED	PUPPING	PURFLER
PUNCHOUT	PUNISHING	PUNTEE	PUPPODUM	PURFLERS
PUNCHOUTS	PUNITION	PUNTEES	PUPPODUMS	PURFLES
PUNCHY	PUNITIONS	PUNTER	PUPPY	PURFLING
PUNCING	PUNITIVE	PUNTERS	PUPPYDOM	PURFLINGS
PUNCTA	PUNITORY	PUNTIES	PUPPYDOMS	PURFLY
PUNCTATE	PUNJI	PUNTING	PUPPYHOOD	PURGATION
PUNCTATED	PUNJIED	PUNTO	PUPPYING	PURGATIVE
PUNCTATOR	PUNJIES	PUNTOS	PUPPYISH	PURGATORY
PUNCTILIO	PUNJIING	PUNTS	PUPPYISM	PURGE
PUNCTO	PUNJIS	PUNTSMAN	PUPPYISMS	PURGEABLE
PUNCTOS	PUNK	PUNTSMEN	PUPPYLIKE	PURGED
PUNCTUAL	PUNKA	PUNTY	PUPS	PURGER
PUNCTUATE	PUNKAH	PUNY	PUPU	PURGERS
PUNCTULE	PUNKAHS	PUP	PUPUNHA	PURGES
PUNCTULES	PUNKAS	PUPA	PUPUNHAS	PURGING
PUNCTUM	PUNKER	PUPAE	PUPUS	PURGINGS
PUNCTUMS	PUNKERS	PUPAL	PUR	PURI
PUNCTURE	PUNKEST	PUPARIA	PURANA	PURIFIED
PUNCTURED	PUNKETTE	PUPARIAL	PURANAS	PURIFIER
PUNCTURER	PUNKETTES	PUPARIUM	PURANIC	PURIFIERS
PUNCTURES	PUNKEY	PUPAS	PURBLIND	PURIFIES
PUNDIT	PUNKEYS	PUPATE	PURCHASE	PURIFY
PUNDITIC	PUNKIE	PUPATED	PURCHASED	PURIFYING
PUNDITRY	PUNKIER	PUPATES	PURCHASER	PURIN
PUNDITS	PUNKIES	PUPATING	PURCHASES	PURINE
PUNDONOR	PUNKIEST	PUPATION	PURDA	PURINES
PUNG	PUNKIN	PUPATIONS	PURDAH	PURING
PUNGA	PUNKINESS	PUPFISH	PURDAHED	PURINS
PUNGAS	PUNKINS	PUPFISHES	PURDAHS	PURIRI
PUNGENCE	PUNKISH	PUPIL	PURDAS	PURIRIS

PURIS	PURPOSE	PURSUE	PUSHILY	PUT
PURISM	PURPOSED	PURSUED	PUSHINESS	PUTAMEN
PURISMS	PURPOSELY	PURSUER	PUSHING	PUTAMENS
PURIST	PURPOSES	PURSUERS	PUSHINGLY	PUTAMINA
PURISTIC	PURPOSING	PURSUES	PUSHOVER	PUTATIVE
PURISTS	PURPOSIVE	PURSUING	PUSHOVERS	PUTCHEON
PURITAN	PURPURA	PURSUINGS	PUSHPIN	PUTCHEONS
PURITANIC	PURPURAS	PURSUIT	PUSHPINS	PUTCHER
PURITANS	PURPURE	PURSUITS	PUSHPIT	PUTCHERS
PURITIES	PURPUREAL	PURSY	PUSHPITS	PUTCHOCK
PURITY	PURPURES	PURTIER	PUSHROD	PUTCHOCKS
PURL	PURPURIC	PURTIEST	PUSHRODS	PUTCHUK
PURLED	PURPURIN	PURTRAID	PUSHUP	PUTCHUKS
PURLER	PURPURINS	PURTRAYD	PUSHUPS	PUTDOWN
PURLERS	PURPY	PURTY	PUSHY	PUTDOWNS
PURLICUE	PURR	PURULENCE	PUSLE	PUTEAL
PURLICUED	PURRED	PURULENCY	PUSLED	PUTEALS
PURLICUES	PURRING	PURULENT	PUSLES	PUTELI
PURLIEU	PURRINGLY	PURVEY	PUSLEY	PUTELIS
PURLIEUS	PURRINGS	PURVEYED	PUSLEYS	PUTID
PURLIEUX	PURRS	PURVEYING	PUSLIKE	PUTLOCK
PURLIN	PURS	PURVEYOR	PUSLING	PUTLOCKS
PURLINE	PURSE	PURVEYORS	PUSS	PUTLOG
PURLINES	PURSED	PURVEYS	PUSSEL	PUTLOGS
PURLING	PURSEFUL	PURVIEW	PUSSELS	PUTOFF
PURLINGS	PURSEFULS	PURVIEWS	PUSSER	PUTOFFS
PURLINS	PURSELIKE	PUS	PUSSERS	PUTOIS
PURLOIN	PURSER	PUSES	PUSSES	PUTON
PURLOINED	PURSERS	PUSH	PUSSIER	PUTONGHUA
PURLOINER	PURSES	PUSHBACK	PUSSIES	PUTONS
PURLOINS	PURSEW	PUSHBACKS	PUSSIEST	PUTOUT
PURLS	PURSEWED	PUSHBALL	PUSSLEY	PUTOUTS
PUROMYCIN	PURSEWING	PUSHBALLS	PUSSLEYS	PUTREFIED
PURPIE	PURSEWS	PUSHBIKE	PUSSLIES	PUTREFIER
PURPIES	PURSIER	PUSHBIKES	PUSSLIKE	PUTREFIES
PURPLE	PURSIEST	PUSHCART	PUSSLY	PUTREFY
PURPLED	PURSILY	PUSHCARTS	PUSSY	PUTRID
PURPLER	PURSINESS	PUSHCHAIR	PUSSYCAT	PUTRIDER
PURPLES	PURSING	PUSHDOWN	PUSSYCATS	PUTRIDEST
PURPLEST	PURSLAIN	PUSHDOWNS	PUSSYFOOT	PUTRIDITY
PURPLIER	PURSLAINS	PUSHED	PUSSYTOES	PUTRIDLY
PURPLIEST	PURSLANE	PUSHER	PUSTULANT	PUTS
PURPLING	PURSLANES	PUSHERS	PUSTULAR	PUTSCH
PURPLISH	PURSUABLE	PUSHES	PUSTULATE	PUTSCHES
PURPLY	PURSUAL	PUSHFUL	PUSTULE	PUTSCHIST
PURPORT	PURSUALS	PUSHFULLY	PUSTULED	PUTT
PURPORTED	PURSUANCE	PUSHIER	PUSTULES	PUTTED
PURPORTS	PURSUANT	PUSHIEST	PUSTULOUS	PUTTEE

PUTTEES	PWNING	PYGMOIDS	PYRAL	PYRITIC
PUTTEN	PWNS	PYGMY	PYRALID	PYRITICAL
PUTTER	PYA	PYGMYISH	PYRALIDID	PYRITISE
PUTTERED	PYAEMIA	PYGMYISM	PYRALIDS	PYRITISED
PUTTERER	PYAEMIAS	PYGMYISMS	PYRALIS	PYRITISES
PUTTERERS	PYAEMIC	PYGOSTYLE	PYRALISES	PYRITIZE
PUTTERING	PYAS	PYIC	PYRAMID	PYRITIZED
PUTTERS	PYAT	PYIN	PYRAMIDAL	PYRITIZES
PUTTI	PYATS	PYINKADO	PYRAMIDED	PYRITOUS
PUTTIE	PYCNIC	PYINKADOS	PYRAMIDES	PYRO
PUTTIED	PYCNIDIA	PYINS	PYRAMIDIA	PYROBORIC
PUTTIER	PYCNIDIAL	PYJAMA	PYRAMIDIC	PYROCERAM
PUTTIERS	PYCNIDIUM	PYJAMAED	PYRAMIDON	PYROCLAST
PUTTIES	PYCNITE	PYJAMAS	PYRAMIDS	PYROGEN
PUTTING	PYCNITES	PYKNIC	PYRAMIS	PYROGENIC
PUTTINGS	PYCNON	PYKNICS	PYRAMISES	PYROGENS
PUTTO	PYCNONS	PYKNOSES	PYRAN	PYROGIES
PUTTOCK	PYCNOSES	PYKNOSIS	PYRANOID	PYROGY
PUTTOCKS	PYCNOSIS	PYKNOSOME	PYRANOSE	PYROHIES
PUTTS	PYCNOSOME	PYKNOTIC	PYRANOSES	PYROHY
PUTTY	PYCNOTIC	PYLON	PYRANS	PYROLA
PUTTYING	PYE	PYLONS	PYRAZOLE	PYROLAS
PUTTYLESS	PYEBALD	PYLORI	PYRAZOLES	PYROLATER
PUTTYLIKE	PYEBALDS	PYLORIC	PYRE	PYROLATRY
PUTTYROOT	PYEING	PYLORUS	PYRENE	PYROLISE
PUTURE	PYELITIC	PYLORUSES	PYRENEITE	PYROLISED
PUTURES	PYELITIS	PYNE	PYRENES	PYROLISES
PUTZ	PYELOGRAM	PYNED	PYRENOID	PYROLIZE
PUTZED	PYEMIA	PYNES	PYRENOIDS	PYROLIZED
PUTZES	PYEMIAS	PYNING	PYRES	PYROLIZES
PUTZING	PYEMIC	PYODERMA	PYRETHRIN	PYROLOGY
PUY	PYENGADU	PYODERMAS	PYRETHRUM	PYROLYSE
PUYS	PYENGADUS	PYODERMIC	PYRETIC	PYROLYSED
PUZEL	PYES	PYOGENIC	PYREX	PYROLYSER
PUZELS	PYET	PYOID	PYREXES	PYROLYSES
PUZZEL	PYETS	PYONER	PYREXIA	PYROLYSIS
PUZZELS	PYGAL	PYONERS	PYREXIAL	PYROLYTIC
PUZZLE	PYGALS	PYONINGS	PYREXIAS	PYROLYZE
PUZZLED	PYGARG	PYORRHEA	PYREXIC	PYROLYZED
PUZZLEDLY	PYGARGS	PYORRHEAL	PYRIC	PYROLYZER
PUZZLEDOM	PYGARGUS	PYORRHEAS	PYRIDIC	PYROLYZES
PUZZLER	PYGIDIA	PYORRHEIC	PYRIDINE	PYROMANCY
PUZZLERS	PYGIDIAL	PYORRHOEA	PYRIDINES	PYROMANIA
PUZZLES	PYGIDIUM	PYOSES	PYRIDOXAL	PYROMETER
PUZZLING	PYGMAEAN	PYOSIS	PYRIDOXIN	PYROMETRY
PUZZOLANA	PYGMEAN	PYOT	PYRIFORM	PYRONE
PWN	PYGMIES	PYOTS	PYRITE	PYRONES
PWNED	PYGMOID	PYRACANTH	PYRITES	PYRONIN

PYRONINE
PYRONINES
PYRONINS
PYROPE
PYROPES
PYROPHONE
PYROPUS
PYROPUSES
PYROS
PYROSCOPE
PYROSES
PYROSIS

PYROSISES
PYROSOME
PYROSOMES
PYROSTAT
PYROSTATS
PYROXENE
PYROXENES
PYROXENIC
PYROXYLE
PYROXYLES
PYROXYLIC
PYROXYLIN

PYRRHIC
PYRRHICS
PYRRHOUS
PYRROL
PYRROLE
PYRROLES
PYRROLIC
PYRROLS
PYRUVATE
PYRUVATES
PYRUVIC
PYSANKA

PYSANKY
PYTHIUM
PYTHIUMS
PYTHON
PYTHONESS
PYTHONIC
PYTHONS
PYURIA
PYURIAS
PYX
PYXED
PYXES

PYXIDES
PYXIDIA
PYXIDIUM
PYXIE
PYXIES
PYXING
PYXIS
PZAZZ
PZAZZES

P

Q

QABALA	QINS	QUADRATE	QUAGGIER	QUAKY
QABALAH	QINTAR	QUADRATED	QUAGGIEST	QUALE
QABALAHS	QINTARKA	QUADRATES	QUAGGY	QUALIA
QABALAS	QINTARS	QUADRATI	QUAGMIRE	QUALIFIED
QABALISM	QIS	QUADRATIC	QUAGMIRED	QUALIFIER
QABALISMS	QIVIUT	QUADRATS	QUAGMIRES	QUALIFIES
QABALIST	QIVIUTS	QUADRATUS	QUAGMIRY	QUALIFY
QABALISTS	QOPH	QUADRELLA	QUAGS	QUALITIED
QADI	QOPHS	QUADRIC	QUAHAUG	QUALITIES
QADIS	QORMA	QUADRICEP	QUAHAUGS	QUALITY
QAID	QORMAS	QUADRICS	QUAHOG	QUALM
QAIDS	QUA	QUADRIFID	QUAHOGS	QUALMIER
QAIMAQAM	QUAALUDE	QUADRIGA	QUAI	QUALMIEST
QAIMAQAMS	QUAALUDES	QUADRIGAE	QUAICH	QUALMING
QAJAQ	QUACK	QUADRIGAS	QUAICHES	QUALMINGS
QAJAQS	QUACKED	QUADRILLE	QUAICHS	QUALMISH
QALAMDAN	QUACKER	QUADRIVIA	QUAIGH	QUALMLESS
QALAMDANS	QUACKERS	QUADROON	QUAIGHS	QUALMS
QAMUTIK	QUACKERY	QUADROONS	QUAIL	QUALMY
QAMUTIKS	QUACKIER	QUADRUMAN	QUAILED	QUAMASH
QANAT	QUACKIEST	QUADRUPED	QUAILING	QUAMASHES
QANATS	QUACKING	QUADRUPLE	QUAILINGS	QUANDANG
QAPIK	QUACKISH	QUADRUPLY	QUAILS	QUANDANGS
QAPIKS	QUACKISM	QUADS	QUAINT	QUANDARY
QASIDA	QUACKISMS	QUAERE	QUAINTER	QUANDONG
QASIDAS	QUACKLE	QUAERED	QUAINTEST	QUANDONGS
QAT	QUACKLED	QUAEREING	QUAINTLY	QUANGO
QATS	QUACKLES	QUAERES	QUAIR	QUANGOS
QAWWAL	QUACKLING	QUAERITUR	QUAIRS	QUANNET
QAWWALI	QUACKS	QUAESITUM	QUAIS	QUANNETS
QAWWALIS	QUACKY	QUAESTOR	QUAKE	QUANT
QAWWALS	QUAD	QUAESTORS	QUAKED	QUANTA
QI	QUADDED	QUAFF	QUAKER	QUANTAL
QIBLA	QUADDING	QUAFFABLE	QUAKERS	QUANTALLY
QIBLAS	QUADDINGS	QUAFFED	QUAKES	QUANTED
QIGONG	QUADPLAY	QUAFFER	QUAKIER	QUANTIC
QIGONGS	QUADPLAYS	QUAFFERS	QUAKIEST	QUANTICAL
QIN	QUADPLEX	QUAFFING	QUAKILY	QUANTICS
QINDAR	QUADRANS	QUAFFS	QUAKINESS	QUANTIFY
QINDARKA	QUADRANT	QUAG	QUAKING	QUANTILE
QINDARS	QUADRANTS	QUAGGA	QUAKINGLY	QUANTILES
QINGHAOSU	QUADRAT	QUAGGAS	QUAKINGS	QUANTING

QUANTISE	QUARTES	QUATE	QUEBECS	QUELCHED
QUANTISED	QUARTET	QUATES	QUEBRACHO	QUELCHES
QUANTISER	QUARTETS	QUATORZE	QUEECHIER	QUELCHING
QUANTISES	QUARTETT	QUATORZES	QUEECHY	QUELEA
QUANTITY	QUARTETTE	QUATRAIN	QUEEN	QUELEAS
QUANTIZE	QUARTETTI	QUATRAINS	QUEENCAKE	QUELL
QUANTIZED	QUARTETTO	QUATRE	QUEENCUP	QUELLABLE
QUANTIZER	QUARTETTS	QUATRES	QUEENCUPS	QUELLED
QUANTIZES	QUARTIC	QUATS	QUEENDOM	QUELLER
QUANTONG	QUARTICS	QUATTED	QUEENDOMS	QUELLERS
QUANTONGS	QUARTIER	QUATTING	QUEENED	QUELLING
QUANTS	QUARTIERS	QUAVER	QUEENFISH	QUELLS
QUANTUM	QUARTILE	QUAVERED	QUEENHOOD	QUEME
QUANTUMS	QUARTILES	QUAVERER	QUEENIE	QUEMED
QUARE	QUARTO	QUAVERERS	QUEENIER	QUEMES
QUARENDEN	QUARTOS	QUAVERIER	QUEENIES	QUEMING
QUARENDER	QUARTS	QUAVERING	QUEENIEST	QUENA
QUARER	QUARTZ	QUAVERS	QUEENING	QUENAS
QUAREST	QUARTZES	QUAVERY	QUEENINGS	QUENCH
QUARK	QUARTZIER	QUAY	QUEENITE	QUENCHED
QUARKS	QUARTZITE	QUAYAGE	QUEENITES	QUENCHER
QUARREL	QUARTZOSE	QUAYAGES	QUEENLESS	QUENCHERS
QUARRELED	QUARTZOUS	QUAYD	QUEENLET	QUENCHES
QUARRELER	QUARTZY	QUAYLIKE	QUEENLETS	QUENCHING
QUARRELS	QUASAR	QUAYS	QUEENLIER	QUENELLE
QUARRIAN	QUASARS	QUAYSIDE	QUEENLIKE	QUENELLES
QUARRIANS	QUASH	QUAYSIDES	QUEENLY	QUEP
QUARRIED	QUASHED	QUAZZIER	QUEENS	QUERCETIC
QUARRIER	QUASHEE	QUAZZIEST	QUEENSHIP	QUERCETIN
QUARRIERS	QUASHEES	QUAZZY	QUEENSIDE	QUERCETUM
QUARRIES	QUASHER	QUBIT	QUEENY	QUERCINE
QUARRION	QUASHERS	QUBITS	QUEER	QUERCITIN
QUARRIONS	QUASHES	QUBYTE	QUEERCORE	QUERIDA
QUARRY	QUASHIE	QUBYTES	QUEERDOM	QUERIDAS
QUARRYING	QUASHIES	QUEACH	QUEERDOMS	QUERIED
QUARRYMAN	QUASHING	QUEACHES	QUEERED	QUERIER
QUARRYMEN	QUASI	QUEACHIER	QUEERER	QUERIERS
QUART	QUASS	QUEACHY	QUEEREST	QUERIES
QUARTAN	QUASSES	QUEAN	QUEERING	QUERIMONY
QUARTANS	QUASSIA	QUEANS	QUEERISH	QUERIST
QUARTE	QUASSIAS	QUEASIER	QUEERITY	QUERISTS
QUARTER	QUASSIN	QUEASIEST	QUEERLY	QUERN
QUARTERED	QUASSINS	QUEASILY	QUEERNESS	QUERNS
QUARTERER	QUAT	QUEASY	QUEERS	QUERULOUS
QUARTERLY	QUATCH	QUEAZIER	QUEEST	QUERY
QUARTERN	QUATCHED	QUEAZIEST	QUEESTS	QUERYING
QUARTERNS	QUATCHES	QUEAZY	QUEINT	QUERYINGS
QUARTERS	QUATCHING	QUEBEC	QUELCH	QUEST

Q

QUESTANT	QUIBBLING	QUIESCES	QUILLMEN	QUINNAT
QUESTANTS	QUIBLIN	QUIESCING	QUILLON	QUINNATS
QUESTED	QUIBLINS	QUIET	QUILLONS	QUINO
QUESTER	QUICH	QUIETED	QUILLOW	QUINOA
QUESTERS	QUICHE	QUIETEN	QUILLOWS	QUINOAS
QUESTING	QUICHED	QUIETENED	QUILLS	QUINOID
QUESTINGS	QUICHES	QUIETENER	QUILLWORK	QUINOIDAL
QUESTION	QUICHING	QUIETENS	QUILLWORT	QUINOIDS
QUESTIONS	QUICK	QUIETER	QUILT	QUINOL
QUESTOR	QUICKBEAM	QUIETERS	QUILTED	QUINOLIN
QUESTORS	QUICKEN	QUIETEST	QUILTER	QUINOLINE
QUESTRIST	QUICKENED	QUIETING	QUILTERS	QUINOLINS
QUESTS	QUICKENER	QUIETINGS	QUILTING	QUINOLONE
QUETCH	QUICKENS	QUIETISM	QUILTINGS	QUINOLS
QUETCHED	QUICKER	QUIETISMS	QUILTS	QUINONE
QUETCHES	QUICKEST	QUIETIST	QUIM	QUINONES
QUETCHING	QUICKFIRE	QUIETISTS	QUIMS	QUINONOID
QUETHE	QUICKIE	QUIETIVE	QUIN	QUINOS
QUETHES	QUICKIES	QUIETIVES	QUINA	QUINQUINA
QUETHING	QUICKLIME	QUIETLY	QUINARIES	QUINS
QUETSCH	QUICKLY	QUIETNESS	QUINARY	QUINSIED
QUETSCHES	QUICKNESS	QUIETS	QUINAS	QUINSIES
QUETZAL	QUICKS	QUIETSOME	QUINATE	QUINSY
QUETZALES	QUICKSAND	QUIETUDE	QUINCE	QUINT
QUETZALS	QUICKSET	QUIETUDES	QUINCES	QUINTA
QUEUE	QUICKSETS	QUIETUS	QUINCHE	QUINTAIN
QUEUED	QUICKSTEP	QUIETUSES	QUINCHED	QUINTAINS
QUEUEING	QUICKY	QUIFF	QUINCHES	QUINTAL
QUEUEINGS	QUID	QUIFFED	QUINCHING	QUINTALS
QUEUER	QUIDAM	QUIFFS	QUINCUNX	QUINTAN
QUEUERS	QUIDAMS	QUIGHT	QUINE	QUINTANS
QUEUES	QUIDDANY	QUIGHTED	QUINELA	QUINTAR
QUEUING	QUIDDIT	QUIGHTING	QUINELAS	QUINTARS
QUEUINGS	QUIDDITCH	QUIGHTS	QUINELLA	QUINTAS
QUEY	QUIDDITS	QUILL	QUINELLAS	QUINTE
QUEYN	QUIDDITY	QUILLAI	QUINES	QUINTES
QUEYNIE	QUIDDLE	QUILLAIA	QUINIC	QUINTET
QUEYNIES	QUIDDLED	QUILLAIAS	QUINIDINE	QUINTETS
QUEYNS	QUIDDLER	QUILLAIS	QUINIE	QUINTETT
QUEYS	QUIDDLERS	QUILLAJA	QUINIELA	QUINTETTE
QUEZAL	QUIDDLES	QUILLAJAS	QUINIELAS	QUINTETTI
QUEZALES	QUIDDLING	QUILLBACK	QUINIES	QUINTETTO
QUEZALS	QUIDNUNC	QUILLED	QUININ	QUINTETTS
QUIBBLE	QUIDNUNCS	QUILLET	QUININA	QUINTIC
QUIBBLED	QUIDS	QUILLETS	QUININAS	QUINTICS
QUIBBLER	QUIESCE	QUILLING	QUININE	QUINTILE
QUIBBLERS	QUIESCED	QUILLINGS	QUININES	QUINTILES
QUIBBLES	QUIESCENT	QUILLMAN	QUININS	QUINTIN

QUINTINS	QUIRKIER	QUITTORS	QUOHOG	QUORUM
QUINTROON	QUIRKIEST	QUIVER	QUOHOGS	QUORUMS
QUINTS	QUIRKILY	QUIVERED	QUOIF	QUOTA
QUINTUPLE	QUIRKING	QUIVERER	QUOIFED	QUOTABLE
QUINTUPLY	QUIRKISH	QUIVERERS	QUOIFING	QUOTABLY
QUINZE	QUIRKS	QUIVERFUL	QUOIFS	QUOTAS
QUINZES	QUIRKY	QUIVERIER	QUOIN	QUOTATION
QUINZHEE	QUIRT	QUIVERING	QUOINED	QUOTATIVE
QUINZHEES	QUIRTED	QUIVERISH	QUOINING	QUOTE
QUINZIE	QUIRTING	QUIVERS	QUOININGS	QUOTED
QUINZIES	QUIRTS	QUIVERY	QUOINS	QUOTER
QUIP	QUISLING	QUIXOTE	QUOIST	QUOTERS
QUIPO	QUISLINGS	QUIXOTES	QUOISTS	QUOTES
QUIPOS	QUIST	QUIXOTIC	QUOIT	QUOTH
QUIPPED	QUISTS	QUIXOTISM	QUOITED	QUOTHA
QUIPPER	QUIT	QUIXOTRY	QUOITER	QUOTIDIAN
QUIPPERS	QUITCH	QUIZ	QUOITERS	QUOTIENT
QUIPPIER	QUITCHED	QUIZZED	QUOITING	QUOTIENTS
QUIPPIEST	QUITCHES	QUIZZER	QUOITS	QUOTING
QUIPPING	QUITCHING	QUIZZERS	QUOKKA	QUOTITION
QUIPPISH	QUITCLAIM	QUIZZERY	QUOKKAS	QUOTUM
QUIPPU	QUITE	QUIZZES	QUOLL	QUOTUMS
QUIPPUS	QUITED	QUIZZICAL	QUOLLS	QURSH
QUIPPY	QUITES	QUIZZIFY	QUOMODO	QURSHES
QUIPS	QUITING	QUIZZING	QUOMODOS	QURUSH
QUIPSTER	QUITRENT	QUIZZINGS	QUONDAM	QURUSHES
QUIPSTERS	QUITRENTS	QULLIQ	QUONK	QUYTE
QUIPU	QUITS	QULLIQS	QUONKED	QUYTED
QUIPUS	QUITTAL	QUOAD	QUONKING	QUYTES
QUIRE	QUITTALS	QUOD	QUONKS	QUYTING
QUIRED	QUITTANCE	QUODDED	QUOOKE	QWERTIES
QUIRES	QUITTED	QUODDING	QUOP	QWERTY
QUIRING	QUITTER	QUODLIBET	QUOPPED	QWERTYS
QUIRISTER	QUITTERS	QUODLIN	QUOPPING	
QUIRK	QUITTING	QUODLINS	QUOPS	
QUIRKED	QUITTOR	QUODS	QUORATE	

Q

R

RABANNA	RABBITS	RACEMED	RACIAL	RACKS
RABANNAS	RABBITY	RACEMES	RACIALISE	RACKWORK
RABASKA	RABBLE	RACEMIC	RACIALISM	RACKWORKS
RABASKAS	RABBLED	RACEMISE	RACIALIST	RACLETTE
RABAT	RABBLER	RACEMISED	RACIALIZE	RACLETTES
RABATINE	RABBLERS	RACEMISES	RACIALLY	RACLOIR
RABATINES	RABBLES	RACEMISM	RACIATION	RACLOIRS
RABATMENT	RABBLING	RACEMISMS	RACIER	RACON
RABATO	RABBLINGS	RACEMIZE	RACIEST	RACONS
RABATOES	RABBONI	RACEMIZED	RACILY	RACONTEUR
RABATOS	RABBONIS	RACEMIZES	RACINESS	RACOON
RABATS	RABI	RACEMOID	RACING	RACOONS
RABATTE	RABIC	RACEMOSE	RACINGS	RACQUET
RABATTED	RABID	RACEMOUS	RACINO	RACQUETED
RABATTES	RABIDER	RACEPATH	RACINOS	RACQUETS
RABATTING	RABIDEST	RACEPATHS	RACISM	RACY
RABBET	RABIDITY	RACER	RACISMS	RAD
RABBETED	RABIDLY	RACERS	RACIST	RADAR
RABBETING	RABIDNESS	RACES	RACISTS	RADARS
RABBETS	RABIES	RACETRACK	RACK	RADDED
RABBI	RABIETIC	RACEWALK	RACKED	RADDER
RABBIES	RABIS	RACEWALKS	RACKER	RADDEST
RABBIN	RABONA	RACEWAY	RACKERS	RADDING
RABBINATE	RABONAS	RACEWAYS	RACKET	RADDLE
RABBINIC	RACA	RACH	RACKETED	RADDLED
RABBINICS	RACAHOUT	RACHE	RACKETEER	RADDLEMAN
RABBINISM	RACAHOUTS	RACHES	RACKETER	RADDLEMEN
RABBINIST	RACCAHOUT	RACHET	RACKETERS	RADDLES
RABDINITE	RACCOON	RACHETED	RACKETIER	RADDLING
RABBINS	RACCOONS	RACHETING	RACKETING	RADDOCKE
RABBIS	RACE	RACHETS	RACKETRY	RADDOCKES
RABBIT	RACEABLE	RACHIAL	RACKETS	RADE
RABBITED	RACECARD	RACHIDES	RACKETT	RADGE
RABBITER	RACECARDS	RACHIDIAL	RACKETTS	RADGER
RABBITERS	RACED	RACHIDIAN	RACKETY	RADGES
RABBITIER	RACEGOER	RACHILLA	RACKFUL	RADGEST
RABBITING	RACEGOERS	RACHILLAE	RACKFULS	RADIABLE
RABBITO	RACEGOING	RACHILLAS	RACKING	RADIAL
RABBITOH	RACEHORSE	RACHIS	RACKINGLY	RADIALE
RABBITOHS	RACEMATE	RACHISES	RACKINGS	RADIALIA
RABBITOS	RACEMATES	RACHITIC	RACKLE	RADIALISE
RABBITRY	RACEME	RACHITIS	RACKLES	RADIALITY

RADIALIZE	RADIOLOGY	RAFTERED	RAGGLES	RAGWORMS
RADIALLY	RADIOMAN	RAFTERING	RAGGLING	RAGWORT
RADIALS	RADIOMEN	RAFTERS	RAGGS	RAGWORTS
RADIAN	RADIONICS	RAFTING	RAGGY	RAH
RADIANCE	RADIOS	RAFTINGS	RAGHEAD	RAHED
RADIANCES	RADIOTHON	RAFTMAN	RAGHEADS	RAHING
RADIANCY	RADISH	RAFTMEN	RAGI	RAHS
RADIANS	RADISHES	RAFTS	RAGING	RAHUI
RADIANT	RADIUM	RAFTSMAN	RAGINGLY	RAHUIS
RADIANTLY	RADIUMS	RAFTSMEN	RAGINGS	RAI
RADIANTS	RADIUS	RAG	RAGINI	RAIA
RADIATA	RADIUSED	RAGA	RAGINIS	RAIAS
RADIATAS	RADIUSES	RAGAS	RAGIS	RAID
RADIATE	RADIUSING	RAGBAG	RAGLAN	RAIDED
RADIATED	RADIX	RAGBAGS	RAGLANS	RAIDER
RADIATELY	RADIXES	RAGBOLT	RAGMAN	RAIDERS
RADIATES	RADOME	RAGBOLTS	RAGMANS	RAIDING
RADIATING	RADOMES	RAGDE	RAGMEN	RAIDINGS
RADIATION	RADON	RAGDOLL	RAGMENT	RAIDS
RADIATIVE	RADONS	RAGDOLLS	RAGMENTS	RAIK
RADIATOR	RADS	RAGE	RAGOUT	RAIKED
RADIATORS	RADULA	RAGED	RAGOUTED	RAIKING
RADIATORY	RADULAE	RAGEE	RAGOUTING	RAIKS
RADICAL	RADULAR	RAGEES	RAGOUTS	RAIL
RADICALLY	RADULAS	RAGEFUL	RAGPICKER	RAILAGE
RADICALS	RADULATE	RAGER	RAGS	RAILAGES
RADICAND	RADWASTE	RAGERS	RAGSTONE	RAILBED
RADICANDS	RADWASTES	RAGES	RAGSTONES	RAILBEDS
RADICANT	RAFALE	RAGG	RAGTAG	RAILBIRD
RADICATE	RAFALES	RAGGA	RAGTAGS	RAILBIRDS
RADICATED	RAFF	RAGGAS	RAGTAIL	RAILBUS
RADICATES	RAFFIA	RAGGED	RAGTIME	RAILBUSES
RADICCHIO	RAFFIAS	RAGGEDER	RAGTIMER	RAILCAR
RADICEL	RAFFINATE	RAGGEDEST	RAGTIMERS	RAILCARD
RADICELS	RAFFINOSE	RAGGEDIER	RAGTIMES	RAILCARDS
RADICES	RAFFISH	RAGGEDLY	RAGTOP	RAILCARS
RADICLE	RAFFISHLY	RAGGEDY	RAGTOPS	RAILE
RADICLES	RAFFLE	RAGGEE	RAGU	RAILED
RADICULAR	RAFFLED	RAGGEES	RAGULED	RAILER
RADICULE	RAFFLER	RAGGERIES	RAGULY	RAILERS
RADICULES	RAFFLERS	RAGGERY	RAGUS	RAILES
RADII	RAFFLES	RAGGIER	RAGWEED	RAILHEAD
RADIO	RAFFLESIA	RAGGIES	RAGWEEDS	RAILHEADS
RADIOED	RAFFLING	RAGGIEST	RAGWHEEL	RAILING
RADIOES	RAFFS	RAGGING	RAGWHEELS	RAILINGLY
RADIOGOLD	RAFT	RAGGINGS	RAGWORK	RAILINGS
RADIOGRAM	RAFTED	RAGGLE	RAGWORKS	RAILLERY
RADIOING	RAFTER	RAGGLED	RAGWORM	RAILLESS

R

RAILLIES	RAINSUIT	RAKEHELLS	RAMADAS	RAMJETS
RAILLY	RAINSUITS	RAKEHELLY	RAMAKIN	RAMMED
RAILMAN	RAINSWEPT	RAKELIKE	RAMAKINS	RAMMEL
RAILMEN	RAINTIGHT	RAKEOFF	RAMAL	RAMMELS
RAILROAD	RAINWASH	RAKEOFFS	RAMATE	RAMMER
RAILROADS	RAINWATER	RAKER	RAMBLA	RAMMERS
RAILS	RAINWEAR	RAKERIES	RAMBLAS	RAMMIER
RAILWAY	RAINWEARS	RAKERS	RAMBLE	RAMMIES
RAILWAYS	RAINY	RAKERY	RAMBLED	RAMMIEST
RAILWOMAN	RAIRD	RAKES	RAMBLER	RAMMING
RAILWOMEN	RAIRDS	RAKESHAME	RAMBLERS	RAMMISH
RAIMENT	RAIS	RAKI	RAMBLES	RAMMISHLY
RAIMENTS	RAISABLE	RAKIA	RAMBLING	RAMMLE
RAIN	RAISE	RAKIAS	RAMBLINGS	RAMMLES
RAINBAND	RAISEABLE	RAKIJA	RAMBUTAN	RAMMY
RAINBANDS	RAISED	RAKIJAS	RAMBUTANS	RAMONA
RAINBIRD	RAISER	RAKING	RAMCAT	RAMONAS
RAINBIRDS	RAISERS	RAKINGS	RAMCATS	RAMOSE
RAINBOW	RAISES	RAKIS	RAMEAL	RAMOSELY
RAINBOWED	RAISIN	RAKISH	RAMEE	RAMOSITY
RAINBOWS	RAISING	RAKISHLY	RAMEES	RAMOUS
RAINBOWY	RAISINGS	RAKSHAS	RAMEKIN	RAMOUSLY
RAINCHECK	RAISINIER	RAKSHASA	RAMEKINS	RAMP
RAINCOAT	RAISINS	RAKSHASAS	RAMEN	RAMPAGE
RAINCOATS	RAISINY	RAKSHASES	RAMENS	RAMPAGED
RAINDATE	RAISONNE	RAKU	RAMENTA	RAMPAGER
RAINDATES	RAIT	RAKUS	RAMENTUM	RAMPAGERS
RAINDROP	RAITA	RALE	RAMEOUS	RAMPAGES
RAINDROPS	RAITAS	RALES	RAMEQUIN	RAMPAGING
RAINE	RAITED	RALLIED	RAMEQUINS	RAMPANCY
RAINED	RAITING	RALLIER	RAMET	RAMPANT
RAINES	RAITS	RALLIERS	RAMETS	RAMPANTLY
RAINFALL	RAIYAT	RALLIES	RAMI	RAMPART
RAINFALLS	RAIYATS	RALLIFORM	RAMIE	RAMPARTED
RAINIER	RAJ	RALLINE	RAMIES	RAMPARTS
RAINIEST	RAJA	RALLY	RAMIFIED	RAMPAUGE
RAINILY	RAJAH	RALLYE	RAMIFIES	RAMPAUGED
RAININESS	RAJAHS	RALLYES	RAMIFORM	RAMPAUGES
RAINING	RAJAHSHIP	RALLYING	RAMIFY	RAMPED
RAINLESS	RAJAS	RALLYINGS	RAMIFYING	RAMPER
RAINMAKER	RAJASHIP	RALLYIST	RAMILIE	RAMPERS
RAINOUT	RAJASHIPS	RALLYISTS	RAMILIES	RAMPICK
RAINOUTS	RAJES	RALPH	RAMILLIE	RAMPICKED
RAINPROOF	RAKE	RALPHED	RAMILLIES	RAMPICKS
RAINS	RAKED	RALPHING	RAMIN	RAMPIKE
RAINSPOUT	RAKEE	RALPHS	RAMINS	RAMPIKES
RAINSTICK	RAKEES	RAM	RAMIS	RAMPING
RAINSTORM	RAKEHELL	RAMADA	RAMJET	RAMPINGS

RAMPION	RANCHERO	RANDONS	RANKISTS	RAPE
RAMPIONS	RANCHEROS	RANDS	RANKLE	RAPED
RAMPIRE	RANCHERS	RANDY	RANKLED	RAPER
RAMPIRED	RANCHES	RANEE	RANKLES	RAPERS
RAMPIRES	RANCHETTE	RANEES	RANKLESS	RAPES
RAMPOLE	RANCHING	RANG	RANKLING	RAPESEED
RAMPOLES	RANCHINGS	RANGA	RANKLY	RAPESEEDS
RAMPS	RANCHLAND	RANGAS	RANKNESS	RAPHAE
RAMPSMAN	RANCHLESS	RANGATIRA	RANKS	RAPHANIA
RAMPSMEN	RANCHLIKE	RANGE	RANKSHIFT	RAPHANIAS
RAMROD	RANCHMAN	RANGED	RANPIKE	RAPHE
RAMRODDED	RANCHMEN	RANGELAND	RANPIKES	RAPHES
RAMRODS	RANCHO	RANGER	RANSACK	RAPHIA
RAMS	RANCHOS	RANGERS	RANSACKED	RAPHIAS
RAMSHORN	RANCID	RANGES	RANSACKER	RAPHIDE
RAMSHORNS	RANCIDER	RANGI	RANSACKS	RAPHIDES
RAMSON	RANCIDEST	RANGIER	RANSEL	RAPHIS
RAMSONS	RANCIDITY	RANGIEST	RANSELS	RAPID
RAMSTAM	RANCIDLY	RANGILY	RANSHAKLE	RAPIDER
RAMTIL	RANCING	RANGINESS	RANSOM	RAPIDEST
RAMTILLA	RANCOR	RANGING	RANSOMED	RAPIDITY
RAMTILLAS	RANCORED	RANGINGS	RANSOMER	RAPIDLY
RAMTILS	RANCOROUS	RANGIORA	RANSOMERS	RAPIDNESS
RAMULAR	RANCORS	RANGIORAS	RANSOMING	RAPIDS
RAMULI	RANCOUR	RANGIS	RANSOMS	RAPIER
RAMULOSE	RANCOURED	RANGOLI	RANT	RAPIERED
RAMULOUS	RANCOURS	RANGOLIS	RANTED	RAPIERS
RAMULUS	RAND	RANGS	RANTER	RAPINE
RAMUS	RANDAN	RANGY	RANTERISM	RAPINES
RAN	RANDANS	RANI	RANTERS	RAPING
RANA	RANDED	RANID	RANTING	RAPINI
RANARIAN	RANDEM	RANIDS	RANTINGLY	RAPINIS
RANARIUM	RANDEMS	RANIFORM	RANTINGS	RAPIST
RANARIUMS	RANDIE	RANINE	RANTIPOLE	RAPISTS
RANAS	RANDIER	RANIS	RANTS	RAPLOCH
RANCE	RANDIES	RANK	RANULA	RAPLOCHS
RANCED	RANDIEST	RANKE	RANULAR	RAPPAREE
RANCEL	RANDILY	RANKED	RANULAS	RAPPAREES
RANCELLED	RANDINESS	RANKER	RANUNCULI	RAPPE
RANCELS	RANDING	RANKERS	RANZEL	RAPPED
RANCES	RANDLORD	RANKES	RANZELMAN	RAPPEE
RANCH	RANDLORDS	RANKEST	RANZELMEN	RAPPEES
RANCHED	RANDOM	RANKING	RANZELS	RAPPEL
RANCHER	RANDOMISE	RANKINGS	RAOULIA	RAPPELED
RANCHERA	RANDOMIZE	RANKISH	RAOULIAS	RAPPELING
RANCHERAS	RANDOMLY	RANKISM	RAP	RAPPELLED
RANCHERIA	RANDOMS	RANKISMS	RAPACIOUS	RAPPELS
RANCHERIE	RANDON	RANKIST	RAPACITY	RAPPEN

RAPPER	RARK	RASPING	RATBAGS	RATIFIES
RAPPERS	RARKED	RASPINGLY	RATBITE	RATIFY
RAPPES	RARKING	RASPINGS	RATCH	RATIFYING
RAPPING	RARKS	RASPISH	RATCHED	RATINE
RAPPINGS	RAS	RASPS	RATCHES	RATINES
RAPPINI	RASBORA	RASPY	RATCHET	RATING
RAPPORT	RASBORAS	RASSE	RATCHETED	RATINGS
RAPPORTS	RASCAILLE	RASSES	RATCHETS	RATIO
RAPS	RASCAL	RASSLE	RATCHING	RATION
RAPT	RASCALDOM	RASSLED	RATE	RATIONAL
RAPTLY	RASCALISM	RASSLER	RATEABLE	RATIONALE
RAPTNESS	RASCALITY	RASSLERS	RATEABLES	RATIONALS
RAPTOR	RASCALLY	RASSLES	RATEABLY	RATIONED
RAPTORIAL	RASCALS	RASSLING	RATED	RATIONING
RAPTORS	RASCASSE	RAST	RATEEN	RATIONS
RAPTURE	RASCASSES	RASTA	RATEENS	RATIOS
RAPTURED	RASCHEL	RASTAFARI	RATEL	RATITE
RAPTURES	RASCHELS	RASTER	RATELS	RATITES
RAPTURING	RASE	RASTERED	RATEMETER	RATLIKE
RAPTURISE	RASED	RASTERING	RATEPAYER	RATLIN
RAPTURIST	RASER	RASTERISE	RATER	RATLINE
RAPTURIZE	RASERS	RASTERIZE	RATERS	RATLINES
RAPTUROUS	RASES	RASTERS	RATES	RATLING
RARE	RASH	RASTRUM	RATFINK	RATLINGS
RAREBIT	RASHED	RASTRUMS	RATFINKS	RATLINS
RAREBITS	RASHER	RASURE	RATFISH	RATO
RARED	RASHERS	RASURES	RATFISHES	RATOO
RAREE	RASHES	RAT	RATH	RATOON
RAREFIED	RASHEST	RATA	RATHA	RATOONED
RAREFIER	RASHIE	RATABLE	RATHAS	RATOONER
RAREFIERS	RASHIES	RATABLES	RATHE	RATOONERS
RAREFIES	RASHING	RATABLY	RATHER	RATOONING
RAREFY	RASHLIKE	RATAFEE	RATHEREST	RATOONS
RAREFYING	RASHLY	RATAFEES	RATHERIPE	RATOOS
RARELY	RASHNESS	RATAFIA	RATHERISH	RATOS
RARENESS	RASING	RATAFIAS	RATHEST	RATPACK
RARER	RASMALAI	RATAL	RATHOLE	RATPACKS
RARERIPE	RASMALAIS	RATALS	RATHOLES	RATPROOF
RARERIPES	RASORIAL	RATAN	RATHOUSE	RATS
RARES	RASP	RATANIES	RATHOUSES	RATSBANE
RAREST	RASPATORY	RATANS	RATHRIPE	RATSBANES
RARIFIED	RASPBERRY	RATANY	RATHRIPES	RATTAIL
RARIFIES	RASPED	RATAPLAN	RATHS	RATTAILED
RARIFY	RASPER	RATAPLANS	RATICIDE	RATTAILS
RARIFYING	RASPERS	RATAS	RATICIDES	RATTAN
RARING	RASPIER	RATATAT	RATIFIED	RATTANS
RARITIES	RASPIEST	RATATATS	RATIFIER	RATTED
RARITY	RASPINESS	RATBAG	RATIFIERS	RATTEEN

RATTEENS	RAUCLER	RAVELMENT	RAWHIDE	RAZER
RATTEN	RAUCLEST	RAVELS	RAWHIDED	RAZERS
RATTENED	RAUCOUS	RAVEN	RAWHIDES	RAZES
RATTENER	RAUCOUSLY	RAVENED	RAWHIDING	RAZING
RATTENERS	RAUGHT	RAVENER	RAWIN	RAZMATAZ
RATTENING	RAUN	RAVENERS	RAWING	RAZOO
RATTENS	RAUNCH	RAVENEST	RAWINGS	RAZOOS
RATTER	RAUNCHED	RAVENING	RAWINS	RAZOR
RATTERIES	RAUNCHES	RAVENINGS	RAWISH	RAZORABLE
RATTERS	RAUNCHIER	RAVENLIKE	RAWLY	RAZORBACK
RATTERY	RAUNCHILY	RAVENOUS	RAWMAISH	RAZORBILL
RATTIER	RAUNCHING	RAVENS	RAWN	RAZORCLAM
RATTIEST	RAUNCHY	RAVER	RAWNESS	RAZORED
RATTILY	RAUNGE	RAVERS	RAWNESSES	RAZORFISH
RATTINESS	RAUNGED	RAVES	RAWNS	RAZORING
RATTING	RAUNGES	RAVEY	RAWS	RAZORS
RATTINGS	RAUNGING	RAVIER	RAX	RAZURE
RATTISH	RAUNS	RAVIEST	RAXED	RAZURES
RATTLE	RAUPATU	RAVIGOTE	RAXES	RAZZ
RATTLEBAG	RAUPATUS	RAVIGOTES	RAXING	RAZZBERRY
RATTLEBOX	RAUPO	RAVIGOTTE	RAY	RAZZED
RATTLED	RAUPOS	RAVIN	RAYA	RAZZES
RATTLER	RAURIKI	RAVINE	RAYAH	RAZZIA
RATTLERS	RAURIKIS	RAVINED	RAYAHS	RAZZIAS
RATTLES	RAUWOLFIA	RAVINES	RAYAS	RAZZING
RATTLIER	RAV	RAVING	RAYED	RAZZINGS
RATTLIEST	RAVAGE	RAVINGLY	RAYGRASS	RAZZLE
RATTLIN	RAVAGED	RAVINGS	RAYING	RAZZLES
RATTLINE	RAVAGER	RAVINING	RAYLE	RE
RATTLINES	RAVAGERS	RAVINS	RAYLED	REABSORB
RATTLING	RAVAGES	RAVIOLI	RAYLES	REABSORBS
RATTLINGS	RAVAGING	RAVIOLIS	RAYLESS	REACCEDE
RATTLINS	RAVE	RAVISH	RAYLESSLY	REACCEDED
RATTLY	RAVED	RAVISHED	RAYLET	REACCEDES
RATTON	RAVEL	RAVISHER	RAYLETS	REACCENT
RATTONS	RAVELED	RAVISHERS	RAYLIKE	REACCENTS
RATTOON	RAVELER	RAVISHES	RAYLING	REACCEPT
RATTOONED	RAVELERS	RAVISHING	RAYNE	REACCEPTS
RATTOONS	RAVELIN	RAVS	RAYNES	REACCLAIM
RATTRAP	RAVELING	RAW	RAYON	REACCUSE
RATTRAPS	RAVELINGS	RAWARU	RAYONS	REACCUSED
RATTY	RAVELINS	RAWARUS	RAYS	REACCUSES
RATU	RAVELLED	RAWBONE	RAZE	REACH
RATUS	RAVELLER	RAWBONED	RAZED	REACHABLE
RAUCID	RAVELLERS	RAWER	RAZEE	REACHED
RAUCITIES	RAVELLIER	RAWEST	RAZEED	REACHER
RAUCITY	RAVELLING	RAWHEAD	RAZEEING	REACHERS
RAUCLE	RAVELLY	RAWHEADS	RAZEES	REACHES

REACHING	READOPTS	REALISM	REAMIEST	REARISES
REACHLESS	READORN	REALISMS	REAMING	REARISING
REACQUIRE	READORNED	REALIST	REAMS	REARLY
REACT	READORNS	REALISTIC	REAMY	REARM
REACTANCE	READOUT	REALISTS	REAN	REARMED
REACTANT	READOUTS	REALITIES	REANALYSE	REARMICE
REACTANTS	READS	REALITY	REANALYZE	REARMING
REACTED	READVANCE	REALIZE	REANIMATE	REARMOST
REACTING	READVISE	REALIZED	REANNEX	REARMOUSE
REACTION	READVISED	REALIZER	REANNEXED	REARMS
REACTIONS	READVISES	REALIZERS	REANNEXES	REAROSE
REACTIVE	READY	REALIZES	REANOINT	REAROUSAL
REACTOR	READYING	REALIZING	REANOINTS	REAROUSE
REACTORS	READYMADE	REALLIE	REANS	REAROUSED
REACTS	REAEDIFY	REALLIED	REANSWER	REAROUSES
REACTUATE	REAEDIFYE	REALLIES	REANSWERS	REARRANGE
READ	REAFFIRM	REALLOT	REAP	REARREST
READABLE	REAFFIRMS	REALLOTS	REAPABLE	REARRESTS
READABLY	REAFFIX	REALLY	REAPED	REARS
READAPT	REAFFIXED	REALLYING	REAPER	REARWARD
READAPTED	REAFFIXES	REALM	REAPERS	REARWARDS
READAPTS	REAGENCY	REALMLESS	REAPHOOK	REASCEND
READD	REAGENT	REALMS	REAPHOOKS	REASCENDS
READDED	REAGENTS	REALNESS	REAPING	REASCENT
READDICT	REAGIN	REALO	REAPINGS	REASCENTS
READDICTS	REAGINIC	REALOS	REAPPAREL	REASON
READDING	REAGINS	REALS	REAPPEAR	REASONED
READDRESS	REAIS	REALTER	REAPPEARS	REASONER
READDS	REAK	REALTERED	REAPPLIED	REASONERS
READER	REAKED	REALTERS	REAPPLIES	REASONING
READERLY	REAKING	REALTIE	REAPPLY	REASONS
READERS	REAKS	REALTIES	REAPPOINT	REASSAIL
READIED	REAL	REALTIME	REAPPROVE	REASSAILS
READIER	REALER	REALTONE	REAPS	REASSERT
READIES	REALES	REALTONES	REAR	REASSERTS
READIEST	REALEST	REALTOR	REARED	REASSESS
READILY	REALGAR	REALTORS	REARER	REASSIGN
READINESS	REALGARS	REALTY	REARERS	REASSIGNS
READING	REALIA	REAM	REARGUARD	REASSORT
READINGS	REALIGN	REAME	REARGUE	REASSORTS
READJUST	REALIGNED	REAMED	REARGUED	REASSUME
READJUSTS	REALIGNS	REAMEND	REARGUES	REASSUMED
README	REALISE	REAMENDED	REARGUING	REASSUMES
READMES	REALISED	REAMENDS	REARHORSE	REASSURE
READMIT	REALISER	REAMER	REARING	REASSURED
READMITS	REALISERS	REAMERS	REARINGS	REASSURER
READOPT	REALISES	REAMES	REARISE	REASSURES
READOPTED	REALISING	REAMIER	REARISEN	REAST

R

REASTED	REBAITING	REBILL	REBORE	REBURIES
REASTIER	REBAITS	REBILLED	REBORED	REBURY
REASTIEST	REBALANCE	REBILLING	REBORES	REBURYING
REASTING	REBAPTISE	REBILLS	REBORING	REBUS
REASTS	REBAPTISM	REBIND	REBORN	REBUSES
REASTY	REBAPTIZE	REBINDING	REBORROW	REBUT
REATA	REBAR	REBINDS	REBORROWS	REBUTMENT
REATAS	REBARS	REBIRTH	REBOTTLE	REBUTS
REATE	REBASE	REBIRTHER	REBOTTLED	REBUTTAL
REATES	REBASED	REBIRTHS	REBOTTLES	REBUTTALS
REATTACH	REBASES	REBIT	REBOUGHT	REBUTTED
REATTACK	REBASING	REBITE	REBOUND	REBUTTER
REATTACKS	REBATABLE	REBITES	REBOUNDED	REBUTTERS
REATTAIN	REBATE	REBITING	REBOUNDER	REBUTTING
REATTAINS	REBATED	REBITTEN	REBOUNDS	REBUTTON
REATTEMPT	REBATER	REBLEND	REBOZO	REBUTTONS
REAVAIL	REBATERS	REBLENDED	REBOZOS	REBUY
REAVAILED	REBATES	REBLENDS	REBRACE	REBUYING
REAVAILS	REBATING	REBLENT	REBRACED	REBUYS
REAVE	REBATO	REBLOCHON	REBRACES	REC
REAVED	REBATOES	REBLOOM	REBRACING	RECAL
REAVER	REBATOS	REBLOOMED	REBRANCH	RECALESCE
REAVERS	REBBE	REBLOOMER	REBRAND	RECALL
REAVES	REBBES	REBLOOMS	REBRANDED	RECALLED
REAVING	REBBETZIN	REBLOSSOM	REBRANDS	RECALLER
REAVOW	REBEC	REBOANT	REBRED	RECALLERS
REAVOWED	REBECK	REBOARD	REBREED	RECALLING
REAVOWING	REBECKS	REBOARDED	REBREEDS	RECALLS
REAVOWS	REBECS	REBOARDS	REBS	RECALMENT
REAWAKE	REBEGAN	REBOATION	REBUFF	RECALS
REAWAKED	REBEGIN	REBODIED	REBUFFED	RECAMIER
REAWAKEN	REBEGINS	REBODIES	REBUFFING	RECAMIERS
REAWAKENS	REBEGUN	REBODY	REBUFFS	RECANE
REAWAKES	REBEL	REBODYING	REBUILD	RECANED
REAWAKING	REBELDOM	REBOIL	REBUILDED	RECANES
REAWOKE	REBELDOMS	REBOILED	REBUILDS	RECANING
REAWOKEN	REBELLED	REBOILING	REBUILT	RECANT
REB	REBELLER	REBOILS	REBUKABLE	RECANTED
REBACK	REBELLERS	REBOOK	REBUKE	RECANTER
REBACKED	REBELLING	REBOOKED	REBUKED	RECANTERS
REBACKING	REBELLION	REBOOKING	REBUKEFUL	RECANTING
REBACKS	REBELLOW	REBOOKS	REBUKER	RECANTS
REBADGE	REBELLOWS	REBOOT	REBUKERS	RECAP
REBADGED	REBELS	REBOOTED	REBUKES	RECAPPED
REBADGES	REBID	REBOOTING	REBUKING	RECAPPING
REBADGING	REBIDDEN	REBOOTS	REBURIAL	RECAPS
REBAIT	REBIDDING	REBOP	REBURIALS	RECAPTION
REBAITED	REBIDS	REBOPS	REBURIED	RECAPTOR

R

RECAPTORS	RECENSES	RECHEWED	RECLADS	RECODE
RECAPTURE	RECENSING	RECHEWING	RECLAIM	RECODED
RECARPET	RECENSION	RECHEWS	RECLAIMED	RECODES
RECARPETS	RECENSOR	RECHIE	RECLAIMER	RECODIFY
RECARRIED	RECENSORS	RECHIP	RECLAIMS	RECODING
RECARRIES	RECENT	RECHIPPED	RECLAME	RECOGNISE
RECARRY	RECENTER	RECHIPS	RECLAMES	RECOGNIZE
RECAST	RECENTEST	RECHLESSE	RECLASP	RECOIL
RECASTING	RECENTLY	RECHOOSE	RECLASPED	RECOILED
RECASTS	RECENTRE	RECHOOSES	RECLASPS	RECOILER
RECATALOG	RECENTRED	RECHOSE	RECLEAN	RECOILERS
RECATCH	RECENTRES	RECHOSEN	RECLEANED	RECOILING
RECATCHES	RECEPT	RECIPE	RECLEANS	RECOILS
RECAUGHT	RECEPTION	RECIPES	RECLIMB	RECOIN
RECAUTION	RECEPTIVE	RECIPIENT	RECLIMBED	RECOINAGE
RECCE	RECEPTOR	RECIRCLE	RECLIMBS	RECOINED
RECCED	RECEPTORS	RECIRCLED	RECLINATE	RECOINING
RECCEED	RECEPTS	RECIRCLES	RECLINE	RECOINS
RECCEING	RECERTIFY	RECISION	RECLINED	RECOLLECT
RECCES	RECESS	RECISIONS	RECLINER	RECOLLET
RECCIED	RECESSED	RECIT	RECLINERS	RECOLLETS
RECCIES	RECESSES	RECITABLE	RECLINES	RECOLOR
RECCO	RECESSING	RECITAL	RECLINING	RECOLORED
RECCOS	RECESSION	RECITALS	RECLOSE	RECOLORS
RECCY	RECESSIVE	RECITE	RECLOSED	RECOLOUR
RECCYING	RECHANGE	RECITED	RECLOSES	RECOLOURS
RECEDE	RECHANGED	RECITER	RECLOSING	RECOMB
RECEDED	RECHANGES	RECITERS	RECLOTHE	RECOMBED
RECEDES	RECHANNEL	RECITES	RECLOTHED	RECOMBINE
RECEDING	RECHARGE	RECITING	RECLOTHES	RECOMBING
RECEIPT	RECHARGED	RECITS	RECLUSE	RECOMBS
RECEIPTED	RECHARGER	RECK	RECLUSELY	RECOMFORT
RECEIPTOR	RECHARGES	RECKAN	RECLUSES	RECOMMEND
RECEIPTS	RECHART	RECKANS	RECLUSION	RECOMMIT
RECEIVAL	RECHARTED	RECKED	RECLUSIVE	RECOMMITS
RECEIVALS	RECHARTER	RECKING	RECLUSORY	RECOMPACT
RECEIVE	RECHARTS	RECKLESS	RECOAL	RECOMPILE
RECEIVED	RECHATE	RECKLING	RECOALED	RECOMPOSE
RECEIVER	RECHATES	RECKLINGS	RECOALING	RECOMPUTE
RECEIVERS	RECHAUFFE	RECKON	RECOALS	RECON
RECEIVES	RECHEAT	RECKONED	RECOAT	RECONCILE
RECEIVING	RECHEATED	RECKONER	RECOATED	RECONDITE
RECEMENT	RECHEATS	RECKONERS	RECOATING	RECONDUCT
RECEMENTS	RECHECK	RECKONING	RECOATS	RECONFER
RECENCIES	RECHECKED	RECKONS	RECOCK	RECONFERS
RECENCY	RECHECKS	RECKS	RECOCKED	RECONFINE
RECENSE	RECHERCHE	RECLAD	RECOCKING	RECONFIRM
RECENSED	RECHEW	RECLADDED	RECOCKS	RECONNECT

RECONNED	RECOURED	RECTANGLE	RECURVATE	REDBAIT
RECONNING	RECOURES	RECTI	RECURVE	REDBAITED
RECONQUER	RECOURING	RECTIFIED	RECURVED	REDBAITER
RECONS	RECOURSE	RECTIFIER	RECURVES	REDBAITS
RECONSIGN	RECOURSED	RECTIFIES	RECURVING	REDBAY
RECONSOLE	RECOURSES	RECTIFY	RECUSAL	REDBAYS
RECONSULT	RECOVER	RECTION	RECUSALS	REDBELLY
RECONTACT	RECOVERED	RECTIONS	RECUSANCE	REDBIRD
RECONTOUR	RECOVEREE	RECTITIC	RECUSANCY	REDBIRDS
RECONVENE	RECOVERER	RECTITIS	RECUSANT	REDBONE
RECONVERT	RECOVEROR	RECTITUDE	RECUSANTS	REDBONES
RECONVEY	RECOVERS	RECTO	RECUSE	REDBREAST
RECONVEYS	RECOVERY	RECTOCELE	RECUSED	REDBRICK
RECONVICT	RECOWER	RECTOR	RECUSES	REDBRICKS
RECOOK	RECOWERED	RECTORAL	RECUSING	REDBUD
RECOOKED	RECOWERS	RECTORATE	RECUT	REDBUDS
RECOOKING	RECOYLE	RECTORESS	RECUTS	REDBUG
RECOOKS	RECOYLED	RECTORIAL	RECUTTING	REDBUGS
RECOPIED	RECOYLES	RECTORIES	RECYCLATE	REDCAP
RECOPIES	RECOYLING	RECTORS	RECYCLE	REDCAPS
RECOPY	RECRATE	RECTORY	RECYCLED	REDCOAT
RECOPYING	RECRATED	RECTOS	RECYCLER	REDCOATS
RECORD	RECRATES	RECTRESS	RECYCLERS	REDD
RECORDED	RECRATING	RECTRICES	RECYCLES	REDDED
RECORDER	RECREANCE	RECTRIX	RECYCLING	REDDEN
RECORDERS	RECREANCY	RECTUM	RECYCLIST	REDDENDA
RECORDING	RECREANT	RECTUMS	RED	REDDENDO
RECORDIST	RECREANTS	RECTUS	REDACT	REDDENDOS
RECORDS	RECREATE	RECUILE	REDACTED	REDDENDUM
RECORK	RECREATED	RECUILED	REDACTING	REDDENED
RECORKED	RECREATES	RECUILES	REDACTION	REDDENING
RECORKING	RECREATOR	RECUILING	REDACTOR	REDDENS
RECORKS	RECREMENT	RECULE	REDACTORS	REDDER
RECOUNT	RECROSS	RECULED	REDACTS	REDDERS
RECOUNTAL	RECROSSED	RECULES	REDAMAGE	REDDEST
RECOUNTED	RECROSSES	RECULING	REDAMAGED	REDDIER
RECOUNTER	RECROWN	RECUMBENT	REDAMAGES	REDDIEST
RECOUNTS	RECROWNED	RECUR	REDAN	REDDING
RECOUP	RECROWNS	RECURE	REDANS	REDDINGS
RECOUPE	RECRUIT	RECURED	REDARGUE	REDDISH
RECOUPED	RECRUITAL	RECURES	REDARGUED	REDDISHLY
RECOUPES	RECRUITED	RECURING	REDARGUES	REDDLE
RECOUPING	RECRUITER	RECURRED	REDATE	REDDLED
RECOUPLE	RECRUITS	RECURRENT	REDATED	REDDLEMAN
RECOUPLED	RECS	RECURRING	REDATES	REDDLEMEN
RECOUPLES	RECTA	RECURS	REDATING	REDDLES
RECOUPS	RECTAL	RECURSION	REDBACK	REDDLING
RECOURE	RECTALLY	RECURSIVE	REDBACKS	REDDS

REDDY	REDFIN	REDLINED	REDRAW	REDTAILS
REDE	REDFINS	REDLINER	REDRAWER	REDTOP
REDEAL	REDFISH	REDLINERS	REDRAWERS	REDTOPS
REDEALING	REDFISHES	REDLINES	REDRAWING	REDUB
REDEALS	REDFOOT	REDLINING	REDRAWN	REDUBBED
REDEALT	REDFOOTS	REDLY	REDRAWS	REDUBBING
REDEAR	REDHANDED	REDNECK	REDREAM	REDUBS
REDEARS	REDHEAD	REDNECKED	REDREAMED	REDUCE
REDECIDE	REDHEADED	REDNECKS	REDREAMS	REDUCED
REDECIDED	REDHEADS	REDNESS	REDREAMT	REDUCER
REDECIDES	REDHORSE	REDNESSES	REDRESS	REDUCERS
REDECRAFT	REDHORSES	REDO	REDRESSAL	REDUCES
REDED	REDIA	REDOCK	REDRESSED	REDUCIBLE
REDEEM	REDIAE	REDOCKED	REDRESSER	REDUCIBLY
REDEEMED	REDIAL	REDOCKING	REDRESSES	REDUCING
REDEEMER	REDIALED	REDOCKS	REDRESSOR	REDUCTANT
REDEEMERS	REDIALING	REDOES	REDREW	REDUCTASE
REDEEMING	REDIALLED	REDOING	REDRIED	REDUCTION
REDEEMS	REDIALS	REDOLENCE	REDRIES	REDUCTIVE
REDEFEAT	REDIAS	REDOLENCY	REDRILL	REDUCTOR
REDEFEATS	REDICTATE	REDOLENT	REDRILLED	REDUCTORS
REDEFECT	REDID	REDON	REDRILLS	REDUIT
REDEFECTS	REDIGEST	REDONE	REDRIVE	REDUITS
REDEFIED	REDIGESTS	REDONNED	REDRIVEN	REDUNDANT
REDEFIES	REDIGRESS	REDONNING	REDRIVES	REDUVIID
REDEFINE	REDING	REDONS	REDRIVING	REDUVIIDS
REDEFINED	REDINGOTE	REDOS	REDROOT	REDUX
REDEFINES	REDIP	REDOUBLE	REDROOTS	REDWARE
REDEFY	REDIPPED	REDOUBLED	REDROVE	REDWARES
REDEFYING	REDIPPING	REDOUBLER	REDRY	REDWATER
REDELESS	REDIPS	REDOUBLES	REDRYING	REDWATERS
REDELIVER	REDIPT	REDOUBT	REDS	REDWING
REDEMAND	REDIRECT	REDOUBTED	REDSEAR	REDWINGS
REDEMANDS	REDIRECTS	REDOUBTS	REDSHANK	REDWOOD
REDENIED	REDISCUSS	REDOUND	REDSHANKS	REDWOODS
REDENIES	REDISPLAY	REDOUNDED	REDSHARF	REDYE
REDENY	REDISPOSE	REDOUNDS	REDSHIFT	REDYED
REDENYING	REDISTIL	REDOUT	REDSHIFTS	REDYEING
REDEPLOY	REDISTILL	REDOUTS	REDSHIRE	REDYES
REDEPLOYS	REDISTILS	REDOWA	REDSHIRT	REE
REDEPOSIT	REDIVIDE	REDOWAS	REDSHIRTS	REEARN
REDES	REDIVIDED	REDOX	REDSHORT	REEARNED
REDESCEND	REDIVIDES	REDOXES	REDSKIN	REEARNING
REDESIGN	REDIVIVUS	REDPOLL	REDSKINS	REEARNS
REDESIGNS	REDIVORCE	REDPOLLS	REDSTART	REEBOK
REDEVELOP	REDLEG	REDRAFT	REDSTARTS	REEBOKS
REDEYE	REDLEGS	REDRAFTED	REDSTREAK	REECH
REDEYES	REDLINE	REDRAFTS	REDTAIL	REECHED

REECHES	REEFABLE	REEMITS	REEVES	REFELLED
REECHIE	REEFED	REEMITTED	REEVESHIP	REFELLING
REECHIER	REEFER	REEMPLOY	REEVING	REFELS
REECHIEST	REEFERS	REEMPLOYS	REEVOKE	REFELT
REECHING	REEFIER	REEN	REEVOKED	REFENCE
REECHO	REEFIEST	REENACT	REEVOKES	REFENCED
REECHOED	REEFING	REENACTED	REEVOKING	REFENCES
REECHOES	REEFINGS	REENACTOR	REEXAMINE	REFENCING
REECHOING	REEFPOINT	REENACTS	REEXECUTE	REFER
REECHY	REEFS	REENDOW	REEXHIBIT	REFERABLE
REED	REEFY	REENDOWED	REEXPEL	REFEREE
REEDBED	REEJECT	REENDOWS	REEXPELS	REFEREED
REEDBEDS	REEJECTED	REENFORCE	REEXPLAIN	REFEREES
REEDBIRD	REEJECTS	REENGAGE	REEXPLORE	REFERENCE
REEDBIRDS	REEK	REENGAGED	REEXPORT	REFERENDA
REEDBUCK	REEKED	REENGAGES	REEXPORTS	REFERENT
REEDBUCKS	REEKER	REENGRAVE	REEXPOSE	REFERENTS
REEDE	REEKERS	REENJOY	REEXPOSED	REFERRAL
REEDED	REEKIE	REENJOYED	REEXPOSES	REFERRALS
REEDEN	REEKIER	REENJOYS	REEXPRESS	REFERRED
REEDER	REEKIEST	REENLARGE	REF	REFERRER
REEDERS	REEKING	REENLIST	REFACE	REFERRERS
REEDES	REEKINGLY	REENLISTS	REFACED	REFERRING
REEDIER	REEKS	REENROLL	REFACES	REFERS
REEDIEST	REEKY	REENROLLS	REFACING	REFFED
REEDIFIED	REEL	REENS	REFALL	REFFING
REEDIFIES	REELABLE	REENSLAVE	REFALLEN	REFFINGS
REEDIFY	REELECT	REENTER	REFALLING	REFFO
REEDILY	REELECTED	REENTERED	REFALLS	REFFOS
REEDINESS	REELECTS	REENTERS	REFASHION	REFI
REEDING	REELED	REENTRANT	REFASTEN	REFIGHT
REEDINGS	REELER	REENTRIES	REFASTENS	REFIGHTS
REEDIT	REELERS	REENTRY	REFECT	REFIGURE
REEDITED	REELEVATE	REEQUIP	REFECTED	REFIGURED
REEDITING	REELING	REEQUIPS	REFECTING	REFIGURES
REEDITION	REELINGLY	REERECT	REFECTION	REFILE
REEDITS	REELINGS	REERECTED	REFECTIVE	REFILED
REEDLIKE	REELMAN	REERECTS	REFECTORY	REFILES
REEDLING	REELMEN	REES	REFECTS	REFILING
REEDLINGS	REELS	REEST	REFED	REFILL
REEDMAN	REEMBARK	REESTED	REFEED	REFILLED
REEDMEN	REEMBARKS	REESTIER	REFEEDING	REFILLING
REEDS	REEMBODY	REESTIEST	REFEEDS	REFILLS
REEDSTOP	REEMBRACE	REESTING	REFEEL	REFILM
REEDSTOPS	REEMERGE	REESTS	REFEELING	REFILMED
REEDUCATE	REEMERGED	REESTY	REFEELS	REFILMING
REEDY	REEMERGES	REEVE	REFEL	REFILMS
REEF	REEMIT	REEVED	REFELL	REFILTER

R

REFILTERS	REFLEXES	REFORMATE	REFUEL	REFUTES
REFINABLE	REFLEXING	REFORMATS	REFUELED	REFUTING
REFINANCE	REFLEXION	REFORMED	REFUELING	REG
REFIND	REFLEXIVE	REFORMER	REFUELLED	REGAIN
REFINDING	REFLEXLY	REFORMERS	REFUELS	REGAINED
REFINDS	REFLIES	REFORMING	REFUGE	REGAINER
REFINE	REFLOAT	REFORMISM	REFUGED	REGAINERS
REFINED	REFLOATED	REFORMIST	REFUGEE	REGAINING
REFINEDLY	REFLOATS	REFORMS	REFUGEES	REGAINS
REFINER	REFLOOD	REFORTIFY	REFUGES	REGAL
REFINERS	REFLOODED	REFOUGHT	REFUGIA	REGALE
REFINERY	REFLOODS	REFOUND	REFUGING	REGALED
REFINES	REFLOW	REFOUNDED	REFUGIUM	REGALER
REFINING	REFLOWED	REFOUNDER	REFULGENT	REGALERS
REFININGS	REFLOWER	REFOUNDS	REFUND	REGALES
REFINISH	REFLOWERS	REFRACT	REFUNDED	REGALIA
REFIRE	REFLOWING	REFRACTED	REFUNDER	REGALIAN
REFIRED	REFLOWN	REFRACTOR	REFUNDERS	REGALIAS
REFIRES	REFLOWS	REFRACTS	REFUNDING	REGALING
REFIRING	REFLUENCE	REFRAIN	REFUNDS	REGALISM
REFIS	REFLUENT	REFRAINED	REFURB	REGALISMS
REFIT	REFLUX	REFRAINER	REFURBED	REGALIST
REFITMENT	REFLUXED	REFRAINS	REFURBING	REGALISTS
REFITS	REFLUXES	REFRAME	REFURBISH	REGALITY
REFITTED	REFLUXING	REFRAMED	REFURBS	REGALLY
REFITTING	REFLY	REFRAMES	REFURNISH	REGALNESS
REFIX	REFLYING	REFRAMING	REFUSABLE	REGALS
REFIXED	REFOCUS	REFREEZE	REFUSAL	REGAR
REFIXES	REFOCUSED	REFREEZES	REFUSALS	REGARD
REFIXING	REFOCUSES	REFRESH	REFUSE	REGARDANT
REFLAG	REFOLD	REFRESHED	REFUSED	REGARDED
REFLAGGED	REFOLDED	REFRESHEN	REFUSENIK	REGARDER
REFLAGS	REFOLDING	REFRESHER	REFUSER	REGARDERS
REFLATE	REFOLDS	REFRESHES	REFUSERS	REGARDFUL
REFLATED	REFOOT	REFRIED	REFUSES	REGARDING
REFLATES	REFOOTED	REFRIES	REFUSING	REGARDS
REFLATING	REFOOTING	REFRINGE	REFUSION	REGARS
REFLATION	REFOOTS	REFRINGED	REFUSIONS	REGATHER
REFLECT	REFOREST	REFRINGES	REFUSNIK	REGATHERS
REFLECTED	REFORESTS	REFRONT	REFUSNIKS	REGATTA
REFLECTER	REFORGE	REFRONTED	REFUTABLE	REGATTAS
REFLECTOR	REFORGED	REFRONTS	REFUTABLY	REGAUGE
REFLECTS	REFORGES	REFROZE	REFUTAL	REGAUGED
REFLET	REFORGING	REFROZEN	REFUTALS	REGAUGES
REFLETS	REFORM	REFRY	REFUTE	REGAUGING
REFLEW	REFORMADE	REFRYING	REFUTED	REGAVE
REFLEX	REFORMADO	REFS	REFUTER	REGEAR
REFLEXED	REFORMAT	REFT	REFUTERS	REGEARED

REGEARING	REGINAS	REGORGES	REGROOVE	REHANDLE
REGEARS	REGION	REGORGING	REGROOVED	REHANDLED
REGELATE	REGIONAL	REGOS	REGROOVES	REHANDLES
REGELATED	REGIONALS	REGOSOL	REGROUND	REHANG
REGELATES	REGIONARY	REGOSOLS	REGROUP	REHANGED
REGENCE	REGIONS	REGRADE	REGROUPED	REHANGING
REGENCES	REGISSEUR	REGRADED	REGROUPS	REHANGS
REGENCIES	REGISTER	REGRADES	REGROW	REHARDEN
REGENCY	REGISTERS	REGRADING	REGROWING	REHARDENS
REGENT	REGISTRAR	REGRAFT	REGROWN	REHASH
REGENTAL	REGISTRY	REGRAFTED	REGROWS	REHASHED
REGENTS	REGIUS	REGRAFTS	REGROWTH	REHASHES
REGES	REGIVE	REGRANT	REGROWTHS	REHASHING
REGEST	REGIVEN	REGRANTED	REGS	REHEAR
REGESTED	REGIVES	REGRANTS	REGUERDON	REHEARD
REGESTING	REGIVING	REGRATE	REGULA	REHEARING
REGESTS	REGLAZE	REGRATED	REGULABLE	REHEARS
REGGAE	REGLAZED	REGRATER	REGULAE	REHEARSAL
REGGAES	REGLAZES	REGRATERS	REGULAR	REHEARSE
REGGAETON	REGLAZING	REGRATES	REGULARLY	REHEARSED
REGGO	REGLET	REGRATING	REGULARS	REHEARSER
REGGOS	REGLETS	REGRATOR	REGULATE	REHEARSES
REGICIDAL	REGLORIFY	REGRATORS	REGULATED	REHEAT
REGICIDE	REGLOSS	REGREDE	REGULATES	REHEATED
REGICIDES	REGLOSSED	REGREDED	REGULATOR	REHEATER
REGIE	REGLOSSES	REGREDES	REGULI	REHEATERS
REGIES	REGLOW	REGREDING	REGULINE	REHEATING
REGIFT	REGLOWED	REGREEN	REGULISE	REHEATS
REGIFTED	REGLOWING	REGREENED	REGULISED	REHEEL
REGIFTER	REGLOWS	REGREENS	REGULISES	REHEELED
REGIFTERS	REGLUE	REGREET	REGULIZE	REHEELING
REGIFTING	REGLUED	REGREETED	REGULIZED	REHEELS
REGIFTS	REGLUES	REGREETS	REGULIZES	REHEM
REGILD	REGLUING	REGRESS	REGULO	REHEMMED
REGILDED	REGMA	REGRESSED	REGULOS	REHEMMING
REGILDING	REGMAKER	REGRESSES	REGULUS	REHEMS
REGILDS	REGMAKERS	REGRESSOR	REGULUSES	REHINGE
REGILT	REGMATA	REGRET	REGUR	REHINGED
REGIME	REGNA	REGRETFUL	REGURS	REHINGES
REGIMEN	REGNAL	REGRETS	REH	REHINGING
REGIMENS	REGNANCY	REGRETTED	REHAB	REHIRE
REGIMENT	REGNANT	REGRETTER	REHABBED	REHIRED
REGIMENTS	REGNUM	REGREW	REHABBER	REHIRES
REGIMES	REGO	REGRIND	REHABBERS	REHIRING
REGIMINAL	REGOLITH	REGRINDS	REHABBING	REHOBOAM
REGINA	REGOLITHS	REGROOM	REHABS	REHOBOAMS
REGINAE	REGORGE	REGROOMED	REHAMMER	REHOME
REGINAL	REGORGED	REGROOMS	REHAMMERS	REHOMED

R

REHOMES	REINCITED	REINSMEN	REITERATE	REJOURNS
REHOMING	REINCITES	REINSPECT	REITERED	REJUDGE
REHOMINGS	REINCUR	REINSPIRE	REITERING	REJUDGED
REHOUSE	REINCURS	REINSTAL	REITERS	REJUDGES
REHOUSED	REINDEER	REINSTALL	REIVE	REJUDGING
REHOUSES	REINDEERS	REINSTALS	REIVED	REJUGGLE
REHOUSING	REINDEX	REINSTATE	REIVER	REJUGGLED
REHS	REINDEXED	REINSURE	REIVERS	REJUGGLES
REHUNG	REINDEXES	REINSURED	REIVES	REJUSTIFY
REHYDRATE	REINDICT	REINSURER	REIVING	REKE
REI	REINDICTS	REINSURES	REIVINGS	REKED
REIF	REINDUCE	REINTER	REJACKET	REKES
REIFIED	REINDUCED	REINTERS	REJACKETS	REKEY
REIFIER	REINDUCES	REINVADE	REJECT	REKEYED
REIFIERS	REINDUCT	REINVADED	REJECTED	REKEYING
REIFIES	REINDUCTS	REINVADES	REJECTEE	REKEYS
REIFS	REINED	REINVENT	REJECTEES	REKINDLE
REIFY	REINETTE	REINVENTS	REJECTER	REKINDLED
REIFYING	REINETTES	REINVEST	REJECTERS	REKINDLES
REIGN	REINFECT	REINVESTS	REJECTING	REKING
REIGNED	REINFECTS	REINVITE	REJECTION	REKNIT
REIGNING	REINFLAME	REINVITED	REJECTIVE	REKNITS
REIGNITE	REINFLATE	REINVITES	REJECTOR	REKNITTED
REIGNITED	REINFORCE	REINVOKE	REJECTORS	REKNOT
REIGNITES	REINFORM	REINVOKED	REJECTS	REKNOTS
REIGNS	REINFORMS	REINVOKES	REJIG	REKNOTTED
REIK	REINFUND	REINVOLVE	REJIGGED	RELABEL
REIKI	REINFUNDS	REIRD	REJIGGER	RELABELED
REIKIS	REINFUSE	REIRDS	REJIGGERS	RELABELS
REIKS	REINFUSED	REIS	REJIGGING	RELACE
REILLUME	REINFUSES	REISES	REJIGS	RELACED
REILLUMED	REINHABIT	REISHI	REJOICE	RELACES
REILLUMES	REINING	REISHIS	REJOICED	RELACHE
REIMAGE	REINJECT	REISSUE	REJOICER	RELACHES
REIMAGED	REINJECTS	REISSUED	REJOICERS	RELACING
REIMAGES	REINJURE	REISSUER	REJOICES	RELACQUER
REIMAGINE	REINJURED	REISSUERS	REJOICING	RELAID
REIMAGING	REINJURES	REISSUES	REJOIN	RELAND
REIMBURSE	REINJURY	REISSUING	REJOINDER	RELANDED
REIMMERSE	REINK	REIST	REJOINED	RELANDING
REIMPLANT	REINKED	REISTAFEL	REJOINING	RELANDS
REIMPORT	REINKING	REISTED	REJOINS	RELAPSE
REIMPORTS	REINKS	REISTING	REJON	RELAPSED
REIMPOSE	REINLESS	REISTS	REJONEO	RELAPSER
REIMPOSED	REINS	REITBOK	REJONEOS	RELAPSERS
REIMPOSES	REINSERT	REITBOKS	REJONES	RELAPSES
REIN	REINSERTS	REITER	REJOURN	RELAPSING
REINCITE	REINSMAN	REITERANT	REJOURNED	RELATA

RELATABLE	RELEGABLE	RELIEVO	RELLISH	REMAILED
RELATE	RELEGATE	RELIEVOS	RELLISHED	REMAILER
RELATED	RELEGATED	RELIGHT	RELLISHES	REMAILERS
RELATEDLY	RELEGATES	RELIGHTED	RELLO	REMAILING
RELATER	RELEND	RELIGHTS	RELLOS	REMAILS
RELATERS	RELENDING	RELIGIEUX	RELOAD	REMAIN
RELATES	RELENDS	RELIGION	RELOADED	REMAINDER
RELATING	RELENT	RELIGIONS	RELOADER	REMAINED
RELATION	RELENTED	RELIGIOSE	RELOADERS	REMAINER
RELATIONS	RELENTING	RELIGIOSO	RELOADING	REMAINERS
RELATIVAL	RELENTS	RELIGIOUS	RELOADS	REMAINING
RELATIVE	RELET	RELINE	RELOAN	REMAINS
RELATIVES	RELETS	RELINED	RELOANED	REMAKE
RELATOR	RELETTER	RELINES	RELOANING	REMAKER
RELATORS	RELETTERS	RELINING	RELOANS	REMAKERS
RELATUM	RELETTING	RELINK	RELOCATE	REMAKES
RELAUNCH	RELEVANCE	RELINKED	RELOCATED	REMAKING
RELAUNDER	RELEVANCY	RELINKING	RELOCATEE	REMAN
RELAX	RELEVANT	RELINKS	RELOCATES	REMAND
RELAXABLE	RELEVE	RELIQUARY	RELOCATOR	REMANDED
RELAXANT	RELEVES	RELIQUE	RELOCK	REMANDING
RELAXANTS	RELIABLE	RELIQUEFY	RELOCKED	REMANDS
RELAXED	RELIABLES	RELIQUES	RELOCKING	REMANENCE
RELAXEDLY	RELIABLY	RELIQUIAE	RELOCKS	REMANENCY
RELAXER	RELIANCE	RELIQUIFY	RELOOK	REMANENT
RELAXERS	RELIANCES	RELISH	RELOOKED	REMANENTS
RELAXES	RELIANT	RELISHED	RELOOKING	REMANET
RELAXIN	RELIANTLY	RELISHES	RELOOKS	REMANETS
RELAXING	RELIC	RELISHING	RELUCENT	REMANIE
RELAXINS	RELICENSE	RELIST	RELUCT	REMANIES
RELAY	RELICS	RELISTED	RELUCTANT	REMANNED
RELAYED	RELICT	RELISTEN	RELUCTATE	REMANNING
RELAYING	RELICTION	RELISTENS	RELUCTED	REMANS
RELAYS	RELICTS	RELISTING	RELUCTING	REMAP
RELEARN	RELIDE	RELISTS	RELUCTS	REMAPPED
RELEARNED	RELIE	RELIT	RELUME	REMAPPING
RELEARNS	RELIED	RELIVABLE	RELUMED	REMAPS
RELEARNT	RELIEF	RELIVE	RELUMES	REMARK
RELEASE	RELIEFS	RELIVED	RELUMINE	REMARKED
RELEASED	RELIER	RELIVER	RELUMINED	REMARKER
RELEASEE	RELIERS	RELIVERED	RELUMINES	REMARKERS
RELEASEES	RELIES	RELIVERS	RELUMING	REMARKET
RELEASER	RELIEVE	RELIVES	RELY	REMARKETS
RELEASERS	RELIEVED	RELIVING	RELYING	REMARKING
RELEASES	RELIEVER	RELLENO	REM	REMARKS
RELEASING	RELIEVERS	RELLENOS	REMADE	REMARQUE
RELEASOR	RELIEVES	RELLIE	REMADES	REMARQUED
RELEASORS	RELIEVING	RELLIES	REMAIL	REMARQUES

R

REMARRIED	REMEND	REMITTEES	REMOULDS	RENDANG
REMARRIES	REMENDED	REMITTENT	REMOUNT	RENDANGS
REMARRY	REMENDING	REMITTER	REMOUNTED	RENDED
REMASTER	REMENDS	REMITTERS	REMOUNTS	RENDER
REMASTERS	REMENS	REMITTING	REMOVABLE	RENDERED
REMATCH	REMERCIED	REMITTOR	REMOVABLY	RENDERER
REMATCHED	REMERCIES	REMITTORS	REMOVAL	RENDERERS
REMATCHES	REMERCY	REMIX	REMOVALS	RENDERING
REMATE	REMERGE	REMIXED	REMOVE	RENDERS
REMATED	REMERGED	REMIXER	REMOVED	RENDIBLE
REMATES	REMERGES	REMIXERS	REMOVEDLY	RENDING
REMATING	REMERGING	REMIXES	REMOVER	RENDITION
REMBLAI	REMET	REMIXING	REMOVERS	RENDS
REMBLAIS	REMEX	REMIXT	REMOVES	RENDZINA
REMBLE	REMIGATE	REMIXTURE	REMOVING	RENDZINAS
REMBLED	REMIGATED	REMNANT	REMS	RENEAGUE
REMBLES	REMIGATES	REMNANTAL	REMUAGE	RENEAGUED
REMBLING	REMIGES	REMNANTS	REMUAGES	RENEAGUES
REMEAD	REMIGIAL	REMODEL	REMUDA	RENEGADE
REMEADED	REMIGRATE	REMODELED	REMUDAS	RENEGADED
REMEADING	REMIND	REMODELER	REMUEUR	RENEGADES
REMEADS	REMINDED	REMODELS	REMUEURS	RENEGADO
REMEASURE	REMINDER	REMODIFY	REMURMUR	RENEGADOS
REMEDE	REMINDERS	REMOISTEN	REMURMURS	RENEGATE
REMEDED	REMINDFUL	REMOLADE	REN	RENEGATES
REMEDES	REMINDING	REMOLADES	RENAGUE	RENEGE
REMEDIAL	REMINDS	REMOLD	RENAGUED	RENEGED
REMEDIAT	REMINISCE	REMOLDED	RENAGUES	RENEGER
REMEDIATE	REMINT	REMOLDING	RENAGUING	RENEGERS
REMEDIED	REMINTED	REMOLDS	RENAIL	RENEGES
REMEDIES	REMINTING	REMONTANT	RENAILED	RENEGING
REMEDING	REMINTS	REMONTOIR	RENAILING	RENEGUE
REMEDY	REMISE	REMORA	RENAILS	RENEGUED
REMEDYING	REMISED	REMORAS	RENAL	RENEGUER
REMEET	REMISES	REMORID	RENAME	RENEGUERS
REMEETING	REMISING	REMORSE	RENAMED	RENEGUES
REMEETS	REMISS	REMORSES	RENAMES	RENEGUING
REMEID	REMISSION	REMOTE	RENAMING	RENEST
REMEIDED	REMISSIVE	REMOTELY	RENASCENT	RENESTED
REMEIDING	REMISSLY	REMOTER	RENATURE	RENESTING
REMEIDS	REMISSORY	REMOTES	RENATURED	RENESTS
REMELT	REMIT	REMOTEST	RENATURES	RENEW
REMELTED	REMITMENT	REMOTION	RENAY	RENEWABLE
REMELTING	REMITS	REMOTIONS	RENAYED	RENEWABLY
REMELTS	REMITTAL	REMOUD	RENAYING	RENEWAL
REMEMBER	REMITTALS	REMOULADE	RENAYS	RENEWALS
REMEMBERS	REMITTED	REMOULD	RENCONTRE	RENEWED
REMEN	REMITTEE	REMOULDED	REND	RENEWEDLY

RENEWER	RENOTIFY	REOBTAINS	REPAINT	REPAYING
RENEWERS	RENOUNCE	REOCCUPY	REPAINTED	REPAYMENT
RENEWING	RENOUNCED	REOCCUR	REPAINTS	REPAYS
RENEWINGS	RENOUNCER	REOCCURS	REPAIR	REPEAL
RENEWS	RENOUNCES	REOFFEND	REPAIRED	REPEALED
RENEY	RENOVATE	REOFFENDS	REPAIRER	REPEALER
RENEYED	RENOVATED	REOFFER	REPAIRERS	REPEALERS
RENEYING	RENOVATES	REOFFERED	REPAIRING	REPEALING
RENEYS	RENOVATOR	REOFFERS	REPAIRMAN	REPEALS
RENFIERST	RENOWN	REOIL	REPAIRMEN	REPEAT
RENFORCE	RENOWNED	REOILED	REPAIRS	REPEATED
RENFORCED	RENOWNER	REOILING	REPAND	REPEATER
RENFORCES	RENOWNERS	REOILS	REPANDLY	REPEATERS
RENFORST	RENOWNING	REOPEN	REPANEL	REPEATING
RENGA	RENOWNS	REOPENED	REPANELED	REPEATS
RENGAS	RENS	REOPENER	REPANELS	REPECHAGE
RENIED	RENT	REOPENERS	REPAPER	REPEG
RENIES	RENTABLE	REOPENING	REPAPERED	REPEGGED
RENIFORM	RENTAL	REOPENS	REPAPERS	REPEGGING
RENIG	RENTALLER	REOPERATE	REPARABLE	REPEGS
RENIGGED	RENTALS	REOPPOSE	REPARABLY	REPEL
RENIGGING	RENTE	REOPPOSED	REPARK	REPELLANT
RENIGS	RENTED	REOPPOSES	REPARKED	REPELLED
RENIN	RENTER	REORDAIN	REPARKING	REPELLENT
RENINS	RENTERS	REORDAINS	REPARKS	REPELLER
RENITENCE	RENTES	REORDER	REPARTEE	REPELLERS
RENITENCY	RENTIER	REORDERED	REPARTEED	REPELLING
RENITENT	RENTIERS	REORDERS	REPARTEES	REPELS
RENK	RENTING	REORG	REPASS	REPENT
RENKER	RENTINGS	REORGED	REPASSAGE	REPENTANT
RENKEST	RENTS	REORGING	REPASSED	REPENTED
RENMINBI	RENUMBER	REORGS	REPASSES	REPENTER
RENMINBIS	RENUMBERS	REORIENT	REPASSING	REPENTERS
RENNASE	RENVERSE	REORIENTS	REPAST	REPENTING
RENNASES	RENVERSED	REOS	REPASTED	REPENTS
RENNE	RENVERSES	REOUTFIT	REPASTING	REPEOPLE
RENNED	RENVERST	REOUTFITS	REPASTS	REPEOPLED
RENNES	RENVOI	REOVIRUS	REPASTURE	REPEOPLES
RENNET	RENVOIS	REOXIDISE	REPATCH	REPERCUSS
RENNETS	RENVOY	REOXIDIZE	REPATCHED	REPEREPE
RENNIN	RENVOYS	REP	REPATCHES	REPEREPES
RENNING	RENY	REPACIFY	REPATTERN	REPERK
RENNINGS	RENYING	REPACK	REPAVE	REPERKED
RENNINS	REO	REPACKAGE	REPAVED	REPERKING
RENO	REOBJECT	REPACKED	REPAVES	REPERKS
RENOGRAM	REOBJECTS	REPACKING	REPAVING	REPERTORY
RENOGRAMS	REOBSERVE	REPACKS	REPAY	REPERUSAL
RENOS	REOBTAIN	REPAID	REPAYABLE	REPERUSE

REPERUSED	REPLEADS	REPOINTED	REPOUR	REPRISES
REPERUSES	REPLED	REPOINTS	REPOURED	REPRISING
REPETEND	REPLEDGE	REPOLISH	REPOURING	REPRIVE
REPETENDS	REPLEDGED	REPOLL	REPOURS	REPRIVED
REPHRASE	REPLEDGES	REPOLLED	REPOUSSE	REPRIVES
REPHRASED	REPLENISH	REPOLLING	REPOUSSES	REPRIVING
REPHRASES	REPLETE	REPOLLS	REPOWER	REPRIZE
REPIGMENT	REPLETED	REPOMAN	REPOWERED	REPRIZED
REPIN	REPLETELY	REPOMEN	REPOWERS	REPRIZES
REPINE	REPLETES	REPONE	REPP	REPRIZING
REPINED	REPLETING	REPONED	REPPED	REPRO
REPINER	REPLETION	REPONES	REPPING	REPROACH
REPINERS	REPLEVIED	REPONING	REPPINGS	REPROBACY
REPINES	REPLEVIES	REPORT	REPPS	REPROBATE
REPINING	REPLEVIN	REPORTAGE	REPREEVE	REPROBE
REPININGS	REPLEVINS	REPORTED	REPREEVED	REPROBED
REPINNED	REPLEVY	REPORTER	REPREEVES	REPROBES
REPINNING	REPLICA	REPORTERS	REPREHEND	REPROBING
REPINS	REPLICANT	REPORTING	REPRESENT	REPROCESS
REPIQUE	REPLICAS	REPORTS	REPRESS	REPRODUCE
REPIQUED	REPLICASE	REPOS	REPRESSED	REPROGRAM
REPIQUES	REPLICATE	REPOSAL	REPRESSER	REPROOF
REPIQUING	REPLICON	REPOSALL	REPRESSES	REPROOFED
REPLA	REPLICONS	REPOSALLS	REPRESSOR	REPROOFS
REPLACE	REPLIED	REPOSALS	REPRICE	REPROS
REPLACED	REPLIER	REPOSE	REPRICED	REPROVAL
REPLACER	REPLIERS	REPOSED	REPRICES	REPROVALS
REPLACERS	REPLIES	REPOSEDLY	REPRICING	REPROVE
REPLACES	REPLOT	REPOSEFUL	REPRIEFE	REPROVED
REPLACING	REPLOTS	REPOSER	REPRIEFES	REPROVER
REPLAN	REPLOTTED	REPOSERS	REPRIEVAL	REPROVERS
REPLANNED	REPLOUGH	REPOSES	REPRIEVE	REPROVES
REPLANS	REPLOUGHS	REPOSING	REPRIEVED	REPROVING
REPLANT	REPLOW	REPOSIT	REPRIEVER	REPRYVE
REPLANTED	REPLOWED	REPOSITED	REPRIEVES	REPRYVED
REPLANTS	REPLOWING	REPOSITOR	REPRIMAND	REPRYVES
REPLASTER	REPLOWS	REPOSITS	REPRIME	REPRYVING
REPLATE	REPLUM	REPOSSESS	REPRIMED	REPS
REPLATED	REPLUMB	REPOST	REPRIMES	REPTANT
REPLATES	REPLUMBED	REPOSTED	REPRIMING	REPTATION
REPLATING	REPLUMBS	REPOSTING	REPRINT	REPTILE
REPLAY	REPLUNGE	REPOSTS	REPRINTED	REPTILES
REPLAYED	REPLUNGED	REPOSURE	REPRINTER	REPTILIA
REPLAYING	REPLUNGES	REPOSURES	REPRINTS	REPTILIAN
REPLAYS	REPLY	REPOT	REPRISAL	REPTILIUM
REPLEAD	REPLYING	REPOTS	REPRISALS	REPTILOID
REPLEADED	REPO	REPOTTED	REPRISE	REPUBLIC
REPLEADER	REPOINT	REPOTTING	REPRISED	REPUBLICS

REPUBLISH	REQUESTED	RERAISED	REROOFED	RESCINDER
REPUDIATE	REQUESTER	RERAISES	REROOFING	RESCINDS
REPUGN	REQUESTOR	RERAISING	REROOFS	RESCORE
REPUGNANT	REQUESTS	RERAN	REROSE	RESCORED
REPUGNED	REQUICKEN	REREAD	REROUTE	RESCORES
REPUGNING	REQUIEM	REREADING	REROUTED	RESCORING
REPUGNS	REQUIEMS	REREADS	REROUTES	RESCREEN
REPULP	REQUIGHT	REREBRACE	REROUTING	RESCREENS
REPULPED	REQUIGHTS	RERECORD	RERUN	RESCRIPT
REPULPING	REQUIN	RERECORDS	RERUNNING	RESCRIPTS
REPULPS	REQUINS	REREDOS	RERUNS	RESCUABLE
REPULSE	REQUINTO	REREDOSES	RES	RESCUE
REPULSED	REQUINTOS	REREDOSSE	RESADDLE	RESCUED
REPULSER	REQUIRE	RERELEASE	RESADDLED	RESCUEE
REPULSERS	REQUIRED	REREMAI	RESADDLES	RESCUEES
REPULSES	REQUIRER	REREMAIS	RESAID	RESCUER
REPULSING	REQUIRERS	REREMICE	RESAIL	RESCUERS
REPULSION	REQUIRES	REREMIND	RESAILED	RESCUES
REPULSIVE	REQUIRING	REREMINDS	RESAILING	RESCUING
REPUMP	REQUISITE	REREMOUSE	RESAILS	RESCULPT
REPUMPED	REQUIT	RERENT	RESALABLE	RESCULPTS
REPUMPING	REQUITAL	RERENTED	RESALE	RESEAL
REPUMPS	REQUITALS	RERENTING	RESALES	RESEALED
REPUNIT	REQUITE	RERENTS	RESALGAR	RESEALING
REPUNITS	REQUITED	REREPEAT	RESALGARS	RESEALS
REPURE	REQUITER	REREPEATS	RESALUTE	RESEARCH
REPURED	REQUITERS	REREVIEW	RESALUTED	RESEASON
REPURES	REQUITES	REREVIEWS	RESALUTES	RESEASONS
REPURIFY	REQUITING	REREVISE	RESAMPLE	RESEAT
REPURING	REQUITS	REREVISED	RESAMPLED	RESEATED
REPURPOSE	REQUITTED	REREVISES	RESAMPLES	RESEATING
REPURSUE	REQUOTE	REREWARD	RESAT	RESEATS
REPURSUED	REQUOTED	REREWARDS	RESAW	RESEAU
REPURSUES	REQUOTES	RERIG	RESAWED	RESEAUS
REPUTABLE	REQUOTING	RERIGGED	RESAWING	RESEAUX
REPUTABLY	REQUOYLE	RERIGGING	RESAWN	RESECT
REPUTE	REQUOYLED	RERIGS	RESAWS	RESECTED
REPUTED	REQUOYLES	RERISE	RESAY	RESECTING
REPUTEDLY	RERACK	RERISEN	RESAYING	RESECTION
REPUTES	RERACKED	RERISES	RESAYS	RESECTS
REPUTING	RERACKING	RERISING	RESCALE	RESECURE
REPUTINGS	RERACKS	REROLL	RESCALED	RESECURED
REQUALIFY	RERADIATE	REROLLED	RESCALES	RESECURES
REQUERE	RERAIL	REROLLER	RESCALING	RESEDA
REQUERED	RERAILED	REROLLERS	RESCHOOL	RESEDAS
REQUERES	RERAILING	REROLLING	RESCHOOLS	RESEE
REQUERING	RERAILS	REROLLS	RESCIND	RESEED
REQUEST	RERAISE	REROOF	RESCINDED	RESEEDED

RESEEDING	RESETTED	RESHOWING	RESILINS	RESITUATE
RESEEDS	RESETTER	RESHOWN	RESILVER	RESIZABLE
RESEEING	RESETTERS	RESHOWS	RESILVERS	RESIZE
RESEEK	RESETTING	RESHUFFLE	RESIN	RESIZED
RESEEKING	RESETTLE	RESIANCE	RESINATA	RESIZES
RESEEKS	RESETTLED	RESIANCES	RESINATAS	RESIZING
RESEEN	RESETTLES	RESIANT	RESINATE	RESKETCH
RESEES	RESEW	RESIANTS	RESINATED	RESKEW
RESEIZE	RESEWED	RESID	RESINATES	RESKEWED
RESEIZED	RESEWING	RESIDE	RESINED	RESKEWING
RESEIZES	RESEWN	RESIDED	RESINER	RESKEWS
RESEIZING	RESEWS	RESIDENCE	RESINERS	RESKILL
RESEIZURE	RESH	RESIDENCY	RESINIER	RESKILLED
RESELECT	RESHAPE	RESIDENT	RESINIEST	RESKILLS
RESELECTS	RESHAPED	RESIDENTS	RESINIFY	RESKIN
RESELL	RESHAPER	RESIDER	RESINING	RESKINNED
RESELLER	RESHAPERS	RESIDERS	RESINISE	RESKINS
RESELLERS	RESHAPES	RESIDES	RESINISED	RESKUE
RESELLING	RESHAPING	RESIDING	RESINISES	RESKUED
RESELLS	RESHARPEN	RESIDS	RESINIZE	RESKUES
RESEMBLE	RESHAVE	RESIDUA	RESINIZED	RESKUING
RESEMBLED	RESHAVED	RESIDUAL	RESINIZES	RESLATE
RESEMBLER	RESHAVEN	RESIDUALS	RESINLIKE	RESLATED
RESEMBLES	RESHAVES	RESIDUARY	RESINOID	RESLATES
RESEND	RESHAVING	RESIDUE	RESINOIDS	RESLATING
RESENDING	RESHES	RESIDUES	RESINOSES	RESMELT
RESENDS	RESHINE	RESIDUOUS	RESINOSIS	RESMELTED
RESENT	RESHINED	RESIDUUM	RESINOUS	RESMELTS
RESENTED	RESHINES	RESIDUUMS	RESINS	RESMOOTH
RESENTER	RESHINGLE	RESIFT	RESINY	RESMOOTHS
RESENTERS	RESHINING	RESIFTED	RESIST	RESNATRON
RESENTFUL	RESHIP	RESIFTING	RESISTANT	RESOAK
RESENTING	RESHIPPED	RESIFTS	RESISTED	RESOAKED
RESENTIVE	RESHIPPER	RESIGHT	RESISTENT	RESOAKING
RESENTS	RESHIPS	RESIGHTED	RESISTER	RESOAKS
RESERPINE	RESHOD	RESIGHTS	RESISTERS	RESOD
RESERVE	RESHOE	RESIGN	RESISTING	RESODDED
RESERVED	RESHOED	RESIGNED	RESISTIVE	RESODDING
RESERVER	RESHOEING	RESIGNER	RESISTOR	RESODS
RESERVERS	RESHOES	RESIGNERS	RESISTORS	RESOFTEN
RESERVES	RESHONE	RESIGNING	RESISTS	RESOFTENS
RESERVICE	RESHOOT	RESIGNS	RESIT	RESOJET
RESERVING	RESHOOTS	RESILE	RESITE	RESOJETS
RESERVIST	RESHOT	RESILED	RESITED	RESOLD
RESERVOIR	RESHOW	RESILES	RESITES	RESOLDER
RESES	RESHOWED	RESILIENT	RESITING	RESOLDERS
RESET	RESHOWER	RESILIN	RESITS	RESOLE
RESETS	RESHOWERS	RESILING	RESITTING	RESOLED

RESOLES
RESOLING
RESOLUBLE
RESOLUTE
RESOLUTER
RESOLUTES
RESOLVE
RESOLVED
RESOLVENT
RESOLVER
RESOLVERS
RESOLVES
RESOLVING
RESONANCE
RESONANT
RESONANTS
RESONATE
RESONATED
RESONATES
RESONATOR
RESORB
RESORBED
RESORBENT
RESORBING
RESORBS
RESORCIN
RESORCINS
RESORT
RESORTED
RESORTER
RESORTERS
RESORTING
RESORTS
RESOUGHT
RESOUND
RESOUNDED
RESOUNDS
RESOURCE
RESOURCED
RESOURCES
RESOW
RESOWED
RESOWING
RESOWN
RESOWS
RESPACE
RESPACED
RESPACES

RESPACING
RESPADE
RESPADED
RESPADES
RESPADING
RESPEAK
RESPEAKS
RESPECIFY
RESPECT
RESPECTED
RESPECTER
RESPECTS
RESPELL
RESPELLED
RESPELLS
RESPELT
RESPIRE
RESPIRED
RESPIRES
RESPIRING
RESPITE
RESPITED
RESPITES
RESPITING
RESPLEND
RESPLENDS
RESPLICE
RESPLICED
RESPLICES
RESPLIT
RESPLITS
RESPOKE
RESPOKEN
RESPOND
RESPONDED
RESPONDER
RESPONDS
RESPONSA
RESPONSE
RESPONSER
RESPONSES
RESPONSOR
RESPONSUM
RESPOOL
RESPOOLED
RESPOOLS
RESPOT
RESPOTS

RESPOTTED
RESPRANG
RESPRAY
RESPRAYED
RESPRAYS
RESPREAD
RESPREADS
RESPRING
RESPRINGS
RESPROUT
RESPROUTS
RESPRUNG
RESSALDAR
REST
RESTABLE
RESTABLED
RESTABLES
RESTACK
RESTACKED
RESTACKS
RESTAFF
RESTAFFED
RESTAFFS
RESTAGE
RESTAGED
RESTAGES
RESTAGING
RESTAMP
RESTAMPED
RESTAMPS
RESTART
RESTARTED
RESTARTER
RESTARTS
RESTATE
RESTATED
RESTATES
RESTATING
RESTATION
RESTED
RESTEM
RESTEMMED
RESTEMS
RESTER
RESTERS
RESTFUL
RESTFULLY
RESTIER

RESTIEST
RESTIFF
RESTIFORM
RESTING
RESTINGS
RESTITCH
RESTITUTE
RESTIVE
RESTIVELY
RESTLESS
RESTO
RESTOCK
RESTOCKED
RESTOCKS
RESTOKE
RESTOKED
RESTOKES
RESTOKING
RESTORAL
RESTORALS
RESTORE
RESTORED
RESTORER
RESTORERS
RESTORES
RESTORING
RESTOS
RESTRAIN
RESTRAINS
RESTRAINT
RESTRESS
RESTRETCH
RESTRICT
RESTRICTS
RESTRIKE
RESTRIKES
RESTRING
RESTRINGE
RESTRINGS
RESTRIVE
RESTRIVEN
RESTRIVES
RESTROOM
RESTROOMS
RESTROVE
RESTRUCK
RESTRUNG
RESTS

RESTUDIED
RESTUDIES
RESTUDY
RESTUFF
RESTUFFED
RESTUFFS
RESTUMP
RESTUMPED
RESTUMPS
RESTY
RESTYLE
RESTYLED
RESTYLES
RESTYLING
RESUBJECT
RESUBMIT
RESUBMITS
RESULT
RESULTANT
RESULTED
RESULTFUL
RESULTING
RESULTS
RESUMABLE
RESUME
RESUMED
RESUMER
RESUMERS
RESUMES
RESUMING
RESUMMON
RESUMMONS
RESUPINE
RESUPPLY
RESURFACE
RESURGE
RESURGED
RESURGENT
RESURGES
RESURGING
RESURRECT
RESURVEY
RESURVEYS
RESUS
RESUSES
RESUSPEND
RESUSSES
RESWALLOW

R

RET	RETARDANT	RETESTED	RETINENES	RETORT
RETABLE	RETARDATE	RETESTIFY	RETINES	RETORTED
RETABLES	RETARDED	RETESTING	RETINITE	RETORTER
RETABLO	RETARDER	RETESTS	RETINITES	RETORTERS
RETABLOS	RETARDERS	RETEXTURE	RETINITIS	RETORTING
RETACK	RETARDING	RETHINK	RETINOIC	RETORTION
RETACKED	RETARDS	RETHINKER	RETINOID	RETORTIVE
RETACKING	RETARGET	RETHINKS	RETINOIDS	RETORTS
RETACKLE	RETARGETS	RETHOUGHT	RETINOL	RETOTAL
RETACKLED	RETASTE	RETHREAD	RETINOLS	RETOTALED
RETACKLES	RETASTED	RETHREADS	RETINT	RETOTALS
RETACKS	RETASTES	RETIA	RETINTED	RETOUCH
RETAG	RETASTING	RETIAL	RETINTING	RETOUCHED
RETAGGED	RETAUGHT	RETIARII	RETINTS	RETOUCHER
RETAGGING	RETAX	RETIARIUS	RETINUE	RETOUCHES
RETAGS	RETAXED	RETIARY	RETINUED	RETOUR
RETAIL	RETAXES	RETICELLA	RETINUES	RETOURED
RETAILED	RETAXING	RETICENCE	RETINULA	RETOURING
RETAILER	RETCH	RETICENCY	RETINULAE	RETOURS
RETAILERS	RETCHED	RETICENT	RETINULAR	RETOX
RETAILING	RETCHES	RETICLE	RETINULAS	RETOXED
RETAILOR	RETCHING	RETICLES	RETIRACY	RETOXES
RETAILORS	RETCHINGS	RETICULA	RETIRAL	RETOXING
RETAILS	RETCHLESS	RETICULAR	RETIRALS	RETRACE
RETAIN	RETE	RETICULE	RETIRANT	RETRACED
RETAINED	RETEACH	RETICULES	RETIRANTS	RETRACER
RETAINER	RETEACHES	RETICULUM	RETIRE	RETRACERS
RETAINERS	RETEAM	RETIE	RETIRED	RETRACES
RETAINING	RETEAMED	RETIED	RETIREDLY	RETRACING
RETAINS	RETEAMING	RETIEING	RETIREE	RETRACK
RETAKE	RETEAMS	RETIES	RETIREES	RETRACKED
RETAKEN	RETEAR	RETIFORM	RETIRER	RETRACKS
RETAKER	RETEARING	RETIGHTEN	RETIRERS	RETRACT
RETAKERS	RETEARS	RETILE	RETIRES	RETRACTED
RETAKES	RETELL	RETILED	RETIRING	RETRACTOR
RETAKING	RETELLER	RETILES	RETITLE	RETRACTS
RETAKINGS	RETELLERS	RETILING	RETITLED	RETRAICT
RETALIATE	RETELLING	RETIME	RETITLES	RETRAICTS
RETALLIED	RETELLS	RETIMED	RETITLING	RETRAIN
RETALLIES	RETEM	RETIMES	RETOLD	RETRAINED
RETALLY	RETEMPER	RETIMING	RETOOK	RETRAINEE
RETAMA	RETEMPERS	RETINA	RETOOL	RETRAINS
RETAMAS	RETEMS	RETINAE	RETOOLED	RETRAIT
RETAPE	RETENE	RETINAL	RETOOLING	RETRAITE
RETAPED	RETENES	RETINALS	RETOOLS	RETRAITES
RETAPES	RETENTION	RETINAS	RETORE	RETRAITS
RETAPING	RETENTIVE	RETINE	RETORN	RETRAITT
RETARD	RETEST	RETINENE	RETORSION	RETRAITTS

RETRAL	RETRY	REUNITE	REVEILLE	REVERIFY
RETRALLY	RETRYING	REUNITED	REVEILLES	REVERING
RETRATE	RETS	REUNITER	REVEL	REVERIST
RETRATED	RETSINA	REUNITERS	REVELATOR	REVERISTS
RETRATES	RETSINAS	REUNITES	REVELED	REVERS
RETRATING	RETTED	REUNITING	REVELER	REVERSAL
RETREAD	RETTERIES	REUPTAKE	REVELERS	REVERSALS
RETREADED	RETTERY	REUPTAKEN	REVELING	REVERSE
RETREADS	RETTING	REUPTAKES	REVELLED	REVERSED
RETREAT	RETUND	REUPTOOK	REVELLER	REVERSELY
RETREATED	RETUNDED	REURGE	REVELLERS	REVERSER
RETREATER	RETUNDING	REURGED	REVELLING	REVERSERS
RETREATS	RETUNDS	REURGES	REVELMENT	REVERSES
RETREE	RETUNE	REURGING	REVELRIES	REVERSI
RETREES	RETUNED	REUSABLE	REVELROUS	REVERSING
RETRENCH	RETUNES	REUSABLES	REVELRY	REVERSION
RETRIAL	RETUNING	REUSE	REVELS	REVERSIS
RETRIALS	RETURF	REUSED	REVENANT	REVERSO
RETRIBUTE	RETURFED	REUSES	REVENANTS	REVERSOS
RETRIED	RETURFING	REUSING	REVENGE	REVERT
RETRIES	RETURFS	REUTILISE	REVENGED	REVERTANT
RETRIEVAL	RETURN	REUTILIZE	REVENGER	REVERTED
RETRIEVE	RETURNED	REUTTER	REVENGERS	REVERTER
RETRIEVED	RETURNEE	REUTTERED	REVENGES	REVERTERS
RETRIEVER	RETURNEES	REUTTERS	REVENGING	REVERTING
RETRIEVES	RETURNER	REV	REVENGIVE	REVERTIVE
RETRIM	RETURNERS	REVALENTA	REVENUAL	REVERTS
RETRIMMED	RETURNIK	REVALUATE	REVENUE	REVERY
RETRIMS	RETURNIKS	REVALUE	REVENUED	REVEST
RETRO	RETURNING	REVALUED	REVENUER	REVESTED
RETROACT	RETURNS	REVALUES	REVENUERS	REVESTING
RETROACTS	RETUSE	REVALUING	REVENUES	REVESTRY
RETROCEDE	RETWEET	REVAMP	REVERABLE	REVESTS
RETROD	RETWEETED	REVAMPED	REVERB	REVET
RETRODDEN	RETWEETS	REVAMPER	REVERBED	REVETMENT
RETRODICT	RETWIST	REVAMPERS	REVERBING	REVETS
RETROFIRE	RETWISTED	REVAMPING	REVERBS	REVETTED
RETROFIT	RETWISTS	REVAMPS	REVERE	REVETTING
RETROFITS	RETYING	REVANCHE	REVERED	REVEUR
RETROFLEX	RETYPE	REVANCHES	REVERENCE	REVEURS
RETROJECT	RETYPED	REVARNISH	REVEREND	REVEUSE
RETRONYM	RETYPES	REVEAL	REVERENDS	REVEUSES
RETRONYMS	RETYPING	REVEALED	REVERENT	REVIBRATE
RETROPACK	REUNIFIED	REVEALER	REVERER	REVICTUAL
RETRORSE	REUNIFIES	REVEALERS	REVERERS	REVIE
RETROS	REUNIFY	REVEALING	REVERES	REVIED
RETROUSSE	REUNION	REVEALS	REVERIE	REVIES
RETROVERT	REUNIONS	REVEHENT	REVERIES	REVIEW

R

REVIEWAL	REVOICE	REWAN	REWIDENED	REWROUGHT
REVIEWALS	REVOICED	REWARD	REWIDENS	REWS
REVIEWED	REVOICES	REWARDED	REWILD	REWTH
REVIEWER	REVOICING	REWARDER	REWILDED	REWTHS
REVIEWERS	REVOKABLE	REWARDERS	REWILDING	REX
REVIEWING	REVOKABLY	REWARDFUL	REWILDS	REXES
REVIEWS	REVOKE	REWARDING	REWIN	REXINE
REVILE	REVOKED	REWARDS	REWIND	REXINES
REVILED	REVOKER	REWAREWA	REWINDED	REYNARD
REVILER	REVOKERS	REWAREWAS	REWINDER	REYNARDS
REVILERS	REVOKES	REWARM	REWINDERS	REZ
REVILES	REVOKING	REWARMED	REWINDING	REZERO
REVILING	REVOLT	REWARMING	REWINDS	REZEROED
REVILINGS	REVOLTED	REWARMS	REWINNING	REZEROES
REVIOLATE	REVOLTER	REWASH	REWINS	REZEROING
REVISABLE	REVOLTERS	REWASHED	REWIRABLE	REZEROS
REVISAL	REVOLTING	REWASHES	REWIRE	REZES
REVISALS	REVOLTS	REWASHING	REWIRED	REZONE
REVISE	REVOLUTE	REWATER	REWIRES	REZONED
REVISED	REVOLVE	REWATERED	REWIRING	REZONES
REVISER	REVOLVED	REWATERS	REWIRINGS	REZONING
REVISERS	REVOLVER	REWAX	REWOKE	REZONINGS
REVISES	REVOLVERS	REWAXED	REWOKEN	REZZES
REVISING	REVOLVES	REWAXES	REWON	RHABDOID
REVISION	REVOLVING	REWAXING	REWORD	RHABDOIDS
REVISIONS	REVOTE	REWEAR	REWORDED	RHABDOM
REVISIT	REVOTED	REWEARING	REWORDING	RHABDOMAL
REVISITED	REVOTES	REWEARS	REWORDS	RHABDOME
REVISITS	REVOTING	REWEAVE	REWORE	RHABDOMES
REVISOR	REVS	REWEAVED	REWORK	RHABDOMS
REVISORS	REVUE	REWEAVES	REWORKED	RHABDUS
REVISORY	REVUES	REWEAVING	REWORKING	RHABDUSES
REVIVABLE	REVUIST	REWED	REWORKS	RHACHIAL
REVIVABLY	REVUISTS	REWEDDED	REWORN	RHACHIDES
REVIVAL	REVULSED	REWEDDING	REWOUND	RHACHILLA
REVIVALS	REVULSION	REWEDS	REWOVE	RHACHIS
REVIVE	REVULSIVE	REWEIGH	REWOVEN	RHACHISES
REVIVED	REVVED	REWEIGHED	REWRAP	RHACHITIS
REVIVER	REVVING	REWEIGHS	REWRAPPED	RHAGADES
REVIVERS	REVYING	REWELD	REWRAPS	RHAMNOSE
REVIVES	REW	REWELDED	REWRAPT	RHAMNOSES
REVIVIFY	REWAKE	REWELDING	REWRITE	RHAMNUS
REVIVING	REWAKED	REWELDS	REWRITER	RHAMNUSES
REVIVINGS	REWAKEN	REWET	REWRITERS	RHAMPHOID
REVIVOR	REWAKENED	REWETS	REWRITES	RHANJA
REVIVORS	REWAKENS	REWETTED	REWRITING	RHANJAS
REVOCABLE	REWAKES	REWETTING	REWRITTEN	RHAPHAE
REVOCABLY	REWAKING	REWIDEN	REWROTE	RHAPHE

RHAPHES	RHEUM	RHIZOPUS	RHOTACISM	RHYTON
RHAPHIDE	RHEUMATIC	RHIZOTOMY	RHOTACIST	RHYTONS
RHAPHIDES	RHEUMATIZ	RHO	RHOTACIZE	RIA
RHAPHIS	RHEUMED	RHODAMIN	RHOTIC	RIAD
RHAPONTIC	RHEUMIC	RHODAMINE	RHOTICITY	RIADS
RHAPSODE	RHEUMIER	RHODAMINS	RHUBARB	RIAL
RHAPSODES	RHEUMIEST	RHODANATE	RHUBARBED	RIALS
RHAPSODIC	RHEUMS	RHODANIC	RHUBARBS	RIALTO
RHAPSODY	RHEUMY	RHODANISE	RHUBARBY	RIALTOS
RHATANIES	RHEXES	RHODANIZE	RHUMB	RIANCIES
RHATANY	RHEXIS	RHODIC	RHUMBA	RIANCY
RHEA	RHEXISES	RHODIE	RHUMBAED	RIANT
RHEAS	RHIES	RHODIES	RHUMBAING	RIANTLY
RHEBOK	RHIGOLENE	RHODINAL	RHUMBAS	RIAS
RHEBOKS	RHIME	RHODINALS	RHUMBS	RIATA
RHEMATIC	RHIMES	RHODIUM	RHUS	RIATAS
RHEME	RHINAL	RHODIUMS	RHUSES	RIB
RHEMES	RHINE	RHODOLITE	RHY	RIBA
RHENIUM	RHINES	RHODONITE	RHYME	RIBALD
RHENIUMS	RHINITIC	RHODOPSIN	RHYMED	RIBALDER
RHEOBASE	RHINITIS	RHODORA	RHYMELESS	RIBALDEST
RHEOBASES	RHINO	RHODORAS	RHYMER	RIBALDLY
RHEOBASIC	RHINOCERI	RHODOUS	RHYMERS	RIBALDRY
RHEOCHORD	RHINOLITH	RHODY	RHYMES	RIBALDS
RHEOCORD	RHINOLOGY	RHOEADINE	RHYMESTER	RIBAND
RHEOCORDS	RHINOS	RHOMB	RHYMING	RIBANDS
RHEOLOGIC	RHIPIDATE	RHOMBI	RHYMIST	RIBAS
RHEOLOGY	RHIPIDION	RHOMBIC	RHYMISTS	RIBATTUTA
RHEOMETER	RHIPIDIUM	RHOMBICAL	RHYNE	RIBAUD
RHEOMETRY	RHIZIC	RHOMBOI	RHYNES	RIBAUDRED
RHEOPHIL	RHIZINE	RHOMBOID	RHYOLITE	RIBAUDRY
RHEOPHILE	RHIZINES	RHOMBOIDS	RHYOLITES	RIBAUDS
RHEOSCOPE	RHIZOBIA	RHOMBOS	RHYOLITIC	RIBAVIRIN
RHEOSTAT	RHIZOBIAL	RHOMBS	RHYTA	RIBBAND
RHEOSTATS	RHIZOBIUM	RHOMBUS	RHYTHM	RIBBANDS
RHEOTAXES	RHIZOCARP	RHOMBUSES	RHYTHMAL	RIBBED
RHEOTAXIS	RHIZOCAUL	RHONCHAL	RHYTHMED	RIBBER
RHEOTOME	RHIZOID	RHONCHI	RHYTHMI	RIBBERS
RHEOTOMES	RHIZOIDAL	RHONCHIAL	RHYTHMIC	RIBBIE
RHEOTROPE	RHIZOIDS	RHONCHUS	RHYTHMICS	RIBBIER
RHESUS	RHIZOMA	RHONCUS	RHYTHMISE	RIBBIES
RHESUSES	RHIZOMATA	RHONCUSES	RHYTHMIST	RIBBIEST
RHETOR	RHIZOME	RHONE	RHYTHMIZE	RIBBING
RHETORIC	RHIZOMES	RHONES	RHYTHMS	RIBBINGS
RHETORICS	RHIZOMIC	RHOPALIC	RHYTHMUS	RIBBIT
RHETORISE	RHIZOPI	RHOPALISM	RHYTIDOME	RIBBITS
RHETORIZE	RHIZOPOD	RHOS	RHYTINA	RIBBON
RHETORS	RHIZOPODS	RHOTACISE	RHYTINAS	RIBBONED

RIBBONIER	RICERCAR	RICKEYS	RIDERED	RIEMS
RIBBONING	RICERCARE	RICKING	RIDERLESS	RIESLING
RIBBONRY	RICERCARI	RICKLE	RIDERS	RIESLINGS
RIBBONS	RICERCARS	RICKLES	RIDERSHIP	RIEVE
RIBBONY	RICERCATA	RICKLIER	RIDES	RIEVED
RIBBY	RICERS	RICKLIEST	RIDGE	RIEVER
RIBCAGE	RICES	RICKLY	RIDGEBACK	RIEVERS
RIBCAGES	RICEY	RICKRACK	RIDGED	RIEVES
RIBES	RICH	RICKRACKS	RIDGEL	RIEVING
RIBEYE	RICHED	RICKS	RIDGELIKE	RIF
RIBEYES	RICHEN	RICKSHA	RIDGELINE	RIFAMPIN
RIBGRASS	RICHENED	RICKSHAS	RIDGELING	RIFAMPINS
RIBIBE	RICHENING	RICKSHAW	RIDGELS	RIFAMYCIN
RIBIBES	RICHENS	RICKSHAWS	RIDGEPOLE	RIFE
RIBIBLE	RICHER	RICKSTAND	RIDGER	RIFELY
RIBIBLES	RICHES	RICKSTICK	RIDGERS	RIFENESS
RIBIER	RICHESSE	RICKYARD	RIDGES	RIFER
RIBIERS	RICHESSES	RICKYARDS	RIDGETOP	RIFEST
RIBLESS	RICHEST	RICOCHET	RIDGETOPS	RIFF
RIBLET	RICHING	RICOCHETS	RIDGETREE	RIFFAGE
RIBLETS	RICHLY	RICOTTA	RIDGEWAY	RIFFAGES
RIBLIKE	RICHNESS	RICOTTAS	RIDGEWAYS	RIFFED
RIBOSE	RICHT	RICRAC	RIDGIER	RIFFING
RIBOSES	RICHTED	RICRACS	RIDGIEST	RIFFLE
RIBOSOMAL	RICHTER	RICTAL	RIDGIL	RIFFLED
RIBOSOME	RICHTEST	RICTUS	RIDGILS	RIFFLER
RIBOSOMES	RICHTING	RICTUSES	RIDGING	RIFFLERS
RIBOZYMAL	RICHTS	RICY	RIDGINGS	RIFFLES
RIBOZYME	RICHWEED	RID	RIDGLING	RIFFLING
RIBOZYMES	RICHWEEDS	RIDABLE	RIDGLINGS	RIFFOLA
RIBS	RICIER	RIDDANCE	RIDGY	RIFFOLAS
RIBSTON	RICIEST	RIDDANCES	RIDIC	RIFFRAFF
RIBSTONE	RICIN	RIDDED	RIDICULE	RIFFRAFFS
RIBSTONES	RICING	RIDDEN	RIDICULED	RIFFS
RIBSTONS	RICINS	RIDDER	RIDICULER	RIFLE
RIBULOSE	RICINUS	RIDDERS	RIDICULES	RIFLEBIRD
RIBULOSES	RICINUSES	RIDDING	RIDING	RIFLED
RIBWORK	RICK	RIDDLE	RIDINGS	RIFLEMAN
RIBWORKS	RICKED	RIDDLED	RIDLEY	RIFLEMEN
RIBWORT	RICKER	RIDDLER	RIDLEYS	RIFLER
RIBWORTS	RICKERS	RIDDLERS	RIDOTTO	RIFLERIES
RICE	RICKET	RIDDLES	RIDOTTOS	RIFLERS
RICEBIRD	RICKETIER	RIDDLING	RIDS	RIFLERY
RICEBIRDS	RICKETILY	RIDDLINGS	RIEL	RIFLES
RICED	RICKETS	RIDE	RIELS	RIFLING
RICEFIELD	RICKETTY	RIDEABLE	RIEM	RIFLINGS
RICEGRASS	RICKETY	RIDENT	RIEMPIE	RIFLIP
RICER	RICKEY	RIDER	RIEMPIES	RIFLIPS

RIFS	RIGHTISTS	RIJSTAFEL	RIMMED	RINGETTES
RIFT	RIGHTLESS	RIKISHA	RIMMER	RINGGIT
RIFTE	RIGHTLY	RIKISHAS	RIMMERS	RINGGITS
RIFTED	RIGHTMOST	RIKISHI	RIMMING	RINGHALS
RIFTIER	RIGHTNESS	RIKSHAW	RIMMINGS	RINGING
RIFTIEST	RIGHTO	RIKSHAWS	RIMOSE	RINGINGLY
RIFTING	RIGHTS	RILE	RIMOSELY	RINGINGS
RIFTLESS	RIGHTSIZE	RILED	RIMOSITY	RINGLESS
RIFTS	RIGHTWARD	RILES	RIMOUS	RINGLET
RIFTY	RIGHTY	RILEY	RIMPLE	RINGLETED
RIG	RIGID	RILIER	RIMPLED	RINGLETS
RIGADOON	RIGIDER	RILIEST	RIMPLES	RINGLETY
RIGADOONS	RIGIDEST	RILIEVI	RIMPLING	RINGLIKE
RIGATONI	RIGIDIFY	RILIEVO	RIMROCK	RINGMAN
RIGATONIS	RIGIDISE	RILING	RIMROCKS	RINGMEN
RIGAUDON	RIGIDISED	RILL	RIMS	RINGNECK
RIGAUDONS	RIGIDISES	RILLE	RIMSHOT	RINGNECKS
RIGG	RIGIDITY	RILLED	RIMSHOTS	RINGS
RIGGALD	RIGIDIZE	RILLES	RIMU	RINGSIDE
RIGGALDS	RIGIDIZED	RILLET	RIMUS	RINGSIDER
RIGGED	RIGIDIZES	RILLETS	RIMY	RINGSIDES
RIGGER	RIGIDLY	RILLETTES	RIN	RINGSTAND
RIGGERS	RIGIDNESS	RILLING	RIND	RINGSTER
RIGGING	RIGIDS	RILLMARK	RINDED	RINGSTERS
RIGGINGS	RIGLIN	RILLMARKS	RINDIER	RINGTAIL
RIGGISH	RIGLING	RILLS	RINDIEST	RINGTAILS
RIGGS	RIGLINGS	RIM	RINDING	RINGTAW
RIGHT	RIGLINS	RIMA	RINDLESS	RINGTAWS
RIGHTABLE	RIGMAROLE	RIMAE	RINDS	RINGTONE
RIGHTABLY	RIGOL	RIMAYE	RINDY	RINGTONES
RIGHTED	RIGOLL	RIMAYES	RINE	RINGTOSS
RIGHTEN	RIGOLLS	RIME	RINES	RINGWAY
RIGHTENED	RIGOLS	RIMED	RING	RINGWAYS
RIGHTENS	RIGOR	RIMELESS	RINGBARK	RINGWISE
RIGHTEOUS	RIGORISM	RIMER	RINGBARKS	RINGWOMB
RIGHTER	RIGORISMS	RIMERS	RINGBIT	RINGWOMBS
RIGHTERS	RIGORIST	RIMES	RINGBITS	RINGWORK
RIGHTEST	RIGORISTS	RIMESTER	RINGBOLT	RINGWORKS
RIGHTFUL	RIGOROUS	RIMESTERS	RINGBOLTS	RINGWORM
RIGHTIER	RIGORS	RIMFIRE	RINGBONE	RINGWORMS
RIGHTIES	RIGOUR	RIMFIRES	RINGBONES	RINK
RIGHTIEST	RIGOURS	RIMIER	RINGDOVE	RINKED
RIGHTING	RIGOUT	RIMIEST	RINGDOVES	RINKHALS
RIGHTINGS	RIGOUTS	RIMINESS	RINGED	RINKING
RIGHTISH	RIGS	RIMING	RINGENT	RINKS
RIGHTISM	RIGSDALER	RIMLAND	RINGER	RINKSIDE
RIGHTISMS	RIGWIDDIE	RIMLANDS	RINGERS	RINKSIDES
RIGHTIST	RIGWOODIE	RIMLESS	RINGETTE	RINNING

RINS	RIPERS	RIPSTOP	RISSOLE	RIVALISE
RINSABLE	RIPES	RIPSTOPS	RISSOLES	RIVALISED
RINSE	RIPEST	RIPT	RISTRA	RIVALISES
RINSEABLE	RIPIENI	RIPTIDE	RISTRAS	RIVALITY
RINSED	RIPIENIST	RIPTIDES	RISTRETTO	RIVALIZE
RINSER	RIPIENO	RIRORIRO	RISUS	RIVALIZED
RINSERS	RIPIENOS	RIRORIROS	RISUSES	RIVALIZES
RINSES	RIPING	RISALDAR	RIT	RIVALLED
RINSIBLE	RIPOFF	RISALDARS	RITARD	RIVALLESS
RINSING	RIPOFFS	RISE	RITARDS	RIVALLING
RINSINGS	RIPOST	RISEN	RITE	RIVALRIES
RIOJA	RIPOSTE	RISER	RITELESS	RIVALROUS
RIOJAS	RIPOSTED	RISERS	RITENUTO	RIVALRY
RIOT	RIPOSTES	RISES	RITENUTOS	RIVALS
RIOTED	RIPOSTING	RISHI	RITES	RIVALSHIP
RIOTER	RIPOSTS	RISHIS	RITONAVIR	RIVAS
RIOTERS	RIPP	RISIBLE	RITORNEL	RIVE
RIOTING	RIPPABLE	RISIBLES	RITORNELL	RIVED
RIOTINGS	RIPPED	RISIBLY	RITORNELS	RIVEL
RIOTISE	RIPPER	RISING	RITS	RIVELLED
RIOTISES	RIPPERS	RISINGS	RITT	RIVELLING
RIOTIZE	RIPPIER	RISK	RITTED	RIVELS
RIOTIZES	RIPPIERS	RISKED	RITTER	RIVEN
RIOTOUS	RIPPING	RISKER	RITTERS	RIVER
RIOTOUSLY	RIPPINGLY	RISKERS	RITTING	RIVERAIN
RIOTRIES	RIPPINGS	RISKFUL	RITTS	RIVERAINS
RIOTRY	RIPPLE	RISKIER	RITUAL	RIVERBANK
RIOTS	RIPPLED	RISKIEST	RITUALISE	RIVERBED
RIP	RIPPLER	RISKILY	RITUALISM	RIVERBEDS
RIPARIAL	RIPPLERS	RISKINESS	RITUALIST	RIVERBOAT
RIPARIALS	RIPPLES	RISKING	RITUALIZE	RIVERED
RIPARIAN	RIPPLET	RISKLESS	RITUALLY	RIVERET
RIPARIANS	RIPPLETS	RISKS	RITUALS	RIVERETS
RIPCORD	RIPPLIER	RISKY	RITUXIMAB	RIVERHEAD
RIPCORDS	RIPPLIEST	RISOLUTO	RITZ	RIVERIER
RIPE	RIPPLING	RISORII	RITZES	RIVERIEST
RIPECK	RIPPLINGS	RISORIUS	RITZIER	RIVERINE
RIPECKS	RIPPLY	RISOTTO	RITZIEST	RIVERLESS
RIPED	RIPPS	RISOTTOS	RITZILY	RIVERLIKE
RIPELY	RIPRAP	RISP	RITZINESS	RIVERMAN
RIPEN	RIPRAPPED	RISPED	RITZY	RIVERMEN
RIPENED	RIPRAPS	RISPETTI	RIVA	RIVERS
RIPENER	RIPS	RISPETTO	RIVAGE	RIVERSIDE
RIPENERS	RIPSAW	RISPING	RIVAGES	RIVERWALK
RIPENESS	RIPSAWED	RISPINGS	RIVAL	RIVERWARD
RIPENING	RIPSAWING	RISPS	RIVALED	RIVERWAY
RIPENS	RIPSAWN	RISQUE	RIVALESS	RIVERWAYS
RIPER	RIPSAWS	RISQUES	RIVALING	RIVERWEED

RIVERY	ROACHING	ROARERS	ROBLE	ROCKED
RIVES	ROAD	ROARIE	ROBLES	ROCKER
RIVET	ROADBED	ROARIER	ROBOCALL	ROCKERIES
RIVETED	ROADBEDS	ROARIEST	ROBOCALLS	ROCKERS
RIVETER	ROADBLOCK	ROARING	ROBORANT	ROCKERY
RIVETERS	ROADCRAFT	ROARINGLY	ROBORANTS	ROCKET
RIVETING	ROADEO	ROARINGS	ROBOT	ROCKETED
RIVETINGS	ROADEOS	ROARMING	ROBOTIC	ROCKETEER
RIVETS	ROADHOG	ROARS	ROBOTICS	ROCKETER
RIVETTED	ROADHOGS	ROARY	ROBOTISE	ROCKETERS
RIVETTING	ROADHOUSE	ROAST	ROBOTISED	ROCKETING
RIVIERA	ROADIE	ROASTED	ROBOTISES	ROCKETRY
RIVIERAS	ROADIES	ROASTER	ROBOTISM	ROCKETS
RIVIERE	ROADING	ROASTERS	ROBOTISMS	ROCKFALL
RIVIERES	ROADINGS	ROASTIE	ROBOTIZE	ROCKFALLS
RIVING	ROADKILL	ROASTIES	ROBOTIZED	ROCKFISH
RIVLIN	ROADKILLS	ROASTING	ROBOTIZES	ROCKHOUND
RIVLINS	ROADLESS	ROASTINGS	ROBOTRIES	ROCKIER
RIVO	ROADMAN	ROASTS	ROBOTRY	ROCKIERS
RIVULET	ROADMEN	ROATE	ROBOTS	ROCKIEST
RIVULETS	ROADS	ROATED	ROBS	ROCKILY
RIVULOSE	ROADSHOW	ROATES	ROBURITE	ROCKINESS
RIVULUS	ROADSHOWS	ROATING	ROBURITES	ROCKING
RIVULUSES	ROADSIDE	ROB	ROBUST	ROCKINGLY
RIYAL	ROADSIDES	ROBALO	ROBUSTA	ROCKINGS
RIYALS	ROADSMAN	ROBALOS	ROBUSTAS	ROCKLAY
RIZ	ROADSMEN	ROBAND	ROBUSTER	ROCKLAYS
RIZA	ROADSTEAD	ROBANDS	ROBUSTEST	ROCKLESS
RIZARD	ROADSTER	ROBATA	ROBUSTLY	ROCKLIKE
RIZARDS	ROADSTERS	ROBATAS	ROC	ROCKLING
RIZAS	ROADWAY	ROBBED	ROCAILLE	ROCKLINGS
RIZZAR	ROADWAYS	ROBBER	ROCAILLES	ROCKOON
RIZZARED	ROADWORK	ROBBERIES	ROCAMBOLE	ROCKOONS
RIZZARING	ROADWORKS	ROBBERS	ROCH	ROCKROSE
RIZZARS	ROAM	ROBBERY	ROCHES	ROCKROSES
RIZZART	ROAMED	ROBBIN	ROCHET	ROCKS
RIZZARTS	ROAMER	ROBBING	ROCHETS	ROCKSHAFT
RIZZER	ROAMERS	ROBBINS	ROCK	ROCKSLIDE
RIZZFRED	ROAMING	ROBE	ROCKABIES	ROCKWATER
RIZZERING	ROAMINGS	ROBED	ROCKABLE	ROCKWEED
RIZZERS	ROAMS	ROBELIKE	ROCKABY	ROCKWEEDS
RIZZOR	ROAN	ROBES	ROCKABYE	ROCKWOOL
RIZZORED	ROANPIPE	ROBIN	ROCKABYES	ROCKWOOLS
RIZZORING	ROANPIPES	ROBING	ROCKAWAY	ROCKWORK
RIZZORS	ROANS	ROBINGS	ROCKAWAYS	ROCKWORKS
ROACH	ROAR	ROBINIA	ROCKBOUND	ROCKY
ROACHED	ROARED	ROBINIAS	ROCKBURST	ROCOCO
ROACHES	ROARER	ROBINS	ROCKCRESS	ROCOCOS

ROCQUET	ROGALLOS	ROISTING	ROLLIE	ROMANS
ROCQUETS	ROGATION	ROISTS	ROLLIES	ROMANTIC
ROCS	ROGATIONS	ROJAK	ROLLING	ROMANTICS
ROD	ROGATORY	ROJAKS	ROLLINGS	ROMANZA
RODDED	ROGER	ROJI	ROLLMOP	ROMANZAS
RODDING	ROGERED	ROJIS	ROLLMOPS	ROMAUNT
RODDINGS	ROGERING	ROK	ROLLNECK	ROMAUNTS
RODE	ROGERINGS	ROKE	ROLLNECKS	ROMCOM
RODED	ROGERS	ROKED	ROLLOCK	ROMCOMS
RODENT	ROGNON	ROKELAY	ROLLOCKS	ROMELDALE
RODENTIAL	ROGNONS	ROKELAYS	ROLLOUT	ROMEO
RODENTS	ROGUE	ROKER	ROLLOUTS	ROMEOS
RODEO	ROGUED	ROKERS	ROLLOVER	ROMNEYA
RODEOED	ROGUEING	ROKES	ROLLOVERS	ROMNEYAS
RODEOING	ROGUER	ROKIER	ROLLS	ROMP
RODEOS	ROGUERIES	ROKIEST	ROLLTOP	ROMPED
RODES	ROGUERS	ROKING	ROLLUP	ROMPER
RODEWAY	ROGUERY	ROKKAKU	ROLLUPS	ROMPERS
RODEWAYS	ROGUES	ROKS	ROLLWAY	ROMPING
RODFISHER	ROGUESHIP	ROKY	ROLLWAYS	ROMPINGLY
RODGERSIA	ROGUIER	ROLAG	ROM	ROMPISH
RODING	ROGUIEST	ROLAGS	ROMA	ROMPISHLY
RODINGS	ROGUING	ROLAMITE	ROMAGE	ROMPS
RODLESS	ROGUISH	ROLAMITES	ROMAGES	ROMS
RODLIKE	ROGUISHLY	ROLE	ROMAIKA	RONCADOR
RODMAN	ROGUY	ROLES	ROMAIKAS	RONCADORS
RODMEN	ROHE	ROLF	ROMAINE	RONDACHE
RODNEY	ROHES	ROLFED	ROMAINES	RONDACHES
RODNEYS	ROID	ROLFER	ROMAJI	RONDAVEL
RODS	ROIDS	ROLFERS	ROMAJIS	RONDAVELS
RODSMAN	ROIL	ROLFING	ROMAL	RONDE
RODSMEN	ROILED	ROLFINGS	ROMALS	RONDEAU
RODSTER	ROILIER	ROLFS	ROMAN	RONDEAUX
RODSTERS	ROILIEST	ROLL	ROMANCE	RONDEL
ROE	ROILING	ROLLABLE	ROMANCED	RONDELET
ROEBUCK	ROILS	ROLLAWAY	ROMANCER	RONDELETS
ROEBUCKS	ROILY	ROLLAWAYS	ROMANCERS	RONDELLE
ROED	ROIN	ROLLBACK	ROMANCES	RONDELLES
ROEMER	ROINED	ROLLBACKS	ROMANCING	RONDELS
ROEMERS	ROINING	ROLLBAR	ROMANESCO	RONDES
ROENTGEN	ROINISH	ROLLBARS	ROMANISE	RONDINO
ROENTGENS	ROINS	ROLLED	ROMANISED	RONDINOS
ROES	ROIST	ROLLER	ROMANISES	RONDO
ROESTI	ROISTED	ROLLERS	ROMANIZE	RONDOS
ROESTIS	ROISTER	ROLLICK	ROMANIZED	RONDURE
ROESTONE	ROISTERED	ROLLICKED	ROMANIZES	RONDURES
ROESTONES	ROISTERER	ROLLICKS	ROMANO	RONE
ROGALLO	ROISTERS	ROLLICKY	ROMANOS	RONEO

ROSEATE

RONEOED	ROOFSCAPE	ROOPED	ROOTLE	ROQUETTE
RONEOING	ROOFTOP	ROOPIER	ROOTLED	ROQUETTES
RONEOS	ROOFTOPS	ROOPIEST	ROOTLES	RORAL
RONEPIPE	ROOFTREE	ROOPING	ROOTLESS	RORE
RONEPIPES	ROOFTREES	ROOPIT	ROOTLET	RORES
RONES	ROOFY	ROOPS	ROOTLETS	RORIC
RONG	ROOIBOS	ROOPY	ROOTLIKE	RORID
RONGGENG	ROOIBOSES	ROORBACH	ROOTLING	RORIE
RONGGENGS	ROOIKAT	ROORBACHS	ROOTS	RORIER
RONIN	ROOIKATS	ROORBACK	ROOTSIER	RORIEST
RONINS	ROOINEK	ROORBACKS	ROOTSIEST	RORQUAL
RONION	ROOINEKS	ROOS	ROOTSTALK	RORQUALS
RONIONS	ROOK	ROOSA	ROOTSTOCK	RORT
RONNE	ROOKED	ROOSAS	ROOTSY	RORTED
RONNEL	ROOKERIES	ROOSE	ROOTWORM	RORTER
RONNELS	ROOKERY	ROOSED	ROOTWORMS	RORTERS
RONNIE	ROOKIE	ROOSER	ROOTY	RORTIER
RONNIES	ROOKIER	ROOSERS	ROPABLE	RORTIEST
RONNING	ROOKIES	ROOSES	ROPE	RORTING
RONT	ROOKIEST	ROOSING	ROPEABLE	RORTINGS
RONTE	ROOKING	ROOST	ROPED	RORTS
RONTES	ROOKISH	ROOSTED	ROPELIKE	RORTY
RONTGEN	ROOKS	ROOSTER	ROPER	RORY
RONTGENS	ROOKY	ROOSTERS	ROPERIES	ROSACE
RONTS	ROOM	ROOSTING	ROPERS	ROSACEA
RONYON	ROOMED	ROOSTS	ROPERY	ROSACEAS
RONYONS	ROOMER	ROOT	ROPES	ROSACEOUS
RONZ	ROOMERS	ROOTAGE	ROPEWALK	ROSACES
RONZER	ROOMETTE	ROOTAGES	ROPEWALKS	ROSAKER
RONZERS	ROOMETTES	ROOTBALL	ROPEWAY	ROSAKERS
ROO	ROOMFUL	ROOTBALLS	ROPEWAYS	ROSALIA
ROOD	ROOMFULS	ROOTBOUND	ROPEWORK	ROSALIAS
ROODS	ROOMIE	ROOTCAP	ROPEWORKS	ROSANILIN
ROOF	ROOMIER	ROOTCAPS	ROPEY	ROSARIA
ROOFED	ROOMIES	ROOTED	ROPIER	ROSARIAN
ROOFER	ROOMIEST	ROOTEDLY	ROPIEST	ROSARIANS
ROOFERS	ROOMILY	ROOTER	ROPILY	ROSARIES
ROOFIE	ROOMINESS	ROOTERS	ROPINESS	ROSARIUM
ROOFIER	ROOMING	ROOTHOLD	ROPING	ROSARIUMS
ROOFIES	ROOMMATE	ROOTHOLDS	ROPINGS	ROSARY
ROOFIEST	ROOMMATES	ROOTIER	ROPY	ROSBIF
ROOFING	ROOMS	ROOTIES	ROQUE	ROSBIFS
ROOFINGS	ROOMSFUL	ROOTIEST	ROQUEFORT	ROSCID
ROOFLESS	ROOMSOME	ROOTINESS	ROQUES	ROSCOE
ROOFLIKE	ROOMY	ROOTING	ROQUET	ROSCOES
ROOFLINE	ROON	ROOTINGS	ROQUETED	ROSE
ROOFLINES	ROONS	ROOTKIT	ROQUETING	ROSEAL
ROOFS	ROOP	ROOTKITS	ROQUETS	ROSEATE

ROSEATELY	ROSHIS	ROSTIS	ROTE	ROTTENEST
ROSEBAY	ROSIED	ROSTRA	ROTED	ROTTENLY
ROSEBAYS	ROSIER	ROSTRAL	ROTELY	ROTTENS
ROSEBED	ROSIERE	ROSTRALLY	ROTENONE	ROTTER
ROSEBEDS	ROSIERES	ROSTRATE	ROTENONES	ROTTERS
ROSEBOWL	ROSIERS	ROSTRATED	ROTES	ROTTES
ROSEBOWLS	ROSIES	ROSTRUM	ROTGRASS	ROTTING
ROSEBUD	ROSIEST	ROSTRUMS	ROTGUT	ROTULA
ROSEBUDS	ROSILY	ROSTS	ROTGUTS	ROTULAE
ROSEBUSH	ROSIN	ROSULA	ROTHER	ROTULAS
ROSED	ROSINATE	ROSULAS	ROTHERS	ROTUND
ROSEFINCH	ROSINATES	ROSULATE	ROTI	ROTUNDA
ROSEFISH	ROSINED	ROSY	ROTIFER	ROTUNDAS
ROSEHIP	ROSINER	ROSYING	ROTIFERAL	ROTUNDATE
ROSEHIPS	ROSINERS	ROT	ROTIFERAN	ROTUNDED
ROSELESS	ROSINESS	ROTA	ROTIFERS	ROTUNDER
ROSELIKE	ROSING	ROTACHUTE	ROTIFORM	ROTUNDEST
ROSELLA	ROSINIER	ROTAL	ROTING	ROTUNDING
ROSELLAS	ROSINIEST	ROTAMETER	ROTINI	ROTUNDITY
ROSELLE	ROSINING	ROTAN	ROTINIS	ROTUNDLY
ROSELLES	ROSINOL	ROTANS	ROTIS	ROTUNDS
ROSEMARY	ROSINOLS	ROTAPLANE	ROTL	ROTURIER
ROSEOLA	ROSINOUS	ROTARIES	ROTLS	ROTURIERS
ROSEOLAR	ROSINS	ROTARY	ROTO	ROUBLE
ROSEOLAS	ROSINWEED	ROTAS	ROTOGRAPH	ROUBLES
ROSERIES	ROSINY	ROTATABLE	ROTOLI	ROUCHE
ROSEROOT	ROSIT	ROTATE	ROTOLO	ROUCHED
ROSEROOTS	ROSITED	ROTATED	ROTOLOS	ROUCHES
ROSERY	ROSITING	ROTATES	ROTON	ROUCHING
ROSES	ROSITS	ROTATING	ROTONS	ROUCHINGS
ROSESLUG	ROSMARINE	ROTATION	ROTOR	ROUCOU
ROSESLUGS	ROSOGLIO	ROTATIONS	ROTORS	ROUCOUS
ROSET	ROSOGLIOS	ROTATIVE	ROTOS	ROUE
ROSETED	ROSOLIO	ROTATOR	ROTOSCOPE	ROUEN
ROSETING	ROSOLIOS	ROTATORES	ROTOTILL	ROUENS
ROSETS	ROSSER	ROTATORS	ROTOTILLS	ROUES
ROSETTE	ROSSERS	ROTATORY	ROTOVATE	ROUGE
ROSETTED	ROST	ROTAVATE	ROTOVATED	ROUGED
ROSETTES	ROSTED	ROTAVATED	ROTOVATES	ROUGES
ROSETTING	ROSTELLA	ROTAVATES	ROTOVATOR	ROUGH
ROSETTY	ROSTELLAR	ROTAVATOR	ROTPROOF	ROUGHAGE
ROSETY	ROSTELLUM	ROTAVIRAL	ROTS	ROUGHAGES
ROSEWATER	ROSTER	ROTAVIRUS	ROTTAN	ROUGHBACK
ROSEWOOD	ROSTERED	ROTCH	ROTTANS	ROUGHCAST
ROSEWOODS	ROSTERING	ROTCHE	ROTTE	ROUGHDRY
ROSHAMBO	ROSTERS	ROTCHES	ROTTED	ROUGHED
ROSHAMBOS	ROSTI	ROTCHIE	ROTTEN	ROUGHEN
ROSHI	ROSTING	ROTCHIES	ROTTENER	ROUGHENED

ROUGHENS
ROUGHER
ROUGHERS
ROUGHEST
ROUGHHEW
ROUGHHEWN
ROUGHHEWS
ROUGHIE
ROUGHIES
ROUGHING
ROUGHINGS
ROUGHISH
ROUGHLEG
ROUGHLEGS
ROUGHLY
ROUGHNECK
ROUGHNESS
ROUGHOUT
ROUGHOUTS
ROUGHS
ROUGHSHOD
ROUGHT
ROUGHY
ROUGING
ROUILLE
ROUILLES
ROUL
ROULADE
ROULADES
ROULE
ROULEAU
ROULEAUS
ROULEAUX
ROULES
ROULETTE
ROULETTED
ROULETTES
ROULS
ROUM
ROUMING
ROUMINGS
ROUMS
ROUNCE
ROUNCES
ROUNCEVAL
ROUNCIES
ROUNCY
ROUND

ROUNDARCH
ROUNDBALL
ROUNDED
ROUNDEDLY
ROUNDEL
ROUNDELAY
ROUNDELS
ROUNDER
ROUNDERS
ROUNDEST
ROUNDHAND
ROUNDHEEL
ROUNDING
ROUNDINGS
ROUNDISH
ROUNDLE
ROUNDLES
ROUNDLET
ROUNDLETS
ROUNDLY
ROUNDNESS
ROUNDS
ROUNDSMAN
ROUNDSMEN
ROUNDTRIP
ROUNDUP
ROUNDUPS
ROUNDURE
ROUNDURES
ROUNDWOOD
ROUNDWORM
ROUP
ROUPED
ROUPET
ROUPIER
ROUPIEST
ROUPILY
ROUPING
ROUPIT
ROUPS
ROUPY
ROUSABLE
ROUSANT
ROUSE
ROUSED
ROUSEMENT
ROUSER
ROUSERS

ROUSES
ROUSING
ROUSINGLY
ROUSSEAU
ROUSSEAUS
ROUSSETTE
ROUST
ROUSTED
ROUSTER
ROUSTERS
ROUSTING
ROUSTS
ROUT
ROUTE
ROUTED
ROUTEING
ROUTEMAN
ROUTEMEN
ROUTER
ROUTERS
ROUTES
ROUTEWAY
ROUTEWAYS
ROUTH
ROUTHIE
ROUTHIER
ROUTHIEST
ROUTHS
ROUTINE
ROUTINEER
ROUTINELY
ROUTINES
ROUTING
ROUTINGS
ROUTINISE
ROUTINISM
ROUTINIST
ROUTINIZE
ROUTOUS
ROUTOUSLY
ROUTS
ROUX
ROVE
ROVED
ROVEN
ROVER
ROVERS
ROVES

ROVING
ROVINGLY
ROVINGS
ROW
ROWABLE
ROWAN
ROWANS
ROWBOAT
ROWBOATS
ROWDEDOW
ROWDEDOWS
ROWDIER
ROWDIES
ROWDIEST
ROWDILY
ROWDINESS
ROWDY
ROWDYDOW
ROWDYDOWS
ROWDYISH
ROWDYISM
ROWDYISMS
ROWED
ROWEL
ROWELED
ROWELING
ROWELLED
ROWELLING
ROWELS
ROWEN
ROWENS
ROWER
ROWERS
ROWIE
ROWIES
ROWING
ROWINGS
ROWLOCK
ROWLOCKS
ROWME
ROWMES
ROWND
ROWNDED
ROWNDELL
ROWNDELLS
ROWNDING
ROWNDS
ROWOVER

ROWOVERS
ROWS
ROWT
ROWTED
ROWTH
ROWTHS
ROWTING
ROWTS
ROYAL
ROYALET
ROYALETS
ROYALISE
ROYALISED
ROYALISES
ROYALISM
ROYALISMS
ROYALIST
ROYALISTS
ROYALIZE
ROYALIZED
ROYALIZES
ROYALLER
ROYALLEST
ROYALLY
ROYALMAST
ROYALS
ROYALTIES
ROYALTY
ROYNE
ROYNED
ROYNES
ROYNING
ROYNISH
ROYST
ROYSTED
ROYSTER
ROYSTERED
ROYSTERER
ROYSTERS
ROYSTING
ROYSTS
ROZELLE
ROZELLES
ROZET
ROZETED
ROZETING
ROZETS
ROZIT

R

ROZITED	RUBBLIER	RUBINEOUS	RUCS	RUDIMENTS
ROZITING	RUBBLIEST	RUBINES	RUCTATION	RUDIS
ROZITS	RUBBLING	RUBINS	RUCTION	RUDISH
ROZZER	RUBBLY	RUBIOUS	RUCTIONS	RUDIST
ROZZERS	RUBBOARD	RUBLE	RUCTIOUS	RUDISTID
RUANA	RUBBOARDS	RUBLES	RUD	RUDISTIDS
RUANAS	RUBBY	RUBLI	RUDACEOUS	RUDISTS
RUB	RUBBYDUB	RUBOFF	RUDAS	RUDS
RUBABOO	RUBBYDUBS	RUBOFFS	RUDASES	RUDY
RUBABOOS	RUBDOWN	RUBOUT	RUDBECKIA	RUE
RUBACE	RUBDOWNS	RUBOUTS	RUDD	RUED
RUBACES	RUBE	RUBRIC	RUDDED	RUEDA
RUBAI	RUBEFIED	RUBRICAL	RUDDER	RUEDAS
RUBAIS	RUBEFIES	RUBRICATE	RUDDERS	RUEFUL
RUBAIYAT	RUBEFY	RUBRICIAN	RUDDIED	RUEFULLY
RUBASSE	RUBEFYING	RUBRICS	RUDDIER	RUEING
RUBASSES	RUBEL	RUBS	RUDDIES	RUEINGS
RUBATI	RUBELLA	RUBSTONE	RUDDIEST	RUELLE
RUBATO	RUBELLAN	RUBSTONES	RUDDILY	RUELLES
RUBATOS	RUBELLANS	RUBUS	RUDDINESS	RUELLIA
RUBBABOO	RUBELLAS	RUBUSES	RUDDING	RUELLIAS
RUBBABOOS	RUBELLITE	RUBY	RUDDLE	RUER
RUBBED	RUBELS	RUBYING	RUDDLED	RUERS
RUBBER	RUBEOLA	RUBYLIKE	RUDDLEMAN	RUES
RUBBERED	RUBEOLAR	RUC	RUDDLEMEN	RUFESCENT
RUBBERIER	RUBEOLAS	RUCHE	RUDDLES	RUFF
RUBBERING	RUBES	RUCHED	RUDDLING	RUFFE
RUBBERISE	RUBESCENT	RUCHES	RUDDOCK	RUFFED
RUBBERIZE	RUBICELLE	RUCHING	RUDDOCKS	RUFFES
RUBBERS	RUBICON	RUCHINGS	RUDDS	RUFFIAN
RUBBERY	RUBICONED	RUCK	RUDDY	RUFFIANED
RUBBET	RUBICONS	RUCKED	RUDDYING	RUFFIANLY
RUBBIDIES	RUBICUND	RUCKING	RUDE	RUFFIANS
RUBBIDY	RUBIDIC	RUCKLE	RUDELY	RUFFIN
RUBBIES	RUBIDIUM	RUCKLED	RUDENESS	RUFFING
RUBBING	RUBIDIUMS	RUCKLES	RUDER	RUFFINS
RUBBINGS	RUBIED	RUCKLING	RUDERAL	RUFFLE
RUBBISH	RUBIER	RUCKMAN	RUDERALS	RUFFLED
RUBBISHED	RUBIES	RUCKMEN	RUDERIES	RUFFLER
RUBBISHES	RUBIEST	RUCKS	RUDERY	RUFFLERS
RUBBISHLY	RUBIFIED	RUCKSACK	RUDES	RUFFLES
RUBBISHY	RUBIFIES	RUCKSACKS	RUDESBIES	RUFFLIER
RUBBIT	RUBIFY	RUCKSEAT	RUDESBY	RUFFLIEST
RUBBITIES	RUBIFYING	RUCKSEATS	RUDEST	RUFFLIKE
RUBBITY	RUBIGO	RUCKUS	RUDI	RUFFLING
RUBBLE	RUBIGOS	RUCKUSES	RUDIE	RUFFLINGS
RUBBLED	RUBIN	RUCOLA	RUDIES	RUFFLY
RUBBLES	RUBINE	RUCOLAS	RUDIMENT	RUFFS

RUFIYAA	RUINED	RUMBLIER	RUMORING	RUNCINATE
RUFIYAAS	RUINER	RUMBLIEST	RUMOROUS	RUND
RUFOUS	RUINERS	RUMBLING	RUMORS	RUNDALE
RUFOUSES	RUING	RUMBLINGS	RUMOUR	RUNDALES
RUG	RUINGS	RUMBLY	RUMOURED	RUNDLE
RUGA	RUINING	RUMBO	RUMOURER	RUNDLED
RUGAE	RUININGS	RUMBOS	RUMOURERS	RUNDLES
RUGAL	RUINOUS	RUMDUM	RUMOURING	RUNDLET
RUGALACH	RUINOUSLY	RUMDUMS	RUMOURS	RUNDLETS
RUGATE	RUINS	RUME	RUMP	RUNDOWN
RUGBIES	RUKH	RUMEN	RUMPED	RUNDOWNS
RUGBY	RUKHS	RUMENS	RUMPIER	RUNDS
RUGELACH	RULABLE	RUMES	RUMPIES	RUNE
RUGELACHS	RULE	RUMINA	RUMPIEST	RUNECRAFT
RUGGED	RULED	RUMINAL	RUMPING	RUNED
RUGGEDER	RULELESS	RUMINANT	RUMPLE	RUNELIKE
RUGGEDEST	RULER	RUMINANTS	RUMPLED	RUNES
RUGGEDISE	RULERED	RUMINATE	RUMPLES	RUNFLAT
RUGGEDIZE	RULERING	RUMINATED	RUMPLESS	RUNFLATS
RUGGEDLY	RULERS	RUMINATES	RUMPLIER	RUNG
RUGGELACH	RULERSHIP	RUMINATOR	RUMPLIEST	RUNGED
RUGGER	RULES	RUMKIN	RUMPLING	RUNGLESS
RUGGERS	RULESSE	RUMKINS	RUMPLY	RUNGS
RUGGIER	RULIER	RUMLY	RUMPO	RUNIC
RUGGIEST	RULIEST	RUMMAGE	RUMPOS	RUNKLE
RUGGING	RULING	RUMMAGED	RUMPOT	RUNKLED
RUGGINGS	RULINGS	RUMMAGER	RUMPOTS	RUNKLES
RUGGY	RULLION	RUMMAGERS	RUMPS	RUNKLING
RUGLIKE	RULLIONS	RUMMAGES	RUMPUS	RUNLESS
RUGOLA	RULLOCK	RUMMAGING	RUMPUSES	RUNLET
RUGOLAS	RULLOCKS	RUMMER	RUMPY	RUNLETS
RUGOSA	RULY	RUMMERS	RUMRUNNER	RUNNABLE
RUGOSAS	RUM	RUMMEST	RUMS	RUNNEL
RUGOSE	RUMAKI	RUMMIER	RUN	RUNNELS
RUGOSELY	RUMAKIS	RUMMIES	RUNABOUT	RUNNER
RUGOSITY	RUMAL	RUMMIEST	RUNABOUTS	RUNNERS
RUGOUS	RUMALS	RUMMILY	RUNAGATE	RUNNET
RUGRAT	RUMBA	RUMMINESS	RUNAGATES	RUNNETS
RUGRATS	RUMBAED	RUMMISH	RUNANGA	RUNNIER
RUGS	RUMBAING	RUMMISHED	RUNANGAS	RUNNIEST
RUGULOSE	RUMBAS	RUMMISHES	RUNAROUND	RUNNINESS
RUIN	RUMBELOW	RUMMY	RUNAWAY	RUNNING
RUINABLE	RUMBELOWS	RUMNESS	RUNAWAYS	RUNNINGLY
RUINATE	RUMBLE	RUMNESSES	RUNBACK	RUNNINGS
RUINATED	RUMBLED	RUMOR	RUNBACKS	RUNNION
RUINATES	RUMBLER	RUMORED	RUNCH	RUNNIONS
RUINATING	RUMBLERS	RUMORER	RUNCHES	RUNNY
RUINATION	RUMBLES	RUMORERS	RUNCIBLE	RUNOFF

RUNOFFS	RURALITES	RUSMAS	RUSTLER	RUTTISHLY
RUNOUT	RURALITY	RUSSE	RUSTLERS	RUTTY
RUNOUTS	RURALIZE	RUSSEL	RUSTLES	RYA
RUNOVER	RURALIZED	RUSSELS	RUSTLESS	RYAL
RUNOVERS	RURALIZES	RUSSET	RUSTLING	RYALS
RUNPROOF	RURALLY	RUSSETED	RUSTLINGS	RYAS
RUNRIG	RURALNESS	RUSSETIER	RUSTPROOF	RYBAT
RUNRIGS	RURALS	RUSSETING	RUSTRE	RYBATS
RUNROUND	RURBAN	RUSSETS	RUSTRED	RYBAUDRYE
RUNROUNDS	RURP	RUSSETY	RUSTRES	RYE
RUNS	RURPS	RUSSIA	RUSTS	RYEBREAD
RUNT	RURU	RUSSIAS	RUSTY	RYEBREADS
RUNTED	RURUS	RUSSIFIED	RUT	RYEFLOUR
RUNTIER	RUSA	RUSSIFIES	RUTABAGA	RYEFLOURS
RUNTIEST	RUSALKA	RUSSIFY	RUTABAGAS	RYEGRASS
RUNTINESS	RUSALKAS	RUSSULA	RUTACEOUS	RYEPECK
RUNTISH	RUSAS	RUSSULAE	RUTH	RYEPECKS
RUNTISHLY	RUSCUS	RUSSULAS	RUTHENIC	RYES
RUNTS	RUSCUSES	RUST	RUTHENIUM	RYFE
RUNTY	RUSE	RUSTABLE	RUTHER	RYKE
RUNWAY	RUSES	RUSTED	RUTHFUL	RYKED
RUNWAYS	RUSH	RUSTIC	RUTHFULLY	RYKES
RUPEE	RUSHED	RUSTICAL	RUTHLESS	RYKING
RUPEES	RUSHEE	RUSTICALS	RUTHS	RYMME
RUPIA	RUSHEES	RUSTICANA	RUTILANT	RYMMED
RUPIAH	RUSHEN	RUSTICATE	RUTILATED	RYMMES
RUPIAHS	RUSHER	RUSTICIAL	RUTILE	RYMMING
RUPIAS	RUSHERS	RUSTICISE	RUTILES	RYND
RUPTURE	RUSHES	RUSTICISM	RUTIN	RYNDS
RUPTURED	RUSHIER	RUSTICITY	RUTINS	RYOKAN
RUPTURES	RUSHIEST	RUSTICIZE	RUTS	RYOKANS
RUPTURING	RUSHINESS	RUSTICLY	RUTTED	RYOT
RURAL	RUSHING	RUSTICS	RUTTER	RYOTS
RURALISE	RUSHINGS	RUSTIER	RUTTERS	RYOTWARI
RURALISED	RUSHLIGHT	RUSTIEST	RUTTIER	RYOTWARIS
RURALISES	RUSHLIKE	RUSTILY	RUTTIEST	RYPE
RURALISM	RUSHY	RUSTINESS	RUTTILY	RYPECK
RURALISMS	RUSINE	RUSTING	RUTTINESS	RYPECKS
RURALIST	RUSK	RUSTINGS	RUTTING	RYPER
RURALISTS	RUSKS	RUSTLE	RUTTINGS	RYU
RURALITE	RUSMA	RUSTLED	RUTTISH	RYUS

S

SAAG	SABIR	SAC	SACKERS	SACRUM
SAAGS	SABIRS	SACATON	SACKFUL	SACRUMS
SAB	SABKHA	SACATONS	SACKFULS	SACS
SABADILLA	SABKHAH	SACBUT	SACKING	SAD
SABAL	SABKHAHS	SACBUTS	SACKINGS	SADDED
SABALS	SABKHAS	SACCADE	SACKLESS	SADDEN
SABATON	SABKHAT	SACCADES	SACKLIKE	SADDENED
SABATONS	SABKHATS	SACCADIC	SACKLOAD	SADDENING
SABAYON	SABLE	SACCATE	SACKLOADS	SADDENS
SABAYONS	SABLED	SACCHARIC	SACKS	SADDER
SABBAT	SABLEFISH	SACCHARIN	SACKSFUL	SADDEST
SABBATH	SABLER	SACCHARUM	SACLESS	SADDHU
SABBATHS	SABLES	SACCIFORM	SACLIKE	SADDHUS
SABBATIC	SABLEST	SACCOI	SACQUE	SADDIE
SABBATICS	SABLING	SACCOS	SACQUES	SADDIES
SABBATINE	SABOT	SACCOSES	SACRA	SADDING
SABBATISE	SABOTAGE	SACCULAR	SACRAL	SADDISH
SABBATISM	SABOTAGED	SACCULATE	SACRALGIA	SADDLE
SABBATIZE	SABOTAGES	SACCULE	SACRALISE	SADDLEBAG
SABBATS	SABOTED	SACCULES	SACRALITY	SADDLEBOW
SABBED	SABOTEUR	SACCULI	SACRALIZE	SADDLED
SABBING	SABOTEURS	SACCULUS	SACRALS	SADDLER
SABBINGS	SABOTIER	SACELLA	SACRAMENT	SADDLERS
SABE	SABOTIERS	SACELLUM	SACRARIA	SADDLERY
SABED	SABOTS	SACHEM	SACRARIAL	SADDLES
SABEING	SABRA	SACHEMDOM	SACRARIUM	SADDLING
SABELLA	SABRAS	SACHEMIC	SACRED	SADDO
SABELLAS	SABRE	SACHEMS	SACREDER	SADDOES
SABER	SABRED	SACHET	SACREDEST	SADDOS
SABERED	SABRELIKE	SACHETED	SACREDLY	SADE
SABERING	SABRES	SACHETS	SACRIFICE	SADES
SABERLIKE	SABREUR	SACK	SACRIFIDE	SADHANA
SABERS	SABREURS	SACKABLE	SACRIFIED	SADHANAS
SABES	SABREWING	SACKAGE	SACRIFIES	SADHE
SABHA	SABRING	SACKAGED	SACRIFY	SADHES
SABHAS	SABS	SACKAGES	SACRILEGE	SADHU
SABICU	SABULINE	SACKAGING	SACRING	SADHUS
SABICUS	SABULOSE	SACKBUT	SACRINGS	SADI
SABIN	SABULOUS	SACKBUTS	SACRIST	SADIRON
SABINE	SABURRA	SACKCLOTH	SACRISTAN	SADIRONS
SABINES	SABURRAL	SACKED	SACRISTS	SADIS
SABINS	SABURRAS	SACKER	SACRISTY	SADISM

SADISMS

SADISMS	SAFRANINE	SAGGERED	SAICE	SAINFOINS
SADIST	SAFRANINS	SAGGERING	SAICES	SAINING
SADISTIC	SAFROL	SAGGERS	SAICK	SAINS
SADISTS	SAFROLE	SAGGIER	SAICKS	SAINT
SADLY	SAFROLES	SAGGIEST	SAICS	SAINTDOM
SADNESS	SAFROLS	SAGGING	SAID	SAINTDOMS
SADNESSES	SAFRONAL	SAGGINGS	SAIDEST	SAINTED
SADO	SAFRONALS	SAGGY	SAIDS	SAINTESS
SADOS	SAFT	SAGIER	SAIDST	SAINTFOIN
SADS	SAFTER	SAGIEST	SAIGA	SAINTHOOD
SADZA	SAFTEST	SAGINATE	SAIGAS	SAINTING
SADZAS	SAG	SAGINATED	SAIKEI	SAINTISH
SAE	SAGA	SAGINATES	SAIKEIS	SAINTISM
SAECULA	SAGACIOUS	SAGITTA	SAIKLESS	SAINTISMS
SAECULUM	SAGACITY	SAGITTAL	SAIL	SAINTLESS
SAECULUMS	SAGAMAN	SAGITTARY	SAILABLE	SAINTLIER
SAETER	SAGAMEN	SAGITTAS	SAILBOARD	SAINTLIKE
SAETERS	SAGAMORE	SAGITTATE	SAILBOAT	SAINTLILY
SAFARI	SAGAMORES	SAGO	SAILBOATS	SAINTLING
SAFARIED	SAGANASH	SAGOIN	SAILCLOTH	SAINTLY
SAFARIING	SAGAPENUM	SAGOINS	SAILED	SAINTS
SAFARIS	SAGAS	SAGOS	SAILER	SAINTSHIP
SAFARIST	SAGATHIES	SAGOUIN	SAILERS	SAIQUE
SAFARISTS	SAGATHY	SAGOUINS	SAILFISH	SAIQUES
SAFE	SAGBUT	SAGRADA	SAILING	SAIR
SAFED	SAGBUTS	SAGS	SAILINGS	SAIRED
SAFEGUARD	SAGE	SAGUARO	SAILLESS	SAIRER
SAFELIGHT	SAGEBRUSH	SAGUAROS	SAILMAKER	SAIREST
SAFELY	SAGEHOOD	SAGUIN	SAILOR	SAIRING
SAFENESS	SAGEHOODS	SAGUINS	SAILORING	SAIRS
SAFER	SAGELY	SAGUM	SAILORLY	SAIS
SAFES	SAGENE	SAGY	SAILORS	SAIST
SAFEST	SAGENES	SAHEB	SAILPAST	SAITH
SAFETIED	SAGENESS	SAHEBS	SAILPASTS	SAITHE
SAFETIES	SAGENITE	SAHIB	SAILPLANE	SAITHES
SAFETY	SAGENITES	SAHIBA	SAILROOM	SAITHS
SAFETYING	SAGENITIC	SAHIBAH	SAILROOMS	SAIYID
SAFETYMAN	SAGER	SAHIBAHS	SAILS	SAIYIDS
SAFETYMEN	SAGES	SAHIBAS	SAIM	SAJOU
SAFFIAN	SAGEST	SAHIBS	SAIMIN	SAJOUS
SAFFIANS	SAGGAR	SAHIWAL	SAIMINS	SAKAI
SAFFLOWER	SAGGARD	SAHIWALS	SAIMIRI	SAKAIS
SAFFRON	SAGGARDS	SAHUARO	SAIMIRIS	SAKE
SAFFRONED	SAGGARED	SAHUAROS	SAIMS	SAKER
SAFFRONS	SAGGARING	SAI	SAIN	SAKERET
SAFFRONY	SAGGARS	SAIBLING	SAINE	SAKERETS
SAFING	SAGGED	SAIBLINGS	SAINED	SAKERS
SAFRANIN	SAGGER	SAIC	SAINFOIN	SAKES

SAKI	SALATS	SALIFY	SALLOWLY	SALSAS
SAKIA	SALBAND	SALIFYING	SALLOWS	SALSE
SAKIAS	SALBANDS	SALIGOT	SALLOWY	SALSES
SAKIEH	SALCHOW	SALIGOTS	SALLY	SALSIFIES
SAKIEHS	SALCHOWS	SALIMETER	SALLYING	SALSIFY
SAKIS	SALE	SALIMETRY	SALLYPORT	SALSILLA
SAKIYEH	SALEABLE	SALINA	SALMI	SALSILLAS
SAKIYEHS	SALEABLY	SALINAS	SALMIS	SALT
SAKKOI	SALEP	SALINE	SALMON	SALTANDO
SAKKOS	SALEPS	SALINES	SALMONET	SALTANDOS
SAKKOSES	SALERATUS	SALINISE	SALMONETS	SALTANT
SAKSAUL	SALERING	SALINISED	SALMONID	SALTANTS
SAKSAULS	SALERINGS	SALINISES	SALMONIDS	SALTATE
SAKTI	SALEROOM	SALINITY	SALMONIER	SALTATED
SAKTIS	SALEROOMS	SALINIZE	SALMONOID	SALTATES
SAL	SALES	SALINIZED	SALMONS	SALTATING
SALAAM	SALESGIRL	SALINIZES	SALMONY	SALTATION
SALAAMED	SALESLADY	SALIVA	SALOL	SALTATO
SALAAMING	SALESMAN	SALIVAL	SALOLS	SALTATORY
SALAAMS	SALESMEN	SALIVARY	SALOMETER	SALTATOS
SALABLE	SALESROOM	SALIVAS	SALON	SALTBOX
SALABLY	SALET	SALIVATE	SALONS	SALTBOXES
SALACIOUS	SALETS	SALIVATED	SALOON	SALTBUSH
SALACITY	SALEWD	SALIVATES	SALOONS	SALTCAT
SALAD	SALEYARD	SALIVATOR	SALOOP	SALTCATS
SALADANG	SALEYARDS	SALIX	SALOOPS	SALTCHUCK
SALADANGS	SALFERN	SALL	SALOP	SALTED
SALADE	SALFERNS	SALLAD	SALOPIAN	SALTER
SALADES	SALIAUNCE	SALLADS	SALOPS	SALTERIES
SALADING	SALIC	SALLAL	SALP	SALTERN
SALADINGS	SALICES	SALLALS	SALPA	SALTERNS
SALADS	SALICET	SALLE	SALPAE	SALTERS
SALAL	SALICETA	SALLEE	SALPAS	SALTERY
SALALS	SALICETS	SALLEES	SALPIAN	SALTEST
SALAMI	SALICETUM	SALLES	SALPIANS	SALTFISH
SALAMIS	SALICIN	SALLET	SALPICON	SALTIE
SALAMON	SALICINE	SALLETS	SALPICONS	SALTIER
SALAMONS	SALICINES	SALLIED	SALPID	SALTIERS
SALANGANE	SALICINS	SALLIER	SALPIDS	SALTIES
SALARIAT	SALICYLIC	SALLIERS	SALPIFORM	SALTIEST
SALARIATS	SALIENCE	SALLIES	SALPINGES	SALTILY
SALARIED	SALIENCES	SALLOW	SALPINX	SALTINE
SALARIES	SALIENCY	SALLOWED	SALPINXES	SALTINES
SALARY	SALIENT	SALLOWER	SALPS	SALTINESS
SALARYING	SALIENTLY	SALLOWEST	SALS	SALTING
SALARYMAN	SALIENTS	SALLOWIER	SALSA	SALTINGS
SALARYMEN	SALIFIED	SALLOWING	SALSAED	SALTIRE
SALAT	SALIFIES	SALLOWISH	SALSAING	SALTIRES

S

SALTISH	SALVAGING	SAMBHARS	SAMMED	SANCAIS
SALTISHLY	SALVARSAN	SAMBHUR	SAMMIE	SANCHO
SALTLESS	SALVATION	SAMBHURS	SAMMIES	SANCHOS
SALTLIKE	SALVATORY	SAMBO	SAMMING	SANCTA
SALTLY	SALVE	SAMBOES	SAMMY	SANCTIFY
SALTNESS	SALVED	SAMBOS	SAMNITIS	SANCTION
SALTO	SALVER	SAMBUCA	SAMOSA	SANCTIONS
SALTOED	SALVERS	SAMBUCAS	SAMOSAS	SANCTITY
SALTOING	SALVES	SAMBUKE	SAMOVAR	SANCTUARY
SALTOS	SALVETE	SAMBUKES	SAMOVARS	SANCTUM
SALTPAN	SALVETES	SAMBUR	SAMOYED	SANCTUMS
SALTPANS	SALVIA	SAMBURS	SAMOYEDS	SAND
SALTPETER	SALVIAS	SAME	SAMP	SANDABLE
SALTPETRE	SALVIFIC	SAMECH	SAMPAN	SANDAL
SALTS	SALVING	SAMECHS	SAMPANS	SANDALED
SALTUS	SALVINGS	SAMEK	SAMPHIRE	SANDALING
SALTUSES	SALVO	SAMEKH	SAMPHIRES	SANDALLED
SALTWATER	SALVOED	SAMEKHS	SAMPI	SANDALS
SALTWORK	SALVOES	SAMEKS	SAMPIRE	SANDARAC
SALTWORKS	SALVOING	SAMEL	SAMPIRES	SANDARACH
SALTWORT	SALVOR	SAMELY	SAMPIS	SANDARACS
SALTWORTS	SALVORS	SAMEN	SAMPLE	SANDBAG
SALTY	SALVOS	SAMENESS	SAMPLED	SANDBAGS
SALUBRITY	SALWAR	SAMES	SAMPLER	SANDBANK
SALUE	SALWARS	SAMEY	SAMPLERS	SANDBANKS
SALUED	SAM	SAMEYNESS	SAMPLERY	SANDBAR
SALUES	SAMA	SAMFOO	SAMPLES	SANDBARS
SALUING	SAMAAN	SAMFOOS	SAMPLING	SANDBLAST
SALUKI	SAMAANS	SAMFU	SAMPLINGS	SANDBOX
SALUKIS	SAMADHI	SAMFUS	SAMPS	SANDBOXES
SALURETIC	SAMADHIS	SAMIEL	SAMS	SANDBOY
SALUT	SAMAN	SAMIELS	SAMSARA	SANDBOYS
SALUTARY	SAMANS	SAMIER	SAMSARAS	SANDBUR
SALUTE	SAMARA	SAMIEST	SAMSARIC	SANDBURR
SALUTED	SAMARAS	SAMISEN	SAMSHOO	SANDBURRS
SALUTER	SAMARITAN	SAMISENS	SAMSHOOS	SANDBURS
SALUTERS	SAMARIUM	SAMITE	SAMSHU	SANDCRACK
SALUTES	SAMARIUMS	SAMITES	SAMSHUS	SANDDAB
SALUTING	SAMAS	SAMITHI	SAMSKARA	SANDDABS
SALVABLE	SAMBA	SAMITHIS	SAMSKARAS	SANDED
SALVABLY	SAMBAED	SAMITI	SAMURAI	SANDEK
SALVAGE	SAMBAING	SAMITIS	SAMURAIS	SANDEKS
SALVAGED	SAMBAL	SAMIZDAT	SAN	SANDER
SALVAGEE	SAMBALS	SAMIZDATS	SANATIVE	SANDERS
SALVAGEES	SAMBAR	SAMLET	SANATORIA	SANDERSES
SALVAGER	SAMBARS	SAMLETS	SANATORY	SANDFISH
SALVAGERS	SAMBAS	SAMLOR	SANBENITO	SANDFLIES
SALVAGES	SAMBHAR	SAMLORS	SANCAI	SANDFLY

SANDGLASS
SANDHEAP
SANDHEAPS
SANDHI
SANDHILL
SANDHILLS
SANDHIS
SANDHOG
SANDHOGS
SANDIER
SANDIEST
SANDINESS
SANDING
SANDINGS
SANDIVER
SANDIVERS
SANDLESS
SANDLIKE
SANDLING
SANDLINGS
SANDLOT
SANDLOTS
SANDMAN
SANDMEN
SANDPAPER
SANDPEEP
SANDPEEPS
SANDPILE
SANDPILES
SANDPIPER
SANDPIT
SANDPITS
SANDPUMP
SANDPUMPS
SANDS
SANDSHOE
SANDSHOES
SANDSOAP
SANDSOAPS
SANDSPIT
SANDSPITS
SANDSPOUT
SANDSPUR
SANDSPURS
SANDSTONE
SANDSTORM
SANDWICH
SANDWORM

SANDWORMS
SANDWORT
SANDWORTS
SANDY
SANDYISH
SANE
SANED
SANELY
SANENESS
SANER
SANES
SANEST
SANG
SANGA
SANGAR
SANGAREE
SANGAREES
SANGARS
SANGAS
SANGEET
SANGEETS
SANGER
SANGERS
SANGFROID
SANGH
SANGHA
SANGHAS
SANGHAT
SANGHATS
SANGHS
SANGLIER
SANGLIERS
SANGO
SANGOMA
SANGOMAS
SANGOS
SANGRAIL
SANGRAILS
SANGREAL
SANGREALS
SANGRIA
SANGRIAS
SANGS
SANGUIFY
SANGUINE
SANGUINED
SANGUINES
SANICLE

SANICLES
SANIDINE
SANIDINES
SANIES
SANIFIED
SANIFIES
SANIFY
SANIFYING
SANING
SANIOUS
SANITARIA
SANITARY
SANITATE
SANITATED
SANITATES
SANITIES
SANITISE
SANITISED
SANITISER
SANITISES
SANITIZE
SANITIZED
SANITIZER
SANITIZES
SANITORIA
SANITY
SANJAK
SANJAKS
SANK
SANKO
SANKOS
SANNIE
SANNIES
SANNOP
SANNOPS
SANNUP
SANNUPS
SANNYASI
SANNYASIN
SANNYASIS
SANPAN
SANPANS
SANPRO
SANPROS
SANS
SANSA
SANSAR
SANSARS

SANSAS
SANSEI
SANSEIS
SANSERIF
SANSERIFS
SANT
SANTAL
SANTALIC
SANTALIN
SANTALINS
SANTALOL
SANTALOLS
SANTALS
SANTERA
SANTERAS
SANTERIA
SANTERIAS
SANTERO
SANTEROS
SANTIM
SANTIMI
SANTIMS
SANTIMU
SANTIR
SANTIRS
SANTO
SANTOKU
SANTOKUS
SANTOL
SANTOLINA
SANTOLS
SANTON
SANTONICA
SANTONIN
SANTONINS
SANTONS
SANTOOR
SANTOORS
SANTOS
SANTOUR
SANTOURS
SANTS
SANTUR
SANTURS
SANYASI
SANYASIS
SAOLA
SAOLAS

SAOUARI
SAOUARIS
SAP
SAPAJOU
SAPAJOUS
SAPAN
SAPANS
SAPANWOOD
SAPEGO
SAPEGOES
SAPELE
SAPELES
SAPFUL
SAPHEAD
SAPHEADED
SAPHEADS
SAPHENA
SAPHENAE
SAPHENAS
SAPHENOUS
SAPID
SAPIDER
SAPIDEST
SAPIDITY
SAPIDLESS
SAPIDNESS
SAPIENCE
SAPIENCES
SAPIENCY
SAPIENS
SAPIENT
SAPIENTLY
SAPIENTS
SAPLESS
SAPLING
SAPLINGS
SAPODILLA
SAPOGENIN
SAPONARIA
SAPONATED
SAPONIFY
SAPONIN
SAPONINE
SAPONINES
SAPONINS
SAPONITE
SAPONITES
SAPOR

S

SAPORIFIC	SAPS	SARDAR	SARMIE	SASHAY
SAPOROUS	SAPSAGO	SARDARS	SARMIES	SASHAYED
SAPORS	SAPSAGOS	SARDEL	SARNEY	SASHAYING
SAPOTA	SAPSUCKER	SARDELLE	SARNEYS	SASHAYS
SAPOTAS	SAPUCAIA	SARDELLES	SARNIE	SASHED
SAPOTE	SAPUCAIAS	SARDELS	SARNIES	SASHES
SAPOTES	SAPWOOD	SARDINE	SAROD	SASHIMI
SAPOUR	SAPWOODS	SARDINED	SARODE	SASHIMIS
SAPOURS	SAR	SARDINES	SARODES	SASHING
SAPPAN	SARABAND	SARDINING	SARODIST	SASHLESS
SAPPANS	SARABANDE	SARDIUS	SARODISTS	SASIN
SAPPED	SARABANDS	SARDIUSES	SARODS	SASINE
SAPPER	SARAFAN	SARDONIAN	SARONG	SASINES
SAPPERS	SARAFANS	SARDONIC	SARONGS	SASINS
SAPPHIC	SARAN	SARDONYX	SARONIC	SASKATOON
SAPPHICS	SARANGI	SARDS	SAROS	SASQUATCH
SAPPHIRE	SARANGIS	SARED	SAROSES	SASS
SAPPHIRED	SARANS	SAREE	SARPANCH	SASSABIES
SAPPHIRES	SARAPE	SAREES	SARRASIN	SASSABY
SAPPHISM	SARAPES	SARGASSA	SARRASINS	SASSAFRAS
SAPPHISMS	SARBACANE	SARGASSO	SARRAZIN	SASSARARA
SAPPHIST	SARCASM	SARGASSOS	SARRAZINS	SASSE
SAPPHISTS	SARCASMS	SARGASSUM	SARS	SASSED
SAPPIER	SARCASTIC	SARGE	SARSAR	SASSES
SAPPIEST	SARCENET	SARGES	SARSARS	SASSIER
SAPPILY	SARCENETS	SARGO	SARSDEN	SASSIES
SAPPINESS	SARCINA	SARGOS	SARSDENS	SASSIEST
SAPPING	SARCINAE	SARGOSES	SARSEN	SASSILY
SAPPINGS	SARCINAS	SARGUS	SARSENET	SASSINESS
SAPPLE	SARCOCARP	SARGUSES	SARSENETS	SASSING
SAPPLED	SARCODE	SARI	SARSENS	SASSOLIN
SAPPLES	SARCODES	SARIN	SARSNET	SASSOLINS
SAPPLING	SARCODIC	SARING	SARSNETS	SASSOLITE
SAPPY	SARCOID	SARINS	SARTOR	SASSWOOD
SAPRAEMIA	SARCOIDS	SARIS	SARTORIAL	SASSWOODS
SAPRAEMIC	SARCOLOGY	SARK	SARTORIAN	SASSY
SAPREMIA	SARCOMA	SARKIER	SARTORII	SASSYWOOD
SAPREMIAS	SARCOMAS	SARKIEST	SARTORIUS	SASTRA
SAPREMIC	SARCOMATA	SARKILY	SARTORS	SASTRAS
SAPROBE	SARCOMERE	SARKINESS	SARUS	SASTRUGA
SAPROBES	SARCONET	SARKING	SARUSES	SASTRUGI
SAPROBIAL	SARCONETS	SARKINGS	SASANQUA	SAT
SAPROBIC	SARCOPTIC	SARKS	SASANQUAS	SATAI
SAPROBITY	SARCOSOME	SARKY	SASARARA	SATAIS
SAPROLITE	SARCOUS	SARMENT	SASARARAS	SATANG
SAPROPEL	SARD	SARMENTA	SASER	SATANGS
SAPROPELS	SARDANA	SARMENTS	SASERS	SATANIC
SAPROZOIC	SARDANAS	SARMENTUM	SASH	SATANICAL

SATANISM	SATINY	SATYR	SAUGH	SAUTOIRS
SATANISMS	SATIRE	SATYRA	SAUGHS	SAUTS
SATANIST	SATIRES	SATYRAL	SAUGHY	SAV
SATANISTS	SATIRIC	SATYRALS	SAUL	SAVABLE
SATANITY	SATIRICAL	SATYRAS	SAULGE	SAVAGE
SATARA	SATIRISE	SATYRE	SAULGES	SAVAGED
SATARAS	SATIRISED	SATYRES	SAULIE	SAVAGEDOM
SATAY	SATIRISER	SATYRESS	SAULIES	SAVAGELY
SATAYS	SATIRISES	SATYRIC	SAULS	SAVAGER
SATCHEL	SATIRIST	SATYRICAL	SAULT	SAVAGERY
SATCHELED	SATIRISTS	SATYRID	SAULTS	SAVAGES
SATCHELS	SATIRIZE	SATYRIDS	SAUNA	SAVAGEST
SATCOM	SATIRIZED	SATYRISK	SAUNAED	SAVAGING
SATCOMS	SATIRIZER	SATYRISKS	SAUNAING	SAVAGISM
SATE	SATIRIZES	SATYRLIKE	SAUNAS	SAVAGISMS
SATED	SATIS	SATYRS	SAUNT	SAVANNA
SATEDNESS	SATISFICE	SAU	SAUNTED	SAVANNAH
SATEEN	SATISFIED	SAUBA	SAUNTER	SAVANNAHS
SATEENS	SATISFIER	SAUBAS	SAUNTERED	SAVANNAS
SATELESS	SATISFIES	SAUCE	SAUNTERER	SAVANT
SATELLES	SATISFY	SAUCEBOAT	SAUNTERS	SAVANTE
SATELLITE	SATIVE	SAUCEBOX	SAUNTING	SAVANTES
SATEM	SATNAV	SAUCED	SAUNTS	SAVANTS
SATES	SATNAVS	SAUCELESS	SAUREL	SAVARIN
SATI	SATORI	SAUCEPAN	SAURELS	SAVARINS
SATIABLE	SATORIS	SAUCEPANS	SAURIAN	SAVASANA
SATIABLY	SATRAP	SAUCEPOT	SAURIANS	SAVASANAS
SATIATE	SATRAPAL	SAUCEPOTS	SAURIES	SAVATE
SATIATED	SATRAPIES	SAUCER	SAUROID	SAVATES
SATIATES	SATRAPS	SAUCERFUL	SAUROIDS	SAVE
SATIATING	SATRAPY	SAUCERS	SAUROPOD	SAVEABLE
SATIATION	SATSANG	SAUCES	SAUROPODS	SAVED
SATIETIES	SATSANGS	SAUCH	SAURY	SAVEGARD
SATIETY	SATSUMA	SAUCHS	SAUSAGE	SAVEGARDS
SATIN	SATSUMAS	SAUCIER	SAUSAGES	SAVELOY
SATINED	SATURABLE	SAUCIERS	SAUT	SAVELOYS
SATINET	SATURANT	SAUCIEST	SAUTE	SAVER
SATINETS	SATURANTS	SAUCILY	SAUTED	SAVERS
SATINETTA	SATURATE	SAUCINESS	SAUTEED	SAVES
SATINETTE	SATURATED	SAUCING	SAUTEEING	SAVEY
SATING	SATURATER	SAUCISSE	SAUTEING	SAVEYED
SATINIER	SATURATES	SAUCISSES	SAUTERNE	SAVEYING
SATINIEST	SATURATOR	SAUCISSON	SAUTERNES	SAVEYS
SATINING	SATURNIC	SAUCY	SAUTES	SAVIN
SATINPOD	SATURNIID	SAUFGARD	SAUTING	SAVINE
SATINPODS	SATURNINE	SAUFGARDS	SAUTOIR	SAVINES
SATINS	SATURNISM	SAUGER	SAUTOIRE	SAVING
SATINWOOD	SATURNIST	SAUGERS	SAUTOIRES	SAVINGLY

S

SAVINGS	SAWAH	SAX	SAZHENS	SCAIL
SAVINS	SAWAHS	SAXATILE	SAZZES	SCAILED
SAVIOR	SAWBILL	SAXAUL	SBIRRI	SCAILING
SAVIORS	SAWBILLS	SAXAULS	SBIRRO	SCAILS
SAVIOUR	SAWBLADE	SAXE	SCAB	SCAITH
SAVIOURS	SAWBLADES	SAXES	SCABBARD	SCAITHED
SAVOR	SAWBONES	SAXHORN	SCABBARDS	SCAITHING
SAVORED	SAWBUCK	SAXHORNS	SCABBED	SCAITHS
SAVORER	SAWBUCKS	SAXICOLE	SCABBIER	SCALA
SAVORERS	SAWDER	SAXIFRAGE	SCABBIEST	SCALABLE
SAVORIER	SAWDERED	SAXIST	SCABBILY	SCALABLY
SAVORIES	SAWDERING	SAXISTS	SCABBING	SCALADE
SAVORIEST	SAWDERS	SAXITOXIN	SCABBLE	SCALADES
SAVORILY	SAWDUST	SAXMAN	SCABBLED	SCALADO
SAVORING	SAWDUSTED	SAXMEN	SCABBLES	SCALADOS
SAVORLESS	SAWDUSTS	SAXONIES	SCABBLING	SCALAE
SAVOROUS	SAWDUSTY	SAXONITE	SCABBY	SCALAGE
SAVORS	SAWED	SAXONITES	SCABIES	SCALAGES
SAVORY	SAWER	SAXONY	SCABIETIC	SCALAR
SAVOUR	SAWERS	SAXOPHONE	SCABIOSA	SCALARE
SAVOURED	SAWFISH	SAXTUBA	SCABIOSAS	SCALARES
SAVOURER	SAWFISHES	SAXTUBAS	SCABIOUS	SCALARS
SAVOURERS	SAWFLIES	SAY	SCABLAND	SCALATION
SAVOURIER	SAWFLY	SAYABLE	SCABLANDS	SCALAWAG
SAVOURIES	SAWGRASS	SAYABLES	SCABLIKE	SCALAWAGS
SAVOURILY	SAWHORSE	SAYED	SCABRID	SCALD
SAVOURING	SAWHORSES	SAYEDS	SCABROUS	SCALDED
SAVOURLY	SAWING	SAYER	SCABS	SCALDER
SAVOURS	SAWINGS	SAYERS	SCAD	SCALDERS
SAVOURY	SAWLIKE	SAYEST	SCADS	SCALDFISH
SAVOY	SAWLOG	SAYID	SCAFF	SCALDHEAD
SAVOYARD	SAWLOGS	SAYIDS	SCAFFED	SCALDIC
SAVOYARDS	SAWMILL	SAYING	SCAFFIE	SCALDING
SAVOYS	SAWMILLER	SAYINGS	SCAFFIER	SCALDINGS
SAVS	SAWMILLS	SAYNE	SCAFFIES	SCALDINI
SAVVEY	SAWN	SAYON	SCAFFIEST	SCALDINO
SAVVEYED	SAWNEY	SAYONARA	SCAFFING	SCALDS
SAVVEYING	SAWNEYS	SAYONARAS	SCAFFOLD	SCALDSHIP
SAVVEYS	SAWPIT	SAYONS	SCAFFOLDS	SCALE
SAVVIED	SAWPITS	SAYS	SCAFFS	SCALEABLE
SAVVIER	SAWS	SAYST	SCAFFY	SCALEABLY
SAVVIES	SAWSHARK	SAYYID	SCAG	SCALED
SAVVIEST	SAWSHARKS	SAYYIDS	SCAGGED	SCALELESS
SAVVILY	SAWTEETH	SAZ	SCAGGING	SCALELIKE
SAVVINESS	SAWTIMBER	SAZERAC	SCAGLIA	SCALENE
SAVVY	SAWTOOTH	SAZERACS	SCAGLIAS	SCALENES
SAVVYING	SAWYER	SAZES	SCAGLIOLA	SCALENI
SAW	SAWYERS	SAZHEN	SCAGS	SCALENUS

S

SCALEPAN	SCAMBLING	SCANTER	SCARABEES	SCARMOGE
SCALEPANS	SCAMEL	SCANTEST	SCARABOID	SCARMOGES
SCALER	SCAMELS	SCANTIER	SCARABS	SCARP
SCALERS	SCAMMED	SCANTIES	SCARCE	SCARPA
SCALES	SCAMMER	SCANTIEST	SCARCELY	SCARPAED
SCALETAIL	SCAMMERS	SCANTILY	SCARCER	SCARPAING
SCALEUP	SCAMMING	SCANTING	SCARCEST	SCARPAS
SCALEUPS	SCAMMONY	SCANTITY	SCARCITY	SCARPED
SCALEWORK	SCAMP	SCANTLE	SCARE	SCARPER
SCALIER	SCAMPED	SCANTLED	SCARECROW	SCARPERED
SCALIEST	SCAMPER	SCANTLES	SCARED	SCARPERS
SCALINESS	SCAMPERED	SCANTLING	SCAREDER	SCARPETTI
SCALING	SCAMPERER	SCANTLY	SCAREDEST	SCARPETTO
SCALINGS	SCAMPERS	SCANTNESS	SCAREDIES	SCARPH
SCALL	SCAMPI	SCANTS	SCAREDY	SCARPHED
SCALLAWAG	SCAMPIES	SCANTY	SCAREHEAD	SCARPHING
SCALLED	SCAMPING	SCAPA	SCARER	SCARPHS
SCALLIES	SCAMPINGS	SCAPAED	SCARERS	SCARPINES
SCALLION	SCAMPIS	SCAPAING	SCARES	SCARPING
SCALLIONS	SCAMPISH	SCAPAS	SCAREWARE	SCARPINGS
SCALLOP	SCAMPS	SCAPE	SCAREY	SCARPS
SCALLOPED	SCAMS	SCAPED	SCARF	SCARRE
SCALLOPER	SCAMSTER	SCAPEGOAT	SCARFED	SCARRED
SCALLOPS	SCAMSTERS	SCAPELESS	SCARFER	SCARRES
SCALLS	SCAMTO	SCAPEMENT	SCARFERS	SCARRIER
SCALLY	SCAMTOS	SCAPES	SCARFING	SCARRIEST
SCALLYWAG	SCAN	SCAPHOID	SCARFINGS	SCARRING
SCALOGRAM	SCAND	SCAPHOIDS	SCARFISH	SCARRINGS
SCALP	SCANDAL	SCAPHOPOD	SCARFPIN	SCARRY
SCALPED	SCANDALED	SCAPI	SCARFPINS	SCARS
SCALPEL	SCANDALS	SCAPING	SCARFS	SCART
SCALPELS	SCANDENT	SCAPOLITE	SCARFSKIN	SCARTED
SCALPER	SCANDIA	SCAPOSE	SCARFWISE	SCARTH
SCALPERS	SCANDIAS	SCAPPLE	SCARIER	SCARTHS
SCALPING	SCANDIC	SCAPPLED	SCARIEST	SCARTING
SCALPINGS	SCANDIUM	SCAPPLES	SCARIFIED	SCARTS
SCALPINS	SCANDIUMS	SCAPPLING	SCARIFIER	SCARVED
SCALPLESS	SCANNABLE	SCAPULA	SCARIFIES	SCARVES
SCALPRUM	SCANNED	SCAPULAE	SCARIFY	SCARY
SCALPRUMS	SCANNER	SCAPULAR	SCARILY	SCAT
SCALPS	SCANNERS	SCAPULARS	SCARINESS	SCATBACK
SCALY	SCANNING	SCAPULARY	SCARING	SCATBACKS
SCAM	SCANNINGS	SCAPULAS	SCARIOSE	SCATCH
SCAMBLE	SCANS	SCAPUS	SCARIOUS	SCATCHES
SCAMBLED	SCANSION	SCAR	SCARLESS	SCATH
SCAMBLER	SCANSIONS	SCARAB	SCARLET	SCATHE
SCAMBLERS	SCANT	SCARABAEI	SCARLETED	SCATHED
SCAMBLES	SCANTED	SCARABEE	SCARLETS	SCATHEFUL

SCATHES	SCAWS	SCENTINGS	SCHEMA	SCHLEP
SCATHING	SCAWTITE	SCENTLESS	SCHEMAS	SCHLEPP
SCATHS	SCAWTITES	SCENTS	SCHEMATA	SCHLEPPED
SCATOLE	SCAZON	SCEPSIS	SCHEMATIC	SCHLEPPER
SCATOLES	SCAZONS	SCEPSISES	SCHEME	SCHLEPPS
SCATOLOGY	SCAZONTES	SCEPTER	SCHEMED	SCHLEPPY
SCATS	SCAZONTIC	SCEPTERED	SCHEMER	SCHLEPS
SCATT	SCEAT	SCEPTERS	SCHEMERS	SCHLICH
SCATTED	SCEATS	SCEPTIC	SCHEMES	SCHLICHS
SCATTER	SCEATT	SCEPTICAL	SCHEMIE	SCHLIERE
SCATTERED	SCEATTAS	SCEPTICS	SCHEMIES	SCHLIEREN
SCATTERER	SCEATTS	SCEPTRAL	SCHEMING	SCHLIERIC
SCATTERS	SCEDULE	SCEPTRE	SCHEMINGS	SCHLOCK
SCATTERY	SCEDULED	SCEPTRED	SCHERZI	SCHLOCKER
SCATTIER	SCEDULES	SCEPTRES	SCHERZO	SCHLOCKEY
SCATTIEST	SCEDULING	SCEPTRING	SCHERZOS	SCHLOCKS
SCATTILY	SCELERAT	SCEPTRY	SCHIAVONE	SCHLOCKY
SCATTING	SCELERATE	SCERNE	SCHIEDAM	SCHLONG
SCATTINGS	SCELERATS	SCERNED	SCHIEDAMS	SCHLONGS
SCATTS	SCENA	SCERNES	SCHILLER	SCHLOSS
SCATTY	SCENARIES	SCERNING	SCHILLERS	SCHLOSSES
SCAUD	SCENARIO	SCHANSE	SCHILLING	SCHLUB
SCAUDED	SCENARIOS	SCHANSES	SCHIMMEL	SCHLUBS
SCAUDING	SCENARISE	SCHANTZE	SCHIMMELS	SCHLUMP
SCAUDS	SCENARIST	SCHANTZES	SCHISM	SCHLUMPED
SCAUP	SCENARIZE	SCHANZE	SCHISMA	SCHLUMPS
SCAUPED	SCENARY	SCHANZES	SCHISMAS	SCHLUMPY
SCAUPER	SCENAS	SCHAPPE	SCHISMS	SCHMALTZ
SCAUPERS	SCEND	SCHAPPED	SCHIST	SCHMALTZY
SCAUPING	SCENDED	SCHAPPES	SCHISTOSE	SCHMALZ
SCAUPS	SCENDING	SCHAPSKA	SCHISTOUS	SCHMALZES
SCAUR	SCENDS	SCHAPSKAS	SCHISTS	SCHMALZY
SCAURED	SCENE	SCHATCHEN	SCHIZIER	SCHMATTE
SCAURIES	SCENED	SCHAV	SCHIZIEST	SCHMATTES
SCAURING	SCENEMAN	SCHAVS	SCHIZO	SCHMEAR
SCAURS	SCENEMEN	SCHECHITA	SCHIZOID	SCHMEARED
SCAURY	SCENERIES	SCHEDULAR	SCHIZOIDS	SCHMEARS
SCAVAGE	SCENERY	SCHEDULE	SCHIZONT	SCHMECK
SCAVAGED	SCENES	SCHEDULED	SCHIZONTS	SCHMECKED
SCAVAGER	SCENESTER	SCHEDULER	SCHIZOPOD	SCHMECKER
SCAVAGERS	SCENIC	SCHEDULES	SCHIZOS	SCHMECKS
SCAVAGES	SCENICAL	SCHEELITE	SCHIZY	SCHMEER
SCAVAGING	SCENICS	SCHELLIES	SCHIZZIER	SCHMEERED
SCAVENGE	SCENING	SCHELLUM	SCHIZZY	SCHMEERS
SCAVENGED	SCENT	SCHELLUMS	SCHLAGER	SCHMELZ
SCAVENGER	SCENTED	SCHELLY	SCHLAGERS	SCHMELZE
SCAVENGES	SCENTFUL	SCHELM	SCHLEMIEL	SCHMELZES
SCAW	SCENTING	SCHELMS	SCHLEMIHL	SCHMICK

SCHMICKER	SCHOLAR	SCHTUPS	SCIMETARS	SCLAFFER
SCHMO	SCHOLARCH	SCHUIT	SCIMITAR	SCLAFFERS
SCHMOCK	SCHOLARLY	SCHUITS	SCIMITARS	SCLAFFING
SCHMOCKS	SCHOLARS	SCHUL	SCIMITER	SCLAFFS
SCHMOE	SCHOLIA	SCHULN	SCIMITERS	SCLATE
SCHMOES	SCHOLIAST	SCHULS	SCINCOID	SCLATED
SCHMOOS	SCHOLION	SCHUSS	SCINCOIDS	SCLATES
SCHMOOSE	SCHOLIUM	SCHUSSED	SCINTILLA	SCLATING
SCHMOOSED	SCHOLIUMS	SCHUSSER	SCIOLISM	SCLAUNDER
SCHMOOSES	SCHOOL	SCHUSSERS	SCIOLISMS	SCLAVE
SCHMOOZ	SCHOOLBAG	SCHUSSES	SCIOLIST	SCLAVES
SCHMOOZE	SCHOOLBOY	SCHUSSING	SCIOLISTS	SCLERA
SCHMOOZED	SCHOOLDAY	SCHUYT	SCIOLOUS	SCLERAE
SCHMOOZER	SCHOOLE	SCHUYTS	SCIOLTO	SCLERAL
SCHMOOZES	SCHOOLED	SCHVARTZE	SCIOMACHY	SCLERAS
SCHMOOZY	SCHOOLER	SCHVITZ	SCIOMANCY	SCLERE
SCHMOS	SCHOOLERS	SCHVITZED	SCION	SCLEREID
SCHMUCK	SCHOOLERY	SCHVITZES	SCIONS	SCLEREIDE
SCHMUCKED	SCHOOLES	SCHWA	SCIOPHYTE	SCLEREIDS
SCHMUCKS	SCHOOLIE	SCHWAG	SCIOSOPHY	SCLEREMA
SCHMUCKY	SCHOOLIES	SCHWAGS	SCIROC	SCLEREMAS
SCHMUTTER	SCHOOLING	SCHWARTZE	SCIROCCO	SCLERES
SCHMUTZ	SCHOOLKID	SCHWAS	SCIROCCOS	SCLERITE
SCHMUTZES	SCHOOLMAN	SCIAENID	SCIROCS	SCLERITES
SCHNAPPER	SCHOOLMEN	SCIAENIDS	SCIRRHI	SCLERITIC
SCHNAPPS	SCHOOLS	SCIAENOID	SCIRRHOID	SCLERITIS
SCHNAPS	SCHOONER	SCIAMACHY	SCIRRHOUS	SCLEROID
SCHNAPSES	SCHOONERS	SCIARID	SCIRRHUS	SCLEROMA
SCHNAUZER	SCHORL	SCIARIDS	SCISSEL	SCLEROMAS
SCHNECKE	SCHORLS	SCIATIC	SCISSELS	SCLEROSAL
SCHNECKEN	SCHOUT	SCIATICA	SCISSIL	SCLEROSE
SCHNEID	SCHOUTS	SCIATICAL	SCISSILE	SCLEROSED
SCHNEIDS	SCHRIK	SCIATICAS	SCISSILS	SCLEROSES
SCHNELL	SCHRIKS	SCIATICS	SCISSION	SCLEROSIS
SCHNITZEL	SCHROD	SCIENCE	SCISSIONS	SCLEROTAL
SCHNOODLE	SCHRODS	SCIENCED	SCISSOR	SCLEROTIA
SCHNOOK	SCHTICK	SCIENCES	SCISSORED	SCLEROTIC
SCHNOOKS	SCHTICKS	SCIENT	SCISSORER	SCLEROTIN
SCHNORKEL	SCHTIK	SCIENTER	SCISSORS	SCLEROUS
SCHNORR	SCHTIKS	SCIENTIAL	SCISSURE	SCLIFF
SCHNORRED	SCHTOOK	SCIENTISE	SCISSURES	SCLIFFS
SCHNORRER	SCHTOOKS	SCIENTISM	SCIURID	SCLIM
SCHNORRS	SCHTOOM	SCIENTIST	SCIURIDS	SCLIMMED
SCHNOZ	SCHTUCK	SCIENTIZE	SCIURINE	SCLIMMING
SCHNOZES	SCHTUCKS	SCILICET	SCIURINES	SCLIMS
SCHNOZZ	SCHTUM	SCILLA	SCIUROID	SCODIER
SCHNOZZES	SCHTUP	SCILLAS	SCLAFF	SCODIEST
SCHNOZZLE	SCHTUPPED	SCIMETAR	SCLAFFED	SCODY

SCOFF	SCONCED	SCOPE	SCORNS	SCOURER
SCOFFED	SCONCES	SCOPED	SCORODITE	SCOURERS
SCOFFER	SCONCHEON	SCOPELID	SCORPER	SCOURGE
SCOFFERS	SCONCING	SCOPELIDS	SCORPERS	SCOURGED
SCOFFING	SCONE	SCOPELOID	SCORPIOID	SCOURGER
SCOFFINGS	SCONES	SCOPES	SCORPION	SCOURGERS
SCOFFLAW	SCONTION	SCOPING	SCORPIONS	SCOURGES
SCOFFLAWS	SCONTIONS	SCOPOLINE	SCORRENDO	SCOURGING
SCOFFS	SCOOBIES	SCOPS	SCORSE	SCOURIE
SCOG	SCOOBY	SCOPULA	SCORSED	SCOURIES
SCOGGED	SCOOCH	SCOPULAE	SCORSER	SCOURING
SCOGGING	SCOOCHED	SCOPULAS	SCORSERS	SCOURINGS
SCOGS	SCOOCHES	SCOPULATE	SCORSES	SCOURS
SCOINSON	SCOOCHING	SCORBUTIC	SCORSING	SCOURSE
SCOINSONS	SCOOG	SCORCH	SCOT	SCOURSED
SCOLD	SCOOGED	SCORCHED	SCOTCH	SCOURSES
SCOLDABLE	SCOOGING	SCORCHER	SCOTCHED	SCOURSING
SCOLDED	SCOOGS	SCORCHERS	SCOTCHES	SCOUSE
SCOLDER	SCOOP	SCORCHES	SCOTCHING	SCOUSER
SCOLDERS	SCOOPABLE	SCORCHING	SCOTER	SCOUSERS
SCOLDING	SCOOPED	SCORDATO	SCOTERS	SCOUSES
SCOLDINGS	SCOOPER	SCORE	SCOTIA	SCOUT
SCOLDS	SCOOPERS	SCORECARD	SCOTIAS	SCOUTED
SCOLECES	SCOOPFUL	SCORED	SCOTOMA	SCOUTER
SCOLECID	SCOOPFULS	SCORELESS	SCOTOMAS	SCOUTERS
SCOLECIDS	SCOOPING	SCORELINE	SCOTOMATA	SCOUTH
SCOLECITE	SCOOPINGS	SCOREPAD	SCOTOMIA	SCOUTHER
SCOLECOID	SCOOPS	SCOREPADS	SCOTOMIAS	SCOUTHERS
SCOLEX	SCOOPSFUL	SCORER	SCOTOMIES	SCOUTHERY
SCOLIA	SCOOSH	SCORERS	SCOTOMY	SCOUTHS
SCOLICES	SCOOSHED	SCORES	SCOTOPHIL	SCOUTING
SCOLIOMA	SCOOSHES	SCORIA	SCOTOPIA	SCOUTINGS
SCOLIOMAS	SCOOSHING	SCORIAC	SCOTOPIAS	SCOUTS
SCOLION	SCOOT	SCORIAE	SCOTOPIC	SCOW
SCOLIOSES	SCOOTCH	SCORIFIED	SCOTS	SCOWDER
SCOLIOSIS	SCOOTCHED	SCORIFIER	SCOTTIE	SCOWDERED
SCOLIOTIC	SCOOTCHES	SCORIFIES	SCOTTIES	SCOWDERS
SCOLLOP	SCOOTED	SCORIFY	SCOUG	SCOWED
SCOLLOPED	SCOOTER	SCORING	SCOUGED	SCOWING
SCOLLOPS	SCOOTERED	SCORINGS	SCOUGING	SCOWL
SCOLYTID	SCOOTERS	SCORIOUS	SCOUGS	SCOWLED
SCOLYTIDS	SCOOTING	SCORN	SCOUNDREL	SCOWLER
SCOLYTOID	SCOOTS	SCORNED	SCOUP	SCOWLERS
SCOMBRID	SCOP	SCORNER	SCOUPED	SCOWLING
SCOMBRIDS	SCOPA	SCORNERS	SCOUPING	SCOWLS
SCOMBROID	SCOPAE	SCORNFUL	SCOUPS	SCOWP
SCOMFISH	SCOPAS	SCORNING	SCOUR	SCOWPED
SCONCE	SCOPATE	SCORNINGS	SCOURED	SCOWPING

SCOWPS
SCOWRER
SCOWRERS
SCOWRIE
SCOWRIES
SCOWS
SCOWTH
SCOWTHER
SCOWTHERS
SCOWTHS
SCOZZA
SCOZZAS
SCRAB
SCRABBED
SCRABBING
SCRABBLE
SCRABBLED
SCRABBLER
SCRABBLES
SCRABBLY
SCRABS
SCRAE
SCRAES
SCRAG
SCRAGGED
SCRAGGIER
SCRAGGILY
SCRAGGING
SCRAGGLY
SCRAGGY
SCRAGS
SCRAICH
SCRAICHED
SCRAICHS
SCRAIGH
SCRAIGHED
SCRAIGHS
SCRAM
SCRAMB
SCRAMBED
SCRAMBING
SCRAMBLE
SCRAMBLED
SCRAMBLER
SCRAMBLES
SCRAMBS
SCRAMJET
SCRAMJETS

SCRAMMED
SCRAMMING
SCRAMS
SCRAN
SCRANCH
SCRANCHED
SCRANCHES
SCRANNEL
SCRANNELS
SCRANNIER
SCRANNY
SCRANS
SCRAP
SCRAPABLE
SCRAPBOOK
SCRAPE
SCRAPED
SCRAPEGUT
SCRAPER
SCRAPERS
SCRAPES
SCRAPHEAP
SCRAPIE
SCRAPIES
SCRAPING
SCRAPINGS
SCRAPPAGE
SCRAPPED
SCRAPPER
SCRAPPERS
SCRAPPIER
SCRAPPILY
SCRAPPING
SCRAPPLE
SCRAPPLES
SCRAPPY
SCRAPS
SCRAPYARD
SCRAT
SCRATCH
SCRATCHED
SCRATCHER
SCRATCHES
SCRATCHIE
SCRATCHY
SCRATS
SCRATTED
SCRATTING

SCRATTLE
SCRATTLED
SCRATTLES
SCRAUCH
SCRAUCHED
SCRAUCHS
SCRAUGH
SCRAUGHED
SCRAUGHS
SCRAVEL
SCRAVELED
SCRAVELS
SCRAW
SCRAWB
SCRAWBED
SCRAWBING
SCRAWBS
SCRAWL
SCRAWLED
SCRAWLER
SCRAWLERS
SCRAWLIER
SCRAWLING
SCRAWLS
SCRAWLY
SCRAWM
SCRAWMED
SCRAWMING
SCRAWMS
SCRAWNIER
SCRAWNILY
SCRAWNY
SCRAWP
SCRAWPED
SCRAWPING
SCRAWPS
SCRAWS
SCRAY
SCRAYE
SCRAYES
SCRAYS
SCREAK
SCREAKED
SCREAKIER
SCREAKING
SCREAKS
SCREAKY
SCREAM

SCREAMED
SCREAMER
SCREAMERS
SCREAMING
SCREAMO
SCREAMOS
SCREAMS
SCREE
SCREECH
SCREECHED
SCREECHER
SCREECHES
SCREECHY
SCREED
SCREEDED
SCREEDER
SCREEDERS
SCREEDING
SCREEDS
SCREEN
SCREENED
SCREENER
SCREENERS
SCREENFUL
SCREENIE
SCREENIES
SCREENING
SCREENS
SCREES
SCREET
SCREETED
SCREETING
SCREETS
SCREEVE
SCREEVED
SCREEVER
SCREEVERS
SCREEVES
SCREEVING
SCREICH
SCREICHED
SCREICHS
SCREIGH
SCREIGHED
SCREIGHS
SCREW
SCREWABLE
SCREWBALL

SCREWBEAN
SCREWED
SCREWER
SCREWERS
SCREWHEAD
SCREWIER
SCREWIEST
SCREWING
SCREWINGS
SCREWLIKE
SCREWS
SCREWTOP
SCREWTOPS
SCREWUP
SCREWUPS
SCREWWORM
SCREWY
SCRIBABLE
SCRIBAL
SCRIBBLE
SCRIBBLED
SCRIBBLER
SCRIBBLES
SCRIBBLY
SCRIBE
SCRIBED
SCRIBER
SCRIBERS
SCRIBES
SCRIBING
SCRIBINGS
SCRIBISM
SCRIBISMS
SCRIECH
SCRIECHED
SCRIECHS
SCRIED
SCRIENE
SCRIENES
SCRIES
SCRIEVE
SCRIEVED
SCRIEVES
SCRIEVING
SCRIGGLE
SCRIGGLED
SCRIGGLES
SCRIGGLY

S

SCRIKE	SCROBE	SCROUGERS	SCRUMPED	SCUCHIN
SCRIKED	SCROBES	SCROUGES	SCRUMPIES	SCUCHINS
SCRIKES	SCROBS	SCROUGING	SCRUMPING	SCUD
SCRIKING	SCROD	SCROUNGE	SCRUMPLE	SCUDDALER
SCRIM	SCRODDLED	SCROUNGED	SCRUMPLED	SCUDDED
SCRIMMAGE	SCRODS	SCROUNGER	SCRUMPLES	SCUDDER
SCRIMP	SCROFULA	SCROUNGES	SCRUMPOX	SCUDDERS
SCRIMPED	SCROFULAS	SCROUNGY	SCRUMPS	SCUDDING
SCRIMPER	SCROG	SCROW	SCRUMPY	SCUDDLE
SCRIMPERS	SCROGGIE	SCROWDGE	SCRUMS	SCUDDLED
SCRIMPIER	SCROGGIER	SCROWDGED	SCRUNCH	SCUDDLES
SCRIMPILY	SCROGGIN	SCROWDGES	SCRUNCHED	SCUDDLING
SCRIMPING	SCROGGINS	SCROWL	SCRUNCHES	SCUDI
SCRIMPIT	SCROGGY	SCROWLE	SCRUNCHIE	SCUDLER
SCRIMPLY	SCROGS	SCROWLED	SCRUNCHIN	SCUDLERS
SCRIMPS	SCROLL	SCROWLES	SCRUNCHY	SCUDO
SCRIMPY	SCROLLED	SCROWLING	SCRUNT	SCUDS
SCRIMS	SCROLLER	SCROWLS	SCRUNTIER	SCUFF
SCRIMSHAW	SCROLLERS	SCROWS	SCRUNTS	SCUFFED
SCRIMURE	SCROLLING	SCROYLE	SCRUNTY	SCUFFER
SCRIMURES	SCROLLS	SCROYLES	SCRUPLE	SCUFFERS
SCRINE	SCROME	SCRUB	SCRUPLED	SCUFFING
SCRINES	SCROMED	SCRUBBED	SCRUPLER	SCUFFLE
SCRIP	SCROMES	SCRUBBER	SCRUPLERS	SCUFFLED
SCRIPPAGE	SCROMING	SCRUBBERS	SCRUPLES	SCUFFLER
SCRIPS	SCROOCH	SCRUBBIER	SCRUPLING	SCUFFLERS
SCRIPT	SCROOCHED	SCRUBBILY	SCRUTABLE	SCUFFLES
SCRIPTED	SCROOCHES	SCRUBBING	SCRUTATOR	SCUFFLING
SCRIPTER	SCROOGE	SCRUBBY	SCRUTINY	SCUFFS
SCRIPTERS	SCROOGED	SCRUBLAND	SCRUTO	SCUFT
SCRIPTING	SCROOGES	SCRUBS	SCRUTOIRE	SCUFTS
SCRIPTORY	SCROOGING	SCRUFF	SCRUTOS	SCUG
SCRIPTS	SCROOP	SCRUFFED	SCRUZE	SCUGGED
SCRIPTURE	SCROOPED	SCRUFFIER	SCRUZED	SCUGGING
SCRITCH	SCROOPING	SCRUFFILY	SCRUZES	SCUGS
SCRITCHED	SCROOPS	SCRUFFING	SCRUZING	SCUL
SCRITCHES	SCROOTCH	SCRUFFS	SCRY	SCULCH
SCRIVE	SCRORP	SCRUFFY	SCRYDE	SCULCHES
SCRIVED	SCRORPS	SCRUM	SCRYER	SCULK
SCRIVENER	SCROTA	SCRUMDOWN	SCRYERS	SCULKED
SCRIVES	SCROTAL	SCRUMMAGE	SCRYING	SCULKER
SCRIVING	SCROTE	SCRUMMED	SCRYINGS	SCULKERS
SCROB	SCROTES	SCRUMMIE	SCRYNE	SCULKING
SCROBBED	SCROTUM	SCRUMMIER	SCRYNES	SCULKS
SCROBBING	SCROTUMS	SCRUMMIES	SCUBA	SCULL
SCROBBLE	SCROUGE	SCRUMMING	SCUBAED	SCULLE
SCROBBLED	SCROUGED	SCRUMMY	SCUBAING	SCULLED
SCROBBLES	SCROUGER	SCRUMP	SCUBAS	SCULLER

SCULLERS	SCUMMY	SCUSE	SCYBALOUS	SEABOARDS
SCULLERY	SCUMS	SCUSED	SCYBALUM	SEABOOT
SCULLES	SCUNCHEON	SCUSES	SCYE	SEABOOTS
SCULLING	SCUNDERED	SCUSING	SCYES	SEABORNE
SCULLINGS	SCUNGE	SCUT	SCYPHATE	SEABOTTLE
SCULLION	SCUNGED	SCUTA	SCYPHI	SEABREAM
SCULLIONS	SCUNGES	SCUTAGE	SCYPHUS	SEABREAMS
SCULLS	SCUNGIER	SCUTAGES	SCYTALE	SEACOAST
SCULP	SCUNGIEST	SCUTAL	SCYTALES	SEACOASTS
SCULPED	SCUNGILE	SCUTATE	SCYTHE	SEACOCK
SCULPIN	SCUNGILI	SCUTATION	SCYTHED	SEACOCKS
SCULPING	SCUNGILLE	SCUTCH	SCYTHEMAN	SEACRAFT
SCULPINS	SCUNGILLI	SCUTCHED	SCYTHEMEN	SEACRAFTS
SCULPS	SCUNGING	SCUTCHEON	SCYTHER	SEACUNNY
SCULPSIT	SCUNGY	SCUTCHER	SCYTHERS	SEADOG
SCULPT	SCUNNER	SCUTCHERS	SCYTHES	SEADOGS
SCULPTED	SCUNNERED	SCUTCHES	SCYTHING	SEADROME
SCULPTING	SCUNNERS	SCUTCHING	SDAINE	SEADROMES
SCULPTOR	SCUP	SCUTE	SDAINED	SEAFARER
SCULPTORS	SCUPPAUG	SCUTELLA	SDAINES	SEAFARERS
SCULPTS	SCUPPAUGS	SCUTELLAR	SDAINING	SEAFARING
SCULPTURE	SCUPPER	SCUTELLUM	SDAYN	SEAFLOOR
SCULS	SCUPPERED	SCUTES	SDAYNED	SEAFLOORS
SCULTCH	SCUPPERS	SCUTIFORM	SDAYNING	SEAFOAM
SCULTCHES	SCUPS	SCUTIGER	SDAYNS	SEAFOAMS
SCUM	SCUR	SCUTIGERS	SDEIGN	SEAFOLK
SCUMBAG	SCURF	SCUTS	SDEIGNE	SEAFOLKS
SCUMBAGS	SCURFIER	SCUTTER	SDEIGNED	SEAFOOD
SCUMBALL	SCURFIEST	SCUTTERED	SDEIGNES	SEAFOODS
SCUMBALLS	SCURFS	SCUTTERS	SDEIGNING	SEAFOWL
SCUMBER	SCURFY	SCUTTLE	SDEIGNS	SEAFOWLS
SCUMBERED	SCURRED	SCUTTLED	SDEIN	SEAFRONT
SCUMBERS	SCURRIED	SCUTTLER	SDEINED	SEAFRONTS
SCUMBLE	SCURRIER	SCUTTLERS	SDEINING	SEAGIRT
SCUMBLED	SCURRIERS	SCUTTLES	SDEINS	SEAGOING
SCUMBLES	SCURRIES	SCUTTLING	SEA	SEAGRASS
SCUMBLING	SCURRIL	SCUTUM	SEABAG	SEAGULL
SCUMFISH	SCURRILE	SCUTWORK	SEABAGS	SEAGULLS
SCUMLESS	SCURRING	SCUTWORKS	SEABANK	SEAHAWK
SCUMLIKE	SCURRIOUR	SCUZZ	SEABANKS	SEAHAWKS
SCUMMED	SCURRY	SCUZZBAG	SEABEACH	SEAHOG
SCUMMER	SCURRYING	SCUZZBAGS	SEABED	SEAHOGS
SCUMMERS	SCURS	SCUZZBALL	SEABEDS	SEAHORSE
SCUMMIER	SCURVIER	SCUZZES	SEABIRD	SEAHORSES
SCUMMIEST	SCURVIES	SCUZZIER	SEABIRDS	SEAHOUND
SCUMMILY	SCURVIEST	SCUZZIEST	SEABLITE	SEAHOUNDS
SCUMMING	SCURVILY	SCUZZY	SEABLITES	SEAKALE
SCUMMINGS	SCURVY	SCYBALA	SEABOARD	SEAKALES

S

SEAKINDLY	SEAMINGS	SEAROBIN	SEATROUT	SEC
SEAL	SEAMLESS	SEAROBINS	SEATROUTS	SECALOSE
SEALABLE	SEAMLIKE	SEARS	SEATS	SECALOSES
SEALANT	SEAMOUNT	SEAS	SEATWORK	SECANT
SEALANTS	SEAMOUNTS	SEASCAPE	SEATWORKS	SECANTLY
SEALCH	SEAMS	SEASCAPES	SEAWALL	SECANTS
SEALCHS	SEAMSET	SEASCOUT	SEAWALLED	SECATEUR
SEALED	SEAMSETS	SEASCOUTS	SEAWALLS	SECATEURS
SEALER	SEAMSTER	SEASE	SEAWAN	SECCO
SEALERIES	SEAMSTERS	SEASED	SEAWANS	SECCOS
SEALERS	SEAMY	SEASES	SEAWANT	SECEDE
SEALERY	SEAN	SEASHELL	SEAWANTS	SECEDED
SEALGH	SEANCE	SEASHELLS	SEAWARD	SECEDER
SEALGHS	SEANCES	SEASHORE	SEAWARDLY	SECEDERS
SEALIFT	SEANED	SEASHORES	SEAWARDS	SECEDES
SEALIFTED	SEANING	SEASICK	SEAWARE	SECEDING
SEALIFTS	SEANNACHY	SEASICKER	SEAWARES	SECERN
SEALINE	SEANS	SEASIDE	SEAWATER	SECERNED
SEALINES	SEAPIECE	SEASIDES	SEAWATERS	SECERNENT
SEALING	SEAPIECES	SEASING	SEAWAY	SECERNING
SEALINGS	SEAPLANE	SEASON	SEAWAYS	SECERNS
SEALLIKE	SEAPLANES	SEASONAL	SEAWEED	SECESH
SEALPOINT	SEAPORT	SEASONALS	SEAWEEDS	SECESHER
SEALS	SEAPORTS	SEASONED	SEAWEEDY	SECESHERS
SEALSKIN	SEAQUAKE	SEASONER	SEAWIFE	SECESHES
SEALSKINS	SEAQUAKES	SEASONERS	SEAWIVES	SECESSION
SEALWAX	SEAQUARIA	SEASONING	SEAWOMAN	SECH
SEALWAXES	SEAR	SEASONS	SEAWOMEN	SECHS
SEALYHAM	SEARAT	SEASPEAK	SEAWORM	SECKEL
SEALYHAMS	SEARATS	SEASPEAKS	SEAWORMS	SECKELS
SEAM	SEARCE	SEASTRAND	SEAWORTHY	SECKLE
SEAMAID	SEARCED	SEASURE	SEAZE	SECKLES
SEAMAIDS	SEARCES	SEASURES	SEAZED	SECLUDE
SEAMAN	SEARCH	SEAT	SEAZES	SECLUDED
SEAMANLY	SEARCHED	SEATBACK	SEAZING	SECLUDES
SEAMARK	SEARCHER	SEATBACKS	SEBACEOUS	SECLUDING
SEAMARKS	SEARCHERS	SEATBELT	SEBACIC	SECLUSION
SEAME	SEARCHES	SEATBELTS	SEBASIC	SECLUSIVE
SEAMED	SEARCHING	SEATED	SEBATE	SECO
SEAMEN	SEARCING	SEATER	SEBATES	SECODONT
SEAMER	SEARE	SEATERS	SEBESTEN	SECODONTS
SEAMERS	SEARED	SEATING	SEBESTENS	SECONAL
SEAMES	SEARER	SEATINGS	SEBIFIC	SECONALS
SEAMFREE	SEAREST	SEATLESS	SEBORRHEA	SECOND
SEAMIER	SEARING	SEATMATE	SEBUM	SECONDARY
SEAMIEST	SEARINGLY	SEATMATES	SEBUMS	SECONDE
SEAMINESS	SEARINGS	SEATRAIN	SEBUNDIES	SECONDED
SEAMING	SEARNESS	SEATRAINS	SEBUNDY	SECONDEE

SECONDEES	SECTORED	SEDERUNT	SEEDED	SEEMER
SECONDER	SECTORIAL	SEDERUNTS	SEEDER	SEEMERS
SECONDERS	SECTORING	SEDES	SEEDERS	SEEMING
SECONDES	SECTORISE	SEDGE	SEEDHEAD	SEEMINGLY
SECONDI	SECTORIZE	SEDGED	SEEDHEADS	SEEMINGS
SECONDING	SECTORS	SEDGELAND	SEEDIER	SEEMLESS
SECONDLY	SECTS	SEDGES	SEEDIEST	SEEMLIER
SECONDO	SECULA	SEDGIER	SEEDILY	SEEMLIEST
SECONDS	SECULAR	SEDGIEST	SEEDINESS	SEEMLIHED
SECPAR	SECULARLY	SEDGY	SEEDING	SEEMLY
SECPARS	SECULARS	SEDILE	SEEDINGS	SEEMLYHED
SECRECIES	SECULUM	SEDILIA	SEEDLESS	SEEMS
SECRECY	SECULUMS	SEDILIUM	SEEDLIKE	SEEN
SECRET	SECUND	SEDIMENT	SEEDLING	SEEP
SECRETA	SECUNDINE	SEDIMENTS	SEEDLINGS	SEEPAGE
SECRETAGE	SECUNDLY	SEDITION	SEEDLIP	SEEPAGES
SECRETARY	SECUNDUM	SEDITIONS	SEEDLIPS	SEEPED
SECRETE	SECURABLE	SEDITIOUS	SEEDMAN	SEEPIER
SECRETED	SECURANCE	SEDUCE	SEEDMEN	SEEPIEST
SECRETER	SECURE	SEDUCED	SEEDNESS	SEEPING
SECRETES	SECURED	SEDUCER	SEEDPOD	SEEPS
SECRETEST	SECURELY	SEDUCERS	SEEDPODS	SEEPY
SECRETIN	SECURER	SEDUCES	SEEDS	SEER
SECRETING	SECURERS	SEDUCIBLE	SEEDSMAN	SEERESS
SECRETINS	SECURES	SEDUCING	SEEDSMEN	SEERESSES
SECRETION	SECUREST	SEDUCINGS	SEEDSTOCK	SEERS
SECRETIVE	SECURING	SEDUCIVE	SEEDTIME	SEES
SECRETLY	SECURITAN	SEDUCTION	SEEDTIMES	SEESAW
SECRETOR	SECURITY	SEDUCTIVE	SEEDY	SEESAWED
SECRETORS	SED	SEDUCTOR	SEEING	SEESAWING
SECRETORY	SEDAN	SEDUCTORS	SEEINGS	SEESAWS
SECRETS	SEDANS	SEDULITY	SEEK	SEETHE
SECS	SEDARIM	SEDULOUS	SEEKER	SEETHED
SECT	SEDATE	SEDUM	SEEKERS	SEETHER
SECTARIAL	SEDATED	SEDUMS	SEEKING	SEETHERS
SECTARIAN	SEDATELY	SEE	SEEKS	SEETHES
SECTARIES	SEDATER	SEEABLE	SEEL	SEETHING
SECTARY	SEDATES	SEECATCH	SEELD	SEETHINGS
SECTATOR	SEDATEST	SEED	SEELED	SEEWING
SECTATORS	SEDATING	SEEDBED	SEELIE	SEEWINGS
SECTILE	SEDATION	SEEDBEDS	SEELIER	SEFER
SECTILITY	SEDATIONS	SEEDBOX	SEELIEST	SEG
SECTION	SEDATIVE	SEEDBOXES	SEELING	SEGAR
SECTIONAL	SEDATIVES	SEEDCAKE	SEELINGS	SEGARS
SECTIONED	SEDENT	SEEDCAKES	SEELS	SEGETAL
SECTIONS	SEDENTARY	SEEDCASE	SEELY	SEGGAR
SECTOR	SEDER	SEEDCASES	SEEM	SEGGARS
SECTORAL	SEDERS	SEEDEATER	SEEMED	SEGHOL

SEGHOLATE	SEILED	SEIZIN	SELENIDE	SELLES
SEGHOLS	SEILING	SEIZING	SELENIDES	SELLING
SEGMENT	SEILS	SEIZINGS	SELENIOUS	SELLINGS
SEGMENTAL	SEINE	SEIZINS	SELENITE	SELLOFF
SEGMENTED	SEINED	SEIZOR	SELENITES	SELLOFFS
SEGMENTS	SEINER	SEIZORS	SELENITIC	SELLOTAPE
SEGNI	SEINERS	SEIZURE	SELENIUM	SELLOUT
SEGNO	SEINES	SEIZURES	SELENIUMS	SELLOUTS
SEGNOS	SEINING	SEJANT	SELENOSES	SELLS
SEGO	SEININGS	SEJEANT	SELENOSIS	SELS
SEGOL	SEIR	SEKOS	SELENOUS	SELSYN
SEGOLATE	SEIRS	SEKOSES	SELES	SELSYNS
SEGOLATES	SEIS	SEKT	SELF	SELTZER
SEGOLS	SEISABLE	SEKTS	SELFDOM	SELTZERS
SEGOS	SEISE	SEL	SELFDOMS	SELVA
SEGREANT	SEISED	SELACHIAN	SELFED	SELVAGE
SEGREGANT	SEISER	SELADANG	SELFHEAL	SELVAGED
SEGREGATE	SEISERS	SELADANGS	SELFHEALS	SELVAGEE
SEGS	SEISES	SELAH	SELFHOOD	SELVAGEES
SEGUE	SEISIN	SELAHS	SELFHOODS	SELVAGES
SEGUED	SEISING	SELAMLIK	SELFIE	SELVAGING
SEGUEING	SEISINGS	SELAMLIKS	SELFIES	SELVAS
SEGUES	SEISINS	SELCOUTH	SELFING	SELVEDGE
SEGUGIO	SEISM	SELD	SELFINGS	SELVEDGED
SEGUGIOS	SEISMAL	SELDOM	SELFISH	SELVEDGES
SEHRI	SEISMIC	SELDOMLY	SELFISHLY	SELVES
SEHRIS	SEISMICAL	SELDSEEN	SELFISM	SEMAINIER
SEI	SEISMISM	SELDSHOWN	SELFISMS	SEMANTEME
SEICENTO	SEISMISMS	SELE	SELFIST	SEMANTIC
SEICENTOS	SEISMS	SELECT	SELFISTS	SEMANTICS
SEICHE	SEISOR	SELECTA	SELFLESS	SEMANTIDE
SEICHES	SEISORS	SELECTAS	SELFNESS	SEMANTRA
SEIDEL	SEISURE	SELECTED	SELFS	SEMANTRON
SEIDELS	SEISURES	SELECTEE	SELFSAME	SEMAPHORE
SEIF	SEITAN	SELECTEES	SELFWARD	SEMATIC
SEIFS	SEITANS	SELECTING	SELFWARDS	SEMBLABLE
SEIGNEUR	SEITEN	SELECTION	SELICTAR	SEMBLABLY
SEIGNEURS	SEITENS	SELECTIVE	SELICTARS	SEMBLANCE
SEIGNEURY	SEITIES	SELECTLY	SELKIE	SEMBLANT
SEIGNIOR	SEITY	SELECTMAN	SELKIES	SEMBLANTS
SEIGNIORS	SEIZA	SELECTMEN	SELL	SEMBLE
SEIGNIORY	SEIZABLE	SELECTOR	SELLA	SEMBLED
SEIGNORAL	SEIZAS	SELECTORS	SELLABLE	SEMBLES
SEIGNORY	SEIZE	SELECTS	SELLAE	SEMBLING
SEIK	SEIZED	SELENATE	SELLAS	SEME
SEIKER	SEIZER	SELENATES	SELLE	SEMEE
SEIKEST	SEIZERS	SELENIAN	SELLER	SEMEED
SEIL	SEIZES	SELENIC	SELLERS	SEMEIA

S

SEMEION	SEMILLONS	SEMISOLID	SENATOR	SENITIS
SEMEIOTIC	SEMILOG	SEMISOLUS	SENATORS	SENNA
SEMEME	SEMILUNAR	SEMISTIFF	SEND	SENNACHIE
SEMEMES	SEMILUNE	SEMISWEET	SENDABLE	SENNAS
SEMEMIC	SEMILUNES	SEMITAR	SENDAL	SENNET
SEMEN	SEMIMAT	SEMITARS	SENDALS	SENNETS
SEMENS	SEMIMATT	SEMITAUR	SENDED	SENNIGHT
SEMES	SEMIMATTE	SEMITAURS	SENDER	SENNIGHTS
SEMESTER	SEMIMETAL	SEMITIST	SENDERS	SENNIT
SEMESTERS	SEMIMICRO	SEMITISTS	SENDING	SENNITS
SEMESTRAL	SEMIMILD	SEMITONAL	SENDINGS	SENOPIA
SEMI	SEMIMOIST	SEMITONE	SENDOFF	SENOPIAS
SEMIANGLE	SEMIMUTE	SEMITONES	SENDOFFS	SENOR
SEMIARID	SEMIMUTES	SEMITONIC	SENDS	SENORA
SEMIBALD	SEMINA	SEMITRUCK	SENDUP	SENORAS
SEMIBOLD	SEMINAL	SEMIURBAN	SENDUPS	SENORES
SEMIBOLDS	SEMINALLY	SEMIVOCAL	SENE	SENORITA
SEMIBREVE	SEMINAR	SEMIVOWEL	SENECA	SENORITAS
SEMIBULL	SEMINARS	SEMIWATER	SENECAS	SENORS
SEMIBULLS	SEMINARY	SEMIWILD	SENECIO	SENRYU
SEMICOLON	SEMINATE	SEMIWORKS	SENECIOS	SENS
SEMICOMA	SEMINATED	SEMMIT	SENEGA	SENSA
SEMICOMAS	SEMINATES	SEMMITS	SENEGAS	SENSATE
SEMICURED	SEMINOMA	SEMOLINA	SENES	SENSATED
SEMIDEAF	SEMINOMAD	SEMOLINAS	SENESCE	SENSATELY
SEMIDEIFY	SEMINOMAS	SEMPER	SENESCED	SENSATES
SEMIDOME	SEMINUDE	SEMPLE	SENESCENT	SENSATING
SEMIDOMED	SEMIOLOGY	SEMPLER	SENESCES	SENSATION
SEMIDOMES	SEMIOPEN	SEMPLEST	SENESCHAL	SENSE
SEMIDRIER	SEMIOSES	SEMPLICE	SENESCING	SENSED
SEMIDRY	SEMIOSIS	SEMPRE	SENGI	SENSEFUL
SEMIDWARF	SEMIOTIC	SEMPSTER	SENGIS	SENSEI
SEMIE	SEMIOTICS	SEMPSTERS	SENGREEN	SENSEIS
SEMIERECT	SEMIOVAL	SEMSEM	SENGREENS	SENSELESS
SEMIES	SEMIPED	SEMSEMS	SENHOR	SENSES
SEMIFINAL	SEMIPEDS	SEMUNCIA	SENHORA	SENSI
SEMIFIT	SEMIPIOUS	SEMUNCIAE	SENHORAS	SENSIBLE
SEMIFLUID	SEMIPLUME	SEMUNCIAL	SENHORES	SENSIBLER
SEMIGALA	SEMIPOLAR	SEMUNCIAS	SENHORITA	SENSIBLES
SEMIGALAS	SEMIPRO	SEN	SENHORS	SENSIBLY
SEMIGLOBE	SEMIPROS	SENA	SENILE	SENSILE
SEMIGLOSS	SEMIRAW	SENARIES	SENILELY	SENSILLA
SEMIGROUP	SEMIRIGID	SENARII	SENILES	SENSILLAE
SEMIHARD	SEMIROUND	SENARIUS	SENILITY	SENSILLUM
SEMIHIGH	SEMIRURAL	SENARY	SENIOR	SENSING
SEMIHOBO	SEMIS	SENAS	SENIORITY	SENSINGS
SEMIHOBOS	SEMISES	SENATE	SENIORS	SENSIS
SEMILLON	SEMISOFT	SENATES	SENITI	SENSISM

S

SENSISMS	SEPALINE	SEPTET	SEQUINING	SERENATED
SENSIST	SEPALLED	SEPTETS	SEQUINNED	SERENATES
SENSISTS	SEPALODY	SEPTETTE	SEQUINS	SERENE
SENSITISE	SEPALOID	SEPTETTES	SEQUITUR	SERENED
SENSITIVE	SEPALOUS	SEPTIC	SEQUITURS	SERENELY
SENSITIZE	SEPALS	SEPTICAL	SEQUOIA	SERENER
SENSOR	SEPARABLE	SEPTICITY	SEQUOIAS	SERENES
SENSORIA	SEPARABLY	SEPTICS	SER	SERENEST
SENSORIAL	SEPARATA	SEPTIFORM	SERA	SERENING
SENSORILY	SEPARATE	SEPTIMAL	SERAC	SERENITY
SENSORIUM	SEPARATED	SEPTIME	SERACS	SERER
SENSORS	SEPARATES	SEPTIMES	SERAFILE	SERES
SENSORY	SEPARATOR	SEPTIMOLE	SERAFILES	SEREST
SENSUAL	SEPARATUM	SEPTLEVA	SERAFIN	SERF
SENSUALLY	SEPHEN	SEPTLEVAS	SERAFINS	SERFAGE
SENSUM	SEPHENS	SEPTORIA	SERAGLIO	SERFAGES
SENSUOUS	SEPIA	SEPTORIAS	SERAGLIOS	SERFDOM
SENT	SEPIAS	SEPTS	SERAI	SERFDOMS
SENTE	SEPIC	SEPTUM	SERAIL	SERFHOOD
SENTED	SEPIMENT	SEPTUMS	SERAILS	SERFHOODS
SENTENCE	SEPIMENTS	SEPTUOR	SERAIS	SERFISH
SENTENCED	SEPIOLITE	SEPTUORS	SERAL	SERFLIKE
SENTENCER	SEPIOST	SEPTUPLE	SERANG	SERFS
SENTENCES	SEPIOSTS	SEPTUPLED	SERANGS	SERFSHIP
SENTENTIA	SEPIUM	SEPTUPLES	SERAPE	SERFSHIPS
SENTI	SEPIUMS	SEPTUPLET	SERAPES	SERGE
SENTIENCE	SEPMAG	SEPULCHER	SERAPH	SERGEANCY
SENTIENCY	SEPOY	SEPULCHRE	SERAPHIC	SERGEANT
SENTIENT	SEPOYS	SEPULTURE	SERAPHIM	SERGEANTS
SENTIENTS	SEPPUKU	SEQUACITY	SERAPHIMS	SERGEANTY
SENTIMENT	SEPPUKUS	SEQUEL	SERAPHIN	SERGED
SENTIMO	SEPS	SEQUELA	SERAPHINE	SERGER
SENTIMOS	SEPSES	SEQUELAE	SERAPHINS	SERGERS
SENTINEL	SEPSIS	SEQUELISE	SERAPHS	SERGES
SENTINELS	SEPT	SEQUELIZE	SERASKIER	SERGING
SENTING	SEPTA	SEQUELS	SERDAB	SERGINGS
SENTRIES	SEPTAGE	SEQUENCE	SERDABS	SERIAL
SENTRY	SEPTAGES	SEQUENCED	SERE	SERIALISE
SENTS	SEPTAL	SEQUENCER	SERED	SERIALISM
SENVIES	SEPTARIA	SEQUENCES	SEREIN	SERIALIST
SENVY	SEPTARIAN	SEQUENCY	SEREINS	SERIALITY
SENZA	SEPTARIUM	SEQUENT	SERENADE	SERIALIZE
SEPAD	SEPTATE	SEQUENTLY	SERENADED	SERIALLY
SEPADDED	SEPTATION	SEQUENTS	SERENADER	SERIALS
SEPADDING	SEPTEMFID	SEQUESTER	SERENADES	SERIATE
SEPADS	SEPTEMVIR	SEQUESTRA	SERENATA	SERIATED
SEPAL	SEPTENARY	SEQUIN	SERENATAS	SERIATELY
SEPALED	SEPTENNIA	SEQUINED	SERENATE	SERIATES

SERIATIM	SERMONING	SERRAE	SERVED	SESSES
SERIATING	SERMONISE	SERRAN	SERVER	SESSILE
SERIATION	SERMONIZE	SERRANID	SERVERIES	SESSILITY
SERIC	SERMONS	SERRANIDS	SERVERS	SESSING
SERICEOUS	SEROGROUP	SERRANO	SERVERY	SESSION
SERICIN	SEROLOGIC	SERRANOID	SERVES	SESSIONAL
SERICINS	SEROLOGY	SERRANOS	SERVEWARE	SESSIONS
SERICITE	SEROMA	SERRANS	SERVEWE	SESSPOOL
SERICITES	SEROMAS	SERRAS	SERVEWED	SESSPOOLS
SERICITIC	SERON	SERRATE	SERVEWES	SESTERCE
SERICON	SERONS	SERRATED	SERVEWING	SESTERCES
SERICONS	SEROON	SERRATES	SERVICE	SESTERTIA
SERIEMA	SEROONS	SERRATI	SERVICED	SESTERTII
SERIEMAS	SEROPUS	SERRATING	SERVICER	SESTET
SERIES	SEROPUSES	SERRATION	SERVICERS	SESTETS
SERIF	SEROSA	SERRATURE	SERVICES	SESTETT
SERIFED	SEROSAE	SERRATUS	SERVICING	SESTETTE
SERIFFED	SEROSAL	SERRE	SERVIENT	SESTETTES
SERIFS	SEROSAS	SERRED	SERVIETTE	SESTETTO
SERIGRAPH	SEROSITY	SERREFILE	SERVILE	SESTETTOS
SERIN	SEROTINAL	SERRES	SERVILELY	SESTETTS
SERINE	SEROTINE	SERRICORN	SERVILES	SESTINA
SERINES	SEROTINES	SERRIED	SERVILISM	SESTINAS
SERINETTE	SEROTINY	SERRIEDLY	SERVILITY	SESTINE
SERING	SEROTONIN	SERRIES	SERVING	SESTINES
SERINGA	SEROTYPE	SERRIFORM	SERVINGS	SESTON
SERINGAS	SEROTYPED	SERRING	SERVITOR	SESTONS
SERINS	SEROTYPES	SERRS	SERVITORS	SET
SERIOUS	SEROTYPIC	SERRULATE	SERVITUDE	SETA
SERIOUSLY	SEROUS	SERRY	SERVLET	SETACEOUS
SERIPH	SEROVAR	SERRYING	SERVLETS	SETAE
SERIPHS	SEROVARS	SERS	SERVO	SETAL
SERJEANCY	SEROW	SERUEWE	SERVOS	SETBACK
SERJEANT	SEROWS	SERUEWED	SERVQUAL	SETBACKS
SERJEANTS	SERPENT	SERUEWES	SERVQUALS	SETENANT
SERJEANTY	SERPENTRY	SERUEWING	SESAME	SETENANTS
SERK	SERPENTS	SERUM	SESAMES	SETIFORM
SERKALI	SERPIGO	SERUMAL	SESAMOID	SETLINE
SERKALIS	SERPIGOES	SERUMS	SESAMOIDS	SETLINES
SERKS	SERPIGOS	SERVABLE	SESE	SETNESS
SERMON	SERPULA	SERVAL	SESELI	SETNESSES
SERMONED	SERPULAE	SERVALS	SESELIS	SETOFF
SERMONEER	SERPULAS	SERVANT	SESEY	SETOFFS
SERMONER	SERPULID	SERVANTED	SESH	SETON
SERMONERS	SERPULIDS	SERVANTRY	SESHES	SETONS
SERMONET	SERPULITE	SERVANTS	SESS	SETOSE
SERMONETS	SERR	SERVE	SESSA	SETOUS
SERMONIC	SERRA	SERVEABLE	SESSED	SETOUT

S

SETOUTS	SEVERALS	SEX	SEXTETTS	SHABASH
SETS	SEVERALTY	SEXAHOLIC	SEXTILE	SHABBATOT
SETSCREW	SEVERANCE	SEXCAPADE	SEXTILES	SHABBIER
SETSCREWS	SEVERE	SEXED	SEXTING	SHABBIEST
SETT	SEVERED	SEXENNIAL	SEXTINGS	SHABBILY
SETTEE	SEVERELY	SEXER	SEXTO	SHABBLE
SETTEES	SEVERER	SEXERCISE	SEXTOLET	SHABBLES
SETTER	SEVEREST	SEXERS	SEXTOLETS	SHABBY
SETTERED	SEVERIES	SEXES	SEXTON	SHABRACK
SETTERING	SEVERING	SEXFID	SEXTONESS	SHABRACKS
SETTERS	SEVERITY	SEXFOIL	SEXTONS	SHACK
SETTING	SEVERS	SEXFOILS	SEXTOS	SHACKED
SETTINGS	SEVERY	SEXIER	SEXTS	SHACKIER
SETTLE	SEVICHE	SEXIEST	SEXTUOR	SHACKIEST
SETTLED	SEVICHES	SEXILY	SEXTUORS	SHACKING
SETTLER	SEVRUGA	SEXINESS	SEXTUPLE	SHACKLE
SETTLERS	SEVRUGAS	SEXING	SEXTUPLED	SHACKLED
SETTLES	SEVS	SEXINGS	SEXTUPLES	SHACKLER
SETTLING	SEW	SEXISM	SEXTUPLET	SHACKLERS
SETTLINGS	SEWABLE	SEXISMS	SEXTUPLY	SHACKLES
SETTLOR	SEWAGE	SEXIST	SEXUAL	SHACKLING
SETTLORS	SEWAGES	SEXISTS	SEXUALISE	SHACKO
SETTS	SEWAN	SEXLESS	SEXUALISM	SHACKOES
SETUALE	SEWANS	SEXLESSLY	SEXUALIST	SHACKOS
SETUALES	SEWAR	SEXLINKED	SEXUALITY	SHACKS
SETULE	SEWARS	SEXOLOGIC	SEXUALIZE	SHACKTOWN
SETULES	SEWED	SEXOLOGY	SEXUALLY	SHACKY
SETULOSE	SEWEL	SEXPERT	SEXVALENT	SHAD
SETULOUS	SEWELLEL	SEXPERTS	SEXY	SHADBERRY
SETUP	SEWELLELS	SEXPOT	SEY	SHADBLOW
SETUPS	SEWELS	SEXPOTS	SEYEN	SHADBLOWS
SETWALL	SEWEN	SEXT	SEYENS	SHADBUSH
SETWALLS	SEWENS	SEXTAIN	SEYS	SHADCHAN
SEV	SEWER	SEXTAINS	SEYSURE	SHADCHANS
SEVEN	SEWERAGE	SEXTAN	SEYSURES	SHADDOCK
SEVENFOLD	SEWERAGES	SEXTANS	SEZ	SHADDOCKS
SEVENISH	SEWERED	SEXTANSES	SFERICS	SHADDUP
SEVENS	SEWERING	SEXTANT	SFORZANDI	SHADE
SEVENTEEN	SEWERINGS	SEXTANTAL	SFORZANDO	SHADED
SEVENTH	SEWERLESS	SEXTANTS	SFORZATI	SHADELESS
SEVENTHLY	SEWERLIKE	SEXTARII	SFORZATO	SHADER
SEVENTHS	SEWERS	SEXTARIUS	SFORZATOS	SHADERS
SEVENTIES	SEWIN	SEXTED	SFUMATO	SHADES
SEVENTY	SEWING	SEXTET	SFUMATOS	SHADFLIES
SEVER	SEWINGS	SEXTETS	SGRAFFITI	SHADFLY
SEVERABLE	SEWINS	SEXTETT	SGRAFFITO	SHADIER
SEVERAL	SEWN	SEXTETTE	SH	SHADIEST
SEVERALLY	SEWS	SEXTETTES	SHA	SHADILY

S

SHADINESS	SHAGS	SHALE	SHAMBAS	SHAMOYING
SHADING	SHAH	SHALED	SHAMBLE	SHAMOYS
SHADINGS	SHAHADA	SHALELIKE	SHAMBLED	SHAMPOO
SHADKHAN	SHAHADAH	SHALES	SHAMBLES	SHAMPOOED
SHADKHANS	SHAHADAHS	SHALEY	SHAMBLIER	SHAMPOOER
SHADOOF	SHAHADAS	SHALIER	SHAMBLING	SHAMPOOS
SHADOOFS	SHAHDOM	SHALIEST	SHAMBLY	SHAMROCK
SHADOW	SHAHDOMS	SHALING	SHAMBOLIC	SHAMROCKS
SHADOWBOX	SHAHEED	SHALL	SHAME	SHAMS
SHADOWED	SHAHEEDS	SHALLI	SHAMEABLE	SHAMUS
SHADOWER	SHAHID	SHALLIS	SHAMEABLY	SHAMUSES
SHADOWERS	SHAHIDS	SHALLON	SHAMED	SHAN
SHADOWIER	SHAHS	SHALLONS	SHAMEFAST	SHANACHIE
SHADOWILY	SHAHTOOSH	SHALLOON	SHAMEFUL	SHAND
SHADOWING	SHAIKH	SHALLOONS	SHAMELESS	SHANDIES
SHADOWS	SHAIKHS	SHALLOP	SHAMER	SHANDRIES
SHADOWY	SHAIRD	SHALLOPS	SHAMERS	SHANDRY
SHADRACH	SHAIRDS	SHALLOT	SHAMES	SHANDS
SHADRACHS	SHAIRN	SHALLOTS	SHAMIANA	SHANDY
SHADS	SHAIRNS	SHALLOW	SHAMIANAH	SHANGHAI
SHADUF	SHAITAN	SHALLOWED	SHAMIANAS	SHANGHAIS
SHADUFS	SHAITANS	SHALLOWER	SHAMINA	SHANK
SHADY	SHAKABLE	SHALLOWLY	SHAMINAS	SHANKBONE
SHAFT	SHAKE	SHALLOWS	SHAMING	SHANKED
SHAFTED	SHAKEABLE	SHALM	SHAMINGS	SHANKING
SHAFTER	SHAKED	SHALMS	SHAMISEN	SHANKS
SHAFTERS	SHAKEDOWN	SHALOM	SHAMISENS	SHANNIES
SHAFTING	SHAKEN	SHALOMS	SHAMMAS	SHANNY
SHAFTINGS	SHAKEOUT	SHALOT	SHAMMASH	SHANS
SHAFTLESS	SHAKEOUTS	SHALOTS	SHAMMASIM	SHANTEY
SHAFTS	SHAKER	SHALT	SHAMMED	SHANTEYS
SHAG	SHAKERS	SHALWAR	SHAMMER	SHANTI
SHAGBARK	SHAKES	SHALWARS	SHAMMERS	SHANTIES
SHAGBARKS	SHAKEUP	SHALY	SHAMMES	SHANTIH
SHAGGABLE	SHAKEUPS	SHAM	SHAMMIED	SHANTIHS
SHAGGED	SHAKIER	SHAMA	SHAMMIES	SHANTIS
SHAGGER	SHAKIEST	SHAMABLE	SHAMMING	SHANTUNG
SHAGGERS	SHAKILY	SHAMABLY	SHAMMOS	SHANTUNGS
SHAGGIER	SHAKINESS	SHAMAL	SHAMMOSIM	SHANTY
SHAGGIEST	SHAKING	SHAMALS	SHAMMY	SHANTYMAN
SHAGGILY	SHAKINGS	SHAMAN	SHAMMYING	SHANTYMEN
SHAGGING	SHAKO	SHAMANIC	SHAMOIS	SHAPABLE
SHAGGY	SHAKOES	SHAMANISM	SHAMOISED	SHAPE
SHAGPILE	SHAKOS	SHAMANIST	SHAMOISES	SHAPEABLE
SHAGREEN	SHAKT	SHAMANS	SHAMOS	SHAPED
SHAGREENS	SHAKUDO	SHAMAS	SHAMOSIM	SHAPELESS
SHAGROON	SHAKUDOS	SHAMATEUR	SHAMOY	SHAPELIER
SHAGROONS	SHAKY	SHAMBA	SHAMOYED	SHAPELY

S

SHAPEN	SHARKS	SHATTERS	SHAYAS	SHEAVE
SHAPENED	SHARKSKIN	SHATTERY	SHAYKH	SHEAVED
SHAPENING	SHARN	SHAUCHLE	SHAYKHS	SHEAVES
SHAPENS	SHARNIER	SHAUCHLED	SHAYS	SHEAVING
SHAPER	SHARNIES	SHAUCHLES	SHAZAM	SHEBANG
SHAPERS	SHARNIEST	SHAUCHLY	SHCHI	SHEBANGS
SHAPES	SHARNS	SHAUGH	SHCHIS	SHEBEAN
SHAPEUP	SHARNY	SHAUGHS	SHE	SHEBEANS
SHAPEUPS	SHARON	SHAUL	SHEA	SHEBEEN
SHAPEWEAR	SHARP	SHAULED	SHEADING	SHEBEENED
SHAPING	SHARPED	SHAULING	SHEADINGS	SHEBEENER
SHAPINGS	SHARPEN	SHAULS	SHEAF	SHEBEENS
SHAPS	SHARPENED	SHAVABLE	SHEAFED	SHECHITA
SHARABLE	SHARPENER	SHAVASANA	SHEAFIER	SHECHITAH
SHARD	SHARPENS	SHAVE	SHEAFIEST	SHECHITAS
SHARDED	SHARPER	SHAVEABLE	SHEAFING	SHED
SHARDS	SHARPERS	SHAVED	SHEAFLIKE	SHEDABLE
SHARE	SHARPEST	SHAVELING	SHEAFS	SHEDDABLE
SHAREABLE	SHARPIE	SHAVEN	SHEAFY	SHEDDED
SHARECROP	SHARPIES	SHAVER	SHEAL	SHEDDER
SHARED	SHARPING	SHAVERS	SHEALED	SHEDDERS
SHAREMAN	SHARPINGS	SHAVES	SHEALING	SHEDDING
SHAREMEN	SHARPISH	SHAVETAIL	SHEALINGS	SHEDDINGS
SHARER	SHARPLY	SHAVIE	SHEALS	SHEDFUL
SHARERS	SHARPNESS	SHAVIES	SHEAR	SHEDFULS
SHARES	SHARPS	SHAVING	SHEARED	SHEDHAND
SHARESMAN	SHARPTAIL	SHAVINGS	SHEARER	SHEDHANDS
SHARESMEN	SHARPY	SHAW	SHEARERS	SHEDLIKE
SHAREWARE	SHASH	SHAWARMA	SHEARING	SHEDLOAD
SHARIA	SHASHED	SHAWARMAS	SHEARINGS	SHEDLOADS
SHARIAH	SHASHES	SHAWED	SHEARLEG	SHEDS
SHARIAHS	SHASHING	SHAWING	SHEARLEGS	SHEEL
SHARIAS	SHASHLICK	SHAWL	SHEARLING	SHEELED
SHARIAT	SHASHLIK	SHAWLED	SHEARMAN	SHEELING
SHARIATS	SHASHLIKS	SHAWLEY	SHEARMEN	SHEELS
SHARIF	SHASLIK	SHAWLEYS	SHEARS	SHEEN
SHARIFIAN	SHASLIKS	SHAWLIE	SHEAS	SHEENED
SHARIFS	SHASTA	SHAWLIES	SHEATFISH	SHEENEY
SHARING	SHASTAS	SHAWLING	SHEATH	SHEENEYS
SHARINGS	SHASTER	SHAWLINGS	SHEATHE	SHEENFUL
SHARK	SHASTERS	SHAWLLESS	SHEATHED	SHEENIE
SHARKED	SHASTRA	SHAWLS	SHEATHER	SHEENIER
SHARKER	SHASTRAS	SHAWM	SHEATHERS	SHEENIES
SHARKERS	SHAT	SHAWMS	SHEATHES	SHEENIEST
SHARKING	SHATOOSH	SHAWN	SHEATHIER	SHEENING
SHARKINGS	SHATTER	SHAWS	SHEATHING	SHEENS
SHARKISH	SHATTERED	SHAY	SHEATHS	SHEENY
SHARKLIKE	SHATTERER	SHAYA	SHEATHY	SHEEP

SHEEPCOT	SHEEVES	SHELLACS	SHEOL	SHEUCH
SHEEPCOTE	SHEGETZ	SHELLBACK	SHEOLS	SHEUCHED
SHEEPCOTS	SHEHITA	SHELLBARK	SHEPHERD	SHEUCHING
SHEEPDOG	SHEHITAH	SHELLDUCK	SHEPHERDS	SHEUCHS
SHEEPDOGS	SHEHITAHS	SHELLED	SHEQALIM	SHEUGH
SHEEPFOLD	SHEHITAS	SHELLER	SHEQEL	SHEUGHED
SHEEPHEAD	SHEHNAI	SHELLERS	SHEQELS	SHEUGHING
SHEEPIER	SHEHNAIS	SHELLFIRE	SHERANG	SHEUGHS
SHEEPIEST	SHEIK	SHELLFISH	SHERANGS	SHEVA
SHEEPISH	SHEIKDOM	SHELLFUL	SHERBERT	SHEVAS
SHEEPLE	SHEIKDOMS	SHELLFULS	SHERBERTS	SHEW
SHEEPLES	SHEIKH	SHELLIER	SHERBET	SHEWBREAD
SHEEPLIKE	SHEIKHA	SHELLIEST	SHERBETS	SHEWED
SHEEPMAN	SHEIKHAS	SHELLING	SHERD	SHEWEL
SHEEPMEN	SHEIKHDOM	SHELLINGS	SHERDS	SHEWELS
SHEEPO	SHEIKHS	SHELLS	SHERE	SHEWER
SHEEPOS	SHEIKS	SHELLWORK	SHEREEF	SHEWERS
SHEEPSKIN	SHEILA	SHELLY	SHEREEFS	SHEWING
SHEEPWALK	SHEILAS	SHELTA	SHERIA	SHEWN
SHEEPY	SHEILING	SHELTAS	SHERIAS	SHEWS
SHEER	SHEILINGS	SHELTER	SHERIAT	SHH
SHEERED	SHEITAN	SHELTERED	SHERIATS	SHHH
SHEERER	SHEITANS	SHELTERER	SHERIF	SHIAI
SHEEREST	SHEITEL	SHELTERS	SHERIFF	SHIAIS
SHEERING	SHEITELS	SHELTERY	SHERIFFS	SHIATSU
SHEERLEG	SHEKALIM	SHELTIE	SHERIFIAN	SHIATSUS
SHEERLEGS	SHEKEL	SHELTIES	SHERIFS	SHIATZU
SHEERLY	SHEKELIM	SHELTY	SHERLOCK	SHIATZUS
SHEERNESS	SHEKELS	SHELVE	SHERLOCKS	SHIBAH
SHEERS	SHELDDUCK	SHELVED	SHERO	SHIBAHS
SHEESH	SHELDRAKE	SHELVER	SHEROES	SHIBUICHI
SHEESHA	SHELDUCK	SHELVERS	SHEROOT	SHICKER
SHEESHAS	SHELDUCKS	SHELVES	SHEROOTS	SHICKERED
SHEET	SHELF	SHELVIER	SHERPA	SHICKERS
SHEETED	SHELFED	SHELVIEST	SHERPAS	SHICKSA
SHEETER	SHELFFUL	SHELVING	SHERRIED	SHICKSAS
SHEETERS	SHELFFULS	SHELVINGS	SHERRIES	SHIDDER
SHEETFED	SHELFIER	SHELVY	SHERRIS	SHIDDERS
SHEETIER	SHELFIEST	SHEMALE	SHERRISES	SHIDDUCH
SHEETIEST	SHELFING	SHEMALES	SHERRY	SHIED
SHEETING	SHELFLIKE	SHEMOZZLE	SHERWANI	SHIEL
SHEETINGS	SHELFROOM	SHEN	SHERWANIS	SHIELD
SHEETLESS	SHELFS	SHENAI	SHES	SHIELDED
SHEETLIKE	SHELFY	SHENAIS	SHET	SHIELDER
SHEETROCK	SHELL	SHEND	SHETLAND	SHIELDERS
SHEETS	SHELLAC	SHENDING	SHETLANDS	SHIELDING
SHEETY	SHELLACK	SHENDS	SHETS	SHIELDS
SHEEVE	SHELLACKS	SHENT	SHETTING	SHIELED

S

SHIELING	SHILL	SHINGLERS	SHIPLOADS	SHIRK
SHIELINGS	SHILLABER	SHINGLES	SHIPMAN	SHIRKED
SHIELS	SHILLALA	SHINGLIER	SHIPMATE	SHIRKER
SHIER	SHILLALAH	SHINGLING	SHIPMATES	SHIRKERS
SHIERS	SHILLALAS	SHINGLY	SHIPMEN	SHIRKING
SHIES	SHILLED	SHINGUARD	SHIPMENT	SHIRKS
SHIEST	SHILLELAH	SHINIER	SHIPMENTS	SHIRR
SHIFT	SHILLING	SHINIES	SHIPOWNER	SHIRRA
SHIFTABLE	SHILLINGS	SHINIEST	SHIPPABLE	SHIRRALEE
SHIFTED	SHILLS	SHINILY	SHIPPED	SHIRRAS
SHIFTER	SHILPIT	SHININESS	SHIPPEN	SHIRRED
SHIFTERS	SHILY	SHINING	SHIPPENS	SHIRRING
SHIFTIER	SHIM	SHININGLY	SHIPPER	SHIRRINGS
SHIFTIEST	SHIMAAL	SHINJU	SHIPPERS	SHIRRS
SHIFTILY	SHIMAALS	SHINJUS	SHIPPIE	SHIRS
SHIFTING	SHIMMED	SHINKIN	SHIPPIES	SHIRT
SHIFTINGS	SHIMMER	SHINKINS	SHIPPING	SHIRTBAND
SHIFTLESS	SHIMMERED	SHINLEAF	SHIPPINGS	SHIRTED
SHIFTS	SHIMMERS	SHINLEAFS	SHIPPO	SHIRTIER
SHIFTWORK	SHIMMERY	SHINNE	SHIPPON	SHIRTIEST
SHIFTY	SHIMMEY	SHINNED	SHIPPONS	SHIRTILY
SHIGELLA	SHIMMEYS	SHINNERY	SHIPPOS	SHIRTING
SHIGELLAE	SHIMMIED	SHINNES	SHIPPOUND	SHIRTINGS
SHIGELLAS	SHIMMIES	SHINNEY	SHIPS	SHIRTLESS
SHIITAKE	SHIMMING	SHINNEYED	SHIPSHAPE	SHIRTLIKE
SHIITAKES	SHIMMY	SHINNEYS	SHIPSIDE	SHIRTS
SHIKAR	SHIMMYING	SHINNIED	SHIPSIDES	SHIRTTAIL
SHIKARA	SHIMOZZLE	SHINNIES	SHIPTIME	SHIRTY
SHIKARAS	SHIMS	SHINNING	SHIPTIMES	SHISH
SHIKAREE	SHIN	SHINNY	SHIPWAY	SHISHA
SHIKAREES	SHINBONE	SHINNYING	SHIPWAYS	SHISHAS
SHIKARI	SHINBONES	SHINOLA	SHIPWORM	SHISO
SHIKARIS	SHINDIES	SHINOLAS	SHIPWORMS	SHISOS
SHIKARRED	SHINDIG	SHINS	SHIPWRECK	SHIST
SHIKARS	SHINDIGS	SHINTIED	SHIPYARD	SHISTS
SHIKKER	SHINDY	SHINTIES	SHIPYARDS	SHIT
SHIKKERED	SHINDYS	SHINTY	SHIR	SHITAKE
SHIKKERS	SHINE	SHINTYING	SHIRALEE	SHITAKES
SHIKRA	SHINED	SHINY	SHIRALEES	SHITBAG
SHIKRAS	SHINELESS	SHIP	SHIRAZ	SHITBAGS
SHIKSA	SHINER	SHIPBOARD	SHIRAZES	SHITCAN
SHIKSAS	SHINERS	SHIPBORNE	SHIRE	SHITCANS
SHIKSE	SHINES	SHIPFUL	SHIRED	SHITE
SHIKSEH	SHINESS	SHIPFULS	SHIREMAN	SHITED
SHIKSEHS	SHINESSES	SHIPLAP	SHIREMEN	SHITES
SHIKSES	SHINGLE	SHIPLAPS	SHIRES	SHITFACE
SHILINGI	SHINGLED	SHIPLESS	SHIRETOWN	SHITFACED
SHILINGIS	SHINGLER	SHIPLOAD	SHIRING	SHITFACES

SHITHEAD	SHIVERS	SHMEAR	SHOALWISE	SHOESHINE
SHITHEADS	SHIVERY	SHMEARED	SHOALY	SHOETREE
SHITHEEL	SHIVES	SHMEARING	SHOAT	SHOETREES
SHITHEELS	SHIVITI	SHMEARS	SHOATS	SHOFAR
SHITHOLE	SHIVITIS	SHMEER	SHOCHET	SHOFARS
SHITHOLES	SHIVOO	SHMEERED	SHOCHETIM	SHOFROTH
SHITHOUSE	SHIVOOS	SHMEERING	SHOCHETS	SHOG
SHITING	SHIVS	SHMEERS	SHOCHU	SHOGGED
SHITLESS	SHIVVED	SHMEK	SHOCHUS	SHOGGING
SHITLIST	SHIVVING	SHMEKS	SHOCK	SHOGGLE
SHITLISTS	SHIZZLE	SHMO	SHOCKABLE	SHOGGLED
SHITLOAD	SHIZZLES	SHMOCK	SHOCKED	SHOGGLES
SHITLOADS	SHKOTZIM	SHMOCKS	SHOCKER	SHOGGLIER
SHITS	SHLEMIEHL	SHMOE	SHOCKERS	SHOGGLING
SHITSTORM	SHLEMIEL	SHMOES	SHOCKING	SHOGGLY
SHITTAH	SHLEMIELS	SHMOOSE	SHOCKS	SHOGI
SHITTAHS	SHLEP	SHMOOSED	SHOD	SHOGIS
SHITTED	SHLEPP	SHMOOSES	SHODDEN	SHOGS
SHITTER	SHLEPPED	SHMOOSING	SHODDIER	SHOGUN
SHITTERS	SHLEPPER	SHMOOZE	SHODDIES	SHOGUNAL
SHITTIER	SHLEPPERS	SHMOOZED	SHODDIEST	SHOGUNATE
SHITTIEST	SHLEPPIER	SHMOOZER	SHODDILY	SHOGUNS
SHITTILY	SHLEPPING	SHMOOZERS	SHODDY	SHOJI
SHITTIM	SHLEPPS	SHMOOZES	SHODER	SHOJIS
SHITTIMS	SHLEPPY	SHMOOZIER	SHODERS	SHOJO
SHITTING	SHLEPS	SHMOOZING	SHOE	SHOLA
SHITTY	SHLIMAZEL	SHMOOZY	SHOEBILL	SHOLAS
SHITWORK	SHLOCK	SHMUCK	SHOEBILLS	SHOLOM
SHITWORKS	SHLOCKIER	SHMUCKIER	SHOEBLACK	SHOLOMS
SHITZU	SHLOCKS	SHMUCKS	SHOEBOX	SHONE
SHITZUS	SHLOCKY	SHMUCKY	SHOEBOXES	SHONEEN
SHIUR	SHLONG	SHNAPPS	SHOEBRUSH	SHONEENS
SHIURIM	SHLONGS	SHNAPS	SHOED	SHONKIER
SHIV	SHLOSHIM	SHNOOK	SHOEHORN	SHONKIEST
SHIVA	SHLOSHIMS	SHNOOKS	SHOEHORNS	SHONKY
SHIVAH	SHLUB	SHNORRER	SHOEING	SHOO
SHIVAHS	SHLUBS	SHNORRERS	SHOEINGS	SHOOED
SHIVAREE	SHLUMP	SHO	SHOELACE	SHOOFLIES
SHIVAREED	SHLUMPED	SHOAL	SHOELACES	SHOOFLY
SHIVAREES	SHLUMPIER	SHOALED	SHOELESS	SHOOGIE
SHIVAS	SHLUMPING	SHOALER	SHOEMAKER	SHOOGIED
SHIVE	SHLUMPS	SHOALEST	SHOEPAC	SHOOGIES
SHIVER	SHLUMPY	SHOALIER	SHOEPACK	SHOOGLE
SHIVERED	SHMALTZ	SHOALIEST	SHOEPACKS	SHOOGLED
SHIVERER	SHMALTZES	SHOALING	SHOEPACS	SHOOGLES
SHIVERERS	SHMALTZY	SHOALINGS	SHOER	SHOOGLIER
SHIVERIER	SHMATTE	SHOALNESS	SHOERS	SHOOGLING
SHIVERING	SHMATTES	SHOALS	SHOES	SHOOGLY

S

SHOOING

SHOOING	SHOPLIFT	SHORTARSE	SHOTTING	SHOWBOAT
SHOOK	SHOPLIFTS	SHORTCAKE	SHOTTLE	SHOWBOATS
SHOOKS	SHOPMAN	SHORTCUT	SHOTTLES	SHOWBOX
SHOOL	SHOPMEN	SHORTCUTS	SHOTTS	SHOWBOXES
SHOOLE	SHOPPE	SHORTED	SHOUGH	SHOWBREAD
SHOOLED	SHOPPED	SHORTEN	SHOUGHS	SHOWCASE
SHOOLES	SHOPPER	SHORTENED	SHOULD	SHOWCASED
SHOOLING	SHOPPERS	SHORTENER	SHOULDER	SHOWCASES
SHOOLS	SHOPPES	SHORTENS	SHOULDERS	SHOWD
SHOON	SHOPPIER	SHORTER	SHOULDEST	SHOWDED
SHOORA	SHOPPIES	SHORTEST	SHOULDST	SHOWDING
SHOORAS	SHOPPIEST	SHORTFALL	SHOUSE	SHOWDOWN
SHOOS	SHOPPING	SHORTGOWN	SHOUSES	SHOWDOWNS
SHOOSH	SHOPPINGS	SHORTHAIR	SHOUT	SHOWDS
SHOOSHED	SHOPPY	SHORTHAND	SHOUTED	SHOWED
SHOOSHES	SHOPS	SHORTHEAD	SHOUTER	SHOWER
SHOOSHING	SHOPTALK	SHORTHOLD	SHOUTERS	SHOWERED
SHOOT	SHOPTALKS	SHORTHORN	SHOUTHER	SHOWERER
SHOOTABLE	SHOPWOMAN	SHORTIA	SHOUTHERS	SHOWERERS
SHOOTDOWN	SHOPWOMEN	SHORTIAS	SHOUTIER	SHOWERFUL
SHOOTER	SHOPWORN	SHORTIE	SHOUTIEST	SHOWERIER
SHOOTERS	SHORAN	SHORTIES	SHOUTING	SHOWERING
SHOOTIE	SHORANS	SHORTING	SHOUTINGS	SHOWERS
SHOOTIES	SHORE	SHORTISH	SHOUTLINE	SHOWERY
SHOOTING	SHOREBIRD	SHORTLIST	SHOUTOUT	SHOWGHE
SHOOTINGS	SHORED	SHORTLY	SHOUTOUTS	SHOWGHES
SHOOTIST	SHOREFAST	SHORTNESS	SHOUTS	SHOWGIRL
SHOOTISTS	SHORELESS	SHORTS	SHOUTY	SHOWGIRLS
SHOOTOUT	SHORELINE	SHORTSTOP	SHOVE	SHOWGOER
SHOOTOUTS	SHOREMAN	SHORTWAVE	SHOVED	SHOWGOERS
SHOOTS	SHOREMEN	SHORTY	SHOVEL	SHOWIER
SHOP	SHORER	SHOT	SHOVELED	SHOWIEST
SHOPBOARD	SHORERS	SHOTCRETE	SHOVELER	SHOWILY
SHOPBOT	SHORES	SHOTE	SHOVELERS	SHOWINESS
SHOPBOTS	SHORESIDE	SHOTES	SHOVELFUL	SHOWING
SHOPBOY	SHORESMAN	SHOTFIRER	SHOVELING	SHOWINGS
SHOPBOYS	SHORESMEN	SHOTGUN	SHOVELLED	SHOWJUMP
SHOPE	SHOREWARD	SHOTGUNS	SHOVELLER	SHOWJUMPS
SHOPFRONT	SHOREWEED	SHOTHOLE	SHOVELS	SHOWMAN
SHOPFUL	SHORING	SHOTHOLES	SHOVER	SHOWMANCE
SHOPFULS	SHORINGS	SHOTMAKER	SHOVERS	SHOWMANLY
SHOPGIRL	SHORL	SHOTPROOF	SHOVES	SHOWMEN
SHOPGIRLS	SHORLS	SHOTS	SHOVING	SHOWN
SHOPHAR	SHORN	SHOTT	SHOVINGS	SHOWOFF
SHOPHARS	SHORT	SHOTTE	SHOW	SHOWOFFS
SHOPHOUSE	SHORTAGE	SHOTTED	SHOWABLE	SHOWPIECE
SHOPHROTH	SHORTAGES	SHOTTEN	SHOWBIZ	SHOWPLACE
SHOPLESS	SHORTARM	SHOTTES	SHOWBIZZY	SHOWRING

SHOWRINGS	SHRIECHED	SHRINKING	SHRUBBY	SHUDDER
SHOWROOM	SHRIECHES	SHRINKS	SHRUBLAND	SHUDDERED
SHOWROOMS	SHRIEK	SHRIS	SHRUBLESS	SHUDDERS
SHOWS	SHRIEKED	SHRITCH	SHRUBLIKE	SHUDDERY
SHOWTIME	SHRIEKER	SHRITCHED	SHRUBS	SHUFFLE
SHOWTIMES	SHRIEKERS	SHRITCHES	SHRUG	SHUFFLED
SHOWY	SHRIEKIER	SHRIVE	SHRUGGED	SHUFFLER
SHOWYARD	SHRIEKING	SHRIVED	SHRUGGING	SHUFFLERS
SHOWYARDS	SHRIEKS	SHRIVEL	SHRUGS	SHUFFLES
SHOYU	SHRIEKY	SHRIVELED	SHRUNK	SHUFFLING
SHOYUS	SHRIEVAL	SHRIVELS	SHRUNKEN	SHUFTI
SHRADDHA	SHRIEVE	SHRIVEN	SHTCHI	SHUFTIES
SHRADDHAS	SHRIEVED	SHRIVER	SHTCHIS	SHUFTIS
SHRANK	SHRIEVES	SHRIVERS	SHTETEL	SHUFTY
SHRAPNEL	SHRIEVING	SHRIVES	SHTETELS	SHUGGIES
SHRAPNELS	SHRIFT	SHRIVING	SHTETL	SHUGGY
SHRED	SHRIFTS	SHRIVINGS	SHTETLACH	SHUL
SHREDDED	SHRIGHT	SHROFF	SHTETLS	SHULE
SHREDDER	SHRIGHTS	SHROFFAGE	SHTICK	SHULED
SHREDDERS	SHRIKE	SHROFFED	SHTICKIER	SHULES
SHREDDIER	SHRIKED	SHROFFING	SHTICKS	SHULING
SHREDDING	SHRIKES	SHROFFS	SHTICKY	SHULN
SHREDDY	SHRIKING	SHROOM	SHTIK	SHULS
SHREDLESS	SHRILL	SHROOMED	SHTIKS	SHUMAI
SHREDS	SHRILLED	SHROOMER	SHTOOK	SHUN
SHREEK	SHRILLER	SHROOMERS	SHTOOKS	SHUNLESS
SHREEKED	SHRILLEST	SHROOMING	SHTOOM	SHUNNABLE
SHREEKING	SHRILLIER	SHROOMS	SHTOOMER	SHUNNED
SHREEKS	SHRILLING	SHROUD	SHTOOMEST	SHUNNER
SHREIK	SHRILLS	SHROUDED	SHTREIMEL	SHUNNERS
SHREIKED	SHRILLY	SHROUDIER	SHTUCK	SHUNNING
SHREIKING	SHRIMP	SHROUDING	SHTUCKS	SHUNPIKE
SHREIKS	SHRIMPED	SHROUDS	SHTUM	SHUNPIKED
SHREW	SHRIMPER	SHROUDY	SHTUMM	SHUNPIKER
SHREWD	SHRIMPERS	SHROVE	SHTUMMER	SHUNPIKES
SHREWDER	SHRIMPIER	SHROVED	SHTUMMEST	SHUNS
SHREWDEST	SHRIMPING	SHROVES	SHTUP	SHUNT
SHREWDIE	SHRIMPS	SHROVING	SHTUPPED	SHUNTED
SHREWDIES	SHRIMPY	SHROW	SHTUPPING	SHUNTER
SHREWDLY	SHRINAL	SHROWD	SHTUPS	SHUNTERS
SHREWED	SHRINE	SHROWED	SHUBUNKIN	SHUNTING
SHREWING	SHRINED	SHROWING	SHUCK	SHUNTINGS
SHREWISH	SHRINES	SHROWS	SHUCKED	SHUNTS
SHREWLIKE	SHRINING	SHRUB	SHUCKER	SHURA
SHREWMICE	SHRINK	SHRUBBED	SHUCKERS	SHURAS
SHREWS	SHRINKAGE	SHRUBBERY	SHUCKING	SHURIKEN
SHRI	SHRINKER	SHRUBBIER	SHUCKINGS	SHURIKENS
SHRIECH	SHRINKERS	SHRUBBING	SHUCKS	SHUSH

SHUSHED	SHYLOCKED	SIBSHIPS	SICKLE	SIDEBOARD
SHUSHER	SHYLOCKS	SIBYL	SICKLED	SIDEBONE
SHUSHERS	SHYLY	SIBYLIC	SICKLEMAN	SIDEBONES
SHUSHES	SHYNESS	SIBYLLIC	SICKLEMEN	SIDEBURN
SHUSHING	SHYNESSES	SIBYLLINE	SICKLEMIA	SIDEBURNS
SHUT	SHYPOO	SIBYLS	SICKLEMIC	SIDECAR
SHUTDOWN	SHYPOOS	SIC	SICKLES	SIDECARS
SHUTDOWNS	SHYSTER	SICARIO	SICKLIED	SIDECHAIR
SHUTE	SHYSTERS	SICARIOS	SICKLIER	SIDECHECK
SHUTED	SI	SICCAN	SICKLIES	SIDED
SHUTES	SIAL	SICCAR	SICKLIEST	SIDEDLY
SHUTEYE	SIALIC	SICCATIVE	SICKLILY	SIDEDNESS
SHUTEYES	SIALID	SICCED	SICKLING	SIDEDRESS
SHUTING	SIALIDAN	SICCING	SICKLY	SIDEHILL
SHUTOFF	SIALIDANS	SICCITIES	SICKLYING	SIDEHILLS
SHUTOFFS	SIALIDS	SICCITY	SICKNESS	SIDEKICK
SHUTOUT	SIALOGRAM	SICE	SICKNURSE	SIDEKICKS
SHUTOUTS	SIALOID	SICES	SICKO	SIDELESS
SHUTS	SIALOLITH	SICH	SICKOS	SIDELIGHT
SHUTTER	SIALON	SICHT	SICKOUT	SIDELINE
SHUTTERED	SIALONS	SICHTED	SICKOUTS	SIDELINED
SHUTTERS	SIALS	SICHTING	SICKROOM	SIDELINER
SHUTTING	SIAMANG	SICHTS	SICKROOMS	SIDELINES
SHUTTLE	SIAMANGS	SICILIANA	SICKS	SIDELING
SHUTTLED	SIAMESE	SICILIANE	SICKY	SIDELINGS
SHUTTLER	SIAMESED	SICILIANO	SICLIKE	SIDELOCK
SHUTTLERS	SIAMESES	SICK	SICS	SIDELOCKS
SHUTTLES	SIAMESING	SICKBAY	SIDA	SIDELONG
SHUTTLING	SIAMEZE	SICKBAYS	SIDALCEA	SIDEMAN
SHVARTZE	SIAMEZED	SICKBED	SIDALCEAS	SIDEMEAT
SHVARTZES	SIAMEZES	SICKBEDS	SIDAS	SIDEMEATS
SHVITZ	SIAMEZING	SICKED	SIDDHA	SIDEMEN
SHVITZED	SIB	SICKEE	SIDDHAS	SIDENOTE
SHVITZES	SIBB	SICKEES	SIDDHI	SIDENOTES
SHVITZING	SIBBS	SICKEN	SIDDHIS	SIDEPATH
SHWA	SIBILANCE	SICKENED	SIDDHUISM	SIDEPATHS
SHWANPAN	SIBILANCY	SICKENER	SIDDUR	SIDEPIECE
SHWANPANS	SIBILANT	SICKENERS	SIDDURIM	SIDER
SHWAS	SIBILANTS	SICKENING	SIDDURS	SIDERAL
SHWESHWE	SIBILATE	SICKENS	SIDE	SIDERATE
SHWESHWES	SIBILATED	SICKER	SIDEARM	SIDERATED
SHY	SIBILATES	SICKERLY	SIDEARMED	SIDERATES
SHYER	SIBILATOR	SICKEST	SIDEARMER	SIDEREAL
SHYERS	SIBILOUS	SICKIE	SIDEARMS	SIDERITE
SHYEST	SIBLING	SICKIES	SIDEBAND	SIDERITES
SHYING	SIBLINGS	SICKING	SIDEBANDS	SIDERITIC
SHYISH	SIBS	SICKISH	SIDEBAR	SIDEROAD
SHYLOCK	SIBSHIP	SICKISHLY	SIDEBARS	SIDEROADS

SIDEROSES	SIEGED	SIFTER	SIGLOS	SIGNEURIE
SIDEROSIS	SIEGER	SIFTERS	SIGLUM	SIGNIEUR
SIDEROTIC	SIEGERS	SIFTING	SIGMA	SIGNIEURS
SIDERS	SIEGES	SIFTINGLY	SIGMAS	SIGNIFICS
SIDES	SIEGING	SIFTINGS	SIGMATE	SIGNIFIED
SIDESHOOT	SIELD	SIFTS	SIGMATED	SIGNIFIER
SIDESHOW	SIEMENS	SIG	SIGMATES	SIGNIFIES
SIDESHOWS	SIEMENSES	SIGANID	SIGMATIC	SIGNIFY
SIDESLIP	SIEN	SIGANIDS	SIGMATING	SIGNING
SIDESLIPS	SIENITE	SIGH	SIGMATION	SIGNINGS
SIDESMAN	SIENITES	SIGHED	SIGMATISM	SIGNIOR
SIDESMEN	SIENNA	SIGHER	SIGMATRON	SIGNIORI
SIDESPIN	SIENNAS	SIGHERS	SIGMOID	SIGNIORS
SIDESPINS	SIENS	SIGHFUL	SIGMOIDAL	SIGNIORY
SIDESPLIT	SIENT	SIGHING	SIGMOIDS	SIGNLESS
SIDESTEP	SIENTS	SIGHINGLY	SIGN	SIGNOR
SIDESTEPS	SIEROZEM	SIGHINGS	SIGNA	SIGNORA
SIDESWIPE	SIEROZEMS	SIGHLESS	SIGNABLE	SIGNORAS
SIDETABLE	SIERRA	SIGHLIKE	SIGNAGE	SIGNORE
SIDETRACK	SIERRAN	SIGHS	SIGNAGES	SIGNORES
SIDEWALK	SIERRAS	SIGHT	SIGNAL	SIGNORI
SIDEWALKS	SIES	SIGHTABLE	SIGNALED	SIGNORIA
SIDEWALL	SIESTA	SIGHTED	SIGNALER	SIGNORIAL
SIDEWALLS	SIESTAS	SIGHTER	SIGNALERS	SIGNORIAS
SIDEWARD	SIETH	SIGHTERS	SIGNALING	SIGNORIES
SIDEWARDS	SIETHS	SIGHTING	SIGNALISE	SIGNORINA
SIDEWAY	SIEUR	SIGHTINGS	SIGNALIZE	SIGNORINE
SIDEWAYS	SIEURS	SIGHTLESS	SIGNALLED	SIGNORINI
SIDEWHEEL	SIEVE	SIGHTLIER	SIGNALLER	SIGNORINO
SIDEWISE	SIEVED	SIGHTLINE	SIGNALLY	SIGNORS
SIDH	SIEVELIKE	SIGHTLY	SIGNALMAN	SIGNORY
SIDHA	SIEVERT	SIGHTS	SIGNALMEN	SIGNPOST
SIDHAS	SIEVERTS	SIGHTSAW	SIGNALS	SIGNPOSTS
SIDHE	SIEVES	SIGHTSEE	SIGNARIES	SIGNS
SIDHUISM	SIEVING	SIGHTSEEN	SIGNARY	SIGS
SIDHUISMS	SIF	SIGHTSEER	SIGNATORY	SIJO
SIDING	SIFAKA	SIGHTSEES	SIGNATURE	SIJOS
SIDINGS	SIFAKAS	SIGHTSMAN	SIGNBOARD	SIK
SIDLE	SIFFLE	SIGHTSMEN	SIGNED	SIKA
SIDLED	SIFFLED	SIGIL	SIGNEE	SIKAS
SIDLER	SIFFLES	SIGILLARY	SIGNEES	SIKE
SIDLERS	SIFFLEUR	SIGILLATE	SIGNER	SIKER
SIDLES	SIFFLEURS	SIGILS	SIGNERS	SIKES
SIDLING	SIFFLEUSE	SIGISBEI	SIGNET	SIKORSKY
SIDLINGLY	SIFFLING	SIGISBEO	SIGNETED	SIKSIK
SIECLE	SIFREI	SIGLA	SIGNETING	SIKSIKS
SIECLES	SIFT	SIGLAS	SIGNETS	SILAGE
SIEGE	SIFTED	SIGLOI	SIGNEUR	SILAGED

SILAGEING	SILICLE	SILLABUB	SILVER	SIMILIZED
SILAGES	SILICLES	SILLABUBS	SILVERED	SIMILIZES
SILAGING	SILICON	SILLADAR	SILVERER	SIMILOR
SILANE	SILICONE	SILLADARS	SILVERERS	SIMILORS
SILANES	SILICONES	SILLER	SILVEREYE	SIMIOID
SILASTIC	SILICONS	SILLERS	SILVERIER	SIMIOUS
SILASTICS	SILICOSES	SILLIBUB	SILVERING	SIMIS
SILD	SILICOSIS	SILLIBUBS	SILVERISE	SIMITAR
SILDS	SILICOTIC	SILLIER	SILVERIZE	SIMITARS
SILE	SILICULA	SILLIES	SILVERLY	SIMKIN
SILED	SILICULAE	SILLIEST	SILVERN	SIMKINS
SILEN	SILICULAS	SILLILY	SILVERS	SIMLIN
SILENCE	SILICULE	SILLINESS	SILVERTIP	SIMLINS
SILENCED	SILICULES	SILLOCK	SILVERY	SIMMER
SILENCER	SILING	SILLOCKS	SILVEX	SIMMERED
SILENCERS	SILIQUA	SILLS	SILVEXES	SIMMERING
SILENCES	SILIQUAE	SILLY	SILVICAL	SIMMERS
SILENCING	SILIQUAS	SILO	SILVICS	SIMNEL
SILENE	SILIQUE	SILOED	SILYMARIN	SIMNELS
SILENES	SILIQUES	SILOING	SIM	SIMOLEON
SILENI	SILIQUOSE	SILOS	SIMA	SIMOLEONS
SILENS	SILIQUOUS	SILOXANE	SIMAR	SIMONIAC
SILENT	SILK	SILOXANES	SIMAROUBA	SIMONIACS
SILENTER	SILKALENE	SILPHIA	SIMARRE	SIMONIES
SILENTEST	SILKALINE	SILPHIUM	SIMARRES	SIMONIOUS
SILENTLY	SILKED	SILPHIUMS	SIMARS	SIMONISE
SILENTS	SILKEN	SILT	SIMARUBA	SIMONISED
SILENUS	SILKENED	SILTATION	SIMARUBAS	SIMONISES
SILER	SILKENING	SILTED	SIMAS	SIMONIST
SILERS	SILKENS	SILTIER	SIMATIC	SIMONISTS
SILES	SILKIE	SILTIEST	SIMAZINE	SIMONIZE
SILESIA	SILKIER	SILTING	SIMAZINES	SIMONIZED
SILESIAS	SILKIES	SILTS	SIMBA	SIMONIZES
SILEX	SILKIEST	SILTSTONE	SIMBAS	SIMONY
SILEXES	SILKILY	SILTY	SIMCHA	SIMOOM
SILICA	SILKINESS	SILURIAN	SIMCHAS	SIMOOMS
SILICAS	SILKING	SILURID	SIMI	SIMOON
SILICATE	SILKLIKE	SILURIDS	SIMIAL	SIMOONS
SILICATED	SILKOLINE	SILURIST	SIMIAN	SIMORG
SILICATES	SILKS	SILURISTS	SIMIANS	SIMORGS
SILICEOUS	SILKTAIL	SILUROID	SIMILAR	SIMP
SILICIC	SILKTAILS	SILUROIDS	SIMILARLY	SIMPAI
SILICIDE	SILKWEED	SILVA	SIMILE	SIMPAIS
SILICIDES	SILKWEEDS	SILVAE	SIMILES	SIMPATICO
SILICIFY	SILKWORM	SILVAN	SIMILISE	SIMPER
SILICIOUS	SILKWORMS	SILVANS	SIMILISED	SIMPERED
SILICIUM	SILKY	SILVAS	SIMILISES	SIMPERER
SILICIUMS	SILL	SILVATIC	SIMILIZE	SIMPERERS

SIMPERING	SINAPISMS	SINGLED	SINLESS	SIPES
SIMPERS	SINCE	SINGLEDOM	SINLESSLY	SIPHON
SIMPKIN	SINCERE	SINGLES	SINNED	SIPHONAGE
SIMPKINS	SINCERELY	SINGLET	SINNER	SIPHONAL
SIMPLE	SINCERER	SINGLETON	SINNERED	SIPHONATE
SIMPLED	SINCEREST	SINGLETS	SINNERING	SIPHONED
SIMPLER	SINCERITY	SINGLING	SINNERS	SIPHONET
SIMPLERS	SINCIPITA	SINGLINGS	SINNET	SIPHONETS
SIMPLES	SINCIPUT	SINGLY	SINNETS	SIPHONIC
SIMPLESSE	SINCIPUTS	SINGS	SINNING	SIPHONING
SIMPLEST	SIND	SINGSONG	SINNINGIA	SIPHONS
SIMPLETON	SINDED	SINGSONGS	SINOLOGUE	SIPHUNCLE
SIMPLEX	SINDING	SINGSONGY	SINOLOGY	SIPING
SIMPLEXES	SINDINGS	SINGSPIEL	SINOPIA	SIPPABLE
SIMPLICES	SINDON	SINGULAR	SINOPIAS	SIPPED
SIMPLICIA	SINDONS	SINGULARS	SINOPIE	SIPPER
SIMPLIFY	SINDS	SINGULARY	SINOPIS	SIPPERS
SIMPLING	SINE	SINGULT	SINOPISES	SIPPET
SIMPLINGS	SINECURE	SINGULTS	SINOPITE	SIPPETS
SIMPLISM	SINECURES	SINGULTUS	SINOPITES	SIPPING
SIMPLISMS	SINED	SINH	SINS	SIPPLE
SIMPLIST	SINES	SINHS	SINSYNE	SIPPLED
SIMPLISTE	SINEW	SINICAL	SINTER	SIPPLES
SIMPLISTS	SINEWED	SINICISE	SINTERED	SIPPLING
SIMPLY	SINEWIER	SINICISED	SINTERIER	SIPPY
SIMPS	SINEWIEST	SINICISES	SINTERING	SIPS
SIMS	SINEWING	SINICIZE	SINTERS	SIR
SIMUL	SINEWLESS	SINICIZED	SINTERY	SIRCAR
SIMULACRA	SINEWS	SINICIZES	SINUATE	SIRCARS
SIMULACRE	SINEWY	SINING	SINUATED	SIRDAR
SIMULANT	SINFONIA	SINISTER	SINUATELY	SIRDARS
SIMULANTS	SINFONIAS	SINISTRAL	SINUATES	SIRE
SIMULAR	SINFONIE	SINK	SINUATING	SIRED
SIMULARS	SINFUL	SINKABLE	SINUATION	SIREE
SIMULATE	SINFULLY	SINKAGE	SINUITIS	SIREES
SIMULATED	SING	SINKAGES	SINUOSE	SIREN
SIMULATES	SINGABLE	SINKER	SINUOSITY	SIRENIAN
SIMULATOR	SINGALONG	SINKERS	STNUOUS	SIRENIANS
SIMULCAST	SINGE	SINKFUL	SINUOUSLY	SIRENIC
SIMULIUM	SINGED	SINKFULS	SINUS	SIRENISE
SIMULIUMS	SINGEING	SINKHOLE	SINUSES	SIRENISED
SIMULS	SINGER	SINKHOLES	SINUSITIS	SIRENISES
SIMURG	SINGERS	SINKIER	SINUSLIKE	SIRENIZE
SIMURGH	SINGES	SINKIEST	SINUSOID	SIRENIZED
SIMURGHS	SINGING	SINKING	SINUSOIDS	SIRENIZES
SIMURGS	SINGINGLY	SINKINGS	SIP	SIRENS
SIN	SINGINGS	SINKS	SIPE	SIRES
SINAPISM	SINGLE	SINKY	SIPED	SIRGANG

S

SIRGANGS	SIS	SITFASTS	SIVERS	SIZEISMS
SIRI	SISAL	SITH	SIWASH	SIZEIST
SIRIASES	SISALS	SITHE	SIWASHED	SIZEISTS
SIRIASIS	SISERARY	SITHED	SIWASHES	SIZEL
SIRIH	SISES	SITHEE	SIWASHING	SIZELS
SIRIHS	SISKIN	SITHEN	SIX	SIZER
SIRING	SISKINS	SITHENCE	SIXAIN	SIZERS
SIRINGS	SISS	SITHENS	SIXAINE	SIZES
SIRIS	SISSES	SITHES	SIXAINES	SIZIER
SIRKAR	SISSIER	SITHING	SIXAINS	SIZIEST
SIRKARS	SISSIES	SITING	SIXER	SIZINESS
SIRLOIN	SISSIEST	SITINGS	SIXERS	SIZING
SIRLOINS	SISSIFIED	SITIOLOGY	SIXES	SIZINGS
SIRNAME	SISSINESS	SITKA	SIXFOLD	SIZISM
SIRNAMED	SISSOO	SITKAMER	SIXISH	SIZISMS
SIRNAMES	SISSOOS	SITKAMERS	SIXMO	SIZIST
SIRNAMING	SISSY	SITOLOGY	SIXMOS	SIZISTS
SIROC	SISSYISH	SITREP	SIXPENCE	SIZY
SIROCCO	SISSYNESS	SITREPS	SIXPENCES	SIZZLE
SIROCCOS	SIST	SITS	SIXPENNY	SIZZLED
SIROCS	SISTA	SITTAR	SIXSCORE	SIZZLER
SIRONISE	SISTAS	SITTARS	SIXSCORES	SIZZLERS
SIRONISED	SISTED	SITTELLA	SIXTE	SIZZLES
SIRONISES	SISTER	SITTELLAS	SIXTEEN	SIZZLING
SIRONIZE	SISTERED	SITTEN	SIXTEENER	SIZZLINGS
SIRONIZED	SISTERING	SITTER	SIXTEENMO	SJAMBOK
SIRONIZES	SISTERLY	SITTERS	SIXTEENS	SJAMBOKED
SIROSET	SISTERS	SITTINE	SIXTEENTH	SJAMBOKS
SIRRA	SISTING	SITTINES	SIXTES	SJOE
SIRRAH	SISTRA	SITTING	SIXTH	SKA
SIRRAHS	SISTROID	SITTINGS	SIXTHLY	SKAG
SIRRAS	SISTRUM	SITUATE	SIXTHS	SKAGS
SIRRED	SISTRUMS	SITUATED	SIXTIES	SKAIL
SIRREE	SISTS	SITUATES	SIXTIETH	SKAILED
SIRREES	SIT	SITUATING	SIXTIETHS	SKAILING
SIRRING	SITAR	SITUATION	SIXTY	SKAILS
SIRS	SITARIST	SITULA	SIXTYFOLD	SKAITH
SIRTUIN	SITARISTS	SITULAE	SIXTYISH	SKAITHED
SIRTUINS	SITARS	SITUP	SIZABLE	SKAITHING
SIRUP	SITATUNGA	SITUPS	SIZABLY	SKAITHS
SIRUPED	SITCOM	SITUS	SIZAR	SKALD
SIRUPIER	SITCOMS	SITUSES	SIZARS	SKALDIC
SIRUPIEST	SITE	SITUTUNGA	SIZARSHIP	SKALDS
SIRUPING	SITED	SITZ	SIZE	SKALDSHIP
SIRUPS	SITELLA	SITZKRIEG	SIZEABLE	SKANGER
SIRUPY	SITELLAS	SITZMARK	SIZEABLY	SKANGERS
SIRVENTE	SITES	SITZMARKS	SIZED	SKANK
SIRVENTES	SITFAST	SIVER	SIZEISM	SKANKED

SKANKER	SKEE	SKELL	SKERRICK	SKIBOBS
SKANKERS	SKEECHAN	SKELLIE	SKERRICKS	SKID
SKANKIER	SKEECHANS	SKELLIED	SKERRIES	SKIDDED
SKANKIEST	SKEED	SKELLIER	SKERRING	SKIDDER
SKANKING	SKEEF	SKELLIES	SKERRY	SKIDDERS
SKANKINGS	SKEEING	SKELLIEST	SKERS	SKIDDIER
SKANKS	SKEELIER	SKELLOCH	SKET	SKIDDIEST
SKANKY	SKEELIEST	SKELLOCHS	SKETCH	SKIDDING
SKART	SKEELY	SKELLS	SKETCHED	SKIDDINGS
SKARTH	SKEEN	SKELLUM	SKETCHER	SKIDDOO
SKARTHS	SKEENS	SKELLUMS	SKETCHERS	SKIDDOOED
SKARTS	SKEER	SKELLY	SKETCHES	SKIDDOOS
SKAS	SKEERED	SKELLYING	SKETCHIER	SKIDDY
SKAT	SKEERIER	SKELM	SKETCHILY	SKIDLID
SKATE	SKEERIEST	SKELMS	SKETCHING	SKIDLIDS
SKATED	SKEERING	SKELP	SKETCHPAD	SKIDMARK
SKATEPARK	SKEERS	SKELPED	SKETCHY	SKIDMARKS
SKATEPUNK	SKEERY	SKELPING	SKETS	SKIDOO
SKATER	SKEES	SKELPINGS	SKETTED	SKIDOOED
SKATERS	SKEESICKS	SKELPIT	SKETTING	SKIDOOER
SKATES	SKEET	SKELPS	SKEW	SKIDOOERS
SKATING	SKEETER	SKELTER	SKEWBACK	SKIDOOING
SKATINGS	SKEETERS	SKELTERED	SKEWBACKS	SKIDOOS
SKATOL	SKEETS	SKELTERS	SKEWBALD	SKIDPAD
SKATOLE	SKEEVIER	SKELUM	SKEWBALDS	SKIDPADS
SKATOLES	SKEEVIEST	SKELUMS	SKEWED	SKIDPAN
SKATOLS	SKEEVY	SKEN	SKEWER	SKIDPANS
SKATS	SKEG	SKENE	SKEWERED	SKIDPROOF
SKATT	SKEGG	SKENES	SKEWERING	SKIDS
SKATTS	SKEGGER	SKENNED	SKEWERS	SKIDWAY
SKAW	SKEGGERS	SKENNING	SKEWEST	SKIDWAYS
SKAWS	SKEGGS	SKENS	SKEWING	SKIED
SKEAN	SKEGS	SKEO	SKEWNESS	SKIER
SKEANE	SKEIGH	SKEOES	SKEWS	SKIERS
SKEANES	SKEIGHER	SKEOS	SKEWWHIFF	SKIES
SKEANS	SKEIGHEST	SKEP	SKI	SKIEY
SKEAR	SKEIN	SKEPFUL	SKIABLE	SKIEYER
SKEARED	SKEINED	SKEPFULS	SKIAGRAM	SKIEYEST
SKEARIER	SKEINING	SKEPPED	SKIAGRAMS	SKIFF
SKEARIEST	SKEINS	SKEPPING	SKIAGRAPH	SKIFFED
SKEARING	SKELDER	SKEPS	SKIAMACHY	SKIFFING
SKEARS	SKELDERED	SKEPSIS	SKIASCOPE	SKIFFLE
SKEARY	SKELDERS	SKEPSISES	SKIASCOPY	SKIFFLED
SKED	SKELETAL	SKEPTIC	SKIATRON	SKIFFLES
SKEDADDLE	SKELETON	SKEPTICAL	SKIATRONS	SKIFFLESS
SKEDDED	SKELETONS	SKEPTICS	SKIBOB	SKIFFLING
SKEDDING	SKELF	SKER	SKIBOBBED	SKIFFS
SKEDS	SKELFS	SKERRED	SKIBOBBER	SKIING

S

SKIINGS	SKINFLICK	SKIPPET	SKITTLING	SKOGGED
SKIJORER	SKINFLINT	SKIPPETS	SKIVE	SKOGGING
SKIJORERS	SKINFOOD	SKIPPIER	SKIVED	SKOGS
SKIJORING	SKINFOODS	SKIPPIEST	SKIVER	SKOKIAAN
SKIJUMPER	SKINFUL	SKIPPING	SKIVERED	SKOKIAANS
SKIKJORER	SKINFULS	SKIPPINGS	SKIVERING	SKOL
SKILFUL	SKINHEAD	SKIPPY	SKIVERS	SKOLED
SKILFULL	SKINHEADS	SKIPS	SKIVES	SKOLIA
SKILFULLY	SKINK	SKIRL	SKIVIE	SKOLING
SKILL	SKINKED	SKIRLED	SKIVIER	SKOLION
SKILLED	SKINKER	SKIRLING	SKIVIEST	SKOLLED
SKILLESS	SKINKERS	SKIRLINGS	SKIVING	SKOLLIE
SKILLET	SKINKING	SKIRLS	SKIVINGS	SKOLLIES
SKILLETS	SKINKS	SKIRMISH	SKIVVIED	SKOLLING
SKILLFUL	SKINLESS	SKIRR	SKIVVIES	SKOLLY
SKILLIER	SKINLIKE	SKIRRED	SKIVVY	SKOLS
SKILLIES	SKINNED	SKIRRET	SKIVVYING	SKOOKUM
SKILLIEST	SKINNER	SKIRRETS	SKIVY	SKOOKUMS
SKILLING	SKINNERS	SKIRRING	SKIWEAR	SKOOL
SKILLINGS	SKINNIER	SKIRRS	SKIWEARS	SKOOLS
SKILLION	SKINNIES	SKIRT	SKLATE	SKOOSH
SKILLIONS	SKINNIEST	SKIRTED	SKLATED	SKOOSHED
SKILLS	SKINNING	SKIRTER	SKLATES	SKOOSHES
SKILLY	SKINNY	SKIRTERS	SKLATING	SKOOSHING
SKIM	SKINS	SKIRTING	SKLENT	SKORDALIA
SKIMBOARD	SKINSUIT	SKIRTINGS	SKLENTED	SKORT
SKIMMED	SKINSUITS	SKIRTLESS	SKLENTING	SKORTS
SKIMMER	SKINT	SKIRTLIKE	SKLENTS	SKOSH
SKIMMERS	SKINTER	SKIRTS	SKLIFF	SKOSHES
SKIMMIA	SKINTEST	SKIS	SKLIFFED	SKRAN
SKIMMIAS	SKINTIGHT	SKIT	SKLIFFING	SKRANS
SKIMMING	SKIO	SKITCH	SKLIFFS	SKREEGH
SKIMMINGS	SKIOES	SKITCHED	SKLIM	SKREEGHED
SKIMO	SKIORER	SKITCHES	SKLIMMED	SKREEGHS
SKIMOBILE	SKIORERS	SKITCHING	SKLIMMING	SKREEN
SKIMOS	SKIORING	SKITE	SKLIMS	SKREENS
SKIMP	SKIORINGS	SKITED	SKOAL	SKREIGH
SKIMPED	SKIOS	SKITES	SKOALED	SKREIGHED
SKIMPIER	SKIP	SKITING	SKOALING	SKREIGHS
SKIMPIEST	SKIPJACK	SKITS	SKOALS	SKRIECH
SKIMPILY	SKIPJACKS	SKITTER	SKODIER	SKRIECHED
SKIMPING	SKIPLANE	SKITTERED	SKODIEST	SKRIECHS
SKIMPS	SKIPLANES	SKITTERS	SKODY	SKRIED
SKIMPY	SKIPPABLE	SKITTERY	SKOFF	SKRIEGH
SKIMS	SKIPPED	SKITTISH	SKOFFED	SKRIEGHED
SKIN	SKIPPER	SKITTLE	SKOFFING	SKRIEGHS
SKINCARE	SKIPPERED	SKITTLED	SKOFFS	SKRIES
SKINCARES	SKIPPERS	SKITTLES	SKOG	SKRIK

SKRIKE	SKUNKED	SKYHOOKS	SKYWALKS	SLAGGIEST
SKRIKED	SKUNKIER	SKYIER	SKYWARD	SLAGGING
SKRIKES	SKUNKIEST	SKYIEST	SKYWARDS	SLAGGINGS
SKRIKING	SKUNKING	SKYING	SKYWATCH	SLAGGY
SKRIKS	SKUNKS	SKYISH	SKYWAY	SLAGHEAP
SKRIMMAGE	SKUNKWEED	SKYJACK	SKYWAYS	SLAGHEAPS
SKRIMP	SKUNKY	SKYJACKED	SKYWRITE	SLAGS
SKRIMPED	SKURRIED	SKYJACKER	SKYWRITER	SLAHAL
SKRIMPING	SKURRIES	SKYJACKS	SKYWRITES	SLAHALS
SKRIMPS	SKURRY	SKYLAB	SKYWROTE	SLAID
SKRONK	SKURRYING	SKYLABS	SLAB	SLAIDS
SKRONKS	SKUTTLE	SKYLARK	SLABBED	SLAIN
SKRUMP	SKUTTLED	SKYLARKED	SLABBER	SLAINTE
SKRUMPED	SKUTTLES	SKYLARKER	SLABBERED	SLAIRG
SKRUMPING	SKUTTLING	SKYLARKS	SLABBERER	SLAIRGED
SKRUMPS	SKY	SKYLESS	SLABBERS	SLAIRGING
SKRY	SKYBOARD	SKYLIGHT	SLABBERY	SLAIRGS
SKRYER	SKYBOARDS	SKYLIGHTS	SLABBIER	SLAISTER
SKRYERS	SKYBORN	SKYLIKE	SLABBIES	SLAISTERS
SKRYING	SKYBORNE	SKYLINE	SLABBIEST	SLAISTERY
SKUA	SKYBOX	SKYLINES	SLABBING	SLAKABLE
SKUAS	SKYBOXES	SKYLIT	SLABBINGS	SLAKE
SKUDLER	SKYBRIDGE	SKYMAN	SLABBY	SLAKEABLE
SKUDLERS	SKYCAP	SKYMEN	SLABLIKE	SLAKED
SKUG	SKYCAPS	SKYPHOI	SLABS	SLAKELESS
SKUGGED	SKYCLAD	SKYPHOS	SLABSTONE	SLAKER
SKUGGING	SKYDIVE	SKYR	SLACK	SLAKERS
SKUGS	SKYDIVED	SKYRE	SLACKED	SLAKES
SKULK	SKYDIVER	SKYRED	SLACKEN	SLAKING
SKULKED	SKYDIVERS	SKYRES	SLACKENED	SLALOM
SKULKER	SKYDIVES	SKYRING	SLACKENER	SLALOMED
SKULKERS	SKYDIVING	SKYRMION	SLACKENS	SLALOMER
SKULKING	SKYDOVE	SKYRMIONS	SLACKER	SLALOMERS
SKULKINGS	SKYED	SKYROCKET	SLACKERS	SLALOMING
SKULKS	SKYER	SKYRS	SLACKEST	SLALOMIST
SKULL	SKYERS	SKYSAIL	SLACKING	SLALOMS
SKULLCAP	SKYEY	SKYSAILS	SLACKLY	SLAM
SKULLCAPS	SKYEYER	SKYSCAPE	SLACKNESS	SLAMDANCE
SKULLED	SKYEYEST	SKYSCAPES	SLACKS	SLAMMAKIN
SKULLING	SKYF	SKYSURF	SLADANG	SLAMMED
SKULLS	SKYFED	SKYSURFED	SLADANGS	SLAMMER
SKULPIN	SKYFING	SKYSURFER	SLADE	SLAMMERS
SKULPINS	SKYFS	SKYSURFS	SLADES	SLAMMING
SKUMMER	SKYGLOW	SKYTE	SLAE	SLAMMINGS
SKUMMERED	SKYGLOWS	SKYTED	SLAES	SLAMS
SKUMMERS	SKYHOME	SKYTES	SLAG	SLANDER
SKUNK	SKYHOMES	SKYTING	SLAGGED	SLANDERED
SKUNKBIRD	SKYHOOK	SKYWALK	SLAGGIER	SLANDERER

SLANDERS	SLARTING	SLAVERS	SLEDGER	SLEEPY
SLANE	SLARTS	SLAVERY	SLEDGERS	SLEER
SLANES	SLASH	SLAVES	SLEDGES	SLEEST
SLANG	SLASHED	SLAVEY	SLEDGING	SLEET
SLANGED	SLASHER	SLAVEYS	SLEDGINGS	SLEETED
SLANGER	SLASHERS	SLAVING	SLEDS	SLEETIER
SLANGERS	SLASHES	SLAVISH	SLEE	SLEETIEST
SLANGIER	SLASHFEST	SLAVISHLY	SLEECH	SLEETING
SLANGIEST	SLASHING	SLAVOCRAT	SLEECHES	SLEETS
SLANGILY	SLASHINGS	SLAVOPHIL	SLEECHIER	SLEETY
SLANGING	SLAT	SLAW	SLEECHY	SLEEVE
SLANGINGS	SLATCH	SLAWS	SLEEK	SLEEVED
SLANGISH	SLATCHES	SLAY	SLEEKED	SLEEVEEN
SLANGS	SLATE	SLAYABLE	SLEEKEN	SLEEVEENS
SLANGUAGE	SLATED	SLAYED	SLEEKENED	SLEEVELET
SLANGULAR	SLATELIKE	SLAYER	SLEEKENS	SLEEVER
SLANGY	SLATER	SLAYERS	SLEEKER	SLEEVERS
SLANK	SLATERS	SLAYING	SLEEKERS	SLEEVES
SLANT	SLATES	SLAYINGS	SLEEKEST	SLEEVING
SLANTED	SLATEY	SLAYS	SLEEKIER	SLEEVINGS
SLANTER	SLATHER	SLEAVE	SLEEKIEST	SLEEZIER
SLANTERS	SLATHERED	SLEAVED	SLEEKING	SLEEZIEST
SLANTIER	SLATHERS	SLEAVES	SLEEKINGS	SLEEZY
SLANTIEST	SLATIER	SLEAVING	SLEEKIT	SLEIDED
SLANTING	SLATIEST	SLEAZE	SLEEKLY	SLEIGH
SLANTLY	SLATINESS	SLEAZEBAG	SLEEKNESS	SLEIGHED
SLANTS	SLATING	SLEAZED	SLEEKS	SLEIGHER
SLANTWAYS	SLATINGS	SLEAZES	SLEEKY	SLEIGHERS
SLANTWISE	SLATS	SLEAZIER	SLEEP	SLEIGHING
SLANTY	SLATTED	SLEAZIEST	SLEEPAWAY	SLEIGHS
SLAP	SLATTER	SLEAZILY	SLEEPER	SLEIGHT
SLAPDASH	SLATTERED	SLEAZING	SLEEPERS	SLEIGHTS
SLAPHAPPY	SLATTERN	SLEAZO	SLEEPERY	SLENDER
SLAPHEAD	SLATTERNS	SLEAZOID	SLEEPIER	SLENDERER
SLAPHEADS	SLATTERS	SLEAZOIDS	SLEEPIEST	SLENDERLY
SLAPJACK	SLATTERY	SLEAZOS	SLEEPILY	SLENTER
SLAPJACKS	SLATTING	SLEAZY	SLEEPING	SLENTERS
SLAPPED	SLATTINGS	SLEB	SLEEPINGS	SLEPT
SLAPPER	SLATY	SLEBS	SLEEPLESS	SLEUTH
SLAPPERS	SLAUGHTER	SLED	SLEEPLIKE	SLEUTHED
SLAPPING	SLAVE	SLEDDED	SLEEPOUT	SLEUTHING
SLAPPINGS	SLAVED	SLEDDER	SLEEPOUTS	SLEUTHS
SLAPS	SLAVER	SLEDDERS	SLEEPOVER	SLEW
SLAPSHOT	SLAVERED	SLEDDING	SLEEPRY	SLEWED
SLAPSHOTS	SLAVERER	SLEDDINGS	SLEEPS	SLEWING
SLAPSTICK	SLAVERERS	SLEDED	SLEEPSUIT	SLEWS
SLART	SLAVERIES	SLEDGE	SLEEPWALK	SLEY
SLARTED	SLAVERING	SLEDGED	SLEEPWEAR	SLEYS

SLICE	SLIGHTED	SLINGSHOT	SLIPPING	SLIVOVITZ
SLICEABLE	SLIGHTER	SLINGY	SLIPPY	SLIVOWITZ
SLICED	SLIGHTERS	SLINK	SLIPRAIL	SLOAN
SLICER	SLIGHTEST	SLINKED	SLIPRAILS	SLOANS
SLICERS	SLIGHTING	SLINKER	SLIPS	SLOB
SLICES	SLIGHTISH	SLINKERS	SLIPSHEET	SLOBBED
SLICING	SLIGHTLY	SLINKIER	SLIPSHOD	SLOBBER
SLICINGS	SLIGHTS	SLINKIEST	SLIPSLOP	SLOBBERED
SLICK	SLILY	SLINKILY	SLIPSLOPS	SLOBBERER
SLICKED	SLIM	SLINKING	SLIPSOLE	SLOBBERS
SLICKEN	SLIMDOWN	SLINKS	SLIPSOLES	SLOBBERY
SLICKENED	SLIMDOWNS	SLINKSKIN	SLIPT	SLOBBIER
SLICKENER	SLIME	SLINKWEED	SLIPUP	SLOBBIEST
SLICKENS	SLIMEBAG	SLINKY	SLIPUPS	SLOBBING
SLICKER	SLIMEBAGS	SLINTER	SLIPWARE	SLOBBISH
SLICKERED	SLIMEBALL	SLINTERS	SLIPWARES	SLOBBY
SLICKERS	SLIMED	SLIOTAR	SLIPWAY	SLOBLAND
SLICKEST	SLIMES	SLIOTARS	SLIPWAYS	SLOBLANDS
SLICKING	SLIMIER	SLIP	SLISH	SLOBS
SLICKINGS	SLIMIEST	SLIPCASE	SLISHES	SLOCKEN
SLICKLY	SLIMILY	SLIPCASED	SLIT	SLOCKENED
SLICKNESS	SLIMINESS	SLIPCASES	SLITHER	SLOCKENS
SLICKROCK	SLIMING	SLIPCOVER	SLITHERED	SLOE
SLICKS	SLIMLINE	SLIPDRESS	SLITHERS	SLOEBUSH
SLICKSTER	SLIMLY	SLIPE	SLITHERY	SLOES
SLID	SLIMMED	SLIPED	SLITLESS	SLOETHORN
SLIDABLE	SLIMMER	SLIPES	SLITLIKE	SLOETREE
SLIDDEN	SLIMMERS	SLIPFORM	SLITS	SLOETREES
SLIDDER	SLIMMEST	SLIPFORMS	SLITTED	SLOG
SLIDDERED	SLIMMING	SLIPING	SLITTER	SLOGAN
SLIDDERS	SLIMMINGS	SLIPKNOT	SLITTERS	SLOGANED
SLIDDERY	SLIMMISH	SLIPKNOTS	SLITTIER	SLOGANEER
SLIDE	SLIMNESS	SLIPLESS	SLITTIEST	SLOGANISE
SLIDED	SLIMPSIER	SLIPNOOSE	SLITTING	SLOGANIZE
SLIDER	SLIMPSY	SLIPOUT	SLITTY	SLOGANS
SLIDERS	SLIMS	SLIPOUTS	SLIVE	SLOGGED
SLIDES	SLIMSIER	SLIPOVER	SLIVED	SLOGGER
SLIDESHOW	SLIMSIEST	SLIPOVERS	SLIVEN	SLOGGERS
SLIDEWAY	SLIMSY	SLIPPAGE	SLIVER	SLOGGING
SLIDEWAYS	SLIMY	SLIPPAGES	SLIVERED	SLOGS
SLIDING	SLING	SLIPPED	SLIVERER	SLOID
SLIDINGLY	SLINGBACK	SLIPPER	SLIVERERS	SLOIDS
SLIDINGS	SLINGER	SLIPPERED	SLIVERING	SLOJD
SLIER	SLINGERS	SLIPPERS	SLIVERS	SLOJDS
SLIEST	SLINGIER	SLIPPERY	SLIVES	SLOKEN
SLIEVE	SLINGIEST	SLIPPIER	SLIVING	SLOKENED
SLIEVES	SLINGING	SLIPPIEST	SLIVOVIC	SLOKENING
SLIGHT	SLINGS	SLIPPILY	SLIVOVICA	SLOKENS

S

SLOMMOCK

SLOMMOCK	SLOSHIER	SLOWEST	SLUGGARD	SLUMPED
SLOMMOCKS	SLOSHIEST	SLOWING	SLUGGARDS	SLUMPIER
SLOMO	SLOSHING	SLOWINGS	SLUGGED	SLUMPIEST
SLOMOS	SLOSHINGS	SLOWISH	SLUGGER	SLUMPING
SLOOM	SLOSHY	SLOWLY	SLUGGERS	SLUMPS
SLOOMED	SLOT	SLOWNESS	SLUGGING	SLUMPY
SLOOMIER	SLOTBACK	SLOWPOKE	SLUGGISH	SLUMS
SLOOMIEST	SLOTBACKS	SLOWPOKES	SLUGHORN	SLUNG
SLOOMING	SLOTH	SLOWS	SLUGHORNE	SLUNGSHOT
SLOOMS	SLOTHED	SLOWWORM	SLUGHORNS	SLUNK
SLOOMY	SLOTHFUL	SLOWWORMS	SLUGLIKE	SLUR
SLOOP	SLOTHING	SLOYD	SLUGS	SLURB
SLOOPS	SLOTHS	SLOYDS	SLUICE	SLURBAN
SLOOSH	SLOTS	SLUB	SLUICED	SLURBS
SLOOSHED	SLOTTED	SLUBB	SLUICES	SLURP
SLOOSHES	SLOTTER	SLUBBED	SLUICEWAY	SLURPED
SLOOSHING	SLOTTERS	SLUBBER	SLUICIER	SLURPER
SLOOT	SLOTTING	SLUBBERED	SLUICIEST	SLURPERS
SLOOTS	SLOUCH	SLUBBERS	SLUICING	SLURPIER
SLOP	SLOUCHED	SLUBBEST	SLUICY	SLURPIEST
SLOPE	SLOUCHER	SLUBBIER	SLUING	SLURPING
SLOPED	SLOUCHERS	SLUBBIEST	SLUIT	SLURPS
SLOPER	SLOUCHES	SLUBBING	SLUITS	SLURPY
SLOPERS	SLOUCHIER	SLUBBINGS	SLUM	SLURRED
SLOPES	SLOUCHILY	SLUBBS	SLUMBER	SLURRIED
SLOPESIDE	SLOUCHING	SLUBBY	SLUMBERED	SLURRIES
SLOPEWISE	SLOUCHY	SLUBS	SLUMBERER	SLURRING
SLOPIER	SLOUGH	SLUDGE	SLUMBERS	SLURRY
SLOPIEST	SLOUGHED	SLUDGED	SLUMBERY	SLURRYING
SLOPING	SLOUGHI	SLUDGES	SLUMBROUS	SLURS
SLOPINGLY	SLOUGHIER	SLUDGIER	SLUMBRY	SLURVE
SLOPPED	SLOUGHING	SLUDGIEST	SLUMGUM	SLURVES
SLOPPIER	SLOUGHIS	SLUDGING	SLUMGUMS	SLUSE
SLOPPIEST	SLOUGHS	SLUDGY	SLUMISM	SLUSES
SLOPPILY	SLOUGHY	SLUE	SLUMISMS	SLUSH
SLOPPING	SLOVE	SLUED	SLUMLORD	SLUSHED
SLOPPY	SLOVEN	SLUEING	SLUMLORDS	SLUSHES
SLOPS	SLOVENLY	SLUES	SLUMMED	SLUSHIER
SLOPWORK	SLOVENRY	SLUFF	SLUMMER	SLUSHIES
SLOPWORKS	SLOVENS	SLUFFED	SLUMMERS	SLUSHIEST
SLOPY	SLOW	SLUFFING	SLUMMIER	SLUSHILY
SLORM	SLOWBACK	SLUFFS	SLUMMIEST	SLUSHING
SLORMED	SLOWBACKS	SLUG	SLUMMING	SLUSHY
SLORMING	SLOWCOACH	SLUGABED	SLUMMINGS	SLUT
SLORMS	SLOWDOWN	SLUGABEDS	SLUMMOCK	SLUTCH
SLOSH	SLOWDOWNS	SLUGFEST	SLUMMOCKS	SLUTCHES
SLOSHED	SLOWED	SLUGFESTS	SLUMMY	SLUTCHIER
SLOSHES	SLOWER	SLUGGABED	SLUMP	SLUTCHY

SLUTS	SMALLSATS	SMARTY	SMEEKING	SMICKET
SLUTTERY	SMALLTIME	SMASH	SMEEKS	SMICKETS
SLUTTIER	SMALM	SMASHABLE	SMEES	SMICKLY
SLUTTIEST	SMALMED	SMASHED	SMEETH	SMIDDIED
SLUTTILY	SMALMIER	SMASHER	SMEETHED	SMIDDIES
SLUTTISH	SMALMIEST	SMASHEROO	SMEETHING	SMIDDY
SLUTTY	SMALMILY	SMASHERS	SMEETHS	SMIDDYING
SLY	SMALMING	SMASHES	SMEGMA	SMIDGE
SLYBOOTS	SMALMS	SMASHING	SMEGMAS	SMIDGEN
SLYER	SMALMY	SMASHINGS	SMEIK	SMIDGENS
SLYEST	SMALT	SMASHUP	SMEIKED	SMIDGEON
SLYISH	SMALTI	SMASHUPS	SMEIKING	SMIDGEONS
SLYLY	SMALTINE	SMATCH	SMEIKS	SMIDGES
SLYNESS	SMALTINES	SMATCHED	SMEKE	SMIDGIN
SLYNESSES	SMALTITE	SMATCHES	SMEKED	SMIDGINS
SLYPE	SMALTITES	SMATCHING	SMEKES	SMIERCASE
SLYPES	SMALTO	SMATTER	SMEKING	SMIGHT
SMA	SMALTOS	SMATTERED	SMELL	SMIGHTING
SMAAK	SMALTS	SMATTERER	SMELLABLE	SMIGHTS
SMAAKED	SMARAGD	SMATTERS	SMELLED	SMILAX
SMAAKING	SMARAGDE	SMAZE	SMELLER	SMILAXES
SMAAKS	SMARAGDES	SMAZES	SMELLERS	SMILE
SMACK	SMARAGDS	SMEAR	SMELLIER	SMILED
SMACKDOWN	SMARM	SMEARCASE	SMELLIES	SMILEFUL
SMACKED	SMARMED	SMEARED	SMELLIEST	SMILELESS
SMACKER	SMARMIER	SMEARER	SMELLING	SMILER
SMACKEROO	SMARMIEST	SMEARERS	SMELLINGS	SMILERS
SMACKERS	SMARMILY	SMEARIER	SMELLS	SMILES
SMACKHEAD	SMARMING	SMEARIEST	SMELLY	SMILET
SMACKING	SMARMS	SMEARILY	SMELT	SMILETS
SMACKINGS	SMARMY	SMEARING	SMELTED	SMILEY
SMACKS	SMART	SMEARS	SMELTER	SMILEYS
SMAIK	SMARTARSE	SMEARY	SMELTERS	SMILIER
SMAIKS	SMARTASS	SMEATH	SMELTERY	SMILIES
SMALL	SMARTED	SMEATHS	SMELTING	SMILIEST
SMALLAGE	SMARTEN	SMECTIC	SMELTINGS	SMILING
SMALLAGES	SMARTENED	SMECTITE	SMELTS	SMILINGLY
SMALLBOY	SMARTENS	SMECTITES	SMERK	SMILINGS
SMALLBOYS	SMARTER	SMECTITIC	SMERKED	SMILODON
SMALLED	SMARTEST	SMEDDUM	SMERKING	SMILODONS
SMALLER	SMARTIE	SMEDDUMS	SMERKS	SMIR
SMALLEST	SMARTIES	SMEE	SMEUSE	SMIRCH
SMALLING	SMARTING	SMEECH	SMEUSES	SMIRCHED
SMALLISH	SMARTISH	SMEECHED	SMEW	SMIRCHER
SMALLNESS	SMARTLY	SMEECHES	SMEWS	SMIRCHERS
SMALLPOX	SMARTNESS	SMEECHING	SMICKER	SMIRCHES
SMALLS	SMARTS	SMEEK	SMICKERED	SMIRCHING
SMALLSAT	SMARTWEED	SMEEKED	SMICKERS	SMIRK

SMIRKED	SMOCKS	SMOOCHER	SMORGS	SMUGGED
SMIRKER	SMOG	SMOOCHERS	SMORING	SMUGGER
SMIRKERS	SMOGGIER	SMOOCHES	SMORZANDO	SMUGGERY
SMIRKIER	SMOGGIEST	SMOOCHIER	SMORZATO	SMUGGEST
SMIRKIEST	SMOGGY	SMOOCHING	SMOTE	SMUGGING
SMIRKILY	SMOGLESS	SMOOCHY	SMOTHER	SMUGGLE
SMIRKING	SMOGS	SMOODGE	SMOTHERED	SMUGGLED
SMIRKS	SMOILE	SMOODGED	SMOTHERER	SMUGGLER
SMIRKY	SMOILED	SMOODGES	SMOTHERS	SMUGGLERS
SMIRR	SMOILES	SMOODGING	SMOTHERY	SMUGGLES
SMIRRED	SMOILING	SMOOGE	SMOUCH	SMUGGLING
SMIRRIER	SMOKABLE	SMOOGED	SMOUCHED	SMUGLY
SMIRRIEST	SMOKE	SMOOGES	SMOUCHES	SMUGNESS
SMIRRING	SMOKEABLE	SMOOGING	SMOUCHING	SMUGS
SMIRRS	SMOKEBOX	SMOOR	SMOULDER	SMUR
SMIRRY	SMOKEBUSH	SMOORED	SMOULDERS	SMURFING
SMIRS	SMOKED	SMOORING	SMOULDRY	SMURFINGS
SMIRTING	SMOKEHO	SMOORS	SMOUSE	SMURRED
SMIRTINGS	SMOKEHOOD	SMOOSH	SMOUSED	SMURRIER
SMISHING	SMOKEHOS	SMOOSHED	SMOUSER	SMURRIEST
SMISHINGS	SMOKEJACK	SMOOSHES	SMOUSERS	SMURRING
SMIT	SMOKELESS	SMOOSHING	SMOUSES	SMURRY
SMITE	SMOKELIKE	SMOOT	SMOUSING	SMURS
SMITER	SMOKEPOT	SMOOTED	SMOUT	SMUSH
SMITERS	SMOKEPOTS	SMOOTH	SMOUTED	SMUSHED
SMITES	SMOKER	SMOOTHE	SMOUTING	SMUSHES
SMITH	SMOKERS	SMOOTHED	SMOUTS	SMUSHING
SMITHED	SMOKES	SMOOTHEN	SMOWT	SMUT
SMITHERS	SMOKEY	SMOOTHENS	SMOWTS	SMUTCH
SMITHERY	SMOKEYS	SMOOTHER	SMOYLE	SMUTCHED
SMITHIED	SMOKIE	SMOOTHERS	SMOYLED	SMUTCHES
SMITHIES	SMOKIER	SMOOTHES	SMOYLES	SMUTCHIER
SMITHING	SMOKIES	SMOOTHEST	SMOYLING	SMUTCHING
SMITHINGS	SMOKIEST	SMOOTHIE	SMRITI	SMUTCHY
SMITHS	SMOKILY	SMOOTHIES	SMRITIS	SMUTS
SMITHY	SMOKINESS	SMOOTHING	SMUDGE	SMUTTED
SMITHYING	SMOKING	SMOOTHISH	SMUDGED	SMUTTIER
SMITING	SMOKINGS	SMOOTHLY	SMUDGEDLY	SMUTTIEST
SMITS	SMOKO	SMOOTHS	SMUDGER	SMUTTILY
SMITTED	SMOKOS	SMOOTHY	SMUDGERS	SMUTTING
SMITTEN	SMOKY	SMOOTING	SMUDGES	SMUTTY
SMITTING	SMOLDER	SMOOTS	SMUDGIER	SMYTRIE
SMITTLE	SMOLDERED	SMORBROD	SMUDGIEST	SMYTRIES
SMOCK	SMOLDERS	SMORBRODS	SMUDGILY	SNAB
SMOCKED	SMOLT	SMORE	SMUDGING	SNABBLE
SMOCKING	SMOLTS	SMORED	SMUDGINGS	SNABBLED
SMOCKINGS	SMOOCH	SMORES	SMUDGY	SNABBLES
SMOCKLIKE	SMOOCHED	SMORG	SMUG	SNABBLING

SNABS	SNAKELIKE	SNARERS	SNATCHY	SNEDDED
SNACK	SNAKEPIT	SNARES	SNATH	SNEDDING
SNACKED	SNAKEPITS	SNARF	SNATHE	SNEDS
SNACKER	SNAKEROOT	SNARFED	SNATHES	SNEE
SNACKERS	SNAKES	SNARFING	SNATHS	SNEED
SNACKETTE	SNAKESKIN	SNARFLE	SNAW	SNEEING
SNACKIER	SNAKEWEED	SNARFLED	SNAWED	SNEER
SNACKIEST	SNAKEWISE	SNARFLES	SNAWING	SNEERED
SNACKING	SNAKEWOOD	SNARFLING	SNAWS	SNEERER
SNACKS	SNAKEY	SNARFS	SNAZZIER	SNEERERS
SNACKY	SNAKIER	SNARIER	SNAZZIEST	SNEERFUL
SNAFFLE	SNAKIEST	SNARIEST	SNAZZILY	SNEERIER
SNAFFLED	SNAKILY	SNARING	SNAZZY	SNEERIEST
SNAFFLES	SNAKINESS	SNARINGS	SNEAD	SNEERING
SNAFFLING	SNAKING	SNARK	SNEADS	SNEERINGS
SNAFU	SNAKISH	SNARKIER	SNEAK	SNEERS
SNAFUED	SNAKY	SNARKIEST	SNEAKBOX	SNEERY
SNAFUING	SNAP	SNARKILY	SNEAKED	SNEES
SNAFUS	SNAPBACK	SNARKS	SNEAKER	SNEESH
SNAG	SNAPBACKS	SNARKY	SNEAKERED	SNEESHAN
SNAGGED	SNAPHANCE	SNARL	SNEAKERS	SNEESHANS
SNAGGER	SNAPLESS	SNARLED	SNEAKEUP	SNEESHED
SNAGGERS	SNAPLINK	SNARLER	SNEAKEUPS	SNEESHES
SNAGGIER	SNAPLINKS	SNARLERS	SNEAKIER	SNEESHIN
SNAGGIEST	SNAPPABLE	SNARLIER	SNEAKIEST	SNEESHING
SNAGGING	SNAPPED	SNARLIEST	SNEAKILY	SNEESHINS
SNAGGLE	SNAPPER	SNARLING	SNEAKING	SNEEZE
SNAGGLES	SNAPPERED	SNARLINGS	SNEAKISH	SNEEZED
SNAGGY	SNAPPERS	SNARLS	SNEAKS	SNEEZER
SNAGLIKE	SNAPPIER	SNARLY	SNEAKSBY	SNEEZERS
SNAGS	SNAPPIEST	SNARRED	SNEAKY	SNEEZES
SNAIL	SNAPPILY	SNARRING	SNEAP	SNEEZIER
SNAILED	SNAPPING	SNARS	SNEAPED	SNEEZIEST
SNAILERY	SNAPPINGS	SNARY	SNEAPING	SNEEZING
SNAILFISH	SNAPPISH	SNASH	SNEAPS	SNEEZINGS
SNAILIER	SNAPPY	SNASHED	SNEATH	SNEEZY
SNAILIEST	SNAPS	SNASHES	SNEATHS	SNELL
SNAILING	SNAPSHOT	SNASHING	SNEB	SNELLED
SNAILLIKE	SNAPSHOTS	SNASTE	SNEBBE	SNELLER
SNAILS	SNAPTIN	SNASTES	SNEBBED	SNELLEST
SNAILY	SNAPTINS	SNATCH	SNEBBES	SNELLING
SNAKE	SNAPWEED	SNATCHED	SNEBBING	SNELLS
SNAKEBIRD	SNAPWEEDS	SNATCHER	SNEBS	SNELLY
SNAKEBIT	SNAR	SNATCHERS	SNECK	SNIB
SNAKEBITE	SNARE	SNATCHES	SNECKED	SNIBBED
SNAKED	SNARED	SNATCHIER	SNECKING	SNIBBING
SNAKEFISH	SNARELESS	SNATCHILY	SNECKS	SNIBS
SNAKEHEAD	SNARER	SNATCHING	SNED	SNICK

S

SNICKED	SNIFTIER	SNIRTED	SNODDING	SNOOTIEST
SNICKER	SNIFTIEST	SNIRTING	SNODDIT	SNOOTILY
SNICKERED	SNIFTING	SNIRTLE	SNODS	SNOOTING
SNICKERER	SNIFTS	SNIRTLED	SNOEK	SNOOTS
SNICKERS	SNIFTY	SNIRTLES	SNOEKS	SNOOTY
SNICKERY	SNIG	SNIRTLING	SNOEP	SNOOZE
SNICKET	SNIGGED	SNIRTS	SNOG	SNOOZED
SNICKETS	SNIGGER	SNIT	SNOGGED	SNOOZER
SNICKING	SNIGGERED	SNITCH	SNOGGER	SNOOZERS
SNICKS	SNIGGERER	SNITCHED	SNOGGERS	SNOOZES
SNIDE	SNIGGERS	SNITCHER	SNOGGING	SNOOZIER
SNIDED	SNIGGING	SNITCHERS	SNOGS	SNOOZIEST
SNIDELY	SNIGGLE	SNITCHES	SNOKE	SNOOZING
SNIDENESS	SNIGGLED	SNITCHIER	SNOKED	SNOOZLE
SNIDER	SNIGGLER	SNITCHING	SNOKES	SNOOZLED
SNIDES	SNIGGLERS	SNITCHY	SNOKING	SNOOZLES
SNIDEST	SNIGGLES	SNITS	SNOOD	SNOOZLING
SNIDEY	SNIGGLING	SNITTIER	SNOODED	SNOOZY
SNIDIER	SNIGLET	SNITTIEST	SNOODING	SNORE
SNIDIEST	SNIGLETS	SNITTY	SNOODS	SNORED
SNIDING	SNIGS	SNIVEL	SNOOK	SNORER
SNIES	SNIP	SNIVELED	SNOOKED	SNORERS
SNIFF	SNIPE	SNIVELER	SNOOKER	SNORES
SNIFFABLE	SNIPED	SNIVELERS	SNOOKERED	SNORING
SNIFFED	SNIPEFISH	SNIVELIER	SNOOKERS	SNORINGS
SNIFFER	SNIPELIKE	SNIVELING	SNOOKING	SNORKEL
SNIFFERS	SNIPER	SNIVELLED	SNOOKS	SNORKELED
SNIFFIER	SNIPERS	SNIVELLER	SNOOL	SNORKELER
SNIFFIEST	SNIPES	SNIVELLY	SNOOLED	SNORKELS
SNIFFILY	SNIPIER	SNIVELS	SNOOLING	SNORT
SNIFFING	SNIPIEST	SNIVELY	SNOOLS	SNORTED
SNIFFINGS	SNIPING	SNOB	SNOOP	SNORTER
SNIFFISH	SNIPINGS	SNOBBERY	SNOOPED	SNORTERS
SNIFFLE	SNIPPED	SNOBBIER	SNOOPER	SNORTIER
SNIFFLED	SNIPPER	SNOBBIEST	SNOOPERS	SNORTIEST
SNIFFLER	SNIPPERS	SNOBBILY	SNOOPIER	SNORTING
SNIFFLERS	SNIPPET	SNOBBISH	SNOOPIEST	SNORTINGS
SNIFFLES	SNIPPETS	SNOBBISM	SNOOPILY	SNORTS
SNIFFLIER	SNIPPETY	SNOBBISMS	SNOOPING	SNORTY
SNIFFLING	SNIPPIER	SNOBBY	SNOOPS	SNOT
SNIFFLY	SNIPPIEST	SNOBLING	SNOOPY	SNOTRAG
SNIFFS	SNIPPILY	SNOBLINGS	SNOOSE	SNOTRAGS
SNIFFY	SNIPPING	SNOBS	SNOOSES	SNOTS
SNIFT	SNIPPINGS	SNOCOACH	SNOOT	SNOTTED
SNIFTED	SNIPPY	SNOD	SNOOTED	SNOTTER
SNIFTER	SNIPS	SNODDED	SNOOTFUL	SNOTTERED
SNIFTERED	SNIPY	SNODDER	SNOOTFULS	SNOTTERS
SNIFTERS	SNIRT	SNODDEST	SNOOTIER	SNOTTERY

S

SNOTTIE	SNOWFALL	SNOWSNAKE	SNUGGER	SOAPED
SNOTTIER	SNOWFALLS	SNOWSTORM	SNUGGERIE	SOAPER
SNOTTIES	SNOWFIELD	SNOWSUIT	SNUGGERY	SOAPERS
SNOTTIEST	SNOWFLAKE	SNOWSUITS	SNUGGEST	SOAPFISH
SNOTTILY	SNOWFLEA	SNOWY	SNUGGIES	SOAPIE
SNOTTING	SNOWFLEAS	SNUB	SNUGGING	SOAPIER
SNOTTY	SNOWFLECK	SNUBBE	SNUGGLE	SOAPIES
SNOUT	SNOWFLICK	SNUBBED	SNUGGLED	SOAPIEST
SNOUTED	SNOWGLOBE	SNUBBER	SNUGGLES	SOAPILY
SNOUTIER	SNOWIER	SNUBBERS	SNUGGLIER	SOAPINESS
SNOUTIEST	SNOWIEST	SNUBBES	SNUGGLING	SOAPING
SNOUTING	SNOWILY	SNUBBEST	SNUGGLY	SOAPLAND
SNOUTISH	SNOWINESS	SNUBBIER	SNUGLY	SOAPLANDS
SNOUTLESS	SNOWING	SNUBBIEST	SNUGNESS	SOAPLESS
SNOUTLIKE	SNOWISH	SNUBBING	SNUGS	SOAPLIKE
SNOUTS	SNOWK	SNUBBINGS	SNUSH	SOAPROOT
SNOUTY	SNOWKED	SNUBBISH	SNUSHED	SOAPROOTS
SNOW	SNOWKING	SNUBBY	SNUSHES	SOAPS
SNOWBALL	SNOWKS	SNUBFIN	SNUSHING	SOAPSTONE
SNOWBALLS	SNOWLAND	SNUBNESS	SNUZZLE	SOAPSUDS
SNOWBANK	SNOWLANDS	SNUBS	SNUZZLED	SOAPSUDSY
SNOWBANKS	SNOWLESS	SNUCK	SNUZZLES	SOAPWORT
SNOWBELL	SNOWLIKE	SNUDGE	SNUZZLING	SOAPWORTS
SNOWBELLS	SNOWLINE	SNUDGED	SNY	SOAPY
SNOWBELT	SNOWLINES	SNUDGES	SNYE	SOAR
SNOWBELTS	SNOWMAKER	SNUDGING	SNYES	SOARAWAY
SNOWBERRY	SNOWMAN	SNUFF	SO	SOARE
SNOWBIRD	SNOWMELT	SNUFFBOX	SOAK	SOARED
SNOWBIRDS	SNOWMELTS	SNUFFED	SOAKAGE	SOARER
SNOWBLINK	SNOWMEN	SNUFFER	SOAKAGES	SOARERS
SNOWBOARD	SNOWMOLD	SNUFFERS	SOAKAWAY	SOARES
SNOWBOOT	SNOWMOLDS	SNUFFIER	SOAKAWAYS	SOARING
SNOWBOOTS	SNOWMOULD	SNUFFIEST	SOAKED	SOARINGLY
SNOWBOUND	SNOWPACK	SNUFFILY	SOAKEN	SOARINGS
SNOWBRUSH	SNOWPACKS	SNUFFING	SOAKER	SOARS
SNOWBUSH	SNOWPLOW	SNUFFINGS	SOAKERS	SOAVE
SNOWCAP	SNOWPLOWS	SNUFFLE	SOAKING	SOAVES
SNOWCAPS	SNOWS	SNUFFLED	SOAKINGLY	SOB
SNOWCAT	SNOWSCAPE	SNUFFLER	SOAKINGS	SOBA
SNOWCATS	SNOWSHED	SNUFFLERS	SOAKS	SOBAS
SNOWCLONE	SNOWSHEDS	SNUFFLES	SOAP	SOBBED
SNOWCOACH	SNOWSHOE	SNUFFLIER	SOAPBARK	SOBBER
SNOWDOME	SNOWSHOED	SNUFFLING	SOAPBARKS	SOBBERS
SNOWDOMES	SNOWSHOER	SNUFFLY	SOAPBERRY	SOBBING
SNOWDRIFT	SNOWSHOES	SNUFFS	SOAPBOX	SOBBINGLY
SNOWDROP	SNOWSLIDE	SNUFFY	SOAPBOXED	SOBBINGS
SNOWDROPS	SNOWSLIP	SNUG	SOAPBOXES	SOBEIT
SNOWED	SNOWSLIPS	SNUGGED	SOAPDISH	SOBER

S

SOBERED	SOCIETIES	SODDIE	SOFTCORE	SOIGNE
SOBERER	SOCIETY	SODDIER	SOFTCOVER	SOIGNEE
SOBEREST	SOCIOGRAM	SODDIES	SOFTED	SOIL
SOBERING	SOCIOLECT	SODDIEST	SOFTEN	SOILAGE
SOBERISE	SOCIOLOGY	SODDING	SOFTENED	SOILAGES
SOBERISED	SOCIOPATH	SODDY	SOFTENER	SOILBORNE
SOBERISES	SOCK	SODGER	SOFTENERS	SOILED
SOBERIZE	SOCKED	SODGERED	SOFTENING	SOILIER
SOBERIZED	SOCKET	SODGERING	SOFTENS	SOILIEST
SOBERIZES	SOCKETED	SODGERS	SOFTER	SOILINESS
SOBERLY	SOCKETING	SODIC	SOFTEST	SOILING
SOBERNESS	SOCKETS	SODICITY	SOFTGOODS	SOILINGS
SOBERS	SOCKETTE	SODIUM	SOFTHEAD	SOILLESS
SOBFUL	SOCKETTES	SODIUMS	SOFTHEADS	SOILS
SOBOLE	SOCKEYE	SODOM	SOFTIE	SOILURE
SOBOLES	SOCKEYES	SODOMIES	SOFTIES	SOILURES
SOBRIETY	SOCKING	SODOMISE	SOFTING	SOILY
SOBRIQUET	SOCKLESS	SODOMISED	SOFTISH	SOIREE
SOBS	SOCKMAN	SODOMISES	SOFTLING	SOIREES
SOC	SOCKMEN	SODOMIST	SOFTLINGS	SOJA
SOCA	SOCKO	SODOMISTS	SOFTLY	SOJAS
SOCAGE	SOCKS	SODOMITE	SOFTNESS	SOJOURN
SOCAGER	SOCLE	SODOMITES	SOFTPASTE	SOJOURNED
SOCAGERS	SOCLES	SODOMITIC	SOFTS	SOJOURNER
SOCAGES	SOCMAN	SODOMIZE	SOFTSCAPE	SOJOURNS
SOCAS	SOCMEN	SODOMIZED	SOFTSHELL	SOJU
SOCCAGE	SOCS	SODOMIZES	SOFTWARE	SOJUS
SOCCAGES	SOD	SODOMS	SOFTWARES	SOKAH
SOCCER	SODA	SODOMY	SOFTWOOD	SOKAHS
SOCCERS	SODAIC	SODS	SOFTWOODS	SOKAIYA
SOCES	SODAIN	SOEVER	SOFTY	SOKE
SOCIABLE	SODAINE	SOFA	SOG	SOKEMAN
SOCIABLES	SODALESS	SOFABED	SOGER	SOKEMANRY
SOCIABLY	SODALIST	SOFABEDS	SOGERS	SOKEMEN
SOCIAL	SODALISTS	SOFAR	SOGGED	SOKEN
SOCIALISE	SODALITE	SOFARS	SOGGIER	SOKENS
SOCIALISM	SODALITES	SOFAS	SOGGIEST	SOKES
SOCIALIST	SODALITY	SOFFIONI	SOGGILY	SOKOL
SOCIALITE	SODAMIDE	SOFFIT	SOGGINESS	SOKOLS
SOCIALITY	SODAMIDES	SOFFITS	SOGGING	SOL
SOCIALIZE	SODAS	SOFT	SOGGINGS	SOLA
SOCIALLY	SODBUSTER	SOFTA	SOGGY	SOLACE
SOCIALS	SODDED	SOFTAS	SOGS	SOLACED
SOCIATE	SODDEN	SOFTBACK	SOH	SOLACER
SOCIATES	SODDENED	SOFTBACKS	SOHO	SOLACERS
SOCIATION	SODDENING	SOFTBALL	SOHS	SOLACES
SOCIATIVE	SODDENLY	SOFTBALLS	SOHUR	SOLACING
SOCIETAL	SODDENS	SOFTBOUND	SOHURS	SOLACIOUS

SOLAH	SOLDERED	SOLERAS	SOLIONS	SOLUNAR
SOLAHS	SOLDERER	SOLERET	SOLIPED	SOLUS
SOLAN	SOLDERERS	SOLERETS	SOLIPEDS	SOLUSES
SOLAND	SOLDERING	SOLERS	SOLIPSISM	SOLUTAL
SOLANDER	SOLDERS	SOLES	SOLIPSIST	SOLUTE
SOLANDERS	SOLDES	SOLEUS	SOLIQUID	SOLUTES
SOLANDS	SOLDI	SOLEUSES	SOLIQUIDS	SOLUTION
SOLANIN	SOLDIER	SOLFATARA	SOLITAIRE	SOLUTIONS
SOLANINE	SOLDIERED	SOLFEGE	SOLITARY	SOLUTIVE
SOLANINES	SOLDIERLY	SOLFEGES	SOLITO	SOLUTIVES
SOLANINS	SOLDIERS	SOLFEGGI	SOLITON	SOLVABLE
SOLANO	SOLDIERY	SOLFEGGIO	SOLITONS	SOLVATE
SOLANOS	SOLDO	SOLFERINO	SOLITUDE	SOLVATED
SOLANS	SOLDS	SOLGEL	SOLITUDES	SOLVATES
SOLANUM	SOLE	SOLI	SOLIVE	SOLVATING
SOLANUMS	SOLECISE	SOLICIT	SOLIVES	SOLVATION
SOLAR	SOLECISED	SOLICITED	SOLLAR	SOLVE
SOLARIA	SOLECISES	SOLICITOR	SOLLARED	SOLVED
SOLARISE	SOLECISM	SOLICITS	SOLLARING	SOLVENCY
SOLARISED	SOLECISMS	SOLICITY	SOLLARS	SOLVENT
SOLARISES	SOLECIST	SOLID	SOLLER	SOLVENTLY
SOLARISM	SOLECISTS	SOLIDAGO	SOLLERET	SOLVENTS
SOLARISMS	SOLECIZE	SOLIDAGOS	SOLLERETS	SOLVER
SOLARIST	SOLECIZED	SOLIDARE	SOLLERS	SOLVERS
SOLARISTS	SOLECIZES	SOLIDARES	SOLLICKER	SOLVES
SOLARIUM	SOLED	SOLIDARY	SOLO	SOLVING
SOLARIUMS	SOLEI	SOLIDATE	SOLOED	SOM
SOLARIZE	SOLEIN	SOLIDATED	SOLOES	SOMA
SOLARIZED	SOLELESS	SOLIDATES	SOLOING	SOMAN
SOLARIZES	SOLELY	SOLIDER	SOLOIST	SOMANS
SOLARS	SOLEMN	SOLIDEST	SOLOISTIC	SOMAS
SOLAS	SOLEMNER	SOLIDI	SOLOISTS	SOMASCOPE
SOLATE	SOLEMNESS	SOLIDIFY	SOLON	SOMATA
SOLATED	SOLEMNEST	SOLIDISH	SOLONCHAK	SOMATIC
SOLATES	SOLEMNIFY	SOLIDISM	SOLONETS	SOMATISM
SOLATIA	SOLEMNISE	SOLIDISMS	SOLONETZ	SOMATISMS
SOLATING	SOLEMNITY	SOLIDIST	SOLONS	SOMATIST
SOLATION	SOLEMNIZE	SOLIDISTS	SOLOS	SOMATISTS
SOLATIONS	SOLEMNLY	SOLIDITY	SOLPUGID	SOMBER
SOLATIUM	SOLENESS	SOLIDLY	SOLPUGIDS	SOMBERED
SOLD	SOLENETTE	SOLIDNESS	SOLS	SOMBERER
SOLDADO	SOLENODON	SOLIDS	SOLSTICE	SOMBEREST
SOLDADOES	SOLENOID	SOLIDUM	SOLSTICES	SOMBERING
SOLDADOS	SOLENOIDS	SOLIDUMS	SOLUBLE	SOMBERLY
SOLDAN	SOLEPLATE	SOLIDUS	SOLUBLES	SOMBERS
SOLDANS	SOLEPRINT	SOLILOQUY	SOLUBLY	SOMBRE
SOLDE	SOLER	SOLING	SOLUM	SOMBRED
SOLDER	SOLERA	SOLION	SOLUMS	SOMBRELY

SOMBRER	SONANCE	SONGS	SONSHIPS	SOOPINGS
SOMBRERO	SONANCES	SONGSHEET	SONSIE	SOOPS
SOMBREROS	SONANCIES	SONGSMITH	SONSIER	SOOPSTAKE
SOMBRES	SONANCY	SONGSTER	SONSIEST	SOOT
SOMBREST	SONANT	SONGSTERS	SONSY	SOOTE
SOMBRING	SONANTAL	SONHOOD	SONTAG	SOOTED
SOMBROUS	SONANTIC	SONHOODS	SONTAGS	SOOTERKIN
SOME	SONANTS	SONIC	SONTIES	SOOTES
SOMEBODY	SONAR	SONICALLY	SOOCHONG	SOOTFLAKE
SOMEDAY	SONARMAN	SONICATE	SOOCHONGS	SOOTH
SOMEDEAL	SONARMEN	SONICATED	SOOEY	SOOTHE
SOMEDEALS	SONARS	SONICATES	SOOGEE	SOOTHED
SOMEDELE	SONATA	SONICATOR	SOOGEED	SOOTHER
SOMEGATE	SONATAS	SONICS	SOOGEEING	SOOTHERED
SOMEHOW	SONATINA	SONLESS	SOOGEES	SOOTHERS
SOMEONE	SONATINAS	SONLIER	SOOGIE	SOOTHES
SOMEONES	SONATINE	SONLIEST	SOOGIED	SOOTHEST
SOMEPLACE	SONCE	SONLIKE	SOOGIEING	SOOTHFAST
SOMERSET	SONCES	SONLY	SOOGIES	SOOTHFUL
SOMERSETS	SONDAGE	SONNE	SOOJEY	SOOTHING
SOMETHING	SONDAGES	SONNES	SOOJEYS	SOOTHINGS
SOMETIME	SONDE	SONNET	SOOK	SOOTHLICH
SOMETIMES	SONDELI	SONNETARY	SOOKED	SOOTHLY
SOMEWAY	SONDELIS	SONNETED	SOOKIER	SOOTHS
SOMEWAYS	SONDER	SONNETEER	SOOKIEST	SOOTHSAID
SOMEWHAT	SONDERS	SONNETING	SOOKING	SOOTHSAY
SOMEWHATS	SONDES	SONNETISE	SOOKS	SOOTHSAYS
SOMEWHEN	SONE	SONNETIZE	SOOKY	SOOTIER
SOMEWHERE	SONERI	SONNETS	SOOL	SOOTIEST
SOMEWHILE	SONERIS	SONNETTED	SOOLE	SOOTILY
SOMEWHY	SONES	SONNIES	SOOLED	SOOTINESS
SOMEWISE	SONG	SONNY	SOOLER	SOOTING
SOMITAL	SONGBIRD	SONOBUOY	SOOLERS	SOOTINGS
SOMITE	SONGBIRDS	SONOBUOYS	SOOLES	SOOTLESS
SOMITES	SONGBOOK	SONOGRAM	SOOLING	SOOTS
SOMITIC	SONGBOOKS	SONOGRAMS	SOOLS	SOOTY
SOMMELIER	SONGCRAFT	SONOGRAPH	SOOM	SOP
SOMNIAL	SONGFEST	SONOMETER	SOOMED	SOPAPILLA
SOMNIATE	SONGFESTS	SONORANT	SOOMING	SOPH
SOMNIATED	SONGFUL	SONORANTS	SOOMS	SOPHERIC
SOMNIATES	SONGFULLY	SONORITY	SOON	SOPHERIM
SOMNIFIC	SONGKOK	SONOROUS	SOONER	SOPHIES
SOMNOLENT	SONGKOKS	SONOVOX	SOONERS	SOPHISM
SOMONI	SONGLESS	SONOVOXES	SOONEST	SOPHISMS
SOMONIS	SONGLIKE	SONS	SOONISH	SOPHIST
SOMS	SONGMAN	SONSE	SOOP	SOPHISTER
SOMY	SONGMEN	SONSES	SOOPED	SOPHISTIC
SON	SONGOLOLO	SONSHIP	SOOPING	SOPHISTRY

SOPHISTS	SORBITANS	SOREHONS	SORORIZES	SORTS
SOPHOMORE	SORBITE	SOREL	SOROSES	SORUS
SOPHS	SORBITES	SORELL	SOROSIS	SOS
SOPHY	SORBITIC	SORELLS	SOROSISES	SOSATIE
SOPITE	SORBITISE	SORELS	SORPTION	SOSATIES
SOPITED	SORBITIZE	SORELY	SORPTIONS	SOSS
SOPITES	SORBITOL	SORENESS	SORPTIVE	SOSSED
SOPITING	SORBITOLS	SORER	SORRA	SOSSES
SOPOR	SORBO	SORES	SORRAS	SOSSING
SOPORIFIC	SORBOSE	SOREST	SORREL	SOSSINGS
SOPOROSE	SORBOSES	SOREX	SORRELS	SOSTENUTI
SOPOROUS	SORBS	SOREXES	SORRIER	SOSTENUTO
SOPORS	SORBUS	SORGHO	SORRIEST	SOT
SOPPED	SORBUSES	SORGHOS	SORRILY	SOTERIAL
SOPPIER	SORCERER	SORGHUM	SORRINESS	SOTH
SOPPIEST	SORCERERS	SORGHUMS	SORROW	SOTHS
SOPPILY	SORCERESS	SORGO	SORROWED	SOTOL
SOPPINESS	SORCERIES	SORGOS	SORROWER	SOTOLS
SOPPING	SORCEROUS	SORI	SORROWERS	SOTS
SOPPINGS	SORCERY	SORICINE	SORROWFUL	SOTTED
SOPPY	SORD	SORICOID	SORROWING	SOTTEDLY
SOPRA	SORDA	SORING	SORROWS	SOTTING
SOPRANI	SORDED	SORINGS	SORRY	SOTTINGS
SOPRANINI	SORDES	SORITES	SORRYISH	SOTTISH
SOPRANINO	SORDID	SORITIC	SORT	SOTTISHLY
SOPRANIST	SORDIDER	SORITICAL	SORTA	SOTTISIER
SOPRANO	SORDIDEST	SORN	SORTABLE	SOU
SOPRANOS	SORDIDLY	SORNED	SORTABLY	SOUARI
SOPS	SORDINE	SORNER	SORTAL	SOUARIS
SORA	SORDINES	SORNERS	SORTALS	SOUBISE
SORAGE	SORDING	SORNING	SORTANCE	SOUBISES
SORAGES	SORDINI	SORNINGS	SORTANCES	SOUBRETTE
SORAL	SORDINO	SORNS	SORTATION	SOUCAR
SORAS	SORDO	SOROBAN	SORTED	SOUCARS
SORB	SORDOR	SOROBANS	SORTER	SOUCE
SORBABLE	SORDORS	SOROCHE	SORTERS	SOUCED
SORBARIA	SORDS	SOROCHES	SORTES	SOUCES
SORBARIAS	SORE	SORORAL	SORTIE	SOUCHONG
SORBATE	SORED	SORORALLY	SORTIED	SOUCHONGS
SORBATES	SOREDIA	SORORATE	SORTIEING	SOUCING
SORBED	SOREDIAL	SORORATES	SORTIES	SOUCT
SORBENT	SOREDIATE	SORORIAL	SORTILEGE	SOUDAN
SORBENTS	SOREDIUM	SORORISE	SORTILEGY	SOUDANS
SORBET	SOREE	SORORISED	SORTING	SOUFFLE
SORBETS	SOREES	SORORISES	SORTINGS	SOUFFLED
SORBIC	SOREHEAD	SORORITY	SORTITION	SOUFFLEED
SORBING	SOREHEADS	SORORIZE	SORTMENT	SOUFFLES
SORBITAN	SOREHON	SORORIZED	SORTMENTS	SOUGH

S

SOUGHED	SOUNDPOST	SOUROCKS	SOUTHRONS	SOWBREADS
SOUGHING	SOUNDS	SOURPUSS	SOUTHS	SOWBUG
SOUGHS	SOUP	SOURS	SOUTHSAID	SOWBUGS
SOUGHT	SOUPCON	SOURSE	SOUTHSAY	SOWCAR
SOUK	SOUPCONS	SOURSES	SOUTHSAYS	SOWCARS
SOUKED	SOUPED	SOURSOP	SOUTHWARD	SOWCE
SOUKING	SOUPER	SOURSOPS	SOUTHWEST	SOWCED
SOUKOUS	SOUPERS	SOURVELD	SOUTIE	SOWCES
SOUKOUSES	SOUPFIN	SOURVELDS	SOUTIES	SOWCING
SOUKS	SOUPFINS	SOURWOOD	SOUTPIEL	SOWDER
SOUL	SOUPIER	SOURWOODS	SOUTPIELS	SOWDERS
SOULDAN	SOUPIEST	SOUS	SOUTS	SOWED
SOULDANS	SOUPILY	SOUSE	SOUVENIR	SOWENS
SOULDIER	SOUPINESS	SOUSED	SOUVENIRS	SOWER
SOULDIERS	SOUPING	SOUSER	SOUVLAKI	SOWERS
SOULED	SOUPLE	SOUSERS	SOUVLAKIA	SOWF
SOULFUL	SOUPLED	SOUSES	SOUVLAKIS	SOWFED
SOULFULLY	SOUPLES	SOUSING	SOV	SOWFF
SOULLESS	SOUPLESS	SOUSINGS	SOVENANCE	SOWFFED
SOULLIKE	SOUPLIKE	SOUSLIK	SOVEREIGN	SOWFFING
SOULMATE	SOUPLING	SOUSLIKS	SOVIET	SOWFFS
SOULMATES	SOUPS	SOUT	SOVIETIC	SOWFING
SOULS	SOUPSPOON	SOUTACHE	SOVIETISE	SOWFS
SOULSTER	SOUPY	SOUTACHES	SOVIETISM	SOWING
SOULSTERS	SOUR	SOUTANE	SOVIETIST	SOWINGS
SOUM	SOURBALL	SOUTANES	SOVIETIZE	SOWL
SOUMED	SOURBALLS	SOUTAR	SOVIETS	SOWLE
SOUMING	SOURCE	SOUTARS	SOVKHOZ	SOWLED
SOUMINGS	SOURCED	SOUTENEUR	SOVKHOZES	SOWLES
SOUMS	SOURCEFUL	SOUTER	SOVKHOZY	SOWLING
SOUND	SOURCES	SOUTERLY	SOVRAN	SOWLS
SOUNDABLE	SOURCING	SOUTERS	SOVRANLY	SOWM
SOUNDBAR	SOURCINGS	SOUTH	SOVRANS	SOWMED
SOUNDBARS	SOURDINE	SOUTHEAST	SOVRANTY	SOWMING
SOUNDBITE	SOURDINES	SOUTHED	SOVS	SOWMS
SOUNDBOX	SOURDOUGH	SOUTHER	SOW	SOWN
SOUNDCARD	SOURED	SOUTHERED	SOWABLE	SOWND
SOUNDED	SOURER	SOUTHERLY	SOWANS	SOWNDED
SOUNDER	SOUREST	SOUTHERN	SOWAR	SOWNDING
SOUNDERS	SOURGUM	SOUTHERNS	SOWARREE	SOWNDS
SOUNDEST	SOURGUMS	SOUTHERS	SOWARREES	SOWNE
SOUNDING	SOURING	SOUTHING	SOWARRIES	SOWNES
SOUNDINGS	SOURINGS	SOUTHINGS	SOWARRY	SOWP
SOUNDLESS	SOURISH	SOUTHLAND	SOWARS	SOWPED
SOUNDLY	SOURISHLY	SOUTHMOST	SOWBACK	SOWPING
SOUNDMAN	SOURLY	SOUTHPAW	SOWBACKS	SOWPS
SOUNDMEN	SOURNESS	SOUTHPAWS	SOWBELLY	SOWS
SOUNDNESS	SOUROCK	SOUTHRON	SOWBREAD	SOWSE

SOWSED	SPACELABS	SPADILLES	SPAINS	SPANCELED
SOWSES	SPACELESS	SPADILLIO	SPAIRGE	SPANCELS
SOWSING	SPACEMAN	SPADILLO	SPAIRGED	SPANDEX
SOWSSE	SPACEMEN	SPADILLOS	SPAIRGES	SPANDEXED
SOWSSED	SPACEPORT	SPADING	SPAIRGING	SPANDEXES
SOWSSES	SPACER	SPADIX	SPAIT	SPANDREL
SOWSSING	SPACERS	SPADIXES	SPAITS	SPANDRELS
SOWTER	SPACES	SPADO	SPAKE	SPANDRIL
SOWTERS	SPACESHIP	SPADOES	SPALD	SPANDRILS
SOWTH	SPACESUIT	SPADONES	SPALDEEN	SPANE
SOWTHED	SPACETIME	SPADOS	SPALDEENS	SPANED
SOWTHING	SPACEWALK	SPADROON	SPALDS	SPANES
SOWTHS	SPACEWARD	SPADROONS	SPALE	SPANG
SOX	SPACEY	SPAE	SPALES	SPANGED
SOY	SPACIAL	SPAED	SPALL	SPANGHEW
SOYA	SPACIALLY	SPAEING	SPALLABLE	SPANGHEWS
SOYAS	SPACIER	SPAEINGS	SPALLE	SPANGING
SOYBEAN	SPACIEST	SPAEMAN	SPALLED	SPANGLE
SOYBEANS	SPACINESS	SPAEMEN	SPALLER	SPANGLED
SOYBURGER	SPACING	SPAER	SPALLERS	SPANGLER
SOYLE	SPACINGS	SPAERS	SPALLES	SPANGLERS
SOYLED	SPACIOUS	SPAES	SPALLING	SPANGLES
SOYLES	SPACKLE	SPAETZLE	SPALLINGS	SPANGLET
SOYLING	SPACKLED	SPAETZLES	SPALLS	SPANGLETS
SOYMEAL	SPACKLES	SPAEWIFE	SPALPEEN	SPANGLIER
SOYMEALS	SPACKLING	SPAEWIVES	SPALPEENS	SPANGLING
SOYMILK	SPACY	SPAG	SPALT	SPANGLY
SOYMILKS	SPADASSIN	SPAGERIC	SPALTED	SPANGS
SOYS	SPADE	SPAGGED	SPALTING	SPANIEL
SOYUZ	SPADED	SPAGGING	SPALTS	SPANIELS
SOYUZES	SPADEFEET	SPAGHETTI	SPAM	SPANING
SOZ	SPADEFISH	SPAGIRIC	SPAMBOT	SPANK
SOZIN	SPADEFOOT	SPAGIRIST	SPAMBOTS	SPANKED
SOZINE	SPADEFUL	SPAGS	SPAMMED	SPANKER
SOZINES	SPADEFULS	SPAGYRIC	SPAMMER	SPANKERS
SOZINS	SPADELIKE	SPAGYRICS	SPAMMERS	SPANKING
SOZZLE	SPADEMAN	SPAGYRIST	SPAMMIE	SPANKINGS
SOZZLED	SPADEMEN	SPAHEE	SPAMMIER	SPANKS
SOZZLES	SPADER	SPAHEES	SPAMMIES	SPANLESS
SOZZLIER	SPADERS	SPAHI	SPAMMIEST	SPANNED
SOZZLIEST	SPADES	SPAHIS	SPAMMING	SPANNER
SOZZLING	SPADESMAN	SPAIL	SPAMMINGS	SPANNERS
SOZZLY	SPADESMEN	SPAILS	SPAMMY	SPANNING
SPA	SPADEWORK	SPAIN	SPAMS	SPANS
SPACE	SPADGER	SPAINED	SPAN	SPANSPEK
SPACEBAND	SPADGERS	SPAING	SPANAEMIA	SPANSPEKS
SPACED	SPADICES	SPAINGS	SPANAEMIC	SPANSULE
SPACELAB	SPADILLE	SPAINING	SPANCEL	SPANSULES

S

SPANWORM

SPANWORM	SPARKLET	SPASMATIC	SPAVINED	SPEAR
SPANWORMS	SPARKLETS	SPASMED	SPAVINS	SPEARED
SPAR	SPARKLIER	SPASMIC	SPAW	SPEARER
SPARABLE	SPARKLIES	SPASMING	SPAWL	SPEARERS
SPARABLES	SPARKLING	SPASMODIC	SPAWLED	SPEARFISH
SPARAXIS	SPARKLY	SPASMS	SPAWLING	SPEARGUN
SPARD	SPARKPLUG	SPASTIC	SPAWLS	SPEARGUNS
SPARE	SPARKS	SPASTICS	SPAWN	SPEARHEAD
SPAREABLE	SPARKY	SPAT	SPAWNED	SPEARIER
SPARED	SPARLIKE	SPATE	SPAWNER	SPEARIEST
SPARELESS	SPARLING	SPATES	SPAWNERS	SPEARING
SPARELY	SPARLINGS	SPATFALL	SPAWNIER	SPEARINGS
SPARENESS	SPAROID	SPATFALLS	SPAWNIEST	SPEARLIKE
SPARER	SPAROIDS	SPATHAL	SPAWNING	SPEARMAN
SPARERIB	SPARRE	SPATHE	SPAWNINGS	SPEARMEN
SPARERIBS	SPARRED	SPATHED	SPAWNS	SPEARMINT
SPARERS	SPARRER	SPATHES	SPAWNY	SPEARS
SPARES	SPARRERS	SPATHIC	SPAWS	SPEARWORT
SPAREST	SPARRES	SPATHOSE	SPAY	SPEARY
SPARGE	SPARRIER	SPATIAL	SPAYAD	SPEAT
SPARGED	SPARRIEST	SPATIALLY	SPAYADS	SPEATS
SPARGER	SPARRING	SPATLESE	SPAYD	SPEC
SPARGERS	SPARRINGS	SPATLESEN	SPAYDS	SPECCED
SPARGES	SPARROW	SPATLESES	SPAYED	SPECCIER
SPARGING	SPARROWS	SPATS	SPAYING	SPECCIES
SPARID	SPARRY	SPATTED	SPAYS	SPECCIEST
SPARIDS	SPARS	SPATTEE	SPAZ	SPECCING
SPARING	SPARSE	SPATTEES	SPAZA	SPECCY
SPARINGLY	SPARSEDLY	SPATTER	SPAZZ	SPECIAL
SPARK	SPARSELY	SPATTERED	SPAZZED	SPECIALER
SPARKE	SPARSER	SPATTERS	SPAZZES	SPECIALLY
SPARKED	SPARSEST	SPATTING	SPAZZING	SPECIALS
SPARKER	SPARSITY	SPATULA	SPEAK	SPECIALTY
SPARKERS	SPART	SPATULAR	SPEAKABLE	SPECIATE
SPARKES	SPARTAN	SPATULAS	SPEAKEASY	SPECIATED
SPARKIE	SPARTANS	SPATULATE	SPEAKER	SPECIATES
SPARKIER	SPARTEINE	SPATULE	SPEAKERS	SPECIE
SPARKIES	SPARTERIE	SPATULES	SPEAKING	SPECIES
SPARKIEST	SPARTH	SPATZLE	SPEAKINGS	SPECIFIC
SPARKILY	SPARTHE	SPATZLES	SPEAKOUT	SPECIFICS
SPARKING	SPARTHES	SPAUL	SPEAKOUTS	SPECIFIED
SPARKISH	SPARTHS	SPAULD	SPEAKS	SPECIFIER
SPARKLE	SPARTICLE	SPAULDS	SPEAL	SPECIFIES
SPARKLED	SPARTINA	SPAULS	SPEALS	SPECIFY
SPARKLER	SPARTINAS	SPAVIE	SPEAN	SPECIMEN
SPARKLERS	SPARTS	SPAVIES	SPEANED	SPECIMENS
SPARKLES	SPAS	SPAVIET	SPEANING	SPECIOUS
SPARKLESS	SPASM	SPAVIN	SPEANS	SPECK

S

SPECKED	SPEEDER	SPEKS	SPENDER	SPEW
SPECKIER	SPEEDERS	SPELAEAN	SPENDERS	SPEWED
SPECKIES	SPEEDFUL	SPELD	SPENDIER	SPEWER
SPECKIEST	SPEEDIER	SPELDED	SPENDIEST	SPEWERS
SPECKING	SPEEDIEST	SPELDER	SPENDING	SPEWIER
SPECKLE	SPEEDILY	SPELDERED	SPENDINGS	SPEWIEST
SPECKLED	SPEEDING	SPELDERS	SPENDS	SPEWINESS
SPECKLES	SPEEDINGS	SPELDIN	SPENDY	SPEWING
SPECKLESS	SPEEDLESS	SPELDING	SPENSE	SPEWS
SPECKLING	SPEEDO	SPELDINGS	SPENSES	SPEWY
SPECKS	SPEEDOS	SPELDINS	SPENT	SPHACELUS
SPECKY	SPEEDREAD	SPELDRIN	SPEOS	SPHAER
SPECS	SPEEDS	SPELDRING	SPEOSES	SPHAERE
SPECT	SPEEDSTER	SPELDRINS	SPERLING	SPHAERES
SPECTACLE	SPEEDUP	SPELDS	SPERLINGS	SPHAERITE
SPECTATE	SPEEDUPS	SPELEAN	SPERM	SPHAERS
SPECTATED	SPEEDWALK	SPELK	SPERMARIA	SPHAGNOUS
SPECTATES	SPEEDWAY	SPELKS	SPERMARY	SPHAGNUM
SPECTATOR	SPEEDWAYS	SPELL	SPERMATIA	SPHAGNUMS
SPECTED	SPEEDWELL	SPELLABLE	SPERMATIC	SPHAIREE
SPECTER	SPEEDY	SPELLBIND	SPERMATID	SPHAIREES
SPECTERS	SPEEL	SPELLDOWN	SPERMIC	SPHEAR
SPECTING	SPEELED	SPELLED	SPERMINE	SPHEARE
SPECTRA	SPEELER	SPELLER	SPERMINES	SPHEARES
SPECTRAL	SPEELERS	SPELLERS	SPERMOUS	SPHEARS
SPECTRE	SPEELING	SPELLFUL	SPERMS	SPHENDONE
SPECTRES	SPEELS	SPELLICAN	SPERRE	SPHENE
SPECTRIN	SPEER	SPELLING	SPERRED	SPHENES
SPECTRINS	SPEERED	SPELLINGS	SPERRES	SPHENIC
SPECTRUM	SPEERING	SPELLS	SPERRING	SPHENODON
SPECTRUMS	SPEERINGS	SPELT	SPERSE	SPHENOID
SPECTS	SPEERS	SPELTER	SPERSED	SPHENOIDS
SPECULA	SPEIL	SPELTERS	SPERSES	SPHERAL
SPECULAR	SPEILED	SPELTS	SPERSING	SPHERE
SPECULATE	SPEILING	SPELTZ	SPERST	SPHERED
SPECULUM	SPEILS	SPELTZES	SPERTHE	SPHERES
SPECULUMS	SPEIR	SPELUNK	SPERTHES	SPHERIC
SPED	SPEIRED	SPELUNKED	SPET	SPHERICAL
SPEECH	SPEIRING	SPELUNKER	SPETCH	SPHERICS
SPEECHED	SPEIRINGS	SPELUNKS	SPETCHED	SPHERIER
SPEECHES	SPEIRS	SPENCE	SPETCHES	SPHERIEST
SPEECHFUL	SPEISE	SPENCER	SPETCHING	SPHERING
SPEECHIFY	SPEISES	SPENCERS	SPETS	SPHEROID
SPEECHING	SPEISS	SPENCES	SPETSNAZ	SPHEROIDS
SPEED	SPEISSES	SPEND	SPETTING	SPHERULAR
SPEEDBALL	SPEK	SPENDABLE	SPETZNAZ	SPHERULE
SPEEDBOAT	SPEKBOOM	SPENDALL	SPEUG	SPHERULES
SPEEDED	SPEKBOOMS	SPENDALLS	SPEUGS	SPHERY

SPHINCTER	SPICULE	SPIGNEL	SPILLWAYS	SPINETTE
SPHINGES	SPICULES	SPIGNELS	SPILOSITE	SPINETTES
SPHINGID	SPICULUM	SPIGOT	SPILT	SPINIER
SPHINGIDS	SPICY	SPIGOTS	SPILTH	SPINIEST
SPHINX	SPIDE	SPIK	SPILTHS	SPINIFEX
SPHINXES	SPIDER	SPIKE	SPIM	SPINIFORM
SPHYGMIC	SPIDERED	SPIKED	SPIMMER	SPININESS
SPHYGMOID	SPIDERIER	SPIKEFISH	SPIMMERS	SPINK
SPHYGMUS	SPIDERING	SPIKELET	SPIMMING	SPINKED
SPHYNX	SPIDERISH	SPIKELETS	SPIMMINGS	SPINKING
SPHYNXES	SPIDERMAN	SPIKELIKE	SPIMS	SPINKS
SPIAL	SPIDERMEN	SPIKENARD	SPIN	SPINLESS
SPIALS	SPIDERS	SPIKER	SPINA	SPINNAKER
SPIC	SPIDERWEB	SPIKERIES	SPINACENE	SPINNER
SPICA	SPIDERY	SPIKERS	SPINACH	SPINNERET
SPICAE	SPIDES	SPIKERY	SPINACHES	SPINNERS
SPICAS	SPIE	SPIKES	SPINACHY	SPINNERY
SPICATE	SPIED	SPIKEY	SPINAE	SPINNET
SPICATED	SPIEGEL	SPIKIER	SPINAGE	SPINNETS
SPICCATO	SPIEGELS	SPIKIEST	SPINAGES	SPINNEY
SPICCATOS	SPIEL	SPIKILY	SPINAL	SPINNEYS
SPICE	SPIELED	SPIKINESS	SPINALLY	SPINNIER
SPICEBUSH	SPIELER	SPIKING	SPINALS	SPINNIES
SPICED	SPIELERS	SPIKS	SPINAR	SPINNIEST
SPICELESS	SPIELING	SPIKY	SPINARAMA	SPINNING
SPICER	SPIELS	SPILE	SPINARS	SPINNINGS
SPICERIES	SPIER	SPILED	SPINAS	SPINNY
SPICERS	SPIERED	SPILES	SPINATE	SPINODE
SPICERY	SPIERING	SPILIKIN	SPINDLE	SPINODES
SPICES	SPIERS	SPILIKINS	SPINDLED	SPINOFF
SPICEY	SPIES	SPILING	SPINDLER	SPINOFFS
SPICIER	SPIF	SPILINGS	SPINDLERS	SPINONE
SPICIEST	SPIFF	SPILITE	SPINDLES	SPINONI
SPICILEGE	SPIFFED	SPILITES	SPINDLIER	SPINOR
SPICILY	SPIFFIED	SPILITIC	SPINDLING	SPINORS
SPICINESS	SPIFFIER	SPILL	SPINDLY	SPINOSE
SPICING	SPIFFIES	SPILLABLE	SPINDRIFT	SPINOSELY
SPICK	SPIFFIEST	SPILLAGE	SPINE	SPINOSITY
SPICKER	SPIFFILY	SPILLAGES	SPINED	SPINOUS
SPICKEST	SPIFFING	SPILLED	SPINEL	SPINOUT
SPICKNEL	SPIFFS	SPILLER	SPINELESS	SPINOUTS
SPICKNELS	SPIFFY	SPILLERS	SPINELIKE	SPINS
SPICKS	SPIFFYING	SPILLIKIN	SPINELLE	SPINSTER
SPICS	SPIFS	SPILLING	SPINELLES	SPINSTERS
SPICULA	SPIGHT	SPILLINGS	SPINELS	SPINTEXT
SPICULAE	SPIGHTED	SPILLOVER	SPINES	SPINTEXTS
SPICULAR	SPIGHTING	SPILLS	SPINET	SPINTO
SPICULATE	SPIGHTS	SPILLWAY	SPINETS	SPINTOS

SPINULA	SPIRIT	SPITTIER	SPLEENIER	SPLITTER
SPINULAE	SPIRITED	SPITTIEST	SPLEENISH	SPLITTERS
SPINULATE	SPIRITFUL	SPITTING	SPLEENS	SPLITTING
SPINULE	SPIRITING	SPITTINGS	SPLEENY	SPLITTISM
SPINULES	SPIRITISM	SPITTLE	SPLENDENT	SPLITTIST
SPINULOSE	SPIRITIST	SPITTLES	SPLENDID	SPLODGE
SPINULOUS	SPIRITOSO	SPITTLIER	SPLENDOR	SPLODGED
SPINY	SPIRITOUS	SPITTLY	SPLENDORS	SPLODGES
SPIRACLE	SPIRITS	SPITTOON	SPLENDOUR	SPLODGIER
SPIRACLES	SPIRITUAL	SPITTOONS	SPLENETIC	SPLODGILY
SPIRACULA	SPIRITUEL	SPITTY	SPLENIA	SPLODGING
SPIRAEA	SPIRITUS	SPITZ	SPLENIAL	SPLODGY
SPIRAEAS	SPIRITY	SPITZES	SPLENIC	SPLOG
SPIRAL	SPIRLING	SPIV	SPLENII	SPLOGS
SPIRALED	SPIRLINGS	SPIVS	SPLENITIS	SPLOOSH
SPIRALING	SPIROGRAM	SPIVVERY	SPLENIUM	SPLOOSHED
SPIRALISM	SPIROGYRA	SPIVVIER	SPLENIUMS	SPLOOSHES
SPIRALIST	SPIROID	SPIVVIEST	SPLENIUS	SPLORE
SPIRALITY	SPIRT	SPIVVISH	SPLENT	SPLORES
SPIRALLED	SPIRTED	SPIVVY	SPLENTS	SPLOSH
SPIRALLY	SPIRTING	SPLAKE	SPLEUCHAN	SPLOSHED
SPIRALS	SPIRTLE	SPLAKES	SPLICE	SPLOSHES
SPIRANT	SPIRTLES	SPLASH	SPLICED	SPLOSHING
SPIRANTS	SPIRTS	SPLASHED	SPLICER	SPLOTCH
SPIRASTER	SPIRULA	SPLASHER	SPLICERS	SPLOTCHED
SPIRATED	SPIRULAE	SPLASHERS	SPLICES	SPLOTCHES
SPIRATION	SPIRULAS	SPLASHES	SPLICING	SPLOTCHY
SPIRE	SPIRULINA	SPLASHIER	SPLICINGS	SPLURGE
SPIREA	SPIRY	SPLASHILY	SPLIFF	SPLURGED
SPIREAS	SPIT	SPLASHING	SPLIFFS	SPLURGER
SPIRED	SPITAL	SPLASHY	SPLINE	SPLURGERS
SPIRELESS	SPITALS	SPLAT	SPLINED	SPLURGES
SPIRELET	SPITBALL	SPLATCH	SPLINES	SPLURGIER
SPIRELETS	SPITBALLS	SPLATCHED	SPLINING	SPLURGING
SPIREM	SPITCHER	SPLATCHES	SPLINT	SPLURGY
SPIREME	SPITCHERS	SPLATS	SPLINTED	SPLURT
SPIREMES	SPITE	SPLATTED	SPLINTER	SPLURTED
SPIREMS	SPITED	SPLATTER	SPLINTERS	SPLURTING
SPIRES	SPITEFUL	SPLATTERS	SPLINTERY	SPLURTS
SPIREWISE	SPITES	SPLATTING	SPLINTING	SPLUTTER
SPIRIC	SPITFIRE	SPLAY	SPLINTS	SPLUTTERS
SPIRICS	SPITFIRES	SPLAYED	SPLISH	SPLUTTERY
SPIRIER	SPITING	SPLAYFEET	SPLISHED	SPOD
SPIRIEST	SPITS	SPLAYFOOT	SPLISHES	SPODDIER
SPIRILLA	SPITTED	SPLAYING	SPLISHING	SPODDIEST
SPIRILLAR	SPITTEN	SPLAYS	SPLIT	SPODDY
SPIRILLUM	SPITTER	SPLEEN	SPLITS	SPODE
SPIRING	SPITTERS	SPLEENFUL	SPLITTED	SPODES

SPODIUM	SPONGERS	SPOOLED	SPORES	SPORULES
SPODIUMS	SPONGES	SPOOLER	SPORICIDE	SPOSH
SPODOGRAM	SPONGIER	SPOOLERS	SPORIDESM	SPOSHES
SPODOSOL	SPONGIEST	SPOOLING	SPORIDIA	SPOSHIER
SPODOSOLS	SPONGILY	SPOOLINGS	SPORIDIAL	SPOSHIEST
SPODS	SPONGIN	SPOOLS	SPORIDIUM	SPOSHY
SPODUMENE	SPONGING	SPOOM	SPORING	SPOT
SPOFFISH	SPONGINS	SPOOMED	SPORK	SPOTLESS
SPOFFY	SPONGIOSE	SPOOMING	SPORKS	SPOTLIGHT
SPOIL	SPONGIOUS	SPOOMS	SPOROCARP	SPOTLIT
SPOILABLE	SPONGOID	SPOON	SPOROCYST	SPOTS
SPOILAGE	SPONGY	SPOONBAIT	SPOROCYTE	SPOTTABLE
SPOILAGES	SPONSAL	SPOONBILL	SPOROGENY	SPOTTED
SPOILED	SPONSALIA	SPOONED	SPOROGONY	SPOTTER
SPOILER	SPONSIBLE	SPOONER	SPOROID	SPOTTERS
SPOILERS	SPONSING	SPOONERS	SPOROPHYL	SPOTTIE
SPOILFIVE	SPONSINGS	SPOONEY	SPOROZOA	SPOTTIER
SPOILFUL	SPONSION	SPOONEYS	SPOROZOAL	SPOTTIES
SPOILING	SPONSIONS	SPOONFED	SPOROZOAN	SPOTTIEST
SPOILS	SPONSON	SPOONFUL	SPOROZOIC	SPOTTILY
SPOILSMAN	SPONSONS	SPOONFULS	SPOROZOON	SPOTTING
SPOILSMEN	SPONSOR	SPOONHOOK	SPORRAN	SPOTTINGS
SPOILT	SPONSORED	SPOONIER	SPORRANS	SPOTTY
SPOKE	SPONSORS	SPOONIES	SPORT	SPOUSAGE
SPOKED	SPONTOON	SPOONIEST	SPORTABLE	SPOUSAGES
SPOKEN	SPONTOONS	SPOONILY	SPORTANCE	SPOUSAL
SPOKES	SPOOF	SPOONING	SPORTBIKE	SPOUSALLY
SPOKESMAN	SPOOFED	SPOONLIKE	SPORTCOAT	SPOUSALS
SPOKESMEN	SPOOFER	SPOONS	SPORTED	SPOUSE
SPOKEWISE	SPOOFERS	SPOONSFUL	SPORTER	SPOUSED
SPOKING	SPOOFERY	SPOONWAYS	SPORTERS	SPOUSES
SPOLIATE	SPOOFIER	SPOONWISE	SPORTFUL	SPOUSING
SPOLIATED	SPOOFIEST	SPOONWORM	SPORTIER	SPOUT
SPOLIATES	SPOOFING	SPOONY	SPORTIES	SPOUTED
SPOLIATOR	SPOOFINGS	SPOOR	SPORTIEST	SPOUTER
SPONDAIC	SPOOFS	SPOORED	SPORTIF	SPOUTERS
SPONDAICS	SPOOFY	SPOORER	SPORTIFS	SPOUTIER
SPONDEE	SPOOK	SPOORERS	SPORTILY	SPOUTIEST
SPONDEES	SPOOKED	SPOORING	SPORTING	SPOUTING
SPONDULIX	SPOOKERY	SPOORS	SPORTIVE	SPOUTINGS
SPONDYL	SPOOKIER	SPOOT	SPORTLESS	SPOUTLESS
SPONDYLS	SPOOKIEST	SPOOTS	SPORTS	SPOUTS
SPONGE	SPOOKILY	SPORADIC	SPORTSMAN	SPOUTY
SPONGEBAG	SPOOKING	SPORAL	SPORTSMEN	SPRACK
SPONGED	SPOOKISH	SPORANGIA	SPORTY	SPRACKLE
SPONGEING	SPOOKS	SPORE	SPORULAR	SPRACKLED
SPONGEOUS	SPOOKY	SPORED	SPORULATE	SPRACKLES
SPONGER	SPOOL	SPORELIKE	SPORULE	SPRAD

S

SPRADDLE	SPREADS	SPRIGHTED	SPRITZING	SPUDDED
SPRADDLED	SPREAGH	SPRIGHTLY	SPRITZY	SPUDDER
SPRADDLES	SPREAGHS	SPRIGHTS	SPROCKET	SPUDDERS
SPRAG	SPREATHE	SPRIGS	SPROCKETS	SPUDDIER
SPRAGGED	SPREATHED	SPRIGTAIL	SPROD	SPUDDIEST
SPRAGGING	SPREATHES	SPRING	SPRODS	SPUDDING
SPRAGS	SPREAZE	SPRINGAL	SPROG	SPUDDINGS
SPRAID	SPREAZED	SPRINGALD	SPROGLET	SPUDDLE
SPRAIN	SPREAZES	SPRINGALS	SPROGLETS	SPUDDLES
SPRAINED	SPREAZING	SPRINGBOK	SPROGS	SPUDDY
SPRAINING	SPRECHERY	SPRINGE	SPRONG	SPUDGEL
SPRAINS	SPRECKLED	SPRINGED	SPROUT	SPUDGELS
SPRAINT	SPRED	SPRINGER	SPROUTED	SPUDS
SPRAINTS	SPREDD	SPRINGERS	SPROUTING	SPUE
SPRANG	SPREDDE	SPRINGES	SPROUTS	SPUED
SPRANGLE	SPREDDEN	SPRINGIER	SPRUCE	SPUEING
SPRANGLED	SPREDDES	SPRINGILY	SPRUCED	SPUER
SPRANGLES	SPREDDING	SPRINGING	SPRUCELY	SPUERS
SPRANGS	SPREDDS	SPRINGLE	SPRUCER	SPUES
SPRAT	SPREDS	SPRINGLES	SPRUCES	SPUG
SPRATS	SPREE	SPRINGLET	SPRUCEST	SPUGGIES
SPRATTLE	SPREED	SPRINGS	SPRUCIER	SPUGGY
SPRATTLED	SPREEING	SPRINGY	SPRUCIEST	SPUGS
SPRATTLES	SPREES	SPRINKLE	SPRUCING	SPUILZIE
SPRAUCHLE	SPREETHE	SPRINKLED	SPRUCY	SPUILZIED
SPRAUNCY	SPREETHED	SPRINKLER	SPRUE	SPUILZIES
SPRAWL	SPREETHES	SPRINKLES	SPRUES	SPUING
SPRAWLED	SPREEZE	SPRINT	SPRUG	SPULE
SPRAWLER	SPREEZED	SPRINTED	SPRUGS	SPULES
SPRAWLERS	SPREEZES	SPRINTER	SPRUIK	SPULYE
SPRAWLIER	SPREEZING	SPRINTERS	SPRUIKED	SPULYED
SPRAWLING	SPREKELIA	SPRINTING	SPRUIKER	SPULYEING
SPRAWLS	SPRENT	SPRINTS	SPRUIKERS	SPULYES
SPRAWLY	SPRENTED	SPRIT	SPRUIKING	SPULYIE
SPRAY	SPRENTING	SPRITE	SPRUIKS	SPULYIED
SPRAYED	SPRENTS	SPRITEFUL	SPRUIT	SPULYIES
SPRAYER	SPREW	SPRITELY	SPRUITS	SPULZIE
SPRAYERS	SPREWS	SPRITES	SPRUNG	SPULZIED
SPRAYEY	SPRIER	SPRITS	SPRUSH	SPULZIES
SPRAYIER	SPRIESI	SPRITSAIL	SPRUSHED	SPUMANTE
SPRAYIEST	SPRIG	SPRITZ	SPRUSHES	SPUMANTES
SPRAYING	SPRIGGED	SPRITZED	SPRUSHING	SPUME
SPRAYINGS	SPRIGGER	SPRITZER	SPRY	SPUMED
SPRAYS	SPRIGGERS	SPRITZERS	SPRYER	SPUMES
SPREAD	SPRIGGIER	SPRITZES	SPRYEST	SPUMIER
SPREADER	SPRIGGING	SPRITZIER	SPRYLY	SPUMIEST
SPREADERS	SPRIGGY	SPRITZIG	SPRYNESS	SPUMING
SPREADING	SPRIGHT	SPRITZIGS	SPUD	SPUMONE

SPUMONES	SPURRIERS	SQUABBEST	SQUAMATE	SQUATTIER
SPUMONI	SPURRIES	SQUABBIER	SQUAMATES	SQUATTILY
SPUMONIS	SPURRIEST	SQUABBING	SQUAME	SQUATTING
SPUMOUS	SPURRING	SQUABBISH	SQUAMELLA	SQUATTLE
SPUMY	SPURRINGS	SQUABBLE	SQUAMES	SQUATTLED
SPUN	SPURRY	SQUABBLED	SQUAMOSAL	SQUATTLES
SPUNGE	SPURS	SQUABBLER	SQUAMOSE	SQUATTY
SPUNGES	SPURT	SQUABBLES	SQUAMOUS	SQUAW
SPUNK	SPURTED	SQUABBY	SQUAMULA	SQUAWBUSH
SPUNKED	SPURTER	SQUABS	SQUAMULAS	SQUAWFISH
SPUNKIE	SPURTERS	SQUACCO	SQUAMULE	SQUAWK
SPUNKIER	SPURTING	SQUACCOS	SQUAMULES	SQUAWKED
SPUNKIES	SPURTLE	SQUAD	SQUANDER	SQUAWKER
SPUNKIEST	SPURTLES	SQUADDED	SQUANDERS	SQUAWKERS
SPUNKILY	SPURTS	SQUADDIE	SQUARE	SQUAWKIER
SPUNKING	SPURWAY	SQUADDIES	SQUARED	SQUAWKING
SPUNKS	SPURWAYS	SQUADDING	SQUARELY	SQUAWKS
SPUNKY	SPUTA	SQUADDY	SQUARER	SQUAWKY
SPUNYARN	SPUTNIK	SQUADOOSH	SQUARERS	SQUAWMAN
SPUNYARNS	SPUTNIKS	SQUADRON	SQUARES	SQUAWMEN
SPUR	SPUTTER	SQUADRONE	SQUAREST	SQUAWROOT
SPURDOG	SPUTTERED	SQUADRONS	SQUARIAL	SQUAWS
SPURDOGS	SPUTTERER	SQUADS	SQUARIALS	SQUEAK
SPURGALL	SPUTTERS	SQUAIL	SQUARING	SQUEAKED
SPURGALLS	SPUTTERY	SQUAILED	SQUARINGS	SQUEAKER
SPURGE	SPUTUM	SQUAILER	SQUARISH	SQUEAKERS
SPURGES	SPUTUMS	SQUAILERS	SQUARK	SQUEAKERY
SPURIAE	SPY	SQUAILING	SQUARKS	SQUEAKIER
SPURIOUS	SPYAL	SQUAILS	SQUARROSE	SQUEAKILY
SPURLESS	SPYALS	SQUALENE	SQUARSON	SQUEAKING
SPURLIKE	SPYCAM	SQUALENES	SQUARSONS	SQUEAKS
SPURLING	SPYCAMS	SQUALID	SQUASH	SQUEAKY
SPURLINGS	SPYGLASS	SQUALIDER	SQUASHED	SQUEAL
SPURN	SPYHOLE	SQUALIDLY	SQUASHER	SQUEALED
SPURNE	SPYHOLES	SQUALL	SQUASHERS	SQUEALER
SPURNED	SPYING	SQUALLED	SQUASHES	SQUEALERS
SPURNER	SPYINGS	SQUALLER	SQUASHIER	SQUEALING
SPURNERS	SPYMASTER	SQUALLERS	SQUASHILY	SQUEALS
SPURNES	SPYPLANE	SQUALLIER	SQUASHING	SQUEAMISH
SPURNING	SPYPLANES	SQUALLING	SQUASHY	SQUEEGEE
SPURNINGS	SPYRE	SQUALLISH	SQUAT	SQUEEGEED
SPURNS	SPYRES	SQUALLS	SQUATLY	SQUEEGEES
SPURRED	SPYWARE	SQUALLY	SQUATNESS	SQUEEZE
SPURRER	SPYWARES	SQUALOID	SQUATS	SQUEEZED
SPURRERS	SQUAB	SQUALOR	SQUATTED	SQUEEZER
SPURREY	SQUABASH	SQUALORS	SQUATTER	SQUEEZERS
SPURREYS	SQUABBED	SQUAMA	SQUATTERS	SQUEEZES
SPURRIER	SQUABBER	SQUAMAE	SQUATTEST	SQUEEZIER

SQUEEZING	SQUILLAE	SQUIRMS	STABBERS	STADDLE
SQUEEZY	SQUILLAS	SQUIRMY	STABBING	STADDLES
SQUEG	SQUILLION	SQUIRR	STABBINGS	STADE
SQUEGGED	SQUILLS	SQUIRRED	STABILATE	STADES
SQUEGGER	SQUINANCY	SQUIRREL	STABILE	STADIA
SQUEGGERS	SQUINCH	SQUIRRELS	STABILES	STADIAL
SQUEGGING	SQUINCHED	SQUIRRELY	STABILISE	STADIALS
SQUEGS	SQUINCHES	SQUIRRING	STABILITY	STADIAS
SQUELCH	SQUINIED	SQUIRRS	STABILIZE	STADIUM
SQUELCHED	SQUINIES	SQUIRT	STABLE	STADIUMS
SQUELCHER	SQUINNIED	SQUIRTED	STABLEBOY	STAFF
SQUELCHES	SQUINNIER	SQUIRTER	STABLED	STAFFAGE
SQUELCHY	SQUINNIES	SQUIRTERS	STABLEMAN	STAFFAGES
SQUIB	SQUINNY	SQUIRTING	STABLEMEN	STAFFED
SQUIBBED	SQUINT	SQUIRTS	STABLER	STAFFER
SQUIBBER	SQUINTED	SQUISH	STABLERS	STAFFERS
SQUIBBERS	SQUINTER	SQUISHED	STABLES	STAFFING
SQUIBBING	SQUINTERS	SQUISHES	STABLEST	STAFFINGS
SQUIBS	SQUINTEST	SQUISHIER	STABLING	STAFFMAN
SQUID	SQUINTIER	SQUISHING	STABLINGS	STAFFMEN
SQUIDDED	SQUINTING	SQUISHY	STABLISH	STAFFROOM
SQUIDDING	SQUINTS	SQUIT	STABLY	STAFFS
SQUIDGE	SQUINTY	SQUITCH	STABS	STAG
SQUIDGED	SQUINY	SQUITCHES	STACATION	STAGE
SQUIDGES	SQUINYING	SQUITS	STACCATI	STAGEABLE
SQUIDGIER	SQUIRAGE	SQUITTERS	STACCATO	STAGED
SQUIDGING	SQUIRAGES	SQUIZ	STACCATOS	STAGEFUL
SQUIDGY	SQUIRALTY	SQUIZZES	STACHYS	STAGEFULS
SQUIDLIKE	SQUIRARCH	SQUOOSH	STACHYSES	STAGEHAND
SQUIDS	SQUIRE	SQUOOSHED	STACK	STAGEHEAD
SQUIER	SQUIREAGE	SQUOOSHES	STACKABLE	STAGELIKE
SQUIERS	SQUIRED	SQUOOSHY	STACKED	STAGER
SQUIFF	SQUIREDOM	SQUUSH	STACKER	STAGERIES
SQUIFFED	SQUIREEN	SQUUSHED	STACKERS	STAGERS
SQUIFFER	SQUIREENS	SQUUSHES	STACKET	STAGERY
SQUIFFERS	SQUIRELY	SQUUSHING	STACKETS	STAGES
SQUIFFIER	SQUIRES	SRADDHA	STACKING	STAGEY
SQUIFFY	SQUIRESS	SRADDHAS	STACKINGS	STAGFTTE
SQUIGGLE	SQUIRING	SRADHA	STACKLESS	STAGETTES
SQUIGGLED	SQUIRISH	SRADHAS	STACKROOM	STAGGARD
SQUIGGLER	SQUIRL	SRI	STACKS	STAGGARDS
SQUIGGLES	SQUIRLS	SRIRACHA	STACKUP	STAGGART
SQUIGGLY	SQUIRM	SRIRACHAS	STACKUPS	STAGGARTS
SQUILGEE	SQUIRMED	SRIS	STACKYARD	STAGGED
SQUILGEED	SQUIRMER	ST	STACTE	STAGGER
SQUILGEES	SQUIRMERS	STAB	STACTES	STAGGERED
SQUILL	SQUIRMIER	STABBED	STADDA	STAGGERER
SQUILLA	SQUIRMING	STABBER	STADDAS	STAGGERS

S

STAGGERY	STAIRS	STALKY	STANCE	STANHOPE
STAGGIE	STAIRSTEP	STALL	STANCES	STANHOPES
STAGGIER	STAIRWAY	STALLAGE	STANCH	STANIEL
STAGGIES	STAIRWAYS	STALLAGES	STANCHED	STANIELS
STAGGIEST	STAIRWELL	STALLED	STANCHEL	STANINE
STAGGING	STAIRWISE	STALLING	STANCHELS	STANINES
STAGGY	STAIRWORK	STALLINGS	STANCHER	STANING
STAGHORN	STAITH	STALLION	STANCHERS	STANK
STAGHORNS	STAITHE	STALLIONS	STANCHES	STANKED
STAGHOUND	STAITHES	STALLMAN	STANCHEST	STANKING
STAGIER	STAITHS	STALLMEN	STANCHING	STANKS
STAGIEST	STAKE	STALLS	STANCHION	STANNARY
STAGILY	STAKED	STALWART	STANCHLY	STANNATE
STAGINESS	STAKEOUT	STALWARTS	STANCK	STANNATES
STAGING	STAKEOUTS	STALWORTH	STAND	STANNATOR
STAGINGS	STAKER	STAMEN	STANDARD	STANNEL
STAGNANCE	STAKERS	STAMENED	STANDARDS	STANNELS
STAGNANCY	STAKES	STAMENS	STANDAWAY	STANNIC
STAGNANT	STAKING	STAMINA	STANDBY	STANNITE
STAGNATE	STALACTIC	STAMINAL	STANDBYS	STANNITES
STAGNATED	STALAG	STAMINAS	STANDDOWN	STANNOUS
STAGNATES	STALAGMA	STAMINATE	STANDEE	STANNUM
STAGS	STALAGMAS	STAMINEAL	STANDEES	STANNUMS
STAGY	STALAGS	STAMINODE	STANDEN	STANOL
STAID	STALE	STAMINODY	STANDER	STANOLS
STAIDER	STALED	STAMINOID	STANDERS	STANYEL
STAIDEST	STALELY	STAMMEL	STANDFAST	STANYELS
STAIDLY	STALEMATE	STAMMELS	STANDGALE	STANZA
STAIDNESS	STALENESS	STAMMER	STANDING	STANZAED
STAIG	STALER	STAMMERED	STANDINGS	STANZAIC
STAIGS	STALES	STAMMERER	STANDISH	STANZAS
STAIN	STALEST	STAMMERS	STANDOFF	STANZE
STAINABLE	STALING	STAMNOI	STANDOFFS	STANZES
STAINED	STALK	STAMNOS	STANDOUT	STANZO
STAINER	STALKED	STAMP	STANDOUTS	STANZOES
STAINERS	STALKER	STAMPED	STANDOVER	STANZOS
STAINING	STALKERS	STAMPEDE	STANDPAT	STAP
STAININGS	STALKIER	STAMPEDED	STANDPIPE	STAPEDES
STAINLESS	STALKIEST	STAMPEDER	STANDS	STAPEDIAL
STAINS	STALKILY	STAMPEDES	STANDUP	STAPEDII
STAIR	STALKING	STAMPEDO	STANDUPS	STAPEDIUS
STAIRCASE	STALKINGS	STAMPEDOS	STANE	STAPELIA
STAIRED	STALKLESS	STAMPER	STANED	STAPELIAS
STAIRFOOT	STALKLIKE	STAMPERS	STANES	STAPES
STAIRHEAD	STALKO	STAMPING	STANG	STAPH
STAIRLESS	STALKOES	STAMPINGS	STANGED	STAPHS
STAIRLIFT	STALKOS	STAMPLESS	STANGING	STAPLE
STAIRLIKE	STALKS	STAMPS	STANGS	STAPLED

S

STAPLER	STARK	STARTED	STATEHOOD	STATUE
STAPLERS	STARKED	STARTER	STATELESS	STATUED
STAPLES	STARKEN	STARTERS	STATELET	STATUES
STAPLING	STARKENED	STARTFUL	STATELETS	STATUETTE
STAPLINGS	STARKENS	STARTING	STATELIER	STATURE
STAPPED	STARKER	STARTINGS	STATELILY	STATURED
STAPPING	STARKERS	STARTISH	STATELY	STATURES
STAPPLE	STARKEST	STARTLE	STATEMENT	STATUS
STAPPLES	STARKING	STARTLED	STATER	STATUSES
STAPS	STARKLY	STARTLER	STATEROOM	STATUSIER
STAR	STARKNESS	STARTLERS	STATERS	STATUSY
STARAGEN	STARKS	STARTLES	STATES	STATUTE
STARAGENS	STARLESS	STARTLIER	STATESIDE	STATUTES
STARBOARD	STARLET	STARTLING	STATESMAN	STATUTORY
STARBURST	STARLETS	STARTLISH	STATESMEN	STAUMREL
STARCH	STARLIGHT	STARTLY	STATEWIDE	STAUMRELS
STARCHED	STARLIKE	STARTS	STATIC	STAUN
STARCHER	STARLING	STARTSY	STATICAL	STAUNCH
STARCHERS	STARLINGS	STARTUP	STATICE	STAUNCHED
STARCHES	STARLIT	STARTUPS	STATICES	STAUNCHER
STARCHIER	STARN	STARVE	STATICKY	STAUNCHES
STARCHILY	STARNED	STARVED	STATICS	STAUNCHLY
STARCHING	STARNIE	STARVER	STATIM	STAUNING
STARCHY	STARNIES	STARVERS	STATIN	STAUNS
STARDOM	STARNING	STARVES	STATING	STAVE
STARDOMS	STARNOSE	STARVING	STATINS	STAVED
STARDRIFT	STARNOSES	STARVINGS	STATION	STAVES
STARDUST	STARNS	STARWORT	STATIONAL	STAVING
STARDUSTS	STAROSTA	STARWORTS	STATIONED	STAVUDINE
STARE	STAROSTAS	STASES	STATIONER	STAW
STARED	STAROSTY	STASH	STATIONS	STAWED
STARER	STARR	STASHED	STATISM	STAWING
STARERS	STARRED	STASHES	STATISMS	STAWS
STARES	STARRIER	STASHIE	STATIST	STAY
STARETS	STARRIEST	STASHIES	STATISTIC	STAYAWAY
STARETSES	STARRILY	STASHING	STATISTS	STAYAWAYS
STARETZ	STARRING	STASIDION	STATIVE	STAYED
STARETZES	STARRINGS	STASIMA	STATIVES	STAYER
STARFISH	STARRS	STASIMON	STATOCYST	STAYERS
STARFRUIT	STARRY	STASIS	STATOLITH	STAYING
STARGAZE	STARS	STAT	STATOR	STAYLESS
STARGAZED	STARSHINE	STATABLE	STATORS	STAYMAKER
STARGAZER	STARSHIP	STATAL	STATS	STAYNE
STARGAZES	STARSHIPS	STATANT	STATTO	STAYNED
STARGAZEY	STARSPOT	STATE	STATTOS	STAYNES
STARING	STARSPOTS	STATEABLE	STATUA	STAYNING
STARINGLY	STARSTONE	STATED	STATUARY	STAYRE
STARINGS	START	STATEDLY	STATUAS	STAYRES

STAYS	STEAMING	STEDDING	STEENBOK	STEEVE
STAYSAIL	STEAMINGS	STEDDS	STEENBOKS	STEEVED
STAYSAILS	STEAMPUNK	STEDDY	STEENBRAS	STEEVELY
STEAD	STEAMROLL	STEDDYING	STEENBUCK	STEEVER
STEADED	STEAMS	STEDE	STEENED	STEEVES
STEADFAST	STEAMSHIP	STEDED	STEENING	STEEVEST
STEADIED	STEAMY	STEDES	STEENINGS	STEEVING
STEADIER	STEAN	STEDFAST	STEENKIRK	STEEVINGS
STEADIERS	STEANE	STEDING	STEENS	STEGNOSES
STEADIES	STEANED	STEDS	STEEP	STEGNOSIS
STEADIEST	STEANES	STEED	STEEPED	STEGNOTIC
STEADILY	STEANING	STEEDED	STEEPEN	STEGODON
STEADING	STEANINGS	STEEDIED	STEEPENED	STEGODONS
STEADINGS	STEANS	STEEDIES	STEEPENS	STEGODONT
STEADS	STEAPSIN	STEEDING	STEEPER	STEGOMYIA
STEADY	STEAPSINS	STEEDLIKE	STEEPERS	STEGOSAUR
STEADYING	STEAR	STEEDS	STEEPEST	STEIL
STEAK	STEARAGE	STEEDY	STEEPEUP	STEILS
STEAKETTE	STEARAGES	STEEDYING	STEEPIER	STEIN
STEAKS	STEARATE	STEEK	STEEPIEST	STEINBOCK
STEAL	STEARATES	STEEKED	STEEPING	STEINBOK
STEALABLE	STEARD	STEEKING	STEEPISH	STEINBOKS
STEALAGE	STEARE	STEEKIT	STEEPLE	STEINED
STEALAGES	STEARED	STEEKS	STEEPLED	STEINING
STEALE	STEARES	STEEL	STEEPLES	STEININGS
STEALED	STEARIC	STEELBOW	STEEPLING	STEINKIRK
STEALER	STEARIN	STEELBOWS	STEEPLY	STEINS
STEALERS	STEARINE	STEELD	STEEPNESS	STELA
STEALES	STEARINES	STEELED	STEEPS	STELAE
STEALING	STEARING	STEELHEAD	STEEPUP	STELAI
STEALINGS	STEARINS	STEELIE	STEEPY	STELAR
STEALS	STEARS	STEELIER	STEER	STELE
STEALT	STEARSMAN	STEELIES	STEERABLE	STELENE
STEALTH	STEARSMEN	STEELIEST	STEERAGE	STELES
STEALTHED	STEATITE	STEELING	STEERAGES	STELIC
STEALTHS	STEATITES	STEELINGS	STEERED	STELL
STEALTHY	STEATITIC	STEELMAN	STEERER	STELLA
STEAM	STEATOMA	STEELMEN	STEERERS	STELLAR
STEAMBOAT	STEATOMAS	STEELS	STEERIER	STELLAS
STEAMED	STEATOSES	STEELWARE	STEERIES	STELLATE
STEAMER	STEATOSIS	STEELWORK	STEERIEST	STELLATED
STEAMERED	STED	STEELY	STEERING	STELLED
STEAMERS	STEDD	STEELYARD	STEERINGS	STELLERID
STEAMIE	STEDDE	STEEM	STEERLING	STELLIFY
STEAMIER	STEDDED	STEEMED	STEERS	STELLING
STEAMIES	STEDDES	STEEMING	STEERSMAN	STELLIO
STEAMIEST	STEDDIED	STEEMS	STEERSMEN	STELLION
STEAMILY	STEDDIES	STEEN	STEERY	STELLIONS

S

STELLITE
STELLITES
STELLS
STELLULAR
STEM
STEMBOK
STEMBOKS
STEMBUCK
STEMBUCKS
STEME
STEMED
STEMES
STEMHEAD
STEMHEADS
STEMING
STEMLESS
STEMLET
STEMLETS
STEMLIKE
STEMMA
STEMMAS
STEMMATA
STEMMATIC
STEMME
STEMMED
STEMMER
STEMMERS
STEMMERY
STEMMES
STEMMIER
STEMMIEST
STEMMING
STEMMINGS
STEMMY
STEMPEL
STEMPELS
STEMPLE
STEMPLES
STEMS
STEMSON
STEMSONS
STEMWARE
STEMWARES
STEN
STENCH
STENCHED
STENCHES
STENCHFUL

STENCHIER
STENCHING
STENCHY
STENCIL
STENCILED
STENCILER
STENCILS
STEND
STENDED
STENDING
STENDS
STENGAH
STENGAHS
STENLOCK
STENLOCKS
STENNED
STENNING
STENO
STENOBATH
STENOKIES
STENOKOUS
STENOKY
STENOPAIC
STENOS
STENOSED
STENOSES
STENOSING
STENOSIS
STENOTIC
STENOTYPE
STENOTYPY
STENS
STENT
STENTED
STENTING
STENTOR
STENTORS
STENTOUR
STENTOURS
STENTS
STEP
STEPBAIRN
STEPCHILD
STEPDAD
STEPDADS
STEPDAME
STEPDAMES
STEPHANE

STEPHANES
STEPLESS
STEPLIKE
STEPMOM
STEPMOMS
STEPNEY
STEPNEYS
STEPOVER
STEPOVERS
STEPPE
STEPPED
STEPPER
STEPPERS
STEPPES
STEPPING
STEPS
STEPSON
STEPSONS
STEPSTOOL
STEPT
STEPWISE
STERADIAN
STERANE
STERANES
STERCORAL
STERCULIA
STERE
STEREO
STEREOED
STEREOING
STEREOME
STEREOMES
STEREOS
STERES
STERIC
STERICAL
STERIGMA
STERIGMAS
STERILANT
STERILE
STERILELY
STERILISE
STERILITY
STERILIZE
STERLET
STERLETS
STERLING
STERLINGS

STERN
STERNA
STERNAGE
STERNAGES
STERNAL
STERNEBRA
STERNED
STERNER
STERNEST
STERNFAST
STERNING
STERNITE
STERNITES
STERNITIC
STERNLY
STERNMOST
STERNNESS
STERNPORT
STERNPOST
STERNS
STERNSON
STERNSONS
STERNUM
STERNUMS
STERNWARD
STERNWAY
STERNWAYS
STEROID
STEROIDAL
STEROIDS
STEROL
STEROLS
STERTOR
STERTORS
STERVE
STERVED
STERVES
STERVING
STET
STETS
STETSON
STETSONS
STETTED
STETTING
STEVEDORE
STEVEN
STEVENS
STEVIA

STEVIAS
STEW
STEWABLE
STEWARD
STEWARDED
STEWARDRY
STEWARDS
STEWARTRY
STEWBUM
STEWBUMS
STEWED
STEWER
STEWERS
STEWIER
STEWIEST
STEWING
STEWINGS
STEWPAN
STEWPANS
STEWPOND
STEWPONDS
STEWPOT
STEWPOTS
STEWS
STEWY
STEY
STEYER
STEYEST
STEYS
STHENIA
STHENIAS
STHENIC
STIBBLE
STIBBLER
STIBBLERS
STIBBLES
STIBIAL
STIBINE
STIBINES
STIBIUM
STIBIUMS
STIBNITE
STIBNITES
STICCADO
STICCADOS
STICCATO
STICCATOS
STICH

S

STICHARIA	STICKWORK	STILBENES	STIM	STINKIEST
STICHERA	STICKY	STILBITE	STIME	STINKING
STICHERON	STICKYING	STILBITES	STIMED	STINKO
STICHIC	STICTION	STILBS	STIMES	STINKPOT
STICHIDIA	STICTIONS	STILE	STIMIE	STINKPOTS
STICHOI	STIDDIE	STILED	STIMIED	STINKS
STICHOS	STIDDIED	STILES	STIMIES	STINKWEED
STICHS	STIDDIES	STILET	STIMING	STINKWOOD
STICK	STIE	STILETS	STIMS	STINKY
STICKABLE	STIED	STILETTO	STIMULANT	STINT
STICKBALL	STIES	STILETTOS	STIMULATE	STINTED
STICKED	STIEVE	STILING	STIMULI	STINTEDLY
STICKER	STIEVELY	STILL	STIMULUS	STINTER
STICKERED	STIEVER	STILLAGE	STIMY	STINTERS
STICKERS	STIEVEST	STILLAGES	STIMYING	STINTIER
STICKFUL	STIFF	STILLBORN	STING	STINTIEST
STICKFULS	STIFFED	STILLED	STINGAREE	STINTING
STICKIE	STIFFEN	STILLER	STINGBULL	STINTINGS
STICKIED	STIFFENED	STILLERS	STINGE	STINTLESS
STICKIER	STIFFENER	STILLEST	STINGED	STINTS
STICKIES	STIFFENS	STILLIER	STINGER	STINTY
STICKIEST	STIFFER	STILLIEST	STINGERS	STIPA
STICKILY	STIFFEST	STILLING	STINGES	STIPAS
STICKING	STIFFIE	STILLINGS	STINGFISH	STIPE
STICKINGS	STIFFIES	STILLION	STINGIER	STIPED
STICKIT	STIFFING	STILLIONS	STINGIES	STIPEL
STICKJAW	STIFFISH	STILLMAN	STINGIEST	STIPELS
STICKJAWS	STIFFLY	STILLMEN	STINGILY	STIPEND
STICKLE	STIFFNESS	STILLNESS	STINGING	STIPENDS
STICKLED	STIFFS	STILLROOM	STINGINGS	STIPES
STICKLER	STIFFWARE	STILLS	STINGLESS	STIPIFORM
STICKLERS	STIFFY	STILLSON	STINGO	STIPITATE
STICKLES	STIFLE	STILLSONS	STINGOS	STIPITES
STICKLIKE	STIFLED	STILLY	STINGRAY	STIPPLE
STICKLING	STIFLER	STILT	STINGRAYS	STIPPLED
STICKMAN	STIFLERS	STILTBIRD	STINGS	STIPPLER
STICKMEN	STIFLES	STILTED	STINGY	STIPPLERS
STICKOUT	STIFLING	STILTEDLY	STINK	STIPPLES
STICKOUTS	STIFLINGS	STILTER	STINKARD	STIPPLING
STICKPIN	STIGMA	STILTERS	STINKARDS	STIPULAR
STICKPINS	STIGMAL	STILTIER	STINKBIRD	STIPULARY
STICKS	STIGMAS	STILTIEST	STINKBUG	STIPULATE
STICKSEED	STIGMATA	STILTING	STINKBUGS	STIPULE
STICKUM	STIGMATIC	STILTINGS	STINKER	STIPULED
STICKUMS	STIGME	STILTISH	STINKEROO	STIPULES
STICKUP	STIGMES	STILTLIKE	STINKERS	STIR
STICKUPS	STILB	STILTS	STINKHORN	STIRABOUT
STICKWEED	STILBENE	STILTY	STINKIER	STIRE

STIRED	STOAI	STOCKWORK	STOLES	STOMPING
STIRES	STOAS	STOCKY	STOLID	STOMPS
STIRING	STOAT	STOCKYARD	STOLIDER	STOMPY
STIRK	STOATS	STODGE	STOLIDEST	STONABLE
STIRKS	STOB	STODGED	STOLIDITY	STOND
STIRLESS	STOBBED	STODGER	STOLIDLY	STONDS
STIRP	STOBBING	STODGERS	STOLLEN	STONE
STIRPES	STOBIE	STODGES	STOLLENS	STONEABLE
STIRPS	STOBS	STODGIER	STOLN	STONEBOAT
STIRRA	STOCCADO	STODGIEST	STOLON	STONECAST
STIRRABLE	STOCCADOS	STODGILY	STOLONATE	STONECHAT
STIRRAH	STOCCATA	STODGING	STOLONIC	STONECROP
STIRRAHS	STOCCATAS	STODGY	STOLONS	STONECUT
STIRRAS	STOCIOUS	STOEP	STOLPORT	STONECUTS
STIRRE	STOCK	STOEPS	STOLPORTS	STONED
STIRRED	STOCKADE	STOGEY	STOMA	STONEFISH
STIRRER	STOCKADED	STOGEYS	STOMACH	STONEFLY
STIRRERS	STOCKADES	STOGIE	STOMACHAL	STONEHAND
STIRRES	STOCKAGE	STOGIES	STOMACHED	STONELESS
STIRRING	STOCKAGES	STOGY	STOMACHER	STONELIKE
STIRRINGS	STOCKCAR	STOIC	STOMACHIC	STONEN
STIRRUP	STOCKCARS	STOICAL	STOMACHS	STONER
STIRRUPS	STOCKED	STOICALLY	STOMACHY	STONERAG
STIRS	STOCKER	STOICISM	STOMACK	STONERAGS
STISHIE	STOCKERS	STOICISMS	STOMACKS	STONERAW
STISHIES	STOCKFISH	STOICS	STOMAL	STONERAWS
STITCH	STOCKHORN	STOIT	STOMAS	STONERN
STITCHED	STOCKIER	STOITED	STOMATA	STONERS
STITCHER	STOCKIEST	STOITER	STOMATAL	STONES
STITCHERS	STOCKILY	STOITERED	STOMATE	STONESHOT
STITCHERY	STOCKINET	STOITERS	STOMATES	STONEWALL
STITCHES	STOCKING	STOITING	STOMATIC	STONEWARE
STITCHING	STOCKINGS	STOITS	STOMATOUS	STONEWASH
STITHIED	STOCKISH	STOKE	STOMIA	STONEWORK
STITHIES	STOCKIST	STOKED	STOMIUM	STONEWORT
STITHY	STOCKISTS	STOKEHOLD	STOMIUMS	STONEY
STITHYING	STOCKLESS	STOKEHOLE	STOMODAEA	STONG
STIVE	STOCKLIST	STOKER	STOMODEA	STONIED
STIVED	STOCKLOCK	STOKERS	STOMODEAL	STONIER
STIVER	STOCKMAN	STOKES	STOMODEUM	STONIES
STIVERS	STOCKMEN	STOKESIA	STOMP	STONIEST
STIVES	STOCKPILE	STOKESIAS	STOMPED	STONILY
STIVIER	STOCKPOT	STOKING	STOMPER	STONINESS
STIVIEST	STOCKPOTS	STOKVEL	STOMPERS	STONING
STIVING	STOCKROOM	STOKVELS	STOMPIE	STONINGS
STIVY	STOCKS	STOLE	STOMPIER	STONISH
STOA	STOCKTAKE	STOLED	STOMPIES	STONISHED
STOAE	STOCKTOOK	STOLEN	STOMPIEST	STONISHES

S

STONK	STOORS	STOPWORD	STORNELLO	STOUSHED
STONKED	STOOSHIE	STOPWORDS	STORY	STOUSHES
STONKER	STOOSHIES	STORABLE	STORYBOOK	STOUSHIE
STONKERED	STOOZE	STORABLES	STORYETTE	STOUSHIES
STONKERS	STOOZED	STORAGE	STORYING	STOUSHING
STONKING	STOOZER	STORAGES	STORYINGS	STOUT
STONKS	STOOZERS	STORAX	STORYLESS	STOUTEN
STONN	STOOZES	STORAXES	STORYLINE	STOUTENED
STONNE	STOOZING	STORE	STORYTIME	STOUTENS
STONNED	STOOZINGS	STORECARD	STOSS	STOUTER
STONNES	STOP	STORED	STOSSES	STOUTEST
STONNING	STOPBAND	STOREMAN	STOT	STOUTH
STONNS	STOPBANDS	STOREMEN	STOTIN	STOUTHS
STONY	STOPBANK	STORER	STOTINKA	STOUTISH
STONYING	STOPBANKS	STOREROOM	STOTINKAS	STOUTLY
STOOD	STOPCOCK	STORERS	STOTINKI	STOUTNESS
STOODEN	STOPCOCKS	STORES	STOTINOV	STOUTS
STOOGE	STOPE	STORESHIP	STOTINS	STOVAINE
STOOGED	STOPED	STOREWIDE	STOTIOUS	STOVAINES
STOOGES	STOPER	STOREY	STOTS	STOVE
STOOGING	STOPERS	STOREYED	STOTT	STOVED
STOOK	STOPES	STOREYS	STOTTED	STOVEPIPE
STOOKED	STOPGAP	STORGE	STOTTER	STOVER
STOOKER	STOPGAPS	STORGES	STOTTERED	STOVERS
STOOKERS	STOPING	STORIATED	STOTTERS	STOVES
STOOKIE	STOPINGS	STORIED	STOTTIE	STOVETOP
STOOKIES	STOPLESS	STORIES	STOTTIES	STOVETOPS
STOOKING	STOPLIGHT	STORIETTE	STOTTING	STOVEWOOD
STOOKINGS	STOPOFF	STORING	STOTTS	STOVIES
STOOKS	STOPOFFS	STORK	STOTTY	STOVING
STOOL	STOPOVER	STORKS	STOUN	STOVINGS
STOOLBALL	STOPOVERS	STORM	STOUND	STOW
STOOLED	STOPPABLE	STORMBIRD	STOUNDED	STOWABLE
STOOLIE	STOPPAGE	STORMCOCK	STOUNDING	STOWAGE
STOOLIES	STOPPAGES	STORMED	STOUNDS	STOWAGES
STOOLING	STOPPED	STORMER	STOUNING	STOWAWAY
STOOLS	STOPPER	STORMERS	STOUNS	STOWAWAYS
STOOLY	STOPPERED	STORMFUL	STOUP	STOWDOWN
STOOP	STOPPERS	STORMIER	STOUPS	STOWDOWNS
STOOPBALL	STOPPING	STORMIEST	STOUR	STOWED
STOOPE	STOPPINGS	STORMILY	STOURE	STOWER
STOOPED	STOPPLE	STORMING	STOURES	STOWERS
STOOPER	STOPPLED	STORMINGS	STOURIE	STOWING
STOOPERS	STOPPLES	STORMLESS	STOURIER	STOWINGS
STOOPES	STOPPLING	STORMLIKE	STOURIEST	STOWLINS
STOOPING	STOPS	STORMS	STOURS	STOWN
STOOPS	STOPT	STORMY	STOURY	STOWND
STOOR	STOPWATCH	STORNELLI	STOUSH	STOWNDED

STOWNDING	STRAINER	STRAPHANG	STRAWIEST	STREELS
STOWNDS	STRAINERS	STRAPHUNG	STRAWING	STREET
STOWNLINS	STRAINING	STRAPLESS	STRAWLESS	STREETAGE
STOWP	STRAINS	STRAPLIKE	STRAWLIKE	STREETBOY
STOWPS	STRAINT	STRAPLINE	STRAWN	STREETCAR
STOWRE	STRAINTS	STRAPPADO	STRAWS	STREETED
STOWRES	STRAIT	STRAPPED	STRAWWORM	STREETFUL
STOWS	STRAITED	STRAPPER	STRAWY	STREETIER
STRABISM	STRAITEN	STRAPPERS	STRAY	STREETING
STRABISMS	STRAITENS	STRAPPIER	STRAYED	STREETS
STRACK	STRAITER	STRAPPING	STRAYER	STREETY
STRAD	STRAITEST	STRAPPY	STRAYERS	STREIGHT
STRADDLE	STRAITING	STRAPS	STRAYING	STREIGHTS
STRADDLED	STRAITLY	STRAPWORT	STRAYINGS	STREIGNE
STRADDLER	STRAITS	STRASS	STRAYLING	STREIGNED
STRADDLES	STRAK	STRASSES	STRAYS	STREIGNES
STRADIOT	STRAKE	STRATA	STRAYVE	STRELITZ
STRADIOTS	STRAKED	STRATAGEM	STRAYVED	STRELITZI
STRADS	STRAKES	STRATAL	STRAYVES	STRENE
STRAE	STRAMACON	STRATAS	STRAYVING	STRENES
STRAES	STRAMASH	STRATEGIC	STREAK	STRENGTH
STRAFE	STRAMAZON	STRATEGY	STREAKED	STRENGTHS
STRAFED	STRAMMEL	STRATH	STREAKER	STRENUITY
STRAFER	STRAMMELS	STRATHS	STREAKERS	STRENUOUS
STRAFERS	STRAMONY	STRATI	STREAKIER	STREP
STRAFES	STRAMP	STRATIFY	STREAKILY	STREPENT
STRAFF	STRAMPED	STRATONIC	STREAKING	STREPS
STRAFFED	STRAMPING	STRATOSE	STREAKS	STRESS
STRAFFING	STRAMPS	STRATOUS	STREAKY	STRESSED
STRAFFS	STRAND	STRATUM	STREAM	STRESSES
STRAFING	STRANDED	STRATUMS	STREAMBED	STRESSFUL
STRAFINGS	STRANDER	STRATUS	STREAMED	STRESSIER
STRAG	STRANDERS	STRATUSES	STREAMER	STRESSING
STRAGGLE	STRANDING	STRAUCHT	STREAMERS	STRESSOR
STRAGGLED	STRANDS	STRAUCHTS	STREAMIER	STRESSORS
STRAGGLER	STRANG	STRAUGHT	STREAMING	STRESSY
STRAGGLES	STRANGE	STRAUGHTS	STREAMLET	STRETCH
STRAGGLY	STRANGELY	STRAUNGE	STRFAMS	STRETCHED
STRAGS	STRANGER	STRAVAGE	STREAMY	STRETCHER
STRAICHT	STRANGERS	STRAVAGED	STREEK	STRETCHES
STRAIGHT	STRANGES	STRAVAGES	STREEKED	STRETCHY
STRAIGHTS	STRANGEST	STRAVAIG	STREEKER	STRETTA
STRAIK	STRANGLE	STRAVAIGS	STREEKERS	STRETTAS
STRAIKED	STRANGLED	STRAW	STREEKING	STRETTE
STRAIKING	STRANGLER	STRAWED	STREEKS	STRETTI
STRAIKS	STRANGLES	STRAWEN	STREEL	STRETTO
STRAIN	STRANGURY	STRAWHAT	STREELED	STRETTOS
STRAINED	STRAP	STRAWIER	STREELING	STREUSEL

S

STREUSELS	STRIDER	STRINKLED	STRODDLE	STRONTIUM
STREW	STRIDERS	STRINKLES	STRODDLED	STROOK
STREWAGE	STRIDES	STRIP	STRODDLES	STROOKE
STREWAGES	STRIDING	STRIPE	STRODE	STROOKEN
STREWED	STRIDLING	STRIPED	STRODLE	STROOKES
STREWER	STRIDOR	STRIPER	STRODLED	STROP
STREWERS	STRIDORS	STRIPERS	STRODLES	STROPHE
STREWING	STRIFE	STRIPES	STRODLING	STROPHES
STREWINGS	STRIFEFUL	STRIPEY	STROKABLE	STROPHIC
STREWMENT	STRIFES	STRIPIER	STROKE	STROPHOID
STREWN	STRIFT	STRIPIEST	STROKED	STROPHULI
STREWS	STRIFTS	STRIPING	STROKEN	STROPPED
STREWTH	STRIG	STRIPINGS	STROKER	STROPPER
STRIA	STRIGA	STRIPLING	STROKERS	STROPPERS
STRIAE	STRIGAE	STRIPPED	STROKES	STROPPIER
STRIATA	STRIGATE	STRIPPER	STROKING	STROPPILY
STRIATAL	STRIGGED	STRIPPERS	STROKINGS	STROPPING
STRIATE	STRIGGING	STRIPPING	STROLL	STROPPY
STRIATED	STRIGIL	STRIPS	STROLLED	STROPS
STRIATES	STRIGILS	STRIPT	STROLLER	STROSSERS
STRIATING	STRIGINE	STRIPY	STROLLERS	STROUD
STRIATION	STRIGOSE	STRIVE	STROLLING	STROUDING
STRIATUM	STRIGS	STRIVED	STROLLS	STROUDS
STRIATUMS	STRIKABLE	STRIVEN	STROMA	STROUP
STRIATURE	STRIKE	STRIVER	STROMAL	STROUPACH
STRICH	STRIKEOUT	STRIVERS	STROMATA	STROUPAN
STRICHES	STRIKER	STRIVES	STROMATIC	STROUPANS
STRICK	STRIKERS	STRIVING	STROMB	STROUPS
STRICKEN	STRIKES	STRIVINGS	STROMBS	STROUT
STRICKLE	STRIKING	STROAM	STROMBUS	STROUTED
STRICKLED	STRIKINGS	STROAMED	STROND	STROUTING
STRICKLES	STRIM	STROAMING	STRONDS	STROUTS
STRICKS	STRIMMED	STROAMS	STRONG	STROVE
STRICT	STRIMMING	STROBE	STRONGARM	STROW
STRICTER	STRIMS	STROBED	STRONGBOX	STROWED
STRICTEST	STRINE	STROBES	STRONGER	STROWER
STRICTION	STRINES	STROBIC	STRONGEST	STROWERS
STRICTISH	STRING	STROBIL	STRONGISH	STROWING
STRICTLY	STRINGED	STROBILA	STRONGLY	STROWINGS
STRICTURE	STRINGENT	STROBILAE	STRONGMAN	STROWN
STRIDDEN	STRINGER	STROBILAR	STRONGMEN	STROWS
STRIDDLE	STRINGERS	STROBILE	STRONGYL	STROY
STRIDDLED	STRINGIER	STROBILES	STRONGYLE	STROYED
STRIDDLES	STRINGILY	STROBILI	STRONGYLS	STROYER
STRIDE	STRINGING	STROBILS	STRONTIA	STROYERS
STRIDENCE	STRINGS	STROBILUS	STRONTIAN	STROYING
STRIDENCY	STRINGY	STROBING	STRONTIAS	STROYS
STRIDENT	STRINKLE	STROBINGS	STRONTIC	STRUCK

STRUCKEN	STUBBLES	STUDS	STUMPER	STUPOROUS
STRUCTURE	STUBBLIER	STUDWORK	STUMPERS	STUPORS
STRUDEL	STUBBLY	STUDWORKS	STUMPIER	STUPRATE
STRUDELS	STUBBORN	STUDY	STUMPIES	STUPRATED
STRUGGLE	STUBBORNS	STUDYING	STUMPIEST	STUPRATES
STRUGGLED	STUBBY	STUFF	STUMPILY	STURDIED
STRUGGLER	STUBS	STUFFED	STUMPING	STURDIER
STRUGGLES	STUCCO	STUFFER	STUMPINGS	STURDIES
STRUM	STUCCOED	STUFFERS	STUMPS	STURDIEST
STRUMA	STUCCOER	STUFFIER	STUMPWORK	STURDILY
STRUMAE	STUCCOERS	STUFFIEST	STUMPY	STURDY
STRUMAS	STUCCOES	STUFFILY	STUMS	STURE
STRUMATIC	STUCCOING	STUFFING	STUN	STURGEON
STRUMITIS	STUCCOS	STUFFINGS	STUNG	STURGEONS
STRUMMED	STUCK	STUFFLESS	STUNK	STURMER
STRUMMEL	STUCKS	STUFFS	STUNKARD	STURMERS
STRUMMELS	STUD	STUFFY	STUNNED	STURNINE
STRUMMER	STUDBOOK	STUGGIER	STUNNER	STURNOID
STRUMMERS	STUDBOOKS	STUGGIEST	STUNNERS	STURNUS
STRUMMING	STUDDED	STUGGY	STUNNING	STURNUSES
STRUMOSE	STUDDEN	STUIVER	STUNNINGS	STURT
STRUMOUS	STUDDIE	STUIVERS	STUNS	STURTED
STRUMPET	STUDDIES	STUKKEND	STUNSAIL	STURTING
STRUMPETS	STUDDING	STULL	STUNSAILS	STURTS
STRUMS	STUDDINGS	STULLS	STUNT	STUSHIE
STRUNG	STUDDLE	STULM	STUNTED	STUSHIES
STRUNT	STUDDLES	STULMS	STUNTING	STUTTER
STRUNTED	STUDE	STULTIFY	STUNTMAN	STUTTERED
STRUNTING	STUDENT	STUM	STUNTMEN	STUTTERER
STRUNTS	STUDENTRY	STUMBLE	STUNTS	STUTTERS
STRUT	STUDENTS	STUMBLED	STUPA	STY
STRUTS	STUDENTY	STUMBLER	STUPAS	STYE
STRUTTED	STUDFARM	STUMBLERS	STUPE	STYED
STRUTTER	STUDFARMS	STUMBLES	STUPED	STYES
STRUTTERS	STUDFISH	STUMBLIER	STUPEFIED	STYGIAN
STRUTTING	STUDHORSE	STUMBLING	STUPEFIER	STYING
STRYCHNIA	STUDIED	STUMBLY	STUPEFIES	STYLAR
STRYCHNIC	STUDIEDLY	STUMER	STUPEFY	STYLATE
STUB	STUDIER	STUMERS	STUPENT	STYLE
STUBBED	STUDIERS	STUMM	STUPES	STYLEBOOK
STUBBIE	STUDIES	STUMMED	STUPID	STYLED
STUBBIER	STUDIO	STUMMEL	STUPIDER	STYLEE
STUBBIES	STUDIOS	STUMMELS	STUPIDEST	STYLEES
STUBBIEST	STUDIOUS	STUMMING	STUPIDITY	STYLELESS
STUBBILY	STUDLIER	STUMP	STUPIDLY	STYLER
STUBBING	STUDLIEST	STUMPAGE	STUPIDS	STYLERS
STUBBLE	STUDLIKE	STUMPAGES	STUPING	STYLES
STUBBLED	STUDLY	STUMPED	STUPOR	STYLET

S

STYLETS	STYMIEING	SUBACTING	SUBBLOCKS	SUBCUTES
STYLI	STYMIES	SUBACTION	SUBBRANCH	SUBCUTIS
STYLIE	STYMING	SUBACTS	SUBBREED	SUBDEACON
STYLIER	STYMY	SUBACUTE	SUBBREEDS	SUBDEALER
STYLIEST	STYMYING	SUBADAR	SUBBUREAU	SUBDEAN
STYLIFORM	STYPSIS	SUBADARS	SUBBY	SUBDEANS
STYLING	STYPSISES	SUBADULT	SUBCANTOR	SUBDEB
STYLINGS	STYPTIC	SUBADULTS	SUBCASTE	SUBDEBS
STYLISE	STYPTICAL	SUBAERIAL	SUBCASTES	SUBDEPOT
STYLISED	STYPTICS	SUBAGENCY	SUBCAUDAL	SUBDEPOTS
STYLISER	STYRAX	SUBAGENT	SUBCAUSE	SUBDEPUTY
STYLISERS	STYRAXES	SUBAGENTS	SUBCAUSES	SUBDERMAL
STYLISES	STYRE	SUBAH	SUBCAVITY	SUBDEW
STYLISH	STYRED	SUBAHDAR	SUBCELL	SUBDEWED
STYLISHLY	STYRENE	SUBAHDARS	SUBCELLAR	SUBDEWING
STYLISING	STYRENES	SUBAHDARY	SUBCELLS	SUBDEWS
STYLIST	STYRES	SUBAHS	SUBCENTER	SUBDIVIDE
STYLISTIC	STYRING	SUBAHSHIP	SUBCENTRE	SUBDOLOUS
STYLISTS	STYROFOAM	SUBALAR	SUBCHASER	SUBDORSAL
STYLITE	STYTE	SUBALPINE	SUBCHIEF	SUBDUABLE
STYLITES	STYTED	SUBALTERN	SUBCHIEFS	SUBDUABLY
STYLITIC	STYTES	SUBAPICAL	SUBCHORD	SUBDUAL
STYLITISM	STYTING	SUBAQUA	SUBCHORDS	SUBDUALS
STYLIZE	SUABILITY	SUBARCTIC	SUBCLAIM	SUBDUCE
STYLIZED	SUABLE	SUBAREA	SUBCLAIMS	SUBDUCED
STYLIZER	SUABLY	SUBAREAS	SUBCLAN	SUBDUCES
STYLIZERS	SUASIBLE	SUBARID	SUBCLANS	SUBDUCING
STYLIZES	SUASION	SUBAS	SUBCLASS	SUBDUCT
STYLIZING	SUASIONS	SUBASTRAL	SUBCLAUSE	SUBDUCTED
STYLO	SUASIVE	SUBATOM	SUBCLERK	SUBDUCTS
STYLOBATE	SUASIVELY	SUBATOMIC	SUBCLERKS	SUBDUE
STYLOID	SUASORY	SUBATOMS	SUBCLIMAX	SUBDUED
STYLOIDS	SUAVE	SUBAUDIO	SUBCODE	SUBDUEDLY
STYLOLITE	SUAVELY	SUBAURAL	SUBCODES	SUBDUER
STYLOPES	SUAVENESS	SUBAXIAL	SUBCOLONY	SUBDUERS
STYLOPID	SUAVER	SUBBASAL	SUBCONSUL	SUBDUES
STYLOPIDS	SUAVEST	SUBBASE	SUBCOOL	SUBDUING
STYLOPISE	SUAVITIES	SUBBASES	SUBCOOLED	SUBDUPLE
STYLOPIZE	SUAVITY	SUBBASIN	SUBCOOLS	SUBDURAL
STYLOPS	SUB	SUBBASINS	SUBCORTEX	SUBDWARF
STYLOS	SUBA	SUBBASS	SUBCOSTA	SUBDWARFS
STYLUS	SUBABBOT	SUBBASSES	SUBCOSTAE	SUBECHO
STYLUSES	SUBABBOTS	SUBBED	SUBCOSTAL	SUBECHOES
STYME	SUBACID	SUBBIE	SUBCOUNTY	SUBEDAR
STYMED	SUBACIDLY	SUBBIES	SUBCRUST	SUBEDARS
STYMES	SUBACRID	SUBBING	SUBCRUSTS	SUBEDIT
STYMIE	SUBACT	SUBBINGS	SUBCULT	SUBEDITED
STYMIED	SUBACTED	SUBBLOCK	SUBCULTS	SUBEDITOR

S

SUBEDITS	SUBGENUS	SUBLEASE	SUBMERSED	SUBPENAED
SUBENTIRE	SUBGOAL	SUBLEASED	SUBMERSES	SUBPENAS
SUBENTRY	SUBGOALS	SUBLEASES	SUBMICRON	SUBPERIOD
SUBEPOCH	SUBGRADE	SUBLESSEE	SUBMISS	SUBPHASE
SUBEPOCHS	SUBGRADES	SUBLESSOR	SUBMISSLY	SUBPHASES
SUBEQUAL	SUBGRAPH	SUBLET	SUBMIT	SUBPHYLA
SUBER	SUBGRAPHS	SUBLETHAL	SUBMITS	SUBPHYLAR
SUBERATE	SUBGROUP	SUBLETS	SUBMITTAL	SUBPHYLUM
SUBERATES	SUBGROUPS	SUBLETTER	SUBMITTED	SUBPLOT
SUBERECT	SUBGUM	SUBLEVEL	SUBMITTER	SUBPLOTS
SUBEREOUS	SUBGUMS	SUBLEVELS	SUBMUCOSA	SUBPOENA
SUBERIC	SUBHA	SUBLIMATE	SUBMUCOUS	SUBPOENAS
SUBERIN	SUBHAS	SUBLIME	SUBNASAL	SUBPOLAR
SUBERINS	SUBHEAD	SUBLIMED	SUBNET	SUBPOTENT
SUBERISE	SUBHEADS	SUBLIMELY	SUBNETS	SUBPRIME
SUBERISED	SUBHEDRAL	SUBLIMER	SUBNEURAL	SUBPRIMES
SUBERISES	SUBHUMAN	SUBLIMERS	SUBNICHE	SUBPRIOR
SUBERIZE	SUBHUMANS	SUBLIMES	SUBNICHES	SUBPRIORS
SUBERIZED	SUBHUMID	SUBLIMEST	SUBNIVEAL	SUBPUBIC
SUBERIZES	SUBIDEA	SUBLIMING	SUBNIVEAN	SUBRACE
SUBEROSE	SUBIDEAS	SUBLIMISE	SUBNODAL	SUBRACES
SUBEROUS	SUBIMAGO	SUBLIMIT	SUBNORMAL	SUBREGION
SUBERS	SUBIMAGOS	SUBLIMITS	SUBNUCLEI	SUBRENT
SUBFAMILY	SUBINCISE	SUBLIMITY	SUBOCEAN	SUBRENTED
SUBFEU	SUBINDEX	SUBLIMIZE	SUBOCTAVE	SUBRENTS
SUBFEUED	SUBINFEUD	SUBLINE	SUBOCULAR	SUBRING
SUBFEUING	SUBITEM	SUBLINEAR	SUBOFFICE	SUBRINGS
SUBFEUS	SUBITEMS	SUBLINES	SUBOPTIC	SUBROGATE
SUBFIELD	SUBITISE	SUBLOT	SUBORAL	SUBRULE
SUBFIELDS	SUBITISED	SUBLOTS	SUBORDER	SUBRULES
SUBFILE	SUBITISES	SUBLUNAR	SUBORDERS	SUBS
SUBFILES	SUBITIZE	SUBLUNARY	SUBORN	SUBSACRAL
SUBFIX	SUBITIZED	SUBLUNATE	SUBORNED	SUBSALE
SUBFIXES	SUBITIZES	SUBLUXATE	SUBORNER	SUBSALES
SUBFLOOR	SUBITO	SUBMAN	SUBORNERS	SUBSAMPLE
SUBFLOORS	SUBJACENT	SUBMARINE	SUBORNING	SUBSCALE
SUBFLUID	SUBJECT	SUBMARKET	SUBORNS	SUBSCALES
SUBFOLDER	SUBJECTED	SUBMATRIX	SUBOSCINE	SUBSCHEMA
SUBFOSSIL	SUBJECTS	SUBMEN	SUBOVAL	SUBSCRIBE
SUBFRAME	SUBJOIN	SUBMENTA	SUBOVATE	SUBSCRIPT
SUBFRAMES	SUBJOINED	SUBMENTAL	SUBOXIDE	SUBSEA
SUBFUSC	SUBJOINS	SUBMENTUM	SUBOXIDES	SUBSECIVE
SUBFUSCS	SUBJUGATE	SUBMENU	SUBPANEL	SUBSECT
SUBFUSK	SUBLATE	SUBMENUS	SUBPANELS	SUBSECTOR
SUBFUSKS	SUBLATED	SUBMERGE	SUBPAR	SUBSECTS
SUBGENERA	SUBLATES	SUBMERGED	SUBPART	SUBSELLIA
SUBGENRE	SUBLATING	SUBMERGES	SUBPARTS	SUBSENSE
SUBGENRES	SUBLATION	SUBMERSE	SUBPENA	SUBSENSES

S

SUBSERE	SUBSTATE	SUBTILISE	SUBURB	SUCCEEDER
SUBSERES	SUBSTATES	SUBTILITY	SUBURBAN	SUCCEEDS
SUBSERIES	SUBSTORM	SUBTILIZE	SUBURBANS	SUCCENTOR
SUBSERVE	SUBSTORMS	SUBTILTY	SUBURBED	SUCCES
SUBSERVED	SUBSTRACT	SUBTITLE	SUBURBIA	SUCCESS
SUBSERVES	SUBSTRATA	SUBTITLED	SUBURBIAS	SUCCESSES
SUBSET	SUBSTRATE	SUBTITLES	SUBURBS	SUCCESSOR
SUBSETS	SUBSTRUCT	SUBTLE	SUBURSINE	SUCCI
SUBSHAFT	SUBSTYLAR	SUBTLER	SUBVASSAL	SUCCINATE
SUBSHAFTS	SUBSTYLE	SUBTLEST	SUBVENE	SUCCINCT
SUBSHELL	SUBSTYLES	SUBTLETY	SUBVENED	SUCCINIC
SUBSHELLS	SUBSULTUS	SUBTLY	SUBVENES	SUCCINITE
SUBSHRUB	SUBSUME	SUBTONE	SUBVENING	SUCCINYL
SUBSHRUBS	SUBSUMED	SUBTONES	SUBVERSAL	SUCCINYLS
SUBSIDE	SUBSUMES	SUBTONIC	SUBVERSE	SUCCISE
SUBSIDED	SUBSUMING	SUBTONICS	SUBVERSED	SUCCOR
SUBSIDER	SUBSYSTEM	SUBTOPIA	SUBVERSES	SUCCORED
SUBSIDERS	SUBTACK	SUBTOPIAN	SUBVERST	SUCCORER
SUBSIDES	SUBTACKS	SUBTOPIAS	SUBVERT	SUCCORERS
SUBSIDIES	SUBTALAR	SUBTOPIC	SUBVERTED	SUCCORIES
SUBSIDING	SUBTASK	SUBTOPICS	SUBVERTER	SUCCORING
SUBSIDISE	SUBTASKS	SUBTORRID	SUBVERTS	SUCCORS
SUBSIDIZE	SUBTAXA	SUBTOTAL	SUBVICAR	SUCCORY
SUBSIDY	SUBTAXON	SUBTOTALS	SUBVICARS	SUCCOS
SUBSIST	SUBTAXONS	SUBTRACT	SUBVIRAL	SUCCOSE
SUBSISTED	SUBTEEN	SUBTRACTS	SUBVIRUS	SUCCOT
SUBSISTER	SUBTEENS	SUBTRADE	SUBVISUAL	SUCCOTASH
SUBSISTS	SUBTENANT	SUBTRADES	SUBVOCAL	SUCCOTH
SUBSITE	SUBTEND	SUBTREND	SUBWARDEN	SUCCOUR
SUBSITES	SUBTENDED	SUBTRENDS	SUBWAY	SUCCOURED
SUBSIZAR	SUBTENDS	SUBTRIBE	SUBWAYED	SUCCOURER
SUBSIZARS	SUBTENSE	SUBTRIBES	SUBWAYING	SUCCOURS
SUBSKILL	SUBTENSES	SUBTRIST	SUBWAYS	SUCCOUS
SUBSKILLS	SUBTENURE	SUBTROPIC	SUBWOOFER	SUCCUBA
SUBSOCIAL	SUBTEST	SUBTRUDE	SUBWORLD	SUCCUBAE
SUBSOIL	SUBTESTS	SUBTRUDED	SUBWORLDS	SUCCUBAS
SUBSOILED	SUBTEXT	SUBTRUDES	SUBWRITER	SUCCUBI
SUBSOILER	SUBTEXTS	SUBTUNIC	SUBZERO	SUCCUBINE
SUBSOILS	SUBTHEME	SUBTUNICS	SUBZONAL	SUCCUBOUS
SUBSOLAR	SUBTHEMES	SUBTWEET	SUBZONE	SUCCUBUS
SUBSONG	SUBTIDAL	SUBTWEETS	SUBZONES	SUCCULENT
SUBSONGS	SUBTIL	SUBTYPE	SUCCADE	SUCCUMB
SUBSONIC	SUBTILE	SUBTYPES	SUCCADES	SUCCUMBED
SUBSPACE	SUBTILELY	SUBUCULA	SUCCAH	SUCCUMBER
SUBSPACES	SUBTILER	SUBUCULAS	SUCCAHS	SUCCUMBS
SUBSTAGE	SUBTILEST	SUBULATE	SUCCEDENT	SUCCURSAL
SUBSTAGES	SUBTILIN	SUBUNIT	SUCCEED	SUCCUS
SUBSTANCE	SUBTILINS	SUBUNITS	SUCCEEDED	SUCCUSS

S

SUCCUSSED	SUCTIONAL	SUDSY	SUFFIXION	SUGS
SUCCUSSES	SUCTIONED	SUE	SUFFLATE	SUHUR
SUCH	SUCTIONS	SUEABLE	SUFFLATED	SUHURS
SUCHLIKE	SUCTORIAL	SUED	SUFFLATES	SUI
SUCHLIKES	SUCTORIAN	SUEDE	SUFFOCATE	SUICIDAL
SUCHNESS	SUCURUJU	SUEDED	SUFFRAGAN	SUICIDE
SUCHWISE	SUCURUJUS	SUEDELIKE	SUFFRAGE	SUICIDED
SUCK	SUD	SUEDES	SUFFRAGES	SUICIDES
SUCKED	SUDAMEN	SUEDETTE	SUFFUSE	SUICIDING
SUCKEN	SUDAMENS	SUEDETTES	SUFFUSED	SUID
SUCKENER	SUDAMINA	SUEDING	SUFFUSES	SUIDIAN
SUCKENERS	SUDAMINAL	SUENT	SUFFUSING	SUIDIANS
SUCKENS	SUDARIA	SUER	SUFFUSION	SUIDS
SUCKER	SUDARIES	SUERS	SUFFUSIVE	SUILLINE
SUCKERED	SUDARIUM	SUES	SUG	SUING
SUCKERING	SUDARY	SUET	SUGAN	SUINGS
SUCKERS	SUDATE	SUETE	SUGANS	SUINT
SUCKET	SUDATED	SUETES	SUGAR	SUINTS
SUCKETS	SUDATES	SUETIER	SUGARALLY	SUIPLAP
SUCKFISH	SUDATING	SUETIEST	SUGARBUSH	SUIPLAPS
SUCKHOLE	SUDATION	SUETS	SUGARCANE	SUIT
SUCKHOLED	SUDATIONS	SUETTIER	SUGARCOAT	SUITABLE
SUCKHOLES	SUDATORIA	SUETTIEST	SUGARED	SUITABLY
SUCKIER	SUDATORY	SUETTY	SUGARER	SUITCASE
SUCKIEST	SUDD	SUETY	SUGARERS	SUITCASES
SUCKINESS	SUDDEN	SUFFARI	SUGARIER	SUITE
SUCKING	SUDDENLY	SUFFARIS	SUGARIEST	SUITED
SUCKINGS	SUDDENS	SUFFECT	SUGARING	SUITER
SUCKLE	SUDDENTY	SUFFECTS	SUGARINGS	SUITERS
SUCKLED	SUDDER	SUFFER	SUGARLESS	SUITES
SUCKLER	SUDDERS	SUFFERED	SUGARLIKE	SUITING
SUCKLERS	SUDDS	SUFFERER	SUGARLOAF	SUITINGS
SUCKLES	SUDOKU	SUFFERERS	SUGARPLUM	SUITLIKE
SUCKLESS	SUDOKUS	SUFFERING	SUGARS	SUITOR
SUCKLING	SUDOR	SUFFERS	SUGARY	SUITORED
SUCKLINGS	SUDORAL	SUFFETE	SUGGED	SUITORING
SUCKS	SUDORIFIC	SUFFETES	SUGGEST	SUITORS
SUCKY	SUDOROUS	SUFFICE	SUGGESTED	SUITRESS
SUCRALOSE	SUDORS	SUFFICED	SUGGESTER	SUITS
SUCRASE	SUDS	SUFFICER	SUGGESTS	SUIVANTE
SUCRASES	SUDSED	SUFFICERS	SUGGING	SUIVANTES
SUCRE	SUDSER	SUFFICES	SUGGINGS	SUIVEZ
SUCRES	SUDSERS	SUFFICING	SUGH	SUJEE
SUCRIER	SUDSES	SUFFIX	SUGHED	SUJEES
SUCRIERS	SUDSIER	SUFFIXAL	SUGHING	SUK
SUCROSE	SUDSIEST	SUFFIXED	SUGHS	SUKH
SUCROSES	SUDSING	SUFFIXES	SUGO	SUKHS
SUCTION	SUDSLESS	SUFFIXING	SUGOS	SUKIYAKI

S

SUKIYAKIS	SULFURED	SULPHINYL	SUMMARISE	SUMPH
SUKKAH	SULFURET	SULPHITE	SUMMARIST	SUMPHISH
SUKKAHS	SULFURETS	SULPHITES	SUMMARIZE	SUMPHS
SUKKOS	SULFURIC	SULPHITIC	SUMMARY	SUMPIT
SUKKOT	SULFURIER	SULPHONE	SUMMAS	SUMPITAN
SUKKOTH	SULFURING	SULPHONES	SUMMAT	SUMPITANS
SUKS	SULFURISE	SULPHONIC	SUMMATE	SUMPITS
SUKUK	SULFURIZE	SULPHONYL	SUMMATED	SUMPS
SUKUKS	SULFUROUS	SULPHS	SUMMATES	SUMPSIMUS
SULCAL	SULFURS	SULPHUR	SUMMATING	SUMPTER
SULCALISE	SULFURY	SULPHURED	SUMMATION	SUMPTERS
SULCALIZE	SULFURYL	SULPHURET	SUMMATIVE	SUMPTUARY
SULCATE	SULFURYLS	SULPHURIC	SUMMATS	SUMPTUOUS
SULCATED	SULK	SULPHURS	SUMMED	SUMPWEED
SULCATION	SULKED	SULPHURY	SUMMER	SUMPWEEDS
SULCI	SULKER	SULPHURYL	SUMMERED	SUMS
SULCUS	SULKERS	SULTAN	SUMMERIER	SUMY
SULDAN	SULKIER	SULTANA	SUMMERING	SUN
SULDANS	SULKIES	SULTANAS	SUMMERLY	SUNBACK
SULFA	SULKIEST	SULTANATE	SUMMERS	SUNBAKE
SULFAS	SULKILY	SULTANESS	SUMMERSET	SUNBAKED
SULFATASE	SULKINESS	SULTANIC	SUMMERY	SUNBAKES
SULFATE	SULKING	SULTANS	SUMMING	SUNBAKING
SULFATED	SULKS	SULTRIER	SUMMINGS	SUNBATH
SULFATES	SULKY	SULTRIEST	SUMMIST	SUNBATHE
SULFATIC	SULLAGE	SULTRILY	SUMMISTS	SUNBATHED
SULFATING	SULLAGES	SULTRY	SUMMIT	SUNBATHER
SULFATION	SULLEN	SULU	SUMMITAL	SUNBATHES
SULFID	SULLENER	SULUS	SUMMITED	SUNBATHS
SULFIDE	SULLENEST	SUM	SUMMITEER	SUNBEAM
SULFIDES	SULLENLY	SUMAC	SUMMITING	SUNBEAMED
SULFIDS	SULLENS	SUMACH	SUMMITRY	SUNBEAMS
SULFINYL	SULLIABLE	SUMACHS	SUMMITS	SUNBEAMY
SULFINYLS	SULLIED	SUMACS	SUMMON	SUNBEAT
SULFITE	SULLIES	SUMATRA	SUMMONED	SUNBEATEN
SULFITES	SULLY	SUMATRAS	SUMMONER	SUNBED
SULFITIC	SULLYING	SUMBITCH	SUMMONERS	SUNBEDS
SULFO	SULPH	SUMI	SUMMONING	SUNBELT
SULFONATE	SULPHA	SUMIS	SUMMONS	SUNBELTS
SULFONE	SULPHAS	SUMLESS	SUMMONSED	SUNBERRY
SULFONES	SULPHATE	SUMMA	SUMMONSES	SUNBIRD
SULFONIC	SULPHATED	SUMMABLE	SUMO	SUNBIRDS
SULFONIUM	SULPHATES	SUMMAE	SUMOIST	SUNBLIND
SULFONYL	SULPHATIC	SUMMAND	SUMOISTS	SUNBLINDS
SULFONYLS	SULPHID	SUMMANDS	SUMOS	SUNBLOCK
SULFOXIDE	SULPHIDE	SUMMAR	SUMOTORI	SUNBLOCKS
SULFUR	SULPHIDES	SUMMARIES	SUMOTORIS	SUNBONNET
SULFURATE	SULPHIDS	SUMMARILY	SUMP	SUNBOW

SUNBOWS	SUNGAR	SUNPROOF	SUPER	SUPERFIX
SUNBRIGHT	SUNGARS	SUNRAY	SUPERABLE	SUPERFLUX
SUNBURN	SUNGAZER	SUNRAYS	SUPERABLY	SUPERFLY
SUNBURNED	SUNGAZERS	SUNRISE	SUPERADD	SUPERFOOD
SUNBURNS	SUNGAZING	SUNRISES	SUPERADDS	SUPERFUND
SUNBURNT	SUNGLASS	SUNRISING	SUPERATE	SUPERFUSE
SUNBURST	SUNGLOW	SUNROOF	SUPERATED	SUPERGENE
SUNBURSTS	SUNGLOWS	SUNROOFS	SUPERATES	SUPERGLUE
SUNCARE	SUNGREBE	SUNROOM	SUPERATOM	SUPERGOOD
SUNCARES	SUNGREBES	SUNROOMS	SUPERB	SUPERGUN
SUNCHOKE	SUNHAT	SUNS	SUPERBAD	SUPERGUNS
SUNCHOKES	SUNHATS	SUNSCALD	SUPERBANK	SUPERHARD
SUNDAE	SUNI	SUNSCALDS	SUPERBER	SUPERHEAT
SUNDAES	SUNIS	SUNSCREEN	SUPERBEST	SUPERHERO
SUNDARI	SUNK	SUNSEEKER	SUPERBIKE	SUPERHET
SUNDARIS	SUNKEN	SUNSET	SUPERBITY	SUPERHETS
SUNDECK	SUNKER	SUNSETS	SUPERBLY	SUPERHIGH
SUNDECKS	SUNKERS	SUNSETTED	SUPERBOLD	SUPERHIT
SUNDER	SUNKET	SUNSHADE	SUPERBOMB	SUPERHITS
SUNDERED	SUNKETS	SUNSHADES	SUPERBRAT	SUPERHIVE
SUNDERER	SUNKIE	SUNSHINE	SUPERBUG	SUPERHOT
SUNDERERS	SUNKIES	SUNSHINES	SUPERBUGS	SUPERHYPE
SUNDERING	SUNKS	SUNSHINY	SUPERCAR	SUPERING
SUNDERS	SUNLAMP	SUNSPECS	SUPERCARS	SUPERIOR
SUNDEW	SUNLAMPS	SUNSPOT	SUPERCEDE	SUPERIORS
SUNDEWS	SUNLAND	SUNSPOTS	SUPERCELL	SUPERJET
SUNDIAL	SUNLANDS	SUNSTAR	SUPERCHIC	SUPERJETS
SUNDIALS	SUNLESS	SUNSTARS	SUPERCITY	SUPERJOCK
SUNDOG	SUNLESSLY	SUNSTONE	SUPERCLUB	SUPERLAIN
SUNDOGS	SUNLIGHT	SUNSTONES	SUPERCOIL	SUPERLAY
SUNDOWN	SUNLIGHTS	SUNSTROKE	SUPERCOLD	SUPERLIE
SUNDOWNED	SUNLIKE	SUNSTRUCK	SUPERCOOL	SUPERLIES
SUNDOWNER	SUNLIT	SUNSUIT	SUPERCOP	SUPERLOAD
SUNDOWNS	SUNN	SUNSUITS	SUPERCOPS	SUPERLONG
SUNDRA	SUNNA	SUNTAN	SUPERCOW	SUPERLOO
SUNDRAS	SUNNAH	SUNTANNED	SUPERCOWS	SUPERLOOS
SUNDRESS	SUNNAHS	SUNTANS	SUPERCUTE	SUPERMALE
SUNDRI	SUNNAS	SUNTRAP	SUPERFD	SUPERMAN
SUNDRIES	SUNNED	SUNTRAPS	SUPEREGO	SUPERMART
SUNDRILY	SUNNIER	SUNUP	SUPEREGOS	SUPERMAX
SUNDRIS	SUNNIES	SUNUPS	SUPERETTE	SUPERMEN
SUNDROPS	SUNNIEST	SUNWARD	SUPERFAN	SUPERMIND
SUNDRY	SUNNILY	SUNWARDS	SUPERFANS	SUPERMINI
SUNFAST	SUNNINESS	SUNWISE	SUPERFARM	SUPERMOM
SUNFISH	SUNNING	SUP	SUPERFAST	SUPERMOMS
SUNFISHES	SUNNS	SUPAWN	SUPERFINE	SUPERMOON
SUNFLOWER	SUNNY	SUPAWNS	SUPERFIRM	SUPERMOTO
SUNG	SUNPORCH	SUPE	SUPERFIT	SUPERNAL

S

SUPERNATE	SUPLEX	SUPREMELY	SURDITIES	SURFRIDER
SUPERNOVA	SUPLEXES	SUPREMER	SURDITY	SURFRIDES
SUPERPIMP	SUPPAWN	SUPREMES	SURDS	SURFRODE
SUPERPLUS	SUPPAWNS	SUPREMEST	SURE	SURFS
SUPERPORT	SUPPEAGO	SUPREMITY	SURED	SURFSIDE
SUPERPOSE	SUPPED	SUPREMO	SUREFIRE	SURFY
SUPERPRO	SUPPER	SUPREMOS	SURELY	SURGE
SUPERPROS	SUPPERED	SUPREMUM	SURENESS	SURGED
SUPERRACE	SUPPERING	SUPREMUMS	SURER	SURGEFUL
SUPERREAL	SUPPERS	SUPS	SURES	SURGELESS
SUPERRICH	SUPPING	SUQ	SUREST	SURGENT
SUPERROAD	SUPPLANT	SUQS	SURETIED	SURGEON
SUPERS	SUPPLANTS	SUR	SURETIES	SURGEONCY
SUPERSAFE	SUPPLE	SURA	SURETY	SURGEONS
SUPERSALE	SUPPLED	SURAH	SURETYING	SURGER
SUPERSALT	SUPPLELY	SURAHS	SURF	SURGERIES
SUPERSAUR	SUPPLER	SURAL	SURFABLE	SURGERS
SUPERSEDE	SUPPLES	SURAMIN	SURFACE	SURGERY
SUPERSELL	SUPPLEST	SURAMINS	SURFACED	SURGES
SUPERSET	SUPPLIAL	SURANCE	SURFACER	SURGICAL
SUPERSETS	SUPPLIALS	SURANCES	SURFACERS	SURGIER
SUPERSEX	SUPPLIANT	SURAS	SURFACES	SURGIEST
SUPERSHOW	SUPPLICAT	SURAT	SURFACING	SURGING
SUPERSIZE	SUPPLIED	SURATS	SURFBIRD	SURGINGS
SUPERSOFT	SUPPLIER	SURBAHAR	SURFBIRDS	SURGY
SUPERSOLD	SUPPLIERS	SURBAHARS	SURFBOARD	SURICATE
SUPERSPY	SUPPLIES	SURBASE	SURFBOAT	SURICATES
SUPERSTAR	SUPPLING	SURBASED	SURFBOATS	SURIMI
SUPERSTUD	SUPPLY	SURBASES	SURFED	SURIMIS
SUPERTAX	SUPPLYING	SURBATE	SURFEIT	SURING
SUPERTHIN	SUPPORT	SURBATED	SURFEITED	SURLIER
SUPERTRAM	SUPPORTED	SURBATES	SURFEITER	SURLIEST
SUPERUSER	SUPPORTER	SURBATING	SURFEITS	SURLILY
SUPERVENE	SUPPORTS	SURBED	SURFER	SURLINESS
SUPERVISE	SUPPOSAL	SURBEDDED	SURFERS	SURLOIN
SUPERWAIF	SUPPOSALS	SURBEDS	SURFFISH	SURLOINS
SUPERWAVE	SUPPOSE	SURBET	SURFICIAL	SURLY
SUPERWEED	SUPPOSED	SURCEASE	SURFIE	SURMASTER
SUPERWIDE	SUPPOSER	SURCEASED	SURFIER	SURMISAL
SUPERWIFE	SUPPOSERS	SURCEASES	SURFIES	SURMISALS
SUPES	SUPPOSES	SURCHARGE	SURFIEST	SURMISE
SUPINATE	SUPPOSING	SURCINGLE	SURFING	SURMISED
SUPINATED	SUPPRESS	SURCOAT	SURFINGS	SURMISER
SUPINATES	SUPPURATE	SURCOATS	SURFLIKE	SURMISERS
SUPINATOR	SUPRA	SURCULI	SURFMAN	SURMISES
SUPINE	SUPREMA	SURCULOSE	SURFMEN	SURMISING
SUPINELY	SUPREMACY	SURCULUS	SURFPERCH	SURMOUNT
SUPINES	SUPREME	SURD	SURFRIDE	SURMOUNTS

S

SURMULLET	SURTAX	SUSPECTS	SUTTLED	SWAG
SURNAME	SURTAXED	SUSPENCE	SUTTLES	SWAGE
SURNAMED	SURTAXES	SUSPEND	SUTTLETIE	SWAGED
SURNAMER	SURTAXING	SUSPENDED	SUTTLING	SWAGER
SURNAMERS	SURTITLE	SUSPENDER	SUTTLY	SWAGERS
SURNAMES	SURTITLES	SUSPENDS	SUTURAL	SWAGES
SURNAMING	SURTOUT	SUSPENS	SUTURALLY	SWAGGED
SURPASS	SURTOUTS	SUSPENSE	SUTURE	SWAGGER
SURPASSED	SURUCUCU	SUSPENSER	SUTURED	SWAGGERED
SURPASSER	SURUCUCUS	SUSPENSES	SUTURES	SWAGGERER
SURPASSES	SURVEIL	SUSPENSOR	SUTURING	SWAGGERS
SURPLICE	SURVEILED	SUSPICION	SUZERAIN	SWAGGIE
SURPLICED	SURVEILLE	SUSPIRE	SUZERAINS	SWAGGIES
SURPLICES	SURVEILS	SUSPIRED	SVARAJ	SWAGGING
SURPLUS	SURVEY	SUSPIRES	SVARAJES	SWAGING
SURPLUSED	SURVEYAL	SUSPIRING	SVASTIKA	SWAGMAN
SURPLUSES	SURVEYALS	SUSS	SVASTIKAS	SWAGMEN
SURPRINT	SURVEYED	SUSSED	SVEDBERG	SWAGS
SURPRINTS	SURVEYING	SUSSES	SVEDBERGS	SWAGSHOP
SURPRISAL	SURVEYOR	SUSSING	SVELTE	SWAGSHOPS
SURPRISE	SURVEYORS	SUSTAIN	SVELTELY	SWAGSMAN
SURPRISED	SURVEYS	SUSTAINED	SVELTER	SWAGSMEN
SURPRISER	SURVIEW	SUSTAINER	SVELTEST	SWAIL
SURPRISES	SURVIEWED	SUSTAINS	SWAB	SWAILS
SURPRIZE	SURVIEWS	SUSTINENT	SWABBED	SWAIN
SURPRIZED	SURVIVAL	SUSU	SWABBER	SWAINING
SURPRIZES	SURVIVALS	SUSURRANT	SWABBERS	SWAININGS
SURQUEDRY	SURVIVE	SUSURRATE	SWABBIE	SWAINISH
SURQUEDY	SURVIVED	SUSURROUS	SWABBIES	SWAINS
SURRA	SURVIVER	SUSURRUS	SWABBING	SWALE
SURRAS	SURVIVERS	SUSUS	SWABBY	SWALED
SURREAL	SURVIVES	SUTILE	SWABS	SWALES
SURREALLY	SURVIVING	SUTLER	SWACHH	SWALIER
SURREALS	SURVIVOR	SUTLERIES	SWACK	SWALIEST
SURREBUT	SURVIVORS	SUTLERS	SWACKED	SWALING
SURREBUTS	SUS	SUTLERY	SWACKING	SWALINGS
SURREINED	SUSCEPTOR	SUTOR	SWACKS	SWALLET
SURREJOIN	SUSCITATE	SUTORIAL	SWAD	SWALLETS
SURRENDER	SUSED	SUTORIAN	SWADDIE	SWALLIES
SURRENDRY	SUSES	SUTORS	SWADDIES	SWALLOW
SURREY	SUSHI	SUTRA	SWADDLE	SWALLOWED
SURREYS	SUSHIS	SUTRAS	SWADDLED	SWALLOWER
SURROGACY	SUSING	SUTTA	SWADDLER	SWALLOWS
SURROGATE	SUSLIK	SUTTAS	SWADDLERS	SWALLY
SURROUND	SUSLIKS	SUTTEE	SWADDLES	SWALY
SURROUNDS	SUSPECT	SUTTEEISM	SWADDLING	SWAM
SURROYAL	SUSPECTED	SUTTEES	SWADDY	SWAMI
SURROYALS	SUSPECTER	SUTTLE	SWADS	SWAMIES

S

SWAMIS	SWANSDOWN	SWARTIEST	SWAY	SWEATS
SWAMP	SWANSKIN	SWARTNESS	SWAYABLE	SWEATSHOP
SWAMPED	SWANSKINS	SWARTY	SWAYBACK	SWEATSUIT
SWAMPER	SWANSONG	SWARVE	SWAYBACKS	SWEATY
SWAMPERS	SWANSONGS	SWARVED	SWAYED	SWEDE
SWAMPIER	SWAP	SWARVES	SWAYER	SWEDES
SWAMPIEST	SWAPFILE	SWARVING	SWAYERS	SWEDGER
SWAMPING	SWAPFILES	SWASH	SWAYFUL	SWEDGERS
SWAMPISH	SWAPPABLE	SWASHED	SWAYING	SWEE
SWAMPLAND	SWAPPED	SWASHER	SWAYINGS	SWEED
SWAMPLESS	SWAPPER	SWASHERS	SWAYL	SWEEING
SWAMPS	SWAPPERS	SWASHES	SWAYLED	SWEEL
SWAMPY	SWAPPING	SWASHIER	SWAYLING	SWEELED
SWAMY	SWAPPINGS	SWASHIEST	SWAYLINGS	SWEELING
SWAN	SWAPS	SWASHING	SWAYLS	SWEELS
SWANG	SWAPT	SWASHINGS	SWAYS	SWEENEY
SWANHERD	SWAPTION	SWASHWORK	SWAZZLE	SWEENEYS
SWANHERDS	SWAPTIONS	SWASHY	SWAZZLES	SWEENIES
SWANK	SWARAJ	SWASTICA	SWEAL	SWEENY
SWANKED	SWARAJES	SWASTICAS	SWEALED	SWEEP
SWANKER	SWARAJISM	SWASTIKA	SWEALING	SWEEPBACK
SWANKERS	SWARAJIST	SWASTIKAS	SWEALINGS	SWEEPER
SWANKEST	SWARD	SWAT	SWEALS	SWEEPERS
SWANKEY	SWARDED	SWATCH	SWEAR	SWEEPIER
SWANKEYS	SWARDIER	SWATCHES	SWEARD	SWEEPIEST
SWANKIE	SWARDIEST	SWATH	SWEARDS	SWEEPING
SWANKIER	SWARDING	SWATHABLE	SWEARER	SWEEPINGS
SWANKIES	SWARDS	SWATHE	SWEARERS	SWEEPS
SWANKIEST	SWARDY	SWATHED	SWEARIER	SWEEPY
SWANKILY	SWARE	SWATHER	SWEARIEST	SWEER
SWANKING	SWARF	SWATHERS	SWEARING	SWEERED
SWANKPOT	SWARFED	SWATHES	SWEARINGS	SWEERING
SWANKPOTS	SWARFING	SWATHIER	SWEARS	SWEERS
SWANKS	SWARFS	SWATHIEST	SWEARWORD	SWEERT
SWANKY	SWARM	SWATHING	SWEARY	SWEES
SWANLIKE	SWARMED	SWATHINGS	SWEAT	SWEET
SWANNED	SWARMER	SWATHS	SWEATBAND	SWEETCORN
SWANNERY	SWARMERS	SWATHY	SWEATBOX	SWEETED
SWANNIE	SWARMING	SWATS	SWEATED	SWEETEN
SWANNIER	SWARMINGS	SWATTED	SWEATER	SWEETENED
SWANNIES	SWARMS	SWATTER	SWEATERED	SWEETENER
SWANNIEST	SWART	SWATTERED	SWEATERS	SWEETENS
SWANNING	SWARTH	SWATTERS	SWEATIER	SWEETER
SWANNINGS	SWARTHIER	SWATTIER	SWEATIEST	SWEETEST
SWANNY	SWARTHILY	SWATTIEST	SWEATILY	SWEETFISH
SWANPAN	SWARTHS	SWATTING	SWEATING	SWEETIE
SWANPANS	SWARTHY	SWATTINGS	SWEATINGS	SWEETIES
SWANS	SWARTIER	SWATTY	SWEATLESS	SWEETING

SWEETINGS	SWELTS	SWILES	SWINGBIN	SWIPPLE
SWEETISH	SWEPT	SWILING	SWINGBINS	SWIPPLES
SWEETLIP	SWEPTBACK	SWILINGS	SWINGBOAT	SWIRE
SWEETLIPS	SWEPTWING	SWILL	SWINGBY	SWIRES
SWEETLY	SWERF	SWILLED	SWINGBYS	SWIRL
SWEETMAN	SWERFED	SWILLER	SWINGE	SWIRLED
SWEETMEAL	SWERFING	SWILLERS	SWINGED	SWIRLIER
SWEETMEAT	SWERFS	SWILLING	SWINGEING	SWIRLIEST
SWEETMEN	SWERVABLE	SWILLINGS	SWINGER	SWIRLING
SWEETNESS	SWERVE	SWILLS	SWINGERS	SWIRLS
SWEETS	SWERVED	SWIM	SWINGES	SWIRLY
SWEETSHOP	SWERVER	SWIMMABLE	SWINGIER	SWISH
SWEETSOP	SWERVERS	SWIMMER	SWINGIEST	SWISHED
SWEETSOPS	SWERVES	SWIMMERET	SWINGING	SWISHER
SWEETVELD	SWERVING	SWIMMERS	SWINGINGS	SWISHERS
SWEETWOOD	SWERVINGS	SWIMMIER	SWINGISM	SWISHES
SWEETY	SWEVEN	SWIMMIEST	SWINGISMS	SWISHEST
SWEIR	SWEVENS	SWIMMILY	SWINGLE	SWISHIER
SWEIRED	SWEY	SWIMMING	SWINGLED	SWISHIEST
SWEIRER	SWEYED	SWIMMINGS	SWINGLES	SWISHING
SWEIREST	SWEYING	SWIMMY	SWINGLING	SWISHINGS
SWEIRING	SWEYS	SWIMS	SWINGMAN	SWISHY
SWEIRNESS	SWIDDEN	SWIMSUIT	SWINGMEN	SWISS
SWEIRS	SWIDDENS	SWIMSUITS	SWINGS	SWISSES
SWEIRT	SWIES	SWIMWEAR	SWINGTAIL	SWISSING
SWELCHIE	SWIFT	SWIMWEARS	SWINGTREE	SWISSINGS
SWELCHIES	SWIFTED	SWINDGE	SWINGY	SWITCH
SWELL	SWIFTER	SWINDGED	SWINISH	SWITCHED
SWELLDOM	SWIFTERS	SWINDGES	SWINISHLY	SWITCHEL
SWELLDOMS	SWIFTEST	SWINDGING	SWINK	SWITCHELS
SWELLED	SWIFTIE	SWINDLE	SWINKED	SWITCHER
SWELLER	SWIFTIES	SWINDLED	SWINKER	SWITCHERS
SWELLERS	SWIFTING	SWINDLER	SWINKERS	SWITCHES
SWELLEST	SWIFTLET	SWINDLERS	SWINKING	SWITCHIER
SWELLFISH	SWIFTLETS	SWINDLES	SWINKS	SWITCHING
SWELLHEAD	SWIFTLY	SWINDLING	SWINNEY	SWITCHMAN
SWELLING	SWIFTNESS	SWINE	SWINNEYS	SWITCHMEN
SWELLINGS	SWIFTS	SWINEHERD	SWIPE	SWITCHY
SWELLISH	SWIFTY	SWINEHOOD	SWIPED	SWITH
SWELLS	SWIG	SWINELIKE	SWIPER	SWITHE
SWELT	SWIGGED	SWINEPOX	SWIPERS	SWITHER
SWELTED	SWIGGER	SWINERIES	SWIPES	SWITHERED
SWELTER	SWIGGERS	SWINERY	SWIPEY	SWITHERS
SWELTERED	SWIGGING	SWINES	SWIPIER	SWITHLY
SWELTERS	SWIGS	SWING	SWIPIEST	SWITS
SWELTING	SWILE	SWINGARM	SWIPING	SWITSES
SWELTRIER	SWILER	SWINGARMS	SWIPLE	SWIVE
SWELTRY	SWILERS	SWINGBEAT	SWIPLES	SWIVED

SWIVEL	SWOOPER	SWOTTY	SYCONOID	SYLPHIER
SWIVELED	SWOOPERS	SWOUN	SYCONS	SYLPHIEST
SWIVELING	SWOOPIER	SWOUND	SYCOPHANT	SYLPHINE
SWIVELLED	SWOOPIEST	SWOUNDED	SYCOSES	SYLPHISH
SWIVELS	SWOOPING	SWOUNDING	SYCOSIS	SYLPHLIKE
SWIVES	SWOOPS	SWOUNDS	SYE	SYLPHS
SWIVET	SWOOPY	SWOUNE	SYED	SYLPHY
SWIVETS	SWOOSH	SWOUNED	SYEING	SYLVA
SWIVING	SWOOSHED	SWOUNES	SYEN	SYLVAE
SWIZ	SWOOSHES	SWOUNING	SYENITE	SYLVAN
SWIZZ	SWOOSHING	SWOUNS	SYENITES	SYLVANER
SWIZZED	SWOP	SWOWND	SYENITIC	SYLVANERS
SWIZZES	SWOPPABLE	SWOWNDS	SYENS	SYLVANITE
SWIZZING	SWOPPED	SWOWNE	SYES	SYLVANS
SWIZZLE	SWOPPER	SWOWNES	SYKE	SYLVAS
SWIZZLED	SWOPPERS	SWOZZLE	SYKER	SYLVATIC
SWIZZLER	SWOPPING	SWOZZLES	SYKES	SYLVIA
SWIZZLERS	SWOPPINGS	SWUM	SYLI	SYLVIAS
SWIZZLES	SWOPS	SWUNG	SYLIS	SYLVIINE
SWIZZLING	SWOPT	SWY	SYLLABARY	SYLVIN
SWOB	SWORD	SYBARITE	SYLLABI	SYLVINE
SWOBBED	SWORDBILL	SYBARITES	SYLLABIC	SYLVINES
SWOBBER	SWORDED	SYBARITIC	SYLLABICS	SYLVINITE
SWOBBERS	SWORDER	SYBBE	SYLLABIFY	SYLVINS
SWOBBING	SWORDERS	SYBBES	SYLLABISE	SYLVITE
SWOBS	SWORDFERN	SYBIL	SYLLABISM	SYLVITES
SWOFFER	SWORDFISH	SYBILS	SYLLABIZE	SYMAR
SWOFFERS	SWORDING	SYBO	SYLLABLE	SYMARS
SWOFFING	SWORDLESS	SYBOE	SYLLABLED	SYMBION
SWOFFINGS	SWORDLIKE	SYBOES	SYLLABLES	SYMBIONS
SWOLE	SWORDMAN	SYBOTIC	SYLLABUB	SYMBIONT
SWOLER	SWORDMEN	SYBOTISM	SYLLABUBS	SYMBIONTS
SWOLEST	SWORDPLAY	SYBOTISMS	SYLLABUS	SYMBIOSES
SWOLLEN	SWORDS	SYBOW	SYLLEPSES	SYMBIOSIS
SWOLLENLY	SWORDSMAN	SYBOWS	SYLLEPSIS	SYMBIOT
SWOLN	SWORDSMEN	SYCAMINE	SYLLEPTIC	SYMBIOTE
SWOON	SWORDTAIL	SYCAMINES	SYLLOGE	SYMBIOTES
SWOONED	SWORE	SYCAMORE	SYLLOGES	SYMBIOTIC
SWOONER	SWORN	SYCAMORES	SYLLOGISE	SYMBIOTS
SWOONERS	SWOT	SYCE	SYLLOGISM	SYMBOL
SWOONIER	SWOTS	SYCEE	SYLLOGIST	SYMBOLE
SWOONIEST	SWOTTED	SYCEES	SYLLOGIZE	SYMBOLED
SWOONING	SWOTTER	SYCES	SYLPH	SYMBOLES
SWOONINGS	SWOTTERS	SYCOMORE	SYLPHIC	SYMBOLIC
SWOONS	SWOTTIER	SYCOMORES	SYLPHID	SYMBOLICS
SWOONY	SWOTTIEST	SYCON	SYLPHIDE	SYMBOLING
SWOOP	SWOTTING	SYCONIA	SYLPHIDES	SYMBOLISE
SWOOPED	SWOTTINGS	SYCONIUM	SYLPHIDS	SYMBOLISM

SYMBOLIST	SYNANDRIA	SYNCOPATE	SYNERGIES	SYNOPSES
SYMBOLIZE	SYNANGIA	SYNCOPE	SYNERGISE	SYNOPSIS
SYMBOLLED	SYNANGIUM	SYNCOPES	SYNERGISM	SYNOPSISE
SYMBOLOGY	SYNANON	SYNCOPIC	SYNERGIST	SYNOPSIZE
SYMBOLS	SYNANONS	SYNCOPTIC	SYNERGIZE	SYNOPTIC
SYMITAR	SYNANTHIC	SYNCRETIC	SYNERGY	SYNOPTICS
SYMITARE	SYNANTHY	SYNCS	SYNES	SYNOPTIST
SYMITARES	SYNAPHEA	SYNCYTIA	SYNESES	SYNOVIA
SYMITARS	SYNAPHEAS	SYNCYTIAL	SYNESIS	SYNOVIAL
SYMMETRAL	SYNAPHEIA	SYNCYTIUM	SYNESISES	SYNOVIAS
SYMMETRIC	SYNAPSE	SYND	SYNFUEL	SYNOVITIC
SYMMETRY	SYNAPSED	SYNDACTYL	SYNFUELS	SYNOVITIS
SYMPATHIN	SYNAPSES	SYNDED	SYNGAMIC	SYNROC
SYMPATHY	SYNAPSID	SYNDESES	SYNGAMIES	SYNROCS
SYMPATICO	SYNAPSIDS	SYNDESIS	SYNGAMOUS	SYNTACTIC
SYMPATRIC	SYNAPSING	SYNDET	SYNGAMY	SYNTAGM
SYMPATRY	SYNAPSIS	SYNDETIC	SYNGAS	SYNTAGMA
SYMPETALY	SYNAPTASE	SYNDETON	SYNGASES	SYNTAGMAS
SYMPHILE	SYNAPTE	SYNDETONS	SYNGASSES	SYNTAGMIC
SYMPHILES	SYNAPTES	SYNDETS	SYNGENEIC	SYNTAGMS
SYMPHILY	SYNAPTIC	SYNDIC	SYNGENIC	SYNTAN
SYMPHONIC	SYNARCHY	SYNDICAL	SYNGRAPH	SYNTANS
SYMPHONY	SYNASTRY	SYNDICATE	SYNGRAPHS	SYNTAX
SYMPHYSES	SYNAXARIA	SYNDICS	SYNING	SYNTAXES
SYMPHYSIS	SYNAXES	SYNDING	SYNIZESES	SYNTECTIC
SYMPHYTIC	SYNAXIS	SYNDINGS	SYNIZESIS	SYNTENIC
SYMPLAST	SYNBIOTIC	SYNDROME	SYNKARYA	SYNTENIES
SYMPLASTS	SYNC	SYNDROMES	SYNKARYON	SYNTENY
SYMPLOCE	SYNCARP	SYNDROMIC	SYNOD	SYNTEXIS
SYMPLOCES	SYNCARPS	SYNDS	SYNODAL	SYNTH
SYMPODIA	SYNCARPY	SYNE	SYNODALS	SYNTHASE
SYMPODIAL	SYNCED	SYNECHIA	SYNODIC	SYNTHASES
SYMPODIUM	SYNCH	SYNECHIAS	SYNODICAL	SYNTHESES
SYMPOSIA	SYNCHED	SYNECIOUS	SYNODS	SYNTHESIS
SYMPOSIAC	SYNCHING	SYNECTIC	SYNODSMAN	SYNTHETIC
SYMPOSIAL	SYNCHRO	SYNECTICS	SYNODSMEN	SYNTHON
SYMPOSIUM	SYNCHRONY	SYNED	SYNOECETE	SYNTHONS
SYMPTOM	SYNCHROS	SYNEDRIA	SYNOECISE	SYNTHPOP
SYMPTOMS	SYNCHS	SYNEDRIAL	SYNOECISM	SYNTHPOPS
SYMPTOSES	SYNCHYSES	SYNEDRION	SYNOECIZE	SYNTHRONI
SYMPTOSIS	SYNCHYSIS	SYNEDRIUM	SYNOEKETE	SYNTHS
SYMPTOTIC	SYNCING	SYNERESES	SYNOICOUS	SYNTONE
SYN	SYNCLINAL	SYNERESIS	SYNONYM	SYNTONES
SYNAGOG	SYNCLINE	SYNERGIA	SYNONYME	SYNTONIC
SYNAGOGAL	SYNCLINES	SYNERGIAS	SYNONYMES	SYNTONIES
SYNAGOGS	SYNCOM	SYNERGIC	SYNONYMIC	SYNTONIN
SYNAGOGUE	SYNCOMS	SYNERGID	SYNONYMS	SYNTONINS
SYNALEPHA	SYNCOPAL	SYNERGIDS	SYNONYMY	SYNTONISE

S

SYNTONIZE
SYNTONOUS
SYNTONY
SYNTYPE
SYNTYPES
SYNURA
SYNURAE
SYPE
SYPED
SYPES
SYPH
SYPHER
SYPHERED
SYPHERING
SYPHERS
SYPHILIS
SYPHILISE
SYPHILIZE

SYPHILOID
SYPHILOMA
SYPHON
SYPHONAGE
SYPHONAL
SYPHONED
SYPHONIC
SYPHONING
SYPHONS
SYPHS
SYPING
SYRAH
SYRAHS
SYREN
SYRENS
SYRETTE
SYRETTES
SYRINGA

SYRINGAS
SYRINGE
SYRINGEAL
SYRINGED
SYRINGES
SYRINGING
SYRINX
SYRINXES
SYRPHIAN
SYRPHIANS
SYRPHID
SYRPHIDS
SYRTES
SYRTIS
SYRUP
SYRUPED
SYRUPIER
SYRUPIEST

SYRUPING
SYRUPLIKE
SYRUPS
SYRUPY
SYSADMIN
SYSADMINS
SYSOP
SYSOPS
SYSSITIA
SYSSITIAS
SYSTALTIC
SYSTEM
SYSTEMED
SYSTEMIC
SYSTEMICS
SYSTEMISE
SYSTEMIZE
SYSTEMS

SYSTOLE
SYSTOLES
SYSTOLIC
SYSTYLE
SYSTYLES
SYTHE
SYTHES
SYVER
SYVERS
SYZYGAL
SYZYGETIC
SYZYGIAL
SYZYGIES
SYZYGY

S

T

TA	TABERDS	TABLING	TABRETS	TACHOGRAM
TAAL	TABERED	TABLINGS	TABS	TACHOS
TAALS	TABERING	TABLOID	TABU	TACHS
TAATA	TABERS	TABLOIDS	TABUED	TACHYLITE
TAATAS	TABES	TABLOIDY	TABUING	TACHYLYTE
TAB	TABESCENT	TABOGGAN	TABULA	TACHYON
TABANID	TABETIC	TABOGGANS	TABULABLE	TACHYONIC
TABANIDS	TABETICS	TABOO	TABULAE	TACHYONS
TABARD	TABI	TABOOED	TABULAR	TACHYPNEA
TABARDED	TABID	TABOOING	TABULARLY	TACIT
TABARDS	TABINET	TABOOLEY	TABULATE	TACITLY
TABARET	TABINETS	TABOOLEYS	TABULATED	TACITNESS
TABARETS	TABIS	TABOOS	TABULATES	TACITURN
TABASHEER	TABLA	TABOR	TABULATOR	TACK
TABASHIR	TABLAS	TABORED	TABULI	TACKBOARD
TABASHIRS	TABLATURE	TABORER	TABULIS	TACKED
TABBED	TABLE	TABORERS	TABUN	TACKER
TABBIED	TABLEAU	TABORET	TABUNS	TACKERS
TABBIER	TABLEAUS	TABORETS	TABUS	TACKET
TABBIES	TABLEAUX	TABORIN	TACAHOUT	TACKETIER
TABBIEST	TABLED	TABORINE	TACAHOUTS	TACKETS
TABBINET	TABLEFUL	TABORINES	TACAMAHAC	TACKETY
TABBINETS	TABLEFULS	TABORING	TACAN	TACKEY
TABBING	TABLELAND	TABORINS	TACANS	TACKIER
TABBINGS	TABLELESS	TABORS	TACE	TACKIES
TABBIS	TABLEMAT	TABOULEH	TACES	TACKIEST
TABBISES	TABLEMATE	TABOULEHS	TACET	TACKIFIED
TABBOULEH	TABLEMATS	TABOULI	TACH	TACKIFIER
TABBOULI	TABLES	TABOULIS	TACHE	TACKIFIES
TABBOULIS	TABLESFUL	TABOUR	TACHES	TACKIFY
TABBY	TABLESIDE	TABOURED	TACHINA	TACKILY
TABBYHOOD	TABLET	TABOURER	TACHINID	TACKINESS
TABBYING	TABLETED	TABOURERS	TACHINIDS	TACKING
TABEFIED	TABLETING	TABOURET	TACHISM	TACKINGS
TABEFIES	TABLETOP	TABOURETS	TACHISME	TACKLE
TABEFY	TABLETOPS	TABOURIN	TACHISMES	TACKLED
TABEFYING	TABLETS	TABOURING	TACHISMS	TACKLER
TABELLION	TABLETTED	TABOURINS	TACHIST	TACKLERS
TABER	TABLEWARE	TABOURS	TACHISTE	TACKLES
TABERD	TABLEWISE	TABRERE	TACHISTES	TACKLESS
TABERDAR	TABLIER	TABRERES	TACHISTS	TACKLING
TABERDARS	TABLIERS	TABRET	TACHO	TACKLINGS

TACKS	TAENIA	TAGINE	TAIKOS	TAILPIPE
TACKSMAN	TAENIAE	TAGINES	TAIL	TAILPIPED
TACKSMEN	TAENIAS	TAGLESS	TAILARD	TAILPIPES
TACKY	TAENIASES	TAGLIKE	TAILARDS	TAILPLANE
TACMAHACK	TAENIASIS	TAGLINE	TAILBACK	TAILRACE
TACNODE	TAENIATE	TAGLINES	TAILBACKS	TAILRACES
TACNODES	TAENIOID	TAGLIONI	TAILBOARD	TAILS
TACO	TAENITE	TAGLIONIS	TAILBONE	TAILSKID
TACONITE	TAENITES	TAGMA	TAILBONES	TAILSKIDS
TACONITES	TAES	TAGMATA	TAILCOAT	TAILSLIDE
TACOS	TAFFAREL	TAGMEME	TAILCOATS	TAILSPIN
TACRINE	TAFFARELS	TAGMEMES	TAILED	TAILSPINS
TACRINES	TAFFEREL	TAGMEMIC	TAILENDER	TAILSPUN
TACT	TAFFERELS	TAGMEMICS	TAILER	TAILSTOCK
TACTFUL	TAFFETA	TAGRAG	TAILERON	TAILWATER
TACTFULLY	TAFFETAS	TAGRAGS	TAILERONS	TAILWHEEL
TACTIC	TAFFETIER	TAGS	TAILERS	TAILWIND
TACTICAL	TAFFETY	TAGUAN	TAILFAN	TAILWINDS
TACTICIAN	TAFFIA	TAGUANS	TAILFANS	TAILYE
TACTICITY	TAFFIAS	TAHA	TAILFIN	TAILYES
TACTICS	TAFFIES	TAHAS	TAILFINS	TAILZIE
TACTILE	TAFFRAIL	TAHINA	TAILFLIES	TAILZIES
TACTILELY	TAFFRAILS	TAHINAS	TAILFLY	TAIN
TACTILIST	TAFFY	TAHINI	TAILGATE	TAINS
TACTILITY	TAFIA	TAHINIS	TAILGATED	TAINT
TACTION	TAFIAS	TAHR	TAILGATER	TAINTED
TACTIONS	TAG	TAHRS	TAILGATES	TAINTING
TACTISM	TAGALONG	TAHSIL	TAILHOOK	TAINTLESS
TACTISMS	TAGALONGS	TAHSILDAR	TAILHOOKS	TAINTS
TACTLESS	TAGAREEN	TAHSILS	TAILING	TAINTURE
TACTS	TAGAREENS	TAI	TAILINGS	TAINTURES
TACTUAL	TAGBOARD	TAIAHA	TAILLAMP	TAIPAN
TACTUALLY	TAGBOARDS	TAIAHAS	TAILLAMPS	TAIPANS
TAD	TAGETES	TAIG	TAILLE	TAIRA
TADALAFIL	TAGGANT	TAIGA	TAILLES	TAIRAS
TADDIE	TAGGANTS	TAIGAS	TAILLESS	TAIS
TADDIES	TAGGED	TAIGLACH	TAILLEUR	TAISCH
TADPOLE	TAGGEE	TAIGLE	TAILLEURS	TAISCHES
TADPOLES	TAGGEES	TAIGLED	TAILLIE	TAISH
TADS	TAGGER	TAIGLES	TAILLIES	TAISHES
TAE	TAGGERS	TAIGLING	TAILLIGHT	TAIT
TAED	TAGGIER	TAIGS	TAILLIKE	TAITS
TAEDIUM	TAGGIEST	TAIHOA	TAILOR	TAIVER
TAEDIUMS	TAGGING	TAIHOAED	TAILORED	TAIVERED
TAEING	TAGGINGS	TAIHOAING	TAILORESS	TAIVERING
TAEKWONDO	TAGGY	TAIHOAS	TAILORING	TAIVERS
TAEL	TAGHAIRM	TAIKO	TAILORS	TAIVERT
TAELS	TAGHAIRMS	TAIKONAUT	TAILPIECE	TAJ

TAJES	TALANTS	TALESMEN	TALLBOY	TALLYHOS
TAJINE	TALAPOIN	TALEYSIM	TALLBOYS	TALLYING
TAJINES	TALAPOINS	TALI	TALLENT	TALLYMAN
TAK	TALAQ	TALIGRADE	TALLENTS	TALLYMEN
TAKA	TALAQS	TALION	TALLER	TALLYSHOP
TAKABLE	TALAR	TALIONIC	TALLEST	TALMA
TAKAHE	TALARIA	TALIONS	TALLET	TALMAS
TAKAHES	TALARS	TALIPAT	TALLETS	TALMUD
TAKAMAKA	TALAS	TALIPATS	TALLGRASS	TALMUDIC
TAKAMAKAS	TALAUNT	TALIPED	TALLIABLE	TALMUDISM
TAKAS	TALAUNTS	TALIPEDS	TALLIATE	TALMUDS
TAKE	TALAYOT	TALIPES	TALLIATED	TALON
TAKEABLE	TALAYOTS	TALIPOT	TALLIATES	TALONED
TAKEAWAY	TALBOT	TALIPOTS	TALLIED	TALONS
TAKEAWAYS	TALBOTS	TALISMAN	TALLIER	TALOOKA
TAKEDOWN	TALBOTYPE	TALISMANS	TALLIERS	TALOOKAS
TAKEDOWNS	TALC	TALK	TALLIES	TALPA
TAKEN	TALCED	TALKABLE	TALLIS	TALPAE
TAKEOFF	TALCIER	TALKATHON	TALLISES	TALPAS
TAKEOFFS	TALCIEST	TALKATIVE	TALLISH	TALUK
TAKEOUT	TALCING	TALKBACK	TALLISIM	TALUKA
TAKEOUTS	TALCKED	TALKBACKS	TALLIT	TALUKAS
TAKEOVER	TALCKIER	TALKBOX	TALLITES	TALUKDAR
TAKEOVERS	TALCKIEST	TALKBOXES	TALLITH	TALUKDARS
TAKER	TALCKING	TALKED	TALLITHES	TALUKS
TAKERS	TALCKY	TALKER	TALLITHIM	TALUS
TAKES	TALCOSE	TALKERS	TALLITHS	TALUSES
TAKEUP	TALCOUS	TALKFEST	TALLITIM	TALWEG
TAKEUPS	TALCS	TALKFESTS	TALLITOT	TALWEGS
TAKHI	TALCUM	TALKIE	TALLITOTH	TAM
TAKHIS	TALCUMED	TALKIER	TALLITS	TAMABLE
TAKI	TALCUMING	TALKIES	TALLNESS	TAMAL
TAKIER	TALCUMS	TALKIEST	TALLOL	TAMALE
TAKIEST	TALCY	TALKINESS	TALLOLS	TAMALES
TAKIN	TALE	TALKING	TALLOT	TAMALS
TAKING	TALEA	TALKINGS	TALLOTS	TAMANDU
TAKINGLY	TALEAE	TALKS	TALLOW	TAMANDUA
TAKINGS	TALEFUL	TALKTIME	TALLOWED	TAMANDUAS
TAKINS	TALEGALLA	TALKTIMES	TALLOWIER	TAMANDUS
TAKIS	TALEGGIO	TALKY	TALLOWING	TAMANOIR
TAKKIES	TALEGGIOS	TALL	TALLOWISH	TAMANOIRS
TAKKY	TALENT	TALLAGE	TALLOWS	TAMANU
TAKS	TALENTED	TALLAGED	TALLOWY	TAMANUS
TAKY	TALENTS	TALLAGES	TALLS	TAMARA
TALA	TALER	TALLAGING	TALLY	TAMARACK
TALAK	TALERS	TALLAISIM	TALLYHO	TAMARACKS
TALAKS	TALES	TALLAT	TALLYHOED	TAMARAO
TALANT	TALESMAN	TALLATS	TALLYHOES	TAMARAOS

TAMARAS	TAMINE	TANAGRA	TANGLES	TANKLESS
TAMARAU	TAMINES	TANAGRAS	TANGLIER	TANKLIKE
TAMARAUS	TAMING	TANAGRINE	TANGLIEST	TANKS
TAMARI	TAMINGS	TANAISTE	TANGLING	TANKSHIP
TAMARILLO	TAMINS	TANAISTES	TANGLINGS	TANKSHIPS
TAMARIN	TAMIS	TANALISED	TANGLY	TANKY
TAMARIND	TAMISE	TANALIZED	TANGO	TANLING
TAMARINDS	TAMISES	TANAS	TANGOED	TANLINGS
TAMARINS	TAMMAR	TANBARK	TANGOES	TANNA
TAMARIS	TAMMARS	TANBARKS	TANGOING	TANNABLE
TAMARISK	TAMMIE	TANDEM	TANGOIST	TANNAGE
TAMARISKS	TAMMIED	TANDEMS	TANGOISTS	TANNAGES
TAMASHA	TAMMIES	TANDOOR	TANGOLIKE	TANNAH
TAMASHAS	TAMMY	TANDOORI	TANGOS	TANNAHS
TAMBAC	TAMMYING	TANDOORIS	TANGRAM	TANNAS
TAMBACS	TAMOXIFEN	TANDOORS	TANGRAMS	TANNATE
TAMBAK	TAMP	TANE	TANGS	TANNATES
TAMBAKS	TAMPALA	TANG	TANGUN	TANNED
TAMBALA	TAMPALAS	TANGA	TANGUNS	TANNER
TAMBALAS	TAMPAN	TANGAS	TANGY	TANNERIES
TAMBER	TAMPANS	TANGED	TANH	TANNERS
TAMBERS	TAMPED	TANGELO	TANHS	TANNERY
TAMBOUR	TAMPER	TANGELOS	TANIST	TANNEST
TAMBOURA	TAMPERED	TANGENCE	TANISTRY	TANNIC
TAMBOURAS	TAMPERER	TANGENCES	TANISTS	TANNIE
TAMBOURED	TAMPERERS	TANGENCY	TANIWHA	TANNIES
TAMBOURER	TAMPERING	TANGENT	TANIWHAS	TANNIN
TAMBOURIN	TAMPERS	TANGENTAL	TANK	TANNING
TAMBOURS	TAMPING	TANGENTS	TANKA	TANNINGS
TAMBUR	TAMPINGS	TANGERINE	TANKAGE	TANNINS
TAMBURA	TAMPION	TANGHIN	TANKAGES	TANNISH
TAMBURAS	TAMPIONS	TANGHINTN	TANKARD	TANNOY
TAMBURIN	TAMPON	TANGHINS	TANKARDS	TANNOYED
TAMBURINS	TAMPONADE	TANGI	TANKAS	TANNOYING
TAMBURS	TAMPONAGE	TANGIBLE	TANKED	TANNOYS
TAME	TAMPONED	TANGIBLES	TANKER	TANOREXIC
TAMEABLE	TAMPONING	TANGIBLY	TANKERED	TANREC
TAMED	TAMPONS	TANGIE	TANKERING	TANRECS
TAMEIN	TAMPS	TANGIER	TANKERS	TANS
TAMEINS	TAMS	TANGIES	TANKFUL	TANSIES
TAMELESS	TAMWORTH	TANGIEST	TANKFULS	TANSY
TAMELY	TAMWORTHS	TANGINESS	TANKIA	TANTALATE
TAMENESS	TAN	TANGING	TANKIAS	TANTALIC
TAMER	TANA	TANGIS	TANKIES	TANTALISE
TAMERS	TANADAR	TANGLE	TANKING	TANTALISM
TAMES	TANADARS	TANGLED	TANKINGS	TANTALITE
TAMEST	TANAGER	TANGLER	TANKINI	TANTALIZE
TAMIN	TANAGERS	TANGLERS	TANKINIS	TANTALOUS

TANTALUM	TAPED	TAPLASH	TARAND	TARIFFING
TANTALUMS	TAPELESS	TAPLASHES	TARANDS	TARIFFS
TANTALUS	TAPELIKE	TAPLESS	TARANTARA	TARING
TANTARA	TAPELINE	TAPPA	TARANTAS	TARINGS
TANTARARA	TAPELINES	TAPPABLE	TARANTASS	TARLATAN
TANTARAS	TAPEN	TAPPAS	TARANTISM	TARLATANS
TANTI	TAPENADE	TAPPED	TARANTIST	TARLETAN
TANTIES	TAPENADES	TAPPER	TARANTULA	TARLETANS
TANTIVIES	TAPER	TAPPERS	TARAS	TARMAC
TANTIVY	TAPERED	TAPPET	TARAXACUM	TARMACKED
TANTO	TAPERER	TAPPETS	TARBOGGIN	TARMACS
TANTONIES	TAPERERS	TAPPICE	TARBOOSH	TARN
TANTONY	TAPERING	TAPPICED	TARBOUCHE	TARNAL
TANTOS	TAPERINGS	TAPPICES	TARBOUSH	TARNALLY
TANTRA	TAPERNESS	TAPPICING	TARBOY	TARNATION
TANTRAS	TAPERS	TAPPING	TARBOYS	TARNISH
TANTRIC	TAPERWISE	TAPPINGS	TARBUSH	TARNISHED
TANTRISM	TAPES	TAPPIT	TARBUSHES	TARNISHER
TANTRISMS	TAPESTRY	TAPROOM	TARCEL	TARNISHES
TANTRIST	TAPET	TAPROOMS	TARCELS	TARNS
TANTRISTS	TAPETA	TAPROOT	TARDIED	TARO
TANTRUM	TAPETAL	TAPROOTED	TARDIER	TAROC
TANTRUMS	TAPETED	TAPROOTS	TARDIES	TAROCS
TANTY	TAPETI	TAPS	TARDIEST	TAROK
TANUKI	TAPETING	TAPSMAN	TARDILY	TAROKS
TANUKIS	TAPETIS	TAPSMEN	TARDINESS	TAROS
TANYARD	TAPETS	TAPSTER	TARDIVE	TAROT
TANYARDS	TAPETUM	TAPSTERS	TARDO	TAROTS
TANZANITE	TAPETUMS	TAPSTRESS	TARDY	TARP
TAO	TAPEWORM	TAPSTRIES	TARDYING	TARPAN
TAONGA	TAPEWORMS	TAPSTRY	TARDYON	TARPANS
TAONGAS	TAPHOLE	TAPU	TARDYONS	TARPAPER
TAOS	TAPHOLES	TAPUED	TARE	TARPAPERS
TAP	TAPHONOMY	TAPUING	TARED	TARPAULIN
TAPA	TAPHOUSE	TAPUS	TARES	TARPON
TAPACOLO	TAPHOUSES	TAQUERIA	TARGA	TARPONS
TAPACOLOS	TAPING	TAQUERIAS	TARGAS	TARPS
TAPACULO	TAPINGS	TAR	TARGE	TARRAGON
TAPACULOS	TAPIOCA	TARA	TARGED	TARRAGONS
TAPADERA	TAPIOCAS	TARABISH	TARGES	TARRAS
TAPADERAS	TAPIR	TARAIRE	TARGET	TARRASES
TAPADERO	TAPIROID	TARAIRES	TARGETED	TARRE
TAPADEROS	TAPIROIDS	TARAKIHI	TARGETEER	TARRED
TAPALO	TAPIRS	TARAKIHIS	TARGETING	TARRES
TAPALOS	TAPIS	TARAMA	TARGETS	TARRIANCE
TAPAS	TAPISES	TARAMAS	TARGING	TARRIED
TAPE	TAPIST	TARAMEA	TARIFF	TARRIER
TAPEABLE	TAPISTS	TARAMEAS	TARIFFED	TARRIERS

TARRIES	TARTARS	TASHED	TASTER	TATTIER
TARRIEST	TARTED	TASHES	TASTERS	TATTIES
TARRINESS	TARTER	TASHING	TASTES	TATTIEST
TARRING	TARTEST	TASIMETER	TASTEVIN	TATTILY
TARRINGS	TARTIER	TASIMETRY	TASTEVINS	TATTINESS
TARROCK	TARTIEST	TASING	TASTIER	TATTING
TARROCKS	TARTILY	TASK	TASTIEST	TATTINGS
TARROW	TARTINE	TASKBAR	TASTILY	TATTLE
TARROWED	TARTINES	TASKBARS	TASTINESS	TATTLED
TARROWING	TARTINESS	TASKED	TASTING	TATTLER
TARROWS	TARTING	TASKER	TASTINGS	TATTLERS
TARRY	TARTISH	TASKERS	TASTY	TATTLES
TARRYING	TARTISHLY	TASKING	TAT	TATTLING
TARS	TARTLET	TASKINGS	TATAHASH	TATTLINGS
TARSAL	TARTLETS	TASKLESS	TATAMI	TATTOO
TARSALGIA	TARTLY	TASKS	TATAMIS	TATTOOED
TARSALS	TARTNESS	TASKWORK	TATAR	TATTOOER
TARSEAL	TARTRATE	TASKWORKS	TATARS	TATTOOERS
TARSEALS	TARTRATED	TASLET	TATE	TATTOOING
TARSEL	TARTRATES	TASLETS	TATER	TATTOOIST
TARSELS	TARTS	TASS	TATERS	TATTOOS
TARSI	TARTUFE	TASSA	TATES	TATTOW
TARSIA	TARTUFES	TASSAS	TATH	TATTOWED
TARSIAS	TARTUFFE	TASSE	TATHATA	TATTOWING
TARSIER	TARTUFFES	TASSEL	TATHATAS	TATTOWS
TARSIERS	TARTUFI	TASSELED	TATHED	TATTS
TARSIOID	TARTUFO	TASSELIER	TATHING	TATTY
TARSIOIDS	TARTUFOS	TASSELING	TATHS	TATU
TARSIPED	TARTY	TASSELL	TATIE	TATUED
TARSIPEDS	TARWEED	TASSELLED	TATIES	TATUING
TARSUS	TARWEFDS	TASSELLS	TATLER	TATUS
TART	TARWHINE	TASSELLY	TATLERS	TAU
TARTAN	TARWHINES	TASSELS	TATOU	TAUBE
TARTANA	TARZAN	TASSELY	TATOUAY	TAUBES
TARTANAS	TARZANS	TASSES	TATOUAYS	TAUGHT
TARTANE	TAS	TASSET	TATOUS	TAUHINU
TARTANED	TASAR	TASSETS	TATS	TAUHINUS
TARTANES	TASARS	TASSIE	TATSOI	TAUHOU
TARTANRY	TASBIH	TASSIES	TATSOIS	TAUHOUS
TARTANS	TASBIHS	TASSO	TATT	TAUIWI
TARTAR	TASE	TASSOS	TATTED	TAUIWIS
TARTARE	TASED	TASSWAGE	TATTER	TAULD
TARTARES	TASER	TASTABLE	TATTERED	TAUNT
TARTARIC	TASERED	TASTE	TATTERIER	TAUNTED
TARTARISE	TASERING	TASTEABLE	TATTERING	TAUNTER
TARTARIZE	TASERS	TASTED	TATTERS	TAUNTERS
TARTARLY	TASES	TASTEFUL	TATTERY	TAUNTING
TARTAROUS	TASH	TASTELESS	TATTIE	TAUNTINGS

TAUNTS	TAVERNAS	TAWTIE	TAXOL	TEACHABLE
TAUON	TAVERNER	TAWTIER	TAXOLS	TEACHABLY
TAUONS	TAVERNERS	TAWTIEST	TAXON	TEACHER
TAUPATA	TAVERNS	TAWTING	TAXONOMER	TEACHERLY
TAUPATAS	TAVERS	TAWTS	TAXONOMIC	TEACHERS
TAUPE	TAVERT	TAX	TAXONOMY	TEACHES
TAUPES	TAVS	TAXA	TAXONS	TEACHIE
TAUPIE	TAW	TAXABLE	TAXOR	TEACHING
TAUPIES	TAWA	TAXABLES	TAXORS	TEACHINGS
TAUREAN	TAWAI	TAXABLY	TAXPAID	TEACHLESS
TAURIC	TAWAIS	TAXACEOUS	TAXPAYER	TEACUP
TAURIFORM	TAWAS	TAXAMETER	TAXPAYERS	TEACUPFUL
TAURINE	TAWDRIER	TAXATION	TAXPAYING	TEACUPS
TAURINES	TAWDRIES	TAXATIONS	TAXUS	TEAD
TAUS	TAWDRIEST	TAXATIVE	TAXWISE	TEADE
TAUT	TAWDRILY	TAXED	TAXYING	TEADES
TAUTAUG	TAWDRY	TAXEME	TAY	TEADS
TAUTAUGS	TAWED	TAXEMES	TAYASSUID	TEAED
TAUTED	TAWER	TAXEMIC	TAYBERRY	TEAGLE
TAUTEN	TAWERIES	TAXER	TAYRA	TEAGLED
TAUTENED	TAWERS	TAXERS	TAYRAS	TEAGLES
TAUTENING	TAWERY	TAXES	TAYS	TEAGLING
TAUTENS	TAWHAI	TAXI	TAZZA	TEAHOUSE
TAUTER	TAWHAIS	TAXIARCH	TAZZAS	TEAHOUSES
TAUTEST	TAWHIRI	TAXIARCHS	TAZZE	TEAING
TAUTING	TAWHIRIS	TAXICAB	TCHICK	TEAK
TAUTIT	TAWIE	TAXICABS	TCHICKED	TEAKETTLE
TAUTLY	TAWIER	TAXIDERMY	TCHICKING	TEAKS
TAUTNESS	TAWIEST	TAXIED	TCHICKS	TEAKWOOD
TAUTOG	TAWING	TAXIES	TCHOTCHKE	TEAKWOODS
TAUTOGS	TAWINGS	TAXIING	TE	TEAL
TAUTOLOGY	TAWNEY	TAXIMAN	TEA	TEALIGHT
TAUTOMER	TAWNEYS	TAXIMEN	TEABAG	TEALIGHTS
TAUTOMERS	TAWNIER	TAXIMETER	TEABAGS	TEALIKE
TAUTONYM	TAWNIES	TAXING	TEABERRY	TEALS
TAUTONYMS	TAWNIEST	TAXINGLY	TEABOARD	TEAM
TAUTONYMY	TAWNILY	TAXINGS	TEABOARDS	TEAMAKER
TAUTS	TAWNINESS	TAXIPLANE	TEABOWL	TEAMAKERS
TAV	TAWNY	TAXIS	TEABOWLS	TEAMED
TAVA	TAWPIE	TAXISES	TEABOX	TEAMER
TAVAH	TAWPIES	TAXITE	TEABOXES	TEAMERS
TAVAHS	TAWS	TAXITES	TEABREAD	TEAMING
TAVAS	TAWSE	TAXITIC	TEABREADS	TEAMINGS
TAVER	TAWSED	TAXIWAY	TEACAKE	TEAMMATE
TAVERED	TAWSES	TAXIWAYS	TEACAKES	TEAMMATES
TAVERING	TAWSING	TAXLESS	TEACART	TEAMS
TAVERN	TAWT	TAXMAN	TEACARTS	TEAMSTER
TAVERNA	TAWTED	TAXMEN	TEACH	TEAMSTERS

TEAMWISE	TEASER	TECHNIQUE	TEEL	TEERS
TEAMWORK	TEASERS	TECHNO	TEELS	TEES
TEAMWORKS	TEASES	TECHNOID	TEEM	TEETER
TEAPOT	TEASHOP	TECHNOIDS	TEEMED	TEETERED
TEAPOTS	TEASHOPS	TECHNOPOP	TEEMER	TEETERING
TEAPOY	TEASING	TECHNOS	TEEMERS	TEETERS
TEAPOYS	TEASINGLY	TECHS	TEEMFUL	TEETH
TEAR	TEASINGS	TECHY	TEEMING	TEETHE
TEARABLE	TEASPOON	TECKEL	TEEMINGLY	TEETHED
TEARAWAY	TEASPOONS	TECKELS	TEEMLESS	TEETHER
TEARAWAYS	TEAT	TECS	TEEMS	TEETHERS
TEARDOWN	TEATASTER	TECTA	TEEN	TEETHES
TEARDOWNS	TEATED	TECTAL	TEENAGE	TEETHING
TEARDROP	TEATIME	TECTIFORM	TEENAGED	TEETHINGS
TEARDROPS	TEATIMES	TECTITE	TEENAGER	TEETHLESS
TEARED	TEATS	TECTITES	TEENAGERS	TEETOTAL
TEARER	TEAWARE	TECTONIC	TEENAGES	TEETOTALS
TEARERS	TEAWARES	TECTONICS	TEEND	TEETOTUM
TEARFUL	TEAZE	TECTONISM	TEENDED	TEETOTUMS
TEARFULLY	TEAZED	TECTORIAL	TEENDING	TEEVEE
TEARGAS	TEAZEL	TECTRICES	TEENDOM	TEEVEES
TEARGASES	TEAZELED	TECTRIX	TEENDOMS	TEF
TEARIER	TEAZELING	TECTUM	TEENDS	TEFF
TEARIEST	TEAZELLED	TECTUMS	TEENE	TEFFS
TEARILY	TEAZELS	TED	TEENED	TEFILLAH
TEARINESS	TEAZES	TEDDED	TEENER	TEFILLIN
TEARING	TEAZING	TEDDER	TEENERS	TEFLON
TEARLESS	TEAZLE	TEDDERED	TEENES	TEFLONS
TEARLIKE	TEAZLED	TEDDERING	TEENFUL	TEFS
TEAROOM	TEAZLES	TEDDERS	TEENIER	TEG
TEAROOMS	TEAZLING	TEDDIE	TEENIEST	TEGG
TEARS	TEBBAD	TEDDIES	TEENING	TEGGS
TEARSHEET	TEBBADS	TEDDING	TEENS	TEGMEN
TEARSTAIN	TEBIBYTE	TEDDY	TEENSIER	TEGMENTA
TEARSTRIP	TEBIBYTES	TEDIER	TEENSIEST	TEGMENTAL
TEARY	TEC	TEDIEST	TEENSY	TEGMENTUM
TEAS	TECH	TEDIOSITY	TEENTIER	TEGMINA
TEASABLE	TECHED	TEDIOUS	TEENTIEST	TEGMINAL
TEASE	TECHIE	TEDIOUSLY	TEENTSIER	TEGS
TEASED	TECHIER	TEDISOME	TEENTSY	TEGU
TEASEL	TECHIES	TEDIUM	TEENTY	TEGUA
TEASELED	TECHIEST	TEDIUMS	TEENY	TEGUAS
TEASELER	TECHILY	TEDS	TEENYBOP	TEGUEXIN
TEASELERS	TECHINESS	TEDY	TEEPEE	TEGUEXINS
TEASELING	TECHNIC	TEE	TEEPEES	TEGULA
TEASELLED	TECHNICAL	TEED	TEER	TEGULAE
TEASELLER	TECHNICS	TEEING	TEERED	TEGULAR
TEASELS	TECHNIKON	TEEK	TEERING	TEGULARLY

TEGULATED
TEGUMEN
TEGUMENT
TEGUMENTS
TEGUMINA
TEGUS
TEHR
TEHRS
TEHSIL
TEHSILDAR
TEHSILS
TEIGLACH
TEIID
TEIIDS
TEIL
TEILS
TEIN
TEIND
TEINDED
TEINDING
TEINDS
TEINS
TEKKIE
TEKKIES
TEKNONYMY
TEKTITE
TEKTITES
TEKTITIC
TEL
TELA
TELAE
TELAMON
TELAMONES
TELAMONS
TELARY
TELCO
TELCOS
TELD
TELE
TELECAST
TELECASTS
TELECHIR
TELECHIRS
TELECINE
TELECINES
TELECOM
TELECOMM
TELECOMMS

TELECOMS
TELECON
TELECONS
TELECOPY
TELEDU
TELEDUS
TELEFAX
TELEFAXED
TELEFAXES
TELEFILM
TELEFILMS
TELEGA
TELEGAS
TELEGENIC
TELEGONIC
TELEGONY
TELEGRAM
TELEGRAMS
TELEGRAPH
TELEMAN
TELEMARK
TELEMARKS
TELEMATIC
TELEMEN
TELEMETER
TELEMETRY
TELEOLOGY
TELEONOMY
TELEOSAUR
TELEOST
TELEOSTS
TELEPATH
TELEPATHS
TELEPATHY
TELEPHEME
TELEPHONE
TELEPHONY
TELEPHOTO
TELEPIC
TELEPICS
TELEPLAY
TELEPLAYS
TELEPOINT
TELEPORT
TELEPORTS
TELEPRINT
TELERAN
TELERANS

TELERGIC
TELERGIES
TELERGY
TELEROBOT
TELES
TELESALE
TELESALES
TELESCOPE
TELESCOPY
TELESEME
TELESEMES
TELESES
TELESHOP
TELESHOPS
TELESIS
TELESM
TELESMS
TELESTIC
TELESTICH
TELESTICS
TELETEX
TELETEXES
TELETEXT
TELETEXTS
TELETHON
TELETHONS
TELETRON
TELETRONS
TELETYPE
TELETYPED
TELETYPES
TELEVIEW
TELEVIEWS
TELEVISE
TELEVISED
TELEVISER
TELEVISES
TELEVISOR
TELEWORK
TELEWORKS
TELEX
TELEXED
TELEXES
TELEXING
TELFER
TELFERAGE
TELFERED
TELFERIC

TELFERING
TELFERS
TELFORD
TELFORDS
TELIA
TELIAL
TELIC
TELICALLY
TELICITY
TELIUM
TELL
TELLABLE
TELLAR
TELLARED
TELLARING
TELLARS
TELLEN
TELLENS
TELLER
TELLERED
TELLERING
TELLERS
TELLIES
TELLIN
TELLING
TELLINGLY
TELLINGS
TELLINOID
TELLINS
TELLS
TELLTALE
TELLTALES
TELLURAL
TELLURATE
TELLURIAN
TELLURIC
TELLURIDE
TELLURION
TELLURISE
TELLURITE
TELLURIUM
TELLURIZE
TELLUROUS
TELLUS
TELLUSES
TELLY
TELLYS
TELNET

TELNETED
TELNETING
TELNETS
TELNETTED
TELOGEN
TELOGENS
TELOI
TELOME
TELOMERE
TELOMERES
TELOMES
TELOMIC
TELOPHASE
TELOS
TELOTAXES
TELOTAXIS
TELPHER
TELPHERED
TELPHERIC
TELPHERS
TELS
TELSON
TELSONIC
TELSONS
TELT
TEMAZEPAM
TEMBLOR
TEMBLORES
TEMBLORS
TEME
TEMED
TEMENE
TEMENOS
TEMERITY
TEMEROUS
TEMES
TEMP
TEMPED
TEMPEH
TEMPEHS
TEMPER
TEMPERA
TEMPERAS
TEMPERATE
TEMPERED
TEMPERER
TEMPERERS
TEMPERING

TEMPERS

TEMPERS
TEMPEST
TEMPESTED
TEMPESTS
TEMPI
TEMPING
TEMPINGS
TEMPLAR
TEMPLARS
TEMPLATE
TEMPLATES
TEMPLE
TEMPLED
TEMPLES
TEMPLET
TEMPLETS
TEMPO
TEMPORAL
TEMPORALS
TEMPORARY
TEMPORE
TEMPORISE
TEMPORIZE
TEMPOS
TEMPS
TEMPT
TEMPTABLE
TEMPTED
TEMPTER
TEMPTERS
TEMPTING
TEMPTINGS
TEMPTRESS
TEMPTS
TEMPURA
TEMPURAS
TEMS
TEMSE
TEMSED
TEMSES
TEMSING
TEMULENCE
TEMULENCY
TEMULENT
TEN
TENABLE
TENABLY
TENACE

TENACES
TENACIOUS
TENACITY
TENACULA
TENACULUM
TENAIL
TENAILLE
TENAILLES
TENAILLON
TENAILS
TENANCIES
TENANCY
TENANT
TENANTED
TENANTING
TENANTRY
TENANTS
TENCH
TENCHES
TEND
TENDANCE
TENDANCES
TENDED
TENDENCE
TENDENCES
TENDENCY
TENDENZ
TENDENZEN
TENDER
TENDERED
TENDERER
TENDERERS
TENDEREST
TENDERING
TENDERISE
TENDERIZE
TENDERLY
TENDERS
TENDING
TENDINOUS
TENDON
TENDONS
TENDRE
TENDRES
TENDRESSE
TENDRIL
TENDRILED
TENDRILLY

TENDRILS
TENDRON
TENDRONS
TENDS
TENDU
TENDUS
TENE
TENEBRAE
TENEBRIO
TENEBRIOS
TENEBRISM
TENEBRIST
TENEBRITY
TENEBROSE
TENEBROUS
TENEMENT
TENEMENTS
TENENDA
TENENDUM
TENENDUMS
TENES
TENESI
TENESMIC
TENESMUS
TENET
TENETS
TENFOLD
TENFOLDS
TENGE
TENGES
TENIA
TENIACIDE
TENIAE
TENIAFUGE
TENIAS
TENIASES
TENIASIS
TENIOID
TENNE
TENNER
TENNERS
TENNES
TENNESI
TENNIES
TENNIS
TENNISES
TENNIST
TENNISTS

TENNO
TENNOS
TENNY
TENON
TENONED
TENONER
TENONERS
TENONING
TENONS
TENOR
TENORINI
TENORINO
TENORIST
TENORISTS
TENORITE
TENORITES
TENORLESS
TENORMAN
TENORMEN
TENOROON
TENOROONS
TENORS
TENOTOMY
TENOUR
TENOURS
TENPENCE
TENPENCES
TENPENNY
TENPIN
TENPINNER
TENPINS
TENREC
TENRECS
TENS
TENSE
TENSED
TENSELESS
TENSELY
TENSENESS
TENSER
TENSES
TENSEST
TENSIBLE
TENSIBLY
TENSILE
TENSILELY
TENSILITY
TENSING

TENSION
TENSIONAL
TENSIONED
TENSIONER
TENSIONS
TENSITIES
TENSITY
TENSIVE
TENSON
TENSONS
TENSOR
TENSORIAL
TENSORS
TENT
TENTACLE
TENTACLED
TENTACLES
TENTACULA
TENTAGE
TENTAGES
TENTATION
TENTATIVE
TENTED
TENTER
TENTERED
TENTERING
TENTERS
TENTFUL
TENTFULS
TENTH
TENTHLY
TENTHS
TENTIE
TENTIER
TENTIEST
TENTIGO
TENTIGOS
TENTING
TENTINGS
TENTLESS
TENTLIKE
TENTMAKER
TENTORIA
TENTORIAL
TENTORIUM
TENTPOLE
TENTPOLES
TENTS

TENTWISE	TEPID	TERCELETS	TERMING	TERRAMARA
TENTY	TEPIDARIA	TERCELS	TERMINI	TERRAMARE
TENUE	TEPIDER	TERCES	TERMINISM	TERRANE
TENUES	TEPIDEST	TERCET	TERMINIST	TERRANES
TENUIOUS	TEPIDITY	TERCETS	TERMINUS	TERRAPIN
TENUIS	TEPIDLY	TERCIO	TERMITARY	TERRAPINS
TENUITIES	TEPIDNESS	TERCIOS	TERMITE	TERRARIA
TENUITY	TEPOY	TEREBENE	TERMITES	TERRARIUM
TENUOUS	TEPOYS	TEREBENES	TERMITIC	TERRAS
TENUOUSLY	TEQUILA	TEREBIC	TERMLESS	TERRASES
TENURABLE	TEQUILAS	TEREBINTH	TERMLIES	TERRASSE
TENURE	TEQUILLA	TEREBRA	TERMLY	TERRASSES
TENURED	TEQUILLAS	TEREBRAE	TERMOR	TERRAZZO
TENURES	TERABYTE	TEREBRANT	TERMORS	TERRAZZOS
TENURIAL	TERABYTES	TEREBRAS	TERMS	TERREEN
TENURING	TERAFLOP	TEREBRATE	TERMTIME	TERREENS
TENUTI	TERAFLOPS	TEREDINES	TERMTIMES	TERRELLA
TENUTO	TERAGLIN	TEREDO	TERN	TERRELLAS
TENUTOS	TERAGLINS	TEREDOS	TERNAL	TERRENE
TENZON	TERAHERTZ	TEREFA	TERNARIES	TERRENELY
TENZONS	TERAI	TEREFAH	TERNARY	TERRENES
TEOCALLI	TERAIS	TEREK	TERNATE	TERRET
TEOCALLIS	TERAKIHI	TEREKS	TERNATELY	TERRETS
TEOPAN	TERAKIHIS	TERES	TERNE	TERRIBLE
TEOPANS	TERAMETER	TERESES	TERNED	TERRIBLES
TEOSINTE	TERAOHM	TERETE	TERNES	TERRIBLY
TEOSINTES	TERAOHMS	TERETES	TERNING	TERRICOLE
TEPA	TERAPH	TERF	TERNION	TERRIER
TEPACHE	TERAPHIM	TERFE	TERNIONS	TERRIERS
TEPACHES	TERAPHIMS	TERFES	TERNS	TERRIES
TEPAL	TERAS	TERFS	TERPENE	TERRIFIC
TEPALS	TERATA	TERGA	TERPENES	TERRIFIED
TEPAS	TERATISM	TERGAL	TERPENIC	TERRIFIER
TEPEE	TERATISMS	TERGITE	TERPENOID	TERRIFIES
TEPEES	TERATOGEN	TERGITES	TERPINE	TERRIFY
TEPEFIED	TERATOID	TERGUM	TERPINEOL	TERRINE
TEPEFIES	TERATOMA	TERIYAKI	TERPINES	TERRINES
TEPEFY	TERATOMAS	TERIYAKIS	TERPINOL	TERRIT
TEPEFYING	TERAWATT	TERM	TERPINOLS	TERRITORY
TEPHIGRAM	TERAWATTS	TERMAGANT	TERRA	TERRITS
TEPHILLAH	TERBIA	TERMED	TERRACE	TERROIR
TEPHILLIN	TERBIAS	TERMER	TERRACED	TERROIRS
TEPHRA	TERBIC	TERMERS	TERRACES	TERROR
TEPHRAS	TERBIUM	TERMINAL	TERRACING	TERRORFUL
TEPHRITE	TERBIUMS	TERMINALS	TERRAE	TERRORISE
TEPHRITES	TERCE	TERMINATE	TERRAFORM	TERRORISM
TEPHRITIC	TERCEL	TERMINER	TERRAIN	TERRORIST
TEPHROITE	TERCELET	TERMINERS	TERRAINS	TERRORIZE

TERRORS	TESTAMENT	TESTY	TETRAPLAS	TEWARTS
TERRY	TESTAMUR	TET	TETRAPOD	TEWED
TERSE	TESTAMURS	TETANAL	TETRAPODS	TEWEL
TERSELY	TESTATA	TETANIC	TETRAPODY	TEWELS
TERSENESS	TESTATE	TETANICAL	TETRARCH	TEWHIT
TERSER	TESTATES	TETANICS	TETRARCHS	TEWHITS
TERSEST	TESTATION	TETANIES	TETRARCHY	TEWING
TERSION	TESTATOR	TETANISE	TETRAS	TEWIT
TERSIONS	TESTATORS	TETANISED	TETRAXON	TEWITS
TERTIA	TESTATRIX	TETANISES	TETRAXONS	TEWS
TERTIAL	TESTATUM	TETANIZE	TETRI	TEX
TERTIALS	TESTATUMS	TETANIZED	TETRIS	TEXAS
TERTIAN	TESTCROSS	TETANIZES	TETRODE	TEXASES
TERTIANS	TESTE	TETANOID	TETRODES	TEXES
TERTIARY	TESTED	TETANUS	TETRONAL	TEXT
TERTIAS	TESTEE	TETANUSES	TETRONALS	TEXTBOOK
TERTIUM	TESTEES	TETANY	TETROSE	TEXTBOOKS
TERTIUS	TESTER	TETCHED	TETROSES	TEXTED
TERTIUSES	TESTERN	TETCHIER	TETROXID	TEXTER
TERTS	TESTERNED	TETCHIEST	TETROXIDE	TEXTERS
TERVALENT	TESTERNS	TETCHILY	TETROXIDS	TEXTILE
TERYLENE	TESTERS	TETCHY	TETRYL	TEXTILES
TERYLENES	TESTES	TETE	TETRYLS	TEXTING
TERZETTA	TESTICLE	TETES	TETS	TEXTINGS
TERZETTAS	TESTICLES	TETH	TETTER	TEXTISM
TERZETTI	TESTIER	TETHER	TETTERED	TEXTISMS
TERZETTO	TESTIEST	TETHERED	TETTERING	TEXTLESS
TERZETTOS	TESTIFIED	TETHERING	TETTEROUS	TEXTONYM
TES	TESTIFIER	TETHERS	TETTERS	TEXTONYMS
TESLA	TESTIFIES	TETHS	TETTIX	TEXTORIAL
TESLAS	TESTIFY	TETOTUM	TETTIXES	TEXTPHONE
TESSELATE	TESTILY	TETOTUMS	TEUCH	TEXTS
TESSELLA	TESTIMONY	TETRA	TEUCHAT	TEXTSPEAK
TESSELLAE	TESTINESS	TETRACID	TEUCHATS	TEXTUAL
TESSELLAR	TESTING	TETRACIDS	TEUCHER	TEXTUALLY
TESSERA	TESTINGS	TETRACT	TEUCHEST	TEXTUARY
TESSERACT	TESTIS	TETRACTS	TEUCHTER	TEXTURAL
TESSERAE	TESTON	TETRAD	TEUCHTERS	TEXTURE
TESSERAL	TESTONS	TETRADIC	TEUGH	TEXTURED
TESSITURA	TESTOON	TETRADITE	TEUGHER	TEXTURES
TESSITURE	TESTOONS	TETRADS	TEUGHEST	TEXTURING
TEST	TESTRIL	TETRAGON	TEUGHLY	TEXTURISE
TESTA	TESTRILL	TETRAGONS	TEUTONISE	TEXTURIZE
TESTABLE	TESTRILLS	TETRAGRAM	TEUTONIZE	TEXTUROUS
TESTACEAN	TESTRILS	TETRALOGY	TEVATRON	THACK
TESTACIES	TESTS	TETRAMER	TEVATRONS	THACKED
TESTACY	TESTUDO	TETRAMERS	TEW	THACKING
TESTAE	TESTUDOS	TETRAPLA	TEWART	THACKS

THAE	THANG	THAWLESS	THEGNS	THEODICY
THAGI	THANGKA	THAWS	THEIC	THEOGONIC
THAGIS	THANGKAS	THAWY	THEICS	THEOGONY
THAIM	THANGS	THE	THEIN	THEOLOG
THAIRM	THANK	THEACEOUS	THEINE	THEOLOGER
THAIRMS	THANKED	THEANDRIC	THEINES	THEOLOGIC
THALAMI	THANKEE	THEANINE	THEINS	THEOLOGS
THALAMIC	THANKER	THEANINES	THEIR	THEOLOGUE
THALAMUS	THANKERS	THEARCHIC	THEIRS	THEOLOGY
THALASSIC	THANKFUL	THEARCHY	THEIRSELF	THEOMACHY
THALE	THANKING	THEATER	THEISM	THEOMANCY
THALER	THANKINGS	THEATERS	THEISMS	THEOMANIA
THALERS	THANKIT	THEATRAL	THEIST	THEONOMY
THALI	THANKLESS	THEATRE	THEISTIC	THEOPATHY
THALIAN	THANKS	THEATRES	THEISTS	THEOPHAGY
THALIS	THANKYOU	THEATRIC	THELEMENT	THEOPHANY
THALLI	THANKYOUS	THEATRICS	THELF	THEORBIST
THALLIC	THANNA	THEAVE	THELITIS	THEORBO
THALLINE	THANNAH	THEAVES	THELVES	THEORBOS
THALLINES	THANNAHS	THEBAINE	THELYTOKY	THEOREM
THALLIOUS	THANNAS	THEBAINES	THEM	THEOREMIC
THALLIUM	THANS	THEBE	THEMA	THEOREMS
THALLIUMS	THANX	THEBES	THEMATA	THEORETIC
THALLOID	THAR	THECA	THEMATIC	THEORIC
THALLOUS	THARM	THECAE	THEMATICS	THEORICS
THALLUS	THARMS	THECAL	THEMATISE	THEORIES
THALLUSES	THARS	THECATE	THEMATIZE	THEORIQUE
THALWEG	THAT	THECODONT	THEME	THEORISE
THALWEGS	THATAWAY	THEE	THEMED	THEORISED
THAN	THATCH	THEED	THEMELESS	THEORISER
THANA	THATCHED	THEEING	THEMES	THEORISES
THANADAR	THATCHER	THEEK	THEMING	THEORIST
THANADARS	THATCHERS	THEEKED	THEMSELF	THEORISTS
THANAGE	THATCHES	THEEKING	THEN	THEORIZE
THANAGES	THATCHIER	THEEKS	THENABOUT	THEORIZED
THANAH	THATCHING	THEELIN	THENAGE	THEORIZER
THANAHS	THATCHT	THEELINS	THENAGES	THEORIZES
THANAS	THATCHY	THEELOL	THENAL	THEORY
THANATISM	THATNESS	THEELOLS	THENAR	THEOSOPH
THANATIST	THAUMATIN	THEES	THENARS	THEOSOPHS
THANATOID	THAW	THEFT	THENCE	THEOSOPHY
THANATOS	THAWED	THEFTLESS	THENS	THEOTOKOI
THANE	THAWER	THEFTS	THEOCON	THEOTOKOS
THANEDOM	THAWERS	THEFTUOUS	THEOCONS	THEOW
THANEDOMS	THAWIER	THEGITHER	THEOCRACY	THEOWS
THANEHOOD	THAWIEST	THEGN	THEOCRASY	THERALITE
THANES	THAWING	THEGNLIER	THEOCRAT	THERAPIES
THANESHIP	THAWINGS	THEGNLY	THEOCRATS	THERAPISE

THERAPIST	THERMIT	THEY	THICKY	THINGY
THERAPIZE	THERMITE	THIAMIN	THIEF	THINK
THERAPSID	THERMITES	THIAMINE	THIEFLIKE	THINKABLE
THERAPY	THERMITS	THIAMINES	THIEVE	THINKABLY
THERBLIG	THERMOS	THIAMINS	THIEVED	THINKER
THERBLIGS	THERMOSES	THIASUS	THIEVERY	THINKERS
THERE	THERMOSET	THIASUSES	THIEVES	THINKING
THEREAT	THERMOTIC	THIAZIDE	THIEVING	THINKINGS
THEREAWAY	THERMS	THIAZIDES	THIEVINGS	THINKS
THEREBY	THEROID	THIAZIN	THIEVISH	THINLY
THEREFOR	THEROLOGY	THIAZINE	THIG	THINNED
THEREFORE	THEROPOD	THIAZINES	THIGGED	THINNER
THEREFROM	THEROPODS	THIAZINS	THIGGER	THINNERS
THEREIN	THESAURAL	THIAZOL	THIGGERS	THINNESS
THEREINTO	THESAURI	THIAZOLE	THIGGING	THINNEST
THEREMIN	THESAURUS	THIAZOLES	THIGGINGS	THINNING
THEREMINS	THESE	THIAZOLS	THIGGIT	THINNINGS
THERENESS	THESES	THIBET	THIGH	THINNISH
THEREOF	THESIS	THIBETS	THIGHBONE	THINS
THEREON	THESP	THIBLE	THIGHED	THIO
THEREOUT	THESPIAN	THIBLES	THIGHS	THIOFURAN
THERES	THESPIANS	THICK	THIGS	THIOL
THERETO	THESPS	THICKED	THILK	THIOLIC
THEREUNTO	THETA	THICKEN	THILL	THIOLS
THEREUPON	THETAS	THICKENED	THILLER	THIONATE
THEREWITH	THETCH	THICKENER	THILLERS	THIONATES
THERIAC	THETCHED	THICKENS	THILLS	THIONIC
THERIACA	THETCHES	THICKER	THIMBLE	THIONIN
THERIACAL	THETCHING	THICKEST	THIMBLED	THIONINE
THERIACAS	THETE	THICKET	THIMBLES	THIONINES
THERIACS	THETES	THICKETED	THIMBLING	THIONINS
THERIAN	THETHER	THICKETS	THIN	THIONYL
THERIANS	THETIC	THICKETY	THINCLAD	THIONYLS
THERM	THETICAL	THICKHEAD	THINCLADS	THIOPHEN
THERMAE	THETRI	THICKIE	THINDOWN	THIOPHENE
THERMAL	THETRIS	THICKIES	THINDOWNS	THIOPHENS
THERMALLY	THEURGIC	THICKING	THINE	THIOPHIL
THERMALS	THEURGIES	THICKISH	THING	THIOTEPA
THERME	THEURGIST	THICKLEAF	THINGAMY	THIOTEPAS
THERMEL	THEURGY	THICKLY	THINGHOOD	THIOUREA
THERMELS	THEW	THICKNESS	THINGIER	THIOUREAS
THERMES	THEWED	THICKO	THINGIES	THIR
THERMETTE	THEWES	THICKOES	THINGIEST	THIRAM
THERMIC	THEWIER	THICKOS	THINGNESS	THIRAMS
THERMICAL	THEWIEST	THICKS	THINGO	THIRD
THERMIDOR	THEWLESS	THICKSET	THINGOS	THIRDED
THERMION	THEWS	THICKSETS	THINGS	THIRDHAND
THERMIONS	THEWY	THICKSKIN	THINGUMMY	THIRDING

T

THIRDINGS	THOLES	THOROUGH	THRASONIC	THREEQUEL
THIRDLY	THOLI	THOROUGHS	THRAVE	THREES
THIRDS	THOLING	THORP	THRAVES	THREESOME
THIRDSMAN	THOLOBATE	THORPE	THRAW	THRENE
THIRDSMEN	THOLOI	THORPES	THRAWARD	THRENES
THIRL	THOLOS	THORPS	THRAWART	THRENETIC
THIRLAGE	THOLUS	THOSE	THRAWED	THRENODE
THIRLAGES	THON	THOTHER	THRAWING	THRENODES
THIRLED	THONDER	THOU	THRAWN	THRENODIC
THIRLING	THONG	THOUED	THRAWNLY	THRENODY
THIRLS	THONGED	THOUGH	THRAWS	THRENOS
THIRST	THONGIER	THOUGHT	THREAD	THRENOSES
THIRSTED	THONGIEST	THOUGHTED	THREADED	THREONINE
THIRSTER	THONGING	THOUGHTEN	THREADEN	THRESH
THIRSTERS	THONGS	THOUGHTS	THREADER	THRESHED
THIRSTFUL	THONGY	THOUING	THREADERS	THRESHEL
THIRSTIER	THORACAL	THOUS	THREADFIN	THRESHELS
THIRSTILY	THORACES	THOUSAND	THREADIER	THRESHER
THIRSTING	THORACIC	THOUSANDS	THREADING	THRESHERS
THIRSTS	THORAX	THOWEL	THREADS	THRESHES
THIRSTY	THORAXES	THOWELS	THREADY	THRESHING
THIRTEEN	THORIA	THOWL	THREAP	THRESHOLD
THIRTEENS	THORIAS	THOWLESS	THREAPED	THRETTIES
THIRTIES	THORIC	THOWLS	THREAPER	THRETTY
THIRTIETH	THORITE	THRAE	THREAPERS	THREW
THIRTY	THORITES	THRAIPING	THREAPING	THRICE
THIRTYISH	THORIUM	THRALDOM	THREAPIT	THRID
THIS	THORIUMS	THRALDOMS	THREAPS	THRIDACE
THISAWAY	THORN	THRALL	THREAT	THRIDACES
THISNESS	THORNBACK	THRALLDOM	THREATED	THRIDDED
THISTLE	THORNBILL	THRALLED	THREATEN	THRIDDING
THISTLES	THORNBIRD	THRALLING	THREATENS	THRIDS
THISTLIER	THORNBUSH	THRALLS	THREATFUL	THRIFT
THISTLY	THORNED	THRANG	THREATING	THRIFTIER
THITHER	THORNIER	THRANGED	THREATS	THRIFTILY
THITHERTO	THORNIEST	THRANGING	THREAVE	THRIFTS
THIVEL	THORNILY	THRANGS	THREAVES	THRIFTY
THIVELS	THORNING	THRAPPLE	THREE	THRILL
THLIPSES	THORNLESS	THRAPPlED	THREEFOLD	THRILLANT
THLIPSIS	THORNLIKE	THRAPPLES	THREENESS	THRILLED
THO	THORNS	THRASH	THREEP	THRILLER
THOFT	THORNSET	THRASHED	THREEPEAT	THRILLERS
THOFTS	THORNTAIL	THRASHER	THREEPED	THRILLIER
THOLE	THORNTREE	THRASHERS	THREEPER	THRILLING
THOLED	THORNY	THRASHES	THREEPERS	THRILLS
THOLEIITE	THORO	THRASHIER	THREEPING	THRILLY
THOLEPIN	THORON	THRASHING	THREEPIT	THRIMSA
THOLEPINS	THORONS	THRASHY	THREEPS	THRIMSAS

THRIP	THRONGED	THRUST	THUMBLIKE	THWAITE
THRIPS	THRONGFUL	THRUSTED	THUMBLING	THWAITES
THRIPSES	THRONGING	THRUSTER	THUMBNAIL	THWART
THRISSEL	THRONGS	THRUSTERS	THUMBNUT	THWARTED
THRISSELS	THRONING	THRUSTFUL	THUMBNUTS	THWARTER
THRIST	THRONNER	THRUSTING	THUMBPOT	THWARTERS
THRISTED	THRONNERS	THRUSTOR	THUMBPOTS	THWARTING
THRISTING	THROPPLE	THRUSTORS	THUMBS	THWARTLY
THRISTLE	THROPPLED	THRUSTS	THUMBTACK	THWARTS
THRISTLES	THROPPLES	THRUTCH	THUMBY	THY
THRISTS	THROSTLE	THRUTCHED	THUMP	THYINE
THRISTY	THROSTLES	THRUTCHES	THUMPED	THYLACINE
THRIVE	THROTTLE	THRUWAY	THUMPER	THYLAKOID
THRIVED	THROTTLED	THRUWAYS	THUMPERS	THYLOSE
THRIVEN	THROTTLER	THRYMSA	THUMPING	THYLOSES
THRIVER	THROTTLES	THRYMSAS	THUMPS	THYLOSIS
THRIVERS	THROUGH	THUD	THUNDER	THYME
THRIVES	THROUGHLY	THUDDED	THUNDERED	THYMES
THRIVING	THROVE	THUDDING	THUNDERER	THYMEY
THRIVINGS	THROW	THUDDINGS	THUNDERS	THYMI
THRO	THROWABLE	THUDS	THUNDERY	THYMIC
THROAT	THROWAWAY	THUG	THUNDROUS	THYMIDINE
THROATED	THROWBACK	THUGGEE	THUNK	THYMIER
THROATIER	THROWDOWN	THUGGEES	THUNKED	THYMIEST
THROATILY	THROWE	THUGGERY	THUNKING	THYMINE
THROATING	THROWER	THUGGISH	THUNKS	THYMINES
THROATS	THROWERS	THUGGISM	THURIBLE	THYMOCYTE
THROATY	THROWES	THUGGISMS	THURIBLES	THYMOL
THROB	THROWING	THUGGO	THURIFER	THYMOLS
THROBBED	THROWINGS	THUGGOS	THURIFERS	THYMOMA
THROBBER	THROWN	THUGS	THURIFIED	THYMOMAS
THROBBERS	THROWOVER	THUJA	THURIFIES	THYMOMATA
THROBBING	THROWS	THUJAS	THURIFY	THYMOSIN
THROBLESS	THROWSTER	THULIA	THURL	THYMOSINS
THROBS	THRU	THULIAS	THURLS	THYMUS
THROE	THRUM	THULITE	THUS	THYMUSES
THROED	THRUMMED	THULITES	THUSES	THYMY
THROEING	THRUMMER	THULIUM	THUSLY	THYRATRON
THROES	THRUMMERS	THULIUMS	THUSNESS	THYREOID
THROMBI	THRUMMIER	THUMB	THUSWISE	THYREOIDS
THROMBIN	THRUMMING	THUMBED	THUYA	THYRISTOR
THROMBINS	THRUMMY	THUMBHOLE	THUYAS	THYROID
THROMBOSE	THRUMS	THUMBIER	THWACK	THYROIDAL
THROMBUS	THRUPENNY	THUMBIEST	THWACKED	THYROIDS
THRONE	THRUPUT	THUMBING	THWACKER	THYROXIN
THRONED	THRUPUTS	THUMBKIN	THWACKERS	THYROXINE
THRONES	THRUSH	THUMBKINS	THWACKING	THYROXINS
THRONG	THRUSHES	THUMBLESS	THWACKS	THYRSE

THYRSES	TICKINGS	TIDDLING	TIED	TIGERIER
THYRSI	TICKLACE	TIDDLY	TIEING	TIGERIEST
THYRSOID	TICKLACES	TIDDY	TIELESS	TIGERISH
THYRSUS	TICKLE	TIDE	TIEPIN	TIGERISM
THYSELF	TICKLEASS	TIDED	TIEPINS	TIGERISMS
TI	TICKLED	TIDELAND	TIER	TIGERLIER
TIAN	TICKLER	TIDELANDS	TIERCE	TIGERLIKE
TIANS	TICKLERS	TIDELESS	TIERCED	TIGERLY
TIAR	TICKLES	TIDELIKE	TIERCEL	TIGERS
TIARA	TICKLIER	TIDELINE	TIERCELET	TIGERWOOD
TIARAED	TICKLIEST	TIDELINES	TIERCELS	TIGERY
TIARAS	TICKLING	TIDEMARK	TIERCERON	TIGES
TIARS	TICKLINGS	TIDEMARKS	TIERCES	TIGGED
TIBIA	TICKLISH	TIDEMILL	TIERCET	TIGGER
TIBIAE	TICKLY	TIDEMILLS	TIERCETS	TIGGERED
TIBIAL	TICKS	TIDERIP	TIERED	TIGGERING
TIBIALES	TICKSEED	TIDERIPS	TIERING	TIGGERS
TIBIALIS	TICKSEEDS	TIDES	TIERS	TIGGING
TIBIAS	TICKTACK	TIDESMAN	TIES	TIGHT
TIC	TICKTACKS	TIDESMEN	TIETAC	TIGHTASS
TICAL	TICKTOCK	TIDEWATER	TIETACK	TIGHTEN
TICALS	TICKTOCKS	TIDEWAVE	TIETACKS	TIGHTENED
TICCA	TICKY	TIDEWAVES	TIETACS	TIGHTENER
TICCED	TICS	TIDEWAY	TIFF	TIGHTENS
TICCING	TICTAC	TIDEWAYS	TIFFANIES	TIGHTER
TICE	TICTACKED	TIDIED	TIFFANY	TIGHTEST
TICED	TICTACS	TIDIER	TIFFED	TIGHTISH
TICES	TICTOC	TIDIERS	TIFFIN	TIGHTKNIT
TICH	TICTOCKED	TIDIES	TIFFINED	TIGHTLY
TICHES	TICTOCS	TIDIEST	TIFFING	TIGHTNESS
TICHIER	TID	TIDILY	TIFFINGS	TIGHTROPE
TICHIEST	TIDAL	TIDINESS	TIFFINING	TIGHTS
TICHY	TIDALLY	TIDING	TIFFINS	TIGHTWAD
TICING	TIDBIT	TIDINGS	TIFFS	TIGHTWADS
TICK	TIDBITS	TIDIVATE	TIFO	TIGHTWIRE
TICKED	TIDDIER	TIDIVATED	TIFOS	TIGLIC
TICKEN	TIDDIES	TIDIVATES	TIFOSI	TIGLON
TICKENS	TIDDIEST	TIDS	TIFOSO	TIGLONS
TICKER	TIDDLE	TIDY	TIFOSOS	TIGNON
TICKERS	TIDDLED	TIDYING	TIFT	TIGNONS
TICKET	TIDDLER	TIDYTIPS	TIFTED	TIGON
TICKETED	TIDDLERS	TIE	TIFTING	TIGONS
TICKETING	TIDDLES	TIEBACK	TIFTS	TIGRESS
TICKETS	TIDDLEY	TIEBACKS	TIG	TIGRESSES
TICKEY	TIDDLEYS	TIEBREAK	TIGE	TIGRIDIA
TICKEYS	TIDDLIER	TIEBREAKS	TIGER	TIGRIDIAS
TICKIES	TIDDLIES	TIECLASP	TIGEREYE	TIGRINE
TICKING	TIDDLIEST	TIECLASPS	TIGEREYES	TIGRISH

TIGRISHLY	TILLERMAN	TIMBREL	TIMON	TINEA
TIGROID	TILLERMEN	TIMBRELS	TIMONEER	TINEAL
TIGS	TILLERS	TIMBRES	TIMONEERS	TINEAS
TIK	TILLICUM	TIME	TIMONS	TINED
TIKA	TILLICUMS	TIMEBOMB	TIMOROUS	TINEID
TIKANGA	TILLIER	TIMEBOMBS	TIMORSOME	TINEIDS
TIKANGAS	TILLIEST	TIMECARD	TIMOTHIES	TINES
TIKAS	TILLING	TIMECARDS	TIMOTHY	TINFOIL
TIKE	TILLINGS	TIMED	TIMOUS	TINFOILS
TIKES	TILLITE	TIMEFRAME	TIMOUSLY	TINFUL
TIKI	TILLITES	TIMELESS	TIMPANA	TINFULS
TIKIED	TILLS	TIMELIER	TIMPANAS	TING
TIKIING	TILLY	TIMELIEST	TIMPANI	TINGE
TIKINAGAN	TILS	TIMELINE	TIMPANIST	TINGED
TIKIS	TILT	TIMELINES	TIMPANO	TINGEING
TIKKA	TILTABLE	TIMELY	TIMPANUM	TINGES
TIKKAS	TILTED	TIMENOGUY	TIMPANUMS	TINGING
TIKOLOSHE	TILTER	TIMEOUS	TIMPS	TINGLE
TIKS	TILTERS	TIMEOUSLY	TIN	TINGLED
TIKTAALIK	TILTH	TIMEOUT	TINA	TINGLER
TIL	TILTHS	TIMEOUTS	TINAJA	TINGLERS
TILAK	TILTING	TIMEPASS	TINAJAS	TINGLES
TILAKS	TILTINGS	TIMEPIECE	TINAMOU	TINGLIER
TILAPIA	TILTMETER	TIMER	TINAMOUS	TINGLIEST
TILAPIAS	TILTROTOR	TIMERS	TINAS	TINGLING
TILBURIES	TILTS	TIMES	TINCAL	TINGLINGS
TILBURY	TILTYARD	TIMESAVER	TINCALS	TINGLISH
TILDE	TILTYARDS	TIMESCALE	TINCHEL	TINGLY
TILDES	TIMARAU	TIMESHARE	TINCHELS	TINGS
TILE	TIMARAUS	TIMESHIFT	TINCT	TINGUAITE
TILED	TIMARIOT	TIMESTAMP	TINCTED	TINHORN
TILEFISH	TIMARIOTS	TIMETABLE	TINCTING	TINHORNS
TILELIKE	TIMBAL	TIMEWORK	TINCTS	TINIER
TILER	TIMBALE	TIMEWORKS	TINCTURE	TINIES
TILERIES	TIMBALES	TIMEWORN	TINCTURED	TINIEST
TILERS	TIMBALS	TIMID	TINCTURES	TINILY
TILERY	TIMBER	TIMIDER	TIND	TININESS
TILES	TIMBERED	TIMIDEST	TINDAL	TINING
TILING	TIMBERIER	TIMIDITY	TINDALS	TINK
TILINGS	TIMBERING	TIMIDLY	TINDED	TINKED
TILL	TIMBERMAN	TIMIDNESS	TINDER	TINKER
TILLABLE	TIMBERMEN	TIMING	TINDERBOX	TINKERED
TILLAGE	TIMBERS	TIMINGS	TINDERIER	TINKERER
TILLAGES	TIMBERY	TIMIST	TINDERS	TINKERERS
TILLED	TIMBO	TIMISTS	TINDERY	TINKERING
TILLER	TIMBOS	TIMOCRACY	TINDING	TINKERMAN
TILLERED	TIMBRAL	TIMOLOL	TINDS	TINKERMEN
TILLERING	TIMBRE	TIMOLOLS	TINE	TINKERS

TINKERTOY	TINSNIPS	TIPPLED	TIRED	TISSULAR
TINKING	TINSTONE	TIPPLER	TIREDER	TISWAS
TINKLE	TINSTONES	TIPPLERS	TIREDEST	TISWASES
TINKLED	TINT	TIPPLES	TIREDLY	TIT
TINKLER	TINTACK	TIPPLING	TIREDNESS	TITAN
TINKLERS	TINTACKS	TIPPY	TIRELESS	TITANATE
TINKLES	TINTED	TIPPYTOE	TIRELING	TITANATES
TINKLIER	TINTER	TIPPYTOED	TIRELINGS	TITANESS
TINKLIEST	TINTERS	TIPPYTOES	TIREMAKER	TITANIA
TINKLING	TINTIER	TIPS	TIRES	TITANIAS
TINKLINGS	TINTIEST	TIPSHEET	TIRESOME	TITANIC
TINKLY	TINTINESS	TIPSHEETS	TIREWOMAN	TITANIS
TINKS	TINTING	TIPSIER	TIREWOMEN	TITANISES
TINLIKE	TINTINGS	TIPSIEST	TIRING	TITANISM
TINMAN	TINTLESS	TIPSIFIED	TIRINGS	TITANISMS
TINMEN	TINTOOKIE	TIPSIFIES	TIRITI	TITANITE
TINNED	TINTS	TIPSIFY	TIRITIS	TITANITES
TINNER	TINTY	TIPSILY	TIRL	TITANIUM
TINNERS	TINTYPE	TIPSINESS	TIRLED	TITANIUMS
TINNIE	TINTYPES	TIPSTAFF	TIRLING	TITANOUS
TINNIER	TINWARE	TIPSTAFFS	TIRLS	TITANS
TINNIES	TINWARES	TIPSTAVES	TIRO	TITBIT
TINNIEST	TINWORK	TIPSTER	TIROES	TITBITS
TINNILY	TINWORKS	TIPSTERS	TIRONIC	TITCH
TINNINESS	TINY	TIPSTOCK	TIROS	TITCHES
TINNING	TIP	TIPSTOCKS	TIRR	TITCHIE
TINNINGS	TIPCART	TIPSY	TIRRED	TITCHIER
TINNITUS	TIPCARTS	TIPT	TIRRING	TITCHIEST
TINNY	TIPCAT	TIPTOE	TIRRIT	TITCHY
TINPLATE	TIPCATS	TIPTOED	TIRRITS	TITE
TINPLATED	TIPI	TIPTOEING	TIRRIVEE	TITELY
TINPLATES	TIPIS	TIPTOES	TIRRIVEES	TITER
TINPOT	TIPLESS	TIPTOP	TIRRIVIE	TITERS
TINPOTS	TIPOFF	TIPTOPS	TIRRIVIES	TITFER
TINS	TIPOFFS	TIPTRONIC	TIRRS	TITFERS
TINSEL	TIPPABLE	TIPULA	TIS	TITHABLE
TINSELED	TIPPED	TIPULAS	TISANE	TITHE
TINSELIER	TIPPEE	TIPUNA	TISANES	TITHIED
TINSELING	TIPPEES	TIPUNAS	TISICK	TITHER
TINSELLED	TIPPER	TIRADE	TISICKS	TITHERS
TINSELLY	TIPPERS	TIRADES	TISSUAL	TITHES
TINSELRY	TIPPET	TIRAGE	TISSUE	TITHING
TINSELS	TIPPETS	TIRAGES	TISSUED	TITHINGS
TINSELY	TIPPIER	TIRAMISU	TISSUES	TITHONIA
TINSEY	TIPPIEST	TIRAMISUS	TISSUEY	TITHONIAS
TINSEYS	TIPPING	TIRASSE	TISSUIER	TITI
TINSMITH	TIPPINGS	TIRASSES	TISSUIEST	TITIAN
TINSMITHS	TIPPLE	TIRE	TISSUING	TITIANS

TITILLATE	TITTING	TIZES	TOAZES	TODDLING
TITIS	TITTISH	TIZWAS	TOAZING	TODDY
TITIVATE	TITTIVATE	TIZWASES	TOBACCO	TODGER
TITIVATED	TITTLE	TIZZ	TOBACCOES	TODGERS
TITIVATES	TITTLEBAT	TIZZES	TOBACCOS	TODIES
TITIVATOR	TITTLED	TIZZIES	TOBIES	TODS
TITLARK	TITTLES	TIZZY	TOBOGGAN	TODY
TITLARKS	TITTLING	TJANTING	TOBOGGANS	TOE
TITLE	TITTUP	TJANTINGS	TOBOGGIN	TOEA
TITLED	TITTUPED	TMESES	TOBOGGINS	TOEAS
TITLELESS	TITTUPIER	TMESIS	TOBY	TOEBIE
TITLER	TITTUPING	TO	TOC	TOEBIES
TITLERS	TITTUPPED	TOAD	TOCCATA	TOECAP
TITLES	TITTUPPY	TOADEATER	TOCCATAS	TOECAPS
TITLIKE	TITTUPS	TOADFISH	TOCCATE	TOECLIP
TITLING	TITTUPY	TOADFLAX	TOCCATINA	TOECLIPS
TITLINGS	TITTY	TOADGRASS	TOCHER	TOED
TITLIST	TITUBANCY	TOADIED	TOCHERED	TOEHOLD
TITLISTS	TITUBANT	TOADIES	TOCHERING	TOEHOLDS
TITMAN	TITUBATE	TOADISH	TOCHERS	TOEIER
TITMEN	TITUBATED	TOADLESS	TOCK	TOEIEST
TITMICE	TITUBATES	TOADLET	TOCKED	TOEING
TITMOSE	TITULAR	TOADLETS	TOCKIER	TOELESS
TITMOUSE	TITULARLY	TOADLIKE	TOCKIEST	TOELIKE
TITOKI	TITULARS	TOADRUSH	TOCKING	TOENAIL
TITOKIS	TITULARY	TOADS	TOCKLEY	TOENAILED
TITRABLE	TITULE	TOADSTONE	TOCKLEYS	TOENAILS
TITRANT	TITULED	TOADSTOOL	TOCKS	TOEPIECE
TITRANTS	TITULES	TOADY	TOCKY	TOEPIECES
TITRATE	TITULI	TOADYING	TOCO	TOEPLATE
TITRATED	TITULING	TOADYINGS	TOCOLOGY	TOEPLATES
TITRATES	TITULUS	TOADYISH	TOCOS	TOERAG
TITRATING	TITUP	TOADYISM	TOCS	TOERAGGER
TITRATION	TITUPED	TOADYISMS	TOCSIN	TOERAGS
TITRATOR	TITUPIER	TOAST	TOCSINS	TOES
TITRATORS	TITUPIEST	TOASTED	TOD	TOESHOE
TITRE	TITUPING	TOASTER	TODAY	TOESHOES
TITRES	TITUPPED	TOASTERS	TODAYS	TOETOE
TITS	TITUPPING	TOASTIE	TODDE	TOETOES
TITTED	TITUPS	TOASTIER	TODDED	TOEY
TITTER	TITUPY	TOASTIES	TODDES	TOFF
TITTERED	TIVY	TOASTIEST	TODDIES	TOFFEE
TITTERER	TIX	TOASTING	TODDING	TOFFEES
TITTERERS	TIYIN	TOASTINGS	TODDLE	TOFFIER
TITTERING	TIYINS	TOASTS	TODDLED	TOFFIES
TITTERS	TIYN	TOASTY	TODDLER	TOFFIEST
TITTIE	TIYNS	TOAZE	TODDLERS	TOFFISH
TITTIES	TIZ	TOAZED	TODDLES	TOFFS

TOFFY	TOILER	TOKER	TOLING	TOLUIDIDE
TOFORE	TOILERS	TOKERS	TOLINGS	TOLUIDIN
TOFT	TOILES	TOKES	TOLL	TOLUIDINE
TOFTS	TOILET	TOKING	TOLLABLE	TOLUIDINS
TOFU	TOILETED	TOKO	TOLLAGE	TOLUIDS
TOFUS	TOILETING	TOKOLOGY	TOLLAGES	TOLUOL
TOFUTTI	TOILETRY	TOKOLOSHE	TOLLBAR	TOLUOLE
TOFUTTIS	TOILETS	TOKOLOSHI	TOLLBARS	TOLUOLES
TOG	TOILETTE	TOKOMAK	TOLLBOOTH	TOLUOLS
TOGA	TOILETTES	TOKOMAKS	TOLLDISH	TOLUS
TOGAE	TOILFUL	TOKONOMA	TOLLED	TOLUYL
TOGAED	TOILFULLY	TOKONOMAS	TOLLER	TOLUYLS
TOGAS	TOILINET	TOKOS	TOLLERS	TOLYL
TOGATE	TOILINETS	TOKOTOKO	TOLLEY	TOLYLS
TOGATED	TOILING	TOKOTOKOS	TOLLEYS	TOLZEY
TOGAVIRUS	TOILINGS	TOKTOKKIE	TOLLGATE	TOLZEYS
TOGE	TOILLESS	TOLA	TOLLGATED	TOM
TOGED	TOILS	TOLAN	TOLLGATES	TOMAHAWK
TOGES	TOILSOME	TOLANE	TOLLHOUSE	TOMAHAWKS
TOGETHER	TOILWORN	TOLANES	TOLLIE	TOMALLEY
TOGGED	TOING	TOLANS	TOLLIES	TOMALLEYS
TOGGER	TOINGS	TOLAR	TOLLING	TOMAN
TOGGERED	TOISE	TOLARJEV	TOLLINGS	TOMANS
TOGGERIES	TOISEACH	TOLARJI	TOLLMAN	TOMATILLO
TOGGERING	TOISEACHS	TOLARS	TOLLMEN	TOMATO
TOGGERS	TOISECH	TOLAS	TOLLS	TOMATOES
TOGGERY	TOISECHS	TOLBOOTH	TOLLWAY	TOMATOEY
TOGGING	TOISES	TOLBOOTHS	TOLLWAYS	TOMATOIER
TOGGLE	TOISON	TOLD	TOLLY	TOMB
TOGGLED	TOISONS	TOLE	TOLSEL	TOMBAC
TOGGLER	TOIT	TOLED	TOLSELS	TOMBACK
TOGGLERS	TOITED	TOLEDO	TOLSEY	TOMBACKS
TOGGLES	TOITING	TOLEDOS	TOLSEYS	TOMBACS
TOGGLING	TOITOI	TOLERABLE	TOLT	TOMBAK
TOGROG	TOITOIS	TOLERABLY	TOLTER	TOMBAKS
TOGROGS	TOITS	TOLERANCE	TOLTERED	TOMBAL
TOGS	TOKAMAK	TOLERANT	TOLTERING	TOMBED
TOGUE	TOKAMAKS	TOLERATE	TOLTERS	TOMBIC
TOGUES	TOKAY	TOLERATED	TOLTS	TOMBING
TOHEROA	TOKAYS	TOLERATFS	TOLU	TOMBLESS
TOHEROAS	TOKE	TOLERATOR	TOLUATE	TOMBLIKE
TOHO	TOKED	TOLES	TOLUATES	TOMBOC
TOHOS	TOKEN	TOLEWARE	TOLUENE	TOMBOCS
TOHUNGA	TOKENED	TOLEWARES	TOLUENES	TOMBOLA
TOHUNGAS	TOKENING	TOLIDIN	TOLUIC	TOMBOLAS
TOIL	TOKENISM	TOLIDINE	TOLUID	TOMBOLO
TOILE	TOKENISMS	TOLIDINES	TOLUIDE	TOMBOLOS
TOILED	TOKENS	TOLIDINS	TOLUIDES	TOMBOY

T

TOMBOYISH	TON	TONGUING	TONS	TOOLKITS
TOMBOYS	TONAL	TONGUINGS	TONSIL	TOOLLESS
TOMBS	TONALITE	TONIC	TONSILAR	TOOLMAKER
TOMBSTONE	TONALITES	TONICALLY	TONSILLAR	TOOLMAN
TOMCAT	TONALITIC	TONICITY	TONSILS	TOOLMEN
TOMCATS	TONALITY	TONICS	TONSOR	TOOLPUSH
TOMCATTED	TONALLY	TONIER	TONSORIAL	TOOLROOM
TOMCOD	TONANT	TONIES	TONSORS	TOOLROOMS
TOMCODS	TONDI	TONIEST	TONSURE	TOOLS
TOME	TONDINI	TONIFIED	TONSURED	TOOLSET
TOMENTA	TONDINO	TONIFIES	TONSURES	TOOLSETS
TOMENTOSE	TONDINOS	TONIFY	TONSURING	TOOLSHED
TOMENTOUS	TONDO	TONIFYING	TONTINE	TOOLSHEDS
TOMENTUM	TONDOS	TONIGHT	TONTINER	TOOLTIP
TOMES	TONE	TONIGHTS	TONTINERS	TOOLTIPS
TOMFOOL	TONEARM	TONING	TONTINES	TOOM
TOMFOOLED	TONEARMS	TONINGS	TONUS	TOOMED
TOMFOOLS	TONED	TONISH	TONUSES	TOOMER
TOMIA	TONELESS	TONISHLY	TONY	TOOMEST
TOMIAL	TONEME	TONITE	TOO	TOOMING
TOMIUM	TONEMES	TONITES	TOOART	TOOMS
TOMMED	TONEMIC	TONK	TOOARTS	TOON
TOMMIED	TONEPAD	TONKA	TOODLE	TOONIE
TOMMIES	TONEPADS	TONKED	TOODLED	TOONIES
TOMMING	TONER	TONKER	TOODLES	TOONS
TOMMY	TONERS	TONKERS	TOODLING	TOORIE
TOMMYCOD	TONES	TONKING	TOOK	TOORIES
TOMMYCODS	TONETIC	TONKS	TOOL	TOOSHIE
TOMMYING	TONETICS	TONLET	TOOLBAG	TOOSHIER
TOMMYROT	TONETTE	TONLETS	TOOLBAGS	TOOSHIEST
TOMMYROTS	TONETTES	TONNAG	TOOLBAR	TOOT
TOMO	TONEY	TONNAGE	TOOLBARS	TOOTED
TOMOGRAM	TONG	TONNAGES	TOOLBOX	TOOTER
TOMOGRAMS	TONGA	TONNAGS	TOOLBOXES	TOOTERS
TOMOGRAPH	TONGAS	TONNE	TOOLCASE	TOOTH
TOMORROW	TONGED	TONNEAU	TOOLCASES	TOOTHACHE
TOMORROWS	TONGER	TONNEAUS	TOOLCHEST	TOOTHCOMB
TOMOS	TONGERS	TONNEAUX	TOOLED	TOOTHED
TOMPION	TONGING	TONNELL	TOOLER	TOOTHFISH
TOMPIONS	TONGMAN	TONNELLS	TOOLERS	TOOTHFUL
TOMPON	TONGMEN	TONNER	TOOLHEAD	TOOTHFULS
TOMPONED	TONGS	TONNERS	TOOLHEADS	TOOTHIER
TOMPONING	TONGSTER	TONNES	TOOLHOUSE	TOOTHIEST
TOMPONS	TONGSTERS	TONNISH	TOOLIE	TOOTHILY
TOMPOT	TONGUE	TONNISHLY	TOOLIES	TOOTHING
TOMS	TONGUED	TONOMETER	TOOLING	TOOTHINGS
TOMTIT	TONGUELET	TONOMETRY	TOOLINGS	TOOTHLESS
TOMTITS	TONGUES	TONOPLAST	TOOLKIT	TOOTHLIKE

TOOTHPICK	TOPHI	TOPOS	TOR	TORICS
TOOTHS	TOPHS	TOPOTYPE	TORA	TORIES
TOOTHSOME	TOPHUS	TOPOTYPES	TORAH	TORII
TOOTHWASH	TOPI	TOPPED	TORAHS	TORMENT
TOOTHWORT	TOPIARIAN	TOPPER	TORAN	TORMENTA
TOOTHY	TOPIARIES	TOPPERS	TORANA	TORMENTED
TOOTING	TOPIARIST	TOPPIER	TORANAS	TORMENTER
TOOTLE	TOPIARY	TOPPIEST	TORANS	TORMENTIL
TOOTLED	TOPIC	TOPPING	TORAS	TORMENTOR
TOOTLER	TOPICAL	TOPPINGLY	TORBANITE	TORMENTS
TOOTLERS	TOPICALLY	TOPPINGS	TORC	TORMENTUM
TOOTLES	TOPICALS	TOPPLE	TORCH	TORMINA
TOOTLING	TOPICS	TOPPLED	TORCHABLE	TORMINAL
TOOTS	TOPING	TOPPLES	TORCHED	TORMINOUS
TOOTSED	TOPIS	TOPPLING	TORCHER	TORN
TOOTSES	TOPKICK	TOPPY	TORCHERE	TORNADE
TOOTSIE	TOPKICKS	TOPRAIL	TORCHERES	TORNADES
TOOTSIES	TOPKNOT	TOPRAILS	TORCHERS	TORNADIC
TOOTSING	TOPKNOTS	TOPS	TORCHES	TORNADO
TOOTSY	TOPLESS	TOPSAIL	TORCHIER	TORNADOES
TOP	TOPLINE	TOPSAILS	TORCHIERE	TORNADOS
TOPALGIA	TOPLINED	TOPSCORE	TORCHIERS	TORNILLO
TOPALGIAS	TOPLINER	TOPSCORED	TORCHIEST	TORNILLOS
TOPARCH	TOPLINERS	TOPSCORES	TORCHING	TORO
TOPARCHS	TOPLINES	TOPSIDE	TORCHINGS	TOROID
TOPARCHY	TOPLINING	TOPSIDER	TORCHLIKE	TOROIDAL
TOPAZ	TOPLOFTY	TOPSIDERS	TORCHLIT	TOROIDS
TOPAZES	TOPMAKER	TOPSIDES	TORCHON	TOROS
TOPAZINE	TOPMAKERS	TOPSMAN	TORCHONS	TOROSE
TOPCOAT	TOPMAKING	TOPSMEN	TORCHWOOD	TOROSITY
TOPCOATS	TOPMAN	TOPSOIL	TORCHY	TOROT
TOPCROSS	TOPMAST	TOPSOILED	TORCS	TOROTH
TOPE	TOPMASTS	TOPSOILS	TORCULAR	TOROUS
TOPECTOMY	TOPMEN	TOPSPIN	TORCULARS	TORPEDO
TOPED	TOPMINNOW	TOPSPINS	TORDION	TORPEDOED
TOPEE	TOPMOST	TOPSTITCH	TORDIONS	TORPEDOER
TOPEES	TOPNOTCH	TOPSTONE	TORE	TORPEDOES
TOPEK	TOPO	TOPSTONES	TOREADOR	TORPEDOS
TOPEKS	TOPOGRAPH	TOPWATER	TOREADORS	TORPEFIED
TOPER	TOPOI	TOPWORK	TORERO	TORPEFIES
TOPERS	TOPOLOGIC	TOPWORKED	TOREROS	TORPEFY
TOPES	TOPOLOGY	TOPWORKS	TORES	TORPID
TOPFLIGHT	TOPOMETRY	TOQUE	TOREUTIC	TORPIDITY
TOPFUL	TOPONYM	TOQUES	TOREUTICS	TORPIDLY
TOPFULL	TOPONYMAL	TOQUET	TORGOCH	TORPIDS
TOPH	TOPONYMIC	TOQUETS	TORGOCHS	TORPITUDE
TOPHE	TOPONYMS	TOQUILLA	TORI	TORPOR
TOPHES	TOPONYMY	TOQUILLAS	TORIC	TORPORS

TORQUATE	TORTE	TOSES	TOTALISTS	TOTTIER
TORQUATED	TORTELLI	TOSH	TOTALITY	TOTTIES
TORQUE	TORTELLIS	TOSHACH	TOTALIZE	TOTTIEST
TORQUED	TORTEN	TOSHACHS	TOTALIZED	TOTTING
TORQUER	TORTES	TOSHED	TOTALIZER	TOTTINGS
TORQUERS	TORTIE	TOSHER	TOTALIZES	TOTTRING
TORQUES	TORTIES	TOSHERS	TOTALLED	TOTTY
TORQUESES	TORTILE	TOSHES	TOTALLING	TOUCAN
TORQUEY	TORTILITY	TOSHIER	TOTALLY	TOUCANET
TORQUIER	TORTILLA	TOSHIEST	TOTALS	TOUCANETS
TORQUIEST	TORTILLAS	TOSHING	TOTANUS	TOUCANS
TORQUING	TORTILLON	TOSHY	TOTANUSES	TOUCH
TORR	TORTIOUS	TOSING	TOTAQUINE	TOUCHABLE
TORREFIED	TORTIVE	TOSS	TOTARA	TOUCHABLY
TORREFIES	TORTOISE	TOSSED	TOTARAS	TOUCHBACK
TORREFY	TORTOISES	TOSSEN	TOTE	TOUCHDOWN
TORRENT	TORTONI	TOSSER	TOTEABLE	TOUCHE
TORRENTS	TORTONIS	TOSSERS	TOTED	TOUCHED
TORRET	TORTRICES	TOSSES	TOTEM	TOUCHER
TORRETS	TORTRICID	TOSSIER	TOTEMIC	TOUCHERS
TORRID	TORTRIX	TOSSIEST	TOTEMISM	TOUCHES
TORRIDER	TORTRIXES	TOSSILY	TOTEMISMS	TOUCHHOLE
TORRIDEST	TORTS	TOSSING	TOTEMIST	TOUCHIER
TORRIDITY	TORTUOUS	TOSSINGS	TOTEMISTS	TOUCHIEST
TORRIDLY	TORTURE	TOSSPOT	TOTEMITE	TOUCHILY
TORRIFIED	TORTURED	TOSSPOTS	TOTEMITES	TOUCHING
TORRIFIES	TORTURER	TOSSUP	TOTEMS	TOUCHINGS
TORRIFY	TORTURERS	TOSSUPS	TOTER	TOUCHLESS
TORRS	TORTURES	TOSSY	TOTERS	TOUCHLINE
TORS	TORTURING	TOST	TOTES	TOUCHMARK
TORSADE	TORTUROUS	TOSTADA	TOTHER	TOUCHPAD
TORSADES	TORULA	TOSTADAS	TOTHERS	TOUCHPADS
TORSE	TORULAE	TOSTADO	TOTIENT	TOUCHTONE
TORSEL	TORULAS	TOSTADOS	TOTIENTS	TOUCHUP
TORSELS	TORULI	TOSTONE	TOTING	TOUCHUPS
TORSES	TORULIN	TOSTONES	TOTITIVE	TOUCHWOOD
TORSI	TORULINS	TOT	TOTITIVES	TOUCHY
TORSION	TORULOSE	TOTABLE	TOTS	TOUGH
TORSIONAL	TORULOSES	TOTAL	TOTTED	TOUGHED
TORSIONS	TORULOSIS	TOTALED	TOTTER	TOUGHEN
TORSIVE	TORULUS	TOTALING	TOTTERED	TOUGHENED
TORSK	TORUS	TOTALISE	TOTTERER	TOUGHENER
TORSKS	TORUSES	TOTALISED	TOTTERERS	TOUGHENS
TORSO	TORY	TOTALISER	TOTTERIER	TOUGHER
TORSOS	TOSA	TOTALISES	TOTTERING	TOUGHEST
TORT	TOSAS	TOTALISM	TOTTERS	TOUGHIE
TORTA	TOSE	TOTALISMS	TOTTERY	TOUGHIES
TORTAS	TOSED	TOTALIST	TOTTIE	TOUGHING

TOYBOX

TOUGHISH	TOUSE	TOWARDS	TOWNEE	TOWSER
TOUGHLY	TOUSED	TOWAWAY	TOWNEES	TOWSERS
TOUGHNESS	TOUSER	TOWAWAYS	TOWNFOLK	TOWSES
TOUGHS	TOUSERS	TOWBAR	TOWNHALL	TOWSIER
TOUGHY	TOUSES	TOWBARS	TOWNHOME	TOWSIEST
TOUK	TOUSIER	TOWBOAT	TOWNHOMES	TOWSING
TOUKED	TOUSIEST	TOWBOATS	TOWNHOUSE	TOWSY
TOUKING	TOUSING	TOWED	TOWNIE	TOWT
TOUKS	TOUSINGS	TOWEL	TOWNIER	TOWTED
TOULADI	TOUSLE	TOWELED	TOWNIES	TOWTING
TOULADIS	TOUSLED	TOWELETTE	TOWNIEST	TOWTS
TOUN	TOUSLES	TOWELHEAD	TOWNISH	TOWY
TOUNS	TOUSLING	TOWELING	TOWNLAND	TOWZE
TOUPEE	TOUSTIE	TOWELINGS	TOWNLANDS	TOWZED
TOUPEED	TOUSTIER	TOWELLED	TOWNLESS	TOWZES
TOUPEES	TOUSTIEST	TOWELLING	TOWNLET	TOWZIER
TOUPET	TOUSY	TOWELS	TOWNLETS	TOWZIEST
TOUPETS	TOUT	TOWER	TOWNLIER	TOWZING
TOUPIE	TOUTED	TOWERED	TOWNLIEST	TOWZY
TOUPIES	TOUTER	TOWERIER	TOWNLING	TOXAEMIA
TOUR	TOUTERS	TOWERIEST	TOWNLINGS	TOXAEMIAS
TOURACO	TOUTIE	TOWERING	TOWNLY	TOXAEMIC
TOURACOS	TOUTIER	TOWERLESS	TOWNS	TOXAPHENE
TOURED	TOUTIEST	TOWERLIKE	TOWNSCAPE	TOXEMIA
TOURER	TOUTING	TOWERS	TOWNSFOLK	TOXEMIAS
TOURERS	TOUTON	TOWERY	TOWNSHIP	TOXEMIC
TOURIE	TOUTONS	TOWHEAD	TOWNSHIPS	TOXIC
TOURIES	TOUTS	TOWHEADED	TOWNSITE	TOXICAL
TOURING	TOUZE	TOWHEADS	TOWNSITES	TOXICALLY
TOURINGS	TOUZED	TOWHEE	TOWNSKIP	TOXICANT
TOURISM	TOUZES	TOWHEES	TOWNSKIPS	TOXICANTS
TOURISMS	TOUZIER	TOWIE	TOWNSMAN	TOXICITY
TOURIST	TOUZIEST	TOWIER	TOWNSMEN	TOXICOSES
TOURISTA	TOUZING	TOWIES	TOWNWARD	TOXICOSIS
TOURISTAS	TOUZLE	TOWIEST	TOWNWEAR	TOXICS
TOURISTED	TOUZLED	TOWING	TOWNWEARS	TOXIGENIC
TOURISTIC	TOUZLES	TOWINGS	TOWNY	TOXIN
TOURISTS	TOUZLING	TOWKAY	TOWPATH	TOXTNE
TOURISTY	TOUZY	TOWKAYS	TOWPATHS	TOXINES
TOURNEDOS	TOVARICH	TOWLINE	TOWPLANE	TOXINS
TOURNEY	TOVARISCH	TOWLINES	TOWPLANES	TOXOCARA
TOURNEYED	TOVARISH	TOWMON	TOWROPE	TOXOCARAL
TOURNEYER	TOW	TOWMOND	TOWROPES	TOXOCARAS
TOURNEYS	TOWABLE	TOWMONDS	TOWS	TOXOID
TOURNURE	TOWAGE	TOWMONS	TOWSACK	TOXOIDS
TOURNURES	TOWAGES	TOWMONT	TOWSACKS	TOXOPHILY
TOURS	TOWARD	TOWMONTS	TOWSE	TOY
TOURTIERE	TOWARDLY	TOWN	TOWSED	TOYBOX

TOYBOXES

TOYBOXES	TRACERIES	TRACKROAD	TRADS	TRAINEE
TOYCHEST	TRACERS	TRACKS	TRADUCE	TRAINEES
TOYCHESTS	TRACERY	TRACKSIDE	TRADUCED	TRAINER
TOYED	TRACES	TRACKSUIT	TRADUCER	TRAINERS
TOYER	TRACEUR	TRACKWAY	TRADUCERS	TRAINFUL
TOYERS	TRACEURS	TRACKWAYS	TRADUCES	TRAINFULS
TOYETIC	TRACHEA	TRACT	TRADUCIAN	TRAINING
TOYING	TRACHEAE	TRACTABLE	TRADUCING	TRAININGS
TOYINGS	TRACHEAL	TRACTABLY	TRAFFIC	TRAINLESS
TOYISH	TRACHEARY	TRACTATE	TRAFFICKY	TRAINLOAD
TOYISHLY	TRACHEAS	TRACTATES	TRAFFICS	TRAINMAN
TOYLAND	TRACHEATE	TRACTATOR	TRAGAL	TRAINMEN
TOYLANDS	TRACHEID	TRACTED	TRAGEDIAN	TRAINS
TOYLESOME	TRACHEIDE	TRACTILE	TRAGEDIES	TRAINWAY
TOYLESS	TRACHEIDS	TRACTING	TRAGEDY	TRAINWAYS
TOYLIKE	TRACHEOLE	TRACTION	TRAGELAPH	TRAIPSE
TOYLSOM	TRACHINUS	TRACTIONS	TRAGI	TRAIPSED
TOYMAN	TRACHITIS	TRACTIVE	TRAGIC	TRAIPSES
TOYMEN	TRACHLE	TRACTOR	TRAGICAL	TRAIPSING
TOYO	TRACHLED	TRACTORS	TRAGICS	TRAIT
TOYON	TRACHLES	TRACTRIX	TRAGOPAN	TRAITOR
TOYONS	TRACHLING	TRACTS	TRAGOPANS	TRAITORLY
TOYOS	TRACHOMA	TRACTUS	TRAGULE	TRAITORS
TOYS	TRACHOMAS	TRACTUSES	TRAGULES	TRAITRESS
TOYSHOP	TRACHYTE	TRAD	TRAGULINE	TRAITS
TOYSHOPS	TRACHYTES	TRADABLE	TRAGUS	TRAJECT
TOYSOME	TRACHYTIC	TRADE	TRAHISON	TRAJECTED
TOYTOWN	TRACING	TRADEABLE	TRAHISONS	TRAJECTS
TOYTOWNS	TRACINGS	TRADED	TRAIK	TRAM
TOYWOMAN	TRACK	TRADEFUL	TRAIKED	TRAMCAR
TOYWOMEN	TRACKABLE	TRADELESS	TRAIKING	TRAMCARS
TOZE	TRACKAGE	TRADEMARK	TRAIKIT	TRAMEL
TOZED	TRACKAGES	TRADENAME	TRAIKS	TRAMELED
TOZES	TRACKBALL	TRADEOFF	TRAIL	TRAMELING
TOZIE	TRACKBED	TRADEOFFS	TRAILABLE	TRAMELL
TOZIES	TRACKBEDS	TRADER	TRAILED	TRAMELLED
TOZING	TRACKED	TRADERS	TRAILER	TRAMELLS
TRABEATE	TRACKER	TRADES	TRAILERED	TRAMELS
TRABEATED	TRACKERS	TRADESMAN	TRAILERS	TRAMLESS
TRABECULA	TRACKIE	TRADESMEN	TRAILHEAD	TRAMLINE
TRABS	TRACKIES	TRADIE	TRAILING	TRAMLINED
TRACE	TRACKING	TRADIES	TRAILLESS	TRAMLINES
TRACEABLE	TRACKINGS	TRADING	TRAILS	TRAMMED
TRACEABLY	TRACKLESS	TRADINGS	TRAILSIDE	TRAMMEL
TRACED	TRACKMAN	TRADITION	TRAIN	TRAMMELED
TRACELESS	TRACKMEN	TRADITIVE	TRAINABLE	TRAMMELER
TRACER	TRACKPAD	TRADITOR	TRAINBAND	TRAMMELS
TRACERIED	TRACKPADS	TRADITORS	TRAINED	TRAMMIE

TRAMMIES	TRANKING	TRANSMIT	TRAPEZIST	TRASHY
TRAMMING	TRANKS	TRANSMITS	TRAPEZIUM	TRASS
TRAMP	TRANKUM	TRANSMOVE	TRAPEZIUS	TRASSES
TRAMPED	TRANKUMS	TRANSMUTE	TRAPEZOID	TRAT
TRAMPER	TRANNIE	TRANSOM	TRAPFALL	TRATS
TRAMPERS	TRANNIES	TRANSOMED	TRAPFALLS	TRATT
TRAMPET	TRANNY	TRANSOMS	TRAPING	TRATTORIA
TRAMPETS	TRANQ	TRANSONIC	TRAPLIKE	TRATTORIE
TRAMPETTE	TRANQS	TRANSPIRE	TRAPLINE	TRATTS
TRAMPIER	TRANQUIL	TRANSPORT	TRAPLINES	TRAUCHLE
TRAMPIEST	TRANS	TRANSPOSE	TRAPNEST	TRAUCHLED
TRAMPING	TRANSACT	TRANSSHIP	TRAPNESTS	TRAUCHLES
TRAMPINGS	TRANSACTS	TRANSUDE	TRAPPEAN	TRAUMA
TRAMPISH	TRANSAXLE	TRANSUDED	TRAPPED	TRAUMAS
TRAMPLE	TRANSCEND	TRANSUDES	TRAPPER	TRAUMATA
TRAMPLED	TRANSCODE	TRANSUME	TRAPPERS	TRAUMATIC
TRAMPLER	TRANSDUCE	TRANSUMED	TRAPPIER	TRAVAIL
TRAMPLERS	TRANSE	TRANSUMES	TRAPPIEST	TRAVAILED
TRAMPLES	TRANSECT	TRANSUMPT	TRAPPING	TRAVAILS
TRAMPLING	TRANSECTS	TRANSVEST	TRAPPINGS	TRAVE
TRAMPOLIN	TRANSENNA	TRANT	TRAPPOSE	TRAVEL
TRAMPS	TRANSEPT	TRANTED	TRAPPOUS	TRAVELED
TRAMPY	TRANSEPTS	TRANTER	TRAPPY	TRAVELER
TRAMROAD	TRANSES	TRANTERS	TRAPROCK	TRAVELERS
TRAMROADS	TRANSEUNT	TRANTING	TRAPROCKS	TRAVELING
TRAMS	TRANSFARD	TRANTS	TRAPS	TRAVELLED
TRAMWAY	TRANSFECT	TRAP	TRAPSE	TRAVELLER
TRAMWAYS	TRANSFER	TRAPAN	TRAPSED	TRAVELOG
TRANCE	TRANSFERS	TRAPANNED	TRAPSES	TRAVELOGS
TRANCED	TRANSFIX	TRAPANNER	TRAPSING	TRAVELS
TRANCEDLY	TRANSFIXT	TRAPANS	TRAPT	TRAVERSAL
TRANCES	TRANSFORM	TRAPBALL	TRAPUNTO	TRAVERSE
TRANCEY	TRANSFUSE	TRAPBALLS	TRAPUNTOS	TRAVERSED
TRANCHE	TRANSGENE	TRAPDOOR	TRASH	TRAVERSER
TRANCHES	TRANSHIP	TRAPDOORS	TRASHCAN	TRAVERSES
TRANCHET	TRANSHIPS	TRAPE	TRASHCANS	TRAVERTIN
TRANCHETS	TRANSHUME	TRAPED	TRASHED	TRAVES
TRANCIER	TRANSIENT	TRAPES	TRASHER	TRAVESTY
TRANCIEST	TRANSIRE	TRAPESED	TRASHERS	TRAVIS
TRANCING	TRANSIRES	TRAPESES	TRASHERY	TRAVISES
TRANECT	TRANSIT	TRAPESING	TRASHES	TRAVOIS
TRANECTS	TRANSITED	TRAPEZE	TRASHIER	TRAVOISE
TRANGAM	TRANSITS	TRAPEZED	TRASHIEST	TRAVOISES
TRANGAMS	TRANSLATE	TRAPEZES	TRASHILY	TRAWL
TRANGLE	TRANSMAN	TRAPEZIA	TRASHING	TRAWLED
TRANGLES	TRANSMEN	TRAPEZIAL	TRASHMAN	TRAWLER
TRANK	TRANSMEW	TRAPEZII	TRASHMEN	TRAWLERS
TRANKED	TRANSMEWS	TRAPEZING	TRASHTRIE	TRAWLEY

TRAWLEYS	TREASON	TREELAWN	TREMAS	TRENDING
TRAWLING	TREASONS	TREELAWNS	TREMATIC	TRENDOID
TRAWLINGS	TREASURE	TREELESS	TREMATODE	TRENDOIDS
TRAWLNET	TREASURED	TREELIKE	TREMATOID	TRENDS
TRAWLNETS	TREASURER	TREELINE	TREMBLANT	TRENDY
TRAWLS	TREASURES	TREELINES	TREMBLE	TRENDYISM
TRAY	TREASURY	TREEN	TREMBLED	TRENISE
TRAYBAKE	TREAT	TREENAIL	TREMBLER	TRENISES
TRAYBAKES	TREATABLE	TREENAILS	TREMBLERS	TRENTAL
TRAYBIT	TREATED	TREENS	TREMBLES	TRENTALS
TRAYBITS	TREATER	TREENWARE	TREMBLIER	TREPAN
TRAYCLOTH	TREATERS	TREES	TREMBLING	TREPANG
TRAYF	TREATIES	TREESHIP	TREMBLOR	TREPANGS
TRAYFUL	TREATING	TREESHIPS	TREMBLORS	TREPANNED
TRAYFULS	TREATINGS	TREETOP	TREMBLY	TREPANNER
TRAYNE	TREATISE	TREETOPS	TREMIE	TREPANS
TRAYNED	TREATISES	TREEWARE	TREMIES	TREPHINE
TRAYNES	TREATMENT	TREEWARES	TREMOLANT	TREPHINED
TRAYNING	TREATS	TREEWAX	TREMOLITE	TREPHINER
TRAYS	TREATY	TREEWAXES	TREMOLO	TREPHINES
TRAZODONE	TREBBIANO	TREF	TREMOLOS	TREPID
TREACHER	TREBLE	TREFA	TREMOR	TREPIDANT
TREACHERS	TREBLED	TREFAH	TREMORED	TREPONEMA
TREACHERY	TREBLES	TREFOIL	TREMORING	TREPONEME
TREACHOUR	TREBLIER	TREFOILED	TREMOROUS	TRES
TREACLE	TREBLIEST	TREFOILS	TREMORS	TRESPASS
TREACLED	TREBLING	TREGETOUR	TREMS	TRESS
TREACLES	TREBLINGS	TREGGINGS	TREMULANT	TRESSED
TREACLIER	TREBLY	TREHALA	TREMULATE	TRESSEL
TREACLING	TREBUCHET	TREHALAS	TREMULOUS	TRESSELS
TREACLY	TREBUCKET	TREHALOSE	TRENAIL	TRESSES
TREAD	TRECENTO	TREIF	TRENAILS	TRESSIER
TREADED	TRECENTOS	TREIFA	TRENCH	TRESSIEST
TREADER	TRECK	TREILLAGE	TRENCHAND	TRESSING
TREADERS	TRECKED	TREILLE	TRENCHANT	TRESSOUR
TREADING	TRECKING	TREILLES	TRENCHARD	TRESSOURS
TREADINGS	TRECKS	TREK	TRENCHED	TRESSURE
TREADLE	TREDDLE	TREKKED	TRENCHER	TRESSURED
TREADLED	TREDDLED	TREKKER	TRENCHERS	TRESSURES
TREADLER	TREDDLES	TREKKERS	TRENCHES	TRESSY
TREADLERS	TREDDLING	TREKKING	TRENCHING	TREST
TREADLES	TREDILLE	TREKKINGS	TREND	TRESTLE
TREADLESS	TREDILLES	TREKS	TRENDED	TRESTLES
TREADLING	TREDRILLE	TRELLIS	TRENDIER	TRESTS
TREADMILL	TREE	TRELLISED	TRENDIES	TRET
TREADS	TREED	TRELLISES	TRENDIEST	TRETINOIN
TREAGUE	TREEHOUSE	TREM	TRENDIFY	TRETS
TREAGUES	TREEING	TREMA	TRENDILY	TREVALLY

TREVALLYS	TRIALITY	TRIBESMEN	TRICKED	TRICYCLER
TREVET	TRIALLED	TRIBLET	TRICKER	TRICYCLES
TREVETS	TRIALLING	TRIBLETS	TRICKERS	TRICYCLIC
TREVIS	TRIALLIST	TRIBOLOGY	TRICKERY	TRIDACNA
TREVISES	TRIALOGUE	TRIBRACH	TRICKIE	TRIDACNAS
TREVISS	TRIALS	TRIBRACHS	TRICKIER	TRIDACTYL
TREVISSES	TRIALWARE	TRIBULATE	TRICKIEST	TRIDARN
TREW	TRIANGLE	TRIBUNAL	TRICKILY	TRIDARNS
TREWS	TRIANGLED	TRIBUNALS	TRICKING	TRIDE
TREWSMAN	TRIANGLES	TRIBUNARY	TRICKINGS	TRIDENT
TREWSMEN	TRIAPSAL	TRIBUNATE	TRICKISH	TRIDENTAL
TREY	TRIARCH	TRIBUNE	TRICKLE	TRIDENTED
TREYBIT	TRIARCHS	TRIBUNES	TRICKLED	TRIDENTS
TREYBITS	TRIARCHY	TRIBUTARY	TRICKLES	TRIDUAN
TREYF	TRIASSIC	TRIBUTE	TRICKLESS	TRIDUUM
TREYFA	TRIATHLON	TRIBUTER	TRICKLET	TRIDUUMS
TREYS	TRIATIC	TRIBUTERS	TRICKLETS	TRIDYMITE
TREZ	TRIATICS	TRIBUTES	TRICKLIER	TRIE
TREZES	TRIATOMIC	TRICAR	TRICKLING	TRIECIOUS
TRIABLE	TRIAXIAL	TRICARS	TRICKLY	TRIED
TRIAC	TRIAXIALS	TRICE	TRICKS	TRIELLA
TRIACID	TRIAXON	TRICED	TRICKSIER	TRIELLAS
TRIACIDS	TRIAXONS	TRICEP	TRICKSILY	TRIENE
TRIACS	TRIAZIN	TRICEPS	TRICKSOME	TRIENES
TRIACT	TRIAZINE	TRICEPSES	TRICKSTER	TRIENNIA
TRIACTINE	TRIAZINES	TRICERION	TRICKSY	TRIENNIAL
TRIACTOR	TRIAZINS	TRICES	TRICKY	TRIENNIUM
TRIACTORS	TRIAZOLE	TRICHINA	TRICLAD	TRIENS
TRIACTS	TRIAZOLES	TRICHINAE	TRICLADS	TRIENTES
TRIAD	TRIAZOLIC	TRICHINAL	TRICLINIA	TRIER
TRIADIC	TRIBADE	TRICHINAS	TRICLINIC	TRIERARCH
TRIADICS	TRIBADES	TRICHITE	TRICLOSAN	TRIERS
TRIADISM	TRIBADIC	TRICHITES	TRICOLOR	TRIES
TRIADISMS	TRIBADIES	TRICHITIC	TRICOLORS	TRIETERIC
TRIADIST	TRIBADISM	TRICHOID	TRICOLOUR	TRIETHYL
TRIADISTS	TRIBADY	TRICHOME	TRICORN	TRIFACIAL
TRIADS	TRIBAL	TRICHOMES	TRICORNE	TRIFECTA
TRIAGE	TRIBALISM	TRICHOMIC	TRICORNES	TRIFECTAS
TRIAGED	TRIBALIST	TRICHORD	TRICORNS	TRIFF
TRIAGES	TRIBALLY	TRICHORDS	TRICOT	TRIFFER
TRIAGING	TRIBALS	TRICHOSES	TRICOTINE	TRIFFEST
TRIAL	TRIBASIC	TRICHOSIS	TRICOTS	TRIFFIC
TRIALED	TRIBBLE	TRICHROIC	TRICROTIC	TRIFFID
TRIALING	TRIBBLES	TRICHROME	TRICTRAC	TRIFFIDS
TRIALISM	TRIBE	TRICING	TRICTRACS	TRIFFIDY
TRIALISMS	TRIBELESS	TRICITIES	TRICUSPID	TRIFID
TRIALIST	TRIBES	TRICITY	TRICYCLE	TRIFLE
TRIALISTS	TRIBESMAN	TRICK	TRICYCLED	TRIFLED

TRIFLER	TRIGYNOUS	TRIMER	TRINKETER	TRIPLANES
TRIFLERS	TRIHEDRA	TRIMERIC	TRINKETRY	TRIPLE
TRIFLES	TRIHEDRAL	TRIMERISM	TRINKETS	TRIPLED
TRIFLING	TRIHEDRON	TRIMEROUS	TRINKUM	TRIPLES
TRIFLINGS	TRIHYBRID	TRIMERS	TRINKUMS	TRIPLET
TRIFOCAL	TRIHYDRIC	TRIMESTER	TRINODAL	TRIPLETS
TRIFOCALS	TRIJET	TRIMETER	TRINOMIAL	TRIPLEX
TRIFOLD	TRIJETS	TRIMETERS	TRINS	TRIPLEXED
TRIFOLIA	TRIJUGATE	TRIMETHYL	TRIO	TRIPLEXES
TRIFOLIES	TRIJUGOUS	TRIMETRIC	TRIODE	TRIPLIED
TRIFOLIUM	TRIKE	TRIMIX	TRIODES	TRIPLIES
TRIFOLY	TRIKES	TRIMIXES	TRIOL	TRIPLING
TRIFORIA	TRILBIED	TRIMLY	TRIOLEIN	TRIPLINGS
TRIFORIAL	TRILBIES	TRIMMED	TRIOLEINS	TRIPLITE
TRIFORIUM	TRILBY	TRIMMER	TRIOLET	TRIPLITES
TRIFORM	TRILBYS	TRIMMERS	TRIOLETS	TRIPLOID
TRIFORMED	TRILD	TRIMMEST	TRIOLS	TRIPLOIDS
TRIG	TRILEMMA	TRIMMING	TRIONES	TRIPLOIDY
TRIGAMIES	TRILEMMAS	TRIMMINGS	TRIONYM	TRIPLY
TRIGAMIST	TRILINEAR	TRIMNESS	TRIONYMAL	TRIPLYING
TRIGAMOUS	TRILITH	TRIMORPH	TRIONYMS	TRIPMAN
TRIGAMY	TRILITHIC	TRIMORPHS	TRIOR	TRIPMEN
TRIGEMINI	TRILITHON	TRIMOTOR	TRIORS	TRIPMETER
TRIGGED	TRILITHS	TRIMOTORS	TRIOS	TRIPOD
TRIGGER	TRILL	TRIMPHONE	TRIOSE	TRIPODAL
TRIGGERED	TRILLED	TRIMPOT	TRIOSES	TRIPODIC
TRIGGERS	TRILLER	TRIMPOTS	TRIOXID	TRIPODIES
TRIGGEST	TRILLERS	TRIMS	TRIOXIDE	TRIPODS
TRIGGING	TRILLING	TRIMTAB	TRIOXIDES	TRIPODY
TRIGLOT	TRILLINGS	TRIMTABS	TRIOXIDS	TRIPOLI
TRIGLOTS	TRILLION	TRIN	TRIOXYGEN	TRIPOLIS
TRIGLY	TRILLIONS	TRINAL	TRIP	TRIPOS
TRIGLYPH	TRILLIUM	TRINARY	TRIPACK	TRIPOSES
TRIGLYPHS	TRILLIUMS	TRINDLE	TRIPACKS	TRIPPANT
TRIGNESS	TRILLO	TRINDLED	TRIPART	TRIPPED
TRIGO	TRILLOES	TRINDLES	TRIPE	TRIPPER
TRIGON	TRILLS	TRINDLING	TRIPEDAL	TRIPPERS
TRIGONAL	TRILOBAL	TRINE	TRIPERIES	TRIPPERY
TRIGONIC	TRILOBATE	TRINED	TRIPERY	TRIPPET
TRIGONOUS	TRILOBE	TRINES	TRIPES	TRIPPETS
TRIGONS	TRILOBED	TRINGLE	TRIPEY	TRIPPIER
TRIGOS	TRILOBES	TRINGLES	TRIPHASE	TRIPPIEST
TRIGRAM	TRILOBITE	TRINING	TRIPHONE	TRIPPING
TRIGRAMS	TRILOGIES	TRINITIES	TRIPHONES	TRIPPINGS
TRIGRAPH	TRILOGY	TRINITRIN	TRIPIER	TRIPPLE
TRIGRAPHS	TRIM	TRINITY	TRIPIEST	TRIPPLED
TRIGS	TRIMARAN	TRINKET	TRIPITAKA	TRIPPLER
TRIGYNIAN	TRIMARANS	TRINKETED	TRIPLANE	TRIPPLERS

TRIPPLES	TRISOMIC	TRITURATE	TROCHEE	TROILIST
TRIPPLING	TRISOMICS	TRIUMPH	TROCHEES	TROILISTS
TRIPPY	TRISOMIES	TRIUMPHAL	TROCHES	TROILITE
TRIPS	TRISOMY	TRIUMPHED	TROCHI	TROILITES
TRIPSES	TRIST	TRIUMPHER	TROCHIL	TROILUS
TRIPSIS	TRISTATE	TRIUMPHS	TROCHILI	TROILUSES
TRIPTAN	TRISTE	TRIUMVIR	TROCHILIC	TROIS
TRIPTANE	TRISTESSE	TRIUMVIRI	TROCHILS	TROJAN
TRIPTANES	TRISTEZA	TRIUMVIRS	TROCHILUS	TROJANS
TRIPTANS	TRISTEZAS	TRIUMVIRY	TROCHISCI	TROKE
TRIPTOTE	TRISTFUL	TRIUNE	TROCHISK	TROKED
TRIPTOTES	TRISTICH	TRIUNES	TROCHISKS	TROKES
TRIPTYCA	TRISTICHS	TRIUNITY	TROCHITE	TROKING
TRIPTYCAS	TRISUL	TRIVALENT	TROCHITES	TROLAND
TRIPTYCH	TRISULA	TRIVALVE	TROCHLEA	TROLANDS
TRIPTYCHS	TRISULAS	TRIVALVED	TROCHLEAE	TROLL
TRIPTYQUE	TRISULS	TRIVALVES	TROCHLEAR	TROLLED
TRIPUDIA	TRITANOPE	TRIVET	TROCHLEAS	TROLLER
TRIPUDIUM	TRITE	TRIVETS	TROCHOID	TROLLERS
TRIPWIRE	TRITELY	TRIVIA	TROCHOIDS	TROLLEY
TRIPWIRES	TRITENESS	TRIVIAL	TROCHUS	TROLLEYED
TRIPY	TRITER	TRIVIALLY	TROCHUSES	TROLLEYS
TRIQUETRA	TRITES	TRIVIUM	TROCK	TROLLIED
TRIRADIAL	TRITEST	TRIVIUMS	TROCKED	TROLLIES
TRIREME	TRITHEISM	TRIWEEKLY	TROCKEN	TROLLING
TRIREMES	TRITHEIST	TRIZONAL	TROCKING	TROLLINGS
TRISAGION	TRITHING	TRIZONE	TROCKS	TROLLISH
TRISCELE	TRITHINGS	TRIZONES	TROD	TROLLIUS
TRISCELES	TRITIATE	TROAD	TRODDEN	TROLLOP
TRISECT	TRITIATED	TROADE	TRODE	TROLLOPED
TRISECTED	TRITIATES	TROADES	TRODES	TROLLOPEE
TRISECTOR	TRITICAL	TROADS	TRODS	TROLLOPS
TRISECTS	TRITICALE	TROAK	TROELIE	TROLLOPY
TRISEME	TRITICISM	TROAKED	TROELIES	TROLLS
TRISEMES	TRITICUM	TROAKING	TROELY	TROLLY
TRISEMIC	TRITICUMS	TROAKS	TROFFER	TROLLYING
TRISERIAL	TRITIDE	TROAT	TROFFERS	TROMBONE
TRISHAW	TRITIDES	TROATED	TROG	TROMBONES
TRISHAWS	TRITIUM	TROATING	TROGGED	TROMINO
TRISKELE	TRITIUMS	TROATS	TROGGING	TROMINOES
TRISKELES	TRITOMA	TROCAR	TROGGS	TROMINOS
TRISKELIA	TRITOMAS	TROCARS	TROGON	TROMMEL
TRISMIC	TRITON	TROCHAIC	TROGONS	TROMMELS
TRISMUS	TRITONE	TROCHAICS	TROGS	TROMP
TRISMUSES	TRITONES	TROCHAL	TROIKA	TROMPE
TRISODIUM	TRITONIA	TROCHAR	TROIKAS	TROMPED
TRISOME	TRITONIAS	TROCHARS	TROILISM	TROMPES
TRISOMES	TRITONS	TROCHE	TROILISMS	TROMPING

T

TROMPS	TROPISM	TROUNCED	TROWELING	TRUCKLINE
TRON	TROPISMS	TROUNCER	TROWELLED	TRUCKLING
TRONA	TROPIST	TROUNCERS	TROWELLER	TRUCKLOAD
TRONAS	TROPISTIC	TROUNCES	TROWELS	TRUCKMAN
TRONC	TROPISTS	TROUNCING	TROWING	TRUCKMEN
TRONCS	TROPOLOGY	TROUPE	TROWS	TRUCKS
TRONE	TROPONIN	TROUPED	TROWSERS	TRUCKSTOP
TRONES	TROPONINS	TROUPER	TROWTH	TRUCULENT
TRONK	TROPPO	TROUPERS	TROWTHS	TRUDGE
TRONKS	TROSSERS	TROUPES	TROY	TRUDGED
TRONS	TROT	TROUPIAL	TROYS	TRUDGEN
TROOLIE	TROTH	TROUPIALS	TRUANCIES	TRUDGENS
TROOLIES	TROTHED	TROUPING	TRUANCY	TRUDGEON
TROOP	TROTHFUL	TROUSE	TRUANT	TRUDGEONS
TROOPED	TROTHING	TROUSER	TRUANTED	TRUDGER
TROOPER	TROTHLESS	TROUSERED	TRUANTING	TRUDGERS
TROOPERS	TROTHS	TROUSERS	TRUANTLY	TRUDGES
TROOPIAL	TROTLINE	TROUSES	TRUANTRY	TRUDGING
TROOPIALS	TROTLINES	TROUSSEAU	TRUANTS	TRUDGINGS
TROOPING	TROTS	TROUT	TRUCAGE	TRUE
TROOPS	TROTTED	TROUTER	TRUCAGES	TRUEBLUE
TROOPSHIP	TROTTER	TROUTERS	TRUCE	TRUEBLUES
TROOSTITE	TROTTERS	TROUTFUL	TRUCED	TRUEBORN
TROOZ	TROTTING	TROUTIER	TRUCELESS	TRUEBRED
TROP	TROTTINGS	TROUTIEST	TRUCES	TRUED
TROPAEOLA	TROTTOIR	TROUTING	TRUCHMAN	TRUEING
TROPARIA	TROTTOIRS	TROUTINGS	TRUCHMANS	TRUELOVE
TROPARION	TROTYL	TROUTLESS	TRUCHMEN	TRUELOVES
TROPE	TROTYLS	TROUTLET	TRUCIAL	TRUEMAN
TROPED	TROU	TROUTLETS	TRUCING	TRUEMEN
TROPEOLIN	TROUBLE	TROUTLIKE	TRUCK	TRUENESS
TROPES	TROUBLED	TROUTLING	TRUCKABLE	TRUEPENNY
TROPHESY	TROUBLER	TROUTS	TRUCKAGE	TRUER
TROPHI	TROUBLERS	TROUTY	TRUCKAGES	TRUES
TROPHIC	TROUBLES	TROUVERE	TRUCKED	TRUEST
TROPHIED	TROUBLING	TROUVERES	TRUCKER	TRUFFE
TROPHIES	TROUBLOUS	TROUVEUR	TRUCKERS	TRUFFES
TROPHY	TROUCH	TROUVEURS	TRUCKFUL	TRUFFLE
TROPHYING	TROUCHES	TROVE	TRUCKFULS	TRUFFLED
TROPIC	TROUGH	TROVER	TRUCKIE	TRUFFLES
TROPICAL	TROUGHED	TROVERS	TRUCKIES	TRUFFLING
TROPICALS	TROUGHING	TROVES	TRUCKING	TRUG
TROPICS	TROUGHS	TROW	TRUCKINGS	TRUGO
TROPIN	TROULE	TROWED	TRUCKLE	TRUGOS
TROPINE	TROULED	TROWEL	TRUCKLED	TRUGS
TROPINES	TROULES	TROWELED	TRUCKLER	TRUING
TROPING	TROULING	TROWELER	TRUCKLERS	TRUISM
TROPINS	TROUNCE	TROWELERS	TRUCKLES	TRUISMS

TRUISTIC	TRUSSED	TRYP	TSARITZAS	TUATHS
TRULL	TRUSSER	TRYPAN	TSARS	TUATUA
TRULLS	TRUSSERS	TRYPS	TSATSKE	TUATUAS
TRULY	TRUSSES	TRYPSIN	TSATSKES	TUB
TRUMEAU	TRUSSING	TRYPSINS	TSESSEBE	TUBA
TRUMEAUX	TRUSSINGS	TRYPTIC	TSESSEBES	TUBAE
TRUMP	TRUST	TRYSAIL	TSETSE	TUBAGE
TRUMPED	TRUSTABLE	TRYSAILS	TSETSES	TUBAGES
TRUMPERY	TRUSTED	TRYST	TSIGANE	TUBAIST
TRUMPET	TRUSTEE	TRYSTE	TSIGANES	TUBAISTS
TRUMPETED	TRUSTEED	TRYSTED	TSIMMES	TUBAL
TRUMPETER	TRUSTEES	TRYSTER	TSITSITH	TUBAR
TRUMPETS	TRUSTER	TRYSTERS	TSK	TUBAS
TRUMPING	TRUSTERS	TRYSTES	TSKED	TUBATE
TRUMPINGS	TRUSTFUL	TRYSTING	TSKING	TUBBABLE
TRUMPLESS	TRUSTIER	TRYSTS	TSKS	TUBBED
TRUMPS	TRUSTIES	TRYWORKS	TSKTSK	TUBBER
TRUNCAL	TRUSTIEST	TSADDIK	TSKTSKED	TUBBERS
TRUNCATE	TRUSTILY	TSADDIKIM	TSKTSKING	TUBBIER
TRUNCATED	TRUSTING	TSADDIKS	TSKTSKS	TUBBIEST
TRUNCATES	TRUSTLESS	TSADDIQ	TSOORIS	TUBBINESS
TRUNCHEON	TRUSTOR	TSADDIQIM	TSORES	TUBBING
TRUNDLE	TRUSTORS	TSADDIQS	TSORIS	TUBBINGS
TRUNDLED	TRUSTS	TSADE	TSORRISS	TUBBISH
TRUNDLER	TRUSTY	TSADES	TSOTSI	TUBBY
TRUNDLERS	TRUTH	TSADI	TSOTSIS	TUBE
TRUNDLES	TRUTHER	TSADIK	TSOURIS	TUBECTOMY
TRUNDLING	TRUTHERS	TSADIKS	TSOURISES	TUBED
TRUNK	TRUTHFUL	TSADIS	TSUBA	TUBEFUL
TRUNKED	TRUTHIER	TSAMBA	TSUBAS	TUBEFULS
TRUNKFISH	TRUTHIEST	TSAMBAS	TSUBO	TUBELESS
TRUNKFUL	TRUTHLESS	TSANTSA	TSUBOS	TUBELIKE
TRUNKFULS	TRUTHLIKE	TSANTSAS	TSUNAMI	TUBENOSE
TRUNKING	TRUTHS	TSAR	TSUNAMIC	TUBENOSES
TRUNKINGS	TRUTHY	TSARDOM	TSUNAMIS	TUBER
TRUNKLESS	TRY	TSARDOMS	TSURIS	TUBERCLE
TRUNKLIKE	TRYE	TSAREVICH	TSURISES	TUBERCLED
TRUNKS	TRYER	TSAREVNA	TSUTSUMU	TUBERCLES
TRUNKWORK	TRYERS	TSAREVNAS	TSUTSUMUS	TUBERCULA
TRUNNEL	TRYING	TSARINA	TUAN	TUBERCULE
TRUNNELS	TRYINGLY	TSARINAS	TUANS	TUBEROID
TRUNNION	TRYINGS	TSARISM	TUART	TUBEROIDS
TRUNNIONS	TRYKE	TSARISMS	TUARTS	TUBEROSE
TRUQUAGE	TRYKES	TSARIST	TUATARA	TUBEROSES
TRUQUAGES	TRYMA	TSARISTS	TUATARAS	TUBEROUS
TRUQUEUR	TRYMATA	TSARITSA	TUATERA	TUBERS
TRUQUEURS	TRYOUT	TSARITSAS	TUATERAS	TUBES
TRUSS	TRYOUTS	TSARITZA	TUATH	TUBEWELL

TUBEWELLS	TUCKAMORE	TUGGED	TULE	TUMMY
TUBEWORK	TUCKBOX	TUGGER	TULES	TUMOR
TUBEWORKS	TUCKBOXES	TUGGERS	TULIP	TUMORAL
TUBEWORM	TUCKED	TUGGING	TULIPANT	TUMORLIKE
TUBEWORMS	TUCKER	TUGGINGLY	TULIPANTS	TUMOROUS
TUBFAST	TUCKERBAG	TUGGINGS	TULIPLIKE	TUMORS
TUBFASTS	TUCKERBOX	TUGHRA	TULIPS	TUMOUR
TUBFISH	TUCKERED	TUGHRAS	TULIPWOOD	TUMOURS
TUBFISHES	TUCKERING	TUGHRIK	TULLE	TUMP
TUBFUL	TUCKERS	TUGHRIKS	TULLES	TUMPED
TUBFULS	TUCKET	TUGLESS	TULLIBEE	TUMPHIES
TUBICOLAR	TUCKETS	TUGRA	TULLIBEES	TUMPHY
TUBICOLE	TUCKING	TUGRAS	TULPA	TUMPIER
TUBICOLES	TUCKINGS	TUGRIK	TULPAS	TUMPIEST
TUBIFEX	TUCKS	TUGRIKS	TULSI	TUMPING
TUBIFEXES	TUCKSHOP	TUGS	TULSIS	TUMPLINE
TUBIFICID	TUCKSHOPS	TUI	TULWAR	TUMPLINES
TUBIFORM	TUCOTUCO	TUILE	TULWARS	TUMPS
TUBING	TUCOTUCOS	TUILES	TUM	TUMPY
TUBINGS	TUCUTUCO	TUILLE	TUMBLE	TUMS
TUBIST	TUCUTUCOS	TUILLES	TUMBLEBUG	TUMSHIE
TUBISTS	TUCUTUCU	TUILLETTE	TUMBLED	TUMSHIES
TUBLIKE	TUCUTUCUS	TUILYIE	TUMBLER	TUMULAR
TUBS	TUFA	TUILYIED	TUMBLERS	TUMULARY
TUBULAR	TUFACEOUS	TUILYIES	TUMBLES	TUMULI
TUBULARLY	TUFAS	TUILZIE	TUMBLESET	TUMULOSE
TUBULARS	TUFF	TUILZIED	TUMBLING	TUMULOUS
TUBULATE	TUFFE	TUILZIES	TUMBLINGS	TUMULT
TUBULATED	TUFFES	TUINA	TUMBREL	TUMULTED
TUBULATES	TUFFET	TUINAS	TUMBRELS	TUMULTING
TUBULATOR	TUFFETS	TUIS	TUMBRIL	TUMULTS
TUBULE	TUFFS	TUISM	TUMBRILS	TUMULUS
TUBULES	TUFOLI	TUISMS	TUMEFIED	TUMULUSES
TUBULIN	TUFOLIS	TUITION	TUMEFIES	TUN
TUBULINS	TUFT	TUITIONAL	TUMEFY	TUNA
TUBULOSE	TUFTED	TUITIONS	TUMEFYING	TUNABLE
TUBULOUS	TUFTER	TUKTOO	TUMESCE	TUNABLY
TUBULURE	TUFTERS	TUKTOOS	TUMESCED	TUNAS
TUBULURES	TUFTIER	TUKTU	TUMESCENT	TUNBELLY
TUCHIS	TUFTIEST	TUKTUS	TUMESCES	TUND
TUCHISES	TUFTILY	TULADI	TUMESCING	TUNDED
TUCHUN	TUFTING	TULADIS	TUMID	TUNDING
TUCHUNS	TUFTINGS	TULAREMIA	TUMIDITY	TUNDISH
TUCHUS	TUFTS	TULAREMIC	TUMIDLY	TUNDISHES
TUCHUSES	TUFTY	TULBAN	TUMIDNESS	TUNDRA
TUCK	TUG	TULBANS	TUMMIES	TUNDRAS
TUCKAHOE	TUGBOAT	TULCHAN	TUMMLER	TUNDS
TUCKAHOES	TUGBOATS	TULCHANS	TUMMLERS	TUNDUN

TUNDUNS	TUNNELERS	TURBETH	TURFINGS	TURN
TUNE	TUNNELING	TURBETHS	TURFITE	TURNABLE
TUNEABLE	TUNNELLED	TURBID	TURFITES	TURNABOUT
TUNEABLY	TUNNELLER	TURBIDITE	TURFLESS	TURNAGAIN
TUNEAGE	TUNNELS	TURBIDITY	TURFLIKE	TURNBACK
TUNEAGES	TUNNIES	TURBIDLY	TURFMAN	TURNBACKS
TUNED	TUNNING	TURBINAL	TURFMEN	TURNCOAT
TUNEFUL	TUNNINGS	TURBINALS	TURFS	TURNCOATS
TUNEFULLY	TUNNY	TURBINATE	TURFSKI	TURNCOCK
TUNELESS	TUNS	TURBINE	TURFSKIS	TURNCOCKS
TUNER	TUNY	TURBINED	TURFY	TURNDOWN
TUNERS	TUP	TURBINES	TURGENCY	TURNDOWNS
TUNES	TUPEK	TURBIT	TURGENT	TURNDUN
TUNESMITH	TUPEKS	TURBITH	TURGENTLY	TURNDUNS
TUNEUP	TUPELO	TURBITHS	TURGID	TURNED
TUNEUPS	TUPELOS	TURBITS	TURGIDER	TURNER
TUNG	TUPIK	TURBO	TURGIDEST	TURNERIES
TUNGS	TUPIKS	TURBOCAR	TURGIDITY	TURNERS
TUNGSTATE	TUPLE	TURBOCARS	TURGIDLY	TURNERY
TUNGSTEN	TUPLES	TURBOFAN	TURGITE	TURNHALL
TUNGSTENS	TUPPED	TURBOFANS	TURGITES	TURNHALLS
TUNGSTIC	TUPPENCE	TURBOJET	TURGOR	TURNING
TUNGSTITE	TUPPENCES	TURBOJETS	TURGORS	TURNINGS
TUNGSTOUS	TUPPENNY	TURBOND	TURION	TURNIP
TUNIC	TUPPING	TURBONDS	TURIONS	TURNIPED
TUNICA	TUPPINGS	TURBOPROP	TURISTA	TURNIPIER
TUNICAE	TUPS	TURBOS	TURISTAS	TURNIPING
TUNICATE	TUPTOWING	TURBOT	TURK	TURNIPS
TUNICATED	TUPUNA	TURBOTS	TURKEY	TURNIPY
TUNICATES	TUPUNAS	TURBULENT	TURKEYS	TURNKEY
TUNICIN	TUQUE	TURCOPOLE	TURKIES	TURNKEYS
TUNICINS	TUQUES	TURD	TURKIESES	TURNOFF
TUNICKED	TURACIN	TURDINE	TURKIS	TURNOFFS
TUNICLE	TURACINS	TURDION	TURKISES	TURNON
TUNICLES	TURACO	TURDIONS	TURKOIS	TURNONS
TUNICS	TURACOS	TURDOID	TURKOISES	TURNOUT
TUNIER	TURACOU	TURDS	TURKS	TURNOUTS
TUNIEST	TURACOUS	TURDUCKEN	TURLOUGH	TURNOVER
TUNING	TURBAN	TUREEN	TURLOUGHS	TURNOVERS
TUNINGS	TURBAND	TUREENS	TURM	TURNPIKE
TUNKET	TURBANDS	TURF	TURME	TURNPIKES
TUNKETS	TURBANED	TURFED	TURMERIC	TURNROUND
TUNNAGE	TURBANNED	TURFEN	TURMERICS	TURNS
TUNNAGES	TURBANS	TURFGRASS	TURMES	TURNSKIN
TUNNED	TURBANT	TURFIER	TURMOIL	TURNSKINS
TUNNEL	TURBANTS	TURFIEST	TURMOILED	TURNSOLE
TUNNELED	TURBARIES	TURFINESS	TURMOILS	TURNSOLES
TUNNELER	TURBARY	TURFING	TURMS	TURNSPIT

TURNSPITS	TUSKER	TUTELARS	TUTTY	TWANGLER
TURNSTILE	TUSKERS	TUTELARY	TUTU	TWANGLERS
TURNSTONE	TUSKIER	TUTENAG	TUTUED	TWANGLES
TURNT	TUSKIEST	TUTENAGS	TUTUS	TWANGLING
TURNTABLE	TUSKING	TUTIORISM	TUTWORK	TWANGS
TURNUP	TUSKINGS	TUTIORIST	TUTWORKER	TWANGY
TURNUPS	TUSKLESS	TUTMAN	TUTWORKS	TWANK
TUROPHILE	TUSKLIKE	TUTMEN	TUX	TWANKAY
TURPETH	TUSKS	TUTOR	TUXEDO	TWANKAYS
TURPETHS	TUSKY	TUTORAGE	TUXEDOED	TWANKED
TURPITUDE	TUSSAC	TUTORAGES	TUXEDOES	TWANKIES
TURPS	TUSSAH	TUTORED	TUXEDOS	TWANKING
TURQUOIS	TUSSAHS	TUTORESS	TUXES	TWANKS
TURQUOISE	TUSSAL	TUTORIAL	TUYER	TWANKY
TURR	TUSSAR	TUTORIALS	TUYERE	TWAS
TURRET	TUSSARS	TUTORING	TUYERES	TWASOME
TURRETED	TUSSEH	TUTORINGS	TUYERS	TWASOMES
TURRETS	TUSSEHS	TUTORISE	TUZZ	TWAT
TURRIBANT	TUSSER	TUTORISED	TUZZES	TWATS
TURRICAL	TUSSERS	TUTORISES	TWA	TWATTED
TURRS	TUSSES	TUTORISM	TWADDLE	TWATTING
TURTLE	TUSSIS	TUTORISMS	TWADDLED	TWATTLE
TURTLED	TUSSISES	TUTORIZE	TWADDLER	TWATTLED
TURTLER	TUSSIVE	TUTORIZED	TWADDLERS	TWATTLER
TURTLERS	TUSSLE	TUTORIZES	TWADDLES	TWATTLERS
TURTLES	TUSSLED	TUTORS	TWADDLIER	TWATTLES
TURTLING	TUSSLES	TUTORSHIP	TWADDLING	TWATTLING
TURTLINGS	TUSSLING	TUTOYED	TWADDLY	TWAY
TURVES	TUSSOCK	TUTOYER	TWAE	TWAYBLADE
TUSCHE	TUSSOCKED	TUTOYERED	TWAES	TWAYS
TUSCHES	TUSSOCKS	TUTOYERS	TWAFALD	TWEAK
TUSH	TUSSOCKY	TUTRESS	TWAIN	TWEAKED
TUSHED	TUSSOR	TUTRESSES	TWAINS	TWEAKER
TUSHERIES	TUSSORE	TUTRICES	TWAITE	TWEAKERS
TUSHERY	TUSSORES	TUTRIX	TWAITES	TWEAKIER
TUSHES	TUSSORS	TUTRIXES	TWAL	TWEAKIEST
TUSHIE	TUSSUCK	TUTS	TWALPENNY	TWEAKING
TUSHIES	TUSSUCKS	TUTSAN	TWALS	TWEAKINGS
TUSHING	TUSSUR	TUTSANS	TWANG	TWEAKS
TUSHKAR	TUSSURS	TUTSED	TWANGED	TWEAKY
TUSHKARS	TUT	TUTSES	TWANGER	TWEE
TUSHKER	TUTANIA	TUTSING	TWANGERS	TWEED
TUSHKERS	TUTANIAS	TUTTED	TWANGIER	TWEEDIER
TUSHY	TUTEE	TUTTI	TWANGIEST	TWEEDIEST
TUSK	TUTEES	TUTTIES	TWANGING	TWEEDILY
TUSKAR	TUTELAGE	TUTTING	TWANGINGS	TWEEDLE
TUSKARS	TUTELAGES	TUTTINGS	TWANGLE	TWEEDLED
TUSKED	TUTELAR	TUTTIS	TWANGLED	TWEEDLER

TWEEDLERS	TWELVEMOS	TWIGHTING	TWINKIES	TWISTER
TWEEDLES	TWELVES	TWIGHTS	TWINKING	TWISTERS
TWEEDLING	TWENTIES	TWIGLESS	TWINKLE	TWISTIER
TWEEDS	TWENTIETH	TWIGLET	TWINKLED	TWISTIEST
TWEEDY	TWENTY	TWIGLETS	TWINKLER	TWISTING
TWEEL	TWENTYISH	TWIGLIKE	TWINKLERS	TWISTINGS
TWEELED	TWERK	TWIGLOO	TWINKLES	TWISTOR
TWEELING	TWERKED	TWIGLOOS	TWINKLIER	TWISTORS
TWEELS	TWERKING	TWIGS	TWINKLING	TWISTS
TWEELY	TWERKINGS	TWIGSOME	TWINKLY	TWISTY
TWEEN	TWERKS	TWILIGHT	TWINKS	TWIT
TWEENAGE	TWERP	TWILIGHTS	TWINKY	TWITCH
TWEENAGER	TWERPIER	TWILIT	TWINLING	TWITCHED
TWEENER	TWERPIEST	TWILL	TWINLINGS	TWITCHER
TWEENERS	TWERPS	TWILLED	TWINNED	TWITCHERS
TWEENESS	TWERPY	TWILLIES	TWINNING	TWITCHES
TWEENIE	TWIBIL	TWILLING	TWINNINGS	TWITCHIER
TWEENIES	TWIBILL	TWILLINGS	TWINS	TWITCHILY
TWEENS	TWIBILLS	TWILLS	TWINSET	TWITCHING
TWEENY	TWIBILS	TWILLY	TWINSETS	TWITCHY
TWEEP	TWICE	TWILT	TWINSHIP	TWITE
TWEEPLE	TWICER	TWILTED	TWINSHIPS	TWITES
TWEEPS	TWICERS	TWILTING	TWINTER	TWITS
TWEER	TWICHILD	TWILTS	TWINTERS	TWITTED
TWEERED	TWIDDLE	TWIN	TWINY	TWITTEN
TWEERING	TWIDDLED	TWINBERRY	TWIRE	TWITTENS
TWEERS	TWIDDLER	TWINBORN	TWIRED	TWITTER
TWEEST	TWIDDLERS	TWINE	TWIRES	TWITTERED
TWEET	TWIDDLES	TWINED	TWIRING	TWITTERER
TWEETABLE	TWIDDLIER	TWINER	TWIRL	TWITTERS
TWEETED	TWIDDLING	TWINERS	TWIRLED	TWITTERY
TWEETER	TWIDDLY	TWINES	TWIRLER	TWITTING
TWEETERS	TWIER	TWINGE	TWIRLERS	TWITTINGS
TWEETING	TWIERS	TWINGED	TWIRLIER	TWITTISH
TWEETS	TWIFOLD	TWINGEING	TWIRLIEST	TWIXT
TWEETUP	TWIFORKED	TWINGES	TWIRLING	TWIZZLE
TWEETUPS	TWIFORMED	TWINGING	TWIRLS	TWIZZLED
TWEEZE	TWIG	TWINIER	TWIRLY	TWIZZLES
TWEEZED	TWIGGED	TWINIEST	TWIRP	TWIZZLING
TWEEZER	TWIGGEN	TWINIGHT	TWIRPIER	TWO
TWEEZERS	TWIGGER	TWINING	TWIRPIEST	TWOCCER
TWEEZES	TWIGGERS	TWININGLY	TWIRPS	TWOCCERS
TWEEZING	TWIGGIER	TWININGS	TWIRPY	TWOCCING
TWELFTH	TWIGGIEST	TWINJET	TWISCAR	TWOCCINGS
TWELFTHLY	TWIGGING	TWINJETS	TWISCARS	TWOCKER
TWELFTHS	TWIGGY	TWINK	TWIST	TWOCKERS
TWELVE	TWIGHT	TWINKED	TWISTABLE	TWOCKING
TWELVEMO	TWIGHTED	TWINKIE	TWISTED	TWOCKINGS

TWOER	TYKES	TYPEFACES	TYPTOED	TYTHES
TWOERS	TYKISH	TYPES	TYPTOING	TYTHING
TWOFER	TYLECTOMY	TYPESET	TYPTOS	TZADDI
TWOFERS	TYLER	TYPESETS	TYPY	TZADDIK
TWOFOLD	TYLERS	TYPESTYLE	TYRAMINE	TZADDIKIM
TWOFOLDS	TYLOPOD	TYPEWRITE	TYRAMINES	TZADDIKS
TWONESS	TYLOPODS	TYPEWROTE	TYRAN	TZADDIQ
TWONESSES	TYLOSES	TYPEY	TYRANED	TZADDIQIM
TWONIE	TYLOSIN	TYPHLITIC	TYRANING	TZADDIQS
TWONIES	TYLOSINS	TYPHLITIS	TYRANNE	TZADDIS
TWOONIE	TYLOSIS	TYPHOID	TYRANNED	TZADIK
TWOONIES	TYLOTE	TYPHOIDAL	TYRANNES	TZADIKS
TWOPENCE	TYLOTES	TYPHOIDIN	TYRANNESS	TZAR
TWOPENCES	TYMBAL	TYPHOIDS	TYRANNIC	TZARDOM
TWOPENNY	TYMBALS	TYPHON	TYRANNIES	TZARDOMS
TWOS	TYMP	TYPHONIAN	TYRANNING	TZAREVNA
TWOSEATER	TYMPAN	TYPHONIC	TYRANNIS	TZAREVNAS
TWOSOME	TYMPANA	TYPHONS	TYRANNISE	TZARINA
TWOSOMES	TYMPANAL	TYPHOON	TYRANNIZE	TZARINAS
TWOSTROKE	TYMPANI	TYPHOONS	TYRANNOUS	TZARISM
TWP	TYMPANIC	TYPHOSE	TYRANNY	TZARISMS
TWYER	TYMPANICS	TYPHOUS	TYRANS	TZARIST
TWYERE	TYMPANIES	TYPHUS	TYRANT	TZARISTS
TWYERES	TYMPANIST	TYPHUSES	TYRANTED	TZARITZA
TWYERS	TYMPANO	TYPIC	TYRANTING	TZARITZAS
TWYFOLD	TYMPANS	TYPICAL	TYRANTS	TZARS
TYCHISM	TYMPANUM	TYPICALLY	TYRE	TZATZIKI
TYCHISMS	TYMPANUMS	TYPIER	TYRED	TZATZIKIS
TYCOON	TYMPANY	TYPIEST	TYRELESS	TZEDAKAH
TYCOONATE	TYMPS	TYPIFIED	TYREMAKER	TZEDAKAHS
TYCOONERY	TYND	TYPIFIER	TYRES	TZETSE
TYCOONS	TYNDE	TYPIFIERS	TYRING	TZETSES
TYDE	TYNE	TYPIFIES	TYRO	TZETZE
TYE	TYNED	TYPIFY	TYROCIDIN	TZETZES
TYED	TYNES	TYPIFYING	TYROES	TZIGANE
TYEE	TYNING	TYPING	TYRONES	TZIGANES
TYEES	TYPABLE	TYPINGS	TYRONIC	TZIGANIES
TYEING	TYPAL	TYPIST	TYROPITA	TZIGANY
TYER	TYPE	TYPISTS	TYROPITAS	TZIMMES
TYERS	TYPEABLE	TYPO	TYROPITTA	TZITZIS
TYES	TYPEBAR	TYPOGRAPH	TYROS	TZITZIT
TYG	TYPEBARS	TYPOLOGIC	TYROSINE	TZITZITH
TYGS	TYPECASE	TYPOLOGY	TYROSINES	TZURIS
TYIN	TYPECASES	TYPOMANIA	TYSTIE	TZURISES
TYING	TYPECAST	TYPOS	TYSTIES	
TYIYN	TYPECASTS	TYPP	TYTE	
TYIYNS	TYPED	TYPPS	TYTHE	
TYKE	TYPEFACE	TYPTO	TYTHED	

U

UAKARI	UGGED	ULAMAS	ULNARIA	ULTRAPURE
UAKARIS	UGGING	ULAN	ULNAS	ULTRARARE
UBEROUS	UGH	ULANS	ULOSES	ULTRARED
UBERTIES	UGHS	ULCER	ULOSIS	ULTRAREDS
UBERTY	UGLIED	ULCERATE	ULOTRICHY	ULTRARICH
UBIETIES	UGLIER	ULCERATED	ULPAN	ULTRAS
UBIETY	UGLIES	ULCERATES	ULPANIM	ULTRASAFE
UBIQUE	UGLIEST	ULCERED	ULSTER	ULTRASLOW
UBIQUITIN	UGLIFIED	ULCERING	ULSTERED	ULTRASOFT
UBIQUITY	UGLIFIER	ULCEROUS	ULSTERS	ULTRATHIN
UBUNTU	UGLIFIERS	ULCERS	ULTERIOR	ULTRATINY
UBUNTUS	UGLIFIES	ULE	ULTIMA	ULTRAWIDE
UCKERS	UGLIFY	ULEMA	ULTIMACY	ULU
UDAL	UGLIFYING	ULEMAS	ULTIMAS	ULULANT
UDALLER	UGLILY	ULES	ULTIMATA	ULULATE
UDALLERS	UGLINESS	ULEX	ULTIMATE	ULULATED
UDALS	UGLY	ULEXES	ULTIMATED	ULULATES
UDDER	UGLYING	ULEXITE	ULTIMATES	ULULATING
UDDERED	UGS	ULEXITES	ULTIMATUM	ULULATION
UDDERFUL	UH	ULICES	ULTIMO	ULUS
UDDERFULS	UHLAN	ULICON	ULTION	ULVA
UDDERLESS	UHLANS	ULICONS	ULTIONS	ULVAS
UDDERS	UHURU	ULIGINOSE	ULTISOL	ULYIE
UDO	UHURUS	ULIGINOUS	ULTISOLS	ULYIES
UDOMETER	UILLEAN	ULIKON	ULTRA	ULZIE
UDOMETERS	UILLEANN	ULIKONS	ULTRACHIC	ULZIES
UDOMETRIC	UINTAHITE	ULITIS	ULTRACOLD	UM
UDOMETRY	UINTAITE	ULITISES	ULTRACOOL	UMAMI
UDON	UINTAITES	ULLAGE	ULTRADRY	UMAMIS
UDONS	UITLANDER	ULLAGED	ULTRAFAST	UMANGITE
UDOS	UJAMAA	ULLAGES	ULTRAFINE	UMANGITES
UDS	UJAMAAS	ULLAGING	ULTRAHEAT	UMBEL
UEY	UKASE	ULLING	ULTRAHIGH	UMBELED
UEYS	UKASES	ULLINGS	ULTRAHIP	UMBELLAR
UFO	UKE	ULMACEOUS	ULTRAHOT	UMBELLATE
UFOLOGIES	UKELELE	ULMIN	ULTRAISM	UMBELLED
UFOLOGIST	UKELELES	ULMINS	ULTRAISMS	UMBELLET
UFOLOGY	UKES	ULNA	ULTRAIST	UMBELLETS
UFOS	UKULELE	ULNAD	ULTRAISTS	UMBELLULE
UG	UKULELES	ULNAE	ULTRALEFT	UMBELS
UGALI	ULAMA	ULNAR	ULTRALOW	UMBELULE
UGALIS	ULAMA	ULNARE	ULTRAPOSH	UMBELULES

UMBER	UME	UMQUHILE	UNAGILE	UNARGUED
UMBERED	UMEBOSHI	UMRA	UNAGING	UNARISEN
UMBERIER	UMEBOSHIS	UMRAH	UNAGREED	UNARM
UMBERIEST	UMES	UMRAHS	UNAI	UNARMED
UMBERING	UMFAZI	UMRAS	UNAIDABLE	UNARMING
UMBERS	UMFAZIS	UMS	UNAIDED	UNARMORED
UMBERY	UMIAC	UMTEENTH	UNAIDEDLY	UNARMS
UMBILICAL	UMIACK	UMU	UNAIMED	UNAROUSED
UMBILICI	UMIACKS	UMUS	UNAIRED	UNARRAYED
UMBILICUS	UMIACS	UMWELT	UNAIS	UNARTFUL
UMBLE	UMIAK	UMWELTS	UNAKIN	UNARY
UMBLES	UMIAKS	UMWHILE	UNAKING	UNASHAMED
UMBO	UMIAQ	UN	UNAKITE	UNASKED
UMBONAL	UMIAQS	UNABASHED	UNAKITES	UNASSAYED
UMBONATE	UMLAUT	UNABATED	UNALARMED	UNASSUMED
UMBONES	UMLAUTED	UNABATING	UNALERTED	UNASSURED
UMBONIC	UMLAUTING	UNABETTED	UNALIGNED	UNATONED
UMBOS	UMLAUTS	UNABIDING	UNALIKE	UNATTIRED
UMBRA	UMLUNGU	UNABJURED	UNALIST	UNATTUNED
UMBRACULA	UMLUNGUS	UNABLE	UNALISTS	UNAU
UMBRAE	UMM	UNABORTED	UNALIVE	UNAUDITED
UMBRAGE	UMMA	UNABRADED	UNALLAYED	UNAUS
UMBRAGED	UMMAH	UNABUSED	UNALLEGED	UNAVENGED
UMBRAGES	UMMAHS	UNABUSIVE	UNALLIED	UNAVERAGE
UMBRAGING	UMMAS	UNACCRUED	UNALLOWED	UNAVERTED
UMBRAL	UMMED	UNACCUSED	UNALLOYED	UNAVOIDED
UMBRAS	UMMING	UNACERBIC	UNALTERED	UNAVOWED
UMBRATED	UMP	UNACHING	UNAMASSED	UNAWAKE
UMBRATIC	UMPED	UNACIDIC	UNAMAZED	UNAWAKED
UMBRATILE	UMPH	UNACTABLE	UNAMENDED	UNAWARDED
UMBRE	UMPHS	UNACTED	UNAMERCED	UNAWARE
UMBREL	UMPIE	UNACTIVE	UNAMIABLE	UNAWARELY
UMBRELLA	UMPIES	UNACTIVED	UNAMUSED	UNAWARES
UMBRELLAS	UMPING	UNACTIVES	UNAMUSING	UNAWED
UMBRELLO	UMPIRAGE	UNADAPTED	UNANCHOR	UNAWESOME
UMBRELLOS	UMPIRAGES	UNADDED	UNANCHORS	UNAXED
UMBRELS	UMPIRE	UNADEPT	UNANELED	UNBACKED
UMBRERE	UMPIRED	UNADEPTLY	UNANIMITY	UNBAFFLED
UMBRERES	UMPIRES	UNADEPTS	UNANIMOUS	UNBAG
UMBRES	UMPIRING	UNADMIRED	UNANNEXED	UNBAGGED
UMBRETTE	UMPS	UNADOPTED	UNANNOYED	UNBAGGING
UMBRETTES	UMPTEEN	UNADORED	UNANXIOUS	UNBAGS
UMBRIERE	UMPTEENTH	UNADORNED	UNAPPAREL	UNBAITED
UMBRIERES	UMPTIER	UNADULT	UNAPPLIED	UNBAKED
UMBRIL	UMPTIEST	UNADVISED	UNAPT	UNBALANCE
UMBRILS	UMPTIETH	UNAFRAID	UNAPTLY	UNBALE
UMBROSE	UMPTY	UNAGED	UNAPTNESS	UNBALED
UMBROUS	UMPY	UNAGEING	UNARCHED	UNBALES

UNBALING	UNBEKNOWN	UNBLESSES	UNBOUNCY	UNBUNDLE
UNBAN	UNBELIEF	UNBLEST	UNBOUND	UNBUNDLED
UNBANDAGE	UNBELIEFS	UNBLIND	UNBOUNDED	UNBUNDLER
UNBANDED	UNBELIEVE	UNBLINDED	UNBOWED	UNBUNDLES
UNBANKED	UNBELOVED	UNBLINDS	UNBOWING	UNBURDEN
UNBANNED	UNBELT	UNBLOCK	UNBOX	UNBURDENS
UNBANNING	UNBELTED	UNBLOCKED	UNBOXED	UNBURIED
UNBANS	UNBELTING	UNBLOCKS	UNBOXES	UNBURIES
UNBAPTISE	UNBELTS	UNBLOODED	UNBOXING	UNBURNED
UNBAPTIZE	UNBEMUSED	UNBLOODY	UNBRACE	UNBURNT
UNBAR	UNBEND	UNBLOTTED	UNBRACED	UNBURROW
UNBARBED	UNBENDED	UNBLOWED	UNBRACES	UNBURROWS
UNBARE	UNBENDING	UNBLOWN	UNBRACING	UNBURTHEN
UNBARED	UNBENDS	UNBLUNTED	UNBRAID	UNBURY
UNBARES	UNBENIGN	UNBLURRED	UNBRAIDED	UNBURYING
UNBARING	UNBENT	UNBOARDED	UNBRAIDS	UNBUSIED
UNBARK	UNBEREFT	UNBOBBED	UNBRAKE	UNBUSIER
UNBARKED	UNBERUFEN	UNBODIED	UNBRAKED	UNBUSIES
UNBARKING	UNBESEEM	UNBODING	UNBRAKES	UNBUSIEST
UNBARKS	UNBESEEMS	UNBOILED	UNBRAKING	UNBUSTED
UNBARRED	UNBESPEAK	UNBOLT	UNBRANDED	UNBUSY
UNBARRING	UNBESPOKE	UNBOLTED	UNBRASTE	UNBUSYING
UNBARS	UNBIAS	UNBOLTING	UNBRED	UNBUTTON
UNBASED	UNBIASED	UNBOLTS	UNBREECH	UNBUTTONS
UNBASHFUL	UNBIASES	UNBONDED	UNBRIDGED	UNCAGE
UNBASTED	UNBIASING	UNBONE	UNBRIDLE	UNCAGED
UNBATED	UNBIASSED	UNBONED	UNBRIDLED	UNCAGES
UNBATHED	UNBIASSES	UNBONES	UNBRIDLES	UNCAGING
UNBE	UNBID	UNBONING	UNBRIEFED	UNCAKE
UNBEAR	UNBIDDEN	UNBONNET	UNBRIGHT	UNCAKED
UNBEARDED	UNBIGOTED	UNBONNETS	UNBRIZZED	UNCAKES
UNBEARED	UNBILLED	UNBOOKED	UNBROILED	UNCAKING
UNBEARING	UNBIND	UNBOOKISH	UNBROKE	UNCALLED
UNBEARS	UNBINDING	UNBOOT	UNBROKEN	UNCANDID
UNBEATEN	UNBINDS	UNBOOTED	UNBROWNED	UNCANDLED
UNBED	UNBISHOP	UNBOOTING	UNBRUISED	UNCANDOR
UNBEDDED	UNBISHOPS	UNBOOTS	UNBRUSED	UNCANDORS
UNBEDDING	UNBITT	UNBORE	UNBRUSHED	UNCANDOUR
UNBEDS	UNBITTED	UNBORN	UNBUCKLE	UNCANNED
UNBEEN	UNBITTEN	UNBORNE	UNBUCKLED	UNCANNIER
UNBEGET	UNBITTER	UNBOSOM	UNBUCKLES	UNCANNILY
UNBEGETS	UNBITTING	UNBOSOMED	UNBUDDED	UNCANNY
UNBEGGED	UNBITTS	UNBOSOMER	UNBUDGING	UNCANONIC
UNBEGOT	UNBLAMED	UNBOSOMS	UNBUILD	UNCAP
UNBEGUILE	UNBLENDED	UNBOTTLE	UNBUILDS	UNCAPABLE
UNBEGUN	UNBLENT	UNBOTTLED	UNBUILT	UNCAPE
UNBEING	UNBLESS	UNBOTTLES	UNBULKIER	UNCAPED
UNBEINGS	UNBLESSED	UNBOUGHT	UNBULKY	UNCAPES

UNCAPING	UNCHARMED	UNCLAMPED	UNCLOTHES	UNCOOL
UNCAPPED	UNCHARMS	UNCLAMPS	UNCLOUD	UNCOOLED
UNCAPPING	UNCHARNEL	UNCLARITY	UNCLOUDED	UNCOPE
UNCAPS	UNCHARRED	UNCLASP	UNCLOUDS	UNCOPED
UNCARDED	UNCHARTED	UNCLASPED	UNCLOUDY	UNCOPES
UNCARED	UNCHARY	UNCLASPS	UNCLOVEN	UNCOPING
UNCAREFUL	UNCHASTE	UNCLASSED	UNCLOYED	UNCORD
UNCARING	UNCHASTER	UNCLASSY	UNCLOYING	UNCORDED
UNCART	UNCHECK	UNCLAWED	UNCLUTCH	UNCORDIAL
UNCARTED	UNCHECKED	UNCLE	UNCLUTTER	UNCORDING
UNCARTING	UNCHECKS	UNCLEAN	UNCO	UNCORDS
UNCARTS	UNCHEERED	UNCLEANED	UNCOATED	UNCORK
UNCARVED	UNCHEWED	UNCLEANER	UNCOATING	UNCORKED
UNCASE	UNCHIC	UNCLEANLY	UNCOBBLED	UNCORKING
UNCASED	UNCHICLY	UNCLEAR	UNCOCK	UNCORKS
UNCASES	UNCHILD	UNCLEARED	UNCOCKED	UNCORRUPT
UNCASHED	UNCHILDED	UNCLEARER	UNCOCKING	UNCOS
UNCASING	UNCHILDS	UNCLEARLY	UNCOCKS	UNCOSTLY
UNCASKED	UNCHILLED	UNCLED	UNCODED	UNCOUNTED
UNCAST	UNCHOKE	UNCLEFT	UNCOER	UNCOUPLE
UNCASTED	UNCHOKED	UNCLENCH	UNCOERCED	UNCOUPLED
UNCASTING	UNCHOKES	UNCLES	UNCOES	UNCOUPLER
UNCASTS	UNCHOKING	UNCLESHIP	UNCOEST	UNCOUPLES
UNCATCHY	UNCHOSEN	UNCLEW	UNCOFFIN	UNCOURTLY
UNCATE	UNCHRISOM	UNCLEWED	UNCOFFINS	UNCOUTH
UNCATERED	UNCHURCH	UNCLEWING	UNCOIL	UNCOUTHER
UNCAUGHT	UNCI	UNCLEWS	UNCOILED	UNCOUTHLY
UNCAUSED	UNCIA	UNCLICHED	UNCOILING	UNCOVER
UNCE	UNCIAE	UNCLIMBED	UNCOILS	UNCOVERED
UNCEASING	UNCIAL	UNCLINCH	UNCOINED	UNCOVERS
UNCEDED	UNCIALLY	UNCLING	UNCOLORED	UNCOWL
UNCERTAIN	UNCIALS	UNCLIP	UNCOLT	UNCOWLED
UNCES	UNCIFORM	UNCLIPPED	UNCOLTED	UNCOWLING
UNCESSANT	UNCIFORMS	UNCLIPS	UNCOLTING	UNCOWLS
UNCHAIN	UNCINAL	UNCLIPT	UNCOLTS	UNCOY
UNCHAINED	UNCINARIA	UNCLOAK	UNCOMBED	UNCOYNED
UNCHAINS	UNCINATE	UNCLOAKED	UNCOMBINE	UNCRACKED
UNCHAIR	UNCINATED	UNCLOAKS	UNCOMELY	UNCRATE
UNCHAIRED	UNCINI	UNCLOG	UNCOMFIER	UNCRATED
UNCHAIRS	UNCINUS	UNCLOGGED	UNCOMFY	UNCRATES
UNCHANCY	UNCIPHER	UNCLOGS	UNCOMIC	UNCRATING
UNCHANGED	UNCIPHERS	UNCLONED	UNCOMMON	UNCRAZIER
UNCHARGE	UNCITED	UNCLOSE	UNCONCERN	UNCRAZY
UNCHARGED	UNCIVIL	UNCLOSED	UNCONFINE	UNCREASED
UNCHARGES	UNCIVILLY	UNCLOSES	UNCONFORM	UNCREATE
UNCHARIER	UNCLAD	UNCLOSING	UNCONFUSE	UNCREATED
UNCHARITY	UNCLAIMED	UNCLOTHE	UNCONGEAL	UNCREATES
UNCHARM	UNCLAMP	UNCLOTHED	UNCOOKED	UNCREWED

UNCROPPED	UNDAMPED	UNDELIGHT	UNDERDONE	UNDERLIER
UNCROSS	UNDAMS	UNDELUDED	UNDERDOSE	UNDERLIES
UNCROSSED	UNDARING	UNDENIED	UNDERDRAW	UNDERLINE
UNCROSSES	UNDASHED	UNDENTED	UNDERDREW	UNDERLING
UNCROWDED	UNDATABLE	UNDER	UNDEREAT	UNDERLIP
UNCROWN	UNDATE	UNDERACT	UNDEREATS	UNDERLIPS
UNCROWNED	UNDATED	UNDERACTS	UNDERFED	UNDERLIT
UNCROWNS	UNDATES	UNDERAGE	UNDERFEED	UNDERLOAD
UNCRUDDED	UNDATING	UNDERAGED	UNDERFELT	UNDERMAN
UNCRUMPLE	UNDAUNTED	UNDERAGES	UNDERFIRE	UNDERMANS
UNCRUSHED	UNDAWNING	UNDERARM	UNDERFISH	UNDERMEN
UNCTION	UNDAZZLE	UNDERARMS	UNDERFLOW	UNDERMINE
UNCTIONS	UNDAZZLED	UNDERATE	UNDERFONG	UNDERMOST
UNCTUOUS	UNDAZZLES	UNDERBAKE	UNDERFOOT	UNDERN
UNCUFF	UNDE	UNDERBEAR	UNDERFUND	UNDERNOTE
UNCUFFED	UNDEAD	UNDERBID	UNDERFUR	UNDERNS
UNCUFFING	UNDEAF	UNDERBIDS	UNDERFURS	UNDERPAD
UNCUFFS	UNDEAFED	UNDERBIT	UNDERGIRD	UNDERPADS
UNCULLED	UNDEAFING	UNDERBITE	UNDERGIRT	UNDERPAID
UNCURABLE	UNDEAFS	UNDERBODY	UNDERGO	UNDERPART
UNCURABLY	UNDEALT	UNDERBORE	UNDERGOD	UNDERPASS
UNCURB	UNDEAR	UNDERBOSS	UNDERGODS	UNDERPAY
UNCURBED	UNDEBASED	UNDERBRED	UNDERGOER	UNDERPAYS
UNCURBING	UNDEBATED	UNDERBRIM	UNDERGOES	UNDERPEEP
UNCURBS	UNDECAGON	UNDERBUD	UNDERGONE	UNDERPIN
UNCURDLED	UNDECAYED	UNDERBUDS	UNDERGOWN	UNDERPINS
UNCURED	UNDECEIVE	UNDERBUSH	UNDERGRAD	UNDERPLAY
UNCURIOUS	UNDECENT	UNDERBUY	UNDERHAIR	UNDERPLOT
UNCURL	UNDECIDED	UNDERBUYS	UNDERHAND	UNDERPROP
UNCURLED	UNDECIMAL	UNDERCARD	UNDERHEAT	UNDERRAN
UNCURLING	UNDECK	UNDERCART	UNDERHUNG	UNDERRATE
UNCURLS	UNDECKED	UNDERCAST	UNDERIVED	UNDERRIPE
UNCURRENT	UNDECKING	UNDERCLAD	UNDERJAW	UNDERRUN
UNCURSE	UNDECKS	UNDERCLAY	UNDERJAWS	UNDERRUNS
UNCURSED	UNDEE	UNDERCLUB	UNDERKEEP	UNDERSAID
UNCURSES	UNDEEDED	UNDERCOAT	UNDERKEPT	UNDERSAY
UNCURSING	UNDEFACED	UNDERCOOK	UNDERKILL	UNDERSAYS
UNCURTAIN	UNDEFIDE	UNDERCOOL	UNDERKING	UNDERSEA
UNCURVED	UNDEFIED	UNDERCUT	UNDERLAID	UNDERSEAL
UNCUS	UNDEFILED	UNDERCUTS	UNDERLAIN	UNDERSEAS
UNCUT	UNDEFINED	UNDERDAKS	UNDERLAP	UNDERSELF
UNCUTE	UNDEIFIED	UNDERDECK	UNDERLAPS	UNDERSELL
UNCYNICAL	UNDEIFIES	UNDERDID	UNDERLAY	UNDERSET
UNDAM	UNDEIFY	UNDERDO	UNDERLAYS	UNDERSETS
UNDAMAGED	UNDELAYED	UNDERDOER	UNDERLEAF	UNDERSHOT
UNDAMMED	UNDELETE	UNDERDOES	UNDERLET	UNDERSIDE
UNDAMMING	UNDELETED	UNDERDOG	UNDERLETS	UNDERSIGN
UNDAMNED	UNDELETES	UNDERDOGS	UNDERLIE	UNDERSIZE

UNDERSKY
UNDERSOIL
UNDERSOLD
UNDERSONG
UNDERSOW
UNDERSOWN
UNDERSOWS
UNDERSPIN
UNDERTAKE
UNDERTANE
UNDERTAX
UNDERTIME
UNDERTINT
UNDERTONE
UNDERTOOK
UNDERTOW
UNDERTOWS
UNDERUSE
UNDERUSED
UNDERUSES
UNDERVEST
UNDERVOTE
UNDERWAY
UNDERWEAR
UNDERWENT
UNDERWING
UNDERWIRE
UNDERWIT
UNDERWITS
UNDERWOOD
UNDERWOOL
UNDERWORK
UNDESERT
UNDESERTS
UNDESERVE
UNDESIRED
UNDEVOUT
UNDID
UNDIES
UNDIGHT
UNDIGHTS
UNDIGNIFY
UNDILUTED
UNDIMMED
UNDINE
UNDINES
UNDINISM
UNDINISMS

UNDINTED
UNDIPPED
UNDIVIDED
UNDIVINE
UNDO
UNDOABLE
UNDOCILE
UNDOCK
UNDOCKED
UNDOCKING
UNDOCKS
UNDOER
UNDOERS
UNDOES
UNDOING
UNDOINGS
UNDONE
UNDOOMED
UNDOS
UNDOTTED
UNDOUBLE
UNDOUBLED
UNDOUBLES
UNDOUBTED
UNDOWERED
UNDRAINED
UNDRAPE
UNDRAPED
UNDRAPES
UNDRAPING
UNDRAW
UNDRAWING
UNDRAWN
UNDRAWS
UNDREADED
UNDREAMED
UNDREAMT
UNDRESS
UNDRESSED
UNDRESSES
UNDREST
UNDREW
UNDRIED
UNDRILLED
UNDRIVEN
UNDROSSY
UNDROWNED
UNDRUNK

UNDUBBED
UNDUE
UNDUG
UNDULANCE
UNDULANCY
UNDULANT
UNDULAR
UNDULATE
UNDULATED
UNDULATES
UNDULATOR
UNDULLED
UNDULOSE
UNDULOUS
UNDULY
UNDUTEOUS
UNDUTIFUL
UNDY
UNDYED
UNDYING
UNDYINGLY
UNDYNAMIC
UNEAGER
UNEAGERLY
UNEARED
UNEARNED
UNEARTH
UNEARTHED
UNEARTHLY
UNEARTHS
UNEASE
UNEASES
UNEASIER
UNEASIEST
UNEASILY
UNEASY
UNEATABLE
UNEATEN
UNEATH
UNEATHES
UNEDGE
UNEDGED
UNEDGES
UNEDGING
UNEDIBLE
UNEDITED
UNEFFACED
UNELATED

UNELECTED
UNEMPTIED
UNENDED
UNENDING
UNENDOWED
UNENGAGED
UNENJOYED
UNENSURED
UNENTERED
UNENVIED
UNENVIOUS
UNENVYING
UNEQUABLE
UNEQUAL
UNEQUALED
UNEQUALLY
UNEQUALS
UNERASED
UNEROTIC
UNERRING
UNERUPTED
UNESPIED
UNESSAYED
UNESSENCE
UNETH
UNETHICAL
UNEVADED
UNEVEN
UNEVENER
UNEVENEST
UNEVENLY
UNEVOLVED
UNEXALTED
UNEXCITED
UNEXCUSED
UNEXOTIC
UNEXPERT
UNEXPIRED
UNEXPOSED
UNEXTINCT
UNEXTREME
UNEYED
UNFABLED
UNFACETED
UNFACT
UNFACTS
UNFADABLE
UNFADED

UNFADING
UNFAILING
UNFAIR
UNFAIRED
UNFAIRER
UNFAIREST
UNFAIRING
UNFAIRLY
UNFAIRS
UNFAITH
UNFAITHS
UNFAKED
UNFALLEN
UNFAMED
UNFAMOUS
UNFANCIED
UNFANCIER
UNFANCY
UNFANNED
UNFASTEN
UNFASTENS
UNFAULTY
UNFAVORED
UNFAZABLE
UNFAZED
UNFEARED
UNFEARFUL
UNFEARING
UNFED
UNFEED
UNFEELING
UNFEIGNED
UNFELLED
UNFELT
UNFELTED
UNFENCE
UNFENCED
UNFENCES
UNFENCING
UNFERTILE
UNFETTER
UNFETTERS
UNFEUDAL
UNFEUED
UNFIGURED
UNFILDE
UNFILED
UNFILIAL

U

UNFILLED	UNFOOLED	UNFURNISH	UNGIRDS	UNGROUPS
UNFILMED	UNFOOLING	UNFURRED	UNGIRT	UNGROWN
UNFINE	UNFOOLS	UNFUSED	UNGIRTH	UNGRUDGED
UNFIRED	UNFOOTED	UNFUSSED	UNGIRTHED	UNGUAL
UNFIRM	UNFORBID	UNFUSSIER	UNGIRTHS	UNGUARD
UNFISHED	UNFORCED	UNFUSSILY	UNGIVING	UNGUARDED
UNFIT	UNFORGED	UNFUSSY	UNGLAD	UNGUARDS
UNFITLY	UNFORGOT	UNGAG	UNGLAZED	UNGUENT
UNFITNESS	UNFORKED	UNGAGGED	UNGLITZY	UNGUENTA
UNFITS	UNFORM	UNGAGGING	UNGLOSSED	UNGUENTS
UNFITTED	UNFORMAL	UNGAGS	UNGLOVE	UNGUENTUM
UNFITTER	UNFORMED	UNGAIN	UNGLOVED	UNGUES
UNFITTEST	UNFORMING	UNGAINFUL	UNGLOVES	UNGUESSED
UNFITTING	UNFORMS	UNGAINLY	UNGLOVING	UNGUIDED
UNFIX	UNFORTUNE	UNGALLANT	UNGLUE	UNGUIFORM
UNFIXED	UNFOUGHT	UNGALLED	UNGLUED	UNGUILTY
UNFIXES	UNFOUND	UNGARBED	UNGLUES	UNGUINOUS
UNFIXING	UNFOUNDED	UNGARBLED	UNGLUING	UNGUIS
UNFIXITY	UNFRAMED	UNGATED	UNGOD	UNGULA
UNFIXT	UNFRANKED	UNGAUGED	UNGODDED	UNGULAE
UNFLAPPED	UNFRAUGHT	UNGAZED	UNGODDING	UNGULAR
UNFLASHY	UNFREE	UNGAZING	UNGODLIER	UNGULATE
UNFLAWED	UNFREED	UNGEAR	UNGODLIKE	UNGULATES
UNFLEDGED	UNFREEDOM	UNGEARED	UNGODLILY	UNGULED
UNFLESH	UNFREEING	UNGEARING	UNGODLY	UNGUM
UNFLESHED	UNFREEMAN	UNGEARS	UNGODS	UNGUMMED
UNFLESHES	UNFREEMEN	UNGELDED	UNGORD	UNGUMMING
UNFLESHLY	UNFREES	UNGENIAL	UNGORED	UNGUMS
UNFLEXED	UNFREEZE	UNGENTEEL	UNGORGED	UNGYVE
UNFLOORED	UNFREEZES	UNGENTLE	UNGOT	UNGYVED
UNFLUSH	UNFRETTED	UNGENTLER	UNGOTTEN	UNGYVES
UNFLUSHED	UNFRIEND	UNGENTLY	UNGOWN	UNGYVING
UNFLUSHES	UNFRIENDS	UNGENUINE	UNGOWNED	UNHABLE
UNFLUTED	UNFROCK	UNGERMANE	UNGOWNING	UNHACKED
UNFLYABLE	UNFROCKED	UNGET	UNGOWNS	UNHAILED
UNFOCUSED	UNFROCKS	UNGETS	UNGRACED	UNHAIR
UNFOILED	UNFROZE	UNGETTING	UNGRADED	UNHAIRED
UNFOLD	UNFROZEN	UNGHOSTED	UNGRASSED	UNHATRER
UNFOLDED	UNFUELLED	UNGHOSTLY	UNGRAVELY	UNHAIRERS
UNFOLDER	UNFUMED	UNGIFTED	UNGRAZED	UNHAIRING
UNFOLDERS	UNFUNDED	UNGILD	UNGREASED	UNHAIRS
UNFOLDING	UNFUNNIER	UNGILDED	UNGREEDY	UNHALLOW
UNFOLDS	UNFUNNILY	UNGILDING	UNGREEN	UNHALLOWS
UNFOLLOW	UNFUNNY	UNGILDS	UNGREENER	UNHALSED
UNFOLLOWS	UNFURL	UNGILT	UNGROOMED	UNHALVED
UNFOND	UNFURLED	UNGIRD	UNGROUND	UNHAND
UNFONDLY	UNFURLING	UNGIRDED	UNGROUP	UNHANDED
UNFOOL	UNFURLS	UNGIRDING	UNGROUPED	UNHANDIER

U

UNHANDILY	UNHEARD	UNHOARDED	UNIAXIAL	UNIMPOSED
UNHANDING	UNHEARSE	UNHOARDS	UNIBODIES	UNINCITED
UNHANDLED	UNHEARSED	UNHOLIER	UNIBODY	UNINDEXED
UNHANDS	UNHEARSES	UNHOLIEST	UNIBROW	UNINJURED
UNHANDY	UNHEART	UNHOLILY	UNIBROWS	UNINSTAL
UNHANG	UNHEARTED	UNHOLPEN	UNICA	UNINSTALL
UNHANGED	UNHEARTS	UNHOLSTER	UNICED	UNINSTALS
UNHANGING	UNHEATED	UNHOLY	UNICITIES	UNINSURED
UNHANGS	UNHEDGED	UNHOMELY	UNICITY	UNINURED
UNHAPPEN	UNHEEDED	UNHONEST	UNICOLOR	UNINVITED
UNHAPPENS	UNHEEDFUL	UNHONORED	UNICOLOUR	UNINVOKED
UNHAPPIED	UNHEEDIER	UNHOOD	UNICOM	UNION
UNHAPPIER	UNHEEDILY	UNHOODED	UNICOMS	UNIONISE
UNHAPPIES	UNHEEDING	UNHOODING	UNICORN	UNIONISED
UNHAPPILY	UNHEEDY	UNHOODS	UNICORNS	UNIONISER
UNHAPPY	UNHELE	UNHOOK	UNICUM	UNIONISES
UNHARBOUR	UNHELED	UNHOOKED	UNICYCLE	UNIONISM
UNHARDIER	UNHELES	UNHOOKING	UNICYCLED	UNIONISMS
UNHARDY	UNHELING	UNHOOKS	UNICYCLES	UNIONIST
UNHARMED	UNHELM	UNHOOP	UNIDEAED	UNIONISTS
UNHARMFUL	UNHELMED	UNHOOPED	UNIDEAL	UNIONIZE
UNHARMING	UNHELMING	UNHOOPING	UNIFACE	UNIONIZED
UNHARNESS	UNHELMS	UNHOOPS	UNIFACES	UNIONIZER
UNHARRIED	UNHELPED	UNHOPED	UNIFIABLE	UNIONIZES
UNHASP	UNHELPFUL	UNHOPEFUL	UNIFIC	UNIONS
UNHASPED	UNHEMMED	UNHORSE	UNIFIED	UNIPAROUS
UNHASPING	UNHEPPEN	UNHORSED	UNIFIER	UNIPED
UNHASPS	UNHEROIC	UNHORSES	UNIFIERS	UNIPEDS
UNHASTIER	UNHERST	UNHORSING	UNIFIES	UNIPLANAR
UNHASTING	UNHEWN	UNHOSTILE	UNIFILAR	UNIPOD
UNHASTY	UNHIDDEN	UNHOUSE	UNIFORM	UNIPODS
UNHAT	UNHINGE	UNHOUSED	UNIFORMED	UNIPOLAR
UNHATCHED	UNHINGED	UNHOUSES	UNIFORMER	UNIPOTENT
UNHATS	UNHINGES	UNHOUSING	UNIFORMLY	UNIQUE
UNHATTED	UNHINGING	UNHUMAN	UNIFORMS	UNIQUELY
UNHATTING	UNHIP	UNHUMANLY	UNIFY	UNIQUER
UNHAUNTED	UNHIPPER	UNHUMBLED	UNIFYING	UNIQUES
UNHEAD	UNHIPPEST	UNHUNG	UNIFYINGS	UNIQUEST
UNHEADED	UNHIRABLE	UNHUNTED	UNIGNITED	UNIRAMOSE
UNHEADING	UNHIRED	UNHURRIED	UNIJUGATE	UNIRAMOUS
UNHEADS	UNHITCH	UNHURT	UNILINEAL	UNIRONED
UNHEAL	UNHITCHED	UNHURTFUL	UNILINEAR	UNIRONIC
UNHEALED	UNHITCHES	UNHUSK	UNILLUMED	UNIS
UNHEALING	UNHIVE	UNHUSKED	UNILOBAR	UNISERIAL
UNHEALS	UNHIVED	UNHUSKING	UNILOBED	UNISEX
UNHEALTH	UNHIVES	UNHUSKS	UNIMBUED	UNISEXES
UNHEALTHS	UNHIVING	UNI	UNIMODAL	UNISEXUAL
UNHEALTHY	UNHOARD	UNIALGAL	UNIMPEDED	UNISIZE

UNISON	UNIVALVES	UNKINKS	UNLEAD	UNLINKED
UNISONAL	UNIVERSAL	UNKISS	UNLEADED	UNLINKING
UNISONANT	UNIVERSE	UNKISSED	UNLEADEDS	UNLINKS
UNISONOUS	UNIVERSES	UNKISSES	UNLEADING	UNLISTED
UNISONS	UNIVOCAL	UNKISSING	UNLEADS	UNLIT
UNISSUED	UNIVOCALS	UNKNELLED	UNLEAL	UNLIVABLE
UNIT	UNJADED	UNKNIGHT	UNLEARN	UNLIVE
UNITAGE	UNJAM	UNKNIGHTS	UNLEARNED	UNLIVED
UNITAGES	UNJAMMED	UNKNIT	UNLEARNS	UNLIVELY
UNITAL	UNJAMMING	UNKNITS	UNLEARNT	UNLIVES
UNITARD	UNJAMS	UNKNITTED	UNLEASED	UNLIVING
UNITARDS	UNJEALOUS	UNKNOT	UNLEASH	UNLOAD
UNITARIAN	UNJOINED	UNKNOTS	UNLEASHED	UNLOADED
UNITARILY	UNJOINT	UNKNOTTED	UNLEASHES	UNLOADER
UNITARITY	UNJOINTED	UNKNOWING	UNLED	UNLOADERS
UNITARY	UNJOINTS	UNKNOWN	UNLESS	UNLOADING
UNITE	UNJOYFUL	UNKNOWNS	UNLET	UNLOADS
UNITED	UNJOYOUS	UNKOSHER	UNLETHAL	UNLOBED
UNITEDLY	UNJUDGED	UNLABELED	UNLETTED	UNLOCATED
UNITER	UNJUST	UNLABORED	UNLEVEL	UNLOCK
UNITERS	UNJUSTER	UNLACE	UNLEVELED	UNLOCKED
UNITES	UNJUSTEST	UNLACED	UNLEVELS	UNLOCKING
UNITIES	UNJUSTLY	UNLACES	UNLEVIED	UNLOCKS
UNITING	UNKED	UNLACING	UNLICH	UNLOGICAL
UNITINGS	UNKEELED	UNLADE	UNLICKED	UNLOOKED
UNITION	UNKEMPT	UNLADED	UNLID	UNLOOSE
UNITIONS	UNKEMPTLY	UNLADEN	UNLIDDED	UNLOOSED
UNITISE	UNKEND	UNLADES	UNLIDDING	UNLOOSEN
UNITISED	UNKENNED	UNLADING	UNLIDS	UNLOOSENS
UNITISER	UNKENNEL	UNLADINGS	UNLIGHTED	UNLOOSES
UNITISERS	UNKENNELS	UNLAID	UNLIKABLE	UNLOOSING
UNITISES	UNKENT	UNLASH	UNLIKE	UNLOPPED
UNITISING	UNKEPT	UNLASHED	UNLIKED	UNLORD
UNITIVE	UNKET	UNLASHES	UNLIKELY	UNLORDED
UNITIVELY	UNKID	UNLASHING	UNLIKES	UNLORDING
UNITIZE	UNKIND	UNLAST	UNLIMBER	UNLORDLY
UNITIZED	UNKINDER	UNLASTE	UNLIMBERS	UNLORDS
UNITIZER	UNKINDEST	UNLATCH	UNLIME	UNIOSABLE
UNITIZERS	UNKINDLED	UNLATCHED	UNLIMED	UNLOST
UNITIZES	UNKINDLY	UNLATCHES	UNLIMES	UNLOVABLE
UNITIZING	UNKING	UNLAW	UNLIMING	UNLOVE
UNITRUST	UNKINGED	UNLAWED	UNLIMITED	UNLOVED
UNITRUSTS	UNKINGING	UNLAWFUL	UNLINE	UNLOVELY
UNITS	UNKINGLY	UNLAWING	UNLINEAL	UNLOVES
UNITY	UNKINGS	UNLAWS	UNLINED	UNLOVING
UNIVALENT	UNKINK	UNLAY	UNLINES	UNLUCKIER
UNIVALVE	UNKINKED	UNLAYING	UNLINING	UNLUCKILY
UNIVALVED	UNKINKING	UNLAYS	UNLINK	UNLUCKY

U

UNLYRICAL	UNMEETLY	UNMOLDING	UNNERVED	UNPAINTS
UNMACHO	UNMELLOW	UNMOLDS	UNNERVES	UNPAIRED
UNMADE	UNMELTED	UNMOLTEN	UNNERVING	UNPALSIED
UNMAILED	UNMENDED	UNMONEYED	UNNEST	UNPANEL
UNMAIMED	UNMERITED	UNMONIED	UNNESTED	UNPANELS
UNMAKABLE	UNMERRIER	UNMOOR	UNNESTING	UNPANGED
UNMAKE	UNMERRY	UNMOORED	UNNESTS	UNPANNEL
UNMAKER	UNMESH	UNMOORING	UNNETHES	UNPANNELS
UNMAKERS	UNMESHED	UNMOORS	UNNETTED	UNPAPER
UNMAKES	UNMESHES	UNMORAL	UNNOBLE	UNPAPERED
UNMAKING	UNMESHING	UNMORALLY	UNNOBLED	UNPAPERS
UNMAKINGS	UNMET	UNMORTISE	UNNOBLES	UNPARED
UNMAN	UNMETED	UNMOTIVED	UNNOBLING	UNPARTED
UNMANACLE	UNMETERED	UNMOULD	UNNOISIER	UNPARTIAL
UNMANAGED	UNMEW	UNMOULDED	UNNOISY	UNPATCHED
UNMANFUL	UNMEWED	UNMOULDS	UNNOTED	UNPATHED
UNMANLIER	UNMEWING	UNMOUNT	UNNOTICED	UNPAVED
UNMANLIKE	UNMEWS	UNMOUNTED	UNNUANCED	UNPAY
UNMANLY	UNMILKED	UNMOUNTS	UNOAKED	UNPAYABLE
UNMANNED	UNMILLED	UNMOURNED	UNOBEYED	UNPAYING
UNMANNING	UNMINDED	UNMOVABLE	UNOBVIOUS	UNPAYS
UNMANNISH	UNMINDFUL	UNMOVABLY	UNOFFERED	UNPEELED
UNMANS	UNMINED	UNMOVED	UNOFTEN	UNPEERED
UNMANTLE	UNMINGLE	UNMOVEDLY	UNOILED	UNPEG
UNMANTLED	UNMINGLED	UNMOVING	UNOPEN	UNPEGGED
UNMANTLES	UNMINGLES	UNMOWN	UNOPENED	UNPEGGING
UNMANURED	UNMIRIER	UNMUFFLE	UNOPPOSED	UNPEGS
UNMAPPED	UNMIRIEST	UNMUFFLED	UNORDER	UNPEN
UNMARD	UNMIRY	UNMUFFLES	UNORDERED	UNPENNED
UNMARKED	UNMISSED	UNMUSICAL	UNORDERLY	UNPENNIED
UNMARRED	UNMITER	UNMUZZLE	UNORDERS	UNPENNING
UNMARRIED	UNMITERED	UNMUZZLED	UNORNATE	UNPENS
UNMARRIES	UNMITERS	UNMUZZLES	UNOWED	UNPENT
UNMARRY	UNMITRE	UNNAIL	UNOWNED	UNPEOPLE
UNMASK	UNMITRED	UNNAILED	UNPACED	UNPEOPLED
UNMASKED	UNMITRES	UNNAILING	UNPACK	IJNPEOPLES
UNMASKER	UNMITRING	UNNAILS	UNPACKED	UNPERCH
UNMASKERS	UNMIX	UNNAMABLE	UNPACKER	UNPERCHED
UNMASKING	UNMIXABLE	UNNAMED	UNPACKERS	UNPERCHES
UNMASKS	UNMIXED	UNNANELD	UNPACKING	UNPERFECT
UNMATCHED	UNMIXEDLY	UNNATIVE	UNPACKS	UNPERPLEX
UNMATED	UNMIXES	UNNATIVED	UNPADDED	UNPERSON
UNMATTED	UNMIXING	UNNATIVES	UNPAGED	UNPERSONS
UNMATURED	UNMIXT	UNNATURAL	UNPAID	UNPERVERT
UNMEANING	UNMOANED	UNNEATH	UNPAINED	UNPICK
UNMEANT	UNMODISH	UNNEEDED	UNPAINFUL	UNPICKED
UNMEEK	UNMOLD	UNNEEDFUL	UNPAINT	UNPICKING
UNMEET	UNMOLDED	UNNERVE	UNPAINTED	UNPICKS

UNPIERCED	UNPOINTED	UNPROVIDE	UNREACHED	UNREPAIR
UNPILE	UNPOISED	UNPROVOKE	UNREAD	UNREPAIRS
UNPILED	UNPOISON	UNPRUNED	UNREADIER	UNRESERVE
UNPILES	UNPOISONS	UNPUCKER	UNREADILY	UNREST
UNPILING	UNPOLICED	UNPUCKERS	UNREADY	UNRESTED
UNPILOTED	UNPOLISH	UNPULLED	UNREAL	UNRESTFUL
UNPIN	UNPOLITE	UNPURE	UNREALISE	UNRESTING
UNPINKED	UNPOLITIC	UNPURELY	UNREALISM	UNRESTS
UNPINKT	UNPOLLED	UNPURGED	UNREALITY	UNRETIRE
UNPINNED	UNPOPE	UNPURSE	UNREALIZE	UNRETIRED
UNPINNING	UNPOPED	UNPURSED	UNREALLY	UNRETIRES
UNPINS	UNPOPES	UNPURSES	UNREAPED	UNREVISED
UNPITIED	UNPOPING	UNPURSING	UNREASON	UNREVOKED
UNPITIFUL	UNPOPULAR	UNPURSUED	UNREASONS	UNRHYMED
UNPITTED	UNPOSED	UNPUZZLE	UNREAVE	UNRIBBED
UNPITYING	UNPOSTED	UNPUZZLED	UNREAVED	UNRID
UNPLACE	UNPOTABLE	UNPUZZLES	UNREAVES	UNRIDABLE
UNPLACED	UNPOTTED	UNQUAKING	UNREAVING	UNRIDDEN
UNPLACES	UNPOURED	UNQUALIFY	UNREBATED	UNRIDDLE
UNPLACING	UNPOWERED	UNQUEEN	UNREBUKED	UNRIDDLED
UNPLAGUED	UNPRAISE	UNQUEENED	UNRECKED	UNRIDDLER
UNPLAINED	UNPRAISED	UNQUEENLY	UNRED	UNRIDDLES
UNPLAIT	UNPRAISES	UNQUEENS	UNREDREST	UNRIDGED
UNPLAITED	UNPRAY	UNQUELLED	UNREDUCED	UNRIFLED
UNPLAITS	UNPRAYED	UNQUIET	UNREDY	UNRIG
UNPLANKED	UNPRAYING	UNQUIETED	UNREEL	UNRIGGED
UNPLANNED	UNPRAYS	UNQUIETER	UNREELED	UNRIGGING
UNPLANTED	UNPREACH	UNQUIETLY	UNREELER	UNRIGHT
UNPLAYED	UNPRECISE	UNQUIETS	UNREELERS	UNRIGHTED
UNPLEASED	UNPREDICT	UNQUOTE	UNREELING	UNRIGHTS
UNPLEATED	UNPREPARE	UNQUOTED	UNREELS	UNRIGS
UNPLEDGED	UNPRESSED	UNQUOTES	UNREEVE	UNRIMED
UNPLIABLE	UNPRETTY	UNQUOTING	UNREEVED	UNRINGED
UNPLIABLY	UNPRICED	UNRACED	UNREEVES	UNRINSED
UNPLIANT	UNPRIEST	UNRACKED	UNREEVING	UNRIP
UNPLOWED	UNPRIESTS	UNRAISED	UNREFINED	UNRIPE
UNPLUCKED	UNPRIMED	UNRAKE	UNREFUTED	UNRIPELY
UNPLUG	UNPRINTED	UNRAKED	UNREIN	UNRTPENED
UNPLUGGED	UNPRISON	UNRAKES	UNREINED	UNRIPER
UNPLUGS	UNPRISONS	UNRAKING	UNREINING	UNRIPEST
UNPLUMB	UNPRIZED	UNRANKED	UNREINS	UNRIPPED
UNPLUMBED	UNPROBED	UNRATED	UNRELATED	UNRIPPING
UNPLUMBS	UNPROP	UNRAVAGED	UNRELAXED	UNRIPS
UNPLUME	UNPROPER	UNRAVEL	UNREMOVED	UNRISEN
UNPLUMED	UNPROPPED	UNRAVELED	UNRENEWED	UNRIVALED
UNPLUMES	UNPROPS	UNRAVELS	UNRENT	UNRIVEN
UNPLUMING	UNPROVED	UNRAZED	UNRENTED	UNRIVET
UNPOETIC	UNPROVEN	UNRAZORED	UNREPAID	UNRIVETED

UNRIVETS	UNRULIEST	UNSCARRED	UNSELFISH	UNSHAPELY
UNROASTED	UNRULY	UNSCARY	UNSELFS	UNSHAPEN
UNROBE	UNRUMPLED	UNSCATHED	UNSELL	UNSHAPES
UNROBED	UNRUSHED	UNSCENTED	UNSELLING	UNSHAPING
UNROBES	UNRUSTED	UNSCOURED	UNSELLS	UNSHARED
UNROBING	UNS	UNSCREW	UNSELVES	UNSHARP
UNROLL	UNSADDLE	UNSCREWED	UNSENSE	UNSHAVED
UNROLLED	UNSADDLED	UNSCREWS	UNSENSED	UNSHAVEN
UNROLLING	UNSADDLES	UNSCYTHED	UNSENSES	UNSHEATHE
UNROLLS	UNSAFE	UNSEAL	UNSENSING	UNSHED
UNROOF	UNSAFELY	UNSEALED	UNSENT	UNSHELL
UNROOFED	UNSAFER	UNSEALING	UNSERIOUS	UNSHELLED
UNROOFING	UNSAFEST	UNSEALS	UNSERVED	UNSHELLS
UNROOFS	UNSAFETY	UNSEAM	UNSET	UNSHENT
UNROOST	UNSAID	UNSEAMED	UNSETS	UNSHEWN
UNROOSTED	UNSAILED	UNSEAMING	UNSETTING	UNSHIFT
UNROOSTS	UNSAINED	UNSEAMS	UNSETTLE	UNSHIFTED
UNROOT	UNSAINT	UNSEARED	UNSETTLED	UNSHIFTS
UNROOTED	UNSAINTED	UNSEASON	UNSETTLES	UNSHIP
UNROOTING	UNSAINTLY	UNSEASONS	UNSEVERED	UNSHIPPED
UNROOTS	UNSAINTS	UNSEAT	UNSEW	UNSHIPS
UNROPE	UNSALABLE	UNSEATED	UNSEWED	UNSHIRTED
UNROPED	UNSALABLY	UNSEATING	UNSEWING	UNSHOCKED
UNROPES	UNSALTED	UNSEATS	UNSEWN	UNSHOD
UNROPING	UNSALUTED	UNSECRET	UNSEWS	UNSHOE
UNROSINED	UNSAMPLED	UNSECRETS	UNSEX	UNSHOED
UNROTTED	UNSAPPED	UNSECULAR	UNSEXED	UNSHOEING
UNROTTEN	UNSASHED	UNSECURED	UNSEXES	UNSHOES
UNROUGED	UNSATABLE	UNSEDUCED	UNSEXIER	UNSHOOT
UNROUGH	UNSATED	UNSEE	UNSEXIEST	UNSHOOTED
UNROUND	UNSATIATE	UNSEEABLE	UNSEXILY	UNSHOOTS
UNROUNDED	UNSATING	UNSEFDED	UNSEXING	UNSHORN
UNROUNDS	UNSAVED	UNSEEING	UNSEXIST	UNSHOT
UNROUSED	UNSAVORY	UNSEEL	UNSEXUAL	UNSHOTS
UNROVE	UNSAVOURY	UNSEELED	UNSEXY	UNSHOTTED
UNROVEN	UNSAW	UNSEELIE	UNSHACKLE	UNSHOUT
UNROYAL	UNSAWED	UNSEELING	UNSHADED	UNSHOUTED
UNROYALLY	UNSAWN	UNSEELS	UNSHADOW	UNSHOUTS
UNRUBBED	UNSAY	UNSEEMING	UNSHADOWS	UNSHOWIER
UNRUDE	UNSAYABLE	UNSEEMLY	UNSHAKED	UNSHOWN
UNRUFFE	UNSAYING	UNSEEN	UNSHAKEN	UNSHOWY
UNRUFFLE	UNSAYS	UNSEENS	UNSHALE	UNSHRIVED
UNRUFFLED	UNSCALE	UNSEES	UNSHALED	UNSHRIVEN
UNRUFFLES	UNSCALED	UNSEIZED	UNSHALES	UNSHROUD
UNRULE	UNSCALES	UNSELDOM	UNSHALING	UNSHROUDS
UNRULED	UNSCALING	UNSELF	UNSHAMED	UNSHRUBD
UNRULES	UNSCANNED	UNSELFED	UNSHAPE	UNSHRUNK
UNRULIER	UNSCARIER	UNSELFING	UNSHAPED	UNSHUNNED

UNSHUT	UNSNARL	UNSPAR	UNSTATES	UNSTUNG
UNSHUTS	UNSNARLED	UNSPARED	UNSTATING	UNSTYLISH
UNSHUTTER	UNSNARLS	UNSPARING	UNSTAYED	UNSUBDUED
UNSICKER	UNSNECK	UNSPARRED	UNSTAYING	UNSUBJECT
UNSICKLED	UNSNECKED	UNSPARS	UNSTEADY	UNSUBTLE
UNSIFTED	UNSNECKS	UNSPEAK	UNSTEEL	UNSUBTLER
UNSIGHING	UNSNUFFED	UNSPEAKS	UNSTEELED	UNSUBTLY
UNSIGHT	UNSOAKED	UNSPED	UNSTEELS	UNSUCCESS
UNSIGHTED	UNSOAPED	UNSPELL	UNSTEMMED	UNSUCKED
UNSIGHTLY	UNSOBER	UNSPELLED	UNSTEP	UNSUIT
UNSIGHTS	UNSOBERED	UNSPELLS	UNSTEPPED	UNSUITED
UNSIGNED	UNSOBERLY	UNSPENT	UNSTEPS	UNSUITING
UNSILENT	UNSOBERS	UNSPHERE	UNSTERILE	UNSUITS
UNSIMILAR	UNSOCIAL	UNSPHERED	UNSTICK	UNSULLIED
UNSINEW	UNSOCKET	UNSPHERES	UNSTICKS	UNSUMMED
UNSINEWED	UNSOCKETS	UNSPIDE	UNSTIFFEN	UNSUNG
UNSINEWS	UNSOD	UNSPIED	UNSTIFLED	UNSUNK
UNSINFUL	UNSODDEN	UNSPILLED	UNSTILLED	UNSUNNED
UNSISTING	UNSOFT	UNSPILT	UNSTINTED	UNSUNNIER
UNSIZABLE	UNSOILED	UNSPLIT	UNSTIRRED	UNSUNNY
UNSIZED	UNSOLACED	UNSPOILED	UNSTITCH	UNSUPPLE
UNSKILFUL	UNSOLD	UNSPOILT	UNSTOCK	UNSURE
UNSKILLED	UNSOLDER	UNSPOKE	UNSTOCKED	UNSURED
UNSKIMMED	UNSOLDERS	UNSPOKEN	UNSTOCKS	UNSURELY
UNSKINNED	UNSOLEMN	UNSPOOL	UNSTONED	UNSURER
UNSLAIN	UNSOLID	UNSPOOLED	UNSTOP	UNSUREST
UNSLAKED	UNSOLIDLY	UNSPOOLS	UNSTOPPED	UNSUSPECT
UNSLICED	UNSOLVED	UNSPOTTED	UNSTOPPER	UNSWADDLE
UNSLICK	UNSONCY	UNSPRAYED	UNSTOPS	UNSWATHE
UNSLING	UNSONSIE	UNSPRUNG	UNSTOW	UNSWATHED
UNSLINGS	UNSONSIER	UNSPUN	UNSTOWED	UNSWATHES
UNSLUICE	UNSONSY	UNSQUARED	UNSTOWING	UNSWAYED
UNSLUICED	UNSOOTE	UNSTABLE	UNSTOWS	UNSWEAR
UNSLUICES	UNSOOTHED	UNSTABLER	UNSTRAP	UNSWEARS
UNSLUNG	UNSORTED	UNSTABLY	UNSTRAPS	UNSWEET
UNSMART	UNSOUGHT	UNSTACK	UNSTRESS	UNSWEPT
UNSMILING	UNSOUL	UNSTACKED	UNSTRING	UNSWOLLEN
UNSMITTEN	UNSOULED	UNSTACKS	UNSTRINGS	UNSWORE
UNSMOKED	UNSOULING	UNSTAGED	UNSTRIP	UNSWORN
UNSMOOTH	UNSOULS	UNSTAID	UNSTRIPED	UNTACK
UNSMOOTHS	UNSOUND	UNSTAINED	UNSTRIPS	UNTACKED
UNSMOTE	UNSOUNDED	UNSTALKED	UNSTRUCK	UNTACKING
UNSNAG	UNSOUNDER	UNSTAMPED	UNSTRUNG	UNTACKLE
UNSNAGGED	UNSOUNDLY	UNSTARCH	UNSTUCK	UNTACKLED
UNSNAGS	UNSOURCED	UNSTARRED	UNSTUDIED	UNTACKLES
UNSNAP	UNSOURED	UNSTARRY	UNSTUFFED	UNTACKS
UNSNAPPED	UNSOWED	UNSTATE	UNSTUFFY	UNTACTFUL
UNSNAPS	UNSOWN	UNSTATED	UNSTUFT	UNTAGGED

UNTAILED	UNTHATCH	UNTOILING	UNTRUSTY	UNUSUAL
UNTAINTED	UNTHAW	UNTOLD	UNTRUTH	UNUSUALLY
UNTAKEN	UNTHAWED	UNTOMB	UNTRUTHS	UNUTTERED
UNTAMABLE	UNTHAWING	UNTOMBED	UNTUCK	UNVAIL
UNTAMABLY	UNTHAWS	UNTOMBING	UNTUCKED	UNVAILE
UNTAME	UNTHINK	UNTOMBS	UNTUCKING	UNVAILED
UNTAMED	UNTHINKS	UNTONED	UNTUCKS	UNVAILES
UNTAMES	UNTHOUGHT	UNTOOLED	UNTUFTED	UNVAILING
UNTAMING	UNTHREAD	UNTOOTHED	UNTUMBLED	UNVAILS
UNTANGLE	UNTHREADS	UNTORN	UNTUNABLE	UNVALUED
UNTANGLED	UNTHRIFT	UNTOUCHED	UNTUNABLY	UNVARIED
UNTANGLES	UNTHRIFTS	UNTOWARD	UNTUNE	UNVARYING
UNTANNED	UNTHRIFTY	UNTRACE	UNTUNED	UNVEIL
UNTAPPED	UNTHRONE	UNTRACED	UNTUNEFUL	UNVEILED
UNTARRED	UNTHRONED	UNTRACES	UNTUNES	UNVEILER
UNTASTED	UNTHRONES	UNTRACING	UNTUNING	UNVEILERS
UNTAUGHT	UNTIDIED	UNTRACK	UNTURBID	UNVEILING
UNTAX	UNTIDIER	UNTRACKED	UNTURF	UNVEILS
UNTAXABLE	UNTIDIES	UNTRACKS	UNTURFED	UNVEINED
UNTAXED	UNTIDIEST	UNTRADED	UNTURFING	UNVENTED
UNTAXES	UNTIDILY	UNTRAINED	UNTURFS	UNVERSED
UNTAXING	UNTIDY	UNTRAPPED	UNTURN	UNVESTED
UNTEACH	UNTIDYING	UNTREAD	UNTURNED	UNVETTED
UNTEACHES	UNTIE	UNTREADED	UNTURNING	UNVEXED
UNTEAM	UNTIED	UNTREADS	UNTURNS	UNVEXT
UNTEAMED	UNTIEING	UNTREATED	UNTUTORED	UNVIABLE
UNTEAMING	UNTIES	UNTRENDY	UNTWILLED	UNVIEWED
UNTEAMS	UNTIL	UNTRESSED	UNTWINE	UNVIRTUE
UNTEMPER	UNTILE	UNTRIDE	UNTWINED	UNVIRTUES
UNTEMPERS	UNTILED	UNTRIED	UNTWINES	UNVISITED
UNTEMPTED	UNTILES	UNTRIM	UNTWINING	UNVISOR
UNTENABLE	UNTILING	UNTRIMMED	UNTWIST	UNVISORED
UNTENABLY	UNTILLED	UNTRIMS	UNTWISTED	UNVISORS
UNTENANT	UNTILTED	UNTROD	UNTWISTS	UNVITAL
UNTENANTS	UNTIMED	UNTRODDEN	UNTYING	UNVIZARD
UNTENDED	UNTIMELY	UNTRUE	UNTYINGS	UNVIZARDS
UNTENDER	UNTIMEOUS	UNTRUER	UNTYPABLE	UNVOCAL
UNTENT	UNTIN	UNTRUEST	UNTYPICAL	UNVOICE
UNTENTED	UNTINGED	UNTRUISM	UNUNBIUM	UNVOICED
UNTENTIER	UNTINNED	UNTRUISMS	UNUNBIUMS	UNVOICES
UNTENTING	UNTINNING	UNTRULY	UNUNITED	UNVOICING
UNTENTS	UNTINS	UNTRUSS	UNUNUNIUM	UNVULGAR
UNTENTY	UNTIPPED	UNTRUSSED	UNURGED	UNWAGED
UNTENURED	UNTIRABLE	UNTRUSSER	UNUSABLE	UNWAISTED
UNTESTED	UNTIRED	UNTRUSSES	UNUSABLY	UNWAKED
UNTETHER	UNTIRING	UNTRUST	UNUSED	UNWAKENED
UNTETHERS	UNTITLED	UNTRUSTED	UNUSEFUL	UNWALLED
UNTHANKED	UNTO	UNTRUSTS	UNUSHERED	UNWANING

UNWANTED	UNWELDED	UNWITTIER	UNYOKE	UPBRAY
UNWARDED	UNWELDY	UNWITTILY	UNYOKED	UPBRAYED
UNWARE	UNWELL	UNWITTING	UNYOKES	UPBRAYING
UNWARELY	UNWEPT	UNWITTY	UNYOKING	UPBRAYS
UNWARES	UNWET	UNWIVE	UNYOUNG	UPBREAK
UNWARIE	UNWETTED	UNWIVED	UNZEALOUS	UPBREAKS
UNWARIER	UNWHIPPED	UNWIVES	UNZIP	UPBRING
UNWARIEST	UNWHIPT	UNWIVING	UNZIPPED	UPBRINGS
UNWARILY	UNWHITE	UNWOMAN	UNZIPPING	UPBROKE
UNWARLIKE	UNWIELDLY	UNWOMANED	UNZIPS	UPBROKEN
UNWARMED	UNWIELDY	UNWOMANLY	UNZONED	UPBROUGHT
UNWARNED	UNWIFELY	UNWOMANS	UP	UPBUILD
UNWARPED	UNWIGGED	UNWON	UPADAISY	UPBUILDER
UNWARY	UNWILFUL	UNWONT	UPAITHRIC	UPBUILDS
UNWASHED	UNWILL	UNWONTED	UPALONG	UPBUILT
UNWASHEDS	UNWILLED	UNWOODED	UPALONGS	UPBURNING
UNWASHEN	UNWILLING	UNWOOED	UPAS	UPBURST
UNWASTED	UNWILLS	UNWORDED	UPASES	UPBURSTS
UNWASTING	UNWIND	UNWORK	UPBEAR	UPBY
UNWATCHED	UNWINDER	UNWORKED	UPBEARER	UPBYE
UNWATER	UNWINDERS	UNWORKING	UPBEARERS	UPCAST
UNWATERED	UNWINDING	UNWORKS	UPBEARING	UPCASTING
UNWATERS	UNWINDS	UNWORLDLY	UPBEARS	UPCASTS
UNWATERY	UNWINGED	UNWORMED	UPBEAT	UPCATCH
UNWAXED	UNWINKING	UNWORN	UPBEATS	UPCATCHES
UNWAYED	UNWIPED	UNWORRIED	UPBIND	UPCAUGHT
UNWEAL	UNWIRE	UNWORTH	UPBINDING	UPCHEER
UNWEALS	UNWIRED	UNWORTHS	UPBINDS	UPCHEERED
UNWEANED	UNWIRES	UNWORTHY	UPBLEW	UPCHEERS
UNWEAPON	UNWIRING	UNWOUND	UPBLOW	UPCHUCK
UNWEAPONS	UNWISDOM	UNWOUNDED	UPBLOWING	UPCHUCKED
UNWEARIED	UNWISDOMS	UNWOVE	UPBLOWN	UPCHUCKS
UNWEARIER	UNWISE	UNWOVEN	UPBLOWS	UPCLIMB
UNWEARIES	UNWISELY	UNWRAP	UPBOIL	UPCLIMBED
UNWEARY	UNWISER	UNWRAPPED	UPBOILED	UPCLIMBS
UNWEAVE	UNWISEST	UNWRAPS	UPBOILING	UPCLOSE
UNWEAVES	UNWISH	UNWREAKED	UPBOILS	UPCLOSED
UNWEAVING	UNWISHED	UNWREATHE	UPBORE	UPCLOSES
UNWEBBED	UNWISHES	UNWRINKLE	UPBORNE	UPCLOSING
UNWED	UNWISHFUL	UNWRITE	UPBOUND	UPCOAST
UNWEDDED	UNWISHING	UNWRITES	UPBOUNDEN	UPCOIL
UNWEEDED	UNWIST	UNWRITING	UPBOW	UPCOILED
UNWEENED	UNWIT	UNWRITTEN	UPBOWS	UPCOILING
UNWEETING	UNWITCH	UNWROTE	UPBRAID	UPCOILS
UNWEIGHED	UNWITCHED	UNWROUGHT	UPBRAIDED	UPCOME
UNWEIGHT	UNWITCHES	UNWRUNG	UPBRAIDER	UPCOMES
UNWEIGHTS	UNWITS	UNYEANED	UPBRAIDS	UPCOMING
UNWELCOME	UNWITTED	UNYIELDED	UPBRAST	UPCOUNTRY

UPCOURT	UPEND	UPGRADE	UPHOLDERS	UPLIFT
UPCURL	UPENDED	UPGRADED	UPHOLDING	UPLIFTED
UPCURLED	UPENDING	UPGRADER	UPHOLDS	UPLIFTER
UPCURLING	UPENDS	UPGRADERS	UPHOLSTER	UPLIFTERS
UPCURLS	UPFIELD	UPGRADES	UPHOORD	UPLIFTING
UPCURVE	UPFILL	UPGRADING	UPHOORDED	UPLIFTS
UPCURVED	UPFILLED	UPGREW	UPHOORDS	UPLIGHT
UPCURVES	UPFILLING	UPGROW	UPHOVE	UPLIGHTED
UPCURVING	UPFILLS	UPGROWING	UPHROE	UPLIGHTER
UPCYCLE	UPFLING	UPGROWN	UPHROES	UPLIGHTS
UPCYCLED	UPFLINGS	UPGROWS	UPHUDDEN	UPLINK
UPCYCLES	UPFLOW	UPGROWTH	UPHUNG	UPLINKED
UPCYCLING	UPFLOWED	UPGROWTHS	UPHURL	UPLINKING
UPDART	UPFLOWING	UPGUSH	UPHURLED	UPLINKS
UPDARTED	UPFLOWS	UPGUSHED	UPHURLING	UPLIT
UPDARTING	UPFLUNG	UPGUSHES	UPHURLS	UPLOAD
UPDARTS	UPFOLD	UPGUSHING	UPJET	UPLOADED
UPDATABLE	UPFOLDED	UPHAND	UPJETS	UPLOADING
UPDATE	UPFOLDING	UPHANG	UPJETTED	UPLOADS
UPDATED	UPFOLDS	UPHANGING	UPJETTING	UPLOCK
UPDATER	UPFOLLOW	UPHANGS	UPKEEP	UPLOCKED
UPDATERS	UPFOLLOWS	UPHAUD	UPKEEPS	UPLOCKING
UPDATES	UPFRONT	UPHAUDING	UPKNIT	UPLOCKS
UPDATING	UPFURL	UPHAUDS	UPKNITS	UPLOOK
UPDIVE	UPFURLED	UPHEAP	UPKNITTED	UPLOOKED
UPDIVED	UPFURLING	UPHEAPED	UPLAID	UPLOOKING
UPDIVES	UPFURLS	UPHEAPING	UPLAND	UPLOOKS
UPDIVING	UPGANG	UPHEAPS	UPLANDER	UPLYING
UPDO	UPGANGS	UPHEAVAL	UPLANDERS	UPMADE
UPDOMING	UPGATHER	UPHEAVALS	UPLANDISH	UPMAKE
UPDOMINGS	UPGATHERS	UPHEAVE	UPLANDS	UPMAKER
UPDOS	UPGAZE	UPHEAVED	UPLAY	UPMAKERS
UPDOVE	UPGAZED	UPHEAVER	UPLAYING	UPMAKES
UPDRAFT	UPGAZES	UPHEAVERS	UPLAYS	UPMAKING
UPDRAFTS	UPGAZING	UPHEAVES	UPLEAD	UPMAKINGS
UPDRAG	UPGIRD	UPHEAVING	UPLEADING	UPMANSHIP
UPDRAGGED	UPGIRDED	UPHELD	UPLEADS	UPMARKET
UPDRAGS	UPGIRDING	UPHILD	UPLEAN	UPMARKETS
UPDRAUGHT	UPGIRDS	UPHILL	UPLEANED	UPMOST
UPDRAW	UPGIRT	UPHILLS	UPLEANING	UPO
UPDRAWING	UPGIRTED	UPHOARD	UPLEANS	UPON
UPDRAWN	UPGIRTING	UPHOARDED	UPLEANT	UPPED
UPDRAWS	UPGIRTS	UPHOARDS	UPLEAP	UPPER
UPDREW	UPGO	UPHOIST	UPLEAPED	UPPERCASE
UPDRIED	UPGOES	UPHOISTED	UPLEAPING	UPPERCUT
UPDRIES	UPGOING	UPHOISTS	UPLEAPS	UPPERCUTS
UPDRY	UPGOINGS	UPHOLD	UPLEAPT	UPPERMOST
UPDRYING	UPGONE	UPHOLDER	UPLED	UPPERPART

UPPERS	UPRIST	UPSET	UPSTAGE	UPSWEEPS
UPPILE	UPRISTS	UPSETS	UPSTAGED	UPSWELL
UPPILED	UPRIVER	UPSETTER	UPSTAGER	UPSWELLED
UPPILES	UPRIVERS	UPSETTERS	UPSTAGERS	UPSWELLS
UPPILING	UPROAR	UPSETTING	UPSTAGES	UPSWEPT
UPPING	UPROARED	UPSEY	UPSTAGING	UPSWING
UPPINGS	UPROARING	UPSEYS	UPSTAIR	UPSWINGS
UPPISH	UPROARS	UPSHIFT	UPSTAIRS	UPSWOLLEN
UPPISHLY	UPROLL	UPSHIFTED	UPSTAND	UPSWUNG
UPPITIER	UPROLLED	UPSHIFTS	UPSTANDS	UPSY
UPPITIEST	UPROLLING	UPSHOOT	UPSTARE	UPTA
UPPITY	UPROLLS	UPSHOOTS	UPSTARED	UPTAK
UPPROP	UPROOT	UPSHOT	UPSTARES	UPTAKE
UPPROPPED	UPROOTAL	UPSHOTS	UPSTARING	UPTAKEN
UPPROPS	UPROOTALS	UPSIDE	UPSTART	UPTAKES
UPRAISE	UPROOTED	UPSIDES	UPSTARTED	UPTAKING
UPRAISED	UPROOTER	UPSIES	UPSTARTS	UPTAKS
UPRAISER	UPROOTERS	UPSILON	UPSTATE	UPTALK
UPRAISERS	UPROOTING	UPSILONS	UPSTATER	UPTALKED
UPRAISES	UPROOTS	UPSITTING	UPSTATERS	UPTALKING
UPRAISING	UPROSE	UPSIZE	UPSTATES	UPTALKS
UPRAN	UPROUSE	UPSIZED	UPSTAY	UPTEAR
UPRATE	UPROUSED	UPSIZES	UPSTAYED	UPTEARING
UPRATED	UPROUSES	UPSIZING	UPSTAYING	UPTEARS
UPRATES	UPROUSING	UPSKILL	UPSTAYS	UPTEMPO
UPRATING	UPRUN	UPSKILLED	UPSTEP	UPTEMPOS
UPREACH	UPRUNNING	UPSKILLS	UPSTEPPED	UPTER
UPREACHED	UPRUNS	UPSKIRT	UPSTEPS	UPTHREW
UPREACHES	UPRUSH	UPSKIRTS	UPSTIR	UPTHROW
UPREAR	UPRUSHED	UPSLOPE	UPSTIRRED	UPTHROWN
UPREARED	UPRUSHES	UPSLOPES	UPSTIRS	UPTHROWS
UPREARING	UPRUSHING	UPSOAR	UPSTOOD	UPTHRUST
UPREARS	UPRYST	UPSOARED	UPSTREAM	UPTHRUSTS
UPREST	UPS	UPSOARING	UPSTREAMS	UPTHUNDER
UPRESTS	UPSADAISY	UPSOARS	UPSTROKE	UPTICK
UPRIGHT	UPSCALE	UPSOLD	UPSTROKES	UPTICKS
UPRIGHTED	UPSCALED	UPSPAKE	UPSURGE	UPTIE
UPRIGHTLY	UPSCALES	UPSPEAK	UPSURGED	UPTIED
UPRIGHTS	UPSCALING	UPSPEAKS	UPSURGES	UPTIES
UPRISAL	UPSEE	UPSPEAR	UPSURGING	UPTIGHT
UPRISALS	UPSEES	UPSPEARED	UPSWARM	UPTIGHTER
UPRISE	UPSELL	UPSPEARS	UPSWARMED	UPTILT
UPRISEN	UPSELLING	UPSPOKE	UPSWARMS	UPTILTED
UPRISER	UPSELLS	UPSPOKEN	UPSWAY	UPTILTING
UPRISERS	UPSEND	UPSPRANG	UPSWAYED	UPTILTS
UPRISES	UPSENDING	UPSPRING	UPSWAYING	UPTIME
UPRISING	UPSENDS	UPSPRINGS	UPSWAYS	UPTIMES
UPRISINGS	UPSENT	UPSPRUNG	UPSWEEP	UPTITLING

U

UPTOOK	UPWOUND	URARE	UREASES	URGER
UPTORE	UPWRAP	URARES	UREDIA	URGERS
UPTORN	UPWRAPS	URARI	UREDIAL	URGES
UPTOSS	UPWROUGHT	URARIS	UREDINE	URGING
UPTOSSED	UR	URASE	UREDINES	URGINGLY
UPTOSSES	URACHI	URASES	UREDINIA	URGINGS
UPTOSSING	URACHUS	URATE	UREDINIAL	URIAL
UPTOWN	URACHUSES	URATES	UREDINIUM	URIALS
UPTOWNER	URACIL	URATIC	UREDINOUS	URIC
UPTOWNERS	URACILS	URB	UREDIUM	URICASE
UPTOWNS	URAEI	URBAN	UREDO	URICASES
UPTRAIN	URAEMIA	URBANE	UREDOS	URIDINE
UPTRAINED	URAEMIAS	URBANELY	UREDOSORI	URIDINES
UPTRAINS	URAEMIC	URBANER	UREIC	URIDYLIC
UPTREND	URAEUS	URBANEST	UREIDE	URINAL
UPTRENDS	URAEUSES	URBANISE	UREIDES	URINALS
UPTRILLED	URALI	URBANISED	UREMIA	URINANT
UPTURN	URALIS	URBANISES	UREMIAS	URINARIES
UPTURNED	URALITE	URBANISM	UREMIC	URINARY
UPTURNING	URALITES	URBANISMS	URENA	URINATE
UPTURNS	URALITIC	URBANIST	URENAS	URINATED
UPTYING	URALITISE	URBANISTS	URENT	URINATES
UPVALUE	URALITIZE	URBANITE	UREOTELIC	URINATING
UPVALUED	URANIA	URBANITES	URES	URINATION
UPVALUES	URANIAN	URBANITY	URESES	URINATIVE
UPVALUING	URANIAS	URBANIZE	URESIS	URINATOR
UPVOTE	URANIC	URBANIZED	URETER	URINATORS
UPVOTED	URANIDE	URBANIZES	URETERAL	URINE
UPVOTES	URANIDES	URBEX	URETERIC	URINED
UPVOTING	URANIN	URBEXES	URETERS	URINEMIA
UPWAFT	URANINITE	URBIA	URETHAN	URINEMIAS
UPWAFTED	URANINS	URBIAS	URETHANE	URINEMIC
UPWAFTING	URANISCI	URBS	URETHANED	URINES
UPWAFTS	URANISCUS	URCEOLATE	URETHANES	URINING
UPWARD	URANISM	URCEOLI	URETHANS	URINOLOGY
UPWARDLY	URANISMS	URCEOLUS	URETHRA	URINOSE
UPWARDS	URANITE	URCHIN	URETHRAE	URINOUS
UPWELL	URANITES	URCHINS	URETHRAL	URITE
UPWELLED	URANITIC	URD	URETHRAS	URITES
UPWELLING	URANIUM	URDE	URETIC	URMAN
UPWELLS	URANIUMS	URDEE	URGE	URMANS
UPWENT	URANOLOGY	URDS	URGED	URN
UPWHIRL	URANOUS	URDY	URGENCE	URNAL
UPWHIRLED	URANYL	URE	URGENCES	URNED
UPWHIRLS	URANYLIC	UREA	URGENCIES	URNFIELD
UPWIND	URANYLS	UREAL	URGENCY	URNFIELDS
UPWINDING	URAO	UREAS	URGENT	URNFUL
UPWINDS	URAOS	UREASE	URGENTLY	URNFULS

URNING
URNINGS
URNLIKE
URNS
UROBILIN
UROBILINS
UROBORIC
UROBOROS
UROCHORD
UROCHORDS
UROCHROME
URODELAN
URODELANS
URODELE
URODELES
URODELOUS
UROGENOUS
UROGRAM
UROGRAMS
UROGRAPHY
UROKINASE
UROLAGNIA
UROLITH
UROLITHIC
UROLITHS
UROLOGIC
UROLOGIES
UROLOGIST
UROLOGY
UROMERE
UROMERES
UROPOD
UROPODAL
UROPODOUS
UROPODS
UROPYGIA
UROPYGIAL
UROPYGIUM
UROSCOPIC
UROSCOPY
UROSES
UROSIS
UROSOME
UROSOMES
UROSTEGE
UROSTEGES
UROSTOMY
UROSTYLE

UROSTYLES
URP
URPED
URPING
URPS
URSA
URSAE
URSID
URSIDS
URSIFORM
URSINE
URSON
URSONS
URTEXT
URTEXTE
URTEXTS
URTICA
URTICANT
URTICANTS
URTICARIA
URTICAS
URTICATE
URTICATED
URTICATES
URUBU
URUBUS
URUS
URUSES
URUSHIOL
URUSHIOLS
URVA
URVAS
US
USABILITY
USABLE
USABLY
USAGE
USAGER
USAGERS
USAGES
USANCE
USANCES
USAUNCE
USAUNCES
USE
USEABLE
USEABLY
USED

USEFUL
USEFULLY
USEFULS
USELESS
USELESSLY
USER
USERNAME
USERNAMES
USERS
USES
USHER
USHERED
USHERESS
USHERETTE
USHERING
USHERINGS
USHERS
USHERSHIP
USING
USNEA
USNEAS
USQUABAE
USQUABAES
USQUE
USQUEBAE
USQUEBAES
USQUES
USTION
USTIONS
USTULATE
USTULATED
USTULATES
USUAL
USUALLY
USUALNESS
USUALS
USUCAPION
USUCAPT
USUCAPTED
USUCAPTS
USUFRUCT
USUFRUCTS
USURE
USURED
USURER
USURERS
USURES
USURESS

USURESSES
USURIES
USURING
USURIOUS
USUROUS
USURP
USURPED
USURPEDLY
USURPER
USURPERS
USURPING
USURPINGS
USURPS
USURY
USWARD
USWARDS
UT
UTA
UTAS
UTASES
UTE
UTENSIL
UTENSILS
UTERI
UTERINE
UTERITIS
UTEROTOMY
UTERUS
UTERUSES
UTES
UTILE
UTILES
UTILIDOR
UTILIDORS
UTILISE
UTILISED
UTILISER
UTILISERS
UTILISES
UTILISING
UTILITIES
UTILITY
UTILIZE
UTILIZED
UTILIZER
UTILIZERS
UTILIZES
UTILIZING

UTIS
UTISES
UTMOST
UTMOSTS
UTOPIA
UTOPIAN
UTOPIANS
UTOPIAS
UTOPIAST
UTOPIASTS
UTOPISM
UTOPISMS
UTOPIST
UTOPISTIC
UTOPISTS
UTRICLE
UTRICLES
UTRICULAR
UTRICULI
UTRICULUS
UTS
UTTER
UTTERABLE
UTTERANCE
UTTERED
UTTERER
UTTERERS
UTTEREST
UTTERING
UTTERINGS
UTTERLESS
UTTERLY
UTTERMOST
UTTERNESS
UTTERS
UTU
UTUS
UVA
UVAE
UVAROVITE
UVAS
UVEA
UVEAL
UVEAS
UVEITIC
UVEITIS
UVEITISES
UVEOUS

U

UVULA

UVULA	UVULARLY	UVULITIS	UXORICIDE
UVULAE	UVULARS	UXORIAL	UXORIOUS
UVULAR	UVULAS	UXORIALLY	

V

VAC	VACUISTS	VAGINITIS	VAINLY	VALETE
VACANCE	VACUITIES	VAGINOSES	VAINNESS	VALETED
VACANCES	VACUITY	VAGINOSIS	VAIR	VALETES
VACANCIES	VACUOLAR	VAGINULA	VAIRE	VALETING
VACANCY	VACUOLATE	VAGINULAE	VAIRIER	VALETINGS
VACANT	VACUOLE	VAGINULE	VAIRIEST	VALETS
VACANTLY	VACUOLES	VAGINULES	VAIRS	VALGOID
VACATABLE	VACUOUS	VAGITUS	VAIRY	VALGOUS
VACATE	VACUOUSLY	VAGITUSES	VAIVODE	VALGUS
VACATED	VACUUM	VAGOTOMY	VAIVODES	VALGUSES
VACATES	VACUUMED	VAGOTONIA	VAJAZZLE	VALI
VACATING	VACUUMING	VAGOTONIC	VAJAZZLED	VALIANCE
VACATION	VACUUMS	VAGRANCY	VAJAZZLES	VALIANCES
VACATIONS	VADE	VAGRANT	VAKAS	VALIANCY
VACATUR	VADED	VAGRANTLY	VAKASES	VALIANT
VACATURS	VADES	VAGRANTS	VAKASS	VALIANTLY
VACCINA	VADING	VAGROM	VAKASSES	VALIANTS
VACCINAL	VADOSE	VAGS	VAKEEL	VALID
VACCINAS	VAE	VAGUE	VAKEELS	VALIDATE
VACCINATE	VAES	VAGUED	VAKIL	VALIDATED
VACCINE	VAG	VAGUELY	VAKILS	VALIDATES
VACCINEE	VAGABOND	VAGUENESS	VALANCE	VALIDATOR
VACCINEES	VAGABONDS	VAGUER	VALANCED	VALIDER
VACCINES	VAGAL	VAGUES	VALANCES	VALIDEST
VACCINIA	VAGALLY	VAGUEST	VALANCING	VALIDITY
VACCINIAL	VAGARIES	VAGUING	VALE	VALIDLY
VACCINIAS	VAGARIOUS	VAGUISH	VALENCE	VALIDNESS
VACCINIUM	VAGARISH	VAGUS	VALENCES	VALINE
VACHERIN	VAGARY	VAHANA	VALENCIA	VALINES
VACHERINS	VAGGED	VAHANAS	VALENCIAS	VALIS
VACILLANT	VAGGING	VAHINE	VALENCIES	VALISE
VACILLATE	VAGI	VAHINES	VALENCY	VALISES
VACKED	VAGILE	VAIL	VALENTINE	VALIUM
VACKING	VAGILITY	VAILED	VALERATE	VALIUMS
VACS	VAGINA	VAILING	VALERATES	VALKYR
VACUA	VAGINAE	VAILS	VALERIAN	VALKYRIE
VACUATE	VAGINAL	VAIN	VALERIANS	VALKYRIES
VACUATED	VAGINALLY	VAINER	VALERIC	VALKYRS
VACUATES	VAGINANT	VAINESSE	VALES	VALLAR
VACUATING	VAGINAS	VAINESSES	VALET	VALLARIES
VACUATION	VAGINATE	VAINEST	VALETA	VALLARS
VACUIST	VAGINATED	VAINGLORY	VALETAS	VALLARY

VALLATE	VALUES	VAMPIRIZE	VANISHER	VAPORED
VALLATION	VALUING	VAMPISH	VANISHERS	VAPORER
VALLECULA	VALUTA	VAMPISHLY	VANISHES	VAPORERS
VALLEY	VALUTAS	VAMPLATE	VANISHING	VAPORETTI
VALLEYED	VALVAL	VAMPLATES	VANITAS	VAPORETTO
VALLEYS	VALVAR	VAMPS	VANITASES	VAPORIER
VALLHUND	VALVASSOR	VAMPY	VANITIED	VAPORIEST
VALLHUNDS	VALVATE	VAN	VANITIES	VAPORIFIC
VALLONIA	VALVE	VANADATE	VANITORY	VAPORING
VALLONIAS	VALVED	VANADATES	VANITY	VAPORINGS
VALLUM	VALVELESS	VANADIATE	VANLIKE	VAPORISE
VALLUMS	VALVELET	VANADIC	VANLOAD	VAPORISED
VALONEA	VALVELETS	VANADIUM	VANLOADS	VAPORISER
VALONEAS	VALVELIKE	VANADIUMS	VANMAN	VAPORISES
VALONIA	VALVES	VANADOUS	VANMEN	VAPORISH
VALONIAS	VALVING	VANASPATI	VANNED	VAPORIZE
VALOR	VALVULA	VANDA	VANNER	VAPORIZED
VALORISE	VALVULAE	VANDAL	VANNERS	VAPORIZER
VALORISED	VALVULAR	VANDALIC	VANNING	VAPORIZES
VALORISES	VALVULE	VANDALISE	VANNINGS	VAPORLESS
VALORIZE	VALVULES	VANDALISH	VANPOOL	VAPORLIKE
VALORIZED	VAMBRACE	VANDALISM	VANPOOLS	VAPOROUS
VALORIZES	VAMBRACED	VANDALIZE	VANQUISH	VAPORS
VALOROUS	VAMBRACES	VANDALS	VANS	VAPORWARE
VALORS	VAMOOSE	VANDAS	VANT	VAPORY
VALOUR	VAMOOSED	VANDYKE	VANTAGE	VAPOUR
VALOURS	VAMOOSES	VANDYKED	VANTAGED	VAPOURED
VALPROATE	VAMOOSING	VANDYKES	VANTAGES	VAPOURER
VALPROIC	VAMOSE	VANDYKING	VANTAGING	VAPOURERS
VALSE	VAMOSED	VANE	VANTBRACE	VAPOURIER
VALSED	VAMOSES	VANED	VANTBRASS	VAPOURING
VALSES	VAMOSING	VANELESS	VANTS	VAPOURISH
VALSING	VAMP	VANES	VANWARD	VAPOUROUS
VALUABLE	VAMPED	VANESSA	VAPE	VAPOURS
VALUABLES	VAMPER	VANESSAS	VAPED	VAPOURY
VALUABLY	VAMPERS	VANESSID	VAPER	VAPULATE
VALUATE	VAMPIER	VANESSIDS	VAPERS	VAPULATED
VALUATED	VAMPIEST	VANG	VAPES	VAPULATES
VALUATES	VAMPING	VANGS	VAPID	VAQUERO
VALUATING	VAMPINGS	VANGUARD	VAPIDER	VAQUEROS
VALUATION	VAMPIRE	VANGUARDS	VAPIDEST	VAR
VALUATOR	VAMPIRED	VANILLA	VAPIDITY	VARA
VALUATORS	VAMPIRES	VANILLAS	VAPIDLY	VARACTOR
VALUE	VAMPIRIC	VANILLIC	VAPIDNESS	VARACTORS
VALUED	VAMPIRING	VANILLIN	VAPING	VARAN
VALUELESS	VAMPIRISE	VANILLINS	VAPINGS	VARANS
VALUER	VAMPIRISH	VANISH	VAPOR	VARAS
VALUERS	VAMPIRISM	VANISHED	VAPORABLE	VARDIES

VARDY	VARIOLAR	VARTABEDS	VASTIDITY	VAULTY
VARE	VARIOLAS	VARUS	VASTIER	VAUNCE
VAREC	VARIOLATE	VARUSES	VASTIEST	VAUNCED
VARECH	VARIOLE	VARVE	VASTITIES	VAUNCES
VARECHS	VARIOLES	VARVED	VASTITUDE	VAUNCING
VARECS	VARIOLITE	VARVEL	VASTITY	VAUNT
VARENYKY	VARIOLOID	VARVELLED	VASTLY	VAUNTAGE
VARES	VARIOLOUS	VARVELS	VASTNESS	VAUNTAGES
VAREUSE	VARIORUM	VARVES	VASTS	VAUNTED
VAREUSES	VARIORUMS	VARY	VASTY	VAUNTER
VARGUENO	VARIOUS	VARYING	VAT	VAUNTERS
VARGUENOS	VARIOUSLY	VARYINGLY	VATABLE	VAUNTERY
VARIA	VARISCITE	VARYINGS	VATFUL	VAUNTFUL
VARIABLE	VARISIZED	VAS	VATFULS	VAUNTIE
VARIABLES	VARISTOR	VASA	VATIC	VAUNTIER
VARIABLY	VARISTORS	VASAL	VATICAL	VAUNTIEST
VARIANCE	VARITYPE	VASCULA	VATICIDE	VAUNTING
VARIANCES	VARITYPED	VASCULAR	VATICIDES	VAUNTINGS
VARIANT	VARITYPES	VASCULUM	VATICINAL	VAUNTS
VARIANTS	VARIX	VASCULUMS	VATMAN	VAUNTY
VARIAS	VARLET	VASE	VATMEN	VAURIEN
VARIATE	VARLETESS	VASECTOMY	VATS	VAURIENS
VARIATED	VARLETRY	VASEFUL	VATTED	VAUS
VARIATES	VARLETS	VASEFULS	VATTER	VAUT
VARIATING	VARLETTO	VASELIKE	VATTERS	VAUTE
VARIATION	VARLETTOS	VASELINE	VATTING	VAUTED
VARIATIVE	VARMENT	VASELINED	VATU	VAUTES
VARICEAL	VARMENTS	VASELINES	VATUS	VAUTING
VARICELLA	VARMINT	VASES	VAU	VAUTS
VARICES	VARMINTS	VASIFORM	VAUCH	VAV
VARICOID	VARNA	VASOMOTOR	VAUCHED	VAVASOR
VARICOSE	VARNAS	VASOSPASM	VAUCHES	VAVASORS
VARICOSED	VARNISH	VASOTOCIN	VAUCHING	VAVASORY
VARICOSES	VARNISHED	VASOTOMY	VAUDOO	VAVASOUR
VARICOSIS	VARNISHER	VASOVAGAL	VAUDOOS	VAVASOURS
VARIED	VARNISHES	VASSAIL	VAUDOUX	VAVASSOR
VARIEDLY	VARNISHY	VASSAILS	VAULT	VAVASSORS
VARIEGATE	VAROOM	VASSAL	VAULTAGE	VAVS
VARIER	VAROOMED	VASSALAGE	VAULTAGES	VAW
VARIERS	VAROOMING	VASSALESS	VAULTED	VAWARD
VARIES	VAROOMS	VASSALISE	VAULTER	VAWARDS
VARIETAL	VARROA	VASSALIZE	VAULTERS	VAWNTIE
VARIETALS	VARROAS	VASSALLED	VAULTIER	VAWNTIER
VARIETIES	VARS	VASSALRY	VAULTIEST	VAWNTIEST
VARIETY	VARSAL	VASSALS	VAULTING	VAWS
VARIFOCAL	VARSITIES	VAST	VAULTINGS	VAWTE
VARIFORM	VARSITY	VASTER	VAULTLIKE	VAWTED
VARIOLA	VARTABED	VASTEST	VAULTS	VAWTES

VAWTING
VAX
VAXES
VEAL
VEALE
VEALED
VEALER
VEALERS
VEALES
VEALIER
VEALIEST
VEALING
VEALS
VEALY
VECTOR
VECTORED
VECTORIAL
VECTORING
VECTORISE
VECTORIZE
VECTORS
VEDALIA
VEDALIAS
VEDETTE
VEDETTES
VEDUTA
VEDUTAS
VEDUTE
VEDUTISTA
VEDUTISTE
VEDUTISTI
VEE
VEEJAY
VEEJAYS
VEENA
VEENAS
VEEP
VEEPEE
VEEPEES
VEEPS
VEER
VEERED
VEERIES
VEERING
VEERINGLY
VEERINGS
VEERS
VEERY

VEES
VEG
VEGA
VEGAN
VEGANIC
VEGANISM
VEGANISMS
VEGANS
VEGAS
VEGELATE
VEGELATES
VEGEMITE
VEGEMITES
VEGES
VEGETABLE
VEGETABLY
VEGETAL
VEGETALLY
VEGETALS
VEGETANT
VEGETATE
VEGETATED
VEGETATES
VEGETE
VEGETIST
VEGETISTS
VEGETIVE
VEGETIVES
VEGGED
VEGGES
VEGGIE
VEGGIER
VEGGIES
VEGGIEST
VEGGING
VEGIE
VEGIER
VEGIES
VEGIEST
VEGO
VEGOS
VEHEMENCE
VEHEMENCY
VEHEMENT
VEHICLE
VEHICLES
VEHICULAR
VEHM

VEHME
VEHMIC
VEHMIQUE
VEIL
VEILED
VEILEDLY
VEILER
VEILERS
VEILIER
VEILIEST
VEILING
VEILINGS
VEILLESS
VEILLEUSE
VEILLIKE
VEILS
VEILY
VEIN
VEINAL
VEINED
VEINER
VEINERS
VEINIER
VEINIEST
VEINING
VEININGS
VEINLESS
VEINLET
VEINLETS
VEINLIKE
VEINOUS
VEINS
VEINSTONE
VEINSTUFF
VEINULE
VEINULES
VEINULET
VEINULETS
VEINY
VELA
VELAMEN
VELAMINA
VELAR
VELARIA
VELARIC
VELARISE
VELARISED
VELARISES

VELARIUM
VELARIZE
VELARIZED
VELARIZES
VELARS
VELATE
VELATED
VELATURA
VELATURAS
VELCRO
VELCROS
VELD
VELDS
VELDSKOEN
VELDT
VELDTS
VELE
VELES
VELETA
VELETAS
VELIGER
VELIGERS
VELITES
VELL
VELLEITY
VELLENAGE
VELLET
VELLETS
VELLICATE
VELLON
VELLONS
VELLS
VELLUM
VELLUMS
VELLUS
VELOCE
VELOCITY
VELODROME
VELOUR
VELOURS
VELOUTE
VELOUTES
VELOUTINE
VELSKOEN
VELSKOENS
VELUM
VELURE
VELURED

VELURES
VELURING
VELVERET
VELVERETS
VELVET
VELVETED
VELVETEEN
VELVETIER
VELVETING
VELVETS
VELVETY
VENA
VENAE
VENAL
VENALITY
VENALLY
VENATIC
VENATICAL
VENATION
VENATIONS
VENATOR
VENATORS
VEND
VENDABLE
VENDABLES
VENDACE
VENDACES
VENDAGE
VENDAGES
VENDANGE
VENDANGES
VENDED
VENDEE
VENDEES
VENDER
VENDERS
VENDETTA
VENDETTAS
VENDEUSE
VENDEUSES
VENDIBLE
VENDIBLES
VENDIBLY
VENDING
VENDINGS
VENDIS
VENDISES
VENDISS

VENDISSES
VENDITION
VENDOR
VENDORS
VENDS
VENDU
VENDUE
VENDUES
VENDUS
VENEER
VENEERED
VENEERER
VENEERERS
VENEERING
VENEERS
VENEFIC
VENEFICAL
VENENATE
VENENATED
VENENATES
VENENE
VENENES
VENENOSE
VENERABLE
VENERABLY
VENERATE
VENERATED
VENERATES
VENERATOR
VENEREAL
VENEREAN
VENEREANS
VENEREOUS
VENERER
VENERERS
VENERIES
VENERY
VENETIAN
VENETIANS
VENEWE
VENEWES
VENEY
VENEYS
VENGE
VENGEABLE
VENGEABLY
VENGEANCE
VENGED

VENGEFUL
VENGEMENT
VENGER
VENGERS
VENGES
VENGING
VENIAL
VENIALITY
VENIALLY
VENIDIUM
VENIDIUMS
VENIN
VENINE
VENINES
VENINS
VENIRE
VENIREMAN
VENIREMEN
VENIRES
VENISON
VENISONS
VENITE
VENITES
VENNEL
VENNELS
VENOGRAM
VENOGRAMS
VENOLOGY
VENOM
VENOMED
VENOMER
VENOMERS
VENOMING
VENOMLESS
VENOMOUS
VENOMS
VENOSE
VENOSITY
VENOUS
VENOUSLY
VENT
VENTAGE
VENTAGES
VENTAIL
VENTAILE
VENTAILES
VENTAILS
VENTANA

VENTANAS
VENTAYLE
VENTAYLES
VENTED
VENTER
VENTERS
VENTIDUCT
VENTIFACT
VENTIGE
VENTIGES
VENTIL
VENTILATE
VENTILS
VENTING
VENTINGS
VENTLESS
VENTOSE
VENTOSES
VENTOSITY
VENTOUSE
VENTOUSES
VENTRAL
VENTRALLY
VENTRALS
VENTRE
VENTRED
VENTRES
VENTRICLE
VENTRING
VENTRINGS
VENTROUS
VENTS
VENTURE
VENTURED
VENTURER
VENTURERS
VENTURES
VENTURI
VENTURING
VENTURIS
VENTUROUS
VENUE
VENUES
VENULAR
VENULE
VENULES
VENULOSE
VENULOUS

VENUS
VENUSES
VENVILLE
VENVILLES
VERA
VERACIOUS
VERACITY
VERANDA
VERANDAED
VERANDAH
VERANDAHS
VERANDAS
VERAPAMIL
VERATRIA
VERATRIAS
VERATRIN
VERATRINE
VERATRINS
VERATRUM
VERATRUMS
VERB
VERBAL
VERBALISE
VERBALISM
VERBALIST
VERBALITY
VERBALIZE
VERBALLED
VERBALLY
VERBALS
VERBARIAN
VERBASCUM
VERBATIM
VERBENA
VERBENAS
VERBERATE
VERBIAGE
VERBIAGES
VERBICIDE
VERBID
VERBIDS
VERBIFIED
VERBIFIES
VERBIFY
VERBILE
VERBILES
VERBING
VERBINGS

VERBLESS
VERBOSE
VERBOSELY
VERBOSER
VERBOSEST
VERBOSITY
VERBOTEN
VERBS
VERD
VERDANCY
VERDANT
VERDANTLY
VERDELHO
VERDELHOS
VERDERER
VERDERERS
VERDEROR
VERDERORS
VERDET
VERDETS
VERDICT
VERDICTS
VERDIGRIS
VERDIN
VERDINS
VERDIT
VERDITE
VERDITER
VERDITERS
VERDITES
VERDITS
VERDOY
VERDOYS
VERDURE
VERDURED
VERDURES
VERDUROUS
VERECUND
VERGE
VERGED
VERGENCE
VERGENCES
VERGENCY
VERGER
VERGERS
VERGES
VERGING
VERGLAS

VERGLASES
VERIDIC
VERIDICAL
VERIER
VERIEST
VERIFIED
VERIFIER
VERIFIERS
VERIFIES
VERIFY
VERIFYING
VERILY
VERISM
VERISMO
VERISMOS
VERISMS
VERIST
VERISTIC
VERISTS
VERITABLE
VERITABLY
VERITAS
VERITATES
VERITE
VERITES
VERITIES
VERITY
VERJUICE
VERJUICED
VERJUICES
VERJUS
VERJUSES
VERKLEMPT
VERKRAMP
VERLAN
VERLANS
VERLIG
VERLIGTE
VERLIGTES
VERMAL
VERMEIL
VERMEILED
VERMEILLE
VERMEILS
VERMELL
VERMELLS
VERMES
VERMIAN

VERMICIDE
VERMICULE
VERMIFORM
VERMIFUGE
VERMIL
VERMILIES
VERMILION
VERMILLED
VERMILS
VERMILY
VERMIN
VERMINATE
VERMINED
VERMINIER
VERMINOUS
VERMINS
VERMINY
VERMIS
VERMOULU
VERMOUTH
VERMOUTHS
VERMUTH
VERMUTHS
VERNACLE
VERNACLES
VERNAL
VERNALISE
VERNALITY
VERNALIZE
VERNALLY
VERNANT
VERNATION
VERNICLE
VERNICLES
VERNIER
VERNIERS
VERNIX
VERNIXES
VERONAL
VERONALS
VERONICA
VERONICAS
VERONIQUE
VERQUERE
VERQUERES
VERQUIRE
VERQUIRES
VERRA

VERREL
VERRELS
VERREY
VERRINE
VERRINES
VERRUCA
VERRUCAE
VERRUCAS
VERRUCOSE
VERRUCOUS
VERRUGA
VERRUGAS
VERRY
VERS
VERSAL
VERSALS
VERSANT
VERSANTS
VERSATILE
VERSE
VERSED
VERSELET
VERSELETS
VERSEMAN
VERSEMEN
VERSER
VERSERS
VERSES
VERSET
VERSETS
VERSICLE
VERSICLES
VERSIFIED
VERSIFIER
VERSIFIES
VERSIFORM
VERSIFY
VERSIN
VERSINE
VERSINES
VERSING
VERSINGS
VERSINS
VERSION
VERSIONAL
VERSIONED
VERSIONER
VERSIONS

VERSO
VERSOS
VERST
VERSTE
VERSTES
VERSTS
VERSUS
VERSUTE
VERT
VERTEBRA
VERTEBRAE
VERTEBRAL
VERTEBRAS
VERTED
VERTEX
VERTEXES
VERTICAL
VERTICALS
VERTICES
VERTICIL
VERTICILS
VERTICITY
VERTIGO
VERTIGOES
VERTIGOS
VERTING
VERTIPORT
VERTISOL
VERTISOLS
VERTS
VERTU
VERTUE
VERTUES
VERTUOUS
VERTUS
VERVAIN
VERVAINS
VERVE
VERVEL
VERVELLED
VERVELS
VERVEN
VERVENS
VERVES
VERVET
VERVETS
VERY
VESICA

VESICAE
VESICAL
VESICANT
VESICANTS
VESICAS
VESICATE
VESICATED
VESICATES
VESICLE
VESICLES
VESICULA
VESICULAE
VESICULAR
VESPA
VESPAS
VESPER
VESPERAL
VESPERALS
VESPERS
VESPIARY
VESPID
VESPIDS
VESPINE
VESPOID
VESSAIL
VESSAILS
VESSEL
VESSELED
VESSELS
VEST
VESTA
VESTAL
VESTALLY
VESTALS
VESTAS
VESTED
VESTEE
VESTEES
VESTIARY
VESTIBULA
VESTIBULE
VESTIGE
VESTIGES
VESTIGIA
VESTIGIAL
VESTIGIUM
VESTIMENT
VESTING

V

VESTINGS	VETTINGS	VIAS	VIBRISSA	VICIOUS
VESTITURE	VETTURA	VIATIC	VIBRISSAE	VICIOUSLY
VESTLESS	VETTURAS	VIATICA	VIBRISSAL	VICOMTE
VESTLIKE	VETTURINI	VIATICAL	VIBRONIC	VICOMTES
VESTMENT	VETTURINO	VIATICALS	VIBS	VICTIM
VESTMENTS	VEX	VIATICUM	VIBURNUM	VICTIMISE
VESTRAL	VEXATION	VIATICUMS	VIBURNUMS	VICTIMIZE
VESTRIES	VEXATIONS	VIATOR	VICAR	VICTIMS
VESTRY	VEXATIOUS	VIATORES	VICARAGE	VICTOR
VESTRYMAN	VEXATORY	VIATORIAL	VICARAGES	VICTORESS
VESTRYMEN	VEXED	VIATORS	VICARATE	VICTORIA
VESTS	VEXEDLY	VIBE	VICARATES	VICTORIAS
VESTURAL	VEXEDNESS	VIBES	VICARESS	VICTORIES
VESTURE	VEXER	VIBEX	VICARIAL	VICTORINE
VESTURED	VEXERS	VIBEY	VICARIANT	VICTORS
VESTURER	VEXES	VIBICES	VICARIATE	VICTORY
VESTURERS	VEXIL	VIBIER	VICARIES	VICTRESS
VESTURES	VEXILLA	VIBIEST	VICARIOUS	VICTRIX
VESTURING	VEXILLAR	VIBIST	VICARLIER	VICTRIXES
VESUVIAN	VEXILLARY	VIBISTS	VICARLY	VICTROLA
VESUVIANS	VEXILLATE	VIBRACULA	VICARS	VICTROLAS
VET	VEXILLUM	VIBRAHARP	VICARSHIP	VICTUAL
VETCH	VEXILS	VIBRANCE	VICARY	VICTUALED
VETCHES	VEXING	VIBRANCES	VICE	VICTUALER
VETCHIER	VEXINGLY	VIBRANCY	VICED	VICTUALS
VETCHIEST	VEXINGS	VIBRANT	VICEGERAL	VICUGNA
VETCHLING	VEXT	VIBRANTLY	VICELESS	VICUGNAS
VETCHY	VEZIR	VIBRANTS	VICELIKE	VICUNA
VETERAN	VEZIRS	VIBRATE	VICENARY	VICUNAS
VETERANS	VIA	VIBRATED	VICENNIAL	VID
VETIVER	VIABILITY	VIBRATES	VICEREGAL	VIDALIA
VETIVERS	VIABLE	VIBRATILE	VICEREINE	VIDALIAS
VETIVERT	VIABLY	VIBRATING	VICEROY	VIDAME
VETIVERTS	VIADUCT	VIBRATION	VICEROYS	VIDAMES
VETKOEK	VIADUCTS	VIBRATIVE	VICES	VIDE
VETKOEKS	VIAE	VIBRATO	VICESIMAL	VIDELICET
VETO	VIAL	VIBRATOR	VICHIES	VIDENDA
VETOED	VIALED	VIBRATORS	VICHY	VIDENDUM
VETOER	VIALFUL	VIBRATORY	VICIATE	VIDEO
VETOERS	VIALFULS	VIBRATOS	VICIATED	VIDEOCAM
VETOES	VIALING	VIBRIO	VICIATES	VIDEOCAMS
VETOING	VIALLED	VIBRIOID	VICIATING	VIDEODISC
VETOLESS	VIALLING	VIBRION	VICINAGE	VIDEODISK
VETS	VIALS	VIBRIONIC	VICINAGES	VIDEOED
VETTED	VIAMETER	VIBRIONS	VICINAL	VIDEOFIT
VETTER	VIAMETERS	VIBRIOS	VICING	VIDEOFITS
VETTERS	VIAND	VIBRIOSES	VICINITY	VIDEOGRAM
VETTING	VIANDS	VIBRIOSIS	VICIOSITY	VIDEOING

VIDEOLAND
VIDEOS
VIDEOTAPE
VIDEOTEX
VIDEOTEXT
VIDETTE
VIDETTES
VIDICON
VIDICONS
VIDIMUS
VIDIMUSES
VIDIOT
VIDIOTS
VIDS
VIDSCREEN
VIDUAGE
VIDUAGES
VIDUAL
VIDUITIES
VIDUITY
VIDUOUS
VIE
VIED
VIELLE
VIELLES
VIENNA
VIER
VIERS
VIES
VIEW
VIEWABLE
VIEWBOOK
VIEWBOOKS
VIEWDATA
VIEWDATAS
VIEWED
VIEWER
VIEWERS
VIEWIER
VIEWIEST
VIEWINESS
VIEWING
VIEWINGS
VIEWLESS
VIEWLY
VIEWPHONE
VIEWPOINT
VIEWPORT

VIEWPORTS
VIEWS
VIEWSHED
VIEWSHEDS
VIEWY
VIFDA
VIFDAS
VIFF
VIFFED
VIFFING
VIFFS
VIG
VIGA
VIGAS
VIGESIMAL
VIGIA
VIGIAS
VIGIL
VIGILANCE
VIGILANT
VIGILANTE
VIGILS
VIGNERON
VIGNERONS
VIGNETTE
VIGNETTED
VIGNETTER
VIGNETTES
VIGOR
VIGORISH
VIGORO
VIGOROS
VIGOROSO
VIGOROUS
VIGORS
VIGOUR
VIGOURS
VIGS
VIHARA
VIHARAS
VIHUELA
VIHUELAS
VIKING
VIKINGISM
VIKINGS
VILAYET
VILAYETS
VILD

VILDE
VILDLY
VILDNESS
VILE
VILELY
VILENESS
VILER
VILEST
VILIACO
VILIACOES
VILIACOS
VILIAGO
VILIAGOES
VILIAGOS
VILIFIED
VILIFIER
VILIFIERS
VILIFIES
VILIFY
VILIFYING
VILIPEND
VILIPENDS
VILL
VILLA
VILLADOM
VILLADOMS
VILLAE
VILLAGE
VILLAGER
VILLAGERS
VILLAGERY
VILLAGES
VILLAGEY
VILLAGIER
VILLAGIO
VILLAGIOS
VILLAGREE
VILLAIN
VILLAINS
VILLAINY
VILLAN
VILLANAGE
VILLANIES
VILLANOUS
VILLANS
VILLANY
VILLAR
VILLAS

VILLATIC
VILLEIN
VILLEINS
VILLENAGE
VILLI
VILLIACO
VILLIACOS
VILLIAGO
VILLIAGOS
VILLIFORM
VILLOSE
VILLOSITY
VILLOUS
VILLOUSLY
VILLS
VILLUS
VIM
VIMANA
VIMANAS
VIMEN
VIMINA
VIMINAL
VIMINEOUS
VIMS
VIN
VINA
VINACEOUS
VINAL
VINALS
VINAS
VINASSE
VINASSES
VINCA
VINCAS
VINCIBLE
VINCIBLY
VINCULA
VINCULAR
VINCULUM
VINCULUMS
VINDALOO
VINDALOOS
VINDEMIAL
VINDICATE
VINE
VINEAL
VINED
VINEGAR

VINEGARED
VINEGARS
VINEGARY
VINELESS
VINELIKE
VINER
VINERIES
VINERS
VINERY
VINES
VINEW
VINEWED
VINEWING
VINEWS
VINEYARD
VINEYARDS
VINIC
VINIER
VINIEST
VINIFERA
VINIFERAS
VINIFIED
VINIFIES
VINIFY
VINIFYING
VINING
VINO
VINOLENT
VINOLOGY
VINOS
VINOSITY
VINOUS
VINOUSLY
VINS
VINT
VINTAGE
VINTAGED
VINTAGER
VINTAGERS
VINTAGES
VINTAGING
VINTED
VINTING
VINTNER
VINTNERS
VINTRIES
VINTRY
VINTS

VINY	VIPERS	VIRGINIA	VIRTU	VISCIN
VINYL	VIRAEMIA	VIRGINIAS	VIRTUAL	VISCINS
VINYLIC	VIRAEMIAS	VIRGINING	VIRTUALLY	VISCOID
VINYLS	VIRAEMIC	VIRGINITY	VIRTUE	VISCOIDAL
VIOL	VIRAGO	VIRGINIUM	VIRTUES	VISCOSE
VIOLA	VIRAGOES	VIRGINLY	VIRTUOSA	VISCOSES
VIOLABLE	VIRAGOISH	VIRGINS	VIRTUOSAS	VISCOSITY
VIOLABLY	VIRAGOS	VIRGULATE	VIRTUOSE	VISCOUNT
VIOLAS	VIRAL	VIRGULE	VIRTUOSI	VISCOUNTS
VIOLATE	VIRALITY	VIRGULES	VIRTUOSIC	VISCOUNTY
VIOLATED	VIRALLY	VIRICIDAL	VIRTUOSO	VISCOUS
VIOLATER	VIRALS	VIRICIDE	VIRTUOSOS	VISCOUSLY
VIOLATERS	VIRANDA	VIRICIDES	VIRTUOUS	VISCUM
VIOLATES	VIRANDAS	VIRID	VIRTUS	VISCUMS
VIOLATING	VIRANDO	VIRIDIAN	VIRUCIDAL	VISCUS
VIOLATION	VIRANDOS	VIRIDIANS	VIRUCIDE	VISE
VIOLATIVE	VIRE	VIRIDITE	VIRUCIDES	VISED
VIOLATOR	VIRED	VIRIDITES	VIRULENCE	VISEED
VIOLATORS	VIRELAI	VIRIDITY	VIRULENCY	VISEING
VIOLD	VIRELAIS	VIRILE	VIRULENT	VISELIKE
VIOLENCE	VIRELAY	VIRILELY	VIRUS	VISES
VIOLENCES	VIRELAYS	VIRILISE	VIRUSES	VISHING
VIOLENT	VIREMENT	VIRILISED	VIRUSLIKE	VISHINGS
VIOLENTED	VIREMENTS	VIRILISES	VIRUSOID	VISIBLE
VIOLENTLY	VIREMIA	VIRILISM	VIRUSOIDS	VISIBLES
VIOLENTS	VIREMIAS	VIRILISMS	VIS	VISIBLY
VIOLER	VIREMIC	VIRILITY	VISA	VISIE
VIOLERS	VIRENT	VIRILIZE	VISAED	VISIED
VIOLET	VIREO	VIRILIZED	VISAGE	VISIEING
VIOLETS	VIREONINE	VIRILIZES	VISAGED	VISIER
VIOLIN	VIREOS	VIRILOCAL	VISAGES	VISIERS
VIOLINIST	VIRES	VIRING	VISAGIST	VISIES
VIOLINS	VIRESCENT	VIRINO	VISAGISTE	VISILE
VIOLIST	VIRETOT	VIRINOS	VISAGISTS	VISILES
VIOLISTS	VIRETOTS	VIRION	VISAING	VISING
VIOLONE	VIRGA	VIRIONS	VISARD	VISION
VIOLONES	VIRGAE	VIRL	VISARDS	VISIONAL
VIOLS	VIRGAS	VIRLS	VISAS	VISTONARY
VIOMYCIN	VIRGATE	VIROGENE	VISCACHA	VISIONED
VIOMYCINS	VIRGATES	VIROGENES	VISCACHAS	VISIONER
VIOSTEROL	VIRGE	VIROID	VISCARIA	VISIONERS
VIPASSANA	VIRGER	VIROIDS	VISCARIAS	VISIONING
VIPER	VIRGERS	VIROLOGIC	VISCERA	VISIONIST
VIPERFISH	VIRGES	VIROLOGY	VISCERAL	VISIONS
VIPERINE	VIRGIN	VIROSE	VISCERATE	VISIT
VIPERISH	VIRGINAL	VIROSES	VISCID	VISITABLE
VIPERLIKE	VIRGINALS	VIROSIS	VISCIDITY	VISITANT
VIPEROUS	VIRGINED	VIROUS	VISCIDLY	VISITANTS

V

VISITATOR	VITALISER	VITILIGOS	VIVAS	VIZCACHAS
VISITE	VITALISES	VITIOSITY	VIVAT	VIZIED
VISITED	VITALISM	VITIOUS	VIVATS	VIZIER
VISITEE	VITALISMS	VITRAGE	VIVDA	VIZIERATE
VISITEES	VITALIST	VITRAGES	VIVDAS	VIZIERIAL
VISITER	VITALISTS	VITRAIL	VIVE	VIZIERS
VISITERS	VITALITY	VITRAIN	VIVELY	VIZIES
VISITES	VITALIZE	VITRAINS	VIVENCIES	VIZIR
VISITING	VITALIZED	VITRAUX	VIVENCY	VIZIRATE
VISITINGS	VITALIZER	VITREOUS	VIVER	VIZIRATES
VISITOR	VITALIZES	VITREUM	VIVERRA	VIZIRIAL
VISITORS	VITALLY	VITREUMS	VIVERRAS	VIZIRS
VISITRESS	VITALNESS	VITRIC	VIVERRID	VIZIRSHIP
VISITS	VITALS	VITRICS	VIVERRIDS	VIZOR
VISIVE	VITAMER	VITRIFIED	VIVERRINE	VIZORED
VISNE	VITAMERS	VITRIFIES	VIVERS	VIZORING
VISNES	VITAMIN	VITRIFORM	VIVES	VIZORLESS
VISNOMIE	VITAMINE	VITRIFY	VIVIANITE	VIZORS
VISNOMIES	VITAMINES	VITRINE	VIVID	VIZSLA
VISNOMY	VITAMINIC	VITRINES	VIVIDER	VIZSLAS
VISON	VITAMINS	VITRIOL	VIVIDEST	VIZY
VISONS	VITAS	VITRIOLED	VIVIDITY	VIZYING
VISOR	VITASCOPE	VITRIOLIC	VIVIDLY	VIZZIE
VISORED	VITATIVE	VITRIOLS	VIVIDNESS	VIZZIED
VISORING	VITE	VITRO	VIVIFIC	VIZZIEING
VISORLESS	VITELLARY	VITTA	VIVIFIED	VIZZIES
VISORS	VITELLI	VITTAE	VIVIFIER	VLEI
VISTA	VITELLIN	VITTATE	VIVIFIERS	VLEIS
VISTAED	VITELLINE	VITTLE	VIVIFIES	VLIES
VISTAING	VITELLINS	VITTLED	VIVIFY	VLOG
VISTAL	VITELLUS	VITTLES	VIVIFYING	VLOGGED
VISTALESS	VITESSE	VITTLING	VIVIPARA	VLOGGER
VISTAS	VITESSES	VITULAR	VIVIPARY	VLOGGERS
VISTO	VITEX	VITULINE	VIVISECT	VLOGGING
VISTOS	VITEXES	VIVA	VIVISECTS	VLOGGINGS
VISUAL	VITIABLE	VIVACE	VIVO	VLOGS
VISUALISE	VITIATE	VIVACES	VIVRES	VLY
VISUALIST	VITIATED	VIVACIOUS	VIXEN	VOAR
VISUALITY	VITIATES	VIVACITY	VIXENISH	VOARS
VISUALIZE	VITIATING	VIVAED	VIXENLY	VOCAB
VISUALLY	VITIATION	VIVAING	VIXENS	VOCABLE
VISUALS	VITIATOR	VIVAMENTE	VIZAMENT	VOCABLES
VITA	VITIATORS	VIVANDIER	VIZAMENTS	VOCABLY
VITACEOUS	VITICETA	VIVARIA	VIZARD	VOCABS
VITAE	VITICETUM	VIVARIES	VIZARDED	VOCABULAR
VITAL	VITICIDE	VIVARIUM	VIZARDING	VOCAL
VITALISE	VITICIDES	VIVARIUMS	VIZARDS	VOCALESE
VITALISED	VITILIGO	VIVARY	VIZCACHA	VOCALESES

VOCALIC	VOERTSAK	VOILA	VOLITATED	VOLUMES
VOCALICS	VOERTSEK	VOILE	VOLITATES	VOLUMETER
VOCALION	VOES	VOILES	VOLITIENT	VOLUMETRY
VOCALIONS	VOETSAK	VOIP	VOLITION	VOLUMINAL
VOCALISE	VOETSEK	VOIPS	VOLITIONS	VOLUMING
VOCALISED	VOG	VOISINAGE	VOLITIVE	VOLUMISE
VOCALISER	VOGIE	VOITURE	VOLITIVES	VOLUMISED
VOCALISES	VOGIER	VOITURES	VOLK	VOLUMISER
VOCALISM	VOGIEST	VOITURIER	VOLKS	VOLUMISES
VOCALISMS	VOGS	VOIVODE	VOLKSLIED	VOLUMIST
VOCALIST	VOGUE	VOIVODES	VOLKSRAAD	VOLUMISTS
VOCALISTS	VOGUED	VOL	VOLLEY	VOLUMIZE
VOCALITY	VOGUEING	VOLA	VOLLEYED	VOLUMIZED
VOCALIZE	VOGUEINGS	VOLABLE	VOLLEYER	VOLUMIZER
VOCALIZED	VOGUER	VOLAE	VOLLEYERS	VOLUMIZES
VOCALIZER	VOGUERS	VOLAGE	VOLLEYING	VOLUNTARY
VOCALIZES	VOGUES	VOLANT	VOLLEYS	VOLUNTEER
VOCALLY	VOGUEY	VOLANTE	VOLOST	VOLUSPA
VOCALNESS	VOGUIER	VOLANTES	VOLOSTS	VOLUSPAS
VOCALS	VOGUIEST	VOLAR	VOLPINO	VOLUTE
VOCATION	VOGUING	VOLARIES	VOLPINOS	VOLUTED
VOCATIONS	VOGUINGS	VOLARY	VOLPLANE	VOLUTES
VOCATIVE	VOGUISH	VOLATIC	VOLPLANED	VOLUTIN
VOCATIVES	VOGUISHLY	VOLATICS	VOLPLANES	VOLUTINS
VOCES	VOICE	VOLATILE	VOLS	VOLUTION
VOCODER	VOICED	VOLATILES	VOLT	VOLUTIONS
VOCODERED	VOICEFUL	VOLCANIAN	VOLTA	VOLUTOID
VOCODERS	VOICELESS	VOLCANIC	VOLTAGE	VOLVA
VOCULAR	VOICEMAIL	VOLCANICS	VOLTAGES	VOLVAE
VOCULE	VOICEOVER	VOLCANISE	VOLTAIC	VOLVAS
VOCULES	VOICER	VOLCANISM	VOLTAISM	VOLVATE
VODCAST	VOICERS	VOLCANIST	VOLTAISMS	VOLVE
VODCASTED	VOICES	VOLCANIZE	VOLTE	VOLVED
VODCASTER	VOICING	VOLCANO	VOLTED	VOLVES
VODCASTS	VOICINGS	VOLCANOES	VOLTES	VOLVING
VODDIES	VOID	VOLCANOS	VOLTI	VOLVOX
VODDY	VOIDABLE	VOLE	VOLTIGEUR	VOLVOXES
VODKA	VOIDANCE	VOLED	VOLTING	VOLVULI
VODKAS	VOIDANCES	VOLELIKE	VOLTINISM	VOLVULUS
VODOU	VOIDED	VOLENS	VOLTIS	VOM
VODOUN	VOIDEE	VOLERIES	VOLTMETER	VOMER
VODOUNS	VOIDEES	VOLERY	VOLTS	VOMERINE
VODOUS	VOIDER	VOLES	VOLUBIL	VOMERS
VODUN	VOIDERS	VOLET	VOLUBLE	VOMICA
VODUNS	VOIDING	VOLETS	VOLUBLY	VOMICAE
VOE	VOIDINGS	VOLING	VOLUCRINE	VOMICAS
VOEMA	VOIDNESS	VOLITANT	VOLUME	VOMIT
VOEMAS	VOIDS	VOLITATE	VOLUMED	VOMITED

V

VOMITER
VOMITERS
VOMITIER
VOMITIEST
VOMITING
VOMITINGS
VOMITIVE
VOMITIVES
VOMITO
VOMITORIA
VOMITORY
VOMITOS
VOMITOUS
VOMITS
VOMITUS
VOMITUSES
VOMITY
VOMMED
VOMMING
VOMS
VONGOLE
VOODOO
VOODOOED
VOODOOING
VOODOOISM
VOODOOIST
VOODOOS
VOORKAMER
VOORSKOT
VOORSKOTS
VOR
VORACIOUS
VORACITY
VORAGO
VORAGOES
VORAGOS
VORANT
VORLAGE
VORLAGES
VORPAL
VORRED
VORRING
VORS
VORTEX
VORTEXES
VORTICAL
VORTICES
VORTICISM

VORTICIST
VORTICITY
VORTICOSE
VOSTRO
VOTABLE
VOTARESS
VOTARIES
VOTARIST
VOTARISTS
VOTARY
VOTE
VOTEABLE
VOTED
VOTEEN
VOTEENS
VOTELESS
VOTER
VOTERS
VOTES
VOTING
VOTINGS
VOTIVE
VOTIVELY
VOTIVES
VOTRESS
VOTRESSES
VOUCH
VOUCHED
VOUCHEE
VOUCHEES
VOUCHER
VOUCHERED
VOUCHERS
VOUCHES
VOUCHING
VOUCHSAFE
VOUDON
VOUDONS
VOUDOU
VOUDOUED
VOUDOUING
VOUDOUN
VOUDOUNS
VOUDOUS
VOUGE
VOUGES
VOULGE
VOULGES

VOULU
VOUSSOIR
VOUSSOIRS
VOUTSAFE
VOUTSAFED
VOUTSAFES
VOUVRAY
VOUVRAYS
VOW
VOWED
VOWEL
VOWELED
VOWELISE
VOWELISED
VOWELISES
VOWELIZE
VOWELIZED
VOWELIZES
VOWELLED
VOWELLESS
VOWELLIER
VOWELLING
VOWELLY
VOWELS
VOWER
VOWERS
VOWESS
VOWESSES
VOWING
VOWLESS
VOWS
VOX
VOXEL
VOXELS
VOYAGE
VOYAGED
VOYAGER
VOYAGERS
VOYAGES
VOYAGEUR
VOYAGEURS
VOYAGING
VOYAGINGS
VOYEUR
VOYEURISM
VOYEURS
VOZHD
VOZHDS

VRAIC
VRAICKER
VRAICKERS
VRAICKING
VRAICS
VRIL
VRILS
VROOM
VROOMED
VROOMING
VROOMS
VROT
VROU
VROUS
VROUW
VROUWS
VROW
VROWS
VRYSTATER
VUG
VUGG
VUGGIER
VUGGIEST
VUGGS
VUGGY
VUGH
VUGHIER
VUGHIEST
VUGHS
VUGHY
VUGS
VUGULAR
VULCAN
VULCANIAN
VULCANIC
VULCANISE
VULCANISM
VULCANIST
VULCANITE
VULCANIZE
VULCANS
VULGAR
VULGARER
VULGAREST
VULGARIAN
VULGARISE
VULGARISM
VULGARITY

VULGARIZE
VULGARLY
VULGARS
VULGATE
VULGATES
VULGO
VULGUS
VULGUSES
VULN
VULNED
VULNERARY
VULNERATE
VULNING
VULNS
VULPICIDE
VULPINE
VULPINISM
VULPINITE
VULSELLA
VULSELLAE
VULSELLUM
VULTURE
VULTURES
VULTURINE
VULTURISH
VULTURISM
VULTURN
VULTURNS
VULTUROUS
VULVA
VULVAE
VULVAL
VULVAR
VULVAS
VULVATE
VULVIFORM
VULVITIS
VUM
VUMMED
VUMMING
VUMS
VUTTIER
VUTTIEST
VUTTY
VUVUZELA
VUVUZELAS
VYING
VYINGLY
VYINGS

V

W

WAAC	WADDED	WADMOLS	WAFT	WAGGLY
WAACS	WADDER	WADS	WAFTAGE	WAGGON
WAAH	WADDERS	WADSET	WAFTAGES	WAGGONED
WAB	WADDIE	WADSETS	WAFTED	WAGGONER
WABAIN	WADDIED	WADSETT	WAFTER	WAGGONERS
WABAINS	WADDIES	WADSETTED	WAFTERS	WAGGONING
WABBIT	WADDING	WADSETTER	WAFTING	WAGGONS
WABBLE	WADDINGS	WADSETTS	WAFTINGS	WAGHALTER
WABBLED	WADDLE	WADT	WAFTS	WAGING
WABBLER	WADDLED	WADTS	WAFTURE	WAGMOIRE
WABBLERS	WADDLER	WADY	WAFTURES	WAGMOIRES
WABBLES	WADDLERS	WAE	WAG	WAGON
WABBLIER	WADDLES	WAEFUL	WAGE	WAGONAGE
WABBLIEST	WADDLIER	WAENESS	WAGED	WAGONAGES
WABBLING	WADDLIEST	WAENESSES	WAGELESS	WAGONED
WABBLY	WADDLING	WAES	WAGENBOOM	WAGONER
WABOOM	WADDLY	WAESOME	WAGER	WAGONERS
WABOOMS	WADDS	WAESUCK	WAGERED	WAGONETTE
WABS	WADDY	WAESUCKS	WAGERER	WAGONFUL
WABSTER	WADDYING	WAFER	WAGERERS	WAGONFULS
WABSTERS	WADE	WAFERED	WAGERING	WAGONING
WACK	WADEABLE	WAFERIER	WAGERINGS	WAGONLESS
WACKE	WADED	WAFERIEST	WAGERS	WAGONLOAD
WACKED	WADER	WAFERING	WAGES	WAGONS
WACKER	WADERS	WAFERS	WAGGA	WAGS
WACKERS	WADES	WAFERY	WAGGAS	WAGSOME
WACKES	WADGE	WAFF	WAGGED	WAGTAIL
WACKEST	WADGES	WAFFED	WAGGER	WAGTAILS
WACKIER	WADI	WAFFIE	WAGGERIES	WAGYU
WACKIEST	WADIES	WAFFIES	WAGGERS	WAGYUS
WACKILY	WADING	WAFFING	WAGGERY	WAHCONDA
WACKINESS	WADINGS	WAFFLE	WAGGING	WAHCONDAS
WACKO	WADIS	WAFFLED	WAGGISH	WAHINE
WACKOES	WADMAAL	WAFFLER	WAGGISHLY	WAHINES
WACKOS	WADMAALS	WAFFLERS	WAGGLE	WAHOO
WACKS	WADMAL	WAFFLES	WAGGLED	WAHOOS
WACKY	WADMALS	WAFFLIER	WAGGLER	WAI
WACONDA	WADMEL	WAFFLIEST	WAGGLERS	WAIATA
WACONDAS	WADMELS	WAFFLING	WAGGLES	WAIATAS
WAD	WADMOL	WAFFLINGS	WAGGLIER	WAID
WADABLE	WADMOLL	WAFFLY	WAGGLIEST	WAIDE
WADD	WADMOLLS	WAFFS	WAGGLING	WAIF

W

WAIFED	WAIT	WAKENERS	WALKIES	WALLOPER
WAIFING	WAITE	WAKENING	WALKING	WALLOPERS
WAIFISH	WAITED	WAKENINGS	WALKINGS	WALLOPING
WAIFLIKE	WAITER	WAKENS	WALKMILL	WALLOPS
WAIFS	WAITERAGE	WAKER	WALKMILLS	WALLOW
WAIFT	WAITERED	WAKERIFE	WALKOUT	WALLOWED
WAIFTS	WAITERING	WAKERS	WALKOUTS	WALLOWER
WAIL	WAITERS	WAKES	WALKOVER	WALLOWERS
WAILED	WAITES	WAKF	WALKOVERS	WALLOWING
WAILER	WAITING	WAKFS	WALKS	WALLOWS
WAILERS	WAITINGLY	WAKIKI	WALKUP	WALLPAPER
WAILFUL	WAITINGS	WAKIKIS	WALKUPS	WALLS
WAILFULLY	WAITLIST	WAKING	WALKWAY	WALLSEND
WAILING	WAITLISTS	WAKINGS	WALKWAYS	WALLSENDS
WAILINGLY	WAITRESS	WALD	WALKYRIE	WALLWORT
WAILINGS	WAITRON	WALDFLUTE	WALKYRIES	WALLWORTS
WAILS	WAITRONS	WALDGRAVE	WALL	WALLY
WAILSOME	WAITS	WALDHORN	WALLA	WALLYBALL
WAIN	WAITSTAFF	WALDHORNS	WALLABA	WALLYDRAG
WAINAGE	WAIVE	WALDO	WALLABAS	WALNUT
WAINAGES	WAIVED	WALDOES	WALLABIES	WALNUTS
WAINED	WAIVER	WALDOS	WALLABY	WALRUS
WAINING	WAIVERS	WALDRAPP	WALLAH	WALRUSES
WAINS	WAIVES	WALDRAPPS	WALLAHS	WALTIER
WAINSCOT	WAIVING	WALDS	WALLAROO	WALTIEST
WAINSCOTS	WAIVODE	WALE	WALLAROOS	WALTY
WAIR	WAIVODES	WALED	WALLAS	WALTZ
WAIRED	WAIWODE	WALER	WALLBOARD	WALTZED
WAIRING	WAIWODES	WALERS	WALLCHART	WALTZER
WAIRS	WAKA	WALES	WALLED	WALTZERS
WAIRSH	WAKAME	WALI	WALLER	WALTZES
WAIRSHER	WAKAMES	WALIE	WALLERS	WALTZING
WAIRSHEST	WAKANDA	WALIER	WALLET	WALTZINGS
WAIRUA	WAKANDAS	WALIES	WALLETS	WALTZLIKE
WAIRUAS	WAKANE	WALIEST	WALLEY	WALY
WAIS	WAKANES	WALING	WALLEYE	WAMBENGER
WAIST	WAKAS	WALIS	WALLEYED	WAMBLE
WAISTBAND	WAKE	WALISE	WALLEYES	WAMBLED
WAISTBELT	WAKEBOARD	WALISES	WALLEYS	WAMBLES
WAISTCOAT	WAKED	WALK	WALLFISH	WAMBLIER
WAISTED	WAKEFUL	WALKABLE	WALLIE	WAMBLIEST
WAISTER	WAKEFULLY	WALKABOUT	WALLIER	WAMBLING
WAISTERS	WAKELESS	WALKATHON	WALLIES	WAMBLINGS
WAISTING	WAKEMAN	WALKAWAY	WALLIEST	WAMBLY
WAISTINGS	WAKEMEN	WALKAWAYS	WALLING	WAME
WAISTLESS	WAKEN	WALKED	WALLINGS	WAMED
WAISTLINE	WAKENED	WALKER	WALLOP	WAMEFOU
WAISTS	WAKENER	WALKERS	WALLOPED	WAMEFOUS

WAMEFUL	WANGLES	WANT	WAR	WARDRESS
WAMEFULS	WANGLING	WANTAGE	WARAGI	WARDROBE
WAMES	WANGLINGS	WANTAGES	WARAGIS	WARDROBED
WAMMUL	WANGS	WANTAWAY	WARATAH	WARDROBER
WAMMULS	WANGUN	WANTAWAYS	WARATAHS	WARDROBES
WAMMUS	WANGUNS	WANTED	WARB	WARDROOM
WAMMUSES	WANHOPE	WANTER	WARBIER	WARDROOMS
WAMPEE	WANHOPES	WANTERS	WARBIEST	WARDROP
WAMPEES	WANIER	WANTHILL	WARBIRD	WARDROPS
WAMPISH	WANIEST	WANTHILLS	WARBIRDS	WARDS
WAMPISHED	WANIGAN	WANTIES	WARBLE	WARDSHIP
WAMPISHES	WANIGANS	WANTING	WARBLED	WARDSHIPS
WAMPUM	WANING	WANTON	WARBLER	WARE
WAMPUMS	WANINGS	WANTONED	WARBLERS	WARED
WAMPUS	WANION	WANTONER	WARBLES	WAREHOU
WAMPUSES	WANIONS	WANTONERS	WARBLIER	WAREHOUS
WAMUS	WANK	WANTONEST	WARBLIEST	WAREHOUSE
WAMUSES	WANKED	WANTONING	WARBLING	WARELESS
WAN	WANKER	WANTONISE	WARBLINGS	WAREROOM
WANCHANCY	WANKERS	WANTONIZE	WARBLY	WAREROOMS
WAND	WANKIER	WANTONLY	WARBONNET	WARES
WANDER	WANKIEST	WANTONS	WARBOT	WAREZ
WANDERED	WANKING	WANTS	WARBOTS	WARFARE
WANDERER	WANKLE	WANTY	WARBS	WARFARED
WANDERERS	WANKS	WANWORDY	WARBY	WARFARER
WANDERING	WANKSTA	WANWORTH	WARCRAFT	WARFARERS
WANDEROO	WANKSTAS	WANWORTHS	WARCRAFTS	WARFARES
WANDEROOS	WANKY	WANY	WARD	WARFARIN
WANDERS	WANLE	WANZE	WARDCORN	WARFARING
WANDLE	WANLY	WANZED	WARDCORNS	WARFARINS
WANDLED	WANNA	WANZES	WARDED	WARGAME
WANDLES	WANNABE	WANZING	WARDEN	WARGAMED
WANDLIKE	WANNABEE	WAP	WARDENED	WARGAMER
WANDLING	WANNABEES	WAPENSHAW	WARDENING	WARGAMERS
WANDOO	WANNABES	WAPENTAKE	WARDENRY	WARGAMES
WANDOOS	WANNED	WAPINSHAW	WARDENS	WARGAMING
WANDS	WANNEL	WAPITI	WARDER	WARHABLE
WANE	WANNER	WAPITIS	WARDERED	WARHEAD
WANED	WANNESS	WAPPED	WARDERING	WARHEADS
WANES	WANNESSES	WAPPEND	WARDERS	WARHORSE
WANEY	WANNEST	WAPPER	WARDIAN	WARHORSES
WANG	WANNIGAN	WAPPERED	WARDING	WARIBASHI
WANGAN	WANNIGANS	WAPPERING	WARDINGS	WARIER
WANGANS	WANNING	WAPPERS	WARDLESS	WARIEST
WANGLE	WANNION	WAPPING	WARDMOTE	WARILY
WANGLED	WANNIONS	WAPS	WARDMOTES	WARIMENT
WANGLER	WANNISH	WAQF	WARDOG	WARIMENTS
WANGLERS	WANS	WAQFS	WARDOGS	WARINESS

W

WARING	WARNS	WARRENS	WARWORK	WASHING
WARISON	WARP	WARREY	WARWORKS	WASHINGS
WARISONS	WARPAGE	WARREYED	WARWORN	WASHINS
WARK	WARPAGES	WARREYING	WARY	WASHLAND
WARKED	WARPAINT	WARREYS	WARZONE	WASHLANDS
WARKING	WARPAINTS	WARRIGAL	WARZONES	WASHOUT
WARKS	WARPATH	WARRIGALS	WAS	WASHOUTS
WARLESS	WARPATHS	WARRING	WASABI	WASHPOT
WARLIKE	WARPED	WARRIOR	WASABIS	WASHPOTS
WARLING	WARPER	WARRIORS	WASE	WASHRAG
WARLINGS	WARPERS	WARRISON	WASES	WASHRAGS
WARLOCK	WARPING	WARRISONS	WASH	WASHROOM
WARLOCKRY	WARPINGS	WARS	WASHABLE	WASHROOMS
WARLOCKS	WARPLANE	WARSAW	WASHABLES	WASHSTAND
WARLORD	WARPLANES	WARSAWS	WASHAWAY	WASHTUB
WARLORDS	WARPOWER	WARSHIP	WASHAWAYS	WASHTUBS
WARM	WARPOWERS	WARSHIPS	WASHBAG	WASHUP
WARMAKER	WARPS	WARSLE	WASHBAGS	WASHUPS
WARMAKERS	WARPWISE	WARSLED	WASHBALL	WASHWIPE
WARMAN	WARRAGAL	WARSLER	WASHBALLS	WASHWIPES
WARMBLOOD	WARRAGALS	WARSLERS	WASHBASIN	WASHWOMAN
WARMED	WARRAGLE	WARSLES	WASHBOARD	WASHWOMEN
WARMEN	WARRAGLES	WARSLING	WASHBOWL	WASHY
WARMER	WARRAGUL	WARST	WASHBOWLS	WASM
WARMERS	WARRAGULS	WARSTLE	WASHCLOTH	WASMS
WARMEST	WARRAN	WARSTLED	WASHDAY	WASP
WARMING	WARRAND	WARSTLER	WASHDAYS	WASPIE
WARMINGS	WARRANDED	WARSTLERS	WASHDOWN	WASPIER
WARMISH	WARRANDS	WARSTLES	WASHDOWNS	WASPIES
WARMIST	WARRANED	WARSTLING	WASHED	WASPIEST
WARMISTS	WARRANING	WART	WASHEN	WASPILY
WARMLY	WARRANS	WARTED	WASHER	WASPINESS
WARMNESS	WARRANT	WARTHOG	WASHERED	WASPISH
WARMONGER	WARRANTED	WARTHOGS	WASHERIES	WASPISHLY
WARMOUTH	WARRANTEE	WARTIER	WASHERING	WASPLIKE
WARMOUTHS	WARRANTER	WARTIEST	WASHERMAN	WASPNEST
WARMS	WARRANTOR	WARTIME	WASHERMEN	WASPNESTS
WARMTH	WARRANTS	WARTIMES	WASHERS	WASPS
WARMTHS	WARRANTY	WARTLESS	WASHERY	WASPY
WARMUP	WARRAY	WARTLIKE	WASHES	WASSAIL
WARMUPS	WARRAYED	WARTS	WASHFAST	WASSAILED
WARN	WARRAYING	WARTWEED	WASHHAND	WASSAILER
WARNED	WARRAYS	WARTWEEDS	WASHHOUSE	WASSAILRY
WARNER	WARRE	WARTWORT	WASHIER	WASSAILS
WARNERS	WARRED	WARTWORTS	WASHIEST	WASSERMAN
WARNING	WARREN	WARTY	WASHILY	WASSERMEN
WARNINGLY	WARRENER	WARWOLF	WASHIN	WASSUP
WARNINGS	WARRENERS	WARWOLVES	WASHINESS	WAST

WASTABLE	WATCHBOX	WATERJET	WAUCHTS	WAVELET
WASTAGE	WATCHCASE	WATERJETS	WAUFF	WAVELETS
WASTAGES	WATCHCRY	WATERLEAF	WAUFFED	WAVELIKE
WASTE	WATCHDOG	WATERLESS	WAUFFING	WAVELLITE
WASTEBIN	WATCHDOGS	WATERLILY	WAUFFS	WAVEMETER
WASTEBINS	WATCHED	WATERLINE	WAUGH	WAVEOFF
WASTED	WATCHER	WATERLOG	WAUGHED	WAVEOFFS
WASTEFUL	WATCHERS	WATERLOGS	WAUGHING	WAVER
WASTEL	WATCHES	WATERLOO	WAUGHS	WAVERED
WASTELAND	WATCHET	WATERLOOS	WAUGHT	WAVERER
WASTELOT	WATCHETS	WATERMAN	WAUGHTED	WAVERERS
WASTELOTS	WATCHEYE	WATERMARK	WAUGHTING	WAVERIER
WASTELS	WATCHEYES	WATERMEN	WAUGHTS	WAVERIEST
WASTENESS	WATCHFUL	WATERMILL	WAUK	WAVERING
WASTER	WATCHING	WATERPOX	WAUKED	WAVERINGS
WASTERED	WATCHLIST	WATERS	WAUKER	WAVEROUS
WASTERFUL	WATCHMAN	WATERSHED	WAUKERS	WAVERS
WASTERIE	WATCHMEN	WATERSIDE	WAUKING	WAVERY
WASTERIES	WATCHOUT	WATERSKI	WAUKMILL	WAVES
WASTERING	WATCHOUTS	WATERSKIS	WAUKMILLS	WAVESHAPE
WASTERS	WATCHWORD	WATERWAY	WAUKRIFE	WAVESON
WASTERY	WATE	WATERWAYS	WAUKS	WAVESONS
WASTES	WATER	WATERWEED	WAUL	WAVETABLE
WASTEWAY	WATERAGE	WATERWORK	WAULED	WAVEY
WASTEWAYS	WATERAGES	WATERWORN	WAULING	WAVEYS
WASTEWEIR	WATERBED	WATERY	WAULINGS	WAVICLE
WASTFULL	WATERBEDS	WATERZOOI	WAULK	WAVICLES
WASTING	WATERBIRD	WATS	WAULKED	WAVIER
WASTINGLY	WATERBUCK	WATT	WAULKER	WAVIES
WASTINGS	WATERBUS	WATTAGE	WAULKERS	WAVIEST
WASTNESS	WATERDOG	WATTAGES	WAULKING	WAVILY
WASTREL	WATERDOGS	WATTAPE	WAULKMILL	WAVINESS
WASTRELS	WATERED	WATTAPES	WAULKS	WAVING
WASTRIE	WATERER	WATTER	WAULS	WAVINGS
WASTRIES	WATERERS	WATTEST	WAUR	WAVY
WASTRIFE	WATERFALL	WATTHOUR	WAURED	WAW
WASTRIFES	WATERFOWL	WATTHOURS	WAURING	WAWA
WASTRY	WATERGATE	WATTLE	WAURS	WAWAED
WASTS	WATERHEAD	WATTLED	WAURST	WAWAING
WAT	WATERHEN	WATTLES	WAVE	WAWAS
WATAP	WATERHENS	WATTLESS	WAVEBAND	WAWE
WATAPE	WATERHOLE	WATTLING	WAVEBANDS	WAWES
WATAPES	WATERIER	WATTLINGS	WAVED	WAWL
WATAPS	WATERIEST	WATTMETER	WAVEFORM	WAWLED
WATCH	WATERILY	WATTS	WAVEFORMS	WAWLING
WATCHA	WATERING	WAUCHT	WAVEFRONT	WAWLINGS
WATCHABLE	WATERINGS	WAUCHTED	WAVEGUIDE	WAWLS
WATCHBAND	WATERISH	WAUCHTING	WAVELESS	WAWS

W

WAX	WAYFARER	WAZZES	WEANLING	WEASONS
WAXABLE	WAYFARERS	WAZZING	WEANLINGS	WEATHER
WAXBERRY	WAYFARES	WAZZOCK	WEANS	WEATHERED
WAXBILL	WAYFARING	WAZZOCKS	WEAPON	WEATHERER
WAXBILLS	WAYGOING	WE	WEAPONED	WEATHERLY
WAXCLOTH	WAYGOINGS	WEAK	WEAPONEER	WEATHERS
WAXCLOTHS	WAYGONE	WEAKEN	WEAPONING	WEAVE
WAXED	WAYGOOSE	WEAKENED	WEAPONISE	WEAVED
WAXEN	WAYGOOSES	WEAKENER	WEAPONIZE	WEAVER
WAXER	WAYING	WEAKENERS	WEAPONRY	WEAVERS
WAXERS	WAYLAID	WEAKENING	WEAPONS	WEAVES
WAXES	WAYLAY	WEAKENS	WEAR	WEAVING
WAXEYE	WAYLAYER	WEAKER	WEARABLE	WEAVINGS
WAXEYES	WAYLAYERS	WEAKEST	WEARABLES	WEAZAND
WAXFLOWER	WAYLAYING	WEAKFISH	WEARED	WEAZANDS
WAXIER	WAYLAYS	WEAKISH	WEARER	WEAZEN
WAXIEST	WAYLEAVE	WEAKISHLY	WEARERS	WEAZENED
WAXILY	WAYLEAVES	WEAKLIER	WEARIED	WEAZENING
WAXINESS	WAYLEGGO	WEAKLIEST	WEARIER	WEAZENS
WAXING	WAYLESS	WEAKLING	WEARIES	WEB
WAXINGS	WAYMARK	WEAKLINGS	WEARIEST	WEBAPP
WAXLIKE	WAYMARKED	WEAKLY	WEARIFUL	WEBAPPS
WAXPLANT	WAYMARKS	WEAKNESS	WEARILESS	WEBBED
WAXPLANTS	WAYMENT	WEAKON	WEARILY	WEBBIE
WAXWEED	WAYMENTED	WEAKONS	WEARINESS	WEBBIER
WAXWEEDS	WAYMENTS	WEAKSIDE	WEARING	WEBBIES
WAXWING	WAYPOINT	WEAKSIDES	WEARINGLY	WEBBIEST
WAXWINGS	WAYPOINTS	WEAL	WEARINGS	WEBBING
WAXWORK	WAYPOST	WEALD	WEARISH	WEBBINGS
WAXWORKER	WAYPOSTS	WEALDS	WEARISOME	WEBBY
WAXWORKS	WAYS	WEALS	WEARPROOF	WEBCAM
WAXWORM	WAYSIDE	WEALSMAN	WEARS	WEBCAMS
WAXWORMS	WAYSIDES	WEALSMEN	WEARY	WEBCAST
WAXY	WAYWARD	WEALTH	WEARYING	WEBCASTED
WAY	WAYWARDLY	WEALTHIER	WEASAND	WEBCASTER
WAYANG	WAYWISER	WEALTHILY	WEASANDS	WEBCASTS
WAYANGS	WAYWISERS	WEALTHS	WEASEL	WEBCHAT
WAYBACK	WAYWODE	WEALTHY	WEASELED	WEBCHATS
WAYBACKS	WAYWODES	WEAMB	WEASELER	WEBER
WAYBILL	WAYWORN	WEAMBS	WEASELERS	WEBERS
WAYBILLS	WAYZGOOSE	WEAN	WEASELIER	WEBFED
WAYBOARD	WAZ	WEANED	WEASELING	WEBFEET
WAYBOARDS	WAZIR	WEANEL	WEASELLED	WEBFOOT
WAYBREAD	WAZIRS	WEANELS	WEASELLER	WEBFOOTED
WAYBREADS	WAZOO	WEANER	WEASELLY	WEBHEAD
WAYED	WAZOOS	WEANERS	WEASELS	WEBHEADS
WAYFARE	WAZZ	WEANING	WEASELY	WEBIFIED
WAYFARED	WAZZED	WEANINGS	WEASON	WEBIFIES

WEBIFY	WEDELED	WEEK	WEEST	WEIGHMAN
WEBIFYING	WEDELING	WEEKDAY	WEET	WEIGHMEN
WEBINAR	WEDELN	WEEKDAYS	WEETE	WEIGHS
WEBINARS	WEDELNED	WEEKE	WEETED	WEIGHT
WEBISODE	WEDELNING	WEEKEND	WEETEN	WEIGHTAGE
WEBISODES	WEDELNS	WEEKENDED	WEETER	WEIGHTED
WEBLESS	WEDELS	WEEKENDER	WEETEST	WEIGHTER
WEBLIKE	WEDGE	WEEKENDS	WEETING	WEIGHTERS
WEBLISH	WEDGED	WEEKES	WEETINGLY	WEIGHTIER
WEBLISHES	WEDGELIKE	WEEKLIES	WEETLESS	WEIGHTILY
WEBLOG	WEDGES	WEEKLONG	WEETS	WEIGHTING
WEBLOGGER	WEDGEWISE	WEEKLY	WEEVER	WEIGHTS
WEBLOGS	WEDGIE	WEEKNIGHT	WEEVERS	WEIGHTY
WEBMAIL	WEDGIER	WEEKS	WEEVIL	WEIL
WEBMAILS	WEDGIES	WEEL	WEEVILED	WEILS
WEBMASTER	WEDGIEST	WEELS	WEEVILIER	WEINER
WEBPAGE	WEDGING	WEEM	WEEVILLED	WEINERS
WEBPAGES	WEDGINGS	WEEMS	WEEVILLY	WEIR
WEBRING	WEDGY	WEEN	WEEVILS	WEIRD
WEBRINGS	WEDLOCK	WEENED	WEEVILY	WEIRDED
WEBS	WEDLOCKS	WEENIE	WEEWEE	WEIRDER
WEBSITE	WEDS	WEENIER	WEEWEED	WEIRDEST
WEBSITES	WEE	WEENIES	WEEWEEING	WEIRDIE
WEBSPACE	WEED	WEENIEST	WEEWEES	WEIRDIES
WEBSPACES	WEEDBED	WEENING	WEFT	WEIRDING
WEBSTER	WEEDBEDS	WEENS	WEFTAGE	WEIRDLY
WEBSTERS	WEEDED	WEENSIER	WEFTAGES	WEIRDNESS
WEBWHEEL	WEEDER	WEENSIEST	WEFTE	WEIRDO
WEBWHEELS	WEEDERIES	WEENSY	WEFTED	WEIRDOES
WEBWORK	WEEDERS	WEENY	WEFTES	WEIRDOS
WEBWORKS	WEEDERY	WEEP	WEFTING	WEIRDS
WEBWORM	WEEDHEAD	WEEPER	WEFTS	WEIRDY
WEBWORMS	WEEDHEADS	WEEPERS	WEFTWISE	WEIRED
WEBZINE	WEEDICIDE	WEEPHOLE	WEID	WEIRING
WEBZINES	WEEDIER	WEEPHOLES	WEIDS	WEIRS
WECHT	WEEDIEST	WEEPIE	WEIGELA	WEISE
WECHTED	WEEDILY	WEEPIER	WEIGELAS	WEISED
WECHTING	WEEDINESS	WEEPIES	WEIGELIA	WEISES
WECHTS	WEEDING	WEEPIEST	WEIGELIAS	WEISING
WED	WEEDINGS	WEEPILY	WEIGH	WEIZE
WEDDED	WEEDLESS	WEEPINESS	WEIGHABLE	WEIZED
WEDDER	WEEDLIKE	WEEPING	WEIGHAGE	WEIZES
WEDDERED	WEEDLINE	WEEPINGLY	WEIGHAGES	WEIZING
WEDDERING	WEEDLINES	WEEPINGS	WEIGHED	WEKA
WEDDERS	WEEDS	WEEPS	WEIGHER	WEKAS
WEDDING	WEEDY	WEEPY	WEIGHERS	WELAWAY
WEDDINGS	WEEING	WEER	WEIGHING	WELCH
WEDEL	WEEJUNS	WEES	WEIGHINGS	WELCHED

WELCHER	WELLCURBS	WENDIGO	WESTERING	WEXING
WELCHERS	WELLDOER	WENDIGOES	WESTERLY	WEY
WELCHES	WELLDOERS	WENDIGOS	WESTERN	WEYARD
WELCHING	WELLED	WENDING	WESTERNER	WEYS
WELCOME	WELLHEAD	WENDS	WESTERNS	WEYWARD
WELCOMED	WELLHEADS	WENGE	WESTERS	WEZAND
WELCOMELY	WELLHOLE	WENGES	WESTIE	WEZANDS
WELCOMER	WELLHOLES	WENNIER	WESTIES	WHA
WELCOMERS	WELLHOUSE	WENNIEST	WESTING	WHACK
WELCOMES	WELLIE	WENNISH	WESTINGS	WHACKED
WELCOMING	WELLIES	WENNY	WESTLIN	WHACKER
WELD	WELLING	WENS	WESTLINS	WHACKERS
WELDABLE	WELLINGS	WENT	WESTMOST	WHACKIER
WELDED	WELLNESS	WENTS	WESTS	WHACKIEST
WELDER	WELLS	WEPT	WESTWARD	WHACKING
WELDERS	WELLSITE	WERE	WESTWARDS	WHACKINGS
WELDING	WELLSITES	WEREGILD	WET	WHACKO
WELDINGS	WELLY	WEREGILDS	WETA	WHACKOES
WELDLESS	WELS	WEREWOLF	WETAS	WHACKOS
WELDMENT	WELSH	WERGELD	WETBACK	WHACKS
WELDMENTS	WELSHED	WERGELDS	WETBACKS	WHACKY
WELDMESH	WELSHER	WERGELT	WETHER	WHAE
WELDOR	WELSHERS	WERGELTS	WETHERS	WHAISLE
WELDORS	WELSHES	WERGILD	WETLAND	WHAISLED
WELDS	WELSHING	WERGILDS	WETLANDS	WHAISLES
WELFARE	WELT	WERNERITE	WETLY	WHAISLING
WELFARES	WELTED	WERO	WETNESS	WHAIZLE
WELFARISM	WELTER	WEROS	WETNESSES	WHAIZLED
WELFARIST	WELTERED	WERRIS	WETPROOF	WHAIZLES
WELFARITE	WELTERING	WERRISES	WETS	WHAIZLING
WELK	WELTERS	WERSH	WETSUIT	WHAKAIRO
WELKE	WELTING	WERSHER	WETSUITS	WHAKAIROS
WELKED	WELTINGS	WERSHEST	WETTABLE	WHAKAPAPA
WELKES	WELTS	WERT	WETTED	WHALE
WELKIN	WEM	WERWOLF	WETTER	WHALEBACK
WELKING	WEMB	WERWOLVES	WETTERS	WHALEBOAT
WELKINS	WEMBS	WESAND	WETTEST	WHALEBONE
WELKS	WEMS	WESANDS	WETTIE	WHALED
WELKT	WEN	WESKIT	WETTIES	WHALELIKE
WELL	WENA	WESKITS	WETTING	WHALEMAN
WELLADAY	WENCH	WESSAND	WETTINGS	WHALEMEN
WELLADAYS	WENCHED	WESSANDS	WETTISH	WHALER
WELLANEAR	WENCHER	WEST	WETWARE	WHALERIES
WELLAWAY	WENCHERS	WESTABOUT	WETWARES	WHALERS
WELLAWAYS	WENCHES	WESTBOUND	WEX	WHALERY
WELLBEING	WENCHING	WESTED	WEXE	WHALES
WELLBORN	WEND	WESTER	WEXED	WHALING
WELLCURB	WENDED	WESTERED	WEXES	WHALINGS

WHALLY	WHATEN	WHEEL	WHEEZILY	WHEREFROM
WHAM	WHATEVER	WHEELBASE	WHEEZING	WHEREIN
WHAMMED	WHATEVS	WHEELED	WHEEZINGS	WHEREINTO
WHAMMIES	WHATNA	WHEELER	WHEEZLE	WHERENESS
WHAMMING	WHATNESS	WHEELERS	WHEEZLED	WHEREOF
WHAMMO	WHATNOT	WHEELIE	WHEEZLES	WHEREON
WHAMMOS	WHATNOTS	WHEELIER	WHEEZLING	WHEREOUT
WHAMMY	WHATS	WHEELIES	WHEEZY	WHERES
WHAMO	WHATSIS	WHEELIEST	WHEFT	WHERESO
WHAMPLE	WHATSISES	WHEELING	WHEFTS	WHERETO
WHAMPLES	WHATSIT	WHEELINGS	WHELK	WHEREUNTO
WHAMS	WHATSITS	WHEELLESS	WHELKED	WHEREUPON
WHANAU	WHATSO	WHEELMAN	WHELKIER	WHEREVER
WHANAUS	WHATTEN	WHEELMEN	WHELKIEST	WHEREWITH
WHANG	WHAUP	WHEELS	WHELKS	WHERRET
WHANGAM	WHAUPS	WHEELSMAN	WHELKY	WHERRETED
WHANGAMS	WHAUR	WHEELSMEN	WHELM	WHERRETS
WHANGED	WHAURS	WHEELSPIN	WHELMED	WHERRIED
WHANGEE	WHEAL	WHEELWORK	WHELMING	WHERRIES
WHANGEES	WHEALS	WHEELY	WHELMS	WHERRIT
WHANGING	WHEAR	WHEEN	WHELP	WHERRITED
WHANGS	WHEARE	WHEENGE	WHELPED	WHERRITS
WHAP	WHEAT	WHEENGED	WHELPING	WHERRY
WHAPPED	WHEATEAR	WHEENGES	WHELPLESS	WHERRYING
WHAPPER	WHEATEARS	WHEENGING	WHELPS	WHERRYMAN
WHAPPERS	WHEATEN	WHEENS	WHEMMLE	WHERRYMEN
WHAPPING	WHEATENS	WHEEP	WHEMMLED	WHERVE
WHAPS	WHEATGERM	WHEEPED	WHEMMLES	WHERVES
WHARE	WHEATIER	WHEEPING	WHEMMLING	WHET
WHARENUI	WHEATIEST	WHEEPLE	WHEN	WHETHER
WHARENUIS	WHEATLAND	WHEEPLED	WHENAS	WHETS
WHAREPUNI	WHEATLESS	WHEEPLES	WHENCE	WHETSTONE
WHARES	WHEATLIKE	WHEEPLING	WHENCES	WHETTED
WHARF	WHEATMEAL	WHEEPS	WHENCEVER	WHETTER
WHARFAGE	WHEATS	WHEESH	WHENEVER	WHETTERS
WHARFAGES	WHEATWORM	WHEESHED	WHENS	WHETTING
WHARFED	WHEATY	WHEESHES	WHENUA	WHEUGH
WHARFIE	WHEE	WHEESHING	WHENUAS	WHEUGHED
WHARFIES	WHEECH	WHEESHT	WHENWE	WHEUGHING
WHARFING	WHEECHED	WHEESHTED	WHENWES	WHEUGHS
WHARFINGS	WHEECHING	WHEESHTS	WHERE	WHEW
WHARFS	WHEECHS	WHEEZE	WHEREAS	WHEWED
WHARVE	WHEEDLE	WHEEZED	WHEREASES	WHEWING
WHARVES	WHEEDLED	WHEEZER	WHEREAT	WHEWS
WHAT	WHEEDLER	WHEEZERS	WHEREBY	WHEY
WHATA	WHEEDLERS	WHEEZES	WHEREFOR	WHEYEY
WHATAS	WHEEDLES	WHEEZIER	WHEREFORE	WHEYFACE
WHATCHA	WHEEDLING	WHEEZIEST	WHEREFORS	WHEYFACED

W

WHEYFACES	WHILES	WHINGDING	WHIPPERS	WHIRRET
WHEYIER	WHILEVER	WHINGE	WHIPPET	WHIRRETED
WHEYIEST	WHILING	WHINGED	WHIPPETS	WHIRRETS
WHEYISH	WHILK	WHINGEING	WHIPPIER	WHIRRIED
WHEYLIKE	WHILLIED	WHINGER	WHIPPIEST	WHIRRIER
WHEYS	WHILLIES	WHINGERS	WHIPPING	WHIRRIES
WHICH	WHILLY	WHINGES	WHIPPINGS	WHIRRIEST
WHICHEVER	WHILLYING	WHINGIER	WHIPPIT	WHIRRING
WHICKER	WHILLYWHA	WHINGIEST	WHIPPITS	WHIRRINGS
WHICKERED	WHILOM	WHINGING	WHIPPY	WHIRRS
WHICKERS	WHILST	WHINGY	WHIPRAY	WHIRRY
WHID	WHIM	WHINIARD	WHIPRAYS	WHIRRYING
WHIDAH	WHIMBERRY	WHINIARDS	WHIPS	WHIRS
WHIDAHS	WHIMBREL	WHINIER	WHIPSAW	WHIRTLE
WHIDDED	WHIMBRELS	WHINIEST	WHIPSAWED	WHIRTLES
WHIDDER	WHIMMED	WHININESS	WHIPSAWN	WHISH
WHIDDERED	WHIMMIER	WHINING	WHIPSAWS	WHISHED
WHIDDERS	WHIMMIEST	WHININGLY	WHIPSNAKE	WHISHES
WHIDDING	WHIMMING	WHININGS	WHIPSTAFF	WHISHING
WHIDS	WHIMMY	WHINNIED	WHIPSTALL	WHISHT
WHIFF	WHIMPER	WHINNIER	WHIPSTER	WHISHTED
WHIFFED	WHIMPERED	WHINNIES	WHIPSTERS	WHISHTING
WHIFFER	WHIMPERER	WHINNIEST	WHIPSTOCK	WHISHTS
WHIFFERS	WHIMPERS	WHINNY	WHIPT	WHISK
WHIFFET	WHIMPLE	WHINNYING	WHIPTAIL	WHISKED
WHIFFETS	WHIMPLED	WHINS	WHIPTAILS	WHISKER
WHIFFIER	WHIMPLES	WHINSTONE	WHIPWORM	WHISKERED
WHIFFIEST	WHIMPLING	WHINY	WHIPWORMS	WHISKERS
WHIFFING	WHIMS	WHINYARD	WHIR	WHISKERY
WHIFFINGS	WHIMSEY	WHINYARDS	WHIRL	WHISKET
WHIFFLE	WHIMSEYS	WHIO	WHIRLBAT	WHISKETS
WHIFFLED	WHIMSICAL	WHIOS	WHIRLBATS	WHISKEY
WHIFFLER	WHIMSIED	WHIP	WHIRLED	WHISKEYS
WHIFFLERS	WHIMSIER	WHIPBIRD	WHIRLER	WHISKIES
WHIFFLERY	WHIMSIES	WHIPBIRDS	WHIRLERS	WHISKING
WHIFFLES	WHIMSIEST	WHIPCAT	WHIRLIER	WHISKS
WHIFFLING	WHIMSILY	WHIPCATS	WHIRLIES	WHISKY
WHIFFS	WHIMSY	WHIPCORD	WHIRLIEST	WHISPER
WHIFFY	WHIN	WHIPCORDS	WHIRLIGIG	WHISPERED
WHIFT	WHINBERRY	WHIPCORDY	WHIRLING	WHISPERER
WHIFTS	WHINCHAT	WHIPCRACK	WHIRLINGS	WHISPERS
WHIG	WHINCHATS	WHIPJACK	WHIRLPOOL	WHISPERY
WHIGGED	WHINE	WHIPJACKS	WHIRLS	WHISS
WHIGGING	WHINED	WHIPLASH	WHIRLWIND	WHISSED
WHIGS	WHINER	WHIPLESS	WHIRLY	WHISSES
WHILE	WHINERS	WHIPLIKE	WHIRR	WHISSING
WHILED	WHINES	WHIPPED	WHIRRA	WHIST
WHILERE	WHINEY	WHIPPER	WHIRRED	WHISTED

WHISTING	WHITHERED	WHIZZINGS	WHOOMPS	WHORLBATS
WHISTLE	WHITHERS	WHIZZO	WHOONGA	WHORLED
WHISTLED	WHITIER	WHIZZY	WHOONGAS	WHORLING
WHISTLER	WHITIES	WHO	WHOOP	WHORLS
WHISTLERS	WHITIEST	WHOA	WHOOPED	WHORT
WHISTLES	WHITING	WHODUNIT	WHOOPEE	WHORTLE
WHISTLING	WHITINGS	WHODUNITS	WHOOPEES	WHORTLES
WHISTS	WHITISH	WHODUNNIT	WHOOPER	WHORTS
WHIT	WHITLING	WHOEVER	WHOOPERS	WHOSE
WHITE	WHITLINGS	WHOLE	WHOOPIE	WHOSESO
WHITEBAIT	WHITLOW	WHOLEFOOD	WHOOPIES	WHOSEVER
WHITEBASS	WHITLOWS	WHOLEMEAL	WHOOPING	WHOSIS
WHITEBEAM	WHITRACK	WHOLENESS	WHOOPINGS	WHOSISES
WHITECAP	WHITRACKS	WHOLES	WHOOPLA	WHOSIT
WHITECAPS	WHITRET	WHOLESALE	WHOOPLAS	WHOSITS
WHITECOAT	WHITRETS	WHOLESOME	WHOOPS	WHOSO
WHITECOMB	WHITRICK	WHOLISM	WHOOPSIE	WHOSOEVER
WHITED	WHITRICKS	WHOLISMS	WHOOPSIES	WHOT
WHITEDAMP	WHITS	WHOLIST	WHOOSH	WHOW
WHITEFACE	WHITSTER	WHOLISTIC	WHOOSHED	WHOWED
WHITEFISH	WHITSTERS	WHOLISTS	WHOOSHES	WHOWING
WHITEFLY	WHITTAW	WHOLLY	WHOOSHING	WHOWS
WHITEHEAD	WHITTAWER	WHOLPHIN	WHOOSIS	WHUMMLE
WHITELIST	WHITTAWS	WHOLPHINS	WHOOSISES	WHUMMLED
WHITELY	WHITTER	WHOM	WHOOT	WHUMMLES
WHITEN	WHITTERED	WHOMBLE	WHOOTED	WHUMMLING
WHITENED	WHITTERS	WHOMBLED	WHOOTING	WHUMP
WHITENER	WHITTLE	WHOMBLES	WHOOTS	WHUMPED
WHITENERS	WHITTLED	WHOMBLING	WHOP	WHUMPING
WHITENESS	WHITTLER	WHOMEVER	WHOPPED	WHUMPS
WHITENING	WHITTLERS	WHOMMLE	WHOPPER	WHUNSTANE
WHITENS	WHITTLES	WHOMMLED	WHOPPERS	WHUP
WHITEOUT	WHITTLING	WHOMMLES	WHOPPING	WHUPPED
WHITEOUTS	WHITTRET	WHOMMLING	WHOPPINGS	WHUPPING
WHITEPOT	WHITTRETS	WHOMP	WHOPS	WHUPPINGS
WHITEPOTS	WHITY	WHOMPED	WHORE	WHUPS
WHITER	WHIZ	WHOMPING	WHORED	WHY
WHITES	WHIZBANG	WHOMPS	WHOREDOM	WHYDA
WHITEST	WHIZBANGS	WHOMSO	WHOREDOMS	WHYDAH
WHITETAIL	WHIZZ	WHOOBUB	WHORES	WHYDAHS
WHITEWALL	WHIZZBANG	WHOOBUBS	WHORESON	WHYDAS
WHITEWARE	WHIZZED	WHOOF	WHORESONS	WHYDUNIT
WHITEWASH	WHIZZER	WHOOFED	WHORING	WHYDUNITS
WHITEWING	WHIZZERS	WHOOFING	WHORINGS	WHYDUNNIT
WHITEWOOD	WHIZZES	WHOOFS	WHORISH	WHYEVER
WHITEY	WHIZZIER	WHOOMP	WHORISHLY	WHYS
WHITEYS	WHIZZIEST	WHOOMPH	WHORL	WIBBLE
WHITHER	WHIZZING	WHOOMPHS	WHORLBAT	WIBBLED

WIBBLES

WIBBLES	WIDEBAND	WIELDING	WIGGLERS	WILDINGS
WIBBLING	WIDEBANDS	WIELDLESS	WIGGLES	WILDISH
WICCA	WIDEBODY	WIELDS	WIGGLIER	WILDLAND
WICCAN	WIDELY	WIELDY	WIGGLIEST	WILDLANDS
WICCANS	WIDEN	WIELS	WIGGLING	WILDLIFE
WICCAS	WIDENED	WIENER	WIGGLY	WILDLIFES
WICE	WIDENER	WIENERS	WIGGY	WILDLING
WICH	WIDENERS	WIENIE	WIGHT	WILDLINGS
WICHES	WIDENESS	WIENIES	WIGHTED	WILDLY
WICK	WIDENING	WIFE	WIGHTING	WILDMAN
WICKAPE	WIDENINGS	WIFED	WIGHTLY	WILDMEN
WICKAPES	WIDENS	WIFEDOM	WIGHTS	WILDNESS
WICKED	WIDEOUT	WIFEDOMS	WIGLESS	WILDS
WICKEDER	WIDEOUTS	WIFEHOOD	WIGLET	WILDWOOD
WICKEDEST	WIDER	WIFEHOODS	WIGLETS	WILDWOODS
WICKEDLY	WIDES	WIFELESS	WIGLIKE	WILE
WICKEDS	WIDEST	WIFELIER	WIGMAKER	WILED
WICKEN	WIDGEON	WIFELIEST	WIGMAKERS	WILEFUL
WICKENS	WIDGEONS	WIFELIKE	WIGS	WILES
WICKER	WIDGET	WIFELY	WIGWAG	WILFUL
WICKERED	WIDGETS	WIFES	WIGWAGGED	WILFULLY
WICKERS	WIDGIE	WIFEY	WIGWAGGER	WILGA
WICKET	WIDGIES	WIFEYS	WIGWAGS	WILGAS
WICKETS	WIDISH	WIFIE	WIGWAM	WILI
WICKIES	WIDOW	WIFIES	WIGWAMS	WILIER
WICKING	WIDOWBIRD	WIFING	WIKI	WILIEST
WICKINGS	WIDOWED	WIFTIER	WIKIALITY	WILILY
WICKIUP	WIDOWER	WIFTIEST	WIKIS	WILINESS
WICKIUPS	WIDOWERED	WIFTY	WIKIUP	WILING
WICKLESS	WIDOWERS	WIG	WIKIUPS	WILIS
WICKS	WIDOWHOOD	WIGAN	WILCO	WILJA
WICKTHING	WIDOWING	WIGANS	WILD	WILJAS
WICKY	WIDOWMAN	WIGEON	WILDCARD	WILL
WICKYUP	WIDOWMEN	WIGEONS	WILDCARDS	WILLABLE
WICKYUPS	WIDOWS	WIGGA	WILDCAT	WILLED
WICOPIES	WIDTH	WIGGAS	WILDCATS	WILLEMITE
WICOPY	WIDTHS	WIGGED	WILDED	WILLER
WIDDER	WIDTHWAY	WIGGER	WILDER	WILLERS
WIDDERS	WIDTHWAYS	WIGGERIES	WILDERED	WILLEST
WIDDIE	WIDTHWISE	WIGGERS	WILDERING	WILLET
WIDDIES	WIEL	WIGGERY	WILDERS	WILLETS
WIDDLE	WIELD	WIGGIER	WILDEST	WILLEY
WIDDLED	WIELDABLE	WIGGIEST	WILDFIRE	WILLEYED
WIDDLES	WIELDED	WIGGING	WILDFIRES	WILLEYING
WIDDLING	WIELDER	WIGGINGS	WILDFOWL	WILLEYS
WIDDY	WIELDERS	WIGGLE	WILDFOWLS	WILLFUL
WIDE	WIELDIER	WIGGLED	WILDGRAVE	WILLFULLY
WIDEAWAKE	WIELDIEST	WIGGLER	WILDING	WILLIAM

WILLIAMS	WIMPISH	WINDBREAK	WINDPACK	WINESKIN
WILLIE	WIMPISHLY	WINDBURN	WINDPACKS	WINESKINS
WILLIED	WIMPLE	WINDBURNS	WINDPIPE	WINESOP
WILLIES	WIMPLED	WINDBURNT	WINDPIPES	WINESOPS
WILLING	WIMPLES	WINDCHILL	WINDPROOF	WINEY
WILLINGER	WIMPLING	WINDED	WINDRING	WING
WILLINGLY	WIMPS	WINDER	WINDROW	WINGBACK
WILLIWAU	WIMPY	WINDERS	WINDROWED	WINGBACKS
WILLIWAUS	WIN	WINDFALL	WINDROWER	WINGBEAT
WILLIWAW	WINCE	WINDFALLS	WINDROWS	WINGBEATS
WILLIWAWS	WINCED	WINDFLAW	WINDS	WINGBOW
WILLOW	WINCER	WINDFLAWS	WINDSAIL	WINGBOWS
WILLOWED	WINCERS	WINDGALL	WINDSAILS	WINGCHAIR
WILLOWER	WINCES	WINDGALLS	WINDSES	WINGDING
WILLOWERS	WINCEY	WINDGUN	WINDSHAKE	WINGDINGS
WILLOWIER	WINCEYS	WINDGUNS	WINDSHIP	WINGE
WILLOWING	WINCH	WINDHOVER	WINDSHIPS	WINGED
WILLOWISH	WINCHED	WINDIER	WINDSLAB	WINGEDLY
WILLOWS	WINCHER	WINDIEST	WINDSLABS	WINGEING
WILLOWY	WINCHERS	WINDIGO	WINDSOCK	WINGER
WILLPOWER	WINCHES	WINDIGOES	WINDSOCKS	WINGERS
WILLS	WINCHING	WINDIGOS	WINDSTORM	WINGES
WILLY	WINCHMAN	WINDILY	WINDSURF	WINGIER
WILLYARD	WINCHMEN	WINDINESS	WINDSURFS	WINGIEST
WILLYART	WINCING	WINDING	WINDSWEPT	WINGING
WILLYING	WINCINGLY	WINDINGLY	WINDTHROW	WINGLESS
WILLYWAW	WINCINGS	WINDINGS	WINDTIGHT	WINGLET
WILLYWAWS	WINCOPIPE	WINDLASS	WINDUP	WINGLETS
WILT	WIND	WINDLE	WINDUPS	WINGLIKE
WILTED	WINDABLE	WINDLED	WINDWARD	WINGMAN
WILTING	WINDAC	WINDLES	WINDWARDS	WINGMEN
WILTJA	WINDACS	WINDLESS	WINDWAY	WINGNUT
WILTJAS	WINDAGE	WINDLING	WINDWAYS	WINGNUTS
WILTS	WINDAGES	WINDLINGS	WINDY	WINGOVER
WILY	WINDAS	WINDLOAD	WINE	WINGOVERS
WIMBLE	WINDASES	WINDLOADS	WINEBERRY	WINGS
WIMBLED	WINDBAG	WINDMILL	WINED	WINGSPAN
WIMBLES	WINDBAGS	WINDMILLS	WINEGLASS	WINGSPANS
WIMBLING	WINDBELL	WINDOCK	WINELESS	WINGSUIT
WIMBREL	WINDDELLS	WINDOCKS	WINEMAKER	WINGSUITS
WIMBRELS	WINDBILL	WINDORE	WINEPRESS	WINGTIP
WIMMIN	WINDBILLS	WINDORES	WINERIES	WINGTIPS
WIMP	WINDBLAST	WINDOW	WINERY	WINGY
WIMPED	WINDBLOW	WINDOWED	WINES	WINIER
WIMPIER	WINDBLOWN	WINDOWIER	WINESAP	WINIEST
WIMPIEST	WINDBLOWS	WINDOWING	WINESAPS	WINING
WIMPINESS	WINDBORNE	WINDOWS	WINESHOP	WINISH
WIMPING	WINDBOUND	WINDOWY	WINESHOPS	WINK

WINKED	WINTERER	WIRELINES	WISELY	WISTFULLY
WINKER	WINTERERS	WIREMAN	WISENESS	WISTING
WINKERS	WINTERFED	WIREMEN	WISENT	WISTITI
WINKING	WINTERIER	WIREPHOTO	WISENTS	WISTITIS
WINKINGLY	WINTERING	WIRER	WISER	WISTLY
WINKINGS	WINTERISE	WIRERS	WISES	WISTS
WINKLE	WINTERISH	WIRES	WISEST	WIT
WINKLED	WINTERIZE	WIRETAP	WISEWOMAN	WITAN
WINKLER	WINTERLY	WIRETAPS	WISEWOMEN	WITANS
WINKLERS	WINTERS	WIREWAY	WISH	WITBLITS
WINKLES	WINTERY	WIREWAYS	WISHA	WITCH
WINKLING	WINTLE	WIREWORK	WISHBONE	WITCHED
WINKS	WINTLED	WIREWORKS	WISHBONES	WITCHEN
WINLESS	WINTLES	WIREWORM	WISHED	WITCHENS
WINN	WINTLING	WIREWORMS	WISHER	WITCHERY
WINNA	WINTRIER	WIREWOVE	WISHERS	WITCHES
WINNABLE	WINTRIEST	WIRIER	WISHES	WITCHETTY
WINNARD	WINTRILY	WIRIEST	WISHFUL	WITCHHOOD
WINNARDS	WINTRY	WIRILDA	WISHFULLY	WITCHIER
WINNED	WINY	WIRILDAS	WISHING	WITCHIEST
WINNER	WINZE	WIRILY	WISHINGS	WITCHING
WINNERS	WINZES	WIRINESS	WISHLESS	WITCHINGS
WINNING	WIPE	WIRING	WISHT	WITCHKNOT
WINNINGLY	WIPEABLE	WIRINGS	WISING	WITCHLIKE
WINNINGS	WIPED	WIRRA	WISKET	WITCHWEED
WINNLE	WIPEOUT	WIRRAH	WISKETS	WITCHY
WINNLES	WIPEOUTS	WIRRAHS	WISP	WITE
WINNOCK	WIPER	WIRRICOW	WISPED	WITED
WINNOCKS	WIPERS	WIRRICOWS	WISPIER	WITELESS
WINNOW	WIPES	WIRY	WISPIEST	WITES
WINNOWED	WIPING	WIS	WISPILY	WITGAT
WINNOWER	WIPINGS	WISARD	WISPINESS	WITGATS
WINNOWERS	WIPPEN	WISARDS	WISPING	WITH
WINNOWING	WIPPENS	WISDOM	WISPISH	WITHAL
WINNOWS	WIRABLE	WISDOMS	WISPLIKE	WITHDRAW
WINNS	WIRE	WISE	WISPS	WITHDRAWN
WINO	WIRED	WISEACRE	WISPY	WITHDRAWS
WINOES	WIREDRAW	WISEACRES	WISS	WITHDREW
WINOS	WIREDRAWN	WISEASS	WISSED	WITHE
WINS	WIREDRAWS	WISEASSES	WISSES	WITHED
WINSEY	WIREDREW	WISECRACK	WISSING	WITHER
WINSEYS	WIREFRAME	WISED	WIST	WITHERED
WINSOME	WIREGRASS	WISEGUY	WISTARIA	WITHERER
WINSOMELY	WIREHAIR	WISEGUYS	WISTARIAS	WITHERERS
WINSOMER	WIREHAIRS	WISELIER	WISTED	WITHERING
WINSOMEST	WIRELESS	WISELIEST	WISTERIA	WITHERITE
WINTER	WIRELIKE	WISELING	WISTERIAS	WITHEROD
WINTERED	WIRELINE	WISELINGS	WISTFUL	WITHERODS

WITHERS	WITTINGS	WOBBLE	WOLDS	WOMANISTS
WITHES	WITTOL	WOBBLED	WOLF	WOMANIZE
WITHHAULT	WITTOLLY	WOBBLER	WOLFBERRY	WOMANIZED
WITHHELD	WITTOLS	WOBBLERS	WOLFED	WOMANIZER
WITHHOLD	WITTY	WOBBLES	WOLFER	WOMANIZES
WITHHOLDS	WITWALL	WOBBLIER	WOLFERS	WOMANKIND
WITHIER	WITWALLS	WOBBLIES	WOLFFISH	WOMANLESS
WITHIES	WITWANTON	WOBBLIEST	WOLFHOUND	WOMANLIER
WITHIEST	WIVE	WOBBLING	WOLFING	WOMANLIKE
WITHIN	WIVED	WOBBLINGS	WOLFINGS	WOMANLY
WITHING	WIVEHOOD	WOBBLY	WOLFISH	WOMANNED
WITHINS	WIVEHOODS	WOBEGONE	WOLFISHLY	WOMANNESS
WITHOUT	WIVER	WOCK	WOLFKIN	WOMANNING
WITHOUTEN	WIVERN	WOCKS	WOLFKINS	WOMANS
WITHOUTS	WIVERNS	WODGE	WOLFLIKE	WOMB
WITHS	WIVERS	WODGES	WOLFLING	WOMBAT
WITHSTAND	WIVES	WOE	WOLFLINGS	WOMBATS
WITHSTOOD	WIVING	WOEBEGONE	WOLFRAM	WOMBED
WITHWIND	WIZ	WOEFUL	WOLFRAMS	WOMBIER
WITHWINDS	WIZARD	WOEFULLER	WOLFS	WOMBIEST
WITHY	WIZARDER	WOEFULLY	WOLFSBANE	WOMBING
WITHYWIND	WIZARDEST	WOENESS	WOLFSKIN	WOMBLIKE
WITING	WIZARDLY	WOENESSES	WOLFSKINS	WOMBS
WITLESS	WIZARDRY	WOES	WOLLIES	WOMBY
WITLESSLY	WIZARDS	WOESOME	WOLLY	WOMEN
WITLING	WIZEN	WOF	WOLVE	WOMENFOLK
WITLINGS	WIZENED	WOFS	WOLVED	WOMENKIND
WITLOOF	WIZENER	WOFUL	WOLVER	WOMERA
WITLOOFS	WIZENEST	WOFULLER	WOLVERENE	WOMERAS
WITNESS	WIZENING	WOFULLEST	WOLVERINE	WOMMERA
WITNESSED	WIZENS	WOFULLY	WOLVERS	WOMMERAS
WITNESSER	WIZES	WOFULNESS	WOLVES	WOMMIT
WITNESSES	WIZIER	WOG	WOLVING	WOMMITS
WITNEY	WIZIERS	WOGGISH	WOLVINGS	WOMYN
WITNEYS	WIZZEN	WOGGLE	WOLVISH	WON
WITS	WIZZENS	WOGGLES	WOLVISHLY	WONDER
WITTED	WIZZES	WOGS	WOMAN	WONDERED
WITTER	WO	WOIWODE	WOMANED	WONDERER
WITTERED	WOAD	WOIWODES	WOMANHOOD	WONDERERS
WITTERING	WOADED	WOJUS	WOMANING	WONDERFUL
WITTERS	WOADS	WOK	WOMANISE	WONDERING
WITTICISM	WOADWAX	WOKE	WOMANISED	WONDERKID
WITTIER	WOADWAXEN	WOKEN	WOMANISER	WONDEROUS
WITTIEST	WOADWAXES	WOKER	WOMANISES	WONDERS
WITTILY	WOAH	WOKEST	WOMANISH	WONDRED
WITTINESS	WOALD	WOKKA	WOMANISM	WONDROUS
WITTING	WOALDS	WOKS	WOMANISMS	WONGA
WITTINGLY	WOBBEGONG	WOLD	WOMANIST	WONGAS

W

WONGI	WOODCHIPS	WOODMEN	WOODWORK	WOOLIE
WONGIED	WOODCHOP	WOODMICE	WOODWORKS	WOOLIER
WONGIING	WOODCHOPS	WOODMOUSE	WOODWORM	WOOLIES
WONGIS	WOODCHUCK	WOODNESS	WOODWORMS	WOOLIEST
WONING	WOODCOCK	WOODNOTE	WOODWOSE	WOOLILY
WONINGS	WOODCOCKS	WOODNOTES	WOODWOSES	WOOLINESS
WONK	WOODCRAFT	WOODPILE	WOODY	WOOLLED
WONKERIES	WOODCUT	WOODPILES	WOODYARD	WOOLLEN
WONKERY	WOODCUTS	WOODPRINT	WOODYARDS	WOOLLENS
WONKIER	WOODED	WOODRAT	WOOED	WOOLLIER
WONKIEST	WOODEN	WOODRATS	WOOER	WOOLLIES
WONKILY	WOODENED	WOODREEVE	WOOERS	WOOLLIEST
WONKINESS	WOODENER	WOODROOF	WOOF	WOOLLIKE
WONKISH	WOODENEST	WOODROOFS	WOOFED	WOOLLILY
WONKS	WOODENING	WOODRUFF	WOOFER	WOOLLY
WONKY	WOODENLY	WOODRUFFS	WOOFERS	WOOLMAN
WONNED	WOODENS	WOODRUSH	WOOFIER	WOOLMEN
WONNER	WOODENTOP	WOODS	WOOFIEST	WOOLPACK
WONNERS	WOODFERN	WOODSCREW	WOOFING	WOOLPACKS
WONNING	WOODFERNS	WOODSHED	WOOFS	WOOLS
WONNINGS	WOODFREE	WOODSHEDS	WOOFTAH	WOOLSACK
WONS	WOODGRAIN	WOODSHOCK	WOOFTAHS	WOOLSACKS
WONT	WOODHEN	WOODSIA	WOOFTER	WOOLSEY
WONTED	WOODHENS	WOODSIAS	WOOFTERS	WOOLSEYS
WONTEDLY	WOODHOLE	WOODSIER	WOOFY	WOOLSHED
WONTING	WOODHOLES	WOODSIEST	WOOHOO	WOOLSHEDS
WONTLESS	WOODHORSE	WOODSKIN	WOOING	WOOLSKIN
WONTON	WOODHOUSE	WOODSKINS	WOOINGLY	WOOLSKINS
WONTONS	WOODIE	WOODSMAN	WOOINGS	WOOLWARD
WONTS	WOODIER	WOODSMEN	WOOL	WOOLWORK
WOO	WOODIES	WOODSMOKE	WOOLD	WOOLWORKS
WOOABLE	WOODIEST	WOODSPITE	WOOLDED	WOOLY
WOOBUT	WOODINESS	WOODSTONE	WOOLDER	WOOMERA
WOOBUTS	WOODING	WOODSTOVE	WOOLDERS	WOOMERANG
WOOD	WOODLAND	WOODSY	WOOLDING	WOOMERAS
WOODBIN	WOODLANDS	WOODTONE	WOOLDINGS	WOON
WOODBIND	WOODLARK	WOODTONES	WOOLDS	WOONED
WOODBINDS	WOODLARKS	WOODWALE	WOOLED	WOONERF
WOODBINE	WOODLESS	WOODWALES	WOOLEN	WOONERFS
WOODBINES	WOODLICE	WOODWARD	WOOLENS	WOONING
WOODBINS	WOODLORE	WOODWARDS	WOOLER	WOONS
WOODBLOCK	WOODLORES	WOODWASP	WOOLERS	WOOPIE
WOODBORER	WOODLOT	WOODWASPS	WOOLFAT	WOOPIES
WOODBOX	WOODLOTS	WOODWAX	WOOLFATS	WOOPS
WOODBOXES	WOODLOUSE	WOODWAXEN	WOOLFELL	WOOPSED
WOODCHAT	WOODMAN	WOODWAXES	WOOLFELLS	WOOPSES
WOODCHATS	WOODMEAL	WOODWIND	WOOLHAT	WOOPSING
WOODCHIP	WOODMEALS	WOODWINDS	WOOLHATS	WOOPY

WOORALI	WORDINGS	WORKHOURS	WORLDIES	WORRIEDLY
WOORALIS	WORDISH	WORKHOUSE	WORLDLIER	WORRIER
WOORARA	WORDLESS	WORKING	WORLDLING	WORRIERS
WOORARAS	WORDLORE	WORKINGS	WORLDLY	WORRIES
WOORARI	WORDLORES	WORKLESS	WORLDS	WORRIMENT
WOORARIS	WORDPLAY	WORKLOAD	WORLDVIEW	WORRISOME
WOOS	WORDPLAYS	WORKLOADS	WORLDWIDE	WORRIT
WOOSE	WORDS	WORKMAN	WORM	WORRITED
WOOSEL	WORDSMITH	WORKMANLY	WORMCAST	WORRITING
WOOSELL	WORDWRAP	WORKMATE	WORMCASTS	WORRITS
WOOSELLS	WORDWRAPS	WORKMATES	WORMED	WORRY
WOOSELS	WORDY	WORKMEN	WORMER	WORRYCOW
WOOSES	WORE	WORKOUT	WORMERIES	WORRYCOWS
WOOSH	WORK	WORKOUTS	WORMERS	WORRYGUTS
WOOSHED	WORKABLE	WORKPIECE	WORMERY	WORRYING
WOOSHES	WORKABLY	WORKPLACE	WORMFLIES	WORRYINGS
WOOSHING	WORKADAY	WORKPRINT	WORMFLY	WORRYWART
WOOT	WORKADAYS	WORKROOM	WORMGEAR	WORSE
WOOTZ	WORKBAG	WORKROOMS	WORMGEARS	WORSED
WOOTZES	WORKBAGS	WORKS	WORMHOLE	WORSEN
WOOZIER	WORKBENCH	WORKSAFE	WORMHOLED	WORSENED
WOOZIEST	WORKBOAT	WORKSHEET	WORMHOLES	WORSENESS
WOOZILY	WORKBOATS	WORKSHOP	WORMIER	WORSENING
WOOZINESS	WORKBOOK	WORKSHOPS	WORMIEST	WORSENS
WOOZY	WORKBOOKS	WORKSHY	WORMIL	WORSER
WOP	WORKBOOT	WORKSITE	WORMILS	WORSES
WOPPED	WORKBOOTS	WORKSITES	WORMINESS	WORSET
WOPPING	WORKBOX	WORKSOME	WORMING	WORSETS
WOPS	WORKBOXES	WORKSONG	WORMISH	WORSHIP
WORCESTER	WORKDAY	WORKSONGS	WORMLIKE	WORSHIPED
WORD	WORKDAYS	WORKSPACE	WORMROOT	WORSHIPER
WORDAGE	WORKED	WORKTABLE	WORMROOTS	WORSHIPS
WORDAGES	WORKER	WORKTOP	WORMS	WORSING
WORDBOOK	WORKERIST	WORKTOPS	WORMSEED	WORST
WORDBOOKS	WORKERS	WORKUP	WORMSEEDS	WORSTED
WORDBOUND	WORKFARE	WORKUPS	WORMWHEEL	WORSTEDS
WORDBREAK	WORKFARES	WORKWEAR	WORMWOOD	WORSTING
WORDCOUNT	WORKFLOW	WORKWEARS	WORMWOODS	WORSTS
WORDED	WORKFLOWS	WORKWEEK	WORMY	WORT
WORDGAME	WORKFOLK	WORKWEEKS	WORN	WORTH
WORDGAMES	WORKFOLKS	WORKWOMAN	WORNNESS	WORTHED
WORDIE	WORKFORCE	WORKWOMEN	WORRAL	WORTHFUL
WORDIER	WORKFUL	WORLD	WORRALS	WORTHIED
WORDIES	WORKGIRL	WORLDBEAT	WORREL	WORTHIER
WORDIEST	WORKGIRLS	WORLDED	WORRELS	WORTHIES
WORDILY	WORKGROUP	WORLDER	WORRICOW	WORTHIEST
WORDINESS	WORKHORSE	WORLDERS	WORRICOWS	WORTHILY
WORDING	WORKHOUR	WORLDIE	WORRIED	WORTHING

W

WORTHLESS	WOWF	WRASTING	WRECKED	WRIGGLERS
WORTHS	WOWFER	WRASTLE	WRECKER	WRIGGLES
WORTHY	WOWFEST	WRASTLED	WRECKERS	WRIGGLIER
WORTHYING	WOWING	WRASTLES	WRECKFISH	WRIGGLING
WORTLE	WOWS	WRASTLING	WRECKFUL	WRIGGLY
WORTLES	WOWSER	WRASTS	WRECKING	WRIGHT
WORTS	WOWSERS	WRATE	WRECKINGS	WRIGHTS
WOS	WOX	WRATH	WRECKS	WRING
WOSBIRD	WOXEN	WRATHED	WREN	WRINGED
WOSBIRDS	WRACK	WRATHFUL	WRENCH	WRINGER
WOST	WRACKED	WRATHIER	WRENCHED	WRINGERS
WOT	WRACKFUL	WRATHIEST	WRENCHER	WRINGING
WOTCHA	WRACKING	WRATHILY	WRENCHERS	WRINGS
WOTCHER	WRACKS	WRATHING	WRENCHES	WRINKLE
WOTS	WRAITH	WRATHLESS	WRENCHING	WRINKLED
WOTTED	WRAITHS	WRATHS	WRENS	WRINKLES
WOTTEST	WRANG	WRATHY	WRENTIT	WRINKLIE
WOTTETH	WRANGED	WRAWL	WRENTITS	WRINKLIER
WOTTING	WRANGING	WRAWLED	WREST	WRINKLIES
WOUBIT	WRANGLE	WRAWLING	WRESTED	WRINKLING
WOUBITS	WRANGLED	WRAWLS	WRESTER	WRINKLY
WOULD	WRANGLER	WRAXLE	WRESTERS	WRIST
WOULDEST	WRANGLERS	WRAXLED	WRESTING	WRISTBAND
WOULDS	WRANGLES	WRAXLES	WRESTLE	WRISTED
WOULDST	WRANGLING	WRAXLING	WRESTLED	WRISTER
WOUND	WRANGS	WRAXLINGS	WRESTLER	WRISTERS
WOUNDABLE	WRAP	WREAK	WRESTLERS	WRISTIER
WOUNDED	WRAPOVER	WREAKED	WRESTLES	WRISTIEST
WOUNDEDLY	WRAPOVERS	WREAKER	WRESTLING	WRISTING
WOUNDER	WRAPPAGE	WREAKERS	WRESTS	WRISTLET
WOUNDERS	WRAPPAGES	WREAKFUL	WRETCH	WRISTLETS
WOUNDIER	WRAPPED	WREAKING	WRETCHED	WRISTLOCK
WOUNDIEST	WRAPPER	WREAKLESS	WRETCHES	WRISTS
WOUNDILY	WRAPPERED	WREAKS	WRETHE	WRISTY
WOUNDING	WRAPPERS	WREATH	WRETHED	WRIT
WOUNDINGS	WRAPPING	WREATHE	WRETHES	WRITABLE
WOUNDLESS	WRAPPINGS	WREATHED	WRETHING	WRITATIVE
WOUNDS	WRAPROUND	WREATHEN	WRICK	WRITE
WOUNDWORT	WRAPS	WREATHER	WRICKED	WRITEABLE
WOUNDY	WRAPT	WREATHERS	WRICKING	WRITEDOWN
WOURALI	WRASSE	WREATHES	WRICKS	WRITEOFF
WOURALIS	WRASSES	WREATHIER	WRIED	WRITEOFFS
WOVE	WRASSLE	WREATHING	WRIER	WRITER
WOVEN	WRASSLED	WREATHS	WRIES	WRITERESS
WOVENS	WRASSLES	WREATHY	WRIEST	WRITERLY
WOW	WRASSLING	WRECK	WRIGGLE	WRITERS
WOWED	WRAST	WRECKAGE	WRIGGLED	WRITES
WOWEE	WRASTED	WRECKAGES	WRIGGLER	WRITHE

WRITHED	WRONGLY	WUD	WURTZITES	WYCH
WRITHEN	WRONGNESS	WUDDED	WURZEL	WYCHES
WRITHER	WRONGOUS	WUDDIES	WURZELS	WYE
WRITHERS	WRONGS	WUDDING	WUS	WYES
WRITHES	WROOT	WUDDY	WUSES	WYLE
WRITHING	WROOTED	WUDJULA	WUSHU	WYLED
WRITHINGS	WROOTING	WUDJULAS	WUSHUS	WYLES
WRITHLED	WROOTS	WUDS	WUSS	WYLIECOAT
WRITING	WROTE	WUDU	WUSSES	WYLING
WRITINGS	WROTH	WUDUS	WUSSIER	WYN
WRITS	WROTHFUL	WUKKAS	WUSSIES	WYND
WRITTEN	WROUGHT	WULFENITE	WUSSIEST	WYNDS
WRIZLED	WRUNG	WULL	WUSSY	WYNN
WROATH	WRY	WULLED	WUTHER	WYNNS
WROATHS	WRYBILL	WULLING	WUTHERED	WYNS
WROKE	WRYBILLS	WULLS	WUTHERING	WYSIWYG
WROKEN	WRYER	WUNNER	WUTHERS	WYTE
WRONG	WRYEST	WUNNERS	WUXIA	WYTED
WRONGDOER	WRYING	WURLEY	WUXIAS	WYTES
WRONGED	WRYLY	WURLEYS	WUZ	WYTING
WRONGER	WRYNECK	WURLIE	WUZZLE	WYVERN
WRONGERS	WRYNECKS	WURLIES	WUZZLED	WYVERNS
WRONGEST	WRYNESS	WURST	WUZZLES	
WRONGFUL	WRYNESSES	WURSTS	WUZZLING	
WRONGING	WRYTHEN	WURTZITE	WYANDOTTE	

W

X

XANTHAM	XENIUM	XERARCH	XIPHOID	XYLOID
XANTHAMS	XENOBLAST	XERASIA	XIPHOIDAL	XYLOIDIN
XANTHAN	XENOCRYST	XERASIAS	XIPHOIDS	XYLOIDINE
XANTHANS	XENOGAMY	XERIC	XIPHOPAGI	XYLOIDINS
XANTHATE	XENOGENIC	XERICALLY	XIS	XYLOL
XANTHATES	XENOGENY	XERISCAPE	XOANA	XYLOLOGY
XANTHEIN	XENOGRAFT	XEROCHASY	XOANON	XYLOLS
XANTHEINS	XENOLITH	XERODERMA	XRAY	XYLOMA
XANTHENE	XENOLITHS	XEROMA	XRAYS	XYLOMAS
XANTHENES	XENOMANIA	XEROMAS	XU	XYLOMATA
XANTHIC	XENOMENIA	XEROMATA	XYLAN	XYLOMETER
XANTHIN	XENON	XEROMORPH	XYLANS	XYLONIC
XANTHINE	XENONS	XEROPHAGY	XYLEM	XYLONITE
XANTHINES	XENOPHILE	XEROPHILE	XYLEMS	XYLONITES
XANTHINS	XENOPHOBE	XEROPHILY	XYLENE	XYLOPHAGE
XANTHISM	XENOPHOBY	XEROPHYTE	XYLENES	XYLOPHONE
XANTHISMS	XENOPHYA	XEROSERE	XYLENOL	XYLORIMBA
XANTHOMA	XENOPUS	XEROSERES	XYLENOLS	XYLOSE
XANTHOMAS	XENOPUSES	XEROSES	XYLIC	XYLOSES
XANTHONE	XENOTIME	XEROSIS	XYLIDIN	XYLOTOMY
XANTHONES	XENOTIMES	XEROSTOMA	XYLIDINE	XYLYL
XANTHOUS	XENURINE	XEROTES	XYLIDINES	XYLYLS
XANTHOXYL	XENURINES	XEROTIC	XYLIDINS	XYST
XEBEC	XERAFIN	XEROX	XYLITOL	XYSTER
XEBECS	XERAFINS	XEROXED	XYLITOLS	XYSTERS
XED	XERANSES	XEROXES	XYLOCARP	XYSTI
XENIA	XERANSIS	XEROXING	XYLOCARPS	XYSTOI
XENIAL	XERANTIC	XERUS	XYLOGEN	XYSTOS
XENIAS	XERAPHIN	XERUSES	XYLOGENS	XYSTS
XENIC	XERAPHINS	XI	XYLOGRAPH	XYSTUS

X

Y

YA	YAFF	YAKUZA	YAPOCKS	YARDLAND
YAAR	YAFFED	YALD	YAPOK	YARDLANDS
YAARS	YAFFING	YALE	YAPOKS	YARDLIGHT
YABA	YAFFLE	YALES	YAPON	YARDMAN
YABAS	YAFFLES	YAM	YAPONS	YARDMEN
YABBA	YAFFS	YAMALKA	YAPP	YARDS
YABBAS	YAG	YAMALKAS	YAPPED	YARDSTICK
YABBER	YAGE	YAMEN	YAPPER	YARDWAND
YABBERED	YAGER	YAMENS	YAPPERS	YARDWANDS
YABBERING	YAGERS	YAMMER	YAPPIE	YARDWORK
YABBERS	YAGES	YAMMERED	YAPPIER	YARDWORKS
YABBIE	YAGGER	YAMMERER	YAPPIES	YARE
YABBIED	YAGGERS	YAMMERERS	YAPPIEST	YARELY
YABBIES	YAGI	YAMMERING	YAPPING	YARER
YABBY	YAGIS	YAMMERS	YAPPINGLY	YAREST
YABBYING	YAGS	YAMPIES	YAPPINGS	YARFA
YACCA	YAH	YAMPY	YAPPS	YARFAS
YACCAS	YAHOO	YAMS	YAPPY	YARK
YACHT	YAHOOISM	YAMULKA	YAPS	YARKED
YACHTED	YAHOOISMS	YAMULKAS	YAPSTER	YARKING
YACHTER	YAHOOS	YAMUN	YAPSTERS	YARKS
YACHTERS	YAHRZEIT	YAMUNS	YAQONA	YARMELKE
YACHTIE	YAHRZEITS	YANG	YAQONAS	YARMELKES
YACHTIES	YAHS	YANGS	YAR	YARMULKA
YACHTING	YAIRD	YANK	YARAK	YARMULKAS
YACHTINGS	YAIRDS	YANKED	YARAKS	YARMULKE
YACHTMAN	YAK	YANKEE	YARCO	YARMULKES
YACHTMEN	YAKHDAN	YANKEES	YARCOS	YARN
YACHTS	YAKHDANS	YANKER	YARD	YARNED
YACHTSMAN	YAKIMONO	YANKERS	YARDAGE	YARNER
YACHTSMEN	YAKIMONOS	YANKIE	YARDAGES	YARNERS
YACK	YAKITORI	YANKIES	YARDANG	YARNING
YACKA	YAKITORIS	YANKING	YARDANGS	YARNS
YACKAS	YAKKA	YANKS	YARDARM	YARPHA
YACKED	YAKKAS	YANQUI	YARDARMS	YARPHAS
YACKER	YAKKED	YANQUIS	YARDBIRD	YARR
YACKERS	YAKKER	YANTRA	YARDBIRDS	YARRAMAN
YACKING	YAKKERS	YANTRAS	YARDED	YARRAMANS
YACKS	YAKKING	YAOURT	YARDER	YARRAMEN
YAD	YAKOW	YAOURTS	YARDERS	YARRAN
YADS	YAKOWS	YAP	YARDING	YARRANS
YAE	YAKS	YAPOCK	YARDINGS	YARRED

YARRING	YAWMETER	YEAHS	YEASTS	YELLOWLY
YARROW	YAWMETERS	YEALDON	YEASTY	YELLOWS
YARROWS	YAWN	YEALDONS	YEBO	YELLOWY
YARRS	YAWNED	YEALING	YECCH	YELLS
YARTA	YAWNER	YEALINGS	YECCHS	YELM
YARTAS	YAWNERS	YEALM	YECH	YELMED
YARTO	YAWNIER	YEALMED	YECHIER	YELMING
YARTOS	YAWNIEST	YEALMING	YECHIEST	YELMS
YAS	YAWNING	YEALMS	YECHS	YELP
YASHMAC	YAWNINGLY	YEAN	YECHY	YELPED
YASHMACS	YAWNINGS	YEANED	YEDE	YELPER
YASHMAK	YAWNS	YEANING	YEDES	YELPERS
YASHMAKS	YAWNSOME	YEANLING	YEDING	YELPING
YASMAK	YAWNY	YEANLINGS	YEED	YELPINGS
YASMAKS	YAWP	YEANS	YEEDING	YELPS
YATAGAN	YAWPED	YEAR	YEEDS	YELT
YATAGANS	YAWPER	YEARBOOK	YEELIN	YELTS
YATAGHAN	YAWPERS	YEARBOOKS	YEELINS	YEMMER
YATAGHANS	YAWPING	YEARD	YEESH	YEMMERS
YATE	YAWPINGS	YEARDED	YEGG	YEN
YATES	YAWPS	YEARDING	YEGGMAN	YENNED
YATTER	YAWS	YEARDS	YEGGMEN	YENNING
YATTERED	YAWY	YEAREND	YEGGS	YENS
YATTERING	YAY	YEARENDS	YEH	YENTA
YATTERS	YAYS	YEARLIES	YELD	YENTAS
YAUD	YBET	YEARLING	YELDRING	YENTE
YAUDS	YBLENT	YEARLINGS	YELDRINGS	YENTES
YAULD	YBORE	YEARLONG	YELDROCK	YEOMAN
YAUP	YBOUND	YEARLY	YELDROCKS	YEOMANLY
YAUPED	YBOUNDEN	YEARN	YELK	YEOMANRY
YAUPER	YBRENT	YEARNED	YELKS	YEOMEN
YAUPERS	YCLAD	YEARNER	YELL	YEOW
YAUPING	YCLED	YEARNERS	YELLED	YEP
YAUPON	YCLEEPE	YEARNING	YELLER	YEPS
YAUPONS	YCLEEPED	YEARNINGS	YELLERS	YER
YAUPS	YCLEEPES	YEARNS	YELLING	YERBA
YAUTIA	YCLEEPING	YEARS	YELLINGS	YERBAS
YAUTIAS	YCLEPED	YEAS	YELLOCH	YERD
YAW	YCLEPT	YEASAYER	YELLOCHED	YERDED
YAWED	YCOND	YEASAYERS	YELLOCHS	YERDING
YAWEY	YDRAD	YEAST	YELLOW	YERDS
YAWIER	YDRED	YEASTED	YELLOWED	YERK
YAWIEST	YE	YEASTIER	YELLOWER	YERKED
YAWING	YEA	YEASTIEST	YELLOWEST	YERKING
YAWL	YEAD	YEASTILY	YELLOWFIN	YERKS
YAWLED	YEADING	YEASTING	YELLOWIER	YERSINIA
YAWLING	YEADS	YEASTLESS	YELLOWING	YERSINIAE
YAWLS	YEAH	YEASTLIKE	YELLOWISH	YERSINIAS

YES	YEX	YIPES	YOBBISH	YOGINI
YESES	YEXED	YIPPED	YOBBISHLY	YOGINIS
YESHIVA	YEXES	YIPPEE	YOBBISM	YOGINS
YESHIVAH	YEXING	YIPPER	YOBBISMS	YOGIS
YESHIVAHS	YEZ	YIPPERS	YOBBO	YOGISM
YESHIVAS	YFERE	YIPPIE	YOBBOES	YOGISMS
YESHIVOT	YFERES	YIPPIES	YOBBOS	YOGOURT
YESHIVOTH	YGLAUNST	YIPPING	YOBBY	YOGOURTS
YESK	YGO	YIPPY	YOBS	YOGURT
YESKED	YGOE	YIPS	YOCK	YOGURTS
YESKING	YIBBLES	YIRD	YOCKED	YOHIMBE
YESKS	YICKER	YIRDED	YOCKING	YOHIMBES
YESSED	YICKERED	YIRDING	YOCKS	YOHIMBINE
YESSES	YICKERING	YIRDS	YOD	YOICK
YESSING	YICKERS	YIRK	YODE	YOICKED
YESSIR	YID	YIRKED	YODEL	YOICKING
YESSIREE	YIDAKI	YIRKING	YODELED	YOICKS
YESSUM	YIDAKIS	YIRKS	YODELER	YOICKSED
YEST	YIDS	YIRR	YODELERS	YOICKSES
YESTER	YIELD	YIRRED	YODELING	YOICKSING
YESTERDAY	YIELDABLE	YIRRING	YODELINGS	YOJAN
YESTEREVE	YIELDED	YIRRS	YODELLED	YOJANA
YESTERN	YIELDER	YIRTH	YODELLER	YOJANAS
YESTREEN	YIELDERS	YIRTHS	YODELLERS	YOJANS
YESTREENS	YIELDING	YITE	YODELLING	YOK
YESTS	YIELDINGS	YITES	YODELS	YOKE
YESTY	YIELDS	YITIE	YODH	YOKED
YET	YIKE	YITIES	YODHS	YOKEL
YETI	YIKED	YITTEN	YODLE	YOKELESS
YETIS	YIKES	YLEM	YODLED	YOKELISH
YETT	YIKING	YLEMS	YODLER	YOKELS
YETTIE	YIKKER	YLIKE	YODLERS	YOKEMATE
YETTIES	YIKKERED	YLKE	YODLES	YOKEMATES
YETTS	YIKKERING	YLKES	YODLING	YOKER
YEUK	YIKKERS	YMOLT	YODS	YOKERED
YEUKED	YILL	YMOLTEN	YOGA	YOKERING
YEUKIER	YILLED	YMPE	YOGAS	YOKERS
YEUKIEST	YILLING	YMPES	YOGEE	YOKES
YEUKING	YILLS	YMPING	YOGEES	YOKING
YEUKS	YIN	YMPT	YOGH	YOKINGS
YEUKY	YINCE	YNAMBU	YOGHOURT	YOKKED
YEVE	YINDIE	YNAMBUS	YOGHOURTS	YOKKING
YEVEN	YINDIES	YO	YOGHS	YOKOZUNA
YEVES	YINGYANG	YOB	YOGHURT	YOKOZUNAS
YEVING	YINGYANGS	YOBBERIES	YOGHURTS	YOKS
YEW	YINS	YOBBERY	YOGI	YOKUL
YEWEN	YIP	YOBBIER	YOGIC	YOLD
YEWS	YIPE	YOBBIEST	YOGIN	YOLDRING

YOLDRINGS	YORPING	YOWE	YTTRIUM	YULAN
YOLK	YORPS	YOWED	YTTRIUMS	YULANS
YOLKED	YOTTABYTE	YOWES	YU	YULE
YOLKIER	YOU	YOWIE	YUAN	YULES
YOLKIEST	YOUK	YOWIES	YUANS	YULETIDE
YOLKLESS	YOUKED	YOWING	YUCA	YULETIDES
YOLKS	YOUKING	YOWL	YUCAS	YUM
YOLKY	YOUKS	YOWLED	YUCCA	YUMBERRY
YOM	YOUNG	YOWLER	YUCCAS	YUMMIER
YOMIM	YOUNGER	YOWLERS	YUCCH	YUMMIES
YOMP	YOUNGERS	YOWLEY	YUCH	YUMMIEST
YOMPED	YOUNGEST	YOWLEYS	YUCK	YUMMINESS
YOMPING	YOUNGISH	YOWLING	YUCKED	YUMMO
YOMPS	YOUNGLING	YOWLINGS	YUCKER	YUMMY
YON	YOUNGLY	YOWLS	YUCKERS	YUMP
YOND	YOUNGNESS	YOWS	YUCKIER	YUMPED
YONDER	YOUNGS	YOWZA	YUCKIEST	YUMPIE
YONDERLY	YOUNGSTER	YPERITE	YUCKINESS	YUMPIES
YONDERS	YOUNGTH	YPERITES	YUCKING	YUMPING
YONI	YOUNGTHLY	YPIGHT	YUCKO	YUMPS
YONIC	YOUNGTHS	YPLAST	YUCKS	YUNX
YONIS	YOUNKER	YPLIGHT	YUCKY	YUNXES
YONKER	YOUNKERS	YPSILOID	YUFT	YUP
YONKERS	YOUPON	YPSILON	YUFTS	YUPON
YONKS	YOUPONS	YPSILONS	YUG	YUPONS
YONNIE	YOUR	YRAPT	YUGA	YUPPIE
YONNIES	YOURN	YRAVISHED	YUGARIE	YUPPIEDOM
YONT	YOURS	YRENT	YUGARIES	YUPPIEISH
YOOF	YOURSELF	YRIVD	YUGAS	YUPPIES
YOOFS	YOURT	YRNEH	YUGS	YUPPIFIED
YOOP	YOURTS	YRNEHS	YUK	YUPPIFIES
YOOPS	YOUS	YSAME	YUKATA	YUPPIFY
YOPPER	YOUSE	YSHEND	YUKATAS	YUPPY
YOPPERS	YOUTH	YSHENDING	YUKE	YUPPYDOM
YORE	YOUTHEN	YSHENDS	YUKED	YUPPYDOMS
YORES	YOUTHENED	YSHENT	YUKES	YUPS
YORK	YOUTHENS	YSLAKED	YUKIER	YUPSTER
YORKED	YOUTHFUL	YTOST	YUKIEST	YUPSTERS
YORKER	YOUTHHEAD	YTTERBIA	YUKING	YURT
YORKERS	YOUTHHOOD	YTTERBIAS	YUKKED	YURTA
YORKIE	YOUTHIER	YTTERBIC	YUKKIER	YURTAS
YORKIES	YOUTHIEST	YTTERBITE	YUKKIEST	YURTS
YORKING	YOUTHLESS	YTTERBIUM	YUKKING	YUS
YORKS	YOUTHLY	YTTERBOUS	YUKKY	YUTZ
YORLING	YOUTHS	YTTRIA	YUKO	YUTZES
YORLINGS	YOUTHSOME	YTTRIAS	YUKOS	YUZU
YORP	YOUTHY	YTTRIC	YUKS	YUZUS
YORPED	YOW	YTTRIOUS	YUKY	YWIS
				YWROKE

Z

ZA	ZAIKAIS	ZANANA	ZAPS	ZEALLESS
ZABAIONE	ZAIRE	ZANANAS	ZAPTIAH	ZEALOT
ZABAIONES	ZAIRES	ZANDER	ZAPTIAHS	ZEALOTISM
ZABAJONE	ZAITECH	ZANDERS	ZAPTIEH	ZEALOTRY
ZABAJONES	ZAITECHS	ZANELLA	ZAPTIEHS	ZEALOTS
ZABETA	ZAKAT	ZANELLAS	ZARAPE	ZEALOUS
ZABETAS	ZAKATS	ZANIED	ZARAPES	ZEALOUSLY
ZABRA	ZAKOUSKA	ZANIER	ZARATITE	ZEALS
ZABRAS	ZAKOUSKI	ZANIES	ZARATITES	ZEAS
ZABTIEH	ZAKUSKA	ZANIEST	ZAREBA	ZEATIN
ZABTIEHS	ZAKUSKI	ZANILY	ZAREBAS	ZEATINS
ZACATON	ZAMAN	ZANINESS	ZAREEBA	ZEBEC
ZACATONS	ZAMANG	ZANJA	ZAREEBAS	ZEBECK
ZACK	ZAMANGS	ZANJAS	ZARF	ZEBECKS
ZACKS	ZAMANS	ZANJERO	ZARFS	ZEBECS
ZADDICK	ZAMARRA	ZANJEROS	ZARI	ZEBRA
ZADDICKS	ZAMARRAS	ZANTE	ZARIBA	ZEBRAFISH
ZADDIK	ZAMARRO	ZANTES	ZARIBAS	ZEBRAIC
ZADDIKIM	ZAMARROS	ZANTEWOOD	ZARIS	ZEBRANO
ZADDIKS	ZAMBO	ZANTHOXYL	ZARNEC	ZEBRANOS
ZAFFAR	ZAMBOMBA	ZANY	ZARNECS	ZEBRAS
ZAFFARS	ZAMBOMBAS	ZANYING	ZARNICH	ZEBRASS
ZAFFER	ZAMBOORAK	ZANYISH	ZARNICHS	ZEBRASSES
ZAFFERS	ZAMBOS	ZANYISM	ZARZUELA	ZEBRAWOOD
ZAFFIR	ZAMBUCK	ZANYISMS	ZARZUELAS	ZEBRINA
ZAFFIRS	ZAMBUCKS	ZANZA	ZAS	ZEBRINAS
ZAFFRE	ZAMBUK	ZANZAS	ZASTRUGA	ZEBRINE
ZAFFRES	ZAMBUKS	ZANZE	ZASTRUGI	ZEBRINES
ZAFTIG	ZAMIA	ZANZES	ZATI	ZEBRINNY
ZAG	ZAMIAS	ZAP	ZATIS	ZEBROID
ZAGGED	ZAMINDAR	ZAPATA	ZAX	ZEBRULA
ZAGGING	ZAMINDARI	ZAPATEADO	ZAXES	ZEBRULAS
ZAGS	ZAMINDARS	ZAPATEO	ZAYIN	ZEBRULE
ZAIBATSU	ZAMINDARY	ZAPATEOS	ZAYINS	ZEBRULES
ZAIBATSUS	ZAMOUSE	ZAPOTILLA	ZAZEN	ZEBU
ZAIDA	ZAMOUSES	ZAPPED	ZAZENS	ZEBUB
ZAIDAS	ZAMPOGNA	ZAPPER	ZE	ZEBUBS
ZAIDEH	ZAMPOGNAS	ZAPPERS	ZEA	ZEBUS
ZAIDEHS	ZAMPONE	ZAPPIER	ZEAL	ZECCHIN
ZAIDIES	ZAMPONI	ZAPPIEST	ZEALANT	ZECCHINE
ZAIDY	ZAMZAWED	ZAPPING	ZEALANTS	ZECCHINES
ZAIKAI	ZANAMIVIR	ZAPPY	ZEALFUL	ZECCHINI

ZECCHINO	ZENITHAL	ZETETICS	ZIKURATS	ZINDABAD
ZECCHINOS	ZENITHS	ZETTABYTE	ZILA	ZINE
ZECCHINS	ZENS	ZEUGMA	ZILAS	ZINEB
ZECHIN	ZEOLITE	ZEUGMAS	ZILCH	ZINEBS
ZECHINS	ZEOLITES	ZEUGMATIC	ZILCHES	ZINES
ZED	ZEOLITIC	ZEUXITE	ZILL	ZINFANDEL
ZEDA	ZEP	ZEUXITES	ZILLA	ZING
ZEDAS	ZEPHYR	ZEX	ZILLAH	ZINGANI
ZEDOARIES	ZEPHYRS	ZEXES	ZILLAHS	ZINGANO
ZEDOARY	ZEPPELIN	ZEZE	ZILLAS	ZINGARA
ZEDS	ZEPPELINS	ZEZES	ZILLION	ZINGARE
ZEE	ZEPPOLE	ZHO	ZILLIONS	ZINGARI
ZEES	ZEPPOLES	ZHOMO	ZILLIONTH	ZINGARO
ZEIN	ZEPPOLI	ZHOMOS	ZILLS	ZINGED
ZEINS	ZEPS	ZHOOSH	ZIMB	ZINGEL
ZEITGEBER	ZERDA	ZHOOSHED	ZIMBI	ZINGELS
ZEITGEIST	ZERDAS	ZHOOSHES	ZIMBIS	ZINGER
ZEREBA	ZEREBA	ZHOOSHING	ZIMBS	ZINGERS
ZEKS	ZEREBAS	ZHOS	ZIMOCCA	ZINGIBER
ZEL	ZERIBA	ZIBELINE	ZIMOCCAS	ZINGIBERS
ZELANT	ZERIBAS	ZIBELINES	ZIN	ZINGIER
ZELANTS	ZERK	ZIBELLINE	ZINC	ZINGIEST
ZELATOR	ZERKS	ZIBET	ZINCATE	ZINGING
ZELATORS	ZERO	ZIBETH	ZINCATES	ZINGS
ZELATRICE	ZEROED	ZIBETHS	ZINCED	ZINGY
ZELATRIX	ZEROES	ZIBETS	ZINCIC	ZINKE
ZELKOVA	ZEROING	ZIFF	ZINCIER	ZINKED
ZELKOVAS	ZEROS	ZIFFIUS	ZINCIEST	ZINKENITE
ZELOSO	ZEROTH	ZIFFIUSES	ZINCIFIED	ZINKES
ZELOTYPIA	ZERUMBET	ZIFFS	ZINCIFIES	ZINKIER
ZELS	ZERUMBETS	ZIG	ZINCIFY	ZINKIEST
ZEMINDAR	ZEST	ZIGAN	ZINCING	ZINKIFIED
ZEMINDARI	ZESTED	ZIGANKA	ZINCITE	ZINKIFIFS
ZEMINDARS	ZESTER	ZIGANKAS	ZINCITES	ZINKIFY
ZEMINDARY	ZESTERS	ZIGANS	ZINCKED	ZINKING
ZEMSTVA	ZESTFUL	ZIGGED	ZINCKIER	ZINKY
ZEMSTVO	ZESTFULLY	ZIGGING	ZINCKIEST	ZINNIA
ZEMSTVOS	ZESTIER	ZIGGURAT	ZINCKIFY	ZINNIAS
ZEN	ZESTIEST	ZIGGURATS	ZINCKING	ZINS
ZENAIDA	ZESTILY	ZIGS	ZINCKY	ZIP
ZENAIDAS	ZESTINESS	ZIGZAG	ZINCO	ZIPLESS
ZENANA	ZESTING	ZIGZAGGED	ZINCODE	ZIPLINE
ZENANAS	ZESTLESS	ZIGZAGGER	ZINCODES	ZIPLINES
ZENDIK	ZESTS	ZIGZAGGY	ZINCOID	ZIPLOCK
ZENDIKS	ZESTY	ZIGZAGS	ZINCOS	ZIPLOCKED
ZENDO	ZETA	ZIKKURAT	ZINCOUS	ZIPLOCKS
ZENDOS	ZETAS	ZIKKURATS	ZINCS	ZIPOLA
ZENITH	ZETETIC	ZIKURAT	ZINCY	ZIPOLAS

ZIPPED	ZIZZES	ZOIC	ZONOID	ZOOGRAFT
ZIPPER	ZIZZING	ZOISITE	ZONOIDS	ZOOGRAFTS
ZIPPERED	ZIZZLE	ZOISITES	ZONULA	ZOOGRAPHY
ZIPPERING	ZIZZLED	ZOISM	ZONULAE	ZOOID
ZIPPERS	ZIZZLES	ZOISMS	ZONULAR	ZOOIDAL
ZIPPIER	ZIZZLING	ZOIST	ZONULAS	ZOOIDS
ZIPPIEST	ZLOTE	ZOISTS	ZONULE	ZOOIER
ZIPPILY	ZLOTIES	ZOL	ZONULES	ZOOIEST
ZIPPINESS	ZLOTY	ZOLPIDEM	ZONULET	ZOOKEEPER
ZIPPING	ZLOTYCH	ZOLPIDEMS	ZONULETS	ZOOKS
ZIPPO	ZLOTYS	ZOLS	ZONURE	ZOOLATER
ZIPPOS	ZO	ZOMBI	ZONURES	ZOOLATERS
ZIPPY	ZOA	ZOMBIE	ZOO	ZOOLATRIA
ZIPS	ZOAEA	ZOMBIES	ZOOBIOTIC	ZOOLATRY
ZIPTOP	ZOAEAE	ZOMBIFIED	ZOOBLAST	ZOOLITE
ZIPWIRE	ZOAEAS	ZOMBIFIES	ZOOBLASTS	ZOOLITES
ZIPWIRES	ZOARIA	ZOMBIFY	ZOOCHORE	ZOOLITH
ZIRAM	ZOARIAL	ZOMBIISM	ZOOCHORES	ZOOLITHIC
ZIRAMS	ZOARIUM	ZOMBIISMS	ZOOCHORY	ZOOLITHS
ZIRCALLOY	ZOBO	ZOMBIS	ZOOCYTIA	ZOOLITIC
ZIRCALOY	ZOBOS	ZOMBOID	ZOOCYTIUM	ZOOLOGIC
ZIRCALOYS	ZOBU	ZOMBORUK	ZOOEA	ZOOLOGIES
ZIRCON	ZOBUS	ZOMBORUKS	ZOOEAE	ZOOLOGIST
ZIRCONIA	ZOCALO	ZONA	ZOOEAL	ZOOLOGY
ZIRCONIAS	ZOCALOS	ZONAE	ZOOEAS	ZOOM
ZIRCONIC	ZOCCO	ZONAL	ZOOECIA	ZOOMABLE
ZIRCONIUM	ZOCCOLO	ZONALLY	ZOOECIUM	ZOOMANCY
ZIRCONS	ZOCCOLOS	ZONARY	ZOOEY	ZOOMANIA
ZIT	ZOCCOS	ZONATE	ZOOGAMETE	ZOOMANIAS
ZITE	ZODIAC	ZONATED	ZOOGAMIES	ZOOMANTIC
ZITHER	ZODIACAL	ZONATION	ZOOGAMOUS	ZOOMED
ZITHERIST	ZODIACS	ZONATIONS	ZOOGAMY	ZOOMETRIC
ZITHERN	ZOEA	ZONDA	ZOOGENIC	ZOOMETRY
ZITHERNS	ZOEAE	ZONDAS	ZOOGENIES	ZOOMING
ZITHERS	ZOEAL	ZONE	ZOOGENOUS	ZOOMORPH
ZITI	ZOEAS	ZONED	ZOOGENY	ZOOMORPHS
ZITIS	ZOECHROME	ZONELESS	ZOOGLEA	ZOOMORPHY
ZITS	ZOECIA	ZONER	ZOOGLEAE	ZOOMS
ZIZ	ZOECIUM	ZONERS	ZOOGLEAL	ZOON
ZIZANIA	ZOEFORM	ZONES	ZOOGLEAS	ZOONAL
ZIZANIAS	ZOETIC	ZONETIME	ZOOGLOEA	ZOONED
ZIZEL	ZOETROPE	ZONETIMES	ZOOGLOEAE	ZOONIC
ZIZELS	ZOETROPES	ZONING	ZOOGLOEAL	ZOONING
ZIZIT	ZOETROPIC	ZONINGS	ZOOGLOEAS	ZOONITE
ZIZITH	ZOFTIG	ZONK	ZOOGLOEIC	ZOONITES
ZIZYPHUS	ZOIATRIA	ZONKED	ZOOGONIES	ZOONITIC
ZIZZ	ZOIATRIAS	ZONKING	ZOOGONOUS	ZOONOMIA
ZIZZED	ZOIATRICS	ZONKS	ZOOGONY	ZOONOMIAS

Z

ZOONOMIC	ZOOTAXIES	ZORILLO	ZUPANS	ZYLONITE
ZOONOMIES	ZOOTAXY	ZORILLOS	ZUPAS	ZYLONITES
ZOONOMIST	ZOOTECHNY	ZORILS	ZUPPA	ZYMASE
ZOONOMY	ZOOTHECIA	ZORINO	ZUPPAS	ZYMASES
ZOONOSES	ZOOTHEISM	ZORINOS	ZURF	ZYME
ZOONOSIS	ZOOTHOME	ZORIS	ZURFS	ZYMES
ZOONOTIC	ZOOTHOMES	ZORRO	ZUZ	ZYMIC
ZOONS	ZOOTIER	ZORROS	ZUZIM	ZYMITE
ZOOPATHY	ZOOTIEST	ZOS	ZUZZIM	ZYMITES
ZOOPERAL	ZOOTOMIC	ZOSTER	ZWANZIGER	ZYMOGEN
ZOOPERIES	ZOOTOMIES	ZOSTERS	ZWIEBACK	ZYMOGENE
ZOOPERIST	ZOOTOMIST	ZOUAVE	ZWIEBACKS	ZYMOGENES
ZOOPERY	ZOOTOMY	ZOUAVES	ZYDECO	ZYMOGENIC
ZOOPHAGAN	ZOOTOXIC	ZOUK	ZYDECOS	ZYMOGENS
ZOOPHAGY	ZOOTOXIN	ZOUKS	ZYGA	ZYMOGRAM
ZOOPHILE	ZOOTOXINS	ZOUNDS	ZYGAENID	ZYMOGRAMS
ZOOPHILES	ZOOTROPE	ZOWEE	ZYGAENOID	ZYMOID
ZOOPHILIA	ZOOTROPES	ZOWIE	ZYGAL	ZYMOLOGIC
ZOOPHILIC	ZOOTROPHY	ZOYSIA	ZYGANTRA	ZYMOLOGY
ZOOPHILY	ZOOTY	ZOYSIAS	ZYGANTRUM	ZYMOLYSES
ZOOPHOBE	ZOOTYPE	ZUCCHETTI	ZYGOCACTI	ZYMOLYSIS
ZOOPHOBES	ZOOTYPES	ZUCCHETTO	ZYGODONT	ZYMOLYTIC
ZOOPHOBIA	ZOOTYPIC	ZUCCHINI	ZYGOID	ZYMOME
ZOOPHORI	ZOOZOO	ZUCCHINIS	ZYGOMA	ZYMOMES
ZOOPHORIC	ZOOZOOS	ZUCHETTA	ZYGOMAS	ZYMOMETER
ZOOPHORUS	ZOPILOTE	ZUCHETTAS	ZYGOMATA	ZYMOSAN
ZOOPHYTE	ZOPILOTES	ZUCHETTO	ZYGOMATIC	ZYMOSANS
ZOOPHYTES	ZOPPA	ZUCHETTOS	ZYGON	ZYMOSES
ZOOPHYTIC	ZOPPO	ZUFFOLI	ZYGOPHYTE	ZYMOSIS
ZOOPLASTY	ZORBING	ZUFFOLO	ZYGOSE	ZYMOTIC
ZOOS	ZORBINGS	ZUFOLI	ZYGOSES	ZYMOTICS
ZOOSCOPIC	ZORBONAUT	ZUFOLO	ZYGOSIS	ZYMURGIES
ZOOSCOPY	ZORGITE	ZUFOLOS	ZYGOSITY	ZYMURGY
ZOOSPERM	ZORGITES	ZUGZWANG	ZYGOSPERM	ZYTHUM
ZOOSPERMS	ZORI	ZUGZWANGS	ZYGOSPORE	ZYTHUMS
ZOOSPORE	ZORIL	ZULU	ZYGOTE	ZYZZYVA
ZOOSPORES	ZORILLA	ZULUS	ZYGOTENE	ZYZZYVAS
ZOOSPORIC	ZORILLAS	ZUMBOORUK	ZYGOTENES	ZZZ
ZOOSTEROL	ZORILLE	ZUPA	ZYGOTES	ZZZS
ZOOT	ZORILLES	ZUPAN	ZYGOTIC	

Z

ten to fifteen letter words

A

AARDWOLVES	ABERDEVINES	ABJUNCTIONS	ABOMINATORS	ABROGATING
ABACTERIAL	ABERNETHIES	ABJURATION	ABONDANCES	ABROGATION
ABACTINALLY	ABERRANCES	ABJURATIONS	ABONNEMENT	ABROGATIONS
ABANDONEDLY	ABERRANCIES	ABLACTATION	ABONNEMENTS	ABROGATIVE
ABANDONEES	ABERRANTLY	ABLACTATIONS	ABORIGINAL	ABROGATORS
ABANDONERS	ABERRATING	ABLATITIOUS	ABORIGINALISM	ABRUPTIONS
ABANDONING	ABERRATION	ABLATIVELY	ABORIGINALISMS	ABRUPTNESS
ABANDONMENT	ABERRATIONAL	ABLUTIONARY	ABORIGINALITIES	ABRUPTNESSES
ABANDONMENTS	ABERRATIONS	ABLUTOMANE	ABORIGINALITY	ABSCESSING
ABANDONWARE	ABEYANCIES	ABLUTOMANES	ABORIGINALLY	ABSCINDING
ABANDONWARES	ABHOMINABLE	ABNEGATING	ABORIGINALS	ABSCISSINS
ABASEMENTS	ABHORRENCE	ABNEGATION	ABORIGINES	ABSCISSION
ABASHMENTS	ABHORRENCES	ABNEGATIONS	ABORTICIDE	ABSCISSIONS
ABATEMENTS	ABHORRENCIES	ABNEGATORS	ABORTICIDES	ABSCONDENCE
ABBOTSHIPS	ABHORRENCY	ABNORMALISM	ABORTIFACIENT	ABSCONDENCES
ABBREVIATE	ABHORRENTLY	ABNORMALISMS	ABORTIFACIENTS	ABSCONDERS
ABBREVIATED	ABHORRINGS	ABNORMALITIES	ABORTIONAL	ABSCONDING
ABBREVIATES	ABIOGENESES	ABNORMALITY	ABORTIONIST	ABSCONDINGS
ABBREVIATING	ABIOGENESIS	ABNORMALLY	ABORTIONISTS	ABSEILINGS
ABBREVIATION	ABIOGENETIC	ABNORMITIES	ABORTIVELY	ABSENTEEISM
ABBREVIATIONS	ABIOGENETICALLY	ABODEMENTS	ABORTIVENESS	ABSENTEEISMS
ABBREVIATOR	ABIOGENICALLY	ABOLISHABLE	ABORTIVENESSES	ABSENTMINDED
ABBREVIATORS	ABIOGENIST	ABOLISHERS	ABORTUARIES	ABSENTMINDEDLY
ABBREVIATORY	ABIOGENISTS	ABOLISHING	ABOVEBOARD	ABSINTHIATED
ABBREVIATURE	ABIOLOGICAL	ABOLISHMENT	ABOVEGROUND	ABSINTHISM
ABBREVIATURES	ABIOTICALLY	ABOLISHMENTS	ABRACADABRA	ABSINTHISMS
ABCOULOMBS	ABIOTROPHIC	ABOLITIONAL	ABRACADABRAS	ABSOLUTELY
ABDICATING	ABIOTROPHIES	ABOLITIONARY	ABRANCHIAL	ABSOLUTENESS
ABDICATION	ABIOTROPHY	ABOLITIONISM	ABRANCHIATE	ABSOLUTENESSES
ABDICATIONS	ABIRRITANT	ABOLITIONISMS	ABRASIVELY	ABSOLUTEST
ABDICATIVE	ABIRRITANTS	ABOLITIONIST	ABRASIVENESS	ABSOLUTION
ABDICATORS	ABIRRITATE	ABOLITIONISTS	ABRASIVENESSES	ABSOLUTIONS
ABDOMINALLY	ABIRRITATED	ABOLITIONS	ABREACTING	ABSOLUTISE
ABDOMINALS	ABIRRITATES	ABOMINABLE	ABREACTION	ABSOLUTISED
ABDOMINOPLASTY	ABIRRITATING	ABOMINABLENESS	ABREACTIONS	ABSOLUTISES
ABDOMINOUS	ABITURIENT	ABOMINABLY	ABREACTIVE	ABSOLUTISING
ABDUCENTES	ABITURIENTS	ABOMINATED	ABRIDGABLE	ABSOLUTISM
ABDUCTIONS	ABJECTIONS	ABOMINATES	ABRIDGEABLE	ABSOLUTISMS
ABDUCTORES	ABJECTNESS	ABOMINATING	ABRIDGEMENT	ABSOLUTIST
ABECEDARIAN	ABJECTNESSES	ABOMINATION	ABRIDGEMENTS	ABSOLUTISTIC
ABECEDARIANS	ABJOINTING	ABOMINATIONS	ABRIDGMENT	ABSOLUTISTS
ABERDEVINE	ABJUNCTION	ABOMINATOR	ABRIDGMENTS	ABSOLUTIVE

ABSOLUTIVES	ABSTENTIONIST	ABSTRUSITY	ACATALEPTIC	ACCEPTEDLY
ABSOLUTIZE	ABSTENTIONISTS	ABSURDISMS	ACATALEPTICS	ACCEPTILATION
ABSOLUTIZED	ABSTENTIONS	ABSURDISTS	ACATAMATHESIA	ACCEPTILATIONS
ABSOLUTIZES	ABSTENTIOUS	ABSURDITIES	ACATAMATHESIAS	ACCEPTINGLY
ABSOLUTIZING	ABSTERGENT	ABSURDNESS	ACATHISIAS	ACCEPTINGNESS
ABSOLUTORY	ABSTERGENTS	ABSURDNESSES	ACAULESCENT	ACCEPTINGNESSES
ABSOLVABLE	ABSTERGING	ABUNDANCES	ACCEDENCES	ACCEPTIVITIES
ABSOLVENTS	ABSTERSION	ABUNDANCIES	ACCELERABLE	ACCEPTIVITY
ABSOLVITOR	ABSTERSIONS	ABUNDANTLY	ACCELERANDO	ACCESSARIES
ABSOLVITORS	ABSTERSIVE	ABUSIVENESS	ACCELERANDOS	ACCESSARILY
ABSORBABILITIES	ABSTERSIVES	ABUSIVENESSES	ACCELERANT	ACCESSARINESS
ABSORBABILITY	ABSTINENCE	ABYSSOPELAGIC	ACCELERANTS	ACCESSARINESSES
ABSORBABLE	ABSTINENCES	ACADEMICAL	ACCELERATE	ACCESSIBILITIES
ABSORBANCE	ABSTINENCIES	ACADEMICALISM	ACCELERATED	ACCESSIBILITY
ABSORBANCES	ABSTINENCY	ACADEMICALISMS	ACCELERATES	ACCESSIBLE
ABSORBANCIES	ABSTINENTLY	ACADEMICALLY	ACCELERATING	ACCESSIBLENESS
ABSORBANCY	ABSTRACTABLE	ACADEMICALS	ACCELERATINGLY	ACCESSIBLY
ABSORBANTS	ABSTRACTED	ACADEMICIAN	ACCELERATION	ACCESSIONAL
ABSORBATES	ABSTRACTEDLY	ACADEMICIANS	ACCELERATIONS	ACCESSIONED
ABSORBEDLY	ABSTRACTEDNESS	ACADEMICISM	ACCELERATIVE	ACCESSIONING
ABSORBEFACIENT	ABSTRACTER	ACADEMICISMS	ACCELERATOR	ACCESSIONS
ABSORBEFACIENTS	ABSTRACTERS	ACADEMISMS	ACCELERATORS	ACCESSORIAL
ABSORBENCIES	ABSTRACTEST	ACADEMISTS	ACCELERATORY	ACCESSORIES
ABSORBENCY	ABSTRACTING	ACALCULIAS	ACCELEROMETER	ACCESSORII
ABSORBENTS	ABSTRACTION	ACALEPHANS	ACCELEROMETERS	ACCESSORILY
ABSORBINGLY	ABSTRACTIONAL	ACANACEOUS	ACCENSIONS	ACCESSORINESS
ABSORPTANCE	ABSTRACTIONISM	ACANTHACEOUS	ACCENTLESS	ACCESSORINESSES
ABSORPTANCES	ABSTRACTIONISMS	ACANTHOCEPHALAN	ACCENTUALITIES	ACCESSORISE
ABSORPTIOMETER	ABSTRACTIONIST	ACANTHUSES	ACCENTUALITY	ACCESSORISED
ABSORPTIOMETERS	ABSTRACTIONISTS	ACARICIDAL	ACCENTUALLY	ACCESSORISES
ABSORPTION	ABSTRACTIONS	ACARICIDES	ACCENTUATE	ACCESSORISING
ABSORPTIONS	ABSTRACTIVE	ACARIDEANS	ACCENTUATED	ACCESSORIUS
ABSORPTIVE	ABSTRACTIVELY	ACARIDIANS	ACCENTUATES	ACCESSORIZE
ABSORPTIVENESS	ABSTRACTIVES	ACARIDOMATIA	ACCENTUATING	ACCESSORIZED
ABSORPTIVITIES	ABSTRACTLY	ACARIDOMATIUM	ACCENTUATION	ACCESSORIZES
ABSORPTIVITY	ABSTRACTNESS	ACARODOMATIA	ACCENTUATIONS	ACCESSORIZING
ABSQUATULATE	ABSTRACTNESSES	ACARODOMATIUM	ACCEPTABILITIES	ACCIACCATURA
ABSQUATULATED	ABSTRACTOR	ACAROLOGIES	ACCEPTABILITY	ACCIACCATURAS
ABSQUATULATES	ABSTRACTORS	ACAROLOGIST	ACCEPTABLE	ACCIACCATURE
ABSQUATULATING	ABSTRICTED	ACAROLOGISTS	ACCEPTABLENESS	ACCIDENCES
ABSTAINERS	ABSTRICTING	ACAROPHILIES	ACCEPTABLY	ACCIDENTAL
ABSTAINING	ABSTRICTION	ACAROPHILY	ACCEPTANCE	ACCIDENTALISM
ABSTEMIOUS	ABSTRICTIONS	ACARPELLOUS	ACCEPTANCES	ACCIDENTALISMS
ABSTEMIOUSLY	ABSTRUSELY	ACARPELOUS	ACCEPTANCIES	ACCIDENTALITIES
ABSTEMIOUSNESS	ABSTRUSENESS	ACATALECTIC	ACCEPTANCY	ACCIDENTALITY
ABSTENTION	ABSTRUSENESSES	ACATALECTICS	ACCEPTANTS	ACCIDENTALLY
ABSTENTIONISM	ABSTRUSEST	ACATALEPSIES	ACCEPTATION	ACCIDENTALNESS
ABSTENTIONISMS	ABSTRUSITIES	ACATALEPSY	ACCEPTATIONS	ACCIDENTALS

ACCIDENTED	ACCOMMODATIONAL	ACCOUCHEUSES	ACCULTURATIONAL	ACERVATION
ACCIDENTLY	ACCOMMODATIONS	ACCOUNTABILITY	ACCULTURATIONS	ACERVATIONS
ACCIDENTOLOGIES	ACCOMMODATIVE	ACCOUNTABLE	ACCULTURATIVE	ACESCENCES
ACCIDENTOLOGY	ACCOMMODATOR	ACCOUNTABLENESS	ACCUMBENCIES	ACESCENCIES
ACCIPITERS	ACCOMMODATORS	ACCOUNTABLY	ACCUMBENCY	ACETABULAR
ACCIPITRAL	ACCOMPANIED	ACCOUNTANCIES	ACCUMULABLE	ACETABULUM
ACCIPITRINE	ACCOMPANIER	ACCOUNTANCY	ACCUMULATE	ACETABULUMS
ACCIPITRINES	ACCOMPANIERS	ACCOUNTANT	ACCUMULATED	ACETALDEHYDE
ACCLAIMERS	ACCOMPANIES	ACCOUNTANTS	ACCUMULATES	ACETALDEHYDES
ACCLAIMING	ACCOMPANIMENT	ACCOUNTANTSHIP	ACCUMULATING	ACETAMIDES
ACCLAMATION	ACCOMPANIMENTS	ACCOUNTANTSHIPS	ACCUMULATION	ACETAMINOPHEN
ACCLAMATIONS	ACCOMPANIST	ACCOUNTING	ACCUMULATIONS	ACETAMINOPHENS
ACCLAMATORY	ACCOMPANISTS	ACCOUNTINGS	ACCUMULATIVE	ACETANILID
ACCLIMATABLE	ACCOMPANYING	ACCOUPLEMENT	ACCUMULATIVELY	ACETANILIDE
ACCLIMATATION	ACCOMPANYIST	ACCOUPLEMENTS	ACCUMULATOR	ACETANILIDES
ACCLIMATATIONS	ACCOMPANYISTS	ACCOURAGED	ACCUMULATORS	ACETANILIDS
ACCLIMATED	ACCOMPLICE	ACCOURAGES	ACCURACIES	ACETAZOLAMIDE
ACCLIMATES	ACCOMPLICES	ACCOURAGING	ACCURATELY	ACETAZOLAMIDES
ACCLIMATING	ACCOMPLISH	ACCOURTING	ACCURATENESS	ACETIFICATION
ACCLIMATION	ACCOMPLISHABLE	ACCOUSTREMENT	ACCURATENESSES	ACETIFICATIONS
ACCLIMATIONS	ACCOMPLISHED	ACCOUSTREMENTS	ACCURSEDLY	ACETIFIERS
ACCLIMATISABLE	ACCOMPLISHER	ACCOUTERED	ACCURSEDNESS	ACETIFYING
ACCLIMATISATION	ACCOMPLISHERS	ACCOUTERING	ACCURSEDNESSES	ACETOACETIC
ACCLIMATISE	ACCOMPLISHES	ACCOUTERMENT	ACCUSATION	ACETOMETER
ACCLIMATISED	ACCOMPLISHING	ACCOUTERMENTS	ACCUSATIONS	ACETOMETERS
ACCLIMATISER	ACCOMPLISHMENT	ACCOUTREMENT	ACCUSATIVAL	ACETONAEMIA
ACCLIMATISERS	ACCOMPLISHMENTS	ACCOUTREMENTS	ACCUSATIVE	ACETONAEMIAS
ACCLIMATISES	ACCOMPTABLE	ACCOUTRING	ACCUSATIVELY	ACETONEMIA
ACCLIMATISING	ACCOMPTANT	ACCREDITABLE	ACCUSATIVES	ACETONEMIAS
ACCLIMATIZABLE	ACCOMPTANTS	ACCREDITATION	ACCUSATORIAL	ACETONITRILE
ACCLIMATIZATION	ACCOMPTING	ACCREDITATIONS	ACCUSATORY	ACETONITRILES
ACCLIMATIZE	ACCORAGING	ACCREDITED	ACCUSEMENT	ACETONURIA
ACCLIMATIZED	ACCORDABLE	ACCREDITING	ACCUSEMENTS	ACETONURIAS
ACCLIMATIZER	ACCORDANCE	ACCRESCENCE	ACCUSINGLY	ACETOPHENETIDIN
ACCLIMATIZERS	ACCORDANCES	ACCRESCENCES	ACCUSTOMARY	ACETYLATED
ACCLIMATIZES	ACCORDANCIES	ACCRESCENT	ACCUSTOMATION	ACETYLATES
ACCLIMATIZING	ACCORDANCY	ACCRETIONARY	ACCUSTOMATIONS	ACETYLATING
ACCLIVITIES	ACCORDANTLY	ACCRETIONS	ACCUSTOMED	ACETYLATION
ACCLIVITOUS	ACCORDINGLY	ACCRUEMENT	ACCUSTOMEDNESS	ACETYLATIONS
ACCOASTING	ACCORDIONIST	ACCRUEMENTS	ACCUSTOMING	ACETYLATIVE
ACCOLADING	ACCORDIONISTS	ACCUBATION	ACCUSTREMENT	ACETYLCHOLINE
ACCOMMODABLE	ACCORDIONS	ACCUBATIONS	ACCUSTREMENTS	ACETYLCHOLINES
ACCOMMODATE	ACCOSTABLE	ACCULTURAL	ACEPHALOUS	ACETYLENES
ACCOMMODATED	ACCOUCHEMENT	ACCULTURATE	ACERACEOUS	ACETYLENIC
ACCOMMODATES	ACCOUCHEMENTS	ACCULTURATED	ACERBATING	ACETYLIDES
ACCOMMODATING	ACCOUCHEUR	ACCULTURATES	ACERBICALLY	ACETYLSALICYLIC
ACCOMMODATINGLY	ACCOUCHEURS	ACCULTURATING	ACERBITIES	ACHAENIUMS
ACCOMMODATION	ACCOUCHEUSE	ACCULTURATION	ACERVATELY	ACHAENOCARP

ACHAENOCARPS

ACHAENOCARPS	ACIDIMETERS	ACOTYLEDON	ACRIFLAVINS	ACROTERION
ACHALASIAS	ACIDIMETRIC	ACOTYLEDONOUS	ACRIMONIES	ACROTERIUM
ACHIEVABLE	ACIDIMETRICAL	ACOTYLEDONS	ACRIMONIOUS	ACRYLAMIDE
ACHIEVEMENT	ACIDIMETRICALLY	ACOUSTICAL	ACRIMONIOUSLY	ACRYLAMIDES
ACHIEVEMENTS	ACIDIMETRIES	ACOUSTICALLY	ACRIMONIOUSNESS	ACRYLONITRILE
ACHINESSES	ACIDIMETRY	ACOUSTICIAN	ACRITARCHS	ACRYLONITRILES
ACHLAMYDEOUS	ACIDNESSES	ACOUSTICIANS	ACROAMATIC	ACTABILITIES
ACHLORHYDRIA	ACIDOMETER	ACQUAINTANCE	ACROAMATICAL	ACTABILITY
ACHLORHYDRIAS	ACIDOMETERS	ACQUAINTANCES	ACROBATICALLY	ACTINICALLY
ACHLORHYDRIC	ACIDOPHILE	ACQUAINTED	ACROBATICS	ACTINIFORM
ACHONDRITE	ACIDOPHILES	ACQUAINTING	ACROBATISM	ACTINOBACILLI
ACHONDRITES	ACIDOPHILIC	ACQUIESCED	ACROBATISMS	ACTINOBACILLUS
ACHONDRITIC	ACIDOPHILOUS	ACQUIESCENCE	ACROCARPOUS	ACTINOBIOLOGIES
ACHONDROPLASIA	ACIDOPHILS	ACQUIESCENCES	ACROCENTRIC	ACTINOBIOLOGY
ACHONDROPLASIAS	ACIDOPHILUS	ACQUIESCENT	ACROCENTRICS	ACTINOCHEMISTRY
ACHONDROPLASTIC	ACIDOPHILUSES	ACQUIESCENTLY	ACROCYANOSES	ACTINOLITE
ACHROMATIC	ACIDULATED	ACQUIESCENTS	ACROCYANOSIS	ACTINOLITES
ACHROMATICALLY	ACIDULATES	ACQUIESCES	ACRODROMOUS	ACTINOMERE
ACHROMATICITIES	ACIDULATING	ACQUIESCING	ACROGENOUS	ACTINOMERES
ACHROMATICITY	ACIDULATION	ACQUIESCINGLY	ACROGENOUSLY	ACTINOMETER
ACHROMATIN	ACIDULATIONS	ACQUIGHTING	ACROLITHIC	ACTINOMETERS
ACHROMATINS	ACIERATING	ACQUIRABILITIES	ACROMEGALIC	ACTINOMETRIC
ACHROMATISATION	ACIERATION	ACQUIRABILITY	ACROMEGALICS	ACTINOMETRICAL
ACHROMATISE	ACIERATIONS	ACQUIRABLE	ACROMEGALIES	ACTINOMETRIES
ACHROMATISED	ACINACEOUS	ACQUIREMENT	ACROMEGALY	ACTINOMETRY
ACHROMATISES	ACINACIFORM	ACQUIREMENTS	ACRONICALLY	ACTINOMORPHIC
ACHROMATISING	ACINETOBACTER	ACQUISITION	ACRONYCALLY	ACTINOMORPHIES
ACHROMATISM	ACINETOBACTERS	ACQUISITIONAL	ACRONYCHAL	ACTINOMORPHOUS
ACHROMATISMS	ACKNOWLEDGE	ACQUISITIONS	ACRONYCHALLY	ACTINOMORPHY
ACHROMATIZATION	ACKNOWLEDGEABLE	ACQUISITIVE	ACRONYMANIA	ACTINOMYCES
ACHROMATIZE	ACKNOWLEDGEABLY	ACQUISITIVELY	ACRONYMANIAS	ACTINOMYCETE
ACHROMATIZED	ACKNOWLEDGED	ACQUISITIVENESS	ACRONYMICALLY	ACTINOMYCETES
ACHROMATIZES	ACKNOWLEDGEDLY	ACQUISITOR	ACRONYMOUS	ACTINOMYCETOUS
ACHROMATIZING	ACKNOWLEDGEMENT	ACQUISITORS	ACROPARESTHESIA	ACTINOMYCIN
ACHROMATOPSIA	ACKNOWLEDGER	ACQUITMENT	ACROPETALLY	ACTINOMYCINS
ACHROMATOPSIAS	ACKNOWLEDGERS	ACQUITMENTS	ACROPHOBES	ACTINOMYCOSES
ACHROMATOUS	ACKNOWLEDGES	ACQUITTALS	ACROPHOBIA	ACTINOMYCOSIS
ACICLOVIRS	ACKNOWLEDGING	ACQUITTANCE	ACROPHOBIAS	ACTINOMYCOTIC
ACICULATED	ACKNOWLEDGMENT	ACQUITTANCED	ACROPHOBIC	ACTINOPODS
ACIDANTHERA	ACKNOWLEDGMENTS	ACQUITTANCES	ACROPHOBICS	ACTINOTHERAPIES
ACIDANTHERAS	ACOELOMATE	ACQUITTANCING	ACROPHONETIC	ACTINOTHERAPY
ACIDICALLY	ACOELOMATES	ACQUITTERS	ACROPHONIC	ACTINOURANIUM
ACIDIFIABLE	ACOLOUTHIC	ACQUITTING	ACROPHONIES	ACTINOURANIUMS
ACIDIFICATION	ACOLOUTHITE	ACRIDITIES	ACROPOLISES	ACTINOZOAN
ACIDIFICATIONS	ACOLOUTHITES	ACRIDNESSES	ACROSPIRES	ACTINOZOANS
ACIDIFIERS	ACOLOUTHOS	ACRIFLAVIN	ACROSTICAL	ACTIONABLE
ACIDIFYING	ACOLOUTHOSES	ACRIFLAVINE	ACROSTICALLY	ACTIONABLY
ACIDIMETER	ACONITINES	ACRIFLAVINES	ACROTERIAL	ACTIONISTS

ACTIONLESS	ADAMANTEAN	ADDUCEABLE	ADIATHERMANCIES	ADMEASURED
ACTIVATING	ADAMANTINE	ADDUCTIONS	ADIATHERMANCY	ADMEASUREMENT
ACTIVATION	ADAPTABILITIES	ADELANTADO	ADIATHERMANOUS	ADMEASUREMENTS
ACTIVATIONS	ADAPTABILITY	ADELANTADOS	ADIATHERMIC	ADMEASURES
ACTIVATORS	ADAPTABLENESS	ADEMPTIONS	ADIPOCERES	ADMEASURING
ACTIVENESS	ADAPTABLENESSES	ADENECTOMIES	ADIPOCEROUS	ADMINICLES
ACTIVENESSES	ADAPTATION	ADENECTOMY	ADIPOCYTES	ADMINICULAR
ACTIVISING	ADAPTATIONAL	ADENITISES	ADIPOSITIES	ADMINICULATE
ACTIVISTIC	ADAPTATIONALLY	ADENOCARCINOMA	ADJACENCES	ADMINICULATED
ACTIVITIES	ADAPTATIONS	ADENOCARCINOMAS	ADJACENCIES	ADMINICULATES
ACTIVIZING	ADAPTATIVE	ADENOHYPOPHYSES	ADJACENTLY	ADMINICULATING
ACTOMYOSIN	ADAPTEDNESS	ADENOHYPOPHYSIS	ADJECTIVAL	ADMINISTER
ACTOMYOSINS	ADAPTEDNESSES	ADENOIDECTOMIES	ADJECTIVALLY	ADMINISTERED
ACTORLIEST	ADAPTIVELY	ADENOIDECTOMY	ADJECTIVELY	ADMINISTERING
ACTRESSIER	ADAPTIVENESS	ADENOMATOUS	ADJECTIVES	ADMINISTERS
ACTRESSIEST	ADAPTIVENESSES	ADENOPATHIES	ADJOURNING	ADMINISTRABLE
ACTUALISATION	ADAPTIVITIES	ADENOPATHY	ADJOURNMENT	ADMINISTRANT
ACTUALISATIONS	ADAPTIVITY	ADENOSINES	ADJOURNMENTS	ADMINISTRANTS
ACTUALISED	ADAPTOGENIC	ADENOVIRAL	ADJUDGEMENT	ADMINISTRATE
ACTUALISES	ADAPTOGENS	ADENOVIRUS	ADJUDGEMENTS	ADMINISTRATED
ACTUALISING	ADDERBEADS	ADENOVIRUSES	ADJUDGMENT	ADMINISTRATES
ACTUALISTS	ADDERSTONE	ADENYLATES	ADJUDGMENTS	ADMINISTRATING
ACTUALITES	ADDERSTONES	ADEPTNESSES	ADJUDICATE	ADMINISTRATION
ACTUALITIES	ADDERWORTS	ADEQUACIES	ADJUDICATED	ADMINISTRATIONS
ACTUALIZATION	ADDICTEDNESS	ADEQUATELY	ADJUDICATES	ADMINISTRATIVE
ACTUALIZATIONS	ADDICTEDNESSES	ADEQUATENESS	ADJUDICATING	ADMINISTRATOR
ACTUALIZED	ADDICTIONS	ADEQUATENESSES	ADJUDICATION	ADMINISTRATORS
ACTUALIZES	ADDICTIVENESS	ADEQUATIVE	ADJUDICATIONS	ADMINISTRATRIX
ACTUALIZING	ADDICTIVENESSES	ADHERENCES	ADJUDICATIVE	ADMIRABILITIES
ACTUARIALLY	ADDITAMENT	ADHERENTLY	ADJUDICATOR	ADMIRABILITY
ACTUATIONS	ADDITAMENTS	ADHESIONAL	ADJUDICATORS	ADMIRABLENESS
ACUMINATED	ADDITIONAL	ADHESIVELY	ADJUDICATORY	ADMIRABLENESSES
ACUMINATES	ADDITIONALITIES	ADHESIVENESS	ADJUNCTION	ADMIRALSHIP
ACUMINATING	ADDITIONALITY	ADHESIVENESSES	ADJUNCTIONS	ADMIRALSHIPS
ACUMINATION	ADDITIONALLY	ADHIBITING	ADJUNCTIVE	ADMIRALTIES
ACUMINATIONS	ADDITITIOUS	ADHIBITION	ADJUNCTIVELY	ADMIRANCES
ACUPRESSURE	ADDITIVELY	ADHIBITIONS	ADJURATION	ADMIRATION
ACUPRESSURES	ADDITIVITIES	ADHOCRACIES	ADJURATIONS	ADMIRATIONS
ACUPUNCTURAL	ADDITIVITY	ADIABATICALLY	ADJURATORY	ADMIRATIVE
ACUPUNCTURE	ADDLEMENTS	ADIABATICS	ADJUSTABILITIES	ADMIRAUNCE
ACUPUNCTURES	ADDLEPATED	ADIACTINIC	ADJUSTABILITY	ADMIRAUNCES
ACUPUNCTURIST	ADDRESSABILITY	ADIAPHORISM	ADJUSTABLE	ADMIRINGLY
ACUPUNCTURISTS	ADDRESSABLE	ADIAPHORISMS	ADJUSTABLY	ADMISSIBILITIES
ACUTENESSES	ADDRESSEES	ADIAPHORIST	ADJUSTMENT	ADMISSIBILITY
ACYCLOVIRS	ADDRESSERS	ADIAPHORISTIC	ADJUSTMENTAL	ADMISSIBLE
ACYLATIONS	ADDRESSING	ADIAPHORISTS	ADJUSTMENTS	ADMISSIBLENESS
ADACTYLOUS	ADDRESSINGS	ADIAPHORON	ADJUTANCIES	ADMISSIONS
ADAMANCIES	ADDRESSORS	ADIAPHOROUS	ADJUVANCIES	ADMITTABLE

ADMITTANCE	ADRENALIZED	ADULTERIZE	ADVENTURISTIC	ADVERTIZINGS
ADMITTANCES	ADRENERGIC	ADULTERIZED	ADVENTURISTS	ADVERTORIAL
ADMITTEDLY	ADRENERGICALLY	ADULTERIZES	ADVENTUROUS	ADVERTORIALS
ADMIXTURES	ADRENOCEPTOR	ADULTERIZING	ADVENTUROUSLY	ADVISABILITIES
ADMONISHED	ADRENOCEPTORS	ADULTEROUS	ADVENTUROUSNESS	ADVISABILITY
ADMONISHER	ADRENOCHROME	ADULTEROUSLY	ADVERBIALISE	ADVISABLENESS
ADMONISHERS	ADRENOCHROMES	ADULTESCENT	ADVERBIALISED	ADVISABLENESSES
ADMONISHES	ADRENOCORTICAL	ADULTESCENTS	ADVERBIALISES	ADVISATORY
ADMONISHING	ADRIAMYCIN	ADULTHOODS	ADVERBIALISING	ADVISEDNESS
ADMONISHINGLY	ADRIAMYCINS	ADULTNESSES	ADVERBIALIZE	ADVISEDNESSES
ADMONISHMENT	ADROITNESS	ADULTRESSES	ADVERBIALIZED	ADVISEMENT
ADMONISHMENTS	ADROITNESSES	ADUMBRATED	ADVERBIALIZES	ADVISEMENTS
ADMONITION	ADSCITITIOUS	ADUMBRATES	ADVERBIALIZING	ADVISERSHIP
ADMONITIONS	ADSCITITIOUSLY	ADUMBRATING	ADVERBIALLY	ADVISERSHIPS
ADMONITIVE	ADSCRIPTION	ADUMBRATION	ADVERBIALS	ADVISORATE
ADMONITORILY	ADSCRIPTIONS	ADUMBRATIONS	ADVERGAMING	ADVISORATES
ADMONITORS	ADSORBABILITIES	ADUMBRATIVE	ADVERGAMINGS	ADVISORIES
ADMONITORY	ADSORBABILITY	ADUMBRATIVELY	ADVERSARIA	ADVOCACIES
ADNOMINALS	ADSORBABLE	ADUNCITIES	ADVERSARIAL	ADVOCATING
ADOLESCENCE	ADSORBATES	ADVANCEMENT	ADVERSARIES	ADVOCATION
ADOLESCENCES	ADSORBENTS	ADVANCEMENTS	ADVERSARINESS	ADVOCATIONS
ADOLESCENT	ADSORPTION	ADVANCINGLY	ADVERSARINESSES	ADVOCATIVE
ADOLESCENTLY	ADSORPTIONS	ADVANTAGEABLE	ADVERSATIVE	ADVOCATORS
ADOLESCENTS	ADSORPTIVE	ADVANTAGED	ADVERSATIVELY	ADVOCATORY
ADOPTABILITIES	ADULARESCENCE	ADVANTAGEOUS	ADVERSATIVES	ADVOUTRERS
ADOPTABILITY	ADULARESCENCES	ADVANTAGEOUSLY	ADVERSENESS	ADVOUTRIES
ADOPTIANISM	ADULARESCENT	ADVANTAGES	ADVERSENESSES	AECIDIOSPORE
ADOPTIANISMS	ADULATIONS	ADVANTAGING	ADVERSITIES	AECIDIOSPORES
ADOPTIANIST	ADULTERANT	ADVECTIONS	ADVERTENCE	AECIDOSPORE
ADOPTIANISTS	ADULTERANTS	ADVENTITIA	ADVERTENCES	AECIDOSPORES
ADOPTIONISM	ADULTERATE	ADVENTITIAL	ADVERTENCIES	AECIOSPORE
ADOPTIONISMS	ADULTERATED	ADVENTITIAS	ADVERTENCY	AECIOSPORES
ADOPTIONIST	ADULTERATES	ADVENTITIOUS	ADVERTED	AEDILESHIP
ADOPTIONISTS	ADULTERATING	ADVENTITIOUSLY	ADVERTENTLY	AEDILESHIPS
ADOPTIVELY	ADULTERATION	ADVENTIVES	ADVERTISED	AEOLIPILES
ADORABILITIES	ADULTERATIONS	ADVENTURED	ADVERTISEMENT	AEOLIPYLES
ADORABILITY	ADULTERATOR	ADVENTUREFUL	ADVERTISEMENTS	AEOLOTROPIC
ADORABLENESS	ADULTERATORS	ADVENTURER	ADVERTISER	AEOLOTROPIES
ADORABLENESSES	ADULTERERS	ADVENTURERS	ADVERTISERS	AEOLOTROPY
ADORATIONS	ADULTERESS	ADVENTURES	ADVERTISES	AEPYORNISES
ADORNMENTS	ADULTERESSES	ADVENTURESOME	ADVERTISING	AERENCHYMA
ADPRESSING	ADULTERIES	ADVENTURESS	ADVERTISINGS	AERENCHYMAS
ADRENALECTOMIES	ADULTERINE	ADVENTURESSES	ADVERTIZED	AERENCHYMATOUS
ADRENALECTOMY	ADULTERINES	ADVENTURING	ADVERTIZEMENT	AERIALISTS
ADRENALINE	ADULTERISE	ADVENTURINGS	ADVERTIZEMENTS	AERIALITIES
ADRENALINES	ADULTERISED	ADVENTURISM	ADVERTIZER	AERIFICATION
ADRENALINS	ADULTERISES	ADVENTURISMS	ADVERTIZERS	AERIFICATIONS
ADRENALISED	ADULTERISING	ADVENTURIST	ADVERTIZES	AEROACOUSTICS

AEROBALLISTICS	AEROGRAPHS	AEROPLANKTONS	AESTHETICISMS	AFFECTIVITY
AEROBATICS	AEROGRAPHY	AEROPULSES	AESTHETICIST	AFFECTLESS
AEROBICALLY	AEROHYDROPLANE	AEROSCOPES	AESTHETICISTS	AFFECTLESSNESS
AEROBICISE	AEROHYDROPLANES	AEROSHELLS	AESTHETICIZE	AFFEERMENT
AEROBICISED	AEROLITHOLOGIES	AEROSIDERITE	AESTHETICIZED	AFFEERMENTS
AEROBICISES	AEROLITHOLOGY	AEROSIDERITES	AESTHETICIZES	AFFENPINSCHER
AEROBICISING	AEROLOGICAL	AEROSOLISATION	AESTHETICIZING	AFFENPINSCHERS
AEROBICIST	AEROLOGIES	AEROSOLISATIONS	AESTHETICS	AFFERENTLY
AEROBICISTS	AEROLOGIST	AEROSOLISE	AESTIVATED	AFFETTUOSO
AEROBICIZE	AEROLOGISTS	AEROSOLISED	AESTIVATES	AFFIANCING
AEROBICIZED	AEROMAGNETIC	AEROSOLISES	AESTIVATING	AFFICIONADO
AEROBICIZES	AEROMANCIES	AEROSOLISING	AESTIVATION	AFFICIONADOS
AEROBICIZING	AEROMECHANIC	AEROSOLIZATION	AESTIVATIONS	AFFIDAVITS
AEROBIOLOGICAL	AEROMECHANICAL	AEROSOLIZATIONS	AESTIVATOR	AFFILIABLE
AEROBIOLOGIES	AEROMECHANICS	AEROSOLIZE	AESTIVATORS	AFFILIATED
AEROBIOLOGIST	AEROMEDICAL	AEROSOLIZED	AETHEREALITIES	AFFILIATES
AEROBIOLOGISTS	AEROMEDICINE	AEROSOLIZES	AETHEREALITY	AFFILIATING
AEROBIOLOGY	AEROMEDICINES	AEROSOLIZING	AETHEREALLY	AFFILIATION
AEROBIONTS	AEROMETERS	AEROSPACES	AETHRIOSCOPE	AFFILIATIONS
AEROBIOSES	AEROMETRIC	AEROSPHERE	AETHRIOSCOPES	AFFINITIES
AEROBIOSIS	AEROMETRIES	AEROSPHERES	AETIOLOGICAL	AFFINITIVE
AEROBIOTIC	AEROMODELLING	AEROSPIKES	AETIOLOGICALLY	AFFIRMABLE
AEROBIOTICALLY	AEROMODELLINGS	AEROSTATIC	AETIOLOGIES	AFFIRMANCE
AEROBRAKED	AEROMOTORS	AEROSTATICAL	AETIOLOGIST	AFFIRMANCES
AEROBRAKES	AERONAUTIC	AEROSTATICS	AETIOLOGISTS	AFFIRMANTS
AEROBRAKING	AERONAUTICAL	AEROSTATION	AFFABILITIES	AFFIRMATION
AEROBRAKINGS	AERONAUTICALLY	AEROSTATIONS	AFFABILITY	AFFIRMATIONS
AEROBUSSES	AERONAUTICS	AEROSTRUCTURE	AFFECTABILITIES	AFFIRMATIVE
AERODIGESTIVE	AERONEUROSES	AEROSTRUCTURES	AFFECTABILITY	AFFIRMATIVELY
AERODONETICS	AERONEUROSIS	AEROTACTIC	AFFECTABLE	AFFIRMATIVES
AERODROMES	AERONOMERS	AEROTRAINS	AFFECTATION	AFFIRMATORY
AERODYNAMIC	AERONOMICAL	AEROTROPIC	AFFECTATIONS	AFFIRMINGLY
AERODYNAMICAL	AERONOMIES	AEROTROPISM	AFFECTEDLY	AFFIXATION
AERODYNAMICALLY	AERONOMIST	AEROTROPISMS	AFFECTEDNESS	AFFIXATIONS
AERODYNAMICIST	AERONOMISTS	AERUGINOUS	AFFECTEDNESSES	AFFIXMENTS
AERODYNAMICISTS	AEROPAUSES	AESTHESIAS	AFFECTINGLY	AFFIXTURES
AERODYNAMICS	AEROPHAGIA	AESTHESIOGEN	AFFECTIONAL	AFFLATIONS
AEROELASTIC	AEROPHAGIAS	AESTHESIOGENIC	AFFECTIONALLY	AFFLATUSES
AEROELASTICIAN	AEROPHAGIES	AESTHESIOGENS	AFFECTIONATE	AFFLICTERS
AEROELASTICIANS	AEROPHOBES	AESTHETICAL	AFFECTIONATELY	AFFLICTING
AEROELASTICITY	AEROPHOBIA	AESTHETICALLY	AFFECTIONED	AFFLICTINGS
AEROEMBOLISM	AEROPHOBIAS	AESTHETICIAN	AFFECTIONING	AFFLICTION
AEROEMBOLISMS	AEROPHOBIC	AESTHETICIANS	AFFECTIONLESS	AFFLICTIONS
AEROGENERATOR	AEROPHONES	AESTHETICISE	AFFECTIONS	AFFLICTIVE
AEROGENERATORS	AEROPHORES	AESTHETICISED	AFFECTIVELY	AFFLICTIVELY
AEROGRAMME	AEROPHYTES	AESTHETICISES	AFFECTIVENESS	AFFLUENCES
AEROGRAMMES	AEROPLANES	AESTHETICISING	AFFECTIVENESSES	AFFLUENCIES
AEROGRAPHIES	AEROPLANKTON	AESTHETICISM	AFFECTIVITIES	AFFLUENTIAL

AFFLUENTIALS	AFICIONADAS	AFTERPEAKS	AGENTIVITIES	AGGRAVATES
AFFLUENTLY	AFICIONADO	AFTERPIECE	AGENTIVITY	AGGRAVATING
AFFLUENTNESS	AFICIONADOS	AFTERPIECES	AGFLATIONS	AGGRAVATINGLY
AFFLUENTNESSES	AFLATOXINS	AFTERSALES	AGGIORNAMENTI	AGGRAVATION
AFFLUENZAS	AFOREMENTIONED	AFTERSENSATION	AGGIORNAMENTO	AGGRAVATIONS
AFFLUXIONS	AFORETHOUGHT	AFTERSENSATIONS	AGGIORNAMENTOS	AGGREGATED
AFFOORDING	AFORETHOUGHTS	AFTERSHAFT	AGGLOMERATE	AGGREGATELY
AFFORCEMENT	AFRORMOSIA	AFTERSHAFTS	AGGLOMERATED	AGGREGATENESS
AFFORCEMENTS	AFRORMOSIAS	AFTERSHAVE	AGGLOMERATES	AGGREGATENESSES
AFFORDABILITIES	AFTERBIRTH	AFTERSHAVES	AGGLOMERATING	AGGREGATES
AFFORDABILITY	AFTERBIRTHS	AFTERSHOCK	AGGLOMERATION	AGGREGATING
AFFORDABLE	AFTERBODIES	AFTERSHOCKS	AGGLOMERATIONS	AGGREGATION
AFFORDABLY	AFTERBRAIN	AFTERSHOWS	AGGLOMERATIVE	AGGREGATIONAL
AFFORESTABLE	AFTERBRAINS	AFTERSUPPER	AGGLUTINABILITY	AGGREGATIONS
AFFORESTATION	AFTERBURNER	AFTERSUPPERS	AGGLUTINABLE	AGGREGATIVE
AFFORESTATIONS	AFTERBURNERS	AFTERSWARM	AGGLUTINANT	AGGREGATIVELY
AFFORESTED	AFTERBURNING	AFTERSWARMS	AGGLUTINANTS	AGGREGATOR
AFFORESTING	AFTERBURNINGS	AFTERTASTE	AGGLUTINATE	AGGREGATORS
AFFRANCHISE	AFTERBURNS	AFTERTASTES	AGGLUTINATED	AGGRESSING
AFFRANCHISED	AFTERCARES	AFTERTHOUGHT	AGGLUTINATES	AGGRESSION
AFFRANCHISEMENT	AFTERCLAPS	AFTERTHOUGHTS	AGGLUTINATING	AGGRESSIONS
AFFRANCHISES	AFTERDAMPS	AFTERTIMES	AGGLUTINATION	AGGRESSIVE
AFFRANCHISING	AFTERDECKS	AFTERTREATMENT	AGGLUTINATIONS	AGGRESSIVELY
AFFRAPPING	AFTEREFFECT	AFTERTREATMENTS	AGGLUTINATIVE	AGGRESSIVENESS
AFFREIGHTMENT	AFTEREFFECTS	AFTERWARDS	AGGLUTININ	AGGRESSIVITIES
AFFREIGHTMENTS	AFTEREYEING	AFTERWORDS	AGGLUTININS	AGGRESSIVITY
AFFRICATED	AFTEREYING	AFTERWORLD	AGGLUTINOGEN	AGGRESSORS
AFFRICATES	AFTERGAMES	AFTERWORLDS	AGGLUTINOGENIC	AGGRIEVEDLY
AFFRICATING	AFTERGLOWS	AGALACTIAS	AGGLUTINOGENS	AGGRIEVEMENT
AFFRICATION	AFTERGRASS	AGALMATOLITE	AGGRADATION	AGGRIEVEMENTS
AFFRICATIONS	AFTERGRASSES	AGALMATOLITES	AGGRADATIONS	AGGRIEVING
AFFRICATIVE	AFTERGROWTH	AGAMICALLY	AGGRANDISE	AGILENESSES
AFFRICATIVES	AFTERGROWTHS	AGAMOGENESES	AGGRANDISED	AGISTMENTS
AFFRIGHTED	AFTERGUARD	AGAMOGENESIS	AGGRANDISEMENT	AGITATEDLY
AFFRIGHTEDLY	AFTERGUARDS	AGAMOGENETIC	AGGRANDISEMENTS	AGITATIONAL
AFFRIGHTEN	AFTERHEATS	AGAMOGONIES	AGGRANDISER	AGITATIONS
AFFRIGHTENED	AFTERIMAGE	AGAMOSPERMIES	AGGRANDISERS	AGNATICALLY
AFFRIGHTENING	AFTERIMAGES	AGAMOSPERMY	AGGRANDISES	AGNOIOLOGIES
AFFRIGHTENS	AFTERLIFES	AGAPANTHUS	AGGRANDISING	AGNOIOLOGY
AFFRIGHTFUL	AFTERLIVES	AGAPANTHUSES	AGGRANDIZE	AGNOLOTTIS
AFFRIGHTING	AFTERMARKET	AGARICACEOUS	AGGRANDIZED	AGNOSTICISM
AFFRIGHTMENT	AFTERMARKETS	AGATEWARES	AGGRANDIZEMENT	AGNOSTICISMS
AFFRIGHTMENTS	AFTERMASTS	AGATHODAIMON	AGGRANDIZEMENTS	AGONISEDLY
AFFRONTING	AFTERMATHS	AGATHODAIMONS	AGGRANDIZER	AGONISINGLY
AFFRONTINGLY	AFTERNOONS	AGEDNESSES	AGGRANDIZERS	AGONISTICAL
AFFRONTINGS	AFTERPAINS	AGELESSNESS	AGGRANDIZES	AGONISTICALLY
AFFRONTIVE	AFTERPARTIES	AGELESSNESSES	AGGRANDIZING	AGONISTICS
AFICIONADA	AFTERPARTY	AGENDALESS	AGGRAVATED	AGONIZEDLY

AGONIZINGLY	AGROBIOLOGIST	AHURUHURUS	AIRFREIGHTED	ALBINOISMS
AGONOTHETES	AGROBIOLOGISTS	AICHMOPHOBIA	AIRFREIGHTING	ALBITISING
AGORAPHOBE	AGROBIOLOGY	AICHMOPHOBIAS	AIRFREIGHTS	ALBITIZING
AGORAPHOBES	AGROBUSINESS	AIGUILLETTE	AIRINESSES	ALBUGINEOUS
AGORAPHOBIA	AGROBUSINESSES	AIGUILLETTES	AIRLESSNESS	ALBUMBLATT
AGORAPHOBIAS	AGROCHEMICAL	AILANTHUSES	AIRLESSNESSES	ALBUMBLATTER
AGORAPHOBIC	AGROCHEMICALS	AILOUROPHILE	AIRLIFTING	ALBUMBLATTS
AGORAPHOBICS	AGRODOLCES	AILOUROPHILES	AIRMAILING	ALBUMENISE
AGRAMMATICAL	AGROFORESTER	AILOUROPHILIA	AIRMANSHIP	ALBUMENISED
AGRANULOCYTE	AGROFORESTERS	AILOUROPHILIAS	AIRMANSHIPS	ALBUMENISES
AGRANULOCYTES	AGROFORESTRIES	AILOUROPHILIC	AIRPROOFED	ALBUMENISING
AGRANULOCYTOSES	AGROFORESTRY	AILOUROPHOBE	AIRPROOFING	ALBUMENIZE
AGRANULOCYTOSIS	AGROINDUSTRIAL	AILOUROPHOBES	AIRSICKNESS	ALBUMENIZED
AGRANULOSES	AGROINDUSTRIES	AILOUROPHOBIA	AIRSICKNESSES	ALBUMENIZES
AGRANULOSIS	AGROINDUSTRY	AILOUROPHOBIAS	AIRSTREAMS	ALBUMENIZING
AGRARIANISM	AGROLOGICAL	AILOUROPHOBIC	AIRSTRIKES	ALBUMINATE
AGRARIANISMS	AGROLOGIES	AILUROPHILE	AIRTIGHTNESS	ALBUMINATES
AGREEABILITIES	AGROLOGIST	AILUROPHILES	AIRTIGHTNESSES	ALBUMINISE
AGREEABILITY	AGROLOGISTS	AILUROPHILIA	AIRWORTHIER	ALBUMINISED
AGREEABLENESS	AGRONOMIAL	AILUROPHILIAS	AIRWORTHIEST	ALBUMINISES
AGREEABLENESSES	AGRONOMICAL	AILUROPHILIC	AIRWORTHINESS	ALBUMINISING
AGREEMENTS	AGRONOMICALLY	AILUROPHOBE	AIRWORTHINESSES	ALBUMINIZE
AGREGATION	AGRONOMICS	AILUROPHOBES	AITCHBONES	ALBUMINIZED
AGREGATIONS	AGRONOMIES	AILUROPHOBIA	AKATHISIAS	ALBUMINIZES
AGRIBUSINESS	AGRONOMIST	AILUROPHOBIAS	AKOLOUTHOS	ALBUMINIZING
AGRIBUSINESSES	AGRONOMISTS	AILUROPHOBIC	AKOLOUTHOSES	ALBUMINOID
AGRIBUSINESSMAN	AGROSTEMMA	AIMLESSNESS	AKOLUTHOSES	ALBUMINOIDS
AGRIBUSINESSMEN	AGROSTEMMAS	AIMLESSNESSES	ALABAMINES	ALBUMINOUS
AGRICHEMICAL	AGROSTEMMATA	AIRBALLING	ALABANDINE	ALBUMINURIA
AGRICHEMICALS	AGROSTOLOGIC	AIRBOARDING	ALABANDINES	ALBUMINURIAS
AGRICULTURAL	AGROSTOLOGICAL	AIRBOARDINGS	ALABANDITE	ALBUMINURIC
AGRICULTURALIST	AGROSTOLOGIES	AIRBRUSHED	ALABANDITES	ALBUTEROLS
AGRICULTURALLY	AGROSTOLOGIST	AIRBRUSHES	ALABASTERS	ALCAICERIA
AGRICULTURE	AGROSTOLOGISTS	AIRBRUSHING	ALABASTRINE	ALCAICERIAS
AGRICULTURES	AGROSTOLOGY	AIRBURSTED	ALABLASTER	ALCARRAZAS
AGRICULTURIST	AGROTERRORISM	AIRBURSTING	ALABLASTERS	ALCATRASES
AGRICULTURISTS	AGROTERRORISMS	AIRCOACHES	ALACRITIES	ALCHEMICAL
AGRIFOODSTUFFS	AGROTOURISM	AIRCRAFTMAN	ALACRITOUS	ALCHEMICALLY
AGRIMONIES	AGROTOURISMS	AIRCRAFTMEN	ALARMINGLY	ALCHEMISED
AGRIOLOGIES	AGROTOURIST	AIRCRAFTSMAN	ALBARELLOS	ALCHEMISES
AGRIPRODUCT	AGROTOURISTS	AIRCRAFTSMEN	ALBATROSSES	ALCHEMISING
AGRIPRODUCTS	AGRYPNOTIC	AIRCRAFTSWOMAN	ALBERTITES	ALCHEMISTIC
AGRITOURISM	AGRYPNOTICS	AIRCRAFTSWOMEN	ALBESCENCE	ALCHEMISTICAL
AGRITOURISMS	AGTERSKOTS	AIRCRAFTWOMAN	ALBESCENCES	ALCHEMISTS
AGRITOURIST	AGUARDIENTE	AIRCRAFTWOMEN	ALBESPINES	ALCHEMIZED
AGRITOURISTS	AGUARDIENTES	AIRDROPPED	ALBESPYNES	ALCHEMIZES
AGROBIOLOGICAL	AHISTORICAL	AIRDROPPING	ALBINESSES	ALCHEMIZING
AGROBIOLOGIES	AHORSEBACK	AIRFREIGHT	ALBINISTIC	ALCHERINGA

ALCHERINGAS	ALDOSTERONES	ALGOMETERS	ALKALINISATIONS	ALLEGORISING
ALCOHOLICALLY	ALDOSTERONISM	ALGOMETRIES	ALKALINISE	ALLEGORIST
ALCOHOLICITIES	ALDOSTERONISMS	ALGOPHOBIA	ALKALINISED	ALLEGORISTS
ALCOHOLICITY	ALEATORIES	ALGOPHOBIAS	ALKALINISES	ALLEGORIZATION
ALCOHOLICS	ALEBENCHES	ALGORISMIC	ALKALINISING	ALLEGORIZATIONS
ALCOHOLISATION	ALECTRYONS	ALGORITHMIC	ALKALINITIES	ALLEGORIZE
ALCOHOLISATIONS	ALEGGEAUNCE	ALGORITHMICALLY	ALKALINITY	ALLEGORIZED
ALCOHOLISE	ALEGGEAUNCES	ALGORITHMS	ALKALINIZATION	ALLEGORIZER
ALCOHOLISED	ALEMBICATED	ALIENABILITIES	ALKALINIZATIONS	ALLEGORIZERS
ALCOHOLISES	ALEMBICATION	ALIENABILITY	ALKALINIZE	ALLEGORIZES
ALCOHOLISING	ALEMBICATIONS	ALIENATING	ALKALINIZED	ALLEGORIZING
ALCOHOLISM	ALEMBROTHS	ALIENATION	ALKALINIZES	ALLEGRETTO
ALCOHOLISMS	ALERTNESSES	ALIENATIONS	ALKALINIZING	ALLEGRETTOS
ALCOHOLIZATION	ALEXANDERS	ALIENATORS	ALKALISABLE	ALLELOMORPH
ALCOHOLIZATIONS	ALEXANDERSES	ALIENNESSES	ALKALISERS	ALLELOMORPHIC
ALCOHOLIZE	ALEXANDRINE	ALIGHTMENT	ALKALISING	ALLELOMORPHISM
ALCOHOLIZED	ALEXANDRINES	ALIGHTMENTS	ALKALIZABLE	ALLELOMORPHISMS
ALCOHOLIZES	ALEXANDRITE	ALIGNMENTS	ALKALIZERS	ALLELOMORPHS
ALCOHOLIZING	ALEXANDRITES	ALIKENESSES	ALKALIZING	ALLELOPATHIC
ALCOHOLOMETER	ALEXIPHARMAKON	ALIMENTARY	ALKALOIDAL	ALLELOPATHIES
ALCOHOLOMETERS	ALEXIPHARMAKONS	ALIMENTATION	ALKYLATING	ALLELOPATHY
ALCOHOLOMETRIES	ALEXIPHARMIC	ALIMENTATIONS	ALKYLATION	ALLELUIAHS
ALCOHOLOMETRY	ALEXIPHARMICS	ALIMENTATIVE	ALKYLATIONS	ALLEMANDES
ALCYONARIAN	ALEXITHYMIA	ALIMENTING	ALLANTOIDAL	ALLERGENIC
ALCYONARIANS	ALEXITHYMIAS	ALIMENTIVENESS	ALLANTOIDES	ALLERGENICITIES
ALDERFLIES	ALFILARIAS	ALINEATION	ALLANTOIDS	ALLERGENICITY
ALDERMANIC	ALFILERIAS	ALINEATIONS	ALLANTOINS	ALLERGISTS
ALDERMANITIES	ALGAECIDES	ALINEMENTS	ALLANTOISES	ALLETHRINS
ALDERMANITY	ALGARROBAS	ALISMACEOUS	ALLARGANDO	ALLEVIANTS
ALDERMANLIER	ALGARROBOS	ALITERACIES	ALLAYMENTS	ALLEVIATED
ALDERMANLIEST	ALGEBRAICAL	ALITERATES	ALLEGATION	ALLEVIATES
ALDERMANLIKE	ALGEBRAICALLY	ALIVENESSES	ALLEGATIONS	ALLEVIATING
ALDERMANLY	ALGEBRAIST	ALIZARINES	ALLEGEANCE	ALLEVIATION
ALDERMANRIES	ALGEBRAISTS	ALKAHESTIC	ALLEGEANCES	ALLEVIATIONS
ALDERMANRY	ALGIDITIES	ALKALESCENCE	ALLEGIANCE	ALLEVIATIVE
ALDERMANSHIP	ALGIDNESSES	ALKALESCENCES	ALLEGIANCES	ALLEVIATOR
ALDERMANSHIPS	ALGOLAGNIA	ALKALESCENCIES	ALLEGIANTS	ALLEVIATORS
ALDERWOMAN	ALGOLAGNIAC	ALKALESCENCY	ALLEGORICAL	ALLEVIATORY
ALDERWOMEN	ALGOLAGNIACS	ALKALESCENT	ALLEGORICALLY	ALLHALLOND
ALDOHEXOSE	ALGOLAGNIAS	ALKALIFIED	ALLEGORICALNESS	ALLHALLOWEN
ALDOHEXOSES	ALGOLAGNIC	ALKALIFIES	ALLEGORIES	ALLHALLOWN
ALDOLISATION	ALGOLAGNIST	ALKALIFYING	ALLEGORISATION	ALLHOLLOWN
ALDOLISATIONS	ALGOLAGNISTS	ALKALIMETER	ALLEGORISATIONS	ALLIACEOUS
ALDOLIZATION	ALGOLOGICAL	ALKALIMETERS	ALLEGORISE	ALLICHOLIES
ALDOLIZATIONS	ALGOLOGICALLY	ALKALIMETRIC	ALLEGORISED	ALLIGARTAS
ALDOPENTOSE	ALGOLOGIES	ALKALIMETRIES	ALLEGORISER	ALLIGATING
ALDOPENTOSES	ALGOLOGIST	ALKALIMETRY	ALLEGORISERS	ALLIGATION
ALDOSTERONE	ALGOLOGISTS	ALKALINISATION	ALLEGORISES	ALLIGATIONS

ALLIGATORS
ALLINEATION
ALLINEATIONS
ALLITERATE
ALLITERATED
ALLITERATES
ALLITERATING
ALLITERATION
ALLITERATIONS
ALLITERATIVE
ALLITERATIVELY
ALLNIGHTER
ALLNIGHTERS
ALLOANTIBODIES
ALLOANTIBODY
ALLOANTIGEN
ALLOANTIGENS
ALLOCARPIES
ALLOCATABLE
ALLOCATING
ALLOCATION
ALLOCATIONS
ALLOCATORS
ALLOCHEIRIA
ALLOCHEIRIAS
ALLOCHIRIA
ALLOCHIRIAS
ALLOCHTHONOUS
ALLOCUTION
ALLOCUTIONS
ALLODYNIAS
ALLOGAMIES
ALLOGAMOUS
ALLOGENEIC
ALLOGRAFTED
ALLOGRAFTING
ALLOGRAFTS
ALLOGRAPHIC
ALLOGRAPHS
ALLOIOSTROPHOS
ALLOMERISM
ALLOMERISMS
ALLOMEROUS
ALLOMETRIC
ALLOMETRIES
ALLOMORPHIC
ALLOMORPHISM
ALLOMORPHISMS

ALLOMORPHS
ALLONYMOUS
ALLOPATHIC
ALLOPATHICALLY
ALLOPATHIES
ALLOPATHIST
ALLOPATHISTS
ALLOPATRIC
ALLOPATRICALLY
ALLOPATRIES
ALLOPHANES
ALLOPHONES
ALLOPHONIC
ALLOPLASMIC
ALLOPLASMS
ALLOPLASTIC
ALLOPOLYPLOID
ALLOPOLYPLOIDS
ALLOPOLYPLOIDY
ALLOPURINOL
ALLOPURINOLS
ALLOSAURUS
ALLOSAURUSES
ALLOSTERIC
ALLOSTERICALLY
ALLOSTERIES
ALLOTETRAPLOID
ALLOTETRAPLOIDS
ALLOTETRAPLOIDY
ALLOTHEISM
ALLOTHEISMS
ALLOTMENTS
ALLOTRIOMORPHIC
ALLOTROPES
ALLOTROPIC
ALLOTROPICALLY
ALLOTROPIES
ALLOTROPISM
ALLOTROPISMS
ALLOTROPOUS
ALLOTTERIES
ALLOTYPICALLY
ALLOTYPIES
ALLOWABILITIES
ALLOWABILITY
ALLOWABLENESS
ALLOWABLENESSES
ALLOWABLES

ALLOWANCED
ALLOWANCES
ALLOWANCING
ALLUREMENT
ALLUREMENTS
ALLURINGLY
ALLUSIVELY
ALLUSIVENESS
ALLUSIVENESSES
ALLWEATHER
ALLWEATHERS
ALLYCHOLLIES
ALLYCHOLLY
ALMACANTAR
ALMACANTARS
ALMANDINES
ALMANDITES
ALMIGHTIER
ALMIGHTIEST
ALMIGHTILY
ALMIGHTINESS
ALMIGHTINESSES
ALMONDIEST
ALMONDITES
ALMSGIVERS
ALMSGIVING
ALMSGIVINGS
ALMSHOUSES
ALMUCANTAR
ALMUCANTARS
ALOESWOODS
ALOGICALLY
ALONENESSES
ALONGSHORE
ALONGSHOREMAN
ALONGSHOREMEN
ALOOFNESSES
ALOPECOIDS
ALPARGATAS
ALPENGLOWS
ALPENHORNS
ALPENSTOCK
ALPENSTOCKS
ALPESTRINE
ALPHABETARIAN
ALPHABETARIANS
ALPHABETED
ALPHABETIC

ALPHABETICAL
ALPHABETICALLY
ALPHABETIFORM
ALPHABETING
ALPHABETISATION
ALPHABETISE
ALPHABETISED
ALPHABETISER
ALPHABETISERS
ALPHABETISES
ALPHABETISING
ALPHABETIZATION
ALPHABETIZE
ALPHABETIZED
ALPHABETIZER
ALPHABETIZERS
ALPHABETIZES
ALPHABETIZING
ALPHAMERIC
ALPHAMERICAL
ALPHAMERICALLY
ALPHAMETIC
ALPHAMETICS
ALPHANUMERIC
ALPHANUMERICAL
ALPHANUMERICS
ALPHASORTED
ALPHASORTING
ALPHASORTS
ALPHATESTED
ALPHATESTING
ALPHATESTS
ALPHOSISES
ALSTROEMERIA
ALSTROEMERIAS
ALTALTISSIMO
ALTALTISSIMOS
ALTARPIECE
ALTARPIECES
ALTAZIMUTH
ALTAZIMUTHS
ALTERABILITIES
ALTERABILITY
ALTERATION
ALTERATIONS
ALTERATIVE
ALTERATIVES
ALTERCATED

ALTERCATES
ALTERCATING
ALTERCATION
ALTERCATIONS
ALTERCATIVE
ALTERITIES
ALTERNANCE
ALTERNANCES
ALTERNANTS
ALTERNATED
ALTERNATELY
ALTERNATES
ALTERNATIM
ALTERNATING
ALTERNATION
ALTERNATIONS
ALTERNATIVE
ALTERNATIVELY
ALTERNATIVENESS
ALTERNATIVES
ALTERNATOR
ALTERNATORS
ALTIGRAPHS
ALTIMETERS
ALTIMETRICAL
ALTIMETRICALLY
ALTIMETRIES
ALTIPLANOS
ALTISONANT
ALTISSIMOS
ALTITONANT
ALTITUDINAL
ALTITUDINARIAN
ALTITUDINARIANS
ALTITUDINOUS
ALTOCUMULI
ALTOCUMULUS
ALTOGETHER
ALTOGETHERS
ALTORUFFLED
ALTOSTRATI
ALTOSTRATUS
ALTRICIALS
ALTRUISTIC
ALTRUISTICALLY
ALUMINATES
ALUMINIDES
ALUMINIFEROUS

ALUMINISED	AMATEURISMS	AMBITIONLESS	AMELIORATE	AMIANTHUSES
ALUMINISES	AMATEURSHIP	AMBITIOUSLY	AMELIORATED	AMIANTUSES
ALUMINISING	AMATEURSHIPS	AMBITIOUSNESS	AMELIORATES	AMICABILITIES
ALUMINIUMS	AMATIVENESS	AMBITIOUSNESSES	AMELIORATING	AMICABILITY
ALUMINIZED	AMATIVENESSES	AMBIVALENCE	AMELIORATION	AMICABLENESS
ALUMINIZES	AMATORIALLY	AMBIVALENCES	AMELIORATIONS	AMICABLENESSES
ALUMINIZING	AMATORIOUS	AMBIVALENCIES	AMELIORATIVE	AMINOACETIC
ALUMINOSILICATE	AMAZEBALLS	AMBIVALENCY	AMELIORATOR	AMINOACIDURIA
ALUMINOSITIES	AMAZEDNESS	AMBIVALENT	AMELIORATORS	AMINOACIDURIAS
ALUMINOSITY	AMAZEDNESSES	AMBIVALENTLY	AMELIORATORY	AMINOBENZOIC
ALUMINOTHERMIES	AMAZEMENTS	AMBIVERSION	AMELOBLAST	AMINOBUTENE
ALUMINOTHERMY	AMAZONIANS	AMBIVERSIONS	AMELOBLASTS	AMINOBUTENES
ALUMSTONES	AMAZONITES	AMBLYGONITE	AMELOGENESES	AMINOPEPTIDASE
ALVEOLARLY	AMAZONSTONE	AMBLYGONITES	AMELOGENESIS	AMINOPEPTIDASES
ALVEOLATION	AMAZONSTONES	AMBLYOPIAS	AMENABILITIES	AMINOPHENAZONE
ALVEOLATIONS	AMBAGITORY	AMBOCEPTOR	AMENABILITY	AMINOPHENAZONES
ALVEOLITIS	AMBASSADOR	AMBOCEPTORS	AMENABLENESS	AMINOPHENOL
ALVEOLITISES	AMBASSADORIAL	AMBOSEXUAL	AMENABLENESSES	AMINOPHENOLS
ALYCOMPAINE	AMBASSADORS	AMBROSIALLY	AMENAUNCES	AMINOPHYLLINE
ALYCOMPAINES	AMBASSADORSHIP	AMBROTYPES	AMENDATORY	AMINOPHYLLINES
AMAKWEREKWERE	AMBASSADORSHIPS	AMBULACRAL	AMENDMENTS	AMINOPTERIN
AMALGAMATE	AMBASSADRESS	AMBULACRUM	AMENORRHEA	AMINOPTERINS
AMALGAMATED	AMBASSADRESSES	AMBULANCEMAN	AMENORRHEAS	AMINOPYRINE
AMALGAMATES	AMBASSAGES	AMBULANCEMEN	AMENORRHEIC	AMINOPYRINES
AMALGAMATING	AMBERGRISES	AMBULANCES	AMENORRHOEA	AMINOTOLUENE
AMALGAMATION	AMBERJACKS	AMBULANCEWOMAN	AMENORRHOEAS	AMINOTOLUENES
AMALGAMATIONS	AMBIDENTATE	AMBULANCEWOMEN	AMENTACEOUS	AMISSIBILITIES
AMALGAMATIVE	AMBIDEXTER	AMBULATING	AMENTIFEROUS	AMISSIBILITY
AMALGAMATOR	AMBIDEXTERITIES	AMBULATION	AMERCEABLE	AMITOTICALLY
AMALGAMATORS	AMBIDEXTERITY	AMBULATIONS	AMERCEMENT	AMITRIPTYLINE
AMANTADINE	AMBIDEXTEROUS	AMBULATORIES	AMERCEMENTS	AMITRIPTYLINES
AMANTADINES	AMBIDEXTERS	AMBULATORILY	AMERCIABLE	AMITRYPTYLINE
AMANUENSES	AMBIDEXTROUS	AMBULATORS	AMERCIAMENT	AMITRYPTYLINES
AMANUENSIS	AMBIDEXTROUSLY	AMBULATORY	AMERCIAMENTS	AMMOCOETES
AMARACUSES	AMBIGUITIES	AMBULETTES	AMERICIUMS	AMMONIACAL
AMARANTACEOUS	AMBIGUOUSLY	AMBUSCADED	AMETABOLIC	AMMONIACUM
AMARANTHACEOUS	AMBIGUOUSNESS	AMBUSCADER	AMETABOLISM	AMMONIACUMS
AMARANTHINE	AMBIGUOUSNESSES	AMBUSCADERS	AMETABOLISMS	AMMONIATED
AMARANTINE	AMBILATERAL	AMBUSCADES	AMETABOLOUS	AMMONIATES
AMARANTINS	AMBIOPHONIES	AMBUSCADING	AMETHYSTINE	AMMONIATING
AMARYLLIDACEOUS	AMBIOPHONY	AMBUSCADOES	AMETROPIAS	AMMONIATION
AMARYLLIDS	AMBISEXUAL	AMBUSCADOS	AMIABILITIES	AMMONIATIONS
AMARYLLISES	AMBISEXUALITIES	AMBUSHMENT	AMIABILITY	AMMONIFICATION
AMASSMENTS	AMBISEXUALITY	AMBUSHMENTS	AMIABLENESS	AMMONIFICATIONS
AMATEURISH	AMBISEXUALS	AMEBOCYTES	AMIABLENESSES	AMMONIFIED
AMATEURISHLY	AMBISONICS	AMELIORABLE	AMIANTHINE	AMMONIFIES
AMATEURISHNESS	AMBITIONED	AMELIORANT	AMIANTHOID	AMMONIFYING
AMATEURISM	AMBITIONING	AMELIORANTS	AMIANTHOIDAL	AMMONOLYSES

AMMONOLYSIS	AMPELOGRAPHY	AMPHIGORIC	AMPICILLIN	AMYLOPECTINS
AMMOPHILOUS	AMPELOPSES	AMPHIGORIES	AMPICILLINS	AMYLOPLAST
AMMUNITION	AMPELOPSIS	AMPHIGOURI	AMPLENESSES	AMYLOPLASTS
AMMUNITIONED	AMPELOPSISES	AMPHIGOURIS	AMPLEXICAUL	AMYLOPSINS
AMMUNITIONING	AMPEROMETRIC	AMPHIMACER	AMPLEXUSES	AMYOTONIAS
AMMUNITIONS	AMPERSANDS	AMPHIMACERS	AMPLIATION	AMYOTROPHIC
AMNESTYING	AMPERZANDS	AMPHIMICTIC	AMPLIATIONS	AMYOTROPHIES
AMNIOCENTESES	AMPHETAMINE	AMPHIMIXES	AMPLIATIVE	AMYOTROPHY
AMNIOCENTESIS	AMPHETAMINES	AMPHIMIXIS	AMPLIDYNES	ANABANTIDS
AMNIOTOMIES	AMPHIARTHROSES	AMPHIOXUSES	AMPLIFIABLE	ANABAPTISE
AMOBARBITAL	AMPHIARTHROSIS	AMPHIPATHIC	AMPLIFICATION	ANABAPTISED
AMOBARBITALS	AMPHIASTER	AMPHIPHILE	AMPLIFICATIONS	ANABAPTISES
AMOEBIASES	AMPHIASTERS	AMPHIPHILES	AMPLIFIERS	ANABAPTISING
AMOEBIASIS	AMPHIBIANS	AMPHIPHILIC	AMPLIFYING	ANABAPTISM
AMOEBIFORM	AMPHIBIOTIC	AMPHIPLOID	AMPLITUDES	ANABAPTISMS
AMOEBOCYTE	AMPHIBIOUS	AMPHIPLOIDIES	AMPLOSOMES	ANABAPTIST
AMOEBOCYTES	AMPHIBIOUSLY	AMPHIPLOIDS	AMPULLACEAL	ANABAPTISTIC
AMONTILLADO	AMPHIBIOUSNESS	AMPHIPLOIDY	AMPULLACEOUS	ANABAPTISTS
AMONTILLADOS	AMPHIBLASTIC	AMPHIPODOUS	AMPULLOSITIES	ANABAPTIZE
AMORALISMS	AMPHIBLASTULA	AMPHIPROSTYLAR	AMPULLOSITY	ANABAPTIZED
AMORALISTS	AMPHIBLASTULAE	AMPHIPROSTYLE	AMPUTATING	ANABAPTIZES
AMORALITIES	AMPHIBOLES	AMPHIPROSTYLES	AMPUTATION	ANABAPTIZING
AMOROSITIES	AMPHIBOLIC	AMPHIPROTIC	AMPUTATIONS	ANABLEPSES
AMOROUSNESS	AMPHIBOLIES	AMPHISBAENA	AMPUTATORS	ANABOLISMS
AMOROUSNESSES	AMPHIBOLITE	AMPHISBAENAE	AMRITATTVA	ANABOLITES
AMORPHISMS	AMPHIBOLITES	AMPHISBAENAS	AMRITATTVAS	ANABOLITIC
AMORPHOUSLY	AMPHIBOLOGICAL	AMPHISBAENIC	AMSINCKIAS	ANABRANCHES
AMORPHOUSNESS	AMPHIBOLOGIES	AMPHISCIAN	AMUSEMENTS	ANACARDIACEOUS
AMORPHOUSNESSES	AMPHIBOLOGY	AMPHISCIANS	AMUSINGNESS	ANACARDIUM
AMORTISABLE	AMPHIBOLOUS	AMPHISTOMATAL	AMUSINGNESSES	ANACARDIUMS
AMORTISATION	AMPHIBRACH	AMPHISTOMATIC	AMUSIVENESS	ANACATHARSES
AMORTISATIONS	AMPHIBRACHIC	AMPHISTOMOUS	AMUSIVENESSES	ANACATHARSIS
AMORTISEMENT	AMPHIBRACHS	AMPHISTYLAR	AMYGDALACEOUS	ANACATHARTIC
AMORTISEMENTS	AMPHICHROIC	AMPHISTYLARS	AMYGDALATE	ANACATHARTICS
AMORTISING	AMPHICHROMATIC	AMPHITHEATER	AMYGDALINE	ANACHARISES
AMORTIZABLE	AMPHICOELOUS	AMPHITHEATERS	AMYGDALINS	ANACHORISM
AMORTIZATION	AMPHICTYON	AMPHITHEATRAL	AMYGDALOID	ANACHORISMS
AMORTIZATIONS	AMPHICTYONIC	AMPHITHEATRE	AMYGDALOIDAL	ANACHRONIC
AMORTIZEMENT	AMPHICTYONIES	AMPHITHEATRES	AMYGDALOIDS	ANACHRONICAL
AMORTIZEMENTS	AMPHICTYONS	AMPHITHEATRIC	AMYLACEOUS	ANACHRONICALLY
AMORTIZING	AMPHICTYONY	AMPHITHEATRICAL	AMYLOBARBITONE	ANACHRONISM
AMOURETTES	AMPHIDENTATE	AMPHITHECIA	AMYLOBARBITONES	ANACHRONISMS
AMOXICILLIN	AMPHIDIPLOID	AMPHITHECIUM	AMYLOIDOSES	ANACHRONISTIC
AMOXICILLINS	AMPHIDIPLOIDIES	AMPHITRICHA	AMYLOIDOSIS	ANACHRONOUS
AMOXYCILLIN	AMPHIDIPLOIDS	AMPHITRICHOUS	AMYLOLYSES	ANACHRONOUSLY
AMOXYCILLINS	AMPHIDIPLOIDY	AMPHITROPOUS	AMYLOLYSIS	ANACLASTIC
AMPACITIES	AMPHIGASTRIA	AMPHOLYTES	AMYLOLYTIC	ANACOLUTHA
AMPELOGRAPHIES	AMPHIGASTRIUM	AMPHOTERIC	AMYLOPECTIN	ANACOLUTHIA

ANACOLUTHIAS	ANAGNORISIS	ANALYSABILITIES	ANAPLASMOSIS	ANATHEMATIZED
ANACOLUTHIC	ANAGOGICAL	ANALYSABILITY	ANAPLASTIC	ANATHEMATIZES
ANACOLUTHICALLY	ANAGOGICALLY	ANALYSABLE	ANAPLASTIES	ANATHEMATIZING
ANACOLUTHON	ANAGRAMMATIC	ANALYSANDS	ANAPLEROSES	ANATOMICAL
ANACOLUTHONS	ANAGRAMMATICAL	ANALYSATION	ANAPLEROSIS	ANATOMICALLY
ANACOUSTIC	ANAGRAMMATISE	ANALYSATIONS	ANAPLEROTIC	ANATOMISATION
ANACREONTIC	ANAGRAMMATISED	ANALYTICAL	ANAPTYCTIC	ANATOMISATIONS
ANACREONTICALLY	ANAGRAMMATISES	ANALYTICALLY	ANAPTYCTICAL	ANATOMISED
ANACREONTICS	ANAGRAMMATISING	ANALYTICITIES	ANARCHICAL	ANATOMISER
ANACRUSTIC	ANAGRAMMATISM	ANALYTICITY	ANARCHICALLY	ANATOMISERS
ANADIPLOSES	ANAGRAMMATISMS	ANALYZABILITIES	ANARCHISED	ANATOMISES
ANADIPLOSIS	ANAGRAMMATIST	ANALYZABILITY	ANARCHISES	ANATOMISING
ANADROMOUS	ANAGRAMMATISTS	ANALYZABLE	ANARCHISING	ANATOMISTS
ANADYOMENE	ANAGRAMMATIZE	ANALYZATION	ANARCHISMS	ANATOMIZATION
ANAEMICALLY	ANAGRAMMATIZED	ANALYZATIONS	ANARCHISTIC	ANATOMIZATIONS
ANAEROBICALLY	ANAGRAMMATIZES	ANAMNESTIC	ANARCHISTICALLY	ANATOMIZED
ANAEROBIONT	ANAGRAMMATIZING	ANAMNESTICALLY	ANARCHISTS	ANATOMIZER
ANAEROBIONTS	ANAGRAMMED	ANAMNIOTES	ANARCHIZED	ANATOMIZERS
ANAEROBIOSES	ANAGRAMMER	ANAMNIOTIC	ANARCHIZES	ANATOMIZES
ANAEROBIOSIS	ANAGRAMMERS	ANAMORPHIC	ANARCHIZING	ANATOMIZING
ANAEROBIOTIC	ANAGRAMMING	ANAMORPHISM	ANARTHRIAS	ANATROPIES
ANAEROBIUM	ANALEMMATA	ANAMORPHISMS	ANARTHROUS	ANATROPOUS
ANAESTHESES	ANALEMMATIC	ANAMORPHOSCOPE	ANARTHROUSLY	ANCESTORED
ANAESTHESIA	ANALEPTICS	ANAMORPHOSCOPES	ANARTHROUSNESS	ANCESTORIAL
ANAESTHESIAS	ANALGESIAS	ANAMORPHOSES	ANASARCOUS	ANCESTORING
ANAESTHESIOLOGY	ANALGESICS	ANAMORPHOSIS	ANASTIGMAT	ANCESTRALLY
ANAESTHESIS	ANALGETICS	ANAMORPHOUS	ANASTIGMATIC	ANCESTRALS
ANAESTHETIC	ANALOGICAL	ANANDAMIDE	ANASTIGMATISM	ANCESTRESS
ANAESTHETICALLY	ANALOGICALLY	ANANDAMIDES	ANASTIGMATISMS	ANCESTRESSES
ANAESTHETICS	ANALOGISED	ANAPAESTIC	ANASTIGMATS	ANCESTRIES
ANAESTHETISE	ANALOGISES	ANAPAESTICAL	ANASTOMOSE	ANCHORAGES
ANAESTHETISED	ANALOGISING	ANAPESTICS	ANASTOMOSED	ANCHORESSES
ANAESTHETISES	ANALOGISMS	ANAPHORESES	ANASTOMOSES	ANCHORETIC
ANAESTHETISING	ANALOGISTS	ANAPHORESIS	ANASTOMOSING	ANCHORETICAL
ANAESTHETIST	ANALOGIZED	ANAPHORICAL	ANASTOMOSIS	ANCHORETTE
ANAESTHETISTS	ANALOGIZES	ANAPHORICALLY	ANASTOMOTIC	ANCHORETTES
ANAESTHETIZE	ANALOGIZING	ANAPHRODISIA	ANASTROPHE	ANCHORITES
ANAESTHETIZED	ANALOGOUSLY	ANAPHRODISIAC	ANASTROPHES	ANCHORITIC
ANAESTHETIZES	ANALOGOUSNESS	ANAPHRODISIACS	ANASTROZOLE	ANCHORITICAL
ANAESTHETIZING	ANALOGOUSNESSES	ANAPHRODISIAS	ANASTROZOLES	ANCHORITICALLY
ANAGENESES	ANALPHABET	ANAPHYLACTIC	ANATHEMATA	ANCHORLESS
ANAGENESIS	ANALPHABETE	ANAPHYLACTOID	ANATHEMATICAL	ANCHORPEOPLE
ANAGLYPHIC	ANALPHABETES	ANAPHYLAXES	ANATHEMATICALS	ANCHORPERSON
ANAGLYPHICAL	ANALPHABETIC	ANAPHYLAXIES	ANATHEMATISE	ANCHORPERSONS
ANAGLYPHIES	ANALPHABETICS	ANAPHYLAXIS	ANATHEMATISED	ANCHORWOMAN
ANAGLYPTIC	ANALPHABETISM	ANAPHYLAXY	ANATHEMATISES	ANCHORWOMEN
ANAGLYPTICAL	ANALPHABETISMS	ANAPLASIAS	ANATHEMATISING	ANCHOVETAS
ANAGNORISES	ANALPHABETS	ANAPLASMOSES	ANATHEMATIZE	ANCHOVETTA

ANCHOVETTAS
ANCHYLOSED
ANCHYLOSES
ANCHYLOSING
ANCHYLOSIS
ANCHYLOTIC
ANCIENTEST
ANCIENTNESS
ANCIENTNESSES
ANCIENTRIES
ANCILLARIES
ANCIPITOUS
ANCYLOSTOMIASES
ANCYLOSTOMIASIS
ANDALUSITE
ANDALUSITES
ANDANTINOS
ANDOUILLES
ANDOUILLETTE
ANDOUILLETTES
ANDRADITES
ANDROCENTRIC
ANDROCENTRISM
ANDROCENTRISMS
ANDROCEPHALOUS
ANDROCLINIA
ANDROCLINIUM
ANDRODIOECIOUS
ANDRODIOECISM
ANDRODIOECISMS
ANDROECIAL
ANDROECIUM
ANDROGENESES
ANDROGENESIS
ANDROGENETIC
ANDROGENIC
ANDROGENOUS
ANDROGYNES
ANDROGYNIES
ANDROGYNOPHORE
ANDROGYNOPHORES
ANDROGYNOUS
ANDROLOGIES
ANDROLOGIST
ANDROLOGISTS
ANDROMEDAS
ANDROMEDOTOXIN
ANDROMEDOTOXINS

ANDROMONOECIOUS
ANDROMONOECISM
ANDROMONOECISMS
ANDROPAUSE
ANDROPAUSES
ANDROPHORE
ANDROPHORES
ANDROSPHINGES
ANDROSPHINX
ANDROSPHINXES
ANDROSTERONE
ANDROSTERONES
ANECDOTAGE
ANECDOTAGES
ANECDOTALISM
ANECDOTALISMS
ANECDOTALIST
ANECDOTALISTS
ANECDOTALLY
ANECDOTICAL
ANECDOTICALLY
ANECDOTIST
ANECDOTISTS
ANELASTICITIES
ANELASTICITY
ANEMICALLY
ANEMOCHORE
ANEMOCHORES
ANEMOCHOROUS
ANEMOGRAMS
ANEMOGRAPH
ANEMOGRAPHIC
ANEMOGRAPHIES
ANEMOGRAPHS
ANEMOGRAPHY
ANEMOLOGIES
ANEMOMETER
ANEMOMETERS
ANEMOMETRIC
ANEMOMETRICAL
ANEMOMETRIES
ANEMOMETRY
ANEMOPHILIES
ANEMOPHILOUS
ANEMOPHILY
ANEMOPHOBIA
ANEMOPHOBIAS
ANEMOSCOPE

ANEMOSCOPES
ANENCEPHALIA
ANENCEPHALIAS
ANENCEPHALIC
ANENCEPHALIES
ANENCEPHALY
ANESTHESIA
ANESTHESIAS
ANESTHESIOLOGY
ANESTHETIC
ANESTHETICALLY
ANESTHETICS
ANESTHETISATION
ANESTHETISE
ANESTHETISED
ANESTHETISES
ANESTHETISING
ANESTHETIST
ANESTHETISTS
ANESTHETIZATION
ANESTHETIZE
ANESTHETIZED
ANESTHETIZES
ANESTHETIZING
ANEUPLOIDIES
ANEUPLOIDS
ANEUPLOIDY
ANEURISMAL
ANEURISMALLY
ANEURISMATIC
ANEURYSMAL
ANEURYSMALLY
ANEURYSMATIC
ANFRACTUOSITIES
ANFRACTUOSITY
ANFRACTUOUS
ANGASHORES
ANGELFISHES
ANGELHOODS
ANGELICALLY
ANGELOLATRIES
ANGELOLATRY
ANGELOLOGIES
ANGELOLOGIST
ANGELOLOGISTS
ANGELOLOGY
ANGELOPHANIES
ANGELOPHANY

ANGIOCARPOUS
ANGIOGENESES
ANGIOGENESIS
ANGIOGENIC
ANGIOGRAMS
ANGIOGRAPHIC
ANGIOGRAPHIES
ANGIOGRAPHY
ANGIOLOGIES
ANGIOMATOUS
ANGIOPLASTIES
ANGIOPLASTY
ANGIOSARCOMA
ANGIOSARCOMAS
ANGIOSARCOMATA
ANGIOSPERM
ANGIOSPERMAL
ANGIOSPERMOUS
ANGIOSPERMS
ANGIOSTOMATOUS
ANGIOSTOMOUS
ANGIOTENSIN
ANGIOTENSINS
ANGISHORES
ANGLEBERRIES
ANGLEBERRY
ANGLEDOZER
ANGLEDOZERS
ANGLERFISH
ANGLERFISHES
ANGLESITES
ANGLETWITCH
ANGLETWITCHES
ANGLEWORMS
ANGLICISATION
ANGLICISATIONS
ANGLICISED
ANGLICISES
ANGLICISING
ANGLICISMS
ANGLICISTS
ANGLICIZATION
ANGLICIZATIONS
ANGLICIZED
ANGLICIZES
ANGLICIZING
ANGLIFYING
ANGLISTICS

ANGLOMANIA
ANGLOMANIAC
ANGLOMANIACS
ANGLOMANIAS
ANGLOPHILE
ANGLOPHILES
ANGLOPHILIA
ANGLOPHILIAS
ANGLOPHILIC
ANGLOPHILS
ANGLOPHOBE
ANGLOPHOBES
ANGLOPHOBIA
ANGLOPHOBIAC
ANGLOPHOBIACS
ANGLOPHOBIAS
ANGLOPHOBIC
ANGLOPHONE
ANGLOPHONES
ANGLOPHONIC
ANGOPHORAS
ANGOSTURAS
ANGRINESSES
ANGUIFAUNA
ANGUIFAUNAE
ANGUIFAUNAS
ANGUILLIFORM
ANGUIPEDES
ANGUISHING
ANGULARITIES
ANGULARITY
ANGULARNESS
ANGULARNESSES
ANGULATING
ANGULATION
ANGULATIONS
ANGUSTIFOLIATE
ANGUSTIROSTRATE
ANGWANTIBO
ANGWANTIBOS
ANHARMONIC
ANHEDONIAS
ANHELATION
ANHELATIONS
ANHIDROSES
ANHIDROSIS
ANHIDROTIC
ANHIDROTICS

A

ANHUNGERED

ANHUNGERED	ANIMATISMS	ANNEXATIONISM	ANNULATIONS	ANORTHITES
ANHYDRASES	ANIMATISTS	ANNEXATIONISMS	ANNULLABLE	ANORTHITIC
ANHYDRIDES	ANIMATRONIC	ANNEXATIONIST	ANNULMENTS	ANORTHOSITE
ANHYDRITES	ANIMATRONICALLY	ANNEXATIONISTS	ANNUNCIATE	ANORTHOSITES
ANICONISMS	ANIMATRONICS	ANNEXATIONS	ANNUNCIATED	ANORTHOSITIC
ANICONISTS	ANIMOSITIES	ANNEXMENTS	ANNUNCIATES	ANOTHERGUESS
ANILINCTUS	ANISEIKONIA	ANNIHILABLE	ANNUNCIATING	ANOVULANTS
ANILINCTUSES	ANISEIKONIAS	ANNIHILATE	ANNUNCIATION	ANOVULATION
ANILINGUSES	ANISEIKONIC	ANNIHILATED	ANNUNCIATIONS	ANOVULATIONS
ANIMADVERSION	ANISOCERCAL	ANNIHILATES	ANNUNCIATIVE	ANOVULATORY
ANIMADVERSIONS	ANISODACTYL	ANNIHILATING	ANNUNCIATOR	ANOXAEMIAS
ANIMADVERT	ANISODACTYLOUS	ANNIHILATION	ANNUNCIATORS	ANSAPHONES
ANIMADVERTED	ANISODACTYLS	ANNIHILATIONISM	ANNUNCIATORY	ANSWERABILITIES
ANIMADVERTER	ANISOGAMIES	ANNIHILATIONS	ANNUNTIATE	ANSWERABILITY
ANIMADVERTERS	ANISOGAMOUS	ANNIHILATIVE	ANNUNTIATED	ANSWERABLE
ANIMADVERTING	ANISOMERIC	ANNIHILATOR	ANNUNTIATES	ANSWERABLENESS
ANIMADVERTS	ANISOMEROUS	ANNIHILATORS	ANNUNTIATING	ANSWERABLY
ANIMALCULA	ANISOMETRIC	ANNIHILATORY	ANODICALLY	ANSWERLESS
ANIMALCULAR	ANISOMETROPIA	ANNIVERSARIES	ANODISATION	ANSWERPHONE
ANIMALCULE	ANISOMETROPIAS	ANNIVERSARY	ANODISATIONS	ANSWERPHONES
ANIMALCULES	ANISOMETROPIC	ANNOTATABLE	ANODIZATION	ANTAGONISABLE
ANIMALCULISM	ANISOMORPHIC	ANNOTATING	ANODIZATIONS	ANTAGONISATION
ANIMALCULISMS	ANISOPHYLLIES	ANNOTATION	ANODONTIAS	ANTAGONISATIONS
ANIMALCULIST	ANISOPHYLLOUS	ANNOTATIONS	ANOESTROUS	ANTAGONISE
ANIMALCULISTS	ANISOPHYLLY	ANNOTATIVE	ANOINTINGS	ANTAGONISED
ANIMALCULUM	ANISOTROPIC	ANNOTATORS	ANOINTMENT	ANTAGONISES
ANIMALIERS	ANISOTROPICALLY	ANNOUNCEMENT	ANOINTMENTS	ANTAGONISING
ANIMALISATION	ANISOTROPIES	ANNOUNCEMENTS	ANOMALISTIC	ANTAGONISM
ANIMALISATIONS	ANISOTROPISM	ANNOUNCERS	ANOMALISTICAL	ANTAGONISMS
ANIMALISED	ANISOTROPISMS	ANNOUNCING	ANOMALISTICALLY	ANTAGONIST
ANIMALISES	ANISOTROPY	ANNOYANCES	ANOMALOUSLY	ANTAGONISTIC
ANIMALISING	ANKLEBONES	ANNOYINGLY	ANOMALOUSNESS	ANTAGONISTS
ANIMALISMS	ANKYLOSAUR	ANNUALISED	ANOMALOUSNESSES	ANTAGONIZABLE
ANIMALISTIC	ANKYLOSAURS	ANNUALISES	ANONACEOUS	ANTAGONIZATION
ANIMALISTS	ANKYLOSAURUS	ANNUALISING	ANONYMISED	ANTAGONIZATIONS
ANIMALITIES	ANKYLOSAURUSES	ANNUALIZED	ANONYMISES	ANTAGONIZE
ANIMALIZATION	ANKYLOSING	ANNUALIZES	ANONYMISING	ANTAGONIZED
ANIMALIZATIONS	ANKYLOSTOMIASES	ANNUALIZING	ANONYMITIES	ANTAGONIZES
ANIMALIZED	ANKYLOSTOMIASIS	ANNUITANTS	ANONYMIZED	ANTAGONIZING
ANIMALIZES	ANNABERGITE	ANNUITISED	ANONYMIZES	ANTALKALIES
ANIMALIZING	ANNABERGITES	ANNUITISES	ANONYMIZING	ANTALKALINE
ANIMALLIKE	ANNALISING	ANNUITISING	ANONYMOUSLY	ANTALKALINES
ANIMATEDLY	ANNALISTIC	ANNUITIZED	ANONYMOUSNESS	ANTALKALIS
ANIMATENESS	ANNALIZING	ANNUITIZES	ANONYMOUSNESSES	ANTAPHRODISIAC
ANIMATENESSES	ANNEALINGS	ANNUITIZING	ANOPHELINE	ANTAPHRODISIACS
ANIMATEURS	ANNELIDANS	ANNULARITIES	ANOPHELINES	ANTARTHRITIC
ANIMATINGLY	ANNEXATION	ANNULARITY	ANORECTICS	ANTARTHRITICS
ANIMATIONS	ANNEXATIONAL	ANNULATION	ANOREXIGENIC	ANTASTHMATIC

ANTASTHMATICS	ANTEVERSION	ANTHOMANIAS	ANTHROPOLOGY	ANTIANDROGENS
ANTEBELLUM	ANTEVERSIONS	ANTHOPHILOUS	ANTHROPOMETRIC	ANTIANEMIA
ANTECEDENCE	ANTEVERTED	ANTHOPHORE	ANTHROPOMETRIES	ANTIANXIETY
ANTECEDENCES	ANTEVERTING	ANTHOPHORES	ANTHROPOMETRIST	ANTIAPARTHEID
ANTECEDENT	ANTHELICES	ANTHOPHYLLITE	ANTHROPOMETRY	ANTIAPHRODISIAC
ANTECEDENTLY	ANTHELIONS	ANTHOPHYLLITES	ANTHROPOMORPH	ANTIARMOUR
ANTECEDENTS	ANTHELIXES	ANTHOTAXIES	ANTHROPOMORPHIC	ANTIARRHYTHMIC
ANTECEDING	ANTHELMINTHIC	ANTHOXANTHIN	ANTHROPOMORPHS	ANTIARRHYTHMICS
ANTECESSOR	ANTHELMINTHICS	ANTHOXANTHINS	ANTHROPOPATHIC	ANTIARTHRITIC
ANTECESSORS	ANTHELMINTIC	ANTHOZOANS	ANTHROPOPATHIES	ANTIARTHRITICS
ANTECHAMBER	ANTHELMINTICS	ANTHRACENE	ANTHROPOPATHISM	ANTIARTHRITIS
ANTECHAMBERS	ANTHEMISES	ANTHRACENES	ANTHROPOPATHY	ANTIASTHMA
ANTECHAPEL	ANTHEMWISE	ANTHRACITE	ANTHROPOPHAGI	ANTIASTHMATIC
ANTECHAPELS	ANTHERIDIA	ANTHRACITES	ANTHROPOPHAGIC	ANTIASTHMATICS
ANTECHOIRS	ANTHERIDIAL	ANTHRACITIC	ANTHROPOPHAGIES	ANTIAUTHORITY
ANTEDATING	ANTHERIDIUM	ANTHRACNOSE	ANTHROPOPHAGITE	ANTIAUXINS
ANTEDATINGS	ANTHEROZOID	ANTHRACNOSES	ANTHROPOPHAGOUS	ANTIBACCHII
ANTEDILUVIAL	ANTHEROZOIDS	ANTHRACOID	ANTHROPOPHAGUS	ANTIBACCHIUS
ANTEDILUVIALLY	ANTHEROZOOID	ANTHRACOSES	ANTHROPOPHAGY	ANTIBACKLASH
ANTEDILUVIAN	ANTHEROZOOIDS	ANTHRACOSIS	ANTHROPOPHOBIA	ANTIBACTERIAL
ANTEDILUVIANS	ANTHERSMUT	ANTHRACYCLINE	ANTHROPOPHOBIAS	ANTIBACTERIALS
ANTEMERIDIAN	ANTHERSMUTS	ANTHRACYCLINES	ANTHROPOPHOBIC	ANTIBALLISTIC
ANTEMORTEM	ANTHOCARPOUS	ANTHRANILATE	ANTHROPOPHOBICS	ANTIBARBARUS
ANTEMUNDANE	ANTHOCARPS	ANTHRANILATES	ANTHROPOPHUISM	ANTIBARBARUSES
ANTENATALLY	ANTHOCHLORE	ANTHRANILIC	ANTHROPOPHUISMS	ANTIBARYON
ANTENATALS	ANTHOCHLORES	ANTHRAQUINONE	ANTHROPOPHYTE	ANTIBARYONS
ANTENNIFEROUS	ANTHOCYANIN	ANTHRAQUINONES	ANTHROPOPHYTES	ANTIBILIOUS
ANTENNIFORM	ANTHOCYANINS	ANTHROPICAL	ANTHROPOPSYCHIC	ANTIBILLBOARD
ANTENNULAR	ANTHOCYANS	ANTHROPOBIOLOGY	ANTHROPOSOPHIC	ANTIBIOSES
ANTENNULES	ANTHOLOGICAL	ANTHROPOCENTRIC	ANTHROPOSOPHIES	ANTIBIOSIS
ANTENUPTIAL	ANTHOLOGIES	ANTHROPOGENESES	ANTHROPOSOPHIST	ANTIBIOTIC
ANTENUPTIALS	ANTHOLOGISE	ANTHROPOGENESIS	ANTHROPOSOPHY	ANTIBIOTICALLY
ANTEORBITAL	ANTHOLOGISED	ANTHROPOGENETIC	ANTHROPOTOMIES	ANTIBIOTICS
ANTEPENDIA	ANTHOLOGISER	ANTHROPOGENIC	ANTHROPOTOMY	ANTIBLACKISM
ANTEPENDIUM	ANTHOLOGISERS	ANTHROPOGENIES	ANTHURIUMS	ANTIBLACKISMS
ANTEPENDIUMS	ANTHOLOGISES	ANTHROPOGENY	ANTIABORTION	ANTIBODIES
ANTEPENULT	ANTHOLOGISING	ANTHROPOGONIES	ANTIABORTIONIST	ANTIBOURGEOIS
ANTEPENULTIMA	ANTHOLOGIST	ANTHROPOGONY	ANTIACADEMIC	ANTIBOYCOTT
ANTEPENULTIMAS	ANTHOLOGISTS	ANTHROPOGRAPHY	ANTIADITIS	ANTIBURGLAR
ANTEPENULTIMATE	ANTHOLOGIZE	ANTHROPOID	ANTIADITISES	ANTIBURGLARY
ANTEPENULTS	ANTHOLOGIZED	ANTHROPOIDAL	ANTIAGGRESSION	ANTIBUSERS
ANTEPOSITION	ANTHOLOGIZER	ANTHROPOIDS	ANTIAIRCRAFT	ANTIBUSINESS
ANTEPOSITIONS	ANTHOLOGIZERS	ANTHROPOLATRIES	ANTIAIRCRAFTS	ANTIBUSING
ANTEPRANDIAL	ANTHOLOGIZES	ANTHROPOLATRY	ANTIALCOHOL	ANTICAKING
ANTERIORITIES	ANTHOLOGIZING	ANTHROPOLOGICAL	ANTIALCOHOLISM	ANTICANCER
ANTERIORITY	ANTHOMANIA	ANTHROPOLOGIES	ANTIALCOHOLISMS	ANTICAPITALISM
ANTERIORLY	ANTHOMANIAC	ANTHROPOLOGIST	ANTIALLERGENIC	ANTICAPITALISMS
ANTEROGRADE	ANTHOMANIACS	ANTHROPOLOGISTS	ANTIANDROGEN	ANTICAPITALIST

ANTICAPITALISTS

ANTICAPITALISTS ANTICLERICALS ANTIDEPRESSANT ANTIFASCIST ANTIHELICES
ANTICARCINOGEN ANTICLIMACTIC ANTIDEPRESSANTS ANTIFASCISTS ANTIHELIXES
ANTICARCINOGENS ANTICLIMACTICAL ANTIDEPRESSION ANTIFASHION ANTIHELMINTHIC
ANTICARIES ANTICLIMAX ANTIDERIVATIVE ANTIFASHIONABLE ANTIHELMINTHICS
ANTICATALYST ANTICLIMAXES ANTIDERIVATIVES ANTIFASHIONS ANTIHEROES
ANTICATALYSTS ANTICLINAL ANTIDESICCANT ANTIFATIGUE ANTIHEROIC
ANTICATHODE ANTICLINALS ANTIDESICCANTS ANTIFEBRILE ANTIHEROINE
ANTICATHODES ANTICLINES ANTIDEVELOPMENT ANTIFEBRILES ANTIHEROINES
ANTICATHOLIC ANTICLINORIA ANTIDIABETIC ANTIFEDERALIST ANTIHERPES
ANTICELLULITE ANTICLINORIUM ANTIDIABETICS ANTIFEDERALISTS ANTIHIJACK
ANTICENSORSHIP ANTICLOCKWISE ANTIDIARRHEAL ANTIFEMALE ANTIHISTAMINE
ANTICHLORISTIC ANTICLOTTING ANTIDIARRHEALS ANTIFEMININE ANTIHISTAMINES
ANTICHLORS ANTICOAGULANT ANTIDIARRHOEAL ANTIFEMINISM ANTIHISTAMINIC
ANTICHOICE ANTICOAGULANTS ANTIDIARRHOEALS ANTIFEMINISMS ANTIHISTAMINICS
ANTICHOICER ANTICODONS ANTIDILUTION ANTIFEMINIST ANTIHISTORICAL
ANTICHOICERS ANTICOINCIDENCE ANTIDIURETIC ANTIFEMINISTS ANTIHOMOSEXUAL
ANTICHOLESTEROL ANTICOLLISION ANTIDIURETICS ANTIFERROMAGNET ANTIHUMANISM
ANTICHOLINERGIC ANTICOLONIAL ANTIDOGMATIC ANTIFERTILITY ANTIHUMANISMS
ANTICHRIST ANTICOLONIALISM ANTIDOTALLY ANTIFILIBUSTER ANTIHUMANISTIC
ANTICHRISTIAN ANTICOLONIALIST ANTIDOTING ANTIFILIBUSTERS ANTIHUNTER
ANTICHRISTIANLY ANTICOLONIALS ANTIDROMIC ANTIFOAMING ANTIHUNTERS
ANTICHRISTS ANTICOMMERCIAL ANTIDROMICALLY ANTIFOGGING ANTIHUNTING
ANTICHTHONES ANTICOMMUNISM ANTIDUMPING ANTIFORECLOSURE ANTIHYDROGEN
ANTICHURCH ANTICOMMUNISMS ANTIDUMPINGS ANTIFOREIGN ANTIHYDROGENS
ANTICIGARETTE ANTICOMMUNIST ANTIECONOMIC ANTIFOREIGNER ANTIHYSTERIC
ANTICIPANT ANTICOMMUNISTS ANTIEDUCATIONAL ANTIFORMALIST ANTIHYSTERICS
ANTICIPANTS ANTICOMPETITIVE ANTIEGALITARIAN ANTIFOULING ANTIJACOBIN
ANTICIPATABLE ANTICONSUMER ANTIELECTRON ANTIFOULINGS ANTIJACOBINS
ANTICIPATE ANTICONVULSANT ANTIELECTRONS ANTIFREEZE ANTIJAMMING
ANTICIPATED ANTICONVULSANTS ANTIELITES ANTIFREEZES ANTIJAMMINGS
ANTICIPATES ANTICONVULSIVE ANTIELITISM ANTIFRICTION ANTIKICKBACK
ANTICIPATING ANTICONVULSIVES ANTIELITISMS ANTIFUNGAL ANTIKNOCKS
ANTICIPATION ANTICORPORATE ANTIELITIST ANTIFUNGALS ANTILEGOMENA
ANTICIPATIONS ANTICORROSION ANTIELITISTS ANTIGAMBLING ANTILEPROSY
ANTICIPATIVE ANTICORROSIONS ANTIEMETIC ANTIGENICALLY ANTILEPTON
ANTICIPATIVELY ANTICORROSIVE ANTIEMETICS ANTIGENICITIES ANTILEPTONS
ANTICIPATOR ANTICORROSIVES ANTIENTROPIC ANTIGENICITY ANTILEUKEMIC
ANTICIPATORILY ANTICORRUPTION ANTIEPILEPSY ANTIGLOBULIN ANTILIBERAL
ANTICIPATORS ANTICREATIVE ANTIEPILEPTIC ANTIGLOBULINS ANTILIBERALISM
ANTICIPATORY ANTICRUELTY ANTIEPILEPTICS ANTIGOVERNMENT ANTILIBERALISMS
ANTICISING ANTICULTURAL ANTIEROTIC ANTIGRAVITIES ANTILIBERALS
ANTICIVISM ANTICYCLONE ANTIESTROGEN ANTIGRAVITY ANTILIBERTARIAN
ANTICIVISMS ANTICYCLONES ANTIESTROGENS ANTIGROPELOES ANTILIFERS
ANTICIZING ANTICYCLONIC ANTIEVOLUTION ANTIGROPELOS ANTILITERATE
ANTICLASSICAL ANTIDANDRUFF ANTIEVOLUTIONS ANTIGROWTH ANTILITTER
ANTICLASTIC ANTIDAZZLE ANTIFAMILY ANTIGUERRILLA ANTILITTERING
ANTICLERICAL ANTIDEFAMATION ANTIFASCISM ANTIHALATION ANTILOGARITHM
ANTICLERICALISM ANTIDEMOCRATIC ANTIFASCISMS ANTIHALATIONS ANTILOGARITHMIC

ANTILOGARITHMS	ANTIMODERN	ANTINOMIANISM	ANTIPERSPIRANTS	ANTIPSYCHOTICS
ANTILOGICAL	ANTIMODERNIST	ANTINOMIANISMS	ANTIPESTICIDE	ANTIPYRESES
ANTILOGIES	ANTIMODERNISTS	ANTINOMIANS	ANTIPETALOUS	ANTIPYRESIS
ANTILOGOUS	ANTIMONARCHICAL	ANTINOMICAL	ANTIPHLOGISTIC	ANTIPYRETIC
ANTILOPINE	ANTIMONARCHIST	ANTINOMICALLY	ANTIPHLOGISTICS	ANTIPYRETICS
ANTILYNCHING	ANTIMONARCHISTS	ANTINOMIES	ANTIPHONAL	ANTIPYRINE
ANTIMACASSAR	ANTIMONATE	ANTINOVELIST	ANTIPHONALLY	ANTIPYRINES
ANTIMACASSARS	ANTIMONATES	ANTINOVELISTS	ANTIPHONALS	ANTIQUARIAN
ANTIMAGNETIC	ANTIMONIAL	ANTINOVELS	ANTIPHONARIES	ANTIQUARIANISM
ANTIMALARIA	ANTIMONIALS	ANTINUCLEAR	ANTIPHONARY	ANTIQUARIANISMS
ANTIMALARIAL	ANTIMONIATE	ANTINUCLEARIST	ANTIPHONER	ANTIQUARIANS
ANTIMALARIALS	ANTIMONIATES	ANTINUCLEARISTS	ANTIPHONERS	ANTIQUARIES
ANTIMANAGEMENT	ANTIMONIDE	ANTINUCLEON	ANTIPHONIC	ANTIQUARKS
ANTIMARIJUANA	ANTIMONIDES	ANTINUCLEONS	ANTIPHONICAL	ANTIQUATED
ANTIMARKET	ANTIMONIES	ANTINUKERS	ANTIPHONICALLY	ANTIQUATEDNESS
ANTIMARKETEER	ANTIMONIOUS	ANTIOBESITY	ANTIPHONIES	ANTIQUATES
ANTIMARKETEERS	ANTIMONITE	ANTIOBSCENITY	ANTIPHRASES	ANTIQUATING
ANTIMASQUE	ANTIMONITES	ANTIODONTALGIC	ANTIPHRASIS	ANTIQUATION
ANTIMASQUES	ANTIMONOPOLIST	ANTIODONTALGICS	ANTIPHRASTIC	ANTIQUATIONS
ANTIMATERIALISM	ANTIMONOPOLISTS	ANTIOESTROGEN	ANTIPHRASTICAL	ANTIQUENESS
ANTIMATERIALIST	ANTIMONOPOLY	ANTIOESTROGENS	ANTIPIRACY	ANTIQUENESSES
ANTIMATTER	ANTIMONOUS	ANTIOXIDANT	ANTIPLAGUE	ANTIQUIEST
ANTIMATTERS	ANTIMONYLS	ANTIOXIDANTS	ANTIPLAQUE	ANTIQUITARIAN
ANTIMECHANIST	ANTIMOSQUITO	ANTIOZONANT	ANTIPLEASURE	ANTIQUITARIANS
ANTIMECHANISTS	ANTIMUSICAL	ANTIOZONANTS	ANTIPOACHING	ANTIQUITIES
ANTIMERGER	ANTIMUSICS	ANTIPARALLEL	ANTIPODALS	ANTIRABIES
ANTIMERISM	ANTIMUTAGEN	ANTIPARALLELS	ANTIPODEAN	ANTIRACHITIC
ANTIMERISMS	ANTIMUTAGENS	ANTIPARASITIC	ANTIPODEANS	ANTIRACHITICS
ANTIMETABOLE	ANTIMYCINS	ANTIPARASITICS	ANTIPOETIC	ANTIRACISM
ANTIMETABOLES	ANTIMYCOTIC	ANTIPARTICLE	ANTIPOLICE	ANTIRACISMS
ANTIMETABOLIC	ANTINARRATIVE	ANTIPARTICLES	ANTIPOLITICAL	ANTIRACIST
ANTIMETABOLITE	ANTINARRATIVES	ANTIPARTIES	ANTIPOLITICS	ANTIRACISTS
ANTIMETABOLITES	ANTINATIONAL	ANTIPASTOS	ANTIPOLLUTION	ANTIRADARS
ANTIMETATHESES	ANTINATIONALIST	ANTIPATHETIC	ANTIPOLLUTIONS	ANTIRADICAL
ANTIMETATHESIS	ANTINATURAL	ANTIPATHETICAL	ANTIPOPULAR	ANTIRADICALISM
ANTIMICROBIAL	ANTINATURE	ANTIPATHIC	ANTIPORNOGRAPHY	ANTIRADICALISMS
ANTIMICROBIALS	ANTINAUSEA	ANTIPATHIES	ANTIPORTER	ANTIRATIONAL
ANTIMILITARISM	ANTINEOPLASTIC	ANTIPATHIST	ANTIPORTERS	ANTIRATIONALISM
ANTIMILITARISMS	ANTINEOPLASTICS	ANTIPATHISTS	ANTIPOVERTY	ANTIRATIONALIST
ANTIMILITARIST	ANTINEPHRITIC	ANTIPERIODIC	ANTIPREDATOR	ANTIRATIONALITY
ANTIMILITARISTS	ANTINEPHRITICS	ANTIPERIODICS	ANTIPRIESTLY	ANTIREALISM
ANTIMILITARY	ANTINEPOTISM	ANTIPERISTALSES	ANTIPROGRESSIVE	ANTIREALISMS
ANTIMISSILE	ANTINEUTRINO	ANTIPERISTALSIS	ANTIPROTON	ANTIREALIST
ANTIMISSILES	ANTINEUTRINOS	ANTIPERISTALTIC	ANTIPROTONS	ANTIREALISTS
ANTIMITOTIC	ANTINEUTRON	ANTIPERISTASES	ANTIPRURITIC	ANTIRECESSION
ANTIMITOTICS	ANTINEUTRONS	ANTIPERISTASIS	ANTIPRURITICS	ANTIREFLECTION
ANTIMNEMONIC	ANTINOISES	ANTIPERSONNEL	ANTIPSYCHIATRY	ANTIREFLECTIVE
ANTIMNEMONICS	ANTINOMIAN	ANTIPERSPIRANT	ANTIPSYCHOTIC	ANTIREFORM

ANTIREGULATORY	ANTISEPTICIZING	ANTISUBVERSION	ANTITUSSIVES	APARTHOTELS
ANTIREJECTION	ANTISEPTICS	ANTISUBVERSIVE	ANTITYPHOID	APARTMENTAL
ANTIRELIGION	ANTISERUMS	ANTISUICIDE	ANTITYPICAL	APARTMENTS
ANTIRELIGIONS	ANTISEXIST	ANTISYMMETRIC	ANTITYPICALLY	APARTNESSES
ANTIRELIGIOUS	ANTISEXISTS	ANTISYPHILITIC	ANTIUNIVERSITY	APATHATONS
ANTIREPUBLICAN	ANTISEXUAL	ANTISYPHILITICS	ANTIVAXERS	APATHETICAL
ANTIREPUBLICANS	ANTISEXUALITIES	ANTISYZYGIES	ANTIVAXXER	APATHETICALLY
ANTIRETROVIRAL	ANTISEXUALITY	ANTISYZYGY	ANTIVAXXERS	APATOSAURS
ANTIRETROVIRALS	ANTISEXUALS	ANTITAKEOVER	ANTIVENENE	APATOSAURUS
ANTIRHEUMATIC	ANTISHAKES	ANTITARNISH	ANTIVENENES	APATOSAURUSES
ANTIRHEUMATICS	ANTISHOCKS	ANTITECHNOLOGY	ANTIVENINS	APERIODICALLY
ANTIRITUALISM	ANTISHOPLIFTING	ANTITERRORISM	ANTIVENOMS	APERIODICITIES
ANTIRITUALISMS	ANTISLAVERY	ANTITERRORISMS	ANTIVIOLENCE	APERIODICITY
ANTIROMANTIC	ANTISMOKER	ANTITERRORIST	ANTIVIRALS	APERITIVES
ANTIROMANTICISM	ANTISMOKERS	ANTITERRORISTS	ANTIVIRUSES	APERTNESSES
ANTIROMANTICS	ANTISMOKING	ANTITHALIAN	ANTIVITAMIN	APFELSTRUDEL
ANTIROYALIST	ANTISMUGGLING	ANTITHEISM	ANTIVITAMINS	APFELSTRUDELS
ANTIROYALISTS	ANTISOCIAL	ANTITHEISMS	ANTIVIVISECTION	APHAERESES
ANTIRRHINUM	ANTISOCIALISM	ANTITHEIST	ANTIWELFARE	APHAERESIS
ANTIRRHINUMS	ANTISOCIALISMS	ANTITHEISTIC	ANTIWHALING	APHAERETIC
ANTISATELLITE	ANTISOCIALIST	ANTITHEISTS	ANTIWORLDS	APHANIPTEROUS
ANTISCIANS	ANTISOCIALISTS	ANTITHEORETICAL	ANTIWRINKLE	APHELANDRA
ANTISCIENCE	ANTISOCIALITIES	ANTITHESES	ANTONINIANUS	APHELANDRAS
ANTISCIENCES	ANTISOCIALITY	ANTITHESIS	ANTONINIANUSES	APHELIOTROPIC
ANTISCIENTIFIC	ANTISOCIALLY	ANTITHETIC	ANTONOMASIA	APHELIOTROPISM
ANTISCORBUTIC	ANTISOCIALS	ANTITHETICAL	ANTONOMASIAS	APHELIOTROPISMS
ANTISCORBUTICS	ANTISPASMODIC	ANTITHETICALLY	ANTONOMASTIC	APHETICALLY
ANTISCRIPTURAL	ANTISPASMODICS	ANTITHROMBIN	ANTONYMIES	APHETISING
ANTISECRECY	ANTISPASTIC	ANTITHROMBINS	ANTONYMOUS	APHETIZING
ANTISEGREGATION	ANTISPASTICS	ANTITHROMBOTIC	ANTRORSELY	APHIDICIDE
ANTISEIZURE	ANTISPASTS	ANTITHROMBOTICS	ANTSINESSES	APHIDICIDES
ANTISENTIMENTAL	ANTISPECULATION	ANTITHYROID	ANUCLEATED	APHORISERS
ANTISEPALOUS	ANTISPECULATIVE	ANTITOBACCO	ANXIOLYTIC	APHORISING
ANTISEPARATIST	ANTISPENDING	ANTITOXINS	ANXIOLYTICS	APHORISTIC
ANTISEPARATISTS	ANTISTATIC	ANTITRADES	ANXIOUSNESS	APHORISTICALLY
ANTISEPSES	ANTISTATICS	ANTITRADITIONAL	ANXIOUSNESSES	APHORIZERS
ANTISEPSIS	ANTISTORIES	ANTITRAGUS	ANYTHINGARIAN	APHORIZING
ANTISEPTIC	ANTISTRESS	ANTITRANSPIRANT	ANYTHINGARIANS	APHRODISIA
ANTISEPTICALLY	ANTISTRIKE	ANTITRINITARIAN	ANYWHITHER	APHRODISIAC
ANTISEPTICISE	ANTISTROPHE	ANTITRUSTER	AORISTICALLY	APHRODISIACAL
ANTISEPTICISED	ANTISTROPHES	ANTITRUSTERS	AORTITISES	APHRODISIACS
ANTISEPTICISES	ANTISTROPHIC	ANTITUBERCULAR	AORTOGRAPHIC	APHRODISIAS
ANTISEPTICISING	ANTISTROPHON	ANTITUBERCULOUS	AORTOGRAPHIES	APHRODITES
ANTISEPTICISM	ANTISTROPHONS	ANTITUMORAL	AORTOGRAPHY	APICULTURAL
ANTISEPTICISMS	ANTISTUDENT	ANTITUMORS	APAGOGICAL	APICULTURE
ANTISEPTICIZE	ANTISTYLES	ANTITUMOUR	APAGOGICALLY	APICULTURES
ANTISEPTICIZED	ANTISUBMARINE	ANTITUMOURAL	APARTHEIDS	APICULTURIST
ANTISEPTICIZES	ANTISUBSIDY	ANTITUSSIVE	APARTHOTEL	APICULTURISTS

APIOLOGIES	APODICTICAL	APOPHENIAS	APOSTOLICISM	APOTHEOSIZED
APISHNESSES	APODICTICALLY	APOPHLEGMATIC	APOSTOLICISMS	APOTHEOSIZES
APITHERAPIES	APODYTERIUM	APOPHLEGMATICS	APOSTOLICITIES	APOTHEOSIZING
APITHERAPY	APODYTERIUMS	APOPHONIES	APOSTOLICITY	APOTROPAIC
APLACENTAL	APOENZYMES	APOPHTHEGM	APOSTOLISE	APOTROPAICALLY
APLANATICALLY	APOGAMOUSLY	APOPHTHEGMATIC	APOSTOLISED	APOTROPAISM
APLANATISM	APOGEOTROPIC	APOPHTHEGMATISE	APOSTOLISES	APOTROPAISMS
APLANATISMS	APOGEOTROPISM	APOPHTHEGMATIST	APOSTOLISING	APOTROPOUS
APLANOGAMETE	APOGEOTROPISMS	APOPHTHEGMATIZE	APOSTOLIZE	APPALLINGLY
APLANOGAMETES	APOLAUSTIC	APOPHTHEGMS	APOSTOLIZED	APPALOOSAS
APLANOSPORE	APOLAUSTICS	APOPHYLLITE	APOSTOLIZES	APPARATCHIK
APLANOSPORES	APOLIPOPROTEIN	APOPHYLLITES	APOSTOLIZING	APPARATCHIKI
APOAPSIDES	APOLIPOPROTEINS	APOPHYSATE	APOSTROPHE	APPARATCHIKS
APOCALYPSE	APOLITICAL	APOPHYSEAL	APOSTROPHES	APPARATUSES
APOCALYPSES	APOLITICALITIES	APOPHYSIAL	APOSTROPHIC	APPARELING
APOCALYPTIC	APOLITICALITY	APOPLECTIC	APOSTROPHISE	APPARELLED
APOCALYPTICAL	APOLITICALLY	APOPLECTICAL	APOSTROPHISED	APPARELLING
APOCALYPTICALLY	APOLITICISM	APOPLECTICALLY	APOSTROPHISES	APPARELMENT
APOCALYPTICISM	APOLITICISMS	APOPLECTICS	APOSTROPHISING	APPARELMENTS
APOCALYPTICISMS	APOLLONIAN	APOPLEXIES	APOSTROPHIZE	APPARENCIES
APOCALYPTISM	APOLLONICON	APOPLEXING	APOSTROPHIZED	APPARENTLY
APOCALYPTISMS	APOLLONICONS	APOPROTEIN	APOSTROPHIZES	APPARENTNESS
APOCALYPTIST	APOLOGETIC	APOPROTEINS	APOSTROPHIZING	APPARENTNESSES
APOCALYPTISTS	APOLOGETICAL	APOSEMATIC	APOSTROPHUS	APPARITION
APOCARPIES	APOLOGETICALLY	APOSEMATICALLY	APOSTROPHUSES	APPARITIONAL
APOCARPOUS	APOLOGETICS	APOSIOPESES	APOTHECARIES	APPARITIONS
APOCATASTASES	APOLOGISED	APOSIOPESIS	APOTHECARY	APPARITORS
APOCATASTASIS	APOLOGISER	APOSIOPETIC	APOTHECIAL	APPARTEMENT
APOCHROMAT	APOLOGISERS	APOSPORIES	APOTHECIUM	APPARTEMENTS
APOCHROMATIC	APOLOGISES	APOSPOROUS	APOTHEGMATIC	APPASSIONATO
APOCHROMATISM	APOLOGISING	APOSTACIES	APOTHEGMATICAL	APPEACHING
APOCHROMATISMS	APOLOGISTS	APOSTASIES	APOTHEGMATISE	APPEACHMENT
APOCHROMATS	APOLOGIZED	APOSTATICAL	APOTHEGMATISED	APPEACHMENTS
APOCOPATED	APOLOGIZER	APOSTATISE	APOTHEGMATISES	APPEALABILITIES
APOCOPATES	APOLOGIZERS	APOSTATISED	APOTHEGMATISING	APPEALABILITY
APOCOPATING	APOLOGIZES	APOSTATISES	APOTHEGMATIST	APPEALABLE
APOCOPATION	APOLOGIZING	APOSTATISING	APOTHEGMATISTS	APPEALINGLY
APOCOPATIONS	APOMICTICAL	APOSTATIZE	APOTHEGMATIZE	APPEALINGNESS
APOCRYPHAL	APOMICTICALLY	APOSTATIZED	APOTHEGMATIZED	APPEALINGNESSES
APOCRYPHALLY	APOMORPHIA	APOSTATIZES	APOTHEGMATIZES	APPEARANCE
APOCRYPHALNESS	APOMORPHIAS	APOSTATIZING	APOTHEGMATIZING	APPEARANCES
APOCRYPHON	APOMORPHINE	APOSTILLES	APOTHEOSES	APPEASABLE
APOCYNACEOUS	APOMORPHINES	APOSTLESHIP	APOTHEOSIS	APPEASEMENT
APOCYNTHION	APONEUROSES	APOSTLESHIPS	APOTHEOSISE	APPEASEMENTS
APOCYNTHIONS	APONEUROSIS	APOSTOLATE	APOTHEOSISED	APPEASINGLY
APODEICTIC	APONEUROTIC	APOSTOLATES	APOTHEOSISES	APPELLANTS
APODEICTICAL	APOPEMPTIC	APOSTOLICAL	APOTHEOSISING	APPELLATION
APODEICTICALLY	APOPEMPTICS	APOSTOLICALLY	APOTHEOSIZE	APPELLATIONAL

APPELLATIONS

APPELLATIONS	APPETIZERS	APPORTIONING	APPRENTICEHOOD	APPROPRIATOR
APPELLATIVE	APPETIZING	APPORTIONMENT	APPRENTICEHOODS	APPROPRIATORS
APPELLATIVELY	APPETIZINGLY	APPORTIONMENTS	APPRENTICEMENT	APPROVABLE
APPELLATIVES	APPLAUDABLE	APPORTIONS	APPRENTICEMENTS	APPROVABLY
APPENDAGES	APPLAUDABLY	APPOSITELY	APPRENTICES	APPROVANCE
APPENDANTS	APPLAUDERS	APPOSITENESS	APPRENTICESHIP	APPROVANCES
APPENDECTOMIES	APPLAUDING	APPOSITENESSES	APPRENTICESHIPS	APPROVINGLY
APPENDECTOMY	APPLAUDINGLY	APPOSITION	APPRENTICING	APPROXIMAL
APPENDENTS	APPLAUSIVE	APPOSITIONAL	APPRESSING	APPROXIMATE
APPENDICECTOMY	APPLAUSIVELY	APPOSITIONS	APPRESSORIA	APPROXIMATED
APPENDICES	APPLECARTS	APPOSITIVE	APPRESSORIUM	APPROXIMATELY
APPENDICITIS	APPLEDRAIN	APPOSITIVELY	APPRISINGS	APPROXIMATES
APPENDICITISES	APPLEDRAINS	APPOSITIVES	APPRIZINGS	APPROXIMATING
APPENDICLE	APPLEJACKS	APPRAISABLE	APPROACHABILITY	APPROXIMATION
APPENDICLES	APPLERINGIE	APPRAISALS	APPROACHABLE	APPROXIMATIONS
APPENDICULAR	APPLERINGIES	APPRAISEES	APPROACHED	APPROXIMATIVE
APPENDICULARIAN	APPLESAUCE	APPRAISEMENT	APPROACHES	APPROXIMEETING
APPENDICULATE	APPLESAUCES	APPRAISEMENTS	APPROACHING	APPROXIMEETINGS
APPENDIXES	APPLETINIS	APPRAISERS	APPROBATED	APPULSIVELY
APPERCEIVE	APPLIANCES	APPRAISING	APPROBATES	APPURTENANCE
APPERCEIVED	APPLICABILITIES	APPRAISINGLY	APPROBATING	APPURTENANCES
APPERCEIVES	APPLICABILITY	APPRAISIVE	APPROBATION	APPURTENANT
APPERCEIVING	APPLICABLE	APPRAISIVELY	APPROBATIONS	APPURTENANTS
APPERCEPTION	APPLICABLENESS	APPRECIABLE	APPROBATIVE	APRICATING
APPERCEPTIONS	APPLICABLY	APPRECIABLY	APPROBATORY	APRICATION
APPERCEPTIVE	APPLICANTS	APPRECIATE	APPROPINQUATE	APRICATIONS
APPERCIPIENT	APPLICATION	APPRECIATED	APPROPINQUATED	APRIORISMS
APPERTAINANCE	APPLICATIONS	APPRECIATES	APPROPINQUATES	APRIORISTS
APPERTAINANCES	APPLICATIVE	APPRECIATING	APPROPINQUATING	APRIORITIES
APPERTAINED	APPLICATIVELY	APPRECIATION	APPROPINQUATION	APSIDIOLES
APPERTAINING	APPLICATOR	APPRECIATIONS	APPROPINQUE	APTERYGIAL
APPERTAINMENT	APPLICATORS	APPRECIATIVE	APPROPINQUED	APTITUDINAL
APPERTAINMENTS	APPLICATORY	APPRECIATIVELY	APPROPINQUES	APTITUDINALLY
APPERTAINS	APPLIQUEING	APPRECIATOR	APPROPINQUING	AQUABATICS
APPERTINENT	APPOGGIATURA	APPRECIATORILY	APPROPINQUITIES	AQUABOARDS
APPERTINENTS	APPOGGIATURAS	APPRECIATORS	APPROPINQUITY	AQUACEUTICAL
APPETEEZEMENT	APPOGGIATURE	APPRECIATORY	APPROPRIABLE	AQUACEUTICALS
APPETEEZEMENTS	APPOINTEES	APPREHENDED	APPROPRIACIES	AQUACULTURAL
APPETENCES	APPOINTERS	APPREHENDING	APPROPRIACY	AQUACULTURE
APPETENCIES	APPOINTING	APPREHENDS	APPROPRIATE	AQUACULTURES
APPETISEMENT	APPOINTIVE	APPREHENSIBLE	APPROPRIATED	AQUACULTURIST
APPETISEMENTS	APPOINTMENT	APPREHENSIBLY	APPROPRIATELY	AQUACULTURISTS
APPETISERS	APPOINTMENTS	APPREHENSION	APPROPRIATENESS	AQUADROMES
APPETISING	APPOINTORS	APPREHENSIONS	APPROPRIATES	AQUAEROBICS
APPETISINGLY	APPORTIONABLE	APPREHENSIVE	APPROPRIATING	AQUAFARMED
APPETITION	APPORTIONED	APPREHENSIVELY	APPROPRIATION	AQUAFARMING
APPETITIONS	APPORTIONER	APPRENTICE	APPROPRIATIONS	AQUAFARMINGS
APPETITIVE	APPORTIONERS	APPRENTICED	APPROPRIATIVE	AQUAFITNESS

AQUAFITNESSES	AQUILINITIES	ARAEOSYSTYLE	ARBORICULTURE	ARCHBISHOP
AQUAFORTIS	AQUILINITY	ARAEOSYSTYLES	ARBORICULTURES	ARCHBISHOPRIC
AQUAFORTISES	ARABESQUED	ARAGONITES	ARBORICULTURIST	ARCHBISHOPRICS
AQUAFORTIST	ARABESQUES	ARAGONITIC	ARBORISATION	ARCHBISHOPS
AQUAFORTISTS	ARABICISATION	ARALIACEOUS	ARBORISATIONS	ARCHDEACON
AQUALEATHER	ARABICISATIONS	ARAUCARIAN	ARBORISING	ARCHDEACONRIES
AQUALEATHERS	ARABICISED	ARAUCARIAS	ARBORIZATION	ARCHDEACONRY
AQUAMANALE	ARABICISES	ARBALESTER	ARBORIZATIONS	ARCHDEACONS
AQUAMANALES	ARABICISING	ARBALESTERS	ARBORIZING	ARCHDIOCESAN
AQUAMANILE	ARABICIZATION	ARBALISTER	ARBORVITAE	ARCHDIOCESE
AQUAMANILES	ARABICIZATIONS	ARBALISTERS	ARBORVITAES	ARCHDIOCESES
AQUAMARINE	ARABICIZED	ARBITRABLE	ARBOVIRUSES	ARCHDRUIDS
AQUAMARINES	ARABICIZES	ARBITRAGED	ARBUSCULAR	ARCHDUCHESS
AQUANAUTICS	ARABICIZING	ARBITRAGER	ARCANENESS	ARCHDUCHESSES
AQUAPHOBES	ARABILITIES	ARBITRAGERS	ARCANENESSES	ARCHDUCHIES
AQUAPHOBIA	ARABINOSES	ARBITRAGES	ARCCOSINES	ARCHDUKEDOM
AQUAPHOBIAS	ARABINOSIDE	ARBITRAGEUR	ARCHAEBACTERIA	ARCHDUKEDOMS
AQUAPHOBIC	ARABINOSIDES	ARBITRAGEURS	ARCHAEBACTERIUM	ARCHEGONIA
AQUAPHOBICS	ARABISATION	ARBITRAGING	ARCHAEOBOTANIES	ARCHEGONIAL
AQUAPLANED	ARABISATIONS	ARBITRAMENT	ARCHAEOBOTANIST	ARCHEGONIATE
AQUAPLANER	ARABIZATION	ARBITRAMENTS	ARCHAEOBOTANY	ARCHEGONIATES
AQUAPLANERS	ARABIZATIONS	ARBITRARILY	ARCHAEOLOGICAL	ARCHEGONIUM
AQUAPLANES	ARACHIDONIC	ARBITRARINESS	ARCHAEOLOGIES	ARCHENEMIES
AQUAPLANING	ARACHNIDAN	ARBITRARINESSES	ARCHAEOLOGIST	ARCHENTERA
AQUAPLANINGS	ARACHNIDANS	ARBITRATED	ARCHAEOLOGISTS	ARCHENTERIC
AQUAPORINS	ARACHNOIDAL	ARBITRATES	ARCHAEOLOGY	ARCHENTERON
AQUARELLES	ARACHNOIDITIS	ARBITRATING	ARCHAEOMETRIC	ARCHENTERONS
AQUARELLIST	ARACHNOIDITISES	ARBITRATION	ARCHAEOMETRIES	ARCHEOASTRONOMY
AQUARELLISTS	ARACHNOIDS	ARBITRATIONAL	ARCHAEOMETRIST	ARCHEOBOTANIES
AQUARIISTS	ARACHNOLOGICAL	ARBITRATIONS	ARCHAEOMETRISTS	ARCHEOBOTANIST
AQUAROBICS	ARACHNOLOGIES	ARBITRATIVE	ARCHAEOMETRY	ARCHEOBOTANISTS
AQUASCAPES	ARACHNOLOGIST	ARBITRATOR	ARCHAEOPTERYX	ARCHEOBOTANY
AQUATICALLY	ARACHNOLOGISTS	ARBITRATORS	ARCHAEOPTERYXES	ARCHEOLOGICAL
AQUATINTAS	ARACHNOLOGY	ARBITRATRICES	ARCHAEORNIS	ARCHEOLOGICALLY
AQUATINTED	ARACHNOPHOBE	ARBITRATRIX	ARCHAEORNISES	ARCHEOLOGIES
AQUATINTER	ARACHNOPHOBES	ARBITRATRIXES	ARCHAEOZOOLOGY	ARCHEOLOGIST
AQUATINTERS	ARACHNOPHOBIA	ARBITREMENT	ARCHAEZOOLOGIES	ARCHEOLOGISTS
AQUATINTING	ARACHNOPHOBIAS	ARBITREMENTS	ARCHAEZOOLOGY	ARCHEOLOGY
AQUATINTIST	ARACHNOPHOBIC	ARBITRESSES	ARCHAICALLY	ARCHEOMAGNETISM
AQUATINTISTS	ARACHNOPHOBICS	ARBITRIUMS	ARCHAICISM	ARCHEOMETRIES
AQUICULTURAL	ARAEOMETER	ARBLASTERS	ARCHAICISMS	ARCHEOMETRY
AQUICULTURE	ARAEOMETERS	ARBORACEOUS	ARCHAISERS	ARCHEOZOOLOGIES
AQUICULTURES	ARAEOMETRIC	ARBOREALLY	ARCHAISING	ARCHEOZOOLOGIST
AQUICULTURIST	ARAEOMETRICAL	ARBORESCENCE	ARCHAISTIC	ARCHEOZOOLOGY
AQUICULTURISTS	ARAEOMETRIES	ARBORESCENCES	ARCHAIZERS	ARCHERESSES
AQUIFEROUS	ARAEOMETRY	ARBORESCENT	ARCHAIZING	ARCHERFISH
AQUIFOLIACEOUS	ARAEOSTYLE	ARBORETUMS	ARCHANGELIC	ARCHERFISHES
AQUILEGIAS	ARAEOSTYLES	ARBORICULTURAL	ARCHANGELS	ARCHESPORE

ARCHESPORES

ARCHESPORES	ARCHNESSES	AREOGRAPHIC	ARISTOLOGY	ARPEGGIATED
ARCHESPORIA	ARCHOLOGIES	AREOGRAPHIES	ARISTOTLES	ARPEGGIATES
ARCHESPORIAL	ARCHONSHIP	AREOGRAPHY	ARITHMETIC	ARPEGGIATING
ARCHESPORIUM	ARCHONSHIPS	AREOLATION	ARITHMETICAL	ARPEGGIATION
ARCHETYPAL	ARCHONTATE	AREOLATIONS	ARITHMETICALLY	ARPEGGIATIONS
ARCHETYPALLY	ARCHONTATES	AREOLOGIES	ARITHMETICIAN	ARPEGGIONE
ARCHETYPES	ARCHOPLASM	AREOMETERS	ARITHMETICIANS	ARPEGGIONES
ARCHETYPICAL	ARCHOPLASMIC	AREOMETRIES	ARITHMETICS	ARPILLERAS
ARCHETYPICALLY	ARCHOPLASMS	AREOSTYLES	ARITHMOMANIA	ARQUEBUSADE
ARCHFIENDS	ARCHOSAURIAN	AREOSYSTILE	ARITHMOMANIAS	ARQUEBUSADES
ARCHGENETHLIAC	ARCHOSAURIANS	AREOSYSTILES	ARITHMOMETER	ARQUEBUSES
ARCHGENETHLIACS	ARCHOSAURS	ARFVEDSONITE	ARITHMOMETERS	ARQUEBUSIER
ARCHICARPS	ARCHPRIEST	ARFVEDSONITES	ARITHMOPHOBIA	ARQUEBUSIERS
ARCHIDIACONAL	ARCHPRIESTHOOD	ARGENTIFEROUS	ARITHMOPHOBIAS	ARRACACHAS
ARCHIDIACONATE	ARCHPRIESTHOODS	ARGENTINES	ARMADILLOS	ARRAGONITE
ARCHIDIACONATES	ARCHPRIESTS	ARGENTITES	ARMAMENTARIA	ARRAGONITES
ARCHIEPISCOPACY	ARCHPRIESTSHIP	ARGILLACEOUS	ARMAMENTARIUM	ARRAGONITIC
ARCHIEPISCOPAL	ARCHPRIESTSHIPS	ARGILLIFEROUS	ARMAMENTARIUMS	ARRAIGNERS
ARCHIEPISCOPATE	ARCHRIVALS	ARGILLITES	ARMATURING	ARRAIGNING
ARCHILOWES	ARCHSTONES	ARGILLITIC	ARMIGEROUS	ARRAIGNINGS
ARCHIMAGES	ARCMINUTES	ARGONAUTIC	ARMILLARIA	ARRAIGNMENT
ARCHIMANDRITE	ARCOGRAPHS	ARGUMENTATION	ARMILLARIAS	ARRAIGNMENTS
ARCHIMANDRITES	ARCOLOGIES	ARGUMENTATIONS	ARMIPOTENCE	ARRANGEABLE
ARCHIPELAGIAN	ARCSECONDS	ARGUMENTATIVE	ARMIPOTENCES	ARRANGEMENT
ARCHIPELAGIC	ARCTANGENT	ARGUMENTATIVELY	ARMIPOTENT	ARRANGEMENTS
ARCHIPELAGO	ARCTANGENTS	ARGUMENTIVE	ARMISTICES	ARRAYMENTS
ARCHIPELAGOES	ARCTICALLY	ARGUMENTUM	ARMLOCKING	ARREARAGES
ARCHIPELAGOS	ARCTOPHILE	ARGUMENTUMS	ARMORIALLY	ARRESTABLE
ARCHIPHONEME	ARCTOPHILES	ARGUTENESS	ARMOURLESS	ARRESTANTS
ARCHIPHONEMES	ARCTOPHILIA	ARGUTENESSES	AROMATASES	ARRESTATION
ARCHIPLASM	ARCTOPHILIAS	ARGYRODITE	AROMATHERAPIES	ARRESTATIONS
ARCHIPLASMIC	ARCTOPHILIES	ARGYRODITES	AROMATHERAPIST	ARRESTINGLY
ARCHIPLASMS	ARCTOPHILIST	ARHATSHIPS	AROMATHERAPISTS	ARRESTMENT
ARCHITECTED	ARCTOPHILISTS	ARHYTHMIAS	AROMATHERAPY	ARRESTMENTS
ARCHITECTING	ARCTOPHILS	ARIBOFLAVINOSES	AROMATICALLY	ARRHENOTOKIES
ARCHITECTONIC	ARCTOPHILY	ARIBOFLAVINOSIS	AROMATICITIES	ARRHENOTOKY
ARCHITECTONICS	ARCUATIONS	ARIDNESSES	AROMATICITY	ARRHYTHMIA
ARCHITECTS	ARCUBALIST	ARISTOCRACIES	AROMATISATION	ARRHYTHMIAS
ARCHITECTURAL	ARCUBALISTS	ARISTOCRACY	AROMATISATIONS	ARRHYTHMIC
ARCHITECTURALLY	ARDUOUSNESS	ARISTOCRAT	AROMATISED	ARRIVANCES
ARCHITECTURE	ARDUOUSNESSES	ARISTOCRATIC	AROMATISES	ARRIVANCIES
ARCHITECTURES	ARECOLINES	ARISTOCRATICAL	AROMATISING	ARRIVEDERCI
ARCHITRAVE	AREFACTION	ARISTOCRATISM	AROMATIZATION	ARRIVISMES
ARCHITRAVED	AREFACTIONS	ARISTOCRATISMS	AROMATIZATIONS	ARRIVISTES
ARCHITRAVES	ARENACEOUS	ARISTOCRATS	AROMATIZED	ARROGANCES
ARCHITYPES	ARENATIONS	ARISTOLOCHIA	AROMATIZES	ARROGANCIES
ARCHIVISTS	ARENICOLOUS	ARISTOLOCHIAS	AROMATIZING	ARROGANTLY
ARCHIVOLTS	AREOCENTRIC	ARISTOLOGIES	ARPEGGIATE	ARROGATING

ARROGATION	ARTFULNESSES	ARTICULATIVE	ASAFOETIDA	ASCOSPORES
ARROGATIONS	ARTHRALGIA	ARTICULATOR	ASAFOETIDAS	ASCOSPORIC
ARROGATIVE	ARTHRALGIAS	ARTICULATORS	ASARABACCA	ASCRIBABLE
ARROGATORS	ARTHRALGIC	ARTICULATORY	ASARABACCAS	ASCRIPTION
ARRONDISSEMENT	ARTHRECTOMIES	ARTIFACTUAL	ASBESTIFORM	ASCRIPTIONS
ARRONDISSEMENTS	ARTHRECTOMY	ARTIFICERS	ASBESTOSES	ASCRIPTIVE
ARROWGRASS	ARTHRITICALLY	ARTIFICIAL	ASBESTOSIS	ASEPTICALLY
ARROWGRASSES	ARTHRITICS	ARTIFICIALISE	ASBESTUSES	ASEPTICISE
ARROWHEADS	ARTHRITIDES	ARTIFICIALISED	ASCARIASES	ASEPTICISED
ARROWROOTS	ARTHRITISES	ARTIFICIALISES	ASCARIASIS	ASEPTICISES
ARROWWOODS	ARTHRODESES	ARTIFICIALISING	ASCENDABLE	ASEPTICISING
ARROWWORMS	ARTHRODESIS	ARTIFICIALITIES	ASCENDANCE	ASEPTICISM
ARSENIATES	ARTHRODIAE	ARTIFICIALITY	ASCENDANCES	ASEPTICISMS
ARSENICALS	ARTHRODIAL	ARTIFICIALIZE	ASCENDANCIES	ASEPTICIZE
ARSENOPYRITE	ARTHROGRAPHIES	ARTIFICIALIZED	ASCENDANCY	ASEPTICIZED
ARSENOPYRITES	ARTHROGRAPHY	ARTIFICIALIZES	ASCENDANTLY	ASEPTICIZES
ARSMETRICK	ARTHROMERE	ARTIFICIALIZING	ASCENDANTS	ASEPTICIZING
ARSMETRICKS	ARTHROMERES	ARTIFICIALLY	ASCENDENCE	ASEXUALITIES
ARSPHENAMINE	ARTHROMERIC	ARTIFICIALNESS	ASCENDENCES	ASEXUALITY
ARSPHENAMINES	ARTHROPATHIES	ARTILLERIES	ASCENDENCIES	ASHAMEDNESS
ARTEFACTUAL	ARTHROPATHY	ARTILLERIST	ASCENDENCY	ASHAMEDNESSES
ARTEMISIAS	ARTHROPLASTIES	ARTILLERISTS	ASCENDENTS	ASHINESSES
ARTEMISININ	ARTHROPLASTY	ARTILLERYMAN	ASCENDEURS	ASHLARINGS
ARTEMISININS	ARTHROPODAL	ARTILLERYMEN	ASCENDIBLE	ASHLERINGS
ARTERIALISATION	ARTHROPODAN	ARTINESSES	ASCENSIONAL	ASHRAMITES
ARTERIALISE	ARTHROPODOUS	ARTIODACTYL	ASCENSIONIST	ASININITIES
ARTERIALISED	ARTHROPODS	ARTIODACTYLOUS	ASCENSIONISTS	ASKEWNESSES
ARTERIALISES	ARTHROSCOPE	ARTIODACTYLS	ASCENSIONS	ASPARAGINASE
ARTERIALISING	ARTHROSCOPES	ARTISANSHIP	ASCERTAINABLE	ASPARAGINASES
ARTERIALIZATION	ARTHROSCOPIC	ARTISANSHIPS	ASCERTAINABLY	ASPARAGINE
ARTERIALIZE	ARTHROSCOPIES	ARTISTICAL	ASCERTAINED	ASPARAGINES
ARTERIALIZED	ARTHROSCOPY	ARTISTICALLY	ASCERTAINING	ASPARAGUSES
ARTERIALIZES	ARTHROSPORE	ARTISTRIES	ASCERTAINMENT	ASPARTAMES
ARTERIALIZING	ARTHROSPORES	ARTLESSNESS	ASCERTAINMENTS	ASPARTATES
ARTERIALLY	ARTHROSPORIC	ARTLESSNESSES	ASCERTAINS	ASPECTABLE
ARTERIOGRAM	ARTHROSPOROUS	ARTMAKINGS	ASCETICALLY	ASPERATING
ARTERIOGRAMS	ARTICHOKES	ARTOCARPUS	ASCETICISM	ASPERGATION
ARTERIOGRAPHIC	ARTICULABLE	ARTOCARPUSES	ASCETICISMS	ASPERGATIONS
ARTERIOGRAPHIES	ARTICULACIES	ARTSINESSES	ASCITITIOUS	ASPERGILLA
ARTERIOGRAPHY	ARTICULACY	ARUNDINACEOUS	ASCLEPIADACEOUS	ASPERGILLI
ARTERIOLAR	ARTICULATE	ARVICOLINE	ASCLEPIADS	ASPERGILLOSES
ARTERIOLES	ARTICULATED	ARYBALLOID	ASCLEPIASES	ASPERGILLOSIS
ARTERIOTOMIES	ARTICULATELY	ARYBALLOSES	ASCOCARPIC	ASPERGILLS
ARTERIOTOMY	ARTICULATENESS	ARYTAENOID	ASCOGONIUM	ASPERGILLUM
ARTERIOVENOUS	ARTICULATES	ARYTAENOIDS	ASCOMYCETE	ASPERGILLUMS
ARTERITIDES	ARTICULATING	ARYTENOIDAL	ASCOMYCETES	ASPERGILLUS
ARTERITISES	ARTICULATION	ARYTENOIDS	ASCOMYCETOUS	ASPERITIES
ARTFULNESS	ARTICULATIONS	ASAFETIDAS	ASCORBATES	ASPERSIONS

ASPERSIVELY	ASSAFETIDA	ASSENTIVENESS	ASSIMILATES	ASSORTEDNESS
ASPERSOIRS	ASSAFETIDAS	ASSENTIVENESSES	ASSIMILATING	ASSORTEDNESSES
ASPERSORIA	ASSAFOETIDA	ASSERTABLE	ASSIMILATION	ASSORTMENT
ASPERSORIES	ASSAFOETIDAS	ASSERTEDLY	ASSIMILATIONISM	ASSORTMENTS
ASPERSORIUM	ASSAGAIING	ASSERTIBLE	ASSIMILATIONIST	ASSUAGEMENT
ASPERSORIUMS	ASSAILABLE	ASSERTIONS	ASSIMILATIONS	ASSUAGEMENTS
ASPHALTERS	ASSAILANTS	ASSERTIVELY	ASSIMILATIVE	ASSUAGINGS
ASPHALTING	ASSAILMENT	ASSERTIVENESS	ASSIMILATIVELY	ASSUBJUGATE
ASPHALTITE	ASSAILMENTS	ASSERTIVENESSES	ASSIMILATOR	ASSUBJUGATED
ASPHALTITES	ASSASSINATE	ASSERTORIC	ASSIMILATORS	ASSUBJUGATES
ASPHALTUMS	ASSASSINATED	ASSESSABLE	ASSIMILATORY	ASSUBJUGATING
ASPHERICAL	ASSASSINATES	ASSESSMENT	ASSISTANCE	ASSUEFACTION
ASPHETERISE	ASSASSINATING	ASSESSMENTS	ASSISTANCES	ASSUEFACTIONS
ASPHETERISED	ASSASSINATION	ASSESSORIAL	ASSISTANTS	ASSUETUDES
ASPHETERISES	ASSASSINATIONS	ASSESSORSHIP	ASSISTANTSHIP	ASSUMABILITIES
ASPHETERISING	ASSASSINATOR	ASSESSORSHIPS	ASSISTANTSHIPS	ASSUMABILITY
ASPHETERISM	ASSASSINATORS	ASSEVERATE	ASSOCIABILITIES	ASSUMINGLY
ASPHETERISMS	ASSAULTERS	ASSEVERATED	ASSOCIABILITY	ASSUMPSITS
ASPHETERIZE	ASSAULTING	ASSEVERATES	ASSOCIABLE	ASSUMPTION
ASPHETERIZED	ASSAULTIVE	ASSEVERATING	ASSOCIATED	ASSUMPTIONS
ASPHETERIZES	ASSAULTIVELY	ASSEVERATINGLY	ASSOCIATES	ASSUMPTIVE
ASPHETERIZING	ASSAULTIVENESS	ASSEVERATION	ASSOCIATESHIP	ASSUMPTIVELY
ASPHYXIANT	ASSEGAAIED	ASSEVERATIONS	ASSOCIATESHIPS	ASSURANCES
ASPHYXIANTS	ASSEGAAIING	ASSEVERATIVE	ASSOCIATING	ASSUREDNESS
ASPHYXIATE	ASSEGAIING	ASSEVERING	ASSOCIATION	ASSUREDNESSES
ASPHYXIATED	ASSEMBLAGE	ASSIBILATE	ASSOCIATIONAL	ASSURGENCIES
ASPHYXIATES	ASSEMBLAGES	ASSIBILATED	ASSOCIATIONISM	ASSURGENCY
ASPHYXIATING	ASSEMBLAGIST	ASSIBILATES	ASSOCIATIONISMS	ASSYTHMENT
ASPHYXIATION	ASSEMBLAGISTS	ASSIBILATING	ASSOCIATIONIST	ASSYTHMENTS
ASPHYXIATIONS	ASSEMBLANCE	ASSIBILATION	ASSOCIATIONISTS	ASTACOLOGICAL
ASPHYXIATOR	ASSEMBLANCES	ASSIBILATIONS	ASSOCIATIONS	ASTACOLOGIES
ASPHYXIATORS	ASSEMBLAUNCE	ASSIDUITIES	ASSOCIATIVE	ASTACOLOGIST
ASPHYXYING	ASSEMBLAUNCES	ASSIDUOUSLY	ASSOCIATIVELY	ASTACOLOGISTS
ASPIDISTRA	ASSEMBLERS	ASSIDUOUSNESS	ASSOCIATIVITIES	ASTACOLOGY
ASPIDISTRAS	ASSEMBLIES	ASSIDUOUSNESSES	ASSOCIATIVITY	ASTARBOARD
ASPIRATING	ASSEMBLING	ASSIGNABILITIES	ASSOCIATOR	ASTATICALLY
ASPIRATION	ASSEMBLYMAN	ASSIGNABILITY	ASSOCIATORS	ASTATICISM
ASPIRATIONAL	ASSEMBLYMEN	ASSIGNABLE	ASSOCIATORY	ASTATICISMS
ASPIRATIONS	ASSEMBLYWOMAN	ASSIGNABLY	ASSOILMENT	ASTEREOGNOSES
ASPIRATORS	ASSEMBLYWOMEN	ASSIGNATION	ASSOILMENTS	ASTEREOGNOSIS
ASPIRATORY	ASSENTANEOUS	ASSIGNATIONS	ASSOILZIED	ASTERIATED
ASPIRINGLY	ASSENTATION	ASSIGNMENT	ASSOILZIEING	ASTERIDIAN
ASPIRINGNESS	ASSENTATIONS	ASSIGNMENTS	ASSOILZIES	ASTERIDIANS
ASPIRINGNESSES	ASSENTATOR	ASSIMILABILITY	ASSONANCES	ASTERISKED
ASPLANCHNIC	ASSENTATORS	ASSIMILABLE	ASSONANTAL	ASTERISKING
ASPLENIUMS	ASSENTIENT	ASSIMILABLY	ASSONATING	ASTERISKLESS
ASPORTATION	ASSENTIENTS	ASSIMILATE	ASSORTATIVE	ASTEROIDAL
ASPORTATIONS	ASSENTINGLY	ASSIMILATED	ASSORTATIVELY	ASTEROIDEAN

A

ASTEROIDEANS	ASTRINGING	ASTRONAVIGATOR	ASYMPTOTICALLY	ATHLEISURES
ASTHENOPIA	ASTROBIOLOGIES	ASTRONAVIGATORS	ASYNARTETE	ATHLETICALLY
ASTHENOPIAS	ASTROBIOLOGIST	ASTRONOMER	ASYNARTETES	ATHLETICISM
ASTHENOPIC	ASTROBIOLOGISTS	ASTRONOMERS	ASYNARTETIC	ATHLETICISMS
ASTHENOSPHERE	ASTROBIOLOGY	ASTRONOMIC	ASYNCHRONIES	ATHROCYTES
ASTHENOSPHERES	ASTROBLEME	ASTRONOMICAL	ASYNCHRONISM	ATHROCYTOSES
ASTHENOSPHERIC	ASTROBLEMES	ASTRONOMICALLY	ASYNCHRONISMS	ATHROCYTOSIS
ASTHMATICAL	ASTROBOTANIES	ASTRONOMIES	ASYNCHRONOUS	ATHWARTSHIP
ASTHMATICALLY	ASTROBOTANY	ASTRONOMISE	ASYNCHRONOUSLY	ATHWARTSHIPS
ASTHMATICS	ASTROCHEMISTRY	ASTRONOMISED	ASYNCHRONY	ATMOLOGIES
ASTIGMATIC	ASTROCOMPASS	ASTRONOMISES	ASYNDETICALLY	ATMOLOGIST
ASTIGMATICALLY	ASTROCOMPASSES	ASTRONOMISING	ASYNDETONS	ATMOLOGISTS
ASTIGMATICS	ASTROCYTES	ASTRONOMIZE	ASYNERGIAS	ATMOLYSING
ASTIGMATISM	ASTROCYTIC	ASTRONOMIZED	ASYNERGIES	ATMOLYZING
ASTIGMATISMS	ASTROCYTOMA	ASTRONOMIZES	ASYNTACTIC	ATMOMETERS
ASTOMATOUS	ASTROCYTOMAS	ASTRONOMIZING	ASYSTOLISM	ATMOMETRIES
ASTONISHED	ASTROCYTOMATA	ASTROPHELS	ASYSTOLISMS	ATMOSPHERE
ASTONISHES	ASTRODOMES	ASTROPHOBIA	ATACAMITES	ATMOSPHERED
ASTONISHING	ASTRODYNAMICIST	ASTROPHOBIAS	ATARACTICS	ATMOSPHERES
ASTONISHINGLY	ASTRODYNAMICS	ASTROPHOBIC	ATAVISTICALLY	ATMOSPHERIC
ASTONISHMENT	ASTROFELLS	ASTROPHOTOGRAPH	ATCHIEVING	ATMOSPHERICAL
ASTONISHMENTS	ASTROGEOLOGIES	ASTROPHYSICAL	ATELECTASES	ATMOSPHERICALLY
ASTOUNDING	ASTROGEOLOGIST	ASTROPHYSICALLY	ATELECTASIS	ATMOSPHERICS
ASTOUNDINGLY	ASTROGEOLOGISTS	ASTROPHYSICIST	ATELECTATIC	ATOMICALLY
ASTOUNDMENT	ASTROGEOLOGY	ASTROPHYSICISTS	ATELEIOSES	ATOMICITIES
ASTOUNDMENTS	ASTROHATCH	ASTROPHYSICS	ATELEIOSIS	ATOMISATION
ASTRACHANS	ASTROHATCHES	ASTROSPHERE	ATHANASIES	ATOMISATIONS
ASTRAGALUS	ASTROLABES	ASTROSPHERES	ATHEISTICAL	ATOMISTICAL
ASTRAKHANS	ASTROLATRIES	ASTROTOURISM	ATHEISTICALLY	ATOMISTICALLY
ASTRANTIAS	ASTROLATRY	ASTROTOURISMS	ATHEMATICALLY	ATOMIZATION
ASTRAPHOBIA	ASTROLOGER	ASTROTOURIST	ATHENAEUMS	ATOMIZATIONS
ASTRAPHOBIAS	ASTROLOGERS	ASTROTOURISTS	ATHEOLOGICAL	ATONALISMS
ASTRAPHOBIC	ASTROLOGIC	ASTROTURFER	ATHEOLOGIES	ATONALISTS
ASTRAPOPHOBIA	ASTROLOGICAL	ASTROTURFERS	ATHEORETICAL	ATONALITIES
ASTRAPOPHOBIAS	ASTROLOGICALLY	ASTROTURFING	ATHERMANCIES	ATONEMENTS
ASTRICTING	ASTROLOGIES	ASTROTURFINGS	ATHERMANCY	ATONICITIES
ASTRICTION	ASTROLOGIST	ASTUCIOUSLY	ATHERMANOUS	ATORVASTATIN
ASTRICTIONS	ASTROLOGISTS	ASTUCITIES	ATHEROGENESES	ATORVASTATINS
ASTRICTIVE	ASTROMETRIC	ASTUTENESS	ATHEROGENESIS	ATRABILIAR
ASTRICTIVELY	ASTROMETRICAL	ASTUTENESSES	ATHEROGENIC	ATRABILIOUS
ASTRINGENCE	ASTROMETRIES	ASYMMETRIC	ATHEROMATA	ATRABILIOUSNESS
ASTRINGENCES	ASTROMETRY	ASYMMETRICAL	ATHEROMATOUS	ATRACURIUM
ASTRINGENCIES	ASTRONAUTIC	ASYMMETRICALLY	ATHEROSCLEROSES	ATRACURIUMS
ASTRINGENCY	ASTRONAUTICAL	ASYMMETRIES	ATHEROSCLEROSIS	ATRAMENTAL
ASTRINGENT	ASTRONAUTICALLY	ASYMPTOMATIC	ATHEROSCLEROTIC	ATRAMENTOUS
ASTRINGENTLY	ASTRONAUTICS	ASYMPTOTES	ATHETISING	ATROCIOUSLY
ASTRINGENTS	ASTRONAUTS	ASYMPTOTIC	ATHETIZING	ATROCIOUSNESS
ASTRINGERS	ASTRONAVIGATION	ASYMPTOTICAL	ATHLEISURE	ATROCIOUSNESSES

ATROCITIES	ATTENUATORS	ATTRACTABLE	AUBRIETIAS	AUDIOTYPISTS
ATROPHYING	ATTESTABLE	ATTRACTANCE	AUCTIONARY	AUDIOVISUAL
ATTACHABLE	ATTESTANTS	ATTRACTANCES	AUCTIONEER	AUDIOVISUALLY
ATTACHMENT	ATTESTATION	ATTRACTANCIES	AUCTIONEERED	AUDIOVISUALS
ATTACHMENTS	ATTESTATIONS	ATTRACTANCY	AUCTIONEERING	AUDIPHONES
ATTACKABLE	ATTESTATIVE	ATTRACTANT	AUCTIONEERS	AUDITIONED
ATTAINABILITIES	ATTESTATOR	ATTRACTANTS	AUCTIONING	AUDITIONER
ATTAINABILITY	ATTESTATORS	ATTRACTERS	AUDACIOUSLY	AUDITIONERS
ATTAINABLE	ATTICISING	ATTRACTING	AUDACIOUSNESS	AUDITIONING
ATTAINABLENESS	ATTICIZING	ATTRACTINGLY	AUDACIOUSNESSES	AUDITORIAL
ATTAINDERS	ATTIREMENT	ATTRACTION	AUDACITIES	AUDITORIES
ATTAINMENT	ATTIREMENTS	ATTRACTIONS	AUDIBILITIES	AUDITORILY
ATTAINMENTS	ATTITUDINAL	ATTRACTIVE	AUDIBILITY	AUDITORIUM
ATTAINTING	ATTITUDINALLY	ATTRACTIVELY	AUDIBLENESS	AUDITORIUMS
ATTAINTMENT	ATTITUDINARIAN	ATTRACTIVENESS	AUDIBLENESSES	AUDITORSHIP
ATTAINTMENTS	ATTITUDINARIANS	ATTRACTORS	AUDIENCIAS	AUDITORSHIPS
ATTAINTURE	ATTITUDINISE	ATTRAHENTS	AUDIOBOOKS	AUDITRESSES
ATTAINTURES	ATTITUDINISED	ATTRAPPING	AUDIOCASSETTE	AUGMENTABLE
ATTEMPERED	ATTITUDINISER	ATTRIBUTABLE	AUDIOCASSETTES	AUGMENTATION
ATTEMPERING	ATTITUDINISERS	ATTRIBUTED	AUDIOGENIC	AUGMENTATIONS
ATTEMPERMENT	ATTITUDINISES	ATTRIBUTER	AUDIOGRAMS	AUGMENTATIVE
ATTEMPERMENTS	ATTITUDINISING	ATTRIBUTERS	AUDIOGRAPH	AUGMENTATIVELY
ATTEMPTABILITY	ATTITUDINISINGS	ATTRIBUTES	AUDIOGRAPHS	AUGMENTATIVES
ATTEMPTABLE	ATTITUDINIZE	ATTRIBUTING	AUDIOLOGIC	AUGMENTERS
ATTEMPTERS	ATTITUDINIZED	ATTRIBUTION	AUDIOLOGICAL	AUGMENTING
ATTEMPTING	ATTITUDINIZER	ATTRIBUTIONAL	AUDIOLOGICALLY	AUGMENTORS
ATTENDANCE	ATTITUDINIZERS	ATTRIBUTIONS	AUDIOLOGIES	AUGURSHIPS
ATTENDANCES	ATTITUDINIZES	ATTRIBUTIVE	AUDIOLOGIST	AUGUSTNESS
ATTENDANCIES	ATTITUDINIZING	ATTRIBUTIVELY	AUDIOLOGISTS	AUGUSTNESSES
ATTENDANCY	ATTITUDINIZINGS	ATTRIBUTIVENESS	AUDIOMETER	AURALITIES
ATTENDANTS	ATTOLASERS	ATTRIBUTIVES	AUDIOMETERS	AUREATENESS
ATTENDEMENT	ATTOLLENTS	ATTRIBUTOR	AUDIOMETRIC	AUREATENESSES
ATTENDEMENTS	ATTOMETERS	ATTRIBUTORS	AUDIOMETRICALLY	AURICULARLY
ATTENDINGS	ATTOMETRES	ATTRISTING	AUDIOMETRICIAN	AURICULARS
ATTENDMENT	ATTOPHYSICS	ATTRITIONAL	AUDIOMETRICIANS	AURICULATE
ATTENDMENTS	ATTORNEYDOM	ATTRITIONS	AUDIOMETRIES	AURICULATED
ATTENTIONAL	ATTORNEYDOMS	ATTRITTING	AUDIOMETRIST	AURICULATELY
ATTENTIONS	ATTORNEYED	ATTUITIONAL	AUDIOMETRISTS	AURIFEROUS
ATTENTIVELY	ATTORNEYING	ATTUITIONS	AUDIOMETRY	AURISCOPES
ATTENTIVENESS	ATTORNEYISM	ATTUITIVELY	AUDIOPHILE	AURISCOPIC
ATTENTIVENESSES	ATTORNEYISMS	ATTUNEMENT	AUDIOPHILES	AUSCULTATE
ATTENUANTS	ATTORNEYSHIP	ATTUNEMENTS	AUDIOPHILS	AUSCULTATED
ATTENUATED	ATTORNEYSHIPS	ATYPICALITIES	AUDIOTAPED	AUSCULTATES
ATTENUATES	ATTORNMENT	ATYPICALITY	AUDIOTAPES	AUSCULTATING
ATTENUATING	ATTORNMENTS	ATYPICALLY	AUDIOTAPING	AUSCULTATION
ATTENUATION	ATTOSECOND	AUBERGINES	AUDIOTYPING	AUSCULTATIONS
ATTENUATIONS	ATTOSECONDS	AUBERGISTE	AUDIOTYPINGS	AUSCULTATIVE
ATTENUATOR	ATTOTESLAS	AUBERGISTES	AUDIOTYPIST	AUSCULTATOR

AUSCULTATORS	AUTHORINGS	AUTOCATALYZING	AUTODIDACTICISM	AUTOIONISATIONS
AUSCULTATORY	AUTHORISABLE	AUTOCEPHALIC	AUTODIDACTS	AUTOIONIZATION
AUSFORMING	AUTHORISATION	AUTOCEPHALIES	AUTODROMES	AUTOIONIZATIONS
AUSFORMINGS	AUTHORISATIONS	AUTOCEPHALOUS	AUTOECIOUS	AUTOJUMBLE
AUSLANDERS	AUTHORISED	AUTOCEPHALY	AUTOECIOUSLY	AUTOJUMBLES
AUSPICATED	AUTHORISER	AUTOCHANGER	AUTOECISMS	AUTOKINESES
AUSPICATES	AUTHORISERS	AUTOCHANGERS	AUTOEROTIC	AUTOKINESIS
AUSPICATING	AUTHORISES	AUTOCHTHON	AUTOEROTICISM	AUTOKINETIC
AUSPICIOUS	AUTHORISING	AUTOCHTHONAL	AUTOEROTICISMS	AUTOLATRIES
AUSPICIOUSLY	AUTHORISMS	AUTOCHTHONES	AUTOEROTISM	AUTOLOADED
AUSPICIOUSNESS	AUTHORITARIAN	AUTOCHTHONIC	AUTOEROTISMS	AUTOLOADING
AUSTENITES	AUTHORITARIANS	AUTOCHTHONIES	AUTOEXPOSURE	AUTOLOGIES
AUSTENITIC	AUTHORITATIVE	AUTOCHTHONISM	AUTOEXPOSURES	AUTOLOGOUS
AUSTERENESS	AUTHORITATIVELY	AUTOCHTHONISMS	AUTOFLARES	AUTOLYSATE
AUSTERENESSES	AUTHORITIES	AUTOCHTHONOUS	AUTOFOCUSES	AUTOLYSATES
AUSTERITIES	AUTHORIZABLE	AUTOCHTHONOUSLY	AUTOGAMIES	AUTOLYSING
AUSTRALITE	AUTHORIZATION	AUTOCHTHONS	AUTOGAMOUS	AUTOLYSINS
AUSTRALITES	AUTHORIZATIONS	AUTOCHTHONY	AUTOGENESES	AUTOLYZATE
AUSTRINGER	AUTHORIZED	AUTOCLAVED	AUTOGENESIS	AUTOLYZATES
AUSTRINGERS	AUTHORIZER	AUTOCLAVES	AUTOGENETIC	AUTOLYZING
AUTARCHICAL	AUTHORIZERS	AUTOCLAVING	AUTOGENICS	AUTOMAGICALLY
AUTARCHIES	AUTHORIZES	AUTOCOMPLETE	AUTOGENIES	AUTOMAKERS
AUTARCHIST	AUTHORIZING	AUTOCOMPLETES	AUTOGENOUS	AUTOMATABLE
AUTARCHISTS	AUTHORLESS	AUTOCOPROPHAGY	AUTOGENOUSLY	AUTOMATICAL
AUTARKICAL	AUTHORSHIP	AUTOCORRECT	AUTOGRAFTED	AUTOMATICALLY
AUTARKISTS	AUTHORSHIPS	AUTOCORRECTS	AUTOGRAFTING	AUTOMATICITIES
AUTECOLOGIC	AUTISTICALLY	AUTOCORRELATION	AUTOGRAFTS	AUTOMATICITY
AUTECOLOGICAL	AUTOALLOGAMIES	AUTOCRACIES	AUTOGRAPHED	AUTOMATICS
AUTECOLOGIES	AUTOALLOGAMY	AUTOCRATIC	AUTOGRAPHIC	AUTOMATING
AUTECOLOGY	AUTOANTIBODIES	AUTOCRATICAL	AUTOGRAPHICAL	AUTOMATION
AUTEURISMS	AUTOANTIBODY	AUTOCRATICALLY	AUTOGRAPHICALLY	AUTOMATIONS
AUTEURISTS	AUTOBAHNEN	AUTOCRIMES	AUTOGRAPHIES	AUTOMATISATION
AUTHENTICAL	AUTOBIOGRAPHER	AUTOCRITIQUE	AUTOGRAPHING	AUTOMATISATIONS
AUTHENTICALLY	AUTOBIOGRAPHERS	AUTOCRITIQUES	AUTOGRAPHS	AUTOMATISE
AUTHENTICATE	AUTOBIOGRAPHIC	AUTOCROSSES	AUTOGRAPHY	AUTOMATISED
AUTHENTICATED	AUTOBIOGRAPHIES	AUTOCUTIES	AUTOGRAVURE	AUTOMATISES
AUTHENTICATES	AUTOBIOGRAPHY	AUTOCYCLES	AUTOGRAVURES	AUTOMATISING
AUTHENTICATING	AUTOBODIES	AUTODESTRUCT	AUTOGUIDES	AUTOMATISM
AUTHENTICATION	AUTOBUSSES	AUTODESTRUCTED	AUTOHYPNOSES	AUTOMATISMS
AUTHENTICATIONS	AUTOCATALYSE	AUTODESTRUCTING	AUTOHYPNOSIS	AUTOMATIST
AUTHENTICATOR	AUTOCATALYSED	AUTODESTRUCTIVE	AUTOHYPNOTIC	AUTOMATISTS
AUTHENTICATORS	AUTOCATALYSES	AUTODESTRUCTS	AUTOIMMUNE	AUTOMATIZATION
AUTHENTICITIES	AUTOCATALYSING	AUTODIALED	AUTOIMMUNITIES	AUTOMATIZATIONS
AUTHENTICITY	AUTOCATALYSIS	AUTODIALING	AUTOIMMUNITY	AUTOMATIZE
AUTHIGENIC	AUTOCATALYTIC	AUTODIALLED	AUTOINFECTION	AUTOMATIZED
AUTHORCRAFT	AUTOCATALYZE	AUTODIALLING	AUTOINFECTIONS	AUTOMATIZES
AUTHORCRAFTS	AUTOCATALYZED	AUTODIDACT	AUTOINOCULATION	AUTOMATIZING
AUTHORESSES	AUTOCATALYZES	AUTODIDACTIC	AUTOIONISATION	AUTOMATONS

AUTOMATOUS	AUTOPSISTS	AUTOTELLER	AUXOMETERS	AVERTIMENTS
AUTOMETERS	AUTOPSYING	AUTOTELLERS	AUXOSPORES	AVGOLEMONO
AUTOMOBILE	AUTOPTICAL	AUTOTETRAPLOID	AUXOTROPHIC	AVGOLEMONOS
AUTOMOBILED	AUTOPTICALLY	AUTOTETRAPLOIDS	AUXOTROPHIES	AVIANISING
AUTOMOBILES	AUTORADIOGRAM	AUTOTETRAPLOIDY	AUXOTROPHS	AVIANIZING
AUTOMOBILIA	AUTORADIOGRAMS	AUTOTHEISM	AUXOTROPHY	AVIATRESSES
AUTOMOBILING	AUTORADIOGRAPH	AUTOTHEISMS	AVAILABILITIES	AVIATRICES
AUTOMOBILISM	AUTORADIOGRAPHS	AUTOTHEIST	AVAILABILITY	AVIATRIXES
AUTOMOBILISMS	AUTORADIOGRAPHY	AUTOTHEISTS	AVAILABLENESS	AVICULTURE
AUTOMOBILIST	AUTOREPLIES	AUTOTIMERS	AVAILABLENESSES	AVICULTURES
AUTOMOBILISTS	AUTOREVERSE	AUTOTOMIES	AVAILINGLY	AVICULTURIST
AUTOMOBILITIES	AUTOREVERSES	AUTOTOMISE	AVALANCHED	AVICULTURISTS
AUTOMOBILITY	AUTORICKSHAW	AUTOTOMISED	AVALANCHES	AVIDNESSES
AUTOMORPHIC	AUTORICKSHAWS	AUTOTOMISES	AVALANCHING	AVISANDUMS
AUTOMORPHICALLY	AUTOROTATE	AUTOTOMISING	AVALEMENTS	AVISEMENTS
AUTOMORPHISM	AUTOROTATED	AUTOTOMIZE	AVANTURINE	AVITAMINOSES
AUTOMORPHISMS	AUTOROTATES	AUTOTOMIZED	AVANTURINES	AVITAMINOSIS
AUTOMOTIVE	AUTOROTATING	AUTOTOMIZES	AVARICIOUS	AVITAMINOTIC
AUTONOMICAL	AUTOROTATION	AUTOTOMIZING	AVARICIOUSLY	AVIZANDUMS
AUTONOMICALLY	AUTOROTATIONS	AUTOTOMOUS	AVARICIOUSNESS	AVOCATIONAL
AUTONOMICS	AUTOROUTES	AUTOTOXAEMIA	AVASCULARITIES	AVOCATIONALLY
AUTONOMIES	AUTOSAVING	AUTOTOXAEMIAS	AVASCULARITY	AVOCATIONS
AUTONOMIST	AUTOSCHEDIASM	AUTOTOXEMIA	AVENACEOUS	AVOIDANCES
AUTONOMISTS	AUTOSCHEDIASMS	AUTOTOXEMIAS	AVENGEMENT	AVOIRDUPOIS
AUTONOMOUS	AUTOSCHEDIASTIC	AUTOTOXINS	AVENGEMENTS	AVOIRDUPOISES
AUTONOMOUSLY	AUTOSCHEDIAZE	AUTOTRANSFORMER	AVENGERESS	AVOPARCINS
AUTONYMOUS	AUTOSCHEDIAZED	AUTOTRANSFUSION	AVENGERESSES	AVOUCHABLE
AUTOPHAGIA	AUTOSCHEDIAZES	AUTOTROPHIC	AVENTAILES	AVOUCHMENT
AUTOPHAGIAS	AUTOSCHEDIAZING	AUTOTROPHICALLY	AVENTURINE	AVOUCHMENTS
AUTOPHAGIES	AUTOSCOPIC	AUTOTROPHIES	AVENTURINES	AVOUTERERS
AUTOPHAGOUS	AUTOSCOPIES	AUTOTROPHS	AVENTURINS	AVOWABLENESS
AUTOPHANOUS	AUTOSEXING	AUTOTROPHY	AVERAGENESS	AVOWABLENESSES
AUTOPHOBIA	AUTOSEXINGS	AUTOTYPIES	AVERAGENESSES	AVUNCULARITIES
AUTOPHOBIAS	AUTOSOMALLY	AUTOTYPING	AVERAGINGS	AVUNCULARITY
AUTOPHOBIES	AUTOSPORES	AUTOTYPOGRAPHY	AVERRUNCATE	AVUNCULARLY
AUTOPHONIES	AUTOSPORTS	AUTOWINDER	AVERRUNCATED	AVUNCULATE
AUTOPHYTES	AUTOSTABILITIES	AUTOWINDERS	AVERRUNCATES	AVUNCULATES
AUTOPHYTIC	AUTOSTABILITY	AUTOWORKER	AVERRUNCATING	AVVOGADORE
AUTOPHYTICALLY	AUTOSTRADA	AUTOWORKERS	AVERRUNCATION	AVVOGADORES
AUTOPILOTS	AUTOSTRADAS	AUTOXIDATION	AVERRUNCATIONS	AWAKENINGS
AUTOPISTAS	AUTOSTRADE	AUTOXIDATIONS	AVERRUNCATOR	AWARENESSES
AUTOPLASTIC	AUTOSUGGEST	AUTUMNALLY	AVERRUNCATORS	AWAYNESSES
AUTOPLASTIES	AUTOSUGGESTED	AUTUMNIEST	AVERSENESS	AWELESSNESS
AUTOPLASTY	AUTOSUGGESTING	AUXANOMETER	AVERSENESSES	AWELESSNESSES
AUTOPOINTS	AUTOSUGGESTION	AUXANOMETERS	AVERSIVELY	AWESOMENESS
AUTOPOLYPLOID	AUTOSUGGESTIONS	AUXILIARIES	AVERSIVENESS	AWESOMENESSES
AUTOPOLYPLOIDS	AUTOSUGGESTIVE	AUXOCHROME	AVERSIVENESSES	AWESTRICKEN
AUTOPOLYPLOIDY	AUTOSUGGESTS	AUXOCHROMES	AVERTIMENT	AWESTRIKES

AWESTRIKING
AWFULNESSES
AWKWARDEST
AWKWARDISH
AWKWARDNESS
AWKWARDNESSES
AXENICALLY
AXEROPHTHOL
AXEROPHTHOLS
AXIALITIES
AXILLARIES
AXINOMANCIES
AXINOMANCY
AXIOLOGICAL

AXIOLOGICALLY
AXIOLOGIES
AXIOLOGIST
AXIOLOGISTS
AXIOMATICAL
AXIOMATICALLY
AXIOMATICS
AXIOMATISATION
AXIOMATISATIONS
AXIOMATISE
AXIOMATISED
AXIOMATISES
AXIOMATISING
AXIOMATIZATION

AXIOMATIZATIONS
AXIOMATIZE
AXIOMATIZED
AXIOMATIZES
AXIOMATIZING
AXISYMMETRIC
AXISYMMETRICAL
AXISYMMETRIES
AXISYMMETRY
AXOLEMMATA
AXONOMETRIC
AXONOMETRIES
AXONOMETRY
AXOPLASMIC

AYAHUASCAS
AYAHUASCOS
AYATOLLAHS
AYUNTAMIENTO
AYUNTAMIENTOS
AYURVEDICS
AZATHIOPRINE
AZATHIOPRINES
AZEDARACHS
AZEOTROPES
AZEOTROPIC
AZEOTROPIES
AZIDOTHYMIDINE
AZIDOTHYMIDINES

AZIMUTHALLY
AZOBENZENE
AZOBENZENES
AZOOSPERMIA
AZOOSPERMIAS
AZOOSPERMIC
AZOTAEMIAS
AZOTOBACTER
AZOTOBACTERS
AZYGOSPORE
AZYGOSPORES

A

B

BAALEBATIM
BABACOOTES
BABBITRIES
BABBITTING
BABBITTRIES
BABBLATIVE
BABBLEMENT
BABBLEMENTS
BABELESQUE
BABESIASES
BABESIASIS
BABESIOSES
BABESIOSIS
BABINGTONITE
BABINGTONITES
BABIROUSSA
BABIROUSSAS
BABIRUSSAS
BABOONERIES
BABYCCINOS
BABYDADDIES
BABYPROOFED
BABYPROOFING
BABYPROOFS
BABYSITTING
BACCALAUREAN
BACCALAUREATE
BACCALAUREATES
BACCHANALIA
BACCHANALIAN
BACCHANALIANISM
BACCHANALIANS
BACCHANALS
BACCHANTES
BACCIFEROUS
BACCIVOROUS
BACHARACHS
BACHELORDOM
BACHELORDOMS
BACHELORETTE
BACHELORETTES
BACHELORHOOD

BACHELORHOODS
BACHELORISM
BACHELORISMS
BACHELORSHIP
BACHELORSHIPS
BACILLAEMIA
BACILLAEMIAS
BACILLEMIA
BACILLEMIAS
BACILLICIDE
BACILLICIDES
BACILLIFORM
BACILLURIA
BACILLURIAS
BACITRACIN
BACITRACINS
BACKACTERS
BACKBENCHER
BACKBENCHERS
BACKBENCHES
BACKBITERS
BACKBITING
BACKBITINGS
BACKBITTEN
BACKBLOCKER
BACKBLOCKERS
BACKBLOCKS
BACKBOARDS
BACKBONELESS
BACKBREAKER
BACKBREAKERS
BACKBREAKING
BACKBURNED
BACKBURNING
BACKCASTING
BACKCHANNEL
BACKCHANNELS
BACKCHATTED
BACKCHATTING
BACKCHECKED
BACKCHECKING
BACKCHECKS

BACKCLOTHS
BACKCOMBED
BACKCOMBING
BACKCOUNTRIES
BACKCOUNTRY
BACKCOURTMAN
BACKCOURTMEN
BACKCOURTS
BACKCROSSED
BACKCROSSES
BACKCROSSING
BACKDATING
BACKDRAFTS
BACKDRAUGHT
BACKDRAUGHTS
BACKDROPPED
BACKDROPPING
BACKFIELDS
BACKFILLED
BACKFILLING
BACKFILLINGS
BACKFIRING
BACKFISCHES
BACKFITTED
BACKFITTING
BACKFITTINGS
BACKFLIPPED
BACKFLIPPING
BACKFLIPPINGS
BACKGAMMON
BACKGAMMONED
BACKGAMMONING
BACKGAMMONS
BACKGROUND
BACKGROUNDED
BACKGROUNDER
BACKGROUNDERS
BACKGROUNDING
BACKGROUNDS
BACKHANDED
BACKHANDEDLY
BACKHANDEDNESS

BACKHANDER
BACKHANDERS
BACKHANDING
BACKHAULED
BACKHAULING
BACKHOEING
BACKHOUSES
BACKLASHED
BACKLASHER
BACKLASHERS
BACKLASHES
BACKLASHING
BACKLIGHTED
BACKLIGHTING
BACKLIGHTS
BACKLINERS
BACKLISTED
BACKLISTING
BACKLOADED
BACKLOADING
BACKLOGGED
BACKLOGGING
BACKMARKER
BACKMARKERS
BACKPACKED
BACKPACKER
BACKPACKERS
BACKPACKING
BACKPACKINGS
BACKPEDALED
BACKPEDALING
BACKPEDALLED
BACKPEDALLING
BACKPEDALS
BACKPIECES
BACKPLANES
BACKPLATES
BACKRONYMS
BACKRUSHES
BACKSCATTER
BACKSCATTERED
BACKSCATTERING

BACKSCATTERINGS
BACKSCATTERS
BACKSCRATCH
BACKSCRATCHED
BACKSCRATCHER
BACKSCRATCHERS
BACKSCRATCHES
BACKSCRATCHING
BACKSCRATCHINGS
BACKSETTING
BACKSHEESH
BACKSHEESHED
BACKSHEESHES
BACKSHEESHING
BACKSHISHED
BACKSHISHES
BACKSHISHING
BACKSHORES
BACKSIGHTS
BACKSLAPPED
BACKSLAPPER
BACKSLAPPERS
BACKSLAPPING
BACKSLASHES
BACKSLIDDEN
BACKSLIDER
BACKSLIDERS
BACKSLIDES
BACKSLIDING
BACKSLIDINGS
BACKSPACED
BACKSPACER
BACKSPACERS
BACKSPACES
BACKSPACING
BACKSPEERED
BACKSPEERING
BACKSPEERS
BACKSPEIRED
BACKSPEIRING
BACKSPEIRS
BACKSPLASH

BACKSPLASHES	BACKWARDATIONS	BACTERIOPHAGOUS	BAGPIPINGS	BALDERLOCKSES
BACKSPLITS	BACKWARDLY	BACTERIOPHAGY	BAGSWINGER	BALDHEADED
BACKSTABBED	BACKWARDNESS	BACTERIOSES	BAGSWINGERS	BALDICOOTS
BACKSTABBER	BACKWARDNESSES	BACTERIOSIS	BAHUVRIHIS	BALDMONEYS
BACKSTABBERS	BACKWASHED	BACTERIOSTASES	BAIGNOIRES	BALDNESSES
BACKSTABBING	BACKWASHES	BACTERIOSTASIS	BAILIESHIP	BALECTIONS
BACKSTABBINGS	BACKWASHING	BACTERIOSTAT	BAILIESHIPS	BALEFULNESS
BACKSTAGES	BACKWATERS	BACTERIOSTATIC	BAILIFFSHIP	BALEFULNESSES
BACKSTAIRS	BACKWINDED	BACTERIOSTATS	BAILIFFSHIPS	BALIBUNTAL
BACKSTALLED	BACKWINDING	BACTERIOTOXIN	BAILIWICKS	BALIBUNTALS
BACKSTALLING	BACKWOODSIER	BACTERIOTOXINS	BAILLIAGES	BALKANISATION
BACKSTALLS	BACKWOODSIEST	BACTERISATION	BAILLIESHIP	BALKANISATIONS
BACKSTAMPED	BACKWOODSMAN	BACTERISATIONS	BAILLIESHIPS	BALKANISED
BACKSTAMPING	BACKWOODSMEN	BACTERISED	BAIRNLIEST	BALKANISES
BACKSTAMPS	BACKWOODSY	BACTERISES	BAISEMAINS	BALKANISING
BACKSTARTING	BACKWORKER	BACTERISING	BAITFISHES	BALKANIZATION
BACKSTARTINGS	BACKWORKERS	BACTERIURIA	BAJILLIONS	BALKANIZATIONS
BACKSTITCH	BACTERAEMIA	BACTERIURIAS	BAKEAPPLES	BALKANIZED
BACKSTITCHED	BACTERAEMIAS	BACTERIZATION	BAKEBOARDS	BALKANIZES
BACKSTITCHES	BACTERAEMIC	BACTERIZATIONS	BAKEHOUSES	BALKANIZING
BACKSTITCHING	BACTEREMIA	BACTERIZED	BAKESTONES	BALKINESSES
BACKSTOPPED	BACTEREMIAS	BACTERIZES	BAKHSHISHED	BALLABILES
BACKSTOPPING	BACTEREMIC	BACTERIZING	BAKHSHISHES	BALLADEERED
BACKSTORIES	BACTERIALLY	BACTEROIDS	BAKHSHISHING	BALLADEERING
BACKSTRAPS	BACTERIALS	BACTERURIA	BAKSHEESHED	BALLADEERS
BACKSTREET	BACTERICIDAL	BACTERURIAS	BAKSHEESHES	BALLADINES
BACKSTREETS	BACTERICIDALLY	BACULIFORM	BAKSHEESHING	BALLADISTS
BACKSTRETCH	BACTERICIDE	BACULOVIRUS	BAKSHISHED	BALLADMONGER
BACKSTRETCHES	BACTERICIDES	BACULOVIRUSES	BAKSHISHES	BALLADMONGERS
BACKSTROKE	BACTERIOCIN	BADDELEYITE	BAKSHISHING	BALLADRIES
BACKSTROKED	BACTERIOCINS	BADDELEYITES	BALACLAVAS	BALLANTING
BACKSTROKES	BACTERIOID	BADDERLOCK	BALALAIKAS	BALLANWRASSE
BACKSTROKING	BACTERIOIDS	BADDERLOCKS	BALANCEABLE	BALLANWRASSES
BACKSWIMMER	BACTERIOLOGIC	BADGERLIER	BALANCINGS	BALLASTERS
BACKSWIMMERS	BACTERIOLOGICAL	BADGERLIEST	BALANITISES	BALLASTING
BACKSWINGS	BACTERIOLOGIES	BADINAGING	BALAYAGING	BALLBREAKER
BACKSWORDMAN	BACTERIOLOGIST	BADINERIES	BALBRIGGAN	BALLBREAKERS
BACKSWORDMEN	BACTERIOLOGISTS	BADMINTONS	BALBRIGGANS	BALLCARRIER
BACKSWORDS	BACTERIOLOGY	BADMOUTHED	BALBUTIENT	BALLCARRIERS
BACKSWORDSMAN	BACTERIOLYSES	BADMOUTHING	BALCONETTE	BALLERINAS
BACKSWORDSMEN	BACTERIOLYSIN	BAFFLEGABS	BALCONETTES	BALLETICALLY
BACKTRACKED	BACTERIOLYSINS	BAFFLEMENT	BALDACHINO	BALLETOMANE
BACKTRACKING	BACTERIOLYSIS	BAFFLEMENTS	BALDACHINOS	BALLETOMANES
BACKTRACKINGS	BACTERIOLYTIC	BAFFLINGLY	BALDACHINS	BALLETOMANIA
BACKTRACKS	BACTERIOPHAGE	BAGASSOSES	BALDAQUINS	BALLETOMANIAS
BACKVELDER	BACTERIOPHAGES	BAGASSOSIS	BALDERDASH	BALLFIELDS
BACKVELDERS	BACTERIOPHAGIC	BAGATELLES	BALDERDASHES	BALLFLOWER
BACKWARDATION	BACTERIOPHAGIES	BAGGINESSES	BALDERLOCKS	BALLFLOWERS

B

BALLHANDLING

BALLHANDLING	BALSAWOODS	BANDMASTERS	BANNISTERS	BARBASTELLES
BALLHANDLINGS	BALTHASARS	BANDOBASTS	BANQUETEER	BARBASTELS
BALLHAWKED	BALTHAZARS	BANDOBUSTS	BANQUETEERS	BARBECUERS
BALLHAWKING	BALUSTERED	BANDOLEERED	BANQUETERS	BARBECUING
BALLICATTER	BALUSTRADE	BANDOLEERS	BANQUETING	BARBELLATE
BALLICATTERS	BALUSTRADED	BANDOLEONS	BANQUETINGS	BARBEQUING
BALLISTICALLY	BALUSTRADES	BANDOLEROS	BANQUETTES	BARBERRIES
BALLISTICS	BALZARINES	BANDOLIERED	BANTAMWEIGHT	BARBERSHOP
BALLISTITE	BAMBOOZLED	BANDOLIERS	BANTAMWEIGHTS	BARBERSHOPS
BALLISTITES	BAMBOOZLEMENT	BANDOLINED	BANTERINGLY	BARBITONES
BALLISTOSPORE	BAMBOOZLEMENTS	BANDOLINES	BANTERINGS	BARBITURATE
BALLISTOSPORES	BAMBOOZLER	BANDOLINING	BANTINGISM	BARBITURATES
BALLOCKSED	BAMBOOZLERS	BANDONEONS	BANTINGISMS	BARBITURIC
BALLOCKSES	BAMBOOZLES	BANDONIONS	BAPHOMETIC	BARBOTINES
BALLOCKSING	BAMBOOZLING	BANDPASSES	BAPTISMALLY	BARCAROLES
BALLOONING	BANALISATION	BANDSAWING	BAPTISTERIES	BARCAROLLE
BALLOONINGS	BANALISATIONS	BANDSHELLS	BAPTISTERY	BARCAROLLES
BALLOONIST	BANALISING	BANDSPREADING	BAPTISTRIES	BARDOLATER
BALLOONISTS	BANALITIES	BANDSPREADINGS	BARACHOISES	BARDOLATERS
BALLOTINGS	BANALIZATION	BANDSTANDS	BARAESTHESIA	BARDOLATRIES
BALLOTTEMENT	BANALIZATIONS	BANDURISTS	BARAESTHESIAS	BARDOLATROUS
BALLOTTEMENTS	BANALIZING	BANDWAGONS	BARAGOUINS	BARDOLATRY
BALLPLAYER	BANCASSURANCE	BANDWIDTHS	BARASINGAS	BAREBACKED
BALLPLAYERS	BANCASSURANCES	BANEBERRIES	BARASINGHA	BAREBACKING
BALLPOINTS	BANCASSURER	BANEFULNESS	BARASINGHAS	BAREBACKINGS
BALLSINESS	BANCASSURERS	BANEFULNESSES	BARATHRUMS	BAREFACEDLY
BALLSINESSES	BANDAGINGS	BANGBELLIES	BARBARESQUE	BAREFACEDNESS
BALLYHOOED	BANDALORES	BANGSRINGS	BARBARIANISM	BAREFACEDNESSES
BALLYHOOING	BANDBRAKES	BANISHMENT	BARBARIANISMS	BAREFOOTED
BALLYRAGGED	BANDEIRANTE	BANISHMENTS	BARBARIANS	BAREHANDED
BALLYRAGGING	BANDEIRANTES	BANISTERED	BARBARICALLY	BAREHANDING
BALMACAANS	BANDELIERS	BANJOLELES	BARBARISATION	BAREHEADED
BALMINESSES	BANDERILLA	BANJULELES	BARBARISATIONS	BARELEGGED
BALMORALITIES	BANDERILLAS	BANKABILITIES	BARBARISED	BARENESSES
BALMORALITY	BANDERILLERO	BANKABILITY	BARBARISES	BARESTHESIA
BALNEARIES	BANDERILLEROS	BANKERLIER	BARBARISING	BARESTHESIAS
BALNEATION	BANDEROLES	BANKERLIEST	BARBARISMS	BARGAINERS
BALNEATIONS	BANDERSNATCH	BANKROLLED	BARBARITIES	BARGAINING
BALNEOLOGICAL	BANDERSNATCHES	BANKROLLER	BARBARIZATION	BARGAININGS
BALNEOLOGIES	BANDFISHES	BANKROLLERS	BARBARIZATIONS	BARGANDERS
BALNEOLOGIST	BANDICOOTED	BANKROLLING	BARBARIZED	BARGEBOARD
BALNEOLOGISTS	BANDICOOTING	BANKRUPTCIES	BARBARIZES	BARGEBOARDS
BALNEOLOGY	BANDICOOTS	BANKRUPTCY	BARBARIZING	BARGEMASTER
BALNEOTHERAPIES	BANDINESSES	BANKRUPTED	BARBAROUSLY	BARGEMASTERS
BALNEOTHERAPY	BANDITRIES	BANKRUPTING	BARBAROUSNESS	BARGEPOLES
BALSAMIEST	BANDLEADER	BANNERALLS	BARBAROUSNESSES	BARHOPPING
BALSAMIFEROUS	BANDLEADERS	BANNERETTE	BARBASCOES	BARIATRICS
BALSAMINACEOUS	BANDMASTER	BANNERETTES	BARBASTELLE	BARKANTINE

BARKANTINES	BAROSCOPES	BARRICADING	BASICITIES	BASTARDIZED
BARKEEPERS	BAROSCOPIC	BARRICADOED	BASICRANIAL	BASTARDIZES
BARKENTINE	BAROTITISES	BARRICADOES	BASIDIOCARP	BASTARDIZING
BARKENTINES	BAROTRAUMA	BARRICADOING	BASIDIOCARPS	BASTARDLIER
BARLEYCORN	BAROTRAUMAS	BARRICADOS	BASIDIOMYCETE	BASTARDLIEST
BARLEYCORNS	BAROTRAUMATA	BARRIERING	BASIDIOMYCETES	BASTARDRIES
BARMBRACKS	BARPERSONS	BARRISTERIAL	BASIDIOMYCETOUS	BASTINADED
BARMINESSES	BARQUANTINE	BARRISTERS	BASIDIOSPORE	BASTINADES
BARMITSVAH	BARQUANTINES	BARRISTERSHIP	BASIDIOSPORES	BASTINADING
BARMITSVAHS	BARQUENTINE	BARRISTERSHIPS	BASIDIOSPOROUS	BASTINADOED
BARMITZVAH	BARQUENTINES	BARROWFULS	BASIFICATION	BASTINADOES
BARMITZVAHS	BARQUETTES	BARTENDERS	BASIFICATIONS	BASTINADOING
BARNBOARDS	BARRACKERS	BARTENDING	BASILICONS	BASTNAESITE
BARNBRACKS	BARRACKING	BARTENDINGS	BASIPETALLY	BASTNAESITES
BARNSBREAKING	BARRACKINGS	BARTIZANED	BASKETBALL	BASTNASITE
BARNSBREAKINGS	BARRACOONS	BARYCENTRE	BASKETBALLS	BASTNASITES
BARNSTORMED	BARRACOUTA	BARYCENTRES	BASKETFULS	BATFOWLERS
BARNSTORMER	BARRACOUTAS	BARYCENTRIC	BASKETLIKE	BATFOWLING
BARNSTORMERS	BARRACUDAS	BARYSPHERE	BASKETRIES	BATFOWLINGS
BARNSTORMING	BARRAMUNDA	BARYSPHERES	BASKETSFUL	BATHETICALLY
BARNSTORMINGS	BARRAMUNDAS	BASALTINES	BASKETWEAVE	BATHHOUSES
BARNSTORMS	BARRAMUNDI	BASALTWARE	BASKETWEAVER	BATHMITSVAH
BAROCEPTOR	BARRAMUNDIES	BASALTWARES	BASKETWEAVERS	BATHMITSVAHS
BAROCEPTORS	BARRAMUNDIS	BASEBALLER	BASKETWEAVES	BATHMITZVAH
BARODYNAMICS	BARRASWAYS	BASEBALLERS	BASKETWORK	BATHMITZVAHS
BAROGNOSES	BARRATRIES	BASEBOARDS	BASKETWORKS	BATHMIZVAH
BAROGNOSIS	BARRATROUS	BASEBURNER	BASMITZVAH	BATHMIZVAHS
BAROGRAPHIC	BARRATROUSLY	BASEBURNERS	BASMITZVAHS	BATHOCHROME
BAROGRAPHS	BARRELAGES	BASELESSLY	BASOPHILES	BATHOCHROMES
BAROMETERS	BARRELFULS	BASELESSNESS	BASOPHILIA	BATHOCHROMIC
BAROMETRIC	BARRELHEAD	BASELESSNESSES	BASOPHILIAS	BATHOLITES
BAROMETRICAL	BARRELHEADS	BASELINERS	BASOPHILIC	BATHOLITHIC
BAROMETRICALLY	BARRELHOUSE	BASEMENTLESS	BASSETTING	BATHOLITHS
BAROMETRIES	BARRELHOUSES	BASENESSES	BASSNESSES	BATHOLITIC
BAROMETZES	BARRELLING	BASEPLATES	BASSOONIST	BATHOMETER
BARONESSES	BARRELSFUL	BASERUNNER	BASSOONISTS	BATHOMETERS
BARONETAGE	BARRENNESS	BASERUNNERS	BASTARDIES	BATHOMETRIC
BARONETAGES	BARRENNESSES	BASERUNNING	BASTARDISATION	BATHOMETRICALLY
BARONETCIES	BARRENWORT	BASERUNNINGS	BASTARDISATIONS	BATHOMETRIES
BARONETESS	BARRENWORTS	BASHAWISMS	BASTARDISE	BATHOMETRY
BARONETESSES	BARRETRIES	BASHAWSHIP	BASTARDISED	BATHOPHILOUS
BARONETICAL	BARRETROUS	BASHAWSHIPS	BASTARDISES	BATHOPHOBIA
BAROPHILES	BARRETROUSLY	BASHFULLER	BASTARDISING	BATHOPHOBIAS
BAROPHILIC	BARRETTERS	BASHFULLEST	BASTARDISM	BATHWATERS
BAROPHORESES	BARRICADED	BASHFULNESS	BASTARDISMS	BATHYBIUSES
BAROPHORESIS	BARRICADER	BASHFULNESSES	BASTARDIZATION	BATHYGRAPHIC
BARORECEPTOR	BARRICADERS	BASHIBAZOUK	BASTARDIZATIONS	BATHYGRAPHICAL
BARORECEPTORS	BARRICADES	BASHIBAZOUKS	BASTARDIZE	BATHYLIMNETIC

BATHYLITES
BATHYLITHIC
BATHYLITHS
BATHYLITIC
BATHYMETER
BATHYMETERS
BATHYMETRIC
BATHYMETRICAL
BATHYMETRICALLY
BATHYMETRIES
BATHYMETRY
BATHYPELAGIC
BATHYSCAPE
BATHYSCAPES
BATHYSCAPH
BATHYSCAPHE
BATHYSCAPHES
BATHYSCAPHS
BATHYSPHERE
BATHYSPHERES
BATMITZVAH
BATMITZVAHS
BATOLOGICAL
BATOLOGIES
BATOLOGIST
BATOLOGISTS
BATONNIERS
BATRACHIAN
BATRACHIANS
BATRACHOPHOBIA
BATRACHOPHOBIAS
BATRACHOPHOBIC
BATSMANSHIP
BATSMANSHIPS
BATTAILOUS
BATTALIONS
BATTEILANT
BATTELLING
BATTEMENTS
BATTENINGS
BATTERINGS
BATTILLING
BATTINESSES
BATTLEAXES
BATTLEBUSES
BATTLEBUSSES
BATTLEDOOR
BATTLEDOORS

BATTLEDORE
BATTLEDORES
BATTLEDRESS
BATTLEDRESSES
BATTLEFIELD
BATTLEFIELDS
BATTLEFRONT
BATTLEFRONTS
BATTLEGROUND
BATTLEGROUNDS
BATTLEMENT
BATTLEMENTED
BATTLEMENTS
BATTLEPIECE
BATTLEPIECES
BATTLEPLANE
BATTLEPLANES
BATTLESHIP
BATTLESHIPS
BATTLESPACE
BATTLESPACES
BATTLEWAGON
BATTLEWAGONS
BATTOLOGICAL
BATTOLOGIES
BAUDRICKES
BAUDRONSES
BAULKINESS
BAULKINESSES
BAULKINGLY
BAULKLINES
BAVARDAGES
BAVAROISES
BAWDINESSES
BAWDYHOUSE
BAWDYHOUSES
BAYBERRIES
BAYNODDIES
BAYONETING
BAYONETTED
BAYONETTING
BAZILLIONS
BEACHBALLS
BEACHCOMBED
BEACHCOMBER
BEACHCOMBERS
BEACHCOMBING
BEACHCOMBINGS

BEACHCOMBS
BEACHFRONT
BEACHFRONTS
BEACHGOERS
BEACHHEADS
BEACHWEARS
BEADBLASTED
BEADBLASTER
BEADBLASTERS
BEADBLASTING
BEADBLASTS
BEADHOUSES
BEADINESSES
BEADLEDOMS
BEADLEHOOD
BEADLEHOODS
BEADLESHIP
BEADLESHIPS
BEADSWOMAN
BEADSWOMEN
BEAKERFULS
BEAMINESSES
BEANFEASTS
BEANSPROUT
BEANSPROUTS
BEANSTALKS
BEARABILITIES
BEARABILITY
BEARABLENESS
BEARABLENESSES
BEARBAITING
BEARBAITINGS
BEARBERRIES
BEARDEDNESS
BEARDEDNESSES
BEARDLESSNESS
BEARDLESSNESSES
BEARDTONGUE
BEARDTONGUES
BEARGRASSES
BEARHUGGED
BEARHUGGING
BEARISHNESS
BEARISHNESSES
BEARNAISES
BEASTHOODS
BEASTLIEST
BEASTLINESS

BEASTLINESSES
BEATBOXERS
BEATBOXING
BEATBOXINGS
BEATIFICAL
BEATIFICALLY
BEATIFICATION
BEATIFICATIONS
BEATIFYING
BEATITUDES
BEAUJOLAIS
BEAUJOLAISES
BEAUMONTAGE
BEAUMONTAGES
BEAUMONTAGUE
BEAUMONTAGUES
BEAUTEOUSLY
BEAUTEOUSNESS
BEAUTEOUSNESSES
BEAUTICIAN
BEAUTICIANS
BEAUTIFICATION
BEAUTIFICATIONS
BEAUTIFIED
BEAUTIFIER
BEAUTIFIERS
BEAUTIFIES
BEAUTIFULLER
BEAUTIFULLEST
BEAUTIFULLY
BEAUTIFULNESS
BEAUTIFULNESSES
BEAUTIFYING
BEAVERBOARD
BEAVERBOARDS
BEBEERINES
BEBLOODING
BEBLUBBERED
BECARPETED
BECARPETING
BECCACCIAS
BECCAFICOS
BECHALKING
BECHANCING
BECHARMING
BECKONINGLY
BECKONINGS
BECLAMORED

BECLAMORING
BECLAMOURED
BECLAMOURING
BECLAMOURS
BECLASPING
BECLOAKING
BECLOGGING
BECLOTHING
BECLOUDING
BECLOWNING
BECOMINGLY
BECOMINGNESS
BECOMINGNESSES
BECOWARDED
BECOWARDING
BECQUERELS
BECRAWLING
BECROWDING
BECRUSTING
BECUDGELED
BECUDGELING
BECUDGELLED
BECUDGELLING
BEDABBLING
BEDAGGLING
BEDARKENED
BEDARKENING
BEDAZZLEMENT
BEDAZZLEMENTS
BEDAZZLING
BEDCHAMBER
BEDCHAMBERS
BEDCLOTHES
BEDCOVERING
BEDCOVERINGS
BEDEAFENED
BEDEAFENING
BEDEHOUSES
BEDELLSHIP
BEDELLSHIPS
BEDELSHIPS
BEDEVILING
BEDEVILLED
BEDEVILLING
BEDEVILMENT
BEDEVILMENTS
BEDFELLOWS
BEDIAPERED

BEDIAPERING	BEETLEHEAD	BEGLAMOURS	BELABORING	BELLHANGERS
BEDIGHTING	BEETLEHEADED	BEGLERBEGS	BELABOURED	BELLIBONES
BEDIMMINGS	BEETLEHEADS	BEGLOOMING	BELABOURING	BELLICOSELY
BEDIMPLING	BEETMASTER	BEGRIMMING	BELAMOURES	BELLICOSITIES
BEDIRTYING	BEETMASTERS	BEGROANING	BELATEDNESS	BELLICOSITY
BEDIZENING	BEETMISTER	BEGRUDGERIES	BELATEDNESSES	BELLIGERATI
BEDIZENMENT	BEETMISTERS	BEGRUDGERS	BELEAGUERED	BELLIGERENCE
BEDIZENMENTS	BEFINGERED	BEGRUDGERY	BELEAGUERING	BELLIGERENCES
BEDLAMISMS	BEFINGERING	BEGRUDGING	BELEAGUERMENT	BELLIGERENCIES
BEDLAMITES	BEFITTINGLY	BEGRUDGINGLY	BELEAGUERMENTS	BELLIGERENCY
BEDPRESSER	BEFLAGGING	BEGUILEMENT	BELEAGUERS	BELLIGERENT
BEDPRESSERS	BEFLECKING	BEGUILEMENTS	BELEMNITES	BELLIGERENTLY
BEDRAGGLED	BEFLOWERED	BEGUILINGLY	BELGICISMS	BELLIGERENTS
BEDRAGGLES	BEFLOWERING	BEGUINAGES	BELIEFLESS	BELLOCKING
BEDRAGGLING	BEFLUMMING	BEHAPPENED	BELIEVABILITIES	BELLOWINGS
BEDRENCHED	BEFOREHAND	BEHAPPENING	BELIEVABILITY	BELLWETHER
BEDRENCHES	BEFORETIME	BEHAVIORAL	BELIEVABLE	BELLWETHERS
BEDRENCHING	BEFORTUNED	BEHAVIORALLY	BELIEVABLY	BELLYACHED
BEDRIVELED	BEFORTUNES	BEHAVIORISM	BELIEVINGLY	BELLYACHER
BEDRIVELING	BEFORTUNING	BEHAVIORISMS	BELIEVINGS	BELLYACHERS
BEDRIVELLED	BEFOULMENT	BEHAVIORIST	BELIQUORED	BELLYACHES
BEDRIVELLING	BEFOULMENTS	BEHAVIORISTIC	BELIQUORING	BELLYACHING
BEDROPPING	BEFRETTING	BEHAVIORISTS	BELITTLEMENT	BELLYACHINGS
BEDRUGGING	BEFRIENDED	BEHAVIOURAL	BELITTLEMENTS	BELLYBANDS
BEDSITTERS	BEFRIENDER	BEHAVIOURALLY	BELITTLERS	BELLYBOATS
BEDSITTING	BEFRIENDERS	BEHAVIOURISM	BELITTLING	BELLYBUTTON
BEDSPREADS	BEFRIENDING	BEHAVIOURISMS	BELITTLINGLY	BELLYBUTTONS
BEDSPRINGS	BEFRINGING	BEHAVIOURIST	BELLADONNA	BELLYFLOPPED
BEDWARFING	BEFUDDLEMENT	BEHAVIOURISTIC	BELLADONNAS	BELLYFLOPPING
BEDWARMERS	BEFUDDLEMENTS	BEHAVIOURISTS	BELLAMOURE	BELLYFLOPS
BEDWETTERS	BEFUDDLING	BEHAVIOURS	BELLAMOURES	BELOMANCIES
BEECHDROPS	BEGGARDOMS	BEHEADINGS	BELLARMINE	BELONGINGNESS
BEECHMASTS	BEGGARHOOD	BEHIGHTING	BELLARMINES	BELONGINGNESSES
BEECHWOODS	BEGGARHOODS	BEHINDHAND	BELLETRISM	BELONGINGS
BEEFBURGER	BEGGARLIER	BEHOLDINGS	BELLETRISMS	BELOWDECKS
BEEFBURGERS	BEGGARLIEST	BEINGNESSES	BELLETRIST	BELOWGROUND
BEEFEATERS	BEGGARLINESS	BEINNESSES	BELLETRISTIC	BELOWSTAIRS
BEEFINESSES	BEGGARLINESSES	BEJABERSES	BELLETRISTICAL	BELSHAZZAR
BEEFSTEAKS	BEGGARWEED	BEJEEZUSES	BELLETRISTS	BELSHAZZARS
BEEKEEPERS	BEGGARWEEDS	BEJESUITED	BELLETTRIST	BELTCOURSE
BEEKEEPING	BEGINNINGLESS	BEJESUITING	BELLETTRISTS	BELTCOURSES
BEEKEEPINGS	BEGINNINGS	BEJEWELING	BELLFLOWER	BELVEDERES
BEERINESSES	BEGIRDLING	BEJEWELLED	BELLFLOWERS	BEMADAMING
BEESWAXING	BEGLADDING	BEJEWELLING	BELLFOUNDER	BEMADDENED
BEESWINGED	BEGLAMORED	BEJUMBLING	BELLFOUNDERS	BEMADDENING
BEETLEBRAIN	BEGLAMORING	BEKNIGHTED	BELLFOUNDRIES	BEMEDALING
BEETLEBRAINED	BEGLAMOURED	BEKNIGHTING	BELLFOUNDRY	BEMEDALLED
BEETLEBRAINS	BEGLAMOURING	BEKNOTTING	BELLHANGER	BEMEDALLING

BEMINGLING	BENEFICIALLY	BENUMBMENT	BEQUEATHERS	BESEECHINGLY
BEMOANINGS	BENEFICIALNESS	BENUMBMENTS	BEQUEATHING	BESEECHINGNESS
BEMONSTERED	BENEFICIALS	BENZALDEHYDE	BEQUEATHMENT	BESEECHINGS
BEMONSTERING	BENEFICIARIES	BENZALDEHYDES	BEQUEATHMENTS	BESEEMINGLY
BEMONSTERS	BENEFICIARY	BENZANTHRACENE	BERASCALED	BESEEMINGNESS
BEMOUTHING	BENEFICIATE	BENZANTHRACENES	BERASCALING	BESEEMINGNESSES
BEMUDDLING	BENEFICIATED	BENZENECARBONYL	BERBERIDACEOUS	BESEEMINGS
BEMUFFLING	BENEFICIATES	BENZENOIDS	BERBERINES	BESEEMLIER
BEMURMURED	BENEFICIATING	BENZIDINES	BERBERISES	BESEEMLIEST
BEMURMURING	BENEFICIATION	BENZIMIDAZOLE	BEREAVEMENT	BESETMENTS
BEMUSEMENT	BENEFICIATIONS	BENZIMIDAZOLES	BEREAVEMENTS	BESHADOWED
BEMUSEMENTS	BENEFICING	BENZOAPYRENE	BERGAMASKO	BESHADOWING
BEMUZZLING	BENEFITERS	BENZOAPYRENES	BERGAMASKOS	BESHIVERED
BENCHERSHIP	BENEFITING	BENZOCAINE	BERGAMASKS	BESHIVERING
BENCHERSHIPS	BENEFITTED	BENZOCAINES	BERGANDERS	BESHOUTING
BENCHLANDS	BENEFITTING	BENZODIAZEPINE	BERGOMASKS	BESHREWING
BENCHMARKED	BENEPLACITO	BENZODIAZEPINES	BERGSCHRUND	BESHROUDED
BENCHMARKING	BENEVOLENCE	BENZOFURAN	BERGSCHRUNDS	BESHROUDING
BENCHMARKINGS	BENEVOLENCES	BENZOFURANS	BERIBBONED	BESIEGEMENT
BENCHMARKS	BENEVOLENT	BENZOLINES	BERKELIUMS	BESIEGEMENTS
BENCHWARMER	BENEVOLENTLY	BENZOPHENONE	BERRYFRUIT	BESIEGINGLY
BENCHWARMERS	BENEVOLENTNESS	BENZOPHENONES	BERRYFRUITS	BESIEGINGS
BENDINESSES	BENGALINES	BENZOQUINONE	BERSAGLIERE	BESLAVERED
BENEDICITE	BENIGHTEDLY	BENZOQUINONES	BERSAGLIERI	BESLAVERING
BENEDICITES	BENIGHTEDNESS	BENZPYRENE	BERSERKERS	BESLOBBERED
BENEDICTION	BENIGHTEDNESSES	BENZPYRENES	BERTILLONAGE	BESLOBBERING
BENEDICTIONAL	BENIGHTENED	BENZYLIDINE	BERTILLONAGES	BESLOBBERS
BENEDICTIONALS	BENIGHTENING	BENZYLIDINES	BERYLLIOSES	BESLUBBERED
BENEDICTIONS	BENIGHTENINGS	BEPAINTING	BERYLLIOSIS	BESLUBBERING
BENEDICTIVE	BENIGHTENS	BEPEARLING	BERYLLIUMS	BESLUBBERS
BENEDICTORY	BENIGHTERS	BEPEPPERED	BESAINTING	BESMEARERS
BENEDICTUS	BENIGHTING	BEPEPPERING	BESCATTERED	BESMEARING
BENEDICTUSES	BENIGHTINGS	BEPESTERED	BESCATTERING	BESMIRCHED
BENEFACTED	BENIGHTMENT	BEPESTERING	BESCATTERS	BESMIRCHES
BENEFACTING	BENIGHTMENTS	BEPIMPLING	BESCORCHED	BESMIRCHING
BENEFACTION	BENIGNANCIES	BEPLASTERED	BESCORCHES	BESMOOTHED
BENEFACTIONS	BENIGNANCY	BEPLASTERING	BESCORCHING	BESMOOTHING
BENEFACTOR	BENIGNANTLY	BEPLASTERS	BESCOURING	BESMUDGING
BENEFACTORS	BENIGNITIES	BEPOMMELLED	BESCRAWLED	BESMUTCHED
BENEFACTORY	BENTGRASSES	BEPOMMELLING	BESCRAWLING	BESMUTCHES
BENEFACTRESS	BENTHOPELAGIC	BEPOWDERED	BESCREENED	BESMUTTING
BENEFACTRESSES	BENTHOSCOPE	BEPOWDERING	BESCREENING	BESOOTHING
BENEFICENCE	BENTHOSCOPES	BEPRAISING	BESCRIBBLE	BESOTTEDLY
BENEFICENCES	BENTONITES	BEQUEATHABLE	BESCRIBBLED	BESOTTEDNESS
BENEFICENT	BENTONITIC	BEQUEATHAL	BESCRIBBLES	BESOTTEDNESSES
BENEFICENTIAL	BENUMBEDNESS	BEQUEATHALS	BESCRIBBLING	BESPANGLED
BENEFICENTLY	BENUMBEDNESSES	BEQUEATHED	BESEECHERS	BESPANGLES
BENEFICIAL	BENUMBINGLY	BEQUEATHER	BESEECHING	

BESPANGLING	BESTRAUGHT	BETWEENITIES	BIBLIOLATERS	BIBLIOPOLY
BESPATTERED	BESTREAKED	BETWEENITY	BIBLIOLATRIES	BIBLIOTHECA
BESPATTERING	BESTREAKING	BETWEENNESS	BIBLIOLATRIST	BIBLIOTHECAE
BESPATTERS	BESTREWING	BETWEENNESSES	BIBLIOLATRISTS	BIBLIOTHECAL
BESPEAKING	BESTRIDABLE	BETWEENTIME	BIBLIOLATROUS	BIBLIOTHECARIES
BESPECKLED	BESTRIDDEN	BETWEENTIMES	BIBLIOLATRY	BIBLIOTHECARY
BESPECKLES	BESTRIDING	BETWEENWHILES	BIBLIOLOGICAL	BIBLIOTHECAS
BESPECKLING	BESTROWING	BEVELLINGS	BIBLIOLOGIES	BIBLIOTHERAPIES
BESPECTACLED	BESTSELLER	BEVELMENTS	BIBLIOLOGIST	BIBLIOTHERAPY
BESPEEDING	BESTSELLERDOM	BEVOMITING	BIBLIOLOGISTS	BIBLIOTICS
BESPITTING	BESTSELLERDOMS	BEWAILINGLY	BIBLIOLOGY	BIBLIOTIST
BESPORTING	BESTSELLERS	BEWAILINGS	BIBLIOMANCIES	BIBLIOTISTS
BESPOTTEDNESS	BESTSELLING	BEWEARYING	BIBLIOMANCY	BIBULOUSLY
BESPOTTEDNESSES	BESTUDDING	BEWELTERED	BIBLIOMANE	BIBULOUSNESS
BESPOTTING	BESWARMING	BEWHISKERED	BIBLIOMANES	BIBULOUSNESSES
BESPOUSING	BETACAROTENE	BEWILDERED	BIBLIOMANIA	BICAMERALISM
BESPOUTING	BETACAROTENES	BEWILDEREDLY	BIBLIOMANIAC	BICAMERALISMS
BESPREADING	BETACYANIN	BEWILDEREDNESS	BIBLIOMANIACAL	BICAMERALIST
BESPRINKLE	BETACYANINS	BEWILDERING	BIBLIOMANIACS	BICAMERALISTS
BESPRINKLED	BETATTERED	BEWILDERINGLY	BIBLIOMANIAS	BICAPSULAR
BESPRINKLES	BETATTERING	BEWILDERMENT	BIBLIOPEGIC	BICARBONATE
BESPRINKLING	BETHANKING	BEWILDERMENTS	BIBLIOPEGIES	BICARBONATES
BESTAINING	BETHANKITS	BEWITCHERIES	BIBLIOPEGIST	BICARPELLARY
BESTARRING	BETHINKING	BEWITCHERS	BIBLIOPEGISTS	BICENTENARIES
BESTEADING	BETHORNING	BEWITCHERY	BIBLIOPEGY	BICENTENARY
BESTIALISE	BETHRALLED	BEWITCHING	BIBLIOPHAGIST	BICENTENNIAL
BESTIALISED	BETHRALLING	BEWITCHINGLY	BIBLIOPHAGISTS	BICENTENNIALS
BESTIALISES	BETHUMBING	BEWITCHMENT	BIBLIOPHIL	BICEPHALOUS
BESTIALISING	BETHUMPING	BEWITCHMENTS	BIBLIOPHILE	BICHLORIDE
BESTIALISM	BETHWACKED	BEWORRYING	BIBLIOPHILES	BICHLORIDES
BESTIALISMS	BETHWACKING	BEWRAPPING	BIBLIOPHILIC	BICHROMATE
BESTIALITIES	BETOKENING	BHIKKHUNIS	BIBLIOPHILIES	BICHROMATED
BESTIALITY	BETREADING	BIANNUALLY	BIBLIOPHILISM	BICHROMATES
BESTIALIZE	BETRIMMING	BIANNULATE	BIBLIOPHILISMS	BICKERINGS
BESTIALIZED	BETROTHALS	BIASNESSES	BIBLIOPHILIST	BICOLLATERAL
BESTIALIZES	BETROTHEDS	BIATHLETES	BIBLIOPHILISTIC	BICOLOURED
BESTIALIZING	BETROTHING	BIAURICULAR	BIBLIOPHILISTS	BICOMPONENT
BESTIARIES	BETROTHMENT	BIAURICULATE	BIBLIOPHILS	BICOMPONENTS
BESTICKING	BETROTHMENTS	BIBLICALLY	BIBLIOPHILY	BICONCAVITIES
BESTILLING	BETTERINGS	BIBLICISMS	BIBLIOPHOBIA	BICONCAVITY
BESTIRRING	BETTERMENT	BIBLICISTS	BIBLIOPHOBIAS	BICONDITIONAL
BESTORMING	BETTERMENTS	BIBLIOGRAPHER	BIBLIOPOLE	BICONDITIONALS
BESTOWMENT	BETTERMOST	BIBLIOGRAPHERS	BIBLIOPOLES	BICONVEXITIES
BESTOWMENTS	BETTERNESS	BIBLIOGRAPHIC	BIBLIOPOLIC	BICONVEXITY
BESTRADDLE	BETTERNESSES	BIBLIOGRAPHICAL	BIBLIOPOLICAL	BICORNUATE
BESTRADDLED	BETULACEOUS	BIBLIOGRAPHIES	BIBLIOPOLIES	BICORPORATE
BESTRADDLES	BETWEENBRAIN	BIBLIOGRAPHY	BIBLIOPOLIST	BICULTURAL
BESTRADDLING	BETWEENBRAINS	BIBLIOLATER	BIBLIOPOLISTS	BICULTURALISM

BICULTURALISMS
BICUSPIDATE
BICUSPIDATES
BICYCLICAL
BICYCLISTS
BIDDABILITIES
BIDDABILITY
BIDDABLENESS
BIDDABLENESSES
BIDENTATED
BIDIALECTAL
BIDIALECTALISM
BIDIALECTALISMS
BIDIRECTIONAL
BIDIRECTIONALLY
BIDONVILLE
BIDONVILLES
BIENNIALLY
BIENSEANCE
BIENSEANCES
BIERKELLER
BIERKELLERS
BIERWURSTS
BIFACIALLY
BIFARIOUSLY
BIFIDITIES
BIFLAGELLATE
BIFOLIOLATE
BIFUNCTIONAL
BIFURCATED
BIFURCATES
BIFURCATING
BIFURCATION
BIFURCATIONS
BIGAMOUSLY
BIGARREAUS
BIGEMINIES
BIGFOOTING
BIGGETIEST
BIGGITIEST
BIGHEADEDLY
BIGHEADEDNESS
BIGHEADEDNESSES
BIGHEARTED
BIGHEARTEDLY
BIGHEARTEDNESS
BIGMOUTHED
BIGNONIACEOUS

BIGUANIDES
BIJECTIONS
BIJOUTERIE
BIJOUTERIES
BILATERALISM
BILATERALISMS
BILATERALLY
BILBERRIES
BILDUNGSROMAN
BILDUNGSROMANS
BILECTIONS
BILESTONES
BILGEWATER
BILGEWATERS
BILHARZIAL
BILHARZIAS
BILHARZIASES
BILHARZIASIS
BILHARZIOSES
BILHARZIOSIS
BILIMBINGS
BILINGUALISM
BILINGUALISMS
BILINGUALLY
BILINGUALS
BILINGUIST
BILINGUISTS
BILIOUSNESS
BILIOUSNESSES
BILIRUBINS
BILIVERDIN
BILIVERDINS
BILLABONGS
BILLBOARDED
BILLBOARDING
BILLBOARDS
BILLETINGS
BILLFISHES
BILLINGSGATE
BILLINGSGATES
BILLIONAIRE
BILLIONAIRES
BILLIONTHS
BILLOWIEST
BILLOWINESS
BILLOWINESSES
BILLOWINGS
BILLPOSTER

BILLPOSTERS
BILLPOSTING
BILLPOSTINGS
BILLSTICKER
BILLSTICKERS
BILLSTICKING
BILLSTICKINGS
BILLYCOCKS
BILOCATION
BILOCATIONS
BILOCULATE
BIMANUALLY
BIMATERNAL
BIMESTRIAL
BIMESTRIALLY
BIMETALLIC
BIMETALLICS
BIMETALLISM
BIMETALLISMS
BIMETALLIST
BIMETALLISTIC
BIMETALLISTS
BIMILLENARIES
BIMILLENARY
BIMILLENNIA
BIMILLENNIAL
BIMILLENNIALS
BIMILLENNIUM
BIMILLENNIUMS
BIMODALITIES
BIMODALITY
BIMOLECULAR
BIMOLECULARLY
BIMONTHLIES
BIMORPHEMIC
BINATIONAL
BINAURALLY
BINDINGNESS
BINDINGNESSES
BINOCULARITIES
BINOCULARITY
BINOCULARLY
BINOCULARS
BINOMIALLY
BINOMINALS
BINTURONGS
BINUCLEATE
BINUCLEATED

BIOACCUMULATE
BIOACCUMULATED
BIOACCUMULATES
BIOACCUMULATING
BIOACCUMULATION
BIOACOUSTICS
BIOACTIVITIES
BIOACTIVITY
BIOAERATION
BIOAERATIONS
BIOAERONAUTICS
BIOARCHAEOLOGY
BIOASSAYED
BIOASSAYING
BIOASTRONAUTICS
BIOASTRONOMIES
BIOASTRONOMY
BIOAVAILABILITY
BIOAVAILABLE
BIOBANKING
BIOBANKINGS
BIOCATALYST
BIOCATALYSTS
BIOCATALYTIC
BIOCELLATE
BIOCENOLOGIES
BIOCENOLOGY
BIOCENOSES
BIOCENOSIS
BIOCENOTIC
BIOCHEMICAL
BIOCHEMICALLY
BIOCHEMICALS
BIOCHEMIST
BIOCHEMISTRIES
BIOCHEMISTRY
BIOCHEMISTS
BIOCLASTIC
BIOCLIMATIC
BIOCLIMATOLOGY
BIOCOENOLOGIES
BIOCOENOLOGY
BIOCOENOSES
BIOCOENOSIS
BIOCOENOTIC
BIOCOMPATIBLE
BIOCOMPUTING
BIOCOMPUTINGS

BIOCONTROL
BIOCONTROLS
BIOCONVERSION
BIOCONVERSIONS
BIODEGRADABLE
BIODEGRADABLES
BIODEGRADATION
BIODEGRADATIONS
BIODEGRADE
BIODEGRADED
BIODEGRADES
BIODEGRADING
BIODESTRUCTIBLE
BIODIESELS
BIODIVERSE
BIODIVERSITIES
BIODIVERSITY
BIODYNAMIC
BIODYNAMICAL
BIODYNAMICS
BIOECOLOGICAL
BIOECOLOGICALLY
BIOECOLOGIES
BIOECOLOGIST
BIOECOLOGISTS
BIOECOLOGY
BIOELECTRIC
BIOELECTRICAL
BIOELECTRICITY
BIOENERGETIC
BIOENERGETICS
BIOENERGIES
BIOENGINEER
BIOENGINEERED
BIOENGINEERING
BIOENGINEERINGS
BIOENGINEERS
BIOETHANOL
BIOETHANOLS
BIOETHICAL
BIOETHICIST
BIOETHICISTS
BIOFEEDBACK
BIOFEEDBACKS
BIOFLAVONOID
BIOFLAVONOIDS
BIOFOULERS
BIOFOULING

BIOFOULINGS	BIOLUMINESCENT	BIOPOLYMER	BIOSYNTHESES	BIPOLARIZE
BIOFUELLED	BIOMAGNETICS	BIOPOLYMERS	BIOSYNTHESIS	BIPOLARIZED
BIOGENESES	BIOMARKERS	BIOPRINTING	BIOSYNTHETIC	BIPOLARIZES
BIOGENESIS	BIOMATERIAL	BIOPRINTINGS	BIOSYSTEMATIC	BIPOLARIZING
BIOGENETIC	BIOMATERIALS	BIOPRIVACIES	BIOSYSTEMATICS	BIPROPELLANT
BIOGENETICAL	BIOMATHEMATICAL	BIOPRIVACY	BIOSYSTEMATIST	BIPROPELLANTS
BIOGENETICALLY	BIOMATHEMATICS	BIOPROSPECTING	BIOSYSTEMATISTS	BIPYRAMIDAL
BIOGENETICS	BIOMECHANICAL	BIOPROSPECTINGS	BIOTECHNICAL	BIPYRAMIDS
BIOGEOCHEMICAL	BIOMECHANICALLY	BIOPSYCHOLOGIES	BIOTECHNOLOGIES	BIQUADRATE
BIOGEOCHEMICALS	BIOMECHANICS	BIOPSYCHOLOGY	BIOTECHNOLOGIST	BIQUADRATES
BIOGEOCHEMISTRY	BIOMEDICAL	BIOREACTOR	BIOTECHNOLOGY	BIQUADRATIC
BIOGEOGRAPHER	BIOMEDICINE	BIOREACTORS	BIOTELEMETRIC	BIQUADRATICS
BIOGEOGRAPHERS	BIOMEDICINES	BIOREAGENT	BIOTELEMETRIES	BIQUARTERLY
BIOGEOGRAPHIC	BIOMETEOROLOGY	BIOREAGENTS	BIOTELEMETRY	BIQUINTILE
BIOGEOGRAPHICAL	BIOMETRICAL	BIOREGIONAL	BIOTERRORS	BIQUINTILES
BIOGEOGRAPHIES	BIOMETRICALLY	BIOREGIONALISM	BIOTICALLY	BIRACIALISM
BIOGEOGRAPHY	BIOMETRICIAN	BIOREGIONALISMS	BIOTURBATION	BIRACIALISMS
BIOGRAPHED	BIOMETRICIANS	BIOREGIONALIST	BIOTURBATIONS	BIRACIALLY
BIOGRAPHEE	BIOMETRICS	BIOREGIONALISTS	BIOWEAPONS	BIRADICALS
BIOGRAPHEES	BIOMETRIES	BIOREGIONS	BIPARENTAL	BIRCHBARKS
BIOGRAPHER	BIOMIMETIC	BIOREMEDIATION	BIPARENTALLY	BIRCHWOODS
BIOGRAPHERS	BIOMIMETICS	BIOREMEDIATIONS	BIPARIETAL	BIRDBRAINED
BIOGRAPHIC	BIOMIMICRIES	BIORHYTHMIC	BIPARTISAN	BIRDBRAINS
BIOGRAPHICAL	BIOMIMICRY	BIORHYTHMICALLY	BIPARTISANISM	BIRDDOGGED
BIOGRAPHICALLY	BIOMININGS	BIORHYTHMICS	BIPARTISANISMS	BIRDDOGGING
BIOGRAPHIES	BIOMOLECULAR	BIORHYTHMS	BIPARTISANSHIP	BIRDDOGGINGS
BIOGRAPHING	BIOMOLECULE	BIOSAFETIES	BIPARTISANSHIPS	BIRDHOUSES
BIOGRAPHISE	BIOMOLECULES	BIOSATELLITE	BIPARTITELY	BIRDLIMING
BIOGRAPHISED	BIOMORPHIC	BIOSATELLITES	BIPARTITION	BIRDSFOOTS
BIOGRAPHISES	BIONOMICALLY	BIOSCIENCE	BIPARTITIONS	BIRDWATCHED
BIOGRAPHISING	BIONOMISTS	BIOSCIENCES	BIPEDALISM	BIRDWATCHER
BIOGRAPHIZE	BIOPARENTS	BIOSCIENTIFIC	BIPEDALISMS	BIRDWATCHERS
BIOGRAPHIZED	BIOPESTICIDAL	BIOSCIENTIST	BIPEDALITIES	BIRDWATCHES
BIOGRAPHIZES	BIOPESTICIDE	BIOSCIENTISTS	BIPEDALITY	BIRDWATCHING
BIOGRAPHIZING	BIOPESTICIDES	BIOSCOPIES	BIPETALOUS	BIRDWATCHINGS
BIOHACKERS	BIOPHILIAS	BIOSENSORS	BIPINNARIA	BIREFRINGENCE
BIOHAZARDOUS	BIOPHYSICAL	BIOSOCIALLY	BIPINNARIAS	BIREFRINGENCES
BIOHAZARDS	BIOPHYSICALLY	BIOSPHERES	BIPINNATELY	BIREFRINGENT
BIOINDUSTRIES	BIOPHYSICIST	BIOSPHERIC	BIPOLARISATION	BIROSTRATE
BIOINDUSTRY	BIOPHYSICISTS	BIOSTATICALLY	BIPOLARISATIONS	BIRTHDATES
BIOINFORMATICS	BIOPHYSICS	BIOSTATICS	BIPOLARISE	BIRTHMARKS
BIOLOGICAL	BIOPIRACIES	BIOSTATISTICAL	BIPOLARISED	BIRTHNAMES
BIOLOGICALLY	BIOPIRATES	BIOSTATISTICIAN	BIPOLARISES	BIRTHNIGHT
BIOLOGICALS	BIOPLASMIC	BIOSTATISTICS	BIPOLARISING	BIRTHNIGHTS
BIOLOGISMS	BIOPLASTIC	BIOSTRATIGRAPHY	BIPOLARITIES	BIRTHPLACE
BIOLOGISTIC	BIOPLASTICS	BIOSTROMES	BIPOLARITY	BIRTHPLACES
BIOLOGISTS	BIOPOIESES	BIOSURGERIES	BIPOLARIZATION	BIRTHRATES
BIOLUMINESCENCE	BIOPOIESIS	BIOSURGERY	BIPOLARIZATIONS	BIRTHRIGHT

BIRTHRIGHTS

BIRTHRIGHTS	BISYMMETRY	BITUMINIZES	BLACKENING	BLACKSMITHING
BIRTHROOTS	BITARTRATE	BITUMINIZING	BLACKENINGS	BLACKSMITHINGS
BIRTHSTONE	BITARTRATES	BITUMINOUS	BLACKFACED	BLACKSMITHS
BIRTHSTONES	BITCHERIES	BIUNIQUENESS	BLACKFACES	BLACKSNAKE
BIRTHWORTS	BITCHFESTS	BIUNIQUENESSES	BLACKFELLA	BLACKSNAKES
BISCUITIER	BITCHINESS	BIVALENCES	BLACKFELLAS	BLACKSPOTS
BISCUITIEST	BITCHINESSES	BIVALENCIES	BLACKFISHES	BLACKSTRAP
BISECTIONAL	BITEPLATES	BIVALVULAR	BLACKFLIES	BLACKSTRAPS
BISECTIONALLY	BITMAPPING	BIVARIANTS	BLACKGAMES	BLACKTAILS
BISECTIONS	BITONALITIES	BIVARIATES	BLACKGUARD	BLACKTHORN
BISECTRICES	BITONALITY	BIVOUACKED	BLACKGUARDED	BLACKTHORNS
BISEXUALISM	BITSTREAMS	BIVOUACKING	BLACKGUARDING	BLACKTOPPED
BISEXUALISMS	BITTERBARK	BIWEEKLIES	BLACKGUARDISM	BLACKTOPPING
BISEXUALITIES	BITTERBARKS	BIZARRENESS	BLACKGUARDISMS	BLACKWASHED
BISEXUALITY	BITTERBRUSH	BIZARRENESSES	BLACKGUARDLIER	BLACKWASHES
BISEXUALLY	BITTERBRUSHES	BIZARRERIE	BLACKGUARDLIEST	BLACKWASHING
BISHOPBIRD	BITTERCRESS	BIZARRERIES	BLACKGUARDLY	BLACKWATER
BISHOPBIRDS	BITTERCRESSES	BLABBERING	BLACKGUARDS	BLACKWATERS
BISHOPDOMS	BITTERLING	BLABBERMOUTH	BLACKHANDER	BLACKWOODS
BISHOPESSES	BITTERLINGS	BLABBERMOUTHS	BLACKHANDERS	BLADDERIER
BISHOPRICS	BITTERNESS	BLACKAMOOR	BLACKHEADED	BLADDERIEST
BISHOPWEED	BITTERNESSES	BLACKAMOORS	BLACKHEADS	BLADDERLIKE
BISHOPWEEDS	BITTERNUTS	BLACKBALLED	BLACKHEART	BLADDERNOSE
BISMUTHINITE	BITTERROOT	BLACKBALLING	BLACKHEARTS	BLADDERNOSES
BISMUTHINITES	BITTERROOTS	BLACKBALLINGS	BLACKISHLY	BLADDERNUT
BISMUTHOUS	BITTERSWEET	BLACKBALLS	BLACKJACKED	BLADDERNUTS
BISOCIATION	BITTERSWEETLY	BLACKBANDS	BLACKJACKING	BLADDERWORT
BISOCIATIONS	BITTERSWEETNESS	BLACKBERRIED	BLACKJACKS	BLADDERWORTS
BISOCIATIVE	BITTERSWEETS	BLACKBERRIES	BLACKLANDS	BLADDERWRACK
BISPHENOLS	BITTERWEED	BLACKBERRY	BLACKLEADED	BLADDERWRACKS
BISPHOSPHONATE	BITTERWEEDS	BLACKBERRYING	BLACKLEADING	BLADEWORKS
BISPHOSPHONATES	BITTERWOOD	BLACKBERRYINGS	BLACKLEADS	BLAEBERRIES
BISSEXTILE	BITTERWOODS	BLACKBIRDED	BLACKLEGGED	BLAMABLENESS
BISSEXTILES	BITTINESSES	BLACKBIRDER	BLACKLEGGING	BLAMABLENESSES
BISTOURIES	BITUMINATE	BLACKBIRDERS	BLACKLISTED	BLAMEABLENESS
BISULFATES	BITUMINATED	BLACKBIRDING	BLACKLISTER	BLAMEABLENESSES
BISULFIDES	BITUMINATES	BLACKBIRDINGS	BLACKLISTERS	BLAMEFULLY
BISULFITES	BITUMINATING	BLACKBIRDS	BLACKLISTING	BLAMEFULNESS
BISULPHATE	BITUMINISATION	BLACKBOARD	BLACKLISTINGS	BLAMEFULNESSES
BISULPHATES	BITUMINISATIONS	BLACKBOARDS	BLACKLISTS	BLAMELESSLY
BISULPHIDE	BITUMINISE	BLACKBODIES	BLACKMAILED	BLAMELESSNESS
BISULPHIDES	BITUMINISED	BLACKBUCKS	BLACKMAILER	BLAMELESSNESSES
BISULPHITE	BITUMINISES	BLACKBUTTS	BLACKMAILERS	BLAMESTORM
BISULPHITES	BITUMINISING	BLACKCOCKS	BLACKMAILING	BLAMESTORMED
BISYMMETRIC	BITUMINIZATION	BLACKCURRANT	BLACKMAILS	BLAMESTORMING
BISYMMETRICAL	BITUMINIZATIONS	BLACKCURRANTS	BLACKNESSES	BLAMESTORMINGS
BISYMMETRICALLY	BITUMINIZE	BLACKDAMPS	BLACKPOLLS	BLAMESTORMS
BISYMMETRIES	BITUMINIZED	BLACKENERS	BLACKSMITH	BLAMEWORTHIER

BLAMEWORTHIEST
BLAMEWORTHINESS
BLAMEWORTHY
BLANCHISSEUSE
BLANCHISSEUSES
BLANCMANGE
BLANCMANGES
BLANDISHED
BLANDISHER
BLANDISHERS
BLANDISHES
BLANDISHING
BLANDISHMENT
BLANDISHMENTS
BLANDNESSES
BLANKETFLOWER
BLANKETFLOWERS
BLANKETIES
BLANKETING
BLANKETINGS
BLANKETLIKE
BLANKETWEED
BLANKETWEEDS
BLANKNESSES
BLANQUETTE
BLANQUETTES
BLARNEYING
BLASPHEMED
BLASPHEMER
BLASPHEMERS
BLASPHEMES
BLASPHEMIES
BLASPHEMING
BLASPHEMOUS
BLASPHEMOUSLY
BLASPHEMOUSNESS
BLASTEMATA
BLASTEMATIC
BLASTHOLES
BLASTMENTS
BLASTOCHYLE
BLASTOCHYLES
BLASTOCOEL
BLASTOCOELE
BLASTOCOELES
BLASTOCOELIC
BLASTOCOELS
BLASTOCYST

BLASTOCYSTS
BLASTODERM
BLASTODERMIC
BLASTODERMS
BLASTODISC
BLASTODISCS
BLASTOGENESES
BLASTOGENESIS
BLASTOGENETIC
BLASTOGENIC
BLASTOMATA
BLASTOMERE
BLASTOMERES
BLASTOMERIC
BLASTOMYCOSES
BLASTOMYCOSIS
BLASTOPORAL
BLASTOPORE
BLASTOPORES
BLASTOPORIC
BLASTOPORS
BLASTOSPHERE
BLASTOSPHERES
BLASTOSPORE
BLASTOSPORES
BLASTULATION
BLASTULATIONS
BLATANCIES
BLATHERERS
BLATHERING
BLATHERINGS
BLATHERSKITE
BLATHERSKITES
BLATTERING
BLAXPLOITATION
BLAXPLOITATIONS
BLAZONINGS
BLAZONRIES
BLEACHABLE
BLEACHERIES
BLEACHERITE
BLEACHERITES
BLEACHINGS
BLEAKNESSES
BLEARINESS
BLEARINESSES
BLEMISHERS
BLEMISHING

BLEMISHMENT
BLEMISHMENTS
BLENNIOIDS
BLENNORRHEA
BLENNORRHEAS
BLENNORRHOEA
BLENNORRHOEAS
BLEOMYCINS
BLEPHARISM
BLEPHARISMS
BLEPHARITIC
BLEPHARITIS
BLEPHARITISES
BLEPHAROPLAST
BLEPHAROPLASTS
BLEPHAROPLASTY
BLEPHAROSPASM
BLEPHAROSPASMS
BLESSEDEST
BLESSEDNESS
BLESSEDNESSES
BLETHERANSKATE
BLETHERANSKATES
BLETHERATION
BLETHERATIONS
BLETHERERS
BLETHERING
BLETHERINGS
BLETHERSKATE
BLETHERSKATES
BLIGHTINGLY
BLIGHTINGS
BLIMPERIES
BLIMPISHLY
BLIMPISHNESS
BLIMPISHNESSES
BLINDFISHES
BLINDFOLDED
BLINDFOLDING
BLINDFOLDS
BLINDINGLY
BLINDNESSES
BLINDSIDED
BLINDSIDES
BLINDSIDING
BLINDSIGHT
BLINDSIGHTS
BLINDSTOREY

BLINDSTOREYS
BLINDSTORIES
BLINDSTORY
BLINDWORMS
BLINGLISHES
BLINKERING
BLISSFULLY
BLISSFULNESS
BLISSFULNESSES
BLISTERIER
BLISTERIEST
BLISTERING
BLISTERINGLY
BLITHENESS
BLITHENESSES
BLITHERING
BLITHESOME
BLITHESOMELY
BLITHESOMENESS
BLITZKRIEG
BLITZKRIEGS
BLIZZARDED
BLIZZARDIER
BLIZZARDIEST
BLIZZARDING
BLIZZARDLY
BLOATEDNESS
BLOATEDNESSES
BLOATWARES
BLOCKADERS
BLOCKADING
BLOCKBOARD
BLOCKBOARDS
BLOCKBUSTED
BLOCKBUSTER
BLOCKBUSTERS
BLOCKBUSTING
BLOCKBUSTINGS
BLOCKBUSTS
BLOCKCHAIN
BLOCKCHAINS
BLOCKHEADED
BLOCKHEADEDLY
BLOCKHEADEDNESS
BLOCKHEADS
BLOCKHOLES
BLOCKHOUSE
BLOCKHOUSES

BLOCKINESS
BLOCKINESSES
BLOCKISHLY
BLOCKISHNESS
BLOCKISHNESSES
BLOCKSHIPS
BLOCKWORKS
BLOGGERATI
BLOGJACKING
BLOGJACKINGS
BLOGOSPHERE
BLOGOSPHERES
BLOGSTREAM
BLOGSTREAMS
BLOKARTING
BLOKARTINGS
BLOKEISHNESS
BLOKEISHNESSES
BLOKISHNESS
BLOKISHNESSES
BLONDENESS
BLONDENESSES
BLONDINING
BLONDNESSES
BLOODBATHS
BLOODCURDLING
BLOODCURDLINGLY
BLOODGUILT
BLOODGUILTIER
BLOODGUILTIEST
BLOODGUILTINESS
BLOODGUILTS
BLOODGUILTY
BLOODHOUND
BLOODHOUNDS
BLOODINESS
BLOODINESSES
BLOODLESSLY
BLOODLESSNESS
BLOODLESSNESSES
BLOODLETTER
BLOODLETTERS
BLOODLETTING
BLOODLETTINGS
BLOODLINES
BLOODLUSTS
BLOODMOBILE
BLOODMOBILES

BLOODROOTS

BLOODROOTS	BLUBBERIER	BLUNDERERS	BOBBLEHEAD	BODYWASHES
BLOODSHEDS	BLUBBERIEST	BLUNDERING	BOBBLEHEADS	BODYWORKER
BLOODSPRENT	BLUBBERING	BLUNDERINGLY	BOBBYSOCKS	BODYWORKERS
BLOODSTAIN	BLUDGEONED	BLUNDERINGS	BOBBYSOXER	BOEREMUSIEK
BLOODSTAINED	BLUDGEONER	BLUNTHEADS	BOBBYSOXERS	BOEREMUSIEKS
BLOODSTAINS	BLUDGEONERS	BLUNTNESSES	BOBSLEDDED	BOEREWORSES
BLOODSTOCK	BLUDGEONING	BLURREDNESS	BOBSLEDDER	BOFFINIEST
BLOODSTOCKS	BLUFBEARDS	BLURREDNESSES	BOBSLEDDERS	BOGGINESSES
BLOODSTONE	BLUEBERRIES	BLURRINESS	BOBSLEDDING	BOGTROTTER
BLOODSTONES	BLUEBLOODS	BLURRINESSES	BOBSLEDDINGS	BOGTROTTERS
BLOODSTREAM	BLUEBONNET	BLURRINGLY	BOBSLEIGHED	BOGTROTTING
BLOODSTREAMS	BLUEBONNETS	BLUSHINGLY	BOBSLEIGHING	BOGTROTTINGS
BLOODSUCKER	BLUEBOTTLE	BLUSHLESSLY	BOBSLEIGHINGS	BOGUSNESSES
BLOODSUCKERS	BLUEBOTTLES	BLUSTERERS	BOBSLEIGHS	BOHEMIANISM
BLOODSUCKING	BLUEBREAST	BLUSTERIER	BOBTAILING	BOHEMIANISMS
BLOODTHIRSTIER	BLUEBREASTS	BLUSTERIEST	BOBWEIGHTS	BOILERMAKER
BLOODTHIRSTIEST	BLUEBUSHES	BLUSTERING	BOCCONCINI	BOILERMAKERS
BLOODTHIRSTILY	BLUEFISHES	BLUSTERINGLY	BODACIOUSLY	BOILERMAKING
BLOODTHIRSTY	BLUEGRASSES	BLUSTERINGS	BODDHISATTVA	BOILERMAKINGS
BLOODWOODS	BLUEISHNESS	BLUSTEROUS	BODDHISATTVAS	BOILERPLATE
BLOODWORMS	BLUEISHNESSES	BLUSTEROUSLY	BODEGUEROS	BOILERPLATED
BLOODWORTS	BLUEJACKET	BLUTWURSTS	BODHISATTVA	BOILERPLATES
BLOOMERIES	BLUEJACKETS	BOARDINGHOUSE	BODHISATTVAS	BOILERPLATING
BLOQUISTES	BLUEJACKING	BOARDINGHOUSES	BODYBOARDED	BOILERSUIT
BLOSSOMIER	BLUEJACKINGS	BOARDROOMS	BODYBOARDING	BOILERSUITS
BLOSSOMIEST	BLUELINERS	BOARDSAILING	BODYBOARDINGS	BOISTEROUS
BLOSSOMING	BLUEMOUTHS	BOARDSAILINGS	BODYBOARDS	BOISTEROUSLY
BLOSSOMINGS	BLUENESSES	BOARDSAILOR	BODYBUILDER	BOISTEROUSNESS
BLOSSOMLESS	BLUEPOINTS	BOARDSAILORS	BODYBUILDERS	BOKMAKIERIE
BLOTCHIEST	BLUEPRINTED	BOARDWALKS	BODYBUILDING	BOKMAKIERIES
BLOTCHINESS	BLUEPRINTING	BOARFISHES	BODYBUILDINGS	BOLDFACING
BLOTCHINESSES	BLUEPRINTS	BOARHOUNDS	BODYBUILDS	BOLDNESSES
BLOTCHINGS	BLUESHIFTED	BOARISHNESS	BODYCHECKED	BOLECTIONS
BLOTTESQUE	BLUESHIFTS	BOARISHNESSES	BODYCHECKING	BOLIVIANOS
BLOTTESQUES	BLUESNARFING	BOASTFULLY	BODYCHECKS	BOLLETRIES
BLOVIATING	BLUESNARFINGS	BOASTFULNESS	BODYGUARDED	BOLLOCKING
BLOVIATION	BLUESTOCKING	BOASTFULNESSES	BODYGUARDING	BOLLOCKINGS
BLOVIATIONS	BLUESTOCKINGS	BOASTINGLY	BODYGUARDS	BOLLOCKSED
BLOWFISHES	BLUESTONES	BOATBUILDER	BODYSHAPER	BOLLOCKSES
BLOWINESSES	BLUETHROAT	BOATBUILDERS	BODYSHAPERS	BOLLOCKSING
BLOWSINESS	BLUETHROATS	BOATBUILDING	BODYSHELLS	BOLOGNESES
BLOWSINESSES	BLUETONGUE	BOATBUILDINGS	BODYSNATCHER	BOLOGRAPHS
BLOWTORCHED	BLUETONGUES	BOATHOUSES	BODYSNATCHERS	BOLOMETERS
BLOWTORCHES	BLUFFNESSES	BOATLIFTED	BODYSURFED	BOLOMETRIC
BLOWTORCHING	BLUISHNESS	BOATLIFTING	BODYSURFER	BOLOMETRICALLY
BLOWZINESS	BLUISHNESSES	BOATSWAINS	BODYSURFERS	BOLOMETRIES
BLOWZINESSES	BLUNDERBUSS	BOBBEJAANS	BODYSURFING	BOLSHEVIKI
BLUBBERERS	BLUNDERBUSSES	BOBBITTING	BODYSURFINGS	BOLSHEVIKS

BOLSHEVISE	BONDMANSHIP	BOOKMAKERS	BOOTLICKINGS	BOTANIZING
BOLSHEVISED	BONDMANSHIPS	BOOKMAKING	BOOTLOADER	BOTANOMANCIES
BOLSHEVISES	BONDSERVANT	BOOKMAKINGS	BOOTLOADERS	BOTANOMANCY
BOLSHEVISING	BONDSERVANTS	BOOKMARKED	BOOTMAKERS	BOTCHERIES
BOLSHEVISM	BONDSTONES	BOOKMARKER	BOOTMAKING	BOTCHINESS
BOLSHEVISMS	BONDSWOMAN	BOOKMARKERS	BOOTMAKINGS	BOTCHINESSES
BOLSHEVIZE	BONDSWOMEN	BOOKMARKING	BOOTSTRAPPED	BOTHERATION
BOLSHEVIZED	BONEBLACKS	BOOKMOBILE	BOOTSTRAPPING	BOTHERATIONS
BOLSHEVIZES	BONEFISHES	BOOKMOBILES	BOOTSTRAPS	BOTHERSOME
BOLSHEVIZING	BONEFISHING	BOOKPLATES	BOOTYLICIOUS	BOTRYOIDAL
BOLSTERERS	BONEFISHINGS	BOOKSELLER	BOOZEHOUND	BOTRYTISES
BOLSTERING	BONEHEADED	BOOKSELLERS	BOOZEHOUNDS	BOTTLEBRUSH
BOLSTERINGS	BONEHEADEDNESS	BOOKSELLING	BOOZINESSES	BOTTLEBRUSHES
BOMBACACEOUS	BONESETTER	BOOKSELLINGS	BORAGINACEOUS	BOTTLEFULS
BOMBARDERS	BONESETTERS	BOOKSHELVES	BORBORYGMAL	BOTTLENECK
BOMBARDIER	BONESHAKER	BOOKSTALLS	BORBORYGMI	BOTTLENECKED
BOMBARDIERS	BONESHAKERS	BOOKSTANDS	BORBORYGMIC	BOTTLENECKING
BOMBARDING	BONHOMMIES	BOOKSTORES	BORBORYGMUS	BOTTLENECKS
BOMBARDMENT	BONILASSES	BOOMERANGED	BORDEREAUX	BOTTLENOSE
BOMBARDMENTS	BONINESSES	BOOMERANGING	BORDERLAND	BOTTLENOSES
BOMBARDONS	BONKBUSTER	BOOMERANGS	BORDERLANDS	BOTTOMINGS
BOMBASINES	BONKBUSTERS	BOOMSLANGS	BORDERLESS	BOTTOMLAND
BOMBASTERS	BONNIBELLS	BOOMSTICKS	BORDERLINE	BOTTOMLANDS
BOMBASTICALLY	BONNILASSE	BOONDOGGLE	BORDERLINES	BOTTOMLESS
BOMBASTING	BONNILASSES	BOONDOGGLED	BORDRAGING	BOTTOMLESSLY
BOMBAZINES	BONNINESSES	BOONDOGGLER	BORDRAGINGS	BOTTOMLESSNESS
BOMBILATED	BONNYCLABBER	BOONDOGGLERS	BORESCOPES	BOTTOMMOST
BOMBILATES	BONNYCLABBERS	BOONDOGGLES	BORGHETTOS	BOTTOMNESS
BOMBILATING	BOOBIALLAS	BOONDOGGLING	BORINGNESS	BOTTOMNESSES
BOMBILATION	BOOBOISIES	BOONGARIES	BORINGNESSES	BOTTOMRIES
BOMBILATIONS	BOOGALOOED	BOORISHNESS	BOROHYDRIDE	BOTULINUMS
BOMBINATED	BOOGALOOING	BOORISHNESSES	BOROHYDRIDES	BOTULINUSES
BOMBINATES	BOOKBINDER	BOOSTERISH	BOROSILICATE	BOUGAINVILIA
BOMBINATING	BOOKBINDERIES	BOOSTERISM	BOROSILICATES	BOUGAINVILIAS
BOMBINATION	BOOKBINDERS	BOOSTERISMS	BORROWINGS	BOUGAINVILLAEA
BOMBINATIONS	BOOKBINDERY	BOOTBLACKS	BOSBERAADS	BOUGAINVILLAEAS
BOMBPROOFED	BOOKBINDING	BOOTLEGGED	BUSCIIVARKS	BOUGAINVILLEA
BOMBPROOFING	BOOKBINDINGS	BOOTLEGGER	BOSCHVELDS	BUUGAINVILLEAS
BOMBPROOFS	BOOKCROSSING	BOOTLEGGERS	BOSKINESSES	BOUILLABAISSE
BOMBSHELLS	BOOKCROSSINGS	BOOTLEGGING	BOSSINESSES	BOUILLABAISSES
BOMBSIGHTS	BOOKENDING	BOOTLEGGINGS	BOSSNAPPING	BOUILLOTTE
BONAMIASES	BOOKISHNESS	BOOTLESSLY	BOSSNAPPINGS	BOUILLOTTES
BONAMIASIS	BOOKISHNESSES	BOOTLESSNESS	BOSSYBOOTS	BOULDERERS
BONASSUSES	BOOKKEEPER	BOOTLESSNESSES	BOTANICALLY	BOULDERIER
BONBONNIERE	BOOKKEEPERS	BOOTLICKED	BOTANICALS	BOULDERIEST
BONBONNIERES	BOOKKEEPING	BOOTLICKER	BOTANISERS	BOULDERING
BONDHOLDER	BOOKKEEPINGS	BOOTLICKERS	BOTANISING	BOULDERINGS
BONDHOLDERS	BOOKLIGHTS	BOOTLICKING	BOTANIZERS	BOULEVARDIER

BOULEVARDIERS	BOUSTROPHEDONIC	BOYSENBERRIES	BRACHYPRISM	BRAILLEWRITER
BOULEVARDS	BOUSTROPHEDONS	BOYSENBERRY	BRACHYPRISMS	BRAILLEWRITERS
BOULEVERSEMENT	BOUTIQUIER	BRAAIVLEIS	BRACHYPTERISM	BRAILLISTS
BOULEVERSEMENTS	BOUTIQUIEST	BRAAIVLEISES	BRACHYPTERISMS	BRAINBOXES
BOULLEWORK	BOUTONNIERE	BRABBLEMENT	BRACHYPTEROUS	BRAINCASES
BOULLEWORKS	BOUTONNIERES	BRABBLEMENTS	BRACHYTHERAPIES	BRAINCHILD
BOUNCEDOWN	BOUVARDIAS	BRACHIATED	BRACHYTHERAPY	BRAINCHILDREN
BOUNCEDOWNS	BOVINITIES	BRACHIATES	BRACHYURAL	BRAINFARTS
BOUNCINESS	BOWDLERISATION	BRACHIATING	BRACHYURAN	BRAINFOODS
BOUNCINESSES	BOWDLERISATIONS	BRACHIATION	BRACHYURANS	BRAININESS
BOUNCINGLY	BOWDLERISE	BRACHIATIONS	BRACHYUROUS	BRAININESSES
BOUNDARIES	BOWDLERISED	BRACHIATOR	BRACKETING	BRAINLESSLY
BOUNDEDNESS	BOWDLERISER	BRACHIATORS	BRACKETINGS	BRAINLESSNESS
BOUNDEDNESSES	BOWDLERISERS	BRACHIOCEPHALIC	BRACKISHNESS	BRAINLESSNESSES
BOUNDERISH	BOWDLERISES	BRACHIOPOD	BRACKISHNESSES	BRAINPOWER
BOUNDLESSLY	BOWDLERISING	BRACHIOPODS	BRACTEATES	BRAINPOWERS
BOUNDLESSNESS	BOWDLERISM	BRACHIOSAURUS	BRACTEOLATE	BRAINSICKLY
BOUNDLESSNESSES	BOWDLERISMS	BRACHIOSAURUSES	BRACTEOLES	BRAINSICKNESS
BOUNDNESSES	BOWDLERIZATION	BRACHISTOCHRONE	BRADYCARDIA	BRAINSICKNESSES
BOUNTEOUSLY	BOWDLERIZATIONS	BRACHYAXES	BRADYCARDIAC	BRAINSTEMS
BOUNTEOUSNESS	BOWDLERIZE	BRACHYAXIS	BRADYCARDIAS	BRAINSTORM
BOUNTEOUSNESSES	BOWDLERIZED	BRACHYCEPHAL	BRADYKINESIA	BRAINSTORMED
BOUNTIFULLY	BOWDLERIZER	BRACHYCEPHALIC	BRADYKINESIAS	BRAINSTORMER
BOUNTIFULNESS	BOWDLERIZERS	BRACHYCEPHALICS	BRADYKININ	BRAINSTORMERS
BOUNTIFULNESSES	BOWDLERIZES	BRACHYCEPHALIES	BRADYKININS	BRAINSTORMING
BOUNTYHEDS	BOWDLERIZING	BRACHYCEPHALISM	BRADYPEPTIC	BRAINSTORMINGS
BOUQUETIERE	BOWERBIRDS	BRACHYCEPHALOUS	BRADYPEPTICS	BRAINSTORMS
BOUQUETIERES	BOWERWOMAN	BRACHYCEPHALS	BRADYSEISM	BRAINTEASER
BOURASQUES	BOWERWOMEN	BRACHYCEPHALY	BRADYSEISMS	BRAINTEASERS
BOURBONISM	BOWHUNTERS	BRACHYCEROUS	BRAGADISME	BRAINWASHED
BOURBONISMS	BOWHUNTING	BRACHYDACTYL	BRAGADISMES	BRAINWASHER
BOURGEOISE	BOWHUNTINGS	BRACHYDACTYLIC	BRAGGADOCIO	BRAINWASHERS
BOURGEOISES	BOWLINGUAL	BRACHYDACTYLIES	BRAGGADOCIOS	BRAINWASHES
BOURGEOISIE	BOWLINGUALS	BRACHYDACTYLISM	BRAGGADOCIOUS	BRAINWASHING
BOURGEOISIES	BOWSTRINGED	BRACHYDACTYLOUS	BRAGGARTISM	BRAINWASHINGS
BOURGEOISIFIED	BOWSTRINGING	BRACHYDACTYLY	BRAGGARTISMS	BRAINWAVES
BOURGEOISIFIES	BOWSTRINGS	BRACHYDIAGONAL	BRAGGARTLIER	BRAINWORKS
BOURGEOISIFY	BOXBERRIES	BRACHYDIAGONALS	BRAGGARTLIEST	BRAMBLIEST
BOURGEOISIFYING	BOXERCISES	BRACHYDOME	BRAGGARTLY	BRAMBLINGS
BOURGEONED	BOXHAULING	BRACHYDOMES	BRAGGINGLY	BRANCHERIES
BOURGEONING	BOXINESSES	BRACHYGRAPHIES	BRAHMANISM	BRANCHIATE
BOURGUIGNON	BOXKEEPERS	BRACHYGRAPHY	BRAHMANISMS	BRANCHIEST
BOURGUIGNONNE	BOXWALLAHS	BRACHYLOGIES	BRAHMANIST	BRANCHINGS
BOURGUIGNONNES	BOYCOTTERS	BRACHYLOGOUS	BRAHMANISTS	BRANCHIOPOD
BOURGUIGNONS	BOYCOTTING	BRACHYLOGY	BRAHMINISM	BRANCHIOPODS
BOUSINGKEN	BOYFRIENDS	BRACHYODONT	BRAHMINISMS	BRANCHIOSTEGAL
BOUSINGKENS	BOYISHNESS	BRACHYPINAKOID	BRAHMINIST	BRANCHLESS
BOUSTROPHEDON	BOYISHNESSES	BRACHYPINAKOIDS	BRAHMINISTS	BRANCHLETS

BRANCHLIKE	BRAVENESSES	BREAKDANCED	BREATHALYSED	BRETTICING
BRANCHLINE	BRAVISSIMO	BREAKDANCER	BREATHALYSER	BREUNNERITE
BRANCHLINES	BRAWNINESS	BREAKDANCERS	BREATHALYSERS	BREUNNERITES
BRANDERING	BRAWNINESSES	BREAKDANCES	BREATHALYSES	BREVETCIES
BRANDISHED	BRAZENNESS	BREAKDANCING	BREATHALYSING	BREVETTING
BRANDISHER	BRAZENNESSES	BREAKDANCINGS	BREATHALYZE	BREVIARIES
BRANDISHERS	BRAZENRIES	BREAKDOWNS	BREATHALYZED	BREVIPENNATE
BRANDISHES	BRAZIERIES	BREAKEVENS	BREATHALYZER	BREWHOUSES
BRANDISHING	BRAZILEINS	BREAKFASTED	BREATHALYZERS	BREWMASTER
BRANDLINGS	BRAZILWOOD	BREAKFASTER	BREATHALYZES	BREWMASTERS
BRANDRETHS	BRAZILWOODS	BREAKFASTERS	BREATHALYZING	BRIARROOTS
BRANFULNESS	BREADBASKET	BREAKFASTING	BREATHARIAN	BRIARWOODS
BRANFULNESSES	BREADBASKETS	BREAKFASTS	BREATHARIANISM	BRICABRACS
BRANGLINGS	BREADBERRIES	BREAKFRONT	BREATHARIANISMS	BRICKCLAYS
BRANKURSINE	BREADBERRY	BREAKFRONTS	BREATHARIANS	BRICKEARTH
BRANKURSINES	BREADBOARD	BREAKPOINT	BREATHIEST	BRICKEARTHS
BRANNIGANS	BREADBOARDED	BREAKPOINTS	BREATHINESS	BRICKFIELD
BRASHINESS	BREADBOARDING	BREAKTHROUGH	BREATHINESSES	BRICKFIELDER
BRASHINESSES	BREADBOARDS	BREAKTHROUGHS	BREATHINGS	BRICKFIELDERS
BRASHNESSES	BREADBOXES	BREAKTIMES	BREATHLESS	BRICKFIELDS
BRASILEINS	BREADCRUMB	BREAKWALLS	BREATHLESSLY	BRICKKILNS
BRASSBOUND	BREADCRUMBED	BREAKWATER	BREATHLESSNESS	BRICKLAYER
BRASSERIES	BREADCRUMBING	BREAKWATERS	BREATHTAKING	BRICKLAYERS
BRASSFOUNDER	BREADCRUMBS	BREASTBONE	BREATHTAKINGLY	BRICKLAYING
BRASSFOUNDERS	BREADFRUIT	BREASTBONES	BRECCIATED	BRICKLAYINGS
BRASSFOUNDING	BREADFRUITS	BREASTFEED	BRECCIATES	BRICKMAKER
BRASSFOUNDINGS	BREADHEADS	BREASTFEEDING	BRECCIATING	BRICKMAKERS
BRASSICACEOUS	BREADKNIFE	BREASTFEEDINGS	BRECCIATION	BRICKMAKING
BRASSIERES	BREADKNIVES	BREASTFEEDS	BRECCIATIONS	BRICKMAKINGS
BRASSINESS	BREADLINES	BREASTPINS	BREECHBLOCK	BRICKSHAPED
BRASSINESSES	BREADROOMS	BREASTPLATE	BREECHBLOCKS	BRICKWALLS
BRASSWARES	BREADROOTS	BREASTPLATES	BREECHCLOTH	BRICKWORKS
BRATPACKER	BREADSTICK	BREASTPLOUGH	BREECHCLOTHS	BRICKYARDS
BRATPACKERS	BREADSTICKS	BREASTPLOUGHS	BREECHCLOUT	BRICOLAGES
BRATTICING	BREADSTUFF	BREASTRAIL	BREECHCLOUTS	BRICOLEURS
BRATTICINGS	BREADSTUFFS	BREASTRAILS	BREECHINGS	BRIDECAKES
BRATTINESS	BREADTHWAYS	BREASTSTROKE	BREECHLESS	BRIDEGROOM
BRATTINESSES	BREADTHWISE	BREASTSTROKER	BREECHLOADER	BRIDEGROOMS
BRATTISHED	BREADWINNER	BREASTSTROKERS	BREECHLOADERS	BRIDEMAIDEN
BRATTISHES	BREADWINNERS	BREASTSTROKES	BREEZELESS	BRIDEMAIDENS
BRATTISHING	BREADWINNING	BREASTSUMMER	BREEZEWAYS	BRIDEMAIDS
BRATTISHINGS	BREADWINNINGS	BREASTSUMMERS	BREEZINESS	BRIDESMAID
BRATTLINGS	BREAKABLENESS	BREASTWORK	BREEZINESSES	BRIDESMAIDS
BRATWURSTS	BREAKABLENESSES	BREASTWORKS	BREMSSTRAHLUNG	BRIDEWEALTH
BRAUNCHING	BREAKABLES	BREATHABILITIES	BREMSSTRAHLUNGS	BRIDEWEALTHS
BRAUNSCHWEIGER	BREAKAWAYS	BREATHABILITY	BRESSUMMER	BRIDEWELLS
BRAUNSCHWEIGERS	BREAKBEATS	BREATHABLE	BRESSUMMERS	BRIDEZILLA
BRAVADOING	BREAKDANCE	BREATHALYSE	BRETASCHES	BRIDEZILLAS

BRIDGEABLE	BRIMFULNESS	BROADLEAVED	BROMINISMS	BROODINGLY
BRIDGEBOARD	BRIMFULNESSES	BROADLEAVES	BROMOCRIPTINE	BROODMARES
BRIDGEBOARDS	BRIMSTONES	BROADLINES	BROMOCRIPTINES	BROOKLIMES
BRIDGEHEAD	BRIMSTONIER	BROADLOOMS	BROMOFORMS	BROOKWEEDS
BRIDGEHEADS	BRIMSTONIEST	BROADNESSES	BROMOURACIL	BROOMBALLER
BRIDGELESS	BRINELLING	BROADPIECE	BROMOURACILS	BROOMBALLERS
BRIDGELIKE	BRINELLINGS	BROADPIECES	BRONCHIALLY	BROOMBALLS
BRIDGEWORK	BRINGDOWNS	BROADSCALE	BRONCHIECTASES	BROOMCORNS
BRIDGEWORKS	BRININESSES	BROADSHEET	BRONCHIECTASIS	BROOMRAPES
BRIDLEWAYS	BRINJARRIES	BROADSHEETS	BRONCHIOLAR	BROOMSTAFF
BRIDLEWISE	BRINKMANSHIP	BROADSIDED	BRONCHIOLE	BROOMSTAFFS
BRIEFCASES	BRINKMANSHIPS	BROADSIDES	BRONCHIOLES	BROOMSTICK
BRIEFNESSES	BRINKSMANSHIP	BROADSIDING	BRONCHIOLITIS	BROOMSTICKS
BRIERROOTS	BRINKSMANSHIPS	BROADSWORD	BRONCHIOLITISES	BROTHERHOOD
BRIERWOODS	BRIOLETTES	BROADSWORDS	BRONCHITIC	BROTHERHOODS
BRIGADIERS	BRIQUETTED	BROADTAILS	BRONCHITICS	BROTHERING
BRIGANDAGE	BRIQUETTES	BROBDINGNAGIAN	BRONCHITIS	BROTHERLIER
BRIGANDAGES	BRIQUETTING	BROCATELLE	BRONCHITISES	BROTHERLIEST
BRIGANDINE	BRISKENING	BROCATELLES	BRONCHODILATOR	BROTHERLIKE
BRIGANDINES	BRISKNESSES	BROCCOLINI	BRONCHODILATORS	BROTHERLINESS
BRIGANDRIES	BRISTLECONE	BROCCOLINIS	BRONCHOGENIC	BROTHERLINESSES
BRIGANTINE	BRISTLECONES	BROCHETTES	BRONCHOGRAPHIES	BROUGHTASES
BRIGANTINES	BRISTLELIKE	BROGUERIES	BRONCHOGRAPHY	BROWALLIAS
BRIGHTENED	BRISTLETAIL	BROIDERERS	BRONCHOSCOPE	BROWBEATEN
BRIGHTENER	BRISTLETAILS	BROIDERIES	BRONCHOSCOPES	BROWBEATER
BRIGHTENERS	BRISTLIEST	BROIDERING	BRONCHOSCOPIC	BROWBEATERS
BRIGHTENING	BRISTLINESS	BROIDERINGS	BRONCHOSCOPICAL	BROWBEATING
BRIGHTNESS	BRISTLINESSES	BROKENHEARTED	BRONCHOSCOPIES	BROWBEATINGS
BRIGHTNESSES	BRITANNIAS	BROKENHEARTEDLY	BRONCHOSCOPIST	BROWNFIELD
BRIGHTSOME	BRITSCHKAS	BROKENNESS	BRONCHOSCOPISTS	BROWNFIELDS
BRIGHTWORK	BRITTANIAS	BROKENNESSES	BRONCHOSCOPY	BROWNNESSES
BRIGHTWORKS	BRITTLENESS	BROKERAGES	BRONCHOSPASM	BROWNNOSED
BRILLIANCE	BRITTLENESSES	BROKERINGS	BRONCHOSPASMS	BROWNNOSER
BRILLIANCES	BROADBANDS	BROMEGRASS	BRONCHOSPASTIC	BROWNNOSERS
BRILLIANCIES	BROADBEANS	BROMEGRASSES	BRONCOBUSTER	BROWNNOSES
BRILLIANCY	BROADBILLS	BROMELAINS	BRONCOBUSTERS	BROWNNOSING
BRILLIANTE	BROADBRIMS	BROMELIACEOUS	BRONDYRONS	BROWNSHIRT
BRILLIANTED	BROADBRUSH	BROMELIADS	BRONTOBYTE	BROWNSHIRTS
BRILLIANTINE	BROADCASTED	BROMEOSINS	BRONTOBYTES	BROWNSTONE
BRILLIANTINED	BROADCASTER	BROMHIDROSES	BRONTOSAUR	BROWNSTONES
BRILLIANTINES	BROADCASTERS	BROMHIDROSIS	BRONTOSAURS	BROWRIDGES
BRILLIANTING	BROADCASTING	BROMIDROSES	BRONTOSAURUS	BROWSABLES
BRILLIANTLY	BROADCASTINGS	BROMIDROSIS	BRONTOSAURUSES	BRUCELLOSES
BRILLIANTNESS	BROADCASTS	BROMINATED	BRONZIFIED	BRUCELLOSIS
BRILLIANTNESSES	BROADCLOTH	BROMINATES	BRONZIFIES	BRUGMANSIA
BRILLIANTS	BROADCLOTHS	BROMINATING	BRONZIFYING	BRUGMANSIAS
BRIMFULLNESS	BROADENERS	BROMINATION	BROODINESS	BRUMMAGEMS
BRIMFULLNESSES	BROADENING	BROMINATIONS	BROODINESSES	BRUSCHETTA

BRUSCHETTAS	BUBONOCELES	BUFFLEHEAD	BULLIONIST	BUMFUZZLED
BRUSCHETTE	BUCCANEERED	BUFFLEHEADS	BULLIONISTS	BUMFUZZLES
BRUSHABILITIES	BUCCANEERING	BUFFOONERIES	BULLISHNESS	BUMFUZZLING
BRUSHABILITY	BUCCANEERINGS	BUFFOONERY	BULLISHNESSES	BUMMALOTIS
BRUSHBACKS	BUCCANEERISH	BUFFOONISH	BULLMASTIFF	BUMPINESSES
BRUSHFIRES	BUCCANEERS	BUFOTALINS	BULLMASTIFFS	BUMPKINISH
BRUSHLANDS	BUCCANIERED	BUFOTENINE	BULLNECKED	BUMPKINLIER
BRUSHMARKS	BUCCANIERING	BUFOTENINES	BULLOCKIER	BUMPKINLIEST
BRUSHSTROKE	BUCCANIERS	BUGGINESSES	BULLOCKIES	BUMPOLOGIES
BRUSHSTROKES	BUCCINATOR	BUGLEWEEDS	BULLOCKIEST	BUMPSADAISY
BRUSHWHEEL	BUCCINATORS	BUHRSTONES	BULLOCKING	BUMPTIOUSLY
BRUSHWHEELS	BUCCINATORY	BUILDDOWNS	BULLROARER	BUMPTIOUSNESS
BRUSHWOODS	BUCELLASES	BUIRDLIEST	BULLROARERS	BUMPTIOUSNESSES
BRUSHWORKS	BUCENTAURS	BULBIFEROUS	BULLRUSHES	BUMSUCKERS
BRUSQUENESS	BUCKBOARDS	BULBOSITIES	BULLSHITTED	BUMSUCKING
BRUSQUENESSES	BUCKBRUSHES	BULBOUSNESS	BULLSHITTER	BUMSUCKINGS
BRUSQUERIE	BUCKETFULS	BULBOUSNESSES	BULLSHITTERS	BUNBURYING
BRUSQUERIES	BUCKETINGS	BULGINESSES	BULLSHITTING	BUNCHBERRIES
BRUTALISATION	BUCKETSFUL	BULKHEADED	BULLSHITTINGS	BUNCHBERRY
BRUTALISATIONS	BUCKHOUNDS	BULKINESSES	BULLSNAKES	BUNCHGRASS
BRUTALISED	BUCKJUMPER	BULLBAITING	BULLTERRIER	BUNCHGRASSES
BRUTALISES	BUCKJUMPERS	BULLBAITINGS	BULLTERRIERS	BUNCHINESS
BRUTALISING	BUCKJUMPING	BULLBRIERS	BULLWADDIE	BUNCHINESSES
BRUTALISMS	BUCKJUMPINGS	BULLDOGGED	BULLWADDIES	BUNDOBUSTS
BRUTALISTS	BUCKLERING	BULLDOGGER	BULLWHACKED	BUNGALOIDS
BRUTALITIES	BUCKRAMING	BULLDOGGERS	BULLWHACKING	BUNGLESOME
BRUTALIZATION	BUCKSHISHED	BULLDOGGING	BULLWHACKS	BUNGLINGLY
BRUTALIZATIONS	BUCKSHISHES	BULLDOGGINGS	BULLWHIPPED	BUNKHOUSES
BRUTALIZED	BUCKSHISHING	BULLDOZERS	BULLWHIPPING	BUOYANCIES
BRUTALIZES	BUCKSKINNED	BULLDOZING	BULLYCIDES	BUOYANTNESS
BRUTALIZING	BUCKTHORNS	BULLETINED	BULLYRAGGED	BUOYANTNESSES
BRUTENESSES	BUCKTOOTHED	BULLETINING	BULLYRAGGING	BUPIVACAINE
BRUTIFYING	BUCKWHEATS	BULLETPROOF	BULRUSHIER	BUPIVACAINES
BRUTISHNESS	BUCKYBALLS	BULLETPROOFED	BULRUSHIEST	BUPRENORPHINE
BRUTISHNESSES	BUCKYTUBES	BULLETPROOFING	BULWADDEES	BUPRENORPHINES
BRYOLOGICAL	BUCOLICALLY	BULLETPROOFS	BULWADDIES	BUPRESTIDS
BRYOLOGIES	BUDGERIGAR	BULLETRIES	BULWARKING	BUPROPIONS
BRYOLOGIST	BUDGERIGARS	BULLETWOOD	BUMBAILIFF	BURDENSOME
BRYOLOGISTS	BUDGETEERS	BULLETWOODS	BUMBAILIFFS	BUREAUCRACIES
BRYOPHYLLUM	BUDGETINGS	BULLFIGHTER	BUMBERSHOOT	BUREAUCRACY
BRYOPHYLLUMS	BUDTENDERS	BULLFIGHTERS	BUMBERSHOOTS	BUREAUCRAT
BRYOPHYTES	BUFFALOBERRIES	BULLFIGHTING	BUMBLEBEES	BUREAUCRATESE
BRYOPHYTIC	BUFFALOBERRY	BULLFIGHTINGS	BUMBLEBERRIES	BUREAUCRATESES
BUBBLEGUMS	BUFFALOFISH	BULLFIGHTS	BUMBLEBERRY	BUREAUCRATIC
BUBBLEHEAD	BUFFALOFISHES	BULLFINCHES	BUMBLEDOMS	BUREAUCRATISE
BUBBLEHEADED	BUFFALOING	BULLHEADED	BUMBLINGLY	BUREAUCRATISED
BUBBLEHEADS	BUFFERINGS	BULLHEADEDLY	BUMFREEZER	BUREAUCRATISES
BUBONOCELE	BUFFETINGS	BULLHEADEDNESS	BUMFREEZERS	BUREAUCRATISING

BUREAUCRATISM

BUREAUCRATISM
BUREAUCRATISMS
BUREAUCRATIST
BUREAUCRATISTS
BUREAUCRATIZE
BUREAUCRATIZED
BUREAUCRATIZES
BUREAUCRATIZING
BUREAUCRATS
BURGEONING
BURGLARIES
BURGLARING
BURGLARIOUS
BURGLARIOUSLY
BURGLARISE
BURGLARISED
BURGLARISES
BURGLARISING
BURGLARIZE
BURGLARIZED
BURGLARIZES
BURGLARIZING
BURGLARPROOF
BURGOMASTER
BURGOMASTERS
BURGUNDIES
BURLADEROS
BURLESQUED
BURLESQUELY
BURLESQUER
BURLESQUERS
BURLESQUES
BURLESQUING
BURLEYCUES
BURLINESSES
BURNETTISE
BURNETTISED
BURNETTISES
BURNETTISING
BURNETTIZE
BURNETTIZED
BURNETTIZES
BURNETTIZING
BURNISHABLE

BURNISHERS
BURNISHING
BURNISHINGS
BURNISHMENT
BURNISHMENTS
BURRAMUNDI
BURRAMUNDIS
BURRAMYSES
BURRAWANGS
BURRFISHES
BURROWSTOWN
BURROWSTOWNS
BURRSTONES
BURSARSHIP
BURSARSHIPS
BURSERACEOUS
BURSICULATE
BURSITISES
BURTHENING
BURTHENSOME
BUSHBABIES
BUSHBASHING
BUSHBASHINGS
BUSHCRAFTS
BUSHELFULS
BUSHELLERS
BUSHELLING
BUSHELLINGS
BUSHELWOMAN
BUSHELWOMEN
BUSHFIGHTING
BUSHFIGHTINGS
BUSHHAMMER
BUSHHAMMERS
BUSHINESSES
BUSHMANSHIP
BUSHMANSHIPS
BUSHMASTER
BUSHMASTERS
BUSHRANGER
BUSHRANGERS
BUSHRANGING
BUSHRANGINGS
BUSHWALKED

BUSHWALKER
BUSHWALKERS
BUSHWALKING
BUSHWALKINGS
BUSHWHACKED
BUSHWHACKER
BUSHWHACKERS
BUSHWHACKING
BUSHWHACKINGS
BUSHWHACKS
BUSINESSES
BUSINESSIER
BUSINESSIEST
BUSINESSLIKE
BUSINESSMAN
BUSINESSMEN
BUSINESSPEOPLE
BUSINESSPERSON
BUSINESSPERSONS
BUSINESSWOMAN
BUSINESSWOMEN
BUSTICATED
BUSTICATES
BUSTICATING
BUSTINESSES
BUSTLINGLY
BUSYBODIED
BUSYBODIES
BUSYBODYING
BUSYBODYINGS
BUSYNESSES
BUTADIENES
BUTCHERBIRD
BUTCHERBIRDS
BUTCHERERS
BUTCHERIES
BUTCHERING
BUTCHERINGS
BUTCHERLIER
BUTCHERLIEST
BUTCHNESSES
BUTENEDIOIC
BUTEONINES
BUTLERAGES

BUTLERSHIP
BUTLERSHIPS
BUTTERBALL
BUTTERBALLS
BUTTERBURS
BUTTERCREAM
BUTTERCREAMS
BUTTERCUPS
BUTTERDOCK
BUTTERDOCKS
BUTTERFATS
BUTTERFINGERED
BUTTERFINGERS
BUTTERFISH
BUTTERFISHES
BUTTERFLIED
BUTTERFLIES
BUTTERFLYER
BUTTERFLYERS
BUTTERFLYFISH
BUTTERFLYFISHES
BUTTERFLYING
BUTTERIEST
BUTTERINES
BUTTERINESS
BUTTERINESSES
BUTTERLESS
BUTTERMILK
BUTTERMILKS
BUTTERNUTS
BUTTERSCOTCH
BUTTERSCOTCHES
BUTTERWEED
BUTTERWEEDS
BUTTERWORT
BUTTERWORTS
BUTTINSKIES
BUTTINSKIS
BUTTOCKING
BUTTONBALL
BUTTONBALLS
BUTTONBUSH
BUTTONBUSHES
BUTTONHELD

BUTTONHOLD
BUTTONHOLDING
BUTTONHOLDS
BUTTONHOLE
BUTTONHOLED
BUTTONHOLER
BUTTONHOLERS
BUTTONHOLES
BUTTONHOLING
BUTTONHOOK
BUTTONHOOKED
BUTTONHOOKING
BUTTONHOOKS
BUTTONIEST
BUTTONLESS
BUTTONMOULD
BUTTONMOULDS
BUTTONWOOD
BUTTONWOODS
BUTTRESSED
BUTTRESSES
BUTTRESSING
BUTTSTOCKS
BUTYLATING
BUTYLATION
BUTYLATIONS
BUTYRACEOUS
BUTYRALDEHYDE
BUTYRALDEHYDES
BUTYROPHENONE
BUTYROPHENONES
BUXOMNESSES
BUZZKILLER
BUZZKILLERS
BYPRODUCTS
BYSSACEOUS
BYSSINOSES
BYSSINOSIS
BYSTANDERS
BYTOWNITES

C

CABALETTAS	CACIQUISMS	CADAVERINES	CAJOLEMENTS	CALCICOLES
CABALISTIC	CACKERMANDER	CADAVEROUS	CAJOLERIES	CALCICOLOUS
CABALISTICAL	CACKERMANDERS	CADAVEROUSLY	CAJOLINGLY	CALCIFEROL
CABALLEROS	CACKLEBERRIES	CADAVEROUSNESS	CAKEWALKED	CALCIFEROLS
CABBAGETOWN	CACKLEBERRY	CADDISFLIES	CAKEWALKER	CALCIFEROUS
CABBAGETOWNS	CACODAEMON	CADDISHNESS	CAKEWALKERS	CALCIFICATION
CABBAGEWORM	CACODAEMONS	CADDISHNESSES	CAKEWALKING	CALCIFICATIONS
CABBAGEWORMS	CACODEMONIC	CADDISWORM	CAKINESSES	CALCIFUGAL
CABBAGIEST	CACODEMONS	CADDISWORMS	CALABASHES	CALCIFUGES
CABBALISMS	CACODOXIES	CADETSHIPS	CALABOGUSES	CALCIFUGOUS
CABBALISTIC	CACOEPISTIC	CADUCITIES	CALABOOSES	CALCIFYING
CABBALISTICAL	CACOGASTRIC	CAECILIANS	CALABRESES	CALCIGEROUS
CABBALISTS	CACOGENICS	CAECITISES	CALAMANCOES	CALCIMINED
CABDRIVERS	CACOGRAPHER	CAENOGENESES	CALAMANCOS	CALCIMINES
CABINETMAKER	CACOGRAPHERS	CAENOGENESIS	CALAMANDER	CALCIMINING
CABINETMAKERS	CACOGRAPHIC	CAENOGENETIC	CALAMANDERS	CALCINABLE
CABINETMAKING	CACOGRAPHICAL	CAESALPINOID	CALAMARIES	CALCINATION
CABINETMAKINGS	CACOGRAPHIES	CAESAREANS	CALAMINING	CALCINATIONS
CABINETRIES	CACOGRAPHY	CAESARIANS	CALAMITIES	CALCINOSES
CABINETWORK	CACOLOGIES	CAESARISMS	CALAMITOUS	CALCINOSIS
CABINETWORKS	CACOMISTLE	CAESAROPAPISM	CALAMITOUSLY	CALCITONIN
CABINMATES	CACOMISTLES	CAESAROPAPISMS	CALAMITOUSNESS	CALCITONINS
CABLECASTED	CACOMIXLES	CAESPITOSE	CALAMONDIN	CALCSINTER
CABLECASTING	CACONYMIES	CAESPITOSELY	CALAMONDINS	CALCSINTERS
CABLECASTS	CACOPHONIC	CAFETERIAS	CALANDRIAS	CALCULABILITIES
CABLEGRAMS	CACOPHONICAL	CAFETIERES	CALAVANCES	CALCULABILITY
CABLEVISION	CACOPHONICALLY	CAFETORIUM	CALAVERITE	CALCULABLE
CABLEVISIONS	CACOPHONIES	CAFETORIUMS	CALAVERITES	CALCULABLY
CABRIOLETS	CACOPHONIOUS	CAFFEINATED	CALCAREOUS	CALCULATED
CACAFUEGOS	CACOPHONOUS	CAFFEINISM	CALCAREOUSLY	CALCULATEDLY
CACCIATORA	CACOPHONOUSLY	CAFFEINISMS	CALCARIFEROUS	CALCULATEDNESS
CACCIATORE	CACOTOPIAN	CAGEYNESSES	CALCARIFORM	CALCULATES
CACHAEMIAS	CACOTOPIAS	CAGINESSES	CALCEAMENTA	CALCULATING
CACHECTICAL	CACOTROPHIES	CAGMAGGING	CALCEAMENTUM	CALCULATINGLY
CACHINNATE	CACOTROPHY	CAGYNESSES	CALCEATING	CALCULATION
CACHINNATED	CACTACEOUS	CAILLEACHS	CALCEDONIES	CALCULATIONAL
CACHINNATES	CACTOBLASTES	CAILLIACHS	CALCEDONIO	CALCULATIONS
CACHINNATING	CACTOBLASTIS	CAINOGENESES	CALCEDONIOS	CALCULATIVE
CACHINNATION	CACUMINALS	CAINOGENESIS	CALCEIFORM	CALCULATOR
CACHINNATIONS	CACUMINOUS	CAINOGENETIC	CALCEOLARIA	CALCULATORS
CACHINNATORY	CADASTRALLY	CAIRNGORMS	CALCEOLARIAS	CALCULUSES
CACHOLONGS	CADAVERINE	CAJOLEMENT	CALCEOLATE	CALEFACIENT

CALEFACIENTS	CALIDITIES	CALMATIVES	CALYCULATE	CAMOUFLEUR
CALEFACTION	CALIFORNIUM	CALMNESSES	CALYPSONIAN	CAMOUFLEURS
CALEFACTIONS	CALIFORNIUMS	CALMODULIN	CALYPSONIANS	CAMPAIGNED
CALEFACTIVE	CALIGINOSITIES	CALMODULINS	CALYPTERAS	CAMPAIGNER
CALEFACTOR	CALIGINOSITY	CALMSTANES	CALYPTRATE	CAMPAIGNERS
CALEFACTORIES	CALIGINOUS	CALMSTONES	CALYPTROGEN	CAMPAIGNING
CALEFACTORS	CALIMOCHOS	CALORESCENCE	CALYPTROGENS	CAMPANEROS
CALEFACTORY	CALIOLOGIES	CALORESCENCES	CAMANACHDS	CAMPANIFORM
CALEMBOURS	CALIPASHES	CALORESCENT	CAMARADERIE	CAMPANILES
CALENDARED	CALIPERING	CALORICALLY	CAMARADERIES	CAMPANISTS
CALENDARER	CALIPHATES	CALORICITIES	CAMARILLAS	CAMPANOLOGER
CALENDARERS	CALISTHENIC	CALORICITY	CAMBERINGS	CAMPANOLOGERS
CALENDARING	CALISTHENICS	CALORIFICALLY	CAMBISTRIES	CAMPANOLOGICAL
CALENDARISATION	CALLBOARDS	CALORIFICATION	CAMCORDERS	CAMPANOLOGIES
CALENDARISE	CALLIATURE	CALORIFICATIONS	CAMCORDING	CAMPANOLOGIST
CALENDARISED	CALLIATURES	CALORIFIER	CAMELBACKS	CAMPANOLOGISTS
CALENDARISES	CALLIDITIES	CALORIFIERS	CAMELEOPARD	CAMPANOLOGY
CALENDARISING	CALLIGRAMME	CALORIMETER	CAMELEOPARDS	CAMPANULACEOUS
CALENDARIST	CALLIGRAMMES	CALORIMETERS	CAMELHAIRS	CAMPANULAR
CALENDARISTS	CALLIGRAMS	CALORIMETRIC	CAMELOPARD	CAMPANULAS
CALENDARIZATION	CALLIGRAPHER	CALORIMETRICAL	CAMELOPARDS	CAMPANULATE
CALENDARIZE	CALLIGRAPHERS	CALORIMETRIES	CAMERAPERSON	CAMPCRAFTS
CALENDARIZED	CALLIGRAPHIC	CALORIMETRY	CAMERAPERSONS	CAMPEADORS
CALENDARIZES	CALLIGRAPHICAL	CALORISING	CAMERAPHONE	CAMPESINOS
CALENDARIZING	CALLIGRAPHIES	CALORIZING	CAMERAPHONES	CAMPESTRAL
CALENDERED	CALLIGRAPHIST	CALOTYPIST	CAMERATION	CAMPESTRIAN
CALENDERER	CALLIGRAPHISTS	CALOTYPISTS	CAMERATIONS	CAMPGROUND
CALENDERERS	CALLIGRAPHY	CALUMNIABLE	CAMERAWOMAN	CAMPGROUNDS
CALENDERING	CALLIOPSIS	CALUMNIATE	CAMERAWOMEN	CAMPHORACEOUS
CALENDERINGS	CALLIPASHES	CALUMNIATED	CAMERAWORK	CAMPHORATE
CALENDRERS	CALLIPERED	CALUMNIATES	CAMERAWORKS	CAMPHORATED
CALENDRICAL	CALLIPERING	CALUMNIATING	CAMERLENGO	CAMPHORATES
CALENDRIES	CALLIPYGEAN	CALUMNIATION	CAMERLENGOS	CAMPHORATING
CALENDULAS	CALLIPYGIAN	CALUMNIATIONS	CAMERLINGO	CAMPIMETRIES
CALENTURES	CALLIPYGOUS	CALUMNIATOR	CAMERLINGOS	CAMPIMETRY
CALESCENCE	CALLISTEMON	CALUMNIATORS	CAMIKNICKERS	CAMPINESSES
CALESCENCES	CALLISTEMONS	CALUMNIATORY	CAMIKNICKS	CAMPNESSES
CALFDOZERS	CALLISTHENIC	CALUMNIOUS	CAMISADOES	CAMPODEIDS
CALIATOURS	CALLISTHENICS	CALUMNIOUSLY	CAMORRISTA	CAMPODEIFORM
CALIBRATED	CALLITHUMP	CALUMNYING	CAMORRISTI	CAMPSHIRTS
CALIBRATER	CALLITHUMPIAN	CALVADOSES	CAMORRISTS	CAMPSTOOLS
CALIBRATERS	CALLITHUMPS	CALVARIUMS	CAMOUFLAGE	CAMPYLOBACTER
CALIBRATES	CALLOSITIES	CALYCANTHEMIES	CAMOUFLAGEABLE	CAMPYLOBACTERS
CALIBRATING	CALLOUSING	CALYCANTHEMY	CAMOUFLAGED	CAMPYLOTROPOUS
CALIBRATION	CALLOUSNESS	CALYCANTHUS	CAMOUFLAGES	CAMSTEERIE
CALIBRATIONS	CALLOUSNESSES	CALYCANTHUSES	CAMOUFLAGIC	CAMWHORING
CALIBRATOR	CALLOWNESS	CALYCIFORM	CAMOUFLAGING	CANALBOATS
CALIBRATORS	CALLOWNESSES	CALYCOIDEOUS	CAMOUFLETS	CANALICULAR

CANALICULATE	CANDELABRUM	CANEPHORES	CANNISTERS	CANTALOUPS
CANALICULATED	CANDELABRUMS	CANEPHORUS	CANNONADED	CANTANKEROUS
CANALICULI	CANDELILLA	CANEPHORUSES	CANNONADES	CANTANKEROUSLY
CANALICULUS	CANDELILLAS	CANESCENCE	CANNONADING	CANTATRICE
CANALISATION	CANDESCENCE	CANESCENCES	CANNONBALL	CANTATRICES
CANALISATIONS	CANDESCENCES	CANINITIES	CANNONBALLED	CANTATRICI
CANALISING	CANDESCENT	CANISTERED	CANNONBALLING	CANTERBURIES
CANALIZATION	CANDESCENTLY	CANISTERING	CANNONBALLS	CANTERBURY
CANALIZATIONS	CANDIDACIES	CANISTERISATION	CANNONEERS	CANTERBURYS
CANALIZING	CANDIDATES	CANISTERISE	CANNONIERS	CANTHARIDAL
CANCELABLE	CANDIDATESHIP	CANISTERISED	CANNONRIES	CANTHARIDES
CANCELATION	CANDIDATESHIPS	CANISTERISES	CANNULATED	CANTHARIDIAN
CANCELATIONS	CANDIDATURE	CANISTERISING	CANNULATES	CANTHARIDIC
CANCELBOTS	CANDIDATURES	CANISTERIZATION	CANNULATING	CANTHARIDIN
CANCELEERED	CANDIDIASES	CANISTERIZE	CANNULATION	CANTHARIDINS
CANCELEERING	CANDIDIASIS	CANISTERIZED	CANNULATIONS	CANTHARIDS
CANCELEERS	CANDIDNESS	CANISTERIZES	CANOEWOODS	CANTHAXANTHIN
CANCELIERED	CANDIDNESSES	CANISTERIZING	CANONESSES	CANTHAXANTHINE
CANCELIERING	CANDLEBERRIES	CANKEREDLY	CANONICALLY	CANTHAXANTHINES
CANCELIERS	CANDLEBERRY	CANKEREDNESS	CANONICALS	CANTHAXANTHINS
CANCELLABLE	CANDLEFISH	CANKEREDNESSES	CANONICATE	CANTHITISES
CANCELLARIAL	CANDLEFISHES	CANKERIEST	CANONICATES	CANTICOING
CANCELLARIAN	CANDLEHOLDER	CANKERWORM	CANONICITIES	CANTICOYED
CANCELLARIATE	CANDLEHOLDERS	CANKERWORMS	CANONICITY	CANTICOYING
CANCELLARIATES	CANDLELIGHT	CANNABINOID	CANONISATION	CANTILENAS
CANCELLATE	CANDLELIGHTED	CANNABINOIDS	CANONISATIONS	CANTILEVER
CANCELLATED	CANDLELIGHTER	CANNABINOL	CANONISERS	CANTILEVERED
CANCELLATION	CANDLELIGHTERS	CANNABINOLS	CANONISING	CANTILEVERING
CANCELLATIONS	CANDLELIGHTS	CANNABISES	CANONISTIC	CANTILEVERS
CANCELLERS	CANDLENUTS	CANNELLINI	CANONIZATION	CANTILLATE
CANCELLING	CANDLEPINS	CANNELLINIS	CANONIZATIONS	CANTILLATED
CANCELLOUS	CANDLEPOWER	CANNELLONI	CANONIZERS	CANTILLATES
CANCERATED	CANDLEPOWERS	CANNELURES	CANONIZING	CANTILLATING
CANCERATES	CANDLESNUFFER	CANNIBALISATION	CANOODLERS	CANTILLATION
CANCERAIING	CANDLESNUFFERS	CANNIBALISE	CANOODLING	CANTILLATIONS
CANCERATION	CANDLESTICK	CANNIBALISED	CANOPHILIA	CANTILLATORY
CANCERATIONS	CANDLESTICKS	CANNIBALISES	CANOPHILIAS	CANTINESSES
CANCEROPHOBIA	CANDLEWICK	CANNIBALISING	CANOPHILIST	CANTONISATION
CANCEROPHOBIAS	CANDLEWICKS	CANNIBALISM	CANOPHILISTS	CANTONISATIONS
CANCEROUSLY	CANDLEWOOD	CANNIBALISMS	CANOPHOBIA	CANTONISED
CANCERPHOBIA	CANDLEWOODS	CANNIBALISTIC	CANOPHOBIAS	CANTONISES
CANCERPHOBIAS	CANDYFLOSS	CANNIBALIZATION	CANOROUSLY	CANTONISING
CANCIONERO	CANDYFLOSSES	CANNIBALIZE	CANOROUSNESS	CANTONIZATION
CANCIONEROS	CANDYGRAMS	CANNIBALIZED	CANOROUSNESSES	CANTONIZATIONS
CANCRIFORM	CANDYTUFTS	CANNIBALIZES	CANTABANKS	CANTONIZED
CANCRIZANS	CANEBRAKES	CANNIBALIZING	CANTABILES	CANTONIZES
CANDELABRA	CANEFRUITS	CANNIBALLY	CANTALOUPE	CANTONIZING
CANDELABRAS	CANEPHORAS	CANNINESSES	CANTALOUPES	CANTONMENT

CANTONMENTS	CAPERNOITED	CAPITULATIONS	CAPTAINCIES	CARAMELISING
CANULATING	CAPERNOITIE	CAPITULATOR	CAPTAINING	CARAMELIZATION
CANULATION	CAPERNOITIES	CAPITULATORS	CAPTAINRIES	CARAMELIZATIONS
CANULATIONS	CAPERNOITY	CAPITULATORY	CAPTAINSHIP	CARAMELIZE
CANVASBACK	CAPICOLLAS	CAPNOMANCIES	CAPTAINSHIPS	CARAMELIZED
CANVASBACKS	CAPICOLLOS	CAPNOMANCY	CAPTIONING	CARAMELIZES
CANVASLIKE	CAPILLACEOUS	CAPOCCHIAS	CAPTIONLESS	CARAMELIZING
CANVASSERS	CAPILLAIRE	CAPODASTRO	CAPTIOUSLY	CARAMELLED
CANVASSING	CAPILLAIRES	CAPODASTROS	CAPTIOUSNESS	CARAMELLING
CANVASSINGS	CAPILLARIES	CAPONIERES	CAPTIOUSNESSES	CARANGOIDS
CANYONEERS	CAPILLARITIES	CAPONISING	CAPTIVANCE	CARAPACIAL
CANYONINGS	CAPILLARITY	CAPONIZING	CAPTIVANCES	CARAVANCES
CANZONETTA	CAPILLITIA	CAPOTASTOS	CAPTIVATED	CARAVANEER
CANZONETTAS	CAPILLITIUM	CAPPARIDACEOUS	CAPTIVATES	CARAVANEERS
CANZONETTE	CAPITALISATION	CAPPELLETTI	CAPTIVATING	CARAVANERS
CAOUTCHOUC	CAPITALISATIONS	CAPPERNOITIES	CAPTIVATINGLY	CARAVANETTE
CAOUTCHOUCS	CAPITALISE	CAPPERNOITY	CAPTIVATION	CARAVANETTES
CAPABILITIES	CAPITALISED	CAPPUCCINI	CAPTIVATIONS	CARAVANING
CAPABILITY	CAPITALISES	CAPPUCCINO	CAPTIVATOR	CARAVANINGS
CAPABLENESS	CAPITALISING	CAPPUCCINOS	CAPTIVATORS	CARAVANNED
CAPABLENESSES	CAPITALISM	CAPREOLATE	CAPTIVAUNCE	CARAVANNER
CAPACIOUSLY	CAPITALISMS	CAPRICCIOS	CAPTIVAUNCES	CARAVANNERS
CAPACIOUSNESS	CAPITALIST	CAPRICCIOSO	CAPTIVITIES	CARAVANNING
CAPACIOUSNESSES	CAPITALISTIC	CAPRICIOUS	CAPTOPRILS	CARAVANNINGS
CAPACITANCE	CAPITALISTS	CAPRICIOUSLY	CARABINEER	CARAVANSARAI
CAPACITANCES	CAPITALIZATION	CAPRICIOUSNESS	CARABINEERS	CARAVANSARAIS
CAPACITATE	CAPITALIZATIONS	CAPRIFICATION	CARABINERO	CARAVANSARIES
CAPACITATED	CAPITALIZE	CAPRIFICATIONS	CARABINEROS	CARAVANSARY
CAPACITATES	CAPITALIZED	CAPRIFOILS	CARABINERS	CARAVANSERAI
CAPACITATING	CAPITALIZES	CAPRIFOLES	CARABINIER	CARAVANSERAIS
CAPACITATION	CAPITALIZING	CAPRIFOLIACEOUS	CARABINIERE	CARAVELLES
CAPACITATIONS	CAPITATION	CAPRIFYING	CARABINIERI	CARBACHOLS
CAPACITIES	CAPITATIONS	CAPRIOLING	CARABINIERS	CARBAMATES
CAPACITIVE	CAPITATIVE	CAPROLACTAM	CARACOLERS	CARBAMAZEPINE
CAPACITIVELY	CAPITELLUM	CAPROLACTAMS	CARACOLING	CARBAMAZEPINES
CAPACITORS	CAPITOLIAN	CAPRYLATES	CARACOLLED	CARBAMIDES
CAPARISONED	CAPITOLINE	CAPSAICINS	CARACOLLING	CARBAMIDINE
CAPARISONING	CAPITULANT	CAPSIZABLE	CARAGEENAN	CARBAMIDINES
CAPARISONS	CAPITULANTS	CAPSOMERES	CARAGEENANS	CARBAMOYLS
CAPELLINES	CAPITULARIES	CAPSULATED	CARAMBOLAS	CARBANIONS
CAPELLINIS	CAPITULARLY	CAPSULATION	CARAMBOLED	CARBAZOLES
CAPELLMEISTER	CAPITULARS	CAPSULATIONS	CARAMBOLES	CARBIDOPAS
CAPELLMEISTERS	CAPITULARY	CAPSULISED	CARAMBOLING	CARBIMAZOLE
CAPERCAILLIE	CAPITULATE	CAPSULISES	CARAMELISATION	CARBIMAZOLES
CAPERCAILLIES	CAPITULATED	CAPSULISING	CARAMELISATIONS	CARBINEERS
CAPERCAILZIE	CAPITULATES	CAPSULIZED	CARAMELISE	CARBINIERS
CAPERCAILZIES	CAPITULATING	CAPSULIZES	CARAMELISED	CARBOCYCLIC
CAPERINGLY	CAPITULATION	CAPSULIZING	CARAMELISES	CARBOHYDRASE

CARBOHYDRASES	CARBONYLATING	CARBYLAMINES	CARDIOCENTESIS	CAREFULLER
CARBOHYDRATE	CARBONYLATION	CARCASSING	CARDIOGENIC	CAREFULLEST
CARBOHYDRATES	CARBONYLATIONS	CARCINOGEN	CARDIOGRAM	CAREFULNESS
CARBOLATED	CARBONYLIC	CARCINOGENESES	CARDIOGRAMS	CAREFULNESSES
CARBOLISED	CARBOREXIC	CARCINOGENESIS	CARDIOGRAPH	CAREGIVERS
CARBOLISES	CARBOREXICS	CARCINOGENIC	CARDIOGRAPHER	CAREGIVING
CARBOLISING	CARBOXYLASE	CARCINOGENICITY	CARDIOGRAPHERS	CAREGIVINGS
CARBOLIZED	CARBOXYLASES	CARCINOGENS	CARDIOGRAPHIC	CARELESSLY
CARBOLIZES	CARBOXYLATE	CARCINOIDS	CARDIOGRAPHICAL	CARELESSNESS
CARBOLIZING	CARBOXYLATED	CARCINOLOGICAL	CARDIOGRAPHIES	CARELESSNESSES
CARBONACEOUS	CARBOXYLATES	CARCINOLOGIES	CARDIOGRAPHS	CARESSINGLY
CARBONADES	CARBOXYLATING	CARCINOLOGIST	CARDIOGRAPHY	CARESSINGS
CARBONADOED	CARBOXYLATION	CARCINOLOGISTS	CARDIOLOGICAL	CARESSIVELY
CARBONADOES	CARBOXYLATIONS	CARCINOLOGY	CARDIOLOGIES	CARETAKERS
CARBONADOING	CARBOXYLIC	CARCINOMAS	CARDIOLOGIST	CARETAKING
CARBONADOS	CARBUNCLED	CARCINOMATA	CARDIOLOGISTS	CARETAKINGS
CARBONARAS	CARBUNCLES	CARCINOMATOID	CARDIOLOGY	CAREWORKER
CARBONATED	CARBUNCULAR	CARCINOMATOSES	CARDIOMEGALIES	CAREWORKERS
CARBONATES	CARBURATED	CARCINOMATOSIS	CARDIOMEGALY	CARFUFFLED
CARBONATING	CARBURATES	CARCINOMATOUS	CARDIOMOTOR	CARFUFFLES
CARBONATION	CARBURATING	CARCINOSARCOMA	CARDIOMYOPATHY	CARFUFFLING
CARBONATIONS	CARBURATION	CARCINOSARCOMAS	CARDIOPATHIES	CARHOPPING
CARBONATITE	CARBURATIONS	CARCINOSES	CARDIOPATHY	CARHOPPINGS
CARBONATITES	CARBURETED	CARCINOSIS	CARDIOPLEGIA	CARICATURA
CARBONETTE	CARBURETER	CARDAMINES	CARDIOPLEGIAS	CARICATURAL
CARBONETTES	CARBURETERS	CARDBOARDIER	CARDIOPULMONARY	CARICATURAS
CARBONIFEROUS	CARBURETING	CARDBOARDIEST	CARDIOTHORACIC	CARICATURE
CARBONISATION	CARBURETION	CARDBOARDS	CARDIOTONIC	CARICATURED
CARBONISATIONS	CARBURETIONS	CARDBOARDY	CARDIOTONICS	CARICATURES
CARBONISED	CARBURETOR	CARDCASTLE	CARDIOVASCULAR	CARICATURING
CARBONISER	CARBURETORS	CARDCASTLES	CARDITISES	CARICATURIST
CARBONISERS	CARBURETTED	CARDHOLDER	CARDOPHAGI	CARICATURISTS
CARBONISES	CARBURETTER	CARDHOLDERS	CARDOPHAGUS	CARILLONED
CARBONISING	CARBURETTERS	CARDIALGIA	CARDPHONES	CARILLONING
CARBONIUMS	CARBURETTING	CARDIALGIAS	CARDPLAYER	CARILLONIST
CARBONIZATION	CARBURETTOR	CARDIALGIC	CARDPLAYERS	CARILLONISTS
CARBONIZATIONS	CARBURETTORS	CARDIALGIES	CARDPUNCHES	CARILLONNED
CARBONIZED	CARBURISATION	CARDIGANED	CARDSHARPER	CARILLONNEUR
CARBONIZER	CARBURISATIONS	CARDINALATE	CARDSHARPERS	CARILLONNEURS
CARBONIZERS	CARBURISED	CARDINALATES	CARDSHARPING	CARILLONNING
CARBONIZES	CARBURISES	CARDINALATIAL	CARDSHARPINGS	CARIOGENIC
CARBONIZING	CARBURISING	CARDINALITIAL	CARDSHARPS	CARIOSITIES
CARBONLESS	CARBURIZATION	CARDINALITIES	CARDUACEOUS	CARIOUSNESS
CARBONNADE	CARBURIZATIONS	CARDINALITY	CAREENAGES	CARIOUSNESSES
CARBONNADES	CARBURIZED	CARDINALLY	CAREERISMS	CARJACKERS
CARBONYLATE	CARBURIZES	CARDINALSHIP	CAREERISTS	CARJACKING
CARBONYLATED	CARBURIZING	CARDINALSHIPS	CAREFREENESS	CARJACKINGS
CARBONYLATES	CARBYLAMINE	CARDIOCENTESES	CAREFREENESSES	CARMAGNOLE

CARMAGNOLES	CARPACCIOS	CARRAGHEEN	CARTOGRAPHICAL	CARYOPTERISES
CARMELITES	CARPELLARY	CARRAGHEENAN	CARTOGRAPHIES	CASCADURAS
CARMINATIVE	CARPELLATE	CARRAGHEENANS	CARTOGRAPHY	CASCARILLA
CARMINATIVES	CARPELLATES	CARRAGHEENIN	CARTOLOGICAL	CASCARILLAS
CARNAHUBAS	CARPENTARIA	CARRAGHEENINS	CARTOLOGIES	CASEATIONS
CARNALISED	CARPENTARIAS	CARRAGHEENS	CARTOMANCIES	CASEBEARER
CARNALISES	CARPENTERED	CARREFOURS	CARTOMANCY	CASEBEARERS
CARNALISING	CARPENTERING	CARRIAGEABLE	CARTONAGES	CASEINATES
CARNALISMS	CARPENTERS	CARRIAGEWAY	CARTONNAGE	CASEINOGEN
CARNALISTS	CARPENTRIES	CARRIAGEWAYS	CARTONNAGES	CASEINOGENS
CARNALITIES	CARPETBAGGED	CARRITCHES	CARTOONIER	CASEMAKERS
CARNALIZED	CARPETBAGGER	CARRIWITCHET	CARTOONIEST	CASEMENTED
CARNALIZES	CARPETBAGGERIES	CARRIWITCHETS	CARTOONING	CASEVACING
CARNALIZING	CARPETBAGGERS	CARRONADES	CARTOONINGS	CASEWORKER
CARNALLING	CARPETBAGGERY	CARROTIEST	CARTOONISH	CASEWORKERS
CARNALLITE	CARPETBAGGING	CARROTTOPPED	CARTOONISHLY	CASHIERERS
CARNALLITES	CARPETBAGGINGS	CARROTTOPS	CARTOONIST	CASHIERING
CARNAPTIOUS	CARPETBAGS	CARROUSELS	CARTOONISTS	CASHIERINGS
CARNAROLIS	CARPETINGS	CARRYBACKS	CARTOONLIKE	CASHIERMENT
CARNASSIAL	CARPETLIKE	CARRYFORWARD	CARTOPHILE	CASHIERMENTS
CARNASSIALS	CARPETMONGER	CARRYFORWARDS	CARTOPHILES	CASHMOBBING
CARNATIONED	CARPETMONGERS	CARRYOVERS	CARTOPHILIC	CASHMOBBINGS
CARNATIONS	CARPETWEED	CARRYTALES	CARTOPHILIES	CASHPOINTS
CARNELIANS	CARPETWEEDS	CARSHARING	CARTOPHILIST	CASHSPIELS
CARNIFEXES	CARPHOLOGIES	CARSHARINGS	CARTOPHILISTS	CASINGHEAD
CARNIFICATION	CARPHOLOGY	CARSICKNESS	CARTOPHILY	CASINGHEADS
CARNIFICATIONS	CARPOGONIA	CARSICKNESSES	CARTOPPERS	CASKSTANDS
CARNIFICIAL	CARPOGONIAL	CARTELISATION	CARTOUCHES	CASSAREEPS
CARNIFYING	CARPOGONIUM	CARTELISATIONS	CARTRIDGES	CASSATIONS
CARNITINES	CARPOLOGICAL	CARTELISED	CARTULARIES	CASSEROLED
CARNIVALESQUE	CARPOLOGIES	CARTELISES	CARTWHEELED	CASSEROLES
CARNIVORES	CARPOLOGIST	CARTELISING	CARTWHEELER	CASSEROLING
CARNIVORIES	CARPOLOGISTS	CARTELISMS	CARTWHEELERS	CASSIMERES
CARNIVOROUS	CARPOMETACARPI	CARTELISTS	CARTWHEELING	CASSINGLES
CARNIVOROUSLY	CARPOMETACARPUS	CARTELIZATION	CARTWHEELS	CASSIOPEIUM
CARNIVOROUSNESS	CARPOOLERS	CARTELIZATIONS	CARTWRIGHT	CASSIOPEIUMS
CARNOSAURS	CARPOOLING	CARTELIZED	CARTWRIGHTS	CASSITERITE
CARNOSITIES	CARPOOLINGS	CARTELIZES	CARUNCULAR	CASSITERITES
CARNOTITES	CARPOPHAGOUS	CARTELIZING	CARUNCULATE	CASSOLETTE
CAROLLINGS	CARPOPHORE	CARTHAMINE	CARUNCULATED	CASSOLETTES
CAROMELLED	CARPOPHORES	CARTHAMINES	CARUNCULOUS	CASSONADES
CAROMELLING	CARPOSPORE	CARTHORSES	CARVACROLS	CASSOULETS
CAROTENOID	CARPOSPORES	CARTILAGES	CARYATIDAL	CASSOWARIES
CAROTENOIDS	CARRAGEENAN	CARTILAGINOUS	CARYATIDEAN	CASSUMUNAR
CAROTINOID	CARRAGEENANS	CARTOGRAMS	CARYATIDES	CASSUMUNARS
CAROTINOIDS	CARRAGEENIN	CARTOGRAPHER	CARYATIDIC	CASTABILITIES
CAROUSINGLY	CARRAGEENINS	CARTOGRAPHERS	CARYOPSIDES	CASTABILITY
CAROUSINGS	CARRAGEENS	CARTOGRAPHIC	CARYOPTERIS	CASTANOSPERMINE

CASTELLANS	CATABOLITES	CATALOGNES	CATAPLEXIES	CATECHETICAL
CASTELLATED	CATABOLIZE	CATALOGUED	CATAPULTED	CATECHETICALLY
CASTELLATION	CATABOLIZED	CATALOGUER	CATAPULTIC	CATECHETICS
CASTELLATIONS	CATABOLIZES	CATALOGUERS	CATAPULTIER	CATECHISATION
CASTELLUMS	CATABOLIZING	CATALOGUES	CATAPULTIERS	CATECHISATIONS
CASTIGATED	CATACAUSTIC	CATALOGUING	CATAPULTING	CATECHISED
CASTIGATES	CATACAUSTICS	CATALOGUISE	CATARACTOUS	CATECHISER
CASTIGATING	CATACHRESES	CATALOGUISED	CATARHINES	CATECHISERS
CASTIGATION	CATACHRESIS	CATALOGUISES	CATARRHALLY	CATECHISES
CASTIGATIONS	CATACHRESTIC	CATALOGUISING	CATARRHINE	CATECHISING
CASTIGATOR	CATACHRESTICAL	CATALOGUIST	CATARRHINES	CATECHISINGS
CASTIGATORS	CATACLASES	CATALOGUISTS	CATARRHOUS	CATECHISMAL
CASTIGATORY	CATACLASIS	CATALOGUIZE	CATASTASES	CATECHISMS
CASTOREUMS	CATACLASMIC	CATALOGUIZED	CATASTASIS	CATECHISTIC
CASTRAMETATION	CATACLASMS	CATALOGUIZES	CATASTROPHE	CATECHISTICAL
CASTRAMETATIONS	CATACLASTIC	CATALOGUIZING	CATASTROPHES	CATECHISTICALLY
CASTRATERS	CATACLINAL	CATALYSERS	CATASTROPHIC	CATECHISTS
CASTRATING	CATACLYSMAL	CATALYSING	CATASTROPHISM	CATECHIZATION
CASTRATION	CATACLYSMIC	CATALYTICAL	CATASTROPHISMS	CATECHIZATIONS
CASTRATIONS	CATACLYSMICALLY	CATALYTICALLY	CATASTROPHIST	CATECHIZED
CASTRATORS	CATACLYSMS	CATALYZERS	CATASTROPHISTS	CATECHIZER
CASTRATORY	CATACOUSTICS	CATALYZING	CATATONIAS	CATECHIZERS
CASUALISATION	CATACUMBAL	CATAMARANS	CATATONICALLY	CATECHIZES
CASUALISATIONS	CATADIOPTRIC	CATAMENIAL	CATATONICS	CATECHIZING
CASUALISED	CATADIOPTRICAL	CATAMOUNTAIN	CATATONIES	CATECHIZINGS
CASUALISES	CATADROMOUS	CATAMOUNTAINS	CATCALLERS	CATECHOLAMINE
CASUALISING	CATAFALCOES	CATAMOUNTS	CATCALLING	CATECHOLAMINES
CASUALISMS	CATAFALQUE	CATANANCHE	CATCHCRIES	CATECHUMEN
CASUALIZATION	CATAFALQUES	CATANANCHES	CATCHFLIES	CATECHUMENAL
CASUALIZATIONS	CATALECTIC	CATAPHONIC	CATCHINESS	CATECHUMENATE
CASUALIZED	CATALECTICS	CATAPHONICS	CATCHINESSES	CATECHUMENATES
CASUALIZES	CATALEPSIES	CATAPHORAS	CATCHLINES	CATECHUMENICAL
CASUALIZING	CATALEPTIC	CATAPHORESES	CATCHMENTS	CATECHUMENISM
CASUALNESS	CATALEPTICALLY	CATAPHORESIS	CATCHPENNIES	CATECHUMENISMS
CASUALNESSES	CATALEPTICS	CATAPHORETIC	CATCHPENNY	CATECHUMENS
CASUALTIES	CATALLACTIC	CATAPHORIC	CATCHPHRASE	CATECHUMENSHIP
CASUARINAS	CATALLACTICALLY	CATAPHORICALLY	CATCHPHRASES	CATECHUMENSHIPS
CASUISTICAL	CATALLACTICS	CATAPHRACT	CATCHPOLES	CATEGOREMATIC
CASUISTICALLY	CATALOGERS	CATAPHRACTIC	CATCHPOLLS	CATEGORIAL
CASUISTRIES	CATALOGING	CATAPHRACTS	CATCHWATER	CATEGORIALLY
CATABOLICALLY	CATALOGISE	CATAPHYLLARY	CATCHWATERS	CATEGORICAL
CATABOLISE	CATALOGISED	CATAPHYLLS	CATCHWEEDS	CATEGORICALLY
CATABOLISED	CATALOGISES	CATAPHYSICAL	CATCHWEIGHT	CATEGORICALNESS
CATABOLISES	CATALOGISING	CATAPLASIA	CATCHWORDS	CATEGORIES
CATABOLISING	CATALOGIZE	CATAPLASIAS	CATECHESES	CATEGORISATION
CATABOLISM	CATALOGIZED	CATAPLASMS	CATECHESIS	CATEGORISATIONS
CATABOLISMS	CATALOGIZES	CATAPLASTIC	CATECHESISES	CATEGORISE
CATABOLITE	CATALOGIZING	CATAPLECTIC	CATECHETIC	CATEGORISED

CATEGORISES

CATEGORISES	CATHETERISING	CATLINITES	CAUSTICALLY	CEANOTHUSES
CATEGORISING	CATHETERISM	CATNAPPERS	CAUSTICITIES	CEASEFIRES
CATEGORIST	CATHETERISMS	CATNAPPING	CAUSTICITY	CEASELESSLY
CATEGORISTS	CATHETERIZATION	CATOPTRICAL	CAUSTICNESS	CEASELESSNESS
CATEGORIZATION	CATHETERIZE	CATOPTRICS	CAUSTICNESSES	CEASELESSNESSES
CATEGORIZATIONS	CATHETERIZED	CATTINESSES	CAUTERANTS	CEBADILLAS
CATEGORIZE	CATHETERIZES	CATTISHNESS	CAUTERISATION	CECUTIENCIES
CATEGORIZED	CATHETERIZING	CATTISHNESSES	CAUTERISATIONS	CECUTIENCY
CATEGORIZES	CATHETOMETER	CAUCHEMARS	CAUTERISED	CEDARBIRDS
CATEGORIZING	CATHETOMETERS	CAUCUSSING	CAUTERISES	CEDARWOODS
CATENACCIO	CATHETUSES	CAUCUSSINGS	CAUTERISING	CEDRELACEOUS
CATENACCIOS	CATHINONES	CAUDATIONS	CAUTERISMS	CEILOMETER
CATENARIAN	CATHIODERMIE	CAUDILLISMO	CAUTERIZATION	CEILOMETERS
CATENARIES	CATHIODERMIES	CAUDILLISMOS	CAUTERIZATIONS	CELANDINES
CATENATING	CATHODALLY	CAULESCENT	CAUTERIZED	CELEBRANTS
CATENATION	CATHODICAL	CAULICOLOUS	CAUTERIZES	CELEBRATED
CATENATIONS	CATHODICALLY	CAULICULATE	CAUTERIZING	CELEBRATEDNESS
CATENULATE	CATHODOGRAPH	CAULICULUS	CAUTIONARY	CELEBRATES
CATERCORNER	CATHODOGRAPHER	CAULICULUSES	CAUTIONERS	CELEBRATING
CATERCORNERED	CATHODOGRAPHERS	CAULIFLORIES	CAUTIONING	CELEBRATION
CATERESSES	CATHODOGRAPHIES	CAULIFLOROUS	CAUTIONRIES	CELEBRATIONS
CATERPILLAR	CATHODOGRAPHS	CAULIFLORY	CAUTIOUSLY	CELEBRATIVE
CATERPILLARS	CATHODOGRAPHY	CAULIFLOWER	CAUTIOUSNESS	CELEBRATOR
CATERWAULED	CATHOLICALLY	CAULIFLOWERET	CAUTIOUSNESSES	CELEBRATORS
CATERWAULER	CATHOLICATE	CAULIFLOWERETS	CAVALCADED	CELEBRATORY
CATERWAULERS	CATHOLICATES	CAULIFLOWERS	CAVALCADES	CELEBREALITIES
CATERWAULING	CATHOLICISATION	CAULIGENOUS	CAVALCADING	CELEBREALITY
CATERWAULINGS	CATHOLICISE	CAUMSTANES	CAVALIERED	CELEBRITIES
CATERWAULS	CATHOLICISED	CAUMSTONES	CAVALIERING	CELEBUTANTE
CATFACINGS	CATHOLICISES	CAUSABILITIES	CAVALIERISH	CELEBUTANTES
CATFISHING	CATHOLICISING	CAUSABILITY	CAVALIERISM	CELECOXIBS
CATHARISED	CATHOLICISM	CAUSALGIAS	CAVALIERISMS	CELERITIES
CATHARISES	CATHOLICISMS	CAUSALITIES	CAVALIERLY	CELERYLIKE
CATHARISING	CATHOLICITIES	CAUSATIONAL	CAVALLETTI	CELESTIALLY
CATHARIZED	CATHOLICITY	CAUSATIONISM	CAVALRYMAN	CELESTIALS
CATHARIZES	CATHOLICIZATION	CAUSATIONISMS	CAVALRYMEN	CELESTINES
CATHARIZING	CATHOLICIZE	CAUSATIONIST	CAVEFISHES	CELESTITES
CATHARTICAL	CATHOLICIZED	CAUSATIONISTS	CAVENDISHES	CELIBACIES
CATHARTICALLY	CATHOLICIZES	CAUSATIONS	CAVERNICOLOUS	CELIBATARIAN
CATHARTICS	CATHOLICIZING	CAUSATIVELY	CAVERNOUSLY	CELIBATARIANS
CATHECTING	CATHOLICLY	CAUSATIVENESS	CAVERNULOUS	CELLARAGES
CATHEDRALS	CATHOLICOI	CAUSATIVENESSES	CAVILLATION	CELLARETTE
CATHEDRATIC	CATHOLICON	CAUSATIVES	CAVILLATIONS	CELLARETTES
CATHEPSINS	CATHOLICONS	CAUSELESSLY	CAVILLINGS	CELLARISTS
CATHETERISATION	CATHOLICOS	CAUSELESSNESS	CAVITATING	CELLARWAYS
CATHETERISE	CATHOLICOSES	CAUSELESSNESSES	CAVITATION	CELLBLOCKS
CATHETERISED	CATHOLYTES	CAUSEWAYED	CAVITATIONS	CELLENTANI
CATHETERISES	CATIONICALLY	CAUSEWAYING	CAVORTINGS	CELLENTANIS

CELLIFEROUS	CENSURABLE	CENTIMETRIC	CENTRICALNESSES	CENTUPLING
CELLOBIOSE	CENSURABLENESS	CENTIMORGAN	CENTRICITIES	CENTURIATION
CELLOBIOSES	CENSURABLY	CENTIMORGANS	CENTRICITY	CENTURIATIONS
CELLOIDINS	CENTAUREAS	CENTINELLS	CENTRIFUGAL	CENTURIATOR
CELLOPHANE	CENTAURIAN	CENTIPEDES	CENTRIFUGALISE	CENTURIATORS
CELLOPHANES	CENTAURIES	CENTIPOISE	CENTRIFUGALISED	CENTURIONS
CELLPHONES	CENTENARIAN	CENTIPOISES	CENTRIFUGALISES	CEPHALAGRA
CELLULARITIES	CENTENARIANISM	CENTONATES	CENTRIFUGALIZE	CEPHALAGRAS
CELLULARITY	CENTENARIANISMS	CENTONELLS	CENTRIFUGALIZED	CEPHALALGIA
CELLULASES	CENTENARIANS	CENTONISTS	CENTRIFUGALIZES	CEPHALALGIAS
CELLULATED	CENTENARIES	CENTRALEST	CENTRIFUGALLY	CEPHALALGIC
CELLULIFEROUS	CENTENIERS	CENTRALISATION	CENTRIFUGALS	CEPHALALGICS
CELLULITES	CENTENNIAL	CENTRALISATIONS	CENTRIFUGATION	CEPHALEXIN
CELLULITIS	CENTENNIALLY	CENTRALISE	CENTRIFUGATIONS	CEPHALEXINS
CELLULITISES	CENTENNIALS	CENTRALISED	CENTRIFUGE	CEPHALICALLY
CELLULOIDS	CENTERBOARD	CENTRALISER	CENTRIFUGED	CEPHALISATION
CELLULOLYTIC	CENTERBOARDS	CENTRALISERS	CENTRIFUGENCE	CEPHALISATIONS
CELLULOSES	CENTEREDNESS	CENTRALISES	CENTRIFUGENCES	CEPHALITIS
CELLULOSIC	CENTEREDNESSES	CENTRALISING	CENTRIFUGES	CEPHALITISES
CELLULOSICS	CENTERFOLD	CENTRALISM	CENTRIFUGING	CEPHALIZATION
CELSITUDES	CENTERFOLDS	CENTRALISMS	CENTRIOLES	CEPHALIZATIONS
CEMBALISTS	CENTERINGS	CENTRALIST	CENTRIPETAL	CEPHALOCELE
CEMENTATION	CENTERLESS	CENTRALISTIC	CENTRIPETALISM	CEPHALOCELES
CEMENTATIONS	CENTERLINE	CENTRALISTS	CENTRIPETALISMS	CEPHALOCHORDATE
CEMENTATORY	CENTERLINES	CENTRALITIES	CENTRIPETALLY	CEPHALOMETER
CEMENTITES	CENTERPIECE	CENTRALITY	CENTROBARIC	CEPHALOMETERS
CEMENTITIOUS	CENTERPIECES	CENTRALIZATION	CENTROCLINAL	CEPHALOMETRIC
CEMETERIES	CENTESIMAL	CENTRALIZATIONS	CENTROIDAL	CEPHALOMETRIES
CENESTHESES	CENTESIMALLY	CENTRALIZE	CENTROLECITHAL	CEPHALOMETRY
CENESTHESIA	CENTESIMALS	CENTRALIZED	CENTROMERE	CEPHALOPOD
CENESTHESIAS	CENTESIMOS	CENTRALIZER	CENTROMERES	CEPHALOPODAN
CENESTHESIS	CENTIGRADE	CENTRALIZERS	CENTROMERIC	CEPHALOPODANS
CENESTHETIC	CENTIGRADES	CENTRALIZES	CENTROSOME	CEPHALOPODIC
CENOBITICAL	CENTIGRAMME	CENTRALIZING	CENTROSOMES	CEPHALOPODOUS
CENOGENESES	CENTIGRAMMES	CENTREBOARD	CENTROSOMIC	CEPHALOPODS
CENOGENESIS	CENTIGRAMS	CENTREBOARDS	CENTROSPHERE	CEPHALORIDINE
CENOGENETIC	CENTILITER	CENTREDNESS	CENTROSPHERES	CEPHALORIDINES
CENOGENETICALLY	CENTILITERS	CENTREDNESSES	CENTROSYMMETRIC	CEPHALOSPORIN
CENOSPECIES	CENTILITRE	CENTREFOLD	CENTUMVIRATE	CEPHALOSPORINS
CENOTAPHIC	CENTILITRES	CENTREFOLDS	CENTUMVIRATES	CEPHALOTHIN
CENSORABLE	CENTILLION	CENTREINGS	CENTUMVIRI	CEPHALOTHINS
CENSORIOUS	CENTILLIONS	CENTRELESS	CENTUMVIRS	CEPHALOTHORACES
CENSORIOUSLY	CENTILLIONTH	CENTRELINE	CENTUPLICATE	CEPHALOTHORACIC
CENSORIOUSNESS	CENTILLIONTHS	CENTRELINES	CENTUPLICATED	CEPHALOTHORAX
CENSORSHIP	CENTIMETER	CENTREPIECE	CENTUPLICATES	CEPHALOTHORAXES
CENSORSHIPS	CENTIMETERS	CENTREPIECES	CENTUPLICATING	CEPHALOTOMIES
CENSURABILITIES	CENTIMETRE	CENTRICALLY	CENTUPLICATION	CEPHALOTOMY
CENSURABILITY	CENTIMETRES	CENTRICALNESS	CENTUPLICATIONS	CERAMICIST

CERAMICISTS	CEREMONIALISM	CESAREVICHES	CHAINSAWING	CHALCOGRAPHISTS
CERAMOGRAPHIES	CEREMONIALISMS	CESAREVITCH	CHAINSHOTS	CHALCOGRAPHY
CERAMOGRAPHY	CEREMONIALIST	CESAREVITCHES	CHAINSTITCH	CHALCOLITHIC
CERARGYRITE	CEREMONIALISTS	CESAREVNAS	CHAINSTITCHES	CHALCOPYRITE
CERARGYRITES	CEREMONIALLY	CESAREWICH	CHAINWHEEL	CHALCOPYRITES
CERASTIUMS	CEREMONIALS	CESAREWICHES	CHAINWHEELS	CHALICOTHERE
CERATITISES	CEREMONIES	CESAREWITCH	CHAINWORKS	CHALICOTHERES
CERATODUSES	CEREMONIOUS	CESAREWITCHES	CHAIRBACKS	CHALKBOARD
CERATOPSIAN	CEREMONIOUSLY	CESPITOSELY	CHAIRBORNE	CHALKBOARDS
CERATOPSIANS	CEREMONIOUSNESS	CESSATIONS	CHAIRBOUND	CHALKFACES
CERATOPSID	CERIFEROUS	CESSIONARIES	CHAIRLIFTS	CHALKINESS
CERATOPSIDS	CEROGRAPHIC	CESSIONARY	CHAIRMANED	CHALKINESSES
CERAUNOGRAPH	CEROGRAPHICAL	CESTOIDEAN	CHAIRMANING	CHALKLANDS
CERAUNOGRAPHS	CEROGRAPHIES	CESTOIDEANS	CHAIRMANNED	CHALKMARKS
CERCARIANS	CEROGRAPHIST	CETEOSAURUS	CHAIRMANNING	CHALKSTONE
CERCOPITHECID	CEROGRAPHISTS	CETEOSAURUSES	CHAIRMANSHIP	CHALKSTONES
CERCOPITHECIDS	CEROGRAPHS	CETOLOGICAL	CHAIRMANSHIPS	CHALKSTRIPE
CERCOPITHECOID	CEROGRAPHY	CETOLOGIES	CHAIRPERSON	CHALKSTRIPES
CERCOPITHECOIDS	CEROMANCIES	CETOLOGIST	CHAIRPERSONS	CHALLENGEABLE
CEREALISTS	CEROPLASTIC	CETOLOGISTS	CHAIRWARMER	CHALLENGED
CEREBELLAR	CEROPLASTICS	CETRIMIDES	CHAIRWARMERS	CHALLENGER
CEREBELLIC	CERTAINEST	CETUXIMABS	CHAIRWOMAN	CHALLENGERS
CEREBELLOUS	CERTAINTIES	CEVADILLAS	CHAIRWOMEN	CHALLENGES
CEREBELLUM	CERTIFIABLE	CEYLANITES	CHAISELESS	CHALLENGING
CEREBELLUMS	CERTIFIABLY	CEYLONITES	CHAKALAKAS	CHALLENGINGLY
CEREBRALISM	CERTIFICATE	CHABAZITES	CHALANNING	CHALUMEAUS
CEREBRALISMS	CERTIFICATED	CHACONINES	CHALAZIONS	CHALUMEAUX
CEREBRALIST	CERTIFICATES	CHAENOMELES	CHALAZOGAMIC	CHALYBEATE
CEREBRALISTS	CERTIFICATING	CHAENOMELESES	CHALAZOGAMIES	CHALYBEATES
CEREBRALLY	CERTIFICATION	CHAETIFEROUS	CHALAZOGAMY	CHALYBITES
CEREBRATED	CERTIFICATIONS	CHAETODONS	CHALCANTHITE	CHAMAELEON
CEREBRATES	CERTIFICATORIES	CHAETOGNATH	CHALCANTHITES	CHAMAELEONS
CEREBRATING	CERTIFICATORY	CHAETOGNATHS	CHALCEDONIC	CHAMAEPHYTE
CEREBRATION	CERTIFIERS	CHAETOPODS	CHALCEDONIES	CHAMAEPHYTES
CEREBRATIONS	CERTIFYING	CHAFFERERS	CHALCEDONY	CHAMBERERS
CEREBRIFORM	CERTIORARI	CHAFFERIES	CHALCEDONYX	CHAMBERHAND
CEREBRITIS	CERTIORARIS	CHAFFERING	CHALCEDONYXES	CHAMBERHANDS
CEREBRITISES	CERTITUDES	CHAFFINCHES	CHALCOCITE	CHAMBERING
CEREBROSIDE	CERULOPLASMIN	CHAFFINGLY	CHALCOCITES	CHAMBERINGS
CEREBROSIDES	CERULOPLASMINS	CHAGRINING	CHALCOGENIDE	CHAMBERLAIN
CEREBROSPINAL	CERUMINOUS	CHAGRINNED	CHALCOGENIDES	CHAMBERLAINS
CEREBROTONIA	CERUSSITES	CHAGRINNING	CHALCOGENS	CHAMBERLAINSHIP
CEREBROTONIAS	CERVELASES	CHAINBRAKE	CHALCOGRAPHER	CHAMBERMAID
CEREBROTONIC	CERVICITIS	CHAINBRAKES	CHALCOGRAPHERS	CHAMBERMAIDS
CEREBROTONICS	CERVICITISES	CHAINFALLS	CHALCOGRAPHIC	CHAMBERPOT
CEREBROVASCULAR	CERVICOGRAPHIES	CHAINPLATE	CHALCOGRAPHICAL	CHAMBERPOTS
CERECLOTHS	CERVICOGRAPHY	CHAINPLATES	CHALCOGRAPHIES	CHAMBRANLE
CEREMONIAL	CESAREVICH	CHAINSAWED	CHALCOGRAPHIST	CHAMBRANLES

CHAMELEONIC	CHANGEABLENESS	CHANTRESSES	CHARACTERIES	CHARGESHEETS
CHAMELEONLIKE	CHANGEABLY	CHANUKIAHS	CHARACTERING	CHARGRILLED
CHAMELEONS	CHANGEAROUND	CHAOLOGIES	CHARACTERISABLE	CHARGRILLING
CHAMFERERS	CHANGEAROUNDS	CHAOLOGIST	CHARACTERISE	CHARGRILLS
CHAMFERING	CHANGEFULLY	CHAOLOGISTS	CHARACTERISED	CHARINESSES
CHAMFRAINS	CHANGEFULNESS	CHAOTICALLY	CHARACTERISER	CHARIOTEER
CHAMOISING	CHANGEFULNESSES	CHAPARAJOS	CHARACTERISERS	CHARIOTEERED
CHAMOMILES	CHANGELESS	CHAPAREJOS	CHARACTERISES	CHARIOTEERING
CHAMPAGNES	CHANGELESSLY	CHAPARRALS	CHARACTERISING	CHARIOTEERS
CHAMPAIGNS	CHANGELESSNESS	CHAPATTIES	CHARACTERISM	CHARIOTING
CHAMPERTIES	CHANGELING	CHAPELRIES	CHARACTERISMS	CHARISMATA
CHAMPERTOUS	CHANGELINGS	CHAPERONAGE	CHARACTERISTIC	CHARISMATIC
CHAMPIGNON	CHANGEOVER	CHAPERONAGES	CHARACTERISTICS	CHARISMATICS
CHAMPIGNONS	CHANGEOVERS	CHAPERONED	CHARACTERIZABLE	CHARITABLE
CHAMPIONED	CHANGEROUND	CHAPERONES	CHARACTERIZE	CHARITABLENESS
CHAMPIONESS	CHANGEROUNDS	CHAPERONING	CHARACTERIZED	CHARITABLY
CHAMPIONESSES	CHANNELERS	CHAPFALLEN	CHARACTERIZER	CHARIVARIED
CHAMPIONING	CHANNELING	CHAPLAINCIES	CHARACTERIZERS	CHARIVARIING
CHAMPIONSHIP	CHANNELISATION	CHAPLAINCY	CHARACTERIZES	CHARIVARIS
CHAMPIONSHIPS	CHANNELISATIONS	CHAPLAINRIES	CHARACTERIZING	CHARLADIES
CHAMPLEVES	CHANNELISE	CHAPLAINRY	CHARACTERLESS	CHARLATANIC
CHANCELESS	CHANNELISED	CHAPLAINSHIP	CHARACTEROLOGY	CHARLATANICAL
CHANCELLERIES	CHANNELISES	CHAPLAINSHIPS	CHARACTERS	CHARLATANISM
CHANCELLERY	CHANNELISING	CHAPMANSHIP	CHARACTERY	CHARLATANISMS
CHANCELLOR	CHANNELIZATION	CHAPMANSHIPS	CHARBROILED	CHARLATANISTIC
CHANCELLORIES	CHANNELIZATIONS	CHAPPESSES	CHARBROILER	CHARLATANRIES
CHANCELLORS	CHANNELIZE	CHAPRASSIES	CHARBROILERS	CHARLATANRY
CHANCELLORSHIP	CHANNELIZED	CHAPRASSIS	CHARBROILING	CHARLATANS
CHANCELLORSHIPS	CHANNELIZES	CHAPSTICKS	CHARBROILS	CHARLESTON
CHANCELLORY	CHANNELIZING	CHAPTALISATION	CHARCOALED	CHARLESTONED
CHANCERIES	CHANNELLED	CHAPTALISATIONS	CHARCOALIER	CHARLESTONING
CHANCINESS	CHANNELLER	CHAPTALISE	CHARCOALIEST	CHARLESTONS
CHANCINESSES	CHANNELLERS	CHAPTALISED	CHARCOALING	CHARLOTTES
CHANCROIDAL	CHANNELLING	CHAPTALISES	CHARCUTERIE	CHARMEUSES
CHANCROIDS	CHANSONETTE	CHAPTALISING	CHARCUTERIES	CHARMINGER
CHANDELIER	CHANSONETTES	CHAPTALIZATION	CHARDONNAY	CHARMINGEST
CHANDELIERED	CHANSONNIER	CHAPTALIZATIONS	CHARDONNAYS	CHARMINGLY
CHANDELIERS	CHANSONNIERS	CHAPTALIZE	CHARGEABILITIES	CHARMLESSLY
CHANDELLED	CHANTARELLE	CHAPTALIZED	CHARGEABILITY	CHARMONIUM
CHANDELLES	CHANTARELLES	CHAPTALIZES	CHARGEABLE	CHAROSETHS
CHANDELLING	CHANTECLER	CHAPTALIZING	CHARGEABLENESS	CHARREADAS
CHANDLERIES	CHANTECLERS	CHAPTERHOUSE	CHARGEABLY	CHARTACEOUS
CHANDLERING	CHANTERELLE	CHAPTERHOUSES	CHARGEBACK	CHARTERERS
CHANDLERINGS	CHANTERELLES	CHAPTERING	CHARGEBACKS	CHARTERING
CHANDLERLY	CHANTEUSES	CHARABANCS	CHARGEHAND	CHARTERPARTIES
CHANGEABILITIES	CHANTICLEER	CHARACINOID	CHARGEHANDS	CHARTERPARTY
CHANGEABILITY	CHANTICLEERS	CHARACTERED	CHARGELESS	CHARTHOUSE
CHANGEABLE	CHANTINGLY	CHARACTERFUL	CHARGESHEET	CHARTHOUSES

CHARTOGRAPHER

CHARTOGRAPHER	CHATTINESSES	CHECKERBOARD	CHEERISHNESS	CHEIROMANCIES
CHARTOGRAPHERS	CHAUDFROID	CHECKERBOARDS	CHEERISHNESSES	CHEIROMANCY
CHARTOGRAPHIC	CHAUDFROIDS	CHECKERING	CHEERLEADER	CHELASHIPS
CHARTOGRAPHICAL	CHAUFFEURED	CHECKLATON	CHEERLEADERS	CHELATABLE
CHARTOGRAPHIES	CHAUFFEURING	CHECKLATONS	CHEERLEADING	CHELATIONS
CHARTOGRAPHY	CHAUFFEURS	CHECKLISTED	CHEERLEADS	CHELICERAE
CHARTREUSE	CHAUFFEUSE	CHECKLISTING	CHEERLESSLY	CHELICERAL
CHARTREUSES	CHAUFFEUSED	CHECKLISTS	CHEERLESSNESS	CHELICERATE
CHARTULARIES	CHAUFFEUSES	CHECKMARKED	CHEERLESSNESSES	CHELICERATES
CHARTULARY	CHAUFFEUSING	CHECKMARKING	CHEESEBOARD	CHELIFEROUS
CHASEPORTS	CHAULMOOGRA	CHECKMARKS	CHEESEBOARDS	CHELONIANS
CHASMOGAMIC	CHAULMOOGRAS	CHECKMATED	CHEESEBURGER	CHELUVIATION
CHASMOGAMIES	CHAULMUGRA	CHECKMATES	CHEESEBURGERS	CHELUVIATIONS
CHASMOGAMOUS	CHAULMUGRAS	CHECKMATING	CHEESECAKE	CHEMAUTOTROPH
CHASMOGAMY	CHAUNTRESS	CHECKPOINT	CHEESECAKES	CHEMAUTOTROPHIC
CHASSEPOTS	CHAUNTRESSES	CHECKPOINTS	CHEESECLOTH	CHEMAUTOTROPHS
CHASTENERS	CHAUNTRIES	CHECKRAILS	CHEESECLOTHS	CHEMIATRIC
CHASTENESS	CHAUSSURES	CHECKREINS	CHEESECUTTER	CHEMICALLY
CHASTENESSES	CHAUTAUQUA	CHECKROOMS	CHEESECUTTERS	CHEMICKING
CHASTENING	CHAUTAUQUAS	CHECKROWED	CHEESEHOPPER	CHEMICKINGS
CHASTENINGLY	CHAUVINISM	CHECKROWING	CHEESEHOPPERS	CHEMICOPHYSICAL
CHASTENMENT	CHAUVINISMS	CHECKSTOPS	CHEESELIKE	CHEMIOSMOSES
CHASTENMENTS	CHAUVINIST	CHECKWEIGHER	CHEESEMITE	CHEMIOSMOSIS
CHASTISABLE	CHAUVINISTIC	CHECKWEIGHERS	CHEESEMITES	CHEMIOSMOTIC
CHASTISEMENT	CHAUVINISTS	CHEDDARIER	CHEESEMONGER	CHEMISETTE
CHASTISEMENTS	CHAVENDERS	CHEDDARIEST	CHEESEMONGERS	CHEMISETTES
CHASTISERS	CHAVTASTIC	CHEECHAKOES	CHEESEPARER	CHEMISORBED
CHASTISING	CHAWBACONS	CHEECHAKOS	CHEESEPARERS	CHEMISORBING
CHASTITIES	CHEAPENERS	CHEECHALKO	CHEESEPARING	CHEMISORBS
CHATEAUBRIAND	CHEAPENING	CHEECHALKOES	CHEESEPARINGS	CHEMISORPTION
CHATEAUBRIANDS	CHEAPISHLY	CHEECHALKOS	CHEESEPRESS	CHEMISORPTIONS
CHATELAINE	CHEAPJACKS	CHEEKBONES	CHEESEPRESSES	CHEMISTRIES
CHATELAINES	CHEAPNESSES	CHEEKINESS	CHEESESTEAK	CHEMITYPES
CHATELAINS	CHEAPSHOTS	CHEEKINESSES	CHEESESTEAKS	CHEMITYPIES
CHATOYANCE	CHEAPSKATE	CHEEKPIECE	CHEESETASTER	CHEMOATTRACTANT
CHATOYANCES	CHEAPSKATES	CHEEKPIECES	CHEESETASTERS	CHEMOAUTOTROPH
CHATOYANCIES	CHEATERIES	CHEEKPOUCH	CHEESEVATS	CHEMOAUTOTROPHS
CHATOYANCY	CHEATINGLY	CHEEKPOUCHES	CHEESEWIRE	CHEMOAUTOTROPHY
CHATOYANTS	CHECHAKOES	CHEEKTEETH	CHEESEWIRES	CHEMOAUTROPH
CHATTERATI	CHECHAQUOS	CHEEKTOOTH	CHEESEWOOD	CHEMOAUTROPHS
CHATTERBOX	CHECKBOOKS	CHEERFULLER	CHEESEWOODS	CHEMOCEPTOR
CHATTERBOXES	CHECKBOXES	CHEERFULLEST	CHEESEWRING	CHEMOCEPTORS
CHATTERERS	CHECKCLERK	CHEERFULLY	CHEESEWRINGS	CHEMOKINES
CHATTERIER	CHECKCLERKS	CHEERFULNESS	CHEESINESS	CHEMOKINESES
CHATTERIEST	CHECKERBERRIES	CHEERFULNESSES	CHEESINESSES	CHEMOKINESIS
CHATTERING	CHECKERBERRY	CHEERINESS	CHEILITISES	CHEMOLITHOTROPH
CHATTERINGS	CHECKERBLOOM	CHEERINESSES	CHEIROMANCER	CHEMONASTIES
CHATTINESS	CHECKERBLOOMS	CHEERINGLY	CHEIROMANCERS	CHEMONASTY

CHEMOPREVENTION	CHEQUERBOARD	CHEVISANCES	CHIEFTAINSHIPS	CHILIARCHIES
CHEMOPSYCHIATRY	CHEQUERBOARDS	CHEVRETTES	CHIFFCHAFF	CHILIARCHS
CHEMORECEPTION	CHEQUERING	CHEVROTAIN	CHIFFCHAFFS	CHILIARCHY
CHEMORECEPTIONS	CHEQUERWISE	CHEVROTAINS	CHIFFONADE	CHILIASTIC
CHEMORECEPTIVE	CHEQUERWORK	CHEVROTINS	CHIFFONADES	CHILLAXING
CHEMORECEPTOR	CHEQUERWORKS	CHEWINESSES	CHIFFONIER	CHILLINESS
CHEMORECEPTORS	CHERALITES	CHIACKINGS	CHIFFONIERS	CHILLINESSES
CHEMOSMOSES	CHERIMOYAS	CHIAREZZAS	CHIFFONNIER	CHILLINGLY
CHEMOSMOSIS	CHERIMOYER	CHIAROSCURISM	CHIFFONNIERS	CHILLNESSES
CHEMOSMOTIC	CHERIMOYERS	CHIAROSCURISMS	CHIFFONNIEST	CHILOPODAN
CHEMOSORBED	CHERISHABLE	CHIAROSCURIST	CHIFFOROBE	CHILOPODANS
CHEMOSORBING	CHERISHERS	CHIAROSCURISTS	CHIFFOROBES	CHILOPODOUS
CHEMOSORBS	CHERISHING	CHIAROSCURO	CHIHUAHUAS	CHILTEPINS
CHEMOSPHERE	CHERISHINGLY	CHIAROSCUROS	CHILBLAINED	CHIMAERISM
CHEMOSPHERES	CHERISHMENT	CHIASMATIC	CHILBLAINS	CHIMAERISMS
CHEMOSPHERIC	CHERISHMENTS	CHIASTOLITE	CHILDBEARING	CHIMERICAL
CHEMOSTATS	CHERMOULAS	CHIASTOLITES	CHILDBEARINGS	CHIMERICALLY
CHEMOSURGERIES	CHERNOZEMIC	CHIBOUQUES	CHILDBIRTH	CHIMERICALNESS
CHEMOSURGERY	CHERNOZEMS	CHICALOTES	CHILDBIRTHS	CHIMERISMS
CHEMOSURGICAL	CHERRYLIKE	CHICANERIES	CHILDCARES	CHIMICHANGA
CHEMOSYNTHESES	CHERRYSTONE	CHICANINGS	CHILDCROWING	CHIMICHANGAS
CHEMOSYNTHESIS	CHERRYSTONES	CHICCORIES	CHILDCROWINGS	CHIMNEYBOARD
CHEMOSYNTHETIC	CHERSONESE	CHICKABIDDIES	CHILDERMAS	CHIMNEYBOARDS
CHEMOTACTIC	CHERSONESES	CHICKABIDDY	CHILDERMASES	CHIMNEYBREAST
CHEMOTACTICALLY	CHERUBICAL	CHICKADEES	CHILDHOODS	CHIMNEYBREASTS
CHEMOTAXES	CHERUBICALLY	CHICKAREES	CHILDISHLY	CHIMNEYING
CHEMOTAXIS	CHERUBIMIC	CHICKENHEARTED	CHILDISHNESS	CHIMNEYLIKE
CHEMOTAXISES	CHERUBLIKE	CHICKENING	CHILDISHNESSES	CHIMNEYPIECE
CHEMOTAXONOMIC	CHERVONETS	CHICKENPOX	CHILDLESSNESS	CHIMNEYPIECES
CHEMOTAXONOMIES	CHESSBOARD	CHICKENPOXES	CHILDLESSNESSES	CHIMNEYPOT
CHEMOTAXONOMIST	CHESSBOARDS	CHICKENSHIT	CHILDLIEST	CHIMNEYPOTS
CHEMOTAXONOMY	CHESSBOXING	CHICKENSHITS	CHILDLIKENESS	CHIMPANZEE
CHEMOTHERAPIES	CHESSBOXINGS	CHICKLINGS	CHILDLIKENESSES	CHIMPANZEES
CHEMOTHERAPIST	CHESSPIECE	CHICKORIES	CHILDMINDER	CHINABERRIES
CHEMOTHERAPISTS	CHESSPIECES	CHICKWEEDS	CHILDMINDERS	CHINABERRY
CHEMOTHERAPY	CHESSPLAYER	CHICNESSES	CHILDMINDING	CHINACHINA
CHEMOTROPIC	CHESSPLAYERS	CHIEFERIES	CHILDMINDINGS	CHINACHINAS
CHEMOTROPICALLY	CHESSYLITE	CHIEFESSES	CHILDNESSES	CHINAROOTS
CHEMOTROPISM	CHESSYLITES	CHIEFLINGS	CHILDPROOF	CHINAWARES
CHEMOTROPISMS	CHESTERFIELD	CHIEFSHIPS	CHILDPROOFED	CHINCAPINS
CHEMPADUKS	CHESTERFIELDS	CHIEFTAINCIES	CHILDPROOFING	CHINCHERINCHEE
CHEMTRAILS	CHESTINESS	CHIEFTAINCY	CHILDPROOFS	CHINCHERINCHEES
CHEMURGICAL	CHESTINESSES	CHIEFTAINESS	CHILDRENSWEAR	CHINCHIEST
CHEMURGIES	CHEVALIERS	CHIEFTAINESSES	CHILDRENSWEARS	CHINCHILLA
CHENOPODIACEOUS	CHEVELURES	CHIEFTAINRIES	CHILIAGONS	CHINCHILLAS
CHEONGSAMS	CHEVESAILE	CHIEFTAINRY	CHILIAHEDRA	CHINCOUGHS
CHEQUEBOOK	CHEVESAILES	CHIEFTAINS	CHILIAHEDRON	CHINKAPINS
CHEQUEBOOKS	CHEVISANCE	CHIEFTAINSHIP	CHILIAHEDRONS	CHINKERINCHEE

CHINKERINCHEES

CHINKERINCHEES	CHIRONOMER	CHIVAREEING	CHLORIMETER	CHLOROFORMIST
CHINOISERIE	CHIRONOMERS	CHIVARIING	CHLORIMETERS	CHLOROFORMISTS
CHINOISERIES	CHIRONOMIC	CHIWEENIES	CHLORIMETRIC	CHLOROFORMS
CHINOVNIKS	CHIRONOMID	CHIYOGAMIS	CHLORIMETRIES	CHLOROHYDRIN
CHINQUAPIN	CHIRONOMIDS	CHLAMYDATE	CHLORIMETRY	CHLOROHYDRINS
CHINQUAPINS	CHIRONOMIES	CHLAMYDEOUS	CHLORINATE	CHLOROMETER
CHINSTRAPS	CHIROPODIAL	CHLAMYDIAE	CHLORINATED	CHLOROMETERS
CHINTZIEST	CHIROPODIES	CHLAMYDIAL	CHLORINATES	CHLOROMETHANE
CHINWAGGED	CHIROPODIST	CHLAMYDIAS	CHLORINATING	CHLOROMETHANES
CHINWAGGING	CHIROPODISTS	CHLAMYDOMONADES	CHLORINATION	CHLOROMETRIC
CHIONODOXA	CHIROPRACTIC	CHLAMYDOMONAS	CHLORINATIONS	CHLOROMETRIES
CHIONODOXAS	CHIROPRACTICS	CHLAMYDOSPORE	CHLORINATOR	CHLOROMETRY
CHIPBOARDS	CHIROPRACTOR	CHLAMYDOSPORES	CHLORINATORS	CHLOROPHYL
CHIPMAKERS	CHIROPRACTORS	CHLOANTHITE	CHLORINISE	CHLOROPHYLL
CHIPOCHIAS	CHIROPTERAN	CHLOANTHITES	CHLORINISED	CHLOROPHYLLOID
CHIPOLATAS	CHIROPTERANS	CHLOASMATA	CHLORINISES	CHLOROPHYLLOUS
CHIPPEREST	CHIROPTEROUS	CHLORACETIC	CHLORINISING	CHLOROPHYLLS
CHIPPERING	CHIROPTERS	CHLORACNES	CHLORINITIES	CHLOROPHYLS
CHIPPINESS	CHIRPINESS	CHLORALISM	CHLORINITY	CHLOROPHYTUM
CHIPPINESSES	CHIRPINESSES	CHLORALISMS	CHLORINIZE	CHLOROPHYTUMS
CHIQUICHIQUI	CHIRRUPERS	CHLORALOSE	CHLORINIZED	CHLOROPICRIN
CHIQUICHIQUIS	CHIRRUPIER	CHLORALOSED	CHLORINIZES	CHLOROPICRINS
CHIRAGRICAL	CHIRRUPIEST	CHLORALOSES	CHLORINIZING	CHLOROPLAST
CHIRALITIES	CHIRRUPING	CHLORAMBUCIL	CHLORITISATION	CHLOROPLASTAL
CHIRIMOYAS	CHIRURGEON	CHLORAMBUCILS	CHLORITISATIONS	CHLOROPLASTIC
CHIROGNOMIES	CHIRURGEONLY	CHLORAMINE	CHLORITIZATION	CHLOROPLASTS
CHIROGNOMIST	CHIRURGEONS	CHLORAMINES	CHLORITIZATIONS	CHLOROPRENE
CHIROGNOMISTS	CHIRURGERIES	CHLORAMPHENICOL	CHLOROACETIC	CHLOROPRENES
CHIROGNOMY	CHIRURGERY	CHLORARGYRITE	CHLOROARGYRITE	CHLOROQUIN
CHIROGRAPH	CHIRURGICAL	CHLORARGYRITES	CHLOROBENZENE	CHLOROQUINE
CHIROGRAPHER	CHISELLERS	CHLORDANES	CHLOROBENZENES	CHLOROQUINES
CHIROGRAPHERS	CHISELLING	CHLORELLAS	CHLOROBROMIDE	CHLOROQUINS
CHIROGRAPHIC	CHISELLINGS	CHLORENCHYMA	CHLOROBROMIDES	CHLOROSISES
CHIROGRAPHICAL	CHITARRONE	CHLORENCHYMAS	CHLOROCALCITE	CHLOROTHIAZIDE
CHIROGRAPHIES	CHITARRONI	CHLORHEXIDINE	CHLOROCALCITES	CHLOROTHIAZIDES
CHIROGRAPHIST	CHITCHATTED	CHLORHEXIDINES	CHLOROCRUORIN	CHLORPICRIN
CHIROGRAPHISTS	CHITCHATTING	CHLORIDATE	CHLOROCRUORINS	CHLORPICRINS
CHIROGRAPHS	CHITTAGONG	CHLORIDATED	CHLORODYNE	CHLORPROMAZINE
CHIROGRAPHY	CHITTAGONGS	CHLORIDATES	CHLORODYNES	CHLORPROMAZINES
CHIROLOGIES	CHITTERING	CHLORIDATING	CHLOROETHENE	CHLORPROPAMIDE
CHIROLOGIST	CHITTERINGS	CHLORIDISE	CHLOROETHENES	CHLORPROPAMIDES
CHIROLOGISTS	CHITTERLING	CHLORIDISED	CHLOROETHYLENE	CHLORTHALIDONE
CHIROMANCER	CHITTERLINGS	CHLORIDISES	CHLOROETHYLENES	CHLORTHALIDONES
CHIROMANCERS	CHIVALRESQUE	CHLORIDISING	CHLOROFORM	CHOANOCYTE
CHIROMANCIES	CHIVALRIES	CHLORIDIZE	CHLOROFORMED	CHOANOCYTES
CHIROMANCY	CHIVALROUS	CHLORIDIZED	CHLOROFORMER	CHOCAHOLIC
CHIROMANTIC	CHIVALROUSLY	CHLORIDIZES	CHLOROFORMERS	CHOCAHOLICS
CHIROMANTICAL	CHIVALROUSNESS	CHLORIDIZING	CHLOROFORMING	CHOCKABLOCK

CHOCKSTONE	CHOLESTASIS	CHONDROMATOUS	CHOREOGRAPHS	CHOWHOUNDS
CHOCKSTONES	CHOLESTATIC	CHONDROPHORE	CHOREOGRAPHY	CHOWKIDARS
CHOCOHOLIC	CHOLESTERATE	CHONDROPHORES	CHOREOLOGIES	CHREMATIST
CHOCOHOLICS	CHOLESTERATES	CHONDROPHORINE	CHOREOLOGIST	CHREMATISTIC
CHOCOLATES	CHOLESTERIC	CHONDROPHORINES	CHOREOLOGISTS	CHREMATISTICS
CHOCOLATEY	CHOLESTERIN	CHONDROSAMINE	CHOREOLOGY	CHREMATISTS
CHOCOLATIER	CHOLESTERINS	CHONDROSAMINES	CHOREPISCOPAL	CHRESTOMATHIC
CHOCOLATIERS	CHOLESTEROL	CHONDROSKELETON	CHORIAMBIC	CHRESTOMATHICAL
CHOCOLATIEST	CHOLESTEROLEMIA	CHONDROSTIAN	CHORIAMBICS	CHRESTOMATHIES
CHOICENESS	CHOLESTEROLS	CHONDROSTIANS	CHORIAMBUS	CHRESTOMATHY
CHOICENESSES	CHOLESTYRAMINE	CHONDRULES	CHORIAMBUSES	CHRISMATION
CHOIRGIRLS	CHOLESTYRAMINES	CHOPFALLEN	CHORIOALLANTOIC	CHRISMATIONS
CHOIRMASTER	CHOLIAMBIC	CHOPHOUSES	CHORIOALLANTOIS	CHRISMATORIES
CHOIRMASTERS	CHOLIAMBICS	CHOPLOGICS	CHORIOCARCINOMA	CHRISMATORY
CHOIRSCREEN	CHOLINERGIC	CHOPPERING	CHORISATION	CHRISTCROSS
CHOIRSCREENS	CHOLINERGICALLY	CHOPPINESS	CHORISATIONS	CHRISTCROSSES
CHOIRSTALL	CHOLINESTERASE	CHOPPINESSES	CHORISTERS	CHRISTENED
CHOIRSTALLS	CHOLINESTERASES	CHOPSOCKIES	CHORIZATION	CHRISTENER
CHOKEBERRIES	CHOMOPHYTE	CHOPSTICKS	CHORIZATIONS	CHRISTENERS
CHOKEBERRY	CHOMOPHYTES	CHORAGUSES	CHORIZONTIST	CHRISTENING
CHOKEBORES	CHONDRICHTHYAN	CHORALISTS	CHORIZONTISTS	CHRISTENINGS
CHOKECHERRIES	CHONDRICHTHYANS	CHORDAMESODERM	CHORIZONTS	CHRISTIANIA
CHOKECHERRY	CHONDRIFICATION	CHORDAMESODERMS	CHOROGRAPHER	CHRISTIANIAS
CHOKECOILS	CHONDRIFIED	CHORDOPHONE	CHOROGRAPHERS	CHRISTOPHANIES
CHOKEDAMPS	CHONDRIFIES	CHORDOPHONES	CHOROGRAPHIC	CHRISTOPHANY
CHOKEHOLDS	CHONDRIFYING	CHORDOPHONIC	CHOROGRAPHICAL	CHROMAFFIN
CHOLAEMIAS	CHONDRIOSOMAL	CHORDOTOMIES	CHOROGRAPHIES	CHROMAKEYS
CHOLAGOGIC	CHONDRIOSOME	CHORDOTOMY	CHOROGRAPHY	CHROMATICALLY
CHOLAGOGUE	CHONDRIOSOMES	CHOREGRAPH	CHOROIDITIS	CHROMATICISM
CHOLAGOGUES	CHONDRITES	CHOREGRAPHED	CHOROIDITISES	CHROMATICISMS
CHOLANGIOGRAM	CHONDRITIC	CHOREGRAPHER	CHOROLOGICAL	CHROMATICITIES
CHOLANGIOGRAMS	CHONDRITIS	CHOREGRAPHERS	CHOROLOGIES	CHROMATICITY
CHOLANGIOGRAPHY	CHONDRITISES	CHOREGRAPHIC	CHOROLOGIST	CHROMATICNESS
CHOLECALCIFEROL	CHONDROBLAST	CHOREGRAPHIES	CHOROLOGISTS	CHROMATICNESSES
CHOLECYSTECTOMY	CHONDROBLASTS	CHOREGRAPHING	CHOROPLETH	CHROMATICS
CHOLECYSTITIDES	CHONDROCRANIA	CHOREGRAPHS	CHOROPLETHS	CHROMATIDS
CHOLECYSTITIS	CHONDROCRANIUM	CHOREGRAPHY	CHORUSMASTER	CHROMATINIC
CHOLECYSTITISES	CHONDROCRANIUMS	CHOREGUSES	CHORUSMASTERS	CHROMATINS
CHOLECYSTOKININ	CHONDROCYTE	CHOREIFORM	CHORUSSING	CHROMATIST
CHOLECYSTOSTOMY	CHONDROCYTES	CHOREODRAMA	CHOUCROUTE	CHROMATISTS
CHOLECYSTOTOMY	CHONDROGENESES	CHOREODRAMAS	CHOUCROUTES	CHROMATOGRAM
CHOLECYSTS	CHONDROGENESIS	CHOREOGRAPH	CHOULTRIES	CHROMATOGRAMS
CHOLELITHIASES	CHONDROITIN	CHOREOGRAPHED	CHOUNTERED	CHROMATOGRAPH
CHOLELITHIASIS	CHONDROITINS	CHOREOGRAPHER	CHOUNTERING	CHROMATOGRAPHED
CHOLELITHS	CHONDROMAS	CHOREOGRAPHERS	CHOWDERHEAD	CHROMATOGRAPHER
CHOLERICALLY	CHONDROMATA	CHOREOGRAPHIC	CHOWDERHEADED	CHROMATOGRAPHIC
CHOLERICLY	CHONDROMATOSES	CHOREOGRAPHIES	CHOWDERHEADS	CHROMATOGRAPHS
CHOLESTASES	CHONDROMATOSIS	CHOREOGRAPHING	CHOWDERING	CHROMATOGRAPHY

CHROMATOID	CHROMOPHORIC	CHRONOLOGIES	CHRYSOPHILITES	CHURCHMANLIER
CHROMATOLOGIES	CHROMOPHOROUS	CHRONOLOGISE	CHRYSOPHYTE	CHURCHMANLIEST
CHROMATOLOGIST	CHROMOPLAST	CHRONOLOGISED	CHRYSOPHYTES	CHURCHMANLY
CHROMATOLOGISTS	CHROMOPLASTS	CHRONOLOGISES	CHRYSOPRASE	CHURCHMANSHIP
CHROMATOLOGY	CHROMOPROTEIN	CHRONOLOGISING	CHRYSOPRASES	CHURCHMANSHIPS
CHROMATOLYSES	CHROMOPROTEINS	CHRONOLOGIST	CHRYSOTILE	CHURCHPEOPLE
CHROMATOLYSIS	CHROMOSCOPE	CHRONOLOGISTS	CHRYSOTILES	CHURCHWARD
CHROMATOLYTIC	CHROMOSCOPES	CHRONOLOGIZE	CHUBBINESS	CHURCHWARDEN
CHROMATOPHORE	CHROMOSOMAL	CHRONOLOGIZED	CHUBBINESSES	CHURCHWARDENS
CHROMATOPHORES	CHROMOSOMALLY	CHRONOLOGIZES	CHUCKAWALLA	CHURCHWARDS
CHROMATOPHORIC	CHROMOSOME	CHRONOLOGIZING	CHUCKAWALLAS	CHURCHWAYS
CHROMATOPHOROUS	CHROMOSOMES	CHRONOLOGY	CHUCKHOLES	CHURCHWOMAN
CHROMATOPSIA	CHROMOSPHERE	CHRONOMETER	CHUCKLEHEAD	CHURCHWOMEN
CHROMATOPSIAS	CHROMOSPHERES	CHRONOMETERS	CHUCKLEHEADED	CHURCHYARD
CHROMATOSPHERE	CHROMOSPHERIC	CHRONOMETRIC	CHUCKLEHEADS	CHURCHYARDS
CHROMATOSPHERES	CHROMOTHERAPIES	CHRONOMETRICAL	CHUCKLESOME	CHURLISHLY
CHROMATYPE	CHROMOTHERAPY	CHRONOMETRIES	CHUCKLINGLY	CHURLISHNESS
CHROMATYPES	CHROMOTYPE	CHRONOMETRY	CHUCKLINGS	CHURLISHNESSES
CHROMIDIUM	CHROMOTYPES	CHRONOSCOPE	CHUCKWALLA	CHURNALISM
CHROMINANCE	CHROMOXYLOGRAPH	CHRONOSCOPES	CHUCKWALLAS	CHURNALISMS
CHROMINANCES	CHRONAXIES	CHRONOSCOPIC	CHUFFINESS	CHURNMILKS
CHROMISING	CHRONICALLY	CHRONOTHERAPIES	CHUFFINESSES	CHURRIGUERESCO
CHROMIZING	CHRONICITIES	CHRONOTHERAPY	CHUGALUGGED	CHURRIGUERESQUE
CHROMOCENTER	CHRONICITY	CHRONOTRON	CHUGALUGGING	CHYLACEOUS
CHROMOCENTERS	CHRONICLED	CHRONOTRONS	CHUMMINESS	CHYLIFEROUS
CHROMOCENTRE	CHRONICLER	CHRYSALIDAL	CHUMMINESSES	CHYLIFICATION
CHROMOCENTRES	CHRONICLERS	CHRYSALIDES	CHUNDERING	CHYLIFICATIONS
CHROMODYNAMICS	CHRONICLES	CHRYSALIDS	CHUNDEROUS	CHYLIFYING
CHROMOGENIC	CHRONICLING	CHRYSALISES	CHUNKINESS	CHYLOMICRON
CHROMOGENS	CHRONOBIOLOGIC	CHRYSANTHEMUM	CHUNKINESSES	CHYLOMICRONS
CHROMOGRAM	CHRONOBIOLOGIES	CHRYSANTHEMUMS	CHUNNERING	CHYMIFEROUS
CHROMOGRAMS	CHRONOBIOLOGIST	CHRYSANTHS	CHUNTERING	CHYMIFICATION
CHROMOLIES	CHRONOBIOLOGY	CHRYSAROBIN	CHUPATTIES	CHYMIFICATIONS
CHROMOMERE	CHRONOGRAM	CHRYSAROBINS	CHUPRASSIES	CHYMIFYING
CHROMOMERES	CHRONOGRAMMATIC	CHRYSOBERYL	CHURCHGOER	CHYMISTRIES
CHROMOMERIC	CHRONOGRAMS	CHRYSOBERYLS	CHURCHGOERS	CHYMOTRYPSIN
CHROMONEMA	CHRONOGRAPH	CHRYSOCOLLA	CHURCHGOING	CHYMOTRYPSINS
CHROMONEMAL	CHRONOGRAPHER	CHRYSOCOLLAS	CHURCHGOINGS	CHYMOTRYPTIC
CHROMONEMATA	CHRONOGRAPHERS	CHRYSOCRACIES	CHURCHIANITIES	CIBACHROME
CHROMONEMATIC	CHRONOGRAPHIC	CHRYSOCRACY	CHURCHIANITY	CIBACHROMES
CHROMONEMIC	CHRONOGRAPHIES	CHRYSOLITE	CHURCHIEST	CICADELLID
CHROMOPHIL	CHRONOGRAPHS	CHRYSOLITES	CHURCHINGS	CICADELLIDS
CHROMOPHILIC	CHRONOGRAPHY	CHRYSOLITIC	CHURCHISMS	CICATRICES
CHROMOPHILS	CHRONOLOGER	CHRYSOMELID	CHURCHLESS	CICATRICHULE
CHROMOPHOBE	CHRONOLOGERS	CHRYSOMELIDS	CHURCHLIER	CICATRICHULES
CHROMOPHOBES	CHRONOLOGIC	CHRYSOPHAN	CHURCHLIEST	CICATRICIAL
CHROMOPHORE	CHRONOLOGICAL	CHRYSOPHANS	CHURCHLINESS	CICATRICLE
CHROMOPHORES	CHRONOLOGICALLY	CHRYSOPHILITE	CHURCHLINESSES	CICATRICLES

CICATRICOSE	CINCHONISM	CINNARIZINE	CIRCULARLY	CIRCUMDUCTIONS
CICATRICULA	CINCHONISMS	CINNARIZINES	CIRCULARNESS	CIRCUMDUCTORY
CICATRICULAS	CINCHONIZATION	CINQUECENTIST	CIRCULARNESSES	CIRCUMDUCTS
CICATRISANT	CINCHONIZATIONS	CINQUECENTISTS	CIRCULATABLE	CIRCUMFERENCE
CICATRISATION	CINCHONIZE	CINQUECENTO	CIRCULATED	CIRCUMFERENCES
CICATRISATIONS	CINCHONIZED	CINQUECENTOS	CIRCULATES	CIRCUMFERENTIAL
CICATRISED	CINCHONIZES	CINQUEFOIL	CIRCULATING	CIRCUMFERENTOR
CICATRISER	CINCHONIZING	CINQUEFOILS	CIRCULATINGS	CIRCUMFERENTORS
CICATRISERS	CINCINNATE	CIPHERINGS	CIRCULATION	CIRCUMFLECT
CICATRISES	CINCINNUSES	CIPHERTEXT	CIRCULATIONS	CIRCUMFLECTED
CICATRISING	CINCTURING	CIPHERTEXTS	CIRCULATIVE	CIRCUMFLECTING
CICATRIXES	CINDERIEST	CIPOLLINOS	CIRCULATOR	CIRCUMFLECTS
CICATRIZANT	CINEANGIOGRAPHY	CIPROFLOXACIN	CIRCULATORS	CIRCUMFLEX
CICATRIZATION	CINEMAGOER	CIPROFLOXACINS	CIRCULATORY	CIRCUMFLEXES
CICATRIZATIONS	CINEMAGOERS	CIRCASSIAN	CIRCUMAMBAGES	CIRCUMFLEXION
CICATRIZED	CINEMATHEQUE	CIRCASSIANS	CIRCUMAMBAGIOUS	CIRCUMFLEXIONS
CICATRIZER	CINEMATHEQUES	CIRCASSIENNE	CIRCUMAMBIENCE	CIRCUMFLUENCE
CICATRIZERS	CINEMATICALLY	CIRCASSIENNES	CIRCUMAMBIENCES	CIRCUMFLUENCES
CICATRIZES	CINEMATISE	CIRCENSIAL	CIRCUMAMBIENCY	CIRCUMFLUENT
CICATRIZING	CINEMATISED	CIRCENSIAN	CIRCUMAMBIENT	CIRCUMFLUOUS
CICERONEING	CINEMATISES	CIRCINATELY	CIRCUMAMBIENTLY	CIRCUMFORANEAN
CICHORACEOUS	CINEMATISING	CIRCUITEER	CIRCUMAMBULATE	CIRCUMFORANEOUS
CICINNUSES	CINEMATIZE	CIRCUITEERED	CIRCUMAMBULATED	CIRCUMFUSE
CICISBEISM	CINEMATIZED	CIRCUITEERING	CIRCUMAMBULATES	CIRCUMFUSED
CICISBEISMS	CINEMATIZES	CIRCUITEERS	CIRCUMAMBULATOR	CIRCUMFUSES
CICLATOUNS	CINEMATIZING	CIRCUITIES	CIRCUMBENDIBUS	CIRCUMFUSILE
CICLOSPORIN	CINEMATOGRAPH	CIRCUITING	CIRCUMCENTER	CIRCUMFUSING
CICLOSPORINS	CINEMATOGRAPHED	CIRCUITOUS	CIRCUMCENTERS	CIRCUMFUSION
CIGARETTES	CINEMATOGRAPHER	CIRCUITOUSLY	CIRCUMCENTRE	CIRCUMFUSIONS
CIGARILLOS	CINEMATOGRAPHIC	CIRCUITOUSNESS	CIRCUMCENTRES	CIRCUMGYRATE
CIGUATERAS	CINEMATOGRAPHS	CIRCUITRIES	CIRCUMCIRCLE	CIRCUMGYRATED
CIGUATOXIN	CINEMATOGRAPHY	CIRCULABLE	CIRCUMCIRCLES	CIRCUMGYRATES
CIGUATOXINS	CINEMICROGRAPHY	CIRCULARISATION	CIRCUMCISE	CIRCUMGYRATING
CILIATIONS	CINEPHILES	CIRCULARISE	CIRCUMCISED	CIRCUMGYRATION
CIMETIDINE	CINEPLEXES	CIRCULARISED	CIRCUMCISER	CIRCUMGYRATIONS
CIMETIDINES	CINERARIAS	CIRCULARISER	CIRCUMCISERS	CIRCUMGYRATORY
CINCHONACEOUS	CINERARIUM	CIRCULARISERS	CIRCUMCISES	CIRCUMINCESSION
CINCHONIDINE	CINERARIUMS	CIRCULARISES	CIRCUMCISING	CIRCUMINSESSION
CINCHONIDINES	CINERATION	CIRCULARISING	CIRCUMCISION	CIRCUMJACENCIES
CINCHONINE	CINERATIONS	CIRCULARITIES	CIRCUMCISIONS	CIRCUMJACENCY
CINCHONINES	CINERATORS	CIRCULARITY	CIRCUMDUCE	CIRCUMJACENT
CINCHONINIC	CINERITIOUS	CIRCULARIZATION	CIRCUMDUCED	CIRCUMLITTORAL
CINCHONISATION	CINGULATED	CIRCULARIZE	CIRCUMDUCES	CIRCUMLOCUTE
CINCHONISATIONS	CINNABARIC	CIRCULARIZED	CIRCUMDUCING	CIRCUMLOCUTED
CINCHONISE	CINNABARINE	CIRCULARIZER	CIRCUMDUCT	CIRCUMLOCUTES
CINCHONISED	CINNAMONIC	CIRCULARIZERS	CIRCUMDUCTED	CIRCUMLOCUTING
CINCHONISES	CINNAMONIER	CIRCULARIZES	CIRCUMDUCTING	CIRCUMLOCUTION
CINCHONISING	CINNAMONIEST	CIRCULARIZING	CIRCUMDUCTION	CIRCUMLOCUTIONS

CIRCUMLOCUTORY	CIRCUMSTANCES	CITHARISTIC	CIVILISATION	CLAMJAMFRIES
CIRCUMLUNAR	CIRCUMSTANCING	CITHARISTS	CIVILISATIONAL	CLAMJAMFRY
CIRCUMMURE	CIRCUMSTANTIAL	CITIFICATION	CIVILISATIONS	CLAMJAMPHRIE
CIRCUMMURED	CIRCUMSTANTIALS	CITIFICATIONS	CIVILISERS	CLAMJAMPHRIES
CIRCUMMURES	CIRCUMSTANTIATE	CITIZENESS	CIVILISING	CLAMMINESS
CIRCUMMURING	CIRCUMSTELLAR	CITIZENESSES	CIVILITIES	CLAMMINESSES
CIRCUMNAVIGABLE	CIRCUMVALLATE	CITIZENISE	CIVILIZABLE	CLAMOROUSLY
CIRCUMNAVIGATE	CIRCUMVALLATED	CITIZENISED	CIVILIZATION	CLAMOROUSNESS
CIRCUMNAVIGATED	CIRCUMVALLATES	CITIZENISES	CIVILIZATIONAL	CLAMOROUSNESSES
CIRCUMNAVIGATES	CIRCUMVALLATING	CITIZENISING	CIVILIZATIONS	CLAMOURERS
CIRCUMNAVIGATOR	CIRCUMVALLATION	CITIZENIZE	CIVILIZERS	CLAMOURING
CIRCUMNUTATE	CIRCUMVENT	CITIZENIZED	CIVILIZING	CLAMPDOWNS
CIRCUMNUTATED	CIRCUMVENTED	CITIZENIZES	CIVILNESSES	CLAMPERING
CIRCUMNUTATES	CIRCUMVENTER	CITIZENIZING	CLABBERING	CLAMSHELLS
CIRCUMNUTATING	CIRCUMVENTERS	CITIZENLIER	CLACKBOXES	CLANDESTINE
CIRCUMNUTATION	CIRCUMVENTING	CITIZENLIEST	CLACKDISHES	CLANDESTINELY
CIRCUMNUTATIONS	CIRCUMVENTION	CITIZENRIES	CLADISTICALLY	CLANDESTINENESS
CIRCUMNUTATORY	CIRCUMVENTIONS	CITIZENSHIP	CLADISTICS	CLANDESTINITIES
CIRCUMPOLAR	CIRCUMVENTIVE	CITIZENSHIPS	CLADOCERAN	CLANDESTINITY
CIRCUMPOSE	CIRCUMVENTOR	CITRICULTURE	CLADOCERANS	CLANGBOXES
CIRCUMPOSED	CIRCUMVENTORS	CITRICULTURES	CLADOGENESES	CLANGORING
CIRCUMPOSES	CIRCUMVENTS	CITRICULTURIST	CLADOGENESIS	CLANGOROUS
CIRCUMPOSING	CIRCUMVOLUTION	CITRICULTURISTS	CLADOGENETIC	CLANGOROUSLY
CIRCUMPOSITION	CIRCUMVOLUTIONS	CITRONELLA	CLADOGRAMS	CLANGOURED
CIRCUMPOSITIONS	CIRCUMVOLUTORY	CITRONELLAL	CLADOPHYLL	CLANGOURING
CIRCUMROTATE	CIRCUMVOLVE	CITRONELLALS	CLADOPHYLLS	CLANJAMFRAY
CIRCUMROTATED	CIRCUMVOLVED	CITRONELLAS	CLADOSPORIA	CLANJAMFRAYS
CIRCUMROTATES	CIRCUMVOLVES	CITRONELLOL	CLADOSPORIUM	CLANKINGLY
CIRCUMROTATING	CIRCUMVOLVING	CITRONELLOLS	CLAIRAUDIENCE	CLANNISHLY
CIRCUMSCISSILE	CIRCUSIEST	CITRULLINE	CLAIRAUDIENCES	CLANNISHNESS
CIRCUMSCRIBABLE	CIRCUSSIER	CITRULLINES	CLAIRAUDIENT	CLANNISHNESSES
CIRCUMSCRIBE	CIRCUSSIEST	CITRUSIEST	CLAIRAUDIENTLY	CLANSWOMAN
CIRCUMSCRIBED	CIRRHIPEDE	CITRUSSIER	CLAIRAUDIENTS	CLANSWOMEN
CIRCUMSCRIBER	CIRRHIPEDES	CITRUSSIEST	CLAIRCOLLE	CLAPBOARDED
CIRCUMSCRIBERS	CIRRHOTICS	CITYFICATION	CLAIRCOLLES	CLAPBOARDING
CIRCUMSCRIBES	CIRRIGRADE	CITYFICATIONS	CLAIRSCHACH	CLAPBOARDS
CIRCUMSCRIBING	CIRRIPEDES	CITYSCAPES	CLAIRSCHACHS	CLAPBREADS
CIRCUMSCRIPTION	CIRROCUMULI	CIVILIANISATION	CLAIRVOYANCE	CLAPDISHES
CIRCUMSCRIPTIVE	CIRROCUMULUS	CIVILIANISE	CLAIRVOYANCES	CLAPOMETER
CIRCUMSOLAR	CIRROSTRATI	CIVILIANISED	CLAIRVOYANCIES	CLAPOMETERS
CIRCUMSPECT	CIRROSTRATIVE	CIVILIANISES	CLAIRVOYANCY	CLAPPERBOARD
CIRCUMSPECTION	CIRROSTRATUS	CIVILIANISING	CLAIRVOYANT	CLAPPERBOARDS
CIRCUMSPECTIONS	CISGENDERED	CIVILIANIZATION	CLAIRVOYANTLY	CLAPPERBOY
CIRCUMSPECTIVE	CISMONTANE	CIVILIANIZE	CLAIRVOYANTS	CLAPPERBOYS
CIRCUMSPECTLY	CISPLATINS	CIVILIANIZED	CLAMANCIES	CLAPPERCLAW
CIRCUMSPECTNESS	CISPONTINE	CIVILIANIZES	CLAMATORIAL	CLAPPERCLAWED
CIRCUMSTANCE	CISTACEOUS	CIVILIANIZING	CLAMBERERS	CLAPPERCLAWER
CIRCUMSTANCED	CITATIONAL	CIVILISABLE	CLAMBERING	CLAPPERCLAWERS

CLAPPERCLAWING	CLASSIFIABLE	CLAVICULATE	CLEISTOGAMOUS	CLEVERNESSES
CLAPPERCLAWS	CLASSIFICATION	CLAVICYTHERIA	CLEISTOGAMOUSLY	CLIANTHUSES
CLAPPERING	CLASSIFICATIONS	CLAVICYTHERIUM	CLEISTOGAMY	CLICKBAITS
CLAPPERINGS	CLASSIFICATORY	CLAVIERIST	CLEMATISES	CLICKETING
CLAPTRAPPERIES	CLASSIFIED	CLAVIERISTIC	CLEMENCIES	CLICKJACKING
CLAPTRAPPERY	CLASSIFIEDS	CLAVIERISTS	CLEMENTINE	CLICKJACKINGS
CLARABELLA	CLASSIFIER	CLAVIGEROUS	CLEMENTINES	CLICKSTREAM
CLARABELLAS	CLASSIFIERS	CLAWHAMMER	CLENBUTEROL	CLICKSTREAMS
CLARENDONS	CLASSIFIES	CLAWHAMMERS	CLENBUTEROLS	CLICKTIVISM
CLARIBELLA	CLASSIFYING	CLAYMATION	CLEOPATRAS	CLICKTIVISMS
CLARIBELLAS	CLASSINESS	CLAYMATIONS	CLEPSYDRAE	CLICKWRAPS
CLARICHORD	CLASSINESSES	CLAYSTONES	CLEPSYDRAS	CLIENTAGES
CLARICHORDS	CLASSLESSNESS	CLAYTONIAS	CLEPTOCRACIES	CLIENTELES
CLARIFICATION	CLASSLESSNESSES	CLEANABILITIES	CLEPTOCRACY	CLIENTLESS
CLARIFICATIONS	CLASSMATES	CLEANABILITY	CLEPTOMANIA	CLIENTSHIP
CLARIFIERS	CLASSROOMS	CLEANHANDED	CLEPTOMANIAC	CLIENTSHIPS
CLARIFYING	CLASSWORKS	CLEANLIEST	CLEPTOMANIACS	CLIFFHANGER
CLARINETIST	CLATHRATES	CLEANLINESS	CLEPTOMANIAS	CLIFFHANGERS
CLARINETISTS	CLATTERERS	CLEANLINESSES	CLERESTORIED	CLIFFHANGING
CLARINETTIST	CLATTERIER	CLEANNESSES	CLERESTORIES	CLIFFHANGINGS
CLARINETTISTS	CLATTERIEST	CLEANSABLE	CLERESTORY	CLIFFHANGS
CLARIONETS	CLATTERING	CLEANSINGS	CLERGIABLE	CLIFFSIDES
CLARIONING	CLATTERINGLY	CLEANSKINS	CLERGYABLE	CLIMACTERIC
CLARTHEADS	CLAUCHTING	CLEANTECHS	CLERGYWOMAN	CLIMACTERICAL
CLASHINGLY	CLAUDICATION	CLEARANCES	CLERGYWOMEN	CLIMACTERICALLY
CLASSICALISM	CLAUDICATIONS	CLEARCOLED	CLERICALISM	CLIMACTERICS
CLASSICALISMS	CLAUGHTING	CLEARCOLES	CLERICALISMS	CLIMACTICAL
CLASSICALIST	CLAUSTRATION	CLEARCOLING	CLERICALIST	CLIMACTICALLY
CLASSICALISTS	CLAUSTRATIONS	CLEARCUTTING	CLERICALISTS	CLIMATICAL
CLASSICALITIES	CLAUSTROPHILIA	CLEARCUTTINGS	CLERICALLY	CLIMATICALLY
CLASSICALITY	CLAUSTROPHILIAS	CLEARHEADED	CLERICATES	CLIMATISED
CLASSICALLY	CLAUSTROPHOBE	CLEARHEADEDLY	CLERICITIES	CLIMATISES
CLASSICALNESS	CLAUSTROPHOBES	CLEARHEADEDNESS	CLERKESSES	CLIMATISING
CLASSICALNESSES	CLAUSTROPHOBIA	CLEARINGHOUSE	CLERKLIEST	CLIMATIZED
CLASSICALS	CLAUSTROPHOBIAS	CLEARINGHOUSES	CLERKLINESS	CLIMATIZES
CLASSICISE	CLAUSTROPHOBIC	CLEARNESSES	CLERKLINESSES	CLIMATIZING
CLASSICISED	CLAVATIONS	CLEARSKINS	CLERKLINGS	CLIMATOGRAPHIES
CLASSICISES	CLAVECINIST	CLEARSTORIED	CLERKSHIPS	CLIMATOGRAPHY
CLASSICISING	CLAVECINISTS	CLEARSTORIES	CLEROMANCIES	CLIMATOLOGIC
CLASSICISM	CLAVICEMBALO	CLEARSTORY	CLEROMANCY	CLIMATOLOGICAL
CLASSICISMS	CLAVICEMBALOS	CLEARWEEDS	CLERUCHIAL	CLIMATOLOGIES
CLASSICIST	CLAVICHORD	CLEARWINGS	CLERUCHIAS	CLIMATOLOGIST
CLASSICISTIC	CLAVICHORDIST	CLEAVABILITIES	CLERUCHIES	CLIMATOLOGISTS
CLASSICISTS	CLAVICHORDISTS	CLEAVABILITY	CLEVERALITIES	CLIMATOLOGY
CLASSICIZE	CLAVICHORDS	CLEAVABLENESS	CLEVERALITY	CLIMATURES
CLASSICIZED	CLAVICORNS	CLEAVABLENESSES	CLEVERDICK	CLIMAXLESS
CLASSICIZES	CLAVICULAE	CLEISTOGAMIC	CLEVERDICKS	CLIMBDOWNS
CLASSICIZING	CLAVICULAR	CLEISTOGAMIES	CLEVERNESS	CLINANDRIA

CLINANDRIUM	CLIPSHEETS	CLOISTERING	CLOUDTOWNS	CNIDOBLASTS
CLINCHINGLY	CLIQUINESS	CLOISTRESS	CLOVERGRASS	COACERVATE
CLINDAMYCIN	CLIQUINESSES	CLOISTRESSES	CLOVERGRASSES	COACERVATED
CLINDAMYCINS	CLIQUISHLY	CLOMIPHENE	CLOVERIEST	COACERVATES
CLINGFILMS	CLIQUISHNESS	CLOMIPHENES	CLOVERLEAF	COACERVATING
CLINGFISHES	CLIQUISHNESSES	CLONAZEPAM	CLOVERLEAFS	COACERVATION
CLINGINESS	CLISHMACLAVER	CLONAZEPAMS	CLOVERLEAVES	COACERVATIONS
CLINGINESSES	CLISHMACLAVERS	CLONICITIES	CLOVERLIKE	COACHBUILDER
CLINGINGLY	CLISTOGAMIES	CLONIDINES	CLOWNERIES	COACHBUILDERS
CLINGINGNESS	CLISTOGAMY	CLOSEDOWNS	CLOWNFISHES	COACHBUILDING
CLINGINGNESSES	CLITICISED	CLOSEFISTED	CLOWNISHLY	COACHBUILDINGS
CLINGSTONE	CLITICISES	CLOSEHEADS	CLOWNISHNESS	COACHBUILT
CLINGSTONES	CLITICISING	CLOSEMOUTHED	CLOWNISHNESSES	COACHLINES
CLINGWRAPS	CLITICIZED	CLOSENESSES	CLOXACILLIN	COACHLOADS
CLINICALLY	CLITICIZES	CLOSESTOOL	CLOXACILLINS	COACHROOFS
CLINICALNESS	CLITICIZING	CLOSESTOOLS	CLOZAPINES	COACHWHIPS
CLINICALNESSES	CLITORECTOMIES	CLOSETFULS	CLUBABILITIES	COACHWOODS
CLINICIANS	CLITORECTOMY	CLOSTRIDIA	CLUBABILITY	COACHWORKS
CLINKERING	CLITORIDECTOMY	CLOSTRIDIAL	CLUBBABILITIES	COACTIVELY
CLINKSTONE	CLITORIDES	CLOSTRIDIAN	CLUBBABILITY	COACTIVITIES
CLINKSTONES	CLITORISES	CLOSTRIDIUM	CLUBBINESS	COACTIVITY
CLINOCHLORE	CLITTERING	CLOSTRIDIUMS	CLUBBINESSES	COADAPTATION
CLINOCHLORES	CLOACALINE	CLOTHBOUND	CLUBFOOTED	COADAPTATIONS
CLINODIAGONAL	CLOACITISES	CLOTHESHORSE	CLUBHAULED	COADJACENCIES
CLINODIAGONALS	CLOAKROOMS	CLOTHESHORSES	CLUBHAULING	COADJACENCY
CLINOMETER	CLOBBERING	CLOTHESLINE	CLUBHOUSES	COADJACENT
CLINOMETERS	CLOCKFACES	CLOTHESLINED	CLUBMANSHIP	COADJACENTS
CLINOMETRIC	CLOCKMAKER	CLOTHESLINES	CLUBMANSHIPS	COADJUTANT
CLINOMETRICAL	CLOCKMAKERS	CLOTHESLINING	CLUBMASTER	COADJUTANTS
CLINOMETRIES	CLOCKWORKS	CLOTHESPIN	CLUBMASTERS	COADJUTORS
CLINOMETRY	CLODDISHLY	CLOTHESPINS	CLUBMOSSES	COADJUTORSHIP
CLINOPINACOID	CLODDISHNESS	CLOTHESPRESS	CLUBRUSHES	COADJUTORSHIPS
CLINOPINACOIDS	CLODDISHNESSES	CLOTHESPRESSES	CLUMPERING	COADJUTRESS
CLINOPINAKOID	CLODHOPPER	CLOTTERING	CLUMPINESS	COADJUTRESSES
CLINOPINAKOIDS	CLODHOPPERS	CLOTTINESS	CLUMPINESSES	COADJUTRICES
CLINOPYROXENE	CLODHOPPING	CLOTTINESSES	CLUMSINESS	COADJUTRIX
CLINOPYROXENES	CLOFIBRATE	CLOUDBERRIES	CLUMSINESSES	COADJUTRIXES
CLINOSTATS	CLOFIBRATES	CLOUDBERRY	CLUSTERIER	COADMIRING
CLINQUANTS	CLOGDANCES	CLOUDBURST	CLUSTERIEST	COADMITTED
CLINTONIAS	CLOGGINESS	CLOUDBURSTS	CLUSTERING	COADMITTING
CLIOMETRIC	CLOGGINESSES	CLOUDINESS	CLUSTERINGLY	COADUNATED
CLIOMETRICAL	CLOGMAKERS	CLOUDINESSES	CLUTCHIEST	COADUNATES
CLIOMETRICIAN	CLOISONNAGE	CLOUDLANDS	CLUTTERIER	COADUNATING
CLIOMETRICIANS	CLOISONNAGES	CLOUDLESSLY	CLUTTERIEST	COADUNATION
CLIOMETRICS	CLOISONNES	CLOUDLESSNESS	CLUTTERING	COADUNATIONS
CLIOMETRIES	CLOISTERED	CLOUDLESSNESSES	CLYPEIFORM	COADUNATIVE
CLIPBOARDS	CLOISTERER	CLOUDSCAPE	CNIDARIANS	COAGENCIES
CLIPSHEARS	CLOISTERERS	CLOUDSCAPES	CNIDOBLAST	COAGULABILITIES

COAGULABILITY	COARSENING	COCAINISMS	COCKAMAMIER	COCKSINESS
COAGULABLE	COASSISTED	COCAINISTS	COCKAMAMIEST	COCKSINESSES
COAGULANTS	COASSISTING	COCAINIZATION	COCKATEELS	COCKSUCKER
COAGULASES	COASSUMING	COCAINIZATIONS	COCKATIELS	COCKSUCKERS
COAGULATED	COASTEERING	COCAINIZED	COCKATRICE	COCKSURELY
COAGULATES	COASTEERINGS	COCAINIZES	COCKATRICES	COCKSURENESS
COAGULATING	COASTGUARD	COCAINIZING	COCKBILLED	COCKSURENESSES
COAGULATION	COASTGUARDMAN	COCAPTAINED	COCKBILLING	COCKSWAINED
COAGULATIONS	COASTGUARDMEN	COCAPTAINING	COCKCHAFER	COCKSWAINING
COAGULATIVE	COASTGUARDS	COCAPTAINS	COCKCHAFERS	COCKSWAINS
COAGULATOR	COASTGUARDSMAN	COCARBOXYLASE	COCKCROWING	COCKTAILED
COAGULATORS	COASTGUARDSMEN	COCARBOXYLASES	COCKCROWINGS	COCKTAILING
COAGULATORY	COASTLANDS	COCARCINOGEN	COCKERNONIES	COCKTEASER
COALESCENCE	COASTLINES	COCARCINOGENIC	COCKERNONY	COCKTEASERS
COALESCENCES	COASTWARDS	COCARCINOGENS	COCKEYEDLY	COCKTHROWING
COALESCENT	COATDRESSES	COCATALYST	COCKEYEDNESS	COCKTHROWINGS
COALESCING	COATIMUNDI	COCATALYSTS	COCKEYEDNESSES	COCKYLEEKIES
COALFIELDS	COATIMUNDIS	COCCIDIANS	COCKFIGHTING	COCKYLEEKY
COALFISHES	COATSTANDS	COCCIDIOSES	COCKFIGHTINGS	COCOMPOSER
COALHOUSES	COATTENDED	COCCIDIOSIS	COCKFIGHTS	COCOMPOSERS
COALIFICATION	COATTENDING	COCCIDIOSTAT	COCKHORSES	COCONSCIOUS
COALIFICATIONS	COATTESTED	COCCIDIOSTATS	COCKIELEEKIE	COCONSCIOUSES
COALIFYING	COATTESTING	COCCIFEROUS	COCKIELEEKIES	COCONSCIOUSNESS
COALITIONAL	COAUTHORED	COCCINEOUS	COCKINESSES	COCONSPIRATOR
COALITIONER	COAUTHORING	COCCOLITES	COCKLEBOAT	COCONSPIRATORS
COALITIONERS	COAUTHORSHIP	COCCOLITHS	COCKLEBOATS	COCONUTTIER
COALITIONISM	COAUTHORSHIPS	COCHAIRING	COCKLEBURS	COCONUTTIEST
COALITIONISMS	COBALAMINS	COCHAIRMAN	COCKLEERTS	COCOONERIES
COALITIONIST	COBALTIFEROUS	COCHAIRMANSHIP	COCKLESHELL	COCOONINGS
COALITIONISTS	COBALTINES	COCHAIRMANSHIPS	COCKLESHELLS	COCOUNSELED
COALITIONS	COBALTITES	COCHAIRMEN	COCKMATCHES	COCOUNSELING
COALMASTER	COBBLERIES	COCHAIRPERSON	COCKNEYDOM	COCOUNSELLED
COALMASTERS	COBBLESTONE	COCHAIRPERSONS	COCKNEYDOMS	COCOUNSELLING
COALMINERS	COBBLESTONED	COCHAIRWOMAN	COCKNEYFICATION	COCOUNSELS
COANCHORED	COBBLESTONES	COCHAIRWOMEN	COCKNEYFIED	COCOZELLES
COANCHORING	COBBLESTONING	COCHAMPION	COCKNEYFIES	COCREATING
COANNEXING	COBELLIGERENT	COCHAMPIONS	COCKNEYFYING	COCREATORS
COAPPEARED	COBELLIGERENTS	COCHINEALS	COCKNEYISH	COCULTIVATE
COAPPEARING	COBWEBBERIES	COCHLEARES	COCKNEYISM	COCULTIVATED
COAPTATION	COBWEBBERY	COCHLEARIFORM	COCKNEYISMS	COCULTIVATES
COAPTATIONS	COBWEBBIER	COCHLEATED	COCKNIFICATION	COCULTIVATING
COARCTATED	COBWEBBIEST	COCKABULLIES	COCKNIFICATIONS	COCULTIVATION
COARCTATES	COBWEBBING	COCKABULLY	COCKNIFIED	COCULTIVATIONS
COARCTATING	COCAINISATION	COCKALEEKIE	COCKNIFIES	COCULTURED
COARCTATION	COCAINISATIONS	COCKALEEKIES	COCKNIFYING	COCULTURES
COARCTATIONS	COCAINISED	COCKALORUM	COCKROACHES	COCULTURING
COARSENESS	COCAINISES	COCKALORUMS	COCKSCOMBS	COCURATING
COARSENESSES	COCAINISING	COCKAMAMIE	COCKSFOOTS	COCURATORS

COCURRICULAR	CODOMINANTS	COENENCHYMES	COEVOLVING	COGNATENESS
COCUSWOODS	CODSWALLOP	COENESTHESES	COEXECUTOR	COGNATENESSES
CODEBREAKER	CODSWALLOPS	COENESTHESIA	COEXECUTORS	COGNATIONS
CODEBREAKERS	COECILIANS	COENESTHESIAS	COEXECUTRICES	COGNISABLE
CODECLINATION	COEDUCATION	COENESTHESIS	COEXECUTRIX	COGNISABLY
CODECLINATIONS	COEDUCATIONAL	COENESTHETIC	COEXECUTRIXES	COGNISANCE
CODEFENDANT	COEDUCATIONALLY	COENOBITES	COEXERTING	COGNISANCES
CODEFENDANTS	COEDUCATIONS	COENOBITIC	COEXISTENCE	COGNITIONAL
CODEPENDENCE	COEFFICIENT	COENOBITICAL	COEXISTENCES	COGNITIONS
CODEPENDENCES	COEFFICIENTS	COENOBITISM	COEXISTENT	COGNITIVELY
CODEPENDENCIES	COELACANTH	COENOBITISMS	COEXISTING	COGNITIVISM
CODEPENDENCY	COELACANTHIC	COENOCYTES	COEXTENDED	COGNITIVISMS
CODEPENDENT	COELACANTHS	COENOCYTIC	COEXTENDING	COGNITIVITIES
CODEPENDENTS	COELANAGLYPHIC	COENOSARCS	COEXTENSION	COGNITIVITY
CODERIVING	COELENTERA	COENOSPECIES	COEXTENSIONS	COGNIZABLE
CODESIGNED	COELENTERATE	COENOSTEUM	COEXTENSIVE	COGNIZABLY
CODESIGNING	COELENTERATES	COENOSTEUMS	COEXTENSIVELY	COGNIZANCE
CODETERMINATION	COELENTERIC	COENZYMATIC	COFAVORITE	COGNIZANCES
CODEVELOPED	COELENTERON	COENZYMATICALLY	COFAVORITES	COGNOMINAL
CODEVELOPER	COELENTERONS	COEQUALITIES	COFEATURED	COGNOMINALLY
CODEVELOPERS	COELIOSCOPIES	COEQUALITY	COFEATURES	COGNOMINATE
CODEVELOPING	COELIOSCOPY	COEQUALNESS	COFEATURING	COGNOMINATED
CODEVELOPS	COELOMATES	COEQUALNESSES	COFFEEHOUSE	COGNOMINATES
CODICILLARY	COELOMATIC	COEQUATING	COFFEEHOUSES	COGNOMINATING
CODICOLOGICAL	COELOSTATS	COERCIMETER	COFFEEMAKER	COGNOMINATION
CODICOLOGIES	COELUROSAUR	COERCIMETERS	COFFEEMAKERS	COGNOMINATIONS
CODICOLOGY	COELUROSAURS	COERCIONIST	COFFEEPOTS	COGNOSCENTE
CODIFIABILITIES	COEMBODIED	COERCIONISTS	COFFERDAMS	COGNOSCENTI
CODIFIABILITY	COEMBODIES	COERCIVELY	COFFINITES	COGNOSCIBLE
CODIFIABLE	COEMBODYING	COERCIVENESS	COFINANCED	COGNOSCING
CODIFICATION	COEMPLOYED	COERCIVENESSES	COFINANCES	COHABITANT
CODIFICATIONS	COEMPLOYING	COERCIVITIES	COFINANCING	COHABITANTS
CODIRECTED	COEMPTIONS	COERCIVITY	COFOUNDERS	COHABITATION
CODIRECTING	COENACTING	COERECTING	COFOUNDING	COHABITATIONS
CODIRECTION	COENAESTHESES	COESSENTIAL	COFUNCTION	COHABITEES
CODIRECTIONS	COENAESTHESIA	COESSENTIALITY	COFUNCTIONS	COHABITERS
CODIRECTOR	COENAESTHESIAS	COESSENTIALLY	COGENERATION	COHABITING
CODIRECTORS	COENAESTHESIS	COESSENTIALNESS	COGENERATIONS	COHABITORS
CODISCOVER	COENAMORED	COETANEOUS	COGENERATOR	COHEIRESSES
CODISCOVERED	COENAMORING	COETANEOUSLY	COGENERATORS	COHERENCES
CODISCOVERER	COENAMOURED	COETANEOUSNESS	COGITATING	COHERENCIES
CODISCOVERERS	COENAMOURING	COETERNALLY	COGITATINGLY	COHERENTLY
CODISCOVERING	COENAMOURS	COETERNITIES	COGITATION	COHERITORS
CODISCOVERS	COENDURING	COETERNITY	COGITATIONS	COHESIBILITIES
CODOLOGIES	COENENCHYMA	COEVALITIES	COGITATIVE	COHESIBILITY
CODOMINANCE	COENENCHYMAS	COEVOLUTION	COGITATIVELY	COHESIONLESS
CODOMINANCES	COENENCHYMATA	COEVOLUTIONARY	COGITATIVENESS	COHESIVELY
CODOMINANT	COENENCHYME	COEVOLUTIONS	COGITATORS	COHESIVENESS

COHESIVENESSES	COINTREAUS	COLICKIEST	COLLATERALS	COLLEGIANER
COHIBITING	COINVENTED	COLICROOTS	COLLATIONS	COLLEGIANERS
COHIBITION	COINVENTING	COLICWEEDS	COLLEAGUED	COLLEGIANS
COHIBITIONS	COINVENTOR	COLINEARITIES	COLLEAGUES	COLLEGIATE
COHIBITIVE	COINVENTORS	COLINEARITY	COLLEAGUESHIP	COLLEGIATELY
COHOBATING	COINVESTED	COLIPHAGES	COLLEAGUESHIPS	COLLEGIATES
COHOMOLOGICAL	COINVESTIGATOR	COLLABORATE	COLLEAGUING	COLLEGIUMS
COHOMOLOGIES	COINVESTIGATORS	COLLABORATED	COLLECTABLE	COLLEMBOLAN
COHOMOLOGY	COINVESTING	COLLABORATES	COLLECTABLES	COLLEMBOLANS
COHORTATIVE	COINVESTOR	COLLABORATING	COLLECTANEA	COLLEMBOLOUS
COHORTATIVES	COINVESTORS	COLLABORATION	COLLECTEDLY	COLLENCHYMA
COHOSTESSED	COKULORISES	COLLABORATIONS	COLLECTEDNESS	COLLENCHYMAS
COHOSTESSES	COLATITUDE	COLLABORATIVE	COLLECTEDNESSES	COLLENCHYMATA
COHOSTESSING	COLATITUDES	COLLABORATIVELY	COLLECTIBLE	COLLENCHYMATOUS
COHOUSINGS	COLCANNONS	COLLABORATIVES	COLLECTIBLES	COLLETERIAL
COHYPONYMS	COLCHICINE	COLLABORATOR	COLLECTING	COLLICULUS
COIFFEUSES	COLCHICINES	COLLABORATORS	COLLECTINGS	COLLIERIES
COIFFURING	COLCHICUMS	COLLAGENASE	COLLECTION	COLLIESHANGIE
COILABILITIES	COLCOTHARS	COLLAGENASES	COLLECTIONS	COLLIESHANGIES
COILABILITY	COLDBLOODS	COLLAGENIC	COLLECTIVE	COLLIGATED
COINCIDENCE	COLDCOCKED	COLLAGENOUS	COLLECTIVELY	COLLIGATES
COINCIDENCES	COLDCOCKING	COLLAGISTS	COLLECTIVENESS	COLLIGATING
COINCIDENCIES	COLDHEARTED	COLLAPSABILITY	COLLECTIVES	COLLIGATION
COINCIDENCY	COLDHEARTEDLY	COLLAPSABLE	COLLECTIVISE	COLLIGATIONS
COINCIDENT	COLDHEARTEDNESS	COLLAPSARS	COLLECTIVISED	COLLIGATIVE
COINCIDENTAL	COLDHOUSES	COLLAPSIBILITY	COLLECTIVISES	COLLIMATED
COINCIDENTALLY	COLDNESSES	COLLAPSIBLE	COLLECTIVISING	COLLIMATES
COINCIDENTLY	COLECTOMIES	COLLAPSING	COLLECTIVISM	COLLIMATING
COINCIDING	COLEMANITE	COLLARBONE	COLLECTIVISMS	COLLIMATION
COINFECTED	COLEMANITES	COLLARBONES	COLLECTIVIST	COLLIMATIONS
COINFECTING	COLEOPTERA	COLLARETTE	COLLECTIVISTIC	COLLIMATOR
COINFERRED	COLEOPTERAL	COLLARETTES	COLLECTIVISTS	COLLIMATORS
COINFERRING	COLEOPTERAN	COLLARLESS	COLLECTIVITIES	COLLINEARITIES
COINHERENCE	COLEOPTERANS	COLLARSTUD	COLLECTIVITY	COLLINEARITY
COINHERENCES	COLEOPTERIST	COLLARSTUDS	COLLECTIVIZE	COLLINEARLY
COINHERING	COLEOPTERISTS	COLLATABLE	COLLECTIVIZED	COLLINSIAS
COINHERITANCE	COLEOPTERON	COLLATERAL	COLLECTIVIZES	COLLIQUABLE
COINHERITANCES	COLEOPTERONS	COLLATERALISE	COLLECTIVIZING	COLLIQUANT
COINHERITOR	COLEOPTEROUS	COLLATERALISED	COLLECTORATE	COLLIQUATE
COINHERITORS	COLEOPTERS	COLLATERALISES	COLLECTORATES	COLLIQUATED
COINSTANTANEITY	COLEOPTILE	COLLATERALISING	COLLECTORS	COLLIQUATES
COINSTANTANEOUS	COLEOPTILES	COLLATERALITIES	COLLECTORSHIP	COLLIQUATING
COINSURANCE	COLEORHIZA	COLLATERALITY	COLLECTORSHIPS	COLLIQUATION
COINSURANCES	COLEORHIZAE	COLLATERALIZE	COLLEGIALISM	COLLIQUATIONS
COINSURERS	COLEORRHIZA	COLLATERALIZED	COLLEGIALISMS	COLLIQUATIVE
COINSURING	COLEORRHIZAE	COLLATERALIZES	COLLEGIALITIES	COLLIQUESCENCE
COINTERRED	COLESTIPOL	COLLATERALIZING	COLLEGIALITY	COLLIQUESCENCES
COINTERRING	COLESTIPOLS	COLLATERALLY	COLLEGIALLY	COLLISIONAL

COLLISIONALLY	COLLUSIONS	COLONOSCOPES	COLORPOINTS	COLOURIZER
COLLISIONS	COLLUSIVELY	COLONOSCOPIES	COLORWASHED	COLOURIZERS
COLLOCATED	COLLUVIUMS	COLONOSCOPY	COLORWASHES	COLOURIZES
COLLOCATES	COLLYRIUMS	COLOPHONIES	COLORWASHING	COLOURIZING
COLLOCATING	COLLYWOBBLES	COLOQUINTIDA	COLOSSALLY	COLOURLESS
COLLOCATION	COLOBOMATA	COLOQUINTIDAS	COLOSSEUMS	COLOURLESSLY
COLLOCATIONAL	COLOCATING	COLORABILITIES	COLOSSUSES	COLOURLESSNESS
COLLOCATIONS	COLOCYNTHS	COLORABILITY	COLOSTOMIES	COLOURPOINT
COLLOCUTOR	COLOGARITHM	COLORABLENESS	COLOSTROUS	COLOURPOINTS
COLLOCUTORS	COLOGARITHMS	COLORABLENESSES	COLOSTRUMS	COLOURWASH
COLLOCUTORY	COLOMBARDS	COLORATION	COLOTOMIES	COLOURWASHED
COLLODIONS	COLONELCIES	COLORATIONS	COLOURABILITIES	COLOURWASHES
COLLODIUMS	COLONELLING	COLORATURA	COLOURABILITY	COLOURWASHING
COLLOGUING	COLONELLINGS	COLORATURAS	COLOURABLE	COLOURWAYS
COLLOIDALITIES	COLONELSHIP	COLORATURE	COLOURABLENESS	COLPITISES
COLLOIDALITY	COLONELSHIPS	COLORATURES	COLOURABLY	COLPORTAGE
COLLOIDALLY	COLONIALISE	COLORBREED	COLOURANTS	COLPORTAGES
COLLOQUIAL	COLONIALISED	COLORBREEDING	COLOURATION	COLPORTEUR
COLLOQUIALISM	COLONIALISES	COLORBREEDS	COLOURATIONS	COLPORTEURS
COLLOQUIALISMS	COLONIALISING	COLORCASTED	COLOURBRED	COLPOSCOPE
COLLOQUIALIST	COLONIALISM	COLORCASTING	COLOURBREED	COLPOSCOPES
COLLOQUIALISTS	COLONIALISMS	COLORCASTS	COLOURBREEDING	COLPOSCOPICAL
COLLOQUIALITIES	COLONIALIST	COLORECTAL	COLOURBREEDS	COLPOSCOPICALLY
COLLOQUIALITY	COLONIALISTIC	COLORFASTNESS	COLOURCAST	COLPOSCOPIES
COLLOQUIALLY	COLONIALISTS	COLORFASTNESSES	COLOURCASTED	COLPOSCOPY
COLLOQUIALNESS	COLONIALIZE	COLORFULLY	COLOURCASTING	COLPOTOMIES
COLLOQUIALS	COLONIALIZED	COLORFULNESS	COLOURCASTS	COLTISHNESS
COLLOQUIED	COLONIALIZES	COLORFULNESSES	COLOURFAST	COLTISHNESSES
COLLOQUIES	COLONIALIZING	COLORIMETER	COLOURFASTNESS	COLTSFOOTS
COLLOQUING	COLONIALLY	COLORIMETERS	COLOURFULLY	COLUBRIADS
COLLOQUISE	COLONIALNESS	COLORIMETRIC	COLOURFULNESS	COLUBRIFORM
COLLOQUISED	COLONIALNESSES	COLORIMETRICAL	COLOURFULNESSES	COLUMBARIA
COLLOQUISES	COLONISABLE	COLORIMETRIES	COLOURIEST	COLUMBARIES
COLLOQUISING	COLONISATION	COLORIMETRY	COLOURINGS	COLUMBARIUM
COLLOQUIST	COLONISATIONIST	COLORISATION	COLOURISATION	COLUMBATES
COLLOQUISTS	COLONISATIONS	COLORISATIONS	COLOURISATIONS	COLUMBINES
COLLOQUIUM	COLONISERS	COLORISERS	COLOURISED	COLUMBITES
COLLOQUIUMS	COLONISING	COLORISING	COLOURISER	COLUMBIUMS
COLLOQUIZE	COLONITISES	COLORISTIC	COLOURISERS	COLUMELLAE
COLLOQUIZED	COLONIZABLE	COLORISTICALLY	COLOURISES	COLUMELLAR
COLLOQUIZES	COLONIZATION	COLORIZATION	COLOURISING	COLUMNARITIES
COLLOQUIZING	COLONIZATIONIST	COLORIZATIONS	COLOURISMS	COLUMNARITY
COLLOQUYING	COLONIZATIONS	COLORIZERS	COLOURISTIC	COLUMNATED
COLLOTYPES	COLONIZERS	COLORIZING	COLOURISTICALLY	COLUMNIATED
COLLOTYPIC	COLONIZING	COLORLESSLY	COLOURISTS	COLUMNIATION
COLLOTYPIES	COLONNADED	COLORLESSNESS	COLOURIZATION	COLUMNIATIONS
COLLUCTATION	COLONNADES	COLORLESSNESSES	COLOURIZATIONS	COLUMNISTIC
COLLUCTATIONS	COLONOSCOPE	COLORPOINT	COLOURIZED	COLUMNISTS

COMANAGEMENT	COMELINESS	COMMANDOES	COMMENTARIAT	COMMINUTED
COMANAGEMENTS	COMELINESSES	COMMEASURABLE	COMMENTARIATS	COMMINUTES
COMANAGERS	COMESTIBLE	COMMEASURE	COMMENTARIES	COMMINUTING
COMANAGING	COMESTIBLES	COMMEASURED	COMMENTARY	COMMINUTION
COMANCHERO	COMETOGRAPHIES	COMMEASURES	COMMENTATE	COMMINUTIONS
COMANCHEROS	COMETOGRAPHY	COMMEASURING	COMMENTATED	COMMISERABLE
COMATOSELY	COMETOLOGIES	COMMEMORABLE	COMMENTATES	COMMISERATE
COMATULIDS	COMETOLOGY	COMMEMORATE	COMMENTATING	COMMISERATED
COMBATABLE	COMEUPPANCE	COMMEMORATED	COMMENTATION	COMMISERATES
COMBATANTS	COMEUPPANCES	COMMEMORATES	COMMENTATIONS	COMMISERATING
COMBATIVELY	COMFINESSES	COMMEMORATING	COMMENTATOR	COMMISERATINGLY
COMBATIVENESS	COMFITURES	COMMEMORATION	COMMENTATORIAL	COMMISERATION
COMBATIVENESSES	COMFORTABLE	COMMEMORATIONAL	COMMENTATORS	COMMISERATIONS
COMBATTING	COMFORTABLENESS	COMMEMORATIONS	COMMENTERS	COMMISERATIVE
COMBINABILITIES	COMFORTABLY	COMMEMORATIVE	COMMENTING	COMMISERATIVELY
COMBINABILITY	COMFORTERS	COMMEMORATIVELY	COMMENTORS	COMMISERATOR
COMBINABLE	COMFORTING	COMMEMORATIVES	COMMERCIAL	COMMISERATORS
COMBINATION	COMFORTINGLY	COMMEMORATOR	COMMERCIALESE	COMMISSAIRE
COMBINATIONAL	COMFORTLESS	COMMEMORATORS	COMMERCIALESES	COMMISSAIRES
COMBINATIONS	COMFORTLESSLY	COMMEMORATORY	COMMERCIALISE	COMMISSARIAL
COMBINATIVE	COMFORTLESSNESS	COMMENCEMENT	COMMERCIALISED	COMMISSARIAT
COMBINATORIAL	COMICALITIES	COMMENCEMENTS	COMMERCIALISES	COMMISSARIATS
COMBINATORIALLY	COMICALITY	COMMENCERS	COMMERCIALISING	COMMISSARIES
COMBINATORICS	COMICALNESS	COMMENCING	COMMERCIALISM	COMMISSARS
COMBINATORY	COMICALNESSES	COMMENDABLE	COMMERCIALISMS	COMMISSARY
COMBININGS	COMINGLING	COMMENDABLENESS	COMMERCIALIST	COMMISSARYSHIP
COMBRETUMS	COMITADJIS	COMMENDABLY	COMMERCIALISTIC	COMMISSARYSHIPS
COMBURGESS	COMITATIVE	COMMENDAMS	COMMERCIALISTS	COMMISSION
COMBURGESSES	COMITATIVES	COMMENDATION	COMMERCIALITIES	COMMISSIONAIRE
COMBUSTIBILITY	COMITATUSES	COMMENDATIONS	COMMERCIALITY	COMMISSIONAIRES
COMBUSTIBLE	COMMANDABLE	COMMENDATOR	COMMERCIALIZE	COMMISSIONAL
COMBUSTIBLENESS	COMMANDANT	COMMENDATORS	COMMERCIALIZED	COMMISSIONARY
COMBUSTIBLES	COMMANDANTS	COMMENDATORY	COMMERCIALIZES	COMMISSIONED
COMBUSTIBLY	COMMANDANTSHIP	COMMENDERS	COMMERCIALIZING	COMMISSIONER
COMBUSTING	COMMANDANTSHIPS	COMMENDING	COMMERCIALLY	COMMISSIONERS
COMBUSTION	COMMANDEER	COMMENSALISM	COMMERCIALS	COMMISSIONING
COMBUSTIONS	COMMANDEERED	COMMENSALISMS	COMMERCING	COMMISSIONS
COMBUSTIOUS	COMMANDEERING	COMMENSALITIES	COMMERGING	COMMISSURAL
COMBUSTIVE	COMMANDEERS	COMMENSALITY	COMMINATED	COMMISSURE
COMBUSTIVES	COMMANDERIES	COMMENSALLY	COMMINATES	COMMISSURES
COMBUSTORS	COMMANDERS	COMMENSALS	COMMINATING	COMMITMENT
COMEDDLING	COMMANDERSHIP	COMMENSURABLE	COMMINATION	COMMITMENTS
COMEDICALLY	COMMANDERSHIPS	COMMENSURABLY	COMMINATIONS	COMMITTABLE
COMEDIENNE	COMMANDERY	COMMENSURATE	COMMINATIVE	COMMITTALS
COMEDIENNES	COMMANDING	COMMENSURATELY	COMMINATORY	COMMITTEEMAN
COMEDIETTA	COMMANDINGLY	COMMENSURATION	COMMINGLED	COMMITTEEMEN
COMEDIETTAS	COMMANDMENT	COMMENSURATIONS	COMMINGLES	COMMITTEES
COMEDOGENIC	COMMANDMENTS	COMMENTARIAL	COMMINGLING	COMMITTEESHIP

COMMITTEESHIPS	COMMONWEALTHS	COMMUNICATORY	COMPACTERS	COMPARATIVENESS
COMMITTEEWOMAN	COMMORANTS	COMMUNINGS	COMPACTEST	COMPARATIVES
COMMITTEEWOMEN	COMMORIENTES	COMMUNIONAL	COMPACTIBLE	COMPARATIVIST
COMMITTERS	COMMOTIONAL	COMMUNIONALLY	COMPACTIFIED	COMPARATIVISTS
COMMITTING	COMMOTIONS	COMMUNIONS	COMPACTIFIES	COMPARATOR
COMMIXTION	COMMUNALISATION	COMMUNIQUE	COMPACTIFY	COMPARATORS
COMMIXTIONS	COMMUNALISE	COMMUNIQUES	COMPACTIFYING	COMPARISON
COMMIXTURE	COMMUNALISED	COMMUNISATION	COMPACTING	COMPARISONS
COMMIXTURES	COMMUNALISER	COMMUNISATIONS	COMPACTION	COMPARTING
COMMODIFICATION	COMMUNALISERS	COMMUNISED	COMPACTIONS	COMPARTMENT
COMMODIFIED	COMMUNALISES	COMMUNISES	COMPACTNESS	COMPARTMENTAL
COMMODIFIES	COMMUNALISING	COMMUNISING	COMPACTNESSES	COMPARTMENTALLY
COMMODIFYING	COMMUNALISM	COMMUNISMS	COMPACTORS	COMPARTMENTED
COMMODIOUS	COMMUNALISMS	COMMUNISTIC	COMPACTURE	COMPARTMENTING
COMMODIOUSLY	COMMUNALIST	COMMUNISTICALLY	COMPACTURES	COMPARTMENTS
COMMODIOUSNESS	COMMUNALISTIC	COMMUNISTS	COMPAGINATE	COMPASSABLE
COMMODITIES	COMMUNALISTS	COMMUNITAIRE	COMPAGINATED	COMPASSING
COMMODITISE	COMMUNALITIES	COMMUNITAIRES	COMPAGINATES	COMPASSINGS
COMMODITISED	COMMUNALITY	COMMUNITARIAN	COMPAGINATING	COMPASSION
COMMODITISES	COMMUNALIZATION	COMMUNITARIANS	COMPAGINATION	COMPASSIONABLE
COMMODITISING	COMMUNALIZE	COMMUNITIES	COMPAGINATIONS	COMPASSIONATE
COMMODITIZE	COMMUNALIZED	COMMUNIZATION	COMPANDERS	COMPASSIONATED
COMMODITIZED	COMMUNALIZER	COMMUNIZATIONS	COMPANDING	COMPASSIONATELY
COMMODITIZES	COMMUNALIZERS	COMMUNIZED	COMPANDORS	COMPASSIONATES
COMMODITIZING	COMMUNALIZES	COMMUNIZES	COMPANIABLE	COMPASSIONATING
COMMODORES	COMMUNALIZING	COMMUNIZING	COMPANIONABLE	COMPASSIONED
COMMONABLE	COMMUNALLY	COMMUTABILITIES	COMPANIONABLY	COMPASSIONING
COMMONAGES	COMMUNARDS	COMMUTABILITY	COMPANIONATE	COMPASSIONLESS
COMMONALITIES	COMMUNAUTAIRE	COMMUTABLE	COMPANIONED	COMPASSIONS
COMMONALITY	COMMUNAUTAIRES	COMMUTABLENESS	COMPANIONHOOD	COMPATIBILITIES
COMMONALTIES	COMMUNICABILITY	COMMUTATED	COMPANIONHOODS	COMPATIBILITY
COMMONALTY	COMMUNICABLE	COMMUTATES	COMPANIONING	COMPATIBLE
COMMONHOLD	COMMUNICABLY	COMMUTATING	COMPANIONLESS	COMPATIBLENESS
COMMONHOLDS	COMMUNICANT	COMMUTATION	COMPANIONS	COMPATIBLES
COMMONINGS	COMMUNICANTS	COMMUTATIONS	COMPANIONSHIP	COMPATIBLY
COMMONNESS	COMMUNICATE	COMMUTATIVE	COMPANIONSHIPS	COMPATRIOT
COMMONNESSES	COMMUNICATED	COMMUTATIVELY	COMPANIONWAY	COMPATRIOTIC
COMMONPLACE	COMMUNICATEE	COMMUTATIVITIES	COMPANIONWAYS	COMPATRIOTISM
COMMONPLACED	COMMUNICATEES	COMMUTATIVITY	COMPANYING	COMPATRIOTISMS
COMMONPLACENESS	COMMUNICATES	COMMUTATOR	COMPARABILITIES	COMPATRIOTS
COMMONPLACES	COMMUNICATING	COMMUTATORS	COMPARABILITY	COMPEARANCE
COMMONPLACING	COMMUNICATION	COMMUTINGS	COMPARABLE	COMPEARANCES
COMMONSENSE	COMMUNICATIONAL	COMONOMERS	COMPARABLENESS	COMPEARANT
COMMONSENSIBLE	COMMUNICATIONS	COMORBIDITIES	COMPARABLY	COMPEARANTS
COMMONSENSICAL	COMMUNICATIVE	COMORBIDITY	COMPARATIST	COMPEARING
COMMONWEAL	COMMUNICATIVELY	COMPACTEDLY	COMPARATISTS	COMPEERING
COMMONWEALS	COMMUNICATOR	COMPACTEDNESS	COMPARATIVE	COMPELLABLE
COMMONWEALTH	COMMUNICATORS	COMPACTEDNESSES	COMPARATIVELY	COMPELLABLY

COMPELLATION	COMPLACENCES	COMPLETING	COMPLICATES	COMPOSITIONALLY
COMPELLATIONS	COMPLACENCIES	COMPLETION	COMPLICATING	COMPOSITIONS
COMPELLATIVE	COMPLACENCY	COMPLETIONS	COMPLICATION	COMPOSITIVE
COMPELLATIVES	COMPLACENT	COMPLETIST	COMPLICATIONS	COMPOSITOR
COMPELLERS	COMPLACENTLY	COMPLETISTS	COMPLICATIVE	COMPOSITORIAL
COMPELLING	COMPLAINANT	COMPLETIVE	COMPLICITIES	COMPOSITORS
COMPELLINGLY	COMPLAINANTS	COMPLETORIES	COMPLICITLY	COMPOSITOUS
COMPENDIOUS	COMPLAINED	COMPLETORY	COMPLICITOUS	COMPOSSIBILITY
COMPENDIOUSLY	COMPLAINER	COMPLEXATION	COMPLICITY	COMPOSSIBLE
COMPENDIOUSNESS	COMPLAINERS	COMPLEXATIONS	COMPLIMENT	COMPOSTABLE
COMPENDIUM	COMPLAINING	COMPLEXEDNESS	COMPLIMENTAL	COMPOSTERS
COMPENDIUMS	COMPLAININGLY	COMPLEXEDNESSES	COMPLIMENTARILY	COMPOSTING
COMPENSABILITY	COMPLAININGS	COMPLEXEST	COMPLIMENTARY	COMPOSTINGS
COMPENSABLE	COMPLAINTS	COMPLEXIFIED	COMPLIMENTED	COMPOSTURE
COMPENSATE	COMPLAISANCE	COMPLEXIFIES	COMPLIMENTER	COMPOSTURED
COMPENSATED	COMPLAISANCES	COMPLEXIFY	COMPLIMENTERS	COMPOSTURES
COMPENSATES	COMPLAISANT	COMPLEXIFYING	COMPLIMENTING	COMPOSTURING
COMPENSATING	COMPLAISANTLY	COMPLEXING	COMPLIMENTS	COMPOSURES
COMPENSATION	COMPLANATE	COMPLEXION	COMPLISHED	COMPOTATION
COMPENSATIONAL	COMPLANATION	COMPLEXIONAL	COMPLISHES	COMPOTATIONS
COMPENSATIONS	COMPLANATIONS	COMPLEXIONED	COMPLISHING	COMPOTATIONSHIP
COMPENSATIVE	COMPLEATED	COMPLEXIONLESS	COMPLOTTED	COMPOTATOR
COMPENSATOR	COMPLEATING	COMPLEXIONS	COMPLOTTER	COMPOTATORS
COMPENSATORS	COMPLECTED	COMPLEXITIES	COMPLOTTERS	COMPOTATORY
COMPENSATORY	COMPLECTING	COMPLEXITY	COMPLOTTING	COMPOTIERS
COMPESCING	COMPLEMENT	COMPLEXNESS	COMPLUVIUM	COMPOUNDABLE
COMPETENCE	COMPLEMENTAL	COMPLEXNESSES	COMPLUVIUMS	COMPOUNDED
COMPETENCES	COMPLEMENTALLY	COMPLEXOMETRIC	COMPONENCIES	COMPOUNDER
COMPETENCIES	COMPLEMENTARIES	COMPLEXONE	COMPONENCY	COMPOUNDERS
COMPETENCY	COMPLEMENTARILY	COMPLEXONES	COMPONENTAL	COMPOUNDING
COMPETENTLY	COMPLEMENTARITY	COMPLEXUSES	COMPONENTIAL	COMPOUNDINGS
COMPETENTNESS	COMPLEMENTARY	COMPLIABLE	COMPONENTS	COMPRADORE
COMPETENTNESSES	COMPLEMENTATION	COMPLIABLENESS	COMPORTANCE	COMPRADORES
COMPETITION	COMPLEMENTED	COMPLIABLY	COMPORTANCES	COMPRADORS
COMPETITIONS	COMPLEMENTING	COMPLIANCE	COMPORTING	COMPREHEND
COMPETITIVE	COMPLEMENTISER	COMPLIANCES	COMPORTMENT	COMPREHENDED
COMPETITIVELY	COMPLEMENTISERS	COMPLIANCIES	COMPORTMENTS	COMPREHENDIBLE
COMPETITIVENESS	COMPLEMENTIZER	COMPLIANCY	COMPOSEDLY	COMPREHENDING
COMPETITOR	COMPLEMENTIZERS	COMPLIANTLY	COMPOSEDNESS	COMPREHENDS
COMPETITORS	COMPLEMENTS	COMPLIANTNESS	COMPOSEDNESSES	COMPREHENSIBLE
COMPILATION	COMPLETABLE	COMPLIANTNESSES	COMPOSITED	COMPREHENSIBLY
COMPILATIONS	COMPLETEDNESS	COMPLICACIES	COMPOSITELY	COMPREHENSION
COMPILATOR	COMPLETEDNESSES	COMPLICACY	COMPOSITENESS	COMPREHENSIONS
COMPILATORS	COMPLETELY	COMPLICANT	COMPOSITENESSES	COMPREHENSIVE
COMPILATORY	COMPLETENESS	COMPLICATE	COMPOSITES	COMPREHENSIVELY
COMPILEMENT	COMPLETENESSES	COMPLICATED	COMPOSITING	COMPREHENSIVES
COMPILEMENTS	COMPLETERS	COMPLICATEDLY	COMPOSITION	COMPREHENSIVISE
COMPLACENCE	COMPLETEST	COMPLICATEDNESS	COMPOSITIONAL	COMPREHENSIVIZE

COMPRESSED	COMPULSIVELY	COMPUTERIZATION	CONCEALMENT	CONCEPTIONAL
COMPRESSEDLY	COMPULSIVENESS	COMPUTERIZE	CONCEALMENTS	CONCEPTIONS
COMPRESSES	COMPULSIVES	COMPUTERIZED	CONCEDEDLY	CONCEPTIOUS
COMPRESSIBILITY	COMPULSIVITIES	COMPUTERIZES	CONCEITEDLY	CONCEPTIVE
COMPRESSIBLE	COMPULSIVITY	COMPUTERIZING	CONCEITEDNESS	CONCEPTUAL
COMPRESSIBLY	COMPULSORIES	COMPUTERLESS	CONCEITEDNESSES	CONCEPTUALISE
COMPRESSING	COMPULSORILY	COMPUTERLIKE	CONCEITFUL	CONCEPTUALISED
COMPRESSION	COMPULSORINESS	COMPUTERNIK	CONCEITING	CONCEPTUALISER
COMPRESSIONAL	COMPULSORY	COMPUTERNIKS	CONCEITLESS	CONCEPTUALISERS
COMPRESSIONS	COMPUNCTION	COMPUTERPHOBE	CONCEIVABILITY	CONCEPTUALISES
COMPRESSIVE	COMPUNCTIONS	COMPUTERPHOBES	CONCEIVABLE	CONCEPTUALISING
COMPRESSIVELY	COMPUNCTIOUS	COMPUTERPHOBIA	CONCEIVABLENESS	CONCEPTUALISM
COMPRESSOR	COMPUNCTIOUSLY	COMPUTERPHOBIAS	CONCEIVABLY	CONCEPTUALISMS
COMPRESSORS	COMPURGATION	COMPUTERPHOBIC	CONCEIVERS	CONCEPTUALIST
COMPRESSURE	COMPURGATIONS	COMPUTERPHOBICS	CONCEIVING	CONCEPTUALISTIC
COMPRESSURES	COMPURGATOR	COMPUTINGS	CONCELEBRANT	CONCEPTUALISTS
COMPRIMARIO	COMPURGATORIAL	COMPUTISTS	CONCELEBRANTS	CONCEPTUALITIES
COMPRIMARIOS	COMPURGATORS	COMRADELIER	CONCELEBRATE	CONCEPTUALITY
COMPRINTED	COMPURGATORY	COMRADELIEST	CONCELEBRATED	CONCEPTUALIZE
COMPRINTING	COMPURSION	COMRADELINESS	CONCELEBRATES	CONCEPTUALIZED
COMPRISABLE	COMPURSIONS	COMRADELINESSES	CONCELEBRATING	CONCEPTUALIZER
COMPRISALS	COMPUTABILITIES	COMRADERIES	CONCELEBRATION	CONCEPTUALIZERS
COMPRISING	COMPUTABILITY	COMRADESHIP	CONCELEBRATIONS	CONCEPTUALIZES
COMPRIZING	COMPUTABLE	COMRADESHIPS	CONCENTERED	CONCEPTUALIZING
COMPROMISE	COMPUTANTS	COMSTOCKER	CONCENTERING	CONCEPTUALLY
COMPROMISED	COMPUTATION	COMSTOCKERIES	CONCENTERS	CONCEPTUSES
COMPROMISER	COMPUTATIONAL	COMSTOCKERS	CONCENTRATE	CONCERNANCIES
COMPROMISERS	COMPUTATIONALLY	COMSTOCKERY	CONCENTRATED	CONCERNANCY
COMPROMISES	COMPUTATIONS	COMSTOCKISM	CONCENTRATEDLY	CONCERNEDLY
COMPROMISING	COMPUTATIVE	COMSTOCKISMS	CONCENTRATES	CONCERNEDNESS
COMPROMISINGLY	COMPUTATOR	CONACREISM	CONCENTRATING	CONCERNEDNESSES
COMPROVINCIAL	COMPUTATORS	CONACREISMS	CONCENTRATION	CONCERNING
COMPTROLLED	COMPUTERATE	CONATIONAL	CONCENTRATIONS	CONCERNMENT
COMPTROLLER	COMPUTERDOM	CONCANAVALIN	CONCENTRATIVE	CONCERNMENTS
COMPTROLLERS	COMPUTERDOMS	CONCANAVALINS	CONCENTRATIVELY	CONCERTANTE
COMPTROLLERSHIP	COMPUTERESE	CONCATENATE	CONCENTRATOR	CONCERTANTES
COMPTROLLING	COMPUTERESES	CONCATENATED	CONCENTRATORS	CONCERTANTI
COMPTROLLS	COMPUTERISABLE	CONCATENATES	CONCENTRED	CONCERTEDLY
COMPULSATIVE	COMPUTERISATION	CONCATENATING	CONCENTRES	CONCERTEDNESS
COMPULSATORY	COMPUTERISE	CONCATENATION	CONCENTRIC	CONCERTEDNESSES
COMPULSING	COMPUTERISED	CONCATENATIONS	CONCENTRICAL	CONCERTGOER
COMPULSION	COMPUTERISES	CONCAVENESS	CONCENTRICALLY	CONCERTGOERS
COMPULSIONIST	COMPUTERISING	CONCAVENESSES	CONCENTRICITIES	CONCERTGOING
COMPULSIONISTS	COMPUTERIST	CONCAVITIES	CONCENTRICITY	CONCERTGOINGS
COMPULSIONS	COMPUTERISTS	CONCEALABLE	CONCENTRING	CONCERTINA
COMPULSITOR	COMPUTERITIS	CONCEALERS	CONCEPTACLE	CONCERTINAED
COMPULSITORS	COMPUTERITISES	CONCEALING	CONCEPTACLES	CONCERTINAING
COMPULSIVE	COMPUTERIZABLE	CONCEALINGLY	CONCEPTION	CONCERTINAS

CONCERTING	CONCHOLOGICAL	CONCOCTIVE	CONCRETIVE	CONDENSATED
CONCERTINI	CONCHOLOGIES	CONCOCTORS	CONCRETIVELY	CONDENSATES
CONCERTINIST	CONCHOLOGIST	CONCOLORATE	CONCRETIZATION	CONDENSATING
CONCERTINISTS	CONCHOLOGISTS	CONCOLOROUS	CONCRETIZATIONS	CONDENSATION
CONCERTINO	CONCHOLOGY	CONCOMITANCE	CONCRETIZE	CONDENSATIONAL
CONCERTINOS	CONCIERGES	CONCOMITANCES	CONCRETIZED	CONDENSATIONS
CONCERTISE	CONCILIABLE	CONCOMITANCIES	CONCRETIZES	CONDENSERIES
CONCERTISED	CONCILIARLY	CONCOMITANCY	CONCRETIZING	CONDENSERS
CONCERTISES	CONCILIARY	CONCOMITANT	CONCREWING	CONDENSERY
CONCERTISING	CONCILIATE	CONCOMITANTLY	CONCUBINAGE	CONDENSIBILITY
CONCERTIZE	CONCILIATED	CONCOMITANTS	CONCUBINAGES	CONDENSIBLE
CONCERTIZED	CONCILIATES	CONCORDANCE	CONCUBINARIES	CONDENSING
CONCERTIZES	CONCILIATING	CONCORDANCES	CONCUBINARY	CONDESCEND
CONCERTIZING	CONCILIATION	CONCORDANT	CONCUBINES	CONDESCENDED
CONCERTMASTER	CONCILIATIONS	CONCORDANTLY	CONCUBITANCIES	CONDESCENDENCE
CONCERTMASTERS	CONCILIATIVE	CONCORDATS	CONCUBITANCY	CONDESCENDENCES
CONCERTMEISTER	CONCILIATOR	CONCORDIAL	CONCUBITANT	CONDESCENDING
CONCERTMEISTERS	CONCILIATORILY	CONCORDING	CONCUBITANTS	CONDESCENDINGLY
CONCERTMISTRESS	CONCILIATORS	CONCORPORATE	CONCUPISCENCE	CONDESCENDS
CONCERTSTUCK	CONCILIATORY	CONCORPORATED	CONCUPISCENCES	CONDESCENSION
CONCERTSTUCKS	CONCINNITIES	CONCORPORATES	CONCUPISCENT	CONDESCENSIONS
CONCESSIBLE	CONCINNITY	CONCORPORATING	CONCUPISCIBLE	CONDIDDLED
CONCESSION	CONCINNOUS	CONCOURSES	CONCURRENCE	CONDIDDLES
CONCESSIONAIRE	CONCIPIENCIES	CONCREATED	CONCURRENCES	CONDIDDLING
CONCESSIONAIRES	CONCIPIENCY	CONCREATES	CONCURRENCIES	CONDIGNNESS
CONCESSIONAL	CONCIPIENT	CONCREATING	CONCURRENCY	CONDIGNNESSES
CONCESSIONARIES	CONCISENESS	CONCREMATION	CONCURRENT	CONDIMENTAL
CONCESSIONARY	CONCISENESSES	CONCREMATIONS	CONCURRENTLY	CONDIMENTED
CONCESSIONER	CONCISIONS	CONCRESCENCE	CONCURRENTS	CONDIMENTING
CONCESSIONERS	CONCLAMATION	CONCRESCENCES	CONCURRING	CONDIMENTS
CONCESSIONIST	CONCLAMATIONS	CONCRESCENT	CONCURRINGLY	CONDISCIPLE
CONCESSIONISTS	CONCLAVISM	CONCRETELY	CONCUSSING	CONDISCIPLES
CONCESSIONNAIRE	CONCLAVISMS	CONCRETENESS	CONCUSSION	CONDITIONABLE
CONCESSIONS	CONCLAVIST	CONCRETENESSES	CONCUSSIONS	CONDITIONAL
CONCESSIVE	CONCLAVISTS	CONCRETING	CONCUSSIVE	CONDITIONALITY
CONCESSIVELY	CONCLUDERS	CONCRETION	CONCYCLICALLY	CONDITIONALLY
CONCETTISM	CONCLUDING	CONCRETIONARY	CONDEMNABLE	CONDITIONALS
CONCETTISMS	CONCLUSION	CONCRETIONS	CONDEMNABLY	CONDITIONATE
CONCETTIST	CONCLUSIONARY	CONCRETISATION	CONDEMNATION	CONDITIONATED
CONCETTISTS	CONCLUSIONS	CONCRETISATIONS	CONDEMNATIONS	CONDITIONATES
CONCHIFEROUS	CONCLUSIVE	CONCRETISE	CONDEMNATORY	CONDITIONATING
CONCHIFORM	CONCLUSIVELY	CONCRETISED	CONDEMNERS	CONDITIONED
CONCHIGLIE	CONCLUSIVENESS	CONCRETISES	CONDEMNING	CONDITIONER
CONCHIOLIN	CONCLUSORY	CONCRETISING	CONDEMNINGLY	CONDITIONERS
CONCHIOLINS	CONCOCTERS	CONCRETISM	CONDEMNORS	CONDITIONING
CONCHITISES	CONCOCTING	CONCRETISMS	CONDENSABILITY	CONDITIONINGS
CONCHOIDAL	CONCOCTION	CONCRETIST	CONDENSABLE	CONDITIONS
CONCHOIDALLY	CONCOCTIONS	CONCRETISTS	CONDENSATE	CONDOLATORY

CONDOLEMENT

CONDOLEMENT
CONDOLEMENTS
CONDOLENCE
CONDOLENCES
CONDOLINGLY
CONDOMINIA
CONDOMINIUM
CONDOMINIUMS
CONDONABLE
CONDONATION
CONDONATIONS
CONDOTTIERE
CONDOTTIERI
CONDUCEMENT
CONDUCEMENTS
CONDUCIBLE
CONDUCINGLY
CONDUCIVENESS
CONDUCIVENESSES
CONDUCTANCE
CONDUCTANCES
CONDUCTIBILITY
CONDUCTIBLE
CONDUCTIMETRIC
CONDUCTING
CONDUCTIOMETRIC
CONDUCTION
CONDUCTIONAL
CONDUCTIONS
CONDUCTIVE
CONDUCTIVELY
CONDUCTIVITIES
CONDUCTIVITY
CONDUCTOMETRIC
CONDUCTORIAL
CONDUCTORS
CONDUCTORSHIP
CONDUCTORSHIPS
CONDUCTRESS
CONDUCTRESSES
CONDUPLICATE
CONDUPLICATION
CONDUPLICATIONS
CONDYLOMAS
CONDYLOMATA
CONDYLOMATOUS
CONEFLOWER
CONEFLOWERS

CONFABBING
CONFABULAR
CONFABULATE
CONFABULATED
CONFABULATES
CONFABULATING
CONFABULATION
CONFABULATIONS
CONFABULATOR
CONFABULATORS
CONFABULATORY
CONFARREATE
CONFARREATION
CONFARREATIONS
CONFECTING
CONFECTION
CONFECTIONARIES
CONFECTIONARY
CONFECTIONER
CONFECTIONERIES
CONFECTIONERS
CONFECTIONERY
CONFECTIONS
CONFEDERACIES
CONFEDERACY
CONFEDERAL
CONFEDERATE
CONFEDERATED
CONFEDERATES
CONFEDERATING
CONFEDERATION
CONFEDERATIONS
CONFEDERATIVE
CONFERENCE
CONFERENCES
CONFERENCIER
CONFERENCIERS
CONFERENCING
CONFERENCINGS
CONFERENTIAL
CONFERMENT
CONFERMENTS
CONFERRABLE
CONFERRALS
CONFERREES
CONFERRENCE
CONFERRENCES
CONFERRERS

CONFERRING
CONFERVOID
CONFERVOIDS
CONFESSABLE
CONFESSANT
CONFESSANTS
CONFESSEDLY
CONFESSING
CONFESSION
CONFESSIONAL
CONFESSIONALISM
CONFESSIONALIST
CONFESSIONALLY
CONFESSIONALS
CONFESSIONARIES
CONFESSIONARY
CONFESSIONS
CONFESSORESS
CONFESSORESSES
CONFESSORS
CONFESSORSHIP
CONFESSORSHIPS
CONFIDANTE
CONFIDANTES
CONFIDANTS
CONFIDENCE
CONFIDENCES
CONFIDENCIES
CONFIDENCY
CONFIDENTIAL
CONFIDENTIALITY
CONFIDENTIALLY
CONFIDENTLY
CONFIDENTS
CONFIDINGLY
CONFIDINGNESS
CONFIDINGNESSES
CONFIGURATE
CONFIGURATED
CONFIGURATES
CONFIGURATING
CONFIGURATION
CONFIGURATIONAL
CONFIGURATIONS
CONFIGURATIVE
CONFIGURATOR
CONFIGURATORS
CONFIGURED

CONFIGURES
CONFIGURING
CONFINABLE
CONFINEABLE
CONFINEDLY
CONFINEDNESS
CONFINEDNESSES
CONFINELESS
CONFINEMENT
CONFINEMENTS
CONFIRMABILITY
CONFIRMABLE
CONFIRMAND
CONFIRMANDS
CONFIRMATION
CONFIRMATIONAL
CONFIRMATIONS
CONFIRMATIVE
CONFIRMATOR
CONFIRMATORS
CONFIRMATORY
CONFIRMEDLY
CONFIRMEDNESS
CONFIRMEDNESSES
CONFIRMEES
CONFIRMERS
CONFIRMING
CONFIRMINGS
CONFIRMORS
CONFISCABLE
CONFISCATABLE
CONFISCATE
CONFISCATED
CONFISCATES
CONFISCATING
CONFISCATION
CONFISCATIONS
CONFISCATOR
CONFISCATORS
CONFISCATORY
CONFISERIE
CONFISERIES
CONFISEURS
CONFITEORS
CONFITURES
CONFLAGRANT
CONFLAGRATE
CONFLAGRATED

CONFLAGRATES
CONFLAGRATING
CONFLAGRATION
CONFLAGRATIONS
CONFLAGRATIVE
CONFLATING
CONFLATION
CONFLATIONS
CONFLICTED
CONFLICTFUL
CONFLICTING
CONFLICTINGLY
CONFLICTION
CONFLICTIONS
CONFLICTIVE
CONFLICTORY
CONFLICTUAL
CONFLUENCE
CONFLUENCES
CONFLUENTLY
CONFLUENTS
CONFOCALLY
CONFORMABILITY
CONFORMABLE
CONFORMABLENESS
CONFORMABLY
CONFORMANCE
CONFORMANCES
CONFORMATION
CONFORMATIONAL
CONFORMATIONS
CONFORMERS
CONFORMING
CONFORMINGLY
CONFORMISM
CONFORMISMS
CONFORMIST
CONFORMISTS
CONFORMITIES
CONFORMITY
CONFOUNDABLE
CONFOUNDED
CONFOUNDEDLY
CONFOUNDEDNESS
CONFOUNDER
CONFOUNDERS
CONFOUNDING
CONFOUNDINGLY

CONFRATERNAL	CONGENIALLY	CONGRATULABLE	CONGRUOUSNESSES	CONJUNCTIVAE
CONFRATERNITIES	CONGENIALNESS	CONGRATULANT	CONICITIES	CONJUNCTIVAL
CONFRATERNITY	CONGENIALNESSES	CONGRATULANTS	CONIDIOPHORE	CONJUNCTIVAS
CONFRERIES	CONGENITAL	CONGRATULATE	CONIDIOPHORES	CONJUNCTIVE
CONFRONTAL	CONGENITALLY	CONGRATULATED	CONIDIOPHOROUS	CONJUNCTIVELY
CONFRONTALS	CONGENITALNESS	CONGRATULATES	CONIDIOSPORE	CONJUNCTIVENESS
CONFRONTATION	CONGESTIBLE	CONGRATULATING	CONIDIOSPORES	CONJUNCTIVES
CONFRONTATIONAL	CONGESTING	CONGRATULATION	CONIFEROUS	CONJUNCTIVITIS
CONFRONTATIONS	CONGESTION	CONGRATULATIONS	CONIOLOGIES	CONJUNCTLY
CONFRONTED	CONGESTIONS	CONGRATULATIVE	CONIROSTRAL	CONJUNCTURAL
CONFRONTER	CONGESTIVE	CONGRATULATOR	CONJECTING	CONJUNCTURE
CONFRONTERS	CONGIARIES	CONGRATULATORS	CONJECTURABLE	CONJUNCTURES
CONFRONTING	CONGLOBATE	CONGRATULATORY	CONJECTURABLY	CONJURATION
CONFRONTMENT	CONGLOBATED	CONGREEING	CONJECTURAL	CONJURATIONS
CONFRONTMENTS	CONGLOBATES	CONGREETED	CONJECTURALLY	CONJURATOR
CONFUSABILITIES	CONGLOBATING	CONGREETING	CONJECTURE	CONJURATORS
CONFUSABILITY	CONGLOBATION	CONGREGANT	CONJECTURED	CONJUREMENT
CONFUSABLE	CONGLOBATIONS	CONGREGANTS	CONJECTURER	CONJUREMENTS
CONFUSABLES	CONGLOBING	CONGREGATE	CONJECTURERS	CONJURINGS
CONFUSEDLY	CONGLOBULATE	CONGREGATED	CONJECTURES	CONLANGERS
CONFUSEDNESS	CONGLOBULATED	CONGREGATES	CONJECTURING	CONNASCENCE
CONFUSEDNESSES	CONGLOBULATES	CONGREGATING	CONJOINERS	CONNASCENCES
CONFUSIBLE	CONGLOBULATING	CONGREGATION	CONJOINING	CONNASCENCIES
CONFUSIBLES	CONGLOBULATION	CONGREGATIONAL	CONJOINTLY	CONNASCENCY
CONFUSINGLY	CONGLOBULATIONS	CONGREGATIONS	CONJUGABLE	CONNASCENT
CONFUSIONAL	CONGLOMERATE	CONGREGATIVE	CONJUGALITIES	CONNATENESS
CONFUSIONS	CONGLOMERATED	CONGREGATOR	CONJUGALITY	CONNATENESSES
CONFUTABLE	CONGLOMERATES	CONGREGATORS	CONJUGALLY	CONNATIONS
CONFUTATION	CONGLOMERATEUR	CONGRESSED	CONJUGANTS	CONNATURAL
CONFUTATIONS	CONGLOMERATEURS	CONGRESSES	CONJUGATED	CONNATURALISE
CONFUTATIVE	CONGLOMERATIC	CONGRESSING	CONJUGATELY	CONNATURALISED
CONFUTEMENT	CONGLOMERATING	CONGRESSIONAL	CONJUGATENESS	CONNATURALISES
CONFUTEMENTS	CONGLOMERATION	CONGRESSIONALLY	CONJUGATENESSES	CONNATURALISING
CONGEALABLE	CONGLOMERATIONS	CONGRESSMAN	CONJUGATES	CONNATURALITIES
CONGEALABLENESS	CONGLOMERATIVE	CONGRESSMEN	CONJUGATING	CONNATURALITY
CONGEALERS	CONGLOMERATOR	CONGRESSPEOPLE	CONJUGATINGS	CONNATURALIZE
CONGEALING	CONGLOMERATORS	CONGRESSPERSON	CONJUGATION	CONNATURALIZED
CONGEALMENT	CONGLUTINANT	CONGRESSPERSONS	CONJUGATIONAL	CONNATURALIZES
CONGEALMENTS	CONGLUTINATE	CONGRESSWOMAN	CONJUGATIONALLY	CONNATURALIZING
CONGELATION	CONGLUTINATED	CONGRESSWOMEN	CONJUGATIONS	CONNATURALLY
CONGELATIONS	CONGLUTINATES	CONGRUENCE	CONJUGATIVE	CONNATURALNESS
CONGENERIC	CONGLUTINATING	CONGRUENCES	CONJUGATOR	CONNATURES
CONGENERICAL	CONGLUTINATION	CONGRUENCIES	CONJUGATORS	CONNECTABLE
CONGENERICS	CONGLUTINATIONS	CONGRUENCY	CONJUNCTION	CONNECTEDLY
CONGENEROUS	CONGLUTINATIVE	CONGRUENTLY	CONJUNCTIONAL	CONNECTEDNESS
CONGENETIC	CONGLUTINATOR	CONGRUITIES	CONJUNCTIONALLY	CONNECTEDNESSES
CONGENIALITIES	CONGLUTINATORS	CONGRUOUSLY	CONJUNCTIONS	CONNECTERS
CONGENIALITY	CONGRATTERS	CONGRUOUSNESS	CONJUNCTIVA	CONNECTIBLE

CONNECTING	CONNUMERATING	CONSCRIPTING	CONSEQUENT	CONSIDERATELY
CONNECTION	CONNUMERATION	CONSCRIPTION	CONSEQUENTIAL	CONSIDERATENESS
CONNECTIONAL	CONNUMERATIONS	CONSCRIPTIONAL	CONSEQUENTIALLY	CONSIDERATION
CONNECTIONISM	CONOIDALLY	CONSCRIPTIONIST	CONSEQUENTLY	CONSIDERATIONS
CONNECTIONISMS	CONOIDICAL	CONSCRIPTIONS	CONSEQUENTS	CONSIDERATIVE
CONNECTIONS	CONOMINEES	CONSCRIPTS	CONSERVABLE	CONSIDERATIVELY
CONNECTIVE	CONOSCENTE	CONSECRATE	CONSERVANCIES	CONSIDERED
CONNECTIVELY	CONOSCENTI	CONSECRATED	CONSERVANCY	CONSIDERER
CONNECTIVES	CONQUERABILITY	CONSECRATEDNESS	CONSERVANT	CONSIDERERS
CONNECTIVITIES	CONQUERABLE	CONSECRATES	CONSERVATION	CONSIDERING
CONNECTIVITY	CONQUERABLENESS	CONSECRATING	CONSERVATIONAL	CONSIDERINGLY
CONNECTORS	CONQUERERS	CONSECRATION	CONSERVATIONIST	CONSIGLIERE
CONNEXIONAL	CONQUERESS	CONSECRATIONS	CONSERVATIONS	CONSIGLIERES
CONNEXIONS	CONQUERESSES	CONSECRATIVE	CONSERVATISE	CONSIGLIERI
CONNIPTION	CONQUERING	CONSECRATOR	CONSERVATISED	CONSIGNABLE
CONNIPTIONS	CONQUERINGLY	CONSECRATORS	CONSERVATISES	CONSIGNATION
CONNIVANCE	CONQUERORS	CONSECRATORY	CONSERVATISING	CONSIGNATIONS
CONNIVANCES	CONQUISTADOR	CONSECTANEOUS	CONSERVATISM	CONSIGNATORIES
CONNIVANCIES	CONQUISTADORES	CONSECTARIES	CONSERVATISMS	CONSIGNATORY
CONNIVANCY	CONQUISTADORS	CONSECTARY	CONSERVATIVE	CONSIGNEES
CONNIVENCE	CONSANGUINE	CONSECUTION	CONSERVATIVELY	CONSIGNERS
CONNIVENCES	CONSANGUINEOUS	CONSECUTIONS	CONSERVATIVES	CONSIGNIFIED
CONNIVENCIES	CONSANGUINITIES	CONSECUTIVE	CONSERVATIZE	CONSIGNIFIES
CONNIVENCY	CONSANGUINITY	CONSECUTIVELY	CONSERVATIZED	CONSIGNIFY
CONNIVENTLY	CONSCIENCE	CONSECUTIVENESS	CONSERVATIZES	CONSIGNIFYING
CONNIVERIES	CONSCIENCELESS	CONSENESCENCE	CONSERVATIZING	CONSIGNING
CONNIVINGLY	CONSCIENCES	CONSENESCENCES	CONSERVATOIRE	CONSIGNMENT
CONNIVINGS	CONSCIENTIOUS	CONSENESCENCIES	CONSERVATOIRES	CONSIGNMENTS
CONNOISSEUR	CONSCIENTIOUSLY	CONSENESCENCY	CONSERVATOR	CONSIGNORS
CONNOISSEURS	CONSCIENTISE	CONSENSION	CONSERVATORIA	CONSILIENCE
CONNOISSEURSHIP	CONSCIENTISED	CONSENSIONS	CONSERVATORIAL	CONSILIENCES
CONNOTATED	CONSCIENTISES	CONSENSUAL	CONSERVATORIES	CONSILIENT
CONNOTATES	CONSCIENTISING	CONSENSUALLY	CONSERVATORIUM	CONSIMILAR
CONNOTATING	CONSCIENTIZE	CONSENSUSES	CONSERVATORIUMS	CONSIMILARITIES
CONNOTATION	CONSCIENTIZED	CONSENTANEITIES	CONSERVATORS	CONSIMILARITY
CONNOTATIONAL	CONSCIENTIZES	CONSENTANEITY	CONSERVATORSHIP	CONSIMILITIES
CONNOTATIONS	CONSCIENTIZING	CONSENTANEOUS	CONSERVATORY	CONSIMILITUDE
CONNOTATIVE	CONSCIONABILITY	CONSENTANEOUSLY	CONSERVATRICES	CONSIMILITUDES
CONNOTATIVELY	CONSCIONABLE	CONSENTERS	CONSERVATRIX	CONSIMILITY
CONNOTIVELY	CONSCIONABLY	CONSENTIENCE	CONSERVATRIXES	CONSISTENCE
CONNUBIALISM	CONSCIOUSES	CONSENTIENCES	CONSERVERS	CONSISTENCES
CONNUBIALISMS	CONSCIOUSLY	CONSENTIENT	CONSERVING	CONSISTENCIES
CONNUBIALITIES	CONSCIOUSNESS	CONSENTING	CONSIDERABLE	CONSISTENCY
CONNUBIALITY	CONSCIOUSNESSES	CONSENTINGLY	CONSIDERABLES	CONSISTENT
CONNUBIALLY	CONSCRIBED	CONSEQUENCE	CONSIDERABLY	CONSISTENTLY
CONNUMERATE	CONSCRIBES	CONSEQUENCED	CONSIDERANCE	CONSISTING
CONNUMERATED	CONSCRIBING	CONSEQUENCES	CONSIDERANCES	CONSISTORIAL
CONNUMERATES	CONSCRIPTED	CONSEQUENCING	CONSIDERATE	CONSISTORIAN

CONSISTORIES	CONSPECIFIC	CONSTELLATING	CONSTRICTING	CONSTUPRATION
CONSISTORY	CONSPECIFICS	CONSTELLATION	CONSTRICTION	CONSTUPRATIONS
CONSOCIATE	CONSPECTUITIES	CONSTELLATIONAL	CONSTRICTIONS	CONSUBSIST
CONSOCIATED	CONSPECTUITY	CONSTELLATIONS	CONSTRICTIVE	CONSUBSISTED
CONSOCIATES	CONSPECTUS	CONSTELLATORY	CONSTRICTIVELY	CONSUBSISTING
CONSOCIATING	CONSPECTUSES	CONSTERING	CONSTRICTOR	CONSUBSISTS
CONSOCIATION	CONSPICUITIES	CONSTERNATE	CONSTRICTORS	CONSUBSTANTIAL
CONSOCIATIONAL	CONSPICUITY	CONSTERNATED	CONSTRICTS	CONSUBSTANTIATE
CONSOCIATIONS	CONSPICUOUS	CONSTERNATES	CONSTRINGE	CONSUETUDE
CONSOLABLE	CONSPICUOUSLY	CONSTERNATING	CONSTRINGED	CONSUETUDES
CONSOLATED	CONSPICUOUSNESS	CONSTERNATION	CONSTRINGENCE	CONSUETUDINARY
CONSOLATES	CONSPIRACIES	CONSTERNATIONS	CONSTRINGENCES	CONSULAGES
CONSOLATING	CONSPIRACY	CONSTIPATE	CONSTRINGENCIES	CONSULATES
CONSOLATION	CONSPIRANT	CONSTIPATED	CONSTRINGENCY	CONSULSHIP
CONSOLATIONS	CONSPIRANTS	CONSTIPATES	CONSTRINGENT	CONSULSHIPS
CONSOLATORIES	CONSPIRATION	CONSTIPATING	CONSTRINGES	CONSULTABLE
CONSOLATORY	CONSPIRATIONAL	CONSTIPATION	CONSTRINGING	CONSULTANCIES
CONSOLATRICES	CONSPIRATIONS	CONSTIPATIONS	CONSTRUABILITY	CONSULTANCY
CONSOLATRIX	CONSPIRATOR	CONSTITUENCIES	CONSTRUABLE	CONSULTANT
CONSOLATRIXES	CONSPIRATORIAL	CONSTITUENCY	CONSTRUALS	CONSULTANTS
CONSOLEMENT	CONSPIRATORS	CONSTITUENT	CONSTRUCTABLE	CONSULTANTSHIP
CONSOLEMENTS	CONSPIRATORY	CONSTITUENTLY	CONSTRUCTED	CONSULTANTSHIPS
CONSOLIDATE	CONSPIRATRESS	CONSTITUENTS	CONSTRUCTER	CONSULTATION
CONSOLIDATED	CONSPIRATRESSES	CONSTITUTE	CONSTRUCTERS	CONSULTATIONS
CONSOLIDATES	CONSPIRERS	CONSTITUTED	CONSTRUCTIBLE	CONSULTATIVE
CONSOLIDATING	CONSPIRING	CONSTITUTER	CONSTRUCTING	CONSULTATIVELY
CONSOLIDATION	CONSPIRINGLY	CONSTITUTERS	CONSTRUCTION	CONSULTATORY
CONSOLIDATIONS	CONSPURCATION	CONSTITUTES	CONSTRUCTIONAL	CONSULTEES
CONSOLIDATIVE	CONSPURCATIONS	CONSTITUTING	CONSTRUCTIONISM	CONSULTERS
CONSOLIDATOR	CONSTABLES	CONSTITUTION	CONSTRUCTIONIST	CONSULTING
CONSOLIDATORS	CONSTABLESHIP	CONSTITUTIONAL	CONSTRUCTIONS	CONSULTINGS
CONSOLINGLY	CONSTABLESHIPS	CONSTITUTIONALS	CONSTRUCTIVE	CONSULTIVE
CONSONANCE	CONSTABLEWICK	CONSTITUTIONIST	CONSTRUCTIVELY	CONSULTORS
CONSONANCES	CONSTABLEWICKS	CONSTITUTIONS	CONSTRUCTIVISM	CONSULTORY
CONSONANCIES	CONSTABULARIES	CONSTITUTIVE	CONSTRUCTIVISMS	CONSUMABLE
CONSONANCY	CONSTABULARY	CONSTITUTIVELY	CONSTRUCTIVIST	CONSUMABLES
CONSONANTAL	CONSTANCIES	CONSTITUTOR	CONSTRUCTIVISTS	CONSUMEDLY
CONSONANTALLY	CONSTANTAN	CONSTITUTORS	CONSTRUCTOR	CONSUMERISM
CONSONANTLY	CONSTANTANS	CONSTRAINABLE	CONSTRUCTORS	CONSUMERISMS
CONSONANTS	CONSTANTLY	CONSTRAINED	CONSTRUCTS	CONSUMERIST
CONSORTABLE	CONSTATATION	CONSTRAINEDLY	CONSTRUCTURE	CONSUMERISTIC
CONSORTERS	CONSTATATIONS	CONSTRAINER	CONSTRUCTURES	CONSUMERISTS
CONSORTIAL	CONSTATING	CONSTRAINERS	CONSTRUERS	CONSUMERSHIP
CONSORTING	CONSTATIVE	CONSTRAINING	CONSTRUING	CONSUMERSHIPS
CONSORTISM	CONSTATIVES	CONSTRAINS	CONSTUPRATE	CONSUMINGLY
CONSORTISMS	CONSTELLATE	CONSTRAINT	CONSTUPRATED	CONSUMINGS
CONSORTIUM	CONSTELLATED	CONSTRAINTS	CONSTUPRATES	CONSUMMATE
CONSORTIUMS	CONSTELLATES	CONSTRICTED	CONSTUPRATING	CONSUMMATED

CONSUMMATELY	CONTAINERPORTS	CONTEMPLATOR	CONTERMINOUS	CONTINENTS
CONSUMMATES	CONTAINERS	CONTEMPLATORS	CONTERMINOUSLY	CONTINGENCE
CONSUMMATING	CONTAINERSHIP	CONTEMPORANEAN	CONTESSERATION	CONTINGENCES
CONSUMMATION	CONTAINERSHIPS	CONTEMPORANEANS	CONTESSERATIONS	CONTINGENCIES
CONSUMMATIONS	CONTAINING	CONTEMPORANEITY	CONTESTABILITY	CONTINGENCY
CONSUMMATIVE	CONTAINMENT	CONTEMPORANEOUS	CONTESTABLE	CONTINGENT
CONSUMMATOR	CONTAINMENTS	CONTEMPORARIES	CONTESTABLENESS	CONTINGENTLY
CONSUMMATORS	CONTAMINABLE	CONTEMPORARILY	CONTESTABLY	CONTINGENTS
CONSUMMATORY	CONTAMINANT	CONTEMPORARY	CONTESTANT	CONTINUABLE
CONSUMPTION	CONTAMINANTS	CONTEMPORISE	CONTESTANTS	CONTINUALITIES
CONSUMPTIONS	CONTAMINATE	CONTEMPORISED	CONTESTATION	CONTINUALITY
CONSUMPTIVE	CONTAMINATED	CONTEMPORISES	CONTESTATIONS	CONTINUALLY
CONSUMPTIVELY	CONTAMINATES	CONTEMPORISING	CONTESTERS	CONTINUALNESS
CONSUMPTIVENESS	CONTAMINATING	CONTEMPORIZE	CONTESTING	CONTINUALNESSES
CONSUMPTIVES	CONTAMINATION	CONTEMPORIZED	CONTESTINGLY	CONTINUANCE
CONSUMPTIVITIES	CONTAMINATIONS	CONTEMPORIZES	CONTEXTLESS	CONTINUANCES
CONSUMPTIVITY	CONTAMINATIVE	CONTEMPORIZING	CONTEXTUAL	CONTINUANT
CONTABESCENCE	CONTAMINATOR	CONTEMPTIBILITY	CONTEXTUALISE	CONTINUANTS
CONTABESCENCES	CONTAMINATORS	CONTEMPTIBLE	CONTEXTUALISED	CONTINUATE
CONTABESCENT	CONTANGOED	CONTEMPTIBLY	CONTEXTUALISES	CONTINUATION
CONTACTABLE	CONTANGOES	CONTEMPTUOUS	CONTEXTUALISING	CONTINUATIONS
CONTACTEES	CONTANGOING	CONTEMPTUOUSLY	CONTEXTUALIZE	CONTINUATIVE
CONTACTING	CONTEMNERS	CONTENDENT	CONTEXTUALIZED	CONTINUATIVELY
CONTACTLESS	CONTEMNIBLE	CONTENDENTS	CONTEXTUALIZES	CONTINUATIVES
CONTACTORS	CONTEMNIBLY	CONTENDERS	CONTEXTUALIZING	CONTINUATOR
CONTACTUAL	CONTEMNING	CONTENDING	CONTEXTUALLY	CONTINUATORS
CONTACTUALLY	CONTEMNORS	CONTENDINGLY	CONTEXTURAL	CONTINUEDLY
CONTADINAS	CONTEMPERATION	CONTENDINGS	CONTEXTURE	CONTINUEDNESS
CONTADINOS	CONTEMPERATIONS	CONTENEMENT	CONTEXTURES	CONTINUEDNESSES
CONTAGIONIST	CONTEMPERATURE	CONTENEMENTS	CONTIGNATION	CONTINUERS
CONTAGIONISTS	CONTEMPERATURES	CONTENTATION	CONTIGNATIONS	CONTINUING
CONTAGIONS	CONTEMPERED	CONTENTATIONS	CONTIGUITIES	CONTINUINGLY
CONTAGIOUS	CONTEMPERING	CONTENTEDLY	CONTIGUITY	CONTINUITIES
CONTAGIOUSLY	CONTEMPERS	CONTENTEDNESS	CONTIGUOUS	CONTINUITY
CONTAGIOUSNESS	CONTEMPLABLE	CONTENTEDNESSES	CONTIGUOUSLY	CONTINUOUS
CONTAINABLE	CONTEMPLANT	CONTENTING	CONTIGUOUSNESS	CONTINUOUSLY
CONTAINERBOARD	CONTEMPLANTS	CONTENTION	CONTINENCE	CONTINUOUSNESS
CONTAINERBOARDS	CONTEMPLATE	CONTENTIONS	CONTINENCES	CONTINUUMS
CONTAINERISE	CONTEMPLATED	CONTENTIOUS	CONTINENCIES	CONTORNIATE
CONTAINERISED	CONTEMPLATES	CONTENTIOUSLY	CONTINENCY	CONTORNIATES
CONTAINERISES	CONTEMPLATING	CONTENTIOUSNESS	CONTINENTAL	CONTORTEDLY
CONTAINERISING	CONTEMPLATION	CONTENTLESS	CONTINENTALISM	CONTORTEDNESS
CONTAINERIZE	CONTEMPLATIONS	CONTENTMENT	CONTINENTALISMS	CONTORTEDNESSES
CONTAINERIZED	CONTEMPLATIST	CONTENTMENTS	CONTINENTALIST	CONTORTING
CONTAINERIZES	CONTEMPLATISTS	CONTERMINAL	CONTINENTALISTS	CONTORTION
CONTAINERIZING	CONTEMPLATIVE	CONTERMINALLY	CONTINENTALLY	CONTORTIONAL
CONTAINERLESS	CONTEMPLATIVELY	CONTERMINANT	CONTINENTALS	CONTORTIONATE
CONTAINERPORT	CONTEMPLATIVES	CONTERMINATE	CONTINENTLY	CONTORTIONED

CONTORTIONISM	CONTRACTIVE	CONTRANATANT	CONTRAVENED	CONTRIVEMENTS
CONTORTIONISMS	CONTRACTIVELY	CONTRAOCTAVE	CONTRAVENER	CONTRIVERS
CONTORTIONIST	CONTRACTIVENESS	CONTRAOCTAVES	CONTRAVENERS	CONTRIVING
CONTORTIONISTIC	CONTRACTOR	CONTRAPLEX	CONTRAVENES	CONTROLLABILITY
CONTORTIONISTS	CONTRACTORS	CONTRAPOSITION	CONTRAVENING	CONTROLLABLE
CONTORTIONS	CONTRACTUAL	CONTRAPOSITIONS	CONTRAVENTION	CONTROLLABLY
CONTORTIVE	CONTRACTUALLY	CONTRAPOSITIVE	CONTRAVENTIONS	CONTROLLED
CONTOURING	CONTRACTURAL	CONTRAPOSITIVES	CONTRAYERVA	CONTROLLER
CONTRABAND	CONTRACTURE	CONTRAPPOSTO	CONTRAYERVAS	CONTROLLERS
CONTRABANDISM	CONTRACTURES	CONTRAPPOSTOS	CONTRECOUP	CONTROLLERSHIP
CONTRABANDISMS	CONTRACYCLICAL	CONTRAPROP	CONTRECOUPS	CONTROLLERSHIPS
CONTRABANDIST	CONTRADANCE	CONTRAPROPELLER	CONTREDANCE	CONTROLLING
CONTRABANDISTS	CONTRADANCES	CONTRAPROPS	CONTREDANCES	CONTROLMENT
CONTRABANDS	CONTRADICT	CONTRAPTION	CONTREDANSE	CONTROLMENTS
CONTRABASS	CONTRADICTABLE	CONTRAPTIONS	CONTREDANSES	CONTROULED
CONTRABASSES	CONTRADICTED	CONTRAPUNTAL	CONTRETEMPS	CONTROULING
CONTRABASSI	CONTRADICTER	CONTRAPUNTALIST	CONTRIBUTABLE	CONTROVERSE
CONTRABASSIST	CONTRADICTERS	CONTRAPUNTALLY	CONTRIBUTARIES	CONTROVERSES
CONTRABASSISTS	CONTRADICTING	CONTRAPUNTIST	CONTRIBUTARY	CONTROVERSIAL
CONTRABASSO	CONTRADICTION	CONTRAPUNTISTS	CONTRIBUTE	CONTROVERSIALLY
CONTRABASSOON	CONTRADICTIONS	CONTRARIAN	CONTRIBUTED	CONTROVERSIES
CONTRABASSOONS	CONTRADICTIOUS	CONTRARIANS	CONTRIBUTES	CONTROVERSY
CONTRABASSOS	CONTRADICTIVE	CONTRARIED	CONTRIBUTING	CONTROVERT
CONTRABBASSI	CONTRADICTIVELY	CONTRARIES	CONTRIBUTION	CONTROVERTED
CONTRABBASSO	CONTRADICTOR	CONTRARIETIES	CONTRIBUTIONS	CONTROVERTER
CONTRABBASSOS	CONTRADICTORIES	CONTRARIETY	CONTRIBUTIVE	CONTROVERTERS
CONTRACEPTION	CONTRADICTORILY	CONTRARILY	CONTRIBUTIVELY	CONTROVERTIBLE
CONTRACEPTIONS	CONTRADICTORS	CONTRARINESS	CONTRIBUTOR	CONTROVERTIBLY
CONTRACEPTIVE	CONTRADICTORY	CONTRARINESSES	CONTRIBUTORIES	CONTROVERTING
CONTRACEPTIVES	CONTRADICTS	CONTRARIOUS	CONTRIBUTORS	CONTROVERTIST
CONTRACLOCKWISE	CONTRAFAGOTTI	CONTRARIOUSLY	CONTRIBUTORY	CONTROVERTISTS
CONTRACTABILITY	CONTRAFAGOTTO	CONTRARIOUSNESS	CONTRISTATION	CONTROVERTS
CONTRACTABLE	CONTRAFAGOTTOS	CONTRARIWISE	CONTRISTATIONS	CONTUBERNAL
CONTRACTABLY	CONTRAFLOW	CONTRARYING	CONTRISTED	CONTUBERNYAL
CONTRACTED	CONTRAFLOWS	CONTRASEXUAL	CONTRISTING	CONTUMACIES
CONTRACTEDLY	CONTRAGESTION	CONTRASEXUALS	CONTRITELY	CONTUMACIOUS
CONTRACTEDNESS	CONTRAGESTIONS	CONTRASTABLE	CONTRITENESS	CONTUMACIOUSLY
CONTRACTIBILITY	CONTRAGESTIVE	CONTRASTABLY	CONTRITENESSES	CONTUMACITIES
CONTRACTIBLE	CONTRAGESTIVES	CONTRASTED	CONTRITION	CONTUMACITY
CONTRACTIBLY	CONTRAHENT	CONTRASTIER	CONTRITIONS	CONTUMELIES
CONTRACTILE	CONTRAHENTS	CONTRASTIEST	CONTRITURATE	CONTUMELIOUS
CONTRACTILITIES	CONTRAINDICANT	CONTRASTING	CONTRITURATED	CONTUMELIOUSLY
CONTRACTILITY	CONTRAINDICANTS	CONTRASTINGLY	CONTRITURATES	CONTUNDING
CONTRACTING	CONTRAINDICATE	CONTRASTIVE	CONTRITURATING	CONTUSIONED
CONTRACTION	CONTRAINDICATED	CONTRASTIVELY	CONTRIVABLE	CONTUSIONS
CONTRACTIONAL	CONTRAINDICATES	CONTRATERRENE	CONTRIVANCE	CONUNDRUMS
CONTRACTIONARY	CONTRALATERAL	CONTRAVALLATION	CONTRIVANCES	CONURBATION
CONTRACTIONS	CONTRALTOS	CONTRAVENE	CONTRIVEMENT	CONURBATIONS

CONVALESCE	CONVENTIONEER	CONVERTIBLENESS	CONVINCIBLE	CONVULSIVENESS
CONVALESCED	CONVENTIONEERS	CONVERTIBLES	CONVINCING	COOKHOUSES
CONVALESCENCE	CONVENTIONER	CONVERTIBLY	CONVINCINGLY	COOKSHACKS
CONVALESCENCES	CONVENTIONERS	CONVERTING	CONVINCINGNESS	COOKSTOVES
CONVALESCENCIES	CONVENTIONIST	CONVERTIPLANE	CONVIVIALIST	COOLHEADED
CONVALESCENCY	CONVENTIONISTS	CONVERTIPLANES	CONVIVIALISTS	COOLHOUSES
CONVALESCENT	CONVENTIONS	CONVERTITE	CONVIVIALITIES	COOLINGNESS
CONVALESCENTLY	CONVENTUAL	CONVERTITES	CONVIVIALITY	COOLINGNESSES
CONVALESCENTS	CONVENTUALLY	CONVERTIVE	CONVIVIALLY	COOLNESSES
CONVALESCES	CONVENTUALS	CONVERTOPLANE	CONVOCATED	COOMCEILED
CONVALESCING	CONVERGENCE	CONVERTOPLANES	CONVOCATES	COONHOUNDS
CONVECTING	CONVERGENCES	CONVERTORS	CONVOCATING	COOPERAGES
CONVECTION	CONVERGENCIES	CONVEXEDLY	CONVOCATION	COOPERATED
CONVECTIONAL	CONVERGENCY	CONVEXITIES	CONVOCATIONAL	COOPERATES
CONVECTIONS	CONVERGENT	CONVEXNESS	CONVOCATIONIST	COOPERATING
CONVECTIVE	CONVERGING	CONVEXNESSES	CONVOCATIONISTS	COOPERATION
CONVECTORS	CONVERSABLE	CONVEYABLE	CONVOCATIONS	COOPERATIONIST
CONVENABLE	CONVERSABLENESS	CONVEYANCE	CONVOCATIVE	COOPERATIONISTS
CONVENANCE	CONVERSABLY	CONVEYANCER	CONVOCATOR	COOPERATIONS
CONVENANCES	CONVERSANCE	CONVEYANCERS	CONVOCATORS	COOPERATIVE
CONVENERSHIP	CONVERSANCES	CONVEYANCES	CONVOLUTED	COOPERATIVELY
CONVENERSHIPS	CONVERSANCIES	CONVEYANCING	CONVOLUTEDLY	COOPERATIVENESS
CONVENIENCE	CONVERSANCY	CONVEYANCINGS	CONVOLUTEDNESS	COOPERATIVES
CONVENIENCES	CONVERSANT	CONVEYORISATION	CONVOLUTELY	COOPERATIVITIES
CONVENIENCIES	CONVERSANTLY	CONVEYORISE	CONVOLUTES	COOPERATIVITY
CONVENIENCY	CONVERSATION	CONVEYORISED	CONVOLUTING	COOPERATOR
CONVENIENT	CONVERSATIONAL	CONVEYORISES	CONVOLUTION	COOPERATORS
CONVENIENTLY	CONVERSATIONISM	CONVEYORISING	CONVOLUTIONAL	COOPERINGS
CONVENINGS	CONVERSATIONIST	CONVEYORIZATION	CONVOLUTIONARY	COOPTATION
CONVENORSHIP	CONVERSATIONS	CONVEYORIZE	CONVOLUTIONS	COOPTATIONS
CONVENORSHIPS	CONVERSATIVE	CONVEYORIZED	CONVOLVING	COOPTATIVE
CONVENTICLE	CONVERSAZIONE	CONVEYORIZES	CONVOLVULACEOUS	COORDINANCE
CONVENTICLED	CONVERSAZIONES	CONVEYORIZING	CONVOLVULI	COORDINANCES
CONVENTICLER	CONVERSAZIONI	CONVICINITIES	CONVOLVULUS	COORDINATE
CONVENTICLERS	CONVERSELY	CONVICINITY	CONVOLVULUSES	COORDINATED
CONVENTICLES	CONVERSERS	CONVICTABLE	CONVULSANT	COORDINATELY
CONVENTICLING	CONVERSING	CONVICTIBLE	CONVULSANTS	COORDINATENESS
CONVENTING	CONVERSION	CONVICTING	CONVULSIBLE	COORDINATES
CONVENTION	CONVERSIONAL	CONVICTION	CONVULSING	COORDINATING
CONVENTIONAL	CONVERSIONARY	CONVICTIONAL	CONVULSION	COORDINATION
CONVENTIONALISE	CONVERSIONS	CONVICTIONS	CONVULSIONAL	COORDINATIONS
CONVENTIONALISM	CONVERTAPLANE	CONVICTISM	CONVULSIONARIES	COORDINATIVE
CONVENTIONALIST	CONVERTAPLANES	CONVICTISMS	CONVULSIONARY	COORDINATOR
CONVENTIONALITY	CONVERTEND	CONVICTIVE	CONVULSIONIST	COORDINATORS
CONVENTIONALIZE	CONVERTENDS	CONVICTIVELY	CONVULSIONISTS	COPARCENARIES
CONVENTIONALLY	CONVERTERS	CONVINCEMENT	CONVULSIONS	COPARCENARY
CONVENTIONALS	CONVERTIBILITY	CONVINCEMENTS	CONVULSIVE	COPARCENER
CONVENTIONARY	CONVERTIBLE	CONVINCERS	CONVULSIVELY	COPARCENERIES

COPARCENERS	COPPERSMITH	COPROPHILIA	COPYTAKERS	CORDIALIZING
COPARCENERY	COPPERSMITHS	COPROPHILIAC	COPYWRITER	CORDIALNESS
COPARCENIES	COPPERWORK	COPROPHILIACS	COPYWRITERS	CORDIALNESSES
COPARENTED	COPPERWORKS	COPROPHILIAS	COPYWRITING	CORDIERITE
COPARENTING	COPPERWORM	COPROPHILIC	COPYWRITINGS	CORDIERITES
COPARTNERED	COPPERWORMS	COPROPHILOUS	COQUELICOT	CORDILLERA
COPARTNERIES	COPPICINGS	COPROPRIETOR	COQUELICOTS	CORDILLERAN
COPARTNERING	COPRAEMIAS	COPROPRIETORS	COQUETRIES	CORDILLERAS
COPARTNERS	COPRESENCE	COPROSPERITIES	COQUETTING	CORDLESSES
COPARTNERSHIP	COPRESENCES	COPROSPERITY	COQUETTISH	CORDOCENTESES
COPARTNERSHIPS	COPRESENTED	COPROSTEROL	COQUETTISHLY	CORDOCENTESIS
COPARTNERY	COPRESENTING	COPROSTEROLS	COQUETTISHNESS	CORDONNETS
COPATRIOTS	COPRESENTS	COPSEWOODS	COQUIMBITE	CORDOTOMIES
COPAYMENTS	COPRESIDENT	COPUBLISHED	COQUIMBITES	CORDUROYED
COPERNICIUM	COPRESIDENTS	COPUBLISHER	CORACIIFORM	CORDUROYING
COPERNICIUMS	COPRINCIPAL	COPUBLISHERS	CORADICATE	CORDWAINER
COPESETTIC	COPRINCIPALS	COPUBLISHES	CORALBELLS	CORDWAINERIES
COPESTONES	COPRISONER	COPUBLISHING	CORALBERRIES	CORDWAINERS
COPILOTING	COPRISONERS	COPULATING	CORALBERRY	CORDWAINERY
COPINGSTONE	COPROCESSING	COPULATION	CORALLACEOUS	CORDYLINES
COPINGSTONES	COPROCESSINGS	COPULATIONS	CORALLIFEROUS	CORECIPIENT
COPIOUSNESS	COPROCESSOR	COPULATIVE	CORALLIFORM	CORECIPIENTS
COPIOUSNESSES	COPROCESSORS	COPULATIVELY	CORALLIGENOUS	COREDEEMED
COPLAINTIFF	COPRODUCED	COPULATIVES	CORALLINES	COREDEEMING
COPLAINTIFFS	COPRODUCER	COPULATORY	CORALLITES	COREFERENTIAL
COPLANARITIES	COPRODUCERS	COPURIFIED	CORALLOIDAL	COREGONINE
COPLANARITY	COPRODUCES	COPURIFIES	CORALLOIDS	CORELATING
COPLOTTING	COPRODUCING	COPURIFYING	CORALROOTS	CORELATION
COPLOTTINGS	COPRODUCTION	COPYCATTED	CORALWORTS	CORELATIONS
COPOLYMERIC	COPRODUCTIONS	COPYCATTING	CORBEILLES	CORELATIVE
COPOLYMERISE	COPRODUCTS	COPYEDITED	CORBELINGS	CORELATIVES
COPOLYMERISED	COPROLALIA	COPYEDITING	CORBELLING	CORELIGIONIST
COPOLYMERISES	COPROLALIAC	COPYFIGHTS	CORBELLINGS	CORELIGIONISTS
COPOLYMERISING	COPROLALIAS	COPYGRAPHS	CORBICULAE	COREOPSISES
COPOLYMERIZE	COPROLITES	COPYHOLDER	CORBICULATE	COREPRESSOR
COPOLYMERIZED	COPROLITHS	COPYHOLDERS	CORDECTOMIES	COREPRESSORS
COPOLYMERIZES	COPROLITIC	COPYLEFTED	CORDECTOMY	COREQUISITE
COPOLYMERIZING	COPROLOGIES	COPYLEFTING	CORDELLING	COREQUISITES
COPOLYMERS	COPROMOTER	COPYREADER	CORDGRASSES	CORESEARCHER
COPPERASES	COPROMOTERS	COPYREADERS	CORDIALISE	CORESEARCHERS
COPPERHEAD	COPROPHAGAN	COPYREADING	CORDIALISED	CORESIDENT
COPPERHEADS	COPROPHAGANS	COPYREADINGS	CORDIALISES	CORESIDENTIAL
COPPERIEST	COPROPHAGIC	COPYRIGHTABLE	CORDIALISING	CORESIDENTS
COPPERINGS	COPROPHAGIES	COPYRIGHTED	CORDIALITIES	CORESPONDENT
COPPERPLATE	COPROPHAGIST	COPYRIGHTER	CORDIALITY	CORESPONDENTS
COPPERPLATES	COPROPHAGISTS	COPYRIGHTERS	CORDIALIZE	CORFHOUSES
COPPERSKIN	COPROPHAGOUS	COPYRIGHTING	CORDIALIZED	CORIACEOUS
COPPERSKINS	COPROPHAGY	COPYRIGHTS	CORDIALIZES	CORIANDERS

C

CORINTHIANISE	CORNETTINO	CORONERSHIP	CORPOREALIZED	CORRELATABLE
CORINTHIANISED	CORNETTINOS	CORONERSHIPS	CORPOREALIZES	CORRELATED
CORINTHIANISES	CORNETTIST	CORONOGRAPH	CORPOREALIZING	CORRELATES
CORINTHIANISING	CORNETTISTS	CORONOGRAPHS	CORPOREALLY	CORRELATING
CORINTHIANIZE	CORNFIELDS	COROTATING	CORPOREALNESS	CORRELATION
CORINTHIANIZED	CORNFLAKES	COROTATION	CORPOREALNESSES	CORRELATIONAL
CORINTHIANIZES	CORNFLOURS	COROTATIONS	CORPOREITIES	CORRELATIONS
CORINTHIANIZING	CORNFLOWER	CORPORALES	CORPOREITY	CORRELATIVE
CORIVALLED	CORNFLOWERS	CORPORALITIES	CORPORIFICATION	CORRELATIVELY
CORIVALLING	CORNHUSKER	CORPORALITY	CORPORIFIED	CORRELATIVENESS
CORIVALRIES	CORNHUSKERS	CORPORALLY	CORPORIFIES	CORRELATIVES
CORIVALSHIP	CORNHUSKING	CORPORALSHIP	CORPORIFYING	CORRELATIVITIES
CORIVALSHIPS	CORNHUSKINGS	CORPORALSHIPS	CORPOSANTS	CORRELATIVITY
CORKBOARDS	CORNICHONS	CORPORASES	CORPSELIKE	CORRELATOR
CORKBORERS	CORNICINGS	CORPORATELY	CORPULENCE	CORRELATORS
CORKINESSES	CORNICULATE	CORPORATENESS	CORPULENCES	CORRELIGIONIST
CORKSCREWED	CORNICULUM	CORPORATENESSES	CORPULENCIES	CORRELIGIONISTS
CORKSCREWING	CORNICULUMS	CORPORATES	CORPULENCY	CORREPTION
CORKSCREWS	CORNIFEROUS	CORPORATION	CORPULENTLY	CORREPTIONS
CORMOPHYTE	CORNIFICATION	CORPORATIONS	CORPUSCLES	CORRESPOND
CORMOPHYTES	CORNIFICATIONS	CORPORATISE	CORPUSCULAR	CORRESPONDED
CORMOPHYTIC	CORNIFYING	CORPORATISED	CORPUSCULARIAN	CORRESPONDENCE
CORMORANTS	CORNIGEROUS	CORPORATISES	CORPUSCULARIANS	CORRESPONDENCES
CORNACEOUS	CORNINESSES	CORPORATISING	CORPUSCULARITY	CORRESPONDENCY
CORNBORERS	CORNOPEANS	CORPORATISM	CORPUSCULE	CORRESPONDENT
CORNBRAIDED	CORNROWING	CORPORATISMS	CORPUSCULES	CORRESPONDENTLY
CORNBRAIDING	CORNSTALKS	CORPORATIST	CORRALLING	CORRESPONDENTS
CORNBRAIDS	CORNSTARCH	CORPORATISTS	CORRASIONS	CORRESPONDING
CORNBRANDIES	CORNSTARCHES	CORPORATIVE	CORRECTABLE	CORRESPONDINGLY
CORNBRANDY	CORNSTONES	CORPORATIVISM	CORRECTEST	CORRESPONDS
CORNBRASHES	CORNUCOPIA	CORPORATIVISMS	CORRECTIBLE	CORRESPONSIVE
CORNBREADS	CORNUCOPIAN	CORPORATIZE	CORRECTING	CORRIGENDA
CORNCOCKLE	CORNUCOPIAS	CORPORATIZED	CORRECTION	CORRIGENDUM
CORNCOCKLES	COROLLACEOUS	CORPORATIZES	CORRECTIONAL	CORRIGENTS
CORNCRAKES	COROLLARIES	CORPORATIZING	CORRECTIONER	CORRIGIBILITIES
CORNEITISES	COROLLIFLORAL	CORPORATOR	CORRECTIONERS	CORRIGIBILITY
CORNELIANS	COROLLIFLOROUS	CORPORATORS	CORRECTIONS	CORRIGIBLE
CORNEMUSES	COROLLIFORM	CORPOREALISE	CORRECTITUDE	CORRIGIBLY
CORNERBACK	COROMANDEL	CORPOREALISED	CORRECTITUDES	CORRIVALLED
CORNERBACKS	COROMANDELS	CORPOREALISES	CORRECTIVE	CORRIVALLING
CORNERINGS	CORONAGRAPH	CORPOREALISING	CORRECTIVELY	CORRIVALRIES
CORNERSTONE	CORONAGRAPHS	CORPOREALISM	CORRECTIVES	CORRIVALRY
CORNERSTONES	CORONARIES	CORPOREALISMS	CORRECTNESS	CORRIVALSHIP
CORNERWAYS	CORONATING	CORPOREALIST	CORRECTNESSES	CORRIVALSHIPS
CORNERWISE	CORONATION	CORPOREALISTS	CORRECTORS	CORROBORABLE
CORNETCIES	CORONATIONS	CORPOREALITIES	CORRECTORY	CORROBORANT
CORNETISTS	CORONAVIRUS	CORPOREALITY	CORREGIDOR	CORROBORATE
CORNETTINI	CORONAVIRUSES	CORPOREALIZE	CORREGIDORS	CORROBORATED

CORROBORATES	CORRUPTNESSES	COSCINOMANCY	COSMOGONIST	COSPONSORSHIP
CORROBORATING	CORRUPTORS	COSCRIPTED	COSMOGONISTS	COSPONSORSHIPS
CORROBORATION	CORSELETTE	COSCRIPTING	COSMOGRAPHER	COSSETTING
CORROBORATIONS	CORSELETTES	COSEISMALS	COSMOGRAPHERS	COSTALGIAS
CORROBORATIVE	CORSETIERE	COSEISMICS	COSMOGRAPHIC	COSTARDMONGER
CORROBORATIVELY	CORSETIERES	COSENTIENT	COSMOGRAPHICAL	COSTARDMONGERS
CORROBORATIVES	CORSETIERS	COSHERINGS	COSMOGRAPHIES	COSTARRING
CORROBORATOR	CORSETRIES	COSIGNATORIES	COSMOGRAPHIST	COSTEANING
CORROBORATORS	CORTICALLY	COSIGNATORY	COSMOGRAPHISTS	COSTEANINGS
CORROBORATORY	CORTICATED	COSIGNIFICATIVE	COSMOGRAPHY	COSTERMONGER
CORROBOREE	CORTICATION	COSINESSES	COSMOLATRIES	COSTERMONGERS
CORROBOREED	CORTICATIONS	COSMECEUTICAL	COSMOLATRY	COSTIVENESS
CORROBOREEING	CORTICOIDS	COSMECEUTICALS	COSMOLINED	COSTIVENESSES
CORROBOREES	CORTICOLOUS	COSMETICAL	COSMOLINES	COSTLESSLY
CORRODANTS	CORTICOSTEROID	COSMETICALLY	COSMOLINING	COSTLINESS
CORRODENTS	CORTICOSTEROIDS	COSMETICIAN	COSMOLOGIC	COSTLINESSES
CORRODIBILITIES	CORTICOSTERONE	COSMETICIANS	COSMOLOGICAL	COSTMARIES
CORRODIBILITY	CORTICOSTERONES	COSMETICISE	COSMOLOGICALLY	COSTOTOMIES
CORRODIBLE	CORTICOTROPHIC	COSMETICISED	COSMOLOGIES	COSTUMERIES
CORROSIBILITIES	CORTICOTROPHIN	COSMETICISES	COSMOLOGIST	COSTUMIERS
CORROSIBILITY	CORTICOTROPHINS	COSMETICISING	COSMOLOGISTS	COSTUMINGS
CORROSIBLE	CORTICOTROPIC	COSMETICISM	COSMONAUTICS	COSURFACTANT
CORROSIONS	CORTICOTROPIN	COSMETICISMS	COSMONAUTS	COSURFACTANTS
CORROSIVELY	CORTICOTROPINS	COSMETICIZE	COSMOPLASTIC	COTANGENTIAL
CORROSIVENESS	CORTISONES	COSMETICIZED	COSMOPOLIS	COTANGENTS
CORROSIVENESSES	CORUSCATED	COSMETICIZES	COSMOPOLISES	COTELETTES
CORROSIVES	CORUSCATES	COSMETICIZING	COSMOPOLITAN	COTEMPORANEOUS
CORRUGATED	CORUSCATING	COSMETICOLOGIES	COSMOPOLITANISM	COTEMPORARY
CORRUGATES	CORUSCATION	COSMETICOLOGY	COSMOPOLITANS	COTENANCIES
CORRUGATING	CORUSCATIONS	COSMETOLOGIES	COSMOPOLITE	COTERMINOUS
CORRUGATION	CORVETTING	COSMETOLOGIST	COSMOPOLITES	COTERMINOUSLY
CORRUGATIONS	CORYBANTES	COSMETOLOGISTS	COSMOPOLITIC	COTILLIONS
CORRUGATOR	CORYBANTIC	COSMETOLOGY	COSMOPOLITICAL	COTONEASTER
CORRUGATORS	CORYBANTISM	COSMICALLY	COSMOPOLITICS	COTONEASTERS
CORRUPTERS	CORYBANTISMS	COSMOCHEMICAL	COSMOPOLITISM	COTRANSDUCE
CORRUPTEST	CORYDALINE	COSMOCHEMIST	COSMOPOLITISMS	COTRANSDUCED
CORRUPTIBILITY	CORYDALINES	COSMOCHEMISTRY	COSMORAMAS	COTRANSDUCES
CORRUPTIBLE	CORYDALISES	COSMOCHEMISTS	COSMORAMIC	COTRANSDUCING
CORRUPTIBLENESS	CORYLOPSES	COSMOCRATIC	COSMOSPHERE	COTRANSDUCTION
CORRUPTIBLY	CORYLOPSIS	COSMOCRATS	COSMOSPHERES	COTRANSDUCTIONS
CORRUPTING	CORYMBOSELY	COSMODROME	COSMOTHEISM	COTRANSFER
CORRUPTION	CORYNEBACTERIA	COSMODROMES	COSMOTHEISMS	COTRANSFERS
CORRUPTIONIST	CORYNEBACTERIAL	COSMOGENIC	COSMOTHETIC	COTRANSPORT
CORRUPTIONISTS	CORYNEBACTERIUM	COSMOGENIES	COSMOTHETICAL	COTRANSPORTED
CORRUPTIONS	CORYNEFORM	COSMOGONAL	COSMOTRONS	COTRANSPORTING
CORRUPTIVE	CORYPHAEUS	COSMOGONIC	COSPONSORED	COTRANSPORTS
CORRUPTIVELY	CORYPHENES	COSMOGONICAL	COSPONSORING	COTRUSTEES
CORRUPTNESS	COSCINOMANCIES	COSMOGONIES	COSPONSORS	COTTABUSES

COTTAGIEST	COUNCILLORSHIP	COUNTERARGUED	COUNTERCHARGING	COUNTERFESAUNCE
COTTAGINGS	COUNCILLORSHIPS	COUNTERARGUES	COUNTERCHARM	COUNTERFIRE
COTTERLESS	COUNCILMAN	COUNTERARGUING	COUNTERCHARMED	COUNTERFIRES
COTTIERISM	COUNCILMANIC	COUNTERARGUMENT	COUNTERCHARMING	COUNTERFLOW
COTTIERISMS	COUNCILMEN	COUNTERASSAULT	COUNTERCHARMS	COUNTERFLOWS
COTTONADES	COUNCILORS	COUNTERASSAULTS	COUNTERCHECK	COUNTERFOIL
COTTONIEST	COUNCILORSHIP	COUNTERATTACK	COUNTERCHECKED	COUNTERFOILS
COTTONMOUTH	COUNCILORSHIPS	COUNTERATTACKED	COUNTERCHECKING	COUNTERFORCE
COTTONMOUTHS	COUNCILWOMAN	COUNTERATTACKER	COUNTERCHECKS	COUNTERFORCES
COTTONOCRACIES	COUNCILWOMEN	COUNTERATTACKS	COUNTERCLAIM	COUNTERFORT
COTTONOCRACY	COUNSELABLE	COUNTERBALANCE	COUNTERCLAIMANT	COUNTERFORTS
COTTONSEED	COUNSELEES	COUNTERBALANCED	COUNTERCLAIMED	COUNTERGLOW
COTTONSEEDS	COUNSELING	COUNTERBALANCES	COUNTERCLAIMING	COUNTERGLOWS
COTTONTAIL	COUNSELINGS	COUNTERBASE	COUNTERCLAIMS	COUNTERGUERILLA
COTTONTAILS	COUNSELLABLE	COUNTERBASES	COUNTERCOUP	COUNTERIMAGE
COTTONWEED	COUNSELLED	COUNTERBID	COUNTERCOUPS	COUNTERIMAGES
COTTONWEEDS	COUNSELLEE	COUNTERBIDDER	COUNTERCRIES	COUNTERING
COTTONWOOD	COUNSELLEES	COUNTERBIDDERS	COUNTERCRY	COUNTERINSTANCE
COTTONWOODS	COUNSELLING	COUNTERBIDS	COUNTERCULTURAL	COUNTERION
COTURNIXES	COUNSELLINGS	COUNTERBLAST	COUNTERCULTURE	COUNTERIONS
COTYLEDONAL	COUNSELLOR	COUNTERBLASTS	COUNTERCULTURES	COUNTERIRRITANT
COTYLEDONARY	COUNSELLORS	COUNTERBLOCKADE	COUNTERCURRENT	COUNTERLIGHT
COTYLEDONOID	COUNSELLORSHIP	COUNTERBLOW	COUNTERCURRENTS	COUNTERLIGHTS
COTYLEDONOUS	COUNSELLORSHIPS	COUNTERBLOWS	COUNTERCYCLICAL	COUNTERMAN
COTYLEDONS	COUNSELORS	COUNTERBLUFF	COUNTERDEMAND	COUNTERMAND
COTYLIFORM	COUNSELORSHIP	COUNTERBLUFFS	COUNTERDEMANDS	COUNTERMANDABLE
COTYLOIDAL	COUNSELORSHIPS	COUNTERBOND	COUNTERDRAW	COUNTERMANDED
COTYLOIDALS	COUNTABILITIES	COUNTERBONDS	COUNTERDRAWING	COUNTERMANDING
COTYLOSAUR	COUNTABILITY	COUNTERBORE	COUNTERDRAWN	COUNTERMANDS
COTYLOSAURS	COUNTBACKS	COUNTERBORED	COUNTERDRAWS	COUNTERMARCH
COUCHETTES	COUNTDOWNS	COUNTERBORES	COUNTERDREW	COUNTERMARCHED
COUCHSURFING	COUNTENANCE	COUNTERBORING	COUNTEREFFORT	COUNTERMARCHES
COUCHSURFINGS	COUNTENANCED	COUNTERBRACE	COUNTEREFFORTS	COUNTERMARCHING
COULIBIACA	COUNTENANCER	COUNTERBRACED	COUNTEREVIDENCE	COUNTERMARK
COULIBIACAS	COUNTENANCERS	COUNTERBRACES	COUNTEREXAMPLE	COUNTERMARKS
COULIBIACS	COUNTENANCES	COUNTERBRACING	COUNTEREXAMPLES	COUNTERMEASURE
COULOMBMETER	COUNTENANCING	COUNTERBUFF	COUNTERFACTUAL	COUNTERMEASURES
COULOMBMETERS	COUNTERACT	COUNTERBUFFED	COUNTERFACTUALS	COUNTERMELODIES
COULOMETER	COUNTERACTED	COUNTERBUFFING	COUNTERFECT	COUNTERMELODY
COULOMETERS	COUNTERACTING	COUNTERBUFFS	COUNTERFEISANCE	COUNTERMEMO
COULOMETRIC	COUNTERACTION	COUNTERCAMPAIGN	COUNTERFEIT	COUNTERMEMOS
COULOMETRICALLY	COUNTERACTIONS	COUNTERCHANGE	COUNTERFEITED	COUNTERMEN
COULOMETRIES	COUNTERACTIVE	COUNTERCHANGED	COUNTERFEITER	COUNTERMINE
COULOMETRY	COUNTERACTIVELY	COUNTERCHANGES	COUNTERFEITERS	COUNTERMINED
COUMARILIC	COUNTERACTS	COUNTERCHANGING	COUNTERFEITING	COUNTERMINES
COUMARONES	COUNTERAGENT	COUNTERCHARGE	COUNTERFEITINGS	COUNTERMINING
COUNCILLOR	COUNTERAGENTS	COUNTERCHARGED	COUNTERFEITLY	COUNTERMOTION
COUNCILLORS	COUNTERARGUE	COUNTERCHARGES	COUNTERFEITS	COUNTERMOTIONS

COUNTERMOVE	COUNTERPLEAS	COUNTERREFORMER	COUNTERSTROKE	COUNTERWEIGHTED
COUNTERMOVED	COUNTERPLED	COUNTERREFORMS	COUNTERSTROKES	COUNTERWEIGHTS
COUNTERMOVEMENT	COUNTERPLOT	COUNTERRESPONSE	COUNTERSTRUCK	COUNTERWORD
COUNTERMOVES	COUNTERPLOTS	COUNTERSANK	COUNTERSTYLE	COUNTERWORDS
COUNTERMOVING	COUNTERPLOTTED	COUNTERSCARP	COUNTERSTYLES	COUNTERWORK
COUNTERMURE	COUNTERPLOTTING	COUNTERSCARPS	COUNTERSUBJECT	COUNTERWORKED
COUNTERMURED	COUNTERPLOY	COUNTERSEAL	COUNTERSUBJECTS	COUNTERWORKER
COUNTERMURES	COUNTERPLOYS	COUNTERSEALED	COUNTERSUE	COUNTERWORKERS
COUNTERMURING	COUNTERPOINT	COUNTERSEALING	COUNTERSUED	COUNTERWORKING
COUNTERMYTH	COUNTERPOINTED	COUNTERSEALS	COUNTERSUES	COUNTERWORKS
COUNTERMYTHS	COUNTERPOINTING	COUNTERSHADING	COUNTERSUING	COUNTERWORLD
COUNTEROFFER	COUNTERPOINTS	COUNTERSHADINGS	COUNTERSUIT	COUNTERWORLDS
COUNTEROFFERS	COUNTERPOISE	COUNTERSHAFT	COUNTERSUITS	COUNTESSES
COUNTERORDER	COUNTERPOISED	COUNTERSHAFTS	COUNTERSUNK	COUNTINGHOUSE
COUNTERORDERED	COUNTERPOISES	COUNTERSHOT	COUNTERTACTIC	COUNTINGHOUSES
COUNTERORDERING	COUNTERPOISING	COUNTERSHOTS	COUNTERTACTICS	COUNTLESSLY
COUNTERORDERS	COUNTERPOSE	COUNTERSIGN	COUNTERTENDENCY	COUNTLINES
COUNTERPACE	COUNTERPOSED	COUNTERSIGNED	COUNTERTENOR	COUNTRIFIED
COUNTERPACES	COUNTERPOSES	COUNTERSIGNING	COUNTERTENORS	COUNTROLLED
COUNTERPANE	COUNTERPOSING	COUNTERSIGNS	COUNTERTERROR	COUNTROLLING
COUNTERPANES	COUNTERPOWER	COUNTERSINK	COUNTERTERRORS	COUNTRYFIED
COUNTERPART	COUNTERPOWERS	COUNTERSINKING	COUNTERTHREAT	COUNTRYISH
COUNTERPARTIES	COUNTERPRESSURE	COUNTERSINKS	COUNTERTHREATS	COUNTRYMAN
COUNTERPARTS	COUNTERPROJECT	COUNTERSNIPER	COUNTERTHRUST	COUNTRYMEN
COUNTERPARTY	COUNTERPROJECTS	COUNTERSNIPERS	COUNTERTHRUSTS	COUNTRYSEAT
COUNTERPEISE	COUNTERPROOF	COUNTERSPELL	COUNTERTOP	COUNTRYSEATS
COUNTERPEISED	COUNTERPROOFS	COUNTERSPELLS	COUNTERTOPS	COUNTRYSIDE
COUNTERPEISES	COUNTERPROPOSAL	COUNTERSPIES	COUNTERTRADE	COUNTRYSIDES
COUNTERPEISING	COUNTERPROTEST	COUNTERSPY	COUNTERTRADED	COUNTRYWIDE
COUNTERPETITION	COUNTERPROTESTS	COUNTERSPYING	COUNTERTRADES	COUNTRYWOMAN
COUNTERPICKET	COUNTERPUNCH	COUNTERSPYINGS	COUNTERTRADING	COUNTRYWOMEN
COUNTERPICKETED	COUNTERPUNCHED	COUNTERSTAIN	COUNTERTREND	COUNTSHIPS
COUNTERPICKETS	COUNTERPUNCHER	COUNTERSTAINED	COUNTERTRENDS	COUPLEDOMS
COUNTERPLAN	COUNTERPUNCHERS	COUNTERSTAINING	COUNTERTYPE	COUPLEMENT
COUNTERPLANNED	COUNTERPUNCHES	COUNTERSTAINS	COUNTERTYPES	COUPLEMENTS
COUNTERPLANNING	COUNTERPUNCHING	COUNTERSTATE	COUNTERVAIL	COUPONINGS
COUNTERPLANS	COUNTERQUESTION	COUNTERSTATED	COUNTERVAILABLE	COURAGEFUL
COUNTERPLAY	COUNTERRAID	COUNTERSTATES	COUNTERVAILED	COURAGEOUS
COUNTERPLAYED	COUNTERRAIDED	COUNTERSTATING	COUNTERVAILING	COURAGEOUSLY
COUNTERPLAYER	COUNTERRAIDING	COUNTERSTEP	COUNTERVAILS	COURAGEOUSNESS
COUNTERPLAYERS	COUNTERRAIDS	COUNTERSTEPS	COUNTERVIEW	COURANTOES
COUNTERPLAYING	COUNTERRALLIED	COUNTERSTRATEGY	COUNTERVIEWS	COURBARILS
COUNTERPLAYS	COUNTERRALLIES	COUNTERSTREAM	COUNTERVIOLENCE	COURBETTES
COUNTERPLEA	COUNTERRALLY	COUNTERSTREAMS	COUNTERWEIGH	COURGETTES
COUNTERPLEAD	COUNTERRALLYING	COUNTERSTRICKEN	COUNTERWEIGHED	COURIERING
COUNTERPLEADED	COUNTERREACTION	COUNTERSTRIKE	COUNTERWEIGHING	COURSEBOOK
COUNTERPLEADING	COUNTERREFORM	COUNTERSTRIKES	COUNTERWEIGHS	COURSEBOOKS
COUNTERPLEADS	COUNTERREFORMED	COUNTERSTRIKING	COUNTERWEIGHT	COURSEWARE

COURSEWARES

COURSEWARES	COVELLINES	COWPUNCHERS	CRAFTSMANLY	CRANIOMETRIST
COURSEWORK	COVELLITES	COXCOMBICAL	CRAFTSMANSHIP	CRANIOMETRISTS
COURSEWORKS	COVENANTAL	COXCOMBICALITY	CRAFTSMANSHIPS	CRANIOMETRY
COURTCRAFT	COVENANTALLY	COXCOMBICALLY	CRAFTSPEOPLE	CRANIOPAGI
COURTCRAFTS	COVENANTED	COXCOMBRIES	CRAFTSPERSON	CRANIOPAGUS
COURTEOUSLY	COVENANTEE	COXCOMICAL	CRAFTSPERSONS	CRANIOSACRAL
COURTEOUSNESS	COVENANTEES	COXINESSES	CRAFTSWOMAN	CRANIOSCOPIES
COURTEOUSNESSES	COVENANTER	COXSWAINED	CRAFTSWOMEN	CRANIOSCOPIST
COURTESANS	COVENANTERS	COXSWAINING	CRAFTWORKS	CRANIOSCOPISTS
COURTESIED	COVENANTING	COYISHNESS	CRAGGEDNESS	CRANIOSCOPY
COURTESIES	COVENANTOR	COYISHNESSES	CRAGGEDNESSES	CRANIOTOMIES
COURTESYING	COVENANTORS	COYOTILLOS	CRAGGINESS	CRANIOTOMY
COURTEZANS	COVERALLED	COZINESSES	CRAGGINESSES	CRANKBAITS
COURTHOUSE	COVERMOUNT	CRABAPPLES	CRAIGFLUKE	CRANKCASES
COURTHOUSES	COVERMOUNTED	CRABBEDNESS	CRAIGFLUKES	CRANKHANDLE
COURTIERISM	COVERMOUNTING	CRABBEDNESSES	CRAKEBERRIES	CRANKHANDLES
COURTIERISMS	COVERMOUNTS	CRABBINESS	CRAKEBERRY	CRANKINESS
COURTIERLIKE	COVERSINES	CRABBINESSES	CRAMBOCLINK	CRANKINESSES
COURTIERLY	COVERSLIPS	CRABEATERS	CRAMBOCLINKS	CRANKNESSES
COURTLIEST	COVERTNESS	CRABGRASSES	CRAMOISIES	CRANKSHAFT
COURTLINESS	COVERTNESSES	CRABSTICKS	CRAMPBARKS	CRANKSHAFTS
COURTLINESSES	COVERTURES	CRACKAJACK	CRAMPFISHES	CRANREUCHS
COURTLINGS	COVETINGLY	CRACKAJACKS	CRAMPONING	CRAPEHANGER
COURTROOMS	COVETIVENESS	CRACKBACKS	CRAMPONNED	CRAPEHANGERS
COURTSHIPS	COVETIVENESSES	CRACKBERRIES	CRAMPONNING	CRAPEHANGING
COURTSIDES	COVETOUSLY	CRACKBERRY	CRAMPONNINGS	CRAPEHANGINGS
COURTYARDS	COVETOUSNESS	CRACKBRAIN	CRANACHANS	CRAPSHOOTER
COUSCOUSES	COVETOUSNESSES	CRACKBRAINED	CRANBERRIES	CRAPSHOOTERS
COUSCOUSOU	COWARDICES	CRACKBRAINS	CRANEFLIES	CRAPSHOOTS
COUSCOUSOUS	COWARDLIER	CRACKDOWNS	CRANESBILL	CRAPULENCE
COUSINAGES	COWARDLIEST	CRACKERJACK	CRANESBILLS	CRAPULENCES
COUSINHOOD	COWARDLINESS	CRACKERJACKS	CRANIECTOMIES	CRAPULENTLY
COUSINHOODS	COWARDLINESSES	CRACKHEADS	CRANIECTOMY	CRAPULOSITIES
COUSINRIES	COWARDRIES	CRACKLEWARE	CRANIOCEREBRAL	CRAPULOSITY
COUSINSHIP	COWARDSHIP	CRACKLEWARES	CRANIOFACIAL	CRAPULOUSLY
COUSINSHIPS	COWARDSHIPS	CRACKLIEST	CRANIOGNOMIES	CRAPULOUSNESS
COUTURIERE	COWBERRIES	CRACKLINGS	CRANIOGNOMY	CRAPULOUSNESSES
COUTURIERES	COWBOYINGS	CRACOVIENNE	CRANIOLOGICAL	CRAQUELURE
COUTURIERS	COWCATCHER	CRACOVIENNES	CRANIOLOGICALLY	CRAQUELURES
COVALENCES	COWCATCHERS	CRADLESONG	CRANIOLOGIES	CRASHINGLY
COVALENCIES	COWERINGLY	CRADLESONGS	CRANIOLOGIST	CRASHWORTHIER
COVALENTLY	COWFEEDERS	CRADLEWALK	CRANIOLOGISTS	CRASHWORTHIEST
COVARIANCE	COWFETERIA	CRADLEWALKS	CRANIOLOGY	CRASHWORTHINESS
COVARIANCES	COWFETERIAS	CRAFTINESS	CRANIOMETER	CRASHWORTHY
COVARIANTS	COWGRASSES	CRAFTINESSES	CRANIOMETERS	CRASSAMENTA
COVARIATES	COWLSTAFFS	CRAFTMANSHIP	CRANIOMETRIC	CRASSAMENTUM
COVARIATION	COWLSTAVES	CRAFTMANSHIPS	CRANIOMETRICAL	CRASSITUDE
COVARIATIONS	COWPUNCHER	CRAFTSMANLIKE	CRANIOMETRIES	CRASSITUDES

CRASSNESSES	CREATIVENESSES	CREESHIEST	CREPITATING	CRICKETING
CRASSULACEAN	CREATIVITIES	CREMAILLERE	CREPITATION	CRICKETINGS
CRASSULACEOUS	CREATIVITY	CREMAILLERES	CREPITATIONS	CRIMEWAVES
CRATERIFORM	CREATORSHIP	CREMASTERS	CREPITATIVE	CRIMINALESE
CRATERINGS	CREATORSHIPS	CREMATIONISM	CREPITUSES	CRIMINALESES
CRATERLESS	CREATRESSES	CREMATIONISMS	CREPOLINES	CRIMINALISATION
CRATERLETS	CREATRIXES	CREMATIONIST	CREPUSCLES	CRIMINALISE
CRATERLIKE	CREATUREHOOD	CREMATIONISTS	CREPUSCULAR	CRIMINALISED
CRAUNCHABLE	CREATUREHOODS	CREMATIONS	CREPUSCULE	CRIMINALISES
CRAUNCHIER	CREATURELINESS	CREMATORIA	CREPUSCULES	CRIMINALISING
CRAUNCHIEST	CREATURELY	CREMATORIAL	CREPUSCULOUS	CRIMINALIST
CRAUNCHINESS	CREATURESHIP	CREMATORIES	CRESCENDOED	CRIMINALISTICS
CRAUNCHINESSES	CREATURESHIPS	CREMATORIUM	CRESCENDOES	CRIMINALISTS
CRAUNCHING	CREDENTIAL	CREMATORIUMS	CRESCENDOING	CRIMINALITIES
CRAVATTING	CREDENTIALED	CREMOCARPS	CRESCENDOS	CRIMINALITY
CRAVENNESS	CREDENTIALING	CRENATIONS	CRESCENTADE	CRIMINALIZATION
CRAVENNESSES	CREDENTIALINGS	CRENATURES	CRESCENTADES	CRIMINALIZE
CRAWDADDIES	CREDENTIALISM	CRENELATED	CRESCENTED	CRIMINALIZED
CRAWFISHED	CREDENTIALISMS	CRENELATES	CRESCENTIC	CRIMINALIZES
CRAWFISHES	CREDENTIALLED	CRENELATING	CRESCIVELY	CRIMINALIZING
CRAWFISHING	CREDENTIALLING	CRENELATION	CRESCOGRAPH	CRIMINALLY
CRAWLINGLY	CREDENTIALLINGS	CRENELATIONS	CRESCOGRAPHS	CRIMINATED
CRAYFISHES	CREDENTIALS	CRENELLATE	CRESTFALLEN	CRIMINATES
CRAYONISTS	CREDIBILITIES	CRENELLATED	CRESTFALLENLY	CRIMINATING
CRAZINESSES	CREDIBILITY	CRENELLATES	CRESTFALLENNESS	CRIMINATION
CRAZYWEEDS	CREDIBLENESS	CRENELLATING	CRETACEOUS	CRIMINATIONS
CREAKINESS	CREDIBLENESSES	CRENELLATION	CRETACEOUSES	CRIMINATIVE
CREAKINESSES	CREDITABILITIES	CRENELLATIONS	CRETACEOUSLY	CRIMINATOR
CREAKINGLY	CREDITABILITY	CRENELLING	CRETINISED	CRIMINATORS
CREAMERIES	CREDITABLE	CRENULATED	CRETINISES	CRIMINATORY
CREAMINESS	CREDITABLENESS	CRENULATION	CRETINISING	CRIMINOGENIC
CREAMINESSES	CREDITABLY	CRENULATIONS	CRETINISMS	CRIMINOLOGIC
CREAMPUFFS	CREDITLESS	CREOLISATION	CRETINIZED	CRIMINOLOGICAL
CREAMWARES	CREDITORSHIP	CREOLISATIONS	CRETINIZES	CRIMINOLOGIES
CREASELESS	CREDITORSHIPS	CREOLISING	CRETINIZING	CRIMINOLOGIST
CREASOTING	CREDITWORTHIER	CREOLIZATION	CRETINOIDS	CRIMINOLOGISTS
CREATIANISM	CREDITWORTHIEST	CREOLIZATIONS	CREVASSING	CRIMINOLOGY
CREATIANISMS	CREDITWORTHY	CREOLIZING	CREWELISTS	CRIMINOUSNESS
CREATININE	CREDULITIES	CREOPHAGIES	CREWELLERIES	CRIMINOUSNESSES
CREATININES	CREDULOUSLY	CREOPHAGOUS	CREWELLERY	CRIMSONING
CREATIONAL	CREDULOUSNESS	CREOSOTING	CREWELLING	CRIMSONNESS
CREATIONISM	CREDULOUSNESSES	CREPEHANGER	CREWELLINGS	CRIMSONNESSES
CREATIONISMS	CREEKSIDES	CREPEHANGERS	CREWELWORK	CRINGELING
CREATIONIST	CREEPINESS	CREPEHANGING	CREWELWORKS	CRINGELINGS
CREATIONISTIC	CREEPINESSES	CREPEHANGINGS	CRIBRATION	CRINGEWORTHIER
CREATIONISTS	CREEPINGLY	CREPINESSES	CRIBRATIONS	CRINGEWORTHIEST
CREATIVELY	CREEPMOUSE	CREPITATED	CRIBRIFORM	CRINGEWORTHY
CREATIVENESS	CREEPMOUSES	CREPITATES	CRICKETERS	CRINGINGLY

CRINICULTURAL	CRITICISED	CROSSABILITIES	CROSSFIELD	CROWBARRED
CRINIGEROUS	CRITICISER	CROSSABILITY	CROSSFIRES	CROWBARRING
CRINKLEROOT	CRITICISERS	CROSSANDRA	CROSSFISHES	CROWBERRIES
CRINKLEROOTS	CRITICISES	CROSSANDRAS	CROSSHAIRS	CROWDEDNESS
CRINKLIEST	CRITICISING	CROSSBANDED	CROSSHATCH	CROWDEDNESSES
CRINOIDEAN	CRITICISINGLY	CROSSBANDING	CROSSHATCHED	CROWDFUNDED
CRINOIDEANS	CRITICISMS	CROSSBANDINGS	CROSSHATCHES	CROWDFUNDING
CRINOLETTE	CRITICIZABLE	CROSSBANDS	CROSSHATCHING	CROWDFUNDINGS
CRINOLETTES	CRITICIZED	CROSSBARRED	CROSSHATCHINGS	CROWDFUNDS
CRINOLINED	CRITICIZER	CROSSBARRING	CROSSHEADS	CROWDSOURCE
CRINOLINES	CRITICIZERS	CROSSBARRINGS	CROSSJACKS	CROWDSOURCED
CRIPPLEDOM	CRITICIZES	CROSSBEAMS	CROSSLIGHT	CROWDSOURCES
CRIPPLEDOMS	CRITICIZING	CROSSBEARER	CROSSLIGHTS	CROWDSOURCING
CRIPPLEWARE	CRITICIZINGLY	CROSSBEARERS	CROSSLINGUISTIC	CROWDSOURCINGS
CRIPPLEWARES	CRITIQUING	CROSSBENCH	CROSSNESSES	CROWKEEPER
CRIPPLINGLY	CROAKINESS	CROSSBENCHER	CROSSOPTERYGIAN	CROWKEEPERS
CRIPPLINGS	CROAKINESSES	CROSSBENCHERS	CROSSOVERS	CROWNLANDS
CRISPATION	CROCHETERS	CROSSBENCHES	CROSSPATCH	CROWNPIECE
CRISPATIONS	CROCHETING	CROSSBILLS	CROSSPATCHES	CROWNPIECES
CRISPATURE	CROCHETINGS	CROSSBIRTH	CROSSPIECE	CROWNWORKS
CRISPATURES	CROCIDOLITE	CROSSBIRTHS	CROSSPIECES	CROWSTEPPED
CRISPBREAD	CROCIDOLITES	CROSSBITES	CROSSROADS	CRUCIATELY
CRISPBREADS	CROCKERIES	CROSSBITING	CROSSRUFFED	CRUCIFEROUS
CRISPENING	CROCODILES	CROSSBITTEN	CROSSRUFFING	CRUCIFIERS
CRISPHEADS	CROCODILIAN	CROSSBONES	CROSSRUFFS	CRUCIFIXES
CRISPINESS	CROCODILIANS	CROSSBOWER	CROSSTALKS	CRUCIFIXION
CRISPINESSES	CROCOISITE	CROSSBOWERS	CROSSTREES	CRUCIFIXIONS
CRISPNESSES	CROCOISITES	CROSSBOWMAN	CROSSWALKS	CRUCIFORMLY
CRISSCROSS	CROCOSMIAS	CROSSBOWMEN	CROSSWINDS	CRUCIFORMS
CRISSCROSSED	CROISSANTS	CROSSBREDS	CROSSWIRES	CRUCIFYING
CRISSCROSSES	CROKINOLES	CROSSBREED	CROSSWORDS	CRUCIVERBAL
CRISSCROSSING	CROOKBACKED	CROSSBREEDING	CROSSWORTS	CRUCIVERBALISM
CRISTIFORM	CROOKBACKS	CROSSBREEDINGS	CROTALARIA	CRUCIVERBALISMS
CRISTOBALITE	CROOKEDEST	CROSSBREEDS	CROTALARIAS	CRUCIVERBALIST
CRISTOBALITES	CROOKEDNESS	CROSSBUCKS	CROTALISMS	CRUCIVERBALISTS
CRITERIONS	CROOKEDNESSES	CROSSCHECK	CROTCHETED	CRUDENESSES
CRITERIUMS	CROOKERIES	CROSSCHECKED	CROTCHETEER	CRUELNESSES
CRITHIDIAL	CROOKNECKS	CROSSCHECKING	CROTCHETEERS	CRUISERWEIGHT
CRITHOMANCIES	CROPDUSTER	CROSSCHECKS	CROTCHETIER	CRUISERWEIGHTS
CRITHOMANCY	CROPDUSTERS	CROSSCLAIM	CROTCHETIEST	CRUISEWAYS
CRITICALITIES	CROPDUSTING	CROSSCLAIMS	CROTCHETINESS	CRUISEWEAR
CRITICALITY	CROPDUSTINGS	CROSSCOURT	CROTCHETINESSES	CRUISEWEARS
CRITICALLY	CROQUANTES	CROSSCURRENT	CROTONALDEHYDE	CRUMBCLOTH
CRITICALNESS	CROQUETING	CROSSCURRENTS	CROTONALDEHYDES	CRUMBCLOTHS
CRITICALNESSES	CROQUETTES	CROSSCUTTING	CROTONBUGS	CRUMBLIEST
CRITICASTER	CROQUIGNOLE	CROSSCUTTINGS	CROUPINESS	CRUMBLINESS
CRITICASTERS	CROQUIGNOLES	CROSSETTES	CROUPINESSES	CRUMBLINESSES
CRITICISABLE	CROREPATIS	CROSSFALLS	CROUSTADES	CRUMBLINGS

CRUMMINESS	CRYOPLANKTONS	CRYPTOGAMIC	CRYPTOZOITES	CRYSTALLOID
CRUMMINESSES	CRYOPRECIPITATE	CRYPTOGAMIES	CRYPTOZOOLOGIES	CRYSTALLOIDAL
CRUMPLIEST	CRYOPRESERVE	CRYPTOGAMIST	CRYPTOZOOLOGIST	CRYSTALLOIDS
CRUMPLINGS	CRYOPRESERVED	CRYPTOGAMISTS	CRYPTOZOOLOGY	CRYSTALLOMANCY
CRUNCHABLE	CRYOPRESERVES	CRYPTOGAMOUS	CRYSTALISABLE	CTENOPHORAN
CRUNCHIEST	CRYOPRESERVING	CRYPTOGAMS	CRYSTALISATION	CTENOPHORANS
CRUNCHINESS	CRYOPROBES	CRYPTOGAMY	CRYSTALISATIONS	CTENOPHORE
CRUNCHINESSES	CRYOPROTECTANT	CRYPTOGENIC	CRYSTALISE	CTENOPHORES
CRUNCHINGS	CRYOPROTECTANTS	CRYPTOGRAM	CRYSTALISED	CUADRILLAS
CRUSHABILITIES	CRYOPROTECTIVE	CRYPTOGRAMS	CRYSTALISER	CUBANELLES
CRUSHABILITY	CRYOSCOPES	CRYPTOGRAPH	CRYSTALISERS	CUBBYHOLES
CRUSHINGLY	CRYOSCOPIC	CRYPTOGRAPHER	CRYSTALISES	CUBICALNESS
CRUSHPROOF	CRYOSCOPIES	CRYPTOGRAPHERS	CRYSTALISING	CUBICALNESSES
CRUSTACEAN	CRYOSTATIC	CRYPTOGRAPHIC	CRYSTALIZABLE	CUBICITIES
CRUSTACEANS	CRYOSURGEON	CRYPTOGRAPHICAL	CRYSTALIZATION	CUBISTICALLY
CRUSTACEOUS	CRYOSURGEONS	CRYPTOGRAPHIES	CRYSTALIZATIONS	CUCKOLDING
CRUSTATION	CRYOSURGERIES	CRYPTOGRAPHIST	CRYSTALIZE	CUCKOLDISE
CRUSTATIONS	CRYOSURGERY	CRYPTOGRAPHISTS	CRYSTALIZED	CUCKOLDISED
CRUSTINESS	CRYOSURGICAL	CRYPTOGRAPHS	CRYSTALIZER	CUCKOLDISES
CRUSTINESSES	CRYOTHERAPIES	CRYPTOGRAPHY	CRYSTALIZERS	CUCKOLDISING
CRUTCHINGS	CRYOTHERAPY	CRYPTOLOGIC	CRYSTALIZES	CUCKOLDIZE
CRYMOTHERAPIES	CRYPTAESTHESIA	CRYPTOLOGICAL	CRYSTALIZING	CUCKOLDIZED
CRYMOTHERAPY	CRYPTAESTHESIAS	CRYPTOLOGIES	CRYSTALLINE	CUCKOLDIZES
CRYOBIOLOGICAL	CRYPTAESTHETIC	CRYPTOLOGIST	CRYSTALLINES	CUCKOLDIZING
CRYOBIOLOGIES	CRYPTANALYSES	CRYPTOLOGISTS	CRYSTALLINITIES	CUCKOLDOMS
CRYOBIOLOGIST	CRYPTANALYSIS	CRYPTOLOGY	CRYSTALLINITY	CUCKOLDRIES
CRYOBIOLOGISTS	CRYPTANALYST	CRYPTOMERIA	CRYSTALLISABLE	CUCKOOFLOWER
CRYOBIOLOGY	CRYPTANALYSTS	CRYPTOMERIAS	CRYSTALLISATION	CUCKOOFLOWERS
CRYOCABLES	CRYPTANALYTIC	CRYPTOMETER	CRYSTALLISE	CUCKOOPINT
CRYOCONITE	CRYPTANALYTICAL	CRYPTOMETERS	CRYSTALLISED	CUCKOOPINTS
CRYOCONITES	CRYPTARITHM	CRYPTOMNESIA	CRYSTALLISER	CUCULIFORM
CRYOGENICALLY	CRYPTARITHMS	CRYPTOMNESIAS	CRYSTALLISERS	CUCULLATED
CRYOGENICS	CRYPTESTHESIA	CRYPTOMNESIC	CRYSTALLISES	CUCULLATELY
CRYOGENIES	CRYPTESTHESIAS	CRYPTONYMOUS	CRYSTALLISING	CUCUMIFORM
CRYOGLOBULIN	CRYPTESTHETIC	CRYPTONYMS	CRYSTALLITE	CUCURBITACEOUS
CRYOGLOBULINS	CRYPTICALLY	CRYPTOPHYTE	CRYSTALLITES	CUCURBITAL
CRYOHYDRATE	CRYPTOBIONT	CRYPTOPHYTES	CRYSTALLITIC	CUDDLESOME
CRYOHYDRATES	CRYPTOBIONTS	CRYPTOPHYTIC	CRYSTALLITIS	CUDGELINGS
CRYOMETERS	CRYPTOBIOSES	CRYPTORCHID	CRYSTALLITISES	CUDGELLERS
CRYOMETRIC	CRYPTOBIOSIS	CRYPTORCHIDISM	CRYSTALLIZABLE	CUDGELLING
CRYOMETRIES	CRYPTOCLASTIC	CRYPTORCHIDISMS	CRYSTALLIZATION	CUDGELLINGS
CRYONICALLY	CRYPTOCOCCAL	CRYPTORCHIDS	CRYSTALLIZE	CUFFUFFLES
CRYOPHILIC	CRYPTOCOCCI	CRYPTORCHISM	CRYSTALLIZED	CUIRASSIER
CRYOPHORUS	CRYPTOCOCCOSES	CRYPTORCHISMS	CRYSTALLIZER	CUIRASSIERS
CRYOPHORUSES	CRYPTOCOCCOSIS	CRYPTOSPORIDIA	CRYSTALLIZERS	CUIRASSING
CRYOPHYSICS	CRYPTOCOCCUS	CRYPTOSPORIDIUM	CRYSTALLIZES	CUISINARTS
CRYOPHYTES	CRYPTOCURRENCY	CRYPTOZOIC	CRYSTALLIZING	CUISINIERS
CRYOPLANKTON	CRYPTOGAMIAN	CRYPTOZOITE	CRYSTALLOGRAPHY	CULICIFORM

CULINARIAN	CUMBROUSNESS	CUPRONICKEL	CURMUDGEONLIER	CURVACIOUSLY
CULINARIANS	CUMBROUSNESSES	CUPRONICKELS	CURMUDGEONLIEST	CURVACIOUSNESS
CULINARILY	CUMMERBUND	CUPULIFEROUS	CURMUDGEONLY	CURVATIONS
CULLENDERS	CUMMERBUNDS	CURABILITIES	CURMUDGEONS	CURVATURES
CULMIFEROUS	CUMMINGTONITE	CURABILITY	CURMURRING	CURVEBALLED
CULMINATED	CUMMINGTONITES	CURABLENESS	CURMURRINGS	CURVEBALLING
CULMINATES	CUMULATELY	CURABLENESSES	CURNAPTIOUS	CURVEBALLS
CULMINATING	CUMULATING	CURANDERAS	CURRAJONGS	CURVEDNESS
CULMINATION	CUMULATION	CURANDEROS	CURRANTIER	CURVEDNESSES
CULMINATIONS	CUMULATIONS	CURARISATION	CURRANTIEST	CURVETTING
CULPABILITIES	CUMULATIVE	CURARISATIONS	CURRAWONGS	CURVICAUDATE
CULPABILITY	CUMULATIVELY	CURARISING	CURREJONGS	CURVICOSTATE
CULPABLENESS	CUMULATIVENESS	CURARIZATION	CURRENCIES	CURVIFOLIATE
CULPABLENESSES	CUMULIFORM	CURARIZATIONS	CURRENTNESS	CURVILINEAL
CULTISHNESS	CUMULOCIRRI	CURARIZING	CURRENTNESSES	CURVILINEALLY
CULTISHNESSES	CUMULOCIRRUS	CURATESHIP	CURRICULAR	CURVILINEAR
CULTIVABILITIES	CUMULONIMBI	CURATESHIPS	CURRICULUM	CURVILINEARITY
CULTIVABILITY	CUMULONIMBUS	CURATIVELY	CURRICULUMS	CURVILINEARLY
CULTIVABLE	CUMULONIMBUSES	CURATIVENESS	CURRIERIES	CURVINESSES
CULTIVATABLE	CUMULOSTRATI	CURATIVENESSES	CURRIJONGS	CURVIROSTRAL
CULTIVATED	CUMULOSTRATUS	CURATORIAL	CURRISHNESS	CUSHINESSES
CULTIVATES	CUNCTATION	CURATORSHIP	CURRISHNESSES	CUSHIONETS
CULTIVATING	CUNCTATIONS	CURATORSHIPS	CURRYCOMBED	CUSHIONIER
CULTIVATION	CUNCTATIOUS	CURATRIXES	CURRYCOMBING	CUSHIONIEST
CULTIVATIONS	CUNCTATIVE	CURBSTONES	CURRYCOMBS	CUSHIONING
CULTIVATOR	CUNCTATORS	CURCUMINES	CURSEDNESS	CUSHIONINGS
CULTIVATORS	CUNCTATORY	CURDINESSES	CURSEDNESSES	CUSHIONLESS
CULTRIFORM	CUNEIFORMS	CURETTAGES	CURSELARIE	CUSPIDATED
CULTURABLE	CUNNILINCTUS	CURETTEMENT	CURSIVENESS	CUSPIDATION
CULTURALLY	CUNNILINCTUSES	CURETTEMENTS	CURSIVENESSES	CUSPIDATIONS
CULTURELESS	CUNNILINGUS	CURFUFFLED	CURSORINESS	CUSPIDORES
CULTURISTS	CUNNILINGUSES	CURFUFFLES	CURSORINESSES	CUSSEDNESS
CULVERINEER	CUNNINGEST	CURFUFFLING	CURSTNESSES	CUSSEDNESSES
CULVERINEERS	CUNNINGNESS	CURIALISMS	CURTAILERS	CUSTARDIER
CULVERTAGE	CUNNINGNESSES	CURIALISTIC	CURTAILING	CUSTARDIEST
CULVERTAGES	CUPBEARERS	CURIALISTS	CURTAILMENT	CUSTODIANS
CULVERTAILED	CUPBOARDED	CURIETHERAPIES	CURTAILMENTS	CUSTODIANSHIP
CULVERTING	CUPBOARDING	CURIETHERAPY	CURTAINING	CUSTODIANSHIPS
CUMBERBUND	CUPELLATION	CURIOSITIES	CURTAINLESS	CUSTODIERS
CUMBERBUNDS	CUPELLATIONS	CURIOUSEST	CURTALAXES	CUSTOMABLE
CUMBERLESS	CUPFERRONS	CURIOUSNESS	CURTATIONS	CUSTOMARIES
CUMBERMENT	CUPHOLDERS	CURIOUSNESSES	CURTILAGES	CUSTOMARILY
CUMBERMENTS	CUPIDINOUS	CURLICUING	CURTNESSES	CUSTOMARINESS
CUMBERSOME	CUPIDITIES	CURLIEWURLIE	CURTSEYING	CUSTOMARINESSES
CUMBERSOMELY	CUPRAMMONIUM	CURLIEWURLIES	CURVACEOUS	CUSTOMHOUSE
CUMBERSOMENESS	CUPRAMMONIUMS	CURLINESSES	CURVACEOUSLY	CUSTOMHOUSES
CUMBRANCES	CUPRESSUSES	CURLPAPERS	CURVACEOUSNESS	CUSTOMISATION
CUMBROUSLY	CUPRIFEROUS	CURMUDGEON	CURVACIOUS	CUSTOMISATIONS

CUSTOMISED	CYANOETHYLATES	CYBERNETICIST	CYCLOADDITIONS	CYCLOPEDIC
CUSTOMISER	CYANOETHYLATING	CYBERNETICISTS	CYCLOALIPHATIC	CYCLOPEDIST
CUSTOMISERS	CYANOETHYLATION	CYBERNETICS	CYCLOALKANE	CYCLOPEDISTS
CUSTOMISES	CYANOGENAMIDE	CYBERPHOBIA	CYCLOALKANES	CYCLOPENTADIENE
CUSTOMISING	CYANOGENAMIDES	CYBERPHOBIAS	CYCLOBARBITONE	CYCLOPENTANE
CUSTOMIZATION	CYANOGENESES	CYBERPHOBIC	CYCLOBARBITONES	CYCLOPENTANES
CUSTOMIZATIONS	CYANOGENESIS	CYBERPORNS	CYCLODEXTRIN	CYCLOPENTOLATE
CUSTOMIZED	CYANOGENETIC	CYBERPUNKS	CYCLODEXTRINS	CYCLOPENTOLATES
CUSTOMIZER	CYANOGENIC	CYBERSECURITIES	CYCLODIALYSES	CYCLOPLEGIA
CUSTOMIZERS	CYANOHYDRIN	CYBERSECURITY	CYCLODIALYSIS	CYCLOPLEGIAS
CUSTOMIZES	CYANOHYDRINS	CYBERSEXES	CYCLODIENE	CYCLOPLEGIC
CUSTOMIZING	CYANOMETER	CYBERSPACE	CYCLODIENES	CYCLOPROPANE
CUSTOMSHOUSE	CYANOMETERS	CYBERSPACES	CYCLOGENESES	CYCLOPROPANES
CUSTOMSHOUSES	CYANOPHYTE	CYBERSQUATTER	CYCLOGENESIS	CYCLORAMAS
CUSTUMARIES	CYANOPHYTES	CYBERSQUATTERS	CYCLOGIROS	CYCLORAMIC
CUTABILITIES	CYANOTYPES	CYBERSQUATTING	CYCLOGRAPH	CYCLOSERINE
CUTABILITY	CYANURATES	CYBERSQUATTINGS	CYCLOGRAPHIC	CYCLOSERINES
CUTANEOUSLY	CYATHIFORM	CYBERSTALKER	CYCLOGRAPHS	CYCLOSPERMOUS
CUTCHERIES	CYBERATHLETE	CYBERSTALKERS	CYCLOHEXANE	CYCLOSPORIN
CUTCHERRIES	CYBERATHLETES	CYBERSTALKING	CYCLOHEXANES	CYCLOSPORINE
CUTENESSES	CYBERATHLETICS	CYBERSTALKINGS	CYCLOHEXANONE	CYCLOSPORINES
CUTGRASSES	CYBERATTACK	CYBERTERRORISM	CYCLOHEXANONES	CYCLOSPORINS
CUTINISATION	CYBERATTACKS	CYBERTERRORISMS	CYCLOHEXIMIDE	CYCLOSTOMATE
CUTINISATIONS	CYBERBULLIES	CYBERTERRORIST	CYCLOHEXIMIDES	CYCLOSTOMATOUS
CUTINISING	CYBERBULLY	CYBERTERRORISTS	CYCLOHEXYLAMINE	CYCLOSTOME
CUTINIZATION	CYBERBULLYING	CYBRARIANS	CYCLOIDALLY	CYCLOSTOMES
CUTINIZATIONS	CYBERBULLYINGS	CYCADACEOUS	CYCLOIDIAN	CYCLOSTOMOUS
CUTINIZING	CYBERCAFES	CYCADEOIDS	CYCLOIDIANS	CYCLOSTYLE
CUTTHROATS	CYBERCASTS	CYCADOPHYTE	CYCLOLITHS	CYCLOSTYLED
CUTTLEBONE	CYBERCHONDRIA	CYCADOPHYTES	CYCLOMETER	CYCLOSTYLES
CUTTLEBONES	CYBERCHONDRIAC	CYCLAMATES	CYCLOMETERS	CYCLOSTYLING
CUTTLEFISH	CYBERCHONDRIACS	CYCLANDELATE	CYCLOMETRIES	CYCLOTHYME
CUTTLEFISHES	CYBERCHONDRIAS	CYCLANDELATES	CYCLOMETRY	CYCLOTHYMES
CYANAMIDES	CYBERCRIME	CYCLANTHACEOUS	CYCLONICAL	CYCLOTHYMIA
CYANIDATION	CYBERCRIMES	CYCLAZOCINE	CYCLONICALLY	CYCLOTHYMIAC
CYANIDATIONS	CYBERCRIMINAL	CYCLAZOCINES	CYCLONITES	CYCLOTHYMIACS
CYANIDINGS	CYBERCRIMINALS	CYCLEPATHS	CYCLOOLEFIN	CYCLOTHYMIAS
CYANOACETYLENE	CYBERNATED	CYCLICALITIES	CYCLOOLEFINIC	CYCLOTHYMIC
CYANOACETYLENES	CYBERNATES	CYCLICALITY	CYCLOOLEFINS	CYCLOTHYMICS
CYANOACRYLATE	CYBERNATING	CYCLICALLY	CYCLOPAEDIA	CYCLOTOMIC
CYANOACRYLATES	CYBERNATION	CYCLICISMS	CYCLOPAEDIAS	CYCLOTRONS
CYANOBACTERIA	CYBERNATIONS	CYCLICITIES	CYCLOPAEDIC	CYLINDERED
CYANOBACTERIUM	CYBERNAUTS	CYCLISATION	CYCLOPAEDIST	CYLINDERING
CYANOCOBALAMIN	CYBERNETIC	CYCLISATIONS	CYCLOPAEDISTS	CYLINDRACEOUS
CYANOCOBALAMINE	CYBERNETICAL	CYCLIZATION	CYCLOPARAFFIN	CYLINDRICAL
CYANOCOBALAMINS	CYBERNETICALLY	CYCLIZATIONS	CYCLOPARAFFINS	CYLINDRICALITY
CYANOETHYLATE	CYBERNETICIAN	CYCLIZINES	CYCLOPEDIA	CYLINDRICALLY
CYANOETHYLATED	CYBERNETICIANS	CYCLOADDITION	CYCLOPEDIAS	CYLINDRICALNESS

CYLINDRICITIES

CYLINDRICITIES
CYLINDRICITY
CYLINDRIFORM
CYLINDRITE
CYLINDRITES
CYLINDROID
CYLINDROIDS
CYMAGRAPHS
CYMBALEERS
CYMBALISTS
CYMBIDIUMS
CYMIFEROUS
CYMOGRAPHIC
CYMOGRAPHS
CYMOPHANES
CYMOPHANOUS
CYMOTRICHIES
CYMOTRICHOUS
CYMOTRICHY
CYNGHANEDD
CYNGHANEDDS
CYNICALNESS
CYNICALNESSES
CYNOMOLGUS
CYNOMOLGUSES
CYNOPHILIA
CYNOPHILIAS
CYNOPHILIST
CYNOPHILISTS

CYNOPHOBIA
CYNOPHOBIAS
CYNOPODOUS
CYPERACEOUS
CYPRINODONT
CYPRINODONTS
CYPRINOIDS
CYPRIPEDIA
CYPRIPEDIUM
CYPRIPEDIUMS
CYPROHEPTADINE
CYPROHEPTADINES
CYPROTERONE
CYPROTERONES
CYSTEAMINE
CYSTEAMINES
CYSTECTOMIES
CYSTECTOMY
CYSTICERCI
CYSTICERCOID
CYSTICERCOIDS
CYSTICERCOSES
CYSTICERCOSIS
CYSTICERCUS
CYSTIDEANS
CYSTINOSES
CYSTINOSIS
CYSTINURIA
CYSTINURIAS

CYSTITIDES
CYSTITISES
CYSTOCARPIC
CYSTOCARPS
CYSTOCELES
CYSTOGENOUS
CYSTOGRAPHIES
CYSTOGRAPHY
CYSTOLITHIASES
CYSTOLITHIASIS
CYSTOLITHS
CYSTOSCOPE
CYSTOSCOPES
CYSTOSCOPIC
CYSTOSCOPIES
CYSTOSCOPY
CYSTOSTOMIES
CYSTOSTOMY
CYSTOTOMIES
CYTOCHALASIN
CYTOCHALASINS
CYTOCHEMICAL
CYTOCHEMISTRIES
CYTOCHEMISTRY
CYTOCHROME
CYTOCHROMES
CYTODIAGNOSES
CYTODIAGNOSIS
CYTOGENESES

CYTOGENESIS
CYTOGENETIC
CYTOGENETICAL
CYTOGENETICALLY
CYTOGENETICIST
CYTOGENETICISTS
CYTOGENETICS
CYTOGENIES
CYTOKINESES
CYTOKINESIS
CYTOKINETIC
CYTOKININS
CYTOLOGICAL
CYTOLOGICALLY
CYTOLOGIES
CYTOLOGIST
CYTOLOGISTS
CYTOLYSINS
CYTOMEGALIC
CYTOMEGALOVIRUS
CYTOMEMBRANE
CYTOMEMBRANES
CYTOMETERS
CYTOMETRIC
CYTOMETRIES
CYTOPATHIC
CYTOPATHIES
CYTOPATHOGENIC
CYTOPATHOLOGIES

CYTOPATHOLOGY
CYTOPENIAS
CYTOPHILIC
CYTOPHOTOMETRIC
CYTOPHOTOMETRY
CYTOPLASMIC
CYTOPLASMICALLY
CYTOPLASMS
CYTOPLASTIC
CYTOPLASTS
CYTOSKELETAL
CYTOSKELETON
CYTOSKELETONS
CYTOSTATIC
CYTOSTATICALLY
CYTOSTATICS
CYTOTAXONOMIC
CYTOTAXONOMIES
CYTOTAXONOMIST
CYTOTAXONOMISTS
CYTOTAXONOMY
CYTOTECHNOLOGY
CYTOTOXICITIES
CYTOTOXICITY
CYTOTOXINS
CZAREVICHES
CZAREVITCH
CZAREVITCHES

D

DABBLINGLY	DAHABEEYAHS	DAMNIFICATION	DAREDEVILTRY	DAUGHTERHOOD
DACHSHUNDS	DAHABIYAHS	DAMNIFICATIONS	DARINGNESS	DAUGHTERHOODS
DACOITAGES	DAHABIYEHS	DAMNIFYING	DARINGNESSES	DAUGHTERLESS
DACQUOISES	DAILINESSES	DAMOISELLE	DARKNESSES	DAUGHTERLIER
DACTYLICALLY	DAILYNESSES	DAMOISELLES	DARLINGNESS	DAUGHTERLIEST
DACTYLIOGRAPHY	DAINTINESS	DAMPCOURSE	DARLINGNESSES	DAUGHTERLINESS
DACTYLIOLOGIES	DAINTINESSES	DAMPCOURSES	DARMSTADTIUM	DAUGHTERLING
DACTYLIOLOGY	DAIRYMAIDS	DAMPISHNESS	DARMSTADTIUMS	DAUGHTERLINGS
DACTYLIOMANCIES	DAISYWHEEL	DAMPISHNESSES	DARNATIONS	DAUGHTERLY
DACTYLIOMANCY	DAISYWHEELS	DAMPNESSES	DARNEDESTS	DAUNDERING
DACTYLISTS	DALLIANCES	DAMSELFISH	DARRAIGNED	DAUNOMYCIN
DACTYLOGRAM	DALMATIANS	DAMSELFISHES	DARRAIGNES	DAUNOMYCINS
DACTYLOGRAMS	DALTONIANS	DAMSELFLIES	DARRAIGNING	DAUNORUBICIN
DACTYLOGRAPHER	DALTONISMS	DANCECORES	DARRAIGNMENT	DAUNORUBICINS
DACTYLOGRAPHERS	DAMAGEABILITIES	DANCEHALLS	DARRAIGNMENTS	DAUNTINGLY
DACTYLOGRAPHIC	DAMAGEABILITY	DANCEWEARS	DARRAINING	DAUNTLESSLY
DACTYLOGRAPHIES	DAMAGEABLE	DANDELIONS	DARRAYNING	DAUNTLESSNESS
DACTYLOGRAPHY	DAMAGINGLY	DANDIFICATION	DARTBOARDS	DAUNTLESSNESSES
DACTYLOLOGIES	DAMASCEENE	DANDIFICATIONS	DARTITISES	DAUNTONING
DACTYLOLOGY	DAMASCEENED	DANDIFYING	DASHBOARDS	DAUPHINESS
DACTYLOSCOPIES	DAMASCEENES	DANDIPRATS	DASHLIGHTS	DAUPHINESSES
DACTYLOSCOPY	DAMASCEENING	DANDRUFFIER	DASTARDIES	DAVENPORTS
DAFFADOWNDILLY	DAMASCENED	DANDRUFFIEST	DASTARDLIER	DAWDLINGLY
DAFFINESSES	DAMASCENES	DANDYFUNKS	DASTARDLIEST	DAWSONITES
DAFFODILLIES	DAMASCENING	DANDYISHLY	DASTARDLINESS	DAYCATIONS
DAFFODILLY	DAMASCENINGS	DANDYPRATS	DASTARDLINESSES	DAYCENTRES
DAFTNESSES	DAMASKEENED	DANGERLESS	DASTARDNESS	DAYDREAMED
DAGGERBOARD	DAMASKEENING	DANGEROUSLY	DASTARDNESSES	DAYDREAMER
DAGGERBOARDS	DAMASKEENS	DANGEROUSNESS	DASYMETERS	DAYDREAMERS
DAGGERLIKE	DAMASKINED	DANGEROUSNESSES	DASYPAEDAL	DAYDREAMIER
DAGUERREAN	DAMASKINING	DANGLINGLY	DASYPHYLLOUS	DAYDREAMIEST
DAGUERREOTYPE	DAMASQUINED	DANKNESSES	DATABASING	DAYDREAMING
DAGUERREOTYPED	DAMASQUINING	DANNEBROGS	DATABUSSES	DAYDREAMINGS
DAGUERREOTYPER	DAMASQUINS	DANTHONIAS	DATAGLOVES	DAYDREAMLIKE
DAGUERREOTYPERS	DAMINOZIDE	DAPPERLING	DATAMATION	DAYFLOWERS
DAGUERREOTYPES	DAMINOZIDES	DAPPERLINGS	DATAMATIONS	DAYLIGHTED
DAGUERREOTYPIES	DAMNABILITIES	DAPPERNESS	DATAVEILLANCE	DAYLIGHTING
DAGUERREOTYPING	DAMNABILITY	DAPPERNESSES	DATAVEILLANCES	DAYLIGHTINGS
DAGUERREOTYPIST	DAMNABLENESS	DAREDEVILRIES	DATEDNESSES	DAYSAILERS
DAGUERREOTYPY	DAMNABLENESSES	DAREDEVILRY	DATELINING	DAYSAILING
DAHABEEAHS	DAMNATIONS	DAREDEVILS	DAUGHTERBOARD	DAYSAILORS
DAHABEEYAH	DAMNEDESTS	DAREDEVILTRIES	DAUGHTERBOARDS	DAYSPRINGS

DAYWORKERS

DAYWORKERS	DEAERATIONS	DEATHLESSNESSES	DEBILITATIONS	DECALESCENT
DAZEDNESSES	DEAERATORS	DEATHLIEST	DEBILITATIVE	DECALITERS
DAZZLEMENT	DEAFENINGLY	DEATHLINESS	DEBILITIES	DECALITRES
DAZZLEMENTS	DEAFENINGS	DEATHLINESSES	DEBONAIRLY	DECALOGIST
DAZZLINGLY	DEAFNESSES	DEATHTRAPS	DEBONAIRNESS	DECALOGISTS
DEACIDIFICATION	DEALATIONS	DEATHWARDS	DEBONAIRNESSES	DECALOGUES
DEACIDIFIED	DEALBATION	DEATHWATCH	DEBONNAIRE	DECAMERONIC
DEACIDIFIES	DEALBATIONS	DEATHWATCHES	DEBOUCHING	DECAMEROUS
DEACIDIFYING	DEALBREAKER	DEATTRIBUTE	DEBOUCHMENT	DECAMETERS
DEACONESSES	DEALBREAKERS	DEATTRIBUTED	DEBOUCHMENTS	DECAMETHONIUM
DEACONHOOD	DEALERSHIP	DEATTRIBUTES	DEBOUCHURE	DECAMETHONIUMS
DEACONHOODS	DEALERSHIPS	DEATTRIBUTING	DEBOUCHURES	DECAMETRES
DEACONRIES	DEALFISHES	DEBAGGINGS	DEBRIDEMENT	DECAMETRIC
DEACONSHIP	DEALIGNING	DEBARCATION	DEBRIDEMENTS	DECAMPMENT
DEACONSHIPS	DEALMAKERS	DEBARCATIONS	DEBRIEFERS	DECAMPMENTS
DEACTIVATE	DEAMBULATORIES	DEBARKATION	DEBRIEFING	DECANDRIAN
DEACTIVATED	DEAMBULATORY	DEBARKATIONS	DEBRIEFINGS	DECANDROUS
DEACTIVATES	DEAMINASES	DEBARMENTS	DEBRUISING	DECANEDIOIC
DEACTIVATING	DEAMINATED	DEBARRASSED	DEBUGGINGS	DECANICALLY
DEACTIVATION	DEAMINATES	DEBARRASSES	DEBUTANTES	DECANTATED
DEACTIVATIONS	DEAMINATING	DEBARRASSING	DECACHORDS	DECANTATES
DEACTIVATOR	DEAMINATION	DEBASEDNESS	DECADENCES	DECANTATING
DEACTIVATORS	DEAMINATIONS	DEBASEDNESSES	DECADENCIES	DECANTATION
DEADENINGLY	DEAMINISATION	DEBASEMENT	DECADENTLY	DECANTATIONS
DEADENINGS	DEAMINISATIONS	DEBASEMENTS	DECAFFEINATE	DECAPITALISE
DEADHEADED	DEAMINISED	DEBASINGLY	DECAFFEINATED	DECAPITALISED
DEADHEADING	DEAMINISES	DEBATEABLE	DECAFFEINATES	DECAPITALISES
DEADHOUSES	DEAMINISING	DEBATEMENT	DECAFFEINATING	DECAPITALISING
DEADLIFTED	DEAMINIZATION	DEBATEMENTS	DECAGONALLY	DECAPITALIZE
DEADLIFTING	DEAMINIZATIONS	DEBATINGLY	DECAGRAMME	DECAPITALIZED
DEADLIGHTS	DEAMINIZED	DEBAUCHEDLY	DECAGRAMMES	DECAPITALIZES
DEADLINESS	DEAMINIZES	DEBAUCHEDNESS	DECAGYNIAN	DECAPITALIZING
DEADLINESSES	DEAMINIZING	DEBAUCHEDNESSES	DECAGYNOUS	DECAPITATE
DEADLINING	DEARBOUGHT	DEBAUCHEES	DECAHEDRAL	DECAPITATED
DEADLOCKED	DEARNESSES	DEBAUCHERIES	DECAHEDRON	DECAPITATES
DEADLOCKING	DEARTICULATE	DEBAUCHERS	DECAHEDRONS	DECAPITATING
DEADNESSES	DEARTICULATED	DEBAUCHERY	DECAHYDRATE	DECAPITATION
DEADPANNED	DEARTICULATES	DEBAUCHING	DECAHYDRATES	DECAPITATIONS
DEADPANNER	DEARTICULATING	DEBAUCHMENT	DECALCIFICATION	DECAPITATOR
DEADPANNERS	DEASPIRATE	DEBAUCHMENTS	DECALCIFIED	DECAPITATORS
DEADPANNING	DEASPIRATED	DEBEARDING	DECALCIFIER	DECAPODANS
DEADSTOCKS	DEASPIRATES	DEBENTURED	DECALCIFIERS	DECAPODOUS
DEADSTROKE	DEASPIRATING	DEBENTURES	DECALCIFIES	DECAPSULATE
DEADWATERS	DEASPIRATION	DEBILITATE	DECALCIFYING	DECAPSULATED
DEADWEIGHT	DEASPIRATIONS	DEBILITATED	DECALCOMANIA	DECAPSULATES
DEADWEIGHTS	DEATHBLOWS	DEBILITATES	DECALCOMANIAS	DECAPSULATING
DEAERATING	DEATHLESSLY	DEBILITATING	DECALESCENCE	DECAPSULATION
DEAERATION	DEATHLESSNESS	DEBILITATION	DECALESCENCES	DECAPSULATIONS

DECARBONATE
DECARBONATED
DECARBONATES
DECARBONATING
DECARBONATION
DECARBONATIONS
DECARBONATOR
DECARBONATORS
DECARBONISATION
DECARBONISE
DECARBONISED
DECARBONISER
DECARBONISERS
DECARBONISES
DECARBONISING
DECARBONIZATION
DECARBONIZE
DECARBONIZED
DECARBONIZER
DECARBONIZERS
DECARBONIZES
DECARBONIZING
DECARBOXYLASE
DECARBOXYLASES
DECARBOXYLATE
DECARBOXYLATED
DECARBOXYLATES
DECARBOXYLATING
DECARBOXYLATION
DECARBURATION
DECARBURATIONS
DECARBURISATION
DECARBURISE
DECARBURISED
DECARBURISES
DECARBURISING
DECARBURIZATION
DECARBURIZE
DECARBURIZED
DECARBURIZES
DECARBURIZING
DECARTELISE
DECARTELISED
DECARTELISES
DECARTELISING
DECARTELIZE
DECARTELIZED
DECARTELIZES

DECARTELIZING
DECASTERES
DECASTICHS
DECASTYLES
DECASUALISATION
DECASUALISE
DECASUALISED
DECASUALISES
DECASUALISING
DECASUALIZATION
DECASUALIZE
DECASUALIZED
DECASUALIZES
DECASUALIZING
DECASYLLABIC
DECASYLLABICS
DECASYLLABLE
DECASYLLABLES
DECATHLETE
DECATHLETES
DECATHLONS
DECAUDATED
DECAUDATES
DECAUDATING
DECEITFULLY
DECEITFULNESS
DECEITFULNESSES
DECEIVABILITIES
DECEIVABILITY
DECEIVABLE
DECEIVABLENESS
DECEIVABLY
DECEIVINGLY
DECEIVINGS
DECELERATE
DECELERATED
DECELERATES
DECELERATING
DECELERATION
DECELERATIONS
DECELERATOR
DECELERATORS
DECELEROMETER
DECELEROMETERS
DECELERONS
DECEMVIRAL
DECEMVIRATE
DECEMVIRATES

DECENARIES
DECENNARIES
DECENNIALLY
DECENNIALS
DECENNIUMS
DECENNOVAL
DECENTERED
DECENTERING
DECENTERINGS
DECENTNESS
DECENTNESSES
DECENTRALISE
DECENTRALISED
DECENTRALISES
DECENTRALISING
DECENTRALIST
DECENTRALISTS
DECENTRALIZE
DECENTRALIZED
DECENTRALIZES
DECENTRALIZING
DECENTRING
DECEPTIBILITIES
DECEPTIBILITY
DECEPTIBLE
DECEPTIONAL
DECEPTIONS
DECEPTIOUS
DECEPTIVELY
DECEPTIVENESS
DECEPTIVENESSES
DECEREBRATE
DECEREBRATED
DECEREBRATES
DECEREBRATING
DECEREBRATION
DECEREBRATIONS
DECEREBRISE
DECEREBRISED
DECEREBRISES
DECEREBRISING
DECEREBRIZE
DECEREBRIZED
DECEREBRIZES
DECEREBRIZING
DECERTIFICATION
DECERTIFIED
DECERTIFIES

DECERTIFYING
DECESSIONS
DECHEANCES
DECHLORINATE
DECHLORINATED
DECHLORINATES
DECHLORINATING
DECHLORINATION
DECHLORINATIONS
DECHRISTIANISE
DECHRISTIANISED
DECHRISTIANISES
DECHRISTIANIZE
DECHRISTIANIZED
DECHRISTIANIZES
DECIDABILITIES
DECIDABILITY
DECIDEDNESS
DECIDEDNESSES
DECIDUOUSLY
DECIDUOUSNESS
DECIDUOUSNESSES
DECIGRAMME
DECIGRAMMES
DECILITERS
DECILITRES
DECILLIONS
DECILLIONTH
DECILLIONTHS
DECIMALISATION
DECIMALISATIONS
DECIMALISE
DECIMALISED
DECIMALISES
DECIMALISING
DECIMALISM
DECIMALISMS
DECIMALIST
DECIMALISTS
DECIMALIZATION
DECIMALIZATIONS
DECIMALIZE
DECIMALIZED
DECIMALIZES
DECIMALIZING
DECIMATING
DECIMATION
DECIMATIONS

DECIMATORS
DECIMETERS
DECIMETRES
DECIMETRIC
DECINORMAL
DECIPHERABILITY
DECIPHERABLE
DECIPHERED
DECIPHERER
DECIPHERERS
DECIPHERING
DECIPHERMENT
DECIPHERMENTS
DECISIONAL
DECISIONED
DECISIONING
DECISIVELY
DECISIVENESS
DECISIVENESSES
DECISTERES
DECITIZENISE
DECITIZENISED
DECITIZENISES
DECITIZENISING
DECITIZENIZE
DECITIZENIZED
DECITIZENIZES
DECITIZENIZING
DECIVILISE
DECIVILISED
DECIVILISES
DECIVILISING
DECIVILIZE
DECIVILIZED
DECIVILIZES
DECIVILIZING
DECKCHAIRS
DECKHOUSES
DECLAIMANT
DECLAIMANTS
DECLAIMERS
DECLAIMING
DECLAIMINGS
DECLAMATION
DECLAMATIONS
DECLAMATORILY
DECLAMATORY
DECLARABLE

DECLARANTS

DECLARANTS	DECOLLATED	DECOLOURING	DECOMPOUNDED	DECONTAMINATES
DECLARATION	DECOLLATES	DECOLOURISATION	DECOMPOUNDING	DECONTAMINATING
DECLARATIONS	DECOLLATING	DECOLOURISE	DECOMPOUNDS	DECONTAMINATION
DECLARATIVE	DECOLLATION	DECOLOURISED	DECOMPRESS	DECONTAMINATIVE
DECLARATIVELY	DECOLLATIONS	DECOLOURISES	DECOMPRESSED	DECONTAMINATOR
DECLARATOR	DECOLLATOR	DECOLOURISING	DECOMPRESSES	DECONTAMINATORS
DECLARATORILY	DECOLLATORS	DECOLOURIZATION	DECOMPRESSING	DECONTEXTUALISE
DECLARATORS	DECOLLETAGE	DECOLOURIZE	DECOMPRESSION	DECONTEXTUALIZE
DECLARATORY	DECOLLETAGES	DECOLOURIZED	DECOMPRESSIONS	DECONTROLLED
DECLAREDLY	DECOLLETES	DECOLOURIZES	DECOMPRESSIVE	DECONTROLLING
DECLASSIFIABLE	DECOLONISATION	DECOLOURIZING	DECOMPRESSOR	DECONTROLS
DECLASSIFIED	DECOLONISATIONS	DECOMMISSION	DECOMPRESSORS	DECORATING
DECLASSIFIES	DECOLONISE	DECOMMISSIONED	DECONCENTRATE	DECORATINGS
DECLASSIFY	DECOLONISED	DECOMMISSIONER	DECONCENTRATED	DECORATION
DECLASSIFYING	DECOLONISES	DECOMMISSIONERS	DECONCENTRATES	DECORATIONS
DECLASSING	DECOLONISING	DECOMMISSIONING	DECONCENTRATING	DECORATIVE
DECLENSION	DECOLONIZATION	DECOMMISSIONS	DECONCENTRATION	DECORATIVELY
DECLENSIONAL	DECOLONIZATIONS	DECOMMITTED	DECONDITION	DECORATIVENESS
DECLENSIONALLY	DECOLONIZE	DECOMMITTING	DECONDITIONED	DECORATORS
DECLENSIONS	DECOLONIZED	DECOMMUNISATION	DECONDITIONING	DECOROUSLY
DECLINABLE	DECOLONIZES	DECOMMUNISE	DECONDITIONS	DECOROUSNESS
DECLINANTS	DECOLONIZING	DECOMMUNISED	DECONGESTANT	DECOROUSNESSES
DECLINATION	DECOLORANT	DECOMMUNISES	DECONGESTANTS	DECORTICATE
DECLINATIONAL	DECOLORANTS	DECOMMUNISING	DECONGESTED	DECORTICATED
DECLINATIONS	DECOLORATE	DECOMMUNIZATION	DECONGESTING	DECORTICATES
DECLINATOR	DECOLORATED	DECOMMUNIZE	DECONGESTION	DECORTICATING
DECLINATORIES	DECOLORATES	DECOMMUNIZED	DECONGESTIONS	DECORTICATION
DECLINATORS	DECOLORATING	DECOMMUNIZES	DECONGESTIVE	DECORTICATIONS
DECLINATORY	DECOLORATION	DECOMMUNIZING	DECONGESTS	DECORTICATOR
DECLINATURE	DECOLORATIONS	DECOMPENSATE	DECONSECRATE	DECORTICATORS
DECLINATURES	DECOLORING	DECOMPENSATED	DECONSECRATED	DECOUPAGED
DECLINISTS	DECOLORISATION	DECOMPENSATES	DECONSECRATES	DECOUPAGES
DECLINOMETER	DECOLORISATIONS	DECOMPENSATING	DECONSECRATING	DECOUPAGING
DECLINOMETERS	DECOLORISE	DECOMPENSATION	DECONSECRATION	DECOUPLERS
DECLIVITIES	DECOLORISED	DECOMPENSATIONS	DECONSECRATIONS	DECOUPLING
DECLIVITOUS	DECOLORISER	DECOMPOSABILITY	DECONSTRUCT	DECOUPLINGS
DECLUTCHED	DECOLORISERS	DECOMPOSABLE	DECONSTRUCTED	DECRASSIFIED
DECLUTCHES	DECOLORISES	DECOMPOSED	DECONSTRUCTING	DECRASSIFIES
DECLUTCHING	DECOLORISING	DECOMPOSER	DECONSTRUCTION	DECRASSIFY
DECLUTTERED	DECOLORIZATION	DECOMPOSERS	DECONSTRUCTIONS	DECRASSIFYING
DECLUTTERING	DECOLORIZATIONS	DECOMPOSES	DECONSTRUCTIVE	DECREASING
DECLUTTERS	DECOLORIZE	DECOMPOSING	DECONSTRUCTOR	DECREASINGLY
DECOCTIBLE	DECOLORIZED	DECOMPOSITE	DECONSTRUCTORS	DECREASINGS
DECOCTIONS	DECOLORIZER	DECOMPOSITES	DECONSTRUCTS	DECREEABLE
DECOCTURES	DECOLORIZERS	DECOMPOSITION	DECONTAMINANT	DECREMENTAL
DECOHERENCE	DECOLORIZES	DECOMPOSITIONS	DECONTAMINANTS	DECREMENTED
DECOHERENCES	DECOLORIZING	DECOMPOUND	DECONTAMINATE	DECREMENTING
DECOHERERS	DECOLOURED	DECOMPOUNDABLE	DECONTAMINATED	DECREMENTS

DECREPITATE
DECREPITATED
DECREPITATES
DECREPITATING
DECREPITATION
DECREPITATIONS
DECREPITLY
DECREPITNESS
DECREPITNESSES
DECREPITUDE
DECREPITUDES
DECRESCENCE
DECRESCENCES
DECRESCENDO
DECRESCENDOS
DECRESCENT
DECRETALIST
DECRETALISTS
DECRETISTS
DECRIMINALISE
DECRIMINALISED
DECRIMINALISES
DECRIMINALISING
DECRIMINALIZE
DECRIMINALIZED
DECRIMINALIZES
DECRIMINALIZING
DECROWNING
DECRUSTATION
DECRUSTATIONS
DECRYPTING
DECRYPTION
DECRYPTIONS
DECUMBENCE
DECUMBENCES
DECUMBENCIES
DECUMBENCY
DECUMBENTLY
DECUMBITURE
DECUMBITURES
DECUMULATION
DECUMULATIONS
DECURIONATE
DECURIONATES
DECURRENCIES
DECURRENCY
DECURRENTLY
DECURSIONS

DECURSIVELY
DECURVATION
DECURVATIONS
DECUSSATED
DECUSSATELY
DECUSSATES
DECUSSATING
DECUSSATION
DECUSSATIONS
DEDICATEDLY
DEDICATEES
DEDICATING
DEDICATION
DEDICATIONAL
DEDICATIONS
DEDICATIVE
DEDICATORIAL
DEDICATORS
DEDICATORY
DEDIFFERENTIATE
DEDRAMATISE
DEDRAMATISED
DEDRAMATISES
DEDRAMATISING
DEDRAMATIZE
DEDRAMATIZED
DEDRAMATIZES
DEDRAMATIZING
DEDUCEMENT
DEDUCEMENTS
DEDUCIBILITIES
DEDUCIBILITY
DEDUCIBLENESS
DEDUCIBLENESSES
DEDUCTIBILITIES
DEDUCTIBILITY
DEDUCTIBLE
DEDUCTIBLES
DEDUCTIONS
DEDUCTIVELY
DEDUPLICATE
DEDUPLICATED
DEDUPLICATES
DEDUPLICATING
DEDUPLICATION
DEDUPLICATIONS
DEEJAYINGS
DEEMSTERSHIP

DEEMSTERSHIPS
DEEPENINGS
DEEPFREEZE
DEEPFREEZES
DEEPFREEZING
DEEPFROZEN
DEEPNESSES
DEEPWATERMAN
DEEPWATERMEN
DEERBERRIES
DEERGRASSES
DEERHOUNDS
DEERSTALKER
DEERSTALKERS
DEERSTALKING
DEERSTALKINGS
DEFACEABLE
DEFACEMENT
DEFACEMENTS
DEFACINGLY
DEFAECATED
DEFAECATES
DEFAECATING
DEFAECATION
DEFAECATIONS
DEFAECATOR
DEFAECATORS
DEFALCATED
DEFALCATES
DEFALCATING
DEFALCATION
DEFALCATIONS
DEFALCATOR
DEFALCATORS
DEFAMATION
DEFAMATIONS
DEFAMATORILY
DEFAMATORY
DEFAULTERS
DEFAULTING
DEFEASANCE
DEFEASANCED
DEFEASANCES
DEFEASIBILITIES
DEFEASIBILITY
DEFEASIBLE
DEFEASIBLENESS
DEFEATISMS

DEFEATISTS
DEFEATURED
DEFEATURES
DEFEATURING
DEFECATING
DEFECATION
DEFECATIONS
DEFECATORS
DEFECTIBILITIES
DEFECTIBILITY
DEFECTIBLE
DEFECTIONIST
DEFECTIONISTS
DEFECTIONS
DEFECTIVELY
DEFECTIVENESS
DEFECTIVENESSES
DEFECTIVES
DEFEMINISATION
DEFEMINISATIONS
DEFEMINISE
DEFEMINISED
DEFEMINISES
DEFEMINISING
DEFEMINIZATION
DEFEMINIZATIONS
DEFEMINIZE
DEFEMINIZED
DEFEMINIZES
DEFEMINIZING
DEFENCELESS
DEFENCELESSLY
DEFENCELESSNESS
DEFENCEMAN
DEFENCEMEN
DEFENDABLE
DEFENDANTS
DEFENESTRATE
DEFENESTRATED
DEFENESTRATES
DEFENESTRATING
DEFENESTRATION
DEFENESTRATIONS
DEFENSATIVE
DEFENSATIVES
DEFENSELESS
DEFENSELESSLY
DEFENSELESSNESS

DEFENSEMAN
DEFENSEMEN
DEFENSIBILITIES
DEFENSIBILITY
DEFENSIBLE
DEFENSIBLENESS
DEFENSIBLY
DEFENSIVELY
DEFENSIVENESS
DEFENSIVENESSES
DEFENSIVES
DEFERENCES
DEFERENTIAL
DEFERENTIALLY
DEFERMENTS
DEFERRABLE
DEFERRABLES
DEFERVESCENCE
DEFERVESCENCES
DEFERVESCENCIES
DEFERVESCENCY
DEFEUDALISE
DEFEUDALISED
DEFEUDALISES
DEFEUDALISING
DEFEUDALIZE
DEFEUDALIZED
DEFEUDALIZES
DEFEUDALIZING
DEFIANTNESS
DEFIANTNESSES
DEFIBRILLATE
DEFIBRILLATED
DEFIBRILLATES
DEFIBRILLATING
DEFIBRILLATION
DEFIBRILLATIONS
DEFIBRILLATOR
DEFIBRILLATORS
DEFIBRINATE
DEFIBRINATED
DEFIBRINATES
DEFIBRINATING
DEFIBRINATION
DEFIBRINATIONS
DEFIBRINISE
DEFIBRINISED
DEFIBRINISES

D

DEFIBRINISING	DEFLAGRATED	DEFOLIATIONS	DEFRAYMENT	DEGLAMORIZED
DEFIBRINIZE	DEFLAGRATES	DEFOLIATOR	DEFRAYMENTS	DEGLAMORIZES
DEFIBRINIZED	DEFLAGRATING	DEFOLIATORS	DEFREEZING	DEGLAMORIZING
DEFIBRINIZES	DEFLAGRATION	DEFORCEMENT	DEFRIENDED	DEGLUTINATE
DEFIBRINIZING	DEFLAGRATIONS	DEFORCEMENTS	DEFRIENDING	DEGLUTINATED
DEFICIENCE	DEFLAGRATOR	DEFORCIANT	DEFROCKING	DEGLUTINATES
DEFICIENCES	DEFLAGRATORS	DEFORCIANTS	DEFROSTERS	DEGLUTINATING
DEFICIENCIES	DEFLATIONARY	DEFORCIATION	DEFROSTING	DEGLUTINATION
DEFICIENCY	DEFLATIONIST	DEFORCIATIONS	DEFROSTINGS	DEGLUTINATIONS
DEFICIENTLY	DEFLATIONISTS	DEFORESTATION	DEFTNESSES	DEGLUTITION
DEFICIENTNESS	DEFLATIONS	DEFORESTATIONS	DEFUELLING	DEGLUTITIONS
DEFICIENTNESSES	DEFLECTABLE	DEFORESTED	DEFUNCTION	DEGLUTITIVE
DEFICIENTS	DEFLECTING	DEFORESTER	DEFUNCTIONS	DEGLUTITORY
DEFILADING	DEFLECTION	DEFORESTERS	DEFUNCTIVE	DEGRADABILITIES
DEFILEMENT	DEFLECTIONAL	DEFORESTING	DEFUNCTNESS	DEGRADABILITY
DEFILEMENTS	DEFLECTIONS	DEFORMABILITIES	DEFUNCTNESSES	DEGRADABLE
DEFILIATION	DEFLECTIVE	DEFORMABILITY	DEGARNISHED	DEGRADATION
DEFILIATIONS	DEFLECTORS	DEFORMABLE	DEGARNISHES	DEGRADATIONS
DEFINABILITIES	DEFLEXIONAL	DEFORMALISE	DEGARNISHING	DEGRADATIVE
DEFINABILITY	DEFLEXIONS	DEFORMALISED	DEGAUSSERS	DEGRADEDLY
DEFINEMENT	DEFLEXURES	DEFORMALISES	DEGAUSSING	DEGRADINGLY
DEFINEMENTS	DEFLOCCULANT	DEFORMALISING	DEGAUSSINGS	DEGRADINGNESS
DEFINIENDA	DEFLOCCULANTS	DEFORMALIZE	DEGEARINGS	DEGRADINGNESSES
DEFINIENDUM	DEFLOCCULATE	DEFORMALIZED	DEGENDERED	DEGRANULATION
DEFINIENTIA	DEFLOCCULATED	DEFORMALIZES	DEGENDERING	DEGRANULATIONS
DEFINITELY	DEFLOCCULATES	DEFORMALIZING	DEGENERACIES	DEGREASANT
DEFINITENESS	DEFLOCCULATING	DEFORMATION	DEGENERACY	DEGREASANTS
DEFINITENESSES	DEFLOCCULATION	DEFORMATIONAL	DEGENERATE	DEGREASERS
DEFINITION	DEFLOCCULATIONS	DEFORMATIONS	DEGENERATED	DEGREASING
DEFINITIONAL	DEFLORATED	DEFORMATIVE	DEGENERATELY	DEGREASINGS
DEFINITIONS	DEFLORATES	DEFORMEDLY	DEGENERATENESS	DEGREELESS
DEFINITISE	DEFLORATING	DEFORMEDNESS	DEGENERATES	DEGRESSION
DEFINITISED	DEFLORATION	DEFORMEDNESSES	DEGENERATING	DEGRESSIONS
DEFINITISES	DEFLORATIONS	DEFORMITIES	DEGENERATION	DEGRESSIVE
DEFINITISING	DEFLOWERED	DEFRAGGERS	DEGENERATIONIST	DEGRESSIVELY
DEFINITIVE	DEFLOWERER	DEFRAGGING	DEGENERATIONS	DEGRINGOLADE
DEFINITIVELY	DEFLOWERERS	DEFRAGGINGS	DEGENERATIVE	DEGRINGOLADED
DEFINITIVENESS	DEFLOWERING	DEFRAGMENT	DEGENEROUS	DEGRINGOLADES
DEFINITIVES	DEFLUXIONS	DEFRAGMENTED	DEGLACIATED	DEGRINGOLADING
DEFINITIZE	DEFOCUSING	DEFRAGMENTING	DEGLACIATION	DEGRINGOLER
DEFINITIZED	DEFOCUSSED	DEFRAGMENTS	DEGLACIATIONS	DEGRINGOLERED
DEFINITIZES	DEFOCUSSES	DEFRAUDATION	DEGLAMORISATION	DEGRINGOLERING
DEFINITIZING	DEFOCUSSING	DEFRAUDATIONS	DEGLAMORISE	DEGRINGOLERS
DEFINITUDE	DEFOLIANTS	DEFRAUDERS	DEGLAMORISED	DEGUSTATED
DEFINITUDES	DEFOLIATED	DEFRAUDING	DEGLAMORISES	DEGUSTATES
DEFLAGRABILITY	DEFOLIATES	DEFRAUDMENT	DEGLAMORISING	DEGUSTATING
DEFLAGRABLE	DEFOLIATING	DEFRAUDMENTS	DEGLAMORIZATION	DEGUSTATION
DEFLAGRATE	DEFOLIATION	DEFRAYABLE	DEGLAMORIZE	DEGUSTATIONS

DEGUSTATORY	DEHYDROGENIZING	DEKAMETERS	DELEVERAGING	DELINEABLE
DEHISCENCE	DEHYDRORETINOL	DEKAMETRES	DELEVERAGINGS	DELINEATED
DEHISCENCES	DEHYDRORETINOLS	DEKAMETRIC	DELFTWARES	DELINEATES
DEHORTATION	DEHYPNOTISATION	DELAMINATE	DELIBATING	DELINEATING
DEHORTATIONS	DEHYPNOTISE	DELAMINATED	DELIBATION	DELINEATION
DEHORTATIVE	DEHYPNOTISED	DELAMINATES	DELIBATIONS	DELINEATIONS
DEHORTATORY	DEHYPNOTISES	DELAMINATING	DELIBERATE	DELINEATIVE
DEHUMANISATION	DEHYPNOTISING	DELAMINATION	DELIBERATED	DELINEATOR
DEHUMANISATIONS	DEHYPNOTIZATION	DELAMINATIONS	DELIBERATELY	DELINEATORS
DEHUMANISE	DEHYPNOTIZE	DELAPSIONS	DELIBERATENESS	DELINEAVIT
DEHUMANISED	DEHYPNOTIZED	DELASSEMENT	DELIBERATES	DELINQUENCIES
DEHUMANISES	DEHYPNOTIZES	DELASSEMENTS	DELIBERATING	DELINQUENCY
DEHUMANISING	DEHYPNOTIZING	DELAYERING	DELIBERATION	DELINQUENT
DEHUMANIZATION	DEICTICALLY	DELAYERINGS	DELIBERATIONS	DELINQUENTLY
DEHUMANIZATIONS	DEIFICATION	DELAYINGLY	DELIBERATIVE	DELINQUENTS
DEHUMANIZE	DEIFICATIONS	DELECTABILITIES	DELIBERATIVELY	DELIQUESCE
DEHUMANIZED	DEINDEXATION	DELECTABILITY	DELIBERATOR	DELIQUESCED
DEHUMANIZES	DEINDEXATIONS	DELECTABLE	DELIBERATORS	DELIQUESCENCE
DEHUMANIZING	DEINDEXING	DELECTABLENESS	DELICACIES	DELIQUESCENCES
DEHUMIDIFIED	DEINDIVIDUATION	DELECTABLES	DELICATELY	DELIQUESCENT
DEHUMIDIFIER	DEINDUSTRIALISE	DELECTABLY	DELICATENESS	DELIQUESCES
DEHUMIDIFIERS	DEINDUSTRIALIZE	DELECTATED	DELICATENESSES	DELIQUESCING
DEHUMIDIFIES	DEINONYCHUS	DELECTATES	DELICATESSEN	DELIQUIUMS
DEHUMIDIFY	DEINONYCHUSES	DELECTATING	DELICATESSENS	DELIRATION
DEHUMIDIFYING	DEINOSAURS	DELECTATION	DELICIOUSLY	DELIRATIONS
DEHYDRATED	DEINOTHERE	DELECTATIONS	DELICIOUSNESS	DELIRIFACIENT
DEHYDRATER	DEINOTHERES	DELEGACIES	DELICIOUSNESSES	DELIRIFACIENTS
DEHYDRATERS	DEINOTHERIA	DELEGATEES	DELIGATION	DELIRIOUSLY
DEHYDRATES	DEINOTHERIUM	DELEGATING	DELIGATIONS	DELIRIOUSNESS
DEHYDRATING	DEINOTHERIUMS	DELEGATION	DELIGHTEDLY	DELIRIOUSNESSES
DEHYDRATION	DEIONISATION	DELEGATIONS	DELIGHTEDNESS	DELITESCENCE
DEHYDRATIONS	DEIONISATIONS	DELEGATORS	DELIGHTEDNESSES	DELITESCENCES
DEHYDRATOR	DEIONISERS	DELEGITIMATION	DELIGHTERS	DELITESCENT
DEHYDRATORS	DEIONISING	DELEGITIMATIONS	DELIGHTFUL	DELIVERABILITY
DEHYDROGENASE	DEIONIZATION	DELEGITIMISE	DELIGHTFULLY	DELIVERABLE
DEHYDROGENASES	DEIONIZATIONS	DELEGITIMISED	DELIGHTFULNESS	DELIVERABLES
DEHYDROGENATE	DEIONIZERS	DELEGITIMISES	DELIGHTING	DELIVERANCE
DEHYDROGENATED	DEIONIZING	DELEGITIMISING	DELIGHTLESS	DELIVERANCES
DEHYDROGENATES	DEIPNOSOPHIST	DELEGITIMIZE	DELIGHTSOME	DELIVERERS
DEHYDROGENATING	DEIPNOSOPHISTS	DELEGITIMIZED	DELIMITATE	DELIVERIES
DEHYDROGENATION	DEISTICALLY	DELEGITIMIZES	DELIMITATED	DELIVERING
DEHYDROGENISE	DEJECTEDLY	DELEGITIMIZING	DELIMITATES	DELIVERYMAN
DEHYDROGENISED	DEJECTEDNESS	DELETERIOUS	DELIMITATING	DELIVERYMEN
DEHYDROGENISES	DEJECTEDNESSES	DELETERIOUSLY	DELIMITATION	DELOCALISATION
DEHYDROGENISING	DEJECTIONS	DELETERIOUSNESS	DELIMITATIONS	DELOCALISATIONS
DEHYDROGENIZE	DEKALITERS	DELEVERAGE	DELIMITATIVE	DELOCALISE
DEHYDROGENIZED	DEKALITRES	DELEVERAGED	DELIMITERS	DELOCALISED
DEHYDROGENIZES	DEKALOGIES	DELEVERAGES	DELIMITING	DELOCALISES

DELOCALISING

DELOCALISING	DEMAGOGING	DEMERITORIOUS	DEMIVEGGES	DEMOGRAPHERS
DELOCALIZATION	DEMAGOGISM	DEMERITORIOUSLY	DEMIVIERGE	DEMOGRAPHIC
DELOCALIZATIONS	DEMAGOGISMS	DEMERSIONS	DEMIVIERGES	DEMOGRAPHICAL
DELOCALIZE	DEMAGOGUED	DEMIBASTION	DEMIVOLTES	DEMOGRAPHICALLY
DELOCALIZED	DEMAGOGUERIES	DEMIBASTIONS	DEMIWORLDS	DEMOGRAPHICS
DELOCALIZES	DEMAGOGUERY	DEMICANTON	DEMOBILISATION	DEMOGRAPHIES
DELOCALIZING	DEMAGOGUES	DEMICANTONS	DEMOBILISATIONS	DEMOGRAPHIST
DELPHICALLY	DEMAGOGUING	DEMIGODDESS	DEMOBILISE	DEMOGRAPHISTS
DELPHINIUM	DEMAGOGUISM	DEMIGODDESSES	DEMOBILISED	DEMOGRAPHY
DELPHINIUMS	DEMAGOGUISMS	DEMIGRATION	DEMOBILISES	DEMOISELLE
DELPHINOID	DEMANDABLE	DEMIGRATIONS	DEMOBILISING	DEMOISELLES
DELPHINOIDS	DEMANDANTS	DEMILITARISE	DEMOBILIZATION	DEMOLISHED
DELTIOLOGIES	DEMANDINGLY	DEMILITARISED	DEMOBILIZATIONS	DEMOLISHER
DELTIOLOGIST	DEMANDINGNESS	DEMILITARISES	DEMOBILIZE	DEMOLISHERS
DELTIOLOGISTS	DEMANDINGNESSES	DEMILITARISING	DEMOBILIZED	DEMOLISHES
DELTIOLOGY	DEMANNINGS	DEMILITARIZE	DEMOBILIZES	DEMOLISHING
DELTOIDEUS	DEMANTOIDS	DEMILITARIZED	DEMOBILIZING	DEMOLISHMENT
DELUDINGLY	DEMARCATED	DEMILITARIZES	DEMOCRACIES	DEMOLISHMENTS
DELUNDUNGS	DEMARCATES	DEMILITARIZING	DEMOCRATIC	DEMOLITION
DELUSIONAL	DEMARCATING	DEMIMONDAINE	DEMOCRATICAL	DEMOLITIONIST
DELUSIONARY	DEMARCATION	DEMIMONDAINES	DEMOCRATICALLY	DEMOLITIONISTS
DELUSIONIST	DEMARCATIONS	DEMIMONDES	DEMOCRATIES	DEMOLITIONS
DELUSIONISTS	DEMARCATOR	DEMINERALISE	DEMOCRATIFIABLE	DEMOLOGIES
DELUSIVELY	DEMARCATORS	DEMINERALISED	DEMOCRATISATION	DEMONESSES
DELUSIVENESS	DEMARKATION	DEMINERALISER	DEMOCRATISE	DEMONETARISE
DELUSIVENESSES	DEMARKATIONS	DEMINERALISERS	DEMOCRATISED	DEMONETARISED
DELUSTERED	DEMARKETED	DEMINERALISES	DEMOCRATISER	DEMONETARISES
DELUSTERING	DEMARKETING	DEMINERALISING	DEMOCRATISERS	DEMONETARISING
DELUSTRANT	DEMATERIALISE	DEMINERALIZE	DEMOCRATISES	DEMONETARIZE
DELUSTRANTS	DEMATERIALISED	DEMINERALIZED	DEMOCRATISING	DEMONETARIZED
DELUSTRING	DEMATERIALISES	DEMINERALIZER	DEMOCRATIST	DEMONETARIZES
DEMAGNETISATION	DEMATERIALISING	DEMINERALIZERS	DEMOCRATISTS	DEMONETARIZING
DEMAGNETISE	DEMATERIALIZE	DEMINERALIZES	DEMOCRATIZATION	DEMONETISATION
DEMAGNETISED	DEMATERIALIZED	DEMINERALIZING	DEMOCRATIZE	DEMONETISATIONS
DEMAGNETISER	DEMATERIALIZES	DEMIPIQUES	DEMOCRATIZED	DEMONETISE
DEMAGNETISERS	DEMATERIALIZING	DEMIRELIEF	DEMOCRATIZER	DEMONETISED
DEMAGNETISES	DEMEANOURS	DEMIRELIEFS	DEMOCRATIZERS	DEMONETISES
DEMAGNETISING	DEMEASNURE	DEMIREPDOM	DEMOCRATIZES	DEMONETISING
DEMAGNETIZATION	DEMEASNURES	DEMIREPDOMS	DEMOCRATIZING	DEMONETIZATION
DEMAGNETIZE	DEMENTATED	DEMISEMIQUAVER	DEMODULATE	DEMONETIZATIONS
DEMAGNETIZED	DEMENTATES	DEMISEMIQUAVERS	DEMODULATED	DEMONETIZE
DEMAGNETIZER	DEMENTATING	DEMISSIONS	DEMODULATES	DEMONETIZED
DEMAGNETIZERS	DEMENTEDLY	DEMISTINGS	DEMODULATING	DEMONETIZES
DEMAGNETIZES	DEMENTEDNESS	DEMITASSES	DEMODULATION	DEMONETIZING
DEMAGNETIZING	DEMENTEDNESSES	DEMIURGEOUS	DEMODULATIONS	DEMONIACAL
DEMAGOGICAL	DEMERGERED	DEMIURGICAL	DEMODULATOR	DEMONIACALLY
DEMAGOGICALLY	DEMERGERING	DEMIURGICALLY	DEMODULATORS	DEMONIACISM
DEMAGOGIES	DEMERITING	DEMIURGUSES	DEMOGRAPHER	DEMONIACISMS

DEMONIANISM	DEMORALIZATION	DEMYELINATIONS	DENATURIZES	DENIGRATIVE
DEMONIANISMS	DEMORALIZATIONS	DEMYSTIFICATION	DENATURIZING	DENIGRATOR
DEMONICALLY	DEMORALIZE	DEMYSTIFIED	DENAZIFICATION	DENIGRATORS
DEMONISATION	DEMORALIZED	DEMYSTIFIES	DENAZIFICATIONS	DENIGRATORY
DEMONISATIONS	DEMORALIZER	DEMYSTIFYING	DENAZIFIED	DENISATION
DEMONISING	DEMORALIZERS	DEMYTHIFICATION	DENAZIFIES	DENISATIONS
DEMONIZATION	DEMORALIZES	DEMYTHIFIED	DENAZIFYING	DENITRATED
DEMONIZATIONS	DEMORALIZING	DEMYTHIFIES	DENDRACHATE	DENITRATES
DEMONIZING	DEMORALIZINGLY	DEMYTHIFYING	DENDRACHATES	DENITRATING
DEMONOCRACIES	DEMOSCENES	DEMYTHOLOGISE	DENDRIFORM	DENITRATION
DEMONOCRACY	DEMOTICIST	DEMYTHOLOGISED	DENDRIMERS	DENITRATIONS
DEMONOLATER	DEMOTICISTS	DEMYTHOLOGISER	DENDRITICAL	DENITRIFICATION
DEMONOLATERS	DEMOTIVATE	DEMYTHOLOGISERS	DENDRITICALLY	DENITRIFICATOR
DEMONOLATRIES	DEMOTIVATED	DEMYTHOLOGISES	DENDROBIUM	DENITRIFICATORS
DEMONOLATRY	DEMOTIVATES	DEMYTHOLOGISING	DENDROBIUMS	DENITRIFIED
DEMONOLOGIC	DEMOTIVATING	DEMYTHOLOGIZE	DENDROGLYPH	DENITRIFIER
DEMONOLOGICAL	DEMOTIVATION	DEMYTHOLOGIZED	DENDROGLYPHS	DENITRIFIERS
DEMONOLOGIES	DEMOTIVATIONS	DEMYTHOLOGIZER	DENDROGRAM	DENITRIFIES
DEMONOLOGIST	DEMOUNTABLE	DEMYTHOLOGIZERS	DENDROGRAMS	DENITRIFYING
DEMONOLOGISTS	DEMOUNTING	DEMYTHOLOGIZES	DENDROIDAL	DENIZATION
DEMONOLOGY	DEMULCENTS	DEMYTHOLOGIZING	DENDROLATRIES	DENIZATIONS
DEMONOMANIA	DEMULSIFICATION	DENATIONALISE	DENDROLATRY	DENIZENING
DEMONOMANIAS	DEMULSIFIED	DENATIONALISED	DENDROLOGIC	DENIZENSHIP
DEMONSTRABILITY	DEMULSIFIER	DENATIONALISES	DENDROLOGICAL	DENIZENSHIPS
DEMONSTRABLE	DEMULSIFIERS	DENATIONALISING	DENDROLOGIES	DENOMINABLE
DEMONSTRABLY	DEMULSIFIES	DENATIONALIZE	DENDROLOGIST	DENOMINATE
DEMONSTRATE	DEMULSIFYING	DENATIONALIZED	DENDROLOGISTS	DENOMINATED
DEMONSTRATED	DEMULTIPLEXER	DENATIONALIZES	DENDROLOGOUS	DENOMINATES
DEMONSTRATES	DEMULTIPLEXERS	DENATIONALIZING	DENDROLOGY	DENOMINATING
DEMONSTRATING	DEMURENESS	DENATURALISE	DENDROMETER	DENOMINATION
DEMONSTRATION	DEMURENESSES	DENATURALISED	DENDROMETERS	DENOMINATIONAL
DEMONSTRATIONAL	DEMURRABLE	DENATURALISES	DENDROPHIS	DENOMINATIONS
DEMONSTRATIONS	DEMURRAGES	DENATURALISING	DENDROPHISES	DENOMINATIVE
DEMONSTRATIVE	DEMUTUALISATION	DENATURALIZE	DENEGATION	DENOMINATIVELY
DEMONSTRATIVELY	DEMUTUALISE	DENATURALIZED	DENEGATIONS	DENOMINATIVES
DEMONSTRATIVES	DEMUTUALISED	DENATURALIZES	DENERVATED	DENOMINATOR
DEMONSTRATOR	DEMUTUALISES	DENATURALIZING	DENERVATES	DENOMINATORS
DEMONSTRATORS	DEMUTUALISING	DENATURANT	DENERVATING	DENOTATING
DEMONSTRATORY	DEMUTUALIZATION	DENATURANTS	DENERVATION	DENOTATION
DEMORALISATION	DEMUTUALIZE	DENATURATION	DENERVATIONS	DENOTATIONS
DEMORALISATIONS	DEMUTUALIZED	DENATURATIONS	DENIABILITIES	DENOTATIVE
DEMORALISE	DEMUTUALIZES	DENATURING	DENIABILITY	DENOTATIVELY
DEMORALISED	DEMUTUALIZING	DENATURISE	DENIALISTS	DENOTEMENT
DEMORALISER	DEMYELINATE	DENATURISED	DENIGRATED	DENOTEMENTS
DEMORALISERS	DEMYELINATED	DENATURISES	DENIGRATES	DENOUEMENT
DEMORALISES	DEMYELINATES	DENATURISING	DENIGRATING	DENOUEMENTS
DEMORALISING	DEMYELINATING	DENATURIZE	DENIGRATION	DENOUNCEMENT
DEMORALISINGLY	DEMYELINATION	DENATURIZED	DENIGRATIONS	DENOUNCEMENTS

DENOUNCERS

DENOUNCERS	DENUCLEARIZED	DEOPPILATIONS	DEPARTMENTALISE	DEPERSONALIZING
DENOUNCING	DENUCLEARIZES	DEOPPILATIVE	DEPARTMENTALISM	DEPHLEGMATE
DENSENESSES	DENUCLEARIZING	DEOPPILATIVES	DEPARTMENTALIZE	DEPHLEGMATED
DENSIFICATION	DENUDATING	DEORBITING	DEPARTMENTALLY	DEPHLEGMATES
DENSIFICATIONS	DENUDATION	DEOXIDATED	DEPARTMENTS	DEPHLEGMATING
DENSIFIERS	DENUDATIONS	DEOXIDATES	DEPARTURES	DEPHLEGMATION
DENSIFYING	DENUDEMENT	DEOXIDATING	DEPASTURED	DEPHLEGMATIONS
DENSIMETER	DENUDEMENTS	DEOXIDATION	DEPASTURES	DEPHLEGMATOR
DENSIMETERS	DENUMERABILITY	DEOXIDATIONS	DEPASTURING	DEPHLEGMATORS
DENSIMETRIC	DENUMERABLE	DEOXIDISATION	DEPAUPERATE	DEPHLOGISTICATE
DENSIMETRIES	DENUMERABLY	DEOXIDISATIONS	DEPAUPERATED	DEPHOSPHORYLATE
DENSIMETRY	DENUNCIATE	DEOXIDISED	DEPAUPERATES	DEPICTIONS
DENSITOMETER	DENUNCIATED	DEOXIDISER	DEPAUPERATING	DEPICTURED
DENSITOMETERS	DENUNCIATES	DEOXIDISERS	DEPAUPERISE	DEPICTURES
DENSITOMETRIC	DENUNCIATING	DEOXIDISES	DEPAUPERISED	DEPICTURING
DENSITOMETRIES	DENUNCIATION	DEOXIDISING	DEPAUPERISES	DEPIGMENTATION
DENSITOMETRY	DENUNCIATIONS	DEOXIDIZATION	DEPAUPERISING	DEPIGMENTATIONS
DENTALISED	DENUNCIATIVE	DEOXIDIZATIONS	DEPAUPERIZE	DEPIGMENTED
DENTALISES	DENUNCIATOR	DEOXIDIZED	DEPAUPERIZED	DEPIGMENTING
DENTALISING	DENUNCIATORS	DEOXIDIZER	DEPAUPERIZES	DEPIGMENTS
DENTALITIES	DENUNCIATORY	DEOXIDIZERS	DEPAUPERIZING	DEPILATING
DENTALIUMS	DEOBSTRUENT	DEOXIDIZES	DEPEINCTED	DEPILATION
DENTALIZED	DEOBSTRUENTS	DEOXIDIZING	DEPEINCTING	DEPILATIONS
DENTALIZES	DEODORANTS	DEOXYCORTONE	DEPENDABILITIES	DEPILATORIES
DENTALIZING	DEODORISATION	DEOXYCORTONES	DEPENDABILITY	DEPILATORS
DENTATIONS	DEODORISATIONS	DEOXYGENATE	DEPENDABLE	DEPILATORY
DENTICARES	DEODORISED	DEOXYGENATED	DEPENDABLENESS	DEPLENISHED
DENTICULATE	DEODORISER	DEOXYGENATES	DEPENDABLY	DEPLENISHES
DENTICULATED	DEODORISERS	DEOXYGENATING	DEPENDANCE	DEPLENISHING
DENTICULATELY	DEODORISES	DEOXYGENATION	DEPENDANCES	DEPLETABLE
DENTICULATION	DEODORISING	DEOXYGENATIONS	DEPENDANCIES	DEPLETIONS
DENTICULATIONS	DEODORIZATION	DEOXYGENISE	DEPENDANCY	DEPLORABILITIES
DENTIFRICE	DEODORIZATIONS	DEOXYGENISED	DEPENDANTS	DEPLORABILITY
DENTIFRICES	DEODORIZED	DEOXYGENISES	DEPENDENCE	DEPLORABLE
DENTIGEROUS	DEODORIZER	DEOXYGENISING	DEPENDENCES	DEPLORABLENESS
DENTILABIAL	DEODORIZERS	DEOXYGENIZE	DEPENDENCIES	DEPLORABLY
DENTILINGUAL	DEODORIZES	DEOXYGENIZED	DEPENDENCY	DEPLORATION
DENTILINGUALS	DEODORIZING	DEOXYGENIZES	DEPENDENTLY	DEPLORATIONS
DENTIROSTRAL	DEONTOLOGICAL	DEOXYGENIZING	DEPENDENTS	DEPLORINGLY
DENTISTRIES	DEONTOLOGIES	DEOXYRIBOSE	DEPENDINGLY	DEPLOYABLE
DENTITIONS	DEONTOLOGIST	DEOXYRIBOSES	DEPEOPLING	DEPLOYMENT
DENTURISMS	DEONTOLOGISTS	DEPAINTING	DEPERSONALISE	DEPLOYMENTS
DENTURISTS	DEONTOLOGY	DEPANNEURS	DEPERSONALISED	DEPLUMATION
DENUCLEARISE	DEOPPILATE	DEPARTEMENT	DEPERSONALISES	DEPLUMATIONS
DENUCLEARISED	DEOPPILATED	DEPARTEMENTS	DEPERSONALISING	DEPOLARISATION
DENUCLEARISES	DEOPPILATES	DEPARTINGS	DEPERSONALIZE	DEPOLARISATIONS
DENUCLEARISING	DEOPPILATING	DEPARTMENT	DEPERSONALIZED	DEPOLARISE
DENUCLEARIZE	DEOPPILATION	DEPARTMENTAL	DEPERSONALIZES	DEPOLARISED

DEPOLARISER	DEPOSITING	DEPREDATORS	DEPURATORY	DERECOGNIZING
DEPOLARISERS	DEPOSITION	DEPREDATORY	DEPUTATION	DEREGISTER
DEPOLARISES	DEPOSITIONAL	DEPREHENDED	DEPUTATIONS	DEREGISTERED
DEPOLARISING	DEPOSITIONS	DEPREHENDING	DEPUTISATION	DEREGISTERING
DEPOLARIZATION	DEPOSITIVE	DEPREHENDS	DEPUTISATIONS	DEREGISTERS
DEPOLARIZATIONS	DEPOSITORIES	DEPRESSANT	DEPUTISING	DEREGISTRATION
DEPOLARIZE	DEPOSITORS	DEPRESSANTS	DEPUTIZATION	DEREGISTRATIONS
DEPOLARIZED	DEPOSITORY	DEPRESSIBLE	DEPUTIZATIONS	DEREGULATE
DEPOLARIZER	DEPRAVATION	DEPRESSING	DEPUTIZING	DEREGULATED
DEPOLARIZERS	DEPRAVATIONS	DEPRESSINGLY	DEQUEUEING	DEREGULATES
DEPOLARIZES	DEPRAVEDLY	DEPRESSION	DERACIALISE	DEREGULATING
DEPOLARIZING	DEPRAVEDNESS	DEPRESSIONS	DERACIALISED	DEREGULATION
DEPOLISHED	DEPRAVEDNESSES	DEPRESSIVE	DERACIALISES	DEREGULATIONS
DEPOLISHES	DEPRAVEMENT	DEPRESSIVELY	DERACIALISING	DEREGULATOR
DEPOLISHING	DEPRAVEMENTS	DEPRESSIVENESS	DERACIALIZE	DEREGULATORS
DEPOLITICISE	DEPRAVINGLY	DEPRESSIVES	DERACIALIZED	DEREGULATORY
DEPOLITICISED	DEPRAVITIES	DEPRESSOMOTOR	DERACIALIZES	DERELICTION
DEPOLITICISES	DEPRECABLE	DEPRESSOMOTORS	DERACIALIZING	DERELICTIONS
DEPOLITICISING	DEPRECATED	DEPRESSORS	DERACINATE	DERELIGIONISE
DEPOLITICIZE	DEPRECATES	DEPRESSURISE	DERACINATED	DERELIGIONISED
DEPOLITICIZED	DEPRECATING	DEPRESSURISED	DERACINATES	DERELIGIONISES
DEPOLITICIZES	DEPRECATINGLY	DEPRESSURISES	DERACINATING	DERELIGIONISING
DEPOLITICIZING	DEPRECATION	DEPRESSURISING	DERACINATION	DERELIGIONIZE
DEPOLYMERISE	DEPRECATIONS	DEPRESSURIZE	DERACINATIONS	DERELIGIONIZED
DEPOLYMERISED	DEPRECATIVE	DEPRESSURIZED	DERAIGNING	DERELIGIONIZES
DEPOLYMERISES	DEPRECATIVELY	DEPRESSURIZES	DERAIGNMENT	DERELIGIONIZING
DEPOLYMERISING	DEPRECATOR	DEPRESSURIZING	DERAIGNMENTS	DEREPRESSED
DEPOLYMERIZE	DEPRECATORILY	DEPRIVABLE	DERAILLEUR	DEREPRESSES
DEPOLYMERIZED	DEPRECATORS	DEPRIVATION	DERAILLEURS	DEREPRESSING
DEPOLYMERIZES	DEPRECATORY	DEPRIVATIONS	DERAILMENT	DEREPRESSION
DEPOLYMERIZING	DEPRECIABLE	DEPRIVATIVE	DERAILMENTS	DEREPRESSIONS
DEPOPULATE	DEPRECIATE	DEPRIVEMENT	DERANGEMENT	DEREQUISITION
DEPOPULATED	DEPRECIATED	DEPRIVEMENTS	DERANGEMENTS	DEREQUISITIONED
DEPOPULATES	DEPRECIATES	DEPROGRAMED	DERATIONED	DEREQUISITIONS
DEPOPULATING	DEPRECIATING	DEPROGRAMING	DERATIONING	DERESTRICT
DEPOPULATION	DEPRECIATINGLY	DEPROGRAMME	DEREALISATION	DERESTRICTED
DEPOPULATIONS	DEPRECIATION	DEPROGRAMMED	DEREALISATIONS	DERESTRICTING
DEPOPULATOR	DEPRECIATIONS	DEPROGRAMMER	DEREALIZATION	DERESTRICTION
DEPOPULATORS	DEPRECIATIVE	DEPROGRAMMERS	DEREALIZATIONS	DERESTRICTIONS
DEPORTABLE	DEPRECIATOR	DEPROGRAMMES	DERECOGNISE	DERESTRICTS
DEPORTATION	DEPRECIATORS	DEPROGRAMMING	DERECOGNISED	DERIDINGLY
DEPORTATIONS	DEPRECIATORY	DEPROGRAMS	DERECOGNISES	DERISIVELY
DEPORTMENT	DEPREDATED	DEPURATING	DERECOGNISING	DERISIVENESS
DEPORTMENTS	DEPREDATES	DEPURATION	DERECOGNITION	DERISIVENESSES
DEPOSITARIES	DEPREDATING	DEPURATIONS	DERECOGNITIONS	DERIVATING
DEPOSITARY	DEPREDATION	DEPURATIVE	DERECOGNIZE	DERIVATION
DEPOSITATION	DEPREDATIONS	DEPURATIVES	DERECOGNIZED	DERIVATIONAL
DEPOSITATIONS	DEPREDATOR	DEPURATORS	DERECOGNIZES	DERIVATIONIST

DERIVATIONISTS	DERMATOPHYTIC	DESALINIZATION	DESCRIPTIVISM	DESERTIZATION
DERIVATIONS	DERMATOPHYTOSES	DESALINIZATIONS	DESCRIPTIVISMS	DESERTIZATIONS
DERIVATISATION	DERMATOPHYTOSIS	DESALINIZE	DESCRIPTIVIST	DESERTLESS
DERIVATISATIONS	DERMATOPLASTIC	DESALINIZED	DESCRIPTOR	DESERVEDLY
DERIVATISE	DERMATOPLASTIES	DESALINIZES	DESCRIPTORS	DESERVEDNESS
DERIVATISED	DERMATOPLASTY	DESALINIZING	DESCRIVING	DESERVEDNESSES
DERIVATISES	DERMATOSES	DESALTINGS	DESECRATED	DESERVINGLY
DERIVATISING	DERMATOSIS	DESATURATE	DESECRATER	DESERVINGNESS
DERIVATIVE	DERMESTIDS	DESATURATED	DESECRATERS	DESERVINGNESSES
DERIVATIVELY	DERMOGRAPHIES	DESATURATES	DESECRATES	DESERVINGS
DERIVATIVENESS	DERMOGRAPHY	DESATURATING	DESECRATING	DESEXUALISATION
DERIVATIVES	DEROGATELY	DESATURATION	DESECRATION	DESEXUALISE
DERIVATIZATION	DEROGATING	DESATURATIONS	DESECRATIONS	DESEXUALISED
DERIVATIZATIONS	DEROGATION	DESCANTERS	DESECRATOR	DESEXUALISES
DERIVATIZE	DEROGATIONS	DESCANTING	DESECRATORS	DESEXUALISING
DERIVATIZED	DEROGATIVE	DESCENDABLE	DESEGREGATE	DESEXUALIZATION
DERIVATIZES	DEROGATIVELY	DESCENDANT	DESEGREGATED	DESEXUALIZE
DERIVATIZING	DEROGATORILY	DESCENDANTS	DESEGREGATES	DESEXUALIZED
DERMABRASION	DEROGATORINESS	DESCENDENT	DESEGREGATING	DESEXUALIZES
DERMABRASIONS	DEROGATORY	DESCENDENTS	DESEGREGATION	DESEXUALIZING
DERMAPLANING	DERRICKING	DESCENDERS	DESEGREGATIONS	DESHABILLE
DERMAPLANINGS	DERRINGERS	DESCENDEUR	DESELECTED	DESHABILLES
DERMAPTERAN	DESACRALISATION	DESCENDEURS	DESELECTING	DESICCANTS
DERMAPTERANS	DESACRALISE	DESCENDIBLE	DESELECTION	DESICCATED
DERMATITIDES	DESACRALISED	DESCENDING	DESELECTIONS	DESICCATES
DERMATITIS	DESACRALISES	DESCENDINGS	DESENSITISATION	DESICCATING
DERMATITISES	DESACRALISING	DESCENSION	DESENSITISE	DESICCATION
DERMATOGEN	DESACRALIZATION	DESCENSIONAL	DESENSITISED	DESICCATIONS
DERMATOGENS	DESACRALIZE	DESCENSIONS	DESENSITISER	DESICCATIVE
DERMATOGLYPHIC	DESACRALIZED	DESCHOOLED	DESENSITISERS	DESICCATIVES
DERMATOGLYPHICS	DESACRALIZES	DESCHOOLER	DESENSITISES	DESICCATOR
DERMATOGRAPHIA	DESACRALIZING	DESCHOOLERS	DESENSITISING	DESICCATORS
DERMATOGRAPHIAS	DESAGREMENT	DESCHOOLING	DESENSITIZATION	DESIDERATA
DERMATOGRAPHIC	DESAGREMENTS	DESCHOOLINGS	DESENSITIZE	DESIDERATE
DERMATOGRAPHIES	DESALINATE	DESCRAMBLE	DESENSITIZED	DESIDERATED
DERMATOGRAPHY	DESALINATED	DESCRAMBLED	DESENSITIZER	DESIDERATES
DERMATOLOGIC	DESALINATES	DESCRAMBLER	DESENSITIZERS	DESIDERATING
DERMATOLOGICAL	DESALINATING	DESCRAMBLERS	DESENSITIZES	DESIDERATION
DERMATOLOGIES	DESALINATION	DESCRAMBLES	DESENSITIZING	DESIDERATIONS
DERMATOLOGIST	DESALINATIONS	DESCRAMBLING	DESERPIDINE	DESIDERATIVE
DERMATOLOGISTS	DESALINATOR	DESCRIBABLE	DESERPIDINES	DESIDERATIVES
DERMATOLOGY	DESALINATORS	DESCRIBERS	DESERTIFICATION	DESIDERATUM
DERMATOMAL	DESALINISATION	DESCRIBING	DESERTIFIED	DESIDERIUM
DERMATOMES	DESALINISATIONS	DESCRIPTION	DESERTIFIES	DESIDERIUMS
DERMATOMIC	DESALINISE	DESCRIPTIONS	DESERTIFYING	DESIGNABLE
DERMATOMYOSITIS	DESALINISED	DESCRIPTIVE	DESERTIONS	DESIGNATED
DERMATOPHYTE	DESALINISES	DESCRIPTIVELY	DESERTISATION	DESIGNATES
DERMATOPHYTES	DESALINISING	DESCRIPTIVENESS	DESERTISATIONS	DESIGNATING

DESIGNATION	DESMOSOMES	DESPISEDNESSES	DESSERTSPOONFUL	DESTRUCTED
DESIGNATIONS	DESNOODING	DESPISEMENT	DESSERTSPOONS	DESTRUCTIBILITY
DESIGNATIVE	DESOBLIGEANTE	DESPISEMENTS	DESSIATINE	DESTRUCTIBLE
DESIGNATOR	DESOBLIGEANTES	DESPISINGLY	DESSIATINES	DESTRUCTING
DESIGNATORS	DESOLATELY	DESPITEFUL	DESSIGNMENT	DESTRUCTION
DESIGNATORY	DESOLATENESS	DESPITEFULLY	DESSIGNMENTS	DESTRUCTIONAL
DESIGNEDLY	DESOLATENESSES	DESPITEFULNESS	DESSYATINE	DESTRUCTIONIST
DESIGNINGLY	DESOLATERS	DESPITEOUS	DESSYATINES	DESTRUCTIONISTS
DESIGNINGS	DESOLATING	DESPITEOUSLY	DESSYATINS	DESTRUCTIONS
DESIGNLESS	DESOLATINGLY	DESPITEOUSNESS	DESTABILISATION	DESTRUCTIVE
DESIGNMENT	DESOLATION	DESPOILERS	DESTABILISE	DESTRUCTIVELY
DESIGNMENTS	DESOLATIONS	DESPOILING	DESTABILISED	DESTRUCTIVENESS
DESILVERED	DESOLATORS	DESPOILINGS	DESTABILISER	DESTRUCTIVES
DESILVERING	DESOLATORY	DESPOILMENT	DESTABILISERS	DESTRUCTIVISM
DESILVERISATION	DESORIENTE	DESPOILMENTS	DESTABILISES	DESTRUCTIVISMS
DESILVERISE	DESORPTION	DESPOLIATION	DESTABILISING	DESTRUCTIVIST
DESILVERISED	DESORPTIONS	DESPOLIATIONS	DESTABILIZATION	DESTRUCTIVISTS
DESILVERISES	DESOXYRIBOSE	DESPONDENCE	DESTABILIZE	DESTRUCTIVITIES
DESILVERISING	DESOXYRIBOSES	DESPONDENCES	DESTABILIZED	DESTRUCTIVITY
DESILVERIZATION	DESPAIRERS	DESPONDENCIES	DESTABILIZER	DESTRUCTOR
DESILVERIZE	DESPAIRFUL	DESPONDENCY	DESTABILIZERS	DESTRUCTORS
DESILVERIZED	DESPAIRING	DESPONDENT	DESTABILIZES	DESTRUCTOS
DESILVERIZES	DESPAIRINGLY	DESPONDENTLY	DESTABILIZING	DESUETUDES
DESILVERIZING	DESPATCHED	DESPONDING	DESTAINING	DESUGARING
DESINENCES	DESPATCHER	DESPONDINGLY	DESTEMPERED	DESULFURATE
DESINENTIAL	DESPATCHERS	DESPONDINGS	DESTEMPERING	DESULFURATED
DESIPIENCE	DESPATCHES	DESPOTATES	DESTEMPERS	DESULFURATES
DESIPIENCES	DESPATCHING	DESPOTICAL	DESTINATED	DESULFURATING
DESIPRAMINE	DESPERADOES	DESPOTICALLY	DESTINATES	DESULFURATION
DESIPRAMINES	DESPERADOS	DESPOTICALNESS	DESTINATING	DESULFURATIONS
DESIRABILITIES	DESPERATELY	DESPOTISMS	DESTINATION	DESULFURED
DESIRABILITY	DESPERATENESS	DESPOTOCRACIES	DESTINATIONS	DESULFURING
DESIRABLENESS	DESPERATENESSES	DESPOTOCRACY	DESTITUTED	DESULFURISATION
DESIRABLENESSES	DESPERATION	DESPUMATED	DESTITUTENESS	DESULFURISE
DESIRABLES	DESPERATIONS	DESPUMATES	DESTITUTENESSES	DESULFURISED
DESIRELESS	DESPICABILITIES	DESPUMATING	DESTITUTES	DESULFURISER
DESIROUSLY	DESPICABILITY	DESPUMATION	DESTITUTING	DESULFURISERS
DESIROUSNESS	DESPICABLE	DESPUMATIONS	DESTITUTION	DESULFURISES
DESIROUSNESSES	DESPICABLENESS	DESQUAMATE	DESTITUTIONS	DESULFURISING
DESISTANCE	DESPICABLY	DESQUAMATED	DESTOCKING	DESULFURIZATION
DESISTANCES	DESPIRITUALISE	DESQUAMATES	DESTREAMED	DESULFURIZE
DESISTENCE	DESPIRITUALISED	DESQUAMATING	DESTREAMING	DESULFURIZED
DESISTENCES	DESPIRITUALISES	DESQUAMATION	DESTRESSED	DESULFURIZER
DESKILLING	DESPIRITUALIZE	DESQUAMATIONS	DESTRESSES	DESULFURIZERS
DESKILLINGS	DESPIRITUALIZED	DESQUAMATIVE	DESTRESSING	DESULFURIZES
DESMODIUMS	DESPIRITUALIZES	DESQUAMATORIES	DESTROYABLE	DESULFURIZING
DESMODROMIC	DESPISABLE	DESQUAMATORY	DESTROYERS	DESULPHURATE
DESMOSOMAL	DESPISEDNESS	DESSERTSPOON	DESTROYING	DESULPHURATED

DESULPHURATES	DETECTIONS	DETERMINATORS	DETONATING	DETRIMENTS
DESULPHURATING	DETECTIVELIKE	DETERMINED	DETONATION	DETRITIONS
DESULPHURATION	DETECTIVES	DETERMINEDLY	DETONATIONS	DETRITOVORE
DESULPHURATIONS	DETECTIVIST	DETERMINEDNESS	DETONATIVE	DETRITOVORES
DESULPHURED	DETECTIVISTS	DETERMINER	DETONATORS	DETRUNCATE
DESULPHURING	DETECTOPHONE	DETERMINERS	DETORSIONS	DETRUNCATED
DESULPHURISE	DETECTOPHONES	DETERMINES	DETORTIONS	DETRUNCATES
DESULPHURISED	DETECTORIST	DETERMINING	DETOXICANT	DETRUNCATING
DESULPHURISER	DETECTORISTS	DETERMINISM	DETOXICANTS	DETRUNCATION
DESULPHURISERS	DETENTIONS	DETERMINISMS	DETOXICATE	DETRUNCATIONS
DESULPHURISES	DETENTISTS	DETERMINIST	DETOXICATED	DETRUSIONS
DESULPHURISING	DETERGENCE	DETERMINISTIC	DETOXICATES	DETUMESCENCE
DESULPHURIZE	DETERGENCES	DETERMINISTS	DETOXICATING	DETUMESCENCES
DESULPHURIZED	DETERGENCIES	DETERRABILITIES	DETOXICATION	DETUMESCENT
DESULPHURIZER	DETERGENCY	DETERRABILITY	DETOXICATIONS	DEUTERAGONIST
DESULPHURIZERS	DETERGENTS	DETERRABLE	DETOXIFICATION	DEUTERAGONISTS
DESULPHURIZES	DETERIORATE	DETERRENCE	DETOXIFICATIONS	DEUTERANOMALIES
DESULPHURIZING	DETERIORATED	DETERRENCES	DETOXIFIED	DEUTERANOMALOUS
DESULPHURS	DETERIORATES	DETERRENTLY	DETOXIFIES	DEUTERANOMALY
DESULTORILY	DETERIORATING	DETERRENTS	DETOXIFYING	DEUTERANOPE
DESULTORINESS	DETERIORATION	DETERSIONS	DETRACTING	DEUTERANOPES
DESULTORINESSES	DETERIORATIONS	DETERSIVES	DETRACTINGLY	DEUTERANOPIA
DETACHABILITIES	DETERIORATIVE	DETESTABILITIES	DETRACTINGS	DEUTERANOPIAS
DETACHABILITY	DETERIORISM	DETESTABILITY	DETRACTION	DEUTERANOPIC
DETACHABLE	DETERIORISMS	DETESTABLE	DETRACTIONS	DEUTERATED
DETACHABLY	DETERIORITIES	DETESTABLENESS	DETRACTIVE	DEUTERATES
DETACHEDLY	DETERIORITY	DETESTABLY	DETRACTIVELY	DEUTERATING
DETACHEDNESS	DETERMENTS	DETESTATION	DETRACTORS	DEUTERATION
DETACHEDNESSES	DETERMINABILITY	DETESTATIONS	DETRACTORY	DEUTERATIONS
DETACHMENT	DETERMINABLE	DETHATCHED	DETRACTRESS	DEUTERIDES
DETACHMENTS	DETERMINABLY	DETHATCHES	DETRACTRESSES	DEUTERIUMS
DETAILEDLY	DETERMINACIES	DETHATCHING	DETRAINING	DEUTEROGAMIES
DETAILEDNESS	DETERMINACY	DETHRONEMENT	DETRAINMENT	DEUTEROGAMIST
DETAILEDNESSES	DETERMINANT	DETHRONEMENTS	DETRAINMENTS	DEUTEROGAMISTS
DETAILINGS	DETERMINANTAL	DETHRONERS	DETRAQUEES	DEUTEROGAMY
DETAINABLE	DETERMINANTS	DETHRONING	DETRIBALISATION	DEUTEROPLASM
DETAINMENT	DETERMINATE	DETHRONINGS	DETRIBALISE	DEUTEROPLASMS
DETAINMENTS	DETERMINATED	DETHRONISE	DETRIBALISED	DEUTEROSCOPIC
DETANGLERS	DETERMINATELY	DETHRONISED	DETRIBALISES	DEUTEROSCOPIES
DETANGLING	DETERMINATENESS	DETHRONISES	DETRIBALISING	DEUTEROSCOPY
DETASSELED	DETERMINATES	DETHRONISING	DETRIBALIZATION	DEUTEROSTOME
DETASSELING	DETERMINATING	DETHRONIZE	DETRIBALIZE	DEUTEROSTOMES
DETASSELLED	DETERMINATION	DETHRONIZED	DETRIBALIZED	DEUTEROTOKIES
DETASSELLING	DETERMINATIONS	DETHRONIZES	DETRIBALIZES	DEUTEROTOKY
DETECTABILITIES	DETERMINATIVE	DETHRONIZING	DETRIBALIZING	DEUTOPLASM
DETECTABILITY	DETERMINATIVELY	DETONABILITIES	DETRIMENTAL	DEUTOPLASMIC
DETECTABLE	DETERMINATIVES	DETONABILITY	DETRIMENTALLY	DEUTOPLASMS
DETECTIBLE	DETERMINATOR	DETONATABLE	DETRIMENTALS	DEUTOPLASTIC

DEVALORISATION	DEVILISHLY	DEVOTIONALISTS	DEXTROUSNESS	DIACTINISM
DEVALORISATIONS	DEVILISHNESS	DEVOTIONALITIES	DEXTROUSNESSES	DIACTINISMS
DEVALORISE	DEVILISHNESSES	DEVOTIONALITY	DEZINCKING	DIADELPHOUS
DEVALORISED	DEVILMENTS	DEVOTIONALLY	DHARMSALAS	DIADOCHIES
DEVALORISES	DEVILSHIPS	DEVOTIONALNESS	DHARMSHALA	DIADROMOUS
DEVALORISING	DEVILTRIES	DEVOTIONALS	DHARMSHALAS	DIAGENESES
DEVALORIZATION	DEVILWOODS	DEVOTIONIST	DIABETICAL	DIAGENESIS
DEVALORIZATIONS	DEVIOUSNESS	DEVOTIONISTS	DIABETOGENIC	DIAGENETIC
DEVALORIZE	DEVIOUSNESSES	DEVOURINGLY	DIABETOLOGIST	DIAGENETICALLY
DEVALORIZED	DEVITALISATION	DEVOURMENT	DIABETOLOGISTS	DIAGEOTROPIC
DEVALORIZES	DEVITALISATIONS	DEVOURMENTS	DIABLERIES	DIAGEOTROPISM
DEVALORIZING	DEVITALISE	DEVOUTNESS	DIABOLICAL	DIAGEOTROPISMS
DEVALUATED	DEVITALISED	DEVOUTNESSES	DIABOLICALLY	DIAGNOSABILITY
DEVALUATES	DEVITALISES	DEVVELLING	DIABOLICALNESS	DIAGNOSABLE
DEVALUATING	DEVITALISING	DEWATERERS	DIABOLISED	DIAGNOSEABLE
DEVALUATION	DEVITALIZATION	DEWATERING	DIABOLISES	DIAGNOSING
DEVALUATIONS	DEVITALIZATIONS	DEWATERINGS	DIABOLISING	DIAGNOSTIC
DEVANAGARI	DEVITALIZE	DEWBERRIES	DIABOLISMS	DIAGNOSTICAL
DEVANAGARIS	DEVITALIZED	DEWINESSES	DIABOLISTS	DIAGNOSTICALLY
DEVASTATED	DEVITALIZES	DEXAMETHASONE	DIABOLIZED	DIAGNOSTICIAN
DEVASTATES	DEVITALIZING	DEXAMETHASONES	DIABOLIZES	DIAGNOSTICIANS
DEVASTATING	DEVITRIFICATION	DEXAMPHETAMINE	DIABOLIZING	DIAGNOSTICS
DEVASTATINGLY	DEVITRIFIED	DEXAMPHETAMINES	DIABOLOGIES	DIAGOMETER
DEVASTATION	DEVITRIFIES	DEXIOTROPIC	DIABOLOLOGIES	DIAGOMETERS
DEVASTATIONS	DEVITRIFYING	DEXTERITIES	DIABOLOLOGY	DIAGONALISABLE
DEVASTATIVE	DEVOCALISE	DEXTEROUSLY	DIACATHOLICON	DIAGONALISATION
DEVASTATOR	DEVOCALISED	DEXTEROUSNESS	DIACATHOLICONS	DIAGONALISE
DEVASTATORS	DEVOCALISES	DEXTEROUSNESSES	DIACAUSTIC	DIAGONALISED
DEVASTAVIT	DEVOCALISING	DEXTERWISE	DIACAUSTICS	DIAGONALISES
DEVASTAVITS	DEVOCALIZE	DEXTRALITIES	DIACHRONIC	DIAGONALISING
DEVELOPABLE	DEVOCALIZED	DEXTRALITY	DIACHRONICALLY	DIAGONALIZABLE
DEVELOPERS	DEVOCALIZES	DEXTRANASE	DIACHRONIES	DIAGONALIZATION
DEVELOPING	DEVOCALIZING	DEXTRANASES	DIACHRONISM	DIAGONALIZE
DEVELOPMENT	DEVOICINGS	DEXTROCARDIA	DIACHRONISMS	DIAGONALIZED
DEVELOPMENTAL	DEVOLUTION	DEXTROCARDIAC	DIACHRONISTIC	DIAGONALIZES
DEVELOPMENTALLY	DEVOLUTIONARY	DEXTROCARDIACS	DIACHRONOUS	DIAGONALIZING
DEVELOPMENTS	DEVOLUTIONIST	DEXTROCARDIAS	DIACHYLONS	DIAGONALLY
DEVELOPPES	DEVOLUTIONISTS	DEXTROGLUCOSE	DIACHYLUMS	DIAGRAMING
DEVERBATIVE	DEVOLVEMENT	DEXTROGLUCOSES	DIACODIONS	DIAGRAMMABLE
DEVERBATIVES	DEVOLVEMENTS	DEXTROGYRATE	DIACODIUMS	DIAGRAMMATIC
DEVIANCIES	DEVONPORTS	DEXTROGYRE	DIACONATES	DIAGRAMMATICAL
DEVIATIONISM	DEVOTEDNESS	DEXTROROTARY	DIACONICON	DIAGRAMMED
DEVIATIONISMS	DEVOTEDNESSES	DEXTROROTATION	DIACONICONS	DIAGRAMMING
DEVIATIONIST	DEVOTEMENT	DEXTROROTATIONS	DIACOUSTIC	DIAGRAPHIC
DEVIATIONISTS	DEVOTEMENTS	DEXTROROTATORY	DIACOUSTICS	DIAHELIOTROPIC
DEVIATIONS	DEVOTIONAL	DEXTRORSAL	DIACRITICAL	DIAHELIOTROPISM
DEVILESSES	DEVOTIONALIST	DEXTRORSELY	DIACRITICALLY	DIAKINESES
DEVILFISHES		DEXTROUSLY	DIACRITICS	DIAKINESIS

DIALECTALLY	DIAMANTIFEROUS	DIAPOPHYSES	DIATOMISTS	DICHLOROMETHANE
DIALECTICAL	DIAMANTINE	DIAPOPHYSIAL	DIATOMITES	DICHLORVOS
DIALECTICALLY	DIAMETRALLY	DIAPOPHYSIS	DIATONICALLY	DICHLORVOSES
DIALECTICIAN	DIAMETRICAL	DIAPOSITIVE	DIATONICISM	DICHOGAMIC
DIALECTICIANS	DIAMETRICALLY	DIAPOSITIVES	DIATONICISMS	DICHOGAMIES
DIALECTICISM	DIAMONDBACK	DIAPYETICS	DIATRETUMS	DICHOGAMOUS
DIALECTICISMS	DIAMONDBACKS	DIARCHICAL	DIATRIBIST	DICHONDRAS
DIALECTICS	DIAMONDIFEROUS	DIARRHETIC	DIATRIBISTS	DICHOTICALLY
DIALECTOLOGICAL	DIAMONDING	DIARRHOEAL	DIATROPISM	DICHOTOMIC
DIALECTOLOGIES	DIAMORPHINE	DIARRHOEAS	DIATROPISMS	DICHOTOMIES
DIALECTOLOGIST	DIAMORPHINES	DIARRHOEIC	DIAZEUCTIC	DICHOTOMISATION
DIALECTOLOGISTS	DIANTHUSES	DIARTHRODIAL	DIAZOMETHANE	DICHOTOMISE
DIALECTOLOGY	DIAPASONAL	DIARTHROSES	DIAZOMETHANES	DICHOTOMISED
DIALLAGOID	DIAPASONIC	DIARTHROSIS	DIAZONIUMS	DICHOTOMISES
DIALOGICAL	DIAPAUSING	DIASCORDIUM	DIAZOTISATION	DICHOTOMISING
DIALOGICALLY	DIAPEDESES	DIASCORDIUMS	DIAZOTISATIONS	DICHOTOMIST
DIALOGISED	DIAPEDESIS	DIASKEUAST	DIAZOTISED	DICHOTOMISTS
DIALOGISES	DIAPEDETIC	DIASKEUASTS	DIAZOTISES	DICHOTOMIZATION
DIALOGISING	DIAPERINGS	DIASTALSES	DIAZOTISING	DICHOTOMIZE
DIALOGISMS	DIAPHANEITIES	DIASTALSIS	DIAZOTIZATION	DICHOTOMIZED
DIALOGISTIC	DIAPHANEITY	DIASTALTIC	DIAZOTIZATIONS	DICHOTOMIZES
DIALOGISTICAL	DIAPHANOMETER	DIASTEMATA	DIAZOTIZED	DICHOTOMIZING
DIALOGISTS	DIAPHANOMETERS	DIASTEMATIC	DIAZOTIZES	DICHOTOMOUS
DIALOGITES	DIAPHANOUS	DIASTEREOISOMER	DIAZOTIZING	DICHOTOMOUSLY
DIALOGIZED	DIAPHANOUSLY	DIASTEREOMER	DIBASICITIES	DICHOTOMOUSNESS
DIALOGIZES	DIAPHANOUSNESS	DIASTEREOMERIC	DIBASICITY	DICHROISCOPE
DIALOGIZING	DIAPHONIES	DIASTEREOMERS	DIBENZOFURAN	DICHROISCOPES
DIALOGUERS	DIAPHORASE	DIASTROPHIC	DIBENZOFURANS	DICHROISCOPIC
DIALOGUING	DIAPHORASES	DIASTROPHICALLY	DIBRANCHIATE	DICHROISMS
DIALYPETALOUS	DIAPHORESES	DIASTROPHISM	DIBRANCHIATES	DICHROITES
DIALYSABILITIES	DIAPHORESIS	DIASTROPHISMS	DIBROMIDES	DICHROITIC
DIALYSABILITY	DIAPHORETIC	DIATESSARON	DICACITIES	DICHROMATE
DIALYSABLE	DIAPHORETICS	DIATESSARONS	DICACODYLS	DICHROMATES
DIALYSATES	DIAPHOTOTROPIC	DIATHERMACIES	DICARBOXYLIC	DICHROMATIC
DIALYSATION	DIAPHOTOTROPIES	DIATHERMACY	DICARPELLARY	DICHROMATICISM
DIALYSATIONS	DIAPHOTOTROPISM	DIATHERMAL	DICASTERIES	DICHROMATICISMS
DIALYTICALLY	DIAPHOTOTROPY	DIATHERMANCIES	DICENTRICS	DICHROMATICS
DIALYZABILITIES	DIAPHRAGMAL	DIATHERMANCY	DICEPHALISM	DICHROMATISM
DIALYZABILITY	DIAPHRAGMATIC	DIATHERMANEITY	DICEPHALISMS	DICHROMATISMS
DIALYZABLE	DIAPHRAGMATITIS	DIATHERMANOUS	DICEPHALOUS	DICHROMATS
DIALYZATES	DIAPHRAGMED	DIATHERMIA	DICHASIALLY	DICHROMISM
DIALYZATION	DIAPHRAGMING	DIATHERMIAS	DICHLAMYDEOUS	DICHROMISMS
DIALYZATIONS	DIAPHRAGMITIS	DIATHERMIC	DICHLORACETIC	DICHROOSCOPE
DIAMAGNETIC	DIAPHRAGMITISES	DIATHERMIES	DICHLORIDE	DICHROOSCOPES
DIAMAGNETICALLY	DIAPHRAGMS	DIATHERMOUS	DICHLORIDES	DICHROOSCOPIC
DIAMAGNETISM	DIAPHYSEAL	DIATOMACEOUS	DICHLOROBENZENE	DICHROSCOPE
DIAMAGNETISMS	DIAPHYSIAL	DIATOMICITIES	DICHLOROETHANE	DICHROSCOPES
DIAMAGNETS	DIAPIRISMS	DIATOMICITY	DICHLOROETHANES	DICHROSCOPIC

DIGRESSING

DICKCISSEL	DIDELPHIDS	DIETICIANS	DIFFRACTOMETRY	DIGITALIZE
DICKCISSELS	DIDELPHINE	DIETITIANS	DIFFRANGIBILITY	DIGITALIZED
DICKEYBIRD	DIDELPHOUS	DIEZEUGMENON	DIFFRANGIBLE	DIGITALIZES
DICKEYBIRDS	DIDGERIDOO	DIEZEUGMENONS	DIFFUSEDLY	DIGITALIZING
DICKYBIRDS	DIDGERIDOOS	DIFFARREATION	DIFFUSEDNESS	DIGITATELY
DICLINISMS	DIDJERIDOO	DIFFARREATIONS	DIFFUSEDNESSES	DIGITATION
DICOTYLEDON	DIDJERIDOOS	DIFFERENCE	DIFFUSENESS	DIGITATIONS
DICOTYLEDONOUS	DIDJERIDUS	DIFFERENCED	DIFFUSENESSES	DIGITIFORM
DICOTYLEDONS	DIDRACHMAS	DIFFERENCES	DIFFUSIBILITIES	DIGITIGRADE
DICOUMARIN	DIDYNAMIAN	DIFFERENCIED	DIFFUSIBILITY	DIGITIGRADES
DICOUMARINS	DIDYNAMIES	DIFFERENCIES	DIFFUSIBLE	DIGITISATION
DICOUMAROL	DIDYNAMOUS	DIFFERENCING	DIFFUSIBLENESS	DIGITISATIONS
DICOUMAROLS	DIECIOUSLY	DIFFERENCY	DIFFUSIONAL	DIGITISERS
DICROTISMS	DIECIOUSNESS	DIFFERENCYING	DIFFUSIONISM	DIGITISING
DICTATIONAL	DIECIOUSNESSES	DIFFERENTIA	DIFFUSIONISMS	DIGITIZATION
DICTATIONS	DIEFFENBACHIA	DIFFERENTIABLE	DIFFUSIONIST	DIGITIZATIONS
DICTATORIAL	DIEFFENBACHIAS	DIFFERENTIAE	DIFFUSIONISTS	DIGITIZERS
DICTATORIALLY	DIELECTRIC	DIFFERENTIAL	DIFFUSIONS	DIGITIZING
DICTATORIALNESS	DIELECTRICALLY	DIFFERENTIALLY	DIFFUSIVELY	DIGITONINS
DICTATORSHIP	DIELECTRICS	DIFFERENTIALS	DIFFUSIVENESS	DIGITORIUM
DICTATORSHIPS	DIENCEPHALA	DIFFERENTIATE	DIFFUSIVENESSES	DIGITORIUMS
DICTATRESS	DIENCEPHALIC	DIFFERENTIATED	DIFFUSIVITIES	DIGITOXIGENIN
DICTATRESSES	DIENCEPHALON	DIFFERENTIATES	DIFFUSIVITY	DIGITOXIGENINS
DICTATRICES	DIENCEPHALONS	DIFFERENTIATING	DIFUNCTIONAL	DIGITOXINS
DICTATRIXES	DIESELINGS	DIFFERENTIATION	DIFUNCTIONALS	DIGLADIATE
DICTATURES	DIESELISATION	DIFFERENTIATOR	DIGASTRICS	DIGLADIATED
DICTIONALLY	DIESELISATIONS	DIFFERENTIATORS	DIGESTANTS	DIGLADIATES
DICTIONARIES	DIESELISED	DIFFERENTLY	DIGESTEDLY	DIGLADIATING
DICTIONARY	DIESELISES	DIFFERENTNESS	DIGESTIBILITIES	DIGLADIATION
DICTYOGENS	DIESELISING	DIFFERENTNESSES	DIGESTIBILITY	DIGLADIATIONS
DICTYOPTERAN	DIESELIZATION	DIFFICULTIES	DIGESTIBLE	DIGLADIATOR
DICTYOPTERANS	DIESELIZATIONS	DIFFICULTLY	DIGESTIBLENESS	DIGLADIATORS
DICTYOSOME	DIESELIZED	DIFFICULTY	DIGESTIBLY	DIGLOSSIAS
DICTYOSOMES	DIESELIZES	DIFFIDENCE	DIGESTIONAL	DIGLYCERIDE
DICTYOSTELE	DIESELIZING	DIFFIDENCES	DIGESTIONS	DIGLYCERIDES
DICTYOSTELES	DIESELLING	DIFFIDENTLY	DIGESTIVELY	DIGNIFICATION
DICUMAROLS	DIESELLINGS	DIFFORMITIES	DIGESTIVES	DIGNIFICATIONS
DICYNODONT	DIESINKERS	DIFFORMITY	DIGITALINS	DIGNIFIEDLY
DICYNODONTS	DIESTRUSES	DIFFRACTED	DIGITALISATION	DIGNIFIEDNESS
DIDACTICAL	DIETARIANS	DIFFRACTING	DIGITALISATIONS	DIGNIFIEDNESSES
DIDACTICALLY	DIETETICAL	DIFFRACTION	DIGITALISE	DIGNIFYING
DIDACTICISM	DIETETICALLY	DIFFRACTIONS	DIGITALISED	DIGNITARIES
DIDACTICISMS	DIETHYLAMIDE	DIFFRACTIVE	DIGITALISES	DIGONEUTIC
DIDACTYLISM	DIETHYLAMIDES	DIFFRACTIVELY	DIGITALISING	DIGONEUTISM
DIDACTYLISMS	DIETHYLAMINE	DIFFRACTIVENESS	DIGITALISM	DIGONEUTISMS
DIDACTYLOUS	DIETHYLAMINES	DIFFRACTOMETER	DIGITALISMS	DIGRAPHICALLY
DIDASCALIC	DIETHYLENE	DIFFRACTOMETERS	DIGITALIZATION	DIGRESSERS
DIDELPHIAN	DIETHYLENES	DIFFRACTOMETRIC	DIGITALIZATIONS	DIGRESSING

DIGRESSION	DILATORINESSES	DIMERIZING	DINNERTIME	DIOXONITRIC
DIGRESSIONAL	DILEMMATIC	DIMETHOATE	DINNERTIMES	DIPEPTIDASE
DIGRESSIONARY	DILETTANTE	DIMETHOATES	DINNERWARE	DIPEPTIDASES
DIGRESSIONS	DILETTANTEISH	DIMETHYLAMINE	DINNERWARES	DIPEPTIDES
DIGRESSIVE	DILETTANTEISM	DIMETHYLAMINES	DINOCERASES	DIPETALOUS
DIGRESSIVELY	DILETTANTEISMS	DIMETHYLANILINE	DINOFLAGELLATE	DIPHENHYDRAMINE
DIGRESSIVENESS	DILETTANTES	DIMIDIATED	DINOFLAGELLATES	DIPHENYLAMINE
DIHYBRIDISM	DILETTANTI	DIMIDIATES	DINOMANIAS	DIPHENYLAMINES
DIHYBRIDISMS	DILETTANTISH	DIMIDIATING	DINOSAURIAN	DIPHENYLENE
DIHYDROCODEINE	DILETTANTISM	DIMIDIATION	DINOSAURIC	DIPHENYLENIMINE
DIHYDROCODEINES	DILETTANTISMS	DIMIDIATIONS	DINOTHERES	DIPHENYLKETONE
DIHYDROGEN	DILIGENCES	DIMINISHABLE	DINOTHERIA	DIPHENYLKETONES
DIJUDICATE	DILIGENTLY	DIMINISHED	DINOTHERIUM	DIPHOSGENE
DIJUDICATED	DILLYDALLIED	DIMINISHES	DINOTHERIUMS	DIPHOSGENES
DIJUDICATES	DILLYDALLIES	DIMINISHING	DINOTURBATION	DIPHOSPHATE
DIJUDICATING	DILLYDALLY	DIMINISHINGLY	DINOTURBATIONS	DIPHOSPHATES
DIJUDICATION	DILLYDALLYING	DIMINISHINGS	DINUCLEOTIDE	DIPHTHERIA
DIJUDICATIONS	DILTIAZEMS	DIMINISHMENT	DINUCLEOTIDES	DIPHTHERIAL
DILACERATE	DILUCIDATE	DIMINISHMENTS	DIOECIOUSLY	DIPHTHERIAS
DILACERATED	DILUCIDATED	DIMINUENDO	DIOECIOUSNESS	DIPHTHERIC
DILACERATES	DILUCIDATES	DIMINUENDOES	DIOECIOUSNESSES	DIPHTHERITIC
DILACERATING	DILUCIDATING	DIMINUENDOS	DIOESTRUSES	DIPHTHERITIS
DILACERATION	DILUCIDATION	DIMINUTION	DIOICOUSLY	DIPHTHERITISES
DILACERATIONS	DILUCIDATIONS	DIMINUTIONS	DIOICOUSNESS	DIPHTHEROID
DILAPIDATE	DILUTABLES	DIMINUTIVAL	DIOICOUSNESSES	DIPHTHEROIDS
DILAPIDATED	DILUTENESS	DIMINUTIVE	DIOPHYSITE	DIPHTHONGAL
DILAPIDATES	DILUTENESSES	DIMINUTIVELY	DIOPHYSITES	DIPHTHONGALLY
DILAPIDATING	DILUTIONARY	DIMINUTIVENESS	DIOPTOMETER	DIPHTHONGED
DILAPIDATION	DILUVIALISM	DIMINUTIVES	DIOPTOMETERS	DIPHTHONGIC
DILAPIDATIONS	DILUVIALISMS	DIMORPHISM	DIOPTOMETRIES	DIPHTHONGING
DILAPIDATOR	DILUVIALIST	DIMORPHISMS	DIOPTOMETRY	DIPHTHONGISE
DILAPIDATORS	DILUVIALISTS	DIMORPHOUS	DIOPTRICAL	DIPHTHONGISED
DILATABILITIES	DIMENHYDRINATE	DIMPLEMENT	DIOPTRICALLY	DIPHTHONGISES
DILATABILITY	DIMENHYDRINATES	DIMPLEMENTS	DIORISTICAL	DIPHTHONGISING
DILATABLENESS	DIMENSIONAL	DINANDERIE	DIORISTICALLY	DIPHTHONGIZE
DILATABLENESSES	DIMENSIONALITY	DINANDERIES	DIORTHOSES	DIPHTHONGIZED
DILATANCIES	DIMENSIONALLY	DINARCHIES	DIORTHOSIS	DIPHTHONGIZES
DILATATION	DIMENSIONED	DINGDONGED	DIORTHOTIC	DIPHTHONGIZING
DILATATIONAL	DIMENSIONING	DINGDONGING	DIOSCOREACEOUS	DIPHTHONGS
DILATATIONS	DIMENSIONLESS	DINGINESSES	DIOSGENINS	DIPHYCERCAL
DILATATORS	DIMENSIONS	DINGLEBERRIES	DIOTHELETE	DIPHYLETIC
DILATOMETER	DIMERCAPROL	DINGLEBERRY	DIOTHELETES	DIPHYLLOUS
DILATOMETERS	DIMERCAPROLS	DINITROBENZENE	DIOTHELETIC	DIPHYODONT
DILATOMETRIC	DIMERISATION	DINITROBENZENES	DIOTHELETICAL	DIPHYODONTS
DILATOMETRIES	DIMERISATIONS	DINITROGEN	DIOTHELISM	DIPHYSITES
DILATOMETRY	DIMERISING	DINITROPHENOL	DIOTHELISMS	DIPHYSITISM
DILATORILY	DIMERIZATION	DINITROPHENOLS	DIOTHELITE	DIPHYSITISMS
DILATORINESS	DIMERIZATIONS	DINNERLESS	DIOTHELITES	DIPLEIDOSCOPE

DIPLEIDOSCOPES	DIPRIONIDIAN	DIRENESSES	DISADVANTAGING	DISALLOWING
DIPLOBIONT	DIPROPELLANT	DIRIGIBILITIES	DISADVENTURE	DISALLYING
DIPLOBIONTIC	DIPROPELLANTS	DIRIGIBILITY	DISADVENTURES	DISAMBIGUATE
DIPLOBIONTS	DIPROTODON	DIRIGIBLES	DISADVENTUROUS	DISAMBIGUATED
DIPLOBLASTIC	DIPROTODONS	DIRIGISMES	DISAFFECTED	DISAMBIGUATES
DIPLOCARDIAC	DIPROTODONT	DIRTINESSES	DISAFFECTEDLY	DISAMBIGUATING
DIPLOCOCCAL	DIPROTODONTID	DISABILITIES	DISAFFECTEDNESS	DISAMBIGUATION
DIPLOCOCCI	DIPROTODONTIDS	DISABILITY	DISAFFECTING	DISAMBIGUATIONS
DIPLOCOCCIC	DIPROTODONTS	DISABLEMENT	DISAFFECTION	DISAMENITIES
DIPLOCOCCUS	DIPSOMANIA	DISABLEMENTS	DISAFFECTIONATE	DISAMENITY
DIPLODOCUS	DIPSOMANIAC	DISABLISMS	DISAFFECTIONS	DISANALOGIES
DIPLODOCUSES	DIPSOMANIACAL	DISABLISTS	DISAFFECTS	DISANALOGOUS
DIPLOGENESES	DIPSOMANIACS	DISABUSALS	DISAFFILIATE	DISANALOGY
DIPLOGENESIS	DIPSOMANIAS	DISABUSING	DISAFFILIATED	DISANCHORED
DIPLOIDIES	DIPSWITCHES	DISACCHARID	DISAFFILIATES	DISANCHORING
DIPLOMACIES	DIPTERISTS	DISACCHARIDASE	DISAFFILIATING	DISANCHORS
DIPLOMAING	DIPTEROCARP	DISACCHARIDASES	DISAFFILIATION	DISANIMATE
DIPLOMATED	DIPTEROCARPOUS	DISACCHARIDE	DISAFFILIATIONS	DISANIMATED
DIPLOMATES	DIPTEROCARPS	DISACCHARIDES	DISAFFIRMANCE	DISANIMATES
DIPLOMATESE	DIPTEROSES	DISACCHARIDS	DISAFFIRMANCES	DISANIMATING
DIPLOMATESES	DIRECTEDNESS	DISACCOMMODATE	DISAFFIRMATION	DISANNEXED
DIPLOMATIC	DIRECTEDNESSES	DISACCOMMODATED	DISAFFIRMATIONS	DISANNEXES
DIPLOMATICAL	DIRECTIONAL	DISACCOMMODATES	DISAFFIRMED	DISANNEXING
DIPLOMATICALLY	DIRECTIONALITY	DISACCORDANT	DISAFFIRMING	DISANNULLED
DIPLOMATICS	DIRECTIONLESS	DISACCORDED	DISAFFIRMS	DISANNULLER
DIPLOMATING	DIRECTIONS	DISACCORDING	DISAFFOREST	DISANNULLERS
DIPLOMATISE	DIRECTIVES	DISACCORDS	DISAFFORESTED	DISANNULLING
DIPLOMATISED	DIRECTIVITIES	DISACCREDIT	DISAFFORESTING	DISANNULLINGS
DIPLOMATISES	DIRECTIVITY	DISACCREDITED	DISAFFORESTMENT	DISANNULMENT
DIPLOMATISING	DIRECTNESS	DISACCREDITING	DISAFFORESTS	DISANNULMENTS
DIPLOMATIST	DIRECTNESSES	DISACCREDITS	DISAGGREGATE	DISANOINTED
DIPLOMATISTS	DIRECTORATE	DISACCUSTOM	DISAGGREGATED	DISANOINTING
DIPLOMATIZE	DIRECTORATES	DISACCUSTOMED	DISAGGREGATES	DISANOINTS
DIPLOMATIZED	DIRECTORIAL	DISACCUSTOMING	DISAGGREGATING	DISAPPAREL
DIPLOMATIZES	DIRECTORIALLY	DISACCUSTOMS	DISAGGREGATION	DISAPPARELLED
DIPLOMATIZING	DIRECTORIES	DISACKNOWLEDGE	DISAGGREGATIONS	DISAPPARELLING
DIPLOMATOLOGIES	DIRECTORSHIP	DISACKNOWLEDGED	DISAGGREGATIVE	DISAPPARELS
DIPLOMATOLOGY	DIRECTORSHIPS	DISACKNOWLEDGES	DISAGREEABILITY	DISAPPEARANCE
DIPLONEMAS	DIRECTRESS	DISADORNED	DISAGREEABLE	DISAPPEARANCES
DIPLOPHASE	DIRECTRESSES	DISADORNING	DISAGREEABLES	DISAPPEARED
DIPLOPHASES	DIRECTRICE	DISADVANCE	DISAGREEABLY	DISAPPEARING
DIPLOSPEAK	DIRECTRICES	DISADVANCED	DISAGREEING	DISAPPEARS
DIPLOSPEAKS	DIRECTRIXES	DISADVANCES	DISAGREEMENT	DISAPPLICATION
DIPLOSTEMONOUS	DIREFULNESS	DISADVANCING	DISAGREEMENTS	DISAPPLICATIONS
DIPLOTENES	DIREFULNESSES	DISADVANTAGE	DISALLOWABLE	DISAPPLIED
DIPNETTING	DIREMPTING	DISADVANTAGED	DISALLOWANCE	DISAPPLIES
DIPPERFULS	DIREMPTION	DISADVANTAGEOUS	DISALLOWANCES	DISAPPLYING
DIPPINESSES	DIREMPTIONS	DISADVANTAGES	DISALLOWED	DISAPPOINT

DISAPPOINTED

DISAPPOINTED	DISASSEMBLY	DISBANDMENTS	DISCANDIES	DISCHURCHES
DISAPPOINTEDLY	DISASSIMILATE	DISBARKING	DISCANDYING	DISCHURCHING
DISAPPOINTING	DISASSIMILATED	DISBARMENT	DISCANDYINGS	DISCIPLESHIP
DISAPPOINTINGLY	DISASSIMILATES	DISBARMENTS	DISCANTERS	DISCIPLESHIPS
DISAPPOINTMENT	DISASSIMILATING	DISBARRING	DISCANTING	DISCIPLINABLE
DISAPPOINTMENTS	DISASSIMILATION	DISBELIEFS	DISCAPACITATE	DISCIPLINAL
DISAPPOINTS	DISASSIMILATIVE	DISBELIEVE	DISCAPACITATED	DISCIPLINANT
DISAPPROBATION	DISASSOCIATE	DISBELIEVED	DISCAPACITATES	DISCIPLINANTS
DISAPPROBATIONS	DISASSOCIATED	DISBELIEVER	DISCAPACITATING	DISCIPLINARIAN
DISAPPROBATIVE	DISASSOCIATES	DISBELIEVERS	DISCARDABLE	DISCIPLINARIANS
DISAPPROBATORY	DISASSOCIATING	DISBELIEVES	DISCARDERS	DISCIPLINARILY
DISAPPROPRIATE	DISASSOCIATION	DISBELIEVING	DISCARDING	DISCIPLINARITY
DISAPPROPRIATED	DISASSOCIATIONS	DISBELIEVINGLY	DISCARDMENT	DISCIPLINARIUM
DISAPPROPRIATES	DISASTROUS	DISBENCHED	DISCARDMENTS	DISCIPLINARIUMS
DISAPPROVAL	DISASTROUSLY	DISBENCHES	DISCARNATE	DISCIPLINARY
DISAPPROVALS	DISATTIRED	DISBENCHING	DISCEPTATION	DISCIPLINE
DISAPPROVE	DISATTIRES	DISBENEFIT	DISCEPTATIONS	DISCIPLINED
DISAPPROVED	DISATTIRING	DISBENEFITS	DISCEPTATIOUS	DISCIPLINER
DISAPPROVER	DISATTRIBUTION	DISBOSOMED	DISCEPTATOR	DISCIPLINERS
DISAPPROVERS	DISATTRIBUTIONS	DISBOSOMING	DISCEPTATORIAL	DISCIPLINES
DISAPPROVES	DISATTUNED	DISBOWELED	DISCEPTATORS	DISCIPLING
DISAPPROVING	DISATTUNES	DISBOWELING	DISCEPTING	DISCIPLINING
DISAPPROVINGLY	DISATTUNING	DISBOWELLED	DISCERNABLE	DISCIPULAR
DISARMAMENT	DISAUTHORISE	DISBOWELLING	DISCERNABLY	DISCISSION
DISARMAMENTS	DISAUTHORISED	DISBRANCHED	DISCERNERS	DISCISSIONS
DISARMINGLY	DISAUTHORISES	DISBRANCHES	DISCERNIBLE	DISCLAIMED
DISARRANGE	DISAUTHORISING	DISBRANCHING	DISCERNIBLY	DISCLAIMER
DISARRANGED	DISAUTHORIZE	DISBUDDING	DISCERNING	DISCLAIMERS
DISARRANGEMENT	DISAUTHORIZED	DISBURDENED	DISCERNINGLY	DISCLAIMING
DISARRANGEMENTS	DISAUTHORIZES	DISBURDENING	DISCERNMENT	DISCLAMATION
DISARRANGES	DISAUTHORIZING	DISBURDENMENT	DISCERNMENTS	DISCLAMATIONS
DISARRANGING	DISAVAUNCE	DISBURDENMENTS	DISCERPIBILITY	DISCLIMAXES
DISARRAYED	DISAVAUNCED	DISBURDENS	DISCERPIBLE	DISCLOSERS
DISARRAYING	DISAVAUNCES	DISBURSABLE	DISCERPING	DISCLOSING
DISARTICULATE	DISAVAUNCING	DISBURSALS	DISCERPTIBLE	DISCLOSURE
DISARTICULATED	DISAVENTROUS	DISBURSEMENT	DISCERPTION	DISCLOSURES
DISARTICULATES	DISAVENTURE	DISBURSEMENTS	DISCERPTIONS	DISCOBOLOS
DISARTICULATING	DISAVENTURES	DISBURSERS	DISCERPTIVE	DISCOBOLUS
DISARTICULATION	DISAVOUCHED	DISBURSING	DISCHARGEABLE	DISCOBOLUSES
DISARTICULATOR	DISAVOUCHES	DISBURTHEN	DISCHARGED	DISCOGRAPHER
DISARTICULATORS	DISAVOUCHING	DISBURTHENED	DISCHARGEE	DISCOGRAPHERS
DISASSEMBLE	DISAVOWABLE	DISBURTHENING	DISCHARGEES	DISCOGRAPHIC
DISASSEMBLED	DISAVOWALS	DISBURTHENS	DISCHARGER	DISCOGRAPHICAL
DISASSEMBLER	DISAVOWEDLY	DISCALCEATE	DISCHARGERS	DISCOGRAPHIES
DISASSEMBLERS	DISAVOWERS	DISCALCEATES	DISCHARGES	DISCOGRAPHY
DISASSEMBLES	DISAVOWING	DISCANDERING	DISCHARGING	DISCOLOGIES
DISASSEMBLIES	DISBANDING	DISCANDERINGS	DISCHUFFED	DISCOLOGIST
DISASSEMBLING	DISBANDMENT	DISCANDIED	DISCHURCHED	DISCOLOGISTS

DISCOLORATION DISCOMMODITIES DISCONSENT DISCORPORATING DISCREDITED
DISCOLORATIONS DISCOMMODITY DISCONSENTED DISCOTHEQUE DISCREDITING
DISCOLORED DISCOMMONED DISCONSENTING DISCOTHEQUES DISCREDITS
DISCOLORING DISCOMMONING DISCONSENTS DISCOUNSEL DISCREETER
DISCOLORMENT DISCOMMONS DISCONSOLATE DISCOUNSELLED DISCREETEST
DISCOLORMENTS DISCOMMUNITIES DISCONSOLATELY DISCOUNSELLING DISCREETLY
DISCOLOURATION DISCOMMUNITY DISCONSOLATION DISCOUNSELS DISCREETNESS
DISCOLOURATIONS DISCOMPOSE DISCONSOLATIONS DISCOUNTABLE DISCREETNESSES
DISCOLOURED DISCOMPOSED DISCONTENT DISCOUNTED DISCREPANCE
DISCOLOURING DISCOMPOSEDLY DISCONTENTED DISCOUNTENANCE DISCREPANCES
DISCOLOURMENT DISCOMPOSES DISCONTENTEDLY DISCOUNTENANCED DISCREPANCIES
DISCOLOURMENTS DISCOMPOSING DISCONTENTFUL DISCOUNTENANCES DISCREPANCY
DISCOLOURS DISCOMPOSINGLY DISCONTENTING DISCOUNTER DISCREPANT
DISCOMBOBERATE DISCOMPOSURE DISCONTENTMENT DISCOUNTERS DISCREPANTLY
DISCOMBOBERATED DISCOMPOSURES DISCONTENTMENTS DISCOUNTING DISCRETELY
DISCOMBOBERATES DISCOMYCETE DISCONTENTS DISCOURAGE DISCRETENESS
DISCOMBOBULATE DISCOMYCETES DISCONTIGUITIES DISCOURAGEABLE DISCRETENESSES
DISCOMBOBULATED DISCOMYCETOUS DISCONTIGUITY DISCOURAGED DISCRETEST
DISCOMBOBULATES DISCONCERT DISCONTIGUOUS DISCOURAGEMENT DISCRETION
DISCOMEDUSAN DISCONCERTED DISCONTINUANCE DISCOURAGEMENTS DISCRETIONAL
DISCOMEDUSANS DISCONCERTEDLY DISCONTINUANCES DISCOURAGER DISCRETIONALLY
DISCOMFITED DISCONCERTEDLY DISCONTINUATION DISCOURAGERS DISCRETIONARILY
DISCOMFITER DISCONCERTING DISCONTINUE DISCOURAGES DISCRETIONARY
DISCOMFITERS DISCONCERTION DISCONTINUED DISCOURAGING DISCRETIONS
DISCOMFITING DISCONCERTIONS DISCONTINUER DISCOURAGINGLY DISCRETIVE
DISCOMFITS DISCONCERTMENT DISCONTINUERS DISCOURING DISCRETIVELY
DISCOMFITURE DISCONCERTMENTS DISCONTINUES DISCOURSAL DISCRETIVES
DISCOMFITURES DISCONCERTS DISCONTINUING DISCOURSED DISCRIMINABLE
DISCOMFORT DISCONFIRM DISCONTINUITIES DISCOURSER DISCRIMINABLY
DISCOMFORTABLE DISCONFIRMATION DISCONTINUITY DISCOURSERS DISCRIMINANT
DISCOMFORTED DISCONFIRMED DISCONTINUOUS DISCOURSES DISCRIMINANTS
DISCOMFORTING DISCONFIRMING DISCONTINUOUSLY DISCOURSING DISCRIMINATE
DISCOMFORTS DISCONFIRMS DISCOPHILE DISCOURSIVE DISCRIMINATED
DISCOMMEND DISCONFORMABLE DISCOPHILES DISCOURTEISE DISCRIMINATELY
DISCOMMENDABLE DISCONFORMITIES DISCOPHORAN DISCOURTEOUS DISCRIMINATES
DISCOMMENDATION DISCONFORMITY DISCOPHORANS DISCOURTEOUSLY DISCRIMINATING
DISCOMMENDED DISCONNECT DISCOPHOROUS DISCOURTESIES DISCRIMINATION
DISCOMMENDING DISCONNECTED DISCORDANCE DISCOURTESY DISCRIMINATIONS
DISCOMMENDS DISCONNECTEDLY DISCORDANCES DISCOVERABLE DISCRIMINATIVE
DISCOMMISSION DISCONNECTER DISCORDANCIES DISCOVERED DISCRIMINATOR
DISCOMMISSIONED DISCONNECTERS DISCORDANCY DISCOVERER DISCRIMINATORS
DISCOMMISSIONS DISCONNECTING DISCORDANT DISCOVERERS DISCRIMINATORY
DISCOMMODE DISCONNECTION DISCORDANTLY DISCOVERIES DISCROWNED
DISCOMMODED DISCONNECTIONS DISCORDFUL DISCOVERING DISCROWNING
DISCOMMODES DISCONNECTIVE DISCORDING DISCOVERTURE DISCULPATE
DISCOMMODING DISCONNECTS DISCORPORATE DISCOVERTURES DISCULPATED
DISCOMMODIOUS DISCONNEXION DISCORPORATED DISCREDITABLE DISCULPATES
DISCOMMODIOUSLY DISCONNEXIONS DISCORPORATES DISCREDITABLY DISCULPATING

DISCUMBERED

DISCUMBERED	DISEMBELLISHING	DISEMPOWERMENT	DISENGAGEMENT	DISENTOMBS
DISCUMBERING	DISEMBITTER	DISEMPOWERMENTS	DISENGAGEMENTS	DISENTRAIL
DISCUMBERS	DISEMBITTERED	DISEMPOWERS	DISENGAGES	DISENTRAILED
DISCURSION	DISEMBITTERING	DISEMVOWEL	DISENGAGING	DISENTRAILING
DISCURSIONS	DISEMBITTERS	DISEMVOWELLED	DISENNOBLE	DISENTRAILS
DISCURSIST	DISEMBODIED	DISEMVOWELLING	DISENNOBLED	DISENTRAIN
DISCURSISTS	DISEMBODIES	DISEMVOWELS	DISENNOBLES	DISENTRAINED
DISCURSIVE	DISEMBODIMENT	DISENABLED	DISENNOBLING	DISENTRAINING
DISCURSIVELY	DISEMBODIMENTS	DISENABLEMENT	DISENROLLED	DISENTRAINMENT
DISCURSIVENESS	DISEMBODYING	DISENABLEMENTS	DISENROLLING	DISENTRAINMENTS
DISCURSORY	DISEMBOGUE	DISENABLES	DISENROLLINGS	DISENTRAINS
DISCURSUSES	DISEMBOGUED	DISENABLING	DISENSHROUD	DISENTRANCE
DISCUSSABLE	DISEMBOGUEMENT	DISENCHAIN	DISENSHROUDED	DISENTRANCED
DISCUSSANT	DISEMBOGUEMENTS	DISENCHAINED	DISENSHROUDING	DISENTRANCEMENT
DISCUSSANTS	DISEMBOGUES	DISENCHAINING	DISENSHROUDS	DISENTRANCES
DISCUSSERS	DISEMBOGUING	DISENCHAINS	DISENSLAVE	DISENTRANCING
DISCUSSIBLE	DISEMBOSOM	DISENCHANT	DISENSLAVED	DISENTRAYLE
DISCUSSING	DISEMBOSOMED	DISENCHANTED	DISENSLAVES	DISENTRAYLED
DISCUSSION	DISEMBOSOMING	DISENCHANTER	DISENSLAVING	DISENTRAYLES
DISCUSSIONAL	DISEMBOSOMS	DISENCHANTERS	DISENTAILED	DISENTRAYLING
DISCUSSIONS	DISEMBOWEL	DISENCHANTING	DISENTAILING	DISENTWINE
DISCUSSIVE	DISEMBOWELED	DISENCHANTINGLY	DISENTAILMENT	DISENTWINED
DISCUSSIVES	DISEMBOWELING	DISENCHANTMENT	DISENTAILMENTS	DISENTWINES
DISCUTIENT	DISEMBOWELLED	DISENCHANTMENTS	DISENTAILS	DISENTWINING
DISCUTIENTS	DISEMBOWELLING	DISENCHANTRESS	DISENTANGLE	DISENVELOP
DISDAINFUL	DISEMBOWELMENT	DISENCHANTS	DISENTANGLED	DISENVELOPED
DISDAINFULLY	DISEMBOWELMENTS	DISENCLOSE	DISENTANGLEMENT	DISENVELOPING
DISDAINFULNESS	DISEMBOWELS	DISENCLOSED	DISENTANGLES	DISENVELOPS
DISDAINING	DISEMBRANGLE	DISENCLOSES	DISENTANGLING	DISENVIRON
DISEASEDNESS	DISEMBRANGLED	DISENCLOSING	DISENTHRAL	DISENVIRONED
DISEASEDNESSES	DISEMBRANGLES	DISENCUMBER	DISENTHRALL	DISENVIRONING
DISEASEFUL	DISEMBRANGLING	DISENCUMBERED	DISENTHRALLED	DISENVIRONS
DISECONOMIES	DISEMBROIL	DISENCUMBERING	DISENTHRALLING	DISEPALOUS
DISECONOMY	DISEMBROILED	DISENCUMBERMENT	DISENTHRALLMENT	DISEQUILIBRATE
DISEMBARKATION	DISEMBROILING	DISENCUMBERS	DISENTHRALS	DISEQUILIBRATED
DISEMBARKATIONS	DISEMBROILS	DISENCUMBRANCE	DISENTHRALMENT	DISEQUILIBRATES
DISEMBARKED	DISEMBURDEN	DISENCUMBRANCES	DISENTHRALMENTS	DISEQUILIBRIA
DISEMBARKING	DISEMBURDENED	DISENDOWED	DISENTHRALS	DISEQUILIBRIUM
DISEMBARKMENT	DISEMBURDENING	DISENDOWER	DISENTHRONE	DISEQUILIBRIUMS
DISEMBARKMENTS	DISEMBURDENS	DISENDOWERS	DISENTHRONED	DISESPOUSE
DISEMBARKS	DISEMPLOYED	DISENDOWING	DISENTHRONES	DISESPOUSED
DISEMBARRASS	DISEMPLOYING	DISENDOWMENT	DISENTHRONING	DISESPOUSES
DISEMBARRASSED	DISEMPLOYMENT	DISENDOWMENTS	DISENTITLE	DISESPOUSING
DISEMBARRASSES	DISEMPLOYMENTS	DISENFRANCHISE	DISENTITLED	DISESTABLISH
DISEMBARRASSING	DISEMPLOYS	DISENFRANCHISED	DISENTITLES	DISESTABLISHED
DISEMBELLISH	DISEMPOWER	DISENFRANCHISES	DISENTITLING	DISESTABLISHES
DISEMBELLISHED	DISEMPOWERED	DISENGAGED	DISENTOMBED	DISESTABLISHING
DISEMBELLISHES	DISEMPOWERING	DISENGAGEDNESS	DISENTOMBING	DISESTEEMED

DISESTEEMING	DISFUNCTIONS	DISGUISABLE	DISHDASHES	DISHWASHERS
DISESTEEMS	DISFURNISH	DISGUISEDLY	DISHEARTEN	DISHWATERS
DISESTIMATION	DISFURNISHED	DISGUISEDNESS	DISHEARTENED	DISILLUDED
DISESTIMATIONS	DISFURNISHES	DISGUISEDNESSES	DISHEARTENING	DISILLUDES
DISFAVORED	DISFURNISHING	DISGUISELESS	DISHEARTENINGLY	DISILLUDING
DISFAVORING	DISFURNISHMENT	DISGUISEMENT	DISHEARTENMENT	DISILLUMINATE
DISFAVOURED	DISFURNISHMENTS	DISGUISEMENTS	DISHEARTENMENTS	DISILLUMINATED
DISFAVOURER	DISGARNISH	DISGUISERS	DISHEARTENS	DISILLUMINATES
DISFAVOURERS	DISGARNISHED	DISGUISING	DISHELMING	DISILLUMINATING
DISFAVOURING	DISGARNISHES	DISGUISINGS	DISHERISON	DISILLUSION
DISFAVOURS	DISGARNISHING	DISGUSTEDLY	DISHERISONS	DISILLUSIONARY
DISFEATURE	DISGARRISON	DISGUSTEDNESS	DISHERITED	DISILLUSIONED
DISFEATURED	DISGARRISONED	DISGUSTEDNESSES	DISHERITING	DISILLUSIONING
DISFEATUREMENT	DISGARRISONING	DISGUSTFUL	DISHERITOR	DISILLUSIONISE
DISFEATUREMENTS	DISGARRISONS	DISGUSTFULLY	DISHERITORS	DISILLUSIONISED
DISFEATURES	DISGAVELLED	DISGUSTFULNESS	DISHEVELED	DISILLUSIONISES
DISFEATURING	DISGAVELLING	DISGUSTING	DISHEVELING	DISILLUSIONIZE
DISFELLOWSHIP	DISGAVELLINGS	DISGUSTINGLY	DISHEVELLED	DISILLUSIONIZED
DISFELLOWSHIPED	DISGESTING	DISGUSTINGNESS	DISHEVELLING	DISILLUSIONIZES
DISFELLOWSHIPS	DISGESTION	DISHABILITATE	DISHEVELMENT	DISILLUSIONMENT
DISFIGURATION	DISGESTIONS	DISHABILITATED	DISHEVELMENTS	DISILLUSIONS
DISFIGURATIONS	DISGLORIFIED	DISHABILITATES	DISHOARDED	DISILLUSIVE
DISFIGURED	DISGLORIFIES	DISHABILITATING	DISHOARDING	DISIMAGINE
DISFIGUREMENT	DISGLORIFY	DISHABILITATION	DISHONESTIES	DISIMAGINED
DISFIGUREMENTS	DISGLORIFYING	DISHABILLE	DISHONESTLY	DISIMAGINES
DISFIGURER	DISGORGEMENT	DISHABILLES	DISHONESTY	DISIMAGINING
DISFIGURERS	DISGORGEMENTS	DISHABITED	DISHONORABLE	DISIMMURED
DISFIGURES	DISGORGERS	DISHABITING	DISHONORABLY	DISIMMURES
DISFIGURING	DISGORGING	DISHABLING	DISHONORARY	DISIMMURING
DISFLESHED	DISGOSPELLING	DISHALLOWED	DISHONORED	DISIMPASSIONED
DISFLESHES	DISGOWNING	DISHALLOWING	DISHONORER	DISIMPRISON
DISFLESHING	DISGRACEFUL	DISHALLOWS	DISHONORERS	DISIMPRISONED
DISFLUENCIES	DISGRACEFULLY	DISHARMONIC	DISHONORING	DISIMPRISONING
DISFLUENCY	DISGRACEFULNESS	DISHARMONIES	DISHONOURABLE	DISIMPRISONMENT
DISFORESTATION	DISGRACERS	DISHARMONIOUS	DISHONOURABLY	DISIMPRISONS
DISFORESTATIONS	DISGRACING	DISHARMONIOUSLY	DISHONOURED	DISIMPROVE
DISFORESTED	DISGRACIOUS	DISHARMONISE	DISHONOURER	DISIMPROVED
DISFORESTING	DISGRADATION	DISHARMONISED	DISHONOURERS	DISIMPROVES
DISFORESTS	DISGRADATIONS	DISHARMONISES	DISHONOURING	DISIMPROVING
DISFORMING	DISGRADING	DISHARMONISING	DISHONOURS	DISINCARCERATE
DISFRANCHISE	DISGREGATION	DISHARMONIZE	DISHORNING	DISINCARCERATED
DISFRANCHISED	DISGREGATIONS	DISHARMONIZED	DISHORSING	DISINCARCERATES
DISFRANCHISES	DISGRUNTLE	DISHARMONIZES	DISHOUSING	DISINCENTIVE
DISFRANCHISING	DISGRUNTLED	DISHARMONIZING	DISHTOWELS	DISINCENTIVES
DISFROCKED	DISGRUNTLEMENT	DISHARMONY	DISHUMOURED	DISINCLINATION
DISFROCKING	DISGRUNTLEMENTS	DISHCLOTHS	DISHUMOURING	DISINCLINATIONS
DISFUNCTION	DISGRUNTLES	DISHCLOUTS	DISHUMOURS	DISINCLINE
DISFUNCTIONAL	DISGRUNTLING	DISHDASHAS	DISHWASHER	DISINCLINED

DISINCLINES	DISINHIBITION	DISINVESTMENT	DISLOCATING	DISMISSION
DISINCLINING	DISINHIBITIONS	DISINVESTMENTS	DISLOCATION	DISMISSIONS
DISINCLOSE	DISINHIBITORY	DISINVESTS	DISLOCATIONS	DISMISSIVE
DISINCLOSED	DISINHIBITS	DISINVIGORATE	DISLODGEMENT	DISMISSIVELY
DISINCLOSES	DISINHUMED	DISINVIGORATED	DISLODGEMENTS	DISMISSORY
DISINCLOSING	DISINHUMES	DISINVIGORATES	DISLODGING	DISMOUNTABLE
DISINCORPORATE	DISINHUMING	DISINVIGORATING	DISLODGMENT	DISMOUNTED
DISINCORPORATED	DISINTEGRABLE	DISINVITED	DISLODGMENTS	DISMOUNTING
DISINCORPORATES	DISINTEGRATE	DISINVITES	DISLOIGNED	DISMUTATION
DISINFECTANT	DISINTEGRATED	DISINVITING	DISLOIGNING	DISMUTATIONS
DISINFECTANTS	DISINTEGRATES	DISINVOLVE	DISLOYALLY	DISNATURALISE
DISINFECTED	DISINTEGRATING	DISINVOLVED	DISLOYALTIES	DISNATURALISED
DISINFECTING	DISINTEGRATION	DISINVOLVES	DISLOYALTY	DISNATURALISES
DISINFECTION	DISINTEGRATIONS	DISINVOLVING	DISLUSTRED	DISNATURALISING
DISINFECTIONS	DISINTEGRATIVE	DISJECTING	DISLUSTRES	DISNATURALIZE
DISINFECTOR	DISINTEGRATOR	DISJECTION	DISLUSTRING	DISNATURALIZED
DISINFECTORS	DISINTEGRATORS	DISJECTIONS	DISMALITIES	DISNATURALIZES
DISINFECTS	DISINTEREST	DISJOINABLE	DISMALLEST	DISNATURALIZING
DISINFESTANT	DISINTERESTED	DISJOINING	DISMALNESS	DISNATURED
DISINFESTANTS	DISINTERESTEDLY	DISJOINTED	DISMALNESSES	DISNATURES
DISINFESTATION	DISINTERESTING	DISJOINTEDLY	DISMANNING	DISNATURING
DISINFESTATIONS	DISINTERESTS	DISJOINTEDNESS	DISMANTLED	DISNESTING
DISINFESTED	DISINTERMENT	DISJOINTING	DISMANTLEMENT	DISOBEDIENCE
DISINFESTING	DISINTERMENTS	DISJUNCTION	DISMANTLEMENTS	DISOBEDIENCES
DISINFESTS	DISINTERRED	DISJUNCTIONS	DISMANTLER	DISOBEDIENT
DISINFLATION	DISINTERRING	DISJUNCTIVE	DISMANTLERS	DISOBEDIENTLY
DISINFLATIONARY	DISINTHRAL	DISJUNCTIVELY	DISMANTLES	DISOBEYERS
DISINFLATIONS	DISINTHRALLED	DISJUNCTIVES	DISMANTLING	DISOBEYING
DISINFORMATION	DISINTHRALLING	DISJUNCTOR	DISMANTLINGS	DISOBLIGATION
DISINFORMATIONS	DISINTHRALLINGS	DISJUNCTORS	DISMASKING	DISOBLIGATIONS
DISINFORMED	DISINTHRALS	DISJUNCTURE	DISMASTING	DISOBLIGATORY
DISINFORMING	DISINTOXICATE	DISJUNCTURES	DISMASTMENT	DISOBLIGED
DISINFORMS	DISINTOXICATED	DISLEAFING	DISMASTMENTS	DISOBLIGEMENT
DISINGENUITIES	DISINTOXICATES	DISLEAVING	DISMAYEDNESS	DISOBLIGEMENTS
DISINGENUITY	DISINTOXICATING	DISLIKABLE	DISMAYEDNESSES	DISOBLIGES
DISINGENUOUS	DISINTOXICATION	DISLIKEABLE	DISMAYFULLY	DISOBLIGING
DISINGENUOUSLY	DISINTRICATE	DISLIKEFUL	DISMAYINGLY	DISOBLIGINGLY
DISINHERISON	DISINTRICATED	DISLIKENED	DISMAYLING	DISOBLIGINGNESS
DISINHERISONS	DISINTRICATES	DISLIKENESS	DISMEMBERED	DISOPERATION
DISINHERIT	DISINTRICATING	DISLIKENESSES	DISMEMBERER	DISOPERATIONS
DISINHERITANCE	DISINURING	DISLIKENING	DISMEMBERERS	DISORDERED
DISINHERITANCES	DISINVENTED	DISLIMBING	DISMEMBERING	DISORDEREDLY
DISINHERITED	DISINVENTING	DISLIMNING	DISMEMBERMENT	DISORDEREDNESS
DISINHERITING	DISINVENTS	DISLINKING	DISMEMBERMENTS	DISORDERING
DISINHERITS	DISINVESTED	DISLOADING	DISMEMBERS	DISORDERLIES
DISINHIBIT	DISINVESTING	DISLOCATED	DISMISSALS	DISORDERLINESS
DISINHIBITED	DISINVESTITURE	DISLOCATEDLY	DISMISSIBLE	DISORDERLY
DISINHIBITING	DISINVESTITURES	DISLOCATES	DISMISSING	DISORDINATE

DISORDINATELY	DISPATCHERS	DISPERSERS	DISPLEASURING	DISPRAISES
DISORGANIC	DISPATCHES	DISPERSIBLE	DISPLENISH	DISPRAISING
DISORGANISATION	DISPATCHFUL	DISPERSING	DISPLENISHED	DISPRAISINGLY
DISORGANISE	DISPATCHING	DISPERSION	DISPLENISHES	DISPREADING
DISORGANISED	DISPATHIES	DISPERSIONS	DISPLENISHING	DISPREDDEN
DISORGANISER	DISPAUPERED	DISPERSIVE	DISPLENISHMENT	DISPREDDING
DISORGANISERS	DISPAUPERING	DISPERSIVELY	DISPLENISHMENTS	DISPRINCED
DISORGANISES	DISPAUPERISE	DISPERSIVENESS	DISPLODING	DISPRISONED
DISORGANISING	DISPAUPERISED	DISPERSOID	DISPLOSION	DISPRISONING
DISORGANIZATION	DISPAUPERISES	DISPERSOIDS	DISPLOSIONS	DISPRISONS
DISORGANIZE	DISPAUPERISING	DISPIRITED	DISPLUMING	DISPRIVACIED
DISORGANIZED	DISPAUPERIZE	DISPIRITEDLY	DISPONDAIC	DISPRIVILEGE
DISORGANIZER	DISPAUPERIZED	DISPIRITEDNESS	DISPONDEES	DISPRIVILEGED
DISORGANIZERS	DISPAUPERIZES	DISPIRITING	DISPONGING	DISPRIVILEGES
DISORGANIZES	DISPAUPERIZING	DISPIRITINGLY	DISPORTING	DISPRIVILEGING
DISORGANIZING	DISPAUPERS	DISPIRITMENT	DISPORTMENT	DISPRIZING
DISORIENTATE	DISPELLERS	DISPIRITMENTS	DISPORTMENTS	DISPROFESS
DISORIENTATED	DISPELLING	DISPITEOUS	DISPOSABILITIES	DISPROFESSED
DISORIENTATES	DISPENCING	DISPITEOUSLY	DISPOSABILITY	DISPROFESSES
DISORIENTATING	DISPENDING	DISPITEOUSNESS	DISPOSABLE	DISPROFESSING
DISORIENTATION	DISPENSABILITY	DISPLACEABLE	DISPOSABLENESS	DISPROFITED
DISORIENTATIONS	DISPENSABLE	DISPLACEMENT	DISPOSABLES	DISPROFITING
DISORIENTED	DISPENSABLENESS	DISPLACEMENTS	DISPOSEDLY	DISPROFITS
DISORIENTING	DISPENSABLY	DISPLACERS	DISPOSINGLY	DISPROOVED
DISORIENTS	DISPENSARIES	DISPLACING	DISPOSINGS	DISPROOVES
DISOWNMENT	DISPENSARY	DISPLANTATION	DISPOSITION	DISPROOVING
DISOWNMENTS	DISPENSATION	DISPLANTATIONS	DISPOSITIONAL	DISPROPERTIED
DISPARAGED	DISPENSATIONAL	DISPLANTED	DISPOSITIONED	DISPROPERTIES
DISPARAGEMENT	DISPENSATIONS	DISPLANTING	DISPOSITIONS	DISPROPERTY
DISPARAGEMENTS	DISPENSATIVE	DISPLAYABLE	DISPOSITIVE	DISPROPERTYING
DISPARAGER	DISPENSATIVELY	DISPLAYERS	DISPOSITIVELY	DISPROPORTION
DISPARAGERS	DISPENSATOR	DISPLAYING	DISPOSITIVES	DISPROPORTIONAL
DISPARAGES	DISPENSATORIES	DISPLEASANCE	DISPOSITOR	DISPROPORTIONED
DISPARAGING	DISPENSATORILY	DISPLEASANCES	DISPOSITORS	DISPROPORTIONS
DISPARAGINGLY	DISPENSATORS	DISPLEASANT	DISPOSSESS	DISPROPRIATE
DISPARATELY	DISPENSATORY	DISPLEASANTED	DISPOSSESSED	DISPROPRIATED
DISPARATENESS	DISPENSERS	DISPLEASANTING	DISPOSSESSES	DISPROPRIATES
DISPARATENESSES	DISPENSING	DISPLEASANTS	DISPOSSESSING	DISPROPRIATING
DISPARATES	DISPEOPLED	DISPLEASED	DISPOSSESSION	DISPROVABLE
DISPARITIES	DISPEOPLES	DISPLEASEDLY	DISPOSSESSIONS	DISPROVALS
DISPARKING	DISPEOPLING	DISPLEASEDNESS	DISPOSSESSOR	DISPROVERS
DISPARTING	DISPERMOUS	DISPLEASES	DISPOSSESSORS	DISPROVIDE
DISPASSION	DISPERSALS	DISPLEASING	DISPOSSESSORY	DISPROVIDED
DISPASSIONATE	DISPERSANT	DISPLEASINGLY	DISPOSTING	DISPROVIDES
DISPASSIONATELY	DISPERSANTS	DISPLEASINGNESS	DISPOSURES	DISPROVIDING
DISPASSIONS	DISPERSEDLY	DISPLEASURE	DISPRAISED	DISPROVING
DISPATCHED	DISPERSEDNESS	DISPLEASURED	DISPRAISER	DISPUNGING
DISPATCHER	DISPERSEDNESSES	DISPLEASURES	DISPRAISERS	DISPURSING

DISPURVEYANCE	DISQUISITIONARY	DISSATISFACTORY	DISSENSUSES	DISSHIVERED
DISPURVEYANCES	DISQUISITIONS	DISSATISFIED	DISSENTERISH	DISSHIVERING
DISPURVEYED	DISQUISITIVE	DISSATISFIEDLY	DISSENTERISM	DISSHIVERS
DISPURVEYING	DISQUISITORY	DISSATISFIES	DISSENTERISMS	DISSIDENCE
DISPURVEYS	DISRANKING	DISSATISFY	DISSENTERS	DISSIDENCES
DISPUTABILITIES	DISREGARDED	DISSATISFYING	DISSENTIENCE	DISSIDENTLY
DISPUTABILITY	DISREGARDER	DISSAVINGS	DISSENTIENCES	DISSIDENTS
DISPUTABLE	DISREGARDERS	DISSEATING	DISSENTIENCIES	DISSILIENCE
DISPUTABLENESS	DISREGARDFUL	DISSECTIBLE	DISSENTIENCY	DISSILIENCES
DISPUTABLY	DISREGARDFULLY	DISSECTING	DISSENTIENT	DISSILIENT
DISPUTANTS	DISREGARDING	DISSECTINGS	DISSENTIENTLY	DISSIMILAR
DISPUTATION	DISREGARDS	DISSECTION	DISSENTIENTS	DISSIMILARITIES
DISPUTATIONS	DISRELATED	DISSECTIONS	DISSENTING	DISSIMILARITY
DISPUTATIOUS	DISRELATION	DISSECTIVE	DISSENTINGLY	DISSIMILARLY
DISPUTATIOUSLY	DISRELATIONS	DISSECTORS	DISSENTION	DISSIMILARS
DISPUTATIVE	DISRELISHED	DISSEISEES	DISSENTIONS	DISSIMILATE
DISPUTATIVELY	DISRELISHES	DISSEISING	DISSENTIOUS	DISSIMILATED
DISPUTATIVENESS	DISRELISHING	DISSEISINS	DISSEPIMENT	DISSIMILATES
DISQUALIFIABLE	DISREMEMBER	DISSEISORS	DISSEPIMENTAL	DISSIMILATING
DISQUALIFIED	DISREMEMBERED	DISSEIZEES	DISSEPIMENTS	DISSIMILATION
DISQUALIFIER	DISREMEMBERING	DISSEIZING	DISSERTATE	DISSIMILATIONS
DISQUALIFIERS	DISREMEMBERS	DISSEIZINS	DISSERTATED	DISSIMILATIVE
DISQUALIFIES	DISREPAIRS	DISSEIZORS	DISSERTATES	DISSIMILATORY
DISQUALIFY	DISREPUTABILITY	DISSELBOOM	DISSERTATING	DISSIMILES
DISQUALIFYING	DISREPUTABLE	DISSELBOOMS	DISSERTATION	DISSIMILITUDE
DISQUANTITIED	DISREPUTABLY	DISSEMBLANCE	DISSERTATIONAL	DISSIMILITUDES
DISQUANTITIES	DISREPUTATION	DISSEMBLANCES	DISSERTATIONIST	DISSIMULATE
DISQUANTITY	DISREPUTATIONS	DISSEMBLED	DISSERTATIONS	DISSIMULATED
DISQUANTITYING	DISREPUTES	DISSEMBLER	DISSERTATIVE	DISSIMULATES
DISQUIETED	DISRESPECT	DISSEMBLERS	DISSERTATOR	DISSIMULATING
DISQUIETEDLY	DISRESPECTABLE	DISSEMBLES	DISSERTATORS	DISSIMULATION
DISQUIETEDNESS	DISRESPECTED	DISSEMBLIES	DISSERTING	DISSIMULATIONS
DISQUIETEN	DISRESPECTFUL	DISSEMBLING	DISSERVICE	DISSIMULATIVE
DISQUIETENED	DISRESPECTFULLY	DISSEMBLINGLY	DISSERVICEABLE	DISSIMULATOR
DISQUIETENING	DISRESPECTING	DISSEMBLINGS	DISSERVICES	DISSIMULATORS
DISQUIETENS	DISRESPECTS	DISSEMINATE	DISSERVING	DISSIPABLE
DISQUIETFUL	DISROBEMENT	DISSEMINATED	DISSEVERANCE	DISSIPATED
DISQUIETING	DISROBEMENTS	DISSEMINATES	DISSEVERANCES	DISSIPATEDLY
DISQUIETINGLY	DISROOTING	DISSEMINATING	DISSEVERATION	DISSIPATEDNESS
DISQUIETIVE	DISRUPTERS	DISSEMINATION	DISSEVERATIONS	DISSIPATER
DISQUIETLY	DISRUPTING	DISSEMINATIONS	DISSEVERED	DISSIPATERS
DISQUIETNESS	DISRUPTION	DISSEMINATIVE	DISSEVERING	DISSIPATES
DISQUIETNESSES	DISRUPTIONS	DISSEMINATOR	DISSEVERMENT	DISSIPATING
DISQUIETOUS	DISRUPTIVE	DISSEMINATORS	DISSEVERMENTS	DISSIPATION
DISQUIETUDE	DISRUPTIVELY	DISSEMINULE	DISSHEATHE	DISSIPATIONS
DISQUIETUDES	DISRUPTIVENESS	DISSEMINULES	DISSHEATHED	DISSIPATIVE
DISQUISITION	DISRUPTORS	DISSENSION	DISSHEATHES	DISSIPATOR
DISQUISITIONAL	DISSATISFACTION	DISSENSIONS	DISSHEATHING	DISSIPATORS

DISSOCIABILITY	DISSONANTLY	DISTENSIBLE	DISTINGUEE	DISTRAUGHTLY
DISSOCIABLE	DISSUADABLE	DISTENSILE	DISTINGUISH	DISTRESSED
DISSOCIABLENESS	DISSUADERS	DISTENSION	DISTINGUISHABLE	DISTRESSER
DISSOCIABLY	DISSUADING	DISTENSIONS	DISTINGUISHABLY	DISTRESSERS
DISSOCIALISE	DISSUASION	DISTENSIVE	DISTINGUISHED	DISTRESSES
DISSOCIALISED	DISSUASIONS	DISTENTION	DISTINGUISHER	DISTRESSFUL
DISSOCIALISES	DISSUASIVE	DISTENTIONS	DISTINGUISHERS	DISTRESSFULLY
DISSOCIALISING	DISSUASIVELY	DISTHRONED	DISTINGUISHES	DISTRESSFULNESS
DISSOCIALITIES	DISSUASIVENESS	DISTHRONES	DISTINGUISHING	DISTRESSING
DISSOCIALITY	DISSUASIVES	DISTHRONING	DISTINGUISHMENT	DISTRESSINGLY
DISSOCIALIZE	DISSUASORIES	DISTHRONISE	DISTORTEDLY	DISTRESSINGS
DISSOCIALIZED	DISSUASORY	DISTHRONISED	DISTORTEDNESS	DISTRIBUEND
DISSOCIALIZES	DISSUNDERED	DISTHRONISES	DISTORTEDNESSES	DISTRIBUENDS
DISSOCIALIZING	DISSUNDERING	DISTHRONISING	DISTORTERS	DISTRIBUTABLE
DISSOCIATE	DISSUNDERS	DISTHRONIZE	DISTORTING	DISTRIBUTARIES
DISSOCIATED	DISSYLLABIC	DISTHRONIZED	DISTORTION	DISTRIBUTARY
DISSOCIATES	DISSYLLABIFIED	DISTHRONIZES	DISTORTIONAL	DISTRIBUTE
DISSOCIATING	DISSYLLABIFIES	DISTHRONIZING	DISTORTIONS	DISTRIBUTED
DISSOCIATION	DISSYLLABIFY	DISTICHOUS	DISTORTIVE	DISTRIBUTEE
DISSOCIATIONS	DISSYLLABIFYING	DISTICHOUSLY	DISTRACTABLE	DISTRIBUTEES
DISSOCIATIVE	DISSYLLABISM	DISTILLABLE	DISTRACTED	DISTRIBUTER
DISSOLUBILITIES	DISSYLLABISMS	DISTILLAND	DISTRACTEDLY	DISTRIBUTERS
DISSOLUBILITY	DISSYLLABLE	DISTILLANDS	DISTRACTEDNESS	DISTRIBUTES
DISSOLUBLE	DISSYLLABLES	DISTILLATE	DISTRACTER	DISTRIBUTING
DISSOLUBLENESS	DISSYMMETRIC	DISTILLATES	DISTRACTERS	DISTRIBUTION
DISSOLUTELY	DISSYMMETRICAL	DISTILLATION	DISTRACTIBILITY	DISTRIBUTIONAL
DISSOLUTENESS	DISSYMMETRIES	DISTILLATIONS	DISTRACTIBLE	DISTRIBUTIONS
DISSOLUTENESSES	DISSYMMETRY	DISTILLATORY	DISTRACTING	DISTRIBUTIVE
DISSOLUTES	DISTAINING	DISTILLERIES	DISTRACTINGLY	DISTRIBUTIVELY
DISSOLUTION	DISTANCELESS	DISTILLERS	DISTRACTION	DISTRIBUTIVES
DISSOLUTIONISM	DISTANCING	DISTILLERY	DISTRACTIONS	DISTRIBUTIVITY
DISSOLUTIONISMS	DISTANTNESS	DISTILLING	DISTRACTIVE	DISTRIBUTOR
DISSOLUTIONIST	DISTANTNESSES	DISTILLINGS	DISTRACTIVELY	DISTRIBUTORS
DISSOLUTIONISTS	DISTASTEFUL	DISTILMENT	DISTRACTOR	DISTRIBUTORSHIP
DISSOLUTIONS	DISTASTEFULLY	DISTILMENTS	DISTRACTORS	DISTRICTED
DISSOLUTIVE	DISTASTEFULNESS	DISTINCTER	DISTRAINABLE	DISTRICTING
DISSOLVABILITY	DISTASTING	DISTINCTEST	DISTRAINED	DISTRINGAS
DISSOLVABLE	DISTELFINK	DISTINCTION	DISTRAINEE	DISTRINGASES
DISSOLVABLENESS	DISTELFINKS	DISTINCTIONS	DISTRAINEES	DISTROUBLE
DISSOLVENT	DISTEMPERATE	DISTINCTIVE	DISTRAINER	DISTROUBLED
DISSOLVENTS	DISTEMPERATURE	DISTINCTIVELY	DISTRAINERS	DISTROUBLES
DISSOLVERS	DISTEMPERATURES	DISTINCTIVENESS	DISTRAINING	DISTROUBLING
DISSOLVING	DISTEMPERED	DISTINCTIVES	DISTRAINMENT	DISTRUSTED
DISSOLVINGS	DISTEMPERING	DISTINCTLY	DISTRAINMENTS	DISTRUSTER
DISSONANCE	DISTEMPERS	DISTINCTNESS	DISTRAINOR	DISTRUSTERS
DISSONANCES	DISTENDERS	DISTINCTNESSES	DISTRAINORS	DISTRUSTFUL
DISSONANCIES	DISTENDING	DISTINCTURE	DISTRAINTS	DISTRUSTFULLY
DISSONANCY	DISTENSIBILITY	DISTINCTURES	DISTRAUGHT	DISTRUSTFULNESS

DISTRUSTING

DISTRUSTING	DISYLLABLE	DIUTURNITIES	DIVERTIBILITY	DIVISIBLENESS
DISTRUSTLESS	DISYLLABLES	DIUTURNITY	DIVERTIBLE	DIVISIBLENESSES
DISTURBANCE	DITCHDIGGER	DIVAGATING	DIVERTICULA	DIVISIONAL
DISTURBANCES	DITCHDIGGERS	DIVAGATION	DIVERTICULAR	DIVISIONALLY
DISTURBANT	DITCHWATER	DIVAGATIONS	DIVERTICULATE	DIVISIONARY
DISTURBANTS	DITCHWATERS	DIVALENCES	DIVERTICULATED	DIVISIONISM
DISTURBATIVE	DITHEISTIC	DIVALENCIES	DIVERTICULITIS	DIVISIONISMS
DISTURBERS	DITHEISTICAL	DIVARICATE	DIVERTICULOSES	DIVISIONIST
DISTURBING	DITHELETES	DIVARICATED	DIVERTICULOSIS	DIVISIONISTS
DISTURBINGLY	DITHELETIC	DIVARICATELY	DIVERTICULUM	DIVISIVELY
DISUBSTITUTED	DITHELETICAL	DIVARICATES	DIVERTIMENTI	DIVISIVENESS
DISULFATES	DITHELETISM	DIVARICATING	DIVERTIMENTO	DIVISIVENESSES
DISULFIDES	DITHELETISMS	DIVARICATINGLY	DIVERTIMENTOS	DIVORCEABLE
DISULFIRAM	DITHELISMS	DIVARICATION	DIVERTINGLY	DIVORCEMENT
DISULFIRAMS	DITHELITISM	DIVARICATIONS	DIVERTISEMENT	DIVORCEMENTS
DISULFOTON	DITHELITISMS	DIVARICATOR	DIVERTISEMENTS	DIVULGATED
DISULFOTONS	DITHERIEST	DIVARICATORS	DIVERTISSEMENT	DIVULGATER
DISULPHATE	DITHERINGS	DIVEBOMBED	DIVERTISSEMENTS	DIVULGATERS
DISULPHATES	DITHIOCARBAMATE	DIVEBOMBING	DIVESTIBLE	DIVULGATES
DISULPHIDE	DITHIOCARBAMIC	DIVELLICATE	DIVESTITURE	DIVULGATING
DISULPHIDES	DITHIONATE	DIVELLICATED	DIVESTITURES	DIVULGATION
DISULPHURET	DITHIONATES	DIVELLICATES	DIVESTMENT	DIVULGATIONS
DISULPHURETS	DITHIONITE	DIVELLICATING	DIVESTMENTS	DIVULGATOR
DISULPHURIC	DITHIONITES	DIVERGEMENT	DIVESTURES	DIVULGATORS
DISUNIONIST	DITHIONOUS	DIVERGEMENTS	DIVIDEDNESS	DIVULGEMENT
DISUNIONISTS	DITHYRAMBIC	DIVERGENCE	DIVIDEDNESSES	DIVULGEMENTS
DISUNITERS	DITHYRAMBICALLY	DIVERGENCES	DIVIDENDLESS	DIVULGENCE
DISUNITIES	DITHYRAMBIST	DIVERGENCIES	DIVINATION	DIVULGENCES
DISUNITING	DITHYRAMBISTS	DIVERGENCY	DIVINATIONS	DIVULSIONS
DISUTILITIES	DITHYRAMBS	DIVERGENTLY	DIVINATORIAL	DIZENMENTS
DISUTILITY	DITRANSITIVE	DIVERGINGLY	DIVINATORS	DIZZINESSES
DISVALUING	DITRANSITIVES	DIVERSENESS	DIVINATORY	DIZZYINGLY
DISVOUCHED	DITRIGLYPH	DIVERSENESSES	DIVINENESS	DJELLABAHS
DISVOUCHES	DITRIGLYPHIC	DIVERSIFIABLE	DIVINENESSES	DOBSONFLIES
DISVOUCHING	DITRIGLYPHS	DIVERSIFICATION	DIVINERESS	DOCENTSHIP
DISWORSHIP	DITROCHEAN	DIVERSIFIED	DIVINERESSES	DOCENTSHIPS
DISWORSHIPED	DITROCHEES	DIVERSIFIER	DIVINIFIED	DOCHMIACAL
DISWORSHIPING	DITSINESSES	DIVERSIFIERS	DIVINIFIES	DOCHMIUSES
DISWORSHIPPED	DITTANDERS	DIVERSIFIES	DIVINIFYING	DOCIBILITIES
DISWORSHIPPING	DITTOGRAPHIC	DIVERSIFORM	DIVINISATION	DOCIBILITY
DISWORSHIPS	DITTOGRAPHIES	DIVERSIFYING	DIVINISATIONS	DOCIBLENESS
DISYLLABIC	DITTOGRAPHY	DIVERSIONAL	DIVINISING	DOCIBLENESSES
DISYLLABIFIED	DITTOLOGIES	DIVERSIONARY	DIVINITIES	DOCILITIES
DISYLLABIFIES	DITZINESSES	DIVERSIONIST	DIVINIZATION	DOCIMASIES
DISYLLABIFY	DIURETICALLY	DIVERSIONISTS	DIVINIZATIONS	DOCIMASTIC
DISYLLABIFYING	DIURETICALNESS	DIVERSIONS	DIVINIZING	DOCIMOLOGIES
DISYLLABISM	DIURNALIST	DIVERSITIES	DIVISIBILITIES	DOCIMOLOGY
DISYLLABISMS	DIURNALISTS	DIVERTIBILITIES	DIVISIBILITY	DOCKISATION

DOCKISATIONS	DOCUMENTARISING	DOGFIGHTING	DOLABRIFORM	DOLOMITIZATION
DOCKIZATION	DOCUMENTARIST	DOGFIGHTINGS	DOLCELATTE	DOLOMITIZATIONS
DOCKIZATIONS	DOCUMENTARISTS	DOGGEDNESS	DOLCELATTES	DOLOMITIZE
DOCKMASTER	DOCUMENTARIZE	DOGGEDNESSES	DOLCEMENTE	DOLOMITIZED
DOCKMASTERS	DOCUMENTARIZED	DOGGINESSES	DOLEFULLER	DOLOMITIZES
DOCKWALLOPER	DOCUMENTARIZES	DOGGISHNESS	DOLEFULLEST	DOLOMITIZING
DOCKWALLOPERS	DOCUMENTARIZING	DOGGISHNESSES	DOLEFULNESS	DOLORIFEROUS
DOCKWORKER	DOCUMENTARY	DOGGONEDER	DOLEFULNESSES	DOLORIMETRIES
DOCKWORKERS	DOCUMENTATION	DOGGONEDEST	DOLESOMELY	DOLORIMETRY
DOCQUETING	DOCUMENTATIONAL	DOGLEGGING	DOLICHOCEPHAL	DOLOROUSLY
DOCTORANDS	DOCUMENTATIONS	DOGMATICAL	DOLICHOCEPHALIC	DOLOROUSNESS
DOCTORATED	DOCUMENTED	DOGMATICALLY	DOLICHOCEPHALS	DOLOROUSNESSES
DOCTORATES	DOCUMENTER	DOGMATICALNESS	DOLICHOCEPHALY	DOLOSTONES
DOCTORATING	DOCUMENTERS	DOGMATISATION	DOLICHOSAURUS	DOLPHINARIA
DOCTORESSES	DOCUMENTING	DOGMATISATIONS	DOLICHOSAURUSES	DOLPHINARIUM
DOCTORINGS	DODDERIEST	DOGMATISED	DOLICHOSES	DOLPHINARIUMS
DOCTORLESS	DODDIPOLLS	DOGMATISER	DOLICHURUS	DOLPHINETS
DOCTORSHIP	DODDYPOLLS	DOGMATISERS	DOLICHURUSES	DOLPHINFISH
DOCTORSHIPS	DODECAGONAL	DOGMATISES	DOLLARBIRD	DOLPHINFISHES
DOCTRESSES	DODECAGONS	DOGMATISING	DOLLARBIRDS	DOLTISHNESS
DOCTRINAIRE	DODECAGYNIAN	DOGMATISMS	DOLLARFISH	DOLTISHNESSES
DOCTRINAIRES	DODECAGYNOUS	DOGMATISTS	DOLLARFISHES	DOMESTICABLE
DOCTRINAIRISM	DODECAHEDRA	DOGMATIZATION	DOLLARISATION	DOMESTICAL
DOCTRINAIRISMS	DODECAHEDRAL	DOGMATIZATIONS	DOLLARISATIONS	DOMESTICALLY
DOCTRINALITIES	DODECAHEDRON	DOGMATIZED	DOLLARISED	DOMESTICATE
DOCTRINALITY	DODECAHEDRONS	DOGMATIZER	DOLLARISES	DOMESTICATED
DOCTRINALLY	DODECANDROUS	DOGMATIZERS	DOLLARISING	DOMESTICATES
DOCTRINARIAN	DODECANOIC	DOGMATIZES	DOLLARIZATION	DOMESTICATING
DOCTRINARIANISM	DODECAPHONIC	DOGMATIZING	DOLLARIZATIONS	DOMESTICATION
DOCTRINARIANS	DODECAPHONIES	DOGMATOLOGIES	DOLLARIZED	DOMESTICATIONS
DOCTRINARISM	DODECAPHONISM	DOGMATOLOGY	DOLLARIZES	DOMESTICATIVE
DOCTRINARISMS	DODECAPHONISMS	DOGNAPINGS	DOLLARIZING	DOMESTICATOR
DOCTRINISM	DODECAPHONIST	DOGNAPPERS	DOLLARLESS	DOMESTICATORS
DOCTRINISMS	DODECAPHONISTS	DOGNAPPING	DOLLAROCRACIES	DOMESTICISE
DOCTRINIST	DODECAPHONY	DOGNAPPINGS	DOLLAROCRACY	DOMESTICISED
DOCTRINISTS	DODECASTYLE	DOGROBBERS	DOLLARSHIP	DOMESTICISES
DOCUDRAMAS	DODECASTYLES	DOGSBODIED	DOLLARSHIPS	DOMESTICISING
DOCUMENTABLE	DODECASYLLABIC	DOGSBODIES	DOLLHOUSES	DOMESTICITIES
DOCUMENTAL	DODECASYLLABLE	DOGSBODYING	DOLLINESSES	DOMESTICITY
DOCUMENTALIST	DODECASYLLABLES	DOGSBODYINGS	DOLLISHNESS	DOMESTICIZE
DOCUMENTALISTS	DODGEBALLS	DOGSLEDDED	DOLLISHNESSES	DOMESTICIZED
DOCUMENTARIAN	DODGINESSES	DOGSLEDDER	DOLLYBIRDS	DOMESTICIZES
DOCUMENTARIANS	DOGARESSAS	DOGSLEDDERS	DOLOMITISATION	DOMESTICIZING
DOCUMENTARIES	DOGBERRIES	DOGSLEDDING	DOLOMITISATIONS	DOMESTIQUE
DOCUMENTARILY	DOGBERRYISM	DOGSLEDDINGS	DOLOMITISE	DOMESTIQUES
DOCUMENTARISE	DOGBERRYISMS	DOGTROTTED	DOLOMITISED	DOMICILIARY
DOCUMENTARISED	DOGCATCHER	DOGTROTTING	DOLOMITISES	DOMICILIATE
DOCUMENTARISES	DOGCATCHERS	DOGWATCHES	DOLOMITISING	DOMICILIATED

DOMICILIATES

DOMICILIATES	DOOMWATCHERS	DORSOLUMBAR	DOUGHNUTLIKE	DOWNLOADING
DOMICILIATING	DOOMWATCHES	DORSOVENTRAL	DOUGHNUTTED	DOWNLOADINGS
DOMICILIATION	DOOMWATCHING	DORSOVENTRALITY	DOUGHNUTTING	DOWNLOOKED
DOMICILIATIONS	DOOMWATCHINGS	DORSOVENTRALLY	DOUGHNUTTINGS	DOWNPLAYED
DOMICILING	DOORFRAMES	DORTINESSES	DOUGHTIEST	DOWNPLAYING
DOMINANCES	DOORKEEPER	DOSEMETERS	DOUGHTINESS	DOWNRATING
DOMINANCIES	DOORKEEPERS	DOSIMETERS	DOUGHTINESSES	DOWNREGULATION
DOMINANTLY	DOORKNOCKED	DOSIMETRIC	DOULOCRACIES	DOWNREGULATIONS
DOMINATING	DOORKNOCKER	DOSIMETRICIAN	DOULOCRACY	DOWNRIGHTLY
DOMINATINGLY	DOORKNOCKERS	DOSIMETRICIANS	DOUPPIONIS	DOWNRIGHTNESS
DOMINATION	DOORKNOCKING	DOSIMETRIES	DOURNESSES	DOWNRIGHTNESSES
DOMINATIONS	DOORKNOCKS	DOSIMETRIST	DOUROUCOULI	DOWNRUSHES
DOMINATIVE	DOORNBOOMS	DOSIMETRISTS	DOUROUCOULIS	DOWNSCALED
DOMINATORS	DOORPLATES	DOSIOLOGIES	DOVEISHNESS	DOWNSCALES
DOMINATRICES	DOORSTEPPED	DOSOLOGIES	DOVEISHNESSES	DOWNSCALING
DOMINATRIX	DOORSTEPPER	DOSSHOUSES	DOVETAILED	DOWNSHIFTED
DOMINATRIXES	DOORSTEPPERS	DOTARDLIER	DOVETAILING	DOWNSHIFTER
DOMINEERED	DOORSTEPPING	DOTARDLIEST	DOVETAILINGS	DOWNSHIFTERS
DOMINEERING	DOORSTEPPINGS	DOTCOMMERS	DOVISHNESS	DOWNSHIFTING
DOMINEERINGLY	DOORSTONES	DOTTINESSES	DOVISHNESSES	DOWNSHIFTINGS
DOMINEERINGNESS	DOPAMINERGIC	DOUBLEHEADER	DOWDINESSES	DOWNSHIFTS
DOMINICKER	DOPESHEETS	DOUBLEHEADERS	DOWELLINGS	DOWNSIZERS
DOMINICKERS	DOPEYNESSES	DOUBLENESS	DOWFNESSES	DOWNSIZING
DOMINIQUES	DOPINESSES	DOUBLENESSES	DOWITCHERS	DOWNSIZINGS
DONATARIES	DOPPELGANGER	DOUBLESPEAK	DOWNBURSTS	DOWNSLIDES
DONATISTIC	DOPPELGANGERS	DOUBLESPEAKER	DOWNCOMERS	DOWNSLOPES
DONATISTICAL	DOPPLERITE	DOUBLESPEAKERS	DOWNCRYING	DOWNSPOUTS
DONATORIES	DOPPLERITES	DOUBLESPEAKS	DOWNDRAFTS	DOWNSTAGES
DONENESSES	DORBEETLES	DOUBLETHINK	DOWNDRAUGHT	DOWNSTAIRS
DONEPEZILS	DORKINESSES	DOUBLETHINKS	DOWNDRAUGHTS	DOWNSTAIRSES
DONKEYWORK	DORMANCIES	DOUBLETONS	DOWNFALLEN	DOWNSTATER
DONKEYWORKS	DORMITIONS	DOUBLETREE	DOWNFORCES	DOWNSTATERS
DONNICKERS	DORMITIVES	DOUBLETREES	DOWNGRADED	DOWNSTATES
DONNISHNESS	DORMITORIES	DOUBTFULLY	DOWNGRADES	DOWNSTREAM
DONNISHNESSES	DORONICUMS	DOUBTFULNESS	DOWNGRADING	DOWNSTROKE
DONNYBROOK	DORSIBRANCHIATE	DOUBTFULNESSES	DOWNHEARTED	DOWNSTROKES
DONNYBROOKS	DORSIFEROUS	DOUBTINGLY	DOWNHEARTEDLY	DOWNSWINGS
DONORSHIPS	DORSIFIXED	DOUBTLESSLY	DOWNHEARTEDNESS	DOWNTHROWS
DOODLEBUGS	DORSIFLEXED	DOUBTLESSNESS	DOWNHILLER	DOWNTOWNER
DOOHICKEYS	DORSIFLEXES	DOUBTLESSNESSES	DOWNHILLERS	DOWNTOWNERS
DOOHICKIES	DORSIFLEXING	DOUCENESSES	DOWNINESSES	DOWNTRENDED
DOOMSAYERS	DORSIFLEXION	DOUCEPERES	DOWNLIGHTER	DOWNTRENDING
DOOMSAYING	DORSIFLEXIONS	DOUCHEBAGS	DOWNLIGHTERS	DOWNTRENDS
DOOMSAYINGS	DORSIGRADE	DOUGHBALLS	DOWNLIGHTS	DOWNTRODDEN
DOOMSDAYER	DORSIVENTRAL	DOUGHFACED	DOWNLINKED	DOWNTURNED
DOOMSDAYERS	DORSIVENTRALITY	DOUGHFACES	DOWNLINKING	DOWNVOTING
DOOMWATCHED	DORSIVENTRALLY	DOUGHINESS	DOWNLOADABLE	DOWNWARDLY
DOOMWATCHER	DORSOLATERAL	DOUGHINESSES	DOWNLOADED	DOWNWARDNESS

DOWNWARDNESSES	DRAGONISING	DRAMATURGIC	DRAWSTRINGS	DRERIHEADS
DOWNWASHES	DRAGONISMS	DRAMATURGICAL	DRAYHORSES	DRESSGUARD
DOWNZONING	DRAGONIZED	DRAMATURGICALLY	DREADFULLY	DRESSGUARDS
DOXOGRAPHER	DRAGONIZES	DRAMATURGIES	DREADFULNESS	DRESSINESS
DOXOGRAPHERS	DRAGONIZING	DRAMATURGIST	DREADFULNESSES	DRESSINESSES
DOXOGRAPHIC	DRAGONLIKE	DRAMATURGISTS	DREADLESSLY	DRESSMAKER
DOXOGRAPHIES	DRAGONNADE	DRAMATURGS	DREADLESSNESS	DRESSMAKERS
DOXOGRAPHY	DRAGONNADED	DRAMATURGY	DREADLESSNESSES	DRESSMAKES
DOXOLOGICAL	DRAGONNADES	DRAPABILITIES	DREADLOCKED	DRESSMAKING
DOXOLOGICALLY	DRAGONNADING	DRAPABILITY	DREADLOCKS	DRESSMAKINGS
DOXOLOGIES	DRAGONROOT	DRAPEABILITIES	DREADNAUGHT	DRIBBLIEST
DOXORUBICIN	DRAGONROOTS	DRAPEABILITY	DREADNAUGHTS	DRIBBLINGS
DOXORUBICINS	DRAGOONAGE	DRAPERYING	DREADNOUGHT	DRICKSIEST
DOXYCYCLINE	DRAGOONAGES	DRASTICALLY	DREADNOUGHTS	DRIFTINGLY
DOXYCYCLINES	DRAGOONING	DRATCHELLS	DREAMBOATS	DRIFTWOODS
DOZINESSES	DRAGSTRIPS	DRAUGHTBOARD	DREAMERIES	DRILLABILITIES
DRABBINESS	DRAGSVILLE	DRAUGHTBOARDS	DREAMFULLY	DRILLABILITY
DRABBINESSES	DRAGSVILLES	DRAUGHTERS	DREAMFULNESS	DRILLHOLES
DRABBLINGS	DRAINBOARD	DRAUGHTIER	DREAMFULNESSES	DRILLMASTER
DRABNESSES	DRAINBOARDS	DRAUGHTIEST	DREAMHOLES	DRILLMASTERS
DRACONIANISM	DRAINLAYER	DRAUGHTILY	DREAMINESS	DRILLSHIPS
DRACONIANISMS	DRAINLAYERS	DRAUGHTINESS	DREAMINESSES	DRILLSTOCK
DRACONICALLY	DRAINPIPES	DRAUGHTINESSES	DREAMINGLY	DRILLSTOCKS
DRACONISMS	DRAKESTONE	DRAUGHTING	DREAMLANDS	DRINKABILITIES
DRACONITES	DRAKESTONES	DRAUGHTMAN	DREAMLESSLY	DRINKABILITY
DRACONTIASES	DRAMATICAL	DRAUGHTMEN	DREAMLESSNESS	DRINKABLENESS
DRACONTIASIS	DRAMATICALLY	DRAUGHTPROOF	DREAMLESSNESSES	DRINKABLENESSES
DRACUNCULIASES	DRAMATICISM	DRAUGHTPROOFED	DREAMTIMES	DRINKABLES
DRACUNCULIASIS	DRAMATICISMS	DRAUGHTPROOFING	DREAMWHILE	DRIPSTONES
DRACUNCULUS	DRAMATISABLE	DRAUGHTPROOFS	DREAMWHILES	DRIVABILITIES
DRACUNCULUSES	DRAMATISATION	DRAUGHTSMAN	DREAMWORLD	DRIVABILITY
DRAFTINESS	DRAMATISATIONS	DRAUGHTSMANSHIP	DREAMWORLDS	DRIVEABILITIES
DRAFTINESSES	DRAMATISED	DRAUGHTSMEN	DREARIHEAD	DRIVEABILITY
DRAFTSMANSHIP	DRAMATISER	DRAUGHTSPERSON	DREARIHEADS	DRIVELINES
DRAFTSMANSHIPS	DRAMATISERS	DRAUGHTSPERSONS	DREARIHOOD	DRIVELLERS
DRAFTSPERSON	DRAMATISES	DRAUGHTSWOMAN	DREARIHOODS	DRIVELLING
DRAFTSPERSONS	DRAMATISING	DRAUGHTSWOMEN	DREARIMENT	DRIVENNESS
DRAFTSWOMAN	DRAMATISTS	DRAWBRIDGE	DREARIMENTS	DRIVENNESSES
DRAFTSWOMEN	DRAMATIZABLE	DRAWBRIDGES	DREARINESS	DRIVERLESS
DRAGGINGLY	DRAMATIZATION	DRAWERFULS	DREARINESSES	DRIVESHAFT
DRAGGLETAILED	DRAMATIZATIONS	DRAWKNIVES	DREARISOME	DRIVESHAFTS
DRAGHOUNDS	DRAMATIZED	DRAWLINGLY	DRECKSILLS	DRIVETHROUGH
DRAGONESSES	DRAMATIZER	DRAWLINGNESS	DREGGINESS	DRIVETHROUGHS
DRAGONFLIES	DRAMATIZERS	DRAWLINGNESSES	DREGGINESSES	DRIVETRAIN
DRAGONHEAD	DRAMATIZES	DRAWNWORKS	DREIKANTER	DRIVETRAINS
DRAGONHEADS	DRAMATIZING	DRAWPLATES	DREIKANTERS	DRIZZLIEST
DRAGONISED	DRAMATURGE	DRAWSHAVES	DRENCHINGS	DRIZZLINGLY
DRAGONISES	DRAMATURGES	DRAWSTRING	DREPANIUMS	DROICHIEST

DROLLERIES	DRUCKENNESS	DUCKBOARDS	DUMBWAITER	DUOPOLISTS
DROLLNESSES	DRUCKENNESSES	DUCKSHOVED	DUMBWAITERS	DUOPSONIES
DROMEDARES	DRUDGERIES	DUCKSHOVER	DUMFOUNDED	DUPABILITIES
DROMEDARIES	DRUDGINGLY	DUCKSHOVERS	DUMFOUNDER	DUPABILITY
DROMOPHOBIA	DRUGMAKERS	DUCKSHOVES	DUMFOUNDERED	DUPLEXINGS
DROMOPHOBIAS	DRUGSTORES	DUCKSHOVING	DUMFOUNDERING	DUPLEXITIES
DRONISHNESS	DRUIDESSES	DUCKSHOVINGS	DUMFOUNDERS	DUPLICABILITIES
DRONISHNESSES	DRUMBEATER	DUCKWALKED	DUMFOUNDING	DUPLICABILITY
DRONKVERDRIET	DRUMBEATERS	DUCKWALKING	DUMMELHEAD	DUPLICABLE
DROOLWORTHIER	DRUMBEATING	DUCTILENESS	DUMMELHEADS	DUPLICANDS
DROOLWORTHIEST	DRUMBEATINGS	DUCTILENESSES	DUMMINESSES	DUPLICATED
DROOLWORTHY	DRUMBLEDOR	DUCTILITIES	DUMORTIERITE	DUPLICATELY
DROOPINESS	DRUMBLEDORS	DUDENESSES	DUMORTIERITES	DUPLICATES
DROOPINESSES	DRUMBLEDRANE	DUENNASHIP	DUMOSITIES	DUPLICATING
DROOPINGLY	DRUMBLEDRANES	DUENNASHIPS	DUMPINESSES	DUPLICATION
DROPCLOTHS	DRUMFISHES	DUFFERDOMS	DUMPISHNESS	DUPLICATIONS
DROPFORGED	DRUMSTICKS	DUFFERISMS	DUMPISHNESSES	DUPLICATIVE
DROPFORGES	DRUNKALOGUE	DUIKERBOKS	DUMPTRUCKS	DUPLICATOR
DROPFORGING	DRUNKALOGUES	DUKKERIPEN	DUNDERFUNK	DUPLICATORS
DROPKICKER	DRUNKATHON	DUKKERIPENS	DUNDERFUNKS	DUPLICATURE
DROPKICKERS	DRUNKATHONS	DULCAMARAS	DUNDERHEAD	DUPLICATURES
DROPLIGHTS	DRUNKENNESS	DULCETNESS	DUNDERHEADED	DUPLICIDENT
DROPPERFUL	DRUNKENNESSES	DULCETNESSES	DUNDERHEADISM	DUPLICITIES
DROPPERFULS	DRUNKOMETER	DULCIFICATION	DUNDERHEADISMS	DUPLICITOUS
DROPPERSFUL	DRUNKOMETERS	DULCIFICATIONS	DUNDERHEADS	DUPLICITOUSLY
DROPSICALLY	DRUPACEOUS	DULCIFLUOUS	DUNDERPATE	DURABILITIES
DROPSONDES	DRYASDUSTS	DULCIFYING	DUNDERPATES	DURABILITY
DROPSTONES	DRYBEATING	DULCILOQUIES	DUNDREARIES	DURABLENESS
DROSERACEOUS	DRYOPITHECINE	DULCILOQUY	DUNGEONERS	DURABLENESSES
DROSOMETER	DRYOPITHECINES	DULCIMORES	DUNGEONING	DURALUMINIUM
DROSOMETERS	DRYSALTERIES	DULCITUDES	DUNIEWASSAL	DURALUMINIUMS
DROSOPHILA	DRYSALTERS	DULLNESSES	DUNIEWASSALS	DURALUMINS
DROSOPHILAE	DRYSALTERY	DULLSVILLE	DUNIWASSAL	DURATIONAL
DROSOPHILAS	DRYWALLERS	DULLSVILLES	DUNIWASSALS	DURCHKOMPONIERT
DROSSINESS	DRYWALLING	DULOCRACIES	DUNNIEWASSAL	DURCHKOMPONIRT
DROSSINESSES	DRYWALLINGS	DUMBFOUNDED	DUNNIEWASSALS	DURICRUSTS
DROUGHTIER	DUALISTICALLY	DUMBFOUNDER	DUODECENNIAL	DUROMETERS
DROUGHTIEST	DUATHLETES	DUMBFOUNDERED	DUODECILLION	DUSKINESSES
DROUGHTINESS	DUBIOSITIES	DUMBFOUNDERING	DUODECILLIONS	DUSKISHNESS
DROUGHTINESSES	DUBIOUSNESS	DUMBFOUNDERS	DUODECIMAL	DUSKISHNESSES
DROUTHIEST	DUBIOUSNESSES	DUMBFOUNDING	DUODECIMALLY	DUSKNESSES
DROUTHINESS	DUBITANCIES	DUMBFOUNDS	DUODECIMALS	DUSTCLOTHS
DROUTHINESSES	DUBITATING	DUMBLEDORE	DUODECIMOS	DUSTCOVERS
DROWSIHEAD	DUBITATION	DUMBLEDORES	DUODENECTOMIES	DUSTINESSES
DROWSIHEADS	DUBITATIONS	DUMBNESSES	DUODENECTOMY	DUSTSHEETS
DROWSIHEDS	DUBITATIVE	DUMBSIZING	DUODENITIS	DUSTSTORMS
DROWSINESS	DUBITATIVELY	DUMBSTRICKEN	DUODENITISES	DUTEOUSNESS
DROWSINESSES	DUCHESSING	DUMBSTRUCK	DUOPOLISTIC	DUTEOUSNESSES

DUTIABILITIES
DUTIABILITY
DUTIFULNESS
DUTIFULNESSES
DUUMVIRATE
DUUMVIRATES
DWARFISHLY
DWARFISHNESS
DWARFISHNESSES
DWARFNESSES
DWINDLEMENT
DWINDLEMENTS
DYADICALLY
DYARCHICAL
DYEABILITIES
DYEABILITY
DYINGNESSES
DYNAMETERS
DYNAMICALLY
DYNAMICIST
DYNAMICISTS
DYNAMISING
DYNAMISTIC
DYNAMITARD
DYNAMITARDS
DYNAMITERS
DYNAMITING
DYNAMIZING
DYNAMOELECTRIC
DYNAMOGENESES
DYNAMOGENESIS

DYNAMOGENIES
DYNAMOGENY
DYNAMOGRAPH
DYNAMOGRAPHS
DYNAMOMETER
DYNAMOMETERS
DYNAMOMETRIC
DYNAMOMETRICAL
DYNAMOMETRIES
DYNAMOMETRY
DYNAMOTORS
DYNASTICAL
DYNASTICALLY
DYNASTICISM
DYNASTICISMS
DYNORPHINS
DYOPHYSITE
DYOPHYSITES
DYOTHELETE
DYOTHELETES
DYOTHELETIC
DYOTHELETICAL
DYOTHELETISM
DYOTHELETISMS
DYOTHELISM
DYOTHELISMS
DYOTHELITE
DYOTHELITES
DYOTHELITIC
DYOTHELITICAL
DYSAESTHESIA

DYSAESTHESIAS
DYSAESTHETIC
DYSARTHRIA
DYSARTHRIAS
DYSBINDINS
DYSCALCULIA
DYSCALCULIAS
DYSCHROIAS
DYSCRASIAS
DYSCRASITE
DYSCRASITES
DYSENTERIC
DYSENTERIES
DYSFUNCTION
DYSFUNCTIONAL
DYSFUNCTIONS
DYSGENESES
DYSGENESIS
DYSGRAPHIA
DYSGRAPHIAS
DYSGRAPHIC
DYSGRAPHICS
DYSHARMONIC
DYSKINESIA
DYSKINESIAS
DYSKINETIC
DYSLECTICS
DYSLOGISTIC
DYSLOGISTICALLY
DYSMENORRHEA
DYSMENORRHEAL

DYSMENORRHEAS
DYSMENORRHEIC
DYSMENORRHOEA
DYSMENORRHOEAL
DYSMENORRHOEAS
DYSMENORRHOEIC
DYSMORPHIC
DYSMORPHOPHOBIA
DYSMORPHOPHOBIC
DYSPAREUNIA
DYSPAREUNIAS
DYSPATHETIC
DYSPATHIES
DYSPEPSIAS
DYSPEPSIES
DYSPEPTICAL
DYSPEPTICALLY
DYSPEPTICS
DYSPHAGIAS
DYSPHAGIES
DYSPHASIAS
DYSPHASICS
DYSPHEMISM
DYSPHEMISMS
DYSPHEMISTIC
DYSPHONIAS
DYSPHORIAS
DYSPLASIAS
DYSPLASTIC
DYSPRACTIC
DYSPRAXIAS

DYSPROSIUM
DYSPROSIUMS
DYSRHYTHMIA
DYSRHYTHMIAS
DYSRHYTHMIC
DYSRHYTHMICS
DYSSYNERGIA
DYSSYNERGIAS
DYSSYNERGIC
DYSSYNERGIES
DYSSYNERGY
DYSTELEOLOGICAL
DYSTELEOLOGIES
DYSTELEOLOGIST
DYSTELEOLOGISTS
DYSTELEOLOGY
DYSTHESIAS
DYSTHYMIAC
DYSTHYMIACS
DYSTHYMIAS
DYSTHYMICS
DYSTOPIANS
DYSTROPHIA
DYSTROPHIAS
DYSTROPHIC
DYSTROPHIES
DYSTROPHIN
DYSTROPHINS
DZIGGETAIS

D

E

EAGERNESSES
EAGLEHAWKS
EAGLESTONE
EAGLESTONES
EAGLEWOODS
EARBASHERS
EARBASHING
EARBASHINGS
EARLIERISE
EARLIERISED
EARLIERISES
EARLIERISING
EARLIERIZE
EARLIERIZED
EARLIERIZES
EARLIERIZING
EARLINESSES
EARLYWOODS
EARMARKING
EARNESTNESS
EARNESTNESSES
EARSPLITTING
EARTHBOUND
EARTHENWARE
EARTHENWARES
EARTHFALLS
EARTHFLAXES
EARTHINESS
EARTHINESSES
EARTHLIEST
EARTHLIGHT
EARTHLIGHTS
EARTHLINESS
EARTHLINESSES
EARTHLINGS
EARTHMOVER
EARTHMOVERS
EARTHMOVING
EARTHMOVINGS
EARTHQUAKE
EARTHQUAKED
EARTHQUAKES

EARTHQUAKING
EARTHRISES
EARTHSHAKER
EARTHSHAKERS
EARTHSHAKING
EARTHSHAKINGLY
EARTHSHATTERING
EARTHSHINE
EARTHSHINES
EARTHSTARS
EARTHWARDS
EARTHWAXES
EARTHWOLVES
EARTHWOMAN
EARTHWOMEN
EARTHWORKS
EARTHWORMS
EARWIGGIER
EARWIGGIEST
EARWIGGING
EARWIGGINGS
EARWITNESS
EARWITNESSES
EASEFULNESS
EASEFULNESSES
EASINESSES
EASSELGATE
EASSELWARD
EASTERLIES
EASTERLING
EASTERLINGS
EASTERMOST
EASTERNERS
EASTERNMOST
EASTWARDLY
EASYGOINGNESS
EASYGOINGNESSES
EAVESDRIPS
EAVESDROPPED
EAVESDROPPER
EAVESDROPPERS
EAVESDROPPING

EAVESDROPPINGS
EAVESDROPS
EAVESTROUGH
EAVESTROUGHS
EBIONISING
EBIONITISM
EBIONITISMS
EBIONIZING
EBOULEMENT
EBOULEMENTS
EBRACTEATE
EBRACTEOLATE
EBRILLADES
EBRIOSITIES
EBULLIENCE
EBULLIENCES
EBULLIENCIES
EBULLIENCY
EBULLIENTLY
EBULLIOMETER
EBULLIOMETERS
EBULLIOMETRIES
EBULLIOMETRY
EBULLIOSCOPE
EBULLIOSCOPES
EBULLIOSCOPIC
EBULLIOSCOPICAL
EBULLIOSCOPIES
EBULLIOSCOPY
EBULLITION
EBULLITIONS
EBURNATION
EBURNATIONS
EBURNIFICATION
EBURNIFICATIONS
ECARDINATE
ECBLASTESES
ECBLASTESIS
ECCALEOBION
ECCALEOBIONS
ECCENTRICAL
ECCENTRICALLY

ECCENTRICITIES
ECCENTRICITY
ECCENTRICS
ECCHYMOSED
ECCHYMOSES
ECCHYMOSIS
ECCHYMOTIC
ECCLESIARCH
ECCLESIARCHS
ECCLESIAST
ECCLESIASTIC
ECCLESIASTICAL
ECCLESIASTICISM
ECCLESIASTICS
ECCLESIASTS
ECCLESIOLATER
ECCLESIOLATERS
ECCLESIOLATRIES
ECCLESIOLATRY
ECCLESIOLOGICAL
ECCLESIOLOGIES
ECCLESIOLOGIST
ECCLESIOLOGISTS
ECCLESIOLOGY
ECCOPROTIC
ECCOPROTICS
ECCREMOCARPUS
ECCREMOCARPUSES
ECCRINOLOGIES
ECCRINOLOGY
ECDYSIASTS
ECHELONING
ECHEVERIAS
ECHIDNINES
ECHINACEAS
ECHINOCOCCI
ECHINOCOCCOSES
ECHINOCOCCOSIS
ECHINOCOCCUS
ECHINODERM
ECHINODERMAL
ECHINODERMATOUS

ECHINODERMS
ECHIUROIDS
ECHOCARDIOGRAM
ECHOCARDIOGRAMS
ECHOGRAPHIES
ECHOGRAPHS
ECHOGRAPHY
ECHOICALLY
ECHOLALIAS
ECHOLOCATION
ECHOLOCATIONS
ECHOPRAXES
ECHOPRAXIA
ECHOPRAXIAS
ECHOPRAXIS
ECHOVIRUSES
ECLAIRCISSEMENT
ECLAMPSIAS
ECLAMPSIES
ECLECTICALLY
ECLECTICISM
ECLECTICISMS
ECLIPSISES
ECLIPTICALLY
ECOCATASTROPHE
ECOCATASTROPHES
ECOCENTRIC
ECOCLIMATE
ECOCLIMATES
ECOFEMINISM
ECOFEMINISMS
ECOFEMINIST
ECOFEMINISTS
ECOFRIENDLIER
ECOFRIENDLIEST
ECOFRIENDLY
ECOLOGICAL
ECOLOGICALLY
ECOLOGISTS
ECOMMERCES
ECOMOVEMENT
ECOMOVEMENTS

ECOMUSEUMS	ECOTERRORISTS	ECTOPHYTES	EDITORIALISER	EDUTAINMENTS
ECONOBOXES	ECOTOURING	ECTOPHYTIC	EDITORIALISERS	EELGRASSES
ECONOMETER	ECOTOURISM	ECTOPICALLY	EDITORIALISES	EERINESSES
ECONOMETERS	ECOTOURISMS	ECTOPLASMIC	EDITORIALISING	EFFACEABLE
ECONOMETRIC	ECOTOURIST	ECTOPLASMS	EDITORIALIST	EFFACEMENT
ECONOMETRICAL	ECOTOURISTS	ECTOPLASTIC	EDITORIALISTS	EFFACEMENTS
ECONOMETRICALLY	ECOTOXICOLOGIES	ECTOPROCTS	EDITORIALIZE	EFFECTIBLE
ECONOMETRICIAN	ECOTOXICOLOGIST	ECTOSARCOUS	EDITORIALIZED	EFFECTIVELY
ECONOMETRICIANS	ECOTOXICOLOGY	ECTOTHERMIC	EDITORIALIZER	EFFECTIVENESS
ECONOMETRICS	ECOTYPICALLY	ECTOTHERMS	EDITORIALIZERS	EFFECTIVENESSES
ECONOMETRIST	ECPHONESES	ECTOTROPHIC	EDITORIALIZES	EFFECTIVES
ECONOMETRISTS	ECPHONESIS	ECTROPIONS	EDITORIALIZING	EFFECTIVITIES
ECONOMICAL	ECPHRACTIC	ECTROPIUMS	EDITORIALLY	EFFECTIVITY
ECONOMICALLY	ECPHRACTICS	ECTYPOGRAPHIES	EDITORIALS	EFFECTLESS
ECONOMISATION	ECRITOIRES	ECTYPOGRAPHY	EDITORSHIP	EFFECTUALITIES
ECONOMISATIONS	ECSTASISED	ECUMENICAL	EDITORSHIPS	EFFECTUALITY
ECONOMISED	ECSTASISES	ECUMENICALISM	EDITRESSES	EFFECTUALLY
ECONOMISER	ECSTASISING	ECUMENICALISMS	EDRIOPHTHALMIAN	EFFECTUALNESS
ECONOMISERS	ECSTASIZED	ECUMENICALLY	EDRIOPHTHALMIC	EFFECTUALNESSES
ECONOMISES	ECSTASIZES	ECUMENICISM	EDRIOPHTHALMOUS	EFFECTUATE
ECONOMISING	ECSTASIZING	ECUMENICISMS	EDUCABILITIES	EFFECTUATED
ECONOMISMS	ECSTASYING	ECUMENICIST	EDUCABILITY	EFFECTUATES
ECONOMISTIC	ECSTATICALLY	ECUMENICISTS	EDUCATABILITIES	EFFECTUATING
ECONOMISTS	ECTHLIPSES	ECUMENICITIES	EDUCATABILITY	EFFECTUATION
ECONOMIZATION	ECTHLIPSIS	ECUMENICITY	EDUCATABLE	EFFECTUATIONS
ECONOMIZATIONS	ECTOBLASTIC	ECUMENISMS	EDUCATEDNESS	EFFEMINACIES
ECONOMIZED	ECTOBLASTS	ECUMENISTS	EDUCATEDNESSES	EFFEMINACY
ECONOMIZER	ECTOCRINES	ECZEMATOUS	EDUCATIONAL	EFFEMINATE
ECONOMIZERS	ECTODERMAL	EDACIOUSLY	EDUCATIONALIST	EFFEMINATED
ECONOMIZES	ECTODERMIC	EDACIOUSNESS	EDUCATIONALISTS	EFFEMINATELY
ECONOMIZING	ECTOENZYME	EDACIOUSNESSES	EDUCATIONALLY	EFFEMINATENESS
ECOPHOBIAS	ECTOENZYMES	EDAPHICALLY	EDUCATIONESE	EFFEMINATES
ECOPHYSIOLOGIES	ECTOGENESES	EDAPHOLOGIES	EDUCATIONESES	EFFEMINATING
ECOPHYSIOLOGY	ECTOGENESIS	EDAPHOLOGY	EDUCATIONIST	EFFEMINISE
ECOREGIONS	ECTOGENETIC	EDELWEISSES	EDUCATIONISTS	EFFEMINISED
ECOSPECIES	ECTOGENICALLY	EDENTULATE	EDUCATIONS	EFFEMINISES
ECOSPECIFIC	ECTOGENIES	EDENTULOUS	EDUCEMENTS	EFFEMINISING
ECOSPHERES	ECTOGENOUS	EDGINESSES	EDULCORANT	EFFEMINIZE
ECOSSAISES	ECTOMORPHIC	EDIBILITIES	EDULCORATE	EFFEMINIZED
ECOSYSTEMS	ECTOMORPHIES	EDIBLENESS	EDULCORATED	EFFEMINIZES
ECOTARIANISM	ECTOMORPHS	EDIBLENESSES	EDULCORATES	EFFEMINIZING
ECOTARIANISMS	ECTOMORPHY	EDIFICATION	EDULCORATING	EFFERENCES
ECOTARIANS	ECTOMYCORRHIZA	EDIFICATIONS	EDULCORATION	EFFERENTLY
ECOTECTURE	ECTOMYCORRHIZAE	EDIFICATORY	EDULCORATIONS	EFFERVESCE
ECOTECTURES	ECTOMYCORRHIZAS	EDIFYINGLY	EDULCORATIVE	EFFERVESCED
ECOTERRORISM	ECTOPARASITE	EDITIONING	EDULCORATOR	EFFERVESCENCE
ECOTERRORISMS	ECTOPARASITES	EDITORIALISE	EDULCORATORS	EFFERVESCENCES
ECOTERRORIST	ECTOPARASITIC	EDITORIALISED	EDUTAINMENT	EFFERVESCENCIES

EFFERVESCENCY EFFULGENCES EIDOGRAPHS ELABORATENESS ELDERBERRY
EFFERVESCENT EFFULGENTLY EIGENFREQUENCY ELABORATENESSES ELDERCARES
EFFERVESCENTLY EFFUSIOMETER EIGENFUNCTION ELABORATES ELDERFLOWER
EFFERVESCES EFFUSIOMETERS EIGENFUNCTIONS ELABORATING ELDERFLOWERS
EFFERVESCIBLE EFFUSIVELY EIGENMODES ELABORATION ELDERLINESS
EFFERVESCING EFFUSIVENESS EIGENTONES ELABORATIONS ELDERLINESSES
EFFERVESCINGLY EFFUSIVENESSES EIGENVALUE ELABORATIVE ELDERSHIPS
EFFETENESS EGALITARIAN EIGENVALUES ELABORATOR ELECAMPANE
EFFETENESSES EGALITARIANISM EIGENVECTOR ELABORATORIES ELECAMPANES
EFFICACIES EGALITARIANISMS EIGENVECTORS ELABORATORS ELECTABILITIES
EFFICACIOUS EGALITARIANS EIGHTBALLS ELABORATORY ELECTABILITY
EFFICACIOUSLY EGAREMENTS EIGHTEENMO ELAEAGNUSES ELECTIONEER
EFFICACIOUSNESS EGGBEATERS EIGHTEENMOS ELAEOLITES ELECTIONEERED
EFFICACITIES EGGHEADEDNESS EIGHTEENTH ELAEOPTENE ELECTIONEERER
EFFICACITY EGGHEADEDNESSES EIGHTEENTHLY ELAEOPTENES ELECTIONEERERS
EFFICIENCE EGLANDULAR EIGHTEENTHS ELAIOSOMES ELECTIONEERING
EFFICIENCES EGLANDULOSE EIGHTFOILS ELASMOBRANCH ELECTIONEERINGS
EFFICIENCIES EGLANTINES EIGHTIETHS ELASMOBRANCHS ELECTIONEERS
EFFICIENCY EGOCENTRIC EIGHTPENCE ELASMOSAUR ELECTIVELY
EFFICIENTLY EGOCENTRICAL EIGHTPENCES ELASMOSAURS ELECTIVENESS
EFFICIENTS EGOCENTRICALLY EIGHTPENNY ELASTANCES ELECTIVENESSES
EFFIERCING EGOCENTRICITIES EIGHTSCORE ELASTICALLY ELECTIVITIES
EFFIGURATE EGOCENTRICITY EIGHTSCORES ELASTICATE ELECTIVITY
EFFIGURATION EGOCENTRICS EIGHTSOMES ELASTICATED ELECTORALLY
EFFIGURATIONS EGOCENTRISM EINSTEINIUM ELASTICATES ELECTORATE
EFFLEURAGE EGOCENTRISMS EINSTEINIUMS ELASTICATING ELECTORATES
EFFLEURAGED EGOISTICAL EIRENICALLY ELASTICATION ELECTORESS
EFFLEURAGES EGOISTICALLY EIRENICONS ELASTICATIONS ELECTORESSES
EFFLEURAGING EGOMANIACAL EISTEDDFOD ELASTICISE ELECTORIAL
EFFLORESCE EGOMANIACALLY EISTEDDFODAU ELASTICISED ELECTORIALLY
EFFLORESCED EGOMANIACS EISTEDDFODIC ELASTICISES ELECTORSHIP
EFFLORESCENCE EGOSURFING EISTEDDFODS ELASTICISING ELECTORSHIPS
EFFLORESCENCES EGOTHEISMS EJACULATED ELASTICITIES ELECTRESSES
EFFLORESCENT EGOTISTICAL EJACULATES ELASTICITY ELECTRICAL
EFFLORESCES EGOTISTICALLY EJACULATING ELASTICIZE ELECTRICALLY
EFFLORESCING EGREGIOUSLY EJACULATION ELASTICIZED ELECTRICALS
EFFLUENCES EGREGIOUSNESS EJACULATIONS ELASTICIZES ELECTRICIAN
EFFLUVIUMS EGREGIOUSNESSES EJACULATIVE ELASTICIZING ELECTRICIANS
EFFLUXIONS EGRESSIONS EJACULATOR ELASTICNESS ELECTRICITIES
EFFORTFULLY EGRESSIVES EJACULATORS ELASTICNESSES ELECTRICITY
EFFORTFULNESS EGURGITATE EJACULATORY ELASTOMERIC ELECTRIFIABLE
EFFORTFULNESSES EGURGITATED EJECTAMENTA ELASTOMERS ELECTRIFICATION
EFFORTLESS EGURGITATES EJECTIVELY ELATEDNESS ELECTRIFIED
EFFORTLESSLY EGURGITATING EJECTMENTS ELATEDNESSES ELECTRIFIER
EFFORTLESSNESS EICOSANOID EKISTICIAN ELATERITES ELECTRIFIERS
EFFRONTERIES EICOSANOIDS EKISTICIANS ELATERIUMS ELECTRIFIES
EFFRONTERY EIDERDOWNS ELABORATED ELBOWROOMS ELECTRIFYING
EFFULGENCE EIDETICALLY ELABORATELY ELDERBERRIES ELECTRIFYINGLY

ELECTRISATION	ELECTROFLUORS	ELECTROLYZERS	ELECTROPHORUS	ELECTROTYPISTS
ELECTRISATIONS	ELECTROFORM	ELECTROLYZES	ELECTROPHORUSES	ELECTROTYPY
ELECTRISED	ELECTROFORMED	ELECTROLYZING	ELECTROPLATE	ELECTROVALENCE
ELECTRISES	ELECTROFORMING	ELECTROMAGNET	ELECTROPLATED	ELECTROVALENCES
ELECTRISING	ELECTROFORMINGS	ELECTROMAGNETIC	ELECTROPLATER	ELECTROVALENCY
ELECTRIZATION	ELECTROFORMS	ELECTROMAGNETS	ELECTROPLATERS	ELECTROVALENT
ELECTRIZATIONS	ELECTROGEN	ELECTROMER	ELECTROPLATES	ELECTROVALENTLY
ELECTRIZED	ELECTROGENESES	ELECTROMERIC	ELECTROPLATING	ELECTROWEAK
ELECTRIZES	ELECTROGENESIS	ELECTROMERISM	ELECTROPLATINGS	ELECTROWINNING
ELECTRIZING	ELECTROGENIC	ELECTROMERISMS	ELECTROPOLAR	ELECTROWINNINGS
ELECTROACOUSTIC	ELECTROGENS	ELECTROMERS	ELECTROPOP	ELECTUARIES
ELECTROACTIVE	ELECTROGILDING	ELECTROMETER	ELECTROPOPS	ELEDOISINS
ELECTROACTIVITY	ELECTROGILDINGS	ELECTROMETERS	ELECTROPOSITIVE	ELEEMOSYNARY
ELECTROANALYSES	ELECTROGRAM	ELECTROMETRIC	ELECTROPUNCTURE	ELEGANCIES
ELECTROANALYSIS	ELECTROGRAMS	ELECTROMETRICAL	ELECTRORECEPTOR	ELEGIACALLY
ELECTROANALYTIC	ELECTROGRAPH	ELECTROMETRIES	ELECTRORHEOLOGY	ELEMENTALISM
ELECTROBIOLOGY	ELECTROGRAPHIC	ELECTROMETRY	ELECTROSCOPE	ELEMENTALISMS
ELECTROCAUTERY	ELECTROGRAPHIES	ELECTROMOTANCE	ELECTROSCOPES	ELEMENTALLY
ELECTROCEMENT	ELECTROGRAPHS	ELECTROMOTANCES	ELECTROSCOPIC	ELEMENTALS
ELECTROCEMENTS	ELECTROGRAPHY	ELECTROMOTIVE	ELECTROSHOCK	ELEMENTARILY
ELECTROCHEMIC	ELECTROING	ELECTROMOTOR	ELECTROSHOCKS	ELEMENTARINESS
ELECTROCHEMICAL	ELECTROJET	ELECTROMOTORS	ELECTROSONDE	ELEMENTARY
ELECTROCHEMIST	ELECTROJETS	ELECTROMYOGRAM	ELECTROSONDES	ELEOPTENES
ELECTROCHEMISTS	ELECTROKINETIC	ELECTROMYOGRAMS	ELECTROSTATIC	ELEPHANTIASES
ELECTROCLASH	ELECTROKINETICS	ELECTROMYOGRAPH	ELECTROSTATICS	ELEPHANTIASIC
ELECTROCLASHES	ELECTROLESS	ELECTRONEGATIVE	ELECTROSURGERY	ELEPHANTIASIS
ELECTROCULTURE	ELECTROLIER	ELECTRONIC	ELECTROSURGICAL	ELEPHANTINE
ELECTROCULTURES	ELECTROLIERS	ELECTRONICA	ELECTROTECHNICS	ELEPHANTOID
ELECTROCUTE	ELECTROLOGIES	ELECTRONICALLY	ELECTROTHERAPY	ELEPIDOTES
ELECTROCUTED	ELECTROLOGIST	ELECTRONICAS	ELECTROTHERMAL	ELEUTHERARCH
ELECTROCUTES	ELECTROLOGISTS	ELECTRONICS	ELECTROTHERMIC	ELEUTHERARCHS
ELECTROCUTING	ELECTROLOGY	ELECTRONVOLT	ELECTROTHERMICS	ELEUTHERIAN
ELECTROCUTION	ELECTROLYSATION	ELECTRONVOLTS	ELECTROTHERMIES	ELEUTHEROCOCCI
ELECTROCUTIONS	ELECTROLYSE	ELECTROOSMOSES	ELECTROTHERMY	ELEUTHEROCOCCUS
ELECTROCYTE	ELECTROLYSED	ELECTROOSMOSIS	ELECTROTINT	ELEUTHERODACTYL
ELECTROCYTES	ELECTROLYSER	ELECTROOSMOTIC	ELECTROTINTS	ELEUTHEROMANIA
ELECTRODEPOSIT	ELECTROLYSERS	ELECTROPHILE	ELECTROTONIC	ELEUTHEROMANIAS
ELECTRODEPOSITS	ELECTROLYSES	ELECTROPHILES	ELECTROTONUS	ELEUTHEROPHOBIA
ELECTRODERMAL	ELECTROLYSING	ELECTROPHILIC	ELECTROTONUSES	ELEUTHEROPHOBIC
ELECTRODES	ELECTROLYSIS	ELECTROPHONE	ELECTROTYPE	ELEVATIONAL
ELECTRODIALYSES	ELECTROLYTE	ELECTROPHONES	ELECTROTYPED	ELEVATIONS
ELECTRODIALYSIS	ELECTROLYTES	ELECTROPHONIC	ELECTROTYPER	ELEVENTHLY
ELECTRODIALYTIC	ELECTROLYTIC	ELECTROPHORESE	ELECTROTYPERS	ELFISHNESS
ELECTRODYNAMIC	ELECTROLYTICS	ELECTROPHORESED	ELECTROTYPES	ELFISHNESSES
ELECTRODYNAMICS	ELECTROLYZATION	ELECTROPHORESES	ELECTROTYPIC	ELICITABLE
ELECTROFISHING	ELECTROLYZE	ELECTROPHORESIS	ELECTROTYPIES	ELICITATION
ELECTROFISHINGS	ELECTROLYZED	ELECTROPHORETIC	ELECTROTYPING	ELICITATIONS
ELECTROFLUOR	ELECTROLYZER	ELECTROPHORI	ELECTROTYPIST	ELIGIBILITIES

ELIGIBILITY	ELUCIDATORY	EMARGINATES	EMBATTLING	EMBLEMISES
ELIMINABILITIES	ELUCUBRATE	EMARGINATING	EMBAYMENTS	EMBLEMISING
ELIMINABILITY	ELUCUBRATED	EMARGINATION	EMBEDDINGS	EMBLEMIZED
ELIMINABLE	ELUCUBRATES	EMARGINATIONS	EMBEDMENTS	EMBLEMIZES
ELIMINANTS	ELUCUBRATING	EMASCULATE	EMBELLISHED	EMBLEMIZING
ELIMINATED	ELUCUBRATION	EMASCULATED	EMBELLISHER	EMBLOOMING
ELIMINATES	ELUCUBRATIONS	EMASCULATES	EMBELLISHERS	EMBLOSSOMED
ELIMINATING	ELUSIVENESS	EMASCULATING	EMBELLISHES	EMBLOSSOMING
ELIMINATION	ELUSIVENESSES	EMASCULATION	EMBELLISHING	EMBLOSSOMS
ELIMINATIONS	ELUSORINESS	EMASCULATIONS	EMBELLISHINGLY	EMBODIMENT
ELIMINATIVE	ELUSORINESSES	EMASCULATIVE	EMBELLISHMENT	EMBODIMENTS
ELIMINATIVISM	ELUTRIATED	EMASCULATOR	EMBELLISHMENTS	EMBOITEMENT
ELIMINATIVISMS	ELUTRIATES	EMASCULATORS	EMBEZZLEMENT	EMBOITEMENTS
ELIMINATOR	ELUTRIATING	EMASCULATORY	EMBEZZLEMENTS	EMBOLDENED
ELIMINATORS	ELUTRIATION	EMBALLINGS	EMBEZZLERS	EMBOLDENER
ELIMINATORY	ELUTRIATIONS	EMBALMINGS	EMBEZZLING	EMBOLDENERS
ELLIPSOGRAPH	ELUTRIATOR	EMBALMMENT	EMBIGGENED	EMBOLDENING
ELLIPSOGRAPHS	ELUTRIATORS	EMBALMMENTS	EMBIGGENING	EMBOLECTOMIES
ELLIPSOIDAL	ELUVIATING	EMBANKMENT	EMBITTERED	EMBOLECTOMY
ELLIPSOIDS	ELUVIATION	EMBANKMENTS	EMBITTERER	EMBOLISATION
ELLIPTICAL	ELUVIATIONS	EMBARCADERO	EMBITTERERS	EMBOLISATIONS
ELLIPTICALLY	ELVISHNESS	EMBARCADEROS	EMBITTERING	EMBOLISING
ELLIPTICALNESS	ELVISHNESSES	EMBARCATION	EMBITTERINGS	EMBOLISMAL
ELLIPTICALS	ELYTRIFORM	EMBARCATIONS	EMBITTERMENT	EMBOLISMIC
ELLIPTICITIES	ELYTRIGEROUS	EMBARGOING	EMBITTERMENTS	EMBOLIZATION
ELLIPTICITY	EMACIATING	EMBARKATION	EMBLAZONED	EMBOLIZATIONS
ELOCUTIONARY	EMACIATION	EMBARKATIONS	EMBLAZONER	EMBOLIZING
ELOCUTIONIST	EMACIATIONS	EMBARKMENT	EMBLAZONERS	EMBONPOINT
ELOCUTIONISTS	EMALANGENI	EMBARKMENTS	EMBLAZONING	EMBONPOINTS
ELOCUTIONS	EMANATIONAL	EMBARQUEMENT	EMBLAZONMENT	EMBORDERED
ELOIGNMENT	EMANATIONS	EMBARQUEMENTS	EMBLAZONMENTS	EMBORDERING
ELOIGNMENTS	EMANATISTS	EMBARRASSABLE	EMBLAZONRIES	EMBOSCATAS
ELOINMENTS	EMANCIPATE	EMBARRASSED	EMBLAZONRY	EMBOSOMING
ELONGATING	EMANCIPATED	EMBARRASSEDLY	EMBLEMATIC	EMBOSSABLE
ELONGATION	EMANCIPATES	EMBARRASSES	EMBLEMATICAL	EMBOSSINGS
ELONGATIONS	EMANCIPATING	EMBARRASSING	EMBLEMATICALLY	EMBOSSMENT
ELOPEMENTS	EMANCIPATION	EMBARRASSINGLY	EMBLEMATISE	EMBOSSMENTS
ELOQUENCES	EMANCIPATIONIST	EMBARRASSMENT	EMBLEMATISED	EMBOTHRIUM
ELOQUENTLY	EMANCIPATIONS	EMBARRASSMENTS	EMBLEMATISES	EMBOTHRIUMS
ELSEWHITHER	EMANCIPATIVE	EMBARRINGS	EMBLEMATISING	EMBOUCHURE
ELUCIDATED	EMANCIPATOR	EMBASEMENT	EMBLEMATIST	EMBOUCHURES
ELUCIDATES	EMANCIPATORS	EMBASEMENTS	EMBLEMATISTS	EMBOUNDING
ELUCIDATING	EMANCIPATORY	EMBASSADES	EMBLEMATIZE	EMBOURGEOISE
ELUCIDATION	EMANCIPIST	EMBASSADOR	EMBLEMATIZED	EMBOURGEOISED
ELUCIDATIONS	EMANCIPISTS	EMBASSADORS	EMBLEMATIZES	EMBOURGEOISES
ELUCIDATIVE	EMARGINATE	EMBASSAGES	EMBLEMATIZING	EMBOURGEOISING
ELUCIDATOR	EMARGINATED	EMBATTLEMENT	EMBLEMENTS	EMBOWELING
ELUCIDATORS	EMARGINATELY	EMBATTLEMENTS	EMBLEMISED	EMBOWELLED

EMBOWELLING	EMBROILERS	EMIGRATIONISTS	EMOTIONALLY	EMPERORSHIP
EMBOWELMENT	EMBROILING	EMIGRATIONS	EMOTIONLESS	EMPERORSHIPS
EMBOWELMENTS	EMBROILMENT	EMIGRATORY	EMOTIONLESSLY	EMPHASISED
EMBOWERING	EMBROILMENTS	EMINENCIES	EMOTIONLESSNESS	EMPHASISES
EMBOWERMENT	EMBROWNING	EMINENTIAL	EMOTIVENESS	EMPHASISING
EMBOWERMENTS	EMBRUEMENT	EMISSARIES	EMOTIVENESSES	EMPHASIZED
EMBOWMENTS	EMBRUEMENTS	EMISSIVITIES	EMOTIVISMS	EMPHASIZES
EMBRACEABLE	EMBRYECTOMIES	EMISSIVITY	EMOTIVITIES	EMPHASIZING
EMBRACEMENT	EMBRYECTOMY	EMITTANCES	EMPACKETED	EMPHATICAL
EMBRACEMENTS	EMBRYOGENESES	EMMARBLING	EMPACKETING	EMPHATICALLY
EMBRACEORS	EMBRYOGENESIS	EMMENAGOGIC	EMPALEMENT	EMPHATICALNESS
EMBRACERIES	EMBRYOGENETIC	EMMENAGOGUE	EMPALEMENTS	EMPHRACTIC
EMBRACINGLY	EMBRYOGENIC	EMMENAGOGUES	EMPANELING	EMPHRACTICS
EMBRACINGNESS	EMBRYOGENIES	EMMENOLOGIES	EMPANELLED	EMPHYSEMAS
EMBRACINGNESSES	EMBRYOGENY	EMMENOLOGY	EMPANELLING	EMPHYSEMATOUS
EMBRAIDING	EMBRYOLOGIC	EMMETROPES	EMPANELMENT	EMPHYSEMIC
EMBRANCHMENT	EMBRYOLOGICAL	EMMETROPIA	EMPANELMENTS	EMPHYSEMICS
EMBRANCHMENTS	EMBRYOLOGICALLY	EMMETROPIAS	EMPANOPLIED	EMPHYTEUSES
EMBRANGLED	EMBRYOLOGIES	EMMETROPIC	EMPANOPLIES	EMPHYTEUSIS
EMBRANGLEMENT	EMBRYOLOGIST	EMOLLESCENCE	EMPANOPLYING	EMPHYTEUTIC
EMBRANGLEMENTS	EMBRYOLOGISTS	EMOLLESCENCES	EMPARADISE	EMPIECEMENT
EMBRANGLES	EMBRYOLOGY	EMOLLIATED	EMPARADISED	EMPIECEMENTS
EMBRANGLING	EMBRYONATE	EMOLLIATES	EMPARADISES	EMPIERCING
EMBRASURED	EMBRYONATED	EMOLLIATING	EMPARADISING	EMPIGHTING
EMBRASURES	EMBRYONICALLY	EMOLLIENCE	EMPARLAUNCE	EMPIRICALLY
EMBRAZURES	EMBRYOPHYTE	EMOLLIENCES	EMPARLAUNCES	EMPIRICALNESS
EMBREADING	EMBRYOPHYTES	EMOLLIENTS	EMPASSIONATE	EMPIRICALNESSES
EMBREATHED	EMBRYOTICALLY	EMOLLITION	EMPASSIONED	EMPIRICALS
EMBREATHES	EMBRYOTOMIES	EMOLLITIONS	EMPATHETIC	EMPIRICISM
EMBREATHING	EMBRYOTOMY	EMOLUMENTAL	EMPATHETICALLY	EMPIRICISMS
EMBRITTLED	EMBRYULCIA	EMOLUMENTARY	EMPATHICALLY	EMPIRICIST
EMBRITTLEMENT	EMBRYULCIAS	EMOLUMENTS	EMPATHISED	EMPIRICISTS
EMBRITTLEMENTS	EMENDATING	EMOTIONABLE	EMPATHISES	EMPIRICUTIC
EMBRITTLES	EMENDATION	EMOTIONALISE	EMPATHISING	EMPLACEMENT
EMBRITTLING	EMENDATIONS	EMOTIONALISED	EMPATHISTS	EMPLACEMENTS
EMBROCATED	EMENDATORS	EMOTIONALISES	EMPATHIZED	EMPLASTERED
EMBROCATES	EMENDATORY	EMOTIONALISING	EMPATHIZES	EMPLASTERING
EMBROCATING	EMERGENCES	EMOTIONALISM	EMPATHIZING	EMPLASTERS
EMBROCATION	EMERGENCIES	EMOTIONALISMS	EMPATRONED	EMPLASTICS
EMBROCATIONS	EMERGENTLY	EMOTIONALIST	EMPATRONING	EMPLASTRON
EMBROGLIOS	EMETICALLY	EMOTIONALISTIC	EMPEACHING	EMPLASTRONS
EMBROIDERED	EMETOPHOBIA	EMOTIONALISTS	EMPENNAGES	EMPLASTRUM
EMBROIDERER	EMETOPHOBIAS	EMOTIONALITIES	EMPEOPLING	EMPLASTRUMS
EMBROIDERERS	EMICATIONS	EMOTIONALITY	EMPERISHED	EMPLEACHED
EMBROIDERIES	EMIGRATING	EMOTIONALIZE	EMPERISHES	EMPLEACHES
EMBROIDERING	EMIGRATION	EMOTIONALIZED	EMPERISHING	EMPLEACHING
EMBROIDERS	EMIGRATIONAL	EMOTIONALIZES	EMPERISING	EMPLECTONS
EMBROIDERY	EMIGRATIONIST	EMOTIONALIZING	EMPERIZING	EMPLECTUMS

EMPLONGING	EMULSIFICATIONS	ENANTIOPATHIES	ENCEPHALINES	ENCHONDROMAS
EMPLOYABILITIES	EMULSIFIED	ENANTIOPATHY	ENCEPHALINS	ENCHONDROMATA
EMPLOYABILITY	EMULSIFIER	ENANTIOSES	ENCEPHALITIC	ENCHONDROMATOUS
EMPLOYABLE	EMULSIFIERS	ENANTIOSIS	ENCEPHALITIDES	ENCINCTURE
EMPLOYABLES	EMULSIFIES	ENANTIOSTYLIES	ENCEPHALITIS	ENCINCTURED
EMPLOYMENT	EMULSIFYING	ENANTIOSTYLOUS	ENCEPHALITISES	ENCINCTURES
EMPLOYMENTS	EMULSIONISE	ENANTIOSTYLY	ENCEPHALITOGEN	ENCINCTURING
EMPOISONED	EMULSIONISED	ENANTIOTROPIC	ENCEPHALITOGENS	ENCIPHERED
EMPOISONING	EMULSIONISES	ENANTIOTROPIES	ENCEPHALOCELE	ENCIPHERER
EMPOISONMENT	EMULSIONISING	ENANTIOTROPY	ENCEPHALOCELES	ENCIPHERERS
EMPOISONMENTS	EMULSIONIZE	ENARRATION	ENCEPHALOGRAM	ENCIPHERING
EMPOLDERED	EMULSIONIZED	ENARRATIONS	ENCEPHALOGRAMS	ENCIPHERMENT
EMPOLDERING	EMULSIONIZES	ENARTHRODIAL	ENCEPHALOGRAPH	ENCIPHERMENTS
EMPOVERISH	EMULSIONIZING	ENARTHROSES	ENCEPHALOGRAPHS	ENCIRCLEMENT
EMPOVERISHED	EMULSOIDAL	ENARTHROSIS	ENCEPHALOGRAPHY	ENCIRCLEMENTS
EMPOVERISHER	EMUNCTIONS	ENCAMPMENT	ENCEPHALOID	ENCIRCLING
EMPOVERISHERS	EMUNCTORIES	ENCAMPMENTS	ENCEPHALOMA	ENCLASPING
EMPOVERISHES	ENABLEMENT	ENCANTHISES	ENCEPHALOMAS	ENCLITICALLY
EMPOVERISHING	ENABLEMENTS	ENCAPSULATE	ENCEPHALOMATA	ENCLOISTER
EMPOVERISHMENT	ENACTMENTS	ENCAPSULATED	ENCEPHALON	ENCLOISTERED
EMPOVERISHMENTS	ENALAPRILS	ENCAPSULATES	ENCEPHALONS	ENCLOISTERING
EMPOWERING	ENAMELINGS	ENCAPSULATING	ENCEPHALOPATHIC	ENCLOISTERS
EMPOWERMENT	ENAMELISTS	ENCAPSULATION	ENCEPHALOPATHY	ENCLOSABLE
EMPOWERMENTS	ENAMELLERS	ENCAPSULATIONS	ENCEPHALOTOMIES	ENCLOSURES
EMPRESSEMENT	ENAMELLING	ENCAPSULED	ENCEPHALOTOMY	ENCLOTHING
EMPRESSEMENTS	ENAMELLINGS	ENCAPSULES	ENCEPHALOUS	ENCLOUDING
EMPTINESSES	ENAMELLIST	ENCAPSULING	ENCHAINING	ENCODEMENT
EMPURPLING	ENAMELLISTS	ENCARNALISE	ENCHAINMENT	ENCODEMENTS
EMPYREUMATA	ENAMELWARE	ENCARNALISED	ENCHAINMENTS	ENCOIGNURE
EMPYREUMATIC	ENAMELWARES	ENCARNALISES	ENCHANTERS	ENCOIGNURES
EMPYREUMATICAL	ENAMELWORK	ENCARNALISING	ENCHANTING	ENCOLOURED
EMPYREUMATISE	ENAMELWORKS	ENCARNALIZE	ENCHANTINGLY	ENCOLOURING
EMPYREUMATISED	ENAMORADOS	ENCARNALIZED	ENCHANTMENT	ENCOLPIONS
EMPYREUMATISES	ENAMOURING	ENCARNALIZES	ENCHANTMENTS	ENCOLPIUMS
EMPYREUMATISING	ENANTHEMAS	ENCARNALIZING	ENCHANTRESS	ENCOMENDERO
EMPYREUMATIZE	ENANTIODROMIA	ENCARPUSES	ENCHANTRESSES	ENCOMENDEROS
EMPYREUMATIZED	ENANTIODROMIAS	ENCASEMENT	ENCHARGING	ENCOMIASTIC
EMPYREUMATIZES	ENANTIODROMIC	ENCASEMENTS	ENCHARMING	ENCOMIASTICAL
EMPYREUMATIZING	ENANTIOMER	ENCASHABLE	ENCHEASONS	ENCOMIASTICALLY
EMULATIONS	ENANTIOMERIC	ENCASHMENT	ENCHEERING	ENCOMIASTS
EMULATIVELY	ENANTIOMERS	ENCASHMENTS	ENCHEIRIDIA	ENCOMIENDA
EMULATRESS	ENANTIOMORPH	ENCAUSTICALLY	ENCHEIRIDION	ENCOMIENDAS
EMULATRESSES	ENANTIOMORPHIC	ENCAUSTICS	ENCHEIRIDIONS	ENCOMPASSED
EMULGENCES	ENANTIOMORPHIES	ENCEPHALALGIA	ENCHILADAS	ENCOMPASSES
EMULOUSNESS	ENANTIOMORPHISM	ENCEPHALALGIAS	ENCHIRIDIA	ENCOMPASSING
EMULOUSNESSES	ENANTIOMORPHOUS	ENCEPHALIC	ENCHIRIDION	ENCOMPASSMENT
EMULSIFIABLE	ENANTIOMORPHS	ENCEPHALIN	ENCHIRIDIONS	ENCOMPASSMENTS
EMULSIFICATION	ENANTIOMORPHY	ENCEPHALINE	ENCHONDROMA	ENCOPRESES

ENCOPRESIS	ENCUMBERING	ENDEARINGLY	ENDOCRANIAL	ENDOMIXISES
ENCOPRETIC	ENCUMBERINGLY	ENDEARINGNESS	ENDOCRANIUM	ENDOMORPHIC
ENCOUNTERED	ENCUMBERMENT	ENDEARINGNESSES	ENDOCRINAL	ENDOMORPHIES
ENCOUNTERER	ENCUMBERMENTS	ENDEARMENT	ENDOCRINES	ENDOMORPHISM
ENCOUNTERERS	ENCUMBRANCE	ENDEARMENTS	ENDOCRINIC	ENDOMORPHISMS
ENCOUNTERING	ENCUMBRANCER	ENDEAVORED	ENDOCRINOLOGIC	ENDOMORPHS
ENCOUNTERS	ENCUMBRANCERS	ENDEAVORER	ENDOCRINOLOGIES	ENDOMORPHY
ENCOURAGED	ENCUMBRANCES	ENDEAVORERS	ENDOCRINOLOGIST	ENDOMYCORRHIZA
ENCOURAGEMENT	ENCURTAINED	ENDEAVORING	ENDOCRINOLOGY	ENDONEURIA
ENCOURAGEMENTS	ENCURTAINING	ENDEAVOURED	ENDOCRINOPATHIC	ENDONEURIUM
ENCOURAGER	ENCURTAINS	ENDEAVOURER	ENDOCRINOPATHY	ENDONUCLEASE
ENCOURAGERS	ENCYCLICAL	ENDEAVOURERS	ENDOCRINOUS	ENDONUCLEASES
ENCOURAGES	ENCYCLICALS	ENDEAVOURING	ENDOCRITIC	ENDONUCLEOLYTIC
ENCOURAGING	ENCYCLOPAEDIA	ENDEAVOURMENT	ENDOCUTICLE	ENDOPARASITE
ENCOURAGINGLY	ENCYCLOPAEDIAS	ENDEAVOURMENTS	ENDOCUTICLES	ENDOPARASITES
ENCOURAGINGS	ENCYCLOPAEDIC	ENDEAVOURS	ENDOCYTOSES	ENDOPARASITIC
ENCRADLING	ENCYCLOPAEDICAL	ENDECAGONS	ENDOCYTOSIS	ENDOPARASITISM
ENCREASING	ENCYCLOPAEDISM	ENDEIXISES	ENDOCYTOTIC	ENDOPARASITISMS
ENCRIMSONED	ENCYCLOPAEDISMS	ENDEMICALLY	ENDODERMAL	ENDOPEPTIDASE
ENCRIMSONING	ENCYCLOPAEDIST	ENDEMICITIES	ENDODERMIC	ENDOPEPTIDASES
ENCRIMSONS	ENCYCLOPAEDISTS	ENDEMICITY	ENDODERMIS	ENDOPEROXIDE
ENCRINITAL	ENCYCLOPEDIA	ENDEMIOLOGIES	ENDODERMISES	ENDOPEROXIDES
ENCRINITES	ENCYCLOPEDIAN	ENDEMIOLOGY	ENDODONTAL	ENDOPHAGIES
ENCRINITIC	ENCYCLOPEDIAS	ENDENIZENED	ENDODONTIC	ENDOPHAGOUS
ENCROACHED	ENCYCLOPEDIC	ENDENIZENING	ENDODONTICALLY	ENDOPHITIC
ENCROACHER	ENCYCLOPEDICAL	ENDENIZENS	ENDODONTICS	ENDOPHYLLOUS
ENCROACHERS	ENCYCLOPEDISM	ENDERGONIC	ENDODONTIST	ENDOPHYTES
ENCROACHES	ENCYCLOPEDISMS	ENDERMATIC	ENDODONTISTS	ENDOPHYTIC
ENCROACHING	ENCYCLOPEDIST	ENDERMICAL	ENDOENZYME	ENDOPHYTICALLY
ENCROACHINGLY	ENCYCLOPEDISTS	ENDLESSNESS	ENDOENZYMES	ENDOPLASMIC
ENCROACHMENT	ENCYSTATION	ENDLESSNESSES	ENDOGAMIES	ENDOPLASMS
ENCROACHMENTS	ENCYSTATIONS	ENDOBIOTIC	ENDOGAMOUS	ENDOPLASTIC
ENCRUSTATION	ENCYSTMENT	ENDOBLASTIC	ENDOGENIES	ENDOPLEURA
ENCRUSTATIONS	ENCYSTMENTS	ENDOBLASTS	ENDOGENOUS	ENDOPLEURAS
ENCRUSTING	ENDAMAGEMENT	ENDOCARDIA	ENDOGENOUSLY	ENDOPODITE
ENCRUSTMENT	ENDAMAGEMENTS	ENDOCARDIAC	ENDOLITHIC	ENDOPODITES
ENCRUSTMENTS	ENDAMAGING	ENDOCARDIAL	ENDOLYMPHATIC	ENDOPOLYPLOID
ENCRYPTING	ENDAMOEBAE	ENDOCARDITIC	ENDOLYMPHS	ENDOPOLYPLOIDY
ENCRYPTION	ENDAMOEBAS	ENDOCARDITIDES	ENDOMETRIA	ENDOPROCTS
ENCRYPTIONS	ENDAMOEBIC	ENDOCARDITIS	ENDOMETRIAL	ENDORADIOSONDE
ENCULTURATE	ENDANGERED	ENDOCARDITISES	ENDOMETRIOSES	ENDORADIOSONDES
ENCULTURATED	ENDANGERER	ENDOCARDIUM	ENDOMETRIOSIS	ENDORHIZAL
ENCULTURATES	ENDANGERERS	ENDOCARPAL	ENDOMETRITIS	ENDORPHINS
ENCULTURATING	ENDANGERING	ENDOCARPIC	ENDOMETRITISES	ENDORSABLE
ENCULTURATION	ENDANGERMENT	ENDOCENTRIC	ENDOMETRIUM	ENDORSATION
ENCULTURATIONS	ENDANGERMENTS	ENDOCHONDRAL	ENDOMITOSES	ENDORSATIONS
ENCULTURATIVE	ENDARCHIES	ENDOCHYLOUS	ENDOMITOSIS	ENDORSEMENT
ENCUMBERED	ENDARTERECTOMY	ENDOCRANIA	ENDOMITOTIC	ENDORSEMENTS

ENDOSCOPES

ENDOSCOPES	ENDOTHERMY	ENFIERCING	ENGENDRURE	ENGYSCOPES
ENDOSCOPIC	ENDOTOXINS	ENFILADING	ENGENDRURES	ENHANCEMENT
ENDOSCOPICALLY	ENDOTRACHEAL	ENFLESHING	ENGENDURES	ENHANCEMENTS
ENDOSCOPIES	ENDOTROPHIC	ENFLEURAGE	ENGINEERED	ENHARMONIC
ENDOSCOPIST	ENDOWMENTS	ENFLEURAGES	ENGINEERING	ENHARMONICAL
ENDOSCOPISTS	ENDPLAYING	ENFLOWERED	ENGINEERINGS	ENHARMONICALLY
ENDOSKELETAL	ENDUNGEONED	ENFLOWERING	ENGINERIES	ENHEARSING
ENDOSKELETON	ENDUNGEONING	ENFOLDMENT	ENGIRDLING	ENHEARTENED
ENDOSKELETONS	ENDUNGEONS	ENFOLDMENTS	ENGLACIALLY	ENHEARTENING
ENDOSMOMETER	ENDURABILITIES	ENFORCEABILITY	ENGLISHING	ENHEARTENS
ENDOSMOMETERS	ENDURABILITY	ENFORCEABLE	ENGLOOMING	ENHUNGERED
ENDOSMOMETRIC	ENDURABLENESS	ENFORCEDLY	ENGLUTTING	ENHUNGERING
ENDOSMOSES	ENDURABLENESSES	ENFORCEMENT	ENGORGEMENT	ENHYDRITES
ENDOSMOSIS	ENDURANCES	ENFORCEMENTS	ENGORGEMENTS	ENHYDRITIC
ENDOSMOTIC	ENDURINGLY	ENFORESTED	ENGOUEMENT	ENHYDROSES
ENDOSMOTICALLY	ENDURINGNESS	ENFORESTING	ENGOUEMENTS	ENHYPOSTASIA
ENDOSPERMIC	ENDURINGNESSES	ENFOULDERED	ENGOUMENTS	ENHYPOSTASIAS
ENDOSPERMS	ENERGETICAL	ENFRAMEMENT	ENGRAFFING	ENHYPOSTATIC
ENDOSPORES	ENERGETICALLY	ENFRAMEMENTS	ENGRAFTATION	ENHYPOSTATISE
ENDOSPOROUS	ENERGETICS	ENFRANCHISE	ENGRAFTATIONS	ENHYPOSTATISED
ENDOSTEALLY	ENERGISATION	ENFRANCHISED	ENGRAFTING	ENHYPOSTATISES
ENDOSTOSES	ENERGISATIONS	ENFRANCHISEMENT	ENGRAFTMENT	ENHYPOSTATISING
ENDOSTOSIS	ENERGISERS	ENFRANCHISER	ENGRAFTMENTS	ENHYPOSTATIZE
ENDOSTYLES	ENERGISING	ENFRANCHISERS	ENGRAILING	ENHYPOSTATIZED
ENDOSULFAN	ENERGIZATION	ENFRANCHISES	ENGRAILMENT	ENHYPOSTATIZES
ENDOSULFANS	ENERGIZATIONS	ENFRANCHISING	ENGRAILMENTS	ENHYPOSTATIZING
ENDOSYMBIONT	ENERGIZERS	ENFREEDOMED	ENGRAINEDLY	ENIGMATICAL
ENDOSYMBIONTS	ENERGIZING	ENFREEDOMING	ENGRAINEDNESS	ENIGMATICALLY
ENDOSYMBIOSES	ENERGUMENS	ENFREEDOMS	ENGRAINEDNESSES	ENIGMATISE
ENDOSYMBIOSIS	ENERVATING	ENFREEZING	ENGRAINERS	ENIGMATISED
ENDOSYMBIOTIC	ENERVATION	ENGAGEMENT	ENGRAINING	ENIGMATISES
ENDOTHECIA	ENERVATIONS	ENGAGEMENTS	ENGRAMMATIC	ENIGMATISING
ENDOTHECIAL	ENERVATIVE	ENGAGINGLY	ENGRASPING	ENIGMATIST
ENDOTHECIUM	ENERVATORS	ENGAGINGNESS	ENGRAVERIES	ENIGMATISTS
ENDOTHELIA	ENFACEMENT	ENGAGINGNESSES	ENGRAVINGS	ENIGMATIZE
ENDOTHELIAL	ENFACEMENTS	ENGARLANDED	ENGRENAGES	ENIGMATIZED
ENDOTHELIOID	ENFEEBLEMENT	ENGARLANDING	ENGRIEVING	ENIGMATIZES
ENDOTHELIOMA	ENFEEBLEMENTS	ENGARLANDS	ENGROOVING	ENIGMATIZING
ENDOTHELIOMAS	ENFEEBLERS	ENGARRISON	ENGROSSEDLY	ENIGMATOGRAPHY
ENDOTHELIOMATA	ENFEEBLING	ENGARRISONED	ENGROSSERS	ENJAMBEMENT
ENDOTHELIUM	ENFELONING	ENGARRISONING	ENGROSSING	ENJAMBEMENTS
ENDOTHERMAL	ENFEOFFING	ENGARRISONS	ENGROSSINGLY	ENJAMBMENT
ENDOTHERMIC	ENFEOFFMENT	ENGENDERED	ENGROSSMENT	ENJAMBMENTS
ENDOTHERMICALLY	ENFEOFFMENTS	ENGENDERER	ENGROSSMENTS	ENJOINDERS
ENDOTHERMIES	ENFESTERED	ENGENDERERS	ENGUARDING	ENJOINMENT
ENDOTHERMISM	ENFETTERED	ENGENDERING	ENGULFMENT	ENJOINMENTS
ENDOTHERMISMS	ENFETTERING	ENGENDERMENT	ENGULFMENTS	ENJOYABLENESS
ENDOTHERMS	ENFEVERING	ENGENDERMENTS	ENGULPHING	ENJOYABLENESSES

ENJOYMENTS	ENNEATHLONS	ENSANGUINED	ENSORCELLMENTS	ENTEROCENTESES
ENKEPHALIN	ENNOBLEMENT	ENSANGUINES	ENSORCELLS	ENTEROCENTESIS
ENKEPHALINE	ENNOBLEMENTS	ENSOULMENT	ENSOULMENT	ENTEROCOCCAL
ENKEPHALINES	ENOKIDAKES	ENSCHEDULE	ENSOULMENTS	ENTEROCOCCI
ENKEPHALINS	ENOKITAKES	ENSCHEDULED	ENSPHERING	ENTEROCOCCUS
ENKERNELLED	ENOLOGICAL	ENSCHEDULES	ENSTAMPING	ENTEROCOEL
ENKERNELLING	ENOLOGISTS	ENSCHEDULING	ENSTATITES	ENTEROCOELE
ENKINDLERS	ENORMITIES	ENSCONCING	ENSTEEPING	ENTEROCOELES
ENKINDLING	ENORMOUSLY	ENSCROLLED	ENSTRUCTURED	ENTEROCOELIC
ENLACEMENT	ENORMOUSNESS	ENSCROLLING	ENSWATHEMENT	ENTEROCOELOUS
ENLACEMENTS	ENORMOUSNESSES	ENSEPULCHRE	ENSWATHEMENTS	ENTEROCOELS
ENLARGEABLE	ENOUNCEMENT	ENSEPULCHRED	ENSWATHING	ENTEROCOLITIDES
ENLARGEDLY	ENOUNCEMENTS	ENSEPULCHRES	ENSWEEPING	ENTEROCOLITIS
ENLARGEDNESS	ENPHYTOTIC	ENSEPULCHRING	ENTABLATURE	ENTEROCOLITISES
ENLARGEDNESSES	ENQUEUEING	ENSERFMENT	ENTABLATURES	ENTEROGASTRONE
ENLARGEMENT	ENQUIRATION	ENSERFMENTS	ENTABLEMENT	ENTEROGASTRONES
ENLARGEMENTS	ENQUIRATIONS	ENSHEATHED	ENTABLEMENTS	ENTEROHEPATITIS
ENLARGENED	ENRAGEMENT	ENSHEATHES	ENTAILMENT	ENTEROKINASE
ENLARGENING	ENRAGEMENTS	ENSHEATHING	ENTAILMENTS	ENTEROKINASES
ENLEVEMENT	ENRANCKLED	ENSHELLING	ENTAMOEBAE	ENTEROLITH
ENLEVEMENTS	ENRANCKLES	ENSHELTERED	ENTAMOEBAS	ENTEROLITHS
ENLIGHTENED	ENRANCKLING	ENSHELTERING	ENTANGLEMENT	ENTEROPATHIES
ENLIGHTENER	ENRAPTURED	ENSHELTERS	ENTANGLEMENTS	ENTEROPATHY
ENLIGHTENERS	ENRAPTURES	ENSHIELDED	ENTANGLERS	ENTEROPNEUST
ENLIGHTENING	ENRAPTURING	ENSHIELDING	ENTANGLING	ENTEROPNEUSTAL
ENLIGHTENMENT	ENRAUNGING	ENSHRINEES	ENTELECHIES	ENTEROPNEUSTS
ENLIGHTENMENTS	ENRAVISHED	ENSHRINEMENT	ENTELLUSES	ENTEROPTOSES
ENLIGHTENS	ENRAVISHES	ENSHRINEMENTS	ENTENDERED	ENTEROPTOSIS
ENLIGHTING	ENRAVISHING	ENSHRINING	ENTENDERING	ENTEROSTOMAL
ENLISTMENT	ENREGIMENT	ENSHROUDED	ENTERCHAUNGE	ENTEROSTOMIES
ENLISTMENTS	ENREGIMENTED	ENSHROUDING	ENTERCHAUNGED	ENTEROSTOMY
ENLIVENERS	ENREGIMENTING	ENSIGNCIES	ENTERCHAUNGES	ENTEROTOMIES
ENLIVENING	ENREGIMENTS	ENSIGNSHIP	ENTERCHAUNGING	ENTEROTOMY
ENLIVENMENT	ENREGISTER	ENSIGNSHIPS	ENTERDEALE	ENTEROTOXIN
ENLIVENMENTS	ENREGISTERED	ENSILABILITIES	ENTERDEALED	ENTEROTOXINS
ENLUMINING	ENREGISTERING	ENSILABILITY	ENTERDEALES	ENTEROVIRAL
ENMESHMENT	ENREGISTERS	ENSILAGEING	ENTERDEALING	ENTEROVIRUS
ENMESHMENTS	ENRHEUMING	ENSILAGING	ENTERECTOMIES	ENTEROVIRUSES
ENNEAGONAL	ENRICHMENT	ENSLAVEMENT	ENTERECTOMY	ENTERPRISE
ENNEAGRAMS	ENRICHMENTS	ENSLAVEMENTS	ENTERITIDES	ENTERPRISED
ENNEAHEDRA	ENROLLMENT	ENSNAREMENT	ENTERITISES	ENTERPRISER
ENNEAHEDRAL	ENROLLMENTS	ENSNAREMENTS	ENTEROBACTERIA	ENTERPRISERS
ENNEAHEDRON	ENROLMENTS	ENSNARLING	ENTEROBACTERIAL	ENTERPRISES
ENNEAHEDRONS	ENROUGHING	ENSORCELED	ENTEROBACTERIUM	ENTERPRISING
ENNEANDRIAN	ENROUNDING	ENSORCELING	ENTEROBIASES	ENTERPRISINGLY
ENNEANDROUS	ENSAMPLING	ENSORCELLED	ENTEROBIASIS	ENTERTAINED
ENNEASTYLE	ENSANGUINATED	ENSORCELLING	ENTEROCELE	ENTERTAINER
ENNEATHLON	ENSANGUINE	ENSORCELLMENT	ENTEROCELES	ENTERTAINERS

ENTERTAINING	ENTICINGLY	ENTOPLASTRA	ENTRENCHMENT	ENVASSALLING
ENTERTAININGLY	ENTICINGNESS	ENTOPLASTRAL	ENTRENCHMENTS	ENVAULTING
ENTERTAININGS	ENTICINGNESSES	ENTOPLASTRON	ENTREPRENEUR	ENVEIGLING
ENTERTAINMENT	ENTIRENESS	ENTOPROCTS	ENTREPRENEURIAL	ENVELOPERS
ENTERTAINMENTS	ENTIRENESSES	ENTOURAGES	ENTREPRENEURS	ENVELOPING
ENTERTAINS	ENTIRETIES	ENTRAILING	ENTREPRENEUSE	ENVELOPMENT
ENTERTAKEN	ENTITATIVE	ENTRAINEMENT	ENTREPRENEUSES	ENVELOPMENTS
ENTERTAKES	ENTITLEMENT	ENTRAINEMENTS	ENTROPICALLY	ENVENOMING
ENTERTAKING	ENTITLEMENTS	ENTRAINERS	ENTROPIONS	ENVENOMISATION
ENTERTISSUED	ENTOBLASTIC	ENTRAINING	ENTROPIUMS	ENVENOMISATIONS
ENTHALPIES	ENTOBLASTS	ENTRAINMENT	ENTRUSTING	ENVENOMIZATION
ENTHRALDOM	ENTODERMAL	ENTRAINMENTS	ENTRUSTMENT	ENVENOMIZATIONS
ENTHRALDOMS	ENTODERMIC	ENTRAMMELED	ENTRUSTMENTS	ENVERMEILED
ENTHRALLED	ENTOILMENT	ENTRAMMELING	ENTWINEMENT	ENVERMEILING
ENTHRALLER	ENTOILMENTS	ENTRAMMELLED	ENTWINEMENTS	ENVERMEILS
ENTHRALLERS	ENTOMBMENT	ENTRAMMELLING	ENTWISTING	ENVIABLENESS
ENTHRALLING	ENTOMBMENTS	ENTRAMMELS	ENUCLEATED	ENVIABLENESSES
ENTHRALLMENT	ENTOMOFAUNA	ENTRANCEMENT	ENUCLEATES	ENVIOUSNESS
ENTHRALLMENTS	ENTOMOFAUNAE	ENTRANCEMENTS	ENUCLEATING	ENVIOUSNESSES
ENTHRALMENT	ENTOMOFAUNAS	ENTRANCEWAY	ENUCLEATION	ENVIRONICS
ENTHRALMENTS	ENTOMOLOGIC	ENTRANCEWAYS	ENUCLEATIONS	ENVIRONING
ENTHRONEMENT	ENTOMOLOGICAL	ENTRANCING	ENUMERABILITIES	ENVIRONMENT
ENTHRONEMENTS	ENTOMOLOGICALLY	ENTRANCINGLY	ENUMERABILITY	ENVIRONMENTAL
ENTHRONING	ENTOMOLOGIES	ENTRAPMENT	ENUMERABLE	ENVIRONMENTALLY
ENTHRONISATION	ENTOMOLOGISE	ENTRAPMENTS	ENUMERATED	ENVIRONMENTS
ENTHRONISATIONS	ENTOMOLOGISED	ENTRAPPERS	ENUMERATES	ENVISAGEMENT
ENTHRONISE	ENTOMOLOGISES	ENTRAPPING	ENUMERATING	ENVISAGEMENTS
ENTHRONISED	ENTOMOLOGISING	ENTREASURE	ENUMERATION	ENVISAGING
ENTHRONISES	ENTOMOLOGIST	ENTREASURED	ENUMERATIONS	ENVISIONED
ENTHRONISING	ENTOMOLOGISTS	ENTREASURES	ENUMERATIVE	ENVISIONING
ENTHRONIZATION	ENTOMOLOGIZE	ENTREASURING	ENUMERATOR	ENVOYSHIPS
ENTHRONIZATIONS	ENTOMOLOGIZED	ENTREATABLE	ENUMERATORS	ENWALLOWED
ENTHRONIZE	ENTOMOLOGIZES	ENTREATIES	ENUNCIABLE	ENWALLOWING
ENTHRONIZED	ENTOMOLOGIZING	ENTREATING	ENUNCIATED	ENWHEELING
ENTHRONIZES	ENTOMOLOGY	ENTREATINGLY	ENUNCIATES	ENWRAPMENT
ENTHRONIZING	ENTOMOPHAGIES	ENTREATINGS	ENUNCIATING	ENWRAPMENTS
ENTHUSIASM	ENTOMOPHAGOUS	ENTREATIVE	ENUNCIATION	ENWRAPPING
ENTHUSIASMS	ENTOMOPHAGY	ENTREATMENT	ENUNCIATIONS	ENWRAPPINGS
ENTHUSIAST	ENTOMOPHILIES	ENTREATMENTS	ENUNCIATIVE	ENWREATHED
ENTHUSIASTIC	ENTOMOPHILOUS	ENTRECHATS	ENUNCIATIVELY	ENWREATHES
ENTHUSIASTICAL	ENTOMOPHILY	ENTRECOTES	ENUNCIATOR	ENWREATHING
ENTHUSIASTS	ENTOMOSTRACAN	ENTREMESSE	ENUNCIATORS	ENZOOTICALLY
ENTHYMEMATIC	ENTOMOSTRACANS	ENTREMESSES	ENUNCIATORY	ENZYMATICALLY
ENTHYMEMATICAL	ENTOMOSTRACOUS	ENTRENCHED	ENUREDNESS	ENZYMICALLY
ENTHYMEMES	ENTOPHYTAL	ENTRENCHER	ENUREDNESSES	ENZYMOLOGICAL
ENTICEABLE	ENTOPHYTES	ENTRENCHERS	ENUREMENTS	ENZYMOLOGIES
ENTICEMENT	ENTOPHYTIC	ENTRENCHES	ENURESISES	ENZYMOLOGIST
ENTICEMENTS	ENTOPHYTOUS	ENTRENCHING	ENVASSALLED	ENZYMOLOGISTS

ENZYMOLOGY	EPEXEGETIC	EPICRANIUM	EPIDOSITES	EPIGRAPHER
ENZYMOLYSES	EPEXEGETICAL	EPICRANIUMS	EPIDOTISATION	EPIGRAPHERS
ENZYMOLYSIS	EPEXEGETICALLY	EPICUREANISM	EPIDOTISATIONS	EPIGRAPHIC
ENZYMOLYTIC	EPHEBOPHILE	EPICUREANISMS	EPIDOTISED	EPIGRAPHICAL
EOHIPPUSES	EPHEBOPHILES	EPICUREANS	EPIDOTIZATION	EPIGRAPHICALLY
EOSINOPHIL	EPHEBOPHILIA	EPICURISED	EPIDOTIZATIONS	EPIGRAPHIES
EOSINOPHILE	EPHEBOPHILIAS	EPICURISES	EPIDOTIZED	EPIGRAPHING
EOSINOPHILES	EPHEDRINES	EPICURISING	EPIGASTRIA	EPIGRAPHIST
EOSINOPHILIA	EPHEMERALITIES	EPICURISMS	EPIGASTRIAL	EPIGRAPHISTS
EOSINOPHILIAS	EPHEMERALITY	EPICURIZED	EPIGASTRIC	EPILATIONS
EOSINOPHILIC	EPHEMERALLY	EPICURIZES	EPIGASTRIUM	EPILEPSIES
EOSINOPHILOUS	EPHEMERALNESS	EPICURIZING	EPIGENESES	EPILEPTICAL
EOSINOPHILS	EPHEMERALNESSES	EPICUTICLE	EPIGENESIS	EPILEPTICALLY
EPAGOMENAL	EPHEMERALS	EPICUTICLES	EPIGENESIST	EPILEPTICS
EPANADIPLOSES	EPHEMERIDES	EPICUTICULAR	EPIGENESISTS	EPILEPTIFORM
EPANADIPLOSIS	EPHEMERIDIAN	EPICYCLICAL	EPIGENETIC	EPILEPTOGENIC
EPANALEPSES	EPHEMERIDS	EPICYCLOID	EPIGENETICALLY	EPILEPTOID
EPANALEPSIS	EPHEMERIST	EPICYCLOIDAL	EPIGENETICIST	EPILIMNION
EPANALEPTIC	EPHEMERISTS	EPICYCLOIDS	EPIGENETICISTS	EPILIMNIONS
EPANAPHORA	EPHEMERONS	EPIDEICTIC	EPIGENETICS	EPILOBIUMS
EPANAPHORAL	EPHEMEROPTERAN	EPIDEICTICAL	EPIGENISTS	EPILOGISED
EPANAPHORAS	EPHEMEROPTERANS	EPIDEMICAL	EPIGENOMES	EPILOGISES
EPANODOSES	EPHEMEROUS	EPIDEMICALLY	EPIGLOTTAL	EPILOGISING
EPANORTHOSES	EPHORALTIES	EPIDEMICITIES	EPIGLOTTIC	EPILOGISTIC
EPANORTHOSIS	EPIBLASTIC	EPIDEMICITY	EPIGLOTTIDES	EPILOGISTS
EPANORTHOTIC	EPICALYCES	EPIDEMIOLOGIC	EPIGLOTTIS	EPILOGIZED
EPARCHATES	EPICALYXES	EPIDEMIOLOGICAL	EPIGLOTTISES	EPILOGIZES
EPAULEMENT	EPICANTHIC	EPIDEMIOLOGIES	EPIGNATHOUS	EPILOGIZING
EPAULEMENTS	EPICANTHUS	EPIDEMIOLOGIST	EPIGONISMS	EPILOGUING
EPAULETTED	EPICARDIAC	EPIDEMIOLOGISTS	EPIGRAMMATIC	EPILOGUISE
EPAULETTES	EPICARDIAL	EPIDEMIOLOGY	EPIGRAMMATICAL	EPILOGUISED
EPEIROGENESES	EPICARDIUM	EPIDENDRONE	EPIGRAMMATISE	EPILOGUISES
EPEIROGENESIS	EPICARDIUMS	EPIDENDRONES	EPIGRAMMATISED	EPILOGUISING
EPEIROGENETIC	EPICEDIANS	EPIDENDRUM	EPIGRAMMATISER	EPILOGUIZE
EPEIROGENIC	EPICENISMS	EPIDENDRUMS	EPIGRAMMATISERS	EPILOGUIZED
EPEIROGENICALLY	EPICENTERS	EPIDERMISES	EPIGRAMMATISES	EPILOGUIZES
EPEIROGENIES	EPICENTRAL	EPIDERMOID	EPIGRAMMATISING	EPILOGUIZING
EPEIROGENY	EPICENTRES	EPIDERMOLYSES	EPIGRAMMATISM	EPIMELETIC
EPENCEPHALA	EPICENTRUM	EPIDERMOLYSIS	EPIGRAMMATISMS	EPIMERASES
EPENCEPHALIC	EPICHEIREMA	EPIDIASCOPE	EPIGRAMMATIST	EPIMERISED
EPENCEPHALON	EPICHEIREMAS	EPIDIASCOPES	EPIGRAMMATISTS	EPIMERISES
EPENCEPHALONS	EPICHEIREMATA	EPIDIDYMAL	EPIGRAMMATIZE	EPIMERISING
EPENTHESES	EPICHLOROHYDRIN	EPIDIDYMIDES	EPIGRAMMATIZED	EPIMERISMS
EPENTHESIS	EPICONDYLE	EPIDIDYMIS	EPIGRAMMATIZER	EPIMERIZED
EPENTHETIC	EPICONDYLES	EPIDIDYMITIS	EPIGRAMMATIZERS	EPIMERIZES
EPEOLATRIES	EPICONDYLITIS	EPIDIDYMITISES	EPIGRAMMATIZES	EPIMERIZING
EPEXEGESES	EPICONDYLITISES	EPIDIORITE	EPIGRAMMATIZING	EPIMORPHIC
EPEXEGESIS	EPICONTINENTAL	EPIDIORITES	EPIGRAPHED	EPIMORPHOSES

EPIMORPHOSIS

EPIMORPHOSIS	EPISCOPALIANISM	EPISTOLERS	EPITHELIUM	EPOXIDISES
EPINASTICALLY	EPISCOPALIANS	EPISTOLETS	EPITHELIUMS	EPOXIDISING
EPINASTIES	EPISCOPALISM	EPISTOLICAL	EPITHELIZATION	EPOXIDIZED
EPINEPHRIN	EPISCOPALISMS	EPISTOLISE	EPITHELIZATIONS	EPOXIDIZES
EPINEPHRINE	EPISCOPALLY	EPISTOLISED	EPITHELIZE	EPOXIDIZING
EPINEPHRINES	EPISCOPANT	EPISTOLISES	EPITHELIZED	EPROUVETTE
EPINEPHRINS	EPISCOPANTS	EPISTOLISING	EPITHELIZES	EPROUVETTES
EPINEURIAL	EPISCOPATE	EPISTOLIST	EPITHELIZING	EPULATIONS
EPINEURIUM	EPISCOPATED	EPISTOLISTS	EPITHEMATA	EPURATIONS
EPINEURIUMS	EPISCOPATES	EPISTOLIZE	EPITHERMAL	EQUABILITIES
EPINICIONS	EPISCOPATING	EPISTOLIZED	EPITHETICAL	EQUABILITY
EPINIKIANS	EPISCOPIES	EPISTOLIZES	EPITHETICALLY	EQUABLENESS
EPINIKIONS	EPISCOPISE	EPISTOLIZING	EPITHETING	EQUABLENESSES
EPIPELAGIC	EPISCOPISED	EPISTOLOGRAPHY	EPITHETONS	EQUALISATION
EPIPETALOUS	EPISCOPISES	EPISTROPHE	EPITHYMETIC	EQUALISATIONS
EPIPHANIES	EPISCOPISING	EPISTROPHES	EPITOMICAL	EQUALISERS
EPIPHANOUS	EPISCOPIZE	EPITAPHERS	EPITOMISATION	EQUALISING
EPIPHENOMENA	EPISCOPIZED	EPITAPHIAL	EPITOMISATIONS	EQUALITARIAN
EPIPHENOMENAL	EPISCOPIZES	EPITAPHIAN	EPITOMISED	EQUALITARIANISM
EPIPHENOMENALLY	EPISCOPIZING	EPITAPHING	EPITOMISER	EQUALITARIANS
EPIPHENOMENON	EPISEMATIC	EPITAPHIST	EPITOMISERS	EQUALITIES
EPIPHONEMA	EPISEPALOUS	EPITAPHISTS	EPITOMISES	EQUALIZATION
EPIPHONEMAS	EPISIOTOMIES	EPITAXIALLY	EPITOMISING	EQUALIZATIONS
EPIPHRAGMS	EPISIOTOMY	EPITHALAMIA	EPITOMISTS	EQUALIZERS
EPIPHYLLOUS	EPISODICAL	EPITHALAMIC	EPITOMIZATION	EQUALIZING
EPIPHYSEAL	EPISODICALLY	EPITHALAMION	EPITOMIZATIONS	EQUALNESSES
EPIPHYSIAL	EPISOMALLY	EPITHALAMIUM	EPITOMIZED	EQUANIMITIES
EPIPHYTICAL	EPISPASTIC	EPITHALAMIUMS	EPITOMIZER	EQUANIMITY
EPIPHYTICALLY	EPISPASTICS	EPITHELIAL	EPITOMIZERS	EQUANIMOUS
EPIPHYTISM	EPISTASIES	EPITHELIALISE	EPITOMIZES	EQUANIMOUSLY
EPIPHYTISMS	EPISTAXISES	EPITHELIALISED	EPITOMIZING	EQUATABILITIES
EPIPHYTOLOGIES	EPISTEMICALLY	EPITHELIALISES	EPITRACHELION	EQUATABILITY
EPIPHYTOLOGY	EPISTEMICS	EPITHELIALISING	EPITRACHELIONS	EQUATIONAL
EPIPHYTOTIC	EPISTEMOLOGICAL	EPITHELIALIZE	EPITROCHOID	EQUATIONALLY
EPIPHYTOTICS	EPISTEMOLOGIES	EPITHELIALIZED	EPITROCHOIDS	EQUATORIAL
EPIPLASTRA	EPISTEMOLOGIST	EPITHELIALIZES	EPIZEUXISES	EQUATORIALLY
EPIPLASTRAL	EPISTEMOLOGISTS	EPITHELIALIZING	EPIZOOTICALLY	EQUATORIALS
EPIPLASTRON	EPISTEMOLOGY	EPITHELIOID	EPIZOOTICS	EQUATORWARD
EPIPOLISMS	EPISTERNAL	EPITHELIOMA	EPIZOOTIES	EQUESTRIAN
EPIROGENETIC	EPISTERNUM	EPITHELIOMAS	EPIZOOTIOLOGIC	EQUESTRIANISM
EPIROGENIC	EPISTERNUMS	EPITHELIOMATA	EPIZOOTIOLOGIES	EQUESTRIANISMS
EPIROGENIES	EPISTILBITE	EPITHELIOMATOUS	EPIZOOTIOLOGY	EQUESTRIANS
EPIRRHEMAS	EPISTILBITES	EPITHELISATION	EPONYCHIUM	EQUESTRIENNE
EPIRRHEMATA	EPISTOLARIAN	EPITHELISATIONS	EPONYCHIUMS	EQUESTRIENNES
EPIRRHEMATIC	EPISTOLARIANS	EPITHELISE	EPONYMOUSLY	EQUIANGULAR
EPISCOPACIES	EPISTOLARIES	EPITHELISED	EPOXIDATION	EQUIANGULARITY
EPISCOPACY	EPISTOLARY	EPITHELISES	EPOXIDATIONS	EQUIBALANCE
EPISCOPALIAN	EPISTOLATORY	EPITHELISING	EPOXIDISED	EQUIBALANCED

EQUIBALANCES	EQUIPMENTS	EQUIVOCATED	ERGATOMORPH	EROTICISES
EQUIBALANCING	EQUIPOISED	EQUIVOCATES	ERGATOMORPHIC	EROTICISING
EQUICALORIC	EQUIPOISES	EQUIVOCATING	ERGATOMORPHS	EROTICISMS
EQUIDIFFERENT	EQUIPOISING	EQUIVOCATINGLY	ERGODICITIES	EROTICISTS
EQUIDISTANCE	EQUIPOLLENCE	EQUIVOCATION	ERGODICITY	EROTICIZATION
EQUIDISTANCES	EQUIPOLLENCES	EQUIVOCATIONS	ERGOGRAPHS	EROTICIZATIONS
EQUIDISTANT	EQUIPOLLENCIES	EQUIVOCATOR	ERGOMANIAC	EROTICIZED
EQUIDISTANTLY	EQUIPOLLENCY	EQUIVOCATORS	ERGOMANIACS	EROTICIZES
EQUIFINALLY	EQUIPOLLENT	EQUIVOCATORY	ERGOMANIAS	EROTICIZING
EQUILATERAL	EQUIPOLLENTLY	EQUIVOQUES	ERGOMETERS	EROTISATION
EQUILATERALLY	EQUIPOLLENTS	ERADIATING	ERGOMETRIC	EROTISATIONS
EQUILATERALS	EQUIPONDERANCE	ERADIATION	ERGOMETRIES	EROTIZATION
EQUILIBRANT	EQUIPONDERANCES	ERADIATIONS	ERGONOMICALLY	EROTIZATIONS
EQUILIBRANTS	EQUIPONDERANCY	ERADICABLE	ERGONOMICS	EROTOGENIC
EQUILIBRATE	EQUIPONDERANT	ERADICABLY	ERGONOMIST	EROTOGENOUS
EQUILIBRATED	EQUIPONDERATE	ERADICANTS	ERGONOMISTS	EROTOLOGICAL
EQUILIBRATES	EQUIPONDERATED	ERADICATED	ERGONOVINE	EROTOLOGIES
EQUILIBRATING	EQUIPONDERATES	ERADICATES	ERGONOVINES	EROTOLOGIST
EQUILIBRATION	EQUIPONDERATING	ERADICATING	ERGOPHOBIA	EROTOLOGISTS
EQUILIBRATIONS	EQUIPOTENT	ERADICATION	ERGOPHOBIAS	EROTOMANIA
EQUILIBRATOR	EQUIPOTENTIAL	ERADICATIONS	ERGOSTEROL	EROTOMANIAC
EQUILIBRATORS	EQUIPOTENTIALS	ERADICATIVE	ERGOSTEROLS	EROTOMANIACS
EQUILIBRATORY	EQUIPROBABILITY	ERADICATOR	ERGOTAMINE	EROTOMANIAS
EQUILIBRIA	EQUIPROBABLE	ERADICATORS	ERGOTAMINES	EROTOPHOBIA
EQUILIBRIST	EQUISETACEOUS	ERASABILITIES	ERGOTISING	EROTOPHOBIAS
EQUILIBRISTIC	EQUISETIFORM	ERASABILITY	ERGOTIZING	ERRANTRIES
EQUILIBRISTS	EQUISETUMS	ERASEMENTS	ERICACEOUS	ERRATICALLY
EQUILIBRITIES	EQUITABILITIES	ERECTILITIES	ERINACEOUS	ERRATICISM
EQUILIBRITY	EQUITABILITY	ERECTILITY	ERIOMETERS	ERRATICISMS
EQUILIBRIUM	EQUITABLENESS	ERECTNESSES	ERIOPHOROUS	ERRONEOUSLY
EQUILIBRIUMS	EQUITABLENESSES	EREMACAUSES	ERIOPHORUM	ERRONEOUSNESS
EQUIMOLECULAR	EQUITATION	EREMACAUSIS	ERIOPHORUMS	ERRONEOUSNESSES
EQUIMULTIPLE	EQUITATIONS	EREMITICAL	ERIOPHYIDS	ERUBESCENCE
EQUIMULTIPLES	EQUIVALENCE	EREMITISMS	ERIOSTEMON	ERUBESCENCES
EQUINITIES	EQUIVALENCES	EREMURUSES	ERIOSTEMONS	ERUBESCENCIES
EQUINOCTIAL	EQUIVALENCIES	ERETHISMIC	ERISTICALLY	ERUBESCENCY
EQUINOCTIALLY	EQUIVALENCY	ERETHISTIC	ERODIBILITIES	ERUBESCENT
EQUINOCTIALS	EQUIVALENT	ERGASTOPLASM	ERODIBILITY	ERUBESCITE
EQUINUMEROUS	EQUIVALENTLY	ERGASTOPLASMIC	EROGENEITIES	ERUBESCITES
EQUIPAGING	EQUIVALENTS	ERGASTOPLASMS	EROGENEITY	ERUCTATING
EQUIPARATE	EQUIVOCACIES	ERGATANDROMORPH	EROSIONALLY	ERUCTATION
EQUIPARATED	EQUIVOCACY	ERGATANERS	EROSIVENESS	ERUCTATIONS
EQUIPARATES	EQUIVOCALITIES	ERGATIVITIES	EROSIVENESSES	ERUCTATIVE
EQUIPARATING	EQUIVOCALITY	ERGATIVITY	EROSIVITIES	ERUDITENESS
EQUIPARATION	EQUIVOCALLY	ERGATOCRACIES	EROSIVITIES	ERUDITENESSES
EQUIPARATIONS	EQUIVOCALNESS	ERGATOCRACY	EROTICALLY	ERUDITIONS
EQUIPARTITION	EQUIVOCALNESSES	ERGATOGYNE	EROTICISATION	ERUPTIONAL
EQUIPARTITIONS	EQUIVOCATE	ERGATOGYNES	EROTICISATIONS	ERUPTIVELY

ERUPTIVENESS	ERYTHROPSIAS	ESCHEATMENTS	ESPLANADES	ESTHESISES
ERUPTIVENESSES	ERYTHROSIN	ESCHEATORS	ESPRESSIVO	ESTHETICAL
ERUPTIVITIES	ERYTHROSINE	ESCHSCHOLTZIA	ESQUIRESSES	ESTHETICALLY
ERUPTIVITY	ERYTHROSINES	ESCHSCHOLTZIAS	ESSAYETTES	ESTHETICIAN
ERVALENTAS	ERYTHROSINS	ESCHSCHOLZIA	ESSAYISTIC	ESTHETICIANS
ERYSIPELAS	ESCABECHES	ESCHSCHOLZIAS	ESSENTIALISE	ESTHETICISM
ERYSIPELASES	ESCADRILLE	ESCLANDRES	ESSENTIALISED	ESTHETICISMS
ERYSIPELATOUS	ESCADRILLES	ESCOPETTES	ESSENTIALISES	ESTIMABLENESS
ERYSIPELOID	ESCALADERS	ESCORTAGES	ESSENTIALISING	ESTIMABLENESSES
ERYSIPELOIDS	ESCALADING	ESCRIBANOS	ESSENTIALISM	ESTIMATING
ERYTHEMATIC	ESCALADOES	ESCRITOIRE	ESSENTIALISMS	ESTIMATION
ERYTHEMATOUS	ESCALATING	ESCRITOIRES	ESSENTIALIST	ESTIMATIONS
ERYTHORBATE	ESCALATION	ESCRITORIAL	ESSENTIALISTS	ESTIMATIVE
ERYTHORBATES	ESCALATIONS	ESCUTCHEON	ESSENTIALITIES	ESTIMATORS
ERYTHORBIC	ESCALATORS	ESCUTCHEONED	ESSENTIALITY	ESTIPULATE
ERYTHRAEMIA	ESCALATORY	ESCUTCHEONS	ESSENTIALIZE	ESTIVATING
ERYTHRAEMIAS	ESCALLONIA	ESEMPLASIES	ESSENTIALIZED	ESTIVATION
ERYTHREMIA	ESCALLONIAS	ESEMPLASTIC	ESSENTIALIZES	ESTIVATIONS
ERYTHREMIAS	ESCALLOPED	ESEMPLASTICALLY	ESSENTIALIZING	ESTIVATORS
ERYTHRINAS	ESCALLOPING	ESOPHAGEAL	ESSENTIALLY	ESTOPPAGES
ERYTHRISMAL	ESCALOPING	ESOPHAGITIDES	ESSENTIALNESS	ESTRADIOLS
ERYTHRISMS	ESCAMOTAGE	ESOPHAGITIS	ESSENTIALNESSES	ESTRAMAZONE
ERYTHRISTIC	ESCAMOTAGES	ESOPHAGITISES	ESSENTIALS	ESTRAMAZONES
ERYTHRITES	ESCAPADOES	ESOPHAGOSCOPE	ESTABLISHABLE	ESTRANGEDNESS
ERYTHRITIC	ESCAPELESS	ESOPHAGOSCOPES	ESTABLISHED	ESTRANGEDNESSES
ERYTHRITOL	ESCAPEMENT	ESOPHAGOSCOPIES	ESTABLISHER	ESTRANGELO
ERYTHRITOLS	ESCAPEMENTS	ESOPHAGOSCOPY	ESTABLISHERS	ESTRANGELOS
ERYTHROBLAST	ESCAPOLOGIES	ESOPHAGUSES	ESTABLISHES	ESTRANGEMENT
ERYTHROBLASTIC	ESCAPOLOGIST	ESOTERICALLY	ESTABLISHING	ESTRANGEMENTS
ERYTHROBLASTS	ESCAPOLOGISTS	ESOTERICAS	ESTABLISHMENT	ESTRANGERS
ERYTHROCYTE	ESCAPOLOGY	ESOTERICISM	ESTABLISHMENTS	ESTRANGHELO
ERYTHROCYTES	ESCARMOUCHE	ESOTERICISMS	ESTAFETTES	ESTRANGHELOS
ERYTHROCYTIC	ESCARMOUCHES	ESOTERICIST	ESTAMINETS	ESTRANGING
ERYTHROMELALGIA	ESCARPMENT	ESOTERICISTS	ESTANCIERO	ESTRAPADES
ERYTHROMYCIN	ESCARPMENTS	ESOTERISMS	ESTANCIEROS	ESTREATING
ERYTHROMYCINS	ESCHAROTIC	ESOTROPIAS	ESTATESMAN	ESTREPEMENT
ERYTHRONIUM	ESCHAROTICS	ESPADRILLE	ESTATESMEN	ESTREPEMENTS
ERYTHRONIUMS	ESCHATOLOGIC	ESPADRILLES	ESTERIFICATION	ESTRIBUTOR
ERYTHROPENIA	ESCHATOLOGICAL	ESPAGNOLES	ESTERIFICATIONS	ESTRIBUTORS
ERYTHROPENIAS	ESCHATOLOGIES	ESPAGNOLETTE	ESTERIFIED	ESTRILDIDS
ERYTHROPHOBIA	ESCHATOLOGIST	ESPAGNOLETTES	ESTERIFIES	ESTROGENIC
ERYTHROPHOBIAS	ESCHATOLOGISTS	ESPALIERED	ESTERIFYING	ESTROGENICALLY
ERYTHROPOIESES	ESCHATOLOGY	ESPALIERING	ESTERISATION	ESURIENCES
ERYTHROPOIESIS	ESCHEATABLE	ESPECIALLY	ESTERISATIONS	ESURIENCIES
ERYTHROPOIETIC	ESCHEATAGE	ESPERANCES	ESTERIZATION	ESURIENTLY
ERYTHROPOIETIN	ESCHEATAGES	ESPIEGLERIE	ESTERIZATIONS	ETEPIMELETIC
ERYTHROPOIETINS	ESCHEATING	ESPIEGLERIES	ESTHESIOGEN	ETERNALISATION
ERYTHROPSIA	ESCHEATMENT	ESPIONAGES	ESTHESIOGENS	ETERNALISATIONS

ETERNALISE	ETHERIFICATIONS	ETHNOGRAPHICA	ETONOGESTRELS	EUDAEMONISMS
ETERNALISED	ETHERIFIED	ETHNOGRAPHICAL	ETOURDERIE	EUDAEMONIST
ETERNALISES	ETHERIFIES	ETHNOGRAPHIES	ETOURDERIES	EUDAEMONISTIC
ETERNALISING	ETHERIFYING	ETHNOGRAPHY	ETRANGERES	EUDAEMONISTICAL
ETERNALIST	ETHERISATION	ETHNOHISTORIAN	ETYMOLOGICA	EUDAEMONISTS
ETERNALISTS	ETHERISATIONS	ETHNOHISTORIANS	ETYMOLOGICAL	EUDAIMONISM
ETERNALITIES	ETHERISERS	ETHNOHISTORIC	ETYMOLOGICALLY	EUDAIMONISMS
ETERNALITY	ETHERISING	ETHNOHISTORICAL	ETYMOLOGICON	EUDEMONIAS
ETERNALIZATION	ETHERIZATION	ETHNOHISTORIES	ETYMOLOGICUM	EUDEMONICS
ETERNALIZATIONS	ETHERIZATIONS	ETHNOHISTORY	ETYMOLOGIES	EUDEMONISM
ETERNALIZE	ETHERIZERS	ETHNOLINGUIST	ETYMOLOGISE	EUDEMONISMS
ETERNALIZED	ETHERIZING	ETHNOLINGUISTIC	ETYMOLOGISED	EUDEMONIST
ETERNALIZES	ETHEROMANIA	ETHNOLINGUISTS	ETYMOLOGISES	EUDEMONISTIC
ETERNALIZING	ETHEROMANIAC	ETHNOLOGIC	ETYMOLOGISING	EUDEMONISTICAL
ETERNALNESS	ETHEROMANIACS	ETHNOLOGICAL	ETYMOLOGIST	EUDEMONISTS
ETERNALNESSES	ETHEROMANIAS	ETHNOLOGICALLY	ETYMOLOGISTS	EUDIALYTES
ETERNISATION	ETHICALITIES	ETHNOLOGIES	ETYMOLOGIZE	EUDICOTYLEDON
ETERNISATIONS	ETHICALITY	ETHNOLOGIST	ETYMOLOGIZED	EUDICOTYLEDONS
ETERNISING	ETHICALNESS	ETHNOLOGISTS	ETYMOLOGIZES	EUDIOMETER
ETERNITIES	ETHICALNESSES	ETHNOMEDICINE	ETYMOLOGIZING	EUDIOMETERS
ETERNIZATION	ETHICISING	ETHNOMEDICINES	EUBACTERIA	EUDIOMETRIC
ETERNIZATIONS	ETHICIZING	ETHNOMUSICOLOGY	EUBACTERIUM	EUDIOMETRICAL
ETERNIZING	ETHIONAMIDE	ETHNOSCIENCE	EUCALYPTOL	EUDIOMETRICALLY
ETHAMBUTOL	ETHIONAMIDES	ETHNOSCIENCES	EUCALYPTOLE	EUDIOMETRIES
ETHAMBUTOLS	ETHIONINES	ETHOLOGICAL	EUCALYPTOLES	EUDIOMETRY
ETHANEDIOIC	ETHNARCHIES	ETHOLOGICALLY	EUCALYPTOLS	EUGENECIST
ETHANEDIOL	ETHNICALLY	ETHOLOGIES	EUCALYPTUS	EUGENECISTS
ETHANEDIOLS	ETHNICISMS	ETHOLOGIST	EUCALYPTUSES	EUGENICALLY
ETHANOATES	ETHNICITIES	ETHOLOGISTS	EUCARYOTES	EUGENICIST
ETHANOLAMINE	ETHNOBIOLOGIES	ETHOXYETHANE	EUCARYOTIC	EUGENICISTS
ETHANOLAMINES	ETHNOBIOLOGY	ETHOXYETHANES	EUCHARISES	EUGEOSYNCLINAL
ETHEOSTOMINE	ETHNOBOTANICAL	ETHYLAMINE	EUCHARISTIC	EUGEOSYNCLINE
ETHEREALISATION	ETHNOBOTANIES	ETHYLAMINES	EUCHLORINE	EUGEOSYNCLINES
ETHEREALISE	ETHNOBOTANIST	ETHYLATING	EUCHLORINES	EUGLENOIDS
ETHEREALISED	ETHNOBOTANISTS	ETHYLATION	EUCHLORINS	EUGLOBULIN
ETHEREALISES	ETHNOBOTANY	ETHYLATIONS	EUCHOLOGIA	EUGLOBULINS
ETHEREALISING	ETHNOCENTRIC	ETHYLBENZENE	EUCHOLOGIES	EUHARMONIC
ETHEREALITIES	ETHNOCENTRICITY	ETHYLBENZENES	EUCHOLOGION	EUHEMERISE
ETHEREALITY	ETHNOCENTRISM	ETIOLATING	EUCHROMATIC	EUHEMERISED
ETHEREALIZATION	ETHNOCENTRISMS	ETIOLATION	EUCHROMATIN	EUHEMERISES
ETHEREALIZE	ETHNOCIDES	ETIOLATIONS	EUCHROMATINS	EUHEMERISING
ETHEREALIZED	ETHNOGENIC	ETIOLOGICAL	EUCRYPHIAS	EUHEMERISM
ETHEREALIZES	ETHNOGENIES	ETIOLOGICALLY	EUDAEMONIA	EUHEMERISMS
ETHEREALIZING	ETHNOGENIST	ETIOLOGIES	EUDAEMONIAS	EUHEMERIST
ETHEREALLY	ETHNOGENISTS	ETIOLOGIST	EUDAEMONIC	EUHEMERISTIC
ETHEREALNESS	ETHNOGRAPHER	ETIOLOGISTS	EUDAEMONICS	EUHEMERISTS
ETHEREALNESSES	ETHNOGRAPHERS	ETIQUETTES	EUDAEMONIES	EUHEMERIZE
ETHERIFICATION	ETHNOGRAPHIC	ETONOGESTREL	EUDAEMONISM	EUHEMERIZED

EUHEMERIZES

EUHEMERIZES	EUPHONICALLY	EUROPHILIA	EUTHANISES	EVANGELICALISMS
EUHEMERIZING	EUPHONIOUS	EUROPHILIAS	EUTHANISING	EVANGELICALLY
EUKARYOTES	EUPHONIOUSLY	EUROPHOBIA	EUTHANIZED	EVANGELICALNESS
EUKARYOTIC	EUPHONIOUSNESS	EUROPHOBIAS	EUTHANIZES	EVANGELICALS
EULOGISERS	EUPHONISED	EUROPHOBIC	EUTHANIZING	EVANGELICISM
EULOGISING	EUPHONISES	EUROTERMINAL	EUTHENISTS	EVANGELICISMS
EULOGISTIC	EUPHONISING	EUROTERMINALS	EUTHERIANS	EVANGELIES
EULOGISTICAL	EUPHONISMS	EURYBATHIC	EUTHYROIDS	EVANGELISATION
EULOGISTICALLY	EUPHONIUMS	EURYHALINE	EUTRAPELIA	EVANGELISATIONS
EULOGIZERS	EUPHONIZED	EURYOECIOUS	EUTRAPELIAS	EVANGELISE
EULOGIZING	EUPHONIZES	EURYPTERID	EUTRAPELIES	EVANGELISED
EUMELANINS	EUPHONIZING	EURYPTERIDS	EUTROPHICATION	EVANGELISER
EUNUCHISED	EUPHORBIACEOUS	EURYPTEROID	EUTROPHICATIONS	EVANGELISERS
EUNUCHISES	EUPHORBIAS	EURYPTEROIDS	EUTROPHIES	EVANGELISES
EUNUCHISING	EUPHORBIUM	EURYTHERMAL	EVACUATING	EVANGELISING
EUNUCHISMS	EUPHORBIUMS	EURYTHERMIC	EVACUATION	EVANGELISM
EUNUCHIZED	EUPHORIANT	EURYTHERMOUS	EVACUATIONS	EVANGELISMS
EUNUCHIZES	EUPHORIANTS	EURYTHERMS	EVACUATIVE	EVANGELIST
EUNUCHIZING	EUPHORICALLY	EURYTHMICAL	EVACUATIVES	EVANGELISTARIES
EUNUCHOIDISM	EUPHRASIAS	EURYTHMICS	EVACUATORS	EVANGELISTARION
EUNUCHOIDISMS	EUPHRASIES	EURYTHMIES	EVAGATIONS	EVANGELISTARY
EUNUCHOIDS	EUPHUISING	EURYTHMIST	EVAGINATED	EVANGELISTIC
EUONYMUSES	EUPHUISTIC	EURYTHMISTS	EVAGINATES	EVANGELISTS
EUPATORIUM	EUPHUISTICAL	EUSPORANGIATE	EVAGINATING	EVANGELIZATION
EUPATORIUMS	EUPHUISTICALLY	EUSTATICALLY	EVAGINATION	EVANGELIZATIONS
EUPATRIDAE	EUPHUIZING	EUSTRESSES	EVAGINATIONS	EVANGELIZE
EUPEPTICITIES	EUPLASTICS	EUTECTOIDS	EVALUATING	EVANGELIZED
EUPEPTICITY	EUPLOIDIES	EUTHANASED	EVALUATION	EVANGELIZER
EUPHAUSIACEAN	EURHYTHMIC	EUTHANASES	EVALUATIONS	EVANGELIZERS
EUPHAUSIACEANS	EURHYTHMICAL	EUTHANASIA	EVALUATIVE	EVANGELIZES
EUPHAUSIDS	EURHYTHMICS	EUTHANASIAS	EVALUATORS	EVANGELIZING
EUPHAUSIID	EURHYTHMIES	EUTHANASIAST	EVANESCENCE	EVANISHING
EUPHAUSIIDS	EURHYTHMIST	EUTHANASIASTS	EVANESCENCES	EVANISHMENT
EUPHEMISED	EURHYTHMISTS	EUTHANASIC	EVANESCENT	EVANISHMENTS
EUPHEMISER	EUROCHEQUE	EUTHANASIES	EVANESCENTLY	EVANITIONS
EUPHEMISERS	EUROCHEQUES	EUTHANASING	EVANESCING	EVAPORABILITIES
EUPHEMISES	EUROCREDIT	EUTHANATISE	EVANGELARIUM	EVAPORABILITY
EUPHEMISING	EUROCREDITS	EUTHANATISED	EVANGELARIUMS	EVAPORABLE
EUPHEMISMS	EUROCREEPS	EUTHANATISES	EVANGELIAR	EVAPORATED
EUPHEMISTIC	EUROCURRENCIES	EUTHANATISING	EVANGELIARIES	EVAPORATES
EUPHEMISTICALLY	EUROCURRENCY	EUTHANATIZE	EVANGELIARION	EVAPORATING
EUPHEMISTS	EURODEPOSIT	EUTHANATIZED	EVANGELIARIONS	EVAPORATION
EUPHEMIZED	EURODEPOSITS	EUTHANATIZES	EVANGELIARIUM	EVAPORATIONS
EUPHEMIZER	EURODOLLAR	EUTHANATIZING	EVANGELIARIUMS	EVAPORATIVE
EUPHEMIZERS	EURODOLLARS	EUTHANAZED	EVANGELIARS	EVAPORATOR
EUPHEMIZES	EUROMARKET	EUTHANAZES	EVANGELIARY	EVAPORATORS
EUPHEMIZING	EUROMARKETS	EUTHANAZING	EVANGELICAL	EVAPORIMETER
EUPHONICAL	EUROPHILES	EUTHANISED	EVANGELICALISM	EVAPORIMETERS

EVAPORITES	EVERYPLACE	EXACERBATION	EXANTHEMATOUS	EXCEPTIONS
EVAPORITIC	EVERYTHING	EXACERBATIONS	EXARATIONS	EXCEPTIOUS
EVAPOROGRAPH	EVERYWHENCE	EXACERBESCENCE	EXARCHATES	EXCEPTLESS
EVAPOROGRAPHS	EVERYWHERE	EXACERBESCENCES	EXARCHISTS	EXCERPTERS
EVAPOROMETER	EVERYWHITHER	EXACTINGLY	EXASPERATE	EXCERPTIBLE
EVAPOROMETERS	EVERYWOMAN	EXACTINGNESS	EXASPERATED	EXCERPTING
EVASIVENESS	EVERYWOMEN	EXACTINGNESSES	EXASPERATEDLY	EXCERPTINGS
EVASIVENESSES	EVIDENCING	EXACTITUDE	EXASPERATER	EXCERPTION
EVECTIONAL	EVIDENTIAL	EXACTITUDES	EXASPERATERS	EXCERPTIONS
EVENEMENTS	EVIDENTIALLY	EXACTMENTS	EXASPERATES	EXCERPTORS
EVENHANDED	EVIDENTIARY	EXACTNESSES	EXASPERATING	EXCESSIVELY
EVENHANDEDLY	EVILDOINGS	EXACTRESSES	EXASPERATINGLY	EXCESSIVENESS
EVENHANDEDNESS	EVILNESSES	EXAGGERATE	EXASPERATION	EXCESSIVENESSES
EVENNESSES	EVINCEMENT	EXAGGERATED	EXASPERATIONS	EXCHANGEABILITY
EVENTFULLY	EVINCEMENTS	EXAGGERATEDLY	EXASPERATIVE	EXCHANGEABLE
EVENTFULNESS	EVISCERATE	EXAGGERATEDNESS	EXASPERATOR	EXCHANGEABLY
EVENTFULNESSES	EVISCERATED	EXAGGERATES	EXASPERATORS	EXCHANGERS
EVENTRATED	EVISCERATES	EXAGGERATING	EXCAMBIONS	EXCHANGING
EVENTRATES	EVISCERATING	EXAGGERATINGLY	EXCAMBIUMS	EXCHEQUERED
EVENTRATING	EVISCERATION	EXAGGERATION	EXCARNATED	EXCHEQUERING
EVENTRATION	EVISCERATIONS	EXAGGERATIONS	EXCARNATES	EXCHEQUERS
EVENTRATIONS	EVISCERATOR	EXAGGERATIVE	EXCARNATING	EXCIPIENTS
EVENTUALISE	EVISCERATORS	EXAGGERATOR	EXCARNATION	EXCISIONAL
EVENTUALISED	EVITATIONS	EXAGGERATORS	EXCARNATIONS	EXCITABILITIES
EVENTUALISES	EVITERNALLY	EXAGGERATORY	EXCAVATING	EXCITABILITY
EVENTUALISING	EVITERNITIES	EXAHERTZES	EXCAVATION	EXCITABLENESS
EVENTUALITIES	EVITERNITY	EXALBUMINOUS	EXCAVATIONAL	EXCITABLENESSES
EVENTUALITY	EVOCATIONS	EXALTATION	EXCAVATIONS	EXCITANCIES
EVENTUALIZE	EVOCATIVELY	EXALTATIONS	EXCAVATORS	EXCITATION
EVENTUALIZED	EVOCATIVENESS	EXALTEDNESS	EXCEEDABLE	EXCITATIONS
EVENTUALIZES	EVOCATIVENESSES	EXALTEDNESSES	EXCEEDINGLY	EXCITATIVE
EVENTUALIZING	EVOLUTIONAL	EXAMINABILITIES	EXCELLENCE	EXCITATORY
EVENTUALLY	EVOLUTIONARILY	EXAMINABILITY	EXCELLENCES	EXCITEDNESS
EVENTUATED	EVOLUTIONARY	EXAMINABLE	EXCELLENCIES	EXCITEDNESSES
EVENTUATES	EVOLUTIONISM	EXAMINANTS	EXCELLENCY	EXCITEMENT
EVENTUATING	EVOLUTIONISMS	EXAMINATES	EXCELLENTLY	EXCITEMENTS
EVENTUATION	EVOLUTIONIST	EXAMINATION	EXCELSIORS	EXCITINGLY
EVENTUATIONS	EVOLUTIONISTIC	EXAMINATIONAL	EXCENTRICS	EXCLAIMERS
EVERBLOOMING	EVOLUTIONISTS	EXAMINATIONS	EXCEPTANTS	EXCLAIMING
EVERDURING	EVOLUTIONS	EXAMINATOR	EXCEPTIONABLE	EXCLAMATION
EVERGLADES	EVOLVEMENT	EXAMINATORS	EXCEPTIONABLY	EXCLAMATIONAL
EVERGREENS	EVOLVEMENTS	EXAMINERSHIP	EXCEPTIONAL	EXCLAMATIONS
EVERLASTING	EVONYMUSES	EXAMINERSHIPS	EXCEPTIONALISM	EXCLAMATIVE
EVERLASTINGLY	EVULGATING	EXANIMATION	EXCEPTIONALISMS	EXCLAMATIVES
EVERLASTINGNESS	EXACERBATE	EXANIMATIONS	EXCEPTIONALITY	EXCLAMATORILY
EVERLASTINGS	EXACERBATED	EXANTHEMAS	EXCEPTIONALLY	EXCLAMATORY
EVERYDAYNESS	EXACERBATES	EXANTHEMATA	EXCEPTIONALNESS	EXCLAUSTRATION
EVERYDAYNESSES	EXACERBATING	EXANTHEMATIC	EXCEPTIONALS	EXCLAUSTRATIONS

EXCLOSURES

EXCLOSURES EXCORTICATE EXCURSIVELY EXEMPLIFIERS EXHAUSTIVITY
EXCLUDABILITIES EXCORTICATED EXCURSIVENESS EXEMPLIFIES EXHAUSTLESS
EXCLUDABILITY EXCORTICATES EXCURSIVENESSES EXEMPLIFYING EXHAUSTLESSLY
EXCLUDABLE EXCORTICATING EXCURSUSES EXEMPTIONS EXHAUSTLESSNESS
EXCLUDIBLE EXCORTICATION EXCUSABLENESS EXENTERATE EXHEREDATE
EXCLUSIONARY EXCORTICATIONS EXCUSABLENESSES EXENTERATED EXHEREDATED
EXCLUSIONISM EXCREMENTA EXCUSATORY EXENTERATES EXHEREDATES
EXCLUSIONISMS EXCREMENTAL EXECRABLENESS EXENTERATING EXHEREDATING
EXCLUSIONIST EXCREMENTITIAL EXECRABLENESSES EXENTERATION EXHEREDATION
EXCLUSIONISTS EXCREMENTITIOUS EXECRATING EXENTERATIONS EXHEREDATIONS
EXCLUSIONS EXCREMENTS EXECRATION EXEQUATURS EXHIBITERS
EXCLUSIVELY EXCREMENTUM EXECRATIONS EXERCISABLE EXHIBITING
EXCLUSIVENESS EXCRESCENCE EXECRATIVE EXERCISERS EXHIBITION
EXCLUSIVENESSES EXCRESCENCES EXECRATIVELY EXERCISING EXHIBITIONER
EXCLUSIVES EXCRESCENCIES EXECRATORS EXERCITATION EXHIBITIONERS
EXCLUSIVISM EXCRESCENCY EXECRATORY EXERCITATIONS EXHIBITIONISM
EXCLUSIVISMS EXCRESCENT EXECUTABLE EXERCYCLES EXHIBITIONISMS
EXCLUSIVIST EXCRESCENTIAL EXECUTABLES EXERGAMING EXHIBITIONIST
EXCLUSIVISTS EXCRESCENTLY EXECUTANCIES EXERGAMINGS EXHIBITIONISTIC
EXCLUSIVITIES EXCRETIONS EXECUTANCY EXERTAINMENT EXHIBITIONISTS
EXCLUSIVITY EXCRETORIES EXECUTANTS EXERTAINMENTS EXHIBITIONS
EXCOGITABLE EXCRUCIATE EXECUTARIES EXFILTRATE EXHIBITIVE
EXCOGITATE EXCRUCIATED EXECUTIONER EXFILTRATED EXHIBITIVELY
EXCOGITATED EXCRUCIATES EXECUTIONERS EXFILTRATES EXHIBITORS
EXCOGITATES EXCRUCIATING EXECUTIONS EXFILTRATING EXHIBITORY
EXCOGITATING EXCRUCIATINGLY EXECUTIVELY EXFOLIANTS EXHILARANT
EXCOGITATION EXCRUCIATION EXECUTIVES EXFOLIATED EXHILARANTS
EXCOGITATIONS EXCRUCIATIONS EXECUTORIAL EXFOLIATES EXHILARATE
EXCOGITATIVE EXCULPABLE EXECUTORSHIP EXFOLIATING EXHILARATED
EXCOGITATOR EXCULPATED EXECUTORSHIPS EXFOLIATION EXHILARATES
EXCOGITATORS EXCULPATES EXECUTRESS EXFOLIATIONS EXHILARATING
EXCOMMUNICABLE EXCULPATING EXECUTRESSES EXFOLIATIVE EXHILARATINGLY
EXCOMMUNICATE EXCULPATION EXECUTRICES EXFOLIATOR EXHILARATION
EXCOMMUNICATED EXCULPATIONS EXECUTRIES EXFOLIATORS EXHILARATIONS
EXCOMMUNICATES EXCULPATORY EXECUTRIXES EXHALATION EXHILARATIVE
EXCOMMUNICATING EXCURSIONED EXEGETICAL EXHALATIONS EXHILARATOR
EXCOMMUNICATION EXCURSIONING EXEGETICALLY EXHAUSTEDLY EXHILARATORS
EXCOMMUNICATIVE EXCURSIONISE EXEGETISTS EXHAUSTERS EXHILARATORY
EXCOMMUNICATOR EXCURSIONISED EXEMPLARILY EXHAUSTIBILITY EXHORTATION
EXCOMMUNICATORS EXCURSIONISES EXEMPLARINESS EXHAUSTIBLE EXHORTATIONS
EXCOMMUNICATORY EXCURSIONISING EXEMPLARINESSES EXHAUSTING EXHORTATIVE
EXCOMMUNION EXCURSIONIST EXEMPLARITIES EXHAUSTINGLY EXHORTATORY
EXCOMMUNIONS EXCURSIONISTS EXEMPLARITY EXHAUSTION EXHUMATING
EXCORIATED EXCURSIONIZE EXEMPLIFIABLE EXHAUSTIONS EXHUMATION
EXCORIATES EXCURSIONIZED EXEMPLIFICATION EXHAUSTIVE EXHUMATIONS
EXCORIATING EXCURSIONIZES EXEMPLIFICATIVE EXHAUSTIVELY EXIGENCIES
EXCORIATION EXCURSIONIZING EXEMPLIFIED EXHAUSTIVENESS EXIGUITIES
EXCORIATIONS EXCURSIONS EXEMPLIFIER EXHAUSTIVITIES EXIGUOUSLY

EXIGUOUSNESS	EXOPARASITIC	EXOTHERMIC	EXPATRIATING	EXPEDITATIONS
EXIGUOUSNESSES	EXOPEPTIDASE	EXOTHERMICALLY	EXPATRIATION	EXPEDITELY
EXILEMENTS	EXOPEPTIDASES	EXOTHERMICITIES	EXPATRIATIONS	EXPEDITERS
EXIMIOUSLY	EXOPHAGIES	EXOTHERMICITY	EXPATRIATISM	EXPEDITING
EXISTENCES	EXOPHAGOUS	EXOTICALLY	EXPATRIATISMS	EXPEDITION
EXISTENTIAL	EXOPHTHALMIA	EXOTICISED	EXPECTABLE	EXPEDITIONARY
EXISTENTIALISM	EXOPHTHALMIAS	EXOTICISES	EXPECTABLY	EXPEDITIONS
EXISTENTIALISMS	EXOPHTHALMIC	EXOTICISING	EXPECTANCE	EXPEDITIOUS
EXISTENTIALIST	EXOPHTHALMOS	EXOTICISMS	EXPECTANCES	EXPEDITIOUSLY
EXISTENTIALISTS	EXOPHTHALMOSES	EXOTICISTS	EXPECTANCIES	EXPEDITIOUSNESS
EXISTENTIALLY	EXOPHTHALMUS	EXOTICIZED	EXPECTANCY	EXPEDITIVE
EXISTENTIALS	EXOPHTHALMUSES	EXOTICIZES	EXPECTANTLY	EXPEDITORS
EXOBIOLOGICAL	EXOPLANETS	EXOTICIZING	EXPECTANTS	EXPELLABLE
EXOBIOLOGIES	EXOPODITES	EXOTICNESS	EXPECTATION	EXPELLANTS
EXOBIOLOGIST	EXOPODITIC	EXOTICNESSES	EXPECTATIONAL	EXPELLENTS
EXOBIOLOGISTS	EXORABILITIES	EXOTROPIAS	EXPECTATIONS	EXPENDABILITIES
EXOBIOLOGY	EXORABILITY	EXPANDABILITIES	EXPECTATIVE	EXPENDABILITY
EXOCENTRIC	EXORATIONS	EXPANDABILITY	EXPECTATIVES	EXPENDABLE
EXOCUTICLE	EXORBITANCE	EXPANDABLE	EXPECTEDLY	EXPENDABLES
EXOCUTICLES	EXORBITANCES	EXPANSIBILITIES	EXPECTEDNESS	EXPENDABLY
EXOCYTOSED	EXORBITANCIES	EXPANSIBILITY	EXPECTEDNESSES	EXPENDITURE
EXOCYTOSES	EXORBITANCY	EXPANSIBLE	EXPECTINGLY	EXPENDITURES
EXOCYTOSING	EXORBITANT	EXPANSIBLY	EXPECTINGS	EXPENSIVELY
EXOCYTOSIS	EXORBITANTLY	EXPANSIONAL	EXPECTORANT	EXPENSIVENESS
EXOCYTOTIC	EXORBITATE	EXPANSIONARY	EXPECTORANTS	EXPENSIVENESSES
EXODERMISES	EXORBITATED	EXPANSIONISM	EXPECTORATE	EXPERIENCE
EXODONTIAS	EXORBITATES	EXPANSIONISMS	EXPECTORATED	EXPERIENCEABLE
EXODONTICS	EXORBITATING	EXPANSIONIST	EXPECTORATES	EXPERIENCED
EXODONTIST	EXORCISERS	EXPANSIONISTIC	EXPECTORATING	EXPERIENCELESS
EXODONTISTS	EXORCISING	EXPANSIONISTS	EXPECTORATION	EXPERIENCER
EXOENZYMES	EXORCISTIC	EXPANSIONS	EXPECTORATIONS	EXPERIENCERS
EXOERYTHROCYTIC	EXORCISTICAL	EXPANSIVELY	EXPECTORATIVE	EXPERIENCES
EXOGENETIC	EXORCIZERS	EXPANSIVENESS	EXPECTORATIVES	EXPERIENCING
EXOGENISMS	EXORCIZING	EXPANSIVENESSES	EXPECTORATOR	EXPERIENTIAL
EXOGENOUSLY	EXOSKELETAL	EXPANSIVITIES	EXPECTORATORS	EXPERIENTIALISM
EXONERATED	EXOSKELETON	EXPANSIVITY	EXPEDIENCE	EXPERIENTIALIST
EXONERATES	EXOSKELETONS	EXPATIATED	EXPEDIENCES	EXPERIENTIALLY
EXONERATING	EXOSPHERES	EXPATIATES	EXPEDIENCIES	EXPERIMENT
EXONERATION	EXOSPHERIC	EXPATIATING	EXPEDIENCY	EXPERIMENTAL
EXONERATIONS	EXOSPHERICAL	EXPATIATION	EXPEDIENTIAL	EXPERIMENTALISE
EXONERATIVE	EXOSPORIUM	EXPATIATIONS	EXPEDIENTIALLY	EXPERIMENTALISM
EXONERATOR	EXOSPOROUS	EXPATIATIVE	EXPEDIENTLY	EXPERIMENTALIST
EXONERATORS	EXOTERICAL	EXPATIATOR	EXPEDIENTS	EXPERIMENTALIZE
EXONUCLEASE	EXOTERICALLY	EXPATIATORS	EXPEDITATE	EXPERIMENTALLY
EXONUCLEASES	EXOTERICISM	EXPATIATORY	EXPEDITATED	EXPERIMENTATION
EXONUMISTS	EXOTERICISMS	EXPATRIATE	EXPEDITATES	EXPERIMENTATIVE
EXOPARASITE	EXOTHERMAL	EXPATRIATED	EXPEDITATING	EXPERIMENTED
EXOPARASITES	EXOTHERMALLY	EXPATRIATES	EXPEDITATION	EXPERIMENTER

EXPERIMENTERS

EXPERIMENTERS	EXPLICATORS	EXPOSITORS	EXPROBRATING	EXSANGUINITY
EXPERIMENTING	EXPLICATORY	EXPOSITORY	EXPROBRATION	EXSANGUINOUS
EXPERIMENTIST	EXPLICITLY	EXPOSITRESS	EXPROBRATIONS	EXSCINDING
EXPERIMENTISTS	EXPLICITNESS	EXPOSITRESSES	EXPROBRATIVE	EXSECTIONS
EXPERIMENTS	EXPLICITNESSES	EXPOSTULATE	EXPROBRATORY	EXSERTIONS
EXPERTISED	EXPLOITABLE	EXPOSTULATED	EXPROMISSION	EXSICCANTS
EXPERTISES	EXPLOITAGE	EXPOSTULATES	EXPROMISSIONS	EXSICCATED
EXPERTISING	EXPLOITAGES	EXPOSTULATING	EXPROMISSOR	EXSICCATES
EXPERTISMS	EXPLOITATION	EXPOSTULATINGLY	EXPROMISSORS	EXSICCATING
EXPERTIZED	EXPLOITATIONS	EXPOSTULATION	EXPROPRIABLE	EXSICCATION
EXPERTIZES	EXPLOITATIVE	EXPOSTULATIONS	EXPROPRIATE	EXSICCATIONS
EXPERTIZING	EXPLOITATIVELY	EXPOSTULATIVE	EXPROPRIATED	EXSICCATIVE
EXPERTNESS	EXPLOITERS	EXPOSTULATOR	EXPROPRIATES	EXSICCATOR
EXPERTNESSES	EXPLOITING	EXPOSTULATORS	EXPROPRIATING	EXSICCATORS
EXPIATIONS	EXPLOITIVE	EXPOSTULATORY	EXPROPRIATION	EXSOLUTION
EXPIRATION	EXPLORATION	EXPOSTURES	EXPROPRIATIONS	EXSOLUTIONS
EXPIRATIONS	EXPLORATIONAL	EXPOUNDERS	EXPROPRIATOR	EXSTIPULATE
EXPIRATORY	EXPLORATIONIST	EXPOUNDING	EXPROPRIATORS	EXSTROPHIES
EXPISCATED	EXPLORATIONISTS	EXPRESSAGE	EXPUGNABLE	EXSUFFLATE
EXPISCATES	EXPLORATIONS	EXPRESSAGES	EXPUGNATION	EXSUFFLATED
EXPISCATING	EXPLORATIVE	EXPRESSERS	EXPUGNATIONS	EXSUFFLATES
EXPISCATION	EXPLORATIVELY	EXPRESSIBLE	EXPULSIONS	EXSUFFLATING
EXPISCATIONS	EXPLORATORY	EXPRESSING	EXPUNCTING	EXSUFFLATION
EXPISCATORY	EXPLOSIBLE	EXPRESSION	EXPUNCTION	EXSUFFLATIONS
EXPLAINABLE	EXPLOSIONS	EXPRESSIONAL	EXPUNCTIONS	EXSUFFLICATE
EXPLAINERS	EXPLOSIVELY	EXPRESSIONISM	EXPURGATED	EXTEMPORAL
EXPLAINING	EXPLOSIVENESS	EXPRESSIONISMS	EXPURGATES	EXTEMPORALLY
EXPLANATION	EXPLOSIVENESSES	EXPRESSIONIST	EXPURGATING	EXTEMPORANEITY
EXPLANATIONS	EXPLOSIVES	EXPRESSIONISTIC	EXPURGATION	EXTEMPORANEOUS
EXPLANATIVE	EXPONENTIAL	EXPRESSIONISTS	EXPURGATIONS	EXTEMPORARILY
EXPLANATIVELY	EXPONENTIALLY	EXPRESSIONLESS	EXPURGATOR	EXTEMPORARINESS
EXPLANATORILY	EXPONENTIALS	EXPRESSIONS	EXPURGATORIAL	EXTEMPORARY
EXPLANATORY	EXPONENTIATION	EXPRESSIVE	EXPURGATORS	EXTEMPORES
EXPLANTATION	EXPONENTIATIONS	EXPRESSIVELY	EXPURGATORY	EXTEMPORISATION
EXPLANTATIONS	EXPORTABILITIES	EXPRESSIVENESS	EXQUISITELY	EXTEMPORISE
EXPLANTING	EXPORTABILITY	EXPRESSIVITIES	EXQUISITENESS	EXTEMPORISED
EXPLETIVELY	EXPORTABLE	EXPRESSIVITY	EXQUISITENESSES	EXTEMPORISER
EXPLETIVES	EXPORTATION	EXPRESSMAN	EXQUISITES	EXTEMPORISERS
EXPLICABLE	EXPORTATIONS	EXPRESSMEN	EXSANGUINATE	EXTEMPORISES
EXPLICABLY	EXPOSEDNESS	EXPRESSNESS	EXSANGUINATED	EXTEMPORISING
EXPLICATED	EXPOSEDNESSES	EXPRESSNESSES	EXSANGUINATES	EXTEMPORIZATION
EXPLICATES	EXPOSITING	EXPRESSURE	EXSANGUINATING	EXTEMPORIZE
EXPLICATING	EXPOSITION	EXPRESSURES	EXSANGUINATION	EXTEMPORIZED
EXPLICATION	EXPOSITIONAL	EXPRESSWAY	EXSANGUINATIONS	EXTEMPORIZER
EXPLICATIONS	EXPOSITIONS	EXPRESSWAYS	EXSANGUINE	EXTEMPORIZERS
EXPLICATIVE	EXPOSITIVE	EXPROBRATE	EXSANGUINED	EXTEMPORIZES
EXPLICATIVELY	EXPOSITIVELY	EXPROBRATED	EXSANGUINEOUS	EXTEMPORIZING
EXPLICATOR	EXPOSITORILY	EXPROBRATES	EXSANGUINITIES	EXTENDABILITIES

EXTENDABILITY	EXTERIORITIES	EXTINCTIONS	EXTRACTION	EXTRAORDINARY
EXTENDABLE	EXTERIORITY	EXTINCTIVE	EXTRACTIONS	EXTRAPOLATE
EXTENDEDLY	EXTERIORIZATION	EXTINCTURE	EXTRACTIVE	EXTRAPOLATED
EXTENDEDNESS	EXTERIORIZE	EXTINCTURES	EXTRACTIVELY	EXTRAPOLATES
EXTENDEDNESSES	EXTERIORIZED	EXTINGUISH	EXTRACTIVES	EXTRAPOLATING
EXTENDIBILITIES	EXTERIORIZES	EXTINGUISHABLE	EXTRACTORS	EXTRAPOLATION
EXTENDIBILITY	EXTERIORIZING	EXTINGUISHANT	EXTRACURRICULAR	EXTRAPOLATIONS
EXTENDIBLE	EXTERIORLY	EXTINGUISHANTS	EXTRADITABLE	EXTRAPOLATIVE
EXTENSIBILITIES	EXTERMINABLE	EXTINGUISHED	EXTRADITED	EXTRAPOLATOR
EXTENSIBILITY	EXTERMINATE	EXTINGUISHER	EXTRADITES	EXTRAPOLATORS
EXTENSIBLE	EXTERMINATED	EXTINGUISHERS	EXTRADITING	EXTRAPOLATORY
EXTENSIBLENESS	EXTERMINATES	EXTINGUISHES	EXTRADITION	EXTRAPOSED
EXTENSIFICATION	EXTERMINATING	EXTINGUISHING	EXTRADITIONS	EXTRAPOSES
EXTENSIMETER	EXTERMINATION	EXTINGUISHMENT	EXTRADOSES	EXTRAPOSING
EXTENSIMETERS	EXTERMINATIONS	EXTINGUISHMENTS	EXTRADOTAL	EXTRAPOSITION
EXTENSIONAL	EXTERMINATIVE	EXTIRPABLE	EXTRADURAL	EXTRAPOSITIONS
EXTENSIONALISM	EXTERMINATOR	EXTIRPATED	EXTRADURALS	EXTRAPYRAMIDAL
EXTENSIONALISMS	EXTERMINATORS	EXTIRPATES	EXTRAEMBRYONIC	EXTRASENSORY
EXTENSIONALITY	EXTERMINATORY	EXTIRPATING	EXTRAFLORAL	EXTRASOLAR
EXTENSIONALLY	EXTERMINED	EXTIRPATION	EXTRAFORANEOUS	EXTRASYSTOLE
EXTENSIONIST	EXTERMINES	EXTIRPATIONS	EXTRAGALACTIC	EXTRASYSTOLES
EXTENSIONISTS	EXTERMINING	EXTIRPATIVE	EXTRAHEPATIC	EXTRATEXTUAL
EXTENSIONS	EXTERNALISATION	EXTIRPATOR	EXTRAJUDICIAL	EXTRATROPICAL
EXTENSITIES	EXTERNALISE	EXTIRPATORS	EXTRAJUDICIALLY	EXTRAUTERINE
EXTENSIVELY	EXTERNALISED	EXTIRPATORY	EXTRALEGAL	EXTRAVAGANCE
EXTENSIVENESS	EXTERNALISES	EXTOLLINGLY	EXTRALEGALLY	EXTRAVAGANCES
EXTENSIVENESSES	EXTERNALISING	EXTOLMENTS	EXTRALIMITAL	EXTRAVAGANCIES
EXTENSIVISATION	EXTERNALISM	EXTORSIVELY	EXTRALIMITARY	EXTRAVAGANCY
EXTENSIVIZATION	EXTERNALISMS	EXTORTIONARY	EXTRALINGUISTIC	EXTRAVAGANT
EXTENSOMETER	EXTERNALIST	EXTORTIONATE	EXTRALITERARY	EXTRAVAGANTLY
EXTENSOMETERS	EXTERNALISTS	EXTORTIONATELY	EXTRALITIES	EXTRAVAGANZA
EXTENUATED	EXTERNALITIES	EXTORTIONER	EXTRALOGICAL	EXTRAVAGANZAS
EXTENUATES	EXTERNALITY	EXTORTIONERS	EXTRAMARITAL	EXTRAVAGATE
EXTENUATING	EXTERNALIZATION	EXTORTIONIST	EXTRAMARITALLY	EXTRAVAGATED
EXTENUATINGLY	EXTERNALIZE	EXTORTIONISTS	EXTRAMETRICAL	EXTRAVAGATES
EXTENUATINGS	EXTERNALIZED	EXTORTIONS	EXTRAMUNDANE	EXTRAVAGATING
EXTENUATION	EXTERNALIZES	EXTRABOLDS	EXTRAMURAL	EXTRAVAGATION
EXTENUATIONS	EXTERNALIZING	EXTRACANONICAL	EXTRAMURALLY	EXTRAVAGATIONS
EXTENUATIVE	EXTERNALLY	EXTRACELLULAR	EXTRAMUSICAL	EXTRAVASATE
EXTENUATIVES	EXTERNSHIP	EXTRACELLULARLY	EXTRANEITIES	EXTRAVASATED
EXTENUATOR	EXTERNSHIPS	EXTRACORPOREAL	EXTRANEITY	EXTRAVASATES
EXTENUATORS	EXTEROCEPTIVE	EXTRACRANIAL	EXTRANEOUS	EXTRAVASATING
EXTENUATORY	EXTEROCEPTOR	EXTRACTABILITY	EXTRANEOUSLY	EXTRAVASATION
EXTERIORISATION	EXTEROCEPTORS	EXTRACTABLE	EXTRANEOUSNESS	EXTRAVASATIONS
EXTERIORISE	EXTERRITORIAL	EXTRACTANT	EXTRANUCLEAR	EXTRAVASCULAR
EXTERIORISED	EXTERRITORIALLY	EXTRACTANTS	EXTRAORDINAIRE	EXTRAVEHICULAR
EXTERIORISES	EXTINCTING	EXTRACTIBLE	EXTRAORDINARIES	EXTRAVERSION
EXTERIORISING	EXTINCTION	EXTRACTING	EXTRAORDINARILY	EXTRAVERSIONS

EXTRAVERSIVE	EXTRICATING	EXTRUDABILITY	EXULCERATING	EYEBROWLESS
EXTRAVERSIVELY	EXTRICATION	EXTRUDABLE	EXULCERATION	EYEDNESSES
EXTRAVERTED	EXTRICATIONS	EXTRUSIBLE	EXULCERATIONS	EYEDROPPER
EXTRAVERTING	EXTRINSICAL	EXTRUSIONS	EXULTANCES	EYEDROPPERS
EXTRAVERTLY	EXTRINSICALITY	EXTUBATING	EXULTANCIES	EYEGLASSES
EXTRAVERTS	EXTRINSICALLY	EXUBERANCE	EXULTANTLY	EYELETEERS
EXTREATING	EXTRINSICALS	EXUBERANCES	EXULTATION	EYELETTING
EXTREMENESS	EXTROPIANS	EXUBERANCIES	EXULTATIONS	EYEOPENERS
EXTREMENESSES	EXTROVERSION	EXUBERANCY	EXULTINGLY	EYEPATCHES
EXTREMISMS	EXTROVERSIONS	EXUBERANTLY	EXURBANITE	EYEPOPPERS
EXTREMISTS	EXTROVERSIVE	EXUBERATED	EXURBANITES	EYESHADOWS
EXTREMITIES	EXTROVERSIVELY	EXUBERATES	EXUVIATING	EYESTRAINS
EXTREMOPHILE	EXTROVERTED	EXUBERATING	EXUVIATION	EYESTRINGS
EXTREMOPHILES	EXTROVERTING	EXUDATIONS	EXUVIATIONS	EYEWITNESS
EXTRICABLE	EXTROVERTLY	EXULCERATE	EYEBALLING	EYEWITNESSED
EXTRICATED	EXTROVERTS	EXULCERATED	EYEBRIGHTS	EYEWITNESSES
EXTRICATES	EXTRUDABILITIES	EXULCERATES	EYEBROWING	EYEWITNESSING

F

FABRICANTS	FACILENESS	FACTITIOUS	FADOMETERS	FAITHWORTHINESS
FABRICATED	FACILENESSES	FACTITIOUSLY	FAGGOTIEST	FAITHWORTHY
FABRICATES	FACILITATE	FACTITIOUSNESS	FAGGOTINGS	FALANGISMS
FABRICATING	FACILITATED	FACTITIVELY	FAGGOTRIES	FALANGISTS
FABRICATION	FACILITATES	FACTORABILITIES	FAGOTTISTS	FALCATIONS
FABRICATIONS	FACILITATING	FACTORABILITY	FAINEANCES	FALCONIFORM
FABRICATIVE	FACILITATION	FACTORABLE	FAINEANCIES	FALCONOIDS
FABRICATOR	FACILITATIONS	FACTORAGES	FAINEANTISE	FALCONRIES
FABRICATORS	FACILITATIVE	FACTORIALLY	FAINEANTISES	FALDERALED
FABRICKING	FACILITATOR	FACTORIALS	FAINNESSES	FALDERALING
FABRICKINGS	FACILITATORS	FACTORINGS	FAINTHEARTED	FALDISTORIES
FABULATING	FACILITATORY	FACTORISATION	FAINTHEARTEDLY	FALDISTORY
FABULATORS	FACILITIES	FACTORISATIONS	FAINTINGLY	FALDSTOOLS
FABULISING	FACINERIOUS	FACTORISED	FAINTISHNESS	FALLACIOUS
FABULISTIC	FACINOROUS	FACTORISES	FAINTISHNESSES	FALLACIOUSLY
FABULIZING	FACINOROUSNESS	FACTORISING	FAINTNESSES	FALLACIOUSNESS
FABULOSITIES	FACSIMILED	FACTORIZATION	FAIRGROUND	FALLALERIES
FABULOSITY	FACSIMILEING	FACTORIZATIONS	FAIRGROUNDS	FALLALISHLY
FABULOUSLY	FACSIMILES	FACTORIZED	FAIRLEADER	FALLBOARDS
FABULOUSNESS	FACSIMILIST	FACTORIZES	FAIRLEADERS	FALLFISHES
FABULOUSNESSES	FACSIMILISTS	FACTORIZING	FAIRNESSES	FALLIBILISM
FACEBOOKED	FACTICITIES	FACTORSHIP	FAIRNITICKLE	FALLIBILISMS
FACEBOOKING	FACTIONALISE	FACTORSHIPS	FAIRNITICKLES	FALLIBILIST
FACECLOTHS	FACTIONALISED	FACTORYLIKE	FAIRNITICLE	FALLIBILISTS
FACELESSNESS	FACTIONALISES	FACTSHEETS	FAIRNITICLES	FALLIBILITIES
FACELESSNESSES	FACTIONALISING	FACTUALISM	FAIRNYTICKLE	FALLIBILITY
FACELIFTED	FACTIONALISM	FACTUALISMS	FAIRNYTICKLES	FALLIBLENESS
FACELIFTING	FACTIONALISMS	FACTUALIST	FAIRNYTICLE	FALLIBLENESSES
FACEPALMED	FACTIONALIST	FACTUALISTIC	FAIRNYTICLES	FALLOWNESS
FACEPALMING	FACTIONALISTS	FACTUALISTS	FAIRYFLOSS	FALLOWNESSES
FACEPLANTED	FACTIONALIZE	FACTUALITIES	FAIRYFLOSSES	FALSEFACES
FACEPLANTING	FACTIONALIZED	FACTUALITY	FAIRYHOODS	FALSEHOODS
FACEPLANTS	FACTIONALIZES	FACTUALNESS	FAIRYLANDS	FALSENESSES
FACEPLATES	FACTIONALIZING	FACTUALNESSES	FAITHCURES	FALSEWORKS
FACEPRINTS	FACTIONALLY	FACULTATIVE	FAITHFULLY	FALSIDICAL
FACETIMING	FACTIONARIES	FACULTATIVELY	FAITHFULNESS	FALSIFIABILITY
FACETIOUSLY	FACTIONARY	FACUNDITIES	FAITHFULNESSES	FALSIFIABLE
FACETIOUSNESS	FACTIONIST	FADDINESSES	FAITHLESSLY	FALSIFICATION
FACETIOUSNESSES	FACTIONISTS	FADDISHNESS	FAITHLESSNESS	FALSIFICATIONS
FACEWORKER	FACTIOUSLY	FADDISHNESSES	FAITHLESSNESSES	FALSIFIERS
FACEWORKERS	FACTIOUSNESS	FADEDNESSES	FAITHWORTHIER	FALSIFYING
FACIALISTS	FACTIOUSNESSES	FADELESSLY	FAITHWORTHIEST	FALTERINGLY

FALTERINGS	FANDABIDOZI	FARADISING	FARTHINGLAND	FASHIOUSNESS
FAMILIARISATION	FANDANGLES	FARADIZATION	FARTHINGLANDS	FASHIOUSNESSES
FAMILIARISE	FANDANGOES	FARADIZATIONS	FARTHINGLESS	FASTBALLER
FAMILIARISED	FANFARADES	FARADIZERS	FARTHINGSWORTH	FASTBALLERS
FAMILIARISER	FANFARONADE	FARADIZING	FARTHINGSWORTHS	FASTENINGS
FAMILIARISERS	FANFARONADED	FARANDINES	FASCIATELY	FASTIDIOUS
FAMILIARISES	FANFARONADES	FARANDOLES	FASCIATION	FASTIDIOUSLY
FAMILIARISING	FANFARONADING	FARAWAYNESS	FASCIATIONS	FASTIDIOUSNESS
FAMILIARITIES	FANFARONAS	FARAWAYNESSES	FASCICULAR	FASTIGIATE
FAMILIARITY	FANFOLDING	FARBOROUGH	FASCICULARLY	FASTIGIATED
FAMILIARIZATION	FANTABULOUS	FARBOROUGHS	FASCICULATE	FASTIGIUMS
FAMILIARIZE	FANTASISED	FARCEMEATS	FASCICULATED	FASTNESSES
FAMILIARIZED	FANTASISER	FARCICALITIES	FASCICULATELY	FATALISTIC
FAMILIARIZER	FANTASISERS	FARCICALITY	FASCICULATION	FATALISTICALLY
FAMILIARIZERS	FANTASISES	FARCICALLY	FASCICULATIONS	FATALITIES
FAMILIARIZES	FANTASISING	FARCICALNESS	FASCICULES	FATALNESSES
FAMILIARIZING	FANTASISTS	FARCICALNESSES	FASCICULUS	FATBRAINED
FAMILIARLY	FANTASIZED	FARCIFYING	FASCIITISES	FATEFULNESS
FAMILIARNESS	FANTASIZER	FAREWELLED	FASCINATED	FATEFULNESSES
FAMILIARNESSES	FANTASIZERS	FAREWELLING	FASCINATEDLY	FATHEADEDLY
FAMILISTIC	FANTASIZES	FARFETCHEDNESS	FASCINATES	FATHEADEDNESS
FAMISHMENT	FANTASIZING	FARINACEOUS	FASCINATING	FATHEADEDNESSES
FAMISHMENTS	FANTASMALLY	FARINOSELY	FASCINATINGLY	FATHERHOOD
FAMOUSNESS	FANTASMICALLY	FARKLEBERRIES	FASCINATION	FATHERHOODS
FAMOUSNESSES	FANTASQUES	FARKLEBERRY	FASCINATIONS	FATHERINGS
FANATICALLY	FANTASTICAL	FARMERESSES	FASCINATIVE	FATHERLAND
FANATICALNESS	FANTASTICALITY	FARMERETTE	FASCINATOR	FATHERLANDS
FANATICALNESSES	FANTASTICALLY	FARMERETTES	FASCINATORS	FATHERLESS
FANATICISATION	FANTASTICALNESS	FARMHOUSES	FASCIOLIASES	FATHERLESSNESS
FANATICISATIONS	FANTASTICATE	FARMSTEADS	FASCIOLIASIS	FATHERLIER
FANATICISE	FANTASTICATED	FARMWORKER	FASCISTICALLY	FATHERLIEST
FANATICISED	FANTASTICATES	FARMWORKERS	FASCITISES	FATHERLIKE
FANATICISES	FANTASTICATING	FARNARKELED	FASHIONABILITY	FATHERLINESS
FANATICISING	FANTASTICATION	FARNARKELING	FASHIONABLE	FATHERLINESSES
FANATICISM	FANTASTICATIONS	FARNARKELINGS	FASHIONABLENESS	FATHERSHIP
FANATICISMS	FANTASTICISM	FARNARKELS	FASHIONABLES	FATHERSHIPS
FANATICIZATION	FANTASTICISMS	FARRAGINOUS	FASHIONABLY	FATHOMABLE
FANATICIZATIONS	FANTASTICO	FARRANDINE	FASHIONERS	FATHOMETER
FANATICIZE	FANTASTICOES	FARRANDINES	FASHIONIER	FATHOMETERS
FANATICIZED	FANTASTICS	FARRIERIES	FASHIONIEST	FATHOMLESS
FANATICIZES	FANTASTRIES	FARROWINGS	FASHIONING	FATHOMLESSLY
FANATICIZING	FANTASYING	FARSIGHTED	FASHIONIST	FATHOMLESSNESS
FANCIFULLY	FANTASYLAND	FARSIGHTEDLY	FASHIONISTA	FATIDICALLY
FANCIFULNESS	FANTASYLANDS	FARSIGHTEDNESS	FASHIONISTAS	FATIGABILITIES
FANCIFULNESSES	FANTOCCINI	FARTHERMORE	FASHIONISTS	FATIGABILITY
FANCIFYING	FARADISATION	FARTHERMOST	FASHIONMONGER	FATIGABLENESS
FANCINESSES	FARADISATIONS	FARTHINGALE	FASHIONMONGERS	FATIGABLENESSES
FANCYWORKS	FARADISERS	FARTHINGALES	FASHIONMONGING	FATIGATING

FATIGUABLE	FAZENDEIRO	FEATHERSTITCH	FEDERALIZATION	FELICITIES
FATIGUABLENESS	FAZENDEIROS	FEATHERSTITCHED	FEDERALIZATIONS	FELICITOUS
FATIGUELESS	FEARFULLER	FEATHERSTITCHES	FEDERALIZE	FELICITOUSLY
FATIGUINGLY	FEARFULLEST	FEATHERWEIGHT	FEDERALIZED	FELICITOUSNESS
FATISCENCE	FEARFULNESS	FEATHERWEIGHTS	FEDERALIZES	FELINENESS
FATISCENCES	FEARFULNESSES	FEATLINESS	FEDERALIZING	FELINENESSES
FATSHEDERA	FEARLESSLY	FEATLINESSES	FEDERARIES	FELINITIES
FATSHEDERAS	FEARLESSNESS	FEATURELESS	FEDERATING	FELLATIONS
FATTENABLE	FEARLESSNESSES	FEATURELESSNESS	FEDERATION	FELLATRICES
FATTENINGS	FEARMONGER	FEATURETTE	FEDERATIONS	FELLATRIXES
FATTINESSES	FEARMONGERING	FEATURETTES	FEDERATIVE	FELLFIELDS
FATUOUSNESS	FEARMONGERINGS	FEBRICITIES	FEDERATIVELY	FELLMONGER
FATUOUSNESSES	FEARMONGERS	FEBRICULAS	FEDERATORS	FELLMONGERED
FAUCETRIES	FEARNAUGHT	FEBRICULES	FEEBLEMINDED	FELLMONGERIES
FAULCHIONS	FEARNAUGHTS	FEBRIFACIENT	FEEBLEMINDEDLY	FELLMONGERING
FAULTFINDER	FEARNOUGHT	FEBRIFACIENTS	FEEBLENESS	FELLMONGERINGS
FAULTFINDERS	FEARNOUGHTS	FEBRIFEROUS	FEEBLENESSES	FELLMONGERS
FAULTFINDING	FEARSOMELY	FEBRIFUGAL	FEEDGRAINS	FELLMONGERY
FAULTFINDINGS	FEARSOMENESS	FEBRIFUGES	FEEDINGSTUFF	FELLNESSES
FAULTINESS	FEARSOMENESSES	FEBRILITIES	FEEDINGSTUFFS	FELLOWSHIP
FAULTINESSES	FEASIBILITIES	FECKLESSLY	FEEDSTOCKS	FELLOWSHIPED
FAULTLESSLY	FEASIBILITY	FECKLESSNESS	FEEDSTUFFS	FELLOWSHIPING
FAULTLESSNESS	FEASIBLENESS	FECKLESSNESSES	FEEDTHROUGH	FELLOWSHIPPED
FAULTLESSNESSES	FEASIBLENESSES	FECULENCES	FEEDTHROUGHS	FELLOWSHIPPING
FAULTLINES	FEATEOUSLY	FECULENCIES	FEEDWATERS	FELLOWSHIPS
FAUNISTICALLY	FEATHERBED	FECUNDATED	FEELINGLESS	FELLWALKER
FAUXBOURDON	FEATHERBEDDED	FECUNDATES	FEELINGNESS	FELLWALKERS
FAUXBOURDONS	FEATHERBEDDING	FECUNDATING	FEELINGNESSES	FELONIOUSLY
FAUXMANCES	FEATHERBEDDINGS	FECUNDATION	FEIGNEDNESS	FELONIOUSNESS
FAVORABLENESS	FEATHERBEDS	FECUNDATIONS	FEIGNEDNESSES	FELONIOUSNESSES
FAVORABLENESSES	FEATHERBRAIN	FECUNDATOR	FEIGNINGLY	FELQUISTES
FAVOREDNESS	FEATHERBRAINED	FECUNDATORS	FEISTINESS	FELSPATHIC
FAVOREDNESSES	FEATHERBRAINS	FECUNDATORY	FEISTINESSES	FELSPATHOID
FAVORINGLY	FEATHEREDGE	FECUNDITIES	FELDSCHARS	FELSPATHOIDS
FAVORITISM	FEATHEREDGED	FEDERACIES	FELDSCHERS	FELSPATHOSE
FAVORITISMS	FEATHEREDGES	FEDERALESE	FELDSPATHIC	FEMALENESS
FAVOURABLE	FEATHEREDGING	FEDERALESES	FELDSPATHOID	FEMALENESSES
FAVOURABLENESS	FEATHERHEAD	FEDERALISATION	FELDSPATHOIDS	FEMALITIES
FAVOURABLY	FEATHERHEADED	FEDERALISATIONS	FELDSPATHOSE	FEMETARIES
FAVOUREDNESS	FEATHERHEADS	FEDERALISE	FELDSPATHS	FEMINACIES
FAVOUREDNESSES	FEATHERIER	FEDERALISED	FELICITATE	FEMINALITIES
FAVOURINGLY	FEATHERIEST	FEDERALISES	FELICITATED	FEMINALITY
FAVOURITES	FEATHERINESS	FEDERALISING	FELICITATES	FEMINEITIES
FAVOURITISM	FEATHERINESSES	FEDERALISM	FELICITATING	FEMINILITIES
FAVOURITISMS	FEATHERING	FEDERALISMS	FELICITATION	FEMINILITY
FAVOURLESS	FEATHERINGS	FEDERALIST	FELICITATIONS	FEMININELY
FAWNINGNESS	FEATHERLESS	FEDERALISTIC	FELICITATOR	FEMININENESS
FAWNINGNESSES	FEATHERLIGHT	FEDERALISTS	FELICITATORS	FEMININENESSES

FEMININISM	FERNITICKLE	FERROELECTRICS	FERTILIZATIONS	FETISHISATION
FEMININISMS	FERNITICKLES	FERROGRAMS	FERTILIZED	FETISHISATIONS
FEMININITIES	FERNITICLE	FERROGRAPHIES	FERTILIZER	FETISHISED
FEMININITY	FERNITICLES	FERROGRAPHY	FERTILIZERS	FETISHISES
FEMINISATION	FERNTICKLE	FERROMAGNESIAN	FERTILIZES	FETISHISING
FEMINISATIONS	FERNTICKLED	FERROMAGNET	FERTILIZING	FETISHISMS
FEMINISING	FERNTICKLES	FERROMAGNETIC	FERULACEOUS	FETISHISTIC
FEMINISTIC	FERNTICLED	FERROMAGNETISM	FERVENCIES	FETISHISTICALLY
FEMINITIES	FERNTICLES	FERROMAGNETISMS	FERVENTEST	FETISHISTS
FEMINIZATION	FERNYTICKLE	FERROMAGNETS	FERVENTNESS	FETISHIZATION
FEMINIZATIONS	FERNYTICKLES	FERROMANGANESE	FERVENTNESSES	FETISHIZATIONS
FEMINIZING	FERNYTICLE	FERROMANGANESES	FERVESCENT	FETISHIZED
FEMTOSECOND	FERNYTICLES	FERROMOLYBDENUM	FERVIDITIES	FETISHIZES
FEMTOSECONDS	FEROCIOUSLY	FERRONICKEL	FERVIDNESS	FETISHIZING
FENCELESSNESS	FEROCIOUSNESS	FERRONICKELS	FERVIDNESSES	FETOLOGIES
FENCELESSNESSES	FEROCIOUSNESSES	FERRONIERE	FESCENNINE	FETOLOGIST
FENCELINES	FEROCITIES	FERRONIERES	FESTILOGIES	FETOLOGISTS
FENCEWIRES	FERRANDINE	FERRONNIERE	FESTINATED	FETOPROTEIN
FENDERLESS	FERRANDINES	FERRONNIERES	FESTINATELY	FETOPROTEINS
FENESTELLA	FERREDOXIN	FERROPRUSSIATE	FESTINATES	FETOSCOPES
FENESTELLAE	FERREDOXINS	FERROPRUSSIATES	FESTINATING	FETOSCOPIES
FENESTELLAS	FERRELLING	FERROSILICON	FESTINATION	FETTERLESS
FENESTRALS	FERRETIEST	FERROSILICONS	FESTINATIONS	FETTERLOCK
FENESTRATE	FERRETINGS	FERROSOFERRIC	FESTIVALGOER	FETTERLOCKS
FENESTRATED	FERRICYANIC	FERROTYPED	FESTIVALGOERS	FETTUCCINE
FENESTRATES	FERRICYANIDE	FERROTYPES	FESTIVENESS	FETTUCCINES
FENESTRATING	FERRICYANIDES	FERROTYPING	FESTIVENESSES	FETTUCCINI
FENESTRATION	FERRICYANOGEN	FERRUGINEOUS	FESTIVITIES	FETTUCCINIS
FENESTRATIONS	FERRICYANOGENS	FERRUGINOUS	FESTOLOGIES	FETTUCINES
FENNELFLOWER	FERRIFEROUS	FERRYBOATS	FESTOONERIES	FETTUCINIS
FENNELFLOWERS	FERRIMAGNET	FERTIGATED	FESTOONERY	FEUDALISATION
FENUGREEKS	FERRIMAGNETIC	FERTIGATES	FESTOONING	FEUDALISATIONS
FEOFFMENTS	FERRIMAGNETISM	FERTIGATING	FESTSCHRIFT	FEUDALISED
FERACITIES	FERRIMAGNETISMS	FERTIGATION	FESTSCHRIFTEN	FEUDALISES
FERETORIES	FERRIMAGNETS	FERTIGATIONS	FESTSCHRIFTS	FEUDALISING
FERMENTABILITY	FERROCENES	FERTILENESS	FETCHINGLY	FEUDALISMS
FERMENTABLE	FERROCHROME	FERTILENESSES	FETICHISED	FEUDALISTIC
FERMENTATION	FERROCHROMES	FERTILISABLE	FETICHISES	FEUDALISTS
FERMENTATIONS	FERROCHROMIUM	FERTILISATION	FETICHISING	FEUDALITIES
FERMENTATIVE	FERROCHROMIUMS	FERTILISATIONS	FETICHISMS	FEUDALIZATION
FERMENTATIVELY	FERROCONCRETE	FERTILISED	FETICHISTIC	FEUDALIZATIONS
FERMENTERS	FERROCONCRETES	FERTILISER	FETICHISTS	FEUDALIZED
FERMENTESCIBLE	FERROCYANIC	FERTILISERS	FETICHIZED	FEUDALIZES
FERMENTING	FERROCYANIDE	FERTILISES	FETICHIZES	FEUDALIZING
FERMENTITIOUS	FERROCYANIDES	FERTILISING	FETICHIZING	FEUDATORIES
FERMENTIVE	FERROCYANOGEN	FERTILITIES	FETIDITIES	FEUILLETES
FERMENTORS	FERROCYANOGENS	FERTILIZABLE	FETIDNESSES	FEUILLETON
FERNALLIES	FERROELECTRIC	FERTILIZATION	FETIPAROUS	FEUILLETONISM

FEUILLETONISMS	FIBRILLATING	FICTIONALISING	FIDEICOMMISSUM	FIGUREHEAD
FEUILLETONIST	FIBRILLATION	FICTIONALITIES	FIDELISMOS	FIGUREHEADS
FEUILLETONISTIC	FIBRILLATIONS	FICTIONALITY	FIDELISTAS	FIGURELESS
FEUILLETONISTS	FIBRILLIFORM	FICTIONALIZE	FIDELITIES	FIGUREWORK
FEUILLETONS	FIBRILLINS	FICTIONALIZED	FIDGETIEST	FIGUREWORKS
FEVERISHLY	FIBRILLOSE	FICTIONALIZES	FIDGETINESS	FILAGGRINS
FEVERISHNESS	FIBRILLOUS	FICTIONALIZING	FIDGETINESSES	FILAGREEING
FEVERISHNESSES	FIBRINOGEN	FICTIONALLY	FIDGETINGLY	FILAMENTARY
FEVEROUSLY	FIBRINOGENIC	FICTIONEER	FIDUCIALLY	FILAMENTOUS
FEVERROOTS	FIBRINOGENOUS	FICTIONEERING	FIDUCIARIES	FILARIASES
FEVERWEEDS	FIBRINOGENS	FICTIONEERINGS	FIDUCIARILY	FILARIASIS
FEVERWORTS	FIBRINOIDS	FICTIONEERS	FIELDBOOTS	FILATORIES
FIANCAILLES	FIBRINOLYSES	FICTIONISATION	FIELDCRAFT	FILCHINGLY
FIANCHETTI	FIBRINOLYSIN	FICTIONISATIONS	FIELDCRAFTS	FILEFISHES
FIANCHETTO	FIBRINOLYSINS	FICTIONISE	FIELDFARES	FILIALNESS
FIANCHETTOED	FIBRINOLYSIS	FICTIONISED	FIELDMOUSE	FILIALNESSES
FIANCHETTOES	FIBRINOLYTIC	FICTIONISES	FIELDPIECE	FILIATIONS
FIANCHETTOING	FIBRINOPEPTIDE	FICTIONISING	FIELDPIECES	FILIBUSTER
FIANCHETTOS	FIBRINOPEPTIDES	FICTIONIST	FIELDSTONE	FILIBUSTERED
FIBERBOARD	FIBROBLAST	FICTIONISTS	FIELDSTONES	FILIBUSTERER
FIBERBOARDS	FIBROBLASTIC	FICTIONIZATION	FIELDSTRIP	FILIBUSTERERS
FIBERFILLS	FIBROBLASTS	FICTIONIZATIONS	FIELDSTRIPPED	FILIBUSTERING
FIBERGLASS	FIBROCARTILAGE	FICTIONIZE	FIELDSTRIPPING	FILIBUSTERINGS
FIBERGLASSED	FIBROCARTILAGES	FICTIONIZED	FIELDSTRIPS	FILIBUSTERISM
FIBERGLASSES	FIBROCEMENT	FICTIONIZES	FIELDVOLES	FILIBUSTERISMS
FIBERGLASSING	FIBROCEMENTS	FICTIONIZING	FIELDWARDS	FILIBUSTEROUS
FIBERISATION	FIBROCYSTIC	FICTITIOUS	FIELDWORKER	FILIBUSTERS
FIBERISATIONS	FIBROCYTES	FICTITIOUSLY	FIELDWORKERS	FILICINEAN
FIBERISING	FIBROLINES	FICTITIOUSNESS	FIELDWORKS	FILIGRAINS
FIBERIZATION	FIBROLITES	FICTIVENESS	FIENDISHLY	FILIGRANES
FIBERIZATIONS	FIBROMATOUS	FICTIVENESSES	FIENDISHNESS	FILIGREEING
FIBERIZING	FIBROMYALGIA	FIDDIOUSED	FIENDISHNESSES	FILIOPIETISTIC
FIBERSCOPE	FIBROMYALGIAS	FIDDIOUSES	FIERCENESS	FILIPENDULOUS
FIBERSCOPES	FIBRONECTIN	FIDDIOUSING	FIERCENESSES	FILLAGREED
FIBREBOARD	FIBRONECTINS	FIDDLEBACK	FIERINESSES	FILLAGREEING
FIBREBOARDS	FIBROSARCOMA	FIDDLEBACKS	FIFTEENERS	FILLAGREES
FIBREFILLS	FIBROSARCOMAS	FIDDLEDEDEE	FIFTEENTHLY	FILLESTERS
FIBREGLASS	FIBROSARCOMATA	FIDDLEDEEDEE	FIFTEENTHS	FILLIPEENS
FIBREGLASSED	FIBROSITIS	FIDDLEHEAD	FIGHTBACKS	FILLISTERS
FIBREGLASSES	FIBROSITISES	FIDDLEHEADS	FIGURABILITIES	FILMGOINGS
FIBREGLASSING	FIBROUSNESS	FIDDLENECK	FIGURABILITY	FILMICALLY
FIBREOPTIC	FIBROUSNESSES	FIDDLENECKS	FIGURANTES	FILMINESSES
FIBRESCOPE	FIBROVASCULAR	FIDDLESTICK	FIGURATELY	FILMMAKERS
FIBRESCOPES	FICKLENESS	FIDDLESTICKS	FIGURATION	FILMMAKING
FIBRILLARY	FICKLENESSES	FIDDLEWOOD	FIGURATIONS	FILMMAKINGS
FIBRILLATE	FICTIONALISE	FIDDLEWOODS	FIGURATIVE	FILMOGRAPHIES
FIBRILLATED	FICTIONALISED	FIDEICOMMISSA	FIGURATIVELY	FILMOGRAPHY
FIBRILLATES	FICTIONALISES	FIDEICOMMISSARY	FIGURATIVENESS	FILMSETTER

FILMSETTERS	FINANCIERS	FINICALNESS	FIRELIGHTS	FISHWIFELIEST
FILMSETTING	FINANCINGS	FINICALNESSES	FIREPLACED	FISHWIFELY
FILMSETTINGS	FINEABLENESS	FINICKETIER	FIREPLACES	FISHYBACKS
FILMSTRIPS	FINEABLENESSES	FINICKETIEST	FIREPOWERS	FISSICOSTATE
FILOPLUMES	FINENESSES	FINICKIEST	FIREPROOFED	FISSILINGUAL
FILOPODIUM	FINESSINGS	FINICKINESS	FIREPROOFING	FISSILITIES
FILOSELLES	FINGERBOARD	FINICKINESSES	FIREPROOFINGS	FISSIONABILITY
FILOVIRUSES	FINGERBOARDS	FINICKINGS	FIREPROOFS	FISSIONABLE
FILTERABILITIES	FINGERBOWL	FINISHINGS	FIRESCAPED	FISSIONABLES
FILTERABILITY	FINGERBOWLS	FINITENESS	FIRESCAPES	FISSIONING
FILTERABLE	FINGERBREADTH	FINITENESSES	FIRESCAPING	FISSIPALMATE
FILTERABLENESS	FINGERBREADTHS	FINNICKIER	FIRESCAPINGS	FISSIPARISM
FILTHINESS	FINGERGLASS	FINNICKIEST	FIRESCREEN	FISSIPARISMS
FILTHINESSES	FINGERGLASSES	FINNOCHIOS	FIRESCREENS	FISSIPARITIES
FILTRABILITIES	FINGERGUARD	FINOCCHIOS	FIRESTONES	FISSIPARITY
FILTRABILITY	FINGERGUARDS	FIORATURAE	FIRESTORMS	FISSIPAROUS
FILTRABLENESS	FINGERHOLD	FIREBALLER	FIRETHORNS	FISSIPAROUSLY
FILTRABLENESSES	FINGERHOLDS	FIREBALLERS	FIRETRUCKS	FISSIPAROUSNESS
FILTRATABLE	FINGERHOLE	FIREBALLING	FIREWALLED	FISSIPEDAL
FILTRATING	FINGERHOLES	FIREBOARDS	FIREWALLING	FISSIPEDES
FILTRATION	FINGERINGS	FIREBOMBED	FIREWARDEN	FISSIROSTRAL
FILTRATIONS	FINGERLESS	FIREBOMBER	FIREWARDENS	FISTFIGHTS
FIMBRIATED	FINGERLIKE	FIREBOMBERS	FIREWATERS	FISTICUFFED
FIMBRIATES	FINGERLING	FIREBOMBING	FIRMAMENTAL	FISTICUFFING
FIMBRIATING	FINGERLINGS	FIREBOMBINGS	FIRMAMENTS	FISTICUFFS
FIMBRIATION	FINGERMARK	FIREBRANDS	FIRMNESSES	FITFULNESS
FIMBRIATIONS	FINGERMARKS	FIREBREAKS	FIRSTBORNS	FITFULNESSES
FIMBRILLATE	FINGERNAIL	FIREBRICKS	FIRSTFRUITS	FITTINGNESS
FIMICOLOUS	FINGERNAILS	FIREBUSHES	FIRSTLINGS	FITTINGNESSES
FINABLENESS	FINGERPICK	FIRECRACKER	FIRSTNESSES	FIVEFINGER
FINABLENESSES	FINGERPICKED	FIRECRACKERS	FISCALISTS	FIVEFINGERS
FINAGLINGS	FINGERPICKING	FIRECRESTS	FISHABILITIES	FIVEPENCES
FINALISATION	FINGERPICKINGS	FIREDRAGON	FISHABILITY	FIXEDNESSES
FINALISATIONS	FINGERPICKS	FIREDRAGONS	FISHBURGER	FIXTURELESS
FINALISERS	FINGERPLATE	FIREDRAKES	FISHBURGERS	FIZGIGGING
FINALISING	FINGERPLATES	FIREFANGED	FISHERFOLK	FIZZENLESS
FINALISTIC	FINGERPOST	FIREFANGING	FISHERWOMAN	FIZZINESSES
FINALITIES	FINGERPOSTS	FIREFIGHTER	FISHERWOMEN	FLABBERGAST
FINALIZATION	FINGERPRINT	FIREFIGHTERS	FISHFINGER	FLABBERGASTED
FINALIZATIONS	FINGERPRINTED	FIREFIGHTING	FISHFINGERS	FLABBERGASTING
FINALIZERS	FINGERPRINTING	FIREFIGHTINGS	FISHIFYING	FLABBERGASTS
FINALIZING	FINGERPRINTINGS	FIREFIGHTS	FISHINESSES	FLABBINESS
FINANCIALIST	FINGERPRINTS	FIREFLOATS	FISHMONGER	FLABBINESSES
FINANCIALISTS	FINGERSTALL	FIREFLOODS	FISHMONGERS	FLABELLATE
FINANCIALLY	FINGERSTALLS	FIREGUARDS	FISHPLATES	FLABELLATION
FINANCIALS	FINGERTIPS	FIREHOUSES	FISHTAILED	FLABELLATIONS
FINANCIERED	FINICALITIES	FIRELIGHTER	FISHTAILING	FLABELLIFORM
FINANCIERING	FINICALITY	FIRELIGHTERS	FISHWIFELIER	FLACCIDEST

FLACCIDITIES	FLAGSTICKS	FLAPDOODLE	FLATTERERS	FLAVOURLESS
FLACCIDITY	FLAGSTONES	FLAPDOODLES	FLATTERIES	FLAVOURSOME
FLACCIDNESS	FLAKINESSES	FLAPPERHOOD	FLATTERING	FLAWLESSLY
FLACCIDNESSES	FLAMBEEING	FLAPPERHOODS	FLATTERINGLY	FLAWLESSNESS
FLACKERIES	FLAMBOYANCE	FLAPPERISH	FLATTEROUS	FLAWLESSNESSES
FLACKERING	FLAMBOYANCES	FLAPTRACKS	FLATTEROUSLY	FLEAHOPPER
FLACKETING	FLAMBOYANCIES	FLAREBACKS	FLATULENCE	FLEAHOPPERS
FLAFFERING	FLAMBOYANCY	FLASHBACKED	FLATULENCES	FLECHETTES
FLAGELLANT	FLAMBOYANT	FLASHBACKING	FLATULENCIES	FLECKERING
FLAGELLANTISM	FLAMBOYANTE	FLASHBACKS	FLATULENCY	FLECTIONAL
FLAGELLANTISMS	FLAMBOYANTES	FLASHBANGS	FLATULENTLY	FLECTIONLESS
FLAGELLANTS	FLAMBOYANTLY	FLASHBOARD	FLATWASHES	FLEDGELING
FLAGELLATE	FLAMBOYANTS	FLASHBOARDS	FLATWATERS	FLEDGELINGS
FLAGELLATED	FLAMEPROOF	FLASHBULBS	FLAUGHTERED	FLEDGLINGS
FLAGELLATES	FLAMEPROOFED	FLASHCARDS	FLAUGHTERING	FLEECELESS
FLAGELLATING	FLAMEPROOFER	FLASHCUBES	FLAUGHTERS	FLEECHINGS
FLAGELLATION	FLAMEPROOFERS	FLASHFORWARD	FLAUGHTING	FLEECHMENT
FLAGELLATIONS	FLAMEPROOFING	FLASHFORWARDS	FLAUNCHING	FLEECHMENTS
FLAGELLATOR	FLAMEPROOFS	FLASHINESS	FLAUNCHINGS	FLEECINESS
FLAGELLATORS	FLAMETHROWER	FLASHINESSES	FLAUNTIEST	FLEECINESSES
FLAGELLATORY	FLAMETHROWERS	FLASHLAMPS	FLAUNTINESS	FLEERINGLY
FLAGELLIFEROUS	FLAMINGOES	FLASHLIGHT	FLAUNTINESSES	FLEETINGLY
FLAGELLIFORM	FLAMINICAL	FLASHLIGHTS	FLAUNTINGLY	FLEETINGNESS
FLAGELLINS	FLAMMABILITIES	FLASHMOBBING	FLAVANONES	FLEETINGNESSES
FLAGELLOMANIA	FLAMMABILITY	FLASHMOBBINGS	FLAVESCENT	FLEETNESSES
FLAGELLOMANIAC	FLAMMABLES	FLASHOVERS	FLAVIVIRUS	FLEHMENING
FLAGELLOMANIACS	FLAMMIFEROUS	FLASHPACKER	FLAVIVIRUSES	FLEMISHING
FLAGELLOMANIAS	FLAMMULATED	FLASHPACKERS	FLAVONOIDS	FLEROVIUMS
FLAGELLUMS	FLAMMULATION	FLASHPOINT	FLAVOPROTEIN	FLESHHOODS
FLAGEOLETS	FLAMMULATIONS	FLASHPOINTS	FLAVOPROTEINS	FLESHINESS
FLAGGINESS	FLANCHINGS	FLASHTUBES	FLAVOPURPURIN	FLESHINESSES
FLAGGINESSES	FLANCONADE	FLATBREADS	FLAVOPURPURINS	FLESHLIEST
FLAGGINGLY	FLANCONADES	FLATFISHES	FLAVORFULLY	FLESHLINESS
FLAGITATED	FLANGELESS	FLATFOOTED	FLAVORIEST	FLESHLINESSES
FLAGITATES	FLANKERING	FLATFOOTING	FLAVORINGS	FLESHLINGS
FLAGITATING	FLANNELBOARD	FLATLANDER	FLAVORISTS	FLESHMENTS
FLAGITATION	FLANNELBOARDS	FLATLANDERS	FLAVORLESS	FLESHMONGER
FLAGITATIONS	FLANNELETS	FLATLINERS	FLAVORSOME	FLESHMONGERS
FLAGITIOUS	FLANNELETTE	FLATLINING	FLAVOURDYNAMICS	FLESHWORMS
FLAGITIOUSLY	FLANNELETTES	FLATNESSES	FLAVOURERS	FLETCHINGS
FLAGITIOUSNESS	FLANNELGRAPH	FLATPICKED	FLAVOURFUL	FLEURETTES
FLAGRANCES	FLANNELGRAPHS	FLATPICKING	FLAVOURFULLY	FLEXECUTIVE
FLAGRANCIES	FLANNELING	FLATSCREEN	FLAVOURIER	FLEXECUTIVES
FLAGRANTLY	FLANNELLED	FLATSCREENS	FLAVOURIEST	FLEXIBILITIES
FLAGRANTNESS	FLANNELLIER	FLATSHARES	FLAVOURING	FLEXIBILITY
FLAGRANTNESSES	FLANNELLIEST	FLATTENERS	FLAVOURINGS	FLEXIBLENESS
FLAGSTAFFS	FLANNELLING	FLATTENING	FLAVOURIST	FLEXIBLENESSES
FLAGSTAVES	FLANNELMOUTHED	FLATTERABLE	FLAVOURISTS	FLEXICURITIES

FLEXICURITY	FLIPFLOPPED	FLOODPLAIN	FLOSCULOUS	FLUFFINESSES
FLEXIHOURS	FLIPFLOPPING	FLOODPLAINS	FLOTATIONS	FLUGELHORN
FLEXIONLESS	FLIPPANCIES	FLOODTIDES	FLOUNCIEST	FLUGELHORNIST
FLEXITARIAN	FLIPPANTLY	FLOODWALLS	FLOUNCINGS	FLUGELHORNISTS
FLEXITARIANISM	FLIPPANTNESS	FLOODWATER	FLOUNDERED	FLUGELHORNS
FLEXITARIANISMS	FLIPPANTNESSES	FLOODWATERS	FLOUNDERING	FLUIDEXTRACT
FLEXITARIANS	FLIRTATION	FLOORBOARD	FLOURISHED	FLUIDEXTRACTS
FLEXITIMES	FLIRTATIONS	FLOORBOARDS	FLOURISHER	FLUIDIFIED
FLEXOGRAPHIC	FLIRTATIOUS	FLOORCLOTH	FLOURISHERS	FLUIDIFIES
FLEXOGRAPHIES	FLIRTATIOUSLY	FLOORCLOTHS	FLOURISHES	FLUIDIFYING
FLEXOGRAPHY	FLIRTATIOUSNESS	FLOORDROBE	FLOURISHIER	FLUIDISATION
FLEXTIMERS	FLIRTINGLY	FLOORDROBES	FLOURISHIEST	FLUIDISATIONS
FLEXUOUSLY	FLITTERING	FLOORHEADS	FLOURISHING	FLUIDISERS
FLIBBERTIGIBBET	FLITTERMICE	FLOORSHOWS	FLOURISHINGLY	FLUIDISING
FLICHTERED	FLITTERMOUSE	FLOORWALKER	FLOUTINGLY	FLUIDITIES
FLICHTERING	FLOATABILITIES	FLOORWALKERS	FLOUTINGSTOCK	FLUIDIZATION
FLICKERIER	FLOATABILITY	FLOPHOUSES	FLOUTINGSTOCKS	FLUIDIZATIONS
FLICKERIEST	FLOATATION	FLOPPINESS	FLOWCHARTING	FLUIDIZERS
FLICKERING	FLOATATIONS	FLOPPINESSES	FLOWCHARTINGS	FLUIDIZING
FLICKERINGLY	FLOATBASES	FLOPTICALS	FLOWCHARTS	FLUIDNESSES
FLICKERTAIL	FLOATINGLY	FLORENTINE	FLOWERAGES	FLUKINESSES
FLICKERTAILS	FLOATPLANE	FLORENTINES	FLOWERBEDS	FLUMMERIES
FLIGHTIEST	FLOATPLANES	FLORESCENCE	FLOWERETTE	FLUMMOXING
FLIGHTINESS	FLOCCILLATION	FLORESCENCES	FLOWERETTES	FLUNITRAZEPAM
FLIGHTINESSES	FLOCCILLATIONS	FLORESCENT	FLOWERHORN	FLUNITRAZEPAMS
FLIGHTLESS	FLOCCULANT	FLORIATION	FLOWERIEST	FLUNKEYDOM
FLIMFLAMMED	FLOCCULANTS	FLORIATIONS	FLOWERINESS	FLUNKEYDOMS
FLIMFLAMMER	FLOCCULATE	FLORIBUNDA	FLOWERINESSES	FLUNKEYISH
FLIMFLAMMERIES	FLOCCULATED	FLORIBUNDAS	FLOWERINGS	FLUNKEYISM
FLIMFLAMMERS	FLOCCULATES	FLORICANES	FLOWERLESS	FLUNKEYISMS
FLIMFLAMMERY	FLOCCULATING	FLORICULTURAL	FLOWERLIKE	FLUNKYISMS
FLIMFLAMMING	FLOCCULATION	FLORICULTURE	FLOWERPOTS	FLUORAPATITE
FLIMSINESS	FLOCCULATIONS	FLORICULTURES	FLOWINGNESS	FLUORAPATITES
FLIMSINESSES	FLOCCULATOR	FLORICULTURIST	FLOWINGNESSES	FLUORESCED
FLINCHINGLY	FLOCCULATORS	FLORICULTURISTS	FLOWMETERS	FLUORESCEIN
FLINCHINGS	FLOCCULENCE	FLORIDEANS	FLOWSTONES	FLUORESCEINE
FLINDERING	FLOCCULENCES	FLORIDEOUS	FLUCTUATED	FLUORESCEINES
FLINDERSIA	FLOCCULENCIES	FLORIDITIES	FLUCTUATES	FLUORESCEINS
FLINDERSIAS	FLOCCULENCY	FLORIDNESS	FLUCTUATING	FLUORESCENCE
FLINTHEADS	FLOCCULENT	FLORIDNESSES	FLUCTUATION	FLUORESCENCES
FLINTIFIED	FLOCCULENTLY	FLORIFEROUS	FLUCTUATIONAL	FLUORESCENT
FLINTIFIES	FLOODGATES	FLORIFEROUSNESS	FLUCTUATIONS	FLUORESCENTS
FLINTIFYING	FLOODLIGHT	FLORIGENIC	FLUEGELHORN	FLUORESCER
FLINTINESS	FLOODLIGHTED	FLORILEGIA	FLUEGELHORNS	FLUORESCERS
FLINTINESSES	FLOODLIGHTING	FLORILEGIUM	FLUENTNESS	FLUORESCES
FLINTLOCKS	FLOODLIGHTINGS	FLORISTICALLY	FLUENTNESSES	FLUORESCING
FLIPBOARDS	FLOODLIGHTS	FLORISTICS	FLUFFBALLS	FLUORIDATE
FLIPCHARTS	FLOODMARKS	FLORISTRIES	FLUFFINESS	FLUORIDATED

FLUORIDATES	FLUOROSCOPY	FLYFISHERS	FOLKLORISH	FOOLHARDINESS
FLUORIDATING	FLUOROTYPE	FLYPITCHER	FOLKLORIST	FOOLHARDINESSES
FLUORIDATION	FLUOROTYPES	FLYPITCHERS	FOLKLORISTIC	FOOLHARDISE
FLUORIDATIONS	FLUOROURACIL	FLYPITCHES	FOLKLORISTS	FOOLHARDISES
FLUORIDISE	FLUOROURACILS	FLYPOSTERS	FOLKSINESS	FOOLHARDIZE
FLUORIDISED	FLUORSPARS	FLYPOSTING	FOLKSINESSES	FOOLHARDIZES
FLUORIDISES	FLUOXETINE	FLYPOSTINGS	FOLKSINGER	FOOLISHEST
FLUORIDISING	FLUOXETINES	FLYRODDERS	FOLKSINGERS	FOOLISHNESS
FLUORIDIZE	FLUPHENAZINE	FLYSCREENS	FOLKSINGING	FOOLISHNESSES
FLUORIDIZED	FLUPHENAZINES	FLYSPECKED	FOLKSINGINGS	FOOTBALLENE
FLUORIDIZES	FLUSHNESSES	FLYSPECKING	FOLKSONOMIES	FOOTBALLENES
FLUORIDIZING	FLUSHWORKS	FLYSTRIKES	FOLKSONOMY	FOOTBALLER
FLUORIMETER	FLUSTEREDLY	FLYSWATTER	FOLKTRONICA	FOOTBALLERS
FLUORIMETERS	FLUSTERIER	FLYSWATTERS	FOLKTRONICAS	FOOTBALLING
FLUORIMETRIC	FLUSTERIEST	FLYWEIGHTS	FOLLICULAR	FOOTBALLIST
FLUORIMETRIES	FLUSTERING	FOAMFLOWER	FOLLICULATE	FOOTBALLISTS
FLUORIMETRY	FLUSTERMENT	FOAMFLOWERS	FOLLICULATED	FOOTBOARDS
FLUORINATE	FLUSTERMENTS	FOAMINESSES	FOLLICULIN	FOOTBRAKES
FLUORINATED	FLUSTRATED	FOCALISATION	FOLLICULINS	FOOTBREADTH
FLUORINATES	FLUSTRATES	FOCALISATIONS	FOLLICULITIS	FOOTBREADTHS
FLUORINATING	FLUSTRATING	FOCALISING	FOLLICULITISES	FOOTBRIDGE
FLUORINATION	FLUSTRATION	FOCALIZATION	FOLLICULOSE	FOOTBRIDGES
FLUORINATIONS	FLUSTRATIONS	FOCALIZATIONS	FOLLICULOUS	FOOTCLOTHS
FLUOROACETATE	FLUTEMOUTH	FOCALIZING	FOLLOWABLE	FOOTDRAGGER
FLUOROACETATES	FLUTEMOUTHS	FOCIMETERS	FOLLOWERSHIP	FOOTDRAGGERS
FLUOROCARBON	FLUTTERBOARD	FOCOMETERS	FOLLOWERSHIPS	FOOTDRAGGING
FLUOROCARBONS	FLUTTERBOARDS	FODDERINGS	FOLLOWINGS	FOOTDRAGGINGS
FLUOROCHROME	FLUTTERERS	FOEDERATUS	FOLLOWSHIP	FOOTFAULTED
FLUOROCHROMES	FLUTTERIER	FOETATIONS	FOLLOWSHIPS	FOOTFAULTING
FLUOROGRAPHIC	FLUTTERIEST	FOETICIDAL	FOMENTATION	FOOTFAULTS
FLUOROGRAPHIES	FLUTTERING	FOETICIDES	FOMENTATIONS	FOOTGUARDS
FLUOROGRAPHY	FLUTTERINGLY	FOETIDNESS	FONCTIONNAIRE	FOOTLAMBERT
FLUOROMETER	FLUTTERINGS	FOETIDNESSES	FONCTIONNAIRES	FOOTLAMBERTS
FLUOROMETERS	FLUVIALIST	FOETIPAROUS	FONDLINGLY	FOOTLESSLY
FLUOROMETRIC	FLUVIALISTS	FOETOSCOPIES	FONDNESSES	FOOTLESSNESS
FLUOROMETRIES	FLUVIATILE	FOETOSCOPY	FONTANELLE	FOOTLESSNESSES
FLUOROMETRY	FLUVIOMARINE	FOGGINESSES	FONTANELLES	FOOTLIGHTS
FLUOROPHORE	FLUVOXAMINE	FOGRAMITES	FONTICULUS	FOOTLOCKER
FLUOROPHORES	FLUVOXAMINES	FOGRAMITIES	FONTINALIS	FOOTLOCKERS
FLUOROPHOSPHATE	FLUXIONALLY	FOILSWOMAN	FONTINALISES	FOOTNOTING
FLUOROSCOPE	FLUXIONARY	FOILSWOMEN	FOODLESSNESS	FOOTPLATEMAN
FLUOROSCOPED	FLUXIONIST	FOISONLESS	FOODLESSNESSES	FOOTPLATEMEN
FLUOROSCOPES	FLUXIONISTS	FOLIACEOUS	FOODSTUFFS	FOOTPLATES
FLUOROSCOPIC	FLUXMETERS	FOLIATIONS	FOOLBEGGED	FOOTPLATEWOMAN
FLUOROSCOPIES	FLYBLOWING	FOLIATURES	FOOLFISHES	FOOTPLATEWOMEN
FLUOROSCOPING	FLYBRIDGES	FOLKINESSES	FOOLHARDIER	FOOTPRINTS
FLUOROSCOPIST	FLYCATCHER	FOLKISHNESS	FOOLHARDIEST	FOOTSLOGGED
FLUOROSCOPISTS	FLYCATCHERS	FOLKISHNESSES	FOOLHARDILY	FOOTSLOGGER

FOOTSLOGGERS	FORCIBLENESS	FOREDOOMED	FORELAYING	FORESEEINGLY
FOOTSLOGGING	FORCIBLENESSES	FOREDOOMING	FORELENDING	FORESHADOW
FOOTSLOGGINGS	FORCIPATED	FOREFATHER	FORELIFTED	FORESHADOWED
FOOTSORENESS	FORCIPATION	FOREFATHERLY	FORELIFTING	FORESHADOWER
FOOTSORENESSES	FORCIPATIONS	FOREFATHERS	FORELOCKED	FORESHADOWERS
FOOTSTALKS	FOREARMING	FOREFEELING	FORELOCKING	FORESHADOWING
FOOTSTALLS	FOREBITTER	FOREFEELINGLY	FOREMANSHIP	FORESHADOWINGS
FOOTSTOCKS	FOREBITTERS	FOREFENDED	FOREMANSHIPS	FORESHADOWS
FOOTSTONES	FOREBODEMENT	FOREFENDING	FOREMASTMAN	FORESHANKS
FOOTSTOOLED	FOREBODEMENTS	FOREFINGER	FOREMASTMEN	FORESHEETS
FOOTSTOOLS	FOREBODERS	FOREFINGERS	FOREMEANING	FORESHEWED
FOOTWEARIER	FOREBODIES	FOREFRONTS	FOREMENTIONED	FORESHEWING
FOOTWEARIEST	FOREBODING	FOREGATHER	FOREMOTHER	FORESHOCKS
FOPPISHNESS	FOREBODINGLY	FOREGATHERED	FOREMOTHERS	FORESHORES
FOPPISHNESSES	FOREBODINGNESS	FOREGATHERING	FORENIGHTS	FORESHORTEN
FORAMINATED	FOREBODINGS	FOREGATHERS	FORENSICALITIES	FORESHORTENED
FORAMINIFER	FOREBRAINS	FOREGLEAMS	FORENSICALITY	FORESHORTENING
FORAMINIFERA	FORECABINS	FOREGOINGS	FORENSICALLY	FORESHORTENINGS
FORAMINIFERAL	FORECADDIE	FOREGONENESS	FOREORDAIN	FORESHORTENS
FORAMINIFERAN	FORECADDIES	FOREGONENESSES	FOREORDAINED	FORESHOWED
FORAMINIFERANS	FORECARRIAGE	FOREGROUND	FOREORDAINING	FORESHOWING
FORAMINIFEROUS	FORECARRIAGES	FOREGROUNDED	FOREORDAINMENT	FORESIGHTED
FORAMINIFERS	FORECASTABLE	FOREGROUNDING	FOREORDAINMENTS	FORESIGHTEDLY
FORAMINOUS	FORECASTED	FOREGROUNDS	FOREORDAINS	FORESIGHTEDNESS
FORBEARANCE	FORECASTER	FOREHANDED	FOREORDINATION	FORESIGHTFUL
FORBEARANCES	FORECASTERS	FOREHANDEDLY	FOREORDINATIONS	FORESIGHTLESS
FORBEARANT	FORECASTING	FOREHANDEDNESS	FOREPASSED	FORESIGHTS
FORBEARERS	FORECASTINGS	FOREHANDING	FOREPAYMENT	FORESIGNIFIED
FORBEARING	FORECASTLE	FOREHENTING	FOREPAYMENTS	FORESIGNIFIES
FORBEARINGLY	FORECASTLES	FOREHOOVES	FOREPLANNED	FORESIGNIFY
FORBIDDALS	FORECHECKED	FOREIGNERS	FOREPLANNING	FORESIGNIFYING
FORBIDDANCE	FORECHECKER	FOREIGNISM	FOREPOINTED	FORESKIRTS
FORBIDDANCES	FORECHECKERS	FOREIGNISMS	FOREPOINTING	FORESLACKED
FORBIDDENLY	FORECHECKING	FOREIGNNESS	FOREPOINTS	FORESLACKING
FORBIDDERS	FORECHECKS	FOREIGNNESSES	FOREQUARTER	FORESLACKS
FORBIDDING	FORECHOSEN	FOREJUDGED	FOREQUARTERS	FORESLOWED
FORBIDDINGLY	FORECLOSABLE	FOREJUDGEMENT	FOREREACHED	FORESLOWING
FORBIDDINGNESS	FORECLOSED	FOREJUDGEMENTS	FOREREACHES	FORESPEAKING
FORBIDDINGS	FORECLOSES	FOREJUDGES	FOREREACHING	FORESPEAKS
FORCEDNESS	FORECLOSING	FOREJUDGING	FOREREADING	FORESPENDING
FORCEDNESSES	FORECLOSURE	FOREJUDGMENT	FOREREADINGS	FORESPENDS
FORCEFULLY	FORECLOSURES	FOREJUDGMENTS	FORERUNNER	FORESPOKEN
FORCEFULNESS	FORECLOTHS	FOREKNOWABLE	FORERUNNERS	FORESTAGES
FORCEFULNESSES	FORECOURSE	FOREKNOWING	FORERUNNING	FORESTAIRS
FORCEMEATS	FORECOURSES	FOREKNOWINGLY	FORESAYING	FORESTALLED
FORCEPSLIKE	FORECOURTS	FOREKNOWLEDGE	FORESEEABILITY	FORESTALLER
FORCIBILITIES	FOREDAMNED	FOREKNOWLEDGES	FORESEEABLE	FORESTALLERS
FORCIBILITY	FOREDATING	FORELADIES	FORESEEING	FORESTALLING

FORESTALLINGS	FOREWARNED	FORHENTING	FORMATIONAL	FORMULATOR
FORESTALLMENT	FOREWARNER	FORHOOIEING	FORMATIONS	FORMULATORS
FORESTALLMENTS	FOREWARNERS	FORINSECAL	FORMATIVELY	FORMULISED
FORESTALLS	FOREWARNING	FORISFAMILIATE	FORMATIVENESS	FORMULISES
FORESTALMENT	FOREWARNINGLY	FORISFAMILIATED	FORMATIVENESSES	FORMULISING
FORESTALMENTS	FOREWARNINGS	FORISFAMILIATES	FORMATIVES	FORMULISMS
FORESTATION	FOREWEIGHED	FORJUDGING	FORMATTERS	FORMULISTIC
FORESTATIONS	FOREWEIGHING	FORJUDGMENT	FORMATTING	FORMULISTS
FORESTAYSAIL	FOREWEIGHS	FORJUDGMENTS	FORMATTINGS	FORMULIZED
FORESTAYSAILS	FORFAIRING	FORKEDNESS	FORMFITTING	FORMULIZES
FORESTLAND	FORFAITERS	FORKEDNESSES	FORMICARIA	FORMULIZING
FORESTLANDS	FORFAITING	FORKINESSES	FORMICARIES	FORNICATED
FORESTLESS	FORFAITINGS	FORKLIFTED	FORMICARIUM	FORNICATES
FORESTRIES	FORFEITABLE	FORKLIFTING	FORMICATED	FORNICATING
FORESWEARING	FORFEITERS	FORLENDING	FORMICATES	FORNICATION
FORESWEARS	FORFEITING	FORLORNEST	FORMICATING	FORNICATIONS
FORETASTED	FORFEITURE	FORLORNNESS	FORMICATION	FORNICATOR
FORETASTES	FORFEITURES	FORLORNNESSES	FORMICATIONS	FORNICATORS
FORETASTING	FORFENDING	FORMABILITIES	FORMIDABILITIES	FORNICATRESS
FORETAUGHT	FORFEUCHEN	FORMABILITY	FORMIDABILITY	FORNICATRESSES
FORETEACHES	FORFICULATE	FORMALDEHYDE	FORMIDABLE	FORSAKENLY
FORETEACHING	FORFOUGHEN	FORMALDEHYDES	FORMIDABLENESS	FORSAKENNESS
FORETELLER	FORFOUGHTEN	FORMALINES	FORMIDABLY	FORSAKENNESSES
FORETELLERS	FORGATHERED	FORMALISABLE	FORMLESSLY	FORSAKINGS
FORETELLING	FORGATHERING	FORMALISATION	FORMLESSNESS	FORSLACKED
FORETHINKER	FORGATHERS	FORMALISATIONS	FORMLESSNESSES	FORSLACKING
FORETHINKERS	FORGEABILITIES	FORMALISED	FORMULAICALLY	FORSLOEING
FORETHINKING	FORGEABILITY	FORMALISER	FORMULARIES	FORSLOWING
FORETHINKS	FORGETFULLY	FORMALISERS	FORMULARISATION	FORSPEAKING
FORETHOUGHT	FORGETFULNESS	FORMALISES	FORMULARISE	FORSPENDING
FORETHOUGHTFUL	FORGETFULNESSES	FORMALISING	FORMULARISED	FORSTERITE
FORETHOUGHTS	FORGETTABLE	FORMALISMS	FORMULARISER	FORSTERITES
FORETOKENED	FORGETTERIES	FORMALISTIC	FORMULARISERS	FORSWEARER
FORETOKENING	FORGETTERS	FORMALISTICALLY	FORMULARISES	FORSWEARERS
FORETOKENINGS	FORGETTERY	FORMALISTS	FORMULARISING	FORSWEARING
FORETOKENS	FORGETTING	FORMALITER	FORMULARISTIC	FORSWINKED
FORETOPMAN	FORGETTINGLY	FORMALITIES	FORMULARIZATION	FORSWINKING
FORETOPMAST	FORGETTINGS	FORMALIZABLE	FORMULARIZE	FORSWORNNESS
FORETOPMASTS	FORGIVABLE	FORMALIZATION	FORMULARIZED	FORSWORNNESSES
FORETOPMEN	FORGIVABLY	FORMALIZATIONS	FORMULARIZER	FORSYTHIAS
FORETRIANGLE	FORGIVENESS	FORMALIZED	FORMULARIZERS	FORTALICES
FORETRIANGLES	FORGIVENESSES	FORMALIZER	FORMULARIZES	FORTEPIANIST
FOREVERMORE	FORGIVINGLY	FORMALIZERS	FORMULARIZING	FORTEPIANISTS
FOREVERNESS	FORGIVINGNESS	FORMALIZES	FORMULATED	FORTEPIANO
FOREVERNESSES	FORGIVINGNESSES	FORMALIZING	FORMULATES	FORTEPIANOS
FOREVOUCHED	FORGOTTENNESS	FORMALNESS	FORMULATING	FORTHCOMES
FOREWARDED	FORGOTTENNESSES	FORMALNESSES	FORMULATION	FORTHCOMING
FOREWARDING	FORHAILING	FORMAMIDES	FORMULATIONS	FORTHCOMINGNESS

FORTHGOING	FORWANDERING	FOUNDATIONERS	FRACTIONALISING	FRAGMENTAL
FORTHGOINGS	FORWANDERS	FOUNDATIONLESS	FRACTIONALISM	FRAGMENTALLY
FORTHINKING	FORWARDERS	FOUNDATIONS	FRACTIONALISMS	FRAGMENTARILY
FORTHOUGHT	FORWARDEST	FOUNDERING	FRACTIONALIST	FRAGMENTARINESS
FORTHRIGHT	FORWARDING	FOUNDEROUS	FRACTIONALISTS	FRAGMENTARY
FORTHRIGHTLY	FORWARDINGS	FOUNDLINGS	FRACTIONALIZE	FRAGMENTATE
FORTHRIGHTNESS	FORWARDNESS	FOUNDRESSES	FRACTIONALIZED	FRAGMENTATED
FORTHRIGHTS	FORWARDNESSES	FOUNTAINED	FRACTIONALIZES	FRAGMENTATES
FORTIFIABLE	FORWARNING	FOUNTAINHEAD	FRACTIONALIZING	FRAGMENTATING
FORTIFICATION	FORWASTING	FOUNTAINHEADS	FRACTIONALLY	FRAGMENTATION
FORTIFICATIONS	FORWEARIED	FOUNTAINING	FRACTIONARY	FRAGMENTATIONS
FORTIFIERS	FORWEARIES	FOUNTAINLESS	FRACTIONATE	FRAGMENTED
FORTIFYING	FORWEARYING	FOURCHETTE	FRACTIONATED	FRAGMENTING
FORTIFYINGLY	FOSCARNETS	FOURCHETTES	FRACTIONATES	FRAGMENTISE
FORTILAGES	FOSSICKERS	FOURDRINIER	FRACTIONATING	FRAGMENTISED
FORTISSIMI	FOSSICKING	FOURDRINIERS	FRACTIONATION	FRAGMENTISES
FORTISSIMO	FOSSICKINGS	FOURFOLDNESS	FRACTIONATIONS	FRAGMENTISING
FORTISSIMOS	FOSSILIFEROUS	FOURFOLDNESSES	FRACTIONATOR	FRAGMENTIZE
FORTISSISSIMO	FOSSILISABLE	FOURPENCES	FRACTIONATORS	FRAGMENTIZED
FORTITUDES	FOSSILISATION	FOURPENNIES	FRACTIONED	FRAGMENTIZES
FORTITUDINOUS	FOSSILISATIONS	FOURPLEXES	FRACTIONING	FRAGMENTIZING
FORTNIGHTLIES	FOSSILISED	FOURRAGERE	FRACTIONISATION	FRAGRANCED
FORTNIGHTLY	FOSSILISES	FOURRAGERES	FRACTIONISE	FRAGRANCES
FORTNIGHTS	FOSSILISING	FOURSCORTH	FRACTIONISED	FRAGRANCIES
FORTRESSED	FOSSILIZABLE	FOURSQUARE	FRACTIONISES	FRAGRANCING
FORTRESSES	FOSSILIZATION	FOURSQUARELY	FRACTIONISING	FRAGRANTLY
FORTRESSING	FOSSILIZATIONS	FOURSQUARENESS	FRACTIONIZATION	FRAGRANTNESS
FORTRESSLIKE	FOSSILIZED	FOURTEENER	FRACTIONIZE	FRAGRANTNESSES
FORTUITIES	FOSSILIZES	FOURTEENERS	FRACTIONIZED	FRAICHEURS
FORTUITISM	FOSSILIZING	FOURTEENTH	FRACTIONIZES	FRAILNESSES
FORTUITISMS	FOSTERAGES	FOURTEENTHLY	FRACTIONIZING	FRAMBESIAS
FORTUITIST	FOSTERINGS	FOURTEENTHS	FRACTIONLET	FRAMBOESIA
FORTUITISTS	FOSTERLING	FOVEOLATED	FRACTIONLETS	FRAMBOESIAS
FORTUITOUS	FOSTERLINGS	FOXBERRIES	FRACTIOUSLY	FRAMBOISES
FORTUITOUSLY	FOSTRESSES	FOXHUNTERS	FRACTIOUSNESS	FRAMESHIFT
FORTUITOUSNESS	FOTHERGILLA	FOXHUNTING	FRACTIOUSNESSES	FRAMESHIFTS
FORTUNATELY	FOTHERGILLAS	FOXHUNTINGS	FRACTOCUMULI	FRAMEWORKS
FORTUNATENESS	FOUDROYANT	FOXINESSES	FRACTOCUMULUS	FRANCHISED
FORTUNATENESSES	FOUGHTIEST	FOXTROTTED	FRACTOGRAPHIES	FRANCHISEES
FORTUNATES	FOULBROODS	FOXTROTTING	FRACTOGRAPHY	FRANCHISEMENT
FORTUNELESS	FOULDERING	FOZINESSES	FRACTOSTRATI	FRANCHISEMENTS
FORTUNISED	FOULMOUTHED	FRABJOUSLY	FRACTOSTRATUS	FRANCHISER
FORTUNISES	FOULNESSES	FRACTALITIES	FRACTURABLE	FRANCHISERS
FORTUNISING	FOUNDATION	FRACTALITY	FRACTURERS	FRANCHISES
FORTUNIZED	FOUNDATIONAL	FRACTIONAL	FRACTURING	FRANCHISING
FORTUNIZES	FOUNDATIONALLY	FRACTIONALISE	FRAGILENESS	FRANCHISOR
FORTUNIZING	FOUNDATIONARY	FRACTIONALISED	FRAGILENESSES	FRANCHISORS
FORWANDERED	FOUNDATIONER	FRACTIONALISES	FRAGILITIES	

FRANCISATION	FRATERNALISM	FREEBASING	FREESTANDING	FREQUENTATIONS
FRANCISATIONS	FRATERNALISMS	FREEBOARDS	FREESTONES	FREQUENTATIVE
FRANCISING	FRATERNALLY	FREEBOOTED	FREESTYLED	FREQUENTATIVES
FRANCIZATION	FRATERNISATION	FREEBOOTER	FREESTYLER	FREQUENTED
FRANCIZATIONS	FRATERNISATIONS	FREEBOOTERIES	FREESTYLERS	FREQUENTER
FRANCIZING	FRATERNISE	FREEBOOTERS	FREESTYLES	FREQUENTERS
FRANCOLINS	FRATERNISED	FREEBOOTERY	FREESTYLING	FREQUENTEST
FRANCOMANIA	FRATERNISER	FREEBOOTIES	FREESTYLINGS	FREQUENTING
FRANCOMANIAS	FRATERNISERS	FREEBOOTING	FREETHINKER	FREQUENTLY
FRANCOPHIL	FRATERNISES	FREEBOOTINGS	FREETHINKERS	FREQUENTNESS
FRANCOPHILE	FRATERNISING	FREECOOLING	FREETHINKING	FREQUENTNESSES
FRANCOPHILES	FRATERNITIES	FREECOOLINGS	FREETHINKINGS	FRESCOINGS
FRANCOPHILS	FRATERNITY	FREECYCLED	FREEWHEELED	FRESCOISTS
FRANCOPHOBE	FRATERNIZATION	FREECYCLES	FREEWHEELER	FRESHENERS
FRANCOPHOBES	FRATERNIZATIONS	FREECYCLING	FREEWHEELERS	FRESHENING
FRANCOPHOBIA	FRATERNIZE	FREEDIVERS	FREEWHEELING	FRESHERDOM
FRANCOPHOBIAS	FRATERNIZED	FREEDIVING	FREEWHEELINGLY	FRESHERDOMS
FRANCOPHONE	FRATERNIZER	FREEDIVINGS	FREEWHEELINGS	FRESHMANSHIP
FRANCOPHONES	FRATERNIZERS	FREEDWOMAN	FREEWHEELS	FRESHMANSHIPS
FRANGIBILITIES	FRATERNIZES	FREEDWOMEN	FREEWRITES	FRESHNESSES
FRANGIBILITY	FRATERNIZING	FREEGANISM	FREEWRITING	FRESHWATER
FRANGIBLENESS	FRATRICIDAL	FREEGANISMS	FREEWRITINGS	FRESHWATERS
FRANGIBLENESSES	FRATRICIDE	FREEHANDED	FREEWRITTEN	FRETBOARDS
FRANGIPANE	FRATRICIDES	FREEHANDEDLY	FREEZINGLY	FRETFULNESS
FRANGIPANES	FRAUDFULLY	FREEHANDEDNESS	FREIGHTAGE	FRETFULNESSES
FRANGIPANI	FRAUDSTERS	FREEHEARTED	FREIGHTAGES	FRIABILITIES
FRANGIPANIS	FRAUDULENCE	FREEHEARTEDLY	FREIGHTERS	FRIABILITY
FRANGIPANNI	FRAUDULENCES	FREEHOLDER	FREIGHTING	FRIABLENESS
FRANKALMOIGN	FRAUDULENCIES	FREEHOLDERS	FREIGHTLESS	FRIABLENESSES
FRANKALMOIGNS	FRAUDULENCY	FREELANCED	FREMESCENCE	FRIARBIRDS
FRANKFORTS	FRAUDULENT	FREELANCER	FREMESCENCES	FRICANDEAU
FRANKFURTER	FRAUDULENTLY	FREELANCERS	FREMESCENT	FRICANDEAUS
FRANKFURTERS	FRAUDULENTNESS	FREELANCES	FREMITUSES	FRICANDEAUX
FRANKFURTS	FRAUGHTAGE	FREELANCING	FRENCHIFICATION	FRICANDOES
FRANKINCENSE	FRAUGHTAGES	FREELOADED	FRENCHIFIED	FRICASSEED
FRANKINCENSES	FRAUGHTEST	FREELOADER	FRENCHIFIES	FRICASSEEING
FRANKLINITE	FRAUGHTING	FREELOADERS	FRENCHIFYING	FRICASSEES
FRANKLINITES	FRAXINELLA	FREELOADING	FRENETICAL	FRICATIVES
FRANKNESSES	FRAXINELLAS	FREELOADINGS	FRENETICALLY	FRICTIONAL
FRANKPLEDGE	FREAKERIES	FREEMARTIN	FRENETICISM	FRICTIONALLY
FRANKPLEDGES	FREAKINESS	FREEMARTINS	FRENETICISMS	FRICTIONLESS
FRANSERIAS	FREAKINESSES	FREEMASONIC	FRENETICNESS	FRICTIONLESSLY
FRANTICALLY	FREAKISHLY	FREEMASONRIES	FRENETICNESSES	FRIEDCAKES
FRANTICNESS	FREAKISHNESS	FREEMASONRY	FRENZIEDLY	FRIENDINGS
FRANTICNESSES	FREAKISHNESSES	FREEMASONS	FREQUENCES	FRIENDLESS
FRATCHETIER	FRECKLIEST	FREENESSES	FREQUENCIES	FRIENDLESSNESS
FRATCHETIEST	FRECKLINGS	FREEPHONES	FREQUENTABLE	FRIENDLIER
FRATCHIEST	FREEBASERS	FREESHEETS	FREQUENTATION	FRIENDLIES

FRIENDLIEST	FRITILLARIAS	FRONTIERSMEN	FROWZINESSES	FRUITLESSNESS
FRIENDLILY	FRITILLARIES	FRONTIERSWOMAN	FROZENNESS	FRUITLESSNESSES
FRIENDLINESS	FRITILLARY	FRONTIERSWOMEN	FROZENNESSES	FRUITWOODS
FRIENDLINESSES	FRITTERERS	FRONTISPIECE	FRUCTIFEROUS	FRUITWORMS
FRIENDSHIP	FRITTERING	FRONTISPIECED	FRUCTIFEROUSLY	FRUMENTACEOUS
FRIENDSHIPS	FRIVOLITIES	FRONTISPIECES	FRUCTIFICATION	FRUMENTARIOUS
FRIEZELIKE	FRIVOLLERS	FRONTISPIECING	FRUCTIFICATIONS	FRUMENTATION
FRIGATOONS	FRIVOLLING	FRONTLESSLY	FRUCTIFIED	FRUMENTATIONS
FRIGHTENED	FRIVOLOUSLY	FRONTLINES	FRUCTIFIER	FRUMENTIES
FRIGHTENER	FRIVOLOUSNESS	FRONTLISTS	FRUCTIFIERS	FRUMPINESS
FRIGHTENERS	FRIVOLOUSNESSES	FRONTOGENESES	FRUCTIFIES	FRUMPINESSES
FRIGHTENING	FRIZZINESS	FRONTOGENESIS	FRUCTIFYING	FRUMPISHLY
FRIGHTENINGLY	FRIZZINESSES	FRONTOGENETIC	FRUCTIVOROUS	FRUMPISHNESS
FRIGHTFULLY	FRIZZLIEST	FRONTOLYSES	FRUCTUARIES	FRUMPISHNESSES
FRIGHTFULNESS	FRIZZLINESS	FRONTOLYSIS	FRUCTUATED	FRUSEMIDES
FRIGHTFULNESSES	FRIZZLINESSES	FRONTPAGED	FRUCTUATES	FRUSTRATED
FRIGHTSOME	FROGFISHES	FRONTPAGES	FRUCTUATING	FRUSTRATER
FRIGIDARIA	FROGGERIES	FRONTPAGING	FRUCTUATION	FRUSTRATERS
FRIGIDARIUM	FROGHOPPER	FRONTRUNNER	FRUCTUATIONS	FRUSTRATES
FRIGIDITIES	FROGHOPPERS	FRONTRUNNERS	FRUCTUOUSLY	FRUSTRATING
FRIGIDNESS	FROGMARCHED	FRONTRUNNING	FRUCTUOUSNESS	FRUSTRATINGLY
FRIGIDNESSES	FROGMARCHES	FRONTRUNNINGS	FRUCTUOUSNESSES	FRUSTRATION
FRIGORIFIC	FROGMARCHING	FRONTWARDS	FRUGALISTA	FRUSTRATIONS
FRIGORIFICO	FROGMOUTHS	FROSTBITES	FRUGALISTAS	FRUTESCENCE
FRIGORIFICOS	FROGSPAWNS	FROSTBITING	FRUGALISTS	FRUTESCENCES
FRIKKADELS	FROLICKERS	FROSTBITINGS	FRUGALITIES	FRUTESCENT
FRILLERIES	FROLICKIER	FROSTBITTEN	FRUGALNESS	FRUTIFYING
FRILLINESS	FROLICKIEST	FROSTBOUND	FRUGALNESSES	FUCIVOROUS
FRILLINESSES	FROLICKING	FROSTFISHES	FRUGIFEROUS	FUCOXANTHIN
FRINGELESS	FROLICSOME	FROSTINESS	FRUGIVORES	FUCOXANTHINS
FRINGELIKE	FROLICSOMELY	FROSTINESSES	FRUGIVOROUS	FUGACIOUSLY
FRINGILLACEOUS	FROLICSOMENESS	FROSTLINES	FRUITARIAN	FUGACIOUSNESS
FRINGILLID	FROMENTIES	FROSTWORKS	FRUITARIANISM	FUGACIOUSNESSES
FRINGILLIFORM	FRONDESCENCE	FROTHERIES	FRUITARIANISMS	FUGACITIES
FRINGILLINE	FRONDESCENCES	FROTHINESS	FRUITARIANS	FUGGINESSES
FRIPONNERIE	FRONDESCENT	FROTHINESSES	FRUITCAKES	FUGITATION
FRIPONNERIES	FRONDIFEROUS	FROUGHIEST	FRUITERERS	FUGITATIONS
FRIPPERERS	FRONTAGERS	FROUZINESS	FRUITERESS	FUGITIVELY
FRIPPERIES	FRONTALITIES	FROUZINESSES	FRUITERESSES	FUGITIVENESS
FRISKINESS	FRONTALITY	FROWARDNESS	FRUITERIES	FUGITIVENESSES
FRISKINESSES	FRONTBENCHER	FROWARDNESSES	FRUITFULLER	FUGITOMETER
FRISKINGLY	FRONTBENCHERS	FROWNINGLY	FRUITFULLEST	FUGITOMETERS
FRITHBORHS	FRONTCOURT	FROWSINESS	FRUITFULLY	FULFILLERS
FRITHSOKEN	FRONTCOURTS	FROWSINESSES	FRUITFULNESS	FULFILLING
FRITHSOKENS	FRONTENISES	FROWSTIEST	FRUITFULNESSES	FULFILLINGS
FRITHSTOOL	FRONTIERED	FROWSTINESS	FRUITINESS	FULFILLMENT
FRITHSTOOLS	FRONTIERING	FROWSTINESSES	FRUITINESSES	FULFILLMENTS
FRITILLARIA	FRONTIERSMAN	FROWZINESS	FRUITLESSLY	FULFILMENT

FULFILMENTS	FUNAMBULATION	FUNEREALLY	FURNISHMENTS	FUSTIANISED
FULGENCIES	FUNAMBULATIONS	FUNGIBILITIES	FURNITURES	FUSTIANISES
FULGURATED	FUNAMBULATOR	FUNGIBILITY	FUROSEMIDE	FUSTIANISING
FULGURATES	FUNAMBULATORS	FUNGICIDAL	FUROSEMIDES	FUSTIANIST
FULGURATING	FUNAMBULATORY	FUNGICIDALLY	FURRIERIES	FUSTIANISTS
FULGURATION	FUNAMBULISM	FUNGICIDES	FURRINESSES	FUSTIANIZE
FULGURATIONS	FUNAMBULISMS	FUNGISTATIC	FURROWIEST	FUSTIANIZED
FULGURITES	FUNAMBULIST	FUNGISTATICALLY	FURROWLESS	FUSTIANIZES
FULIGINOSITIES	FUNAMBULISTS	FUNGISTATS	FURSHLUGGINER	FUSTIANIZING
FULIGINOSITY	FUNCTIONAL	FUNGOSITIES	FURTHCOMING	FUSTIGATED
FULIGINOUS	FUNCTIONALISM	FUNICULARS	FURTHCOMINGS	FUSTIGATES
FULIGINOUSLY	FUNCTIONALISMS	FUNICULATE	FURTHERANCE	FUSTIGATING
FULIGINOUSNESS	FUNCTIONALIST	FUNKINESSES	FURTHERANCES	FUSTIGATION
FULLBLOODS	FUNCTIONALISTIC	FUNNELFORM	FURTHERERS	FUSTIGATIONS
FULLERENES	FUNCTIONALISTS	FUNNELLING	FURTHERING	FUSTIGATOR
FULLERIDES	FUNCTIONALITIES	FUNNINESSES	FURTHERMORE	FUSTIGATORS
FULLERITES	FUNCTIONALITY	FURACIOUSNESS	FURTHERMOST	FUSTIGATORY
FULLMOUTHED	FUNCTIONALLY	FURACIOUSNESSES	FURTHERSOME	FUSTILARIAN
FULLNESSES	FUNCTIONALS	FURACITIES	FURTIVENESS	FUSTILARIANS
FULMINANTS	FUNCTIONARIES	FURALDEHYDE	FURTIVENESSES	FUSTILIRIAN
FULMINATED	FUNCTIONARY	FURALDEHYDES	FURUNCULAR	FUSTILIRIANS
FULMINATES	FUNCTIONATE	FURANOSIDE	FURUNCULOSES	FUSTILLIRIAN
FULMINATING	FUNCTIONATED	FURANOSIDES	FURUNCULOSIS	FUSTILLIRIANS
FULMINATION	FUNCTIONATES	FURAZOLIDONE	FURUNCULOUS	FUSTINESSES
FULMINATIONS	FUNCTIONATING	FURAZOLIDONES	FUSHIONLESS	FUSULINIDS
FULMINATOR	FUNCTIONED	FURBEARERS	FUSIBILITIES	FUTILENESS
FULMINATORS	FUNCTIONING	FURBELOWED	FUSIBILITY	FUTILENESSES
FULMINATORY	FUNCTIONLESS	FURBELOWING	FUSIBLENESS	FUTILITARIAN
FULMINEOUS	FUNDAMENTAL	FURBISHERS	FUSIBLENESSES	FUTILITARIANISM
FULSOMENESS	FUNDAMENTALISM	FURBISHING	FUSILLADED	FUTILITARIANS
FULSOMENESSES	FUNDAMENTALISMS	FURCATIONS	FUSILLADES	FUTILITIES
FUMATORIES	FUNDAMENTALIST	FURCIFEROUS	FUSILLADING	FUTURELESS
FUMATORIUM	FUNDAMENTALISTS	FURFURACEOUS	FUSILLATION	FUTURELESSNESS
FUMATORIUMS	FUNDAMENTALITY	FURFURACEOUSLY	FUSILLATIONS	FUTURISTIC
FUMBLINGLY	FUNDAMENTALLY	FURFURALDEHYDE	FUSIONISMS	FUTURISTICALLY
FUMBLINGNESS	FUNDAMENTALNESS	FURFURALDEHYDES	FUSIONISTS	FUTURISTICS
FUMBLINGNESSES	FUNDAMENTALS	FURFUROLES	FUSIONLESS	FUTURITIES
FUMIGATING	FUNDAMENTS	FURIOSITIES	FUSSBUDGET	FUTURITION
FUMIGATION	FUNDHOLDER	FURIOUSNESS	FUSSBUDGETIER	FUTURITIONS
FUMIGATIONS	FUNDHOLDERS	FURIOUSNESSES	FUSSBUDGETIEST	FUTUROLOGICAL
FUMIGATORS	FUNDHOLDING	FURLOUGHED	FUSSBUDGETS	FUTUROLOGIES
FUMIGATORY	FUNDHOLDINGS	FURLOUGHING	FUSSBUDGETY	FUTUROLOGIST
FUMITORIES	FUNDRAISED	FURMENTIES	FUSSINESSES	FUTUROLOGISTS
FUMOSITIES	FUNDRAISER	FURNIMENTS	FUSTANELLA	FUTUROLOGY
FUNAMBULATE	FUNDRAISERS	FURNISHERS	FUSTANELLAS	FUZZINESSES
FUNAMBULATED	FUNDRAISES	FURNISHING	FUSTANELLE	
FUNAMBULATES	FUNDRAISING	FURNISHINGS	FUSTANELLES	
FUNAMBULATING	FUNDRAISINGS	FURNISHMENT	FUSTIANISE	

G

GABAPENTIN	GAINSAYERS	GALACTOSYL	GALLIAMBICS	GALLOWGLASSES
GABAPENTINS	GAINSAYING	GALACTOSYLS	GALLIARDISE	GALLOWSNESS
GABARDINES	GAINSAYINGS	GALANTAMINE	GALLIARDISES	GALLOWSNESSES
GABBINESSES	GAINSHARING	GALANTAMINES	GALLIASSES	GALLSICKNESS
GABBLEMENT	GAINSHARINGS	GALANTINES	GALLICISATION	GALLSICKNESSES
GABBLEMENTS	GAINSTRIVE	GALAVANTED	GALLICISATIONS	GALLSTONES
GABBROITIC	GAINSTRIVED	GALAVANTING	GALLICISED	GALLUMPHED
GABERDINES	GAINSTRIVEN	GALDRAGONS	GALLICISES	GALLUMPHING
GABERLUNZIE	GAINSTRIVES	GALENGALES	GALLICISING	GALLYGASKINS
GABERLUNZIES	GAINSTRIVING	GALENICALS	GALLICISMS	GALRAVAGED
GABIONADES	GAINSTROVE	GALEOPITHECINE	GALLICIZATION	GALRAVAGES
GABIONAGES	GAITERLESS	GALEOPITHECOID	GALLICIZATIONS	GALRAVAGING
GABIONNADE	GALABIYAHS	GALIMATIAS	GALLICIZED	GALRAVITCH
GABIONNADES	GALACTAGOGUE	GALIMATIASES	GALLICIZES	GALRAVITCHED
GADGETEERS	GALACTAGOGUES	GALINGALES	GALLICIZING	GALRAVITCHES
GADGETIEST	GALACTICOS	GALIONGEES	GALLIGASKINS	GALRAVITCHING
GADGETRIES	GALACTOMETER	GALIVANTED	GALLIMAUFRIES	GALUMPHERS
GADOLINITE	GALACTOMETERS	GALIVANTING	GALLIMAUFRY	GALUMPHING
GADOLINITES	GALACTOMETRIES	GALLABEAHS	GALLINACEAN	GALVANICAL
GADOLINIUM	GALACTOMETRY	GALLABIAHS	GALLINACEANS	GALVANICALLY
GADOLINIUMS	GALACTOPHOROUS	GALLABIEHS	GALLINACEOUS	GALVANISATION
GADROONING	GALACTOPOIESES	GALLABIYAH	GALLINAZOS	GALVANISATIONS
GADROONINGS	GALACTOPOIESIS	GALLABIYAHS	GALLINIPPER	GALVANISED
GADZOOKERIES	GALACTOPOIETIC	GALLABIYAS	GALLINIPPERS	GALVANISER
GADZOOKERY	GALACTOPOIETICS	GALLABIYEH	GALLINULES	GALVANISERS
GAELICISED	GALACTORRHEA	GALLABIYEHS	GALLISISED	GALVANISES
GAELICISES	GALACTORRHEAS	GALLAMINES	GALLISISES	GALVANISING
GAELICISING	GALACTORRHOEA	GALLANTEST	GALLISISING	GALVANISMS
GAELICISMS	GALACTORRHOEAS	GALLANTING	GALLISIZED	GALVANISTS
GAELICIZED	GALACTOSAEMIA	GALLANTNESS	GALLISIZES	GALVANIZATION
GAELICIZES	GALACTOSAEMIAS	GALLANTNESSES	GALLISIZING	GALVANIZATIONS
GAELICIZING	GALACTOSAEMIC	GALLANTRIES	GALLIVANTED	GALVANIZED
GAILLARDIA	GALACTOSAMINE	GALLBLADDER	GALLIVANTING	GALVANIZER
GAILLARDIAS	GALACTOSAMINES	GALLBLADDERS	GALLIVANTS	GALVANIZERS
GAINFULNESS	GALACTOSEMIA	GALLEASSES	GALLIWASPS	GALVANIZES
GAINFULNESSES	GALACTOSEMIAS	GALLERISTS	GALLOGLASS	GALVANIZING
GAINGIVING	GALACTOSEMIC	GALLERYGOER	GALLOGLASSES	GALVANOMETER
GAINGIVINGS	GALACTOSES	GALLERYGOERS	GALLONAGES	GALVANOMETERS
GAINLESSNESS	GALACTOSIDASE	GALLERYING	GALLOPADED	GALVANOMETRIC
GAINLESSNESSES	GALACTOSIDASES	GALLERYITE	GALLOPADES	GALVANOMETRICAL
GAINLINESS	GALACTOSIDE	GALLERYITES	GALLOPADING	GALVANOMETRIES
GAINLINESSES	GALACTOSIDES	GALLIAMBIC	GALLOWGLASS	GALVANOMETRY

GASTRONOMES

GALVANOPLASTIC	GAMETOPHYTES	GANGSTERDOMS	GARLICKING	GASLIGHTED
GALVANOPLASTIES	GAMETOPHYTIC	GANGSTERISH	GARMENTING	GASLIGHTING
GALVANOPLASTY	GAMEYNESSES	GANGSTERISM	GARMENTLESS	GASOMETERS
GALVANOSCOPE	GAMIFICATION	GANGSTERISMS	GARMENTURE	GASOMETRIC
GALVANOSCOPES	GAMIFICATIONS	GANGSTERLAND	GARMENTURES	GASOMETRICAL
GALVANOSCOPIC	GAMINERIES	GANGSTERLANDS	GARNETIFEROUS	GASOMETRIES
GALVANOSCOPIES	GAMINESQUE	GANNETRIES	GARNIERITE	GASPEREAUS
GALVANOSCOPY	GAMINESSES	GANNISTERS	GARNIERITES	GASPEREAUX
GALVANOTROPIC	GAMMERSTANG	GANTELOPES	GARNISHEED	GASPINESSES
GALVANOTROPISM	GAMMERSTANGS	GANTLETING	GARNISHEEING	GASSINESSES
GALVANOTROPISMS	GAMMOCKING	GAOLBREAKING	GARNISHEEMENT	GASTEROPOD
GAMAHUCHED	GAMMONINGS	GAOLBREAKS	GARNISHEEMENTS	GASTEROPODOUS
GAMAHUCHES	GAMOGENESES	GAOLBROKEN	GARNISHEES	GASTEROPODS
GAMAHUCHING	GAMOGENESIS	GAOLERESSES	GARNISHERS	GASTHAUSER
GAMARUCHED	GAMOGENETIC	GARAGISTES	GARNISHING	GASTHAUSES
GAMARUCHES	GAMOGENETICAL	GARBAGEMAN	GARNISHINGS	GASTIGHTNESS
GAMARUCHING	GAMOGENETICALLY	GARBAGEMEN	GARNISHMENT	GASTIGHTNESSES
GAMBADOING	GAMOPETALOUS	GARBAGIEST	GARNISHMENTS	GASTNESSES
GAMBOLLING	GAMOPHYLLOUS	GARBOLOGIES	GARNISHORS	GASTRAEUMS
GAMEBREAKER	GAMOSEPALOUS	GARBOLOGIST	GARNISHRIES	GASTRALGIA
GAMEBREAKERS	GAMOTROPIC	GARBOLOGISTS	GARNITURES	GASTRALGIAS
GAMEFISHES	GAMOTROPISM	GARBURATOR	GAROTTINGS	GASTRALGIC
GAMEKEEPER	GAMOTROPISMS	GARBURATORS	GARRETEERS	GASTRECTOMIES
GAMEKEEPERS	GAMYNESSES	GARDENFULS	GARRISONED	GASTRECTOMY
GAMEKEEPING	GANDERISMS	GARDENINGS	GARRISONING	GASTRITIDES
GAMEKEEPINGS	GANGBANGED	GARDENLESS	GARROTTERS	GASTRITISES
GAMENESSES	GANGBANGER	GARDEROBES	GARROTTING	GASTROCNEMII
GAMESMANSHIP	GANGBANGERS	GARGANTUAN	GARROTTINGS	GASTROCNEMIUS
GAMESMANSHIPS	GANGBANGING	GARGANTUAS	GARRULITIES	GASTROCOLIC
GAMESOMELY	GANGBOARDS	GARGARISED	GARRULOUSLY	GASTRODUODENAL
GAMESOMENESS	GANGBUSTER	GARGARISES	GARRULOUSNESS	GASTROENTERIC
GAMESOMENESSES	GANGBUSTERS	GARGARISING	GARRULOUSNESSES	GASTROENTERITIC
GAMETANGIA	GANGBUSTING	GARGARISMS	GARRYOWENS	GASTROENTERITIS
GAMETANGIAL	GANGBUSTINGS	GARGARIZED	GASBAGGING	GASTROLITH
GAMETANGIUM	GANGLIATED	GARGARIZES	GASCONADED	GASTROLITHS
GAMETICALLY	GANGLIFORM	GARGARIZING	GASCONADER	GASTROLOGER
GAMETOCYTE	GANGLIONATED	GARGOYLISM	GASCONADERS	GASTROLOGERS
GAMETOCYTES	GANGLIONIC	GARGOYLISMS	GASCONADES	GASTROLOGICAL
GAMETOGENESES	GANGLIOSIDE	GARIBALDIS	GASCONADING	GASTROLOGIES
GAMETOGENESIS	GANGLIOSIDES	GARISHNESS	GASCONISMS	GASTROLOGIST
GAMETOGENIC	GANGMASTER	GARISHNESSES	GASEOUSNESS	GASTROLOGISTS
GAMETOGENIES	GANGMASTERS	GARLANDAGE	GASEOUSNESSES	GASTROLOGY
GAMETOGENOUS	GANGPLANKS	GARLANDAGES	GASHLINESS	GASTROMANCIES
GAMETOGENY	GANGRENING	GARLANDING	GASHLINESSES	GASTROMANCY
GAMETOPHORE	GANGRENOUS	GARLANDLESS	GASHOLDERS	GASTRONOME
GAMETOPHORES	GANGSHAGGED	GARLANDRIES	GASIFIABLE	GASTRONOMER
GAMETOPHORIC	GANGSHAGGING	GARLICKIER	GASIFICATION	GASTRONOMERS
GAMETOPHYTE	GANGSTERDOM	GARLICKIEST	GASIFICATIONS	GASTRONOMES

GASTRONOMIC	GATEKEEPERS	GEARWHEELS	GEMEINSCHAFT	GENEALOGISTS
GASTRONOMICAL	GATEKEEPING	GEEKINESSES	GEMEINSCHAFTEN	GENEALOGIZE
GASTRONOMICALLY	GATEKEEPINGS	GEEKSPEAKS	GEMEINSCHAFTS	GENEALOGIZED
GASTRONOMICS	GATHERABLE	GEFUFFLING	GEMFIBROZIL	GENEALOGIZES
GASTRONOMIES	GATHERINGS	GEGENSCHEIN	GEMFIBROZILS	GENEALOGIZING
GASTRONOMIST	GAUCHENESS	GEGENSCHEINS	GEMINATELY	GENECOLOGIES
GASTRONOMISTS	GAUCHENESSES	GEHLENITES	GEMINATING	GENECOLOGY
GASTRONOMY	GAUCHERIES	GEITONOGAMIES	GEMINATION	GENERALATE
GASTROPODAN	GAUDEAMUSES	GEITONOGAMOUS	GEMINATIONS	GENERALATES
GASTROPODANS	GAUDINESSES	GEITONOGAMY	GEMMACEOUS	GENERALCIES
GASTROPODOUS	GAUFFERING	GELANDESPRUNG	GEMMATIONS	GENERALISABLE
GASTROPODS	GAUFFERINGS	GELANDESPRUNGS	GEMMIFEROUS	GENERALISATION
GASTROPORN	GAULEITERS	GELATINATE	GEMMINESSES	GENERALISATIONS
GASTROPORNS	GAULTHERIA	GELATINATED	GEMMIPAROUS	GENERALISE
GASTROPUBS	GAULTHERIAS	GELATINATES	GEMMIPAROUSLY	GENERALISED
GASTROSCOPE	GAUNTLETED	GELATINATING	GEMMOLOGICAL	GENERALISER
GASTROSCOPES	GAUNTLETING	GELATINATION	GEMMOLOGIES	GENERALISERS
GASTROSCOPIC	GAUNTNESSES	GELATINATIONS	GEMMOLOGIST	GENERALISES
GASTROSCOPIES	GAUSSMETER	GELATINISATION	GEMMOLOGISTS	GENERALISING
GASTROSCOPIST	GAUSSMETERS	GELATINISATIONS	GEMMULATION	GENERALISM
GASTROSCOPISTS	GAUZINESSES	GELATINISE	GEMMULATIONS	GENERALISMS
GASTROSCOPY	GAVELKINDS	GELATINISED	GEMOLOGICAL	GENERALISSIMO
GASTROSOPH	GAWKIHOODS	GELATINISER	GEMOLOGIES	GENERALISSIMOS
GASTROSOPHER	GAWKINESSES	GELATINISERS	GEMOLOGIST	GENERALIST
GASTROSOPHERS	GAWKISHNESS	GELATINISES	GEMOLOGISTS	GENERALISTS
GASTROSOPHIES	GAWKISHNESSES	GELATINISING	GEMUTLICHKEIT	GENERALITIES
GASTROSOPHS	GAYCATIONS	GELATINIZATION	GEMUTLICHKEITS	GENERALITY
GASTROSOPHY	GAZEHOUNDS	GELATINIZATIONS	GENDARMERIE	GENERALIZABLE
GASTROSTOMIES	GAZETTEERED	GELATINIZE	GENDARMERIES	GENERALIZATION
GASTROSTOMY	GAZETTEERING	GELATINIZED	GENDARMERY	GENERALIZATIONS
GASTROTOMIES	GAZETTEERISH	GELATINIZER	GENDERISED	GENERALIZE
GASTROTOMY	GAZETTEERS	GELATINIZERS	GENDERISES	GENERALIZED
GASTROTRICH	GAZILLIONAIRE	GELATINIZES	GENDERISING	GENERALIZER
GASTROTRICHS	GAZILLIONAIRES	GELATINIZING	GENDERIZED	GENERALIZERS
GASTROVASCULAR	GAZILLIONS	GELATINOID	GENDERIZES	GENERALIZES
GASTRULATE	GAZUMPINGS	GELATINOIDS	GENDERIZING	GENERALIZING
GASTRULATED	GAZUNDERED	GELATINOUS	GENDERLESS	GENERALLED
GASTRULATES	GAZUNDERER	GELATINOUSLY	GENDERQUEER	GENERALLING
GASTRULATING	GAZUNDERERS	GELATINOUSNESS	GENDERQUEERS	GENERALNESS
GASTRULATION	GAZUNDERING	GELIDITIES	GENEALOGIC	GENERALNESSES
GASTRULATIONS	GEALOUSIES	GELIDNESSES	GENEALOGICAL	GENERALSHIP
GATECRASHED	GEANTICLINAL	GELIGNITES	GENEALOGICALLY	GENERALSHIPS
GATECRASHER	GEANTICLINE	GELLIFLOWRE	GENEALOGIES	GENERATING
GATECRASHERS	GEANTICLINES	GELLIFLOWRES	GENEALOGISE	GENERATION
GATECRASHES	GEARCHANGE	GELSEMINES	GENEALOGISED	GENERATIONAL
GATECRASHING	GEARCHANGES	GELSEMININE	GENEALOGISES	GENERATIONALLY
GATEHOUSES	GEARSHIFTS	GELSEMININES	GENEALOGISING	GENERATIONISM
GATEKEEPER	GEARSTICKS	GELSEMIUMS	GENEALOGIST	GENERATIONISMS

GENERATIONS	GENITIVALLY	GENTILITIOUS	GEOBOTANIST	GEOHYDROLOGISTS
GENERATIVE	GENITIVELY	GENTILIZED	GEOBOTANISTS	GEOHYDROLOGY
GENERATORS	GENITOURINARY	GENTILIZES	GEOCACHERS	GEOLATRIES
GENERATRICES	GENITRICES	GENTILIZING	GEOCACHING	GEOLINGUISTICS
GENERATRIX	GENITRIXES	GENTILSHOMMES	GEOCACHINGS	GEOLOCATION
GENERICALLY	GENLOCKING	GENTLEFOLK	GEOCARPIES	GEOLOCATIONS
GENERICNESS	GENLOCKINGS	GENTLEFOLKS	GEOCENTRIC	GEOLOGIANS
GENERICNESSES	GENOCIDAIRE	GENTLEHOOD	GEOCENTRICAL	GEOLOGICAL
GENEROSITIES	GENOCIDAIRES	GENTLEHOODS	GEOCENTRICALLY	GEOLOGICALLY
GENEROSITY	GENOPHOBIA	GENTLEMANHOOD	GEOCENTRICISM	GEOLOGISED
GENEROUSLY	GENOPHOBIAS	GENTLEMANHOODS	GEOCENTRICISMS	GEOLOGISES
GENEROUSNESS	GENOTYPICAL	GENTLEMANLIER	GEOCHEMICAL	GEOLOGISING
GENEROUSNESSES	GENOTYPICALLY	GENTLEMANLIEST	GEOCHEMICALLY	GEOLOGISTS
GENETHLIAC	GENOTYPICITIES	GENTLEMANLIKE	GEOCHEMIST	GEOLOGIZED
GENETHLIACAL	GENOTYPICITY	GENTLEMANLINESS	GEOCHEMISTRIES	GEOLOGIZES
GENETHLIACALLY	GENOTYPING	GENTLEMANLY	GEOCHEMISTRY	GEOLOGIZING
GENETHLIACON	GENOUILLERE	GENTLEMANSHIP	GEOCHEMISTS	GEOMAGNETIC
GENETHLIACONS	GENOUILLERES	GENTLEMANSHIPS	GEOCHRONOLOGIC	GEOMAGNETICALLY
GENETHLIACS	GENSDARMES	GENTLENESS	GEOCHRONOLOGIES	GEOMAGNETISM
GENETHLIALOGIC	GENTAMICIN	GENTLENESSE	GEOCHRONOLOGIST	GEOMAGNETISMS
GENETHLIALOGIES	GENTAMICINS	GENTLENESSES	GEOCHRONOLOGY	GEOMAGNETIST
GENETHLIALOGY	GENTEELEST	GENTLEPERSON	GEOCORONAE	GEOMAGNETISTS
GENETICALLY	GENTEELISE	GENTLEPERSONS	GEOCORONAS	GEOMANCERS
GENETICIST	GENTEELISED	GENTLEWOMAN	GEODEMOGRAPHICS	GEOMANCIES
GENETICISTS	GENTEELISES	GENTLEWOMANLIER	GEODESICAL	GEOMECHANICS
GENETOTROPHIC	GENTEELISH	GENTLEWOMANLY	GEODESISTS	GEOMEDICAL
GENETRICES	GENTEELISING	GENTLEWOMEN	GEODETICAL	GEOMEDICINE
GENETRIXES	GENTEELISM	GENTRIFICATION	GEODETICALLY	GEOMEDICINES
GENEVRETTE	GENTEELISMS	GENTRIFICATIONS	GEODYNAMIC	GEOMETRICAL
GENEVRETTES	GENTEELIZE	GENTRIFIED	GEODYNAMICAL	GEOMETRICALLY
GENIALISED	GENTEELIZED	GENTRIFIER	GEODYNAMICIST	GEOMETRICIAN
GENIALISES	GENTEELIZES	GENTRIFIERS	GEODYNAMICISTS	GEOMETRICIANS
GENIALISING	GENTEELIZING	GENTRIFIES	GEODYNAMICS	GEOMETRICS
GENIALITIES	GENTEELNESS	GENTRIFYING	GEOENGINEERING	GEOMETRIDS
GENIALIZED	GENTEELNESSES	GENUFLECTED	GEOENGINEERINGS	GEOMETRIES
GENIALIZES	GENTIANACEOUS	GENUFLECTING	GEOGNOSIES	GEOMETRISATION
GENIALIZING	GENTIANELLA	GENUFLECTION	GEOGNOSTIC	GEOMETRISATIONS
GENIALNESS	GENTIANELLAS	GENUFLECTIONS	GEOGNOSTICAL	GEOMETRISE
GENIALNESSES	GENTILESSE	GENUFLECTOR	GEOGNOSTICALLY	GEOMETRISED
GENICULATE	GENTILESSES	GENUFLECTORS	GEOGRAPHER	GEOMETRISES
GENICULATED	GENTILHOMME	GENUFLECTS	GEOGRAPHERS	GEOMETRISING
GENICULATELY	GENTILISED	GENUFLEXION	GEOGRAPHIC	GEOMETRIST
GENICULATES	GENTILISES	GENUFLEXIONS	GEOGRAPHICAL	GEOMETRISTS
GENICULATING	GENTILISING	GENUINENESS	GEOGRAPHICALLY	GEOMETRIZATION
GENICULATION	GENTILISMS	GENUINENESSES	GEOGRAPHIES	GEOMETRIZATIONS
GENICULATIONS	GENTILITIAL	GEOBOTANIC	GEOHYDROLOGIC	GEOMETRIZE
GENISTEINS	GENTILITIAN	GEOBOTANICAL	GEOHYDROLOGIES	GEOMETRIZED
GENITALIAL	GENTILITIES	GEOBOTANIES	GEOHYDROLOGIST	GEOMETRIZES

G

GEOMETRIZING	GEOSYNCHRONOUS	GERMANIZATIONS	GERRYMANDERS	GHOSTLIEST
GEOMORPHIC	GEOSYNCLINAL	GERMANIZED	GERUNDIVAL	GHOSTLINESS
GEOMORPHOGENIC	GEOSYNCLINE	GERMANIZES	GERUNDIVELY	GHOSTLINESSES
GEOMORPHOGENIES	GEOSYNCLINES	GERMANIZING	GERUNDIVES	GHOSTWRITE
GEOMORPHOGENIST	GEOTACTICAL	GERMICIDAL	GESELLSCHAFT	GHOSTWRITER
GEOMORPHOGENY	GEOTACTICALLY	GERMICIDES	GESELLSCHAFTEN	GHOSTWRITERS
GEOMORPHOLOGIC	GEOTAGGING	GERMINABILITIES	GESELLSCHAFTS	GHOSTWRITES
GEOMORPHOLOGIES	GEOTECHNIC	GERMINABILITY	GESNERIADS	GHOSTWRITING
GEOMORPHOLOGIST	GEOTECHNICAL	GERMINABLE	GESSAMINES	GHOSTWRITTEN
GEOMORPHOLOGY	GEOTECHNICS	GERMINALLY	GESTALTISM	GHOSTWROTE
GEOPHAGIAS	GEOTECHNOLOGIES	GERMINATED	GESTALTISMS	GHOULISHLY
GEOPHAGIES	GEOTECHNOLOGY	GERMINATES	GESTALTIST	GHOULISHNESS
GEOPHAGISM	GEOTECTONIC	GERMINATING	GESTALTISTS	GHOULISHNESSES
GEOPHAGISMS	GEOTECTONICALLY	GERMINATION	GESTATIONAL	GIANTESSES
GEOPHAGIST	GEOTECTONICS	GERMINATIONS	GESTATIONS	GIANTHOODS
GEOPHAGISTS	GEOTEXTILE	GERMINATIVE	GESTATORIAL	GIANTLIEST
GEOPHAGOUS	GEOTEXTILES	GERMINATOR	GESTICULANT	GIANTSHIPS
GEOPHILOUS	GEOTHERMAL	GERMINATORS	GESTICULATE	GIARDIASES
GEOPHYSICAL	GEOTHERMALLY	GERMINESSES	GESTICULATED	GIARDIASIS
GEOPHYSICALLY	GEOTHERMIC	GERMPLASMS	GESTICULATES	GIBBERELLIC
GEOPHYSICIST	GEOTHERMOMETER	GERONTOCRACIES	GESTICULATING	GIBBERELLIN
GEOPHYSICISTS	GEOTHERMOMETERS	GERONTOCRACY	GESTICULATION	GIBBERELLINS
GEOPHYSICS	GEOTROPICALLY	GERONTOCRAT	GESTICULATIONS	GIBBERINGS
GEOPOLITICAL	GEOTROPISM	GERONTOCRATIC	GESTICULATIVE	GIBBERISHES
GEOPOLITICALLY	GEOTROPISMS	GERONTOCRATS	GESTICULATOR	GIBBETTING
GEOPOLITICIAN	GERANIACEOUS	GERONTOLOGIC	GESTICULATORS	GIBBOSITIES
GEOPOLITICIANS	GERATOLOGICAL	GERONTOLOGICAL	GESTICULATORY	GIBBOUSNESS
GEOPOLITICS	GERATOLOGIES	GERONTOLOGIES	GESTURALLY	GIBBOUSNESSES
GEOPONICAL	GERATOLOGIST	GERONTOLOGIST	GESUNDHEIT	GIDDINESSES
GEOPRESSURED	GERATOLOGISTS	GERONTOLOGISTS	GETTERINGS	GIFTEDNESS
GEORGETTES	GERATOLOGY	GERONTOLOGY	GEWURZTRAMINER	GIFTEDNESSES
GEOSCIENCE	GERFALCONS	GERONTOMORPHIC	GEWURZTRAMINERS	GIFTWRAPPED
GEOSCIENCES	GERIATRICIAN	GERONTOPHIL	GEYSERITES	GIFTWRAPPING
GEOSCIENTIFIC	GERIATRICIANS	GERONTOPHILE	GHASTFULLY	GIFTWRAPPINGS
GEOSCIENTIST	GERIATRICS	GERONTOPHILES	GHASTLIEST	GIGACYCLES
GEOSCIENTISTS	GERIATRIST	GERONTOPHILIA	GHASTLINESS	GIGAHERTZES
GEOSPATIAL	GERIATRISTS	GERONTOPHILIAS	GHASTLINESSES	GIGANTESQUE
GEOSPHERES	GERMANDERS	GERONTOPHILS	GHASTNESSES	GIGANTICALLY
GEOSTATICS	GERMANENESS	GERONTOPHOBE	GHETTOISATION	GIGANTICIDE
GEOSTATIONARY	GERMANENESSES	GERONTOPHOBES	GHETTOISATIONS	GIGANTICIDES
GEOSTRATEGIC	GERMANISATION	GERONTOPHOBIA	GHETTOISED	GIGANTICNESS
GEOSTRATEGICAL	GERMANISATIONS	GERONTOPHOBIAS	GHETTOISES	GIGANTICNESSES
GEOSTRATEGIES	GERMANISED	GERRYMANDER	GHETTOISING	GIGANTISMS
GEOSTRATEGIST	GERMANISES	GERRYMANDERED	GHETTOIZATION	GIGANTOLOGIES
GEOSTRATEGISTS	GERMANISING	GERRYMANDERER	GHETTOIZATIONS	GIGANTOLOGY
GEOSTRATEGY	GERMANITES	GERRYMANDERERS	GHETTOIZED	GIGANTOMACHIA
GEOSTROPHIC	GERMANIUMS	GERRYMANDERING	GHETTOIZES	GIGANTOMACHIAS
GEOSTROPHICALLY	GERMANIZATION	GERRYMANDERINGS	GHETTOIZING	GIGANTOMACHIES

GIGANTOMACHY	GINGERIEST	GLADDENERS	GLAMOURIZED	GLASSWORKS
GIGGLESOME	GINGERLIER	GLADDENING	GLAMOURIZES	GLASSWORMS
GIGGLINGLY	GINGERLIEST	GLADFULNESS	GLAMOURIZING	GLASSWORTS
GIGMANITIES	GINGERLINESS	GLADFULNESSES	GLAMOURLESS	GLASSYHEADED
GILDSWOMAN	GINGERLINESSES	GLADIATORIAL	GLAMOUROUS	GLAUBERITE
GILDSWOMEN	GINGERROOT	GLADIATORIAN	GLAMOUROUSLY	GLAUBERITES
GILLFLIRTS	GINGERROOTS	GLADIATORS	GLAMOUROUSNESS	GLAUCESCENCE
GILLIFLOWER	GINGERSNAP	GLADIATORSHIP	GLAMOURPUSS	GLAUCESCENCES
GILLIFLOWERS	GINGERSNAPS	GLADIATORSHIPS	GLAMOURPUSSES	GLAUCESCENT
GILLNETTED	GINGIVECTOMIES	GLADIATORY	GLANCINGLY	GLAUCOMATOUS
GILLNETTER	GINGIVECTOMY	GLADIOLUSES	GLANDEROUS	GLAUCONITE
GILLNETTERS	GINGIVITIS	GLADNESSES	GLANDIFEROUS	GLAUCONITES
GILLNETTING	GINGIVITISES	GLADSOMELY	GLANDIFORM	GLAUCONITIC
GILLRAVAGE	GINGLIMOID	GLADSOMENESS	GLANDULARLY	GLAUCOUSLY
GILLRAVAGED	GIPSYHOODS	GLADSOMENESSES	GLANDULIFEROUS	GLAUCOUSNESS
GILLRAVAGES	GIPSYWORTS	GLADSOMEST	GLANDULOUS	GLAUCOUSNESSES
GILLRAVAGING	GIRANDOLAS	GLADSTONES	GLANDULOUSLY	GLAZIERIES
GILLRAVITCH	GIRANDOLES	GLADWRAPPED	GLARINESSES	GLAZINESSES
GILLRAVITCHED	GIRDLECAKE	GLADWRAPPING	GLARINGNESS	GLEAMINGLY
GILLRAVITCHES	GIRDLECAKES	GLAIKETNESS	GLARINGNESSES	GLEEFULNESS
GILLRAVITCHING	GIRDLESCONE	GLAIKETNESSES	GLASNOSTIAN	GLEEFULNESSES
GILLYFLOWER	GIRDLESCONES	GLAIKITNESS	GLASNOSTIC	GLEEMAIDEN
GILLYFLOWERS	GIRDLESTEAD	GLAIKITNESSES	GLASSBLOWER	GLEEMAIDENS
GILRAVAGED	GIRDLESTEADS	GLAIRINESS	GLASSBLOWERS	GLEGNESSES
GILRAVAGER	GIRLFRIEND	GLAIRINESSES	GLASSBLOWING	GLEISATION
GILRAVAGERS	GIRLFRIENDS	GLAMORISATION	GLASSBLOWINGS	GLEISATIONS
GILRAVAGES	GIRLISHNESS	GLAMORISATIONS	GLASSCLOTH	GLEIZATION
GILRAVAGING	GIRLISHNESSES	GLAMORISED	GLASSCLOTHS	GLEIZATIONS
GILRAVITCH	GIRTHLINES	GLAMORISER	GLASSCUTTER	GLENDOVEER
GILRAVITCHED	GISMOLOGIES	GLAMORISERS	GLASSCUTTERS	GLENDOVEERS
GILRAVITCHES	GITTARONES	GLAMORISES	GLASSHOUSE	GLENGARRIES
GILRAVITCHING	GITTERNING	GLAMORISING	GLASSHOUSES	GLIBNESSES
GILSONITES	GIVENNESSES	GLAMORIZATION	GLASSIFIED	GLIDEPATHS
GIMBALLING	GIZMOLOGIES	GLAMORIZATIONS	GLASSIFIES	GLIMMERIER
GIMCRACKERIES	GLABRESCENT	GLAMORIZED	GLASSIFYING	GLIMMERIEST
GIMCRACKERY	GLABROUSNESS	GLAMORIZER	GLASSINESS	GLIMMERING
GIMMICKIER	GLABROUSNESSES	GLAMORIZERS	GLASSINESSES	GLIMMERINGLY
GIMMICKIEST	GLACIALIST	GLAMORIZES	GLASSMAKER	GLIMMERINGS
GIMMICKING	GLACIALISTS	GLAMORIZING	GLASSMAKERS	GLIOBLASTOMA
GIMMICKRIES	GLACIATING	GLAMOROUSLY	GLASSMAKING	GLIOBLASTOMAS
GINGELLIES	GLACIATION	GLAMOROUSNESS	GLASSMAKINGS	GLIOBLASTOMATA
GINGERADES	GLACIATIONS	GLAMOROUSNESSES	GLASSPAPER	GLIOMATOSES
GINGERBREAD	GLACIOLOGIC	GLAMOURING	GLASSPAPERED	GLIOMATOSIS
GINGERBREADED	GLACIOLOGICAL	GLAMOURISE	GLASSPAPERING	GLIOMATOUS
GINGERBREADIER	GLACIOLOGIES	GLAMOURISED	GLASSPAPERS	GLISSADERS
GINGERBREADIEST	GLACIOLOGIST	GLAMOURISES	GLASSWARES	GLISSADING
GINGERBREADS	GLACIOLOGISTS	GLAMOURISING	GLASSWORKER	GLISSANDOS
GINGERBREADY	GLACIOLOGY	GLAMOURIZE	GLASSWORKERS	GLISTENING

GLISTENINGLY
GLISTERING
GLISTERINGLY
GLITCHIEST
GLITTERAND
GLITTERATI
GLITTERIER
GLITTERIEST
GLITTERING
GLITTERINGLY
GLITTERINGS
GLITZINESS
GLITZINESSES
GLOATINGLY
GLOBALISATION
GLOBALISATIONS
GLOBALISED
GLOBALISES
GLOBALISING
GLOBALISMS
GLOBALISTS
GLOBALIZATION
GLOBALIZATIONS
GLOBALIZED
GLOBALIZES
GLOBALIZING
GLOBEFISHES
GLOBEFLOWER
GLOBEFLOWERS
GLOBESITIES
GLOBETROTS
GLOBETROTTED
GLOBETROTTER
GLOBETROTTERS
GLOBETROTTING
GLOBETROTTINGS
GLOBIGERINA
GLOBIGERINAE
GLOBIGERINAS
GLOBOSENESS
GLOBOSENESSES
GLOBOSITIES
GLOBULARITIES
GLOBULARITY
GLOBULARLY
GLOBULARNESS
GLOBULARNESSES
GLOBULIFEROUS

GLOBULITES
GLOCHIDIATE
GLOCHIDIUM
GLOCKENSPIEL
GLOCKENSPIELS
GLOMERATED
GLOMERATES
GLOMERATING
GLOMERATION
GLOMERATIONS
GLOMERULAR
GLOMERULATE
GLOMERULES
GLOMERULUS
GLOOMFULLY
GLOOMINESS
GLOOMINESSES
GLOOMSTERS
GLORIFIABLE
GLORIFICATION
GLORIFICATIONS
GLORIFIERS
GLORIFYING
GLORIOUSLY
GLORIOUSNESS
GLORIOUSNESSES
GLOSSARIAL
GLOSSARIALLY
GLOSSARIES
GLOSSARIST
GLOSSARISTS
GLOSSATORS
GLOSSECTOMIES
GLOSSECTOMY
GLOSSEMATICS
GLOSSINESS
GLOSSINESSES
GLOSSINGLY
GLOSSITISES
GLOSSODYNIA
GLOSSODYNIAS
GLOSSOGRAPHER
GLOSSOGRAPHERS
GLOSSOGRAPHICAL
GLOSSOGRAPHIES
GLOSSOGRAPHY
GLOSSOLALIA
GLOSSOLALIAS

GLOSSOLALIST
GLOSSOLALISTS
GLOSSOLARYNGEAL
GLOSSOLOGICAL
GLOSSOLOGIES
GLOSSOLOGIST
GLOSSOLOGISTS
GLOSSOLOGY
GLOTTIDEAN
GLOTTOGONIC
GLOTTOLOGIES
GLOTTOLOGY
GLOVEBOXES
GLOWERINGLY
GLOWSTICKS
GLUCINIUMS
GLUCOCORTICOID
GLUCOCORTICOIDS
GLUCOKINASE
GLUCOKINASES
GLUCONATES
GLUCONEOGENESES
GLUCONEOGENESIS
GLUCONEOGENIC
GLUCOPHORE
GLUCOPHORES
GLUCOPROTEIN
GLUCOPROTEINS
GLUCOSAMINE
GLUCOSAMINES
GLUCOSIDAL
GLUCOSIDASE
GLUCOSIDASES
GLUCOSIDES
GLUCOSIDIC
GLUCOSURIA
GLUCOSURIAS
GLUCOSURIC
GLUCURONIC
GLUCURONIDASE
GLUCURONIDASES
GLUCURONIDE
GLUCURONIDES
GLUEYNESSES
GLUINESSES
GLUMACEOUS
GLUMIFEROUS
GLUMNESSES

GLUTAMATES
GLUTAMINASE
GLUTAMINASES
GLUTAMINES
GLUTAMINIC
GLUTARALDEHYDE
GLUTARALDEHYDES
GLUTATHIONE
GLUTATHIONES
GLUTETHIMIDE
GLUTETHIMIDES
GLUTINOSITIES
GLUTINOSITY
GLUTINOUSLY
GLUTINOUSNESS
GLUTINOUSNESSES
GLUTTINGLY
GLUTTONIES
GLUTTONISE
GLUTTONISED
GLUTTONISES
GLUTTONISH
GLUTTONISING
GLUTTONIZE
GLUTTONIZED
GLUTTONIZES
GLUTTONIZING
GLUTTONOUS
GLUTTONOUSLY
GLUTTONOUSNESS
GLYCAEMIAS
GLYCATIONS
GLYCERALDEHYDE
GLYCERALDEHYDES
GLYCERIDES
GLYCERIDIC
GLYCERINATE
GLYCERINATED
GLYCERINATES
GLYCERINATING
GLYCERINES
GLYCOCOLLS
GLYCOGENESES
GLYCOGENESIS
GLYCOGENETIC
GLYCOGENIC
GLYCOGENOLYSES
GLYCOGENOLYSIS

GLYCOGENOLYTIC
GLYCOLIPID
GLYCOLIPIDS
GLYCOLYSES
GLYCOLYSIS
GLYCOLYTIC
GLYCONEOGENESES
GLYCONEOGENESIS
GLYCOPEPTIDE
GLYCOPEPTIDES
GLYCOPHYTE
GLYCOPHYTES
GLYCOPHYTIC
GLYCOPROTEIN
GLYCOPROTEINS
GLYCOSIDASE
GLYCOSIDASES
GLYCOSIDES
GLYCOSIDIC
GLYCOSIDICALLY
GLYCOSURIA
GLYCOSURIAS
GLYCOSURIC
GLYCOSYLATE
GLYCOSYLATED
GLYCOSYLATES
GLYCOSYLATING
GLYCOSYLATION
GLYCOSYLATIONS
GLYOXALINE
GLYOXALINES
GLYPHOGRAPH
GLYPHOGRAPHER
GLYPHOGRAPHERS
GLYPHOGRAPHIC
GLYPHOGRAPHICAL
GLYPHOGRAPHIES
GLYPHOGRAPHS
GLYPHOGRAPHY
GLYPHOSATE
GLYPHOSATES
GLYPTODONT
GLYPTODONTS
GLYPTOGRAPHER
GLYPTOGRAPHERS
GLYPTOGRAPHIC
GLYPTOGRAPHICAL
GLYPTOGRAPHIES

GLYPTOGRAPHY	GOALSCORER	GOGGLEBOXES	GOLLIWOGGS	GONORRHOEIC
GLYPTOTHECA	GOALSCORERS	GOITROGENIC	GOLOMYNKAS	GOODFELLAS
GLYPTOTHECAE	GOALTENDER	GOITROGENICITY	GOLOPTIOUS	GOODFELLOW
GMELINITES	GOALTENDERS	GOITROGENS	GOLUPTIOUS	GOODFELLOWS
GNAPHALIUM	GOALTENDING	GOLDARNING	GOMBEENISM	GOODFELLOWSHIP
GNAPHALIUMS	GOALTENDINGS	GOLDBEATER	GOMBEENISMS	GOODFELLOWSHIPS
GNASHINGLY	GOATFISHES	GOLDBEATERS	GONADECTOMIES	GOODINESSES
GNATCATCHER	GOATISHNESS	GOLDBRICKED	GONADECTOMISED	GOODLIHEAD
GNATCATCHERS	GOATISHNESSES	GOLDBRICKING	GONADECTOMIZED	GOODLIHEADS
GNATHONICAL	GOATSBEARD	GOLDBRICKS	GONADECTOMY	GOODLINESS
GNATHONICALLY	GOATSBEARDS	GOLDCRESTS	GONADOTROPHIC	GOODLINESSES
GNATHOSTOMATOUS	GOATSUCKER	GOLDENBERRIES	GONADOTROPHIN	GOODLYHEAD
GNATHOSTOME	GOATSUCKERS	GOLDENBERRY	GONADOTROPHINS	GOODLYHEADS
GNATHOSTOMES	GOBBELINES	GOLDENEYES	GONADOTROPIC	GOODNESSES
GNEISSITIC	GOBBLEDEGOOK	GOLDENNESS	GONADOTROPIN	GOODNIGHTS
GNETOPHYTE	GOBBLEDEGOOKS	GOLDENNESSES	GONADOTROPINS	GOODWILLED
GNETOPHYTES	GOBBLEDYGOOK	GOLDENRODS	GONDOLIERS	GOOEYNESSES
GNOMICALLY	GOBBLEDYGOOKS	GOLDENSEAL	GONENESSES	GOOFINESSES
GNOMONICAL	GOBSMACKED	GOLDENSEALS	GONFALONIER	GOOGLEWHACK
GNOMONICALLY	GOBSTOPPER	GOLDFIELDS	GONFALONIERS	GOOGLEWHACKS
GNOMONOLOGIES	GOBSTOPPERS	GOLDFINCHES	GONGORISTIC	GOOGOLPLEX
GNOMONOLOGY	GOCHUJANGS	GOLDFINNIES	GONIATITES	GOOGOLPLEXES
GNOSEOLOGIES	GODAMNDEST	GOLDFISHES	GONIATITOID	GOOINESSES
GNOSEOLOGY	GODCHILDREN	GOLDILOCKS	GONIATITOIDS	GOONEYBIRD
GNOSIOLOGIES	GODDAMMING	GOLDILOCKSES	GONIMOBLAST	GOONEYBIRDS
GNOSIOLOGY	GODDAMNDEST	GOLDMINERS	GONIMOBLASTS	GOOPINESSES
GNOSTICALLY	GODDAMNEDEST	GOLDSINNIES	GONIOMETER	GOOSANDERS
GNOSTICISM	GODDAMNING	GOLDSMITHERIES	GONIOMETERS	GOOSEBERRIES
GNOSTICISMS	GODDAUGHTER	GOLDSMITHERY	GONIOMETRIC	GOOSEBERRY
GNOTOBIOLOGICAL	GODDAUGHTERS	GOLDSMITHRIES	GONIOMETRICAL	GOOSEFISHES
GNOTOBIOLOGIES	GODDESSHOOD	GOLDSMITHRY	GONIOMETRICALLY	GOOSEFLESH
GNOTOBIOLOGY	GODDESSHOODS	GOLDSMITHS	GONIOMETRIES	GOOSEFLESHES
GNOTOBIOSES	GODFATHERED	GOLDSPINKS	GONIOMETRY	GOOSEFOOTS
GNOTOBIOSIS	GODFATHERING	GOLDSTICKS	GONIOSCOPE	GOOSEGRASS
GNOTOBIOTE	GODFATHERS	GOLDSTONES	GONIOSCOPES	GOOSEGRASSES
GNOTOBIOTES	GODFORSAKEN	GOLDTHREAD	GONOCOCCAL	GOOSEHERDS
GNOTOBIOTIC	GODLESSNESS	GOLDTHREADS	GONOCOCCIC	GOOSENECKED
GNOTOBIOTICALLY	GODLESSNESSES	GOLIARDERIES	GONOCOCCOID	GOOSENECKS
GNOTOBIOTICS	GODLIKENESS	GOLIARDERY	GONOCOCCUS	GOOSINESSES
GOALKEEPER	GODLIKENESSES	GOLIARDIES	GONOPHORES	GOPHERWOOD
GOALKEEPERS	GODLINESSES	GOLIATHISE	GONOPHORIC	GOPHERWOODS
GOALKEEPING	GODMOTHERED	GOLIATHISED	GONOPHOROUS	GORBELLIES
GOALKEEPINGS	GODMOTHERING	GOLIATHISES	GONORRHEAL	GORBLIMEYS
GOALKICKER	GODMOTHERS	GOLIATHISING	GONORRHEAS	GORBLIMIES
GOALKICKERS	GODPARENTS	GOLIATHIZE	GONORRHEIC	GOREHOUNDS
GOALKICKING	GODROONING	GOLIATHIZED	GONORRHOEA	GORGEOUSLY
GOALKICKINGS	GODROONINGS	GOLIATHIZES	GONORRHOEAL	GORGEOUSNESS
GOALMOUTHS	GOFFERINGS	GOLIATHIZING	GONORRHOEAS	GORGEOUSNESSES

GORGONEION	GOSSAMERIEST	GOVERNMENTAL	GRADUALIST	GRAMMATICISED
GORGONIANS	GOSSIPIEST	GOVERNMENTALISE	GRADUALISTIC	GRAMMATICISES
GORGONISED	GOSSIPINGLY	GOVERNMENTALISM	GRADUALISTS	GRAMMATICISING
GORGONISES	GOSSIPINGS	GOVERNMENTALIST	GRADUALITIES	GRAMMATICISM
GORGONISING	GOSSIPMONGER	GOVERNMENTALIZE	GRADUALITY	GRAMMATICISMS
GORGONIZED	GOSSIPMONGERS	GOVERNMENTALLY	GRADUALNESS	GRAMMATICIZE
GORGONIZES	GOSSIPPERS	GOVERNMENTESE	GRADUALNESSES	GRAMMATICIZED
GORGONIZING	GOSSIPPING	GOVERNMENTESES	GRADUATESHIP	GRAMMATICIZES
GORILLAGRAM	GOSSIPRIES	GOVERNMENTS	GRADUATESHIPS	GRAMMATICIZING
GORILLAGRAMS	GOTHICALLY	GOVERNORATE	GRADUATING	GRAMMATIST
GORINESSES	GOTHICISED	GOVERNORATES	GRADUATION	GRAMMATISTS
GORMANDISE	GOTHICISES	GOVERNORSHIP	GRADUATIONS	GRAMMATOLOGIES
GORMANDISED	GOTHICISING	GOVERNORSHIPS	GRADUATORS	GRAMMATOLOGIST
GORMANDISER	GOTHICISMS	GOWDSPINKS	GRAECISING	GRAMMATOLOGISTS
GORMANDISERS	GOTHICIZED	GOWPENFULS	GRAECIZING	GRAMMATOLOGY
GORMANDISES	GOTHICIZES	GRACEFULLER	GRAFFITIED	GRAMOPHONE
GORMANDISING	GOTHICIZING	GRACEFULLEST	GRAFFITIING	GRAMOPHONES
GORMANDISINGS	GOURDINESS	GRACEFULLY	GRAFFITING	GRAMOPHONIC
GORMANDISM	GOURDINESSES	GRACEFULNESS	GRAFFITIST	GRAMOPHONICALLY
GORMANDISMS	GOURMANDISE	GRACEFULNESSES	GRAFFITISTS	GRAMOPHONIES
GORMANDIZE	GOURMANDISED	GRACELESSLY	GRAINFIELD	GRAMOPHONIST
GORMANDIZED	GOURMANDISES	GRACELESSNESS	GRAINFIELDS	GRAMOPHONISTS
GORMANDIZER	GOURMANDISING	GRACELESSNESSES	GRAININESS	GRAMOPHONY
GORMANDIZERS	GOURMANDISM	GRACILENESS	GRAININESSES	GRANADILLA
GORMANDIZES	GOURMANDISMS	GRACILENESSES	GRALLATORIAL	GRANADILLAS
GORMANDIZING	GOURMANDIZE	GRACILITIES	GRALLOCHED	GRANDADDIES
GORMANDIZINGS	GOURMANDIZED	GRACIOSITIES	GRALLOCHING	GRANDAUNTS
GOSLARITES	GOURMANDIZES	GRACIOSITY	GRAMERCIES	GRANDBABIES
GOSPELISED	GOURMANDIZING	GRACIOUSLY	GRAMICIDIN	GRANDCHILD
GOSPELISES	GOUTINESSES	GRACIOUSNESS	GRAMICIDINS	GRANDCHILDREN
GOSPELISING	GOUVERNANTE	GRACIOUSNESSES	GRAMINACEOUS	GRANDDDADDIES
GOSPELIZED	GOUVERNANTES	GRADABILITIES	GRAMINEOUS	GRANDDDADDY
GOSPELIZES	GOVERNABILITIES	GRADABILITY	GRAMINICOLOUS	GRANDDAUGHTER
GOSPELIZING	GOVERNABILITY	GRADABLENESS	GRAMINIVOROUS	GRANDDAUGHTERS
GOSPELLERS	GOVERNABLE	GRADABLENESSES	GRAMINOLOGIES	GRANDEESHIP
GOSPELLIER	GOVERNABLENESS	GRADATIONAL	GRAMINOLOGY	GRANDEESHIPS
GOSPELLIEST	GOVERNALLS	GRADATIONALLY	GRAMMALOGUE	GRANDFATHER
GOSPELLING	GOVERNANCE	GRADATIONED	GRAMMALOGUES	GRANDFATHERED
GOSPELLINGS	GOVERNANCES	GRADATIONS	GRAMMARIAN	GRANDFATHERING
GOSPELLISE	GOVERNANTE	GRADATORIES	GRAMMARIANS	GRANDFATHERLIER
GOSPELLISED	GOVERNANTES	GRADDANING	GRAMMARLESS	GRANDFATHERLY
GOSPELLISES	GOVERNESSED	GRADELIEST	GRAMMATICAL	GRANDFATHERS
GOSPELLISING	GOVERNESSES	GRADIENTER	GRAMMATICALITY	GRANDIFLORA
GOSPELLIZE	GOVERNESSIER	GRADIENTERS	GRAMMATICALLY	GRANDIFLORAS
GOSPELLIZED	GOVERNESSIEST	GRADIOMETER	GRAMMATICALNESS	GRANDILOQUENCE
GOSPELLIZES	GOVERNESSING	GRADIOMETERS	GRAMMATICASTER	GRANDILOQUENCES
GOSPELLIZING	GOVERNESSY	GRADUALISM	GRAMMATICASTERS	GRANDILOQUENT
GOSSAMERIER	GOVERNMENT	GRADUALISMS	GRAMMATICISE	GRANDILOQUENTLY

GRANDILOQUOUS	GRANGERIZE	GRANULATOR	GRAPHITOID	GRATIFIERS
GRANDIOSELY	GRANGERIZED	GRANULATORS	GRAPHOLECT	GRATIFYING
GRANDIOSENESS	GRANGERIZER	GRANULIFEROUS	GRAPHOLECTS	GRATIFYINGLY
GRANDIOSENESSES	GRANGERIZERS	GRANULIFORM	GRAPHOLOGIC	GRATILLITIES
GRANDIOSITIES	GRANGERIZES	GRANULITES	GRAPHOLOGICAL	GRATILLITY
GRANDIOSITY	GRANGERIZING	GRANULITIC	GRAPHOLOGIES	GRATINATED
GRANDMAMAS	GRANITELIKE	GRANULITISATION	GRAPHOLOGIST	GRATINATES
GRANDMAMMA	GRANITEWARE	GRANULITIZATION	GRAPHOLOGISTS	GRATINATING
GRANDMAMMAS	GRANITEWARES	GRANULOCYTE	GRAPHOLOGY	GRATINEEING
GRANDMASTER	GRANITIFICATION	GRANULOCYTES	GRAPHOMANIA	GRATITUDES
GRANDMASTERS	GRANITIFORM	GRANULOCYTIC	GRAPHOMANIAS	GRATUITIES
GRANDMOTHER	GRANITISATION	GRANULOMAS	GRAPHOMOTOR	GRATUITOUS
GRANDMOTHERLIER	GRANITISATIONS	GRANULOMATA	GRAPHOPHOBIA	GRATUITOUSLY
GRANDMOTHERLY	GRANITISED	GRANULOMATOUS	GRAPHOPHOBIAS	GRATUITOUSNESS
GRANDMOTHERS	GRANITISES	GRANULOSES	GRAPINESSES	GRATULATED
GRANDNEPHEW	GRANITISING	GRANULOSIS	GRAPLEMENT	GRATULATES
GRANDNEPHEWS	GRANITITES	GRAPEFRUIT	GRAPLEMENTS	GRATULATING
GRANDNESSES	GRANITIZATION	GRAPEFRUITS	GRAPPLINGS	GRATULATION
GRANDNIECE	GRANITIZATIONS	GRAPELOUSE	GRAPTOLITE	GRATULATIONS
GRANDNIECES	GRANITIZED	GRAPESEEDS	GRAPTOLITES	GRATULATORY
GRANDPAPAS	GRANITIZES	GRAPESHOTS	GRAPTOLITIC	GRAUNCHERS
GRANDPARENT	GRANITIZING	GRAPESTONE	GRASPINGLY	GRAUNCHING
GRANDPARENTAL	GRANITOIDS	GRAPESTONES	GRASPINGNESS	GRAVADLAXES
GRANDPARENTHOOD	GRANIVORES	GRAPETREES	GRASPINGNESSES	GRAVEDIGGER
GRANDPARENTS	GRANIVOROUS	GRAPEVINES	GRASSBIRDS	GRAVEDIGGERS
GRANDSIRES	GRANNIEING	GRAPHEMICALLY	GRASSFINCH	GRAVELLIER
GRANDSTAND	GRANODIORITE	GRAPHEMICS	GRASSFINCHES	GRAVELLIEST
GRANDSTANDED	GRANODIORITES	GRAPHICACIES	GRASSHOOKS	GRAVELLING
GRANDSTANDER	GRANODIORITIC	GRAPHICACY	GRASSHOPPER	GRAVENESSES
GRANDSTANDERS	GRANOLITHIC	GRAPHICALLY	GRASSHOPPERS	GRAVEOLENT
GRANDSTANDING	GRANOLITHICS	GRAPHICALNESS	GRASSINESS	GRAVEROBBER
GRANDSTANDINGS	GRANOLITHS	GRAPHICALNESSES	GRASSINESSES	GRAVEROBBERS
GRANDSTANDS	GRANOPHYRE	GRAPHICNESS	GRASSLANDS	GRAVESIDES
GRANDSTOOD	GRANOPHYRES	GRAPHICNESSES	GRASSPLOTS	GRAVESITES
GRANDUNCLE	GRANOPHYRIC	GRAPHITISABLE	GRASSQUITS	GRAVESTONE
GRANDUNCLES	GRANTSMANSHIP	GRAPHITISATION	GRASSROOTS	GRAVESTONES
GRANGERISATION	GRANTSMANSHIPS	GRAPHITISATIONS	GRASSWRACK	GRAVEYARDS
GRANGERISATIONS	GRANULARITIES	GRAPHITISE	GRASSWRACKS	GRAVIDITIES
GRANGERISE	GRANULARITY	GRAPHITISED	GRATEFULLER	GRAVIDNESS
GRANGERISED	GRANULARLY	GRAPHITISES	GRATEFULLEST	GRAVIDNESSES
GRANGERISER	GRANULATED	GRAPHITISING	GRATEFULLY	GRAVIMETER
GRANGERISERS	GRANULATER	GRAPHITIZABLE	GRATEFULNESS	GRAVIMETERS
GRANGERISES	GRANULATERS	GRAPHITIZATION	GRATEFULNESSES	GRAVIMETRIC
GRANGERISING	GRANULATES	GRAPHITIZATIONS	GRATICULATION	GRAVIMETRICAL
GRANGERISM	GRANULATING	GRAPHITIZE	GRATICULATIONS	GRAVIMETRICALLY
GRANGERISMS	GRANULATION	GRAPHITIZED	GRATICULES	GRAVIMETRIES
GRANGERIZATION	GRANULATIONS	GRAPHITIZES	GRATIFICATION	GRAVIMETRY
GRANGERIZATIONS	GRANULATIVE	GRAPHITIZING	GRATIFICATIONS	GRAVIPERCEPTION

GRAVITASES	GRECIANISE	GREENLIGHTING	GREISENISING	GRILLSTEAKS
GRAVITATED	GRECIANISED	GREENLIGHTS	GREISENIZATION	GRILLWORKS
GRAVITATER	GRECIANISES	GREENLINGS	GREISENIZATIONS	GRIMACINGLY
GRAVITATERS	GRECIANISING	GREENMAILED	GREISENIZE	GRIMALKINS
GRAVITATES	GRECIANIZE	GREENMAILER	GREISENIZED	GRIMINESSES
GRAVITATING	GRECIANIZED	GREENMAILERS	GREISENIZES	GRIMLOOKED
GRAVITATION	GRECIANIZES	GREENMAILING	GREISENIZING	GRIMNESSES
GRAVITATIONAL	GRECIANIZING	GREENMAILS	GREMOLATAS	GRINDELIAS
GRAVITATIONALLY	GREEDHEADS	GREENNESSES	GRENADIERS	GRINDERIES
GRAVITATIONS	GREEDINESS	GREENOCKITE	GRENADILLA	GRINDHOUSE
GRAVITATIVE	GREEDINESSES	GREENOCKITES	GRENADILLAS	GRINDHOUSES
GRAVITINOS	GREENBACKER	GREENROOMS	GRENADINES	GRINDINGLY
GRAVITOMETER	GREENBACKERS	GREENSANDS	GRESSORIAL	GRINDSTONE
GRAVITOMETERS	GREENBACKISM	GREENSHANK	GRESSORIOUS	GRINDSTONES
GRAYBEARDED	GREENBACKISMS	GREENSHANKS	GREVILLEAS	GRINNINGLY
GRAYBEARDS	GREENBACKS	GREENSICKNESS	GREWHOUNDS	GRIPPINGLY
GRAYFISHES	GREENBELTS	GREENSICKNESSES	GREWSOMEST	GRISAILLES
GRAYHEADED	GREENBONES	GREENSKEEPER	GREYBEARDED	GRISEOFULVIN
GRAYHOUNDS	GREENBOTTLE	GREENSKEEPERS	GREYBEARDS	GRISEOFULVINS
GRAYLISTED	GREENBOTTLES	GREENSOMES	GREYHEADED	GRISLINESS
GRAYLISTING	GREENBRIER	GREENSPEAK	GREYHOUNDS	GRISLINESSES
GRAYNESSES	GREENBRIERS	GREENSPEAKS	GREYLISTED	GRISTLIEST
GRAYSTONES	GREENCLOTH	GREENSTICK	GREYLISTING	GRISTLINESS
GRAYWACKES	GREENCLOTHS	GREENSTONE	GREYNESSES	GRISTLINESSES
GRAYWATERS	GREENERIES	GREENSTONES	GREYSCALES	GRISTMILLS
GRAYWETHER	GREENFIELD	GREENSTUFF	GREYSTONES	GRITSTONES
GRAYWETHERS	GREENFIELDS	GREENSTUFFS	GREYWACKES	GRITTINESS
GREASEBALL	GREENFINCH	GREENSWARD	GREYWETHER	GRITTINESSES
GREASEBALLS	GREENFINCHES	GREENSWARDS	GREYWETHERS	GRIVATIONS
GREASEBAND	GREENFLIES	GREENWASHED	GRIDDLEBREAD	GRIZZLIEST
GREASEBANDS	GREENGAGES	GREENWASHES	GRIDDLEBREADS	GROANINGLY
GREASEBUSH	GREENGROCER	GREENWASHING	GRIDDLECAKE	GROATSWORTH
GREASEBUSHES	GREENGROCERIES	GREENWASHINGS	GRIDDLECAKES	GROATSWORTHS
GREASELESS	GREENGROCERS	GREENWEEDS	GRIDIRONED	GROCETERIA
GREASEPAINT	GREENGROCERY	GREENWINGS	GRIDIRONING	GROCETERIAS
GREASEPAINTS	GREENHANDS	GREENWOODS	GRIDLOCKED	GROGGERIES
GREASEPROOF	GREENHEADS	GREGARIANISM	GRIDLOCKING	GROGGINESS
GREASEPROOFS	GREENHEART	GREGARIANISMS	GRIEVANCES	GROGGINESSES
GREASEWOOD	GREENHEARTS	GREGARINES	GRIEVINGLY	GROMMETING
GREASEWOODS	GREENHORNS	GREGARINIAN	GRIEVOUSLY	GROOVELESS
GREASINESS	GREENHOUSE	GREGARIOUS	GRIEVOUSNESS	GROOVELIKE
GREASINESSES	GREENHOUSES	GREGARIOUSLY	GRIEVOUSNESSES	GROOVINESS
GREATCOATED	GREENISHNESS	GREGARIOUSNESS	GRIFFINISH	GROOVINESSES
GREATCOATS	GREENISHNESSES	GREISENISATION	GRIFFINISM	GROSGRAINS
GREATENING	GREENKEEPER	GREISENISATIONS	GRIFFINISMS	GROSSIERETE
GREATHEARTED	GREENKEEPERS	GREISENISE	GRILLERIES	GROSSIERETES
GREATHEARTEDLY	GREENLIGHT	GREISENISED	GRILLROOMS	GROSSNESSES
GREATNESSES	GREENLIGHTED	GREISENISES	GRILLSTEAK	GROSSULARITE

GROSSULARITES	GROUNDSHARE	GRUBSTAKES	GUARDRAILS	GUILEFULLY
GROSSULARS	GROUNDSHARED	GRUBSTAKING	GUARDROOMS	GUILEFULNESS
GROTESQUELY	GROUNDSHARES	GRUBSTREET	GUARDSHIPS	GUILEFULNESSES
GROTESQUENESS	GROUNDSHARING	GRUDGELESS	GUARISHING	GUILELESSLY
GROTESQUENESSES	GROUNDSHEET	GRUDGINGLY	GUAYABERAS	GUILELESSNESS
GROTESQUER	GROUNDSHEETS	GRUELINGLY	GUBERNACULA	GUILELESSNESSES
GROTESQUERIE	GROUNDSILL	GRUELLINGLY	GUBERNACULAR	GUILLEMETS
GROTESQUERIES	GROUNDSILLS	GRUELLINGS	GUBERNACULUM	GUILLEMOTS
GROTESQUERY	GROUNDSKEEPER	GRUESOMELY	GUBERNATION	GUILLOCHED
GROTESQUES	GROUNDSKEEPERS	GRUESOMENESS	GUBERNATIONS	GUILLOCHES
GROTESQUEST	GROUNDSMAN	GRUESOMENESSES	GUBERNATOR	GUILLOCHING
GROTTINESS	GROUNDSMEN	GRUESOMEST	GUBERNATORIAL	GUILLOTINE
GROTTINESSES	GROUNDSPEED	GRUFFNESSES	GUBERNATORS	GUILLOTINED
GROUCHIEST	GROUNDSPEEDS	GRUMBLIEST	GUBERNIYAS	GUILLOTINER
GROUCHINESS	GROUNDSWELL	GRUMBLINGLY	GUDGEONING	GUILLOTINERS
GROUCHINESSES	GROUNDSWELLS	GRUMBLINGS	GUERDONERS	GUILLOTINES
GROUNDAGES	GROUNDWATER	GRUMMETING	GUERDONING	GUILLOTINING
GROUNDBAIT	GROUNDWATERS	GRUMNESSES	GUERILLAISM	GUILTINESS
GROUNDBAITED	GROUNDWOOD	GRUMPINESS	GUERILLAISMS	GUILTINESSES
GROUNDBAITING	GROUNDWOODS	GRUMPINESSES	GUERRILLAISM	GUILTLESSLY
GROUNDBAITS	GROUNDWORK	GRUMPISHLY	GUERRILLAISMS	GUILTLESSNESS
GROUNDBREAKER	GROUNDWORKS	GRUMPISHNESS	GUERRILLAS	GUILTLESSNESSES
GROUNDBREAKERS	GROUPTHINK	GRUMPISHNESSES	GUERRILLERO	GUITARFISH
GROUNDBREAKING	GROUPTHINKS	GRUNTINGLY	GUERRILLEROS	GUITARFISHES
GROUNDBREAKINGS	GROUPUSCULE	GUACAMOLES	GUESSINGLY	GUITARISTS
GROUNDBURST	GROUPUSCULES	GUACHAMOLE	GUESSTIMATE	GULLIBILITIES
GROUNDBURSTS	GROUPWARES	GUACHAMOLES	GUESSTIMATED	GULLIBILITY
GROUNDEDLY	GROUPWORKS	GUACHAROES	GUESSTIMATES	GULOSITIES
GROUNDFISH	GROUSELIKE	GUANABANAS	GUESSTIMATING	GUMMIFEROUS
GROUNDFISHES	GROVELINGLY	GUANAZOLOS	GUESSWORKS	GUMMINESSES
GROUNDHOGS	GROVELINGS	GUANETHIDINE	GUESTBOOKS	GUMMOSITIES
GROUNDINGS	GROVELLERS	GUANETHIDINES	GUESTENING	GUMSHIELDS
GROUNDLESS	GROVELLING	GUANIDINES	GUESTHOUSE	GUMSHOEING
GROUNDLESSLY	GROVELLINGLY	GUANIFEROUS	GUESTHOUSES	GUMSUCKERS
GROUNDLESSNESS	GROVELLINGS	GUANOSINES	GUESTIMATE	GUNCOTTONS
GROUNDLING	GROWLERIES	GUARANTEED	GUESTIMATED	GUNFIGHTER
GROUNDLINGS	GROWLINESS	GUARANTEEING	GUESTIMATES	GUNFIGHTERS
GROUNDMASS	GROWLINESSES	GUARANTEES	GUESTIMATING	GUNFIGHTING
GROUNDMASSES	GROWLINGLY	GUARANTIED	GUIDEBOOKS	GUNFIGHTINGS
GROUNDNUTS	GROWTHIEST	GUARANTIES	GUIDELINES	GUNKHOLING
GROUNDOUTS	GROWTHINESS	GUARANTORS	GUIDEPOSTS	GUNMANSHIP
GROUNDPLOT	GROWTHINESSES	GUARANTYING	GUIDESHIPS	GUNMANSHIPS
GROUNDPLOTS	GROWTHISTS	GUARDEDNESS	GUIDEWORDS	GUNNERSHIP
GROUNDPROX	GRUBBINESS	GUARDEDNESSES	GUIDWILLIE	GUNNERSHIPS
GROUNDPROXES	GRUBBINESSES	GUARDHOUSE	GUILDHALLS	GUNNYSACKS
GROUNDSELL	GRUBSTAKED	GUARDHOUSES	GUILDSHIPS	GUNPOWDERIER
GROUNDSELLS	GRUBSTAKER	GUARDIANSHIP	GUILDSWOMAN	GUNPOWDERIEST
GROUNDSELS	GRUBSTAKERS	GUARDIANSHIPS	GUILDSWOMEN	GUNPOWDERS

G

GUNPOWDERY	GUTTURALISED	GYMNOSPERMS	GYNECOLOGIES	GYPSOPHILAS
GUNRUNNERS	GUTTURALISES	GYMNOSPERMY	GYNECOLOGIST	GYPSYHOODS
GUNRUNNING	GUTTURALISING	GYNAECEUMS	GYNECOLOGISTS	GYPSYWORTS
GUNRUNNINGS	GUTTURALISM	GYNAECOCRACIES	GYNECOLOGY	GYRATIONAL
GUNSLINGER	GUTTURALISMS	GYNAECOCRACY	GYNECOMASTIA	GYRFALCONS
GUNSLINGERS	GUTTURALITIES	GYNAECOCRATIC	GYNECOMASTIAS	GYROCOMPASS
GUNSLINGING	GUTTURALITY	GYNAECOLOGIC	GYNIATRICS	GYROCOMPASSES
GUNSLINGINGS	GUTTURALIZATION	GYNAECOLOGICAL	GYNIATRIES	GYROCOPTER
GUNSMITHING	GUTTURALIZE	GYNAECOLOGIES	GYNIOLATRIES	GYROCOPTERS
GUNSMITHINGS	GUTTURALIZED	GYNAECOLOGIST	GYNIOLATRY	GYROFREQUENCIES
GURGITATION	GUTTURALIZES	GYNAECOLOGISTS	GYNOCRACIES	GYROFREQUENCY
GURGITATIONS	GUTTURALIZING	GYNAECOLOGY	GYNOCRATIC	GYROMAGNETIC
GUSHINESSES	GUTTURALLY	GYNAECOMAST	GYNODIOECIOUS	GYROMAGNETISM
GUSSETINGS	GUTTURALNESS	GYNAECOMASTIA	GYNODIOECISM	GYROMAGNETISMS
GUSTATIONS	GUTTURALNESSES	GYNAECOMASTIAS	GYNODIOECISMS	GYROMANCIES
GUSTATORILY	GYMNASIARCH	GYNAECOMASTIES	GYNOGENESES	GYROPILOTS
GUSTINESSES	GYMNASIARCHS	GYNAECOMASTS	GYNOGENESIS	GYROPLANES
GUTBUCKETS	GYMNASIAST	GYNAECOMASTY	GYNOGENETIC	GYROSCOPES
GUTLESSNESS	GYMNASIASTS	GYNANDRIES	GYNOMONOECIOUS	GYROSCOPIC
GUTLESSNESSES	GYMNASIUMS	GYNANDRISM	GYNOMONOECISM	GYROSCOPICALLY
GUTSINESSES	GYMNASTICAL	GYNANDRISMS	GYNOMONOECISMS	GYROSCOPICS
GUTTATIONS	GYMNASTICALLY	GYNANDROMORPH	GYNOPHOBES	GYROSTABILISER
GUTTERBLOOD	GYMNASTICS	GYNANDROMORPHIC	GYNOPHOBIA	GYROSTABILISERS
GUTTERBLOODS	GYMNORHINAL	GYNANDROMORPHS	GYNOPHOBIAS	GYROSTABILIZER
GUTTERIEST	GYMNOSOPHIES	GYNANDROMORPHY	GYNOPHOBIC	GYROSTABILIZERS
GUTTERINGS	GYMNOSOPHIST	GYNANDROUS	GYNOPHOBICS	GYROSTATIC
GUTTERSNIPE	GYMNOSOPHISTS	GYNARCHIES	GYNOPHORES	GYROSTATICALLY
GUTTERSNIPES	GYMNOSOPHS	GYNECOCRACIES	GYNOPHORIC	GYROSTATICS
GUTTERSNIPISH	GYMNOSOPHY	GYNECOCRACY	GYNOSTEMIA	GYROVAGUES
GUTTIFEROUS	GYMNOSPERM	GYNECOCRATIC	GYNOSTEMIUM	
GUTTURALISATION	GYMNOSPERMIES	GYNECOLOGIC	GYPSIFEROUS	
GUTTURALISE	GYMNOSPERMOUS	GYNECOLOGICAL	GYPSOPHILA	

H

HAANEPOOTS	HACKBUTEERS	HAEMATOBLAST	HAEMOCOELS	HAEMOPHILIOID
HABERDASHER	HACKBUTTER	HAEMATOBLASTIC	HAEMOCONIA	HAEMOPHOBIA
HABERDASHERIES	HACKBUTTERS	HAEMATOBLASTS	HAEMOCONIAS	HAEMOPHOBIAS
HABERDASHERS	HACKERAZZI	HAEMATOCELE	HAEMOCYANIN	HAEMOPOIESES
HABERDASHERY	HACKERAZZIS	HAEMATOCELES	HAEMOCYANINS	HAEMOPOIESIS
HABERDINES	HACKERAZZO	HAEMATOCRIT	HAEMOCYTES	HAEMOPOIETIC
HABERGEONS	HACKMATACK	HAEMATOCRITS	HAEMOCYTOMETER	HAEMOPROTEIN
HABILATORY	HACKMATACKS	HAEMATOCRYAL	HAEMOCYTOMETERS	HAEMOPROTEINS
HABILIMENT	HACKNEYING	HAEMATOGENESES	HAEMODIALYSER	HAEMOPTYSES
HABILIMENTS	HACKNEYISM	HAEMATOGENESIS	HAEMODIALYSERS	HAEMOPTYSIS
HABILITATE	HACKNEYISMS	HAEMATOGENETIC	HAEMODIALYSES	HAEMORRHAGE
HABILITATED	HACKNEYMAN	HAEMATOGENIC	HAEMODIALYSIS	HAEMORRHAGED
HABILITATES	HACKNEYMEN	HAEMATOGENOUS	HAEMODIALYZER	HAEMORRHAGES
HABILITATING	HACKSAWING	HAEMATOLOGIC	HAEMODIALYZERS	HAEMORRHAGIC
HABILITATION	HACKTIVISM	HAEMATOLOGICAL	HAEMODILUTION	HAEMORRHAGING
HABILITATIONS	HACKTIVISMS	HAEMATOLOGIES	HAEMODILUTIONS	HAEMORRHAGINGS
HABILITATOR	HACKTIVIST	HAEMATOLOGIST	HAEMODYNAMIC	HAEMORRHOID
HABILITATORS	HACKTIVISTS	HAEMATOLOGISTS	HAEMODYNAMICS	HAEMORRHOIDAL
HABITABILITIES	HACQUETONS	HAEMATOLOGY	HAEMOFLAGELLATE	HAEMORRHOIDS
HABITABILITY	HADROSAURS	HAEMATOLYSES	HAEMOGLOBIN	HAEMOSIDERIN
HABITABLENESS	HADROSAURUS	HAEMATOLYSIS	HAEMOGLOBINS	HAEMOSIDERINS
HABITABLENESSES	HADROSAURUSES	HAEMATOMAS	HAEMOGLOBINURIA	HAEMOSTASES
HABITATION	HAECCEITIES	HAEMATOMATA	HAEMOGLOBINURIC	HAEMOSTASIA
HABITATIONAL	HAEMACHROME	HAEMATOPHAGOUS	HAEMOLYMPH	HAEMOSTASIAS
HABITATIONS	HAEMACHROMES	HAEMATOPOIESES	HAEMOLYMPHS	HAEMOSTASIS
HABITAUNCE	HAEMACYTOMETER	HAEMATOPOIESIS	HAEMOLYSED	HAEMOSTATIC
HABITAUNCES	HAEMACYTOMETERS	HAEMATOPOIETIC	HAEMOLYSES	HAEMOSTATICS
HABITUALLY	HAEMAGGLUTINATE	HAEMATOSES	HAEMOLYSIN	HAEMOSTATS
HABITUALNESS	HAEMAGGLUTININ	HAEMATOSIS	HAEMOLYSING	HAEMOTOXIC
HABITUALNESSES	HAEMAGGLUTININS	HAEMATOTHERMAL	HAEMOLYSINS	HAEMOTOXIN
HABITUATED	HAEMAGOGUE	HAEMATOXYLIC	HAEMOLYSIS	HAEMOTOXINS
HABITUATES	HAEMAGOGUES	HAEMATOXYLIN	HAEMOLYTIC	HAGBERRIES
HABITUATING	HAEMANGIOMA	HAEMATOXYLINS	HAEMOLYZED	HAGBUTEERS
HABITUATION	HAEMANGIOMAS	HAEMATOXYLON	HAEMOLYZES	HAGBUTTERS
HABITUATIONS	HAEMANGIOMATA	HAEMATOXYLONS	HAEMOLYZING	HAGGADICAL
HABITUDINAL	HAEMATEINS	HAEMATOZOA	HAEMOPHILE	HAGGADISTIC
HACENDADOS	HAEMATEMESES	HAEMATOZOON	HAEMOPHILES	HAGGADISTS
HACIENDADO	HAEMATEMESIS	HAEMATURIA	HAEMOPHILIA	HAGGARDNESS
HACIENDADOS	HAEMATINIC	HAEMATURIAS	HAEMOPHILIAC	HAGGARDNESSES
HACKAMORES	HAEMATINICS	HAEMATURIC	HAEMOPHILIACS	HAGGISHNESS
HACKBERRIES	HAEMATITES	HAEMOCHROME	HAEMOPHILIAS	HAGGISHNESSES
HACKBUTEER	HAEMATITIC	HAEMOCHROMES	HAEMOPHILIC	HAGIARCHIES

HAGIOCRACIES	HAIRSPLITTERS	HALLOWEDNESS	HALOPHYTIC	HAMSHACKLES
HAGIOCRACY	HAIRSPLITTING	HALLOWEDNESSES	HALOPHYTISM	HAMSHACKLING
HAGIOGRAPHER	HAIRSPLITTINGS	HALLOYSITE	HALOPHYTISMS	HAMSTRINGED
HAGIOGRAPHERS	HAIRSPRAYS	HALLOYSITES	HALOTHANES	HAMSTRINGING
HAGIOGRAPHIC	HAIRSPRING	HALLSTANDS	HALTERBREAK	HAMSTRINGS
HAGIOGRAPHICAL	HAIRSPRINGS	HALLUCINANT	HALTERBREAKING	HANDBAGGED
HAGIOGRAPHIES	HAIRSTREAK	HALLUCINANTS	HALTERBREAKS	HANDBAGGING
HAGIOGRAPHIST	HAIRSTREAKS	HALLUCINATE	HALTERBROKE	HANDBAGGINGS
HAGIOGRAPHISTS	HAIRSTYLES	HALLUCINATED	HALTERBROKEN	HANDBALLED
HAGIOGRAPHY	HAIRSTYLING	HALLUCINATES	HALTERNECK	HANDBALLER
HAGIOLATER	HAIRSTYLINGS	HALLUCINATING	HALTERNECKS	HANDBALLERS
HAGIOLATERS	HAIRSTYLIST	HALLUCINATION	HALTINGNESS	HANDBALLING
HAGIOLATRIES	HAIRSTYLISTS	HALLUCINATIONAL	HALTINGNESSES	HANDBARROW
HAGIOLATROUS	HAIRWEAVING	HALLUCINATIONS	HAMADRYADES	HANDBARROWS
HAGIOLATRY	HAIRWEAVINGS	HALLUCINATIVE	HAMADRYADS	HANDBASKET
HAGIOLOGIC	HAIRYBACKS	HALLUCINATOR	HAMADRYASES	HANDBASKETS
HAGIOLOGICAL	HALACHISTS	HALLUCINATORS	HAMAMELIDACEOUS	HANDBRAKES
HAGIOLOGIES	HALAKHISTS	HALLUCINATORY	HAMAMELISES	HANDBREADTH
HAGIOLOGIST	HALBERDIER	HALLUCINOGEN	HAMANTASCH	HANDBREADTHS
HAGIOLOGISTS	HALBERDIERS	HALLUCINOGENIC	HAMANTASCHEN	HANDCLASPS
HAGIOSCOPE	HALCYONIAN	HALLUCINOGENICS	HAMARTHRITIS	HANDCRAFTED
HAGIOSCOPES	HALENESSES	HALLUCINOGENS	HAMARTHRITISES	HANDCRAFTING
HAGIOSCOPIC	HALFENDEALE	HALLUCINOSES	HAMARTIOLOGIES	HANDCRAFTS
HAILSTONES	HALFENDEALES	HALLUCINOSIS	HAMARTIOLOGY	HANDCRAFTSMAN
HAILSTORMS	HALFHEARTED	HALOBIONTIC	HAMBURGERS	HANDCRAFTSMEN
HAIRBRAINED	HALFHEARTEDLY	HALOBIONTS	HAMESUCKEN	HANDCUFFED
HAIRBREADTH	HALFHEARTEDNESS	HALOBIOTIC	HAMESUCKENS	HANDCUFFING
HAIRBREADTHS	HALFNESSES	HALOCARBON	HAMFATTERED	HANDEDNESS
HAIRBRUSHES	HALFPENNIES	HALOCARBONS	HAMFATTERING	HANDEDNESSES
HAIRCLOTHS	HALFPENNYWORTH	HALOCLINES	HAMFATTERS	HANDFASTED
HAIRCUTTER	HALFPENNYWORTHS	HALOGENATE	HAMMERCLOTH	HANDFASTING
HAIRCUTTERS	HALFSERIOUSLY	HALOGENATED	HAMMERCLOTHS	HANDFASTINGS
HAIRCUTTING	HALFTRACKS	HALOGENATES	HAMMERHEAD	HANDFEEDING
HAIRCUTTINGS	HALFWITTED	HALOGENATING	HAMMERHEADED	HANDGLASSES
HAIRDRESSER	HALFWITTEDLY	HALOGENATION	HAMMERHEADS	HANDICAPPED
HAIRDRESSERS	HALFWITTEDNESS	HALOGENATIONS	HAMMERINGS	HANDICAPPER
HAIRDRESSING	HALIEUTICS	HALOGENOID	HAMMERKOPS	HANDICAPPERS
HAIRDRESSINGS	HALIPLANKTON	HALOGENOUS	HAMMERLESS	HANDICAPPING
HAIRDRIERS	HALIPLANKTONS	HALOGETONS	HAMMERLOCK	HANDICRAFT
HAIRDRYERS	HALLALLING	HALOMORPHIC	HAMMERLOCKS	HANDICRAFTER
HAIRINESSES	HALLEFLINTA	HALOPERIDOL	HAMMERSTONE	HANDICRAFTERS
HAIRLESSES	HALLEFLINTAS	HALOPERIDOLS	HAMMERSTONES	HANDICRAFTS
HAIRLESSNESS	HALLELUIAH	HALOPHILES	HAMMERTOES	HANDICRAFTSMAN
HAIRLESSNESSES	HALLELUIAHS	HALOPHILIC	HAMMINESSES	HANDICRAFTSMEN
HAIRPIECES	HALLELUJAH	HALOPHILIES	HAMPEREDNESS	HANDICUFFS
HAIRSBREADTH	HALLELUJAHS	HALOPHILOUS	HAMPEREDNESSES	HANDINESSES
HAIRSBREADTHS	HALLMARKED	HALOPHOBES	HAMSHACKLE	HANDIWORKS
HAIRSPLITTER	HALLMARKING	HALOPHYTES	HAMSHACKLED	HANDKERCHER

HANDKERCHERS	HANDWORKERS	HAPPENCHANCE	HARDHEADED	HARMOLODICS
HANDKERCHIEF	HANDWRINGER	HAPPENCHANCES	HARDHEADEDLY	HARMONICAL
HANDKERCHIEFS	HANDWRINGERS	HAPPENINGS	HARDHEADEDNESS	HARMONICALLY
HANDKERCHIEVES	HANDWRITES	HAPPENSTANCE	HARDHEARTED	HARMONICAS
HANDLANGER	HANDWRITING	HAPPENSTANCES	HARDHEARTEDLY	HARMONICHORD
HANDLANGERS	HANDWRITINGS	HAPPINESSES	HARDHEARTEDNESS	HARMONICHORDS
HANDLEABLE	HANDWRITTEN	HAPTOGLOBIN	HARDIHEADS	HARMONICIST
HANDLEBARS	HANDWROUGHT	HAPTOGLOBINS	HARDIHOODS	HARMONICISTS
HANDLELESS	HANDYPERSON	HAPTOTROPIC	HARDIMENTS	HARMONICON
HANDLINERS	HANDYPERSONS	HAPTOTROPISM	HARDINESSES	HARMONICONS
HANDMAIDEN	HANDYWORKS	HAPTOTROPISMS	HARDINGGRASS	HARMONIOUS
HANDMAIDENS	HANGABILITIES	HARAMZADAS	HARDINGGRASSES	HARMONIOUSLY
HANDPASSED	HANGABILITY	HARAMZADIS	HARDLINERS	HARMONIOUSNESS
HANDPASSES	HANGARAGES	HARANGUERS	HARDMOUTHED	HARMONIPHON
HANDPASSING	HANKERINGS	HARANGUING	HARDNESSES	HARMONIPHONE
HANDPHONES	HANSARDISE	HARASSEDLY	HARDSCAPES	HARMONIPHONES
HANDPICKED	HANSARDISED	HARASSINGLY	HARDSCRABBLE	HARMONIPHONS
HANDPICKING	HANSARDISES	HARASSINGS	HARDSCRABBLES	HARMONISABLE
HANDPRESSES	HANSARDISING	HARASSMENT	HARDSTANDING	HARMONISATION
HANDPRINTS	HANSARDIZE	HARASSMENTS	HARDSTANDINGS	HARMONISATIONS
HANDSBREADTH	HANSARDIZED	HARBINGERED	HARDSTANDS	HARMONISED
HANDSBREADTHS	HANSARDIZES	HARBINGERING	HARDWAREMAN	HARMONISER
HANDSELING	HANSARDIZING	HARBINGERS	HARDWAREMEN	HARMONISERS
HANDSELLED	HANSELLING	HARBORAGES	HARDWIRING	HARMONISES
HANDSELLING	HANTAVIRUS	HARBORFULS	HARDWORKING	HARMONISING
HANDSHAKES	HANTAVIRUSES	HARBORLESS	HAREBRAINED	HARMONISTIC
HANDSHAKING	HAPAXANTHIC	HARBORMASTER	HARELIPPED	HARMONISTICALLY
HANDSHAKINGS	HAPAXANTHOUS	HARBORMASTERS	HARESTAILS	HARMONISTS
HANDSOMELY	HAPHAZARDLY	HARBORSIDE	HARIOLATED	HARMONIUMIST
HANDSOMENESS	HAPHAZARDNESS	HARBOURAGE	HARIOLATES	HARMONIUMISTS
HANDSOMENESSES	HAPHAZARDNESSES	HARBOURAGES	HARIOLATING	HARMONIUMS
HANDSOMEST	HAPHAZARDRIES	HARBOURERS	HARIOLATION	HARMONIZABLE
HANDSPIKES	HAPHAZARDRY	HARBOURFUL	HARIOLATIONS	HARMONIZATION
HANDSPRING	HAPHAZARDS	HARBOURFULS	HARLEQUINADE	HARMONIZATIONS
HANDSPRINGS	HAPHTARAHS	HARBOURING	HARLEQUINADES	HARMONIZED
HANDSTAFFS	HAPHTAROTH	HARBOURLESS	HARLEQUINED	HARMONIZER
HANDSTAMPED	HAPLESSNESS	HARBOURSIDE	HARLEQUINING	HARMONIZERS
HANDSTAMPING	HAPLESSNESSES	HARBOURSIDES	HARLEQUINS	HARMONIZES
HANDSTAMPS	HAPLOBIONT	HARDBACKED	HARLOTRIES	HARMONIZING
HANDSTANDS	HAPLOBIONTIC	HARDBOARDS	HARMALINES	HARMONOGRAM
HANDSTAVES	HAPLOBIONTS	HARDBODIES	HARMATTANS	HARMONOGRAMS
HANDSTROKE	HAPLOGRAPHIES	HARDBOUNDS	HARMDOINGS	HARMONOGRAPH
HANDSTROKES	HAPLOGRAPHY	HARDCOVERS	HARMFULNESS	HARMONOGRAPHS
HANDSTURNS	HAPLOIDIES	HARDENINGS	HARMFULNESSES	HARMONOMETER
HANDTOWELS	HAPLOLOGIC	HARDFISTED	HARMLESSLY	HARMONOMETERS
HANDWHEELS	HAPLOLOGIES	HARDGRASSES	HARMLESSNESS	HARMOSTIES
HANDWORKED	HAPLOSTEMONOUS	HARDHANDED	HARMLESSNESSES	HARMOTOMES
HANDWORKER	HAPLOTYPES	HARDHANDEDNESS	HARMOLODIC	HARNESSERS

HARNESSING	HASENPFEFFER	HAUSTELLATE	HEADHUNTINGS	HEADSTRONGNESS
HARNESSLESS	HASENPFEFFERS	HAUSTELLUM	HEADINESSES	HEADTEACHER
HARPOONEER	HASHEESHES	HAUSTORIAL	HEADLEASES	HEADTEACHERS
HARPOONEERS	HASSOCKIER	HAUSTORIUM	HEADLESSNESS	HEADWAITER
HARPOONERS	HASSOCKIEST	HAVERSACKS	HEADLESSNESSES	HEADWAITERS
HARPOONING	HASTEFULLY	HAVERSINES	HEADLIGHTS	HEADWATERS
HARPSICHORD	HASTINESSES	HAWFINCHES	HEADLINERS	HEADWORKER
HARPSICHORDIST	HATBRUSHES	HAWKISHNESS	HEADLINING	HEADWORKERS
HARPSICHORDISTS	HATCHABILITIES	HAWKISHNESSES	HEADMASTER	HEALTHCARE
HARPSICHORDS	HATCHABILITY	HAWKSBEARD	HEADMASTERLIER	HEALTHCARES
HARQUEBUSE	HATCHBACKS	HAWKSBEARDS	HEADMASTERLIEST	HEALTHFULLY
HARQUEBUSES	HATCHELING	HAWKSBILLS	HEADMASTERLY	HEALTHFULNESS
HARQUEBUSIER	HATCHELLED	HAWSEHOLES	HEADMASTERS	HEALTHFULNESSES
HARQUEBUSIERS	HATCHELLER	HAWSEPIPES	HEADMASTERSHIP	HEALTHIEST
HARQUEBUSS	HATCHELLERS	HAWTHORNIER	HEADMASTERSHIPS	HEALTHINESS
HARQUEBUSSES	HATCHELLING	HAWTHORNIEST	HEADMISTRESS	HEALTHINESSES
HARROWINGLY	HATCHERIES	HAYCATIONS	HEADMISTRESSES	HEALTHISMS
HARROWINGS	HATCHETIER	HAYMAKINGS	HEADMISTRESSIER	HEALTHLESS
HARROWMENT	HATCHETIEST	HAZARDABLE	HEADMISTRESSY	HEALTHLESSNESS
HARROWMENTS	HATCHETTITE	HAZARDIZES	HEADPEACES	HEALTHSOME
HARRUMPHED	HATCHETTITES	HAZARDOUSLY	HEADPHONES	HEAPSTEADS
HARRUMPHING	HATCHLINGS	HAZARDOUSNESS	HEADPIECES	HEARKENERS
HARSHENING	HATCHMENTS	HAZARDOUSNESSES	HEADQUARTER	HEARKENING
HARSHNESSES	HATEFULNESS	HAZARDRIES	HEADQUARTERED	HEARTACHES
HARTBEESES	HATEFULNESSES	HAZELWOODS	HEADQUARTERING	HEARTBEATS
HARTBEESTS	HATELESSNESS	HAZINESSES	HEADQUARTERS	HEARTBREAK
HARTEBEEST	HATELESSNESSES	HEADACHIER	HEADREACHED	HEARTBREAKER
HARTEBEESTS	HATEWORTHIER	HEADACHIEST	HEADREACHES	HEARTBREAKERS
HARTSHORNS	HATEWORTHIEST	HEADBANGED	HEADREACHING	HEARTBREAKING
HARUMPHING	HATEWORTHY	HEADBANGING	HEADSCARVES	HEARTBREAKINGLY
HARUSPICAL	HATINATORS	HEADBANGINGS	HEADSHAKES	HEARTBREAKS
HARUSPICATE	HATLESSNESS	HEADBOARDS	HEADSHEETS	HEARTBROKE
HARUSPICATED	HATLESSNESSES	HEADBOROUGH	HEADSHRINKER	HEARTBROKEN
HARUSPICATES	HAUBERGEON	HEADBOROUGHS	HEADSHRINKERS	HEARTBROKENLY
HARUSPICATING	HAUBERGEONS	HEADCHAIRS	HEADSPACES	HEARTBROKENNESS
HARUSPICATION	HAUGHTIEST	HEADCHEESE	HEADSPRING	HEARTBURNING
HARUSPICATIONS	HAUGHTINESS	HEADCHEESES	HEADSPRINGS	HEARTBURNINGS
HARUSPICES	HAUGHTINESSES	HEADCLOTHS	HEADSQUARE	HEARTBURNS
HARUSPICIES	HAUNTINGLY	HEADCOUNTS	HEADSQUARES	HEARTENERS
HARVESTABLE	HAUSFRAUEN	HEADDRESSES	HEADSTALLS	HEARTENING
HARVESTERS	HAUSSMANNISE	HEADFISHES	HEADSTANDS	HEARTENINGLY
HARVESTING	HAUSSMANNISED	HEADFOREMOST	HEADSTICKS	HEARTHRUGS
HARVESTINGS	HAUSSMANNISES	HEADFRAMES	HEADSTOCKS	HEARTHSTONE
HARVESTLESS	HAUSSMANNISING	HEADGUARDS	HEADSTONES	HEARTHSTONES
HARVESTMAN	HAUSSMANNIZE	HEADHUNTED	HEADSTREAM	HEARTIKINS
HARVESTMEN	HAUSSMANNIZED	HEADHUNTER	HEADSTREAMS	HEARTINESS
HARVESTTIME	HAUSSMANNIZES	HEADHUNTERS	HEADSTRONG	HEARTINESSES
HARVESTTIMES	HAUSSMANNIZING	HEADHUNTING	HEADSTRONGLY	HEARTLANDS

HEARTLESSLY	HEATHENNESS	HECOGENINS	HEFTINESSES	HELIOCHROME
HEARTLESSNESS	HEATHENNESSES	HECTICALLY	HEGEMONIAL	HELIOCHROMES
HEARTLESSNESSES	HEATHENRIES	HECTOCOTYLI	HEGEMONICAL	HELIOCHROMIC
HEARTLINGS	HEATHERIER	HECTOCOTYLUS	HEGEMONIES	HELIOCHROMIES
HEARTRENDING	HEATHERIEST	HECTOGRAMME	HEGEMONISM	HELIOCHROMY
HEARTRENDINGLY	HEATHFOWLS	HECTOGRAMMES	HEGEMONISMS	HELIOGRAMS
HEARTSEASE	HEATHLANDS	HECTOGRAMS	HEGEMONIST	HELIOGRAPH
HEARTSEASES	HEATSTROKE	HECTOGRAPH	HEGEMONISTS	HELIOGRAPHED
HEARTSEEDS	HEATSTROKES	HECTOGRAPHED	HEGUMENIES	HELIOGRAPHER
HEARTSICKNESS	HEAVENLIER	HECTOGRAPHIC	HEGUMENOSES	HELIOGRAPHERS
HEARTSICKNESSES	HEAVENLIEST	HECTOGRAPHIES	HEIGHTENED	HELIOGRAPHIC
HEARTSINKS	HEAVENLINESS	HECTOGRAPHING	HEIGHTENER	HELIOGRAPHICAL
HEARTSOMELY	HEAVENLINESSES	HECTOGRAPHS	HEIGHTENERS	HELIOGRAPHIES
HEARTSOMENESS	HEAVENWARD	HECTOGRAPHY	HEIGHTENING	HELIOGRAPHING
HEARTSOMENESSES	HEAVENWARDS	HECTOLITER	HEIGHTISMS	HELIOGRAPHS
HEARTSORES	HEAVINESSES	HECTOLITERS	HEINOUSNESS	HELIOGRAPHY
HEARTSTRING	HEAVYHEARTED	HECTOLITRE	HEINOUSNESSES	HELIOGRAVURE
HEARTSTRINGS	HEAVYHEARTEDLY	HECTOLITRES	HEKTOGRAMS	HELIOGRAVURES
HEARTTHROB	HEAVYWEIGHT	HECTOMETER	HELDENTENOR	HELIOLATER
HEARTTHROBS	HEAVYWEIGHTS	HECTOMETERS	HELDENTENORS	HELIOLATERS
HEARTWARMING	HEBDOMADAL	HECTOMETRE	HELIACALLY	HELIOLATRIES
HEARTWATER	HEBDOMADALLY	HECTOMETRES	HELIANTHEMUM	HELIOLATROUS
HEARTWATERS	HEBDOMADAR	HECTORINGLY	HELIANTHEMUMS	HELIOLATRY
HEARTWOODS	HEBDOMADARIES	HECTORINGS	HELIANTHUS	HELIOLITHIC
HEARTWORMS	HEBDOMADARS	HECTORISMS	HELIANTHUSES	HELIOLOGIES
HEATEDNESS	HEBDOMADARY	HECTORSHIP	HELIBUSSES	HELIOMETER
HEATEDNESSES	HEBDOMADER	HECTORSHIPS	HELICHRYSUM	HELIOMETERS
HEATHBERRIES	HEBDOMADERS	HECTOSTERE	HELICHRYSUMS	HELIOMETRIC
HEATHBERRY	HEBEPHRENIA	HECTOSTERES	HELICITIES	HELIOMETRICAL
HEATHBIRDS	HEBEPHRENIAC	HEDGEBILLS	HELICLINES	HELIOMETRICALLY
HEATHCOCKS	HEBEPHRENIACS	HEDGEHOPPED	HELICOGRAPH	HELIOMETRIES
HEATHENDOM	HEBEPHRENIAS	HEDGEHOPPER	HELICOGRAPHS	HELIOMETRY
HEATHENDOMS	HEBEPHRENIC	HEDGEHOPPERS	HELICOIDAL	HELIOPAUSE
HEATHENESSE	HEBEPHRENICS	HEDGEHOPPING	HELICOIDALLY	HELIOPAUSES
HEATHENESSES	HEBETATING	HEDGEHOPPINGS	HELICONIAS	HELIOPHILOUS
HEATHENISE	HEBETATION	HEDONICALLY	HELICOPTED	HELIOPHOBIC
HEATHENISED	HEBETATIONS	HEDONISTIC	HELICOPTER	HELIOPHYTE
HEATHENISES	HEBETATIVE	HEDONISTICALLY	HELICOPTERED	HELIOPHYTES
HEATHENISH	HEBETUDINOSITY	HEDYPHANES	HELICOPTERING	HELIOSCIOPHYTE
HEATHENISHLY	HEBETUDINOUS	HEDYSARUMS	HELICOPTERS	HELIOSCIOPHYTES
HEATHENISHNESS	HEBRAISATION	HEEDFULNESS	HELICOPTING	HELIOSCOPE
HEATHENISING	HEBRAISATIONS	HEEDFULNESSES	HELICTITES	HELIOSCOPES
HEATHENISM	HEBRAISING	HEEDINESSES	HELIDROMES	HELIOSCOPIC
HEATHENISMS	HEBRAIZATION	HEEDLESSLY	HELILIFTED	HELIOSPHERE
HEATHENIZE	HEBRAIZATIONS	HEEDLESSNESS	HELILIFTING	HELIOSPHERES
HEATHENIZED	HEBRAIZING	HEEDLESSNESSES	HELIOCENTRIC	HELIOSTATIC
HEATHENIZES	HECKELPHONE	HEELPIECES	HELIOCENTRICISM	HELIOSTATS
HEATHENIZING	HECKELPHONES	HEELPLATES	HELIOCENTRICITY	HELIOTACTIC

HELIOTAXES	HELLGRAMMITES	HEMATOCRITS	HEMICHORDATES	HEMISPHEROIDAL
HELIOTAXIS	HELLHOUNDS	HEMATOCRYAL	HEMICRANIA	HEMISPHEROIDS
HELIOTHERAPIES	HELLISHNESS	HEMATOGENESES	HEMICRANIAS	HEMISTICHAL
HELIOTHERAPY	HELLISHNESSES	HEMATOGENESIS	HEMICRYPTOPHYTE	HEMISTICHS
HELIOTROPE	HELLSCAPES	HEMATOGENETIC	HEMICRYSTALLINE	HEMITERPENE
HELIOTROPES	HELMETINGS	HEMATOGENIC	HEMICYCLES	HEMITERPENES
HELIOTROPIC	HELMETLIKE	HEMATOGENOUS	HEMICYCLIC	HEMITROPAL
HELIOTROPICAL	HELMINTHIASES	HEMATOLOGIC	HEMIELYTRA	HEMITROPES
HELIOTROPICALLY	HELMINTHIASIS	HEMATOLOGICAL	HEMIELYTRAL	HEMITROPIC
HELIOTROPIES	HELMINTHIC	HEMATOLOGIES	HEMIELYTRON	HEMITROPIES
HELIOTROPIN	HELMINTHICS	HEMATOLOGIST	HEMIHEDRAL	HEMITROPISM
HELIOTROPINS	HELMINTHOID	HEMATOLOGISTS	HEMIHEDRIES	HEMITROPISMS
HELIOTROPISM	HELMINTHOLOGIC	HEMATOLOGY	HEMIHEDRISM	HEMITROPOUS
HELIOTROPISMS	HELMINTHOLOGIES	HEMATOLYSES	HEMIHEDRISMS	HEMIZYGOUS
HELIOTROPY	HELMINTHOLOGIST	HEMATOLYSIS	HEMIHEDRON	HEMOCHROMATOSES
HELIOTYPED	HELMINTHOLOGY	HEMATOMATA	HEMIHEDRONS	HEMOCHROMATOSIS
HELIOTYPES	HELMINTHOUS	HEMATOPHAGOUS	HEMIHYDRATE	HEMOCHROME
HELIOTYPIC	HELMSMANSHIP	HEMATOPOIESES	HEMIHYDRATED	HEMOCHROMES
HELIOTYPIES	HELMSMANSHIPS	HEMATOPOIESIS	HEMIHYDRATES	HEMOCONIAS
HELIOTYPING	HELOPHYTES	HEMATOPOIETIC	HEMIMETABOLOUS	HEMOCYANIN
HELIOZOANS	HELPFULNESS	HEMATOPORPHYRIN	HEMIMORPHIC	HEMOCYANINS
HELIPILOTS	HELPFULNESSES	HEMATOTHERMAL	HEMIMORPHIES	HEMOCYTOMETER
HELISKIING	HELPLESSLY	HEMATOXYLIN	HEMIMORPHISM	HEMOCYTOMETERS
HELISKIINGS	HELPLESSNESS	HEMATOXYLINS	HEMIMORPHISMS	HEMODIALYSES
HELISPHERIC	HELPLESSNESSES	HEMATOZOON	HEMIMORPHITE	HEMODIALYSIS
HELISPHERICAL	HELVETIUMS	HEMATURIAS	HEMIMORPHITES	HEMODIALYZER
HELLACIOUS	HEMACHROME	HEMELYTRAL	HEMIMORPHY	HEMODIALYZERS
HELLACIOUSLY	HEMACHROMES	HEMELYTRON	HEMIONUSES	HEMODILUTION
HELLBENDER	HEMACYTOMETER	HEMELYTRUM	HEMIOPSIAS	HEMODILUTIONS
HELLBENDERS	HEMACYTOMETERS	HEMERALOPIA	HEMIPARASITE	HEMODYNAMIC
HELLBROTHS	HEMAGGLUTINATE	HEMERALOPIAS	HEMIPARASITES	HEMODYNAMICALLY
HELLDIVERS	HEMAGGLUTINATED	HEMERALOPIC	HEMIPARASITIC	HEMODYNAMICS
HELLEBORES	HEMAGGLUTINATES	HEMEROCALLIS	HEMIPLEGIA	HEMOFLAGELLATE
HELLEBORINE	HEMAGGLUTININ	HEMEROCALLISES	HEMIPLEGIAS	HEMOFLAGELLATES
HELLEBORINES	HEMAGGLUTININS	HEMERYTHRIN	HEMIPLEGIC	HEMOGLOBIN
HELLENISATION	HEMAGOGUES	HEMERYTHRINS	HEMIPLEGICS	HEMOGLOBINS
HELLENISATIONS	HEMANGIOMA	HEMIACETAL	HEMIPTERAL	HEMOGLOBINURIA
HELLENISED	HEMANGIOMAS	HEMIACETALS	HEMIPTERAN	HEMOGLOBINURIAS
HELLENISES	HEMANGIOMATA	HEMIALGIAS	HEMIPTERANS	HEMOGLOBINURIC
HELLENISING	HEMATEMESES	HEMIANOPIA	HEMIPTERON	HEMOLYMPHS
HELLENIZATION	HEMATEMESIS	HEMIANOPIAS	HEMIPTERONS	HEMOLYSING
HELLENIZATIONS	HEMATINICS	HEMIANOPIC	HEMIPTEROUS	HEMOLYSINS
HELLENIZED	HEMATOBLAST	HEMIANOPSIA	HEMISPACES	HEMOLYZING
HELLENIZES	HEMATOBLASTIC	HEMIANOPSIAS	HEMISPHERE	HEMOPHILES
HELLENIZING	HEMATOBLASTS	HEMIANOPTIC	HEMISPHERES	HEMOPHILIA
HELLGRAMITE	HEMATOCELE	HEMICELLULOSE	HEMISPHERIC	HEMOPHILIAC
HELLGRAMITES	HEMATOCELES	HEMICELLULOSES	HEMISPHERICAL	HEMOPHILIACS
HELLGRAMMITE	HEMATOCRIT	HEMICHORDATE	HEMISPHEROID	HEMOPHILIAS

HEMOPHILIC	HENDECASYLLABLE	HEPATOSCOPY	HERBALISTS	HERENESSES
HEMOPHILICS	HENDIADYSES	HEPATOTOXIC	HERBARIANS	HERESIARCH
HEMOPHILIOID	HENOTHEISM	HEPATOTOXICITY	HERBARIUMS	HERESIARCHS
HEMOPOIESES	HENOTHEISMS	HEPHTHEMIMER	HERBICIDAL	HERESIOGRAPHER
HEMOPOIESIS	HENOTHEIST	HEPHTHEMIMERAL	HERBICIDALLY	HERESIOGRAPHERS
HEMOPOIETIC	HENOTHEISTIC	HEPHTHEMIMERS	HERBICIDES	HERESIOGRAPHIES
HEMOPROTEIN	HENOTHEISTS	HEPTACHLOR	HERBIVORES	HERESIOGRAPHY
HEMOPROTEINS	HENPECKERIES	HEPTACHLORS	HERBIVORIES	HERESIOLOGIES
HEMOPTYSES	HENPECKERY	HEPTACHORD	HERBIVOROUS	HERESIOLOGIST
HEMOPTYSIS	HENPECKING	HEPTACHORDS	HERBIVOROUSLY	HERESIOLOGISTS
HEMORRHAGE	HEORTOLOGICAL	HEPTADECANOIC	HERBIVOROUSNESS	HERESIOLOGY
HEMORRHAGED	HEORTOLOGIES	HEPTAGLOTS	HERBOLOGIES	HERESTHETIC
HEMORRHAGES	HEORTOLOGIST	HEPTAGONAL	HERBORISATION	HERESTHETICAL
HEMORRHAGIC	HEORTOLOGISTS	HEPTAGYNOUS	HERBORISATIONS	HERESTHETICIAN
HEMORRHAGING	HEORTOLOGY	HEPTAHEDRA	HERBORISED	HERESTHETICIANS
HEMORRHAGINGS	HEPARINISED	HEPTAHEDRAL	HERBORISES	HERESTHETICS
HEMORRHOID	HEPARINIZED	HEPTAHEDRON	HERBORISING	HERETICALLY
HEMORRHOIDAL	HEPARINOID	HEPTAHEDRONS	HERBORISTS	HERETICATE
HEMORRHOIDALS	HEPATECTOMIES	HEPTAMEROUS	HERBORIZATION	HERETICATED
HEMORRHOIDS	HEPATECTOMISED	HEPTAMETER	HERBORIZATIONS	HERETICATES
HEMOSIDERIN	HEPATECTOMIZED	HEPTAMETERS	HERBORIZED	HERETICATING
HEMOSIDERINS	HEPATECTOMY	HEPTAMETRICAL	HERBORIZES	HERETOFORE
HEMOSTASES	HEPATICOLOGICAL	HEPTANDROUS	HERBORIZING	HERETOFORES
HEMOSTASIA	HEPATICOLOGIES	HEPTANGULAR	HERCOGAMIES	HERETRICES
HEMOSTASIAS	HEPATICOLOGIST	HEPTAPODIC	HERCOGAMOUS	HERETRIXES
HEMOSTASIS	HEPATICOLOGISTS	HEPTAPODIES	HERCULESES	HERIOTABLE
HEMOSTATIC	HEPATICOLOGY	HEPTARCHAL	HERCYNITES	HERITABILITIES
HEMOSTATICS	HEPATISATION	HEPTARCHIC	HEREABOUTS	HERITABILITY
HEMOTOXINS	HEPATISATIONS	HEPTARCHIES	HEREAFTERS	HERITRESSES
HEMSTITCHED	HEPATISING	HEPTARCHIST	HEREDITABILITY	HERITRICES
HEMSTITCHER	HEPATITIDES	HEPTARCHISTS	HEREDITABLE	HERITRIXES
HEMSTITCHERS	HEPATITISES	HEPTASTICH	HEREDITABLY	HERKOGAMIES
HEMSTITCHES	HEPATIZATION	HEPTASTICHS	HEREDITAMENT	HERMANDADS
HEMSTITCHING	HEPATIZATIONS	HEPTASYLLABIC	HEREDITAMENTS	HERMAPHRODITE
HENCEFORTH	HEPATIZING	HEPTATHLETE	HEREDITARIAN	HERMAPHRODITES
HENCEFORWARD	HEPATOCELLULAR	HEPTATHLETES	HEREDITARIANISM	HERMAPHRODITIC
HENCEFORWARDS	HEPATOCYTE	HEPTATHLON	HEREDITARIANIST	HERMAPHRODITISM
HENCHPERSON	HEPATOCYTES	HEPTATHLONS	HEREDITARIANS	HERMATYPIC
HENCHPERSONS	HEPATOGENOUS	HEPTATONIC	HEREDITARILY	HERMENEUTIC
HENCHWOMAN	HEPATOLOGIES	HEPTAVALENT	HEREDITARINESS	HERMENEUTICAL
HENCHWOMEN	HEPATOLOGIST	HERALDICALLY	HEREDITARY	HERMENEUTICALLY
HENDECAGON	HEPATOLOGISTS	HERALDISTS	HEREDITIES	HERMENEUTICS
HENDECAGONAL	HEPATOLOGY	HERALDRIES	HEREDITIST	HERMENEUTIST
HENDECAGONS	HEPATOMATA	HERALDSHIP	HEREDITISTS	HERMENEUTISTS
HENDECAHEDRA	HEPATOMEGALIES	HERALDSHIPS	HEREINABOVE	HERMETICAL
HENDECAHEDRON	HEPATOMEGALY	HERBACEOUS	HEREINAFTER	HERMETICALLY
HENDECAHEDRONS	HEPATOPANCREAS	HERBACEOUSLY	HEREINBEFORE	HERMETICISM
HENDECASYLLABIC	HEPATOSCOPIES	HERBALISMS	HEREINBELOW	HERMETICISMS

HERMETICITIES	HERRINGBONES	HETEROCHROMOUS	HETEROGENEOUSLY	HETERONYMOUS
HERMETICITY	HERRINGBONING	HETEROCHRONIC	HETEROGENESES	HETERONYMOUSLY
HERMETISMS	HERRINGERS	HETEROCHRONIES	HETEROGENESIS	HETERONYMS
HERMETISTS	HERRYMENTS	HETEROCHRONISM	HETEROGENETIC	HETEROOUSIAN
HERMITAGES	HERSTORIES	HETEROCHRONISMS	HETEROGENIC	HETEROOUSIANS
HERMITESSES	HESITANCES	HETEROCHRONOUS	HETEROGENIES	HETEROPHIL
HERMITICAL	HESITANCIES	HETEROCHRONY	HETEROGENOUS	HETEROPHILE
HERMITICALLY	HESITANTLY	HETEROCLITE	HETEROGENY	HETEROPHILES
HERMITISMS	HESITATERS	HETEROCLITES	HETEROGONIC	HETEROPHILS
HERMITRIES	HESITATING	HETEROCLITIC	HETEROGONIES	HETEROPHONIES
HERNIATING	HESITATINGLY	HETEROCLITOUS	HETEROGONOUS	HETEROPHONY
HERNIATION	HESITATION	HETEROCONT	HETEROGONOUSLY	HETEROPHYLLIES
HERNIATIONS	HESITATIONS	HETEROCONTS	HETEROGONY	HETEROPHYLLOUS
HERNIORRHAPHIES	HESITATIVE	HETEROCYCLE	HETEROGRAFT	HETEROPHYLLY
HERNIORRHAPHY	HESITATORS	HETEROCYCLES	HETEROGRAFTS	HETEROPLASIA
HERNIOTOMIES	HESITATORY	HETEROCYCLIC	HETEROGRAPHIC	HETEROPLASIAS
HERNIOTOMY	HESPERIDIA	HETEROCYCLICS	HETEROGRAPHICAL	HETEROPLASTIC
HEROICALLY	HESPERIDIN	HETEROCYST	HETEROGRAPHIES	HETEROPLASTIES
HEROICALNESS	HESPERIDINS	HETEROCYSTOUS	HETEROGRAPHY	HETEROPLASTY
HEROICALNESSES	HESPERIDIUM	HETEROCYSTS	HETEROGYNOUS	HETEROPLOID
HEROICISED	HESSONITES	HETERODACTYL	HETEROKARYON	HETEROPLOIDIES
HEROICISES	HETAERISMIC	HETERODACTYLOUS	HETEROKARYONS	HETEROPLOIDS
HEROICISING	HETAERISMS	HETERODACTYLS	HETEROKARYOSES	HETEROPLOIDY
HEROICIZED	HETAERISTIC	HETERODONT	HETEROKARYOSIS	HETEROPODS
HEROICIZES	HETAERISTS	HETERODOXIES	HETEROKARYOTIC	HETEROPOLAR
HEROICIZING	HETAIRISMIC	HETERODOXY	HETEROKONT	HETEROPOLARITY
HEROICNESS	HETAIRISMS	HETERODUPLEX	HETEROKONTAN	HETEROPTERAN
HEROICNESSES	HETAIRISTIC	HETERODUPLEXES	HETEROKONTS	HETEROPTERANS
HEROICOMIC	HETAIRISTS	HETERODYNE	HETEROLECITHAL	HETEROPTEROUS
HEROICOMICAL	HETERARCHIES	HETERODYNED	HETEROLOGIES	HETEROSCEDASTIC
HEROINISMS	HETERARCHY	HETERODYNES	HETEROLOGOUS	HETEROSCIAN
HERONSHAWS	HETERAUXESES	HETERODYNING	HETEROLOGOUSLY	HETEROSCIANS
HERPESVIRUS	HETERAUXESIS	HETEROECIOUS	HETEROLOGY	HETEROSEXISM
HERPESVIRUSES	HETEROAROMATIC	HETEROECISM	HETEROLYSES	HETEROSEXISMS
HERPETOFAUNA	HETEROATOM	HETEROECISMS	HETEROLYSIS	HETEROSEXIST
HERPETOFAUNAE	HETEROATOMS	HETEROFLEXIBLE	HETEROLYTIC	HETEROSEXISTS
HERPETOFAUNAS	HETEROAUXIN	HETEROFLEXIBLES	HETEROMEROUS	HETEROSEXUAL
HERPETOLOGIC	HETEROAUXINS	HETEROGAMETE	HETEROMORPHIC	HETEROSEXUALITY
HERPETOLOGICAL	HETEROBLASTIC	HETEROGAMETES	HETEROMORPHIES	HETEROSEXUALLY
HERPETOLOGIES	HETEROBLASTIES	HETEROGAMETIC	HETEROMORPHISM	HETEROSEXUALS
HERPETOLOGIST	HETEROBLASTY	HETEROGAMETIES	HETEROMORPHISMS	HETEROSOCIAL
HERPETOLOGISTS	HETEROCARPOUS	HETEROGAMETY	HETEROMORPHOUS	HETEROSOCIALITY
HERPETOLOGY	HETEROCERCAL	HETEROGAMIES	HETEROMORPHY	HETEROSOMATOUS
HERRENVOLK	HETEROCERCALITY	HETEROGAMOUS	HETERONOMIES	HETEROSPECIFIC
HERRENVOLKS	HETEROCERCIES	HETEROGAMY	HETERONOMOUS	HETEROSPECIFICS
HERRIMENTS	HETEROCERCY	HETEROGENEITIES	HETERONOMOUSLY	HETEROSPORIES
HERRINGBONE	HETEROCHROMATIC	HETEROGENEITY	HETERONOMY	HETEROSPOROUS
HERRINGBONED	HETEROCHROMATIN	HETEROGENEOUS	HETERONORMATIVE	HETEROSPORY

HETEROSTROPHIC	HETMANSHIPS	HEXAMETRAL	HIBERNATIONS	HIERARCHISED
HETEROSTROPHIES	HEULANDITE	HEXAMETRIC	HIBERNATOR	HIERARCHISES
HETEROSTROPHY	HEULANDITES	HEXAMETRICAL	HIBERNATORS	HIERARCHISING
HETEROSTYLED	HEURISTICALLY	HEXAMETRISE	HIBERNICISATION	HIERARCHISM
HETEROSTYLIES	HEURISTICS	HEXAMETRISED	HIBERNICISE	HIERARCHISMS
HETEROSTYLISM	HEXACHLORETHANE	HEXAMETRISES	HIBERNICISED	HIERARCHIZE
HETEROSTYLISMS	HEXACHLORIDE	HEXAMETRISING	HIBERNICISES	HIERARCHIZED
HETEROSTYLOUS	HEXACHLORIDES	HEXAMETRIST	HIBERNICISING	HIERARCHIZES
HETEROSTYLY	HEXACHLOROPHANE	HEXAMETRISTS	HIBERNICIZATION	HIERARCHIZING
HETEROTACTIC	HEXACHLOROPHENE	HEXAMETRIZE	HIBERNICIZE	HIERATICAL
HETEROTACTOUS	HEXACHORDS	HEXAMETRIZED	HIBERNICIZED	HIERATICALLY
HETEROTAXES	HEXACOSANOIC	HEXAMETRIZES	HIBERNICIZES	HIERATICAS
HETEROTAXIA	HEXACTINAL	HEXAMETRIZING	HIBERNICIZING	HIEROCRACIES
HETEROTAXIAS	HEXACTINELLID	HEXANDRIAN	HIBERNISATION	HIEROCRACY
HETEROTAXIC	HEXACTINELLIDS	HEXANDROUS	HIBERNISATIONS	HIEROCRATIC
HETEROTAXIES	HEXADACTYLIC	HEXANGULAR	HIBERNISED	HIEROCRATICAL
HETEROTAXIS	HEXADACTYLOUS	HEXAPLARIAN	HIBERNISES	HIEROCRATS
HETEROTAXY	HEXADECANE	HEXAPLARIC	HIBERNISING	HIERODULES
HETEROTHALLIC	HEXADECANES	HEXAPLOIDIES	HIBERNIZATION	HIERODULIC
HETEROTHALLIES	HEXADECANOIC	HEXAPLOIDS	HIBERNIZATIONS	HIEROGLYPH
HETEROTHALLISM	HEXADECIMAL	HEXAPLOIDY	HIBERNIZED	HIEROGLYPHED
HETEROTHALLISMS	HEXADECIMALS	HEXAPODIES	HIBERNIZES	HIEROGLYPHIC
HETEROTHALLY	HEXADECYLS	HEXARCHIES	HIBERNIZING	HIEROGLYPHICAL
HETEROTHERMAL	HEXAEMERIC	HEXASTICHAL	HIBISCUSES	HIEROGLYPHICS
HETEROTOPIA	HEXAEMERON	HEXASTICHIC	HICCOUGHED	HIEROGLYPHING
HETEROTOPIAS	HEXAEMERONS	HEXASTICHON	HICCOUGHING	HIEROGLYPHIST
HETEROTOPIC	HEXAFLUORIDE	HEXASTICHONS	HICCUPIEST	HIEROGLYPHISTS
HETEROTOPIES	HEXAFLUORIDES	HEXASTICHS	HICCUPPING	HIEROGLYPHS
HETEROTOPOUS	HEXAGONALLY	HEXASTYLES	HIDALGOISH	HIEROGRAMMAT
HETEROTOPY	HEXAGRAMMOID	HEXATEUCHAL	HIDALGOISM	HIEROGRAMMATE
HETEROTROPH	HEXAGRAMMOIDS	HEXATHLONS	HIDALGOISMS	HIEROGRAMMATES
HETEROTROPHIC	HEXAGYNIAN	HEXAVALENT	HIDDENITES	HIEROGRAMMATIC
HETEROTROPHIES	HEXAGYNOUS	HEXOBARBITAL	HIDDENMOST	HIEROGRAMMATIST
HETEROTROPHS	HEXAHEDRAL	HEXOBARBITALS	HIDDENNESS	HIEROGRAMMATS
HETEROTROPHY	HEXAHEDRON	HEXOKINASE	HIDDENNESSES	HIEROGRAMS
HETEROTYPIC	HEXAHEDRONS	HEXOKINASES	HIDEOSITIES	HIEROGRAPH
HETEROTYPICAL	HEXAHEMERIC	HEXOSAMINIDASE	HIDEOUSNESS	HIEROGRAPHER
HETEROUSIAN	HEXAHEMERON	HEXOSAMINIDASES	HIDEOUSNESSES	HIEROGRAPHERS
HETEROUSIANS	HEXAHEMERONS	HEXYLRESORCINOL	HIERACIUMS	HIEROGRAPHIC
HETEROZYGOSES	HEXAHYDRATE	HIBAKUSHAS	HIERACOSPHINGES	HIEROGRAPHICAL
HETEROZYGOSIS	HEXAHYDRATED	HIBERNACLE	HIERACOSPHINX	HIEROGRAPHIES
HETEROZYGOSITY	HEXAHYDRATES	HIBERNACLES	HIERACOSPHINXES	HIEROGRAPHS
HETEROZYGOTE	HEXAMERISM	HIBERNACULA	HIERARCHAL	HIEROGRAPHY
HETEROZYGOTES	HEXAMERISMS	HIBERNACULUM	HIERARCHIC	HIEROLATRIES
HETEROZYGOUS	HEXAMEROUS	HIBERNATED	HIERARCHICAL	HIEROLATRY
HETHERWARD	HEXAMETERS	HIBERNATES	HIERARCHICALLY	HIEROLOGIC
HETMANATES	HEXAMETHONIUM	HIBERNATING	HIERARCHIES	HIEROLOGICAL
HETMANSHIP	HEXAMETHONIUMS	HIBERNATION	HIERARCHISE	HIEROLOGIES

HIEROLOGIST

HIEROLOGIST	HIGHWAYMEN	HIPPIENESSES	HIRSUTENESS	HISTOCOMPATIBLE
HIEROLOGISTS	HIGHWROUGHT	HIPPINESSES	HIRSUTENESSES	HISTOGENESES
HIEROMANCIES	HIJACKINGS	HIPPOCAMPAL	HIRSUTISMS	HISTOGENESIS
HIEROMANCY	HILARIOUSLY	HIPPOCAMPI	HIRUDINEAN	HISTOGENETIC
HIEROPHANT	HILARIOUSNESS	HIPPOCAMPUS	HIRUDINEANS	HISTOGENIC
HIEROPHANTIC	HILARIOUSNESSES	HIPPOCENTAUR	HIRUDINOID	HISTOGENICALLY
HIEROPHANTS	HILARITIES	HIPPOCENTAURS	HIRUDINOUS	HISTOGENIES
HIEROPHOBIA	HILLBILLIES	HIPPOCRASES	HISPANICISE	HISTOGRAMS
HIEROPHOBIAS	HILLCRESTS	HIPPOCREPIAN	HISPANICISED	HISTOLOGIC
HIEROPHOBIC	HILLINESSES	HIPPOCREPIANS	HISPANICISES	HISTOLOGICAL
HIEROPHOBICS	HILLOCKIER	HIPPODAMES	HISPANICISING	HISTOLOGICALLY
HIEROSCOPIES	HILLOCKIEST	HIPPODAMIST	HISPANICISM	HISTOLOGIES
HIEROSCOPY	HILLSLOPES	HIPPODAMISTS	HISPANICISMS	HISTOLOGIST
HIERURGICAL	HILLWALKER	HIPPODAMOUS	HISPANICIZE	HISTOLOGISTS
HIERURGIES	HILLWALKERS	HIPPODROME	HISPANICIZED	HISTOLYSES
HIGHBALLED	HILLWALKING	HIPPODROMES	HISPANICIZES	HISTOLYSIS
HIGHBALLING	HILLWALKINGS	HIPPODROMIC	HISPANICIZING	HISTOLYTIC
HIGHBINDER	HINDBERRIES	HIPPOGRIFF	HISPANIDAD	HISTOLYTICALLY
HIGHBINDERS	HINDBRAINS	HIPPOGRIFFS	HISPANIDADS	HISTOPATHOLOGIC
HIGHBLOODED	HINDCASTED	HIPPOGRYPH	HISPANIOLISE	HISTOPATHOLOGY
HIGHBROWED	HINDCASTING	HIPPOGRYPHS	HISPANIOLISED	HISTOPHYSIOLOGY
HIGHBROWISM	HINDERANCE	HIPPOLOGIES	HISPANIOLISES	HISTOPLASMOSES
HIGHBROWISMS	HINDERANCES	HIPPOLOGIST	HISPANIOLISING	HISTOPLASMOSIS
HIGHBUSHES	HINDERINGLY	HIPPOLOGISTS	HISPANIOLIZE	HISTORIANS
HIGHCHAIRS	HINDERINGS	HIPPOMANES	HISPANIOLIZED	HISTORIATED
HIGHERMOST	HINDERLAND	HIPPOPHAGIES	HISPANIOLIZES	HISTORICAL
HIGHFALUTIN	HINDERLANDS	HIPPOPHAGIST	HISPANIOLIZING	HISTORICALLY
HIGHFALUTING	HINDERLANS	HIPPOPHAGISTS	HISPANISMS	HISTORICALNESS
HIGHFALUTINGS	HINDERLINGS	HIPPOPHAGOUS	HISPIDITIES	HISTORICISE
HIGHFALUTINS	HINDERLINS	HIPPOPHAGY	HISTAMINASE	HISTORICISED
HIGHFLIERS	HINDERMOST	HIPPOPHILE	HISTAMINASES	HISTORICISES
HIGHFLYERS	HINDFOREMOST	HIPPOPHILES	HISTAMINERGIC	HISTORICISING
HIGHJACKED	HINDQUARTER	HIPPOPHOBE	HISTAMINES	HISTORICISM
HIGHJACKER	HINDQUARTERS	HIPPOPHOBES	HISTAMINIC	HISTORICISMS
HIGHJACKERS	HINDRANCES	HIPPOPOTAMI	HISTIDINES	HISTORICIST
HIGHJACKING	HINDSHANKS	HIPPOPOTAMIAN	HISTIOCYTE	HISTORICISTS
HIGHJACKINGS	HINDSIGHTS	HIPPOPOTAMIC	HISTIOCYTES	HISTORICITIES
HIGHLANDER	HINTERLAND	HIPPOPOTAMUS	HISTIOCYTIC	HISTORICITY
HIGHLANDERS	HINTERLANDS	HIPPOPOTAMUSES	HISTIOLOGIES	HISTORICIZE
HIGHLIGHTED	HIPPEASTRUM	HIPPURITES	HISTIOLOGY	HISTORICIZED
HIGHLIGHTER	HIPPEASTRUMS	HIPPURITIC	HISTIOPHOROID	HISTORICIZES
HIGHLIGHTERS	HIPPIATRIC	HIPSTERISM	HISTOBLAST	HISTORICIZING
HIGHLIGHTING	HIPPIATRICS	HIPSTERISMS	HISTOBLASTS	HISTORIETTE
HIGHLIGHTS	HIPPIATRIES	HIRCOCERVUS	HISTOCHEMICAL	HISTORIETTES
HIGHNESSES	HIPPIATRIST	HIRCOCERVUSES	HISTOCHEMICALLY	HISTORIFIED
HIGHTAILED	HIPPIATRISTS	HIRCOSITIES	HISTOCHEMIST	HISTORIFIES
HIGHTAILING	HIPPIEDOMS	HIRSELLING	HISTOCHEMISTRY	HISTORIFYING
HIGHWAYMAN	HIPPIENESS	HIRSELLINGS	HISTOCHEMISTS	HISTORIOGRAPHER

HISTORIOGRAPHIC	HOBGOBLINISM	HOLLOWARES	HOLOPLANKTON	HOMEOTELEUTONS
HISTORIOGRAPHY	HOBGOBLINISMS	HOLLOWNESS	HOLOPLANKTONS	HOMEOTHERM
HISTORIOLOGIES	HOBGOBLINRIES	HOLLOWNESSES	HOLOSTERIC	HOMEOTHERMAL
HISTORIOLOGY	HOBGOBLINRY	HOLLOWWARE	HOLOTHURIAN	HOMEOTHERMIC
HISTORISMS	HOBGOBLINS	HOLLOWWARES	HOLOTHURIANS	HOMEOTHERMIES
HISTORYING	HOBJOBBERS	HOLLYHOCKS	HOLSTERING	HOMEOTHERMISM
HISTRIONIC	HOBJOBBING	HOLOBENTHIC	HOLYSTONED	HOMEOTHERMISMS
HISTRIONICAL	HOBJOBBINGS	HOLOBLASTIC	HOLYSTONES	HOMEOTHERMOUS
HISTRIONICALLY	HOBNAILING	HOLOBLASTICALLY	HOLYSTONING	HOMEOTHERMS
HISTRIONICISM	HOBNOBBERS	HOLOCAINES	HOMALOGRAPHIC	HOMEOTHERMY
HISTRIONICISMS	HOBNOBBIER	HOLOCAUSTAL	HOMALOIDAL	HOMEOTYPIC
HISTRIONICS	HOBNOBBIEST	HOLOCAUSTIC	HOMEBIRTHS	HOMEOTYPICAL
HISTRIONISM	HOBNOBBING	HOLOCAUSTS	HOMEBODIES	HOMEOWNERS
HISTRIONISMS	HOCHMAGANDIES	HOLOCRYSTALLINE	HOMEBUYERS	HOMEOWNERSHIP
HITCHHIKED	HOCHMAGANDY	HOLODISCUS	HOMECOMERS	HOMEOWNERSHIPS
HITCHHIKER	HODGEPODGE	HOLODISCUSES	HOMECOMING	HOMEPLACES
HITCHHIKERS	HODGEPODGES	HOLOENZYME	HOMECOMINGS	HOMEPORTED
HITCHHIKES	HODMANDODS	HOLOENZYMES	HOMECRAFTS	HOMEPORTING
HITCHHIKING	HODOGRAPHIC	HOLOGAMIES	HOMELESSNESS	HOMESCHOOL
HITCHHIKINGS	HODOGRAPHS	HOLOGRAPHED	HOMELESSNESSES	HOMESCHOOLED
HITHERMOST	HODOMETERS	HOLOGRAPHER	HOMELINESS	HOMESCHOOLER
HITHERSIDE	HODOMETRIES	HOLOGRAPHERS	HOMELINESSES	HOMESCHOOLERS
HITHERSIDES	HODOSCOPES	HOLOGRAPHIC	HOMEMAKERS	HOMESCHOOLING
HITHERWARD	HOGGISHNESS	HOLOGRAPHICALLY	HOMEMAKING	HOMESCHOOLS
HITHERWARDS	HOGGISHNESSES	HOLOGRAPHIES	HOMEMAKINGS	HOMESCREETCH
HOACTZINES	HOIDENISHNESS	HOLOGRAPHING	HOMEOBOXES	HOMESCREETCHES
HOARFROSTS	HOIDENISHNESSES	HOLOGRAPHS	HOMEOMERIC	HOMESHORING
HOARHOUNDS	HOJATOLESLAM	HOLOGRAPHY	HOMEOMERIES	HOMESHORINGS
HOARINESSES	HOJATOLESLAMS	HOLOGYNIES	HOMEOMEROUS	HOMESICKNESS
HOARSENESS	HOJATOLISLAM	HOLOHEDRAL	HOMEOMORPH	HOMESICKNESSES
HOARSENESSES	HOJATOLISLAMS	HOLOHEDRISM	HOMEOMORPHIC	HOMESOURCING
HOARSENING	HOKEYNESSES	HOLOHEDRISMS	HOMEOMORPHIES	HOMESOURCINGS
HOBBITRIES	HOKEYPOKEY	HOLOHEDRON	HOMEOMORPHISM	HOMESTALLS
HOBBLEBUSH	HOKEYPOKEYS	HOLOHEDRONS	HOMEOMORPHISMS	HOMESTANDS
HOBBLEBUSHES	HOKINESSES	HOLOMETABOLIC	HOMEOMORPHOUS	HOMESTEADED
HOBBLEDEHOY	HOKYPOKIES	HOLOMETABOLISM	HOMEOMORPHS	HOMESTEADER
HOBBLEDEHOYDOM	HOLARCHIES	HOLOMETABOLISMS	HOMEOMORPHY	HOMESTEADERS
HOBBLEDEHOYDOMS	HOLDERBATS	HOLOMETABOLOUS	HOMEOPATHIC	HOMESTEADING
HOBBLEDEHOYHOOD	HOLDERSHIP	HOLOMORPHIC	HOMEOPATHICALLY	HOMESTEADINGS
HOBBLEDEHOYISH	HOLDERSHIPS	HOLOPHOTAL	HOMEOPATHIES	HOMESTEADS
HOBBLEDEHOYISM	HOLIDAYERS	HOLOPHOTES	HOMEOPATHIST	HOMESTRETCH
HOBBLEDEHOYISMS	HOLIDAYING	HOLOPHRASE	HOMEOPATHISTS	HOMESTRETCHES
HOBBLEDEHOYS	HOLIDAYMAKER	HOLOPHRASES	HOMEOPATHS	HOMEWORKER
HOBBLINGLY	HOLIDAYMAKERS	HOLOPHRASTIC	HOMEOPATHY	HOMEWORKERS
HOBBYHORSE	HOLINESSES	HOLOPHYTES	HOMEOSTASES	HOMEWORKING
HOBBYHORSED	HOLISTICALLY	HOLOPHYTIC	HOMEOSTASIS	HOMEWORKINGS
HOBBYHORSES	HOLLANDAISE	HOLOPHYTISM	HOMEOSTATIC	HOMEYNESSES
HOBBYHORSING	HOLLANDAISES	HOLOPHYTISMS	HOMEOTELEUTON	HOMICIDALLY

HOMILETICAL	HOMOEOSTATIC	HOMOGONOUS	HOMOMORPHOSIS	HOMOSEXUALLY
HOMILETICALLY	HOMOEOTELEUTON	HOMOGONOUSLY	HOMOMORPHOUS	HOMOSEXUALS
HOMILETICS	HOMOEOTELEUTONS	HOMOGRAFTS	HOMOMORPHS	HOMOSOCIAL
HOMINESSES	HOMOEOTHERM	HOMOGRAPHIC	HOMOMORPHY	HOMOSOCIALITIES
HOMINISATION	HOMOEOTHERMAL	HOMOGRAPHIES	HOMONUCLEAR	HOMOSOCIALITY
HOMINISATIONS	HOMOEOTHERMIC	HOMOGRAPHS	HOMONYMIES	HOMOSPORIES
HOMINISING	HOMOEOTHERMOUS	HOMOGRAPHY	HOMONYMITIES	HOMOSPOROUS
HOMINIZATION	HOMOEOTHERMS	HOMOIOMEROUS	HOMONYMITY	HOMOSTYLIES
HOMINIZATIONS	HOMOEOTYPIC	HOMOIOTHERM	HOMONYMOUS	HOMOTAXIAL
HOMINIZING	HOMOEOTYPICAL	HOMOIOTHERMAL	HOMONYMOUSLY	HOMOTAXIALLY
HOMOBLASTIC	HOMOEROTIC	HOMOIOTHERMIC	HOMOOUSIAN	HOMOTHALLIC
HOMOBLASTIES	HOMOEROTICISM	HOMOIOTHERMIES	HOMOOUSIANS	HOMOTHALLIES
HOMOBLASTY	HOMOEROTICISMS	HOMOIOTHERMS	HOMOPHILES	HOMOTHALLISM
HOMOCENTRIC	HOMOEROTISM	HOMOIOTHERMY	HOMOPHOBES	HOMOTHALLISMS
HOMOCENTRICALLY	HOMOEROTISMS	HOMOIOUSIAN	HOMOPHOBIA	HOMOTHALLY
HOMOCERCAL	HOMOGAMETIC	HOMOIOUSIANS	HOMOPHOBIAS	HOMOTHERMAL
HOMOCERCIES	HOMOGAMIES	HOMOLOGATE	HOMOPHOBIC	HOMOTHERMIC
HOMOCHLAMYDEOUS	HOMOGAMOUS	HOMOLOGATED	HOMOPHONES	HOMOTHERMIES
HOMOCHROMATIC	HOMOGENATE	HOMOLOGATES	HOMOPHONIC	HOMOTHERMOUS
HOMOCHROMATISM	HOMOGENATES	HOMOLOGATING	HOMOPHONICALLY	HOMOTHERMY
HOMOCHROMATISMS	HOMOGENEITIES	HOMOLOGATION	HOMOPHONIES	HOMOTONIES
HOMOCHROMIES	HOMOGENEITY	HOMOLOGATIONS	HOMOPHONOUS	HOMOTONOUS
HOMOCHROMOUS	HOMOGENEOUS	HOMOLOGICAL	HOMOPHYLIES	HOMOTRANSPLANT
HOMOCHROMY	HOMOGENEOUSLY	HOMOLOGICALLY	HOMOPHYLLIC	HOMOTRANSPLANTS
HOMOCYCLIC	HOMOGENEOUSNESS	HOMOLOGIES	HOMOPLASIES	HOMOTYPIES
HOMOCYSTEINE	HOMOGENESES	HOMOLOGISE	HOMOPLASMIES	HOMOUSIANS
HOMOCYSTEINES	HOMOGENESIS	HOMOLOGISED	HOMOPLASMY	HOMOZYGOSES
HOMOEOMERIC	HOMOGENETIC	HOMOLOGISER	HOMOPLASTIC	HOMOZYGOSIS
HOMOEOMERIES	HOMOGENETICAL	HOMOLOGISERS	HOMOPLASTICALLY	HOMOZYGOSITIES
HOMOEOMEROUS	HOMOGENIES	HOMOLOGISES	HOMOPLASTIES	HOMOZYGOSITY
HOMOEOMERY	HOMOGENISATION	HOMOLOGISING	HOMOPLASTY	HOMOZYGOTE
HOMOEOMORPH	HOMOGENISATIONS	HOMOLOGIZE	HOMOPOLARITIES	HOMOZYGOTES
HOMOEOMORPHIC	HOMOGENISE	HOMOLOGIZED	HOMOPOLARITY	HOMOZYGOTIC
HOMOEOMORPHIES	HOMOGENISED	HOMOLOGIZER	HOMOPOLYMER	HOMOZYGOUS
HOMOEOMORPHISM	HOMOGENISER	HOMOLOGIZERS	HOMOPOLYMERIC	HOMOZYGOUSLY
HOMOEOMORPHISMS	HOMOGENISERS	HOMOLOGIZES	HOMOPOLYMERS	HOMUNCULAR
HOMOEOMORPHOUS	HOMOGENISES	HOMOLOGIZING	HOMOPTERAN	HOMUNCULES
HOMOEOMORPHS	HOMOGENISING	HOMOLOGOUMENA	HOMOPTERANS	HOMUNCULUS
HOMOEOMORPHY	HOMOGENIZATION	HOMOLOGOUS	HOMOPTEROUS	HONESTNESS
HOMOEOPATH	HOMOGENIZATIONS	HOMOLOGRAPHIC	HOMORGANIC	HONESTNESSES
HOMOEOPATHIC	HOMOGENIZE	HOMOLOGUES	HOMOSCEDASTIC	HONEYBELLS
HOMOEOPATHIES	HOMOGENIZED	HOMOLOGUMENA	HOMOSEXUAL	HONEYBUNCH
HOMOEOPATHIST	HOMOGENIZER	HOMOLOSINE	HOMOSEXUALISM	HONEYBUNCHES
HOMOEOPATHISTS	HOMOGENIZERS	HOMOMORPHIC	HOMOSEXUALISMS	HONEYCOMBED
HOMOEOPATHS	HOMOGENIZES	HOMOMORPHIES	HOMOSEXUALIST	HONEYCOMBING
HOMOEOPATHY	HOMOGENIZING	HOMOMORPHISM	HOMOSEXUALISTS	HONEYCOMBINGS
HOMOEOSTASES	HOMOGENOUS	HOMOMORPHISMS	HOMOSEXUALITIES	HONEYCOMBS
HOMOEOSTASIS	HOMOGONIES	HOMOMORPHOSES	HOMOSEXUALITY	HONEYCREEPER

HONEYCREEPERS
HONEYDEWED
HONEYEATER
HONEYEATERS
HONEYGUIDE
HONEYGUIDES
HONEYMONTH
HONEYMONTHED
HONEYMONTHING
HONEYMONTHS
HONEYMOONED
HONEYMOONER
HONEYMOONERS
HONEYMOONING
HONEYMOONS
HONEYSUCKER
HONEYSUCKERS
HONEYSUCKLE
HONEYSUCKLED
HONEYSUCKLES
HONEYTRAPS
HONORABILITIES
HONORABILITY
HONORABLENESS
HONORABLENESSES
HONORARIES
HONORARILY
HONORARIUM
HONORARIUMS
HONORIFICAL
HONORIFICALLY
HONORIFICS
HONOURABILITIES
HONOURABILITY
HONOURABLE
HONOURABLENESS
HONOURABLY
HONOURLESS
HOODEDNESS
HOODEDNESSES
HOODLUMISH
HOODLUMISM
HOODLUMISMS
HOODOOISMS
HOODWINKED
HOODWINKER
HOODWINKERS
HOODWINKING

HOOFPRINTS
HOOKCHECKS
HOOKEDNESS
HOOKEDNESSES
HOOLACHANS
HOOLIGANISM
HOOLIGANISMS
HOOPSKIRTS
HOOTANANNIE
HOOTANANNIES
HOOTANANNY
HOOTENANNIE
HOOTENANNIES
HOOTENANNY
HOOTNANNIE
HOOTNANNIES
HOOVERINGS
HOPEFULNESS
HOPEFULNESSES
HOPELESSLY
HOPELESSNESS
HOPELESSNESSES
HOPLOLOGIES
HOPLOLOGIST
HOPLOLOGISTS
HOPPERCARS
HOPPINESSES
HOPSACKING
HOPSACKINGS
HOPSCOTCHED
HOPSCOTCHES
HOPSCOTCHING
HOREHOUNDS
HORIATIKIS
HORIZONLESS
HORIZONTAL
HORIZONTALITIES
HORIZONTALITY
HORIZONTALLY
HORIZONTALNESS
HORIZONTALS
HORMOGONIA
HORMOGONIUM
HORMONALLY
HORMONELIKE
HORNBLENDE
HORNBLENDES
HORNBLENDIC

HORNEDNESS
HORNEDNESSES
HORNFELSES
HORNFISHES
HORNINESSES
HORNLESSNESS
HORNLESSNESSES
HORNSTONES
HORNSWOGGLE
HORNSWOGGLED
HORNSWOGGLES
HORNSWOGGLING
HORNWRACKS
HORNYHEADS
HORNYWINKS
HOROGRAPHER
HOROGRAPHERS
HOROGRAPHIES
HOROGRAPHY
HOROLOGERS
HOROLOGICAL
HOROLOGIES
HOROLOGION
HOROLOGIONS
HOROLOGIST
HOROLOGISTS
HOROLOGIUM
HOROMETRICAL
HOROMETRIES
HOROSCOPES
HOROSCOPIC
HOROSCOPIES
HOROSCOPIST
HOROSCOPISTS
HORRENDOUS
HORRENDOUSLY
HORRENDOUSNESS
HORRIBLENESS
HORRIBLENESSES
HORRIDNESS
HORRIDNESSES
HORRIFICALLY
HORRIFICATION
HORRIFICATIONS
HORRIFYING
HORRIFYINGLY
HORRIPILANT
HORRIPILATE

HORRIPILATED
HORRIPILATES
HORRIPILATING
HORRIPILATION
HORRIPILATIONS
HORRISONANT
HORRISONOUS
HORSEBACKS
HORSEBEANS
HORSEBOXES
HORSEFEATHERS
HORSEFLESH
HORSEFLESHES
HORSEFLIES
HORSEHAIRS
HORSEHEADS
HORSEHIDES
HORSELAUGH
HORSELAUGHS
HORSELEECH
HORSELEECHES
HORSEMANSHIP
HORSEMANSHIPS
HORSEMEATS
HORSEMINTS
HORSEPLAYER
HORSEPLAYERS
HORSEPLAYS
HORSEPONDS
HORSEPOWER
HORSEPOWERS
HORSEPOXES
HORSERACES
HORSERADISH
HORSERADISHES
HORSESHITS
HORSESHOED
HORSESHOEING
HORSESHOEINGS
HORSESHOER
HORSESHOERS
HORSESHOES
HORSETAILS
HORSEWEEDS
HORSEWHIPPED
HORSEWHIPPER
HORSEWHIPPERS
HORSEWHIPPING

HORSEWHIPS
HORSEWOMAN
HORSEWOMEN
HORSINESSES
HORTATIONS
HORTATIVELY
HORTATORILY
HORTENSIAS
HORTICULTURAL
HORTICULTURALLY
HORTICULTURE
HORTICULTURES
HORTICULTURIST
HORTICULTURISTS
HOSANNAING
HOSPITABLE
HOSPITABLENESS
HOSPITABLY
HOSPITAGES
HOSPITALER
HOSPITALERS
HOSPITALES
HOSPITALISATION
HOSPITALISE
HOSPITALISED
HOSPITALISES
HOSPITALISING
HOSPITALIST
HOSPITALISTS
HOSPITALITIES
HOSPITALITY
HOSPITALIZATION
HOSPITALIZE
HOSPITALIZED
HOSPITALIZES
HOSPITALIZING
HOSPITALLER
HOSPITALLERS
HOSTELINGS
HOSTELLERS
HOSTELLING
HOSTELLINGS
HOSTELRIES
HOSTESSING
HOSTILITIES
HOTCHPOTCH
HOTCHPOTCHES
HOTDOGGERS

HOTDOGGING	HOUSEHOLDERS	HOUSEWIFESKEPS	HUFFINESSES	HUMDUDGEON
HOTELLINGS	HOUSEHOLDERSHIP	HOUSEWIFEY	HUFFISHNESS	HUMDUDGEONS
HOTFOOTING	HOUSEHOLDS	HOUSEWIFIER	HUFFISHNESSES	HUMDURGEON
HOTHEADEDLY	HOUSEHUSBAND	HOUSEWIFIEST	HUGENESSES	HUMDURGEONS
HOTHEADEDNESS	HOUSEHUSBANDS	HOUSEWIVES	HUGEOUSNESS	HUMECTANTS
HOTHEADEDNESSES	HOUSEKEEPER	HOUSEWORKER	HUGEOUSNESSES	HUMECTATED
HOTHOUSING	HOUSEKEEPERS	HOUSEWORKERS	HULLABALLOO	HUMECTATES
HOTHOUSINGS	HOUSEKEEPING	HOUSEWORKS	HULLABALLOOS	HUMECTATING
HOTPRESSED	HOUSEKEEPINGS	HOUSEWRAPS	HULLABALOO	HUMECTATION
HOTPRESSES	HOUSEKEEPS	HOUSTONIAS	HULLABALOOS	HUMECTATIONS
HOTPRESSING	HOUSELEEKS	HOVERBOARD	HUMANENESS	HUMECTIVES
HOTTENTOTS	HOUSELESSNESS	HOVERBOARDS	HUMANENESSES	HUMGRUFFIAN
HOUGHMAGANDIE	HOUSELESSNESSES	HOVERCRAFT	HUMANHOODS	HUMGRUFFIANS
HOUGHMAGANDIES	HOUSELIGHTS	HOVERCRAFTS	HUMANISATION	HUMGRUFFIN
HOUNDFISHES	HOUSELINES	HOVERFLIES	HUMANISATIONS	HUMGRUFFINS
HOURGLASSES	HOUSELINGS	HOVERINGLY	HUMANISERS	HUMICOLOUS
HOURPLATES	HOUSELLING	HOVERPORTS	HUMANISING	HUMIDIFICATION
HOUSEBOATER	HOUSELLINGS	HOVERTRAIN	HUMANISTIC	HUMIDIFICATIONS
HOUSEBOATERS	HOUSEMAIDS	HOVERTRAINS	HUMANISTICALLY	HUMIDIFIED
HOUSEBOATS	HOUSEMASTER	HOWLROUNDS	HUMANITARIAN	HUMIDIFIER
HOUSEBOUND	HOUSEMASTERS	HOWSOMDEVER	HUMANITARIANISM	HUMIDIFIERS
HOUSEBREAK	HOUSEMATES	HOWSOMEVER	HUMANITARIANIST	HUMIDIFIES
HOUSEBREAKER	HOUSEMISTRESS	HOWTOWDIES	HUMANITARIANS	HUMIDIFYING
HOUSEBREAKERS	HOUSEMISTRESSES	HOYDENHOOD	HUMANITIES	HUMIDISTAT
HOUSEBREAKING	HOUSEMOTHER	HOYDENHOODS	HUMANIZATION	HUMIDISTATS
HOUSEBREAKINGS	HOUSEMOTHERS	HOYDENISHNESS	HUMANIZATIONS	HUMIDITIES
HOUSEBREAKS	HOUSEPAINTER	HOYDENISHNESSES	HUMANIZERS	HUMIDNESSES
HOUSEBROKE	HOUSEPAINTERS	HOYDENISMS	HUMANIZING	HUMIFICATION
HOUSEBROKEN	HOUSEPARENT	HUBRISTICALLY	HUMANKINDS	HUMIFICATIONS
HOUSECARLS	HOUSEPARENTS	HUCKABACKS	HUMANNESSES	HUMILIATED
HOUSECLEAN	HOUSEPERSON	HUCKLEBERRIES	HUMBLEBEES	HUMILIATES
HOUSECLEANED	HOUSEPERSONS	HUCKLEBERRY	HUMBLEBRAG	HUMILIATING
HOUSECLEANING	HOUSEPLANT	HUCKLEBERRYING	HUMBLEBRAGGED	HUMILIATINGLY
HOUSECLEANINGS	HOUSEPLANTS	HUCKLEBERRYINGS	HUMBLEBRAGGING	HUMILIATION
HOUSECLEANS	HOUSEROOMS	HUCKLEBONE	HUMBLEBRAGS	HUMILIATIONS
HOUSECOATS	HOUSESITTING	HUCKLEBONES	HUMBLENESS	HUMILIATIVE
HOUSECRAFT	HOUSEWARES	HUCKSTERAGE	HUMBLENESSES	HUMILIATOR
HOUSECRAFTS	HOUSEWARMING	HUCKSTERAGES	HUMBLESSES	HUMILIATORS
HOUSEDRESS	HOUSEWARMINGS	HUCKSTERED	HUMBLINGLY	HUMILIATORY
HOUSEDRESSES	HOUSEWIFELIER	HUCKSTERESS	HUMBUCKERS	HUMILITIES
HOUSEFATHER	HOUSEWIFELIEST	HUCKSTERESSES	HUMBUGGABLE	HUMMELLERS
HOUSEFATHERS	HOUSEWIFELINESS	HUCKSTERIES	HUMBUGGERIES	HUMMELLING
HOUSEFLIES	HOUSEWIFELY	HUCKSTERING	HUMBUGGERS	HUMMELLINGS
HOUSEFRONT	HOUSEWIFERIES	HUCKSTERISM	HUMBUGGERY	HUMMINGBIRD
HOUSEFRONTS	HOUSEWIFERY	HUCKSTERISMS	HUMBUGGING	HUMMINGBIRDS
HOUSEGUEST	HOUSEWIFESHIP	HUCKSTRESS	HUMDINGERS	HUMMOCKIER
HOUSEGUESTS	HOUSEWIFESHIPS	HUCKSTRESSES	HUMDRUMNESS	HUMMOCKIEST
HOUSEHOLDER	HOUSEWIFESKEP	HUDIBRASTIC	HUMDRUMNESSES	HUMMOCKING

HUMORALISM	HURRYINGLY	HYBRIDISABLE	HYDRATIONS	HYDROCRACK
HUMORALISMS	HURTFULNESS	HYBRIDISATION	HYDRAULICALLY	HYDROCRACKED
HUMORALIST	HURTFULNESSES	HYBRIDISATIONS	HYDRAULICKED	HYDROCRACKER
HUMORALISTS	HURTLEBERRIES	HYBRIDISED	HYDRAULICKING	HYDROCRACKERS
HUMORESQUE	HURTLEBERRY	HYBRIDISER	HYDRAULICKINGS	HYDROCRACKING
HUMORESQUES	HURTLESSLY	HYBRIDISERS	HYDRAULICS	HYDROCRACKINGS
HUMORISTIC	HURTLESSNESS	HYBRIDISES	HYDRAZIDES	HYDROCRACKS
HUMORLESSLY	HURTLESSNESSES	HYBRIDISING	HYDRAZINES	HYDROCYANIC
HUMORLESSNESS	HUSBANDAGE	HYBRIDISMS	HYDRICALLY	HYDRODYNAMIC
HUMORLESSNESSES	HUSBANDAGES	HYBRIDISTS	HYDROACOUSTICS	HYDRODYNAMICAL
HUMOROUSLY	HUSBANDERS	HYBRIDITIES	HYDROBIOLOGICAL	HYDRODYNAMICIST
HUMOROUSNESS	HUSBANDING	HYBRIDIZABLE	HYDROBIOLOGIES	HYDRODYNAMICS
HUMOROUSNESSES	HUSBANDLAND	HYBRIDIZATION	HYDROBIOLOGIST	HYDROELASTIC
HUMORSOMENESS	HUSBANDLANDS	HYBRIDIZATIONS	HYDROBIOLOGISTS	HYDROELECTRIC
HUMORSOMENESSES	HUSBANDLESS	HYBRIDIZED	HYDROBIOLOGY	HYDROEXTRACTOR
HUMOURLESS	HUSBANDLIER	HYBRIDIZER	HYDROBROMIC	HYDROEXTRACTORS
HUMOURLESSLY	HUSBANDLIEST	HYBRIDIZERS	HYDROCARBON	HYDROFLUORIC
HUMOURLESSNESS	HUSBANDLIKE	HYBRIDIZES	HYDROCARBONS	HYDROFOILS
HUMOURSOME	HUSBANDMAN	HYBRIDIZING	HYDROCASTS	HYDROFORMING
HUMOURSOMENESS	HUSBANDMEN	HYBRIDOMAS	HYDROCELES	HYDROFORMINGS
HUMPBACKED	HUSBANDRIES	HYBRIDOMATA	HYDROCELLULOSE	HYDROGENASE
HUMPINESSES	HUSHABYING	HYDANTOINS	HYDROCELLULOSES	HYDROGENASES
HUNCHBACKED	HUSHPUPPIES	HYDATHODES	HYDROCEPHALI	HYDROGENATE
HUNCHBACKS	HUSKINESSES	HYDATIDIFORM	HYDROCEPHALIC	HYDROGENATED
HUNDREDERS	HYACINTHINE	HYDNOCARPATE	HYDROCEPHALICS	HYDROGENATES
HUNDREDFOLD	HYALINISATION	HYDNOCARPATES	HYDROCEPHALIES	HYDROGENATING
HUNDREDFOLDS	HYALINISATIONS	HYDNOCARPIC	HYDROCEPHALOID	HYDROGENATION
HUNDREDORS	HYALINISED	HYDRAEMIAS	HYDROCEPHALOUS	HYDROGENATIONS
HUNDREDTHS	HYALINISES	HYDRAGOGUE	HYDROCEPHALUS	HYDROGENATOR
HUNDREDWEIGHT	HYALINISING	HYDRAGOGUES	HYDROCEPHALUSES	HYDROGENATORS
HUNDREDWEIGHTS	HYALINIZATION	HYDRALAZINE	HYDROCEPHALY	HYDROGENISATION
HUNGERINGLY	HYALINIZATIONS	HYDRALAZINES	HYDROCHLORIC	HYDROGENISE
HUNGRINESS	HYALINIZED	HYDRANGEAS	HYDROCHLORIDE	HYDROGENISED
HUNGRINESSES	HYALINIZES	HYDRARGYRAL	HYDROCHLORIDES	HYDROGENISES
HUNTIEGOWK	HYALINIZING	HYDRARGYRIA	HYDROCHORE	HYDROGENISING
HUNTIEGOWKED	HYALOMELAN	HYDRARGYRIAS	HYDROCHORES	HYDROGENIZATION
HUNTIEGOWKING	HYALOMELANE	HYDRARGYRIC	HYDROCHORIC	HYDROGENIZE
HUNTIEGOWKS	HYALOMELANES	HYDRARGYRISM	HYDROCODONE	HYDROGENIZED
HUNTRESSES	HYALOMELANS	HYDRARGYRISMS	HYDROCODONES	HYDROGENIZES
HUNTSMANSHIP	HYALONEMAS	HYDRARGYRUM	HYDROCOLLOID	HYDROGENIZING
HUNTSMANSHIPS	HYALOPHANE	HYDRARGYRUMS	HYDROCOLLOIDAL	HYDROGENOLYSES
HUPAITHRIC	HYALOPHANES	HYDRARTHROSES	HYDROCOLLOIDS	HYDROGENOLYSIS
HURLBARROW	HYALOPLASM	HYDRARTHROSIS	HYDROCORAL	HYDROGENOUS
HURLBARROWS	HYALOPLASMIC	HYDRASTINE	HYDROCORALLINE	HYDROGEOLOGICAL
HURRICANES	HYALOPLASMS	HYDRASTINES	HYDROCORALLINES	HYDROGEOLOGIES
HURRICANOES	HYALURONIC	HYDRASTININE	HYDROCORALS	HYDROGEOLOGIST
HURRIEDNESS	HYALURONIDASE	HYDRASTININES	HYDROCORTISONE	HYDROGEOLOGISTS
HURRIEDNESSES	HYALURONIDASES	HYDRASTISES	HYDROCORTISONES	HYDROGEOLOGY

HYDROGRAPH	HYDROMANIA	HYDROPHILITE	HYDROSPHERES	HYDROXYLASE
HYDROGRAPHER	HYDROMANIAS	HYDROPHILITES	HYDROSPHERIC	HYDROXYLASES
HYDROGRAPHERS	HYDROMANTIC	HYDROPHILOUS	HYDROSTATIC	HYDROXYLATE
HYDROGRAPHIC	HYDROMECHANICAL	HYDROPHILY	HYDROSTATICAL	HYDROXYLATED
HYDROGRAPHICAL	HYDROMECHANICS	HYDROPHOBIA	HYDROSTATICALLY	HYDROXYLATES
HYDROGRAPHIES	HYDROMEDUSA	HYDROPHOBIAS	HYDROSTATICS	HYDROXYLATING
HYDROGRAPHS	HYDROMEDUSAE	HYDROPHOBIC	HYDROSTATS	HYDROXYLATION
HYDROGRAPHY	HYDROMEDUSAN	HYDROPHOBICITY	HYDROSULPHATE	HYDROXYLATIONS
HYDROKINETIC	HYDROMEDUSANS	HYDROPHOBOUS	HYDROSULPHATES	HYDROXYLIC
HYDROKINETICAL	HYDROMEDUSAS	HYDROPHONE	HYDROSULPHIDE	HYDROXYPROLINE
HYDROKINETICS	HYDROMEDUSOID	HYDROPHONES	HYDROSULPHIDES	HYDROXYPROLINES
HYDROLASES	HYDROMEDUSOIDS	HYDROPHYTE	HYDROSULPHITE	HYDROXYUREA
HYDROLOGIC	HYDROMETALLURGY	HYDROPHYTES	HYDROSULPHITES	HYDROXYUREAS
HYDROLOGICAL	HYDROMETEOR	HYDROPHYTIC	HYDROSULPHURIC	HYDROXYZINE
HYDROLOGICALLY	HYDROMETEORS	HYDROPHYTON	HYDROSULPHUROUS	HYDROXYZINES
HYDROLOGIES	HYDROMETER	HYDROPHYTONS	HYDROTACTIC	HYDROXYZINES
HYDROLOGIST	HYDROMETERS	HYDROPHYTOUS	HYDROTAXES	HYDROZINCITE
HYDROLOGISTS	HYDROMETRIC	HYDROPLANE	HYDROTAXIS	HYDROZINCITES
HYDROLYSABLE	HYDROMETRICAL	HYDROPLANED	HYDROTHECA	HYDROZOANS
HYDROLYSATE	HYDROMETRICALLY	HYDROPLANES	HYDROTHECAE	HYETOGRAPH
HYDROLYSATES	HYDROMETRIES	HYDROPLANING	HYDROTHERAPIC	HYETOGRAPHIC
HYDROLYSATION	HYDROMETRY	HYDROPNEUMATIC	HYDROTHERAPIES	HYETOGRAPHICAL
HYDROLYSATIONS	HYDROMORPHIC	HYDROPOLYP	HYDROTHERAPIST	HYETOGRAPHIES
HYDROLYSED	HYDRONAUTS	HYDROPOLYPS	HYDROTHERAPISTS	HYETOGRAPHS
HYDROLYSER	HYDRONEPHROSES	HYDROPONIC	HYDROTHERAPY	HYETOGRAPHY
HYDROLYSERS	HYDRONEPHROSIS	HYDROPONICALLY	HYDROTHERMAL	HYETOLOGIES
HYDROLYSES	HYDRONEPHROTIC	HYDROPONICS	HYDROTHERMALLY	HYETOMETER
HYDROLYSING	HYDRONICALLY	HYDROPOWER	HYDROTHORACES	HYETOMETERS
HYDROLYSIS	HYDRONIUMS	HYDROPOWERS	HYDROTHORACIC	HYETOMETROGRAPH
HYDROLYTES	HYDROPATHIC	HYDROPSIES	HYDROTHORAX	HYGIENICALLY
HYDROLYTIC	HYDROPATHICAL	HYDROPULTS	HYDROTHORAXES	HYGIENISTS
HYDROLYTICALLY	HYDROPATHICALLY	HYDROQUINOL	HYDROTROPIC	HYGRISTORS
HYDROLYZABLE	HYDROPATHICS	HYDROQUINOLS	HYDROTROPICALLY	HYGROCHASIES
HYDROLYZATE	HYDROPATHIES	HYDROQUINONE	HYDROTROPISM	HYGROCHASTIC
HYDROLYZATES	HYDROPATHIST	HYDROQUINONES	HYDROTROPISMS	HYGROCHASY
HYDROLYZATION	HYDROPATHISTS	HYDROSCOPE	HYDROVANES	HYGRODEIKS
HYDROLYZATIONS	HYDROPATHS	HYDROSCOPES	HYDROXIDES	HYGROGRAPH
HYDROLYZED	HYDROPATHY	HYDROSCOPIC	HYDROXIUMS	HYGROGRAPHIC
HYDROLYZER	HYDROPEROXIDE	HYDROSCOPICAL	HYDROXONIUM	HYGROGRAPHICAL
HYDROLYZERS	HYDROPEROXIDES	HYDROSERES	HYDROXONIUMS	HYGROGRAPHS
HYDROLYZES	HYDROPHANE	HYDROSOLIC	HYDROXYACETIC	HYGROLOGIES
HYDROLYZING	HYDROPHANES	HYDROSOMAL	HYDROXYAPATITE	HYGROMETER
HYDROMAGNETIC	HYDROPHANOUS	HYDROSOMATA	HYDROXYAPATITES	HYGROMETERS
HYDROMAGNETICS	HYDROPHILE	HYDROSOMATOUS	HYDROXYBUTYRATE	HYGROMETRIC
HYDROMANCER	HYDROPHILES	HYDROSOMES	HYDROXYCITRIC	HYGROMETRICAL
HYDROMANCERS	HYDROPHILIC	HYDROSPACE	HYDROXYLAMINE	HYGROMETRICALLY
HYDROMANCIES	HYDROPHILICITY	HYDROSPACES	HYDROXYLAMINES	HYGROMETRIES
HYDROMANCY	HYDROPHILIES	HYDROSPHERE	HYDROXYLAPATITE	HYGROMETRY
				HYGROPHILE

HYGROPHILES	HYMNODISTS	HYPERAEMIAS	HYPERCALCAEMIC	HYPERDULICAL
HYGROPHILOUS	HYMNOGRAPHER	HYPERAEMIC	HYPERCALCEMIA	HYPEREFFICIENT
HYGROPHOBE	HYMNOGRAPHERS	HYPERAESTHESIA	HYPERCALCEMIAS	HYPEREMESES
HYGROPHOBES	HYMNOGRAPHIES	HYPERAESTHESIAS	HYPERCALCEMIC	HYPEREMESIS
HYGROPHYTE	HYMNOGRAPHY	HYPERAESTHESIC	HYPERCAPNIA	HYPEREMETIC
HYGROPHYTES	HYMNOLOGIC	HYPERAESTHETIC	HYPERCAPNIAS	HYPEREMIAS
HYGROPHYTIC	HYMNOLOGICAL	HYPERAGGRESSIVE	HYPERCAPNIC	HYPEREMOTIONAL
HYGROSCOPE	HYMNOLOGIES	HYPERALERT	HYPERCARBIA	HYPERENDEMIC
HYGROSCOPES	HYMNOLOGIST	HYPERALGESIA	HYPERCARBIAS	HYPERENERGETIC
HYGROSCOPIC	HYMNOLOGISTS	HYPERALGESIAS	HYPERCATABOLISM	HYPERESTHESIA
HYGROSCOPICAL	HYOPLASTRA	HYPERALGESIC	HYPERCATALECTIC	HYPERESTHESIAS
HYGROSCOPICALLY	HYOPLASTRAL	HYPERAROUSAL	HYPERCATALEXES	HYPERESTHETIC
HYGROSCOPICITY	HYOPLASTRON	HYPERAROUSALS	HYPERCATALEXIS	HYPEREUTECTIC
HYGROSTATS	HYOSCYAMINE	HYPERAWARE	HYPERCAUTIOUS	HYPEREUTECTOID
HYLOGENESES	HYOSCYAMINES	HYPERAWARENESS	HYPERCHARGE	HYPEREXCITABLE
HYLOGENESIS	HYOSCYAMUS	HYPERBARIC	HYPERCHARGED	HYPEREXCITED
HYLOMORPHIC	HYOSCYAMUSES	HYPERBARICALLY	HYPERCHARGES	HYPEREXCITEMENT
HYLOMORPHISM	HYPABYSSAL	HYPERBATIC	HYPERCHARGING	HYPEREXCRETION
HYLOMORPHISMS	HYPABYSSALLY	HYPERBATICALLY	HYPERCIVILISED	HYPEREXCRETIONS
HYLOPATHISM	HYPAESTHESIA	HYPERBATON	HYPERCIVILIZED	HYPEREXTEND
HYLOPATHISMS	HYPAESTHESIAS	HYPERBATONS	HYPERCOAGULABLE	HYPEREXTENDED
HYLOPATHIST	HYPAESTHESIC	HYPERBOLAE	HYPERCOLOUR	HYPEREXTENDING
HYLOPATHISTS	HYPAETHRAL	HYPERBOLAEON	HYPERCOLOURS	HYPEREXTENDS
HYLOPHAGOUS	HYPAETHRON	HYPERBOLAEONS	HYPERCOMPLEX	HYPEREXTENSION
HYLOPHYTES	HYPAETHRONS	HYPERBOLAS	HYPERCONSCIOUS	HYPEREXTENSIONS
HYLOTHEISM	HYPALGESIA	HYPERBOLES	HYPERCORRECT	HYPERFASTIDIOUS
HYLOTHEISMS	HYPALGESIAS	HYPERBOLIC	HYPERCORRECTION	HYPERFOCAL
HYLOTHEIST	HYPALGESIC	HYPERBOLICAL	HYPERCORRECTLY	HYPERFUNCTION
HYLOTHEISTS	HYPALLACTIC	HYPERBOLICALLY	HYPERCRITIC	HYPERFUNCTIONAL
HYLOTOMOUS	HYPALLAGES	HYPERBOLISE	HYPERCRITICAL	HYPERFUNCTIONS
HYLOZOICAL	HYPANTHIAL	HYPERBOLISED	HYPERCRITICALLY	HYPERGAMIES
HYLOZOISMS	HYPANTHIUM	HYPERBOLISES	HYPERCRITICISE	HYPERGAMOUS
HYLOZOISTIC	HYPERACIDITIES	HYPERBOLISING	HYPERCRITICISED	HYPERGEOMETRIC
HYLOZOISTICALLY	HYPERACIDITY	HYPERBOLISM	HYPERCRITICISES	HYPERGLYCAEMIA
HYLOZOISTS	HYPERACTION	HYPERBOLISMS	HYPERCRITICISM	HYPERGLYCAEMIAS
HYMENAEANS	HYPERACTIONS	HYPERBOLIST	HYPERCRITICISMS	HYPERGLYCAEMIC
HYMENEALLY	HYPERACTIVE	HYPERBOLISTS	HYPERCRITICIZE	HYPERGLYCEMIA
HYMENOPHORE	HYPERACTIVES	HYPERBOLIZE	HYPERCRITICIZED	HYPERGLYCEMIAS
HYMENOPHORES	HYPERACTIVITIES	HYPERBOLIZED	HYPERCRITICIZES	HYPERGLYCEMIC
HYMENOPLASTIES	HYPERACTIVITY	HYPERBOLIZES	HYPERCRITICS	HYPERGOLIC
HYMENOPLASTY	HYPERACUITIES	HYPERBOLIZING	HYPERCUBES	HYPERGOLICALLY
HYMENOPTERA	HYPERACUITY	HYPERBOLOID	HYPERDACTYL	HYPERHIDROSES
HYMENOPTERAN	HYPERACUSES	HYPERBOLOIDAL	HYPERDACTYLIES	HYPERHIDROSIS
HYMENOPTERANS	HYPERACUSIS	HYPERBOLOIDS	HYPERDACTYLY	HYPERICINS
HYMENOPTERON	HYPERACUTE	HYPERBOREAN	HYPERDORIAN	HYPERICUMS
HYMENOPTERONS	HYPERACUTENESS	HYPERBOREANS	HYPERDULIA	HYPERIDROSES
HYMENOPTEROUS	HYPERADRENALISM	HYPERCALCAEMIA	HYPERDULIAS	HYPERIDROSIS
HYMNODICAL	HYPERAEMIA	HYPERCALCAEMIAS	HYPERDULIC	HYPERIMMUNE

HYPERIMMUNISE	HYPERMETERS	HYPERPHYSICALLY	HYPERRESPONSIVE	HYPERTENSE
HYPERIMMUNISED	HYPERMETRIC	HYPERPIGMENTED	HYPERROMANTIC	HYPERTENSION
HYPERIMMUNISES	HYPERMETRICAL	HYPERPITUITARY	HYPERROMANTICS	HYPERTENSIONS
HYPERIMMUNISING	HYPERMETROPIA	HYPERPLANE	HYPERSALINE	HYPERTENSIVE
HYPERIMMUNIZE	HYPERMETROPIAS	HYPERPLANES	HYPERSALINITIES	HYPERTENSIVES
HYPERIMMUNIZED	HYPERMETROPIC	HYPERPLASIA	HYPERSALINITY	HYPERTEXTS
HYPERIMMUNIZES	HYPERMETROPICAL	HYPERPLASIAS	HYPERSALIVATION	HYPERTHERMAL
HYPERIMMUNIZING	HYPERMETROPIES	HYPERPLASTIC	HYPERSARCOMA	HYPERTHERMIA
HYPERINFLATED	HYPERMETROPY	HYPERPLOID	HYPERSARCOMAS	HYPERTHERMIAS
HYPERINFLATION	HYPERMILING	HYPERPLOIDIES	HYPERSARCOMATA	HYPERTHERMIC
HYPERINFLATIONS	HYPERMILINGS	HYPERPLOIDS	HYPERSARCOSES	HYPERTHERMIES
HYPERINOSES	HYPERMNESIA	HYPERPLOIDY	HYPERSARCOSIS	HYPERTHERMY
HYPERINOSIS	HYPERMNESIAS	HYPERPNEAS	HYPERSECRETION	HYPERTHYMIA
HYPERINOTIC	HYPERMNESIC	HYPERPNEIC	HYPERSECRETIONS	HYPERTHYMIAS
HYPERINSULINISM	HYPERMOBILITIES	HYPERPNOEA	HYPERSENSITISE	HYPERTHYROID
HYPERINTENSE	HYPERMOBILITY	HYPERPNOEAS	HYPERSENSITISED	HYPERTHYROIDISM
HYPERINVOLUTION	HYPERMODERN	HYPERPOLARISE	HYPERSENSITISES	HYPERTHYROIDS
HYPERIRRITABLE	HYPERMODERNISM	HYPERPOLARISED	HYPERSENSITIVE	HYPERTONIA
HYPERKERATOSES	HYPERMODERNISMS	HYPERPOLARISES	HYPERSENSITIZE	HYPERTONIAS
HYPERKERATOSIS	HYPERMODERNIST	HYPERPOLARISING	HYPERSENSITIZED	HYPERTONIC
HYPERKERATOTIC	HYPERMODERNISTS	HYPERPOLARIZE	HYPERSENSITIZES	HYPERTONICITIES
HYPERKINESES	HYPERMUTABILITY	HYPERPOLARIZED	HYPERSENSUAL	HYPERTONICITY
HYPERKINESIA	HYPERMUTABLE	HYPERPOLARIZES	HYPERSEXUAL	HYPERTROPHIC
HYPERKINESIAS	HYPERNATRAEMIA	HYPERPOLARIZING	HYPERSEXUALITY	HYPERTROPHICAL
HYPERKINESIS	HYPERNATRAEMIAS	HYPERPOWER	HYPERSOMNIA	HYPERTROPHIED
HYPERKINETIC	HYPERNOVAE	HYPERPOWERS	HYPERSOMNIAS	HYPERTROPHIES
HYPERLINKED	HYPERNOVAS	HYPERPRODUCER	HYPERSOMNOLENCE	HYPERTROPHOUS
HYPERLINKING	HYPERNYMIES	HYPERPRODUCERS	HYPERSONIC	HYPERTROPHY
HYPERLINKS	HYPEROPIAS	HYPERPRODUCTION	HYPERSONICALLY	HYPERTROPHYING
HYPERLIPEMIA	HYPEROREXIA	HYPERPROSEXIA	HYPERSONICS	HYPERTYPICAL
HYPERLIPEMIAS	HYPEROREXIAS	HYPERPROSEXIAS	HYPERSPACE	HYPERURBANISM
HYPERLIPEMIC	HYPEROSMIA	HYPERPYRETIC	HYPERSPACES	HYPERURBANISMS
HYPERLIPIDAEMIA	HYPEROSMIAS	HYPERPYREXIA	HYPERSPATIAL	HYPERURICAEMIA
HYPERLIPIDEMIA	HYPEROSTOSES	HYPERPYREXIAL	HYPERSTATIC	HYPERURICAEMIAS
HYPERLIPIDEMIAS	HYPEROSTOSIS	HYPERPYREXIAS	HYPERSTHENE	HYPERURICEMIA
HYPERLYDIAN	HYPEROSTOSISES	HYPERRATIONAL	HYPERSTHENES	HYPERURICEMIAS
HYPERMANIA	HYPEROSTOTIC	HYPERREACTIVE	HYPERSTHENIA	HYPERVELOCITIES
HYPERMANIAS	HYPEROXIDE	HYPERREACTIVITY	HYPERSTHENIAS	HYPERVELOCITY
HYPERMANIC	HYPEROXIDES	HYPERREACTOR	HYPERSTHENIC	HYPERVENTILATE
HYPERMARKET	HYPERPARASITE	HYPERREACTORS	HYPERSTHENITE	HYPERVENTILATED
HYPERMARKETS	HYPERPARASITES	HYPERREALISM	HYPERSTHENITES	HYPERVENTILATES
HYPERMARTS	HYPERPARASITIC	HYPERREALISMS	HYPERSTIMULATE	HYPERVIGILANCE
HYPERMASCULINE	HYPERPARASITISM	HYPERREALIST	HYPERSTIMULATED	HYPERVIGILANCES
HYPERMEDIA	HYPERPHAGIA	HYPERREALISTIC	HYPERSTIMULATES	HYPERVIGILANT
HYPERMEDIAS	HYPERPHAGIAS	HYPERREALISTS	HYPERSTRESS	HYPERVIRULENT
HYPERMETABOLIC	HYPERPHAGIC	HYPERREALITIES	HYPERSTRESSES	HYPERVISCOSITY
HYPERMETABOLISM	HYPERPHRYGIAN	HYPERREALITY	HYPERSURFACE	HYPESTHESIA
HYPERMETER	HYPERPHYSICAL	HYPERREALS	HYPERSURFACES	HYPESTHESIAS

HYPESTHESIC	HYPNOPOMPIC	HYPOCHONDRIA	HYPOGLOSSALS	HYPOPHOSPHORIC
HYPHENATED	HYPNOTHERAPIES	HYPOCHONDRIAC	HYPOGLYCAEMIA	HYPOPHOSPHOROUS
HYPHENATES	HYPNOTHERAPIST	HYPOCHONDRIACAL	HYPOGLYCAEMIAS	HYPOPHRYGIAN
HYPHENATING	HYPNOTHERAPISTS	HYPOCHONDRIACS	HYPOGLYCAEMIC	HYPOPHYGES
HYPHENATION	HYPNOTHERAPY	HYPOCHONDRIAS	HYPOGLYCEMIA	HYPOPHYSEAL
HYPHENATIONS	HYPNOTICALLY	HYPOCHONDRIASES	HYPOGLYCEMIAS	HYPOPHYSECTOMY
HYPHENISATION	HYPNOTISABILITY	HYPOCHONDRIASIS	HYPOGLYCEMIC	HYPOPHYSES
HYPHENISATIONS	HYPNOTISABLE	HYPOCHONDRIASM	HYPOGLYCEMICS	HYPOPHYSIAL
HYPHENISED	HYPNOTISATION	HYPOCHONDRIASMS	HYPOGNATHISM	HYPOPHYSIS
HYPHENISES	HYPNOTISATIONS	HYPOCHONDRIAST	HYPOGNATHISMS	HYPOPITUITARISM
HYPHENISING	HYPNOTISED	HYPOCHONDRIASTS	HYPOGNATHOUS	HYPOPITUITARY
HYPHENISMS	HYPNOTISER	HYPOCHONDRIUM	HYPOGYNIES	HYPOPLASIA
HYPHENIZATION	HYPNOTISERS	HYPOCORISM	HYPOGYNOUS	HYPOPLASIAS
HYPHENIZATIONS	HYPNOTISES	HYPOCORISMA	HYPOKALEMIA	HYPOPLASTIC
HYPHENIZED	HYPNOTISING	HYPOCORISMAS	HYPOKALEMIAS	HYPOPLASTIES
HYPHENIZES	HYPNOTISMS	HYPOCORISMS	HYPOKALEMIC	HYPOPLASTRA
HYPHENIZING	HYPNOTISTIC	HYPOCORISTIC	HYPOLIMNIA	HYPOPLASTRON
HYPHENLESS	HYPNOTISTS	HYPOCORISTICAL	HYPOLIMNION	HYPOPLASTY
HYPNAGOGIC	HYPNOTIZABILITY	HYPOCOTYLOUS	HYPOLIMNIONS	HYPOPLOIDIES
HYPNOANALYSES	HYPNOTIZABLE	HYPOCOTYLS	HYPOLYDIAN	HYPOPLOIDS
HYPNOANALYSIS	HYPNOTIZATION	HYPOCRISIES	HYPOMAGNESAEMIA	HYPOPLOIDY
HYPNOANALYTIC	HYPNOTIZATIONS	HYPOCRITES	HYPOMAGNESEMIA	HYPOPNOEAS
HYPNOBIRTHING	HYPNOTIZED	HYPOCRITIC	HYPOMAGNESEMIAS	HYPOSENSITISE
HYPNOBIRTHINGS	HYPNOTIZER	HYPOCRITICAL	HYPOMANIAS	HYPOSENSITISED
HYPNOGENESES	HYPNOTIZERS	HYPOCRITICALLY	HYPOMANICS	HYPOSENSITISES
HYPNOGENESIS	HYPNOTIZES	HYPOCRYSTALLINE	HYPOMENORRHEA	HYPOSENSITISING
HYPNOGENETIC	HYPNOTIZING	HYPOCYCLOID	HYPOMENORRHEAS	HYPOSENSITIZE
HYPNOGENIC	HYPOACIDITIES	HYPOCYCLOIDAL	HYPOMENORRHOEA	HYPOSENSITIZED
HYPNOGENIES	HYPOACIDITY	HYPOCYCLOIDS	HYPOMENORRHOEAS	HYPOSENSITIZES
HYPNOGENOUS	HYPOAEOLIAN	HYPODERMAL	HYPOMIXOLYDIAN	HYPOSENSITIZING
HYPNOGOGIC	HYPOALLERGENIC	HYPODERMAS	HYPOMORPHIC	HYPOSPADIAS
HYPNOIDISE	HYPOBLASTIC	HYPODERMIC	HYPOMORPHS	HYPOSPADIASES
HYPNOIDISED	HYPOBLASTS	HYPODERMICALLY	HYPONASTIC	HYPOSTASES
HYPNOIDISES	HYPOCALCAEMIA	HYPODERMICS	HYPONASTICALLY	HYPOSTASIS
HYPNOIDISING	HYPOCALCAEMIAS	HYPODERMIS	HYPONASTIES	HYPOSTASISATION
HYPNOIDIZE	HYPOCALCAEMIC	HYPODERMISES	HYPONATRAEMIA	HYPOSTASISE
HYPNOIDIZED	HYPOCALCEMIA	HYPODIPLOID	HYPONATRAEMIAS	HYPOSTASISED
HYPNOIDIZES	HYPOCALCEMIAS	HYPODIPLOIDIES	HYPONITRITE	HYPOSTASISES
HYPNOIDIZING	HYPOCALCEMIC	HYPODIPLOIDY	HYPONITRITES	HYPOSTASISING
HYPNOLOGIC	HYPOCAUSTS	HYPODORIAN	HYPONITROUS	HYPOSTASIZATION
HYPNOLOGICAL	HYPOCENTER	HYPOEUTECTIC	HYPONYMIES	HYPOSTASIZE
HYPNOLOGIES	HYPOCENTERS	HYPOEUTECTOID	HYPOPHARYNGES	HYPOSTASIZED
HYPNOLOGIST	HYPOCENTRAL	HYPOGAEOUS	HYPOPHARYNX	HYPOSTASIZES
HYPNOLOGISTS	HYPOCENTRE	HYPOGASTRIA	HYPOPHARYNXES	HYPOSTASIZING
HYPNOPAEDIA	HYPOCENTRES	HYPOGASTRIC	HYPOPHOSPHATE	HYPOSTATIC
HYPNOPAEDIAS	HYPOCHLORITE	HYPOGASTRIUM	HYPOPHOSPHATES	HYPOSTATICAL
HYPNOPHOBIA	HYPOCHLORITES	HYPOGENOUS	HYPOPHOSPHITE	HYPOSTATICALLY
HYPNOPHOBIAS	HYPOCHLOROUS	HYPOGLOSSAL	HYPOPHOSPHITES	HYPOSTATISATION

HYPOSTATISE	HYPOTHALAMI	HYPOTHESIZER	HYPOXAEMIC	HYSTERECTOMISE
HYPOSTATISED	HYPOTHALAMIC	HYPOTHESIZERS	HYPOXANTHINE	HYSTERECTOMISED
HYPOSTATISES	HYPOTHALAMUS	HYPOTHESIZES	HYPOXANTHINES	HYSTERECTOMISES
HYPOSTATISING	HYPOTHECAE	HYPOTHESIZING	HYPOXEMIAS	HYSTERECTOMIZE
HYPOSTATIZATION	HYPOTHECARY	HYPOTHETIC	HYPSOCHROME	HYSTERECTOMIZED
HYPOSTATIZE	HYPOTHECATE	HYPOTHETICAL	HYPSOCHROMES	HYSTERECTOMIZES
HYPOSTATIZED	HYPOTHECATED	HYPOTHETICALLY	HYPSOCHROMIC	HYSTERECTOMY
HYPOSTATIZES	HYPOTHECATES	HYPOTHETISE	HYPSOGRAPHIC	HYSTERESES
HYPOSTATIZING	HYPOTHECATING	HYPOTHETISED	HYPSOGRAPHICAL	HYSTERESIAL
HYPOSTHENIA	HYPOTHECATION	HYPOTHETISES	HYPSOGRAPHIES	HYSTERESIS
HYPOSTHENIAS	HYPOTHECATIONS	HYPOTHETISING	HYPSOGRAPHY	HYSTERETIC
HYPOSTHENIC	HYPOTHECATOR	HYPOTHETIZE	HYPSOMETER	HYSTERETICALLY
HYPOSTOMES	HYPOTHECATORS	HYPOTHETIZED	HYPSOMETERS	HYSTERICAL
HYPOSTRESS	HYPOTHENUSE	HYPOTHETIZES	HYPSOMETRIC	HYSTERICALLY
HYPOSTRESSES	HYPOTHENUSES	HYPOTHETIZING	HYPSOMETRICAL	HYSTERICKY
HYPOSTROPHE	HYPOTHERMAL	HYPOTHYMIA	HYPSOMETRICALLY	HYSTERITIS
HYPOSTROPHES	HYPOTHERMIA	HYPOTHYMIAS	HYPSOMETRIES	HYSTERITISES
HYPOSTYLES	HYPOTHERMIAS	HYPOTHYROID	HYPSOMETRIST	HYSTEROGENIC
HYPOSULPHATE	HYPOTHERMIC	HYPOTHYROIDISM	HYPSOMETRISTS	HYSTEROGENIES
HYPOSULPHATES	HYPOTHESES	HYPOTHYROIDISMS	HYPSOMETRY	HYSTEROGENY
HYPOSULPHITE	HYPOTHESIS	HYPOTHYROIDS	HYPSOPHOBE	HYSTEROIDAL
HYPOSULPHITES	HYPOTHESISE	HYPOTONIAS	HYPSOPHOBES	HYSTEROMANIA
HYPOSULPHURIC	HYPOTHESISED	HYPOTONICITIES	HYPSOPHOBIA	HYSTEROMANIAS
HYPOSULPHUROUS	HYPOTHESISER	HYPOTONICITY	HYPSOPHOBIAS	HYSTEROTOMIES
HYPOTACTIC	HYPOTHESISERS	HYPOTROCHOID	HYPSOPHYLL	HYSTEROTOMY
HYPOTENSION	HYPOTHESISES	HYPOTROCHOIDS	HYPSOPHYLLARY	HYSTRICOMORPH
HYPOTENSIONS	HYPOTHESISING	HYPOTYPOSES	HYPSOPHYLLS	HYSTRICOMORPHIC
HYPOTENSIVE	HYPOTHESIST	HYPOTYPOSIS	HYRACOIDEAN	HYSTRICOMORPHS
HYPOTENSIVES	HYPOTHESISTS	HYPOVENTILATION	HYRACOIDEANS	
HYPOTENUSE	HYPOTHESIZE	HYPOXAEMIA	HYSTERANTHOUS	
HYPOTENUSES	HYPOTHESIZED	HYPOXAEMIAS	HYSTERECTOMIES	

I

IAMBICALLY	ICHTHYOLATRY	ICONOGRAPHIC	IDEALISATIONS	IDEOLOGICAL
IAMBOGRAPHER	ICHTHYOLITE	ICONOGRAPHICAL	IDEALISERS	IDEOLOGICALLY
IAMBOGRAPHERS	ICHTHYOLITES	ICONOGRAPHIES	IDEALISING	IDEOLOGIES
IATROCHEMICAL	ICHTHYOLITIC	ICONOGRAPHY	IDEALISTIC	IDEOLOGISE
IATROCHEMIST	ICHTHYOLOGIC	ICONOLATER	IDEALISTICALLY	IDEOLOGISED
IATROCHEMISTRY	ICHTHYOLOGICAL	ICONOLATERS	IDEALITIES	IDEOLOGISES
IATROCHEMISTS	ICHTHYOLOGIES	ICONOLATRIES	IDEALIZATION	IDEOLOGISING
IATROGENIC	ICHTHYOLOGIST	ICONOLATROUS	IDEALIZATIONS	IDEOLOGIST
IATROGENICALLY	ICHTHYOLOGISTS	ICONOLATRY	IDEALIZERS	IDEOLOGISTS
IATROGENICITIES	ICHTHYOLOGY	ICONOLOGICAL	IDEALIZING	IDEOLOGIZE
IATROGENICITY	ICHTHYOPHAGIES	ICONOLOGIES	IDEALNESSES	IDEOLOGIZED
IATROGENIES	ICHTHYOPHAGIST	ICONOLOGIST	IDEALOGIES	IDEOLOGIZES
IBUPROFENS	ICHTHYOPHAGISTS	ICONOLOGISTS	IDEALOGUES	IDEOLOGIZING
ICEBOATERS	ICHTHYOPHAGOUS	ICONOMACHIES	IDEATIONAL	IDEOLOGUES
ICEBOATING	ICHTHYOPHAGY	ICONOMACHIST	IDEATIONALLY	IDEOPHONES
ICEBOATINGS	ICHTHYOPSID	ICONOMACHISTS	IDEMPOTENCIES	IDEOPOLISES
ICEBREAKER	ICHTHYOPSIDAN	ICONOMACHY	IDEMPOTENCY	IDEOPRAXIST
ICEBREAKERS	ICHTHYOPSIDANS	ICONOMATIC	IDEMPOTENT	IDEOPRAXISTS
ICEBREAKING	ICHTHYOPSIDS	ICONOMATICISM	IDEMPOTENTS	IDIOBLASTIC
ICEFISHING	ICHTHYORNIS	ICONOMATICISMS	IDENTICALLY	IDIOBLASTS
ICHNEUMONS	ICHTHYORNISES	ICONOMETER	IDENTICALNESS	IDIOGLOSSIA
ICHNOFOSSIL	ICHTHYOSAUR	ICONOMETERS	IDENTICALNESSES	IDIOGLOSSIAS
ICHNOFOSSILS	ICHTHYOSAURI	ICONOMETRIES	IDENTIFIABLE	IDIOGRAPHIC
ICHNOGRAPHIC	ICHTHYOSAURIAN	ICONOMETRY	IDENTIFIABLY	IDIOGRAPHS
ICHNOGRAPHICAL	ICHTHYOSAURIANS	ICONOPHILISM	IDENTIFICATION	IDIOLECTAL
ICHNOGRAPHIES	ICHTHYOSAURS	ICONOPHILISMS	IDENTIFICATIONS	IDIOLECTIC
ICHNOGRAPHY	ICHTHYOSAURUS	ICONOPHILIST	IDENTIFIED	IDIOMATICAL
ICHNOLITES	ICHTHYOSAURUSES	ICONOPHILISTS	IDENTIFIER	IDIOMATICALLY
ICHNOLOGICAL	ICHTHYOSES	ICONOSCOPE	IDENTIFIERS	IDIOMATICALNESS
ICHNOLOGIES	ICHTHYOSIS	ICONOSCOPES	IDENTIFIES	IDIOMATICNESS
ICHTHYOCOLLA	ICHTHYOTIC	ICONOSTASES	IDENTIFYING	IDIOMATICNESSES
ICHTHYOCOLLAS	ICKINESSES	ICONOSTASIS	IDENTIKITS	IDIOMORPHIC
ICHTHYODORULITE	ICONICALLY	ICOSAHEDRA	IDENTITIES	IDIOMORPHICALLY
ICHTHYODORYLITE	ICONICITIES	ICOSAHEDRAL	IDEOGRAMIC	IDIOMORPHISM
ICHTHYOFAUNA	ICONIFYING	ICOSAHEDRON	IDEOGRAMMATIC	IDIOMORPHISMS
ICHTHYOFAUNAE	ICONOCLASM	ICOSAHEDRONS	IDEOGRAMMIC	IDIOPATHIC
ICHTHYOFAUNAL	ICONOCLASMS	ICOSANDRIAN	IDEOGRAPHIC	IDIOPATHICALLY
ICHTHYOFAUNAS	ICONOCLAST	ICOSANDROUS	IDEOGRAPHICAL	IDIOPATHIES
ICHTHYOIDAL	ICONOCLASTIC	ICOSITETRAHEDRA	IDEOGRAPHICALLY	IDIOPHONES
ICHTHYOIDS	ICONOCLASTS	ICTERICALS	IDEOGRAPHIES	IDIOPHONIC
ICHTHYOLATRIES	ICONOGRAPHER	ICTERITIOUS	IDEOGRAPHS	IDIOPLASMATIC
ICHTHYOLATROUS	ICONOGRAPHERS	IDEALISATION	IDEOGRAPHY	IDIOPLASMIC

IDIOPLASMS

IDIOPLASMS	IGNITIBILITIES	ILLEGITIMACIES	ILLOGICALNESS	ILLUSTRATIONS
IDIORHYTHMIC	IGNITIBILITY	ILLEGITIMACY	ILLOGICALNESSES	ILLUSTRATIVE
IDIORRHYTHMIC	IGNOBILITIES	ILLEGITIMATE	ILLUMINABLE	ILLUSTRATIVELY
IDIOSYNCRASIES	IGNOBILITY	ILLEGITIMATED	ILLUMINANCE	ILLUSTRATOR
IDIOSYNCRASY	IGNOBLENESS	ILLEGITIMATELY	ILLUMINANCES	ILLUSTRATORS
IDIOSYNCRATIC	IGNOBLENESSES	ILLEGITIMATES	ILLUMINANT	ILLUSTRATORY
IDIOSYNCRATICAL	IGNOMINIES	ILLEGITIMATING	ILLUMINANTS	ILLUSTRIOUS
IDIOTHERMOUS	IGNOMINIOUS	ILLEGITIMATION	ILLUMINATE	ILLUSTRIOUSLY
IDIOTICALLY	IGNOMINIOUSLY	ILLEGITIMATIONS	ILLUMINATED	ILLUSTRIOUSNESS
IDIOTICALNESS	IGNOMINIOUSNESS	ILLIBERALISE	ILLUMINATES	ILLUSTRISSIMO
IDIOTICALNESSES	IGNORAMUSES	ILLIBERALISED	ILLUMINATI	ILLUVIATED
IDIOTICONS	IGNORANCES	ILLIBERALISES	ILLUMINATING	ILLUVIATES
IDLENESSES	IGNORANTLY	ILLIBERALISING	ILLUMINATINGLY	ILLUVIATING
IDOLATRESS	IGNORANTNESS	ILLIBERALISM	ILLUMINATION	ILLUVIATION
IDOLATRESSES	IGNORANTNESSES	ILLIBERALISMS	ILLUMINATIONAL	ILLUVIATIONS
IDOLATRIES	IGNORATION	ILLIBERALITIES	ILLUMINATIONS	IMAGINABLE
IDOLATRISE	IGNORATIONS	ILLIBERALITY	ILLUMINATIVE	IMAGINABLENESS
IDOLATRISED	IGUANODONS	ILLIBERALIZE	ILLUMINATO	IMAGINABLY
IDOLATRISER	ILEOSTOMIES	ILLIBERALIZED	ILLUMINATOR	IMAGINARIES
IDOLATRISERS	ILLAQUEABLE	ILLIBERALIZES	ILLUMINATORS	IMAGINARILY
IDOLATRISES	ILLAQUEATE	ILLIBERALIZING	ILLUMINERS	IMAGINARINESS
IDOLATRISING	ILLAQUEATED	ILLIBERALLY	ILLUMINING	IMAGINARINESSES
IDOLATRIZE	ILLAQUEATES	ILLIBERALNESS	ILLUMINISM	IMAGINATION
IDOLATRIZED	ILLAQUEATING	ILLIBERALNESSES	ILLUMINISMS	IMAGINATIONAL
IDOLATRIZER	ILLAQUEATION	ILLICITNESS	ILLUMINIST	IMAGINATIONS
IDOLATRIZERS	ILLAQUEATIONS	ILLICITNESSES	ILLUMINISTS	IMAGINATIVE
IDOLATRIZES	ILLATIVELY	ILLIMITABILITY	ILLUSIONAL	IMAGINATIVELY
IDOLATRIZING	ILLAUDABLE	ILLIMITABLE	ILLUSIONARY	IMAGINATIVENESS
IDOLATROUS	ILLAUDABLY	ILLIMITABLENESS	ILLUSIONED	IMAGINEERED
IDOLATROUSLY	ILLAWARRAS	ILLIMITABLY	ILLUSIONISM	IMAGINEERING
IDOLATROUSNESS	ILLEGALISATION	ILLIMITATION	ILLUSIONISMS	IMAGINEERS
IDOLISATION	ILLEGALISATIONS	ILLIMITATIONS	ILLUSIONIST	IMAGININGS
IDOLISATIONS	ILLEGALISE	ILLIQUATION	ILLUSIONISTIC	IMAGINISTS
IDOLIZATION	ILLEGALISED	ILLIQUATIONS	ILLUSIONISTS	IMAGISTICALLY
IDOLIZATIONS	ILLEGALISES	ILLIQUIDITIES	ILLUSIVELY	IMBALANCED
IDOLOCLAST	ILLEGALISING	ILLIQUIDITY	ILLUSIVENESS	IMBALANCES
IDOLOCLASTS	ILLEGALITIES	ILLITERACIES	ILLUSIVENESSES	IMBECILELY
IDONEITIES	ILLEGALITY	ILLITERACY	ILLUSORILY	IMBECILICALLY
IDOXURIDINE	ILLEGALIZATION	ILLITERATE	ILLUSORINESS	IMBECILITIES
IDOXURIDINES	ILLEGALIZATIONS	ILLITERATELY	ILLUSORINESSES	IMBECILITY
IDYLLICALLY	ILLEGALIZE	ILLITERATENESS	ILLUSTRATABLE	IMBIBITION
IFFINESSES	ILLEGALIZED	ILLITERATES	ILLUSTRATE	IMBIBITIONAL
IGNESCENTS	ILLEGALIZES	ILLOCUTION	ILLUSTRATED	IMBIBITIONS
IGNIMBRITE	ILLEGALIZING	ILLOCUTIONARY	ILLUSTRATEDS	IMBITTERED
IGNIMBRITES	ILLEGIBILITIES	ILLOCUTIONS	ILLUSTRATES	IMBITTERING
IGNIPOTENT	ILLEGIBILITY	ILLOGICALITIES	ILLUSTRATING	IMBOLDENED
IGNITABILITIES	ILLEGIBLENESS	ILLOGICALITY	ILLUSTRATION	IMBOLDENING
IGNITABILITY	ILLEGIBLENESSES	ILLOGICALLY	ILLUSTRATIONAL	IMBORDERED

IMBORDERING	IMMANENTISMS	IMMENSENESSES	IMMISERIZATIONS	IMMORALISM
IMBOSOMING	IMMANENTIST	IMMENSITIES	IMMISERIZE	IMMORALISMS
IMBOWERING	IMMANENTISTIC	IMMENSURABILITY	IMMISERIZED	IMMORALIST
IMBRANGLED	IMMANENTISTS	IMMENSURABLE	IMMISERIZES	IMMORALISTS
IMBRANGLES	IMMANENTLY	IMMERGENCE	IMMISERIZING	IMMORALITIES
IMBRANGLING	IMMANITIES	IMMERGENCES	IMMISSIONS	IMMORALITY
IMBRICATED	IMMANTLING	IMMERITOUS	IMMITIGABILITY	IMMORTALISATION
IMBRICATELY	IMMARCESCIBLE	IMMERSIBLE	IMMITIGABLE	IMMORTALISE
IMBRICATES	IMMARGINATE	IMMERSIONISM	IMMITIGABLY	IMMORTALISED
IMBRICATING	IMMATERIAL	IMMERSIONISMS	IMMITTANCE	IMMORTALISER
IMBRICATION	IMMATERIALISE	IMMERSIONIST	IMMITTANCES	IMMORTALISERS
IMBRICATIONS	IMMATERIALISED	IMMERSIONISTS	IMMIXTURES	IMMORTALISES
IMBROCCATA	IMMATERIALISES	IMMERSIONS	IMMOBILISATION	IMMORTALISING
IMBROCCATAS	IMMATERIALISING	IMMETHODICAL	IMMOBILISATIONS	IMMORTALITIES
IMBROGLIOS	IMMATERIALISM	IMMETHODICALLY	IMMOBILISE	IMMORTALITY
IMBROWNING	IMMATERIALISMS	IMMIGRANCIES	IMMOBILISED	IMMORTALIZATION
IMBRUEMENT	IMMATERIALIST	IMMIGRANCY	IMMOBILISER	IMMORTALIZE
IMBRUEMENTS	IMMATERIALISTS	IMMIGRANTS	IMMOBILISERS	IMMORTALIZED
IMBUEMENTS	IMMATERIALITIES	IMMIGRATED	IMMOBILISES	IMMORTALIZER
IMIDAZOLES	IMMATERIALITY	IMMIGRATES	IMMOBILISING	IMMORTALIZERS
IMINAZOLES	IMMATERIALIZE	IMMIGRATING	IMMOBILISM	IMMORTALIZES
IMINOUREAS	IMMATERIALIZED	IMMIGRATION	IMMOBILISMS	IMMORTALIZING
IMIPRAMINE	IMMATERIALIZES	IMMIGRATIONAL	IMMOBILITIES	IMMORTALLY
IMIPRAMINES	IMMATERIALIZING	IMMIGRATIONS	IMMOBILITY	IMMORTELLE
IMITABILITIES	IMMATERIALLY	IMMIGRATOR	IMMOBILIZATION	IMMORTELLES
IMITABILITY	IMMATERIALNESS	IMMIGRATORS	IMMOBILIZATIONS	IMMOTILITIES
IMITABLENESS	IMMATURELY	IMMIGRATORY	IMMOBILIZE	IMMOTILITY
IMITABLENESSES	IMMATURENESS	IMMINENCES	IMMOBILIZED	IMMOVABILITIES
IMITANCIES	IMMATURENESSES	IMMINENCIES	IMMOBILIZER	IMMOVABILITY
IMITATIONAL	IMMATUREST	IMMINENTLY	IMMOBILIZERS	IMMOVABLENESS
IMITATIONS	IMMATURITIES	IMMINENTNESS	IMMOBILIZES	IMMOVABLENESSES
IMITATIVELY	IMMATURITY	IMMINENTNESSES	IMMOBILIZING	IMMOVABLES
IMITATIVENESS	IMMEASURABILITY	IMMINGLING	IMMODERACIES	IMMOVEABILITIES
IMITATIVENESSES	IMMEASURABLE	IMMINUTION	IMMODERACY	IMMOVEABILITY
IMMACULACIES	IMMEASURABLY	IMMINUTIONS	IMMODERATE	IMMOVEABLE
IMMACULACY	IMMEASURED	IMMISCIBILITIES	IMMODERATELY	IMMOVEABLENESS
IMMACULATE	IMMEDIACIES	IMMISCIBILITY	IMMODERATENESS	IMMOVEABLES
IMMACULATELY	IMMEDIATELY	IMMISCIBLE	IMMODERATION	IMMOVEABLY
IMMACULATENESS	IMMEDIATENESS	IMMISCIBLY	IMMODERATIONS	IMMUNIFACIENT
IMMANACLED	IMMEDIATENESSES	IMMISERATION	IMMODESTER	IMMUNISATION
IMMANACLES	IMMEDIATISM	IMMISERATIONS	IMMODESTEST	IMMUNISATIONS
IMMANACLING	IMMEDIATISMS	IMMISERISATION	IMMODESTIES	IMMUNISERS
IMMANATION	IMMEDICABLE	IMMISERISATIONS	IMMODESTLY	IMMUNISING
IMMANATIONS	IMMEDICABLENESS	IMMISERISE	IMMOLATING	IMMUNITIES
IMMANENCES	IMMEDICABLY	IMMISERISED	IMMOLATION	IMMUNIZATION
IMMANENCIES	IMMEMORIAL	IMMISERISES	IMMOLATIONS	IMMUNIZATIONS
IMMANENTAL	IMMEMORIALLY	IMMISERISING	IMMOLATORS	IMMUNIZERS
IMMANENTISM	IMMENSENESS	IMMISERIZATION	IMMOMENTOUS	IMMUNIZING

IMMUNOASSAY	IMMUNOSUPPRESS	IMPARTABLE	IMPECCABILITY	IMPERATORSHIP
IMMUNOASSAYABLE	IMMUNOTHERAPIES	IMPARTATION	IMPECCABLE	IMPERATORSHIPS
IMMUNOASSAYIST	IMMUNOTHERAPY	IMPARTATIONS	IMPECCABLY	IMPERCEABLE
IMMUNOASSAYISTS	IMMUNOTOXIC	IMPARTIALITIES	IMPECCANCIES	IMPERCEIVABLE
IMMUNOASSAYS	IMMUNOTOXIN	IMPARTIALITY	IMPECCANCY	IMPERCEPTIBLE
IMMUNOBLOT	IMMUNOTOXINS	IMPARTIALLY	IMPECUNIOSITIES	IMPERCEPTIBLY
IMMUNOBLOTS	IMMUREMENT	IMPARTIALNESS	IMPECUNIOSITY	IMPERCEPTION
IMMUNOBLOTTING	IMMUREMENTS	IMPARTIALNESSES	IMPECUNIOUS	IMPERCEPTIONS
IMMUNOBLOTTINGS	IMMUTABILITIES	IMPARTIBILITIES	IMPECUNIOUSLY	IMPERCEPTIVE
IMMUNOCHEMICAL	IMMUTABILITY	IMPARTIBILITY	IMPECUNIOUSNESS	IMPERCEPTIVELY
IMMUNOCHEMIST	IMMUTABLENESS	IMPARTIBLE	IMPEDANCES	IMPERCEPTIVITY
IMMUNOCHEMISTRY	IMMUTABLENESSES	IMPARTIBLY	IMPEDIMENT	IMPERCIPIENCE
IMMUNOCHEMISTS	IMPACTIONS	IMPARTMENT	IMPEDIMENTA	IMPERCIPIENCES
IMMUNOCOMPETENT	IMPACTITES	IMPARTMENTS	IMPEDIMENTAL	IMPERCIPIENT
IMMUNOCOMPLEX	IMPAINTING	IMPASSABILITIES	IMPEDIMENTARY	IMPERCIPIENTLY
IMMUNOCOMPLEXES	IMPAIRABLE	IMPASSABILITY	IMPEDIMENTS	IMPERFECTER
IMMUNODEFICIENT	IMPAIRINGS	IMPASSABLE	IMPEDINGLY	IMPERFECTEST
IMMUNODIAGNOSES	IMPAIRMENT	IMPASSABLENESS	IMPEDITIVE	IMPERFECTIBLE
IMMUNODIAGNOSIS	IMPAIRMENTS	IMPASSABLY	IMPELLENTS	IMPERFECTION
IMMUNODIFFUSION	IMPALEMENT	IMPASSIBILITIES	IMPENDENCE	IMPERFECTIONS
IMMUNOGENESES	IMPALEMENTS	IMPASSIBILITY	IMPENDENCES	IMPERFECTIVE
IMMUNOGENESIS	IMPALPABILITIES	IMPASSIBLE	IMPENDENCIES	IMPERFECTIVELY
IMMUNOGENETIC	IMPALPABILITY	IMPASSIBLENESS	IMPENDENCY	IMPERFECTIVES
IMMUNOGENETICAL	IMPALPABLE	IMPASSIBLY	IMPENETRABILITY	IMPERFECTLY
IMMUNOGENETICS	IMPALPABLY	IMPASSIONATE	IMPENETRABLE	IMPERFECTNESS
IMMUNOGENIC	IMPALUDISM	IMPASSIONED	IMPENETRABLY	IMPERFECTNESSES
IMMUNOGENICALLY	IMPALUDISMS	IMPASSIONEDLY	IMPENETRATE	IMPERFECTS
IMMUNOGENICITY	IMPANATION	IMPASSIONEDNESS	IMPENETRATED	IMPERFORABLE
IMMUNOGENS	IMPANATIONS	IMPASSIONING	IMPENETRATES	IMPERFORATE
IMMUNOGLOBULIN	IMPANELING	IMPASSIONS	IMPENETRATING	IMPERFORATED
IMMUNOGLOBULINS	IMPANELLED	IMPASSIVELY	IMPENETRATION	IMPERFORATION
IMMUNOLOGIC	IMPANELLING	IMPASSIVENESS	IMPENETRATIONS	IMPERFORATIONS
IMMUNOLOGICAL	IMPANELMENT	IMPASSIVENESSES	IMPENITENCE	IMPERIALISE
IMMUNOLOGICALLY	IMPANELMENTS	IMPASSIVITIES	IMPENITENCES	IMPERIALISED
IMMUNOLOGIES	IMPANNELLED	IMPASSIVITY	IMPENITENCIES	IMPERIALISES
IMMUNOLOGIST	IMPANNELLING	IMPASTATION	IMPENITENCY	IMPERIALISING
IMMUNOLOGISTS	IMPARADISE	IMPASTATIONS	IMPENITENT	IMPERIALISM
IMMUNOLOGY	IMPARADISED	IMPATIENCE	IMPENITENTLY	IMPERIALISMS
IMMUNOMODULATOR	IMPARADISES	IMPATIENCES	IMPENITENTNESS	IMPERIALIST
IMMUNOPATHOLOGY	IMPARADISING	IMPATIENTLY	IMPENITENTS	IMPERIALISTIC
IMMUNOPHORESES	IMPARIDIGITATE	IMPEACHABILITY	IMPERATIVAL	IMPERIALISTS
IMMUNOPHORESIS	IMPARIPINNATE	IMPEACHABLE	IMPERATIVE	IMPERIALITIES
IMMUNOREACTION	IMPARISYLLABIC	IMPEACHERS	IMPERATIVELY	IMPERIALITY
IMMUNOREACTIONS	IMPARITIES	IMPEACHING	IMPERATIVENESS	IMPERIALIZE
IMMUNOREACTIVE	IMPARKATION	IMPEACHMENT	IMPERATIVES	IMPERIALIZED
IMMUNOSORBENT	IMPARKATIONS	IMPEACHMENTS	IMPERATORIAL	IMPERIALIZES
IMMUNOSORBENTS	IMPARLANCE	IMPEARLING	IMPERATORIALLY	IMPERIALIZING
IMMUNOSTIMULANT	IMPARLANCES	IMPECCABILITIES	IMPERATORS	IMPERIALLY

IMPERIALNESS	IMPERSONATORS	IMPISHNESS	IMPLICITIES	IMPORTUNATE
IMPERIALNESSES	IMPERTINENCE	IMPISHNESSES	IMPLICITLY	IMPORTUNATELY
IMPERILING	IMPERTINENCES	IMPLACABILITIES	IMPLICITNESS	IMPORTUNATENESS
IMPERILLED	IMPERTINENCIES	IMPLACABILITY	IMPLICITNESSES	IMPORTUNED
IMPERILLING	IMPERTINENCY	IMPLACABLE	IMPLODENTS	IMPORTUNELY
IMPERILMENT	IMPERTINENT	IMPLACABLENESS	IMPLORATION	IMPORTUNER
IMPERILMENTS	IMPERTINENTLY	IMPLACABLY	IMPLORATIONS	IMPORTUNERS
IMPERIOUSLY	IMPERTURBABLE	IMPLACENTAL	IMPLORATOR	IMPORTUNES
IMPERIOUSNESS	IMPERTURBABLY	IMPLANTABLE	IMPLORATORS	IMPORTUNING
IMPERIOUSNESSES	IMPERTURBATION	IMPLANTATION	IMPLORATORY	IMPORTUNINGS
IMPERISHABILITY	IMPERTURBATIONS	IMPLANTATIONS	IMPLORINGLY	IMPORTUNITIES
IMPERISHABLE	IMPERVIABILITY	IMPLANTERS	IMPLOSIONS	IMPORTUNITY
IMPERISHABLES	IMPERVIABLE	IMPLANTING	IMPLOSIVELY	IMPOSINGLY
IMPERISHABLY	IMPERVIABLENESS	IMPLAUSIBILITY	IMPLOSIVES	IMPOSINGNESS
IMPERMANENCE	IMPERVIOUS	IMPLAUSIBLE	IMPLUNGING	IMPOSINGNESSES
IMPERMANENCES	IMPERVIOUSLY	IMPLAUSIBLENESS	IMPOCKETED	IMPOSITION
IMPERMANENCIES	IMPERVIOUSNESS	IMPLAUSIBLY	IMPOCKETING	IMPOSITIONS
IMPERMANENCY	IMPETICOSSED	IMPLEACHED	IMPOLDERED	IMPOSSIBILISM
IMPERMANENT	IMPETICOSSES	IMPLEACHES	IMPOLDERING	IMPOSSIBILISMS
IMPERMANENTLY	IMPETICOSSING	IMPLEACHING	IMPOLICIES	IMPOSSIBILIST
IMPERMEABILITY	IMPETIGINES	IMPLEADABLE	IMPOLITELY	IMPOSSIBILISTS
IMPERMEABLE	IMPETIGINOUS	IMPLEADERS	IMPOLITENESS	IMPOSSIBILITIES
IMPERMEABLENESS	IMPETRATED	IMPLEADING	IMPOLITENESSES	IMPOSSIBILITY
IMPERMEABLY	IMPETRATES	IMPLEDGING	IMPOLITEST	IMPOSSIBLE
IMPERMISSIBLE	IMPETRATING	IMPLEMENTAL	IMPOLITICAL	IMPOSSIBLENESS
IMPERMISSIBLY	IMPETRATION	IMPLEMENTATION	IMPOLITICALLY	IMPOSSIBLES
IMPERSCRIPTIBLE	IMPETRATIONS	IMPLEMENTATIONS	IMPOLITICLY	IMPOSSIBLY
IMPERSEVERANT	IMPETRATIVE	IMPLEMENTED	IMPOLITICNESS	IMPOSTHUMATE
IMPERSISTENT	IMPETRATOR	IMPLEMENTER	IMPOLITICNESSES	IMPOSTHUMATED
IMPERSONAL	IMPETRATORS	IMPLEMENTERS	IMPONDERABILIA	IMPOSTHUMATES
IMPERSONALISE	IMPETRATORY	IMPLEMENTING	IMPONDERABILITY	IMPOSTHUMATING
IMPERSONALISED	IMPETUOSITIES	IMPLEMENTOR	IMPONDERABLE	IMPOSTHUMATION
IMPERSONALISES	IMPETUOSITY	IMPLEMENTORS	IMPONDERABLES	IMPOSTHUMATIONS
IMPERSONALISING	IMPETUOUSLY	IMPLEMENTS	IMPONDERABLY	IMPOSTHUME
IMPERSONALITIES	IMPETUOUSNESS	IMPLETIONS	IMPONDEROUS	IMPOSTHUMED
IMPERSONALITY	IMPETUOUSNESSES	IMPLEXIONS	IMPORTABILITIES	IMPOSTHUMES
IMPERSONALIZE	IMPICTURED	IMPLEXUOUS	IMPORTABILITY	IMPOSTOROUS
IMPERSONALIZED	IMPIERCEABLE	IMPLICATED	IMPORTABLE	IMPOSTROUS
IMPERSONALIZES	IMPIGNORATE	IMPLICATES	IMPORTANCE	IMPOSTUMATE
IMPERSONALIZING	IMPIGNORATED	IMPLICATING	IMPORTANCES	IMPOSTUMATED
IMPERSONALLY	IMPIGNORATES	IMPLICATION	IMPORTANCIES	IMPOSTUMATES
IMPERSONATE	IMPIGNORATING	IMPLICATIONAL	IMPORTANCY	IMPOSTUMATING
IMPERSONATED	IMPIGNORATION	IMPLICATIONS	IMPORTANTLY	IMPOSTUMATION
IMPERSONATES	IMPIGNORATIONS	IMPLICATIVE	IMPORTATION	IMPOSTUMATIONS
IMPERSONATING	IMPINGEMENT	IMPLICATIVELY	IMPORTATIONS	IMPOSTUMED
IMPERSONATION	IMPINGEMENTS	IMPLICATIVENESS	IMPORTINGS	IMPOSTUMES
IMPERSONATIONS	IMPIOUSNESS	IMPLICATURE	IMPORTUNACIES	IMPOSTURES
IMPERSONATOR	IMPIOUSNESSES	IMPLICATURES	IMPORTUNACY	IMPOSTUROUS

IMPOTENCES	IMPREGNATES	IMPROBABLY	IMPROVISATRIX	IMPUTATIONS
IMPOTENCIES	IMPREGNATING	IMPROBATION	IMPROVISATRIXES	IMPUTATIVE
IMPOTENTLY	IMPREGNATION	IMPROBATIONS	IMPROVISED	IMPUTATIVELY
IMPOTENTNESS	IMPREGNATIONS	IMPROBITIES	IMPROVISER	INABILITIES
IMPOTENTNESSES	IMPREGNATOR	IMPROMPTUS	IMPROVISERS	INABSTINENCE
IMPOUNDABLE	IMPREGNATORS	IMPROPERER	IMPROVISES	INABSTINENCES
IMPOUNDAGE	IMPREGNING	IMPROPEREST	IMPROVISING	INACCESSIBILITY
IMPOUNDAGES	IMPRESARIO	IMPROPERLY	IMPROVISOR	INACCESSIBLE
IMPOUNDERS	IMPRESARIOS	IMPROPERNESS	IMPROVISORS	INACCESSIBLY
IMPOUNDING	IMPRESCRIPTIBLE	IMPROPERNESSES	IMPROVVISATORE	INACCURACIES
IMPOUNDMENT	IMPRESCRIPTIBLY	IMPROPRIATE	IMPROVVISATORES	INACCURACY
IMPOUNDMENTS	IMPRESSERS	IMPROPRIATED	IMPROVVISATRICE	INACCURATE
IMPOVERISH	IMPRESSIBILITY	IMPROPRIATES	IMPRUDENCE	INACCURATELY
IMPOVERISHED	IMPRESSIBLE	IMPROPRIATING	IMPRUDENCES	INACCURATENESS
IMPOVERISHER	IMPRESSING	IMPROPRIATION	IMPRUDENTLY	INACTIVATE
IMPOVERISHERS	IMPRESSION	IMPROPRIATIONS	IMPSONITES	INACTIVATED
IMPOVERISHES	IMPRESSIONABLE	IMPROPRIATOR	IMPUDENCES	INACTIVATES
IMPOVERISHING	IMPRESSIONAL	IMPROPRIATORS	IMPUDENCIES	INACTIVATING
IMPOVERISHMENT	IMPRESSIONALLY	IMPROPRIETIES	IMPUDENTLY	INACTIVATION
IMPOVERISHMENTS	IMPRESSIONISM	IMPROPRIETY	IMPUDENTNESS	INACTIVATIONS
IMPOWERING	IMPRESSIONISMS	IMPROVABILITIES	IMPUDENTNESSES	INACTIVELY
IMPRACTICABLE	IMPRESSIONIST	IMPROVABILITY	IMPUDICITIES	INACTIVENESS
IMPRACTICABLY	IMPRESSIONISTIC	IMPROVABLE	IMPUDICITY	INACTIVENESSES
IMPRACTICAL	IMPRESSIONISTS	IMPROVABLENESS	IMPUGNABLE	INACTIVITIES
IMPRACTICALITY	IMPRESSIONS	IMPROVABLY	IMPUGNATION	INACTIVITY
IMPRACTICALLY	IMPRESSIVE	IMPROVEMENT	IMPUGNATIONS	INADAPTABLE
IMPRACTICALNESS	IMPRESSIVELY	IMPROVEMENTS	IMPUGNMENT	INADAPTATION
IMPRECATED	IMPRESSIVENESS	IMPROVIDENCE	IMPUGNMENTS	INADAPTATIONS
IMPRECATES	IMPRESSMENT	IMPROVIDENCES	IMPUISSANCE	INADAPTIVE
IMPRECATING	IMPRESSMENTS	IMPROVIDENT	IMPUISSANCES	INADEQUACIES
IMPRECATION	IMPRESSURE	IMPROVIDENTLY	IMPUISSANT	INADEQUACY
IMPRECATIONS	IMPRESSURES	IMPROVINGLY	IMPULSIONS	INADEQUATE
IMPRECATORY	IMPRIMATUR	IMPROVISATE	IMPULSIVELY	INADEQUATELY
IMPRECISELY	IMPRIMATURS	IMPROVISATED	IMPULSIVENESS	INADEQUATENESS
IMPRECISENESS	IMPRINTERS	IMPROVISATES	IMPULSIVENESSES	INADEQUATES
IMPRECISENESSES	IMPRINTING	IMPROVISATING	IMPULSIVITIES	INADMISSIBILITY
IMPRECISION	IMPRINTINGS	IMPROVISATION	IMPULSIVITY	INADMISSIBLE
IMPRECISIONS	IMPRISONABLE	IMPROVISATIONAL	IMPUNDULUS	INADMISSIBLY
IMPREDICATIVE	IMPRISONED	IMPROVISATIONS	IMPUNITIES	INADVERTENCE
IMPREGNABILITY	IMPRISONER	IMPROVISATOR	IMPURENESS	INADVERTENCES
IMPREGNABLE	IMPRISONERS	IMPROVISATORE	IMPURENESSES	INADVERTENCIES
IMPREGNABLENESS	IMPRISONING	IMPROVISATORES	IMPURITIES	INADVERTENCY
IMPREGNABLY	IMPRISONMENT	IMPROVISATORI	IMPURPLING	INADVERTENT
IMPREGNANT	IMPRISONMENTS	IMPROVISATORIAL	IMPUTABILITIES	INADVERTENTLY
IMPREGNANTS	IMPROBABILITIES	IMPROVISATORS	IMPUTABILITY	INADVISABILITY
IMPREGNATABLE	IMPROBABILITY	IMPROVISATORY	IMPUTABLENESS	INADVISABLE
IMPREGNATE	IMPROBABLE	IMPROVISATRICE	IMPUTABLENESSES	INADVISABLENESS
IMPREGNATED	IMPROBABLENESS	IMPROVISATRICES	IMPUTATION	INADVISABLY

INALIENABILITY	INARGUABLE	INCALCULABLE	INCARCERATING	INCENTIVISATION
INALIENABLE	INARGUABLY	INCALCULABLY	INCARCERATION	INCENTIVISE
INALIENABLENESS	INARTICULACIES	INCALESCENCE	INCARCERATIONS	INCENTIVISED
INALIENABLY	INARTICULACY	INCALESCENCES	INCARCERATOR	INCENTIVISES
INALTERABILITY	INARTICULATE	INCALESCENT	INCARCERATORS	INCENTIVISING
INALTERABLE	INARTICULATELY	INCANDESCE	INCARDINATE	INCENTIVIZATION
INALTERABLENESS	INARTICULATES	INCANDESCED	INCARDINATED	INCENTIVIZE
INALTERABLY	INARTICULATION	INCANDESCENCE	INCARDINATES	INCENTIVIZED
INAMORATAS	INARTICULATIONS	INCANDESCENCES	INCARDINATING	INCENTIVIZES
INAMORATOS	INARTIFICIAL	INCANDESCENCIES	INCARDINATION	INCENTIVIZING
INANENESSES	INARTIFICIALLY	INCANDESCENCY	INCARDINATIONS	INCEPTIONS
INANIMATELY	INARTISTIC	INCANDESCENT	INCARNADINE	INCEPTIVELY
INANIMATENESS	INARTISTICALLY	INCANDESCENTLY	INCARNADINED	INCEPTIVES
INANIMATENESSES	INATTENTION	INCANDESCENTS	INCARNADINES	INCERTAINTIES
INANIMATION	INATTENTIONS	INCANDESCES	INCARNADINING	INCERTAINTY
INANIMATIONS	INATTENTIVE	INCANDESCING	INCARNATED	INCERTITUDE
INANITIONS	INATTENTIVELY	INCANTATION	INCARNATES	INCERTITUDES
INAPPARENT	INATTENTIVENESS	INCANTATIONAL	INCARNATING	INCESSANCIES
INAPPARENTLY	INAUDIBILITIES	INCANTATIONS	INCARNATION	INCESSANCY
INAPPEASABLE	INAUDIBILITY	INCANTATOR	INCARNATIONS	INCESSANTLY
INAPPELLABLE	INAUDIBLENESS	INCANTATORS	INCARVILLEA	INCESSANTNESS
INAPPETENCE	INAUDIBLENESSES	INCANTATORY	INCARVILLEAS	INCESSANTNESSES
INAPPETENCES	INAUGURALS	INCAPABILITIES	INCASEMENT	INCESTUOUS
INAPPETENCIES	INAUGURATE	INCAPABILITY	INCASEMENTS	INCESTUOUSLY
INAPPETENCY	INAUGURATED	INCAPABLENESS	INCATENATE	INCESTUOUSNESS
INAPPETENT	INAUGURATES	INCAPABLENESSES	INCATENATED	INCHARITABLE
INAPPLICABILITY	INAUGURATING	INCAPABLES	INCATENATES	INCHOATELY
INAPPLICABLE	INAUGURATION	INCAPACIOUS	INCATENATING	INCHOATENESS
INAPPLICABLY	INAUGURATIONS	INCAPACIOUSNESS	INCATENATION	INCHOATENESSES
INAPPOSITE	INAUGURATOR	INCAPACITANT	INCATENATIONS	INCHOATING
INAPPOSITELY	INAUGURATORS	INCAPACITANTS	INCAUTIONS	INCHOATION
INAPPOSITENESS	INAUGURATORY	INCAPACITATE	INCAUTIOUS	INCHOATIONS
INAPPRECIABLE	INAURATING	INCAPACITATED	INCAUTIOUSLY	INCHOATIVE
INAPPRECIABLY	INAUSPICIOUS	INCAPACITATES	INCAUTIOUSNESS	INCHOATIVELY
INAPPRECIATION	INAUSPICIOUSLY	INCAPACITATING	INCEDINGLY	INCHOATIVES
INAPPRECIATIONS	INAUTHENTIC	INCAPACITATION	INCENDIARIES	INCIDENCES
INAPPRECIATIVE	INAUTHENTICITY	INCAPACITATIONS	INCENDIARISM	INCIDENTAL
INAPPREHENSIBLE	INBOUNDING	INCAPACITIES	INCENDIARISMS	INCIDENTALLY
INAPPREHENSION	INBREATHED	INCAPACITY	INCENDIARY	INCIDENTALNESS
INAPPREHENSIONS	INBREATHES	INCAPSULATE	INCENDIVITIES	INCIDENTALS
INAPPREHENSIVE	INBREATHING	INCAPSULATED	INCENDIVITY	INCINERATE
INAPPROACHABLE	INBREEDERS	INCAPSULATES	INCENSATION	INCINERATED
INAPPROACHABLY	INBREEDING	INCAPSULATING	INCENSATIONS	INCINERATES
INAPPROPRIATE	INBREEDINGS	INCAPSULATION	INCENSEMENT	INCINERATING
INAPPROPRIATELY	INBRINGING	INCAPSULATIONS	INCENSEMENTS	INCINERATION
INAPTITUDE	INBRINGINGS	INCARCERATE	INCENSORIES	INCINERATIONS
INAPTITUDES	INBURSTING	INCARCERATED	INCENTIVELY	INCINERATOR
INAPTNESSES	INCALCULABILITY	INCARCERATES	INCENTIVES	INCINERATORS

INCIPIENCE

INCIPIENCE	INCLUSIVITY	INCOMPARABILITY	INCONDENSIBLE	INCONSTRUABLE
INCIPIENCES	INCOAGULABLE	INCOMPARABLE	INCONDITELY	INCONSUMABLE
INCIPIENCIES	INCOERCIBLE	INCOMPARABLY	INCONFORMITIES	INCONSUMABLY
INCIPIENCY	INCOGITABILITY	INCOMPARED	INCONFORMITY	INCONTESTABLE
INCIPIENTLY	INCOGITABLE	INCOMPATIBILITY	INCONGRUENCE	INCONTESTABLY
INCISIFORM	INCOGITANCIES	INCOMPATIBLE	INCONGRUENCES	INCONTIGUOUS
INCISIVELY	INCOGITANCY	INCOMPATIBLES	INCONGRUENT	INCONTIGUOUSLY
INCISIVENESS	INCOGITANT	INCOMPATIBLY	INCONGRUENTLY	INCONTINENCE
INCISIVENESSES	INCOGITATIVE	INCOMPETENCE	INCONGRUITIES	INCONTINENCES
INCISORIAL	INCOGNISABLE	INCOMPETENCES	INCONGRUITY	INCONTINENCIES
INCITATION	INCOGNISANCE	INCOMPETENCIES	INCONGRUOUS	INCONTINENCY
INCITATIONS	INCOGNISANCES	INCOMPETENCY	INCONGRUOUSLY	INCONTINENT
INCITATIVE	INCOGNISANT	INCOMPETENT	INCONGRUOUSNESS	INCONTINENTLY
INCITATIVES	INCOGNITAS	INCOMPETENTLY	INCONSCIENT	INCONTROLLABLE
INCITEMENT	INCOGNITOS	INCOMPETENTS	INCONSCIENTLY	INCONTROLLABLY
INCITEMENTS	INCOGNIZABLE	INCOMPLETE	INCONSCIONABLE	INCONVENIENCE
INCITINGLY	INCOGNIZANCE	INCOMPLETELY	INCONSCIOUS	INCONVENIENCED
INCIVILITIES	INCOGNIZANCES	INCOMPLETENESS	INCONSECUTIVE	INCONVENIENCES
INCIVILITY	INCOGNIZANT	INCOMPLETION	INCONSECUTIVELY	INCONVENIENCIES
INCLASPING	INCOHERENCE	INCOMPLETIONS	INCONSEQUENCE	INCONVENIENCING
INCLEMENCIES	INCOHERENCES	INCOMPLIANCE	INCONSEQUENCES	INCONVENIENCY
INCLEMENCY	INCOHERENCIES	INCOMPLIANCES	INCONSEQUENT	INCONVENIENT
INCLEMENTLY	INCOHERENCY	INCOMPLIANCIES	INCONSEQUENTIAL	INCONVENIENTLY
INCLEMENTNESS	INCOHERENT	INCOMPLIANCY	INCONSEQUENTLY	INCONVERSABLE
INCLEMENTNESSES	INCOHERENTLY	INCOMPLIANT	INCONSIDERABLE	INCONVERSANT
INCLINABLE	INCOHERENTNESS	INCOMPLIANTLY	INCONSIDERABLY	INCONVERTIBLE
INCLINABLENESS	INCOHESIVE	INCOMPOSED	INCONSIDERATE	INCONVERTIBLY
INCLINATION	INCOMBUSTIBLE	INCOMPOSITE	INCONSIDERATELY	INCONVINCIBLE
INCLINATIONAL	INCOMBUSTIBLES	INCOMPOSSIBLE	INCONSIDERATION	INCONVINCIBLY
INCLINATIONS	INCOMBUSTIBLY	INCOMPREHENSION	INCONSISTENCE	INCOORDINATE
INCLINATORIA	INCOMMENSURABLE	INCOMPREHENSIVE	INCONSISTENCES	INCOORDINATION
INCLINATORIUM	INCOMMENSURABLY	INCOMPRESSIBLE	INCONSISTENCIES	INCOORDINATIONS
INCLINATORY	INCOMMENSURATE	INCOMPRESSIBLY	INCONSISTENCY	INCORONATE
INCLININGS	INCOMMISCIBLE	INCOMPUTABILITY	INCONSISTENT	INCORONATED
INCLINOMETER	INCOMMODED	INCOMPUTABLE	INCONSISTENTLY	INCORONATION
INCLINOMETERS	INCOMMODES	INCOMPUTABLY	INCONSOLABILITY	INCORONATIONS
INCLIPPING	INCOMMODING	INCOMUNICADO	INCONSOLABLE	INCORPORABLE
INCLOSABLE	INCOMMODIOUS	INCONCEIVABLE	INCONSOLABLY	INCORPORAL
INCLOSURES	INCOMMODIOUSLY	INCONCEIVABLES	INCONSONANCE	INCORPORALL
INCLUDABLE	INCOMMODITIES	INCONCEIVABLY	INCONSONANCES	INCORPORATE
INCLUDEDNESS	INCOMMODITY	INCONCINNITIES	INCONSONANT	INCORPORATED
INCLUDEDNESSES	INCOMMUNICABLE	INCONCINNITY	INCONSONANTLY	INCORPORATES
INCLUDIBLE	INCOMMUNICABLY	INCONCINNOUS	INCONSPICUOUS	INCORPORATING
INCLUSIONS	INCOMMUNICADO	INCONCLUSION	INCONSPICUOUSLY	INCORPORATION
INCLUSIVELY	INCOMMUNICATIVE	INCONCLUSIONS	INCONSTANCIES	INCORPORATIONS
INCLUSIVENESS	INCOMMUTABILITY	INCONCLUSIVE	INCONSTANCY	INCORPORATIVE
INCLUSIVENESSES	INCOMMUTABLE	INCONCLUSIVELY	INCONSTANT	INCORPORATOR
INCLUSIVITIES	INCOMMUTABLY	INCONDENSABLE	INCONSTANTLY	INCORPORATORS

INCORPOREAL	INCREDULOUS	INCUBATORS	INCURIOUSNESS	INDEFEASIBLY
INCORPOREALITY	INCREDULOUSLY	INCUBATORY	INCURIOUSNESSES	INDEFECTIBILITY
INCORPOREALLY	INCREDULOUSNESS	INCULCATED	INCURRABLE	INDEFECTIBLE
INCORPOREITIES	INCREMATED	INCULCATES	INCURRENCE	INDEFECTIBLY
INCORPOREITY	INCREMATES	INCULCATING	INCURRENCES	INDEFENSIBILITY
INCORPSING	INCREMATING	INCULCATION	INCURSIONS	INDEFENSIBLE
INCORRECTLY	INCREMATION	INCULCATIONS	INCURVATED	INDEFENSIBLY
INCORRECTNESS	INCREMATIONS	INCULCATIVE	INCURVATES	INDEFINABILITY
INCORRECTNESSES	INCREMENTAL	INCULCATOR	INCURVATING	INDEFINABLE
INCORRIGIBILITY	INCREMENTALISM	INCULCATORS	INCURVATION	INDEFINABLENESS
INCORRIGIBLE	INCREMENTALISMS	INCULCATORY	INCURVATIONS	INDEFINABLES
INCORRIGIBLES	INCREMENTALIST	INCULPABILITIES	INCURVATURE	INDEFINABLY
INCORRIGIBLY	INCREMENTALISTS	INCULPABILITY	INCURVATURES	INDEFINITE
INCORRODIBLE	INCREMENTALLY	INCULPABLE	INCURVITIES	INDEFINITELY
INCORROSIBLE	INCREMENTALS	INCULPABLENESS	INDAGATING	INDEFINITENESS
INCORRUPTED	INCREMENTED	INCULPABLY	INDAGATION	INDEFINITES
INCORRUPTIBLE	INCREMENTING	INCULPATED	INDAGATIONS	INDEHISCENCE
INCORRUPTIBLES	INCREMENTS	INCULPATES	INDAGATIVE	INDEHISCENCES
INCORRUPTIBLY	INCRESCENT	INCULPATING	INDAGATORS	INDEHISCENT
INCORRUPTION	INCRETIONARY	INCULPATION	INDAGATORY	INDELIBILITIES
INCORRUPTIONS	INCRETIONS	INCULPATIONS	INDAPAMIDE	INDELIBILITY
INCORRUPTIVE	INCRIMINATE	INCULPATIVE	INDAPAMIDES	INDELIBLENESS
INCORRUPTLY	INCRIMINATED	INCULPATORY	INDEBTEDNESS	INDELIBLENESSES
INCORRUPTNESS	INCRIMINATES	INCUMBENCIES	INDEBTEDNESSES	INDELICACIES
INCORRUPTNESSES	INCRIMINATING	INCUMBENCY	INDECENCIES	INDELICACY
INCRASSATE	INCRIMINATION	INCUMBENTLY	INDECENTER	INDELICATE
INCRASSATED	INCRIMINATIONS	INCUMBENTS	INDECENTEST	INDELICATELY
INCRASSATES	INCRIMINATOR	INCUMBERED	INDECENTLY	INDELICATENESS
INCRASSATING	INCRIMINATORS	INCUMBERING	INDECIDUATE	INDEMNIFICATION
INCRASSATION	INCRIMINATORY	INCUMBERINGLY	INDECIDUOUS	INDEMNIFIED
INCRASSATIONS	INCROSSBRED	INCUMBRANCE	INDECIPHERABLE	INDEMNIFIER
INCRASSATIVE	INCROSSBREDS	INCUMBRANCER	INDECIPHERABLY	INDEMNIFIERS
INCRASSATIVES	INCROSSBREED	INCUMBRANCERS	INDECISION	INDEMNIFIES
INCREASABLE	INCROSSBREEDING	INCUMBRANCES	INDECISIONS	INDEMNIFYING
INCREASEDLY	INCROSSBREEDS	INCUNABLES	INDECISIVE	INDEMNITIES
INCREASEFUL	INCROSSING	INCUNABULA	INDECISIVELY	INDEMONSTRABLE
INCREASERS	INCRUSTANT	INCUNABULAR	INDECISIVENESS	INDEMONSTRABLY
INCREASING	INCRUSTANTS	INCUNABULIST	INDECLINABLE	INDENTATION
INCREASINGLY	INCRUSTATION	INCUNABULISTS	INDECLINABLY	INDENTATIONS
INCREASINGS	INCRUSTATIONS	INCUNABULUM	INDECOMPOSABLE	INDENTIONS
INCREATELY	INCRUSTING	INCURABILITIES	INDECOROUS	INDENTURED
INCREDIBILITIES	INCRUSTMENT	INCURABILITY	INDECOROUSLY	INDENTURES
INCREDIBILITY	INCRUSTMENTS	INCURABLENESS	INDECOROUSNESS	INDENTURESHIP
INCREDIBLE	INCUBATING	INCURABLENESSES	INDECORUMS	INDENTURESHIPS
INCREDIBLENESS	INCUBATION	INCURABLES	INDEFATIGABLE	INDENTURING
INCREDIBLY	INCUBATIONAL	INCURIOSITIES	INDEFATIGABLY	INDEPENDENCE
INCREDULITIES	INCUBATIONS	INCURIOSITY	INDEFEASIBILITY	INDEPENDENCES
INCREDULITY	INCUBATIVE	INCURIOUSLY	INDEFEASIBLE	INDEPENDENCIES

INDEPENDENCY	INDICTMENTS	INDIGNIFYING	INDISSOLUBLY	INDIVISIBILITY
INDEPENDENT	INDIFFERENCE	INDIGNITIES	INDISSOLVABLE	INDIVISIBLE
INDEPENDENTLY	INDIFFERENCES	INDIGOLITE	INDISSUADABLE	INDIVISIBLENESS
INDEPENDENTS	INDIFFERENCIES	INDIGOLITES	INDISSUADABLY	INDIVISIBLES
INDESCRIBABLE	INDIFFERENCY	INDIGOTINS	INDISTINCT	INDIVISIBLY
INDESCRIBABLES	INDIFFERENT	INDINAVIRS	INDISTINCTION	INDOCILITIES
INDESCRIBABLY	INDIFFERENTISM	INDIRECTION	INDISTINCTIONS	INDOCILITY
INDESIGNATE	INDIFFERENTISMS	INDIRECTIONS	INDISTINCTIVE	INDOCTRINATE
INDESTRUCTIBLE	INDIFFERENTIST	INDIRECTLY	INDISTINCTIVELY	INDOCTRINATED
INDESTRUCTIBLY	INDIFFERENTISTS	INDIRECTNESS	INDISTINCTLY	INDOCTRINATES
INDETECTABLE	INDIFFERENTLY	INDIRECTNESSES	INDISTINCTNESS	INDOCTRINATING
INDETECTIBLE	INDIFFERENTS	INDIRUBINS	INDISTRIBUTABLE	INDOCTRINATION
INDETERMINABLE	INDIGENCES	INDISCERNIBLE	INDITEMENT	INDOCTRINATIONS
INDETERMINABLY	INDIGENCIES	INDISCERNIBLY	INDITEMENTS	INDOCTRINATOR
INDETERMINACIES	INDIGENISATION	INDISCERPTIBLE	INDIVERTIBLE	INDOCTRINATORS
INDETERMINACY	INDIGENISATIONS	INDISCIPLINABLE	INDIVERTIBLY	INDOLEACETIC
INDETERMINATE	INDIGENISE	INDISCIPLINE	INDIVIDABLE	INDOLEBUTYRIC
INDETERMINATELY	INDIGENISED	INDISCIPLINED	INDIVIDUAL	INDOLENCES
INDETERMINATION	INDIGENISES	INDISCIPLINES	INDIVIDUALISE	INDOLENCIES
INDETERMINED	INDIGENISING	INDISCOVERABLE	INDIVIDUALISED	INDOLENTLY
INDETERMINISM	INDIGENITIES	INDISCREET	INDIVIDUALISER	INDOMETACIN
INDETERMINISMS	INDIGENITY	INDISCREETER	INDIVIDUALISERS	INDOMETACINS
INDETERMINIST	INDIGENIZATION	INDISCREETEST	INDIVIDUALISES	INDOMETHACIN
INDETERMINISTIC	INDIGENIZATIONS	INDISCREETLY	INDIVIDUALISING	INDOMETHACINS
INDETERMINISTS	INDIGENIZE	INDISCREETNESS	INDIVIDUALISM	INDOMITABILITY
INDEXATION	INDIGENIZED	INDISCRETE	INDIVIDUALISMS	INDOMITABLE
INDEXATIONS	INDIGENIZES	INDISCRETELY	INDIVIDUALIST	INDOMITABLENESS
INDEXICALS	INDIGENIZING	INDISCRETENESS	INDIVIDUALISTIC	INDOMITABLY
INDEXTERITIES	INDIGENOUS	INDISCRETION	INDIVIDUALISTS	INDOPHENOL
INDEXTERITY	INDIGENOUSLY	INDISCRETIONARY	INDIVIDUALITIES	INDOPHENOLS
INDEXTROUS	INDIGENOUSNESS	INDISCRETIONS	INDIVIDUALITY	INDORSABLE
INDICATABLE	INDIGENTLY	INDISCRIMINATE	INDIVIDUALIZE	INDORSATION
INDICATING	INDIGESTED	INDISPENSABLE	INDIVIDUALIZED	INDORSATIONS
INDICATION	INDIGESTIBILITY	INDISPENSABLES	INDIVIDUALIZER	INDORSEMENT
INDICATIONAL	INDIGESTIBLE	INDISPENSABLY	INDIVIDUALIZERS	INDORSEMENTS
INDICATIONS	INDIGESTIBLES	INDISPOSED	INDIVIDUALIZES	INDRAUGHTS
INDICATIVE	INDIGESTIBLY	INDISPOSEDNESS	INDIVIDUALIZING	INDRENCHED
INDICATIVELY	INDIGESTING	INDISPOSES	INDIVIDUALLY	INDRENCHES
INDICATIVES	INDIGESTION	INDISPOSING	INDIVIDUALS	INDRENCHING
INDICATORS	INDIGESTIONS	INDISPOSITION	INDIVIDUATE	INDUBITABILITY
INDICATORY	INDIGESTIVE	INDISPOSITIONS	INDIVIDUATED	INDUBITABLE
INDICOLITE	INDIGNANCE	INDISPUTABILITY	INDIVIDUATES	INDUBITABLENESS
INDICOLITES	INDIGNANCES	INDISPUTABLE	INDIVIDUATING	INDUBITABLY
INDICTABLE	INDIGNANTLY	INDISPUTABLY	INDIVIDUATION	INDUCEMENT
INDICTABLY	INDIGNATION	INDISSOCIABLE	INDIVIDUATIONS	INDUCEMENTS
INDICTIONAL	INDIGNATIONS	INDISSOCIABLY	INDIVIDUATOR	INDUCIBILITIES
INDICTIONS	INDIGNIFIED	INDISSOLUBILITY	INDIVIDUATORS	INDUCIBILITY
INDICTMENT	INDIGNIFIES	INDISSOLUBLE	INDIVIDUUM	INDUCTANCE

INDUCTANCES	INDWELLERS	INELASTICALLY	INERRABILITY	INEXORABILITY
INDUCTILITIES	INDWELLING	INELASTICITIES	INERRABLENESS	INEXORABLE
INDUCTILITY	INDWELLINGS	INELASTICITY	INERRABLENESSES	INEXORABLENESS
INDUCTIONAL	INEARTHING	INELEGANCE	INERRANCIES	INEXORABLY
INDUCTIONS	INEBRIANTS	INELEGANCES	INERTIALLY	INEXPANSIBLE
INDUCTIVELY	INEBRIATED	INELEGANCIES	INERTNESSES	INEXPECTANCIES
INDUCTIVENESS	INEBRIATES	INELEGANCY	INESCAPABLE	INEXPECTANCY
INDUCTIVENESSES	INEBRIATING	INELEGANTLY	INESCAPABLY	INEXPECTANT
INDUCTIVITIES	INEBRIATION	INELIGIBILITIES	INESCULENT	INEXPECTATION
INDUCTIVITY	INEBRIATIONS	INELIGIBILITY	INESCUTCHEON	INEXPECTATIONS
INDULGENCE	INEBRIETIES	INELIGIBLE	INESCUTCHEONS	INEXPEDIENCE
INDULGENCED	INEDIBILITIES	INELIGIBLENESS	INESSENTIAL	INEXPEDIENCES
INDULGENCES	INEDIBILITY	INELIGIBLES	INESSENTIALITY	INEXPEDIENCIES
INDULGENCIES	INEDUCABILITIES	INELIGIBLY	INESSENTIALS	INEXPEDIENCY
INDULGENCING	INEDUCABILITY	INELOQUENCE	INESTIMABILITY	INEXPEDIENT
INDULGENCY	INEDUCABLE	INELOQUENCES	INESTIMABLE	INEXPEDIENTLY
INDULGENTLY	INEFFABILITIES	INELOQUENT	INESTIMABLENESS	INEXPENSIVE
INDULGINGLY	INEFFABILITY	INELOQUENTLY	INESTIMABLY	INEXPENSIVELY
INDUMENTUM	INEFFABLENESS	INELUCTABILITY	INEVITABILITIES	INEXPENSIVENESS
INDUMENTUMS	INEFFABLENESSES	INELUCTABLE	INEVITABILITY	INEXPERIENCE
INDUPLICATE	INEFFACEABILITY	INELUCTABLY	INEVITABLE	INEXPERIENCED
INDUPLICATED	INEFFACEABLE	INELUDIBILITIES	INEVITABLENESS	INEXPERIENCES
INDUPLICATION	INEFFACEABLY	INELUDIBILITY	INEVITABLES	INEXPERTLY
INDUPLICATIONS	INEFFECTIVE	INELUDIBLE	INEVITABLY	INEXPERTNESS
INDURATING	INEFFECTIVELY	INELUDIBLY	INEXACTITUDE	INEXPERTNESSES
INDURATION	INEFFECTIVENESS	INENARRABLE	INEXACTITUDES	INEXPIABLE
INDURATIONS	INEFFECTUAL	INEPTITUDE	INEXACTNESS	INEXPIABLENESS
INDURATIVE	INEFFECTUALITY	INEPTITUDES	INEXACTNESSES	INEXPIABLY
INDUSTRIAL	INEFFECTUALLY	INEPTNESSES	INEXCITABLE	INEXPLAINABLE
INDUSTRIALISE	INEFFECTUALNESS	INEQUALITIES	INEXCUSABILITY	INEXPLAINABLY
INDUSTRIALISED	INEFFICACIES	INEQUALITY	INEXCUSABLE	INEXPLICABILITY
INDUSTRIALISES	INEFFICACIOUS	INEQUATION	INEXCUSABLENESS	INEXPLICABLE
INDUSTRIALISING	INEFFICACIOUSLY	INEQUATIONS	INEXCUSABLY	INEXPLICABLY
INDUSTRIALISM	INEFFICACITIES	INEQUIPOTENT	INEXECRABLE	INEXPLICIT
INDUSTRIALISMS	INEFFICACITY	INEQUITABLE	INEXECUTABLE	INEXPLICITLY
INDUSTRIALIST	INEFFICACY	INEQUITABLENESS	INEXECUTION	INEXPLICITNESS
INDUSTRIALISTS	INEFFICIENCIES	INEQUITABLY	INEXECUTIONS	INEXPRESSIBLE
INDUSTRIALIZE	INEFFICIENCY	INEQUITIES	INEXHAUSTED	INEXPRESSIBLES
INDUSTRIALIZED	INEFFICIENT	INEQUIVALVE	INEXHAUSTIBLE	INEXPRESSIBLY
INDUSTRIALIZES	INEFFICIENTLY	INEQUIVALVED	INEXHAUSTIBLY	INEXPRESSIVE
INDUSTRIALIZING	INEFFICIENTS	INERADICABILITY	INEXHAUSTIVE	INEXPRESSIVELY
INDUSTRIALLY	INEGALITARIAN	INERADICABLE	INEXISTANT	INEXPUGNABILITY
INDUSTRIALS	INEGALITARIANS	INERADICABLY	INEXISTENCE	INEXPUGNABLE
INDUSTRIES	INELABORATE	INERASABLE	INEXISTENCES	INEXPUGNABLY
INDUSTRIOUS	INELABORATED	INERASABLY	INEXISTENCIES	INEXPUNGIBLE
INDUSTRIOUSLY	INELABORATELY	INERASIBLE	INEXISTENCY	INEXTENDED
INDUSTRIOUSNESS	INELABORATES	INERASIBLY	INEXISTENT	INEXTENSIBILITY
INDUSTRYWIDE	INELABORATING	INERRABILITIES	INEXORABILITIES	INEXTENSIBLE

INEXTENSION	INFANTILIZED	INFERRABLE	INFINITIVALLY	INFLECTIONS
INEXTENSIONS	INFANTILIZES	INFERRIBLE	INFINITIVE	INFLECTIVE
INEXTIRPABLE	INFANTILIZING	INFERTILELY	INFINITIVELY	INFLECTORS
INEXTRICABILITY	INFANTRIES	INFERTILITIES	INFINITIVES	INFLEXIBILITIES
INEXTRICABLE	INFANTRYMAN	INFERTILITY	INFINITUDE	INFLEXIBILITY
INEXTRICABLY	INFANTRYMEN	INFESTANTS	INFINITUDES	INFLEXIBLE
INFALLIBISM	INFARCTION	INFESTATION	INFIRMARER	INFLEXIBLENESS
INFALLIBISMS	INFARCTIONS	INFESTATIONS	INFIRMARERS	INFLEXIBLY
INFALLIBIST	INFATUATED	INFEUDATION	INFIRMARIAN	INFLEXIONAL
INFALLIBISTS	INFATUATEDLY	INFEUDATIONS	INFIRMARIANS	INFLEXIONALLY
INFALLIBILITIES	INFATUATES	INFIBULATE	INFIRMARIES	INFLEXIONLESS
INFALLIBILITY	INFATUATING	INFIBULATED	INFIRMITIES	INFLEXIONS
INFALLIBLE	INFATUATION	INFIBULATES	INFIRMNESS	INFLEXURES
INFALLIBLENESS	INFATUATIONS	INFIBULATING	INFIRMNESSES	INFLICTABLE
INFALLIBLES	INFEASIBILITIES	INFIBULATION	INFIXATION	INFLICTERS
INFALLIBLY	INFEASIBILITY	INFIBULATIONS	INFIXATIONS	INFLICTING
INFAMISING	INFEASIBLE	INFIDELITIES	INFLAMABLE	INFLICTION
INFAMIZING	INFEASIBLENESS	INFIDELITY	INFLAMINGLY	INFLICTIONS
INFAMONISE	INFECTANTS	INFIELDERS	INFLAMMABILITY	INFLICTIVE
INFAMONISED	INFECTIONS	INFIELDSMAN	INFLAMMABLE	INFLICTORS
INFAMONISES	INFECTIOUS	INFIELDSMEN	INFLAMMABLENESS	INFLORESCENCE
INFAMONISING	INFECTIOUSLY	INFIGHTERS	INFLAMMABLES	INFLORESCENCES
INFAMONIZE	INFECTIOUSNESS	INFIGHTING	INFLAMMABLY	INFLORESCENT
INFAMONIZED	INFECTIVELY	INFIGHTINGS	INFLAMMATION	INFLOWINGS
INFAMONIZES	INFECTIVENESS	INFILLINGS	INFLAMMATIONS	INFLUENCEABLE
INFAMONIZING	INFECTIVENESSES	INFILTRATE	INFLAMMATORILY	INFLUENCED
INFAMOUSLY	INFECTIVITIES	INFILTRATED	INFLAMMATORY	INFLUENCER
INFAMOUSNESS	INFECTIVITY	INFILTRATES	INFLATABLE	INFLUENCERS
INFAMOUSNESSES	INFECUNDITIES	INFILTRATING	INFLATABLES	INFLUENCES
INFANGTHIEF	INFECUNDITY	INFILTRATION	INFLATEDLY	INFLUENCING
INFANGTHIEFS	INFEFTMENT	INFILTRATIONS	INFLATEDNESS	INFLUENTIAL
INFANTEERS	INFEFTMENTS	INFILTRATIVE	INFLATEDNESSES	INFLUENTIALLY
INFANTHOOD	INFELICITIES	INFILTRATOR	INFLATINGLY	INFLUENTIALS
INFANTHOODS	INFELICITOUS	INFILTRATORS	INFLATIONARY	INFLUENZAL
INFANTICIDAL	INFELICITOUSLY	INFINITANT	INFLATIONISM	INFLUENZAS
INFANTICIDE	INFELICITY	INFINITARY	INFLATIONISMS	INFLUXIONS
INFANTICIDES	INFEOFFING	INFINITATE	INFLATIONIST	INFOGRAPHIC
INFANTILISATION	INFERENCES	INFINITATED	INFLATIONISTS	INFOGRAPHICS
INFANTILISE	INFERENCING	INFINITATES	INFLATIONS	INFOLDINGS
INFANTILISED	INFERENCINGS	INFINITATING	INFLATUSES	INFOLDMENT
INFANTILISES	INFERENTIAL	INFINITELY	INFLECTABLE	INFOLDMENTS
INFANTILISING	INFERENTIALLY	INFINITENESS	INFLECTEDNESS	INFOMANIAS
INFANTILISM	INFERIORITIES	INFINITENESSES	INFLECTEDNESSES	INFOMERCIAL
INFANTILISMS	INFERIORITY	INFINITESIMAL	INFLECTING	INFOMERCIALS
INFANTILITIES	INFERIORLY	INFINITESIMALLY	INFLECTION	INFOPRENEURIAL
INFANTILITY	INFERNALITIES	INFINITESIMALS	INFLECTIONAL	INFORMABLE
INFANTILIZATION	INFERNALITY	INFINITIES	INFLECTIONALLY	INFORMALITIES
INFANTILIZE	INFERNALLY	INFINITIVAL	INFLECTIONLESS	INFORMALITY

INHUMANITY

INFORMALLY	INFRAPOSED	INGATHERER	INGRATIATORY	INHALATORIUMS
INFORMANTS	INFRAPOSITION	INGATHERERS	INGRATITUDE	INHALATORS
INFORMATICIAN	INFRAPOSITIONS	INGATHERING	INGRATITUDES	INHARMONIC
INFORMATICIANS	INFRASONIC	INGATHERINGS	INGRAVESCENCE	INHARMONICAL
INFORMATICS	INFRASOUND	INGEMINATE	INGRAVESCENCES	INHARMONICITIES
INFORMATION	INFRASOUNDS	INGEMINATED	INGRAVESCENT	INHARMONICITY
INFORMATIONAL	INFRASPECIFIC	INGEMINATES	INGREDIENT	INHARMONIES
INFORMATIONALLY	INFRASTRUCTURAL	INGEMINATING	INGREDIENTS	INHARMONIOUS
INFORMATIONS	INFRASTRUCTURE	INGEMINATION	INGRESSION	INHARMONIOUSLY
INFORMATISATION	INFRASTRUCTURES	INGEMINATIONS	INGRESSIONS	INHAUSTING
INFORMATISE	INFREQUENCE	INGENERATE	INGRESSIVE	INHEARSING
INFORMATISED	INFREQUENCES	INGENERATED	INGRESSIVENESS	INHERENCES
INFORMATISES	INFREQUENCIES	INGENERATES	INGRESSIVES	INHERENCIES
INFORMATISING	INFREQUENCY	INGENERATING	INGROOVING	INHERENTLY
INFORMATIVE	INFREQUENT	INGENERATION	INGROSSING	INHERITABILITY
INFORMATIVELY	INFREQUENTLY	INGENERATIONS	INGROUNDED	INHERITABLE
INFORMATIVENESS	INFRINGEMENT	INGENIOUSLY	INGROUNDING	INHERITABLENESS
INFORMATIZATION	INFRINGEMENTS	INGENIOUSNESS	INGROWNNESS	INHERITABLY
INFORMATIZE	INFRINGERS	INGENIOUSNESSES	INGROWNNESSES	INHERITANCE
INFORMATIZED	INFRINGING	INGENUITIES	INGULFMENT	INHERITANCES
INFORMATIZES	INFRUCTUOUS	INGENUOUSLY	INGULFMENTS	INHERITING
INFORMATIZING	INFRUCTUOUSLY	INGENUOUSNESS	INGULPHING	INHERITORS
INFORMATORILY	INFUNDIBULA	INGENUOUSNESSES	INGURGITATE	INHERITRESS
INFORMATORY	INFUNDIBULAR	INGESTIBLE	INGURGITATED	INHERITRESSES
INFORMEDLY	INFUNDIBULATE	INGESTIONS	INGURGITATES	INHERITRICES
INFORMIDABLE	INFUNDIBULIFORM	INGLENEUKS	INGURGITATING	INHERITRIX
INFORMINGLY	INFUNDIBULUM	INGLENOOKS	INGURGITATION	INHERITRIXES
INFORTUNES	INFURIATED	INGLORIOUS	INGURGITATIONS	INHIBITABLE
INFOSPHERE	INFURIATELY	INGLORIOUSLY	INHABITABILITY	INHIBITEDLY
INFOSPHERES	INFURIATES	INGLORIOUSNESS	INHABITABLE	INHIBITERS
INFOTAINMENT	INFURIATING	INGRAFTATION	INHABITANCE	INHIBITING
INFOTAINMENTS	INFURIATINGLY	INGRAFTATIONS	INHABITANCES	INHIBITION
INFRACOSTAL	INFURIATION	INGRAFTING	INHABITANCIES	INHIBITIONS
INFRACTING	INFURIATIONS	INGRAFTMENT	INHABITANCY	INHIBITIVE
INFRACTION	INFUSCATED	INGRAFTMENTS	INHABITANT	INHIBITORS
INFRACTIONS	INFUSIBILITIES	INGRAINEDLY	INHABITANTS	INHIBITORY
INFRACTORS	INFUSIBILITY	INGRAINEDNESS	INHABITATION	INHOLDINGS
INFRAGRANT	INFUSIBLENESS	INGRAINEDNESSES	INHABITATIONS	INHOMOGENEITIES
INFRAHUMAN	INFUSIBLENESSES	INGRAINERS	INHABITERS	INHOMOGENEITY
INFRAHUMANS	INFUSIONISM	INGRAINING	INHABITING	INHOMOGENEOUS
INFRALAPSARIAN	INFUSIONISMS	INGRATEFUL	INHABITIVENESS	INHOSPITABLE
INFRALAPSARIANS	INFUSIONIST	INGRATIATE	INHABITORS	INHOSPITABLY
INFRAMAXILLARY	INFUSIONISTS	INGRATIATED	INHABITRESS	INHOSPITALITIES
INFRANGIBILITY	INFUSORIAL	INGRATIATES	INHABITRESSES	INHOSPITALITY
INFRANGIBLE	INFUSORIAN	INGRATIATING	INHALATION	INHUMANELY
INFRANGIBLENESS	INFUSORIANS	INGRATIATINGLY	INHALATIONAL	INHUMANEST
INFRANGIBLY	INFUSORIES	INGRATIATION	INHALATIONS	INHUMANITIES
INFRAORBITAL	INGATHERED	INGRATIATIONS	INHALATORIUM	INHUMANITY

INHUMANNESS	INITIATORIES	INNKEEPERS	INOBSERVANCE	INORDINACY
INHUMANNESSES	INITIATORS	INNOCENCES	INOBSERVANCES	INORDINATE
INHUMATING	INITIATORY	INNOCENCIES	INOBSERVANT	INORDINATELY
INHUMATION	INITIATRESS	INNOCENTER	INOBSERVANTLY	INORDINATENESS
INHUMATIONS	INITIATRESSES	INNOCENTEST	INOBSERVATION	INORDINATION
INIMICALITIES	INITIATRICES	INNOCENTLY	INOBSERVATIONS	INORDINATIONS
INIMICALITY	INITIATRIX	INNOCUITIES	INOBTRUSIVE	INORGANICALLY
INIMICALLY	INITIATRIXES	INNOCUOUSLY	INOBTRUSIVELY	INORGANICS
INIMICALNESS	INJECTABLE	INNOCUOUSNESS	INOBTRUSIVENESS	INORGANISATION
INIMICALNESSES	INJECTABLES	INNOCUOUSNESSES	INOCCUPATION	INORGANISATIONS
INIMICITIOUS	INJECTANTS	INNOMINABLE	INOCCUPATIONS	INORGANISED
INIMITABILITIES	INJECTIONS	INNOMINABLES	INOCULABILITIES	INORGANIZATION
INIMITABILITY	INJELLYING	INNOMINATE	INOCULABILITY	INORGANIZATIONS
INIMITABLE	INJOINTING	INNOVATING	INOCULABLE	INORGANIZED
INIMITABLENESS	INJUDICIAL	INNOVATION	INOCULANTS	INOSCULATE
INIMITABLY	INJUDICIALLY	INNOVATIONAL	INOCULATED	INOSCULATED
INIQUITIES	INJUDICIOUS	INNOVATIONIST	INOCULATES	INOSCULATES
INIQUITOUS	INJUDICIOUSLY	INNOVATIONISTS	INOCULATING	INOSCULATING
INIQUITOUSLY	INJUDICIOUSNESS	INNOVATIONS	INOCULATION	INOSCULATION
INIQUITOUSNESS	INJUNCTING	INNOVATIVE	INOCULATIONS	INOSCULATIONS
INITIALERS	INJUNCTION	INNOVATIVELY	INOCULATIVE	INOSILICATE
INITIALING	INJUNCTIONS	INNOVATIVENESS	INOCULATOR	INOSILICATES
INITIALISATION	INJUNCTIVE	INNOVATORS	INOCULATORS	INPATIENTS
INITIALISATIONS	INJUNCTIVELY	INNOVATORY	INOCULATORY	INPAYMENTS
INITIALISE	INJURIOUSLY	INNOXIOUSLY	INODOROUSLY	INPOURINGS
INITIALISED	INJURIOUSNESS	INNOXIOUSNESS	INODOROUSNESS	INQUIETING
INITIALISES	INJURIOUSNESSES	INNOXIOUSNESSES	INODOROUSNESSES	INQUIETUDE
INITIALISING	INJUSTICES	INNUENDOED	INOFFENSIVE	INQUIETUDES
INITIALISM	INKBERRIES	INNUENDOES	INOFFENSIVELY	INQUILINES
INITIALISMS	INKHOLDERS	INNUENDOING	INOFFENSIVENESS	INQUILINIC
INITIALIZATION	INKINESSES	INNUMERABILITY	INOFFICIOUS	INQUILINICS
INITIALIZATIONS	INMARRIAGE	INNUMERABLE	INOFFICIOUSLY	INQUILINISM
INITIALIZE	INMARRIAGES	INNUMERABLENESS	INOFFICIOUSNESS	INQUILINISMS
INITIALIZED	INMIGRANTS	INNUMERABLY	INOPERABILITIES	INQUILINITIES
INITIALIZES	INNATENESS	INNUMERACIES	INOPERABILITY	INQUILINITY
INITIALIZING	INNATENESSES	INNUMERACY	INOPERABLE	INQUILINOUS
INITIALLED	INNAVIGABLE	INNUMERATE	INOPERABLENESS	INQUINATED
INITIALLER	INNAVIGABLY	INNUMERATES	INOPERABLY	INQUINATES
INITIALLERS	INNERMOSTS	INNUMEROUS	INOPERATIVE	INQUINATING
INITIALLING	INNERNESSES	INNUTRIENT	INOPERATIVENESS	INQUINATION
INITIALNESS	INNERSOLES	INNUTRITION	INOPERCULATE	INQUINATIONS
INITIALNESSES	INNERSPRING	INNUTRITIONS	INOPERCULATES	INQUIRATION
INITIATING	INNERVATED	INNUTRITIOUS	INOPPORTUNE	INQUIRATIONS
INITIATION	INNERVATES	INOBEDIENCE	INOPPORTUNELY	INQUIRENDO
INITIATIONS	INNERVATING	INOBEDIENCES	INOPPORTUNENESS	INQUIRENDOS
INITIATIVE	INNERVATION	INOBEDIENT	INOPPORTUNITIES	INQUIRINGLY
INITIATIVELY	INNERVATIONS	INOBEDIENTLY	INOPPORTUNITY	INQUISITION
INITIATIVES	INNERWEARS	INOBSERVABLE	INORDINACIES	INQUISITIONAL

INQUISITIONIST	INSCRIPTIONAL	INSEMINATOR	INSIGNIFICANCE	INSOLENTLY
INQUISITIONISTS	INSCRIPTIONS	INSEMINATORS	INSIGNIFICANCES	INSOLIDITIES
INQUISITIONS	INSCRIPTIVE	INSENSATELY	INSIGNIFICANCY	INSOLIDITY
INQUISITIVE	INSCRIPTIVELY	INSENSATENESS	INSIGNIFICANT	INSOLUBILISE
INQUISITIVELY	INSCROLLED	INSENSATENESSES	INSIGNIFICANTLY	INSOLUBILISED
INQUISITIVENESS	INSCROLLING	INSENSIBILITIES	INSIGNIFICATIVE	INSOLUBILISES
INQUISITOR	INSCRUTABILITY	INSENSIBILITY	INSINCERELY	INSOLUBILISING
INQUISITORIAL	INSCRUTABLE	INSENSIBLE	INSINCERER	INSOLUBILITIES
INQUISITORIALLY	INSCRUTABLENESS	INSENSIBLENESS	INSINCEREST	INSOLUBILITY
INQUISITORS	INSCRUTABLY	INSENSIBLY	INSINCERITIES	INSOLUBILIZE
INQUISITRESS	INSCULPING	INSENSITIVE	INSINCERITY	INSOLUBILIZED
INQUISITRESSES	INSCULPTURE	INSENSITIVELY	INSINEWING	INSOLUBILIZES
INQUISITURIENT	INSCULPTURED	INSENSITIVENESS	INSINUATED	INSOLUBILIZING
INRUSHINGS	INSCULPTURES	INSENSITIVITIES	INSINUATES	INSOLUBLENESS
INSALIVATE	INSCULPTURING	INSENSITIVITY	INSINUATING	INSOLUBLENESSES
INSALIVATED	INSECTARIA	INSENSUOUS	INSINUATINGLY	INSOLUBLES
INSALIVATES	INSECTARIES	INSENTIENCE	INSINUATION	INSOLVABILITIES
INSALIVATING	INSECTARIUM	INSENTIENCES	INSINUATIONS	INSOLVABILITY
INSALIVATION	INSECTARIUMS	INSENTIENCIES	INSINUATIVE	INSOLVABLE
INSALIVATIONS	INSECTICIDAL	INSENTIENCY	INSINUATOR	INSOLVABLY
INSALUBRIOUS	INSECTICIDALLY	INSENTIENT	INSINUATORS	INSOLVENCIES
INSALUBRIOUSLY	INSECTICIDE	INSEPARABILITY	INSINUATORY	INSOLVENCY
INSALUBRITIES	INSECTICIDES	INSEPARABLE	INSIPIDEST	INSOLVENTS
INSALUBRITY	INSECTIFORM	INSEPARABLENESS	INSIPIDITIES	INSOMNIACS
INSALUTARY	INSECTIFUGE	INSEPARABLES	INSIPIDITY	INSOMNIOUS
INSANENESS	INSECTIFUGES	INSEPARABLY	INSIPIDNESS	INSOMNOLENCE
INSANENESSES	INSECTIONS	INSEPARATE	INSIPIDNESSES	INSOMNOLENCES
INSANITARINESS	INSECTIVORE	INSERTABLE	INSIPIENCE	INSOUCIANCE
INSANITARY	INSECTIVORES	INSERTIONAL	INSIPIENCES	INSOUCIANCES
INSANITATION	INSECTIVOROUS	INSERTIONS	INSIPIENTLY	INSOUCIANT
INSANITATIONS	INSECTOLOGIES	INSESSORIAL	INSISTENCE	INSOUCIANTLY
INSANITIES	INSECTOLOGIST	INSEVERABLE	INSISTENCES	INSOULMENT
INSATIABILITIES	INSECTOLOGISTS	INSHEATHED	INSISTENCIES	INSOULMENTS
INSATIABILITY	INSECTOLOGY	INSHEATHES	INSISTENCY	INSOURCING
INSATIABLE	INSECURELY	INSHEATHING	INSISTENTLY	INSOURCINGS
INSATIABLENESS	INSECURENESS	INSHELLING	INSISTINGLY	INSPANNING
INSATIABLY	INSECURENESSES	INSHELTERED	INSNAREMENT	INSPECTABLE
INSATIATELY	INSECUREST	INSHELTERING	INSNAREMENTS	INSPECTING
INSATIATENESS	INSECURITIES	INSHELTERS	INSOBRIETIES	INSPECTINGLY
INSATIATENESSES	INSECURITY	INSHIPPING	INSOBRIETY	INSPECTION
INSATIETIES	INSELBERGE	INSHRINEMENT	INSOCIABILITIES	INSPECTIONAL
INSCIENCES	INSELBERGS	INSHRINEMENTS	INSOCIABILITY	INSPECTIONS
INSCONCING	INSEMINATE	INSHRINING	INSOCIABLE	INSPECTIVE
INSCRIBABLE	INSEMINATED	INSIDIOUSLY	INSOCIABLY	INSPECTORAL
INSCRIBABLENESS	INSEMINATES	INSIDIOUSNESS	INSOLATING	INSPECTORATE
INSCRIBERS	INSEMINATING	INSIDIOUSNESSES	INSOLATION	INSPECTORATES
INSCRIBING	INSEMINATION	INSIGHTFUL	INSOLATIONS	INSPECTORIAL
INSCRIPTION	INSEMINATIONS	INSIGHTFULLY	INSOLENCES	INSPECTORS

INSPECTORSHIP	INSTANCING	INSTITUTES	INSUBORDINATES	INSURGENCE
INSPECTORSHIPS	INSTANTANEITIES	INSTITUTING	INSUBORDINATION	INSURGENCES
INSPHERING	INSTANTANEITY	INSTITUTION	INSUBSTANTIAL	INSURGENCIES
INSPIRABLE	INSTANTANEOUS	INSTITUTIONAL	INSUBSTANTIALLY	INSURGENCY
INSPIRATION	INSTANTANEOUSLY	INSTITUTIONALLY	INSUFFERABLE	INSURGENTLY
INSPIRATIONAL	INSTANTIAL	INSTITUTIONARY	INSUFFERABLY	INSURGENTS
INSPIRATIONALLY	INSTANTIATE	INSTITUTIONS	INSUFFICIENCE	INSURMOUNTABLE
INSPIRATIONISM	INSTANTIATED	INSTITUTIST	INSUFFICIENCES	INSURMOUNTABLY
INSPIRATIONISMS	INSTANTIATES	INSTITUTISTS	INSUFFICIENCIES	INSURRECTION
INSPIRATIONIST	INSTANTIATING	INSTITUTIVE	INSUFFICIENCY	INSURRECTIONAL
INSPIRATIONISTS	INSTANTIATION	INSTITUTIVELY	INSUFFICIENT	INSURRECTIONARY
INSPIRATIONS	INSTANTIATIONS	INSTITUTOR	INSUFFICIENTLY	INSURRECTIONISM
INSPIRATIVE	INSTANTNESS	INSTITUTORS	INSUFFLATE	INSURRECTIONIST
INSPIRATOR	INSTANTNESSES	INSTREAMING	INSUFFLATED	INSURRECTIONS
INSPIRATORS	INSTARRING	INSTREAMINGS	INSUFFLATES	INSUSCEPTIBLE
INSPIRATORY	INSTATEMENT	INSTRESSED	INSUFFLATING	INSUSCEPTIBLY
INSPIRINGLY	INSTATEMENTS	INSTRESSES	INSUFFLATION	INSUSCEPTIVE
INSPIRITED	INSTAURATION	INSTRESSING	INSUFFLATIONS	INSUSCEPTIVELY
INSPIRITER	INSTAURATIONS	INSTRUCTED	INSUFFLATOR	INSWATHING
INSPIRITERS	INSTAURATOR	INSTRUCTIBLE	INSUFFLATORS	INSWINGERS
INSPIRITING	INSTAURATORS	INSTRUCTING	INSULARISM	INTACTNESS
INSPIRITINGLY	INSTIGATED	INSTRUCTION	INSULARISMS	INTACTNESSES
INSPIRITMENT	INSTIGATES	INSTRUCTIONAL	INSULARITIES	INTAGLIATED
INSPIRITMENTS	INSTIGATING	INSTRUCTIONS	INSULARITY	INTAGLIOED
INSPISSATE	INSTIGATINGLY	INSTRUCTIVE	INSULATING	INTAGLIOES
INSPISSATED	INSTIGATION	INSTRUCTIVELY	INSULATION	INTAGLIOING
INSPISSATES	INSTIGATIONS	INSTRUCTIVENESS	INSULATIONS	INTANGIBILITIES
INSPISSATING	INSTIGATIVE	INSTRUCTOR	INSULATORS	INTANGIBILITY
INSPISSATION	INSTIGATOR	INSTRUCTORS	INSULINASE	INTANGIBLE
INSPISSATIONS	INSTIGATORS	INSTRUCTORSHIP	INSULINASES	INTANGIBLENESS
INSPISSATOR	INSTILLATION	INSTRUCTORSHIPS	INSULSITIES	INTANGIBLES
INSPISSATORS	INSTILLATIONS	INSTRUCTRESS	INSULTABLE	INTANGIBLY
INSTABILITIES	INSTILLERS	INSTRUCTRESSES	INSULTINGLY	INTEGRABILITIES
INSTABILITY	INSTILLING	INSTRUMENT	INSULTMENT	INTEGRABILITY
INSTAGRAMMED	INSTILLMENT	INSTRUMENTAL	INSULTMENTS	INTEGRABLE
INSTAGRAMMING	INSTILLMENTS	INSTRUMENTALISM	INSUPERABILITY	INTEGRALITIES
INSTAGRAMS	INSTILMENT	INSTRUMENTALIST	INSUPERABLE	INTEGRALITY
INSTALLANT	INSTILMENTS	INSTRUMENTALITY	INSUPERABLENESS	INTEGRALLY
INSTALLANTS	INSTINCTIVE	INSTRUMENTALLY	INSUPERABLY	INTEGRANDS
INSTALLATION	INSTINCTIVELY	INSTRUMENTALS	INSUPPORTABLE	INTEGRANTS
INSTALLATIONS	INSTINCTIVITIES	INSTRUMENTATION	INSUPPORTABLY	INTEGRATED
INSTALLERS	INSTINCTIVITY	INSTRUMENTED	INSUPPRESSIBLE	INTEGRATES
INSTALLING	INSTINCTUAL	INSTRUMENTING	INSUPPRESSIBLY	INTEGRATING
INSTALLMENT	INSTINCTUALLY	INSTRUMENTS	INSURABILITIES	INTEGRATION
INSTALLMENTS	INSTITORIAL	INSUBJECTION	INSURABILITY	INTEGRATIONIST
INSTALMENT	INSTITUTED	INSUBJECTIONS	INSURANCER	INTEGRATIONISTS
INSTALMENTS	INSTITUTER	INSUBORDINATE	INSURANCERS	INTEGRATIONS
INSTANCIES	INSTITUTERS	INSUBORDINATELY	INSURANCES	INTEGRATIVE

INTEGRATOR	INTENDANCE	INTERABANGS	INTERBREEDINGS	INTERCHANGEMENT
INTEGRATORS	INTENDANCES	INTERACTANT	INTERBREEDS	INTERCHANGER
INTEGRITIES	INTENDANCIES	INTERACTANTS	INTERBROKER	INTERCHANGERS
INTEGUMENT	INTENDANCY	INTERACTED	INTERCALAR	INTERCHANGES
INTEGUMENTAL	INTENDANTS	INTERACTING	INTERCALARILY	INTERCHANGING
INTEGUMENTARY	INTENDEDLY	INTERACTION	INTERCALARY	INTERCHANNEL
INTEGUMENTS	INTENDERED	INTERACTIONAL	INTERCALATE	INTERCHAPTER
INTELLECTED	INTENDERING	INTERACTIONISM	INTERCALATED	INTERCHAPTERS
INTELLECTION	INTENDMENT	INTERACTIONISMS	INTERCALATES	INTERCHURCH
INTELLECTIONS	INTENDMENTS	INTERACTIONIST	INTERCALATING	INTERCIPIENT
INTELLECTIVE	INTENERATE	INTERACTIONISTS	INTERCALATION	INTERCIPIENTS
INTELLECTIVELY	INTENERATED	INTERACTIONS	INTERCALATIONS	INTERCLASS
INTELLECTS	INTENERATES	INTERACTIVE	INTERCALATIVE	INTERCLAVICLE
INTELLECTUAL	INTENERATING	INTERACTIVELY	INTERCAMPUS	INTERCLAVICLES
INTELLECTUALISE	INTENERATION	INTERACTIVITIES	INTERCASTE	INTERCLAVICULAR
INTELLECTUALISM	INTENERATIONS	INTERACTIVITY	INTERCEDED	INTERCLUDE
INTELLECTUALIST	INTENSATED	INTERAGENCY	INTERCEDENT	INTERCLUDED
INTELLECTUALITY	INTENSATES	INTERALLELIC	INTERCEDER	INTERCLUDES
INTELLECTUALIZE	INTENSATING	INTERALLIED	INTERCEDERS	INTERCLUDING
INTELLECTUALLY	INTENSATIVE	INTERAMBULACRA	INTERCEDES	INTERCLUSION
INTELLECTUALS	INTENSATIVES	INTERAMBULACRAL	INTERCEDING	INTERCLUSIONS
INTELLIGENCE	INTENSENESS	INTERAMBULACRUM	INTERCELLULAR	INTERCLUSTER
INTELLIGENCER	INTENSENESSES	INTERANIMATION	INTERCENSAL	INTERCOASTAL
INTELLIGENCERS	INTENSIFICATION	INTERANIMATIONS	INTERCEPTED	INTERCOLLEGIATE
INTELLIGENCES	INTENSIFIED	INTERANNUAL	INTERCEPTER	INTERCOLLINE
INTELLIGENT	INTENSIFIER	INTERARCHED	INTERCEPTERS	INTERCOLONIAL
INTELLIGENTIAL	INTENSIFIERS	INTERARCHES	INTERCEPTING	INTERCOLONIALLY
INTELLIGENTLY	INTENSIFIES	INTERARCHING	INTERCEPTION	INTERCOLUMNAR
INTELLIGENTSIA	INTENSIFYING	INTERATOMIC	INTERCEPTIONS	INTERCOMMUNAL
INTELLIGENTSIAS	INTENSIONAL	INTERBASIN	INTERCEPTIVE	INTERCOMMUNE
INTELLIGENTZIA	INTENSIONALITY	INTERBEDDED	INTERCEPTOR	INTERCOMMUNED
INTELLIGENTZIAS	INTENSIONALLY	INTERBEDDING	INTERCEPTORS	INTERCOMMUNES
INTELLIGIBILITY	INTENSIONS	INTERBEDDINGS	INTERCEPTS	INTERCOMMUNING
INTELLIGIBLE	INTENSITIES	INTERBEHAVIOR	INTERCESSION	INTERCOMMUNION
INTELLIGIBLY	INTENSITIVE	INTERBEHAVIORAL	INTERCESSIONAL	INTERCOMMUNIONS
INTEMERATE	INTENSITIVES	INTERBEHAVIORS	INTERCESSIONS	INTERCOMMUNITY
INTEMERATELY	INTENSIVELY	INTERBEHAVIOUR	INTERCESSOR	INTERCOMPANY
INTEMERATENESS	INTENSIVENESS	INTERBEHAVIOURS	INTERCESSORIAL	INTERCOMPARE
INTEMPERANCE	INTENSIVENESSES	INTERBLEND	INTERCESSORS	INTERCOMPARED
INTEMPERANCES	INTENSIVES	INTERBLENDED	INTERCESSORY	INTERCOMPARES
INTEMPERANT	INTENTIONAL	INTERBLENDING	INTERCHAIN	INTERCOMPARING
INTEMPERANTS	INTENTIONALITY	INTERBLENDS	INTERCHAINED	INTERCOMPARISON
INTEMPERATE	INTENTIONALLY	INTERBOROUGH	INTERCHAINING	INTERCONNECT
INTEMPERATELY	INTENTIONED	INTERBRAIN	INTERCHAINS	INTERCONNECTED
INTEMPERATENESS	INTENTIONS	INTERBRAINS	INTERCHANGE	INTERCONNECTING
INTEMPESTIVE	INTENTNESS	INTERBRANCH	INTERCHANGEABLE	INTERCONNECTION
INTEMPESTIVELY	INTENTNESSES	INTERBREED	INTERCHANGEABLY	INTERCONNECTOR
INTEMPESTIVITY	INTERABANG	INTERBREEDING	INTERCHANGED	INTERCONNECTORS

INTERCONNECTS

INTERCONNECTS	INTERDEALER	INTERESSES	INTERFLUENCE	INTERINFLUENCE
INTERCONNEXION	INTERDEALERS	INTERESSING	INTERFLUENCES	INTERINFLUENCED
INTERCONNEXIONS	INTERDEALING	INTERESTED	INTERFLUENT	INTERINFLUENCES
INTERCONVERSION	INTERDEALS	INTERESTEDLY	INTERFLUOUS	INTERINVOLVE
INTERCONVERT	INTERDEALT	INTERESTEDNESS	INTERFLUVE	INTERINVOLVED
INTERCONVERTED	INTERDENTAL	INTERESTING	INTERFLUVES	INTERINVOLVES
INTERCONVERTING	INTERDENTALLY	INTERESTINGLY	INTERFLUVIAL	INTERINVOLVING
INTERCONVERTS	INTERDEPEND	INTERESTINGNESS	INTERFOLDED	INTERIONIC
INTERCOOLED	INTERDEPENDED	INTERETHNIC	INTERFOLDING	INTERIORISATION
INTERCOOLER	INTERDEPENDENCE	INTERFACED	INTERFOLDS	INTERIORISE
INTERCOOLERS	INTERDEPENDENCY	INTERFACES	INTERFOLIATE	INTERIORISED
INTERCOOLING	INTERDEPENDENT	INTERFACIAL	INTERFOLIATED	INTERIORISES
INTERCOOLS	INTERDEPENDING	INTERFACIALLY	INTERFOLIATES	INTERIORISING
INTERCORPORATE	INTERDEPENDS	INTERFACING	INTERFOLIATING	INTERIORITIES
INTERCORRELATE	INTERDIALECTAL	INTERFACINGS	INTERFRATERNITY	INTERIORITY
INTERCORRELATED	INTERDICTED	INTERFACULTY	INTERFRETTED	INTERIORIZATION
INTERCORRELATES	INTERDICTING	INTERFAITH	INTERFRONTAL	INTERIORIZE
INTERCORTICAL	INTERDICTION	INTERFAMILIAL	INTERFUSED	INTERIORIZED
INTERCOSTAL	INTERDICTIONS	INTERFAMILY	INTERFUSES	INTERIORIZES
INTERCOSTALLY	INTERDICTIVE	INTERFASCICULAR	INTERFUSING	INTERIORIZING
INTERCOSTALS	INTERDICTIVELY	INTERFEMORAL	INTERFUSION	INTERIORLY
INTERCOUNTRY	INTERDICTOR	INTERFERED	INTERFUSIONS	INTERISLAND
INTERCOUNTY	INTERDICTORS	INTERFERENCE	INTERGALACTIC	INTERJACENCIES
INTERCOUPLE	INTERDICTORY	INTERFERENCES	INTERGENERATION	INTERJACENCY
INTERCOURSE	INTERDICTS	INTERFERENTIAL	INTERGENERIC	INTERJACENT
INTERCOURSES	INTERDIFFUSE	INTERFERER	INTERGLACIAL	INTERJACULATE
INTERCRATER	INTERDIFFUSED	INTERFERERS	INTERGLACIALS	INTERJACULATED
INTERCROPPED	INTERDIFFUSES	INTERFERES	INTERGRADATION	INTERJACULATES
INTERCROPPING	INTERDIFFUSING	INTERFERING	INTERGRADATIONS	INTERJACULATING
INTERCROPS	INTERDIFFUSION	INTERFERINGLY	INTERGRADE	INTERJACULATORY
INTERCROSS	INTERDIFFUSIONS	INTERFEROGRAM	INTERGRADED	INTERJECTED
INTERCROSSED	INTERDIGITAL	INTERFEROGRAMS	INTERGRADES	INTERJECTING
INTERCROSSES	INTERDIGITATE	INTERFEROMETER	INTERGRADIENT	INTERJECTION
INTERCROSSING	INTERDIGITATED	INTERFEROMETERS	INTERGRADING	INTERJECTIONAL
INTERCRURAL	INTERDIGITATES	INTERFEROMETRIC	INTERGRAFT	INTERJECTIONARY
INTERCULTURAL	INTERDIGITATING	INTERFEROMETRY	INTERGRAFTED	INTERJECTIONS
INTERCULTURALLY	INTERDIGITATION	INTERFERON	INTERGRAFTING	INTERJECTOR
INTERCULTURE	INTERDINED	INTERFERONS	INTERGRAFTS	INTERJECTORS
INTERCULTURES	INTERDINES	INTERFERTILE	INTERGRANULAR	INTERJECTORY
INTERCURRENCE	INTERDINING	INTERFERTILITY	INTERGROUP	INTERJECTS
INTERCURRENCES	INTERDISTRICT	INTERFIBER	INTERGROUPS	INTERJECTURAL
INTERCURRENT	INTERDIVISIONAL	INTERFIBRE	INTERGROWING	INTERJOINED
INTERCURRENTLY	INTERDOMINION	INTERFILED	INTERGROWN	INTERJOINING
INTERCURRENTS	INTERELECTRODE	INTERFILES	INTERGROWS	INTERJOINS
INTERCUTTING	INTERELECTRON	INTERFILING	INTERGROWTH	INTERKINESES
INTERDASHED	INTERELECTRONIC	INTERFLOWED	INTERGROWTHS	INTERKINESIS
INTERDASHES	INTEREPIDEMIC	INTERFLOWING	INTERINDIVIDUAL	INTERKNITS
INTERDASHING	INTERESSED	INTERFLOWS	INTERINDUSTRY	INTERKNITTED

INTERKNITTING	INTERLINED	INTERLUNATION	INTERMEZZI	INTERNALISING
INTERKNOTS	INTERLINER	INTERLUNATIONS	INTERMEZZO	INTERNALITIES
INTERKNOTTED	INTERLINERS	INTERMARGINAL	INTERMEZZOS	INTERNALITY
INTERKNOTTING	INTERLINES	INTERMARRIAGE	INTERMIGRATION	INTERNALIZATION
INTERLACED	INTERLINGUA	INTERMARRIAGES	INTERMIGRATIONS	INTERNALIZE
INTERLACEDLY	INTERLINGUAL	INTERMARRIED	INTERMINABILITY	INTERNALIZED
INTERLACEMENT	INTERLINGUALLY	INTERMARRIES	INTERMINABLE	INTERNALIZES
INTERLACEMENTS	INTERLINGUAS	INTERMARRY	INTERMINABLY	INTERNALIZING
INTERLACES	INTERLINING	INTERMARRYING	INTERMINGLE	INTERNALLY
INTERLACING	INTERLININGS	INTERMATTED	INTERMINGLED	INTERNALNESS
INTERLACUSTRINE	INTERLINKED	INTERMATTING	INTERMINGLES	INTERNALNESSES
INTERLAMINAR	INTERLINKING	INTERMAXILLA	INTERMINGLING	INTERNATIONAL
INTERLAMINATE	INTERLINKS	INTERMAXILLAE	INTERMISSION	INTERNATIONALLY
INTERLAMINATED	INTERLOANS	INTERMAXILLARY	INTERMISSIONS	INTERNATIONALS
INTERLAMINATES	INTERLOBULAR	INTERMEDDLE	INTERMISSIVE	INTERNECINE
INTERLAMINATING	INTERLOCAL	INTERMEDDLED	INTERMITOTIC	INTERNECIVE
INTERLAMINATION	INTERLOCATION	INTERMEDDLER	INTERMITTED	INTERNEURAL
INTERLAPPED	INTERLOCATIONS	INTERMEDDLERS	INTERMITTENCE	INTERNEURON
INTERLAPPING	INTERLOCKED	INTERMEDDLES	INTERMITTENCES	INTERNEURONAL
INTERLARDED	INTERLOCKER	INTERMEDDLING	INTERMITTENCIES	INTERNEURONS
INTERLARDING	INTERLOCKERS	INTERMEDIA	INTERMITTENCY	INTERNISTS
INTERLARDS	INTERLOCKING	INTERMEDIACIES	INTERMITTENT	INTERNMENT
INTERLAYER	INTERLOCKS	INTERMEDIACY	INTERMITTENTLY	INTERNMENTS
INTERLAYERED	INTERLOCUTION	INTERMEDIAL	INTERMITTER	INTERNODAL
INTERLAYERING	INTERLOCUTIONS	INTERMEDIARIES	INTERMITTERS	INTERNODES
INTERLAYERINGS	INTERLOCUTOR	INTERMEDIARY	INTERMITTING	INTERNODIAL
INTERLAYERS	INTERLOCUTORILY	INTERMEDIATE	INTERMITTINGLY	INTERNSHIP
INTERLAYING	INTERLOCUTORS	INTERMEDIATED	INTERMITTOR	INTERNSHIPS
INTERLEAVE	INTERLOCUTORY	INTERMEDIATELY	INTERMITTORS	INTERNUCLEAR
INTERLEAVED	INTERLOCUTRESS	INTERMEDIATES	INTERMIXED	INTERNUCLEON
INTERLEAVES	INTERLOCUTRICE	INTERMEDIATING	INTERMIXES	INTERNUCLEONIC
INTERLEAVING	INTERLOCUTRICES	INTERMEDIATION	INTERMIXING	INTERNUCLEOTIDE
INTERLENDING	INTERLOCUTRIX	INTERMEDIATIONS	INTERMIXTURE	INTERNUNCIAL
INTERLENDS	INTERLOCUTRIXES	INTERMEDIATOR	INTERMIXTURES	INTERNUNCIO
INTERLEUKIN	INTERLOOPED	INTERMEDIATORS	INTERMODAL	INTERNUNCIOS
INTERLEUKINS	INTERLOOPING	INTERMEDIATORY	INTERMODULATION	INTEROBSERVER
INTERLIBRARY	INTERLOOPS	INTERMEDIN	INTERMOLECULAR	INTEROCEAN
INTERLINEAL	INTERLOPED	INTERMEDINS	INTERMONTANE	INTEROCEANIC
INTERLINEALLY	INTERLOPER	INTERMEDIUM	INTERMOUNTAIN	INTEROCEPTION
INTERLINEAR	INTERLOPERS	INTERMEDIUMS	INTERMUNDANE	INTEROCEPTIONS
INTERLINEARLY	INTERLOPES	INTERMEMBRANE	INTERMURED	INTEROCEPTIVE
INTERLINEARS	INTERLOPING	INTERMENSTRUAL	INTERMURES	INTEROCEPTOR
INTERLINEATE	INTERLUDED	INTERMENTS	INTERMURING	INTEROCEPTORS
INTERLINEATED	INTERLUDES	INTERMESHED	INTERMUSCULAR	INTEROCULAR
INTERLINEATES	INTERLUDIAL	INTERMESHES	INTERNALISATION	INTEROFFICE
INTERLINEATING	INTERLUDING	INTERMESHING	INTERNALISE	INTEROPERABLE
INTERLINEATION	INTERLUNAR	INTERMETALLIC	INTERNALISED	INTEROPERATIVE
INTERLINEATIONS	INTERLUNARY	INTERMETALLICS	INTERNALISES	INTERORBITAL

INTERORGAN

INTERORGAN	INTERPILASTERS	INTERPRETABLY	INTERREGNUM	INTERRUPTS
INTEROSCULANT	INTERPLANETARY	INTERPRETATE	INTERREGNUMS	INTERSCAPULAR
INTEROSCULATE	INTERPLANT	INTERPRETATED	INTERRELATE	INTERSCHOLASTIC
INTEROSCULATED	INTERPLANTED	INTERPRETATES	INTERRELATED	INTERSCHOOL
INTEROSCULATES	INTERPLANTING	INTERPRETATING	INTERRELATEDLY	INTERSCRIBE
INTEROSCULATING	INTERPLANTS	INTERPRETATION	INTERRELATES	INTERSCRIBED
INTEROSCULATION	INTERPLAYED	INTERPRETATIONS	INTERRELATING	INTERSCRIBES
INTEROSSEAL	INTERPLAYING	INTERPRETATIVE	INTERRELATION	INTERSCRIBING
INTEROSSEOUS	INTERPLAYS	INTERPRETED	INTERRELATIONS	INTERSECTED
INTERPAGED	INTERPLEAD	INTERPRETER	INTERRELIGIOUS	INTERSECTING
INTERPAGES	INTERPLEADED	INTERPRETERS	INTERRENAL	INTERSECTION
INTERPAGING	INTERPLEADER	INTERPRETERSHIP	INTERROBANG	INTERSECTIONAL
INTERPANDEMIC	INTERPLEADERS	INTERPRETESS	INTERROBANGS	INTERSECTIONS
INTERPARIETAL	INTERPLEADING	INTERPRETESSES	INTERROGABLE	INTERSECTS
INTERPARISH	INTERPLEADS	INTERPRETING	INTERROGANT	INTERSEGMENT
INTERPAROCHIAL	INTERPLEURAL	INTERPRETIVE	INTERROGANTS	INTERSEGMENTAL
INTERPAROXYSMAL	INTERPLUVIAL	INTERPRETIVELY	INTERROGATE	INTERSEGMENTS
INTERPARTICLE	INTERPLUVIALS	INTERPRETRESS	INTERROGATED	INTERSENSORY
INTERPARTY	INTERPOINT	INTERPRETRESSES	INTERROGATEE	INTERSEPTAL
INTERPELLANT	INTERPOINTS	INTERPRETS	INTERROGATEES	INTERSERTAL
INTERPELLANTS	INTERPOLABLE	INTERPROVINCIAL	INTERROGATES	INTERSERTED
INTERPELLATE	INTERPOLAR	INTERPROXIMAL	INTERROGATING	INTERSERTING
INTERPELLATED	INTERPOLATE	INTERPSYCHIC	INTERROGATINGLY	INTERSERTS
INTERPELLATES	INTERPOLATED	INTERPUNCTION	INTERROGATION	INTERSERVICE
INTERPELLATING	INTERPOLATER	INTERPUNCTIONS	INTERROGATIONAL	INTERSESSION
INTERPELLATION	INTERPOLATERS	INTERPUNCTUATE	INTERROGATIONS	INTERSESSIONS
INTERPELLATIONS	INTERPOLATES	INTERPUNCTUATED	INTERROGATIVE	INTERSEXES
INTERPELLATOR	INTERPOLATING	INTERPUNCTUATES	INTERROGATIVELY	INTERSEXUAL
INTERPELLATORS	INTERPOLATION	INTERPUPILLARY	INTERROGATIVES	INTERSEXUALISM
INTERPENETRABLE	INTERPOLATIONS	INTERQUARTILE	INTERROGATOR	INTERSEXUALISMS
INTERPENETRANT	INTERPOLATIVE	INTERRACIAL	INTERROGATORIES	INTERSEXUALITY
INTERPENETRATE	INTERPOLATOR	INTERRACIALLY	INTERROGATORILY	INTERSEXUALLY
INTERPENETRATED	INTERPOLATORS	INTERRADIAL	INTERROGATORS	INTERSEXUALS
INTERPENETRATES	INTERPONED	INTERRADIALLY	INTERROGATORY	INTERSIDEREAL
INTERPERCEPTUAL	INTERPONES	INTERRADII	INTERROGEE	INTERSOCIETAL
INTERPERMEATE	INTERPONING	INTERRADIUS	INTERROGEES	INTERSOCIETY
INTERPERMEATED	INTERPOPULATION	INTERRADIUSES	INTERRUPTED	INTERSPACE
INTERPERMEATES	INTERPOSABLE	INTERRAILED	INTERRUPTEDLY	INTERSPACED
INTERPERMEATING	INTERPOSAL	INTERRAILER	INTERRUPTER	INTERSPACES
INTERPERSONAL	INTERPOSALS	INTERRAILERS	INTERRUPTERS	INTERSPACING
INTERPERSONALLY	INTERPOSED	INTERRAILING	INTERRUPTIBLE	INTERSPATIAL
INTERPETIOLAR	INTERPOSER	INTERRAILS	INTERRUPTING	INTERSPATIALLY
INTERPHALANGEAL	INTERPOSERS	INTERRAMAL	INTERRUPTION	INTERSPECIES
INTERPHASE	INTERPOSES	INTERREGAL	INTERRUPTIONS	INTERSPECIFIC
INTERPHASES	INTERPOSING	INTERREGES	INTERRUPTIVE	INTERSPERSAL
INTERPHONE	INTERPOSITION	INTERREGIONAL	INTERRUPTIVELY	INTERSPERSALS
INTERPHONES	INTERPOSITIONS	INTERREGNA	INTERRUPTOR	INTERSPERSE
INTERPILASTER	INTERPRETABLE	INTERREGNAL	INTERRUPTORS	INTERSPERSED

INTERSPERSEDLY	INTERTILLAGES	INTERVENORS	INTERZONES	INTONATIONAL
INTERSPERSES	INTERTILLED	INTERVENTION	INTESTACIES	INTONATIONS
INTERSPERSING	INTERTILLING	INTERVENTIONAL	INTESTATES	INTONATORS
INTERSPERSION	INTERTILLS	INTERVENTIONISM	INTESTINAL	INTONINGLY
INTERSPERSIONS	INTERTISSUED	INTERVENTIONIST	INTESTINALLY	INTORSIONS
INTERSPINAL	INTERTRAFFIC	INTERVENTIONS	INTESTINES	INTORTIONS
INTERSPINOUS	INTERTRAFFICS	INTERVENTOR	INTHRALLED	INTOXICABLE
INTERSTADIAL	INTERTRIAL	INTERVENTORS	INTHRALLING	INTOXICANT
INTERSTADIALS	INTERTRIBAL	INTERVERTEBRAL	INTHRONING	INTOXICANTS
INTERSTAGE	INTERTRIGO	INTERVIEWED	INTIFADAHS	INTOXICATE
INTERSTATE	INTERTRIGOS	INTERVIEWEE	INTIFADEHS	INTOXICATED
INTERSTATES	INTERTROOP	INTERVIEWEES	INTIMACIES	INTOXICATEDLY
INTERSTATION	INTERTROPICAL	INTERVIEWER	INTIMATELY	INTOXICATES
INTERSTELLAR	INTERTWINE	INTERVIEWERS	INTIMATENESS	INTOXICATING
INTERSTELLARY	INTERTWINED	INTERVIEWING	INTIMATENESSES	INTOXICATINGLY
INTERSTERILE	INTERTWINEMENT	INTERVIEWS	INTIMATERS	INTOXICATION
INTERSTERILITY	INTERTWINEMENTS	INTERVILLAGE	INTIMATING	INTOXICATIONS
INTERSTICE	INTERTWINES	INTERVISIBILITY	INTIMATION	INTOXICATIVE
INTERSTICES	INTERTWINING	INTERVISIBLE	INTIMATIONS	INTOXICATOR
INTERSTIMULUS	INTERTWININGLY	INTERVISITATION	INTIMIDATE	INTOXICATORS
INTERSTITIAL	INTERTWININGS	INTERVITAL	INTIMIDATED	INTOXIMETER
INTERSTITIALLY	INTERTWIST	INTERVOCALIC	INTIMIDATES	INTOXIMETERS
INTERSTITIALS	INTERTWISTED	INTERVOLVE	INTIMIDATING	INTRACAPSULAR
INTERSTRAIN	INTERTWISTING	INTERVOLVED	INTIMIDATINGLY	INTRACARDIAC
INTERSTRAND	INTERTWISTINGLY	INTERVOLVES	INTIMIDATION	INTRACARDIAL
INTERSTRATIFIED	INTERTWISTS	INTERVOLVING	INTIMIDATIONS	INTRACARDIALLY
INTERSTRATIFIES	INTERUNION	INTERWEAVE	INTIMIDATOR	INTRACAVITARY
INTERSTRATIFY	INTERUNIONS	INTERWEAVED	INTIMIDATORS	INTRACELLULAR
INTERSUBJECTIVE	INTERUNIVERSITY	INTERWEAVEMENT	INTIMIDATORY	INTRACELLULARLY
INTERSYSTEM	INTERURBAN	INTERWEAVEMENTS	INTIMISTES	INTRACEREBRAL
INTERTANGLE	INTERVALES	INTERWEAVER	INTIMITIES	INTRACEREBRALLY
INTERTANGLED	INTERVALLEY	INTERWEAVERS	INTINCTION	INTRACOMPANY
INTERTANGLEMENT	INTERVALLIC	INTERWEAVES	INTINCTIONS	INTRACRANIAL
INTERTANGLES	INTERVALLUM	INTERWEAVING	INTITULING	INTRACRANIALLY
INTERTANGLING	INTERVALLUMS	INTERWINDING	INTOLERABILITY	INTRACTABILITY
INTERTARSAL	INTERVALOMETER	INTERWINDS	INTOLERABLE	INTRACTABLE
INTERTENTACULAR	INTERVALOMETERS	INTERWORKED	INTOLERABLENESS	INTRACTABLENESS
INTERTERMINAL	INTERVARSITY	INTERWORKING	INTOLERABLY	INTRACTABLY
INTERTERMS	INTERVEINED	INTERWORKINGS	INTOLERANCE	INTRACUTANEOUS
INTERTEXTS	INTERVEINING	INTERWORKS	INTOLERANCES	INTRADERMAL
INTERTEXTUAL	INTERVEINS	INTERWOUND	INTOLERANT	INTRADERMALLY
INTERTEXTUALITY	INTERVENED	INTERWOVEN	INTOLERANTLY	INTRADERMIC
INTERTEXTUALLY	INTERVENER	INTERWREATHE	INTOLERANTNESS	INTRADERMICALLY
INTERTEXTURE	INTERVENERS	INTERWREATHED	INTOLERANTS	INTRADOSES
INTERTEXTURES	INTERVENES	INTERWREATHES	INTOLERATION	INTRAFALLOPIAN
INTERTIDAL	INTERVENIENT	INTERWREATHING	INTOLERATIONS	INTRAFASCICULAR
INTERTIDALLY	INTERVENING	INTERWROUGHT	INTONATING	INTRAGALACTIC
INTERTILLAGE	INTERVENOR	INTERZONAL	INTONATION	INTRAGENIC

INTRAMEDULLARY	INTRASPECIFIC	INTRIGUING	INTROSPECTIVELY	INTUMESCENCY
INTRAMERCURIAL	INTRASTATE	INTRIGUINGLY	INTROSPECTS	INTUMESCENT
INTRAMOLECULAR	INTRATELLURIC	INTRINSICAL	INTROSUSCEPTION	INTUMESCES
INTRAMUNDANE	INTRATHECAL	INTRINSICALITY	INTROVERSIBLE	INTUMESCING
INTRAMURAL	INTRATHECALLY	INTRINSICALLY	INTROVERSION	INTURBIDATE
INTRAMURALLY	INTRATHORACIC	INTRINSICALNESS	INTROVERSIONS	INTURBIDATED
INTRAMURALS	INTRAUTERINE	INTRINSICATE	INTROVERSIVE	INTURBIDATES
INTRAMUSCULAR	INTRAVASATION	INTRODUCED	INTROVERSIVELY	INTURBIDATING
INTRAMUSCULARLY	INTRAVASATIONS	INTRODUCER	INTROVERTED	INTUSSUSCEPT
INTRANASAL	INTRAVASCULAR	INTRODUCERS	INTROVERTING	INTUSSUSCEPTED
INTRANASALLY	INTRAVASCULARLY	INTRODUCES	INTROVERTIVE	INTUSSUSCEPTING
INTRANATIONAL	INTRAVENOUS	INTRODUCIBLE	INTROVERTS	INTUSSUSCEPTION
INTRANSIGEANCE	INTRAVENOUSLY	INTRODUCING	INTRUDINGLY	INTUSSUSCEPTIVE
INTRANSIGEANCES	INTRAVERSABLE	INTRODUCTION	INTRUSIONAL	INTUSSUSCEPTS
INTRANSIGEANT	INTRAVITAL	INTRODUCTIONS	INTRUSIONIST	INTWINEMENT
INTRANSIGEANTLY	INTRAVITALLY	INTRODUCTIVE	INTRUSIONISTS	INTWINEMENTS
INTRANSIGEANTS	INTRAVITAM	INTRODUCTORILY	INTRUSIONS	INTWISTING
INTRANSIGENCE	INTRAZONAL	INTRODUCTORY	INTRUSIVELY	INUMBRATED
INTRANSIGENCES	INTREATFULL	INTROFYING	INTRUSIVENESS	INUMBRATES
INTRANSIGENCIES	INTREATING	INTROGRESSANT	INTRUSIVENESSES	INUMBRATING
INTRANSIGENCY	INTREATINGLY	INTROGRESSANTS	INTRUSIVES	INUNCTIONS
INTRANSIGENT	INTREATMENT	INTROGRESSION	INTRUSTING	INUNDATING
INTRANSIGENTISM	INTREATMENTS	INTROGRESSIONS	INTRUSTMENT	INUNDATION
INTRANSIGENTIST	INTRENCHANT	INTROGRESSIVE	INTRUSTMENTS	INUNDATIONS
INTRANSIGENTLY	INTRENCHED	INTROITUSES	INTUBATING	INUNDATORS
INTRANSIGENTS	INTRENCHER	INTROJECTED	INTUBATION	INUNDATORY
INTRANSITIVE	INTRENCHERS	INTROJECTING	INTUBATIONS	INURBANELY
INTRANSITIVELY	INTRENCHES	INTROJECTION	INTUITABLE	INURBANITIES
INTRANSITIVES	INTRENCHING	INTROJECTIONS	INTUITIONAL	INURBANITY
INTRANSITIVITY	INTRENCHMENT	INTROJECTIVE	INTUITIONALISM	INUREDNESS
INTRANSMISSIBLE	INTRENCHMENTS	INTROJECTS	INTUITIONALISMS	INUREDNESSES
INTRANSMUTABLE	INTREPIDITIES	INTROMISSIBLE	INTUITIONALIST	INUREMENTS
INTRANUCLEAR	INTREPIDITY	INTROMISSION	INTUITIONALISTS	INURNMENTS
INTRAOCULAR	INTREPIDLY	INTROMISSIONS	INTUITIONALLY	INUSITATION
INTRAOCULARLY	INTREPIDNESS	INTROMISSIVE	INTUITIONISM	INUSITATIONS
INTRAPARIETAL	INTREPIDNESSES	INTROMITTED	INTUITIONISMS	INUTILITIES
INTRAPARTUM	INTRICACIES	INTROMITTENT	INTUITIONIST	INUTTERABLE
INTRAPERITONEAL	INTRICATELY	INTROMITTER	INTUITIONISTS	INVAGINABLE
INTRAPERSONAL	INTRICATENESS	INTROMITTERS	INTUITIONS	INVAGINATE
INTRAPETIOLAR	INTRICATENESSES	INTROMITTING	INTUITIVELY	INVAGINATED
INTRAPLATE	INTRIGANTE	INTRORSELY	INTUITIVENESS	INVAGINATES
INTRAPOPULATION	INTRIGANTES	INTROSPECT	INTUITIVENESSES	INVAGINATING
INTRAPRENEUR	INTRIGANTS	INTROSPECTED	INTUITIVISM	INVAGINATION
INTRAPRENEURIAL	INTRIGUANT	INTROSPECTING	INTUITIVISMS	INVAGINATIONS
INTRAPRENEURS	INTRIGUANTE	INTROSPECTION	INTUMESCED	INVALIDATE
INTRAPSYCHIC	INTRIGUANTES	INTROSPECTIONAL	INTUMESCENCE	INVALIDATED
INTRASEXUAL	INTRIGUANTS	INTROSPECTIONS	INTUMESCENCES	INVALIDATES
INTRASPECIES	INTRIGUERS	INTROSPECTIVE	INTUMESCENCIES	INVALIDATING

INVALIDATION	INVENTIONAL	INVETERATE	INVISIBLENESS	INWARDNESS
INVALIDATIONS	INVENTIONLESS	INVETERATELY	INVISIBLENESSES	INWARDNESSES
INVALIDATOR	INVENTIONS	INVETERATENESS	INVISIBLES	INWORKINGS
INVALIDATORS	INVENTIVELY	INVIABILITIES	INVITATION	INWRAPMENT
INVALIDEST	INVENTIVENESS	INVIABILITY	INVITATIONAL	INWRAPMENTS
INVALIDHOOD	INVENTIVENESSES	INVIABLENESS	INVITATIONALS	INWRAPPING
INVALIDHOODS	INVENTORIABLE	INVIABLENESSES	INVITATIONS	INWRAPPINGS
INVALIDING	INVENTORIAL	INVIDIOUSLY	INVITATORIES	INWREATHED
INVALIDINGS	INVENTORIALLY	INVIDIOUSNESS	INVITATORY	INWREATHES
INVALIDISM	INVENTORIED	INVIDIOUSNESSES	INVITEMENT	INWREATHING
INVALIDISMS	INVENTORIES	INVIGILATE	INVITEMENTS	IODINATING
INVALIDITIES	INVENTORYING	INVIGILATED	INVITINGLY	IODINATION
INVALIDITY	INVENTRESS	INVIGILATES	INVITINGNESS	IODINATIONS
INVALIDNESS	INVENTRESSES	INVIGILATING	INVITINGNESSES	IODISATION
INVALIDNESSES	INVERACITIES	INVIGILATION	INVOCATING	IODISATIONS
INVALUABLE	INVERACITY	INVIGILATIONS	INVOCATION	IODIZATION
INVALUABLENESS	INVERITIES	INVIGILATOR	INVOCATIONAL	IODIZATIONS
INVALUABLY	INVERNESSES	INVIGILATORS	INVOCATIONS	IODOMETRIC
INVARIABILITIES	INVERSIONS	INVIGORANT	INVOCATIVE	IODOMETRICAL
INVARIABILITY	INVERTASES	INVIGORANTS	INVOCATORS	IODOMETRICALLY
INVARIABLE	INVERTEBRAL	INVIGORATE	INVOCATORY	IODOMETRIES
INVARIABLENESS	INVERTEBRATE	INVIGORATED	INVOICINGS	IONICITIES
INVARIABLES	INVERTEBRATES	INVIGORATES	INVOLUCELLA	IONISATION
INVARIABLY	INVERTEDLY	INVIGORATING	INVOLUCELLATE	IONISATIONS
INVARIANCE	INVERTIBILITIES	INVIGORATINGLY	INVOLUCELLATED	IONIZATION
INVARIANCES	INVERTIBILITY	INVIGORATION	INVOLUCELLUM	IONIZATIONS
INVARIANCIES	INVERTIBLE	INVIGORATIONS	INVOLUCELS	IONOPAUSES
INVARIANCY	INVESTABLE	INVIGORATIVE	INVOLUCRAL	IONOPHORES
INVARIANTS	INVESTIBLE	INVIGORATIVELY	INVOLUCRATE	IONOPHORESES
INVASIVELY	INVESTIGABLE	INVIGORATOR	INVOLUCRES	IONOPHORESIS
INVASIVENESS	INVESTIGATE	INVIGORATORS	INVOLUCRUM	IONOSONDES
INVASIVENESSES	INVESTIGATED	INVINCIBILITIES	INVOLUNTARILY	IONOSPHERE
INVEAGLING	INVESTIGATES	INVINCIBILITY	INVOLUNTARINESS	IONOSPHERES
INVECTIVELY	INVESTIGATING	INVINCIBLE	INVOLUNTARY	IONOSPHERIC
INVECTIVENESS	INVESTIGATION	INVINCIBLENESS	INVOLUTEDLY	IONOSPHERICALLY
INVECTIVENESSES	INVESTIGATIONAL	INVINCIBLY	INVOLUTELY	IONOTROPIC
INVECTIVES	INVESTIGATIONS	INVIOLABILITIES	INVOLUTING	IONOTROPIES
INVEIGHERS	INVESTIGATIVE	INVIOLABILITY	INVOLUTION	IONTOPHORESES
INVEIGHING	INVESTIGATOR	INVIOLABLE	INVOLUTIONAL	IONTOPHORESIS
INVEIGLEMENT	INVESTIGATORS	INVIOLABLENESS	INVOLUTIONS	IONTOPHORETIC
INVEIGLEMENTS	INVESTIGATORY	INVIOLABLY	INVOLVEDLY	IPECACUANHA
INVEIGLERS	INVESTITIVE	INVIOLACIES	INVOLVEMENT	IPECACUANHAS
INVEIGLING	INVESTITURE	INVIOLATED	INVOLVEMENTS	IPRATROPIUM
INVENDIBILITIES	INVESTITURES	INVIOLATELY	INVULNERABILITY	IPRATROPIUMS
INVENDIBILITY	INVESTMENT	INVIOLATENESS	INVULNERABLE	IPRINDOLES
INVENDIBLE	INVESTMENTS	INVIOLATENESSES	INVULNERABLY	IPRONIAZID
INVENTABLE	INVETERACIES	INVISIBILITIES	INVULTUATION	IPRONIAZIDS
INVENTIBLE	INVETERACY	INVISIBILITY	INVULTUATIONS	IPSELATERAL

IPSILATERAL	IRONMONGERS	IRRECEPTIVE	IRREFRANGIBLY	IRREPARABLY
IPSILATERALLY	IRONMONGERY	IRRECIPROCAL	IRREFUTABILITY	IRREPEALABILITY
IRACUNDITIES	IRONNESSES	IRRECIPROCITIES	IRREFUTABLE	IRREPEALABLE
IRACUNDITY	IRONSMITHS	IRRECIPROCITY	IRREFUTABLENESS	IRREPEALABLY
IRACUNDULOUS	IRONSTONES	IRRECLAIMABLE	IRREFUTABLY	IRREPLACEABLE
IRASCIBILITIES	IRONWORKER	IRRECLAIMABLY	IRREGARDLESS	IRREPLACEABLY
IRASCIBILITY	IRONWORKERS	IRRECOGNISABLE	IRREGULARITIES	IRREPLEVIABLE
IRASCIBLENESS	IRRADIANCE	IRRECOGNITION	IRREGULARITY	IRREPLEVISABLE
IRASCIBLENESSES	IRRADIANCES	IRRECOGNITIONS	IRREGULARLY	IRREPREHENSIBLE
IRATENESSES	IRRADIANCIES	IRRECOGNIZABLE	IRREGULARS	IRREPREHENSIBLY
IREFULNESS	IRRADIANCY	IRRECONCILABLE	IRRELATION	IRREPRESSIBLE
IREFULNESSES	IRRADIATED	IRRECONCILABLES	IRRELATIONS	IRREPRESSIBLY
IRENICALLY	IRRADIATES	IRRECONCILABLY	IRRELATIVE	IRREPROACHABLE
IRENICISMS	IRRADIATING	IRRECONCILED	IRRELATIVELY	IRREPROACHABLY
IRENOLOGIES	IRRADIATION	IRRECONCILEMENT	IRRELATIVENESS	IRREPRODUCIBLE
IRIDACEOUS	IRRADIATIONS	IRRECOVERABLE	IRRELEVANCE	IRREPROVABLE
IRIDECTOMIES	IRRADIATIVE	IRRECOVERABLY	IRRELEVANCES	IRREPROVABLY
IRIDECTOMY	IRRADIATOR	IRRECUSABLE	IRRELEVANCIES	IRRESISTANCE
IRIDESCENCE	IRRADIATORS	IRRECUSABLY	IRRELEVANCY	IRRESISTANCES
IRIDESCENCES	IRRADICABLE	IRREDEEMABILITY	IRRELEVANT	IRRESISTIBILITY
IRIDESCENT	IRRADICABLY	IRREDEEMABLE	IRRELEVANTLY	IRRESISTIBLE
IRIDESCENTLY	IRRADICATE	IRREDEEMABLES	IRRELIEVABLE	IRRESISTIBLY
IRIDISATION	IRRADICATED	IRREDEEMABLY	IRRELIGION	IRRESOLUBILITY
IRIDISATIONS	IRRADICATES	IRREDENTAS	IRRELIGIONIST	IRRESOLUBLE
IRIDIZATION	IRRADICATING	IRREDENTISM	IRRELIGIONISTS	IRRESOLUBLY
IRIDIZATIONS	IRRATIONAL	IRREDENTISMS	IRRELIGIONS	IRRESOLUTE
IRIDOCYTES	IRRATIONALISE	IRREDENTIST	IRRELIGIOUS	IRRESOLUTELY
IRIDOLOGIES	IRRATIONALISED	IRREDENTISTS	IRRELIGIOUSLY	IRRESOLUTENESS
IRIDOLOGIST	IRRATIONALISES	IRREDUCIBILITY	IRRELIGIOUSNESS	IRRESOLUTION
IRIDOLOGISTS	IRRATIONALISING	IRREDUCIBLE	IRREMEABLE	IRRESOLUTIONS
IRIDOSMINE	IRRATIONALISM	IRREDUCIBLENESS	IRREMEABLY	IRRESOLVABILITY
IRIDOSMINES	IRRATIONALISMS	IRREDUCIBLY	IRREMEDIABLE	IRRESOLVABLE
IRIDOSMIUM	IRRATIONALIST	IRREDUCTIBILITY	IRREMEDIABLY	IRRESOLVABLY
IRIDOSMIUMS	IRRATIONALISTIC	IRREDUCTION	IRREMISSIBILITY	IRRESPECTIVE
IRIDOTOMIES	IRRATIONALISTS	IRREDUCTIONS	IRREMISSIBLE	IRRESPECTIVELY
IRISATIONS	IRRATIONALITIES	IRREFLECTION	IRREMISSIBLY	IRRESPIRABLE
IRKSOMENESS	IRRATIONALITY	IRREFLECTIONS	IRREMISSION	IRRESPONSIBLE
IRKSOMENESSES	IRRATIONALIZE	IRREFLECTIVE	IRREMISSIONS	IRRESPONSIBLES
IRONFISTED	IRRATIONALIZED	IRREFLEXION	IRREMISSIVE	IRRESPONSIBLY
IRONHANDED	IRRATIONALIZES	IRREFLEXIONS	IRREMOVABILITY	IRRESPONSIVE
IRONHEARTED	IRRATIONALIZING	IRREFLEXIVE	IRREMOVABLE	IRRESPONSIVELY
IRONICALLY	IRRATIONALLY	IRREFORMABILITY	IRREMOVABLENESS	IRRESTRAINABLE
IRONICALNESS	IRRATIONALNESS	IRREFORMABLE	IRREMOVABLY	IRRESUSCITABLE
IRONICALNESSES	IRRATIONALS	IRREFORMABLY	IRRENOWNED	IRRESUSCITABLY
IRONMASTER	IRREALISABLE	IRREFRAGABILITY	IRREPAIRABLE	IRRETENTION
IRONMASTERS	IRREALITIES	IRREFRAGABLE	IRREPARABILITY	IRRETENTIONS
IRONMONGER	IRREALIZABLE	IRREFRAGABLY	IRREPARABLE	IRRETENTIVE
IRONMONGERIES	IRREBUTTABLE	IRREFRANGIBLE	IRREPARABLENESS	IRRETENTIVENESS

IRRETRIEVABLE	ISINGLASSES	ISOCHRONOUS	ISOKINETIC	ISOPERIMETRICAL
IRRETRIEVABLY	ISLOMANIAS	ISOCHRONOUSLY	ISOKONTANS	ISOPERIMETRIES
IRREVERENCE	ISMATICALNESS	ISOCHROOUS	ISOLABILITIES	ISOPERIMETRY
IRREVERENCES	ISMATICALNESSES	ISOCLINALS	ISOLABILITY	ISOPIESTIC
IRREVERENT	ISOAGGLUTININ	ISOCLINICS	ISOLATABLE	ISOPIESTICALLY
IRREVERENTIAL	ISOAGGLUTININS	ISOCRACIES	ISOLATIONISM	ISOPLETHIC
IRREVERENTLY	ISOALLOXAZINE	ISOCRYMALS	ISOLATIONISMS	ISOPLUVIAL
IRREVERSIBILITY	ISOALLOXAZINES	ISOCYANATE	ISOLATIONIST	ISOPLUVIALS
IRREVERSIBLE	ISOAMINILE	ISOCYANATES	ISOLATIONISTS	ISOPOLITIES
IRREVERSIBLY	ISOAMINILES	ISOCYANIDE	ISOLATIONS	ISOPRENALINE
IRREVOCABILITY	ISOANTIBODIES	ISOCYANIDES	ISOLECITHAL	ISOPRENALINES
IRREVOCABLE	ISOANTIBODY	ISODIAMETRIC	ISOLEUCINE	ISOPRENOID
IRREVOCABLENESS	ISOANTIGEN	ISODIAMETRICAL	ISOLEUCINES	ISOPRENOIDS
IRREVOCABLY	ISOANTIGENIC	ISODIAPHERE	ISOMAGNETIC	ISOPROPYLS
IRRIDENTAS	ISOANTIGENS	ISODIAPHERES	ISOMAGNETICS	ISOPROTERENOL
IRRIGATING	ISOBARISMS	ISODIMORPHIC	ISOMERASES	ISOPROTERENOLS
IRRIGATION	ISOBAROMETRIC	ISODIMORPHISM	ISOMERISATION	ISOPTERANS
IRRIGATIONAL	ISOBILATERAL	ISODIMORPHISMS	ISOMERISATIONS	ISOPTEROUS
IRRIGATIONS	ISOBUTANES	ISODIMORPHOUS	ISOMERISED	ISOPYCNALS
IRRIGATIVE	ISOBUTENES	ISODONTALS	ISOMERISES	ISOPYCNICS
IRRIGATORS	ISOBUTYLENE	ISODYNAMIC	ISOMERISING	ISORHYTHMIC
IRRITABILITIES	ISOBUTYLENES	ISODYNAMICS	ISOMERISMS	ISOSEISMAL
IRRITABILITY	ISOCALORIC	ISOELECTRIC	ISOMERIZATION	ISOSEISMALS
IRRITABLENESS	ISOCARBOXAZID	ISOELECTRONIC	ISOMERIZATIONS	ISOSEISMIC
IRRITABLENESSES	ISOCARBOXAZIDS	ISOENZYMATIC	ISOMERIZED	ISOSEISMICS
IRRITANCIES	ISOCHASMIC	ISOENZYMES	ISOMERIZES	ISOSMOTICALLY
IRRITATEDLY	ISOCHEIMAL	ISOENZYMIC	ISOMERIZING	ISOSPONDYLOUS
IRRITATING	ISOCHEIMALS	ISOFLAVONE	ISOMETRICAL	ISOSPORIES
IRRITATINGLY	ISOCHEIMENAL	ISOFLAVONES	ISOMETRICALLY	ISOSPOROUS
IRRITATION	ISOCHEIMENALS	ISOGAMETES	ISOMETRICS	ISOSTACIES
IRRITATIONS	ISOCHEIMIC	ISOGAMETIC	ISOMETRIES	ISOSTASIES
IRRITATIVE	ISOCHIMALS	ISOGENETIC	ISOMETROPIA	ISOSTATICALLY
IRRITATORS	ISOCHROMATIC	ISOGEOTHERM	ISOMETROPIAS	ISOSTEMONOUS
IRROTATIONAL	ISOCHROMOSOME	ISOGEOTHERMAL	ISOMORPHIC	ISOSTHENURIA
IRRUPTIONS	ISOCHROMOSOMES	ISOGEOTHERMALS	ISOMORPHICALLY	ISOSTHENURIAS
IRRUPTIVELY	ISOCHRONAL	ISOGEOTHERMIC	ISOMORPHISM	ISOTENISCOPE
IRUKANDJIS	ISOCHRONALLY	ISOGEOTHERMICS	ISOMORPHISMS	ISOTENISCOPES
ISABELLINE	ISOCHRONES	ISOGEOTHERMS	ISOMORPHOUS	ISOTHERALS
ISABELLINES	ISOCHRONISE	ISOGLOSSAL	ISONIAZIDE	ISOTHERMAL
ISALLOBARIC	ISOCHRONISED	ISOGLOSSES	ISONIAZIDES	ISOTHERMALLY
ISALLOBARS	ISOCHRONISES	ISOGLOSSIC	ISONIAZIDS	ISOTHERMALS
ISAPOSTOLIC	ISOCHRONISING	ISOGLOTTAL	ISONITRILE	ISOTONICALLY
ISCHAEMIAS	ISOCHRONISM	ISOGLOTTIC	ISONITRILES	ISOTONICITIES
ISCHURETIC	ISOCHRONISMS	ISOGRAFTED	ISOOCTANES	ISOTONICITY
ISCHURETICS	ISOCHRONIZE	ISOGRAFTING	ISOPACHYTE	ISOTOPICALLY
ISEIKONIAS	ISOCHRONIZED	ISOHYETALS	ISOPACHYTES	ISOTRETINOIN
ISENTROPIC	ISOCHRONIZES	ISOIMMUNISATION	ISOPERIMETER	ISOTRETINOINS
ISENTROPICALLY	ISOCHRONIZING	ISOIMMUNIZATION	ISOPERIMETERS	ISOTROPICALLY

ISOTROPIES

ISOTROPIES	ITALIANISE	ITALICIZATION	ITERATIVENESSES	ITINERANTS
ISOTROPISM	ITALIANISED	ITALICIZATIONS	ITEROPARITIES	ITINERARIES
ISOTROPISMS	ITALIANISES	ITALICIZED	ITEROPARITY	ITINERATED
ISOTROPOUS	ITALIANISING	ITALICIZES	ITEROPAROUS	ITINERATES
ISOXSUPRINE	ITALIANIZE	ITALICIZING	ITHYPHALLI	ITINERATING
ISOXSUPRINES	ITALIANIZED	ITCHINESSES	ITHYPHALLIC	ITINERATION
ISPAGHULAS	ITALIANIZES	ITEMISATION	ITHYPHALLICS	ITINERATIONS
ITACOLUMITE	ITALIANIZING	ITEMISATIONS	ITHYPHALLUS	IVERMECTIN
ITACOLUMITES	ITALICISATION	ITEMIZATION	ITHYPHALLUSES	IVERMECTINS
ITALIANATE	ITALICISATIONS	ITEMIZATIONS	ITINERACIES	IVORYBILLS
ITALIANATED	ITALICISED	ITERATIONS	ITINERANCIES	IVORYWOODS
ITALIANATES	ITALICISES	ITERATIVELY	ITINERANCY	IZVESTIYAS
ITALIANATING	ITALICISING	ITERATIVENESS	ITINERANTLY	

J

JABBERINGLY	JACKROLLING	JAMAHIRIYAS	JASPERISED	JEJUNOSTOMY
JABBERINGS	JACKSCREWS	JAMBALAYAS	JASPERISES	JELLIFICATION
JABBERWOCK	JACKSHAFTS	JAMBOKKING	JASPERISING	JELLIFICATIONS
JABBERWOCKIES	JACKSMELTS	JAMBOLANAS	JASPERIZED	JELLIFYING
JABBERWOCKS	JACKSMITHS	JAMBUSTERS	JASPERIZES	JELLYBEANS
JABBERWOCKY	JACKSNIPES	JANISARIES	JASPERIZING	JELLYFISHES
JABORANDIS	JACKSTAFFS	JANISSARIES	JASPERWARE	JELLYGRAPH
JABOTICABA	JACKSTAVES	JANITORIAL	JASPERWARES	JELLYGRAPHED
JABOTICABAS	JACKSTONES	JANITORSHIP	JASPIDEOUS	JELLYGRAPHING
JACARANDAS	JACKSTRAWS	JANITORSHIPS	JASPILITES	JELLYGRAPHS
JACKALLING	JACQUERIES	JANITRESSES	JAUNDICING	JELLYROLLS
JACKALOPES	JACTATIONS	JANITRIXES	JAUNTINESS	JEMMINESSES
JACKANAPES	JACTITATION	JANIZARIAN	JAUNTINESSES	JENNETINGS
JACKANAPESES	JACTITATIONS	JANIZARIES	JAUNTINGLY	JEOPARDERS
JACKAROOED	JACULATING	JANNEYINGS	JAVELINING	JEOPARDIED
JACKAROOING	JACULATION	JAPANISING	JAWBATIONS	JEOPARDIES
JACKASSERIES	JACULATIONS	JAPANIZING	JAWBONINGS	JEOPARDING
JACKASSERY	JACULATORS	JAPONAISERIE	JAWBREAKER	JEOPARDISE
JACKBOOTED	JACULATORY	JAPONAISERIES	JAWBREAKERS	JEOPARDISED
JACKBOOTING	JADEDNESSES	JARDINIERE	JAWBREAKING	JEOPARDISES
JACKEROOED	JADISHNESS	JARDINIERES	JAWBREAKINGLY	JEOPARDISING
JACKEROOING	JADISHNESSES	JARGONEERS	JAWCRUSHER	JEOPARDIZE
JACKETLESS	JAGDWURSTS	JARGONELLE	JAWCRUSHERS	JEOPARDIZED
JACKFISHES	JAGGEDNESS	JARGONELLES	JAYHAWKERS	JEOPARDIZES
JACKFRUITS	JAGGEDNESSES	JARGONIEST	JAYWALKERS	JEOPARDIZING
JACKHAMMER	JAGGHERIES	JARGONISATION	JAYWALKING	JEOPARDOUS
JACKHAMMERED	JAGHIRDARS	JARGONISATIONS	JAYWALKINGS	JEOPARDOUSLY
JACKHAMMERING	JAGUARONDI	JARGONISED	JAZZINESSES	JEOPARDYING
JACKHAMMERS	JAGUARONDIS	JARGONISES	JEALOUSEST	JEQUERITIES
JACKKNIFED	JAGUARUNDI	JARGONISING	JEALOUSHOOD	JEQUIRITIES
JACKKNIFES	JAGUARUNDIS	JARGONISTIC	JEALOUSHOODS	JERFALCONS
JACKKNIFING	JAILBREAKER	JARGONISTS	JEALOUSIES	JERKINESSES
JACKKNIVES	JAILBREAKERS	JARGONIZATION	JEALOUSING	JERKINHEAD
JACKLIGHTED	JAILBREAKING	JARGONIZATIONS	JEALOUSNESS	JERKINHEADS
JACKLIGHTING	JAILBREAKS	JARGONIZED	JEALOUSNESSES	JERKWATERS
JACKLIGHTS	JAILBROKEN	JARGONIZES	JEANSWEARS	JERRYMANDER
JACKPLANES	JAILERESSES	JARGONIZING	JEISTIECOR	JERRYMANDERED
JACKPOTTED	JAILHOUSES	JARLSBERGS	JEISTIECORS	JERRYMANDERING
JACKPOTTING	JAILORESSES	JAROVISING	JEJUNENESS	JERRYMANDERS
JACKRABBIT	JALOALLOFANE	JAROVIZING	JEJUNENESSES	JESSAMINES
JACKRABBITS	JALOALLOFANES	JASMONATES	JEJUNITIES	JESSERANTS
JACKROLLED	JAMAHIRIYA	JASPERIEST	JEJUNOSTOMIES	JESUITICAL

JESUITICALLY	JOBSWORTHS	JOSTLEMENT	JOYFULNESSES	JUICEHEADS
JESUITISMS	JOCKEYISMS	JOSTLEMENTS	JOYLESSNESS	JUICINESSES
JESUITRIES	JOCKEYSHIP	JOUISANCES	JOYLESSNESSES	JULIENNING
JETSTREAMS	JOCKEYSHIPS	JOURNALESE	JOYOUSNESS	JUMBLINGLY
JETTATURAS	JOCKSTRAPS	JOURNALESES	JOYOUSNESSES	JUMBOISING
JETTINESSES	JOCKTELEGS	JOURNALING	JOYPOPPERS	JUMBOIZING
JETTISONABLE	JOCOSENESS	JOURNALINGS	JOYPOPPING	JUMHOURIYA
JETTISONED	JOCOSENESSES	JOURNALISATION	JOYRIDINGS	JUMHOURIYAS
JETTISONING	JOCOSERIOUS	JOURNALISATIONS	JUBILANCES	JUMPINESSES
JEWELFISHES	JOCOSITIES	JOURNALISE	JUBILANCIES	JUNCACEOUS
JEWELLERIES	JOCULARITIES	JOURNALISED	JUBILANTLY	JUNCTIONAL
JEWELWEEDS	JOCULARITY	JOURNALISER	JUBILARIAN	JUNEATINGS
JICKAJOGGED	JOCULATORS	JOURNALISERS	JUBILARIANS	JUNGLEGYMS
JICKAJOGGING	JOCUNDITIES	JOURNALISES	JUBILATING	JUNGLELIKE
JICKAJOGGINGS	JOCUNDNESS	JOURNALISING	JUBILATION	JUNIORATES
JIGAJIGGED	JOCUNDNESSES	JOURNALISM	JUBILATIONS	JUNIORITIES
JIGAJIGGING	JOGTROTTED	JOURNALISMS	JUDDERIEST	JUNKERDOMS
JIGAJOGGED	JOGTROTTING	JOURNALIST	JUDGEMENTAL	JUNKETEERED
JIGAJOGGING	JOHANNESES	JOURNALISTIC	JUDGEMENTALLY	JUNKETEERING
JIGAMAREES	JOHNNYCAKE	JOURNALISTS	JUDGEMENTS	JUNKETEERS
JIGGERMAST	JOHNNYCAKES	JOURNALIZATION	JUDGESHIPS	JUNKETINGS
JIGGERMASTS	JOHNSONGRASS	JOURNALIZATIONS	JUDGMATICAL	JUNKETTERS
JIGGUMBOBS	JOHNSONGRASSES	JOURNALIZE	JUDGMATICALLY	JUNKETTING
JILLFLIRTS	JOINTEDNESS	JOURNALIZED	JUDGMENTAI	JUNKINESSES
JIMPNESSES	JOINTEDNESSES	JOURNALIZER	JUDGMENTALLY	JURIDICALLY
JIMSONWEED	JOINTNESSES	JOURNALIZERS	JUDICATION	JURISCONSULT
JIMSONWEEDS	JOINTRESSES	JOURNALIZES	JUDICATIONS	JURISCONSULTS
JINGOISTIC	JOINTURESS	JOURNALIZING	JUDICATIVE	JURISDICTION
JINGOISTICALLY	JOINTURESSES	JOURNALLED	JUDICATORIAL	JURISDICTIONAL
JINRICKSHA	JOINTURING	JOURNALLING	JUDICATORIES	JURISDICTIONS
JINRICKSHAS	JOINTWEEDS	JOURNALLINGS	JUDICATORS	JURISDICTIVE
JINRICKSHAW	JOINTWORMS	JOURNEYERS	JUDICATORY	JURISPRUDENCE
JINRICKSHAWS	JOKESMITHS	JOURNEYING	JUDICATURE	JURISPRUDENCES
JINRIKISHA	JOKINESSES	JOURNEYMAN	JUDICATURES	JURISPRUDENT
JINRIKISHAS	JOLIOTIUMS	JOURNEYMEN	JUDICIALLY	JURISPRUDENTIAL
JINRIKSHAS	JOLLEYINGS	JOURNEYWORK	JUDICIARIES	JURISPRUDENTS
JITTERBUGGED	JOLLIFICATION	JOURNEYWORKS	JUDICIARILY	JURISTICAL
JITTERBUGGING	JOLLIFICATIONS	JOUYSAUNCE	JUDICIOUSLY	JURISTICALLY
JITTERBUGS	JOLLIFYING	JOUYSAUNCES	JUDICIOUSNESS	JUSTICESHIP
JITTERIEST	JOLLIMENTS	JOVIALITIES	JUDICIOUSNESSES	JUSTICESHIPS
JITTERINESS	JOLLINESSES	JOVIALNESS	JUGGERNAUT	JUSTICIABILITY
JITTERINESSES	JOLLYBOATS	JOVIALNESSES	JUGGERNAUTS	JUSTICIABLE
JOBCENTRES	JOLLYHEADS	JOVIALTIES	JUGGLERIES	JUSTICIALISM
JOBERNOWLS	JOLTERHEAD	JOVYSAUNCE	JUGGLINGLY	JUSTICIALISMS
JOBHOLDERS	JOLTERHEADS	JOVYSAUNCES	JUGLANDACEOUS	JUSTICIARIES
JOBLESSNESS	JONNYCAKES	JOWLINESSES	JUGULATING	JUSTICIARS
JOBLESSNESSES	JOSEPHINITE	JOYFULLEST	JUGULATION	JUSTICIARSHIP
JOBSEEKERS	JOSEPHINITES	JOYFULNESS	JUGULATIONS	JUSTICIARSHIPS

JUSTICIARY	JUSTIFICATIONS	JUSTIFYING	JUVENILENESS	JUXTAPOSING
JUSTIFIABILITY	JUSTIFICATIVE	JUSTNESSES	JUVENILENESSES	JUXTAPOSITION
JUSTIFIABLE	JUSTIFICATOR	JUVENESCENCE	JUVENILITIES	JUXTAPOSITIONAL
JUSTIFIABLENESS	JUSTIFICATORS	JUVENESCENCES	JUVENILITY	JUXTAPOSITIONS
JUSTIFIABLY	JUSTIFICATORY	JUVENESCENT	JUXTAPOSED	
JUSTIFICATION	JUSTIFIERS	JUVENILELY	JUXTAPOSES	

J

K

KABALISTIC	KALLITYPES	KARYOLOGICAL	KEELHAULED	KERATINOPHILIC
KABARAGOYA	KALSOMINED	KARYOLOGIES	KEELHAULING	KERATINOUS
KABARAGOYAS	KALSOMINES	KARYOLOGIST	KEELHAULINGS	KERATITIDES
KABBALISMS	KALSOMINING	KARYOLOGISTS	KEELIVINES	KERATITISES
KABBALISTIC	KAMELAUKION	KARYOLYMPH	KEELYVINES	KERATOGENOUS
KABBALISTS	KAMELAUKIONS	KARYOLYMPHS	KEENNESSES	KERATOMATA
KABELJOUWS	KAMERADING	KARYOLYSES	KEEPERLESS	KERATOMETER
KACHUMBERS	KANAMYCINS	KARYOLYSIS	KEEPERSHIP	KERATOMETERS
KADAITCHAS	KANGAROOED	KARYOLYTIC	KEEPERSHIPS	KERATOPHYRE
KAFFEEKLATSCH	KANGAROOING	KARYOMAPPING	KEEPSAKIER	KERATOPHYRES
KAFFEEKLATSCHES	KANTIKOYED	KARYOMAPPINGS	KEEPSAKIEST	KERATOPLASTIC
KAFFIRBOOM	KANTIKOYING	KARYOPLASM	KEESHONDEN	KERATOPLASTIES
KAFFIRBOOMS	KAOLINISED	KARYOPLASMIC	KEFUFFLING	KERATOPLASTY
KAHIKATEAS	KAOLINISES	KARYOPLASMS	KEKERENGUS	KERATOTOMIES
KAHIKATOAS	KAOLINISING	KARYOSOMES	KELPFISHES	KERATOTOMY
KAIKAWAKAS	KAOLINITES	KARYOTYPED	KELYPHITIC	KERAUNOGRAPH
KAIKOMAKOS	KAOLINITIC	KARYOTYPES	KENNELLING	KERAUNOGRAPHS
KAILYAIRDS	KAOLINIZED	KARYOTYPIC	KENNETTING	KERBLOOEYS
KAINOGENESES	KAOLINIZES	KARYOTYPICAL	KENOGENESES	KERBSTONES
KAINOGENESIS	KAOLINIZING	KARYOTYPICALLY	KENOGENESIS	KERCHIEFED
KAINOGENETIC	KAOLINOSES	KARYOTYPING	KENOGENETIC	KERCHIEFING
KAIROMONES	KAOLINOSIS	KATABOLICALLY	KENOGENETICALLY	KERCHIEVES
KAISERDOMS	KAPELLMEISTER	KATABOLISM	KENOPHOBIA	KERFUFFLED
KAISERISMS	KAPELLMEISTERS	KATABOLISMS	KENOPHOBIAS	KERFUFFLES
KAISERSHIP	KARABINERS	KATABOTHRON	KENOTICIST	KERFUFFLING
KAISERSHIPS	KARANGAING	KATABOTHRONS	KENOTICISTS	KERMESITES
KAKISTOCRACIES	KARATEISTS	KATADROMOUS	KENSPECKLE	KERNELLIER
KAKISTOCRACY	KARMICALLY	KATATHERMOMETER	KENTLEDGES	KERNELLIEST
KALAMKARIS	KARSTIFICATION	KATAVOTHRON	KERATECTOMIES	KERNELLING
KALANCHOES	KARSTIFICATIONS	KATAVOTHRONS	KERATECTOMY	KERNICTERUS
KALASHNIKOV	KARSTIFIED	KATHAKALIS	KERATINISATION	KERNICTERUSES
KALASHNIKOVS	KARSTIFIES	KATHAREVOUSA	KERATINISATIONS	KERNMANTEL
KALEIDOPHONE	KARSTIFYING	KATHAREVOUSAS	KERATINISE	KERPLUNKED
KALEIDOPHONES	KARUHIRUHI	KATHAROMETER	KERATINISED	KERPLUNKING
KALEIDOSCOPE	KARUHIRUHIS	KATHAROMETERS	KERATINISES	KERSANTITE
KALEIDOSCOPES	KARYOGAMIC	KATZENJAMMER	KERATINISING	KERSANTITES
KALEIDOSCOPIC	KARYOGAMIES	KATZENJAMMERS	KERATINIZATION	KERSEYMERE
KALENDARED	KARYOGRAMS	KAWANATANGA	KERATINIZATIONS	KERSEYMERES
KALENDARING	KARYOKINESES	KAWANATANGAS	KERATINIZE	KERYGMATIC
KALIPHATES	KARYOKINESIS	KAZATSKIES	KERATINIZED	KETCHUPIER
KALLIKREIN	KARYOKINETIC	KAZILLIONS	KERATINIZES	KETCHUPIEST
KALLIKREINS	KARYOLOGIC	KEELHALING	KERATINIZING	KETOACIDOSES

KETOACIDOSIS	KHITMUTGAR	KILOCALORIE	KINEMATICS	KINGCRAFTS
KETOGENESES	KHITMUTGARS	KILOCALORIES	KINEMATOGRAPH	KINGDOMLESS
KETOGENESIS	KHUSKHUSES	KILOCURIES	KINEMATOGRAPHER	KINGFISHER
KETONAEMIA	KIBBITZERS	KILOCYCLES	KINEMATOGRAPHIC	KINGFISHERS
KETONAEMIAS	KIBBITZING	KILOGAUSSES	KINEMATOGRAPHS	KINGFISHES
KETONEMIAS	KIBBUTZNIK	KILOGRAMME	KINEMATOGRAPHY	KINGLIHOOD
KETONURIAS	KIBBUTZNIKS	KILOGRAMMES	KINESCOPED	KINGLIHOODS
KETOSTEROID	KICKABOUTS	KILOHERTZES	KINESCOPES	KINGLINESS
KETOSTEROIDS	KICKAROUND	KILOJOULES	KINESCOPING	KINGLINESSES
KETTLEBELL	KICKAROUNDS	KILOLITERS	KINESIATRIC	KINGMAKERS
KETTLEBELLS	KICKBOARDS	KILOLITRES	KINESIATRICS	KINGSNAKES
KETTLEDRUM	KICKBOXERS	KILOMETERS	KINESIOLOGIES	KINKINESSES
KETTLEDRUMMER	KICKBOXING	KILOMETRES	KINESIOLOGIST	KINNIKINIC
KETTLEDRUMMERS	KICKBOXINGS	KILOMETRIC	KINESIOLOGISTS	KINNIKINICK
KETTLEDRUMS	KICKFLIPPED	KILOMETRICAL	KINESIOLOGY	KINNIKINICKS
KETTLEFULS	KICKFLIPPING	KILOPARSEC	KINESIPATH	KINNIKINICS
KETTLESTITCH	KICKPLATES	KILOPARSECS	KINESIPATHIC	KINNIKINNICK
KETTLESTITCHES	KICKSHAWSES	KILOPASCAL	KINESIPATHIES	KINNIKINNICKS
KEYBOARDED	KICKSORTER	KILOPASCALS	KINESIPATHIST	KINTLEDGES
KEYBOARDER	KICKSORTERS	KILOTONNES	KINESIPATHISTS	KIRBIGRIPS
KEYBOARDERS	KICKSTANDS	KIMBERLITE	KINESIPATHS	KIRKYAIRDS
KEYBOARDING	KICKSTARTED	KIMBERLITES	KINESIPATHY	KIRSCHWASSER
KEYBOARDINGS	KICKSTARTING	KINAESTHESES	KINESITHERAPIES	KIRSCHWASSERS
KEYBOARDIST	KICKSTARTS	KINAESTHESIA	KINESITHERAPY	KISSAGRAMS
KEYBOARDISTS	KIDDIEWINK	KINAESTHESIAS	KINESTHESES	KISSOGRAMS
KEYBUTTONS	KIDDIEWINKIE	KINAESTHESIS	KINESTHESIA	KISSPEPTIN
KEYLOGGERS	KIDDIEWINKIES	KINAESTHETIC	KINESTHESIAS	KISSPEPTINS
KEYLOGGING	KIDDIEWINKS	KINDERGARTEN	KINESTHESIS	KITCHENALIA
KEYLOGGINGS	KIDDISHNESS	KINDERGARTENER	KINESTHETIC	KITCHENALIAS
KEYPRESSES	KIDDISHNESSES	KINDERGARTENERS	KINESTHETICALLY	KITCHENDOM
KEYPUNCHED	KIDDYWINKS	KINDERGARTENS	KINETHEODOLITE	KITCHENDOMS
KEYPUNCHER	KIDNAPINGS	KINDERGARTNER	KINETHEODOLITES	KITCHENERS
KEYPUNCHERS	KIDNAPPEES	KINDERGARTNERS	KINETICALLY	KITCHENETS
KEYPUNCHES	KIDNAPPERS	KINDERSPIEL	KINETICIST	KITCHENETTE
KEYPUNCHING	KIDNAPPING	KINDERSPIELS	KINETICISTS	KITCHENETTES
KEYSTONING	KIDNAPPINGS	KINDHEARTED	KINETOCHORE	KITCHENING
KEYSTROKED	KIDNEYLIKE	KINDHEARTEDLY	KINETOCHORES	KITCHENMAID
KEYSTROKES	KIDOLOGIES	KINDHEARTEDNESS	KINETOGRAPH	KITCHENMAIDS
KEYSTROKING	KIDOLOGIST	KINDLESSLY	KINETOGRAPHS	KITCHENWARE
KEYSTROKINGS	KIDOLOGISTS	KINDLINESS	KINETONUCLEI	KITCHENWARES
KEYWORKERS	KIESELGUHR	KINDLINESSES	KINETONUCLEUS	KITEBOARDS
KHALIFATES	KIESELGUHRS	KINDNESSES	KINETONUCLEUSES	KITESURFER
KHANSAMAHS	KIESELGURS	KINDREDNESS	KINETOPLAST	KITESURFERS
KHEDIVATES	KIESERITES	KINDREDNESSES	KINETOPLASTS	KITESURFING
KHEDIVIATE	KILDERKINS	KINDREDSHIP	KINETOSCOPE	KITESURFINGS
KHEDIVIATES	KILLIFISHES	KINDREDSHIPS	KINETOSCOPES	KITSCHIEST
KHIDMUTGAR	KILLIKINICK	KINEMATICAL	KINETOSOME	KITSCHIFIED
KHIDMUTGARS	KILLIKINICKS	KINEMATICALLY	KINETOSOMES	KITSCHIFIES

KITSCHIFYING	KLUTZINESSES	KNIPHOFIAS	KNUCKLEHEADS	KREOSOTING
KITSCHNESS	KNACKERIES	KNOBBINESS	KNUCKLIEST	KRIEGSPIEL
KITSCHNESSES	KNACKERING	KNOBBINESSES	KOEKSISTER	KRIEGSPIELS
KITTENIEST	KNACKINESS	KNOBBLIEST	KOEKSISTERS	KRIEGSSPIEL
KITTENISHLY	KNACKINESSES	KNOBKERRIE	KOHLRABIES	KRIEGSSPIELS
KITTENISHNESS	KNACKWURST	KNOBKERRIES	KOHUTUHUTU	KROMESKIES
KITTENISHNESSES	KNACKWURSTS	KNOBSTICKS	KOHUTUHUTUS	KRUGERRAND
KITTIWAKES	KNAGGINESS	KNOCKABOUT	KOLINSKIES	KRUGERRANDS
KIWIFRUITS	KNAGGINESSES	KNOCKABOUTS	KOLKHOZNIK	KRUMMHORNS
KIWISPORTS	KNAPSACKED	KNOCKBACKS	KOLKHOZNIKI	KRYOMETERS
KLANGFARBE	KNAVESHIPS	KNOCKDOWNS	KOLKHOZNIKS	KRYPTONITE
KLANGFARBES	KNAVISHNESS	KNOCKWURST	KOMONDOROCK	KRYPTONITES
KLEBSIELLA	KNAVISHNESSES	KNOCKWURSTS	KOMONDOROK	KUMARAHOUS
KLEBSIELLAS	KNEEBOARDED	KNOTGRASSES	KOMPROMATS	KUMMERBUND
KLEINHUISIE	KNEEBOARDING	KNOTTINESS	KONIMETERS	KUMMERBUNDS
KLEINHUISIES	KNEEBOARDS	KNOTTINESSES	KONIOLOGIES	KUNDALINIS
KLENDUSITIES	KNEECAPPED	KNOWABLENESS	KONISCOPES	KURBASHING
KLENDUSITY	KNEECAPPING	KNOWABLENESSES	KOOKABURRA	KURCHATOVIUM
KLEPHTISMS	KNEECAPPINGS	KNOWINGEST	KOOKABURRAS	KURCHATOVIUMS
KLEPTOCRACIES	KNEEPIECES	KNOWINGNESS	KOOKINESSES	KURDAITCHA
KLEPTOCRACY	KNEVELLING	KNOWINGNESSES	KOTAHITANGA	KURDAITCHAS
KLEPTOCRATIC	KNICKERBOCKER	KNOWLEDGABILITY	KOTAHITANGAS	KURFUFFLED
KLEPTOMANIA	KNICKERBOCKERS	KNOWLEDGABLE	KOTTABOSES	KURFUFFLES
KLEPTOMANIAC	KNICKKNACK	KNOWLEDGABLY	KOTUKUTUKU	KURFUFFLING
KLEPTOMANIACS	KNICKKNACKS	KNOWLEDGEABLE	KOTUKUTUKUS	KURRAJONGS
KLEPTOMANIAS	KNICKPOINT	KNOWLEDGEABLY	KOULIBIACA	KURTOSISES
KLETTERSCHUH	KNICKPOINTS	KNOWLEDGED	KOULIBIACAS	KVETCHIEST
KLETTERSCHUHE	KNIFEPOINT	KNOWLEDGES	KOURBASHED	KVETCHINESS
KLINOSTATS	KNIFEPOINTS	KNOWLEDGING	KOURBASHES	KVETCHINESSES
KLIPSPRINGER	KNIFERESTS	KNUBBLIEST	KOURBASHING	KVETCHINGS
KLIPSPRINGERS	KNIGHTAGES	KNUCKLEBALL	KOUSKOUSES	KWASHIORKOR
KLONDIKERS	KNIGHTHEAD	KNUCKLEBALLER	KOWHAIWHAI	KWASHIORKORS
KLONDIKING	KNIGHTHEADS	KNUCKLEBALLERS	KOWHAIWHAIS	KYANISATION
KLONDYKERS	KNIGHTHOOD	KNUCKLEBALLS	KRAKOWIAKS	KYANISATIONS
KLONDYKING	KNIGHTHOODS	KNUCKLEBONE	KRAUTROCKS	KYANIZATION
KLOOCHMANS	KNIGHTLESS	KNUCKLEBONES	KREASOTING	KYANIZATIONS
KLOOTCHMAN	KNIGHTLIER	KNUCKLEDUSTER	KREMLINOLOGIES	KYMOGRAPHIC
KLOOTCHMANS	KNIGHTLIEST	KNUCKLEDUSTERS	KREMLINOLOGIST	KYMOGRAPHIES
KLOOTCHMEN	KNIGHTLINESS	KNUCKLEHEAD	KREMLINOLOGISTS	KYMOGRAPHS
KLUTZINESS	KNIGHTLINESSES	KNUCKLEHEADED	KREMLINOLOGY	KYMOGRAPHY

L

LABANOTATION	LABOURINGLY	LACHRYMATION	LACTALBUMINS	LADYFISHES
LABANOTATIONS	LABOURISMS	LACHRYMATIONS	LACTARIANS	LADYLIKENESS
LABDACISMS	LABOURISTS	LACHRYMATOR	LACTATIONAL	LADYLIKENESSES
LABEFACTATION	LABOURITES	LACHRYMATORIES	LACTATIONALLY	LADYNESSES
LABEFACTATIONS	LABOURSAVING	LACHRYMATORS	LACTATIONS	LAEOTROPIC
LABEFACTION	LABOURSOME	LACHRYMATORY	LACTESCENCE	LAEVIGATED
LABEFACTIONS	LABRADOODLE	LACHRYMOSE	LACTESCENCES	LAEVIGATES
LABELLABLE	LABRADOODLES	LACHRYMOSELY	LACTESCENT	LAEVIGATING
LABELLINGS	LABRADORESCENT	LACHRYMOSITIES	LACTIFEROUS	LAEVOGYRATE
LABELLISTS	LABRADORITE	LACHRYMOSITY	LACTIFEROUSNESS	LAEVOROTARY
LABELMATES	LABRADORITES	LACINESSES	LACTIFLUOUS	LAEVOROTATION
LABIALISATION	LABYRINTHAL	LACINIATED	LACTIVISMS	LAEVOROTATIONS
LABIALISATIONS	LABYRINTHIAN	LACINIATION	LACTIVISTS	LAEVOROTATORY
LABIALISED	LABYRINTHIC	LACINIATIONS	LACTOBACILLI	LAEVULOSES
LABIALISES	LABYRINTHICAL	LACKADAISICAL	LACTOBACILLUS	LAGENIFORM
LABIALISING	LABYRINTHICALLY	LACKADAISICALLY	LACTOFLAVIN	LAGERPHONE
LABIALISMS	LABYRINTHINE	LACKADAISY	LACTOFLAVINS	LAGERPHONES
LABIALITIES	LABYRINTHITIS	LACKLUSTER	LACTOGENIC	LAGGARDLIER
LABIALIZATION	LABYRINTHITISES	LACKLUSTERS	LACTOGLOBULIN	LAGGARDLIEST
LABIALIZATIONS	LABYRINTHODONT	LACKLUSTRE	LACTOGLOBULINS	LAGGARDNESS
LABIALIZED	LABYRINTHODONTS	LACKLUSTRES	LACTOMETER	LAGGARDNESSES
LABIALIZES	LABYRINTHS	LACONICALLY	LACTOMETERS	LAGNIAPPES
LABIALIZING	LACCOLITES	LACONICISM	LACTOPROTEIN	LAGOMORPHIC
LABILITIES	LACCOLITHIC	LACONICISMS	LACTOPROTEINS	LAGOMORPHOUS
LABIODENTAL	LACCOLITHS	LACQUERERS	LACTOSCOPE	LAGOMORPHS
LABIODENTALS	LACCOLITIC	LACQUERING	LACTOSCOPES	LAICISATION
LABIONASAL	LACEMAKERS	LACQUERINGS	LACTOSURIA	LAICISATIONS
LABIONASALS	LACEMAKING	LACQUERWARE	LACTOSURIAS	LAICIZATION
LABIOVELAR	LACEMAKINGS	LACQUERWARES	LACTOVEGETARIAN	LAICIZATIONS
LABIOVELARS	LACERABILITIES	LACQUERWORK	LACTULOSES	LAIRDLIEST
LABORATORIES	LACERABILITY	LACQUERWORKS	LACUNOSITIES	LAIRDSHIPS
LABORATORY	LACERATING	LACQUEYING	LACUNOSITY	LAKEFRONTS
LABOREDNESS	LACERATION	LACRIMARIES	LACUSTRINE	LAKESHORES
LABOREDNESSES	LACERATIONS	LACRIMATION	LADDERIEST	LALAPALOOZA
LABORINGLY	LACERATIVE	LACRIMATIONS	LADDERLIKE	LALAPALOOZAS
LABORIOUSLY	LACERTIANS	LACRIMATOR	LADDERPROOF	LALLAPALOOZA
LABORIOUSNESS	LACERTILIAN	LACRIMATORS	LADDISHNESS	LALLAPALOOZAS
LABORIOUSNESSES	LACERTILIANS	LACRIMATORY	LADDISHNESSES	LALLATIONS
LABORSAVING	LACERTINES	LACRYMATOR	LADIESWEAR	LALLYGAGGED
LABOUREDLY	LACHRYMALS	LACRYMATORS	LADIESWEARS	LALLYGAGGING
LABOUREDNESS	LACHRYMARIES	LACRYMATORY	LADYFINGER	LAMASERAIS
LABOUREDNESSES	LACHRYMARY	LACTALBUMIN	LADYFINGERS	LAMASERIES

LAMBASTING

LAMBASTING	LAMINARIZING	LANCINATING	LANDOWNERS	LANGUISHMENT
LAMBDACISM	LAMINATING	LANCINATION	LANDOWNERSHIP	LANGUISHMENTS
LAMBDACISMS	LAMINATION	LANCINATIONS	LANDOWNERSHIPS	LANGUOROUS
LAMBDOIDAL	LAMINATIONS	LANDAMMANN	LANDOWNING	LANGUOROUSLY
LAMBENCIES	LAMINATORS	LANDAMMANNS	LANDOWNINGS	LANGUOROUSNESS
LAMBITIVES	LAMINECTOMIES	LANDAMMANS	LANDSCAPED	LANIFEROUS
LAMBREQUIN	LAMINECTOMY	LANDAULETS	LANDSCAPER	LANIGEROUS
LAMBREQUINS	LAMINGTONS	LANDAULETTE	LANDSCAPERS	LANKINESSES
LAMBRUSCOS	LAMINITISES	LANDAULETTES	LANDSCAPES	LANKNESSES
LAMBSWOOLS	LAMMERGEIER	LANDBOARDING	LANDSCAPING	LANOSITIES
LAMEBRAINED	LAMMERGEIERS	LANDBOARDINGS	LANDSCAPINGS	LANSQUENET
LAMEBRAINS	LAMMERGEYER	LANDBOARDS	LANDSCAPIST	LANSQUENETS
LAMELLARLY	LAMMERGEYERS	LANDDAMNED	LANDSCAPISTS	LANTERLOOS
LAMELLATED	LAMPADARIES	LANDDAMNES	LANDSHARKS	LANTERNING
LAMELLATELY	LAMPADEDROMIES	LANDDAMNING	LANDSKIPPED	LANTERNIST
LAMELLATION	LAMPADEDROMY	LANDDROSES	LANDSKIPPING	LANTERNISTS
LAMELLATIONS	LAMPADEPHORIA	LANDDROSTS	LANDSKNECHT	LANTHANIDE
LAMELLIBRANCH	LAMPADEPHORIAS	LANDFILLED	LANDSKNECHTS	LANTHANIDES
LAMELLIBRANCHS	LAMPADISTS	LANDFILLING	LANDSLIDDEN	LANTHANONS
LAMELLICORN	LAMPADOMANCIES	LANDFILLINGS	LANDSLIDES	LANTHANUMS
LAMELLICORNS	LAMPADOMANCY	LANDFORCES	LANDSLIDING	LANUGINOSE
LAMELLIFORM	LAMPBLACKED	LANDGRAVATE	LANDWAITER	LANUGINOUS
LAMELLIROSTRAL	LAMPBLACKING	LANDGRAVATES	LANDWAITERS	LANUGINOUSNESS
LAMELLIROSTRATE	LAMPBLACKS	LANDGRAVES	LANDWASHES	LANZKNECHT
LAMELLOSITIES	LAMPHOLDER	LANDGRAVIATE	LANGBEINITE	LANZKNECHTS
LAMELLOSITY	LAMPHOLDERS	LANDGRAVIATES	LANGBEINITES	LAODICEANS
LAMENESSES	LAMPLIGHTER	LANDGRAVINE	LANGLAUFER	LAPAROSCOPE
LAMENTABLE	LAMPLIGHTERS	LANDGRAVINES	LANGLAUFERS	LAPAROSCOPES
LAMENTABLENESS	LAMPLIGHTS	LANDHOLDER	LANGOSTINO	LAPAROSCOPIC
LAMENTABLY	LAMPOONERIES	LANDHOLDERS	LANGOSTINOS	LAPAROSCOPIES
LAMENTATION	LAMPOONERS	LANDHOLDING	LANGOUSTES	LAPAROSCOPIST
LAMENTATIONS	LAMPOONERY	LANDHOLDINGS	LANGOUSTINE	LAPAROSCOPISTS
LAMENTEDLY	LAMPOONING	LANDLADIES	LANGOUSTINES	LAPAROSCOPY
LAMENTINGLY	LAMPOONIST	LANDLESSNESS	LANGRIDGES	LAPAROTOMIES
LAMENTINGS	LAMPOONISTS	LANDLESSNESSES	LANGSPIELS	LAPAROTOMY
LAMESTREAM	LAMPROPHYRE	LANDLOCKED	LANGUAGELESS	LAPIDARIAN
LAMESTREAMS	LAMPROPHYRES	LANDLOPERS	LANGUAGING	LAPIDARIES
LAMINARIAN	LAMPROPHYRIC	LANDLORDISM	LANGUESCENT	LAPIDARIST
LAMINARIANS	LAMPSHADES	LANDLORDISMS	LANGUETTES	LAPIDARISTS
LAMINARIAS	LAMPSHELLS	LANDLUBBER	LANGUIDNESS	LAPIDATING
LAMINARINS	LAMPSTANDS	LANDLUBBERLY	LANGUIDNESSES	LAPIDATION
LAMINARISE	LANCEJACKS	LANDLUBBERS	LANGUISHED	LAPIDATIONS
LAMINARISED	LANCEOLATE	LANDLUBBING	LANGUISHER	LAPIDESCENCE
LAMINARISES	LANCEOLATED	LANDMARKED	LANGUISHERS	LAPIDESCENCES
LAMINARISING	LANCEOLATELY	LANDMARKING	LANGUISHES	LAPIDESCENT
LAMINARIZE	LANCEWOODS	LANDMASSES	LANGUISHING	LAPIDICOLOUS
LAMINARIZED	LANCINATED	LANDMINING	LANGUISHINGLY	LAPIDIFICATION
LAMINARIZES	LANCINATES	LANDMININGS	LANGUISHINGS	LAPIDIFICATIONS

LAPIDIFIED	LARYNGOLOGY	LATERISATION	LATTICEWORK	LAURUSTINUSES
LAPIDIFIES	LARYNGOPHONIES	LATERISATIONS	LATTICEWORKS	LAURVIKITE
LAPIDIFYING	LARYNGOPHONY	LATERISING	LATTICINGS	LAURVIKITES
LAPILLIFORM	LARYNGOSCOPE	LATERITIOUS	LATTICINIO	LAVALIERES
LAPSTRAKES	LARYNGOSCOPES	LATERIZATION	LAUDABILITIES	LAVALLIERE
LAPSTREAKS	LARYNGOSCOPIC	LATERIZATIONS	LAUDABILITY	LAVALLIERES
LARCENISTS	LARYNGOSCOPIES	LATERIZING	LAUDABLENESS	LAVATIONAL
LARCENOUSLY	LARYNGOSCOPIST	LATEROVERSION	LAUDABLENESSES	LAVATORIAL
LARCHWOODS	LARYNGOSCOPISTS	LATEROVERSIONS	LAUDATIONS	LAVATORIES
LARDACEOUS	LARYNGOSCOPY	LATESCENCE	LAUDATIVES	LAVENDERED
LARDALITES	LARYNGOSPASM	LATESCENCES	LAUDATORIES	LAVENDERING
LARGEHEARTED	LARYNGOSPASMS	LATHERIEST	LAUGHABLENESS	LAVERBREAD
LARGEMOUTH	LARYNGOTOMIES	LATHYRISMS	LAUGHABLENESSES	LAVERBREADS
LARGEMOUTHS	LARYNGOTOMY	LATHYRITIC	LAUGHINGLY	LAVEROCKED
LARGENESSES	LASCIVIOUS	LATHYRUSES	LAUGHINGSTOCK	LAVEROCKING
LARGHETTOS	LASCIVIOUSLY	LATICIFEROUS	LAUGHINGSTOCKS	LAVISHMENT
LARGITIONS	LASCIVIOUSNESS	LATICIFERS	LAUGHLINES	LAVISHMENTS
LARKINESSES	LASERDISCS	LATICLAVES	LAUGHWORTHIER	LAVISHNESS
LARKISHNESS	LASERDISKS	LATIFUNDIA	LAUGHWORTHIEST	LAVISHNESSES
LARKISHNESSES	LASERWORTS	LATIFUNDIO	LAUGHWORTHY	LAVOLTAING
LARRIKINISM	LASSITUDES	LATIFUNDIOS	LAUNCEGAYE	LAWBREAKER
LARRIKINISMS	LASTINGNESS	LATIFUNDIUM	LAUNCEGAYES	LAWBREAKERS
LARVACEOUS	LASTINGNESSES	LATIMERIAS	LAUNCHINGS	LAWBREAKING
LARVICIDAL	LATCHSTRING	LATINISATION	LAUNCHPADS	LAWBREAKINGS
LARVICIDED	LATCHSTRINGS	LATINISATIONS	LAUNDERERS	LAWFULNESS
LARVICIDES	LATECOMERS	LATINISING	LAUNDERETTE	LAWFULNESSES
LARVICIDING	LATEENRIGGED	LATINITIES	LAUNDERETTES	LAWGIVINGS
LARVIKITES	LATENESSES	LATINIZATION	LAUNDERING	LAWLESSNESS
LARVIPAROUS	LATENSIFICATION	LATINIZATIONS	LAUNDERINGS	LAWLESSNESSES
LARYNGEALLY	LATERALING	LATINIZING	LAUNDRESSES	LAWMAKINGS
LARYNGEALS	LATERALISATION	LATIROSTRAL	LAUNDRETTE	LAWMONGERS
LARYNGECTOMEE	LATERALISATIONS	LATIROSTRATE	LAUNDRETTES	LAWNMOWERS
LARYNGECTOMEES	LATERALISE	LATISEPTATE	LAUNDRYMAN	LAWRENCIUM
LARYNGECTOMIES	LATERALISED	LATITANCIES	LAUNDRYMEN	LAWRENCIUMS
LARYNGECTOMISED	LATERALISES	LATITATION	LAUNDRYWOMAN	LAWYERINGS
LARYNGECTOMIZED	LATERALISING	LATITATIONS	LAUNDRYWOMEN	LAWYERLIER
LARYNGECTOMY	LATERALITIES	LATITUDINAL	LAURACEOUS	LAWYERLIEST
LARYNGISMUS	LATERALITY	LATITUDINALLY	LAURDALITE	LAWYERLIKE
LARYNGISMUSES	LATERALIZATION	LATITUDINARIAN	LAURDALITES	LAXATIVENESS
LARYNGITIC	LATERALIZATIONS	LATITUDINARIANS	LAUREATESHIP	LAXATIVENESSES
LARYNGITIDES	LATERALIZE	LATITUDINOUS	LAUREATESHIPS	LAYBACKING
LARYNGITIS	LATERALIZED	LATRATIONS	LAUREATING	LAYMANISED
LARYNGITISES	LATERALIZES	LATROCINIA	LAUREATION	LAYMANISES
LARYNGOLOGIC	LATERALIZING	LATROCINIES	LAUREATIONS	LAYMANISING
LARYNGOLOGICAL	LATERALLED	LATROCINIUM	LAURELLING	LAYMANIZED
LARYNGOLOGIES	LATERALLING	LATTERMATH	LAURUSTINE	LAYMANIZES
LARYNGOLOGIST	LATERBORNS	LATTERMATHS	LAURUSTINES	LAYMANIZING
LARYNGOLOGISTS	LATERIGRADE	LATTERMOST	LAURUSTINUS	LAYPERSONS

LAZARETTES	LEATHERBOUND	LEECHCRAFTS	LEGISLATES	LEGITIMISTS
LAZARETTOS	LEATHERETTE	LEERINESSES	LEGISLATING	LEGITIMIZATION
LAZINESSES	LEATHERETTES	LEETSPEAKS	LEGISLATION	LEGITIMIZATIONS
LEACHABILITIES	LEATHERGOODS	LEFTWARDLY	LEGISLATIONS	LEGITIMIZE
LEACHABILITY	LEATHERHEAD	LEGALISATION	LEGISLATIVE	LEGITIMIZED
LEADENNESS	LEATHERHEADS	LEGALISATIONS	LEGISLATIVELY	LEGITIMIZER
LEADENNESSES	LEATHERIER	LEGALISERS	LEGISLATIVES	LEGITIMIZERS
LEADERBOARD	LEATHERIEST	LEGALISING	LEGISLATOR	LEGITIMIZES
LEADERBOARDS	LEATHERINESS	LEGALISTIC	LEGISLATORIAL	LEGITIMIZING
LEADERENES	LEATHERINESSES	LEGALISTICALLY	LEGISLATORS	LEGLESSNESS
LEADERETTE	LEATHERING	LEGALITIES	LEGISLATORSHIP	LEGLESSNESSES
LEADERETTES	LEATHERINGS	LEGALIZATION	LEGISLATORSHIPS	LEGUMINOUS
LEADERLESS	LEATHERJACKET	LEGALIZATIONS	LEGISLATRESS	LEGWARMERS
LEADERSHIP	LEATHERJACKETS	LEGALIZERS	LEGISLATRESSES	LEIOMYOMAS
LEADERSHIPS	LEATHERLEAF	LEGALIZING	LEGISLATURE	LEIOMYOMATA
LEADPLANTS	LEATHERLEAFS	LEGATARIES	LEGISLATURES	LEIOTRICHIES
LEADSCREWS	LEATHERLEAVES	LEGATESHIP	LEGITIMACIES	LEIOTRICHOUS
LEAFCUTTER	LEATHERLIKE	LEGATESHIPS	LEGITIMACY	LEIOTRICHY
LEAFCUTTERS	LEATHERNECK	LEGATIONARY	LEGITIMATE	LEISHMANIA
LEAFHOPPER	LEATHERNECKS	LEGATISSIMO	LEGITIMATED	LEISHMANIAE
LEAFHOPPERS	LEATHERWOOD	LEGATORIAL	LEGITIMATELY	LEISHMANIAL
LEAFINESSES	LEATHERWOODS	LEGENDARIES	LEGITIMATENESS	LEISHMANIAS
LEAFLESSNESS	LEATHERWORK	LEGENDARILY	LEGITIMATES	LEISHMANIASES
LEAFLESSNESSES	LEATHERWORKS	LEGENDISED	LEGITIMATING	LEISHMANIASIS
LEAFLETEER	LEAVENINGS	LEGENDISES	LEGITIMATION	LEISHMANIOSES
LEAFLETEERS	LEBENSRAUM	LEGENDISING	LEGITIMATIONS	LEISHMANIOSIS
LEAFLETERS	LEBENSRAUMS	LEGENDISTS	LEGITIMATISE	LEISTERING
LEAFLETING	LECHEROUSLY	LEGENDIZED	LEGITIMATISED	LEISURABLE
LEAFLETTED	LECHEROUSNESS	LEGENDIZES	LEGITIMATISES	LEISURABLY
LEAFLETTING	LECHEROUSNESSES	LEGENDIZING	LEGITIMATISING	LEISURELIER
LEAFSTALKS	LECITHINASE	LEGENDRIES	LEGITIMATIZE	LEISURELIEST
LEAGUERING	LECITHINASES	LEGERDEMAIN	LEGITIMATIZED	LEISURELINESS
LEAKINESSES	LECTIONARIES	LEGERDEMAINIST	LEGITIMATIZES	LEISURELINESSES
LEANNESSES	LECTIONARY	LEGERDEMAINISTS	LEGITIMATIZING	LEISUREWEAR
LEAPFROGGED	LECTISTERNIA	LEGERDEMAINS	LEGITIMATOR	LEISUREWEARS
LEAPFROGGING	LECTISTERNIUM	LEGERITIES	LEGITIMATORS	LEITMOTIFS
LEARINESSES	LECTISTERNIUMS	LEGGINESSES	LEGITIMISATION	LEITMOTIVS
LEARNABILITIES	LECTORATES	LEGIBILITIES	LEGITIMISATIONS	LEMMATISATION
LEARNABILITY	LECTORSHIP	LEGIBILITY	LEGITIMISE	LEMMATISATIONS
LEARNEDNESS	LECTORSHIPS	LEGIBLENESS	LEGITIMISED	LEMMATISED
LEARNEDNESSES	LECTOTYPES	LEGIBLENESSES	LEGITIMISER	LEMMATISES
LEASEBACKS	LECTRESSES	LEGIONARIES	LEGITIMISERS	LEMMATISING
LEASEHOLDER	LECTURESHIP	LEGIONELLA	LEGITIMISES	LEMMATIZATION
LEASEHOLDERS	LECTURESHIPS	LEGIONELLAE	LEGITIMISING	LEMMATIZATIONS
LEASEHOLDS	LECYTHIDACEOUS	LEGIONELLAS	LEGITIMISM	LEMMATIZED
LEASTAWAYS	LECYTHISES	LEGIONNAIRE	LEGITIMISMS	LEMMATIZES
LEATHERBACK	LEDERHOSEN	LEGIONNAIRES	LEGITIMIST	LEMMATIZING
LEATHERBACKS	LEECHCRAFT	LEGISLATED	LEGITIMISTIC	LEMMINGLIKE

LEMNISCATE	LEPIDOPTERAN	LESSEESHIP	LEUCOCIDINS	LEUKEMOGENESIS
LEMNISCATES	LEPIDOPTERANS	LESSEESHIPS	LEUCOCRATIC	LEUKEMOGENIC
LEMONFISHES	LEPIDOPTERIST	LESSENINGS	LEUCOCYTES	LEUKEMOGENS
LEMONGRASS	LEPIDOPTERISTS	LESSONINGS	LEUCOCYTHAEMIA	LEUKOBLAST
LEMONGRASSES	LEPIDOPTEROLOGY	LETHALITIES	LEUCOCYTHAEMIAS	LEUKOBLASTS
LEMONWOODS	LEPIDOPTERON	LETHARGICAL	LEUCOCYTIC	LEUKOCIDIN
LENGTHENED	LEPIDOPTERONS	LETHARGICALLY	LEUCOCYTOLYSES	LEUKOCIDINS
LENGTHENER	LEPIDOPTEROUS	LETHARGIED	LEUCOCYTOLYSIS	LEUKOCYTES
LENGTHENERS	LEPIDOSIREN	LETHARGIES	LEUCOCYTOPENIA	LEUKOCYTIC
LENGTHENING	LEPIDOSIRENS	LETHARGISE	LEUCOCYTOPENIAS	LEUKOCYTOLYSES
LENGTHIEST	LEPRECHAUN	LETHARGISED	LEUCOCYTOSES	LEUKOCYTOLYSIS
LENGTHINESS	LEPRECHAUNISH	LETHARGISES	LEUCOCYTOSIS	LEUKOCYTOPENIA
LENGTHINESSES	LEPRECHAUNS	LETHARGISING	LEUCOCYTOTIC	LEUKOCYTOPENIAS
LENGTHSMAN	LEPRECHAWN	LETHARGIZE	LEUCODEPLETED	LEUKOCYTOSES
LENGTHSMEN	LEPRECHAWNS	LETHARGIZED	LEUCODERMA	LEUKOCYTOSIS
LENGTHWAYS	LEPROMATOUS	LETHARGIZES	LEUCODERMAL	LEUKOCYTOTIC
LENGTHWISE	LEPROSARIA	LETHARGIZING	LEUCODERMAS	LEUKODEPLETED
LENIENCIES	LEPROSARIUM	LETHIFEROUS	LEUCODERMIA	LEUKODERMA
LENITIVELY	LEPROSARIUMS	LETROZOLES	LEUCODERMIAS	LEUKODERMAL
LENOCINIUM	LEPROSERIE	LETTERBOXED	LEUCODERMIC	LEUKODERMAS
LENOCINIUMS	LEPROSERIES	LETTERBOXES	LEUCOMAINE	LEUKODERMIC
LENTAMENTE	LEPROSITIES	LETTERBOXING	LEUCOMAINES	LEUKODYSTROPHY
LENTICELLATE	LEPROUSNESS	LETTERBOXINGS	LEUCOPENIA	LEUKOPENIA
LENTICULAR	LEPROUSNESSES	LETTERFORM	LEUCOPENIAS	LEUKOPENIAS
LENTICULARLY	LEPTOCEPHALI	LETTERFORMS	LEUCOPENIC	LEUKOPENIC
LENTICULARS	LEPTOCEPHALIC	LETTERHEAD	LEUCOPLAKIA	LEUKOPLAKIA
LENTICULES	LEPTOCEPHALOUS	LETTERHEADS	LEUCOPLAKIAS	LEUKOPLAKIAS
LENTIGINES	LEPTOCEPHALUS	LETTERINGS	LEUCOPLAKIC	LEUKOPLAKIC
LENTIGINOSE	LEPTOCERCAL	LETTERLESS	LEUCOPLAST	LEUKOPOIESES
LENTIGINOUS	LEPTODACTYL	LETTERPRESS	LEUCOPLASTID	LEUKOPOIESIS
LENTISSIMO	LEPTODACTYLOUS	LETTERPRESSES	LEUCOPLASTIDS	LEUKOPOIETIC
LENTIVIRUS	LEPTODACTYLS	LETTERSETS	LEUCOPLASTS	LEUKORRHEA
LENTIVIRUSES	LEPTOKURTIC	LETTERSPACING	LEUCOPOIESES	LEUKORRHEAL
LEONTIASES	LEPTOPHOSES	LETTERSPACINGS	LEUCOPOIESIS	LEUKORRHEAS
LEONTIASIS	LEPTOPHYLLOUS	LEUCAEMIAS	LEUCOPOIETIC	LEUKOTOMES
LEONTOPODIUM	LEPTORRHINE	LEUCAEMOGEN	LEUCORRHOEA	LEUKOTOMIES
LEONTOPODIUMS	LEPTOSOMATIC	LEUCAEMOGENESES	LEUCORRHOEAL	LEUKOTRIENE
LEOPARDESS	LEPTOSOMES	LEUCAEMOGENESIS	LEUCORRHOEAS	LEUKOTRIENES
LEOPARDESSES	LEPTOSOMIC	LEUCAEMOGENIC	LEUCOTOMES	LEVANTINES
LEOPARDSKIN	LEPTOSPIRAL	LEUCAEMOGENS	LEUCOTOMIES	LEVELHEADED
LEOPARDSKINS	LEPTOSPIRE	LEUCHAEMIA	LEUKAEMIAS	LEVELHEADEDNESS
LEPIDODENDROID	LEPTOSPIRES	LEUCHAEMIAS	LEUKAEMOGEN	LEVELLINGS
LEPIDODENDROIDS	LEPTOSPIROSES	LEUCITOHEDRA	LEUKAEMOGENESES	LEVELNESSES
LEPIDOLITE	LEPTOSPIROSIS	LEUCITOHEDRON	LEUKAEMOGENESIS	LEVERAGING
LEPIDOLITES	LEPTOTENES	LEUCITOHEDRONS	LEUKAEMOGENIC	LEVIATHANS
LEPIDOMELANE	LESBIANISM	LEUCOBLAST	LEUKAEMOGENS	LEVIGATING
LEPIDOMELANES	LESBIANISMS	LEUCOBLASTS	LEUKEMOGEN	LEVIGATION
LEPIDOPTERA	LESPEDEZAS	LEUCOCIDIN	LEUKEMOGENESES	LEVIGATIONS

LEVIGATORS	LIABILITIES	LIBERTICIDAL	LICKPENNIES	LIGHTENINGS
LEVIRATICAL	LIABLENESS	LIBERTICIDE	LICKSPITTLE	LIGHTERAGE
LEVIRATION	LIABLENESSES	LIBERTICIDES	LICKSPITTLES	LIGHTERAGES
LEVIRATIONS	LIBATIONAL	LIBERTINAGE	LIDOCAINES	LIGHTERING
LEVITATING	LIBATIONARY	LIBERTINAGES	LIEBFRAUMILCH	LIGHTERMAN
LEVITATION	LIBECCHIOS	LIBERTINES	LIEBFRAUMILCHS	LIGHTERMEN
LEVITATIONAL	LIBELLANTS	LIBERTINISM	LIENHOLDER	LIGHTFACED
LEVITATIONS	LIBELLINGS	LIBERTINISMS	LIENHOLDERS	LIGHTFACES
LEVITATORS	LIBELLOUSLY	LIBIDINALLY	LIENTERIES	LIGHTFASTNESS
LEVITICALLY	LIBELOUSLY	LIBIDINIST	LIEUTENANCIES	LIGHTFASTNESSES
LEVOROTARY	LIBERALISATION	LIBIDINISTS	LIEUTENANCY	LIGHTHEARTED
LEVOROTATORY	LIBERALISATIONS	LIBIDINOSITIES	LIEUTENANT	LIGHTHEARTEDLY
LEWDNESSES	LIBERALISE	LIBIDINOSITY	LIEUTENANTRIES	LIGHTHOUSE
LEXICALISATION	LIBERALISED	LIBIDINOUS	LIEUTENANTRY	LIGHTHOUSEMAN
LEXICALISATIONS	LIBERALISER	LIBIDINOUSLY	LIEUTENANTS	LIGHTHOUSEMEN
LEXICALISE	LIBERALISERS	LIBIDINOUSNESS	LIEUTENANTSHIP	LIGHTHOUSES
LEXICALISED	LIBERALISES	LIBRAIRIES	LIEUTENANTSHIPS	LIGHTLYING
LEXICALISES	LIBERALISING	LIBRARIANS	LIFEBLOODS	LIGHTNESSES
LEXICALISING	LIBERALISM	LIBRARIANSHIP	LIFEBOATMAN	LIGHTNINGED
LEXICALITIES	LIBERALISMS	LIBRARIANSHIPS	LIFEBOATMEN	LIGHTNINGS
LEXICALITY	LIBERALIST	LIBRATIONAL	LIFEGUARDED	LIGHTPLANE
LEXICALIZATION	LIBERALISTIC	LIBRATIONS	LIFEGUARDING	LIGHTPLANES
LEXICALIZATIONS	LIBERALISTS	LIBRETTIST	LIFEGUARDS	LIGHTPROOF
LEXICALIZE	LIBERALITIES	LIBRETTISTS	LIFEHACKED	LIGHTSHIPS
LEXICALIZED	LIBERALITY	LICENSABLE	LIFEHACKER	LIGHTSOMELY
LEXICALIZES	LIBERALIZATION	LICENSURES	LIFEHACKERS	LIGHTSOMENESS
LEXICALIZING	LIBERALIZATIONS	LICENTIATE	LIFEHACKING	LIGHTSOMENESSES
LEXICOGRAPHER	LIBERALIZE	LICENTIATES	LIFELESSLY	LIGHTTIGHT
LEXICOGRAPHERS	LIBERALIZED	LICENTIATESHIP	LIFELESSNESS	LIGHTWEIGHT
LEXICOGRAPHIC	LIBERALIZER	LICENTIATESHIPS	LIFELESSNESSES	LIGHTWEIGHTS
LEXICOGRAPHICAL	LIBERALIZERS	LICENTIATION	LIFELIKENESS	LIGHTWOODS
LEXICOGRAPHIES	LIBERALIZES	LICENTIATIONS	LIFELIKENESSES	LIGNICOLOUS
LEXICOGRAPHIST	LIBERALIZING	LICENTIOUS	LIFEMANSHIP	LIGNIFICATION
LEXICOGRAPHISTS	LIBERALNESS	LICENTIOUSLY	LIFEMANSHIPS	LIGNIFICATIONS
LEXICOGRAPHY	LIBERALNESSES	LICENTIOUSNESS	LIFESAVERS	LIGNIFYING
LEXICOLOGICAL	LIBERATING	LICHANOSES	LIFESAVING	LIGNIPERDOUS
LEXICOLOGICALLY	LIBERATION	LICHENISMS	LIFESAVINGS	LIGNIVOROUS
LEXICOLOGIES	LIBERATIONISM	LICHENISTS	LIFESTYLER	LIGNOCAINE
LEXICOLOGIST	LIBERATIONISMS	LICHENOLOGICAL	LIFESTYLERS	LIGNOCAINES
LEXICOLOGISTS	LIBERATIONIST	LICHENOLOGIES	LIFESTYLES	LIGNOCELLULOSE
LEXICOLOGY	LIBERATIONISTS	LICHENOLOGIST	LIFEWORLDS	LIGNOCELLULOSES
LEXIGRAPHIC	LIBERATIONS	LICHENOLOGISTS	LIGAMENTAL	LIGNOCELLULOSIC
LEXIGRAPHICAL	LIBERATORS	LICHENOLOGY	LIGAMENTARY	LIGNOSULFONATE
LEXIGRAPHIES	LIBERATORY	LICHTLYING	LIGAMENTOUS	LIGNOSULFONATES
LEXIGRAPHY	LIBERTARIAN	LICITNESSES	LIGATURING	LIGULIFLORAL
LEYLANDIIS	LIBERTARIANISM	LICKERISHLY	LIGHTBULBS	LIGUSTRUMS
LHERZOLITE	LIBERTARIANISMS	LICKERISHNESS	LIGHTENERS	LIKABILITIES
LHERZOLITES	LIBERTARIANS	LICKERISHNESSES	LIGHTENING	LIKABILITY

LIKABLENESS	LIMITEDNESSES	LINEOLATED	LIPOGRAMMATISMS	LIQUIDATES
LIKABLENESSES	LIMITINGLY	LINERBOARD	LIPOGRAMMATIST	LIQUIDATING
LIKEABILITIES	LIMITLESSLY	LINERBOARDS	LIPOGRAMMATISTS	LIQUIDATION
LIKEABILITY	LIMITLESSNESS	LINESCORES	LIPOGRAPHIES	LIQUIDATIONISM
LIKEABLENESS	LIMITLESSNESSES	LINGBERRIES	LIPOGRAPHY	LIQUIDATIONISMS
LIKEABLENESSES	LIMITROPHE	LINGERINGLY	LIPOMATOSES	LIQUIDATIONIST
LIKELIHOOD	LIMIVOROUS	LINGERINGS	LIPOMATOSIS	LIQUIDATIONISTS
LIKELIHOODS	LIMNOLOGIC	LINGONBERRIES	LIPOMATOUS	LIQUIDATIONS
LIKELINESS	LIMNOLOGICAL	LINGONBERRY	LIPOPHILIC	LIQUIDATOR
LIKELINESSES	LIMNOLOGICALLY	LINGUIFORM	LIPOPLASTS	LIQUIDATORS
LIKENESSES	LIMNOLOGIES	LINGUISTER	LIPOPROTEIN	LIQUIDIEST
LILANGENIS	LIMNOLOGIST	LINGUISTERS	LIPOPROTEINS	LIQUIDISED
LILIACEOUS	LIMNOLOGISTS	LINGUISTIC	LIPOSCULPTURE	LIQUIDISER
LILLIPUTIAN	LIMNOPHILOUS	LINGUISTICAL	LIPOSCULPTURES	LIQUIDISERS
LILLIPUTIANS	LIMOUSINES	LINGUISTICALLY	LIPOSUCKED	LIQUIDISES
LILTINGNESS	LIMPIDITIES	LINGUISTICIAN	LIPOSUCKING	LIQUIDISING
LILTINGNESSES	LIMPIDNESS	LINGUISTICIANS	LIPOSUCTION	LIQUIDITIES
LIMACIFORM	LIMPIDNESSES	LINGUISTICS	LIPOSUCTIONS	LIQUIDIZED
LIMACOLOGIES	LIMPNESSES	LINGUISTRIES	LIPOTROPIC	LIQUIDIZER
LIMACOLOGIST	LINCOMYCIN	LINGUISTRY	LIPOTROPIES	LIQUIDIZERS
LIMACOLOGISTS	LINCOMYCINS	LINGULATED	LIPOTROPIN	LIQUIDIZES
LIMACOLOGY	LINCRUSTAS	LINISHINGS	LIPOTROPINS	LIQUIDIZING
LIMBERNESS	LINEALITIES	LINKSLANDS	LIPPINESSES	LIQUIDNESS
LIMBERNESSES	LINEAMENTAL	LINOLEATES	LIPPITUDES	LIQUIDNESSES
LIMBURGITE	LINEAMENTS	LINOTYPERS	LIPREADERS	LIQUIDUSES
LIMBURGITES	LINEARISATION	LINOTYPING	LIPREADING	LIQUIFACTION
LIMELIGHTED	LINEARISATIONS	LINTSTOCKS	LIPREADINGS	LIQUIFACTIONS
LIMELIGHTER	LINEARISED	LINTWHITES	LIPSTICKED	LIQUIFACTIVE
LIMELIGHTERS	LINEARISES	LIONCELLES	LIPSTICKING	LIQUIFIABLE
LIMELIGHTING	LINEARISING	LIONFISHES	LIQUATIONS	LIQUIFIERS
LIMELIGHTS	LINEARITIES	LIONHEARTED	LIQUEFACIENT	LIQUIFYING
LIMERENCES	LINEARIZATION	LIONHEARTEDNESS	LIQUEFACIENTS	LIQUORICES
LIMESCALES	LINEARIZATIONS	LIONISATION	LIQUEFACTION	LIQUORISHLY
LIMESTONES	LINEARIZED	LIONISATIONS	LIQUEFACTIONS	LIQUORISHNESS
LIMEWASHES	LINEARIZES	LIONIZATION	LIQUEFACTIVE	LIQUORISHNESSES
LIMEWATERS	LINEARIZING	LIONIZATIONS	LIQUEFIABLE	LIRIODENDRA
LIMICOLINE	LINEATIONS	LIPECTOMIES	LIQUEFIERS	LIRIODENDRON
LIMICOLOUS	LINEBACKER	LIPGLOSSES	LIQUEFYING	LIRIODENDRONS
LIMINESSES	LINEBACKERS	LIPIDOPLAST	LIQUESCENCE	LISSENCEPHALOUS
LIMITABLENESS	LINEBACKING	LIPIDOPLASTS	LIQUESCENCES	LISSOMENESS
LIMITABLENESSES	LINEBACKINGS	LIPOCHROME	LIQUESCENCIES	LISSOMENESSES
LIMITARIAN	LINEBREEDING	LIPOCHROMES	LIQUESCENCY	LISSOMNESS
LIMITARIANS	LINEBREEDINGS	LIPODYSTROPHIES	LIQUESCENT	LISSOMNESSES
LIMITATION	LINECASTER	LIPODYSTROPHY	LIQUESCING	LISSOTRICHOUS
LIMITATIONAL	LINECASTERS	LIPOGENESES	LIQUEURING	LISTENABILITIES
LIMITATIONS	LINECASTING	LIPOGENESIS	LIQUIDAMBAR	LISTENABILITY
LIMITATIVE	LINECASTINGS	LIPOGRAMMATIC	LIQUIDAMBARS	LISTENABLE
LIMITEDNESS	LINENFOLDS	LIPOGRAMMATISM	LIQUIDATED	LISTENERSHIP

LISTENERSHIPS	LITEROSITIES	LITHONTHRYPTICS	LITHOTRITIES	LIVEABILITY
LISTENINGS	LITEROSITY	LITHONTRIPTIC	LITHOTRITISE	LIVEABLENESS
LISTERIOSES	LITHENESSES	LITHONTRIPTICS	LITHOTRITISED	LIVEABLENESSES
LISTERIOSIS	LITHESOMENESS	LITHONTRIPTIST	LITHOTRITISES	LIVEBLOGGED
LISTLESSLY	LITHESOMENESSES	LITHONTRIPTISTS	LITHOTRITISING	LIVEBLOGGER
LISTLESSNESS	LITHIFICATION	LITHONTRIPTOR	LITHOTRITIST	LIVEBLOGGERS
LISTLESSNESSES	LITHIFICATIONS	LITHONTRIPTORS	LITHOTRITISTS	LIVEBLOGGING
LITENESSES	LITHIFYING	LITHOPHAGOUS	LITHOTRITIZE	LIVEBLOGGINGS
LITERACIES	LITHISTIDS	LITHOPHANE	LITHOTRITIZED	LIVELIHEAD
LITERALISATION	LITHOCHROMATIC	LITHOPHANES	LITHOTRITIZES	LIVELIHEADS
LITERALISATIONS	LITHOCHROMATICS	LITHOPHILOUS	LITHOTRITIZING	LIVELIHOOD
LITERALISE	LITHOCHROMIES	LITHOPHYSA	LITHOTRITOR	LIVELIHOODS
LITERALISED	LITHOCHROMY	LITHOPHYSAE	LITHOTRITORS	LIVELINESS
LITERALISER	LITHOCLAST	LITHOPHYSE	LITHOTRITY	LIVELINESSES
LITERALISERS	LITHOCLASTS	LITHOPHYSES	LITHOTYPES	LIVENESSES
LITERALISES	LITHOCYSTS	LITHOPHYTE	LITIGATING	LIVERISHLY
LITERALISING	LITHODOMOUS	LITHOPHYTES	LITIGATION	LIVERISHNESS
LITERALISM	LITHOGENOUS	LITHOPHYTIC	LITIGATIONS	LIVERISHNESSES
LITERALISMS	LITHOGLYPH	LITHOPONES	LITIGATORS	LIVERLEAVES
LITERALIST	LITHOGLYPHS	LITHOPRINT	LITIGIOUSLY	LIVERMORIUM
LITERALISTIC	LITHOGRAPH	LITHOPRINTS	LITIGIOUSNESS	LIVERMORIUMS
LITERALISTS	LITHOGRAPHED	LITHOSPERMUM	LITIGIOUSNESSES	LIVERWORTS
LITERALITIES	LITHOGRAPHER	LITHOSPERMUMS	LITTERATEUR	LIVERWURST
LITERALITY	LITHOGRAPHERS	LITHOSPHERE	LITTERATEURS	LIVERWURSTS
LITERALIZATION	LITHOGRAPHIC	LITHOSPHERES	LITTERBAGS	LIVESTOCKS
LITERALIZATIONS	LITHOGRAPHICAL	LITHOSPHERIC	LITTERBUGS	LIVESTREAM
LITERALIZE	LITHOGRAPHIES	LITHOSTATIC	LITTERIEST	LIVESTREAMED
LITERALIZED	LITHOGRAPHING	LITHOTOMES	LITTERMATE	LIVESTREAMING
LITERALIZER	LITHOGRAPHS	LITHOTOMIC	LITTERMATES	LIVESTREAMS
LITERALIZERS	LITHOGRAPHY	LITHOTOMICAL	LITTLENECK	LIVETRAPPED
LITERALIZES	LITHOLAPAXIES	LITHOTOMIES	LITTLENECKS	LIVETRAPPING
LITERALIZING	LITHOLAPAXY	LITHOTOMIST	LITTLENESS	LIVIDITIES
LITERALNESS	LITHOLATRIES	LITHOTOMISTS	LITTLENESSES	LIVIDNESSES
LITERALNESSES	LITHOLATROUS	LITHOTOMOUS	LITTLEWORTH	LIVINGNESS
LITERARILY	LITHOLATRY	LITHOTRIPSIES	LITURGICAL	LIVINGNESSES
LITERARINESS	LITHOLOGIC	LITHOTRIPSY	LITURGICALLY	LIVRAISONS
LITERARINESSES	LITHOLOGICAL	LITHOTRIPTER	LITURGIOLOGIES	LIXIVIATED
LITERARYISM	LITHOLOGICALLY	LITHOTRIPTERS	LITURGIOLOGIST	LIXIVIATES
LITERARYISMS	LITHOLOGIES	LITHOTRIPTIC	LITURGIOLOGISTS	LIXIVIATING
LITERATELY	LITHOLOGIST	LITHOTRIPTICS	LITURGIOLOGY	LIXIVIATION
LITERATENESS	LITHOLOGISTS	LITHOTRIPTIST	LITURGISMS	LIXIVIATIONS
LITERATENESSES	LITHOMANCIES	LITHOTRIPTISTS	LITURGISTIC	LOADMASTER
LITERATION	LITHOMANCY	LITHOTRIPTOR	LITURGISTS	LOADMASTERS
LITERATIONS	LITHOMARGE	LITHOTRIPTORS	LIVABILITIES	LOADSAMONEY
LITERATORS	LITHOMARGES	LITHOTRITE	LIVABILITY	LOADSAMONEYS
LITERATURE	LITHOMETEOR	LITHOTRITES	LIVABLENESS	LOADSAMONIES
LITERATURED	LITHOMETEORS	LITHOTRITIC	LIVABLENESSES	LOADSPACES
LITERATURES	LITHONTHRYPTIC	LITHOTRITICS	LIVEABILITIES	LOADSTONES

LOAMINESSES
LOANSHIFTS
LOATHEDNESS
LOATHEDNESSES
LOATHFULNESS
LOATHFULNESSES
LOATHINGLY
LOATHLIEST
LOATHLINESS
LOATHLINESSES
LOATHNESSES
LOATHSOMELY
LOATHSOMENESS
LOATHSOMENESSES
LOBECTOMIES
LOBLOLLIES
LOBOTOMIES
LOBOTOMISE
LOBOTOMISED
LOBOTOMISES
LOBOTOMISING
LOBOTOMIZE
LOBOTOMIZED
LOBOTOMIZES
LOBOTOMIZING
LOBSCOUSES
LOBSTERERS
LOBSTERING
LOBSTERINGS
LOBSTERLIKE
LOBSTERMAN
LOBSTERMEN
LOBTAILING
LOBTAILINGS
LOBULATION
LOBULATIONS
LOCALISABILITY
LOCALISABLE
LOCALISATION
LOCALISATIONS
LOCALISERS
LOCALISING
LOCALISTIC
LOCALITIES
LOCALIZABILITY
LOCALIZABLE
LOCALIZATION
LOCALIZATIONS

LOCALIZERS
LOCALIZING
LOCALNESSES
LOCATEABLE
LOCATIONAL
LOCATIONALLY
LOCKHOUSES
LOCKKEEPER
LOCKKEEPERS
LOCKMAKERS
LOCKSMITHERIES
LOCKSMITHERY
LOCKSMITHING
LOCKSMITHINGS
LOCKSMITHS
LOCKSTITCH
LOCKSTITCHED
LOCKSTITCHES
LOCKSTITCHING
LOCOMOBILE
LOCOMOBILES
LOCOMOBILITIES
LOCOMOBILITY
LOCOMOTING
LOCOMOTION
LOCOMOTIONS
LOCOMOTIVE
LOCOMOTIVELY
LOCOMOTIVENESS
LOCOMOTIVES
LOCOMOTIVITIES
LOCOMOTIVITY
LOCOMOTORS
LOCOMOTORY
LOCOPLANTS
LOCORESTIVE
LOCULAMENT
LOCULAMENTS
LOCULATION
LOCULATIONS
LOCULICIDAL
LOCUTIONARY
LOCUTORIES
LODESTONES
LODGEMENTS
LODGEPOLES
LOFTINESSES
LOGAGRAPHIA

LOGAGRAPHIAS
LOGANBERRIES
LOGANBERRY
LOGANIACEOUS
LOGAOEDICS
LOGARITHMIC
LOGARITHMICAL
LOGARITHMICALLY
LOGARITHMS
LOGGERHEAD
LOGGERHEADED
LOGGERHEADS
LOGICALITIES
LOGICALITY
LOGICALNESS
LOGICALNESSES
LOGICISING
LOGICIZING
LOGINESSES
LOGISTICAL
LOGISTICALLY
LOGISTICIAN
LOGISTICIANS
LOGJAMMING
LOGJAMMINGS
LOGNORMALITIES
LOGNORMALITY
LOGNORMALLY
LOGOCENTRISM
LOGOCENTRISMS
LOGODAEDALIC
LOGODAEDALIES
LOGODAEDALUS
LOGODAEDALUSES
LOGODAEDALY
LOGOGRAMMATIC
LOGOGRAPHER
LOGOGRAPHERS
LOGOGRAPHIC
LOGOGRAPHICAL
LOGOGRAPHICALLY
LOGOGRAPHIES
LOGOGRAPHS
LOGOGRAPHY
LOGOGRIPHIC
LOGOGRIPHS
LOGOMACHIES
LOGOMACHIST

LOGOMACHISTS
LOGOPAEDIC
LOGOPAEDICS
LOGOPEDICS
LOGOPHILES
LOGORRHEAS
LOGORRHEIC
LOGORRHOEA
LOGORRHOEAS
LOGOTHETES
LOGOTYPIES
LOGROLLERS
LOGROLLING
LOGROLLINGS
LOINCLOTHS
LOITERINGLY
LOITERINGS
LOLLAPALOOSA
LOLLAPALOOSAS
LOLLAPALOOZA
LOLLAPALOOZAS
LOLLOPIEST
LOLLYGAGGED
LOLLYGAGGING
LOMENTACEOUS
LONELINESS
LONELINESSES
LONENESSES
LONESOMELY
LONESOMENESS
LONESOMENESSES
LONGAEVOUS
LONGANIMITIES
LONGANIMITY
LONGANIMOUS
LONGBOARDS
LONGBOWMAN
LONGBOWMEN
LONGCLOTHS
LONGEVITIES
LONGHAIRED
LONGHEADED
LONGHEADEDNESS
LONGHOUSES
LONGICAUDATE
LONGICORNS
LONGINQUITIES
LONGINQUITY

LONGIPENNATE
LONGIROSTRAL
LONGITUDES
LONGITUDINAL
LONGITUDINALLY
LONGJUMPED
LONGJUMPING
LONGLEAVES
LONGLINERS
LONGLISTED
LONGLISTING
LONGNESSES
LONGPRIMER
LONGPRIMERS
LONGSHOREMAN
LONGSHOREMEN
LONGSHORING
LONGSHORINGS
LONGSIGHTED
LONGSIGHTEDNESS
LONGSOMELY
LONGSOMENESS
LONGSOMENESSES
LONGWEARING
LOOKALIKES
LOONINESSES
LOOPHOLING
LOOPINESSES
LOOSEBOXES
LOOSENESSES
LOOSENINGS
LOOSESTRIFE
LOOSESTRIFES
LOOYENWORK
LOOYENWORKS
LOPGRASSES
LOPHOBRANCH
LOPHOBRANCHIATE
LOPHOBRANCHS
LOPHOPHORATE
LOPHOPHORE
LOPHOPHORES
LOPSIDEDLY
LOPSIDEDNESS
LOPSIDEDNESSES
LOQUACIOUS
LOQUACIOUSLY
LOQUACIOUSNESS

L

LOQUACITIES

LOQUACITIES
LORAZEPAMS
LORDLINESS
LORDLINESSES
LORDOLATRIES
LORDOLATRY
LORGNETTES
LORICATING
LORICATION
LORICATIONS
LORNNESSES
LOSABLENESS
LOSABLENESSES
LOSSMAKERS
LOSSMAKING
LOSTNESSES
LOTHNESSES
LOTUSLANDS
LOUDHAILER
LOUDHAILERS
LOUDMOUTHED
LOUDMOUTHS
LOUDNESSES
LOUDSPEAKER
LOUDSPEAKERS
LOUNDERING
LOUNDERINGS
LOUNGEWEAR
LOUNGEWEARS
LOUNGINGLY
LOUSEWORTS
LOUSINESSES
LOUTISHNESS
LOUTISHNESSES
LOVABILITIES
LOVABILITY
LOVABLENESS
LOVABLENESSES
LOVASTATIN
LOVASTATINS
LOVEABILITIES
LOVEABILITY
LOVEABLENESS
LOVEABLENESSES
LOVELESSLY
LOVELESSNESS
LOVELESSNESSES
LOVELIGHTS

LOVELIHEAD
LOVELIHEADS
LOVELINESS
LOVELINESSES
LOVELORNNESS
LOVELORNNESSES
LOVEMAKERS
LOVEMAKING
LOVEMAKINGS
LOVESICKNESS
LOVESICKNESSES
LOVESTRUCK
LOVEWORTHIER
LOVEWORTHIES
LOVEWORTHIEST
LOVEWORTHY
LOVINGNESS
LOVINGNESSES
LOWBALLING
LOWBALLINGS
LOWBROWISM
LOWBROWISMS
LOWERCASED
LOWERCASES
LOWERCASING
LOWERCLASSMAN
LOWERCLASSMEN
LOWERINGLY
LOWLANDERS
LOWLIGHTED
LOWLIGHTING
LOWLIHEADS
LOWLINESSES
LOWSENINGS
LOXODROMES
LOXODROMIC
LOXODROMICAL
LOXODROMICALLY
LOXODROMICS
LOXODROMIES
LOYALNESSES
LOZENGIEST
LUBBERLIER
LUBBERLIEST
LUBBERLINESS
LUBBERLINESSES
LUBRICANTS
LUBRICATED

LUBRICATES
LUBRICATING
LUBRICATION
LUBRICATIONAL
LUBRICATIONS
LUBRICATIVE
LUBRICATOR
LUBRICATORS
LUBRICIOUS
LUBRICIOUSLY
LUBRICITIES
LUBRICOUSLY
LUBRITORIA
LUBRITORIUM
LUBRITORIUMS
LUCIDITIES
LUCIDNESSES
LUCIFERASE
LUCIFERASES
LUCIFERINS
LUCIFEROUS
LUCIFUGOUS
LUCKENBOOTH
LUCKENBOOTHS
LUCKENGOWAN
LUCKENGOWANS
LUCKINESSES
LUCKLESSLY
LUCKLESSNESS
LUCKLESSNESSES
LUCKPENNIES
LUCRATIVELY
LUCRATIVENESS
LUCRATIVENESSES
LUCTATIONS
LUCUBRATED
LUCUBRATES
LUCUBRATING
LUCUBRATION
LUCUBRATIONS
LUCUBRATOR
LUCUBRATORS
LUCULENTLY
LUDICROUSLY
LUDICROUSNESS
LUDICROUSNESSES
LUETICALLY
LUFTMENSCH

LUFTMENSCHEN
LUGUBRIOUS
LUGUBRIOUSLY
LUGUBRIOUSNESS
LUKEWARMISH
LUKEWARMLY
LUKEWARMNESS
LUKEWARMNESSES
LUKEWARMTH
LUKEWARMTHS
LULLABYING
LUMBAGINOUS
LUMBERINGLY
LUMBERINGNESS
LUMBERINGNESSES
LUMBERINGS
LUMBERJACK
LUMBERJACKET
LUMBERJACKETS
LUMBERJACKS
LUMBERSOME
LUMBERSOMENESS
LUMBERYARD
LUMBERYARDS
LUMBOSACRAL
LUMBRICALES
LUMBRICALIS
LUMBRICALISES
LUMBRICALS
LUMBRICIFORM
LUMBRICOID
LUMBRICUSES
LUMINAIRES
LUMINANCES
LUMINARIAS
LUMINARIES
LUMINARISM
LUMINARISMS
LUMINARIST
LUMINARISTS
LUMINATION
LUMINATIONS
LUMINESCED
LUMINESCENCE
LUMINESCENCES
LUMINESCENT
LUMINESCES
LUMINESCING

LUMINIFEROUS
LUMINOSITIES
LUMINOSITY
LUMINOUSLY
LUMINOUSNESS
LUMINOUSNESSES
LUMISTEROL
LUMISTEROLS
LUMPECTOMIES
LUMPECTOMY
LUMPFISHES
LUMPINESSES
LUMPISHNESS
LUMPISHNESSES
LUMPSUCKER
LUMPSUCKERS
LUNARNAUTS
LUNATICALLY
LUNCHBOXES
LUNCHBREAK
LUNCHBREAKS
LUNCHEONED
LUNCHEONETTE
LUNCHEONETTES
LUNCHEONING
LUNCHMEATS
LUNCHPAILS
LUNCHROOMS
LUNCHTIMES
LUNGFISHES
LUNINESSES
LUNKHEADED
LURIDNESSES
LUSCIOUSLY
LUSCIOUSNESS
LUSCIOUSNESSES
LUSHNESSES
LUSKISHNESS
LUSKISHNESSES
LUSTERLESS
LUSTERWARE
LUSTERWARES
LUSTFULNESS
LUSTFULNESSES
LUSTIHEADS
LUSTIHOODS
LUSTINESSES
LUSTRATING

LUSTRATION
LUSTRATIONS
LUSTRATIVE
LUSTRELESS
LUSTREWARE
LUSTREWARES
LUSTROUSLY
LUSTROUSNESS
LUSTROUSNESSES
LUTEINISATION
LUTEINISATIONS
LUTEINISED
LUTEINISES
LUTEINISING
LUTEINIZATION
LUTEINIZATIONS
LUTEINIZED
LUTEINIZES
LUTEINIZING
LUTEOTROPHIC
LUTEOTROPHIN
LUTEOTROPHINS
LUTEOTROPIC
LUTEOTROPIN
LUTEOTROPINS
LUTESTRING
LUTESTRINGS
LUVVIEDOMS
LUXULIANITE
LUXULIANITES
LUXULLIANITE

LUXULLIANITES
LUXULYANITE
LUXULYANITES
LUXURIANCE
LUXURIANCES
LUXURIANCIES
LUXURIANCY
LUXURIANTLY
LUXURIATED
LUXURIATES
LUXURIATING
LUXURIATION
LUXURIATIONS
LUXURIOUSLY
LUXURIOUSNESS
LUXURIOUSNESSES
LYCANTHROPE
LYCANTHROPES
LYCANTHROPIC
LYCANTHROPIES
LYCANTHROPIST
LYCANTHROPISTS
LYCANTHROPY
LYCHNOSCOPE
LYCHNOSCOPES
LYCOPODIUM
LYCOPODIUMS
LYMPHADENITIS
LYMPHADENITISES
LYMPHADENOPATHY
LYMPHANGIAL

LYMPHANGIOGRAM
LYMPHANGIOGRAMS
LYMPHANGIOMA
LYMPHANGIOMAS
LYMPHANGIOMATA
LYMPHANGITIC
LYMPHANGITIDES
LYMPHANGITIS
LYMPHANGITISES
LYMPHATICALLY
LYMPHATICS
LYMPHOADENOMA
LYMPHOADENOMAS
LYMPHOADENOMATA
LYMPHOBLAST
LYMPHOBLASTIC
LYMPHOBLASTS
LYMPHOCYTE
LYMPHOCYTES
LYMPHOCYTIC
LYMPHOCYTOPENIA
LYMPHOCYTOSES
LYMPHOCYTOSIS
LYMPHOCYTOTIC
LYMPHOGRAM
LYMPHOGRAMS
LYMPHOGRANULOMA
LYMPHOGRAPHIC
LYMPHOGRAPHIES
LYMPHOGRAPHY
LYMPHOKINE

LYMPHOKINES
LYMPHOMATA
LYMPHOMATOID
LYMPHOMATOSES
LYMPHOMATOSIS
LYMPHOMATOUS
LYMPHOPENIA
LYMPHOPENIAS
LYMPHOPOIESES
LYMPHOPOIESIS
LYMPHOPOIETIC
LYMPHOSARCOMA
LYMPHOSARCOMAS
LYMPHOSARCOMATA
LYMPHOTROPHIC
LYOPHILISATION
LYOPHILISATIONS
LYOPHILISE
LYOPHILISED
LYOPHILISER
LYOPHILISERS
LYOPHILISES
LYOPHILISING
LYOPHILIZATION
LYOPHILIZATIONS
LYOPHILIZE
LYOPHILIZED
LYOPHILIZER
LYOPHILIZERS
LYOPHILIZES
LYOPHILIZING

LYOSORPTION
LYOSORPTIONS
LYRICALNESS
LYRICALNESSES
LYRICISING
LYRICIZING
LYSERGIDES
LYSIGENETIC
LYSIGENOUS
LYSIMETERS
LYSIMETRIC
LYSOGENICITIES
LYSOGENICITY
LYSOGENIES
LYSOGENISATION
LYSOGENISATIONS
LYSOGENISE
LYSOGENISED
LYSOGENISES
LYSOGENISING
LYSOGENIZATION
LYSOGENIZATIONS
LYSOGENIZE
LYSOGENIZED
LYSOGENIZES
LYSOGENIZING
LYSOLECITHIN
LYSOLECITHINS
LYTHRACEOUS

L

M

MACABERESQUE
MACADAMIAS
MACADAMISATION
MACADAMISATIONS
MACADAMISE
MACADAMISED
MACADAMISER
MACADAMISERS
MACADAMISES
MACADAMISING
MACADAMIZATION
MACADAMIZATIONS
MACADAMIZE
MACADAMIZED
MACADAMIZER
MACADAMIZERS
MACADAMIZES
MACADAMIZING
MACARISING
MACARIZING
MACARONICALLY
MACARONICS
MACARONIES
MACCARONIES
MACCARONIS
MACCHERONCINI
MACCHERONCINIS
MACCHIATOS
MACEBEARER
MACEBEARERS
MACEDOINES
MACERANDUBA
MACERANDUBAS
MACERATERS
MACERATING
MACERATION
MACERATIONS
MACERATIVE
MACERATORS
MACHAIRODONT
MACHAIRODONTS
MACHIAVELIAN

MACHIAVELIANS
MACHIAVELLIAN
MACHIAVELLIANS
MACHICOLATE
MACHICOLATED
MACHICOLATES
MACHICOLATING
MACHICOLATION
MACHICOLATIONS
MACHINABILITIES
MACHINABILITY
MACHINABLE
MACHINATED
MACHINATES
MACHINATING
MACHINATION
MACHINATIONS
MACHINATOR
MACHINATORS
MACHINEABILITY
MACHINEABLE
MACHINEGUN
MACHINEGUNNED
MACHINEGUNNING
MACHINEGUNS
MACHINELESS
MACHINELIKE
MACHINEMAN
MACHINEMEN
MACHINERIES
MACHINIMAS
MACHININGS
MACHINISTS
MACHMETERS
MACHTPOLITIK
MACHTPOLITIKS
MACINTOSHES
MACKINTOSH
MACKINTOSHES
MACONOCHIE
MACONOCHIES
MACRENCEPHALIA

MACRENCEPHALIAS
MACRENCEPHALIES
MACRENCEPHALY
MACROAGGREGATE
MACROAGGREGATED
MACROAGGREGATES
MACROBIOTA
MACROBIOTAS
MACROBIOTE
MACROBIOTES
MACROBIOTIC
MACROBIOTICS
MACROCARPA
MACROCARPAS
MACROCEPHALIA
MACROCEPHALIAS
MACROCEPHALIC
MACROCEPHALIES
MACROCEPHALOUS
MACROCEPHALY
MACROCLIMATE
MACROCLIMATES
MACROCLIMATIC
MACROCODES
MACROCOPIES
MACROCOSMIC
MACROCOSMICALLY
MACROCOSMS
MACROCYCLE
MACROCYCLES
MACROCYCLIC
MACROCYSTS
MACROCYTES
MACROCYTIC
MACROCYTOSES
MACROCYTOSIS
MACRODACTYL
MACRODACTYLIC
MACRODACTYLIES
MACRODACTYLOUS
MACRODACTYLS
MACRODACTYLY

MACRODIAGONAL
MACRODIAGONALS
MACRODOMES
MACRODONTIC
MACROECONOMIC
MACROECONOMICS
MACROEVOLUTION
MACROEVOLUTIONS
MACROFAUNA
MACROFAUNAE
MACROFAUNAS
MACROFLORA
MACROFLORAE
MACROFLORAS
MACROFOSSIL
MACROFOSSILS
MACROGAMETE
MACROGAMETES
MACROGLIAS
MACROGLOBULIN
MACROGLOBULINS
MACROGRAPH
MACROGRAPHIC
MACROGRAPHS
MACROLIDES
MACROLOGIES
MACROMARKETING
MACROMARKETINGS
MACROMERES
MACROMOLECULAR
MACROMOLECULE
MACROMOLECULES
MACROMOLES
MACROMUTATION
MACROMUTATIONS
MACRONUCLEAR
MACRONUCLEI
MACRONUCLEUS
MACRONUCLEUSES
MACRONUTRIENT
MACRONUTRIENTS
MACROPHAGE
MACROPHAGES

MACROPHAGIC
MACROPHAGOUS
MACROPHOTOGRAPH
MACROPHYLA
MACROPHYLUM
MACROPHYSICS
MACROPHYTE
MACROPHYTES
MACROPHYTIC
MACROPINACOID
MACROPINACOIDS
MACROPINAKOID
MACROPINAKOIDS
MACROPRISM
MACROPRISMS
MACROPRUDENTIAL
MACROPSIAS
MACROPTEROUS
MACROSCALE
MACROSCALES
MACROSCOPIC
MACROSCOPICALLY
MACROSOCIOLOGY
MACROSPORANGIA
MACROSPORANGIUM
MACROSPORE
MACROSPORES
MACROSTRUCTURAL
MACROSTRUCTURE
MACROSTRUCTURES
MACROZAMIA
MACROZAMIAS
MACTATIONS
MACULATING
MACULATION
MACULATIONS
MACULATURE
MACULATURES
MADBRAINED
MADDENINGLY
MADDENINGNESS
MADDENINGNESSES

MADEFACTION	MAGISTRACY	MAGNETIZED	MAHARISHIS	MAINPRISING
MADEFACTIONS	MAGISTRALITIES	MAGNETIZER	MAHATMAISM	MAINSHEETS
MADELEINES	MAGISTRALITY	MAGNETIZERS	MAHATMAISMS	MAINSPRING
MADEMOISELLE	MAGISTRALLY	MAGNETIZES	MAHLSTICKS	MAINSPRINGS
MADEMOISELLES	MAGISTRALS	MAGNETIZING	MAHOGANIES	MAINSTAGES
MADERISATION	MAGISTRAND	MAGNETOCHEMICAL	MAIASAURAS	MAINSTREAM
MADERISATIONS	MAGISTRANDS	MAGNETOELECTRIC	MAIDENHAIR	MAINSTREAMED
MADERISING	MAGISTRATE	MAGNETOGRAPH	MAIDENHAIRS	MAINSTREAMING
MADERIZATION	MAGISTRATES	MAGNETOGRAPHS	MAIDENHEAD	MAINSTREAMINGS
MADERIZATIONS	MAGISTRATESHIP	MAGNETOMETER	MAIDENHEADS	MAINSTREAMS
MADERIZING	MAGISTRATESHIPS	MAGNETOMETERS	MAIDENHOOD	MAINSTREETING
MADONNAISH	MAGISTRATIC	MAGNETOMETRIC	MAIDENHOODS	MAINSTREETINGS
MADONNAWISE	MAGISTRATICAL	MAGNETOMETRIES	MAIDENLIER	MAINTAINABILITY
MADRASSAHS	MAGISTRATICALLY	MAGNETOMETRY	MAIDENLIEST	MAINTAINABLE
MADREPORAL	MAGISTRATURE	MAGNETOMOTIVE	MAIDENLIKE	MAINTAINED
MADREPORES	MAGISTRATURES	MAGNETOPAUSE	MAIDENLINESS	MAINTAINER
MADREPORIAN	MAGMATISMS	MAGNETOPAUSES	MAIDENLINESSES	MAINTAINERS
MADREPORIANS	MAGNALIUMS	MAGNETOSPHERE	MAIDENWEED	MAINTAINING
MADREPORIC	MAGNANIMITIES	MAGNETOSPHERES	MAIDENWEEDS	MAINTENANCE
MADREPORITE	MAGNANIMITY	MAGNETOSPHERIC	MAIDISHNESS	MAINTENANCED
MADREPORITES	MAGNANIMOUS	MAGNETOSTATIC	MAIDISHNESSES	MAINTENANCES
MADREPORITIC	MAGNANIMOUSLY	MAGNETOSTATICS	MAIDSERVANT	MAINTENANCING
MADRIGALESQUE	MAGNANIMOUSNESS	MAGNETRONS	MAIDSERVANTS	MAINTOPMAST
MADRIGALIAN	MAGNATESHIP	MAGNIFIABLE	MAIEUTICAL	MAINTOPMASTS
MADRIGALIST	MAGNATESHIPS	MAGNIFICAL	MAILABILITIES	MAINTOPSAIL
MADRIGALISTS	MAGNESITES	MAGNIFICALLY	MAILABILITY	MAINTOPSAILS
MADRILENES	MAGNESIUMS	MAGNIFICAT	MAILCOACHES	MAISONETTE
MAELSTROMS	MAGNESSTONE	MAGNIFICATION	MAILGRAMMED	MAISONETTES
MAENADICALLY	MAGNESSTONES	MAGNIFICATIONS	MAILGRAMMING	MAISONNETTE
MAENADISMS	MAGNETICAL	MAGNIFICATS	MAILMERGED	MAISONNETTES
MAFFICKERS	MAGNETICALLY	MAGNIFICENCE	MAILMERGES	MAISTERDOME
MAFFICKING	MAGNETICIAN	MAGNIFICENCES	MAILMERGING	MAISTERDOMES
MAFFICKINGS	MAGNETICIANS	MAGNIFICENT	MAILPOUCHES	MAISTERING
MAGALOGUES	MAGNETISABLE	MAGNIFICENTLY	MAILSHOTTED	MAISTRINGS
MAGAZINIST	MAGNETISATION	MAGNIFICENTNESS	MAILSHOTTING	MAJESTICAL
MAGAZINISTS	MAGNETISATIONS	MAGNIFICOES	MAIMEDNESS	MAJESTICALLY
MAGDALENES	MAGNETISED	MAGNIFICOS	MAIMEDNESSES	MAJESTICALNESS
MAGGOTIEST	MAGNETISER	MAGNIFIERS	MAINBRACES	MAJESTICNESS
MAGGOTORIA	MAGNETISERS	MAGNIFYING	MAINFRAMES	MAJESTICNESSES
MAGGOTORIUM	MAGNETISES	MAGNILOQUENCE	MAINLANDER	MAJOLICAWARE
MAGIANISMS	MAGNETISING	MAGNILOQUENCES	MAINLANDERS	MAJOLICAWARES
MAGISTERIAL	MAGNETISMS	MAGNILOQUENT	MAINLINERS	MAJORDOMOS
MAGISTERIALLY	MAGNETISTS	MAGNILOQUENTLY	MAINLINING	MAJORETTES
MAGISTERIALNESS	MAGNETITES	MAGNITUDES	MAINLININGS	MAJORETTING
MAGISTERIES	MAGNETITIC	MAGNITUDINOUS	MAINPERNOR	MAJORETTINGS
MAGISTERIUM	MAGNETIZABLE	MAGNOLIACEOUS	MAINPERNORS	MAJORITAIRE
MAGISTERIUMS	MAGNETIZATION	MAHARAJAHS	MAINPRISED	MAJORITAIRES
MAGISTRACIES	MAGNETIZATIONS	MAHARANEES	MAINPRISES	MAJORITARIAN

M

MAJORITARIANISM	MALAGUETTAS	MALEFFECTS	MALLEABLENESS	MALVOISIES
MAJORITARIANS	MALAKATOONE	MALEFICALLY	MALLEABLENESSES	MAMAGUYING
MAJORITIES	MALAKATOONES	MALEFICENCE	MALLEATING	MAMILLATED
MAJORSHIPS	MALAPERTLY	MALEFICENCES	MALLEATION	MAMILLATION
MAJUSCULAR	MALAPERTNESS	MALEFICENT	MALLEATIONS	MAMILLATIONS
MAJUSCULES	MALAPERTNESSES	MALEFICIAL	MALLEIFORM	MAMILLIFORM
MAKEREADIES	MALAPPORTIONED	MALENESSES	MALLEMAROKING	MAMMALIANS
MAKESHIFTS	MALAPPROPRIATE	MALENGINES	MALLEMAROKINGS	MAMMALIFEROUS
MAKEWEIGHT	MALAPPROPRIATED	MALENTENDU	MALLEMUCKS	MAMMALITIES
MAKEWEIGHTS	MALAPPROPRIATES	MALENTENDUS	MALLENDERS	MAMMALOGICAL
MAKUNOUCHI	MALAPROPIAN	MALEVOLENCE	MALLEOLUSES	MAMMALOGIES
MAKUNOUCHIS	MALAPROPISM	MALEVOLENCES	MALLOPHAGOUS	MAMMALOGIST
MALABSORPTION	MALAPROPISMS	MALEVOLENT	MALLOWPUFF	MAMMALOGISTS
MALABSORPTIONS	MALAPROPIST	MALEVOLENTLY	MALLOWPUFFS	MAMMAPLASTIES
MALACHITES	MALAPROPISTS	MALFEASANCE	MALMSTONES	MAMMAPLASTY
MALACOLOGICAL	MALAPROPOS	MALFEASANCES	MALNOURISHED	MAMMECTOMIES
MALACOLOGIES	MALARIOLOGIES	MALFEASANT	MALNUTRITION	MAMMECTOMY
MALACOLOGIST	MALARIOLOGIST	MALFEASANTS	MALNUTRITIONS	MAMMETRIES
MALACOLOGISTS	MALARIOLOGISTS	MALFORMATION	MALOCCLUDED	MAMMIFEROUS
MALACOLOGY	MALARIOLOGY	MALFORMATIONS	MALOCCLUSION	MAMMILLARIA
MALACOPHILIES	MALASSIMILATION	MALFUNCTION	MALOCCLUSIONS	MAMMILLARIAS
MALACOPHILOUS	MALATHIONS	MALFUNCTIONED	MALODOROUS	MAMMILLARY
MALACOPHILY	MALAXATING	MALFUNCTIONING	MALODOROUSLY	MAMMILLATE
MALACOPHYLLOUS	MALAXATION	MALFUNCTIONINGS	MALODOROUSNESS	MAMMILLATED
MALACOPTERYGIAN	MALAXATIONS	MALFUNCTIONS	MALOLACTIC	MAMMILLATION
MALACOSTRACAN	MALAXATORS	MALICIOUSLY	MALONYLUREA	MAMMILLATIONS
MALACOSTRACANS	MALCONFORMATION	MALICIOUSNESS	MALONYLUREAS	MAMMILLIFORM
MALACOSTRACOUS	MALCONTENT	MALICIOUSNESSES	MALPIGHIACEOUS	MAMMITIDES
MALADAPTATION	MALCONTENTED	MALIGNANCE	MALPIGHIAS	MAMMOCKING
MALADAPTATIONS	MALCONTENTEDLY	MALIGNANCES	MALPOSITION	MAMMOGENIC
MALADAPTED	MALCONTENTS	MALIGNANCIES	MALPOSITIONS	MAMMOGRAMS
MALADAPTIVE	MALDEPLOYMENT	MALIGNANCY	MALPRACTICE	MAMMOGRAPH
MALADAPTIVELY	MALDEPLOYMENTS	MALIGNANTLY	MALPRACTICES	MAMMOGRAPHIC
MALADDRESS	MALDISTRIBUTION	MALIGNANTS	MALPRACTITIONER	MAMMOGRAPHIES
MALADDRESSES	MALEDICENT	MALIGNITIES	MALPRESENTATION	MAMMOGRAPHS
MALADJUSTED	MALEDICTED	MALIGNMENT	MALTALENTS	MAMMOGRAPHY
MALADJUSTIVE	MALEDICTING	MALIGNMENTS	MALTINESSES	MAMMONISMS
MALADJUSTMENT	MALEDICTION	MALIMPRINTED	MALTODEXTRIN	MAMMONISTIC
MALADJUSTMENTS	MALEDICTIONS	MALIMPRINTING	MALTODEXTRINS	MAMMONISTS
MALADMINISTER	MALEDICTIVE	MALIMPRINTINGS	MALTREATED	MAMMONITES
MALADMINISTERED	MALEDICTORY	MALINGERED	MALTREATER	MAMMOPLASTIES
MALADMINISTERS	MALEFACTION	MALINGERER	MALTREATERS	MAMMOPLASTY
MALADROITLY	MALEFACTIONS	MALINGERERS	MALTREATING	MANAGEABILITIES
MALADROITNESS	MALEFACTOR	MALINGERIES	MALTREATMENT	MANAGEABILITY
MALADROITNESSES	MALEFACTORS	MALINGERING	MALTREATMENTS	MANAGEABLE
MALADROITS	MALEFACTORY	MALLANDERS	MALVACEOUS	MANAGEABLENESS
MALAGUENAS	MALEFACTRESS	MALLEABILITIES	MALVERSATION	MANAGEABLY
MALAGUETTA	MALEFACTRESSES	MALLEABILITY	MALVERSATIONS	MANAGEMENT

MANAGEMENTAL	MANDUCATING	MANICURISTS	MANNERISTICALLY	MANSUETUDE
MANAGEMENTS	MANDUCATION	MANIFESTABLE	MANNERISTS	MANSUETUDES
MANAGERESS	MANDUCATIONS	MANIFESTANT	MANNERLESS	MANTELLETTA
MANAGERESSES	MANDUCATORY	MANIFESTANTS	MANNERLESSNESS	MANTELLETTAS
MANAGERIAL	MANDYLIONS	MANIFESTATION	MANNERLIER	MANTELPIECE
MANAGERIALISM	MANEUVERABILITY	MANIFESTATIONAL	MANNERLIEST	MANTELPIECES
MANAGERIALISMS	MANEUVERABLE	MANIFESTATIONS	MANNERLINESS	MANTELSHELF
MANAGERIALIST	MANEUVERED	MANIFESTATIVE	MANNERLINESSES	MANTELSHELVES
MANAGERIALISTS	MANEUVERER	MANIFESTED	MANNIFEROUS	MANTELTREE
MANAGERIALLY	MANEUVERERS	MANIFESTER	MANNISHNESS	MANTELTREES
MANAGERSHIP	MANEUVERING	MANIFESTERS	MANNISHNESSES	MANTICALLY
MANAGERSHIPS	MANEUVERINGS	MANIFESTIBLE	MANOEUVERED	MANTICORAS
MANCHESTER	MANFULLEST	MANIFESTING	MANOEUVERING	MANTICORES
MANCHESTERS	MANFULNESS	MANIFESTLY	MANOEUVERS	MANTLETREE
MANCHINEEL	MANFULNESSES	MANIFESTNESS	MANOEUVRABILITY	MANTLETREES
MANCHINEELS	MANGABEIRA	MANIFESTNESSES	MANOEUVRABLE	MANTYHOSES
MANCIPATED	MANGABEIRAS	MANIFESTOED	MANOEUVRED	MANUBRIUMS
MANCIPATES	MANGALSUTRA	MANIFESTOES	MANOEUVRER	MANUFACTORIES
MANCIPATING	MANGALSUTRAS	MANIFESTOING	MANOEUVRERS	MANUFACTORY
MANCIPATION	MANGANATES	MANIFESTOS	MANOEUVRES	MANUFACTURABLE
MANCIPATIONS	MANGANESES	MANIFOLDED	MANOEUVRING	MANUFACTURAL
MANCIPATORY	MANGANESIAN	MANIFOLDER	MANOEUVRINGS	MANUFACTURE
MANDAMUSED	MANGANIFEROUS	MANIFOLDERS	MANOMETERS	MANUFACTURED
MANDAMUSES	MANGANITES	MANIFOLDING	MANOMETRIC	MANUFACTURER
MANDAMUSING	MANGELWURZEL	MANIFOLDLY	MANOMETRICAL	MANUFACTURERS
MANDARINATE	MANGELWURZELS	MANIFOLDNESS	MANOMETRICALLY	MANUFACTURES
MANDARINATES	MANGEMANGE	MANIFOLDNESSES	MANOMETRIES	MANUFACTURING
MANDARINES	MANGEMANGES	MANIPULABILITY	MANORIALISM	MANUFACTURINGS
MANDARINIC	MANGETOUTS	MANIPULABLE	MANORIALISMS	MANUMISSION
MANDARINISM	MANGINESSES	MANIPULARS	MANOSCOPIES	MANUMISSIONS
MANDARINISMS	MANGOLDWURZEL	MANIPULATABLE	MANRIKIGUSARI	MANUMITTED
MANDATARIES	MANGOLDWURZELS	MANIPULATE	MANRIKIGUSARIS	MANUMITTER
MANDATORIES	MANGOSTANS	MANIPULATED	MANSCAPING	MANUMITTERS
MANDATORILY	MANGOSTEEN	MANIPULATES	MANSCAPINGS	MANUMITTING
MANDIBULAR	MANGOSTEENS	MANIPULATING	MANSERVANT	MANURANCES
MANDIBULATE	MANGOUSTES	MANIPULATION	MANSIONARIES	MANUSCRIPT
MANDIBULATED	MANGULATED	MANIPULATIONS	MANSIONARY	MANUSCRIPTS
MANDIBULATES	MANGULATES	MANIPULATIVE	MANSLAUGHTER	MANZANILLA
MANDILIONS	MANGULATING	MANIPULATIVELY	MANSLAUGHTERS	MANZANILLAS
MANDIOCCAS	MANHANDLED	MANIPULATIVES	MANSLAYERS	MANZANITAS
MANDOLINES	MANHANDLES	MANIPULATOR	MANSONRIES	MAPMAKINGS
MANDOLINIST	MANHANDLING	MANIPULATORS	MANSPLAINED	MAPPEMONDS
MANDOLINISTS	MANHATTANS	MANIPULATORY	MANSPLAINING	MAQUILADORA
MANDRAGORA	MANHUNTERS	MANLINESSES	MANSPLAININGS	MAQUILADORAS
MANDRAGORAS	MANIACALLY	MANNEQUINS	MANSPLAINS	MAQUILLAGE
MANDUCABLE	MANICOTTIS	MANNERISMS	MANSPREADING	MAQUILLAGES
MANDUCATED	MANICURING	MANNERISTIC	MANSPREADINGS	MAQUISARDS
MANDUCATES	MANICURIST	MANNERISTICAL	MANSPREADS	MARABUNTAS

MARANATHAS	MARGARINES	MARIHUANAS	MARLINSPIKE	MARROWSKIES
MARASCHINO	MARGARITAS	MARIJUANAS	MARLINSPIKES	MARROWSKYING
MARASCHINOS	MARGARITES	MARIMBAPHONE	MARLSTONES	MARSEILLES
MARASMUSES	MARGARITIC	MARIMBAPHONES	MARMALADES	MARSHALCIES
MARATHONER	MARGARITIFEROUS	MARIMBISTS	MARMALISED	MARSHALERS
MARATHONERS	MARGENTING	MARINADING	MARMALISES	MARSHALING
MARATHONING	MARGHERITA	MARINATING	MARMALISING	MARSHALLED
MARATHONINGS	MARGHERITAS	MARINATION	MARMALIZED	MARSHALLER
MARAUDINGS	MARGINALIA	MARINATIONS	MARMALIZES	MARSHALLERS
MARBELISED	MARGINALISATION	MARIONBERRIES	MARMALIZING	MARSHALLING
MARBELISES	MARGINALISE	MARIONBERRY	MARMARISED	MARSHALLINGS
MARBELISING	MARGINALISED	MARIONETTE	MARMARISES	MARSHALSHIP
MARBELIZED	MARGINALISES	MARIONETTES	MARMARISING	MARSHALSHIPS
MARBELIZES	MARGINALISING	MARISCHALLED	MARMARIZED	MARSHBUCKS
MARBELIZING	MARGINALISM	MARISCHALLING	MARMARIZES	MARSHELDER
MARBLEISED	MARGINALISMS	MARISCHALS	MARMARIZING	MARSHELDERS
MARBLEISES	MARGINALIST	MARIVAUDAGE	MARMAROSES	MARSHINESS
MARBLEISING	MARGINALISTS	MARIVAUDAGES	MARMAROSIS	MARSHINESSES
MARBLEIZED	MARGINALITIES	MARKEDNESS	MARMELISED	MARSHLANDER
MARBLEIZES	MARGINALITY	MARKEDNESSES	MARMELISES	MARSHLANDERS
MARBLEIZING	MARGINALIZATION	MARKETABILITIES	MARMELISING	MARSHLANDS
MARBLEWOOD	MARGINALIZE	MARKETABILITY	MARMELIZED	MARSHLOCKS
MARBLEWOODS	MARGINALIZED	MARKETABLE	MARMELIZES	MARSHLOCKSES
MARCANTANT	MARGINALIZES	MARKETABLENESS	MARMELIZING	MARSHMALLOW
MARCANTANTS	MARGINALIZING	MARKETABLY	MARMOREALLY	MARSHMALLOWIER
MARCASITES	MARGINALLY	MARKETEERS	MAROONINGS	MARSHMALLOWIEST
MARCASITICAL	MARGINATED	MARKETINGS	MARPRELATE	MARSHMALLOWS
MARCATISSIMO	MARGINATES	MARKETISATION	MARPRELATED	MARSHMALLOWY
MARCELLERS	MARGINATING	MARKETISATIONS	MARPRELATES	MARSHWORTS
MARCELLING	MARGINATION	MARKETISED	MARPRELATING	MARSIPOBRANCH
MARCESCENCE	MARGINATIONS	MARKETISES	MARQUESSATE	MARSIPOBRANCHS
MARCESCENCES	MARGRAVATE	MARKETISING	MARQUESSATES	MARSQUAKES
MARCESCENT	MARGRAVATES	MARKETIZATION	MARQUESSES	MARSUPIALIAN
MARCESCIBLE	MARGRAVIAL	MARKETIZATIONS	MARQUETERIE	MARSUPIALIANS
MARCHANTIA	MARGRAVIATE	MARKETIZED	MARQUETERIES	MARSUPIALS
MARCHANTIAS	MARGRAVIATES	MARKETIZES	MARQUETRIES	MARSUPIANS
MARCHIONESS	MARGRAVINE	MARKETIZING	MARQUISATE	MARTELLANDO
MARCHIONESSES	MARGRAVINES	MARKETPLACE	MARQUISATES	MARTELLANDOS
MARCHLANDS	MARGUERITA	MARKETPLACES	MARQUISETTE	MARTELLATO
MARCHPANES	MARGUERITAS	MARKSMANSHIP	MARQUISETTES	MARTELLATOS
MARCONIGRAM	MARGUERITE	MARKSMANSHIPS	MARRIAGEABILITY	MARTELLING
MARCONIGRAMS	MARGUERITES	MARKSWOMAN	MARRIAGEABLE	MARTENSITE
MARCONIGRAPH	MARIALITES	MARKSWOMEN	MARROWBONE	MARTENSITES
MARCONIGRAPHED	MARICULTURE	MARLACIOUS	MARROWBONES	MARTENSITIC
MARCONIGRAPHING	MARICULTURES	MARLINESPIKE	MARROWFATS	MARTENSITICALLY
MARCONIGRAPHS	MARICULTURIST	MARLINESPIKES	MARROWIEST	MARTIALISM
MARCONIING	MARICULTURISTS	MARLINGSPIKE	MARROWLESS	MARTIALISMS
MARESCHALS	MARIGRAPHS	MARLINGSPIKES	MARROWSKIED	MARTIALIST

MARTIALISTS	MASCULINIST	MASSOTHERAPIST	MASTICATOR	MATCHMAKINGS
MARTIALNESS	MASCULINISTS	MASSOTHERAPISTS	MASTICATORIES	MATCHMARKED
MARTIALNESSES	MASCULINITIES	MASSOTHERAPY	MASTICATORS	MATCHMARKING
MARTINETISH	MASCULINITY	MASSPRIEST	MASTICATORY	MATCHMARKS
MARTINETISM	MASCULINIZATION	MASSPRIESTS	MASTIGOPHORAN	MATCHPLAYS
MARTINETISMS	MASCULINIZE	MASSYMORES	MASTIGOPHORANS	MATCHSTICK
MARTINGALE	MASCULINIZED	MASTECTOMIES	MASTIGOPHORE	MATCHSTICKS
MARTINGALES	MASCULINIZES	MASTECTOMY	MASTIGOPHORES	MATCHWOODS
MARTINGALS	MASCULINIZING	MASTERATES	MASTIGOPHORIC	MATELASSES
MARTYRDOMS	MASCULISTS	MASTERCLASS	MASTIGOPHOROUS	MATELLASSE
MARTYRISATION	MASHGICHIM	MASTERCLASSES	MASTITIDES	MATELLASSES
MARTYRISATIONS	MASKALLONGE	MASTERDOMS	MASTITISES	MATELOTTES
MARTYRISED	MASKALLONGES	MASTERFULLY	MASTODONIC	MATERFAMILIAS
MARTYRISES	MASKALONGE	MASTERFULNESS	MASTODONTIC	MATERFAMILIASES
MARTYRISING	MASKALONGES	MASTERFULNESSES	MASTODONTS	MATERIALISATION
MARTYRIZATION	MASKANONGE	MASTERHOOD	MASTODYNIA	MATERIALISE
MARTYRIZATIONS	MASKANONGES	MASTERHOODS	MASTODYNIAS	MATERIALISED
MARTYRIZED	MASKINONGE	MASTERINGS	MASTOIDECTOMIES	MATERIALISER
MARTYRIZES	MASKINONGES	MASTERLESS	MASTOIDECTOMY	MATERIALISERS
MARTYRIZING	MASKIROVKA	MASTERLIER	MASTOIDITIDES	MATERIALISES
MARTYROLOGIC	MASKIROVKAS	MASTERLIEST	MASTOIDITIS	MATERIALISING
MARTYROLOGICAL	MASOCHISMS	MASTERLINESS	MASTOIDITISES	MATERIALISM
MARTYROLOGIES	MASOCHISTIC	MASTERLINESSES	MASTOPEXIES	MATERIALISMS
MARTYROLOGIST	MASOCHISTICALLY	MASTERMIND	MASTURBATE	MATERIALIST
MARTYROLOGISTS	MASOCHISTS	MASTERMINDED	MASTURBATED	MATERIALISTIC
MARTYROLOGY	MASONICALLY	MASTERMINDING	MASTURBATES	MATERIALISTICAL
MARVELLERS	MASQUERADE	MASTERMINDS	MASTURBATING	MATERIALISTS
MARVELLING	MASQUERADED	MASTERPIECE	MASTURBATION	MATERIALITIES
MARVELLOUS	MASQUERADER	MASTERPIECES	MASTURBATIONS	MATERIALITY
MARVELLOUSLY	MASQUERADERS	MASTERSHIP	MASTURBATOR	MATERIALIZATION
MARVELLOUSNESS	MASQUERADES	MASTERSHIPS	MASTURBATORS	MATERIALIZE
MARVELOUSLY	MASQUERADING	MASTERSINGER	MASTURBATORY	MATERIALIZED
MARVELOUSNESS	MASSACRERS	MASTERSINGERS	MATACHINAS	MATERIALIZER
MARVELOUSNESSES	MASSACRING	MASTERSTROKE	MATAGOURIS	MATERIALIZERS
MARZIPANNED	MASSAGISTS	MASTERSTROKES	MATCHBOARD	MATERIALIZES
MARZIPANNING	MASSARANDUBA	MASTERWORK	MATCHBOARDING	MATERIALIZING
MASCARAING	MASSARANDUBAS	MASTERWORKS	MATCHBOARDINGS	MATERIALLY
MASCARPONE	MASSASAUGA	MASTERWORT	MATCHBOARDS	MATERIALNESS
MASCARPONES	MASSASAUGAS	MASTERWORTS	MATCHBOOKS	MATERIALNESSES
MASCULINELY	MASSERANDUBA	MASTHEADED	MATCHBOXES	MATERNALISM
MASCULINENESS	MASSERANDUBAS	MASTHEADING	MATCHLESSLY	MATERNALISMS
MASCULINENESSES	MASSETERIC	MASTHOUSES	MATCHLESSNESS	MATERNALISTIC
MASCULINES	MASSIFICATION	MASTICABLE	MATCHLESSNESSES	MATERNALLY
MASCULINISATION	MASSIFICATIONS	MASTICATED	MATCHLOCKS	MATERNITIES
MASCULINISE	MASSINESSES	MASTICATES	MATCHMAKER	MATEYNESSES
MASCULINISED	MASSIVENESS	MASTICATING	MATCHMAKERS	MATFELLONS
MASCULINISES	MASSIVENESSES	MASTICATION	MATCHMAKES	MATGRASSES
MASCULINISING	MASSOTHERAPIES	MASTICATIONS	MATCHMAKING	MATHEMATIC

MATHEMATICAL	MATRICULATION	MATRYOSHKI	MAXIMATION	MEASLINESSES
MATHEMATICALLY	MATRICULATIONS	MATSUTAKES	MAXIMATIONS	MEASURABILITIES
MATHEMATICIAN	MATRICULATOR	MATTAMORES	MAXIMISATION	MEASURABILITY
MATHEMATICIANS	MATRICULATORS	MATTERIEST	MAXIMISATIONS	MEASURABLE
MATHEMATICISE	MATRICULATORY	MATTERLESS	MAXIMISERS	MEASURABLENESS
MATHEMATICISED	MATRIFOCAL	MATTIFYING	MAXIMISING	MEASURABLY
MATHEMATICISES	MATRIFOCALITIES	MATTRASSES	MAXIMIZATION	MEASUREDLY
MATHEMATICISING	MATRIFOCALITY	MATTRESSES	MAXIMIZATIONS	MEASUREDNESS
MATHEMATICISM	MATRILINEAL	MATURATING	MAXIMIZERS	MEASUREDNESSES
MATHEMATICISMS	MATRILINEALLY	MATURATION	MAXIMIZING	MEASURELESS
MATHEMATICIZE	MATRILINEAR	MATURATIONAL	MAYFLOWERS	MEASURELESSLY
MATHEMATICIZED	MATRILINIES	MATURATIONS	MAYONNAISE	MEASURELESSNESS
MATHEMATICIZES	MATRILOCAL	MATURATIVE	MAYONNAISES	MEASUREMENT
MATHEMATICIZING	MATRILOCALITIES	MATURENESS	MAYORALTIES	MEASUREMENTS
MATHEMATICS	MATRILOCALITY	MATURENESSES	MAYORESSES	MEASURINGS
MATHEMATISATION	MATRILOCALLY	MATURITIES	MAYORSHIPS	MEATINESSES
MATHEMATISE	MATRIMONIAL	MATUTINALLY	MAYSTERDOME	MEATLOAVES
MATHEMATISED	MATRIMONIALLY	MAUDLINISM	MAYSTERDOMES	MEATPACKER
MATHEMATISES	MATRIMONIES	MAUDLINISMS	MAZARINADE	MEATPACKERS
MATHEMATISING	MATRIOSHKA	MAUDLINNESS	MAZARINADES	MEATPACKING
MATHEMATIZATION	MATRIOSHKAS	MAUDLINNESSES	MAZEDNESSES	MEATPACKINGS
MATHEMATIZE	MATRIOSHKI	MAULSTICKS	MAZINESSES	MEATSCREEN
MATHEMATIZED	MATROCLINAL	MAUMETRIES	MEADOWIEST	MEATSCREENS
MATHEMATIZES	MATROCLINIC	MAUNDERERS	MEADOWLAND	MEATSPACES
MATHEMATIZING	MATROCLINIES	MAUNDERING	MEADOWLANDS	MECAMYLAMINE
MATINESSES	MATROCLINOUS	MAUNDERINGS	MEADOWLARK	MECAMYLAMINES
MATRESFAMILIAS	MATROCLINY	MAUSOLEUMS	MEADOWLARKS	MECHANICAL
MATRIARCHAL	MATRONAGES	MAVERICKED	MEADOWSWEET	MECHANICALISM
MATRIARCHALISM	MATRONHOOD	MAVERICKING	MEADOWSWEETS	MECHANICALISMS
MATRIARCHALISMS	MATRONHOODS	MAVOURNEEN	MEAGERNESS	MECHANICALLY
MATRIARCHATE	MATRONISED	MAVOURNEENS	MEAGERNESSES	MECHANICALNESS
MATRIARCHATES	MATRONISES	MAVOURNINS	MEAGRENESS	MECHANICALS
MATRIARCHIC	MATRONISING	MAWKISHNESS	MEAGRENESSES	MECHANICIAN
MATRIARCHIES	MATRONIZED	MAWKISHNESSES	MEALINESSES	MECHANICIANS
MATRIARCHS	MATRONIZES	MAWMETRIES	MEALYMOUTHED	MECHANISABLE
MATRIARCHY	MATRONIZING	MAXIDRESSES	MEANDERERS	MECHANISATION
MATRICIDAL	MATRONLIER	MAXILLARIES	MEANDERING	MECHANISATIONS
MATRICIDES	MATRONLIEST	MAXILLIPED	MEANDERINGLY	MECHANISED
MATRICLINIC	MATRONLINESS	MAXILLIPEDARY	MEANDERINGS	MECHANISER
MATRICLINOUS	MATRONLINESSES	MAXILLIPEDE	MEANINGFUL	MECHANISERS
MATRICULANT	MATRONSHIP	MAXILLIPEDES	MEANINGFULLY	MECHANISES
MATRICULANTS	MATRONSHIPS	MAXILLIPEDS	MEANINGFULNESS	MECHANISING
MATRICULAR	MATRONYMIC	MAXILLOFACIAL	MEANINGLESS	MECHANISMS
MATRICULAS	MATRONYMICS	MAXILLULAE	MEANINGLESSLY	MECHANISTIC
MATRICULATE	MATROYSHKA	MAXIMALIST	MEANINGLESSNESS	MECHANISTICALLY
MATRICULATED	MATROYSHKAS	MAXIMALISTS	MEANNESSES	MECHANISTS
MATRICULATES	MATRYOSHKA	MAXIMAPHILIES	MEANWHILES	MECHANIZABLE
MATRICULATING	MATRYOSHKAS	MAXIMAPHILY	MEASLINESS	MECHANIZATION

MECHANIZATIONS	MEDIATIZATION	MEDIEVALISTIC	MEGAFLORAE	MEGAPHONIC
MECHANIZED	MEDIATIZATIONS	MEDIEVALISTS	MEGAFLORAS	MEGAPHONICALLY
MECHANIZER	MEDIATIZED	MEDIEVALLY	MEGAGAMETE	MEGAPHONING
MECHANIZERS	MEDIATIZES	MEDIOCRACIES	MEGAGAMETES	MEGAPHYLLS
MECHANIZES	MEDIATIZING	MEDIOCRACY	MEGAGAMETOPHYTE	MEGAPIXELS
MECHANIZING	MEDIATORIAL	MEDIOCRITIES	MEGAGAUSSES	MEGAPLEXES
MECHANOCHEMICAL	MEDIATORIALLY	MEDIOCRITY	MEGAHERBIVORE	MEGAPROJECT
MECHANOMORPHISM	MEDIATORSHIP	MEDITATING	MEGAHERBIVORES	MEGAPROJECTS
MECHANORECEPTOR	MEDIATORSHIPS	MEDITATION	MEGAHERTZES	MEGAQUAKES
MECHANOTHERAPY	MEDIATRESS	MEDITATIONS	MEGAJOULES	MEGASCOPES
MECHATRONIC	MEDIATRESSES	MEDITATIVE	MEGAKARYOCYTE	MEGASCOPIC
MECHATRONICS	MEDIATRICES	MEDITATIVELY	MEGAKARYOCYTES	MEGASCOPICALLY
MECLIZINES	MEDIATRIXES	MEDITATIVENESS	MEGAKARYOCYTIC	MEGASPORANGIA
MECONOPSES	MEDICALISATION	MEDITATORS	MEGALITHIC	MEGASPORANGIUM
MECONOPSIS	MEDICALISATIONS	MEDITERRANEAN	MEGALITRES	MEGASPORES
MEDAILLONS	MEDICALISE	MEDIUMISTIC	MEGALOBLAST	MEGASPORIC
MEDALLIONED	MEDICALISED	MEDIUMSHIP	MEGALOBLASTIC	MEGASPOROPHYLL
MEDALLIONING	MEDICALISES	MEDIUMSHIPS	MEGALOBLASTS	MEGASPOROPHYLLS
MEDALLIONS	MEDICALISING	MEDIVACING	MEGALOCARDIA	MEGASTORES
MEDALLISTS	MEDICALIZATION	MEDIVACKED	MEGALOCARDIAS	MEGASTORMS
MEDALPLAYS	MEDICALIZATIONS	MEDIVACKING	MEGALOCEPHALIC	MEGASTRUCTURE
MEDDLESOME	MEDICALIZE	MEDRESSEHS	MEGALOCEPHALIES	MEGASTRUCTURES
MEDDLESOMELY	MEDICALIZED	MEDULLATED	MEGALOCEPHALOUS	MEGATECHNOLOGY
MEDDLESOMENESS	MEDICALIZES	MEDULLOBLASTOMA	MEGALOCEPHALY	MEGATHERES
MEDDLINGLY	MEDICALIZING	MEDUSIFORM	MEGALODONS	MEGATHERIAN
MEDEVACING	MEDICAMENT	MEEKNESSES	MEGALOMANIA	MEGATHRUST
MEDEVACKED	MEDICAMENTAL	MEERSCHAUM	MEGALOMANIAC	MEGATONNAGE
MEDEVACKING	MEDICAMENTALLY	MEERSCHAUMS	MEGALOMANIACAL	MEGATONNAGES
MEDIAEVALISM	MEDICAMENTARY	MEETINGHOUSE	MEGALOMANIACS	MEGAVERTEBRATE
MEDIAEVALISMS	MEDICAMENTED	MEETINGHOUSES	MEGALOMANIAS	MEGAVERTEBRATES
MEDIAEVALIST	MEDICAMENTING	MEETNESSES	MEGALOMANIC	MEGAVITAMIN
MEDIAEVALISTIC	MEDICAMENTOUS	MEFLOQUINE	MEGALOPOLIS	MEGAVITAMINS
MEDIAEVALISTS	MEDICAMENTS	MEFLOQUINES	MEGALOPOLISES	MEIOFAUNAE
MEDIAEVALLY	MEDICASTER	MEGACEPHALIC	MEGALOPOLITAN	MEIOFAUNAL
MEDIAEVALS	MEDICASTERS	MEGACEPHALIES	MEGALOPOLITANS	MEIOFAUNAS
MEDIAGENIC	MEDICATING	MEGACEPHALOUS	MEGALOPSES	MEIOSPORES
MEDIASTINA	MEDICATION	MEGACEPHALY	MEGALOSAUR	MEIOTICALLY
MEDIASTINAL	MEDICATIONS	MEGACHURCH	MEGALOSAURI	MEITNERIUM
MEDIASTINUM	MEDICATIVE	MEGACHURCHES	MEGALOSAURIAN	MEITNERIUMS
MEDIATENESS	MEDICINABLE	MEGACITIES	MEGALOSAURIANS	MEKOMETERS
MEDIATENESSES	MEDICINALLY	MEGACORPORATION	MEGALOSAURS	MELACONITE
MEDIATIONAL	MEDICINALS	MEGACURIES	MEGALOSAURUS	MELACONITES
MEDIATIONS	MEDICINERS	MEGACYCLES	MEGANEWTON	MELALEUCAS
MEDIATISATION	MEDICINING	MEGADEATHS	MEGANEWTONS	MELAMPODES
MEDIATISATIONS	MEDICOLEGAL	MEGAFARADS	MEGAPARSEC	MELANAEMIA
MEDIATISED	MEDIEVALISM	MEGAFAUNAE	MEGAPARSECS	MELANAEMIAS
MEDIATISES	MEDIEVALISMS	MEGAFAUNAL	MEGAPHONED	MELANCHOLIA
MEDIATISING	MEDIEVALIST	MEGAFAUNAS	MEGAPHONES	MELANCHOLIAC

M

MELANCHOLIACS	MELIORATES	MELODRAMATISE	MEMORIALIST	MENINGOCOCCI
MELANCHOLIAE	MELIORATING	MELODRAMATISED	MEMORIALISTS	MENINGOCOCCIC
MELANCHOLIAS	MELIORATION	MELODRAMATISES	MEMORIALIZATION	MENINGOCOCCUS
MELANCHOLIC	MELIORATIONS	MELODRAMATISING	MEMORIALIZE	MENISCECTOMIES
MELANCHOLICALLY	MELIORATIVE	MELODRAMATIST	MEMORIALIZED	MENISCECTOMY
MELANCHOLICS	MELIORATIVES	MELODRAMATISTS	MEMORIALIZER	MENISCUSES
MELANCHOLIES	MELIORATOR	MELODRAMATIZE	MEMORIALIZERS	MENISPERMACEOUS
MELANCHOLILY	MELIORATORS	MELODRAMATIZED	MEMORIALIZES	MENISPERMUM
MELANCHOLINESS	MELIORISMS	MELODRAMATIZES	MEMORIALIZING	MENISPERMUMS
MELANCHOLIOUS	MELIORISTIC	MELODRAMATIZING	MEMORIALLY	MENOLOGIES
MELANCHOLY	MELIORISTS	MELODRAMES	MEMORISABLE	MENOMINEES
MELANISATION	MELIORITIES	MELOMANIAC	MEMORISATION	MENOPAUSAL
MELANISATIONS	MELIPHAGOUS	MELOMANIACS	MEMORISATIONS	MENOPAUSES
MELANISING	MELISMATIC	MELOMANIAS	MEMORISERS	MENOPAUSIC
MELANISTIC	MELLIFEROUS	MELONGENES	MEMORISING	MENOPOLISES
MELANIZATION	MELLIFICATION	MELOXICAMS	MEMORIZABLE	MENORRHAGIA
MELANIZATIONS	MELLIFICATIONS	MELPHALANS	MEMORIZATION	MENORRHAGIAS
MELANIZING	MELLIFLUENCE	MELTABILITIES	MEMORIZATIONS	MENORRHAGIC
MELANOBLAST	MELLIFLUENCES	MELTABILITY	MEMORIZERS	MENORRHEAS
MELANOBLASTS	MELLIFLUENT	MELTINGNESS	MEMORIZING	MENORRHOEA
MELANOCHROI	MELLIFLUENTLY	MELTINGNESSES	MEMORIZINGS	MENORRHOEAS
MELANOCHROIC	MELLIFLUOUS	MELTWATERS	MENACINGLY	MENSCHIEST
MELANOCHROOUS	MELLIFLUOUSLY	MELUNGEONS	MENADIONES	MENSERVANTS
MELANOCYTE	MELLIFLUOUSNESS	MEMBERLESS	MENAGERIES	MENSTRUALLY
MELANOCYTES	MELLIPHAGOUS	MEMBERSHIP	MENAQUINONE	MENSTRUATE
MELANOGENESES	MELLIVOROUS	MEMBERSHIPS	MENAQUINONES	MENSTRUATED
MELANOGENESIS	MELLOPHONE	MEMBRANACEOUS	MENARCHEAL	MENSTRUATES
MELANOMATA	MELLOPHONES	MEMBRANEOUS	MENARCHIAL	MENSTRUATING
MELANOPHORE	MELLOTRONS	MEMBRANOUS	MENDACIOUS	MENSTRUATION
MELANOPHORES	MELLOWIEST	MEMBRANOUSLY	MENDACIOUSLY	MENSTRUATIONS
MELANOSITIES	MELLOWNESS	MEMOIRISMS	MENDACIOUSNESS	MENSTRUOUS
MELANOSITY	MELLOWNESSES	MEMOIRISTS	MENDACITIES	MENSTRUUMS
MELANOSOME	MELLOWSPEAK	MEMORABILE	MENDELEVIUM	MENSURABILITIES
MELANOSOMES	MELLOWSPEAKS	MEMORABILIA	MENDELEVIUMS	MENSURABILITY
MELANOTROPIN	MELOCOTONS	MEMORABILITIES	MENDICANCIES	MENSURABLE
MELANOTROPINS	MELOCOTOON	MEMORABILITY	MENDICANCY	MENSURATION
MELANTERITE	MELOCOTOONS	MEMORABLENESS	MENDICANTS	MENSURATIONAL
MELANTERITES	MELODICALLY	MEMORABLENESSES	MENDICITIES	MENSURATIONS
MELANURIAS	MELODIOUSLY	MEMORANDUM	MENINGIOMA	MENSURATIVE
MELAPHYRES	MELODIOUSNESS	MEMORANDUMS	MENINGIOMAS	MENTALESES
MELASTOMACEOUS	MELODIOUSNESSES	MEMORATIVE	MENINGIOMATA	MENTALISMS
MELASTOMES	MELODISERS	MEMORIALISATION	MENINGITIC	MENTALISTIC
MELATONINS	MELODISING	MEMORIALISE	MENINGITIDES	MENTALISTICALLY
MELIACEOUS	MELODIZERS	MEMORIALISED	MENINGITIS	MENTALISTS
MELICOTTON	MELODIZING	MEMORIALISER	MENINGITISES	MENTALITIES
MELICOTTONS	MELODRAMAS	MEMORIALISERS	MENINGOCELE	MENTATIONS
MELIORABLE	MELODRAMATIC	MEMORIALISES	MENINGOCELES	MENTHACEOUS
MELIORATED	MELODRAMATICS	MEMORIALISING	MENINGOCOCCAL	MENTHOLATED

MENTICIDES	MERCERIZERS	MERCURIALITIES	MERONYMIES	MESHUGGENER
MENTIONABLE	MERCERIZES	MERCURIALITY	MEROPIDANS	MESHUGGENERS
MENTIONERS	MERCERIZING	MERCURIALIZE	MEROPLANKTON	MESITYLENE
MENTIONING	MERCHANDISE	MERCURIALIZED	MEROPLANKTONS	MESITYLENES
MENTONNIERE	MERCHANDISED	MERCURIALIZES	MEROZOITES	MESMERICAL
MENTONNIERES	MERCHANDISER	MERCURIALIZING	MERPEOPLES	MESMERICALLY
MENTORINGS	MERCHANDISERS	MERCURIALLY	MERRIMENTS	MESMERISATION
MENTORSHIP	MERCHANDISES	MERCURIALNESS	MERRINESSES	MESMERISATIONS
MENTORSHIPS	MERCHANDISING	MERCURIALNESSES	MERRYMAKER	MESMERISED
MENUISIERS	MERCHANDISINGS	MERCURIALS	MERRYMAKERS	MESMERISER
MEPACRINES	MERCHANDIZE	MERCURISED	MERRYMAKING	MESMERISERS
MEPERIDINE	MERCHANDIZED	MERCURISES	MERRYMAKINGS	MESMERISES
MEPERIDINES	MERCHANDIZER	MERCURISING	MERRYTHOUGHT	MESMERISING
MEPHITICAL	MERCHANDIZERS	MERCURIZED	MERRYTHOUGHTS	MESMERISMS
MEPHITICALLY	MERCHANDIZES	MERCURIZES	MERVEILLEUSE	MESMERISTS
MEPHITISES	MERCHANDIZING	MERCURIZING	MERVEILLEUSES	MESMERIZATION
MEPHITISMS	MERCHANDIZINGS	MERDIVOROUS	MERVEILLEUX	MESMERIZATIONS
MEPROBAMATE	MERCHANTABILITY	MEREOLOGICAL	MERVEILLEUXES	MESMERIZED
MEPROBAMATES	MERCHANTABLE	MEREOLOGIES	MESALLIANCE	MESMERIZER
MERBROMINS	MERCHANTED	MERESTONES	MESALLIANCES	MESMERIZERS
MERCANTILE	MERCHANTING	MERETRICIOUS	MESATICEPHALIC	MESMERIZES
MERCANTILISM	MERCHANTINGS	MERETRICIOUSLY	MESATICEPHALIES	MESMERIZING
MERCANTILISMS	MERCHANTLIKE	MERGANSERS	MESATICEPHALOUS	MESNALTIES
MERCANTILIST	MERCHANTMAN	MERIDIONAL	MESATICEPHALY	MESOAMERICAN
MERCANTILISTIC	MERCHANTMEN	MERIDIONALITIES	MESCALINES	MESOBENTHOS
MERCANTILISTS	MERCHANTRIES	MERIDIONALITY	MESCALISMS	MESOBENTHOSES
MERCAPTANS	MERCHANTRY	MERIDIONALLY	MESDEMOISELLES	MESOBLASTIC
MERCAPTIDE	MERCHILDREN	MERIDIONALS	MESENCEPHALA	MESOBLASTS
MERCAPTIDES	MERCIFULLY	MERISTEMATIC	MESENCEPHALIC	MESOCEPHALIC
MERCAPTOPURINE	MERCIFULNESS	MERISTICALLY	MESENCEPHALON	MESOCEPHALICS
MERCAPTOPURINES	MERCIFULNESSES	MERITOCRACIES	MESENCEPHALONS	MESOCEPHALIES
MERCENARIES	MERCIFYING	MERITOCRACY	MESENCHYMAL	MESOCEPHALISM
MERCENARILY	MERCILESSLY	MERITOCRAT	MESENCHYMATOUS	MESOCEPHALISMS
MERCENARINESS	MERCILESSNESS	MERITOCRATIC	MESENCHYME	MESOCEPHALOUS
MERCENARINESSES	MERCILESSNESSES	MERITOCRATS	MESENCHYMES	MESOCEPHALY
MERCENARISM	MERCURATED	MERITORIOUS	MESENTERIAL	MESOCRANIES
MERCENARISMS	MERCURATES	MERITORIOUSLY	MESENTERIC	MESOCRATIC
MERCERISATION	MERCURATING	MERITORIOUSNESS	MESENTERIES	MESOCYCLONE
MERCERISATIONS	MERCURATION	MERMAIDENS	MESENTERITIS	MESOCYCLONES
MERCERISED	MERCURATIONS	MEROBLASTIC	MESENTERITISES	MESODERMAL
MERCERISER	MERCURIALISE	MEROBLASTICALLY	MESENTERON	MESODERMIC
MERCERISERS	MERCURIALISED	MEROGENESES	MESENTERONIC	MESOGASTRIA
MERCERISES	MERCURIALISES	MEROGENESIS	MESHUGAASEN	MESOGASTRIC
MERCERISING	MERCURIALISING	MEROGENETIC	MESHUGASEN	MESOGASTRIUM
MERCERIZATION	MERCURIALISM	MEROGONIES	MESHUGGENAH	MESOGLOEAS
MERCERIZATIONS	MERCURIALISMS	MEROMORPHIC	MESHUGGENAHS	MESOGNATHIES
MERCERIZED	MERCURIALIST	MEROMYOSIN	MESHUGGENEH	MESOGNATHISM
MERCERIZER	MERCURIALISTS	MEROMYOSINS	MESHUGGENEHS	MESOGNATHISMS

M

MESOGNATHOUS	MESQUINERIE	METACERCARIAL	METAGROBOLIZED	METALLOIDAL
MESOGNATHY	MESQUINERIES	METACERCARIAS	METAGROBOLIZES	METALLOIDS
MESOHIPPUS	MESSAGINGS	METACHROMATIC	METAGROBOLIZING	METALLOPHONE
MESOHIPPUSES	MESSALINES	METACHROMATISM	METALANGUAGE	METALLOPHONES
MESOKURTIC	MESSEIGNEURS	METACHROMATISMS	METALANGUAGES	METALLURGIC
MESOMERISM	MESSENGERED	METACHRONISM	METALDEHYDE	METALLURGICAL
MESOMERISMS	MESSENGERING	METACHRONISMS	METALDEHYDES	METALLURGICALLY
MESOMORPHIC	MESSENGERS	METACHROSES	METALEPSES	METALLURGIES
MESOMORPHIES	MESSIAHSHIP	METACHROSIS	METALEPSIS	METALLURGIST
MESOMORPHISM	MESSIAHSHIPS	METACINNABARITE	METALEPTIC	METALLURGISTS
MESOMORPHISMS	MESSIANICALLY	METACOGNITION	METALEPTICAL	METALLURGY
MESOMORPHOUS	MESSIANISM	METACOGNITIONS	METALHEADS	METALMARKS
MESOMORPHS	MESSIANISMS	METACOMPUTER	METALINGUISTIC	METALSMITH
MESOMORPHY	MESSINESSES	METACOMPUTERS	METALINGUISTICS	METALSMITHS
MESONEPHRIC	MESTRANOLS	METACOMPUTING	METALISATION	METALWARES
MESONEPHROI	METABISULPHITE	METACOMPUTINGS	METALISATIONS	METALWORKER
MESONEPHROS	METABISULPHITES	METAETHICAL	METALISING	METALWORKERS
MESONEPHROSES	METABOLICALLY	METAETHICS	METALIZATION	METALWORKING
MESOPAUSES	METABOLIES	METAFEMALE	METALIZATIONS	METALWORKINGS
MESOPELAGIC	METABOLISABLE	METAFEMALES	METALIZING	METALWORKS
MESOPHILES	METABOLISE	METAFICTION	METALLICALLY	METAMATERIAL
MESOPHILIC	METABOLISED	METAFICTIONAL	METALLIDING	METAMATERIALS
MESOPHYLLIC	METABOLISES	METAFICTIONIST	METALLIDINGS	METAMATHEMATICS
MESOPHYLLOUS	METABOLISING	METAFICTIONISTS	METALLIFEROUS	METAMERICALLY
MESOPHYLLS	METABOLISM	METAFICTIONS	METALLINGS	METAMERISM
MESOPHYTES	METABOLISMS	METAGALACTIC	METALLISATION	METAMERISMS
MESOPHYTIC	METABOLITE	METAGALAXIES	METALLISATIONS	METAMICTISATION
MESOSCAPHE	METABOLITES	METAGALAXY	METALLISED	METAMICTIZATION
MESOSCAPHES	METABOLIZABLE	METAGENESES	METALLISES	METAMORPHIC
MESOSPHERE	METABOLIZE	METAGENESIS	METALLISING	METAMORPHICALLY
MESOSPHERES	METABOLIZED	METAGENETIC	METALLISTS	METAMORPHISM
MESOSPHERIC	METABOLIZES	METAGENETICALLY	METALLIZATION	METAMORPHISMS
MESOTHELIA	METABOLIZING	METAGNATHISM	METALLIZATIONS	METAMORPHIST
MESOTHELIAL	METABOLOME	METAGNATHISMS	METALLIZED	METAMORPHISTS
MESOTHELIOMA	METABOLOMES	METAGNATHOUS	METALLIZES	METAMORPHOSE
MESOTHELIOMAS	METABOLOMICS	METAGRABOLISE	METALLIZING	METAMORPHOSED
MESOTHELIOMATA	METABOTROPIC	METAGRABOLISED	METALLOCENE	METAMORPHOSES
MESOTHELIUM	METACARPAL	METAGRABOLISES	METALLOCENES	METAMORPHOSING
MESOTHELIUMS	METACARPALS	METAGRABOLISING	METALLOGENETIC	METAMORPHOSIS
MESOTHERAPIES	METACARPUS	METAGRABOLIZE	METALLOGENIC	METAMORPHOUS
MESOTHERAPY	METACENTER	METAGRABOLIZED	METALLOGENIES	METANALYSES
MESOTHORACES	METACENTERS	METAGRABOLIZES	METALLOGENY	METANALYSIS
MESOTHORACIC	METACENTRE	METAGRABOLIZING	METALLOGRAPHER	METANARRATIVE
MESOTHORAX	METACENTRES	METAGROBOLISE	METALLOGRAPHERS	METANARRATIVES
MESOTHORAXES	METACENTRIC	METAGROBOLISED	METALLOGRAPHIC	METANEPHRIC
MESOTHORIUM	METACENTRICS	METAGROBOLISES	METALLOGRAPHIES	METANEPHROI
MESOTHORIUMS	METACERCARIA	METAGROBOLISING	METALLOGRAPHIST	METANEPHROS
MESOTROPHIC	METACERCARIAE	METAGROBOLIZE	METALLOGRAPHY	METAPERIODIC

METAPHASES
METAPHORIC
METAPHORICAL
METAPHORICALLY
METAPHORIST
METAPHORISTS
METAPHOSPHATE
METAPHOSPHATES
METAPHOSPHORIC
METAPHRASE
METAPHRASED
METAPHRASES
METAPHRASING
METAPHRASIS
METAPHRAST
METAPHRASTIC
METAPHRASTICAL
METAPHRASTS
METAPHYSIC
METAPHYSICAL
METAPHYSICALLY
METAPHYSICIAN
METAPHYSICIANS
METAPHYSICISE
METAPHYSICISED
METAPHYSICISES
METAPHYSICISING
METAPHYSICIST
METAPHYSICISTS
METAPHYSICIZE
METAPHYSICIZED
METAPHYSICIZES
METAPHYSICIZING
METAPHYSICS
METAPLASES
METAPLASIA
METAPLASIAS
METAPLASIS
METAPLASMIC
METAPLASMS
METAPLASTIC
METAPOLITICAL
METAPOLITICS
METAPROTEIN
METAPROTEINS
METAPSYCHIC
METAPSYCHICAL
METAPSYCHICS

METAPSYCHOLOGY
METARCHONS
METASEQUOIA
METASEQUOIAS
METASILICATE
METASILICATES
METASILICIC
METASOMATA
METASOMATIC
METASOMATISM
METASOMATISMS
METASOMATOSES
METASOMATOSIS
METASTABILITIES
METASTABILITY
METASTABLE
METASTABLES
METASTABLY
METASTASES
METASTASIS
METASTASISE
METASTASISED
METASTASISES
METASTASISING
METASTASIZE
METASTASIZED
METASTASIZES
METASTASIZING
METASTATIC
METASTATICALLY
METATARSAL
METATARSALS
METATARSUS
METATHEORETICAL
METATHEORIES
METATHEORY
METATHERIAN
METATHERIANS
METATHESES
METATHESIS
METATHESISE
METATHESISED
METATHESISES
METATHESISING
METATHESIZE
METATHESIZED
METATHESIZES
METATHESIZING

METATHETIC
METATHETICAL
METATHETICALLY
METATHORACES
METATHORACIC
METATHORAX
METATHORAXES
METATUNGSTIC
METAVANADIC
METAVERSES
METAXYLEMS
METECDYSES
METECDYSIS
METEMPIRIC
METEMPIRICAL
METEMPIRICALLY
METEMPIRICISM
METEMPIRICISMS
METEMPIRICIST
METEMPIRICISTS
METEMPIRICS
METEMPSYCHOSES
METEMPSYCHOSIS
METEMPSYCHOSIST
METENCEPHALA
METENCEPHALIC
METENCEPHALON
METENCEPHALONS
METEORICALLY
METEORISMS
METEORISTS
METEORITAL
METEORITES
METEORITIC
METEORITICAL
METEORITICIST
METEORITICISTS
METEORITICS
METEOROGRAM
METEOROGRAMS
METEOROGRAPH
METEOROGRAPHIC
METEOROGRAPHS
METEOROIDAL
METEOROIDS
METEOROLITE
METEOROLITES
METEOROLOGIC

METEOROLOGICAL
METEOROLOGIES
METEOROLOGIST
METEOROLOGISTS
METEOROLOGY
METERSTICK
METERSTICKS
METESTICKS
METESTROUS
METESTRUSES
METFORMINS
METHACRYLATE
METHACRYLATES
METHACRYLIC
METHADONES
METHAEMOGLOBIN
METHAEMOGLOBINS
METHAMPHETAMINE
METHANAMIDE
METHANAMIDES
METHANATION
METHANATIONS
METHANOMETER
METHANOMETERS
METHANOYLS
METHAQUALONE
METHAQUALONES
METHEDRINE
METHEDRINES
METHEGLINS
METHEMOGLOBIN
METHEMOGLOBINS
METHENAMINE
METHENAMINES
METHICILLIN
METHICILLINS
METHINKETH
METHIONINE
METHIONINES
METHODICAL
METHODICALLY
METHODICALNESS
METHODISATION
METHODISATIONS
METHODISED
METHODISER
METHODISERS
METHODISES

METHODISING
METHODISMS
METHODISTIC
METHODISTS
METHODIZATION
METHODIZATIONS
METHODIZED
METHODIZER
METHODIZERS
METHODIZES
METHODIZING
METHODOLOGICAL
METHODOLOGIES
METHODOLOGIST
METHODOLOGISTS
METHODOLOGY
METHOMANIA
METHOMANIAS
METHOTREXATE
METHOTREXATES
METHOXIDES
METHOXYBENZENE
METHOXYBENZENES
METHOXYCHLOR
METHOXYCHLORS
METHOXYFLURANE
METHOXYFLURANES
METHYLAMINE
METHYLAMINES
METHYLASES
METHYLATED
METHYLATES
METHYLATING
METHYLATION
METHYLATIONS
METHYLATOR
METHYLATORS
METHYLCELLULOSE
METHYLDOPA
METHYLDOPAS
METHYLENES
METHYLMERCURIES
METHYLMERCURY
METHYLPHENIDATE
METHYLPHENOL
METHYLPHENOLS
METHYLTHIONINE
METHYLTHIONINES

M

METHYLXANTHINE	METROLOGIC	MICRIFYING	MICROBURSTS	MICROCOSMS
METHYLXANTHINES	METROLOGICAL	MICROAEROPHILE	MICROBUSES	MICROCRACK
METHYSERGIDE	METROLOGICALLY	MICROAEROPHILES	MICROBUSSES	MICROCRACKED
METHYSERGIDES	METROLOGIES	MICROAEROPHILIC	MICROCAPSULE	MICROCRACKING
METICULOSITIES	METROLOGIST	MICROAGGRESSION	MICROCAPSULES	MICROCRACKINGS
METICULOSITY	METROLOGISTS	MICROAMPERE	MICROCARDS	MICROCRACKS
METICULOUS	METROMANIA	MICROAMPERES	MICROCASSETTE	MICROCRYSTAL
METICULOUSLY	METROMANIAS	MICROANALYSES	MICROCASSETTES	MICROCRYSTALS
METICULOUSNESS	METRONIDAZOLE	MICROANALYSIS	MICROCELEBRITY	MICROCULTURAL
METOCLOPRAMIDE	METRONIDAZOLES	MICROANALYST	MICROCEPHAL	MICROCULTURE
METOCLOPRAMIDES	METRONOMES	MICROANALYSTS	MICROCEPHALIC	MICROCULTURES
METOESTROUS	METRONOMIC	MICROANALYTIC	MICROCEPHALICS	MICROCURIE
METOESTRUS	METRONOMICAL	MICROANALYTICAL	MICROCEPHALIES	MICROCURIES
METOESTRUSES	METRONOMICALLY	MICROANATOMICAL	MICROCEPHALOUS	MICROCYTES
METONYMICAL	METRONYMIC	MICROANATOMIES	MICROCEPHALS	MICROCYTIC
METONYMICALLY	METRONYMICS	MICROANATOMY	MICROCEPHALY	MICRODETECTION
METONYMIES	METROPLEXES	MICROARRAY	MICROCHEMICAL	MICRODETECTIONS
METOPOSCOPIC	METROPOLIS	MICROARRAYS	MICROCHEMISTRY	MICRODETECTOR
METOPOSCOPICAL	METROPOLISES	MICROBALANCE	MICROCHIPPED	MICRODETECTORS
METOPOSCOPIES	METROPOLITAN	MICROBALANCES	MICROCHIPPING	MICRODISSECTION
METOPOSCOPIST	METROPOLITANATE	MICROBAROGRAPH	MICROCHIPS	MICRODONTOUS
METOPOSCOPISTS	METROPOLITANISE	MICROBAROGRAPHS	MICROCIRCUIT	MICRODRIVE
METOPOSCOPY	METROPOLITANISM	MICROBEADS	MICROCIRCUITRY	MICRODRIVES
METRALGIAS	METROPOLITANIZE	MICROBEAMS	MICROCIRCUITS	MICRODRONE
METRESTICK	METROPOLITANS	MICROBIOLOGIC	MICROCLIMATE	MICRODRONES
METRESTICKS	METROPOLITICAL	MICROBIOLOGICAL	MICROCLIMATES	MICROEARTHQUAKE
METRICALLY	METRORRHAGIA	MICROBIOLOGIES	MICROCLIMATIC	MICROECONOMIC
METRICATED	METRORRHAGIAS	MICROBIOLOGIST	MICROCLINE	MICROECONOMICS
METRICATES	METROSEXUAL	MICROBIOLOGISTS	MICROCLINES	MICROELECTRODE
METRICATING	METROSEXUALS	MICROBIOLOGY	MICROCOCCAL	MICROELECTRODES
METRICATION	METROSTYLE	MICROBIOME	MICROCOCCI	MICROELECTRONIC
METRICATIONS	METROSTYLES	MICROBIOMES	MICROCOCCUS	MICROELEMENT
METRICIANS	METTLESOME	MICROBIOTA	MICROCODES	MICROELEMENTS
METRICISED	METTLESOMENESS	MICROBIOTAS	MICROCOMPONENT	MICROEVOLUTION
METRICISES	MEZCALINES	MICROBLOGGER	MICROCOMPONENTS	MICROEVOLUTIONS
METRICISING	MEZZALUNAS	MICROBLOGGERS	MICROCOMPUTER	MICROFARAD
METRICISMS	MEZZANINES	MICROBLOGGING	MICROCOMPUTERS	MICROFARADS
METRICISTS	MEZZOTINTED	MICROBLOGGINGS	MICROCOMPUTING	MICROFAUNA
METRICIZED	MEZZOTINTER	MICROBLOGS	MICROCOMPUTINGS	MICROFAUNAE
METRICIZES	MEZZOTINTERS	MICROBREWER	MICROCOPIED	MICROFAUNAL
METRICIZING	MEZZOTINTING	MICROBREWERIES	MICROCOPIES	MICROFAUNAS
METRIFICATION	MEZZOTINTO	MICROBREWERS	MICROCOPYING	MICROFELSITIC
METRIFICATIONS	MEZZOTINTOS	MICROBREWERY	MICROCOPYINGS	MICROFIBER
METRIFIERS	MEZZOTINTS	MICROBREWING	MICROCOSMIC	MICROFIBERS
METRIFONATE	MIAROLITIC	MICROBREWINGS	MICROCOSMICAL	MICROFIBRE
METRIFONATES	MIASMATICAL	MICROBREWS	MICROCOSMICALLY	MICROFIBRES
METRIFYING	MIASMATOUS	MICROBUBBLES	MICROCOSMOS	MICROFIBRIL
METRITISES	MIASMICALLY	MICROBURST	MICROCOSMOSES	MICROFIBRILLAR

MICROFIBRILS	MICROGRAPHY	MICROMESHES	MICROPARASITIC	MICROPRINTED
MICROFICHE	MICROGRAVITIES	MICROMETEORITE	MICROPARTICLE	MICROPRINTING
MICROFICHES	MICROGRAVITY	MICROMETEORITES	MICROPARTICLES	MICROPRINTINGS
MICROFILAMENT	MICROGREENS	MICROMETEORITIC	MICROPARTIES	MICROPRINTS
MICROFILAMENTS	MICROGROOVE	MICROMETEOROID	MICROPARTY	MICROPRISM
MICROFILARIA	MICROGROOVES	MICROMETEOROIDS	MICROPAYMENT	MICROPRISMS
MICROFILARIAE	MICROHABITAT	MICROMETER	MICROPAYMENTS	MICROPROBE
MICROFILARIAL	MICROHABITATS	MICROMETERS	MICROPEGMATITE	MICROPROBES
MICROFILING	MICROIMAGE	MICROMETHOD	MICROPEGMATITES	MICROPROCESSING
MICROFILINGS	MICROIMAGES	MICROMETHODS	MICROPEGMATITIC	MICROPROCESSOR
MICROFILMABLE	MICROINCHES	MICROMETRE	MICROPHAGE	MICROPROCESSORS
MICROFILMED	MICROINJECT	MICROMETRES	MICROPHAGES	MICROPROGRAM
MICROFILMER	MICROINJECTED	MICROMETRIC	MICROPHAGOUS	MICROPROGRAMS
MICROFILMERS	MICROINJECTING	MICROMETRICAL	MICROPHONE	MICROPROJECTION
MICROFILMING	MICROINJECTION	MICROMETRIES	MICROPHONES	MICROPROJECTOR
MICROFILMS	MICROINJECTIONS	MICROMETRY	MICROPHONIC	MICROPROJECTORS
MICROFILTER	MICROINJECTS	MICROMICROCURIE	MICROPHONICS	MICROPSIAS
MICROFILTERS	MICROLIGHT	MICROMICROFARAD	MICROPHOTOGRAPH	MICROPTEROUS
MICROFLOPPIES	MICROLIGHTING	MICROMILLIMETRE	MICROPHOTOMETER	MICROPUBLISHER
MICROFLOPPY	MICROLIGHTINGS	MICROMINIATURE	MICROPHOTOMETRY	MICROPUBLISHERS
MICROFLORA	MICROLIGHTS	MICROMINIS	MICROPHYLL	MICROPUBLISHING
MICROFLORAE	MICROLITER	MICROMOLAR	MICROPHYLLOUS	MICROPULSATION
MICROFLORAL	MICROLITERS	MICROMOLES	MICROPHYLLS	MICROPULSATIONS
MICROFLORAS	MICROLITES	MICROMORPHOLOGY	MICROPHYSICAL	MICROPUMPS
MICROFORMS	MICROLITHIC	MICROMORTS	MICROPHYSICALLY	MICROPUNCTURE
MICROFOSSIL	MICROLITHS	MICRONATION	MICROPHYSICIST	MICROPUNCTURES
MICROFOSSILS	MICROLITIC	MICRONATIONS	MICROPHYSICISTS	MICROPYLAR
MICROFUNGI	MICROLITRE	MICRONEEDLE	MICROPHYSICS	MICROPYLES
MICROFUNGUS	MICROLITRES	MICRONEEDLES	MICROPHYTE	MICROPYROMETER
MICROFUNGUSES	MICROLOANS	MICRONISATION	MICROPHYTES	MICROPYROMETERS
MICROGAMETE	MICROLOGIC	MICRONISATIONS	MICROPHYTIC	MICROQUAKE
MICROGAMETES	MICROLOGICAL	MICRONISED	MICROPIPET	MICROQUAKES
MICROGAMETOCYTE	MICROLOGICALLY	MICRONISES	MICROPIPETS	MICRORADIOGRAPH
MICROGENERATION	MICROLOGIES	MICRONISING	MICROPIPETTE	MICROREADER
MICROGLIAS	MICROLOGIST	MICRONIZATION	MICROPIPETTES	MICROREADERS
MICROGRAMS	MICROLOGISTS	MICRONIZATIONS	MICROPLANKTON	MICROSATELLITE
MICROGRANITE	MICROLUCES	MICRONIZED	MICROPLANKTONS	MICROSATELLITES
MICROGRANITES	MICROLUXES	MICRONIZES	MICROPLASTIC	MICROSCALE
MICROGRANITIC	MICROMANAGE	MICRONIZING	MICROPLASTICS	MICROSCALES
MICROGRAPH	MICROMANAGED	MICRONUCLEI	MICROPOLIS	MICROSCOPE
MICROGRAPHED	MICROMANAGEMENT	MICRONUCLEUS	MICROPOLISES	MICROSCOPES
MICROGRAPHER	MICROMANAGER	MICRONUCLEUSES	MICROPORES	MICROSCOPIC
MICROGRAPHERS	MICROMANAGERS	MICRONUTRIENT	MICROPOROSITIES	MICROSCOPICAL
MICROGRAPHIC	MICROMANAGES	MICRONUTRIENTS	MICROPOROSITY	MICROSCOPICALLY
MICROGRAPHICS	MICROMANAGING	MICROORGANISM	MICROPOROUS	MICROSCOPIES
MICROGRAPHIES	MICROMARKETING	MICROORGANISMS	MICROPOWER	MICROSCOPIST
MICROGRAPHING	MICROMARKETINGS	MICROPARASITE	MICROPOWERS	MICROSCOPISTS
MICROGRAPHS	MICROMERES	MICROPARASITES	MICROPRINT	MICROSCOPY

MICROSECOND	MICROTOMES	MIDDLEBROWISM	MIGRATIONAL	MILLEFEUILLE
MICROSECONDS	MICROTOMIC	MIDDLEBROWISMS	MIGRATIONIST	MILLEFEUILLES
MICROSEISM	MICROTOMICAL	MIDDLEBROWS	MIGRATIONISTS	MILLEFIORI
MICROSEISMIC	MICROTOMIES	MIDDLEBUSTER	MIGRATIONS	MILLEFIORIS
MICROSEISMICAL	MICROTOMIST	MIDDLEBUSTERS	MILDEWIEST	MILLEFLEUR
MICROSEISMICITY	MICROTOMISTS	MIDDLEMOST	MILDNESSES	MILLEFLEURS
MICROSEISMS	MICROTONAL	MIDDLEWARE	MILEOMETER	MILLENARIAN
MICROSITES	MICROTONALITIES	MIDDLEWARES	MILEOMETERS	MILLENARIANISM
MICROSKIRT	MICROTONALITY	MIDDLEWEIGHT	MILESTONES	MILLENARIANISMS
MICROSKIRTS	MICROTONALLY	MIDDLEWEIGHTS	MILITANCES	MILLENARIANS
MICROSLEEP	MICROTONES	MIDDLINGLY	MILITANCIES	MILLENARIES
MICROSLEEPS	MICROTUBES	MIDFIELDER	MILITANTLY	MILLENARISM
MICROSMATIC	MICROTUBULAR	MIDFIELDERS	MILITANTNESS	MILLENARISMS
MICROSOMAL	MICROTUBULE	MIDIBUSSES	MILITANTNESSES	MILLENNIAL
MICROSOMES	MICROTUBULES	MIDINETTES	MILITARIES	MILLENNIALISM
MICROSPECIES	MICROTUNNELLING	MIDISKIRTS	MILITARILY	MILLENNIALISMS
MICROSPHERE	MICROVASCULAR	MIDLANDERS	MILITARISATION	MILLENNIALIST
MICROSPHERES	MICROVILLAR	MIDLATITUDE	MILITARISATIONS	MILLENNIALISTS
MICROSPHERICAL	MICROVILLI	MIDLATITUDES	MILITARISE	MILLENNIALLY
MICROSPORANGIA	MICROVILLOUS	MIDLITTORAL	MILITARISED	MILLENNIALS
MICROSPORANGIUM	MICROVILLUS	MIDLITTORALS	MILITARISES	MILLENNIANISM
MICROSPORE	MICROVOLTS	MIDNIGHTLY	MILITARISING	MILLENNIANISMS
MICROSPORES	MICROWATTS	MIDRASHOTH	MILITARISM	MILLENNIARISM
MICROSPORIC	MICROWAVABLE	MIDSAGITTAL	MILITARISMS	MILLENNIARISMS
MICROSPORIDIAN	MICROWAVEABLE	MIDSECTION	MILITARIST	MILLENNIUM
MICROSPOROCYTE	MICROWAVED	MIDSECTIONS	MILITARISTIC	MILLENNIUMS
MICROSPOROCYTES	MICROWAVES	MIDSHIPMAN	MILITARISTS	MILLEPEDES
MICROSPOROPHYLL	MICROWAVING	MIDSHIPMATE	MILITARIZATION	MILLEPORES
MICROSPOROUS	MICROWIRES	MIDSHIPMATES	MILITARIZATIONS	MILLERITES
MICROSTATE	MICROWORLD	MIDSHIPMEN	MILITARIZE	MILLESIMAL
MICROSTATES	MICROWORLDS	MIDSTORIES	MILITARIZED	MILLESIMALLY
MICROSTOMATOUS	MICROWRITER	MIDSTREAMS	MILITARIZES	MILLESIMALS
MICROSTOMOUS	MICROWRITERS	MIDSUMMERS	MILITARIZING	MILLHOUSES
MICROSTRUCTURAL	MICRURGIES	MIDWATCHES	MILITATING	MILLIAMPERE
MICROSTRUCTURE	MICTURATED	MIDWESTERN	MILITATION	MILLIAMPERES
MICROSTRUCTURES	MICTURATES	MIDWIFERIES	MILITATIONS	MILLIARIES
MICROSURGEON	MICTURATING	MIDWINTERS	MILITIAMAN	MILLICURIE
MICROSURGEONS	MICTURITION	MIFEPRISTONE	MILITIAMEN	MILLICURIES
MICROSURGERIES	MICTURITIONS	MIFEPRISTONES	MILKFISHES	MILLIDEGREE
MICROSURGERY	MIDDELMANNETJIE	MIFFINESSES	MILKINESSES	MILLIDEGREES
MICROSURGICAL	MIDDELSKOT	MIGHTINESS	MILKSHAKES	MILLIGRAMME
MICROSWITCH	MIDDELSKOTS	MIGHTINESSES	MILKSOPISM	MILLIGRAMMES
MICROSWITCHES	MIDDENSTEAD	MIGMATITES	MILKSOPISMS	MILLIGRAMS
MICROTECHNIC	MIDDENSTEADS	MIGNONETTE	MILKSOPPIER	MILLIHENRIES
MICROTECHNICS	MIDDLEBREAKER	MIGNONETTES	MILKSOPPIEST	MILLIHENRY
MICROTECHNIQUE	MIDDLEBREAKERS	MIGRAINEUR	MILKSOPPING	MILLIHENRYS
MICROTECHNIQUES	MIDDLEBROW	MIGRAINEURS	MILKTOASTS	MILLILAMBERT
MICROTECHNOLOGY	MIDDLEBROWED	MIGRAINOUS	MILLBOARDS	MILLILAMBERTS

MILLILITER	MILLWRIGHT	MINERALISED	MINIATURED	MINIMISING
MILLILITERS	MILLWRIGHTS	MINERALISER	MINIATURES	MINIMIZATION
MILLILITRE	MILOMETERS	MINERALISERS	MINIATURING	MINIMIZATIONS
MILLILITRES	MILQUETOAST	MINERALISES	MINIATURISATION	MINIMIZERS
MILLILUCES	MILQUETOASTS	MINERALISING	MINIATURISE	MINIMIZING
MILLILUXES	MIMEOGRAPH	MINERALIST	MINIATURISED	MINIRUGBIES
MILLIMETER	MIMEOGRAPHED	MINERALISTS	MINIATURISES	MINISCHOOL
MILLIMETERS	MIMEOGRAPHING	MINERALIZABLE	MINIATURISING	MINISCHOOLS
MILLIMETRE	MIMEOGRAPHS	MINERALIZATION	MINIATURIST	MINISCULES
MILLIMETRES	MIMETICALLY	MINERALIZATIONS	MINIATURISTIC	MINISERIES
MILLIMICRON	MIMIVIRUSES	MINERALIZE	MINIATURISTS	MINISKIRTED
MILLIMICRONS	MIMMICKING	MINERALIZED	MINIATURIZATION	MINISKIRTS
MILLIMOLAR	MIMOGRAPHER	MINERALIZER	MINIATURIZE	MINISTATES
MILLIMOLES	MIMOGRAPHERS	MINERALIZERS	MINIATURIZED	MINISTERED
MILLINERIES	MIMOGRAPHIES	MINERALIZES	MINIATURIZES	MINISTERIA
MILLIONAIRE	MIMOGRAPHY	MINERALIZING	MINIATURIZING	MINISTERIAL
MILLIONAIRES	MIMOSACEOUS	MINERALOGIC	MINIBIKERS	MINISTERIALIST
MILLIONAIRESS	MINACIOUSLY	MINERALOGICAL	MINIBREAKS	MINISTERIALISTS
MILLIONAIRESSES	MINACITIES	MINERALOGICALLY	MINIBUDGET	MINISTERIALLY
MILLIONARY	MINATORIAL	MINERALOGIES	MINIBUDGETS	MINISTERING
MILLIONFOLD	MINATORIALLY	MINERALOGISE	MINIBUSSES	MINISTERIUM
MILLIONNAIRE	MINATORILY	MINERALOGISED	MINICABBING	MINISTERSHIP
MILLIONNAIRES	MINAUDERIE	MINERALOGISES	MINICABBINGS	MINISTERSHIPS
MILLIONNAIRESS	MINAUDERIES	MINERALOGISING	MINICALCULATOR	MINISTRANT
MILLIONTHS	MINAUDIERE	MINERALOGIST	MINICALCULATORS	MINISTRANTS
MILLIOSMOL	MINAUDIERES	MINERALOGISTS	MINICASSETTE	MINISTRATION
MILLIOSMOLS	MINCEMEATS	MINERALOGIZE	MINICASSETTES	MINISTRATIONS
MILLIPEDES	MINDBLOWER	MINERALOGIZED	MINICOMPUTER	MINISTRATIVE
MILLIPROBE	MINDBLOWERS	MINERALOGIZES	MINICOMPUTERS	MINISTRESS
MILLIPROBES	MINDEDNESS	MINERALOGIZING	MINICOURSE	MINISTRESSES
MILLIRADIAN	MINDEDNESSES	MINERALOGY	MINICOURSES	MINISTRIES
MILLIRADIANS	MINDFULNESS	MINESHAFTS	MINIDISHES	MINISTROKE
MILLIROENTGEN	MINDFULNESSES	MINESTONES	MINIDRESSES	MINISTROKES
MILLIROENTGENS	MINDLESSLY	MINESTRONE	MINIFICATION	MINISYSTEM
MILLISECOND	MINDLESSNESS	MINESTRONES	MINIFICATIONS	MINISYSTEMS
MILLISECONDS	MINDLESSNESSES	MINESWEEPER	MINIFLOPPIES	MINITOWERS
MILLISIEVERT	MINDSCAPES	MINESWEEPERS	MINIFLOPPY	MINITRACKS
MILLISIEVERTS	MINDSHARES	MINESWEEPING	MINIMALISM	MINIVOLLEY
MILLIVOLTS	MINEFIELDS	MINESWEEPINGS	MINIMALISMS	MINIVOLLEYS
MILLIWATTS	MINEHUNTER	MINEWORKER	MINIMALIST	MINNESINGER
MILLOCRACIES	MINEHUNTERS	MINEWORKERS	MINIMALISTIC	MINNESINGERS
MILLOCRACY	MINELAYERS	MINGIMINGI	MINIMALISTS	MINNICKING
MILLOCRATS	MINELAYING	MINGIMINGIS	MINIMARKET	MINNOCKING
MILLSCALES	MINELAYINGS	MINGINESSES	MINIMARKETS	MINORITAIRE
MILLSTONES	MINERALISABLE	MINGLEMENT	MINIMAXING	MINORITAIRES
MILLSTREAM	MINERALISATION	MINGLEMENTS	MINIMISATION	MINORITIES
MILLSTREAMS	MINERALISATIONS	MINGLINGLY	MINIMISATIONS	MINORSHIPS
MILLWHEELS	MINERALISE	MINIATIONS	MINIMISERS	MINOXIDILS

M

MINSTRELSIES	MISADVERTENCE	MISAPPLIED	MISATTRIBUTING	MISBRANDING
MINSTRELSY	MISADVERTENCES	MISAPPLIES	MISATTRIBUTION	MISBUILDING
MINUSCULAR	MISADVICES	MISAPPLYING	MISATTRIBUTIONS	MISBUTTONED
MINUSCULES	MISADVISED	MISAPPRAISAL	MISAUNTERS	MISBUTTONING
MINUTENESS	MISADVISEDLY	MISAPPRAISALS	MISAVERRED	MISBUTTONS
MINUTENESSES	MISADVISEDNESS	MISAPPRECIATE	MISAVERRING	MISCALCULATE
MIRABELLES	MISADVISES	MISAPPRECIATED	MISAWARDED	MISCALCULATED
MIRABILISES	MISADVISING	MISAPPRECIATES	MISAWARDING	MISCALCULATES
MIRACIDIAL	MISALIGNED	MISAPPRECIATING	MISBALANCE	MISCALCULATING
MIRACIDIUM	MISALIGNING	MISAPPRECIATION	MISBALANCED	MISCALCULATION
MIRACULOUS	MISALIGNMENT	MISAPPRECIATIVE	MISBALANCES	MISCALCULATIONS
MIRACULOUSLY	MISALIGNMENTS	MISAPPREHEND	MISBALANCING	MISCALCULATOR
MIRACULOUSNESS	MISALLEGED	MISAPPREHENDED	MISBECOMES	MISCALCULATORS
MIRANDISED	MISALLEGES	MISAPPREHENDING	MISBECOMING	MISCALLERS
MIRANDISES	MISALLEGING	MISAPPREHENDS	MISBECOMINGNESS	MISCALLING
MIRANDISING	MISALLIANCE	MISAPPREHENSION	MISBEGINNING	MISCANTHUS
MIRANDIZED	MISALLIANCES	MISAPPREHENSIVE	MISBEGOTTEN	MISCANTHUSES
MIRANDIZES	MISALLOCATE	MISAPPROPRIATE	MISBEHAVED	MISCAPTION
MIRANDIZING	MISALLOCATED	MISAPPROPRIATED	MISBEHAVER	MISCAPTIONED
MIRIFICALLY	MISALLOCATES	MISAPPROPRIATES	MISBEHAVERS	MISCAPTIONING
MIRINESSES	MISALLOCATING	MISARRANGE	MISBEHAVES	MISCAPTIONS
MIRKINESSES	MISALLOCATION	MISARRANGED	MISBEHAVING	MISCARRIAGE
MIRRORINGS	MISALLOCATIONS	MISARRANGEMENT	MISBEHAVIOR	MISCARRIAGES
MIRRORLIKE	MISALLOTMENT	MISARRANGEMENTS	MISBEHAVIORS	MISCARRIED
MIRRORWISE	MISALLOTMENTS	MISARRANGES	MISBEHAVIOUR	MISCARRIES
MIRTHFULLY	MISALLOTTED	MISARRANGING	MISBEHAVIOURS	MISCARRYING
MIRTHFULNESS	MISALLOTTING	MISARTICULATE	MISBELIEFS	MISCASTING
MIRTHFULNESSES	MISALLYING	MISARTICULATED	MISBELIEVE	MISCATALOG
MIRTHLESSLY	MISALTERED	MISARTICULATES	MISBELIEVED	MISCATALOGED
MIRTHLESSNESS	MISALTERING	MISARTICULATING	MISBELIEVER	MISCATALOGING
MIRTHLESSNESSES	MISANALYSES	MISASSAYED	MISBELIEVERS	MISCATALOGS
MISACCEPTION	MISANALYSIS	MISASSAYING	MISBELIEVES	MISCEGENATE
MISACCEPTIONS	MISANDRIES	MISASSEMBLE	MISBELIEVING	MISCEGENATED
MISADAPTED	MISANDRIST	MISASSEMBLED	MISBESEEMED	MISCEGENATES
MISADAPTING	MISANDRISTS	MISASSEMBLES	MISBESEEMING	MISCEGENATING
MISADDRESS	MISANDROUS	MISASSEMBLING	MISBESEEMS	MISCEGENATION
MISADDRESSED	MISANTHROPE	MISASSIGNED	MISBESTOWAL	MISCEGENATIONAL
MISADDRESSES	MISANTHROPES	MISASSIGNING	MISBESTOWALS	MISCEGENATIONS
MISADDRESSING	MISANTHROPIC	MISASSIGNS	MISBESTOWED	MISCEGENATOR
MISADJUSTED	MISANTHROPICAL	MISASSUMED	MISBESTOWING	MISCEGENATORS
MISADJUSTING	MISANTHROPIES	MISASSUMES	MISBESTOWS	MISCEGENES
MISADJUSTS	MISANTHROPIST	MISASSUMING	MISBIASING	MISCEGENETIC
MISADVENTURE	MISANTHROPISTS	MISASSUMPTION	MISBIASSED	MISCEGENIST
MISADVENTURED	MISANTHROPOS	MISASSUMPTIONS	MISBIASSES	MISCEGENISTS
MISADVENTURER	MISANTHROPOSES	MISATONING	MISBIASSING	MISCEGINES
MISADVENTURERS	MISANTHROPY	MISATTRIBUTE	MISBILLING	MISCELLANARIAN
MISADVENTURES	MISAPPLICATION	MISATTRIBUTED	MISBINDING	MISCELLANARIANS
MISADVENTUROUS	MISAPPLICATIONS	MISATTRIBUTES	MISBRANDED	MISCELLANEA

MISCELLANEOUS	MISCLASSIFYING	MISCONSTRUCTED	MISCREDITS	MISDISTRIBUTION
MISCELLANEOUSLY	MISCLASSING	MISCONSTRUCTING	MISCUTTING	MISDIVIDED
MISCELLANIES	MISCOINING	MISCONSTRUCTION	MISDEALERS	MISDIVIDES
MISCELLANIST	MISCOLORED	MISCONSTRUCTS	MISDEALING	MISDIVIDING
MISCELLANISTS	MISCOLORING	MISCONSTRUE	MISDEEMFUL	MISDIVISION
MISCELLANY	MISCOLOURED	MISCONSTRUED	MISDEEMING	MISDIVISIONS
MISCHALLENGE	MISCOLOURING	MISCONSTRUES	MISDEEMINGS	MISDOUBTED
MISCHALLENGES	MISCOLOURS	MISCONSTRUING	MISDEFINED	MISDOUBTFUL
MISCHANCED	MISCOMPREHEND	MISCONTENT	MISDEFINES	MISDOUBTING
MISCHANCEFUL	MISCOMPREHENDED	MISCONTENTED	MISDEFINING	MISDRAWING
MISCHANCES	MISCOMPREHENDS	MISCONTENTING	MISDEMEANANT	MISDRAWINGS
MISCHANCIER	MISCOMPUTATION	MISCONTENTMENT	MISDEMEANANTS	MISDREADED
MISCHANCIEST	MISCOMPUTATIONS	MISCONTENTMENTS	MISDEMEANED	MISDREADING
MISCHANCING	MISCOMPUTE	MISCONTENTS	MISDEMEANING	MISDRIVING
MISCHANNEL	MISCOMPUTED	MISCOOKING	MISDEMEANOR	MISEDITING
MISCHANNELED	MISCOMPUTES	MISCOPYING	MISDEMEANORS	MISEDUCATE
MISCHANNELING	MISCOMPUTING	MISCORRECT	MISDEMEANOUR	MISEDUCATED
MISCHANNELLED	MISCONCEIT	MISCORRECTED	MISDEMEANOURS	MISEDUCATES
MISCHANNELLING	MISCONCEITED	MISCORRECTING	MISDEMEANS	MISEDUCATING
MISCHANNELS	MISCONCEITING	MISCORRECTION	MISDESCRIBE	MISEDUCATION
MISCHANTER	MISCONCEITS	MISCORRECTIONS	MISDESCRIBED	MISEDUCATIONS
MISCHANTERS	MISCONCEIVE	MISCORRECTS	MISDESCRIBES	MISEMPHASES
MISCHARACTERISE	MISCONCEIVED	MISCORRELATION	MISDESCRIBING	MISEMPHASIS
MISCHARACTERIZE	MISCONCEIVER	MISCORRELATIONS	MISDESCRIPTION	MISEMPHASISE
MISCHARGED	MISCONCEIVERS	MISCOUNSEL	MISDESCRIPTIONS	MISEMPHASISED
MISCHARGES	MISCONCEIVES	MISCOUNSELLED	MISDESERTS	MISEMPHASISES
MISCHARGING	MISCONCEIVING	MISCOUNSELLING	MISDEVELOP	MISEMPHASISING
MISCHIEFED	MISCONCEPTION	MISCOUNSELLINGS	MISDEVELOPED	MISEMPHASIZE
MISCHIEFING	MISCONCEPTIONS	MISCOUNSELS	MISDEVELOPING	MISEMPHASIZED
MISCHIEVOUS	MISCONDUCT	MISCOUNTED	MISDEVELOPS	MISEMPHASIZES
MISCHIEVOUSLY	MISCONDUCTED	MISCOUNTING	MISDEVOTION	MISEMPHASIZING
MISCHIEVOUSNESS	MISCONDUCTING	MISCREANCE	MISDEVOTIONS	MISEMPLOYED
MISCHMETAL	MISCONDUCTS	MISCREANCES	MISDIAGNOSE	MISEMPLOYING
MISCHMETALS	MISCONJECTURE	MISCREANCIES	MISDIAGNOSED	MISEMPLOYMENT
MISCHOICES	MISCONJECTURED	MISCREANCY	MISDIAGNOSES	MISEMPLOYMENTS
MISCHOOSES	MISCONJECTURES	MISCREANTS	MISDIAGNOSING	MISEMPLOYS
MISCHOOSING	MISCONJECTURING	MISCREATED	MISDIAGNOSIS	MISENROLLED
MISCIBILITIES	MISCONNECT	MISCREATES	MISDIALING	MISENROLLING
MISCIBILITY	MISCONNECTED	MISCREATING	MISDIALLED	MISENROLLS
MISCITATION	MISCONNECTING	MISCREATION	MISDIALLING	MISENTERED
MISCITATIONS	MISCONNECTION	MISCREATIONS	MISDIETING	MISENTERING
MISCLAIMED	MISCONNECTIONS	MISCREATIVE	MISDIGHTED	MISENTREAT
MISCLAIMING	MISCONNECTS	MISCREATOR	MISDIGHTING	MISENTREATED
MISCLASSED	MISCONSTER	MISCREATORS	MISDIRECTED	MISENTREATING
MISCLASSES	MISCONSTERED	MISCREAUNCE	MISDIRECTING	MISENTREATS
MISCLASSIFIED	MISCONSTERING	MISCREAUNCES	MISDIRECTION	MISENTRIES
MISCLASSIFIES	MISCONSTERS	MISCREDITED	MISDIRECTIONS	MISERABILISM
MISCLASSIFY	MISCONSTRUCT	MISCREDITING	MISDIRECTS	MISERABILISMS

MISERABILIST	MISFOCUSING	MISGUIDERS	MISINSTRUCTION	MISLIPPENED
MISERABILISTS	MISFOCUSSED	MISGUIDING	MISINSTRUCTIONS	MISLIPPENING
MISERABLENESS	MISFOCUSSES	MISHALLOWED	MISINSTRUCTS	MISLIPPENS
MISERABLENESSES	MISFOCUSSING	MISHANDLED	MISINTELLIGENCE	MISLOCATED
MISERABLES	MISFOLDING	MISHANDLES	MISINTENDED	MISLOCATES
MISERABLISM	MISFORMATION	MISHANDLING	MISINTENDING	MISLOCATING
MISERABLISMS	MISFORMATIONS	MISHANDLINGS	MISINTENDS	MISLOCATION
MISERABLIST	MISFORMING	MISHANTERS	MISINTERPRET	MISLOCATIONS
MISERABLISTS	MISFORTUNE	MISHAPPENED	MISINTERPRETED	MISLODGING
MISERICORD	MISFORTUNED	MISHAPPENING	MISINTERPRETER	MISLUCKING
MISERICORDE	MISFORTUNES	MISHAPPENS	MISINTERPRETERS	MISMANAGED
MISERICORDES	MISFRAMING	MISHAPPING	MISINTERPRETING	MISMANAGEMENT
MISERICORDS	MISFUNCTION	MISHEARING	MISINTERPRETS	MISMANAGEMENTS
MISERLIEST	MISFUNCTIONED	MISHEGAASEN	MISINTERRED	MISMANAGER
MISERLINESS	MISFUNCTIONING	MISHGUGGLE	MISINTERRING	MISMANAGERS
MISERLINESSES	MISFUNCTIONS	MISHGUGGLED	MISJOINDER	MISMANAGES
MISESTEEMED	MISGAUGING	MISHGUGGLES	MISJOINDERS	MISMANAGING
MISESTEEMING	MISGENDERED	MISHGUGGLING	MISJOINING	MISMANNERS
MISESTEEMS	MISGENDERING	MISHITTING	MISJUDGEMENT	MISMARKING
MISESTIMATE	MISGENDERS	MISHMASHES	MISJUDGEMENTS	MISMARRIAGE
MISESTIMATED	MISGIVINGS	MISHMOSHES	MISJUDGERS	MISMARRIAGES
MISESTIMATES	MISGOVERNANCE	MISHUGASES	MISJUDGING	MISMARRIED
MISESTIMATING	MISGOVERNANCES	MISIDENTIFIED	MISJUDGMENT	MISMARRIES
MISESTIMATION	MISGOVERNAUNCE	MISIDENTIFIES	MISJUDGMENTS	MISMARRYING
MISESTIMATIONS	MISGOVERNAUNCES	MISIDENTIFY	MISKEEPING	MISMATCHED
MISEVALUATE	MISGOVERNED	MISIDENTIFYING	MISKENNING	MISMATCHES
MISEVALUATED	MISGOVERNING	MISIMPRESSION	MISKICKING	MISMATCHING
MISEVALUATES	MISGOVERNMENT	MISIMPRESSIONS	MISKNOWING	MISMATCHMENT
MISEVALUATING	MISGOVERNMENTS	MISIMPROVE	MISKNOWLEDGE	MISMATCHMENTS
MISEVALUATION	MISGOVERNOR	MISIMPROVED	MISKNOWLEDGES	MISMATINGS
MISEVALUATIONS	MISGOVERNORS	MISIMPROVEMENT	MISLABELED	MISMEASURE
MISFALLING	MISGOVERNS	MISIMPROVEMENTS	MISLABELING	MISMEASURED
MISFARINGS	MISGRADING	MISIMPROVES	MISLABELLED	MISMEASUREMENT
MISFEASANCE	MISGRAFTED	MISIMPROVING	MISLABELLING	MISMEASUREMENTS
MISFEASANCES	MISGRAFTING	MISINFERRED	MISLABORED	MISMEASURES
MISFEASORS	MISGROWING	MISINFERRING	MISLABORING	MISMEASURING
MISFEATURE	MISGROWTHS	MISINFORMANT	MISLABOURED	MISMEETING
MISFEATURED	MISGUESSED	MISINFORMANTS	MISLABOURING	MISMETRING
MISFEATURES	MISGUESSES	MISINFORMATION	MISLABOURS	MISNOMERED
MISFEATURING	MISGUESSING	MISINFORMATIONS	MISLEADERS	MISNOMERING
MISFEEDING	MISGUGGLED	MISINFORMED	MISLEADING	MISNUMBERED
MISFEIGNED	MISGUGGLES	MISINFORMER	MISLEADINGLY	MISNUMBERING
MISFEIGNING	MISGUGGLING	MISINFORMERS	MISLEARNED	MISNUMBERS
MISFIELDED	MISGUIDANCE	MISINFORMING	MISLEARNING	MISOBSERVANCE
MISFIELDING	MISGUIDANCES	MISINFORMS	MISLEEKING	MISOBSERVANCES
MISFITTING	MISGUIDEDLY	MISINSTRUCT	MISLIGHTED	MISOBSERVE
MISFOCUSED	MISGUIDEDNESS	MISINSTRUCTED	MISLIGHTING	MISOBSERVED
MISFOCUSES	MISGUIDEDNESSES	MISINSTRUCTING	MISLIKINGS	MISOBSERVES

MISOBSERVING	MISPHRASED	MISPROPORTIONS	MISRENDERS	MISSIONISATION
MISOCAPNIC	MISPHRASES	MISPUNCTUATE	MISREPORTED	MISSIONISATIONS
MISOGAMIES	MISPHRASING	MISPUNCTUATED	MISREPORTER	MISSIONISE
MISOGAMIST	MISPICKELS	MISPUNCTUATES	MISREPORTERS	MISSIONISED
MISOGAMISTS	MISPLACEMENT	MISPUNCTUATING	MISREPORTING	MISSIONISER
MISOGYNIES	MISPLACEMENTS	MISPUNCTUATION	MISREPORTS	MISSIONISERS
MISOGYNIST	MISPLACING	MISPUNCTUATIONS	MISREPRESENT	MISSIONISES
MISOGYNISTIC	MISPLANNED	MISQUOTATION	MISREPRESENTED	MISSIONISING
MISOGYNISTICAL	MISPLANNING	MISQUOTATIONS	MISREPRESENTER	MISSIONIZATION
MISOGYNISTS	MISPLANTED	MISQUOTERS	MISREPRESENTERS	MISSIONIZATIONS
MISOGYNOUS	MISPLANTING	MISQUOTING	MISREPRESENTING	MISSIONIZE
MISOLOGIES	MISPLAYING	MISRAISING	MISREPRESENTS	MISSIONIZED
MISOLOGIST	MISPLEADED	MISREADING	MISROUTEING	MISSIONIZER
MISOLOGISTS	MISPLEADING	MISREADINGS	MISROUTING	MISSIONIZERS
MISONEISMS	MISPLEADINGS	MISRECKONED	MISSAYINGS	MISSIONIZES
MISONEISTIC	MISPLEASED	MISRECKONING	MISSEATING	MISSIONIZING
MISONEISTS	MISPLEASES	MISRECKONINGS	MISSEEMING	MISSISHNESS
MISORDERED	MISPLEASING	MISRECKONS	MISSEEMINGS	MISSISHNESSES
MISORDERING	MISPOINTED	MISRECOLLECTION	MISSELLING	MISSORTING
MISORIENTATION	MISPOINTING	MISRECORDED	MISSELLINGS	MISSOUNDED
MISORIENTATIONS	MISPOISING	MISRECORDING	MISSENDING	MISSOUNDING
MISORIENTED	MISPOSITION	MISRECORDS	MISSENSING	MISSPACING
MISORIENTING	MISPOSITIONED	MISREFERENCE	MISSETTING	MISSPEAKING
MISORIENTS	MISPOSITIONING	MISREFERENCED	MISSHAPENLY	MISSPELLED
MISPACKAGE	MISPOSITIONS	MISREFERENCES	MISSHAPENNESS	MISSPELLING
MISPACKAGED	MISPRAISED	MISREFERENCING	MISSHAPENNESSES	MISSPELLINGS
MISPACKAGES	MISPRAISES	MISREFERRED	MISSHAPERS	MISSPENDER
MISPACKAGING	MISPRAISING	MISREFERRING	MISSHAPING	MISSPENDERS
MISPAINTED	MISPRICING	MISREGARDED	MISSHEATHED	MISSPENDING
MISPAINTING	MISPRINTED	MISREGARDING	MISSILEERS	MISSTAMPED
MISPARSING	MISPRINTING	MISREGARDS	MISSILEMAN	MISSTAMPING
MISPARTING	MISPRISING	MISREGISTER	MISSILEMEN	MISSTARTED
MISPATCHED	MISPRISION	MISREGISTERED	MISSILERIES	MISSTARTING
MISPATCHES	MISPRISIONS	MISREGISTERING	MISSILRIES	MISSTATEMENT
MISPATCHING	MISPRIZERS	MISREGISTERS	MISSIOLOGIES	MISSTATEMENTS
MISPENNING	MISPRIZING	MISREGISTRATION	MISSIOLOGY	MISSTATING
MISPERCEIVE	MISPROGRAM	MISRELATED	MISSIONARIES	MISSTEERED
MISPERCEIVED	MISPROGRAMED	MISRELATES	MISSIONARISE	MISSTEERING
MISPERCEIVES	MISPROGRAMING	MISRELATING	MISSIONARISED	MISSTEPPED
MISPERCEIVING	MISPROGRAMMED	MISRELATION	MISSIONARISES	MISSTEPPING
MISPERCEPTION	MISPROGRAMMING	MISRELATIONS	MISSIONARISING	MISSTOPPED
MISPERCEPTIONS	MISPROGRAMS	MISRELYING	MISSIONARIZE	MISSTOPPING
MISPERSUADE	MISPRONOUNCE	MISREMEMBER	MISSIONARIZED	MISSTRICKEN
MISPERSUADED	MISPRONOUNCED	MISREMEMBERED	MISSIONARIZES	MISSTRIKES
MISPERSUADES	MISPRONOUNCES	MISREMEMBERING	MISSIONARIZING	MISSTRIKING
MISPERSUADING	MISPRONOUNCING	MISREMEMBERS	MISSIONARY	MISSTYLING
MISPERSUASION	MISPROPORTION	MISRENDERED	MISSIONERS	MISSUITING
MISPERSUASIONS	MISPROPORTIONED	MISRENDERING	MISSIONING	MISSUMMATION

MISSUMMATIONS

MISSUMMATIONS	MISTREATMENTS	MITHRIDATE	MIZZONITES	MODERATRIX
MISTAKABLE	MISTRESSED	MITHRIDATES	MNEMONICAL	MODERATRIXES
MISTAKABLY	MISTRESSES	MITHRIDATIC	MNEMONICALLY	MODERNISATION
MISTAKEABLE	MISTRESSING	MITHRIDATISE	MNEMONISTS	MODERNISATIONS
MISTAKEABLY	MISTRESSLESS	MITHRIDATISED	MNEMOTECHNIC	MODERNISED
MISTAKENLY	MISTRESSLIER	MITHRIDATISES	MNEMOTECHNICS	MODERNISER
MISTAKENNESS	MISTRESSLIEST	MITHRIDATISING	MNEMOTECHNIST	MODERNISERS
MISTAKENNESSES	MISTRESSLY	MITHRIDATISM	MNEMOTECHNISTS	MODERNISES
MISTAKINGS	MISTRUSTED	MITHRIDATISMS	MOBCASTING	MODERNISING
MISTEACHES	MISTRUSTER	MITHRIDATIZE	MOBCASTINGS	MODERNISMS
MISTEACHING	MISTRUSTERS	MITHRIDATIZED	MOBILISABLE	MODERNISTIC
MISTELLING	MISTRUSTFUL	MITHRIDATIZES	MOBILISATION	MODERNISTICALLY
MISTEMPERED	MISTRUSTFULLY	MITHRIDATIZING	MOBILISATIONS	MODERNISTS
MISTEMPERING	MISTRUSTFULNESS	MITIGATING	MOBILISERS	MODERNITIES
MISTEMPERS	MISTRUSTING	MITIGATION	MOBILISING	MODERNIZATION
MISTENDING	MISTRUSTINGLY	MITIGATIONS	MOBILITIES	MODERNIZATIONS
MISTERMING	MISTRUSTLESS	MITIGATIVE	MOBILIZABLE	MODERNIZED
MISTHINKING	MISTRYSTED	MITIGATIVES	MOBILIZATION	MODERNIZER
MISTHOUGHT	MISTRYSTING	MITIGATORS	MOBILIZATIONS	MODERNIZERS
MISTHOUGHTS	MISTUTORED	MITIGATORY	MOBILIZERS	MODERNIZES
MISTHROWING	MISTUTORING	MITOCHONDRIA	MOBILIZING	MODERNIZING
MISTIGRISES	MISUNDERSTAND	MITOCHONDRIAL	MOBLOGGERS	MODERNNESS
MISTIMINGS	MISUNDERSTANDS	MITOCHONDRION	MOBOCRACIES	MODERNNESSES
MISTINESSES	MISUNDERSTOOD	MITOGENETIC	MOBOCRATIC	MODIFIABILITIES
MISTITLING	MISUTILISATION	MITOGENICITIES	MOBOCRATICAL	MODIFIABILITY
MISTLETOES	MISUTILISATIONS	MITOGENICITY	MOCHINESSES	MODIFIABLE
MISTOUCHED	MISUTILIZATION	MITOMYCINS	MOCKERNUTS	MODIFIABLENESS
MISTOUCHES	MISUTILIZATIONS	MITOTICALLY	MOCKINGBIRD	MODIFICATION
MISTOUCHING	MISVALUING	MITRAILLES	MOCKINGBIRDS	MODIFICATIONS
MISTRACING	MISVENTURE	MITRAILLEUR	MOCKUMENTARIES	MODIFICATIVE
MISTRAINED	MISVENTURES	MITRAILLEURS	MOCKUMENTARY	MODIFICATORY
MISTRAINING	MISVENTUROUS	MITRAILLEUSE	MODAFINILS	MODILLIONS
MISTRANSCRIBE	MISVOCALISATION	MITRAILLEUSES	MODALISTIC	MODISHNESS
MISTRANSCRIBED	MISVOCALIZATION	MITREWORTS	MODALITIES	MODISHNESSES
MISTRANSCRIBES	MISWANDRED	MITTIMUSES	MODELLINGS	MODULABILITIES
MISTRANSCRIBING	MISWEENING	MIXABILITIES	MODELLISTS	MODULABILITY
MISTRANSLATE	MISWENDING	MIXABILITY	MODERATELY	MODULARISED
MISTRANSLATED	MISWORDING	MIXEDNESSES	MODERATENESS	MODULARITIES
MISTRANSLATES	MISWORDINGS	MIXMASTERS	MODERATENESSES	MODULARITY
MISTRANSLATING	MISWORSHIP	MIXOBARBARIC	MODERATING	MODULARIZED
MISTRANSLATION	MISWORSHIPPED	MIXOLOGIES	MODERATION	MODULATING
MISTRANSLATIONS	MISWORSHIPPING	MIXOLOGIST	MODERATIONS	MODULATION
MISTRAYNED	MISWORSHIPPINGS	MIXOLOGISTS	MODERATISM	MODULATIONS
MISTREADING	MISWORSHIPS	MIXOLYDIAN	MODERATISMS	MODULATIVE
MISTREADINGS	MISWRITING	MIXOTROPHIC	MODERATORS	MODULATORS
MISTREATED	MISWRITTEN	MIZENMASTS	MODERATORSHIP	MODULATORY
MISTREATING	MITERWORTS	MIZZENMAST	MODERATORSHIPS	MOISTENERS
MISTREATMENT	MITHRADATIC	MIZZENMASTS	MODERATRICES	MOISTENING

MOISTIFIED	MOLLUSCOID	MONADOLOGIES	MONEYBELTS	MONITORINGS
MOISTIFIES	MOLLUSCOIDAL	MONADOLOGY	MONEYBOXES	MONITORSHIP
MOISTIFYING	MOLLUSCOIDS	MONANDRIES	MONEYCHANGER	MONITORSHIPS
MOISTNESSES	MOLLUSCOUS	MONANDROUS	MONEYCHANGERS	MONITRESSES
MOISTURELESS	MOLLUSKANS	MONANTHOUS	MONEYGRUBBING	MONKEYGLAND
MOISTURISE	MOLLYCODDLE	MONARCHALLY	MONEYGRUBBINGS	MONKEYISMS
MOISTURISED	MOLLYCODDLED	MONARCHIAL	MONEYLENDER	MONKEYPODS
MOISTURISER	MOLLYCODDLER	MONARCHICAL	MONEYLENDERS	MONKEYPOTS
MOISTURISERS	MOLLYCODDLERS	MONARCHICALLY	MONEYLENDING	MONKEYPOXES
MOISTURISES	MOLLYCODDLES	MONARCHIES	MONEYLENDINGS	MONKEYSHINE
MOISTURISING	MOLLYCODDLING	MONARCHISE	MONEYMAKER	MONKEYSHINES
MOISTURIZE	MOLLYCODDLINGS	MONARCHISED	MONEYMAKERS	MONKFISHES
MOISTURIZED	MOLLYHAWKS	MONARCHISES	MONEYMAKING	MONKISHNESS
MOISTURIZER	MOLLYMAWKS	MONARCHISING	MONEYMAKINGS	MONKISHNESSES
MOISTURIZERS	MOLOCHISED	MONARCHISM	MONEYSPINNING	MONKSHOODS
MOISTURIZES	MOLOCHISES	MONARCHISMS	MONEYWORTS	MONOACIDIC
MOISTURIZING	MOLOCHISING	MONARCHIST	MONGERINGS	MONOAMINERGIC
MOITHERING	MOLOCHIZED	MONARCHISTIC	MONGOLISMS	MONOAMINES
MOLALITIES	MOLOCHIZES	MONARCHISTS	MONGOLOIDS	MONOATOMIC
MOLARITIES	MOLOCHIZING	MONARCHIZE	MONGRELISATION	MONOBLEPSES
MOLASSESES	MOLYBDATES	MONARCHIZED	MONGRELISATIONS	MONOBLEPSIS
MOLDABILITIES	MOLYBDENITE	MONARCHIZES	MONGRELISE	MONOCARBOXYLIC
MOLDABILITY	MOLYBDENITES	MONARCHIZING	MONGRELISED	MONOCARDIAN
MOLDAVITES	MOLYBDENOSES	MONASTERIAL	MONGRELISER	MONOCARDIANS
MOLDBOARDS	MOLYBDENOSIS	MONASTERIES	MONGRELISERS	MONOCARPELLARY
MOLDINESSES	MOLYBDENOUS	MONASTICAL	MONGRELISES	MONOCARPIC
MOLECATCHER	MOLYBDENUM	MONASTICALLY	MONGRELISING	MONOCARPOUS
MOLECATCHERS	MOLYBDENUMS	MONASTICISM	MONGRELISM	MONOCEROSES
MOLECULARITIES	MOLYBDOSES	MONASTICISMS	MONGRELISMS	MONOCEROUS
MOLECULARITY	MOLYBDOSIS	MONAURALLY	MONGRELIZATION	MONOCHASIA
MOLECULARLY	MOMENTANEOUS	MONCHIQUITE	MONGRELIZATIONS	MONOCHASIAL
MOLENDINAR	MOMENTARILY	MONCHIQUITES	MONGRELIZE	MONOCHASIUM
MOLENDINARIES	MOMENTARINESS	MONDEGREEN	MONGRELIZED	MONOCHLAMYDEOUS
MOLENDINARS	MOMENTARINESSES	MONDEGREENS	MONGRELIZER	MONOCHLORIDE
MOLENDINARY	MOMENTOUSLY	MONECIOUSLY	MONGRELIZERS	MONOCHLORIDES
MOLESTATION	MOMENTOUSNESS	MONERGISMS	MONGRELIZES	MONOCHORDS
MOLESTATIONS	MOMENTOUSNESSES	MONESTROUS	MONGRELIZING	MONOCHROIC
MOLIMINOUS	MOMPRENEUR	MONETARILY	MONGRELLIER	MONOCHROICS
MOLLIFIABLE	MOMPRENEURS	MONETARISM	MONGRELLIEST	MONOCHROMASIES
MOLLIFICATION	MONACHISMS	MONETARISMS	MONILIASES	MONOCHROMASY
MOLLIFICATIONS	MONACHISTS	MONETARIST	MONILIASIS	MONOCHROMAT
MOLLIFIERS	MONACTINAL	MONETARISTS	MONILIFORM	MONOCHROMATE
MOLLIFYING	MONACTINES	MONETISATION	MONISTICAL	MONOCHROMATES
MOLLITIOUS	MONADELPHOUS	MONETISATIONS	MONISTICALLY	MONOCHROMATIC
MOLLUSCANS	MONADICALLY	MONETISING	MONITORIAL	MONOCHROMATICS
MOLLUSCICIDAL	MONADIFORM	MONETIZATION	MONITORIALLY	MONOCHROMATISM
MOLLUSCICIDE	MONADISTIC	MONETIZATIONS	MONITORIES	MONOCHROMATISMS
MOLLUSCICIDES	MONADNOCKS	MONETIZING	MONITORING	MONOCHROMATOR

MONOCHROMATORS	MONODRAMATIC	MONOGRAPHS	MONOLOGUISED	MONOPHOBIA
MONOCHROMATS	MONOECIOUS	MONOGRAPHY	MONOLOGUISES	MONOPHOBIAS
MONOCHROME	MONOECIOUSLY	MONOGYNIAN	MONOLOGUISING	MONOPHOBIC
MONOCHROMES	MONOECISMS	MONOGYNIES	MONOLOGUIST	MONOPHOBICS
MONOCHROMIC	MONOESTERS	MONOGYNIST	MONOLOGUISTS	MONOPHONIC
MONOCHROMICAL	MONOFILAMENT	MONOGYNISTS	MONOLOGUIZE	MONOPHONICALLY
MONOCHROMIES	MONOFILAMENTS	MONOGYNOUS	MONOLOGUIZED	MONOPHONIES
MONOCHROMIST	MONOGAMIES	MONOHYBRID	MONOLOGUIZES	MONOPHOSPHATE
MONOCHROMISTS	MONOGAMIST	MONOHYBRIDS	MONOLOGUIZING	MONOPHOSPHATES
MONOCHROMY	MONOGAMISTIC	MONOHYDRATE	MONOMACHIA	MONOPHTHONG
MONOCLINAL	MONOGAMISTS	MONOHYDRATED	MONOMACHIAS	MONOPHTHONGAL
MONOCLINALLY	MONOGAMOUS	MONOHYDRATES	MONOMACHIES	MONOPHTHONGISE
MONOCLINALS	MONOGAMOUSLY	MONOHYDRIC	MONOMANIAC	MONOPHTHONGISED
MONOCLINES	MONOGAMOUSNESS	MONOHYDROGEN	MONOMANIACAL	MONOPHTHONGISES
MONOCLINIC	MONOGASTRIC	MONOHYDROXY	MONOMANIACALLY	MONOPHTHONGIZE
MONOCLINISM	MONOGENEAN	MONOICOUSLY	MONOMANIACS	MONOPHTHONGIZED
MONOCLINISMS	MONOGENEANS	MONOLATERS	MONOMANIAS	MONOPHTHONGIZES
MONOCLINOUS	MONOGENESES	MONOLATRIES	MONOMEROUS	MONOPHTHONGS
MONOCLONAL	MONOGENESIS	MONOLATRIST	MONOMETALLIC	MONOPHYLETIC
MONOCLONALS	MONOGENETIC	MONOLATRISTS	MONOMETALLISM	MONOPHYLIES
MONOCOQUES	MONOGENICALLY	MONOLATROUS	MONOMETALLISMS	MONOPHYLLOUS
MONOCOTYLEDON	MONOGENIES	MONOLAYERS	MONOMETALLIST	MONOPHYODONT
MONOCOTYLEDONS	MONOGENISM	MONOLINGUAL	MONOMETALLISTS	MONOPHYODONTS
MONOCOTYLS	MONOGENISMS	MONOLINGUALISM	MONOMETERS	MONOPHYSITE
MONOCRACIES	MONOGENIST	MONOLINGUALISMS	MONOMETRIC	MONOPHYSITES
MONOCRATIC	MONOGENISTIC	MONOLINGUALS	MONOMETRICAL	MONOPHYSITIC
MONOCROPPED	MONOGENISTS	MONOLINGUIST	MONOMOLECULAR	MONOPHYSITISM
MONOCROPPING	MONOGENOUS	MONOLINGUISTS	MONOMOLECULARLY	MONOPHYSITISMS
MONOCRYSTAL	MONOGLYCERIDE	MONOLITHIC	MONOMORPHEMIC	MONOPITCHES
MONOCRYSTALLINE	MONOGLYCERIDES	MONOLITHICALLY	MONOMORPHIC	MONOPLANES
MONOCRYSTALS	MONOGONIES	MONOLOGGED	MONOMORPHISM	MONOPLEGIA
MONOCULARLY	MONOGRAMED	MONOLOGGING	MONOMORPHISMS	MONOPLEGIAS
MONOCULARS	MONOGRAMING	MONOLOGICAL	MONOMORPHOUS	MONOPLEGIC
MONOCULOUS	MONOGRAMMATIC	MONOLOGIES	MONOMYARIAN	MONOPLEGICS
MONOCULTURAL	MONOGRAMMED	MONOLOGISE	MONOMYARIANS	MONOPLOIDS
MONOCULTURE	MONOGRAMMER	MONOLOGISED	MONONUCLEAR	MONOPODIAL
MONOCULTURES	MONOGRAMMERS	MONOLOGISES	MONONUCLEARS	MONOPODIALLY
MONOCYCLES	MONOGRAMMING	MONOLOGISING	MONONUCLEATE	MONOPODIAS
MONOCYCLIC	MONOGRAPHED	MONOLOGIST	MONONUCLEATED	MONOPODIES
MONOCYTOID	MONOGRAPHER	MONOLOGISTS	MONONUCLEOSES	MONOPODIUM
MONODACTYLOUS	MONOGRAPHERS	MONOLOGIZE	MONONUCLEOSIS	MONOPOLIES
MONODELPHIAN	MONOGRAPHIC	MONOLOGIZED	MONONUCLEOTIDE	MONOPOLISATION
MONODELPHIANS	MONOGRAPHICAL	MONOLOGIZES	MONONUCLEOTIDES	MONOPOLISATIONS
MONODELPHIC	MONOGRAPHICALLY	MONOLOGIZING	MONOPETALOUS	MONOPOLISE
MONODELPHOUS	MONOGRAPHIES	MONOLOGUED	MONOPHAGIES	MONOPOLISED
MONODICALLY	MONOGRAPHING	MONOLOGUES	MONOPHAGOUS	MONOPOLISER
MONODISPERSE	MONOGRAPHIST	MONOLOGUING	MONOPHASES	MONOPOLISERS
MONODRAMAS	MONOGRAPHISTS	MONOLOGUISE	MONOPHASIC	MONOPOLISES

MONOPOLISING	MONOSOMIES	MONOTHELETE	MONSEIGNEUR	MONUMENTED
MONOPOLISM	MONOSPACED	MONOTHELETES	MONSEIGNEURS	MONUMENTING
MONOPOLISMS	MONOSPECIFIC	MONOTHELETIC	MONSIGNORI	MONZONITES
MONOPOLIST	MONOSPECIFICITY	MONOTHELETICAL	MONSIGNORIAL	MONZONITIC
MONOPOLISTIC	MONOSPERMAL	MONOTHELETISM	MONSIGNORS	MOODINESSES
MONOPOLISTS	MONOSPERMOUS	MONOTHELETISMS	MONSTERING	MOONCALVES
MONOPOLIZATION	MONOSTABLE	MONOTHELISM	MONSTERINGS	MOONCHILDREN
MONOPOLIZATIONS	MONOSTELES	MONOTHELISMS	MONSTRANCE	MOONCRAFTS
MONOPOLIZE	MONOSTELIC	MONOTHELITE	MONSTRANCES	MOONFISHES
MONOPOLIZED	MONOSTELIES	MONOTHELITES	MONSTROSITIES	MOONFLOWER
MONOPOLIZER	MONOSTICHIC	MONOTHELITISM	MONSTROSITY	MOONFLOWERS
MONOPOLIZERS	MONOSTICHOUS	MONOTHELITISMS	MONSTROUSLY	MOONINESSES
MONOPOLIZES	MONOSTICHS	MONOTHERAPIES	MONSTROUSNESS	MOONLIGHTED
MONOPOLIZING	MONOSTOMOUS	MONOTHERAPY	MONSTROUSNESSES	MOONLIGHTER
MONOPRINTS	MONOSTROPHE	MONOTOCOUS	MONSTRUOSITIES	MOONLIGHTERS
MONOPRIONIDIAN	MONOSTROPHES	MONOTONICALLY	MONSTRUOSITY	MOONLIGHTING
MONOPROPELLANT	MONOSTROPHIC	MONOTONICITIES	MONSTRUOUS	MOONLIGHTINGS
MONOPROPELLANTS	MONOSTROPHICS	MONOTONICITY	MONTADALES	MOONLIGHTS
MONOPSONIES	MONOSTYLAR	MONOTONIES	MONTAGNARD	MOONPHASES
MONOPSONIST	MONOSTYLOUS	MONOTONING	MONTAGNARDS	MOONQUAKES
MONOPSONISTIC	MONOSYLLABIC	MONOTONISE	MONTBRETIA	MOONRAKERS
MONOPSONISTS	MONOSYLLABICITY	MONOTONISED	MONTBRETIAS	MOONRAKING
MONOPTERAL	MONOSYLLABISM	MONOTONISES	MONTELIMAR	MOONRAKINGS
MONOPTEROI	MONOSYLLABISMS	MONOTONISING	MONTELIMARS	MOONSCAPES
MONOPTERON	MONOSYLLABLE	MONOTONIZE	MONTGOLFIER	MOONSHINED
MONOPTEROS	MONOSYLLABLES	MONOTONIZED	MONTGOLFIERS	MOONSHINER
MONOPTEROSES	MONOSYMMETRIC	MONOTONIZES	MONTHLINGS	MOONSHINERS
MONOPTOTES	MONOSYMMETRICAL	MONOTONIZING	MONTICELLITE	MOONSHINES
MONOPULSES	MONOSYMMETRIES	MONOTONOUS	MONTICELLITES	MOONSHINIER
MONORCHIDISM	MONOSYMMETRY	MONOTONOUSLY	MONTICOLOUS	MOONSHINIEST
MONORCHIDISMS	MONOSYNAPTIC	MONOTONOUSNESS	MONTICULATE	MOONSHINING
MONORCHIDS	MONOTASKED	MONOTREMATOUS	MONTICULES	MOONSHININGS
MONORCHISM	MONOTASKING	MONOTREMES	MONTICULOUS	MOONSTONES
MONORCHISMS	MONOTASKINGS	MONOTRICHIC	MONTICULUS	MOONSTRICKEN
MONORHINAL	MONOTELEPHONE	MONOTRICHOUS	MONTICULUSES	MOONSTRIKE
MONORHINES	MONOTELEPHONES	MONOTROCHS	MONTMORILLONITE	MOONSTRIKES
MONORHYMED	MONOTERPENE	MONOUNSATURATE	MONUMENTAL	MOONSTRUCK
MONORHYMES	MONOTERPENES	MONOUNSATURATED	MONUMENTALISE	MOONWALKED
MONOSACCHARIDE	MONOTHALAMIC	MONOUNSATURATES	MONUMENTALISED	MOONWALKER
MONOSACCHARIDES	MONOTHALAMOUS	MONOVALENCE	MONUMENTALISES	MOONWALKERS
MONOSATURATED	MONOTHECAL	MONOVALENCES	MONUMENTALISING	MOONWALKING
MONOSEMIES	MONOTHECOUS	MONOVALENCIES	MONUMENTALITIES	MOORBUZZARD
MONOSEPALOUS	MONOTHEISM	MONOVALENCY	MONUMENTALITY	MOORBUZZARDS
MONOSKIERS	MONOTHEISMS	MONOVALENT	MONUMENTALIZE	MOOSEBIRDS
MONOSKIING	MONOTHEIST	MONOXYLONS	MONUMENTALIZED	MOOSEHAIRS
MONOSKIINGS	MONOTHEISTIC	MONOXYLOUS	MONUMENTALIZES	MOOSEHIDES
MONOSODIUM	MONOTHEISTICAL	MONOZYGOTIC	MONUMENTALIZING	MOOSEWOODS
MONOSOMICS	MONOTHEISTS	MONOZYGOUS	MONUMENTALLY	MOOSEYARDS

M

MOOTNESSES

MOOTNESSES	MORIGERATED	MORPHOMETRY	MOSAICKING	MOTHERLINESS
MOPINESSES	MORIGERATES	MORPHOPHONEME	MOSAICKINGS	MOTHERLINESSES
MOPISHNESS	MORIGERATING	MORPHOPHONEMES	MOSAICLIKE	MOTHERWORT
MOPISHNESSES	MORIGERATION	MORPHOPHONEMIC	MOSASAURUS	MOTHERWORTS
MORALISATION	MORIGERATIONS	MORPHOPHONEMICS	MOSBOLLETJIE	MOTHPROOFED
MORALISATIONS	MORIGEROUS	MORPHOPHONOLOGY	MOSBOLLETJIES	MOTHPROOFER
MORALISERS	MORONICALLY	MORPHOSYNTAX	MOSCHATELS	MOTHPROOFERS
MORALISING	MORONITIES	MORPHOSYNTAXES	MOSCHIFEROUS	MOTHPROOFING
MORALISINGS	MOROSENESS	MORPHOTROPIC	MOSCOVIUMS	MOTHPROOFS
MORALISTIC	MOROSENESSES	MORPHOTROPIES	MOSKONFYTS	MOTILITIES
MORALISTICALLY	MOROSITIES	MORPHOTROPY	MOSQUITOES	MOTIONISTS
MORALITIES	MORPHACTIN	MORSELLING	MOSQUITOEY	MOTIONLESS
MORALIZATION	MORPHACTINS	MORSELLINGS	MOSQUITOFISH	MOTIONLESSLY
MORALIZATIONS	MORPHALLAXES	MORTADELLA	MOSQUITOFISHES	MOTIONLESSNESS
MORALIZERS	MORPHALLAXIS	MORTADELLAS	MOSQUITOIER	MOTIVATING
MORALIZING	MORPHEMICALLY	MORTADELLE	MOSQUITOIEST	MOTIVATION
MORALIZINGS	MORPHEMICS	MORTALISED	MOSSBACKED	MOTIVATIONAL
MORASSIEST	MORPHINISM	MORTALISES	MOSSBLUITER	MOTIVATIONALLY
MORATORIUM	MORPHINISMS	MORTALISING	MOSSBLUITERS	MOTIVATIONS
MORATORIUMS	MORPHINOMANIA	MORTALITIES	MOSSBUNKER	MOTIVATIVE
MORBIDEZZA	MORPHINOMANIAC	MORTALIZED	MOSSBUNKERS	MOTIVATORS
MORBIDEZZAS	MORPHINOMANIACS	MORTALIZES	MOSSINESSES	MOTIVELESS
MORBIDITIES	MORPHINOMANIAS	MORTALIZING	MOSSPLANTS	MOTIVELESSLY
MORBIDNESS	MORPHOGENESES	MORTARBOARD	MOSSTROOPER	MOTIVELESSNESS
MORBIDNESSES	MORPHOGENESIS	MORTARBOARDS	MOSSTROOPERS	MOTIVITIES
MORBIFEROUS	MORPHOGENETIC	MORTARIEST	MOTETTISTS	MOTOCROSSES
MORBIFICALLY	MORPHOGENIC	MORTARLESS	MOTHBALLED	MOTONEURON
MORBILLIFORM	MORPHOGENIES	MORTCLOTHS	MOTHBALLING	MOTONEURONAL
MORBILLIVIRUS	MORPHOGENS	MORTGAGEABLE	MOTHERBOARD	MOTONEURONS
MORBILLIVIRUSES	MORPHOGENY	MORTGAGEES	MOTHERBOARDS	MOTORBICYCLE
MORBILLOUS	MORPHOGRAPHER	MORTGAGERS	MOTHERCRAFT	MOTORBICYCLES
MORDACIOUS	MORPHOGRAPHERS	MORTGAGING	MOTHERCRAFTS	MOTORBIKED
MORDACIOUSLY	MORPHOGRAPHIES	MORTGAGORS	MOTHERESES	MOTORBIKES
MORDACIOUSNESS	MORPHOGRAPHY	MORTICIANS	MOTHERFUCKER	MOTORBIKING
MORDACITIES	MORPHOLINE	MORTIFEROUS	MOTHERFUCKERS	MOTORBOATED
MORDANCIES	MORPHOLINES	MORTIFEROUSNESS	MOTHERFUCKING	MOTORBOATER
MORDANTING	MORPHOLINO	MORTIFICATION	MOTHERHOOD	MOTORBOATERS
MORENESSES	MORPHOLINOS	MORTIFICATIONS	MOTHERHOODS	MOTORBOATING
MORGANATIC	MORPHOLOGIC	MORTIFIERS	MOTHERHOUSE	MOTORBOATINGS
MORGANATICALLY	MORPHOLOGICAL	MORTIFYING	MOTHERHOUSES	MOTORBOATS
MORGANITES	MORPHOLOGICALLY	MORTIFYINGLY	MOTHERIEST	MOTORBUSES
MORGELLONS	MORPHOLOGIES	MORTIFYINGS	MOTHERINGS	MOTORBUSSES
MORGENSTERN	MORPHOLOGIST	MORTUARIES	MOTHERLAND	MOTORCADED
MORGENSTERNS	MORPHOLOGISTS	MORULATION	MOTHERLANDS	MOTORCADES
MORIBUNDITIES	MORPHOLOGY	MORULATIONS	MOTHERLESS	MOTORCADING
MORIBUNDITY	MORPHOMETRIC	MOSAICALLY	MOTHERLESSNESS	MOTORCOACH
MORIBUNDLY	MORPHOMETRICS	MOSAICISMS	MOTHERLIER	MOTORCOACHES
MORIGERATE	MORPHOMETRIES	MOSAICISTS	MOTHERLIEST	MOTORCYCLE

MOTORCYCLED	MOUNTAINIER	MOUSTACHIO	MRIDANGAMS	MUDDLEMENT
MOTORCYCLES	MOUNTAINIEST	MOUSTACHIOED	MUCEDINOUS	MUDDLEMENTS
MOTORCYCLING	MOUNTAINOUS	MOUSTACHIOS	MUCHNESSES	MUDDLINGLY
MOTORCYCLINGS	MOUNTAINOUSLY	MOUTHBREATHER	MUCIDITIES	MUDHOPPERS
MOTORCYCLIST	MOUNTAINOUSNESS	MOUTHBREATHERS	MUCIDNESSES	MUDLARKING
MOTORCYCLISTS	MOUNTAINSIDE	MOUTHBREEDER	MUCIFEROUS	MUDLOGGERS
MOTORHOMES	MOUNTAINSIDES	MOUTHBREEDERS	MUCILAGINOUS	MUDLOGGING
MOTORICALLY	MOUNTAINTOP	MOUTHBROODER	MUCILAGINOUSLY	MUDLOGGINGS
MOTORISATION	MOUNTAINTOPS	MOUTHBROODERS	MUCINOGENS	MUDPUPPIES
MOTORISATIONS	MOUNTEBANK	MOUTHFEELS	MUCKAMUCKED	MUDSKIPPER
MOTORISING	MOUNTEBANKED	MOUTHPARTS	MUCKAMUCKING	MUDSKIPPERS
MOTORIZATION	MOUNTEBANKERIES	MOUTHPIECE	MUCKAMUCKS	MUDSLINGER
MOTORIZATIONS	MOUNTEBANKERY	MOUTHPIECES	MUCKENDERS	MUDSLINGERS
MOTORIZING	MOUNTEBANKING	MOUTHWASHES	MUCKINESSES	MUDSLINGING
MOTORMOUTH	MOUNTEBANKINGS	MOUTHWATERING	MUCKRAKERS	MUDSLINGINGS
MOTORMOUTHS	MOUNTEBANKISM	MOUTHWATERINGLY	MUCKRAKING	MUFFETTEES
MOTORSHIPS	MOUNTEBANKISMS	MOUVEMENTE	MUCKRAKINGS	MUFFINEERS
MOTORTRUCK	MOUNTEBANKS	MOVABILITIES	MUCKSPREAD	MUGEARITES
MOTORTRUCKS	MOUNTENANCE	MOVABILITY	MUCKSPREADER	MUGGINESSES
MOTOSCAFOS	MOUNTENANCES	MOVABLENESS	MUCKSPREADERS	MUGWUMPERIES
MOUCHARABIES	MOUNTENAUNCE	MOVABLENESSES	MUCKSPREADING	MUGWUMPERY
MOUCHARABY	MOUNTENAUNCES	MOVEABILITIES	MUCKSPREADS	MUGWUMPISH
MOUDIEWART	MOURNFULLER	MOVEABILITY	MUCKSWEATS	MUGWUMPISM
MOUDIEWARTS	MOURNFULLEST	MOVEABLENESS	MUCKYMUCKS	MUGWUMPISMS
MOUDIEWORT	MOURNFULLY	MOVEABLENESSES	MUCOCUTANEOUS	MUJAHEDDIN
MOUDIEWORTS	MOURNFULNESS	MOVELESSLY	MUCOLYTICS	MUJAHEDEEN
MOUDIWARTS	MOURNFULNESSES	MOVELESSNESS	MUCOMEMBRANOUS	MUJAHIDEEN
MOUDIWORTS	MOURNINGLY	MOVELESSNESSES	MUCOPEPTIDE	MUKHABARAT
MOULDABILITIES	MOURNIVALS	MOVIEGOERS	MUCOPEPTIDES	MUKHABARATS
MOULDABILITY	MOURVEDRES	MOVIEGOING	MUCOPROTEIN	MULATRESSES
MOULDBOARD	MOUSEBIRDS	MOVIEGOINGS	MUCOPROTEINS	MULATTRESS
MOULDBOARDS	MOUSEOVERS	MOVIELANDS	MUCOPURULENT	MULATTRESSES
MOULDERING	MOUSEPIECE	MOVIEMAKER	MUCOSANGUINEOUS	MULBERRIES
MOULDINESS	MOUSEPIECES	MOVIEMAKERS	MUCOSITIES	MULIEBRITIES
MOULDINESSES	MOUSETAILS	MOVIEMAKING	MUCOVISCIDOSES	MULIEBRITY
MOULDWARPS	MOUSETRAPPED	MOVIEMAKINGS	MUCOVISCIDOSIS	MULISHNESS
MOULDYWARP	MOUSETRAPPING	MOWBURNING	MUCRONATED	MULISHNESSES
MOULDYWARPS	MOUSETRAPPINGS	MOWBURNINGS	MUCRONATION	MULLAHISMS
MOUNDBIRDS	MOUSETRAPS	MOWDIEWART	MUCRONATIONS	MULLARKIES
MOUNTAINBOARD	MOUSINESSES	MOWDIEWARTS	MUDCAPPING	MULLIGATAWNIES
MOUNTAINBOARDER	MOUSQUETAIRE	MOWDIEWORT	MUDCAPPINGS	MULLIGATAWNY
MOUNTAINBOARDS	MOUSQUETAIRES	MOWDIEWORTS	MUDDINESSES	MULLIGRUBS
MOUNTAINED	MOUSSELIKE	MOXIBUSTION	MUDDLEDNESS	MULLIONING
MOUNTAINEER	MOUSSELINE	MOXIBUSTIONS	MUDDLEDNESSES	MULLOCKIER
MOUNTAINEERED	MOUSSELINES	MOYGASHELS	MUDDLEHEAD	MULLOCKIEST
MOUNTAINEERING	MOUSTACHED	MOZZARELLA	MUDDLEHEADED	MULTANGULAR
MOUNTAINEERINGS	MOUSTACHES	MOZZARELLAS	MUDDLEHEADEDLY	MULTANIMOUS
MOUNTAINEERS	MOUSTACHIAL	MRIDAMGAMS	MUDDLEHEADS	MULTARTICULATE

MULTEITIES   MULTICOSTATE   MULTIFOCALS   MULTILOCATIONAL   MULTIPARTYISMS
MULTIACCESS   MULTICOUNTY   MULTIFOILS   MULTILOCULAR   MULTIPEDES
MULTIACCESSES   MULTICOURSE   MULTIFOLIATE   MULTILOCULATE   MULTIPHASE
MULTIAGENCY   MULTICULTI   MULTIFOLIOLATE   MULTILOCULATE   MULTIPHASIC
MULTIANGULAR   MULTICULTIS   MULTIFORMITIES   MULTILOQUENCE   MULTIPHOTON
MULTIARMED   MULTICULTURAL   MULTIFORMITY   MULTILOQUENCES   MULTIPICTURE
MULTIARTICULATE   MULTICULTURALLY   MULTIFORMS   MULTILOQUENT   MULTIPIECE
MULTIAUTHOR   MULTICURIE   MULTIFREQUENCY   MULTILOQUIES   MULTIPISTON
MULTIAXIAL   MULTICURRENCIES   MULTIFUNCTION   MULTILOQUOUS   MULTIPLANE
MULTIBARREL   MULTICURRENCY   MULTIFUNCTIONAL   MULTILOQUY   MULTIPLANES
MULTIBARRELED   MULTICUSPID   MULTIGENES   MULTIMANNED   MULTIPLANT
MULTIBARRELLED   MULTICUSPIDATE   MULTIGENIC   MULTIMEDIA   MULTIPLAYER
MULTIBARRELS   MULTICUSPIDS   MULTIGRADE   MULTIMEDIAS   MULTIPLAYERS
MULTIBILLION   MULTICYCLE   MULTIGRADES   MULTIMEGATON   MULTIPLETS
MULTIBLADED   MULTICYCLES   MULTIGRAIN   MULTIMEGAWATT   MULTIPLEXED
MULTIBRANCHED   MULTICYLINDER   MULTIGRAVIDA   MULTIMEGAWATTS   MULTIPLEXER
MULTIBUILDING   MULTIDENTATE   MULTIGRAVIDAE   MULTIMEMBER   MULTIPLEXERS
MULTICAMERATE   MULTIDIALECTAL   MULTIGRAVIDAS   MULTIMETALLIC   MULTIPLEXES
MULTICAMPUS   MULTIDIGITATE   MULTIGROUP   MULTIMETER   MULTIPLEXING
MULTICAPITATE   MULTIDISCIPLINE   MULTIHEADED   MULTIMETERS   MULTIPLEXINGS
MULTICARBON   MULTIDIVISIONAL   MULTIHOSPITAL   MULTIMILLENNIAL   MULTIPLEXOR
MULTICASTS   MULTIDOMAIN   MULTIHULLS   MULTIMILLION   MULTIPLEXORS
MULTICAULINE   MULTIELECTRODE   MULTIJUGATE   MULTIMODAL   MULTIPLIABLE
MULTICAUSAL   MULTIELEMENT   MULTIJUGOUS   MULTIMODES   MULTIPLICABLE
MULTICELLED   MULTIEMPLOYER   MULTILANES   MULTIMOLECULAR   MULTIPLICAND
MULTICELLULAR   MULTIEMPLOYERS   MULTILATERAL   MULTINATION   MULTIPLICANDS
MULTICENTER   MULTIENGINE   MULTILATERALISM   MULTINATIONAL   MULTIPLICATE
MULTICENTRAL   MULTIENGINED   MULTILATERALIST   MULTINATIONALS   MULTIPLICATES
MULTICENTRE   MULTIENZYME   MULTILATERALLY   MULTINOMIAL   MULTIPLICATION
MULTICENTRIC   MULTIETHNIC   MULTILAYER   MULTINOMIALS   MULTIPLICATIONS
MULTICHAIN   MULTIETHNICS   MULTILAYERED   MULTINOMINAL   MULTIPLICATIVE
MULTICHAMBERED   MULTIFACED   MULTILAYERS   MULTINUCLEAR   MULTIPLICATOR
MULTICHANNEL   MULTIFACETED   MULTILEVEL   MULTINUCLEATE   MULTIPLICATORS
MULTICHARACTER   MULTIFACTOR   MULTILEVELED   MULTINUCLEATED   MULTIPLICITIES
MULTICIDES   MULTIFACTORIAL   MULTILEVELLED   MULTINUCLEOLAR   MULTIPLICITY
MULTICIPITAL   MULTIFAMILIES   MULTILINEAL   MULTINUCLEOLATE   MULTIPLIED
MULTICLIENT   MULTIFAMILY   MULTILINEAR   MULTIORGASMIC   MULTIPLIER
MULTICOATED   MULTIFARIOUS   MULTILINES   MULTIPACKS   MULTIPLIERS
MULTICOLOR   MULTIFARIOUSLY   MULTILINGUAL   MULTIPANED   MULTIPLIES
MULTICOLORED   MULTIFIDLY   MULTILINGUALISM   MULTIPARAE   MULTIPLYING
MULTICOLORS   MULTIFIDOUS   MULTILINGUALLY   MULTIPARAMETER   MULTIPOINT
MULTICOLOUR   MULTIFILAMENT   MULTILINGUIST   MULTIPARAS   MULTIPOLAR
MULTICOLOURED   MULTIFILAMENTS   MULTILINGUISTS   MULTIPARITIES   MULTIPOLARITIES
MULTICOLOURS   MULTIFLASH   MULTILOBATE   MULTIPARITY   MULTIPOLARITY
MULTICOLUMN   MULTIFLORA   MULTILOBED   MULTIPAROUS   MULTIPOLES
MULTICOMPONENT   MULTIFLORAS   MULTILOBES   MULTIPARTICLE   MULTIPOTENT
MULTICONDUCTOR   MULTIFLOROUS   MULTILOBULAR   MULTIPARTITE   MULTIPOTENTIAL
MULTICOPIES   MULTIFOCAL   MULTILOBULATE   MULTIPARTY   MULTIPOWER
                                                              MULTIPARTYISM

MULTIPRESENCE	MULTISTORIED	MULTIVIBRATOR	MUNICIPALISM	MUSCARINES
MULTIPRESENCES	MULTISTORIES	MULTIVIBRATORS	MUNICIPALISMS	MUSCARINIC
MULTIPRESENT	MULTISTORY	MULTIVIOUS	MUNICIPALIST	MUSCATORIA
MULTIPROBLEM	MULTISTRANDED	MULTIVITAMIN	MUNICIPALISTS	MUSCATORIUM
MULTIPROCESSING	MULTISTRIKE	MULTIVITAMINS	MUNICIPALITIES	MUSCAVADOS
MULTIPROCESSOR	MULTISTRIKES	MULTIVOCAL	MUNICIPALITY	MUSCOLOGIES
MULTIPROCESSORS	MULTISULCATE	MULTIVOCALS	MUNICIPALIZE	MUSCOVADOS
MULTIPRODUCT	MULTISYLLABIC	MULTIVOLTINE	MUNICIPALIZED	MUSCOVITES
MULTIPRONGED	MULTISYSTEM	MULTIVOLUME	MUNICIPALIZES	MUSCULARITIES
MULTIPURPOSE	MULTITALENTED	MULTIWARHEAD	MUNICIPALIZING	MUSCULARITY
MULTIRACIAL	MULTITASKED	MULTIWAVELENGTH	MUNICIPALLY	MUSCULARLY
MULTIRACIALISM	MULTITASKING	MULTIWINDOW	MUNICIPALS	MUSCULATION
MULTIRACIALISMS	MULTITASKINGS	MULTIWINDOWS	MUNIFICENCE	MUSCULATIONS
MULTIRACIALLY	MULTITASKS	MULTOCULAR	MUNIFICENCES	MUSCULATURE
MULTIRAMIFIED	MULTITERMINAL	MULTUNGULATE	MUNIFICENT	MUSCULATURES
MULTIRANGE	MULTITHREADING	MULTUNGULATES	MUNIFICENTLY	MUSCULOSKELETAL
MULTIREGIONAL	MULTITHREADINGS	MUMBLEMENT	MUNIFICENTNESS	MUSEOLOGICAL
MULTIRELIGIOUS	MULTITIERED	MUMBLEMENTS	MUNIFIENCE	MUSEOLOGIES
MULTIROOMED	MULTITONED	MUMBLETYPEG	MUNIFIENCES	MUSEOLOGIST
MULTISCIENCE	MULTITONES	MUMBLETYPEGS	MUNITIONED	MUSEOLOGISTS
MULTISCIENCES	MULTITOOLS	MUMBLINGLY	MUNITIONEER	MUSHINESSES
MULTISCREEN	MULTITOWERED	MUMCHANCES	MUNITIONEERS	MUSHMOUTHS
MULTISCREENS	MULTITRACK	MUMMERINGS	MUNITIONER	MUSHROOMED
MULTISENSE	MULTITRACKED	MUMMICHOGS	MUNITIONERS	MUSHROOMER
MULTISENSORY	MULTITRACKING	MUMMIFICATION	MUNITIONETTE	MUSHROOMERS
MULTISEPTATE	MULTITRACKS	MUMMIFICATIONS	MUNITIONETTES	MUSHROOMIER
MULTISERIAL	MULTITRILLION	MUMMIFORMS	MUNITIONING	MUSHROOMIEST
MULTISERIATE	MULTITRILLIONS	MUMMIFYING	MURDERABILIA	MUSHROOMING
MULTISERVICE	MULTITUDES	MUMPISHNESS	MURDERBALL	MUSHROOMINGS
MULTISIDED	MULTITUDINARY	MUMPISHNESSES	MURDERBALLS	MUSICALISATION
MULTISKILL	MULTITUDINOUS	MUMPRENEUR	MURDERESSES	MUSICALISATIONS
MULTISKILLED	MULTITUDINOUSLY	MUMPRENEURS	MURDEROUSLY	MUSICALISE
MULTISKILLING	MULTIUNION	MUMPSIMUSES	MURDEROUSNESS	MUSICALISED
MULTISKILLINGS	MULTIUTILITIES	MUMSINESSES	MURDEROUSNESSES	MUSICALISES
MULTISKILLS	MULTIUTILITY	MUNCHABLES	MURGEONING	MUSICALISING
MULTISONANT	MULTIVALENCE	MUNDANENESS	MURKINESSES	MUSICALITIES
MULTISOURCE	MULTIVALENCES	MUNDANENESSES	MURMURATION	MUSICALITY
MULTISPECIES	MULTIVALENCIES	MUNDANITIES	MURMURATIONS	MUSICALIZATION
MULTISPECTRAL	MULTIVALENCY	MUNDIFICATION	MURMURINGLY	MUSICALIZATIONS
MULTISPEED	MULTIVALENT	MUNDIFICATIONS	MURMURINGS	MUSICALIZE
MULTISPIRAL	MULTIVALENTS	MUNDIFICATIVE	MURMUROUSLY	MUSICALIZED
MULTISPORT	MULTIVARIABLE	MUNDIFICATIVES	MURTHERERS	MUSICALIZES
MULTISTAGE	MULTIVARIATE	MUNDIFYING	MURTHERING	MUSICALIZING
MULTISTANDARD	MULTIVARIOUS	MUNDUNGUSES	MUSCADELLE	MUSICALNESS
MULTISTATE	MULTIVERSE	MUNICIPALISE	MUSCADELLES	MUSICALNESSES
MULTISTEMMED	MULTIVERSES	MUNICIPALISED	MUSCADINES	MUSICIANER
MULTISTOREY	MULTIVERSITIES	MUNICIPALISES	MUSCARDINE	MUSICIANERS
MULTISTOREYS	MULTIVERSITY	MUNICIPALISING	MUSCARDINES	MUSICIANLIER

M

MUSICIANLIEST	MUTAGENISING	MUTUALITIES	MYCORRHIZAE	MYLONITIZED
MUSICIANLY	MUTAGENIZE	MUTUALIZATION	MYCORRHIZAL	MYLONITIZES
MUSICIANSHIP	MUTAGENIZED	MUTUALIZATIONS	MYCORRHIZAS	MYLONITIZING
MUSICIANSHIPS	MUTAGENIZES	MUTUALIZED	MYCOTOXICOLOGY	MYOBLASTIC
MUSICOLOGICAL	MUTAGENIZING	MUTUALIZES	MYCOTOXICOSES	MYOCARDIAL
MUSICOLOGICALLY	MUTATIONAL	MUTUALIZING	MYCOTOXICOSIS	MYOCARDIOGRAPH
MUSICOLOGIES	MUTATIONALLY	MUTUALNESS	MYCOTOXINS	MYOCARDIOGRAPHS
MUSICOLOGIST	MUTATIONIST	MUTUALNESSES	MYCOTOXOLOGIES	MYOCARDIOPATHY
MUSICOLOGISTS	MUTATIONISTS	MUZZINESSES	MYCOTOXOLOGY	MYOCARDITIS
MUSICOLOGY	MUTENESSES	MYASTHENIA	MYCOTROPHIC	MYOCARDITISES
MUSICOTHERAPIES	MUTESSARIF	MYASTHENIAS	MYCOVIRUSES	MYOCARDIUM
MUSICOTHERAPY	MUTESSARIFAT	MYASTHENIC	MYDRIATICS	MYOCLONUSES
MUSKELLUNGE	MUTESSARIFATS	MYASTHENICS	MYELENCEPHALA	MYOELECTRIC
MUSKELLUNGES	MUTESSARIFS	MYCETOLOGIES	MYELENCEPHALIC	MYOELECTRICAL
MUSKETEERS	MUTILATING	MYCETOLOGY	MYELENCEPHALON	MYOFIBRILLAR
MUSKETOONS	MUTILATION	MYCETOMATA	MYELENCEPHALONS	MYOFIBRILS
MUSKETRIES	MUTILATIONS	MYCETOMATOUS	MYELINATED	MYOFILAMENT
MUSKINESSES	MUTILATIVE	MYCETOPHAGOUS	MYELITIDES	MYOFILAMENTS
MUSKMELONS	MUTILATORS	MYCETOZOAN	MYELITISES	MYOGLOBINS
MUSQUASHES	MUTINEERED	MYCETOZOANS	MYELOBLAST	MYOGRAPHIC
MUSQUETOON	MUTINEERING	MYCOBACTERIA	MYELOBLASTIC	MYOGRAPHICAL
MUSQUETOONS	MUTINOUSLY	MYCOBACTERIAL	MYELOBLASTS	MYOGRAPHICALLY
MUSSELCRACKER	MUTINOUSNESS	MYCOBACTERIUM	MYELOCYTES	MYOGRAPHIES
MUSSELCRACKERS	MUTINOUSNESSES	MYCOBIONTS	MYELOCYTIC	MYOGRAPHIST
MUSSINESSES	MUTOSCOPES	MYCODOMATIA	MYELOFIBROSES	MYOGRAPHISTS
MUSSITATED	MUTTERATION	MYCODOMATIUM	MYELOFIBROSIS	MYOINOSITOL
MUSSITATES	MUTTERATIONS	MYCOFLORAE	MYELOFIBROTIC	MYOINOSITOLS
MUSSITATING	MUTTERINGLY	MYCOFLORAS	MYELOGENOUS	MYOLOGICAL
MUSSITATION	MUTTERINGS	MYCOLOGICAL	MYELOGRAMS	MYOLOGISTS
MUSSITATIONS	MUTTONBIRD	MYCOLOGICALLY	MYELOGRAPHIES	MYOMANCIES
MUSTACHIOED	MUTTONBIRDER	MYCOLOGIES	MYELOGRAPHY	MYOMECTOMIES
MUSTACHIOS	MUTTONBIRDERS	MYCOLOGIST	MYELOMATOID	MYOMECTOMY
MUSTARDIER	MUTTONBIRDS	MYCOLOGISTS	MYELOMATOUS	MYOPATHIES
MUSTARDIEST	MUTTONCHOPS	MYCOPHAGIES	MYELOPATHIC	MYOPHILIES
MUSTELINES	MUTTONFISH	MYCOPHAGIST	MYELOPATHIES	MYOPHILOUS
MUSTINESSES	MUTTONFISHES	MYCOPHAGISTS	MYELOPATHY	MYOPICALLY
MUTABILITIES	MUTTONHEAD	MYCOPHAGOUS	MYIOPHILIES	MYOSITISES
MUTABILITY	MUTTONHEADED	MYCOPHILES	MYIOPHILOUS	MYOSOTISES
MUTABLENESS	MUTTONHEADS	MYCOPLASMA	MYLOHYOIDS	MYOSTATINS
MUTABLENESSES	MUTTONIEST	MYCOPLASMAL	MYLONITISATION	MYRIADFOLD
MUTAGENESES	MUTUALISATION	MYCOPLASMAS	MYLONITISATIONS	MYRIADFOLDS
MUTAGENESIS	MUTUALISATIONS	MYCOPLASMATA	MYLONITISE	MYRIAPODAN
MUTAGENICALLY	MUTUALISED	MYCOPLASMOSES	MYLONITISED	MYRIAPODOUS
MUTAGENICITIES	MUTUALISES	MYCOPLASMOSIS	MYLONITISES	MYRINGITIS
MUTAGENICITY	MUTUALISING	MYCORHIZAE	MYLONITISING	MYRINGITISES
MUTAGENISE	MUTUALISMS	MYCORHIZAL	MYLONITIZATION	MYRINGOSCOPE
MUTAGENISED	MUTUALISTIC	MYCORHIZAS	MYLONITIZATIONS	MYRINGOSCOPES
MUTAGENISES	MUTUALISTS	MYCORRHIZA	MYLONITIZE	MYRINGOTOMIES

MYRINGOTOMY
MYRIORAMAS
MYRIOSCOPE
MYRIOSCOPES
MYRISTICIVOROUS
MYRMECOCHORIES
MYRMECOCHORY
MYRMECOLOGIC
MYRMECOLOGICAL
MYRMECOLOGIES
MYRMECOLOGIST
MYRMECOLOGISTS
MYRMECOLOGY
MYRMECOPHAGOUS
MYRMECOPHILE
MYRMECOPHILES
MYRMECOPHILIES
MYRMECOPHILOUS
MYRMECOPHILY
MYRMIDONES
MYRMIDONIAN
MYROBALANS
MYRTACEOUS
MYSOPHOBIA
MYSOPHOBIAS
MYSTAGOGIC

MYSTAGOGICAL
MYSTAGOGICALLY
MYSTAGOGIES
MYSTAGOGUE
MYSTAGOGUES
MYSTAGOGUS
MYSTAGOGUSES
MYSTERIOUS
MYSTERIOUSLY
MYSTERIOUSNESS
MYSTICALLY
MYSTICALNESS
MYSTICALNESSES
MYSTICETES
MYSTICISMS
MYSTIFICATION
MYSTIFICATIONS
MYSTIFIERS
MYSTIFYING
MYSTIFYINGLY
MYTHICALLY
MYTHICISATION
MYTHICISATIONS
MYTHICISED
MYTHICISER
MYTHICISERS

MYTHICISES
MYTHICISING
MYTHICISMS
MYTHICISTS
MYTHICIZATION
MYTHICIZATIONS
MYTHICIZED
MYTHICIZER
MYTHICIZERS
MYTHICIZES
MYTHICIZING
MYTHMAKERS
MYTHMAKING
MYTHMAKINGS
MYTHOGENESES
MYTHOGENESIS
MYTHOGRAPHER
MYTHOGRAPHERS
MYTHOGRAPHIES
MYTHOGRAPHY
MYTHOLOGER
MYTHOLOGERS
MYTHOLOGIAN
MYTHOLOGIANS
MYTHOLOGIC
MYTHOLOGICAL

MYTHOLOGICALLY
MYTHOLOGIES
MYTHOLOGISATION
MYTHOLOGISE
MYTHOLOGISED
MYTHOLOGISER
MYTHOLOGISERS
MYTHOLOGISES
MYTHOLOGISING
MYTHOLOGIST
MYTHOLOGISTS
MYTHOLOGIZATION
MYTHOLOGIZE
MYTHOLOGIZED
MYTHOLOGIZER
MYTHOLOGIZERS
MYTHOLOGIZES
MYTHOLOGIZING
MYTHOMANES
MYTHOMANIA
MYTHOMANIAC
MYTHOMANIACS
MYTHOMANIAS
MYTHOPOEIA
MYTHOPOEIAS
MYTHOPOEIC

MYTHOPOEISM
MYTHOPOEISMS
MYTHOPOEIST
MYTHOPOEISTS
MYTHOPOESES
MYTHOPOESIS
MYTHOPOETIC
MYTHOPOETICAL
MYTHOPOETS
MYTILIFORM
MYXAMOEBAE
MYXAMOEBAS
MYXEDEMATOUS
MYXOEDEMAS
MYXOEDEMATOUS
MYXOEDEMIC
MYXOMATOSES
MYXOMATOSIS
MYXOMATOUS
MYXOMYCETE
MYXOMYCETES
MYXOMYCETOUS
MYXOVIRUSES

M

N

NABOBERIES	NANOPARTICLE	NARCOANALYSES	NARRATOLOGY	NATIONALISES
NABOBESSES	NANOPARTICLES	NARCOANALYSIS	NARROWBAND	NATIONALISING
NACHTMAALS	NANOPHYSICS	NARCOCATHARSES	NARROWBANDS	NATIONALISM
NAFFNESSES	NANOPLANKTON	NARCOCATHARSIS	NARROWCAST	NATIONALISMS
NAIFNESSES	NANOPLANKTONS	NARCOHYPNOSES	NARROWCASTED	NATIONALIST
NAILBITERS	NANOPUBLISHING	NARCOHYPNOSIS	NARROWCASTING	NATIONALISTIC
NAILBRUSHES	NANOPUBLISHINGS	NARCOLEPSIES	NARROWCASTINGS	NATIONALISTS
NAISSANCES	NANOSECOND	NARCOLEPSY	NARROWCASTS	NATIONALITIES
NAIVENESSES	NANOSECONDS	NARCOLEPTIC	NARROWINGS	NATIONALITY
NAKEDNESSES	NANOTECHNOLOGY	NARCOLEPTICS	NARROWNESS	NATIONALIZATION
NALBUPHINE	NANOTESLAS	NARCOSYNTHESES	NARROWNESSES	NATIONALIZE
NALBUPHINES	NANOWORLDS	NARCOSYNTHESIS	NASALISATION	NATIONALIZED
NALORPHINE	NAPHTHALENE	NARCOTERRORISM	NASALISATIONS	NATIONALIZER
NALORPHINES	NAPHTHALENES	NARCOTERRORISMS	NASALISING	NATIONALIZERS
NALTREXONE	NAPHTHALIC	NARCOTERRORIST	NASALITIES	NATIONALIZES
NALTREXONES	NAPHTHALIN	NARCOTERRORISTS	NASALIZATION	NATIONALIZING
NAMAYCUSHES	NAPHTHALINE	NARCOTICALLY	NASALIZATIONS	NATIONALLY
NAMECHECKED	NAPHTHALINES	NARCOTINES	NASALIZING	NATIONHOOD
NAMECHECKING	NAPHTHALINS	NARCOTISATION	NASCENCIES	NATIONHOODS
NAMECHECKS	NAPHTHALISE	NARCOTISATIONS	NASEBERRIES	NATIONLESS
NAMELESSLY	NAPHTHALISED	NARCOTISED	NASOFRONTAL	NATIONWIDE
NAMELESSNESS	NAPHTHALISES	NARCOTISES	NASOGASTRIC	NATIVENESS
NAMELESSNESSES	NAPHTHALISING	NARCOTISING	NASOLACRYMAL	NATIVENESSES
NAMEPLATES	NAPHTHALIZE	NARCOTISMS	NASOPHARYNGEAL	NATIVISTIC
NAMEWORTHIER	NAPHTHALIZED	NARCOTISTS	NASOPHARYNGES	NATIVITIES
NAMEWORTHIEST	NAPHTHALIZES	NARCOTIZATION	NASOPHARYNX	NATRIURESES
NAMEWORTHY	NAPHTHALIZING	NARCOTIZATIONS	NASOPHARYNXES	NATRIURESIS
NANDROLONE	NAPHTHENES	NARCOTIZED	NASTINESSES	NATRIURESISES
NANDROLONES	NAPHTHENIC	NARCOTIZES	NASTURTIUM	NATRIURETIC
NANISATION	NAPHTHYLAMINE	NARCOTIZING	NASTURTIUMS	NATRIURETICS
NANISATIONS	NAPHTHYLAMINES	NARGHILIES	NATALITIAL	NATROLITES
NANIZATION	NAPOLEONITE	NARGHILLIES	NATALITIES	NATTERIEST
NANIZATIONS	NAPOLEONITES	NARGUILEHS	NATATIONAL	NATTERJACK
NANNOPLANKTON	NAPPINESSES	NARRATABLE	NATATORIAL	NATTERJACKS
NANNOPLANKTONS	NAPRAPATHIES	NARRATIONAL	NATATORIUM	NATTINESSES
NANOGRAMME	NAPRAPATHY	NARRATIONS	NATATORIUMS	NATURALISATION
NANOGRAMMES	NARCISSISM	NARRATIVELY	NATHELESSE	NATURALISATIONS
NANOGRASSES	NARCISSISMS	NARRATIVES	NATIONALISATION	NATURALISE
NANOMATERIAL	NARCISSIST	NARRATOLOGICAL	NATIONALISE	NATURALISED
NANOMATERIALS	NARCISSISTIC	NARRATOLOGIES	NATIONALISED	NATURALISES
NANOMETERS	NARCISSISTS	NARRATOLOGIST	NATIONALISER	NATURALISING
NANOMETRES	NARCISSUSES	NARRATOLOGISTS	NATIONALISERS	NATURALISM

NATURALISMS	NAVIGATIONAL	NECESSAIRES	NECROMANCY	NECROTROPHS
NATURALIST	NAVIGATIONALLY	NECESSARIAN	NECROMANIA	NECTAREOUS
NATURALISTIC	NAVIGATIONS	NECESSARIANISM	NECROMANIAC	NECTAREOUSNESS
NATURALISTS	NAVIGATORS	NECESSARIANISMS	NECROMANIACS	NECTARIFEROUS
NATURALIZATION	NAYSAYINGS	NECESSARIANS	NECROMANIAS	NECTARINES
NATURALIZATIONS	NAZIFICATION	NECESSARIES	NECROMANTIC	NECTARIVOROUS
NATURALIZE	NAZIFICATIONS	NECESSARILY	NECROMANTICAL	NECTOCALYCES
NATURALIZED	NEANDERTAL	NECESSARINESS	NECROMANTICALLY	NECTOCALYX
NATURALIZES	NEANDERTALER	NECESSARINESSES	NECROPHAGOUS	NEEDCESSITIES
NATURALIZING	NEANDERTALERS	NECESSITARIAN	NECROPHILE	NEEDCESSITY
NATURALNESS	NEANDERTALS	NECESSITARIANS	NECROPHILES	NEEDFULNESS
NATURALNESSES	NEANDERTHAL	NECESSITATE	NECROPHILIA	NEEDFULNESSES
NATURISTIC	NEANDERTHALER	NECESSITATED	NECROPHILIAC	NEEDINESSES
NATUROPATH	NEANDERTHALERS	NECESSITATES	NECROPHILIACS	NEEDLECORD
NATUROPATHIC	NEANDERTHALOID	NECESSITATING	NECROPHILIAS	NEEDLECORDS
NATUROPATHIES	NEANDERTHALS	NECESSITATION	NECROPHILIC	NEEDLECRAFT
NATUROPATHS	NEAPOLITAN	NECESSITATIONS	NECROPHILIES	NEEDLECRAFTS
NATUROPATHY	NEAPOLITANS	NECESSITATIVE	NECROPHILISM	NEEDLEFISH
NAUGAHYDES	NEARNESSES	NECESSITIED	NECROPHILISMS	NEEDLEFISHES
NAUGHTIEST	NEARSHORED	NECESSITIES	NECROPHILOUS	NEEDLEFULS
NAUGHTINESS	NEARSHORES	NECESSITOUS	NECROPHILS	NEEDLELESS
NAUGHTINESSES	NEARSHORING	NECESSITOUSLY	NECROPHILY	NEEDLELIKE
NAUMACHIAE	NEARSIGHTED	NECESSITOUSNESS	NECROPHOBE	NEEDLEPOINT
NAUMACHIAS	NEARSIGHTEDLY	NECKCLOTHS	NECROPHOBES	NEEDLEPOINTED
NAUMACHIES	NEARSIGHTEDNESS	NECKERCHIEF	NECROPHOBIA	NEEDLEPOINTING
NAUPLIIFORM	NEARTHROSES	NECKERCHIEFS	NECROPHOBIAS	NEEDLEPOINTS
NAUSEATING	NEARTHROSIS	NECKERCHIEVES	NECROPHOBIC	NEEDLESSLY
NAUSEATINGLY	NEATNESSES	NECKLACING	NECROPHOROUS	NEEDLESSNESS
NAUSEATION	NEBBISHERS	NECKLACINGS	NECROPOLEIS	NEEDLESSNESSES
NAUSEATIONS	NEBBISHIER	NECKPIECES	NECROPOLES	NEEDLESTICK
NAUSEATIVE	NEBBISHIEST	NECKVERSES	NECROPOLIS	NEEDLESTICKS
NAUSEOUSLY	NEBENKERNS	NECROBIOSES	NECROPOLISES	NEEDLEWOMAN
NAUSEOUSNESS	NEBUCHADNEZZAR	NECROBIOSIS	NECROPSIED	NEEDLEWOMEN
NAUSEOUSNESSES	NEBUCHADNEZZARS	NECROBIOTIC	NECROPSIES	NEEDLEWORK
NAUTICALLY	NEBULISATION	NECROGRAPHER	NECROPSYING	NEEDLEWORKER
NAUTILOIDS	NEBULISATIONS	NECROGRAPHERS	NECROSCOPIC	NEEDLEWORKERS
NAUTILUSES	NEBULISERS	NECROLATER	NECROSCOPICAL	NEEDLEWORKS
NAVARCHIES	NEBULISING	NECROLATERS	NECROSCOPIES	NEESBERRIES
NAVELWORTS	NEBULIZATION	NECROLATRIES	NECROSCOPY	NEFARIOUSLY
NAVICULARE	NEBULIZATIONS	NECROLATRY	NECROTISED	NEFARIOUSNESS
NAVICULARES	NEBULIZERS	NECROLOGIC	NECROTISES	NEFARIOUSNESSES
NAVICULARS	NEBULIZING	NECROLOGICAL	NECROTISING	NEGATIONAL
NAVIGABILITIES	NEBULOSITIES	NECROLOGIES	NECROTIZED	NEGATIONIST
NAVIGABILITY	NEBULOSITY	NECROLOGIST	NECROTIZES	NEGATIONISTS
NAVIGABLENESS	NEBULOUSLY	NECROLOGISTS	NECROTIZING	NEGATIVELY
NAVIGABLENESSES	NEBULOUSNESS	NECROMANCER	NECROTOMIES	NEGATIVENESS
NAVIGATING	NEBULOUSNESSES	NECROMANCERS	NECROTROPH	NEGATIVENESSES
NAVIGATION	NECESSAIRE	NECROMANCIES	NECROTROPHIC	NEGATIVING

NEGATIVISM	NEGROHEADS	NEMATODIRUS	NEOLOGICAL	NEOREALISM
NEGATIVISMS	NEGROPHILE	NEMATODIRUSES	NEOLOGICALLY	NEOREALISMS
NEGATIVIST	NEGROPHILES	NEMATOLOGICAL	NEOLOGISED	NEOREALIST
NEGATIVISTIC	NEGROPHILISM	NEMATOLOGIES	NEOLOGISES	NEOREALISTIC
NEGATIVISTS	NEGROPHILISMS	NEMATOLOGIST	NEOLOGISING	NEOREALISTS
NEGATIVITIES	NEGROPHILIST	NEMATOLOGISTS	NEOLOGISMS	NEOSTIGMINE
NEGATIVITY	NEGROPHILISTS	NEMATOLOGY	NEOLOGISTIC	NEOSTIGMINES
NEGLECTABLE	NEGROPHILS	NEMATOPHORE	NEOLOGISTICAL	NEOTEINIAS
NEGLECTEDNESS	NEGROPHOBE	NEMATOPHORES	NEOLOGISTICALLY	NEOTERICAL
NEGLECTEDNESSES	NEGROPHOBES	NEMERTEANS	NEOLOGISTS	NEOTERICALLY
NEGLECTERS	NEGROPHOBIA	NEMERTIANS	NEOLOGIZED	NEOTERICALS
NEGLECTFUL	NEGROPHOBIAS	NEMERTINES	NEOLOGIZES	NEOTERISED
NEGLECTFULLY	NEIGHBORED	NEMOPHILAS	NEOLOGIZING	NEOTERISES
NEGLECTFULNESS	NEIGHBORHOOD	NEOANTHROPIC	NEONATALLY	NEOTERISING
NEGLECTING	NEIGHBORHOODS	NEOARSPHENAMINE	NEONATICIDE	NEOTERISMS
NEGLECTINGLY	NEIGHBORING	NEOCAPITALISM	NEONATICIDES	NEOTERISTS
NEGLECTION	NEIGHBORLESS	NEOCAPITALISMS	NEONATOLOGIES	NEOTERIZED
NEGLECTIONS	NEIGHBORLIER	NEOCAPITALIST	NEONATOLOGIST	NEOTERIZES
NEGLECTIVE	NEIGHBORLIEST	NEOCAPITALISTS	NEONATOLOGISTS	NEOTERIZING
NEGLECTORS	NEIGHBORLINESS	NEOCLASSIC	NEONATOLOGY	NEOTROPICS
NEGLIGEABLE	NEIGHBORLY	NEOCLASSICAL	NEONOMIANISM	NEOVITALISM
NEGLIGENCE	NEIGHBOURED	NEOCLASSICISM	NEONOMIANISMS	NEOVITALISMS
NEGLIGENCES	NEIGHBOURHOOD	NEOCLASSICISMS	NEONOMIANS	NEOVITALIST
NEGLIGENTLY	NEIGHBOURHOODS	NEOCLASSICIST	NEOORTHODOX	NEOVITALISTS
NEGLIGIBILITIES	NEIGHBOURING	NEOCLASSICISTS	NEOORTHODOXIES	NEPENTHEAN
NEGLIGIBILITY	NEIGHBOURLESS	NEOCOLONIAL	NEOORTHODOXY	NEPHALISMS
NEGLIGIBLE	NEIGHBOURLIER	NEOCOLONIALISM	NEOPAGANISE	NEPHALISTS
NEGLIGIBLENESS	NEIGHBOURLIEST	NEOCOLONIALISMS	NEOPAGANISED	NEPHELINES
NEGLIGIBLY	NEIGHBOURLINESS	NEOCOLONIALIST	NEOPAGANISES	NEPHELINIC
NEGOCIANTS	NEIGHBOURLY	NEOCOLONIALISTS	NEOPAGANISING	NEPHELINITE
NEGOTIABILITIES	NEIGHBOURS	NEOCONSERVATISM	NEOPAGANISM	NEPHELINITES
NEGOTIABILITY	NELUMBIUMS	NEOCONSERVATIVE	NEOPAGANISMS	NEPHELINITIC
NEGOTIABLE	NEMATHELMINTH	NEOCORTEXES	NEOPAGANIZE	NEPHELITES
NEGOTIANTS	NEMATHELMINTHIC	NEOCORTICAL	NEOPAGANIZED	NEPHELOMETER
NEGOTIATED	NEMATHELMINTHS	NEOCORTICES	NEOPAGANIZES	NEPHELOMETERS
NEGOTIATES	NEMATICIDAL	NEODYMIUMS	NEOPAGANIZING	NEPHELOMETRIC
NEGOTIATING	NEMATICIDE	NEOGENESES	NEOPHILIAC	NEPHELOMETRIES
NEGOTIATION	NEMATICIDES	NEOGENESIS	NEOPHILIACS	NEPHELOMETRY
NEGOTIATIONS	NEMATOBLAST	NEOGENETIC	NEOPHILIAS	NEPHOGRAMS
NEGOTIATOR	NEMATOBLASTS	NEOGOTHICS	NEOPHOBIAS	NEPHOGRAPH
NEGOTIATORS	NEMATOCIDAL	NEOGRAMMARIAN	NEOPILINAS	NEPHOGRAPHS
NEGOTIATORY	NEMATOCIDE	NEOGRAMMARIANS	NEOPLASIAS	NEPHOLOGIC
NEGOTIATRESS	NEMATOCIDES	NEOLIBERAL	NEOPLASTIC	NEPHOLOGICAL
NEGOTIATRESSES	NEMATOCYST	NEOLIBERALISM	NEOPLASTICISM	NEPHOLOGIES
NEGOTIATRICES	NEMATOCYSTIC	NEOLIBERALISMS	NEOPLASTICISMS	NEPHOLOGIST
NEGOTIATRIX	NEMATOCYSTS	NEOLIBERALS	NEOPLASTICIST	NEPHOLOGISTS
NEGOTIATRIXES	NEMATODIRIASES	NEOLITHICS	NEOPLASTICISTS	NEPHOSCOPE
NEGRITUDES	NEMATODIRIASIS	NEOLOGIANS	NEOPLASTIES	NEPHOSCOPES

NEPHRALGIA	NEPTUNIUMS	NEURASTHENICS	NEUROFIBRIL	NEUROPATHICAL
NEPHRALGIAS	NERDINESSES	NEURATIONS	NEUROFIBRILAR	NEUROPATHICALLY
NEPHRALGIC	NERVATIONS	NEURECTOMIES	NEUROFIBRILLAR	NEUROPATHIES
NEPHRALGIES	NERVATURES	NEURECTOMY	NEUROFIBRILLARY	NEUROPATHIST
NEPHRECTOMIES	NERVELESSLY	NEURILEMMA	NEUROFIBRILS	NEUROPATHISTS
NEPHRECTOMISE	NERVELESSNESS	NEURILEMMAL	NEUROFIBROMA	NEUROPATHOLOGIC
NEPHRECTOMISED	NERVELESSNESSES	NEURILEMMAS	NEUROFIBROMAS	NEUROPATHOLOGY
NEPHRECTOMISES	NERVINESSES	NEURILITIES	NEUROFIBROMATA	NEUROPATHS
NEPHRECTOMISING	NERVOSITIES	NEURITIDES	NEUROGENESES	NEUROPATHY
NEPHRECTOMIZE	NERVOUSNESS	NEURITISES	NEUROGENESIS	NEUROPEPTIDE
NEPHRECTOMIZED	NERVOUSNESSES	NEUROACTIVE	NEUROGENIC	NEUROPEPTIDES
NEPHRECTOMIZES	NERVURATION	NEUROANATOMIC	NEUROGENICALLY	NEUROPHYSIOLOGY
NEPHRECTOMIZING	NERVURATIONS	NEUROANATOMICAL	NEUROGLIAL	NEUROPLASM
NEPHRECTOMY	NESCIENCES	NEUROANATOMIES	NEUROGLIAS	NEUROPLASMS
NEPHRIDIAL	NESHNESSES	NEUROANATOMIST	NEUROGRAMS	NEUROPSYCHIATRY
NEPHRIDIUM	NESSELRODE	NEUROANATOMISTS	NEUROHORMONAL	NEUROPSYCHOLOGY
NEPHRITICAL	NESSELRODES	NEUROANATOMY	NEUROHORMONE	NEUROPTERA
NEPHRITICS	NETBALLERS	NEUROBIOLOGICAL	NEUROHORMONES	NEUROPTERAN
NEPHRITIDES	NETHERLINGS	NEUROBIOLOGIES	NEUROHUMOR	NEUROPTERANS
NEPHRITISES	NETHERMORE	NEUROBIOLOGIST	NEUROHUMORAL	NEUROPTERIST
NEPHROBLASTOMA	NETHERMORES	NEUROBIOLOGISTS	NEUROHUMORS	NEUROPTERISTS
NEPHROBLASTOMAS	NETHERMOST	NEUROBIOLOGY	NEUROHUMOUR	NEUROPTERON
NEPHROLEPIS	NETHERSTOCK	NEUROBLAST	NEUROHUMOURS	NEUROPTERONS
NEPHROLEPISES	NETHERSTOCKS	NEUROBLASTOMA	NEUROHYPNOLOGY	NEUROPTEROUS
NEPHROLOGICAL	NETHERWARD	NEUROBLASTOMAS	NEUROHYPOPHYSES	NEURORADIOLOGY
NEPHROLOGIES	NETHERWARDS	NEUROBLASTOMATA	NEUROHYPOPHYSIS	NEUROSCIENCE
NEPHROLOGIST	NETHERWORLD	NEUROBLASTS	NEUROLEMMA	NEUROSCIENCES
NEPHROLOGISTS	NETHERWORLDS	NEUROCHEMICAL	NEUROLEMMAS	NEUROSCIENTIFIC
NEPHROLOGY	NETIQUETTE	NEUROCHEMICALS	NEUROLEPTIC	NEUROSCIENTIST
NEPHROPATHIC	NETIQUETTES	NEUROCHEMIST	NEUROLEPTICS	NEUROSCIENTISTS
NEPHROPATHIES	NETMINDERS	NEUROCHEMISTRY	NEUROLINGUIST	NEUROSECRETION
NEPHROPATHY	NETSURFERS	NEUROCHEMISTS	NEUROLINGUISTIC	NEUROSECRETIONS
NEPHROPEXIES	NETSURFING	NEUROCHIPS	NEUROLINGUISTS	NEUROSECRETORY
NEPHROPEXY	NETSURFINGS	NEUROCOELE	NEUROLOGIC	NEUROSENSORY
NEPHROPTOSES	NETTLELIKE	NEUROCOELES	NEUROLOGICAL	NEUROSPORA
NEPHROPTOSIS	NETTLESOME	NEUROCOELS	NEUROLOGICALLY	NEUROSPORAS
NEPHROSCOPE	NETWORKERS	NEUROCOGNITIVE	NEUROLOGIES	NEUROSURGEON
NEPHROSCOPES	NETWORKING	NEUROCOMPUTER	NEUROLOGIST	NEUROSURGEONS
NEPHROSCOPIES	NETWORKINGS	NEUROCOMPUTERS	NEUROLOGISTS	NEUROSURGERIES
NEPHROSCOPY	NEURALGIAS	NEUROCOMPUTING	NEUROLYSES	NEUROSURGERY
NEPHROSTOME	NEURAMINIC	NEUROCOMPUTINGS	NEUROLYSIS	NEUROSURGICAL
NEPHROSTOMES	NEURAMINIDASE	NEURODIVERSITY	NEUROMARKETING	NEUROSURGICALLY
NEPHROTICS	NEURAMINIDASES	NEUROECTODERMAL	NEUROMARKETINGS	NEUROSYPHILIS
NEPHROTOMIES	NEURASTHENIA	NEUROENDOCRINE	NEUROMASTS	NEUROSYPHILISES
NEPHROTOMY	NEURASTHENIAC	NEUROETHOLOGIES	NEUROMATOUS	NEUROTICALLY
NEPHROTOXIC	NEURASTHENIACS	NEUROETHOLOGY	NEUROMOTOR	NEUROTICISM
NEPHROTOXICITY	NEURASTHENIAS	NEUROFEEDBACK	NEUROMUSCULAR	NEUROTICISMS
NEPOTISTIC	NEURASTHENIC	NEUROFEEDBACKS	NEUROPATHIC	NEUROTOMIES

NEUROTOMIST	NEUTROPHILE	NEWSPEOPLE	NICOTINISMS	NIGHTBIRDS
NEUROTOMISTS	NEUTROPHILES	NEWSPERSON	NICROSILAL	NIGHTBLIND
NEUROTOXIC	NEUTROPHILIC	NEWSPERSONS	NICROSILALS	NIGHTCLASS
NEUROTOXICITIES	NEUTROPHILS	NEWSPRINTS	NICTATIONS	NIGHTCLASSES
NEUROTOXICITY	NEVERMINDS	NEWSREADER	NICTITATED	NIGHTCLOTHES
NEUROTOXIN	NEVERTHELESS	NEWSREADERS	NICTITATES	NIGHTCLUBBED
NEUROTOXINS	NEVERTHEMORE	NEWSSHEETS	NICTITATING	NIGHTCLUBBER
NEUROTROPHIC	NEWFANGLED	NEWSSTANDS	NICTITATION	NIGHTCLUBBERS
NEUROTROPHIES	NEWFANGLEDLY	NEWSTRADES	NICTITATIONS	NIGHTCLUBBING
NEUROTROPHY	NEWFANGLEDNESS	NEWSWEEKLIES	NIDAMENTAL	NIGHTCLUBBINGS
NEUROTROPIC	NEWFANGLENESS	NEWSWEEKLY	NIDAMENTUM	NIGHTCLUBS
NEUROTYPICAL	NEWFANGLENESSES	NEWSWORTHIER	NIDDERINGS	NIGHTDRESS
NEUROVASCULAR	NEWFANGLES	NEWSWORTHIEST	NIDDERLING	NIGHTDRESSES
NEURULATION	NEWISHNESS	NEWSWORTHINESS	NIDDERLINGS	NIGHTFALLS
NEURULATIONS	NEWISHNESSES	NEWSWORTHY	NIDERLINGS	NIGHTFARING
NEURYPNOLOGIES	NEWMARKETS	NEWSWRITING	NIDICOLOUS	NIGHTFIRES
NEURYPNOLOGY	NEWSAGENCIES	NEWSWRITINGS	NIDIFICATE	NIGHTGEARS
NEUTERINGS	NEWSAGENCY	NEXTNESSES	NIDIFICATED	NIGHTGLOWS
NEUTRALISATION	NEWSAGENTS	NIACINAMIDE	NIDIFICATES	NIGHTGOWNS
NEUTRALISATIONS	NEWSBREAKS	NIACINAMIDES	NIDIFICATING	NIGHTHAWKS
NEUTRALISE	NEWSCASTER	NIAISERIES	NIDIFICATION	NIGHTINGALE
NEUTRALISED	NEWSCASTERS	NIALAMIDES	NIDIFICATIONS	NIGHTINGALES
NEUTRALISER	NEWSCASTING	NIBBLINGLY	NIDIFUGOUS	NIGHTLIFES
NEUTRALISERS	NEWSCASTINGS	NICCOLITES	NIDULATION	NIGHTLIVES
NEUTRALISES	NEWSDEALER	NICENESSES	NIDULATIONS	NIGHTMARES
NEUTRALISING	NEWSDEALERS	NICKELIFEROUS	NIFEDIPINE	NIGHTMARIER
NEUTRALISM	NEWSFLASHES	NICKELINES	NIFEDIPINES	NIGHTMARIEST
NEUTRALISMS	NEWSGROUPS	NICKELISED	NIFFNAFFED	NIGHTMARISH
NEUTRALIST	NEWSHOUNDS	NICKELISES	NIFFNAFFING	NIGHTMARISHLY
NEUTRALISTIC	NEWSINESSES	NICKELISING	NIFTINESSES	NIGHTMARISHNESS
NEUTRALISTS	NEWSLETTER	NICKELIZED	NIGGARDING	NIGHTPIECE
NEUTRALITIES	NEWSLETTERS	NICKELIZES	NIGGARDISE	NIGHTPIECES
NEUTRALITY	NEWSMAGAZINE	NICKELIZING	NIGGARDISES	NIGHTRIDER
NEUTRALIZATION	NEWSMAGAZINES	NICKELLING	NIGGARDIZE	NIGHTRIDERS
NEUTRALIZATIONS	NEWSMAKERS	NICKELODEON	NIGGARDIZES	NIGHTRIDING
NEUTRALIZE	NEWSMONGER	NICKELODEONS	NIGGARDLIER	NIGHTRIDINGS
NEUTRALIZED	NEWSMONGERS	NICKERNUTS	NIGGARDLIEST	NIGHTSCOPE
NEUTRALIZER	NEWSPAPERDOM	NICKNAMERS	NIGGARDLINESS	NIGHTSCOPES
NEUTRALIZERS	NEWSPAPERDOMS	NICKNAMING	NIGGARDLINESSES	NIGHTSHADE
NEUTRALIZES	NEWSPAPERED	NICKPOINTS	NIGGERDOMS	NIGHTSHADES
NEUTRALIZING	NEWSPAPERING	NICKSTICKS	NIGGERHEAD	NIGHTSHIRT
NEUTRALNESS	NEWSPAPERISM	NICKUMPOOP	NIGGERHEADS	NIGHTSHIRTS
NEUTRALNESSES	NEWSPAPERISMS	NICKUMPOOPS	NIGGERIEST	NIGHTSIDES
NEUTRETTOS	NEWSPAPERMAN	NICOMPOOPS	NIGGERISMS	NIGHTSPOTS
NEUTRINOLESS	NEWSPAPERMEN	NICOTIANAS	NIGGERLING	NIGHTSTAND
NEUTROPENIA	NEWSPAPERS	NICOTINAMIDE	NIGGERLINGS	NIGHTSTANDS
NEUTROPENIAS	NEWSPAPERWOMAN	NICOTINAMIDES	NIGGLINGLY	NIGHTSTICK
NEUTROPHIL	NEWSPAPERWOMEN	NICOTINISM	NIGHNESSES	NIGHTSTICKS

NIGHTTIDES	NISBERRIES	NITROGLYCERINE	NOCTILUCENCES	NOMENCLATURES
NIGHTTIMES	NITPICKERS	NITROGLYCERINES	NOCTILUCENT	NOMENKLATURA
NIGHTWALKER	NITPICKIER	NITROGLYCERINS	NOCTILUCOUS	NOMENKLATURAS
NIGHTWALKERS	NITPICKIEST	NITROMETER	NOCTIVAGANT	NOMINALISATION
NIGHTWATCHMAN	NITPICKING	NITROMETERS	NOCTIVAGANTS	NOMINALISATIONS
NIGHTWATCHMEN	NITPICKINGS	NITROMETHANE	NOCTIVAGATION	NOMINALISE
NIGHTWEARS	NITRAMINES	NITROMETHANES	NOCTIVAGATIONS	NOMINALISED
NIGRESCENCE	NITRANILINE	NITROMETRIC	NOCTIVAGOUS	NOMINALISES
NIGRESCENCES	NITRANILINES	NITROPARAFFIN	NOCTUARIES	NOMINALISING
NIGRESCENT	NITRATINES	NITROPARAFFINS	NOCTURNALITIES	NOMINALISM
NIGRIFYING	NITRATIONS	NITROPHILOUS	NOCTURNALITY	NOMINALISMS
NIGRITUDES	NITRAZEPAM	NITROSAMINE	NOCTURNALLY	NOMINALIST
NIGROMANCIES	NITRAZEPAMS	NITROSAMINES	NOCTURNALS	NOMINALISTIC
NIGROMANCY	NITRIDINGS	NITROSATION	NOCUOUSNESS	NOMINALISTS
NIGROSINES	NITRIFIABLE	NITROSATIONS	NOCUOUSNESSES	NOMINALIZATION
NIHILISTIC	NITRIFICATION	NITROTOLUENE	NODALISING	NOMINALIZATIONS
NIHILITIES	NITRIFICATIONS	NITROTOLUENES	NODALITIES	NOMINALIZE
NIKETHAMIDE	NITRIFIERS	NITWITTEDNESS	NODALIZING	NOMINALIZED
NIKETHAMIDES	NITRIFYING	NITWITTEDNESSES	NODOSITIES	NOMINALIZES
NILPOTENTS	NITROBACTERIA	NITWITTERIES	NODULATION	NOMINALIZING
NIMBLENESS	NITROBACTERIUM	NITWITTERY	NODULATIONS	NOMINATELY
NIMBLENESSES	NITROBENZENE	NOBBINESSES	NOEMATICAL	NOMINATING
NIMBLESSES	NITROBENZENES	NOBILESSES	NOEMATICALLY	NOMINATION
NIMBLEWITS	NITROCELLULOSE	NOBILITATE	NOGOODNIKS	NOMINATIONS
NIMBLEWITTED	NITROCELLULOSES	NOBILITATED	NOISELESSLY	NOMINATIVAL
NIMBOSTRATI	NITROCHLOROFORM	NOBILITATES	NOISELESSNESS	NOMINATIVALLY
NIMBOSTRATUS	NITROCOTTON	NOBILITATING	NOISELESSNESSES	NOMINATIVE
NIMBYNESSES	NITROCOTTONS	NOBILITATION .	NOISEMAKER	NOMINATIVELY
NINCOMPOOP	NITROFURAN	NOBILITATIONS	NOISEMAKERS	NOMINATIVES
NINCOMPOOPERIES	NITROFURANS	NOBILITIES	NOISEMAKING	NOMINATORS
NINCOMPOOPERY	NITROGELATIN	NOBLENESSES	NOISEMAKINGS	NOMOCRACIES
NINCOMPOOPS	NITROGELATINE	NOBLEWOMAN	NOISINESSES	NOMOGENIES
NINEPENCES	NITROGELATINES	NOBLEWOMEN	NOISOMENESS	NOMOGRAPHER
NINEPENNIES	NITROGELATINS	NOCHELLING	NOISOMENESSES	NOMOGRAPHERS
NINESCORES	NITROGENASE	NOCICEPTIVE	NOMADICALLY	NOMOGRAPHIC
NINETEENTH	NITROGENASES	NOCICEPTOR	NOMADISATION	NOMOGRAPHICAL
NINETEENTHLIES	NITROGENISATION	NOCICEPTORS	NOMADISATIONS	NOMOGRAPHICALLY
NINETEENTHLY	NITROGENISE	NOCIRECEPTOR	NOMADISING	NOMOGRAPHIES
NINETEENTHS	NITROGENISED	NOCIRECEPTORS	NOMADIZATION	NOMOGRAPHS
NINETIETHS	NITROGENISES	NOCTAMBULATION	NOMADIZATIONS	NOMOGRAPHY
NINHYDRINS	NITROGENISING	NOCTAMBULATIONS	NOMADIZING	NOMOLOGICAL
NINNYHAMMER	NITROGENIZATION	NOCTAMBULISM	NOMARCHIES	NOMOLOGICALLY
NINNYHAMMERS	NITROGENIZE	NOCTAMBULISMS	NOMENCLATIVE	NOMOLOGIES
NIPCHEESES	NITROGENIZED	NOCTAMBULIST	NOMENCLATOR	NOMOLOGIST
NIPPERKINS	NITROGENIZES	NOCTAMBULISTS	NOMENCLATORIAL	NOMOLOGISTS
NIPPINESSES	NITROGENIZING	NOCTILUCAE	NOMENCLATORS	NOMOTHETES
NIPPLEWORT	NITROGENOUS	NOCTILUCAS	NOMENCLATURAL	NOMOTHETIC
NIPPLEWORTS	NITROGLYCERIN	NOCTILUCENCE	NOMENCLATURE	NOMOTHETICAL

NONABRASIVE	NONALLELIC	NONATTENDERS	NONCANDIDACY	NONCLASSIFIED
NONABSORBABLE	NONALLERGENIC	NONATTRIBUTABLE	NONCANDIDATE	NONCLASSROOM
NONABSORBENT	NONALLERGIC	NONAUDITORY	NONCANDIDATES	NONCLERICAL
NONABSORPTIVE	NONALPHABETIC	NONAUTHORS	NONCAPITAL	NONCLINICAL
NONABSTRACT	NONALUMINIUM	NONAUTOMATED	NONCAPITALIST	NONCLOGGING
NONACADEMIC	NONALUMINUM	NONAUTOMATIC	NONCAPITALISTS	NONCOERCIVE
NONACADEMICS	NONAMBIGUOUS	NONAUTOMOTIVE	NONCARBOHYDRATE	NONCOGNITIVE
NONACCEPTANCE	NONANALYTIC	NONAUTONOMOUS	NONCARCINOGEN	NONCOGNITIVISM
NONACCEPTANCES	NONANATOMIC	NONAVAILABILITY	NONCARCINOGENIC	NONCOGNITIVISMS
NONACCIDENTAL	NONANSWERED	NONBACTERIAL	NONCARCINOGENS	NONCOHERENT
NONACCOUNTABLE	NONANSWERING	NONBANKING	NONCARDIAC	NONCOINCIDENCE
NONACCREDITED	NONANSWERS	NONBARBITURATE	NONCARRIER	NONCOINCIDENCES
NONACCRUAL	NONANTAGONISTIC	NONBARBITURATES	NONCARRIERS	NONCOLLECTOR
NONACHIEVEMENT	NONANTIBIOTIC	NONBEARING	NONCELEBRATION	NONCOLLECTORS
NONACHIEVEMENTS	NONANTIBIOTICS	NONBEHAVIORAL	NONCELEBRATIONS	NONCOLLEGE
NONACQUISITIVE	NONANTIGENIC	NONBEHAVIOURAL	NONCELEBRITIES	NONCOLLEGIATE
NONACTINGS	NONAPPEARANCE	NONBELIEFS	NONCELEBRITY	NONCOLLINEAR
NONACTIONS	NONAPPEARANCES	NONBELIEVER	NONCELLULAR	NONCOLORED
NONACTIVATED	NONAQUATIC	NONBELIEVERS	NONCELLULOSIC	NONCOLORFAST
NONADAPTIVE	NONAQUEOUS	NONBELLIGERENCY	NONCELLULOSICS	NONCOLOURED
NONADDICTIVE	NONARBITRARY	NONBELLIGERENT	NONCENTRAL	NONCOLOURFAST
NONADDICTS	NONARCHITECT	NONBELLIGERENTS	NONCERTIFICATED	NONCOLOURS
NONADDITIVE	NONARCHITECTS	NONBETTING	NONCERTIFIED	NONCOMBATANT
NONADDITIVITIES	NONARCHITECTURE	NONBINDING	NONCHALANCE	NONCOMBATANTS
NONADDITIVITY	NONARGUMENT	NONBIOGRAPHICAL	NONCHALANCES	NONCOMBATIVE
NONADHESIVE	NONARGUMENTS	NONBIOLOGICAL	NONCHALANT	NONCOMBUSTIBLE
NONADIABATIC	NONARISTOCRATIC	NONBIOLOGICALLY	NONCHALANTLY	NONCOMBUSTIBLES
NONADJACENT	NONAROMATIC	NONBIOLOGIST	NONCHARACTER	NONCOMMERCIAL
NONADMIRER	NONAROMATICS	NONBIOLOGISTS	NONCHARACTERS	NONCOMMISSIONED
NONADMIRERS	NONARRIVAL	NONBONDING	NONCHARISMATIC	NONCOMMITMENT
NONADMISSION	NONARRIVALS	NONBOTANIST	NONCHARISMATICS	NONCOMMITMENTS
NONADMISSIONS	NONARTISTIC	NONBOTANISTS	NONCHAUVINIST	NONCOMMITTAL
NONAESTHETIC	NONARTISTS	NONBREAKABLE	NONCHAUVINISTS	NONCOMMITTALLY
NONAFFILIATED	NONASCETIC	NONBREATHING	NONCHEMICAL	NONCOMMITTALS
NONAFFLUENT	NONASCETICS	NONBREEDER	NONCHEMICALS	NONCOMMITTED
NONAGENARIAN	NONASPIRIN	NONBREEDERS	NONCHROMOSOMAL	NONCOMMUNICANT
NONAGENARIANS	NONASSERTIVE	NONBREEDING	NONCHURCHED	NONCOMMUNICANTS
NONAGESIMAL	NONASSOCIATED	NONBROADCAST	NONCHURCHES	NONCOMMUNIST
NONAGESIMALS	NONASTRONOMICAL	NONBUILDING	NONCHURCHGOER	NONCOMMUNISTS
NONAGGRESSION	NONATHLETE	NONBURNABLE	NONCHURCHGOERS	NONCOMMUNITY
NONAGGRESSIONS	NONATHLETES	NONBUSINESS	NONCHURCHING	NONCOMMUTATIVE
NONAGGRESSIVE	NONATHLETIC	NONCABINET	NONCIRCULAR	NONCOMPARABLE
NONAGRICULTURAL	NONATTACHED	NONCALLABLE	NONCIRCULATING	NONCOMPATIBLE
NONALCOHOLIC	NONATTACHMENT	NONCALORIC	NONCITIZEN	NONCOMPETITION
NONALGEBRAIC	NONATTACHMENTS	NONCANCELABLE	NONCITIZENS	NONCOMPETITIONS
NONALIGNED	NONATTENDANCE	NONCANCELLABLE	NONCLANDESTINE	NONCOMPETITIVE
NONALIGNMENT	NONATTENDANCES	NONCANCEROUS	NONCLASSES	NONCOMPETITOR
NONALIGNMENTS	NONATTENDER	NONCANDIDACIES	NONCLASSICAL	NONCOMPETITORS

NONCOMPLETION	NONCONFORMISMS	NONCORRELATION	NONDELINQUENT	NONDIVERGENT
NONCOMPLETIONS	NONCONFORMIST	NONCORRELATIONS	NONDELINQUENTS	NONDIVERSIFIED
NONCOMPLEX	NONCONFORMISTS	NONCORRODIBLE	NONDELIVERIES	NONDIVIDING
NONCOMPLIANCE	NONCONFORMITIES	NONCORRODING	NONDELIVERY	NONDOCTORS
NONCOMPLIANCES	NONCONFORMITY	NONCORROSIVE	NONDEMANDING	NONDOCTRINAIRE
NONCOMPLICATED	NONCONFORMS	NONCOUNTRIES	NONDEMANDS	NONDOCUMENTARY
NONCOMPLYING	NONCONGRUENT	NONCOUNTRY	NONDEMOCRATIC	NONDOGMATIC
NONCOMPLYINGS	NONCONJUGATED	NONCOVERAGE	NONDEPARTMENTAL	NONDOMESTIC
NONCOMPOSER	NONCONNECTION	NONCOVERAGES	NONDEPENDENT	NONDOMICILED
NONCOMPOSERS	NONCONNECTIONS	NONCREATIVE	NONDEPENDENTS	NONDOMINANT
NONCOMPOUND	NONCONSCIOUS	NONCREATIVITIES	NONDEPLETABLE	NONDORMANT
NONCOMPRESSIBLE	NONCONSECUTIVE	NONCREATIVITY	NONDEPLETING	NONDRAMATIC
NONCOMPUTER	NONCONSENSUAL	NONCREDENTIALED	NONDEPOSITION	NONDRINKER
NONCOMPUTERISED	NONCONSERVATION	NONCRIMINAL	NONDEPOSITIONS	NONDRINKERS
NONCOMPUTERIZED	NONCONSERVATIVE	NONCRIMINALS	NONDEPRESSED	NONDRINKING
NONCONCEPTUAL	NONCONSOLIDATED	NONCRITICAL	NONDERIVATIVE	NONDRIVERS
NONCONCERN	NONCONSTANT	NONCROSSOVER	NONDESCRIPT	NONDURABLE
NONCONCERNS	NONCONSTRUCTION	NONCROSSOVERS	NONDESCRIPTIVE	NONDURABLES
NONCONCLUSION	NONCONSTRUCTIVE	NONCRUSHABLE	NONDESCRIPTLY	NONEARNING
NONCONCLUSIONS	NONCONSUMER	NONCRYSTALLINE	NONDESCRIPTNESS	NONECONOMIC
NONCONCURRED	NONCONSUMERS	NONCULINARY	NONDESCRIPTS	NONECONOMIST
NONCONCURRENCE	NONCONSUMING	NONCULTIVATED	NONDESTRUCTIVE	NONECONOMISTS
NONCONCURRENCES	NONCONSUMPTION	NONCULTIVATION	NONDETACHABLE	NONEDIBLES
NONCONCURRENT	NONCONSUMPTIONS	NONCULTIVATIONS	NONDEVELOPMENT	NONEDITORIAL
NONCONCURRING	NONCONSUMPTIVE	NONCULTURAL	NONDEVELOPMENTS	NONEDUCATION
NONCONCURS	NONCONTACT	NONCUMULATIVE	NONDEVIANT	NONEDUCATIONAL
NONCONDENSABLE	NONCONTACTS	NONCURRENT	NONDIABETIC	NONEFFECTIVE
NONCONDITIONED	NONCONTAGIOUS	NONCUSTODIAL	NONDIABETICS	NONEFFECTIVES
NONCONDUCTING	NONCONTEMPORARY	NONCUSTOMER	NONDIALYSABLE	NONELASTIC
NONCONDUCTION	NONCONTIGUOUS	NONCUSTOMERS	NONDIALYZABLE	NONELECTED
NONCONDUCTIONS	NONCONTINGENT	NONCYCLICAL	NONDIAPAUSING	NONELECTION
NONCONDUCTIVE	NONCONTINUOUS	NONDANCERS	NONDIDACTIC	NONELECTIONS
NONCONDUCTOR	NONCONTRACT	NONDEALERS	NONDIFFUSIBLE	NONELECTIVE
NONCONDUCTORS	NONCONTRACTUAL	NONDECEPTIVE	NONDIMENSIONAL	NONELECTRIC
NONCONFERENCE	NONCONTRIBUTING	NONDECISION	NONDIPLOMATIC	NONELECTRICAL
NONCONFIDENCE	NONCONTRIBUTORY	NONDECISIONS	NONDIRECTED	NONELECTRICALS
NONCONFIDENCES	NONCONTROLLABLE	NONDECREASING	NONDIRECTIONAL	NONELECTRICS
NONCONFIDENTIAL	NONCONTROLLED	NONDEDUCTIBLE	NONDIRECTIVE	NONELECTROLYTE
NONCONFLICTING	NONCONTROLLING	NONDEDUCTIVE	NONDISABLED	NONELECTROLYTES
NONCONFORM	NONCONVENTIONAL	NONDEFENCE	NONDISCLOSURE	NONELECTRONIC
NONCONFORMANCE	NONCONVERTIBLE	NONDEFENSE	NONDISCLOSURES	NONELEMENTARY
NONCONFORMANCES	NONCOOPERATION	NONDEFERRABLE	NONDISCOUNT	NONEMERGENCIES
NONCONFORMED	NONCOOPERATIONS	NONDEFORMING	NONDISCURSIVE	NONEMERGENCY
NONCONFORMER	NONCOOPERATIVE	NONDEGENERATE	NONDISJUNCTION	NONEMOTIONAL
NONCONFORMERS	NONCOOPERATOR	NONDEGRADABLE	NONDISJUNCTIONS	NONEMPHATIC
NONCONFORMING	NONCOOPERATORS	NONDELEGATE	NONDISPERSIVE	NONEMPIRICAL
NONCONFORMINGS	NONCOPLANAR	NONDELEGATES	NONDISRUPTIVE	NONEMPLOYEE
NONCONFORMISM	NONCORPORATE	NONDELIBERATE	NONDISTINCTIVE	NONEMPLOYEES

N

NONEMPLOYMENT	NONFACTUAL	NONGOVERNMENT	NONIMPLICATIONS	NONINTEREST
NONEMPLOYMENTS	NONFACULTIES	NONGOVERNMENTAL	NONIMPORTATION	NONINTERFERENCE
NONENCAPSULATED	NONFACULTY	NONGRADUATE	NONIMPORTATIONS	NONINTERSECTING
NONENFORCEMENT	NONFAMILIAL	NONGRADUATES	NONINCLUSION	NONINTERVENTION
NONENFORCEMENTS	NONFAMILIES	NONGRAMMATICAL	NONINCLUSIONS	NONINTIMIDATING
NONENGAGEMENT	NONFARMERS	NONGRANULAR	NONINCREASING	NONINTOXICANT
NONENGAGEMENTS	NONFATTENING	NONGREGARIOUS	NONINCUMBENT	NONINTOXICANTS
NONENGINEERING	NONFEASANCE	NONGROWING	NONINCUMBENTS	NONINTOXICATING
NONENTITIES	NONFEASANCES	NONGROWTHS	NONINDEPENDENCE	NONINTRUSIVE
NONENTRIES	NONFEDERAL	NONHAEMOLYTIC	NONINDICTABLE	NONINTUITIVE
NONENZYMATIC	NONFEDERATED	NONHALOGENATED	NONINDIGENOUS	NONINVASIVE
NONENZYMIC	NONFEEDING	NONHANDICAPPED	NONINDIVIDUAL	NONINVOLVED
NONEQUILIBRIA	NONFEMINIST	NONHAPPENING	NONINDIVIDUALS	NONINVOLVEMENT
NONEQUILIBRIUM	NONFEMINISTS	NONHAPPENINGS	NONINDUCTIVE	NONINVOLVEMENTS
NONEQUILIBRIUMS	NONFERROUS	NONHARMONIC	NONINDUSTRIAL	NONIONISING
NONEQUIVALENCE	NONFICTION	NONHAZARDOUS	NONINDUSTRY	NONIONIZING
NONEQUIVALENCES	NONFICTIONAL	NONHEMOLYTIC	NONINFECTED	NONIRRADIATED
NONEQUIVALENT	NONFICTIONALLY	NONHEREDITARY	NONINFECTIOUS	NONIRRIGATED
NONESSENTIAL	NONFICTIONS	NONHIERARCHICAL	NONINFECTIVE	NONIRRITANT
NONESSENTIALS	NONFIGURATIVE	NONHISTONE	NONINFESTED	NONIRRITANTS
NONESTABLISHED	NONFILAMENTOUS	NONHISTORICAL	NONINFLAMMABLE	NONIRRITATING
NONESTERIFIED	NONFILTERABLE	NONHOMOGENEITY	NONINFLAMMATORY	NONJOINDER
NONESUCHES	NONFINANCIAL	NONHOMOGENEOUS	NONINFLATIONARY	NONJOINDERS
NONETHELESS	NONFISSIONABLE	NONHOMOLOGOUS	NONINFLECTIONAL	NONJOINERS
NONETHICAL	NONFLAMMABILITY	NONHOMOSEXUAL	NONINFLUENCE	NONJUDGEMENTAL
NONETHNICS	NONFLAMMABLE	NONHOMOSEXUALS	NONINFLUENCES	NONJUDGMENTAL
NONEVALUATIVE	NONFLOWERING	NONHORMONAL	NONINFORMATION	NONJUDICIAL
NONEVIDENCE	NONFLUENCIES	NONHOSPITAL	NONINFORMATIONS	NONJUSTICIABLE
NONEVIDENCES	NONFLUENCY	NONHOSPITALISED	NONINFRINGEMENT	NONKOSHERS
NONEXCLUSIVE	NONFLUORESCENT	NONHOSPITALIZED	NONINITIAL	NONLADDERING
NONEXECUTIVE	NONFORFEITABLE	NONHOSTILE	NONINITIATE	NONLANDOWNER
NONEXECUTIVES	NONFORFEITURE	NONHOUSING	NONINITIATES	NONLANDOWNERS
NONEXEMPTS	NONFORFEITURES	NONHUNTERS	NONINSECTICIDAL	NONLANGUAGE
NONEXISTENCE	NONFREEZING	NONHUNTING	NONINSECTS	NONLANGUAGES
NONEXISTENCES	NONFRIVOLOUS	NONHYGROSCOPIC	NONINSTALLMENT	NONLAWYERS
NONEXISTENT	NONFULFILLMENT	NONHYSTERICAL	NONINSTALLMENTS	NONLEGUMES
NONEXISTENTIAL	NONFULFILLMENTS	NONIDENTICAL	NONINSTALMENT	NONLEGUMINOUS
NONEXISTENTS	NONFULFILMENT	NONIDENTITIES	NONINSTRUMENTAL	NONLEXICAL
NONEXPENDABLE	NONFULFILMENTS	NONIDENTITY	NONINSURANCE	NONLIBRARIAN
NONEXPERIMENTAL	NONFUNCTIONAL	NONIDEOLOGICAL	NONINSURANCES	NONLIBRARIANS
NONEXPERTS	NONFUNCTIONING	NONILLIONS	NONINSURED	NONLIBRARY
NONEXPLANATORY	NONGASEOUS	NONILLIONTH	NONINTEGRAL	NONLINEARITIES
NONEXPLOITATION	NONGENETIC	NONILLIONTHS	NONINTEGRATED	NONLINEARITY
NONEXPLOITATIVE	NONGENITAL	NONIMITATIVE	NONINTELLECTUAL	NONLINGUISTIC
NONEXPLOITIVE	NONGEOMETRICAL	NONIMMIGRANT	NONINTERACTING	NONLIQUIDS
NONEXPLOSIVE	NONGLAMOROUS	NONIMMIGRANTS	NONINTERACTIVE	NONLITERAL
NONEXPOSED	NONGOLFERS	NONIMPACTS	NONINTERCOURSE	NONLITERARY
NONFACTORS	NONGONOCOCCAL	NONIMPLICATION	NONINTERCOURSES	NONLITERATE

NONLITERATES	NONMONETARY	NONOCCURRENCES	NONPHILOSOPHERS	NONPROSSED
NONLIVINGS	NONMONOGAMOUS	NONOFFICIAL	NONPHONEMIC	NONPROSSES
NONLOGICAL	NONMORTALS	NONOFFICIALS	NONPHONETIC	NONPROSSING
NONLOGICALLY	NONMOTILITIES	NONOPERATIC	NONPHOSPHATE	NONPROTEIN
NONLUMINOUS	NONMOTILITY	NONOPERATING	NONPHOTOGRAPHIC	NONPSYCHIATRIC
NONMAGNETIC	NONMOTORISED	NONOPERATIONAL	NONPHYSICAL	NONPSYCHIATRIST
NONMAINSTREAM	NONMOTORIZED	NONOPERATIVE	NONPHYSICIAN	NONPSYCHOTIC
NONMALICIOUS	NONMUNICIPAL	NONOPTIMAL	NONPHYSICIANS	NONPUNITIVE
NONMALIGNANT	NONMUSICAL	NONORGANIC	NONPLASTIC	NONPURPOSIVE
NONMALLEABLE	NONMUSICALS	NONORGASMIC	NONPLASTICS	NONQUANTIFIABLE
NONMANAGEMENT	NONMUSICIAN	NONORTHODOX	NONPLAYERS	NONQUANTITATIVE
NONMANAGERIAL	NONMUSICIANS	NONOVERLAPPING	NONPLAYING	NONRACIALLY
NONMANDATORY	NONMUTANTS	NONOXIDISING	NONPLUSING	NONRACISMS
NONMARITAL	NONMYELINATED	NONOXIDIZING	NONPLUSSED	NONRADIOACTIVE
NONMARKETS	NONMYSTICAL	NONPAPISTS	NONPLUSSES	NONRAILROAD
NONMATERIAL	NONNARRATIVE	NONPARALLEL	NONPLUSSING	NONRANDOMNESS
NONMATHEMATICAL	NONNATIONAL	NONPARAMETRIC	NONPOISONOUS	NONRANDOMNESSES
NONMATRICULATED	NONNATIONALS	NONPARASITIC	NONPOLARISABLE	NONRATIONAL
NONMEANINGFUL	NONNATIVES	NONPAREILS	NONPOLARIZABLE	NONREACTIVE
NONMEASURABLE	NONNATURAL	NONPARENTS	NONPOLITICAL	NONREACTOR
NONMECHANICAL	NONNECESSITIES	NONPARITIES	NONPOLITICALLY	NONREACTORS
NONMECHANISTIC	NONNECESSITY	NONPARTICIPANT	NONPOLITICIAN	NONREADERS
NONMEDICAL	NONNEGATIVE	NONPARTICIPANTS	NONPOLITICIANS	NONREADING
NONMEETING	NONNEGLIGENT	NONPARTIES	NONPOLLUTING	NONREADINGS
NONMEETINGS	NONNEGOTIABLE	NONPARTISAN	NONPOPULAR	NONREALISTIC
NONMEMBERS	NONNEGOTIABLES	NONPARTISANSHIP	NONPORTABLE	NONRECEIPT
NONMEMBERSHIP	NONNETWORK	NONPARTIZAN	NONPOSSESSION	NONRECEIPTS
NONMEMBERSHIPS	NONNITROGENOUS	NONPARTIZANSHIP	NONPOSSESSIONS	NONRECIPROCAL
NONMERCURIAL	NONNORMATIVE	NONPASSERINE	NONPRACTICAL	NONRECOGNITION
NONMETALLIC	NONNUCLEAR	NONPASSIVE	NONPRACTICING	NONRECOGNITIONS
NONMETAMERIC	NONNUCLEATED	NONPATHOGENIC	NONPRACTISING	NONRECOMBINANT
NONMETAPHORICAL	NONNUMERICAL	NONPAYMENT	NONPREGNANT	NONRECOMBINANTS
NONMETRICAL	NONNUTRITIOUS	NONPAYMENTS	NONPREHENSILE	NONRECOURSE
NONMETROPOLITAN	NONNUTRITIVE	NONPECUNIARY	NONPRESCRIPTION	NONRECOVERABLE
NONMICROBIAL	NONOBJECTIVE	NONPERFORMANCE	NONPRINTING	NONRECURRENT
NONMIGRANT	NONOBJECTIVISM	NONPERFORMANCES	NONPROBLEM	NONRECURRING
NONMIGRANTS	NONOBJECTIVISMS	NONPERFORMER	NONPROBLEMS	NONRECYCLABLE
NONMIGRATORY	NONOBJECTIVIST	NONPERFORMERS	NONPRODUCING	NONRECYCLABLES
NONMILITANT	NONOBJECTIVISTS	NONPERFORMING	NONPRODUCTIVE	NONREDUCING
NONMILITANTS	NONOBJECTIVITY	NONPERISHABLE	NONPRODUCTIVITY	NONREDUNDANT
NONMILITARY	NONOBSCENE	NONPERISHABLES	NONPROFESSIONAL	NONREFILLABLE
NONMIMETIC	NONOBSERVANCE	NONPERMANENT	NONPROFESSORIAL	NONREFLECTING
NONMINORITIES	NONOBSERVANCES	NONPERMISSIVE	NONPROFITS	NONREFLECTIVE
NONMINORITY	NONOBSERVANT	NONPERSISTENT	NONPROGRAM	NONREFLEXIVE
NONMODERNS	NONOBVIOUS	NONPERSONAL	NONPROGRAMMER	NONREFUNDABLE
NONMOLECULAR	NONOBVIOUSES	NONPERSONS	NONPROGRAMMERS	NONREGIMENTAL
NONMONETARIST	NONOCCUPATIONAL	NONPETROLEUM	NONPROGRESSIVE	NONREGULATED
NONMONETARISTS	NONOCCURRENCE	NONPHILOSOPHER	NONPROPRIETARY	NONREGULATION

N

NONREIGNING	NONSALEABLE	NONSOLUTIONS	NONSUPERVISORY	NONTYPICAL
NONRELATIVE	NONSAPONIFIABLE	NONSOLVENT	NONSUPPORT	NONUNANIMOUS
NONRELATIVES	NONSCHEDULED	NONSPATIAL	NONSUPPORTS	NONUNIFORM
NONRELATIVISTIC	NONSCIENCE	NONSPEAKER	NONSURGICAL	NONUNIFORMITIES
NONRELEVANT	NONSCIENCES	NONSPEAKERS	NONSWIMMER	NONUNIFORMITY
NONRELIGIOUS	NONSCIENTIFIC	NONSPEAKING	NONSWIMMERS	NONUNIONISED
NONRENEWABLE	NONSCIENTIST	NONSPECIALIST	NONSYLLABIC	NONUNIONISM
NONRENEWAL	NONSCIENTISTS	NONSPECIALISTS	NONSYLLABICS	NONUNIONISMS
NONRENEWALS	NONSEASONAL	NONSPECIFIC	NONSYMBOLIC	NONUNIONIST
NONREPAYABLE	NONSECRETOR	NONSPECIFICALLY	NONSYMMETRIC	NONUNIONISTS
NONREPRODUCTIVE	NONSECRETORS	NONSPECIFICITY	NONSYMMETRICAL	NONUNIONIZED
NONRESIDENCE	NONSECRETORY	NONSPECTACULAR	NONSYNCHRONOUS	NONUNIQUENESS
NONRESIDENCES	NONSECRETS	NONSPECTRAL	NONSYSTEMATIC	NONUNIQUENESSES
NONRESIDENCIES	NONSECTARIAN	NONSPECULAR	NONSYSTEMIC	NONUNIVERSAL
NONRESIDENCY	NONSEDIMENTABLE	NONSPECULATIVE	NONSYSTEMS	NONUNIVERSITY
NONRESIDENT	NONSEGREGATED	NONSPEECHES	NONTACTICAL	NONUTILITARIAN
NONRESIDENTIAL	NONSEGREGATION	NONSPHERICAL	NONTALKERS	NONUTILITIES
NONRESIDENTS	NONSEGREGATIONS	NONSPORTING	NONTAXABLE	NONUTILITY
NONRESISTANCE	NONSELECTED	NONSTAINING	NONTEACHING	NONUTOPIAN
NONRESISTANCES	NONSELECTIVE	NONSTANDARD	NONTECHNICAL	NONVALIDITIES
NONRESISTANT	NONSENSATIONAL	NONSTAPLES	NONTEMPORAL	NONVALIDITY
NONRESISTANTS	NONSENSICAL	NONSTARTER	NONTENURED	NONVANISHING
NONRESONANT	NONSENSICALITY	NONSTARTERS	NONTERMINAL	NONVASCULAR
NONRESPONDENT	NONSENSICALLY	NONSTATIONARY	NONTERMINALS	NONVECTORS
NONRESPONDENTS	NONSENSICALNESS	NONSTATISTICAL	NONTERMINATING	NONVEGETARIAN
NONRESPONDER	NONSENSITIVE	NONSTATIVE	NONTEXTUAL	NONVEGETARIANS
NONRESPONDERS	NONSENSUOUS	NONSTATIVES	NONTHEATRICAL	NONVENEREAL
NONRESPONSE	NONSENTENCE	NONSTATUTORY	NONTHEISMS	NONVENOMOUS
NONRESPONSES	NONSENTENCES	NONSTELLAR	NONTHEISTIC	NONVERBALLY
NONRESPONSIVE	NONSEPTATE	NONSTEROID	NONTHEISTS	NONVETERAN
NONRESTRICTED	NONSEQUENTIAL	NONSTEROIDAL	NONTHEOLOGICAL	NONVETERANS
NONRESTRICTIVE	NONSERIALS	NONSTEROIDS	NONTHEORETICAL	NONVIEWERS
NONRETRACTILE	NONSERIOUS	NONSTORIES	NONTHERAPEUTIC	NONVINTAGE
NONRETROACTIVE	NONSHRINKABLE	NONSTRATEGIC	NONTHERMAL	NONVINTAGES
NONRETURNABLE	NONSIGNERS	NONSTRIATED	NONTHINKING	NONVIOLENCE
NONRETURNABLES	NONSIGNIFICANT	NONSTRIKING	NONTHINKINGS	NONVIOLENCES
NONREUSABLE	NONSIGNIFICANTS	NONSTRUCTURAL	NONTHREATENING	NONVIOLENT
NONREVERSIBLE	NONSIMULTANEOUS	NONSTRUCTURED	NONTOBACCO	NONVIOLENTLY
NONRHOTICITIES	NONSINKABLE	NONSTUDENT	NONTOTALITARIAN	NONVIRGINS
NONRHOTICITY	NONSINUSOIDAL	NONSTUDENTS	NONTRADING	NONVISCOUS
NONRIOTERS	NONSKATERS	NONSUBJECT	NONTRADITIONAL	NONVOCATIONAL
NONRIOTING	NONSKELETAL	NONSUBJECTIVE	NONTRANSFERABLE	NONVOLATILE
NONROTATING	NONSKILLED	NONSUBJECTS	NONTRANSITIVE	NONVOLCANIC
NONROUTINE	NONSMOKERS	NONSUBSIDISED	NONTREATMENT	NONVOLUNTARY
NONRUMINANT	NONSMOKING	NONSUBSIDIZED	NONTREATMENTS	NONWINNING
NONRUMINANTS	NONSOCIALIST	NONSUCCESS	NONTRIVIAL	NONWORKERS
NONRUNNERS	NONSOCIALISTS	NONSUCCESSES	NONTROPICAL	NONWORKING
NONSALABLE	NONSOLUTION	NONSUITING	NONTURBULENT	NONWRITERS

NONYELLOWING	NORMOTENSIVE	NORTHWESTWARDLY	NOTAPHILISTS	NOTODONTIDS
NOODLEDOMS	NORMOTENSIVES	NORTHWESTWARDS	NOTARIALLY	NOTONECTAL
NOOGENESES	NORMOTHERMIA	NORTRIPTYLINE	NOTARISATION	NOTORIETIES
NOOGENESIS	NORMOTHERMIAS	NORTRIPTYLINES	NOTARISATIONS	NOTORIOUSLY
NOOMETRIES	NORMOTHERMIC	NOSEBANDED	NOTARISING	NOTORIOUSNESS
NOOSPHERES	NOROVIRUSES	NOSEBLEEDING	NOTARIZATION	NOTORIOUSNESSES
NOOTROPICS	NORSELLERS	NOSEBLEEDINGS	NOTARIZATIONS	NOTORNISES
NORADRENALIN	NORSELLING	NOSEBLEEDS	NOTARIZING	NOTOTHERIUM
NORADRENALINE	NORTHBOUND	NOSEDIVING	NOTARYSHIP	NOTOTHERIUMS
NORADRENALINES	NORTHCOUNTRYMAN	NOSEGUARDS	NOTARYSHIPS	NOTOUNGULATE
NORADRENALINS	NORTHCOUNTRYMEN	NOSEPIECES	NOTATIONAL	NOTOUNGULATES
NORADRENERGIC	NORTHEASTER	NOSEWHEELS	NOTCHBACKS	NOTUNGULATE
NORDICITIES	NORTHEASTERLIES	NOSINESSES	NOTCHELING	NOTUNGULATES
NOREPINEPHRINE	NORTHEASTERLY	NOSOCOMIAL	NOTCHELLED	NOTWITHSTANDING
NOREPINEPHRINES	NORTHEASTERN	NOSOGRAPHER	NOTCHELLING	NOTWORKING
NORETHINDRONE	NORTHEASTERS	NOSOGRAPHERS	NOTEBANDIS	NOTWORKINGS
NORETHINDRONES	NORTHEASTS	NOSOGRAPHIC	NOTEDNESSES	NOUGATINES
NORETHISTERONE	NORTHEASTWARD	NOSOGRAPHIES	NOTEPAPERS	NOUMENALISM
NORETHISTERONES	NORTHEASTWARDLY	NOSOGRAPHY	NOTEWORTHIER	NOUMENALISMS
NORMALCIES	NORTHEASTWARDS	NOSOLOGICAL	NOTEWORTHIEST	NOUMENALIST
NORMALISABLE	NORTHERING	NOSOLOGICALLY	NOTEWORTHILY	NOUMENALISTS
NORMALISATION	NORTHERLIES	NOSOLOGIES	NOTEWORTHINESS	NOUMENALITIES
NORMALISATIONS	NORTHERLINESS	NOSOLOGIST	NOTEWORTHY	NOUMENALITY
NORMALISED	NORTHERLINESSES	NOSOLOGISTS	NOTHINGARIAN	NOUMENALLY
NORMALISER	NORTHERMOST	NOSOPHOBIA	NOTHINGARIANISM	NOURISHABLE
NORMALISERS	NORTHERNER	NOSOPHOBIAS	NOTHINGARIANS	NOURISHERS
NORMALISES	NORTHERNERS	NOSTALGIAS	NOTHINGISM	NOURISHING
NORMALISING	NORTHERNISE	NOSTALGICALLY	NOTHINGISMS	NOURISHINGLY
NORMALITIES	NORTHERNISED	NOSTALGICS	NOTHINGNESS	NOURISHMENT
NORMALIZABLE	NORTHERNISES	NOSTALGIST	NOTHINGNESSES	NOURISHMENTS
NORMALIZATION	NORTHERNISING	NOSTALGISTS	NOTICEABILITIES	NOURITURES
NORMALIZATIONS	NORTHERNISM	NOSTOLOGIC	NOTICEABILITY	NOURRITURE
NORMALIZED	NORTHERNISMS	NOSTOLOGICAL	NOTICEABLE	NOURRITURES
NORMALIZER	NORTHERNIZE	NOSTOLOGIES	NOTICEABLY	NOUSELLING
NORMALIZERS	NORTHERNIZED	NOSTOMANIA	NOTICEBOARD	NOVACULITE
NORMALIZES	NORTHERNIZES	NOSTOMANIAS	NOTICEBOARDS	NOVACULITES
NORMALIZING	NORTHERNIZING	NOSTOPATHIES	NOTIFIABLE	NOVELETTES
NORMATIVELY	NORTHERNMOST	NOSTOPATHY	NOTIFICATION	NOVELETTISH
NORMATIVENESS	NORTHLANDS	NOSTRADAMIC	NOTIFICATIONS	NOVELETTIST
NORMATIVENESSES	NORTHWARDLY	NOTABILITIES	NOTIONALIST	NOVELETTISTS
NORMOGLYCAEMIA	NORTHWARDS	NOTABILITY	NOTIONALISTS	NOVELISATION
NORMOGLYCAEMIAS	NORTHWESTER	NOTABLENESS	NOTIONALITIES	NOVELISATIONS
NORMOGLYCAEMIC	NORTHWESTERLIES	NOTABLENESSES	NOTIONALITY	NOVELISERS
NORMOGLYCEMIA	NORTHWESTERLY	NOTAPHILIC	NOTIONALLY	NOVELISING
NORMOGLYCEMIAS	NORTHWESTERN	NOTAPHILIES	NOTIONISTS	NOVELISTIC
NORMOGLYCEMIC	NORTHWESTERS	NOTAPHILISM	NOTOCHORDAL	NOVELISTICALLY
NORMOTENSION	NORTHWESTS	NOTAPHILISMS	NOTOCHORDS	NOVELIZATION
NORMOTENSIONS	NORTHWESTWARD	NOTAPHILIST	NOTODONTID	NOVELIZATIONS

NOVELIZERS	NUCLEONICS	NUMBERABLE	NUMMULITIC	NUTRITIONARY
NOVELIZING	NUCLEOPHILE	NUMBERINGS	NUMSKULLED	NUTRITIONIST
NOVEMDECILLION	NUCLEOPHILES	NUMBERLESS	NUNCIATURE	NUTRITIONISTS
NOVEMDECILLIONS	NUCLEOPHILIC	NUMBERLESSLY	NUNCIATURES	NUTRITIONS
NOVENARIES	NUCLEOPHILICITY	NUMBERLESSNESS	NUNCUPATED	NUTRITIOUS
NOVICEHOOD	NUCLEOPLASM	NUMBERPLATE	NUNCUPATES	NUTRITIOUSLY
NOVICEHOODS	NUCLEOPLASMATIC	NUMBERPLATES	NUNCUPATING	NUTRITIOUSNESS
NOVICESHIP	NUCLEOPLASMIC	NUMBFISHES	NUNCUPATION	NUTRITIVELY
NOVICESHIPS	NUCLEOPLASMS	NUMBNESSES	NUNCUPATIONS	NUTRITIVES
NOVICIATES	NUCLEOPROTEIN	NUMBNUTSES	NUNCUPATIVE	NUTTINESSES
NOVITIATES	NUCLEOPROTEINS	NUMBSKULLED	NUNCUPATORY	NYCHTHEMERAL
NOVOBIOCIN	NUCLEOSIDE	NUMBSKULLS	NUNNATIONS	NYCHTHEMERON
NOVOBIOCINS	NUCLEOSIDES	NUMERABILITIES	NUNNISHNESS	NYCHTHEMERONS
NOVOCAINES	NUCLEOSOMAL	NUMERABILITY	NUNNISHNESSES	NYCTAGINACEOUS
NOVOCENTENARIES	NUCLEOSOME	NUMERACIES	NUPTIALITIES	NYCTALOPES
NOVOCENTENARY	NUCLEOSOMES	NUMERAIRES	NUPTIALITY	NYCTALOPIA
NOVODAMUSES	NUCLEOSYNTHESES	NUMERATING	NURSEHOUND	NYCTALOPIAS
NOWCASTING	NUCLEOSYNTHESIS	NUMERATION	NURSEHOUNDS	NYCTALOPIC
NOWCASTINGS	NUCLEOSYNTHETIC	NUMERATIONS	NURSELINGS	NYCTANTHOUS
NOXIOUSNESS	NUCLEOTIDASE	NUMERATIVE	NURSEMAIDED	NYCTINASTIC
NOXIOUSNESSES	NUCLEOTIDASES	NUMERATORS	NURSEMAIDING	NYCTINASTIES
NUBBINESSES	NUCLEOTIDE	NUMERICALLY	NURSEMAIDS	NYCTINASTY
NUBIFEROUS	NUCLEOTIDES	NUMEROLOGICAL	NURSERYMAID	NYCTITROPIC
NUBIGENOUS	NUDENESSES	NUMEROLOGIES	NURSERYMAIDS	NYCTITROPISM
NUBILITIES	NUDIBRANCH	NUMEROLOGIST	NURSERYMAN	NYCTITROPISMS
NUCIFEROUS	NUDIBRANCHIATE	NUMEROLOGISTS	NURSERYMEN	NYCTOPHOBIA
NUCIVOROUS	NUDIBRANCHIATES	NUMEROLOGY	NURTURABLE	NYCTOPHOBIAS
NUCLEARISATION	NUDIBRANCHS	NUMEROSITIES	NURTURANCE	NYCTOPHOBIC
NUCLEARISATIONS	NUDICAUDATE	NUMEROSITY	NURTURANCES	NYMPHAEACEOUS
NUCLEARISE	NUDICAULOUS	NUMEROUSLY	NUTATIONAL	NYMPHAEUMS
NUCLEARISED	NUGATORINESS	NUMEROUSNESS	NUTBUTTERS	NYMPHALIDS
NUCLEARISES	NUGATORINESSES	NUMEROUSNESSES	NUTCRACKER	NYMPHETTES
NUCLEARISING	NUGGETIEST	NUMINOUSES	NUTCRACKERS	NYMPHLIEST
NUCLEARIZATION	NUGGETTING	NUMINOUSNESS	NUTGRASSES	NYMPHOLEPSIES
NUCLEARIZATIONS	NUISANCERS	NUMINOUSNESSES	NUTHATCHES	NYMPHOLEPSY
NUCLEARIZE	NULLIFICATION	NUMISMATIC	NUTJOBBERS	NYMPHOLEPT
NUCLEARIZED	NULLIFICATIONS	NUMISMATICALLY	NUTMEGGIER	NYMPHOLEPTIC
NUCLEARIZES	NULLIFIDIAN	NUMISMATICS	NUTMEGGIEST	NYMPHOLEPTS
NUCLEARIZING	NULLIFIDIANS	NUMISMATIST	NUTMEGGING	NYMPHOMANIA
NUCLEATING	NULLIFIERS	NUMISMATISTS	NUTPECKERS	NYMPHOMANIAC
NUCLEATION	NULLIFYING	NUMISMATOLOGIES	NUTRACEUTICAL	NYMPHOMANIACAL
NUCLEATIONS	NULLIPARAE	NUMISMATOLOGIST	NUTRACEUTICALS	NYMPHOMANIACS
NUCLEATORS	NULLIPARAS	NUMISMATOLOGY	NUTRIGENETICS	NYMPHOMANIAS
NUCLEOCAPSID	NULLIPARITIES	NUMMULATED	NUTRIGENOMICS	NYSTAGMOID
NUCLEOCAPSIDS	NULLIPARITY	NUMMULATION	NUTRIMENTAL	NYSTAGMUSES
NUCLEOLATE	NULLIPAROUS	NUMMULATIONS	NUTRIMENTS	
NUCLEOLATED	NULLIPORES	NUMMULINES	NUTRITIONAL	
NUCLEONICALLY	NULLNESSES	NUMMULITES	NUTRITIONALLY	

O

OAFISHNESS	OBJECTIONS	OBLATENESSES	OBNOXIOUSNESSES	OBSERVANCY
OAFISHNESSES	OBJECTIVAL	OBLATIONAL	OBNUBILATE	OBSERVANTLY
OAKENSHAWS	OBJECTIVATE	OBLIGATELY	OBNUBILATED	OBSERVANTS
OAKINESSES	OBJECTIVATED	OBLIGATING	OBNUBILATES	OBSERVATION
OARSMANSHIP	OBJECTIVATES	OBLIGATION	OBNUBILATING	OBSERVATIONAL
OARSMANSHIPS	OBJECTIVATING	OBLIGATIONAL	OBNUBILATION	OBSERVATIONALLY
OASTHOUSES	OBJECTIVATION	OBLIGATIONS	OBNUBILATIONS	OBSERVATIONS
OBBLIGATOS	OBJECTIVATIONS	OBLIGATIVE	OBREPTIONS	OBSERVATIVE
OBCOMPRESSED	OBJECTIVELY	OBLIGATORILY	OBREPTITIOUS	OBSERVATOR
OBDURACIES	OBJECTIVENESS	OBLIGATORINESS	OBSCENENESS	OBSERVATORIES
OBDURATELY	OBJECTIVENESSES	OBLIGATORS	OBSCENENESSES	OBSERVATORS
OBDURATENESS	OBJECTIVES	OBLIGATORY	OBSCENITIES	OBSERVATORY
OBDURATENESSES	OBJECTIVISE	OBLIGEMENT	OBSCURANTIC	OBSERVINGLY
OBDURATING	OBJECTIVISED	OBLIGEMENTS	OBSCURANTISM	OBSESSIONAL
OBDURATION	OBJECTIVISES	OBLIGINGLY	OBSCURANTISMS	OBSESSIONALLY
OBDURATIONS	OBJECTIVISING	OBLIGINGNESS	OBSCURANTIST	OBSESSIONIST
OBEDIENCES	OBJECTIVISM	OBLIGINGNESSES	OBSCURANTISTS	OBSESSIONISTS
OBEDIENTIAL	OBJECTIVISMS	OBLIQUATION	OBSCURANTS	OBSESSIONS
OBEDIENTIARIES	OBJECTIVIST	OBLIQUATIONS	OBSCURATION	OBSESSIVELY
OBEDIENTIARY	OBJECTIVISTIC	OBLIQUENESS	OBSCURATIONS	OBSESSIVENESS
OBEDIENTLY	OBJECTIVISTS	OBLIQUENESSES	OBSCUREMENT	OBSESSIVENESSES
OBEISANCES	OBJECTIVITIES	OBLIQUITIES	OBSCUREMENTS	OBSESSIVES
OBEISANTLY	OBJECTIVITY	OBLIQUITOUS	OBSCURENESS	OBSIDIONAL
OBELISCOID	OBJECTIVIZE	OBLITERATE	OBSCURENESSES	OBSIDIONARY
OBELISKOID	OBJECTIVIZED	OBLITERATED	OBSCURITIES	OBSIGNATED
OBESENESSES	OBJECTIVIZES	OBLITERATES	OBSECRATED	OBSIGNATES
OBESOGENIC	OBJECTIVIZING	OBLITERATING	OBSECRATES	OBSIGNATING
OBFUSCATED	OBJECTLESS	OBLITERATION	OBSECRATING	OBSIGNATION
OBFUSCATES	OBJECTLESSNESS	OBLITERATIONS	OBSECRATION	OBSIGNATIONS
OBFUSCATING	OBJURATION	OBLITERATIVE	OBSECRATIONS	OBSIGNATORY
OBFUSCATION	OBJURATIONS	OBLITERATOR	OBSEQUIOUS	OBSOLESCED
OBFUSCATIONS	OBJURGATED	OBLITERATORS	OBSEQUIOUSLY	OBSOLESCENCE
OBFUSCATORY	OBJURGATES	OBLIVIOUSLY	OBSEQUIOUSNESS	OBSOLESCENCES
OBITUARIES	OBJURGATING	OBLIVIOUSNESS	OBSERVABILITIES	OBSOLESCENT
OBITUARIST	OBJURGATION	OBLIVIOUSNESSES	OBSERVABILITY	OBSOLESCENTLY
OBITUARISTS	OBJURGATIONS	OBLIVISCENCE	OBSERVABLE	OBSOLESCES
OBJECTIFICATION	OBJURGATIVE	OBLIVISCENCES	OBSERVABLENESS	OBSOLESCING
OBJECTIFIED	OBJURGATOR	OBMUTESCENCE	OBSERVABLES	OBSOLETELY
OBJECTIFIES	OBJURGATORS	OBMUTESCENCES	OBSERVABLY	OBSOLETENESS
OBJECTIFYING	OBJURGATORY	OBMUTESCENT	OBSERVANCE	OBSOLETENESSES
OBJECTIONABLE	OBLANCEOLATE	OBNOXIOUSLY	OBSERVANCES	OBSOLETING
OBJECTIONABLY	OBLATENESS	OBNOXIOUSNESS	OBSERVANCIES	OBSOLETION

OBSOLETIONS

OBSOLETIONS	OBTAINMENTS	OCCASIONALLY	OCEANGOING	OCTAPODIES
OBSOLETISM	OBTEMPERATE	OCCASIONED	OCEANOGRAPHER	OCTARCHIES
OBSOLETISMS	OBTEMPERATED	OCCASIONER	OCEANOGRAPHERS	OCTASTICHON
OBSTETRICAL	OBTEMPERATES	OCCASIONERS	OCEANOGRAPHIC	OCTASTICHONS
OBSTETRICALLY	OBTEMPERATING	OCCASIONING	OCEANOGRAPHICAL	OCTASTICHOUS
OBSTETRICIAN	OBTEMPERED	OCCIDENTAL	OCEANOGRAPHIES	OCTASTICHS
OBSTETRICIANS	OBTEMPERING	OCCIDENTALISE	OCEANOGRAPHY	OCTASTROPHIC
OBSTETRICS	OBTENTIONS	OCCIDENTALISED	OCEANOLOGICAL	OCTASTYLES
OBSTINACIES	OBTESTATION	OCCIDENTALISES	OCEANOLOGIES	OCTAVALENT
OBSTINATELY	OBTESTATIONS	OCCIDENTALISING	OCEANOLOGIST	OCTENNIALLY
OBSTINATENESS	OBTRUDINGS	OCCIDENTALISM	OCEANOLOGISTS	OCTILLIONS
OBSTINATENESSES	OBTRUNCATE	OCCIDENTALISMS	OCEANOLOGY	OCTILLIONTH
OBSTIPATION	OBTRUNCATED	OCCIDENTALIST	OCELLATION	OCTILLIONTHS
OBSTIPATIONS	OBTRUNCATES	OCCIDENTALISTS	OCELLATIONS	OCTINGENARIES
OBSTREPERATE	OBTRUNCATING	OCCIDENTALIZE	OCHLOCRACIES	OCTINGENARY
OBSTREPERATED	OBTRUSIONS	OCCIDENTALIZED	OCHLOCRACY	OCTINGENTENARY
OBSTREPERATES	OBTRUSIVELY	OCCIDENTALIZES	OCHLOCRATIC	OCTOCENTENARIES
OBSTREPERATING	OBTRUSIVENESS	OCCIDENTALIZING	OCHLOCRATICAL	OCTOCENTENARY
OBSTREPEROUS	OBTRUSIVENESSES	OCCIDENTALLY	OCHLOCRATICALLY	OCTODECILLION
OBSTREPEROUSLY	OBTUNDENTS	OCCIDENTALS	OCHLOCRATS	OCTODECILLIONS
OBSTRICTION	OBTUNDITIES	OCCIPITALLY	OCHLOPHOBIA	OCTODECIMO
OBSTRICTIONS	OBTURATING	OCCIPITALS	OCHLOPHOBIAC	OCTODECIMOS
OBSTROPALOUS	OBTURATION	OCCLUDENTS	OCHLOPHOBIACS	OCTOGENARIAN
OBSTROPULOUS	OBTURATIONS	OCCLUSIONS	OCHLOPHOBIAS	OCTOGENARIANS
OBSTRUCTED	OBTURATORS	OCCLUSIVENESS	OCHLOPHOBIC	OCTOGENARIES
OBSTRUCTER	OBTUSENESS	OCCLUSIVENESSES	OCHLOPHOBICS	OCTOGENARY
OBSTRUCTERS	OBTUSENESSES	OCCLUSIVES	OCHRACEOUS	OCTOGYNOUS
OBSTRUCTING	OBTUSITIES	OCCULTATION	OCHROLEUCOUS	OCTOHEDRON
OBSTRUCTINGLY	OBUMBRATED	OCCULTATIONS	OCTACHORDAL	OCTOHEDRONS
OBSTRUCTION	OBUMBRATES	OCCULTISMS	OCTACHORDS	OCTONARIAN
OBSTRUCTIONAL	OBUMBRATING	OCCULTISTS	OCTAGONALLY	OCTONARIANS
OBSTRUCTIONALLY	OBUMBRATION	OCCULTNESS	OCTAHEDRAL	OCTONARIES
OBSTRUCTIONISM	OBUMBRATIONS	OCCULTNESSES	OCTAHEDRALLY	OCTONARIUS
OBSTRUCTIONISMS	OBVENTIONS	OCCUPANCES	OCTAHEDRITE	OCTONOCULAR
OBSTRUCTIONIST	OBVERSIONS	OCCUPANCIES	OCTAHEDRITES	OCTOPETALOUS
OBSTRUCTIONISTS	OBVIATIONS	OCCUPATING	OCTAHEDRON	OCTOPLOIDS
OBSTRUCTIONS	OBVIOUSNESS	OCCUPATION	OCTAHEDRONS	OCTOPODANS
OBSTRUCTIVE	OBVIOUSNESSES	OCCUPATIONAL	OCTAMEROUS	OCTOPODOUS
OBSTRUCTIVELY	OBVOLUTION	OCCUPATIONALLY	OCTAMETERS	OCTOPUSHER
OBSTRUCTIVENESS	OBVOLUTIONS	OCCUPATIONS	OCTANDRIAN	OCTOPUSHERS
OBSTRUCTIVES	OBVOLUTIVE	OCCUPATIVE	OCTANDROUS	OCTOPUSHES
OBSTRUCTOR	OCCASIONAL	OCCURRENCE	OCTANEDIOIC	OCTOSEPALOUS
OBSTRUCTORS	OCCASIONALISM	OCCURRENCES	OCTANGULAR	OCTOSTICHOUS
OBSTRUENTS	OCCASIONALISMS	OCCURRENTS	OCTAPEPTIDE	OCTOSTYLES
OBTAINABILITIES	OCCASIONALIST	OCEANARIUM	OCTAPEPTIDES	OCTOSYLLABIC
OBTAINABILITY	OCCASIONALISTS	OCEANARIUMS	OCTAPLOIDIES	OCTOSYLLABICS
OBTAINABLE	OCCASIONALITIES	OCEANFRONT	OCTAPLOIDS	OCTOSYLLABLE
OBTAINMENT	OCCASIONALITY	OCEANFRONTS	OCTAPLOIDY	OCTOSYLLABLES

OCTOTHORPS	ODONTOPHORE	OESTROGENICALLY	OFFPRINTING	OLFACTORIES
OCTUPLICATE	ODONTOPHORES	OESTROGENS	OFFSADDLED	OLFACTRONICS
OCTUPLICATES	ODONTOPHOROUS	OFFENCEFUL	OFFSADDLES	OLIGAEMIAS
OCULARISTS	ODONTORHYNCHOUS	OFFENCELESS	OFFSADDLING	OLIGARCHAL
OCULOMOTOR	ODONTORNITHES	OFFENDEDLY	OFFSCOURING	OLIGARCHIC
ODALISQUES	ODONTOSTOMATOUS	OFFENDRESS	OFFSCOURINGS	OLIGARCHICAL
ODDSMAKERS	ODORIFEROUS	OFFENDRESSES	OFFSEASONS	OLIGARCHICALLY
ODIOUSNESS	ODORIFEROUSLY	OFFENSELESS	OFFSETABLE	OLIGARCHIES
ODIOUSNESSES	ODORIFEROUSNESS	OFFENSIVELY	OFFSETTING	OLIGOCHAETE
ODOMETRIES	ODORIMETRIES	OFFENSIVENESS	OFFSETTINGS	OLIGOCHAETES
ODONATISTS	ODORIMETRY	OFFENSIVENESSES	OFFSHORING	OLIGOCHROME
ODONATOLOGIES	ODORIPHORE	OFFENSIVES	OFFSHORINGS	OLIGOCHROMES
ODONATOLOGIST	ODORIPHORES	OFFERTORIES	OFFSPRINGS	OLIGOCLASE
ODONATOLOGISTS	ODOROUSNESS	OFFHANDEDLY	OFTENNESSES	OLIGOCLASES
ODONATOLOGY	ODOROUSNESSES	OFFHANDEDNESS	OFTENTIMES	OLIGOCYTHAEMIA
ODONTALGIA	OECOLOGICAL	OFFHANDEDNESSES	OGANESSONS	OLIGOCYTHAEMIAS
ODONTALGIAS	OECOLOGICALLY	OFFICEHOLDER	OILINESSES	OLIGODENDROCYTE
ODONTALGIC	OECOLOGIES	OFFICEHOLDERS	OINOLOGIES	OLIGODENDROGLIA
ODONTALGIES	OECOLOGIST	OFFICERING	OLDFANGLED	OLIGOGENES
ODONTOBLAST	OECOLOGISTS	OFFICIALDOM	OLEAGINOUS	OLIGOMERIC
ODONTOBLASTIC	OECUMENICAL	OFFICIALDOMS	OLEAGINOUSLY	OLIGOMERISATION
ODONTOBLASTS	OECUMENICALLY	OFFICIALESE	OLEAGINOUSNESS	OLIGOMERIZATION
ODONTOCETE	OEDEMATOSE	OFFICIALESES	OLEANDOMYCIN	OLIGOMEROUS
ODONTOCETES	OEDEMATOUS	OFFICIALISM	OLEANDOMYCINS	OLIGONUCLEOTIDE
ODONTOGENIC	OEDOMETERS	OFFICIALISMS	OLECRANONS	OLIGOPEPTIDE
ODONTOGENIES	OENOLOGICAL	OFFICIALITIES	OLEIFEROUS	OLIGOPEPTIDES
ODONTOGENY	OENOLOGIES	OFFICIALITY	OLEOGRAPHIC	OLIGOPHAGIES
ODONTOGLOSSUM	OENOLOGIST	OFFICIALLY	OLEOGRAPHIES	OLIGOPHAGOUS
ODONTOGLOSSUMS	OENOLOGISTS	OFFICIALTIES	OLEOGRAPHS	OLIGOPHAGY
ODONTOGRAPH	OENOMANCIES	OFFICIALTY	OLEOGRAPHY	OLIGOPOLIES
ODONTOGRAPHIES	OENOMANIAS	OFFICIANTS	OLEOMARGARIN	OLIGOPOLISTIC
ODONTOGRAPHS	OENOMETERS	OFFICIARIES	OLEOMARGARINE	OLIGOPSONIES
ODONTOGRAPHY	OENOPHILES	OFFICIATED	OLEOMARGARINES	OLIGOPSONISTIC
ODONTOLITE	OENOPHILIES	OFFICIATES	OLEOMARGARINS	OLIGOPSONY
ODONTOLITES	OENOPHILIST	OFFICIATING	OLEOPHILIC	OLIGOSACCHARIDE
ODONTOLOGIC	OENOPHILISTS	OFFICIATION	OLEORESINOUS	OLIGOSPERMIA
ODONTOLOGICAL	OENOTHERAS	OFFICIATIONS	OLEORESINS	OLIGOSPERMIAS
ODONTOLOGIES	OESOPHAGEAL	OFFICIATOR	OLERACEOUS	OLIGOTROPHIC
ODONTOLOGIST	OESOPHAGITIS	OFFICIATORS	OLFACTIBLE	OLIGOTROPHIES
ODONTOLOGISTS	OESOPHAGITISES	OFFICINALLY	OLFACTIONS	OLIGOTROPHY
ODONTOLOGY	OESOPHAGOSCOPE	OFFICINALS	OLFACTOLOGIES	OLIGURESES
ODONTOMATA	OESOPHAGOSCOPES	OFFICIOUSLY	OLFACTOLOGIST	OLIGURESIS
ODONTOMATOUS	OESOPHAGOSCOPY	OFFICIOUSNESS	OLFACTOLOGISTS	OLIGURETIC
ODONTOPHOBIA	OESOPHAGUS	OFFICIOUSNESSES	OLFACTOLOGY	OLINGUITOS
ODONTOPHOBIAS	OESOPHAGUSES	OFFISHNESS	OLFACTOMETER	OLIVACEOUS
ODONTOPHORAL	OESTRADIOL	OFFISHNESSES	OLFACTOMETERS	OLIVENITES
ODONTOPHORAN	OESTRADIOLS	OFFLOADING	OLFACTOMETRIES	OLIVEWOODS
ODONTOPHORANS	OESTROGENIC	OFFPRINTED	OLFACTOMETRY	OLIVINITIC

OLOGOANING	OMNIPOTENCY	ONCOTOMIES	ONSHORINGS	OPAQUENESSES
OLOLIUQUIS	OMNIPOTENT	ONCOVIRUSES	ONSLAUGHTS	OPEIDOSCOPE
OMBROGENOUS	OMNIPOTENTLY	ONDOGRAPHS	ONTOGENESES	OPEIDOSCOPES
OMBROMETER	OMNIPOTENTS	ONEIRICALLY	ONTOGENESIS	OPENABILITIES
OMBROMETERS	OMNIPRESENCE	ONEIROCRITIC	ONTOGENETIC	OPENABILITY
OMBROPHILE	OMNIPRESENCES	ONEIROCRITICAL	ONTOGENETICALLY	OPENHANDED
OMBROPHILES	OMNIPRESENT	ONEIROCRITICISM	ONTOGENICALLY	OPENHANDEDLY
OMBROPHILOUS	OMNIRANGES	ONEIROCRITICS	ONTOGENIES	OPENHANDEDNESS
OMBROPHILS	OMNISCIENCE	ONEIRODYNIA	ONTOLOGICAL	OPENHEARTED
OMBROPHOBE	OMNISCIENCES	ONEIRODYNIAS	ONTOLOGICALLY	OPENHEARTEDLY
OMBROPHOBES	OMNISCIENT	ONEIROLOGIES	ONTOLOGIES	OPENHEARTEDNESS
OMBROPHOBOUS	OMNISCIENTLY	ONEIROLOGY	ONTOLOGIST	OPENMOUTHED
OMBUDSMANSHIP	OMNISHAMBLES	ONEIROMANCER	ONTOLOGISTS	OPENMOUTHEDLY
OMBUDSMANSHIPS	OMNIVORIES	ONEIROMANCERS	ONYCHITISES	OPENMOUTHEDNESS
OMINOUSNESS	OMNIVOROUS	ONEIROMANCIES	ONYCHOCRYPTOSES	OPENNESSES
OMINOUSNESSES	OMNIVOROUSLY	ONEIROMANCY	ONYCHOCRYPTOSIS	OPERABILITIES
OMISSIVENESS	OMNIVOROUSNESS	ONEIROSCOPIES	ONYCHOMANCIES	OPERABILITY
OMISSIVENESSES	OMOPHAGIAS	ONEIROSCOPIST	ONYCHOMANCY	OPERAGOERS
OMITTANCES	OMOPHAGIES	ONEIROSCOPISTS	ONYCHOPHAGIES	OPERAGOING
OMMATIDIAL	OMOPHAGOUS	ONEIROSCOPY	ONYCHOPHAGIST	OPERAGOINGS
OMMATIDIUM	OMOPHORION	ONEROUSNESS	ONYCHOPHAGISTS	OPERATICALLY
OMMATOPHORE	OMOPLATOSCOPIES	ONEROUSNESSES	ONYCHOPHAGY	OPERATIONAL
OMMATOPHORES	OMOPLATOSCOPY	ONGOINGNESS	ONYCHOPHORAN	OPERATIONALISM
OMMATOPHOROUS	OMPHACITES	ONGOINGNESSES	ONYCHOPHORANS	OPERATIONALISMS
OMNIBENEVOLENCE	OMPHALOMANCIES	ONIONSKINS	OOGAMOUSLY	OPERATIONALIST
OMNIBENEVOLENT	OMPHALOMANCY	ONOCENTAUR	OOJAMAFLIP	OPERATIONALISTS
OMNIBUSSES	OMPHALOSKEPSES	ONOCENTAURS	OOJAMAFLIPS	OPERATIONALLY
OMNICOMPETENCE	OMPHALOSKEPSIS	ONOMASIOLOGIES	OOMPAHPAHS	OPERATIONISM
OMNICOMPETENCES	ONAGRACEOUS	ONOMASIOLOGY	OOPHORECTOMIES	OPERATIONISMS
OMNICOMPETENT	ONBOARDING	ONOMASTICALLY	OOPHORECTOMISE	OPERATIONIST
OMNIDIRECTIONAL	ONBOARDINGS	ONOMASTICIAN	OOPHORECTOMISED	OPERATIONISTS
OMNIFARIOUS	ONCHOCERCIASES	ONOMASTICIANS	OOPHORECTOMISES	OPERATIONS
OMNIFARIOUSLY	ONCHOCERCIASIS	ONOMASTICON	OOPHORECTOMIZE	OPERATISED
OMNIFARIOUSNESS	ONCOGENESES	ONOMASTICONS	OOPHORECTOMIZED	OPERATISES
OMNIFEROUS	ONCOGENESIS	ONOMASTICS	OOPHORECTOMIZES	OPERATISING
OMNIFICENCE	ONCOGENETICIST	ONOMATOLOGIES	OOPHORECTOMY	OPERATIVELY
OMNIFICENCES	ONCOGENETICISTS	ONOMATOLOGIST	OOPHORITIC	OPERATIVENESS
OMNIFICENT	ONCOGENICITIES	ONOMATOLOGISTS	OOPHORITIS	OPERATIVENESSES
OMNIFORMITIES	ONCOGENICITY	ONOMATOLOGY	OOPHORITISES	OPERATIVES
OMNIFORMITY	ONCOGENOUS	ONOMATOPOEIA	OOZINESSES	OPERATIVITIES
OMNIGENOUS	ONCOLOGICAL	ONOMATOPOEIAS	OPACIFIERS	OPERATIVITY
OMNIPARITIES	ONCOLOGIES	ONOMATOPOEIC	OPACIFYING	OPERATIZED
OMNIPARITY	ONCOLOGIST	ONOMATOPOESES	OPALESCENCE	OPERATIZES
OMNIPAROUS	ONCOLOGISTS	ONOMATOPOESIS	OPALESCENCES	OPERATIZING
OMNIPATIENT	ONCOLYTICS	ONOMATOPOETIC	OPALESCENT	OPERATORLESS
OMNIPOTENCE	ONCOMETERS	ONOMATOPOIESES	OPALESCENTLY	OPERCULARS
OMNIPOTENCES	ONCORNAVIRUS	ONOMATOPOIESIS	OPALESCING	OPERCULATE
OMNIPOTENCIES	ONCORNAVIRUSES	ONSETTINGS	OPAQUENESS	OPERCULATED

OPERCULUMS	OPHTHALMOPLEGIA	OPPIGNERATING	OPPROBRIOUSNESS	OPTIMIZERS
OPERETTIST	OPHTHALMOSCOPE	OPPIGNERATION	OPPROBRIUM	OPTIMIZING
OPERETTISTS	OPHTHALMOSCOPES	OPPIGNERATIONS	OPPROBRIUMS	OPTIONALITIES
OPEROSENESS	OPHTHALMOSCOPIC	OPPIGNORATE	OPPUGNANCIES	OPTIONALITY
OPEROSENESSES	OPHTHALMOSCOPY	OPPIGNORATED	OPPUGNANCY	OPTIONALLY
OPEROSITIES	OPINICUSES	OPPIGNORATES	OPPUGNANTLY	OPTOACOUSTIC
OPHICALCITE	OPINIONATE	OPPIGNORATING	OPPUGNANTS	OPTOELECTRONIC
OPHICALCITES	OPINIONATED	OPPIGNORATION	OPSIMATHIES	OPTOELECTRONICS
OPHICLEIDE	OPINIONATEDLY	OPPIGNORATIONS	OPSIOMETER	OPTOKINETIC
OPHICLEIDES	OPINIONATEDNESS	OPPILATING	OPSIOMETERS	OPTOLOGIES
OPHIDIARIA	OPINIONATELY	OPPILATION	OPSOMANIAC	OPTOLOGIST
OPHIDIARIUM	OPINIONATES	OPPILATIONS	OPSOMANIACS	OPTOLOGISTS
OPHIDIARIUMS	OPINIONATING	OPPILATIVE	OPSOMANIAS	OPTOMETERS
OPHIOLATER	OPINIONATIVE	OPPONENCIES	OPSONIFICATION	OPTOMETRIC
OPHIOLATERS	OPINIONATIVELY	OPPORTUNELY	OPSONIFICATIONS	OPTOMETRICAL
OPHIOLATRIES	OPINIONATOR	OPPORTUNENESS	OPSONIFIED	OPTOMETRIES
OPHIOLATROUS	OPINIONATORS	OPPORTUNENESSES	OPSONIFIES	OPTOMETRIST
OPHIOLATRY	OPINIONIST	OPPORTUNISM	OPSONIFYING	OPTOMETRISTS
OPHIOLITES	OPINIONISTS	OPPORTUNISMS	OPSONISATION	OPTOPHONES
OPHIOLITIC	OPISOMETER	OPPORTUNIST	OPSONISATIONS	OPULENCIES
OPHIOLOGIC	OPISOMETERS	OPPORTUNISTIC	OPSONISING	ORACULARITIES
OPHIOLOGICAL	OPISTHOBRANCH	OPPORTUNISTS	OPSONIZATION	ORACULARITY
OPHIOLOGIES	OPISTHOBRANCHS	OPPORTUNITIES	OPSONIZATIONS	ORACULARLY
OPHIOLOGIST	OPISTHOCOELIAN	OPPORTUNITY	OPSONIZING	ORACULARNESS
OPHIOLOGISTS	OPISTHOCOELOUS	OPPOSABILITIES	OPTATIVELY	ORACULARNESSES
OPHIOMORPH	OPISTHODOMOI	OPPOSABILITY	OPTIMALISATION	ORACULOUSLY
OPHIOMORPHIC	OPISTHODOMOS	OPPOSELESS	OPTIMALISATIONS	ORACULOUSNESS
OPHIOMORPHOUS	OPISTHOGLOSSAL	OPPOSINGLY	OPTIMALISE	ORACULOUSNESSES
OPHIOMORPHS	OPISTHOGNATHISM	OPPOSITELY	OPTIMALISED	ORANGEADES
OPHIOPHAGOUS	OPISTHOGNATHOUS	OPPOSITENESS	OPTIMALISES	ORANGERIES
OPHIOPHILIST	OPISTHOGRAPH	OPPOSITENESSES	OPTIMALISING	ORANGEWOOD
OPHIOPHILISTS	OPISTHOGRAPHIC	OPPOSITION	OPTIMALITIES	ORANGEWOODS
OPHIUROIDS	OPISTHOGRAPHIES	OPPOSITIONAL	OPTIMALITY	ORANGUTANS
OPHTHALMIA	OPISTHOGRAPHS	OPPOSITIONIST	OPTIMALIZATION	ORATORIANS
OPHTHALMIAS	OPISTHOGRAPHY	OPPOSITIONISTS	OPTIMALIZATIONS	ORATORICAL
OPHTHALMIC	OPISTHOSOMA	OPPOSITIONLESS	OPTIMALIZE	ORATORICALLY
OPHTHALMIST	OPISTHOSOMATA	OPPOSITIONS	OPTIMALIZED	ORATRESSES
OPHTHALMISTS	OPISTHOTONIC	OPPOSITIVE	OPTIMALIZES	ORBICULARES
OPHTHALMITIS	OPISTHOTONOS	OPPRESSING	OPTIMALIZING	ORBICULARIS
OPHTHALMITISES	OPISTHOTONOSES	OPPRESSINGLY	OPTIMISATION	ORBICULARITIES
OPHTHALMOLOGIC	OPOBALSAMS	OPPRESSION	OPTIMISATIONS	ORBICULARITY
OPHTHALMOLOGIES	OPODELDOCS	OPPRESSIONS	OPTIMISERS	ORBICULARLY
OPHTHALMOLOGIST	OPOPANAXES	OPPRESSIVE	OPTIMISING	ORBICULATE
OPHTHALMOLOGY	OPOTHERAPIES	OPPRESSIVELY	OPTIMISTIC	ORBICULATED
OPHTHALMOMETER	OPOTHERAPY	OPPRESSIVENESS	OPTIMISTICAL	ORCHARDING
OPHTHALMOMETERS	OPPIGNERATE	OPPRESSORS	OPTIMISTICALLY	ORCHARDINGS
OPHTHALMOMETRY	OPPIGNERATED	OPPROBRIOUS	OPTIMIZATION	ORCHARDIST
OPHTHALMOPHOBIA	OPPIGNERATES	OPPROBRIOUSLY	OPTIMIZATIONS	ORCHARDISTS

O

ORCHARDMAN	ORDINAIRES	ORGANISMIC	ORIENTALISED	ORNAMENTATIONS
ORCHARDMEN	ORDINANCES	ORGANISMICALLY	ORIENTALISES	ORNAMENTED
ORCHESOGRAPHIES	ORDINARIER	ORGANISTRUM	ORIENTALISING	ORNAMENTER
ORCHESOGRAPHY	ORDINARIES	ORGANISTRUMS	ORIENTALISM	ORNAMENTERS
ORCHESTICS	ORDINARIEST	ORGANITIES	ORIENTALISMS	ORNAMENTING
ORCHESTRAL	ORDINARILY	ORGANIZABILITY	ORIENTALIST	ORNAMENTIST
ORCHESTRALIST	ORDINARINESS	ORGANIZABLE	ORIENTALISTS	ORNAMENTISTS
ORCHESTRALISTS	ORDINARINESSES	ORGANIZATION	ORIENTALITIES	ORNATENESS
ORCHESTRALLY	ORDINATELY	ORGANIZATIONAL	ORIENTALITY	ORNATENESSES
ORCHESTRAS	ORDINATING	ORGANIZATIONS	ORIENTALIZE	ORNERINESS
ORCHESTRATE	ORDINATION	ORGANIZERS	ORIENTALIZED	ORNERINESSES
ORCHESTRATED	ORDINATIONS	ORGANIZING	ORIENTALIZES	ORNITHICHNITE
ORCHESTRATER	ORDONNANCE	ORGANIZINGS	ORIENTALIZING	ORNITHICHNITES
ORCHESTRATERS	ORDONNANCES	ORGANOCHLORINE	ORIENTALLY	ORNITHINES
ORCHESTRATES	ORECCHIETTE	ORGANOCHLORINES	ORIENTATED	ORNITHISCHIAN
ORCHESTRATING	ORECCHIETTES	ORGANOGENESES	ORIENTATES	ORNITHISCHIANS
ORCHESTRATION	ORECCHIETTI	ORGANOGENESIS	ORIENTATING	ORNITHODELPHIAN
ORCHESTRATIONAL	OREOGRAPHIC	ORGANOGENETIC	ORIENTATION	ORNITHODELPHIC
ORCHESTRATIONS	OREOGRAPHICAL	ORGANOGENIES	ORIENTATIONAL	ORNITHODELPHOUS
ORCHESTRATOR	OREOGRAPHICALLY	ORGANOGENY	ORIENTATIONALLY	ORNITHOGALUM
ORCHESTRATORS	OREOGRAPHIES	ORGANOGRAM	ORIENTATIONS	ORNITHOGALUMS
ORCHESTRIC	OREOGRAPHY	ORGANOGRAMS	ORIENTATOR	ORNITHOLOGIC
ORCHESTRINA	OREOLOGICAL	ORGANOGRAPHIC	ORIENTATORS	ORNITHOLOGICAL
ORCHESTRINAS	OREOLOGIES	ORGANOGRAPHICAL	ORIENTEERED	ORNITHOLOGIES
ORCHESTRION	OREOLOGIST	ORGANOGRAPHIES	ORIENTEERING	ORNITHOLOGIST
ORCHESTRIONS	OREOLOGISTS	ORGANOGRAPHIST	ORIENTEERINGS	ORNITHOLOGISTS
ORCHIDACEOUS	OREPEARCHED	ORGANOGRAPHISTS	ORIENTEERS	ORNITHOLOGY
ORCHIDECTOMIES	OREPEARCHES	ORGANOGRAPHY	ORIFLAMMES	ORNITHOMANCIES
ORCHIDECTOMY	OREPEARCHING	ORGANOLEPTIC	ORIGINALITIES	ORNITHOMANCY
ORCHIDEOUS	ORGANELLES	ORGANOLOGICAL	ORIGINALITY	ORNITHOMANTIC
ORCHIDISTS	ORGANICALLY	ORGANOLOGIES	ORIGINALLY	ORNITHOMORPH
ORCHIDLIKE	ORGANICISM	ORGANOLOGIST	ORIGINATED	ORNITHOMORPHIC
ORCHIDOLOGIES	ORGANICISMS	ORGANOLOGISTS	ORIGINATES	ORNITHOMORPHS
ORCHIDOLOGIST	ORGANICIST	ORGANOLOGY	ORIGINATING	ORNITHOPHILIES
ORCHIDOLOGISTS	ORGANICISTIC	ORGANOMERCURIAL	ORIGINATION	ORNITHOPHILOUS
ORCHIDOLOGY	ORGANICISTS	ORGANOMETALLIC	ORIGINATIONS	ORNITHOPHILY
ORCHIDOMANIA	ORGANICITIES	ORGANOMETALLICS	ORIGINATIVE	ORNITHOPHOBIA
ORCHIDOMANIAC	ORGANICITY	ORGANOPHOSPHATE	ORIGINATIVELY	ORNITHOPHOBIAS
ORCHIDOMANIACS	ORGANISABILITY	ORGANOSOLS	ORIGINATOR	ORNITHOPOD
ORCHIDOMANIAS	ORGANISABLE	ORGANOTHERAPIES	ORIGINATORS	ORNITHOPODS
ORCHIECTOMIES	ORGANISATION	ORGANOTHERAPY	ORINASALLY	ORNITHOPTER
ORCHIECTOMY	ORGANISATIONAL	ORGANZINES	ORISMOLOGICAL	ORNITHOPTERS
ORCHITISES	ORGANISATIONS	ORGASMICALLY	ORISMOLOGIES	ORNITHORHYNCHUS
ORDAINABLE	ORGANISERS	ORGASTICALLY	ORISMOLOGY	ORNITHOSAUR
ORDAINMENT	ORGANISING	ORGIASTICALLY	ORNAMENTAL	ORNITHOSAURS
ORDAINMENTS	ORGANISINGS	ORICALCHES	ORNAMENTALLY	ORNITHOSCOPIES
ORDERLINESS	ORGANISMAL	ORICHALCEOUS	ORNAMENTALS	ORNITHOSCOPY
ORDERLINESSES	ORGANISMALLY	ORIENTALISE	ORNAMENTATION	ORNITHOSES

ORNITHOSIS	ORTHOCHROMATIC	ORTHOGONALIZES	ORTHOPRAXIS	ORYCTOLOGIES
OROBANCHACEOUS	ORTHOCHROMATISM	ORTHOGONALIZING	ORTHOPRAXY	ORYCTOLOGY
OROGENESES	ORTHOCLASE	ORTHOGONALLY	ORTHOPRISM	OSCILLATED
OROGENESIS	ORTHOCLASES	ORTHOGRADE	ORTHOPRISMS	OSCILLATES
OROGENETIC	ORTHOCLASTIC	ORTHOGRAPH	ORTHOPSYCHIATRY	OSCILLATING
OROGENETICALLY	ORTHOCOUSINS	ORTHOGRAPHER	ORTHOPTERA	OSCILLATION
OROGENICALLY	ORTHODIAGONAL	ORTHOGRAPHERS	ORTHOPTERAN	OSCILLATIONAL
OROGRAPHER	ORTHODIAGONALS	ORTHOGRAPHIC	ORTHOPTERANS	OSCILLATIONS
OROGRAPHERS	ORTHODONTIA	ORTHOGRAPHICAL	ORTHOPTERIST	OSCILLATIVE
OROGRAPHIC	ORTHODONTIAS	ORTHOGRAPHIES	ORTHOPTERISTS	OSCILLATOR
OROGRAPHICAL	ORTHODONTIC	ORTHOGRAPHIST	ORTHOPTEROID	OSCILLATORS
OROGRAPHICALLY	ORTHODONTICALLY	ORTHOGRAPHISTS	ORTHOPTEROIDS	OSCILLATORY
OROGRAPHIES	ORTHODONTICS	ORTHOGRAPHS	ORTHOPTEROLOGY	OSCILLOGRAM
OROLOGICAL	ORTHODONTIST	ORTHOGRAPHY	ORTHOPTERON	OSCILLOGRAMS
OROLOGICALLY	ORTHODONTISTS	ORTHOHYDROGEN	ORTHOPTEROUS	OSCILLOGRAPH
OROLOGISTS	ORTHODOXES	ORTHOHYDROGENS	ORTHOPTERS	OSCILLOGRAPHIC
OROMAXILLARY	ORTHODOXIES	ORTHOMOLECULAR	ORTHOPTICS	OSCILLOGRAPHIES
OROPHARYNGEAL	ORTHODOXLY	ORTHOMORPHIC	ORTHOPTIST	OSCILLOGRAPHS
OROPHARYNGES	ORTHODROMIC	ORTHONORMAL	ORTHOPTISTS	OSCILLOGRAPHY
OROPHARYNX	ORTHODROMICS	ORTHOPAEDIC	ORTHOPYROXENE	OSCILLOSCOPE
OROPHARYNXES	ORTHODROMIES	ORTHOPAEDICAL	ORTHOPYROXENES	OSCILLOSCOPES
OROROTUNDITIES	ORTHODROMY	ORTHOPAEDICALLY	ORTHOREXIA	OSCILLOSCOPIC
OROROTUNDITY	ORTHOEPICAL	ORTHOPAEDICS	ORTHOREXIAS	OSCITANCES
OROTUNDITIES	ORTHOEPICALLY	ORTHOPAEDIES	ORTHORHOMBIC	OSCITANCIES
OROTUNDITY	ORTHOEPIES	ORTHOPAEDIST	ORTHOSCOPE	OSCITANTLY
ORPHANAGES	ORTHOEPIST	ORTHOPAEDISTS	ORTHOSCOPES	OSCITATING
ORPHANHOOD	ORTHOEPISTS	ORTHOPAEDY	ORTHOSCOPIC	OSCITATION
ORPHANHOODS	ORTHOGENESES	ORTHOPEDIA	ORTHOSILICATE	OSCITATIONS
ORPHANISMS	ORTHOGENESIS	ORTHOPEDIAS	ORTHOSILICATES	OSCULATING
ORPHARIONS	ORTHOGENETIC	ORTHOPEDIC	ORTHOSILICIC	OSCULATION
ORPHEOREON	ORTHOGENIC	ORTHOPEDICAL	ORTHOSTATIC	OSCULATIONS
ORPHEOREONS	ORTHOGENICALLY	ORTHOPEDICALLY	ORTHOSTICHIES	OSCULATORIES
ORPHICALLY	ORTHOGENICS	ORTHOPEDICS	ORTHOSTICHOUS	OSCULATORY
ORRISROOTS	ORTHOGNATHIC	ORTHOPEDIES	ORTHOSTICHY	OSMETERIUM
ORTANIQUES	ORTHOGNATHIES	ORTHOPEDIST	ORTHOTISTS	OSMIDROSES
ORTHOBORATE	ORTHOGNATHISM	ORTHOPEDISTS	ORTHOTONES	OSMIDROSIS
ORTHOBORATES	ORTHOGNATHISMS	ORTHOPHOSPHATE	ORTHOTONESES	OSMIRIDIUM
ORTHOBORIC	ORTHOGNATHOUS	ORTHOPHOSPHATES	ORTHOTONESIS	OSMIRIDIUMS
ORTHOCAINE	ORTHOGNATHY	ORTHOPHOSPHORIC	ORTHOTONIC	OSMOLALITIES
ORTHOCAINES	ORTHOGONAL	ORTHOPHYRE	ORTHOTOPIC	OSMOLALITY
ORTHOCENTER	ORTHOGONALISE	ORTHOPHYRES	ORTHOTROPIC	OSMOLARITIES
ORTHOCENTERS	ORTHOGONALISED	ORTHOPHYRIC	ORTHOTROPIES	OSMOLARITY
ORTHOCENTRE	ORTHOGONALISES	ORTHOPINAKOID	ORTHOTROPISM	OSMOMETERS
ORTHOCENTRES	ORTHOGONALISING	ORTHOPINAKOIDS	ORTHOTROPISMS	OSMOMETRIC
ORTHOCEPHALIC	ORTHOGONALITIES	ORTHOPNOEA	ORTHOTROPOUS	OSMOMETRICALLY
ORTHOCEPHALIES	ORTHOGONALITY	ORTHOPNOEAS	ORTHOTROPY	OSMOMETRIES
ORTHOCEPHALOUS	ORTHOGONALIZE	ORTHOPRAXES	ORTHOTUNGSTIC	OSMOREGULATION
ORTHOCEPHALY	ORTHOGONALIZED	ORTHOPRAXIES	ORTHOVANADIC	OSMOREGULATIONS

OSMOREGULATORY	OSTEOGENESES	OSTRACISER	OTOSCLEROSES	OUTBLUFFED
OSMOTICALLY	OSTEOGENESIS	OSTRACISERS	OTOSCLEROSIS	OUTBLUFFING
OSMUNDINES	OSTEOGENETIC	OSTRACISES	OTOSCOPIES	OUTBLUSHED
OSSIFEROUS	OSTEOGENIC	OSTRACISING	OTOTOXICITIES	OUTBLUSHES
OSSIFICATION	OSTEOGENIES	OSTRACISMS	OTOTOXICITY	OUTBLUSHING
OSSIFICATIONS	OSTEOGENOUS	OSTRACIZABLE	OTTERHOUND	OUTBLUSTER
OSSIFRAGAS	OSTEOGRAPHIES	OSTRACIZED	OTTERHOUNDS	OUTBLUSTERED
OSSIFRAGES	OSTEOGRAPHY	OSTRACIZER	OTTRELITES	OUTBLUSTERING
OSSIVOROUS	OSTEOLOGICAL	OSTRACIZERS	OUANANICHE	OUTBLUSTERS
OSTEICHTHYAN	OSTEOLOGICALLY	OSTRACIZES	OUANANICHES	OUTBOASTED
OSTEICHTHYANS	OSTEOLOGIES	OSTRACIZING	OUBLIETTES	OUTBOASTING
OSTEITIDES	OSTEOLOGIST	OSTRACODAN	OUGHTLINGS	OUTBRAGGED
OSTEITISES	OSTEOLOGISTS	OSTRACODERM	OUGHTNESSES	OUTBRAGGING
OSTENSIBILITIES	OSTEOMALACIA	OSTRACODERMS	OUROBOROSES	OUTBRAVING
OSTENSIBILITY	OSTEOMALACIAL	OSTRACODES	OUROLOGIES	OUTBRAWLED
OSTENSIBLE	OSTEOMALACIAS	OSTRACODOUS	OUROSCOPIES	OUTBRAWLING
OSTENSIBLY	OSTEOMALACIC	OSTREACEOUS	OUTACHIEVE	OUTBRAZENED
OSTENSIVELY	OSTEOMYELITIS	OSTREICULTURE	OUTACHIEVED	OUTBRAZENING
OSTENSORIA	OSTEOMYELITISES	OSTREICULTURES	OUTACHIEVES	OUTBRAZENS
OSTENSORIES	OSTEOPATHIC	OSTREICULTURIST	OUTACHIEVING	OUTBREAKING
OSTENSORIUM	OSTEOPATHICALLY	OSTREOPHAGE	OUTARGUING	OUTBREATHE
OSTENTATION	OSTEOPATHIES	OSTREOPHAGES	OUTBACKERS	OUTBREATHED
OSTENTATIONS	OSTEOPATHIST	OSTREOPHAGIES	OUTBALANCE	OUTBREATHES
OSTENTATIOUS	OSTEOPATHISTS	OSTREOPHAGOUS	OUTBALANCED	OUTBREATHING
OSTENTATIOUSLY	OSTEOPATHS	OSTREOPHAGY	OUTBALANCES	OUTBREEDING
OSTEOARTHRITIC	OSTEOPATHY	OSTRICHISM	OUTBALANCING	OUTBREEDINGS
OSTEOARTHRITICS	OSTEOPETROSES	OSTRICHISMS	OUTBARGAIN	OUTBRIBING
OSTEOARTHRITIS	OSTEOPETROSIS	OSTRICHLIKE	OUTBARGAINED	OUTBUILDING
OSTEOARTHROSES	OSTEOPHYTE	OTHERGATES	OUTBARGAINING	OUTBUILDINGS
OSTEOARTHROSIS	OSTEOPHYTES	OTHERGUESS	OUTBARGAINS	OUTBULGING
OSTEOBLAST	OSTEOPHYTIC	OTHERNESSES	OUTBARKING	OUTBULKING
OSTEOBLASTIC	OSTEOPLASTIC	OTHERWHERE	OUTBARRING	OUTBULLIED
OSTEOBLASTS	OSTEOPLASTIES	OTHERWHILE	OUTBAWLING	OUTBULLIES
OSTEOCLASES	OSTEOPLASTY	OTHERWHILES	OUTBEAMING	OUTBULLYING
OSTEOCLASIS	OSTEOPOROSES	OTHERWORLD	OUTBEGGING	OUTBURNING
OSTEOCLAST	OSTEOPOROSIS	OTHERWORLDISH	OUTBIDDERS	OUTBURSTING
OSTEOCLASTIC	OSTEOPOROTIC	OTHERWORLDLIER	OUTBIDDING	OUTCALLING
OSTEOCLASTS	OSTEOSARCOMA	OTHERWORLDLIEST	OUTBITCHED	OUTCAPERED
OSTEOCOLLA	OSTEOSARCOMAS	OTHERWORLDLY	OUTBITCHES	OUTCAPERING
OSTEOCOLLAS	OSTEOSARCOMATA	OTHERWORLDS	OUTBITCHING	OUTCASTEING
OSTEOCYTES	OSTEOSISES	OTIOSENESS	OUTBLAZING	OUTCASTING
OSTEODERMAL	OSTEOTOMES	OTIOSENESSES	OUTBLEATED	OUTCATCHES
OSTEODERMATOUS	OSTEOTOMIES	OTIOSITIES	OUTBLEATING	OUTCATCHING
OSTEODERMIC	OSTLERESSES	OTOLARYNGOLOGY	OUTBLESSED	OUTCAVILED
OSTEODERMOUS	OSTRACEANS	OTOLOGICAL	OUTBLESSES	OUTCAVILING
OSTEODERMS	OSTRACEOUS	OTOLOGISTS	OUTBLESSING	OUTCAVILLED
OSTEOFIBROSES	OSTRACISABLE	OTOPLASTIES	OUTBLOOMED	OUTCAVILLING
OSTEOFIBROSIS	OSTRACISED	OTORRHOEAS	OUTBLOOMING	OUTCHARGED

OUTCHARGES	OUTDEBATES	OUTFEASTING	OUTGENERALLING	OUTINTRIGUES
OUTCHARGING	OUTDEBATING	OUTFEELING	OUTGENERALS	OUTINTRIGUING
OUTCHARMED	OUTDELIVER	OUTFENCING	OUTGIVINGS	OUTJESTING
OUTCHARMING	OUTDELIVERED	OUTFIELDER	OUTGLARING	OUTJETTING
OUTCHEATED	OUTDELIVERING	OUTFIELDERS	OUTGLEAMED	OUTJETTINGS
OUTCHEATING	OUTDELIVERS	OUTFIGHTING	OUTGLEAMING	OUTJINXING
OUTCHIDDEN	OUTDESIGNED	OUTFIGHTINGS	OUTGLITTER	OUTJOCKEYED
OUTCHIDING	OUTDESIGNING	OUTFIGURED	OUTGLITTERED	OUTJOCKEYING
OUTCLASSED	OUTDESIGNS	OUTFIGURES	OUTGLITTERING	OUTJOCKEYS
OUTCLASSES	OUTDISTANCE	OUTFIGURING	OUTGLITTERS	OUTJUGGLED
OUTCLASSING	OUTDISTANCED	OUTFINDING	OUTGLOWING	OUTJUGGLES
OUTCLIMBED	OUTDISTANCES	OUTFISHING	OUTGNAWING	OUTJUGGLING
OUTCLIMBING	OUTDISTANCING	OUTFITTERS	OUTGOINGNESS	OUTJUMPING
OUTCOACHED	OUTDODGING	OUTFITTING	OUTGOINGNESSES	OUTJUTTING
OUTCOACHES	OUTDOORSIER	OUTFITTINGS	OUTGRINNED	OUTJUTTINGS
OUTCOACHING	OUTDOORSIEST	OUTFLANKED	OUTGRINNING	OUTKEEPING
OUTCOMPETE	OUTDOORSMAN	OUTFLANKING	OUTGROSSED	OUTKICKING
OUTCOMPETED	OUTDOORSMANSHIP	OUTFLASHED	OUTGROSSES	OUTKILLING
OUTCOMPETES	OUTDOORSMEN	OUTFLASHES	OUTGROSSING	OUTKISSING
OUTCOMPETING	OUTDRAGGED	OUTFLASHING	OUTGROWING	OUTLANDERS
OUTCOOKING	OUTDRAGGING	OUTFLINGING	OUTGROWTHS	OUTLANDISH
OUTCOUNTED	OUTDRAWING	OUTFLOATED	OUTGUESSED	OUTLANDISHLY
OUTCOUNTING	OUTDREAMED	OUTFLOATING	OUTGUESSES	OUTLANDISHNESS
OUTCRAFTIED	OUTDREAMING	OUTFLOWING	OUTGUESSING	OUTLASHING
OUTCRAFTIES	OUTDRESSED	OUTFLOWINGS	OUTGUIDING	OUTLASTING
OUTCRAFTYING	OUTDRESSES	OUTFLUSHED	OUTGUNNING	OUTLAUGHED
OUTCRAWLED	OUTDRESSING	OUTFLUSHES	OUTGUSHING	OUTLAUGHING
OUTCRAWLING	OUTDRINKING	OUTFLUSHING	OUTHANDLED	OUTLAUNCED
OUTCROPPED	OUTDRIVING	OUTFOOLING	OUTHANDLES	OUTLAUNCES
OUTCROPPING	OUTDROPPED	OUTFOOTING	OUTHANDLING	OUTLAUNCHED
OUTCROPPINGS	OUTDROPPING	OUTFROWNED	OUTHARBORS	OUTLAUNCHES
OUTCROSSED	OUTDUELING	OUTFROWNING	OUTHAULERS	OUTLAUNCHING
OUTCROSSES	OUTDUELLED	OUTFUMBLED	OUTHEARING	OUTLAUNCING
OUTCROSSING	OUTDUELLING	OUTFUMBLES	OUTHITTING	OUTLAWRIES
OUTCROSSINGS	OUTDWELLED	OUTFUMBLING	OUTHOMERED	OUTLEADING
OUTCROWDED	OUTDWELLING	OUTGAINING	OUTHOMERING	OUTLEAPING
OUTCROWDING	OUTEARNING	OUTGALLOPED	OUTHOWLING	OUTLEARNED
OUTCROWING	OUTECHOING	OUTGALLOPING	OUTHUMORED	OUTLEARNING
OUTCURSING	OUTERCOATS	OUTGALLOPS	OUTHUMORING	OUTLODGING
OUTDACIOUS	OUTERCOURSE	OUTGAMBLED	OUTHUMOURED	OUTLODGINGS
OUTDANCING	OUTERCOURSES	OUTGAMBLES	OUTHUMOURING	OUTLOOKING
OUTDATEDLY	OUTERWEARS	OUTGAMBLING	OUTHUMOURS	OUTLUSTERED
OUTDATEDNESS	OUTFABLING	OUTGASSING	OUTHUNTING	OUTLUSTERING
OUTDATEDNESSES	OUTFANGTHIEF	OUTGASSINGS	OUTHUSTLED	OUTLUSTERS
OUTDAZZLED	OUTFANGTHIEVES	OUTGENERAL	OUTHUSTLES	OUTLUSTRED
OUTDAZZLES	OUTFASTING	OUTGENERALED	OUTHUSTLING	OUTLUSTRES
OUTDAZZLING	OUTFAWNING	OUTGENERALING	OUTINTRIGUE	OUTLUSTRING
OUTDEBATED	OUTFEASTED	OUTGENERALLED	OUTINTRIGUED	OUTMANEUVER

O

OUTMANEUVERED	OUTORGANIZES	OUTPOURING	OUTREASONS	OUTSCHEMING
OUTMANEUVERING	OUTORGANIZING	OUTPOURINGS	OUTREBOUND	OUTSCOLDED
OUTMANEUVERS	OUTPAINTED	OUTPOWERED	OUTREBOUNDED	OUTSCOLDING
OUTMANIPULATE	OUTPAINTING	OUTPOWERING	OUTREBOUNDING	OUTSCOOPED
OUTMANIPULATED	OUTPASSING	OUTPRAYING	OUTREBOUNDS	OUTSCOOPING
OUTMANIPULATES	OUTPASSION	OUTPREACHED	OUTRECKONED	OUTSCORING
OUTMANIPULATING	OUTPASSIONED	OUTPREACHES	OUTRECKONING	OUTSCORNED
OUTMANNING	OUTPASSIONING	OUTPREACHING	OUTRECKONS	OUTSCORNING
OUTMANOEUVRE	OUTPASSIONS	OUTPREENED	OUTRECUIDANCE	OUTSCREAMED
OUTMANOEUVRED	OUTPATIENT	OUTPREENING	OUTRECUIDANCES	OUTSCREAMING
OUTMANOEUVRES	OUTPATIENTS	OUTPRESSED	OUTREDDENED	OUTSCREAMS
OUTMANOEUVRING	OUTPEEPING	OUTPRESSES	OUTREDDENING	OUTSELLING
OUTMANTLED	OUTPEERING	OUTPRESSING	OUTREDDENS	OUTSERVING
OUTMANTLES	OUTPEOPLED	OUTPRICING	OUTREDDING	OUTSETTING
OUTMANTLING	OUTPEOPLES	OUTPRIZING	OUTREDDINGS	OUTSETTINGS
OUTMARCHED	OUTPEOPLING	OUTPRODUCE	OUTREIGNED	OUTSETTLEMENT
OUTMARCHES	OUTPERFORM	OUTPRODUCED	OUTREIGNING	OUTSETTLEMENTS
OUTMARCHING	OUTPERFORMED	OUTPRODUCES	OUTRELIEFS	OUTSHAMING
OUTMARRIAGE	OUTPERFORMING	OUTPRODUCING	OUTREPRODUCE	OUTSHINING
OUTMARRIAGES	OUTPERFORMS	OUTPROMISE	OUTREPRODUCED	OUTSHOOTING
OUTMASTERED	OUTPITCHED	OUTPROMISED	OUTREPRODUCES	OUTSHOUTED
OUTMASTERING	OUTPITCHES	OUTPROMISES	OUTREPRODUCING	OUTSHOUTING
OUTMASTERS	OUTPITCHING	OUTPROMISING	OUTRIDINGS	OUTSIDERNESS
OUTMATCHED	OUTPITYING	OUTPSYCHED	OUTRIGGERS	OUTSIDERNESSES
OUTMATCHES	OUTPLACEMENT	OUTPSYCHING	OUTRIGGING	OUTSINGING
OUTMATCHING	OUTPLACEMENTS	OUTPULLING	OUTRIGGINGS	OUTSINNING
OUTMEASURE	OUTPLACERS	OUTPUNCHED	OUTRIGHTLY	OUTSITTING
OUTMEASURED	OUTPLACING	OUTPUNCHES	OUTRINGING	OUTSKATING
OUTMEASURES	OUTPLANNED	OUTPUNCHING	OUTRIVALED	OUTSLEEPING
OUTMEASURING	OUTPLANNING	OUTPURSUED	OUTRIVALING	OUTSLICKED
OUTMODEDLY	OUTPLAYING	OUTPURSUES	OUTRIVALLED	OUTSLICKING
OUTMODEDNESS	OUTPLODDED	OUTPURSUING	OUTRIVALLING	OUTSMARTED
OUTMODEDNESSES	OUTPLODDING	OUTPUSHING	OUTROARING	OUTSMARTING
OUTMUSCLED	OUTPLOTTED	OUTPUTTING	OUTROCKING	OUTSMELLED
OUTMUSCLES	OUTPLOTTING	OUTQUARTERS	OUTROLLING	OUTSMELLING
OUTMUSCLING	OUTPOINTED	OUTQUOTING	OUTROOPERS	OUTSMILING
OUTNIGHTED	OUTPOINTING	OUTRAGEOUS	OUTROOTING	OUTSMOKING
OUTNIGHTING	OUTPOLITICK	OUTRAGEOUSLY	OUTRUNNERS	OUTSNORING
OUTNUMBERED	OUTPOLITICKED	OUTRAGEOUSNESS	OUTRUNNING	OUTSOARING
OUTNUMBERING	OUTPOLITICKING	OUTRAISING	OUTRUSHING	OUTSOURCED
OUTNUMBERS	OUTPOLITICKS	OUTRANGING	OUTSAILING	OUTSOURCES
OUTOFFICES	OUTPOLLING	OUTRANKING	OUTSAVORED	OUTSOURCING
OUTORGANISE	OUTPOPULATE	OUTREACHED	OUTSAVORING	OUTSOURCINGS
OUTORGANISED	OUTPOPULATED	OUTREACHES	OUTSAVOURED	OUTSPANNED
OUTORGANISES	OUTPOPULATES	OUTREACHING	OUTSAVOURING	OUTSPANNING
OUTORGANISING	OUTPOPULATING	OUTREADING	OUTSAVOURS	OUTSPARKLE
OUTORGANIZE	OUTPORTERS	OUTREASONED	OUTSCHEMED	OUTSPARKLED
OUTORGANIZED	OUTPOURERS	OUTREASONING	OUTSCHEMES	OUTSPARKLES

OUTSPARKLING	OUTSTRIPPING	OUTTRAVELED	OUTWORKERS	OVERACHIEVING
OUTSPEAKING	OUTSTRIVEN	OUTTRAVELING	OUTWORKING	OVERACTING
OUTSPECKLE	OUTSTRIVES	OUTTRAVELLED	OUTWORTHED	OVERACTION
OUTSPECKLES	OUTSTRIVING	OUTTRAVELLING	OUTWORTHING	OVERACTIONS
OUTSPEEDED	OUTSTROKES	OUTTRAVELS	OUTWRESTED	OVERACTIVE
OUTSPEEDING	OUTSTUDIED	OUTTRICKED	OUTWRESTING	OVERACTIVITIES
OUTSPELLED	OUTSTUDIES	OUTTRICKING	OUTWRESTLE	OVERACTIVITY
OUTSPELLING	OUTSTUDYING	OUTTROTTED	OUTWRESTLED	OVERADJUSTMENT
OUTSPENDING	OUTSTUNTED	OUTTROTTING	OUTWRESTLES	OVERADJUSTMENTS
OUTSPOKENLY	OUTSTUNTING	OUTTRUMPED	OUTWRESTLING	OVERADVERTISE
OUTSPOKENNESS	OUTSULKING	OUTTRUMPING	OUTWRITING	OVERADVERTISED
OUTSPOKENNESSES	OUTSUMMING	OUTVALUING	OUTWRITTEN	OVERADVERTISES
OUTSPORTED	OUTSWEARING	OUTVAUNTED	OUTWROUGHT	OVERADVERTISING
OUTSPORTING	OUTSWEEPING	OUTVAUNTING	OUTYELLING	OVERADVERTIZE
OUTSPREADING	OUTSWEETEN	OUTVENOMED	OUTYELPING	OVERADVERTIZED
OUTSPREADS	OUTSWEETENED	OUTVENOMING	OUTYIELDED	OVERADVERTIZES
OUTSPRINGING	OUTSWEETENING	OUTVILLAIN	OUTYIELDING	OVERADVERTIZING
OUTSPRINGS	OUTSWEETENS	OUTVILLAINED	OUVIRANDRA	OVERAGGRESSIVE
OUTSPRINTED	OUTSWELLED	OUTVILLAINING	OUVIRANDRAS	OVERAMBITIOUS
OUTSPRINTING	OUTSWELLING	OUTVILLAINS	OVALBUMINS	OVERAMPLIFIED
OUTSPRINTS	OUTSWIMMING	OUTVOICING	OVALNESSES	OVERANALYSE
OUTSTANDING	OUTSWINGER	OUTWAITING	OVARIECTOMIES	OVERANALYSED
OUTSTANDINGLY	OUTSWINGERS	OUTWALKING	OVARIECTOMISED	OVERANALYSES
OUTSTARING	OUTSWINGING	OUTWARDNESS	OVARIECTOMIZED	OVERANALYSING
OUTSTARTED	OUTSWOLLEN	OUTWARDNESSES	OVARIECTOMY	OVERANALYSIS
OUTSTARTING	OUTTALKING	OUTWARRING	OVARIOTOMIES	OVERANALYTICAL
OUTSTATING	OUTTASKING	OUTWASTING	OVARIOTOMIST	OVERANALYZE
OUTSTATION	OUTTELLING	OUTWATCHED	OVARIOTOMISTS	OVERANALYZED
OUTSTATIONS	OUTTHANKED	OUTWATCHES	OVARIOTOMY	OVERANALYZES
OUTSTAYING	OUTTHANKING	OUTWATCHING	OVARITIDES	OVERANALYZING
OUTSTEERED	OUTTHIEVED	OUTWEARIED	OVARITISES	OVERANXIETIES
OUTSTEERING	OUTTHIEVES	OUTWEARIES	OVERABOUND	OVERANXIETY
OUTSTEPPED	OUTTHIEVING	OUTWEARING	OVERABOUNDED	OVERANXIOUS
OUTSTEPPING	OUTTHINKING	OUTWEARYING	OVERABOUNDING	OVERAPPLICATION
OUTSTRAINED	OUTTHOUGHT	OUTWEEDING	OVERABOUNDS	OVERARCHED
OUTSTRAINING	OUTTHROBBED	OUTWEEPING	OVERABSTRACT	OVERARCHES
OUTSTRAINS	OUTTHROBBING	OUTWEIGHED	OVERABUNDANCE	OVERARCHING
OUTSTRETCH	OUTTHROWING	OUTWEIGHING	OVERABUNDANCES	OVERARMING
OUTSTRETCHED	OUTTHRUSTED	OUTWELLING	OVERABUNDANT	OVERAROUSAL
OUTSTRETCHES	OUTTHRUSTING	OUTWHIRLED	OVERACCENTUATE	OVERAROUSALS
OUTSTRETCHING	OUTTHRUSTS	OUTWHIRLING	OVERACCENTUATED	OVERARRANGE
OUTSTRIDDEN	OUTTONGUED	OUTWICKING	OVERACCENTUATES	OVERARRANGED
OUTSTRIDED	OUTTONGUES	OUTWILLING	OVERACHIEVE	OVERARRANGES
OUTSTRIDES	OUTTONGUING	OUTWINDING	OVERACHIEVED	OVERARRANGING
OUTSTRIDING	OUTTOPPING	OUTWINGING	OVERACHIEVEMENT	OVERARTICULATE
OUTSTRIKES	OUTTOWERED	OUTWINNING	OVERACHIEVER	OVERARTICULATED
OUTSTRIKING	OUTTOWERING	OUTWISHING	OVERACHIEVERS	OVERARTICULATES
OUTSTRIPPED	OUTTRADING	OUTWITTING	OVERACHIEVES	OVERASSERT

O

OVERASSERTED	OVERBORROW	OVERBUSIES	OVERCLAIMED	OVERCOMMUNICATE
OVERASSERTING	OVERBORROWED	OVERBUSYING	OVERCLAIMING	OVERCOMPENSATE
OVERASSERTION	OVERBORROWING	OVERBUYING	OVERCLAIMS	OVERCOMPENSATED
OVERASSERTIONS	OVERBORROWS	OVERCALLED	OVERCLASSES	OVERCOMPENSATES
OVERASSERTIVE	OVERBOUGHT	OVERCALLING	OVERCLASSIFIED	OVERCOMPLEX
OVERASSERTS	OVERBOUNDED	OVERCANOPIED	OVERCLASSIFIES	OVERCOMPLIANCE
OVERASSESSMENT	OVERBOUNDING	OVERCANOPIES	OVERCLASSIFY	OVERCOMPLIANCES
OVERASSESSMENTS	OVERBOUNDS	OVERCANOPY	OVERCLASSIFYING	OVERCOMPLICATE
OVERATTENTION	OVERBRAKED	OVERCANOPYING	OVERCLEANED	OVERCOMPLICATED
OVERATTENTIONS	OVERBRAKES	OVERCAPACITIES	OVERCLEANING	OVERCOMPLICATES
OVERATTENTIVE	OVERBRAKING	OVERCAPACITY	OVERCLEANS	OVERCOMPRESS
OVERBAKING	OVERBREATHING	OVERCAPITALISE	OVERCLEARED	OVERCOMPRESSED
OVERBALANCE	OVERBREATHINGS	OVERCAPITALISED	OVERCLEARING	OVERCOMPRESSES
OVERBALANCED	OVERBREEDING	OVERCAPITALISES	OVERCLEARS	OVERCOMPRESSING
OVERBALANCES	OVERBREEDS	OVERCAPITALIZE	OVERCLEVER	OVERCONCERN
OVERBALANCING	OVERBRIDGE	OVERCAPITALIZED	OVERCLOCKED	OVERCONCERNED
OVERBEARING	OVERBRIDGED	OVERCAPITALIZES	OVERCLOCKER	OVERCONCERNING
OVERBEARINGLY	OVERBRIDGES	OVERCAREFUL	OVERCLOCKERS	OVERCONCERNS
OVERBEARINGNESS	OVERBRIDGING	OVERCARRIED	OVERCLOCKING	OVERCONFIDENCE
OVERBEATEN	OVERBRIEFED	OVERCARRIES	OVERCLOCKINGS	OVERCONFIDENCES
OVERBEATING	OVERBRIEFING	OVERCARRYING	OVERCLOCKS	OVERCONFIDENT
OVERBEJEWELED	OVERBRIEFS	OVERCASTED	OVERCLOUDED	OVERCONFIDENTLY
OVERBEJEWELLED	OVERBRIGHT	OVERCASTING	OVERCLOUDING	OVERCONSCIOUS
OVERBETTED	OVERBRIMMED	OVERCASTINGS	OVERCLOUDS	OVERCONSTRUCT
OVERBETTING	OVERBRIMMING	OVERCATCHES	OVERCLOYED	OVERCONSTRUCTED
OVERBETTINGS	OVERBROWED	OVERCATCHING	OVERCLOYING	OVERCONSTRUCTS
OVERBIDDEN	OVERBROWING	OVERCAUGHT	OVERCLUBBED	OVERCONSUME
OVERBIDDER	OVERBROWSE	OVERCAUTION	OVERCLUBBING	OVERCONSUMED
OVERBIDDERS	OVERBROWSED	OVERCAUTIONS	OVERCOACHED	OVERCONSUMES
OVERBIDDING	OVERBROWSES	OVERCAUTIOUS	OVERCOACHES	OVERCONSUMING
OVERBIDDINGS	OVERBROWSING	OVERCAUTIOUSLY	OVERCOACHING	OVERCONSUMPTION
OVERBILLED	OVERBRUTAL	OVERCENTRALISE	OVERCOATING	OVERCONTROL
OVERBILLING	OVERBUILDING	OVERCENTRALISED	OVERCOATINGS	OVERCONTROLLED
OVERBLANKET	OVERBUILDS	OVERCENTRALISES	OVERCOLORED	OVERCONTROLLING
OVERBLANKETS	OVERBULKED	OVERCENTRALIZE	OVERCOLORING	OVERCONTROLS
OVERBLEACH	OVERBULKING	OVERCENTRALIZED	OVERCOLORS	OVERCOOKED
OVERBLEACHED	OVERBURDEN	OVERCENTRALIZES	OVERCOLOUR	OVERCOOKING
OVERBLEACHES	OVERBURDENED	OVERCHARGE	OVERCOLOURED	OVERCOOLED
OVERBLEACHING	OVERBURDENING	OVERCHARGED	OVERCOLOURING	OVERCOOLING
OVERBLOUSE	OVERBURDENS	OVERCHARGES	OVERCOLOURS	OVERCORRECT
OVERBLOUSES	OVERBURDENSOME	OVERCHARGING	OVERCOMERS	OVERCORRECTED
OVERBLOWING	OVERBURNED	OVERCHARGINGS	OVERCOMING	OVERCORRECTING
OVERBOILED	OVERBURNING	OVERCHECKS	OVERCOMMIT	OVERCORRECTION
OVERBOILING	OVERBURTHEN	OVERCHILLED	OVERCOMMITMENT	OVERCORRECTIONS
OVERBOLDLY	OVERBURTHENED	OVERCHILLING	OVERCOMMITMENTS	OVERCORRECTS
OVERBOOKED	OVERBURTHENING	OVERCHILLS	OVERCOMMITS	OVERCOUNTED
OVERBOOKING	OVERBURTHENS	OVERCIVILISED	OVERCOMMITTED	OVERCOUNTING
OVERBOOKINGS	OVERBUSIED	OVERCIVILIZED	OVERCOMMITTING	OVERCOUNTS

OVERCOVERED	OVERDEVELOPS	OVERDRIVING	OVEREMPLOYMENT	OVEREXPANDED
OVERCOVERING	OVERDEVIATE	OVERDRYING	OVEREMPLOYMENTS	OVEREXPANDING
OVERCOVERS	OVERDEVIATED	OVERDUBBED	OVERENAMORED	OVEREXPANDS
OVERCRAMMED	OVERDEVIATES	OVERDUBBING	OVERENAMOURED	OVEREXPANSION
OVERCRAMMING	OVERDEVIATING	OVERDUSTED	OVERENCOURAGE	OVEREXPANSIONS
OVERCRAMMINGS	OVERDIAGNOSES	OVERDUSTING	OVERENCOURAGED	OVEREXPECTATION
OVERCRAWED	OVERDIAGNOSIS	OVERDYEING	OVERENCOURAGES	OVEREXPLAIN
OVERCRAWING	OVERDILUTED	OVEREAGERNESS	OVERENCOURAGING	OVEREXPLAINED
OVERCREDULITIES	OVERDIRECT	OVEREAGERNESSES	OVERENERGETIC	OVEREXPLAINING
OVERCREDULITY	OVERDIRECTED	OVEREARNEST	OVERENGINEER	OVEREXPLAINS
OVERCREDULOUS	OVERDIRECTING	OVEREASIER	OVERENGINEERED	OVEREXPLICIT
OVERCRITICAL	OVERDIRECTS	OVEREASIEST	OVERENGINEERING	OVEREXPLOIT
OVERCROPPED	OVERDISCOUNT	OVEREATERS	OVERENGINEERS	OVEREXPLOITED
OVERCROPPING	OVERDISCOUNTED	OVEREATING	OVERENROLLED	OVEREXPLOITING
OVERCROWDED	OVERDISCOUNTING	OVEREATINGS	OVERENTERTAINED	OVEREXPLOITS
OVERCROWDING	OVERDISCOUNTS	OVEREDITED	OVERENTHUSIASM	OVEREXPOSE
OVERCROWDINGS	OVERDIVERSITIES	OVEREDITING	OVERENTHUSIASMS	OVEREXPOSED
OVERCROWDS	OVERDIVERSITY	OVEREDUCATE	OVEREQUIPPED	OVEREXPOSES
OVERCROWED	OVERDOCUMENT	OVEREDUCATED	OVEREQUIPPING	OVEREXPOSING
OVERCROWING	OVERDOCUMENTED	OVEREDUCATES	OVEREQUIPS	OVEREXPOSURE
OVERCULTIVATION	OVERDOCUMENTING	OVEREDUCATING	OVERESTIMATE	OVEREXPOSURES
OVERCURING	OVERDOCUMENTS	OVEREDUCATION	OVERESTIMATED	OVEREXTEND
OVERCUTTING	OVERDOMINANCE	OVEREDUCATIONS	OVERESTIMATES	OVEREXTENDED
OVERCUTTINGS	OVERDOMINANCES	OVEREFFUSIVE	OVERESTIMATING	OVEREXTENDING
OVERDARING	OVERDOMINANT	OVEREGGING	OVERESTIMATION	OVEREXTENDS
OVERDECKED	OVERDOSAGE	OVERELABORATE	OVERESTIMATIONS	OVEREXTENSION
OVERDECKING	OVERDOSAGES	OVERELABORATED	OVEREVALUATION	OVEREXTENSIONS
OVERDECORATE	OVERDOSING	OVERELABORATES	OVEREVALUATIONS	OVEREXTRACTION
OVERDECORATED	OVERDRAFTS	OVERELABORATING	OVEREXAGGERATE	OVEREXTRACTIONS
OVERDECORATES	OVERDRAMATIC	OVERELABORATION	OVEREXAGGERATED	OVEREXTRAVAGANT
OVERDECORATING	OVERDRAMATISE	OVEREMBELLISH	OVEREXAGGERATES	OVEREXUBERANT
OVERDECORATION	OVERDRAMATISED	OVEREMBELLISHED	OVEREXCITABLE	OVEREYEING
OVERDECORATIONS	OVERDRAMATISES	OVEREMBELLISHES	OVEREXCITE	OVERFACILE
OVERDEEPENING	OVERDRAMATISING	OVEREMOTED	OVEREXCITED	OVERFALLEN
OVERDELICATE	OVERDRAMATIZE	OVEREMOTES	OVEREXCITEMENT	OVERFALLING
OVERDEMANDING	OVERDRAMATIZED	OVEREMOTING	OVEREXCITEMENTS	OVERFAMILIAR
OVERDEPENDENCE	OVERDRAMATIZES	OVEREMOTIONAL	OVEREXCITES	OVERFAMILIARITY
OVERDEPENDENCES	OVERDRAMATIZING	OVEREMPHASES	OVEREXCITING	OVERFASTIDIOUS
OVERDEPENDENT	OVERDRAUGHT	OVEREMPHASIS	OVEREXERCISE	OVERFATIGUE
OVERDESIGN	OVERDRAUGHTS	OVEREMPHASISE	OVEREXERCISED	OVERFATIGUED
OVERDESIGNED	OVERDRAWING	OVEREMPHASISED	OVEREXERCISES	OVERFATIGUES
OVERDESIGNING	OVERDRESSED	OVEREMPHASISES	OVEREXERCISING	OVERFATIGUING
OVERDESIGNS	OVERDRESSES	OVEREMPHASISING	OVEREXERTED	OVERFAVORED
OVERDETERMINED	OVERDRESSING	OVEREMPHASIZE	OVEREXERTING	OVERFAVORING
OVERDEVELOP	OVERDRINKING	OVEREMPHASIZED	OVEREXERTION	OVERFAVORS
OVERDEVELOPED	OVERDRINKS	OVEREMPHASIZES	OVEREXERTIONS	OVERFAVOUR
OVERDEVELOPING	OVERDRIVEN	OVEREMPHASIZING	OVEREXERTS	OVERFAVOURED
OVERDEVELOPMENT	OVERDRIVES	OVEREMPHATIC	OVEREXPAND	OVERFAVOURING

O

OVERFAVOURS	OVERFORWARD	OVERGLAMORISES	OVERGROWING	OVERHONOURED
OVERFEARED	OVERFORWARDNESS	OVERGLAMORISING	OVERGROWTH	OVERHONOURING
OVERFEARING	OVERFRAUGHT	OVERGLAMORIZE	OVERGROWTHS	OVERHONOURS
OVERFEEDING	OVERFREEDOM	OVERGLAMORIZED	OVERHAILED	OVERHOPING
OVERFEEDINGS	OVERFREEDOMS	OVERGLAMORIZES	OVERHAILES	OVERHUNTED
OVERFERTILISE	OVERFREELY	OVERGLAMORIZING	OVERHAILING	OVERHUNTING
OVERFERTILISED	OVERFREIGHT	OVERGLANCE	OVERHALING	OVERHUNTINGS
OVERFERTILISES	OVERFREIGHTING	OVERGLANCED	OVERHANDED	OVERHYPING
OVERFERTILISING	OVERFREIGHTS	OVERGLANCES	OVERHANDING	OVERIDEALISE
OVERFERTILIZE	OVERFULFIL	OVERGLANCING	OVERHANDLE	OVERIDEALISED
OVERFERTILIZED	OVERFULFILL	OVERGLAZED	OVERHANDLED	OVERIDEALISES
OVERFERTILIZES	OVERFULFILLED	OVERGLAZES	OVERHANDLES	OVERIDEALISING
OVERFERTILIZING	OVERFULFILLING	OVERGLAZING	OVERHANDLING	OVERIDEALIZE
OVERFILLED	OVERFULFILLS	OVERGLOOMED	OVERHANGING	OVERIDEALIZED
OVERFILLING	OVERFULFILS	OVERGLOOMING	OVERHAPPIER	OVERIDEALIZES
OVERFINENESS	OVERFULLNESS	OVERGLOOMS	OVERHAPPIEST	OVERIDEALIZING
OVERFINENESSES	OVERFULLNESSES	OVERGOADED	OVERHARVEST	OVERIDENTIFIED
OVERFINISHED	OVERFULNESS	OVERGOADING	OVERHARVESTED	OVERIDENTIFIES
OVERFISHED	OVERFULNESSES	OVERGOINGS	OVERHARVESTING	OVERIDENTIFY
OVERFISHES	OVERFUNDED	OVERGORGED	OVERHARVESTS	OVERIDENTIFYING
OVERFISHING	OVERFUNDING	OVERGORGES	OVERHASTES	OVERIMAGINATIVE
OVERFISHINGS	OVERFUNDINGS	OVERGORGING	OVERHASTILY	OVERIMPRESS
OVERFLIGHT	OVERFUSSIER	OVERGOVERN	OVERHASTINESS	OVERIMPRESSED
OVERFLIGHTS	OVERFUSSIEST	OVERGOVERNED	OVERHASTINESSES	OVERIMPRESSES
OVERFLOODED	OVERGALLED	OVERGOVERNING	OVERHATING	OVERIMPRESSING
OVERFLOODING	OVERGALLING	OVERGOVERNS	OVERHAULED	OVERINCLINED
OVERFLOODS	OVERGANGING	OVERGRADED	OVERHAULING	OVERINDULGE
OVERFLOURISH	OVERGARMENT	OVERGRADES	OVERHEAPED	OVERINDULGED
OVERFLOURISHED	OVERGARMENTS	OVERGRADING	OVERHEAPING	OVERINDULGENCE
OVERFLOURISHES	OVERGEARED	OVERGRAINED	OVERHEARING	OVERINDULGENCES
OVERFLOURISHING	OVERGEARING	OVERGRAINER	OVERHEATED	OVERINDULGENT
OVERFLOWED	OVERGENERALISE	OVERGRAINERS	OVERHEATING	OVERINDULGES
OVERFLOWING	OVERGENERALISED	OVERGRAINING	OVERHEATINGS	OVERINDULGING
OVERFLOWINGLY	OVERGENERALISES	OVERGRAINS	OVERHENTING	OVERINFLATE
OVERFLOWINGS	OVERGENERALIZE	OVERGRASSED	OVERHITTING	OVERINFLATED
OVERFLUSHES	OVERGENERALIZED	OVERGRASSES	OVERHOLDING	OVERINFLATES
OVERFLYING	OVERGENERALIZES	OVERGRASSING	OVERHOLIER	OVERINFLATING
OVERFOCUSED	OVERGENEROSITY	OVERGRAZED	OVERHOLIEST	OVERINFLATION
OVERFOCUSES	OVERGENEROUS	OVERGRAZES	OVERHOMOGENISE	OVERINFLATIONS
OVERFOCUSING	OVERGENEROUSLY	OVERGRAZING	OVERHOMOGENISED	OVERINFORM
OVERFOCUSSED	OVERGETTING	OVERGRAZINGS	OVERHOMOGENISES	OVERINFORMED
OVERFOCUSSES	OVERGILDED	OVERGREEDIER	OVERHOMOGENIZE	OVERINFORMING
OVERFOCUSSING	OVERGILDING	OVERGREEDIEST	OVERHOMOGENIZED	OVERINFORMS
OVERFOLDED	OVERGIRDED	OVERGREEDY	OVERHOMOGENIZES	OVERINGENIOUS
OVERFOLDING	OVERGIRDING	OVERGREENED	OVERHONORED	OVERINGENUITIES
OVERFONDLY	OVERGIVING	OVERGREENING	OVERHONORING	OVERINGENUITY
OVERFONDNESS	OVERGLAMORISE	OVERGREENS	OVERHONORS	OVERINSISTENT
OVERFONDNESSES	OVERGLAMORISED	OVERGROUND	OVERHONOUR	OVERINSURANCE

OVERINSURANCES	OVERLEARNED	OVERMANNING	OVERMULTIPLYING	OVERORNAMENT
OVERINSURE	OVERLEARNING	OVERMANNINGS	OVERMULTITUDE	OVERORNAMENTED
OVERINSURED	OVERLEARNS	OVERMANTEL	OVERMULTITUDED	OVERORNAMENTING
OVERINSURES	OVERLEARNT	OVERMANTELS	OVERMULTITUDES	OVERORNAMENTS
OVERINSURING	OVERLEATHER	OVERMASTED	OVERMULTITUDING	OVERPACKAGE
OVERINTENSE	OVERLEATHERS	OVERMASTER	OVERMUSCLED	OVERPACKAGED
OVERINTENSITIES	OVERLEAVEN	OVERMASTERED	OVERNAMING	OVERPACKAGES
OVERINTENSITY	OVERLEAVENED	OVERMASTERING	OVERNETTED	OVERPACKAGING
OVERINVESTMENT	OVERLEAVENING	OVERMASTERS	OVERNETTING	OVERPACKED
OVERINVESTMENTS	OVERLEAVENS	OVERMASTING	OVERNETTINGS	OVERPACKING
OVERISSUANCE	OVERLENDING	OVERMATCHED	OVERNICELY	OVERPAINTED
OVERISSUANCES	OVERLENGTH	OVERMATCHES	OVERNICENESS	OVERPAINTING
OVERISSUED	OVERLENGTHEN	OVERMATCHING	OVERNICENESSES	OVERPAINTS
OVERISSUES	OVERLENGTHENED	OVERMATTER	OVERNIGHTED	OVERPARTED
OVERISSUING	OVERLENGTHENING	OVERMATTERS	OVERNIGHTER	OVERPARTICULAR
OVERJOYING	OVERLENGTHENS	OVERMATURE	OVERNIGHTERS	OVERPARTING
OVERJUMPED	OVERLENGTHS	OVERMATURITIES	OVERNIGHTING	OVERPASSED
OVERJUMPING	OVERLETTING	OVERMATURITY	OVERNIGHTS	OVERPASSES
OVERKEEPING	OVERLEVERAGED	OVERMEASURE	OVERNOURISH	OVERPASSING
OVERKILLED	OVERLIGHTED	OVERMEASURED	OVERNOURISHED	OVERPAYING
OVERKILLING	OVERLIGHTING	OVERMEASURES	OVERNOURISHES	OVERPAYMENT
OVERKINDNESS	OVERLIGHTS	OVERMEASURING	OVERNOURISHING	OVERPAYMENTS
OVERKINDNESSES	OVERLITERAL	OVERMEDICATE	OVERNUTRITION	OVERPEDALED
OVERLABORED	OVERLITERARY	OVERMEDICATED	OVERNUTRITIONS	OVERPEDALING
OVERLABORING	OVERLIVING	OVERMEDICATES	OVEROBVIOUS	OVERPEDALLED
OVERLABORS	OVERLOADED	OVERMEDICATING	OVEROFFICE	OVERPEDALLING
OVERLABOUR	OVERLOADING	OVERMEDICATION	OVEROFFICED	OVERPEDALLINGS
OVERLABOURED	OVERLOCKED	OVERMEDICATIONS	OVEROFFICES	OVERPEDALS
OVERLABOURING	OVERLOCKER	OVERMELTED	OVEROFFICING	OVERPEERED
OVERLABOURS	OVERLOCKERS	OVERMELTING	OVEROPERATE	OVERPEERING
OVERLADING	OVERLOCKING	OVERMERRIER	OVEROPERATED	OVERPEOPLE
OVERLANDED	OVERLOCKINGS	OVERMERRIEST	OVEROPERATES	OVERPEOPLED
OVERLANDER	OVERLOOKED	OVERMIGHTIER	OVEROPERATING	OVERPEOPLES
OVERLANDERS	OVERLOOKER	OVERMIGHTIEST	OVEROPINIONATED	OVERPEOPLING
OVERLANDING	OVERLOOKERS	OVERMIGHTY	OVEROPTIMISM	OVERPERCHED
OVERLAPPED	OVERLOOKING	OVERMILKED	OVEROPTIMISMS	OVERPERCHES
OVERLAPPING	OVERLORDED	OVERMILKING	OVEROPTIMIST	OVERPERCHING
OVERLARDED	OVERLORDING	OVERMINING	OVEROPTIMISTIC	OVERPERSUADE
OVERLARDING	OVERLORDSHIP	OVERMIXING	OVEROPTIMISTS	OVERPERSUADED
OVERLAUNCH	OVERLORDSHIPS	OVERMODEST	OVERORCHESTRATE	OVERPERSUADES
OVERLAUNCHED	OVERLOVING	OVERMODESTLY	OVERORGANISE	OVERPERSUADING
OVERLAUNCHES	OVERMANAGE	OVERMOUNTED	OVERORGANISED	OVERPERSUASION
OVERLAUNCHING	OVERMANAGED	OVERMOUNTING	OVERORGANISES	OVERPERSUASIONS
OVERLAVISH	OVERMANAGES	OVERMOUNTS	OVERORGANISING	OVERPESSIMISTIC
OVERLAYING	OVERMANAGING	OVERMUCHES	OVERORGANIZE	OVERPICTURE
OVERLAYINGS	OVERMANIES	OVERMULTIPLIED	OVERORGANIZED	OVERPICTURED
OVERLEAPED	OVERMANNED	OVERMULTIPLIES	OVERORGANIZES	OVERPICTURES
OVERLEAPING	OVERMANNERED	OVERMULTIPLY	OVERORGANIZING	OVERPICTURING

OVERPITCHED	OVERPRESCRIBES	OVERPROTECTIONS	OVERREPORT	OVERSCRUPULOUS
OVERPITCHES	OVERPRESCRIBING	OVERPROTECTIVE	OVERREPORTED	OVERSCUTCHED
OVERPITCHING	OVERPRESSED	OVERPROTECTS	OVERREPORTING	OVERSECRETION
OVERPLACED	OVERPRESSES	OVERPUMPED	OVERREPORTS	OVERSECRETIONS
OVERPLAIDED	OVERPRESSING	OVERPUMPING	OVERREPRESENTED	OVERSEEDED
OVERPLAIDS	OVERPRESSURE	OVERQUALIFIED	OVERRESPOND	OVERSEEDING
OVERPLANNED	OVERPRESSURES	OVERRACKED	OVERRESPONDED	OVERSEEING
OVERPLANNING	OVERPRICED	OVERRACKING	OVERRESPONDING	OVERSELLING
OVERPLANNINGS	OVERPRICES	OVERRAKING	OVERRESPONDS	OVERSENSITIVE
OVERPLANTED	OVERPRICING	OVERRANKED	OVERRIDDEN	OVERSENSITIVITY
OVERPLANTING	OVERPRINTED	OVERRANKING	OVERRIDERS	OVERSERIOUS
OVERPLANTS	OVERPRINTING	OVERRASHLY	OVERRIDING	OVERSERIOUSLY
OVERPLAYED	OVERPRINTS	OVERRASHNESS	OVERRIPENED	OVERSERVICE
OVERPLAYING	OVERPRIVILEGED	OVERRASHNESSES	OVERRIPENESS	OVERSERVICED
OVERPLOTTED	OVERPRIZED	OVERRATING	OVERRIPENESSES	OVERSERVICES
OVERPLOTTING	OVERPRIZES	OVERRAUGHT	OVERRIPENING	OVERSERVICING
OVERPLOTTINGS	OVERPRIZING	OVERREACHED	OVERRIPENS	OVERSETTING
OVERPLUSES	OVERPROCESS	OVERREACHER	OVERROASTED	OVERSEWING
OVERPLUSSES	OVERPROCESSED	OVERREACHERS	OVERROASTING	OVERSHADED
OVERPLYING	OVERPROCESSES	OVERREACHES	OVERROASTS	OVERSHADES
OVERPOISED	OVERPROCESSING	OVERREACHING	OVERRUFFED	OVERSHADING
OVERPOISES	OVERPRODUCE	OVERREACTED	OVERRUFFING	OVERSHADOW
OVERPOISING	OVERPRODUCED	OVERREACTING	OVERRULERS	OVERSHADOWED
OVERPOPULATE	OVERPRODUCES	OVERREACTION	OVERRULING	OVERSHADOWING
OVERPOPULATED	OVERPRODUCING	OVERREACTIONS	OVERRULINGS	OVERSHADOWS
OVERPOPULATES	OVERPRODUCTION	OVERREACTS	OVERRUNNER	OVERSHARED
OVERPOPULATING	OVERPRODUCTIONS	OVERREADING	OVERRUNNERS	OVERSHARES
OVERPOPULATION	OVERPROGRAM	OVERRECKON	OVERRUNNING	OVERSHARING
OVERPOPULATIONS	OVERPROGRAMED	OVERRECKONED	OVERSAILED	OVERSHINES
OVERPOSTED	OVERPROGRAMING	OVERRECKONING	OVERSAILING	OVERSHINING
OVERPOSTING	OVERPROGRAMMED	OVERRECKONS	OVERSALTED	OVERSHIRTS
OVERPOTENT	OVERPROGRAMMING	OVERREDDED	OVERSALTING	OVERSHOOTING
OVERPOWERED	OVERPROGRAMS	OVERREDDING	OVERSANGUINE	OVERSHOOTS
OVERPOWERING	OVERPROMISE	OVERREFINE	OVERSATURATE	OVERSHOWER
OVERPOWERINGLY	OVERPROMISED	OVERREFINED	OVERSATURATED	OVERSHOWERED
OVERPOWERS	OVERPROMISES	OVERREFINEMENT	OVERSATURATES	OVERSHOWERING
OVERPRAISE	OVERPROMISING	OVERREFINEMENTS	OVERSATURATING	OVERSHOWERS
OVERPRAISED	OVERPROMOTE	OVERREFINES	OVERSATURATION	OVERSIGHTS
OVERPRAISES	OVERPROMOTED	OVERREFINING	OVERSATURATIONS	OVERSIMPLE
OVERPRAISING	OVERPROMOTES	OVERREGULATE	OVERSAUCED	OVERSIMPLIFIED
OVERPRECISE	OVERPROMOTING	OVERREGULATED	OVERSAUCES	OVERSIMPLIFIES
OVERPREPARATION	OVERPROOFS	OVERREGULATES	OVERSAUCING	OVERSIMPLIFY
OVERPREPARE	OVERPROPORTION	OVERREGULATING	OVERSAVING	OVERSIMPLIFYING
OVERPREPARED	OVERPROPORTIONS	OVERREGULATION	OVERSCALED	OVERSIMPLISTIC
OVERPREPARES	OVERPROTECT	OVERREGULATIONS	OVERSCHUTCHT	OVERSIMPLY
OVERPREPARING	OVERPROTECTED	OVERRELIANCE	OVERSCORED	OVERSIZING
OVERPRESCRIBE	OVERPROTECTING	OVERRELIANCES	OVERSCORES	OVERSKATED
OVERPRESCRIBED	OVERPROTECTION	OVERRENNING	OVERSCORING	OVERSKATES

OVERSKATING	OVERSTAFFED	OVERSTRESSING	OVERSWEARS	OVERTIGHTENING
OVERSKIPPED	OVERSTAFFING	OVERSTRETCH	OVERSWEETEN	OVERTIGHTENS
OVERSKIPPING	OVERSTAFFINGS	OVERSTRETCHED	OVERSWEETENED	OVERTIMELY
OVERSKIRTS	OVERSTAFFS	OVERSTRETCHES	OVERSWEETENING	OVERTIMERS
OVERSLAUGH	OVERSTAINED	OVERSTRETCHING	OVERSWEETENS	OVERTIMING
OVERSLAUGHED	OVERSTAINING	OVERSTREWED	OVERSWEETNESS	OVERTIPPED
OVERSLAUGHING	OVERSTAINS	OVERSTREWING	OVERSWEETNESSES	OVERTIPPING
OVERSLAUGHS	OVERSTANDING	OVERSTREWN	OVERSWELLED	OVERTIRING
OVERSLEEPING	OVERSTANDS	OVERSTREWS	OVERSWELLING	OVERTNESSES
OVERSLEEPS	OVERSTARED	OVERSTRIDDEN	OVERSWELLS	OVERTOILED
OVERSLEEVE	OVERSTARES	OVERSTRIDE	OVERSWIMMING	OVERTOILING
OVERSLEEVES	OVERSTARING	OVERSTRIDES	OVERSWINGING	OVERTOPPED
OVERSLIPPED	OVERSTATED	OVERSTRIDING	OVERSWINGS	OVERTOPPING
OVERSLIPPING	OVERSTATEMENT	OVERSTRIKE	OVERSWOLLEN	OVERTOPPINGS
OVERSMOKED	OVERSTATEMENTS	OVERSTRIKES	OVERTAKING	OVERTOWERED
OVERSMOKES	OVERSTATES	OVERSTRIKING	OVERTAKINGS	OVERTOWERING
OVERSMOKING	OVERSTATING	OVERSTRODE	OVERTALKATIVE	OVERTOWERS
OVERSOAKED	OVERSTAYED	OVERSTRONG	OVERTALKED	OVERTRADED
OVERSOAKING	OVERSTAYER	OVERSTROOKE	OVERTALKING	OVERTRADES
OVERSOLICITOUS	OVERSTAYERS	OVERSTRUCK	OVERTASKED	OVERTRADING
OVERSOWING	OVERSTAYING	OVERSTRUCTURED	OVERTASKING	OVERTRADINGS
OVERSPECIALISE	OVERSTEERED	OVERSTRUNG	OVERTAUGHT	OVERTRAINED
OVERSPECIALISED	OVERSTEERING	OVERSTUDIED	OVERTAXATION	OVERTRAINING
OVERSPECIALISES	OVERSTEERS	OVERSTUDIES	OVERTAXATIONS	OVERTRAINS
OVERSPECIALIZE	OVERSTEPPED	OVERSTUDYING	OVERTAXING	OVERTREATED
OVERSPECIALIZED	OVERSTEPPING	OVERSTUFFED	OVERTEACHES	OVERTREATING
OVERSPECIALIZES	OVERSTIMULATE	OVERSTUFFING	OVERTEACHING	OVERTREATMENT
OVERSPECULATE	OVERSTIMULATED	OVERSTUFFS	OVERTEDIOUS	OVERTREATMENTS
OVERSPECULATED	OVERSTIMULATES	OVERSUBSCRIBE	OVERTEEMED	OVERTREATS
OVERSPECULATES	OVERSTIMULATING	OVERSUBSCRIBED	OVERTEEMING	OVERTRICKS
OVERSPECULATING	OVERSTIMULATION	OVERSUBSCRIBES	OVERTHINKING	OVERTRIMMED
OVERSPECULATION	OVERSTINKING	OVERSUBSCRIBING	OVERTHINKS	OVERTRIMMING
OVERSPENDER	OVERSTINKS	OVERSUBTLE	OVERTHINNED	OVERTRIPPED
OVERSPENDERS	OVERSTIRRED	OVERSUBTLETIES	OVERTHINNING	OVERTRIPPING
OVERSPENDING	OVERSTIRRING	OVERSUBTLETY	OVERTHOUGHT	OVERTRUMPED
OVERSPENDINGS	OVERSTOCKED	OVERSUDSED	OVERTHROWER	OVERTRUMPING
OVERSPENDS	OVERSTOCKING	OVERSUDSES	OVERTHROWERS	OVERTRUMPS
OVERSPICED	OVERSTOCKS	OVERSUDSING	OVERTHROWING	OVERTRUSTED
OVERSPICES	OVERSTOREY	OVERSUPPED	OVERTHROWN	OVERTRUSTING
OVERSPICING	OVERSTOREYS	OVERSUPPING	OVERTHROWS	OVERTRUSTS
OVERSPILLED	OVERSTORIES	OVERSUPPLIED	OVERTHRUST	OVERTURING
OVERSPILLING	OVERSTRAIN	OVERSUPPLIES	OVERTHRUSTS	OVERTURNED
OVERSPILLS	OVERSTRAINED	OVERSUPPLY	OVERTHWART	OVERTURNER
OVERSPREAD	OVERSTRAINING	OVERSUPPLYING	OVERTHWARTED	OVERTURNERS
OVERSPREADING	OVERSTRAINS	OVERSUSPICIOUS	OVERTHWARTING	OVERTURNING
OVERSPREADS	OVERSTRESS	OVERSWAYED	OVERTHWARTS	OVERTYPING
OVERSTABILITIES	OVERSTRESSED	OVERSWAYING	OVERTIGHTEN	OVERURGING
OVERSTABILITY	OVERSTRESSES	OVERSWEARING	OVERTIGHTENED	OVERUTILISATION

OVERUTILISE	OVERWEENED	OVERWRESTING	OXALACETATE	OXYGENISING
OVERUTILISED	OVERWEENING	OVERWRESTLE	OXALACETATES	OXYGENIZED
OVERUTILISES	OVERWEENINGLY	OVERWRESTLED	OXALOACETATE	OXYGENIZER
OVERUTILISING	OVERWEENINGNESS	OVERWRESTLES	OXALOACETATES	OXYGENIZERS
OVERUTILIZATION	OVERWEENINGS	OVERWRESTLING	OXALOACETIC	OXYGENIZES
OVERUTILIZE	OVERWEIGHED	OVERWRESTS	OXIDATIONAL	OXYGENIZING
OVERUTILIZED	OVERWEIGHING	OVERWRITES	OXIDATIONS	OXYGENLESS
OVERUTILIZES	OVERWEIGHS	OVERWRITING	OXIDATIVELY	OXYHAEMOGLOBIN
OVERUTILIZING	OVERWEIGHT	OVERWRITTEN	OXIDIMETRIC	OXYHAEMOGLOBINS
OVERVALUATION	OVERWEIGHTED	OVERWROUGHT	OXIDIMETRIES	OXYHEMOGLOBIN
OVERVALUATIONS	OVERWEIGHTING	OVERYEARED	OXIDIMETRY	OXYHEMOGLOBINS
OVERVALUED	OVERWEIGHTS	OVERYEARING	OXIDISABLE	OXYHYDROGEN
OVERVALUES	OVERWETTED	OVERZEALOUS	OXIDISATION	OXYHYDROGENS
OVERVALUING	OVERWETTING	OVERZEALOUSLY	OXIDISATIONS	OXYMORONIC
OVERVEILED	OVERWHELMED	OVERZEALOUSNESS	OXIDIZABLE	OXYMORONICALLY
OVERVEILING	OVERWHELMING	OVIPARITIES	OXIDIZATION	OXYPHENBUTAZONE
OVERVIOLENT	OVERWHELMINGLY	OVIPAROUSLY	OXIDIZATIONS	OXYRHYNCHUS
OVERVOLTAGE	OVERWHELMINGS	OVIPOSITED	OXIDOREDUCTASE	OXYRHYNCHUSES
OVERVOLTAGES	OVERWHELMS	OVIPOSITING	OXIDOREDUCTASES	OXYSULPHIDE
OVERVOTING	OVERWILIER	OVIPOSITION	OXIMETRIES	OXYSULPHIDES
OVERWARIER	OVERWILIEST	OVIPOSITIONAL	OXYACETYLENE	OXYTETRACYCLINE
OVERWARIEST	OVERWINDED	OVIPOSITIONS	OXYACETYLENES	OXYURIASES
OVERWARMED	OVERWINDING	OVIPOSITOR	OXYCEPHALIC	OXYURIASIS
OVERWARMING	OVERWINGED	OVIPOSITORS	OXYCEPHALIES	OYSTERCATCHER
OVERWASHES	OVERWINGING	OVIRAPTORS	OXYCEPHALOUS	OYSTERCATCHERS
OVERWATCHED	OVERWINTER	OVOVIVIPARITIES	OXYCEPHALY	OYSTERINGS
OVERWATCHES	OVERWINTERED	OVOVIVIPARITY	OXYCODONES	OZOCERITES
OVERWATCHING	OVERWINTERING	OVOVIVIPAROUS	OXYGENASES	OZOKERITES
OVERWATERED	OVERWINTERS	OVOVIVIPAROUSLY	OXYGENATED	OZONATIONS
OVERWATERING	OVERWISELY	OVULATIONS	OXYGENATES	OZONIFEROUS
OVERWATERS	OVERWITHHELD	OVULIFEROUS	OXYGENATING	OZONISATION
OVERWEARIED	OVERWITHHOLD	OWERLOUPEN	OXYGENATION	OZONISATIONS
OVERWEARIES	OVERWITHHOLDING	OWERLOUPING	OXYGENATIONS	OZONIZATION
OVERWEARING	OVERWITHHOLDS	OWERLOUPIT	OXYGENATOR	OZONIZATIONS
OVERWEARYING	OVERWORKED	OWLISHNESS	OXYGENATORS	OZONOLYSES
OVERWEATHER	OVERWORKING	OWLISHNESSES	OXYGENISED	OZONOLYSIS
OVERWEATHERED	OVERWRAPPED	OWNERSHIPS	OXYGENISER	OZONOSPHERE
OVERWEATHERING	OVERWRAPPING	OWRECOMING	OXYGENISERS	OZONOSPHERES
OVERWEATHERS	OVERWRESTED	OXACILLINS	OXYGENISES	

P

PACEMAKERS	PACKAGINGS	PADRONISMS	PAEDOPHILIC	PAINTBOXES
PACEMAKING	PACKBOARDS	PADYMELONS	PAEDOPHILICS	PAINTBRUSH
PACEMAKINGS	PACKCLOTHS	PAEDAGOGIC	PAEDOTRIBE	PAINTBRUSHES
PACESETTER	PACKETISED	PAEDAGOGUE	PAEDOTRIBES	PAINTERLINESS
PACESETTERS	PACKETISES	PAEDAGOGUES	PAEDOTROPHIES	PAINTERLINESSES
PACESETTING	PACKETISING	PAEDERASTIC	PAEDOTROPHY	PAINTINESS
PACESETTINGS	PACKETIZED	PAEDERASTIES	PAGANISATION	PAINTINESSES
PACHYCARPOUS	PACKETIZES	PAEDERASTS	PAGANISATIONS	PAINTRESSES
PACHYDACTYL	PACKETIZING	PAEDERASTY	PAGANISERS	PAINTWORKS
PACHYDACTYLOUS	PACKFRAMES	PAEDEUTICS	PAGANISING	PAKIRIKIRI
PACHYDERMAL	PACKHORSES	PAEDIATRIC	PAGANISTIC	PAKIRIKIRIS
PACHYDERMATOUS	PACKINGHOUSE	PAEDIATRICIAN	PAGANISTICALLY	PALACINKES
PACHYDERMIA	PACKINGHOUSES	PAEDIATRICIANS	PAGANIZATION	PALAEANTHROPIC
PACHYDERMIAS	PACKNESSES	PAEDIATRICS	PAGANIZATIONS	PALAEBIOLOGIES
PACHYDERMIC	PACKSADDLE	PAEDIATRIES	PAGANIZERS	PALAEBIOLOGIST
PACHYDERMOUS	PACKSADDLES	PAEDIATRIST	PAGANIZING	PALAEBIOLOGISTS
PACHYDERMS	PACKSHEETS	PAEDIATRISTS	PAGEANTRIES	PALAEBIOLOGY
PACHYMENINGITIS	PACKSTAFFS	PAEDOBAPTISM	PAGINATING	PALAEETHNOLOGY
PACHYMETER	PACKTHREAD	PAEDOBAPTISMS	PAGINATION	PALAEOANTHROPIC
PACHYMETERS	PACKTHREADS	PAEDOBAPTIST	PAGINATIONS	PALAEOBIOLOGIC
PACHYSANDRA	PACLITAXEL	PAEDOBAPTISTS	PAIDEUTICS	PALAEOBIOLOGIES
PACHYSANDRAS	PACLITAXELS	PAEDODONTIC	PAILLASSES	PALAEOBIOLOGIST
PACHYTENES	PACTIONING	PAEDODONTICS	PAILLETTES	PALAEOBIOLOGY
PACIFIABLE	PADDLEBALL	PAEDOGENESES	PAINFULLER	PALAEOBOTANIC
PACIFICALLY	PADDLEBALLS	PAEDOGENESIS	PAINFULLEST	PALAEOBOTANICAL
PACIFICATE	PADDLEBOARD	PAEDOGENETIC	PAINFULNESS	PALAEOBOTANIES
PACIFICATED	PADDLEBOARDS	PAEDOGENIC	PAINFULNESSES	PALAEOBOTANIST
PACIFICATES	PADDLEBOAT	PAEDOLOGICAL	PAINKILLER	PALAEOBOTANISTS
PACIFICATING	PADDLEBOATS	PAEDOLOGIES	PAINKILLERS	PALAEOBOTANY
PACIFICATION	PADDLEFISH	PAEDOLOGIST	PAINKILLING	PALAEOCLIMATE
PACIFICATIONS	PADDLEFISHES	PAEDOLOGISTS	PAINLESSLY	PALAEOCLIMATES
PACIFICATOR	PADDOCKING	PAEDOMORPHIC	PAINLESSNESS	PALAEOCLIMATIC
PACIFICATORS	PADDYMELON	PAEDOMORPHISM	PAINLESSNESSES	PALAEOCRYSTIC
PACIFICATORY	PADDYMELONS	PAEDOMORPHISMS	PAINSTAKER	PALAEOCURRENT
PACIFICISM	PADDYWACKED	PAEDOMORPHOSES	PAINSTAKERS	PALAEOCURRENTS
PACIFICISMS	PADDYWACKING	PAEDOMORPHOSIS	PAINSTAKING	PALAEOECOLOGIC
PACIFICIST	PADDYWACKS	PAEDOPHILE	PAINSTAKINGLY	PALAEOECOLOGIES
PACIFICISTS	PADDYWHACK	PAEDOPHILES	PAINSTAKINGNESS	PALAEOECOLOGIST
PACIFISTIC	PADDYWHACKS	PAEDOPHILIA	PAINSTAKINGS	PALAEOECOLOGY
PACIFISTICALLY	PADEMELONS	PAEDOPHILIAC	PAINTBALLING	PALAEOETHNOLOGY
PACKABILITIES	PADEREROES	PAEDOPHILIACS	PAINTBALLINGS	PALAEOGAEA
PACKABILITY	PADLOCKING	PAEDOPHILIAS	PAINTBALLS	PALAEOGAEAS

PALAEOGEOGRAPHY	PALATALISATIONS	PALEOLITHS	PALISADING	PALMCORDERS
PALAEOGRAPHER	PALATALISE	PALEOLOGIES	PALISADOED	PALMERWORM
PALAEOGRAPHERS	PALATALISED	PALEOMAGNETIC	PALISADOES	PALMERWORMS
PALAEOGRAPHIC	PALATALISES	PALEOMAGNETISM	PALISADOING	PALMETTOES
PALAEOGRAPHICAL	PALATALISING	PALEOMAGNETISMS	PALISANDER	PALMHOUSES
PALAEOGRAPHIES	PALATALIZATION	PALEOMAGNETIST	PALISANDERS	PALMIFICATION
PALAEOGRAPHIST	PALATALIZATIONS	PALEOMAGNETISTS	PALLADIOUS	PALMIFICATIONS
PALAEOGRAPHISTS	PALATALIZE	PALEONTOLOGIC	PALLADIUMS	PALMIPEDES
PALAEOGRAPHY	PALATALIZED	PALEONTOLOGICAL	PALLASITES	PALMISTERS
PALAEOLIMNOLOGY	PALATALIZES	PALEONTOLOGIES	PALLBEARER	PALMISTRIES
PALAEOLITH	PALATALIZING	PALEONTOLOGIST	PALLBEARERS	PALMITATES
PALAEOLITHIC	PALATIALLY	PALEONTOLOGISTS	PALLESCENCE	PALMPRINTS
PALAEOLITHS	PALATIALNESS	PALEONTOLOGY	PALLESCENCES	PALOVERDES
PALAEOLOGIES	PALATIALNESSES	PALEOPATHOLOGY	PALLESCENT	PALPABILITIES
PALAEOLOGY	PALATINATE	PALEOZOOLOGICAL	PALLETISATION	PALPABILITY
PALAEOMAGNETIC	PALATINATES	PALEOZOOLOGIES	PALLETISATIONS	PALPABLENESS
PALAEOMAGNETISM	PALAVERERS	PALEOZOOLOGIST	PALLETISED	PALPABLENESSES
PALAEOMAGNETIST	PALAVERING	PALEOZOOLOGISTS	PALLETISER	PALPATIONS
PALAEONTOGRAPHY	PALEACEOUS	PALEOZOOLOGY	PALLETISERS	PALPEBRATE
PALAEONTOLOGIES	PALEMPORES	PALFRENIER	PALLETISES	PALPEBRATED
PALAEONTOLOGIST	PALENESSES	PALFRENIERS	PALLETISING	PALPEBRATES
PALAEONTOLOGY	PALEOBIOLOGIC	PALIFICATION	PALLETIZATION	PALPEBRATING
PALAEOPATHOLOGY	PALEOBIOLOGICAL	PALIFICATIONS	PALLETIZATIONS	PALPITATED
PALAEOPEDOLOGY	PALEOBIOLOGIES	PALILALIAS	PALLETIZED	PALPITATES
PALAEOPHYTOLOGY	PALEOBIOLOGIST	PALILLOGIES	PALLETIZER	PALPITATING
PALAEOSOLS	PALEOBIOLOGISTS	PALIMONIES	PALLETIZERS	PALPITATION
PALAEOTYPE	PALEOBIOLOGY	PALIMPSEST	PALLETIZES	PALPITATIONS
PALAEOTYPES	PALEOBOTANIC	PALIMPSESTS	PALLETIZING	PALSGRAVES
PALAEOTYPIC	PALEOBOTANICAL	PALINDROME	PALLIAMENT	PALSGRAVINE
PALAEOZOOLOGIES	PALEOBOTANIES	PALINDROMES	PALLIAMENTS	PALSGRAVINES
PALAEOZOOLOGIST	PALEOBOTANIST	PALINDROMIC	PALLIASSES	PALTRINESS
PALAEOZOOLOGY	PALEOBOTANISTS	PALINDROMICAL	PALLIATING	PALTRINESSES
PALAESTRAE	PALEOBOTANY	PALINDROMIST	PALLIATION	PALUDAMENT
PALAESTRAL	PALEOECOLOGIC	PALINDROMISTS	PALLIATIONS	PALUDAMENTA
PALAESTRAS	PALEOECOLOGICAL	PALINGENESES	PALLIATIVE	PALUDAMENTS
PALAESTRIC	PALEOECOLOGIES	PALINGENESIA	PALLIATIVELY	PALUDAMENTUM
PALAESTRICAL	PALEOECOLOGIST	PALINGENESIAS	PALLIATIVES	PALUDAMENTUMS
PALAFITTES	PALEOECOLOGISTS	PALINGENESIES	PALLIATORS	PALUDICOLOUS
PALAGONITE	PALEOECOLOGY	PALINGENESIS	PALLIATORY	PALUDINOUS
PALAGONITES	PALEOGEOGRAPHIC	PALINGENESIST	PALLIDITIES	PALUSTRIAN
PALAMPORES	PALEOGEOGRAPHY	PALINGENESISTS	PALLIDNESS	PALUSTRINE
PALANKEENS	PALEOGRAPHER	PALINGENESY	PALLIDNESSES	PALYNOLOGIC
PALANQUINS	PALEOGRAPHERS	PALINGENETIC	PALMACEOUS	PALYNOLOGICAL
PALATABILITIES	PALEOGRAPHIC	PALINGENETICAL	PALMATIFID	PALYNOLOGICALLY
PALATABILITY	PALEOGRAPHICAL	PALINODIES	PALMATIONS	PALYNOLOGIES
PALATABLENESS	PALEOGRAPHIES	PALINOPIAS	PALMATIPARTITE	PALYNOLOGIST
PALATABLENESSES	PALEOGRAPHY	PALINOPSIA	PALMATISECT	PALYNOLOGISTS
PALATALISATION	PALEOLITHIC	PALINOPSIAS	PALMCORDER	PALYNOLOGY

PAMPELMOOSE	PANCREOZYMIN	PANELLIZED	PANMIXISES	PANSPERMISMS
PAMPELMOOSES	PANCREOZYMINS	PANENTHEISM	PANNICULUS	PANSPERMIST
PAMPELMOUSE	PANCYTOPENIA	PANENTHEISMS	PANNICULUSES	PANSPERMISTS
PAMPELMOUSES	PANCYTOPENIAS	PANENTHEIST	PANNIKELLS	PANTAGAMIES
PAMPEREDNESS	PANDAEMONIUM	PANENTHEISTS	PANOMPHAEAN	PANTAGRAPH
PAMPEREDNESSES	PANDAEMONIUMS	PANESTHESIA	PANOPHOBIA	PANTAGRAPHS
PAMPERINGS	PANDANACEOUS	PANESTHESIAS	PANOPHOBIAS	PANTALEONS
PAMPHLETED	PANDANUSES	PANETELLAS	PANOPHTHALMIA	PANTALETTED
PAMPHLETEER	PANDATIONS	PANETTONES	PANOPHTHALMIAS	PANTALETTES
PAMPHLETEERED	PANDECTIST	PANFISHING	PANOPHTHALMITIS	PANTALONES
PAMPHLETEERING	PANDECTISTS	PANFISHINGS	PANOPTICAL	PANTALOONED
PAMPHLETEERINGS	PANDEMONIAC	PANGENESES	PANOPTICALLY	PANTALOONERIES
PAMPHLETEERS	PANDEMONIACAL	PANGENESIS	PANOPTICON	PANTALOONERY
PAMPHLETING	PANDEMONIAN	PANGENETIC	PANOPTICONS	PANTALOONS
PAMPOOTIES	PANDEMONIANS	PANGENETICALLY	PANORAMICALLY	PANTDRESSES
PANACHAEAS	PANDEMONIC	PANGRAMMATIST	PANPHARMACON	PANTECHNICON
PANAESTHESIA	PANDEMONIUM	PANGRAMMATISTS	PANPHARMACONS	PANTECHNICONS
PANAESTHESIAS	PANDEMONIUMS	PANHANDLED	PANPSYCHISM	PANTHEISMS
PANAESTHETISM	PANDERESSES	PANHANDLER	PANPSYCHISMS	PANTHEISTIC
PANAESTHETISMS	PANDERINGS	PANHANDLERS	PANPSYCHIST	PANTHEISTICAL
PANARITIUM	PANDERISMS	PANHANDLES	PANPSYCHISTIC	PANTHEISTICALLY
PANARITIUMS	PANDERMITE	PANHANDLING	PANPSYCHISTS	PANTHEISTS
PANARTHRITIS	PANDERMITES	PANHARMONICON	PANRADIOMETER	PANTHENOLS
PANARTHRITISES	PANDICULATION	PANHARMONICONS	PANRADIOMETERS	PANTHEOLOGIES
PANATELLAS	PANDICULATIONS	PANHELLENIC	PANSEXUALISM	PANTHEOLOGIST
PANBROILED	PANDOWDIES	PANHELLENION	PANSEXUALISMS	PANTHEOLOGISTS
PANBROILING	PANDURATED	PANHELLENIONS	PANSEXUALIST	PANTHEOLOGY
PANCHAYATS	PANDURIFORM	PANHELLENIUM	PANSEXUALISTS	PANTHERESS
PANCHROMATIC	PANEGOISMS	PANHELLENIUMS	PANSEXUALITIES	PANTHERESSES
PANCHROMATISM	PANEGYRICA	PANICKIEST	PANSEXUALITY	PANTHERINE
PANCHROMATISMS	PANEGYRICAL	PANICMONGER	PANSEXUALS	PANTHERISH
PANCOSMISM	PANEGYRICALLY	PANICMONGERS	PANSOPHICAL	PANTIHOSES
PANCOSMISMS	PANEGYRICON	PANICULATE	PANSOPHICALLY	PANTILINGS
PANCRATIAN	PANEGYRICS	PANICULATED	PANSOPHIES	PANTISOCRACIES
PANCRATIAST	PANEGYRIES	PANICULATELY	PANSOPHISM	PANTISOCRACY
PANCRATIASTS	PANEGYRISE	PANIDIOMORPHIC	PANSOPHISMS	PANTISOCRAT
PANCRATIST	PANEGYRISED	PANIFICATION	PANSOPHIST	PANTISOCRATIC
PANCRATISTS	PANEGYRISES	PANIFICATIONS	PANSOPHISTS	PANTISOCRATICAL
PANCRATIUM	PANEGYRISING	PANISLAMIST	PANSPERMATIC	PANTISOCRATIST
PANCRATIUMS	PANEGYRIST	PANJANDARUM	PANSPERMATISM	PANTISOCRATISTS
PANCREASES	PANEGYRISTS	PANJANDARUMS	PANSPERMATISMS	PANTISOCRATS
PANCREATECTOMY	PANEGYRIZE	PANJANDRUM	PANSPERMATIST	PANTOFFLES
PANCREATIC	PANEGYRIZED	PANJANDRUMS	PANSPERMATISTS	PANTOGRAPH
PANCREATIN	PANEGYRIZES	PANLEUCOPENIA	PANSPERMIA	PANTOGRAPHER
PANCREATINS	PANEGYRIZING	PANLEUCOPENIAS	PANSPERMIAS	PANTOGRAPHERS
PANCREATITIDES	PANELLINGS	PANLEUKOPENIA	PANSPERMIC	PANTOGRAPHIC
PANCREATITIS	PANELLISED	PANLEUKOPENIAS	PANSPERMIES	PANTOGRAPHICAL
PANCREATITISES	PANELLISTS	PANLOGISMS	PANSPERMISM	PANTOGRAPHIES

PANTOGRAPHS

PANTOGRAPHS	PAPERBACKING	PAPRIKASES	PARACASEIN	PARADOXOLOGY
PANTOGRAPHY	PAPERBACKS	PAPRIKASHES	PARACASEINS	PARADOXURE
PANTOMIMED	PAPERBARKS	PAPULATION	PARACENTESES	PARADOXURES
PANTOMIMES	PAPERBOARD	PAPULATIONS	PARACENTESIS	PARADOXURINE
PANTOMIMIC	PAPERBOARDS	PAPULIFEROUS	PARACETAMOL	PARADOXURINES
PANTOMIMICAL	PAPERBOUND	PAPYRACEOUS	PARACETAMOLS	PARADROPPED
PANTOMIMICALLY	PAPERBOUNDS	PAPYROLOGICAL	PARACHRONISM	PARADROPPING
PANTOMIMING	PAPERCLIPS	PAPYROLOGIES	PARACHRONISMS	PARAENESES
PANTOMIMIST	PAPERGIRLS	PAPYROLOGIST	PARACHUTED	PARAENESIS
PANTOMIMISTS	PAPERHANGER	PAPYROLOGISTS	PARACHUTES	PARAENETIC
PANTOPHAGIES	PAPERHANGERS	PAPYROLOGY	PARACHUTIC	PARAENETICAL
PANTOPHAGIST	PAPERHANGING	PARABAPTISM	PARACHUTING	PARAESTHESIA
PANTOPHAGISTS	PAPERHANGINGS	PARABAPTISMS	PARACHUTINGS	PARAESTHESIAS
PANTOPHAGOUS	PAPERINESS	PARABEMATA	PARACHUTIST	PARAESTHETIC
PANTOPHAGY	PAPERINESSES	PARABEMATIC	PARACHUTISTS	PARAFFINED
PANTOPHOBIA	PAPERKNIFE	PARABIOSES	PARACLETES	PARAFFINES
PANTOPHOBIAS	PAPERKNIVES	PARABIOSIS	PARACROSTIC	PARAFFINIC
PANTOPRAGMATIC	PAPERMAKER	PARABIOTIC	PARACROSTICS	PARAFFINIER
PANTOPRAGMATICS	PAPERMAKERS	PARABIOTICALLY	PARACYANOGEN	PARAFFINIEST
PANTOSCOPE	PAPERMAKING	PARABLASTIC	PARACYANOGENS	PARAFFINING
PANTOSCOPES	PAPERMAKINGS	PARABLASTS	PARADIDDLE	PARAFFINOID
PANTOSCOPIC	PAPERWARES	PARABLEPSES	PARADIDDLED	PARAGENESES
PANTOTHENATE	PAPERWEIGHT	PARABLEPSIES	PARADIDDLES	PARAGENESIA
PANTOTHENATES	PAPERWEIGHTS	PARABLEPSIS	PARADIDDLING	PARAGENESIAS
PANTOTHENIC	PAPERWORKS	PARABLEPSY	PARADIGMATIC	PARAGENESIS
PANTOUFLES	PAPETERIES	PARABLEPTIC	PARADIGMATICAL	PARAGENETIC
PANTROPICAL	PAPILIONACEOUS	PARABOLANUS	PARADISAIC	PARAGENETICALLY
PANTRYMAID	PAPILLATED	PARABOLANUSES	PARADISAICAL	PARAGLIDED
PANTRYMAIDS	PAPILLIFEROUS	PARABOLICAL	PARADISAICALLY	PARAGLIDER
PANTSUITED	PAPILLIFORM	PARABOLICALLY	PARADISEAN	PARAGLIDERS
PANTYHOSES	PAPILLITIS	PARABOLISATION	PARADISIAC	PARAGLIDES
PANTYWAIST	PAPILLITISES	PARABOLISATIONS	PARADISIACAL	PARAGLIDING
PANTYWAISTS	PAPILLOMAS	PARABOLISE	PARADISIACALLY	PARAGLIDINGS
PANZEROTTI	PAPILLOMATA	PARABOLISED	PARADISIAL	PARAGLOSSA
PANZEROTTO	PAPILLOMATOSES	PARABOLISES	PARADISIAN	PARAGLOSSAE
PANZEROTTOS	PAPILLOMATOSIS	PARABOLISING	PARADISICAL	PARAGLOSSAL
PANZOOTICS	PAPILLOMATOUS	PARABOLIST	PARADOCTOR	PARAGLOSSATE
PAPALISING	PAPILLOMAVIRUS	PARABOLISTS	PARADOCTORS	PARAGNATHISM
PAPALIZING	PAPILLOTES	PARABOLIZATION	PARADOXERS	PARAGNATHISMS
PAPAPRELATIST	PAPILLULATE	PARABOLIZATIONS	PARADOXICAL	PARAGNATHOUS
PAPAPRELATISTS	PAPILLULES	PARABOLIZE	PARADOXICALITY	PARAGNOSES
PAPAVERACEOUS	PAPISTICAL	PARABOLIZED	PARADOXICALLY	PARAGNOSIS
PAPAVERINE	PAPISTICALLY	PARABOLIZES	PARADOXICALNESS	PARAGOGICAL
PAPAVERINES	PAPISTRIES	PARABOLIZING	PARADOXIDIAN	PARAGOGICALLY
PAPAVEROUS	PAPOVAVIRUS	PARABOLOID	PARADOXIES	PARAGOGUES
PAPERBACKED	PAPOVAVIRUSES	PARABOLOIDAL	PARADOXIST	PARAGONING
PAPERBACKER	PAPPARDELLE	PARABOLOIDS	PARADOXISTS	PARAGONITE
PAPERBACKERS	PAPPARDELLES	PARABRAKES	PARADOXOLOGIES	PARAGONITES

PARAGRAMMATIST	PARALLAXES	PARALYSATIONS	PARAMETRISING	PARAPENTES
PARAGRAMMATISTS	PARALLELED	PARALYSERS	PARAMETRIZATION	PARAPENTING
PARAGRAPHED	PARALLELEPIPED	PARALYSING	PARAMETRIZE	PARAPENTINGS
PARAGRAPHER	PARALLELEPIPEDA	PARALYSINGLY	PARAMETRIZED	PARAPERIODIC
PARAGRAPHERS	PARALLELEPIPEDS	PARALYTICALLY	PARAMETRIZES	PARAPHASIA
PARAGRAPHIA	PARALLELING	PARALYTICS	PARAMETRIZING	PARAPHASIAS
PARAGRAPHIAS	PARALLELINGS	PARALYZATION	PARAMILITARIES	PARAPHASIC
PARAGRAPHIC	PARALLELISE	PARALYZATIONS	PARAMILITARY	PARAPHERNALIA
PARAGRAPHICAL	PARALLELISED	PARALYZERS	PARAMNESIA	PARAPHILIA
PARAGRAPHICALLY	PARALLELISES	PARALYZING	PARAMNESIAS	PARAPHILIAC
PARAGRAPHING	PARALLELISING	PARALYZINGLY	PARAMOECIA	PARAPHILIACS
PARAGRAPHIST	PARALLELISM	PARAMAECIA	PARAMOECIUM	PARAPHILIAS
PARAGRAPHISTS	PARALLELISMS	PARAMAECIUM	PARAMORPHIC	PARAPHIMOSES
PARAGRAPHS	PARALLELIST	PARAMAGNET	PARAMORPHINE	PARAPHIMOSIS
PARAHELIOTROPIC	PARALLELISTIC	PARAMAGNETIC	PARAMORPHINES	PARAPHONIA
PARAHYDROGEN	PARALLELISTS	PARAMAGNETISM	PARAMORPHISM	PARAPHONIAS
PARAHYDROGENS	PARALLELIZE	PARAMAGNETISMS	PARAMORPHISMS	PARAPHONIC
PARAINFLUENZA	PARALLELIZED	PARAMAGNETS	PARAMORPHOUS	PARAPHRASABLE
PARAINFLUENZAS	PARALLELIZES	PARAMASTOID	PARAMORPHS	PARAPHRASE
PARAJOURNALISM	PARALLELIZING	PARAMASTOIDS	PARAMOUNCIES	PARAPHRASED
PARAJOURNALISMS	PARALLELLED	PARAMATTAS	PARAMOUNCY	PARAPHRASER
PARAKEELYA	PARALLELLING	PARAMECIUM	PARAMOUNTCIES	PARAPHRASERS
PARAKEELYAS	PARALLELLY	PARAMECIUMS	PARAMOUNTCY	PARAPHRASES
PARAKELIAS	PARALLELOGRAM	PARAMEDICAL	PARAMOUNTLY	PARAPHRASING
PARAKITING	PARALLELOGRAMS	PARAMEDICALS	PARAMOUNTS	PARAPHRAST
PARAKITINGS	PARALLELOPIPED	PARAMEDICO	PARAMYLUMS	PARAPHRASTIC
PARALALIAS	PARALLELOPIPEDA	PARAMEDICOS	PARAMYXOVIRUS	PARAPHRASTICAL
PARALANGUAGE	PARALLELOPIPEDS	PARAMEDICS	PARAMYXOVIRUSES	PARAPHRASTS
PARALANGUAGES	PARALLELWISE	PARAMENSTRUA	PARANEPHRIC	PARAPHRAXES
PARALDEHYDE	PARALOGIAS	PARAMENSTRUUM	PARANEPHROS	PARAPHRAXIA
PARALDEHYDES	PARALOGIES	PARAMENSTRUUMS	PARANEPHROSES	PARAPHRAXIAS
PARALEGALS	PARALOGISE	PARAMETERISE	PARANOEICS	PARAPHRAXIS
PARALEIPOMENA	PARALOGISED	PARAMETERISED	PARANOIACS	PARAPHRENIA
PARALEIPOMENON	PARALOGISES	PARAMETERISES	PARANOICALLY	PARAPHRENIAS
PARALEIPSES	PARALOGISING	PARAMETERISING	PARANOIDAL	PARAPHYSATE
PARALEIPSIS	PARALOGISM	PARAMETERIZE	PARANORMAL	PARAPHYSES
PARALEXIAS	PARALOGISMS	PARAMETERIZED	PARANORMALITIES	PARAPHYSIS
PARALIMNION	PARALOGIST	PARAMETERIZES	PARANORMALITY	PARAPINEAL
PARALIMNIONS	PARALOGISTIC	PARAMETERIZING	PARANORMALLY	PARAPLANNER
PARALINGUISTIC	PARALOGISTS	PARAMETERS	PARANORMALS	PARAPLANNERS
PARALINGUISTICS	PARALOGIZE	PARAMETRAL	PARANTHELIA	PARAPLEGIA
PARALIPOMENA	PARALOGIZED	PARAMETRIC	PARANTHELION	PARAPLEGIAS
PARALIPOMENON	PARALOGIZES	PARAMETRICAL	PARANTHROPUS	PARAPLEGIC
PARALIPSES	PARALOGIZING	PARAMETRICALLY	PARANTHROPUSES	PARAPLEGICS
PARALIPSIS	PARALOGUES	PARAMETRISATION	PARANYMPHS	PARAPODIAL
PARALLACTIC	PARALYMPIC	PARAMETRISE	PARAPARESES	PARAPODIUM
PARALLACTICAL	PARALYMPICS	PARAMETRISED	PARAPARESIS	PARAPOPHYSES
PARALLACTICALLY	PARALYSATION	PARAMETRISES	PARAPARETIC	PARAPOPHYSIAL

P

PARAPOPHYSIS

PARAPOPHYSIS	PARASITISE	PARASYNTHETON	PARDONABLE	PARFOCALIZED
PARAPRAXES	PARASITISED	PARATACTIC	PARDONABLENESS	PARFOCALIZES
PARAPRAXIS	PARASITISES	PARATACTICAL	PARDONABLY	PARFOCALIZING
PARAPRAXISES	PARASITISING	PARATACTICALLY	PARDONINGS	PARGASITES
PARAPSYCHIC	PARASITISM	PARATANIWHA	PARDONLESS	PARGETINGS
PARAPSYCHICAL	PARASITISMS	PARATANIWHAS	PAREGORICS	PARGETTERS
PARAPSYCHISM	PARASITIZATION	PARATHESES	PAREIDOLIA	PARGETTING
PARAPSYCHISMS	PARASITIZATIONS	PARATHESIS	PAREIDOLIAS	PARGETTINGS
PARAPSYCHOLOGY	PARASITIZE	PARATHIONS	PARENCEPHALA	PARGYLINES
PARAPSYCHOSES	PARASITIZED	PARATHORMONE	PARENCEPHALON	PARHELIACAL
PARAPSYCHOSIS	PARASITIZES	PARATHORMONES	PARENCHYMA	PARHELIONS
PARAQUADRATE	PARASITIZING	PARATHYROID	PARENCHYMAL	PARHYPATES
PARAQUADRATES	PARASITOID	PARATHYROIDS	PARENCHYMAS	PARIPINNATE
PARAQUITOS	PARASITOIDS	PARATROOPER	PARENCHYMATA	PARISCHANE
PARARHYMES	PARASITOLOGIC	PARATROOPERS	PARENCHYMATOUS	PARISCHANES
PARAROSANILINE	PARASITOLOGICAL	PARATROOPS	PARENTAGES	PARISCHANS
PARAROSANILINES	PARASITOLOGIES	PARATUNGSTIC	PARENTALLY	PARISHIONER
PARARTHRIA	PARASITOLOGIST	PARATYPHOID	PARENTERAL	PARISHIONERS
PARARTHRIAS	PARASITOLOGISTS	PARATYPHOIDS	PARENTERALLY	PARISYLLABIC
PARASAILED	PARASITOLOGY	PARAWALKER	PARENTHESES	PARKINSONIAN
PARASAILING	PARASITOSES	PARAWALKERS	PARENTHESIS	PARKINSONIANS
PARASAILINGS	PARASITOSIS	PARBOILING	PARENTHESISE	PARKINSONISM
PARASCENDER	PARASKIING	PARBREAKED	PARENTHESISED	PARKINSONISMS
PARASCENDERS	PARASKIINGS	PARBREAKING	PARENTHESISES	PARKLEAVES
PARASCENDING	PARASOMNIA	PARBUCKLED	PARENTHESISING	PARLEMENTS
PARASCENDINGS	PARASOMNIAS	PARBUCKLES	PARENTHESIZE	PARLEYVOOED
PARASCENIA	PARASPHENOID	PARBUCKLING	PARENTHESIZED	PARLEYVOOING
PARASCENIUM	PARASPHENOIDS	PARCELLING	PARENTHESIZES	PARLEYVOOS
PARASCEVES	PARASTATAL	PARCELWISE	PARENTHESIZING	PARLIAMENT
PARASCIENCE	PARASTATALS	PARCENARIES	PARENTHETIC	PARLIAMENTARIAN
PARASCIENCES	PARASTICHIES	PARCHEDNESS	PARENTHETICAL	PARLIAMENTARILY
PARASELENAE	PARASTICHOUS	PARCHEDNESSES	PARENTHETICALLY	PARLIAMENTARISM
PARASELENE	PARASTICHY	PARCHEESIS	PARENTHOOD	PARLIAMENTARY
PARASELENIC	PARASUICIDE	PARCHMENTIER	PARENTHOODS	PARLIAMENTING
PARASEXUAL	PARASUICIDES	PARCHMENTIEST	PARENTINGS	PARLIAMENTINGS
PARASEXUALITIES	PARASYMBIONT	PARCHMENTISE	PARENTLESS	PARLIAMENTS
PARASEXUALITY	PARASYMBIONTS	PARCHMENTISED	PARESTHESIA	PARLOURMAID
PARASHIOTH	PARASYMBIOSES	PARCHMENTISES	PARESTHESIAS	PARLOURMAIDS
PARASITAEMIA	PARASYMBIOSIS	PARCHMENTISING	PARESTHETIC	PARLOUSNESS
PARASITAEMIAS	PARASYMBIOTIC	PARCHMENTIZE	PARFLECHES	PARLOUSNESSES
PARASITICAL	PARASYMPATHETIC	PARCHMENTIZED	PARFLESHES	PARMACITIE
PARASITICALLY	PARASYNAPSES	PARCHMENTIZES	PARFOCALISE	PARMACITIES
PARASITICALNESS	PARASYNAPSIS	PARCHMENTIZING	PARFOCALISED	PARMIGIANA
PARASITICIDAL	PARASYNAPTIC	PARCHMENTS	PARFOCALISES	PARMIGIANO
PARASITICIDE	PARASYNTHESES	PARCHMENTY	PARFOCALISING	PARMIGIANOS
PARASITICIDES	PARASYNTHESIS	PARCIMONIES	PARFOCALITIES	PAROCCIPITAL
PARASITISATION	PARASYNTHETA	PARDALISES	PARFOCALITY	PAROCCIPITALS
PARASITISATIONS	PARASYNTHETIC	PARDALOTES	PARFOCALIZE	PAROCHIALISE

PAROCHIALISED	PARQUETTED	PARTIBILITIES	PARTICULARS	PASODOBLES
PAROCHIALISES	PARQUETTING	PARTIBILITY	PARTICULATE	PASQUEFLOWER
PAROCHIALISING	PARRAKEETS	PARTICIPABLE	PARTICULATES	PASQUEFLOWERS
PAROCHIALISM	PARRAMATTA	PARTICIPANT	PARTISANLY	PASQUILANT
PAROCHIALISMS	PARRAMATTAS	PARTICIPANTLY	PARTISANSHIP	PASQUILANTS
PAROCHIALITIES	PARRHESIAS	PARTICIPANTS	PARTISANSHIPS	PASQUILERS
PAROCHIALITY	PARRICIDAL	PARTICIPATE	PARTITIONED	PASQUILLED
PAROCHIALIZE	PARRICIDES	PARTICIPATED	PARTITIONER	PASQUILLING
PAROCHIALIZED	PARRITCHES	PARTICIPATES	PARTITIONERS	PASQUINADE
PAROCHIALIZES	PARROCKING	PARTICIPATING	PARTITIONING	PASQUINADED
PAROCHIALIZING	PARROQUETS	PARTICIPATION	PARTITIONIST	PASQUINADER
PAROCHIALLY	PARROTFISH	PARTICIPATIONAL	PARTITIONISTS	PASQUINADERS
PAROCHINES	PARROTFISHES	PARTICIPATIONS	PARTITIONMENT	PASQUINADES
PARODISTIC	PARROTIEST	PARTICIPATIVE	PARTITIONMENTS	PASQUINADING
PAROECIOUS	PARROTRIES	PARTICIPATOR	PARTITIONS	PASSABLENESS
PAROECISMS	PARSIMONIES	PARTICIPATORS	PARTITIVELY	PASSABLENESSES
PAROEMIACS	PARSIMONIOUS	PARTICIPATORY	PARTITIVES	PASSACAGLIA
PAROEMIOGRAPHER	PARSIMONIOUSLY	PARTICIPIAL	PARTITURAS	PASSACAGLIAS
PAROEMIOGRAPHY	PARSONAGES	PARTICIPIALLY	PARTIZANLY	PASSAGEWAY
PAROEMIOLOGIES	PARSONICAL	PARTICIPIALS	PARTIZANSHIP	PASSAGEWAYS
PAROEMIOLOGY	PARTAKINGS	PARTICIPLE	PARTIZANSHIPS	PASSAGEWORK
PARONOMASIA	PARTHENOCARPIC	PARTICIPLES	PARTNERING	PASSAGEWORKS
PARONOMASIAS	PARTHENOCARPIES	PARTICLEBOARD	PARTNERINGS	PASSALONGS
PARONOMASIES	PARTHENOCARPOUS	PARTICLEBOARDS	PARTNERLESS	PASSAMENTED
PARONOMASTIC	PARTHENOCARPY	PARTICOLORED	PARTNERSHIP	PASSAMENTING
PARONOMASTICAL	PARTHENOGENESES	PARTICOLOURED	PARTNERSHIPS	PASSAMENTS
PARONOMASY	PARTHENOGENESIS	PARTICULAR	PARTRIDGEBERRY	PASSAMEZZO
PARONYCHIA	PARTHENOGENETIC	PARTICULARISE	PARTRIDGES	PASSAMEZZOS
PARONYCHIAL	PARTHENOSPORE	PARTICULARISED	PARTURIENCIES	PASSEMEASURE
PARONYCHIAS	PARTHENOSPORES	PARTICULARISER	PARTURIENCY	PASSEMEASURES
PARONYMIES	PARTIALISE	PARTICULARISERS	PARTURIENT	PASSEMENTED
PARONYMOUS	PARTIALISED	PARTICULARISES	PARTURIENTS	PASSEMENTERIE
PARONYMOUSLY	PARTIALISES	PARTICULARISING	PARTURIFACIENT	PASSEMENTERIES
PAROTIDITIC	PARTIALISING	PARTICULARISM	PARTURIFACIENTS	PASSEMENTING
PAROTIDITIS	PARTIALISM	PARTICULARISMS	PARTURITION	PASSEMENTS
PAROTIDITISES	PARTIALISMS	PARTICULARIST	PARTURITIONS	PASSENGERS
PAROTITIDES	PARTIALIST	PARTICULARISTIC	PARTYGOERS	PASSEPIEDS
PAROTITISES	PARTIALISTS	PARTICULARISTS	PARURETICS	PASSERIFORM
PAROXETINE	PARTIALITIES	PARTICULARITIES	PARVANIMITIES	PASSERINES
PAROXETINES	PARTIALITY	PARTICULARITY	PARVANIMITY	PASSIBILITIES
PAROXYSMAL	PARTIALIZE	PARTICULARIZE	PARVIFOLIATE	PASSIBILITY
PAROXYSMALLY	PARTIALIZED	PARTICULARIZED	PARVOLINES	PASSIBLENESS
PAROXYSMIC	PARTIALIZES	PARTICULARIZER	PARVOVIRUS	PASSIBLENESSES
PAROXYTONE	PARTIALIZING	PARTICULARIZERS	PARVOVIRUSES	PASSIFLORA
PAROXYTONES	PARTIALLED	PARTICULARIZES	PASIGRAPHIC	PASSIFLORACEOUS
PAROXYTONIC	PARTIALLING	PARTICULARIZING	PASIGRAPHICAL	PASSIFLORAS
PARQUETING	PARTIALNESS	PARTICULARLY	PASIGRAPHIES	PASSIMETER
PARQUETRIES	PARTIALNESSES	PARTICULARNESS	PASIGRAPHY	PASSIMETERS

PASSIONALS

PASSIONALS	PASTEURIZATION	PATCHWORKED	PATHOLOGICAL	PATRIARCHATE
PASSIONARIES	PASTEURIZATIONS	PATCHWORKING	PATHOLOGICALLY	PATRIARCHATES
PASSIONARY	PASTEURIZE	PATCHWORKS	PATHOLOGIES	PATRIARCHIES
PASSIONATE	PASTEURIZED	PATELLECTOMIES	PATHOLOGISE	PATRIARCHISM
PASSIONATED	PASTEURIZER	PATELLECTOMY	PATHOLOGISED	PATRIARCHISMS
PASSIONATELY	PASTEURIZERS	PATELLIFORM	PATHOLOGISES	PATRIARCHS
PASSIONATENESS	PASTEURIZES	PATENTABILITIES	PATHOLOGISING	PATRIARCHY
PASSIONATES	PASTEURIZING	PATENTABILITY	PATHOLOGIST	PATRIATING
PASSIONATING	PASTICCIOS	PATENTABLE	PATHOLOGISTS	PATRIATION
PASSIONFLOWER	PASTICHEUR	PATERCOVES	PATHOLOGIZE	PATRIATIONS
PASSIONFLOWERS	PASTICHEURS	PATEREROES	PATHOLOGIZED	PATRICIANLY
PASSIONING	PASTINESSES	PATERFAMILIAS	PATHOLOGIZES	PATRICIANS
PASSIONLESS	PASTITSIOS	PATERFAMILIASES	PATHOLOGIZING	PATRICIATE
PASSIONLESSLY	PASTNESSES	PATERNALISM	PATHOPHOBIA	PATRICIATES
PASSIONLESSNESS	PASTORALES	PATERNALISMS	PATHOPHOBIAS	PATRICIDAL
PASSIVATED	PASTORALISM	PATERNALIST	PATHOPHYSIOLOGY	PATRICIDES
PASSIVATES	PASTORALISMS	PATERNALISTIC	PATIBULARY	PATRICLINIC
PASSIVATING	PASTORALIST	PATERNALISTS	PATIENTEST	PATRICLINOUS
PASSIVATION	PASTORALISTS	PATERNALLY	PATIENTING	PATRIFOCAL
PASSIVATIONS	PASTORALLY	PATERNITIES	PATINATING	PATRIFOCALITIES
PASSIVENESS	PASTORALNESS	PATERNOSTER	PATINATION	PATRIFOCALITY
PASSIVENESSES	PASTORALNESSES	PATERNOSTERS	PATINATIONS	PATRILINEAGE
PASSIVISMS	PASTORATES	PATHBREAKING	PATINISING	PATRILINEAGES
PASSIVISTS	PASTORIUMS	PATHETICAL	PATINIZING	PATRILINEAL
PASSIVITIES	PASTORLIER	PATHETICALLY	PATISSERIE	PATRILINEALLY
PASSMENTED	PASTORLIEST	PATHFINDER	PATISSERIES	PATRILINEAR
PASSMENTING	PASTORSHIP	PATHFINDERS	PATISSIERS	PATRILINEARLY
PASSPORTED	PASTORSHIPS	PATHFINDING	PATRESFAMILIAS	PATRILINIES
PASSPORTING	PASTOURELLE	PATHFINDINGS	PATRIALISATION	PATRILOCAL
PASTEBOARD	PASTOURELLES	PATHLESSNESS	PATRIALISATIONS	PATRILOCALLY
PASTEBOARDS	PASTRYCOOK	PATHLESSNESSES	PATRIALISE	PATRIMONIAL
PASTEDOWNS	PASTRYCOOKS	PATHOBIOLOGIES	PATRIALISED	PATRIMONIALLY
PASTELISTS	PASTURABLE	PATHOBIOLOGY	PATRIALISES	PATRIMONIES
PASTELLIST	PASTURAGES	PATHOGENES	PATRIALISING	PATRIOTICALLY
PASTELLISTS	PASTURELAND	PATHOGENESES	PATRIALISM	PATRIOTISM
PASTEURELLA	PASTURELANDS	PATHOGENESIS	PATRIALISMS	PATRIOTISMS
PASTEURELLAE	PASTURELESS	PATHOGENETIC	PATRIALITIES	PATRISTICAL
PASTEURELLAS	PATAPHYSICS	PATHOGENIC	PATRIALITY	PATRISTICALLY
PASTEURISATION	PATCHBOARD	PATHOGENICITIES	PATRIALIZATION	PATRISTICISM
PASTEURISATIONS	PATCHBOARDS	PATHOGENICITY	PATRIALIZATIONS	PATRISTICISMS
PASTEURISE	PATCHCOCKE	PATHOGENIES	PATRIALIZE	PATRISTICS
PASTEURISED	PATCHCOCKES	PATHOGENOUS	PATRIALIZED	PATROCLINAL
PASTEURISER	PATCHERIES	PATHOGNOMIES	PATRIALIZES	PATROCLINIC
PASTEURISERS	PATCHINESS	PATHOGNOMONIC	PATRIALIZING	PATROCLINIES
PASTEURISES	PATCHINESSES	PATHOGNOMY	PATRIARCHAL	PATROCLINOUS
PASTEURISING	PATCHOCKES	PATHOGRAPHIES	PATRIARCHALISM	PATROCLINY
PASTEURISM	PATCHOULIES	PATHOGRAPHY	PATRIARCHALISMS	PATROLLERS
PASTEURISMS	PATCHOULIS	PATHOLOGIC	PATRIARCHALLY	PATROLLING

PATROLOGICAL	PAUPERISATION	PEACETIMES	PECKISHNESS	PEDAGOGUISHNESS
PATROLOGIES	PAUPERISATIONS	PEACHBLOWS	PECKISHNESSES	PEDAGOGUISM
PATROLOGIST	PAUPERISED	PEACHERINO	PECTINACEOUS	PEDAGOGUISMS
PATROLOGISTS	PAUPERISES	PEACHERINOS	PECTINATED	PEDALBOATS
PATROLWOMAN	PAUPERISING	PEACHINESS	PECTINATELY	PEDALLINGS
PATROLWOMEN	PAUPERISMS	PEACHINESSES	PECTINATION	PEDANTICAL
PATRONAGED	PAUPERIZATION	PEACOCKERIES	PECTINATIONS	PEDANTICALLY
PATRONAGES	PAUPERIZATIONS	PEACOCKERY	PECTINESTERASE	PEDANTICISE
PATRONAGING	PAUPERIZED	PEACOCKIER	PECTINESTERASES	PEDANTICISED
PATRONESSES	PAUPERIZES	PEACOCKIEST	PECTINEUSES	PEDANTICISES
PATRONISATION	PAUPERIZING	PEACOCKING	PECTISABLE	PEDANTICISING
PATRONISATIONS	PAUPIETTES	PEACOCKISH	PECTISATION	PEDANTICISM
PATRONISED	PAUSEFULLY	PEAKEDNESS	PECTISATIONS	PEDANTICISMS
PATRONISER	PAUSELESSLY	PEAKEDNESSES	PECTIZABLE	PEDANTICIZE
PATRONISERS	PAVEMENTED	PEAKINESSES	PECTIZATION	PEDANTICIZED
PATRONISES	PAVEMENTING	PEANUTTIER	PECTIZATIONS	PEDANTICIZES
PATRONISING	PAVILIONED	PEANUTTIEST	PECTOLITES	PEDANTICIZING
PATRONISINGLY	PAVILIONING	PEARLASHES	PECTORALLY	PEDANTISED
PATRONIZATION	PAVONAZZOS	PEARLESCENCE	PECTORILOQUIES	PEDANTISES
PATRONIZATIONS	PAWKINESSES	PEARLESCENCES	PECTORILOQUY	PEDANTISING
PATRONIZED	PAWNBROKER	PEARLESCENT	PECULATING	PEDANTISMS
PATRONIZER	PAWNBROKERS	PEARLINESS	PECULATION	PEDANTIZED
PATRONIZERS	PAWNBROKING	PEARLINESSES	PECULATIONS	PEDANTIZES
PATRONIZES	PAWNBROKINGS	PEARLWARES	PECULATORS	PEDANTIZING
PATRONIZING	PAWNTICKET	PEARLWORTS	PECULIARISE	PEDANTOCRACIES
PATRONIZINGLY	PAWNTICKETS	PEARMONGER	PECULIARISED	PEDANTOCRACY
PATRONLESS	PAYCHEQUES	PEARMONGERS	PECULIARISES	PEDANTOCRAT
PATRONLIER	PAYMASTERS	PEARTNESSES	PECULIARISING	PEDANTOCRATIC
PATRONLIEST	PAYNIMRIES	PEASANTIER	PECULIARITIES	PEDANTOCRATS
PATRONYMIC	PAYSAGISTS	PEASANTIEST	PECULIARITY	PEDANTRIES
PATRONYMICS	PEABERRIES	PEASANTRIES	PECULIARIZE	PEDDLERIES
PATROONSHIP	PEACEABLENESS	PEASHOOTER	PECULIARIZED	PEDERASTIC
PATROONSHIPS	PEACEABLENESSES	PEASHOOTERS	PECULIARIZES	PEDERASTIES
PATTERNING	PEACEFULLER	PEASOUPERS	PECULIARIZING	PEDEREROES
PATTERNINGS	PEACEFULLEST	PEBBLEDASH	PECULIARLY	PEDESTALED
PATTERNLESS	PEACEFULLY	PEBBLEDASHED	PECUNIARILY	PEDESTALING
PATTRESSES	PEACEFULNESS	PEBBLEDASHES	PEDAGOGICAL	PEDESTALLED
PATULOUSLY	PEACEFULNESSES	PEBBLEDASHING	PEDAGOGICALLY	PEDESTALLING
PATULOUSNESS	PEACEKEEPER	PEBBLEWEAVE	PEDAGOGICS	PEDESTRIAN
PATULOUSNESSES	PEACEKEEPERS	PEBBLEWEAVES	PEDAGOGIES	PEDESTRIANISE
PAUCILOQUENT	PEACEKEEPING	PECCABILITIES	PEDAGOGISM	PEDESTRIANISED
PAUGHTIEST	PEACEKEEPINGS	PECCABILITY	PEDAGOGISMS	PEDESTRIANISES
PAULOWNIAS	PEACELESSNESS	PECCADILLO	PEDAGOGUED	PEDESTRIANISING
PAUNCHIEST	PEACELESSNESSES	PECCADILLOES	PEDAGOGUERIES	PEDESTRIANISM
PAUNCHINESS	PEACEMAKER	PECCADILLOS	PEDAGOGUERY	PEDESTRIANISMS
PAUNCHINESSES	PEACEMAKERS	PECCANCIES	PEDAGOGUES	PEDESTRIANIZE
PAUPERDOMS	PEACEMAKING	PECKERWOOD	PEDAGOGUING	PEDESTRIANIZED
PAUPERESSES	PEACEMAKINGS	PECKERWOODS	PEDAGOGUISH	PEDESTRIANIZES

PEDESTRIANIZING

PEDESTRIANIZING	PEERLESSNESS	PELTMONGER	PENEPLANATION	PENINSULAR
PEDESTRIANS	PEERLESSNESSES	PELTMONGERS	PENEPLANATIONS	PENINSULARITIES
PEDETENTOUS	PEEVISHNESS	PELVIMETER	PENEPLANES	PENINSULARITY
PEDIATRICIAN	PEEVISHNESSES	PELVIMETERS	PENETRABILITIES	PENINSULAS
PEDIATRICIANS	PEGMATITES	PELVIMETRIES	PENETRABILITY	PENINSULATE
PEDIATRICS	PEGMATITIC	PELVIMETRY	PENETRABLE	PENINSULATED
PEDIATRIST	PEIRASTICALLY	PELYCOSAUR	PENETRABLENESS	PENINSULATES
PEDIATRISTS	PEJORATING	PELYCOSAURS	PENETRABLY	PENINSULATING
PEDICELLARIA	PEJORATION	PEMPHIGOID	PENETRALIA	PENISTONES
PEDICELLARIAE	PEJORATIONS	PEMPHIGOIDS	PENETRALIAN	PENITENCES
PEDICELLATE	PEJORATIVE	PEMPHIGOUS	PENETRANCE	PENITENCIES
PEDICULATE	PEJORATIVELY	PEMPHIGUSES	PENETRANCES	PENITENTIAL
PEDICULATED	PEJORATIVES	PENALISATION	PENETRANCIES	PENITENTIALLY
PEDICULATES	PELARGONIC	PENALISATIONS	PENETRANCY	PENITENTIALS
PEDICULATION	PELARGONIUM	PENALISING	PENETRANTS	PENITENTIARIES
PEDICULATIONS	PELARGONIUMS	PENALITIES	PENETRATED	PENITENTIARY
PEDICULOSES	PELECYPODS	PENALIZATION	PENETRATES	PENITENTLY
PEDICULOSIS	PELLAGRINS	PENALIZATIONS	PENETRATING	PENMANSHIP
PEDICULOUS	PELLAGROUS	PENALIZING	PENETRATINGLY	PENMANSHIPS
PEDICURING	PELLETIFIED	PENANNULAR	PENETRATION	PENNACEOUS
PEDICURIST	PELLETIFIES	PENCILINGS	PENETRATIONS	PENNALISMS
PEDICURISTS	PELLETIFYING	PENCILLERS	PENETRATIVE	PENNATULACEOUS
PEDIMENTAL	PELLETISATION	PENCILLING	PENETRATIVELY	PENNATULAE
PEDIMENTED	PELLETISATIONS	PENCILLINGS	PENETRATIVENESS	PENNATULAS
PEDIPALPUS	PELLETISED	PENDENCIES	PENETRATOR	PENNILESSLY
PEDOGENESES	PELLETISER	PENDENTIVE	PENETRATORS	PENNILESSNESS
PEDOGENESIS	PELLETISERS	PENDENTIVES	PENETROMETER	PENNILESSNESSES
PEDOGENETIC	PELLETISES	PENDICLERS	PENETROMETERS	PENNILLION
PEDOLOGICAL	PELLETISING	PENDRAGONS	PENFRIENDS	PENNINITES
PEDOLOGIES	PELLETIZATION	PENDRAGONSHIP	PENGUINERIES	PENNONCELLE
PEDOLOGIST	PELLETIZATIONS	PENDRAGONSHIPS	PENGUINERY	PENNONCELLES
PEDOLOGISTS	PELLETIZED	PENDULATED	PENGUINRIES	PENNONCELS
PEDOMETERS	PELLETIZER	PENDULATES	PENHOLDERS	PENNYCRESS
PEDOPHILES	PELLETIZERS	PENDULATING	PENICILLAMINE	PENNYCRESSES
PEDOPHILIA	PELLETIZES	PENDULOSITIES	PENICILLAMINES	PENNYLANDS
PEDOPHILIAC	PELLETIZING	PENDULOSITY	PENICILLATE	PENNYROYAL
PEDOPHILIACS	PELLICULAR	PENDULOUSLY	PENICILLATELY	PENNYROYALS
PEDOPHILIAS	PELLITORIES	PENDULOUSNESS	PENICILLATION	PENNYWEIGHT
PEDOPHILIC	PELLUCIDITIES	PENDULOUSNESSES	PENICILLATIONS	PENNYWEIGHTS
PEDOPHILICS	PELLUCIDITY	PENELOPISE	PENICILLIA	PENNYWHISTLE
PEDUNCULAR	PELLUCIDLY	PENELOPISED	PENICILLIFORM	PENNYWHISTLES
PEDUNCULATE	PELLUCIDNESS	PENELOPISES	PENICILLIN	PENNYWINKLE
PEDUNCULATED	PELLUCIDNESSES	PENELOPISING	PENICILLINASE	PENNYWINKLES
PEDUNCULATION	PELMANISMS	PENELOPIZE	PENICILLINASES	PENNYWORTH
PEDUNCULATIONS	PELOLOGIES	PENELOPIZED	PENICILLINS	PENNYWORTHS
PEELGARLIC	PELOTHERAPIES	PENELOPIZES	PENICILLIUM	PENNYWORTS
PEELGARLICS	PELOTHERAPY	PENELOPIZING	PENICILLIUMS	PENOLOGICAL
PEERLESSLY	PELTATIONS	PENEPLAINS	PENICILLUS	PENOLOGICALLY

PENOLOGIES	PENTAGRAPH	PENTATHLETE	PEOPLELESS	PEPTONISER
PENOLOGIST	PENTAGRAPHS	PENTATHLETES	PEPEROMIAS	PEPTONISERS
PENOLOGISTS	PENTAGYNIAN	PENTATHLON	PEPPERBOXES	PEPTONISES
PENONCELLE	PENTAGYNOUS	PENTATHLONS	PEPPERCORN	PEPTONISING
PENONCELLES	PENTAHEDRA	PENTATHLUM	PEPPERCORNIER	PEPTONIZATION
PENPUSHERS	PENTAHEDRAL	PENTATHLUMS	PEPPERCORNIEST	PEPTONIZATIONS
PENPUSHING	PENTAHEDRON	PENTATOMIC	PEPPERCORNS	PEPTONIZED
PENPUSHINGS	PENTAHEDRONS	PENTATONIC	PEPPERCORNY	PEPTONIZER
PENSEROSOS	PENTAHYDRATE	PENTAVALENCE	PEPPERGRASS	PEPTONIZERS
PENSIEROSO	PENTAHYDRATES	PENTAVALENCES	PEPPERGRASSES	PEPTONIZES
PENSILENESS	PENTALOGIES	PENTAVALENCIES	PEPPERIDGE	PEPTONIZING
PENSILENESSES	PENTALPHAS	PENTAVALENCY	PEPPERIDGES	PERACIDITIES
PENSILITIES	PENTAMERIES	PENTAVALENT	PEPPERIEST	PERACIDITY
PENSIONABLE	PENTAMERISM	PENTAZOCINE	PEPPERINESS	PERADVENTURE
PENSIONARIES	PENTAMERISMS	PENTAZOCINES	PEPPERINESSES	PERADVENTURES
PENSIONARY	PENTAMEROUS	PENTECONTER	PEPPERINGS	PERAEOPODS
PENSIONEER	PENTAMETER	PENTECONTERS	PEPPERMILL	PERAMBULATE
PENSIONERS	PENTAMETERS	PENTETERIC	PEPPERMILLS	PERAMBULATED
PENSIONING	PENTAMIDINE	PENTHEMIMER	PEPPERMINT	PERAMBULATES
PENSIONLESS	PENTAMIDINES	PENTHEMIMERAL	PEPPERMINTIER	PERAMBULATING
PENSIONNAT	PENTANDRIAN	PENTHEMIMERS	PEPPERMINTIEST	PERAMBULATION
PENSIONNATS	PENTANDROUS	PENTHOUSED	PEPPERMINTS	PERAMBULATIONS
PENSIVENESS	PENTANGLES	PENTHOUSES	PEPPERMINTY	PERAMBULATOR
PENSIVENESSES	PENTANGULAR	PENTHOUSING	PEPPERONIS	PERAMBULATORS
PENSTEMONS	PENTAPEPTIDE	PENTIMENTI	PEPPERTREE	PERAMBULATORY
PENTABARBITAL	PENTAPEPTIDES	PENTIMENTO	PEPPERTREES	PERBORATES
PENTABARBITALS	PENTAPLOID	PENTLANDITE	PEPPERWORT	PERCALINES
PENTACHORD	PENTAPLOIDIES	PENTLANDITES	PEPPERWORTS	PERCEIVABILITY
PENTACHORDS	PENTAPLOIDS	PENTOBARBITAL	PEPPINESSES	PERCEIVABLE
PENTACRINOID	PENTAPLOIDY	PENTOBARBITALS	PEPSINATED	PERCEIVABLY
PENTACRINOIDS	PENTAPODIC	PENTOBARBITONE	PEPSINATES	PERCEIVERS
PENTACTINAL	PENTAPODIES	PENTOBARBITONES	PEPSINATING	PERCEIVING
PENTACYCLIC	PENTAPOLIS	PENTOSANES	PEPSINOGEN	PERCEIVINGS
PENTADACTYL	PENTAPOLISES	PENTOSIDES	PEPSINOGENS	PERCENTAGE
PENTADACTYLE	PENTAPOLITAN	PENTOXIDES	PEPTALKING	PERCENTAGES
PENTADACTYLES	PENTAPRISM	PENTSTEMON	PEPTICITIES	PERCENTILE
PENTADACTYLIC	PENTAPRISMS	PENTSTEMONS	PEPTIDASES	PERCENTILES
PENTADACTYLIES	PENTAQUARK	PENTYLENES	PEPTIDOGLYCAN	PERCEPTIBILITY
PENTADACTYLISM	PENTAQUARKS	PENULTIMAS	PEPTIDOGLYCANS	PERCEPTIBLE
PENTADACTYLISMS	PENTARCHICAL	PENULTIMATE	PEPTISABLE	PERCEPTIBLY
PENTADACTYLOUS	PENTARCHIES	PENULTIMATELY	PEPTISATION	PERCEPTION
PENTADACTYLS	PENTASTICH	PENULTIMATES	PEPTISATIONS	PERCEPTIONAL
PENTADACTYLY	PENTASTICHOUS	PENUMBROUS	PEPTIZABLE	PERCEPTIONS
PENTADELPHOUS	PENTASTICHS	PENURIOUSLY	PEPTIZATION	PERCEPTIVE
PENTAGONAL	PENTASTYLE	PENURIOUSNESS	PEPTIZATIONS	PERCEPTIVELY
PENTAGONALLY	PENTASTYLES	PENURIOUSNESSES	PEPTONISATION	PERCEPTIVENESS
PENTAGONALS	PENTASYLLABIC	PEOPLEHOOD	PEPTONISATIONS	PERCEPTIVITIES
PENTAGRAMS	PENTATEUCHAL	PEOPLEHOODS	PEPTONISED	PERCEPTIVITY

P

PERCEPTUAL	PERDITIONABLE	PERFECTIBILISM	PERFORATING	PERICARPIC
PERCEPTUALLY	PERDITIONS	PERFECTIBILISMS	PERFORATION	PERICENTER
PERCHERIES	PERDUELLION	PERFECTIBILIST	PERFORATIONS	PERICENTERS
PERCHERONS	PERDUELLIONS	PERFECTIBILISTS	PERFORATIVE	PERICENTRAL
PERCHLORATE	PERDURABILITIES	PERFECTIBILITY	PERFORATOR	PERICENTRE
PERCHLORATES	PERDURABILITY	PERFECTIBLE	PERFORATORS	PERICENTRES
PERCHLORIC	PERDURABLE	PERFECTING	PERFORATORY	PERICENTRIC
PERCHLORIDE	PERDURABLY	PERFECTION	PERFORATUS	PERICHAETIA
PERCHLORIDES	PERDURANCE	PERFECTIONATE	PERFORATUSES	PERICHAETIAL
PERCHLOROETHENE	PERDURANCES	PERFECTIONATED	PERFORMABILITY	PERICHAETIUM
PERCIFORMS	PERDURATION	PERFECTIONATES	PERFORMABLE	PERICHONDRAL
PERCIPIENCE	PERDURATIONS	PERFECTIONATING	PERFORMANCE	PERICHONDRIA
PERCIPIENCES	PEREGRINATE	PERFECTIONISM	PERFORMANCES	PERICHONDRIAL
PERCIPIENCIES	PEREGRINATED	PERFECTIONISMS	PERFORMATIVE	PERICHONDRIUM
PERCIPIENCY	PEREGRINATES	PERFECTIONIST	PERFORMATIVELY	PERICHORESES
PERCIPIENT	PEREGRINATING	PERFECTIONISTIC	PERFORMATIVES	PERICHORESIS
PERCIPIENTLY	PEREGRINATION	PERFECTIONISTS	PERFORMATORY	PERICHYLOUS
PERCIPIENTS	PEREGRINATIONS	PERFECTIONS	PERFORMERS	PERICLASES
PERCOCTING	PEREGRINATOR	PERFECTIVE	PERFORMING	PERICLASTIC
PERCOIDEAN	PEREGRINATORS	PERFECTIVELY	PERFORMINGS	PERICLINAL
PERCOIDEANS	PEREGRINATORY	PERFECTIVENESS	PERFUMELESS	PERICLINES
PERCOLABLE	PEREGRINES	PERFECTIVES	PERFUMERIES	PERICLITATE
PERCOLATED	PEREGRINITIES	PERFECTIVITIES	PERFUMIERS	PERICLITATED
PERCOLATES	PEREGRINITY	PERFECTIVITY	PERFUMIEST	PERICLITATES
PERCOLATING	PEREIOPODS	PERFECTNESS	PERFUNCTORILY	PERICLITATING
PERCOLATION	PEREMPTORILY	PERFECTNESSES	PERFUNCTORINESS	PERICRANIA
PERCOLATIONS	PEREMPTORINESS	PERFECTORS	PERFUNCTORY	PERICRANIAL
PERCOLATIVE	PEREMPTORY	PERFERVIDITIES	PERFUSATES	PERICRANIUM
PERCOLATOR	PERENNATED	PERFERVIDITY	PERFUSIONIST	PERICRANIUMS
PERCOLATORS	PERENNATES	PERFERVIDLY	PERFUSIONISTS	PERICULOUS
PERCURRENT	PERENNATING	PERFERVIDNESS	PERFUSIONS	PERICYCLES
PERCURSORY	PERENNATION	PERFERVIDNESSES	PERGAMENEOUS	PERICYCLIC
PERCUSSANT	PERENNATIONS	PERFERVORS	PERGAMENTACEOUS	PERICYNTHIA
PERCUSSING	PERENNIALITIES	PERFERVOUR	PERGUNNAHS	PERICYNTHION
PERCUSSION	PERENNIALITY	PERFERVOURS	PERIASTRON	PERICYNTHIONS
PERCUSSIONAL	PERENNIALLY	PERFICIENT	PERIASTRONS	PERIDERMAL
PERCUSSIONIST	PERENNIALS	PERFICIENTS	PERIBLASTS	PERIDERMIC
PERCUSSIONISTS	PERENNIBRANCH	PERFIDIOUS	PERICARDIA	PERIDESMIA
PERCUSSIONS	PERENNIBRANCHS	PERFIDIOUSLY	PERICARDIAC	PERIDESMIUM
PERCUSSIVE	PERENNITIES	PERFIDIOUSNESS	PERICARDIAL	PERIDINIAN
PERCUSSIVELY	PERESTROIKA	PERFLUOROCARBON	PERICARDIAN	PERIDINIANS
PERCUSSIVENESS	PERESTROIKAS	PERFOLIATE	PERICARDITIC	PERIDINIUM
PERCUSSORS	PERFECTATION	PERFOLIATION	PERICARDITIDES	PERIDINIUMS
PERCUTANEOUS	PERFECTATIONS	PERFOLIATIONS	PERICARDITIS	PERIDOTITE
PERCUTANEOUSLY	PERFECTERS	PERFORABLE	PERICARDITISES	PERIDOTITES
PERCUTIENT	PERFECTEST	PERFORANSES	PERICARDIUM	PERIDOTITIC
PERCUTIENTS	PERFECTIBILIAN	PERFORATED	PERICARDIUMS	PERIDROMES
PERDENDOSI	PERFECTIBILIANS	PERFORATES	PERICARPIAL	PERIEGESES

PERIEGESIS
PERIGASTRIC
PERIGASTRITIS
PERIGASTRITISES
PERIGENESES
PERIGENESIS
PERIGLACIAL
PERIGONIAL
PERIGONIUM
PERIGYNIES
PERIGYNOUS
PERIHELIAL
PERIHELION
PERIHEPATIC
PERIHEPATITIS
PERIHEPATITISES
PERIKARYAL
PERIKARYON
PERILOUSLY
PERILOUSNESS
PERILOUSNESSES
PERILYMPHS
PERIMENOPAUSAL
PERIMENOPAUSE
PERIMENOPAUSES
PERIMETERS
PERIMETRAL
PERIMETRIC
PERIMETRICAL
PERIMETRICALLY
PERIMETRIES
PERIMORPHIC
PERIMORPHISM
PERIMORPHISMS
PERIMORPHOUS
PERIMORPHS
PERIMYSIUM
PERINAEUMS
PERINATALLY
PERINEPHRIA
PERINEPHRIC
PERINEPHRITIS
PERINEPHRITISES
PERINEPHRIUM
PERINEURAL
PERINEURIA
PERINEURIAL
PERINEURITIC

PERINEURITIS
PERINEURITISES
PERINEURIUM
PERIODATES
PERIODICAL
PERIODICALIST
PERIODICALISTS
PERIODICALLY
PERIODICALS
PERIODICITIES
PERIODICITY
PERIODIDES
PERIODISATION
PERIODISATIONS
PERIODISED
PERIODISES
PERIODISING
PERIODIZATION
PERIODIZATIONS
PERIODIZED
PERIODIZES
PERIODIZING
PERIODONTAL
PERIODONTALLY
PERIODONTIA
PERIODONTIAS
PERIODONTIC
PERIODONTICALLY
PERIODONTICS
PERIODONTIST
PERIODONTISTS
PERIODONTITIS
PERIODONTITISES
PERIODONTOLOGY
PERIONYCHIA
PERIONYCHIUM
PERIOSTEAL
PERIOSTEUM
PERIOSTITIC
PERIOSTITIDES
PERIOSTITIS
PERIOSTITISES
PERIOSTRACUM
PERIOSTRACUMS
PERIPATETIC
PERIPATETICAL
PERIPATETICALLY
PERIPATETICISM

PERIPATETICISMS
PERIPATETICS
PERIPATUSES
PERIPETEIA
PERIPETEIAN
PERIPETEIAS
PERIPETIAN
PERIPETIAS
PERIPETIES
PERIPHERAL
PERIPHERALITIES
PERIPHERALITY
PERIPHERALLY
PERIPHERALS
PERIPHERIC
PERIPHERICAL
PERIPHERIES
PERIPHONIC
PERIPHRASE
PERIPHRASED
PERIPHRASES
PERIPHRASING
PERIPHRASIS
PERIPHRASTIC
PERIPHRASTICAL
PERIPHYTIC
PERIPHYTON
PERIPHYTONS
PERIPLASMS
PERIPLASTS
PERIPLUSES
PERIPROCTS
PERIPTERAL
PERIPTERIES
PERISARCAL
PERISARCOUS
PERISCIANS
PERISCOPES
PERISCOPIC
PERISCOPICALLY
PERISELENIA
PERISELENIUM
PERISHABILITIES
PERISHABILITY
PERISHABLE
PERISHABLENESS
PERISHABLES
PERISHABLY

PERISHINGLY
PERISPERMAL
PERISPERMIC
PERISPERMS
PERISPOMENA
PERISPOMENON
PERISPOMENONS
PERISSODACTYL
PERISSODACTYLE
PERISSODACTYLES
PERISSODACTYLIC
PERISSODACTYLS
PERISSOLOGIES
PERISSOLOGY
PERISSOSYLLABIC
PERISTALITH
PERISTALITHS
PERISTALSES
PERISTALSIS
PERISTALTIC
PERISTALTICALLY
PERISTERITE
PERISTERITES
PERISTERONIC
PERISTOMAL
PERISTOMATIC
PERISTOMES
PERISTOMIAL
PERISTREPHIC
PERISTYLAR
PERISTYLES
PERITECTIC
PERITECTICS
PERITHECIA
PERITHECIAL
PERITHECIUM
PERITONAEA
PERITONAEAL
PERITONAEUM
PERITONAEUMS
PERITONEAL
PERITONEALLY
PERITONEOSCOPY
PERITONEUM
PERITONEUMS
PERITONITIC
PERITONITIS
PERITONITISES

PERITRACKS
PERITRICHA
PERITRICHOUS
PERITRICHOUSLY
PERITRICHS
PERITYPHLITIS
PERITYPHLITISES
PERIVITELLINE
PERIWIGGED
PERIWIGGING
PERIWINKLE
PERIWINKLES
PERJINKETY
PERJINKITIES
PERJINKITY
PERJURIOUS
PERJURIOUSLY
PERKINESSES
PERLEMOENS
PERLOCUTION
PERLOCUTIONARY
PERLOCUTIONS
PERLUSTRATE
PERLUSTRATED
PERLUSTRATES
PERLUSTRATING
PERLUSTRATION
PERLUSTRATIONS
PERMABEARS
PERMABULLS
PERMACULTURE
PERMACULTURES
PERMAFROST
PERMAFROSTS
PERMALINKS
PERMALLOYS
PERMANENCE
PERMANENCES
PERMANENCIES
PERMANENCY
PERMANENTLY
PERMANENTNESS
PERMANENTNESSES
PERMANENTS
PERMANGANATE
PERMANGANATES
PERMANGANIC
PERMEABILITIES

PERMEABILITY

PERMEABILITY
PERMEABLENESS
PERMEABLENESSES
PERMEAMETER
PERMEAMETERS
PERMEANCES
PERMEATING
PERMEATION
PERMEATIONS
PERMEATIVE
PERMEATORS
PERMETHRIN
PERMETHRINS
PERMILLAGE
PERMILLAGES
PERMISSIBILITY
PERMISSIBLE
PERMISSIBLENESS
PERMISSIBLY
PERMISSION
PERMISSIONS
PERMISSIVE
PERMISSIVELY
PERMISSIVENESS
PERMITTANCE
PERMITTANCES
PERMITTEES
PERMITTERS
PERMITTING
PERMITTIVITIES
PERMITTIVITY
PERMUTABILITIES
PERMUTABILITY
PERMUTABLE
PERMUTABLENESS
PERMUTABLY
PERMUTATED
PERMUTATES
PERMUTATING
PERMUTATION
PERMUTATIONAL
PERMUTATIONS
PERNANCIES
PERNICIOUS
PERNICIOUSLY
PERNICIOUSNESS
PERNICKETIER
PERNICKETIEST

PERNICKETINESS
PERNICKETY
PERNOCTATE
PERNOCTATED
PERNOCTATES
PERNOCTATING
PERNOCTATION
PERNOCTATIONS
PERONEUSES
PERORATING
PERORATION
PERORATIONAL
PERORATIONS
PERORATORS
PEROVSKIAS
PEROVSKITE
PEROVSKITES
PEROXIDASE
PEROXIDASES
PEROXIDATION
PEROXIDATIONS
PEROXIDING
PEROXIDISE
PEROXIDISED
PEROXIDISES
PEROXIDISING
PEROXIDIZE
PEROXIDIZED
PEROXIDIZES
PEROXIDIZING
PEROXISOMAL
PEROXISOME
PEROXISOMES
PEROXYSULPHURIC
PERPENDICULAR
PERPENDICULARLY
PERPENDICULARS
PERPENDING
PERPETRABLE
PERPETRATE
PERPETRATED
PERPETRATES
PERPETRATING
PERPETRATION
PERPETRATIONS
PERPETRATOR
PERPETRATORS
PERPETUABLE

PERPETUALISM
PERPETUALISMS
PERPETUALIST
PERPETUALISTS
PERPETUALITIES
PERPETUALITY
PERPETUALLY
PERPETUALS
PERPETUANCE
PERPETUANCES
PERPETUATE
PERPETUATED
PERPETUATES
PERPETUATING
PERPETUATION
PERPETUATIONS
PERPETUATOR
PERPETUATORS
PERPETUITIES
PERPETUITY
PERPHENAZINE
PERPHENAZINES
PERPLEXEDLY
PERPLEXEDNESS
PERPLEXEDNESSES
PERPLEXERS
PERPLEXING
PERPLEXINGLY
PERPLEXITIES
PERPLEXITY
PERQUISITE
PERQUISITES
PERQUISITION
PERQUISITIONS
PERQUISITOR
PERQUISITORS
PERRUQUIER
PERRUQUIERS
PERSCRUTATION
PERSCRUTATIONS
PERSECUTED
PERSECUTEE
PERSECUTEES
PERSECUTES
PERSECUTING
PERSECUTION
PERSECUTIONS
PERSECUTIVE

PERSECUTOR
PERSECUTORS
PERSECUTORY
PERSEITIES
PERSELINES
PERSEVERANCE
PERSEVERANCES
PERSEVERANT
PERSEVERATE
PERSEVERATED
PERSEVERATES
PERSEVERATING
PERSEVERATION
PERSEVERATIONS
PERSEVERATIVE
PERSEVERATOR
PERSEVERATORS
PERSEVERED
PERSEVERES
PERSEVERING
PERSEVERINGLY
PERSICARIA
PERSICARIAS
PERSIENNES
PERSIFLAGE
PERSIFLAGES
PERSIFLEUR
PERSIFLEURS
PERSIMMONS
PERSISTENCE
PERSISTENCES
PERSISTENCIES
PERSISTENCY
PERSISTENT
PERSISTENTLY
PERSISTENTS
PERSISTERS
PERSISTING
PERSISTINGLY
PERSISTIVE
PERSNICKETIER
PERSNICKETIEST
PERSNICKETINESS
PERSNICKETY
PERSONABLE
PERSONABLENESS
PERSONABLY
PERSONAGES

PERSONALIA
PERSONALISATION
PERSONALISE
PERSONALISED
PERSONALISES
PERSONALISING
PERSONALISM
PERSONALISMS
PERSONALIST
PERSONALISTIC
PERSONALISTS
PERSONALITIES
PERSONALITY
PERSONALIZATION
PERSONALIZE
PERSONALIZED
PERSONALIZES
PERSONALIZING
PERSONALLY
PERSONALTIES
PERSONALTY
PERSONATED
PERSONATES
PERSONATING
PERSONATINGS
PERSONATION
PERSONATIONS
PERSONATIVE
PERSONATOR
PERSONATORS
PERSONHOOD
PERSONHOODS
PERSONIFIABLE
PERSONIFICATION
PERSONIFIED
PERSONIFIER
PERSONIFIERS
PERSONIFIES
PERSONIFYING
PERSONISED
PERSONISES
PERSONISING
PERSONIZED
PERSONIZES
PERSONIZING
PERSONNELS
PERSONPOWER
PERSONPOWERS

PERSPECTIVAL	PERSULFURIC	PERVERSEST	PESTOLOGISTS	PETRODOLLARS
PERSPECTIVE	PERSULPHATE	PERVERSION	PETAHERTZES	PETRODROME
PERSPECTIVELY	PERSULPHATES	PERVERSIONS	PETALIFEROUS	PETRODROMES
PERSPECTIVES	PERSULPHURIC	PERVERSITIES	PETALODIES	PETROGENESES
PERSPECTIVISM	PERSWADING	PERVERSITY	PETALOMANIA	PETROGENESIS
PERSPECTIVISMS	PERTAINING	PERVERSIVE	PETALOMANIAS	PETROGENETIC
PERSPECTIVIST	PERTINACIOUS	PERVERTEDLY	PETAMETERS	PETROGENIES
PERSPECTIVISTS	PERTINACIOUSLY	PERVERTEDNESS	PETAMETRES	PETROGLYPH
PERSPICACIOUS	PERTINACITIES	PERVERTEDNESSES	PETAURINES	PETROGLYPHIC
PERSPICACIOUSLY	PERTINACITY	PERVERTERS	PETAURISTS	PETROGLYPHIES
PERSPICACITIES	PERTINENCE	PERVERTIBLE	PETCHARIES	PETROGLYPHS
PERSPICACITY	PERTINENCES	PERVERTING	PETERSHAMS	PETROGLYPHY
PERSPICUITIES	PERTINENCIES	PERVIATING	PETHIDINES	PETROGRAMS
PERSPICUITY	PERTINENCY	PERVICACIES	PETIOLATED	PETROGRAPHER
PERSPICUOUS	PERTINENTLY	PERVICACIOUS	PETIOLULES	PETROGRAPHERS
PERSPICUOUSLY	PERTINENTS	PERVICACITIES	PETITENESS	PETROGRAPHIC
PERSPICUOUSNESS	PERTNESSES	PERVICACITY	PETITENESSES	PETROGRAPHICAL
PERSPIRABLE	PERTURBABLE	PERVIOUSLY	PETITIONARY	PETROGRAPHIES
PERSPIRATE	PERTURBABLY	PERVIOUSNESS	PETITIONED	PETROGRAPHY
PERSPIRATED	PERTURBANCE	PERVIOUSNESSES	PETITIONER	PETROLAGES
PERSPIRATES	PERTURBANCES	PESCATARIAN	PETITIONERS	PETROLATUM
PERSPIRATING	PERTURBANT	PESCATARIANS	PETITIONING	PETROLATUMS
PERSPIRATION	PERTURBANTS	PESCETARIAN	PETITIONINGS	PETROLEOUS
PERSPIRATIONS	PERTURBATE	PESCETARIANS	PETITIONIST	PETROLEUMS
PERSPIRATORY	PERTURBATED	PESHMERGAS	PETITIONISTS	PETROLEURS
PERSPIRIER	PERTURBATES	PESKINESSES	PETNAPINGS	PETROLEUSE
PERSPIRIEST	PERTURBATING	PESSIMISMS	PETNAPPERS	PETROLEUSES
PERSPIRING	PERTURBATION	PESSIMISTIC	PETNAPPING	PETROLHEAD
PERSPIRINGLY	PERTURBATIONAL	PESSIMISTICAL	PETNAPPINGS	PETROLHEADS
PERSTRINGE	PERTURBATIONS	PESSIMISTICALLY	PETRICHORS	PETROLIFEROUS
PERSTRINGED	PERTURBATIVE	PESSIMISTS	PETRIFACTION	PETROLLING
PERSTRINGES	PERTURBATOR	PESTERINGLY	PETRIFACTIONS	PETROLOGIC
PERSTRINGING	PERTURBATORIES	PESTERMENT	PETRIFACTIVE	PETROLOGICAL
PERSUADABILITY	PERTURBATORS	PESTERMENTS	PETRIFICATION	PETROLOGICALLY
PERSUADABLE	PERTURBATORY	PESTHOUSES	PETRIFICATIONS	PETROLOGIES
PERSUADERS	PERTURBEDLY	PESTICIDAL	PETRIFIERS	PETROLOGIST
PERSUADING	PERTURBERS	PESTICIDES	PETRIFYING	PETROLOGISTS
PERSUASIBILITY	PERTURBING	PESTIFEROUS	PETRISSAGE	PETROMONEY
PERSUASIBLE	PERTURBINGLY	PESTIFEROUSLY	PETRISSAGES	PETROMONEYS
PERSUASION	PERTUSIONS	PESTIFEROUSNESS	PETROCHEMICAL	PETROMONIES
PERSUASIONS	PERTUSSISES	PESTILENCE	PETROCHEMICALLY	PETRONELLA
PERSUASIVE	PERVASIONS	PESTILENCES	PETROCHEMICALS	PETRONELLAS
PERSUASIVELY	PERVASIVELY	PESTILENTIAL	PETROCHEMIST	PETROPHYSICAL
PERSUASIVENESS	PERVASIVENESS	PESTILENTIALLY	PETROCHEMISTRY	PETROPHYSICIST
PERSUASIVES	PERVASIVENESSES	PESTILENTLY	PETROCHEMISTS	PETROPHYSICISTS
PERSUASORY	PERVERSELY	PESTOLOGICAL	PETROCURRENCIES	PETROPHYSICS
PERSULFATE	PERVERSENESS	PESTOLOGIES	PETROCURRENCY	PETROPOUNDS
PERSULFATES	PERVERSENESSES	PESTOLOGIST	PETRODOLLAR	PETROSTATE

P

PETROSTATES	PHAGOCYTISED	PHALLOIDINS	PHARMACEUTICALS	PHARYNGOSCOPIC
PETTEDNESS	PHAGOCYTISES	PHANEROGAM	PHARMACEUTICS	PHARYNGOSCOPIES
PETTEDNESSES	PHAGOCYTISING	PHANEROGAMIC	PHARMACEUTIST	PHARYNGOSCOPY
PETTICHAPS	PHAGOCYTISM	PHANEROGAMOUS	PHARMACEUTISTS	PHARYNGOTOMIES
PETTICHAPSES	PHAGOCYTISMS	PHANEROGAMS	PHARMACIES	PHARYNGOTOMY
PETTICOATED	PHAGOCYTIZE	PHANEROPHYTE	PHARMACIST	PHASCOGALE
PETTICOATS	PHAGOCYTIZED	PHANEROPHYTES	PHARMACISTS	PHASCOGALES
PETTIFOGGED	PHAGOCYTIZES	PHANSIGARS	PHARMACODYNAMIC	PHASEDOWNS
PETTIFOGGER	PHAGOCYTIZING	PHANTASIAST	PHARMACOGENOMIC	PHASEOLINS
PETTIFOGGERIES	PHAGOCYTOSE	PHANTASIASTS	PHARMACOGNOSIES	PHATICALLY
PETTIFOGGERS	PHAGOCYTOSED	PHANTASIED	PHARMACOGNOSIST	PHEASANTRIES
PETTIFOGGERY	PHAGOCYTOSES	PHANTASIES	PHARMACOGNOSTIC	PHEASANTRY
PETTIFOGGING	PHAGOCYTOSING	PHANTASIME	PHARMACOGNOSY	PHELLODERM
PETTIFOGGINGS	PHAGOCYTOSIS	PHANTASIMES	PHARMACOKINETIC	PHELLODERMAL
PETTINESSES	PHAGOCYTOTIC	PHANTASIMS	PHARMACOLOGIC	PHELLODERMS
PETTISHNESS	PHAGOMANIA	PHANTASMAGORIA	PHARMACOLOGICAL	PHELLOGENETIC
PETTISHNESSES	PHAGOMANIAC	PHANTASMAGORIAL	PHARMACOLOGIES	PHELLOGENIC
PETULANCES	PHAGOMANIACS	PHANTASMAGORIAS	PHARMACOLOGIST	PHELLOGENS
PETULANCIES	PHAGOMANIAS	PHANTASMAGORIC	PHARMACOLOGISTS	PHELLOPLASTIC
PETULANTLY	PHAGOPHOBIA	PHANTASMAGORIES	PHARMACOLOGY	PHELLOPLASTICS
PEWHOLDERS	PHAGOPHOBIAS	PHANTASMAGORY	PHARMACOPEIA	PHELONIONS
PEWTERIEST	PHAGOSOMES	PHANTASMAL	PHARMACOPEIAL	PHENACAINE
PHACOLITES	PHALANGEAL	PHANTASMALIAN	PHARMACOPEIAS	PHENACAINES
PHACOLITHS	PHALANGERS	PHANTASMALITIES	PHARMACOPOEIA	PHENACETIN
PHAELONION	PHALANGIDS	PHANTASMALITY	PHARMACOPOEIAL	PHENACETINS
PHAELONIONS	PHALANGIST	PHANTASMALLY	PHARMACOPOEIAN	PHENACITES
PHAENOGAMIC	PHALANGISTS	PHANTASMATA	PHARMACOPOEIANS	PHENAKISMS
PHAENOGAMOUS	PHALANSTERIAN	PHANTASMIC	PHARMACOPOEIAS	PHENAKISTOSCOPE
PHAENOGAMS	PHALANSTERIANS	PHANTASMICAL	PHARMACOPOEIC	PHENAKITES
PHAENOLOGIES	PHALANSTERIES	PHANTASMICALLY	PHARMACOPOEIST	PHENANTHRENE
PHAENOLOGY	PHALANSTERISM	PHANTASTIC	PHARMACOPOEISTS	PHENANTHRENES
PHAENOMENA	PHALANSTERISMS	PHANTASTICS	PHARMACOPOLIST	PHENARSAZINE
PHAENOMENON	PHALANSTERIST	PHANTASTRIES	PHARMACOPOLISTS	PHENARSAZINES
PHAENOTYPE	PHALANSTERISTS	PHANTASTRY	PHARMACOTHERAPY	PHENAZINES
PHAENOTYPED	PHALANSTERY	PHANTASYING	PHARYNGALS	PHENCYCLIDINE
PHAENOTYPES	PHALAROPES	PHANTOMATIC	PHARYNGEAL	PHENCYCLIDINES
PHAENOTYPING	PHALLICALLY	PHANTOMISH	PHARYNGEALS	PHENETICIST
PHAEOMELANIN	PHALLICISM	PHANTOMLIKE	PHARYNGITIC	PHENETICISTS
PHAEOMELANINS	PHALLICISMS	PHANTOSMES	PHARYNGITIDES	PHENETIDINE
PHAGEDAENA	PHALLICIST	PHARISAICAL	PHARYNGITIS	PHENETIDINES
PHAGEDAENAS	PHALLICISTS	PHARISAICALLY	PHARYNGITISES	PHENETOLES
PHAGEDAENIC	PHALLOCENTRIC	PHARISAICALNESS	PHARYNGOLOGICAL	PHENFORMIN
PHAGEDENAS	PHALLOCENTRISM	PHARISAISM	PHARYNGOLOGIES	PHENFORMINS
PHAGEDENIC	PHALLOCENTRISMS	PHARISAISMS	PHARYNGOLOGIST	PHENGOPHOBIA
PHAGOCYTES	PHALLOCRAT	PHARISEEISM	PHARYNGOLOGISTS	PHENGOPHOBIAS
PHAGOCYTIC	PHALLOCRATIC	PHARISEEISMS	PHARYNGOLOGY	PHENMETRAZINE
PHAGOCYTICAL	PHALLOCRATS	PHARMACEUTIC	PHARYNGOSCOPE	PHENMETRAZINES
PHAGOCYTISE	PHALLOIDIN	PHARMACEUTICAL	PHARYNGOSCOPES	PHENOBARBITAL

PHENOBARBITALS	PHENOMENOLOGIST	PHILANTHROPIES	PHILOLOGERS	PHILOSOPHIZERS
PHENOBARBITONE	PHENOMENOLOGY	PHILANTHROPIST	PHILOLOGIAN	PHILOSOPHIZES
PHENOBARBITONES	PHENOMENON	PHILANTHROPISTS	PHILOLOGIANS	PHILOSOPHIZING
PHENOBARBS	PHENOMENONS	PHILANTHROPOID	PHILOLOGIC	PHILOSOPHIZINGS
PHENOCOPIES	PHENOTHIAZINE	PHILANTHROPOIDS	PHILOLOGICAL	PHILOSOPHY
PHENOCRYST	PHENOTHIAZINES	PHILANTHROPY	PHILOLOGICALLY	PHILOXENIA
PHENOCRYSTIC	PHENOTYPED	PHILATELIC	PHILOLOGIES	PHILOXENIAS
PHENOCRYSTS	PHENOTYPES	PHILATELICALLY	PHILOLOGIST	PHILTERING
PHENOLATED	PHENOTYPIC	PHILATELIES	PHILOLOGISTS	PHISNOMIES
PHENOLATES	PHENOTYPICAL	PHILATELIST	PHILOLOGUE	PHLEBECTOMIES
PHENOLATING	PHENOTYPICALLY	PHILATELISTS	PHILOLOGUES	PHLEBECTOMY
PHENOLOGICAL	PHENOTYPING	PHILAVERIES	PHILOMATHIC	PHLEBITIDES
PHENOLOGICALLY	PHENOXIDES	PHILHARMONIC	PHILOMATHICAL	PHLEBITISES
PHENOLOGIES	PHENTOLAMINE	PHILHARMONICS	PHILOMATHIES	PHLEBOGRAM
PHENOLOGIST	PHENTOLAMINES	PHILHELLENE	PHILOMATHS	PHLEBOGRAMS
PHENOLOGISTS	PHENYLALANIN	PHILHELLENES	PHILOMATHY	PHLEBOGRAPHIC
PHENOLPHTHALEIN	PHENYLALANINE	PHILHELLENIC	PHILOMELAS	PHLEBOGRAPHIES
PHENOMENAL	PHENYLALANINES	PHILHELLENISM	PHILOPENAS	PHLEBOGRAPHY
PHENOMENALISE	PHENYLALANINS	PHILHELLENISMS	PHILOPOENA	PHLEBOLITE
PHENOMENALISED	PHENYLAMINE	PHILHELLENIST	PHILOPOENAS	PHLEBOLITES
PHENOMENALISES	PHENYLAMINES	PHILHELLENISTS	PHILOSOPHASTER	PHLEBOLOGIES
PHENOMENALISING	PHENYLBUTAZONE	PHILHORSES	PHILOSOPHASTERS	PHLEBOLOGY
PHENOMENALISM	PHENYLBUTAZONES	PHILIPPICS	PHILOSOPHE	PHLEBOSCLEROSES
PHENOMENALISMS	PHENYLENES	PHILIPPINA	PHILOSOPHER	PHLEBOSCLEROSIS
PHENOMENALIST	PHENYLEPHRINE	PHILIPPINAS	PHILOSOPHERESS	PHLEBOTOMIC
PHENOMENALISTIC	PHENYLEPHRINES	PHILIPPINE	PHILOSOPHERS	PHLEBOTOMICAL
PHENOMENALISTS	PHENYLKETONURIA	PHILIPPINES	PHILOSOPHES	PHLEBOTOMIES
PHENOMENALITIES	PHENYLKETONURIC	PHILISTIAS	PHILOSOPHESS	PHLEBOTOMISE
PHENOMENALITY	PHENYLMETHYL	PHILISTINE	PHILOSOPHESSES	PHLEBOTOMISED
PHENOMENALIZE	PHENYLMETHYLS	PHILISTINES	PHILOSOPHIC	PHLEBOTOMISES
PHENOMENALIZED	PHENYLTHIOUREA	PHILISTINISM	PHILOSOPHICAL	PHLEBOTOMISING
PHENOMENALIZES	PHENYLTHIOUREAS	PHILISTINISMS	PHILOSOPHICALLY	PHLEBOTOMIST
PHENOMENALIZING	PHENYTOINS	PHILLABEGS	PHILOSOPHIES	PHLEBOTOMISTS
PHENOMENALLY	PHEROMONAL	PHILLIBEGS	PHILOSOPHISE	PHLEBOTOMIZE
PHENOMENAS	PHEROMONES	PHILLIPSITE	PHILOSOPHISED	PHLEBOTOMIZED
PHENOMENISE	PHIALIFORM	PHILLIPSITES	PHILOSOPHISER	PHLEBOTOMIZES
PHENOMENISED	PHILADELPHUS	PHILLUMENIES	PHILOSOPHISERS	PHLEBOTOMIZING
PHENOMENISES	PHILADELPHUSES	PHILLUMENIST	PHILOSOPHISES	PHLEBOTOMY
PHENOMENISING	PHILANDERED	PHILLUMENISTS	PHILOSOPHISING	PHLEGMAGOGIC
PHENOMENISM	PHILANDERER	PHILLUMENY	PHILOSOPHISINGS	PHLEGMAGOGICS
PHENOMENISMS	PHILANDERERS	PHILODENDRA	PHILOSOPHISM	PHLEGMAGOGUE
PHENOMENIST	PHILANDERING	PHILODENDRON	PHILOSOPHISMS	PHLEGMAGOGUES
PHENOMENISTS	PHILANDERINGS	PHILODENDRONS	PHILOSOPHIST	PHLEGMASIA
PHENOMENIZE	PHILANDERS	PHILOGYNIES	PHILOSOPHISTIC	PHLEGMASIAS
PHENOMENIZED	PHILANTHROPE	PHILOGYNIST	PHILOSOPHISTS	PHLEGMATIC
PHENOMENIZES	PHILANTHROPES	PHILOGYNISTS	PHILOSOPHIZE	PHLEGMATICAL
PHENOMENIZING	PHILANTHROPIC	PHILOGYNOUS	PHILOSOPHIZED	PHLEGMATICALLY
PHENOMENOLOGIES	PHILANTHROPICAL	PHILOLOGER	PHILOSOPHIZER	PHLEGMATICNESS

PHLEGMIEST	PHONEMICIZING	PHONOGRAPH	PHOSPHATIDE	PHOSPHORET
PHLEGMONIC	PHONENDOSCOPE	PHONOGRAPHER	PHOSPHATIDES	PHOSPHORETS
PHLEGMONOID	PHONENDOSCOPES	PHONOGRAPHERS	PHOSPHATIDIC	PHOSPHORETTED
PHLEGMONOUS	PHONETICAL	PHONOGRAPHIC	PHOSPHATIDYL	PHOSPHORIC
PHLOGISTIC	PHONETICALLY	PHONOGRAPHIES	PHOSPHATIDYLS	PHOSPHORISE
PHLOGISTICATE	PHONETICIAN	PHONOGRAPHIST	PHOSPHATING	PHOSPHORISED
PHLOGISTICATED	PHONETICIANS	PHONOGRAPHISTS	PHOSPHATISATION	PHOSPHORISES
PHLOGISTICATES	PHONETICISATION	PHONOGRAPHS	PHOSPHATISE	PHOSPHORISING
PHLOGISTICATING	PHONETICISE	PHONOGRAPHY	PHOSPHATISED	PHOSPHORISM
PHLOGISTON	PHONETICISED	PHONOLITES	PHOSPHATISES	PHOSPHORISMS
PHLOGISTONS	PHONETICISES	PHONOLITIC	PHOSPHATISING	PHOSPHORITE
PHLOGOPITE	PHONETICISING	PHONOLOGIC	PHOSPHATIZATION	PHOSPHORITES
PHLOGOPITES	PHONETICISM	PHONOLOGICAL	PHOSPHATIZE	PHOSPHORITIC
PHLORIZINS	PHONETICISMS	PHONOLOGICALLY	PHOSPHATIZED	PHOSPHORIZE
PHLYCTAENA	PHONETICIST	PHONOLOGIES	PHOSPHATIZES	PHOSPHORIZED
PHLYCTAENAE	PHONETICISTS	PHONOLOGIST	PHOSPHATIZING	PHOSPHORIZES
PHLYCTENAE	PHONETICIZATION	PHONOLOGISTS	PHOSPHATURIA	PHOSPHORIZING
PHOCOMELIA	PHONETICIZE	PHONOMETER	PHOSPHATURIAS	PHOSPHOROLYSES
PHOCOMELIAS	PHONETICIZED	PHONOMETERS	PHOSPHATURIC	PHOSPHOROLYSIS
PHOCOMELIC	PHONETICIZES	PHONOMETRIC	PHOSPHENES	PHOSPHOROLYTIC
PHOCOMELIES	PHONETICIZING	PHONOMETRICAL	PHOSPHIDES	PHOSPHOROSCOPE
PHOENIXISM	PHONETISATION	PHONOPHOBIA	PHOSPHINES	PHOSPHOROSCOPES
PHOENIXISMS	PHONETISATIONS	PHONOPHOBIAS	PHOSPHITES	PHOSPHOROUS
PHOENIXLIKE	PHONETISED	PHONOPHORE	PHOSPHOCREATIN	PHOSPHORUS
PHOLIDOSES	PHONETISES	PHONOPHORES	PHOSPHOCREATINE	PHOSPHORUSES
PHOLIDOSIS	PHONETISING	PHONOPORES	PHOSPHOCREATINS	PHOSPHORYL
PHONASTHENIA	PHONETISMS	PHONOSCOPE	PHOSPHOKINASE	PHOSPHORYLASE
PHONASTHENIAS	PHONETISTS	PHONOSCOPES	PHOSPHOKINASES	PHOSPHORYLASES
PHONATHONS	PHONETIZATION	PHONOTACTIC	PHOSPHOLIPASE	PHOSPHORYLATE
PHONATIONS	PHONETIZATIONS	PHONOTACTICS	PHOSPHOLIPASES	PHOSPHORYLATED
PHONAUTOGRAPH	PHONETIZED	PHONOTYPED	PHOSPHOLIPID	PHOSPHORYLATES
PHONAUTOGRAPHIC	PHONETIZES	PHONOTYPER	PHOSPHOLIPIDS	PHOSPHORYLATING
PHONAUTOGRAPHS	PHONETIZING	PHONOTYPERS	PHOSPHONIC	PHOSPHORYLATION
PHONECARDS	PHONEYNESS	PHONOTYPES	PHOSPHONIUM	PHOSPHORYLATIVE
PHONEMATIC	PHONEYNESSES	PHONOTYPIC	PHOSPHONIUMS	PHOSPHORYLS
PHONEMATICALLY	PHONICALLY	PHONOTYPICAL	PHOSPHOPROTEIN	PHOSPHURET
PHONEMICALLY	PHONINESSES	PHONOTYPIES	PHOSPHOPROTEINS	PHOSPHURETS
PHONEMICISATION	PHONMETERS	PHONOTYPING	PHOSPHORATE	PHOSPHURETTED
PHONEMICISE	PHONOCAMPTIC	PHONOTYPIST	PHOSPHORATED	PHOTICALLY
PHONEMICISED	PHONOCAMPTICS	PHONOTYPISTS	PHOSPHORATES	PHOTOACTINIC
PHONEMICISES	PHONOCARDIOGRAM	PHORMINGES	PHOSPHORATING	PHOTOACTIVE
PHONEMICISING	PHONOCHEMISTRY	PHOSGENITE	PHOSPHORES	PHOTOAUTOTROPH
PHONEMICIST	PHONOFIDDLE	PHOSGENITES	PHOSPHORESCE	PHOTOAUTOTROPHS
PHONEMICISTS	PHONOFIDDLES	PHOSPHATASE	PHOSPHORESCED	PHOTOBATHIC
PHONEMICIZATION	PHONOGRAMIC	PHOSPHATASES	PHOSPHORESCENCE	PHOTOBIOLOGIC
PHONEMICIZE	PHONOGRAMICALLY	PHOSPHATED	PHOSPHORESCENT	PHOTOBIOLOGICAL
PHONEMICIZED	PHONOGRAMMIC	PHOSPHATES	PHOSPHORESCES	PHOTOBIOLOGIES
PHONEMICIZES	PHONOGRAMS	PHOSPHATIC	PHOSPHORESCING	PHOTOBIOLOGIST

PHOTOBIOLOGISTS	PHOTODETECTOR	PHOTOGENIES	PHOTOLITHO	PHOTONUCLEAR
PHOTOBIOLOGY	PHOTODETECTORS	PHOTOGEOLOGIC	PHOTOLITHOGRAPH	PHOTOOXIDATION
PHOTOBLOGGED	PHOTODIODE	PHOTOGEOLOGICAL	PHOTOLITHOS	PHOTOOXIDATIONS
PHOTOBLOGGING	PHOTODIODES	PHOTOGEOLOGIES	PHOTOLUMINESCE	PHOTOOXIDATIVE
PHOTOBLOGS	PHOTODISKS	PHOTOGEOLOGIST	PHOTOLUMINESCED	PHOTOOXIDISE
PHOTOBOMBED	PHOTODISSOCIATE	PHOTOGEOLOGISTS	PHOTOLUMINESCES	PHOTOOXIDISED
PHOTOBOMBING	PHOTODUPLICATE	PHOTOGEOLOGY	PHOTOLYSABLE	PHOTOOXIDISES
PHOTOBOMBS	PHOTODUPLICATED	PHOTOGLYPH	PHOTOLYSED	PHOTOOXIDISING
PHOTOCALLS	PHOTODUPLICATES	PHOTOGLYPHIC	PHOTOLYSES	PHOTOOXIDIZE
PHOTOCARDS	PHOTODYNAMIC	PHOTOGLYPHIES	PHOTOLYSING	PHOTOOXIDIZED
PHOTOCATALYSES	PHOTODYNAMICS	PHOTOGLYPHS	PHOTOLYSIS	PHOTOOXIDIZES
PHOTOCATALYSIS	PHOTOELASTIC	PHOTOGLYPHY	PHOTOLYTIC	PHOTOOXIDIZING
PHOTOCATALYTIC	PHOTOELASTICITY	PHOTOGRAMMETRIC	PHOTOLYTICALLY	PHOTOPERIOD
PHOTOCATHODE	PHOTOELECTRIC	PHOTOGRAMMETRY	PHOTOLYZABLE	PHOTOPERIODIC
PHOTOCATHODES	PHOTOELECTRICAL	PHOTOGRAMS	PHOTOLYZED	PHOTOPERIODISM
PHOTOCELLS	PHOTOELECTRODE	PHOTOGRAPH	PHOTOLYZES	PHOTOPERIODISMS
PHOTOCHEMICAL	PHOTOELECTRODES	PHOTOGRAPHED	PHOTOLYZING	PHOTOPERIODS
PHOTOCHEMICALLY	PHOTOELECTRON	PHOTOGRAPHER	PHOTOMACHINE	PHOTOPHASE
PHOTOCHEMIST	PHOTOELECTRONIC	PHOTOGRAPHERS	PHOTOMACHINES	PHOTOPHASES
PHOTOCHEMISTRY	PHOTOELECTRONS	PHOTOGRAPHIC	PHOTOMACROGRAPH	PHOTOPHILIC
PHOTOCHEMISTS	PHOTOEMISSION	PHOTOGRAPHICAL	PHOTOMAPPED	PHOTOPHILIES
PHOTOCHROMIC	PHOTOEMISSIONS	PHOTOGRAPHIES	PHOTOMAPPING	PHOTOPHILOUS
PHOTOCHROMICS	PHOTOEMISSIVE	PHOTOGRAPHING	PHOTOMASKS	PHOTOPHILS
PHOTOCHROMIES	PHOTOENGRAVE	PHOTOGRAPHIST	PHOTOMECHANICAL	PHOTOPHILY
PHOTOCHROMISM	PHOTOENGRAVED	PHOTOGRAPHISTS	PHOTOMETER	PHOTOPHOBE
PHOTOCHROMISMS	PHOTOENGRAVER	PHOTOGRAPHS	PHOTOMETERS	PHOTOPHOBES
PHOTOCHROMY	PHOTOENGRAVERS	PHOTOGRAPHY	PHOTOMETRIC	PHOTOPHOBIA
PHOTOCOMPOSE	PHOTOENGRAVES	PHOTOGRAVURE	PHOTOMETRICALLY	PHOTOPHOBIAS
PHOTOCOMPOSED	PHOTOENGRAVING	PHOTOGRAVURES	PHOTOMETRIES	PHOTOPHOBIC
PHOTOCOMPOSER	PHOTOENGRAVINGS	PHOTOINDUCED	PHOTOMETRIST	PHOTOPHONE
PHOTOCOMPOSERS	PHOTOEXCITATION	PHOTOINDUCTION	PHOTOMETRISTS	PHOTOPHONES
PHOTOCOMPOSES	PHOTOEXCITED	PHOTOINDUCTIONS	PHOTOMETRY	PHOTOPHONIC
PHOTOCOMPOSING	PHOTOFINISHER	PHOTOINDUCTIVE	PHOTOMICROGRAPH	PHOTOPHONIES
PHOTOCONDUCTING	PHOTOFINISHERS	PHOTOIONISATION	PHOTOMONTAGE	PHOTOPHONY
PHOTOCONDUCTION	PHOTOFINISHING	PHOTOIONISE	PHOTOMONTAGES	PHOTOPHORE
PHOTOCONDUCTIVE	PHOTOFINISHINGS	PHOTOIONISED	PHOTOMOSAIC	PHOTOPHORES
PHOTOCONDUCTOR	PHOTOFISSION	PHOTOIONISES	PHOTOMOSAICS	PHOTOPHORESES
PHOTOCONDUCTORS	PHOTOFISSIONS	PHOTOIONISING	PHOTOMULTIPLIER	PHOTOPHORESIS
PHOTOCOPIABLE	PHOTOFLASH	PHOTOIONIZATION	PHOTOMURAL	PHOTOPLAYS
PHOTOCOPIED	PHOTOFLASHES	PHOTOIONIZE	PHOTOMURALS	PHOTOPOLYMER
PHOTOCOPIER	PHOTOFLOOD	PHOTOIONIZED	PHOTONASTIC	PHOTOPOLYMERS
PHOTOCOPIERS	PHOTOFLOODS	PHOTOIONIZES	PHOTONASTIES	PHOTOPOSITIVE
PHOTOCOPIES	PHOTOFLUOROGRAM	PHOTOIONIZING	PHOTONASTY	PHOTOPRODUCT
PHOTOCOPYING	PHOTOGELATIN	PHOTOJOURNALISM	PHOTONEGATIVE	PHOTOPRODUCTION
PHOTOCOPYINGS	PHOTOGELATINE	PHOTOJOURNALIST	PHOTONEUTRON	PHOTOPRODUCTS
PHOTOCURRENT	PHOTOGENES	PHOTOKINESES	PHOTONEUTRONS	PHOTOPSIAS
PHOTOCURRENTS	PHOTOGENIC	PHOTOKINESIS	PHOTONOVEL	PHOTOPSIES
PHOTODEGRADABLE	PHOTOGENICALLY	PHOTOKINETIC	PHOTONOVELS	PHOTOREACTION

P

PHOTOREACTIONS

PHOTOREACTIONS	PHOTOSTATIC	PHOTOTUBES	PHRENITIDES	PHYCOPHAEINS
PHOTOREACTIVE	PHOTOSTATING	PHOTOTYPED	PHRENITISES	PHYCOXANTHIN
PHOTOREALISM	PHOTOSTATS	PHOTOTYPES	PHRENOLOGIC	PHYCOXANTHINS
PHOTOREALISMS	PHOTOSTATTED	PHOTOTYPESET	PHRENOLOGICAL	PHYLACTERIC
PHOTOREALIST	PHOTOSTATTING	PHOTOTYPESETS	PHRENOLOGICALLY	PHYLACTERICAL
PHOTOREALISTIC	PHOTOSYNTHATE	PHOTOTYPESETTER	PHRENOLOGIES	PHYLACTERIES
PHOTOREALISTS	PHOTOSYNTHATES	PHOTOTYPIC	PHRENOLOGISE	PHYLACTERY
PHOTORECEPTION	PHOTOSYNTHESES	PHOTOTYPICALLY	PHRENOLOGISED	PHYLARCHIES
PHOTORECEPTIONS	PHOTOSYNTHESIS	PHOTOTYPIES	PHRENOLOGISES	PHYLAXISES
PHOTORECEPTIVE	PHOTOSYNTHESISE	PHOTOTYPING	PHRENOLOGISING	PHYLESISES
PHOTORECEPTOR	PHOTOSYNTHESIZE	PHOTOTYPOGRAPHY	PHRENOLOGIST	PHYLETICALLY
PHOTORECEPTORS	PHOTOSYNTHETIC	PHOTOVOLTAIC	PHRENOLOGISTS	PHYLLARIES
PHOTOREDUCE	PHOTOSYSTEM	PHOTOVOLTAICS	PHRENOLOGIZE	PHYLLOCLAD
PHOTOREDUCED	PHOTOSYSTEMS	PHOTOXYLOGRAPHY	PHRENOLOGIZED	PHYLLOCLADE
PHOTOREDUCES	PHOTOTACTIC	PHOTOZINCOGRAPH	PHRENOLOGIZES	PHYLLOCLADES
PHOTOREDUCING	PHOTOTACTICALLY	PHRAGMOPLAST	PHRENOLOGIZING	PHYLLOCLADS
PHOTOREDUCTION	PHOTOTAXES	PHRAGMOPLASTS	PHRENOLOGY	PHYLLODIAL
PHOTOREDUCTIONS	PHOTOTAXIES	PHRASELESS	PHRENSICAL	PHYLLODIES
PHOTOREFRACTIVE	PHOTOTAXIS	PHRASEMAKER	PHRENSYING	PHYLLODIUM
PHOTORESIST	PHOTOTELEGRAM	PHRASEMAKERS	PHRONTISTERIES	PHYLLOMANIA
PHOTORESISTS	PHOTOTELEGRAMS	PHRASEMAKING	PHRONTISTERY	PHYLLOMANIAS
PHOTOSCANNED	PHOTOTELEGRAPH	PHRASEMAKINGS	PHTHALATES	PHYLLOPHAGOUS
PHOTOSCANNING	PHOTOTELEGRAPHS	PHRASEMONGER	PHTHALEINS	PHYLLOPLANE
PHOTOSCANS	PHOTOTELEGRAPHY	PHRASEMONGERING	PHTHALOCYANIN	PHYLLOPLANES
PHOTOSENSITISE	PHOTOTHERAPIES	PHRASEMONGERS	PHTHALOCYANINE	PHYLLOPODS
PHOTOSENSITISED	PHOTOTHERAPY	PHRASEOGRAM	PHTHALOCYANINES	PHYLLOQUINONE
PHOTOSENSITISER	PHOTOTHERMAL	PHRASEOGRAMS	PHTHALOCYANINS	PHYLLOQUINONES
PHOTOSENSITISES	PHOTOTHERMALLY	PHRASEOGRAPH	PHTHIRIASES	PHYLLOSILICATE
PHOTOSENSITIVE	PHOTOTHERMIC	PHRASEOGRAPHIC	PHTHIRIASIS	PHYLLOSILICATES
PHOTOSENSITIZE	PHOTOTONIC	PHRASEOGRAPHIES	PHTHISICAL	PHYLLOSPHERE
PHOTOSENSITIZED	PHOTOTONUS	PHRASEOGRAPHS	PHTHISICKY	PHYLLOSPHERES
PHOTOSENSITIZER	PHOTOTONUSES	PHRASEOGRAPHY	PHYCOBILIN	PHYLLOTACTIC
PHOTOSENSITIZES	PHOTOTOPOGRAPHY	PHRASEOLOGIC	PHYCOBILINS	PHYLLOTACTICAL
PHOTOSENSOR	PHOTOTOXIC	PHRASEOLOGICAL	PHYCOBIONT	PHYLLOTAXES
PHOTOSENSORS	PHOTOTOXICITIES	PHRASEOLOGIES	PHYCOBIONTS	PHYLLOTAXIES
PHOTOSETTER	PHOTOTOXICITY	PHRASEOLOGIST	PHYCOCYANIN	PHYLLOTAXIS
PHOTOSETTERS	PHOTOTRANSISTOR	PHRASEOLOGISTS	PHYCOCYANINS	PHYLLOTAXY
PHOTOSETTING	PHOTOTROPE	PHRASEOLOGY	PHYCOCYANS	PHYLLOXERA
PHOTOSETTINGS	PHOTOTROPES	PHREAKINGS	PHYCOERYTHRIN	PHYLLOXERAE
PHOTOSHOOT	PHOTOTROPH	PHREATOPHYTE	PHYCOERYTHRINS	PHYLLOXERAS
PHOTOSHOOTS	PHOTOTROPHIC	PHREATOPHYTES	PHYCOLOGICAL	PHYLOGENESES
PHOTOSHOPPED	PHOTOTROPHS	PHREATOPHYTIC	PHYCOLOGIES	PHYLOGENESIS
PHOTOSHOPPING	PHOTOTROPIC	PHRENESIAC	PHYCOLOGIST	PHYLOGENETIC
PHOTOSHOPS	PHOTOTROPICALLY	PHRENETICAL	PHYCOLOGISTS	PHYLOGENIC
PHOTOSPHERE	PHOTOTROPIES	PHRENETICALLY	PHYCOMYCETE	PHYLOGENIES
PHOTOSPHERES	PHOTOTROPISM	PHRENETICNESS	PHYCOMYCETES	PHYSALISES
PHOTOSPHERIC	PHOTOTROPISMS	PHRENETICNESSES	PHYCOMYCETOUS	PHYSHARMONICA
PHOTOSTATED	PHOTOTROPY	PHRENETICS	PHYCOPHAEIN	PHYSHARMONICAS

PHYSIATRIC	PHYSIOLOGIC	PHYTOGRAPHIC	PIANOFORTE	PICKEERERS
PHYSIATRICAL	PHYSIOLOGICAL	PHYTOGRAPHIES	PIANOFORTES	PICKEERING
PHYSIATRICS	PHYSIOLOGICALLY	PHYTOGRAPHY	PIANOLISTS	PICKELHAUBE
PHYSIATRIES	PHYSIOLOGIES	PHYTOHORMONE	PICADILLOS	PICKELHAUBES
PHYSIATRIST	PHYSIOLOGIST	PHYTOHORMONES	PICANINNIES	PICKERELWEED
PHYSIATRISTS	PHYSIOLOGISTS	PHYTOLITHS	PICARESQUE	PICKERELWEEDS
PHYSICALISM	PHYSIOLOGUS	PHYTOLOGICAL	PICARESQUES	PICKETBOAT
PHYSICALISMS	PHYSIOLOGUSES	PHYTOLOGICALLY	PICAROONED	PICKETBOATS
PHYSICALIST	PHYSIOLOGY	PHYTOLOGIES	PICAROONING	PICKETINGS
PHYSICALISTIC	PHYSIOPATHOLOGY	PHYTOLOGIST	PICAYUNISH	PICKINESSES
PHYSICALISTS	PHYSIOTHERAPIES	PHYTOLOGISTS	PICAYUNISHLY	PICKPOCKET
PHYSICALITIES	PHYSIOTHERAPIST	PHYTONADIONE	PICAYUNISHNESS	PICKPOCKETED
PHYSICALITY	PHYSIOTHERAPY	PHYTONADIONES	PICCADILLIES	PICKPOCKETING
PHYSICALLY	PHYSITHEISM	PHYTOPATHOGEN	PICCADILLO	PICKPOCKETS
PHYSICALNESS	PHYSITHEISMS	PHYTOPATHOGENIC	PICCADILLOES	PICKTHANKS
PHYSICALNESSES	PHYSITHEISTIC	PHYTOPATHOGENS	PICCADILLOS	PICNICKERS
PHYSICIANCIES	PHYSOCLISTOUS	PHYTOPATHOLOGY	PICCADILLS	PICNICKIER
PHYSICIANCY	PHYSOSTIGMIN	PHYTOPHAGIC	PICCADILLY	PICNICKIEST
PHYSICIANER	PHYSOSTIGMINE	PHYTOPHAGIES	PICCALILLI	PICNICKING
PHYSICIANERS	PHYSOSTIGMINES	PHYTOPHAGOUS	PICCALILLIS	PICOCURIES
PHYSICIANS	PHYSOSTIGMINS	PHYTOPHAGY	PICCANINNIES	PICOFARADS
PHYSICIANSHIP	PHYSOSTOMOUS	PHYTOPLANKTER	PICCANINNY	PICOMETERS
PHYSICIANSHIPS	PHYTOALEXIN	PHYTOPLANKTERS	PICCOLOIST	PICOMETRES
PHYSICISMS	PHYTOALEXINS	PHYTOPLANKTON	PICCOLOISTS	PICORNAVIRUS
PHYSICISTS	PHYTOBENTHOS	PHYTOPLANKTONIC	PICHICIAGO	PICORNAVIRUSES
PHYSICKING	PHYTOBENTHOSES	PHYTOPLANKTONS	PICHICIAGOS	PICOSECOND
PHYSICOCHEMICAL	PHYTOCHEMICAL	PHYTOSANITARY	PICHICIEGO	PICOSECONDS
PHYSIOCRACIES	PHYTOCHEMICALLY	PHYTOSOCIOLOGY	PICHICIEGOS	PICOWAVING
PHYSIOCRACY	PHYTOCHEMICALS	PHYTOSTEROL	PICHOLINES	PICQUETING
PHYSIOCRAT	PHYTOCHEMIST	PHYTOSTEROLS	PICKABACKED	PICROCARMINE
PHYSIOCRATIC	PHYTOCHEMISTRY	PHYTOTHERAPIES	PICKABACKING	PICROCARMINES
PHYSIOCRATS	PHYTOCHEMISTS	PHYTOTHERAPY	PICKABACKS	PICROTOXIN
PHYSIOGNOMIC	PHYTOCHROME	PHYTOTOMIES	PICKADILLIES	PICROTOXINS
PHYSIOGNOMICAL	PHYTOCHROMES	PHYTOTOMIST	PICKADILLO	PICTARNIES
PHYSIOGNOMIES	PHYTOESTROGEN	PHYTOTOMISTS	PICKADILLOES	PICTOGRAMS
PHYSIOGNOMIST	PHYTOESTROGENS	PHYTOTOXIC	PICKADILLOS	PICTOGRAPH
PHYSIOGNOMISTS	PHYTOFLAGELLATE	PHYTOTOXICITIES	PICKADILLS	PICTOGRAPHIC
PHYSIOGNOMY	PHYTOGENESES	PHYTOTOXICITY	PICKADILLY	PICTOGRAPHIES
PHYSIOGRAPHER	PHYTOGENESIS	PHYTOTOXIN	PICKANINNIES	PICTOGRAPHS
PHYSIOGRAPHERS	PHYTOGENETIC	PHYTOTOXINS	PICKANINNY	PICTOGRAPHY
PHYSIOGRAPHIC	PHYTOGENETICAL	PHYTOTRONS	PICKAPACKED	PICTORIALISE
PHYSIOGRAPHICAL	PHYTOGENIC	PIACULARITIES	PICKAPACKING	PICTORIALISED
PHYSIOGRAPHIES	PHYTOGENIES	PIACULARITY	PICKAPACKS	PICTORIALISES
PHYSIOGRAPHY	PHYTOGEOGRAPHER	PIANISSIMI	PICKAROONS	PICTORIALISING
PHYSIOLATER	PHYTOGEOGRAPHIC	PIANISSIMO	PICKBACKED	PICTORIALISM
PHYSIOLATERS	PHYTOGEOGRAPHY	PIANISSIMOS	PICKBACKING	PICTORIALISMS
PHYSIOLATRIES	PHYTOGRAPHER	PIANISSISSIMO	PICKEDNESS	PICTORIALIST
PHYSIOLATRY	PHYTOGRAPHERS	PIANISTICALLY	PICKEDNESSES	PICTORIALISTS

P

PICTORIALIZE

PICTORIALIZE	PIEMONTITES	PIGNERATING	PILLARLESS	PINCHPOINT
PICTORIALIZED	PIEPOWDERS	PIGNERATION	PILLICOCKS	PINCHPOINTS
PICTORIALIZES	PIERCEABLE	PIGNERATIONS	PILLIONING	PINCUSHION
PICTORIALIZING	PIERCINGLY	PIGNORATED	PILLIONIST	PINCUSHIONS
PICTORIALLY	PIERCINGNESS	PIGNORATES	PILLIONISTS	PINEALECTOMIES
PICTORIALNESS	PIERCINGNESSES	PIGNORATING	PILLIWINKS	PINEALECTOMISE
PICTORIALNESSES	PIERRETTES	PIGNORATION	PILLORISED	PINEALECTOMISED
PICTORIALS	PIETISTICAL	PIGNORATIONS	PILLORISES	PINEALECTOMISES
PICTORICAL	PIETISTICALLY	PIGSCONCES	PILLORISING	PINEALECTOMIZE
PICTORICALLY	PIEZOCHEMISTRY	PIGSTICKED	PILLORIZED	PINEALECTOMIZED
PICTUREGOER	PIEZOELECTRIC	PIGSTICKER	PILLORIZES	PINEALECTOMIZES
PICTUREGOERS	PIEZOMAGNETIC	PIGSTICKERS	PILLORIZING	PINEALECTOMY
PICTUREPHONE	PIEZOMAGNETISM	PIGSTICKING	PILLORYING	PINEAPPLES
PICTUREPHONES	PIEZOMAGNETISMS	PIGSTICKINGS	PILLOWCASE	PINFEATHER
PICTURESQUE	PIEZOMETER	PIKEPERCHES	PILLOWCASES	PINFEATHERS
PICTURESQUELY	PIEZOMETERS	PIKESTAFFS	PILLOWIEST	PINFOLDING
PICTURESQUENESS	PIEZOMETRIC	PIKESTAVES	PILLOWSLIP	PINGRASSES
PICTURISATION	PIEZOMETRICALLY	PILASTERED	PILLOWSLIPS	PINGUEFIED
PICTURISATIONS	PIEZOMETRIES	PILEORHIZA	PILNIEWINKS	PINGUEFIES
PICTURISED	PIEZOMETRY	PILEORHIZAS	PILOCARPIN	PINGUEFYING
PICTURISES	PIFFERAROS	PILFERABLE	PILOCARPINE	PINGUIDITIES
PICTURISING	PIGEONHOLE	PILFERAGES	PILOCARPINES	PINGUIDITY
PICTURIZATION	PIGEONHOLED	PILFERINGLY	PILOCARPINS	PINGUITUDE
PICTURIZATIONS	PIGEONHOLER	PILFERINGS	PILOSITIES	PINGUITUDES
PICTURIZED	PIGEONHOLERS	PILFERPROOF	PILOTFISHES	PINHEADEDNESS
PICTURIZES	PIGEONHOLES	PILGARLICK	PILOTHOUSE	PINHEADEDNESSES
PICTURIZING	PIGEONHOLING	PILGARLICKS	PILOTHOUSES	PINHOOKERS
PIDDLINGLY	PIGEONITES	PILGARLICKY	PIMPERNELS	PINKERTONS
PIDGINISATION	PIGEONRIES	PILGARLICS	PIMPLINESS	PINKINESSES
PIDGINISATIONS	PIGEONWING	PILGRIMAGE	PIMPLINESSES	PINKISHNESS
PIDGINISED	PIGEONWINGS	PILGRIMAGED	PIMPMOBILE	PINKISHNESSES
PIDGINISES	PIGGINESSES	PILGRIMAGER	PIMPMOBILES	PINKNESSES
PIDGINISING	PIGGISHNESS	PILGRIMAGERS	PINACOIDAL	PINNACLING
PIDGINIZATION	PIGGISHNESSES	PILGRIMAGES	PINACOTHECA	PINNATIFID
PIDGINIZATIONS	PIGGYBACKED	PILGRIMAGING	PINACOTHECAE	PINNATIFIDLY
PIDGINIZED	PIGGYBACKING	PILGRIMERS	PINAKOIDAL	PINNATIONS
PIDGINIZES	PIGGYBACKS	PILGRIMING	PINAKOTHEK	PINNATIPARTITE
PIDGINIZING	PIGHEADEDLY	PILGRIMISE	PINAKOTHEKS	PINNATIPED
PIECEMEALED	PIGHEADEDNESS	PILGRIMISED	PINBALLING	PINNATISECT
PIECEMEALING	PIGHEADEDNESSES	PILGRIMISES	PINCERLIKE	PINNIEWINKLE
PIECEMEALS	PIGMENTARY	PILGRIMISING	PINCHBECKS	PINNIEWINKLES
PIECEWORKER	PIGMENTATION	PILGRIMIZE	PINCHCOCKS	PINNIPEDES
PIECEWORKERS	PIGMENTATIONS	PILGRIMIZED	PINCHCOMMONS	PINNIPEDIAN
PIECEWORKS	PIGMENTING	PILGRIMIZES	PINCHCOMMONSES	PINNIPEDIANS
PIEDMONTITE	PIGMENTOSA	PILGRIMIZING	PINCHFISTS	PINNULATED
PIEDMONTITES	PIGMENTOSAS	PILIFEROUS	PINCHINGLY	PINNYWINKLE
PIEDNESSES	PIGNERATED	PILLAGINGS	PINCHPENNIES	PINNYWINKLES
PIEMONTITE	PIGNERATES	PILLARISTS	PINCHPENNY	PINOCYTOSES

PINOCYTOSIS	PIQUANTNESS	PITCHFORKED	PIXELLATING	PLAGIARISES
PINOCYTOTIC	PIQUANTNESSES	PITCHFORKING	PIXELLATION	PLAGIARISING
PINOCYTOTICALLY	PIRACETAMS	PITCHFORKS	PIXELLATIONS	PLAGIARISM
PINPOINTED	PIRATICALLY	PITCHINESS	PIXILATING	PLAGIARISMS
PINPOINTING	PIRLICUING	PITCHINESSES	PIXILATION	PLAGIARIST
PINPRICKED	PIROPLASMA	PITCHOMETER	PIXILATIONS	PLAGIARISTIC
PINPRICKING	PIROPLASMATA	PITCHOMETERS	PIXILLATED	PLAGIARISTS
PINSETTERS	PIROPLASMS	PITCHPERSON	PIXILLATES	PLAGIARIZE
PINSPOTTED	PIROUETTED	PITCHPERSONS	PIXILLATING	PLAGIARIZED
PINSPOTTER	PIROUETTER	PITCHPINES	PIXILLATION	PLAGIARIZER
PINSPOTTERS	PIROUETTERS	PITCHPIPES	PIXILLATIONS	PLAGIARIZERS
PINSPOTTING	PIROUETTES	PITCHPOLED	PIXINESSES	PLAGIARIZES
PINSTRIPED	PIROUETTING	PITCHPOLES	PIZAZZIEST	PLAGIARIZING
PINSTRIPES	PISCATORIAL	PITCHPOLING	PIZZAZZIER	PLAGIOCEPHALIES
PINTADERAS	PISCATORIALLY	PITCHSTONE	PIZZAZZIEST	PLAGIOCEPHALY
PINTUCKING	PISCATRIXES	PITCHSTONES	PIZZICATOS	PLAGIOCLASE
PINTUCKINGS	PISCICOLOUS	PITCHWOMAN	PLACABILITIES	PLAGIOCLASES
PINWHEELED	PISCICULTURAL	PITCHWOMEN	PLACABILITY	PLAGIOCLASTIC
PINWHEELING	PISCICULTURALLY	PITEOUSNESS	PLACABLENESS	PLAGIOCLIMAX
PINWRENCHES	PISCICULTURE	PITEOUSNESSES	PLACABLENESSES	PLAGIOCLIMAXES
PIONEERING	PISCICULTURES	PITHECANTHROPI	PLACARDING	PLAGIOSTOMATOUS
PIOUSNESSES	PISCICULTURIST	PITHECANTHROPUS	PLACATINGLY	PLAGIOSTOME
PIPECLAYED	PISCICULTURISTS	PITHECOIDS	PLACATIONS	PLAGIOSTOMES
PIPECLAYING	PISCIFAUNA	PITHINESSES	PLACEHOLDER	PLAGIOSTOMOUS
PIPEFISHES	PISCIFAUNAE	PITIABLENESS	PLACEHOLDERS	PLAGIOTROPIC
PIPEFITTER	PISCIFAUNAS	PITIABLENESSES	PLACEKICKED	PLAGIOTROPISM
PIPEFITTERS	PISCIVORES	PITIFULLER	PLACEKICKER	PLAGIOTROPISMS
PIPEFITTING	PISCIVOROUS	PITIFULLEST	PLACEKICKERS	PLAGIOTROPOUS
PIPEFITTINGS	PISSASPHALT	PITIFULNESS	PLACEKICKING	PLAGUELIKE
PIPELINING	PISSASPHALTS	PITIFULNESSES	PLACEKICKS	PLAGUESOME
PIPELININGS	PISTACHIOS	PITILESSLY	PLACELESSLY	PLAINCHANT
PIPERACEOUS	PISTAREENS	PITILESSNESS	PLACEMENTS	PLAINCHANTS
PIPERAZINE	PISTILLARY	PITILESSNESSES	PLACENTALS	PLAINCLOTHES
PIPERAZINES	PISTILLATE	PITTOSPORUM	PLACENTATE	PLAINCLOTHESMAN
PIPERIDINE	PISTILLODE	PITTOSPORUMS	PLACENTATION	PLAINCLOTHESMEN
PIPERIDINES	PISTILLODES	PITUITARIES	PLACENTATIONS	PLAINNESSES
PIPERONALS	PISTOLEERS	PITUITRINS	PLACENTIFORM	PLAINSONGS
PIPESTONES	PISTOLEROS	PITYRIASES	PLACENTOLOGIES	PLAINSPOKEN
PIPINESSES	PISTOLIERS	PITYRIASIS	PLACENTOLOGY	PLAINSPOKENNESS
PIPISTRELLE	PISTOLLING	PITYROSPORUM	PLACIDITIES	PLAINSTANES
PIPISTRELLES	PITAPATTED	PITYROSPORUMS	PLACIDNESS	PLAINSTONES
PIPISTRELS	PITAPATTING	PIWAKAWAKA	PLACIDNESSES	PLAINTEXTS
PIPIWHARAUROA	PITCHBENDS	PIWAKAWAKAS	PLACODERMS	PLAINTIFFS
PIPIWHARAUROAS	PITCHBLENDE	PIXELATING	PLAGIARIES	PLAINTIVELY
PIPSISSEWA	PITCHBLENDES	PIXELATION	PLAGIARISE	PLAINTIVENESS
PIPSISSEWAS	PITCHERFUL	PIXELATIONS	PLAGIARISED	PLAINTIVENESSES
PIPSQUEAKS	PITCHERFULS	PIXELLATED	PLAGIARISER	PLAINTLESS
PIQUANCIES	PITCHERSFUL	PIXELLATES	PLAGIARISERS	PLAINWORKS

P

PLAISTERED	PLANLESSNESSES	PLASMOGAMY	PLASTICIZED	PLATINIFEROUS
PLAISTERING	PLANOBLAST	PLASMOLYSE	PLASTICIZER	PLATINIRIDIUM
PLANARIANS	PLANOBLASTS	PLASMOLYSED	PLASTICIZERS	PLATINIRIDIUMS
PLANARITIES	PLANOCONVEX	PLASMOLYSES	PLASTICIZES	PLATINISATION
PLANATIONS	PLANOGAMETE	PLASMOLYSING	PLASTICIZING	PLATINISATIONS
PLANCHETTE	PLANOGAMETES	PLASMOLYSIS	PLASTICKIER	PLATINISED
PLANCHETTES	PLANOGRAMS	PLASMOLYTIC	PLASTICKIEST	PLATINISES
PLANELOADS	PLANOGRAPHIC	PLASMOLYTICALLY	PLASTIDIAL	PLATINISING
PLANENESSES	PLANOGRAPHIES	PLASMOLYZE	PLASTIDULE	PLATINIZATION
PLANESIDES	PLANOGRAPHY	PLASMOLYZED	PLASTIDULES	PLATINIZATIONS
PLANETARIA	PLANOMETER	PLASMOLYZES	PLASTILINA	PLATINIZED
PLANETARIES	PLANOMETERS	PLASMOLYZING	PLASTILINAS	PLATINIZES
PLANETARIUM	PLANOMETRIC	PLASMOSOMA	PLASTINATION	PLATINIZING
PLANETARIUMS	PLANOMETRICALLY	PLASMOSOMATA	PLASTINATIONS	PLATINOCYANIC
PLANETESIMAL	PLANOMETRIES	PLASMOSOME	PLASTIQUES	PLATINOCYANIDE
PLANETESIMALS	PLANOMETRY	PLASMOSOMES	PLASTISOLS	PLATINOCYANIDES
PLANETICAL	PLANTAGINACEOUS	PLASTERBOARD	PLASTOCYANIN	PLATINOIDS
PLANETLIKE	PLANTATION	PLASTERBOARDS	PLASTOCYANINS	PLATINOTYPE
PLANETOIDAL	PLANTATIONS	PLASTERERS	PLASTOGAMIES	PLATINOTYPES
PLANETOIDS	PLANTIGRADE	PLASTERIER	PLASTOGAMY	PLATITUDES
PLANETOLOGICAL	PLANTIGRADES	PLASTERIEST	PLASTOMETER	PLATITUDINAL
PLANETOLOGIES	PLANTLINGS	PLASTERINESS	PLASTOMETERS	PLATITUDINARIAN
PLANETOLOGIST	PLANTOCRACIES	PLASTERINESSES	PLASTOMETRIC	PLATITUDINISE
PLANETOLOGISTS	PLANTOCRACY	PLASTERING	PLASTOMETRIES	PLATITUDINISED
PLANETOLOGY	PLANTSWOMAN	PLASTERINGS	PLASTOMETRY	PLATITUDINISER
PLANETWIDE	PLANTSWOMEN	PLASTERSTONE	PLASTOQUINONE	PLATITUDINISERS
PLANGENCIES	PLANULIFORM	PLASTERSTONES	PLASTOQUINONES	PLATITUDINISES
PLANGENTLY	PLAQUETTES	PLASTERWORK	PLATANACEOUS	PLATITUDINISING
PLANIGRAMS	PLASMAGELS	PLASTERWORKS	PLATEAUING	PLATITUDINIZE
PLANIGRAPH	PLASMAGENE	PLASTICALLY	PLATEGLASS	PLATITUDINIZED
PLANIGRAPHIES	PLASMAGENES	PLASTICATED	PLATEGLASSES	PLATITUDINIZER
PLANIGRAPHS	PLASMAGENIC	PLASTICENE	PLATELAYER	PLATITUDINIZERS
PLANIGRAPHY	PLASMALEMMA	PLASTICENES	PLATELAYERS	PLATITUDINIZES
PLANIMETER	PLASMALEMMAS	PLASTICINE	PLATELAYING	PLATITUDINIZING
PLANIMETERS	PLASMAPHERESES	PLASTICINES	PLATELAYINGS	PLATITUDINOUS
PLANIMETRIC	PLASMAPHERESIS	PLASTICISATION	PLATEMAKER	PLATITUDINOUSLY
PLANIMETRICAL	PLASMASOLS	PLASTICISATIONS	PLATEMAKERS	PLATONICALLY
PLANIMETRICALLY	PLASMATICAL	PLASTICISE	PLATEMAKING	PLATONISMS
PLANIMETRIES	PLASMINOGEN	PLASTICISED	PLATEMAKINGS	PLATOONING
PLANIMETRY	PLASMINOGENS	PLASTICISER	PLATEMARKED	PLATTELAND
PLANISHERS	PLASMODESM	PLASTICISERS	PLATEMARKING	PLATTELANDS
PLANISHING	PLASMODESMA	PLASTICISES	PLATEMARKS	PLATTERFUL
PLANISPHERE	PLASMODESMAS	PLASTICISING	PLATERESQUE	PLATTERFULS
PLANISPHERES	PLASMODESMATA	PLASTICITIES	PLATFORMED	PLATTERSFUL
PLANISPHERIC	PLASMODESMS	PLASTICITY	PLATFORMER	PLATYCEPHALIC
PLANKTONIC	PLASMODIAL	PLASTICIZATION	PLATFORMERS	PLATYCEPHALOUS
PLANLESSLY	PLASMODIUM	PLASTICIZATIONS	PLATFORMING	PLATYFISHES
PLANLESSNESS	PLASMOGAMIES	PLASTICIZE	PLATFORMINGS	PLATYHELMINTH

P

PLATYHELMINTHIC	PLEADINGLY	PLEINAIRIST	PLEONASTICAL	PLEXIMETERS
PLATYHELMINTHS	PLEASANCES	PLEINAIRISTS	PLEONASTICALLY	PLEXIMETRIC
PLATYKURTIC	PLEASANTER	PLEIOCHASIA	PLEONECTIC	PLEXIMETRIES
PLATYPUSES	PLEASANTEST	PLEIOCHASIUM	PLEONEXIAS	PLEXIMETRY
PLATYRRHINE	PLEASANTLY	PLEIOMERIES	PLEROCERCOID	PLIABILITIES
PLATYRRHINES	PLEASANTNESS	PLEIOMEROUS	PLEROCERCOIDS	PLIABILITY
PLATYRRHINIAN	PLEASANTNESSES	PLEIOTAXIES	PLEROMATIC	PLIABLENESS
PLATYRRHINIANS	PLEASANTRIES	PLEIOTROPIC	PLEROPHORIA	PLIABLENESSES
PLAUDITORY	PLEASANTRY	PLEIOTROPIES	PLEROPHORIAS	PLIANTNESS
PLAUSIBILITIES	PLEASINGLY	PLEIOTROPISM	PLEROPHORIES	PLIANTNESSES
PLAUSIBILITY	PLEASINGNESS	PLEIOTROPISMS	PLEROPHORY	PLICATENESS
PLAUSIBLENESS	PLEASINGNESSES	PLEIOTROPY	PLESIOSAUR	PLICATENESSES
PLAUSIBLENESSES	PLEASURABILITY	PLENARTIES	PLESIOSAURIAN	PLICATIONS
PLAYABILITIES	PLEASURABLE	PLENILUNAR	PLESIOSAURIANS	PLICATURES
PLAYABILITY	PLEASURABLENESS	PLENILUNES	PLESIOSAURS	PLODDINGLY
PLAYACTING	PLEASURABLY	PLENIPOTENCE	PLESSIMETER	PLODDINGNESS
PLAYACTINGS	PLEASUREFUL	PLENIPOTENCES	PLESSIMETERS	PLODDINGNESSES
PLAYACTORS	PLEASURELESS	PLENIPOTENCIES	PLESSIMETRIC	PLOTLESSNESS
PLAYBUSSES	PLEASURERS	PLENIPOTENCY	PLESSIMETRIES	PLOTLESSNESSES
PLAYDOUGHS	PLEASURING	PLENIPOTENT	PLESSIMETRY	PLOTTERING
PLAYFELLOW	PLEBEIANISE	PLENIPOTENTIAL	PLETHORICAL	PLOTTINGLY
PLAYFELLOWS	PLEBEIANISED	PLENIPOTENTIARY	PLETHORICALLY	PLOUGHABLE
PLAYFIELDS	PLEBEIANISES	PLENISHERS	PLETHYSMOGRAM	PLOUGHBACK
PLAYFULNESS	PLEBEIANISING	PLENISHING	PLETHYSMOGRAMS	PLOUGHBACKS
PLAYFULNESSES	PLEBEIANISM	PLENISHINGS	PLETHYSMOGRAPH	PLOUGHBOYS
PLAYGOINGS	PLEBEIANISMS	PLENISHMENT	PLETHYSMOGRAPHS	PLOUGHGATE
PLAYGROUND	PLEBEIANIZE	PLENISHMENTS	PLETHYSMOGRAPHY	PLOUGHGATES
PLAYGROUNDS	PLEBEIANIZED	PLENITUDES	PLEURAPOPHYSES	PLOUGHHEAD
PLAYGROUPS	PLEBEIANIZES	PLENITUDINOUS	PLEURAPOPHYSIS	PLOUGHHEADS
PLAYHOUSES	PLEBEIANIZING	PLENTEOUSLY	PLEURISIES	PLOUGHINGS
PLAYLEADER	PLEBEIANLY	PLENTEOUSNESS	PLEURITICAL	PLOUGHLAND
PLAYLEADERS	PLEBIFICATION	PLENTEOUSNESSES	PLEURITICS	PLOUGHLANDS
PLAYLISTED	PLEBIFICATIONS	PLENTIFULLY	PLEURITISES	PLOUGHMANSHIP
PLAYLISTING	PLEBIFYING	PLENTIFULNESS	PLEUROCARPOUS	PLOUGHMANSHIPS
PLAYMAKERS	PLEBISCITARY	PLENTIFULNESSES	PLEUROCENTESES	PLOUGHSHARE
PLAYMAKING	PLEBISCITE	PLENTITUDE	PLEUROCENTESIS	PLOUGHSHARES
PLAYMAKINGS	PLEBISCITES	PLENTITUDES	PLEURODONT	PLOUGHSTAFF
PLAYREADER	PLECOPTERAN	PLEOCHROIC	PLEURODONTS	PLOUGHSTAFFS
PLAYREADERS	PLECOPTERANS	PLEOCHROISM	PLEURODYNIA	PLOUGHTAIL
PLAYSCHOOL	PLECOPTEROUS	PLEOCHROISMS	PLEURODYNIAS	PLOUGHTAILS
PLAYSCHOOLS	PLECTOGNATH	PLEOMORPHIC	PLEURONIAS	PLOUGHWISE
PLAYTHINGS	PLECTOGNATHIC	PLEOMORPHIES	PLEUROPNEUMONIA	PLOUGHWRIGHT
PLAYWRIGHT	PLECTOGNATHOUS	PLEOMORPHISM	PLEUROTOMIES	PLOUGHWRIGHTS
PLAYWRIGHTING	PLECTOGNATHS	PLEOMORPHISMS	PLEUROTOMY	PLOUTERING
PLAYWRIGHTINGS	PLECTOPTEROUS	PLEOMORPHOUS	PLEUSTONIC	PLOVERIEST
PLAYWRIGHTS	PLEDGEABLE	PLEOMORPHY	PLEXIGLASS	PLOWMANSHIP
PLAYWRITING	PLEINAIRISM	PLEONASTES	PLEXIGLASSES	PLOWMANSHIPS
PLAYWRITINGS	PLEINAIRISMS	PLEONASTIC	PLEXIMETER	PLOWSHARES

PLOWSTAFFS	PLURALIZATION	PNEUMATICITY	PNEUMONOLOGY	PODOPHYLIN
PLOWTERING	PLURALIZATIONS	PNEUMATICS	PNEUMOTHORACES	PODOPHYLINS
PLOWWRIGHT	PLURALIZED	PNEUMATOLOGICAL	PNEUMOTHORAX	PODOPHYLLI
PLOWWRIGHTS	PLURALIZER	PNEUMATOLOGIES	PNEUMOTHORAXES	PODOPHYLLIN
PLUCKINESS	PLURALIZERS	PNEUMATOLOGIST	POACHINESS	PODOPHYLLINS
PLUCKINESSES	PLURALIZES	PNEUMATOLOGISTS	POACHINESSES	PODOPHYLLUM
PLUGBOARDS	PLURALIZING	PNEUMATOLOGY	POCKETABLE	PODOPHYLLUMS
PLUGUGLIES	PLURILITERAL	PNEUMATOLYSES	POCKETBIKE	PODOSPHERE
PLUMASSIER	PLURILOCULAR	PNEUMATOLYSIS	POCKETBIKES	PODOSPHERES
PLUMASSIERS	PLURIPARAE	PNEUMATOLYTIC	POCKETBOOK	PODSOLISATION
PLUMBAGINACEOUS	PLURIPARAS	PNEUMATOMETER	POCKETBOOKS	PODSOLISATIONS
PLUMBAGINOUS	PLURIPOTENT	PNEUMATOMETERS	POCKETFULS	PODSOLISED
PLUMBERIES	PLURIPRESENCE	PNEUMATOMETRIES	POCKETKNIFE	PODSOLISES
PLUMBIFEROUS	PLURIPRESENCES	PNEUMATOMETRY	POCKETKNIVES	PODSOLISING
PLUMBISOLVENCY	PLURISERIAL	PNEUMATOPHORE	POCKETLESS	PODSOLIZATION
PLUMBISOLVENT	PLURISERIATE	PNEUMATOPHORES	POCKETPHONE	PODSOLIZATIONS
PLUMBNESSES	PLUSHINESS	PNEUMECTOMIES	POCKETPHONES	PODSOLIZED
PLUMBOSOLVENCY	PLUSHINESSES	PNEUMECTOMY	POCKETSFUL	PODSOLIZES
PLUMBOSOLVENT	PLUSHNESSES	PNEUMOBACILLI	POCKMANKIES	PODSOLIZING
PLUMDAMASES	PLUTOCRACIES	PNEUMOBACILLUS	POCKMANTIE	PODZOLISATION
PLUMIGEROUS	PLUTOCRACY	PNEUMOCOCCAL	POCKMANTIES	PODZOLISATIONS
PLUMMETING	PLUTOCRATIC	PNEUMOCOCCI	POCKMARKED	PODZOLISED
PLUMOSITIES	PLUTOCRATICAL	PNEUMOCOCCUS	POCKMARKING	PODZOLISES
PLUMPENING	PLUTOCRATICALLY	PNEUMOCONIOSES	POCKPITTED	PODZOLISING
PLUMPNESSES	PLUTOCRATS	PNEUMOCONIOSIS	POCOCURANTE	PODZOLIZATION
PLUMULACEOUS	PLUTOLATRIES	PNEUMOCONIOTIC	POCOCURANTEISM	PODZOLIZATIONS
PLUMULARIAN	PLUTOLATRY	PNEUMOCONIOTICS	POCOCURANTEISMS	PODZOLIZED
PLUMULARIANS	PLUTOLOGIES	PNEUMOCYSTIS	POCOCURANTES	PODZOLIZES
PLUNDERABLE	PLUTOLOGIST	PNEUMOCYSTISES	POCOCURANTISM	PODZOLIZING
PLUNDERAGE	PLUTOLOGISTS	PNEUMODYNAMICS	POCOCURANTISMS	POENOLOGIES
PLUNDERAGES	PLUTONISMS	PNEUMOGASTRIC	POCOCURANTIST	POETASTERIES
PLUNDERERS	PLUTONIUMS	PNEUMOGASTRICS	POCOCURANTISTS	POETASTERING
PLUNDERING	PLUTONOMIES	PNEUMOGRAM	POCULIFORM	POETASTERINGS
PLUNDEROUS	PLUTONOMIST	PNEUMOGRAMS	PODAGRICAL	POETASTERS
PLUPERFECT	PLUTONOMISTS	PNEUMOGRAPH	PODARGUSES	POETASTERY
PLUPERFECTS	PLUVIOMETER	PNEUMOGRAPHS	PODCASTERS	POETASTRIES
PLURALISATION	PLUVIOMETERS	PNEUMOKONIOSES	PODCASTING	POETICALLY
PLURALISATIONS	PLUVIOMETRIC	PNEUMOKONIOSIS	PODCASTINGS	POETICALNESS
PLURALISED	PLUVIOMETRICAL	PNEUMONECTOMIES	PODGINESSES	POETICALNESSES
PLURALISER	PLUVIOMETRIES	PNEUMONECTOMY	PODIATRIES	POETICISED
PLURALISERS	PLUVIOMETRY	PNEUMONIAS	PODIATRIST	POETICISES
PLURALISES	PLYOMETRIC	PNEUMONICS	PODIATRISTS	POETICISING
PLURALISING	PLYOMETRICS	PNEUMONITIDES	PODOCONIOSES	POETICISMS
PLURALISMS	PNEUMATHODE	PNEUMONITIS	PODOCONIOSIS	POETICIZED
PLURALISTIC	PNEUMATHODES	PNEUMONITISES	PODOLOGIES	POETICIZES
PLURALISTICALLY	PNEUMATICAL	PNEUMONOLOGIES	PODOLOGIST	POETICIZING
PLURALISTS	PNEUMATICALLY	PNEUMONOLOGIST	PODOLOGISTS	POETICULES
PLURALITIES	PNEUMATICITIES	PNEUMONOLOGISTS	PODOPHTHALMOUS	POETRESSES

POGONOPHORAN	POKELOGANS	POLEMONIUMS	POLITICKED	POLLYANNAISH
POGONOPHORANS	POKERISHLY	POLIANITES	POLITICKER	POLLYANNAISM
POGONOTOMIES	POKERWORKS	POLICEWOMAN	POLITICKERS	POLLYANNAISMS
POGONOTOMY	POKINESSES	POLICEWOMEN	POLITICKING	POLLYANNAS
POGROMISTS	POLARIMETER	POLICYHOLDER	POLITICKINGS	POLLYANNISH
POHUTUKAWA	POLARIMETERS	POLICYHOLDERS	POLITICOES	POLONAISES
POHUTUKAWAS	POLARIMETRIC	POLICYMAKER	POLITIQUES	POLONISING
POIGNADOES	POLARIMETRIES	POLICYMAKERS	POLLARDING	POLONIZING
POIGNANCES	POLARIMETRY	POLIOMYELITIDES	POLLENATED	POLTERGEIST
POIGNANCIES	POLARISABILITY	POLIOMYELITIS	POLLENATES	POLTERGEISTS
POIGNANTLY	POLARISABLE	POLIOMYELITISES	POLLENATING	POLTROONERIES
POIKILITIC	POLARISATION	POLIORCETIC	POLLENIFEROUS	POLTROONERY
POIKILOCYTE	POLARISATIONS	POLIORCETICS	POLLENISER	POLVERINES
POIKILOCYTES	POLARISCOPE	POLIOVIRUS	POLLENISERS	POLYACRYLAMIDE
POIKILOTHERM	POLARISCOPES	POLIOVIRUSES	POLLENIZER	POLYACRYLAMIDES
POIKILOTHERMAL	POLARISCOPIC	POLISHABLE	POLLENIZERS	POLYACTINAL
POIKILOTHERMIC	POLARISERS	POLISHINGS	POLLENOSES	POLYACTINE
POIKILOTHERMIES	POLARISING	POLISHMENT	POLLENOSIS	POLYACTINES
POIKILOTHERMISM	POLARITIES	POLISHMENTS	POLLICITATION	POLYADELPHOUS
POIKILOTHERMS	POLARIZABILITY	POLITBUROS	POLLICITATIONS	POLYALCOHOL
POIKILOTHERMY	POLARIZABLE	POLITENESS	POLLINATED	POLYALCOHOLS
POINCIANAS	POLARIZATION	POLITENESSES	POLLINATES	POLYAMIDES
POINSETTIA	POLARIZATIONS	POLITESSES	POLLINATING	POLYAMINES
POINSETTIAS	POLARIZERS	POLITICALISE	POLLINATION	POLYAMORIES
POINTEDNESS	POLARIZING	POLITICALISED	POLLINATIONS	POLYAMOROUS
POINTEDNESSES	POLAROGRAM	POLITICALISES	POLLINATOR	POLYANDRIES
POINTELLES	POLAROGRAMS	POLITICALISING	POLLINATORS	POLYANDROUS
POINTILLES	POLAROGRAPH	POLITICALIZE	POLLINIFEROUS	POLYANTHAS
POINTILLISM	POLAROGRAPHIC	POLITICALIZED	POLLINISED	POLYANTHUS
POINTILLISME	POLAROGRAPHIES	POLITICALIZES	POLLINISER	POLYANTHUSES
POINTILLISMES	POLAROGRAPHS	POLITICALIZING	POLLINISERS	POLYARCHIES
POINTILLISMS	POLAROGRAPHY	POLITICALLY	POLLINISES	POLYARTHRITIDES
POINTILLIST	POLEMARCHS	POLITICASTER	POLLINISING	POLYARTHRITIS
POINTILLISTE	POLEMICALLY	POLITICASTERS	POLLINIZED	POLYARTHRITISES
POINTILLISTES	POLEMICISE	POLITICIAN	POLLINIZER	POLYATOMIC
POINTILLISTIC	POLEMICISED	POLITICIANS	POLLINIZERS	POLYAXIALS
POINTILLISTS	POLEMICISES	POLITICISATION	POLLINIZES	POLYAXONIC
POINTLESSLY	POLEMICISING	POLITICISATIONS	POLLINIZING	POLYBAGGED
POINTLESSNESS	POLEMICIST	POLITICISE	POLLINOSES	POLYBAGGING
POINTLESSNESSES	POLEMICISTS	POLITICISED	POLLINOSIS	POLYBASITE
POISONABLE	POLEMICIZE	POLITICISES	POLLTAKERS	POLYBASITES
POISONINGS	POLEMICIZED	POLITICISING	POLLUCITES	POLYBUTADIENE
POISONOUSLY	POLEMICIZES	POLITICIZATION	POLLUSIONS	POLYBUTADIENES
POISONOUSNESS	POLEMICIZING	POLITICIZATIONS	POLLUTANTS	POLYCARBONATE
POISONOUSNESSES	POLEMISING	POLITICIZE	POLLUTEDLY	POLYCARBONATES
POISONWOOD	POLEMIZING	POLITICIZED	POLLUTEDNESS	POLYCARBOXYLATE
POISONWOODS	POLEMONIACEOUS	POLITICIZES	POLLUTEDNESSES	POLYCARBOXYLIC
POKEBERRIES	POLEMONIUM	POLITICIZING	POLLUTIONS	POLYCARPELLARY

POLYCARPIC	POLYCRYSTALLINE	POLYGAMIZED	POLYHEDRIC	POLYMERIZED
POLYCARPIES	POLYCRYSTALS	POLYGAMIZES	POLYHEDRON	POLYMERIZES
POLYCARPOUS	POLYCULTURE	POLYGAMIZING	POLYHEDRONS	POLYMERIZING
POLYCENTRIC	POLYCULTURES	POLYGAMOUS	POLYHEDROSES	POLYMEROUS
POLYCENTRICS	POLYCYCLIC	POLYGAMOUSLY	POLYHEDROSIS	POLYMORPHIC
POLYCENTRISM	POLYCYCLICS	POLYGENESES	POLYHISTOR	POLYMORPHICALLY
POLYCENTRISMS	POLYCYSTIC	POLYGENESIS	POLYHISTORIAN	POLYMORPHISM
POLYCHAETE	POLYCYTHAEMIA	POLYGENETIC	POLYHISTORIANS	POLYMORPHISMS
POLYCHAETES	POLYCYTHAEMIAS	POLYGENETICALLY	POLYHISTORIC	POLYMORPHOUS
POLYCHAETOUS	POLYCYTHEMIA	POLYGENIES	POLYHISTORIES	POLYMORPHOUSLY
POLYCHASIA	POLYCYTHEMIAS	POLYGENISM	POLYHISTORS	POLYMORPHS
POLYCHASIUM	POLYCYTHEMIC	POLYGENISMS	POLYHISTORY	POLYMYOSITIS
POLYCHETES	POLYDACTYL	POLYGENIST	POLYHYBRID	POLYMYOSITISES
POLYCHETOUS	POLYDACTYLIES	POLYGENISTS	POLYHYBRIDS	POLYMYXINS
POLYCHLORINATED	POLYDACTYLISM	POLYGENOUS	POLYHYDRIC	POLYNEURITIDES
POLYCHLOROPRENE	POLYDACTYLISMS	POLYGLOTISM	POLYHYDROXY	POLYNEURITIS
POLYCHOTOMIES	POLYDACTYLOUS	POLYGLOTISMS	POLYIMIDES	POLYNEURITISES
POLYCHOTOMOUS	POLYDACTYLS	POLYGLOTTAL	POLYISOPRENE	POLYNOMIAL
POLYCHOTOMY	POLYDACTYLY	POLYGLOTTIC	POLYISOPRENES	POLYNOMIALISM
POLYCHREST	POLYDAEMONISM	POLYGLOTTISM	POLYLEMMAS	POLYNOMIALISMS
POLYCHRESTS	POLYDAEMONISMS	POLYGLOTTISMS	POLYLINGUAL	POLYNOMIALS
POLYCHROIC	POLYDEMONISM	POLYGLOTTOUS	POLYLYSINE	POLYNUCLEAR
POLYCHROISM	POLYDEMONISMS	POLYGLOTTS	POLYLYSINES	POLYNUCLEATE
POLYCHROISMS	POLYDIPSIA	POLYGONACEOUS	POLYMASTIA	POLYNUCLEOTIDE
POLYCHROMATIC	POLYDIPSIAS	POLYGONALLY	POLYMASTIAS	POLYNUCLEOTIDES
POLYCHROMATISM	POLYDIPSIC	POLYGONATUM	POLYMASTIC	POLYOLEFIN
POLYCHROMATISMS	POLYDISPERSE	POLYGONATUMS	POLYMASTICS	POLYOLEFINS
POLYCHROME	POLYDISPERSITY	POLYGONIES	POLYMASTIES	POLYOMINOES
POLYCHROMED	POLYELECTROLYTE	POLYGONUMS	POLYMASTISM	POLYOMINOS
POLYCHROMES	POLYEMBRYONATE	POLYGRAPHED	POLYMASTISMS	POLYONYMIC
POLYCHROMIC	POLYEMBRYONIC	POLYGRAPHER	POLYMATHIC	POLYONYMIES
POLYCHROMIES	POLYEMBRYONIES	POLYGRAPHERS	POLYMATHIES	POLYONYMOUS
POLYCHROMING	POLYEMBRYONY	POLYGRAPHIC	POLYMERASE	POLYPARIES
POLYCHROMOUS	POLYESTERS	POLYGRAPHICALLY	POLYMERASES	POLYPARIUM
POLYCHROMY	POLYESTROUS	POLYGRAPHIES	POLYMERIDE	POLYPEPTIDE
POLYCISTRONIC	POLYETHENE	POLYGRAPHING	POLYMERIDES	POLYPEPTIDES
POLYCLINIC	POLYETHENES	POLYGRAPHIST	POLYMERIES	POLYPEPTIDIC
POLYCLINICS	POLYETHYLENE	POLYGRAPHISTS	POLYMERISATION	POLYPETALOUS
POLYCLONAL	POLYETHYLENES	POLYGRAPHS	POLYMERISATIONS	POLYPHAGIA
POLYCLONALS	POLYGALACEOUS	POLYGRAPHY	POLYMERISE	POLYPHAGIAS
POLYCOTTON	POLYGAMIES	POLYGYNIAN	POLYMERISED	POLYPHAGIES
POLYCOTTONS	POLYGAMISE	POLYGYNIES	POLYMERISES	POLYPHAGOUS
POLYCOTYLEDON	POLYGAMISED	POLYGYNIST	POLYMERISING	POLYPHARMACIES
POLYCOTYLEDONS	POLYGAMISES	POLYGYNISTS	POLYMERISM	POLYPHARMACY
POLYCROTIC	POLYGAMISING	POLYGYNOUS	POLYMERISMS	POLYPHASIC
POLYCROTISM	POLYGAMIST	POLYHALITE	POLYMERIZATION	POLYPHENOL
POLYCROTISMS	POLYGAMISTS	POLYHALITES	POLYMERIZATIONS	POLYPHENOLIC
POLYCRYSTAL	POLYGAMIZE	POLYHEDRAL	POLYMERIZE	POLYPHENOLS

POLYPHLOESBOEAN	POLYSORBATE	POLYTONALITIES	POMPELMOUSE	PONTIFICATIONS
POLYPHLOISBIC	POLYSORBATES	POLYTONALITY	POMPELMOUSES	PONTIFICATOR
POLYPHONES	POLYSTICHOUS	POLYTONALLY	POMPHOLYGOUS	PONTIFICATORS
POLYPHONIC	POLYSTYLAR	POLYTROPHIC	POMPHOLYXES	PONTIFICES
POLYPHONICALLY	POLYSTYLES	POLYTUNNEL	POMPOSITIES	PONTIFYING
POLYPHONIES	POLYSTYRENE	POLYTUNNELS	POMPOUSNESS	PONTLEVISES
POLYPHONIST	POLYSTYRENES	POLYTYPICAL	POMPOUSNESSES	PONTONEERS
POLYPHONISTS	POLYSULFIDE	POLYTYPING	PONDERABILITIES	PONTONIERS
POLYPHONOUS	POLYSULFIDES	POLYUNSATURATE	PONDERABILITY	PONTONNIER
POLYPHONOUSLY	POLYSULPHIDE	POLYUNSATURATED	PONDERABLE	PONTONNIERS
POLYPHOSPHORIC	POLYSULPHIDES	POLYUNSATURATES	PONDERABLES	PONTOONERS
POLYPHYLETIC	POLYSYLLABIC	POLYURETHAN	PONDERABLY	PONTOONING
POLYPHYLLOUS	POLYSYLLABICAL	POLYURETHANE	PONDERANCE	PONYTAILED
POLYPHYODONT	POLYSYLLABICISM	POLYURETHANES	PONDERANCES	POORHOUSES
POLYPIDOMS	POLYSYLLABISM	POLYURETHANS	PONDERANCIES	POORMOUTHED
POLYPLOIDAL	POLYSYLLABISMS	POLYVALENCE	PONDERANCY	POORMOUTHING
POLYPLOIDIC	POLYSYLLABLE	POLYVALENCES	PONDERATED	POORMOUTHS
POLYPLOIDIES	POLYSYLLABLES	POLYVALENCIES	PONDERATES	POORNESSES
POLYPLOIDS	POLYSYLLOGISM	POLYVALENCY	PONDERATING	POPLINETTE
POLYPLOIDY	POLYSYLLOGISMS	POLYVALENT	PONDERATION	POPLINETTES
POLYPODIES	POLYSYNAPTIC	POLYVINYLIDENE	PONDERATIONS	POPMOBILITIES
POLYPODOUS	POLYSYNDETON	POLYVINYLIDENES	PONDERINGLY	POPMOBILITY
POLYPROPENE	POLYSYNDETONS	POLYVINYLS	PONDERMENT	POPPERINGS
POLYPROPENES	POLYSYNTHESES	POLYWATERS	PONDERMENTS	POPPYCOCKS
POLYPROPYLENE	POLYSYNTHESIS	POLYZOARIA	PONDEROSAS	POPPYHEADS
POLYPROPYLENES	POLYSYNTHESISM	POLYZOARIAL	PONDEROSITIES	POPULARISATION
POLYPROTODONT	POLYSYNTHESISMS	POLYZOARIES	PONDEROSITY	POPULARISATIONS
POLYPROTODONTS	POLYSYNTHETIC	POLYZOARIUM	PONDEROUSLY	POPULARISE
POLYPTYCHS	POLYSYNTHETICAL	POMATUMING	PONDEROUSNESS	POPULARISED
POLYRHYTHM	POLYSYNTHETISM	POMEGRANATE	PONDEROUSNESSES	POPULARISER
POLYRHYTHMIC	POLYSYNTHETISMS	POMEGRANATES	PONDOKKIES	POPULARISERS
POLYRHYTHMS	POLYTECHNIC	POMICULTURE	PONEROLOGIES	POPULARISES
POLYRIBOSOMAL	POLYTECHNICAL	POMICULTURES	PONEROLOGY	POPULARISING
POLYRIBOSOME	POLYTECHNICS	POMIFEROUS	PONIARDING	POPULARIST
POLYRIBOSOMES	POLYTENIES	POMMELLING	PONTIANACS	POPULARITIES
POLYSACCHARIDE	POLYTHALAMOUS	POMOERIUMS	PONTIANAKS	POPULARITY
POLYSACCHARIDES	POLYTHEISM	POMOLOGICAL	PONTICELLO	POPULARIZATION
POLYSACCHAROSE	POLYTHEISMS	POMOLOGICALLY	PONTICELLOS	POPULARIZATIONS
POLYSACCHAROSES	POLYTHEIST	POMOLOGIES	PONTIFICAL	POPULARIZE
POLYSEMANT	POLYTHEISTIC	POMOLOGIST	PONTIFICALITIES	POPULARIZED
POLYSEMANTS	POLYTHEISTICAL	POMOLOGISTS	PONTIFICALITY	POPULARIZER
POLYSEMIES	POLYTHEISTS	POMOSEXUAL	PONTIFICALLY	POPULARIZERS
POLYSEMOUS	POLYTHENES	POMOSEXUALS	PONTIFICALS	POPULARIZES
POLYSEPALOUS	POLYTOCOUS	POMPADOURED	PONTIFICATE	POPULARIZING
POLYSILOXANE	POLYTONALISM	POMPADOURS	PONTIFICATED	POPULATING
POLYSILOXANES	POLYTONALISMS	POMPELMOOSE	PONTIFICATES	POPULATION
POLYSOMICS	POLYTONALIST	POMPELMOOSES	PONTIFICATING	POPULATIONAL
POLYSOMIES	POLYTONALISTS	POMPELMOUS	PONTIFICATION	POPULATIONS

P

POPULISTIC	PORNOGRAPHERS	PORTAMENTO	PORTULACACEOUS	POSSIBILISTS
POPULOUSLY	PORNOGRAPHIC	PORTAPACKS	PORTULACAS	POSSIBILITIES
POPULOUSNESS	PORNOGRAPHIES	PORTATIVES	PORWIGGLES	POSSIBILITY
POPULOUSNESSES	PORNOGRAPHY	PORTCULLIS	POSHNESSES	POSSIBLEST
PORBEAGLES	PORNOTOPIA	PORTCULLISED	POSITIONAL	POSTABORTION
PORCELAINEOUS	PORNOTOPIAN	PORTCULLISES	POSITIONALLY	POSTACCIDENT
PORCELAINISE	PORNOTOPIAS	PORTCULLISING	POSITIONED	POSTADOLESCENT
PORCELAINISED	POROGAMIES	PORTENDING	POSITIONING	POSTADOLESCENTS
PORCELAINISES	POROMERICS	PORTENTOUS	POSITIONINGS	POSTAMPUTATION
PORCELAINISING	POROSCOPES	PORTENTOUSLY	POSITIVELY	POSTAPOCALYPTIC
PORCELAINIZE	POROSCOPIC	PORTENTOUSNESS	POSITIVENESS	POSTARREST
PORCELAINIZED	POROSCOPIES	PORTEOUSES	POSITIVENESSES	POSTATOMIC
PORCELAINIZES	POROSITIES	PORTERAGES	POSITIVEST	POSTATTACK
PORCELAINIZING	POROUSNESS	PORTERESSES	POSITIVISM	POSTBELLUM
PORCELAINLIKE	POROUSNESSES	PORTERHOUSE	POSITIVISMS	POSTBIBLICAL
PORCELAINOUS	PORPENTINE	PORTERHOUSES	POSITIVIST	POSTBOURGEOIS
PORCELAINS	PORPENTINES	PORTFOLIOS	POSITIVISTIC	POSTBUSSES
PORCELANEOUS	PORPHYRIAS	PORTHORSES	POSITIVISTS	POSTCAPITALIST
PORCELLANEOUS	PORPHYRIES	PORTHOUSES	POSITIVITIES	POSTCARDED
PORCELLANISE	PORPHYRINS	PORTIONERS	POSITIVITY	POSTCARDING
PORCELLANISED	PORPHYRIOS	PORTIONING	POSITRONIUM	POSTCARDLIKE
PORCELLANISES	PORPHYRITE	PORTIONIST	POSITRONIUMS	POSTCLASSIC
PORCELLANISING	PORPHYRITES	PORTIONISTS	POSOLOGICAL	POSTCLASSICAL
PORCELLANITE	PORPHYRITIC	PORTIONLESS	POSOLOGIES	POSTCODING
PORCELLANITES	PORPHYROGENITE	PORTLINESS	POSSESSABLE	POSTCOITAL
PORCELLANIZE	PORPHYROGENITES	PORTLINESSES	POSSESSEDLY	POSTCOLLEGE
PORCELLANIZED	PORPHYROID	PORTMANTEAU	POSSESSEDNESS	POSTCOLLEGIATE
PORCELLANIZES	PORPHYROIDS	PORTMANTEAUS	POSSESSEDNESSES	POSTCOLONIAL
PORCELLANIZING	PORPHYROPSIN	PORTMANTEAUX	POSSESSING	POSTCONCEPTION
PORCELLANOUS	PORPHYROPSINS	PORTMANTLE	POSSESSION	POSTCONCERT
PORCHETTAS	PORPHYROUS	PORTMANTLES	POSSESSIONAL	POSTCONQUEST
PORCUPINES	PORPOISING	PORTMANTUA	POSSESSIONARY	POSTCONSONANTAL
PORCUPINIER	PORRACEOUS	PORTMANTUAS	POSSESSIONATE	POSTCONVENTION
PORCUPINIEST	PORRECTING	PORTOBELLO	POSSESSIONATES	POSTCOPULATORY
PORCUPINISH	PORRECTION	PORTOBELLOS	POSSESSIONED	POSTCORONARY
PORIFERANS	PORRECTIONS	PORTOLANOS	POSSESSIONLESS	POSTCRANIAL
PORIFEROUS	PORRENGERS	PORTRAITED	POSSESSIONS	POSTCRANIALLY
PORINESSES	PORRIDGIER	PORTRAITING	POSSESSIVE	POSTCRISIS
PORISMATIC	PORRIDGIEST	PORTRAITIST	POSSESSIVELY	POSTDATING
PORISMATICAL	PORRIGINOUS	PORTRAITISTS	POSSESSIVENESS	POSTDEADLINE
PORISTICAL	PORRINGERS	PORTRAITURE	POSSESSIVES	POSTDEBATE
PORKINESSES	PORTABELLA	PORTRAITURES	POSSESSORS	POSTDEBUTANTE
PORLOCKING	PORTABELLAS	PORTRAYABLE	POSSESSORSHIP	POSTDELIVERY
PORNIFICATION	PORTABELLO	PORTRAYALS	POSSESSORSHIPS	POSTDEPRESSION
PORNIFICATIONS	PORTABELLOS	PORTRAYERS	POSSESSORY	POSTDEVALUATION
PORNOCRACIES	PORTABILITIES	PORTRAYING	POSSIBILISM	POSTDILUVIAL
PORNOCRACY	PORTABILITY	PORTREEVES	POSSIBILISMS	POSTDILUVIAN
PORNOGRAPHER	PORTAMENTI	PORTRESSES	POSSIBILIST	POSTDILUVIANS

POSTDIVESTITURE	POSTGRADUATE	POSTLIMINIA	POSTPERSON	POSTTENSION
POSTDIVORCE	POSTGRADUATES	POSTLIMINIARY	POSTPERSONS	POSTTENSIONED
POSTDOCTORAL	POSTGRADUATION	POSTLIMINIES	POSTPOLLINATION	POSTTENSIONING
POSTDOCTORALS	POSTGRADUATIONS	POSTLIMINIOUS	POSTPONABLE	POSTTENSIONS
POSTDOCTORATE	POSTHARVEST	POSTLIMINIUM	POSTPONEMENT	POSTTRANSFUSION
POSTDOCTORATES	POSTHASTES	POSTLIMINOUS	POSTPONEMENTS	POSTTRAUMATIC
POSTEDITING	POSTHEATED	POSTLIMINY	POSTPONENCE	POSTTREATMENT
POSTEDITINGS	POSTHEATING	POSTLITERATE	POSTPONENCES	POSTTREATMENTS
POSTELECTION	POSTHEMORRHAGIC	POSTMARITAL	POSTPONERS	POSTULANCIES
POSTEMBRYONAL	POSTHOLDER	POSTMARKED	POSTPONING	POSTULANCY
POSTEMBRYONIC	POSTHOLDERS	POSTMARKING	POSTPOSING	POSTULANTS
POSTEMERGENCE	POSTHOLIDAY	POSTMASTECTOMY	POSTPOSITION	POSTULANTSHIP
POSTEMERGENCY	POSTHOLOCAUST	POSTMASTER	POSTPOSITIONAL	POSTULANTSHIPS
POSTEPILEPTIC	POSTHORSES	POSTMASTERS	POSTPOSITIONS	POSTULATED
POSTERIORITIES	POSTHOSPITAL	POSTMASTERSHIP	POSTPOSITIVE	POSTULATES
POSTERIORITY	POSTHOUSES	POSTMASTERSHIPS	POSTPOSITIVELY	POSTULATING
POSTERIORLY	POSTHUMOUS	POSTMATING	POSTPOSITIVES	POSTULATION
POSTERIORS	POSTHUMOUSLY	POSTMEDIEVAL	POSTPRANDIAL	POSTULATIONAL
POSTERISATION	POSTHUMOUSNESS	POSTMENOPAUSAL	POSTPRIMARY	POSTULATIONALLY
POSTERISATIONS	POSTHYPNOTIC	POSTMENSTRUAL	POSTPRISON	POSTULATIONS
POSTERISED	POSTILIONS	POSTMERIDIAN	POSTPRODUCTION	POSTULATOR
POSTERISES	POSTILLATE	POSTMIDNIGHT	POSTPRODUCTIONS	POSTULATORS
POSTERISING	POSTILLATED	POSTMILLENARIAN	POSTPUBERTIES	POSTULATORY
POSTERITIES	POSTILLATES	POSTMILLENNIAL	POSTPUBERTY	POSTULATUM
POSTERIZATION	POSTILLATING	POSTMISTRESS	POSTPUBESCENT	POSTURINGS
POSTERIZATIONS	POSTILLATION	POSTMISTRESSES	POSTPUBESCENTS	POSTURISED
POSTERIZED	POSTILLATIONS	POSTMODERN	POSTRECESSION	POSTURISES
POSTERIZES	POSTILLATOR	POSTMODERNISM	POSTRETIREMENT	POSTURISING
POSTERIZING	POSTILLATORS	POSTMODERNISMS	POSTRIDERS	POSTURISTS
POSTEROLATERAL	POSTILLERS	POSTMODERNIST	POSTROMANTIC	POSTURIZED
POSTERUPTIVE	POSTILLING	POSTMODERNISTS	POSTROMANTICS	POSTURIZES
POSTEXERCISE	POSTILLION	POSTMODERNS	POSTSCENIUM	POSTURIZING
POSTEXILIAN	POSTILLIONS	POSTMODIFIED	POSTSCENIUMS	POSTVACCINAL
POSTEXILIC	POSTIMPACT	POSTMODIFIES	POSTSCRIPT	POSTVACCINATION
POSTEXPERIENCE	POSTIMPERIAL	POSTMODIFY	POSTSCRIPTS	POSTVAGOTOMY
POSTEXPOSURE	POSTINAUGURAL	POSTMODIFYING	POSTSEASON	POSTVASECTOMY
POSTFEMINISM	POSTINDUSTRIAL	POSTMORTEM	POSTSEASONS	POSTVOCALIC
POSTFEMINISMS	POSTINFECTION	POSTMORTEMS	POSTSECONDARY	POSTWEANING
POSTFEMINIST	POSTINJECTION	POSTNATALLY	POSTSTIMULATION	POSTWORKSHOP
POSTFEMINISTS	POSTINOCULATION	POSTNEONATAL	POSTSTIMULATORY	POTABILITIES
POSTFIXING	POSTIRRADIATION	POSTNUPTIAL	POSTSTIMULUS	POTABILITY
POSTFLIGHT	POSTISCHEMIC	POSTOCULAR	POSTSTRIKE	POTABLENESS
POSTFORMED	POSTISOLATION	POSTOCULARS	POSTSURGICAL	POTABLENESSES
POSTFORMING	POSTLANDING	POSTOPERATIVE	POSTSYNAPTIC	POTAMOGETON
POSTFRACTURE	POSTLAPSARIAN	POSTOPERATIVELY	POSTSYNCED	POTAMOGETONS
POSTFREEZE	POSTLAUNCH	POSTORBITAL	POSTSYNCHRONISE	POTAMOLOGICAL
POSTGANGLIONIC	POSTLIBERATION	POSTORGASMIC	POSTSYNCHRONIZE	POTAMOLOGIES
POSTGLACIAL	POSTLIMINARY	POSTPARTUM	POSTSYNCING	POTAMOLOGIST

P

POTAMOLOGISTS

POTAMOLOGISTS	POTICHOMANIAS	POWELLIZES	PRACTICUMS	PRAGMATISER
POTAMOLOGY	POTLATCHED	POWELLIZING	PRACTIQUES	PRAGMATISERS
POTASSIUMS	POTLATCHES	POWERBANDS	PRACTISANT	PRAGMATISES
POTATOBUGS	POTLATCHING	POWERBOATING	PRACTISANTS	PRAGMATISING
POTBELLIED	POTOMETERS	POWERBOATINGS	PRACTISERS	PRAGMATISM
POTBELLIES	POTPOURRIS	POWERBOATS	PRACTISING	PRAGMATISMS
POTBOILERS	POTSHOTTING	POWERFULLY	PRACTITIONER	PRAGMATIST
POTBOILING	POTSHOTTINGS	POWERFULNESS	PRACTITIONERS	PRAGMATISTIC
POTBOILINGS	POTTERINGLY	POWERFULNESSES	PRACTOLOLS	PRAGMATISTS
POTENTATES	POTTERINGS	POWERHOUSE	PRAEAMBLES	PRAGMATIZATION
POTENTIALITIES	POTTINESSES	POWERHOUSES	PRAEOCOCIAL	PRAGMATIZATIONS
POTENTIALITY	POTTINGARS	POWERLESSLY	PRAECORDIAL	PRAGMATIZE
POTENTIALLY	POTTINGERS	POWERLESSNESS	PRAEDIALITIES	PRAGMATIZED
POTENTIALS	POTTYMOUTH	POWERLESSNESSES	PRAEDIALITY	PRAGMATIZER
POTENTIARIES	POTTYMOUTHS	POWERLIFTER	PRAEFECTORIAL	PRAGMATIZERS
POTENTIARY	POTWALLERS	POWERLIFTERS	PRAELECTED	PRAGMATIZES
POTENTIATE	POULTERERS	POWERLIFTING	PRAELECTING	PRAGMATIZING
POTENTIATED	POULTICING	POWERLIFTINGS	PRAELUDIUM	PRAISEACHS
POTENTIATES	POULTROONE	POWERPLAYS	PRAEMUNIRE	PRAISELESS
POTENTIATING	POULTROONES	POWERTRAIN	PRAEMUNIRES	PRAISEWORTHIER
POTENTIATION	POULTRYMAN	POWERTRAINS	PRAENOMENS	PRAISEWORTHIEST
POTENTIATIONS	POULTRYMEN	POWSOWDIES	PRAENOMINA	PRAISEWORTHILY
POTENTIATOR	POUNDCAKES	POXVIRUSES	PRAENOMINAL	PRAISEWORTHY
POTENTIATORS	POURBOIRES	POZZOLANAS	PRAENOMINALLY	PRAISINGLY
POTENTILLA	POURPARLER	POZZOLANIC	PRAEPOSTOR	PRALLTRILLER
POTENTILLAS	POURPARLERS	POZZUOLANA	PRAEPOSTORS	PRALLTRILLERS
POTENTIOMETER	POURPOINTS	POZZUOLANAS	PRAESIDIUM	PRANAYAMAS
POTENTIOMETERS	POURSEWING	PRACHARAKS	PRAESIDIUMS	PRANCINGLY
POTENTIOMETRIC	POURTRAHED	PRACTICABILITY	PRAETORIAL	PRANDIALLY
POTENTIOMETRIES	POURTRAICT	PRACTICABLE	PRAETORIAN	PRANKINGLY
POTENTIOMETRY	POURTRAICTS	PRACTICABLENESS	PRAETORIANS	PRANKISHLY
POTENTISED	POURTRAYED	PRACTICABLY	PRAETORIUM	PRANKISHNESS
POTENTISES	POURTRAYING	PRACTICALISM	PRAETORIUMS	PRANKISHNESSES
POTENTISING	POUSOWDIES	PRACTICALISMS	PRAETORSHIP	PRANKSTERS
POTENTIZED	POUSSETTED	PRACTICALIST	PRAETORSHIPS	PRASEODYMIUM
POTENTIZES	POUSSETTES	PRACTICALISTS	PRAGMATICAL	PRASEODYMIUMS
POTENTIZING	POUSSETTING	PRACTICALITIES	PRAGMATICALITY	PRATFALLEN
POTENTNESS	POUTASSOUS	PRACTICALITY	PRAGMATICALLY	PRATFALLING
POTENTNESSES	POUTHERING	PRACTICALLY	PRAGMATICALNESS	PRATINCOLE
POTHECARIES	POWDERIEST	PRACTICALNESS	PRAGMATICISM	PRATINCOLES
POTHERIEST	POWDERINGS	PRACTICALNESSES	PRAGMATICISMS	PRATTLEBOX
POTHOLDERS	POWDERLESS	PRACTICALS	PRAGMATICIST	PRATTLEBOXES
POTHOLINGS	POWDERLIKE	PRACTICERS	PRAGMATICISTS	PRATTLEMENT
POTHUNTERS	POWELLISED	PRACTICIAN	PRAGMATICS	PRATTLEMENTS
POTHUNTING	POWELLISES	PRACTICIANS	PRAGMATISATION	PRATTLINGLY
POTHUNTINGS	POWELLISING	PRACTICING	PRAGMATISATIONS	PRAXEOLOGICAL
POTICARIES	POWELLITES	PRACTICKED	PRAGMATISE	PRAXEOLOGIES
POTICHOMANIA	POWELLIZED	PRACTICKING	PRAGMATISED	PRAXEOLOGY

PRAXINOSCOPE	PREADMONISH	PREARRANGES	PRECANCELS	PRECEPTORSHIP
PRAXINOSCOPES	PREADMONISHED	PREARRANGING	PRECANCEROUS	PRECEPTORSHIPS
PRAYERFULLY	PREADMONISHES	PREASSEMBLED	PRECANCERS	PRECEPTORY
PRAYERFULNESS	PREADMONISHING	PREASSIGNED	PRECAPITALIST	PRECEPTRESS
PRAYERFULNESSES	PREADMONITION	PREASSIGNING	PRECARIATS	PRECEPTRESSES
PRAYERLESS	PREADMONITIONS	PREASSIGNS	PRECARIOUS	PRECESSING
PRAYERLESSLY	PREADOLESCENCE	PREASSURANCE	PRECARIOUSLY	PRECESSION
PRAYERLESSNESS	PREADOLESCENCES	PREASSURANCES	PRECARIOUSNESS	PRECESSIONAL
PREABSORBED	PREADOLESCENT	PREASSURED	PRECASTING	PRECESSIONALLY
PREABSORBING	PREADOLESCENTS	PREASSURES	PRECAUTION	PRECESSIONS
PREABSORBS	PREADOPTED	PREASSURING	PRECAUTIONAL	PRECHARGED
PREACCUSED	PREADOPTING	PREATTUNED	PRECAUTIONARY	PRECHARGES
PREACCUSES	PREAGRICULTURAL	PREATTUNES	PRECAUTIONED	PRECHARGING
PREACCUSING	PREALLOTTED	PREATTUNING	PRECAUTIONING	PRECHECKED
PREACHABLE	PREALLOTTING	PREAUDIENCE	PRECAUTIONS	PRECHECKING
PREACHERSHIP	PREALTERED	PREAUDIENCES	PRECAUTIOUS	PRECHILLED
PREACHERSHIPS	PREALTERING	PREAVERRED	PRECEDENCE	PRECHILLING
PREACHIEST	PREAMBLING	PREAVERRING	PRECEDENCES	PRECHOOSES
PREACHIFIED	PREAMBULARY	PREAXIALLY	PRECEDENCIES	PRECHOOSING
PREACHIFIES	PREAMBULATE	PREBENDARIES	PRECEDENCY	PRECHRISTIAN
PREACHIFYING	PREAMBULATED	PREBENDARY	PRECEDENTED	PRECIEUSES
PREACHIFYINGS	PREAMBULATES	PREBIBLICAL	PRECEDENTIAL	PRECIOSITIES
PREACHINESS	PREAMBULATING	PREBIDDING	PRECEDENTIALLY	PRECIOSITY
PREACHINESSES	PREAMBULATORY	PREBIDDINGS	PRECEDENTLY	PRECIOUSES
PREACHINGLY	PREAMPLIFIER	PREBILLING	PRECEDENTS	PRECIOUSLY
PREACHINGS	PREAMPLIFIERS	PREBINDING	PRECENSORED	PRECIOUSNESS
PREACHMENT	PREANAESTHETIC	PREBIOLOGIC	PRECENSORING	PRECIOUSNESSES
PREACHMENTS	PREANAESTHETICS	PREBIOLOGICAL	PRECENSORS	PRECIPICED
PREACQUAINT	PREANESTHETIC	PREBIOTICS	PRECENTING	PRECIPICES
PREACQUAINTANCE	PREANNOUNCE	PREBLESSED	PRECENTORIAL	PRECIPITABILITY
PREACQUAINTED	PREANNOUNCED	PREBLESSES	PRECENTORS	PRECIPITABLE
PREACQUAINTING	PREANNOUNCES	PREBLESSING	PRECENTORSHIP	PRECIPITANCE
PREACQUAINTS	PREANNOUNCING	PREBOARDED	PRECENTORSHIPS	PRECIPITANCES
PREACQUISITION	PREAPPLIED	PREBOARDING	PRECENTRESS	PRECIPITANCIES
PREADAMITE	PREAPPLIES	PREBOILING	PRECENTRESSES	PRECIPITANCY
PREADAMITES	PREAPPLYING	PREBOOKING	PRECENTRICES	PRECIPITANT
PREADAPTATION	PREAPPOINT	PREBREAKFAST	PRECENTRIX	PRECIPITANTLY
PREADAPTATIONS	PREAPPOINTED	PREBUDGETS	PRECENTRIXES	PRECIPITANTNESS
PREADAPTED	PREAPPOINTING	PREBUILDING	PRECEPTIAL	PRECIPITANTS
PREADAPTING	PREAPPOINTS	PREBUTTALS	PRECEPTIVE	PRECIPITATE
PREADAPTIVE	PREAPPROVE	PRECALCULI	PRECEPTIVELY	PRECIPITATED
PREADJUSTED	PREAPPROVED	PRECALCULUS	PRECEPTORAL	PRECIPITATELY
PREADJUSTING	PREAPPROVES	PRECALCULUSES	PRECEPTORATE	PRECIPITATENESS
PREADJUSTS	PREAPPROVING	PRECANCELED	PRECEPTORATES	PRECIPITATES
PREADMISSION	PREARRANGE	PRECANCELING	PRECEPTORIAL	PRECIPITATING
PREADMISSIONS	PREARRANGED	PRECANCELLATION	PRECEPTORIALS	PRECIPITATION
PREADMITTED	PREARRANGEMENT	PRECANCELLED	PRECEPTORIES	PRECIPITATIONS
PREADMITTING	PREARRANGEMENTS	PRECANCELLING	PRECEPTORS	PRECIPITATIVE

PRECIPITATOR

PRECIPITATOR	PRECOGNITIVE	PRECONDITIONED	PRECURSORS	PREDESTINARIAN
PRECIPITATORS	PRECOGNIZANT	PRECONDITIONING	PRECURSORY	PREDESTINARIANS
PRECIPITIN	PRECOGNIZE	PRECONDITIONS	PRECUTTING	PREDESTINATE
PRECIPITINOGEN	PRECOGNIZED	PRECONISATION	PRECYCLING	PREDESTINATED
PRECIPITINOGENS	PRECOGNIZES	PRECONISATIONS	PREDACEOUS	PREDESTINATES
PRECIPITINS	PRECOGNIZING	PRECONISED	PREDACEOUSNESS	PREDESTINATING
PRECIPITOUS	PRECOGNOSCE	PRECONISES	PREDACIOUS	PREDESTINATION
PRECIPITOUSLY	PRECOGNOSCED	PRECONISING	PREDACIOUSNESS	PREDESTINATIONS
PRECIPITOUSNESS	PRECOGNOSCES	PRECONIZATION	PREDACITIES	PREDESTINATIVE
PRECISENESS	PRECOGNOSCING	PRECONIZATIONS	PREDATIONS	PREDESTINATOR
PRECISENESSES	PRECOLLEGE	PRECONIZED	PREDATISMS	PREDESTINATORS
PRECISIANISM	PRECOLLEGIATE	PRECONIZES	PREDATORILY	PREDESTINE
PRECISIANISMS	PRECOLONIAL	PRECONIZING	PREDATORINESS	PREDESTINED
PRECISIANIST	PRECOMBUSTION	PRECONQUEST	PREDATORINESSES	PREDESTINES
PRECISIANISTS	PRECOMBUSTIONS	PRECONSCIOUS	PREDECEASE	PREDESTINIES
PRECISIANS	PRECOMMITMENT	PRECONSCIOUSES	PREDECEASED	PREDESTINING
PRECISIONISM	PRECOMMITMENTS	PRECONSCIOUSLY	PREDECEASES	PREDESTINY
PRECISIONISMS	PRECOMPETITIVE	PRECONSONANTAL	PREDECEASING	PREDETERMINABLE
PRECISIONIST	PRECOMPOSE	PRECONSTRUCT	PREDECESSOR	PREDETERMINATE
PRECISIONISTS	PRECOMPOSED	PRECONSTRUCTED	PREDECESSORS	PREDETERMINE
PRECISIONS	PRECOMPOSES	PRECONSTRUCTING	PREDEDUCTED	PREDETERMINED
PRECLASSICAL	PRECOMPOSING	PRECONSTRUCTION	PREDEDUCTING	PREDETERMINER
PRECLEANED	PRECOMPUTE	PRECONSTRUCTS	PREDEDUCTS	PREDETERMINERS
PRECLEANING	PRECOMPUTED	PRECONSUME	PREDEFINED	PREDETERMINES
PRECLEARANCE	PRECOMPUTER	PRECONSUMED	PREDEFINES	PREDETERMINING
PRECLEARANCES	PRECOMPUTES	PRECONSUMES	PREDEFINING	PREDETERMINISM
PRECLEARED	PRECOMPUTING	PRECONSUMING	PREDEFINITION	PREDETERMINISMS
PRECLEARING	PRECONCEIT	PRECONTACT	PREDEFINITIONS	PREDEVALUATION
PRECLINICAL	PRECONCEITED	PRECONTACTS	PREDELIVERIES	PREDEVELOP
PRECLINICALLY	PRECONCEITING	PRECONTRACT	PREDELIVERY	PREDEVELOPED
PRECLUDABLE	PRECONCEITS	PRECONTRACTED	PREDENTARY	PREDEVELOPING
PRECLUDING	PRECONCEIVE	PRECONTRACTING	PREDENTATE	PREDEVELOPMENT
PRECLUSION	PRECONCEIVED	PRECONTRACTS	PREDEPARTURE	PREDEVELOPMENTS
PRECLUSIONS	PRECONCEIVES	PRECONVENTION	PREDEPOSIT	PREDEVELOPS
PRECLUSIVE	PRECONCEIVING	PRECONVICTION	PREDEPOSITED	PREDEVOTED
PRECLUSIVELY	PRECONCEPTION	PRECONVICTIONS	PREDEPOSITING	PREDEVOTES
PRECOCIALS	PRECONCEPTIONS	PRECOOKERS	PREDEPOSITS	PREDEVOTING
PRECOCIOUS	PRECONCERT	PRECOOKING	PREDESIGNATE	PREDIABETES
PRECOCIOUSLY	PRECONCERTED	PRECOOLING	PREDESIGNATED	PREDIABETESES
PRECOCIOUSNESS	PRECONCERTEDLY	PRECOPULATORY	PREDESIGNATES	PREDIABETIC
PRECOCITIES	PRECONCERTING	PRECORDIAL	PREDESIGNATING	PREDIABETICS
PRECOGNISANT	PRECONCERTS	PRECREASED	PREDESIGNATION	PREDIALITIES
PRECOGNISE	PRECONCILIAR	PRECREASES	PREDESIGNATIONS	PREDIALITY
PRECOGNISED	PRECONDEMN	PRECREASING	PREDESIGNATORY	PREDICABILITIES
PRECOGNISES	PRECONDEMNED	PRECRITICAL	PREDESIGNED	PREDICABILITY
PRECOGNISING	PRECONDEMNING	PRECURRERS	PREDESIGNING	PREDICABLE
PRECOGNITION	PRECONDEMNS	PRECURSING	PREDESIGNS	PREDICABLENESS
PRECOGNITIONS	PRECONDITION	PRECURSIVE	PREDESTINABLE	PREDICABLES

PREDICAMENT	PREDNISONE	PREERECTING	PREFERENTIALISM	PREFORMATIVE
PREDICAMENTAL	PREDNISONES	PREESTABLISH	PREFERENTIALIST	PREFORMATIVES
PREDICAMENTS	PREDOCTORAL	PREESTABLISHED	PREFERENTIALITY	PREFORMATS
PREDICANTS	PREDOMINANCE	PREESTABLISHES	PREFERENTIALLY	PREFORMATTED
PREDICATED	PREDOMINANCES	PREESTABLISHING	PREFERMENT	PREFORMATTING
PREDICATES	PREDOMINANCIES	PREETHICAL	PREFERMENTS	PREFORMING
PREDICATING	PREDOMINANCY	PREEXCITED	PREFERRABLE	PREFORMULATE
PREDICATION	PREDOMINANT	PREEXCITES	PREFERRERS	PREFORMULATED
PREDICATIONS	PREDOMINANTLY	PREEXCITING	PREFERRING	PREFORMULATES
PREDICATIVE	PREDOMINATE	PREEXEMPTED	PREFIGURATE	PREFORMULATING
PREDICATIVELY	PREDOMINATED	PREEXEMPTING	PREFIGURATED	PREFRANKED
PREDICATOR	PREDOMINATELY	PREEXEMPTS	PREFIGURATES	PREFRANKING
PREDICATORS	PREDOMINATES	PREEXISTED	PREFIGURATING	PREFREEZES
PREDICATORY	PREDOMINATING	PREEXISTENCE	PREFIGURATION	PREFREEZING
PREDICTABILITY	PREDOMINATION	PREEXISTENCES	PREFIGURATIONS	PREFRESHMAN
PREDICTABLE	PREDOMINATIONS	PREEXISTENT	PREFIGURATIVE	PREFRESHMEN
PREDICTABLENESS	PREDOMINATOR	PREEXISTING	PREFIGURATIVELY	PREFRONTAL
PREDICTABLY	PREDOMINATORS	PREEXPERIMENT	PREFIGURED	PREFRONTALS
PREDICTERS	PREDOOMING	PREEXPOSED	PREFIGUREMENT	PREFULGENT
PREDICTING	PREDRILLED	PREEXPOSES	PREFIGUREMENTS	PREFUNDING
PREDICTION	PREDRILLING	PREEXPOSING	PREFIGURES	PREGANGLIONIC
PREDICTIONS	PREDYNASTIC	PREFABBING	PREFIGURING	PREGENITAL
PREDICTIVE	PREECLAMPSIA	PREFABRICATE	PREFINANCE	PREGLACIAL
PREDICTIVELY	PREECLAMPSIAS	PREFABRICATED	PREFINANCED	PREGNABILITIES
PREDICTORS	PREECLAMPTIC	PREFABRICATES	PREFINANCES	PREGNABILITY
PREDIGESTED	PREEDITING	PREFABRICATING	PREFINANCING	PREGNANCES
PREDIGESTING	PREELECTED	PREFABRICATION	PREFINANCINGS	PREGNANCIES
PREDIGESTION	PREELECTING	PREFABRICATIONS	PREFIXALLY	PREGNANTLY
PREDIGESTIONS	PREELECTION	PREFABRICATOR	PREFIXIONS	PREGNENOLONE
PREDIGESTS	PREELECTRIC	PREFABRICATORS	PREFIXTURE	PREGNENOLONES
PREDIKANTS	PREEMBARGO	PREFASCIST	PREFIXTURES	PREGROWTHS
PREDILECTED	PREEMERGENCE	PREFATORIAL	PREFLIGHTED	PREGUIDING
PREDILECTION	PREEMERGENT	PREFATORIALLY	PREFLIGHTING	PREGUSTATION
PREDILECTIONS	PREEMINENCE	PREFATORILY	PREFLIGHTS	PREGUSTATIONS
PREDINNERS	PREEMINENCES	PREFECTORIAL	PREFLORATION	PREHALLUCES
PREDISCHARGE	PREEMINENT	PREFECTSHIP	PREFLORATIONS	PREHANDLED
PREDISCOVERIES	PREEMINENTLY	PREFECTSHIPS	PREFOCUSED	PREHANDLES
PREDISCOVERY	PREEMPLOYMENT	PREFECTURAL	PREFOCUSES	PREHANDLING
PREDISPOSAL	PREEMPTING	PREFECTURE	PREFOCUSING	PREHARDENED
PREDISPOSALS	PREEMPTION	PREFECTURES	PREFOCUSSED	PREHARDENING
PREDISPOSE	PREEMPTIONS	PREFERABILITIES	PREFOCUSSES	PREHARDENS
PREDISPOSED	PREEMPTIVE	PREFERABILITY	PREFOCUSSING	PREHARVEST
PREDISPOSES	PREEMPTIVELY	PREFERABLE	PREFOLIATION	PREHARVESTS
PREDISPOSING	PREEMPTORS	PREFERABLENESS	PREFOLIATIONS	PREHEADACHE
PREDISPOSITION	PREENACTED	PREFERABLY	PREFORMATION	PREHEATERS
PREDISPOSITIONS	PREENACTING	PREFERENCE	PREFORMATIONISM	PREHEATING
PREDNISOLONE	PREENROLLMENT	PREFERENCES	PREFORMATIONIST	PREHEMINENCE
PREDNISOLONES	PREERECTED	PREFERENTIAL	PREFORMATIONS	PREHEMINENCES

PREHENDING	PREJUDGMENT	PRELIMITING	PREMEDICATE	PREMONITOR
PREHENSIBLE	PREJUDGMENTS	PRELINGUAL	PREMEDICATED	PREMONITORILY
PREHENSILE	PREJUDICANT	PRELINGUALLY	PREMEDICATES	PREMONITORS
PREHENSILITIES	PREJUDICATE	PRELITERACIES	PREMEDICATING	PREMONITORY
PREHENSILITY	PREJUDICATED	PRELITERACY	PREMEDICATION	PREMOTIONS
PREHENSION	PREJUDICATES	PRELITERARY	PREMEDICATIONS	PREMOULDED
PREHENSIONS	PREJUDICATING	PRELITERATE	PREMEDIEVAL	PREMOULDING
PREHENSIVE	PREJUDICATION	PRELITERATES	PREMEDITATE	PREMOVEMENT
PREHENSORIAL	PREJUDICATIONS	PRELOADING	PREMEDITATED	PREMOVEMENTS
PREHENSORS	PREJUDICATIVE	PRELOCATED	PREMEDITATEDLY	PREMUNITION
PREHENSORY	PREJUDICED	PRELOCATES	PREMEDITATES	PREMUNITIONS
PREHISTORIAN	PREJUDICES	PRELOCATING	PREMEDITATING	PREMYCOTIC
PREHISTORIANS	PREJUDICIAL	PRELOGICAL	PREMEDITATION	PRENATALLY
PREHISTORIC	PREJUDICIALLY	PRELUDIOUS	PREMEDITATIONS	PRENEGOTIATE
PREHISTORICAL	PREJUDICIALNESS	PRELUNCHEON	PREMEDITATIVE	PRENEGOTIATED
PREHISTORICALLY	PREJUDICING	PRELUNCHEONS	PREMEDITATOR	PRENEGOTIATES
PREHISTORIES	PREJUDIZES	PRELUSIONS	PREMEDITATORS	PRENEGOTIATING
PREHISTORY	PREKINDERGARTEN	PRELUSIVELY	PREMEIOTIC	PRENEGOTIATION
PREHOLIDAY	PRELAPSARIAN	PRELUSORILY	PREMENOPAUSAL	PRENEGOTIATIONS
PREHOMINID	PRELATESHIP	PREMALIGNANT	PREMENSTRUAL	PRENOMINAL
PREHOMINIDS	PRELATESHIPS	PREMANDIBULAR	PREMENSTRUALLY	PRENOMINALLY
PREIGNITION	PRELATESSES	PREMANDIBULARS	PREMIERING	PRENOMINATE
PREIGNITIONS	PRELATICAL	PREMANUFACTURE	PREMIERSHIP	PRENOMINATED
PREIMPLANTATION	PRELATICALLY	PREMANUFACTURED	PREMIERSHIPS	PRENOMINATES
PREIMPOSED	PRELATIONS	PREMANUFACTURES	PREMIGRATION	PRENOMINATING
PREIMPOSES	PRELATISED	PREMARITAL	PREMILLENARIAN	PRENOMINATION
PREIMPOSING	PRELATISES	PREMARITALLY	PREMILLENARIANS	PRENOMINATIONS
PREINAUGURAL	PRELATISING	PREMARKETED	PREMILLENNIAL	PRENOTIFICATION
PREINDUCTION	PRELATISMS	PREMARKETING	PREMILLENNIALLY	PRENOTIFIED
PREINDUSTRIAL	PRELATISTS	PREMARKETS	PREMILLENNIALS	PRENOTIFIES
PREINFORMED	PRELATIZED	PREMARRIAGE	PREMISSING	PRENOTIFYING
PREINFORMING	PRELATIZES	PREMATURELY	PREMODIFICATION	PRENOTIONS
PREINFORMS	PRELATIZING	PREMATURENESS	PREMODIFIED	PRENTICESHIP
PREINSERTED	PRELATURES	PREMATURENESSES	PREMODIFIES	PRENTICESHIPS
PREINSERTING	PRELAUNCHED	PREMATURES	PREMODIFYING	PRENTICING
PREINSERTS	PRELAUNCHES	PREMATURITIES	PREMOISTEN	PRENUMBERED
PREINTERVIEW	PRELAUNCHING	PREMATURITY	PREMOISTENED	PRENUMBERING
PREINTERVIEWED	PRELECTING	PREMAXILLA	PREMOISTENING	PRENUMBERS
PREINTERVIEWING	PRELECTION	PREMAXILLAE	PREMOISTENS	PRENUPTIAL
PREINTERVIEWS	PRELECTIONS	PREMAXILLARIES	PREMOLDING	PRENUPTIALS
PREINVASION	PRELECTORS	PREMAXILLARY	PREMONISHED	PREOBTAINED
PREINVITED	PRELEXICAL	PREMAXILLAS	PREMONISHES	PREOBTAINING
PREINVITES	PRELIBATION	PREMEASURE	PREMONISHING	PREOBTAINS
PREINVITING	PRELIBATIONS	PREMEASURED	PREMONISHMENT	PREOCCUPANCIES
PREJUDGEMENT	PRELIMINARIES	PREMEASURES	PREMONISHMENTS	PREOCCUPANCY
PREJUDGEMENTS	PRELIMINARILY	PREMEASURING	PREMONITION	PREOCCUPANT
PREJUDGERS	PRELIMINARY	PREMEDICAL	PREMONITIONS	PREOCCUPANTS
PREJUDGING	PRELIMITED	PREMEDICALLY	PREMONITIVE	PREOCCUPATE

PREOCCUPATED	PREPENSELY	PREPOSTEROUSLY	PREPUNCTUAL	PRESANCTIFIED
PREOCCUPATES	PREPENSING	PREPOSTORS	PREPURCHASE	PRESANCTIFIES
PREOCCUPATING	PREPENSIVE	PREPOTENCE	PREPURCHASED	PRESANCTIFY
PREOCCUPATION	PREPERFORMANCE	PREPOTENCES	PREPURCHASES	PRESANCTIFYING
PREOCCUPATIONS	PREPLACING	PREPOTENCIES	PREPURCHASING	PRESBYACOUSES
PREOCCUPIED	PREPLANNED	PREPOTENCY	PREQUALIFIED	PRESBYACOUSIS
PREOCCUPIES	PREPLANNING	PREPOTENTLY	PREQUALIFIES	PRESBYACUSES
PREOCCUPYING	PREPLANTING	PREPPINESS	PREQUALIFY	PRESBYACUSIS
PREOCULARS	PREPOLLENCE	PREPPINESSES	PREQUALIFYING	PRESBYCOUSES
PREOPENING	PREPOLLENCES	PREPRANDIAL	PREREADING	PRESBYCOUSIS
PREOPERATIONAL	PREPOLLENCIES	PREPREPARED	PRERECESSION	PRESBYCUSES
PREOPERATIVE	PREPOLLENCY	PREPRESIDENTIAL	PRERECORDED	PRESBYCUSIS
PREOPERATIVELY	PREPOLLENT	PREPRESSES	PRERECORDING	PRESBYOPES
PREOPTIONS	PREPOLLICES	PREPRICING	PRERECORDS	PRESBYOPIA
PREORDAINED	PREPONDERANCE	PREPRIMARIES	PREREGISTER	PRESBYOPIAS
PREORDAINING	PREPONDERANCES	PREPRIMARY	PREREGISTERED	PRESBYOPIC
PREORDAINMENT	PREPONDERANCIES	PREPRINTED	PREREGISTERING	PRESBYOPICS
PREORDAINMENTS	PREPONDERANCY	PREPRINTING	PREREGISTERS	PRESBYOPIES
PREORDAINS	PREPONDERANT	PREPROCESS	PREREGISTRATION	PRESBYTERAL
PREORDERED	PREPONDERANTLY	PREPROCESSED	PREREHEARSAL	PRESBYTERATE
PREORDERING	PREPONDERATE	PREPROCESSES	PREREHEARSALS	PRESBYTERATES
PREORDINANCE	PREPONDERATED	PREPROCESSING	PRERELEASE	PRESBYTERIAL
PREORDINANCES	PREPONDERATELY	PREPROCESSOR	PRERELEASED	PRESBYTERIALLY
PREORDINATION	PREPONDERATES	PREPROCESSORS	PRERELEASES	PRESBYTERIALS
PREORDINATIONS	PREPONDERATING	PREPRODUCTION	PRERELEASING	PRESBYTERIAN
PREOVULATORY	PREPONDERATION	PREPRODUCTIONS	PREREQUIRE	PRESBYTERIANISE
PREPACKAGE	PREPONDERATIONS	PREPROFESSIONAL	PREREQUIRED	PRESBYTERIANISM
PREPACKAGED	PREPORTION	PREPROGRAM	PREREQUIRES	PRESBYTERIANIZE
PREPACKAGES	PREPORTIONED	PREPROGRAMED	PREREQUIRING	PRESBYTERIANS
PREPACKAGING	PREPORTIONING	PREPROGRAMING	PREREQUISITE	PRESBYTERIES
PREPACKING	PREPORTIONS	PREPROGRAMMED	PREREQUISITES	PRESBYTERS
PREPARATION	PREPOSITION	PREPROGRAMMING	PRERETIREMENT	PRESBYTERSHIP
PREPARATIONS	PREPOSITIONAL	PREPROGRAMMINGS	PREREVIEWED	PRESBYTERSHIPS
PREPARATIVE	PREPOSITIONALLY	PREPROGRAMS	PREREVIEWING	PRESBYTERY
PREPARATIVELY	PREPOSITIONS	PREPSYCHEDELIC	PREREVIEWS	PRESBYTISM
PREPARATIVES	PREPOSITIVE	PREPUBERAL	PREREVISIONIST	PRESBYTISMS
PREPARATOR	PREPOSITIVELY	PREPUBERTAL	PREREVOLUTION	PRESCHEDULE
PREPARATORILY	PREPOSITIVES	PREPUBERTIES	PRERINSING	PRESCHEDULED
PREPARATORS	PREPOSITOR	PREPUBERTY	PREROGATIVE	PRESCHEDULES
PREPARATORY	PREPOSITORS	PREPUBESCENCE	PREROGATIVED	PRESCHEDULING
PREPAREDLY	PREPOSSESS	PREPUBESCENCES	PREROGATIVELY	PRESCHOOLER
PREPAREDNESS	PREPOSSESSED	PREPUBESCENT	PREROGATIVES	PRESCHOOLERS
PREPAREDNESSES	PREPOSSESSES	PREPUBESCENTS	PREROMANTIC	PRESCHOOLS
PREPASTING	PREPOSSESSING	PREPUBLICATION	PREROMANTICS	PRESCIENCE
PREPATELLAR	PREPOSSESSINGLY	PREPUBLICATIONS	PRESAGEFUL	PRESCIENCES
PREPAYABLE	PREPOSSESSION	PREPUNCHED	PRESAGEFULLY	PRESCIENTIFIC
PREPAYMENT	PREPOSSESSIONS	PREPUNCHES	PRESAGEMENT	PRESCIENTLY
PREPAYMENTS	PREPOSTEROUS	PREPUNCHING	PRESAGEMENTS	PRESCINDED

PRESCINDENT
PRESCINDING
PRESCISSION
PRESCISSIONS
PRESCORING
PRESCREENED
PRESCREENING
PRESCREENS
PRESCRIBED
PRESCRIBER
PRESCRIBERS
PRESCRIBES
PRESCRIBING
PRESCRIBINGS
PRESCRIPTIBLE
PRESCRIPTION
PRESCRIPTIONS
PRESCRIPTIVE
PRESCRIPTIVELY
PRESCRIPTIVISM
PRESCRIPTIVISMS
PRESCRIPTIVIST
PRESCRIPTIVISTS
PRESCRIPTS
PRESEASONS
PRESELECTED
PRESELECTING
PRESELECTION
PRESELECTIONS
PRESELECTOR
PRESELECTORS
PRESELECTS
PRESELLING
PRESENSION
PRESENSIONS
PRESENTABILITY
PRESENTABLE
PRESENTABLENESS
PRESENTABLY
PRESENTATION
PRESENTATIONAL
PRESENTATIONISM
PRESENTATIONIST
PRESENTATIONS
PRESENTATIVE
PRESENTEEISM
PRESENTEEISMS
PRESENTEES

PRESENTENCE
PRESENTENCED
PRESENTENCES
PRESENTENCING
PRESENTERS
PRESENTIAL
PRESENTIALITIES
PRESENTIALITY
PRESENTIALLY
PRESENTIENT
PRESENTIMENT
PRESENTIMENTAL
PRESENTIMENTS
PRESENTING
PRESENTISM
PRESENTISMS
PRESENTIST
PRESENTISTS
PRESENTIVE
PRESENTIVENESS
PRESENTIVES
PRESENTMENT
PRESENTMENTS
PRESENTNESS
PRESENTNESSES
PRESERVABILITY
PRESERVABLE
PRESERVABLY
PRESERVATION
PRESERVATIONIST
PRESERVATIONS
PRESERVATIVE
PRESERVATIVES
PRESERVATORIES
PRESERVATORY
PRESERVERS
PRESERVICE
PRESERVING
PRESETTING
PRESETTLED
PRESETTLEMENT
PRESETTLES
PRESETTLING
PRESHAPING
PRESHIPPED
PRESHIPPING
PRESHOWING
PRESHRINKING

PRESHRINKS
PRESHRUNKEN
PRESIDENCIES
PRESIDENCY
PRESIDENTESS
PRESIDENTESSES
PRESIDENTIAL
PRESIDENTIALLY
PRESIDENTS
PRESIDENTSHIP
PRESIDENTSHIPS
PRESIDIARY
PRESIDIUMS
PRESIFTING
PRESIGNALED
PRESIGNALING
PRESIGNALLED
PRESIGNALLING
PRESIGNALS
PRESIGNIFIED
PRESIGNIFIES
PRESIGNIFY
PRESIGNIFYING
PRESLAUGHTER
PRESLICING
PRESOAKING
PRESOLVING
PRESORTING
PRESPECIFIED
PRESPECIFIES
PRESPECIFY
PRESPECIFYING
PRESSBOARD
PRESSBOARDS
PRESSGANGS
PRESSINGLY
PRESSINGNESS
PRESSINGNESSES
PRESSMARKS
PRESSROOMS
PRESSURELESS
PRESSURING
PRESSURISATION
PRESSURISATIONS
PRESSURISE
PRESSURISED
PRESSURISER
PRESSURISERS

PRESSURISES
PRESSURISING
PRESSURIZATION
PRESSURIZATIONS
PRESSURIZE
PRESSURIZED
PRESSURIZER
PRESSURIZERS
PRESSURIZES
PRESSURIZING
PRESSWOMAN
PRESSWOMEN
PRESSWORKS
PRESTAMPED
PRESTAMPING
PRESTATION
PRESTATIONS
PRESTERILISE
PRESTERILISED
PRESTERILISES
PRESTERILISING
PRESTERILIZE
PRESTERILIZED
PRESTERILIZES
PRESTERILIZING
PRESTERNUM
PRESTERNUMS
PRESTIDIGITATOR
PRESTIGEFUL
PRESTIGIATOR
PRESTIGIATORS
PRESTIGIOUS
PRESTIGIOUSLY
PRESTIGIOUSNESS
PRESTISSIMO
PRESTISSIMOS
PRESTORAGE
PRESTORING
PRESTRESSED
PRESTRESSES
PRESTRESSING
PRESTRICTION
PRESTRICTIONS
PRESTRUCTURE
PRESTRUCTURED
PRESTRUCTURES
PRESTRUCTURING
PRESUMABLE

PRESUMABLY
PRESUMEDLY
PRESUMINGLY
PRESUMMITS
PRESUMPTION
PRESUMPTIONS
PRESUMPTIVE
PRESUMPTIVELY
PRESUMPTIVENESS
PRESUMPTUOUS
PRESUMPTUOUSLY
PRESUPPOSE
PRESUPPOSED
PRESUPPOSES
PRESUPPOSING
PRESUPPOSITION
PRESUPPOSITIONS
PRESURGERY
PRESURMISE
PRESURMISES
PRESURVEYED
PRESURVEYING
PRESURVEYS
PRESWEETEN
PRESWEETENED
PRESWEETENING
PRESWEETENS
PRESYMPTOMATIC
PRESYNAPTIC
PRESYNAPTICALLY
PRETASTING
PRETELEVISION
PRETELLING
PRETENCELESS
PRETENDANT
PRETENDANTS
PRETENDEDLY
PRETENDENT
PRETENDENTS
PRETENDERS
PRETENDERSHIP
PRETENDERSHIPS
PRETENDING
PRETENDINGLY
PRETENSELESS
PRETENSION
PRETENSIONED
PRETENSIONING

PRETENSIONLESS	PRETTIFIER	PREVENTIBLY	PRIESTCRAFTS	PRIMITIVISM
PRETENSIONS	PRETTIFIERS	PREVENTING	PRIESTESSES	PRIMITIVISMS
PRETENSIVE	PRETTIFIES	PREVENTION	PRIESTHOOD	PRIMITIVIST
PRETENTIOUS	PRETTIFYING	PREVENTIONS	PRIESTHOODS	PRIMITIVISTIC
PRETENTIOUSLY	PRETTINESS	PREVENTIVE	PRIESTLIER	PRIMITIVISTS
PRETENTIOUSNESS	PRETTINESSES	PREVENTIVELY	PRIESTLIEST	PRIMITIVITIES
PRETERHUMAN	PRETTYISMS	PREVENTIVENESS	PRIESTLIKE	PRIMITIVITY
PRETERISTS	PRETZELLED	PREVENTIVES	PRIESTLINESS	PRIMNESSES
PRETERITENESS	PRETZELLING	PREVIEWERS	PRIESTLINESSES	PRIMOGENIAL
PRETERITENESSES	PREUNIFICATION	PREVIEWING	PRIESTLING	PRIMOGENIT
PRETERITES	PREUNITING	PREVIOUSLY	PRIESTLINGS	PRIMOGENITAL
PRETERITION	PREUNIVERSITY	PREVIOUSNESS	PRIESTSHIP	PRIMOGENITARY
PRETERITIONS	PREVAILERS	PREVIOUSNESSES	PRIESTSHIPS	PRIMOGENITIVE
PRETERITIVE	PREVAILING	PREVISIONAL	PRIGGERIES	PRIMOGENITIVES
PRETERMINAL	PREVAILINGLY	PREVISIONARY	PRIGGISHLY	PRIMOGENITOR
PRETERMINATION	PREVAILMENT	PREVISIONED	PRIGGISHNESS	PRIMOGENITORS
PRETERMINATIONS	PREVAILMENTS	PREVISIONING	PRIGGISHNESSES	PRIMOGENITRICES
PRETERMISSION	PREVALENCE	PREVISIONS	PRIMAEVALLY	PRIMOGENITRIX
PRETERMISSIONS	PREVALENCES	PREVISITED	PRIMALITIES	PRIMOGENITRIXES
PRETERMITS	PREVALENCIES	PREVISITING	PRIMAQUINE	PRIMOGENITS
PRETERMITTED	PREVALENCY	PREVOCALIC	PRIMAQUINES	PRIMOGENITURE
PRETERMITTER	PREVALENTLY	PREVOCALICALLY	PRIMARINESS	PRIMOGENITURES
PRETERMITTERS	PREVALENTNESS	PREVOCATIONAL	PRIMARINESSES	PRIMORDIAL
PRETERMITTING	PREVALENTNESSES	PREWARMING	PRIMATESHIP	PRIMORDIALISM
PRETERNATURAL	PREVALENTS	PREWARNING	PRIMATESHIPS	PRIMORDIALISMS
PRETERNATURALLY	PREVALUING	PREWASHING	PRIMATIALS	PRIMORDIALITIES
PRETERPERFECT	PREVARICATE	PREWEANING	PRIMATICAL	PRIMORDIALITY
PRETERPERFECTS	PREVARICATED	PREWEIGHED	PRIMATOLOGICAL	PRIMORDIALLY
PRETESTING	PREVARICATES	PREWEIGHING	PRIMATOLOGIES	PRIMORDIALS
PRETEXTING	PREVARICATING	PREWORKING	PRIMATOLOGIST	PRIMORDIUM
PRETEXTINGS	PREVARICATION	PREWRAPPED	PRIMATOLOGISTS	PRIMROSIER
PRETHEATER	PREVARICATIONS	PREWRAPPING	PRIMATOLOGY	PRIMROSIEST
PRETHEATRE	PREVARICATOR	PREWRITING	PRIMAVERAS	PRIMROSING
PRETORIANS	PREVARICATORS	PREWRITINGS	PRIMENESSES	PRIMULACEOUS
PRETORSHIP	PREVENANCIES	PREWRITTEN	PRIMEVALLY	PRIMULINES
PRETORSHIPS	PREVENANCY	PRICELESSLY	PRIMIGENIAL	PRINCEDOMS
PRETOURNAMENT	PREVENIENCE	PRICELESSNESS	PRIMIGRAVIDA	PRINCEHOOD
PRETRAINED	PREVENIENCES	PRICELESSNESSES	PRIMIGRAVIDAE	PRINCEHOODS
PRETRAINING	PREVENIENT	PRICINESSES	PRIMIGRAVIDAS	PRINCEKINS
PRETREATED	PREVENIENTLY	PRICKLIEST	PRIMIPARAE	PRINCELETS
PRETREATING	PREVENTABILITY	PRICKLINESS	PRIMIPARAS	PRINCELIER
PRETREATMENT	PREVENTABLE	PRICKLINESSES	PRIMIPARITIES	PRINCELIEST
PRETREATMENTS	PREVENTABLY	PRICKLINGS	PRIMIPARITY	PRINCELIKE
PRETRIMMED	PREVENTATIVE	PRICKWOODS	PRIMIPAROUS	PRINCELINESS
PRETRIMMING	PREVENTATIVES	PRIDEFULLY	PRIMITIVELY	PRINCELINESSES
PRETTIFICATION	PREVENTERS	PRIDEFULNESS	PRIMITIVENESS	PRINCELING
PRETTIFICATIONS	PREVENTIBILITY	PRIDEFULNESSES	PRIMITIVENESSES	PRINCELINGS
PRETTIFIED	PREVENTIBLE	PRIESTCRAFT	PRIMITIVES	PRINCESHIP

PRINCESHIPS

PRINCESHIPS	PRIORSHIPS	PRIZEFIGHTERS	PROBOULEUTIC	PROCESSIONARY
PRINCESSES	PRISMATICAL	PRIZEFIGHTING	PROBUSINESS	PROCESSIONED
PRINCESSLIER	PRISMATICALLY	PRIZEFIGHTINGS	PROCACIOUS	PROCESSIONER
PRINCESSLIEST	PRISMATOID	PRIZEFIGHTS	PROCACITIES	PROCESSIONERS
PRINCESSLY	PRISMATOIDAL	PRIZEWINNER	PROCAMBIAL	PROCESSIONING
PRINCIFIED	PRISMATOIDS	PRIZEWINNERS	PROCAMBIUM	PROCESSIONINGS
PRINCIPALITIES	PRISMOIDAL	PRIZEWINNING	PROCAMBIUMS	PROCESSIONS
PRINCIPALITY	PRISONMENT	PRIZEWOMAN	PROCAPITALIST	PROCESSORS
PRINCIPALLY	PRISONMENTS	PRIZEWOMEN	PROCARBAZINE	PROCESSUAL
PRINCIPALNESS	PRISSINESS	PROABORTION	PROCARBAZINES	PROCHRONISM
PRINCIPALNESSES	PRISSINESSES	PROACTIONS	PROCARYONS	PROCHRONISMS
PRINCIPALS	PRISTINELY	PROAIRESES	PROCARYOTE	PROCIDENCE
PRINCIPALSHIP	PRIVATDOCENT	PROAIRESIS	PROCARYOTES	PROCIDENCES
PRINCIPALSHIPS	PRIVATDOCENTS	PROBABILIORISM	PROCARYOTIC	PROCLAIMANT
PRINCIPATE	PRIVATDOZENT	PROBABILIORISMS	PROCATHEDRAL	PROCLAIMANTS
PRINCIPATES	PRIVATDOZENTS	PROBABILIORIST	PROCATHEDRALS	PROCLAIMED
PRINCIPIAL	PRIVATEERED	PROBABILIORISTS	PROCEDURAL	PROCLAIMER
PRINCIPIUM	PRIVATEERING	PROBABILISM	PROCEDURALLY	PROCLAIMERS
PRINCIPLED	PRIVATEERINGS	PROBABILISMS	PROCEDURALS	PROCLAIMING
PRINCIPLES	PRIVATEERS	PROBABILIST	PROCEDURES	PROCLAMATION
PRINCIPLING	PRIVATEERSMAN	PROBABILISTIC	PROCEEDERS	PROCLAMATIONS
PRINTABILITIES	PRIVATEERSMEN	PROBABILISTS	PROCEEDING	PROCLAMATORY
PRINTABILITY	PRIVATENESS	PROBABILITIES	PROCEEDINGS	PROCLITICS
PRINTABLENESS	PRIVATENESSES	PROBABILITY	PROCELEUSMATIC	PROCLIVITIES
PRINTABLENESSES	PRIVATIONS	PROBATIONAL	PROCELEUSMATICS	PROCLIVITY
PRINTERIES	PRIVATISATION	PROBATIONALLY	PROCELLARIAN	PROCOELOUS
PRINTHEADS	PRIVATISATIONS	PROBATIONARIES	PROCELLARIANS	PROCONSULAR
PRINTMAKER	PRIVATISED	PROBATIONARY	PROCEPHALIC	PROCONSULATE
PRINTMAKERS	PRIVATISER	PROBATIONER	PROCERCOID	PROCONSULATES
PRINTMAKING	PRIVATISERS	PROBATIONERS	PROCERCOIDS	PROCONSULS
PRINTMAKINGS	PRIVATISES	PROBATIONERSHIP	PROCEREBRA	PROCONSULSHIP
PRINTWHEEL	PRIVATISING	PROBATIONS	PROCEREBRAL	PROCONSULSHIPS
PRINTWHEELS	PRIVATISMS	PROBATIVELY	PROCEREBRUM	PROCRASTINATE
PRINTWORKS	PRIVATISTS	PROBENECID	PROCEREBRUMS	PROCRASTINATED
PRIORESSES	PRIVATIVELY	PROBENECIDS	PROCERITIES	PROCRASTINATES
PRIORITIES	PRIVATIVES	PROBIOTICS	PROCESSABILITY	PROCRASTINATING
PRIORITISATION	PRIVATIZATION	PROBLEMATIC	PROCESSABLE	PROCRASTINATION
PRIORITISATIONS	PRIVATIZATIONS	PROBLEMATICAL	PROCESSERS	PROCRASTINATIVE
PRIORITISE	PRIVATIZED	PROBLEMATICALLY	PROCESSIBILITY	PROCRASTINATOR
PRIORITISED	PRIVATIZER	PROBLEMATICS	PROCESSIBLE	PROCRASTINATORS
PRIORITISES	PRIVATIZERS	PROBLEMIST	PROCESSING	PROCRASTINATORY
PRIORITISING	PRIVATIZES	PROBLEMISTS	PROCESSINGS	PROCREANTS
PRIORITIZATION	PRIVATIZING	PROBOSCIDEAN	PROCESSION	PROCREATED
PRIORITIZATIONS	PRIVILEGED	PROBOSCIDEANS	PROCESSIONAL	PROCREATES
PRIORITIZE	PRIVILEGES	PROBOSCIDES	PROCESSIONALIST	PROCREATING
PRIORITIZED	PRIVILEGING	PROBOSCIDIAN	PROCESSIONALLY	PROCREATION
PRIORITIZES	PRIZEFIGHT	PROBOSCIDIANS	PROCESSIONALS	PROCREATIONAL
PRIORITIZING	PRIZEFIGHTER	PROBOSCISES	PROCESSIONARIES	PROCREATIONS

PROCREATIVE	PROCURACIES	PRODUCTIVELY	PROFICIENTS	PROGENITURE
PROCREATIVENESS	PROCURANCE	PRODUCTIVENESS	PROFILINGS	PROGENITURES
PROCREATOR	PROCURANCES	PRODUCTIVITIES	PROFILISTS	PROGESTATIONAL
PROCREATORS	PROCURATION	PRODUCTIVITY	PROFITABILITIES	PROGESTERONE
PROCRUSTEAN	PROCURATIONS	PROEMBRYOS	PROFITABILITY	PROGESTERONES
PROCRYPSES	PROCURATOR	PROENZYMES	PROFITABLE	PROGESTINS
PROCRYPSIS	PROCURATORIAL	PROESTRUSES	PROFITABLENESS	PROGESTOGEN
PROCRYPTIC	PROCURATORIES	PROFANATION	PROFITABLY	PROGESTOGENIC
PROCRYPTICALLY	PROCURATORS	PROFANATIONS	PROFITEERED	PROGESTOGENS
PROCTALGIA	PROCURATORSHIP	PROFANATORY	PROFITEERING	PROGGINSES
PROCTALGIAS	PROCURATORSHIPS	PROFANENESS	PROFITEERINGS	PROGLOTTIC
PROCTITIDES	PROCURATORY	PROFANENESSES	PROFITEERS	PROGLOTTID
PROCTITISES	PROCUREMENT	PROFANITIES	PROFITEROLE	PROGLOTTIDEAN
PROCTODAEA	PROCUREMENTS	PROFASCIST	PROFITEROLES	PROGLOTTIDES
PROCTODAEAL	PROCURESSES	PROFECTITIOUS	PROFITINGS	PROGLOTTIDS
PROCTODAEUM	PROCUREURS	PROFEMINIST	PROFITLESS	PROGLOTTIS
PROCTODAEUMS	PROCURINGS	PROFESSEDLY	PROFITLESSLY	PROGNATHIC
PROCTODEAL	PROCYONIDS	PROFESSING	PROFITWISE	PROGNATHISM
PROCTODEUM	PRODIGALISE	PROFESSION	PROFLIGACIES	PROGNATHISMS
PROCTODEUMS	PRODIGALISED	PROFESSIONAL	PROFLIGACY	PROGNATHOUS
PROCTOLOGIC	PRODIGALISES	PROFESSIONALISE	PROFLIGATE	PROGNOSING
PROCTOLOGICAL	PRODIGALISING	PROFESSIONALISM	PROFLIGATELY	PROGNOSTIC
PROCTOLOGIES	PRODIGALITIES	PROFESSIONALIST	PROFLIGATES	PROGNOSTICATE
PROCTOLOGIST	PRODIGALITY	PROFESSIONALIZE	PROFLUENCE	PROGNOSTICATED
PROCTOLOGISTS	PRODIGALIZE	PROFESSIONALLY	PROFLUENCES	PROGNOSTICATES
PROCTOLOGY	PRODIGALIZED	PROFESSIONALS	PROFOUNDER	PROGNOSTICATING
PROCTORAGE	PRODIGALIZES	PROFESSIONS	PROFOUNDEST	PROGNOSTICATION
PROCTORAGES	PRODIGALIZING	PROFESSORATE	PROFOUNDLY	PROGNOSTICATIVE
PROCTORIAL	PRODIGALLY	PROFESSORATES	PROFOUNDNESS	PROGNOSTICATOR
PROCTORIALLY	PRODIGIOSITIES	PROFESSORESS	PROFOUNDNESSES	PROGNOSTICATORS
PROCTORING	PRODIGIOSITY	PROFESSORESSES	PROFULGENT	PROGNOSTICS
PROCTORISE	PRODIGIOUS	PROFESSORIAL	PROFUNDITIES	PROGRADATION
PROCTORISED	PRODIGIOUSLY	PROFESSORIALLY	PROFUNDITY	PROGRADATIONS
PROCTORISES	PRODIGIOUSNESS	PROFESSORIAT	PROFUSENESS	PROGRADING
PROCTORISING	PRODITORIOUS	PROFESSORIATE	PROFUSENESSES	PROGRAMABLE
PROCTORIZE	PRODNOSING	PROFESSORIATES	PROFUSIONS	PROGRAMERS
PROCTORIZED	PRODROMATA	PROFESSORIATS	PROGENITIVE	PROGRAMING
PROCTORIZES	PRODUCEMENT	PROFESSORS	PROGENITIVENESS	PROGRAMINGS
PROCTORIZING	PRODUCEMENTS	PROFESSORSHIP	PROGENITOR	PROGRAMMABILITY
PROCTORSHIP	PRODUCIBILITIES	PROFESSORSHIPS	PROGENITORIAL	PROGRAMMABLE
PROCTORSHIPS	PRODUCIBILITY	PROFFERERS	PROGENITORS	PROGRAMMABLES
PROCTOSCOPE	PRODUCIBLE	PROFFERING	PROGENITORSHIP	PROGRAMMATIC
PROCTOSCOPES	PRODUCTIBILITY	PROFICIENCE	PROGENITORSHIPS	PROGRAMMED
PROCTOSCOPIC	PRODUCTILE	PROFICIENCES	PROGENITRESS	PROGRAMMER
PROCTOSCOPIES	PRODUCTION	PROFICIENCIES	PROGENITRESSES	PROGRAMMERS
PROCTOSCOPY	PRODUCTIONAL	PROFICIENCY	PROGENITRICES	PROGRAMMES
PROCUMBENT	PRODUCTIONS	PROFICIENT	PROGENITRIX	PROGRAMMING
PROCURABLE	PRODUCTIVE	PROFICIENTLY	PROGENITRIXES	PROGRAMMINGS

PROGRESSED	PROINSULINS	PROLETARIANISMS	PROLOGISTS	PROMISCUOUS
PROGRESSES	PROJECTABLE	PROLETARIANIZE	PROLOGIZED	PROMISCUOUSLY
PROGRESSING	PROJECTILE	PROLETARIANIZED	PROLOGIZES	PROMISCUOUSNESS
PROGRESSION	PROJECTILES	PROLETARIANIZES	PROLOGIZING	PROMISEFUL
PROGRESSIONAL	PROJECTING	PROLETARIANNESS	PROLOGUING	PROMISELESS
PROGRESSIONALLY	PROJECTINGS	PROLETARIANS	PROLOGUISE	PROMISINGLY
PROGRESSIONARY	PROJECTION	PROLETARIAT	PROLOGUISED	PROMISSIVE
PROGRESSIONISM	PROJECTIONAL	PROLETARIATE	PROLOGUISES	PROMISSORILY
PROGRESSIONISMS	PROJECTIONIST	PROLETARIATES	PROLOGUISING	PROMISSORS
PROGRESSIONIST	PROJECTIONISTS	PROLETARIATS	PROLOGUIZE	PROMISSORY
PROGRESSIONISTS	PROJECTIONS	PROLETARIES	PROLOGUIZED	PROMONARCHIST
PROGRESSIONS	PROJECTISATION	PROLICIDAL	PROLOGUIZES	PROMONTORIES
PROGRESSISM	PROJECTISATIONS	PROLICIDES	PROLOGUIZING	PROMONTORY
PROGRESSISMS	PROJECTIVE	PROLIFERATE	PROLONGABLE	PROMOTABILITIES
PROGRESSIST	PROJECTIVELY	PROLIFERATED	PROLONGATE	PROMOTABILITY
PROGRESSISTS	PROJECTIVITIES	PROLIFERATES	PROLONGATED	PROMOTABLE
PROGRESSIVE	PROJECTIVITY	PROLIFERATING	PROLONGATES	PROMOTIONAL
PROGRESSIVELY	PROJECTIZATION	PROLIFERATION	PROLONGATING	PROMOTIONS
PROGRESSIVENESS	PROJECTIZATIONS	PROLIFERATIONS	PROLONGATION	PROMOTIVENESS
PROGRESSIVES	PROJECTMENT	PROLIFERATIVE	PROLONGATIONS	PROMOTIVENESSES
PROGRESSIVISM	PROJECTMENTS	PROLIFEROUS	PROLONGERS	PROMPTBOOK
PROGRESSIVISMS	PROJECTORS	PROLIFEROUSLY	PROLONGING	PROMPTBOOKS
PROGRESSIVIST	PROJECTURE	PROLIFICACIES	PROLONGMENT	PROMPTINGS
PROGRESSIVISTIC	PROJECTURES	PROLIFICACY	PROLONGMENTS	PROMPTITUDE
PROGRESSIVISTS	PROKARYONS	PROLIFICAL	PROLUSIONS	PROMPTITUDES
PROGRESSIVITIES	PROKARYOTE	PROLIFICALLY	PROMACHOSES	PROMPTNESS
PROGRESSIVITY	PROKARYOTES	PROLIFICATION	PROMENADED	PROMPTNESSES
PROGYMNASIA	PROKARYOTIC	PROLIFICATIONS	PROMENADER	PROMPTUARIES
PROGYMNASIUM	PROKARYOTS	PROLIFICITIES	PROMENADERS	PROMPTUARY
PROGYMNASIUMS	PROLACTINS	PROLIFICITY	PROMENADES	PROMPTURES
PROHIBITED	PROLAMINES	PROLIFICNESS	PROMENADING	PROMULGATE
PROHIBITER	PROLAPSING	PROLIFICNESSES	PROMETHAZINE	PROMULGATED
PROHIBITERS	PROLAPSUSES	PROLIXIOUS	PROMETHAZINES	PROMULGATES
PROHIBITING	PROLATENESS	PROLIXITIES	PROMETHEUM	PROMULGATING
PROHIBITION	PROLATENESSES	PROLIXNESS	PROMETHEUMS	PROMULGATION
PROHIBITIONARY	PROLATIONS	PROLIXNESSES	PROMETHIUM	PROMULGATIONS
PROHIBITIONISM	PROLEGOMENA	PROLOCUTION	PROMETHIUMS	PROMULGATOR
PROHIBITIONISMS	PROLEGOMENAL	PROLOCUTIONS	PROMILITARY	PROMULGATORS
PROHIBITIONIST	PROLEGOMENARY	PROLOCUTOR	PROMINENCE	PROMULGING
PROHIBITIONISTS	PROLEGOMENON	PROLOCUTORS	PROMINENCES	PROMUSCIDATE
PROHIBITIONS	PROLEGOMENOUS	PROLOCUTORSHIP	PROMINENCIES	PROMUSCIDES
PROHIBITIVE	PROLEPTICAL	PROLOCUTORSHIPS	PROMINENCY	PROMYCELIA
PROHIBITIVELY	PROLEPTICALLY	PROLOCUTRICES	PROMINENTLY	PROMYCELIAL
PROHIBITIVENESS	PROLETARIAN	PROLOCUTRIX	PROMINENTNESS	PROMYCELIUM
PROHIBITOR	PROLETARIANISE	PROLOCUTRIXES	PROMINENTNESSES	PRONATIONS
PROHIBITORS	PROLETARIANISED	PROLOGISED	PROMINENTS	PRONATORES
PROHIBITORY	PROLETARIANISES	PROLOGISES	PROMISCUITIES	PRONENESSES
PROINSULIN	PROLETARIANISM	PROLOGISING	PROMISCUITY	PRONEPHRIC

PRONEPHROI	PROPAGABILITY	PROPENDING	PROPITIATED	PROPOSITUS
PRONEPHROS	PROPAGABLE	PROPENSELY	PROPITIATES	PROPOUNDED
PRONEPHROSES	PROPAGABLENESS	PROPENSENESS	PROPITIATING	PROPOUNDER
PRONGBUCKS	PROPAGANDA	PROPENSENESSES	PROPITIATION	PROPOUNDERS
PRONGHORNS	PROPAGANDAS	PROPENSION	PROPITIATIONS	PROPOUNDING
PRONOMINAL	PROPAGANDISE	PROPENSIONS	PROPITIATIOUS	PROPOXYPHENE
PRONOMINALISE	PROPAGANDISED	PROPENSITIES	PROPITIATIVE	PROPOXYPHENES
PRONOMINALISED	PROPAGANDISER	PROPENSITY	PROPITIATOR	PROPRAETOR
PRONOMINALISES	PROPAGANDISERS	PROPENSIVE	PROPITIATORIES	PROPRAETORIAL
PRONOMINALISING	PROPAGANDISES	PROPERDINS	PROPITIATORILY	PROPRAETORIAN
PRONOMINALIZE	PROPAGANDISING	PROPERISPOMENA	PROPITIATORS	PROPRAETORS
PRONOMINALIZED	PROPAGANDISM	PROPERISPOMENON	PROPITIATORY	PROPRANOLOL
PRONOMINALIZES	PROPAGANDISMS	PROPERNESS	PROPITIOUS	PROPRANOLOLS
PRONOMINALIZING	PROPAGANDIST	PROPERNESSES	PROPITIOUSLY	PROPRETORS
PRONOMINALLY	PROPAGANDISTIC	PROPERTIED	PROPITIOUSNESS	PROPRIETARIES
PRONOUNCEABLE	PROPAGANDISTS	PROPERTIES	PROPLASTID	PROPRIETARILY
PRONOUNCED	PROPAGANDIZE	PROPERTYING	PROPLASTIDS	PROPRIETARY
PRONOUNCEDLY	PROPAGANDIZED	PROPERTYLESS	PROPODEONS	PROPRIETIES
PRONOUNCEMENT	PROPAGANDIZER	PROPHECIES	PROPODEUMS	PROPRIETOR
PRONOUNCEMENTS	PROPAGANDIZERS	PROPHESIABLE	PROPOLISES	PROPRIETORIAL
PRONOUNCER	PROPAGANDIZES	PROPHESIED	PROPONENTS	PROPRIETORIALLY
PRONOUNCERS	PROPAGANDIZING	PROPHESIER	PROPORTION	PROPRIETORS
PRONOUNCES	PROPAGATED	PROPHESIERS	PROPORTIONABLE	PROPRIETORSHIP
PRONOUNCING	PROPAGATES	PROPHESIES	PROPORTIONABLY	PROPRIETORSHIPS
PRONOUNCINGS	PROPAGATING	PROPHESYING	PROPORTIONAL	PROPRIETRESS
PRONUCLEAR	PROPAGATION	PROPHESYINGS	PROPORTIONALITY	PROPRIETRESSES
PRONUCLEARIST	PROPAGATIONAL	PROPHETESS	PROPORTIONALLY	PROPRIETRICES
PRONUCLEARISTS	PROPAGATIONS	PROPHETESSES	PROPORTIONALS	PROPRIETRIX
PRONUCLEUS	PROPAGATIVE	PROPHETHOOD	PROPORTIONATE	PROPRIETRIXES
PRONUCLEUSES	PROPAGATOR	PROPHETHOODS	PROPORTIONATED	PROPRIOCEPTION
PRONUNCIAMENTO	PROPAGATORS	PROPHETICAL	PROPORTIONATELY	PROPRIOCEPTIONS
PRONUNCIAMENTOS	PROPAGULES	PROPHETICALLY	PROPORTIONATES	PROPRIOCEPTIVE
PRONUNCIATION	PROPAGULUM	PROPHETICISM	PROPORTIONATING	PROPRIOCEPTOR
PRONUNCIATIONAL	PROPANEDIOIC	PROPHETICISMS	PROPORTIONED	PROPRIOCEPTORS
PRONUNCIATIONS	PROPANONES	PROPHETISM	PROPORTIONING	PROPROCTOR
PRONUNCIOS	PROPAROXYTONE	PROPHETISMS	PROPORTIONINGS	PROPROCTORS
PROOEMIONS	PROPAROXYTONES	PROPHETSHIP	PROPORTIONLESS	PROPUGNATION
PROOEMIUMS	PROPELLANT	PROPHETSHIPS	PROPORTIONMENT	PROPUGNATIONS
PROOFREADER	PROPELLANTS	PROPHYLACTIC	PROPORTIONMENTS	PROPULSION
PROOFREADERS	PROPELLENT	PROPHYLACTICS	PROPORTIONS	PROPULSIONS
PROOFREADING	PROPELLENTS	PROPHYLAXES	PROPOSABLE	PROPULSIVE
PROOFREADINGS	PROPELLERS	PROPHYLAXIS	PROPOSITAE	PROPULSORS
PROOFREADS	PROPELLING	PROPINQUITIES	PROPOSITION	PROPULSORY
PROOFROOMS	PROPELLINGS	PROPINQUITY	PROPOSITIONAL	PROPYLAEUM
PROPAEDEUTIC	PROPELLORS	PROPIONATE	PROPOSITIONALLY	PROPYLAMINE
PROPAEDEUTICAL	PROPELMENT	PROPIONATES	PROPOSITIONED	PROPYLAMINES
PROPAEDEUTICS	PROPELMENTS	PROPITIABLE	PROPOSITIONING	PROPYLENES
PROPAGABILITIES	PROPENDENT	PROPITIATE	PROPOSITIONS	PROPYLITES

PROPYLITISATION	PROSECTORSHIPS	PROSINESSES	PROSTATECTOMY	PROTANOPES
PROPYLITISE	PROSECUTABLE	PROSLAMBANOMENE	PROSTATISM	PROTANOPIA
PROPYLITISED	PROSECUTED	PROSLAVERY	PROSTATISMS	PROTANOPIAS
PROPYLITISES	PROSECUTES	PROSOBRANCH	PROSTATITIS	PROTANOPIC
PROPYLITISING	PROSECUTING	PROSOBRANCHS	PROSTATITISES	PROTEACEOUS
PROPYLITIZATION	PROSECUTION	PROSODIANS	PROSTERNUM	PROTECTANT
PROPYLITIZE	PROSECUTIONS	PROSODICAL	PROSTERNUMS	PROTECTANTS
PROPYLITIZED	PROSECUTOR	PROSODICALLY	PROSTHESES	PROTECTERS
PROPYLITIZES	PROSECUTORIAL	PROSODISTS	PROSTHESIS	PROTECTING
PROPYLITIZING	PROSECUTORS	PROSOPAGNOSIA	PROSTHETIC	PROTECTINGLY
PRORATABLE	PROSECUTRICES	PROSOPAGNOSIAS	PROSTHETICALLY	PROTECTION
PRORATIONS	PROSECUTRIX	PROSOPOGRAPHER	PROSTHETICS	PROTECTIONISM
PRORECTORS	PROSECUTRIXES	PROSOPOGRAPHERS	PROSTHETIST	PROTECTIONISMS
PROROGATED	PROSELYTED	PROSOPOGRAPHIES	PROSTHETISTS	PROTECTIONIST
PROROGATES	PROSELYTES	PROSOPOGRAPHY	PROSTHODONTIA	PROTECTIONISTS
PROROGATING	PROSELYTIC	PROSOPOPEIA	PROSTHODONTIAS	PROTECTIONS
PROROGATION	PROSELYTING	PROSOPOPEIAL	PROSTHODONTICS	PROTECTIVE
PROROGATIONS	PROSELYTISATION	PROSOPOPEIAS	PROSTHODONTIST	PROTECTIVELY
PROROGUING	PROSELYTISE	PROSOPOPOEIA	PROSTHODONTISTS	PROTECTIVENESS
PROSAICALLY	PROSELYTISED	PROSOPOPOEIAL	PROSTITUTE	PROTECTIVES
PROSAICALNESS	PROSELYTISER	PROSOPOPOEIAS	PROSTITUTED	PROTECTORAL
PROSAICALNESSES	PROSELYTISERS	PROSPECTED	PROSTITUTES	PROTECTORATE
PROSAICISM	PROSELYTISES	PROSPECTING	PROSTITUTING	PROTECTORATES
PROSAICISMS	PROSELYTISING	PROSPECTINGS	PROSTITUTION	PROTECTORIAL
PROSAICNESS	PROSELYTISM	PROSPECTION	PROSTITUTIONS	PROTECTORIES
PROSAICNESSES	PROSELYTISMS	PROSPECTIONS	PROSTITUTOR	PROTECTORLESS
PROSATEURS	PROSELYTIZATION	PROSPECTIVE	PROSTITUTORS	PROTECTORS
PROSAUROPOD	PROSELYTIZE	PROSPECTIVELY	PROSTOMIAL	PROTECTORSHIP
PROSAUROPODS	PROSELYTIZED	PROSPECTIVENESS	PROSTOMIUM	PROTECTORSHIPS
PROSCENIUM	PROSELYTIZER	PROSPECTIVES	PROSTRATED	PROTECTORY
PROSCENIUMS	PROSELYTIZERS	PROSPECTLESS	PROSTRATES	PROTECTRESS
PROSCIUTTI	PROSELYTIZES	PROSPECTOR	PROSTRATING	PROTECTRESSES
PROSCIUTTO	PROSELYTIZING	PROSPECTORS	PROSTRATION	PROTECTRICES
PROSCIUTTOS	PROSEMINAR	PROSPECTUS	PROSTRATIONS	PROTECTRIX
PROSCRIBED	PROSEMINARS	PROSPECTUSES	PROSYLLOGISM	PROTECTRIXES
PROSCRIBER	PROSENCEPHALA	PROSPERING	PROSYLLOGISMS	PROTEIFORM
PROSCRIBERS	PROSENCEPHALIC	PROSPERITIES	PROTACTINIUM	PROTEINACEOUS
PROSCRIBES	PROSENCEPHALON	PROSPERITY	PROTACTINIUMS	PROTEINASE
PROSCRIBING	PROSENCHYMAS	PROSPEROUS	PROTAGONISM	PROTEINASES
PROSCRIPTION	PROSENCHYMATA	PROSPEROUSLY	PROTAGONISMS	PROTEINOUS
PROSCRIPTIONS	PROSENCHYMATOUS	PROSPEROUSNESS	PROTAGONIST	PROTEINURIA
PROSCRIPTIVE	PROSEUCHAE	PROSTACYCLIN	PROTAGONISTS	PROTEINURIAS
PROSCRIPTIVELY	PROSIFYING	PROSTACYCLINS	PROTAMINES	PROTENDING
PROSCRIPTS	PROSILIENCIES	PROSTAGLANDIN	PROTANDRIES	PROTENSION
PROSECTING	PROSILIENCY	PROSTAGLANDINS	PROTANDROUS	PROTENSIONS
PROSECTORIAL	PROSILIENT	PROSTANTHERA	PROTANOMALIES	PROTENSITIES
PROSECTORS	PROSIMIANS	PROSTANTHERAS	PROTANOMALOUS	PROTENSITY
PROSECTORSHIP		PROSTATECTOMIES	PROTANOMALY	PROTENSIVE

P

PROTENSIVELY	PROTHROMBINS	PROTOMORPHIC	PROTOTHERIANS	PROTUBERANCES
PROTEOCLASTIC	PROTISTANS	PROTONATED	PROTOTROPH	PROTUBERANCIES
PROTEOGLYCAN	PROTISTOLOGIES	PROTONATES	PROTOTROPHIC	PROTUBERANCY
PROTEOGLYCANS	PROTISTOLOGIST	PROTONATING	PROTOTROPHIES	PROTUBERANT
PROTEOLYSE	PROTISTOLOGISTS	PROTONATION	PROTOTROPHS	PROTUBERANTLY
PROTEOLYSED	PROTISTOLOGY	PROTONATIONS	PROTOTROPHY	PROTUBERATE
PROTEOLYSES	PROTOACTINIUM	PROTONEMAL	PROTOTYPAL	PROTUBERATED
PROTEOLYSING	PROTOACTINIUMS	PROTONEMATA	PROTOTYPED	PROTUBERATES
PROTEOLYSIS	PROTOAVISES	PROTONEMATAL	PROTOTYPES	PROTUBERATING
PROTEOLYTIC	PROTOCHORDATE	PROTONOTARIAL	PROTOTYPIC	PROTUBERATION
PROTEOLYTICALLY	PROTOCHORDATES	PROTONOTARIAT	PROTOTYPICAL	PROTUBERATIONS
PROTEOMICS	PROTOCOCCAL	PROTONOTARIATS	PROTOTYPICALLY	PROUDHEARTED
PROTERANDRIES	PROTOCOLED	PROTONOTARIES	PROTOTYPING	PROUDNESSES
PROTERANDROUS	PROTOCOLIC	PROTONOTARY	PROTOXIDES	PROUSTITES
PROTERANDRY	PROTOCOLING	PROTOPATHIC	PROTOXYLEM	PROVABILITIES
PROTEROGYNIES	PROTOCOLISE	PROTOPATHIES	PROTOXYLEMS	PROVABILITY
PROTEROGYNOUS	PROTOCOLISED	PROTOPATHY	PROTOZOANS	PROVABLENESS
PROTEROGYNY	PROTOCOLISES	PROTOPHILIC	PROTOZOOLOGICAL	PROVABLENESSES
PROTERVITIES	PROTOCOLISING	PROTOPHLOEM	PROTOZOOLOGIES	PROVANTING
PROTERVITY	PROTOCOLIST	PROTOPHLOEMS	PROTOZOOLOGIST	PROVASCULAR
PROTESTANT	PROTOCOLISTS	PROTOPHYTE	PROTOZOOLOGISTS	PROVEABILITIES
PROTESTANTS	PROTOCOLIZE	PROTOPHYTES	PROTOZOOLOGY	PROVEABILITY
PROTESTATION	PROTOCOLIZED	PROTOPHYTIC	PROTOZOONS	PROVECTION
PROTESTATIONS	PROTOCOLIZES	PROTOPLANET	PROTRACTED	PROVECTIONS
PROTESTERS	PROTOCOLIZING	PROTOPLANETARY	PROTRACTEDLY	PROVEDITOR
PROTESTING	PROTOCOLLED	PROTOPLANETS	PROTRACTEDNESS	PROVEDITORE
PROTESTINGLY	PROTOCOLLING	PROTOPLASM	PROTRACTIBLE	PROVEDITORES
PROTESTORS	PROTOCTIST	PROTOPLASMAL	PROTRACTILE	PROVEDITORS
PROTHALAMIA	PROTOCTISTS	PROTOPLASMATIC	PROTRACTING	PROVEDORES
PROTHALAMION	PROTODERMS	PROTOPLASMIC	PROTRACTION	PROVENANCE
PROTHALAMIUM	PROTOGALAXIES	PROTOPLASMS	PROTRACTIONS	PROVENANCES
PROTHALLIA	PROTOGALAXY	PROTOPLAST	PROTRACTIVE	PROVENDERED
PROTHALLIAL	PROTOGENIC	PROTOPLASTIC	PROTRACTOR	PROVENDERING
PROTHALLIC	PROTOGINES	PROTOPLASTS	PROTRACTORS	PROVENDERS
PROTHALLIUM	PROTOGYNIES	PROTOPORPHYRIN	PROTREPTIC	PROVENIENCE
PROTHALLOID	PROTOGYNOUS	PROTOPORPHYRINS	PROTREPTICAL	PROVENIENCES
PROTHALLUS	PROTOHISTORIAN	PROTOSPATAIRE	PROTREPTICS	PROVENTRICULAR
PROTHALLUSES	PROTOHISTORIANS	PROTOSPATAIRES	PROTRUDABLE	PROVENTRICULI
PROTHETICALLY	PROTOHISTORIC	PROTOSPATHAIRE	PROTRUDENT	PROVENTRICULUS
PROTHONOTARIAL	PROTOHISTORIES	PROTOSPATHAIRES	PROTRUDING	PROVERBIAL
PROTHONOTARIAT	PROTOHISTORY	PROTOSPATHARIUS	PROTRUSIBLE	PROVERBIALISE
PROTHONOTARIATS	PROTOHUMAN	PROTOSTARS	PROTRUSILE	PROVERBIALISED
PROTHONOTARIES	PROTOHUMANS	PROTOSTELE	PROTRUSION	PROVERBIALISES
PROTHONOTARY	PROTOLANGUAGE	PROTOSTELES	PROTRUSIONS	PROVERBIALISING
PROTHORACES	PROTOLANGUAGES	PROTOSTELIC	PROTRUSIVE	PROVERBIALISM
PROTHORACIC	PROTOLITHIC	PROTOSTOME	PROTRUSIVELY	PROVERBIALISMS
PROTHORAXES	PROTOMARTYR	PROTOSTOMES	PROTRUSIVENESS	PROVERBIALIST
PROTHROMBIN	PROTOMARTYRS	PROTOTHERIAN	PROTUBERANCE	PROVERBIALISTS

PROVERBIALIZE	PROVOCATION	PRUSSIANIZE	PSEUDEPIGRAPHIC	PSEUDOMONADS
PROVERBIALIZED	PROVOCATIONS	PRUSSIANIZED	PSEUDEPIGRAPHON	PSEUDOMONAS
PROVERBIALIZES	PROVOCATIVE	PRUSSIANIZES	PSEUDEPIGRAPHS	PSEUDOMORPH
PROVERBIALIZING	PROVOCATIVELY	PRUSSIANIZING	PSEUDEPIGRAPHY	PSEUDOMORPHIC
PROVERBIALLY	PROVOCATIVENESS	PRUSSIATES	PSEUDERIES	PSEUDOMORPHISM
PROVERBING	PROVOCATIVES	PSALIGRAPHIES	PSEUDIMAGINES	PSEUDOMORPHISMS
PROVIDABLE	PROVOCATOR	PSALIGRAPHY	PSEUDIMAGO	PSEUDOMORPHOUS
PROVIDENCE	PROVOCATORS	PSALMBOOKS	PSEUDIMAGOES	PSEUDOMORPHS
PROVIDENCES	PROVOCATORY	PSALMODICAL	PSEUDIMAGOS	PSEUDOMUTUALITY
PROVIDENTIAL	PROVOKABLE	PSALMODIES	PSEUDOACID	PSEUDONYMITIES
PROVIDENTIALLY	PROVOKEMENT	PSALMODISE	PSEUDOACIDS	PSEUDONYMITY
PROVIDENTLY	PROVOKEMENTS	PSALMODISED	PSEUDOALLELE	PSEUDONYMOUS
PROVINCEWIDE	PROVOKINGLY	PSALMODISES	PSEUDOALLELES	PSEUDONYMOUSLY
PROVINCIAL	PROVOLONES	PSALMODISING	PSEUDOARTHROSES	PSEUDONYMS
PROVINCIALISE	PROVOSTRIES	PSALMODIST	PSEUDOARTHROSIS	PSEUDOPODAL
PROVINCIALISED	PROVOSTSHIP	PSALMODISTS	PSEUDOBULB	PSEUDOPODIA
PROVINCIALISES	PROVOSTSHIPS	PSALMODIZE	PSEUDOBULBS	PSEUDOPODIAL
PROVINCIALISING	PROWLINGLY	PSALMODIZED	PSEUDOCARP	PSEUDOPODIUM
PROVINCIALISM	PROXIMALLY	PSALMODIZES	PSEUDOCARPOUS	PSEUDOPODS
PROVINCIALISMS	PROXIMATELY	PSALMODIZING	PSEUDOCARPS	PSEUDOPREGNANCY
PROVINCIALIST	PROXIMATENESS	PSALTERIAN	PSEUDOCIDE	PSEUDOPREGNANT
PROVINCIALISTS	PROXIMATENESSES	PSALTERIES	PSEUDOCIDES	PSEUDORANDOM
PROVINCIALITIES	PROXIMATION	PSALTERIUM	PSEUDOCLASSIC	PSEUDOSCALAR
PROVINCIALITY	PROXIMATIONS	PSALTRESSES	PSEUDOCLASSICS	PSEUDOSCALARS
PROVINCIALIZE	PROXIMITIES	PSAMMOPHIL	PSEUDOCODE	PSEUDOSCIENCE
PROVINCIALIZED	PROZYMITES	PSAMMOPHILE	PSEUDOCODES	PSEUDOSCIENCES
PROVINCIALIZES	PRUDENTIAL	PSAMMOPHILES	PSEUDOCOEL	PSEUDOSCIENTIST
PROVINCIALIZING	PRUDENTIALISM	PSAMMOPHILOUS	PSEUDOCOELOMATE	PSEUDOSCOPE
PROVINCIALLY	PRUDENTIALISMS	PSAMMOPHILS	PSEUDOCOELS	PSEUDOSCOPES
PROVINCIALS	PRUDENTIALIST	PSAMMOPHYTE	PSEUDOCYESES	PSEUDOSCORPION
PROVIRUSES	PRUDENTIALISTS	PSAMMOPHYTES	PSEUDOCYESIS	PSEUDOSCORPIONS
PROVISIONAL	PRUDENTIALITIES	PSAMMOPHYTIC	PSEUDOEPHEDRINE	PSEUDOSOLUTION
PROVISIONALLY	PRUDENTIALITY	PSELLISMUS	PSEUDOGRAPH	PSEUDOSOLUTIONS
PROVISIONALS	PRUDENTIALLY	PSELLISMUSES	PSEUDOGRAPHIES	PSEUDOSYMMETRY
PROVISIONARIES	PRUDENTIALS	PSEPHOANALYSES	PSEUDOGRAPHS	PSEUDOVECTOR
PROVISIONARY	PRUDISHNESS	PSEPHOANALYSIS	PSEUDOGRAPHY	PSEUDOVECTORS
PROVISIONED	PRUDISHNESSES	PSEPHOLOGICAL	PSEUDOLOGIA	PSILANTHROPIC
PROVISIONER	PRURIENCES	PSEPHOLOGICALLY	PSEUDOLOGIAS	PSILANTHROPIES
PROVISIONERS	PRURIENCIES	PSEPHOLOGIES	PSEUDOLOGIES	PSILANTHROPISM
PROVISIONING	PRURIENTLY	PSEPHOLOGIST	PSEUDOLOGUE	PSILANTHROPISMS
PROVISIONS	PRURIGINOUS	PSEPHOLOGISTS	PSEUDOLOGUES	PSILANTHROPIST
PROVISORILY	PRURITUSES	PSEPHOLOGY	PSEUDOLOGY	PSILANTHROPISTS
PROVITAMIN	PRUSSIANISATION	PSEUDAESTHESIA	PSEUDOMARTYR	PSILANTHROPY
PROVITAMINS	PRUSSIANISE	PSEUDAESTHESIAS	PSEUDOMARTYRS	PSILOCYBIN
PROVOCABLE	PRUSSIANISED	PSEUDARTHROSES	PSEUDOMEMBRANE	PSILOCYBINS
PROVOCANTS	PRUSSIANISES	PSEUDARTHROSIS	PSEUDOMEMBRANES	PSILOMELANE
PROVOCATEUR	PRUSSIANISING	PSEUDEPIGRAPH	PSEUDOMONAD	PSILOMELANES
PROVOCATEURS	PRUSSIANIZATION	PSEUDEPIGRAPHA	PSEUDOMONADES	PSILOPHYTE

P

PSILOPHYTES	PSYCHOANALYZER	PSYCHOGRAPHICAL	PSYCHONEUROTIC	PSYCHROMETER
PSILOPHYTIC	PSYCHOANALYZERS	PSYCHOGRAPHICS	PSYCHONEUROTICS	PSYCHROMETERS
PSITTACINE	PSYCHOANALYZES	PSYCHOGRAPHIES	PSYCHONOMIC	PSYCHROMETRIC
PSITTACINES	PSYCHOANALYZING	PSYCHOGRAPHS	PSYCHONOMICS	PSYCHROMETRICAL
PSITTACOSES	PSYCHOBABBLE	PSYCHOGRAPHY	PSYCHOPATH	PSYCHROMETRIES
PSITTACOSIS	PSYCHOBABBLED	PSYCHOHISTORIAN	PSYCHOPATHIC	PSYCHROMETRY
PSITTACOTIC	PSYCHOBABBLER	PSYCHOHISTORIES	PSYCHOPATHICS	PSYCHROPHILIC
PSORIATICS	PSYCHOBABBLERS	PSYCHOHISTORY	PSYCHOPATHIES	PTARMIGANS
PSYCHAGOGUE	PSYCHOBABBLES	PSYCHOKINESES	PSYCHOPATHIST	PTERANODON
PSYCHAGOGUES	PSYCHOBABBLING	PSYCHOKINESIS	PSYCHOPATHISTS	PTERANODONS
PSYCHASTHENIA	PSYCHOBILLIES	PSYCHOKINETIC	PSYCHOPATHOLOGY	PTERIDINES
PSYCHASTHENIAS	PSYCHOBILLY	PSYCHOLINGUIST	PSYCHOPATHS	PTERIDOLOGICAL
PSYCHASTHENIC	PSYCHOBIOGRAPHY	PSYCHOLINGUISTS	PSYCHOPATHY	PTERIDOLOGIES
PSYCHASTHENICS	PSYCHOBIOLOGIC	PSYCHOLOGIC	PSYCHOPHILIES	PTERIDOLOGIST
PSYCHEDELIA	PSYCHOBIOLOGIES	PSYCHOLOGICAL	PSYCHOPHILY	PTERIDOLOGISTS
PSYCHEDELIAS	PSYCHOBIOLOGIST	PSYCHOLOGICALLY	PSYCHOPHYSICAL	PTERIDOLOGY
PSYCHEDELIC	PSYCHOBIOLOGY	PSYCHOLOGIES	PSYCHOPHYSICIST	PTERIDOMANIA
PSYCHEDELICALLY	PSYCHOCHEMICAL	PSYCHOLOGISE	PSYCHOPHYSICS	PTERIDOMANIAS
PSYCHEDELICS	PSYCHOCHEMICALS	PSYCHOLOGISED	PSYCHOPOMP	PTERIDOPHILIST
PSYCHIATER	PSYCHOCHEMISTRY	PSYCHOLOGISES	PSYCHOPOMPS	PTERIDOPHILISTS
PSYCHIATERS	PSYCHODELIA	PSYCHOLOGISING	PSYCHOSEXUAL	PTERIDOPHYTE
PSYCHIATRIC	PSYCHODELIAS	PSYCHOLOGISM	PSYCHOSEXUALITY	PTERIDOPHYTES
PSYCHIATRICAL	PSYCHODELIC	PSYCHOLOGISMS	PSYCHOSEXUALLY	PTERIDOPHYTIC
PSYCHIATRICALLY	PSYCHODELICALLY	PSYCHOLOGIST	PSYCHOSOCIAL	PTERIDOPHYTOUS
PSYCHIATRIES	PSYCHODRAMA	PSYCHOLOGISTIC	PSYCHOSOCIALLY	PTERIDOSPERM
PSYCHIATRIST	PSYCHODRAMAS	PSYCHOLOGISTS	PSYCHOSOCIOLOGY	PTERIDOSPERMS
PSYCHIATRISTS	PSYCHODRAMATIC	PSYCHOLOGIZE	PSYCHOSOMATIC	PTERODACTYL
PSYCHIATRY	PSYCHODYNAMIC	PSYCHOLOGIZED	PSYCHOSOMATICS	PTERODACTYLE
PSYCHICALLY	PSYCHODYNAMICS	PSYCHOLOGIZES	PSYCHOSOMIMETIC	PTERODACTYLES
PSYCHICISM	PSYCHOGALVANIC	PSYCHOLOGIZING	PSYCHOSURGEON	PTERODACTYLS
PSYCHICISMS	PSYCHOGASES	PSYCHOLOGY	PSYCHOSURGEONS	PTEROSAURIAN
PSYCHICIST	PSYCHOGENESES	PSYCHOMACHIA	PSYCHOSURGERIES	PTEROSAURIANS
PSYCHICISTS	PSYCHOGENESIS	PSYCHOMACHIAS	PSYCHOSURGERY	PTEROSAURS
PSYCHOACOUSTIC	PSYCHOGENETIC	PSYCHOMACHIES	PSYCHOSURGICAL	PTERYGIALS
PSYCHOACOUSTICS	PSYCHOGENETICAL	PSYCHOMACHY	PSYCHOSYNTHESES	PTERYGIUMS
PSYCHOACTIVE	PSYCHOGENETICS	PSYCHOMETER	PSYCHOSYNTHESIS	PTERYGOIDS
PSYCHOANALYSE	PSYCHOGENIC	PSYCHOMETERS	PSYCHOTECHNICS	PTERYLOGRAPHIC
PSYCHOANALYSED	PSYCHOGENICALLY	PSYCHOMETRIC	PSYCHOTHERAPIES	PTERYLOGRAPHIES
PSYCHOANALYSER	PSYCHOGERIATRIC	PSYCHOMETRICAL	PSYCHOTHERAPIST	PTERYLOGRAPHY
PSYCHOANALYSERS	PSYCHOGNOSES	PSYCHOMETRICIAN	PSYCHOTHERAPY	PTERYLOSES
PSYCHOANALYSES	PSYCHOGNOSIS	PSYCHOMETRICS	PSYCHOTICALLY	PTERYLOSIS
PSYCHOANALYSING	PSYCHOGNOSTIC	PSYCHOMETRIES	PSYCHOTICISM	PTOCHOCRACIES
PSYCHOANALYSIS	PSYCHOGONIES	PSYCHOMETRIST	PSYCHOTICISMS	PTOCHOCRACY
PSYCHOANALYST	PSYCHOGONY	PSYCHOMETRISTS	PSYCHOTICS	PTYALAGOGIC
PSYCHOANALYSTS	PSYCHOGRAM	PSYCHOMETRY	PSYCHOTOMIMETIC	PTYALAGOGUE
PSYCHOANALYTIC	PSYCHOGRAMS	PSYCHOMOTOR	PSYCHOTOXIC	PTYALAGOGUES
PSYCHOANALYZE	PSYCHOGRAPH	PSYCHONEUROSES	PSYCHOTROPIC	PTYALISING
PSYCHOANALYZED	PSYCHOGRAPHIC	PSYCHONEUROSIS	PSYCHOTROPICS	PTYALIZING

P

PUBCRAWLER	PUGGINESSES	PULSIMETERS	PUNCHBOWLS	PUNISHABILITY
PUBCRAWLERS	PUGILISTIC	PULSOMETER	PUNCHINELLO	PUNISHABLE
PUBERULENT	PUGILISTICAL	PULSOMETERS	PUNCHINELLOES	PUNISHINGLY
PUBERULOUS	PUGILISTICALLY	PULTACEOUS	PUNCHINELLOS	PUNISHMENT
PUBESCENCE	PUGNACIOUS	PULTRUDING	PUNCHINESS	PUNISHMENTS
PUBESCENCES	PUGNACIOUSLY	PULTRUSION	PUNCHINESSES	PUNITIVELY
PUBLICALLY	PUGNACIOUSNESS	PULTRUSIONS	PUNCHLINES	PUNITIVENESS
PUBLICATION	PUGNACITIES	PULVERABLE	PUNCTATION	PUNITIVENESSES
PUBLICATIONS	PUISSANCES	PULVERATION	PUNCTATIONS	PUNKINESSES
PUBLICISED	PUISSANTLY	PULVERATIONS	PUNCTATORS	PUPIGEROUS
PUBLICISES	PUISSAUNCE	PULVERINES	PUNCTILIOS	PUPILABILITIES
PUBLICISING	PUISSAUNCES	PULVERISABLE	PUNCTILIOUS	PUPILABILITY
PUBLICISTS	PULCHRITUDE	PULVERISATION	PUNCTILIOUSLY	PUPILARITIES
PUBLICITIES	PULCHRITUDES	PULVERISATIONS	PUNCTILIOUSNESS	PUPILARITY
PUBLICIZED	PULCHRITUDINOUS	PULVERISED	PUNCTUALIST	PUPILLAGES
PUBLICIZES	PULLULATED	PULVERISER	PUNCTUALISTS	PUPILLARITIES
PUBLICIZING	PULLULATES	PULVERISERS	PUNCTUALITIES	PUPILLARITY
PUBLICNESS	PULLULATING	PULVERISES	PUNCTUALITY	PUPILLATED
PUBLICNESSES	PULLULATION	PULVERISING	PUNCTUALLY	PUPILLATES
PUBLISHABLE	PULLULATIONS	PULVERIZABLE	PUNCTUATED	PUPILLATING
PUBLISHERS	PULMOBRANCH	PULVERIZATION	PUNCTUATES	PUPILSHIPS
PUBLISHING	PULMOBRANCHIATE	PULVERIZATIONS	PUNCTUATING	PUPIPAROUS
PUBLISHINGS	PULMOBRANCHS	PULVERIZED	PUNCTUATION	PUPPETEERED
PUBLISHMENT	PULMONATES	PULVERIZER	PUNCTUATIONIST	PUPPETEERING
PUBLISHMENTS	PULMONOLOGIES	PULVERIZERS	PUNCTUATIONISTS	PUPPETEERS
PUCCINIACEOUS	PULMONOLOGIST	PULVERIZES	PUNCTUATIONS	PUPPETLIKE
PUCKERIEST	PULMONOLOGISTS	PULVERIZING	PUNCTUATIVE	PUPPETRIES
PUCKEROOED	PULMONOLOGY	PULVERULENCE	PUNCTUATOR	PUPPYHOODS
PUCKISHNESS	PULPBOARDS	PULVERULENCES	PUNCTUATORS	PURBLINDLY
PUCKISHNESSES	PULPIFYING	PULVERULENT	PUNCTULATE	PURBLINDNESS
PUDDENINGS	PULPINESSES	PULVILISED	PUNCTULATED	PURBLINDNESSES
PUDDINGIER	PULPITEERED	PULVILIZED	PUNCTULATES	PURCHASABILITY
PUDDINGIEST	PULPITEERING	PULVILLIFORM	PUNCTULATING	PURCHASABLE
PUDGINESSES	PULPITEERS	PULVILLING	PUNCTULATION	PURCHASERS
PUDIBUNDITIES	PULPITRIES	PULVILLIOS	PUNCTULATIONS	PURCHASING
PUDIBUNDITY	PULPSTONES	PULVINATED	PUNCTURABLE	PURCHASINGS
PUDICITIES	PULSATANCE	PULVINULES	PUNCTURATION	PURDONIUMS
PUERILISMS	PULSATANCES	PUMICATING	PUNCTURATIONS	PUREBLOODS
PUERILITIES	PULSATILITIES	PUMMELLING	PUNCTURERS	PURENESSES
PUERPERALLY	PULSATILITY	PUMMELLINGS	PUNCTURING	PURGATIONS
PUERPERIUM	PULSATILLA	PUMPERNICKEL	PUNDIGRION	PURGATIVELY
PUFFERFISH	PULSATILLAS	PUMPERNICKELS	PUNDIGRIONS	PURGATIVES
PUFFERFISHES	PULSATIONS	PUMPHOUSES	PUNDITRIES	PURGATORIAL
PUFFINESSES	PULSATIVELY	PUMPKINSEED	PUNDONORES	PURGATORIALLY
PUFFTALOONAS	PULSEBEATS	PUMPKINSEEDS	PUNGENCIES	PURGATORIAN
PUFTALOONAS	PULSELESSNESS	PUNCHBALLS	PUNICACEOUS	PURGATORIANS
PUFTALOONIES	PULSELESSNESSES	PUNCHBOARD	PUNINESSES	PURGATORIES
PUFTALOONS	PULSIMETER	PUNCHBOARDS	PUNISHABILITIES	PURIFICATION

PURIFICATIONS	PURSUIVANT	PUTRESCIBLE	PYKNOSOMES	PYRIDOXALS
PURIFICATIVE	PURSUIVANTS	PUTRESCIBLES	PYLORECTOMIES	PYRIDOXAMINE
PURIFICATOR	PURTENANCE	PUTRESCINE	PYLORECTOMY	PYRIDOXAMINES
PURIFICATORS	PURTENANCES	PUTRESCINES	PYOGENESES	PYRIDOXINE
PURIFICATORY	PURULENCES	PUTRIDITIES	PYOGENESIS	PYRIDOXINES
PURISTICAL	PURULENCIES	PUTRIDNESS	PYORRHOEAL	PYRIDOXINS
PURISTICALLY	PURULENTLY	PUTRIDNESSES	PYORRHOEAS	PYRIMETHAMINE
PURITANICAL	PURVEYANCE	PUTRIFICATION	PYORRHOEIC	PYRIMETHAMINES
PURITANICALLY	PURVEYANCES	PUTRIFICATIONS	PYRACANTHA	PYRIMIDINE
PURITANICALNESS	PUSCHKINIA	PUTSCHISTS	PYRACANTHAS	PYRIMIDINES
PURITANISE	PUSCHKINIAS	PUTTYROOTS	PYRACANTHS	PYRITHIAMINE
PURITANISED	PUSHCHAIRS	PUZZLEDOMS	PYRALIDIDS	PYRITHIAMINES
PURITANISES	PUSHFULNESS	PUZZLEHEADED	PYRAMIDALLY	PYRITIFEROUS
PURITANISING	PUSHFULNESSES	PUZZLEMENT	PYRAMIDICAL	PYRITISING
PURITANISM	PUSHINESSES	PUZZLEMENTS	PYRAMIDICALLY	PYRITIZING
PURITANISMS	PUSHINGNESS	PUZZLINGLY	PYRAMIDING	PYRITOHEDRA
PURITANIZE	PUSHINGNESSES	PUZZOLANAS	PYRAMIDION	PYRITOHEDRAL
PURITANIZED	PUSILLANIMITIES	PYCNIDIOSPORE	PYRAMIDIONS	PYRITOHEDRON
PURITANIZES	PUSILLANIMITY	PYCNIDIOSPORES	PYRAMIDIST	PYRITOHEDRONS
PURITANIZING	PUSILLANIMOUS	PYCNOCONIDIA	PYRAMIDISTS	PYROBALLOGIES
PURLICUING	PUSILLANIMOUSLY	PYCNOCONIDIUM	PYRAMIDOLOGIES	PYROBALLOGY
PURLOINERS	PUSSYFOOTED	PYCNODYSOSTOSES	PYRAMIDOLOGIST	PYROCATECHIN
PURLOINING	PUSSYFOOTER	PYCNODYSOSTOSIS	PYRAMIDOLOGISTS	PYROCATECHINS
PUROMYCINS	PUSSYFOOTERS	PYCNOGONID	PYRAMIDOLOGY	PYROCATECHOL
PURPLEHEART	PUSSYFOOTING	PYCNOGONIDS	PYRAMIDONS	PYROCATECHOLS
PURPLEHEARTS	PUSSYFOOTINGS	PYCNOGONOID	PYRANOMETER	PYROCERAMS
PURPLENESS	PUSSYFOOTS	PYCNOGONOIDS	PYRANOMETERS	PYROCHEMICAL
PURPLENESSES	PUSTULANTS	PYCNOMETER	PYRANOSIDE	PYROCHEMICALLY
PURPORTEDLY	PUSTULATED	PYCNOMETERS	PYRANOSIDES	PYROCLASTIC
PURPORTING	PUSTULATES	PYCNOMETRIC	PYRARGYRITE	PYROCLASTICS
PURPORTLESS	PUSTULATING	PYCNOSOMES	PYRARGYRITES	PYROCLASTS
PURPOSEFUL	PUSTULATION	PYCNOSPORE	PYRENEITES	PYROELECTRIC
PURPOSEFULLY	PUSTULATIONS	PYCNOSPORES	PYRENOCARP	PYROELECTRICITY
PURPOSEFULNESS	PUTANGITANGI	PYCNOSTYLE	PYRENOCARPS	PYROELECTRICS
PURPOSELESS	PUTANGITANGIS	PYCNOSTYLES	PYRENOMYCETOUS	PYROGALLATE
PURPOSELESSLY	PUTATIVELY	PYELITISES	PYRETHRINS	PYROGALLATES
PURPOSELESSNESS	PUTONGHUAS	PYELOGRAMS	PYRETHROID	PYROGALLIC
PURPOSIVELY	PUTREFACIENT	PYELOGRAPHIC	PYRETHROIDS	PYROGALLOL
PURPOSIVENESS	PUTREFACTION	PYELOGRAPHIES	PYRETHRUMS	PYROGALLOLS
PURPOSIVENESSES	PUTREFACTIONS	PYELOGRAPHY	PYRETOLOGIES	PYROGENETIC
PURPRESTURE	PUTREFACTIVE	PYELONEPHRITIC	PYRETOLOGY	PYROGENICITIES
PURPRESTURES	PUTREFIABLE	PYELONEPHRITIS	PYRETOTHERAPIES	PYROGENICITY
PURSERSHIP	PUTREFIERS	PYGARGUSES	PYRETOTHERAPY	PYROGENOUS
PURSERSHIPS	PUTREFYING	PYGOSTYLES	PYRGEOMETER	PYROGNOSTIC
PURSINESSES	PUTRESCENCE	PYKNODYSOSTOSES	PYRGEOMETERS	PYROGNOSTICS
PURSUANCES	PUTRESCENCES	PYKNODYSOSTOSIS	PYRHELIOMETER	PYROGRAPHER
PURSUANTLY	PUTRESCENT	PYKNOMETER	PYRHELIOMETERS	PYROGRAPHERS
PURSUINGLY	PUTRESCIBILITY	PYKNOMETERS	PYRHELIOMETRIC	PYROGRAPHIC

P

PYROGRAPHIES

PYROGRAPHIES
PYROGRAPHY
PYROGRAVURE
PYROGRAVURES
PYROKINESES
PYROKINESIS
PYROLATERS
PYROLATRIES
PYROLIGNEOUS
PYROLIGNIC
PYROLISING
PYROLIZING
PYROLOGIES
PYROLUSITE
PYROLUSITES
PYROLYSABLE
PYROLYSATE
PYROLYSATES
PYROLYSERS
PYROLYSING
PYROLYTICALLY
PYROLYZABLE

PYROLYZATE
PYROLYZATES
PYROLYZERS
PYROLYZING
PYROMAGNETIC
PYROMANCER
PYROMANCERS
PYROMANCIES
PYROMANIAC
PYROMANIACAL
PYROMANIACS
PYROMANIAS
PYROMANTIC
PYROMERIDE
PYROMERIDES
PYROMETALLURGY
PYROMETERS
PYROMETRIC
PYROMETRICAL
PYROMETRICALLY
PYROMETRIES
PYROMORPHITE

PYROMORPHITES
PYRONINOPHILIC
PYROPHOBIA
PYROPHOBIAS
PYROPHOBIC
PYROPHOBICS
PYROPHONES
PYROPHORIC
PYROPHOROUS
PYROPHORUS
PYROPHORUSES
PYROPHOSPHATE
PYROPHOSPHATES
PYROPHOSPHORIC
PYROPHOTOGRAPH
PYROPHOTOGRAPHS
PYROPHOTOGRAPHY
PYROPHOTOMETER
PYROPHOTOMETERS
PYROPHOTOMETRY
PYROPHYLLITE
PYROPHYLLITES

PYROSCOPES
PYROSTATIC
PYROSULFITE
PYROSULFITES
PYROSULPHATE
PYROSULPHATES
PYROSULPHURIC
PYROTARTARIC
PYROTARTRATE
PYROTARTRATES
PYROTECHNIC
PYROTECHNICAL
PYROTECHNICALLY
PYROTECHNICIAN
PYROTECHNICIANS
PYROTECHNICS
PYROTECHNIES
PYROTECHNIST
PYROTECHNISTS
PYROTECHNY
PYROVANADIC
PYROXENITE

PYROXENITES
PYROXENITIC
PYROXENOID
PYROXENOIDS
PYROXYLINE
PYROXYLINES
PYROXYLINS
PYRRHICIST
PYRRHICISTS
PYRRHOTINE
PYRRHOTINES
PYRRHOTITE
PYRRHOTITES
PYRRHULOXIA
PYRRHULOXIAS
PYRROLIDINE
PYRROLIDINES
PYTHOGENIC
PYTHONESSES
PYTHONOMORPH
PYTHONOMORPHS

P

Q

QABALISTIC	QUADRENNIALLY	QUADRIPLEGIA	QUADRUPLES	QUALIFIEDLY
QINGHAOSUS	QUADRENNIALS	QUADRIPLEGIAS	QUADRUPLET	QUALIFIERS
QUACKERIES	QUADRENNIUM	QUADRIPLEGIC	QUADRUPLETS	QUALIFYING
QUACKSALVER	QUADRENNIUMS	QUADRIPLEGICS	QUADRUPLEX	QUALIFYINGS
QUACKSALVERS	QUADRICEPS	QUADRIPOLE	QUADRUPLEXED	QUALITATIVE
QUACKSALVING	QUADRICEPSES	QUADRIPOLES	QUADRUPLEXES	QUALITATIVELY
QUADCOPTER	QUADRICIPITAL	QUADRIREME	QUADRUPLEXING	QUALMISHLY
QUADCOPTERS	QUADRICONE	QUADRIREMES	QUADRUPLICATE	QUALMISHNESS
QUADPLEXES	QUADRICONES	QUADRISECT	QUADRUPLICATED	QUALMISHNESSES
QUADRAGENARIAN	QUADRIENNIA	QUADRISECTED	QUADRUPLICATES	QUANDARIES
QUADRAGENARIANS	QUADRIENNIAL	QUADRISECTING	QUADRUPLICATING	QUANGOCRACIES
QUADRAGESIMAL	QUADRIENNIUM	QUADRISECTION	QUADRUPLICATION	QUANGOCRACY
QUADRANGLE	QUADRIENNIUMS	QUADRISECTIONS	QUADRUPLICITIES	QUANTIFIABLE
QUADRANGLES	QUADRIFARIOUS	QUADRISECTS	QUADRUPLICITY	QUANTIFICATION
QUADRANGULAR	QUADRIFOLIATE	QUADRISYLLABIC	QUADRUPLIES	QUANTIFICATIONS
QUADRANGULARLY	QUADRIFORM	QUADRISYLLABICS	QUADRUPLING	QUANTIFIED
QUADRANTAL	QUADRIGEMINAL	QUADRISYLLABLE	QUADRUPOLE	QUANTIFIER
QUADRANTES	QUADRIGEMINATE	QUADRISYLLABLES	QUADRUPOLES	QUANTIFIERS
QUADRAPHONIC	QUADRIGEMINOUS	QUADRIVALENCE	QUAESITUMS	QUANTIFIES
QUADRAPHONICS	QUADRILATERAL	QUADRIVALENCES	QUAESTIONARIES	QUANTIFYING
QUADRAPHONIES	QUADRILATERALS	QUADRIVALENCIES	QUAESTIONARY	QUANTISATION
QUADRAPHONY	QUADRILINGUAL	QUADRIVALENCY	QUAESTORIAL	QUANTISATIONS
QUADRAPLEGIA	QUADRILITERAL	QUADRIVALENT	QUAESTORSHIP	QUANTISERS
QUADRAPLEGIAS	QUADRILITERALS	QUADRIVALENTS	QUAESTORSHIPS	QUANTISING
QUADRAPLEGIC	QUADRILLED	QUADRIVIAL	QUAESTUARIES	QUANTITATE
QUADRAPLEGICS	QUADRILLER	QUADRIVIUM	QUAESTUARY	QUANTITATED
QUADRASONIC	QUADRILLERS	QUADRIVIUMS	QUAGGINESS	QUANTITATES
QUADRASONICS	QUADRILLES	QUADROPHONIC	QUAGGINESSES	QUANTITATING
QUADRATICAL	QUADRILLING	QUADROPHONICS	QUAGMIRIER	QUANTITATION
QUADRATICALLY	QUADRILLION	QUADROPHONIES	QUAGMIRIEST	QUANTITATIONS
QUADRATICS	QUADRILLIONS	QUADROPHONY	QUAGMIRING	QUANTITATIVE
QUADRATING	QUADRILLIONTH	QUADRUMANE	QUAINTNESS	QUANTITATIVELY
QUADRATRICES	QUADRILLIONTHS	QUADRUMANES	QUAINTNESSES	QUANTITIES
QUADRATRIX	QUADRILOCULAR	QUADRUMANOUS	QUAKINESSES	QUANTITIVE
QUADRATRIXES	QUADRINGENARIES	QUADRUMANS	QUALIFIABLE	QUANTITIVELY
QUADRATURA	QUADRINGENARY	QUADRUMVIR	QUALIFICATION	QUANTIVALENCE
QUADRATURE	QUADRINOMIAL	QUADRUMVIRATE	QUALIFICATIONS	QUANTIVALENCES
QUADRATURES	QUADRINOMIALS	QUADRUMVIRATES	QUALIFICATIVE	QUANTIVALENT
QUADRATUSES	QUADRIPARTITE	QUADRUMVIRS	QUALIFICATIVES	QUANTIZATION
QUADRELLAS	QUADRIPARTITION	QUADRUPEDAL	QUALIFICATOR	QUANTIZATIONS
QUADRENNIA	QUADRIPHONIC	QUADRUPEDS	QUALIFICATORS	QUANTIZERS
QUADRENNIAL	QUADRIPHONICS	QUADRUPLED	QUALIFICATORY	QUANTIZING

QUANTOMETER	QUARTERINGS	QUATTROCENTIST	QUESADILLAS	QUIDDANIED
QUANTOMETERS	QUARTERLIES	QUATTROCENTISTS	QUESTINGLY	QUIDDANIES
QUAQUAVERSAL	QUARTERLIFE	QUATTROCENTO	QUESTIONABILITY	QUIDDANYING
QUAQUAVERSALLY	QUARTERLIGHT	QUATTROCENTOS	QUESTIONABLE	QUIDDITATIVE
QUARANTINE	QUARTERLIGHTS	QUAVERIEST	QUESTIONABLY	QUIDDITCHES
QUARANTINED	QUARTERMASTER	QUAVERINGLY	QUESTIONARIES	QUIDDITIES
QUARANTINES	QUARTERMASTERS	QUAVERINGS	QUESTIONARY	QUIESCENCE
QUARANTINING	QUARTERMISTRESS	QUEACHIEST	QUESTIONED	QUIESCENCES
QUARENDENS	QUARTEROON	QUEASINESS	QUESTIONEE	QUIESCENCIES
QUARENDERS	QUARTEROONS	QUEASINESSES	QUESTIONEES	QUIESCENCY
QUARRELERS	QUARTERSAW	QUEBRACHOS	QUESTIONER	QUIESCENTLY
QUARRELING	QUARTERSAWED	QUEECHIEST	QUESTIONERS	QUIETENERS
QUARRELINGS	QUARTERSAWING	QUEENCAKES	QUESTIONING	QUIETENING
QUARRELLED	QUARTERSAWN	QUEENCRAFT	QUESTIONINGLY	QUIETENINGS
QUARRELLER	QUARTERSAWS	QUEENCRAFTS	QUESTIONINGS	QUIETISTIC
QUARRELLERS	QUARTERSTAFF	QUEENFISHES	QUESTIONIST	QUIETNESSES
QUARRELLING	QUARTERSTAFFS	QUEENHOODS	QUESTIONISTS	QUILLBACKS
QUARRELLINGS	QUARTERSTAVES	QUEENLIEST	QUESTIONLESS	QUILLWORKS
QUARRELLOUS	QUARTETTES	QUEENLINESS	QUESTIONLESSLY	QUILLWORTS
QUARRELSOME	QUARTODECIMAN	QUEENLINESSES	QUESTIONNAIRE	QUINACRINE
QUARRELSOMELY	QUARTODECIMANS	QUEENSHIPS	QUESTIONNAIRES	QUINACRINES
QUARRELSOMENESS	QUARTZIEST	QUEENSIDES	QUESTORIAL	QUINALBARBITONE
QUARRENDER	QUARTZIFEROUS	QUEERCORES	QUESTORSHIP	QUINAQUINA
QUARRENDERS	QUARTZITES	QUEERITIES	QUESTORSHIPS	QUINAQUINAS
QUARRIABLE	QUARTZITIC	QUEERNESSES	QUESTRISTS	QUINCENTENARIES
QUARRINGTON	QUASICRYSTAL	QUELQUECHOSE	QUIBBLINGLY	QUINCENTENARY
QUARRINGTONS	QUASICRYSTALS	QUELQUECHOSES	QUIBBLINGS	QUINCENTENNIAL
QUARRYINGS	QUASIPARTICLE	QUENCHABLE	QUICKBEAMS	QUINCENTENNIALS
QUARRYMASTER	QUASIPARTICLES	QUENCHINGS	QUICKENERS	QUINCUNCIAL
QUARRYMASTERS	QUASIPERIODIC	QUENCHLESS	QUICKENING	QUINCUNCIALLY
QUARTATION	QUATERCENTENARY	QUENCHLESSLY	QUICKENINGS	QUINCUNXES
QUARTATIONS	QUATERNARIES	QUERCETINS	QUICKLIMES	QUINCUNXIAL
QUARTERAGE	QUATERNARY	QUERCETUMS	QUICKNESSES	QUINDECAGON
QUARTERAGES	QUATERNATE	QUERCITINS	QUICKSANDS	QUINDECAGONS
QUARTERBACK	QUATERNION	QUERCITRON	QUICKSILVER	QUINDECAPLET
QUARTERBACKED	QUATERNIONIST	QUERCITRONS	QUICKSILVERED	QUINDECAPLETS
QUARTERBACKING	QUATERNIONISTS	QUERIMONIES	QUICKSILVERIER	QUINDECENNIAL
QUARTERBACKINGS	QUATERNIONS	QUERIMONIOUS	QUICKSILVERIEST	QUINDECENNIALS
QUARTERBACKS	QUATERNITIES	QUERIMONIOUSLY	QUICKSILVERING	QUINDECILLION
QUARTERDECK	QUATERNITY	QUERNSTONE	QUICKSILVERINGS	QUINDECILLIONS
QUARTERDECKER	QUATORZAIN	QUERNSTONES	QUICKSILVERISH	QUINGENTENARIES
QUARTERDECKERS	QUATORZAINS	QUERSPRUNG	QUICKSILVERS	QUINGENTENARY
QUARTERDECKS	QUATREFEUILLE	QUERSPRUNGS	QUICKSILVERY	QUINIDINES
QUARTERERS	QUATREFEUILLES	QUERULOUSLY	QUICKSTEPPED	QUINOLINES
QUARTERFINAL	QUATREFOIL	QUERULOUSNESS	QUICKSTEPPING	QUINOLONES
QUARTERFINALIST	QUATREFOILS	QUERULOUSNESSES	QUICKSTEPS	QUINQUAGENARIAN
QUARTERFINALS	QUATTROCENTISM	QUERYINGLY	QUICKTHORN	QUINQUAGESIMAL
QUARTERING	QUATTROCENTISMS	QUESADILLA	QUICKTHORNS	QUINQUECOSTATE

QUINQUEFARIOUS QUINQUIVALENCES QUINTUPLICATES QUIVERINGS QUODLIBETARIAN
QUINQUEFOLIATE QUINQUIVALENCY QUINTUPLICATING QUIVERSFUL QUODLIBETARIANS
QUINQUENNIA QUINQUIVALENT QUINTUPLICATION QUIXOTICAL QUODLIBETIC
QUINQUENNIAD QUINTESSENCE QUINTUPLIES QUIXOTICALLY QUODLIBETICAL
QUINQUENNIADS QUINTESSENCES QUINTUPLING QUIXOTISMS QUODLIBETICALLY
QUINQUENNIAL QUINTESSENTIAL QUIRISTERS QUIXOTRIES QUODLIBETS
QUINQUENNIALLY QUINTESSENTIALS QUIRKINESS QUIZMASTER QUOTABILITIES
QUINQUENNIALS QUINTETTES QUIRKINESSES QUIZMASTERS QUOTABILITY
QUINQUENNIUM QUINTILLION QUISLINGISM QUIZZERIES QUOTABLENESS
QUINQUENNIUMS QUINTILLIONS QUISLINGISMS QUIZZICALITIES QUOTABLENESSES
QUINQUEPARTITE QUINTILLIONTH QUITCLAIMED QUIZZICALITY QUOTATIONS
QUINQUEREME QUINTILLIONTHS QUITCLAIMING QUIZZICALLY QUOTATIOUS
QUINQUEREMES QUINTROONS QUITCLAIMS QUIZZIFICATION QUOTATIVES
QUINQUEVALENCE QUINTUPLED QUITTANCED QUIZZIFICATIONS QUOTEWORTHIER
QUINQUEVALENCES QUINTUPLES QUITTANCES QUIZZIFIED QUOTEWORTHIEST
QUINQUEVALENCY QUINTUPLET QUITTANCING QUIZZIFIES QUOTEWORTHY
QUINQUEVALENT QUINTUPLETS QUIVERFULS QUIZZIFYING QUOTIDIANS
QUINQUINAS QUINTUPLICATE QUIVERIEST QUIZZINESS QUOTITIONS
QUINQUIVALENCE QUINTUPLICATED QUIVERINGLY QUIZZINESSES

Q

R

RABATMENTS	RACEWALKERS	RADIALISES	RADIESTHESIST	RADIOGRAPHIES
RABATTEMENT	RACEWALKING	RADIALISING	RADIESTHESISTS	RADIOGRAPHING
RABATTEMENTS	RACEWALKINGS	RADIALITIES	RADIESTHETIC	RADIOGRAPHS
RABATTINGS	RACHIOTOMIES	RADIALIZATION	RADIOACTIVATE	RADIOGRAPHY
RABBINATES	RACHIOTOMY	RADIALIZATIONS	RADIOACTIVATED	RADIOIODINE
RABBINICAL	RACHISCHISES	RADIALIZED	RADIOACTIVATES	RADIOIODINES
RABBINICALLY	RACHISCHISIS	RADIALIZES	RADIOACTIVATING	RADIOISOTOPE
RABBINISMS	RACHITIDES	RADIALIZING	RADIOACTIVATION	RADIOISOTOPES
RABBINISTIC	RACHITISES	RADIANCIES	RADIOACTIVE	RADIOISOTOPIC
RABBINISTS	RACIALISED	RADIATIONAL	RADIOACTIVELY	RADIOLABEL
RABBINITES	RACIALISES	RADIATIONLESS	RADIOACTIVITIES	RADIOLABELED
RABBITBRUSH	RACIALISING	RADIATIONS	RADIOACTIVITY	RADIOLABELING
RABBITBRUSHES	RACIALISMS	RADICALISATION	RADIOAUTOGRAPH	RADIOLABELLED
RABBITFISH	RACIALISTIC	RADICALISATIONS	RADIOAUTOGRAPHS	RADIOLABELLING
RABBITFISHES	RACIALISTS	RADICALISE	RADIOAUTOGRAPHY	RADIOLABELS
RABBITIEST	RACIALIZED	RADICALISED	RADIOBIOLOGIC	RADIOLARIAN
RABBITINGS	RACIALIZES	RADICALISES	RADIOBIOLOGICAL	RADIOLARIANS
RABBITRIES	RACIALIZING	RADICALISING	RADIOBIOLOGIES	RADIOLOCATION
RABBLEMENT	RACIATIONS	RADICALISM	RADIOBIOLOGIST	RADIOLOCATIONAL
RABBLEMENTS	RACINESSES	RADICALISMS	RADIOBIOLOGISTS	RADIOLOCATIONS
RABIDITIES	RACKABONES	RADICALISTIC	RADIOBIOLOGY	RADIOLOGIC
RABIDNESSES	RACKETEERED	RADICALITIES	RADIOCARBON	RADIOLOGICAL
RACCAHOUTS	RACKETEERING	RADICALITY	RADIOCARBONS	RADIOLOGICALLY
RACECOURSE	RACKETEERINGS	RADICALIZATION	RADIOCHEMICAL	RADIOLOGIES
RACECOURSES	RACKETEERS	RADICALIZATIONS	RADIOCHEMICALLY	RADIOLOGIST
RACEGOINGS	RACKETIEST	RADICALIZE	RADIOCHEMIST	RADIOLOGISTS
RACEHORSES	RACKETRIES	RADICALIZED	RADIOCHEMISTRY	RADIOLUCENCIES
RACEMATION	RACONTEURING	RADICALIZES	RADIOCHEMISTS	RADIOLUCENCY
RACEMATIONS	RACONTEURINGS	RADICALIZING	RADIOECOLOGIES	RADIOLUCENT
RACEMISATION	RACONTEURS	RADICALNESS	RADIOECOLOGY	RADIOLYSES
RACEMISATIONS	RACONTEUSE	RADICALNESSES	RADIOELEMENT	RADIOLYSIS
RACEMISING	RACONTEUSES	RADICATING	RADIOELEMENTS	RADIOLYTIC
RACEMIZATION	RACQUETBALL	RADICATION	RADIOGENIC	RADIOMETER
RACEMIZATIONS	RACQUETBALLS	RADICATIONS	RADIOGOLDS	RADIOMETERS
RACEMIZING	RACQUETING	RADICCHIOS	RADIOGONIOMETER	RADIOMETRIC
RACEMOSELY	RACTOPAMINE	RADICELLOSE	RADIOGONIOMETRY	RADIOMETRICALLY
RACEMOUSLY	RACTOPAMINES	RADICICOLOUS	RADIOGRAMS	RADIOMETRIES
RACETRACKER	RADARSCOPE	RADICIFORM	RADIOGRAPH	RADIOMETRY
RACETRACKERS	RADARSCOPES	RADICIVOROUS	RADIOGRAPHED	RADIOMICROMETER
RACETRACKS	RADIALISATION	RADICULOSE	RADIOGRAPHER	RADIOMIMETIC
RACEWALKED	RADIALISATIONS	RADIESTHESIA	RADIOGRAPHERS	RADIONUCLIDE
RACEWALKER	RADIALISED	RADIESTHESIAS	RADIOGRAPHIC	RADIONUCLIDES

RADIOPACITIES	RADIOTELEPHONE	RAINBOWLIKE	RAMIFICATION	RANGATIRATANGAS
RADIOPACITY	RADIOTELEPHONED	RAINCHECKS	RAMIFICATIONS	RANGEFINDER
RADIOPAGER	RADIOTELEPHONES	RAINFOREST	RAMMISHNESS	RANGEFINDERS
RADIOPAGERS	RADIOTELEPHONIC	RAINFORESTS	RAMMISHNESSES	RANGEFINDING
RADIOPAGING	RADIOTELEPHONY	RAININESSES	RAMOSITIES	RANGEFINDINGS
RADIOPAGINGS	RADIOTELETYPE	RAINMAKERS	RAMPACIOUS	RANGELANDS
RADIOPAQUE	RADIOTELETYPES	RAINMAKING	RAMPAGEOUS	RANGERSHIP
RADIOPHONE	RADIOTHERAPIES	RAINMAKINGS	RAMPAGEOUSLY	RANGERSHIPS
RADIOPHONES	RADIOTHERAPIST	RAINPROOFED	RAMPAGEOUSNESS	RANGINESSES
RADIOPHONIC	RADIOTHERAPISTS	RAINPROOFING	RAMPAGINGS	RANIVOROUS
RADIOPHONICALLY	RADIOTHERAPY	RAINPROOFS	RAMPALLIAN	RANKNESSES
RADIOPHONICS	RADIOTHERMIES	RAINSPOUTS	RAMPALLIANS	RANKSHIFTED
RADIOPHONIES	RADIOTHERMY	RAINSQUALL	RAMPANCIES	RANKSHIFTING
RADIOPHONIST	RADIOTHONS	RAINSQUALLS	RAMPARTING	RANKSHIFTS
RADIOPHONISTS	RADIOTHORIUM	RAINSTICKS	RAMPAUGING	RANSACKERS
RADIOPHONY	RADIOTHORIUMS	RAINSTORMS	RAMRODDING	RANSACKING
RADIOPHOSPHORUS	RADIOTOXIC	RAINWASHED	RAMSHACKLE	RANSACKINGS
RADIOPHOTO	RADIOTRACER	RAINWASHES	RANCELLING	RANSHACKLE
RADIOPHOTOS	RADIOTRACERS	RAINWASHING	RANCHERIAS	RANSHACKLED
RADIOPROTECTION	RADULIFORM	RAINWATERS	RANCHERIES	RANSHACKLES
RADIOPROTECTIVE	RAFFINATES	RAISINIEST	RANCHETTES	RANSHACKLING
RADIORESISTANT	RAFFINOSES	RAISONNEUR	RANCHLANDS	RANSHAKLED
RADIOSCOPE	RAFFISHNESS	RAISONNEURS	RANCIDITIES	RANSHAKLES
RADIOSCOPES	RAFFISHNESSES	RAIYATWARI	RANCIDNESS	RANSHAKLING
RADIOSCOPIC	RAFFLESIAS	RAIYATWARIS	RANCIDNESSES	RANSOMABLE
RADIOSCOPICALLY	RAFTERINGS	RAJAHSHIPS	RANCOROUSLY	RANSOMLESS
RADIOSCOPIES	RAGAMUFFIN	RAJPRAMUKH	RANCOROUSNESS	RANSOMWARE
RADIOSCOPY	RAGAMUFFINS	RAJPRAMUKHS	RANCOROUSNESSES	RANSOMWARES
RADIOSENSITISE	RAGGAMUFFIN	RAKEHELLIER	RANDINESSES	RANTERISMS
RADIOSENSITISED	RAGGAMUFFINS	RAKEHELLIEST	RANDOMISATION	RANTIPOLED
RADIOSENSITISES	RAGGEDIEST	RAKESHAMES	RANDOMISATIONS	RANTIPOLES
RADIOSENSITIVE	RAGGEDNESS	RAKISHNESS	RANDOMISED	RANTIPOLING
RADIOSENSITIZE	RAGGEDNESSES	RAKISHNESSES	RANDOMISER	RANUNCULACEOUS
RADIOSENSITIZED	RAGMATICAL	RALLENTANDI	RANDOMISERS	RANUNCULUS
RADIOSENSITIZES	RAGPICKERS	RALLENTANDO	RANDOMISES	RANUNCULUSES
RADIOSONDE	RAILBUSSES	RALLENTANDOS	RANDOMISING	RAPACIOUSLY
RADIOSONDES	RAILLERIES	RALLYCROSS	RANDOMIZATION	RAPACIOUSNESS
RADIOSTRONTIUM	RAILROADED	RALLYCROSSES	RANDOMIZATIONS	RAPACIOUSNESSES
RADIOSTRONTIUMS	RAILROADER	RALLYINGLY	RANDOMIZED	RAPACITIES
RADIOTELEGRAM	RAILROADERS	RAMAPITHECINE	RANDOMIZER	RAPIDITIES
RADIOTELEGRAMS	RAILROADING	RAMAPITHECINES	RANDOMIZERS	RAPIDNESSES
RADIOTELEGRAPH	RAILROADINGS	RAMBLINGLY	RANDOMIZES	RAPIERLIKE
RADIOTELEGRAPHS	RAILWAYMAN	RAMBOUILLET	RANDOMIZING	RAPPELLING
RADIOTELEGRAPHY	RAILWAYMEN	RAMBOUILLETS	RANDOMNESS	RAPPELLINGS
RADIOTELEMETER	RAILWORKER	RAMBUNCTIOUS	RANDOMNESSES	RAPPORTAGE
RADIOTELEMETERS	RAILWORKERS	RAMBUNCTIOUSLY	RANDOMWISE	RAPPORTAGES
RADIOTELEMETRIC	RAINBOWIER	RAMENTACEOUS	RANGATIRAS	RAPPORTEUR
RADIOTELEMETRY	RAINBOWIEST	RAMGUNSHOCH	RANGATIRATANGA	RAPPORTEURS

R

RAPPROCHEMENT	RATABILITY	RATIONALIZABLE	RAYGRASSES	REACCUSTOMS
RAPPROCHEMENTS	RATABLENESS	RATIONALIZATION	RAYLESSNESS	REACQUAINT
RAPSCALLION	RATABLENESSES	RATIONALIZE	RAYLESSNESSES	REACQUAINTANCE
RAPSCALLIONS	RATAPLANNED	RATIONALIZED	RAZMATAZES	REACQUAINTANCES
RAPTATORIAL	RATAPLANNING	RATIONALIZER	RAZORBACKS	REACQUAINTED
RAPTNESSES	RATATOUILLE	RATIONALIZERS	RAZORBILLS	REACQUAINTING
RAPTURELESS	RATATOUILLES	RATIONALIZES	RAZORCLAMS	REACQUAINTS
RAPTURISED	RATBAGGERIES	RATIONALIZING	RAZORFISHES	REACQUIRED
RAPTURISES	RATBAGGERY	RATIONALLY	RAZZAMATAZZ	REACQUIRES
RAPTURISING	RATCHETING	RATIONALNESS	RAZZAMATAZZES	REACQUIRING
RAPTURISTS	RATEABILITIES	RATIONALNESSES	RAZZBERRIES	REACQUISITION
RAPTURIZED	RATEABILITY	RATIONINGS	RAZZMATAZZ	REACQUISITIONS
RAPTURIZES	RATEABLENESS	RATTENINGS	RAZZMATAZZES	REACTANCES
RAPTURIZING	RATEABLENESSES	RATTINESSES	REABSORBED	REACTIONAL
RAPTUROUSLY	RATEMETERS	RATTLEBAGS	REABSORBING	REACTIONARIES
RAPTUROUSNESS	RATEPAYERS	RATTLEBOXES	REABSORPTION	REACTIONARISM
RAPTUROUSNESSES	RATHERIPES	RATTLEBRAIN	REABSORPTIONS	REACTIONARISMS
RAREFACTION	RATHSKELLER	RATTLEBRAINED	REACCEDING	REACTIONARIST
RAREFACTIONAL	RATHSKELLERS	RATTLEBRAINS	REACCELERATE	REACTIONARISTS
RAREFACTIONS	RATIFIABLE	RATTLEPODS	REACCELERATED	REACTIONARY
RAREFACTIVE	RATIFICATION	RATTLESNAKE	REACCELERATES	REACTIONARYISM
RAREFIABLE	RATIFICATIONS	RATTLESNAKES	REACCELERATING	REACTIONARYISMS
RAREFICATION	RATIOCINATE	RATTLETRAP	REACCENTED	REACTIONISM
RAREFICATIONAL	RATIOCINATED	RATTLETRAPS	REACCENTING	REACTIONISMS
RAREFICATIONS	RATIOCINATES	RATTLINGLY	REACCEPTED	REACTIONIST
RARENESSES	RATIOCINATING	RATTOONING	REACCEPTING	REACTIONISTS
RASCAILLES	RATIOCINATION	RAUCOUSNESS	REACCESSION	REACTIVATE
RASCALDOMS	RATIOCINATIONS	RAUCOUSNESSES	REACCESSIONS	REACTIVATED
RASCALISMS	RATIOCINATIVE	RAUNCHIEST	REACCLAIMED	REACTIVATES
RASCALITIES	RATIOCINATOR	RAUNCHINESS	REACCLAIMING	REACTIVATING
RASCALLIER	RATIOCINATORS	RAUNCHINESSES	REACCLAIMS	REACTIVATION
RASCALLIEST	RATIOCINATORY	RAUWOLFIAS	REACCLIMATISE	REACTIVATIONS
RASCALLION	RATIONALES	RAVAGEMENT	REACCLIMATISED	REACTIVELY
RASCALLIONS	RATIONALISABLE	RAVAGEMENTS	REACCLIMATISES	REACTIVENESS
RASHNESSES	RATIONALISATION	RAVELLIEST	REACCLIMATISING	REACTIVENESSES
RASPATORIES	RATIONALISE	RAVELLINGS	REACCLIMATIZE	REACTIVITIES
RASPBERRIES	RATIONALISED	RAVELMENTS	REACCLIMATIZED	REACTIVITY
RASPINESSES	RATIONALISER	RAVENINGLY	REACCLIMATIZES	REACTUATED
RASTAFARIAN	RATIONALISERS	RAVENOUSLY	REACCLIMATIZING	REACTUATES
RASTAFARIANS	RATIONALISES	RAVENOUSNESS	REACCREDIT	REACTUATING
RASTAFARIS	RATIONALISING	RAVENOUSNESSES	REACCREDITATION	READABILITIES
RASTERISED	RATIONALISM	RAVIGOTTES	REACCREDITED	READABILITY
RASTERISES	RATIONALISMS	RAVISHINGLY	REACCREDITING	READABLENESS
RASTERISING	RATIONALIST	RAVISHMENT	REACCREDITS	READABLENESSES
RASTERIZED	RATIONALISTIC	RAVISHMENTS	REACCUSING	READAPTATION
RASTERIZES	RATIONALISTS	RAWINSONDE	REACCUSTOM	READAPTATIONS
RASTERIZING	RATIONALITIES	RAWINSONDES	REACCUSTOMED	READAPTING
RATABILITIES	RATIONALITY	RAWMAISHES	REACCUSTOMING	READDICTED

READDICTING	REAFFIRMED	REAMENDMENT	REAPPRAISEMENTS	REASSEMBLAGE
READDRESSED	REAFFIRMING	REAMENDMENTS	REAPPRAISER	REASSEMBLAGES
READDRESSES	REAFFIXING	REANALYSED	REAPPRAISERS	REASSEMBLE
READDRESSING	REAFFOREST	REANALYSES	REAPPRAISES	REASSEMBLED
READERLIER	REAFFORESTATION	REANALYSING	REAPPRAISING	REASSEMBLES
READERLIEST	REAFFORESTED	REANALYSIS	REAPPROPRIATE	REASSEMBLIES
READERSHIP	REAFFORESTING	REANALYZED	REAPPROPRIATED	REASSEMBLING
READERSHIPS	REAFFORESTS	REANALYZES	REAPPROPRIATES	REASSEMBLY
READINESSES	REAGENCIES	REANALYZING	REAPPROPRIATING	REASSERTED
READJUSTABLE	REAGGREGATE	REANIMATED	REAPPROVED	REASSERTING
READJUSTED	REAGGREGATED	REANIMATES	REAPPROVES	REASSERTION
READJUSTER	REAGGREGATES	REANIMATING	REAPPROVING	REASSERTIONS
READJUSTERS	REAGGREGATING	REANIMATION	REARGUARDS	REASSESSED
READJUSTING	REAGGREGATION	REANIMATIONS	REARGUMENT	REASSESSES
READJUSTMENT	REAGGREGATIONS	REANNEXATION	REARGUMENTS	REASSESSING
READJUSTMENTS	REALIGNING	REANNEXATIONS	REARHORSES	REASSESSMENT
READMISSION	REALIGNMENT	REANNEXING	REARMAMENT	REASSESSMENTS
READMISSIONS	REALIGNMENTS	REANOINTED	REARMAMENTS	REASSIGNED
READMITTANCE	REALISABILITIES	REANOINTING	REAROUSALS	REASSIGNING
READMITTANCES	REALISABILITY	REANSWERED	REAROUSING	REASSIGNMENT
READMITTED	REALISABLE	REANSWERING	REARRANGED	REASSIGNMENTS
READMITTING	REALISABLY	REAPPARELED	REARRANGEMENT	REASSORTED
READOPTING	REALISATION	REAPPARELING	REARRANGEMENTS	REASSORTING
READOPTION	REALISATIONS	REAPPARELLED	REARRANGER	REASSORTMENT
READOPTIONS	REALISTICALLY	REAPPARELLING	REARRANGERS	REASSORTMENTS
READORNING	REALIZABILITIES	REAPPARELS	REARRANGES	REASSUMING
READVANCED	REALIZABILITY	REAPPEARANCE	REARRANGING	REASSUMPTION
READVANCES	REALIZABLE	REAPPEARANCES	REARRESTED	REASSUMPTIONS
READVANCING	REALIZABLY	REAPPEARED	REARRESTING	REASSURANCE
READVERTISE	REALIZATION	REAPPEARING	REARTICULATE	REASSURANCES
READVERTISED	REALIZATIONS	REAPPLICATION	REARTICULATED	REASSURERS
READVERTISEMENT	REALLOCATE	REAPPLICATIONS	REARTICULATES	REASSURING
READVERTISES	REALLOCATED	REAPPLYING	REARTICULATING	REASSURINGLY
READVERTISING	REALLOCATES	REAPPOINTED	REASCENDED	REASTINESS
READVERTIZE	REALLOCATING	REAPPOINTING	REASCENDING	REASTINESSES
READVERTIZED	REALLOCATION	REAPPOINTMENT	REASCENSION	REATTACHED
READVERTIZEMENT	REALLOCATIONS	REAPPOINTMENTS	REASCENSIONS	REATTACHES
READVERTIZES	REALLOTMENT	REAPPOINTS	REASONABILITIES	REATTACHING
READVERTIZING	REALLOTMENTS	REAPPORTION	REASONABILITY	REATTACHMENT
READVISING	REALLOTTED	REAPPORTIONED	REASONABLE	REATTACHMENTS
READYMADES	REALLOTTING	REAPPORTIONING	REASONABLENESS	REATTACKED
READEDIFIED	REALNESSES	REAPPORTIONMENT	REASONABLY	REATTACKING
REAEDIFIES	REALPOLITIK	REAPPORTIONS	REASONEDLY	REATTAINED
REAEDIFYED	REALPOLITIKER	REAPPRAISAL	REASONINGS	REATTAINING
REAEDIFYES	REALPOLITIKERS	REAPPRAISALS	REASONLESS	REATTEMPTED
REAEDIFYING	REALPOLITIKS	REAPPRAISE	REASONLESSLY	REATTEMPTING
REAFFIRMATION	REALTERING	REAPPRAISED	REASSAILED	REATTEMPTS
REAFFIRMATIONS	REAMENDING	REAPPRAISEMENT	REASSAILING	REATTRIBUTE

REATTRIBUTED	REBLOOMING	RECALESCED	RECAPPABLE	RECEPTIBILITIES
REATTRIBUTES	REBLOSSOMED	RECALESCENCE	RECAPTIONS	RECEPTIBILITY
REATTRIBUTING	REBLOSSOMING	RECALESCENCES	RECAPTURED	RECEPTIBLE
REATTRIBUTION	REBLOSSOMS	RECALESCENT	RECAPTURER	RECEPTIONIST
REATTRIBUTIONS	REBOARDING	RECALESCES	RECAPTURERS	RECEPTIONISTS
REAUTHORISATION	REBOATIONS	RECALESCING	RECAPTURES	RECEPTIONS
REAUTHORISE	REBORROWED	RECALIBRATE	RECAPTURING	RECEPTIVELY
REAUTHORISED	REBORROWING	RECALIBRATED	RECARPETED	RECEPTIVENESS
REAUTHORISES	REBOTTLING	RECALIBRATES	RECARPETING	RECEPTIVENESSES
REAUTHORISING	REBOUNDERS	RECALIBRATING	RECARRYING	RECEPTIVITIES
REAUTHORIZATION	REBOUNDING	RECALIBRATION	RECATALOGED	RECEPTIVITY
REAUTHORIZE	REBOUNDINGS	RECALIBRATIONS	RECATALOGING	RECERTIFICATION
REAUTHORIZED	REBRANCHED	RECALLABILITIES	RECATALOGS	RECERTIFIED
REAUTHORIZES	REBRANCHES	RECALLABILITY	RECATALOGUE	RECERTIFIES
REAUTHORIZING	REBRANCHING	RECALLABLE	RECATALOGUED	RECERTIFYING
REAVAILING	REBRANDING	RECALLMENT	RECATALOGUES	RECESSIONAL
REAWAKENED	REBRANDINGS	RECALLMENTS	RECATALOGUING	RECESSIONALS
REAWAKENING	REBREEDING	RECALMENTS	RECATCHING	RECESSIONARY
REAWAKENINGS	REBROADCAST	RECANALISATION	RECAUTIONED	RECESSIONISTA
REBALANCED	REBROADCASTED	RECANALISATIONS	RECAUTIONING	RECESSIONISTAS
REBALANCES	REBROADCASTING	RECANALISE	RECAUTIONS	RECESSIONS
REBALANCING	REBROADCASTS	RECANALISED	RECEIPTING	RECESSIVELY
REBAPTISED	REBUILDING	RECANALISES	RECEIPTORS	RECESSIVENESS
REBAPTISES	REBUILDINGS	RECANALISING	RECEIVABILITIES	RECESSIVENESSES
REBAPTISING	REBUKEFULLY	RECANALIZATION	RECEIVABILITY	RECESSIVES
REBAPTISMS	REBUKINGLY	RECANALIZATIONS	RECEIVABLE	RECHALLENGE
REBAPTIZED	REBUTMENTS	RECANALIZE	RECEIVABLENESS	RECHALLENGED
REBAPTIZES	REBUTTABLE	RECANALIZED	RECEIVABLES	RECHALLENGES
REBAPTIZING	REBUTTONED	RECANALIZES	RECEIVERSHIP	RECHALLENGING
REBARBATIVE	REBUTTONING	RECANALIZING	RECEIVERSHIPS	RECHANGING
REBARBATIVELY	RECALCITRANCE	RECANTATION	RECEIVINGS	RECHANNELED
REBATEABLE	RECALCITRANCES	RECANTATIONS	RECEMENTED	RECHANNELING
REBATEMENT	RECALCITRANCIES	RECAPITALISE	RECEMENTING	RECHANNELLED
REBATEMENTS	RECALCITRANCY	RECAPITALISED	RECENSIONS	RECHANNELLING
REBBETZINS	RECALCITRANT	RECAPITALISES	RECENSORED	RECHANNELS
REBEGINNING	RECALCITRANTS	RECAPITALISING	RECENSORING	RECHARGEABLE
REBELLIONS	RECALCITRATE	RECAPITALIZE	RECENTNESS	RECHARGERS
REBELLIOUS	RECALCITRATED	RECAPITALIZED	RECENTNESSES	RECHARGING
REBELLIOUSLY	RECALCITRATES	RECAPITALIZES	RECENTRIFUGE	RECHARTERED
REBELLIOUSNESS	RECALCITRATING	RECAPITALIZING	RECENTRIFUGED	RECHARTERING
REBELLOWED	RECALCITRATION	RECAPITULATE	RECENTRIFUGES	RECHARTERS
REBELLOWING	RECALCITRATIONS	RECAPITULATED	RECENTRIFUGING	RECHARTING
REBIRTHERS	RECALCULATE	RECAPITULATES	RECENTRING	RECHAUFFES
REBIRTHING	RECALCULATED	RECAPITULATING	RECEPTACLE	RECHEATING
REBIRTHINGS	RECALCULATES	RECAPITULATION	RECEPTACLES	RECHECKING
REBLENDING	RECALCULATING	RECAPITULATIONS	RECEPTACULA	RECHIPPING
REBLOCHONS	RECALCULATION	RECAPITULATIVE	RECEPTACULAR	RECHIPPINGS
REBLOOMERS	RECALCULATIONS	RECAPITULATORY	RECEPTACULUM	RECHOOSING

RECHOREOGRAPH	RECITATIONIST	RECOGNISANCE	RECOLONIZATION	RECOMMITTING
RECHOREOGRAPHED	RECITATIONISTS	RECOGNISANCES	RECOLONIZATIONS	RECOMPACTED
RECHOREOGRAPHS	RECITATIONS	RECOGNISANT	RECOLONIZE	RECOMPACTING
RECHRISTEN	RECITATIVE	RECOGNISED	RECOLONIZED	RECOMPACTS
RECHRISTENED	RECITATIVES	RECOGNISEE	RECOLONIZES	RECOMPENCE
RECHRISTENING	RECITATIVI	RECOGNISEES	RECOLONIZING	RECOMPENCES
RECHRISTENS	RECITATIVO	RECOGNISER	RECOLORING	RECOMPENSABLE
RECHROMATOGRAPH	RECITATIVOS	RECOGNISERS	RECOLOURED	RECOMPENSE
RECIDIVISM	RECKLESSLY	RECOGNISES	RECOLOURING	RECOMPENSED
RECIDIVISMS	RECKLESSNESS	RECOGNISING	RECOMBINANT	RECOMPENSER
RECIDIVIST	RECKLESSNESSES	RECOGNISOR	RECOMBINANTS	RECOMPENSERS
RECIDIVISTIC	RECKONINGS	RECOGNISORS	RECOMBINATION	RECOMPENSES
RECIDIVISTS	RECLADDING	RECOGNITION	RECOMBINATIONAL	RECOMPENSING
RECIDIVOUS	RECLAIMABLE	RECOGNITIONS	RECOMBINATIONS	RECOMPILATION
RECIPIENCE	RECLAIMABLY	RECOGNITIVE	RECOMBINED	RECOMPILATIONS
RECIPIENCES	RECLAIMANT	RECOGNITORY	RECOMBINES	RECOMPILED
RECIPIENCIES	RECLAIMANTS	RECOGNIZABILITY	RECOMBINING	RECOMPILES
RECIPIENCY	RECLAIMERS	RECOGNIZABLE	RECOMFORTED	RECOMPILING
RECIPIENTS	RECLAIMING	RECOGNIZABLY	RECOMFORTING	RECOMPOSED
RECIPROCAL	RECLAMATION	RECOGNIZANCE	RECOMFORTLESS	RECOMPOSES
RECIPROCALITIES	RECLAMATIONS	RECOGNIZANCES	RECOMFORTS	RECOMPOSING
RECIPROCALITY	RECLASPING	RECOGNIZANT	RECOMFORTURE	RECOMPOSITION
RECIPROCALLY	RECLASSIFIED	RECOGNIZED	RECOMFORTURES	RECOMPOSITIONS
RECIPROCALS	RECLASSIFIES	RECOGNIZEE	RECOMMENCE	RECOMPRESS
RECIPROCANT	RECLASSIFY	RECOGNIZEES	RECOMMENCED	RECOMPRESSED
RECIPROCANTS	RECLASSIFYING	RECOGNIZER	RECOMMENCEMENT	RECOMPRESSES
RECIPROCATE	RECLEANING	RECOGNIZERS	RECOMMENCEMENTS	RECOMPRESSING
RECIPROCATED	RECLIMBING	RECOGNIZES	RECOMMENCES	RECOMPRESSION
RECIPROCATES	RECLINABLE	RECOGNIZING	RECOMMENCING	RECOMPRESSIONS
RECIPROCATING	RECLINATION	RECOGNIZOR	RECOMMENDABLE	RECOMPUTATION
RECIPROCATION	RECLINATIONS	RECOGNIZORS	RECOMMENDABLY	RECOMPUTATIONS
RECIPROCATIONS	RECLOSABLE	RECOILLESS	RECOMMENDATION	RECOMPUTED
RECIPROCATIVE	RECLOTHING	RECOINAGES	RECOMMENDATIONS	RECOMPUTES
RECIPROCATOR	RECLUSENESS	RECOLLECTED	RECOMMENDATORY	RECOMPUTING
RECIPROCATORS	RECLUSENESSES	RECOLLECTEDLY	RECOMMENDED	RECONCEIVE
RECIPROCATORY	RECLUSIONS	RECOLLECTEDNESS	RECOMMENDER	RECONCEIVED
RECIPROCITIES	RECLUSIVELY	RECOLLECTING	RECOMMENDERS	RECONCEIVES
RECIPROCITY	RECLUSIVENESS	RECOLLECTION	RECOMMENDING	RECONCEIVING
RECIRCLING	RECLUSIVENESSES	RECOLLECTIONS	RECOMMENDS	RECONCENTRATE
RECIRCULATE	RECLUSORIES	RECOLLECTIVE	RECOMMISSION	RECONCENTRATED
RECIRCULATED	RECODIFICATION	RECOLLECTIVELY	RECOMMISSIONED	RECONCENTRATES
RECIRCULATES	RECODIFICATIONS	RECOLLECTS	RECOMMISSIONING	RECONCENTRATING
RECIRCULATING	RECODIFIED	RECOLONISATION	RECOMMISSIONS	RECONCENTRATION
RECIRCULATION	RECODIFIES	RECOLONISATIONS	RECOMMITMENT	RECONCEPTION
RECIRCULATIONS	RECODIFYING	RECOLONISE	RECOMMITMENTS	RECONCEPTIONS
RECITALIST	RECOGNISABILITY	RECOLONISED	RECOMMITTAL	RECONCEPTUALISE
RECITALISTS	RECOGNISABLE	RECOLONISES	RECOMMITTALS	RECONCEPTUALIZE
RECITATION	RECOGNISABLY	RECOLONISING	RECOMMITTED	RECONCILABILITY

RECONCILABLE	RECONNECTIONS	RECONSTITUTED	RECONVERTS	RECREATIONISTS
RECONCILABLY	RECONNECTS	RECONSTITUTES	RECONVEYANCE	RECREATIONS
RECONCILED	RECONNOISSANCE	RECONSTITUTING	RECONVEYANCES	RECREATIVE
RECONCILEMENT	RECONNOISSANCES	RECONSTITUTION	RECONVEYED	RECREATIVELY
RECONCILEMENTS	RECONNOITER	RECONSTITUTIONS	RECONVEYING	RECREATORS
RECONCILER	RECONNOITERED	RECONSTRUCT	RECONVICTED	RECREMENTAL
RECONCILERS	RECONNOITERER	RECONSTRUCTED	RECONVICTING	RECREMENTITIAL
RECONCILES	RECONNOITERERS	RECONSTRUCTIBLE	RECONVICTION	RECREMENTITIOUS
RECONCILIATION	RECONNOITERING	RECONSTRUCTING	RECONVICTIONS	RECREMENTS
RECONCILIATIONS	RECONNOITERS	RECONSTRUCTION	RECONVICTS	RECRIMINATE
RECONCILIATORY	RECONNOITRE	RECONSTRUCTIONS	RECONVINCE	RECRIMINATED
RECONCILING	RECONNOITRED	RECONSTRUCTIVE	RECONVINCED	RECRIMINATES
RECONDENSATION	RECONNOITRER	RECONSTRUCTOR	RECONVINCES	RECRIMINATING
RECONDENSATIONS	RECONNOITRERS	RECONSTRUCTORS	RECONVINCING	RECRIMINATION
RECONDENSE	RECONNOITRES	RECONSTRUCTS	RECORDABLE	RECRIMINATIONS
RECONDENSED	RECONNOITRING	RECONSULTED	RECORDATION	RECRIMINATIVE
RECONDENSES	RECONNOITRINGS	RECONSULTING	RECORDATIONS	RECRIMINATOR
RECONDENSING	RECONQUERED	RECONSULTS	RECORDERSHIP	RECRIMINATORS
RECONDITELY	RECONQUERING	RECONTACTED	RECORDERSHIPS	RECRIMINATORY
RECONDITENESS	RECONQUERS	RECONTACTING	RECORDINGS	RECROSSING
RECONDITENESSES	RECONQUEST	RECONTACTS	RECORDISTS	RECROWNING
RECONDITION	RECONQUESTS	RECONTAMINATE	RECOUNTALS	RECRUDESCE
RECONDITIONED	RECONSECRATE	RECONTAMINATED	RECOUNTERS	RECRUDESCED
RECONDITIONING	RECONSECRATED	RECONTAMINATES	RECOUNTING	RECRUDESCENCE
RECONDITIONS	RECONSECRATES	RECONTAMINATING	RECOUNTMENT	RECRUDESCENCES
RECONDUCTED	RECONSECRATING	RECONTAMINATION	RECOUNTMENTS	RECRUDESCENCIES
RECONDUCTING	RECONSECRATION	RECONTEXTUALISE	RECOUPABLE	RECRUDESCENCY
RECONDUCTS	RECONSECRATIONS	RECONTEXTUALIZE	RECOUPLING	RECRUDESCENT
RECONFERRED	RECONSIDER	RECONTINUE	RECOUPMENT	RECRUDESCES
RECONFERRING	RECONSIDERATION	RECONTINUED	RECOUPMENTS	RECRUDESCING
RECONFIGURATION	RECONSIDERED	RECONTINUES	RECOURSING	RECRUITABLE
RECONFIGURE	RECONSIDERING	RECONTINUING	RECOVERABILITY	RECRUITALS
RECONFIGURED	RECONSIDERS	RECONTOURED	RECOVERABLE	RECRUITERS
RECONFIGURES	RECONSIGNED	RECONTOURING	RECOVERABLENESS	RECRUITING
RECONFIGURING	RECONSIGNING	RECONTOURS	RECOVEREES	RECRUITINGS
RECONFINED	RECONSIGNS	RECONVALESCE	RECOVERERS	RECRUITMENT
RECONFINES	RECONSOLED	RECONVALESCED	RECOVERIES	RECRUITMENTS
RECONFINING	RECONSOLES	RECONVALESCENCE	RECOVERING	RECRYSTALLISE
RECONFIRMATION	RECONSOLIDATE	RECONVALESCENT	RECOVERORS	RECRYSTALLISED
RECONFIRMATIONS	RECONSOLIDATED	RECONVALESCES	RECOWERING	RECRYSTALLISES
RECONFIRMED	RECONSOLIDATES	RECONVALESCING	RECREANCES	RECRYSTALLISING
RECONFIRMING	RECONSOLIDATING	RECONVENED	RECREANCIES	RECRYSTALLIZE
RECONFIRMS	RECONSOLIDATION	RECONVENES	RECREANTLY	RECRYSTALLIZED
RECONNAISSANCE	RECONSOLING	RECONVENING	RECREATING	RECRYSTALLIZES
RECONNAISSANCES	RECONSTITUENT	RECONVERSION	RECREATION	RECRYSTALLIZING
RECONNECTED	RECONSTITUENTS	RECONVERSIONS	RECREATIONAL	RECTANGLED
RECONNECTING	RECONSTITUTABLE	RECONVERTED	RECREATIONALLY	RECTANGLES
RECONNECTION	RECONSTITUTE	RECONVERTING	RECREATIONIST	RECTANGULAR

RECTANGULARITY	RECUPERATORS	REDEDICATE	REDESCENDS	REDISCOUNT
RECTANGULARLY	RECUPERATORY	REDEDICATED	REDESCRIBE	REDISCOUNTABLE
RECTIFIABILITY	RECURELESS	REDEDICATES	REDESCRIBED	REDISCOUNTED
RECTIFIABLE	RECURRENCE	REDEDICATING	REDESCRIBES	REDISCOUNTING
RECTIFICATION	RECURRENCES	REDEDICATION	REDESCRIBING	REDISCOUNTS
RECTIFICATIONS	RECURRENCIES	REDEDICATIONS	REDESCRIPTION	REDISCOVER
RECTIFIERS	RECURRENCY	REDEEMABILITIES	REDESCRIPTIONS	REDISCOVERED
RECTIFYING	RECURRENTLY	REDEEMABILITY	REDESIGNED	REDISCOVERER
RECTILINEAL	RECURRINGLY	REDEEMABLE	REDESIGNING	REDISCOVERERS
RECTILINEALLY	RECURSIONS	REDEEMABLENESS	REDETERMINATION	REDISCOVERIES
RECTILINEAR	RECURSIVELY	REDEEMABLY	REDETERMINE	REDISCOVERING
RECTILINEARITY	RECURSIVENESS	REDEEMLESS	REDETERMINED	REDISCOVERS
RECTILINEARLY	RECURSIVENESSES	REDEFEATED	REDETERMINES	REDISCOVERY
RECTIPETALIES	RECURVIROSTRAL	REDEFEATING	REDETERMINING	REDISCUSSED
RECTIPETALITIES	RECUSANCES	REDEFECTED	REDEVELOPED	REDISCUSSES
RECTIPETALITY	RECUSANCIES	REDEFECTING	REDEVELOPER	REDISCUSSING
RECTIPETALY	RECUSATION	REDEFINING	REDEVELOPERS	REDISPLAYED
RECTIROSTRAL	RECUSATIONS	REDEFINITION	REDEVELOPING	REDISPLAYING
RECTISERIAL	RECYCLABLE	REDEFINITIONS	REDEVELOPMENT	REDISPLAYS
RECTITISES	RECYCLABLES	REDELIVERANCE	REDEVELOPMENTS	REDISPOSED
RECTITUDES	RECYCLATES	REDELIVERANCES	REDEVELOPS	REDISPOSES
RECTITUDINOUS	RECYCLEABLE	REDELIVERED	REDIALLING	REDISPOSING
RECTOCELES	RECYCLEABLES	REDELIVERER	REDICTATED	REDISPOSITION
RECTORATES	RECYCLINGS	REDELIVERERS	REDICTATES	REDISPOSITIONS
RECTORESSES	RECYCLISTS	REDELIVERIES	REDICTATING	REDISSOLUTION
RECTORIALS	REDACTIONAL	REDELIVERING	REDIGESTED	REDISSOLUTIONS
RECTORSHIP	REDACTIONS	REDELIVERS	REDIGESTING	REDISSOLVE
RECTORSHIPS	REDACTORIAL	REDELIVERY	REDIGESTION	REDISSOLVED
RECTRESSES	REDAMAGING	REDEMANDED	REDIGESTIONS	REDISSOLVES
RECTRICIAL	REDARGUING	REDEMANDING	REDIGRESSED	REDISSOLVING
RECULTIVATE	REDBAITERS	REDEMPTIBLE	REDIGRESSES	REDISTILLATION
RECULTIVATED	REDBAITING	REDEMPTION	REDIGRESSING	REDISTILLATIONS
RECULTIVATES	REDBELLIES	REDEMPTIONAL	REDINGOTES	REDISTILLED
RECULTIVATING	REDBREASTS	REDEMPTIONER	REDINTEGRATE	REDISTILLING
RECUMBENCE	REDCURRANT	REDEMPTIONERS	REDINTEGRATED	REDISTILLS
RECUMBENCES	REDCURRANTS	REDEMPTIONS	REDINTEGRATES	REDISTRIBUTE
RECUMBENCIES	REDDISHNESS	REDEMPTIVE	REDINTEGRATING	REDISTRIBUTED
RECUMBENCY	REDDISHNESSES	REDEMPTIVELY	REDINTEGRATION	REDISTRIBUTES
RECUMBENTLY	REDECIDING	REDEMPTORY	REDINTEGRATIONS	REDISTRIBUTING
RECUPERABLE	REDECORATE	REDEPLOYED	REDINTEGRATIVE	REDISTRIBUTION
RECUPERATE	REDECORATED	REDEPLOYING	REDIRECTED	REDISTRIBUTIONS
RECUPERATED	REDECORATES	REDEPLOYMENT	REDIRECTING	REDISTRIBUTIVE
RECUPERATES	REDECORATING	REDEPLOYMENTS	REDIRECTION	REDISTRICT
RECUPERATING	REDECORATION	REDEPOSITED	REDIRECTIONS	REDISTRICTED
RECUPERATION	REDECORATIONS	REDEPOSITING	REDISBURSE	REDISTRICTING
RECUPERATIONS	REDECORATOR	REDEPOSITS	REDISBURSED	REDISTRICTINGS
RECUPERATIVE	REDECORATORS	REDESCENDED	REDISBURSES	REDISTRICTS
RECUPERATOR	REDECRAFTS	REDESCENDING	REDISBURSING	REDIVIDING

REDIVISION

REDIVISION	REDUCTIVELY	REEMBROIDERS	REENGRAVED	REEVALUATION
REDIVISIONS	REDUCTIVENESS	REEMERGENCE	REENGRAVES	REEVALUATIONS
REDIVORCED	REDUCTIVENESSES	REEMERGENCES	REENGRAVING	REEVESHIPS
REDIVORCES	REDUCTIVES	REEMERGING	REENJOYING	REEXAMINATION
REDIVORCING	REDUNDANCE	REEMISSION	REENLARGED	REEXAMINATIONS
REDLININGS	REDUNDANCES	REEMISSIONS	REENLARGES	REEXAMINED
REDOLENCES	REDUNDANCIES	REEMITTING	REENLARGING	REEXAMINES
REDOLENCIES	REDUNDANCY	REEMPHASES	REENLISTED	REEXAMINING
REDOLENTLY	REDUNDANTLY	REEMPHASIS	REENLISTING	REEXECUTED
REDOUBLEMENT	REDUPLICATE	REEMPHASISE	REENLISTMENT	REEXECUTES
REDOUBLEMENTS	REDUPLICATED	REEMPHASISED	REENLISTMENTS	REEXECUTING
REDOUBLERS	REDUPLICATES	REEMPHASISES	REENROLLED	REEXHIBITED
REDOUBLING	REDUPLICATING	REEMPHASISING	REENROLLING	REEXHIBITING
REDOUBTABLE	REDUPLICATION	REEMPHASIZE	REENSLAVED	REEXHIBITS
REDOUBTABLENESS	REDUPLICATIONS	REEMPHASIZED	REENSLAVES	REEXPELLED
REDOUBTABLY	REDUPLICATIVE	REEMPHASIZES	REENSLAVING	REEXPELLING
REDOUBTING	REDUPLICATIVELY	REEMPHASIZING	REENTERING	REEXPERIENCE
REDOUNDING	REEDIFYING	REEMPLOYED	REENTHRONE	REEXPERIENCED
REDOUNDINGS	REEDINESSES	REEMPLOYING	REENTHRONED	REEXPERIENCES
REDRAFTING	REEDITIONS	REEMPLOYMENT	REENTHRONES	REEXPERIENCING
REDREAMING	REEDUCATED	REEMPLOYMENTS	REENTHRONING	REEXPLAINED
REDRESSABLE	REEDUCATES	REENACTING	REENTRANCE	REEXPLAINING
REDRESSALS	REEDUCATING	REENACTMENT	REENTRANCES	REEXPLAINS
REDRESSERS	REEDUCATION	REENACTMENTS	REENTRANTS	REEXPLORED
REDRESSIBLE	REEDUCATIONS	REENACTORS	REEQUIPMENT	REEXPLORES
REDRESSING	REEDUCATIVE	REENCOUNTER	REEQUIPMENTS	REEXPLORING
REDRESSIVE	REEFPOINTS	REENCOUNTERED	REEQUIPPED	REEXPORTATION
REDRESSORS	REEJECTING	REENCOUNTERING	REEQUIPPING	REEXPORTATIONS
REDRILLING	REELECTING	REENCOUNTERS	REERECTING	REEXPORTED
REDRUTHITE	REELECTION	REENDOWING	REESCALATE	REEXPORTING
REDRUTHITES	REELECTIONS	REENERGISE	REESCALATED	REEXPOSING
REDSHIFTED	REELEVATED	REENERGISED	REESCALATES	REEXPOSURE
REDSHIRTED	REELEVATES	REENERGISES	REESCALATING	REEXPOSURES
REDSHIRTING	REELEVATING	REENERGISING	REESCALATION	REEXPRESSED
REDSTREAKS	REELIGIBILITIES	REENERGIZE	REESCALATIONS	REEXPRESSES
REDUCIBILITIES	REELIGIBILITY	REENERGIZED	REESTABLISH	REEXPRESSING
REDUCIBILITY	REELIGIBLE	REENERGIZES	REESTABLISHED	REFASHIONED
REDUCIBLENESS	REEMBARKED	REENERGIZING	REESTABLISHES	REFASHIONING
REDUCIBLENESSES	REEMBARKING	REENFORCED	REESTABLISHING	REFASHIONMENT
REDUCTANTS	REEMBODIED	REENFORCES	REESTABLISHMENT	REFASHIONMENTS
REDUCTASES	REEMBODIES	REENFORCING	REESTIMATE	REFASHIONS
REDUCTIONAL	REEMBODYING	REENGAGEMENT	REESTIMATED	REFASTENED
REDUCTIONISM	REEMBRACED	REENGAGEMENTS	REESTIMATES	REFASTENING
REDUCTIONISMS	REEMBRACES	REENGAGING	REESTIMATING	REFECTIONER
REDUCTIONIST	REEMBRACING	REENGINEER	REEVALUATE	REFECTIONERS
REDUCTIONISTIC	REEMBROIDER	REENGINEERED	REEVALUATED	REFECTIONS
REDUCTIONISTS	REEMBROIDERED	REENGINEERING	REEVALUATES	REFECTORIAN
REDUCTIONS	REEMBROIDERING	REENGINEERS	REEVALUATING	REFECTORIANS

REFECTORIES	REFLECTION	REFLOWINGS	REFOUNDATION	REFRESHMENT
REFEEDINGS	REFLECTIONAL	REFLUENCES	REFOUNDATIONS	REFRESHMENTS
REFEREEING	REFLECTIONLESS	REFOCILLATE	REFOUNDERS	REFRIGERANT
REFEREEINGS	REFLECTIONS	REFOCILLATED	REFOUNDING	REFRIGERANTS
REFERENCED	REFLECTIVE	REFOCILLATES	REFRACTABLE	REFRIGERATE
REFERENCER	REFLECTIVELY	REFOCILLATING	REFRACTARIES	REFRIGERATED
REFERENCERS	REFLECTIVENESS	REFOCILLATION	REFRACTARY	REFRIGERATES
REFERENCES	REFLECTIVITIES	REFOCILLATIONS	REFRACTILE	REFRIGERATING
REFERENCING	REFLECTIVITY	REFOCUSING	REFRACTING	REFRIGERATION
REFERENCINGS	REFLECTOGRAM	REFOCUSSED	REFRACTION	REFRIGERATIONS
REFERENDARIES	REFLECTOGRAMS	REFOCUSSES	REFRACTIONS	REFRIGERATIVE
REFERENDARY	REFLECTOGRAPH	REFOCUSSING	REFRACTIVE	REFRIGERATOR
REFERENDUM	REFLECTOGRAPHS	REFORESTATION	REFRACTIVELY	REFRIGERATORIES
REFERENDUMS	REFLECTOGRAPHY	REFORESTATIONS	REFRACTIVENESS	REFRIGERATORS
REFERENTIAL	REFLECTOMETER	REFORESTED	REFRACTIVITIES	REFRIGERATORY
REFERENTIALITY	REFLECTOMETERS	REFORESTING	REFRACTIVITY	REFRINGENCE
REFERENTIALLY	REFLECTOMETRIES	REFORMABILITIES	REFRACTOMETER	REFRINGENCES
REFERRABLE	REFLECTOMETRY	REFORMABILITY	REFRACTOMETERS	REFRINGENCIES
REFERRIBLE	REFLECTORISE	REFORMABLE	REFRACTOMETRIC	REFRINGENCY
REFIGHTING	REFLECTORISED	REFORMADES	REFRACTOMETRIES	REFRINGENT
REFIGURING	REFLECTORISES	REFORMADOES	REFRACTOMETRY	REFRINGING
REFILLABLE	REFLECTORISING	REFORMADOS	REFRACTORIES	REFRONTING
REFILTERED	REFLECTORIZE	REFORMATES	REFRACTORILY	REFUELABLE
REFILTERING	REFLECTORIZED	REFORMATION	REFRACTORINESS	REFUELINGS
REFINANCED	REFLECTORIZES	REFORMATIONAL	REFRACTORS	REFUELLABLE
REFINANCES	REFLECTORIZING	REFORMATIONIST	REFRACTORY	REFUELLING
REFINANCING	REFLECTORS	REFORMATIONISTS	REFRACTURE	REFUELLINGS
REFINANCINGS	REFLEXIBILITIES	REFORMATIONS	REFRACTURED	REFUGEEISM
REFINEDNESS	REFLEXIBILITY	REFORMATIVE	REFRACTURES	REFUGEEISMS
REFINEDNESSES	REFLEXIBLE	REFORMATORIES	REFRACTURING	REFULGENCE
REFINEMENT	REFLEXIONAL	REFORMATORY	REFRAINERS	REFULGENCES
REFINEMENTS	REFLEXIONS	REFORMATTED	REFRAINING	REFULGENCIES
REFINERIES	REFLEXIVELY	REFORMATTING	REFRAINMENT	REFULGENCY
REFINISHED	REFLEXIVENESS	REFORMINGS	REFRAINMENTS	REFULGENTLY
REFINISHER	REFLEXIVENESSES	REFORMISMS	REFRANGIBILITY	REFUNDABILITIES
REFINISHERS	REFLEXIVES	REFORMISTS	REFRANGIBLE	REFUNDABILITY
REFINISHES	REFLEXIVITIES	REFORMULATE	REFRANGIBLENESS	REFUNDABLE
REFINISHING	REFLEXIVITY	REFORMULATED	REFREEZING	REFUNDINGS
REFITMENTS	REFLEXOLOGICAL	REFORMULATES	REFRESHENED	REFUNDMENT
REFITTINGS	REFLEXOLOGIES	REFORMULATING	REFRESHENER	REFUNDMENTS
REFLAGGING	REFLEXOLOGIST	REFORMULATION	REFRESHENERS	REFURBISHED
REFLATIONARY	REFLEXOLOGISTS	REFORMULATIONS	REFRESHENING	REFURBISHER
REFLATIONS	REFLEXOLOGY	REFORTIFICATION	REFRESHENS	REFURBISHERS
REFLECTANCE	REFLOATING	REFORTIFIED	REFRESHERS	REFURBISHES
REFLECTANCES	REFLOODING	REFORTIFIES	REFRESHFUL	REFURBISHING
REFLECTERS	REFLOWERED	REFORTIFYING	REFRESHFULLY	REFURBISHINGS
REFLECTING	REFLOWERING	REFOULEMENT	REFRESHING	REFURBISHMENT
REFLECTINGLY	REFLOWERINGS	REFOULEMENTS	REFRESHINGLY	REFURBISHMENTS

R

REFURNISHED	REGIMENTALS	REGREDIENCES	REGULISING	REHUMANIZES
REFURNISHES	REGIMENTATION	REGREENING	REGULIZING	REHUMANIZING
REFURNISHING	REGIMENTATIONS	REGREETING	REGURGITANT	REHYDRATABLE
REFUSENIKS	REGIMENTED	REGRESSING	REGURGITANTS	REHYDRATED
REFUTABILITIES	REGIMENTING	REGRESSION	REGURGITATE	REHYDRATES
REFUTABILITY	REGIONALISATION	REGRESSIONS	REGURGITATED	REHYDRATING
REFUTATION	REGIONALISE	REGRESSIVE	REGURGITATES	REHYDRATION
REFUTATIONS	REGIONALISED	REGRESSIVELY	REGURGITATING	REHYDRATIONS
REGAINABLE	REGIONALISES	REGRESSIVENESS	REGURGITATION	REHYPNOTISE
REGAINMENT	REGIONALISING	REGRESSIVITIES	REGURGITATIONS	REHYPNOTISED
REGAINMENTS	REGIONALISM	REGRESSIVITY	REHABILITANT	REHYPNOTISES
REGALEMENT	REGIONALISMS	REGRESSORS	REHABILITANTS	REHYPNOTISING
REGALEMENTS	REGIONALIST	REGRETFULLY	REHABILITATE	REHYPNOTIZE
REGALITIES	REGIONALISTIC	REGRETFULNESS	REHABILITATED	REHYPNOTIZED
REGALNESSES	REGIONALISTS	REGRETFULNESSES	REHABILITATES	REHYPNOTIZES
REGARDABLE	REGIONALIZATION	REGRETTABLE	REHABILITATING	REHYPNOTIZING
REGARDFULLY	REGIONALIZE	REGRETTABLY	REHABILITATION	REICHSMARK
REGARDFULNESS	REGIONALIZED	REGRETTERS	REHABILITATIONS	REICHSMARKS
REGARDFULNESSES	REGIONALIZES	REGRETTING	REHABILITATIVE	REIDENTIFIED
REGARDLESS	REGIONALIZING	REGRINDING	REHABILITATOR	REIDENTIFIES
REGARDLESSLY	REGIONALLY	REGROOMING	REHABILITATORS	REIDENTIFY
REGARDLESSNESS	REGISSEURS	REGROOVING	REHAMMERED	REIDENTIFYING
REGATHERED	REGISTERABLE	REGROUPING	REHAMMERING	REIFICATION
REGATHERING	REGISTERED	REGROUPINGS	REHANDLING	REIFICATIONS
REGELATING	REGISTERER	REGUERDONED	REHANDLINGS	REIFICATORY
REGELATION	REGISTERERS	REGUERDONING	REHARDENED	REIGNITING
REGELATIONS	REGISTERING	REGUERDONS	REHARDENING	REIGNITION
REGENERABLE	REGISTRABLE	REGULARISATION	REHEARINGS	REIGNITIONS
REGENERACIES	REGISTRANT	REGULARISATIONS	REHEARSALS	REILLUMINE
REGENERACY	REGISTRANTS	REGULARISE	REHEARSERS	REILLUMINED
REGENERATE	REGISTRARIES	REGULARISED	REHEARSING	REILLUMINES
REGENERATED	REGISTRARS	REGULARISES	REHEARSINGS	REILLUMING
REGENERATELY	REGISTRARSHIP	REGULARISING	REHEATINGS	REILLUMINING
REGENERATENESS	REGISTRARSHIPS	REGULARITIES	REHOSPITALISE	REIMAGINED
REGENERATES	REGISTRARY	REGULARITY	REHOSPITALISED	REIMAGINES
REGENERATING	REGISTRATION	REGULARIZATION	REHOSPITALISES	REIMAGINING
REGENERATION	REGISTRATIONAL	REGULARIZATIONS	REHOSPITALISING	REIMBURSABLE
REGENERATIONS	REGISTRATIONS	REGULARIZE	REHOSPITALIZE	REIMBURSED
REGENERATIVE	REGISTRIES	REGULARIZED	REHOSPITALIZED	REIMBURSEMENT
REGENERATIVELY	REGLORIFIED	REGULARIZES	REHOSPITALIZES	REIMBURSEMENTS
REGENERATOR	REGLORIFIES	REGULARIZING	REHOSPITALIZING	REIMBURSER
REGENERATORS	REGLORIFYING	REGULATING	REHOUSINGS	REIMBURSERS
REGENERATORY	REGLOSSING	REGULATION	REHUMANISE	REIMBURSES
REGENTSHIP	REGNANCIES	REGULATIONS	REHUMANISED	REIMBURSING
REGENTSHIPS	REGRAFTING	REGULATIVE	REHUMANISES	REIMMERSED
REGGAETONS	REGRANTING	REGULATIVELY	REHUMANISING	REIMMERSES
REGIMENTAL	REGRATINGS	REGULATORS	REHUMANIZE	REIMMERSING
REGIMENTALLY	REGREDIENCE	REGULATORY	REHUMANIZED	REIMPLANTATION

REIMPLANTATIONS	REINFESTATIONS	REINSERTING	REINTERMENT	REINVOKING
REIMPLANTED	REINFLAMED	REINSERTION	REINTERMENTS	REINVOLVED
REIMPLANTING	REINFLAMES	REINSERTIONS	REINTERPRET	REINVOLVES
REIMPLANTS	REINFLAMING	REINSPECTED	REINTERPRETED	REINVOLVING
REIMPORTATION	REINFLATED	REINSPECTING	REINTERPRETING	REIOYNDURE
REIMPORTATIONS	REINFLATES	REINSPECTION	REINTERPRETS	REIOYNDURES
REIMPORTED	REINFLATING	REINSPECTIONS	REINTERRED	REISSUABLE
REIMPORTER	REINFLATION	REINSPECTS	REINTERRING	REISTAFELS
REIMPORTERS	REINFLATIONS	REINSPIRED	REINTERROGATE	REITERANCE
REIMPORTING	REINFORCEABLE	REINSPIRES	REINTERROGATED	REITERANCES
REIMPOSING	REINFORCED	REINSPIRING	REINTERROGATES	REITERATED
REIMPOSITION	REINFORCEMENT	REINSPIRIT	REINTERROGATING	REITERATEDLY
REIMPOSITIONS	REINFORCEMENTS	REINSPIRITED	REINTERROGATION	REITERATES
REIMPRESSION	REINFORCER	REINSPIRITING	REINTERVIEW	REITERATING
REIMPRESSIONS	REINFORCERS	REINSPIRITS	REINTERVIEWED	REITERATION
REINCARNATE	REINFORCES	REINSTALLATION	REINTERVIEWING	REITERATIONS
REINCARNATED	REINFORCING	REINSTALLATIONS	REINTERVIEWS	REITERATIVE
REINCARNATES	REINFORMED	REINSTALLED	REINTRODUCE	REITERATIVELY
REINCARNATING	REINFORMING	REINSTALLING	REINTRODUCED	REITERATIVES
REINCARNATION	REINFUNDED	REINSTALLS	REINTRODUCES	REJACKETED
REINCARNATIONS	REINFUNDING	REINSTALMENT	REINTRODUCING	REJACKETING
REINCITING	REINFUSING	REINSTALMENTS	REINTRODUCTION	REJECTABLE
REINCORPORATE	REINHABITED	REINSTATED	REINTRODUCTIONS	REJECTAMENTA
REINCORPORATED	REINHABITING	REINSTATEMENT	REINVADING	REJECTIBLE
REINCORPORATES	REINHABITS	REINSTATEMENTS	REINVASION	REJECTINGLY
REINCORPORATING	REINITIATE	REINSTATES	REINVASIONS	REJECTIONIST
REINCORPORATION	REINITIATED	REINSTATING	REINVENTED	REJECTIONISTS
REINCREASE	REINITIATES	REINSTATION	REINVENTING	REJECTIONS
REINCREASED	REINITIATING	REINSTATIONS	REINVENTION	REJIGGERED
REINCREASES	REINJECTED	REINSTATOR	REINVENTIONS	REJIGGERING
REINCREASING	REINJECTING	REINSTATORS	REINVESTED	REJOICEFUL
REINCURRED	REINJECTION	REINSTITUTE	REINVESTIGATE	REJOICEMENT
REINCURRING	REINJECTIONS	REINSTITUTED	REINVESTIGATED	REJOICEMENTS
REINDEXING	REINJURIES	REINSTITUTES	REINVESTIGATES	REJOICINGLY
REINDICTED	REINJURING	REINSTITUTING	REINVESTIGATING	REJOICINGS
REINDICTING	REINNERVATE	REINSTITUTION	REINVESTIGATION	REJOINDERS
REINDICTMENT	REINNERVATED	REINSTITUTIONS	REINVESTING	REJOINDURE
REINDICTMENTS	REINNERVATES	REINSURANCE	REINVESTMENT	REJOINDURES
REINDUCING	REINNERVATING	REINSURANCES	REINVESTMENTS	REJONEADOR
REINDUCTED	REINNERVATION	REINSURERS	REINVIGORATE	REJONEADORA
REINDUCTING	REINNERVATIONS	REINSURING	REINVIGORATED	REJONEADORAS
REINDUSTRIALISE	REINOCULATE	REINTEGRATE	REINVIGORATES	REJONEADORES
REINDUSTRIALIZE	REINOCULATED	REINTEGRATED	REINVIGORATING	REJOURNING
REINFECTED	REINOCULATES	REINTEGRATES	REINVIGORATION	REJUGGLING
REINFECTING	REINOCULATING	REINTEGRATING	REINVIGORATIONS	REJUSTIFIED
REINFECTION	REINOCULATION	REINTEGRATION	REINVIGORATOR	REJUSTIFIES
REINFECTIONS	REINOCULATIONS	REINTEGRATIONS	REINVIGORATORS	REJUSTIFYING
REINFESTATION	REINSERTED	REINTEGRATIVE	REINVITING	REJUVENATE

R

REJUVENATED

REJUVENATED	RELATIONIST	RELEGATIONS	RELIGIOSOS	RELUCTATIONS
REJUVENATES	RELATIONISTS	RELENTINGS	RELIGIOUSES	RELUCTIVITIES
REJUVENATING	RELATIONLESS	RELENTLESS	RELIGIOUSLY	RELUCTIVITY
REJUVENATION	RELATIONSHIP	RELENTLESSLY	RELIGIOUSNESS	RELUMINING
REJUVENATIONS	RELATIONSHIPS	RELENTLESSNESS	RELIGIOUSNESSES	REMAILINGS
REJUVENATOR	RELATIVELY	RELENTMENT	RELINQUISH	REMAINDERED
REJUVENATORS	RELATIVENESS	RELENTMENTS	RELINQUISHED	REMAINDERING
REJUVENESCE	RELATIVENESSES	RELETTERED	RELINQUISHER	REMAINDERMAN
REJUVENESCED	RELATIVISATION	RELETTERING	RELINQUISHERS	REMAINDERMEN
REJUVENESCENCE	RELATIVISATIONS	RELEVANCES	RELINQUISHES	REMAINDERS
REJUVENESCENCES	RELATIVISE	RELEVANCIES	RELINQUISHING	REMANDMENT
REJUVENESCENT	RELATIVISED	RELEVANTLY	RELINQUISHMENT	REMANDMENTS
REJUVENESCES	RELATIVISES	RELIABILITIES	RELINQUISHMENTS	REMANENCES
REJUVENESCING	RELATIVISING	RELIABILITY	RELIQUAIRE	REMANENCIES
REJUVENISE	RELATIVISM	RELIABLENESS	RELIQUAIRES	REMANUFACTURE
REJUVENISED	RELATIVISMS	RELIABLENESSES	RELIQUARIES	REMANUFACTURED
REJUVENISES	RELATIVIST	RELICENSED	RELIQUEFIED	REMANUFACTURER
REJUVENISING	RELATIVISTIC	RELICENSES	RELIQUEFIES	REMANUFACTURERS
REJUVENIZE	RELATIVISTS	RELICENSING	RELIQUEFYING	REMANUFACTURES
REJUVENIZED	RELATIVITIES	RELICENSURE	RELIQUIFIED	REMANUFACTURING
REJUVENIZES	RELATIVITIST	RELICENSURES	RELIQUIFIES	REMARKABILITIES
REJUVENIZING	RELATIVITISTS	RELICTIONS	RELIQUIFYING	REMARKABILITY
REKEYBOARD	RELATIVITY	RELIEFLESS	RELISHABLE	REMARKABLE
REKEYBOARDED	RELATIVIZATION	RELIEVABLE	RELISTENED	REMARKABLENESS
REKEYBOARDING	RELATIVIZATIONS	RELIEVEDLY	RELISTENING	REMARKABLES
REKEYBOARDS	RELATIVIZE	RELIGHTING	RELIVERING	REMARKABLY
REKINDLING	RELATIVIZED	RELIGIEUSE	RELLISHING	REMARKETED
REKINDLINGS	RELATIVIZES	RELIGIEUSES	RELOCATABLE	REMARKETING
REKNITTING	RELATIVIZING	RELIGIONARIES	RELOCATEES	REMARRIAGE
REKNITTINGS	RELAUNCHED	RELIGIONARY	RELOCATING	REMARRIAGES
REKNOTTING	RELAUNCHES	RELIGIONER	RELOCATION	REMARRYING
REKNOTTINGS	RELAUNCHING	RELIGIONERS	RELOCATIONS	REMASTERED
RELABELING	RELAUNDERED	RELIGIONISE	RELOCATORS	REMASTERING
RELABELLED	RELAUNDERING	RELIGIONISED	RELUBRICATE	REMATCHING
RELABELLING	RELAUNDERS	RELIGIONISES	RELUBRICATED	REMATERIALISE
RELACQUERED	RELAXATION	RELIGIONISING	RELUBRICATES	REMATERIALISED
RELACQUERING	RELAXATIONS	RELIGIONISM	RELUBRICATING	REMATERIALISES
RELACQUERS	RELAXATIVE	RELIGIONISMS	RELUBRICATION	REMATERIALISING
RELANDSCAPE	RELAXATIVES	RELIGIONIST	RELUBRICATIONS	REMATERIALIZE
RELANDSCAPED	RELAXEDNESS	RELIGIONISTS	RELUCTANCE	REMATERIALIZED
RELANDSCAPES	RELAXEDNESSES	RELIGIONIZE	RELUCTANCES	REMATERIALIZES
RELANDSCAPING	RELEARNING	RELIGIONIZED	RELUCTANCIES	REMATERIALIZING
RELATEDNESS	RELEASABLE	RELIGIONIZES	RELUCTANCY	REMEASURED
RELATEDNESSES	RELEASEMENT	RELIGIONIZING	RELUCTANTLY	REMEASUREMENT
RELATIONAL	RELEASEMENTS	RELIGIONLESS	RELUCTATED	REMEASUREMENTS
RELATIONALLY	RELEGATABLE	RELIGIOSELY	RELUCTATES	REMEASURES
RELATIONISM	RELEGATING	RELIGIOSITIES	RELUCTATING	REMEASURING
RELATIONISMS	RELEGATION	RELIGIOSITY	RELUCTATION	REMEDIABILITIES

R

REMEDIABILITY	REMINISCED	REMODELLING	REMORALIZATIONS	REMUNERATORY
REMEDIABLE	REMINISCENCE	REMODELLINGS	REMORALIZE	REMURMURED
REMEDIABLY	REMINISCENCES	REMODIFIED	REMORALIZED	REMURMURING
REMEDIALLY	REMINISCENT	REMODIFIES	REMORALIZES	REMYTHOLOGISE
REMEDIATED	REMINISCENTIAL	REMODIFYING	REMORALIZING	REMYTHOLOGISED
REMEDIATES	REMINISCENTLY	REMOISTENED	REMORSEFUL	REMYTHOLOGISES
REMEDIATING	REMINISCENTS	REMOISTENING	REMORSEFULLY	REMYTHOLOGISING
REMEDIATION	REMINISCER	REMOISTENS	REMORSEFULNESS	REMYTHOLOGIZE
REMEDIATIONS	REMINISCERS	REMONETISATION	REMORSELESS	REMYTHOLOGIZED
REMEDILESS	REMINISCES	REMONETISATIONS	REMORSELESSLY	REMYTHOLOGIZES
REMEDILESSLY	REMINISCING	REMONETISE	REMORSELESSNESS	REMYTHOLOGIZING
REMEDILESSNESS	REMISSIBILITIES	REMONETISED	REMORTGAGE	RENAISSANCE
REMEMBERABILITY	REMISSIBILITY	REMONETISES	REMORTGAGED	RENAISSANCES
REMEMBERABLE	REMISSIBLE	REMONETISING	REMORTGAGES	RENASCENCE
REMEMBERABLY	REMISSIBLENESS	REMONETIZATION	REMORTGAGING	RENASCENCES
REMEMBERED	REMISSIBLY	REMONETIZATIONS	REMOTENESS	RENATIONALISE
REMEMBERER	REMISSIONS	REMONETIZE	REMOTENESSES	RENATIONALISED
REMEMBERERS	REMISSIVELY	REMONETIZED	REMOTIVATE	RENATIONALISES
REMEMBERING	REMISSNESS	REMONETIZES	REMOTIVATED	RENATIONALISING
REMEMBRANCE	REMISSNESSES	REMONETIZING	REMOTIVATES	RENATIONALIZE
REMEMBRANCER	REMITMENTS	REMONSTRANCE	REMOTIVATING	RENATIONALIZED
REMEMBRANCERS	REMITTABLE	REMONSTRANCES	REMOTIVATION	RENATIONALIZES
REMEMBRANCES	REMITTANCE	REMONSTRANT	REMOTIVATIONS	RENATIONALIZING
REMERCYING	REMITTANCES	REMONSTRANTLY	REMOULADES	RENATURATION
REMIGATING	REMITTENCE	REMONSTRANTS	REMOULDING	RENATURATIONS
REMIGATION	REMITTENCES	REMONSTRATE	REMOUNTING	RENATURING
REMIGATIONS	REMITTENCIES	REMONSTRATED	REMOUNTINGS	RENCONTRED
REMIGRATED	REMITTENCY	REMONSTRATES	REMOVABILITIES	RENCONTRES
REMIGRATES	REMITTENTLY	REMONSTRATING	REMOVABILITY	RENCONTRING
REMIGRATING	REMIXTURES	REMONSTRATINGLY	REMOVABLENESS	RENCOUNTER
REMIGRATION	REMOBILISATION	REMONSTRATION	REMOVABLENESSES	RENCOUNTERED
REMIGRATIONS	REMOBILISATIONS	REMONSTRATIONS	REMOVALIST	RENCOUNTERING
REMILITARISE	REMOBILISE	REMONSTRATIVE	REMOVALISTS	RENCOUNTERS
REMILITARISED	REMOBILISED	REMONSTRATIVELY	REMOVEABLE	RENDERABLE
REMILITARISES	REMOBILISES	REMONSTRATOR	REMOVEDNESS	RENDERINGS
REMILITARISING	REMOBILISING	REMONSTRATORS	REMOVEDNESSES	RENDEZVOUS
REMILITARIZE	REMOBILIZATION	REMONSTRATORY	REMUNERABILITY	RENDEZVOUSED
REMILITARIZED	REMOBILIZATIONS	REMONTANTS	REMUNERABLE	RENDEZVOUSES
REMILITARIZES	REMOBILIZE	REMONTOIRE	REMUNERATE	RENDEZVOUSING
REMILITARIZING	REMOBILIZED	REMONTOIRES	REMUNERATED	RENDITIONED
REMINERALISE	REMOBILIZES	REMONTOIRS	REMUNERATES	RENDITIONING
REMINERALISED	REMOBILIZING	REMORALISATION	REMUNERATING	RENDITIONS
REMINERALISES	REMODELERS	REMORALISATIONS	REMUNERATION	RENEAGUING
REMINERALISING	REMODELING	REMORALISE	REMUNERATIONS	RENEGADING
REMINERALIZE	REMODELINGS	REMORALISED	REMUNERATIVE	RENEGADOES
REMINERALIZED	REMODELLED	REMORALISES	REMUNERATIVELY	RENEGATION
REMINERALIZES	REMODELLER	REMORALISING	REMUNERATOR	RENEGATIONS
REMINERALIZING	REMODELLERS	REMORALIZATION	REMUNERATORS	RENEGOTIABLE

R

RENEGOTIATE	RENOVATORS	REORCHESTRATING	REPACIFYING	REPEATABILITIES
RENEGOTIATED	RENSSELAERITE	REORCHESTRATION	REPACKAGED	REPEATABILITY
RENEGOTIATES	RENSSELAERITES	REORDAINED	REPACKAGER	REPEATABLE
RENEGOTIATING	RENTABILITIES	REORDAINING	REPACKAGERS	REPEATEDLY
RENEGOTIATION	RENTABILITY	REORDERING	REPACKAGES	REPEATINGS
RENEGOTIATIONS	RENTALLERS	REORDINATION	REPACKAGING	REPECHAGES
RENEWABILITIES	RENUMBERED	REORDINATIONS	REPAGINATE	REPELLANCE
RENEWABILITY	RENUMBERING	REORGANISATION	REPAGINATED	REPELLANCES
RENEWABLES	RENUNCIATE	REORGANISATIONS	REPAGINATES	REPELLANCIES
RENEWEDNESS	RENUNCIATES	REORGANISE	REPAGINATING	REPELLANCY
RENEWEDNESSES	RENUNCIATION	REORGANISED	REPAGINATION	REPELLANTLY
RENFORCING	RENUNCIATIONS	REORGANISER	REPAGINATIONS	REPELLANTS
RENITENCES	RENUNCIATIVE	REORGANISERS	REPAINTING	REPELLENCE
RENITENCIES	RENUNCIATORY	REORGANISES	REPAINTINGS	REPELLENCES
RENOGRAPHIC	RENVERSEMENT	REORGANISING	REPAIRABILITIES	REPELLENCIES
RENOGRAPHIES	RENVERSEMENTS	REORGANIZATION	REPAIRABILITY	REPELLENCY
RENOGRAPHY	RENVERSING	REORGANIZATIONS	REPAIRABLE	REPELLENTLY
RENOMINATE	REOBJECTED	REORGANIZE	REPANELING	REPELLENTS
RENOMINATED	REOBJECTING	REORGANIZED	REPANELLED	REPELLINGLY
RENOMINATES	REOBSERVED	REORGANIZER	REPANELLING	REPENTANCE
RENOMINATING	REOBSERVES	REORGANIZERS	REPAPERING	REPENTANCES
RENOMINATION	REOBSERVING	REORGANIZES	REPARABILITIES	REPENTANTLY
RENOMINATIONS	REOBTAINED	REORGANIZING	REPARABILITY	REPENTANTS
RENORMALISATION	REOBTAINING	REORIENTATE	REPARATION	REPENTINGLY
RENORMALISE	REOCCUPATION	REORIENTATED	REPARATIONS	REPEOPLING
RENORMALISED	REOCCUPATIONS	REORIENTATES	REPARATIVE	REPERCUSSED
RENORMALISES	REOCCUPIED	REORIENTATING	REPARATORY	REPERCUSSES
RENORMALISING	REOCCUPIES	REORIENTATION	REPARTEEING	REPERCUSSING
RENORMALIZATION	REOCCUPYING	REORIENTATIONS	REPARTITION	REPERCUSSION
RENORMALIZE	REOCCURRED	REORIENTED	REPARTITIONED	REPERCUSSIONS
RENORMALIZED	REOCCURRENCE	REORIENTING	REPARTITIONING	REPERCUSSIVE
RENORMALIZES	REOCCURRENCES	REOUTFITTED	REPARTITIONS	REPERTOIRE
RENORMALIZING	REOCCURRING	REOUTFITTING	REPASSAGES	REPERTOIRES
RENOSTERVELD	REOFFENDED	REOVIRUSES	REPASTURES	REPERTORIAL
RENOSTERVELDS	REOFFENDER	REOXIDATION	REPATCHING	REPERTORIES
RENOTIFIED	REOFFENDERS	REOXIDATIONS	REPATRIATE	REPERUSALS
RENOTIFIES	REOFFENDING	REOXIDISED	REPATRIATED	REPERUSING
RENOTIFYING	REOFFERING	REOXIDISES	REPATRIATES	REPETITEUR
RENOUNCEABLE	REOPENINGS	REOXIDISING	REPATRIATING	REPETITEURS
RENOUNCEMENT	REOPERATED	REOXIDIZED	REPATRIATION	REPETITEUSE
RENOUNCEMENTS	REOPERATES	REOXIDIZES	REPATRIATIONS	REPETITEUSES
RENOUNCERS	REOPERATING	REOXIDIZING	REPATRIATOR	REPETITION
RENOUNCING	REOPERATION	REOXYGENATE	REPATRIATORS	REPETITIONAL
RENOVASCULAR	REOPERATIONS	REOXYGENATED	REPATTERNED	REPETITIONARY
RENOVATING	REOPPOSING	REOXYGENATES	REPATTERNING	REPETITIONS
RENOVATION	REORCHESTRATE	REOXYGENATING	REPATTERNS	REPETITIOUS
RENOVATIONS	REORCHESTRATED	REPACIFIED	REPAYMENTS	REPETITIOUSLY
RENOVATIVE	REORCHESTRATES	REPACIFIES	REPEALABLE	REPETITIOUSNESS

REPETITIVE	REPLICANTS	REPORTEDLY	REPRESENTANT	REPRISTINATED
REPETITIVELY	REPLICASES	REPORTINGLY	REPRESENTANTS	REPRISTINATES
REPETITIVENESS	REPLICATED	REPORTINGS	REPRESENTATION	REPRISTINATING
REPHOTOGRAPH	REPLICATES	REPORTORIAL	REPRESENTATIONS	REPRISTINATION
REPHOTOGRAPHED	REPLICATING	REPORTORIALLY	REPRESENTATIVE	REPRISTINATIONS
REPHOTOGRAPHING	REPLICATION	REPOSEDNESS	REPRESENTATIVES	REPRIVATISATION
REPHOTOGRAPHS	REPLICATIONS	REPOSEDNESSES	REPRESENTED	REPRIVATISE
REPHRASING	REPLICATIVE	REPOSEFULLY	REPRESENTEE	REPRIVATISED
REPHRASINGS	REPLICATOR	REPOSEFULNESS	REPRESENTEES	REPRIVATISES
REPIGMENTED	REPLICATORS	REPOSEFULNESSES	REPRESENTER	REPRIVATISING
REPIGMENTING	REPLOTTING	REPOSITING	REPRESENTERS	REPRIVATIZATION
REPIGMENTS	REPLOUGHED	REPOSITION	REPRESENTING	REPRIVATIZE
REPINEMENT	REPLOUGHING	REPOSITIONED	REPRESENTMENT	REPRIVATIZED
REPINEMENTS	REPLUMBING	REPOSITIONING	REPRESENTMENTS	REPRIVATIZES
REPININGLY	REPLUNGING	REPOSITIONS	REPRESENTOR	REPRIVATIZING
REPLACEABILITY	REPOINTING	REPOSITORIES	REPRESENTORS	REPROACHABLE
REPLACEABLE	REPOINTINGS	REPOSITORS	REPRESENTS	REPROACHABLY
REPLACEMENT	REPOLARISATION	REPOSITORY	REPRESSERS	REPROACHED
REPLACEMENTS	REPOLARISATIONS	REPOSSESSED	REPRESSIBILITY	REPROACHER
REPLANNING	REPOLARISE	REPOSSESSES	REPRESSIBLE	REPROACHERS
REPLANTATION	REPOLARISED	REPOSSESSING	REPRESSIBLY	REPROACHES
REPLANTATIONS	REPOLARISES	REPOSSESSION	REPRESSING	REPROACHFUL
REPLANTING	REPOLARISING	REPOSSESSIONS	REPRESSION	REPROACHFULLY
REPLASTERED	REPOLARIZATION	REPOSSESSOR	REPRESSIONIST	REPROACHFULNESS
REPLASTERING	REPOLARIZATIONS	REPOSSESSORS	REPRESSIONISTS	REPROACHING
REPLASTERS	REPOLARIZE	REPOTTINGS	REPRESSIONS	REPROACHINGLY
REPLEADERS	REPOLARIZED	REPOUSSAGE	REPRESSIVE	REPROACHLESS
REPLEADING	REPOLARIZES	REPOUSSAGES	REPRESSIVELY	REPROBACIES
REPLEDGING	REPOLARIZING	REPOUSSOIR	REPRESSIVENESS	REPROBANCE
REPLENISHABLE	REPOLISHED	REPOUSSOIRS	REPRESSORS	REPROBANCES
REPLENISHED	REPOLISHES	REPOWERING	REPRESSURISE	REPROBATED
REPLENISHER	REPOLISHING	REPREEVING	REPRESSURISED	REPROBATER
REPLENISHERS	REPOPULARISE	REPREHENDABLE	REPRESSURISES	REPROBATERS
REPLENISHES	REPOPULARISED	REPREHENDED	REPRESSURISING	REPROBATES
REPLENISHING	REPOPULARISES	REPREHENDER	REPRESSURIZE	REPROBATING
REPLENISHMENT	REPOPULARISING	REPREHENDERS	REPRESSURIZED	REPROBATION
REPLENISHMENTS	REPOPULARIZE	REPREHENDING	REPRESSURIZES	REPROBATIONARY
REPLETENESS	REPOPULARIZED	REPREHENDS	REPRESSURIZING	REPROBATIONS
REPLETENESSES	REPOPULARIZES	REPREHENSIBLE	REPRIEVABLE	REPROBATIVE
REPLETIONS	REPOPULARIZING	REPREHENSIBLY	REPRIEVALS	REPROBATIVELY
REPLEVIABLE	REPOPULATE	REPREHENSION	REPRIEVERS	REPROBATOR
REPLEVINED	REPOPULATED	REPREHENSIONS	REPRIEVING	REPROBATORS
REPLEVINING	REPOPULATES	REPREHENSIVE	REPRIMANDED	REPROBATORY
REPLEVISABLE	REPOPULATING	REPREHENSIVELY	REPRIMANDING	REPROCESSED
REPLEVYING	REPOPULATION	REPREHENSORY	REPRIMANDS	REPROCESSES
REPLICABILITIES	REPOPULATIONS	REPRESENTABLE	REPRINTERS	REPROCESSING
REPLICABILITY	REPORTABLE	REPRESENTAMEN	REPRINTING	REPROCESSINGS
REPLICABLE	REPORTAGES	REPRESENTAMENS	REPRISTINATE	REPRODUCED

REPRODUCER	REPUBLICANISMS	REPUTATION	RERADIATING	RESCINDMENT
REPRODUCERS	REPUBLICANIZE	REPUTATIONAL	RERADIATION	RESCINDMENTS
REPRODUCES	REPUBLICANIZED	REPUTATIONLESS	RERADIATIONS	RESCISSIBLE
REPRODUCIBILITY	REPUBLICANIZES	REPUTATIONS	RERAILINGS	RESCISSION
REPRODUCIBLE	REPUBLICANIZING	REPUTATIVE	REREADINGS	RESCISSIONS
REPRODUCIBLES	REPUBLICANS	REPUTATIVELY	REREBRACES	RESCISSORY
REPRODUCIBLY	REPUBLICATION	REPUTELESS	RERECORDED	RESCREENED
REPRODUCING	REPUBLICATIONS	REQUALIFIED	RERECORDING	RESCREENING
REPRODUCTION	REPUBLISHED	REQUALIFIES	REREDORTER	RESCRIPTED
REPRODUCTIONS	REPUBLISHER	REQUALIFYING	REREDORTERS	RESCRIPTING
REPRODUCTIVE	REPUBLISHERS	REQUESTERS	REREDOSSES	RESCRIPTION
REPRODUCTIVELY	REPUBLISHES	REQUESTING	REREGISTER	RESCRIPTIONS
REPRODUCTIVES	REPUBLISHING	REQUESTORS	REREGISTERED	RESCULPTED
REPRODUCTIVITY	REPUDIABLE	REQUICKENED	REREGISTERING	RESCULPTING
REPROGRAMED	REPUDIATED	REQUICKENING	REREGISTERS	RESEALABLE
REPROGRAMING	REPUDIATES	REQUICKENS	REREGISTRATION	RESEARCHABLE
REPROGRAMMABLE	REPUDIATING	REQUIESCAT	REREGISTRATIONS	RESEARCHED
REPROGRAMME	REPUDIATION	REQUIESCATS	REREGULATE	RESEARCHER
REPROGRAMMED	REPUDIATIONIST	REQUIGHTED	REREGULATED	RESEARCHERS
REPROGRAMMES	REPUDIATIONISTS	REQUIGHTING	REREGULATES	RESEARCHES
REPROGRAMMING	REPUDIATIONS	REQUIRABLE	REREGULATING	RESEARCHFUL
REPROGRAMS	REPUDIATIVE	REQUIREMENT	REREGULATION	RESEARCHING
REPROGRAPHER	REPUDIATOR	REQUIREMENTS	REREGULATIONS	RESEARCHIST
REPROGRAPHERS	REPUDIATORS	REQUIRINGS	RERELEASED	RESEARCHISTS
REPROGRAPHIC	REPUGNANCE	REQUISITELY	RERELEASES	RESEASONED
REPROGRAPHICS	REPUGNANCES	REQUISITENESS	RERELEASING	RESEASONING
REPROGRAPHIES	REPUGNANCIES	REQUISITENESSES	REREMINDED	RESECTABILITIES
REPROGRAPHY	REPUGNANCY	REQUISITES	REREMINDING	RESECTABILITY
REPROOFING	REPUGNANTLY	REQUISITION	REREPEATED	RESECTABLE
REPROVABLE	REPULSIONS	REQUISITIONARY	REREPEATING	RESECTIONAL
REPROVINGLY	REPULSIVELY	REQUISITIONED	REREVIEWED	RESECTIONS
REPROVISION	REPULSIVENESS	REQUISITIONING	REREVIEWING	RESECURING
REPROVISIONED	REPULSIVENESSES	REQUISITIONIST	REREVISING	RESEGREGATE
REPROVISIONING	REPUNCTUATION	REQUISITIONISTS	REROUTEING	RESEGREGATED
REPROVISIONS	REPUNCTUATIONS	REQUISITIONS	RESADDLING	RESEGREGATES
REPTATIONS	REPURCHASE	REQUISITOR	RESALEABLE	RESEGREGATING
REPTILIANLY	REPURCHASED	REQUISITORIES	RESALUTING	RESEGREGATION
REPTILIANS	REPURCHASES	REQUISITORS	RESAMPLING	RESEGREGATIONS
REPTILIFEROUS	REPURCHASING	REQUISITORY	RESCHEDULE	RESEIZURES
REPTILIFORM	REPURIFIED	REQUITABLE	RESCHEDULED	RESELECTED
REPTILIOUS	REPURIFIES	REQUITEFUL	RESCHEDULES	RESELECTING
REPTILOIDS	REPURIFYING	REQUITELESS	RESCHEDULING	RESELECTION
REPUBLICAN	REPURPOSED	REQUITEMENT	RESCHEDULINGS	RESELECTIONS
REPUBLICANISE	REPURPOSES	REQUITEMENTS	RESCHOOLED	RESEMBLANCE
REPUBLICANISED	REPURPOSING	REQUITTING	RESCHOOLING	RESEMBLANCES
REPUBLICANISES	REPURSUING	REQUOYLING	RESCINDABLE	RESEMBLANT
REPUBLICANISING	REPUTABILITIES	RERADIATED	RESCINDERS	RESEMBLERS
REPUBLICANISM	REPUTABILITY	RERADIATES	RESCINDING	RESEMBLING

RESENSITISE	RESHIPMENTS	RESINOUSNESS	RESOFTENED	RESOURCEFULLY
RESENSITISED	RESHIPPERS	RESINOUSNESSES	RESOFTENING	RESOURCEFULNESS
RESENSITISES	RESHIPPING	RESIPISCENCE	RESOLDERED	RESOURCELESS
RESENSITISING	RESHOOTING	RESIPISCENCES	RESOLDERING	RESOURCING
RESENSITIZE	RESHOWERED	RESIPISCENCIES	RESOLIDIFIED	RESOURCINGS
RESENSITIZED	RESHOWERING	RESIPISCENCY	RESOLIDIFIES	RESPEAKING
RESENSITIZES	RESHOWINGS	RESIPISCENT	RESOLIDIFY	RESPECIFIED
RESENSITIZING	RESHUFFLED	RESISTANCE	RESOLIDIFYING	RESPECIFIES
RESENTENCE	RESHUFFLES	RESISTANCES	RESOLUBILITIES	RESPECIFYING
RESENTENCED	RESHUFFLING	RESISTANTS	RESOLUBILITY	RESPECTABILISE
RESENTENCES	RESIDENCES	RESISTENTS	RESOLUBLENESS	RESPECTABILISED
RESENTENCING	RESIDENCIES	RESISTIBILITIES	RESOLUBLENESSES	RESPECTABILISES
RESENTFULLY	RESIDENTER	RESISTIBILITY	RESOLUTELY	RESPECTABILITY
RESENTFULNESS	RESIDENTERS	RESISTIBLE	RESOLUTENESS	RESPECTABILIZE
RESENTFULNESSES	RESIDENTIAL	RESISTIBLY	RESOLUTENESSES	RESPECTABILIZED
RESENTINGLY	RESIDENTIALLY	RESISTINGLY	RESOLUTEST	RESPECTABILIZES
RESENTMENT	RESIDENTIARIES	RESISTIVELY	RESOLUTION	RESPECTABLE
RESENTMENTS	RESIDENTIARY	RESISTIVENESS	RESOLUTIONER	RESPECTABLENESS
RESERPINES	RESIDENTSHIP	RESISTIVENESSES	RESOLUTIONERS	RESPECTABLES
RESERVABLE	RESIDENTSHIPS	RESISTIVITIES	RESOLUTIONIST	RESPECTABLY
RESERVATION	RESIDUALLY	RESISTIVITY	RESOLUTIONISTS	RESPECTANT
RESERVATIONIST	RESIGHTING	RESISTLESS	RESOLUTIONS	RESPECTERS
RESERVATIONISTS	RESIGNATION	RESISTLESSLY	RESOLUTIVE	RESPECTFUL
RESERVATIONS	RESIGNATIONS	RESISTLESSNESS	RESOLVABILITIES	RESPECTFULLY
RESERVATORIES	RESIGNEDLY	RESITTINGS	RESOLVABILITY	RESPECTFULNESS
RESERVATORY	RESIGNEDNESS	RESITUATED	RESOLVABLE	RESPECTING
RESERVEDLY	RESIGNEDNESSES	RESITUATES	RESOLVABLENESS	RESPECTIVE
RESERVEDNESS	RESIGNMENT	RESITUATING	RESOLVEDLY	RESPECTIVELY
RESERVEDNESSES	RESIGNMENTS	RESKETCHED	RESOLVEDNESS	RESPECTIVENESS
RESERVICED	RESILEMENT	RESKETCHES	RESOLVEDNESSES	RESPECTLESS
RESERVICES	RESILEMENTS	RESKETCHING	RESOLVENTS	RESPELLING
RESERVICING	RESILIENCE	RESKILLING	RESONANCES	RESPELLINGS
RESERVISTS	RESILIENCES	RESKILLINGS	RESONANTLY	RESPIRABILITIES
RESERVOIRED	RESILIENCIES	RESKINNING	RESONATING	RESPIRABILITY
RESERVOIRING	RESILIENCY	RESMELTING	RESONATION	RESPIRABLE
RESERVOIRS	RESILIENTLY	RESMOOTHED	RESONATIONS	RESPIRATION
RESETTABLE	RESILVERED	RESMOOTHING	RESONATORS	RESPIRATIONAL
RESETTLEMENT	RESILVERING	RESNATRONS	RESORBENCE	RESPIRATIONS
RESETTLEMENTS	RESINATING	RESOCIALISATION	RESORBENCES	RESPIRATOR
RESETTLING	RESINIFEROUS	RESOCIALISE	RESORCINAL	RESPIRATORS
RESHAPINGS	RESINIFICATION	RESOCIALISED	RESORCINOL	RESPIRATORY
RESHARPENED	RESINIFICATIONS	RESOCIALISES	RESORCINOLS	RESPIRITUALISE
RESHARPENING	RESINIFIED	RESOCIALISING	RESORPTION	RESPIRITUALISED
RESHARPENS	RESINIFIES	RESOCIALIZATION	RESORPTIONS	RESPIRITUALISES
RESHINGLED	RESINIFYING	RESOCIALIZE	RESORPTIVE	RESPIRITUALIZE
RESHINGLES	RESINISING	RESOCIALIZED	RESOUNDING	RESPIRITUALIZED
RESHINGLING	RESINIZING	RESOCIALIZES	RESOUNDINGLY	RESPIRITUALIZES
RESHIPMENT	RESINOUSLY	RESOCIALIZING	RESOURCEFUL	RESPIROLOGIES

R

RESPIROLOGIST	RESPREADING	RESTITCHED	RESTRESSING	RESUMMONED
RESPIROLOGISTS	RESPRINGING	RESTITCHES	RESTRETCHED	RESUMMONING
RESPIROLOGY	RESPROUTED	RESTITCHING	RESTRETCHES	RESUMPTION
RESPIROMETER	RESPROUTING	RESTITUTED	RESTRETCHING	RESUMPTIONS
RESPIROMETERS	RESSALDARS	RESTITUTES	RESTRICKEN	RESUMPTIVE
RESPIROMETRIC	RESSENTIMENT	RESTITUTING	RESTRICTED	RESUMPTIVELY
RESPIROMETRIES	RESSENTIMENTS	RESTITUTION	RESTRICTEDLY	RESUPINATE
RESPIROMETRY	RESTABILISE	RESTITUTIONISM	RESTRICTEDNESS	RESUPINATION
RESPITELESS	RESTABILISED	RESTITUTIONISMS	RESTRICTING	RESUPINATIONS
RESPLENDED	RESTABILISES	RESTITUTIONIST	RESTRICTION	RESUPPLIED
RESPLENDENCE	RESTABILISING	RESTITUTIONISTS	RESTRICTIONISM	RESUPPLIES
RESPLENDENCES	RESTABILIZE	RESTITUTIONS	RESTRICTIONISMS	RESUPPLYING
RESPLENDENCIES	RESTABILIZED	RESTITUTIVE	RESTRICTIONIST	RESURFACED
RESPLENDENCY	RESTABILIZES	RESTITUTOR	RESTRICTIONISTS	RESURFACER
RESPLENDENT	RESTABILIZING	RESTITUTORS	RESTRICTIONS	RESURFACERS
RESPLENDENTLY	RESTABLING	RESTITUTORY	RESTRICTIVE	RESURFACES
RESPLENDING	RESTACKING	RESTIVENESS	RESTRICTIVELY	RESURFACING
RESPLICING	RESTAFFING	RESTIVENESSES	RESTRICTIVENESS	RESURGENCE
RESPLITTING	RESTAMPING	RESTLESSLY	RESTRICTIVES	RESURGENCES
RESPONDENCE	RESTARTABLE	RESTLESSNESS	RESTRIKING	RESURRECTED
RESPONDENCES	RESTARTERS	RESTLESSNESSES	RESTRINGED	RESURRECTING
RESPONDENCIES	RESTARTING	RESTOCKING	RESTRINGEING	RESURRECTION
RESPONDENCY	RESTATEMENT	RESTORABLE	RESTRINGENT	RESURRECTIONAL
RESPONDENT	RESTATEMENTS	RESTORABLENESS	RESTRINGENTS	RESURRECTIONARY
RESPONDENTIA	RESTATIONED	RESTORATION	RESTRINGES	RESURRECTIONISE
RESPONDENTIAS	RESTATIONING	RESTORATIONISM	RESTRINGING	RESURRECTIONISM
RESPONDENTS	RESTATIONS	RESTORATIONISMS	RESTRIVING	RESURRECTIONIST
RESPONDERS	RESTAURANT	RESTORATIONIST	RESTRUCTURE	RESURRECTIONIZE
RESPONDING	RESTAURANTEUR	RESTORATIONISTS	RESTRUCTURED	RESURRECTIONS
RESPONSELESS	RESTAURANTEURS	RESTORATIONS	RESTRUCTURES	RESURRECTIVE
RESPONSERS	RESTAURANTS	RESTORATIVE	RESTRUCTURING	RESURRECTOR
RESPONSIBILITY	RESTAURATEUR	RESTORATIVELY	RESTRUCTURINGS	RESURRECTORS
RESPONSIBLE	RESTAURATEURS	RESTORATIVES	RESTUDYING	RESURRECTS
RESPONSIBLENESS	RESTAURATION	RESTRAINABLE	RESTUFFING	RESURVEYED
RESPONSIBLY	RESTAURATIONS	RESTRAINED	RESTUMPING	RESURVEYING
RESPONSIONS	RESTEMMING	RESTRAINEDLY	RESUBJECTED	RESUSCITABLE
RESPONSIVE	RESTFULLER	RESTRAINEDNESS	RESUBJECTING	RESUSCITANT
RESPONSIVELY	RESTFULLEST	RESTRAINER	RESUBJECTS	RESUSCITANTS
RESPONSIVENESS	RESTFULNESS	RESTRAINERS	RESUBMISSION	RESUSCITATE
RESPONSORIAL	RESTFULNESSES	RESTRAINING	RESUBMISSIONS	RESUSCITATED
RESPONSORIALS	RESTHARROW	RESTRAININGS	RESUBMITTED	RESUSCITATES
RESPONSORIES	RESTHARROWS	RESTRAINTS	RESUBMITTING	RESUSCITATING
RESPONSORS	RESTIMULATE	RESTRENGTHEN	RESULTANTLY	RESUSCITATION
RESPONSORY	RESTIMULATED	RESTRENGTHENED	RESULTANTS	RESUSCITATIONS
RESPONSUMS	RESTIMULATES	RESTRENGTHENING	RESULTATIVE	RESUSCITATIVE
RESPOOLING	RESTIMULATING	RESTRENGTHENS	RESULTATIVES	RESUSCITATOR
RESPOTTING	RESTIMULATION	RESTRESSED	RESULTLESS	RESUSCITATORS
RESPRAYING	RESTIMULATIONS	RESTRESSES	RESULTLESSNESS	RESUSPENDED

RESUSPENDING	RETALIATIONIST	RETICULATE	RETOTALLING	RETRANSMIT
RESUSPENDS	RETALIATIONISTS	RETICULATED	RETOUCHABLE	RETRANSMITS
RESVERATROL	RETALIATIONS	RETICULATELY	RETOUCHERS	RETRANSMITTED
RESVERATROLS	RETALIATIVE	RETICULATES	RETOUCHING	RETRANSMITTING
RESWALLOWED	RETALIATOR	RETICULATING	RETOUCHINGS	RETREADING
RESWALLOWING	RETALIATORS	RETICULATION	RETRACEABLE	RETREATANT
RESWALLOWS	RETALIATORY	RETICULATIONS	RETRACEMENT	RETREATANTS
RESYNCHRONISE	RETALLYING	RETICULOCYTE	RETRACEMENTS	RETREATERS
RESYNCHRONISED	RETARDANTS	RETICULOCYTES	RETRACKING	RETREATING
RESYNCHRONISES	RETARDATES	RETICULUMS	RETRACTABILITY	RETRENCHABLE
RESYNCHRONISING	RETARDATION	RETIGHTENED	RETRACTABLE	RETRENCHED
RESYNCHRONIZE	RETARDATIONS	RETIGHTENING	RETRACTATION	RETRENCHES
RESYNCHRONIZED	RETARDATIVE	RETIGHTENS	RETRACTATIONS	RETRENCHING
RESYNCHRONIZES	RETARDATORY	RETINACULA	RETRACTIBILITY	RETRENCHMENT
RESYNCHRONIZING	RETARDMENT	RETINACULAR	RETRACTIBLE	RETRENCHMENTS
RESYNTHESES	RETARDMENTS	RETINACULUM	RETRACTILE	RETRIBUTED
RESYNTHESIS	RETARGETED	RETINALITE	RETRACTILITIES	RETRIBUTES
RESYNTHESISE	RETARGETING	RETINALITES	RETRACTILITY	RETRIBUTING
RESYNTHESISED	RETEACHING	RETINISPORA	RETRACTING	RETRIBUTION
RESYNTHESISES	RETELLINGS	RETINISPORAS	RETRACTION	RETRIBUTIONS
RESYNTHESISING	RETEMPERED	RETINITIDES	RETRACTIONS	RETRIBUTIVE
RESYNTHESIZE	RETEMPERING	RETINITISES	RETRACTIVE	RETRIBUTIVELY
RESYNTHESIZED	RETENTIONIST	RETINOBLASTOMA	RETRACTIVELY	RETRIBUTOR
RESYNTHESIZES	RETENTIONISTS	RETINOBLASTOMAS	RETRACTORS	RETRIBUTORS
RESYNTHESIZING	RETENTIONS	RETINOPATHIES	RETRAINABLE	RETRIBUTORY
RESYSTEMATISE	RETENTIVELY	RETINOPATHY	RETRAINEES	RETRIEVABILITY
RESYSTEMATISED	RETENTIVENESS	RETINOSCOPE	RETRAINING	RETRIEVABLE
RESYSTEMATISES	RETENTIVENESSES	RETINOSCOPES	RETRAININGS	RETRIEVABLENESS
RESYSTEMATISING	RETENTIVES	RETINOSCOPIC	RETRANSFER	RETRIEVABLY
RESYSTEMATIZE	RETENTIVITIES	RETINOSCOPIES	RETRANSFERRED	RETRIEVALS
RESYSTEMATIZED	RETENTIVITY	RETINOSCOPIST	RETRANSFERRING	RETRIEVEMENT
RESYSTEMATIZES	RETESTIFIED	RETINOSCOPISTS	RETRANSFERS	RETRIEVEMENTS
RESYSTEMATIZING	RETESTIFIES	RETINOSCOPY	RETRANSFORM	RETRIEVERS
RETACKLING	RETESTIFYING	RETINOSPORA	RETRANSFORMED	RETRIEVING
RETAILINGS	RETEXTURED	RETINOSPORAS	RETRANSFORMING	RETRIEVINGS
RETAILMENT	RETEXTURES	RETINOTECTAL	RETRANSFORMS	RETRIMMING
RETAILMENTS	RETEXTURING	RETIRACIES	RETRANSFUSE	RETROACTED
RETAILORED	RETHINKERS	RETIREDNESS	RETRANSFUSED	RETROACTING
RETAILORING	RETHINKING	RETIREDNESSES	RETRANSFUSES	RETROACTION
RETAINABLE	RETHINKINGS	RETIREMENT	RETRANSFUSING	RETROACTIONS
RETAINERSHIP	RETHREADED	RETIREMENTS	RETRANSLATE	RETROACTIVE
RETAINERSHIPS	RETHREADING	RETIRINGLY	RETRANSLATED	RETROACTIVELY
RETAINMENT	RETICELLAS	RETIRINGNESS	RETRANSLATES	RETROACTIVENESS
RETAINMENTS	RETICENCES	RETIRINGNESSES	RETRANSLATING	RETROACTIVITIES
RETALIATED	RETICENCIES	RETORSIONS	RETRANSLATION	RETROACTIVITY
RETALIATES	RETICENTLY	RETORTIONS	RETRANSLATIONS	RETROBULBAR
RETALIATING	RETICULARLY	RETOTALING	RETRANSMISSION	RETROCEDED
RETALIATION	RETICULARY	RETOTALLED	RETRANSMISSIONS	RETROCEDENCE

R

RETROCEDENCES

RETROCEDENCES	RETROGRESSIVELY	RETROVIRUSES	REVALORISATION	REVELLINGS
RETROCEDENT	RETROJECTED	RETURNABILITIES	REVALORISATIONS	REVELMENTS
RETROCEDES	RETROJECTING	RETURNABILITY	REVALORISE	REVENDICATE
RETROCEDING	RETROJECTION	RETURNABLE	REVALORISED	REVENDICATED
RETROCESSION	RETROJECTIONS	RETURNABLES	REVALORISES	REVENDICATES
RETROCESSIONS	RETROJECTS	RETURNLESS	REVALORISING	REVENDICATING
RETROCESSIVE	RETROLENTAL	RETWEETING	REVALORIZATION	REVENDICATION
RETROCHOIR	RETROMINGENCIES	RETWISTING	REVALORIZATIONS	REVENDICATIONS
RETROCHOIRS	RETROMINGENCY	REUNIFICATION	REVALORIZE	REVENGEFUL
RETROCOGNITION	RETROMINGENT	REUNIFICATIONS	REVALORIZED	REVENGEFULLY
RETROCOGNITIONS	RETROMINGENTS	REUNIFYING	REVALORIZES	REVENGEFULNESS
RETRODICTED	RETROPACKS	REUNIONISM	REVALORIZING	REVENGELESS
RETRODICTING	RETROPERITONEAL	REUNIONISMS	REVALUATED	REVENGEMENT
RETRODICTION	RETROPHILIA	REUNIONIST	REVALUATES	REVENGEMENTS
RETRODICTIONS	RETROPHILIAC	REUNIONISTIC	REVALUATING	REVENGINGLY
RETRODICTIVE	RETROPHILIACS	REUNIONISTS	REVALUATION	REVENGINGS
RETRODICTS	RETROPHILIAS	REUNITABLE	REVALUATIONS	REVERBATORIES
RETROENGINE	RETROPULSION	REUPHOLSTER	REVAMPINGS	REVERBATORY
RETROENGINES	RETROPULSIONS	REUPHOLSTERED	REVANCHISM	REVERBERANT
RETROFIRED	RETROPULSIVE	REUPHOLSTERING	REVANCHISMS	REVERBERANTLY
RETROFIRES	RETROREFLECTION	REUPHOLSTERS	REVANCHIST	REVERBERATE
RETROFIRING	RETROREFLECTIVE	REUPTAKING	REVANCHISTS	REVERBERATED
RETROFITTED	RETROREFLECTOR	REUSABILITIES	REVARNISHED	REVERBERATES
RETROFITTING	RETROREFLECTORS	REUSABILITY	REVARNISHES	REVERBERATING
RETROFITTINGS	RETROROCKET	REUTILISATION	REVARNISHING	REVERBERATION
RETROFLECTED	RETROROCKETS	REUTILISATIONS	REVEALABILITIES	REVERBERATIONS
RETROFLECTION	RETRORSELY	REUTILISED	REVEALABILITY	REVERBERATIVE
RETROFLECTIONS	RETROSEXUAL	REUTILISES	REVEALABLE	REVERBERATOR
RETROFLEXED	RETROSEXUALS	REUTILISING	REVEALINGLY	REVERBERATORIES
RETROFLEXES	RETROSPECT	REUTILIZATION	REVEALINGNESS	REVERBERATORS
RETROFLEXING	RETROSPECTED	REUTILIZATIONS	REVEALINGNESSES	REVERBERATORY
RETROFLEXION	RETROSPECTING	REUTILIZED	REVEALINGS	REVERENCED
RETROFLEXIONS	RETROSPECTION	REUTILIZES	REVEALMENT	REVERENCER
RETROGRADATION	RETROSPECTIONS	REUTILIZING	REVEALMENTS	REVERENCERS
RETROGRADATIONS	RETROSPECTIVE	REUTTERING	REVEGETATE	REVERENCES
RETROGRADE	RETROSPECTIVELY	REVACCINATE	REVEGETATED	REVERENCING
RETROGRADED	RETROSPECTIVES	REVACCINATED	REVEGETATES	REVERENTIAL
RETROGRADELY	RETROSPECTS	REVACCINATES	REVEGETATING	REVERENTIALLY
RETROGRADES	RETROUSSAGE	REVACCINATING	REVEGETATION	REVERENTLY
RETROGRADING	RETROUSSAGES	REVACCINATION	REVEGETATIONS	REVERENTNESS
RETROGRESS	RETROVERSE	REVACCINATIONS	REVELATION	REVERENTNESSES
RETROGRESSED	RETROVERSION	REVALENTAS	REVELATIONAL	REVERIFIED
RETROGRESSES	RETROVERSIONS	REVALIDATE	REVELATIONIST	REVERIFIES
RETROGRESSING	RETROVERTED	REVALIDATED	REVELATIONISTS	REVERIFYING
RETROGRESSION	RETROVERTING	REVALIDATES	REVELATIONS	REVERSEDLY
RETROGRESSIONAL	RETROVERTS	REVALIDATING	REVELATIVE	REVERSELESS
RETROGRESSIONS	RETROVIRAL	REVALIDATION	REVELATORS	REVERSIBILITIES
RETROGRESSIVE	RETROVIRUS	REVALIDATIONS	REVELATORY	REVERSIBILITY

REVERSIBLE	REVISITATIONS	REVOKABILITIES	REWINDINGS	RHEOCHORDS
REVERSIBLES	REVISITING	REVOKABILITY	REWORDINGS	RHEOLOGICAL
REVERSIBLY	REVISUALISATION	REVOKEMENT	REWORKINGS	RHEOLOGICALLY
REVERSINGS	REVISUALIZATION	REVOKEMENTS	REWRAPPING	RHEOLOGIES
REVERSIONAL	REVITALISATION	REVOLTINGLY	REWRITABLE	RHEOLOGIST
REVERSIONALLY	REVITALISATIONS	REVOLUTION	REWRITEABLE	RHEOLOGISTS
REVERSIONARIES	REVITALISE	REVOLUTIONAL	RHABDOCOELE	RHEOMETERS
REVERSIONARY	REVITALISED	REVOLUTIONARIES	RHABDOCOELES	RHEOMETRIC
REVERSIONER	REVITALISES	REVOLUTIONARILY	RHABDOLITH	RHEOMETRICAL
REVERSIONERS	REVITALISING	REVOLUTIONARY	RHABDOLITHS	RHEOMETRIES
REVERSIONS	REVITALIZATION	REVOLUTIONER	RHABDOMANCER	RHEOMORPHIC
REVERSISES	REVITALIZATIONS	REVOLUTIONERS	RHABDOMANCERS	RHEOMORPHISM
REVERTANTS	REVITALIZE	REVOLUTIONISE	RHABDOMANCIES	RHEOMORPHISMS
REVERTIBLE	REVITALIZED	REVOLUTIONISED	RHABDOMANCY	RHEOPHILES
REVESTIARIES	REVITALIZES	REVOLUTIONISER	RHABDOMANTIST	RHEORECEPTOR
REVESTIARY	REVITALIZING	REVOLUTIONISERS	RHABDOMANTISTS	RHEORECEPTORS
REVESTRIES	REVIVABILITIES	REVOLUTIONISES	RHABDOMERE	RHEOSCOPES
REVETMENTS	REVIVABILITY	REVOLUTIONISING	RHABDOMERES	RHEOSTATIC
REVIBRATED	REVIVALISM	REVOLUTIONISM	RHABDOMYOMA	RHEOTACTIC
REVIBRATES	REVIVALISMS	REVOLUTIONISMS	RHABDOMYOMAS	RHEOTROPES
REVIBRATING	REVIVALIST	REVOLUTIONIST	RHABDOMYOMATA	RHEOTROPIC
REVICTUALED	REVIVALISTIC	REVOLUTIONISTS	RHABDOSPHERE	RHEOTROPISM
REVICTUALING	REVIVALISTS	REVOLUTIONIZE	RHABDOSPHERES	RHEOTROPISMS
REVICTUALLED	REVIVEMENT	REVOLUTIONIZED	RHABDOVIRUS	RHETORICAL
REVICTUALLING	REVIVEMENTS	REVOLUTIONIZER	RHABDOVIRUSES	RHETORICALLY
REVICTUALS	REVIVESCENCE	REVOLUTIONIZERS	RHACHIDIAL	RHETORICIAN
REVIEWABLE	REVIVESCENCES	REVOLUTIONIZES	RHACHILLAS	RHETORICIANS
REVILEMENT	REVIVESCENCIES	REVOLUTIONIZING	RHACHITISES	RHETORISED
REVILEMENTS	REVIVESCENCY	REVOLUTIONS	RHADAMANTHINE	RHETORISES
REVILINGLY	REVIVESCENT	REVOLVABLE	RHAGADIFORM	RHETORISING
REVINDICATE	REVIVIFICATION	REVOLVABLY	RHAMNACEOUS	RHETORIZED
REVINDICATED	REVIVIFICATIONS	REVOLVENCIES	RHAMPHOTHECA	RHETORIZES
REVINDICATES	REVIVIFIED	REVOLVENCY	RHAMPHOTHECAE	RHETORIZING
REVINDICATING	REVIVIFIES	REVOLVINGLY	RHAPONTICS	RHEUMATEESE
REVINDICATION	REVIVIFYING	REVOLVINGS	RHAPSODICAL	RHEUMATEESES
REVINDICATIONS	REVIVINGLY	REVULSIONARY	RHAPSODICALLY	RHEUMATICAL
REVIOLATED	REVIVISCENCE	REVULSIONS	RHAPSODIES	RHEUMATICALLY
REVIOLATES	REVIVISCENCES	REVULSIVELY	RHAPSODISE	RHEUMATICKY
REVIOLATING	REVIVISCENCIES	REVULSIVES	RHAPSODISED	RHEUMATICS
REVISIONAL	REVIVISCENCY	REWAKENING	RHAPSODISES	RHEUMATISE
REVISIONARY	REVIVISCENT	REWARDABLE	RHAPSODISING	RHEUMATISES
REVISIONISM	REVOCABILITIES	REWARDABLENESS	RHAPSODIST	RHEUMATISM
REVISIONISMS	REVOCABILITY	REWARDINGLY	RHAPSODISTIC	RHEUMATISMAL
REVISIONIST	REVOCABLENESS	REWARDLESS	RHAPSODISTS	RHEUMATISMS
REVISIONISTS	REVOCABLENESSES	REWATERING	RHAPSODIZE	RHEUMATIZE
REVISITANT	REVOCATION	REWEIGHING	RHAPSODIZED	RHEUMATIZES
REVISITANTS	REVOCATIONS	REWIDENING	RHAPSODIZES	RHEUMATOID
REVISITATION	REVOCATORY	REWILDINGS	RHAPSODIZING	RHEUMATOIDALLY

RHEUMATOLOGICAL	RHINOSCOPIES	RHODODAPHNE	RHUBARBINGS	RIBBONWOOD
RHEUMATOLOGIES	RHINOSCOPY	RHODODAPHNES	RHUMBATRON	RIBBONWOODS
RHEUMATOLOGIST	RHINOTHECA	RHODODENDRA	RHUMBATRONS	RIBGRASSES
RHEUMATOLOGISTS	RHINOTHECAE	RHODODENDRON	RHYMESTERS	RIBOFLAVIN
RHEUMATOLOGY	RHINOVIRUS	RHODODENDRONS	RHYNCHOCOEL	RIBOFLAVINE
RHIGOLENES	RHINOVIRUSES	RHODOLITES	RHYNCHOCOELS	RIBOFLAVINES
RHINENCEPHALA	RHIPIDIONS	RHODOMONTADE	RHYNCHODONT	RIBOFLAVINS
RHINENCEPHALIC	RHIPIDIUMS	RHODOMONTADED	RHYNCHOPHORE	RIBONUCLEASE
RHINENCEPHALON	RHIZANTHOUS	RHODOMONTADES	RHYNCHOPHORES	RIBONUCLEASES
RHINENCEPHALONS	RHIZOCARPIC	RHODOMONTADING	RHYNCHOPHOROUS	RIBONUCLEIC
RHINESTONE	RHIZOCARPOUS	RHODONITES	RHYPAROGRAPHER	RIBONUCLEOSIDE
RHINESTONED	RHIZOCARPS	RHODOPHANE	RHYPAROGRAPHERS	RIBONUCLEOSIDES
RHINESTONES	RHIZOCAULS	RHODOPHANES	RHYPAROGRAPHIC	RIBONUCLEOTIDE
RHINITIDES	RHIZOCEPHALAN	RHODOPSINS	RHYPAROGRAPHIES	RIBONUCLEOTIDES
RHINITISES	RHIZOCEPHALANS	RHOEADINES	RHYPAROGRAPHY	RICEFIELDS
RHINOCERICAL	RHIZOCEPHALOUS	RHOICISSUS	RHYTHMICAL	RICEGRASSES
RHINOCEROI	RHIZOCTONIA	RHOICISSUSES	RHYTHMICALLY	RICERCARES
RHINOCEROS	RHIZOCTONIAS	RHOMBENCEPHALA	RHYTHMICITIES	RICERCATAS
RHINOCEROSES	RHIZOGENETIC	RHOMBENCEPHALON	RHYTHMICITY	RICHNESSES
RHINOCEROT	RHIZOGENIC	RHOMBENPORPHYR	RHYTHMISATION	RICINOLEIC
RHINOCEROTE	RHIZOGENOUS	RHOMBENPORPHYRS	RHYTHMISATIONS	RICKBURNER
RHINOCEROTES	RHIZOMATOUS	RHOMBENPORPHYRY	RHYTHMISED	RICKBURNERS
RHINOCEROTIC	RHIZOMORPH	RHOMBOHEDRA	RHYTHMISES	RICKETIEST
RHINOLALIA	RHIZOMORPHOUS	RHOMBOHEDRAL	RHYTHMISING	RICKETINESS
RHINOLALIAS	RHIZOMORPHS	RHOMBOHEDRON	RHYTHMISTS	RICKETINESSES
RHINOLITHS	RHIZOPHAGOUS	RHOMBOHEDRONS	RHYTHMIZATION	RICKETTIER
RHINOLOGICAL	RHIZOPHILOUS	RHOMBOIDAL	RHYTHMIZATIONS	RICKETTIEST
RHINOLOGIES	RHIZOPHORE	RHOMBOIDEI	RHYTHMIZED	RICKETTSIA
RHINOLOGIST	RHIZOPHORES	RHOMBOIDES	RHYTHMIZES	RICKETTSIAE
RHINOLOGISTS	RHIZOPLANE	RHOMBOIDEUS	RHYTHMIZING	RICKETTSIAL
RHINOPHONIA	RHIZOPLANES	RHOMBPORPHYRIES	RHYTHMLESS	RICKETTSIAS
RHINOPHONIAS	RHIZOPODAN	RHOMBPORPHYRY	RHYTHMMOMETER	RICKSTANDS
RHINOPHYMA	RHIZOPODANS	RHOPALISMS	RHYTHMMOMETERS	RICKSTICKS
RHINOPHYMAS	RHIZOPODOUS	RHOPALOCERAL	RHYTHMOPOEIA	RICOCHETED
RHINOPLASTIC	RHIZOPUSES	RHOPALOCEROUS	RHYTHMOPOEIAS	RICOCHETING
RHINOPLASTIES	RHIZOSPHERE	RHOTACISED	RHYTHMUSES	RICOCHETTED
RHINOPLASTY	RHIZOSPHERES	RHOTACISES	RHYTIDECTOMIES	RICOCHETTING
RHINORRHAGIA	RHIZOTOMIES	RHOTACISING	RHYTIDECTOMY	RIDABILITIES
RHINORRHAGIAS	RHODAMINES	RHOTACISMS	RHYTIDOMES	RIDABILITY
RHINORRHOEA	RHODANATES	RHOTACISTIC	RIBALDRIES	RIDDLINGLY
RHINORRHOEAL	RHODANISED	RHOTACISTS	RIBATTUTAS	RIDERSHIPS
RHINORRHOEAS	RHODANISES	RHOTACIZED	RIBAUDRIES	RIDESHARING
RHINOSCLEROMA	RHODANISING	RHOTACIZES	RIBAVIRINS	RIDESHARINGS
RHINOSCLEROMAS	RHODANIZED	RHOTACIZING	RIBBONFISH	RIDGEBACKS
RHINOSCLEROMATA	RHODANIZES	RHOTICITIES	RIBBONFISHES	RIDGELINES
RHINOSCOPE	RHODANIZING	RHUBARBIER	RIBBONIEST	RIDGELINGS
RHINOSCOPES	RHODOCHROSITE	RHUBARBIEST	RIBBONLIKE	RIDGEPOLES
RHINOSCOPIC	RHODOCHROSITES	RHUBARBING	RIBBONRIES	RIDGETREES

RIDICULERS	RIGWIDDIES	RISORGIMENTOS	RIVERWORTHIER	ROCKABILLIES
RIDICULING	RIGWOODIES	RISTRETTOS	RIVERWORTHIEST	ROCKABILLY
RIDICULOUS	RIJKSDAALER	RITARDANDI	RIVERWORTHINESS	ROCKBURSTS
RIDICULOUSLY	RIJKSDAALERS	RITARDANDO	RIVERWORTHY	ROCKCRESSES
RIDICULOUSNESS	RIJSTAFELS	RITARDANDOS	RIVETINGLY	ROCKETEERS
RIEBECKITE	RIJSTTAFEL	RITONAVIRS	ROADABILITIES	ROCKETRIES
RIEBECKITES	RIJSTTAFELS	RITORNELLE	ROADABILITY	ROCKETSONDE
RIFACIMENTI	RIMINESSES	RITORNELLES	ROADBLOCKED	ROCKETSONDES
RIFACIMENTO	RIMOSITIES	RITORNELLI	ROADBLOCKING	ROCKFISHES
RIFACIMENTOS	RINDERPEST	RITORNELLO	ROADBLOCKS	ROCKHOPPER
RIFAMPICIN	RINDERPESTS	RITORNELLOS	ROADCRAFTS	ROCKHOPPERS
RIFAMPICINS	RINFORZANDO	RITORNELLS	ROADHEADER	ROCKHOUNDING
RIFAMYCINS	RINGBARKED	RITOURNELLE	ROADHEADERS	ROCKHOUNDINGS
RIFENESSES	RINGBARKING	RITOURNELLES	ROADHOLDING	ROCKHOUNDS
RIFLEBIRDS	RINGHALSES	RITUALISATION	ROADHOLDINGS	ROCKINESSES
RIGAMAROLE	RINGLEADER	RITUALISATIONS	ROADHOUSES	ROCKSHAFTS
RIGAMAROLES	RINGLEADERS	RITUALISED	ROADMAKING	ROCKSLIDES
RIGHTABLENESS	RINGLETIER	RITUALISES	ROADMAKINGS	ROCKSTEADIES
RIGHTABLENESSES	RINGLETIEST	RITUALISING	ROADMENDER	ROCKSTEADY
RIGHTENING	RINGMASTER	RITUALISMS	ROADMENDERS	ROCKWATERS
RIGHTEOUSLY	RINGMASTERS	RITUALISTIC	ROADROLLER	RODENTICIDE
RIGHTEOUSNESS	RINGSIDERS	RITUALISTICALLY	ROADROLLERS	RODENTICIDES
RIGHTEOUSNESSES	RINGSTANDS	RITUALISTS	ROADRUNNER	RODFISHERS
RIGHTFULLY	RINGSTRAKED	RITUALIZATION	ROADRUNNERS	RODFISHING
RIGHTFULNESS	RINGTOSSES	RITUALIZATIONS	ROADSTEADS	RODFISHINGS
RIGHTFULNESSES	RINKHALSES	RITUALIZED	ROADWORTHIER	RODGERSIAS
RIGHTNESSES	RINSABILITIES	RITUALIZES	ROADWORTHIES	RODOMONTADE
RIGHTSIZED	RINSABILITY	RITUALIZING	ROADWORTHIEST	RODOMONTADED
RIGHTSIZES	RINSIBILITIES	RITUXIMABS	ROADWORTHINESS	RODOMONTADER
RIGHTSIZING	RINSIBILITY	RITZINESSES	ROADWORTHY	RODOMONTADERS
RIGHTSIZINGS	RINTHEREOUT	RIVALESSES	ROBERDSMAN	RODOMONTADES
RIGHTWARDLY	RINTHEREOUTS	RIVALISING	ROBERDSMEN	RODOMONTADING
RIGHTWARDS	RIOTOUSNESS	RIVALITIES	ROBERTSMAN	ROENTGENISATION
RIGIDIFICATION	RIOTOUSNESSES	RIVALIZING	ROBERTSMEN	ROENTGENISE
RIGIDIFICATIONS	RIPENESSES	RIVALSHIPS	ROBORATING	ROENTGENISED
RIGIDIFIED	RIPIDOLITE	RIVERBANKS	ROBOTICALLY	ROENTGENISES
RIGIDIFIES	RIPIDOLITES	RIVERBOATS	ROBOTISATION	ROENTGENISING
RIGIDIFYING	RIPIENISTS	RIVERCRAFT	ROBOTISATIONS	ROENTGENIUM
RIGIDISING	RIPPLINGLY	RIVERCRAFTS	ROBOTISING	ROENTGENIUMS
RIGIDITIES	RIPRAPPING	RIVERFRONT	ROBOTIZATION	ROENTGENIZATION
RIGIDIZING	RIPSNORTER	RIVERFRONTS	ROBOTIZATIONS	ROENTGENIZE
RIGIDNESSES	RIPSNORTERS	RIVERHEADS	ROBOTIZING	ROENTGENIZED
RIGMAROLES	RIPSNORTING	RIVERSCAPE	ROBUSTIOUS	ROENTGENIZES
RIGORISTIC	RIPSNORTINGLY	RIVERSCAPES	ROBUSTIOUSLY	ROENTGENIZING
RIGOROUSLY	RISIBILITIES	RIVERSIDES	ROBUSTIOUSNESS	ROENTGENOGRAM
RIGOROUSNESS	RISIBILITY	RIVERWALKS	ROBUSTNESS	ROENTGENOGRAMS
RIGOROUSNESSES	RISKINESSES	RIVERWARDS	ROBUSTNESSES	ROENTGENOGRAPH
RIGSDALERS	RISORGIMENTO	RIVERWEEDS	ROCAMBOLES	ROENTGENOGRAPHS

R

ROENTGENOGRAPHY	ROMANIZATION	RONTGENOPAQUE	ROSTERINGS	ROUGHCASTERS
ROENTGENOLOGIC	ROMANIZATIONS	RONTGENOSCOPE	ROSTROCARINATE	ROUGHCASTING
ROENTGENOLOGIES	ROMANIZING	RONTGENOSCOPES	ROSTROCARINATES	ROUGHCASTS
ROENTGENOLOGIST	ROMANTICAL	RONTGENOSCOPIC	ROTACHUTES	ROUGHDRIED
ROENTGENOLOGY	ROMANTICALITIES	RONTGENOSCOPIES	ROTAMETERS	ROUGHDRIES
ROENTGENOPAQUE	ROMANTICALITY	RONTGENOSCOPY	ROTAPLANES	ROUGHDRYING
ROENTGENOSCOPE	ROMANTICALLY	RONTGENOTHERAPY	ROTATIONAL	ROUGHENING
ROENTGENOSCOPES	ROMANTICISATION	ROOFLESSNESS	ROTATIVELY	ROUGHHEWED
ROENTGENOSCOPIC	ROMANTICISE	ROOFLESSNESSES	ROTAVATING	ROUGHHEWING
ROENTGENOSCOPY	ROMANTICISED	ROOFSCAPES	ROTAVATORS	ROUGHHOUSE
ROGUESHIPS	ROMANTICISES	ROOMINESSES	ROTAVIRUSES	ROUGHHOUSED
ROGUISHNESS	ROMANTICISING	ROOTEDNESS	ROTGRASSES	ROUGHHOUSES
ROGUISHNESSES	ROMANTICISM	ROOTEDNESSES	ROTIFERANS	ROUGHHOUSING
ROISTERERS	ROMANTICISMS	ROOTINESSES	ROTIFEROUS	ROUGHHOUSINGS
ROISTERING	ROMANTICIST	ROOTLESSNESS	ROTISSERIE	ROUGHNECKED
ROISTERINGS	ROMANTICISTS	ROOTLESSNESSES	ROTISSERIED	ROUGHNECKING
ROISTEROUS	ROMANTICIZATION	ROOTSERVER	ROTISSERIEING	ROUGHNECKS
ROISTEROUSLY	ROMANTICIZE	ROOTSERVERS	ROTISSERIES	ROUGHNESSES
ROLLCOLLAR	ROMANTICIZED	ROOTSINESS	ROTOGRAPHED	ROUGHRIDER
ROLLCOLLARS	ROMANTICIZES	ROOTSINESSES	ROTOGRAPHING	ROUGHRIDERS
ROLLERBALL	ROMANTICIZING	ROOTSTALKS	ROTOGRAPHS	ROULETTING
ROLLERBALLS	ROMELDALES	ROOTSTOCKS	ROTOGRAVURE	ROUNCEVALS
ROLLERBLADE	ROMPISHNESS	ROPEDANCER	ROTOGRAVURES	ROUNDABOUT
ROLLERBLADED	ROMPISHNESSES	ROPEDANCERS	ROTORCRAFT	ROUNDABOUTATION
ROLLERBLADER	RONDOLETTO	ROPEDANCING	ROTORCRAFTS	ROUNDABOUTED
ROLLERBLADERS	RONDOLETTOS	ROPEDANCINGS	ROTOSCOPED	ROUNDABOUTEDLY
ROLLERBLADES	RONTGENISATION	ROPEWALKER	ROTOSCOPES	ROUNDABOUTILITY
ROLLERBLADING	RONTGENISATIONS	ROPEWALKERS	ROTOSCOPING	ROUNDABOUTING
ROLLERBLADINGS	RONTGENISE	ROPINESSES	ROTOTILLED	ROUNDABOUTLY
ROLLERCOASTER	RONTGENISED	ROQUEFORTS	ROTOTILLER	ROUNDABOUTNESS
ROLLERCOASTERED	RONTGENISES	ROQUELAURE	ROTOTILLERS	ROUNDABOUTS
ROLLERCOASTERS	RONTGENISING	ROQUELAURES	ROTOTILLING	ROUNDARCHED
ROLLERDROME	RONTGENIZATION	ROSANILINE	ROTOVATING	ROUNDBALLS
ROLLERDROMES	RONTGENIZATIONS	ROSANILINES	ROTOVATORS	ROUNDEDNESS
ROLLICKIER	RONTGENIZE	ROSANILINS	ROTTENNESS	ROUNDEDNESSES
ROLLICKIEST	RONTGENIZED	ROSEBUSHES	ROTTENNESSES	ROUNDELAYS
ROLLICKING	RONTGENIZES	ROSEFINCHES	ROTTENSTONE	ROUNDHANDS
ROLLICKINGS	RONTGENIZING	ROSEFISHES	ROTTENSTONED	ROUNDHEADED
ROLLOCKING	RONTGENOGRAM	ROSEMALING	ROTTENSTONES	ROUNDHEADEDNESS
ROLLOCKINGS	RONTGENOGRAMS	ROSEMALINGS	ROTTENSTONING	ROUNDHEELS
ROMANCICAL	RONTGENOGRAPH	ROSEMARIES	ROTTWEILER	ROUNDHOUSE
ROMANCINGS	RONTGENOGRAPHS	ROSETTINGS	ROTTWEILERS	ROUNDHOUSES
ROMANESCOS	RONTGENOGRAPHY	ROSEWATERS	ROTUNDITIES	ROUNDNESSES
ROMANICITE	RONTGENOLOGICAL	ROSINESSES	ROTUNDNESS	ROUNDTABLE
ROMANICITES	RONTGENOLOGIES	ROSINWEEDS	ROTUNDNESSES	ROUNDTABLES
ROMANISATION	RONTGENOLOGIST	ROSMARINES	ROUGHBACKS	ROUNDTRIPPING
ROMANISATIONS	RONTGENOLOGISTS	ROSTELLATE	ROUGHCASTED	ROUNDTRIPPINGS
ROMANISING	RONTGENOLOGY	ROSTELLUMS	ROUGHCASTER	ROUNDTRIPS

ROUNDWOODS	RUBBERNECKED	RUDDINESSES	RUMGUMPTION	RUSSIFYING
ROUNDWORMS	RUBBERNECKER	RUDENESSES	RUMGUMPTIONS	RUSTBUCKET
ROUSEABOUT	RUBBERNECKERS	RUDIMENTAL	RUMINANTLY	RUSTBUCKETS
ROUSEABOUTS	RUBBERNECKING	RUDIMENTALLY	RUMINATING	RUSTICALLY
ROUSEDNESS	RUBBERNECKS	RUDIMENTARILY	RUMINATINGLY	RUSTICATED
ROUSEDNESSES	RUBBERWEAR	RUDIMENTARINESS	RUMINATION	RUSTICATES
ROUSEMENTS	RUBBERWEARS	RUDIMENTARY	RUMINATIONS	RUSTICATING
ROUSSETTES	RUBBISHIER	RUEFULNESS	RUMINATIVE	RUSTICATINGS
ROUSTABOUT	RUBBISHIEST	RUEFULNESSES	RUMINATIVELY	RUSTICATION
ROUSTABOUTS	RUBBISHING	RUFESCENCE	RUMINATORS	RUSTICATIONS
ROUTEMARCH	RUBBISHLIER	RUFESCENCES	RUMLEGUMPTION	RUSTICATOR
ROUTEMARCHED	RUBBISHLIEST	RUFFIANING	RUMLEGUMPTIONS	RUSTICATORS
ROUTEMARCHES	RUBBLEWORK	RUFFIANISH	RUMMELGUMPTION	RUSTICISED
ROUTEMARCHING	RUBBLEWORKS	RUFFIANISM	RUMMELGUMPTIONS	RUSTICISES
ROUTINEERS	RUBEFACIENT	RUFFIANISMS	RUMMINESSES	RUSTICISING
ROUTINISATION	RUBEFACIENTS	RUGGEDISATION	RUMMISHING	RUSTICISMS
ROUTINISATIONS	RUBEFACTION	RUGGEDISATIONS	RUMMLEGUMPTION	RUSTICITIES
ROUTINISED	RUBEFACTIONS	RUGGEDISED	RUMMLEGUMPTIONS	RUSTICIZED
ROUTINISES	RUBELLITES	RUGGEDISES	RUMORMONGER	RUSTICIZES
ROUTINISING	RUBESCENCE	RUGGEDISING	RUMORMONGERING	RUSTICIZING
ROUTINISMS	RUBESCENCES	RUGGEDIZATION	RUMORMONGERINGS	RUSTICWORK
ROUTINISTS	RUBIACEOUS	RUGGEDIZATIONS	RUMORMONGERS	RUSTICWORKS
ROUTINIZATION	RUBICELLES	RUGGEDIZED	RUMRUNNERS	RUSTINESSES
ROUTINIZATIONS	RUBICONING	RUGGEDIZES	RUNAROUNDS	RUSTLINGLY
ROUTINIZED	RUBICUNDITIES	RUGGEDIZING	RUNECRAFTS	RUSTPROOFED
ROUTINIZES	RUBICUNDITY	RUGGEDNESS	RUNNINESSES	RUSTPROOFING
ROUTINIZING	RUBIGINOSE	RUGGEDNESSES	RUNTINESSES	RUSTPROOFINGS
ROWANBERRIES	RUBIGINOUS	RUGOSITIES	RUPESTRIAN	RUSTPROOFS
ROWANBERRY	RUBRICALLY	RUINATIONS	RUPICOLINE	RUTHENIOUS
ROWDINESSES	RUBRICATED	RUINOUSNESS	RUPICOLOUS	RUTHENIUMS
ROWDYDOWED	RUBRICATES	RUINOUSNESSES	RUPTURABLE	RUTHERFORD
ROWDYDOWING	RUBRICATING	RULERSHIPS	RUPTUREWORT	RUTHERFORDIUM
ROYALISING	RUBRICATION	RUMBLEDETHUMP	RUPTUREWORTS	RUTHERFORDIUMS
ROYALISTIC	RUBRICATIONS	RUMBLEDETHUMPS	RURALISATION	RUTHERFORDS
ROYALIZING	RUBRICATOR	RUMBLEGUMPTION	RURALISATIONS	RUTHFULNESS
ROYALMASTS	RUBRICATORS	RUMBLEGUMPTIONS	RURALISING	RUTHFULNESSES
ROYSTERERS	RUBRICIANS	RUMBLINGLY	RURALITIES	RUTHLESSLY
ROYSTERING	RUBYTHROAT	RUMBULLION	RURALIZATION	RUTHLESSNESS
ROYSTEROUS	RUBYTHROATS	RUMBULLIONS	RURALIZATIONS	RUTHLESSNESSES
RUBBERIEST	RUCTATIONS	RUMBUNCTIOUS	RURALIZING	RUTTINESSES
RUBBERISED	RUDBECKIAS	RUMBUSTICAL	RURALNESSES	RUTTISHNESS
RUBBERISES	RUDDERHEAD	RUMBUSTIOUS	RURIDECANAL	RUTTISHNESSES
RUBBERISING	RUDDERHEADS	RUMBUSTIOUSLY	RUSHINESSES	RYBAUDRYES
RUBBERIZED	RUDDERLESS	RUMBUSTIOUSNESS	RUSHLIGHTS	RYEGRASSES
RUBBERIZES	RUDDERPOST	RUMELGUMPTION	RUSSETIEST	
RUBBERIZING	RUDDERPOSTS	RUMELGUMPTIONS	RUSSETINGS	
RUBBERLIKE	RUDDERSTOCK	RUMFUSTIAN	RUSSETTING	
RUBBERNECK	RUDDERSTOCKS	RUMFUSTIANS	RUSSETTINGS	

R

S

SABADILLAS	SACCHARIMETRIES	SACERDOTALISMS	SACREDNESSES	SADDLEROOMS
SABBATARIAN	SACCHARIMETRY	SACERDOTALIST	SACRIFICEABLE	SADDLETREE
SABBATICAL	SACCHARINE	SACERDOTALISTS	SACRIFICED	SADDLETREES
SABBATICALS	SACCHARINELY	SACERDOTALIZE	SACRIFICER	SADISTICALLY
SABBATISED	SACCHARINES	SACERDOTALIZED	SACRIFICERS	SADOMASOCHISM
SABBATISES	SACCHARINITIES	SACERDOTALIZES	SACRIFICES	SADOMASOCHISMS
SABBATISING	SACCHARINITY	SACERDOTALIZING	SACRIFICIAL	SADOMASOCHIST
SABBATISMS	SACCHARINS	SACERDOTALLY	SACRIFICIALLY	SADOMASOCHISTIC
SABBATIZED	SACCHARISATION	SACHEMDOMS	SACRIFICING	SADOMASOCHISTS
SABBATIZES	SACCHARISATIONS	SACHEMSHIP	SACRIFYING	SAFECRACKER
SABBATIZING	SACCHARISE	SACHEMSHIPS	SACRILEGES	SAFECRACKERS
SABERMETRICIAN	SACCHARISED	SACKCLOTHS	SACRILEGIOUS	SAFECRACKING
SABERMETRICIANS	SACCHARISES	SACRALGIAS	SACRILEGIOUSLY	SAFECRACKINGS
SABERMETRICS	SACCHARISING	SACRALISATION	SACRILEGIST	SAFEGUARDED
SABLEFISHES	SACCHARIZATION	SACRALISATIONS	SACRILEGISTS	SAFEGUARDING
SABOTAGING	SACCHARIZATIONS	SACRALISED	SACRISTANS	SAFEGUARDS
SABRETACHE	SACCHARIZE	SACRALISES	SACRISTIES	SAFEKEEPING
SABRETACHES	SACCHARIZED	SACRALISING	SACROCOCCYGEAL	SAFEKEEPINGS
SABREWINGS	SACCHARIZES	SACRALITIES	SACROCOSTAL	SAFELIGHTS
SABULOSITIES	SACCHARIZING	SACRALIZATION	SACROCOSTALS	SAFENESSES
SABULOSITY	SACCHAROID	SACRALIZATIONS	SACROILIAC	SAFFLOWERS
SABURRATION	SACCHAROIDAL	SACRALIZED	SACROILIACS	SAFFRONIER
SABURRATIONS	SACCHAROIDS	SACRALIZES	SACROILIITIS	SAFFRONIEST
SACAHUISTA	SACCHAROMETER	SACRALIZING	SACROILIITISES	SAFRANINES
SACAHUISTAS	SACCHAROMETERS	SACRAMENTAL	SACROSANCT	SAGACIOUSLY
SACAHUISTE	SACCHAROMETRIES	SACRAMENTALISM	SACROSANCTITIES	SAGACIOUSNESS
SACAHUISTES	SACCHAROMETRY	SACRAMENTALISMS	SACROSANCTITY	SAGACIOUSNESSES
SACCADICALLY	SACCHAROMYCES	SACRAMENTALIST	SACROSANCTNESS	SAGACITIES
SACCHARASE	SACCHAROMYCETES	SACRAMENTALISTS	SADDLEBACK	SAGANASHES
SACCHARASES	SACCHAROSE	SACRAMENTALITY	SADDLEBACKED	SAGAPENUMS
SACCHARATE	SACCHAROSES	SACRAMENTALLY	SADDLEBACKS	SAGEBRUSHES
SACCHARATED	SACCHARUMS	SACRAMENTALNESS	SADDLEBAGS	SAGENESSES
SACCHARATES	SACCULATED	SACRAMENTALS	SADDLEBILL	SAGINATING
SACCHARIDE	SACCULATION	SACRAMENTARIAN	SADDLEBILLS	SAGINATION
SACCHARIDES	SACCULATIONS	SACRAMENTARIANS	SADDLEBOWS	SAGINATIONS
SACCHARIFEROUS	SACCULIFORM	SACRAMENTARIES	SADDLEBRED	SAGITTALLY
SACCHARIFIED	SACERDOTAL	SACRAMENTARY	SADDLEBREDS	SAGITTARIES
SACCHARIFIES	SACERDOTALISE	SACRAMENTED	SADDLECLOTH	SAGITTIFORM
SACCHARIFY	SACERDOTALISED	SACRAMENTING	SADDLECLOTHS	SAILBOARDED
SACCHARIFYING	SACERDOTALISES	SACRAMENTS	SADDLELESS	SAILBOARDER
SACCHARIMETER	SACERDOTALISING	SACRARIUMS	SADDLERIES	SAILBOARDERS
SACCHARIMETERS	SACERDOTALISM	SACREDNESS	SADDLEROOM	SAILBOARDING

SAILBOARDINGS	SALBUTAMOL	SALINIZATION	SALTARELLO	SALUTATORILY
SAILBOARDS	SALBUTAMOLS	SALINIZATIONS	SALTARELLOS	SALUTATORY
SAILBOATER	SALEABILITIES	SALINIZING	SALTATIONISM	SALUTIFEROUS
SAILBOATERS	SALEABILITY	SALINOMETER	SALTATIONISMS	SALVABILITIES
SAILBOATING	SALEABLENESS	SALINOMETERS	SALTATIONIST	SALVABILITY
SAILBOATINGS	SALEABLENESSES	SALINOMETRIC	SALTATIONISTS	SALVABLENESS
SAILCLOTHS	SALERATUSES	SALINOMETRIES	SALTATIONS	SALVABLENESSES
SAILFISHES	SALESCLERK	SALINOMETRY	SALTATORIAL	SALVAGEABILITY
SAILMAKERS	SALESCLERKS	SALIVATING	SALTATORIOUS	SALVAGEABLE
SAILMAKING	SALESGIRLS	SALIVATION	SALTBUSHES	SALVARSANS
SAILMAKINGS	SALESLADIES	SALIVATIONS	SALTCELLAR	SALVATIONAL
SAILORINGS	SALESMANSHIP	SALIVATORS	SALTCELLARS	SALVATIONISM
SAILORLESS	SALESMANSHIPS	SALLENDERS	SALTCHUCKER	SALVATIONISMS
SAILORLIER	SALESPEOPLE	SALLOWIEST	SALTCHUCKERS	SALVATIONIST
SAILORLIEST	SALESPERSON	SALLOWNESS	SALTCHUCKS	SALVATIONISTS
SAILORLIKE	SALESPERSONS	SALLOWNESSES	SALTFISHES	SALVATIONS
SAILPLANED	SALESROOMS	SALLYPORTS	SALTIGRADE	SALVATORIES
SAILPLANER	SALESWOMAN	SALMAGUNDI	SALTIGRADES	SALVERFORM
SAILPLANERS	SALESWOMEN	SALMAGUNDIES	SALTIMBANCO	SALVIFICAL
SAILPLANES	SALIAUNCES	SALMAGUNDIS	SALTIMBANCOS	SALVIFICALLY
SAILPLANING	SALICACEOUS	SALMAGUNDY	SALTIMBOCCA	SALVINIACEOUS
SAILPLANINGS	SALICETUMS	SALMANASER	SALTIMBOCCAS	SAMARIFORM
SAINTESSES	SALICIONAL	SALMANASERS	SALTINESSES	SAMARITANS
SAINTFOINS	SALICIONALS	SALMANAZAR	SALTIREWISE	SAMARSKITE
SAINTHOODS	SALICORNIA	SALMANAZARS	SALTISHNESS	SAMARSKITES
SAINTLIEST	SALICORNIAS	SALMONBERRIES	SALTISHNESSES	SAMENESSES
SAINTLINESS	SALICYLAMIDE	SALMONBERRY	SALTNESSES	SAMEYNESSES
SAINTLINESSES	SALICYLAMIDES	SALMONELLA	SALTPETERS	SAMNITISES
SAINTLINGS	SALICYLATE	SALMONELLAE	SALTPETREMAN	SAMPLERIES
SAINTPAULIA	SALICYLATED	SALMONELLAS	SALTPETREMEN	SANATORIUM
SAINTPAULIAS	SALICYLATES	SALMONELLOSES	SALTPETRES	SANATORIUMS
SAINTSHIPS	SALICYLATING	SALMONELLOSIS	SALTSHAKER	SANBENITOS
SALABILITIES	SALICYLISM	SALMONIEST	SALTSHAKERS	SANCTIFIABLE
SALABILITY	SALICYLISMS	SALMONOIDS	SALTWATERS	SANCTIFICATION
SALABLENESS	SALIENCIES	SALOMETERS	SALUBRIOUS	SANCTIFICATIONS
SALABLENESSES	SALIENTIAN	SALOPETTES	SALUBRIOUSLY	SANCTIFIED
SALACIOUSLY	SALIENTIANS	SALPIGLOSSES	SALUBRIOUSNESS	SANCTIFIEDLY
SALACIOUSNESS	SALIFEROUS	SALPIGLOSSIS	SALUBRITIES	SANCTIFIER
SALACIOUSNESSES	SALIFIABLE	SALPIGLOSSISES	SALURETICS	SANCTIFIERS
SALACITIES	SALIFICATION	SALPINGECTOMIES	SALUTARILY	SANCTIFIES
SALAMANDER	SALIFICATIONS	SALPINGECTOMY	SALUTARINESS	SANCTIFYING
SALAMANDERS	SALIMETERS	SALPINGIAN	SALUTARINESSES	SANCTIFYINGLY
SALAMANDRIAN	SALIMETRIC	SALPINGITIC	SALUTATION	SANCTIFYINGS
SALAMANDRIANS	SALIMETRIES	SALPINGITIS	SALUTATIONAL	SANCTIMONIES
SALAMANDRINE	SALINISATION	SALPINGITISES	SALUTATIONS	SANCTIMONIOUS
SALAMANDROID	SALINISATIONS	SALSOLACEOUS	SALUTATORIAN	SANCTIMONIOUSLY
SALAMANDROIDS	SALINISING	SALSUGINOUS	SALUTATORIANS	SANCTIMONY
SALANGANES	SALINITIES	SALTARELLI	SALUTATORIES	SANCTIONABLE

SANCTIONED	SANDLOTTERS	SANITARIANS	SAPLESSNESS	SAPSUCKERS
SANCTIONEER	SANDPAINTING	SANITARIES	SAPLESSNESSES	SARABANDES
SANCTIONEERS	SANDPAINTINGS	SANITARILY	SAPODILLAS	SARBACANES
SANCTIONER	SANDPAPERED	SANITARINESS	SAPOGENINS	SARCASTICALLY
SANCTIONERS	SANDPAPERIER	SANITARINESSES	SAPONACEOUS	SARCENCHYMATOUS
SANCTIONING	SANDPAPERIEST	SANITARIST	SAPONACEOUSNESS	SARCENCHYME
SANCTIONLESS	SANDPAPERING	SANITARISTS	SAPONARIAS	SARCENCHYMES
SANCTITIES	SANDPAPERINGS	SANITARIUM	SAPONIFIABLE	SARCOCARPS
SANCTITUDE	SANDPAPERS	SANITARIUMS	SAPONIFICATION	SARCOCOLLA
SANCTITUDES	SANDPAPERY	SANITATING	SAPONIFICATIONS	SARCOCOLLAS
SANCTUARIES	SANDPIPERS	SANITATION	SAPONIFIED	SARCOCYSTIS
SANCTUARISE	SANDSPOUTS	SANITATIONIST	SAPONIFIER	SARCOCYSTISES
SANCTUARISED	SANDSTONES	SANITATIONISTS	SAPONIFIERS	SARCOIDOSES
SANCTUARISES	SANDSTORMS	SANITATIONS	SAPONIFIES	SARCOIDOSIS
SANCTUARISING	SANDSUCKER	SANITISATION	SAPONIFYING	SARCOLEMMA
SANCTUARIZE	SANDSUCKERS	SANITISATIONS	SAPOTACEOUS	SARCOLEMMAL
SANCTUARIZED	SANDWICHED	SANITISERS	SAPPANWOOD	SARCOLEMMAS
SANCTUARIZES	SANDWICHES	SANITISING	SAPPANWOODS	SARCOLEMMATA
SANCTUARIZING	SANDWICHING	SANITIZATION	SAPPERMENT	SARCOLOGIES
SANDALLING	SANENESSES	SANITIZATIONS	SAPPHIRINE	SARCOMATOID
SANDALWOOD	SANGFROIDS	SANITIZERS	SAPPHIRINES	SARCOMATOSES
SANDALWOODS	SANGUIFEROUS	SANITIZING	SAPPINESSES	SARCOMATOSIS
SANDARACHS	SANGUIFICATION	SANITORIUM	SAPRAEMIAS	SARCOMATOUS
SANDBAGGED	SANGUIFICATIONS	SANITORIUMS	SAPROBIONT	SARCOMERES
SANDBAGGER	SANGUIFIED	SANNYASINS	SAPROBIONTS	SARCOPENIA
SANDBAGGERS	SANGUIFIES	SANSCULOTTE	SAPROBIOTIC	SARCOPENIAS
SANDBAGGING	SANGUIFYING	SANSCULOTTERIE	SAPROBITIES	SARCOPHAGAL
SANDBLASTED	SANGUINARIA	SANSCULOTTERIES	SAPROGENIC	SARCOPHAGI
SANDBLASTER	SANGUINARIAS	SANSCULOTTES	SAPROGENICITIES	SARCOPHAGOUS
SANDBLASTERS	SANGUINARILY	SANSCULOTTIC	SAPROGENICITY	SARCOPHAGUS
SANDBLASTING	SANGUINARINESS	SANSCULOTTIDES	SAPROGENOUS	SARCOPHAGUSES
SANDBLASTINGS	SANGUINARY	SANSCULOTTISH	SAPROLEGNIA	SARCOPLASM
SANDBLASTS	SANGUINELY	SANSCULOTTISM	SAPROLEGNIAS	SARCOPLASMIC
SANDCASTLE	SANGUINENESS	SANSCULOTTISMS	SAPROLITES	SARCOPLASMS
SANDCASTLES	SANGUINENESSES	SANSCULOTTIST	SAPROLITIC	SARCOSOMAL
SANDCRACKS	SANGUINEOUS	SANSCULOTTISTS	SAPROPELIC	SARCOSOMES
SANDERLING	SANGUINEOUSNESS	SANSEVIERIA	SAPROPELITE	SARDONIANS
SANDERLINGS	SANGUINING	SANSEVIERIAS	SAPROPELITES	SARDONICAL
SANDERSWOOD	SANGUINITIES	SANTALACEOUS	SAPROPHAGOUS	SARDONICALLY
SANDERSWOODS	SANGUINITY	SANTOLINAS	SAPROPHYTE	SARDONICISM
SANDFISHES	SANGUINIVOROUS	SANTONICAS	SAPROPHYTES	SARDONICISMS
SANDGLASSES	SANGUINOLENCIES	SAPANWOODS	SAPROPHYTIC	SARDONYXES
SANDGROPER	SANGUINOLENCY	SAPIDITIES	SAPROPHYTICALLY	SARGASSOES
SANDGROPERS	SANGUINOLENT	SAPIDNESSES	SAPROPHYTISM	SARGASSUMS
SANDGROUSE	SANGUIVOROUS	SAPIENCIES	SAPROPHYTISMS	SARKINESSES
SANDGROUSES	SANITARIAN	SAPIENTIAL	SAPROTROPH	SARMENTACEOUS
SANDINESSES	SANITARIANISM	SAPIENTIALLY	SAPROTROPHIC	SARMENTOSE
SANDLOTTER	SANITARIANISMS	SAPINDACEOUS	SAPROTROPHS	SARMENTOUS

SARPANCHES	SATIATIONS	SATURNISMS	SAVORINESS	SCAITHLESS
SARRACENIA	SATINETTAS	SATURNISTS	SAVORINESSES	SCALABILITIES
SARRACENIACEOUS	SATINETTES	SATYAGRAHA	SAVOURIEST	SCALABILITY
SARRACENIAS	SATINFLOWER	SATYAGRAHAS	SAVOURINESS	SCALABLENESS
SARRUSOPHONE	SATINFLOWERS	SATYAGRAHI	SAVOURINESSES	SCALABLENESSES
SARRUSOPHONES	SATINWOODS	SATYAGRAHIS	SAVOURLESS	SCALARIFORM
SARSAPARILLA	SATIRICALLY	SATYRESQUE	SAVVINESSES	SCALARIFORMLY
SARSAPARILLAS	SATIRICALNESS	SATYRESSES	SAWBONESES	SCALATIONS
SARTORIALLY	SATIRICALNESSES	SATYRIASES	SAWDUSTIER	SCALDBERRIES
SARTORIUSES	SATIRISABLE	SATYRIASIS	SAWDUSTIEST	SCALDBERRY
SASKATOONS	SATIRISATION	SAUCEBOATS	SAWDUSTING	SCALDFISHES
SASQUATCHES	SATIRISATIONS	SAUCEBOXES	SAWGRASSES	SCALDHEADS
SASSAFRASES	SATIRISERS	SAUCERFULS	SAWMILLERS	SCALDSHIPS
SASSARARAS	SATIRISING	SAUCERLESS	SAWTIMBERS	SCALEBOARD
SASSINESSES	SATIRIZABLE	SAUCERLIKE	SAXICAVOUS	SCALEBOARDS
SASSOLITES	SATIRIZATION	SAUCINESSES	SAXICOLINE	SCALENOHEDRA
SASSYWOODS	SATIRIZATIONS	SAUCISSONS	SAXICOLOUS	SCALENOHEDRON
SATANICALLY	SATIRIZERS	SAUERBRATEN	SAXIFRAGACEOUS	SCALENOHEDRONS
SATANICALNESS	SATIRIZING	SAUERBRATENS	SAXIFRAGES	SCALETAILS
SATANICALNESSES	SATISFACTION	SAUERKRAUT	SAXITOXINS	SCALEWORKS
SATANITIES	SATISFACTIONS	SAUERKRAUTS	SAXOPHONES	SCALINESSES
SATANOLOGIES	SATISFACTORILY	SAUNTERERS	SAXOPHONIC	SCALLAWAGS
SATANOLOGY	SATISFACTORY	SAUNTERING	SAXOPHONIST	SCALLOPERS
SATANOPHANIES	SATISFIABLE	SAUNTERINGLY	SAXOPHONISTS	SCALLOPING
SATANOPHANY	SATISFICED	SAUNTERINGS	SCABBARDED	SCALLOPINGS
SATANOPHOBIA	SATISFICER	SAURISCHIAN	SCABBARDING	SCALLOPINI
SATANOPHOBIAS	SATISFICERS	SAURISCHIANS	SCABBARDLESS	SCALLOPINIS
SATCHELFUL	SATISFICES	SAUROGNATHOUS	SCABBEDNESS	SCALLYWAGS
SATCHELFULS	SATISFICING	SAUROPODOUS	SCABBEDNESSES	SCALOGRAMS
SATCHELLED	SATISFICINGS	SAUROPSIDAN	SCABBINESS	SCALOPPINE
SATCHELSFUL	SATISFIERS	SAUROPSIDANS	SCABBINESSES	SCALOPPINES
SATEDNESSES	SATISFYING	SAUROPTERYGIAN	SCABERULOUS	SCALOPPINI
SATELLITED	SATISFYINGLY	SAUROPTERYGIANS	SCABIOUSES	SCALPELLIC
SATELLITES	SATURABILITIES	SAUSSURITE	SCABRIDITIES	SCALPELLIFORM
SATELLITIC	SATURABILITY	SAUSSURITES	SCABRIDITY	SCALPRIFORM
SATELLITING	SATURATERS	SAUSSURITIC	SCABROUSLY	SCAMBAITING
SATELLITISED	SATURATING	SAVABLENESS	SCABROUSNESS	SCAMBAITINGS
SATELLITISED	SATURATION	SAVABLENESSES	SCABROUSNESSES	SCAMBLINGLY
SATELLITISES	SATURATIONS	SAVAGEDOMS	SCAFFOLAGE	SCAMBLINGS
SATELLITISING	SATURATORS	SAVAGENESS	SCAFFOLAGES	SCAMMONIATE
SATELLITIUM	SATURNALIA	SAVAGENESSES	SCAFFOLDAGE	SCAMMONIES
SATELLITIUMS	SATURNALIAN	SAVAGERIES	SCAFFOLDAGES	SCAMPERERS
SATELLITIZE	SATURNALIANLY	SAVEABLENESS	SCAFFOLDED	SCAMPERING
SATELLITIZED	SATURNALIAS	SAVEABLENESSES	SCAFFOLDER	SCAMPERINGS
SATELLITIZES	SATURNIIDS	SAVEGARDED	SCAFFOLDERS	SCAMPISHLY
SATELLITIZING	SATURNINELY	SAVEGARDING	SCAFFOLDING	SCAMPISHNESS
SATIABILITIES	SATURNINITIES	SAVINGNESS	SCAFFOLDINGS	SCAMPISHNESSES
SATIABILITY	SATURNINITY	SAVINGNESSES	SCAGLIOLAS	SCANDALING

S

SCANDALISATION

SCANDALISATION	SCAPHOCEPHALUS	SCARIFYING	SCATURIENT	SCHALSTEINS
SCANDALISATIONS	SCAPHOCEPHALY	SCARIFYINGLY	SCAVENGERED	SCHAPPEING
SCANDALISE	SCAPHOPODS	SCARINESSES	SCAVENGERIES	SCHATCHENS
SCANDALISED	SCAPIGEROUS	SCARLATINA	SCAVENGERING	SCHECHITAH
SCANDALISER	SCAPOLITES	SCARLATINAL	SCAVENGERINGS	SCHECHITAHS
SCANDALISERS	SCAPULARIES	SCARLATINAS	SCAVENGERS	SCHECHITAS
SCANDALISES	SCAPULATED	SCARLETING	SCAVENGERY	SCHECKLATON
SCANDALISING	SCAPULIMANCIES	SCARPERING	SCAVENGING	SCHECKLATONS
SCANDALIZATION	SCAPULIMANCY	SCATHEFULNESS	SCAVENGINGS	SCHEDULERS
SCANDALIZATIONS	SCAPULIMANTIC	SCATHEFULNESSES	SCAZONTICS	SCHEDULING
SCANDALIZE	SCAPULOMANCIES	SCATHELESS	SCELERATES	SCHEDULINGS
SCANDALIZED	SCAPULOMANCY	SCATHINGLY	SCENARISATION	SCHEELITES
SCANDALIZER	SCAPULOMANTIC	SCATOLOGIC	SCENARISATIONS	SCHEFFLERA
SCANDALIZERS	SCARABAEAN	SCATOLOGICAL	SCENARISED	SCHEFFLERAS
SCANDALIZES	SCARABAEANS	SCATOLOGIES	SCENARISES	SCHEMATICAL
SCANDALIZING	SCARABAEID	SCATOLOGIST	SCENARISING	SCHEMATICALLY
SCANDALLED	SCARABAEIDS	SCATOLOGISTS	SCENARISTS	SCHEMATICS
SCANDALLING	SCARABAEIST	SCATOPHAGIES	SCENARIZATION	SCHEMATISATION
SCANDALMONGER	SCARABAEISTS	SCATOPHAGOUS	SCENARIZATIONS	SCHEMATISATIONS
SCANDALMONGERS	SCARABAEOID	SCATOPHAGY	SCENARIZED	SCHEMATISE
SCANDALOUS	SCARABAEOIDS	SCATTERABLE	SCENARIZES	SCHEMATISED
SCANDALOUSLY	SCARABAEUS	SCATTERATION	SCENARIZING	SCHEMATISES
SCANDALOUSNESS	SCARABAEUSES	SCATTERATIONS	SCENESHIFTER	SCHEMATISING
SCANSORIAL	SCARABOIDS	SCATTERBRAIN	SCENESHIFTERS	SCHEMATISM
SCANTINESS	SCARAMOUCH	SCATTERBRAINED	SCENESTERS	SCHEMATISMS
SCANTINESSES	SCARAMOUCHE	SCATTERBRAINS	SCENICALLY	SCHEMATIST
SCANTITIES	SCARAMOUCHED	SCATTEREDLY	SCENOGRAPHER	SCHEMATISTS
SCANTLINGS	SCARAMOUCHES	SCATTERERS	SCENOGRAPHERS	SCHEMATIZATION
SCANTNESSES	SCARAMOUCHING	SCATTERGOOD	SCENOGRAPHIC	SCHEMATIZATIONS
SCAPEGALLOWS	SCARCEMENT	SCATTERGOODS	SCENOGRAPHICAL	SCHEMATIZE
SCAPEGALLOWSES	SCARCEMENTS	SCATTERGRAM	SCENOGRAPHIES	SCHEMATIZED
SCAPEGOATED	SCARCENESS	SCATTERGRAMS	SCENOGRAPHY	SCHEMATIZES
SCAPEGOATING	SCARCENESSES	SCATTERGUN	SCENTLESSNESS	SCHEMATIZING
SCAPEGOATINGS	SCARCITIES	SCATTERGUNS	SCENTLESSNESSES	SCHEMINGLY
SCAPEGOATISM	SCARECROWS	SCATTERIER	SCEPTERING	SCHEMOZZLE
SCAPEGOATISMS	SCAREHEADS	SCATTERIEST	SCEPTERLESS	SCHEMOZZLED
SCAPEGOATS	SCAREMONGER	SCATTERING	SCEPTICALLY	SCHEMOZZLES
SCAPEGRACE	SCAREMONGERING	SCATTERINGLY	SCEPTICISM	SCHEMOZZLING
SCAPEGRACES	SCAREMONGERINGS	SCATTERINGS	SCEPTICISMS	SCHERZANDI
SCAPEMENTS	SCAREMONGERS	SCATTERLING	SCEPTRELESS	SCHERZANDO
SCAPEWHEEL	SCAREWARES	SCATTERLINGS	SCEUOPHYLACIA	SCHERZANDOS
SCAPEWHEELS	SCARFISHES	SCATTERMOUCH	SCEUOPHYLACIUM	SCHIAVONES
SCAPHOCEPHALI	SCARFSKINS	SCATTERMOUCHES	SCEUOPHYLACIUMS	SCHILLERISATION
SCAPHOCEPHALIC	SCARIFICATION	SCATTEROMETER	SCEUOPHYLAX	SCHILLERISE
SCAPHOCEPHALICS	SCARIFICATIONS	SCATTEROMETERS	SCEUOPHYLAXES	SCHILLERISED
SCAPHOCEPHALIES	SCARIFICATOR	SCATTERSHOT	SCHADENFREUDE	SCHILLERISES
SCAPHOCEPHALISM	SCARIFICATORS	SCATTINESS	SCHADENFREUDES	SCHILLERISING
SCAPHOCEPHALOUS	SCARIFIERS	SCATTINESSES	SCHALSTEIN	SCHILLERIZATION

SCHILLERIZE	SCHIZOMYCETES	SCHMICKEST	SCHOOLCRAFTS	SCHOTTISCHE
SCHILLERIZED	SCHIZOMYCETIC	SCHMOOSING	SCHOOLDAYS	SCHOTTISCHES
SCHILLERIZES	SCHIZOMYCETOUS	SCHMOOZERS	SCHOOLERIES	SCHRECKLICH
SCHILLERIZING	SCHIZOPHRENE	SCHMOOZIER	SCHOOLFELLOW	SCHTUPPING
SCHILLINGS	SCHIZOPHRENES	SCHMOOZIEST	SCHOOLFELLOWS	SCHUSSBOOMER
SCHINDYLESES	SCHIZOPHRENETIC	SCHMOOZING	SCHOOLGIRL	SCHUSSBOOMERS
SCHINDYLESIS	SCHIZOPHRENIA	SCHMUCKIER	SCHOOLGIRLISH	SCHVARTZES
SCHINDYLETIC	SCHIZOPHRENIAS	SCHMUCKIEST	SCHOOLGIRLS	SCHVITZING
SCHIPPERKE	SCHIZOPHRENIC	SCHMUCKING	SCHOOLGOING	SCHWARMEREI
SCHIPPERKES	SCHIZOPHRENICS	SCHMUTTERS	SCHOOLGOINGS	SCHWARMEREIS
SCHISMATIC	SCHIZOPHYCEOUS	SCHNAPPERS	SCHOOLHOUSE	SCHWARMERISCH
SCHISMATICAL	SCHIZOPHYTE	SCHNAPPSES	SCHOOLHOUSES	SCHWARTZES
SCHISMATICALLY	SCHIZOPHYTES	SCHNAUZERS	SCHOOLINGS	SCHWARZLOT
SCHISMATICALS	SCHIZOPHYTIC	SCHNITZELS	SCHOOLKIDS	SCHWARZLOTS
SCHISMATICS	SCHIZOPODAL	SCHNOODLES	SCHOOLMAID	SCIAENOIDS
SCHISMATISE	SCHIZOPODOUS	SCHNORKELED	SCHOOLMAIDS	SCIAMACHIES
SCHISMATISED	SCHIZOPODS	SCHNORKELING	SCHOOLMARM	SCIENTIFIC
SCHISMATISES	SCHIZOTHYMIA	SCHNORKELLED	SCHOOLMARMISH	SCIENTIFICAL
SCHISMATISING	SCHIZOTHYMIAS	SCHNORKELLING	SCHOOLMARMS	SCIENTIFICALLY
SCHISMATIZE	SCHIZOTHYMIC	SCHNORKELS	SCHOOLMASTER	SCIENTIFICITIES
SCHISMATIZED	SCHIZZIEST	SCHNORRERS	SCHOOLMASTERED	SCIENTIFICITY
SCHISMATIZES	SCHLEMIELS	SCHNORRING	SCHOOLMASTERING	SCIENTISED
SCHISMATIZING	SCHLEMIHLS	SCHNOZZLES	SCHOOLMASTERISH	SCIENTISES
SCHISTOSITIES	SCHLEPPERS	SCHOLARCHS	SCHOOLMASTERLY	SCIENTISING
SCHISTOSITY	SCHLEPPIER	SCHOLARLIER	SCHOOLMASTERS	SCIENTISMS
SCHISTOSOMAL	SCHLEPPIEST	SCHOLARLIEST	SCHOOLMATE	SCIENTISTIC
SCHISTOSOME	SCHLEPPING	SCHOLARLINESS	SCHOOLMATES	SCIENTISTS
SCHISTOSOMES	SCHLIERENS	SCHOLARLINESSES	SCHOOLMISTRESS	SCIENTIZED
SCHISTOSOMIASES	SCHLIMAZEL	SCHOLARSHIP	SCHOOLMISTRESSY	SCIENTIZES
SCHISTOSOMIASIS	SCHLIMAZELS	SCHOLARSHIPS	SCHOOLROOM	SCIENTIZING
SCHIZAEACEOUS	SCHLOCKERS	SCHOLASTIC	SCHOOLROOMS	SCINCOIDIAN
SCHIZANTHUS	SCHLOCKEYS	SCHOLASTICAL	SCHOOLTEACHER	SCINCOIDIANS
SCHIZANTHUSES	SCHLOCKIER	SCHOLASTICALLY	SCHOOLTEACHERS	SCINDAPSUS
SCHIZOCARP	SCHLOCKIEST	SCHOLASTICATE	SCHOOLTEACHING	SCINDAPSUSES
SCHIZOCARPIC	SCHLUMBERGERA	SCHOLASTICATES	SCHOOLTEACHINGS	SCINTIGRAM
SCHIZOCARPOUS	SCHLUMBERGERAS	SCHOLASTICISM	SCHOOLTIDE	SCINTIGRAMS
SCHIZOCARPS	SCHLUMPIER	SCHOLASTICISMS	SCHOOLTIDES	SCINTIGRAPHIC
SCHIZOGENESES	SCHLUMPIEST	SCHOLASTICS	SCHOOLTIME	SCINTIGRAPHIES
SCHIZOGENESIS	SCHLUMPING	SCHOLIASTIC	SCHOOLTIMES	SCINTIGRAPHY
SCHIZOGENETIC	SCHMALTZES	SCHOLIASTS	SCHOOLWARD	SCINTILLAE
SCHIZOGENIC	SCHMALTZIER	SCHOOLBAGS	SCHOOLWARDS	SCINTILLANT
SCHIZOGNATHOUS	SCHMALTZIEST	SCHOOLBOOK	SCHOOLWORK	SCINTILLANTLY
SCHIZOGONIC	SCHMALZIER	SCHOOLBOOKS	SCHOOLWORKS	SCINTILLAS
SCHIZOGONIES	SCHMALZIEST	SCHOOLBOYISH	SCHOOLYARD	SCINTILLASCOPE
SCHIZOGONOUS	SCHMEARING	SCHOOLBOYS	SCHOOLYARDS	SCINTILLASCOPES
SCHIZOGONY	SCHMECKERS	SCHOOLCHILD	SCHORLACEOUS	SCINTILLATE
SCHIZOIDAL	SCHMECKING	SCHOOLCHILDREN	SCHORLOMITE	SCINTILLATED
SCHIZOMYCETE	SCHMEERING	SCHOOLCRAFT	SCHORLOMITES	SCINTILLATES

S

SCINTILLATING	SCLEROCAULY	SCLEROTOMY	SCOREBOARDS	SCRABBLIEST
SCINTILLATINGLY	SCLERODERM	SCOFFINGLY	SCORECARDS	SCRABBLING
SCINTILLATION	SCLERODERMA	SCOLDINGLY	SCOREKEEPER	SCRABBLINGS
SCINTILLATIONS	SCLERODERMAS	SCOLECIFORM	SCOREKEEPERS	SCRAGGEDNESS
SCINTILLATOR	SCLERODERMATA	SCOLECITES	SCORELINES	SCRAGGEDNESSES
SCINTILLATORS	SCLERODERMATOUS	SCOLLOPING	SCORESHEET	SCRAGGIEST
SCINTILLISCAN	SCLERODERMIA	SCOLOPACEOUS	SCORESHEETS	SCRAGGINESS
SCINTILLISCANS	SCLERODERMIAS	SCOLOPENDRA	SCORIACEOUS	SCRAGGINESSES
SCINTILLOMETER	SCLERODERMIC	SCOLOPENDRAS	SCORIFICATION	SCRAGGLIER
SCINTILLOMETERS	SCLERODERMITE	SCOLOPENDRID	SCORIFICATIONS	SCRAGGLIEST
SCINTILLON	SCLERODERMITES	SCOLOPENDRIDS	SCORIFIERS	SCRAGGLING
SCINTILLONS	SCLERODERMOUS	SCOLOPENDRIFORM	SCORIFYING	SCRAICHING
SCINTILLOSCOPE	SCLERODERMS	SCOLOPENDRINE	SCORNFULLY	SCRAIGHING
SCINTILLOSCOPES	SCLEROMALACIA	SCOLOPENDRIUM	SCORNFULNESS	SCRAMBLERS
SCINTISCAN	SCLEROMALACIAS	SCOLOPENDRIUMS	SCORNFULNESSES	SCRAMBLING
SCINTISCANNER	SCLEROMATA	SCOLYTOIDS	SCORODITES	SCRAMBLINGLY
SCINTISCANNERS	SCLEROMETER	SCOMBROIDS	SCORPAENID	SCRAMBLINGS
SCINTISCANS	SCLEROMETERS	SCOMFISHED	SCORPAENIDS	SCRANCHING
SCIOLISTIC	SCLEROMETRIC	SCOMFISHES	SCORPAENOID	SCRANNIEST
SCIOMACHIES	SCLEROPHYLL	SCOMFISHING	SCORPAENOIDS	SCRAPBOOKED
SCIOMANCER	SCLEROPHYLLIES	SCONCHEONS	SCORPIOIDS	SCRAPBOOKING
SCIOMANCERS	SCLEROPHYLLOUS	SCOOTCHING	SCORPIONIC	SCRAPBOOKINGS
SCIOMANCIES	SCLEROPHYLLS	SCOOTERING	SCORZONERA	SCRAPBOOKS
SCIOMANTIC	SCLEROPHYLLY	SCOOTERIST	SCORZONERAS	SCRAPEGOOD
SCIOPHYTES	SCLEROPROTEIN	SCOOTERISTS	SCOTODINIA	SCRAPEGOODS
SCIOPHYTIC	SCLEROPROTEINS	SCOPELOIDS	SCOTODINIAS	SCRAPEGUTS
SCIOSOPHIES	SCLEROSING	SCOPOLAMINE	SCOTOMATOUS	SCRAPEPENNIES
SCIRRHOSITIES	SCLEROTALS	SCOPOLAMINES	SCOTOMETER	SCRAPEPENNY
SCIRRHOSITY	SCLEROTIAL	SCOPOLINES	SCOTOMETERS	SCRAPERBOARD
SCIRRHUSES	SCLEROTICS	SCOPOPHILIA	SCOUNDRELLIER	SCRAPERBOARDS
SCISSIPARITIES	SCLEROTINS	SCOPOPHILIAC	SCOUNDRELLIEST	SCRAPHEAPS
SCISSIPARITY	SCLEROTIOID	SCOPOPHILIACS	SCOUNDRELLY	SCRAPPAGES
SCISSORERS	SCLEROTISATION	SCOPOPHILIAS	SCOUNDRELS	SCRAPPIEST
SCISSORING	SCLEROTISATIONS	SCOPOPHILIC	SCOURGINGS	SCRAPPINESS
SCISSORTAIL	SCLEROTISE	SCOPOPHOBIA	SCOUTCRAFT	SCRAPPINESSES
SCISSORTAILS	SCLEROTISED	SCOPOPHOBIAS	SCOUTCRAFTS	SCRAPPINGS
SCISSORWISE	SCLEROTISES	SCOPTOPHILIA	SCOUTHERED	SCRAPYARDS
SCITAMINEOUS	SCLEROTISING	SCOPTOPHILIAS	SCOUTHERING	SCRATCHBACK
SCLAUNDERS	SCLEROTITIS	SCOPTOPHOBIA	SCOUTHERINGS	SCRATCHBACKS
SCLEREIDES	SCLEROTITISES	SCOPTOPHOBIAS	SCOUTMASTER	SCRATCHBOARD
SCLERENCHYMA	SCLEROTIUM	SCORBUTICALLY	SCOUTMASTERS	SCRATCHBOARDS
SCLERENCHYMAS	SCLEROTIZATION	SCORCHINGLY	SCOWDERING	SCRATCHBUILD
SCLERENCHYMATA	SCLEROTIZATIONS	SCORCHINGNESS	SCOWDERINGS	SCRATCHBUILDER
SCLERIASES	SCLEROTIZE	SCORCHINGNESSES	SCOWLINGLY	SCRATCHBUILDERS
SCLERIASIS	SCLEROTIZED	SCORCHINGS	SCOWTHERED	SCRATCHBUILDING
SCLERITISES	SCLEROTIZES	SCORDATURA	SCOWTHERING	SCRATCHBUILDS
SCLEROCAULIES	SCLEROTIZING	SCORDATURAS	SCRABBLERS	SCRATCHBUILT
SCLEROCAULOUS	SCLEROTOMIES	SCOREBOARD	SCRABBLIER	SCRATCHCARD

SCRATCHCARDS SCREENPLAYS SCRIMPNESSES SCRITCHING SCRUMMAGED
SCRATCHERS SCREENSAVER SCRIMSHANDER SCRITCHINGS SCRUMMAGER
SCRATCHIER SCREENSAVERS SCRIMSHANDERED SCRIVEBOARD SCRUMMAGERS
SCRATCHIES SCREENSHOT SCRIMSHANDERING SCRIVEBOARDS SCRUMMAGES
SCRATCHIEST SCREENSHOTS SCRIMSHANDERS SCRIVENERS SCRUMMAGING
SCRATCHILY SCREENSHOTTED SCRIMSHANDIED SCRIVENERSHIP SCRUMMIEST
SCRATCHINESS SCREENSHOTTING SCRIMSHANDIES SCRIVENERSHIPS SCRUMPLING
SCRATCHINESSES SCREENWRITER SCRIMSHANDY SCRIVENING SCRUMPOXES
SCRATCHING SCREENWRITERS SCRIMSHANDYING SCRIVENINGS SCRUMPTIOUS
SCRATCHINGLY SCREENWRITING SCRIMSHANK SCROBBLING SCRUMPTIOUSLY
SCRATCHINGS SCREENWRITINGS SCRIMSHANKED SCROBICULAR SCRUMPTIOUSNESS
SCRATCHLESS SCREEVINGS SCRIMSHANKER SCROBICULATE SCRUNCHEON
SCRATCHPLATE SCREICHING SCRIMSHANKERS SCROBICULATED SCRUNCHEONS
SCRATCHPLATES SCREIGHING SCRIMSHANKING SCROBICULE SCRUNCHIER
SCRATTLING SCREWBALLS SCRIMSHANKS SCROBICULES SCRUNCHIES
SCRAUCHING SCREWBEANS SCRIMSHAWED SCROFULOUS SCRUNCHIEST
SCRAUGHING SCREWDRIVER SCRIMSHAWING SCROFULOUSLY SCRUNCHING
SCRAVELING SCREWDRIVERS SCRIMSHAWS SCROFULOUSNESS SCRUNCHINGS
SCRAVELLED SCREWHEADS SCRIMSHONER SCROGGIEST SCRUNCHINS
SCRAVELLING SCREWINESS SCRIMSHONERS SCROLLABLE SCRUNCHION
SCRAWLIEST SCREWINESSES SCRIPHOLDER SCROLLINGS SCRUNCHIONS
SCRAWLINGLY SCREWWORMS SCRIPHOLDERS SCROLLWISE SCRUNTIEST
SCRAWLINGS SCRIBACIOUS SCRIPOPHILE SCROLLWORK SCRUPLELESS
SCRAWNIEST SCRIBACIOUSNESS SCRIPOPHILES SCROLLWORKS SCRUPULOSITIES
SCRAWNINESS SCRIBBLEMENT SCRIPOPHILIES SCROOCHING SCRUPULOSITY
SCRAWNINESSES SCRIBBLEMENTS SCRIPOPHILIST SCROOTCHED SCRUPULOUS
SCREAKIEST SCRIBBLERS SCRIPOPHILISTS SCROOTCHES SCRUPULOUSLY
SCREAKINGS SCRIBBLIER SCRIPOPHILY SCROOTCHING SCRUPULOUSNESS
SCREAMINGLY SCRIBBLIEST SCRIPPAGES SCROPHULARIA SCRUTABILITIES
SCREAMINGS SCRIBBLING SCRIPTORIA SCROPHULARIAS SCRUTABILITY
SCREECHERS SCRIBBLINGLY SCRIPTORIAL SCROUNGERS SCRUTATORS
SCREECHIER SCRIBBLINGS SCRIPTORIUM SCROUNGIER SCRUTINEER
SCREECHIEST SCRIECHING SCRIPTORIUMS SCROUNGIEST SCRUTINEERS
SCREECHING SCRIEVEBOARD SCRIPTURAL SCROUNGING SCRUTINIES
SCREEDINGS SCRIEVEBOARDS SCRIPTURALISM SCROUNGINGS SCRUTINISE
SCREENABLE SCRIGGLIER SCRIPTURALISMS SCROWDGING SCRUTINISED
SCREENAGER SCRIGGLIEST SCRIPTURALIST SCRUBBABLE SCRUTINISER
SCREENAGERS SCRIGGLING SCRIPTURALISTS SCRUBBIEST SCRUTINISERS
SCREENCAST SCRIMMAGED SCRIPTURALLY SCRUBBINESS SCRUTINISES
SCREENCASTS SCRIMMAGER SCRIPTURES SCRUBBINESSES SCRUTINISING
SCREENCRAFT SCRIMMAGERS SCRIPTURISM SCRUBBINGS SCRUTINISINGLY
SCREENCRAFTS SCRIMMAGES SCRIPTURISMS SCRUBLANDS SCRUTINIZE
SCREENFULS SCRIMMAGING SCRIPTURIST SCRUBWOMAN SCRUTINIZED
SCREENINGS SCRIMPIEST SCRIPTURISTS SCRUBWOMEN SCRUTINIZER
SCREENLAND SCRIMPINESS SCRIPTWRITER SCRUFFIEST SCRUTINIZERS
SCREENLANDS SCRIMPINESSES SCRIPTWRITERS SCRUFFINESS SCRUTINIZES
SCREENLIKE SCRIMPINGS SCRIPTWRITING SCRUFFINESSES SCRUTINIZING
SCREENPLAY SCRIMPNESS SCRIPTWRITINGS SCRUMDOWNS SCRUTINIZINGLY

S

SCRUTINOUS	SCUTELLATE	SEAQUARIUMS	SECESSIONIST	SECTARIANISING
SCRUTINOUSLY	SCUTELLATED	SEARCHABLE	SECESSIONISTS	SECTARIANISM
SCRUTOIRES	SCUTELLATION	SEARCHINGLY	SECESSIONS	SECTARIANISMS
SCUDDALERS	SCUTELLATIONS	SEARCHINGNESS	SECLUDEDLY	SECTARIANIZE
SCUFFLINGS	SCUTTERING	SEARCHINGNESSES	SECLUDEDNESS	SECTARIANIZED
SCULDUDDERIES	SCUTTLEBUTT	SEARCHINGS	SECLUDEDNESSES	SECTARIANIZES
SCULDUDDERY	SCUTTLEBUTTS	SEARCHLESS	SECLUSIONIST	SECTARIANIZING
SCULDUDDRIES	SCUTTLEFUL	SEARCHLIGHT	SECLUSIONISTS	SECTARIANS
SCULDUDDRY	SCUTTLEFULS	SEARCHLIGHTS	SECLUSIONS	SECTILITIES
SCULDUGGERIES	SCUTTLINGS	SEAREDNESS	SECLUSIVELY	SECTIONALISE
SCULDUGGERY	SCUZZBALLS	SEAREDNESSES	SECLUSIVENESS	SECTIONALISED
SCULLERIES	SCYPHIFORM	SEARNESSES	SECLUSIVENESSES	SECTIONALISES
SCULPTINGS	SCYPHISTOMA	SEASICKEST	SECOBARBITAL	SECTIONALISING
SCULPTRESS	SCYPHISTOMAE	SEASICKNESS	SECOBARBITALS	SECTIONALISM
SCULPTRESSES	SCYPHISTOMAS	SEASICKNESSES	SECONDARIES	SECTIONALISMS
SCULPTURAL	SCYPHOZOAN	SEASONABILITIES	SECONDARILY	SECTIONALIST
SCULPTURALLY	SCYPHOZOANS	SEASONABILITY	SECONDARINESS	SECTIONALISTS
SCULPTURED	SCYTHELIKE	SEASONABLE	SECONDARINESSES	SECTIONALIZE
SCULPTURES	SDEIGNFULL	SEASONABLENESS	SECONDHAND	SECTIONALIZED
SCULPTURESQUE	SDEIGNFULLY	SEASONABLY	SECONDINGS	SECTIONALIZES
SCULPTURESQUELY	SDRUCCIOLA	SEASONALITIES	SECONDMENT	SECTIONALIZING
SCULPTURING	SEABEACHES	SEASONALITY	SECONDMENTS	SECTIONALLY
SCULPTURINGS	SEABORGIUM	SEASONALLY	SECRETAGES	SECTIONALS
SCUMBERING	SEABORGIUMS	SEASONALNESS	SECRETAGOGIC	SECTIONING
SCUMBLINGS	SEABOTTLES	SEASONALNESSES	SECRETAGOGUE	SECTIONISATION
SCUMFISHED	SEACHANGER	SEASONINGS	SECRETAGOGUES	SECTIONISATIONS
SCUMFISHES	SEACHANGERS	SEASONLESS	SECRETAIRE	SECTIONISE
SCUMFISHING	SEACUNNIES	SEASTRANDS	SECRETAIRES	SECTIONISED
SCUNCHEONS	SEAFARINGS	SEAWEEDIER	SECRETARIAL	SECTIONISES
SCUNGILLIS	SEAGRASSES	SEAWEEDIEST	SECRETARIAT	SECTIONISING
SCUNNERING	SEALIFTING	SEAWORTHIER	SECRETARIATE	SECTIONIZATION
SCUPPERING	SEALPOINTS	SEAWORTHIEST	SECRETARIATES	SECTIONIZATIONS
SCUPPERNONG	SEAMANLIER	SEAWORTHINESS	SECRETARIATS	SECTIONIZE
SCUPPERNONGS	SEAMANLIEST	SEAWORTHINESSES	SECRETARIES	SECTIONIZED
SCURFINESS	SEAMANLIKE	SEBIFEROUS	SECRETARYSHIP	SECTIONIZES
SCURFINESSES	SEAMANSHIP	SEBORRHEAL	SECRETARYSHIPS	SECTIONIZING
SCURRILITIES	SEAMANSHIPS	SEBORRHEAS	SECRETIONAL	SECTORIALS
SCURRILITY	SEAMINESSES	SEBORRHEIC	SECRETIONARY	SECTORISATION
SCURRILOUS	SEAMLESSLY	SEBORRHOEA	SECRETIONS	SECTORISATIONS
SCURRILOUSLY	SEAMLESSNESS	SEBORRHOEAL	SECRETIVELY	SECTORISED
SCURRILOUSNESS	SEAMLESSNESSES	SEBORRHOEAS	SECRETIVENESS	SECTORISES
SCURRIOURS	SEAMSTRESS	SEBORRHOEIC	SECRETIVENESSES	SECTORISING
SCURVINESS	SEAMSTRESSES	SECERNENTS	SECRETNESS	SECTORIZATION
SCURVINESSES	SEAMSTRESSIES	SECERNMENT	SECRETNESSES	SECTORIZATIONS
SCUTATIONS	SEAMSTRESSY	SECERNMENTS	SECRETORIES	SECTORIZED
SCUTCHEONLESS	SEANNACHIE	SECESSIONAL	SECTARIANISE	SECTORIZES
SCUTCHEONS	SEANNACHIES	SECESSIONISM	SECTARIANISED	SECTORIZING
SCUTCHINGS	SEAQUARIUM	SECESSIONISMS	SECTARIANISES	SECULARISATION

SECULARISATIONS	SEDENTARILY	SEEMLINESS	SEISMOGRAPH	SELENIFEROUS
SECULARISE	SEDENTARINESS	SEEMLINESSES	SEISMOGRAPHER	SELENOCENTRIC
SECULARISED	SEDENTARINESSES	SEEMLYHEDS	SEISMOGRAPHERS	SELENODONT
SECULARISER	SEDGELANDS	SEERSUCKER	SEISMOGRAPHIC	SELENODONTS
SECULARISERS	SEDIGITATED	SEERSUCKERS	SEISMOGRAPHICAL	SELENOGRAPH
SECULARISES	SEDIMENTABLE	SEETHINGLY	SEISMOGRAPHIES	SELENOGRAPHER
SECULARISING	SEDIMENTARILY	SEGHOLATES	SEISMOGRAPHS	SELENOGRAPHERS
SECULARISM	SEDIMENTARY	SEGMENTALLY	SEISMOGRAPHY	SELENOGRAPHIC
SECULARISMS	SEDIMENTATION	SEGMENTARY	SEISMOLOGIC	SELENOGRAPHICAL
SECULARIST	SEDIMENTATIONS	SEGMENTATE	SEISMOLOGICAL	SELENOGRAPHIES
SECULARISTIC	SEDIMENTED	SEGMENTATION	SEISMOLOGICALLY	SELENOGRAPHIST
SECULARISTS	SEDIMENTING	SEGMENTATIONS	SEISMOLOGIES	SELENOGRAPHISTS
SECULARITIES	SEDIMENTOLOGIC	SEGMENTING	SEISMOLOGIST	SELENOGRAPHS
SECULARITY	SEDIMENTOLOGIES	SEGREGABLE	SEISMOLOGISTS	SELENOGRAPHY
SECULARIZATION	SEDIMENTOLOGIST	SEGREGANTS	SEISMOLOGY	SELENOLOGICAL
SECULARIZATIONS	SEDIMENTOLOGY	SEGREGATED	SEISMOMETER	SELENOLOGIES
SECULARIZE	SEDIMENTOUS	SEGREGATES	SEISMOMETERS	SELENOLOGIST
SECULARIZED	SEDITIONARIES	SEGREGATING	SEISMOMETRIC	SELENOLOGISTS
SECULARIZER	SEDITIONARY	SEGREGATION	SEISMOMETRICAL	SELENOLOGY
SECULARIZERS	SEDITIOUSLY	SEGREGATIONAL	SEISMOMETRIES	SELFISHNESS
SECULARIZES	SEDITIOUSNESS	SEGREGATIONIST	SEISMOMETRY	SELFISHNESSES
SECULARIZING	SEDITIOUSNESSES	SEGREGATIONISTS	SEISMONASTIC	SELFLESSLY
SECUNDINES	SEDUCEABLE	SEGREGATIONS	SEISMONASTIES	SELFLESSNESS
SECUNDOGENITURE	SEDUCEMENT	SEGREGATIVE	SEISMONASTY	SELFLESSNESSES
SECURANCES	SEDUCEMENTS	SEGREGATOR	SEISMOSCOPE	SELFNESSES
SECUREMENT	SEDUCINGLY	SEGREGATORS	SEISMOSCOPES	SELFSAMENESS
SECUREMENTS	SEDUCTIONS	SEGUIDILLA	SEISMOSCOPIC	SELFSAMENESSES
SECURENESS	SEDUCTIVELY	SEGUIDILLAS	SELACHIANS	SELLOTAPED
SECURENESSES	SEDUCTIVENESS	SEIGNEURIAL	SELAGINELLA	SELLOTAPES
SECURIFORM	SEDUCTIVENESSES	SEIGNEURIE	SELAGINELLAS	SELLOTAPING
SECURITANS	SEDUCTRESS	SEIGNEURIES	SELDOMNESS	SELTZOGENE
SECURITIES	SEDUCTRESSES	SEIGNIORAGE	SELDOMNESSES	SELTZOGENES
SECURITISATION	SEDULITIES	SEIGNIORAGES	SELECTABLE	SELVEDGING
SECURITISATIONS	SEDULOUSLY	SEIGNIORALTIES	SELECTIONIST	SEMAINIERS
SECURITISE	SEDULOUSNESS	SEIGNIORALTY	SELECTIONISTS	SEMANTEMES
SECURITISED	SEDULOUSNESSES	SEIGNIORIAL	SELECTIONS	SEMANTICAL
SECURITISES	SEECATCHES	SEIGNIORIES	SELECTIVELY	SEMANTICALLY
SECURITISING	SEECATCHIE	SEIGNIORSHIP	SELECTIVENESS	SEMANTICIST
SECURITIZATION	SEEDEATERS	SEIGNIORSHIPS	SELECTIVENESSES	SEMANTICISTS
SECURITIZATIONS	SEEDINESSES	SEIGNORAGE	SELECTIVITIES	SEMANTIDES
SECURITIZE	SEEDNESSES	SEIGNORAGES	SELECTIVITY	SEMANTRONS
SECURITIZED	SEEDSTOCKS	SEIGNORIAL	SELECTNESS	SEMAPHORED
SECURITIZES	SEEMELESSE	SEIGNORIES	SELECTNESSES	SEMAPHORES
SECURITIZING	SEEMINGNESS	SEISMICALLY	SELECTORATE	SEMAPHORIC
SECUROCRAT	SEEMINGNESSES	SEISMICITIES	SELECTORATES	SEMAPHORICAL
SECUROCRATS	SEEMLIHEAD	SEISMICITY	SELECTORIAL	SEMAPHORICALLY
SEDATENESS	SEEMLIHEADS	SEISMOGRAM	SELEGILINE	SEMAPHORING
SEDATENESSES	SEEMLIHEDS	SEISMOGRAMS	SELEGILINES	SEMASIOLOGICAL

S

SEMASIOLOGIES

SEMASIOLOGIES	SEMICHORUS	SEMIDIURNAL	SEMIMONTHLY	SEMIPERIMETERS
SEMASIOLOGIST	SEMICHORUSES	SEMIDIVINE	SEMIMYSTICAL	SEMIPERMANENT
SEMASIOLOGISTS	SEMICIRCLE	SEMIDOCUMENTARY	SEMINALITIES	SEMIPERMEABLE
SEMASIOLOGY	SEMICIRCLED	SEMIDOMINANT	SEMINALITY	SEMIPLUMES
SEMATOLOGIES	SEMICIRCLES	SEMIDRIEST	SEMINARIAL	SEMIPOLITICAL
SEMATOLOGY	SEMICIRCULAR	SEMIDRYING	SEMINARIAN	SEMIPOPULAR
SEMBLABLES	SEMICIRCULARLY	SEMIDWARFS	SEMINARIANS	SEMIPORCELAIN
SEMBLANCES	SEMICIRQUE	SEMIDWARVES	SEMINARIES	SEMIPORCELAINS
SEMBLATIVE	SEMICIRQUES	SEMIELLIPTICAL	SEMINARIST	SEMIPORNOGRAPHY
SEMEIOLOGIC	SEMICIVILISED	SEMIEMPIRICAL	SEMINARISTS	SEMIPOSTAL
SEMEIOLOGICAL	SEMICIVILIZED	SEMIEVERGREEN	SEMINATING	SEMIPOSTALS
SEMEIOLOGIES	SEMICLASSIC	SEMIFEUDAL	SEMINATION	SEMIPRECIOUS
SEMEIOLOGIST	SEMICLASSICAL	SEMIFINALIST	SEMINATIONS	SEMIPRIVATE
SEMEIOLOGISTS	SEMICLASSICS	SEMIFINALISTS	SEMINATURAL	SEMIPUBLIC
SEMEIOLOGY	SEMICOLONIAL	SEMIFINALS	SEMINIFEROUS	SEMIQUAVER
SEMEIOTICALLY	SEMICOLONIALISM	SEMIFINISHED	SEMINOMADIC	SEMIQUAVERS
SEMEIOTICIAN	SEMICOLONIES	SEMIFITTED	SEMINOMADS	SEMIREFINED
SEMEIOTICIANS	SEMICOLONS	SEMIFLEXIBLE	SEMINOMATA	SEMIRELIGIOUS
SEMEIOTICS	SEMICOLONY	SEMIFLUIDIC	SEMINUDITIES	SEMIRETIRED
SEMELPARITIES	SEMICOMATOSE	SEMIFLUIDITIES	SEMINUDITY	SEMIRETIREMENT
SEMELPARITY	SEMICOMMERCIAL	SEMIFLUIDITY	SEMIOCHEMICAL	SEMIRETIREMENTS
SEMELPAROUS	SEMICONDUCTING	SEMIFLUIDS	SEMIOCHEMICALS	SEMIROUNDS
SEMESTERED	SEMICONDUCTION	SEMIFORMAL	SEMIOFFICIAL	SEMISACRED
SEMESTERING	SEMICONDUCTIONS	SEMIFREDDI	SEMIOFFICIALLY	SEMISECRET
SEMESTERINGS	SEMICONDUCTOR	SEMIFREDDO	SEMIOLOGIC	SEMISEDENTARY
SEMESTRIAL	SEMICONDUCTORS	SEMIFREDDOS	SEMIOLOGICAL	SEMISHRUBBY
SEMIABSTRACT	SEMICONSCIOUS	SEMIGLOBES	SEMIOLOGICALLY	SEMISKILLED
SEMIABSTRACTION	SEMICONSCIOUSLY	SEMIGLOBULAR	SEMIOLOGIES	SEMISOLIDS
SEMIANGLES	SEMICONSONANT	SEMIGLOSSES	SEMIOLOGIST	SEMISOLUSES
SEMIANNUAL	SEMICONSONANTS	SEMIGROUPS	SEMIOLOGISTS	SEMISUBMERSIBLE
SEMIANNUALLY	SEMICRYSTALLIC	SEMIHOBOES	SEMIOPAQUE	SEMISYNTHETIC
SEMIAQUATIC	SEMICRYSTALLINE	SEMILEGENDARY	SEMIOTICALLY	SEMITERETE
SEMIARBOREAL	SEMICYLINDER	SEMILETHAL	SEMIOTICIAN	SEMITERRESTRIAL
SEMIARIDITIES	SEMICYLINDERS	SEMILETHALS	SEMIOTICIANS	SEMITONALLY
SEMIARIDITY	SEMICYLINDRICAL	SEMILIQUID	SEMIOTICIST	SEMITONICALLY
SEMIAUTOMATED	SEMIDARKNESS	SEMILIQUIDS	SEMIOTICISTS	SEMITRAILER
SEMIAUTOMATIC	SEMIDARKNESSES	SEMILITERATE	SEMIOVIPAROUS	SEMITRAILERS
SEMIAUTOMATICS	SEMIDEIFIED	SEMILITERATES	SEMIPALMATE	SEMITRANSLUCENT
SEMIAUTONOMOUS	SEMIDEIFIES	SEMILOGARITHMIC	SEMIPALMATED	SEMITRANSPARENT
SEMIBASEMENT	SEMIDEIFYING	SEMILUCENT	SEMIPALMATION	SEMITROPIC
SEMIBASEMENTS	SEMIDEPONENT	SEMILUNATE	SEMIPALMATIONS	SEMITROPICAL
SEMIBREVES	SEMIDEPONENTS	SEMILUSTROUS	SEMIPARASITE	SEMITROPICS
SEMICARBAZIDE	SEMIDESERT	SEMIMANUFACTURE	SEMIPARASITES	SEMITRUCKS
SEMICARBAZIDES	SEMIDESERTS	SEMIMENSTRUAL	SEMIPARASITIC	SEMIVITREOUS
SEMICARBAZONE	SEMIDETACHED	SEMIMETALLIC	SEMIPARASITISM	SEMIVOCALIC
SEMICARBAZONES	SEMIDETACHEDS	SEMIMETALS	SEMIPARASITISMS	SEMIVOWELS
SEMICENTENNIAL	SEMIDIAMETER	SEMIMONASTIC	SEMIPELLUCID	SEMIWEEKLIES
SEMICENTENNIALS	SEMIDIAMETERS	SEMIMONTHLIES	SEMIPERIMETER	SEMIWEEKLY

SEMIYEARLY	SENSATIONISTS	SENSUALISM	SENTINELLED	SEPTENNIUM
SEMPERVIVUM	SENSATIONLESS	SENSUALISMS	SENTINELLING	SEPTENNIUMS
SEMPERVIVUMS	SENSATIONS	SENSUALIST	SEPALODIES	SEPTENTRIAL
SEMPITERNAL	SENSELESSLY	SENSUALISTIC	SEPARABILITIES	SEPTENTRION
SEMPITERNALLY	SENSELESSNESS	SENSUALISTS	SEPARABILITY	SEPTENTRIONAL
SEMPITERNITIES	SENSELESSNESSES	SENSUALITIES	SEPARABLENESS	SEPTENTRIONALLY
SEMPITERNITY	SENSIBILIA	SENSUALITY	SEPARABLENESSES	SEPTENTRIONES
SEMPITERNUM	SENSIBILITIES	SENSUALIZATION	SEPARATELY	SEPTENTRIONS
SEMPITERNUMS	SENSIBILITY	SENSUALIZATIONS	SEPARATENESS	SEPTICAEMIA
SEMPSTERING	SENSIBLENESS	SENSUALIZE	SEPARATENESSES	SEPTICAEMIAS
SEMPSTERINGS	SENSIBLENESSES	SENSUALIZED	SEPARATING	SEPTICAEMIC
SEMPSTRESS	SENSIBLEST	SENSUALIZES	SEPARATION	SEPTICALLY
SEMPSTRESSES	SENSITISATION	SENSUALIZING	SEPARATIONISM	SEPTICEMIA
SEMPSTRESSING	SENSITISATIONS	SENSUALNESS	SEPARATIONISMS	SEPTICEMIAS
SEMPSTRESSINGS	SENSITISED	SENSUALNESSES	SEPARATIONIST	SEPTICEMIC
SENARMONTITE	SENSITISER	SENSUOSITIES	SEPARATIONISTS	SEPTICIDAL
SENARMONTITES	SENSITISERS	SENSUOSITY	SEPARATIONS	SEPTICIDALLY
SENATORIAL	SENSITISES	SENSUOUSLY	SEPARATISM	SEPTICITIES
SENATORIALLY	SENSITISING	SENSUOUSNESS	SEPARATISMS	SEPTIFEROUS
SENATORIAN	SENSITIVELY	SENSUOUSNESSES	SEPARATIST	SEPTIFRAGAL
SENATORSHIP	SENSITIVENESS	SENTENCERS	SEPARATISTIC	SEPTILATERAL
SENATORSHIPS	SENSITIVENESSES	SENTENCING	SEPARATISTS	SEPTILLION
SENECTITUDE	SENSITIVES	SENTENCINGS	SEPARATIVE	SEPTILLIONS
SENECTITUDES	SENSITIVITIES	SENTENTIAE	SEPARATIVELY	SEPTILLIONTH
SENESCENCE	SENSITIVITY	SENTENTIAL	SEPARATIVENESS	SEPTILLIONTHS
SENESCENCES	SENSITIZATION	SENTENTIALLY	SEPARATORIES	SEPTIMOLES
SENESCHALS	SENSITIZATIONS	SENTENTIOUS	SEPARATORS	SEPTIVALENT
SENESCHALSHIP	SENSITIZED	SENTENTIOUSLY	SEPARATORY	SEPTUAGENARIAN
SENESCHALSHIPS	SENSITIZER	SENTENTIOUSNESS	SEPARATRICES	SEPTUAGENARIANS
SENHORITAS	SENSITIZERS	SENTIENCES	SEPARATRIX	SEPTUAGENARIES
SENILITIES	SENSITIZES	SENTIENCIES	SEPARATUMS	SEPTUAGENARY
SENIORITIES	SENSITIZING	SENTIENTLY	SEPIOLITES	SEPTUPLETS
SENNACHIES	SENSITOMETER	SENTIMENTAL	SEPIOSTAIRE	SEPTUPLICATE
SENSATIONAL	SENSITOMETERS	SENTIMENTALISE	SEPIOSTAIRES	SEPTUPLICATES
SENSATIONALISE	SENSITOMETRIC	SENTIMENTALISED	SEPTATIONS	SEPTUPLING
SENSATIONALISED	SENSITOMETRIES	SENTIMENTALISES	SEPTAVALENT	SEPULCHERED
SENSATIONALISES	SENSITOMETRY	SENTIMENTALISM	SEPTEMVIRATE	SEPULCHERING
SENSATIONALISM	SENSOMOTOR	SENTIMENTALISMS	SEPTEMVIRATES	SEPULCHERS
SENSATIONALISMS	SENSORIALLY	SENTIMENTALIST	SEPTEMVIRI	SEPULCHRAL
SENSATIONALIST	SENSORIMOTOR	SENTIMENTALISTS	SEPTEMVIRS	SEPULCHRALLY
SENSATIONALISTS	SENSORINEURAL	SENTIMENTALITY	SEPTENARIES	SEPULCHRED
SENSATIONALIZE	SENSORIUMS	SENTIMENTALIZE	SEPTENARII	SEPULCHRES
SENSATIONALIZED	SENSUALISATION	SENTIMENTALIZED	SEPTENARIUS	SEPULCHRING
SENSATIONALIZES	SENSUALISATIONS	SENTIMENTALIZES	SEPTENDECILLION	SEPULCHROUS
SENSATIONALLY	SENSUALISE	SENTIMENTALLY	SEPTENNATE	SEPULTURAL
SENSATIONISM	SENSUALISED	SENTIMENTS	SEPTENNATES	SEPULTURED
SENSATIONISMS	SENSUALISES	SENTINELED	SEPTENNIAL	SEPULTURES
SENSATIONIST	SENSUALISING	SENTINELING	SEPTENNIALLY	SEPULTURING

S

SEQUACIOUS

SEQUACIOUS	SERENDIPITOUSLY	SERIOUSNESSES	SEROTHERAPY	SERRANOIDS
SEQUACIOUSLY	SERENDIPITY	SERJEANCIES	SEROTINIES	SERRASALMO
SEQUACIOUSNESS	SERENENESS	SERJEANTIES	SEROTINOUS	SERRASALMOS
SEQUACITIES	SERENENESSES	SERJEANTRIES	SEROTONERGIC	SERRATIONS
SEQUELISED	SERENITIES	SERJEANTRY	SEROTONINERGIC	SERRATIROSTRAL
SEQUELISES	SERGEANCIES	SERJEANTSHIP	SEROTONINS	SERRATULATE
SEQUELISING	SERGEANTIES	SERJEANTSHIPS	SEROTYPING	SERRATURES
SEQUELIZED	SERGEANTSHIP	SERMONEERS	SEROTYPINGS	SERRATUSES
SEQUELIZES	SERGEANTSHIPS	SERMONETTE	SEROUSNESS	SERREFILES
SEQUELIZING	SERIALISATION	SERMONETTES	SEROUSNESSES	SERRICORNS
SEQUENCERS	SERIALISATIONS	SERMONICAL	SERPENTIFORM	SERRIEDNESS
SEQUENCIES	SERIALISED	SERMONINGS	SERPENTINE	SERRIEDNESSES
SEQUENCING	SERIALISES	SERMONISED	SERPENTINED	SERRULATED
SEQUENCINGS	SERIALISING	SERMONISER	SERPENTINELY	SERRULATION
SEQUENTIAL	SERIALISMS	SERMONISERS	SERPENTINES	SERRULATIONS
SEQUENTIALITIES	SERIALISTS	SERMONISES	SERPENTINIC	SERTULARIAN
SEQUENTIALITY	SERIALITIES	SERMONISING	SERPENTINING	SERTULARIANS
SEQUENTIALLY	SERIALIZATION	SERMONISINGS	SERPENTININGLY	SERVANTHOOD
SEQUESTERED	SERIALIZATIONS	SERMONIZED	SERPENTININGS	SERVANTHOODS
SEQUESTERING	SERIALIZED	SERMONIZER	SERPENTINISE	SERVANTING
SEQUESTERS	SERIALIZES	SERMONIZERS	SERPENTINISED	SERVANTLESS
SEQUESTRABLE	SERIALIZING	SERMONIZES	SERPENTINISES	SERVANTRIES
SEQUESTRAL	SERIATIONS	SERMONIZING	SERPENTINISING	SERVANTSHIP
SEQUESTRANT	SERICICULTURE	SERMONIZINGS	SERPENTINITE	SERVANTSHIPS
SEQUESTRANTS	SERICICULTURES	SEROCONVERSION	SERPENTINITES	SERVEWARES
SEQUESTRATE	SERICICULTURIST	SEROCONVERSIONS	SERPENTINIZE	SERVICEABILITY
SEQUESTRATED	SERICITISATION	SEROCONVERT	SERPENTINIZED	SERVICEABLE
SEQUESTRATES	SERICITISATIONS	SEROCONVERTED	SERPENTINIZES	SERVICEABLENESS
SEQUESTRATING	SERICITIZATION	SEROCONVERTING	SERPENTINIZING	SERVICEABLY
SEQUESTRATION	SERICITIZATIONS	SEROCONVERTS	SERPENTINOUS	SERVICEBERRIES
SEQUESTRATIONS	SERICTERIA	SERODIAGNOSES	SERPENTISE	SERVICEBERRY
SEQUESTRATOR	SERICTERIUM	SERODIAGNOSIS	SERPENTISED	SERVICELESS
SEQUESTRATORS	SERICULTURAL	SERODIAGNOSTIC	SERPENTISES	SERVICEMAN
SEQUESTRUM	SERICULTURE	SEROGROUPS	SERPENTISING	SERVICEMEN
SEQUESTRUMS	SERICULTURES	SEROLOGICAL	SERPENTIZE	SERVICEWOMAN
SERAPHICAL	SERICULTURIST	SEROLOGICALLY	SERPENTIZED	SERVICEWOMEN
SERAPHICALLY	SERICULTURISTS	SEROLOGIES	SERPENTIZES	SERVICINGS
SERAPHINES	SERIGRAPHER	SEROLOGIST	SERPENTIZING	SERVIETTES
SERASKIERATE	SERIGRAPHERS	SEROLOGISTS	SERPENTLIKE	SERVILENESS
SERASKIERATES	SERIGRAPHIC	SERONEGATIVE	SERPENTRIES	SERVILENESSES
SERASKIERS	SERIGRAPHIES	SERONEGATIVITY	SERPIGINES	SERVILISMS
SERENADERS	SERIGRAPHS	SEROPOSITIVE	SERPIGINOUS	SERVILITIES
SERENADING	SERIGRAPHY	SEROPOSITIVITY	SERPIGINOUSLY	SERVITORIAL
SERENATING	SERINETTES	SEROPURULENT	SERPULITES	SERVITORSHIP
SERENDIPITIES	SERIOCOMIC	SEROSITIES	SERRADELLA	SERVITORSHIPS
SERENDIPITIST	SERIOCOMICAL	SEROTAXONOMIES	SERRADELLAS	SERVITRESS
SERENDIPITISTS	SERIOCOMICALLY	SEROTAXONOMY	SERRADILLA	SERVITRESSES
SERENDIPITOUS	SERIOUSNESS	SEROTHERAPIES	SERRADILLAS	SERVITUDES

SHARECROPS

SERVOCONTROL	SEVENTEENTHS	SEXTILLIONTHS	SHADOWCASTS	SHAMELESSNESSES
SERVOCONTROLS	SEVENTIETH	SEXTODECIMO	SHADOWGRAPH	SHAMEWORTHIER
SERVOMECHANICAL	SEVENTIETHS	SEXTODECIMOS	SHADOWGRAPHIES	SHAMEWORTHIEST
SERVOMECHANISM	SEVERABILITIES	SEXTONESSES	SHADOWGRAPHS	SHAMEWORTHY
SERVOMECHANISMS	SEVERABILITY	SEXTONSHIP	SHADOWGRAPHY	SHAMIANAHS
SERVOMOTOR	SEVERALFOLD	SEXTONSHIPS	SHADOWIEST	SHAMIYANAH
SERVOMOTORS	SEVERALTIES	SEXTUPLETS	SHADOWINESS	SHAMIYANAHS
SESQUIALTER	SEVERANCES	SEXTUPLICATE	SHADOWINESSES	SHAMMASHIM
SESQUIALTERA	SEVERENESS	SEXTUPLICATED	SHADOWINGS	SHAMOISING
SESQUIALTERAS	SEVERENESSES	SEXTUPLICATES	SHADOWLESS	SHAMPOOERS
SESQUIALTERS	SEVERITIES	SEXTUPLICATING	SHADOWLIKE	SHAMPOOING
SESQUICARBONATE	SEWABILITIES	SEXTUPLIED	SHAGGEDNESS	SHANACHIES
SESQUICENTENARY	SEWABILITY	SEXTUPLIES	SHAGGEDNESSES	SHANDRYDAN
SESQUIOXIDE	SEXAGENARIAN	SEXTUPLING	SHAGGINESS	SHANDRYDANS
SESQUIOXIDES	SEXAGENARIANS	SEXTUPLYING	SHAGGINESSES	SHANDYGAFF
SESQUIPEDAL	SEXAGENARIES	SEXUALISATION	SHAGGYMANE	SHANDYGAFFS
SESQUIPEDALIAN	SEXAGENARY	SEXUALISATIONS	SHAGGYMANES	SHANGHAIED
SESQUIPEDALIANS	SEXAGESIMAL	SEXUALISED	SHAGREENED	SHANGHAIER
SESQUIPEDALITY	SEXAGESIMALLY	SEXUALISES	SHAGTASTIC	SHANGHAIERS
SESQUIPEDALS	SEXAGESIMALS	SEXUALISING	SHAHTOOSHES	SHANGHAIING
SESQUIPLICATE	SEXAHOLICS	SEXUALISMS	SHAKEDOWNS	SHANKBONES
SESQUISULPHIDE	SEXANGULAR	SEXUALISTS	SHAKINESSES	SHANKPIECE
SESQUISULPHIDES	SEXANGULARLY	SEXUALITIES	SHAKUHACHI	SHANKPIECES
SESQUITERPENE	SEXAVALENT	SEXUALIZATION	SHAKUHACHIS	SHANTYTOWN
SESQUITERPENES	SEXCAPADES	SEXUALIZATIONS	SHALLOWEST	SHANTYTOWNS
SESQUITERTIA	SEXCENTENARIES	SEXUALIZED	SHALLOWING	SHAPELESSLY
SESQUITERTIAS	SEXCENTENARY	SEXUALIZES	SHALLOWINGS	SHAPELESSNESS
SESSILITIES	SEXDECILLION	SEXUALIZING	SHALLOWNESS	SHAPELESSNESSES
SESSIONALLY	SEXDECILLIONS	SFORZANDOS	SHALLOWNESSES	SHAPELIEST
SESTERTIUM	SEXENNIALLY	SHABBINESS	SHAMANISMS	SHAPELINESS
SESTERTIUS	SEXENNIALS	SHABBINESSES	SHAMANISTIC	SHAPELINESSES
SETACEOUSLY	SEXERCISES	SHABRACQUE	SHAMANISTS	SHAPESHIFTER
SETIFEROUS	SEXINESSES	SHABRACQUES	SHAMATEURISM	SHAPESHIFTERS
SETIGEROUS	SEXIVALENT	SHACKLEBONE	SHAMATEURISMS	SHAPESHIFTING
SETTERWORT	SEXLESSNESS	SHACKLEBONES	SHAMATEURS	SHAPESHIFTINGS
SETTERWORTS	SEXLESSNESSES	SHACKTOWNS	SHAMBLIEST	SHAPEWEARS
SETTLEABLE	SEXLOCULAR	SHADBERRIES	SHAMBLINGS	SHARAWADGI
SETTLEDNESS	SEXOLOGICAL	SHADBUSHES	SHAMBOLICALLY	SHARAWADGIS
SETTLEDNESSES	SEXOLOGIES	SHADCHANIM	SHAMEFACED	SHARAWAGGI
SETTLEMENT	SEXOLOGIST	SHADINESSES	SHAMEFACEDLY	SHARAWAGGIS
SETTLEMENTS	SEXOLOGISTS	SHADKHANIM	SHAMEFACEDNESS	SHAREABILITIES
SEVENPENCE	SEXPARTITE	SHADOWBOXED	SHAMEFASTNESS	SHAREABILITY
SEVENPENCES	SEXPLOITATION	SHADOWBOXES	SHAMEFASTNESSES	SHARECROPPED
SEVENPENNIES	SEXPLOITATIONS	SHADOWBOXING	SHAMEFULLY	SHARECROPPER
SEVENPENNY	SEXTARIUSES	SHADOWCAST	SHAMEFULNESS	SHARECROPPERS
SEVENTEENS	SEXTILLION	SHADOWCASTED	SHAMEFULNESSES	SHARECROPPING
SEVENTEENTH	SEXTILLIONS	SHADOWCASTING	SHAMELESSLY	SHARECROPPINGS
SEVENTEENTHLY	SEXTILLIONTH	SHADOWCASTINGS	SHAMELESSNESS	SHARECROPS

S

SHAREFARMER	SHEATHINGS	SHELLACKING	SHERARDISES	SHILLELAHS
SHAREFARMERS	SHEATHLESS	SHELLACKINGS	SHERARDISING	SHILLINGLESS
SHAREHOLDER	SHEATHLIKE	SHELLBACKS	SHERARDIZATION	SHILLINGSWORTH
SHAREHOLDERS	SHEBAGGING	SHELLBARKS	SHERARDIZATIONS	SHILLINGSWORTHS
SHAREHOLDING	SHEBAGGINGS	SHELLBOUND	SHERARDIZE	SHILLYSHALLIED
SHAREHOLDINGS	SHEBEENERS	SHELLCRACKER	SHERARDIZED	SHILLYSHALLIER
SHAREMILKER	SHEBEENING	SHELLCRACKERS	SHERARDIZES	SHILLYSHALLIERS
SHAREMILKERS	SHEBEENINGS	SHELLDRAKE	SHERARDIZING	SHILLYSHALLIES
SHARENTING	SHECHITAHS	SHELLDRAKES	SHEREEFIAN	SHILLYSHALLY
SHARENTINGS	SHECKLATON	SHELLDUCKS	SHERGOTTITE	SHILLYSHALLYING
SHAREWARES	SHECKLATONS	SHELLFIRES	SHERGOTTITES	SHIMMERIER
SHARKSKINS	SHEEPBERRIES	SHELLFISHERIES	SHERIFFALTIES	SHIMMERIEST
SHARKSUCKER	SHEEPBERRY	SHELLFISHERY	SHERIFFALTY	SHIMMERING
SHARKSUCKERS	SHEEPCOTES	SHELLFISHES	SHERIFFDOM	SHIMMERINGLY
SHARPBENDER	SHEEPFOLDS	SHELLINESS	SHERIFFDOMS	SHIMMERINGS
SHARPBENDERS	SHEEPHEADS	SHELLINESSES	SHERIFFSHIP	SHIMOZZLES
SHARPENERS	SHEEPHERDER	SHELLPROOF	SHERIFFSHIPS	SHINGLIEST
SHARPENING	SHEEPHERDERS	SHELLSHOCK	SHERLOCKED	SHINGLINGS
SHARPENINGS	SHEEPHERDING	SHELLSHOCKED	SHERLOCKING	SHINGUARDS
SHARPNESSES	SHEEPHERDINGS	SHELLSHOCKS	SHEWBREADS	SHININESSES
SHARPSHOOTER	SHEEPISHLY	SHELLWORKS	SHIBBOLETH	SHININGNESS
SHARPSHOOTERS	SHEEPISHNESS	SHELLYCOAT	SHIBBOLETHS	SHININGNESSES
SHARPSHOOTING	SHEEPISHNESSES	SHELLYCOATS	SHIBUICHIS	SHINLEAVES
SHARPSHOOTINGS	SHEEPSHANK	SHELTERBELT	SHIDDUCHIM	SHINNERIES
SHARPTAILS	SHEEPSHANKS	SHELTERBELTS	SHIELDINGS	SHINNEYING
SHASHLICKS	SHEEPSHEAD	SHELTERERS	SHIELDLESS	SHINPLASTER
SHATOOSHES	SHEEPSHEADS	SHELTERIER	SHIELDLIKE	SHINPLASTERS
SHATTERERS	SHEEPSHEARER	SHELTERIEST	SHIELDLING	SHINSPLINTS
SHATTERIER	SHEEPSHEARERS	SHELTERING	SHIELDLINGS	SHIPBOARDS
SHATTERIEST	SHEEPSHEARING	SHELTERINGS	SHIELDRAKE	SHIPBROKER
SHATTERING	SHEEPSHEARINGS	SHELTERLESS	SHIELDRAKES	SHIPBROKERS
SHATTERINGLY	SHEEPSKINS	SHEMOZZLED	SHIELDWALL	SHIPBUILDER
SHATTERPROOF	SHEEPTRACK	SHEMOZZLES	SHIELDWALLS	SHIPBUILDERS
SHAUCHLIER	SHEEPTRACKS	SHEMOZZLING	SHIFTINESS	SHIPBUILDING
SHAUCHLIEST	SHEEPWALKS	SHENANIGAN	SHIFTINESSES	SHIPBUILDINGS
SHAUCHLING	SHEERNESSES	SHENANIGANS	SHIFTLESSLY	SHIPFITTER
SHAVASANAS	SHEETROCKED	SHEPHERDED	SHIFTLESSNESS	SHIPFITTERS
SHAVELINGS	SHEETROCKING	SHEPHERDESS	SHIFTLESSNESSES	SHIPLAPPED
SHAVETAILS	SHEETROCKS	SHEPHERDESSES	SHIFTSTICK	SHIPLAPPING
SHEARLINGS	SHEIKHDOMS	SHEPHERDING	SHIFTSTICKS	SHIPLAPPINGS
SHEARWATER	SHELDDUCKS	SHEPHERDINGS	SHIFTWORKS	SHIPMASTER
SHEARWATERS	SHELDRAKES	SHEPHERDLESS	SHIGELLOSES	SHIPMASTERS
SHEATFISHES	SHELFROOMS	SHEPHERDLING	SHIGELLOSIS	SHIPOWNERS
SHEATHBILL	SHELFTALKER	SHEPHERDLINGS	SHIKARRING	SHIPPOUNDS
SHEATHBILLS	SHELFTALKERS	SHERARDISATION	SHILLABERS	SHIPWRECKED
SHEATHFISH	SHELLACKED	SHERARDISATIONS	SHILLALAHS	SHIPWRECKING
SHEATHFISHES	SHELLACKER	SHERARDISE	SHILLELAGH	SHIPWRECKS
SHEATHIEST	SHELLACKERS	SHERARDISED	SHILLELAGHS	SHIPWRIGHT

SHIPWRIGHTS	SHMALTZIER	SHOPFITTER	SHORTHANDED	SHOWBIZZIEST
SHIRETOWNS	SHMALTZIEST	SHOPFITTERS	SHORTHANDS	SHOWBOATED
SHIRRALEES	SHMOOZIEST	SHOPFRONTS	SHORTHEADS	SHOWBOATER
SHIRTBANDS	SHMUCKIEST	SHOPHOUSES	SHORTHORNS	SHOWBOATERS
SHIRTDRESS	SHOALINESS	SHOPKEEPER	SHORTLISTED	SHOWBOATING
SHIRTDRESSES	SHOALINESSES	SHOPKEEPERS	SHORTLISTING	SHOWBREADS
SHIRTFRONT	SHOALNESSES	SHOPKEEPING	SHORTLISTS	SHOWCASING
SHIRTFRONTED	SHOCKABILITIES	SHOPKEEPINGS	SHORTNESSES	SHOWERHEAD
SHIRTFRONTING	SHOCKABILITY	SHOPLIFTED	SHORTSHEET	SHOWERHEADS
SHIRTFRONTS	SHOCKHEADED	SHOPLIFTER	SHORTSHEETED	SHOWERIEST
SHIRTINESS	SHOCKINGLY	SHOPLIFTERS	SHORTSHEETING	SHOWERINESS
SHIRTINESSES	SHOCKINGNESS	SHOPLIFTING	SHORTSHEETS	SHOWERINESSES
SHIRTLIFTER	SHOCKINGNESSES	SHOPLIFTINGS	SHORTSIGHTED	SHOWERINGS
SHIRTLIFTERS	SHOCKPROOF	SHOPSOILED	SHORTSIGHTEDLY	SHOWERLESS
SHIRTMAKER	SHOCKSTALL	SHOPWALKER	SHORTSTOPS	SHOWERPROOF
SHIRTMAKERS	SHOCKSTALLS	SHOPWALKERS	SHORTSWORD	SHOWERPROOFED
SHIRTSLEEVE	SHOCKUMENTARIES	SHOPWINDOW	SHORTSWORDS	SHOWERPROOFING
SHIRTSLEEVED	SHOCKUMENTARY	SHOPWINDOWS	SHORTWAVED	SHOWERPROOFINGS
SHIRTSLEEVES	SHODDINESS	SHOREBIRDS	SHORTWAVES	SHOWERPROOFS
SHIRTTAILED	SHODDINESSES	SHOREFRONT	SHORTWAVING	SHOWGROUND
SHIRTTAILING	SHOEBLACKS	SHOREFRONTS	SHOTCRETES	SHOWGROUNDS
SHIRTTAILS	SHOEBRUSHES	SHORELINES	SHOTFIRERS	SHOWINESSES
SHIRTWAIST	SHOEHORNED	SHORESIDES	SHOTGUNNED	SHOWJUMPED
SHIRTWAISTED	SHOEHORNING	SHOREWARDS	SHOTGUNNER	SHOWJUMPER
SHIRTWAISTER	SHOEMAKERS	SHOREWEEDS	SHOTGUNNERS	SHOWJUMPERS
SHIRTWAISTERS	SHOEMAKING	SHORTARSES	SHOTGUNNING	SHOWJUMPING
SHIRTWAISTS	SHOEMAKINGS	SHORTBOARD	SHOTMAKERS	SHOWJUMPINGS
SHITCANNED	SHOESHINES	SHORTBOARDS	SHOTMAKING	SHOWMANCES
SHITCANNING	SHOESTRING	SHORTBREAD	SHOTMAKINGS	SHOWMANLIER
SHITHOUSES	SHOESTRINGS	SHORTBREADS	SHOULDERED	SHOWMANLIEST
SHITSTORMS	SHOGGLIEST	SHORTCAKES	SHOULDERING	SHOWMANSHIP
SHITTIMWOOD	SHOGUNATES	SHORTCHANGE	SHOULDERINGS	SHOWMANSHIPS
SHITTIMWOODS	SHONGOLOLO	SHORTCHANGED	SHOUTHERED	SHOWPIECES
SHITTINESS	SHONGOLOLOS	SHORTCHANGER	SHOUTHERING	SHOWPLACES
SHITTINESSES	SHOOGIEING	SHORTCHANGERS	SHOUTINGLY	SHOWROOMING
SHIVAREEING	SHOOGLIEST	SHORTCHANGES	SHOUTLINES	SHOWROOMINGS
SHIVERIEST	SHOOTAROUND	SHORTCHANGING	SHOVELBOARD	SHOWSTOPPER
SHIVERINGLY	SHOOTAROUNDS	SHORTCOMING	SHOVELBOARDS	SHOWSTOPPERS
SHIVERINGS	SHOOTDOWNS	SHORTCOMINGS	SHOVELFULS	SHOWSTOPPING
SHLEMIEHLS	SHOPAHOLIC	SHORTCRUST	SHOVELHEAD	SHREDDIEST
SHLEMOZZLE	SHOPAHOLICS	SHORTCUTTING	SHOVELHEADS	SHREDDINGS
SHLEMOZZLED	SHOPAHOLISM	SHORTENERS	SHOVELLERS	SHREWDNESS
SHLEMOZZLES	SHOPAHOLISMS	SHORTENING	SHOVELLING	SHREWDNESSES
SHLEMOZZLING	SHOPBOARDS	SHORTENINGS	SHOVELNOSE	SHREWISHLY
SHLEPPIEST	SHOPBREAKER	SHORTFALLS	SHOVELNOSES	SHREWISHNESS
SHLIMAZELS	SHOPBREAKERS	SHORTGOWNS	SHOVELSFUL	SHREWISHNESSES
SHLOCKIEST	SHOPBREAKING	SHORTHAIRED	SHOWBIZZES	SHREWMOUSE
SHLUMPIEST	SHOPBREAKINGS	SHORTHAIRS	SHOWBIZZIER	SHRIECHING

S

SHRIEKIEST	SHUNAMITISM	SICKLEBILL	SIDESTEPPED	SIGMATISMS
SHRIEKINGLY	SHUNAMITISMS	SICKLEBILLS	SIDESTEPPER	SIGMATRONS
SHRIEKINGS	SHUNPIKERS	SICKLEMIAS	SIDESTEPPERS	SIGMOIDALLY
SHRIEVALTIES	SHUNPIKING	SICKLINESS	SIDESTEPPING	SIGMOIDECTOMIES
SHRIEVALTY	SHUNPIKINGS	SICKLINESSES	SIDESTEPPINGS	SIGMOIDECTOMY
SHRILLIEST	SHUTTERBUG	SICKNESSES	SIDESTREAM	SIGMOIDOSCOPE
SHRILLINGS	SHUTTERBUGS	SICKNURSED	SIDESTROKE	SIGMOIDOSCOPES
SHRILLNESS	SHUTTERING	SICKNURSES	SIDESTROKES	SIGMOIDOSCOPIC
SHRILLNESSES	SHUTTERINGS	SICKNURSING	SIDESWIPED	SIGMOIDOSCOPIES
SHRIMPIEST	SHUTTERLESS	SICKNURSINGS	SIDESWIPER	SIGMOIDOSCOPY
SHRIMPINGS	SHUTTLECOCK	SIDDHUISMS	SIDESWIPERS	SIGNALINGS
SHRIMPLIKE	SHUTTLECOCKED	SIDEARMERS	SIDESWIPES	SIGNALISATION
SHRINELIKE	SHUTTLECOCKING	SIDEARMING	SIDESWIPING	SIGNALISATIONS
SHRINKABLE	SHUTTLECOCKS	SIDEBOARDS	SIDETABLES	SIGNALISED
SHRINKAGES	SHUTTLELESS	SIDEBURNED	SIDETRACKED	SIGNALISES
SHRINKFLATION	SHUTTLEWISE	SIDECHAIRS	SIDETRACKING	SIGNALISING
SHRINKFLATIONS	SHYLOCKING	SIDECHECKS	SIDETRACKS	SIGNALIZATION
SHRINKINGLY	SIALAGOGIC	SIDEDNESSES	SIDEWHEELER	SIGNALIZATIONS
SHRINKPACK	SIALAGOGUE	SIDEDRESSES	SIDEWHEELERS	SIGNALIZED
SHRINKPACKS	SIALAGOGUES	SIDELEVERS	SIDEWHEELS	SIGNALIZES
SHRITCHING	SIALOGOGIC	SIDELIGHTS	SIDEWINDER	SIGNALIZING
SHRIVELING	SIALOGOGUE	SIDELINERS	SIDEWINDERS	SIGNALLERS
SHRIVELLED	SIALOGOGUES	SIDELINING	SIEGECRAFT	SIGNALLING
SHRIVELLING	SIALOGRAMS	SIDEPIECES	SIEGECRAFTS	SIGNALLINGS
SHROFFAGES	SIALOGRAPHIES	SIDERATING	SIEGEWORKS	SIGNALMENT
SHROUDIEST	SIALOGRAPHY	SIDERATION	SIFFLEUSES	SIGNALMENTS
SHROUDINGS	SIALOLITHS	SIDERATIONS	SIGHTLESSLY	SIGNATORIES
SHROUDLESS	SIALORRHOEA	SIDEREALLY	SIGHTLESSNESS	SIGNATURES
SHRUBBERIED	SIALORRHOEAS	SIDEROLITE	SIGHTLESSNESSES	SIGNBOARDS
SHRUBBERIES	SIBILANCES	SIDEROLITES	SIGHTLIEST	SIGNEURIES
SHRUBBIEST	SIBILANCIES	SIDEROPENIA	SIGHTLINES	SIGNIFIABLE
SHRUBBINESS	SIBILANTLY	SIDEROPENIAS	SIGHTLINESS	SIGNIFICANCE
SHRUBBINESSES	SIBILATING	SIDEROPHILE	SIGHTLINESSES	SIGNIFICANCES
SHRUBLANDS	SIBILATION	SIDEROPHILES	SIGHTSCREEN	SIGNIFICANCIES
SHTETELACH	SIBILATIONS	SIDEROPHILIC	SIGHTSCREENS	SIGNIFICANCY
SHTICKIEST	SIBILATORS	SIDEROPHILIN	SIGHTSEEING	SIGNIFICANT
SHTREIMELS	SIBILATORY	SIDEROPHILINS	SIGHTSEEINGS	SIGNIFICANTLY
SHUBUNKINS	SICCATIVES	SIDEROSTAT	SIGHTSEERS	SIGNIFICANTS
SHUDDERIER	SICILIANAS	SIDEROSTATIC	SIGHTWORTHIER	SIGNIFICATE
SHUDDERIEST	SICILIANOS	SIDEROSTATS	SIGHTWORTHIEST	SIGNIFICATES
SHUDDERING	SICILIENNE	SIDESADDLE	SIGHTWORTHY	SIGNIFICATION
SHUDDERINGLY	SICILIENNES	SIDESADDLES	SIGILLARIAN	SIGNIFICATIONS
SHUDDERINGS	SICKENINGLY	SIDESHOOTS	SIGILLARIANS	SIGNIFICATIVE
SHUDDERSOME	SICKENINGS	SIDESLIPPED	SIGILLARID	SIGNIFICATIVELY
SHUFFLEBOARD	SICKERNESS	SIDESLIPPING	SIGILLARIDS	SIGNIFICATOR
SHUFFLEBOARDS	SICKERNESSES	SIDESPLITS	SIGILLATION	SIGNIFICATORS
SHUFFLINGLY	SICKISHNESS	SIDESPLITTING	SIGILLATIONS	SIGNIFICATORY
SHUFFLINGS	SICKISHNESSES	SIDESPLITTINGLY	SIGMATIONS	SIGNIFIEDS

SIGNIFIERS	SILTSTONES	SILYMARINS	SIMULATING	SINGABLENESSES
SIGNIFYING	SILVERBACK	SIMAROUBACEOUS	SIMULATION	SINGALONGS
SIGNIFYINGS	SILVERBACKS	SIMAROUBAS	SIMULATIONS	SINGLEDOMS
SIGNIORIES	SILVERBERRIES	SIMARUBACEOUS	SIMULATIVE	SINGLEHOOD
SIGNORINAS	SILVERBERRY	SIMILARITIES	SIMULATIVELY	SINGLEHOODS
SIGNPOSTED	SILVERBILL	SIMILARITY	SIMULATORS	SINGLENESS
SIGNPOSTING	SILVERBILLS	SIMILATIVE	SIMULATORY	SINGLENESSES
SIGNPOSTINGS	SILVEREYES	SIMILISING	SIMULCASTED	SINGLESTICK
SIKORSKIES	SILVERFISH	SIMILITUDE	SIMULCASTING	SINGLESTICKS
SILDENAFIL	SILVERFISHES	SIMILITUDES	SIMULCASTS	SINGLETONS
SILDENAFILS	SILVERHORN	SIMILIZING	SIMULTANEITIES	SINGLETRACK
SILENTIARIES	SILVERHORNS	SIMILLIMUM	SIMULTANEITY	SINGLETRACKS
SILENTIARY	SILVERIEST	SIMILLIMUMS	SIMULTANEOUS	SINGLETREE
SILENTNESS	SILVERINESS	SIMONIACAL	SIMULTANEOUSES	SINGLETREES
SILENTNESSES	SILVERINESSES	SIMONIACALLY	SIMULTANEOUSLY	SINGSONGED
SILHOUETTE	SILVERINGS	SIMONISING	SIMVASTATIN	SINGSONGIER
SILHOUETTED	SILVERISED	SIMONIZING	SIMVASTATINS	SINGSONGIEST
SILHOUETTES	SILVERISES	SIMPERINGLY	SINANTHROPUS	SINGSONGING
SILHOUETTING	SILVERISING	SIMPERINGS	SINANTHROPUSES	SINGSPIELS
SILHOUETTIST	SILVERIZED	SIMPLEMINDED	SINARCHISM	SINGULARISATION
SILHOUETTISTS	SILVERIZES	SIMPLEMINDEDLY	SINARCHISMS	SINGULARISE
SILICATING	SILVERIZING	SIMPLENESS	SINARCHIST	SINGULARISED
SILICICOLOUS	SILVERLING	SIMPLENESSES	SINARCHISTS	SINGULARISES
SILICIFEROUS	SILVERLINGS	SIMPLESSES	SINARQUISM	SINGULARISING
SILICIFICATION	SILVERPOINT	SIMPLETONS	SINARQUISMS	SINGULARISM
SILICIFICATIONS	SILVERPOINTS	SIMPLICIAL	SINARQUIST	SINGULARISMS
SILICIFIED	SILVERSIDE	SIMPLICIALLY	SINARQUISTS	SINGULARIST
SILICIFIES	SILVERSIDES	SIMPLICIDENTATE	SINCERENESS	SINGULARISTS
SILICIFYING	SILVERSKIN	SIMPLICITER	SINCERENESSES	SINGULARITIES
SILICONISED	SILVERSKINS	SIMPLICITIES	SINCERITIES	SINGULARITY
SILICONIZED	SILVERSMITH	SIMPLICITY	SINCIPITAL	SINGULARIZATION
SILICOTICS	SILVERSMITHING	SIMPLIFIABLE	SINDONOLOGIES	SINGULARIZE
SILICULOSE	SILVERSMITHINGS	SIMPLIFICATION	SINDONOLOGIST	SINGULARIZED
SILIQUACEOUS	SILVERSMITHS	SIMPLIFICATIONS	SINDONOLOGISTS	SINGULARIZES
SILKALENES	SILVERTAIL	SIMPLIFICATIVE	SINDONOLOGY	SINGULARIZING
SILKALINES	SILVERTAILS	SIMPLIFICATOR	SINDONOPHANIES	SINGULARLY
SILKGROWER	SILVERTIPS	SIMPLIFICATORS	SINDONOPHANY	SINGULARNESS
SILKGROWERS	SILVERWARE	SIMPLIFIED	SINECURISM	SINGULARNESSES
SILKINESSES	SILVERWARES	SIMPLIFIER	SINECURISMS	SINGULTUSES
SILKOLINES	SILVERWEED	SIMPLIFIERS	SINECURIST	SINICISING
SILKSCREEN	SILVERWEEDS	SIMPLIFIES	SINECURISTS	SINICIZING
SILKSCREENED	SILVESTRIAN	SIMPLIFYING	SINEWINESS	SINISTERITIES
SILKSCREENING	SILVICULTURAL	SIMPLISTES	SINEWINESSES	SINISTERITY
SILKSCREENS	SILVICULTURALLY	SIMPLISTIC	SINFONIETTA	SINISTERLY
SILLIMANITE	SILVICULTURE	SIMPLISTICALLY	SINFONIETTAS	SINISTERNESS
SILLIMANITES	SILVICULTURES	SIMULACRES	SINFULNESS	SINISTERNESSES
SILLINESSES	SILVICULTURIST	SIMULACRUM	SINFULNESSES	SINISTERWISE
SILTATIONS	SILVICULTURISTS	SIMULACRUMS	SINGABLENESS	SINISTRALITIES

S

SINISTRALITY	SIPUNCULOID	SKAITHLESS	SKETCHINESS	SKIMPINESS
SINISTRALLY	SIPUNCULOIDS	SKALDSHIPS	SKETCHINESSES	SKIMPINESSES
SINISTRALS	SIRENISING	SKANKINESS	SKETCHPADS	SKIMPINGLY
SINISTRODEXTRAL	SIRENIZING	SKANKINESSES	SKEUOMORPH	SKINFLICKS
SINISTRORSAL	SIRONISING	SKATEBOARD	SKEUOMORPHIC	SKINFLINTIER
SINISTRORSALLY	SIRONIZING	SKATEBOARDED	SKEUOMORPHISM	SKINFLINTIEST
SINISTRORSE	SISERARIES	SKATEBOARDER	SKEUOMORPHISMS	SKINFLINTS
SINISTRORSELY	SISSINESSES	SKATEBOARDERS	SKEUOMORPHS	SKINFLINTY
SINISTROUS	SISSYNESSES	SKATEBOARDING	SKEWBACKED	SKINNINESS
SINISTROUSLY	SISTERHOOD	SKATEBOARDINGS	SKEWNESSES	SKINNINESSES
SINLESSNESS	SISTERHOODS	SKATEBOARDS	SKIAGRAPHS	SKINTIGHTER
SINLESSNESSES	SISTERLESS	SKATEPARKS	SKIAMACHIES	SKINTIGHTEST
SINNINGIAS	SISTERLIER	SKATEPUNKS	SKIASCOPES	SKINTIGHTS
SINOATRIAL	SISTERLIEST	SKEDADDLED	SKIASCOPIES	SKIPPERING
SINOLOGICAL	SISTERLIKE	SKEDADDLER	SKIBOBBERS	SKIPPERINGS
SINOLOGIES	SISTERLINESS	SKEDADDLERS	SKIBOBBING	SKIPPINGLY
SINOLOGIST	SISTERLINESSES	SKEDADDLES	SKIBOBBINGS	SKIRMISHED
SINOLOGISTS	SITATUNGAS	SKEDADDLING	SKIDDOOING	SKIRMISHER
SINOLOGUES	SITIOLOGIES	SKELDERING	SKIDOOINGS	SKIRMISHERS
SINSEMILLA	SITIOPHOBIA	SKELETALLY	SKIJORINGS	SKIRMISHES
SINSEMILLAS	SITIOPHOBIAS	SKELETOGENOUS	SKIJUMPERS	SKIRMISHING
SINTERABILITIES	SITOLOGIES	SKELETONIC	SKIKJORERS	SKIRMISHINGS
SINTERABILITY	SITOPHOBIA	SKELETONISE	SKIKJORING	SKITTERIER
SINTERIEST	SITOPHOBIAS	SKELETONISED	SKIKJORINGS	SKITTERIEST
SINUATIONS	SITOSTEROL	SKELETONISER	SKILFULNESS	SKITTERING
SINUITISES	SITOSTEROLS	SKELETONISERS	SKILFULNESSES	SKITTISHLY
SINUOSITIES	SITUATIONAL	SKELETONISES	SKILLCENTRE	SKITTISHNESS
SINUOUSNESS	SITUATIONALLY	SKELETONISING	SKILLCENTRES	SKITTISHNESSES
SINUOUSNESSES	SITUATIONISM	SKELETONIZE	SKILLESSNESS	SKORDALIAS
SINUPALLIAL	SITUATIONISMS	SKELETONIZED	SKILLESSNESSES	SKREEGHING
SINUPALLIATE	SITUATIONS	SKELETONIZER	SKILLFULLY	SKREIGHING
SINUSITISES	SITUTUNGAS	SKELETONIZERS	SKILLFULNESS	SKRIECHING
SINUSOIDAL	SITZKRIEGS	SKELETONIZES	SKILLFULNESSES	SKRIEGHING
SINUSOIDALLY	SIXPENNIES	SKELETONIZING	SKILLIGALEE	SKRIMMAGED
SIPHONAGES	SIXTEENERS	SKELLOCHED	SKILLIGALEES	SKRIMMAGES
SIPHONOGAM	SIXTEENMOS	SKELLOCHING	SKILLIGOLEE	SKRIMMAGING
SIPHONOGAMIES	SIXTEENTHLY	SKELTERING	SKILLIGOLEES	SKRIMSHANK
SIPHONOGAMS	SIXTEENTHS	SKEPTICALLY	SKIMBOARDED	SKRIMSHANKED
SIPHONOGAMY	SIZABLENESS	SKEPTICALNESS	SKIMBOARDER	SKRIMSHANKER
SIPHONOPHORE	SIZABLENESSES	SKEPTICALNESSES	SKIMBOARDERS	SKRIMSHANKERS
SIPHONOPHORES	SIZEABLENESS	SKEPTICISM	SKIMBOARDING	SKRIMSHANKING
SIPHONOPHOROUS	SIZEABLENESSES	SKEPTICISMS	SKIMBOARDS	SKRIMSHANKS
SIPHONOSTELE	SIZINESSES	SKETCHABILITIES	SKIMMINGLY	SKULDUDDERIES
SIPHONOSTELES	SIZZLINGLY	SKETCHABILITY	SKIMMINGTON	SKULDUDDERY
SIPHONOSTELIC	SJAMBOKING	SKETCHABLE	SKIMMINGTONS	SKULDUGGERIES
SIPHUNCLES	SJAMBOKKED	SKETCHBOOK	SKIMOBILED	SKULDUGGERY
SIPUNCULID	SJAMBOKKING	SKETCHBOOKS	SKIMOBILES	SKULKINGLY
SIPUNCULIDS		SKETCHIEST	SKIMOBILING	SKULLDUGGERIES

SKULLDUGGERY	SLACTIVISMS	SLAUGHTERING	SLEEPWEARS	SLINGBACKS
SKUMMERING	SLACTIVIST	SLAUGHTERMAN	SLEEPYHEAD	SLINGSHOTS
SKUNKBIRDS	SLACTIVISTS	SLAUGHTERMEN	SLEEPYHEADED	SLINGSTONE
SKUNKWEEDS	SLAISTERED	SLAUGHTEROUS	SLEEPYHEADS	SLINGSTONES
SKUTTERUDITE	SLAISTERIES	SLAUGHTEROUSLY	SLEETINESS	SLINKINESS
SKUTTERUDITES	SLAISTERING	SLAUGHTERS	SLEETINESSES	SLINKINESSES
SKYBRIDGES	SLALOMISTS	SLAUGHTERY	SLEEVEHAND	SLINKSKINS
SKYDIVINGS	SLAMDANCED	SLAVEHOLDER	SLEEVEHANDS	SLINKWEEDS
SKYJACKERS	SLAMDANCES	SLAVEHOLDERS	SLEEVELESS	SLIPCOVERED
SKYJACKING	SLAMDANCING	SLAVEHOLDING	SLEEVELETS	SLIPCOVERING
SKYJACKINGS	SLAMMAKINS	SLAVEHOLDINGS	SLEEVELIKE	SLIPCOVERS
SKYLARKERS	SLAMMERKIN	SLAVERINGLY	SLEIGHINGS	SLIPDRESSES
SKYLARKING	SLAMMERKINS	SLAVERINGS	SLENDEREST	SLIPFORMED
SKYLARKINGS	SLANDERERS	SLAVISHNESS	SLENDERISE	SLIPFORMING
SKYLIGHTED	SLANDERING	SLAVISHNESSES	SLENDERISED	SLIPNOOSES
SKYROCKETED	SLANDEROUS	SLAVOCRACIES	SLENDERISES	SLIPPERIER
SKYROCKETING	SLANDEROUSLY	SLAVOCRACY	SLENDERISING	SLIPPERIEST
SKYROCKETS	SLANDEROUSNESS	SLAVOCRATS	SLENDERIZE	SLIPPERILY
SKYSCRAPER	SLANGINESS	SLAVOPHILE	SLENDERIZED	SLIPPERINESS
SKYSCRAPERS	SLANGINESSES	SLAVOPHILES	SLENDERIZES	SLIPPERINESSES
SKYSURFERS	SLANGINGLY	SLAVOPHILS	SLENDERIZING	SLIPPERING
SKYSURFING	SLANGUAGES	SLEAZEBAGS	SLENDERNESS	SLIPPERWORT
SKYSURFINGS	SLANTENDICULAR	SLEAZEBALL	SLENDERNESSES	SLIPPERWORTS
SKYWATCHED	SLANTINDICULAR	SLEAZEBALLS	SLEUTHHOUND	SLIPPINESS
SKYWATCHES	SLANTINGLY	SLEAZINESS	SLEUTHHOUNDS	SLIPPINESSES
SKYWATCHING	SLANTINGWAYS	SLEAZINESSES	SLEUTHINGS	SLIPSHEETED
SKYWRITERS	SLAPDASHED	SLEDGEHAMMER	SLICKENERS	SLIPSHEETING
SKYWRITING	SLAPDASHES	SLEDGEHAMMERED	SLICKENING	SLIPSHEETS
SKYWRITINGS	SLAPDASHING	SLEDGEHAMMERING	SLICKENSIDE	SLIPSHODDINESS
SKYWRITTEN	SLAPHAPPIER	SLEDGEHAMMERS	SLICKENSIDED	SLIPSHODNESS
SLABBERERS	SLAPHAPPIEST	SLEECHIEST	SLICKENSIDES	SLIPSHODNESSES
SLABBERIER	SLAPSTICKS	SLEEKENING	SLICKNESSES	SLIPSLOPPIER
SLABBERIEST	SLASHFESTS	SLEEKNESSES	SLICKROCKS	SLIPSLOPPIEST
SLABBERING	SLASHINGLY	SLEEKSTONE	SLICKSTERS	SLIPSLOPPY
SLABBINESS	SLATHERING	SLEEKSTONES	SLICKSTONE	SLIPSTREAM
SLABBINESSES	SLATINESSES	SLEEPINESS	SLICKSTONES	SLIPSTREAMED
SLABSTONES	SLATTERING	SLEEPINESSES	SLIDDERIER	SLIPSTREAMING
SLACKENERS	SLATTERNLIER	SLEEPLESSLY	SLIDDERIEST	SLIPSTREAMS
SLACKENING	SLATTERNLIEST	SLEEPLESSNESS	SLIDDERING	SLITHERIER
SLACKENINGS	SLATTERNLINESS	SLEEPLESSNESSES	SLIDESHOWS	SLITHERIEST
SLACKLINING	SLATTERNLY	SLEEPOVERS	SLIGHTINGLY	SLITHERING
SLACKLININGS	SLAUGHTERABLE	SLEEPSUITS	SLIGHTNESS	SLIVOVICAS
SLACKNESSES	SLAUGHTERED	SLEEPWALKED	SLIGHTNESSES	SLIVOVICES
SLACKTIVISM	SLAUGHTERER	SLEEPWALKER	SLIMEBALLS	SLIVOVITZES
SLACKTIVISMS	SLAUGHTERERS	SLEEPWALKERS	SLIMINESSES	SLIVOWITZES
SLACKTIVIST	SLAUGHTERHOUSE	SLEEPWALKING	SLIMNASTICS	SLOBBERERS
SLACKTIVISTS	SLAUGHTERHOUSES	SLEEPWALKINGS	SLIMNESSES	SLOBBERIER
SLACTIVISM	SLAUGHTERIES	SLEEPWALKS	SLIMPSIEST	SLOBBERIEST

S

SLOBBERING	SLOWNESSES	SLUMPFLATION	SMASHEROOS	SMOKESTACKS
SLOBBISHNESS	SLUBBERING	SLUMPFLATIONARY	SMASHINGLY	SMOKETIGHT
SLOBBISHNESSES	SLUBBERINGLY	SLUMPFLATIONS	SMASHMOUTH	SMOKINESSES
SLOCKDOLAGER	SLUBBERINGS	SLUNGSHOTS	SMATTERERS	SMOLDERING
SLOCKDOLAGERS	SLUGGABEDS	SLUSHINESS	SMATTERING	SMOOCHIEST
SLOCKDOLIGER	SLUGGARDISE	SLUSHINESSES	SMATTERINGLY	SMOOTHABLE
SLOCKDOLIGERS	SLUGGARDISED	SLUTCHIEST	SMATTERINGS	SMOOTHBORE
SLOCKDOLOGER	SLUGGARDISES	SLUTTERIES	SMEARCASES	SMOOTHBORED
SLOCKDOLOGERS	SLUGGARDISING	SLUTTINESS	SMEARINESS	SMOOTHBORES
SLOCKENING	SLUGGARDIZE	SLUTTINESSES	SMEARINESSES	SMOOTHENED
SLOEBUSHES	SLUGGARDIZED	SLUTTISHLY	SMELLINESS	SMOOTHENING
SLOETHORNS	SLUGGARDIZES	SLUTTISHNESS	SMELLINESSES	SMOOTHINGS
SLOGANEERED	SLUGGARDIZING	SLUTTISHNESSES	SMELTERIES	SMOOTHNESS
SLOGANEERING	SLUGGARDLIER	SMACKDOWNS	SMICKERING	SMOOTHNESSES
SLOGANEERINGS	SLUGGARDLIEST	SMACKEROOS	SMICKERINGS	SMOOTHPATE
SLOGANEERS	SLUGGARDLINESS	SMACKHEADS	SMIERCASES	SMOOTHPATES
SLOGANISED	SLUGGARDLY	SMALLCLOTHES	SMIFLIGATE	SMORGASBORD
SLOGANISES	SLUGGARDNESS	SMALLHOLDER	SMIFLIGATED	SMORGASBORDS
SLOGANISING	SLUGGARDNESSES	SMALLHOLDERS	SMIFLIGATES	SMORREBROD
SLOGANISINGS	SLUGGISHLY	SMALLHOLDING	SMIFLIGATING	SMORREBRODS
SLOGANIZED	SLUGGISHNESS	SMALLHOLDINGS	SMILACACEOUS	SMOTHERERS
SLOGANIZES	SLUGGISHNESSES	SMALLMOUTH	SMILINGNESS	SMOTHERIER
SLOGANIZING	SLUGHORNES	SMALLMOUTHS	SMILINGNESSES	SMOTHERIEST
SLOGANIZINGS	SLUICEGATE	SMALLNESSES	SMIRKINGLY	SMOTHERINESS
SLOMMOCKED	SLUICEGATES	SMALLPOXES	SMITHCRAFT	SMOTHERINESSES
SLOMMOCKING	SLUICELIKE	SMALLSWORD	SMITHCRAFTS	SMOTHERING
SLOPESIDES	SLUICEWAYS	SMALLSWORDS	SMITHEREEN	SMOTHERINGLY
SLOPINGNESS	SLUMBERERS	SMALMINESS	SMITHEREENED	SMOTHERINGS
SLOPINGNESSES	SLUMBERFUL	SMALMINESSES	SMITHEREENING	SMOULDERED
SLOPPINESS	SLUMBERIER	SMARAGDINE	SMITHEREENS	SMOULDERING
SLOPPINESSES	SLUMBERIEST	SMARAGDITE	SMITHERIES	SMOULDERINGLY
SLOPWORKER	SLUMBERING	SMARAGDITES	SMITHSONITE	SMOULDERINGS
SLOPWORKERS	SLUMBERINGLY	SMARMINESS	SMITHSONITES	SMOULDRIER
SLOTHFULLY	SLUMBERINGS	SMARMINESSES	SMOKEBOARD	SMOULDRIEST
SLOTHFULNESS	SLUMBERLAND	SMARTARSED	SMOKEBOARDS	SMUDGELESS
SLOTHFULNESSES	SLUMBERLANDS	SMARTARSES	SMOKEBOXES	SMUDGINESS
SLOUCHIEST	SLUMBERLESS	SMARTASSES	SMOKEBUSHES	SMUDGINESSES
SLOUCHINESS	SLUMBEROUS	SMARTENING	SMOKEHOODS	SMUGGERIES
SLOUCHINESSES	SLUMBEROUSLY	SMARTINGLY	SMOKEHOUSE	SMUGGLINGS
SLOUCHINGLY	SLUMBEROUSNESS	SMARTMOUTH	SMOKEHOUSES	SMUGNESSES
SLOUGHIEST	SLUMBERSOME	SMARTMOUTHS	SMOKEJACKS	SMUTCHIEST
SLOVENLIER	SLUMBROUSLY	SMARTNESSES	SMOKELESSLY	SMUTTINESS
SLOVENLIEST	SLUMBROUSNESS	SMARTPHONE	SMOKELESSNESS	SMUTTINESSES
SLOVENLIKE	SLUMBROUSNESSES	SMARTPHONES	SMOKELESSNESSES	SNACKETTES
SLOVENLINESS	SLUMGULLION	SMARTWATCH	SMOKEPROOF	SNAGGLETEETH
SLOVENLINESSES	SLUMGULLIONS	SMARTWATCHES	SMOKESCREEN	SNAGGLETOOTH
SLOVENRIES	SLUMMOCKED	SMARTWEEDS	SMOKESCREENS	SNAGGLETOOTHED
SLOWCOACHES	SLUMMOCKING	SMARTYPANTS	SMOKESTACK	SNAILERIES

SNAILFISHES	SNEAKINGNESSES	SNIVELIEST	SNOWBLINKS	SNOWTUBING
SNAKEBIRDS	SNEAKISHLY	SNIVELINGS	SNOWBLOWER	SNOWTUBINGS
SNAKEBITES	SNEAKISHNESS	SNIVELLERS	SNOWBLOWERS	SNUBBINESS
SNAKEBITTEN	SNEAKISHNESSES	SNIVELLIER	SNOWBOARDED	SNUBBINESSES
SNAKEFISHES	SNEAKSBIES	SNIVELLIEST	SNOWBOARDER	SNUBBINGLY
SNAKEHEADS	SNEERINGLY	SNIVELLING	SNOWBOARDERS	SNUBNESSES
SNAKEMOUTH	SNEESHINGS	SNIVELLINGS	SNOWBOARDING	SNUFFBOXES
SNAKEMOUTHS	SNEEZELESS	SNOBBERIES	SNOWBOARDINGS	SNUFFINESS
SNAKEROOTS	SNEEZEWEED	SNOBBISHLY	SNOWBOARDS	SNUFFINESSES
SNAKESKINS	SNEEZEWEEDS	SNOBBISHNESS	SNOWBRUSHES	SNUFFLIEST
SNAKESTONE	SNEEZEWOOD	SNOBBISHNESSES	SNOWBUSHES	SNUFFLINGS
SNAKESTONES	SNEEZEWOODS	SNOBBOCRACIES	SNOWCAPPED	SNUGGERIES
SNAKEWEEDS	SNEEZEWORT	SNOBBOCRACY	SNOWCLONES	SNUGGLIEST
SNAKEWOODS	SNEEZEWORTS	SNOBOCRACIES	SNOWCOACHES	SNUGNESSES
SNAKINESSES	SNICKERERS	SNOBOCRACY	SNOWDRIFTS	SOAPBERRIES
SNAKISHNESS	SNICKERIER	SNOBOGRAPHER	SNOWFIELDS	SOAPBOXING
SNAKISHNESSES	SNICKERIEST	SNOBOGRAPHERS	SNOWFLAKES	SOAPDISHES
SNAPDRAGON	SNICKERING	SNOBOGRAPHIES	SNOWFLECKS	SOAPFISHES
SNAPDRAGONS	SNICKERSNEE	SNOBOGRAPHY	SNOWFLICKS	SOAPFLAKES
SNAPHANCES	SNICKERSNEED	SNOCOACHES	SNOWGLOBES	SOAPINESSES
SNAPHAUNCE	SNICKERSNEEING	SNOLLYGOSTER	SNOWINESSES	SOAPOLALLIE
SNAPHAUNCES	SNICKERSNEES	SNOLLYGOSTERS	SNOWMAKERS	SOAPOLALLIES
SNAPHAUNCH	SNIDENESSES	SNOOKERING	SNOWMAKING	SOAPSTONES
SNAPHAUNCHES	SNIFFINESS	SNOOPERSCOPE	SNOWMOBILE	SOAPSUDSIER
SNAPPERING	SNIFFINESSES	SNOOPERSCOPES	SNOWMOBILED	SOAPSUDSIEST
SNAPPINESS	SNIFFINGLY	SNOOTINESS	SNOWMOBILER	SOBERINGLY
SNAPPINESSES	SNIFFISHLY	SNOOTINESSES	SNOWMOBILERS	SOBERISING
SNAPPINGLY	SNIFFISHNESS	SNORKELERS	SNOWMOBILES	SOBERIZING
SNAPPISHLY	SNIFFISHNESSES	SNORKELING	SNOWMOBILING	SOBERNESSES
SNAPPISHNESS	SNIFFLIEST	SNORKELINGS	SNOWMOBILINGS	SOBERSIDED
SNAPPISHNESSES	SNIFTERING	SNORKELLED	SNOWMOBILIST	SOBERSIDEDNESS
SNAPSHOOTER	SNIGGERERS	SNORKELLER	SNOWMOBILISTS	SOBERSIDES
SNAPSHOOTERS	SNIGGERING	SNORKELLERS	SNOWMOULDS	SOBOLIFEROUS
SNAPSHOOTING	SNIGGERINGLY	SNORKELLING	SNOWPLOUGH	SOBRIETIES
SNAPSHOOTINGS	SNIGGERINGS	SNORKELLINGS	SNOWPLOUGHED	SOBRIQUETS
SNAPSHOTTED	SNIGGLINGS	SNORTINGLY	SNOWPLOUGHING	SOCDOLAGER
SNAPSHOTTING	SNIPEFISHES	SNOTTERIES	SNOWPLOUGHS	SOCDOLAGERS
SNARLINGLY	SNIPERSCOPE	SNOTTERING	SNOWPLOWED	SOCDOLIGER
SNATCHIEST	SNIPERSCOPES	SNOTTINESS	SNOWPLOWING	SOCDOLIGERS
SNATCHINGLY	SNIPPERSNAPPER	SNOTTINESSES	SNOWSCAPES	SOCDOLOGER
SNATCHINGS	SNIPPERSNAPPERS	SNOWBALLED	SNOWSHOEING	SOCDOLOGERS
SNAZZINESS	SNIPPETIER	SNOWBALLING	SNOWSHOEINGS	SOCIABILITIES
SNAZZINESSES	SNIPPETIEST	SNOWBERRIES	SNOWSHOERS	SOCIABILITY
SNEAKBOXES	SNIPPETINESS	SNOWBLADER	SNOWSLIDES	SOCIABLENESS
SNEAKINESS	SNIPPETINESSES	SNOWBLADERS	SNOWSNAKES	SOCIABLENESSES
SNEAKINESSES	SNIPPINESS	SNOWBLADES	SNOWSTORMS	SOCIALISABLE
SNEAKINGLY	SNIPPINESSES	SNOWBLADING	SNOWSURFING	SOCIALISATION
SNEAKINGNESS	SNITCHIEST	SNOWBLADINGS	SNOWSURFINGS	SOCIALISATIONS

S

SOCIALISED

SOCIALISED	SOCIOLOGISTIC	SOGDOLOGERS	SOLEMNISER	SOLIDIFIABLE
SOCIALISER	SOCIOLOGISTS	SOGGINESSES	SOLEMNISERS	SOLIDIFICATION
SOCIALISERS	SOCIOMETRIC	SOILINESSES	SOLEMNISES	SOLIDIFICATIONS
SOCIALISES	SOCIOMETRIES	SOJOURNERS	SOLEMNISING	SOLIDIFIED
SOCIALISING	SOCIOMETRIST	SOJOURNING	SOLEMNITIES	SOLIDIFIER
SOCIALISINGS	SOCIOMETRISTS	SOJOURNINGS	SOLEMNIZATION	SOLIDIFIERS
SOCIALISMS	SOCIOMETRY	SOJOURNMENT	SOLEMNIZATIONS	SOLIDIFIES
SOCIALISTIC	SOCIOPATHIC	SOJOURNMENTS	SOLEMNIZED	SOLIDIFYING
SOCIALISTICALLY	SOCIOPATHIES	SOKEMANRIES	SOLEMNIZER	SOLIDITIES
SOCIALISTS	SOCIOPATHS	SOLACEMENT	SOLEMNIZERS	SOLIDNESSES
SOCIALITES	SOCIOPATHY	SOLACEMENTS	SOLEMNIZES	SOLIDUNGULATE
SOCIALITIES	SOCIOPOLITICAL	SOLANACEOUS	SOLEMNIZING	SOLIDUNGULATES
SOCIALIZABLE	SOCIORELIGIOUS	SOLARIMETER	SOLEMNNESS	SOLIDUNGULOUS
SOCIALIZATION	SOCIOSEXUAL	SOLARIMETERS	SOLEMNNESSES	SOLIFIDIAN
SOCIALIZATIONS	SOCKDOLAGER	SOLARISATION	SOLENESSES	SOLIFIDIANISM
SOCIALIZED	SOCKDOLAGERS	SOLARISATIONS	SOLENETTES	SOLIFIDIANISMS
SOCIALIZER	SOCKDOLIGER	SOLARISING	SOLENODONS	SOLIFIDIANS
SOCIALIZERS	SOCKDOLIGERS	SOLARIZATION	SOLENOIDAL	SOLIFLUCTION
SOCIALIZES	SOCKDOLOGER	SOLARIZATIONS	SOLENOIDALLY	SOLIFLUCTIONS
SOCIALIZING	SOCKDOLOGERS	SOLARIZING	SOLEPLATES	SOLIFLUXION
SOCIALIZINGS	SODALITIES	SOLDATESQUE	SOLEPRINTS	SOLIFLUXIONS
SOCIALNESS	SODBUSTERS	SOLDERABILITIES	SOLFATARAS	SOLILOQUIES
SOCIALNESSES	SODDENNESS	SOLDERABILITY	SOLFATARIC	SOLILOQUISE
SOCIATIONS	SODDENNESSES	SOLDERABLE	SOLFEGGIOS	SOLILOQUISED
SOCIETALLY	SODICITIES	SOLDERINGS	SOLFERINOS	SOLILOQUISER
SOCIOBIOLOGICAL	SODOMISING	SOLDIERIES	SOLICITANT	SOLILOQUISERS
SOCIOBIOLOGIES	SODOMITICAL	SOLDIERING	SOLICITANTS	SOLILOQUISES
SOCIOBIOLOGIST	SODOMITICALLY	SOLDIERINGS	SOLICITATION	SOLILOQUISING
SOCIOBIOLOGISTS	SODOMIZING	SOLDIERLIER	SOLICITATIONS	SOLILOQUIST
SOCIOBIOLOGY	SOFTBALLER	SOLDIERLIEST	SOLICITIES	SOLILOQUISTS
SOCIOCULTURAL	SOFTBALLERS	SOLDIERLIKE	SOLICITING	SOLILOQUIZE
SOCIOCULTURALLY	SOFTBOUNDS	SOLDIERLINESS	SOLICITINGS	SOLILOQUIZED
SOCIOECONOMIC	SOFTCOVERS	SOLDIERLINESSES	SOLICITORS	SOLILOQUIZER
SOCIOGRAMS	SOFTENINGS	SOLDIERSHIP	SOLICITORSHIP	SOLILOQUIZERS
SOCIOHISTORICAL	SOFTHEADED	SOLDIERSHIPS	SOLICITORSHIPS	SOLILOQUIZES
SOCIOLECTS	SOFTHEADEDLY	SOLECISING	SOLICITOUS	SOLILOQUIZING
SOCIOLINGUIST	SOFTHEADEDNESS	SOLECISTIC	SOLICITOUSLY	SOLIPEDOUS
SOCIOLINGUISTIC	SOFTHEARTED	SOLECISTICAL	SOLICITOUSNESS	SOLIPSISMS
SOCIOLINGUISTS	SOFTHEARTEDLY	SOLECISTICALLY	SOLICITUDE	SOLIPSISTIC
SOCIOLOGESE	SOFTHEARTEDNESS	SOLECIZING	SOLICITUDES	SOLIPSISTICALLY
SOCIOLOGESES	SOFTNESSES	SOLEMNESSES	SOLIDARISM	SOLIPSISTS
SOCIOLOGIC	SOFTSCAPES	SOLEMNIFICATION	SOLIDARISMS	SOLITAIRES
SOCIOLOGICAL	SOFTSHELLS	SOLEMNIFIED	SOLIDARIST	SOLITARIAN
SOCIOLOGICALLY	SOGDOLAGER	SOLEMNIFIES	SOLIDARISTIC	SOLITARIANS
SOCIOLOGIES	SOGDOLAGERS	SOLEMNIFYING	SOLIDARISTS	SOLITARIES
SOCIOLOGISM	SOGDOLIGER	SOLEMNISATION	SOLIDARITIES	SOLITARILY
SOCIOLOGISMS	SOGDOLIGERS	SOLEMNISATIONS	SOLIDARITY	SOLITARINESS
SOCIOLOGIST	SOGDOLOGER	SOLEMNISED	SOLIDATING	SOLITARINESSES

SOLITUDINARIAN	SOLVOLYSES	SOMBERNESSES	SOMNIATING	SONNETEERING
SOLITUDINARIANS	SOLVOLYSIS	SOMBRENESS	SOMNIATIVE	SONNETEERINGS
SOLITUDINOUS	SOLVOLYTIC	SOMBRENESSES	SOMNIATORY	SONNETEERS
SOLIVAGANT	SOMAESTHESIA	SOMBRERITE	SOMNIFACIENT	SONNETISED
SOLIVAGANTS	SOMAESTHESIAS	SOMBRERITES	SOMNIFACIENTS	SONNETISES
SOLLICKERS	SOMAESTHESIS	SOMEBODIES	SOMNIFEROUS	SONNETISING
SOLMISATION	SOMAESTHESISES	SOMEPLACES	SOMNIFEROUSLY	SONNETIZED
SOLMISATIONS	SOMAESTHETIC	SOMERSAULT	SOMNILOQUENCE	SONNETIZES
SOLMIZATION	SOMASCOPES	SOMERSAULTED	SOMNILOQUENCES	SONNETIZING
SOLMIZATIONS	SOMATICALLY	SOMERSAULTING	SOMNILOQUIES	SONNETTING
SOLONCHAKS	SOMATOGENIC	SOMERSAULTS	SOMNILOQUISE	SONOFABITCH
SOLONETSES	SOMATOLOGIC	SOMERSETED	SOMNILOQUISED	SONOGRAPHER
SOLONETZES	SOMATOLOGICAL	SOMERSETING	SOMNILOQUISES	SONOGRAPHERS
SOLONETZIC	SOMATOLOGICALLY	SOMERSETTED	SOMNILOQUISING	SONOGRAPHIES
SOLONISATION	SOMATOLOGIES	SOMERSETTING	SOMNILOQUISM	SONOGRAPHS
SOLONISATIONS	SOMATOLOGIST	SOMESTHESIA	SOMNILOQUISMS	SONOGRAPHY
SOLONIZATION	SOMATOLOGISTS	SOMESTHESIAS	SOMNILOQUIST	SONOMETERS
SOLONIZATIONS	SOMATOLOGY	SOMESTHESIS	SOMNILOQUISTS	SONORITIES
SOLSTITIAL	SOMATOMEDIN	SOMESTHESISES	SOMNILOQUIZE	SONOROUSLY
SOLSTITIALLY	SOMATOMEDINS	SOMESTHETIC	SOMNILOQUIZED	SONOROUSNESS
SOLUBILISATION	SOMATOPLASM	SOMETHINGS	SOMNILOQUIZES	SONOROUSNESSES
SOLUBILISATIONS	SOMATOPLASMS	SOMEWHENCE	SOMNILOQUIZING	SOOTERKINS
SOLUBILISE	SOMATOPLASTIC	SOMEWHERES	SOMNILOQUOUS	SOOTFLAKES
SOLUBILISED	SOMATOPLEURAL	SOMEWHILES	SOMNILOQUY	SOOTHERING
SOLUBILISES	SOMATOPLEURE	SOMEWHITHER	SOMNOLENCE	SOOTHFASTLY
SOLUBILISING	SOMATOPLEURES	SOMMELIERS	SOMNOLENCES	SOOTHFASTNESS
SOLUBILITIES	SOMATOPLEURIC	SOMNAMBULANCE	SOMNOLENCIES	SOOTHFASTNESSES
SOLUBILITY	SOMATOSENSORY	SOMNAMBULANCES	SOMNOLENCY	SOOTHINGLY
SOLUBILIZATION	SOMATOSTATIN	SOMNAMBULANT	SOMNOLENTLY	SOOTHINGNESS
SOLUBILIZATIONS	SOMATOSTATINS	SOMNAMBULANTS	SOMNOLESCENT	SOOTHINGNESSES
SOLUBILIZE	SOMATOTENSIC	SOMNAMBULAR	SONGCRAFTS	SOOTHSAYER
SOLUBILIZED	SOMATOTONIA	SOMNAMBULARY	SONGFULNESS	SOOTHSAYERS
SOLUBILIZES	SOMATOTONIAS	SOMNAMBULATE	SONGFULNESSES	SOOTHSAYING
SOLUBILIZING	SOMATOTONIC	SOMNAMBULATED	SONGLESSLY	SOOTHSAYINGS
SOLUBLENESS	SOMATOTONICS	SOMNAMBULATES	SONGOLOLOS	SOOTINESSES
SOLUBLENESSES	SOMATOTROPHIC	SOMNAMBULATING	SONGSHEETS	SOPAIPILLA
SOLUTIONAL	SOMATOTROPHIN	SOMNAMBULATION	SONGSMITHS	SOPAIPILLAS
SOLUTIONED	SOMATOTROPHINS	SOMNAMBULATIONS	SONGSTRESS	SOPAPILLAS
SOLUTIONING	SOMATOTROPIC	SOMNAMBULATOR	SONGSTRESSES	SOPHISTERS
SOLUTIONIST	SOMATOTROPIN	SOMNAMBULATORS	SONGWRITER	SOPHISTICAL
SOLUTIONISTS	SOMATOTROPINE	SOMNAMBULE	SONGWRITERS	SOPHISTICALLY
SOLVABILITIES	SOMATOTROPINES	SOMNAMBULES	SONGWRITING	SOPHISTICATE
SOLVABILITY	SOMATOTROPINS	SOMNAMBULIC	SONGWRITINGS	SOPHISTICATED
SOLVABLENESS	SOMATOTYPE	SOMNAMBULISM	SONICATING	SOPHISTICATEDLY
SOLVABLENESSES	SOMATOTYPED	SOMNAMBULISMS	SONICATION	SOPHISTICATES
SOLVATIONS	SOMATOTYPES	SOMNAMBULIST	SONICATIONS	SOPHISTICATING
SOLVENCIES	SOMATOTYPING	SOMNAMBULISTIC	SONICATORS	SOPHISTICATION
SOLVENTLESS	SOMBERNESS	SOMNAMBULISTS	SONIFEROUS	SOPHISTICATIONS

S

SOPHISTICATOR	SORROWLESS	SOUNDTRACK	SOUTHERNMOST	SOYBURGERS
SOPHISTICATORS	SORTATIONS	SOUNDTRACKED	SOUTHERNNESS	SPACEBANDS
SOPHISTRIES	SORTILEGER	SOUNDTRACKING	SOUTHERNNESSES	SPACEBORNE
SOPHOMORES	SORTILEGERS	SOUNDTRACKS	SOUTHERNWOOD	SPACECRAFT
SOPHOMORIC	SORTILEGES	SOUPINESSES	SOUTHERNWOODS	SPACECRAFTS
SOPHOMORICAL	SORTILEGIES	SOUPSPOONS	SOUTHLANDER	SPACEFARING
SOPORIFEROUS	SORTITIONS	SOURCEBOOK	SOUTHLANDERS	SPACEFARINGS
SOPORIFEROUSLY	SOSTENUTOS	SOURCEBOOKS	SOUTHLANDS	SPACEFLIGHT
SOPORIFICALLY	SOTERIOLOGIC	SOURCELESS	SOUTHSAYING	SPACEFLIGHTS
SOPORIFICS	SOTERIOLOGICAL	SOURDELINE	SOUTHWARDLY	SPACEPLANE
SOPPINESSES	SOTERIOLOGIES	SOURDELINES	SOUTHWARDS	SPACEPLANES
SOPRANINOS	SOTERIOLOGY	SOURDOUGHS	SOUTHWESTER	SPACEPORTS
SOPRANISTS	SOTTISHNESS	SOURNESSES	SOUTHWESTERLIES	SPACESHIPS
SORBABILITIES	SOTTISHNESSES	SOURPUSSES	SOUTHWESTERLY	SPACESUITS
SORBABILITY	SOTTISIERS	SOUSAPHONE	SOUTHWESTERN	SPACETIMES
SORBEFACIENT	SOUBRETTES	SOUSAPHONES	SOUTHWESTERS	SPACEWALKED
SORBEFACIENTS	SOUBRETTISH	SOUSAPHONIST	SOUTHWESTS	SPACEWALKER
SORBITISATION	SOUBRIQUET	SOUSAPHONISTS	SOUTHWESTWARD	SPACEWALKERS
SORBITISATIONS	SOUBRIQUETS	SOUTENEURS	SOUTHWESTWARDLY	SPACEWALKING
SORBITISED	SOULDIERED	SOUTERRAIN	SOUTHWESTWARDS	SPACEWALKS
SORBITISES	SOULDIERING	SOUTERRAINS	SOUVENIRED	SPACEWOMAN
SORBITISING	SOULFULNESS	SOUTHBOUND	SOUVENIRING	SPACEWOMEN
SORBITIZATION	SOULFULNESSES	SOUTHEASTER	SOUVLAKIAS	SPACINESSES
SORBITIZATIONS	SOULLESSLY	SOUTHEASTERLIES	SOVENANCES	SPACIOUSLY
SORBITIZED	SOULLESSNESS	SOUTHEASTERLY	SOVEREIGNLY	SPACIOUSNESS
SORBITIZES	SOULLESSNESSES	SOUTHEASTERN	SOVEREIGNS	SPACIOUSNESSES
SORBITIZING	SOUNDALIKE	SOUTHEASTERS	SOVEREIGNTIES	SPADASSINS
SORCERESSES	SOUNDALIKES	SOUTHEASTS	SOVEREIGNTIST	SPADEFISHES
SORDAMENTE	SOUNDBITES	SOUTHEASTWARD	SOVEREIGNTISTS	SPADEFOOTS
SORDIDNESS	SOUNDBOARD	SOUTHEASTWARDS	SOVEREIGNTY	SPADEWORKS
SORDIDNESSES	SOUNDBOARDS	SOUTHERING	SOVIETISATION	SPADICEOUS
SOREHEADED	SOUNDBOXES	SOUTHERLIES	SOVIETISATIONS	SPADICIFLORAL
SOREHEADEDLY	SOUNDCARDS	SOUTHERLINESS	SOVIETISED	SPADILLIOS
SOREHEADEDNESS	SOUNDINGLY	SOUTHERLINESSES	SOVIETISES	SPAGHETTIFIED
SORENESSES	SOUNDLESSLY	SOUTHERMOST	SOVIETISING	SPAGHETTIFIES
SORICIDENT	SOUNDLESSNESS	SOUTHERNER	SOVIETISMS	SPAGHETTIFY
SORORIALLY	SOUNDLESSNESSES	SOUTHERNERS	SOVIETISTIC	SPAGHETTIFYING
SORORICIDAL	SOUNDNESSES	SOUTHERNISE	SOVIETISTS	SPAGHETTILIKE
SORORICIDE	SOUNDPOSTS	SOUTHERNISED	SOVIETIZATION	SPAGHETTINI
SORORICIDES	SOUNDPROOF	SOUTHERNISES	SOVIETIZATIONS	SPAGHETTINIS
SORORISING	SOUNDPROOFED	SOUTHERNISING	SOVIETIZED	SPAGHETTIS
SORORITIES	SOUNDPROOFING	SOUTHERNISM	SOVIETIZES	SPAGIRISTS
SORORIZING	SOUNDPROOFINGS	SOUTHERNISMS	SOVIETIZING	SPAGYRICAL
SORRINESSES	SOUNDPROOFS	SOUTHERNIZE	SOVIETOLOGICAL	SPAGYRICALLY
SORROWFULLY	SOUNDSCAPE	SOUTHERNIZED	SOVIETOLOGIST	SPAGYRISTS
SORROWFULNESS	SOUNDSCAPES	SOUTHERNIZES	SOVIETOLOGISTS	SPALLATION
SORROWFULNESSES	SOUNDSTAGE	SOUTHERNIZING	SOVRANTIES	SPALLATIONS
SORROWINGS	SOUNDSTAGES	SOUTHERNLY	SOWBELLIES	SPANAEMIAS

SPANAKOPITA	SPARROWGRASSES	SPEAKERPHONES	SPECIATIONS	SPECTATRIXES
SPANAKOPITAS	SPARROWHAWK	SPEAKERSHIP	SPECIESISM	SPECTINOMYCIN
SPANCELING	SPARROWHAWKS	SPEAKERSHIPS	SPECIESISMS	SPECTINOMYCINS
SPANCELLED	SPARROWLIKE	SPEAKINGLY	SPECIESIST	SPECTRALITIES
SPANCELLING	SPARSENESS	SPEARCARRIER	SPECIESISTS	SPECTRALITY
SPANGHEWED	SPARSENESSES	SPEARCARRIERS	SPECIFIABLE	SPECTRALLY
SPANGHEWING	SPARSITIES	SPEARFISHED	SPECIFICAL	SPECTRALNESS
SPANGLIEST	SPARTEINES	SPEARFISHES	SPECIFICALLY	SPECTRALNESSES
SPANGLINGS	SPARTERIES	SPEARFISHING	SPECIFICATE	SPECTROGRAM
SPANIELLED	SPARTICLES	SPEARHEADED	SPECIFICATED	SPECTROGRAMS
SPANIELLING	SPASMATICAL	SPEARHEADING	SPECIFICATES	SPECTROGRAPH
SPANIOLATE	SPASMODICAL	SPEARHEADS	SPECIFICATING	SPECTROGRAPHIC
SPANIOLATED	SPASMODICALLY	SPEARMINTS	SPECIFICATION	SPECTROGRAPHIES
SPANIOLATES	SPASMODIST	SPEARWORTS	SPECIFICATIONS	SPECTROGRAPHS
SPANIOLATING	SPASMODISTS	SPECIALEST	SPECIFICATIVE	SPECTROGRAPHY
SPANIOLISE	SPASMOLYTIC	SPECIALISATION	SPECIFICATORY	SPECTROLOGICAL
SPANIOLISED	SPASMOLYTICS	SPECIALISATIONS	SPECIFICITIES	SPECTROLOGIES
SPANIOLISES	SPASTICALLY	SPECIALISE	SPECIFICITY	SPECTROLOGY
SPANIOLISING	SPASTICITIES	SPECIALISED	SPECIFIERS	SPECTROMETER
SPANIOLIZE	SPASTICITY	SPECIALISER	SPECIFYING	SPECTROMETERS
SPANIOLIZED	SPATANGOID	SPECIALISERS	SPECIOCIDE	SPECTROMETRIC
SPANIOLIZES	SPATANGOIDS	SPECIALISES	SPECIOCIDES	SPECTROMETRIES
SPANIOLIZING	SPATCHCOCK	SPECIALISING	SPECIOSITIES	SPECTROMETRY
SPANKINGLY	SPATCHCOCKED	SPECIALISM	SPECIOSITY	SPECTROSCOPE
SPANOKOPITA	SPATCHCOCKING	SPECIALISMS	SPECIOUSLY	SPECTROSCOPES
SPANOKOPITAS	SPATCHCOCKS	SPECIALIST	SPECIOUSNESS	SPECTROSCOPIC
SPARAGMATIC	SPATHACEOUS	SPECIALISTIC	SPECIOUSNESSES	SPECTROSCOPICAL
SPARAGRASS	SPATHIPHYLLUM	SPECIALISTS	SPECKLEDNESS	SPECTROSCOPIES
SPARAGRASSES	SPATHIPHYLLUMS	SPECIALITIES	SPECKLEDNESSES	SPECTROSCOPIST
SPARAXISES	SPATHULATE	SPECIALITY	SPECKSIONEER	SPECTROSCOPISTS
SPARENESSES	SPATIALISATION	SPECIALIZATION	SPECKSIONEERS	SPECTROSCOPY
SPARGANIUM	SPATIALISATIONS	SPECIALIZATIONS	SPECKTIONEER	SPECULARITIES
SPARGANIUMS	SPATIALITIES	SPECIALIZE	SPECKTIONEERS	SPECULARITY
SPARINGNESS	SPATIALITY	SPECIALIZED	SPECTACLED	SPECULARLY
SPARINGNESSES	SPATIALIZATION	SPECIALIZER	SPECTACLES	SPECULATED
SPARKISHLY	SPATIALIZATIONS	SPECIALIZERS	SPECTACULAR	SPECULATES
SPARKLEBERRIES	SPATIOTEMPORAL	SPECIALIZES	SPECTACULARITY	SPECULATING
SPARKLEBERRY	SPATTERDASH	SPECIALIZING	SPECTACULARLY	SPECULATION
SPARKLESSLY	SPATTERDASHES	SPECIALLED	SPECTACULARS	SPECULATIONS
SPARKLIEST	SPATTERDOCK	SPECIALLING	SPECTATING	SPECULATIST
SPARKLINGLY	SPATTERDOCKS	SPECIALNESS	SPECTATORIAL	SPECULATISTS
SPARKLINGS	SPATTERING	SPECIALNESSES	SPECTATORS	SPECULATIVE
SPARKPLUGGED	SPATTERWORK	SPECIALOGUE	SPECTATORSHIP	SPECULATIVELY
SPARKPLUGGING	SPATTERWORKS	SPECIALOGUES	SPECTATORSHIPS	SPECULATIVENESS
SPARKPLUGS	SPEAKEASIES	SPECIALTIES	SPECTATRESS	SPECULATOR
SPARROWFART	SPEAKERINE	SPECIATING	SPECTATRESSES	SPECULATORS
SPARROWFARTS	SPEAKERINES	SPECIATION	SPECTATRICES	SPECULATORY
SPARROWGRASS	SPEAKERPHONE	SPECIATIONAL	SPECTATRIX	SPECULATRICE

SPECULATRICES	SPELAEOLOGY	SPERMATHECAL	SPERMATOZOON	SPHALERITES
SPECULATRIX	SPELAEOTHEM	SPERMATHECAS	SPERMICIDAL	SPHENDONES
SPECULATRIXES	SPELAEOTHEMS	SPERMATIAL	SPERMICIDE	SPHENODONS
SPEECHCRAFT	SPELDERING	SPERMATICAL	SPERMICIDES	SPHENODONT
SPEECHCRAFTS	SPELDRINGS	SPERMATICALLY	SPERMIDUCT	SPHENODONTS
SPEECHFULNESS	SPELEOLOGICAL	SPERMATICS	SPERMIDUCTS	SPHENOGRAM
SPEECHFULNESSES	SPELEOLOGIES	SPERMATIDS	SPERMIOGENESES	SPHENOGRAMS
SPEECHIFICATION	SPELEOLOGIST	SPERMATIUM	SPERMIOGENESIS	SPHENOIDAL
SPEECHIFIED	SPELEOLOGISTS	SPERMATOBLAST	SPERMIOGENETIC	SPHENOPSID
SPEECHIFIER	SPELEOLOGY	SPERMATOBLASTIC	SPERMOGONE	SPHENOPSIDS
SPEECHIFIERS	SPELEOTHEM	SPERMATOBLASTS	SPERMOGONES	SPHERELESS
SPEECHIFIES	SPELEOTHEMS	SPERMATOCELE	SPERMOGONIA	SPHERELIKE
SPEECHIFYING	SPELEOTHERAPIES	SPERMATOCELES	SPERMOGONIUM	SPHERICALITIES
SPEECHIFYINGS	SPELEOTHERAPY	SPERMATOCIDAL	SPERMOPHILE	SPHERICALITY
SPEECHLESS	SPELLBINDER	SPERMATOCIDE	SPERMOPHILES	SPHERICALLY
SPEECHLESSLY	SPELLBINDERS	SPERMATOCIDES	SPERMOPHYTE	SPHERICALNESS
SPEECHLESSNESS	SPELLBINDING	SPERMATOCYTE	SPERMOPHYTES	SPHERICALNESSES
SPEECHMAKER	SPELLBINDINGLY	SPERMATOCYTES	SPERMOPHYTIC	SPHERICITIES
SPEECHMAKERS	SPELLBINDS	SPERMATOGENESES	SPERRYLITE	SPHERICITY
SPEECHMAKING	SPELLBOUND	SPERMATOGENESIS	SPERRYLITES	SPHERISTERION
SPEECHMAKINGS	SPELLCHECK	SPERMATOGENETIC	SPESSARTINE	SPHERISTERIONS
SPEECHWRITER	SPELLCHECKED	SPERMATOGENIC	SPESSARTINES	SPHEROCYTE
SPEECHWRITERS	SPELLCHECKER	SPERMATOGENIES	SPESSARTITE	SPHEROCYTES
SPEEDBALLED	SPELLCHECKERS	SPERMATOGENOUS	SPESSARTITES	SPHEROCYTOSES
SPEEDBALLING	SPELLCHECKING	SPERMATOGENY	SPETSNAZES	SPHEROCYTOSIS
SPEEDBALLINGS	SPELLCHECKS	SPERMATOGONIA	SPETZNAZES	SPHEROIDAL
SPEEDBALLS	SPELLDOWNS	SPERMATOGONIAL	SPEWINESSES	SPHEROIDALLY
SPEEDBOATING	SPELLICANS	SPERMATOGONIUM	SPHACELATE	SPHEROIDICALLY
SPEEDBOATINGS	SPELLINGLY	SPERMATOPHORAL	SPHACELATED	SPHEROIDICITIES
SPEEDBOATS	SPELLSTOPT	SPERMATOPHORE	SPHACELATES	SPHEROIDICITY
SPEEDFREAK	SPELUNKERS	SPERMATOPHORES	SPHACELATING	SPHEROIDISATION
SPEEDFREAKS	SPELUNKING	SPERMATOPHYTE	SPHACELATION	SPHEROIDISE
SPEEDFULLY	SPELUNKINGS	SPERMATOPHYTES	SPHACELATIONS	SPHEROIDISED
SPEEDINESS	SPENDTHRIFT	SPERMATOPHYTIC	SPHACELUSES	SPHEROIDISES
SPEEDINESSES	SPENDTHRIFTS	SPERMATORRHEA	SPHAERIDIA	SPHEROIDISING
SPEEDOMETER	SPERMACETI	SPERMATORRHEAS	SPHAERIDIUM	SPHEROIDIZATION
SPEEDOMETERS	SPERMACETIS	SPERMATORRHOEA	SPHAERITES	SPHEROIDIZE
SPEEDREADING	SPERMADUCT	SPERMATORRHOEAS	SPHAEROCRYSTAL	SPHEROIDIZED
SPEEDREADS	SPERMADUCTS	SPERMATOTHECA	SPHAEROCRYSTALS	SPHEROIDIZES
SPEEDSKATING	SPERMAGONIA	SPERMATOTHECAE	SPHAEROSIDERITE	SPHEROIDIZING
SPEEDSKATINGS	SPERMAGONIUM	SPERMATOTHECAS	SPHAGNICOLOUS	SPHEROMETER
SPEEDSTERS	SPERMAPHYTE	SPERMATOZOA	SPHAGNOLOGIES	SPHEROMETERS
SPEEDWALKS	SPERMAPHYTES	SPERMATOZOAL	SPHAGNOLOGIST	SPHEROPLAST
SPEEDWELLS	SPERMAPHYTIC	SPERMATOZOAN	SPHAGNOLOGISTS	SPHEROPLASTS
SPELAEOLOGICAL	SPERMARIES	SPERMATOZOANS	SPHAGNOLOGY	SPHERULITE
SPELAEOLOGIES	SPERMARIUM	SPERMATOZOIC	SPHAIRISTIKE	SPHERULITES
SPELAEOLOGIST	SPERMATHECA	SPERMATOZOID	SPHAIRISTIKES	SPHERULITIC
SPELAEOLOGISTS	SPERMATHECAE	SPERMATOZOIDS	SPHALERITE	SPHINCTERAL

SPHINCTERIAL	SPIFFLICATED	SPINNERULES	SPIRITOUSNESSES	SPIROGRAPHIES
SPHINCTERIC	SPIFFLICATES	SPINOSITIES	SPIRITUALISE	SPIROGRAPHS
SPHINCTERS	SPIFFLICATING	SPINSTERDOM	SPIRITUALISED	SPIROGRAPHY
SPHINGOMYELIN	SPIFFLICATION	SPINSTERDOMS	SPIRITUALISER	SPIROGYRAS
SPHINGOMYELINS	SPIFFLICATIONS	SPINSTERHOOD	SPIRITUALISERS	SPIROMETER
SPHINGOSINE	SPIFLICATE	SPINSTERHOODS	SPIRITUALISES	SPIROMETERS
SPHINGOSINES	SPIFLICATED	SPINSTERIAL	SPIRITUALISING	SPIROMETRIC
SPHINXLIKE	SPIFLICATES	SPINSTERIAN	SPIRITUALISM	SPIROMETRIES
SPHRAGISTIC	SPIFLICATING	SPINSTERISH	SPIRITUALISMS	SPIROMETRY
SPHRAGISTICS	SPIFLICATION	SPINSTERLIER	SPIRITUALIST	SPIRONOLACTONE
SPHYGMOGRAM	SPIFLICATIONS	SPINSTERLIEST	SPIRITUALISTIC	SPIRONOLACTONES
SPHYGMOGRAMS	SPIKEFISHES	SPINSTERLY	SPIRITUALISTS	SPIROPHORE
SPHYGMOGRAPH	SPIKENARDS	SPINSTERSHIP	SPIRITUALITIES	SPIROPHORES
SPHYGMOGRAPHIC	SPIKINESSES	SPINSTERSHIPS	SPIRITUALITY	SPIRULINAE
SPHYGMOGRAPHIES	SPILLIKINS	SPINSTRESS	SPIRITUALIZE	SPIRULINAS
SPHYGMOGRAPHS	SPILLOVERS	SPINSTRESSES	SPIRITUALIZED	SPISSITUDE
SPHYGMOGRAPHY	SPILOSITES	SPINTHARISCOPE	SPIRITUALIZER	SPISSITUDES
SPHYGMOLOGIES	SPINACENES	SPINTHARISCOPES	SPIRITUALIZERS	SPITBALLED
SPHYGMOLOGY	SPINACEOUS	SPINULESCENT	SPIRITUALIZES	SPITBALLING
SPHYGMOMETER	SPINACHIER	SPINULIFEROUS	SPIRITUALIZING	SPITCHCOCK
SPHYGMOMETERS	SPINACHIEST	SPIRACULAR	SPIRITUALLY	SPITCHCOCKED
SPHYGMOPHONE	SPINACHLIKE	SPIRACULATE	SPIRITUALNESS	SPITCHCOCKING
SPHYGMOPHONES	SPINARAMAS	SPIRACULUM	SPIRITUALNESSES	SPITCHCOCKS
SPHYGMOSCOPE	SPINDLELEGS	SPIRALIFORM	SPIRITUALS	SPITCHERED
SPHYGMOSCOPES	SPINDLESHANKS	SPIRALISER	SPIRITUALTIES	SPITCHERING
SPHYGMUSES	SPINDLIEST	SPIRALISERS	SPIRITUALTY	SPITEFULLER
SPICEBERRIES	SPINDLINGS	SPIRALISMS	SPIRITUELLE	SPITEFULLEST
SPICEBERRY	SPINDRIFTS	SPIRALISTS	SPIRITUOSITIES	SPITEFULLY
SPICEBUSHES	SPINELESSLY	SPIRALITIES	SPIRITUOSITY	SPITEFULNESS
SPICILEGES	SPINELESSNESS	SPIRALIZER	SPIRITUOUS	SPITEFULNESSES
SPICINESSES	SPINELESSNESSES	SPIRALIZERS	SPIRITUOUSNESS	SPITSTICKER
SPICULATED	SPINESCENCE	SPIRALLING	SPIRITUSES	SPITSTICKERS
SPICULATION	SPINESCENCES	SPIRASTERS	SPIRKETTING	SPITTLEBUG
SPICULATIONS	SPINESCENT	SPIRATIONS	SPIRKETTINGS	SPITTLEBUGS
SPIDERIEST	SPINIFEROUS	SPIRIFEROUS	SPIROCHAETAEMIA	SPITTLIEST
SPIDERLIKE	SPINIFEXES	SPIRILLOSES	SPIROCHAETAL	SPIVVERIES
SPIDERWEBS	SPINIGEROUS	SPIRILLOSIS	SPIROCHAETE	SPLANCHNIC
SPIDERWOOD	SPINIGRADE	SPIRITEDLY	SPIROCHAETES	SPLANCHNOCELE
SPIDERWOODS	SPINIGRADES	SPIRITEDNESS	SPIROCHAETOSES	SPLANCHNOCELES
SPIDERWORK	SPININESSES	SPIRITEDNESSES	SPIROCHAETOSIS	SPLANCHNOLOGIES
SPIDERWORKS	SPINMEISTER	SPIRITINGS	SPIROCHETAL	SPLANCHNOLOGY
SPIDERWORT	SPINMEISTERS	SPIRITISMS	SPIROCHETE	SPLASHBACK
SPIDERWORTS	SPINNAKERS	SPIRITISTIC	SPIROCHETES	SPLASHBACKS
SPIEGELEISEN	SPINNERETS	SPIRITISTS	SPIROCHETOSES	SPLASHBOARD
SPIEGELEISENS	SPINNERETTE	SPIRITLESS	SPIROCHETOSIS	SPLASHBOARDS
SPIFFINESS	SPINNERETTES	SPIRITLESSLY	SPIROGRAMS	SPLASHDOWN
SPIFFINESSES	SPINNERIES	SPIRITLESSNESS	SPIROGRAPH	SPLASHDOWNS
SPIFFLICATE	SPINNERULE	SPIRITOUSNESS	SPIROGRAPHIC	SPLASHIEST

S

SPLASHINESS

SPLASHINESS	SPLENITISES	SPOKESPEOPLE	SPONTANEITIES	SPOROPHORES
SPLASHINESSES	SPLENIUSES	SPOKESPERSON	SPONTANEITY	SPOROPHORIC
SPLASHINGS	SPLENIZATION	SPOKESPERSONS	SPONTANEOUS	SPOROPHOROUS
SPLASHPROOF	SPLENIZATIONS	SPOKESWOMAN	SPONTANEOUSLY	SPOROPHYLL
SPLATCHING	SPLENOMEGALIES	SPOKESWOMEN	SPONTANEOUSNESS	SPOROPHYLLS
SPLATTERED	SPLENOMEGALY	SPOLIATING	SPOOFERIES	SPOROPHYLS
SPLATTERING	SPLEUCHANS	SPOLIATION	SPOOKERIES	SPOROPHYTE
SPLATTERPUNK	SPLINTERED	SPOLIATIONS	SPOOKINESS	SPOROPHYTES
SPLATTERPUNKS	SPLINTERIER	SPOLIATIVE	SPOOKINESSES	SPOROPHYTIC
SPLATTINGS	SPLINTERIEST	SPOLIATORS	SPOONBAITS	SPOROPOLLENIN
SPLAYFOOTED	SPLINTERING	SPOLIATORY	SPOONBILLS	SPOROPOLLENINS
SPLAYFOOTEDLY	SPLINTLIKE	SPONDAICAL	SPOONDRIFT	SPOROTRICHOSES
SPLEENFULLY	SPLINTWOOD	SPONDOOLICKS	SPOONDRIFTS	SPOROTRICHOSIS
SPLEENIEST	SPLINTWOODS	SPONDULICKS	SPOONERISM	SPOROZOANS
SPLEENLESS	SPLITTINGS	SPONDYLITIC	SPOONERISMS	SPOROZOITE
SPLEENLIKE	SPLITTISMS	SPONDYLITICS	SPOONHOOKS	SPOROZOITES
SPLEENSTONE	SPLITTISTS	SPONDYLITIDES	SPOONWORMS	SPORTABILITIES
SPLEENSTONES	SPLODGIEST	SPONDYLITIS	SPORADICAL	SPORTABILITY
SPLEENWORT	SPLODGINESS	SPONDYLITISES	SPORADICALLY	SPORTANCES
SPLEENWORTS	SPLODGINESSES	SPONDYLOLYSES	SPORADICALNESS	SPORTBIKES
SPLENATIVE	SPLOOSHING	SPONDYLOLYSIS	SPORANGIAL	SPORTCASTER
SPLENDIDER	SPLOTCHIER	SPONDYLOSES	SPORANGIOLA	SPORTCASTERS
SPLENDIDEST	SPLOTCHIEST	SPONDYLOSIS	SPORANGIOLE	SPORTCOATS
SPLENDIDIOUS	SPLOTCHILY	SPONDYLOSISES	SPORANGIOLES	SPORTFISHERMAN
SPLENDIDLY	SPLOTCHINESS	SPONDYLOUS	SPORANGIOLUM	SPORTFISHERMEN
SPLENDIDNESS	SPLOTCHINESSES	SPONGEABLE	SPORANGIOPHORE	SPORTFISHING
SPLENDIDNESSES	SPLOTCHING	SPONGEBAGS	SPORANGIOPHORES	SPORTFISHINGS
SPLENDIDOUS	SPLURGIEST	SPONGELIKE	SPORANGIOSPORE	SPORTFULLY
SPLENDIFEROUS	SPLUTTERED	SPONGEWARE	SPORANGIOSPORES	SPORTFULNESS
SPLENDIFEROUSLY	SPLUTTERER	SPONGEWARES	SPORANGIUM	SPORTFULNESSES
SPLENDOROUS	SPLUTTERERS	SPONGEWOOD	SPORICIDAL	SPORTINESS
SPLENDOURS	SPLUTTERIER	SPONGEWOODS	SPORICIDES	SPORTINESSES
SPLENDROUS	SPLUTTERIEST	SPONGICOLOUS	SPORIDESMS	SPORTINGLY
SPLENECTOMIES	SPLUTTERING	SPONGIFORM	SPOROCARPS	SPORTIVELY
SPLENECTOMISE	SPLUTTERINGLY	SPONGINESS	SPOROCYSTIC	SPORTIVENESS
SPLENECTOMISED	SPLUTTERINGS	SPONGINESSES	SPOROCYSTS	SPORTIVENESSES
SPLENECTOMISES	SPODOGRAMS	SPONGIOBLAST	SPOROCYTES	SPORTSCAST
SPLENECTOMISING	SPODOMANCIES	SPONGIOBLASTIC	SPOROGENESES	SPORTSCASTER
SPLENECTOMIZE	SPODOMANCY	SPONGIOBLASTS	SPOROGENESIS	SPORTSCASTERS
SPLENECTOMIZED	SPODOMANTIC	SPONGOLOGIES	SPOROGENIC	SPORTSCASTS
SPLENECTOMIZES	SPODUMENES	SPONGOLOGIST	SPOROGENIES	SPORTSMANLIER
SPLENECTOMIZING	SPOILFIVES	SPONGOLOGISTS	SPOROGENOUS	SPORTSMANLIEST
SPLENECTOMY	SPOILSPORT	SPONGOLOGY	SPOROGONIA	SPORTSMANLIKE
SPLENETICAL	SPOILSPORTS	SPONSIONAL	SPOROGONIAL	SPORTSMANLY
SPLENETICALLY	SPOKESHAVE	SPONSORIAL	SPOROGONIC	SPORTSMANSHIP
SPLENETICS	SPOKESHAVES	SPONSORING	SPOROGONIES	SPORTSMANSHIPS
SPLENISATION	SPOKESMANSHIP	SPONSORSHIP	SPOROGONIUM	SPORTSPEOPLE
SPLENISATIONS	SPOKESMANSHIPS	SPONSORSHIPS	SPOROPHORE	SPORTSPERSON

SPORTSPERSONS	SPREAGHERY	SPRINGTIME	SPUTTERINGS	SQUANDERMANIAS
SPORTSWEAR	SPREATHING	SPRINGTIMES	SPYCATCHER	SQUAREHEAD
SPORTSWEARS	SPRECHERIES	SPRINGWATER	SPYCATCHERS	SQUAREHEADS
SPORTSWOMAN	SPRECHGESANG	SPRINGWATERS	SPYGLASSES	SQUARENESS
SPORTSWOMEN	SPRECHGESANGS	SPRINGWOOD	SPYMASTERS	SQUARENESSES
SPORTSWRITER	SPRECHSTIMME	SPRINGWOODS	SQUABASHED	SQUAREWISE
SPORTSWRITERS	SPRECHSTIMMES	SPRINGWORT	SQUABASHER	SQUARISHLY
SPORTSWRITING	SPREETHING	SPRINGWORTS	SQUABASHERS	SQUARISHNESS
SPORTSWRITINGS	SPREKELIAS	SPRINKLERED	SQUABASHES	SQUARISHNESSES
SPORULATED	SPRIGGIEST	SPRINKLERING	SQUABASHING	SQUARSONAGE
SPORULATES	SPRIGHTFUL	SPRINKLERS	SQUABBIEST	SQUARSONAGES
SPORULATING	SPRIGHTFULLY	SPRINKLING	SQUABBLERS	SQUASHABLE
SPORULATION	SPRIGHTFULNESS	SPRINKLINGS	SQUABBLING	SQUASHIEST
SPORULATIONS	SPRIGHTING	SPRINTINGS	SQUABBLINGS	SQUASHINESS
SPORULATIVE	SPRIGHTLESS	SPRITEFULLY	SQUADOOSHES	SQUASHINESSES
SPOTLESSLY	SPRIGHTLIER	SPRITEFULNESS	SQUADRONAL	SQUATNESSES
SPOTLESSNESS	SPRIGHTLIEST	SPRITEFULNESSES	SQUADRONED	SQUATTERED
SPOTLESSNESSES	SPRIGHTLINESS	SPRITELIER	SQUADRONES	SQUATTERING
SPOTLIGHTED	SPRIGHTLINESSES	SPRITELIEST	SQUADRONING	SQUATTIEST
SPOTLIGHTING	SPRIGTAILS	SPRITSAILS	SQUAILINGS	SQUATTINESS
SPOTLIGHTS	SPRINGALDS	SPRITZIEST	SQUALIDEST	SQUATTINESSES
SPOTTEDNESS	SPRINGBOARD	SPROUTINGS	SQUALIDITIES	SQUATTINGS
SPOTTEDNESSES	SPRINGBOARDS	SPRUCENESS	SQUALIDITY	SQUATTLING
SPOTTINESS	SPRINGBOKS	SPRUCENESSES	SQUALIDNESS	SQUATTOCRACIES
SPOTTINESSES	SPRINGBUCK	SPRYNESSES	SQUALIDNESSES	SQUATTOCRACY
SPOUSELESS	SPRINGBUCKS	SPUILZIEING	SQUALLIEST	SQUAWBUSHES
SPOYLEFULL	SPRINGEING	SPULEBLADE	SQUALLINGS	SQUAWFISHES
SPRACHGEFUHL	SPRINGHAAS	SPULEBLADES	SQUAMATION	SQUAWKIEST
SPRACHGEFUHLS	SPRINGHALT	SPULYIEING	SQUAMATIONS	SQUAWKINGS
SPRACKLING	SPRINGHALTS	SPULZIEING	SQUAMELLAS	SQUAWROOTS
SPRADDLING	SPRINGHASE	SPUMESCENCE	SQUAMIFORM	SQUEAKERIES
SPRANGLING	SPRINGHEAD	SPUMESCENCES	SQUAMOSALS	SQUEAKIEST
SPRATTLING	SPRINGHEADS	SPUMESCENT	SQUAMOSELY	SQUEAKINESS
SPRAUCHLED	SPRINGHOUSE	SPUNBONDED	SQUAMOSENESS	SQUEAKINESSES
SPRAUCHLES	SPRINGHOUSES	SPUNKINESS	SQUAMOSENESSES	SQUEAKINGLY
SPRAUCHLING	SPRINGIEST	SPUNKINESSES	SQUAMOSITIES	SQUEAKINGS
SPRAUNCIER	SPRINGINESS	SPURGALLED	SQUAMOSITY	SQUEALINGS
SPRAUNCIEST	SPRINGINESSES	SPURGALLING	SQUAMOUSLY	SQUEAMISHLY
SPRAWLIEST	SPRINGINGS	SPURIOSITIES	SQUAMOUSNESS	SQUEAMISHNESS
SPREADABILITIES	SPRINGKEEPER	SPURIOSITY	SQUAMOUSNESSES	SQUEAMISHNESSES
SPREADABILITY	SPRINGKEEPERS	SPURIOUSLY	SQUAMULOSE	SQUEEGEEING
SPREADABLE	SPRINGLESS	SPURIOUSNESS	SQUANDERED	SQUEEZABILITIES
SPREADEAGLED	SPRINGLETS	SPURIOUSNESSES	SQUANDERER	SQUEEZABILITY
SPREADINGLY	SPRINGLIKE	SPUTTERERS	SQUANDERERS	SQUEEZABLE
SPREADINGS	SPRINGTAIL	SPUTTERIER	SQUANDERING	SQUEEZIEST
SPREADSHEET	SPRINGTAILS	SPUTTERIEST	SQUANDERINGLY	SQUEEZINGS
SPREADSHEETS	SPRINGTIDE	SPUTTERING	SQUANDERINGS	SQUEGGINGS
SPREAGHERIES	SPRINGTIDES	SPUTTERINGLY	SQUANDERMANIA	SQUELCHERS

S

SQUELCHIER	SQUIRRELED	STABLISHMENTS	STAGINESSES	STALAGMITIC
SQUELCHIEST	SQUIRRELFISH	STACATIONS	STAGNANCES	STALAGMITICAL
SQUELCHING	SQUIRRELFISHES	STACCATISSIMO	STAGNANCIES	STALAGMITICALLY
SQUELCHINGS	SQUIRRELIER	STACKROOMS	STAGNANTLY	STALAGMOMETER
SQUETEAGUE	SQUIRRELIEST	STACKYARDS	STAGNATING	STALAGMOMETERS
SQUETEAGUES	SQUIRRELING	STACTOMETER	STAGNATION	STALAGMOMETRIES
SQUIBBINGS	SQUIRRELLED	STACTOMETERS	STAGNATIONS	STALAGMOMETRY
SQUIDGIEST	SQUIRRELLIER	STADDLESTONE	STAIDNESSES	STALEMATED
SQUIFFIEST	SQUIRRELLIEST	STADDLESTONES	STAINABILITIES	STALEMATES
SQUIGGLERS	SQUIRRELLING	STADHOLDER	STAINABILITY	STALEMATING
SQUIGGLIER	SQUIRRELLY	STADHOLDERATE	STAINLESSES	STALENESSES
SQUIGGLIEST	SQUIRTINGS	STADHOLDERATES	STAINLESSLY	STALKINESS
SQUIGGLING	SQUISHIEST	STADHOLDERS	STAINLESSNESS	STALKINESSES
SQUILGEEING	SQUISHINESS	STADHOLDERSHIP	STAINLESSNESSES	STALLENGER
SQUILLIONS	SQUISHINESSES	STADHOLDERSHIPS	STAINPROOF	STALLENGERS
SQUINANCIES	SQUOOSHIER	STADIOMETER	STAIRCASED	STALLHOLDER
SQUINCHING	SQUOOSHIEST	STADIOMETERS	STAIRCASES	STALLHOLDERS
SQUINNIEST	SQUOOSHING	STADTHOLDER	STAIRCASING	STALLINGER
SQUINNYING	STABBINGLY	STADTHOLDERATE	STAIRCASINGS	STALLINGERS
SQUINTIEST	STABILATES	STADTHOLDERATES	STAIRFOOTS	STALLMASTER
SQUINTINGLY	STABILISATION	STADTHOLDERS	STAIRHEADS	STALLMASTERS
SQUINTINGS	STABILISATIONS	STADTHOLDERSHIP	STAIRLIFTS	STALWARTLY
SQUIRALITIES	STABILISATOR	STAFFRIDER	STAIRSTEPPED	STALWARTNESS
SQUIRALITY	STABILISATORS	STAFFRIDERS	STAIRSTEPPING	STALWARTNESSES
SQUIRALTIES	STABILISED	STAFFROOMS	STAIRSTEPS	STALWORTHS
SQUIRARCHAL	STABILISER	STAGECOACH	STAIRWELLS	STAMINEOUS
SQUIRARCHICAL	STABILISERS	STAGECOACHES	STAIRWORKS	STAMINIFEROUS
SQUIRARCHIES	STABILISES	STAGECOACHING	STAKEHOLDER	STAMINODES
SQUIRARCHS	STABILISING	STAGECOACHINGS	STAKEHOLDERS	STAMINODIA
SQUIRARCHY	STABILITIES	STAGECOACHMAN	STAKHANOVISM	STAMINODIES
SQUIREAGES	STABILIZATION	STAGECOACHMEN	STAKHANOVISMS	STAMINODIUM
SQUIREARCH	STABILIZATIONS	STAGECRAFT	STAKHANOVITE	STAMMERERS
SQUIREARCHAL	STABILIZATOR	STAGECRAFTS	STAKHANOVITES	STAMMERING
SQUIREARCHICAL	STABILIZATORS	STAGEHANDS	STAKTOMETER	STAMMERINGLY
SQUIREARCHIES	STABILIZED	STAGEHEADS	STAKTOMETERS	STAMMERINGS
SQUIREARCHS	STABILIZER	STAGESTRUCK	STALACTICAL	STAMPEDERS
SQUIREARCHY	STABILIZERS	STAGFLATION	STALACTIFORM	STAMPEDING
SQUIREDOMS	STABILIZES	STAGFLATIONARY	STALACTITAL	STAMPEDOED
SQUIREHOOD	STABILIZING	STAGFLATIONS	STALACTITE	STAMPEDOING
SQUIREHOODS	STABLEBOYS	STAGGERBUSH	STALACTITED	STANCHABLE
SQUIRELIKE	STABLEMATE	STAGGERBUSHES	STALACTITES	STANCHELLED
SQUIRELING	STABLEMATES	STAGGERERS	STALACTITIC	STANCHELLING
SQUIRELINGS	STABLENESS	STAGGERIER	STALACTITICAL	STANCHERED
SQUIRESHIP	STABLENESSES	STAGGERIEST	STALACTITICALLY	STANCHERING
SQUIRESHIPS	STABLISHED	STAGGERING	STALACTITIFORM	STANCHINGS
SQUIRESSES	STABLISHES	STAGGERINGLY	STALACTITIOUS	STANCHIONED
SQUIRMIEST	STABLISHING	STAGGERINGS	STALAGMITE	STANCHIONING
SQUIRMINGLY	STABLISHMENT	STAGHOUNDS	STALAGMITES	STANCHIONS

STANCHLESS	STAPHYLINE	STARSHINES	STATIONERIES	STAYMAKERS
STANCHNESS	STAPHYLINID	STARSTONES	STATIONERS	STEADFASTLY
STANCHNESSES	STAPHYLINIDS	STARSTRUCK	STATIONERY	STEADFASTNESS
STANDARDBRED	STAPHYLITIS	STARTINGLY	STATIONING	STEADFASTNESSES
STANDARDBREDS	STAPHYLITISES	STARTLEMENT	STATIONMASTER	STEADINESS
STANDARDISATION	STAPHYLOCOCCAL	STARTLEMENTS	STATIONMASTERS	STEADINESSES
STANDARDISE	STAPHYLOCOCCI	STARTLIEST	STATISTICAL	STEAKETTES
STANDARDISED	STAPHYLOCOCCIC	STARTLINGLY	STATISTICALLY	STEAKHOUSE
STANDARDISER	STAPHYLOCOCCUS	STARTLINGS	STATISTICIAN	STEAKHOUSES
STANDARDISERS	STAPHYLOMA	STARVATION	STATISTICIANS	STEALINGLY
STANDARDISES	STAPHYLOMAS	STARVATIONS	STATISTICS	STEALTHFUL
STANDARDISING	STAPHYLOMATA	STARVELING	STATOBLAST	STEALTHIER
STANDARDIZATION	STAPHYLOPLASTIC	STARVELINGS	STATOBLASTS	STEALTHIEST
STANDARDIZE	STAPHYLOPLASTY	STASIDIONS	STATOCYSTS	STEALTHILY
STANDARDIZED	STAPHYLORRHAPHY	STASIMORPHIES	STATOLATRIES	STEALTHINESS
STANDARDIZER	STARBOARDED	STASIMORPHY	STATOLATRY	STEALTHINESSES
STANDARDIZERS	STARBOARDING	STATECRAFT	STATOLITHIC	STEALTHING
STANDARDIZES	STARBOARDS	STATECRAFTS	STATOLITHS	STEALTHINGS
STANDARDIZING	STARBURSTS	STATEHOODS	STATOSCOPE	STEAMBOATS
STANDARDLESS	STARCHEDLY	STATEHOUSE	STATOSCOPES	STEAMERING
STANDARDLY	STARCHEDNESS	STATEHOUSES	STATUARIES	STEAMFITTER
STANDDOWNS	STARCHEDNESSES	STATELESSNESS	STATUESQUE	STEAMFITTERS
STANDFASTS	STARCHIEST	STATELESSNESSES	STATUESQUELY	STEAMINESS
STANDFIRST	STARCHINESS	STATELIEST	STATUESQUENESS	STEAMINESSES
STANDFIRSTS	STARCHINESSES	STATELINESS	STATUETTES	STEAMPUNKS
STANDGALES	STARCHLIKE	STATELINESSES	STATUSIEST	STEAMROLLED
STANDISHES	STARDRIFTS	STATEMENTED	STATUTABLE	STEAMROLLER
STANDOFFISH	STARFISHED	STATEMENTING	STATUTABLY	STEAMROLLERED
STANDOFFISHLY	STARFISHES	STATEMENTINGS	STATUTORILY	STEAMROLLERING
STANDOFFISHNESS	STARFLOWER	STATEMENTS	STAUNCHABLE	STEAMROLLERS
STANDOVERS	STARFLOWERS	STATEROOMS	STAUNCHERS	STEAMROLLING
STANDPATTER	STARFRUITS	STATESMANLIER	STAUNCHEST	STEAMROLLS
STANDPATTERS	STARFUCKER	STATESMANLIEST	STAUNCHING	STEAMSHIPS
STANDPATTISM	STARFUCKERS	STATESMANLIKE	STAUNCHINGS	STEAMTIGHT
STANDPATTISMS	STARFUCKING	STATESMANLY	STAUNCHLESS	STEAMTIGHTNESS
STANDPIPES	STARFUCKINGS	STATESMANSHIP	STAUNCHNESS	STEAROPTENE
STANDPOINT	STARGAZERS	STATESMANSHIPS	STAUNCHNESSES	STEAROPTENES
STANDPOINTS	STARGAZING	STATESPERSON	STAUROLITE	STEARSMATE
STANDSTILL	STARGAZINGS	STATESPERSONS	STAUROLITES	STEARSMATES
STANDSTILLS	STARKENING	STATESWOMAN	STAUROLITIC	STEATOCELE
STANNARIES	STARKNESSES	STATESWOMEN	STAUROSCOPE	STEATOCELES
STANNATORS	STARLIGHTED	STATICALLY	STAUROSCOPES	STEATOLYSES
STANNIFEROUS	STARLIGHTS	STATICKIER	STAUROSCOPIC	STEATOLYSIS
STANNOTYPE	STARMONGER	STATICKIEST	STAVESACRE	STEATOMATOUS
STANNOTYPES	STARMONGERS	STATIONARIES	STAVESACRES	STEATOPYGA
STAPEDECTOMIES	STAROSTIES	STATIONARILY	STAVUDINES	STEATOPYGAS
STAPEDECTOMY	STARRINESS	STATIONARINESS	STAYCATION	STEATOPYGIA
STAPEDIUSES	STARRINESSES	STATIONARY	STAYCATIONS	STEATOPYGIAS

S

STEATOPYGIC	STEGANOGRAM	STEMWINDERS	STENOTYPISTS	STERCORATING
STEATOPYGOUS	STEGANOGRAMS	STENCHIEST	STENTMASTER	STERCORICOLOUS
STEATORRHEA	STEGANOGRAPH	STENCILERS	STENTMASTERS	STERCULIACEOUS
STEATORRHEAS	STEGANOGRAPHER	STENCILING	STENTORIAN	STERCULIAS
STEATORRHOEA	STEGANOGRAPHERS	STENCILINGS	STEPBAIRNS	STEREOACUITIES
STEATORRHOEAS	STEGANOGRAPHIC	STENCILLED	STEPBROTHER	STEREOACUITY
STEDFASTLY	STEGANOGRAPHIES	STENCILLER	STEPBROTHERS	STEREOBATE
STEDFASTNESS	STEGANOGRAPHIST	STENCILLERS	STEPCHILDREN	STEREOBATES
STEDFASTNESSES	STEGANOGRAPHS	STENCILLING	STEPDANCER	STEREOBATIC
STEELHEADS	STEGANOGRAPHY	STENCILLINGS	STEPDANCERS	STEREOBLIND
STEELINESS	STEGANOPOD	STENOBATHIC	STEPDANCING	STEREOCARD
STEELINESSES	STEGANOPODOUS	STENOBATHS	STEPDANCINGS	STEREOCARDS
STEELMAKER	STEGANOPODS	STENOCARDIA	STEPDAUGHTER	STEREOCHEMICAL
STEELMAKERS	STEGNOTICS	STENOCARDIAS	STEPDAUGHTERS	STEREOCHEMISTRY
STEELMAKING	STEGOCARPOUS	STENOCHROME	STEPFAMILIES	STEREOCHROME
STEELMAKINGS	STEGOCEPHALIAN	STENOCHROMES	STEPFAMILY	STEREOCHROMED
STEELWARES	STEGOCEPHALIANS	STENOCHROMIES	STEPFATHER	STEREOCHROMES
STEELWORKER	STEGOCEPHALOUS	STENOCHROMY	STEPFATHERS	STEREOCHROMIES
STEELWORKERS	STEGODONTS	STENOGRAPH	STEPHANITE	STEREOCHROMING
STEELWORKING	STEGOMYIAS	STENOGRAPHED	STEPHANITES	STEREOCHROMY
STEELWORKINGS	STEGOPHILIST	STENOGRAPHER	STEPHANOTIS	STEREOGNOSES
STEELWORKS	STEGOPHILISTS	STENOGRAPHERS	STEPHANOTISES	STEREOGNOSIS
STEELYARDS	STEGOSAURIAN	STENOGRAPHIC	STEPLADDER	STEREOGRAM
STEENBRASES	STEGOSAURIANS	STENOGRAPHICAL	STEPLADDERS	STEREOGRAMS
STEENBUCKS	STEGOSAURS	STENOGRAPHIES	STEPMOTHER	STEREOGRAPH
STEENKIRKS	STEGOSAURUS	STENOGRAPHING	STEPMOTHERLIER	STEREOGRAPHED
STEEPDOWNE	STEGOSAURUSES	STENOGRAPHIST	STEPMOTHERLIEST	STEREOGRAPHIC
STEEPEDOWNE	STEINBOCKS	STENOGRAPHISTS	STEPMOTHERLY	STEREOGRAPHICAL
STEEPENING	STEINKIRKS	STENOGRAPHS	STEPMOTHERS	STEREOGRAPHIES
STEEPINESS	STELLARATOR	STENOGRAPHY	STEPPARENT	STEREOGRAPHING
STEEPINESSES	STELLARATORS	STENOHALINE	STEPPARENTING	STEREOGRAPHS
STEEPLEBUSH	STELLATELY	STENOPAEIC	STEPPARENTINGS	STEREOGRAPHY
STEEPLEBUSHES	STELLERIDAN	STENOPETALOUS	STEPPARENTS	STEREOISOMER
STEEPLECHASE	STELLERIDANS	STENOPHAGOUS	STEPSISTER	STEREOISOMERIC
STEEPLECHASED	STELLERIDS	STENOPHYLLOUS	STEPSISTERS	STEREOISOMERISM
STEEPLECHASER	STELLIFEROUS	STENOTHERM	STEPSTOOLS	STEREOISOMERS
STEEPLECHASERS	STELLIFIED	STENOTHERMAL	STERADIANS	STEREOISOMETRIC
STEEPLECHASES	STELLIFIES	STENOTHERMS	STERCORACEOUS	STEREOLOGICAL
STEEPLECHASING	STELLIFORM	STENOTOPIC	STERCORANISM	STEREOLOGICALLY
STEEPLECHASINGS	STELLIFYING	STENOTROPIC	STERCORANISMS	STEREOLOGIES
STEEPLEJACK	STELLIFYINGS	STENOTYPED	STERCORANIST	STEREOLOGY
STEEPLEJACKS	STELLIONATE	STENOTYPER	STERCORANISTS	STEREOMETER
STEEPNESSES	STELLIONATES	STENOTYPERS	STERCORARIES	STEREOMETERS
STEERAGEWAY	STELLULARLY	STENOTYPES	STERCORARIOUS	STEREOMETRIC
STEERAGEWAYS	STELLULATE	STENOTYPIC	STERCORARY	STEREOMETRICAL
STEERLINGS	STEMMATOUS	STENOTYPIES	STERCORATE	STEREOMETRIES
STEERSMATE	STEMMERIES	STENOTYPING	STERCORATED	STEREOMETRY
STEERSMATES	STEMWINDER	STENOTYPIST	STERCORATES	STEREOPHONIC

STEREOPHONIES	STERIGMATA	STEROIDOGENESIS	STICKBALLS	STIGMATISM
STEREOPHONY	STERILANTS	STEROIDOGENIC	STICKERING	STIGMATISMS
STEREOPSES	STERILISABLE	STERTOROUS	STICKHANDLE	STIGMATIST
STEREOPSIS	STERILISATION	STERTOROUSLY	STICKHANDLED	STIGMATISTS
STEREOPTICON	STERILISATIONS	STERTOROUSNESS	STICKHANDLER	STIGMATIZATION
STEREOPTICONS	STERILISED	STETHOSCOPE	STICKHANDLERS	STIGMATIZATIONS
STEREOPTICS	STERILISER	STETHOSCOPES	STICKHANDLES	STIGMATIZE
STEREOREGULAR	STERILISERS	STETHOSCOPIC	STICKHANDLING	STIGMATIZED
STEREOSCOPE	STERILISES	STETHOSCOPIES	STICKHANDLINGS	STIGMATIZER
STEREOSCOPES	STERILISING	STETHOSCOPIST	STICKINESS	STIGMATIZERS
STEREOSCOPIC	STERILITIES	STETHOSCOPISTS	STICKINESSES	STIGMATIZES
STEREOSCOPICAL	STERILIZABLE	STETHOSCOPY	STICKLEADER	STIGMATIZING
STEREOSCOPIES	STERILIZATION	STEVEDORED	STICKLEADERS	STIGMATOPHILIA
STEREOSCOPIST	STERILIZATIONS	STEVEDORES	STICKLEBACK	STIGMATOPHILIAS
STEREOSCOPISTS	STERILIZED	STEVEDORING	STICKLEBACKS	STIGMATOPHILIST
STEREOSCOPY	STERILIZER	STEVEDORINGS	STICKLINGS	STIGMATOSE
STEREOSONIC	STERILIZERS	STEVENGRAPH	STICKSEEDS	STILBESTROL
STEREOSPECIFIC	STERILIZES	STEVENGRAPHS	STICKTIGHT	STILBESTROLS
STEREOTACTIC	STERILIZING	STEWARDESS	STICKTIGHTS	STILBOESTROL
STEREOTACTICAL	STERLINGLY	STEWARDESSES	STICKWEEDS	STILBOESTROLS
STEREOTAXES	STERLINGNESS	STEWARDING	STICKWORKS	STILETTOED
STEREOTAXIA	STERLINGNESSES	STEWARDRIES	STICKYBEAK	STILETTOES
STEREOTAXIAS	STERNALGIA	STEWARDSHIP	STICKYBEAKED	STILETTOING
STEREOTAXIC	STERNALGIAS	STEWARDSHIPS	STICKYBEAKING	STILLATORIES
STEREOTAXICALLY	STERNALGIC	STEWARTRIES	STICKYBEAKS	STILLATORY
STEREOTAXIS	STERNBOARD	STIACCIATO	STIDDIEING	STILLBIRTH
STEREOTOMIES	STERNBOARDS	STIACCIATOS	STIFFENERS	STILLBIRTHS
STEREOTOMY	STERNEBRAE	STIBIALISM	STIFFENING	STILLBORNS
STEREOTROPIC	STERNFASTS	STIBIALISMS	STIFFENINGS	STILLHOUSE
STEREOTROPISM	STERNFOREMOST	STICCADOES	STIFFNESSES	STILLHOUSES
STEREOTROPISMS	STERNNESSES	STICCATOES	STIFFWARES	STILLICIDE
STEREOTYPE	STERNOCOSTAL	STICHARION	STIFLINGLY	STILLICIDES
STEREOTYPED	STERNOTRIBE	STICHARIONS	STIGMARIAN	STILLIFORM
STEREOTYPER	STERNPORTS	STICHICALLY	STIGMARIANS	STILLNESSES
STEREOTYPERS	STERNPOSTS	STICHIDIUM	STIGMASTEROL	STILLROOMS
STEREOTYPES	STERNSHEET	STICHOLOGIES	STIGMASTEROLS	STILPNOSIDERITE
STEREOTYPIC	STERNSHEETS	STICHOLOGY	STIGMATICAL	STILTBIRDS
STEREOTYPICAL	STERNUTATION	STICHOMETRIC	STIGMATICALLY	STILTEDNESS
STEREOTYPICALLY	STERNUTATIONS	STICHOMETRICAL	STIGMATICS	STILTEDNESSES
STEREOTYPIES	STERNUTATIVE	STICHOMETRIES	STIGMATIFEROUS	STILTINESS
STEREOTYPING	STERNUTATIVES	STICHOMETRY	STIGMATISATION	STILTINESSES
STEREOTYPINGS	STERNUTATOR	STICHOMYTHIA	STIGMATISATIONS	STIMPMETER
STEREOTYPIST	STERNUTATORIES	STICHOMYTHIAS	STIGMATISE	STIMPMETERS
STEREOTYPISTS	STERNUTATORS	STICHOMYTHIC	STIGMATISED	STIMULABLE
STEREOTYPY	STERNUTATORY	STICHOMYTHIES	STIGMATISER	STIMULANCIES
STEREOVISION	STERNWARDS	STICHOMYTHY	STIGMATISERS	STIMULANCY
STEREOVISIONS	STERNWORKS	STICKABILITIES	STIGMATISES	STIMULANTS
STERICALLY	STEROIDOGENESES	STICKABILITY	STIGMATISING	STIMULATED

STIMULATER	STIPULATIONS	STOCKISHNESS	STOITERING	STONEBREAKER
STIMULATERS	STIPULATOR	STOCKISHNESSES	STOKEHOLDS	STONEBREAKERS
STIMULATES	STIPULATORS	STOCKJOBBER	STOKEHOLES	STONEBREAKS
STIMULATING	STIPULATORY	STOCKJOBBERIES	STOLENWISE	STONECASTS
STIMULATINGLY	STIRABOUTS	STOCKJOBBERS	STOLIDITIES	STONECHATS
STIMULATION	STIRPICULTURE	STOCKJOBBERY	STOLIDNESS	STONECROPS
STIMULATIONS	STIRPICULTURES	STOCKJOBBING	STOLIDNESSES	STONECUTTER
STIMULATIVE	STIRRINGLY	STOCKJOBBINGS	STOLONIFEROUS	STONECUTTERS
STIMULATIVES	STITCHCRAFT	STOCKKEEPER	STOMACHACHE	STONECUTTING
STIMULATOR	STITCHCRAFTS	STOCKKEEPERS	STOMACHACHES	STONECUTTINGS
STIMULATORS	STITCHERIES	STOCKLISTS	STOMACHALS	STONEFISHES
STIMULATORY	STITCHINGS	STOCKLOCKS	STOMACHERS	STONEFLIES
STINGAREES	STITCHWORK	STOCKPILED	STOMACHFUL	STONEGROUND
STINGBULLS	STITCHWORKS	STOCKPILER	STOMACHFULNESS	STONEHANDS
STINGFISHES	STITCHWORT	STOCKPILERS	STOMACHFULS	STONEHORSE
STINGINESS	STITCHWORTS	STOCKPILES	STOMACHICAL	STONEHORSES
STINGINESSES	STOCCADOES	STOCKPILING	STOMACHICS	STONELESSNESS
STINGINGLY	STOCHASTIC	STOCKPILINGS	STOMACHIER	STONELESSNESSES
STINGINGNESS	STOCHASTICALLY	STOCKPUNISHT	STOMACHIEST	STONEMASON
STINGINGNESSES	STOCKADING	STOCKROOMS	STOMACHING	STONEMASONRIES
STINKBIRDS	STOCKBREEDER	STOCKROUTE	STOMACHLESS	STONEMASONRY
STINKEROOS	STOCKBREEDERS	STOCKROUTES	STOMACHOUS	STONEMASONS
STINKHORNS	STOCKBREEDING	STOCKTAKEN	STOMATITIC	STONESHOTS
STINKINGLY	STOCKBREEDINGS	STOCKTAKES	STOMATITIDES	STONEWALLED
STINKINGNESS	STOCKBROKER	STOCKTAKING	STOMATITIS	STONEWALLER
STINKINGNESSES	STOCKBROKERAGE	STOCKTAKINGS	STOMATITISES	STONEWALLERS
STINKSTONE	STOCKBROKERAGES	STOCKWORKS	STOMATODAEA	STONEWALLING
STINKSTONES	STOCKBROKERS	STOCKYARDS	STOMATODAEUM	STONEWALLINGS
STINKWEEDS	STOCKBROKING	STODGINESS	STOMATOGASTRIC	STONEWALLS
STINKWOODS	STOCKBROKINGS	STODGINESSES	STOMATOLOGICAL	STONEWARES
STINTEDNESS	STOCKFISHES	STOECHIOLOGICAL	STOMATOLOGIES	STONEWASHED
STINTEDNESSES	STOCKHOLDER	STOECHIOLOGIES	STOMATOLOGIST	STONEWASHES
STINTINGLY	STOCKHOLDERS	STOECHIOLOGY	STOMATOLOGISTS	STONEWASHING
STIPELLATE	STOCKHOLDING	STOECHIOMETRIC	STOMATOLOGY	STONEWORKER
STIPENDIARIES	STOCKHOLDINGS	STOECHIOMETRIES	STOMATOPLASTIES	STONEWORKERS
STIPENDIARY	STOCKHORNS	STOECHIOMETRY	STOMATOPLASTY	STONEWORKS
STIPENDIATE	STOCKHORSE	STOICALNESS	STOMATOPOD	STONEWORTS
STIPENDIATED	STOCKHORSES	STOICALNESSES	STOMATOPODS	STONINESSES
STIPENDIATES	STOCKINESS	STOICHEIOLOGIES	STOMODAEAL	STONISHING
STIPENDIATING	STOCKINESSES	STOICHEIOLOGY	STOMODAEUM	STONKERING
STIPITIFORM	STOCKINETS	STOICHEIOMETRIC	STOMODAEUMS	STONYHEARTED
STIPPLINGS	STOCKINETTE	STOICHEIOMETRY	STOMODEUMS	STOOLBALLS
STIPULABLE	STOCKINETTES	STOICHIOLOGICAL	STONEBOATS	STOOPBALLS
STIPULACEOUS	STOCKINGED	STOICHIOLOGIES	STONEBORER	STOOPINGLY
STIPULATED	STOCKINGER	STOICHIOLOGY	STONEBORERS	STOPLIGHTS
STIPULATES	STOCKINGERS	STOICHIOMETRIC	STONEBRASH	STOPPERING
STIPULATING	STOCKINGLESS	STOICHIOMETRIES	STONEBRASHES	STOPWATCHES
STIPULATION	STOCKISHLY	STOICHIOMETRY	STONEBREAK	STORECARDS

STOREFRONT	STOVEPIPES	STRAIGHTLACED	STRANGULATED	STRATIFIES
STOREFRONTS	STOVEWOODS	STRAIGHTLY	STRANGULATES	STRATIFORM
STOREHOUSE	STRABISMAL	STRAIGHTNESS	STRANGULATING	STRATIFYING
STOREHOUSES	STRABISMIC	STRAIGHTNESSES	STRANGULATION	STRATIGRAPHER
STOREKEEPER	STRABISMICAL	STRAIGHTWAY	STRANGULATIONS	STRATIGRAPHERS
STOREKEEPERS	STRABISMOMETER	STRAIGHTWAYS	STRANGURIES	STRATIGRAPHIC
STOREKEEPING	STRABISMOMETERS	STRAINEDLY	STRAPHANGED	STRATIGRAPHICAL
STOREKEEPINGS	STRABISMUS	STRAININGS	STRAPHANGER	STRATIGRAPHIES
STOREROOMS	STRABISMUSES	STRAITENED	STRAPHANGERS	STRATIGRAPHIST
STORESHIPS	STRABOMETER	STRAITENING	STRAPHANGING	STRATIGRAPHISTS
STORIETTES	STRABOMETERS	STRAITJACKET	STRAPHANGINGS	STRATIGRAPHY
STORIOLOGIES	STRABOTOMIES	STRAITJACKETED	STRAPHANGS	STRATOCRACIES
STORIOLOGIST	STRABOTOMY	STRAITJACKETING	STRAPLESSES	STRATOCRACY
STORIOLOGISTS	STRACCHINI	STRAITJACKETS	STRAPLINES	STRATOCRAT
STORIOLOGY	STRACCHINO	STRAITLACED	STRAPONTIN	STRATOCRATIC
STORKSBILL	STRADDLEBACK	STRAITLACEDLY	STRAPONTINS	STRATOCRATS
STORKSBILLS	STRADDLERS	STRAITLACEDNESS	STRAPPADOED	STRATOCUMULI
STORMBIRDS	STRADDLING	STRAITNESS	STRAPPADOES	STRATOCUMULUS
STORMBOUND	STRAGGLERS	STRAITNESSES	STRAPPADOING	STRATOPAUSE
STORMCOCKS	STRAGGLIER	STRAITWAISTCOAT	STRAPPADOS	STRATOPAUSES
STORMFULLY	STRAGGLIEST	STRAMACONS	STRAPPIEST	STRATOSPHERE
STORMFULNESS	STRAGGLING	STRAMASHED	STRAPPINGS	STRATOSPHERES
STORMFULNESSES	STRAGGLINGLY	STRAMASHES	STRAPWORTS	STRATOSPHERIC
STORMINESS	STRAGGLINGS	STRAMASHING	STRATAGEMS	STRATOSPHERICAL
STORMINESSES	STRAICHTER	STRAMAZONS	STRATEGETIC	STRATOTANKER
STORMPROOF	STRAICHTEST	STRAMINEOUS	STRATEGETICAL	STRATOTANKERS
STORMSTAYED	STRAIGHTAWAY	STRAMONIES	STRATEGICAL	STRATOVOLCANO
STORYBOARD	STRAIGHTAWAYS	STRAMONIUM	STRATEGICALLY	STRATOVOLCANOES
STORYBOARDED	STRAIGHTBRED	STRAMONIUMS	STRATEGICS	STRATOVOLCANOS
STORYBOARDING	STRAIGHTBREDS	STRANDEDNESS	STRATEGIES	STRAUCHTED
STORYBOARDS	STRAIGHTED	STRANDEDNESSES	STRATEGISE	STRAUCHTER
STORYBOOKS	STRAIGHTEDGE	STRANDFLAT	STRATEGISED	STRAUCHTEST
STORYETTES	STRAIGHTEDGED	STRANDFLATS	STRATEGISES	STRAUCHTING
STORYLINES	STRAIGHTEDGES	STRANDLINE	STRATEGISING	STRAUGHTED
STORYTELLER	STRAIGHTEN	STRANDLINES	STRATEGIST	STRAUGHTER
STORYTELLERS	STRAIGHTENED	STRANDWOLF	STRATEGISTS	STRAUGHTEST
STORYTELLING	STRAIGHTENER	STRANDWOLVES	STRATEGIZE	STRAUGHTING
STORYTELLINGS	STRAIGHTENERS	STRANGENESS	STRATEGIZED	STRAVAGING
STORYTIMES	STRAIGHTENING	STRANGENESSES	STRATEGIZES	STRAVAIGED
STOTTERING	STRAIGHTENS	STRANGERED	STRATEGIZING	STRAVAIGER
STOUTENING	STRAIGHTER	STRANGERING	STRATHSPEY	STRAVAIGERS
STOUTHEARTED	STRAIGHTEST	STRANGLEHOLD	STRATHSPEYS	STRAVAIGING
STOUTHEARTEDLY	STRAIGHTFORTH	STRANGLEHOLDS	STRATICULATE	STRAWBERRIES
STOUTHERIE	STRAIGHTFORWARD	STRANGLEMENT	STRATICULATION	STRAWBERRY
STOUTHERIES	STRAIGHTING	STRANGLEMENTS	STRATICULATIONS	STRAWBOARD
STOUTHRIEF	STRAIGHTISH	STRANGLERS	STRATIFICATION	STRAWBOARDS
STOUTHRIEFS	STRAIGHTJACKET	STRANGLING	STRATIFICATIONS	STRAWFLOWER
STOUTNESSES	STRAIGHTJACKETS	STRANGULATE	STRATIFIED	STRAWFLOWERS

S

STRAWWEIGHT	STREETWALKING	STREPTOMYCETES	STRIDULANT	STRINGPIECES
STRAWWEIGHTS	STREETWALKINGS	STREPTOMYCIN	STRIDULANTLY	STRINGYBARK
STRAWWORMS	STREETWARD	STREPTOMYCINS	STRIDULATE	STRINGYBARKS
STRAYLINGS	STREETWARDS	STREPTOSOLEN	STRIDULATED	STRINKLING
STREAKIEST	STREETWEAR	STREPTOSOLENS	STRIDULATES	STRINKLINGS
STREAKINESS	STREETWEARS	STREPTOTHRICIN	STRIDULATING	STRIPAGRAM
STREAKINESSES	STREETWISE	STREPTOTHRICINS	STRIDULATION	STRIPAGRAMS
STREAKINGS	STREIGNING	STRESSBUSTER	STRIDULATIONS	STRIPELESS
STREAKLIKE	STRELITZES	STRESSBUSTERS	STRIDULATOR	STRIPINESS
STREAMBEDS	STRELITZIA	STRESSBUSTING	STRIDULATORS	STRIPINESSES
STREAMERED	STRELITZIAS	STRESSFULLY	STRIDULATORY	STRIPLINGS
STREAMIEST	STRENGTHEN	STRESSFULNESS	STRIDULOUS	STRIPOGRAM
STREAMINESS	STRENGTHENED	STRESSFULNESSES	STRIDULOUSLY	STRIPOGRAMS
STREAMINESSES	STRENGTHENER	STRESSIEST	STRIDULOUSNESS	STRIPPABLE
STREAMINGLY	STRENGTHENERS	STRESSLESS	STRIFELESS	STRIPPAGRAM
STREAMINGS	STRENGTHENING	STRESSLESSNESS	STRIGIFORM	STRIPPAGRAMS
STREAMLESS	STRENGTHENINGS	STRETCHABILITY	STRIKEBOUND	STRIPPERGRAM
STREAMLETS	STRENGTHENS	STRETCHABLE	STRIKEBREAKER	STRIPPERGRAMS
STREAMLIKE	STRENGTHFUL	STRETCHERED	STRIKEBREAKERS	STRIPPINGS
STREAMLINE	STRENGTHLESS	STRETCHERING	STRIKEBREAKING	STRIPTEASE
STREAMLINED	STRENUITIES	STRETCHERS	STRIKEBREAKINGS	STRIPTEASER
STREAMLINER	STRENUOSITIES	STRETCHIER	STRIKELESS	STRIPTEASERS
STREAMLINERS	STRENUOSITY	STRETCHIEST	STRIKEOUTS	STRIPTEASES
STREAMLINES	STRENUOUSLY	STRETCHINESS	STRIKEOVER	STRIVINGLY
STREAMLING	STRENUOUSNESS	STRETCHINESSES	STRIKEOVERS	STROBILACEOUS
STREAMLINGS	STRENUOUSNESSES	STRETCHING	STRIKINGLY	STROBILATE
STREAMLINING	STREPEROUS	STRETCHINGS	STRIKINGNESS	STROBILATED
STREAMLININGS	STREPHOSYMBOLIA	STRETCHLESS	STRIKINGNESSES	STROBILATES
STREAMSIDE	STREPITANT	STRETCHMARKS	STRINGBOARD	STROBILATING
STREAMSIDES	STREPITATION	STREWMENTS	STRINGBOARDS	STROBILATION
STREETAGES	STREPITATIONS	STRIATIONS	STRINGCOURSE	STROBILATIONS
STREETBOYS	STREPITOSO	STRIATURES	STRINGCOURSES	STROBILIFORM
STREETCARS	STREPITOUS	STRICKENLY	STRINGENCIES	STROBILINE
STREETFULS	STREPSIPTEROUS	STRICKLING	STRINGENCY	STROBILISATION
STREETIEST	STREPTOBACILLI	STRICTIONS	STRINGENDO	STROBILISATIONS
STREETKEEPER	STREPTOBACILLUS	STRICTNESS	STRINGENTLY	STROBILIZATION
STREETKEEPERS	STREPTOCARPUS	STRICTNESSES	STRINGENTNESS	STROBILIZATIONS
STREETLAMP	STREPTOCARPUSES	STRICTURED	STRINGENTNESSES	STROBILOID
STREETLAMPS	STREPTOCOCCAL	STRICTURES	STRINGHALT	STROBILUSES
STREETLIGHT	STREPTOCOCCI	STRIDDLING	STRINGHALTED	STROBOSCOPE
STREETLIGHTS	STREPTOCOCCIC	STRIDELEGGED	STRINGHALTS	STROBOSCOPES
STREETROOM	STREPTOCOCCUS	STRIDELEGS	STRINGIEST	STROBOSCOPIC
STREETROOMS	STREPTOKINASE	STRIDENCES	STRINGINESS	STROBOSCOPICAL
STREETSCAPE	STREPTOKINASES	STRIDENCIES	STRINGINESSES	STROBOTRON
STREETSCAPES	STREPTOLYSIN	STRIDENTLY	STRINGINGS	STROBOTRONS
STREETSMART	STREPTOLYSINS	STRIDEWAYS	STRINGLESS	STRODDLING
STREETWALKER	STREPTOMYCES	STRIDULANCE	STRINGLIKE	STROGANOFF
STREETWALKERS	STREPTOMYCETE	STRIDULANCES	STRINGPIECE	STROGANOFFS

STROKEPLAY	STRUCTURAL	STUBBORNLY	STUPENDIOUS	STYLOPODIA
STROLLINGS	STRUCTURALISE	STUBBORNNESS	STUPENDOUS	STYLOPODIUM
STROMATOLITE	STRUCTURALISED	STUBBORNNESSES	STUPENDOUSLY	STYLOSTIXES
STROMATOLITES	STRUCTURALISES	STUCCOWORK	STUPENDOUSNESS	STYLOSTIXIS
STROMATOLITIC	STRUCTURALISING	STUCCOWORKS	STUPIDITIES	STYPTICITIES
STROMATOUS	STRUCTURALISM	STUDDINGSAIL	STUPIDNESS	STYPTICITY
STROMBULIFEROUS	STRUCTURALISMS	STUDDINGSAILS	STUPIDNESSES	STYRACACEOUS
STROMBULIFORM	STRUCTURALIST	STUDENTIER	STUPRATING	STYROFOAMS
STROMBUSES	STRUCTURALISTS	STUDENTIEST	STUPRATION	SUABILITIES
STRONGARMED	STRUCTURALIZE	STUDENTRIES	STUPRATIONS	SUASIVENESS
STRONGARMING	STRUCTURALIZED	STUDENTSHIP	STURDINESS	SUASIVENESSES
STRONGARMS	STRUCTURALIZES	STUDENTSHIPS	STURDINESSES	SUAVENESSES
STRONGBOXES	STRUCTURALIZING	STUDFISHES	STUTTERERS	SUAVEOLENT
STRONGHOLD	STRUCTURALLY	STUDHORSES	STUTTERING	SUBABDOMINAL
STRONGHOLDS	STRUCTURATION	STUDIEDNESS	STUTTERINGLY	SUBACETATE
STRONGNESS	STRUCTURATIONS	STUDIEDNESSES	STUTTERINGS	SUBACETATES
STRONGNESSES	STRUCTURED	STUDIOUSLY	STYLEBOOKS	SUBACIDITIES
STRONGPOINT	STRUCTURELESS	STUDIOUSNESS	STYLELESSNESS	SUBACIDITY
STRONGPOINTS	STRUCTURES	STUDIOUSNESSES	STYLELESSNESSES	SUBACIDNESS
STRONGROOM	STRUCTURING	STUFFINESS	STYLIFEROUS	SUBACIDNESSES
STRONGROOMS	STRUGGLERS	STUFFINESSES	STYLISATION	SUBACTIONS
STRONGYLES	STRUGGLING	STULTIFICATION	STYLISATIONS	SUBACUTELY
STRONGYLOID	STRUGGLINGLY	STULTIFICATIONS	STYLISHNESS	SUBADOLESCENT
STRONGYLOIDOSES	STRUGGLINGS	STULTIFIED	STYLISHNESSES	SUBADOLESCENTS
STRONGYLOIDOSIS	STRUMITISES	STULTIFIER	STYLISTICALLY	SUBAERIALLY
STRONGYLOIDS	STRUMPETED	STULTIFIERS	STYLISTICS	SUBAFFLUENT
STRONGYLOSES	STRUMPETING	STULTIFIES	STYLITISMS	SUBAGENCIES
STRONGYLOSIS	STRUTHIOID	STULTIFYING	STYLIZATION	SUBAGGREGATE
STRONTIANITE	STRUTHIOIDS	STUMBLEBUM	STYLIZATIONS	SUBAGGREGATES
STRONTIANITES	STRUTHIOUS	STUMBLEBUMS	STYLOBATES	SUBAGGREGATION
STRONTIANS	STRUTTINGLY	STUMBLIEST	STYLOGRAPH	SUBAGGREGATIONS
STRONTIUMS	STRUTTINGS	STUMBLINGLY	STYLOGRAPHIC	SUBAHDARIES
STROPHANTHIN	STRYCHNIAS	STUMPINESS	STYLOGRAPHICAL	SUBAHSHIPS
STROPHANTHINS	STRYCHNINE	STUMPINESSES	STYLOGRAPHIES	SUBALLIANCE
STROPHANTHUS	STRYCHNINED	STUMPWORKS	STYLOGRAPHS	SUBALLIANCES
STROPHANTHUSES	STRYCHNINES	STUNNINGLY	STYLOGRAPHY	SUBALLOCATION
STROPHICAL	STRYCHNINING	STUNTEDNESS	STYLOLITES	SUBALLOCATIONS
STROPHIOLATE	STRYCHNINISM	STUNTEDNESSES	STYLOLITIC	SUBALTERNANT
STROPHIOLATED	STRYCHNINISMS	STUNTWOMAN	STYLOMETRIES	SUBALTERNANTS
STROPHIOLE	STRYCHNISM	STUNTWOMEN	STYLOMETRY	SUBALTERNATE
STROPHIOLES	STRYCHNISMS	STUPEFACIENT	STYLOPHONE	SUBALTERNATES
STROPHOIDS	STUBBINESS	STUPEFACIENTS	STYLOPHONES	SUBALTERNATION
STROPHULUS	STUBBINESSES	STUPEFACTION	STYLOPISED	SUBALTERNATIONS
STROPPIEST	STUBBLIEST	STUPEFACTIONS	STYLOPISES	SUBALTERNITIES
STROPPINESS	STUBBORNED	STUPEFACTIVE	STYLOPISING	SUBALTERNITY
STROPPINESSES	STUBBORNER	STUPEFIERS	STYLOPIZED	SUBALTERNS
STROUDINGS	STUBBORNEST	STUPEFYING	STYLOPIZES	SUBANGULAR
STROUPACHS	STUBBORNING	STUPEFYINGLY	STYLOPIZING	SUBANTARCTIC

S

SUBAPOSTOLIC	SUBCARDINAL	SUBCLASSIFIES	SUBCONTRACTORS	SUBDEPUTIES
SUBAPPEARANCE	SUBCARDINALS	SUBCLASSIFY	SUBCONTRACTS	SUBDERMALLY
SUBAPPEARANCES	SUBCARRIER	SUBCLASSIFYING	SUBCONTRAOCTAVE	SUBDEVELOPMENT
SUBAQUATIC	SUBCARRIERS	SUBCLASSING	SUBCONTRARIES	SUBDEVELOPMENTS
SUBAQUEOUS	SUBCATEGORIES	SUBCLAUSES	SUBCONTRARIETY	SUBDIACONAL
SUBARACHNOID	SUBCATEGORISE	SUBCLAVIAN	SUBCONTRARY	SUBDIACONATE
SUBARACHNOIDAL	SUBCATEGORISED	SUBCLAVIANS	SUBCOOLING	SUBDIACONATES
SUBARACHNOIDS	SUBCATEGORISES	SUBCLAVICULAR	SUBCORDATE	SUBDIALECT
SUBARBOREAL	SUBCATEGORISING	SUBCLIMACTIC	SUBCORIACEOUS	SUBDIALECTS
SUBARBORESCENT	SUBCATEGORIZE	SUBCLIMAXES	SUBCORTEXES	SUBDIRECTOR
SUBARCTICS	SUBCATEGORIZED	SUBCLINICAL	SUBCORTICAL	SUBDIRECTORS
SUBARCUATE	SUBCATEGORIZES	SUBCLINICALLY	SUBCORTICES	SUBDISCIPLINE
SUBARCUATION	SUBCATEGORIZING	SUBCLUSTER	SUBCOSTALS	SUBDISCIPLINES
SUBARCUATIONS	SUBCATEGORY	SUBCLUSTERED	SUBCOUNTIES	SUBDISTRICT
SUBARRATION	SUBCAVITIES	SUBCLUSTERING	SUBCRANIAL	SUBDISTRICTS
SUBARRATIONS	SUBCEILING	SUBCLUSTERS	SUBCRITICAL	SUBDIVIDABLE
SUBARRHATION	SUBCEILINGS	SUBCOLLECTION	SUBCRUSTAL	SUBDIVIDED
SUBARRHATIONS	SUBCELESTIAL	SUBCOLLECTIONS	SUBCULTURAL	SUBDIVIDER
SUBARTICLE	SUBCELESTIALS	SUBCOLLEGE	SUBCULTURALLY	SUBDIVIDERS
SUBARTICLES	SUBCELLARS	SUBCOLLEGES	SUBCULTURE	SUBDIVIDES
SUBASSEMBLE	SUBCELLULAR	SUBCOLLEGIATE	SUBCULTURED	SUBDIVIDING
SUBASSEMBLED	SUBCENTERS	SUBCOLONIES	SUBCULTURES	SUBDIVISIBLE
SUBASSEMBLES	SUBCENTRAL	SUBCOMMISSION	SUBCULTURING	SUBDIVISION
SUBASSEMBLIES	SUBCENTRALLY	SUBCOMMISSIONED	SUBCURATIVE	SUBDIVISIONAL
SUBASSEMBLING	SUBCENTRES	SUBCOMMISSIONER	SUBCUTANEOUS	SUBDIVISIONS
SUBASSEMBLY	SUBCEPTION	SUBCOMMISSIONS	SUBCUTANEOUSLY	SUBDIVISIVE
SUBASSOCIATION	SUBCEPTIONS	SUBCOMMITTEE	SUBCUTISES	SUBDOMINANT
SUBASSOCIATIONS	SUBCHANTER	SUBCOMMITTEES	SUBDEACONATE	SUBDOMINANTS
SUBATMOSPHERIC	SUBCHANTERS	SUBCOMMUNITIES	SUBDEACONATES	SUBDUCTING
SUBATOMICS	SUBCHAPTER	SUBCOMMUNITY	SUBDEACONRIES	SUBDUCTION
SUBAUDIBLE	SUBCHAPTERS	SUBCOMPACT	SUBDEACONRY	SUBDUCTIONS
SUBAUDITION	SUBCHARTER	SUBCOMPACTS	SUBDEACONS	SUBDUEDNESS
SUBAUDITIONS	SUBCHARTERED	SUBCOMPONENT	SUBDEACONSHIP	SUBDUEDNESSES
SUBAURICULAR	SUBCHARTERING	SUBCOMPONENTS	SUBDEACONSHIPS	SUBDUEMENT
SUBAVERAGE	SUBCHARTERS	SUBCONSCIOUS	SUBDEALERS	SUBDUEMENTS
SUBAXILLARY	SUBCHASERS	SUBCONSCIOUSES	SUBDEANERIES	SUBDUPLICATE
SUBBASEMENT	SUBCHELATE	SUBCONSCIOUSLY	SUBDEANERY	SUBECONOMIC
SUBBASEMENTS	SUBCHLORIDE	SUBCONSULS	SUBDEBUTANTE	SUBECONOMIES
SUBBITUMINOUS	SUBCHLORIDES	SUBCONTIGUOUS	SUBDEBUTANTES	SUBECONOMY
SUBBRANCHES	SUBCIRCUIT	SUBCONTINENT	SUBDECANAL	SUBEDITING
SUBBUREAUS	SUBCIRCUITS	SUBCONTINENTAL	SUBDECISION	SUBEDITORIAL
SUBBUREAUX	SUBCIVILISATION	SUBCONTINENTS	SUBDECISIONS	SUBEDITORS
SUBCABINET	SUBCIVILISED	SUBCONTINUOUS	SUBDELIRIA	SUBEDITORSHIP
SUBCABINETS	SUBCIVILIZATION	SUBCONTRACT	SUBDELIRIOUS	SUBEDITORSHIPS
SUBCALIBER	SUBCIVILIZED	SUBCONTRACTED	SUBDELIRIUM	SUBEMPLOYED
SUBCALIBRE	SUBCLASSED	SUBCONTRACTING	SUBDELIRIUMS	SUBEMPLOYMENT
SUBCANTORS	SUBCLASSES	SUBCONTRACTINGS	SUBDEPARTMENT	SUBEMPLOYMENTS
SUBCAPSULAR	SUBCLASSIFIED	SUBCONTRACTOR	SUBDEPARTMENTS	SUBENTRIES

SUBEPIDERMAL	SUBINDEXES	SUBJACENCY	SUBJUNCTIVES	SUBLITERACIES
SUBEQUATORIAL	SUBINDICATE	SUBJACENTLY	SUBKINGDOM	SUBLITERACY
SUBERISATION	SUBINDICATED	SUBJECTABILITY	SUBKINGDOMS	SUBLITERARY
SUBERISATIONS	SUBINDICATES	SUBJECTABLE	SUBLANCEOLATE	SUBLITERATE
SUBERISING	SUBINDICATING	SUBJECTIFIED	SUBLANGUAGE	SUBLITERATES
SUBERIZATION	SUBINDICATION	SUBJECTIFIES	SUBLANGUAGES	SUBLITERATURE
SUBERIZATIONS	SUBINDICATIONS	SUBJECTIFY	SUBLAPSARIAN	SUBLITERATURES
SUBERIZING	SUBINDICATIVE	SUBJECTIFYING	SUBLAPSARIANISM	SUBLITTORAL
SUBFACTORIAL	SUBINDICES	SUBJECTING	SUBLAPSARIANS	SUBLITTORALS
SUBFACTORIALS	SUBINDUSTRIES	SUBJECTION	SUBLATIONS	SUBLUXATED
SUBFAMILIES	SUBINDUSTRY	SUBJECTIONS	SUBLEASING	SUBLUXATES
SUBFERTILE	SUBINFEUDATE	SUBJECTIVE	SUBLESSEES	SUBLUXATING
SUBFERTILITIES	SUBINFEUDATED	SUBJECTIVELY	SUBLESSORS	SUBLUXATION
SUBFERTILITY	SUBINFEUDATES	SUBJECTIVENESS	SUBLETHALLY	SUBLUXATIONS
SUBFEUDATION	SUBINFEUDATING	SUBJECTIVES	SUBLETTERS	SUBMANAGER
SUBFEUDATIONS	SUBINFEUDATION	SUBJECTIVISE	SUBLETTING	SUBMANAGERS
SUBFEUDATORY	SUBINFEUDATIONS	SUBJECTIVISED	SUBLETTINGS	SUBMANDIBULAR
SUBFOLDERS	SUBINFEUDATORY	SUBJECTIVISES	SUBLIBRARIAN	SUBMANDIBULARS
SUBFOSSILS	SUBINFEUDED	SUBJECTIVISING	SUBLIBRARIANS	SUBMANIFOLD
SUBFREEZING	SUBINFEUDING	SUBJECTIVISM	SUBLICENSE	SUBMANIFOLDS
SUBFUSCOUS	SUBINFEUDS	SUBJECTIVISMS	SUBLICENSED	SUBMARGINAL
SUBGENERATION	SUBINHIBITORY	SUBJECTIVIST	SUBLICENSES	SUBMARGINALLY
SUBGENERATIONS	SUBINSINUATION	SUBJECTIVISTIC	SUBLICENSING	SUBMARINED
SUBGENERIC	SUBINSINUATIONS	SUBJECTIVISTS	SUBLIEUTENANCY	SUBMARINER
SUBGENERICALLY	SUBINSPECTOR	SUBJECTIVITIES	SUBLIEUTENANT	SUBMARINERS
SUBGENUSES	SUBINSPECTORS	SUBJECTIVITY	SUBLIEUTENANTS	SUBMARINES
SUBGLACIAL	SUBINTELLECTION	SUBJECTIVIZE	SUBLIMABLE	SUBMARINING
SUBGLACIALLY	SUBINTELLIGENCE	SUBJECTIVIZED	SUBLIMATED	SUBMARKETS
SUBGLOBOSE	SUBINTELLIGITUR	SUBJECTIVIZES	SUBLIMATES	SUBMATRICES
SUBGLOBULAR	SUBINTERVAL	SUBJECTIVIZING	SUBLIMATING	SUBMATRIXES
SUBGOVERNMENT	SUBINTERVALS	SUBJECTLESS	SUBLIMATION	SUBMAXILLARIES
SUBGOVERNMENTS	SUBINTRANT	SUBJECTSHIP	SUBLIMATIONS	SUBMAXILLARY
SUBGROUPED	SUBINTRODUCE	SUBJECTSHIPS	SUBLIMENESS	SUBMAXIMAL
SUBGROUPING	SUBINTRODUCED	SUBJOINDER	SUBLIMENESSES	SUBMEDIANT
SUBHARMONIC	SUBINTRODUCES	SUBJOINDERS	SUBLIMINAL	SUBMEDIANTS
SUBHARMONICS	SUBINTRODUCING	SUBJOINING	SUBLIMINALLY	SUBMENTUMS
SUBHASTATION	SUBINVOLUTION	SUBJUGABLE	SUBLIMINALS	SUBMERGEMENT
SUBHASTATIONS	SUBINVOLUTIONS	SUBJUGATED	SUBLIMINGS	SUBMERGEMENTS
SUBHEADING	SUBIRRIGATE	SUBJUGATES	SUBLIMISED	SUBMERGENCE
SUBHEADINGS	SUBIRRIGATED	SUBJUGATING	SUBLIMISES	SUBMERGENCES
SUBIMAGINAL	SUBIRRIGATES	SUBJUGATION	SUBLIMISING	SUBMERGIBILITY
SUBIMAGINES	SUBIRRIGATING	SUBJUGATIONS	SUBLIMITIES	SUBMERGIBLE
SUBIMAGOES	SUBIRRIGATION	SUBJUGATOR	SUBLIMIZED	SUBMERGIBLES
SUBINCISED	SUBIRRIGATIONS	SUBJUGATORS	SUBLIMIZES	SUBMERGING
SUBINCISES	SUBITANEOUS	SUBJUNCTION	SUBLIMIZING	SUBMERSIBILITY
SUBINCISING	SUBITISING	SUBJUNCTIONS	SUBLINEATION	SUBMERSIBLE
SUBINCISION	SUBITIZING	SUBJUNCTIVE	SUBLINEATIONS	SUBMERSIBLES
SUBINCISIONS	SUBJACENCIES	SUBJUNCTIVELY	SUBLINGUAL	SUBMERSING

SUBMERSION

SUBMERSION	SUBNASCENT	SUBORDINATENESS	SUBPROJECT	SUBSECTION
SUBMERSIONS	SUBNATIONAL	SUBORDINATES	SUBPROJECTS	SUBSECTIONS
SUBMETACENTRIC	SUBNATURAL	SUBORDINATING	SUBPROLETARIAT	SUBSECTORS
SUBMETACENTRICS	SUBNETWORK	SUBORDINATION	SUBPROLETARIATS	SUBSEGMENT
SUBMICROGRAM	SUBNETWORKED	SUBORDINATIONS	SUBRATIONAL	SUBSEGMENTS
SUBMICRONS	SUBNETWORKING	SUBORDINATIVE	SUBREFERENCE	SUBSEIZURE
SUBMICROSCOPIC	SUBNETWORKS	SUBORDINATOR	SUBREFERENCES	SUBSEIZURES
SUBMILLIMETER	SUBNORMALITIES	SUBORDINATORS	SUBREGIONAL	SUBSELLIUM
SUBMILLIMETERS	SUBNORMALITY	SUBORGANISATION	SUBREGIONS	SUBSENSIBLE
SUBMILLIMETRE	SUBNORMALLY	SUBORGANIZATION	SUBRENTING	SUBSENTENCE
SUBMILLIMETRES	SUBNORMALS	SUBORNATION	SUBREPTION	SUBSENTENCES
SUBMINIATURE	SUBNUCLEAR	SUBORNATIONS	SUBREPTIONS	SUBSEQUENCE
SUBMINIATURES	SUBNUCLEUS	SUBORNATIVE	SUBREPTITIOUS	SUBSEQUENCES
SUBMINIATURISE	SUBNUCLEUSES	SUBOSCINES	SUBREPTITIOUSLY	SUBSEQUENT
SUBMINIATURISED	SUBOCCIPITAL	SUBPANATION	SUBREPTIVE	SUBSEQUENTIAL
SUBMINIATURISES	SUBOCEANIC	SUBPANATIONS	SUBROGATED	SUBSEQUENTLY
SUBMINIATURIZE	SUBOCTAVES	SUBPARAGRAPH	SUBROGATES	SUBSEQUENTNESS
SUBMINIATURIZED	SUBOCTUPLE	SUBPARAGRAPHS	SUBROGATING	SUBSEQUENTS
SUBMINIATURIZES	SUBOFFICER	SUBPARALLEL	SUBROGATION	SUBSERVIENCE
SUBMINIMAL	SUBOFFICERS	SUBPENAING	SUBROGATIONS	SUBSERVIENCES
SUBMINISTER	SUBOFFICES	SUBPERIODS	SUBROUTINE	SUBSERVIENCIES
SUBMINISTERED	SUBOPERCULA	SUBPHRENIC	SUBROUTINES	SUBSERVIENCY
SUBMINISTERING	SUBOPERCULAR	SUBPHYLUMS	SUBSAMPLED	SUBSERVIENT
SUBMINISTERS	SUBOPERCULUM	SUBPOENAED	SUBSAMPLES	SUBSERVIENTLY
SUBMISSIBLE	SUBOPERCULUMS	SUBPOENAING	SUBSAMPLING	SUBSERVIENTS
SUBMISSION	SUBOPTIMAL	SUBPOPULATION	SUBSATELLITE	SUBSERVING
SUBMISSIONS	SUBOPTIMISATION	SUBPOPULATIONS	SUBSATELLITES	SUBSESSILE
SUBMISSIVE	SUBOPTIMISE	SUBPOTENCIES	SUBSATURATED	SUBSHRUBBY
SUBMISSIVELY	SUBOPTIMISED	SUBPOTENCY	SUBSATURATION	SUBSIDENCE
SUBMISSIVENESS	SUBOPTIMISES	SUBPREFECT	SUBSATURATIONS	SUBSIDENCES
SUBMISSNESS	SUBOPTIMISING	SUBPREFECTS	SUBSCAPULAR	SUBSIDENCIES
SUBMISSNESSES	SUBOPTIMIZATION	SUBPREFECTURE	SUBSCAPULARS	SUBSIDENCY
SUBMITTABLE	SUBOPTIMIZE	SUBPREFECTURES	SUBSCHEMATA	SUBSIDIARIAT
SUBMITTALS	SUBOPTIMIZED	SUBPRIMATE	SUBSCIENCE	SUBSIDIARIATS
SUBMITTERS	SUBOPTIMIZES	SUBPRIMATES	SUBSCIENCES	SUBSIDIARIES
SUBMITTING	SUBOPTIMIZING	SUBPRINCIPAL	SUBSCRIBABLE	SUBSIDIARILY
SUBMITTINGS	SUBOPTIMUM	SUBPRINCIPALS	SUBSCRIBED	SUBSIDIARINESS
SUBMOLECULE	SUBOPTIMUMS	SUBPRIORESS	SUBSCRIBER	SUBSIDIARISM
SUBMOLECULES	SUBORBICULAR	SUBPRIORESSES	SUBSCRIBERS	SUBSIDIARITIES
SUBMONTANE	SUBORBITAL	SUBPROBLEM	SUBSCRIBES	SUBSIDIARITY
SUBMONTANELY	SUBORDINAL	SUBPROBLEMS	SUBSCRIBING	SUBSIDIARY
SUBMUCOSAE	SUBORDINANCIES	SUBPROCESS	SUBSCRIBINGS	SUBSIDISABLE
SUBMUCOSAL	SUBORDINANCY	SUBPROCESSES	SUBSCRIPTION	SUBSIDISATION
SUBMUCOSAS	SUBORDINARIES	SUBPRODUCT	SUBSCRIPTIONS	SUBSIDISATIONS
SUBMULTIPLE	SUBORDINARY	SUBPRODUCTS	SUBSCRIPTIVE	SUBSIDISED
SUBMULTIPLES	SUBORDINATE	SUBPROFESSIONAL	SUBSCRIPTS	SUBSIDISER
SUBMUNITION	SUBORDINATED	SUBPROGRAM	SUBSECRETARIES	SUBSIDISERS
SUBMUNITIONS	SUBORDINATELY	SUBPROGRAMS	SUBSECRETARY	SUBSIDISES
				SUBSIDISING

SUBSIDIZABLE	SUBSTANTIALISMS	SUBSTITUTIONARY	SUBTERFUGES	SUBTOTALLING
SUBSIDIZATION	SUBSTANTIALIST	SUBSTITUTIONS	SUBTERMINAL	SUBTOTALLY
SUBSIDIZATIONS	SUBSTANTIALISTS	SUBSTITUTIVE	SUBTERNATURAL	SUBTRACTED
SUBSIDIZED	SUBSTANTIALITY	SUBSTITUTIVELY	SUBTERRAIN	SUBTRACTER
SUBSIDIZER	SUBSTANTIALIZE	SUBSTITUTIVITY	SUBTERRAINS	SUBTRACTERS
SUBSIDIZERS	SUBSTANTIALIZED	SUBSTRACTED	SUBTERRANE	SUBTRACTING
SUBSIDIZES	SUBSTANTIALIZES	SUBSTRACTING	SUBTERRANEAN	SUBTRACTION
SUBSIDIZING	SUBSTANTIALLY	SUBSTRACTION	SUBTERRANEANLY	SUBTRACTIONS
SUBSISTENCE	SUBSTANTIALNESS	SUBSTRACTIONS	SUBTERRANEANS	SUBTRACTIVE
SUBSISTENCES	SUBSTANTIALS	SUBSTRACTOR	SUBTERRANEOUS	SUBTRACTOR
SUBSISTENT	SUBSTANTIATE	SUBSTRACTORS	SUBTERRANEOUSLY	SUBTRACTORS
SUBSISTENTIAL	SUBSTANTIATED	SUBSTRACTS	SUBTERRANES	SUBTRAHEND
SUBSISTERS	SUBSTANTIATES	SUBSTRATAL	SUBTERRENE	SUBTRAHENDS
SUBSISTING	SUBSTANTIATING	SUBSTRATES	SUBTERRENES	SUBTREASURER
SUBSOCIALLY	SUBSTANTIATION	SUBSTRATIVE	SUBTERRESTRIAL	SUBTREASURERS
SUBSOCIETIES	SUBSTANTIATIONS	SUBSTRATOSPHERE	SUBTERRESTRIALS	SUBTREASURIES
SUBSOCIETY	SUBSTANTIATIVE	SUBSTRATUM	SUBTEXTUAL	SUBTREASURY
SUBSOILERS	SUBSTANTIATOR	SUBSTRATUMS	SUBTHERAPEUTIC	SUBTRIANGULAR
SUBSOILING	SUBSTANTIATORS	SUBSTRUCTED	SUBTHRESHOLD	SUBTRIPLICATE
SUBSOILINGS	SUBSTANTIVAL	SUBSTRUCTING	SUBTILENESS	SUBTROPICAL
SUBSONICALLY	SUBSTANTIVALLY	SUBSTRUCTION	SUBTILENESSES	SUBTROPICALLY
SUBSPECIALISE	SUBSTANTIVE	SUBSTRUCTIONS	SUBTILISATION	SUBTROPICS
SUBSPECIALISED	SUBSTANTIVELY	SUBSTRUCTS	SUBTILISATIONS	SUBTRUDING
SUBSPECIALISES	SUBSTANTIVENESS	SUBSTRUCTURAL	SUBTILISED	SUBTWEETED
SUBSPECIALISING	SUBSTANTIVES	SUBSTRUCTURE	SUBTILISER	SUBTWEETING
SUBSPECIALIST	SUBSTANTIVISE	SUBSTRUCTURES	SUBTILISERS	SUBTYPICAL
SUBSPECIALISTS	SUBSTANTIVISED	SUBSULTIVE	SUBTILISES	SUBUMBRELLA
SUBSPECIALITIES	SUBSTANTIVISES	SUBSULTORILY	SUBTILISIN	SUBUMBRELLAR
SUBSPECIALITY	SUBSTANTIVISING	SUBSULTORY	SUBTILISING	SUBUMBRELLAS
SUBSPECIALIZE	SUBSTANTIVITIES	SUBSULTUSES	SUBTILISINS	SUBUNGULATE
SUBSPECIALIZED	SUBSTANTIVITY	SUBSUMABLE	SUBTILITIES	SUBUNGULATES
SUBSPECIALIZES	SUBSTANTIVIZE	SUBSUMPTION	SUBTILIZATION	SUBURBANISATION
SUBSPECIALIZING	SUBSTANTIVIZED	SUBSUMPTIONS	SUBTILIZATIONS	SUBURBANISE
SUBSPECIALTIES	SUBSTANTIVIZES	SUBSUMPTIVE	SUBTILIZED	SUBURBANISED
SUBSPECIALTY	SUBSTANTIVIZING	SUBSURFACE	SUBTILIZER	SUBURBANISES
SUBSPECIES	SUBSTATION	SUBSURFACES	SUBTILIZERS	SUBURBANISING
SUBSPECIFIC	SUBSTATIONS	SUBSYSTEMS	SUBTILIZES	SUBURBANISM
SUBSPECIFICALLY	SUBSTELLAR	SUBTACKSMAN	SUBTILIZING	SUBURBANISMS
SUBSPINOUS	SUBSTERNAL	SUBTACKSMEN	SUBTILTIES	SUBURBANITE
SUBSPONTANEOUS	SUBSTITUENT	SUBTANGENT	SUBTITLING	SUBURBANITES
SUBSTANCELESS	SUBSTITUENTS	SUBTANGENTS	SUBTITLINGS	SUBURBANITIES
SUBSTANCES	SUBSTITUTABLE	SUBTEMPERATE	SUBTITULAR	SUBURBANITY
SUBSTANDARD	SUBSTITUTE	SUBTENANCIES	SUBTLENESS	SUBURBANIZATION
SUBSTANTIAL	SUBSTITUTED	SUBTENANCY	SUBTLENESSES	SUBURBANIZE
SUBSTANTIALISE	SUBSTITUTES	SUBTENANTS	SUBTLETIES	SUBURBANIZED
SUBSTANTIALISED	SUBSTITUTING	SUBTENDING	SUBTOTALED	SUBURBANIZES
SUBSTANTIALISES	SUBSTITUTION	SUBTENURES	SUBTOTALING	SUBURBANIZING
SUBSTANTIALISM	SUBSTITUTIONAL	SUBTERFUGE	SUBTOTALLED	SUBURBICARIAN

SUBVARIETIES

SUBVARIETIES
SUBVARIETY
SUBVASSALS
SUBVENTION
SUBVENTIONARY
SUBVENTIONS
SUBVERSALS
SUBVERSING
SUBVERSION
SUBVERSIONARIES
SUBVERSIONARY
SUBVERSIONS
SUBVERSIVE
SUBVERSIVELY
SUBVERSIVENESS
SUBVERSIVES
SUBVERTEBRAL
SUBVERTERS
SUBVERTICAL
SUBVERTING
SUBVIRUSES
SUBVISIBLE
SUBVITREOUS
SUBVOCALISATION
SUBVOCALISE
SUBVOCALISED
SUBVOCALISES
SUBVOCALISING
SUBVOCALIZATION
SUBVOCALIZE
SUBVOCALIZED
SUBVOCALIZES
SUBVOCALIZING
SUBVOCALLY
SUBWARDENS
SUBWOOFERS
SUBWRITERS
SUCCEDANEA
SUCCEDANEOUS
SUCCEDANEUM
SUCCEDANEUMS
SUCCEDENTS
SUCCEEDABLE
SUCCEEDERS
SUCCEEDING
SUCCEEDINGLY
SUCCENTORS
SUCCENTORSHIP

SUCCENTORSHIPS
SUCCESSANTLY
SUCCESSFUL
SUCCESSFULLY
SUCCESSFULNESS
SUCCESSION
SUCCESSIONAL
SUCCESSIONALLY
SUCCESSIONIST
SUCCESSIONISTS
SUCCESSIONLESS
SUCCESSIONS
SUCCESSIVE
SUCCESSIVELY
SUCCESSIVENESS
SUCCESSLESS
SUCCESSLESSLY
SUCCESSLESSNESS
SUCCESSORAL
SUCCESSORS
SUCCESSORSHIP
SUCCESSORSHIPS
SUCCINATES
SUCCINCTER
SUCCINCTEST
SUCCINCTLY
SUCCINCTNESS
SUCCINCTNESSES
SUCCINCTORIA
SUCCINCTORIES
SUCCINCTORIUM
SUCCINCTORIUMS
SUCCINCTORY
SUCCINITES
SUCCINYLCHOLINE
SUCCORABLE
SUCCORLESS
SUCCOTASHES
SUCCOURABLE
SUCCOURERS
SUCCOURING
SUCCOURLESS
SUCCUBUSES
SUCCULENCE
SUCCULENCES
SUCCULENCIES
SUCCULENCY
SUCCULENTLY

SUCCULENTS
SUCCUMBERS
SUCCUMBING
SUCCURSALE
SUCCURSALES
SUCCURSALS
SUCCUSSATION
SUCCUSSATIONS
SUCCUSSING
SUCCUSSION
SUCCUSSIONS
SUCCUSSIVE
SUCHNESSES
SUCKERFISH
SUCKERFISHES
SUCKFISHES
SUCKHOLING
SUCKINESSES
SUCRALFATE
SUCRALFATES
SUCRALOSES
SUCTIONING
SUCTORIANS
SUDATORIES
SUDATORIUM
SUDATORIUMS
SUDDENNESS
SUDDENNESSES
SUDDENTIES
SUDORIFEROUS
SUDORIFICS
SUDORIPAROUS
SUEABILITIES
SUEABILITY
SUFFERABLE
SUFFERABLENESS
SUFFERABLY
SUFFERANCE
SUFFERANCES
SUFFERINGLY
SUFFERINGS
SUFFICIENCE
SUFFICIENCES
SUFFICIENCIES
SUFFICIENCY
SUFFICIENT
SUFFICIENTLY
SUFFICIENTS

SUFFICINGNESS
SUFFICINGNESSES
SUFFIGANCE
SUFFIGANCES
SUFFISANCE
SUFFISANCES
SUFFIXATION
SUFFIXATIONS
SUFFIXIONS
SUFFLATING
SUFFLATION
SUFFLATIONS
SUFFOCATED
SUFFOCATES
SUFFOCATING
SUFFOCATINGLY
SUFFOCATINGS
SUFFOCATION
SUFFOCATIONS
SUFFOCATIVE
SUFFRAGANS
SUFFRAGANSHIP
SUFFRAGANSHIPS
SUFFRAGETTE
SUFFRAGETTES
SUFFRAGETTISM
SUFFRAGETTISMS
SUFFRAGISM
SUFFRAGISMS
SUFFRAGIST
SUFFRAGISTS
SUFFRUTESCENT
SUFFRUTICOSE
SUFFUMIGATE
SUFFUMIGATED
SUFFUMIGATES
SUFFUMIGATING
SUFFUMIGATION
SUFFUMIGATIONS
SUFFUSIONS
SUGARALLIE
SUGARALLIES
SUGARBERRIES
SUGARBERRY
SUGARBUSHES
SUGARCANES
SUGARCOATED
SUGARCOATING

SUGARCOATS
SUGARHOUSE
SUGARHOUSES
SUGARINESS
SUGARINESSES
SUGARLOAVES
SUGARPLUMS
SUGGESTERS
SUGGESTIBILITY
SUGGESTIBLE
SUGGESTIBLENESS
SUGGESTIBLY
SUGGESTING
SUGGESTION
SUGGESTIONISE
SUGGESTIONISED
SUGGESTIONISES
SUGGESTIONISING
SUGGESTIONISM
SUGGESTIONISMS
SUGGESTIONIST
SUGGESTIONISTS
SUGGESTIONIZE
SUGGESTIONIZED
SUGGESTIONIZES
SUGGESTIONIZING
SUGGESTIONS
SUGGESTIVE
SUGGESTIVELY
SUGGESTIVENESS
SUICIDALLY
SUICIDOLOGIES
SUICIDOLOGIST
SUICIDOLOGISTS
SUICIDOLOGY
SUITABILITIES
SUITABILITY
SUITABLENESS
SUITABLENESSES
SUITRESSES
SULCALISED
SULCALISES
SULCALISING
SULCALIZED
SULCALIZES
SULCALIZING
SULCATIONS
SULFACETAMIDE

SULFACETAMIDES	SULFURIZATION	SULPHURATED	SUMMARISATION	SUMPHISHNESS
SULFADIAZINE	SULFURIZATIONS	SULPHURATES	SUMMARISATIONS	SUMPHISHNESSES
SULFADIAZINES	SULFURIZED	SULPHURATING	SUMMARISED	SUMPSIMUSES
SULFADIMIDINE	SULFURIZES	SULPHURATION	SUMMARISER	SUMPTUOSITIES
SULFADIMIDINES	SULFURIZING	SULPHURATIONS	SUMMARISERS	SUMPTUOSITY
SULFADOXINE	SULFUROUSLY	SULPHURATOR	SUMMARISES	SUMPTUOUSLY
SULFADOXINES	SULFUROUSNESS	SULPHURATORS	SUMMARISING	SUMPTUOUSNESS
SULFAMETHAZINE	SULFUROUSNESSES	SULPHUREOUS	SUMMARISTS	SUMPTUOUSNESSES
SULFAMETHAZINES	SULKINESSES	SULPHUREOUSLY	SUMMARIZABLE	SUNBATHERS
SULFANILAMIDE	SULLENNESS	SULPHUREOUSNESS	SUMMARIZATION	SUNBATHING
SULFANILAMIDES	SULLENNESSES	SULPHURETED	SUMMARIZATIONS	SUNBATHINGS
SULFATASES	SULPHACETAMIDE	SULPHURETING	SUMMARIZED	SUNBEAMIER
SULFATHIAZOLE	SULPHACETAMIDES	SULPHURETS	SUMMARIZER	SUNBEAMIEST
SULFATHIAZOLES	SULPHADIAZINE	SULPHURETTED	SUMMARIZERS	SUNBERRIES
SULFATIONS	SULPHADIAZINES	SULPHURETTING	SUMMARIZES	SUNBONNETED
SULFHYDRYL	SULPHADOXINE	SULPHURIER	SUMMARIZING	SUNBONNETS
SULFHYDRYLS	SULPHADOXINES	SULPHURIEST	SUMMATIONAL	SUNBURNING
SULFINPYRAZONE	SULPHANILAMIDE	SULPHURING	SUMMATIONS	SUNDERABLE
SULFINPYRAZONES	SULPHANILAMIDES	SULPHURISATION	SUMMERHOUSE	SUNDERANCE
SULFONAMIDE	SULPHATASE	SULPHURISATIONS	SUMMERHOUSES	SUNDERANCES
SULFONAMIDES	SULPHATASES	SULPHURISE	SUMMERIEST	SUNDERINGS
SULFONATED	SULPHATHIAZOLE	SULPHURISED	SUMMERINESS	SUNDERMENT
SULFONATES	SULPHATHIAZOLES	SULPHURISES	SUMMERINESSES	SUNDERMENTS
SULFONATING	SULPHATING	SULPHURISING	SUMMERINGS	SUNDOWNERS
SULFONATION	SULPHATION	SULPHURIZATION	SUMMERLESS	SUNDOWNING
SULFONATIONS	SULPHATIONS	SULPHURIZATIONS	SUMMERLIER	SUNDRENCHED
SULFONIUMS	SULPHHYDRYL	SULPHURIZE	SUMMERLIEST	SUNDRESSES
SULFONMETHANE	SULPHHYDRYLS	SULPHURIZED	SUMMERLIKE	SUNFLOWERS
SULFONMETHANES	SULPHINPYRAZONE	SULPHURIZES	SUMMERLONG	SUNGAZINGS
SULFONYLUREA	SULPHINYLS	SULPHURIZING	SUMMERSAULT	SUNGLASSES
SULFONYLUREAS	SULPHONAMIDE	SULPHUROUS	SUMMERSAULTED	SUNLESSNESS
SULFOXIDES	SULPHONAMIDES	SULPHUROUSLY	SUMMERSAULTING	SUNLESSNESSES
SULFURATED	SULPHONATE	SULPHUROUSNESS	SUMMERSAULTS	SUNLOUNGER
SULFURATES	SULPHONATED	SULPHURWORT	SUMMERSETS	SUNLOUNGERS
SULFURATING	SULPHONATES	SULPHURWORTS	SUMMERSETTED	SUNNINESSES
SULFURATION	SULPHONATING	SULPHURYLS	SUMMERSETTING	SUNPORCHES
SULFURATIONS	SULPHONATION	SULTANATES	SUMMERTIDE	SUNRISINGS
SULFUREOUS	SULPHONATIONS	SULTANESSES	SUMMERTIDES	SUNSCREENING
SULFURETED	SULPHONIUM	SULTANSHIP	SUMMERTIME	SUNSCREENINGS
SULFURETING	SULPHONIUMS	SULTANSHIPS	SUMMERTIMES	SUNSCREENS
SULFURETTED	SULPHONMETHANE	SULTRINESS	SUMMERWEIGHT	SUNSEEKERS
SULFURETTING	SULPHONMETHANES	SULTRINESSES	SUMMERWOOD	SUNSETTING
SULFURIEST	SULPHONYLS	SUMBITCHES	SUMMERWOODS	SUNSETTINGS
SULFURISATION	SULPHONYLUREA	SUMMABILITIES	SUMMITEERS	SUNSHINIER
SULFURISATIONS	SULPHONYLUREAS	SUMMABILITY	SUMMITLESS	SUNSHINIEST
SULFURISED	SULPHOXIDE	SUMMARINESS	SUMMITRIES	SUNSPOTTED
SULFURISES	SULPHOXIDES	SUMMARINESSES	SUMMONABLE	SUNSTROKES
SULFURISING	SULPHURATE	SUMMARISABLE	SUMMONSING	SUNTANNING

SUNTANNINGS	SUPERATHLETE	SUPERCENTERS	SUPERCOOLED	SUPEREROGATORS
SUNWORSHIPPER	SUPERATHLETES	SUPERCHARGE	SUPERCOOLING	SUPEREROGATORY
SUNWORSHIPPERS	SUPERATING	SUPERCHARGED	SUPERCOOLS	SUPERESSENTIAL
SUOVETAURILIA	SUPERATION	SUPERCHARGER	SUPERCOVER	SUPERETTES
SUOVETAURILIAS	SUPERATIONS	SUPERCHARGERS	SUPERCOVERS	SUPEREVIDENT
SUPERABILITIES	SUPERATOMS	SUPERCHARGES	SUPERCRIMINAL	SUPEREXALT
SUPERABILITY	SUPERBANKS	SUPERCHARGING	SUPERCRIMINALS	SUPEREXALTATION
SUPERABLENESS	SUPERBAZAAR	SUPERCHERIE	SUPERCRITICAL	SUPEREXALTED
SUPERABLENESSES	SUPERBAZAARS	SUPERCHERIES	SUPERCURRENT	SUPEREXALTING
SUPERABOUND	SUPERBAZAR	SUPERCHURCH	SUPERCURRENTS	SUPEREXALTS
SUPERABOUNDED	SUPERBAZARS	SUPERCHURCHES	SUPERDAINTIER	SUPEREXCELLENCE
SUPERABOUNDING	SUPERBIKES	SUPERCILIARIES	SUPERDAINTIEST	SUPEREXCELLENT
SUPERABOUNDS	SUPERBITCH	SUPERCILIARY	SUPERDAINTY	SUPEREXPENSIVE
SUPERABSORBENT	SUPERBITCHES	SUPERCILIOUS	SUPERDELEGATE	SUPEREXPRESS
SUPERABSORBENTS	SUPERBITIES	SUPERCILIOUSLY	SUPERDELEGATES	SUPEREXPRESSES
SUPERABUNDANCE	SUPERBLOCK	SUPERCITIES	SUPERDELUXE	SUPERFAMILIES
SUPERABUNDANCES	SUPERBLOCKS	SUPERCIVILISED	SUPERDENSE	SUPERFAMILY
SUPERABUNDANT	SUPERBNESS	SUPERCIVILIZED	SUPERDIPLOMAT	SUPERFARMS
SUPERABUNDANTLY	SUPERBNESSES	SUPERCLASS	SUPERDIPLOMATS	SUPERFATTED
SUPERACHIEVER	SUPERBOARD	SUPERCLASSES	SUPERDOMINANT	SUPERFECTA
SUPERACHIEVERS	SUPERBOARDS	SUPERCLEAN	SUPERDOMINANTS	SUPERFECTAS
SUPERACTIVE	SUPERBOMBER	SUPERCLUBS	SUPEREFFECTIVE	SUPERFEMALE
SUPERACTIVITIES	SUPERBOMBERS	SUPERCLUSTER	SUPEREFFICIENCY	SUPERFEMALES
SUPERACTIVITY	SUPERBOMBS	SUPERCLUSTERS	SUPEREFFICIENT	SUPERFETATE
SUPERACUTE	SUPERBRAIN	SUPERCOILED	SUPEREGOIST	SUPERFETATED
SUPERADDED	SUPERBRAINS	SUPERCOILING	SUPEREGOISTS	SUPERFETATES
SUPERADDING	SUPERBRATS	SUPERCOILS	SUPERELASTIC	SUPERFETATING
SUPERADDITION	SUPERBRIGHT	SUPERCOLLIDER	SUPERELEVATE	SUPERFETATION
SUPERADDITIONAL	SUPERBUREAUCRAT	SUPERCOLLIDERS	SUPERELEVATED	SUPERFETATIONS
SUPERADDITIONS	SUPERCABINET	SUPERCOLOSSAL	SUPERELEVATES	SUPERFICIAL
SUPERAGENCIES	SUPERCABINETS	SUPERCOLUMNAR	SUPERELEVATING	SUPERFICIALISE
SUPERAGENCY	SUPERCALENDER	SUPERCOMPUTER	SUPERELEVATION	SUPERFICIALISED
SUPERAGENT	SUPERCALENDERED	SUPERCOMPUTERS	SUPERELEVATIONS	SUPERFICIALISES
SUPERAGENTS	SUPERCALENDERS	SUPERCOMPUTING	SUPERELITE	SUPERFICIALITY
SUPERALLOY	SUPERCARGO	SUPERCOMPUTINGS	SUPERELITES	SUPERFICIALIZE
SUPERALLOYS	SUPERCARGOES	SUPERCONDUCT	SUPEREMINENCE	SUPERFICIALIZED
SUPERALTAR	SUPERCARGOS	SUPERCONDUCTED	SUPEREMINENCES	SUPERFICIALIZES
SUPERALTARS	SUPERCARGOSHIP	SUPERCONDUCTING	SUPEREMINENT	SUPERFICIALLY
SUPERALTERN	SUPERCARGOSHIPS	SUPERCONDUCTION	SUPEREMINENTLY	SUPERFICIALNESS
SUPERALTERNS	SUPERCARRIER	SUPERCONDUCTIVE	SUPEREROGANT	SUPERFICIALS
SUPERAMBITIOUS	SUPERCARRIERS	SUPERCONDUCTOR	SUPEREROGATE	SUPERFICIES
SUPERANNUABLE	SUPERCAUTIOUS	SUPERCONDUCTORS	SUPEREROGATED	SUPERFINENESS
SUPERANNUATE	SUPERCEDED	SUPERCONDUCTS	SUPEREROGATES	SUPERFINENESSES
SUPERANNUATED	SUPERCEDES	SUPERCONFIDENCE	SUPEREROGATING	SUPERFIRMS
SUPERANNUATES	SUPERCEDING	SUPERCONFIDENT	SUPEREROGATION	SUPERFIXES
SUPERANNUATING	SUPERCELESTIAL	SUPERCONTINENT	SUPEREROGATIONS	SUPERFLACK
SUPERANNUATION	SUPERCELLS	SUPERCONTINENTS	SUPEREROGATIVE	SUPERFLACKS
SUPERANNUATIONS	SUPERCENTER	SUPERCONVENIENT	SUPEREROGATOR	SUPERFLUID

SUPERFLUIDITIES	SUPERHEAVY	SUPERINDUCTIONS	SUPERLUXURIES	SUPERNATURALISE
SUPERFLUIDITY	SUPERHELICAL	SUPERINFECT	SUPERLUXURIOUS	SUPERNATURALISM
SUPERFLUIDS	SUPERHELICES	SUPERINFECTED	SUPERLUXURY	SUPERNATURALIST
SUPERFLUITIES	SUPERHELIX	SUPERINFECTING	SUPERLYING	SUPERNATURALIZE
SUPERFLUITY	SUPERHELIXES	SUPERINFECTION	SUPERMACHO	SUPERNATURALLY
SUPERFLUOUS	SUPERHEROES	SUPERINFECTIONS	SUPERMAJORITIES	SUPERNATURALS
SUPERFLUOUSLY	SUPERHEROINE	SUPERINFECTS	SUPERMAJORITY	SUPERNATURE
SUPERFLUOUSNESS	SUPERHEROINES	SUPERINSULATED	SUPERMALES	SUPERNATURES
SUPERFLUXES	SUPERHETERODYNE	SUPERINTEND	SUPERMARKET	SUPERNORMAL
SUPERFOETATION	SUPERHIGHWAY	SUPERINTENDED	SUPERMARKETS	SUPERNORMALITY
SUPERFOETATIONS	SUPERHIGHWAYS	SUPERINTENDENCE	SUPERMARTS	SUPERNORMALLY
SUPERFOODS	SUPERHIVES	SUPERINTENDENCY	SUPERMASCULINE	SUPERNOVAE
SUPERFRONTAL	SUPERHUMAN	SUPERINTENDENT	SUPERMASSIVE	SUPERNOVAS
SUPERFRONTALS	SUPERHUMANISE	SUPERINTENDENTS	SUPERMAXES	SUPERNUMERARIES
SUPERFUNDS	SUPERHUMANISED	SUPERINTENDING	SUPERMEMBRANE	SUPERNUMERARY
SUPERFUSED	SUPERHUMANISES	SUPERINTENDS	SUPERMEMBRANES	SUPERNURSE
SUPERFUSES	SUPERHUMANISING	SUPERINTENSITY	SUPERMICRO	SUPERNURSES
SUPERFUSING	SUPERHUMANITIES	SUPERIORESS	SUPERMICROS	SUPERNUTRIENT
SUPERFUSION	SUPERHUMANITY	SUPERIORESSES	SUPERMILITANT	SUPERNUTRIENTS
SUPERFUSIONS	SUPERHUMANIZE	SUPERIORITIES	SUPERMILITANTS	SUPERNUTRITION
SUPERGENES	SUPERHUMANIZED	SUPERIORITY	SUPERMINDS	SUPERNUTRITIONS
SUPERGIANT	SUPERHUMANIZES	SUPERIORLY	SUPERMINIS	SUPEROCTAVE
SUPERGIANTS	SUPERHUMANIZING	SUPERIORSHIP	SUPERMINISTER	SUPEROCTAVES
SUPERGLACIAL	SUPERHUMANLY	SUPERIORSHIPS	SUPERMINISTERS	SUPERORDER
SUPERGLUED	SUPERHUMANNESS	SUPERJACENT	SUPERMODEL	SUPERORDERS
SUPERGLUEING	SUPERHUMANS	SUPERJOCKS	SUPERMODELS	SUPERORDINAL
SUPERGLUES	SUPERHUMERAL	SUPERJUMBO	SUPERMODERN	SUPERORDINARY
SUPERGLUING	SUPERHUMERALS	SUPERJUMBOS	SUPERMOONS	SUPERORDINATE
SUPERGOVERNMENT	SUPERHYPED	SUPERKINGDOM	SUPERMOTOS	SUPERORDINATED
SUPERGRAPHICS	SUPERHYPES	SUPERKINGDOMS	SUPERMUNDANE	SUPERORDINATES
SUPERGRASS	SUPERHYPING	SUPERLARGE	SUPERNACULA	SUPERORDINATING
SUPERGRASSES	SUPERIMPORTANT	SUPERLATIVE	SUPERNACULAR	SUPERORDINATION
SUPERGRAVITIES	SUPERIMPOSABLE	SUPERLATIVELY	SUPERNACULUM	SUPERORGANIC
SUPERGRAVITY	SUPERIMPOSE	SUPERLATIVENESS	SUPERNALLY	SUPERORGANICISM
SUPERGROUP	SUPERIMPOSED	SUPERLATIVES	SUPERNANNIES	SUPERORGANICIST
SUPERGROUPS	SUPERIMPOSES	SUPERLAWYER	SUPERNANNY	SUPERORGANISM
SUPERGROWTH	SUPERIMPOSING	SUPERLAWYERS	SUPERNATANT	SUPERORGANISMS
SUPERGROWTHS	SUPERIMPOSITION	SUPERLIGHT	SUPERNATANTS	SUPERORGASM
SUPERHARDEN	SUPERINCUMBENCE	SUPERLINER	SUPERNATATION	SUPERORGASMS
SUPERHARDENED	SUPERINCUMBENCY	SUPERLINERS	SUPERNATATIONS	SUPEROVULATE
SUPERHARDENING	SUPERINCUMBENT	SUPERLOADS	SUPERNATED	SUPEROVULATED
SUPERHARDENS	SUPERINDIVIDUAL	SUPERLOBBYIST	SUPERNATES	SUPEROVULATES
SUPERHEATED	SUPERINDUCE	SUPERLOBBYISTS	SUPERNATING	SUPEROVULATING
SUPERHEATER	SUPERINDUCED	SUPERLOYALIST	SUPERNATION	SUPEROVULATION
SUPERHEATERS	SUPERINDUCEMENT	SUPERLOYALISTS	SUPERNATIONAL	SUPEROVULATIONS
SUPERHEATING	SUPERINDUCES	SUPERLUMINAL	SUPERNATIONALLY	SUPEROXIDE
SUPERHEATS	SUPERINDUCING	SUPERLUNAR	SUPERNATIONS	SUPEROXIDES
SUPERHEAVIES	SUPERINDUCTION	SUPERLUNARY	SUPERNATURAL	SUPERPARASITISM

S

SUPERPARTICLE	SUPERPROFIT	SUPERSECRECY	SUPERSPECIALIST	SUPERSTUDS
SUPERPARTICLES	SUPERPROFITS	SUPERSECRET	SUPERSPECIALS	SUPERSUBTILE
SUPERPATRIOT	SUPERQUALITIES	SUPERSECRETS	SUPERSPECIES	SUPERSUBTLE
SUPERPATRIOTIC	SUPERQUALITY	SUPERSEDABLE	SUPERSPECTACLE	SUPERSUBTLETIES
SUPERPATRIOTISM	SUPERRACES	SUPERSEDEAS	SUPERSPECTACLES	SUPERSUBTLETY
SUPERPATRIOTS	SUPERREALISM	SUPERSEDEASES	SUPERSPEED	SUPERSURGEON
SUPERPEOPLE	SUPERREALISMS	SUPERSEDED	SUPERSPEEDS	SUPERSURGEONS
SUPERPERSON	SUPERREALIST	SUPERSEDENCE	SUPERSPIES	SUPERSWEET
SUPERPERSONAL	SUPERREALISTS	SUPERSEDENCES	SUPERSTARDOM	SUPERSYMMETRIC
SUPERPERSONS	SUPERREFINE	SUPERSEDER	SUPERSTARDOMS	SUPERSYMMETRIES
SUPERPHENOMENA	SUPERREFINED	SUPERSEDERE	SUPERSTARS	SUPERSYMMETRY
SUPERPHENOMENON	SUPERREFINES	SUPERSEDERES	SUPERSTATE	SUPERSYSTEM
SUPERPHONE	SUPERREFINING	SUPERSEDERS	SUPERSTATES	SUPERSYSTEMS
SUPERPHONES	SUPERREGIONAL	SUPERSEDES	SUPERSTATION	SUPERTANKER
SUPERPHOSPHATE	SUPERREGIONALS	SUPERSEDING	SUPERSTATIONS	SUPERTANKERS
SUPERPHOSPHATES	SUPERROADS	SUPERSEDURE	SUPERSTIMULATE	SUPERTAXES
SUPERPHYLA	SUPERROMANTIC	SUPERSEDURES	SUPERSTIMULATED	SUPERTEACHER
SUPERPHYLUM	SUPERSAFETIES	SUPERSELLER	SUPERSTIMULATES	SUPERTEACHERS
SUPERPHYSICAL	SUPERSAFETY	SUPERSELLERS	SUPERSTITION	SUPERTERRANEAN
SUPERPIMPS	SUPERSALES	SUPERSELLING	SUPERSTITIONS	SUPERTERRIFIC
SUPERPLANE	SUPERSALESMAN	SUPERSELLS	SUPERSTITIOUS	SUPERTHICK
SUPERPLANES	SUPERSALESMEN	SUPERSENSIBLE	SUPERSTITIOUSLY	SUPERTHRILLER
SUPERPLASTIC	SUPERSALTS	SUPERSENSIBLY	SUPERSTOCK	SUPERTHRILLERS
SUPERPLASTICITY	SUPERSATURATE	SUPERSENSITIVE	SUPERSTOCKS	SUPERTIGHT
SUPERPLASTICS	SUPERSATURATED	SUPERSENSORY	SUPERSTORE	SUPERTITLE
SUPERPLAYER	SUPERSATURATES	SUPERSENSUAL	SUPERSTORES	SUPERTITLES
SUPERPLAYERS	SUPERSATURATING	SUPERSESSION	SUPERSTORM	SUPERTONIC
SUPERPLUSES	SUPERSATURATION	SUPERSESSIONS	SUPERSTORMS	SUPERTONICS
SUPERPOLITE	SUPERSAURS	SUPERSEXES	SUPERSTRATA	SUPERTRAMS
SUPERPOLYMER	SUPERSAVER	SUPERSEXUALITY	SUPERSTRATUM	SUPERTRUCK
SUPERPOLYMERS	SUPERSAVERS	SUPERSHARP	SUPERSTRATUMS	SUPERTRUCKS
SUPERPORTS	SUPERSCALAR	SUPERSHOWS	SUPERSTRENGTH	SUPERTWIST
SUPERPOSABLE	SUPERSCALE	SUPERSINGER	SUPERSTRENGTHS	SUPERTWISTS
SUPERPOSED	SUPERSCHOOL	SUPERSINGERS	SUPERSTRIKE	SUPERUSERS
SUPERPOSES	SUPERSCHOOLS	SUPERSIZED	SUPERSTRIKES	SUPERVENED
SUPERPOSING	SUPERSCOUT	SUPERSIZES	SUPERSTRING	SUPERVENES
SUPERPOSITION	SUPERSCOUTS	SUPERSIZING	SUPERSTRINGS	SUPERVENIENCE
SUPERPOSITIONS	SUPERSCREEN	SUPERSLEUTH	SUPERSTRONG	SUPERVENIENCES
SUPERPOWER	SUPERSCREENS	SUPERSLEUTHS	SUPERSTRUCT	SUPERVENIENT
SUPERPOWERED	SUPERSCRIBE	SUPERSLICK	SUPERSTRUCTED	SUPERVENING
SUPERPOWERFUL	SUPERSCRIBED	SUPERSMART	SUPERSTRUCTING	SUPERVENTION
SUPERPOWERS	SUPERSCRIBES	SUPERSMOOTH	SUPERSTRUCTION	SUPERVENTIONS
SUPERPRAISE	SUPERSCRIBING	SUPERSONIC	SUPERSTRUCTIONS	SUPERVIRILE
SUPERPRAISED	SUPERSCRIPT	SUPERSONICALLY	SUPERSTRUCTIVE	SUPERVIRTUOSI
SUPERPRAISES	SUPERSCRIPTION	SUPERSONICS	SUPERSTRUCTS	SUPERVIRTUOSO
SUPERPRAISING	SUPERSCRIPTIONS	SUPERSOUND	SUPERSTRUCTURAL	SUPERVIRTUOSOS
SUPERPREMIUM	SUPERSCRIPTS	SUPERSOUNDS	SUPERSTRUCTURE	SUPERVIRULENT
SUPERPREMIUMS	SUPERSECRECIES	SUPERSPECIAL	SUPERSTRUCTURES	SUPERVISAL

SUPERVISALS	SUPPLEMENTARILY	SUPPORTLESS	SUPRACHIASMIC	SURCHARGEMENT
SUPERVISED	SUPPLEMENTARY	SUPPORTMENT	SUPRACHOROIDAL	SURCHARGEMENTS
SUPERVISEE	SUPPLEMENTATION	SUPPORTMENTS	SUPRACILIARY	SURCHARGER
SUPERVISEES	SUPPLEMENTED	SUPPORTRESS	SUPRACOSTAL	SURCHARGERS
SUPERVISES	SUPPLEMENTER	SUPPORTRESSES	SUPRACRUSTAL	SURCHARGES
SUPERVISING	SUPPLEMENTERS	SUPPORTURE	SUPRAGLOTTAL	SURCHARGING
SUPERVISION	SUPPLEMENTING	SUPPORTURES	SUPRALAPSARIAN	SURCINGLED
SUPERVISIONS	SUPPLEMENTS	SUPPOSABLE	SUPRALAPSARIANS	SURCINGLES
SUPERVISOR	SUPPLENESS	SUPPOSABLY	SUPRALIMINAL	SURCINGLING
SUPERVISORS	SUPPLENESSES	SUPPOSEDLY	SUPRALIMINALLY	SURCULUSES
SUPERVISORSHIP	SUPPLETION	SUPPOSINGS	SUPRALUNAR	SUREFOOTED
SUPERVISORSHIPS	SUPPLETIONS	SUPPOSITION	SUPRAMAXILLARY	SUREFOOTEDLY
SUPERVISORY	SUPPLETIVE	SUPPOSITIONAL	SUPRAMOLECULAR	SUREFOOTEDNESS
SUPERVOLUTE	SUPPLETIVES	SUPPOSITIONALLY	SUPRAMOLECULE	SURENESSES
SUPERWAIFS	SUPPLETORILY	SUPPOSITIONARY	SUPRAMOLECULES	SURETYSHIP
SUPERWAVES	SUPPLETORY	SUPPOSITIONLESS	SUPRAMUNDANE	SURETYSHIPS
SUPERWEAPON	SUPPLIABLE	SUPPOSITIONS	SUPRANATIONAL	SURFACELESS
SUPERWEAPONS	SUPPLIANCE	SUPPOSITIOUS	SUPRANATIONALLY	SURFACEMAN
SUPERWEEDS	SUPPLIANCES	SUPPOSITIOUSLY	SUPRAOPTIC	SURFACEMEN
SUPERWIDES	SUPPLIANTLY	SUPPOSITITIOUS	SUPRAORBITAL	SURFACINGS
SUPERWIVES	SUPPLIANTS	SUPPOSITIVE	SUPRAPUBIC	SURFACTANT
SUPERWOMAN	SUPPLICANT	SUPPOSITIVELY	SUPRARATIONAL	SURFACTANTS
SUPERWOMEN	SUPPLICANTS	SUPPOSITIVES	SUPRARENAL	SURFBOARDED
SUPINATING	SUPPLICATE	SUPPOSITORIES	SUPRARENALS	SURFBOARDER
SUPINATION	SUPPLICATED	SUPPOSITORY	SUPRASEGMENTAL	SURFBOARDERS
SUPINATIONS	SUPPLICATES	SUPPRESSANT	SUPRASENSIBLE	SURFBOARDING
SUPINATORS	SUPPLICATING	SUPPRESSANTS	SUPRATEMPORAL	SURFBOARDINGS
SUPINENESS	SUPPLICATINGLY	SUPPRESSED	SUPRAVITAL	SURFBOARDS
SUPINENESSES	SUPPLICATION	SUPPRESSEDLY	SUPRAVITALLY	SURFCASTER
SUPPEAGOES	SUPPLICATIONS	SUPPRESSER	SUPREMACIES	SURFCASTERS
SUPPEDANEA	SUPPLICATORY	SUPPRESSERS	SUPREMACISM	SURFCASTING
SUPPEDANEUM	SUPPLICATS	SUPPRESSES	SUPREMACISMS	SURFCASTINGS
SUPPERLESS	SUPPLICAVIT	SUPPRESSIBILITY	SUPREMACIST	SURFEITERS
SUPPERTIME	SUPPLICAVITS	SUPPRESSIBLE	SUPREMACISTS	SURFEITING
SUPPERTIMES	SUPPLYMENT	SUPPRESSING	SUPREMATISM	SURFEITINGS
SUPPLANTATION	SUPPLYMENTS	SUPPRESSION	SUPREMATISMS	SURFFISHES
SUPPLANTATIONS	SUPPORTABILITY	SUPPRESSIONS	SUPREMATIST	SURFPERCHES
SUPPLANTED	SUPPORTABLE	SUPPRESSIVE	SUPREMATISTS	SURFRIDDEN
SUPPLANTER	SUPPORTABLENESS	SUPPRESSIVENESS	SUPREMENESS	SURFRIDERS
SUPPLANTERS	SUPPORTABLY	SUPPRESSOR	SUPREMENESSES	SURFRIDING
SUPPLANTING	SUPPORTANCE	SUPPRESSORS	SUPREMITIES	SURFRIDINGS
SUPPLEJACK	SUPPORTANCES	SUPPURATED	SURADDITION	SURGEONCIES
SUPPLEJACKS	SUPPORTERS	SUPPURATES	SURADDITIONS	SURGEONFISH
SUPPLEMENT	SUPPORTING	SUPPURATING	SURBASEMENT	SURGEONFISHES
SUPPLEMENTAL	SUPPORTINGS	SUPPURATION	SURBASEMENTS	SURGEONSHIP
SUPPLEMENTALLY	SUPPORTIVE	SUPPURATIONS	SURBEDDING	SURGEONSHIPS
SUPPLEMENTALS	SUPPORTIVELY	SUPPURATIVE	SURCEASING	SURGICALLY
SUPPLEMENTARIES	SUPPORTIVENESS	SUPPURATIVES	SURCHARGED	SURJECTION

SURJECTIONS

SURJECTIONS	SURREBUTTERS	SURVEYORSHIP	SUSPENSELESS	SUSTENTATED
SURJECTIVE	SURREBUTTING	SURVEYORSHIPS	SUSPENSERS	SUSTENTATES
SURLINESSES	SURREJOINDER	SURVIEWING	SUSPENSIBILITY	SUSTENTATING
SURMASTERS	SURREJOINDERS	SURVIVABILITIES	SUSPENSIBLE	SUSTENTATION
SURMISABLE	SURREJOINED	SURVIVABILITY	SUSPENSION	SUSTENTATIONS
SURMISINGS	SURREJOINING	SURVIVABLE	SUSPENSIONS	SUSTENTATIVE
SURMISTRESS	SURREJOINS	SURVIVALISM	SUSPENSIVE	SUSTENTATOR
SURMISTRESSES	SURRENDERED	SURVIVALISMS	SUSPENSIVELY	SUSTENTATORS
SURMOUNTABLE	SURRENDEREE	SURVIVALIST	SUSPENSIVENESS	SUSTENTION
SURMOUNTED	SURRENDEREES	SURVIVALISTS	SUSPENSOID	SUSTENTIONS
SURMOUNTER	SURRENDERER	SURVIVANCE	SUSPENSOIDS	SUSTENTIVE
SURMOUNTERS	SURRENDERERS	SURVIVANCES	SUSPENSORIA	SUSURRATED
SURMOUNTING	SURRENDERING	SURVIVORSHIP	SUSPENSORIAL	SUSURRATES
SURMOUNTINGS	SURRENDEROR	SURVIVORSHIPS	SUSPENSORIES	SUSURRATING
SURMULLETS	SURRENDERORS	SUSCEPTANCE	SUSPENSORIUM	SUSURRATION
SURNOMINAL	SURRENDERS	SUSCEPTANCES	SUSPENSORS	SUSURRATIONS
SURPASSABLE	SURRENDRIES	SUSCEPTIBILITY	SUSPENSORY	SUSURRUSES
SURPASSERS	SURREPTITIOUS	SUSCEPTIBLE	SUSPERCOLLATE	SUTLERSHIP
SURPASSING	SURREPTITIOUSLY	SUSCEPTIBLENESS	SUSPERCOLLATED	SUTLERSHIPS
SURPASSINGLY	SURROGACIES	SUSCEPTIBLY	SUSPERCOLLATES	SUTTEEISMS
SURPASSINGNESS	SURROGATED	SUSCEPTIVE	SUSPERCOLLATING	SUTTLETIES
SURPLUSAGE	SURROGATES	SUSCEPTIVENESS	SUSPICIONAL	SUTURATION
SURPLUSAGES	SURROGATESHIP	SUSCEPTIVITIES	SUSPICIONED	SUTURATIONS
SURPLUSING	SURROGATESHIPS	SUSCEPTIVITY	SUSPICIONING	SUZERAINTIES
SURPLUSSED	SURROGATING	SUSCEPTORS	SUSPICIONLESS	SUZERAINTY
SURPLUSSES	SURROGATION	SUSCIPIENT	SUSPICIONS	SVARABHAKTI
SURPLUSSING	SURROGATIONS	SUSCIPIENTS	SUSPICIOUS	SVARABHAKTIS
SURPRINTED	SURROGATUM	SUSCITATED	SUSPICIOUSLY	SVELTENESS
SURPRINTING	SURROGATUMS	SUSCITATES	SUSPICIOUSNESS	SVELTENESSES
SURPRISALS	SURROUNDED	SUSCITATING	SUSPIRATION	SWAGGERERS
SURPRISEDLY	SURROUNDING	SUSCITATION	SUSPIRATIONS	SWAGGERING
SURPRISERS	SURROUNDINGS	SUSCITATIONS	SUSPIRIOUS	SWAGGERINGLY
SURPRISING	SURTARBRAND	SUSPECTABLE	SUSTAINABILITY	SWAGGERINGS
SURPRISINGLY	SURTARBRANDS	SUSPECTEDLY	SUSTAINABLE	SWAINISHNESS
SURPRISINGNESS	SURTURBRAND	SUSPECTEDNESS	SUSTAINABLY	SWAINISHNESSES
SURPRISINGS	SURTURBRANDS	SUSPECTEDNESSES	SUSTAINEDLY	SWALLOWABLE
SURPRIZING	SURVEILING	SUSPECTERS	SUSTAINERS	SWALLOWERS
SURQUEDIES	SURVEILLANCE	SUSPECTFUL	SUSTAINING	SWALLOWING
SURQUEDRIES	SURVEILLANCES	SUSPECTING	SUSTAININGLY	SWALLOWTAIL
SURREALISM	SURVEILLANT	SUSPECTLESS	SUSTAININGS	SWALLOWTAILS
SURREALISMS	SURVEILLANTS	SUSPENDERED	SUSTAINMENT	SWALLOWWORT
SURREALIST	SURVEILLED	SUSPENDERS	SUSTAINMENTS	SWALLOWWORTS
SURREALISTIC	SURVEILLES	SUSPENDIBILITY	SUSTENANCE	SWAMPINESS
SURREALISTS	SURVEILLING	SUSPENDIBLE	SUSTENANCES	SWAMPINESSES
SURREBUTTAL	SURVEYABLE	SUSPENDING	SUSTENTACULA	SWAMPLANDS
SURREBUTTALS	SURVEYANCE	SUSPENSEFUL	SUSTENTACULAR	SWANKINESS
SURREBUTTED	SURVEYANCES	SUSPENSEFULLY	SUSTENTACULUM	SWANKINESSES
SURREBUTTER	SURVEYINGS	SUSPENSEFULNESS	SUSTENTATE	SWANNERIES

SWANSDOWNS	SWEETENINGS	SWINGINGEST	SWORDCRAFTS	SYLLABICATED
SWARAJISMS	SWEETFISHES	SWINGINGLY	SWORDFERNS	SYLLABICATES
SWARAJISTS	SWEETHEART	SWINGLETREE	SWORDFISHES	SYLLABICATING
SWARTHIEST	SWEETHEARTED	SWINGLETREES	SWORDPLAYER	SYLLABICATION
SWARTHINESS	SWEETHEARTING	SWINGLINGS	SWORDPLAYERS	SYLLABICATIONS
SWARTHINESSES	SWEETHEARTINGS	SWINGOMETER	SWORDPLAYS	SYLLABICITIES
SWARTHNESS	SWEETHEARTS	SWINGOMETERS	SWORDPROOF	SYLLABICITY
SWARTHNESSES	SWEETIEWIFE	SWINGTREES	SWORDSMANSHIP	SYLLABIFICATION
SWARTNESSES	SWEETIEWIVES	SWINISHNESS	SWORDSMANSHIPS	SYLLABIFIED
SWASHBUCKLE	SWEETISHLY	SWINISHNESSES	SWORDSTICK	SYLLABIFIES
SWASHBUCKLED	SWEETISHNESS	SWIRLINGLY	SWORDSTICKS	SYLLABIFYING
SWASHBUCKLER	SWEETISHNESSES	SWISHINGLY	SWORDSWOMAN	SYLLABISED
SWASHBUCKLERS	SWEETMEATS	SWITCHABLE	SWORDSWOMEN	SYLLABISES
SWASHBUCKLES	SWEETNESSES	SWITCHBACK	SWORDTAILS	SYLLABISING
SWASHBUCKLING	SWEETSHOPS	SWITCHBACKED	SYBARITICAL	SYLLABISMS
SWASHWORKS	SWEETVELDS	SWITCHBACKING	SYBARITICALLY	SYLLABIZED
SWATCHBOOK	SWEETWATER	SWITCHBACKS	SYBARITISH	SYLLABIZES
SWATCHBOOKS	SWEETWATERS	SWITCHBLADE	SYBARITISM	SYLLABIZING
SWATHEABLE	SWEETWOODS	SWITCHBLADES	SYBARITISMS	SYLLABLING
SWATTERING	SWEIRNESSES	SWITCHBOARD	SYCOPHANCIES	SYLLABOGRAM
SWAYBACKED	SWELLFISHES	SWITCHBOARDS	SYCOPHANCY	SYLLABOGRAMS
SWEARWORDS	SWELLHEADED	SWITCHEROO	SYCOPHANTIC	SYLLABOGRAPHIES
SWEATBANDS	SWELLHEADEDNESS	SWITCHEROOS	SYCOPHANTICAL	SYLLABOGRAPHY
SWEATBOXES	SWELLHEADS	SWITCHGEAR	SYCOPHANTICALLY	SYLLABUSES
SWEATERDRESS	SWELLINGLY	SWITCHGEARS	SYCOPHANTISE	SYLLEPTICAL
SWEATERDRESSES	SWELTERING	SWITCHGIRL	SYCOPHANTISED	SYLLEPTICALLY
SWEATINESS	SWELTERINGLY	SWITCHGIRLS	SYCOPHANTISES	SYLLOGISATION
SWEATINESSES	SWELTERINGS	SWITCHGRASS	SYCOPHANTISH	SYLLOGISATIONS
SWEATPANTS	SWELTRIEST	SWITCHGRASSES	SYCOPHANTISHLY	SYLLOGISED
SWEATSHIRT	SWEPTWINGS	SWITCHIEST	SYCOPHANTISING	SYLLOGISER
SWEATSHIRTS	SWERVELESS	SWITCHINGS	SYCOPHANTISM	SYLLOGISERS
SWEATSHOPS	SWIFTNESSES	SWITCHLIKE	SYCOPHANTISMS	SYLLOGISES
SWEATSUITS	SWIMFEEDER	SWITCHOVER	SYCOPHANTIZE	SYLLOGISING
SWEEPBACKS	SWIMFEEDERS	SWITCHOVERS	SYCOPHANTIZED	SYLLOGISMS
SWEEPINGLY	SWIMMERETS	SWITCHYARD	SYCOPHANTIZES	SYLLOGISTIC
SWEEPINGNESS	SWIMMINGLY	SWITCHYARDS	SYCOPHANTIZING	SYLLOGISTICAL
SWEEPINGNESSES	SWIMMINGNESS	SWITHERING	SYCOPHANTLIER	SYLLOGISTICALLY
SWEEPSTAKE	SWIMMINGNESSES	SWIVELBLOCK	SYCOPHANTLIEST	SYLLOGISTICS
SWEEPSTAKES	SWINDLINGS	SWIVELBLOCKS	SYCOPHANTLY	SYLLOGISTS
SWEETBREAD	SWINEHERDS	SWIVELLING	SYCOPHANTRIES	SYLLOGIZATION
SWEETBREADS	SWINEHOODS	SWOLLENNESS	SYCOPHANTRY	SYLLOGIZATIONS
SWEETBRIAR	SWINEPOXES	SWOLLENNESSES	SYCOPHANTS	SYLLOGIZED
SWEETBRIARS	SWINESTONE	SWOONINGLY	SYLLABARIA	SYLLOGIZER
SWEETBRIER	SWINESTONES	SWOOPSTAKE	SYLLABARIES	SYLLOGIZERS
SWEETBRIERS	SWINGBEATS	SWORDBEARER	SYLLABARIUM	SYLLOGIZES
SWEETCORNS	SWINGBOATS	SWORDBEARERS	SYLLABICAL	SYLLOGIZING
SWEETENERS	SWINGEINGLY	SWORDBILLS	SYLLABICALLY	SYLPHIDINE
SWEETENING	SWINGINGER	SWORDCRAFT	SYLLABICATE	SYLVANITES

S

SYLVESTRAL	SYMMETRIAN	SYMPHILIES	SYNADELPHITES	SYNCHROMESH
SYLVESTRIAN	SYMMETRIANS	SYMPHILISM	SYNAERESES	SYNCHROMESHES
SYLVICULTURAL	SYMMETRICAL	SYMPHILISMS	SYNAERESIS	SYNCHRONAL
SYLVICULTURE	SYMMETRICALLY	SYMPHILOUS	SYNAESTHESES	SYNCHRONEITIES
SYLVICULTURES	SYMMETRICALNESS	SYMPHONICALLY	SYNAESTHESIA	SYNCHRONEITY
SYLVINITES	SYMMETRIES	SYMPHONIES	SYNAESTHESIAS	SYNCHRONIC
SYMBIONTIC	SYMMETRISATION	SYMPHONION	SYNAESTHESIS	SYNCHRONICAL
SYMBIONTICALLY	SYMMETRISATIONS	SYMPHONIONS	SYNAESTHETIC	SYNCHRONICALLY
SYMBIOTICAL	SYMMETRISE	SYMPHONIOUS	SYNAGOGICAL	SYNCHRONICITIES
SYMBIOTICALLY	SYMMETRISED	SYMPHONIOUSLY	SYNAGOGUES	SYNCHRONICITY
SYMBOLICAL	SYMMETRISES	SYMPHONIST	SYNALEPHAS	SYNCHRONIES
SYMBOLICALLY	SYMMETRISING	SYMPHONISTS	SYNALLAGMATIC	SYNCHRONISATION
SYMBOLICALNESS	SYMMETRIZATION	SYMPHYLOUS	SYNALOEPHA	SYNCHRONISE
SYMBOLISATION	SYMMETRIZATIONS	SYMPHYSEAL	SYNALOEPHAS	SYNCHRONISED
SYMBOLISATIONS	SYMMETRIZE	SYMPHYSEOTOMIES	SYNANDRIUM	SYNCHRONISER
SYMBOLISED	SYMMETRIZED	SYMPHYSEOTOMY	SYNANDROUS	SYNCHRONISERS
SYMBOLISER	SYMMETRIZES	SYMPHYSIAL	SYNANTHEROUS	SYNCHRONISES
SYMBOLISERS	SYMMETRIZING	SYMPHYSIOTOMIES	SYNANTHESES	SYNCHRONISING
SYMBOLISES	SYMMETROPHOBIA	SYMPHYSIOTOMY	SYNANTHESIS	SYNCHRONISM
SYMBOLISING	SYMMETROPHOBIAS	SYMPHYSTIC	SYNANTHETIC	SYNCHRONISMS
SYMBOLISMS	SYMPATHECTOMIES	SYMPIESOMETER	SYNANTHIES	SYNCHRONISTIC
SYMBOLISTIC	SYMPATHECTOMY	SYMPIESOMETERS	SYNANTHOUS	SYNCHRONISTICAL
SYMBOLISTICAL	SYMPATHETIC	SYMPLASTIC	SYNAPHEIAS	SYNCHRONIZATION
SYMBOLISTICALLY	SYMPATHETICAL	SYMPODIALLY	SYNAPOSEMATIC	SYNCHRONIZE
SYMBOLISTS	SYMPATHETICALLY	SYMPOSIACS	SYNAPOSEMATISM	SYNCHRONIZED
SYMBOLIZATION	SYMPATHETICS	SYMPOSIARCH	SYNAPOSEMATISMS	SYNCHRONIZER
SYMBOLIZATIONS	SYMPATHIES	SYMPOSIARCHS	SYNAPTASES	SYNCHRONIZERS
SYMBOLIZED	SYMPATHINS	SYMPOSIAST	SYNAPTICAL	SYNCHRONIZES
SYMBOLIZER	SYMPATHIQUE	SYMPOSIASTS	SYNAPTICALLY	SYNCHRONIZING
SYMBOLIZERS	SYMPATHISE	SYMPOSIUMS	SYNAPTOSOMAL	SYNCHRONOLOGIES
SYMBOLIZES	SYMPATHISED	SYMPTOMATIC	SYNAPTOSOME	SYNCHRONOLOGY
SYMBOLIZING	SYMPATHISER	SYMPTOMATICAL	SYNAPTOSOMES	SYNCHRONOSCOPE
SYMBOLLING	SYMPATHISERS	SYMPTOMATICALLY	SYNARCHIES	SYNCHRONOSCOPES
SYMBOLOGICAL	SYMPATHISES	SYMPTOMATISE	SYNARTHRODIAL	SYNCHRONOUS
SYMBOLOGIES	SYMPATHISING	SYMPTOMATISED	SYNARTHRODIALLY	SYNCHRONOUSLY
SYMBOLOGIST	SYMPATHIZE	SYMPTOMATISES	SYNARTHROSES	SYNCHRONOUSNESS
SYMBOLOGISTS	SYMPATHIZED	SYMPTOMATISING	SYNARTHROSIS	SYNCHROSCOPE
SYMBOLOGRAPHIES	SYMPATHIZER	SYMPTOMATIZE	SYNASTRIES	SYNCHROSCOPES
SYMBOLOGRAPHY	SYMPATHIZERS	SYMPTOMATIZED	SYNAXARION	SYNCHROTRON
SYMBOLOLATRIES	SYMPATHIZES	SYMPTOMATIZES	SYNBIOTICS	SYNCHROTRONS
SYMBOLOLATRY	SYMPATHIZING	SYMPTOMATIZING	SYNCARPIES	SYNCLASTIC
SYMBOLOLOGIES	SYMPATHOLYTIC	SYMPTOMATOLOGIC	SYNCARPOUS	SYNCLINALS
SYMBOLOLOGY	SYMPATHOLYTICS	SYMPTOMATOLOGY	SYNCHONDROSES	SYNCLINORIA
SYMMETALISM	SYMPATHOMIMETIC	SYMPTOMLESS	SYNCHONDROSIS	SYNCLINORIUM
SYMMETALISMS	SYMPATRICALLY	SYMPTOMOLOGICAL	SYNCHORESES	SYNCOPATED
SYMMETALLIC	SYMPATRIES	SYMPTOMOLOGIES	SYNCHORESIS	SYNCOPATES
SYMMETALLISM	SYMPETALIES	SYMPTOMOLOGY	SYNCHROFLASH	SYNCOPATING
SYMMETALLISMS	SYMPETALOUS	SYNADELPHITE	SYNCHROFLASHES	SYNCOPATION

SYNCOPATIONS	SYNDICSHIPS	SYNOECIOSIS	SYNTACTICALLY	SYNTHETISMS
SYNCOPATIVE	SYNDIOTACTIC	SYNOECIOUS	SYNTACTICS	SYNTHETIST
SYNCOPATOR	SYNDYASMIAN	SYNOECISED	SYNTAGMATA	SYNTHETISTS
SYNCOPATORS	SYNECDOCHE	SYNOECISES	SYNTAGMATIC	SYNTHETIZATION
SYNCRETISATION	SYNECDOCHES	SYNOECISING	SYNTAGMATITE	SYNTHETIZATIONS
SYNCRETISATIONS	SYNECDOCHIC	SYNOECISMS	SYNTAGMATITES	SYNTHETIZE
SYNCRETISE	SYNECDOCHICAL	SYNOECIZED	SYNTECTICAL	SYNTHETIZED
SYNCRETISED	SYNECDOCHICALLY	SYNOECIZES	SYNTENOSES	SYNTHETIZER
SYNCRETISES	SYNECDOCHISM	SYNOECIZING	SYNTENOSIS	SYNTHETIZERS
SYNCRETISING	SYNECDOCHISMS	SYNOECOLOGIES	SYNTERESES	SYNTHETIZES
SYNCRETISM	SYNECOLOGIC	SYNOECOLOGY	SYNTERESIS	SYNTHETIZING
SYNCRETISMS	SYNECOLOGICAL	SYNOEKETES	SYNTEXISES	SYNTHRONUS
SYNCRETIST	SYNECOLOGICALLY	SYNONYMATIC	SYNTHESISATION	SYNTONICALLY
SYNCRETISTIC	SYNECOLOGIES	SYNONYMICAL	SYNTHESISATIONS	SYNTONISED
SYNCRETISTS	SYNECOLOGIST	SYNONYMICON	SYNTHESISE	SYNTONISES
SYNCRETIZATION	SYNECOLOGISTS	SYNONYMICONS	SYNTHESISED	SYNTONISING
SYNCRETIZATIONS	SYNECOLOGY	SYNONYMIES	SYNTHESISER	SYNTONIZED
SYNCRETIZE	SYNECPHONESES	SYNONYMISE	SYNTHESISERS	SYNTONIZES
SYNCRETIZED	SYNECPHONESIS	SYNONYMISED	SYNTHESISES	SYNTONIZING
SYNCRETIZES	SYNECTICALLY	SYNONYMISES	SYNTHESISING	SYPHERINGS
SYNCRETIZING	SYNEIDESES	SYNONYMISING	SYNTHESIST	SYPHILISATION
SYNDACTYLIES	SYNEIDESIS	SYNONYMIST	SYNTHESISTS	SYPHILISATIONS
SYNDACTYLISM	SYNERGETIC	SYNONYMISTS	SYNTHESIZATION	SYPHILISED
SYNDACTYLISMS	SYNERGETICALLY	SYNONYMITIES	SYNTHESIZATIONS	SYPHILISES
SYNDACTYLOUS	SYNERGICALLY	SYNONYMITY	SYNTHESIZE	SYPHILISING
SYNDACTYLS	SYNERGISED	SYNONYMIZE	SYNTHESIZED	SYPHILITIC
SYNDACTYLY	SYNERGISES	SYNONYMIZED	SYNTHESIZER	SYPHILITICALLY
SYNDERESES	SYNERGISING	SYNONYMIZES	SYNTHESIZERS	SYPHILITICS
SYNDERESIS	SYNERGISMS	SYNONYMIZING	SYNTHESIZES	SYPHILIZATION
SYNDESISES	SYNERGISTIC	SYNONYMOUS	SYNTHESIZING	SYPHILIZATIONS
SYNDESMOSES	SYNERGISTICALLY	SYNONYMOUSLY	SYNTHESPIAN	SYPHILIZED
SYNDESMOSIS	SYNERGISTS	SYNONYMOUSNESS	SYNTHESPIANS	SYPHILIZES
SYNDESMOTIC	SYNERGIZED	SYNOPSISED	SYNTHETASE	SYPHILIZING
SYNDETICAL	SYNERGIZES	SYNOPSISES	SYNTHETASES	SYPHILOLOGIES
SYNDETICALLY	SYNERGIZING	SYNOPSISING	SYNTHETICAL	SYPHILOLOGIST
SYNDICALISM	SYNESTHESIA	SYNOPSIZED	SYNTHETICALLY	SYPHILOLOGISTS
SYNDICALISMS	SYNESTHESIAS	SYNOPSIZES	SYNTHETICISM	SYPHILOLOGY
SYNDICALIST	SYNESTHETIC	SYNOPSIZING	SYNTHETICISMS	SYPHILOMAS
SYNDICALISTIC	SYNGENESES	SYNOPTICAL	SYNTHETICS	SYPHILOMATA
SYNDICALISTS	SYNGENESIOUS	SYNOPTICALLY	SYNTHETISATION	SYPHILOPHOBIA
SYNDICATED	SYNGENESIS	SYNOPTISTIC	SYNTHETISATIONS	SYPHILOPHOBIAS
SYNDICATES	SYNGENETIC	SYNOPTISTS	SYNTHETISE	SYPHONAGES
SYNDICATING	SYNGNATHOUS	SYNOSTOSES	SYNTHETISED	SYRINGITIS
SYNDICATION	SYNKARYONIC	SYNOSTOSIS	SYNTHETISER	SYRINGITISES
SYNDICATIONS	SYNKARYONS	SYNOVIALLY	SYNTHETISERS	SYRINGOMYELIA
SYNDICATOR	SYNODICALLY	SYNOVITISES	SYNTHETISES	SYRINGOMYELIAS
SYNDICATORS	SYNOECETES	SYNSEPALOUS	SYNTHETISING	SYRINGOMYELIC
SYNDICSHIP	SYNOECIOSES	SYNTACTICAL	SYNTHETISM	SYRINGOTOMIES

S

SYRINGOTOMY

SYRINGOTOMY
SYSSARCOSES
SYSSARCOSIS
SYSSARCOTIC
SYSTEMATIC
SYSTEMATICAL
SYSTEMATICALLY
SYSTEMATICIAN
SYSTEMATICIANS
SYSTEMATICNESS

SYSTEMATICS
SYSTEMATISATION
SYSTEMATISE
SYSTEMATISED
SYSTEMATISER
SYSTEMATISERS
SYSTEMATISES
SYSTEMATISING
SYSTEMATISM
SYSTEMATISMS

SYSTEMATIST
SYSTEMATISTS
SYSTEMATIZATION
SYSTEMATIZE
SYSTEMATIZED
SYSTEMATIZER
SYSTEMATIZERS
SYSTEMATIZES
SYSTEMATIZING
SYSTEMATOLOGIES

SYSTEMATOLOGY
SYSTEMICALLY
SYSTEMISATION
SYSTEMISATIONS
SYSTEMISED
SYSTEMISER
SYSTEMISERS
SYSTEMISES
SYSTEMISING
SYSTEMIZATION

SYSTEMIZATIONS
SYSTEMIZED
SYSTEMIZER
SYSTEMIZERS
SYSTEMIZES
SYSTEMIZING
SYSTEMLESS
SYZYGETICALLY

T

TABASHEERS	TABULARIZE	TACHYGRAPHY	TACTUALITY	TAILSPINNING
TABBOULEHS	TABULARIZED	TACHYLITES	TADALAFILS	TAILSTOCKS
TABBYHOODS	TABULARIZES	TACHYLITIC	TAEKWONDOS	TAILWATERS
TABEFACTION	TABULARIZING	TACHYLYTES	TAENIACIDE	TAILWHEELS
TABEFACTIONS	TABULATING	TACHYLYTIC	TAENIACIDES	TAINTLESSLY
TABELLIONS	TABULATION	TACHYMETER	TAENIAFUGE	TAKINGNESS
TABERNACLE	TABULATIONS	TACHYMETERS	TAENIAFUGES	TAKINGNESSES
TABERNACLED	TABULATORS	TACHYMETRIC	TAFFETASES	TALBOTYPES
TABERNACLES	TABULATORY	TACHYMETRICAL	TAFFETIEST	TALEBEARER
TABERNACLING	TACAMAHACS	TACHYMETRICALLY	TAFFETISED	TALEBEARERS
TABERNACULAR	TACHEOMETER	TACHYMETRIES	TAFFETIZED	TALEBEARING
TABESCENCE	TACHEOMETERS	TACHYMETRY	TAGLIARINI	TALEBEARINGS
TABESCENCES	TACHEOMETRIC	TACHYPHASIA	TAGLIARINIS	TALEGALLAS
TABLANETTE	TACHEOMETRICAL	TACHYPHASIAS	TAGLIATELLE	TALENTLESS
TABLANETTES	TACHEOMETRIES	TACHYPHRASIA	TAGLIATELLES	TALETELLER
TABLATURES	TACHEOMETRY	TACHYPHRASIAS	TAHSILDARS	TALETELLERS
TABLECLOTH	TACHISTOSCOPE	TACHYPHYLAXES	TAIKONAUTS	TALETELLING
TABLECLOTHS	TACHISTOSCOPES	TACHYPHYLAXIS	TAILBOARDS	TALETELLINGS
TABLELANDS	TACHISTOSCOPIC	TACHYPNEAS	TAILCOATED	TALISMANIC
TABLEMATES	TACHOGRAMS	TACHYPNOEA	TAILENDERS	TALISMANICAL
TABLESPOON	TACHOGRAPH	TACHYPNOEAS	TAILGATERS	TALISMANICALLY
TABLESPOONFUL	TACHOGRAPHS	TACITNESSES	TAILGATING	TALKABILITIES
TABLESPOONFULS	TACHOMETER	TACITURNITIES	TAILGATINGS	TALKABILITY
TABLESPOONS	TACHOMETERS	TACITURNITY	TAILHOPPING	TALKATHONS
TABLESPOONSFUL	TACHOMETRIC	TACITURNLY	TAILHOPPINGS	TALKATIVELY
TABLETOPPED	TACHOMETRICAL	TACKBOARDS	TAILLESSLY	TALKATIVENESS
TABLETTING	TACHOMETRICALLY	TACKETIEST	TAILLESSNESS	TALKATIVENESSES
TABLEWARES	TACHOMETRIES	TACKIFIERS	TAILLESSNESSES	TALKINESSES
TABLOIDIER	TACHOMETRY	TACKIFYING	TAILLIGHTS	TALLGRASSES
TABLOIDIEST	TACHYARRHYTHMIA	TACKINESSES	TAILORBIRD	TALLIATING
TABOGGANED	TACHYCARDIA	TACMAHACKS	TAILORBIRDS	TALLNESSES
TABOGGANING	TACHYCARDIAC	TACTFULNESS	TAILORESSES	TALLOWIEST
TABOPARESES	TACHYCARDIAS	TACTFULNESSES	TAILORINGS	TALLYHOING
TABOPARESIS	TACHYGRAPH	TACTICALLY	TAILORMADE	TALLYSHOPS
TABULARISATION	TACHYGRAPHER	TACTICIANS	TAILORMAKE	TALLYWOMAN
TABULARISATIONS	TACHYGRAPHERS	TACTICITIES	TAILORMAKES	TALLYWOMEN
TABULARISE	TACHYGRAPHIC	TACTILISTS	TAILORMAKING	TALMUDISMS
TABULARISED	TACHYGRAPHICAL	TACTILITIES	TAILPIECES	TAMABILITIES
TABULARISES	TACHYGRAPHIES	TACTLESSLY	TAILPIPING	TAMABILITY
TABULARISING	TACHYGRAPHIST	TACTLESSNESS	TAILPLANES	TAMABLENESS
TABULARIZATION	TACHYGRAPHISTS	TACTLESSNESSES	TAILSLIDES	TAMABLENESSES
TABULARIZATIONS	TACHYGRAPHS	TACTUALITIES	TAILSPINNED	TAMARILLOS

TAMBOURERS

TAMBOURERS	TANTALISATION	TAPSALTEERIES	TARNISHERS	TASTELESSLY
TAMBOURINE	TANTALISATIONS	TAPSIETEERIE	TARNISHING	TASTELESSNESS
TAMBOURINES	TANTALISED	TAPSIETEERIES	TARPAULING	TASTELESSNESSES
TAMBOURING	TANTALISER	TAPSTRESSES	TARPAULINGS	TASTEMAKER
TAMBOURINIST	TANTALISERS	TARABISHES	TARPAULINS	TASTEMAKERS
TAMBOURINISTS	TANTALISES	TARADIDDLE	TARRADIDDLE	TASTINESSES
TAMBOURINS	TANTALISING	TARADIDDLES	TARRADIDDLES	TATAHASHES
TAMEABILITIES	TANTALISINGLY	TARAMASALATA	TARRIANCES	TATPURUSHA
TAMEABILITY	TANTALISINGS	TARAMASALATAS	TARRINESSES	TATPURUSHAS
TAMEABLENESS	TANTALISMS	TARANTARAED	TARSALGIAS	TATTERDEMALION
TAMEABLENESSES	TANTALITES	TARANTARAING	TARSOMETATARSAL	TATTERDEMALIONS
TAMELESSNESS	TANTALIZATION	TARANTARAS	TARSOMETATARSI	TATTERDEMALLION
TAMELESSNESSES	TANTALIZATIONS	TARANTASES	TARSOMETATARSUS	TATTERIEST
TAMENESSES	TANTALIZED	TARANTASSES	TARTANALIA	TATTERSALL
TAMOXIFENS	TANTALIZER	TARANTELLA	TARTANALIAS	TATTERSALLS
TAMPERINGS	TANTALIZERS	TARANTELLAS	TARTANRIES	TATTINESSES
TAMPERPROOF	TANTALIZES	TARANTISMS	TARTAREOUS	TATTLETALE
TAMPONADES	TANTALIZING	TARANTISTS	TARTARISATION	TATTLETALED
TAMPONAGES	TANTALIZINGLY	TARANTULAE	TARTARISATIONS	TATTLETALES
TANDEMWISE	TANTALIZINGS	TARANTULAS	TARTARISED	TATTLETALING
TANGENCIES	TANTALUSES	TARATANTARA	TARTARISES	TATTLINGLY
TANGENTALLY	TANTAMOUNT	TARATANTARAED	TARTARISING	TATTOOISTS
TANGENTIAL	TANTARARAS	TARATANTARAING	TARTARIZATION	TAUNTINGLY
TANGENTIALITIES	TANZANITES	TARATANTARAS	TARTARIZATIONS	TAUROBOLIA
TANGENTIALITY	TAPERINGLY	TARAXACUMS	TARTARIZED	TAUROBOLIUM
TANGENTIALLY	TAPERNESSES	TARBOGGINED	TARTARIZES	TAUROMACHIAN
TANGERINES	TAPERSTICK	TARBOGGINING	TARTARIZING	TAUROMACHIES
TANGHININS	TAPERSTICKS	TARBOGGINS	TARTINESSES	TAUROMACHY
TANGIBILITIES	TAPESCRIPT	TARBOOSHES	TARTNESSES	TAUROMORPHOUS
TANGIBILITY	TAPESCRIPTS	TARBOUCHES	TARTRAZINE	TAUTNESSES
TANGIBLENESS	TAPESTRIED	TARBOUSHES	TARTRAZINES	TAUTOCHRONE
TANGIBLENESSES	TAPESTRIES	TARDIGRADE	TASEOMETER	TAUTOCHRONES
TANGINESSES	TAPESTRYING	TARDIGRADES	TASEOMETERS	TAUTOCHRONISM
TANGLEFOOT	TAPHEPHOBIA	TARDINESSES	TASIMETERS	TAUTOCHRONISMS
TANGLEFOOTS	TAPHEPHOBIAS	TARGETABLE	TASIMETRIC	TAUTOCHRONOUS
TANGLEMENT	TAPHEPHOBIC	TARGETEERS	TASIMETRIES	TAUTOLOGIC
TANGLEMENTS	TAPHONOMIC	TARGETINGS	TASKMASTER	TAUTOLOGICAL
TANGLESOME	TAPHONOMICAL	TARGETITIS	TASKMASTERS	TAUTOLOGICALLY
TANGLEWEED	TAPHONOMIES	TARGETITISES	TASKMISTRESS	TAUTOLOGIES
TANGLEWEEDS	TAPHONOMIST	TARGETLESS	TASKMISTRESSES	TAUTOLOGISE
TANGLINGLY	TAPHONOMISTS	TARIFFICATION	TASSELIEST	TAUTOLOGISED
TANISTRIES	TAPHOPHOBIA	TARIFFICATIONS	TASSELLIER	TAUTOLOGISES
TANKBUSTER	TAPHOPHOBIAS	TARIFFLESS	TASSELLIEST	TAUTOLOGISING
TANKBUSTERS	TAPHROGENESES	TARMACADAM	TASSELLING	TAUTOLOGISM
TANKBUSTING	TAPHROGENESIS	TARMACADAMS	TASSELLINGS	TAUTOLOGISMS
TANKBUSTINGS	TAPOTEMENT	TARMACKING	TASTEFULLY	TAUTOLOGIST
TANOREXICS	TAPOTEMENTS	TARNATIONS	TASTEFULNESS	TAUTOLOGISTS
TANTALATES	TAPSALTEERIE	TARNISHABLE	TASTEFULNESSES	TAUTOLOGIZE

TAUTOLOGIZED TAXONOMISTS TECHNICALISES TECHNOLOGISED TEEMINGNESS
TAUTOLOGIZES TAXPAYINGS TECHNICALISING TECHNOLOGISES TEEMINGNESSES
TAUTOLOGIZING TAYASSUIDS TECHNICALITIES TECHNOLOGISING TEENTSIEST
TAUTOLOGOUS TAYBERRIES TECHNICALITY TECHNOLOGIST TEENYBOPPER
TAUTOLOGOUSLY TCHOTCHKES TECHNICALIZE TECHNOLOGISTS TEENYBOPPERS
TAUTOMERIC TCHOUKBALL TECHNICALIZED TECHNOLOGIZE TEETERBOARD
TAUTOMERISM TCHOUKBALLS TECHNICALIZES TECHNOLOGIZED TEETERBOARDS
TAUTOMERISMS TEABERRIES TECHNICALIZING TECHNOLOGIZES TEETHRIDGE
TAUTOMETRIC TEACHABILITIES TECHNICALLY TECHNOLOGIZING TEETHRIDGES
TAUTOMETRICAL TEACHABILITY TECHNICALNESS TECHNOLOGY TEETOTALED
TAUTONYMIC TEACHABLENESS TECHNICALNESSES TECHNOMANIA TEETOTALER
TAUTONYMIES TEACHABLENESSES TECHNICALS TECHNOMANIAC TEETOTALERS
TAUTONYMOUS TEACHERLESS TECHNICIAN TECHNOMANIACS TEETOTALING
TAUTOPHONIC TEACHERLIER TECHNICIANS TECHNOMANIAS TEETOTALISM
TAUTOPHONICAL TEACHERLIEST TECHNICISE TECHNOMUSIC TEETOTALISMS
TAUTOPHONIES TEACHERSHIP TECHNICISED TECHNOMUSICS TEETOTALIST
TAUTOPHONY TEACHERSHIPS TECHNICISES TECHNOPHILE TEETOTALISTS
TAWDRINESS TEACUPFULS TECHNICISING TECHNOPHILES TEETOTALLED
TAWDRINESSES TEACUPSFUL TECHNICISM TECHNOPHILIA TEETOTALLER
TAWHEOWHEO TEAKETTLES TECHNICISMS TECHNOPHILIAS TEETOTALLERS
TAWHEOWHEOS TEARFULNESS TECHNICIST TECHNOPHOBE TEETOTALLING
TAWNINESSES TEARFULNESSES TECHNICISTS TECHNOPHOBES TEETOTALLY
TAXABILITIES TEARGASSED TECHNICIZE TECHNOPHOBIA TEGUMENTAL
TAXABILITY TEARGASSES TECHNICIZED TECHNOPHOBIAS TEGUMENTARY
TAXABLENESS TEARGASSING TECHNICIZES TECHNOPHOBIC TEHSILDARS
TAXABLENESSES TEARINESSES TECHNICIZING TECHNOPHOBICS TEICHOPSIA
TAXAMETERS TEARJERKER TECHNICOLOUR TECHNOPOLE TEICHOPSIAS
TAXATIONAL TEARJERKERS TECHNICOLOURED TECHNOPOLES TEINOSCOPE
TAXIDERMAL TEARLESSLY TECHNIKONS TECHNOPOLIS TEINOSCOPES
TAXIDERMIC TEARSHEETS TECHNIQUES TECHNOPOLISES TEKNONYMIES
TAXIDERMIES TEARSTAINED TECHNOBABBLE TECHNOPOLITAN TEKNONYMOUS
TAXIDERMISE TEARSTAINS TECHNOBABBLES TECHNOPOLITANS TELAESTHESIA
TAXIDERMISED TEARSTRIPS TECHNOCRACIES TECHNOPOPS TELAESTHESIAS
TAXIDERMISES TEASELINGS TECHNOCRACY TECHNOSPEAK TELAESTHETIC
TAXIDERMISING TEASELLERS TECHNOCRAT TECHNOSPEAKS TELANGIECTASES
TAXIDERMIST TEASELLING TECHNOCRATIC TECHNOSTRESS TELANGIECTASIA
TAXIDERMISTS TEASELLINGS TECHNOCRATS TECHNOSTRESSES TELANGIECTASIAS
TAXIDERMIZE TEASPOONFUL TECHNOFEAR TECHNOSTRUCTURE TELANGIECTASIS
TAXIDERMIZED TEASPOONFULS TECHNOFEARS TECTIBRANCH TELANGIECTATIC
TAXIDERMIZES TEASPOONSFUL TECHNOGRAPHIES TECTIBRANCHIATE TELAUTOGRAPHIC
TAXIDERMIZING TEATASTERS TECHNOGRAPHY TECTIBRANCHS TELAUTOGRAPHIES
TAXIMETERS TEAZELLING TECHNOJUNKIE TECTONICALLY TELAUTOGRAPHY
TAXIPLANES TECHINESSES TECHNOJUNKIES TECTONISMS TELEARCHICS
TAXONOMERS TECHNETIUM TECHNOLOGIC TECTRICIAL TELEBANKING
TAXONOMICAL TECHNETIUMS TECHNOLOGICAL TEDIOSITIES TELEBANKINGS
TAXONOMICALLY TECHNETRONIC TECHNOLOGICALLY TEDIOUSNESS TELEBRIDGE
TAXONOMIES TECHNICALISE TECHNOLOGIES TEDIOUSNESSES TELEBRIDGES
TAXONOMIST TECHNICALISED TECHNOLOGISE TEDIOUSOME TELECAMERA

TELECAMERAS

TELECAMERAS	TELEGRAPHERS	TELEOLOGIES	TELEPHOTOS	TELESTHESIA
TELECASTED	TELEGRAPHESE	TELEOLOGISM	TELEPOINTS	TELESTHESIAS
TELECASTER	TELEGRAPHESES	TELEOLOGISMS	TELEPORTATION	TELESTHETIC
TELECASTERS	TELEGRAPHIC	TELEOLOGIST	TELEPORTATIONS	TELESTICHS
TELECASTING	TELEGRAPHICALLY	TELEOLOGISTS	TELEPORTED	TELESURGERIES
TELECHIRIC	TELEGRAPHIES	TELEONOMIC	TELEPORTING	TELESURGERY
TELECOMMAND	TELEGRAPHING	TELEONOMIES	TELEPRESENCE	TELETYPESETTING
TELECOMMANDS	TELEGRAPHIST	TELEOSAURIAN	TELEPRESENCES	TELETYPEWRITER
TELECOMMUTE	TELEGRAPHISTS	TELEOSAURIANS	TELEPRINTED	TELETYPEWRITERS
TELECOMMUTED	TELEGRAPHS	TELEOSAURS	TELEPRINTER	TELETYPING
TELECOMMUTER	TELEGRAPHY	TELEOSTEAN	TELEPRINTERS	TELEUTOSPORE
TELECOMMUTERS	TELEHEALTH	TELEOSTEANS	TELEPRINTING	TELEUTOSPORES
TELECOMMUTES	TELEHEALTHS	TELEOSTOME	TELEPRINTS	TELEUTOSPORIC
TELECOMMUTING	TELEJOURNALISM	TELEOSTOMES	TELEPROCESSING	TELEVANGELICAL
TELECOMMUTINGS	TELEJOURNALISMS	TELEOSTOMOUS	TELEPROCESSINGS	TELEVANGELISM
TELECONFERENCE	TELEJOURNALIST	TELEPATHED	TELERECORD	TELEVANGELISMS
TELECONFERENCES	TELEJOURNALISTS	TELEPATHIC	TELERECORDED	TELEVANGELIST
TELECONNECTION	TELEKINESES	TELEPATHICALLY	TELERECORDING	TELEVANGELISTS
TELECONNECTIONS	TELEKINESIS	TELEPATHIES	TELERECORDINGS	TELEVERITE
TELECONTROL	TELEKINETIC	TELEPATHING	TELERECORDS	TELEVERITES
TELECONTROLS	TELEKINETICALLY	TELEPATHISE	TELERGICALLY	TELEVIEWED
TELECONVERTER	TELEMARKED	TELEPATHISED	TELEROBOTS	TELEVIEWER
TELECONVERTERS	TELEMARKETER	TELEPATHISES	TELESCIENCE	TELEVIEWERS
TELECOPIES	TELEMARKETERS	TELEPATHISING	TELESCIENCES	TELEVIEWING
TELECOTTAGE	TELEMARKETING	TELEPATHIST	TELESCOPED	TELEVIEWINGS
TELECOTTAGES	TELEMARKETINGS	TELEPATHISTS	TELESCOPES	TELEVISERS
TELECOTTAGING	TELEMARKING	TELEPATHIZE	TELESCOPIC	TELEVISING
TELECOTTAGINGS	TELEMATICS	TELEPATHIZED	TELESCOPICAL	TELEVISION
TELECOURSE	TELEMEDICINE	TELEPATHIZES	TELESCOPICALLY	TELEVISIONAL
TELECOURSES	TELEMEDICINES	TELEPATHIZING	TELESCOPIES	TELEVISIONALLY
TELEDILDONICS	TELEMEETING	TELEPHEMES	TELESCOPIFORM	TELEVISIONARY
TELEFACSIMILE	TELEMEETINGS	TELEPHERIQUE	TELESCOPING	TELEVISIONS
TELEFACSIMILES	TELEMESSAGE	TELEPHERIQUES	TELESCOPIST	TELEVISORS
TELEFAXING	TELEMESSAGES	TELEPHONED	TELESCOPISTS	TELEVISUAL
TELEFERIQUE	TELEMETERED	TELEPHONER	TELESCREEN	TELEVISUALLY
TELEFERIQUES	TELEMETERING	TELEPHONERS	TELESCREENS	TELEWORKED
TELEGENICALLY	TELEMETERS	TELEPHONES	TELESELLING	TELEWORKER
TELEGNOSES	TELEMETRIC	TELEPHONIC	TELESELLINGS	TELEWORKERS
TELEGNOSIS	TELEMETRICAL	TELEPHONICALLY	TELESERVICES	TELEWORKING
TELEGNOSTIC	TELEMETRICALLY	TELEPHONIES	TELESHOPPED	TELEWORKINGS
TELEGONIES	TELEMETRIES	TELEPHONING	TELESHOPPING	TELEWRITER
TELEGONOUS	TELENCEPHALA	TELEPHONIST	TELESHOPPINGS	TELEWRITERS
TELEGRAMMATIC	TELENCEPHALIC	TELEPHONISTS	TELESMATIC	TELFERAGES
TELEGRAMMED	TELENCEPHALON	TELEPHONITIS	TELESMATICAL	TELICITIES
TELEGRAMMIC	TELENCEPHALONS	TELEPHONITISES	TELESMATICALLY	TELIOSPORE
TELEGRAMMING	TELEOLOGIC	TELEPHOTOGRAPH	TELESOFTWARE	TELIOSPORES
TELEGRAPHED	TELEOLOGICAL	TELEPHOTOGRAPHS	TELESOFTWARES	TELLERSHIP
TELEGRAPHER	TELEOLOGICALLY	TELEPHOTOGRAPHY	TELESTEREOSCOPE	TELLERSHIPS

TENSIONALLY

TELLURATES	TEMPERAMENTALLY	TEMPORISINGLY	TENDENTIOUS	TENEBRIONIDS
TELLURETTED	TEMPERAMENTFUL	TEMPORISINGS	TENDENTIOUSLY	TENEBRIOUS
TELLURIANS	TEMPERAMENTS	TEMPORIZATION	TENDENTIOUSNESS	TENEBRIOUSNESS
TELLURIDES	TEMPERANCE	TEMPORIZATIONS	TENDERABLE	TENEBRISMS
TELLURIONS	TEMPERANCES	TEMPORIZED	TENDERFEET	TENEBRISTS
TELLURISED	TEMPERATED	TEMPORIZER	TENDERFOOT	TENEBRITIES
TELLURISES	TEMPERATELY	TEMPORIZERS	TENDERFOOTS	TENEBROSITIES
TELLURISING	TEMPERATENESS	TEMPORIZES	TENDERHEARTED	TENEBROSITY
TELLURITES	TEMPERATENESSES	TEMPORIZING	TENDERHEARTEDLY	TENEBROUSNESS
TELLURIUMS	TEMPERATES	TEMPORIZINGLY	TENDERINGS	TENEBROUSNESSES
TELLURIZED	TEMPERATING	TEMPORIZINGS	TENDERISATION	TENEMENTAL
TELLURIZES	TEMPERATIVE	TEMPTABILITIES	TENDERISATIONS	TENEMENTARY
TELLURIZING	TEMPERATURE	TEMPTABILITY	TENDERISED	TENEMENTED
TELLUROMETER	TEMPERATURES	TEMPTABLENESS	TENDERISER	TENESMUSES
TELLUROMETERS	TEMPERINGS	TEMPTABLENESSES	TENDERISERS	TENIACIDES
TELNETTING	TEMPESTING	TEMPTATION	TENDERISES	TENIAFUGES
TELOCENTRIC	TEMPESTIVE	TEMPTATIONS	TENDERISING	TENNANTITE
TELOCENTRICS	TEMPESTUOUS	TEMPTATIOUS	TENDERIZATION	TENNANTITES
TELOMERASE	TEMPESTUOUSLY	TEMPTINGLY	TENDERIZATIONS	TENNESSINE
TELOMERASES	TEMPESTUOUSNESS	TEMPTINGNESS	TENDERIZED	TENNESSINES
TELOMERISATION	TEMPOLABILE	TEMPTINGNESSES	TENDERIZER	TENORRHAPHIES
TELOMERISATIONS	TEMPORALISE	TEMPTRESSES	TENDERIZERS	TENORRHAPHY
TELOMERIZATION	TEMPORALISED	TEMULENCES	TENDERIZES	TENOSYNOVITIS
TELOMERIZATIONS	TEMPORALISES	TEMULENCIES	TENDERIZING	TENOSYNOVITISES
TELOPHASES	TEMPORALISING	TEMULENTLY	TENDERLING	TENOTOMIES
TELOPHASIC	TEMPORALITIES	TENABILITIES	TENDERLINGS	TENOTOMIST
TELPHERAGE	TEMPORALITY	TENABILITY	TENDERLOIN	TENOTOMISTS
TELPHERAGES	TEMPORALIZE	TENABLENESS	TENDERLOINS	TENOVAGINITIS
TELPHERING	TEMPORALIZED	TENABLENESSES	TENDERNESS	TENOVAGINITISES
TELPHERLINE	TEMPORALIZES	TENACIOUSLY	TENDERNESSES	TENPINNERS
TELPHERLINES	TEMPORALIZING	TENACIOUSNESS	TENDEROMETER	TENPOUNDER
TELPHERMAN	TEMPORALLY	TENACIOUSNESSES	TENDEROMETERS	TENPOUNDERS
TELPHERMEN	TEMPORALNESS	TENACITIES	TENDINITIDES	TENSENESSES
TELPHERWAY	TEMPORALNESSES	TENACULUMS	TENDINITIS	TENSIBILITIES
TELPHERWAYS	TEMPORALTIES	TENAILLONS	TENDINITISES	TENSIBILITY
TEMAZEPAMS	TEMPORALTY	TENANTABLE	TENDONITIDES	TENSIBLENESS
TEMERARIOUS	TEMPORANEOUS	TENANTLESS	TENDONITIS	TENSIBLENESSES
TEMERARIOUSLY	TEMPORARIES	TENANTRIES	TENDONITISES	TENSILENESS
TEMERARIOUSNESS	TEMPORARILY	TENANTSHIP	TENDOVAGINITIS	TENSILENESSES
TEMERITIES	TEMPORARINESS	TENANTSHIPS	TENDRESSES	TENSILITIES
TEMEROUSLY	TEMPORARINESSES	TENDENCIAL	TENDRILLAR	TENSIMETER
TEMPERABILITIES	TEMPORISATION	TENDENCIALLY	TENDRILLED	TENSIMETERS
TEMPERABILITY	TEMPORISATIONS	TENDENCIES	TENDRILLIER	TENSIOMETER
TEMPERABLE	TEMPORISED	TENDENCIOUS	TENDRILLIEST	TENSIOMETERS
TEMPERALITIE	TEMPORISER	TENDENCIOUSLY	TENDRILLOUS	TENSIOMETRIC
TEMPERALITIES	TEMPORISERS	TENDENCIOUSNESS	TENDRILOUS	TENSIOMETRIES
TEMPERAMENT	TEMPORISES	TENDENTIAL	TENEBRIFIC	TENSIOMETRY
TEMPERAMENTAL	TEMPORISING	TENDENTIALLY	TENEBRIONID	TENSIONALLY

TENSIONERS	TERATOLOGISTS	TERMINATION	TERRESTRIALLY	TERSANCTUS
TENSIONING	TERATOLOGY	TERMINATIONAL	TERRESTRIALNESS	TERSANCTUSES
TENSIONLESS	TERATOMATA	TERMINATIONS	TERRESTRIALS	TERSENESSES
TENTACULAR	TERATOMATOUS	TERMINATIVE	TERRIBILITIES	TERTIARIES
TENTACULATE	TERATOPHOBIA	TERMINATIVELY	TERRIBILITY	TERVALENCIES
TENTACULIFEROUS	TERATOPHOBIAS	TERMINATOR	TERRIBLENESS	TERVALENCY
TENTACULITE	TERCENTENARIES	TERMINATORS	TERRIBLENESSES	TESCHENITE
TENTACULITES	TERCENTENARY	TERMINATORY	TERRICOLES	TESCHENITES
TENTACULOID	TERCENTENNIAL	TERMINISMS	TERRICOLOUS	TESSARAGLOT
TENTACULUM	TERCENTENNIALS	TERMINISTS	TERRIFICALLY	TESSELATED
TENTATIONS	TEREBINTHINE	TERMINOLOGICAL	TERRIFIERS	TESSELATES
TENTATIVELY	TEREBINTHS	TERMINOLOGIES	TERRIFYING	TESSELATING
TENTATIVENESS	TEREBRANTS	TERMINOLOGIST	TERRIFYINGLY	TESSELLATE
TENTATIVENESSES	TEREBRATED	TERMINOLOGISTS	TERRIGENOUS	TESSELLATED
TENTATIVES	TEREBRATES	TERMINOLOGY	TERRITORIAL	TESSELLATES
TENTERHOOK	TEREBRATING	TERMINUSES	TERRITORIALISE	TESSELLATING
TENTERHOOKS	TEREBRATION	TERMITARIA	TERRITORIALISED	TESSELLATION
TENTIGINOUS	TEREBRATIONS	TERMITARIES	TERRITORIALISES	TESSELLATIONS
TENTMAKERS	TEREBRATULA	TERMITARIUM	TERRITORIALISM	TESSERACTS
TENUIROSTRAL	TEREBRATULAE	TERMITARIUMS	TERRITORIALISMS	TESSITURAS
TENUOUSNESS	TEREBRATULAS	TERNEPLATE	TERRITORIALIST	TESTABILITIES
TENUOUSNESSES	TEREPHTHALATE	TERNEPLATES	TERRITORIALISTS	TESTABILITY
TENURIALLY	TEREPHTHALATES	TEROTECHNOLOGY	TERRITORIALITY	TESTACEANS
TEPEFACTION	TEREPHTHALIC	TERPENELESS	TERRITORIALIZE	TESTACEOUS
TEPEFACTIONS	TERGIVERSANT	TERPENOIDS	TERRITORIALIZED	TESTAMENTAL
TEPHIGRAMS	TERGIVERSANTS	TERPINEOLS	TERRITORIALIZES	TESTAMENTAR
TEPHROITES	TERGIVERSATE	TERPOLYMER	TERRITORIALLY	TESTAMENTARILY
TEPHROMANCIES	TERGIVERSATED	TERPOLYMERS	TERRITORIALS	TESTAMENTARY
TEPHROMANCY	TERGIVERSATES	TERPSICHOREAL	TERRITORIED	TESTAMENTS
TEPIDARIUM	TERGIVERSATING	TERPSICHOREAN	TERRITORIES	TESTATIONS
TEPIDITIES	TERGIVERSATION	TERRACELESS	TERRORISATION	TESTATRICES
TEPIDNESSES	TERGIVERSATIONS	TERRACETTE	TERRORISATIONS	TESTATRIXES
TERAHERTZES	TERGIVERSATOR	TERRACETTES	TERRORISED	TESTCROSSED
TERAMETERS	TERGIVERSATORS	TERRACINGS	TERRORISER	TESTCROSSES
TERATOCARCINOMA	TERGIVERSATORY	TERRACOTTA	TERRORISERS	TESTCROSSING
TERATOGENESES	TERMAGANCIES	TERRACOTTAS	TERRORISES	TESTERNING
TERATOGENESIS	TERMAGANCY	TERRAFORMED	TERRORISING	TESTICULAR
TERATOGENIC	TERMAGANTLY	TERRAFORMING	TERRORISMS	TESTICULATE
TERATOGENICIST	TERMAGANTS	TERRAFORMINGS	TERRORISTIC	TESTICULATED
TERATOGENICISTS	TERMINABILITIES	TERRAFORMS	TERRORISTS	TESTIFICATE
TERATOGENICITY	TERMINABILITY	TERRAMARAS	TERRORIZATION	TESTIFICATES
TERATOGENIES	TERMINABLE	TERRAMARES	TERRORIZATIONS	TESTIFICATION
TERATOGENS	TERMINABLENESS	TERRAQUEOUS	TERRORIZED	TESTIFICATIONS
TERATOGENY	TERMINABLY	TERRARIUMS	TERRORIZER	TESTIFICATOR
TERATOLOGIC	TERMINALLY	TERREMOTIVE	TERRORIZERS	TESTIFICATORS
TERATOLOGICAL	TERMINATED	TERREPLEIN	TERRORIZES	TESTIFICATORY
TERATOLOGIES	TERMINATES	TERREPLEINS	TERRORIZING	TESTIFIERS
TERATOLOGIST	TERMINATING	TERRESTRIAL	TERRORLESS	TESTIFYING

TESTIMONIAL	TETRACHOTOMIES	TETRAMERIC	TETRASTYLES	THALAMICALLY
TESTIMONIALISE	TETRACHOTOMOUS	TETRAMERISM	TETRASYLLABIC	THALAMIFLORAL
TESTIMONIALISED	TETRACHOTOMY	TETRAMERISMS	TETRASYLLABICAL	THALASSAEMIA
TESTIMONIALISES	TETRACTINAL	TETRAMEROUS	TETRASYLLABLE	THALASSAEMIAS
TESTIMONIALIZE	TETRACTINALS	TETRAMETER	TETRASYLLABLES	THALASSAEMIC
TESTIMONIALIZED	TETRACTINE	TETRAMETERS	TETRATHEISM	THALASSAEMICS
TESTIMONIALIZES	TETRACTINES	TETRAMETHYL	TETRATHEISMS	THALASSEMIA
TESTIMONIALS	TETRACYCLIC	TETRAMETHYLLEAD	TETRATHLON	THALASSEMIAS
TESTIMONIED	TETRACYCLINE	TETRAMORPHIC	TETRATHLONS	THALASSEMIC
TESTIMONIES	TETRACYCLINES	TETRANDRIAN	TETRATOMIC	THALASSEMICS
TESTIMONYING	TETRADACTYL	TETRANDROUS	TETRAVALENCE	THALASSIAN
TESTINESSES	TETRADACTYLIES	TETRAPLEGIA	TETRAVALENCES	THALASSIANS
TESTOSTERONE	TETRADACTYLOUS	TETRAPLEGIAS	TETRAVALENCIES	THALASSOCRACIES
TESTOSTERONES	TETRADACTYLS	TETRAPLEGIC	TETRAVALENCY	THALASSOCRACY
TESTUDINAL	TETRADACTYLY	TETRAPLOID	TETRAVALENT	THALASSOCRAT
TESTUDINARY	TETRADITES	TETRAPLOIDIES	TETRAVALENTS	THALASSOCRATS
TESTUDINEOUS	TETRADRACHM	TETRAPLOIDS	TETRAZOLIUM	THALASSOGRAPHER
TESTUDINES	TETRADRACHMS	TETRAPLOIDY	TETRAZOLIUMS	THALASSOGRAPHIC
TETANICALLY	TETRADYMITE	TETRAPODIC	TETRAZZINI	THALASSOGRAPHY
TETANISATION	TETRADYMITES	TETRAPODIES	TETRODOTOXIN	THALASSOTHERAPY
TETANISATIONS	TETRADYNAMOUS	TETRAPODOUS	TETRODOTOXINS	THALATTOCRACIES
TETANISING	TETRAETHYL	TETRAPOLIS	TETROTOXIN	THALATTOCRACY
TETANIZATION	TETRAETHYLLEAD	TETRAPOLISES	TETROTOXINS	THALICTRUM
TETANIZATIONS	TETRAETHYLLEADS	TETRAPOLITAN	TETROXIDES	THALICTRUMS
TETANIZING	TETRAETHYLS	TETRAPTERAN	TEUTONISED	THALIDOMIDE
TETARTOHEDRAL	TETRAFLUORIDE	TETRAPTEROUS	TEUTONISES	THALIDOMIDES
TETARTOHEDRALLY	TETRAFLUORIDES	TETRAPTOTE	TEUTONISING	THALLIFORM
TETARTOHEDRISM	TETRAGONAL	TETRAPTOTES	TEUTONIZED	THALLOPHYTE
TETARTOHEDRISMS	TETRAGONALLY	TETRAPYRROLE	TEUTONIZES	THALLOPHYTES
TETCHINESS	TETRAGONALNESS	TETRAPYRROLES	TEUTONIZING	THALLOPHYTIC
TETCHINESSES	TETRAGONOUS	TETRARCHATE	TEXTBOOKISH	THANATISMS
TETHERBALL	TETRAGRAMMATON	TETRARCHATES	TEXTPHONES	THANATISTS
TETHERBALLS	TETRAGRAMMATONS	TETRARCHIC	TEXTSPEAKS	THANATOGNOMONIC
TETRABASIC	TETRAGRAMS	TETRARCHICAL	TEXTUALISM	THANATOGRAPHIES
TETRABASICITIES	TETRAGYNIAN	TETRARCHIES	TEXTUALISMS	THANATOGRAPHY
TETRABASICITY	TETRAGYNOUS	TETRASEMIC	TEXTUALIST	THANATOLOGICAL
TETRABORATE	TETRAHEDRA	TETRASPORANGIA	TEXTUALISTS	THANATOLOGIES
TETRABORATES	TETRAHEDRAL	TETRASPORANGIUM	TEXTUARIES	THANATOLOGIST
TETRABRACH	TETRAHEDRALLY	TETRASPORE	TEXTURALLY	THANATOLOGISTS
TETRABRACHS	TETRAHEDRITE	TETRASPORES	TEXTURELESS	THANATOLOGY
TETRABRANCHIATE	TETRAHEDRITES	TETRASPORIC	TEXTURINGS	THANATOPHOBIA
TETRACAINE	TETRAHEDRON	TETRASPOROUS	TEXTURISED	THANATOPHOBIAS
TETRACAINES	TETRAHEDRONS	TETRASTICH	TEXTURISES	THANATOPSES
TETRACHLORIDE	TETRAHYDROFURAN	TETRASTICHAL	TEXTURISING	THANATOPSIS
TETRACHLORIDES	TETRAHYMENA	TETRASTICHIC	TEXTURIZED	THANATOSES
TETRACHORD	TETRAHYMENAS	TETRASTICHOUS	TEXTURIZES	THANATOSIS
TETRACHORDAL	TETRALOGIES	TETRASTICHS	TEXTURIZING	THANEHOODS
TETRACHORDS	TETRAMERAL	TETRASTYLE	THALAMENCEPHALA	THANESHIPS

THANKFULLER	THAUMATURGY	THEATROMANIAS	THEODOLITES	THEONOMIES
THANKFULLEST	THEANTHROPIC	THEATROPHONE	THEODOLITIC	THEONOMOUS
THANKFULLY	THEANTHROPIES	THEATROPHONES	THEOGONICAL	THEOPATHETIC
THANKFULNESS	THEANTHROPISM	THECODONTS	THEOGONIES	THEOPATHIC
THANKFULNESSES	THEANTHROPISMS	THEFTUOUSLY	THEOGONIST	THEOPATHIES
THANKLESSLY	THEANTHROPIST	THEGNLIEST	THEOGONISTS	THEOPHAGIES
THANKLESSNESS	THEANTHROPISTS	THEIRSELVES	THEOLOGASTER	THEOPHAGOUS
THANKLESSNESSES	THEANTHROPY	THEISTICAL	THEOLOGASTERS	THEOPHANIC
THANKSGIVER	THEARCHIES	THEISTICALLY	THEOLOGATE	THEOPHANIES
THANKSGIVERS	THEATERGOER	THELEMENTS	THEOLOGATES	THEOPHANOUS
THANKSGIVING	THEATERGOERS	THELITISES	THEOLOGERS	THEOPHOBIA
THANKSGIVINGS	THEATERGOING	THELYTOKIES	THEOLOGIAN	THEOPHOBIAC
THANKWORTHIER	THEATERGOINGS	THELYTOKOUS	THEOLOGIANS	THEOPHOBIACS
THANKWORTHIEST	THEATERLAND	THEMATICALLY	THEOLOGICAL	THEOPHOBIAS
THANKWORTHILY	THEATERLANDS	THEMATISATION	THEOLOGICALLY	THEOPHOBIST
THANKWORTHINESS	THEATREGOER	THEMATISATIONS	THEOLOGIES	THEOPHOBISTS
THANKWORTHY	THEATREGOERS	THEMATISED	THEOLOGISATION	THEOPHORIC
THARBOROUGH	THEATREGOING	THEMATISES	THEOLOGISATIONS	THEOPHYLLINE
THARBOROUGHS	THEATREGOINGS	THEMATISING	THEOLOGISE	THEOPHYLLINES
THATCHIEST	THEATRELAND	THEMATIZATION	THEOLOGISED	THEOPNEUST
THATCHINGS	THEATRELANDS	THEMATIZATIONS	THEOLOGISER	THEOPNEUSTIES
THATCHLESS	THEATRICAL	THEMATIZED	THEOLOGISERS	THEOPNEUSTY
THATNESSES	THEATRICALISE	THEMATIZES	THEOLOGISES	THEORBISTS
THAUMASITE	THEATRICALISED	THEMATIZING	THEOLOGISING	THEOREMATIC
THAUMASITES	THEATRICALISES	THEMSELVES	THEOLOGIST	THEOREMATICAL
THAUMATINS	THEATRICALISING	THENABOUTS	THEOLOGISTS	THEOREMATICALLY
THAUMATOGENIES	THEATRICALISM	THENARDITE	THEOLOGIZATION	THEOREMATIST
THAUMATOGENY	THEATRICALISMS	THENARDITES	THEOLOGIZATIONS	THEOREMATISTS
THAUMATOGRAPHY	THEATRICALITIES	THENCEFORTH	THEOLOGIZE	THEORETICAL
THAUMATOLATRIES	THEATRICALITY	THENCEFORWARD	THEOLOGIZED	THEORETICALLY
THAUMATOLATRY	THEATRICALIZE	THENCEFORWARDS	THEOLOGIZER	THEORETICIAN
THAUMATOLOGIES	THEATRICALIZED	THEOBROMINE	THEOLOGIZERS	THEORETICIANS
THAUMATOLOGY	THEATRICALIZES	THEOBROMINES	THEOLOGIZES	THEORETICS
THAUMATROPE	THEATRICALIZING	THEOCENTRIC	THEOLOGIZING	THEORIQUES
THAUMATROPES	THEATRICALLY	THEOCENTRICISM	THEOLOGOUMENA	THEORISATION
THAUMATROPICAL	THEATRICALNESS	THEOCENTRICISMS	THEOLOGOUMENON	THEORISATIONS
THAUMATURGE	THEATRICALS	THEOCENTRICITY	THEOLOGUES	THEORISERS
THAUMATURGES	THEATRICISE	THEOCENTRISM	THEOMACHIES	THEORISING
THAUMATURGIC	THEATRICISED	THEOCENTRISMS	THEOMACHIST	THEORIZATION
THAUMATURGICAL	THEATRICISES	THEOCRACIES	THEOMACHISTS	THEORIZATIONS
THAUMATURGICS	THEATRICISING	THEOCRASIES	THEOMANCIES	THEORIZERS
THAUMATURGIES	THEATRICISM	THEOCRATIC	THEOMANIAC	THEORIZING
THAUMATURGISM	THEATRICISMS	THEOCRATICAL	THEOMANIACS	THEOSOPHER
THAUMATURGISMS	THEATRICIZE	THEOCRATICALLY	THEOMANIAS	THEOSOPHERS
THAUMATURGIST	THEATRICIZED	THEODICEAN	THEOMANTIC	THEOSOPHIC
THAUMATURGISTS	THEATRICIZES	THEODICEANS	THEOMORPHIC	THEOSOPHICAL
THAUMATURGUS	THEATRICIZING	THEODICIES	THEOMORPHISM	THEOSOPHICALLY
THAUMATURGUSES	THEATROMANIA	THEODOLITE	THEOMORPHISMS	

THEOSOPHIES	THEREWITHIN	THERMOCHROMISMS	THERMOMETRICAL	THERMOSTATTED
THEOSOPHISE	THERIANTHROPIC	THERMOCHROMY	THERMOMETRIES	THERMOSTATTING
THEOSOPHISED	THERIANTHROPISM	THERMOCLINE	THERMOMETRY	THERMOTACTIC
THEOSOPHISES	THERIOLATRIES	THERMOCLINES	THERMOMOTOR	THERMOTAXES
THEOSOPHISING	THERIOLATRY	THERMOCOUPLE	THERMOMOTORS	THERMOTAXIC
THEOSOPHISM	THERIOMORPH	THERMOCOUPLES	THERMONASTIES	THERMOTAXIS
THEOSOPHISMS	THERIOMORPHIC	THERMODURIC	THERMONASTY	THERMOTENSILE
THEOSOPHIST	THERIOMORPHISM	THERMODYNAMIC	THERMONUCLEAR	THERMOTHERAPIES
THEOSOPHISTICAL	THERIOMORPHISMS	THERMODYNAMICAL	THERMOPERIODIC	THERMOTHERAPY
THEOSOPHISTS	THERIOMORPHOSES	THERMODYNAMICS	THERMOPERIODISM	THERMOTICAL
THEOSOPHIZE	THERIOMORPHOSIS	THERMOELECTRIC	THERMOPHIL	THERMOTICS
THEOSOPHIZED	THERIOMORPHOUS	THERMOELECTRON	THERMOPHILE	THERMOTOLERANT
THEOSOPHIZES	THERIOMORPHS	THERMOELECTRONS	THERMOPHILES	THERMOTROPIC
THEOSOPHIZING	THERMAESTHESIA	THERMOELEMENT	THERMOPHILIC	THERMOTROPICS
THEOTECHNIC	THERMAESTHESIAS	THERMOELEMENTS	THERMOPHILOUS	THERMOTROPISM
THEOTECHNIES	THERMALISATION	THERMOFORM	THERMOPHILS	THERMOTROPISMS
THEOTECHNY	THERMALISATIONS	THERMOFORMABLE	THERMOPHYLLOUS	THEROLOGIES
THERALITES	THERMALISE	THERMOFORMED	THERMOPILE	THEROPHYTE
THERAPEUSES	THERMALISED	THERMOFORMING	THERMOPILES	THEROPHYTES
THERAPEUSIS	THERMALISES	THERMOFORMS	THERMOPLASTIC	THEROPODAN
THERAPEUTIC	THERMALISING	THERMOGENESES	THERMOPLASTICS	THEROPODANS
THERAPEUTICAL	THERMALIZATION	THERMOGENESIS	THERMORECEPTOR	THERSITICAL
THERAPEUTICALLY	THERMALIZATIONS	THERMOGENETIC	THERMORECEPTORS	THESAURUSES
THERAPEUTICS	THERMALIZE	THERMOGENIC	THERMOREGULATE	THESMOTHETE
THERAPEUTIST	THERMALIZED	THERMOGENOUS	THERMOREGULATED	THESMOTHETES
THERAPEUTISTS	THERMALIZES	THERMOGRAM	THERMOREGULATES	THETICALLY
THERAPISED	THERMALIZING	THERMOGRAMS	THERMOREGULATOR	THEURGICAL
THERAPISES	THERMESTHESIA	THERMOGRAPH	THERMOREMANENCE	THEURGICALLY
THERAPISING	THERMESTHESIAS	THERMOGRAPHER	THERMOREMANENT	THEURGISTS
THERAPISTS	THERMETTES	THERMOGRAPHERS	THERMOSCOPE	THIABENDAZOLE
THERAPIZED	THERMICALLY	THERMOGRAPHIC	THERMOSCOPES	THIABENDAZOLES
THERAPIZES	THERMIDORS	THERMOGRAPHIES	THERMOSCOPIC	THIAMINASE
THERAPIZING	THERMIONIC	THERMOGRAPHS	THERMOSCOPICAL	THIAMINASES
THERAPSIDS	THERMIONICS	THERMOGRAPHY	THERMOSETS	THICKENERS
THEREABOUT	THERMISTOR	THERMOHALINE	THERMOSETTING	THICKENING
THEREABOUTS	THERMISTORS	THERMOJUNCTION	THERMOSIPHON	THICKENINGS
THEREAFTER	THERMOBALANCE	THERMOJUNCTIONS	THERMOSIPHONS	THICKETIER
THEREAGAINST	THERMOBALANCES	THERMOLABILE	THERMOSPHERE	THICKETIEST
THEREAMONG	THERMOBARIC	THERMOLABILITY	THERMOSPHERES	THICKHEADED
THEREANENT	THERMOBAROGRAPH	THERMOLOGIES	THERMOSPHERIC	THICKHEADEDNESS
THEREBESIDE	THERMOBAROMETER	THERMOLOGY	THERMOSTABILITY	THICKHEADS
THEREINAFTER	THERMOCHEMICAL	THERMOLYSES	THERMOSTABLE	THICKLEAVES
THEREINBEFORE	THERMOCHEMIST	THERMOLYSIS	THERMOSTAT	THICKNESSES
THERENESSES	THERMOCHEMISTRY	THERMOLYTIC	THERMOSTATED	THICKSKINS
THERETHROUGH	THERMOCHEMISTS	THERMOMAGNETIC	THERMOSTATIC	THIEVERIES
THERETOFORE	THERMOCHROMIC	THERMOMETER	THERMOSTATICS	THIEVISHLY
THEREUNDER	THERMOCHROMIES	THERMOMETERS	THERMOSTATING	THIEVISHNESS
THEREWITHAL	THERMOCHROMISM	THERMOMETRIC	THERMOSTATS	THIEVISHNESSES

THIGHBONES

THIGHBONES
THIGMOTACTIC
THIGMOTAXES
THIGMOTAXIS
THIGMOTROPIC
THIGMOTROPISM
THIGMOTROPISMS
THIMBLEBERRIES
THIMBLEBERRY
THIMBLEFUL
THIMBLEFULS
THIMBLERIG
THIMBLERIGGED
THIMBLERIGGER
THIMBLERIGGERS
THIMBLERIGGING
THIMBLERIGGINGS
THIMBLERIGS
THIMBLESFUL
THIMBLEWEED
THIMBLEWEEDS
THIMBLEWIT
THIMBLEWITS
THIMBLEWITTED
THIMEROSAL
THIMEROSALS
THINGAMABOB
THINGAMABOBS
THINGAMAJIG
THINGAMAJIGS
THINGAMIES
THINGAMYBOB
THINGAMYBOBS
THINGAMYJIG
THINGAMYJIGS
THINGHOODS
THINGINESS
THINGINESSES
THINGLINESS
THINGLINESSES
THINGNESSES
THINGUMABOB
THINGUMABOBS
THINGUMAJIG
THINGUMAJIGS
THINGUMBOB
THINGUMBOBS
THINGUMMIES

THINGUMMYBOB
THINGUMMYBOBS
THINGUMMYJIG
THINGUMMYJIGS
THINKABLENESS
THINKABLENESSES
THINKINGLY
THINKINGNESS
THINKINGNESSES
THINKPIECE
THINKPIECES
THINNESSES
THIOALCOHOL
THIOALCOHOLS
THIOBACILLI
THIOBACILLUS
THIOBARBITURATE
THIOCARBAMIDE
THIOCARBAMIDES
THIOCYANATE
THIOCYANATES
THIOCYANIC
THIODIGLYCOL
THIODIGLYCOLS
THIOFURANS
THIOPENTAL
THIOPENTALS
THIOPENTONE
THIOPENTONES
THIOPHENES
THIORIDAZINE
THIORIDAZINES
THIOSINAMINE
THIOSINAMINES
THIOSULFATE
THIOSULFATES
THIOSULFURIC
THIOSULPHATE
THIOSULPHATES
THIOSULPHURIC
THIOURACIL
THIOURACILS
THIRDBOROUGH
THIRDBOROUGHS
THIRDSTREAM
THIRDSTREAMS
THIRSTIEST
THIRSTINESS

THIRSTINESSES
THIRSTLESS
THIRTEENTH
THIRTEENTHLY
THIRTEENTHS
THIRTIETHS
THIRTYFOLD
THIRTYSOMETHING
THISNESSES
THISTLEDOWN
THISTLEDOWNS
THISTLIEST
THITHERWARD
THITHERWARDS
THIXOTROPE
THIXOTROPES
THIXOTROPIC
THIXOTROPIES
THIXOTROPY
THOLEIITES
THOLEIITIC
THOLOBATES
THORACENTESES
THORACENTESIS
THORACICALLY
THORACOCENTESES
THORACOCENTESIS
THORACOPLASTIES
THORACOPLASTY
THORACOSCOPE
THORACOSCOPES
THORACOSTOMIES
THORACOSTOMY
THORACOTOMIES
THORACOTOMY
THORIANITE
THORIANITES
THORNBACKS
THORNBILLS
THORNBIRDS
THORNBUSHES
THORNHEDGE
THORNHEDGES
THORNINESS
THORNINESSES
THORNPROOF
THORNPROOFS
THORNTAILS

THORNTREES
THOROUGHBASS
THOROUGHBASSES
THOROUGHBRACE
THOROUGHBRACED
THOROUGHBRACES
THOROUGHBRED
THOROUGHBREDS
THOROUGHER
THOROUGHEST
THOROUGHFARE
THOROUGHFARES
THOROUGHGOING
THOROUGHGOINGLY
THOROUGHLY
THOROUGHNESS
THOROUGHNESSES
THOROUGHPACED
THOROUGHPIN
THOROUGHPINS
THOROUGHWAX
THOROUGHWAXES
THOROUGHWORT
THOROUGHWORTS
THOUGHTCAST
THOUGHTCASTS
THOUGHTFUL
THOUGHTFULLY
THOUGHTFULNESS
THOUGHTLESS
THOUGHTLESSLY
THOUGHTLESSNESS
THOUGHTWAY
THOUGHTWAYS
THOUSANDFOLD
THOUSANDFOLDS
THOUSANDTH
THOUSANDTHS
THRAIPINGS
THRALLDOMS
THRAPPLING
THRASHIEST
THRASHINGS
THRASONICAL
THRASONICALLY
THREADBARE
THREADBARENESS
THREADBARER

THREADBAREST
THREADFINS
THREADIEST
THREADINESS
THREADINESSES
THREADLESS
THREADLIKE
THREADMAKER
THREADMAKERS
THREADWORM
THREADWORMS
THREATENED
THREATENER
THREATENERS
THREATENING
THREATENINGLY
THREATENINGS
THREEFOLDNESS
THREEFOLDNESSES
THREENESSES
THREEPEATED
THREEPEATING
THREEPEATS
THREEPENCE
THREEPENCES
THREEPENCEWORTH
THREEPENNIES
THREEPENNY
THREEPENNYWORTH
THREEQUELS
THREESCORE
THREESCORES
THREESOMES
THREMMATOLOGIES
THREMMATOLOGY
THRENETICAL
THRENODIAL
THRENODIES
THRENODIST
THRENODISTS
THREONINES
THRESHINGS
THRESHOLDS
THRIFTIEST
THRIFTINESS
THRIFTINESSES
THRIFTLESS
THRIFTLESSLY

THRIFTLESSNESS	THROTTLEABLE	THUMBTACKING	THUSNESSES	THYSANUROUS
THRILLIEST	THROTTLEHOLD	THUMBTACKS	THWACKINGS	TIBIOFIBULA
THRILLINGLY	THROTTLEHOLDS	THUMBWHEEL	THWARTEDLY	TIBIOFIBULAE
THRILLINGNESS	THROTTLERS	THUMBWHEELS	THWARTINGLY	TIBIOFIBULAS
THRILLINGNESSES	THROTTLING	THUMPINGLY	THWARTINGS	TIBIOTARSI
THRIVELESS	THROTTLINGS	THUNBERGIA	THWARTSHIP	TIBIOTARSUS
THRIVINGLY	THROUGHFARE	THUNBERGIAS	THWARTSHIPS	TIBOUCHINA
THRIVINGNESS	THROUGHFARES	THUNDERBIRD	THWARTWAYS	TIBOUCHINAS
THRIVINGNESSES	THROUGHGAUN	THUNDERBIRDS	THWARTWISE	TICHORRHINE
THROATIEST	THROUGHGAUNS	THUNDERBOLT	THYLACINES	TICHORRHINES
THROATINESS	THROUGHITHER	THUNDERBOLTS	THYLAKOIDS	TICKETINGS
THROATINESSES	THROUGHOTHER	THUNDERBOX	THYMECTOMIES	TICKETLESS
THROATLASH	THROUGHOUT	THUNDERBOXES	THYMECTOMISE	TICKETTYBOO
THROATLASHES	THROUGHPUT	THUNDERCLAP	THYMECTOMISED	TICKLEASSES
THROATLATCH	THROUGHPUTS	THUNDERCLAPS	THYMECTOMISES	TICKLISHLY
THROATLATCHES	THROUGHWAY	THUNDERCLOUD	THYMECTOMISING	TICKLISHNESS
THROATWORT	THROUGHWAYS	THUNDERCLOUDS	THYMECTOMIZE	TICKLISHNESSES
THROATWORTS	THROWAWAYS	THUNDERERS	THYMECTOMIZED	TICKTACKED
THROBBINGLY	THROWBACKS	THUNDERFLASH	THYMECTOMIZES	TICKTACKING
THROBBINGS	THROWDOWNS	THUNDERFLASHES	THYMECTOMIZING	TICKTACKTOE
THROMBOCYTE	THROWOVERS	THUNDERHEAD	THYMECTOMY	TICKTACKTOES
THROMBOCYTES	THROWSTERS	THUNDERHEADS	THYMELAEACEOUS	TICKTOCKED
THROMBOCYTIC	THRUMMIEST	THUNDERIER	THYMIDINES	TICKTOCKING
THROMBOEMBOLIC	THRUMMINGLY	THUNDERIEST	THYMIDYLIC	TICTACKING
THROMBOEMBOLISM	THRUMMINGS	THUNDERING	THYMOCYTES	TICTOCKING
THROMBOGEN	THRUPENNIES	THUNDERINGLY	THYRATRONS	TIDDLEDYWINK
THROMBOGENS	THRUPPENCE	THUNDERINGS	THYRISTORS	TIDDLEDYWINKS
THROMBOKINASE	THRUPPENCES	THUNDERLESS	THYROCALCITONIN	TIDDLEYWINK
THROMBOKINASES	THRUPPENNIES	THUNDEROUS	THYROGLOBULIN	TIDDLEYWINKS
THROMBOLYSES	THRUPPENNY	THUNDEROUSLY	THYROGLOBULINS	TIDDLYWINK
THROMBOLYSIS	THRUSHLIKE	THUNDEROUSNESS	THYROIDECTOMIES	TIDDLYWINKS
THROMBOLYTIC	THRUSTINGS	THUNDERSHOWER	THYROIDECTOMY	TIDEWAITER
THROMBOLYTICS	THRUTCHING	THUNDERSHOWERS	THYROIDITIDES	TIDEWAITERS
THROMBOPHILIA	THUDDINGLY	THUNDERSTONE	THYROIDITIS	TIDEWATERS
THROMBOPHILIAS	THUGGERIES	THUNDERSTONES	THYROIDITISES	TIDINESSES
THROMBOPLASTIC	THUMBHOLES	THUNDERSTORM	THYROTOXICOSES	TIDIVATING
THROMBOPLASTIN	THUMBIKINS	THUNDERSTORMS	THYROTOXICOSIS	TIDIVATION
THROMBOPLASTINS	THUMBLINGS	THUNDERSTRICKEN	THYROTROPHIC	TIDIVATIONS
THROMBOSED	THUMBNAILS	THUNDERSTRIKE	THYROTROPHIN	TIEBREAKER
THROMBOSES	THUMBPIECE	THUNDERSTRIKES	THYROTROPHINS	TIEBREAKERS
THROMBOSING	THUMBPIECES	THUNDERSTRIKING	THYROTROPIC	TIEMANNITE
THROMBOSIS	THUMBPRINT	THUNDERSTROKE	THYROTROPIN	TIEMANNITES
THROMBOTIC	THUMBPRINTS	THUNDERSTROKES	THYROTROPINS	TIERCELETS
THROMBOXANE	THUMBSCREW	THUNDERSTRUCK	THYROXINES	TIERCERONS
THROMBOXANES	THUMBSCREWS	THURIFEROUS	THYRSOIDAL	TIGERISHLY
THRONELESS	THUMBSTALL	THURIFICATION	THYSANOPTEROUS	TIGERISHNESS
THRONGINGS	THUMBSTALLS	THURIFICATIONS	THYSANURAN	TIGERISHNESSES
THROPPLING	THUMBTACKED	THURIFYING	THYSANURANS	TIGERLIEST

TIGERWOODS	TIMBROMANIACS	TIMOROUSLY	TIREMAKERS	TITTUPIEST
TIGGYWINKLE	TIMBROMANIAS	TIMOROUSNESS	TIRESOMELY	TITTUPPIER
TIGGYWINKLES	TIMBROPHILIES	TIMOROUSNESSES	TIRESOMENESS	TITTUPPIEST
TIGHTASSED	TIMBROPHILIST	TIMPANISTS	TIRESOMENESSES	TITTUPPING
TIGHTASSES	TIMBROPHILISTS	TINCTORIAL	TIROCINIUM	TITUBANCIES
TIGHTENERS	TIMBROPHILY	TINCTORIALLY	TIROCINIUMS	TITUBATING
TIGHTENING	TIMEFRAMES	TINCTURING	TITANESSES	TITUBATION
TIGHTENINGS	TIMEKEEPER	TINDERBOXES	TITANICALLY	TITUBATIONS
TIGHTFISTED	TIMEKEEPERS	TINDERIEST	TITANIFEROUS	TITULARIES
TIGHTFISTEDNESS	TIMEKEEPING	TINGLINGLY	TITANOSAUR	TITULARITIES
TIGHTISHLY	TIMEKEEPINGS	TINGUAITES	TITANOSAURS	TITULARITY
TIGHTNESSES	TIMELESSLY	TININESSES	TITANOTHERE	TOADEATERS
TIGHTROPES	TIMELESSNESS	TINKERINGS	TITANOTHERES	TOADFISHES
TIGHTWIRES	TIMELESSNESSES	TINKERTOYS	TITARAKURA	TOADFLAXES
TIGRISHNESS	TIMELINESS	TINKLINGLY	TITARAKURAS	TOADGRASSES
TIGRISHNESSES	TIMELINESSES	TINNINESSES	TITHINGMAN	TOADRUSHES
TIKINAGANS	TIMENOGUYS	TINNITUSES	TITHINGMEN	TOADSTONES
TIKOLOSHES	TIMEPASSED	TINPLATING	TITILLATED	TOADSTOOLS
TIKTAALIKS	TIMEPASSES	TINSELIEST	TITILLATES	TOASTMASTER
TILEFISHES	TIMEPASSING	TINSELLIER	TITILLATING	TOASTMASTERS
TILIACEOUS	TIMEPIECES	TINSELLIEST	TITILLATINGLY	TOASTMISTRESS
TILLANDSIA	TIMEPLEASER	TINSELLING	TITILLATION	TOASTMISTRESSES
TILLANDSIAS	TIMEPLEASERS	TINSELRIES	TITILLATIONS	TOBACCANALIAN
TILLERINGS	TIMESAVERS	TINSMITHING	TITILLATIVE	TOBACCANALIANS
TILLERLESS	TIMESAVING	TINSMITHINGS	TITILLATOR	TOBACCOLESS
TILTMETERS	TIMESCALES	TINTINESSES	TITILLATORS	TOBACCONIST
TILTROTORS	TIMESERVER	TINTINNABULA	TITIPOUNAMU	TOBACCONISTS
TIMBERDOODLE	TIMESERVERS	TINTINNABULANT	TITIPOUNAMUS	TOBOGGANED
TIMBERDOODLES	TIMESERVING	TINTINNABULAR	TITIVATING	TOBOGGANER
TIMBERHEAD	TIMESERVINGS	TINTINNABULARY	TITIVATION	TOBOGGANERS
TIMBERHEADS	TIMESHARES	TINTINNABULATE	TITIVATIONS	TOBOGGANING
TIMBERIEST	TIMESHIFTED	TINTINNABULATED	TITIVATORS	TOBOGGANINGS
TIMBERINGS	TIMESHIFTING	TINTINNABULATES	TITLEHOLDER	TOBOGGANIST
TIMBERLAND	TIMESHIFTS	TINTINNABULOUS	TITLEHOLDERS	TOBOGGANISTS
TIMBERLANDS	TIMESTAMPED	TINTINNABULUM	TITLEHOLDING	TOBOGGINED
TIMBERLINE	TIMESTAMPING	TINTOMETER	TITRATABLE	TOBOGGINING
TIMBERLINES	TIMESTAMPS	TINTOMETERS	TITRATIONS	TOCCATELLA
TIMBERWORK	TIMETABLED	TINTOOKIES	TITRIMETRIC	TOCCATELLAS
TIMBERWORKS	TIMETABLES	TIPPYTOEING	TITTERINGLY	TOCCATINAS
TIMBERYARD	TIMETABLING	TIPSIFYING	TITTERINGS	TOCHERLESS
TIMBERYARDS	TIMETABLINGS	TIPSINESSES	TITTIVATED	TOCOLOGIES
TIMBRELLED	TIMEWORKER	TIPTRONICS	TITTIVATES	TOCOPHEROL
TIMBROLOGIES	TIMEWORKERS	TIRAILLEUR	TITTIVATING	TOCOPHEROLS
TIMBROLOGIST	TIMIDITIES	TIRAILLEURS	TITTIVATION	TOCOPHOBIA
TIMBROLOGISTS	TIMIDNESSES	TIREDNESSES	TITTIVATIONS	TOCOPHOBIAS
TIMBROLOGY	TIMOCRACIES	TIRELESSLY	TITTIVATOR	TODDLERHOOD
TIMBROMANIA	TIMOCRATIC	TIRELESSNESS	TITTIVATORS	TODDLERHOODS
TIMBROMANIAC	TIMOCRATICAL	TIRELESSNESSES	TITTLEBATS	TOENAILING

TOERAGGERS
TOFFISHNESS
TOFFISHNESSES
TOGAVIRUSES
TOGETHERNESS
TOGETHERNESSES
TOILETINGS
TOILETRIES
TOILFULNESS
TOILFULNESSES
TOILINETTE
TOILINETTES
TOILSOMELY
TOILSOMENESS
TOILSOMENESSES
TOKENISTIC
TOKOLOGIES
TOKOLOSHES
TOKOLOSHIS
TOKOPHOBIA
TOKOPHOBIAS
TOKTOKKIES
TOLBUTAMIDE
TOLBUTAMIDES
TOLERABILITIES
TOLERABILITY
TOLERABLENESS
TOLERABLENESSES
TOLERANCES
TOLERANTLY
TOLERATING
TOLERATION
TOLERATIONISM
TOLERATIONISMS
TOLERATIONIST
TOLERATIONISTS
TOLERATIONS
TOLERATIVE
TOLERATORS
TOLLBOOTHS
TOLLBRIDGE
TOLLBRIDGES
TOLLDISHES
TOLLGATING
TOLLHOUSES
TOLLKEEPER
TOLLKEEPERS
TOLUIDIDES

TOLUIDINES
TOMAHAWKED
TOMAHAWKING
TOMATILLOES
TOMATILLOS
TOMATOIEST
TOMBOYISHLY
TOMBOYISHNESS
TOMBOYISHNESSES
TOMBSTONES
TOMBSTONING
TOMBSTONINGS
TOMCATTING
TOMCATTINGS
TOMFOOLERIES
TOMFOOLERY
TOMFOOLING
TOMFOOLISH
TOMFOOLISHNESS
TOMOGRAPHIC
TOMOGRAPHIES
TOMOGRAPHS
TOMOGRAPHY
TONALITIES
TONALITIVE
TONELESSLY
TONELESSNESS
TONELESSNESSES
TONETICALLY
TONGUELESS
TONGUELETS
TONGUELIKE
TONGUESTER
TONGUESTERS
TONICITIES
TONISHNESS
TONISHNESSES
TONNISHNESS
TONNISHNESSES
TONOMETERS
TONOMETRIC
TONOMETRIES
TONOPLASTS
TONSILITIS
TONSILITISES
TONSILLARY
TONSILLECTOMIES
TONSILLECTOMY

TONSILLITIC
TONSILLITIDES
TONSILLITIS
TONSILLITISES
TONSILLOTOMIES
TONSILLOTOMY
TOOLCHESTS
TOOLHOLDER
TOOLHOLDERS
TOOLHOUSES
TOOLMAKERS
TOOLMAKING
TOOLMAKINGS
TOOLPUSHER
TOOLPUSHERS
TOOLPUSHES
TOOTHACHES
TOOTHBRUSH
TOOTHBRUSHES
TOOTHBRUSHING
TOOTHBRUSHINGS
TOOTHCOMBS
TOOTHFISHES
TOOTHINESS
TOOTHINESSES
TOOTHPASTE
TOOTHPASTES
TOOTHPICKS
TOOTHSHELL
TOOTHSHELLS
TOOTHSOMELY
TOOTHSOMENESS
TOOTHSOMENESSES
TOOTHWASHES
TOOTHWORTS
TOPAGNOSES
TOPAGNOSIA
TOPAGNOSIAS
TOPAGNOSIS
TOPARCHIES
TOPAZOLITE
TOPAZOLITES
TOPCROSSES
TOPDRESSING
TOPDRESSINGS
TOPECTOMIES
TOPGALLANT
TOPGALLANTS

TOPHACEOUS
TOPIARISTS
TOPICALITIES
TOPICALITY
TOPKNOTTED
TOPLESSNESS
TOPLESSNESSES
TOPLOFTICAL
TOPLOFTIER
TOPLOFTIEST
TOPLOFTILY
TOPLOFTINESS
TOPLOFTINESSES
TOPMAKINGS
TOPMINNOWS
TOPNOTCHER
TOPNOTCHERS
TOPOCENTRIC
TOPOCHEMISTRIES
TOPOCHEMISTRY
TOPOGRAPHER
TOPOGRAPHERS
TOPOGRAPHIC
TOPOGRAPHICAL
TOPOGRAPHICALLY
TOPOGRAPHIES
TOPOGRAPHS
TOPOGRAPHY
TOPOISOMERASE
TOPOISOMERASES
TOPOLOGICAL
TOPOLOGICALLY
TOPOLOGIES
TOPOLOGIST
TOPOLOGISTS
TOPOMETRIES
TOPONYMICAL
TOPONYMICS
TOPONYMIES
TOPONYMIST
TOPONYMISTS
TOPOPHILIA
TOPOPHILIAS
TOPSCORING
TOPSOILING
TOPSOILINGS
TOPSTITCHED
TOPSTITCHES

TOPSTITCHING
TOPWORKING
TORBANITES
TORBERNITE
TORBERNITES
TORCHBEARER
TORCHBEARERS
TORCHIERES
TORCHLIGHT
TORCHLIGHTS
TORCHWOODS
TORMENTEDLY
TORMENTERS
TORMENTILS
TORMENTING
TORMENTINGLY
TORMENTINGS
TORMENTORS
TORMENTUMS
TOROIDALLY
TOROSITIES
TORPEDINOUS
TORPEDOERS
TORPEDOING
TORPEDOIST
TORPEDOISTS
TORPEFYING
TORPESCENCE
TORPESCENCES
TORPESCENT
TORPIDITIES
TORPIDNESS
TORPIDNESSES
TORPITUDES
TORPORIFIC
TORREFACTION
TORREFACTIONS
TORREFYING
TORRENTIAL
TORRENTIALITIES
TORRENTIALITY
TORRENTIALLY
TORRENTUOUS
TORRIDITIES
TORRIDNESS
TORRIDNESSES
TORRIFYING
TORSIBILITIES

TORSIBILITY	TOTALIZERS	TOURNAMENT	TOXIGENICITY	TRACHEOSCOPIES
TORSIOGRAPH	TOTALIZING	TOURNAMENTS	TOXIPHAGOUS	TRACHEOSCOPY
TORSIOGRAPHS	TOTAQUINES	TOURNEYERS	TOXIPHOBIA	TRACHEOSTOMIES
TORSIONALLY	TOTEMICALLY	TOURNEYING	TOXIPHOBIAC	TRACHEOSTOMY
TORTELLINI	TOTEMISTIC	TOURNIQUET	TOXIPHOBIACS	TRACHEOTOMIES
TORTELLINIS	TOTIPALMATE	TOURNIQUETS	TOXIPHOBIAS	TRACHEOTOMY
TORTFEASOR	TOTIPALMATION	TOURTIERES	TOXOCARIASES	TRACHINUSES
TORTFEASORS	TOTIPALMATIONS	TOVARICHES	TOXOCARIASIS	TRACHITISES
TORTICOLLAR	TOTIPOTENCIES	TOVARISCHES	TOXOPHILIES	TRACHOMATOUS
TORTICOLLIS	TOTIPOTENCY	TOVARISHES	TOXOPHILITE	TRACHYPTERUS
TORTICOLLISES	TOTIPOTENT	TOWARDLINESS	TOXOPHILITES	TRACHYPTERUSES
TORTILITIES	TOTTERIEST	TOWARDLINESSES	TOXOPHILITIC	TRACHYTOID
TORTILLONS	TOTTERINGLY	TOWARDNESS	TOXOPLASMA	TRACKBALLS
TORTIOUSLY	TOTTERINGS	TOWARDNESSES	TOXOPLASMAS	TRACKERBALL
TORTOISESHELL	TOUCHABLENESS	TOWELETTES	TOXOPLASMIC	TRACKERBALLS
TORTOISESHELLS	TOUCHABLENESSES	TOWELHEADS	TOXOPLASMOSES	TRACKLAYER
TORTRICIDS	TOUCHBACKS	TOWELLINGS	TOXOPLASMOSIS	TRACKLAYERS
TORTUOSITIES	TOUCHDOWNS	TOWERINGLY	TOYISHNESS	TRACKLAYING
TORTUOSITY	TOUCHHOLES	TOWNHOUSES	TOYISHNESSES	TRACKLAYINGS
TORTUOUSLY	TOUCHINESS	TOWNSCAPED	TRABEATION	TRACKLEMENT
TORTUOUSNESS	TOUCHINESSES	TOWNSCAPES	TRABEATIONS	TRACKLEMENTS
TORTUOUSNESSES	TOUCHINGLY	TOWNSCAPING	TRABECULAE	TRACKLESSLY
TORTUREDLY	TOUCHINGNESS	TOWNSCAPINGS	TRABECULAR	TRACKLESSNESS
TORTURESOME	TOUCHINGNESSES	TOWNSFOLKS	TRABECULAS	TRACKLESSNESSES
TORTURINGLY	TOUCHLINES	TOWNSPEOPLE	TRABECULATE	TRACKROADS
TORTURINGS	TOUCHMARKS	TOWNSPEOPLES	TRABECULATED	TRACKSIDES
TORTUROUSLY	TOUCHPAPER	TOWNSWOMAN	TRACASSERIE	TRACKSUITS
TOSSICATED	TOUCHPAPERS	TOWNSWOMEN	TRACASSERIES	TRACKWALKER
TOSTICATED	TOUCHSCREEN	TOXALBUMIN	TRACEABILITIES	TRACKWALKERS
TOSTICATION	TOUCHSCREENS	TOXALBUMINS	TRACEABILITY	TRACTABILITIES
TOSTICATIONS	TOUCHSTONE	TOXAPHENES	TRACEABLENESS	TRACTABILITY
TOTALISATION	TOUCHSTONES	TOXICATION	TRACEABLENESSES	TRACTABLENESS
TOTALISATIONS	TOUCHTONES	TOXICATIONS	TRACELESSLY	TRACTABLENESSES
TOTALISATOR	TOUCHWOODS	TOXICITIES	TRACHEARIAN	TRACTARIAN
TOTALISATORS	TOUGHENERS	TOXICOGENIC	TRACHEARIANS	TRACTARIANS
TOTALISERS	TOUGHENING	TOXICOLOGIC	TRACHEARIES	TRACTATORS
TOTALISING	TOUGHENINGS	TOXICOLOGICAL	TRACHEATED	TRACTILITIES
TOTALISTIC	TOUGHNESSES	TOXICOLOGICALLY	TRACHEATES	TRACTILITY
TOTALITARIAN	TOURBILLION	TOXICOLOGIES	TRACHEIDAL	TRACTIONAL
TOTALITARIANISE	TOURBILLIONS	TOXICOLOGIST	TRACHEIDES	TRACTORATION
TOTALITARIANISM	TOURBILLON	TOXICOLOGISTS	TRACHEITIDES	TRACTORATIONS
TOTALITARIANIZE	TOURBILLONS	TOXICOLOGY	TRACHEITIS	TRACTORFEED
TOTALITARIANS	TOURISTICALLY	TOXICOMANIA	TRACHEITISES	TRACTORFEEDS
TOTALITIES	TOURISTIER	TOXICOMANIAS	TRACHELATE	TRACTRICES
TOTALIZATION	TOURISTIEST	TOXICOPHAGOUS	TRACHEOLAR	TRADECRAFT
TOTALIZATIONS	TOURMALINE	TOXICOPHOBIA	TRACHEOLES	TRADECRAFTS
TOTALIZATOR	TOURMALINES	TOXICOPHOBIAS	TRACHEOPHYTE	TRADEMARKED
TOTALIZATORS	TOURMALINIC	TOXIGENICITIES	TRACHEOPHYTES	TRADEMARKING

TRADEMARKS	TRADUCTION	TRAINABILITY	TRAMPOLINES	TRANSACTINIDE
TRADENAMES	TRADUCTIONS	TRAINBANDS	TRAMPOLINING	TRANSACTINIDES
TRADERSHIP	TRADUCTIVE	TRAINBEARER	TRAMPOLININGS	TRANSACTION
TRADERSHIPS	TRAFFICABILITY	TRAINBEARERS	TRAMPOLINIST	TRANSACTIONAL
TRADESCANTIA	TRAFFICABLE	TRAINEESHIP	TRAMPOLINISTS	TRANSACTIONALLY
TRADESCANTIAS	TRAFFICATOR	TRAINEESHIPS	TRAMPOLINS	TRANSACTIONS
TRADESFOLK	TRAFFICATORS	TRAINLOADS	TRANCELIKE	TRANSACTOR
TRADESFOLKS	TRAFFICKED	TRAINSPOTTER	TRANQUILER	TRANSACTORS
TRADESMANLIKE	TRAFFICKER	TRAINSPOTTERISH	TRANQUILEST	TRANSALPINE
TRADESPEOPLE	TRAFFICKERS	TRAINSPOTTERS	TRANQUILISATION	TRANSALPINES
TRADESPEOPLES	TRAFFICKIER	TRAIPSINGS	TRANQUILISE	TRANSAMINASE
TRADESPERSON	TRAFFICKIEST	TRAITORESS	TRANQUILISED	TRANSAMINASES
TRADESPERSONS	TRAFFICKING	TRAITORESSES	TRANQUILISER	TRANSAMINATION
TRADESWOMAN	TRAFFICKINGS	TRAITORHOOD	TRANQUILISERS	TRANSAMINATIONS
TRADESWOMEN	TRAFFICLESS	TRAITORHOODS	TRANQUILISES	TRANSANDEAN
TRADITIONAL	TRAGACANTH	TRAITORISM	TRANQUILISING	TRANSANDINE
TRADITIONALISE	TRAGACANTHS	TRAITORISMS	TRANQUILISINGLY	TRANSATLANTIC
TRADITIONALISED	TRAGEDIANS	TRAITOROUS	TRANQUILITIES	TRANSAXLES
TRADITIONALISES	TRAGEDIENNE	TRAITOROUSLY	TRANQUILITY	TRANSCALENCIES
TRADITIONALISM	TRAGEDIENNES	TRAITOROUSNESS	TRANQUILIZATION	TRANSCALENCY
TRADITIONALISMS	TRAGELAPHINE	TRAITORSHIP	TRANQUILIZE	TRANSCALENT
TRADITIONALIST	TRAGELAPHS	TRAITORSHIPS	TRANQUILIZED	TRANSCAUCASIAN
TRADITIONALISTS	TRAGICALLY	TRAITRESSES	TRANQUILIZER	TRANSCEIVER
TRADITIONALITY	TRAGICALNESS	TRAJECTILE	TRANQUILIZERS	TRANSCEIVERS
TRADITIONALIZE	TRAGICALNESSES	TRAJECTING	TRANQUILIZES	TRANSCENDED
TRADITIONALIZED	TRAGICOMEDIES	TRAJECTION	TRANQUILIZING	TRANSCENDENCE
TRADITIONALIZES	TRAGICOMEDY	TRAJECTIONS	TRANQUILIZINGLY	TRANSCENDENCES
TRADITIONALLY	TRAGICOMIC	TRAJECTORIES	TRANQUILLER	TRANSCENDENCIES
TRADITIONARILY	TRAGICOMICAL	TRAJECTORY	TRANQUILLEST	TRANSCENDENCY
TRADITIONARY	TRAGICOMICALLY	TRALATICIOUS	TRANQUILLISE	TRANSCENDENT
TRADITIONER	TRAILBASTON	TRALATITIOUS	TRANQUILLISED	TRANSCENDENTAL
TRADITIONERS	TRAILBASTONS	TRAMELLING	TRANQUILLISER	TRANSCENDENTALS
TRADITIONIST	TRAILBLAZER	TRAMMELERS	TRANQUILLISERS	TRANSCENDENTLY
TRADITIONISTS	TRAILBLAZERS	TRAMMELING	TRANQUILLISES	TRANSCENDENTS
TRADITIONLESS	TRAILBLAZING	TRAMMELLED	TRANQUILLISING	TRANSCENDING
TRADITIONS	TRAILBLAZINGS	TRAMMELLER	TRANQUILLITIES	TRANSCENDINGLY
TRADITORES	TRAILBREAKER	TRAMMELLERS	TRANQUILLITY	TRANSCENDS
TRADUCEMENT	TRAILBREAKERS	TRAMMELLING	TRANQUILLIZE	TRANSCODED
TRADUCEMENTS	TRAILERABLE	TRAMONTANA	TRANQUILLIZED	TRANSCODER
TRADUCIANISM	TRAILERING	TRAMONTANAS	TRANQUILLIZER	TRANSCODERS
TRADUCIANISMS	TRAILERINGS	TRAMONTANE	TRANQUILLIZERS	TRANSCODES
TRADUCIANIST	TRAILERIST	TRAMONTANES	TRANQUILLIZES	TRANSCODING
TRADUCIANISTIC	TRAILERISTS	TRAMPETTES	TRANQUILLIZING	TRANSCRANIAL
TRADUCIANISTS	TRAILERITE	TRAMPLINGS	TRANQUILLY	TRANSCRIBABLE
TRADUCIANS	TRAILERITES	TRAMPOLINE	TRANQUILNESS	TRANSCRIBE
TRADUCIBLE	TRAILHEADS	TRAMPOLINED	TRANQUILNESSES	TRANSCRIBED
TRADUCINGLY	TRAILINGLY	TRAMPOLINER	TRANSACTED	TRANSCRIBER
TRADUCINGS	TRAINABILITIES	TRAMPOLINERS	TRANSACTING	TRANSCRIBERS

TRANSCRIBES

TRANSCRIBES	TRANSFERABILITY	TRANSFORMISTS	TRANSHUMES	TRANSLATED
TRANSCRIBING	TRANSFERABLE	TRANSFORMS	TRANSHUMING	TRANSLATES
TRANSCRIPT	TRANSFERAL	TRANSFUSABLE	TRANSIENCE	TRANSLATING
TRANSCRIPTASE	TRANSFERALS	TRANSFUSED	TRANSIENCES	TRANSLATION
TRANSCRIPTASES	TRANSFERASE	TRANSFUSER	TRANSIENCIES	TRANSLATIONAL
TRANSCRIPTION	TRANSFERASES	TRANSFUSERS	TRANSIENCY	TRANSLATIONALLY
TRANSCRIPTIONAL	TRANSFEREE	TRANSFUSES	TRANSIENTLY	TRANSLATIONS
TRANSCRIPTIONS	TRANSFEREES	TRANSFUSIBLE	TRANSIENTNESS	TRANSLATIVE
TRANSCRIPTIVE	TRANSFERENCE	TRANSFUSING	TRANSIENTNESSES	TRANSLATIVES
TRANSCRIPTIVELY	TRANSFERENCES	TRANSFUSION	TRANSIENTS	TRANSLATOR
TRANSCRIPTOME	TRANSFERENTIAL	TRANSFUSIONAL	TRANSILIENCE	TRANSLATORIAL
TRANSCRIPTOMES	TRANSFEROR	TRANSFUSIONIST	TRANSILIENCES	TRANSLATORS
TRANSCRIPTS	TRANSFERORS	TRANSFUSIONISTS	TRANSILIENCIES	TRANSLATORY
TRANSCULTURAL	TRANSFERRABLE	TRANSFUSIONS	TRANSILIENCY	TRANSLEITHAN
TRANSCURRENT	TRANSFERRAL	TRANSFUSIVE	TRANSILIENT	TRANSLITERATE
TRANSCUTANEOUS	TRANSFERRALS	TRANSFUSIVELY	TRANSILLUMINATE	TRANSLITERATED
TRANSDERMAL	TRANSFERRED	TRANSGENDER	TRANSISTHMIAN	TRANSLITERATES
TRANSDUCED	TRANSFERRER	TRANSGENDERED	TRANSISTOR	TRANSLITERATING
TRANSDUCER	TRANSFERRERS	TRANSGENDERS	TRANSISTORISE	TRANSLITERATION
TRANSDUCERS	TRANSFERRIBLE	TRANSGENES	TRANSISTORISED	TRANSLITERATOR
TRANSDUCES	TRANSFERRIN	TRANSGENESES	TRANSISTORISES	TRANSLITERATORS
TRANSDUCING	TRANSFERRING	TRANSGENESIS	TRANSISTORISING	TRANSLOCATE
TRANSDUCTANT	TRANSFERRINS	TRANSGENIC	TRANSISTORIZE	TRANSLOCATED
TRANSDUCTANTS	TRANSFIGURATION	TRANSGENICS	TRANSISTORIZED	TRANSLOCATES
TRANSDUCTION	TRANSFIGURE	TRANSGRESS	TRANSISTORIZES	TRANSLOCATING
TRANSDUCTIONAL	TRANSFIGURED	TRANSGRESSED	TRANSISTORIZING	TRANSLOCATION
TRANSDUCTIONS	TRANSFIGUREMENT	TRANSGRESSES	TRANSISTORS	TRANSLOCATIONS
TRANSDUCTOR	TRANSFIGURES	TRANSGRESSING	TRANSITABLE	TRANSLUCENCE
TRANSDUCTORS	TRANSFIGURING	TRANSGRESSION	TRANSITING	TRANSLUCENCES
TRANSECTED	TRANSFINITE	TRANSGRESSIONAL	TRANSITION	TRANSLUCENCIES
TRANSECTING	TRANSFIXED	TRANSGRESSIONS	TRANSITIONAL	TRANSLUCENCY
TRANSECTION	TRANSFIXES	TRANSGRESSIVE	TRANSITIONALLY	TRANSLUCENT
TRANSECTIONS	TRANSFIXING	TRANSGRESSIVELY	TRANSITIONALS	TRANSLUCENTLY
TRANSENNAS	TRANSFIXION	TRANSGRESSOR	TRANSITIONARY	TRANSLUCID
TRANSEPTAL	TRANSFIXIONS	TRANSGRESSORS	TRANSITIONED	TRANSLUCIDITIES
TRANSEPTATE	TRANSFORMABLE	TRANSHIPMENT	TRANSITIONING	TRANSLUCIDITY
TRANSEPTED	TRANSFORMATION	TRANSHIPMENTS	TRANSITIONS	TRANSLUMENAL
TRANSEXUAL	TRANSFORMATIONS	TRANSHIPPED	TRANSITIVE	TRANSLUMINAL
TRANSEXUALISM	TRANSFORMATIVE	TRANSHIPPER	TRANSITIVELY	TRANSLUNAR
TRANSEXUALISMS	TRANSFORMED	TRANSHIPPERS	TRANSITIVENESS	TRANSLUNARY
TRANSEXUALITIES	TRANSFORMER	TRANSHIPPING	TRANSITIVES	TRANSMANCHE
TRANSEXUALITY	TRANSFORMERS	TRANSHIPPINGS	TRANSITIVITIES	TRANSMARINE
TRANSEXUALS	TRANSFORMING	TRANSHISTORICAL	TRANSITIVITY	TRANSMEMBRANE
TRANSFECTED	TRANSFORMINGS	TRANSHUMANCE	TRANSITORILY	TRANSMEWED
TRANSFECTING	TRANSFORMISM	TRANSHUMANCES	TRANSITORINESS	TRANSMEWING
TRANSFECTION	TRANSFORMISMS	TRANSHUMANT	TRANSITORY	TRANSMIGRANT
TRANSFECTIONS	TRANSFORMIST	TRANSHUMANTS	TRANSLATABILITY	TRANSMIGRANTS
TRANSFECTS	TRANSFORMISTIC	TRANSHUMED	TRANSLATABLE	TRANSMIGRATE

TRANSMIGRATED	TRANSMUTED	TRANSPLANTED	TRANSSEXUALISM	TRANSVERSAL
TRANSMIGRATES	TRANSMUTER	TRANSPLANTER	TRANSSEXUALISMS	TRANSVERSALITY
TRANSMIGRATING	TRANSMUTERS	TRANSPLANTERS	TRANSSEXUALITY	TRANSVERSALLY
TRANSMIGRATION	TRANSMUTES	TRANSPLANTING	TRANSSEXUALS	TRANSVERSALS
TRANSMIGRATIONS	TRANSMUTING	TRANSPLANTINGS	TRANSSHAPE	TRANSVERSE
TRANSMIGRATIVE	TRANSNATIONAL	TRANSPLANTS	TRANSSHAPED	TRANSVERSED
TRANSMIGRATOR	TRANSNATURAL	TRANSPOLAR	TRANSSHAPES	TRANSVERSELY
TRANSMIGRATORS	TRANSOCEANIC	TRANSPONDER	TRANSSHAPING	TRANSVERSENESS
TRANSMIGRATORY	TRANSONICS	TRANSPONDERS	TRANSSHIPMENT	TRANSVERSES
TRANSMISSIBLE	TRANSPACIFIC	TRANSPONDOR	TRANSSHIPMENTS	TRANSVERSING
TRANSMISSION	TRANSPADANE	TRANSPONDORS	TRANSSHIPPED	TRANSVERSION
TRANSMISSIONAL	TRANSPARENCE	TRANSPONTINE	TRANSSHIPPER	TRANSVERSIONS
TRANSMISSIONS	TRANSPARENCES	TRANSPORTABLE	TRANSSHIPPERS	TRANSVERTER
TRANSMISSIVE	TRANSPARENCIES	TRANSPORTAL	TRANSSHIPPING	TRANSVERTERS
TRANSMISSIVELY	TRANSPARENCY	TRANSPORTALS	TRANSSHIPPINGS	TRANSVESTED
TRANSMISSIVITY	TRANSPARENT	TRANSPORTANCE	TRANSSHIPS	TRANSVESTIC
TRANSMISSOMETER	TRANSPARENTISE	TRANSPORTANCES	TRANSSONIC	TRANSVESTING
TRANSMITTABLE	TRANSPARENTISED	TRANSPORTATION	TRANSTHORACIC	TRANSVESTISM
TRANSMITTAL	TRANSPARENTISES	TRANSPORTATIONS	TRANSUBSTANTIAL	TRANSVESTISMS
TRANSMITTALS	TRANSPARENTIZE	TRANSPORTED	TRANSUDATE	TRANSVESTIST
TRANSMITTANCE	TRANSPARENTIZED	TRANSPORTEDLY	TRANSUDATES	TRANSVESTISTS
TRANSMITTANCES	TRANSPARENTIZES	TRANSPORTEDNESS	TRANSUDATION	TRANSVESTITE
TRANSMITTANCIES	TRANSPARENTLY	TRANSPORTER	TRANSUDATIONS	TRANSVESTITES
TRANSMITTANCY	TRANSPARENTNESS	TRANSPORTERS	TRANSUDATORY	TRANSVESTITISM
TRANSMITTED	TRANSPERSON	TRANSPORTING	TRANSUDING	TRANSVESTITISMS
TRANSMITTER	TRANSPERSONAL	TRANSPORTINGLY	TRANSUMING	TRANSVESTS
TRANSMITTERS	TRANSPERSONS	TRANSPORTINGS	TRANSUMPTION	TRANSWOMAN
TRANSMITTIBLE	TRANSPHOBIA	TRANSPORTIVE	TRANSUMPTIONS	TRANSWOMEN
TRANSMITTING	TRANSPHOBIAS	TRANSPORTS	TRANSUMPTIVE	TRAPANNERS
TRANSMITTIVITY	TRANSPHOBIC	TRANSPOSABILITY	TRANSUMPTS	TRAPANNING
TRANSMOGRIFIED	TRANSPICUOUS	TRANSPOSABLE	TRANSURANIAN	TRAPESINGS
TRANSMOGRIFIES	TRANSPICUOUSLY	TRANSPOSAL	TRANSURANIC	TRAPEZIFORM
TRANSMOGRIFY	TRANSPIERCE	TRANSPOSALS	TRANSURANICS	TRAPEZISTS
TRANSMOGRIFYING	TRANSPIERCED	TRANSPOSED	TRANSURANIUM	TRAPEZIUMS
TRANSMONTANE	TRANSPIERCES	TRANSPOSER	TRANSURETHRAL	TRAPEZIUSES
TRANSMONTANES	TRANSPIERCING	TRANSPOSERS	TRANSVAGINAL	TRAPEZOHEDRA
TRANSMOUNTAIN	TRANSPIRABLE	TRANSPOSES	TRANSVALUATE	TRAPEZOHEDRAL
TRANSMOVED	TRANSPIRATION	TRANSPOSING	TRANSVALUATED	TRAPEZOHEDRON
TRANSMOVES	TRANSPIRATIONAL	TRANSPOSINGS	TRANSVALUATES	TRAPEZOHEDRONS
TRANSMOVING	TRANSPIRATIONS	TRANSPOSITION	TRANSVALUATING	TRAPEZOIDAL
TRANSMUNDANE	TRANSPIRATORY	TRANSPOSITIONAL	TRANSVALUATION	TRAPEZOIDS
TRANSMUTABILITY	TRANSPIRED	TRANSPOSITIONS	TRANSVALUATIONS	TRAPNESTED
TRANSMUTABLE	TRANSPIRES	TRANSPOSITIVE	TRANSVALUE	TRAPNESTING
TRANSMUTABLY	TRANSPIRING	TRANSPOSON	TRANSVALUED	TRAPPINESS
TRANSMUTATION	TRANSPLACENTAL	TRANSPOSONS	TRANSVALUER	TRAPPINESSES
TRANSMUTATIONAL	TRANSPLANT	TRANSPUTER	TRANSVALUERS	TRAPSHOOTER
TRANSMUTATIONS	TRANSPLANTABLE	TRANSPUTERS	TRANSVALUES	TRAPSHOOTERS
TRANSMUTATIVE	TRANSPLANTATION	TRANSSEXUAL	TRANSVALUING	TRAPSHOOTING

T

TRAPSHOOTINGS	TRAVOLATORS	TREEHOPPER	TRENDINESS	TRIALLINGS
TRASHERIES	TRAWLERMAN	TREEHOPPERS	TRENDINESSES	TRIALLISTS
TRASHINESS	TRAWLERMEN	TREEHOUSES	TRENDSETTER	TRIALOGUES
TRASHINESSES	TRAYCLOTHS	TREELESSNESS	TRENDSETTERS	TRIALWARES
TRASHTRIES	TRAYMOBILE	TREELESSNESSES	TRENDSETTING	TRIAMCINOLONE
TRATTORIAS	TRAYMOBILES	TREENWARES	TRENDSETTINGS	TRIAMCINOLONES
TRAUCHLING	TRAZODONES	TREGETOURS	TRENDYISMS	TRIANDRIAN
TRAUMATICALLY	TREACHERER	TREHALOSES	TREPANATION	TRIANDROUS
TRAUMATISATION	TREACHERERS	TREILLAGED	TREPANATIONS	TRIANGULAR
TRAUMATISATIONS	TREACHERIES	TREILLAGES	TREPANNERS	TRIANGULARITIES
TRAUMATISE	TREACHEROUS	TREKSCHUIT	TREPANNING	TRIANGULARITY
TRAUMATISED	TREACHEROUSLY	TREKSCHUITS	TREPANNINGS	TRIANGULARLY
TRAUMATISES	TREACHEROUSNESS	TRELLISING	TREPHINATION	TRIANGULATE
TRAUMATISING	TREACHETOUR	TRELLISWORK	TREPHINATIONS	TRIANGULATED
TRAUMATISM	TREACHETOURS	TRELLISWORKS	TREPHINERS	TRIANGULATELY
TRAUMATISMS	TREACHOURS	TREMATODES	TREPHINING	TRIANGULATES
TRAUMATIZATION	TREACLIEST	TREMATOIDS	TREPHININGS	TRIANGULATING
TRAUMATIZATIONS	TREACLINESS	TREMBLEMENT	TREPIDATION	TRIANGULATION
TRAUMATIZE	TREACLINESSES	TREMBLEMENTS	TREPIDATIONS	TRIANGULATIONS
TRAUMATIZED	TREADLINGS	TREMBLIEST	TREPIDATORY	TRIAPSIDAL
TRAUMATIZES	TREADMILLS	TREMBLINGLY	TREPONEMAL	TRIARCHIES
TRAUMATIZING	TREADWHEEL	TREMBLINGS	TREPONEMAS	TRIATHLETE
TRAUMATOLOGICAL	TREADWHEELS	TREMENDOUS	TREPONEMATA	TRIATHLETES
TRAUMATOLOGIES	TREASONABLE	TREMENDOUSLY	TREPONEMATOSES	TRIATHLONS
TRAUMATOLOGY	TREASONABLENESS	TREMENDOUSNESS	TREPONEMATOSIS	TRIATOMICALLY
TRAUMATONASTIES	TREASONABLY	TREMOLANDI	TREPONEMATOUS	TRIAXIALITIES
TRAUMATONASTY	TREASONOUS	TREMOLANDO	TREPONEMES	TRIAXIALITY
TRAVAILING	TREASURABLE	TREMOLANDOS	TRESPASSED	TRIBADISMS
TRAVELATOR	TREASURELESS	TREMOLANTS	TRESPASSER	TRIBALISMS
TRAVELATORS	TREASURERS	TREMOLITES	TRESPASSERS	TRIBALISTIC
TRAVELINGS	TREASURERSHIP	TREMOLITIC	TRESPASSES	TRIBALISTS
TRAVELLERS	TREASURERSHIPS	TREMORLESS	TRESPASSING	TRIBESPEOPLE
TRAVELLING	TREASURIES	TREMULANTS	TRESTLETREE	TRIBESWOMAN
TRAVELLINGS	TREASURING	TREMULATED	TRESTLETREES	TRIBESWOMEN
TRAVELOGUE	TREATABILITIES	TREMULATES	TRESTLEWORK	TRIBOELECTRIC
TRAVELOGUES	TREATABILITY	TREMULATING	TRESTLEWORKS	TRIBOLOGICAL
TRAVERSABLE	TREATMENTS	TREMULOUSLY	TRETINOINS	TRIBOLOGIES
TRAVERSALS	TREATYLESS	TREMULOUSNESS	TREVALLIES	TRIBOLOGIST
TRAVERSERS	TREBBIANOS	TREMULOUSNESSES	TRIABLENESS	TRIBOLOGISTS
TRAVERSING	TREBLENESS	TRENCHANCIES	TRIABLENESSES	TRIBOMETER
TRAVERSINGS	TREBLENESSES	TRENCHANCY	TRIACETATE	TRIBOMETERS
TRAVERTINE	TREBUCHETS	TRENCHANTLY	TRIACETATES	TRIBRACHIAL
TRAVERTINES	TREBUCKETS	TRENCHARDS	TRIACONTER	TRIBRACHIC
TRAVERTINS	TRECENTIST	TRENCHERMAN	TRIACONTERS	TRIBROMOETHANOL
TRAVESTIED	TRECENTISTS	TRENCHERMEN	TRIACTINAL	TRIBROMOMETHANE
TRAVESTIES	TREDECILLION	TRENDIFIED	TRIADELPHOUS	TRIBULATED
TRAVESTYING	TREDECILLIONS	TRENDIFIES	TRIADICALLY	TRIBULATES
TRAVOLATOR	TREDRILLES	TRENDIFYING	TRIALITIES	TRIBULATING

TRILATERALISMS

TRIBULATION	TRICHINOTIC	TRICHOTOMISES	TRICORPORATE	TRIFOLIATED
TRIBULATIONS	TRICHINOUS	TRICHOTOMISING	TRICORPORATED	TRIFOLIOLATE
TRIBUNATES	TRICHLORACETIC	TRICHOTOMIZE	TRICOSTATE	TRIFOLIUMS
TRIBUNESHIP	TRICHLORFON	TRICHOTOMIZED	TRICOTEUSE	TRIFURCATE
TRIBUNESHIPS	TRICHLORFONS	TRICHOTOMIZES	TRICOTEUSES	TRIFURCATED
TRIBUNICIAL	TRICHLORIDE	TRICHOTOMIZING	TRICOTINES	TRIFURCATES
TRIBUNICIAN	TRICHLORIDES	TRICHOTOMOUS	TRICROTISM	TRIFURCATING
TRIBUNITIAL	TRICHLOROACETIC	TRICHOTOMOUSLY	TRICROTISMS	TRIFURCATION
TRIBUNITIAN	TRICHLOROETHANE	TRICHOTOMY	TRICROTOUS	TRIFURCATIONS
TRIBUTARIES	TRICHLORPHON	TRICHROISM	TRICUSPIDAL	TRIGAMISTS
TRIBUTARILY	TRICHLORPHONS	TRICHROISMS	TRICUSPIDATE	TRIGEMINAL
TRIBUTARINESS	TRICHOBACTERIA	TRICHROMAT	TRICUSPIDS	TRIGEMINALS
TRIBUTARINESSES	TRICHOCYST	TRICHROMATIC	TRICYCLERS	TRIGEMINUS
TRICAMERAL	TRICHOCYSTIC	TRICHROMATISM	TRICYCLICS	TRIGGERFISH
TRICARBOXYLIC	TRICHOCYSTS	TRICHROMATISMS	TRICYCLING	TRIGGERFISHES
TRICARPELLARY	TRICHOGYNE	TRICHROMATS	TRICYCLINGS	TRIGGERING
TRICENTENARIES	TRICHOGYNES	TRICHROMIC	TRICYCLIST	TRIGGERLESS
TRICENTENARY	TRICHOGYNIAL	TRICHROMICS	TRICYCLISTS	TRIGGERMAN
TRICENTENNIAL	TRICHOGYNIC	TRICHRONOUS	TRIDACTYLOUS	TRIGGERMEN
TRICENTENNIALS	TRICHOLOGICAL	TRICHURIASES	TRIDENTATE	TRIGLYCERIDE
TRICEPHALOUS	TRICHOLOGIES	TRICHURIASIS	TRIDIMENSIONAL	TRIGLYCERIDES
TRICERATOPS	TRICHOLOGIST	TRICKERIES	TRIDOMINIA	TRIGLYPHIC
TRICERATOPSES	TRICHOLOGISTS	TRICKINESS	TRIDOMINIUM	TRIGLYPHICAL
TRICERIONS	TRICHOLOGY	TRICKINESSES	TRIDOMINIUMS	TRIGNESSES
TRICHIASES	TRICHOMONACIDAL	TRICKISHLY	TRIDYMITES	TRIGONALLY
TRICHIASIS	TRICHOMONACIDE	TRICKISHNESS	TRIENNIALLY	TRIGONOMETER
TRICHINELLA	TRICHOMONACIDES	TRICKISHNESSES	TRIENNIALS	TRIGONOMETERS
TRICHINELLAE	TRICHOMONAD	TRICKLIEST	TRIENNIUMS	TRIGONOMETRIC
TRICHINELLAS	TRICHOMONADAL	TRICKLINGLY	TRIERARCHAL	TRIGONOMETRICAL
TRICHINIASES	TRICHOMONADS	TRICKLINGS	TRIERARCHIES	TRIGONOMETRIES
TRICHINIASIS	TRICHOMONAL	TRICKSIEST	TRIERARCHS	TRIGONOMETRY
TRICHINISATION	TRICHOMONIASES	TRICKSINESS	TRIERARCHY	TRIGRAMMATIC
TRICHINISATIONS	TRICHOMONIASIS	TRICKSINESSES	TRIETHIODIDE	TRIGRAMMIC
TRICHINISE	TRICHOPHYTON	TRICKSTERING	TRIETHIODIDES	TRIGRAPHIC
TRICHINISED	TRICHOPHYTONS	TRICKSTERINGS	TRIETHYLAMINE	TRIHALOMETHANE
TRICHINISES	TRICHOPHYTOSES	TRICKSTERS	TRIETHYLAMINES	TRIHALOMETHANES
TRICHINISING	TRICHOPHYTOSIS	TRICKTRACK	TRIFACIALS	TRIHEDRALS
TRICHINIZATION	TRICHOPTERAN	TRICKTRACKS	TRIFARIOUS	TRIHEDRONS
TRICHINIZATIONS	TRICHOPTERANS	TRICLINIUM	TRIFFIDIAN	TRIHYBRIDS
TRICHINIZE	TRICHOPTERIST	TRICLOSANS	TRIFFIDIER	TRIHYDRATE
TRICHINIZED	TRICHOPTERISTS	TRICOLETTE	TRIFFIDIEST	TRIHYDRATED
TRICHINIZES	TRICHOPTEROUS	TRICOLETTES	TRIFLINGLY	TRIHYDRATES
TRICHINIZING	TRICHOTHECENE	TRICOLORED	TRIFLINGNESS	TRIHYDROXY
TRICHINOSE	TRICHOTHECENES	TRICOLOURED	TRIFLINGNESSES	TRIIODOMETHANE
TRICHINOSED	TRICHOTOMIC	TRICOLOURS	TRIFLUOPERAZINE	TRIIODOMETHANES
TRICHINOSES	TRICHOTOMIES	TRICONSONANTAL	TRIFLURALIN	TRILATERAL
TRICHINOSING	TRICHOTOMISE	TRICONSONANTIC	TRIFLURALINS	TRILATERALISM
TRICHINOSIS	TRICHOTOMISED	TRICORNERED	TRIFOLIATE	TRILATERALISMS

TRILATERALIST	TRINACRIAN	TRIPERSONALITY	TRIQUETRAL	TRITENESSES
TRILATERALISTS	TRINACRIFORM	TRIPETALOUS	TRIQUETRAS	TRITERNATE
TRILATERALLY	TRINISCOPE	TRIPHAMMER	TRIQUETROUS	TRITHEISMS
TRILATERALS	TRINISCOPES	TRIPHAMMERS	TRIQUETROUSLY	TRITHEISTIC
TRILATERATION	TRINITARIAN	TRIPHENYLAMINE	TRIQUETRUM	TRITHEISTICAL
TRILATERATIONS	TRINITARIANS	TRIPHENYLAMINES	TRIRADIATE	TRITHEISTS
TRILINEATE	TRINITRATE	TRIPHIBIOUS	TRIRADIATELY	TRITHIONATE
TRILINGUAL	TRINITRATES	TRIPHOSPHATE	TRISACCHARIDE	TRITHIONATES
TRILINGUALISM	TRINITRINS	TRIPHOSPHATES	TRISACCHARIDES	TRITHIONIC
TRILINGUALISMS	TRINITROBENZENE	TRIPHTHONG	TRISAGIONS	TRITIATING
TRILINGUALLY	TRINITROCRESOL	TRIPHTHONGAL	TRISECTING	TRITIATION
TRILITERAL	TRINITROCRESOLS	TRIPHTHONGS	TRISECTION	TRITIATIONS
TRILITERALISM	TRINITROPHENOL	TRIPHYLITE	TRISECTIONS	TRITICALES
TRILITERALISMS	TRINITROPHENOLS	TRIPHYLITES	TRISECTORS	TRITICALLY
TRILITERALS	TRINITROTOLUENE	TRIPHYLLOUS	TRISECTRICES	TRITICALNESS
TRILITHONS	TRINITROTOLUOL	TRIPINNATE	TRISECTRIX	TRITICALNESSES
TRILLIONAIRE	TRINITROTOLUOLS	TRIPINNATELY	TRISKELION	TRITICEOUS
TRILLIONAIRES	TRINKETERS	TRIPITAKAS	TRISKELIONS	TRITICISMS
TRILLIONTH	TRINKETING	TRIPLENESS	TRISOCTAHEDRA	TRITUBERCULAR
TRILLIONTHS	TRINKETINGS	TRIPLENESSES	TRISOCTAHEDRAL	TRITUBERCULATE
TRILOBATED	TRINKETRIES	TRIPLETAIL	TRISOCTAHEDRON	TRITUBERCULIES
TRILOBITES	TRINOCULAR	TRIPLETAILS	TRISOCTAHEDRONS	TRITUBERCULISM
TRILOBITIC	TRINOMIALISM	TRIPLEXING	TRISTEARIN	TRITUBERCULISMS
TRILOCULAR	TRINOMIALISMS	TRIPLICATE	TRISTEARINS	TRITUBERCULY
TRIMERISMS	TRINOMIALIST	TRIPLICATED	TRISTESSES	TRITURABLE
TRIMESTERS	TRINOMIALISTS	TRIPLICATES	TRISTFULLY	TRITURATED
TRIMESTRAL	TRINOMIALLY	TRIPLICATING	TRISTFULNESS	TRITURATES
TRIMESTRIAL	TRINOMIALS	TRIPLICATION	TRISTFULNESSES	TRITURATING
TRIMETHADIONE	TRINUCLEOTIDE	TRIPLICATIONS	TRISTICHIC	TRITURATION
TRIMETHADIONES	TRINUCLEOTIDES	TRIPLICITIES	TRISTICHOUS	TRITURATIONS
TRIMETHOPRIM	TRIOECIOUS	TRIPLICITY	TRISTIMULUS	TRITURATOR
TRIMETHOPRIMS	TRIOXOBORIC	TRIPLOBLASTIC	TRISUBSTITUTED	TRITURATORS
TRIMETHYLAMINE	TRIOXYGENS	TRIPLOIDIES	TRISULCATE	TRIUMPHALISM
TRIMETHYLAMINES	TRIPALMITIN	TRIPMETERS	TRISULFIDE	TRIUMPHALISMS
TRIMETHYLENE	TRIPALMITINS	TRIPPERIER	TRISULFIDES	TRIUMPHALIST
TRIMETHYLENES	TRIPARTISM	TRIPPERIEST	TRISULPHIDE	TRIUMPHALISTS
TRIMETRICAL	TRIPARTISMS	TRIPPERISH	TRISULPHIDES	TRIUMPHALS
TRIMETROGON	TRIPARTITE	TRIPPINGLY	TRISYLLABIC	TRIUMPHANT
TRIMETROGONS	TRIPARTITELY	TRIPTEROUS	TRISYLLABICAL	TRIUMPHANTLY
TRIMMINGLY	TRIPARTITION	TRIPTYQUES	TRISYLLABICALLY	TRIUMPHERIES
TRIMNESSES	TRIPARTITIONS	TRIPUDIARY	TRISYLLABLE	TRIUMPHERS
TRIMOLECULAR	TRIPEHOUND	TRIPUDIATE	TRISYLLABLES	TRIUMPHERY
TRIMONTHLY	TRIPEHOUNDS	TRIPUDIATED	TRITAGONIST	TRIUMPHING
TRIMORPHIC	TRIPERSONAL	TRIPUDIATES	TRITAGONISTS	TRIUMPHINGS
TRIMORPHISM	TRIPERSONALISM	TRIPUDIATING	TRITANOPES	TRIUMVIRAL
TRIMORPHISMS	TRIPERSONALISMS	TRIPUDIATION	TRITANOPIA	TRIUMVIRATE
TRIMORPHOUS	TRIPERSONALIST	TRIPUDIATIONS	TRITANOPIAS	TRIUMVIRATES
TRIMPHONES	TRIPERSONALISTS	TRIQUETRAE	TRITANOPIC	TRIUMVIRIES

TRIUNITIES	TROCHOTRON	TROPHOBLASTS	TROPOSPHERES	TRUCKLINES
TRIVALENCE	TROCHOTRONS	TROPHOLOGIES	TROPOSPHERIC	TRUCKLINGS
TRIVALENCES	TROCTOLITE	TROPHOLOGY	TROPOTAXES	TRUCKLOADS
TRIVALENCIES	TROCTOLITES	TROPHONEUROSES	TROPOTAXIS	TRUCKMASTER
TRIVALENCY	TROGLODYTE	TROPHONEUROSIS	TROTHPLIGHT	TRUCKMASTERS
TRIVALVULAR	TROGLODYTES	TROPHOPLASM	TROTHPLIGHTED	TRUCKSTOPS
TRIVIALISATION	TROGLODYTIC	TROPHOPLASMS	TROTHPLIGHTING	TRUCULENCE
TRIVIALISATIONS	TROGLODYTICAL	TROPHOTACTIC	TROTHPLIGHTS	TRUCULENCES
TRIVIALISE	TROGLODYTISM	TROPHOTAXES	TROUBADOUR	TRUCULENCIES
TRIVIALISED	TROGLODYTISMS	TROPHOTAXIS	TROUBADOURS	TRUCULENCY
TRIVIALISES	TROLLEYBUS	TROPHOTROPIC	TROUBLEDLY	TRUCULENTLY
TRIVIALISING	TROLLEYBUSES	TROPHOTROPISM	TROUBLEFREE	TRUEHEARTED
TRIVIALISM	TROLLEYBUSSES	TROPHOTROPISMS	TROUBLEMAKER	TRUEHEARTEDNESS
TRIVIALISMS	TROLLEYING	TROPHOZOITE	TROUBLEMAKERS	TRUENESSES
TRIVIALIST	TROLLIUSES	TROPHOZOITES	TROUBLEMAKING	TRUEPENNIES
TRIVIALISTS	TROLLOPEES	TROPICALISATION	TROUBLEMAKINGS	TRUFFLINGS
TRIVIALITIES	TROLLOPIER	TROPICALISE	TROUBLESHOOT	TRUMPERIES
TRIVIALITY	TROLLOPIEST	TROPICALISED	TROUBLESHOOTER	TRUMPETERS
TRIVIALIZATION	TROLLOPING	TROPICALISES	TROUBLESHOOTERS	TRUMPETING
TRIVIALIZATIONS	TROLLOPISH	TROPICALISING	TROUBLESHOOTING	TRUMPETINGS
TRIVIALIZE	TROMBICULID	TROPICALITIES	TROUBLESHOOTS	TRUMPETLIKE
TRIVIALIZED	TROMBICULIDS	TROPICALITY	TROUBLESHOT	TRUMPETWEED
TRIVIALIZES	TROMBIDIASES	TROPICALIZATION	TROUBLESOME	TRUMPETWEEDS
TRIVIALIZING	TROMBIDIASIS	TROPICALIZE	TROUBLESOMELY	TRUNCATELY
TRIVIALNESS	TROMBONIST	TROPICALIZED	TROUBLESOMENESS	TRUNCATING
TRIVIALNESSES	TROMBONISTS	TROPICALIZES	TROUBLINGS	TRUNCATINGS
TRIWEEKLIES	TROMOMETER	TROPICALIZING	TROUBLOUSLY	TRUNCATION
TROCHAICALLY	TROMOMETERS	TROPICALLY	TROUBLOUSNESS	TRUNCATIONS
TROCHANTER	TROMOMETRIC	TROPICBIRD	TROUBLOUSNESSES	TRUNCHEONED
TROCHANTERAL	TROOPSHIPS	TROPICBIRDS	TROUGHINGS	TRUNCHEONER
TROCHANTERIC	TROOSTITES	TROPISMATIC	TROUGHLIKE	TRUNCHEONERS
TROCHANTERS	TROPAEOLIN	TROPOCOLLAGEN	TROUNCINGS	TRUNCHEONING
TROCHEAMETER	TROPAEOLINS	TROPOCOLLAGENS	TROUSERING	TRUNCHEONS
TROCHEAMETERS	TROPAEOLUM	TROPOLOGIC	TROUSERINGS	TRUNKFISHES
TROCHELMINTH	TROPAEOLUMS	TROPOLOGICAL	TROUSERLESS	TRUNKSLEEVE
TROCHELMINTHS	TROPARIONS	TROPOLOGICALLY	TROUSSEAUS	TRUNKSLEEVES
TROCHILUSES	TROPEOLINS	TROPOLOGIES	TROUSSEAUX	TRUNKWORKS
TROCHISCUS	TROPHALLACTIC	TROPOMYOSIN	TROUTLINGS	TRUNNIONED
TROCHISCUSES	TROPHALLAXES	TROPOMYOSINS	TROUTSTONE	TRUSTABILITIES
TROCHLEARS	TROPHALLAXIS	TROPOPAUSE	TROUTSTONES	TRUSTABILITY
TROCHOIDAL	TROPHESIAL	TROPOPAUSES	TROUVAILLE	TRUSTAFARIAN
TROCHOIDALLY	TROPHESIES	TROPOPHILOUS	TROUVAILLES	TRUSTAFARIANS
TROCHOMETER	TROPHICALLY	TROPOPHYTE	TROWELLERS	TRUSTBUSTER
TROCHOMETERS	TROPHOBIOSES	TROPOPHYTES	TROWELLING	TRUSTBUSTERS
TROCHOPHORE	TROPHOBIOSIS	TROPOPHYTIC	TRUANTINGS	TRUSTBUSTING
TROCHOPHORES	TROPHOBIOTIC	TROPOSCATTER	TRUANTRIES	TRUSTBUSTINGS
TROCHOSPHERE	TROPHOBLAST	TROPOSCATTERS	TRUANTSHIP	TRUSTEEING
TROCHOSPHERES	TROPHOBLASTIC	TROPOSPHERE	TRUANTSHIPS	TRUSTEESHIP

TRUSTEESHIPS	TSAREVITCH	TUBERCULOSED	TULARAEMIC	TUNBELLIED
TRUSTFULLY	TSAREVITCHES	TUBERCULOSES	TULAREMIAS	TUNBELLIES
TRUSTFULNESS	TSCHERNOSEM	TUBERCULOSIS	TULIPOMANIA	TUNEFULNESS
TRUSTFULNESSES	TSCHERNOSEMS	TUBERCULOUS	TULIPOMANIAS	TUNEFULNESSES
TRUSTINESS	TSESAREVICH	TUBERCULOUSLY	TULIPWOODS	TUNELESSLY
TRUSTINESSES	TSESAREVICHES	TUBERCULUM	TUMATAKURU	TUNELESSNESS
TRUSTINGLY	TSESAREVITCH	TUBERIFEROUS	TUMATAKURUS	TUNELESSNESSES
TRUSTINGNESS	TSESAREVITCHES	TUBERIFORM	TUMBLEBUGS	TUNESMITHS
TRUSTINGNESSES	TSESAREVNA	TUBEROSITIES	TUMBLEDOWN	TUNGSTATES
TRUSTLESSLY	TSESAREVNAS	TUBEROSITY	TUMBLEHOME	TUNGSTITES
TRUSTLESSNESS	TSESAREWICH	TUBICOLOUS	TUMBLEHOMES	TUNNELINGS
TRUSTLESSNESSES	TSESAREWICHES	TUBIFICIDS	TUMBLERFUL	TUNNELLERS
TRUSTWORTHIER	TSESAREWITCH	TUBIFLOROUS	TUMBLERFULS	TUNNELLIKE
TRUSTWORTHIEST	TSESAREWITCHES	TUBOCURARINE	TUMBLERSFUL	TUNNELLING
TRUSTWORTHILY	TSOTSITAAL	TUBOCURARINES	TUMBLESETS	TUNNELLINGS
TRUSTWORTHINESS	TSOTSITAALS	TUBOPLASTIES	TUMBLEWEED	TUPPENNIES
TRUSTWORTHY	TSUNAMIGENIC	TUBOPLASTY	TUMBLEWEEDS	TUPTOWINGS
TRUTHFULLY	TSUTSUGAMUSHI	TUBULARIAN	TUMEFACIENT	TURACOVERDIN
TRUTHFULNESS	TSUTSUGAMUSHIS	TUBULARIANS	TUMEFACTION	TURACOVERDINS
TRUTHFULNESSES	TUBBINESSES	TUBULARITIES	TUMEFACTIONS	TURANGAWAEWAE
TRUTHINESS	TUBECTOMIES	TUBULARITY	TUMESCENCE	TURANGAWAEWAES
TRUTHINESSES	TUBERACEOUS	TUBULATING	TUMESCENCES	TURBELLARIAN
TRUTHLESSNESS	TUBERCULAR	TUBULATION	TUMESCENTLY	TURBELLARIANS
TRUTHLESSNESSES	TUBERCULARLY	TUBULATIONS	TUMIDITIES	TURBIDIMETER
TRYINGNESS	TUBERCULARS	TUBULATORS	TUMIDNESSES	TURBIDIMETERS
TRYINGNESSES	TUBERCULATE	TUBULATURE	TUMORGENIC	TURBIDIMETRIC
TRYPAFLAVINE	TUBERCULATED	TUBULATURES	TUMORGENICITIES	TURBIDIMETRIES
TRYPAFLAVINES	TUBERCULATELY	TUBULIFLORAL	TUMORGENICITY	TURBIDIMETRY
TRYPANOCIDAL	TUBERCULATION	TUBULIFLOROUS	TUMORIGENESES	TURBIDITES
TRYPANOCIDE	TUBERCULATIONS	TUBULOUSLY	TUMORIGENESIS	TURBIDITIES
TRYPANOCIDES	TUBERCULES	TUCKAMORES	TUMORIGENIC	TURBIDNESS
TRYPANOSOMAL	TUBERCULIN	TUCKERBAGS	TUMORIGENICITY	TURBIDNESSES
TRYPANOSOME	TUBERCULINS	TUCKERBOXES	TUMULOSITIES	TURBINACIOUS
TRYPANOSOMES	TUBERCULISATION	TUFFACEOUS	TUMULOSITY	TURBINATED
TRYPANOSOMIASES	TUBERCULISE	TUFFTAFFETA	TUMULTUARY	TURBINATES
TRYPANOSOMIASIS	TUBERCULISED	TUFFTAFFETAS	TUMULTUATE	TURBINATION
TRYPANOSOMIC	TUBERCULISES	TUFFTAFFETIES	TUMULTUATED	TURBINATIONS
TRYPARSAMIDE	TUBERCULISING	TUFFTAFFETY	TUMULTUATES	TURBOCHARGED
TRYPARSAMIDES	TUBERCULIZATION	TUFTAFFETA	TUMULTUATING	TURBOCHARGER
TRYPSINOGEN	TUBERCULIZE	TUFTAFFETAS	TUMULTUATION	TURBOCHARGERS
TRYPSINOGENS	TUBERCULIZED	TUFTAFFETIES	TUMULTUATIONS	TURBOCHARGING
TRYPTAMINE	TUBERCULIZES	TUFTAFFETY	TUMULTUOUS	TURBOCHARGINGS
TRYPTAMINES	TUBERCULIZING	TUILLETTES	TUMULTUOUSLY	TURBOELECTRIC
TRYPTOPHAN	TUBERCULOID	TUILYIEING	TUMULTUOUSNESS	TURBOGENERATOR
TRYPTOPHANE	TUBERCULOMA	TUILZIEING	TUNABILITIES	TURBOGENERATORS
TRYPTOPHANES	TUBERCULOMAS	TUITIONARY	TUNABILITY	TURBOMACHINERY
TRYPTOPHANS	TUBERCULOMATA	TULARAEMIA	TUNABLENESS	TURBOPROPS
TSAREVICHES	TUBERCULOSE	TULARAEMIAS	TUNABLENESSES	TURBOSHAFT

TURBOSHAFTS	TURPENTINIER	TWEENESSES	TYPECASTER	TYPOGRAPHISTS
TURBULATOR	TURPENTINIEST	TWELVEFOLD	TYPECASTERS	TYPOGRAPHS
TURBULATORS	TURPENTINING	TWELVEMONTH	TYPECASTING	TYPOGRAPHY
TURBULENCE	TURPENTINY	TWELVEMONTHS	TYPECASTINGS	TYPOLOGICAL
TURBULENCES	TURPITUDES	TWENTIETHS	TYPEFOUNDER	TYPOLOGICALLY
TURBULENCIES	TURQUOISES	TWENTYFOLD	TYPEFOUNDERS	TYPOLOGIES
TURBULENCY	TURRIBANTS	TWENTYFOLDS	TYPEFOUNDING	TYPOLOGIST
TURBULENTLY	TURRICULATE	TWICHILDREN	TYPEFOUNDINGS	TYPOLOGISTS
TURCOPOLES	TURRICULATED	TWIDDLIEST	TYPEFOUNDRIES	TYPOMANIAS
TURCOPOLIER	TURTLEBACK	TWIDDLINGS	TYPEFOUNDRY	TYPOTHETAE
TURCOPOLIERS	TURTLEBACKS	TWILIGHTED	TYPESCRIPT	TYRANNESSES
TURDUCKENS	TURTLEDOVE	TWILIGHTING	TYPESCRIPTS	TYRANNICAL
TURFGRASSES	TURTLEDOVES	TWINBERRIES	TYPESETTER	TYRANNICALLY
TURFINESSES	TURTLEHEAD	TWINFLOWER	TYPESETTERS	TYRANNICALNESS
TURFSKIING	TURTLEHEADS	TWINFLOWERS	TYPESETTING	TYRANNICIDAL
TURFSKIINGS	TURTLENECK	TWINKLIEST	TYPESETTINGS	TYRANNICIDE
TURGENCIES	TURTLENECKED	TWINKLINGS	TYPESTYLES	TYRANNICIDES
TURGESCENCE	TURTLENECKS	TWISTABILITIES	TYPEWRITER	TYRANNISED
TURGESCENCES	TUSSOCKIER	TWISTABILITY	TYPEWRITERS	TYRANNISER
TURGESCENCIES	TUSSOCKIEST	TWITCHIEST	TYPEWRITES	TYRANNISERS
TURGESCENCY	TUTELARIES	TWITCHINGS	TYPEWRITING	TYRANNISES
TURGESCENT	TUTIORISMS	TWITTERATI	TYPEWRITINGS	TYRANNISING
TURGIDITIES	TUTIORISTS	TWITTERERS	TYPEWRITTEN	TYRANNIZED
TURGIDNESS	TUTORESSES	TWITTERIER	TYPHACEOUS	TYRANNIZER
TURGIDNESSES	TUTORIALLY	TWITTERIEST	TYPHLITISES	TYRANNIZERS
TURMOILING	TUTORISING	TWITTERING	TYPHLOLOGIES	TYRANNIZES
TURNABOUTS	TUTORIZING	TWITTERINGLY	TYPHLOLOGY	TYRANNIZING
TURNAGAINS	TUTORSHIPS	TWITTERINGS	TYPHLOSOLE	TYRANNOSAUR
TURNAROUND	TUTOYERING	TWITTINGLY	TYPHLOSOLES	TYRANNOSAURS
TURNAROUNDS	TUTWORKERS	TWOFOLDNESS	TYPHOGENIC	TYRANNOSAURUS
TURNBROACH	TUTWORKMAN	TWOFOLDNESSES	TYPHOIDINS	TYRANNOSAURUSES
TURNBROACHES	TUTWORKMEN	TWOPENCEWORTH	TYPICALITIES	TYRANNOUSLY
TURNBUCKLE	TWADDLIEST	TWOPENCEWORTHS	TYPICALITY	TYRANNOUSNESS
TURNBUCKLES	TWADDLINGS	TWOPENNIES	TYPICALNESS	TYRANNOUSNESSES
TURNIPIEST	TWALPENNIES	TWOSEATERS	TYPICALNESSES	TYREMAKERS
TURNROUNDS	TWANGINGLY	TYCOONATES	TYPIFICATION	TYROCIDINE
TURNSTILES	TWANGLINGLY	TYCOONERIES	TYPIFICATIONS	TYROCIDINES
TURNSTONES	TWANGLINGS	TYLECTOMIES	TYPOGRAPHED	TYROCIDINS
TURNTABLES	TWATTLINGS	TYMPANIFORM	TYPOGRAPHER	TYROGLYPHID
TURNTABLIST	TWAYBLADES	TYMPANISTS	TYPOGRAPHERS	TYROGLYPHIDS
TURNTABLISTS	TWEEDINESS	TYMPANITES	TYPOGRAPHIA	TYROPITTAS
TURNVEREIN	TWEEDINESSES	TYMPANITESES	TYPOGRAPHIC	TYROSINASE
TURNVEREINS	TWEEDLEDEE	TYMPANITIC	TYPOGRAPHICAL	TYROSINASES
TUROPHILES	TWEEDLEDEED	TYMPANITIS	TYPOGRAPHICALLY	TYROTHRICIN
TURPENTINE	TWEEDLEDEEING	TYMPANITISES	TYPOGRAPHIES	TYROTHRICINS
TURPENTINED	TWEEDLEDEES	TYNDALLIMETRIES	TYPOGRAPHING	
TURPENTINES	TWEENAGERS	TYNDALLIMETRY	TYPOGRAPHIST	

U

UBERSEXUAL	ULTIMATELY	ULTRAFILTERING	ULTRAMINIATURE	ULTRAROYALIST
UBERSEXUALS	ULTIMATENESS	ULTRAFILTERS	ULTRAMODERN	ULTRAROYALISTS
UBIQUARIAN	ULTIMATENESSES	ULTRAFILTRATE	ULTRAMODERNISM	ULTRASECRET
UBIQUINONE	ULTIMATING	ULTRAFILTRATES	ULTRAMODERNISMS	ULTRASENSITIVE
UBIQUINONES	ULTIMATUMS	ULTRAFILTRATION	ULTRAMODERNIST	ULTRASENSUAL
UBIQUITARIAN	ULTIMOGENITURE	ULTRAGLAMOROUS	ULTRAMODERNISTS	ULTRASERIOUS
UBIQUITARIANISM	ULTIMOGENITURES	ULTRAHAZARDOUS	ULTRAMONTANE	ULTRASHARP
UBIQUITARIANS	ULTRABASIC	ULTRAHEATED	ULTRAMONTANES	ULTRASHORT
UBIQUITARY	ULTRABASICS	ULTRAHEATING	ULTRAMONTANISM	ULTRASIMPLE
UBIQUITIES	ULTRACAREFUL	ULTRAHEATS	ULTRAMONTANISMS	ULTRASLICK
UBIQUITINATION	ULTRACASUAL	ULTRAHEAVIER	ULTRAMONTANIST	ULTRASMALL
UBIQUITINATIONS	ULTRACAUTIOUS	ULTRAHEAVIEST	ULTRAMONTANISTS	ULTRASMART
UBIQUITINS	ULTRACENTRIFUGE	ULTRAHEAVY	ULTRAMUNDANE	ULTRASMOOTH
UBIQUITOUS	ULTRACIVILISED	ULTRAHUMAN	ULTRANATIONAL	ULTRASONIC
UBIQUITOUSLY	ULTRACIVILIZED	ULTRAISTIC	ULTRAORTHODOX	ULTRASONICALLY
UBIQUITOUSNESS	ULTRACLEAN	ULTRALARGE	ULTRAPATRIOTIC	ULTRASONICS
UDOMETRIES	ULTRACOMMERCIAL	ULTRALEFTISM	ULTRAPHYSICAL	ULTRASONOGRAPHY
UFOLOGICAL	ULTRACOMPACT	ULTRALEFTISMS	ULTRAPOWERFUL	ULTRASOUND
UFOLOGISTS	ULTRACOMPETENT	ULTRALEFTIST	ULTRAPRACTICAL	ULTRASOUNDS
UGLIFICATION	ULTRACONVENIENT	ULTRALEFTISTS	ULTRAPRECISE	ULTRASTRUCTURAL
UGLIFICATIONS	ULTRACREPIDATE	ULTRALEFTS	ULTRAPRECISION	ULTRASTRUCTURE
UGLINESSES	ULTRACREPIDATED	ULTRALIBERAL	ULTRAPRECISIONS	ULTRASTRUCTURES
UGSOMENESS	ULTRACREPIDATES	ULTRALIBERALISM	ULTRAQUIET	ULTRATINIER
UGSOMENESSES	ULTRACRITICAL	ULTRALIBERALS	ULTRARADICAL	ULTRATINIEST
UINTAHITES	ULTRADEMOCRATIC	ULTRALIGHT	ULTRARADICALS	ULTRAVACUA
UINTATHERE	ULTRADENSE	ULTRALIGHTS	ULTRARAPID	ULTRAVACUUM
UINTATHERES	ULTRADISTANCE	ULTRAMAFIC	ULTRARAREFIED	ULTRAVACUUMS
UITLANDERS	ULTRADISTANT	ULTRAMARATHON	ULTRARATIONAL	ULTRAVIOLENCE
ULCERATING	ULTRADRIER	ULTRAMARATHONER	ULTRAREALISM	ULTRAVIOLENCES
ULCERATION	ULTRADRIEST	ULTRAMARATHONS	ULTRAREALISMS	ULTRAVIOLENT
ULCERATIONS	ULTRADRYER	ULTRAMARINE	ULTRAREALIST	ULTRAVIOLET
ULCERATIVE	ULTRADRYEST	ULTRAMARINES	ULTRAREALISTIC	ULTRAVIOLETS
ULCEROGENIC	ULTRAEFFICIENT	ULTRAMASCULINE	ULTRAREALISTS	ULTRAVIRILE
ULCEROUSLY	ULTRAENERGETIC	ULTRAMICRO	ULTRAREFINED	ULTRAVIRILITIES
ULCEROUSNESS	ULTRAEXCLUSIVE	ULTRAMICROMETER	ULTRARELIABLE	ULTRAVIRILITY
ULCEROUSNESSES	ULTRAFAMILIAR	ULTRAMICROSCOPE	ULTRARIGHT	ULTRAVIRUS
ULOTRICHIES	ULTRAFASTIDIOUS	ULTRAMICROSCOPY	ULTRARIGHTISM	ULTRAVIRUSES
ULOTRICHOUS	ULTRAFEMININE	ULTRAMICROTOME	ULTRARIGHTISMS	ULTRAWIDEBAND
ULSTERETTE	ULTRAFICHE	ULTRAMICROTOMES	ULTRARIGHTIST	ULTRAWIDEBANDS
ULSTERETTES	ULTRAFICHES	ULTRAMICROTOMY	ULTRARIGHTISTS	ULTRONEOUS
ULTERIORLY	ULTRAFILTER	ULTRAMILITANT	ULTRARIGHTS	ULTRONEOUSLY
ULTIMACIES	ULTRAFILTERED	ULTRAMILITANTS	ULTRAROMANTIC	ULTRONEOUSNESS

ULULATIONS
UMBELLATED
UMBELLATELY
UMBELLIFER
UMBELLIFEROUS
UMBELLIFERS
UMBELLULATE
UMBELLULES
UMBILICALLY
UMBILICALS
UMBILICATE
UMBILICATED
UMBILICATION
UMBILICATIONS
UMBILICUSES
UMBILIFORM
UMBONATION
UMBONATIONS
UMBRACULATE
UMBRACULIFORM
UMBRACULUM
UMBRAGEOUS
UMBRAGEOUSLY
UMBRAGEOUSNESS
UMBRATICAL
UMBRATILES
UMBRATILOUS
UMBRELLAED
UMBRELLAING
UMBRELLOES
UMBRIFEROUS
UMPIRESHIP
UMPIRESHIPS
UMPTEENTHS
UNABASHEDLY
UNABATEDLY
UNABBREVIATED
UNABOLISHED
UNABRIDGED
UNABROGATED
UNABSOLVED
UNABSORBED
UNABSORBENT
UNACADEMIC
UNACADEMICALLY
UNACCENTED
UNACCENTUATED
UNACCEPTABILITY

UNACCEPTABLE
UNACCEPTABLY
UNACCEPTANCE
UNACCEPTANCES
UNACCEPTED
UNACCLIMATED
UNACCLIMATISED
UNACCLIMATIZED
UNACCOMMODATED
UNACCOMMODATING
UNACCOMPANIED
UNACCOMPLISHED
UNACCOUNTABLE
UNACCOUNTABLY
UNACCOUNTED
UNACCREDITED
UNACCULTURATED
UNACCUSABLE
UNACCUSABLY
UNACCUSTOMED
UNACCUSTOMEDLY
UNACHIEVABLE
UNACHIEVED
UNACKNOWLEDGED
UNACQUAINT
UNACQUAINTANCE
UNACQUAINTANCES
UNACQUAINTED
UNACQUAINTING
UNACQUAINTS
UNACTIVING
UNACTORISH
UNACTUATED
UNADAPTABLE
UNADDRESSED
UNADJUDICATED
UNADJUSTED
UNADMIRING
UNADMITTED
UNADMONISHED
UNADOPTABLE
UNADULTERATE
UNADULTERATED
UNADULTERATEDLY
UNADVENTROUS
UNADVENTUROUS
UNADVENTUROUSLY
UNADVERTISED

UNADVERTIZED
UNADVISABLE
UNADVISABLENESS
UNADVISABLY
UNADVISEDLY
UNADVISEDNESS
UNADVISEDNESSES
UNAESTHETIC
UNAFFECTED
UNAFFECTEDLY
UNAFFECTEDNESS
UNAFFECTING
UNAFFECTIONATE
UNAFFILIATED
UNAFFLUENT
UNAFFORDABLE
UNAGGRESSIVE
UNAGREEABLE
UNALIENABLE
UNALIENABLY
UNALIENATED
UNALLEVIATED
UNALLOCATED
UNALLOTTED
UNALLOWABLE
UNALLURING
UNALTERABILITY
UNALTERABLE
UNALTERABLENESS
UNALTERABLY
UNALTERING
UNAMBIGUOUS
UNAMBIGUOUSLY
UNAMBITIOUS
UNAMBITIOUSLY
UNAMBIVALENT
UNAMBIVALENTLY
UNAMENABLE
UNAMENDABLE
UNAMIABILITIES
UNAMIABILITY
UNAMIABLENESS
UNAMIABLENESSES
UNAMORTISED
UNAMORTIZED
UNAMPLIFIED
UNAMUSABLE
UNAMUSINGLY

UNANAESTHETISED
UNANAESTHETIZED
UNANALYSABLE
UNANALYSED
UNANALYTIC
UNANALYTICAL
UNANALYZABLE
UNANALYZED
UNANCHORED
UNANCHORING
UNANESTHETISED
UNANESTHETIZED
UNANIMATED
UNANIMITIES
UNANIMOUSLY
UNANIMOUSNESS
UNANIMOUSNESSES
UNANNEALED
UNANNOTATED
UNANNOUNCED
UNANSWERABILITY
UNANSWERABLE
UNANSWERABLY
UNANSWERED
UNANTICIPATED
UNANTICIPATEDLY
UNAPOLOGETIC
UNAPOLOGISING
UNAPOLOGIZING
UNAPOSTOLIC
UNAPOSTOLICAL
UNAPOSTOLICALLY
UNAPPALLED
UNAPPARELLED
UNAPPARELLING
UNAPPARELS
UNAPPARENT
UNAPPEALABLE
UNAPPEALABLY
UNAPPEALING
UNAPPEALINGLY
UNAPPEASABLE
UNAPPEASABLY
UNAPPEASED
UNAPPETISING
UNAPPETISINGLY
UNAPPETIZING
UNAPPETIZINGLY

UNAPPLAUSIVE
UNAPPLICABLE
UNAPPOINTED
UNAPPRECIATED
UNAPPRECIATION
UNAPPRECIATIONS
UNAPPRECIATIVE
UNAPPREHENDED
UNAPPREHENSIBLE
UNAPPREHENSIVE
UNAPPRISED
UNAPPROACHABLE
UNAPPROACHABLY
UNAPPROACHED
UNAPPROPRIATE
UNAPPROPRIATED
UNAPPROPRIATES
UNAPPROPRIATING
UNAPPROVED
UNAPPROVING
UNAPPROVINGLY
UNAPTNESSES
UNARGUABLE
UNARGUABLY
UNARMOURED
UNARRANGED
UNARROGANT
UNARTFULLY
UNARTICULATE
UNARTICULATED
UNARTIFICIAL
UNARTIFICIALLY
UNARTISTIC
UNARTISTLIKE
UNASCENDABLE
UNASCENDED
UNASCENDIBLE
UNASCERTAINABLE
UNASCERTAINED
UNASHAMEDLY
UNASHAMEDNESS
UNASHAMEDNESSES
UNASPIRATED
UNASPIRING
UNASPIRINGLY
UNASPIRINGNESS
UNASSAILABILITY
UNASSAILABLE

U

UNASSAILABLY

UNASSAILABLY	UNAVAILINGLY	UNBEFITTING	UNBIASINGS	UNBOUNDEDLY
UNASSAILED	UNAVAILINGNESS	UNBEFRIENDED	UNBIASSEDLY	UNBOUNDEDNESS
UNASSEMBLED	UNAVERTABLE	UNBEGETTING	UNBIASSEDNESS	UNBOUNDEDNESSES
UNASSERTIVE	UNAVERTIBLE	UNBEGINNING	UNBIASSEDNESSES	UNBOWDLERISED
UNASSERTIVELY	UNAVOIDABILITY	UNBEGOTTEN	UNBIASSING	UNBOWDLERIZED
UNASSIGNABLE	UNAVOIDABLE	UNBEGUILED	UNBIASSINGS	UNBRACKETED
UNASSIGNED	UNAVOIDABLENESS	UNBEGUILES	UNBIBLICAL	UNBRAIDING
UNASSIMILABLE	UNAVOIDABLY	UNBEGUILING	UNBINDINGS	UNBRANCHED
UNASSIMILATED	UNAVOWEDLY	UNBEHOLDEN	UNBIRTHDAY	UNBREACHABLE
UNASSISTED	UNAWAKENED	UNBEKNOWNST	UNBIRTHDAYS	UNBREACHED
UNASSISTEDLY	UNAWAKENING	UNBELIEVABILITY	UNBISHOPED	UNBREAKABLE
UNASSISTING	UNAWARENESS	UNBELIEVABLE	UNBISHOPING	UNBREATHABLE
UNASSOCIATED	UNAWARENESSES	UNBELIEVABLY	UNBLAMABLE	UNBREATHED
UNASSUAGEABLE	UNBAILABLE	UNBELIEVED	UNBLAMABLY	UNBREATHING
UNASSUAGED	UNBALANCED	UNBELIEVER	UNBLAMEABLE	UNBREECHED
UNASSUMING	UNBALANCES	UNBELIEVERS	UNBLAMEABLY	UNBREECHES
UNASSUMINGLY	UNBALANCING	UNBELIEVES	UNBLEACHED	UNBREECHING
UNASSUMINGNESS	UNBALLASTED	UNBELIEVING	UNBLEMISHED	UNBRIBABLE
UNATHLETIC	UNBANDAGED	UNBELIEVINGLY	UNBLENCHED	UNBRIDGEABLE
UNATONABLE	UNBANDAGES	UNBELIEVINGNESS	UNBLENCHING	UNBRIDLEDLY
UNATTACHED	UNBANDAGING	UNBELLIGERENT	UNBLESSEDNESS	UNBRIDLEDNESS
UNATTAINABLE	UNBANNINGS	UNBENDABLE	UNBLESSEDNESSES	UNBRIDLEDNESSES
UNATTAINABLY	UNBAPTISED	UNBENDINGLY	UNBLESSING	UNBRIDLING
UNATTAINTED	UNBAPTISES	UNBENDINGNESS	UNBLINDFOLD	UNBRILLIANT
UNATTEMPTED	UNBAPTISING	UNBENDINGNESSES	UNBLINDFOLDED	UNBROKENLY
UNATTENDED	UNBAPTIZED	UNBENDINGS	UNBLINDFOLDING	UNBROKENNESS
UNATTENDING	UNBAPTIZES	UNBENEFICED	UNBLINDFOLDS	UNBROKENNESSES
UNATTENTIVE	UNBAPTIZING	UNBENEFICIAL	UNBLINDING	UNBROTHERLIKE
UNATTENUATED	UNBARBERED	UNBENEFITED	UNBLINKING	UNBROTHERLY
UNATTESTED	UNBARRICADE	UNBENEFITTED	UNBLINKINGLY	UNBUCKLING
UNATTRACTIVE	UNBARRICADED	UNBENIGHTED	UNBLISSFUL	UNBUDGEABLE
UNATTRACTIVELY	UNBARRICADES	UNBENIGNANT	UNBLOCKING	UNBUDGEABLY
UNATTRIBUTABLE	UNBARRICADING	UNBENIGNLY	UNBLOODIED	UNBUDGETED
UNATTRIBUTED	UNBATTERED	UNBESEEMED	UNBLOODIER	UNBUDGINGLY
UNAUGMENTED	UNBEARABLE	UNBESEEMING	UNBLOODIEST	UNBUFFERED
UNAUSPICIOUS	UNBEARABLENESS	UNBESEEMINGLY	UNBLUSHING	UNBUILDABLE
UNAUTHENTIC	UNBEARABLY	UNBESOUGHT	UNBLUSHINGLY	UNBUILDING
UNAUTHENTICATED	UNBEATABLE	UNBESPEAKING	UNBLUSHINGNESS	UNBULKIEST
UNAUTHENTICITY	UNBEATABLY	UNBESPEAKS	UNBOASTFUL	UNBUNDLERS
UNAUTHORISED	UNBEAUTIFUL	UNBESPOKEN	UNBONNETED	UNBUNDLING
UNAUTHORITATIVE	UNBEAUTIFULLY	UNBESTOWED	UNBONNETING	UNBUNDLINGS
UNAUTHORIZED	UNBEAVERED	UNBETRAYED	UNBORROWED	UNBURDENED
UNAUTOMATED	UNBECOMING	UNBETTERABLE	UNBOSOMERS	UNBURDENING
UNAVAILABILITY	UNBECOMINGLY	UNBETTERED	UNBOSOMING	UNBUREAUCRATIC
UNAVAILABLE	UNBECOMINGNESS	UNBEWAILED	UNBOTTLING	UNBURNABLE
UNAVAILABLENESS	UNBECOMINGS	UNBIASEDLY	UNBOTTOMED	UNBURNISHED
UNAVAILABLY	UNBEDIMMED	UNBIASEDNESS	UNBOUNCIER	UNBURROWED
UNAVAILING	UNBEDINNED	UNBIASEDNESSES	UNBOUNCIEST	UNBURROWING

UNBURTHENED	UNCEASINGNESS	UNCHASTEST	UNCIPHERING	UNCLOGGING
UNBURTHENING	UNCEASINGNESSES	UNCHASTISABLE	UNCIRCULATED	UNCLOISTER
UNBURTHENS	UNCELEBRATED	UNCHASTISED	UNCIRCUMCISED	UNCLOISTERED
UNBUSINESSLIKE	UNCENSORED	UNCHASTITIES	UNCIRCUMCISION	UNCLOISTERING
UNBUTTERED	UNCENSORIOUS	UNCHASTITY	UNCIRCUMCISIONS	UNCLOISTERS
UNBUTTONED	UNCENSURED	UNCHASTIZABLE	UNCIRCUMSCRIBED	UNCLOTHING
UNBUTTONING	UNCEREBRAL	UNCHASTIZED	UNCIVILISED	UNCLOUDEDLY
UNCALCIFIED	UNCEREMONIOUS	UNCHAUVINISTIC	UNCIVILISEDLY	UNCLOUDEDNESS
UNCALCINED	UNCEREMONIOUSLY	UNCHECKABLE	UNCIVILISEDNESS	UNCLOUDEDNESSES
UNCALCULATED	UNCERTAINLY	UNCHECKING	UNCIVILITIES	UNCLOUDIER
UNCALCULATING	UNCERTAINNESS	UNCHEERFUL	UNCIVILITY	UNCLOUDIEST
UNCALIBRATED	UNCERTAINNESSES	UNCHEERFULLY	UNCIVILIZED	UNCLOUDING
UNCALLOUSED	UNCERTAINTIES	UNCHEERFULNESS	UNCIVILIZEDLY	UNCLUBABLE
UNCANCELED	UNCERTAINTY	UNCHEWABLE	UNCIVILIZEDNESS	UNCLUBBABLE
UNCANCELLED	UNCERTIFICATED	UNCHILDING	UNCIVILNESS	UNCLUTCHED
UNCANDIDLY	UNCERTIFIED	UNCHILDLIKE	UNCIVILNESSES	UNCLUTCHES
UNCANDIDNESS	UNCHAINING	UNCHIVALROUS	UNCLAMPING	UNCLUTCHING
UNCANDIDNESSES	UNCHAIRING	UNCHIVALROUSLY	UNCLARIFIED	UNCLUTTERED
UNCANDOURS	UNCHALLENGEABLE	UNCHLORINATED	UNCLARITIES	UNCLUTTERING
UNCANNIEST	UNCHALLENGEABLY	UNCHOREOGRAPHED	UNCLASPING	UNCLUTTERS
UNCANNINESS	UNCHALLENGED	UNCHRISTEN	UNCLASSICAL	UNCOALESCE
UNCANNINESSES	UNCHALLENGING	UNCHRISTENED	UNCLASSIER	UNCOALESCED
UNCANONICAL	UNCHANCIER	UNCHRISTENING	UNCLASSIEST	UNCOALESCES
UNCANONICALNESS	UNCHANCIEST	UNCHRISTENS	UNCLASSIFIABLE	UNCOALESCING
UNCANONISE	UNCHANGEABILITY	UNCHRISTIAN	UNCLASSIFIED	UNCOATINGS
UNCANONISED	UNCHANGEABLE	UNCHRISTIANED	UNCLEANEST	UNCODIFIED
UNCANONISES	UNCHANGEABLY	UNCHRISTIANING	UNCLEANLIER	UNCOERCIVE
UNCANONISING	UNCHANGING	UNCHRISTIANISE	UNCLEANLIEST	UNCOERCIVELY
UNCANONIZE	UNCHANGINGLY	UNCHRISTIANISED	UNCLEANLINESS	UNCOFFINED
UNCANONIZED	UNCHANGINGNESS	UNCHRISTIANISES	UNCLEANLINESSES	UNCOFFINING
UNCANONIZES	UNCHANNELED	UNCHRISTIANIZE	UNCLEANNESS	UNCOLLECTABLE
UNCANONIZING	UNCHANNELLED	UNCHRISTIANIZED	UNCLEANNESSES	UNCOLLECTABLES
UNCAPITALISED	UNCHAPERONED	UNCHRISTIANIZES	UNCLEANSED	UNCOLLECTED
UNCAPITALIZED	UNCHARGING	UNCHRISTIANLIKE	UNCLEAREST	UNCOLLECTIBLE
UNCAPSIZABLE	UNCHARIEST	UNCHRISTIANLY	UNCLEARNESS	UNCOLLECTIBLES
UNCAPTIONED	UNCHARISMATIC	UNCHRISTIANS	UNCLEARNESSES	UNCOLOURED
UNCAPTIVATED	UNCHARITABLE	UNCHRONICLED	UNCLENCHED	UNCOMATABLE
UNCAPTURABLE	UNCHARITABLY	UNCHRONOLOGICAL	UNCLENCHES	UNCOMBATIVE
UNCARPETED	UNCHARITIES	UNCHURCHED	UNCLENCHING	UNCOMBINED
UNCASTRATED	UNCHARMING	UNCHURCHES	UNCLERICAL	UNCOMBINES
UNCATALOGED	UNCHARNELLED	UNCHURCHING	UNCLESHIPS	UNCOMBINING
UNCATALOGUED	UNCHARNELLING	UNCHURCHLY	UNCLIMBABLE	UNCOMEATABLE
UNCATCHABLE	UNCHARNELS	UNCILIATED	UNCLIMBABLENESS	UNCOMELIER
UNCATCHIER	UNCHARTERED	UNCINARIAS	UNCLINCHED	UNCOMELIEST
UNCATCHIEST	UNCHASTELY	UNCINARIASES	UNCLINCHES	UNCOMELINESS
UNCATEGORISABLE	UNCHASTENED	UNCINARIASIS	UNCLINCHING	UNCOMELINESSES
UNCATEGORIZABLE	UNCHASTENESS	UNCINEMATIC	UNCLIPPING	UNCOMFIEST
UNCEASINGLY	UNCHASTENESSES	UNCIPHERED	UNCLOAKING	UNCOMFORTABLE

UNCOMFORTABLY	UNCONCEIVABLY	UNCONQUERABLE	UNCONVENTIONAL	UNCRITICAL
UNCOMFORTED	UNCONCEIVED	UNCONQUERABLY	UNCONVERSABLE	UNCRITICALLY
UNCOMMENDABLE	UNCONCERNED	UNCONQUERED	UNCONVERSANT	UNCROSSABLE
UNCOMMENDABLY	UNCONCERNEDLY	UNCONSCIENTIOUS	UNCONVERTED	UNCROSSING
UNCOMMENDED	UNCONCERNEDNESS	UNCONSCIONABLE	UNCONVERTIBLE	UNCROWNING
UNCOMMERCIAL	UNCONCERNING	UNCONSCIONABLY	UNCONVICTED	UNCRUMPLED
UNCOMMITTED	UNCONCERNMENT	UNCONSCIOUS	UNCONVINCED	UNCRUMPLES
UNCOMMONER	UNCONCERNMENTS	UNCONSCIOUSES	UNCONVINCING	UNCRUMPLING
UNCOMMONEST	UNCONCERNS	UNCONSCIOUSLY	UNCONVINCINGLY	UNCRUSHABLE
UNCOMMONLY	UNCONCERTED	UNCONSCIOUSNESS	UNCONVOYED	UNCRYSTALLISED
UNCOMMONNESS	UNCONCILIATORY	UNCONSECRATE	UNCOOPERATIVE	UNCRYSTALLIZED
UNCOMMONNESSES	UNCONCLUSIVE	UNCONSECRATED	UNCOOPERATIVELY	UNCTIONLESS
UNCOMMUNICABLE	UNCONCOCTED	UNCONSECRATES	UNCOORDINATED	UNCTUOSITIES
UNCOMMUNICATED	UNCONDITIONAL	UNCONSECRATING	UNCOPYRIGHTABLE	UNCTUOSITY
UNCOMMUNICATIVE	UNCONDITIONALLY	UNCONSENTANEOUS	UNCOQUETTISH	UNCTUOUSLY
UNCOMMUTED	UNCONDITIONED	UNCONSENTING	UNCORRECTABLE	UNCTUOUSNESS
UNCOMPACTED	UNCONDUCIVE	UNCONSIDERED	UNCORRECTED	UNCTUOUSNESSES
UNCOMPANIED	UNCONFEDERATED	UNCONSIDERING	UNCORRELATED	UNCUCKOLDED
UNCOMPANIONABLE	UNCONFESSED	UNCONSOLED	UNCORROBORATED	UNCULTIVABLE
UNCOMPANIONED	UNCONFINABLE	UNCONSOLIDATED	UNCORRUPTED	UNCULTIVATABLE
UNCOMPASSIONATE	UNCONFINED	UNCONSTANT	UNCORSETED	UNCULTIVATED
UNCOMPELLED	UNCONFINEDLY	UNCONSTRAINABLE	UNCOSTLIER	UNCULTURED
UNCOMPELLING	UNCONFINES	UNCONSTRAINED	UNCOSTLIEST	UNCUMBERED
UNCOMPENSATED	UNCONFINING	UNCONSTRAINEDLY	UNCOUNSELLED	UNCURBABLE
UNCOMPETITIVE	UNCONFIRMED	UNCONSTRAINT	UNCOUNTABLE	UNCURTAILED
UNCOMPLACENT	UNCONFORMABLE	UNCONSTRAINTS	UNCOUPLERS	UNCURTAINED
UNCOMPLAINING	UNCONFORMABLY	UNCONSTRICTED	UNCOUPLING	UNCURTAINING
UNCOMPLAININGLY	UNCONFORMING	UNCONSTRUCTED	UNCOURAGEOUS	UNCURTAINS
UNCOMPLAISANT	UNCONFORMITIES	UNCONSTRUCTIVE	UNCOURTEOUS	UNCUSTOMARILY
UNCOMPLAISANTLY	UNCONFORMITY	UNCONSUMED	UNCOURTLIER	UNCUSTOMARY
UNCOMPLETED	UNCONFOUNDED	UNCONSUMMATED	UNCOURTLIEST	UNCUSTOMED
UNCOMPLIANT	UNCONFUSED	UNCONTAINABLE	UNCOURTLINESS	UNCYNICALLY
UNCOMPLICATED	UNCONFUSEDLY	UNCONTAMINATED	UNCOURTLINESSES	UNDANCEABLE
UNCOMPLIMENTARY	UNCONFUSES	UNCONTEMNED	UNCOUTHEST	UNDAUNTABLE
UNCOMPLYING	UNCONFUSING	UNCONTEMPLATED	UNCOUTHNESS	UNDAUNTEDLY
UNCOMPOSABLE	UNCONGEALED	UNCONTEMPORARY	UNCOUTHNESSES	UNDAUNTEDNESS
UNCOMPOUNDED	UNCONGEALING	UNCONTENTIOUS	UNCOVENANTED	UNDAUNTEDNESSES
UNCOMPREHENDED	UNCONGEALS	UNCONTESTABLE	UNCOVERING	UNDAUNTING
UNCOMPREHENDING	UNCONGENIAL	UNCONTESTED	UNCRAZIEST	UNDAZZLING
UNCOMPREHENSIVE	UNCONGENIALITY	UNCONTRACTED	UNCREATEDNESS	UNDEBARRED
UNCOMPROMISABLE	UNCONJECTURED	UNCONTRADICTED	UNCREATEDNESSES	UNDEBATABLE
UNCOMPROMISING	UNCONJUGAL	UNCONTRIVED	UNCREATING	UNDEBATABLY
UNCOMPUTERISED	UNCONJUGATED	UNCONTROLLABLE	UNCREATIVE	UNDEBAUCHED
UNCOMPUTERIZED	UNCONJUNCTIVE	UNCONTROLLABLY	UNCREDENTIALED	UNDECADENT
UNCONCEALABLE	UNCONNECTED	UNCONTROLLED	UNCREDIBLE	UNDECAGONS
UNCONCEALED	UNCONNECTEDLY	UNCONTROLLEDLY	UNCREDITABLE	UNDECEIVABLE
UNCONCEALING	UNCONNECTEDNESS	UNCONTROVERSIAL	UNCREDITED	UNDECEIVED
UNCONCEIVABLE	UNCONNIVING	UNCONTROVERTED	UNCRIPPLED	UNDECEIVER

UNDECEIVERS
UNDECEIVES
UNDECEIVING
UNDECIDABILITY
UNDECIDABLE
UNDECIDEDLY
UNDECIDEDNESS
UNDECIDEDNESSES
UNDECIDEDS
UNDECILLION
UNDECILLIONS
UNDECIMOLE
UNDECIMOLES
UNDECIPHERABLE
UNDECIPHERED
UNDECISIVE
UNDECLARED
UNDECLINING
UNDECOMPOSABLE
UNDECOMPOSED
UNDECORATED
UNDEDICATED
UNDEFEATABLE
UNDEFEATED
UNDEFENDED
UNDEFINABLE
UNDEFOLIATED
UNDEFORMED
UNDEIFYING
UNDELAYING
UNDELECTABLE
UNDELEGATED
UNDELETING
UNDELIBERATE
UNDELIGHTED
UNDELIGHTFUL
UNDELIGHTS
UNDELIVERABLE
UNDELIVERED
UNDEMANDING
UNDEMARCATED
UNDEMOCRATIC
UNDEMONSTRABLE
UNDEMONSTRATED
UNDEMONSTRATIVE
UNDENIABLE
UNDENIABLENESS
UNDENIABLY

UNDEPENDABLE
UNDEPENDING
UNDEPLORED
UNDEPRAVED
UNDEPRECIATED
UNDEPRESSED
UNDEPRIVED
UNDERACHIEVE
UNDERACHIEVED
UNDERACHIEVER
UNDERACHIEVERS
UNDERACHIEVES
UNDERACHIEVING
UNDERACTED
UNDERACTING
UNDERACTION
UNDERACTIONS
UNDERACTIVE
UNDERACTIVITIES
UNDERACTIVITY
UNDERACTOR
UNDERACTORS
UNDERAGENT
UNDERAGENTS
UNDERBAKED
UNDERBAKES
UNDERBAKING
UNDERBEARER
UNDERBEARERS
UNDERBEARING
UNDERBEARINGS
UNDERBEARS
UNDERBELLIES
UNDERBELLY
UNDERBIDDER
UNDERBIDDERS
UNDERBIDDING
UNDERBITES
UNDERBITING
UNDERBITTEN
UNDERBLANKET
UNDERBLANKETS
UNDERBODIES
UNDERBORNE
UNDERBOSSES
UNDERBOUGH
UNDERBOUGHS
UNDERBOUGHT

UNDERBREATH
UNDERBREATHS
UNDERBREEDING
UNDERBREEDINGS
UNDERBRIDGE
UNDERBRIDGES
UNDERBRIMS
UNDERBRUSH
UNDERBRUSHED
UNDERBRUSHES
UNDERBRUSHING
UNDERBUDDED
UNDERBUDDING
UNDERBUDGET
UNDERBUDGETED
UNDERBUDGETING
UNDERBUDGETS
UNDERBUILD
UNDERBUILDER
UNDERBUILDERS
UNDERBUILDING
UNDERBUILDS
UNDERBUILT
UNDERBURNT
UNDERBUSHED
UNDERBUSHES
UNDERBUSHING
UNDERBUYING
UNDERCAPITALISE
UNDERCAPITALIZE
UNDERCARDS
UNDERCARRIAGE
UNDERCARRIAGES
UNDERCARTS
UNDERCASTS
UNDERCHARGE
UNDERCHARGED
UNDERCHARGES
UNDERCHARGING
UNDERCLASS
UNDERCLASSES
UNDERCLASSMAN
UNDERCLASSMEN
UNDERCLAYS
UNDERCLIFF
UNDERCLIFFS
UNDERCLOTHE
UNDERCLOTHED

UNDERCLOTHES
UNDERCLOTHING
UNDERCLOTHINGS
UNDERCLUBBED
UNDERCLUBBING
UNDERCLUBS
UNDERCOATED
UNDERCOATING
UNDERCOATINGS
UNDERCOATS
UNDERCOOKED
UNDERCOOKING
UNDERCOOKS
UNDERCOOLED
UNDERCOOLING
UNDERCOOLS
UNDERCOUNT
UNDERCOUNTED
UNDERCOUNTING
UNDERCOUNTS
UNDERCOVER
UNDERCOVERT
UNDERCOVERTS
UNDERCRACKERS
UNDERCREST
UNDERCRESTED
UNDERCRESTING
UNDERCRESTS
UNDERCROFT
UNDERCROFTS
UNDERCURRENT
UNDERCURRENTS
UNDERCUTTING
UNDERDAMPER
UNDERDAMPERS
UNDERDECKS
UNDERDELIVER
UNDERDELIVERED
UNDERDELIVERING
UNDERDELIVERS
UNDERDEVELOP
UNDERDEVELOPED
UNDERDEVELOPING
UNDERDEVELOPS
UNDERDOERS
UNDERDOING
UNDERDOSED
UNDERDOSES

UNDERDOSING
UNDERDRAIN
UNDERDRAINAGE
UNDERDRAINAGES
UNDERDRAINED
UNDERDRAINING
UNDERDRAINS
UNDERDRAWERS
UNDERDRAWING
UNDERDRAWINGS
UNDERDRAWN
UNDERDRAWS
UNDERDRESS
UNDERDRESSED
UNDERDRESSES
UNDERDRESSING
UNDERDRIVE
UNDERDRIVES
UNDEREARTH
UNDEREARTHS
UNDEREATEN
UNDEREATING
UNDEREDUCATED
UNDEREMPHASES
UNDEREMPHASIS
UNDEREMPHASISE
UNDEREMPHASISED
UNDEREMPHASISES
UNDEREMPHASIZE
UNDEREMPHASIZED
UNDEREMPHASIZES
UNDEREMPLOYED
UNDEREMPLOYMENT
UNDERESTIMATE
UNDERESTIMATED
UNDERESTIMATES
UNDERESTIMATING
UNDERESTIMATION
UNDEREXPLOIT
UNDEREXPLOITED
UNDEREXPLOITING
UNDEREXPLOITS
UNDEREXPOSE
UNDEREXPOSED
UNDEREXPOSES
UNDEREXPOSING
UNDEREXPOSURE
UNDEREXPOSURES

UNDERFEEDING	UNDERGROUNDS	UNDERLEAVES	UNDERNOURISHES	UNDERPRICINGS
UNDERFEEDINGS	UNDERGROVE	UNDERLETTER	UNDERNOURISHING	UNDERPRISE
UNDERFEEDS	UNDERGROVES	UNDERLETTERS	UNDERNTIME	UNDERPRISED
UNDERFELTS	UNDERGROWN	UNDERLETTING	UNDERNTIMES	UNDERPRISES
UNDERFINANCED	UNDERGROWTH	UNDERLETTINGS	UNDERNUTRITION	UNDERPRISING
UNDERFINISHED	UNDERGROWTHS	UNDERLEVERAGED	UNDERNUTRITIONS	UNDERPRIVILEGED
UNDERFIRED	UNDERHAIRS	UNDERLIERS	UNDEROCCUPIED	UNDERPRIZE
UNDERFIRES	UNDERHANDED	UNDERLINED	UNDERPAINTING	UNDERPRIZED
UNDERFIRING	UNDERHANDEDLY	UNDERLINEN	UNDERPAINTINGS	UNDERPRIZES
UNDERFISHED	UNDERHANDEDNESS	UNDERLINENS	UNDERPANTS	UNDERPRIZING
UNDERFISHES	UNDERHANDING	UNDERLINES	UNDERPARTS	UNDERPRODUCE
UNDERFISHING	UNDERHANDS	UNDERLINGS	UNDERPASSES	UNDERPRODUCED
UNDERFLOOR	UNDERHEATED	UNDERLINING	UNDERPASSION	UNDERPRODUCES
UNDERFLOWS	UNDERHEATING	UNDERLININGS	UNDERPASSIONS	UNDERPRODUCING
UNDERFONGED	UNDERHEATS	UNDERLOADED	UNDERPAYING	UNDERPRODUCTION
UNDERFONGING	UNDERHONEST	UNDERLOADING	UNDERPAYMENT	UNDERPROOF
UNDERFONGS	UNDERINFLATED	UNDERLOADS	UNDERPAYMENTS	UNDERPROPPED
UNDERFOOTED	UNDERINFLATION	UNDERLOOKER	UNDERPEEPED	UNDERPROPPER
UNDERFOOTING	UNDERINFLATIONS	UNDERLOOKERS	UNDERPEEPING	UNDERPROPPERS
UNDERFOOTS	UNDERINSURE	UNDERLYING	UNDERPEEPS	UNDERPROPPING
UNDERFULFIL	UNDERINSURED	UNDERLYINGLY	UNDERPEOPLED	UNDERPROPS
UNDERFULFILL	UNDERINSURES	UNDERMANNED	UNDERPERFORM	UNDERPUBLICISED
UNDERFULFILLED	UNDERINSURING	UNDERMANNING	UNDERPERFORMED	UNDERPUBLICIZED
UNDERFULFILLING	UNDERINVEST	UNDERMANNINGS	UNDERPERFORMING	UNDERQUALIFIED
UNDERFULFILLS	UNDERINVESTED	UNDERMASTED	UNDERPERFORMS	UNDERQUOTE
UNDERFULFILS	UNDERINVESTING	UNDERMEANING	UNDERPINNED	UNDERQUOTED
UNDERFUNDED	UNDERINVESTMENT	UNDERMEANINGS	UNDERPINNING	UNDERQUOTES
UNDERFUNDING	UNDERINVESTS	UNDERMENTIONED	UNDERPINNINGS	UNDERQUOTING
UNDERFUNDINGS	UNDERJAWED	UNDERMINDE	UNDERPITCH	UNDERRATED
UNDERFUNDS	UNDERKEEPER	UNDERMINDED	UNDERPLANT	UNDERRATES
UNDERGARMENT	UNDERKEEPERS	UNDERMINDES	UNDERPLANTED	UNDERRATING
UNDERGARMENTS	UNDERKEEPING	UNDERMINDING	UNDERPLANTING	UNDERREACT
UNDERGIRDED	UNDERKEEPS	UNDERMINED	UNDERPLANTS	UNDERREACTED
UNDERGIRDING	UNDERKILLS	UNDERMINER	UNDERPLAYED	UNDERREACTING
UNDERGIRDS	UNDERKINGDOM	UNDERMINERS	UNDERPLAYING	UNDERREACTION
UNDERGLAZE	UNDERKINGDOMS	UNDERMINES	UNDERPLAYS	UNDERREACTIONS
UNDERGLAZES	UNDERKINGS	UNDERMINING	UNDERPLOTS	UNDERREACTS
UNDERGOERS	UNDERLAPPED	UNDERMININGS	UNDERPOPULATED	UNDERREPORT
UNDERGOING	UNDERLAPPING	UNDERNAMED	UNDERPOWERED	UNDERREPORTED
UNDERGOWNS	UNDERLAYER	UNDERNEATH	UNDERPRAISE	UNDERREPORTING
UNDERGRADS	UNDERLAYERS	UNDERNEATHS	UNDERPRAISED	UNDERREPORTS
UNDERGRADUATE	UNDERLAYING	UNDERNICENESS	UNDERPRAISES	UNDERRUNNING
UNDERGRADUATES	UNDERLAYMENT	UNDERNICENESSES	UNDERPRAISING	UNDERRUNNINGS
UNDERGRADUETTE	UNDERLAYMENTS	UNDERNOTED	UNDERPREPARED	UNDERSATURATED
UNDERGRADUETTES	UNDERLEASE	UNDERNOTES	UNDERPRICE	UNDERSAYING
UNDERGROUND	UNDERLEASED	UNDERNOTING	UNDERPRICED	UNDERSCORE
UNDERGROUNDER	UNDERLEASES	UNDERNOURISH	UNDERPRICES	UNDERSCORED
UNDERGROUNDERS	UNDERLEASING	UNDERNOURISHED	UNDERPRICING	UNDERSCORES

UNDERSCORING	UNDERSPEND	UNDERSTUDY	UNDERUTILIZING	UNDESCENDED
UNDERSCORINGS	UNDERSPENDING	UNDERSTUDYING	UNDERVALUATION	UNDESCENDIBLE
UNDERSCRUB	UNDERSPENDINGS	UNDERSUBSCRIBED	UNDERVALUATIONS	UNDESCRIBABLE
UNDERSCRUBS	UNDERSPENDS	UNDERSUPPLIED	UNDERVALUE	UNDESCRIBED
UNDERSEALED	UNDERSPENT	UNDERSUPPLIES	UNDERVALUED	UNDESCRIED
UNDERSEALING	UNDERSPINS	UNDERSUPPLY	UNDERVALUER	UNDESERVED
UNDERSEALINGS	UNDERSTAFFED	UNDERSUPPLYING	UNDERVALUERS	UNDESERVEDLY
UNDERSEALS	UNDERSTAFFING	UNDERSURFACE	UNDERVALUES	UNDESERVEDNESS
UNDERSECRETARY	UNDERSTAFFINGS	UNDERSURFACES	UNDERVALUING	UNDESERVER
UNDERSELLER	UNDERSTAND	UNDERTAKABLE	UNDERVESTS	UNDESERVERS
UNDERSELLERS	UNDERSTANDABLE	UNDERTAKEN	UNDERVIEWER	UNDESERVES
UNDERSELLING	UNDERSTANDABLY	UNDERTAKER	UNDERVIEWERS	UNDESERVING
UNDERSELLS	UNDERSTANDED	UNDERTAKERS	UNDERVOICE	UNDESERVINGLY
UNDERSELVES	UNDERSTANDER	UNDERTAKES	UNDERVOICES	UNDESIGNATED
UNDERSENSE	UNDERSTANDERS	UNDERTAKING	UNDERVOTES	UNDESIGNED
UNDERSENSES	UNDERSTANDING	UNDERTAKINGS	UNDERWATER	UNDESIGNEDLY
UNDERSERVED	UNDERSTANDINGLY	UNDERTAXED	UNDERWATERS	UNDESIGNEDNESS
UNDERSETTING	UNDERSTANDINGS	UNDERTAXES	UNDERWEARS	UNDESIGNING
UNDERSEXED	UNDERSTANDS	UNDERTAXING	UNDERWEIGHT	UNDESIRABILITY
UNDERSHAPEN	UNDERSTATE	UNDERTENANCIES	UNDERWEIGHTS	UNDESIRABLE
UNDERSHERIFF	UNDERSTATED	UNDERTENANCY	UNDERWHELM	UNDESIRABLENESS
UNDERSHERIFFS	UNDERSTATEDLY	UNDERTENANT	UNDERWHELMED	UNDESIRABLES
UNDERSHIRT	UNDERSTATEMENT	UNDERTENANTS	UNDERWHELMING	UNDESIRABLY
UNDERSHIRTED	UNDERSTATEMENTS	UNDERTHINGS	UNDERWHELMS	UNDESIRING
UNDERSHIRTS	UNDERSTATES	UNDERTHIRST	UNDERWINGS	UNDESIROUS
UNDERSHOOT	UNDERSTATING	UNDERTHIRSTS	UNDERWIRED	UNDESPAIRING
UNDERSHOOTING	UNDERSTEER	UNDERTHRUST	UNDERWIRES	UNDESPAIRINGLY
UNDERSHOOTS	UNDERSTEERED	UNDERTHRUSTING	UNDERWIRING	UNDESPATCHED
UNDERSHORTS	UNDERSTEERING	UNDERTHRUSTS	UNDERWIRINGS	UNDESPOILED
UNDERSHRUB	UNDERSTEERS	UNDERTIMED	UNDERWOODS	UNDESTROYED
UNDERSHRUBS	UNDERSTOCK	UNDERTIMES	UNDERWOOLS	UNDETECTABLE
UNDERSIDES	UNDERSTOCKED	UNDERTINTS	UNDERWORKED	UNDETECTED
UNDERSIGNED	UNDERSTOCKING	UNDERTONED	UNDERWORKER	UNDETERMINABLE
UNDERSIGNING	UNDERSTOCKS	UNDERTONES	UNDERWORKERS	UNDETERMINATE
UNDERSIGNS	UNDERSTOOD	UNDERTRICK	UNDERWORKING	UNDETERMINATION
UNDERSIZED	UNDERSTOREY	UNDERTRICKS	UNDERWORKS	UNDETERMINED
UNDERSKIES	UNDERSTOREYS	UNDERTRUMP	UNDERWORLD	UNDETERRED
UNDERSKINKER	UNDERSTORIES	UNDERTRUMPED	UNDERWORLDS	UNDEVELOPED
UNDERSKINKERS	UNDERSTORY	UNDERTRUMPING	UNDERWRITE	UNDEVIATING
UNDERSKIRT	UNDERSTRAPPER	UNDERTRUMPS	UNDERWRITER	UNDEVIATINGLY
UNDERSKIRTS	UNDERSTRAPPERS	UNDERUSING	UNDERWRITERS	UNDIAGNOSABLE
UNDERSLEEVE	UNDERSTRAPPING	UNDERUTILISE	UNDERWRITES	UNDIAGNOSED
UNDERSLEEVES	UNDERSTRATA	UNDERUTILISED	UNDERWRITING	UNDIALECTICAL
UNDERSLUNG	UNDERSTRATUM	UNDERUTILISES	UNDERWRITINGS	UNDIDACTIC
UNDERSOILS	UNDERSTRATUMS	UNDERUTILISING	UNDERWRITTEN	UNDIFFERENCED
UNDERSONGS	UNDERSTRENGTH	UNDERUTILIZE	UNDERWROTE	UNDIGESTED
UNDERSOWED	UNDERSTUDIED	UNDERUTILIZED	UNDERWROUGHT	UNDIGESTIBLE
UNDERSOWING	UNDERSTUDIES	UNDERUTILIZES	UNDESCENDABLE	UNDIGHTING

U

UNDIGNIFIED

UNDIGNIFIED	UNDISTILLED	UNDRINKABLE	UNEMBODIED	UNEQUIPPED
UNDIGNIFIES	UNDISTINCTIVE	UNDRIVEABLE	UNEMOTIONAL	UNEQUITABLE
UNDIGNIFYING	UNDISTINGUISHED	UNDROOPING	UNEMOTIONALLY	UNEQUIVOCABLE
UNDIMINISHABLE	UNDISTORTED	UNDROSSIER	UNEMOTIONED	UNEQUIVOCABLY
UNDIMINISHED	UNDISTRACTED	UNDROSSIEST	UNEMPHASISED	UNEQUIVOCAL
UNDIPLOMATIC	UNDISTRACTEDLY	UNDULANCES	UNEMPHASIZED	UNEQUIVOCALLY
UNDIRECTED	UNDISTRACTING	UNDULANCIES	UNEMPHATIC	UNEQUIVOCALNESS
UNDISAPPOINTING	UNDISTRIBUTED	UNDULATELY	UNEMPHATICALLY	UNERASABLE
UNDISCERNED	UNDISTURBED	UNDULATING	UNEMPIRICAL	UNERRINGLY
UNDISCERNEDLY	UNDISTURBEDLY	UNDULATINGLY	UNEMPLOYABILITY	UNERRINGNESS
UNDISCERNIBLE	UNDISTURBING	UNDULATION	UNEMPLOYABLE	UNERRINGNESSES
UNDISCERNIBLY	UNDIVERSIFIED	UNDULATIONIST	UNEMPLOYABLES	UNESCAPABLE
UNDISCERNING	UNDIVERTED	UNDULATIONISTS	UNEMPLOYED	UNESCORTED
UNDISCERNINGS	UNDIVERTING	UNDULATIONS	UNEMPLOYEDS	UNESSENCED
UNDISCHARGED	UNDIVESTED	UNDULATORS	UNEMPLOYMENT	UNESSENCES
UNDISCIPLINABLE	UNDIVESTEDLY	UNDULATORY	UNEMPLOYMENTS	UNESSENCING
UNDISCIPLINE	UNDIVIDABLE	UNDUPLICATED	UNENCHANTED	UNESSENTIAL
UNDISCIPLINED	UNDIVIDEDLY	UNDUTIFULLY	UNENCLOSED	UNESSENTIALLY
UNDISCIPLINES	UNDIVIDEDNESS	UNDUTIFULNESS	UNENCOURAGING	UNESSENTIALS
UNDISCLOSED	UNDIVIDEDNESSES	UNDUTIFULNESSES	UNENCUMBERED	UNESTABLISHED
UNDISCOMFITED	UNDIVORCED	UNDYINGNESS	UNENDANGERED	UNESTHETIC
UNDISCORDANT	UNDIVULGED	UNDYINGNESSES	UNENDEARED	UNETHICALLY
UNDISCORDING	UNDOCTORED	UNEARMARKED	UNENDEARING	UNEVALUATED
UNDISCOURAGED	UNDOCTRINAIRE	UNEARTHING	UNENDINGLY	UNEVANGELICAL
UNDISCOVERABLE	UNDOCTRINAIRES	UNEARTHLIER	UNENDINGNESS	UNEVENNESS
UNDISCOVERABLY	UNDOCUMENTED	UNEARTHLIEST	UNENDINGNESSES	UNEVENNESSES
UNDISCOVERED	UNDOGMATIC	UNEARTHLINESS	UNENDURABLE	UNEVENTFUL
UNDISCUSSABLE	UNDOGMATICALLY	UNEARTHLINESSES	UNENDURABLENESS	UNEVENTFULLY
UNDISCUSSED	UNDOMESTIC	UNEASINESS	UNENDURABLY	UNEVENTFULNESS
UNDISCUSSIBLE	UNDOMESTICATE	UNEASINESSES	UNENFORCEABLE	UNEVIDENCED
UNDISGUISABLE	UNDOMESTICATED	UNEATABLENESS	UNENFORCED	UNEXACTING
UNDISGUISED	UNDOMESTICATES	UNEATABLENESSES	UNENJOYABLE	UNEXAGGERATED
UNDISGUISEDLY	UNDOMESTICATING	UNECCENTRIC	UNENLARGED	UNEXAMINED
UNDISHONOURED	UNDOUBLING	UNECLIPSED	UNENLIGHTENED	UNEXAMPLED
UNDISMANTLED	UNDOUBTABLE	UNECOLOGICAL	UNENLIGHTENING	UNEXCAVATED
UNDISMAYED	UNDOUBTEDLY	UNECONOMIC	UNENQUIRING	UNEXCELLED
UNDISORDERED	UNDOUBTFUL	UNECONOMICAL	UNENRICHED	UNEXCEPTIONABLE
UNDISPATCHED	UNDOUBTING	UNEDIFYING	UNENSLAVED	UNEXCEPTIONABLY
UNDISPENSED	UNDOUBTINGLY	UNEDUCABLE	UNENTAILED	UNEXCEPTIONAL
UNDISPOSED	UNDRAINABLE	UNEDUCATED	UNENTERPRISING	UNEXCEPTIONALLY
UNDISPUTABLE	UNDRAMATIC	UNEFFECTED	UNENTERTAINED	UNEXCITABLE
UNDISPUTED	UNDRAMATICALLY	UNELABORATE	UNENTERTAINING	UNEXCITING
UNDISPUTEDLY	UNDRAMATISED	UNELABORATED	UNENTHRALLED	UNEXCLUDED
UNDISSEMBLED	UNDRAMATIZED	UNELECTABLE	UNENTHUSIASTIC	UNEXCLUSIVE
UNDISSOCIATED	UNDREADING	UNELECTRIFIED	UNENTITLED	UNEXCLUSIVELY
UNDISSOLVED	UNDREAMING	UNEMBARRASSED	UNENVIABLE	UNEXECUTED
UNDISSOLVING	UNDRESSING	UNEMBELLISHED	UNENVIABLY	UNEXEMPLIFIED
UNDISTEMPERED	UNDRESSINGS	UNEMBITTERED	UNEQUALLED	UNEXERCISED

UNEXHAUSTED	UNFASHIONED	UNFILLABLE	UNFOREKNOWN	UNFREQUENT
UNEXPANDED	UNFASTENED	UNFILLETED	UNFORESEEABLE	UNFREQUENTED
UNEXPECTANT	UNFASTENING	UNFILTERABLE	UNFORESEEING	UNFREQUENTING
UNEXPECTED	UNFASTIDIOUS	UNFILTERED	UNFORESEEN	UNFREQUENTLY
UNEXPECTEDLY	UNFATHERED	UNFILTRABLE	UNFORESKINNED	UNFREQUENTS
UNEXPECTEDNESS	UNFATHERLIER	UNFINDABLE	UNFORESTED	UNFRIENDED
UNEXPENDED	UNFATHERLIEST	UNFINISHED	UNFORETOLD	UNFRIENDEDNESS
UNEXPENSIVE	UNFATHERLY	UNFINISHING	UNFOREWARNED	UNFRIENDING
UNEXPENSIVELY	UNFATHOMABLE	UNFINISHINGS	UNFORFEITED	UNFRIENDLIER
UNEXPERIENCED	UNFATHOMABLY	UNFITNESSES	UNFORGETTABLE	UNFRIENDLIEST
UNEXPERIENT	UNFATHOMED	UNFITTEDNESS	UNFORGETTABLY	UNFRIENDLILY
UNEXPIATED	UNFAULTIER	UNFITTEDNESSES	UNFORGIVABLE	UNFRIENDLINESS
UNEXPLAINABLE	UNFAULTIEST	UNFITTINGLY	UNFORGIVABLY	UNFRIENDLY
UNEXPLAINED	UNFAVORABLE	UNFIXEDNESS	UNFORGIVEN	UNFRIENDSHIP
UNEXPLODED	UNFAVORABLENESS	UNFIXEDNESSES	UNFORGIVENESS	UNFRIENDSHIPS
UNEXPLOITED	UNFAVORABLY	UNFIXITIES	UNFORGIVENESSES	UNFRIGHTED
UNEXPLORED	UNFAVORITE	UNFLAGGING	UNFORGIVING	UNFRIGHTENED
UNEXPRESSED	UNFAVOURABLE	UNFLAGGINGLY	UNFORGIVINGNESS	UNFRIVOLOUS
UNEXPRESSIBLE	UNFAVOURABLY	UNFLAMBOYANT	UNFORGOTTEN	UNFROCKING
UNEXPRESSIVE	UNFAVOURED	UNFLAPPABILITY	UNFORMALISED	UNFRUCTUOUS
UNEXPUGNABLE	UNFAVOURITE	UNFLAPPABLE	UNFORMALIZED	UNFRUITFUL
UNEXPURGATED	UNFEARFULLY	UNFLAPPABLENESS	UNFORMATTED	UNFRUITFULLY
UNEXTENDED	UNFEASIBLE	UNFLAPPABLY	UNFORMIDABLE	UNFRUITFULNESS
UNEXTENUATED	UNFEATHERED	UNFLASHIER	UNFORMULATED	UNFULFILLABLE
UNEXTINGUISHED	UNFEATURED	UNFLASHIEST	UNFORSAKEN	UNFULFILLED
UNEXTRAORDINARY	UNFEELINGLY	UNFLATTERING	UNFORTHCOMING	UNFULFILLING
UNFADINGLY	UNFEELINGNESS	UNFLATTERINGLY	UNFORTIFIED	UNFUNNIEST
UNFADINGNESS	UNFEELINGNESSES	UNFLAVORED	UNFORTUNATE	UNFURNISHED
UNFADINGNESSES	UNFEIGNEDLY	UNFLAVOURED	UNFORTUNATELY	UNFURNISHES
UNFAILINGLY	UNFEIGNEDNESS	UNFLESHING	UNFORTUNATENESS	UNFURNISHING
UNFAILINGNESS	UNFEIGNEDNESSES	UNFLESHLIER	UNFORTUNATES	UNFURROWED
UNFAILINGNESSES	UNFEIGNING	UNFLESHLIEST	UNFORTUNED	UNFUSSIEST
UNFAIRNESS	UNFELLOWED	UNFLINCHING	UNFORTUNES	UNGAINLIER
UNFAIRNESSES	UNFEMININE	UNFLINCHINGLY	UNFOSSILIFEROUS	UNGAINLIEST
UNFAITHFUL	UNFERMENTED	UNFLUSHING	UNFOSSILISED	UNGAINLINESS
UNFAITHFULLY	UNFERTILISED	UNFLUSTERED	UNFOSSILIZED	UNGAINLINESSES
UNFAITHFULNESS	UNFERTILIZED	UNFOCUSSED	UNFOSTERED	UNGAINSAID
UNFALLIBLE	UNFETTERED	UNFOLDINGS	UNFOUGHTEN	UNGAINSAYABLE
UNFALSIFIABLE	UNFETTERING	UNFOLDMENT	UNFOUNDEDLY	UNGALLANTLY
UNFALTERING	UNFEUDALISE	UNFOLDMENTS	UNFOUNDEDNESS	UNGARMENTED
UNFALTERINGLY	UNFEUDALISED	UNFOLLOWED	UNFOUNDEDNESSES	UNGARNERED
UNFAMILIAR	UNFEUDALISES	UNFOLLOWING	UNFRANCHISED	UNGARNISHED
UNFAMILIARITIES	UNFEUDALISING	UNFORBIDDEN	UNFRAUGHTED	UNGARTERED
UNFAMILIARITY	UNFEUDALIZE	UNFORCEDLY	UNFRAUGHTING	UNGATHERED
UNFAMILIARLY	UNFEUDALIZED	UNFORCIBLE	UNFRAUGHTS	UNGENEROSITIES
UNFANCIEST	UNFEUDALIZES	UNFORDABLE	UNFREEDOMS	UNGENEROSITY
UNFASHIONABLE	UNFEUDALIZING	UNFOREBODING	UNFREEZING	UNGENEROUS
UNFASHIONABLY	UNFILIALLY	UNFOREKNOWABLE	UNFREEZINGS	UNGENEROUSLY

U

UNGENITURED

UNGENITURED	UNGROUNDED	UNHARMONIOUS	UNHOMELIEST	UNIDEALISM
UNGENTEELLY	UNGROUNDEDLY	UNHARNESSED	UNHOMELIKE	UNIDEALISMS
UNGENTILITIES	UNGROUNDEDNESS	UNHARNESSES	UNHOMOGENISED	UNIDEALISTIC
UNGENTILITY	UNGROUPING	UNHARNESSING	UNHOMOGENIZED	UNIDENTIFIABLE
UNGENTLEMANLIER	UNGRUDGING	UNHARVESTED	UNHONOURED	UNIDENTIFIED
UNGENTLEMANLIKE	UNGRUDGINGLY	UNHASTIEST	UNHOPEFULLY	UNIDEOLOGICAL
UNGENTLEMANLY	UNGUARDEDLY	UNHATTINGS	UNHOSPITABLE	UNIDIMENSIONAL
UNGENTLENESS	UNGUARDEDNESS	UNHAZARDED	UNHOUSELED	UNIDIOMATIC
UNGENTLENESSES	UNGUARDEDNESSES	UNHAZARDOUS	UNHOUZZLED	UNIDIOMATICALLY
UNGENTLEST	UNGUARDING	UNHEALABLE	UNHUMANISE	UNIDIRECTIONAL
UNGENTRIFIED	UNGUENTARIA	UNHEALTHFUL	UNHUMANISED	UNIFICATION
UNGENUINENESS	UNGUENTARIES	UNHEALTHFULLY	UNHUMANISES	UNIFICATIONS
UNGENUINENESSES	UNGUENTARIUM	UNHEALTHFULNESS	UNHUMANISING	UNIFLOROUS
UNGERMINATED	UNGUENTARY	UNHEALTHIER	UNHUMANIZE	UNIFOLIATE
UNGETATABLE	UNGUERDONED	UNHEALTHIEST	UNHUMANIZED	UNIFOLIOLATE
UNGHOSTLIER	UNGUESSABLE	UNHEALTHILY	UNHUMANIZES	UNIFORMEST
UNGHOSTLIEST	UNGUICULATE	UNHEALTHINESS	UNHUMANIZING	UNIFORMING
UNGIMMICKY	UNGUICULATED	UNHEALTHINESSES	UNHUMOROUS	UNIFORMITARIAN
UNGIRTHING	UNGUICULATES	UNHEARSING	UNHURRIEDLY	UNIFORMITARIANS
UNGLACIATED	UNGUILTIER	UNHEARTING	UNHURRYING	UNIFORMITIES
UNGLAMORISED	UNGUILTIEST	UNHEEDEDLY	UNHURTFULLY	UNIFORMITY
UNGLAMORIZED	UNGULIGRADE	UNHEEDFULLY	UNHURTFULNESS	UNIFORMNESS
UNGLAMOROUS	UNHABITABLE	UNHEEDIEST	UNHURTFULNESSES	UNIFORMNESSES
UNGLITZIER	UNHABITUATED	UNHEEDINGLY	UNHUSBANDED	UNIGENITURE
UNGLITZIEST	UNHACKNEYED	UNHELMETED	UNHYDROLYSED	UNIGENITURES
UNGODLIEST	UNHALLOWED	UNHELPABLE	UNHYDROLYZED	UNIGNORABLE
UNGODLINESS	UNHALLOWING	UNHELPFULLY	UNHYGIENIC	UNILABIATE
UNGODLINESSES	UNHAMPERED	UNHELPFULNESS	UNHYPHENATED	UNILATERAL
UNGOVERNABLE	UNHANDIEST	UNHELPFULNESSES	UNHYSTERICAL	UNILATERALISM
UNGOVERNABLY	UNHANDINESS	UNHERALDED	UNHYSTERICALLY	UNILATERALISMS
UNGOVERNED	UNHANDINESSES	UNHEROICAL	UNIAXIALLY	UNILATERALIST
UNGRACEFUL	UNHANDSELLED	UNHEROICALLY	UNICAMERAL	UNILATERALISTS
UNGRACEFULLY	UNHANDSOME	UNHESITATING	UNICAMERALISM	UNILATERALITIES
UNGRACEFULNESS	UNHANDSOMELY	UNHESITATINGLY	UNICAMERALISMS	UNILATERALITY
UNGRACIOUS	UNHANDSOMENESS	UNHIDEBOUND	UNICAMERALIST	UNILATERALLY
UNGRACIOUSLY	UNHAPPENED	UNHINDERED	UNICAMERALISTS	UNILINGUAL
UNGRACIOUSNESS	UNHAPPENING	UNHINGEMENT	UNICAMERALLY	UNILINGUALISM
UNGRAMMATIC	UNHAPPENINGS	UNHINGEMENTS	UNICELLULAR	UNILINGUALISMS
UNGRAMMATICAL	UNHAPPIEST	UNHISTORIC	UNICELLULARITY	UNILINGUALIST
UNGRAMMATICALLY	UNHAPPINESS	UNHISTORICAL	UNICENTRAL	UNILINGUALISTS
UNGRASPABLE	UNHAPPINESSES	UNHITCHING	UNICOLORATE	UNILINGUALS
UNGRATEFUL	UNHAPPYING	UNHOARDING	UNICOLORED	UNILITERAL
UNGRATEFULLY	UNHARBOURED	UNHOLINESS	UNICOLOROUS	UNILLUMINATED
UNGRATEFULNESS	UNHARBOURING	UNHOLINESSES	UNICOLOURED	UNILLUMINATING
UNGRATIFIED	UNHARBOURS	UNHOLSTERED	UNICOSTATE	UNILLUMINED
UNGREEDIER	UNHARDENED	UNHOLSTERING	UNICYCLING	UNILLUSIONED
UNGREEDIEST	UNHARDIEST	UNHOLSTERS	UNICYCLIST	UNILLUSTRATED
UNGREENEST	UNHARMFULLY	UNHOMELIER	UNICYCLISTS	UNILOBULAR

U

UNILOCULAR	UNINFORMATIVELY	UNINTERPRETED	UNITEDNESS	UNJUSTNESSES
UNIMAGINABLE	UNINFORMED	UNINTERRUPTED	UNITEDNESSES	UNKEMPTNESS
UNIMAGINABLY	UNINFORMING	UNINTERRUPTEDLY	UNITHOLDER	UNKEMPTNESSES
UNIMAGINATIVE	UNINGRATIATING	UNINTIMIDATED	UNITHOLDERS	UNKENNELED
UNIMAGINATIVELY	UNINHABITABLE	UNINTOXICATING	UNITISATION	UNKENNELING
UNIMAGINED	UNINHABITED	UNINTRODUCED	UNITISATIONS	UNKENNELLED
UNIMMORTAL	UNINHIBITED	UNINUCLEAR	UNITIZATION	UNKENNELLING
UNIMMUNISED	UNINHIBITEDLY	UNINUCLEATE	UNITIZATIONS	UNKINDLIER
UNIMMUNIZED	UNINHIBITEDNESS	UNINVENTIVE	UNIVALENCE	UNKINDLIEST
UNIMOLECULAR	UNINITIATE	UNINVESTED	UNIVALENCES	UNKINDLINESS
UNIMPAIRED	UNINITIATED	UNINVIDIOUS	UNIVALENCIES	UNKINDLINESSES
UNIMPARTED	UNINITIATES	UNINVITING	UNIVALENCY	UNKINDNESS
UNIMPASSIONED	UNINOCULATED	UNINVOLVED	UNIVALENTS	UNKINDNESSES
UNIMPEACHABLE	UNINQUIRING	UNIONISATION	UNIVALVULAR	UNKINGLIER
UNIMPEACHABLY	UNINQUISITIVE	UNIONISATIONS	UNIVARIANT	UNKINGLIEST
UNIMPEACHED	UNINSCRIBED	UNIONISERS	UNIVARIATE	UNKINGLIKE
UNIMPEDEDLY	UNINSPECTED	UNIONISING	UNIVERSALISABLE	UNKNIGHTED
UNIMPLORED	UNINSPIRED	UNIONISTIC	UNIVERSALISE	UNKNIGHTING
UNIMPORTANCE	UNINSPIRING	UNIONIZATION	UNIVERSALISED	UNKNIGHTLIER
UNIMPORTANCES	UNINSTALLED	UNIONIZATIONS	UNIVERSALISES	UNKNIGHTLIEST
UNIMPORTANT	UNINSTALLING	UNIONIZERS	UNIVERSALISING	UNKNIGHTLINESS
UNIMPORTUNED	UNINSTALLS	UNIONIZING	UNIVERSALISM	UNKNIGHTLY
UNIMPOSING	UNINSTRUCTED	UNIPARENTAL	UNIVERSALISMS	UNKNITTING
UNIMPREGNATED	UNINSTRUCTIVE	UNIPARENTALLY	UNIVERSALIST	UNKNOTTING
UNIMPRESSED	UNINSULATED	UNIPARTITE	UNIVERSALISTIC	UNKNOWABILITIES
UNIMPRESSIBLE	UNINSURABLE	UNIPERSONAL	UNIVERSALISTS	UNKNOWABILITY
UNIMPRESSIVE	UNINSUREDS	UNIPERSONALITY	UNIVERSALITIES	UNKNOWABLE
UNIMPRISONED	UNINTEGRATED	UNIPOLARITIES	UNIVERSALITY	UNKNOWABLENESS
UNIMPROVED	UNINTELLECTUAL	UNIPOLARITY	UNIVERSALIZABLE	UNKNOWABLES
UNIMPUGNABLE	UNINTELLIGENCE	UNIQUENESS	UNIVERSALIZE	UNKNOWABLY
UNINAUGURATED	UNINTELLIGENCES	UNIQUENESSES	UNIVERSALIZED	UNKNOWINGLY
UNINCHANTED	UNINTELLIGENT	UNIRONICALLY	UNIVERSALIZES	UNKNOWINGNESS
UNINCLOSED	UNINTELLIGENTLY	UNIRRADIATED	UNIVERSALIZING	UNKNOWINGNESSES
UNINCORPORATED	UNINTELLIGIBLE	UNIRRIGATED	UNIVERSALLY	UNKNOWINGS
UNINCUMBERED	UNINTELLIGIBLY	UNISEPTATE	UNIVERSALNESS	UNKNOWLEDGEABLE
UNINDEARED	UNINTENDED	UNISERIALLY	UNIVERSALNESSES	UNKNOWNNESS
UNINDENTED	UNINTENTIONAL	UNISERIATE	UNIVERSALS	UNKNOWNNESSES
UNINDICTED	UNINTENTIONALLY	UNISERIATELY	UNIVERSITARIAN	UNLABELLED
UNINFECTED	UNINTEREST	UNISEXUALITIES	UNIVERSITIES	UNLABORING
UNINFLAMED	UNINTERESTED	UNISEXUALITY	UNIVERSITY	UNLABORIOUS
UNINFLAMMABLE	UNINTERESTEDLY	UNISEXUALLY	UNIVOCALLY	UNLABOURED
UNINFLATED	UNINTERESTING	UNISONALLY	UNIVOLTINE	UNLABOURING
UNINFLECTED	UNINTERESTINGLY	UNISONANCE	UNJAUNDICED	UNLADYLIKE
UNINFLUENCED	UNINTERESTS	UNISONANCES	UNJOINTING	UNLAMENTED
UNINFLUENTIAL	UNINTERMITTED	UNITARIANISM	UNJUSTIFIABLE	UNLATCHING
UNINFORCEABLE	UNINTERMITTEDLY	UNITARIANISMS	UNJUSTIFIABLY	UNLAUNDERED
UNINFORCED	UNINTERMITTING	UNITARIANS	UNJUSTIFIED	UNLAWFULLY
UNINFORMATIVE	UNINTERPRETABLE	UNITARITIES	UNJUSTNESS	UNLAWFULNESS

U

UNLAWFULNESSES

UNLAWFULNESSES
UNLEARNABLE
UNLEARNEDLY
UNLEARNEDNESS
UNLEARNEDNESSES
UNLEARNING
UNLEASHING
UNLEAVENED
UNLEISURED
UNLEISURELY
UNLESSONED
UNLETTABLE
UNLETTERED
UNLEVELING
UNLEVELLED
UNLEVELLING
UNLIBERATED
UNLIBIDINOUS
UNLICENSED
UNLIFELIKE
UNLIGHTENED
UNLIGHTSOME
UNLIKEABLE
UNLIKELIER
UNLIKELIEST
UNLIKELIHOOD
UNLIKELIHOODS
UNLIKELINESS
UNLIKELINESSES
UNLIKENESS
UNLIKENESSES
UNLIMBERED
UNLIMBERING
UNLIMITEDLY
UNLIMITEDNESS
UNLIMITEDNESSES
UNLIQUEFIED
UNLIQUIDATED
UNLIQUORED
UNLISTENABLE
UNLISTENED
UNLISTENING
UNLITERARY
UNLIVEABLE
UNLIVELIER
UNLIVELIEST
UNLIVELINESS
UNLIVELINESSES

UNLOADINGS
UNLOCALISED
UNLOCALIZED
UNLOCKABLE
UNLOOSENED
UNLOOSENING
UNLORDLIER
UNLORDLIEST
UNLOVEABLE
UNLOVELIER
UNLOVELIEST
UNLOVELINESS
UNLOVELINESSES
UNLOVERLIKE
UNLOVINGLY
UNLOVINGNESS
UNLOVINGNESSES
UNLUCKIEST
UNLUCKINESS
UNLUCKINESSES
UNLUXURIANT
UNLUXURIOUS
UNMACADAMISED
UNMACADAMIZED
UNMAGNIFIED
UNMAIDENLY
UNMAILABLE
UNMAINTAINABLE
UNMAINTAINED
UNMALICIOUS
UNMALICIOUSLY
UNMALLEABILITY
UNMALLEABLE
UNMANACLED
UNMANACLES
UNMANACLING
UNMANAGEABLE
UNMANAGEABLY
UNMANFULLY
UNMANIPULATED
UNMANLIEST
UNMANLINESS
UNMANLINESSES
UNMANNERED
UNMANNEREDLY
UNMANNERLIER
UNMANNERLIEST
UNMANNERLINESS

UNMANNERLY
UNMANTLING
UNMANUFACTURED
UNMARKETABLE
UNMARRIABLE
UNMARRIAGEABLE
UNMARRIEDS
UNMARRYING
UNMASCULINE
UNMASKINGS
UNMASTERED
UNMATCHABLE
UNMATCHING
UNMATERIAL
UNMATERIALISED
UNMATERIALIZED
UNMATERNAL
UNMATHEMATICAL
UNMATRICULATED
UNMEANINGLY
UNMEANINGNESS
UNMEANINGNESSES
UNMEASURABLE
UNMEASURABLY
UNMEASURED
UNMEASUREDLY
UNMECHANIC
UNMECHANICAL
UNMECHANISE
UNMECHANISED
UNMECHANISES
UNMECHANISING
UNMECHANIZE
UNMECHANIZED
UNMECHANIZES
UNMECHANIZING
UNMEDIATED
UNMEDICATED
UNMEDICINABLE
UNMEDITATED
UNMEETNESS
UNMEETNESSES
UNMELLOWED
UNMELODIOUS
UNMELODIOUSNESS
UNMEMORABLE
UNMEMORABLY
UNMENTIONABLE

UNMENTIONABLES
UNMENTIONABLY
UNMENTIONED
UNMERCENARY
UNMERCHANTABLE
UNMERCIFUL
UNMERCIFULLY
UNMERCIFULNESS
UNMERITABLE
UNMERITEDLY
UNMERITING
UNMERRIEST
UNMETABOLISED
UNMETABOLIZED
UNMETALLED
UNMETAPHORICAL
UNMETAPHYSICAL
UNMETHODICAL
UNMETHODISED
UNMETHODIZED
UNMETRICAL
UNMILITARY
UNMINDFULLY
UNMINDFULNESS
UNMINDFULNESSES
UNMINGLING
UNMINISTERIAL
UNMIRACULOUS
UNMISSABLE
UNMISTAKABLE
UNMISTAKABLY
UNMISTAKEABLE
UNMISTAKEABLY
UNMISTRUSTFUL
UNMITERING
UNMITIGABLE
UNMITIGABLY
UNMITIGATED
UNMITIGATEDLY
UNMITIGATEDNESS
UNMODERATED
UNMODERNISED
UNMODERNIZED
UNMODIFIABLE
UNMODIFIED
UNMODULATED
UNMOISTENED
UNMOLESTED

UNMONITORED
UNMORALISED
UNMORALISING
UNMORALITIES
UNMORALITY
UNMORALIZED
UNMORALIZING
UNMORTGAGED
UNMORTIFIED
UNMORTISED
UNMORTISES
UNMORTISING
UNMOTHERLIER
UNMOTHERLIEST
UNMOTHERLY
UNMOTIVATED
UNMOULDING
UNMOUNTING
UNMOVEABLE
UNMOVEABLY
UNMUFFLING
UNMUNITIONED
UNMURMURING
UNMURMURINGLY
UNMUSICALLY
UNMUSICALNESS
UNMUSICALNESSES
UNMUTILATED
UNMUZZLING
UNMUZZLINGS
UNMYELINATED
UNNAMEABLE
UNNATIVING
UNNATURALISE
UNNATURALISED
UNNATURALISES
UNNATURALISING
UNNATURALIZE
UNNATURALIZED
UNNATURALIZES
UNNATURALIZING
UNNATURALLY
UNNATURALNESS
UNNATURALNESSES
UNNAVIGABLE
UNNAVIGATED
UNNECESSARILY
UNNECESSARINESS

UNNECESSARY	UNOBTRUSIVENESS	UNPANNELLING	UNPERCEIVED	UNPLASTICISED
UNNEEDFULLY	UNOCCUPIED	UNPAPERING	UNPERCEIVEDLY	UNPLASTICIZED
UNNEGOTIABLE	UNOFFENDED	UNPARADISE	UNPERCEPTIVE	UNPLAUSIBLE
UNNEIGHBORED	UNOFFENDING	UNPARADISED	UNPERCHING	UNPLAUSIBLY
UNNEIGHBORLY	UNOFFENSIVE	UNPARADISES	UNPERFECTED	UNPLAUSIVE
UNNEIGHBOURED	UNOFFICERED	UNPARADISING	UNPERFECTION	UNPLAYABLE
UNNEIGHBOURLY	UNOFFICIAL	UNPARAGONED	UNPERFECTIONS	UNPLEASANT
UNNERVINGLY	UNOFFICIALLY	UNPARALLEL	UNPERFECTLY	UNPLEASANTLY
UNNEUROTIC	UNOFFICIOUS	UNPARALLELED	UNPERFECTNESS	UNPLEASANTNESS
UNNEWSWORTHIER	UNOPENABLE	UNPARASITISED	UNPERFECTNESSES	UNPLEASANTRIES
UNNEWSWORTHIEST	UNOPERATIVE	UNPARASITIZED	UNPERFORATED	UNPLEASANTRY
UNNEWSWORTHY	UNOPPOSING	UNPARDONABLE	UNPERFORMABLE	UNPLEASING
UNNILHEXIUM	UNOPPRESSIVE	UNPARDONABLY	UNPERFORMED	UNPLEASINGLY
UNNILHEXIUMS	UNORDAINED	UNPARDONED	UNPERFORMING	UNPLEASURABLE
UNNILPENTIUM	UNORDERING	UNPARDONING	UNPERFUMED	UNPLEASURABLY
UNNILPENTIUMS	UNORDINARY	UNPARENTAL	UNPERILOUS	UNPLOUGHED
UNNILQUADIUM	UNORGANISED	UNPARENTED	UNPERISHABLE	UNPLUGGING
UNNILQUADIUMS	UNORGANIZED	UNPARLIAMENTARY	UNPERISHED	UNPLUMBING
UNNILSEPTIUM	UNORIGINAL	UNPASSABLE	UNPERISHING	UNPOETICAL
UNNILSEPTIUMS	UNORIGINALITIES	UNPASSABLENESS	UNPERJURED	UNPOETICALLY
UNNOISIEST	UNORIGINALITY	UNPASSIONATE	UNPERPETRATED	UNPOETICALNESS
UNNOTICEABLE	UNORIGINALS	UNPASSIONED	UNPERPLEXED	UNPOISONED
UNNOTICEABLY	UNORIGINATE	UNPASTEURISED	UNPERPLEXES	UNPOISONING
UNNOTICING	UNORIGINATED	UNPASTEURIZED	UNPERPLEXING	UNPOLARISABLE
UNNOURISHED	UNORNAMENTAL	UNPASTORAL	UNPERSECUTED	UNPOLARISED
UNNOURISHING	UNORNAMENTED	UNPASTURED	UNPERSONED	UNPOLARIZABLE
UNNUMBERED	UNORTHODOX	UNPATENTABLE	UNPERSONING	UNPOLARIZED
UNNURTURED	UNORTHODOXIES	UNPATENTED	UNPERSUADABLE	UNPOLICIED
UNOBEDIENT	UNORTHODOXLY	UNPATHETIC	UNPERSUADED	UNPOLISHABLE
UNOBJECTIONABLE	UNORTHODOXY	UNPATHWAYED	UNPERSUASIVE	UNPOLISHED
UNOBJECTIONABLY	UNOSSIFIED	UNPATRIOTIC	UNPERTURBED	UNPOLISHES
UNOBLIGING	UNOSTENTATIOUS	UNPATRIOTICALLY	UNPERVERTED	UNPOLISHING
UNOBNOXIOUS	UNOVERCOME	UNPATRONISED	UNPERVERTING	UNPOLITELY
UNOBSCURED	UNOVERTHROWN	UNPATRONIZED	UNPERVERTS	UNPOLITENESS
UNOBSERVABLE	UNOXIDISED	UNPATTERNED	UNPHILOSOPHIC	UNPOLITENESSES
UNOBSERVABLES	UNOXIDIZED	UNPAVILIONED	UNPHILOSOPHICAL	UNPOLITICAL
UNOBSERVANCE	UNOXYGENATED	UNPEACEABLE	UNPHONETIC	UNPOLLUTED
UNOBSERVANCES	UNPACIFIED	UNPEACEABLENESS	UNPICKABLE	UNPOPULARITIES
UNOBSERVANT	UNPACKINGS	UNPEACEFUL	UNPICTURESQUE	UNPOPULARITY
UNOBSERVED	UNPAINTABLE	UNPEACEFULLY	UNPIGMENTED	UNPOPULARLY
UNOBSERVEDLY	UNPAINTING	UNPEDANTIC	UNPILLARED	UNPOPULATED
UNOBSERVING	UNPALATABILITY	UNPEDIGREED	UNPILLOWED	UNPOPULOUS
UNOBSTRUCTED	UNPALATABLE	UNPEERABLE	UNPITIFULLY	UNPORTIONED
UNOBSTRUCTIVE	UNPALATABLY	UNPENSIONED	UNPITIFULNESS	UNPOSSESSED
UNOBTAINABLE	UNPAMPERED	UNPEOPLING	UNPITIFULNESSES	UNPOSSESSING
UNOBTAINED	UNPANELLED	UNPEPPERED	UNPITYINGLY	UNPOSSIBLE
UNOBTRUSIVE	UNPANELLING	UNPERCEIVABLE	UNPLAITING	UNPOWDERED
UNOBTRUSIVELY	UNPANNELLED	UNPERCEIVABLY	UNPLASTERED	UNPRACTICABLE

U

UNPRACTICAL

UNPRACTICAL	UNPRETTIER	UNPROJECTED	UNPUNISHABLE	UNRAVELLERS
UNPRACTICALITY	UNPRETTIEST	UNPROLIFIC	UNPUNISHABLY	UNRAVELLING
UNPRACTICALLY	UNPRETTINESS	UNPROMISED	UNPUNISHED	UNRAVELLINGS
UNPRACTICALNESS	UNPRETTINESSES	UNPROMISING	UNPURCHASABLE	UNRAVELMENT
UNPRACTICED	UNPREVAILING	UNPROMISINGLY	UNPURCHASEABLE	UNRAVELMENTS
UNPRACTISED	UNPREVENTABLE	UNPROMPTED	UNPURCHASED	UNRAVISHED
UNPRACTISEDNESS	UNPREVENTED	UNPRONOUNCEABLE	UNPURIFIED	UNREACHABLE
UNPRAISEWORTHY	UNPRIESTED	UNPRONOUNCED	UNPURPOSED	UNREACTIVE
UNPRAISING	UNPRIESTING	UNPROPERLY	UNPURVAIDE	UNREADABILITIES
UNPREACHED	UNPRIESTLIER	UNPROPERTIED	UNPURVEYED	UNREADABILITY
UNPREACHES	UNPRIESTLIEST	UNPROPHETIC	UNPUTDOWNABLE	UNREADABLE
UNPREACHING	UNPRIESTLY	UNPROPHETICAL	UNPUZZLING	UNREADABLENESS
UNPRECEDENTED	UNPRINCELIER	UNPROPITIOUS	UNQUALIFIABLE	UNREADABLY
UNPRECEDENTEDLY	UNPRINCELIEST	UNPROPITIOUSLY	UNQUALIFIED	UNREADIEST
UNPREDESTINED	UNPRINCELY	UNPROPORTIONATE	UNQUALIFIEDLY	UNREADINESS
UNPREDICTABLE	UNPRINCIPLED	UNPROPORTIONED	UNQUALIFIEDNESS	UNREADINESSES
UNPREDICTABLES	UNPRINTABLE	UNPROPOSED	UNQUALIFIES	UNREALISABLE
UNPREDICTABLY	UNPRINTABLENESS	UNPROPPING	UNQUALIFYING	UNREALISED
UNPREDICTED	UNPRINTABLY	UNPROSPEROUS	UNQUALITED	UNREALISES
UNPREDICTING	UNPRISABLE	UNPROSPEROUSLY	UNQUALITIED	UNREALISING
UNPREDICTS	UNPRISONED	UNPROTECTED	UNQUANTIFIABLE	UNREALISMS
UNPREFERRED	UNPRISONING	UNPROTECTEDNESS	UNQUANTIFIED	UNREALISTIC
UNPREGNANT	UNPRIVILEGED	UNPROTESTANTISE	UNQUANTISED	UNREALISTICALLY
UNPREJUDICED	UNPRIZABLE	UNPROTESTANTIZE	UNQUANTIZED	UNREALITIES
UNPREJUDICEDLY	UNPROBLEMATIC	UNPROTESTED	UNQUARRIED	UNREALIZABLE
UNPRELATICAL	UNPROCEDURAL	UNPROTESTING	UNQUEENING	UNREALIZED
UNPREMEDITABLE	UNPROCESSED	UNPROVABLE	UNQUEENLIER	UNREALIZES
UNPREMEDITATED	UNPROCLAIMED	UNPROVIDED	UNQUEENLIEST	UNREALIZING
UNPREMEDITATION	UNPROCURABLE	UNPROVIDEDLY	UNQUEENLIKE	UNREASONABLE
UNPREOCCUPIED	UNPRODUCED	UNPROVIDENT	UNQUENCHABLE	UNREASONABLY
UNPREPARED	UNPRODUCTIVE	UNPROVIDES	UNQUENCHABLY	UNREASONED
UNPREPAREDLY	UNPRODUCTIVELY	UNPROVIDING	UNQUENCHED	UNREASONING
UNPREPAREDNESS	UNPRODUCTIVITY	UNPROVISIONED	UNQUESTIONABLE	UNREASONINGLY
UNPREPARES	UNPROFANED	UNPROVOCATIVE	UNQUESTIONABLY	UNRECALLABLE
UNPREPARING	UNPROFESSED	UNPROVOKED	UNQUESTIONED	UNRECALLED
UNPREPOSSESSED	UNPROFESSIONAL	UNPROVOKEDLY	UNQUESTIONING	UNRECALLING
UNPREPOSSESSING	UNPROFESSIONALS	UNPROVOKES	UNQUESTIONINGLY	UNRECAPTURABLE
UNPRESCRIBED	UNPROFITABILITY	UNPROVOKING	UNQUICKENED	UNRECEIPTED
UNPRESENTABLE	UNPROFITABLE	UNPUBLICISED	UNQUIETEST	UNRECEIVED
UNPRESSURED	UNPROFITABLY	UNPUBLICIZED	UNQUIETING	UNRECEPTIVE
UNPRESSURISED	UNPROFITED	UNPUBLISHABLE	UNQUIETNESS	UNRECIPROCATED
UNPRESSURIZED	UNPROFITING	UNPUBLISHED	UNQUIETNESSES	UNRECKONABLE
UNPRESUMING	UNPROFITINGS	UNPUCKERED	UNQUOTABLE	UNRECKONED
UNPRESUMPTUOUS	UNPROGRAMMABLE	UNPUCKERING	UNRANSOMED	UNRECLAIMABLE
UNPRETENDING	UNPROGRAMMED	UNPUNCTUAL	UNRATIFIED	UNRECLAIMABLY
UNPRETENDINGLY	UNPROGRESSIVE	UNPUNCTUALITIES	UNRAVELING	UNRECLAIMED
UNPRETENTIOUS	UNPROGRESSIVELY	UNPUNCTUALITY	UNRAVELLED	UNRECOGNISABLE
UNPRETENTIOUSLY	UNPROHIBITED	UNPUNCTUATED	UNRAVELLER	UNRECOGNISABLY

UNRECOGNISED	UNREGISTERED	UNREPAIRABLE	UNRESERVES	UNREVOLUTIONARY
UNRECOGNISING	UNREGRETTED	UNREPAIRED	UNRESISTANT	UNREWARDED
UNRECOGNIZABLE	UNREGULATED	UNREPEALABLE	UNRESISTED	UNREWARDEDLY
UNRECOGNIZABLY	UNREHEARSED	UNREPEALED	UNRESISTIBLE	UNREWARDING
UNRECOGNIZED	UNREINFORCED	UNREPEATABLE	UNRESISTING	UNRHETORICAL
UNRECOGNIZING	UNREJOICED	UNREPEATED	UNRESISTINGLY	UNRHYTHMIC
UNRECOLLECTED	UNREJOICING	UNREPELLED	UNRESOLVABLE	UNRHYTHMICAL
UNRECOMMENDABLE	UNRELATIVE	UNREPENTANCE	UNRESOLVED	UNRHYTHMICALLY
UNRECOMMENDED	UNRELEASED	UNREPENTANCES	UNRESOLVEDNESS	UNRIDDLEABLE
UNRECOMPENSED	UNRELENTING	UNREPENTANT	UNRESPECTABLE	UNRIDDLERS
UNRECONCILABLE	UNRELENTINGLY	UNREPENTANTLY	UNRESPECTABLES	UNRIDDLING
UNRECONCILABLY	UNRELENTINGNESS	UNREPENTED	UNRESPECTED	UNRIDEABLE
UNRECONCILED	UNRELENTOR	UNREPENTING	UNRESPECTIVE	UNRIGHTEOUS
UNRECONCILIABLE	UNRELENTORS	UNREPENTINGLY	UNRESPITED	UNRIGHTEOUSLY
UNRECONSTRUCTED	UNRELIABILITIES	UNREPINING	UNRESPONSIVE	UNRIGHTEOUSNESS
UNRECORDED	UNRELIABILITY	UNREPININGLY	UNRESPONSIVELY	UNRIGHTFUL
UNRECOUNTED	UNRELIABLE	UNREPLACEABLE	UNRESTFULNESS	UNRIGHTFULLY
UNRECOVERABLE	UNRELIABLENESS	UNREPLENISHED	UNRESTFULNESSES	UNRIGHTFULNESS
UNRECOVERABLY	UNRELIABLY	UNREPORTABLE	UNRESTINGLY	UNRIGHTING
UNRECOVERED	UNRELIEVABLE	UNREPORTED	UNRESTINGNESS	UNRIPENESS
UNRECTIFIED	UNRELIEVED	UNREPOSEFUL	UNRESTINGNESSES	UNRIPENESSES
UNRECURING	UNRELIEVEDLY	UNREPOSING	UNRESTORED	UNRIPPINGS
UNRECYCLABLE	UNRELIGIOUS	UNREPRESENTED	UNRESTRAINABLE	UNRIVALLED
UNRECYCLABLES	UNRELIGIOUSLY	UNREPRESSED	UNRESTRAINED	UNRIVETING
UNREDEEMABLE	UNRELISHED	UNREPRIEVABLE	UNRESTRAINEDLY	UNRIVETTED
UNREDEEMED	UNRELUCTANT	UNREPRIEVED	UNRESTRAINT	UNRIVETTING
UNREDRESSED	UNREMAINING	UNREPRIMANDED	UNRESTRAINTS	UNROADWORTHY
UNREDUCIBLE	UNREMARKABLE	UNREPROACHED	UNRESTRICTED	UNROMANISED
UNREFLECTED	UNREMARKABLY	UNREPROACHFUL	UNRESTRICTEDLY	UNROMANIZED
UNREFLECTING	UNREMARKED	UNREPROACHING	UNRETARDED	UNROMANTIC
UNREFLECTINGLY	UNREMEDIED	UNREPRODUCIBLE	UNRETENTIVE	UNROMANTICAL
UNREFLECTIVE	UNREMEMBERED	UNREPROVABLE	UNRETIRING	UNROMANTICALLY
UNREFLECTIVELY	UNREMEMBERING	UNREPROVED	UNRETOUCHED	UNROMANTICISED
UNREFORMABLE	UNREMINISCENT	UNREPROVING	UNRETURNABLE	UNROMANTICIZED
UNREFORMED	UNREMITTED	UNREPUGNANT	UNRETURNED	UNROOSTING
UNREFRACTED	UNREMITTEDLY	UNREPULSABLE	UNRETURNING	UNROUNDING
UNREFRESHED	UNREMITTENT	UNREQUESTED	UNRETURNINGLY	UNRUFFABLE
UNREFRESHING	UNREMITTENTLY	UNREQUIRED	UNREVEALABLE	UNRUFFLEDNESS
UNREFRIGERATED	UNREMITTING	UNREQUISITE	UNREVEALED	UNRUFFLEDNESSES
UNREGARDED	UNREMITTINGLY	UNREQUITED	UNREVEALING	UNRUFFLING
UNREGARDING	UNREMITTINGNESS	UNREQUITEDLY	UNREVENGED	UNRULIMENT
UNREGENERACIES	UNREMORSEFUL	UNRESCINDED	UNREVENGEFUL	UNRULIMENTS
UNREGENERACY	UNREMORSEFULLY	UNRESENTED	UNREVEREND	UNRULINESS
UNREGENERATE	UNREMORSELESS	UNRESENTFUL	UNREVERENT	UNRULINESSES
UNREGENERATED	UNREMOVABLE	UNRESENTING	UNREVERSED	UNRUPTURED
UNREGENERATELY	UNREMUNERATIVE	UNRESERVED	UNREVERTED	UNSADDLING
UNREGENERATES	UNRENDERED	UNRESERVEDLY	UNREVIEWABLE	UNSAFENESS
UNREGIMENTED	UNRENOWNED	UNRESERVEDNESS	UNREVIEWED	UNSAFENESSES

UNSAFETIES

UNSAFETIES	UNSAYABLES	UNSECONDED	UNSETTLEDNESS	UNSHUTTING
UNSAILORLIKE	UNSCABBARD	UNSECRETED	UNSETTLEDNESSES	UNSIGHTEDLY
UNSAINTING	UNSCABBARDED	UNSECRETING	UNSETTLEMENT	UNSIGHTING
UNSAINTLIER	UNSCABBARDING	UNSECTARIAN	UNSETTLEMENTS	UNSIGHTLIER
UNSAINTLIEST	UNSCABBARDS	UNSECTARIANISM	UNSETTLING	UNSIGHTLIEST
UNSAINTLINESS	UNSCALABLE	UNSECTARIANISMS	UNSETTLINGLY	UNSIGHTLINESS
UNSAINTLINESSES	UNSCARIEST	UNSECTARIANS	UNSETTLINGS	UNSIGHTLINESSES
UNSALABILITIES	UNSCAVENGERED	UNSEEMINGS	UNSHACKLED	UNSINEWING
UNSALABILITY	UNSCEPTRED	UNSEEMLIER	UNSHACKLES	UNSINKABLE
UNSALARIED	UNSCHEDULED	UNSEEMLIEST	UNSHACKLING	UNSINNOWED
UNSALEABILITIES	UNSCHOLARLIKE	UNSEEMLINESS	UNSHADOWABLE	UNSISTERED
UNSALEABILITY	UNSCHOLARLY	UNSEEMLINESSES	UNSHADOWED	UNSISTERLINESS
UNSALEABLE	UNSCHOOLED	UNSEGMENTED	UNSHADOWING	UNSISTERLY
UNSALEABLY	UNSCIENTIFIC	UNSEGREGATED	UNSHAKABLE	UNSIZEABLE
UNSALVAGEABLE	UNSCISSORED	UNSEISABLE	UNSHAKABLENESS	UNSKILFULLY
UNSANCTIFIED	UNSCORCHED	UNSEIZABLE	UNSHAKABLY	UNSKILFULNESS
UNSANCTIFIES	UNSCOTTIFIED	UNSELECTED	UNSHAKEABLE	UNSKILFULNESSES
UNSANCTIFY	UNSCRAMBLE	UNSELECTIVE	UNSHAKEABLENESS	UNSKILLFUL
UNSANCTIFYING	UNSCRAMBLED	UNSELECTIVELY	UNSHAKEABLY	UNSKILLFULLY
UNSANCTIONED	UNSCRAMBLER	UNSELFCONSCIOUS	UNSHAKENLY	UNSKILLFULNESS
UNSANDALLED	UNSCRAMBLERS	UNSELFISHLY	UNSHAPELIER	UNSLAKABLE
UNSANITARY	UNSCRAMBLES	UNSELFISHNESS	UNSHAPELIEST	UNSLEEPING
UNSATIABLE	UNSCRAMBLING	UNSELFISHNESSES	UNSHARPENED	UNSLEEPINGS
UNSATIATED	UNSCRATCHED	UNSELLABLE	UNSHEATHED	UNSLINGING
UNSATIATING	UNSCREENED	UNSEMINARIED	UNSHEATHES	UNSLIPPING
UNSATIRICAL	UNSCREWING	UNSENSATIONAL	UNSHEATHING	UNSLUICING
UNSATISFACTION	UNSCRIPTED	UNSENSIBLE	UNSHELLING	UNSLUMBERING
UNSATISFACTIONS	UNSCRIPTURAL	UNSENSIBLY	UNSHELTERED	UNSLUMBROUS
UNSATISFACTORY	UNSCRIPTURALLY	UNSENSITISED	UNSHIELDED	UNSMILINGLY
UNSATISFIABLE	UNSCRUPLED	UNSENSITIVE	UNSHIFTING	UNSMIRCHED
UNSATISFIED	UNSCRUPULOSITY	UNSENSITIZED	UNSHINGLED	UNSMOKABLE
UNSATISFIEDNESS	UNSCRUPULOUS	UNSENSUALISE	UNSHIPPING	UNSMOOTHED
UNSATISFYING	UNSCRUPULOUSLY	UNSENSUALISED	UNSHOCKABLE	UNSMOOTHING
UNSATURATE	UNSCRUTINISED	UNSENSUALISES	UNSHOOTING	UNSMOTHERABLE
UNSATURATED	UNSCRUTINIZED	UNSENSUALISING	UNSHOTTING	UNSNAGGING
UNSATURATES	UNSCULPTURED	UNSENSUALIZE	UNSHOUTING	UNSNAPPING
UNSATURATION	UNSEALABLE	UNSENSUALIZED	UNSHOWERED	UNSNARLING
UNSATURATIONS	UNSEARCHABLE	UNSENSUALIZES	UNSHOWIEST	UNSNECKING
UNSAVORIER	UNSEARCHABLES	UNSENSUALIZING	UNSHRINKABLE	UNSOBERING
UNSAVORIEST	UNSEARCHABLY	UNSENTENCED	UNSHRINKING	UNSOCIABILITIES
UNSAVORILY	UNSEARCHED	UNSENTIMENTAL	UNSHRINKINGLY	UNSOCIABILITY
UNSAVORINESS	UNSEASONABLE	UNSEPARABLE	UNSHROUDED	UNSOCIABLE
UNSAVORINESSES	UNSEASONABLY	UNSEPARATED	UNSHROUDING	UNSOCIABLENESS
UNSAVOURIER	UNSEASONED	UNSEPULCHRED	UNSHRUBBED	UNSOCIABLY
UNSAVOURIEST	UNSEASONEDNESS	UNSERIOUSNESS	UNSHUNNABLE	UNSOCIALISED
UNSAVOURTLY	UNSEASONING	UNSERIOUSNESSES	UNSHUTTERED	UNSOCIALISM
UNSAVOURINESS	UNSEAWORTHINESS	UNSERVICEABLE	UNSHUTTERING	UNSOCIALISMS
UNSAVOURINESSES	UNSEAWORTHY	UNSETTLEDLY	UNSHUTTERS	UNSOCIALITIES

UNSOCIALITY	UNSPIRITUALIZED	UNSTERILIZED	UNSUBSCRIBE	UNSUSCEPTIBLE
UNSOCIALIZED	UNSPIRITUALIZES	UNSTICKING	UNSUBSCRIBED	UNSUSPECTED
UNSOCIALLY	UNSPIRITUALLY	UNSTIFFENED	UNSUBSCRIBER	UNSUSPECTEDLY
UNSOCKETED	UNSPLINTERABLE	UNSTIFFENING	UNSUBSCRIBERS	UNSUSPECTEDNESS
UNSOCKETING	UNSPOOLING	UNSTIFFENS	UNSUBSCRIBES	UNSUSPECTING
UNSOFTENED	UNSPORTING	UNSTIGMATISED	UNSUBSCRIBING	UNSUSPECTINGLY
UNSOFTENING	UNSPORTSMANLIKE	UNSTIGMATIZED	UNSUBSIDISED	UNSUSPENDED
UNSOLDERED	UNSPOTTEDNESS	UNSTIMULATED	UNSUBSIDIZED	UNSUSPICION
UNSOLDERING	UNSPOTTEDNESSES	UNSTINTING	UNSUBSTANTIAL	UNSUSPICIONS
UNSOLDIERLIKE	UNSPRINKLED	UNSTINTINGLY	UNSUBSTANTIALLY	UNSUSPICIOUS
UNSOLDIERLY	UNSTABLENESS	UNSTITCHED	UNSUBSTANTIATED	UNSUSPICIOUSLY
UNSOLICITED	UNSTABLENESSES	UNSTITCHES	UNSUBTLEST	UNSUSTAINABLE
UNSOLICITOUS	UNSTABLEST	UNSTITCHING	UNSUCCEEDED	UNSUSTAINABLY
UNSOLIDITIES	UNSTACKING	UNSTOCKING	UNSUCCESSES	UNSUSTAINED
UNSOLIDITY	UNSTAIDNESS	UNSTOCKINGED	UNSUCCESSFUL	UNSUSTAINING
UNSOLVABLE	UNSTAIDNESSES	UNSTOOPING	UNSUCCESSFULLY	UNSWADDLED
UNSONSIEST	UNSTAINABLE	UNSTOPPABLE	UNSUCCESSIVE	UNSWADDLES
UNSOPHISTICATE	UNSTANCHABLE	UNSTOPPABLY	UNSUCCOURED	UNSWADDLING
UNSOPHISTICATED	UNSTANCHED	UNSTOPPERED	UNSUFFERABLE	UNSWALLOWED
UNSOUNDABLE	UNSTANDARDISED	UNSTOPPERING	UNSUFFICIENT	UNSWATHING
UNSOUNDEST	UNSTANDARDIZED	UNSTOPPERS	UNSUITABILITIES	UNSWAYABLE
UNSOUNDNESS	UNSTARCHED	UNSTOPPING	UNSUITABILITY	UNSWEARING
UNSOUNDNESSES	UNSTARCHES	UNSTRAINED	UNSUITABLE	UNSWEARINGS
UNSPARINGLY	UNSTARCHING	UNSTRAPPED	UNSUITABLENESS	UNSWEETENED
UNSPARINGNESS	UNSTARRIER	UNSTRAPPING	UNSUITABLY	UNSWERVING
UNSPARINGNESSES	UNSTARRIEST	UNSTRATIFIED	UNSUMMERED	UNSWERVINGLY
UNSPARRING	UNSTARTLING	UNSTREAMED	UNSUMMONED	UNSYLLABLED
UNSPEAKABLE	UNSTATESMANLIKE	UNSTRENGTHENED	UNSUNNIEST	UNSYMMETRICAL
UNSPEAKABLENESS	UNSTATUTABLE	UNSTRESSED	UNSUPERFLUOUS	UNSYMMETRICALLY
UNSPEAKABLY	UNSTATUTABLY	UNSTRESSES	UNSUPERVISED	UNSYMMETRIES
UNSPEAKING	UNSTAUNCHABLE	UNSTRESSING	UNSUPPLENESS	UNSYMMETRISED
UNSPECIALISED	UNSTAUNCHED	UNSTRIATED	UNSUPPLENESSES	UNSYMMETRIZED
UNSPECIALIZED	UNSTEADFAST	UNSTRINGED	UNSUPPLIED	UNSYMMETRY
UNSPECIFIABLE	UNSTEADFASTLY	UNSTRINGING	UNSUPPORTABLE	UNSYMPATHETIC
UNSPECIFIC	UNSTEADFASTNESS	UNSTRIPPED	UNSUPPORTED	UNSYMPATHIES
UNSPECIFICALLY	UNSTEADIED	UNSTRIPPING	UNSUPPORTEDLY	UNSYMPATHISING
UNSPECIFIED	UNSTEADIER	UNSTRUCTURED	UNSUPPOSABLE	UNSYMPATHIZING
UNSPECTACLED	UNSTEADIES	UNSTUFFIER	UNSUPPRESSED	UNSYMPATHY
UNSPECTACULAR	UNSTEADIEST	UNSTUFFIEST	UNSURFACED	UNSYNCHRONISED
UNSPECULATIVE	UNSTEADILY	UNSUBDUABLE	UNSURMISED	UNSYNCHRONIZED
UNSPELLING	UNSTEADINESS	UNSUBJECTED	UNSURMOUNTABLE	UNSYSTEMATIC
UNSPHERING	UNSTEADINESSES	UNSUBJECTING	UNSURPASSABLE	UNSYSTEMATICAL
UNSPIRITED	UNSTEADYING	UNSUBJECTS	UNSURPASSABLY	UNSYSTEMATISED
UNSPIRITUAL	UNSTEELING	UNSUBLIMATED	UNSURPASSED	UNSYSTEMATIZED
UNSPIRITUALISE	UNSTEPPING	UNSUBLIMED	UNSURPRISED	UNSYSTEMIC
UNSPIRITUALISED	UNSTERCORATED	UNSUBMERGED	UNSURPRISING	UNTACKLING
UNSPIRITUALISES	UNSTEREOTYPED	UNSUBMISSIVE	UNSURPRISINGLY	UNTAILORED
UNSPIRITUALIZE	UNSTERILISED	UNSUBMITTING	UNSURVEYED	UNTAINTEDLY

UNTAINTEDNESS
UNTAINTEDNESSES
UNTAINTING
UNTALENTED
UNTAMABLENESS
UNTAMABLENESSES
UNTAMEABLE
UNTAMEABLENESS
UNTAMEABLY
UNTAMEDNESS
UNTAMEDNESSES
UNTANGIBLE
UNTANGLING
UNTARNISHED
UNTASTEFUL
UNTEACHABLE
UNTEACHABLENESS
UNTEACHING
UNTEARABLE
UNTECHNICAL
UNTELLABLE
UNTEMPERED
UNTEMPERING
UNTENABILITIES
UNTENABILITY
UNTENABLENESS
UNTENABLENESSES
UNTENANTABLE
UNTENANTED
UNTENANTING
UNTENDERED
UNTENDERLY
UNTENTIEST
UNTERMINATED
UNTERRESTRIAL
UNTERRIFIED
UNTERRIFYING
UNTESTABLE
UNTETHERED
UNTETHERING
UNTHANKFUL
UNTHANKFULLY
UNTHANKFULNESS
UNTHATCHED
UNTHATCHES
UNTHATCHING
UNTHEOLOGICAL
UNTHEORETICAL

UNTHICKENED
UNTHINKABILITY
UNTHINKABLE
UNTHINKABLENESS
UNTHINKABLY
UNTHINKING
UNTHINKINGLY
UNTHINKINGNESS
UNTHOROUGH
UNTHOUGHTFUL
UNTHOUGHTFULLY
UNTHREADED
UNTHREADING
UNTHREATENED
UNTHREATENING
UNTHRESHED
UNTHRIFTIER
UNTHRIFTIEST
UNTHRIFTIHEAD
UNTHRIFTIHEADS
UNTHRIFTILY
UNTHRIFTINESS
UNTHRIFTINESSES
UNTHRIFTYHEAD
UNTHRIFTYHEADS
UNTHRIFTYHED
UNTHRIFTYHEDS
UNTHRONING
UNTIDINESS
UNTIDINESSES
UNTILLABLE
UNTIMBERED
UNTIMELIER
UNTIMELIEST
UNTIMELINESS
UNTIMELINESSES
UNTIMEOUSLY
UNTINCTURED
UNTIRINGLY
UNTOCHERED
UNTOGETHER
UNTORMENTED
UNTORTURED
UNTOUCHABILITY
UNTOUCHABLE
UNTOUCHABLES
UNTOWARDLINESS
UNTOWARDLY

UNTOWARDNESS
UNTOWARDNESSES
UNTRACEABLE
UNTRACKING
UNTRACTABLE
UNTRACTABLENESS
UNTRADITIONAL
UNTRADITIONALLY
UNTRAMMELED
UNTRAMMELLED
UNTRAMPLED
UNTRANQUIL
UNTRANSFERABLE
UNTRANSFERRABLE
UNTRANSFORMED
UNTRANSLATABLE
UNTRANSLATABLY
UNTRANSLATED
UNTRANSMIGRATED
UNTRANSMISSIBLE
UNTRANSMITTED
UNTRANSMUTABLE
UNTRANSMUTED
UNTRANSPARENT
UNTRAVELED
UNTRAVELLED
UNTRAVERSABLE
UNTRAVERSED
UNTREADING
UNTREASURE
UNTREASURED
UNTREASURES
UNTREASURING
UNTREATABLE
UNTREMBLING
UNTREMBLINGLY
UNTREMENDOUS
UNTREMULOUS
UNTRENCHED
UNTRENDIER
UNTRENDIEST
UNTRESPASSING
UNTRIMMING
UNTROUBLED
UNTROUBLEDLY
UNTRUENESS
UNTRUENESSES
UNTRUSSERS

UNTRUSSING
UNTRUSSINGS
UNTRUSTFUL
UNTRUSTIER
UNTRUSTIEST
UNTRUSTINESS
UNTRUSTINESSES
UNTRUSTING
UNTRUSTWORTHILY
UNTRUSTWORTHY
UNTRUTHFUL
UNTRUTHFULLY
UNTRUTHFULNESS
UNTUCKERED
UNTUMULTUOUS
UNTUNABLENESS
UNTUNABLENESSES
UNTUNEABLE
UNTUNEFULLY
UNTUNEFULNESS
UNTUNEFULNESSES
UNTURNABLE
UNTWISTING
UNTWISTINGS
UNTYPICALLY
UNTYREABLE
UNUNUNIUMS
UNUPLIFTED
UNUSEFULLY
UNUSEFULNESS
UNUSEFULNESSES
UNUSUALNESS
UNUSUALNESSES
UNUTILISED
UNUTILIZED
UNUTTERABLE
UNUTTERABLENESS
UNUTTERABLES
UNUTTERABLY
UNVACCINATED
UNVALUABLE
UNVANQUISHABLE
UNVANQUISHED
UNVARIABLE
UNVARIEGATED
UNVARNISHED
UNVARYINGLY
UNVEILINGS

UNVENDIBLE
UNVENERABLE
UNVENTILATED
UNVERACIOUS
UNVERACITIES
UNVERACITY
UNVERBALISED
UNVERBALIZED
UNVERIFIABILITY
UNVERIFIABLE
UNVERIFIED
UNVIOLATED
UNVIRTUOUS
UNVIRTUOUSLY
UNVISITABLE
UNVISORING
UNVITIATED
UNVITRIFIABLE
UNVITRIFIED
UNVIZARDED
UNVIZARDING
UNVOCALISED
UNVOCALIZED
UNVOICINGS
UNVOYAGEABLE
UNVULGARISE
UNVULGARISED
UNVULGARISES
UNVULGARISING
UNVULGARIZE
UNVULGARIZED
UNVULGARIZES
UNVULGARIZING
UNVULNERABLE
UNWANDERING
UNWARENESS
UNWARENESSES
UNWARINESS
UNWARINESSES
UNWARRANTABLE
UNWARRANTABLY
UNWARRANTED
UNWARRANTEDLY
UNWASHEDNESS
UNWASHEDNESSES
IINWATCHABLE
UNWATCHFUL
UNWATCHFULLY

UNWATCHFULNESS	UNWIFELIKE	UNWOUNDABLE	UPHEAPINGS	UPROOTEDNESS
UNWATERING	UNWILLINGLY	UNWRAPPING	UPHILLWARD	UPROOTEDNESSES
UNWAVERING	UNWILLINGNESS	UNWREATHED	UPHOARDING	UPROOTINGS
UNWAVERINGLY	UNWILLINGNESSES	UNWREATHES	UPHOISTING	UPSETTABLE
UNWEAKENED	UNWINDABLE	UNWREATHING	UPHOLDINGS	UPSETTINGLY
UNWEAPONED	UNWINDINGS	UNWRINKLED	UPHOLSTERED	UPSETTINGS
UNWEAPONING	UNWINKINGLY	UNWRINKLES	UPHOLSTERER	UPSHIFTING
UNWEARABLE	UNWINNABLE	UNWRINKLING	UPHOLSTERERS	UPSHOOTING
UNWEARABLES	UNWINNOWED	UNYIELDING	UPHOLSTERIES	UPSIDEOWNE
UNWEARIABLE	UNWISENESS	UNYIELDINGLY	UPHOLSTERING	UPSITTINGS
UNWEARIABLY	UNWISENESSES	UNYIELDINGNESS	UPHOLSTERS	UPSKILLING
UNWEARIEDLY	UNWITCHING	UPBRAIDERS	UPHOLSTERY	UPSKIRTING
UNWEARIEDNESS	UNWITHDRAWING	UPBRAIDING	UPHOLSTRESS	UPSKIRTINGS
UNWEARIEDNESSES	UNWITHERED	UPBRAIDINGLY	UPHOLSTRESSES	UPSPEAKING
UNWEARIEST	UNWITHERING	UPBRAIDINGS	UPHOORDING	UPSPEARING
UNWEARYING	UNWITHHELD	UPBREAKING	UPKNITTING	UPSPRINGING
UNWEARYINGLY	UNWITHHOLDEN	UPBRINGING	UPLIFTINGLY	UPSTANDING
UNWEATHERED	UNWITHHOLDING	UPBRINGINGS	UPLIFTINGS	UPSTANDINGNESS
UNWEDGABLE	UNWITHSTOOD	UPBUILDERS	UPLIGHTERS	UPSTARTING
UNWEDGEABLE	UNWITNESSED	UPBUILDING	UPLIGHTING	UPSTEPPING
UNWEETINGLY	UNWITTIEST	UPBUILDINGS	UPLIGHTINGS	UPSTEPPINGS
UNWEIGHING	UNWITTINGLY	UPBUOYANCE	UPLINKINGS	UPSTIRRING
UNWEIGHTED	UNWITTINGNESS	UPBUOYANCES	UPMANSHIPS	UPSTREAMED
UNWEIGHTING	UNWITTINGNESSES	UPBURSTING	UPMARKETED	UPSTREAMING
UNWEIGHTINGS	UNWOMANING	UPCATCHING	UPMARKETING	UPSTRETCHED
UNWELCOMED	UNWOMANLIER	UPCHEERING	UPPERCASED	UPSURGENCE
UNWELCOMELY	UNWOMANLIEST	UPCHUCKING	UPPERCASES	UPSURGENCES
UNWELCOMENESS	UNWOMANLINESS	UPCLIMBING	UPPERCASING	UPSWARMING
UNWELCOMENESSES	UNWOMANLINESSES	UPCOUNTRIES	UPPERCLASSMAN	UPSWEEPING
UNWELCOMING	UNWONTEDLY	UPDATEABLE	UPPERCLASSMEN	UPSWELLING
UNWELLNESS	UNWONTEDNESS	UPDRAGGING	UPPERCUTTING	UPSWINGING
UNWELLNESSES	UNWONTEDNESSES	UPDRAGGINGS	UPPERPARTS	UPTALKINGS
UNWESTERNISED	UNWORKABILITIES	UPDRAUGHTS	UPPERWORKS	UPTHROWING
UNWESTERNIZED	UNWORKABILITY	UPFILLINGS	UPPISHNESS	UPTHRUSTED
UNWHISTLEABLE	UNWORKABLE	UPFLASHING	UPPISHNESSES	UPTHRUSTING
UNWHOLESOME	UNWORKMANLIKE	UPFLINGING	UPPITINESS	UPTHUNDERED
UNWHOLESOMELY	UNWORLDLIER	UPFOLLOWED	UPPITINESSES	UPTHUNDERING
UNWHOLESOMENESS	UNWORLDLIEST	UPFOLLOWING	UPPITYNESS	UPTHUNDERS
UNWIELDIER	UNWORLDLINESS	UPGATHERED	UPPITYNESSES	UPTIGHTEST
UNWIELDIEST	UNWORLDLINESSES	UPGATHERING	UPPROPPING	UPTIGHTNESS
UNWIELDILY	UNWORSHIPFUL	UPGRADABILITIES	UPREACHING	UPTIGHTNESSES
UNWIELDINESS	UNWORSHIPPED	UPGRADABILITY	UPRIGHTEOUSLY	UPTITLINGS
UNWIELDINESSES	UNWORTHIER	UPGRADABLE	UPRIGHTING	UPTRAINING
UNWIELDLILY	UNWORTHIES	UPGRADATION	UPRIGHTNESS	UPTURNINGS
UNWIELDLINESS	UNWORTHIEST	UPGRADATIONS	UPRIGHTNESSES	UPVALUATION
UNWIELDLINESSES	UNWORTHILY	UPGRADEABILITY	UPROARIOUS	UPVALUATIONS
UNWIFELIER	UNWORTHINESS	UPGRADEABLE	UPROARIOUSLY	UPWARDNESS
UNWIFELIEST	UNWORTHINESSES	UPGROWINGS	UPROARIOUSNESS	UPWARDNESSES

U

UPWELLINGS	URCEOLUSES	UROCHORDATES	USHERSHIPS	UTILITARIANISM
UPWHIRLING	UREDINIOSPORE	UROCHROMES	USQUEBAUGH	UTILITARIANISMS
URALITISATION	UREDINIOSPORES	URODYNAMICS	USQUEBAUGHS	UTILITARIANIZE
URALITISATIONS	UREDINIUMS	UROGENITAL	USTILAGINEOUS	UTILITARIANIZED
URALITISED	UREDIOSPORE	UROGENITALS	USTILAGINOUS	UTILITARIANIZES
URALITISES	UREDIOSPORES	UROGRAPHIC	USTULATING	UTILITARIANS
URALITISING	UREDOSORUS	UROGRAPHIES	USTULATION	UTILIZABLE
URALITIZATION	UREDOSPORE	UROKINASES	USTULATIONS	UTILIZATION
URALITIZATIONS	UREDOSPORES	UROLAGNIAS	USUALNESSES	UTILIZATIONS
URALITIZED	UREOTELISM	UROLITHIASES	USUCAPIENT	UTOPIANISE
URALITIZES	UREOTELISMS	UROLITHIASIS	USUCAPIENTS	UTOPIANISED
URALITIZING	URETERITIS	UROLOGICAL	USUCAPIONS	UTOPIANISER
URANALYSES	URETERITISES	UROLOGISTS	USUCAPTIBLE	UTOPIANISERS
URANALYSIS	URETHANING	UROPOIESES	USUCAPTING	UTOPIANISES
URANINITES	URETHRITIC	UROPOIESIS	USUCAPTION	UTOPIANISING
URANOGRAPHER	URETHRITIDES	UROPYGIUMS	USUCAPTIONS	UTOPIANISM
URANOGRAPHERS	URETHRITIS	UROSCOPIES	USUFRUCTED	UTOPIANISMS
URANOGRAPHIC	URETHRITISES	UROSCOPIST	USUFRUCTING	UTOPIANIZE
URANOGRAPHICAL	URETHROSCOPE	UROSCOPISTS	USUFRUCTUARIES	UTOPIANIZED
URANOGRAPHIES	URETHROSCOPES	UROSTEGITE	USUFRUCTUARY	UTOPIANIZER
URANOGRAPHIST	URETHROSCOPIC	UROSTEGITES	USURIOUSLY	UTOPIANIZERS
URANOGRAPHISTS	URETHROSCOPIES	UROSTHENIC	USURIOUSNESS	UTOPIANIZES
URANOGRAPHY	URETHROSCOPY	UROSTOMIES	USURIOUSNESSES	UTOPIANIZING
URANOLOGIES	URICOSURIC	URTICACEOUS	USURPATION	UTRICULARIA
URANOMETRIES	URICOTELIC	URTICARIAL	USURPATIONS	UTRICULARIAS
URANOMETRY	URICOTELISM	URTICARIAS	USURPATIVE	UTRICULATE
URANOPLASTIES	URICOTELISMS	URTICARIOUS	USURPATORY	UTRICULITIS
URANOPLASTY	URINALYSES	URTICATING	USURPATURE	UTRICULITISES
URBANENESS	URINALYSIS	URTICATION	USURPATURES	UTTERABLENESS
URBANENESSES	URINATIONS	URTICATIONS	USURPINGLY	UTTERABLENESSES
URBANISATION	URINIFEROUS	USABILITIES	UTERECTOMIES	UTTERANCES
URBANISATIONS	URINIPAROUS	USABLENESS	UTERECTOMY	UTTERMOSTS
URBANISING	URINOGENITAL	USABLENESSES	UTERITISES	UTTERNESSES
URBANISTIC	URINOLOGIES	USEABILITIES	UTEROGESTATION	UVAROVITES
URBANISTICALLY	URINOMETER	USEABILITY	UTEROGESTATIONS	UVULITISES
URBANITIES	URINOMETERS	USEABLENESS	UTEROTOMIES	UXORICIDAL
URBANIZATION	URINOSCOPIES	USEABLENESSES	UTILISABLE	UXORICIDES
URBANIZATIONS	URINOSCOPY	USEFULNESS	UTILISATION	UXORILOCAL
URBANIZING	UROBILINOGEN	USEFULNESSES	UTILISATIONS	UXORIOUSLY
URBANOLOGIES	UROBILINOGENS	USELESSNESS	UTILITARIAN	UXORIOUSNESS
URBANOLOGIST	UROBOROSES	USELESSNESSES	UTILITARIANISE	UXORIOUSNESSES
URBANOLOGISTS	UROCHORDAL	USHERESSES	UTILITARIANISED	
URBANOLOGY	UROCHORDATE	USHERETTES	UTILITARIANISES	

V

VACANTNESS	VAGABONDING	VALEDICTORIANS	VALVULITIS	VANQUISHES
VACANTNESSES	VAGABONDISE	VALEDICTORIES	VALVULITISES	VANQUISHING
VACATIONED	VAGABONDISED	VALEDICTORY	VAMPIRISED	VANQUISHMENT
VACATIONER	VAGABONDISES	VALENTINES	VAMPIRISES	VANQUISHMENTS
VACATIONERS	VAGABONDISH	VALERIANACEOUS	VAMPIRISING	VANTAGELESS
VACATIONING	VAGABONDISING	VALETUDINARIAN	VAMPIRISMS	VANTBRACES
VACATIONIST	VAGABONDISM	VALETUDINARIANS	VAMPIRIZED	VANTBRASSES
VACATIONISTS	VAGABONDISMS	VALETUDINARIES	VAMPIRIZES	VAPIDITIES
VACATIONLAND	VAGABONDIZE	VALETUDINARY	VAMPIRIZING	VAPIDNESSES
VACATIONLANDS	VAGABONDIZED	VALIANCIES	VANADIATES	VAPORABILITIES
VACATIONLESS	VAGABONDIZES	VALIANTNESS	VANADINITE	VAPORABILITY
VACCINATED	VAGABONDIZING	VALIANTNESSES	VANADINITES	VAPORESCENCE
VACCINATES	VAGARIOUSLY	VALIDATING	VANASPATIS	VAPORESCENCES
VACCINATING	VAGILITIES	VALIDATION	VANCOMYCIN	VAPORESCENT
VACCINATION	VAGINECTOMIES	VALIDATIONS	VANCOMYCINS	VAPORETTOS
VACCINATIONS	VAGINECTOMY	VALIDATORS	VANDALISATION	VAPORIFORM
VACCINATOR	VAGINICOLINE	VALIDATORY	VANDALISATIONS	VAPORIMETER
VACCINATORS	VAGINICOLOUS	VALIDITIES	VANDALISED	VAPORIMETERS
VACCINATORY	VAGINISMUS	VALIDNESSES	VANDALISES	VAPORISABLE
VACCINIUMS	VAGINISMUSES	VALLATIONS	VANDALISING	VAPORISATION
VACILLATED	VAGINITIDES	VALLECULAE	VANDALISMS	VAPORISATIONS
VACILLATES	VAGINITISES	VALLECULAR	VANDALISTIC	VAPORISERS
VACILLATING	VAGOTOMIES	VALLECULAS	VANDALIZATION	VAPORISHNESS
VACILLATINGLY	VAGOTONIAS	VALLECULATE	VANDALIZATIONS	VAPORISHNESSES
VACILLATION	VAGOTROPIC	VALORISATION	VANDALIZED	VAPORISING
VACILLATIONS	VAGRANCIES	VALORISATIONS	VANDALIZES	VAPORIZABLE
VACILLATOR	VAGRANTNESS	VALORISING	VANDALIZING	VAPORIZATION
VACILLATORS	VAGRANTNESSES	VALORIZATION	VANGUARDISM	VAPORIZATIONS
VACILLATORY	VAGUENESSES	VALORIZATIONS	VANGUARDISMS	VAPORIZERS
VACUATIONS	VAINGLORIED	VALORIZING	VANGUARDIST	VAPORIZING
VACUOLATED	VAINGLORIES	VALOROUSLY	VANGUARDISTS	VAPOROSITIES
VACUOLATION	VAINGLORIOUS	VALPOLICELLA	VANISHINGLY	VAPOROSITY
VACUOLATIONS	VAINGLORIOUSLY	VALPOLICELLAS	VANISHINGS	VAPOROUSLY
VACUOLISATION	VAINGLORYING	VALPROATES	VANISHMENT	VAPOROUSNESS
VACUOLISATIONS	VAINNESSES	VALUABLENESS	VANISHMENTS	VAPOROUSNESSES
VACUOLIZATION	VAIVODESHIP	VALUABLENESSES	VANITORIES	VAPORWARES
VACUOLIZATIONS	VAIVODESHIPS	VALUATIONAL	VANPOOLING	VAPOURABILITIES
VACUOUSNESS	VAJAZZLING	VALUATIONALLY	VANPOOLINGS	VAPOURABILITY
VACUOUSNESSES	VAJAZZLINGS	VALUATIONS	VANQUISHABLE	VAPOURABLE
VAGABONDAGE	VALEDICTION	VALUELESSNESS	VANQUISHED	VAPOURIEST
VAGABONDAGES	VALEDICTIONS	VALUELESSNESSES	VANQUISHER	VAPOURINGLY
VAGABONDED	VALEDICTORIAN	VALVASSORS	VANQUISHERS	VAPOURINGS

VAPOURISHNESS	VARIOLATORS	VASECTOMISING	VATICINATOR	VEGETATIVELY
VAPOURISHNESSES	VARIOLISATION	VASECTOMIZE	VATICINATORS	VEGETATIVENESS
VAPOURLESS	VARIOLISATIONS	VASECTOMIZED	VATICINATORY	VEGGIEBURGER
VAPOURWARE	VARIOLITES	VASECTOMIZES	VAUDEVILLE	VEGGIEBURGERS
VAPOURWARES	VARIOLITIC	VASECTOMIZING	VAUDEVILLEAN	VEHEMENCES
VAPULATING	VARIOLIZATION	VASELINING	VAUDEVILLEANS	VEHEMENCIES
VAPULATION	VARIOLIZATIONS	VASOACTIVE	VAUDEVILLES	VEHEMENTLY
VAPULATIONS	VARIOLOIDS	VASOACTIVITIES	VAUDEVILLIAN	VEILLEUSES
VARIABILITIES	VARIOMETER	VASOACTIVITY	VAUDEVILLIANS	VEINSTONES
VARIABILITY	VARIOMETERS	VASOCONSTRICTOR	VAUDEVILLIST	VEINSTUFFS
VARIABLENESS	VARIOUSNESS	VASODILATATION	VAUDEVILLISTS	VELARISATION
VARIABLENESSES	VARIOUSNESSES	VASODILATATIONS	VAULTINGLY	VELARISATIONS
VARIATIONAL	VARISCITES	VASODILATATORY	VAUNTERIES	VELARISING
VARIATIONALLY	VARITYPING	VASODILATION	VAUNTINGLY	VELARIZATION
VARIATIONIST	VARITYPIST	VASODILATIONS	VAVASORIES	VELARIZATIONS
VARIATIONISTS	VARITYPISTS	VASODILATOR	VECTOGRAPH	VELARIZING
VARIATIONS	VARLETESSES	VASODILATORS	VECTOGRAPHS	VELDSCHOEN
VARICELLAR	VARLETRIES	VASODILATORY	VECTORIALLY	VELDSCHOENS
VARICELLAS	VARNISHERS	VASOINHIBITOR	VECTORINGS	VELDSKOENS
VARICELLATE	VARNISHIER	VASOINHIBITORS	VECTORISATION	VELITATION
VARICELLOID	VARNISHIEST	VASOINHIBITORY	VECTORISATIONS	VELITATIONS
VARICELLOUS	VARNISHING	VASOPRESSIN	VECTORISED	VELLEITIES
VARICOCELE	VARNISHINGS	VASOPRESSINS	VECTORISES	VELLENAGES
VARICOCELES	VARSOVIENNE	VASOPRESSOR	VECTORISING	VELLICATED
VARICOLORED	VARSOVIENNES	VASOPRESSORS	VECTORIZATION	VELLICATES
VARICOLOURED	VASCULARISATION	VASOSPASMS	VECTORIZATIONS	VELLICATING
VARICOSITIES	VASCULARISE	VASOSPASTIC	VECTORIZED	VELLICATION
VARICOSITY	VASCULARISED	VASOTOCINS	VECTORIZES	VELLICATIONS
VARICOTOMIES	VASCULARISES	VASOTOMIES	VECTORIZING	VELLICATIVE
VARICOTOMY	VASCULARISING	VASSALAGES	VECTORSCOPE	VELOCIMETER
VARIEDNESS	VASCULARITIES	VASSALESSES	VECTORSCOPES	VELOCIMETERS
VARIEDNESSES	VASCULARITY	VASSALISED	VEDUTISTAS	VELOCIMETRIES
VARIEGATED	VASCULARIZATION	VASSALISES	VEGEBURGER	VELOCIMETRY
VARIEGATES	VASCULARIZE	VASSALISING	VEGEBURGERS	VELOCIPEDE
VARIEGATING	VASCULARIZED	VASSALIZED	VEGETABLES	VELOCIPEDEAN
VARIEGATION	VASCULARIZES	VASSALIZES	VEGETABLIER	VELOCIPEDEANS
VARIEGATIONS	VASCULARIZING	VASSALIZING	VEGETABLIEST	VELOCIPEDED
VARIEGATOR	VASCULARLY	VASSALLING	VEGETARIAN	VELOCIPEDER
VARIEGATORS	VASCULATURE	VASSALRIES	VEGETARIANISM	VELOCIPEDERS
VARIETALLY	VASCULATURES	VASTIDITIES	VEGETARIANISMS	VELOCIPEDES
VARIFOCALS	VASCULIFORM	VASTITUDES	VEGETARIANS	VELOCIPEDIAN
VARIFORMLY	VASCULITIDES	VASTNESSES	VEGETATING	VELOCIPEDIANS
VARIOLATED	VASCULITIS	VATICINATE	VEGETATINGS	VELOCIPEDING
VARIOLATES	VASCULITISES	VATICINATED	VEGETATION	VELOCIPEDIST
VARIOLATING	VASECTOMIES	VATICINATES	VEGETATIONAL	VELOCIPEDISTS
VARIOLATION	VASECTOMISE	VATICINATING	VEGETATIONS	VELOCIRAPTOR
VARIOLATIONS	VASECTOMISED	VATICINATION	VEGETATIOUS	VELOCIRAPTORS
VARIOLATOR	VASECTOMISES	VATICINATIONS	VEGETATIVE	VELOCITIES

V

VELODROMES	VENEREOLOGISTS	VENTRICULE	VERBALISES	VERIDICOUS
VELOUTINES	VENEREOLOGY	VENTRICULES	VERBALISING	VERIFIABILITIES
VELUTINOUS	VENESECTION	VENTRICULI	VERBALISMS	VERIFIABILITY
VELVETEENED	VENESECTIONS	VENTRICULUS	VERBALISTIC	VERIFIABLE
VELVETEENS	VENGEANCES	VENTRILOQUAL	VERBALISTS	VERIFIABLENESS
VELVETIEST	VENGEFULLY	VENTRILOQUIAL	VERBALITIES	VERIFIABLY
VELVETINESS	VENGEFULNESS	VENTRILOQUIALLY	VERBALIZATION	VERIFICATION
VELVETINESSES	VENGEFULNESSES	VENTRILOQUIES	VERBALIZATIONS	VERIFICATIONS
VELVETINGS	VENGEMENTS	VENTRILOQUISE	VERBALIZED	VERIFICATIVE
VELVETLIKE	VENIALITIES	VENTRILOQUISED	VERBALIZER	VERIFICATORY
VENALITIES	VENIALNESS	VENTRILOQUISES	VERBALIZERS	VERISIMILAR
VENATICALLY	VENIALNESSES	VENTRILOQUISING	VERBALIZES	VERISIMILARLY
VENATIONAL	VENIPUNCTURE	VENTRILOQUISM	VERBALIZING	VERISIMILITIES
VENATORIAL	VENIPUNCTURES	VENTRILOQUISMS	VERBALLING	VERISIMILITUDE
VENDETTIST	VENISECTION	VENTRILOQUIST	VERBARIANS	VERISIMILITUDES
VENDETTISTS	VENISECTIONS	VENTRILOQUISTIC	VERBASCUMS	VERISIMILITY
VENDIBILITIES	VENOGRAPHIC	VENTRILOQUISTS	VERBENACEOUS	VERISIMILOUS
VENDIBILITY	VENOGRAPHICAL	VENTRILOQUIZE	VERBERATED	VERITABLENESS
VENDIBLENESS	VENOGRAPHIES	VENTRILOQUIZED	VERBERATES	VERITABLENESSES
VENDIBLENESSES	VENOGRAPHY	VENTRILOQUIZES	VERBERATING	VERJUICING
VENDITATION	VENOLOGIES	VENTRILOQUIZING	VERBERATION	VERKRAMPTE
VENDITATIONS	VENOMOUSLY	VENTRILOQUOUS	VERBERATIONS	VERKRAMPTES
VENDITIONS	VENOMOUSNESS	VENTRILOQUY	VERBICIDES	VERMEILING
VENEERINGS	VENOMOUSNESSES	VENTRIPOTENT	VERBIFICATION	VERMEILLED
VENEFICALLY	VENOSCLEROSES	VENTROLATERAL	VERBIFICATIONS	VERMEILLES
VENEFICIOUS	VENOSCLEROSIS	VENTROMEDIAL	VERBIFYING	VERMEILLING
VENEFICIOUSLY	VENOSITIES	VENTURESOME	VERBIGERATE	VERMICELLI
VENEFICOUS	VENOUSNESS	VENTURESOMELY	VERBIGERATED	VERMICELLIS
VENEFICOUSLY	VENOUSNESSES	VENTURESOMENESS	VERBIGERATES	VERMICIDAL
VENENATING	VENTIDUCTS	VENTURINGLY	VERBIGERATING	VERMICIDES
VENEPUNCTURE	VENTIFACTS	VENTURINGS	VERBIGERATION	VERMICULAR
VENEPUNCTURES	VENTILABLE	VENTUROUSLY	VERBIGERATIONS	VERMICULARLY
VENERABILITIES	VENTILATED	VENTUROUSNESS	VERBOSENESS	VERMICULATE
VENERABILITY	VENTILATES	VENTUROUSNESSES	VERBOSENESSES	VERMICULATED
VENERABLENESS	VENTILATING	VERACIOUSLY	VERBOSITIES	VERMICULATES
VENERABLENESSES	VENTILATION	VERACIOUSNESS	VERDANCIES	VERMICULATING
VENERABLES	VENTILATIONS	VERACIOUSNESSES	VERDIGRISED	VERMICULATION
VENERATING	VENTILATIVE	VERACITIES	VERDIGRISES	VERMICULATIONS
VENERATION	VENTILATOR	VERANDAHED	VERDIGRISING	VERMICULES
VENERATIONAL	VENTILATORS	VERAPAMILS	VERDURELESS	VERMICULITE
VENERATIONS	VENTILATORY	VERATRIDINE	VERGEBOARD	VERMICULITES
VENERATIVE	VENTOSITIES	VERATRIDINES	VERGEBOARDS	VERMICULOUS
VENERATIVENESS	VENTRICLES	VERATRINES	VERGENCIES	VERMICULTURE
VENERATORS	VENTRICOSE	VERBALISATION	VERGERSHIP	VERMICULTURES
VENEREALLY	VENTRICOSITIES	VERBALISATIONS	VERGERSHIPS	VERMIFUGAL
VENEREOLOGICAL	VENTRICOSITY	VERBALISED	VERIDICALITIES	VERMIFUGES
VENEREOLOGIES	VENTRICOUS	VERBALISER	VERIDICALITY	VERMILIONED
VENEREOLOGIST	VENTRICULAR	VERBALISERS	VERIDICALLY	VERMILIONING

VERMILIONS	VERSABILITIES	VERTIGINES	VETERINARIAN	VIBROMETERS
VERMILLING	VERSABILITY	VERTIGINOUS	VETERINARIANS	VICARESSES
VERMILLION	VERSATILELY	VERTIGINOUSLY	VETERINARIES	VICARIANCE
VERMILLIONS	VERSATILENESS	VERTIGINOUSNESS	VETERINARY	VICARIANCES
VERMINATED	VERSATILENESSES	VERTIPORTS	VETTURINOS	VICARIANTS
VERMINATES	VERSATILITIES	VERUMONTANA	VEXATIOUSLY	VICARIATES
VERMINATING	VERSATILITY	VERUMONTANUM	VEXATIOUSNESS	VICARIOUSLY
VERMINATION	VERSICOLOR	VERUMONTANUMS	VEXATIOUSNESSES	VICARIOUSNESS
VERMINATIONS	VERSICOLORED	VESICATING	VEXEDNESSES	VICARIOUSNESSES
VERMINIEST	VERSICOLOUR	VESICATION	VEXILLARIES	VICARLIEST
VERMINOUSLY	VERSICOLOURED	VESICATIONS	VEXILLATION	VICARSHIPS
VERMINOUSNESS	VERSICULAR	VESICATORIES	VEXILLATIONS	VICEGERENCIES
VERMINOUSNESSES	VERSIFICATION	VESICATORY	VEXILLOLOGIC	VICEGERENCY
VERMIVOROUS	VERSIFICATIONS	VESICULARITIES	VEXILLOLOGICAL	VICEGERENT
VERNACULAR	VERSIFICATOR	VESICULARITY	VEXILLOLOGIES	VICEGERENTS
VERNACULARISE	VERSIFICATORS	VESICULARLY	VEXILLOLOGIST	VICEREGALLY
VERNACULARISED	VERSIFIERS	VESICULATE	VEXILLOLOGISTS	VICEREGENT
VERNACULARISES	VERSIFYING	VESICULATED	VEXILLOLOGY	VICEREGENTS
VERNACULARISING	VERSIONERS	VESICULATES	VEXINGNESS	VICEREINES
VERNACULARISM	VERSIONING	VESICULATING	VEXINGNESSES	VICEROYALTIES
VERNACULARISMS	VERSIONINGS	VESICULATION	VIABILITIES	VICEROYALTY
VERNACULARIST	VERSIONIST	VESICULATIONS	VIBRACULAR	VICEROYSHIP
VERNACULARISTS	VERSIONISTS	VESICULOSE	VIBRACULARIA	VICEROYSHIPS
VERNACULARITIES	VERSLIBRIST	VESPERTILIAN	VIBRACULARIUM	VICHYSSOIS
VERNACULARITY	VERSLIBRISTE	VESPERTILIONID	VIBRACULOID	VICHYSSOISE
VERNACULARIZE	VERSLIBRISTES	VESPERTILIONIDS	VIBRACULUM	VICHYSSOISES
VERNACULARIZED	VERSLIBRISTS	VESPERTILIONINE	VIBRAHARPIST	VICINITIES
VERNACULARIZES	VERTEBRALLY	VESPERTINAL	VIBRAHARPISTS	VICIOSITIES
VERNACULARIZING	VERTEBRATE	VESPERTINE	VIBRAHARPS	VICIOUSNESS
VERNACULARLY	VERTEBRATED	VESPIARIES	VIBRANCIES	VICIOUSNESSES
VERNACULARS	VERTEBRATES	VESTIARIES	VIBRAPHONE	VICISSITUDE
VERNALISATION	VERTEBRATION	VESTIBULAR	VIBRAPHONES	VICISSITUDES
VERNALISATIONS	VERTEBRATIONS	VESTIBULED	VIBRAPHONIST	VICISSITUDINARY
VERNALISED	VERTICALITIES	VESTIBULES	VIBRAPHONISTS	VICISSITUDINOUS
VERNALISES	VERTICALITY	VESTIBULING	VIBRATILITIES	VICOMTESSE
VERNALISING	VERTICALLY	VESTIBULITIS	VIBRATILITY	VICOMTESSES
VERNALITIES	VERTICALNESS	VESTIBULITISES	VIBRATINGLY	VICTIMHOOD
VERNALIZATION	VERTICALNESSES	VESTIBULUM	VIBRATIONAL	VICTIMHOODS
VERNALIZATIONS	VERTICILLASTER	VESTIGIALLY	VIBRATIONLESS	VICTIMISATION
VERNALIZED	VERTICILLASTERS	VESTIMENTAL	VIBRATIONS	VICTIMISATIONS
VERNALIZES	VERTICILLATE	VESTIMENTARY	VIBRATIUNCLE	VICTIMISED
VERNALIZING	VERTICILLATED	VESTIMENTS	VIBRATIUNCLES	VICTIMISER
VERNATIONS	VERTICILLATELY	VESTITURES	VIBRATOLESS	VICTIMISERS
VERNISSAGE	VERTICILLATION	VESTMENTAL	VIBROFLOTATION	VICTIMISES
VERNISSAGES	VERTICILLATIONS	VESTMENTED	VIBROFLOTATIONS	VICTIMISING
VERRUCIFORM	VERTICILLIUM	VESUVIANITE	VIBROGRAPH	VICTIMIZATION
VERRUCOSITIES	VERTICILLIUMS	VESUVIANITES	VIBROGRAPHS	VICTIMIZATIONS
VERRUCOSITY	VERTICITIES	VETCHLINGS	VIBROMETER	VICTIMIZED

VICTIMIZER	VIDEOTELEPHONE	VILLAGIZATIONS	VINDICATIVE	VIOLACEOUS
VICTIMIZERS	VIDEOTELEPHONES	VILLAGREES	VINDICATIVENESS	VIOLATIONS
VICTIMIZES	VIDEOTEXES	VILLAINAGE	VINDICATOR	VIOLENTING
VICTIMIZING	VIDEOTEXTS	VILLAINAGES	VINDICATORILY	VIOLINISTIC
VICTIMLESS	VIDEOTHEQUE	VILLAINESS	VINDICATORS	VIOLINISTICALLY
VICTIMOLOGIES	VIDEOTHEQUES	VILLAINESSES	VINDICATORY	VIOLINISTS
VICTIMOLOGIST	VIDSCREENS	VILLAINIES	VINDICATRESS	VIOLONCELLI
VICTIMOLOGISTS	VIEWERSHIP	VILLAINOUS	VINDICATRESSES	VIOLONCELLIST
VICTIMOLOGY	VIEWERSHIPS	VILLAINOUSLY	VINDICTIVE	VIOLONCELLISTS
VICTORESSES	VIEWFINDER	VILLAINOUSNESS	VINDICTIVELY	VIOLONCELLO
VICTORIANA	VIEWFINDERS	VILLANAGES	VINDICTIVENESS	VIOLONCELLOS
VICTORIANAS	VIEWINESSES	VILLANELLA	VINEDRESSER	VIOSTEROLS
VICTORINES	VIEWLESSLY	VILLANELLAS	VINEDRESSERS	VIPASSANAS
VICTORIOUS	VIEWPHONES	VILLANELLE	VINEGARETTE	VIPERFISHES
VICTORIOUSLY	VIEWPOINTS	VILLANELLES	VINEGARETTES	VIPERIFORM
VICTORIOUSNESS	VIGILANCES	VILLANOUSLY	VINEGARIER	VIPERISHLY
VICTORYLESS	VIGILANTES	VILLEGGIATURA	VINEGARIEST	VIPEROUSLY
VICTRESSES	VIGILANTISM	VILLEGGIATURAS	VINEGARING	VIRAGINIAN
VICTUALAGE	VIGILANTISMS	VILLEINAGE	VINEGARISH	VIRAGINOUS
VICTUALAGES	VIGILANTLY	VILLEINAGES	VINEGARRETTE	VIRALITIES
VICTUALERS	VIGILANTNESS	VILLENAGES	VINEGARRETTES	VIREONINES
VICTUALING	VIGILANTNESSES	VILLIACOES	VINEGARROON	VIRESCENCE
VICTUALLAGE	VIGINTILLION	VILLIAGOES	VINEGARROONS	VIRESCENCES
VICTUALLAGES	VIGINTILLIONS	VILLICATION	VINEYARDIST	VIRGINALIST
VICTUALLED	VIGNETTERS	VILLICATIONS	VINEYARDISTS	VIRGINALISTS
VICTUALLER	VIGNETTING	VILLOSITIES	VINICULTURAL	VIRGINALLED
VICTUALLERS	VIGNETTINGS	VINAIGRETTE	VINICULTURE	VIRGINALLING
VICTUALLESS	VIGNETTIST	VINAIGRETTES	VINICULTURES	VIRGINALLY
VICTUALLING	VIGNETTISTS	VINBLASTINE	VINICULTURIST	VIRGINHOOD
VIDEOCASSETTE	VIGORISHES	VINBLASTINES	VINICULTURISTS	VIRGINHOODS
VIDEOCASSETTES	VIGOROUSLY	VINCIBILITIES	VINIFEROUS	VIRGINITIES
VIDEOCONFERENCE	VIGOROUSNESS	VINCIBILITY	VINIFICATION	VIRGINIUMS
VIDEODISCS	VIGOROUSNESSES	VINCIBLENESS	VINIFICATIONS	VIRIDESCENCE
VIDEODISKS	VIKINGISMS	VINCIBLENESSES	VINIFICATOR	VIRIDESCENCES
VIDEOGRAMS	VILDNESSES	VINCRISTINE	VINIFICATORS	VIRIDESCENT
VIDEOGRAPHER	VILENESSES	VINCRISTINES	VINOLOGIES	VIRIDITIES
VIDEOGRAPHERS	VILIFICATION	VINDEMIATE	VINOLOGIST	VIRILESCENCE
VIDEOGRAPHIES	VILIFICATIONS	VINDEMIATED	VINOLOGISTS	VIRILESCENCES
VIDEOGRAPHY	VILIPENDED	VINDEMIATES	VINOSITIES	VIRILESCENT
VIDEOLANDS	VILIPENDER	VINDEMIATING	VINTAGINGS	VIRILISATION
VIDEOPHILE	VILIPENDERS	VINDICABILITIES	VINYLCYANIDE	VIRILISATIONS
VIDEOPHILES	VILIPENDING	VINDICABILITY	VINYLCYANIDES	VIRILISING
VIDEOPHONE	VILLAGERIES	VINDICABLE	VINYLIDENE	VIRILITIES
VIDEOPHONES	VILLAGIEST	VINDICATED	VINYLIDENES	VIRILIZATION
VIDEOPHONIC	VILLAGIOES	VINDICATES	VIOLABILITIES	VIRILIZATIONS
VIDEOTAPED	VILLAGISATION	VINDICATING	VIOLABILITY	VIRILIZING
VIDEOTAPES	VILLAGISATIONS	VINDICATION	VIOLABLENESS	VIROLOGICAL
VIDEOTAPING	VILLAGIZATION	VINDICATIONS	VIOLABLENESSES	VIROLOGICALLY

VIROLOGIES

VIROLOGIES	VISCIDNESSES	VISUALISATIONS	VITICETUMS	VITRIOLATION
VIROLOGIST	VISCOELASTIC	VISUALISED	VITICOLOUS	VITRIOLATIONS
VIROLOGISTS	VISCOELASTICITY	VISUALISER	VITICULTURAL	VITRIOLING
VIRTUALISATION	VISCOMETER	VISUALISERS	VITICULTURALLY	VITRIOLISATION
VIRTUALISATIONS	VISCOMETERS	VISUALISES	VITICULTURE	VITRIOLISATIONS
VIRTUALISE	VISCOMETRIC	VISUALISING	VITICULTURER	VITRIOLISE
VIRTUALISED	VISCOMETRICAL	VISUALISTS	VITICULTURERS	VITRIOLISED
VIRTUALISES	VISCOMETRIES	VISUALITIES	VITICULTURES	VITRIOLISES
VIRTUALISING	VISCOMETRY	VISUALIZATION	VITICULTURIST	VITRIOLISING
VIRTUALISM	VISCOSIMETER	VISUALIZATIONS	VITICULTURISTS	VITRIOLIZATION
VIRTUALISMS	VISCOSIMETERS	VISUALIZED	VITIFEROUS	VITRIOLIZATIONS
VIRTUALIST	VISCOSIMETRIC	VISUALIZER	VITILITIGATE	VITRIOLIZE
VIRTUALISTS	VISCOSIMETRICAL	VISUALIZERS	VITILITIGATED	VITRIOLIZED
VIRTUALITIES	VISCOSIMETRIES	VISUALIZES	VITILITIGATES	VITRIOLIZES
VIRTUALITY	VISCOSIMETRY	VISUALIZING	VITILITIGATING	VITRIOLIZING
VIRTUALIZATION	VISCOSITIES	VITALISATION	VITILITIGATION	VITRIOLLED
VIRTUALIZATIONS	VISCOUNTCIES	VITALISATIONS	VITILITIGATIONS	VITRIOLLING
VIRTUALIZE	VISCOUNTCY	VITALISERS	VITIOSITIES	VITUPERABLE
VIRTUALIZED	VISCOUNTESS	VITALISING	VITRAILLED	VITUPERATE
VIRTUALIZES	VISCOUNTESSES	VITALISTIC	VITRAILLIST	VITUPERATED
VIRTUALIZING	VISCOUNTIES	VITALISTICALLY	VITRAILLISTS	VITUPERATES
VIRTUELESS	VISCOUNTSHIP	VITALITIES	VITRECTOMIES	VITUPERATING
VIRTUOSITIES	VISCOUNTSHIPS	VITALIZATION	VITRECTOMY	VITUPERATION
VIRTUOSITY	VISCOUSNESS	VITALIZATIONS	VITREORETINAL	VITUPERATIONS
VIRTUOSOSHIP	VISCOUSNESSES	VITALIZERS	VITREOSITIES	VITUPERATIVE
VIRTUOSOSHIPS	VISIBILITIES	VITALIZING	VITREOSITY	VITUPERATIVELY
VIRTUOUSLY	VISIBILITY	VITALNESSES	VITREOUSES	VITUPERATOR
VIRTUOUSNESS	VISIBLENESS	VITAMINISE	VITREOUSLY	VITUPERATORS
VIRTUOUSNESSES	VISIBLENESSES	VITAMINISED	VITREOUSNESS	VITUPERATORY
VIRULENCES	VISIOGENIC	VITAMINISES	VITREOUSNESSES	VIVACIOUSLY
VIRULENCIES	VISIONALLY	VITAMINISING	VITRESCENCE	VIVACIOUSNESS
VIRULENTLY	VISIONARIES	VITAMINIZE	VITRESCENCES	VIVACIOUSNESSES
VIRULIFEROUS	VISIONARINESS	VITAMINIZED	VITRESCENT	VIVACISSIMO
VISAGISTES	VISIONARINESSES	VITAMINIZES	VITRESCIBILITY	VIVACITIES
VISCACHERA	VISIONINGS	VITAMINIZING	VITRESCIBLE	VIVANDIERE
VISCACHERAS	VISIONISTS	VITASCOPES	VITRIFACTION	VIVANDIERES
VISCERALLY	VISIONLESS	VITATIVENESS	VITRIFACTIONS	VIVANDIERS
VISCERATED	VISIOPHONE	VITATIVENESSES	VITRIFACTURE	VIVERRINES
VISCERATES	VISIOPHONES	VITELLARIES	VITRIFACTURES	VIVIANITES
VISCERATING	VISITATION	VITELLICLE	VITRIFIABILITY	VIVIDITIES
VISCEROMOTOR	VISITATIONAL	VITELLICLES	VITRIFIABLE	VIVIDNESSES
VISCEROPTOSES	VISITATIONS	VITELLIGENOUS	VITRIFICATION	VIVIFICATION
VISCEROPTOSIS	VISITATIVE	VITELLINES	VITRIFICATIONS	VIVIFICATIONS
VISCEROTONIA	VISITATORIAL	VITELLOGENESES	VITRIFYING	VIVIPARIES
VISCEROTONIAS	VISITATORS	VITELLOGENESIS	VITRIOLATE	VIVIPARISM
VISCEROTONIC	VISITORIAL	VITELLOGENIC	VITRIOLATED	VIVIPARISMS
VISCIDITIES	VISITRESSES	VITELLUSES	VITRIOLATES	VIVIPARITIES
VISCIDNESS	VISUALISATION	VITIATIONS	VITRIOLATING	VIVIPARITY

VIVIPAROUS	VOCATIONALISTS	VOLATILISABLE	VOLLEYBALL	VOLUNTEERED
VIVIPAROUSLY	VOCATIONALLY	VOLATILISATION	VOLLEYBALLS	VOLUNTEERING
VIVIPAROUSNESS	VOCATIVELY	VOLATILISATIONS	VOLPLANING	VOLUNTEERISM
VIVISECTED	VOCICULTURAL	VOLATILISE	VOLTAMETER	VOLUNTEERISMS
VIVISECTING	VOCIFERANCE	VOLATILISED	VOLTAMETERS	VOLUNTEERS
VIVISECTION	VOCIFERANCES	VOLATILISES	VOLTAMETRIC	VOLUNTOURISM
VIVISECTIONAL	VOCIFERANT	VOLATILISING	VOLTAMMETER	VOLUNTOURISMS
VIVISECTIONALLY	VOCIFERANTS	VOLATILITIES	VOLTAMMETERS	VOLUPTUARIES
VIVISECTIONIST	VOCIFERATE	VOLATILITY	VOLTIGEURS	VOLUPTUARY
VIVISECTIONISTS	VOCIFERATED	VOLATILIZABLE	VOLTINISMS	VOLUPTUOSITIES
VIVISECTIONS	VOCIFERATES	VOLATILIZATION	VOLTMETERS	VOLUPTUOSITY
VIVISECTIVE	VOCIFERATING	VOLATILIZATIONS	VOLUBILITIES	VOLUPTUOUS
VIVISECTOR	VOCIFERATION	VOLATILIZE	VOLUBILITY	VOLUPTUOUSLY
VIVISECTORIA	VOCIFERATIONS	VOLATILIZED	VOLUBLENESS	VOLUPTUOUSNESS
VIVISECTORIUM	VOCIFERATOR	VOLATILIZES	VOLUBLENESSES	VOLUTATION
VIVISECTORIUMS	VOCIFERATORS	VOLATILIZING	VOLUMENOMETER	VOLUTATIONS
VIVISECTORS	VOCIFEROSITIES	VOLCANICALLY	VOLUMENOMETERS	VOLVULUSES
VIVISEPULTURE	VOCIFEROSITY	VOLCANICITIES	VOLUMETERS	VOMERONASAL
VIVISEPULTURES	VOCIFEROUS	VOLCANICITY	VOLUMETRIC	VOMITORIES
VIXENISHLY	VOCIFEROUSLY	VOLCANISATION	VOLUMETRICAL	VOMITORIUM
VIXENISHNESS	VOCIFEROUSNESS	VOLCANISATIONS	VOLUMETRICALLY	VOMITURITION
VIXENISHNESSES	VODCASTERS	VOLCANISED	VOLUMETRIES	VOMITURITIONS
VIZIERATES	VODCASTING	VOLCANISES	VOLUMINOSITIES	VOODOOISMS
VIZIERSHIP	VODCASTINGS	VOLCANISING	VOLUMINOSITY	VOODOOISTIC
VIZIERSHIPS	VOETGANGER	VOLCANISMS	VOLUMINOUS	VOODOOISTS
VIZIRSHIPS	VOETGANGERS	VOLCANISTS	VOLUMINOUSLY	VOORKAMERS
VOCABULARIAN	VOETSTOETS	VOLCANIZATION	VOLUMINOUSNESS	VOORTREKKER
VOCABULARIANS	VOETSTOOTS	VOLCANIZATIONS	VOLUMISERS	VOORTREKKERS
VOCABULARIED	VOGUISHNESS	VOLCANIZED	VOLUMISING	VORACIOUSLY
VOCABULARIES	VOGUISHNESSES	VOLCANIZES	VOLUMIZERS	VORACIOUSNESS
VOCABULARY	VOICEFULNESS	VOLCANIZING	VOLUMIZING	VORACIOUSNESSES
VOCABULIST	VOICEFULNESSES	VOLCANOLOGIC	VOLUMOMETER	VORACITIES
VOCABULISTS	VOICELESSLY	VOLCANOLOGICAL	VOLUMOMETERS	VORAGINOUS
VOCALICALLY	VOICELESSNESS	VOLCANOLOGIES	VOLUNTARIES	VORTICALLY
VOCALISATION	VOICELESSNESSES	VOLCANOLOGIST	VOLUNTARILY	VORTICELLA
VOCALISATIONS	VOICEMAILS	VOLCANOLOGISTS	VOLUNTARINESS	VORTICELLAE
VOCALISERS	VOICEOVERS	VOLCANOLOGY	VOLUNTARINESSES	VORTICELLAS
VOCALISING	VOICEPRINT	VOLITATING	VOLUNTARISM	VORTICISMS
VOCALITIES	VOICEPRINTS	VOLITATION	VOLUNTARISMS	VORTICISTS
VOCALIZATION	VOIDABLENESS	VOLITATIONAL	VOLUNTARIST	VORTICITIES
VOCALIZATIONS	VOIDABLENESSES	VOLITATIONS	VOLUNTARISTIC	VORTICULAR
VOCALIZERS	VOIDNESSES	VOLITIONAL	VOLUNTARISTS	VORTIGINOUS
VOCALIZING	VOISINAGES	VOLITIONALLY	VOLUNTARYISM	VOTARESSES
VOCALNESSES	VOITURIERS	VOLITIONARY	VOLUNTARYISMS	VOTIVENESS
VOCATIONAL	VOIVODESHIP	VOLITIONLESS	VOLUNTARYIST	VOTIVENESSES
VOCATIONALISM	VOIVODESHIPS	VOLITORIAL	VOLUNTARYISTS	VOUCHERING
VOCATIONALISMS	VOLATILENESS	VOLKSLIEDER	VOLUNTATIVE	VOUCHSAFED
VOCATIONALIST	VOLATILENESSES	VOLKSRAADS	VOLUNTATIVES	VOUCHSAFEMENT

VOUCHSAFEMENTS

VOUCHSAFEMENTS
VOUCHSAFES
VOUCHSAFING
VOUCHSAFINGS
VOUSSOIRED
VOUSSOIRING
VOUTSAFING
VOWELISATION
VOWELISATIONS
VOWELISING
VOWELIZATION
VOWELIZATIONS
VOWELIZING
VOWELLIEST
VOYAGEABLE
VOYEURISMS
VOYEURISTIC
VOYEURISTICALLY

VRAICKINGS
VRAISEMBLANCE
VRAISEMBLANCES
VRYSTATERS
VULCANICITIES
VULCANICITY
VULCANISABLE
VULCANISATE
VULCANISATES
VULCANISATION
VULCANISATIONS
VULCANISED
VULCANISER
VULCANISERS
VULCANISES
VULCANISING
VULCANISMS
VULCANISTS

VULCANITES
VULCANIZABLE
VULCANIZATE
VULCANIZATES
VULCANIZATION
VULCANIZATIONS
VULCANIZED
VULCANIZER
VULCANIZERS
VULCANIZES
VULCANIZING
VULCANOLOGIC
VULCANOLOGICAL
VULCANOLOGIES
VULCANOLOGIST
VULCANOLOGISTS
VULCANOLOGY
VULGARIANS

VULGARISATION
VULGARISATIONS
VULGARISED
VULGARISER
VULGARISERS
VULGARISES
VULGARISING
VULGARISMS
VULGARITIES
VULGARIZATION
VULGARIZATIONS
VULGARIZED
VULGARIZER
VULGARIZERS
VULGARIZES
VULGARIZING
VULNERABILITIES
VULNERABILITY

VULNERABLE
VULNERABLENESS
VULNERABLY
VULNERARIES
VULNERATED
VULNERATES
VULNERATING
VULNERATION
VULNERATIONS
VULPECULAR
VULPICIDES
VULPINISMS
VULPINITES
VULTURISMS
VULVITISES
VULVOVAGINAL
VULVOVAGINITIS

W

WACKINESSES	WAITERAGES	WALLOPINGS	WAPENTAKES	WARLORDISMS
WADSETTERS	WAITERHOOD	WALLOWINGS	WAPINSCHAW	WARMBLOODS
WADSETTING	WAITERHOODS	WALLPAPERED	WAPINSCHAWS	WARMHEARTED
WAFFLESTOMPER	WAITERINGS	WALLPAPERING	WAPINSHAWS	WARMHEARTEDNESS
WAFFLESTOMPERS	WAITLISTED	WALLPAPERS	WAPPENSCHAW	WARMNESSES
WAGELESSNESS	WAITLISTING	WALLPEPPER	WAPPENSCHAWING	WARMONGERING
WAGELESSNESSES	WAITPEOPLE	WALLPEPPERS	WAPPENSCHAWINGS	WARMONGERINGS
WAGENBOOMS	WAITPERSON	WALLPOSTER	WAPPENSCHAWS	WARMONGERS
WAGEWORKER	WAITPERSONS	WALLPOSTERS	WAPPENSHAW	WARRANDICE
WAGEWORKERS	WAITRESSED	WALLYBALLS	WAPPENSHAWING	WARRANDICES
WAGGISHNESS	WAITRESSES	WALLYDRAGS	WAPPENSHAWINGS	WARRANDING
WAGGISHNESSES	WAITRESSING	WALLYDRAIGLE	WAPPENSHAWS	WARRANTABILITY
WAGGLINGLY	WAITRESSINGS	WALLYDRAIGLES	WARBLINGLY	WARRANTABLE
WAGGONETTE	WAITSTAFFS	WALNUTWOOD	WARBONNETS	WARRANTABLENESS
WAGGONETTES	WAKEBOARDED	WALNUTWOODS	WARCHALKER	WARRANTABLY
WAGGONLESS	WAKEBOARDER	WAMBENGERS	WARCHALKERS	WARRANTEES
WAGGONLOAD	WAKEBOARDERS	WAMBLINESS	WARCHALKING	WARRANTERS
WAGGONLOADS	WAKEBOARDING	WAMBLINESSES	WARCHALKINGS	WARRANTIED
WAGHALTERS	WAKEBOARDINGS	WAMBLINGLY	WARDENRIES	WARRANTIES
WAGONETTES	WAKEBOARDS	WAMPISHING	WARDENSHIP	WARRANTING
WAGONLOADS	WAKEFULNESS	WAMPUMPEAG	WARDENSHIPS	WARRANTINGS
WAGONWRIGHT	WAKEFULNESSES	WAMPUMPEAGS	WARDERSHIP	WARRANTISE
WAGONWRIGHTS	WALDFLUTES	WANCHANCIE	WARDERSHIPS	WARRANTISED
WAINSCOTED	WALDGRAVES	WANDERINGLY	WARDRESSES	WARRANTISES
WAINSCOTING	WALDGRAVINE	WANDERINGS	WARDROBERS	WARRANTISING
WAINSCOTINGS	WALDGRAVINES	WANDERLUST	WARDROBING	WARRANTIZE
WAINSCOTTED	WALDSTERBEN	WANDERLUSTS	WAREHOUSED	WARRANTIZED
WAINSCOTTING	WALDSTERBENS	WANRESTFUL	WAREHOUSEMAN	WARRANTIZES
WAINSCOTTINGS	WALKABOUTS	WANTHRIVEN	WAREHOUSEMEN	WARRANTIZING
WAINWRIGHT	WALKATHONS	WANTONISED	WAREHOUSER	WARRANTLESS
WAINWRIGHTS	WALKINGSTICK	WANTONISES	WAREHOUSERS	WARRANTORS
WAISTBANDS	WALKINGSTICKS	WANTONISING	WAREHOUSES	WARRANTYING
WAISTBELTS	WALKSHORTS	WANTONIZED	WAREHOUSING	WARRIORESS
WAISTCLOTH	WALLBOARDS	WANTONIZES	WAREHOUSINGS	WARRIORESSES
WAISTCLOTHS	WALLCHARTS	WANTONIZING	WARFARINGS	WASHABILITIES
WAISTCOATED	WALLCLIMBER	WANTONNESS	WARGAMINGS	WASHABILITY
WAISTCOATEER	WALLCLIMBERS	WANTONNESSES	WARIBASHIS	WASHATERIA
WAISTCOATEERS	WALLCOVERING	WANWORDIER	WARINESSES	WASHATERIAS
WAISTCOATING	WALLCOVERINGS	WANWORDIEST	WARLIKENESS	WASHBASINS
WAISTCOATINGS	WALLFISHES	WAPENSCHAW	WARLIKENESSES	WASHBOARDS
WAISTCOATS	WALLFLOWER	WAPENSCHAWS	WARLOCKRIES	WASHCLOTHS
WAISTLINES	WALLFLOWERS	WAPENSHAWS	WARLORDISM	WASHERWOMAN

WASHERWOMEN

WASHERWOMEN	WATCHMAKERS	WATERFOWLINGS	WATERSIDES	WEAKFISHES
WASHETERIA	WATCHMAKING	WATERFOWLS	WATERSKIING	WEAKHEARTED
WASHETERIAS	WATCHMAKINGS	WATERFRONT	WATERSKIINGS	WEAKISHNESS
WASHHOUSES	WATCHSPRING	WATERFRONTS	WATERSMEET	WEAKISHNESSES
WASHINESSES	WATCHSPRINGS	WATERGATES	WATERSMEETS	WEAKLINESS
WASHINGTONIA	WATCHSTRAP	WATERGLASS	WATERSPOUT	WEAKLINESSES
WASHINGTONIAS	WATCHSTRAPS	WATERGLASSES	WATERSPOUTS	WEAKNESSES
WASHSTANDS	WATCHTOWER	WATERHEADS	WATERTHRUSH	WEALTHIEST
WASPINESSES	WATCHTOWERS	WATERHOLES	WATERTHRUSHES	WEALTHINESS
WASPISHNESS	WATCHWORDS	WATERINESS	WATERTIGHT	WEALTHINESSES
WASPISHNESSES	WATERBIRDS	WATERINESSES	WATERTIGHTNESS	WEALTHLESS
WASSAILERS	WATERBOARDING	WATERISHNESS	WATERWEEDS	WEAPONEERED
WASSAILING	WATERBOARDINGS	WATERISHNESSES	WATERWHEEL	WEAPONEERING
WASSAILINGS	WATERBORNE	WATERLEAFS	WATERWHEELS	WEAPONEERINGS
WASSAILRIES	WATERBRAIN	WATERLEAVES	WATERWORKS	WEAPONEERS
WASTEBASKET	WATERBRAINS	WATERLESSNESS	WATERZOOIS	WEAPONISED
WASTEBASKETS	WATERBUCKS	WATERLESSNESSES	WATTLEBARK	WEAPONISES
WASTEFULLY	WATERBUSES	WATERLILIES	WATTLEBARKS	WEAPONISING
WASTEFULNESS	WATERBUSSES	WATERLINES	WATTLEBIRD	WEAPONIZED
WASTEFULNESSES	WATERCOLOR	WATERLOGGED	WATTLEBIRDS	WEAPONIZES
WASTELANDS	WATERCOLORIST	WATERLOGGING	WATTLEWORK	WEAPONIZING
WASTENESSES	WATERCOLORISTS	WATERLOGGINGS	WATTLEWORKS	WEAPONLESS
WASTEPAPER	WATERCOLORS	WATERMANSHIP	WATTMETERS	WEAPONRIES
WASTEPAPERS	WATERCOLOUR	WATERMANSHIPS	WAULKMILLS	WEARABILITIES
WASTERFULLY	WATERCOLOURIST	WATERMARKED	WAVEFRONTS	WEARABILITY
WASTERFULNESS	WATERCOLOURISTS	WATERMARKING	WAVEGUIDES	WEARIFULLY
WASTERFULNESSES	WATERCOLOURS	WATERMARKS	WAVELENGTH	WEARIFULNESS
WASTEWATER	WATERCOOLER	WATERMELON	WAVELENGTHS	WEARIFULNESSES
WASTEWATERS	WATERCOOLERS	WATERMELONS	WAVELESSLY	WEARILESSLY
WASTEWEIRS	WATERCOURSE	WATERMILLS	WAVELLITES	WEARINESSES
WASTNESSES	WATERCOURSES	WATERPOWER	WAVEMETERS	WEARISOMELY
WATCHABLES	WATERCRAFT	WATERPOWERS	WAVERINGLY	WEARISOMENESS
WATCHBANDS	WATERCRAFTS	WATERPOXES	WAVERINGNESS	WEARISOMENESSES
WATCHBOXES	WATERCRESS	WATERPROOF	WAVERINGNESSES	WEARYINGLY
WATCHCASES	WATERCRESSES	WATERPROOFED	WAVESHAPES	WEASELIEST
WATCHCRIES	WATERDRIVE	WATERPROOFER	WAVETABLES	WEASELLERS
WATCHDOGGED	WATERDRIVES	WATERPROOFERS	WAVINESSES	WEASELLIER
WATCHDOGGING	WATERFALLS	WATERPROOFING	WAXBERRIES	WEASELLIEST
WATCHDOGGINGS	WATERFINDER	WATERPROOFINGS	WAXFLOWERS	WEASELLING
WATCHFULLY	WATERFINDERS	WATERPROOFNESS	WAXINESSES	WEATHERABILITY
WATCHFULNESS	WATERFLOOD	WATERPROOFS	WAXWORKERS	WEATHERABLE
WATCHFULNESSES	WATERFLOODED	WATERQUAKE	WAYFARINGS	WEATHERBOARD
WATCHGLASS	WATERFLOODING	WATERQUAKES	WAYMARKING	WEATHERBOARDED
WATCHGLASSES	WATERFLOODINGS	WATERSCAPE	WAYMENTING	WEATHERBOARDING
WATCHGUARD	WATERFLOODS	WATERSCAPES	WAYWARDNESS	WEATHERBOARDS
WATCHGUARDS	WATERFOWLER	WATERSHEDS	WAYWARDNESSES	WEATHERCAST
WATCHLISTS	WATERFOWLERS	WATERSIDER	WAYZGOOSES	WEATHERCASTER
WATCHMAKER	WATERFOWLING	WATERSIDERS	WEAKENINGS	WEATHERCASTERS

WEATHERCASTS	WEBCASTINGS	WELDMESHES	WESTERNIZATIONS	WHEEDLINGLY
WEATHERCLOTH	WEBCHATTED	WELFARISMS	WESTERNIZE	WHEEDLINGS
WEATHERCLOTHS	WEBCHATTING	WELFARISTIC	WESTERNIZED	WHEELBARROW
WEATHERCOCK	WEBLIOGRAPHIES	WELFARISTS	WESTERNIZES	WHEELBARROWED
WEATHERCOCKED	WEBLIOGRAPHY	WELFARITES	WESTERNIZING	WHEELBARROWING
WEATHERCOCKING	WEBLOGGERS	WELLBEINGS	WESTERNMOST	WHEELBARROWS
WEATHERCOCKS	WEBLOGGING	WELLHOUSES	WESTWARDLY	WHEELBASES
WEATHERERS	WEBLOGGINGS	WELLINGTON	WETTABILITIES	WHEELCHAIR
WEATHERGIRL	WEBMASTERS	WELLINGTONIA	WETTABILITY	WHEELCHAIRS
WEATHERGIRLS	WEEDICIDES	WELLINGTONIAS	WHAIKORERO	WHEELHORSE
WEATHERGLASS	WEEDINESSES	WELLINGTONS	WHAIKOREROS	WHEELHORSES
WEATHERGLASSES	WEEDKILLER	WELLNESSES	WHAKAPAPAS	WHEELHOUSE
WEATHERING	WEEDKILLERS	WELLSPRING	WHALEBACKS	WHEELHOUSES
WEATHERINGS	WEEKENDERS	WELLSPRINGS	WHALEBOATS	WHEELSPINS
WEATHERISATION	WEEKENDING	WELTANSCHAUUNG	WHALEBONES	WHEELWORKS
WEATHERISATIONS	WEEKENDINGS	WELTANSCHAUUNGS	WHAREPUNIS	WHEELWRIGHT
WEATHERISE	WEEKNIGHTS	WELTERWEIGHT	WHARFINGER	WHEELWRIGHTS
WEATHERISED	WEELDLESSE	WELTERWEIGHTS	WHARFINGERS	WHEESHTING
WEATHERISES	WEEPINESSES	WELTSCHMERZ	WHARFMASTER	WHEEZINESS
WEATHERISING	WEEVILIEST	WELTSCHMERZES	WHARFMASTERS	WHEEZINESSES
WEATHERIZATION	WEEVILLIER	WELWITSCHIA	WHATABOUTERIES	WHEEZINGLY
WEATHERIZATIONS	WEEVILLIEST	WELWITSCHIAS	WHATABOUTERY	WHENCEFORTH
WEATHERIZE	WEIGHBOARD	WENSLEYDALE	WHATABOUTISM	WHENCESOEVER
WEATHERIZED	WEIGHBOARDS	WENSLEYDALES	WHATABOUTISMS	WHENSOEVER
WEATHERIZES	WEIGHBRIDGE	WENTLETRAP	WHATABOUTS	WHEREABOUT
WEATHERIZING	WEIGHBRIDGES	WENTLETRAPS	WHATCHAMACALLIT	WHEREABOUTS
WEATHERLIER	WEIGHTAGES	WEREWOLFERIES	WHATNESSES	WHEREAFTER
WEATHERLIEST	WEIGHTIEST	WEREWOLFERY	WHATSERNAME	WHEREAGAINST
WEATHERLINESS	WEIGHTINESS	WEREWOLFISH	WHATSERNAMES	WHEREFORES
WEATHERLINESSES	WEIGHTINESSES	WEREWOLFISM	WHATSHERNAME	WHEREINSOEVER
WEATHERMAN	WEIGHTINGS	WEREWOLFISMS	WHATSHERNAMES	WHERENESSES
WEATHERMEN	WEIGHTLESS	WEREWOLVES	WHATSHISNAME	WHERESOEVER
WEATHERMOST	WEIGHTLESSLY	WERNERITES	WHATSHISNAMES	WHERETHROUGH
WEATHEROMETER	WEIGHTLESSNESS	WERWOLFISH	WHATSISNAME	WHEREUNDER
WEATHEROMETERS	WEIGHTLIFTER	WESTERINGS	WHATSISNAMES	WHEREUNTIL
WEATHERPERSON	WEIGHTLIFTERS	WESTERLIES	WHATSITSNAME	WHEREWITHAL
WEATHERPERSONS	WEIGHTLIFTING	WESTERLINESS	WHATSITSNAMES	WHEREWITHALS
WEATHERPROOF	WEIGHTLIFTINGS	WESTERLINESSES	WHATSOEVER	WHEREWITHS
WEATHERPROOFED	WEIMARANER	WESTERNERS	WHATSOMEVER	WHERRETING
WEATHERPROOFING	WEIMARANERS	WESTERNISATION	WHEATFIELD	WHERRITING
WEATHERPROOFS	WEIRDNESSES	WESTERNISATIONS	WHEATFIELDS	WHETSTONES
WEATHERWOMAN	WEISENHEIMER	WESTERNISE	WHEATGERMS	WHEWELLITE
WEATHERWOMEN	WEISENHEIMERS	WESTERNISED	WHEATGRASS	WHEWELLITES
WEATHERWORN	WELCOMENESS	WESTERNISES	WHEATGRASSES	WHEYISHNESS
WEAVERBIRD	WELCOMENESSES	WESTERNISING	WHEATLANDS	WHEYISHNESSES
WEAVERBIRDS	WELCOMINGLY	WESTERNISM	WHEATMEALS	WHICHSOEVER
WEBCASTERS	WELDABILITIES	WESTERNISMS	WHEATWORMS	WHICKERING
WEBCASTING	WELDABILITY	WESTERNIZATION	WHEEDLESOME	WHIDDERING

W

WHIFFLERIES

WHIFFLERIES	WHIPPOORWILL	WHITEBEARDS	WHITTERING	WHOSESOEVER
WHIFFLETREE	WHIPPOORWILLS	WHITEBOARD	WHITTLINGS	WHUNSTANES
WHIFFLETREES	WHIPSAWING	WHITEBOARDS	WHIZZBANGS	WHYDUNNITS
WHIFFLINGS	WHIPSNAKES	WHITEBOYISM	WHIZZINGLY	WICKEDNESS
WHIGGAMORE	WHIPSTAFFS	WHITEBOYISMS	WHODUNITRIES	WICKEDNESSES
WHIGGAMORES	WHIPSTALLED	WHITECOATS	WHODUNITRY	WICKERWORK
WHIGMALEERIE	WHIPSTALLING	WHITECOMBS	WHODUNNITRIES	WICKERWORKS
WHIGMALEERIES	WHIPSTALLS	WHITEDAMPS	WHODUNNITRY	WICKETKEEPER
WHIGMALEERY	WHIPSTITCH	WHITEFACES	WHODUNNITS	WICKETKEEPERS
WHILLYWHAED	WHIPSTITCHED	WHITEFISHES	WHOLEFOODS	WICKTHINGS
WHILLYWHAING	WHIPSTITCHES	WHITEFLIES	WHOLEGRAIN	WIDDERSHINS
WHILLYWHAS	WHIPSTITCHING	WHITEHEADS	WHOLEGRAINS	WIDEAWAKES
WHILLYWHAW	WHIPSTOCKS	WHITELISTED	WHOLEHEARTED	WIDEBODIES
WHILLYWHAWED	WHIPTAILED	WHITELISTING	WHOLEHEARTEDLY	WIDECHAPPED
WHILLYWHAWING	WHIRLABOUT	WHITELISTS	WHOLEMEALS	WIDEMOUTHED
WHILLYWHAWS	WHIRLABOUTS	WHITENESSES	WHOLENESSES	WIDENESSES
WHIMBERRIES	WHIRLBLAST	WHITENINGS	WHOLESALED	WIDERSHINS
WHIMPERERS	WHIRLBLASTS	WHITESMITH	WHOLESALER	WIDESCREEN
WHIMPERING	WHIRLIGIGS	WHITESMITHS	WHOLESALERS	WIDESPREAD
WHIMPERINGLY	WHIRLINGLY	WHITETAILS	WHOLESALES	WIDOWBIRDS
WHIMPERINGS	WHIRLPOOLS	WHITETHORN	WHOLESALING	WIDOWERHOOD
WHIMSICALITIES	WHIRLWINDS	WHITETHORNS	WHOLESALINGS	WIDOWERHOODS
WHIMSICALITY	WHIRLYBIRD	WHITETHROAT	WHOLESOMELY	WIDOWHOODS
WHIMSICALLY	WHIRLYBIRDS	WHITETHROATS	WHOLESOMENESS	WIELDINESS
WHIMSICALNESS	WHIRRETING	WHITEWALLS	WHOLESOMENESSES	WIELDINESSES
WHIMSICALNESSES	WHISKERANDO	WHITEWARES	WHOLESOMER	WIENERWURST
WHIMSINESS	WHISKERANDOED	WHITEWASHED	WHOLESOMEST	WIENERWURSTS
WHIMSINESSES	WHISKERANDOS	WHITEWASHER	WHOLESTITCH	WIFELINESS
WHINBERRIES	WHISKERIER	WHITEWASHERS	WHOLESTITCHES	WIFELINESSES
WHINGDINGS	WHISKERIEST	WHITEWASHES	WHOLEWHEAT	WIGWAGGERS
WHINGEINGLY	WHISKEYFIED	WHITEWASHING	WHOMSOEVER	WIGWAGGING
WHINGEINGS	WHISKIFIED	WHITEWASHINGS	WHOREHOUSE	WIKIALITIES
WHININESSES	WHISPERERS	WHITEWATER	WHOREHOUSES	WIKITORIAL
WHINSTONES	WHISPERIER	WHITEWINGS	WHOREMASTER	WIKITORIALS
WHIPCORDIER	WHISPERIEST	WHITEWOODS	WHOREMASTERIES	WILDCATTED
WHIPCORDIEST	WHISPERING	WHITEYWOOD	WHOREMASTERLY	WILDCATTER
WHIPCRACKS	WHISPERINGLY	WHITEYWOODS	WHOREMASTERS	WILDCATTERS
WHIPLASHED	WHISPERINGS	WHITHERING	WHOREMASTERY	WILDCATTING
WHIPLASHES	WHISPEROUSLY	WHITHERSOEVER	WHOREMISTRESS	WILDCATTINGS
WHIPLASHING	WHISTLEABLE	WHITHERWARD	WHOREMISTRESSES	WILDEBEEST
WHIPPERSNAPPER	WHISTLEBLOWING	WHITHERWARDS	WHOREMONGER	WILDEBEESTS
WHIPPERSNAPPERS	WHISTLEBLOWINGS	WHITISHNESS	WHOREMONGERIES	WILDERMENT
WHIPPETING	WHISTLINGLY	WHITISHNESSES	WHOREMONGERS	WILDERMENTS
WHIPPETINGS	WHISTLINGS	WHITLEATHER	WHOREMONGERY	WILDERNESS
WHIPPINESS	WHITEBAITS	WHITLEATHERS	WHORISHNESS	WILDERNESSES
WHIPPINESSES	WHITEBASSES	WHITTAWERS	WHORISHNESSES	WILDFLOWER
WHIPPLETREE	WHITEBEAMS	WHITTERICK	WHORTLEBERRIES	WILDFLOWERS
WHIPPLETREES	WHITEBEARD	WHITTERICKS	WHORTLEBERRY	WILDFOWLER

WILDFOWLERS	WINDJAMMER	WINEGLASSFUL	WINTERKILLED	WISECRACKS
WILDFOWLING	WINDJAMMERS	WINEGLASSFULS	WINTERKILLING	WISENESSES
WILDFOWLINGS	WINDJAMMING	WINEGROWER	WINTERKILLINGS	WISENHEIMER
WILDGRAVES	WINDJAMMINGS	WINEGROWERS	WINTERKILLS	WISENHEIMERS
WILDNESSES	WINDLASSED	WINEGROWING	WINTERLESS	WISHFULNESS
WILFULNESS	WINDLASSES	WINEGROWINGS	WINTERLIER	WISHFULNESSES
WILFULNESSES	WINDLASSING	WINEMAKERS	WINTERLIEST	WISHTONWISH
WILINESSES	WINDLESSLY	WINEMAKING	WINTERLINESS	WISHTONWISHES
WILLEMITES	WINDLESSNESS	WINEMAKINGS	WINTERLINESSES	WISPINESSES
WILLFULNESS	WINDLESSNESSES	WINEPRESSES	WINTERTIDE	WISTFULNESS
WILLFULNESSES	WINDLESTRAE	WINGCHAIRS	WINTERTIDES	WISTFULNESSES
WILLIEWAUGHT	WINDLESTRAES	WINGLESSNESS	WINTERTIME	WITBLITSES
WILLIEWAUGHTS	WINDLESTRAW	WINGLESSNESSES	WINTERTIMES	WITCHBROOM
WILLINGEST	WINDLESTRAWS	WINGSPREAD	WINTERWEIGHT	WITCHBROOMS
WILLINGNESS	WINDMILLED	WINGSPREADS	WINTRINESS	WITCHCRAFT
WILLINGNESSES	WINDMILLING	WINNABILITIES	WINTRINESSES	WITCHCRAFTS
WILLOWHERB	WINDOWIEST	WINNABILITY	WIREDRAWER	WITCHERIES
WILLOWHERBS	WINDOWINGS	WINNINGEST	WIREDRAWERS	WITCHETTIES
WILLOWIEST	WINDOWLESS	WINNINGNESS	WIREDRAWING	WITCHGRASS
WILLOWLIKE	WINDOWPANE	WINNINGNESSES	WIREDRAWINGS	WITCHGRASSES
WILLOWWARE	WINDOWPANES	WINNOWINGS	WIREFRAMES	WITCHHOODS
WILLOWWARES	WINDOWSILL	WINSOMENESS	WIREGRASSES	WITCHINGLY
WILLPOWERS	WINDOWSILLS	WINSOMENESSES	WIREHAIRED	WITCHKNOTS
WIMPINESSES	WINDPROOFED	WINTERBERRIES	WIRELESSED	WITCHWEEDS
WIMPISHNESS	WINDPROOFING	WINTERBERRY	WIRELESSES	WITENAGEMOT
WIMPISHNESSES	WINDPROOFS	WINTERBOURNE	WIRELESSING	WITENAGEMOTE
WINCEYETTE	WINDROWERS	WINTERBOURNES	WIRELESSLY	WITENAGEMOTES
WINCEYETTES	WINDROWING	WINTERCRESS	WIREPHOTOS	WITENAGEMOTS
WINCHESTER	WINDSCREEN	WINTERCRESSES	WIREPULLER	WITGATBOOM
WINCHESTERS	WINDSCREENS	WINTERFEED	WIREPULLERS	WITGATBOOMS
WINCOPIPES	WINDSHAKES	WINTERFEEDING	WIREPULLING	WITHDRAWABLE
WINDBAGGERIES	WINDSHIELD	WINTERFEEDS	WIREPULLINGS	WITHDRAWAL
WINDBAGGERY	WINDSHIELDS	WINTERGREEN	WIRETAPPED	WITHDRAWALS
WINDBLASTS	WINDSTORMS	WINTERGREENS	WIRETAPPER	WITHDRAWER
WINDBREAKER	WINDSUCKER	WINTERIEST	WIRETAPPERS	WITHDRAWERS
WINDBREAKERS	WINDSUCKERS	WINTERINESS	WIRETAPPING	WITHDRAWING
WINDBREAKS	WINDSURFED	WINTERINESSES	WIRETAPPINGS	WITHDRAWMENT
WINDBURNED	WINDSURFER	WINTERISATION	WIREWALKER	WITHDRAWMENTS
WINDBURNING	WINDSURFERS	WINTERISATIONS	WIREWALKERS	WITHDRAWNNESS
WINDCHEATER	WINDSURFING	WINTERISED	WIREWORKER	WITHDRAWNNESSES
WINDCHEATERS	WINDSURFINGS	WINTERISES	WIREWORKERS	WITHEREDNESS
WINDCHILLS	WINDTHROWS	WINTERISING	WIREWORKING	WITHEREDNESSES
WINDFALLEN	WINEBERRIES	WINTERIZATION	WIREWORKINGS	WITHERINGLY
WINDFLOWER	WINEBIBBER	WINTERIZATIONS	WIRINESSES	WITHERINGS
WINDFLOWERS	WINEBIBBERS	WINTERIZED	WISECRACKED	WITHERITES
WINDGALLED	WINEBIBBING	WINTERIZES	WISECRACKER	WITHERSHINS
WINDHOVERS	WINEBIBBINGS	WINTERIZING	WISECRACKERS	WITHHOLDEN
WINDINESSES	WINEGLASSES	WINTERKILL	WISECRACKING	WITHHOLDER

W

WITHHOLDERS	WOMANISERS	WOODCARVERS	WOODSWALLOW	WORKABILITY
WITHHOLDING	WOMANISHLY	WOODCARVING	WOODSWALLOWS	WORKABLENESS
WITHHOLDMENT	WOMANISHNESS	WOODCARVINGS	WOODTHRUSH	WORKABLENESSES
WITHHOLDMENTS	WOMANISHNESSES	WOODCHOPPER	WOODTHRUSHES	WORKAHOLIC
WITHINDOORS	WOMANISING	WOODCHOPPERS	WOODWAXENS	WORKAHOLICS
WITHOUTDOORS	WOMANISINGS	WOODCHUCKS	WOODWORKER	WORKAHOLISM
WITHSTANDER	WOMANIZERS	WOODCRAFTS	WOODWORKERS	WORKAHOLISMS
WITHSTANDERS	WOMANIZING	WOODCRAFTSMAN	WOODWORKING	WORKAROUND
WITHSTANDING	WOMANIZINGS	WOODCRAFTSMEN	WOODWORKINGS	WORKAROUNDS
WITHSTANDS	WOMANKINDS	WOODCUTTER	WOOLGATHERER	WORKBASKET
WITHYWINDS	WOMANLIEST	WOODCUTTERS	WOOLGATHERERS	WORKBASKETS
WITLESSNESS	WOMANLINESS	WOODCUTTING	WOOLGATHERING	WORKBENCHES
WITLESSNESSES	WOMANLINESSES	WOODCUTTINGS	WOOLGATHERINGS	WORKERISTS
WITNESSABLE	WOMANNESSES	WOODENHEAD	WOOLGROWER	WORKERLESS
WITNESSERS	WOMANPOWER	WOODENHEADED	WOOLGROWERS	WORKFELLOW
WITNESSING	WOMANPOWERS	WOODENHEADS	WOOLGROWING	WORKFELLOWS
WITTICISMS	WOMENFOLKS	WOODENNESS	WOOLGROWINGS	WORKFORCES
WITTINESSES	WOMENKINDS	WOODENNESSES	WOOLINESSES	WORKGROUPS
WITWANTONED	WOMENSWEAR	WOODENTOPS	WOOLLINESS	WORKHORSES
WITWANTONING	WOMENSWEARS	WOODENWARE	WOOLLINESSES	WORKHOUSES
WITWANTONS	WONDERFULLY	WOODENWARES	WOOLLYBACK	WORKINGMAN
WIZARDLIER	WONDERFULNESS	WOODGRAINS	WOOLLYBACKS	WORKINGMEN
WIZARDLIEST	WONDERFULNESSES	WOODGROUSE	WOOLLYBUTT	WORKINGWOMAN
WIZARDRIES	WONDERINGLY	WOODGROUSES	WOOLLYBUTTS	WORKINGWOMEN
WOADWAXENS	WONDERINGS	WOODHORSES	WOOLLYFOOT	WORKLESSNESS
WOBBEGONGS	WONDERKIDS	WOODHOUSES	WOOLLYFOOTS	WORKLESSNESSES
WOBBLINESS	WONDERLAND	WOODINESSES	WOOLSORTER	WORKMANLIER
WOBBLINESSES	WONDERLANDS	WOODLANDER	WOOLSORTERS	WORKMANLIEST
WOEBEGONENESS	WONDERLESS	WOODLANDERS	WOOMERANGS	WORKMANLIKE
WOEBEGONENESSES	WONDERMENT	WOODLESSNESS	WOOZINESSES	WORKMANSHIP
WOEFULLEST	WONDERMENTS	WOODLESSNESSES	WORCESTERBERRY	WORKMANSHIPS
WOEFULNESS	WONDERMONGER	WOODNESSES	WORCESTERS	WORKMASTER
WOEFULNESSES	WONDERMONGERING	WOODPECKER	WORDBREAKS	WORKMASTERS
WOFULNESSES	WONDERMONGERS	WOODPECKERS	WORDCOUNTS	WORKMISTRESS
WOLFBERRIES	WONDERSTRUCK	WOODPRINTS	WORDINESSES	WORKMISTRESSES
WOLFFISHES	WONDERWORK	WOODREEVES	WORDISHNESS	WORKPEOPLE
WOLFHOUNDS	WONDERWORKS	WOODRUSHES	WORDISHNESSES	WORKPIECES
WOLFISHNESS	WONDROUSLY	WOODSCREWS	WORDLESSLY	WORKPLACES
WOLFISHNESSES	WONDROUSNESS	WOODSHEDDED	WORDLESSNESS	WORKPRINTS
WOLFRAMITE	WONDROUSNESSES	WOODSHEDDING	WORDLESSNESSES	WORKSHEETS
WOLFRAMITES	WONKINESSES	WOODSHEDDINGS	WORDMONGER	WORKSHOPPED
WOLFSBANES	WONTEDNESS	WOODSHOCKS	WORDMONGERS	WORKSHOPPING
WOLLASTONITE	WONTEDNESSES	WOODSHRIKE	WORDSEARCH	WORKSPACES
WOLLASTONITES	WOODBLOCKS	WOODSHRIKES	WORDSEARCHES	WORKSTATION
WOLVERENES	WOODBORERS	WOODSMOKES	WORDSMITHERIES	WORKSTATIONS
WOLVERINES	WOODBURYTYPE	WOODSPITES	WORDSMITHERY	WORKSTREAM
WOMANFULLY	WOODBURYTYPES	WOODSTONES	WORDSMITHS	WORKSTREAMS
WOMANHOODS	WOODCARVER	WOODSTOVES	WORKABILITIES	WORKTABLES

WORKWATCHER
WORKWATCHERS
WORLDBEATS
WORLDLIEST
WORLDLINESS
WORLDLINESSES
WORLDLINGS
WORLDSCALE
WORLDSCALES
WORLDVIEWS
WORMINESSES
WORMWHEELS
WORNNESSES
WORRIMENTS
WORRISOMELY
WORRISOMENESS
WORRISOMENESSES
WORRYINGLY
WORRYWARTS
WORSENESSES
WORSENINGS

WORSHIPABLE
WORSHIPERS
WORSHIPFUL
WORSHIPFULLY
WORSHIPFULNESS
WORSHIPING
WORSHIPLESS
WORSHIPPED
WORSHIPPER
WORSHIPPERS
WORSHIPPING
WORTHINESS
WORTHINESSES
WORTHLESSLY
WORTHLESSNESS
WORTHLESSNESSES
WORTHWHILE
WORTHWHILENESS
WOUNDINGLY
WOUNDWORTS
WRAITHLIKE

WRANGLERSHIP
WRANGLERSHIPS
WRANGLESOME
WRANGLINGS
WRAPAROUND
WRAPAROUNDS
WRAPPERING
WRAPROUNDS
WRATHFULLY
WRATHFULNESS
WRATHFULNESSES
WRATHINESS
WRATHINESSES
WREATHIEST
WREATHLESS
WREATHLIKE
WRECKFISHES
WRECKMASTER
WRECKMASTERS
WRENCHINGLY
WRENCHINGS

WRESTLINGS
WRETCHEDER
WRETCHEDEST
WRETCHEDLY
WRETCHEDNESS
WRETCHEDNESSES
WRIGGLIEST
WRIGGLINGS
WRINKLELESS
WRINKLIEST
WRISTBANDS
WRISTLOCKS
WRISTWATCH
WRISTWATCHES
WRITEDOWNS
WRITERESSES
WRITERLIER
WRITERLIEST
WRITERSHIP
WRITERSHIPS
WRITHINGLY

WRONGDOERS
WRONGDOING
WRONGDOINGS
WRONGFULLY
WRONGFULNESS
WRONGFULNESSES
WRONGHEADED
WRONGHEADEDLY
WRONGHEADEDNESS
WRONGNESSES
WRONGOUSLY
WULFENITES
WUNDERKIND
WUNDERKINDER
WUNDERKINDS
WYANDOTTES
WYLIECOATS

W

X

XANTHATION	XENODIAGNOSES	XENOTRANSPLANTS	XEROPHYTIC	XYLOGENOUS
XANTHATIONS	XENODIAGNOSIS	XENOTROPIC	XEROPHYTICALLY	XYLOGRAPHED
XANTHOCHROIA	XENODIAGNOSTIC	XERANTHEMUM	XEROPHYTISM	XYLOGRAPHER
XANTHOCHROIAS	XENODOCHIUM	XERANTHEMUMS	XEROPHYTISMS	XYLOGRAPHERS
XANTHOCHROIC	XENODOCHIUMS	XERISCAPED	XERORADIOGRAPHY	XYLOGRAPHIC
XANTHOCHROID	XENOGAMIES	XERISCAPES	XEROSTOMAS	XYLOGRAPHICAL
XANTHOCHROIDS	XENOGAMOUS	XERISCAPING	XEROSTOMATA	XYLOGRAPHIES
XANTHOCHROISM	XENOGENEIC	XEROCHASIES	XEROSTOMIA	XYLOGRAPHING
XANTHOCHROISMS	XENOGENESES	XERODERMAE	XEROSTOMIAS	XYLOGRAPHS
XANTHOCHROMIA	XENOGENESIS	XERODERMAS	XEROTHERMIC	XYLOGRAPHY
XANTHOCHROMIAS	XENOGENETIC	XERODERMATIC	XEROTRIPSES	XYLOIDINES
XANTHOCHROOUS	XENOGENIES	XERODERMATOUS	XEROTRIPSIS	XYLOLOGIES
XANTHOMATA	XENOGENOUS	XERODERMIA	XIPHIHUMERALIS	XYLOMETERS
XANTHOMATOUS	XENOGLOSSIA	XERODERMIAS	XIPHIPLASTRA	XYLOPHAGAN
XANTHOMELANOUS	XENOGLOSSIAS	XERODERMIC	XIPHIPLASTRAL	XYLOPHAGANS
XANTHOPHYL	XENOGLOSSIES	XEROGRAPHER	XIPHIPLASTRALS	XYLOPHAGES
XANTHOPHYLL	XENOGLOSSY	XEROGRAPHERS	XIPHIPLASTRON	XYLOPHAGOUS
XANTHOPHYLLOUS	XENOGRAFTS	XEROGRAPHIC	XIPHISTERNA	XYLOPHILOUS
XANTHOPHYLLS	XENOLITHIC	XEROGRAPHICALLY	XIPHISTERNUM	XYLOPHONES
XANTHOPHYLS	XENOMANIAS	XEROGRAPHIES	XIPHISTERNUMS	XYLOPHONIC
XANTHOPSIA	XENOMENIAS	XEROGRAPHY	XIPHOPAGIC	XYLOPHONIST
XANTHOPSIAS	XENOMORPHIC	XEROMORPHIC	XIPHOPAGOUS	XYLOPHONISTS
XANTHOPTERIN	XENOMORPHICALLY	XEROMORPHOUS	XIPHOPAGUS	XYLOPYROGRAPHY
XANTHOPTERINE	XENOPHILES	XEROMORPHS	XIPHOPAGUSES	XYLORIMBAS
XANTHOPTERINES	XENOPHOBES	XEROPHAGIES	XIPHOPHYLLOUS	XYLOTOMIES
XANTHOPTERINS	XENOPHOBIA	XEROPHILES	XIPHOSURAN	XYLOTOMIST
XANTHOXYLS	XENOPHOBIAS	XEROPHILIES	XIPHOSURANS	XYLOTOMISTS
XENARTHRAL	XENOPHOBIC	XEROPHILOUS	XYLOBALSAMUM	XYLOTOMOUS
XENOBIOTIC	XENOPHOBICALLY	XEROPHTHALMIA	XYLOBALSAMUMS	XYLOTYPOGRAPHIC
XENOBIOTICS	XENOPHOBIES	XEROPHTHALMIAS	XYLOCARPOUS	XYLOTYPOGRAPHY
XENOBLASTS	XENOPLASTIC	XEROPHTHALMIC	XYLOCHROME	XYRIDACEOUS
XENOCRYSTS	XENOTRANSPLANT	XEROPHYTES	XYLOCHROMES	

X

Y

YACHTSMANSHIP	YELLOWBARK	YELLOWWARE	YESTERNIGHT	YOURSELVES
YACHTSMANSHIPS	YELLOWBARKS	YELLOWWARES	YESTERNIGHTS	YOUTHENING
YACHTSWOMAN	YELLOWBIRD	YELLOWWEED	YESTERYEAR	YOUTHFULLY
YACHTSWOMEN	YELLOWBIRDS	YELLOWWEEDS	YESTERYEARS	YOUTHFULNESS
YAFFINGALE	YELLOWCAKE	YELLOWWOOD	YIELDABLENESS	YOUTHFULNESSES
YAFFINGALES	YELLOWCAKES	YELLOWWOODS	YIELDABLENESSES	YOUTHHEADS
YAMMERINGS	YELLOWFINS	YELLOWWORT	YIELDINGLY	YOUTHHOODS
YARBOROUGH	YELLOWHAMMER	YELLOWWORTS	YIELDINGNESS	YOUTHQUAKE
YARBOROUGHS	YELLOWHAMMERS	YEOMANRIES	YIELDINGNESSES	YOUTHQUAKES
YARDLIGHTS	YELLOWHEAD	YERSINIOSES	YOCTOSECOND	YPSILIFORM
YARDMASTER	YELLOWHEADS	YERSINIOSIS	YOCTOSECONDS	YTHUNDERED
YARDMASTERS	YELLOWIEST	YESTERDAYS	YODELLINGS	YTTERBITES
YARDSTICKS	YELLOWISHNESS	YESTEREVEN	YOHIMBINES	YTTERBIUMS
YATTERINGLY	YELLOWISHNESSES	YESTEREVENING	YOKEFELLOW	YTTRIFEROUS
YATTERINGS	YELLOWLEGS	YESTEREVENINGS	YOKEFELLOWS	YUCKINESSES
YEARNINGLY	YELLOWNESS	YESTEREVENS	YOTTABYTES	YUMBERRIES
YEASTINESS	YELLOWNESSES	YESTEREVES	YOUNGBERRIES	YUMMINESSES
YEASTINESSES	YELLOWTAIL	YESTERMORN	YOUNGBERRY	YUPPIEDOMS
YELLOCHING	YELLOWTAILS	YESTERMORNING	YOUNGLINGS	YUPPIFICATION
YELLOWBACK	YELLOWTHROAT	YESTERMORNINGS	YOUNGNESSES	YUPPIFICATIONS
YELLOWBACKS	YELLOWTHROATS	YESTERMORNS	YOUNGSTERS	YUPPIFYING

Z

ZABAGLIONE	ZESTFULNESSES	ZINGIBERACEOUS	ZOOGEOGRAPHY	ZOOPHILIST
ZABAGLIONES	ZESTINESSES	ZINJANTHROPI	ZOOGLOEOID	ZOOPHILISTS
ZALAMBDODONT	ZETTABYTES	ZINJANTHROPUS	ZOOGONIDIA	ZOOPHILOUS
ZALAMBDODONTS	ZEUGLODONT	ZINJANTHROPUSES	ZOOGONIDIUM	ZOOPHOBIAS
ZAMBOORAKS	ZEUGLODONTS	ZINKENITES	ZOOGRAFTING	ZOOPHOBOUS
ZAMINDARIES	ZEUGMATICALLY	ZINKIFEROUS	ZOOGRAFTINGS	ZOOPHYSIOLOGIES
ZAMINDARIS	ZIBELLINES	ZINKIFICATION	ZOOGRAPHER	ZOOPHYSIOLOGIST
ZANAMIVIRS	ZIDOVUDINE	ZINKIFICATIONS	ZOOGRAPHERS	ZOOPHYSIOLOGY
ZANINESSES	ZIDOVUDINES	ZINKIFYING	ZOOGRAPHIC	ZOOPHYTICAL
ZANTEDESCHIA	ZIGZAGGEDNESS	ZINZIBERACEOUS	ZOOGRAPHICAL	ZOOPHYTOID
ZANTEDESCHIAS	ZIGZAGGEDNESSES	ZIPLOCKING	ZOOGRAPHIES	ZOOPHYTOLOGICAL
ZANTEWOODS	ZIGZAGGERIES	ZIPPINESSES	ZOOGRAPHIST	ZOOPHYTOLOGIES
ZANTHOXYLS	ZIGZAGGERS	ZIRCALLOYS	ZOOGRAPHISTS	ZOOPHYTOLOGIST
ZANTHOXYLUM	ZIGZAGGERY	ZIRCONIUMS	ZOOKEEPERS	ZOOPHYTOLOGISTS
ZANTHOXYLUMS	ZIGZAGGIER	ZITHERISTS	ZOOLATRIAS	ZOOPHYTOLOGY
ZAPATEADOS	ZIGZAGGIEST	ZIZYPHUSES	ZOOLATRIES	ZOOPLANKTER
ZAPOTILLAS	ZIGZAGGING	ZOANTHARIAN	ZOOLATROUS	ZOOPLANKTERS
ZEALOTISMS	ZILLIONAIRE	ZOANTHARIANS	ZOOLOGICAL	ZOOPLANKTON
ZEALOTRIES	ZILLIONAIRES	ZOANTHROPIC	ZOOLOGICALLY	ZOOPLANKTONIC
ZEALOUSNESS	ZILLIONTHS	ZOANTHROPIES	ZOOLOGISTS	ZOOPLANKTONS
ZEALOUSNESSES	ZINCIFEROUS	ZOANTHROPY	ZOOMAGNETIC	ZOOPLASTIC
ZEBRAFISHES	ZINCIFICATION	ZOECHROMES	ZOOMAGNETISM	ZOOPLASTIES
ZEBRAWOODS	ZINCIFICATIONS	ZOMBIELIKE	ZOOMAGNETISMS	ZOOPSYCHOLOGIES
ZEBRINNIES	ZINCIFYING	ZOMBIFICATION	ZOOMANCIES	ZOOPSYCHOLOGY
ZEITGEBERS	ZINCKENITE	ZOMBIFICATIONS	ZOOMETRICAL	ZOOSCOPIES
ZEITGEISTIER	ZINCKENITES	ZOMBIFYING	ZOOMETRIES	ZOOSPERMATIC
ZEITGEISTIEST	ZINCKIFICATION	ZOOCEPHALIC	ZOOMORPHIC	ZOOSPERMIA
ZEITGEISTS	ZINCKIFICATIONS	ZOOCHEMICAL	ZOOMORPHIES	ZOOSPERMIUM
ZEITGEISTY	ZINCKIFIED	ZOOCHEMISTRIES	ZOOMORPHISM	ZOOSPORANGIA
ZELATRICES	ZINCKIFIES	ZOOCHEMISTRY	ZOOMORPHISMS	ZOOSPORANGIAL
ZELATRIXES	ZINCKIFYING	ZOOCHORIES	ZOONOMISTS	ZOOSPORANGIUM
ZELOPHOBIA	ZINCOGRAPH	ZOOCHOROUS	ZOOPATHIES	ZOOSPOROUS
ZELOPHOBIAS	ZINCOGRAPHER	ZOOCULTURE	ZOOPATHOLOGIES	ZOOSTEROLS
ZELOPHOBIC	ZINCOGRAPHERS	ZOOCULTURES	ZOOPATHOLOGY	ZOOTECHNICAL
ZELOPHOBICS	ZINCOGRAPHIC	ZOODENDRIA	ZOOPERISTS	ZOOTECHNICS
ZELOTYPIAS	ZINCOGRAPHICAL	ZOODENDRIUM	ZOOPHAGANS	ZOOTECHNIES
ZEMINDARIES	ZINCOGRAPHIES	ZOOGAMETES	ZOOPHAGIES	ZOOTHAPSES
ZEMINDARIS	ZINCOGRAPHS	ZOOGEOGRAPHER	ZOOPHAGOUS	ZOOTHAPSIS
ZEOLITIFORM	ZINCOGRAPHY	ZOOGEOGRAPHERS	ZOOPHILIAS	ZOOTHECIAL
ZEPTOSECOND	ZINCOLYSES	ZOOGEOGRAPHIC	ZOOPHILIES	ZOOTHECIUM
ZEPTOSECONDS	ZINCOLYSIS	ZOOGEOGRAPHICAL	ZOOPHILISM	ZOOTHEISMS
ZESTFULNESS	ZINFANDELS	ZOOGEOGRAPHIES	ZOOPHILISMS	ZOOTHEISTIC

Leabharlanna Fhine Gall